OFFICIAL

METHODS OF ANALYSIS

OF THE

ASSOCIATION OF OFFICIAL ANALYTICAL CHEMISTS

WILLIAM HORWITZ, Editor

THIRTEENTH EDITION, 1980

PUBLISHED BY THE
ASSOCIATION OF OFFICIAL ANALYTICAL CHEMISTS
PO BOX 540, BENJAMIN FRANKLIN STATION
WASHINGTON, DC 20044

Direct inquiries related to the scientific content of *Official Methods of Analysis* to:

Editor, Official Methods of Analysis
Association of Official Analytical Chemists
Box 540, Benjamin Franklin Station
Washington, DC 20044 USA

Direct inquiries related to the procurement of *Official Methods of Analysis*, supplements (Changes in Methods), Journal of the AOAC, or other AOAC publications to:

Assistant Business Manager, Publications
Association of Official Analytical Chemists
1111 N 19th Street (Suite 210)
Arlington, VA 22209 USA (Telephone: 703-522-3032)

Library of Congress Catalog Card Number: 20-21343
ISBN 0-935584-14-5

A copy of the 13th edition of this publication is on file with the Office of the Federal Register. U. S. Government Agencies may apply to the Director of the Office of the Federal Register for approval to incorporate this edition by reference in their regulations. The procedures that Federal agencies must follow in applying for the Director's approval are in Title 1, Part 51 of the *Code of Federal Regulations.*

Composed by
Monotype Composition Company, Inc.
Baltimore, Maryland

Printed and bound by
George Banta Company, Inc.
Menasha, Wisconsin

Preface to Thirteenth Edition

The most noticeable physical change in this thirteenth edition of *Official Methods of Analysis of the Association of Official Analytical Chemists* ("The Book of Methods") is its size. A survey of users of the Book of Methods revealed an overwhelming desire to maintain the compendium as a single volume. The easiest way to do this was to increase the size of the page. Users also expressed a desire for a system that will keep the same reference number for a given method from edition to edition. A practical system that will maintain the continuity of the numbering system and the organizational structure of the methods within a chapter has not yet been devised.

Approximately 175 new methods have been added during the current five year period (1974–1978); 83 methods have been deleted, replaced, or surplused. The approval of an average of only 35 new methods per year represents a marked decline from the 70 per year of the four year period of the previous edition (1970–1973) and the 50 per year of the five year period of the tenth edition (1965–1969). The decline is undoubtedly the result of a number of factors. Chief among them are the greater complexity of modern methods, requiring a large investment in resources that is not readily mobilized to fit an Associate Referee's schedule; and the fact that government agencies are attempting to obtain compliance, especially of the newer statutes, by promulgation of regulations and by auditing rather than by laboratory examinations.

The greatest activity, as measured by approval of new methods, is in the field of pesticide formulations, partly as a result of the active implementation of the cooperative agreement with the Collaborative International Pesticide Analytical Council (CIPAC). Other active areas include extraneous materials, vitamins and other nutrients, dairy products, and microbiological methods. In fact, examination for and by biological constituents (filth, microbiological assays, and examination for food-borne pathogens) comprises approximately 17% of the new methods adopted.

A comparison of the types of methods adopted between this and the previous edition reveals that gas-liquid chromatography has overtaken spectrophotometry in its various forms (visible, ultraviolet, and fluorescent) as the most predominant quantitative technique in *Official Methods.* High pressure (or performance) liquid chromatography has spurted from none to 6% of the adopted methods within the relatively short period of five years. Electrometric methods (potentiometric, polarographic, and ion-selective) are now sufficiently numerous to deserve a separate category. Infrared methods are no longer a major factor in quantitation; they are now mainly used for identification and confirmation. A comparison of the present and previous editions is presented in Table 1. The figures given are only rough approximations because of the arbitrariness often required in classifying a method and in deciding when a new method or revision is sufficiently independent to warrant contributing to the statistics.

Table 1. Classification of new methods approved by the AOAC in the thirteenth and twelfth editions

Method classification	13th edition (1980)	12th edition (1975)
Gas-liquid chromatography	18%	14%
Spectrophotometry	16	20
Titrimetric	10	7
Filth, isolation	8	14
Automated	7	5
Biological and microbiological	9	8
High pressure liquid chromatography	6	—
Atomic absorption	4	9
Electrometric	5	—
Chromatography (thin layer, etc.)	3	3
Gravimetric	2	6
Miscellaneous (physical, qualitative, etc.)	11	13

The most interesting new collaboratively studied method is the mass spectrometric method for the detection of adulteration of honey with high fructose corn sirup. Corn sirups (from a monocotyledonous plant) have a distinctly different $^{13}C/^{12}C$ ratio than sirups from most dicotyledonous plants, which are the source of most honeys. The isotope ratio mass spectrometer required for this determination is a highly specialized instrument, even in the field of mass spectrometry. Despite the rarity of the instrumentation, sufficient laboratories participated in the collaborative study to establish the reproducibility of the method.

A problem that has arisen is how to handle the numerous individual instruments of diverse design and manufacture that have been developed to automate a particular determination. Even if this problem is solved by incorporating all the available instruments into the initial collaborative study, the problem returns with the first "new and improved" modification. Different instrument designs and their subsequent modifications have been handled in the infrared determination of milk constituents by providing performance specifications which must be met by the basic instrument in general, when compared to a reference method or reference sample. In addition, the user must satisfy himself that his particular instrument also meets the performance specifications by frequent comparisons with the reference method or sample. This requirement eliminates the need for repeated collaborative studies every time a manufacturer redesigns or modifies his basic equipment, and in addition provides a continuous quality control technique on the performance of the instrument, method, and laboratory.

It should not be overlooked that automation is not confined to physical and chemical determinations. The microbiological chapter contains three collaboratively studied instrumental methods for somatic cell count and an instrumental method for distributing a liquid sample for plate counting. Biochemical diagnostic kits have also been evaluated collaboratively for their effectiveness in identifying *Salmonella* and other enteric isolates.

A criticism that is often leveled at the AOAC validation mechanism is that it is too slow to keep up with the pace of requirements for methods by regulatory agencies and the regulated industry. This objection overlooks the point that the speed with which a method is validated is almost completely in the hands of those needing the validated method, rather than in the hands of the AOAC. The method must be tested for ruggedness, and the directions tested for clarity; samples must be prepared and distributed; laboratories must analyze the samples and report the results. Dubious results must be investigated and occasionally samples must be reanalyzed. The data must be tabulated and analyzed, and a report written. There is no way to short-cut the process of obtaining intra- and interlaboratory variability except to conduct the necessary experimental work and perform the necessary statistical calculations. Only then is the recommendation subject to the time restrictions of the AOAC mechanism. To ensure that the AOAC mechanism of annual approval is not holding up use of needed methods, a new temporary class of methods has been introduced entitled "Interim First Action." These are methods which, together with their supporting studies, have been received between annual meetings and have been sent through the customary reviewing procedure. To be designated Interim First Action, a method must have been approved by the appropriate Referee and Subcommittee, and by the Chairman of the Committee on Official Methods. The method only lacks the formal vote by those AOAC members having regulatory authority over the commodity involved. Such formal approval is usually provided at the next annual meeting, at which time the method becomes "First Action." Approximately five interim methods are approved annually. Several such methods appear in this volume, depending upon the time of their submission and review in relation to the editorial status of the chapter to which they are assigned. The current status of these Interim First Action methods, as well as the status of any method, can be found by consulting the latest cumulative index to *Changes in Methods,* which appears as the final pages of each March issue of the Journal.

For those users of AOAC methods who may not be familiar with the procedures by which a method is included in this volume, we are reprinting a paper prepared for the Joint International Symposium, "The Harmonization of Collaborative Studies," held in London, England 9–10 March 1978. The document was drafted by the AOAC Committee on Collaborative Studies: Elwyn D. Schall, Chairman; Charles W. Gehrke, William Horwitz, Anthony J. Malonski, James P. Minyard, Jr., Forrest W. Quackenbush, and Ernest S. Windham. This paper appeared in *Analytical Chemistry* (March 1978), **50,** 337A–340A.

The publication of this "Book of Methods" is possible only because of the extensive cooperation of thousands of analysts who have volunteered to direct, participate in, and review the numerous collaborative studies that form the basis for inclusion of the several thousand methods that appear herein. Special recognition is due to Mrs. Betty Johnson who has prepared an entirely new index for this edition.

28 September, 1979

William Horwitz, Ph.D.
Editor

Abstract from

Preface to First Edition

"In presenting this revision of the official and tentative methods of analysis of the Association of Official Agricultural Chemists, it is appropriate to give a brief statement of the organization of the Association, its purpose, and the procedure by which the methods are adopted.

"Membership in the Association is institutional and includes the State Departments of Agriculture, the State Agricultural Colleges and Experiment Stations, the Federal Department of Agriculture, and the Federal, State, and City offices charged with the enforcement of food, feed, drug, fertilizer, insecticide and fungicide control laws.

"The Association was founded at Philadelphia, Pa., September 9, 1884, by the following representative agricultural chemists of that time, the organization being the result of a series of informal meetings held the immediately preceding years:

"Prof. H. W. Wiley, Chemist of the Department of Agriculture, Washington, D.C.

Mr. Clifford Richardson, Assistant Chemist of the Department of Agriculture, Washington, D.C.

Mr. Philip E. Chazal, State Chemist of South Carolina.

Dr. Chas. W. Dabney, Jr., State Chemist of North Carolina.

Dr. W. J. Gascoyne, State Chemist of Virginia.

Dr. E. H. Jenkins, Connecticut Experiment Station.

Prof. John A. Meyers, State Chemist of Mississippi.

Prof. H. C. White, State Chemist of Georgia.

Mr. C. DeGhequier, Secretary National Fertilizer Association.

Dr. Schumann, Dr. Lehmann, Mr. Gaines and others."

Contents

Illustrations

FIGURE PAGE

FIGURE PAGE

Collaborative Study Procedures of the Association of Official Analytical Chemists

The Association of Official Analytical Chemists (AOAC) is a unique, nonprofit scientific organization whose primary purpose is to serve the needs of government regulatory and research agencies for analytical methods. The goal of the Association is to provide methods which will perform with the necessary accuracy and precision under usual laboratory conditions (*1*). Since its formation in 1884 the AOAC has provided a mechanism to select methods of analysis from published literature or develop new methods, collaboratively test them through interlaboratory studies, approve them, and publish the approved methods for a wide variety of materials relating to foods, drugs, cosmetics, agriculture, forensic science, and products affecting the public health and welfare. Its membership is composed of scientists from Federal, State, Provincial, and other regulatory bodies who work within the AOAC's established procedures as researchers, methods collaborators, and committee members. Although most of the members are from North America, many nations throughout the world are represented.

The AOAC has almost a century of experience in utilizing the collaborative study as a means of determining the reliability of analytical methods for general purposes and, especially, for regulatory purposes. In fact, the AOAC's major contribution to analytical science has been to bring the collaborative study technique for the validation of analytical methods to a high degree of perfection. In such a study, laboratories analyze identical sample sets which cover the range of applicability of a method previously selected as being useful and practical. The purpose of the study is to establish the characteristics of the methods with respect to accuracy, precision, sensitivity, range, specificity, limit of detection, limit of reliable measurement, selectivity, practicality, and similar attributes, as required.

ORGANIZATION AND PROCEDURES FOR AOAC COLLABORATIVE STUDIES

The collaborative study is organized and directed by an analyst designated as the Associate Referee for the specific subject under investigation. Currently, some 600 Associate Referees appointed by the Association are responsible for as many topics. An Associate Referee is selected for his knowledge, interest, and experience in the subject matter field. He operates under the scientific guidance, support, and administrative supervision of a General Referee, who is in turn responsible for a product area. The Associate Referee reviews the literature and selects one or two of the better analytical methods available, modifying them as needed. Alternatively, he may develop or adapt a method used in his laboratory for the analyte and matrix under study, testing it thoroughly in his laboratory before designing a collaborative study. The General Referee is kept informed of such preliminary studies.

The samples analyzed in a collaborative study are normally prepared and distributed to the participants by the Associate Referee. The Association follows the recommendations of Youden (*2*) that not fewer than five laboratories participate and that a minimum of six sample materials be sent to each. These are minima and, in practice, both are usually exceeded. In addition, a reference or practice sample is included, where possible.

Laboratories with at least some experience in the general subject matter are selected as collaborators. Because the objective of the study is to standardize the method, as contrasted to standardizing the analyst (*3*), all analysts are instructed to follow the method exactly as written even though they may not concur with the Associate Referee's selection among possible alternatives. The level of the analyte in the samples is usually unknown to the participants.

All individual results obtained by the collaborators are reported to the Associate Referee, who compiles and evaluates them. Since statistical treatment of the data is considered essential in a rigorous evaluation of the method for accuracy, precision, sensitivity, and specificity, it is now required for all studies. The Association considers this of such importance that it provides statistical assistance in all cases where it is otherwise unavailable to the Associate Referee. A statistical manual (*4*) is also provided.

The Associate Referee makes the initial judgment on the performance of the method. If he recommends approval, it passes to the General Referee and then to a committee of experts. If both recommend approval, the method is presented at the Association's annual business meeting for vote by the membership.

Approved methods and supporting data are published in the *Journal of the Association of Official Analytical Chemists.* They are subject to scrutiny and general testing by other analysts for at least a year before final adoption. They may be modified and restudied collaboratively as needed, should feedback from general use reveal flaws in the method or in its written set of directions. Approved methods are included in the Association's "Official Methods of Analysis", a book of some 1000 pages which is updated every 4–5 years.

The preceding summary of AOAC's modus operandi recognizes the need for healthy skepticism toward results obtained by analytical methods which have not undergone such rigorous scrutiny and interlaboratory testing of their accuracy, precision, dependability, specificity, and practicality.

SELECTION OF METHODS FOR STUDY

A certain degree of variability is associated with all measurements. Much of the research on analytical chemistry is an attempt to minimize that variability. But there are many different types of variability in analytical work. We often find that when we attempt to minimize one kind, we must necessarily permit expansion in another kind. In practical analytical chemistry, the problem often comes down to which variability is to be minimized.

Some examples of this point may be helpful. In atomic weight determination, everything—especially *practicality*—is sacrificed for *accuracy.* A high degree of accuracy and practicality is required in the assay of precious metals, but the fire assay used is generally *applicable* to little else besides metals and minerals.

In clinical chemistry, within-laboratory *precision* (repeatability) is critical, and often is of greater interest to clinical laboratories than absolute accuracy or agreement with the values of other laboratories (reproducibility). In drug analysis, a high degree of accuracy is required in the therapeutic *range* because the analytical values determining the identity, strength, quality, and purity of pharmaceutical preparations, as laid down in pharmacopoeial specifications, are directly related to clinical value. With polynuclear hydrocarbons, *specificity* is important, since some of these compounds are carcinogenic while others are not. In applying the famous Delaney clause of the United States Federal Food, Drug, and Cosmetic Act, all attributes of the analytical methods are secondary to the detection of extremely small concentrations (*detectability*), or to exhibiting a high degree of response for small changes in concentration (*sensitivity*).

There is a very special case involving accuracy, where the "true value" is determined by the method of analysis. Many legal specifications and standards for food and agricultural products define ill-defined components such as moisture, fat, protein, and crude fiber in terms of reference methods. Therefore, the precision of these methods becomes the limiting factor for their performance. In fact, most analyses involved in commercial transactions require primarily that the buyer and seller agree on the same value (analytically and economically), regardless of where it stands on an absolute scale.

The point of these examples is that although methods of analysis are characterized by a number of attributes—accuracy, precision, specificity, sensitivity, detectability, dependability, and practicality—no method is so flawless that all these qualities can be maximized simultaneously. For any particular analysis, the analyst must determine, on the basis of the purpose of the analysis, which attributes are essential and which may be compromised.

Unfortunately, the literature is replete with examples indicating that an individual analyst, and especially the originator of a method of analysis, is not an unbiased judge of the relative merits of the methods of analysis which he develops and uses. In our experience, the collaborative study provides impartial data on the suitability of the method. The data, in many cases, speak for themselves.

The collaborative study, or ring test or round robin test, as it is called in other organizations, provides the basic information on the performance of analytical methods. The extent of the information will depend on the number of samples provided, the number of analyses performed, and the number of laboratories participating. The data should be unbiased because the composition of the samples is known only to the administrator of the study. Some of the requirements of the study and their relationship to the characteristics and attributes of the method are as follows:

(1) *Accuracy.* Samples must be of defined composition (by spiking, by formulation, or by analytical consensus).

(2) *Specificity.* Samples should contain related analytes.

(3) *Sensitivity.* Samples should differ from each other or from negative samples by a known amount.

(4) *Applicability.* Samples should include the concentration range and matrix components of interest.

(5) *Blanks.* Samples should include different matrices with "none" of the component of interest.

(6) *Precision.* Instructions should request replicate analyses by the same or different analysts in the same laboratory, preferably on different days. By far a better procedure is to include "blind" (unknown to the analyst) replicate samples in the series.

(7) *Practicality.* Instructions should request information as to the actual and elapsed time required for the analyses; the availability of reagents, equipment, and standards; and any necessary substitutions. When practice samples are included, the number of analyses required to achieve the stated recovery and repeatability, should be reported.

PROCEDURAL DETAILS OF COLLABORATIVE STUDY

As numerous beginners in this field have discovered, much preliminary work must be done before sending out samples:

(1) The method must be chosen and demonstrated to apply to the matrices and concentrations of interest.

(2) The critical variables in the method should have been determined and the need for their control emphasized [a ruggedness test (*5*) is useful for this purpose].

(3) The method should be written in detail by the Associate Referee and tested by an analyst not previously connected with its development.

(4) Unusual standards, reagents, and equipment must be available from usual commercial sources of supply, or sufficient quantities must be prepared or obtained to furnish to the participants.

(5) The samples must be identical and homogeneous so that the analytical sample error is only a negligible fraction of the expected analytical error.

(6) A sufficient number of samples must be prepared to cover typical matrices and the concentration range of interest (tolerance, maximum or minimum specifications, likely levels of occurrence, etc.).

(7) Samples must be stable and capable of surviving the rigors of commercial transportation.

(8) Reserve samples should be prepared and preserved to replace lost samples and to permit reanalysis of samples considered as outliers to attempt to discover the cause of abnormal results.

(9) The instructions must be clear. They should be reviewed by someone not connected with the study to uncover potential misunderstandings and ambiguities.

(10) If the analyte is subject to change (e.g., bacterial levels, nitroglycerin tablets), provision must be made for all participants to begin the analysis at the same time.

(11) Practice samples of a known and declared composition should be furnished with instructions not to analyze the unknowns until a specified degree of recovery and repeatability (or other attribute) has been achieved.

(12) Provision should be made when necessary for submission of standard curves, tracings of recorder charts, or photographs of thin-layer plates in order to assist in determining possible causes of error.

OTHER TYPES OF INTERLABORATORY STUDIES

This type of collaborative study, which is designed to determine the characteristics of a method, must be carefully distinguished from other types of interlaboratory studies which by design or through ignorance provide other kinds of information. The most important types of other studies are:

(1) Those studies which require the collaborators to investigate the variability of parts of methods or applicability to different types of samples. (An interlaboratory study is usually an inefficient way of obtaining this type of information.)

(2) Those studies which permit an analyst to use any method he desires. Such studies invariably produce such a wide scatter of results that the data are of little value for evaluation of methods. They may be useful in selecting a method from a number of apparently equivalent methods, provided the purpose

is emphasized beforehand and the participants provide a description of the method used in order to permit a correlation of the details of the methods with apparent biases and variabilities.

(3) Those studies which are used for quality control purposes, whose participants are not permitted sufficient time to gain familiarity with the method, or who permit deviations to enter into the performance of the analyses on the grounds that the deviation is obviously an improvement which could not possibly affect the results of the analysis, or who claim to have a superior method.

With this background information, it is now appropriate to introduce the following definitions which were agreed upon as part of the guidelines for collaboration between the AOAC and the Collaborative International Pesticide Analytical Council Ltd. (CIPAC) (*6*).

Collaborative study. An analytical study involving a number of laboratories analyzing the same sample(s) by the same method(s) for the purpose of validating the performance of the method(s).

Preliminary interlaboratory study. An analytical study in which two or more laboratories evaluate a method to determine if it is ready for a collaborative study.

Laboratory performance check. The analysis of very carefully prepared and homogeneous samples, normally of known active ingredient content, to establish or verify the performance of a laboratory or analyst.

SUMMARY

The collaborative study is an experiment designed to evaluate the performance of a method of analysis through the analysis of a number of identical samples by a number of different laboratories. With proper design, it provides an unbiased evaluation of the performance of a method in the hands of those analysts who will use it. A collaborative study must be distinguished from those studies designed to choose a method or to determine laboratory or analyst performance.

REFERENCES

(*1*) AOAC, "Handbook of the AOAC", 4th ed., AOAC, Box 540, Benjamin Franklin Station, Washington, D.C. 20044, 1977.

(*2*) W. J. Youden, "Accuracy of Analytical Procedures", *J. Assoc. Off. Anal. Chem.,* **45,** 169–73 (1962).

(*3*) Harold Egan, "Methods of Analysis; An Analysis of Methods", *ibid.,* **60,** 260–7 (1977).

(*4*) W. J. Youden and E. H. Steiner, "Statistical Manual of the AOAC: Statistical Techniques for Collaborative Tests. Planning and Analysis of Results of Collaborative Tests", AOAC, Box 540, Benjamin Franklin Station, Washington, D.C. 20044, 1975.

(*5*) W. J. Youden, "The Collaborative Test", *J. Assoc. Off. Anal. Chem.,* **46,** 55–62 (1963).

(*6*) "Guidelines for Collaboration Between the Association of Official Analytical Chemists (AOAC) and the Collaborative International Pesticide Analytical Council Ltd. (CIPAC)", *ibid.,* **57,** 447–9 (1974).

BIBLIOGRAPHY

Daniel Banes, "The Collaborative Study as a Scientific Concept", *J. Assoc. Off. Anal. Chem.,* **52,** 203–06 (1969).

William Horwitz, "Problems of Sampling and Analytical Methods", *ibid.,* **59,** 1197–203 (1976).

Reprinted with permission from: *Analytical Chemistry* (March 1978) **50,** 337A–340A.
Published 1978 American Chemical Society

Definitions of Terms and Explanatory Notes

Reagents

(1) Term "H_2O" means distilled water, except where otherwise specified, and except where the water does not mix with the detn, as in "H_2O bath."

(2) Term "alcohol" means 95% ethanol by vol. Alcohol of strength *x*% may be prepd by dilg *x* mL 95% alcohol to 95 mL with H_2O. Absolute alcohol is 99.5% by vol. Formulae of specially denatured alcohols (SDA) used as reagents are as follows:

SDA No.	100	parts alcohol plus
1	5	wood alcohol
2-B	0.5	benzene or rubber hydrocarbon solv.
3-A	5	MeOH
12-A	5	benzene
13-A	10	ether
23-A	10	acetone
30	10	MeOH

"Reagent" alcohol is 95 parts SDA 3-A plus 5 parts isopropanol.

(3) Term "ether" means ethyl ether, peroxide-free by following test: To 420 mL ether in separator add 9.0 mL 1% NH_4VO_3 in H_2SO_4 (1+16). Shake 3 min and let sep. Drain lower layer into 25 mL g-s graduate, dil. to 10 mL with H_2SO_4 (1+16), and mix. Any orange color should not exceed that produced by 0.30 mg H_2O_2 (1 mL of soln prepd by dilg 1 mL 30% H_2O_2 to 100 mL with H_2O) and 9.0 mL 1% NH_4VO_3 in H_2SO_4 (1+16). Peroxides may be eliminated by passing ≤700 mL ether thru 10 cm column of Woelm basic alumina in 22 mm id tube.

(4) Reagents listed below, unless otherwise specified, have approx. strength stated and conform in purity with Recommended Specifications for Analytical Reagent Chemicals of American Chemical Society:

	Assay
Sulfuric Acid	95.0–98.0% H_2SO_4
Hydrochloric acid	36.5–38.0% HCl
Nitric acid	69.0–71.0% HNO_3
Fuming nitric acid	≥90% HNO_3
Acetic acid	≥99.7% $HC_2H_3O_2$
Hydrobromic acid	47.0–49.0% HBr
Ammonium hydroxide	28–30% NH_3
Phosphoric acid	≥85% H_3PO_4

Where no indication of diln is given, reagent is of concn given above.

(5) All other reagents and test solns, unless otherwise described in text, conform to requirements of American Chemical Society. Where such specifications have not been prepd, use highest grade reagent. When anhyd. salt is intended, it is so stated; otherwise the crystd product is meant.

(6) Unless otherwise specified, phenolphthalein (phthln) used as indicator is 1% alc. soln; Me orange is 0.1% aq. soln; Me red is 0.1% alc. soln.

(7) Directions for stdzg reagents are given in Chapter **50**.

(8) Unusual reagents not mentioned in reagent sections or cross referenced, other than common reagents normally found in laboratory, are italicized first time they occur in method.

(9) Com. prepd reagent solns must be checked for applicability to specific method. They may contain undeclared buffers, preservatives, chelating agents, etc.

(10) In expressions (1+2), (5+4), etc., used in connection with name of reagent, first numeral indicates vol. reagent used, and second numeral indicates vol. H_2O. For example, HCl (1+2) means reagent prepd by mixing 1 vol. HCl with 2 vols H_2O. When one of reagents is solid, expression means parts by wt, first numeral representing solid reagent and second numeral H_2O. Solns for which the solv. is not specified are aq. solns.

(11) In making up solns of definite percentage, it is understood that *x* g substance is dissolved in H_2O and dild to 100 mL. Altho not theoretically correct, this convention will not result in any appreciable error in any of methods given in this book.

(12) Chromic acid cleaning soln is prepd by (*1*) adding 1 L H_2SO_4 to ca 35 mL satd aq. $Na_2Cr_2O_7$ soln; or (*2*) adding 2220 mL (9 lb) H_2SO_4 to ca 25 mL satd aq. CrO_3 soln (170 g/100 mL). Reagents may be tech. grade. Use only after first cleaning by other means (e.g., detergent) and draining. Mixt. is expensive and hazardous. Use repeatedly until it is dild or has a greenish tinge. Discard carefully with copious amts of H_2O.

(13) All calcns are based on table of international atomic weights, **52.001**.

Apparatus

(14) Burets, vol. flasks, and pipets conform to following Federal specifications (available from General Services Admin., Specification Activity 3F1, Washington Navy Yard, Bldg. 197, Washington, DC 20407):

Buret	NNN-B-00789a	May 19, 1965
Flask, vol.	NNN-F-00289d	Feb 7, 1977
Pipet, vol.	NNN-P-395c	March 13, 1970
Pipet, measuring	NNN-P-350c	July 16, 1973

See also NBS Circular 602, "Testing of Glass Volumetric Apparatus" (available as Com 73-10504 from NTIS, Springfield, VA 22151).

(15) Standard taper (₮) glass joints may be used instead of stoppers where the latter are specified or implied for connecting glass app.

(16) Sieve designations, unless otherwise specified, are those described in Federal Specification RR-S-366e, Nov 9, 1973 (available from General Services Admin.). Designation " '100-mesh' (or other number) powder (material, etc.)" means material ground to pass thru std sieve No. 100 (or other number). Corresponding international std and US std sieves are given in Table 1.

(17) Term "paper" means filter paper, unless otherwise specified.

(18) Term "high-speed blender" designates mixer with 4 canted, sharp-edge, stainless steel blades rotating at the bottom of 4-lobe jar at 10,000–12,000 rpm, or with equiv. shearing action. Suspended solids are reduced to fine pulp by action of blades and by lobular container, which swirls suspended solids into blades. Waring Blendor, or equiv., meets these requirements.

(19) "Flat-end rod" is glass rod with one end flattened by heating to softening in flame and pressing vertically on flat surface to form circular disk with flat bottom at end.

(20) Designation and pore diam. range of fritted glassware are: extra coarse, 170–220 μm; coarse, 40–60; medium, 10–15; fine, 4–5.5; Jena designations and pore diam. are: 1, 110 μm; 2, 45; 3, 25; 4, 8.

(21) Unless otherwise indicated, temps are expressed as degrees Centigrade.

Table 1. Nominal Dimensions of Standard Test Sieves (U.S.A. Standard Series)

Sieve Designation		Nominal Sieve Opening, inches	Nominal Wire Diameter, mm
International Standard[a] (ISO)	U.S.A. Standard		
12.5 mm[b]	1/2 in.[b]	0.500	2.67
11.2 mm	7/16 in.	0.438	2.45
9.5 mm	3/8 in.	0.375	2.27
8.0 mm	5/16 in.	0.312	2.07
6.7 mm	0.265 in.	0.265	1.87
6.3 mm[b]	1/4 in.[b]	0.250	1.82
5.6 mm	No. 3 1/2	0.223	1.68
4.75 mm	No. 4	0.187	1.54
4.00 mm	No. 5	0.157	1.37
3.35 mm	No. 6	0.132	1.23
2.80 mm	No. 7	0.111	1.10
2.38 mm	No. 8	0.0937	1.00
2.00 mm	No. 10	0.0787	0.900
1.70 mm	No. 12	0.0661	0.810
1.40 mm	No. 14	0.0555	0.725
1.18 mm	No. 16	0.0469	0.650
1.00 mm	No. 18	0.0394	0.580
850 μm[c]	No. 20	0.0331	0.510
710 μm	No. 25	0.0278	0.450
600 μm	No. 30	0.0234	0.390
500 μm	No. 35	0.0197	0.340
425 μm	No. 40	0.0165	0.290
355 μm	No. 45	0.0139	0.247
300 μm	No. 50	0.0117	0.215
250 μm	No. 60	0.0098	0.180
212 μm	No. 70	0.0083	0.152
180 μm	No. 80	0.0070	0.131
150 μm	No. 100	0.0059	0.110
125 μm	No. 120	0.0049	0.091
106 μm	No. 140	0.0041	0.076
90 μm	No. 170	0.0035	0.064
75 μm	No. 200	0.0029	0.053
63 μm	No. 230	0.0025	0.044
53 μm	No. 270	0.0021	0.037

[a] These standard designations correspond to the values for test sieve apertures recommended by the International Organization for Standardization, Geneva, Switzerland.

[b] These sieves are not in the standard series but they have been included because they are in common usage.

[c] 1000 μm = 1 mm.

Standard Operations

(22) Operations specified as "wash (rinse, ext. etc.) with two (three, four, etc.) 10 mL (or other vol.) portions H_2O (or other solv.)" mean that the operation is to be performed with indicated vol. of solv. and repeated with same vol. of solv. until number of portions required have been used.

(23) Definitions of terms used in methods involving spectrophotometry are those given in JAOAC **37,** 54(1954). Most important principles and definitions are:

(a) More accurate instrument may be substituted for less accurate instrument (e.g., spectrophtr may replace colorimeter) where latter is specified in method. Wavelength specified in method is understood to be that of max. absorbance (A), unless no peak is present.

(b) *Absorbance(s)* (A).—Neg. logarithm to base 10 of ratio of transmittance (T) of sample to that of ref. or std material. Other names that have been used for quantity represented by this term are optical density, extinction, and absorbancy.

(c) *Absorptivity(ies)* (a).—Absorbance per unit concn and cell length. $a = A/bc$, where b is in cm and c in g/L, or $a = (A/bc) \times 1000$, if c is in mg/L. Other names that have been used for this or related quantities are extinction coefficient, specific absorption, absorbance index, and $E^{1\%}_{1cm}$.

(d) *Transmittance(s)* (T).—Ratio of radiant power transmitted by sample to radiant power incident on sample, when both are measured at same spectral position and with same slit width. Beam is understood to be parallel radiation and incident at right angles to plane parallel surface of sample. If sample is soln, solute transmittance is quantity usually desired and is detd directly as ratio of transmittance of soln in cell to transmittance of solv. in an equal cell. Other names that have been used for this quantity are transmittancy and transmission.

(e) *Standardization.*—Spectrophtr may be checked for accuracy of wavelength scale by ref. to Hg lines: 239.95, 248.3, 253.65, 265.3, 280.4, 302.25, 313.16, 334.15, 365.43, 404.66, 435.83, 546.07, 578.0, and 1014.0 nm. To check consistency of absorbance scale, prep. soln of 0.0400 g K_2CrO_4/L 0.05N KOH and det. absorbance at following wavelengths in 1 cm cell: 230 nm, 0.171; 275, 0.757; 313.2, 0.043; 375, 0.991; 400, 0.396. *See* "Standards for Checking the Calibration of Spectrophotometers," Letter Circular LC-1017, reissued Jan 1967, NBS.

(24) *Least square treatment of data and calculation of regression lines.*—This technic finds the best fitting straight line for set of data such as std curve. It calcs that straight line whose sum of squares of vertical deviations (usually A) of observations from the line is smaller than corresponding sum of squares of deviations from any other line. Equation of straight line is:

$$Y = a + bX,$$

where a is intercept at Y axis ($X = 0$), and b is slope of line.

Least square estimates of constants are:

$$b = \frac{\Sigma(X_iY_i) - [(\Sigma X_i \Sigma Y_i)/n]}{\Sigma X_i^2 - (\Sigma X_i)^2/n}$$

$$a = \bar{Y} - b\bar{X},$$

where Σ = "sum of" the n individual values of indicated operation, and $\bar{X}$ and $\bar{Y}$ are the averages of the X and Y points.

Example: To find "best" straight line relating A (Y) to concn (X):

Observation No. ($_i$)	Concn X_i	Absorbance Y_i	X_i^2	X_iY_i
1	80	1.270	6400	101.6
2	60	1.000	3600	60.0
3	40	0.700	1600	28.0
4	30	0.550	900	16.5
5	20	0.250	400	5.0
6	10	0.100	100	1.0
7	0	0.050	0	0.0
Totals: $n = 7$	$\Sigma X_i = 240$	$\Sigma Y_i = 3.92$	$\Sigma X_i^2 = 13000$	$\Sigma(X_iY_i) = 212.1$

$$\bar{X} = \Sigma X_i/n = 240/7 = 34.29$$

$$\bar{Y} = \Sigma Y_i/n = 3.92/7 = 0.56$$

$$b = \frac{212.1 - (240)(3.92)/7}{13000 - (240)^2/7} = \frac{77.7}{4771} = 0.0163$$

$$a = 0.56 - 0.0163(34.29) = 0.001$$

Best equation is then:

$$Y = 0.00 + 0.0163X$$

If for sample, $A = 0.82$, corresponding concn (X) would be:

$$X = (Y - 0.00)/0.0163 = 0.82/0.0163 = 50.3.$$

Many scientific and statistical calculators are preprogrammed to perform this calcn.

(25) Common safety precautions are given in Chapter **51**.

Editorial Conventions

(26) For sake of simplicity, abbreviations Cl and I instead of Cl_2 and I_2 are used for chlorine and iodine. Similar abbreviations have been used in other cases (O, N, H). The same abbreviation may also be used for the ion where no ambiguity will result.

(27) Reagents and app. referenced with only a letter, e.g., (**c**), will be found in the reagent or apparatus section of that method.

(28) To conserve space, most of the articles and some prepositions have been eliminated.

(29) Names and addresses of manufacturers and suppliers, and trade names of frequently mentioned materials, are furnished below solely as a matter of identification and convenience, without implication of approval, endorsement, or certification. The same products available from other suppliers or other brands from other sources may serve equally well if proper tests indicate their use is satisfactory. These firms when mentioned in a method are given by name only (without addresses).

Manufacturers and Suppliers

Ace Glass, Inc., PO Box 688, 1430 N West Blvd, Vineland, NJ 08360

Aldrich Chemical Co., Inc., 940 W St. Paul Ave, Milwaukee, WI 53233

Allied Chemical Corp., Specialty Chemicals Div., PO Box 1087R, Morristown, NJ 07960

Aluminum Company of America, 1501 Alcoa Bldg, Pittsburgh, PA 15219

American Cyanamid Co., Agricultural Div., PO Box 400, Princeton, NJ 08540

American Instrument Co., Div. of Travenol Laboratories, Inc., 8030 Georgia Ave, Silver Spring, MD 20910

(*ASBC*) American Society of Brewing Chemists, 3340 Pilot Knob Rd, St. Paul, MN 55121

(*ATCC*) American Type Culture Collection, 12301 Parklawn Dr, Rockville, MD 20852

Analabs Inc., 80 Republic Dr, North Haven, CT 06473

Applied Science Laboratories, Inc. (Applied Science Division, Milton Roy Co.), PO Box 440, State College, PA 16801

Baird-Atomic, Inc., 125 Middlesex Tnpk, Bedford, MA 01730

J. T. Baker Chemical Co., 222 Red School Ln, Phillipsburg, NJ 08865

Barber-Colman Co., see *Searle Analytic, Inc.*

Bausch & Lomb, Inc., Analytical Systems Div., 820 Linden Ave, Rochester, NY 14625

BBL, Div. of Bioquest, PO Box 243, Cockeysville, MD 21030

Beckman Instruments, Inc., 2500 Harbor Blvd, Fullerton, CA 92634

Becton, Dickinson, & Co., Rutherford, NJ 07070

Bio-Rad Laboratories, 32nd and Griffin Ave, Richmond, CA 94804

Brinkmann Instruments, Inc., Cantiague Rd, Westbury, NY 11590

Burdick & Jackson Laboratories, Inc., 1953 S Harvey St, Muskegon, MI 49442

Burrell Corp., 2223 Fifth Ave, Pittsburgh, PA 15219

Calbiochem, 10933 N Torrey Pines Rd, La Jolla, CA 92037

Carborundum Co., PO Box 423, Niagara Falls, NY 14302

Cenco Inc., 2600 S Kostner Ave, Chicago, IL 60623

Coleman Instruments Division, Perkin-Elmer Corp., 2000 York Rd, Oak Brook, IL 60521

Corning Glass Works, Laboratory Products Dept., Corning, NY 14830

Curtin Matheson Scientific, Inc., PO Box 1546, Houston, TX 77001

Difco Laboratories, PO Box 1058A, Detroit, MI 48232

Dohrmann Div. of Envirotech Corp., 3240 Scott Blvd, Santa Clara, CA 95050

Dow Chemical Co., Ag-Organics Dept., PO Box 1706, Midland, MI 48640

Dow Corning Corp., Midland, MI 48640

E. I. du Pont de Nemours & Co., Wilmington, DE 19898

Eastman Kodak Co., Eastman Organic Chemicals, 343 State St, Rochester, NY 14650

Eaton-Dikeman Co., Mt. Holly Springs, PA 17065

Elanco Products Co., Div. of Eli Lilly Co., Elanco Analytical Laboratory, Dept. MC757, Indianapolis, IN 46206

Fisher & Porter Co., Lab Crest Scientific Div., County Line Rd, Warminster, PA 18974

Fisher Scientific Co., 711 Forbes Ave, Pittsburgh, PA 15219

Floridin Co., Berkeley Springs, WV 25411

Foss America Inc., PO Box 504, Route 82, Fishkill, NY 12524

GAF Corp., 140 W 51st St, New York, NY 10020

G.B. Fermentation Industries, Inc., 1 N Broadway, Des Plaines, IL 60016

Geigy Chemical Corp., Saw Mill River Rd, Ardsley, NY 10502

Hamilton Co., PO Box 17500, Reno NV 89510

Hess & Clark Laboratories, Div. of Rhodia, Inc., 7th and Orange Sts, Ashland, OH 44805

Hewlett-Packard Co., 1501 Page Mill Rd, Palo Alto, CA 94304

Hoffman-La Roche, Inc., Nutley, NJ 07110

ICI-America, Inc., Chemical Research Dept., Wilmington, DE 19899

ICN—K&K Laboratories, Inc., 121 Express St, Plainview, NY 11803

ICN Pharmaceuticals, Inc., Life Sciences Group, 26201 Miles Rd, Cleveland, OH 44128

Johns-Manville Products Corp., Greenwood Plaza, Denver, CO 80217

Kimble Products, Owens-Illinois, PO Box 1035, Toledo, OH 43666

Kontes Glass Co., Spruce St, Vineland, NJ 08360

Labconco Corp., 8811 Prospect Ave, Kansas City, MO 64132

Eli Lilly & Co., 740 S Alabama St, Indianapolis, IN 46206

Mallinckrodt Chemicals Works, Science Products Div., 2nd & Mallinckrodt Sts, St. Louis, MO 63147

MC/B Manufacturing Chemists, 2909 Highland Ave, Norwood, OH 45212

Matheson Scientific, Inc., see *Curtin Matheson Scientific, Inc.*

Merck & Co., Inc., 126 E Lincoln Ave, Rahway, NJ 07065

Miles Laboratories, Inc., Elkhart, IN 46514

Monsanto Chemical Co., 800 N Lindberg Blvd, St. Louis, MO 63166

(*NBS*) National Bureau of Standards, Washington, DC 20234

(*NF*) National Formulary, *see USP*

New York Laboratory Supply Co., 510 Hempstead Tnpk, West Hempstead, NY 11552

Orion Research Inc., 380 Putnam Ave, Cambridge, MA 02139

Perkin-Elmer Corp., 702-G Main Ave, Norwalk, CT 06856

Phillips Chemical Co., Division of Phillips Petroleum Co., Specialty Chemicals, Drawer 'O', Borger, TX 79007.

Pierce Chemical Co., PO Box 117, Rockford, IL 61105

H. Reeve Angel & Co., Inc., 9 Bridewell Pl, Clifton, NJ 07014

Rohm & Haas Co., Independence Mall West, Philadelphia, PA 19105

Salsbury Laboratories, Charles City, IA 50616

Sargent-Welch Scientific Co., 7300 N Linder Ave, Skokie, IL 60076

(*S&S*) Schleicher & Schuell, Inc., 543 Washington St, Keene, NH 03431

Schoeffel Instrument Corp., 24 Booker St, Westwood, NJ 07675
SGA Scientific, Inc., 735 Broad St, Bloomfield, NJ 07003
Scientific Products, Div. of American Hospital Supply Corp., 1430 Waukegan Rd, McGaw Park, IL 60085
Searle Analytic, Inc., 2000 Nuclear Dr, Des Plaines, IL 60018
Shell Oil Co., PO Box 2463, Houston, TX 77001
Sigma Chemical Co., PO Box 14508, St. Louis, MO 63178
G. Frederick Smith Chemical Co., PO Box 23344, Columbus, OH 43223
Sterwin Chemicals, Inc., 90 Park Ave, New York, NY 10016
Supelco, Bellefonte, PA 16823
Technicon Instruments Corp., 511 Benedict Ave, Tarrytown, NY 10591
Arthur H. Thomas Co., Vine St at 3rd, PO Box 779, Philadelphia, PA 19105
Ultra-Violet Products, Inc., 5100 Walnut Grove Ave, San Gabriel, CA 91778
Union Carbide Corp., Chemicals and Plastics, 270 Park Ave, New York, NY 10017
Union Carbide Corp., Agricultural Products and Services, PO Box 1906, Salinas, CA 93901
Uniroyal Chemical, Elm St, Naugatuck, CT 06770
The Upjohn Co., Kalamazoo, MI 49001
(*USDA*) U.S. Department of Agriculture, Office of Information, Washington, DC 20250
(*USP*) United States Pharmacopeial Convention, Inc., 12601 Twinbrook Pkwy, Rockville, MD 20852
Varian Aerograph, 2700 Mitchell Dr, Walnut Creek, CA 94598
Varian Instrument Div., 611 Hansen Way, Palo Alto. CA 94303
Velsicol Chemical Corp., 341 E Ohio St, Chicago, IL 60611
VWR Scientific, PO Box 3200, San Francisco, CA 94119
Wallerstein Co., see G. B. Fermentation Industries, Inc.
Waters Associates, Inc., Maple St, Milford, MA 01757
Winthrop Laboratories, Special Chemicals Dept., 90 Park Ave, New York, NY 10016

Trade Names

Amberlite. Ion exchange resins. Rohm and Haas Co.
Anakrom. Gas chromatography supports. Analabs, Inc.
Celite. Diatomaceous products. Johns-Manville Products Corp.
Chromosorb. Chromatographic supports and packings. Johns-Manville Products Corp.
Dowex. Ion exchange resins. Dow Chemical Co.
Florisil. Chromatographic adsorbents. Floridin Co.
Gas-Chrom. Gas chromatography solid supports. Applied Science Laboratories, Inc.
Hyflo Super-Cel. Diatomaceous products. Johns-Manville Products Corp.
Skellysolve. Hydrocarbon solvents. Getty Refining and Marketing Co., PO Box 1650, Tulsa, OK 74102
Teflon. Chemically resistant polytetrafluoroethylene. E. I. du Pont de Nemours & Co.
Tygon. Halogenated vinyl plastic. Norton Co., Plastics & Synthetics Div., 12 E Ave, Tallmadge, OH 44278

(30) The folllowing abbreviations, many of which conform with those of *Chemical Abstracts*, are used. In general, principle governing use of periods after abbreviations is that period is used where final letter of abbreviation is not the same as final letter of word it represents. Periods are not used with units, except inch(es) and gallon(s).

Abbreviation	*Word*
a	absorptivity(ies)
A	absorbance(s) thruout (not restricted to formulas); not absorption. *A'* is used for std; A_0 for blank; 3 digit subscript numerals usually denote wavelengths in nm
AA	atomic absorption
Ac	CH_3CO- (acetyl, not acetate)
ACS	American Chemical Society
addn	addition
addnl	additional
alc.	alcoholic (not alcohol)
alk.	alkaline (not alkali)
alky	alkalinity
amp	ampere(s)
amt	amount
anal.	analytical(ly)
anhyd.	anhydrous
AOCS	American Oil Chemists' Society
app.	apparatus
approx.	approximate(ly)
aq.	aqueous
ASTM	American Society for Testing and Materials
atm.	atmosphere, atmospheric
av.	average (except as verb)
Bé.	degree Baumé
bp	boiling point
Bu	butyl
C	degrees Celsius (Centigrade)
ca	about, approximately
calc.	calculate
calcd	calculated
calcg	calculating
calcn	calculation
Cat. No.	Catalog Number
centrf.	centrifuge
centrfd	centrifuged
centrfg	centrifuging
Chap.	Chapter
chem.	chemical(ly)
chromatgc	chromatographic
chromatgd	chromatographed
chromatgy	chromatography
Ci	curie(s)
CI	Color Index
CIPAC	Collaborative International Pesticides Analytical Council
cm	centimeter(s)
compd	compound
com.	commercial(ly)
conc.	concentrate (as verb or noun)
concd	concentrated
concg	concentrating
concn	concentration
const	constant
contg	containing
cP	centipoise
cpm	counts per minute
cryst.	crystalline (not crystallize)
crystd	crystallized
crystg	crystallizing
crystn	crystallization
cu in.	cubic inch(es)
dc	direct current
det.	determine
detd	determined

Abbreviation	*Word*
detg	determining
detn	determination
diam.	diameter
diat. earth	diatomaceous earth
dil.	dilute
dild	diluted
dilg	diluting
diln	dilution
distd	distilled
distg	distilling
distn	distillation
DMF	*N,N*-dimethylformamide
DMSO	dimethyl sulfoxide
EDTA	ethylenedinitrilotetraacetic acid (or -tetra-acetate)
e.g.	for example
elec.	electric(al)
equiv.	equivalent
est.	estimate
estd	estimated
estg	estimating
estn	estimation
Et	ethyl
EtOH	ethanol (the chemical entity C_2H_5OH)
evap.	evaporate
evapd	evaporated
evapg	evaporating
evapn	evaporation
ext	extract
extd	extracted
extg	extracting
extn	extraction
F	degrees Fahrenheit (°C = (5/9) × (°F − 32))
FAO	Food and Agriculture Organization
Fig.	Figure (illustration)
fl oz	fluid ounce(s) (29.57 mL)
fp	freezing point
ft	foot (30.48 cm)
g	gram(s)
g	gravity (in centrfg)
gal.	gallon(s) (3.785 L)
GLC	gas-liquid chromatography
g-s	glass-stoppered
HCHO	formaldehyde
HOAc	acetic acid (not HAc)
HPLC	high pressure (or performance) liquid chromatography
hr	hour(s)
ht	height
id	inner diameter (or dimension)
in.	inch(es) (2.54 cm)
inorg.	inorganic
insol.	insoluble
IR	infrared
ISO	International Organization for Standardization
JAOAC	Journal of the Association of Official Analytical Chemists (after 1965)
	Journal of the Association of Official Agricultural Chemists (before 1966)
kg	kilogram(s)
L	liter(s)
lb	pound(s) (453.6 g)
liq.	liquid
m	meter(s); milli—as prefix

Abbreviation	*Word*
m	molal
M	molar (as applied to concn), not molal
ma	milliampere (cf amp)
mag.	magnetic(ally)
max.	maximum
mech.	mechanical(ly)
Me	methyl
MeOH	methyl alcohol
mg	milligram(s)
min	minute(s)
min.	minimum
mixt.	mixture
mL	milliliter(s)
mm	millimeter(s)
mp	melting point
mμ	millimicron (10^{-6} mm); use nanometer (nm) (10^{-9} m)
mv	millivolt
MW	molecular weight
N	normal (as applied to concn); in equations, normality of titrating reagent
N	Newton (10^5 dynes)
n	refractive index
NBS	National Bureau of Standards
NCA	National Canners Association (now National Food Processors Association)
neg.	negative
neut.	neutral
neutze	neutralize
neutzd	neutralized
neutzg	neutralizing
neutzn	neutralization
NF	National Formulary
ng	nanogram (10^{-9} g)
nm	nanometer (10^{-9} m); formerly mμ
No.	number
-OAc	acetate (cf Ac)
-OCN	cyanate
od	outer diameter (or dimension)
org.	organic
oxidn	oxidation
oz	ounce(s) (28.35 g)
p	pico (10^{-12}) as prefix
Pa	Pascal (1 Newton/m^2; 9.87 × 10^{-6} atm.; 7.5 × 10^{-3} mm Hg (torr); 1.45 × 10^{-4} psi)
par.	paragraph(s)
pet ether	petroleum ether
phthln	phenolphthalein
pos.	positive
powd	powdered (as adjective)
ppb	parts per billion (1/10^9)
ppm	parts per million (1/10^6)
ppt	precipitate
pptd	precipitated
pptg	precipitating
pptn	precipitation
Pr	propyl
prep.	prepare
prepd	prepared
prepg	preparing
prepn	preparation
psi	pounds per square inch (absolute)
psig	pounds per square inch gage (atmospheric pressure = 0)
pt	pint(s) (473 mL)

Abbreviation	*Word*
QAC	quaternary ammonium compound
qt	quart(s) (946 mL)
qual.	qualitative(ly)
quant.	quantitative(ly)
®	Trademark name—(Registered)
R_f	distance spot moved/distance solv. moved (TLC)
r-b	round-bottom (flask)
ref.	reference
resp.	respectively
rpm	revolutions per minute
sat.	saturate
satd	saturated
satg	saturating
satn	saturation
-SCN	thiocyanate
SDF	special denatured formula (applied to alcohol)
sec	second(s)
sep.	separate(ly)
sepd	separated
sepg	separating
sepn	separation
sol.	soluble
soln	solution
solv.	solvent
sp gr	specific gravity (apparent density)
spectrophtr	spectrophotometer
spectrophtric	spectrophotometric(ally)
sq	square
SRM	Standard Reference Material of National Bureau of Standards
std	standard
std dev.	standard deviation
stdzd	standardized
stdze	standardize
stdzg	standardizing
stdzn	standardization
T	transmittance
tech.	technical
temp.	temperature
titr.	titrate
titrd	titrated
titrg	titrating
titrn	itration
TLC	thin layer chromatography
USDA	United States Department of Agriculture

Abbreviation	*Word*
USP	United States Pharmacopeia
UV	ultraviolet
v	volt(s)
v/v	both components measured by vol.
vac.	vacuum
vol.	volume; also volumetric when used with flask
w/w	both components measured by wt
WHO	World Health Organization
wt	weight
μ	micron (0.001 mm); use micrometer (μm) (10^{-6} m)
μg	microgram(s) (10^{-6} g)
μL	microliter(s) (10^{-6} L)
μm	micrometer(s) (10^{-6} m); formerly μ
Δ	difference (*e.g.,* $\Delta A = (A - A')$)
′	foot (feet) (1′ = 30.48 cm)
″	inch(es) (1″ = 2.54 cm)
/	per
%	per cent (parts per 100); percentage
>	more than; greater than; above; exceeds (use with numbers only)
<	less than; under; below (use with numbers only)
≤	not more than; not greater than; equal to or less than
≥	not less than; equal to or greater than; equal to or more than; at least
₸	standard taper
$	standard spherical joint

(31) ★ This symbol indicates a method which is in or is being considered for "surplus" status. Such methods are satisfactory methods, having been subjected to collaborative studies and review. They are thought not to be in current use for various reasons: The purpose for which they were developed no longer exists; the product for which they were developed no longer is marketed; they have been replaced by other methods; etc. These methods retain their official status but are carried in this or next edition only by ref. Any laboratory who uses these methods and wishes the text retained or reprinted in next edition must so notify the AOAC.

(32) Nos. appearing in titles of methods in bold face refer to the Selected References at the end of the Chap. These refs often contain the performance data supporting the adoption of the method.

1. Agricultural Liming Materials

1.001 Sampling (*1*)—Procedure

(*Caution: See* **51.036.**)

Take sample representative of lot or shipment. Avoid disproportionate amt of surface or any modified or damaged zone.

(**a**) *Burnt or lump lime, in bulk.*—Collect composite sample of ≥10 shovelfuls/car, with proportionate amts from smaller lots, taking each shovelful from different part of lot or shipment. Immediately crush to pass 5 cm (2") diam. circular opening, mix thoroly and rapidly, reduce composite to ca 2 kg (5 lb) sample by riffling or quartering, and place in labeled, dry, air-tight container.

(**b**) *Hydrated lime and ground burnt lime, in bags.*—Select 10 bags from different parts of each lot or shipment of ≤20 tons and 1 addnl bag for each addnl 5 tons. Use sampling tube to withdraw top to bottom core from each bag selected. Combine cores, mix thoroly and rapidly, reduce composite to ca 1 kg (2 lb) by riffling or quartering, and place in dry, air-tight container.

(**c**) *Ground limestone and ground marl, in bags.*—Proceed as in (**b**).

(**d**) *Ground limestone, ground burnt lime, ground marl, and slag, in bulk.*—Use slotted sampling tube to withdraw samples to full sampler depth from 10 points in lot or shipment. Proceed as in (**b**), beginning "Combine cores, . . ."

1.002 Mechanical Analysis (*2*)—Procedure

(*Caution: See* **51.036.**)

If entire sample is not to be dried, obtain lesser portions by riffling or quartering. Dry at 110° to const wt and cool to room temp.

Obtain 90–150 g dry sample by riffling or quartering. Break any agglomerates formed during drying by rolling dry sample with hard rubber roller on hard rubber mat, wet sieving as in **2.011(a)**, or by equally effective means that does not result in crushing the limestone. (If wet sieving is used to break agglomerates, do wet sieving on sieve having smallest opening to be used in final testing. After drying, transfer to sieves to be used in final testing. If only 1 sieve is to be used, do not transfer.) Quant. transfer weighed sample to 8" diam. std sieve or set of sieves (e.g., Nos. 10, 20, 40, 60, 80, and 100 or other appropriate combination).

Sieve by lateral and vertical motion accompanied by jarring action. Continue ≥5 min or until addnl 3 min of sieving time fails to change results of any sieve fraction by 0.5% of total sample wt. Do not overload any sieve when assaying closely sized materials.

Det. wt of each sieve fraction and report as % of total sample wt.

1.003 Preparation of Sample (*1*)—Procedure

Reduce dried sample, **1.002**, to amt sufficient for analysis and grind ≥225 g (0.5 lb) reduced sample in mortar, ball mill, or other mech. app. to pass No. 60 sieve. Mix thoroly, and store in air-tight container.

Neutralizing Value—Official Final Action

(Uncorrected for sulfide content)

1.004 ***Reagents***

(**a**) *Sodium hydroxide std soln.*—0.25*N*. Prep. and stdze as in **50.032–50.036**.

(**b**) *Hydrochloric acid std soln.*—0.5*N*. Stdze against (**a**), using phthln.

1.005 *Indicator Titration Method*

Place 0.5 g burnt or hydrated lime (1 g ground limestone or ground marl), prepd as in **1.003**, in 250 mL erlenmeyer; add 50 mL HCl std soln and boil *gently* 5 min. Cool, and titr. excess acid with NaOH std soln, using phthln. For burnt and hydrated lime, report as % CaO; for limestone and marl, report as % $CaCO_3$ equivalence.

% $CaCO_3$ equivalence of sample = 2.5 × (mL HCl − mL NaOH/2).

% CaO equivalence = 2.8 × (mL HCl − mL NaOH/2).

1.006 *Potentiometric Titration Method* (*3*)

(Applicable to liming materials contg large amt of Fe^{+2} or coloring matter, but not to silicate materials)

Proceed as in **1.005** thru "Cool, . . ." Transfer to 250 mL beaker and insert glass and calomel electrodes of pH meter, buret contg 0.25*N* NaOH, and mech. stirrer. Stir at moderate speed to avoid splash. Deliver NaOH rapidly to pH 5, then dropwise until soln attains pH 7 and remains const 1 min while stirring. (If end point is passed, add, from 1 mL Mohr pipet, just enough 0.5*N* HCl to bring pH to <7, and back-titr. slowly to pH 7.) Add mL of excess acid, if used, to initial 50 mL in calcg. Report as % $CaCO_3$ or CaO equivalence as in **1.005**.

1.007 *Approximate Proportions of Calcium and Magnesium in Magnesic Limestone*

Slightly acidify titrd soln, **1.005** or **1.006**, transfer to 250 mL vol. flask, and dil. to vol. Det. Ca in 50 mL aliquot as in **7.096**, beginning ". . . dil. to ca 100 mL . . ." Subtract its $CaCO_3$ equivalence from total $CaCO_3$ equivalence, **1.005** or **1.006**, and assign difference as $CaCO_3$ equivalence of the Mg content of the limestone.

Caustic Value (*4*)—Official Final Action

1.008 ***Apparatus (Figure 1:01)***

Use 500 mL Pyrex erlenmeyer, *A*, and fritted glass filter (Corning Glass Works No. 39535, 30F), *F*. Connect filter to siphon tube *B* with thick-wall rubber tubing. Use receiving flasks *M* and *N* calibrated *to deliver* 50 and 100 mL, resp. *S* is suction flask.

1.009 ***Determination***

Transfer portion of sample, **1.003**, to weighing bottle and det. wt bottle and contents in atm. of min. moisture and CO_2 content. With polished, narrow-point spatula calibrated to hold ca 1.5 g, withdraw sample to be used and det. exact wt by difference. Insert sample directly into dry flask, *A*, fitted with tight rubber stopper.

Prep. *sucrose soln immediately before use* by placing 25 g granulated sucrose in measuring flask calibrated *to deliver* 500 mL. Dissolve sucrose with cold *CO_2-free H_2O* and dil. to vol. Holding both erlenmeyer contg sample and flask contg sucrose soln in slightly inclined position, insert neck of sucrose soln flask short distance into erlenmeyer, and carefully transfer sucrose soln with synchronized rotary motion of both flasks to prevent granulation of lime. Stopper erlenmeyer securely, agitate, and add, if desired, some clean dry beads. Completely dissolve uncoated caustic lime by six 1 min agitations at 2 or 3 min intervals. Invert flask to trap any solid particles between stopper and neck and crush by carefully twisting stopper. Let stand 15 min and filter as follows:

Connect filter cone *F* with siphon *B* and close stopcock *D*. Connect receiving flasks, apply suction, and quickly connect erlenmeyer *A* contg lime soln with stopper *E*. Open stopcock *C* and filter 25–50 mL soln. Close *C* and open *D* to release suction. Remove *M* and replace with similar dry flask. Close *D*, open *C*, and continue filtration until both *M* and *N* are filled at least to marks. To disconnect system, close stopcock *C*, and gently press down outlet of flask *M* and then outlet of flask *N*, to remove any excess liq. above marks. Let intermediate connection empty, open stopcock *D*, and remove *M* and *N*. Titr. first 50 mL, or pilot aliquot, of filtered soln with 0.5*N* HCl, using phthln. To covered 200 mL beaker add twice vol. 0.5*N* acid required for this titrn, add second (100 mL) aliquot of filtered soln to this acid and phthln, and complete titrn.

Calc. caustic value of sample: $X = 7V/W$,
where X = % active CaO; V = mL 0.5*N* acid used/100 mL lime soln; W = g sample.

Carbon Dioxide (*5*)—Official Final Action

1.010 ***Apparatus and Reagents***

Knorr alkalimeter with CO_2 absorption train.—Fill guard tube of alkalimeter with Ascarite. Connect upper end of condenser to absorption train consisting of 5 or 6 U-shape, g-s drying tubes (or equiv.) joined in series. Fill first tube with H_2SO_4 and second with Ag_2SO_4-H_2SO_4 soln (10 g Ag_2SO_4 in 100 mL H_2SO_4) to remove acidic gases other than CO_2. Fill third tube with $Mg(ClO_4)_2$ to absorb H_2O. Fill inlet ⅔ of fourth and succeeding tubes with Ascarite to absorb CO_2, and outlet ⅓ of each tube with $Mg(ClO_4)_2$. Connect last tube in train with aspirating bottle or suction source.

Condition app. daily before use, and also when freshly filled tube is placed in train, by aspirating air at rate of 2–3 bubbles/sec thru dry alkalimeter assembly and absorption train until CO_2 absorption tubes attain const wt (usually 20–30 min). Tare against similarly packed tubes. Use std procedure for wiping tubes with dry, lint-free cloth before each weighing.

1.011 ***Determination***

Transfer 3 g burnt or hydrated lime or 0.5–1.0 g limestone or marl, prepd as in **1.003**, to dry alkalimeter flask. Momentarily open stopcocks of first 2 CO_2 absorption tubes to air to equalize pressure, weigh tubes sep., and place in position in train. With assembled alkalimeter connected to absorption train, adjust rate of aspiration of air thru system to ca 2 bubbles/sec. Close funnel stopcock, remove alkalimeter guard tube, fill funnel with 50 mL HCl (1+4), and replace guard tube. Open funnel stopcock and let acid run slowly into flask, taking care that evolution of gas is so gradual as not to materially increase flow thru tubes. After all acid is added, agitate alkalimeter assembly to ensure complete dispersion of sample in acid soln. Continue aspiration, gradually heat contents of flask to bp, and boil 2–3 min after H_2O begins to condense. Discontinue heating, and continue aspiration 15–20 min or until app. cools. Remove, equalize internal and external pressure, and reweigh absorption tubes.

Increase in wt = wt CO_2. (Material increase in wt of second tube usually indicates exhaustion of first tube, but may result from too rapid evolution of CO_2 in relation to aspiration rate.) Report % $CaCO_3$.

CALCIUM SILICATE SLAGS

1.012 Neutralizing Value (*6*)—Official Final Action

(Uncorrected for sulfide content)

(a) *Blast furnace slag.*—Transfer 0.5 g sample, ground to pass No. 80 sieve, to 250 mL erlenmeyer. Wash down with small

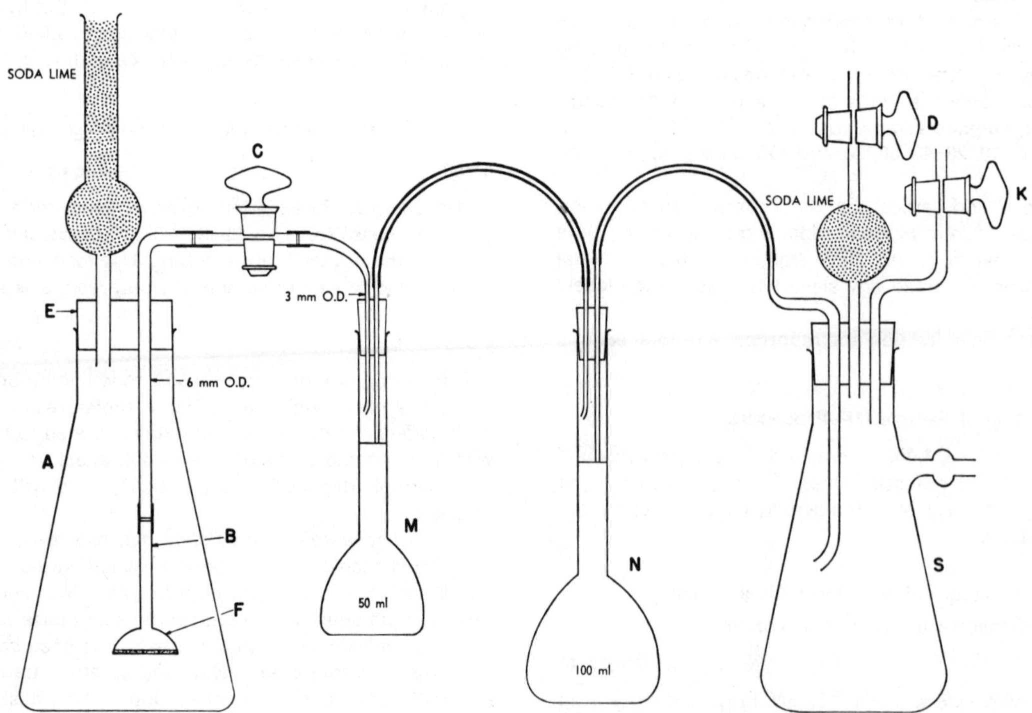

FIG. 1:01—Apparatus for automatic filtration and measurement of lime solutions

portions H_2O and add 35 mL 0.5*N* HCl while swirling. Heat to gentle boil over burner, *agitating suspension continuously* until bulk of sample dissolves. Boil 5 min and cool to room temp.; then dil. with CO_2-free H_2O to ca 150 mL and add 1 mL *30% H_2O_2* and 5 drops bromocresol green, **2.144(c)**. Back-titr. with 0.5*N* NaOH, adding first 15 mL rapidly and titrg dropwise thereafter, vigorously agitating contents of stoppered flask after each addn, until indicator tint matches or slightly exceeds that of pH 5.2 phthalate buffer soln, **50.010**, of like vol. and indicator concn, after 2–3 sec agitation.

(b) *Rock phosphate reduction furnace slag.*—Transfer 0.5 g sample to 250 mL beaker. Wash down with small portions H_2O and add, stirring continuously, 50 mL HOAc (1+4). Heat to bp and boil 5 min, stirring frequently. Evap. to dryness on steam bath. Add 20 mL of the HOAc, dil. to 150 mL, and heat to bp; add NH_4OH (1+1) to distinct yellow of Me red. Digest ca 10 min on hot plate. Filter by gravity thru 9 cm paper, catching filtrate in 100 × 50 mm lipped Pyrex crystg dish; wash beaker 3 times and paper 5 addnl times with *neut. 0.5N NH_4OAc*. Evap. filtrate on hot plate. Adjust heat so bubbles breaking thru viscous surface film are released gently to avoid spattering. (To expedite dehydration, repeat treatments with 25 mL hot H_2O and evapn 2 or 3 times.) Continue heating residue on hot plate until no HOAc odor remains. Heat addnl 10 min at full heat of hot plate; then ignite 10 min at 550°. Cool, wet residue with 15 mL H_2O, place watch glass over dish, and add 25 mL 0.5*N* HCl thru lip of dish. Heat 5 min over burner at gentle simmer. Rinse watch glass, filter suspended matter on 9 cm paper, catching filtrate in 250 mL erlenmeyer, and wash dish and filter 3 times with hot H_2O. Titr. excess acid with 0.5*N* NaOH to distinct yellow of Me red.

Net acid used × 5 = neutzg value of slag in terms of % $CaCO_3$ equivalence.

Sulfide Sulfur (*7*)—Official Final Action

(*Note:* $CdSO_4$ is toxic: *see also* **51.084**.)

1.013 ***Reagents***

(a) *Zinc dust.*—Low in Pb.

(b) *Absorbent soln.*—Dissolve 20 g $CdSO_4.2\frac{2}{3}H_2O$ in H_2O and dil. to 1 L. Adjust to pH 5.6 potentiometrically or colorimetrically. If colorimetrically, match sep. 50 mL aliquot to buffer of same pH, **50.010**.

(c) *Sodium hydroxide std soln.*—0.1*N*. Prep. and stdze as in **50.032–50.036**.

(d) *Std acid.*—0.1*N* HCl. Stdze against std alkali, **(c)**, using Me red.

(e) *Methyl red indicator.*—Dissolve 0.2 g Me red in 100 mL alcohol.

1.014 ***Apparatus***

Fit 250 mL erlenmeyer with 2-hole No. 5.5 stopper. Insert thru stopper 60 mL separator with stem drawn out to 2 mm and bent upward at tip, adjusting separator so stem is 6 mm from bottom of flask. Also insert thru stopper 6 mm glass outlet tube. Connect with amber rubber tubing to inlet of 25 × 150 mm tube half filled with H_2O and heated to near bp before and during detn. Connect in series 2 addnl tubes of same size, each contg 25 mL absorbent soln and held in 600 mL beaker filled with cold H_2O.

1.015 ***Determination***

Fill absorbent tubes with absorbent soln and heat H_2O tube to gentle boiling. Weigh 1 g slag, ground to pass No. 80 sieve, into evolution flask, add 1 g Zn dust, and wash down sides with 5–10 mL H_2O; mix with flat-end rod and connect flask to app. Add 50 mL HCl (1+4) to separator and let acid flow into reaction flask while swirling contents. If necessary, apply pressure to transfer acid and close stopcock while a little of the acid is still above it. Heat to bp; then regulate to maintain active but not too vigorous boiling for 10 min. Swirl flask frequently after adding acid and for first 5 min of boiling. To disconnect, hold inlet in first absorbent tube firmly with one hand and quickly pull off rubber tubing with other hand without pinching.

Filter CdS suspension by gravity thru 9 cm paper into 250 mL erlenmeyer and wash with H_2O to vol. of 100 mL. Add 4 drops Me red indicator and agitate vigorously while titrg slowly with 0.1*N* NaOH to exact tint of *ref. soln* (50 mL absorbent soln dild to 100 mL, with identical indicator concn, in 250 mL erlenmeyer). If end point is passed so that $Cd(OH)_2$ ppts, add 1–2 mL 0.1*N* HCl, let stand until ppt disappears, and complete titrn dropwise, agitating vigorously.

% $CaCO_3$ equivalence of sulfide *S* in sample = net mL 0.1*N* NaOH/2

g Sulfide S/detn = mL 0.1*N* NaOH × 0.0016

% Sulfide S = g sulfide S × 100

ELEMENTAL ANALYSIS

Gravimetric Methods

1.016 Preparation of Sample Solution by Acid Digestion (*8*)—Official Final Action

(*Caution: See* **51.019, 51.026,** and **51.028.**)

Prep. samples as in **1.003**, preferably in agate mortar. Grind silicates to pass No. 100 sieve, and dry all samples at 105°.

Weigh 2 g limestone or 0.5 g silicate. If sample contains org. matter, transfer to Pt crucible and place in cold furnace. Raise temp. gradually to 1000° and hold 15 min. Transfer sample to 400 mL beaker and, if ignited, moisten cautiously with H_2O. Add 10 mL HNO_3 and evap. on hot plate at low heat until mixt. becomes pasty. Cool, and add 10 mL H_2O and 20 mL 60% $HClO_4$. Boil to heavy fumes of $HClO_4$, cover, and fume slowly until soln is colorless or slightly yellow (5–10 min). Do not evap. to dryness. Cool to <100° and add 50 mL H_2O. Filter thru Whatman 41H or finer paper into 250 mL vol. flask. *Wash thoroly with hot H_2O to remove all traces of $HClO_4$.* Reserve filtrate and washings for prepn of *Sample Solns X and Y,* **1.017(a)** and **(b)**.

1.017 Silica (*8*)—Official Final Action

(*See* also **1.041–1.043**.)

(*Caution: See* **51.025** and **51.028.**)

Transfer paper with SiO_2 to uncovered Pt crucible and heat gently with low flame until paper chars without flame. Partially cover crucible and cautiously burn C. Finally cover completely and heat with blast lamp or in furnace at 1150–1200°. Cool in desiccator and weigh. Repeat to const wt (*W*). Treat with ca 1 mL H_2O, 2 drops H_2SO_4 (1+1), and 10 mL HF. Cautiously evap. to dryness in hood. Heat 2 min at 1050–1100°, cool in desiccator, and weigh (*B*).

$W - B$ = g SiO_2 in sample.
g SiO_2 × 0.4674 = g Si.

(a) *Sample Soln X.*–(0.008 g limestone or 0.002 g silicate/mL.) Fuse residue from Si detn with 0.5 g Na_2CO_3 by heating covered crucible 10 min over Meker burner. Cool, fill crucible ⅔ full with H_2O, and add 2 mL 60% $HClO_4$ dropwise, with stirring. Warm if necessary to dissolve melt. Add to filtrate and washings reserved for prepn of *Sample Soln X* in **1.016**. Dil. to 250 mL with H_2O.

(b) *Sample Soln Y.*–(0.00016 g limestone or 0.00004 g silicate/mL.) Dil. 10 mL *Sample Soln X* to 500 mL with H_2O.

1.018 Oxides of Iron, Aluminum, Phosphorus, and Titanium (*9*)—Official Final Action

(Alternatively, Fe, Al, Mn, P, and Ti may be detd colorimetrically as in **1.025–1.040**.)

To 125 mL aliquot *Soln X* from **1.017(a)**, add 10 mL HCl and few drops Me red indicator; heat to gentle boil and add NH_4OH (1+1) until ppt forms and indicator just changes to distinct yellow. Boil ≤2 min and filter rapidly. Wash ppt 6–8 times with hot *2% NH_4NO_3* soln. Return ppt and filter to original beaker, add 10 mL HCl, and macerate filter with policeman. Dil. with H_2O, heat to dissolve ppt, dil. to ca 200 mL, and reppt as above. Wash thoroly with the hot NH_4NO_3 soln until Cl-free. Combine first and second filtrates and save for Ca and Mg detns.

Place ppt in Pt crucible and dry. Ignite gently to oxidize C, heat to bright red ca 10 min, cool in desiccator, and weigh in covered crucible as $Fe_2O_3 + Al_2O_3 + P_2O_5 + TiO_2$.

1.019 Calcium (*9*)—Official Final Action

Conc. combined filtrates and washings from **1.018** to ca 50 mL; make slightly alk. with NH_4OH (1+1); while still hot, add *satd $(NH_4)_2C_2O_4$ soln* dropwise as long as any ppt forms, and then enough excess to convert Mg salts also to oxalate. Heat to bp, let stand ≥3 hr, decant clear soln thru filter, pour 15–20 mL hot H_2O on ppt, and again decant clear soln thru filter. Dissolve any ppt remaining on filter by washing with hot HCl (1+9) into original beaker, wash 6 times with hot H_2O, and then reppt at bp by adding NH_4OH and a little satd $(NH_4)_2C_2O_4$ soln. Let stand as before, filter thru same filter, and wash with hot H_2O until Cl-free. Reserve filtrates and washings from both pptns for detn of Mg, **1.021**.

Complete detn by one of following methods and report as % CaO:

(a) Ignite ppt in crucible, either over S-free blast lamp, or in elec. furnace at 950°, to const wt, cool in desiccator, and weigh as CaO.

(b) Incinerate filter over low flame, mix ignited ppt with finely pulverized and dried mixt. of equal parts of *$(NH_4)_2SO_4$ and NH_4Cl*, and drive off excess sulfate by carefully heating upper portion of crucible. Complete ignition, cool in desiccator, and weigh as $CaSO_4$.

(c) Perforate apex of cone; wash CaC_2O_4 ppt into beaker used for pptn; then wash filter with hot H_2SO_4 (1+4), and titr. at 85–90° with 0.1*N* $KMnO_4$.

Magnesium (*10*)—Official Final Action

1.020 ***Reagent***

Phosphate soln.—Dissolve 100 g $(NH_4)_2HPO_4$ in hot H_2O, dil. to 1 L, and add 5 mL $CHCl_3$.

1.021 ***Determination***

To combined filtrates and washings, **1.019**, add 2 mL 1*M* citric acid, 100 mL NH_4OH, and 50 mL alcohol. Then add 25 mL of the phosphate soln, with const stirring, and let stand 12–24 hr. Filter, wash twice with NH_4OH (1+9), and dissolve ppt in HNO_3 (1+4), washing soln into original beaker to vol. of 100–150 mL. Add 1/10 vol. NH_4OH and 2 drops of the phosphate soln. Stir vigorously and let stand ≥3 hr. Filter thru gooch, wash with NH_4OH (1+9), moisten filter with *satd soln of NH_4NO_3 made slightly ammoniacal*, ignite, and weigh as $Mg_2P_2O_7$. Report as % MgO. Correct wt $Mg_2P_2O_7$ for co-pptd $Mn_2P_2O_7$ by detg Mn as in **33.127**.

EDTA Titration Methods

Calcium and Magnesium (*11*)—Official Final Action

(Not applicable to samples with high phosphate content or contg <2% Mg)

(*Caution: See* **51.050**.)

1.022 ***Reagents***

(a) *Buffer soln.*—pH 10. Dissolve 67.5 g NH_4Cl in 200 mL H_2O, add 570 mL NH_4OH, and dil. to 1 L.

(b) *Potassium hydroxide-potassium cyanide soln.*— Dissolve 280 g KOH and 66 g KCN in 1 L H_2O.

(c) *Potassium cyanide soln.*—2%. Dissolve 2 g KCN in 100 mL H_2O.

(d) *Eriochrome black T indicator soln.*—Dissolve 0.2 g indicator (Eastman Kodak P6361, or equiv.) in 50 mL MeOH contg 2 g $NH_2OH.HCl$. Store ≤1 month.

(e) *Magnesium std solns.*—0.25 and 1.00 mg/mL. Dissolve 0.25 and 1.00 g Mg turnings in HCl (1+10) and dil. each to 1 L with double distd H_2O.

(f) *Calcium std soln.*—1 mg/mL. Dissolve 2.4973 g $CaCO_3$, primary std grade, previously dried 2 hr at 285°, in HCl (1+10). Dil. to 1 L with double distd H_2O.

(g) *Calcein indicator.*—Grind together 1 g indicator, 10 g charcoal (Norite A is satisfactory), and 100 g KCl. (Indicator is described in Anal. Chem. **28**, 882 (1956), and is available from G. Frederick Smith Chemical Co. and Eastman Kodak.)

(h) *Disodium dihydrogen EDTA std solns.*—*(1) 0.4%.*—Dissolve 4 g Na_2H_2EDTA in 1 L H_2O. Stdze against std Ca and Mg solns. *(2) 0.1%.*—Prep. as in *(1)*, using 1 g Na_2H_2EDTA, and stdze against 0.25 mg/mL Mg std soln.

1.023 ***Standardization***

(a) *For calcium.*—Pipet 10 mL std Ca soln into 300 mL erlenmeyer and add 10 mL H_2O. Add 10 mL KOH-KCN soln and ca 35 mg calcein indicator. Using mag. stirrer and artificial light, titr. with 0.4% EDTA std soln to disappearance of all green. Titr. ≥3 aliquots and use av. to calc. titer Ca soln = 10/mL EDTA soln.

(b) *For magnesium.*—Pipet 10 mL 0.25 and 1.00 mg/mL Mg std solns into 300 mL erlenmeyers and add 100 mL H_2O. Add 5 mL pH 10 buffer, 2 mL 2% KCN soln, and 10 drops eriochrome black T indicator. Using mag. stirrer and artificial light, titr. with 0.1 and 0.4% EDTA std solns, resp., until color changes permanently from wine red to pure blue. Titr. ≥3 aliquots and use av. to calc. titer Mg soln = 2.5/mL EDTA soln, or 10/mL EDTA soln, resp.

1.024 ***Determination***

Dry sample at 110° to const wt and cool to room temp. Grind to pass No. 60 or 80 sieve and mix thoroly. Accurately weigh ca 0.5 g into 250 mL beaker, add 20 mL HCl (1+1), and evap. to dryness on hot plate. Dissolve residue in 5 mL HCl (1+10), dil. to ca 100 mL with H_2O, and digest over low flame 1 hr. Cool, transfer to 200 mL vol. flask, dil. to vol., mix, and let settle or filter.

(a) *For calcium.*—Pipet 10 mL aliquot into 300 mL erlenmeyer and titr. as in **1.023(a)**, observing end point thru soln and away from light. % Ca = (Titer EDTA std soln for Ca) × mL EDTA std soln × 2/g sample.

(b) *For magnesium.*—(For agricultural limestones contg >4% Mg.) For Ca + Mg, pipet 10 mL aliquot into 300 mL erlenmeyer and titr. with 0.4% EDTA soln as in **1.023(b)**.

% Mg = (Titer EDTA std soln for Mg) × [(mL EDTA std soln in Ca + Mg titrn) − (mL EDTA std soln in Ca titrn)] × 2/g sample.

(c) *For magnesium.*—(For agricultural limestones contg 2–4%

Mg.) Pipet 10 mL aliquot (0.5–1.0 mg Mg) into 300 mL erlenmeyer and add exact vol. of 0.4% EDTA soln required for Ca detn. Titr. with 0.1% EDTA soln as in **1.023(b)**.

% Mg = (Titer EDTA std soln for Mg) × mL EDTA std 0.1% soln × 2/g sample.

Colorimetric Methods (12)—Official Final Action

(Carry reagent blanks thru detn with stds and samples. Treat aliquots of blank soln (corresponding to aliquot sizes of sample solns taken for analysis) as in *Determination* for appropriate element and correct values for samples accordingly.)

Det. Al, Fe, Mn, P, and Ti in solns prepd by $HClO_4$ digestion, **1.016–1.017**, or NaOH fusion, **1.025**. Det. Si only in soln prepd by NaOH fusion.

1.025 Preparation of Sample Solution by Sodium Hydroxide Fusion

Prep. samples as in **1.003**, preferably in agate mortar. Grind samples to pass No. 100 sieve and dry at 105°.

(**a**) *Sample Soln X.*—(0.005 g limestone or 0.002 g silicate/mL.) Place 0.5 g limestone or 0.2 g silicate in 75 mL Ni crucible. If sample contains org. matter, place uncovered crucible in cold furnace, raise temp. gradually to 900°, and hold 15 min. Remove crucible from furnace and let cool. Mix 0.3 g KNO_3 with sample and add 1.5 g NaOH pellets. Cover crucible with Ni cover and heat 5 min at dull redness over gas flame. (Do not fuse in furnace.) Remove from flame and swirl melt around sides. Cool, add ca 50 mL H_2O, and warm to disintegrate fused cake. Transfer to 150 mL beaker contg 15 mL 5*N* $HClO_4$ (1(60%)+1). Scrub crucible and lid with policeman, and wash any residue into beaker. Transfer to 100 mL vol. flask and dil. to vol. (*Sample Soln X*). (This soln is acidic and is normally clear and free of insol. matter. Occasionally particles of oxidized Ni from crucible appear. When this occurs, let particles settle before taking aliquots.)

(**b**) *Sample Soln Y.*—(0.00015 g limestone or 0.00004 g silicate/mL.) Dil. 15 mL limestone *Sample Soln X* or 10 mL silicate *Sample Soln X* to 500 mL with H_2O.

Aluminum

1.026 *Reagents*

(**a**) *Aluminum std solns.*—(*1*) *Stock soln.*—100 μg Al/mL. To 0.1000 g pure Al metal in 30 mL beaker, add 6 mL HCl (1+1). Cover with watch glass and warm gently until Al completely dissolves. Dil. to 1 L with H_2O. (*2*) *Working soln.*—4 μg Al/mL. Dil. 20 mL stock soln to 500 mL.

(**b**) *Aluminon soln.*—Dissolve sep. in H_2O: 0.5 g NH_4 aurintricarboxylate in 100 mL; 10 g acacia (gum arabic) in 200 mL; and 100 g NH_4OAc in 400 mL. Filter acacia soln. Add 56 mL HCl to NH_4OAc soln and adjust pH to 4.5 with HCl or NH_4OH. Combine 3 solns and dil. to 1 L with H_2O.

(**c**) *Antifoam soln.*—Disperse 0.03 g silicone defoamer (Dow Corning Corp. Antifoam A) in 100 mL H_2O.

(**d**) *Thioglycolic acid soln.*—Dil. 1 mL $HSCH_2COOH$ to 100 mL with H_2O.

1.027 *Preparation of Standard Curve*

Transfer aliquots of std soln contg 0, 4, 20, 40, 60, and 80 μg Al to 100 mL vol. flasks and proceed as in detn. Prep. std curve by plotting %*T* against μg Al on semilog paper.

1.028 *Determination*

Use *Sample Soln X* for limestones contg <0.2% or silicates contg <0.8% Al and adjust pH of aliquot to 4.5 with NH_4OH. For materials contg greater concns of Al, use *Sample Soln Y* and omit pH adjustment.

Transfer aliquot (≤20 mL contg <80 μg Al) of *Sample Soln X* or *Y* to 100 mL vol. flask. Dil. to 20 mL with H_2O. Add 2 mL thioglycolic acid soln, 0.5 mL antifoam soln, and 10 mL aluminon soln. Place flask in boiling H_2O 20 min (250 mL beaker contg 125 mL H_2O holds 100 mL vol. flask conveniently). Remove flask from H_2O and let cool ca 30 min. Dil. to 100 mL with H_2O. Use 0 μg Al soln, **1.027**, to set 100% *T* at 525 nm. Read %*T* for sample soln and det. μg Al from std. curve. Calc. % Al in sample.

Iron

1.029 *Reagents*

(**a**) *Iron std solns.*—(*1*) *Stock soln.*—100 μg Fe/mL. Dissolve 0.1000 g pure Fe metal in 5 mL 2*N* HCl and dil. to 1 L with H_2O. (*2*) *Working soln.*—5 μg Fe/mL. Dil. 25 mL stock soln to 500 mL.

(**b**) *2,4,6-Tripyridyl-s-triazine* (*TPTZ*) *soln.*— (Available from G. Frederick Smith Chemical Co.) Dissolve 0.500 g TPTZ in few drops HCl and dil. to 1 L with H_2O.

(**c**) *Hydroxylamine hydrochloride soln.*—Dissolve 50 g $NH_2OH.HCl$ in H_2O. Add 10 mL TPTZ soln and 0.5 g $NaClO_4.H_2O$, and dil. to 500 mL with H_2O. Transfer to separator, add 25 mL *nitrobenzene,* and shake several min. Let phases sep. and discard lower nitrobenzene phase contg Fe. Repeat extn 2 or 3 times.

(**d**) *Acetate buffer soln.*—Dissolve 164 g anhyd. NaOAc in H_2O. Add 115 mL HOAc, 10 mL $NH_2OH.HCl$ soln, 0.05 g TPTZ, and 1 g $NaClO_4.H_2O$, and dil. to 1 L with H_2O. Transfer to separator, add 25 mL nitrobenzene, and shake several min. Let phases sep. and discard lower nitrobenzene phase. Repeat extn 3 or 4 times.

1.030 *Preparation of Standard Curve*

Treat aliquots of std soln contg 0, 5, 50, and 100 μg Fe as in detn. Prep. std curve by plotting %*T* against μg Fe on semilog paper.

1.031 *Determination*

Use *Sample Soln X* (≤5 mL) for limestones contg <0.05% or silicates contg <0.2% Fe and *Sample Soln Y* for materials contg greater concns of Fe.

Transfer aliquot (<100 μg Fe) of *Sample Soln X* or *Y* to 100 mL vol. flask. Add 3 mL $NH_2OH.HCl$ soln and 10 mL TPTZ soln. Add NH_4OH dropwise until Fe derivative remains violet on mixing. Add 10 mL buffer soln and dil. to 100 mL. Use 0 μg Fe soln, **1.030**, to set 100% *T* at 593 nm. Read %*T* for sample soln and det. μg Fe from std curve. Calc. % Fe in sample.

Manganese

1.032 *Reagents*

(**a**) *Manganese std soln.*—50 μg Mn/mL. Dissolve 0.0500 g pure Mn metal in 20 mL 0.5*N* H_2SO_4 and dil. to 1 L with H_2O.

(**b**) *Acid mixture.*—Add 800 mL HNO_3 and 200 mL H_3PO_4 to H_2O and dil. to 2 L.

1.033 *Preparation of Standard Curve*

Treat aliquots of std soln contg 0, 50, 100, 300, and 500 μg Mn as in detn. Prep. std curve by plotting %*T* against μg Mn on semilog paper.

1.034 ***Determination***

Transfer aliquot (<500 μg Mn) of *Sample Soln X* to 150 mL beaker. Add 25 mL acid mixt. and 0.3 g KIO_4. Bring to bp and keep near boiling temp. 10 min after color develops. Let cool, transfer to 50 mL vol. flask, dil. to vol., and mix. Use 0 μg Mn soln, **1.033**, to set 100% *T* at 525 nm. Read %*T* for sample soln and det. μg Mn from std curve. Calc. % Mn in sample.

Phosphorus

(Do not clean glassware with detergents contg P.)

1.035 ***Reagents***

(**a**) *Phosphorus std solns.*—(*1*) *Stock soln.*—100 μg P/mL. Dissolve 0.4393 g KH_2PO_4 in H_2O and dil. to 1 L. (*2*) *Working soln.*—5 μg P/mL. Dil. 25 mL stock soln to 500 mL.

(**b**) *Ammonium molybdate soln.*—Dissolve 20 g $(NH_4)_6Mo_7O_{24}.4H_2O$ in 500 mL H_2O. Add 285 mL H_2SO_4, cool, and dil. to 1 L with H_2O.

(**c**) *Hydrazine sulfate soln.*—Dissolve 2 g $N_2H_4.H_2SO_4$ in H_2O and dil. to 1 L.

1.036 ***Preparation of Standard Curve***

Treat aliquots of std soln contg 0, 5, 50, and 75 μg P as in detn. Prep. std curve by plotting %*T* against μg P on semilog paper.

1.037 ***Determination***

Transfer aliquot (≤15 mL contg <75 μg P) of *Sample Soln X* to 100 mL vol. flask. Add 5 mL NH_4 molybdate soln and mix. Add 5 mL $N_2H_4.H_2SO_4$ soln, dil. to 70 mL with H_2O, and mix. Place flask in boiling H_2O 9 min. Remove, *cool rapidly,* and dil. to vol. Use 0 μg P soln, **1.036**, to set 100% *T* at 827 nm. Read %*T* for sample soln and det. μg P from std curve. Calc. % P in sample.

Titanium

1.038 ***Reagents***

(**a**) *Titanium std solns.*—(*1*) *Stock soln.*—100 μg Ti/mL. Place 0.1668 g TiO_2 and 2 g $K_2S_2O_7$ in Pt crucible. Heat covered crucible gently at first and then at dull red ca 15 min. Dissolve melt in 50 mL H_2SO_4 (1+1) and dil. to 1 L with H_2O. (*2*) *Working soln.*—5 μg Ti/mL. Dil. 25 mL stock soln to 500 mL.

(**b**) *Acetate buffer soln.*—pH 4.7. Dissolve 41 g anhyd. NaOAc in H_2O, add 30 mL HOAc, and dil. to 1 L.

(**c**) *Disodium-1,2-dihydroxybenzene-3,5-disulfonate* (*Tiron*) *soln.*—Dissolve 4 g Tiron in H_2O and dil. to 100 mL.

1.039 ***Preparation of Standard Curve***

Treat aliquots of std soln contg 0, 5, 50, and 75 μg Ti as in detn, but do not add dithionite to stds. Prep. std curve by plotting %*T* against μg Ti on semilog paper.

1.040 ***Determination***

Transfer aliquot (<75 μg Ti) of *Sample Soln X* to 50 mL beaker. Dil. to ca 25 mL with H_2O. Add 5 mL Tiron soln and then NH_4OH (1+9) dropwise until soln is neut. to Congo Red paper. (Tiron soln must be added before pH is adjusted.) Transfer to 50 mL vol. flask, add 5 mL buffer soln, dil. to vol. with H_2O, and mix thoroly. Add 25 mg *dithionite* ($Na_2S_2O_4$) and dissolve with min. agitation (to avoid reappearance of blue). Use 0 μg Ti soln, **1.039**, to set 100% *T* at 410 nm. Read %*T* for sample soln within 15 min after adding dithionite. Det. μg Ti from std curve. Calc. % Ti in sample.

Silicon

(Clean all glassware with HCl (1+1).)

1.041 ***Reagents***

(**a**) *Silicon std soln.*—20 μg Si/mL. Place 0.0428 g pure SiO_2 in 75 mL Ni crucible and treat as in **1.025(a)**, but dil. with H_2O to 1 L instead of 100 mL.

(**b**) *Tartaric acid soln.*—Dissolve 50 g tartaric acid in H_2O and dil. to 500 mL. Store in plastic bottle.

(**c**) *Ammonium molybdate soln.*—Dissolve 7.5 g $(NH_4)_6Mo_7O_{24}.4H_2O$ in 75 mL H_2O, add 10 mL H_2SO_4 (1+1), and dil. to 100 mL with H_2O. Store in plastic bottle.

(**d**) *Reducing soln.*—Dissolve 0.7 g Na_2SO_3 in 10 mL H_2O. Add 0.15 g 1-amino-2-naphthol-4-sulfonic acid and stir until dissolved. Dissolve 9 g $NaHSO_3$ in 90 mL H_2O, add to first soln, and mix. Store in plastic bottle.

1.042 ***Preparation of Standard Curve***

Treat aliquots of std soln contg 0, 20, 100, and 200 μg Si as in detn. Prep. std curve by plotting %*T* against μg Si on semilog paper.

1.043 ***Determination***

Transfer 10 mL *Sample Soln Y* to 100 mL vol. flask (use *Sample Soln X* for limestones contg <0.2% Si) and add 1 mL NH_4 molybdate soln with swirling. Mix well, and let stand 10 min. Add 4 mL tartaric acid soln with swirling, and mix well. Add 1 mL reducing soln with swirling, dil. to vol., mix well, and let stand ≥30 min. Use 0 μg Si soln, **1.042**, to set 100% *T* at 650 nm. Read %*T* for sample soln and det. μg Si from std curve. Calc. % Si in sample.

SELECTED REFERENCES

(*1*) JAOAC **7**, 252(1924).
(*2*) JAOAC **7**, 252(1924); **55**, 539(1972).
(*3*) JAOAC **38**, 240(1955).
(*4*) Ind. Eng. Chem. **20**, 312(1928); JAOAC **11**, 153 (1928); **14**, 283(1931).
(*5*) JAOAC **38**, 413(1955).
(*6*) JAOAC **27**, 74, 532(1944); **28**, 310(1945); **31**, 71(1948).
(*7*) JAOAC **31**, 715(1948).
(*8*) JAOAC **46**, 603(1963); **47**, 1019(1964).
(*9*) U.S. Geol. Survey Bull. **700**, p. 106; Ind. Eng. Chem. **9**, 1114(1917).
(*10*) Washington, "Chemical Analysis of Rocks," 3rd Ed., 1919, p. 181.
(*11*) JAOAC **45**, 1(1962); **46**, 611(1963); **50**, 190(1967).
(*12*) JAOAC **47**, 1019(1964).

2. Fertilizers

Sampling—Official Final Action

2.001 ***Solid Fertilizers (1)***

(a) *Bagged fertilizers.*—Use slotted single or double tube trier with solid cone tip, constructed of stainless steel or brass. (Do not use unplated brass for samples on which micronutrients are to be detd.) Trier length, exclusive of handle, should be approx. length of filled bag to be sampled, but >25″; length of slot, >23″; width of slot ⩾0.5″; and id ⩾⅝″.

Take sample as follows: Lay bag horizontally and remove core diagonally from end to end. From lots of ⩾10 bags, take core from each of 10 bags. When necessary to sample lots of <10 bags, take 10 cores but at least 1 core from each bag present. For small packages (⩽10 lb), take 1 entire package as sample.

(b) *Bulk fertilizers, including railroad car-size lots.*—Use trier of design represented in Table **2:01**.

Table 2:01 Trier specifications

Trier	Length, in.	od, in.	id, in.	Compartments No.	Compartments Size, in.
Missouri	59	1⅛	⅞	8	3
552 Grain[a]	63	1⅜	1⅛	11	3½
Missouri "D"[b]	52	1¼	1	1	45

Triers available from:
[a] Seedboro Equipment Co., 618 W Jackson Blvd, Chicago, IL 60606.
[b] American Tool and Die, Inc., 1105 Maple St, West Des Moines, IA 50265.

Draw 10 vertical cores distributed in std concentric sampling pattern (Fig. **2:01**) of such design that each core represents approx. equal fractions of lot.

Bulk shipments may be sampled at time of loading or unloading by passing sampling cup, Fig. **2:02** (mouth dimensions: width ¾″, length 16″ or as long as max. diam. of stream), thru entire stream of material as it drops from belt or chute. Make sampling such as to assure ⩾10 equal-timed-spaced passes thruout transfer operation. Stream samples are not applicable unless uniform continuous flow of fertilizer is maintained for >3 min while lot is being sampled.

(c) *Preparation of sample.*—Place composite sample in air-tight container and deliver entire sample to laboratory. Reduce composite sample in laboratory, using riffle.

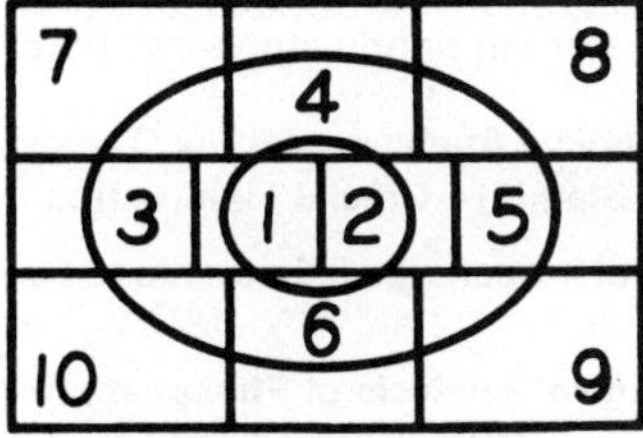

FIG. 2:01—Sampling pattern

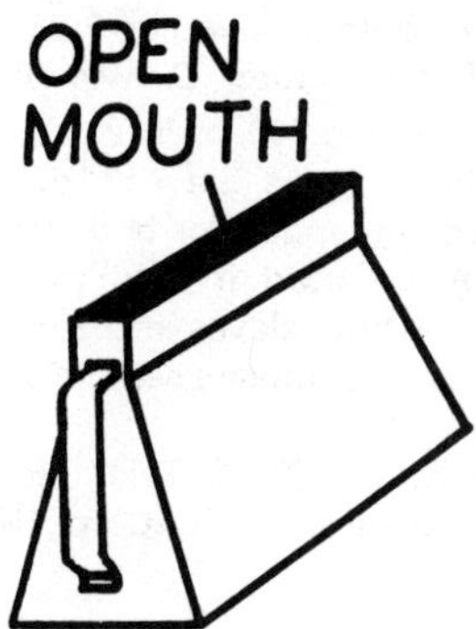

FIG. 2:02—Sampling cup

2.002 ***Liquid Fertilizers (2)***
(In Absence of Free Ammonia)

(a) *Clear solns.*—(Mixed liqs and N solns.) Secure sample directly from mixing vat, storage tank, or delivery tank after thoro mixing. Take sample from surface or thru direct tap. Flush direct tap, or delivery line and faucet, and collect sample in glass or polyethylene container. Alternatively, lower sample container into well mixed material thru port in top of tank and let fill. Seal container tightly.

(b) *Fluid fertilizers with suspended material.*—(Salt suspensions and slurries.) Agitate material in storage until thoroly mixed (15 min usually adequate) before taking sample. Sample directly as in **(a)**, or use 500 mL Missouri or Indiana sampling bottle, Fig. **2:03**. Lower sampling bottle from top opening to bottom of tank and raise slowly while filling. Transfer to sample bottle and seal tightly.

Alternatively, secure sample from tap on recirculation line after agitating *and* recirculating simultaneously until thoroly mixed. Draw sample while recirculating. If recirculation line is

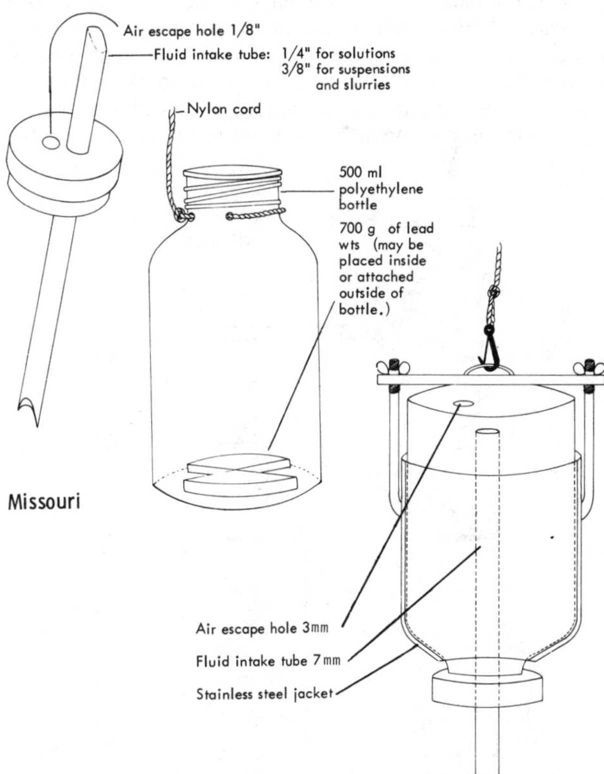

FIG. 2:03—Missouri and Indiana weighted restricted-fill fluid fertilizer sampling bottles designed to fill while being lowered (and raised) in storage tanks

attached to manifold delivery line, allowing cross-contamination, pump ca 30 cm (1′) or 2000 L (500 gal.) into temporary storage tank, then sample from recirculation line as above or from delivery line. Transfer to sample bottle and seal tightly.

Ammoniacal Solutions (3)

2.003 ***Apparatus***

(**a**) *Container.*—Polyethylene reagent-form bottle with buttress-type cap, 1 L (1 qt) capacity.

(**b**) *Sample flow control apparatus.*—Construct from following fittings: 1½ × ¼″ reducing bushing; ¼″ tee; ¼″ nipple 12–18″ long (length not critical); two ¼″ stainless steel, blunt-nose needle valves with hose connections (Hoke No. 328; Hoke Inc., 1 Tenakill Pk, Cresskill, NJ 07626). All fittings except valves can be either Al or stainless steel. (*See* Fig. **2:04**.)

Attach valves directly to tee which is then attached to reducing bushing thru nipple. To both valves attach ¼″ id Tygon tubing (Hoke No. 314A hose connection), 12″ length to sample valve and sufficient length to vent valve to reach disposal area or container. To free end of sample tubing attach 3″ length of ¼″ glass or stainless steel tubing inserted thru No. 4 rubber stopper. To exit end of metal tube attach addnl 6″ length of Tygon tubing. Make certain all connections are tight. App. can be attached directly to tank cars, but requires addnl coupling, which varies with installation, to attach to storage tanks. 1½″ "quick coupler" (Ever-Tite Coupling Co., 254 W 54th St, New York, NY 10019) suffices in most cases.

2.004 ***Sampling***

Prep. sample bottle in laboratory by adding ca 500 mL H_2O, replacing cap, and weighing accurately (±0.1 g). Attach sampling app. to car or tank and, with sample valve closed, flush line thru vent valve. Partially collapse sample bottle, insert sample tube with stopper, and seat tightly. With sample tube dipping below surface of H_2O in bottle, throttle vent valve to maintain small flow of soln and partially open sample valve, collecting ca 100 mL sample. (Bottle should not expand to full size during this time.) Close sample valve, remove sample tube, partially collapse bottle, and cap tightly. Reweigh (±0.1 g) and calc. wt sample. Cool to 20°, transfer to 1 or 2 L vol. flask, dil. to vol. with H_2O, mix thoroly, and take aliquots for analysis.

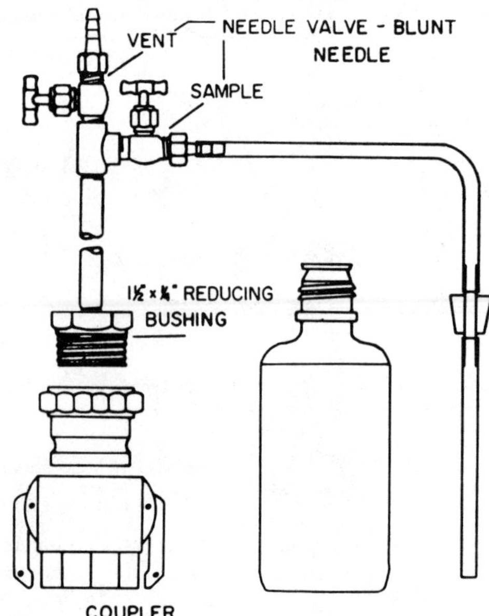

FIG. 2:04—Sampling apparatus for ammoniacal solutions, including "quick coupler" for attaching to storage tanks

Anhydrous Ammonia (3)

(*Caution:* Use extreme care in handling anhyd. NH_3. Suitable gas mask and rubber gloves are required. *See* **51.032**.)

2.005 ***Sampling***

Use sample tube of thermal shock-resistant glass calibrated to contain 100 mL and graduated in 0.05 mL subdivisions up to 0.5 mL. (Dupont special oil centrf. tube or ASTM long-form oil tube is satisfactory.) Flush line and fill tube to 100 mL mark with sample in such manner that condensing moisture will not enter sample tube. (Skirt attached to end of sample line will drain moisture away.)

2.006 ***Water and Nitrogen***

Immediately close sample tube with tight-fitting rubber stopper into which is inserted tight-fitting piece of 6 mm id glass tubing 5–8 cm long, bent at its exit from outer end of stopper to let gases escape but to exclude entrance of moisture or moisture-laden air. Place in H_2O bath at approx. air temp. and let NH_3 evap. When temp. of sample tube is ca that of bath, remove tube, wipe outer surface, and det. vol. of residue.

$$\% \, H_2O \text{ in sample} = \text{mL residue} \times C,$$

where C = 0.74, 0.70, or 0.66 for pressures in original containers of 100, 150, or 200 psi, resp.

$$\% \, N = (100 - \% \, H_2O) \times 0.8224.$$

2.007 Preparation of Sample (*4*)—Official Final Action

Reduce gross sample to amt sufficient for analysis or grind ⩾225 g (0.5 lb) of reduced sample without previous sieving. For fertilizer materials and moist fertilizer mixts, grind to pass sieve with 1 mm circular openings, or No. 20 sieve; for dry mixts that tend to segregate, grind to pass No. 40 sieve. Grind as rapidly as possible to avoid loss or gain of moisture during operation. Mix thoroly and store in tightly stoppered bottles.

2.008 ★ Mechanical Analysis of Bone, Tankage, and ★ Basic Slag (*5*)—Official Final Action

Sieve thru circular openings 0.5 mm diam. *See* **2.008**, 11th ed.

Mechanical Analysis of Phosphate Rock (*6*) Official Final Action

2.009 ***Apparatus***

(**a**) *Water pressure control.*—*See* Fig. **2:05**. Connect valve, *A*, std pressure gage, *B*, and aerator, *C*, with ⅜″ diam. pipe.

(**b**) *Sieves.*—Nos. 100 and 200, bronze or stainless steel cloth, checked against certified sieves. Sieves 8″ diam. and 2″ in depth to sieve cloth are recommended for both wet and dry sieving, but other sizes may be used if detd to be suitable under conditions of method. (Other sieves in U.S. series may be used, with precaution to ensure complete sepn of sample into desired fractions.)

(**c**) *Sieve shaker.*—Ro-Tap (W. S. Tyler, Inc., 8200 Tyler Blvd, Mentor, OH 44060), Syntron (FMC Corp., Material Handling

★ Surplus method—*see* inside front cover.

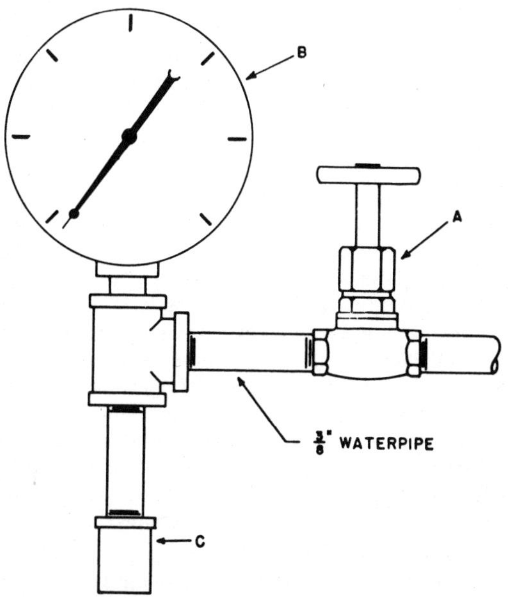

FIG. 2:05—Apparatus for control of water pressure

Equipment Div., Homer City, PA 15748), or other suitable machine.

2.010 ***Reagent***

Dispersing agent.—Dissolve 36 g Na hexametaphosphate and 8 g Na_2CO_3 in H_2O and dil. to 1 L.

2.011 ***Determination***

(**a**) *Ground phosphate rock.*—Place 100 g sample on No. 200 sieve and wash with moderate stream of tap H_2O at max. gage pressure of 0.28 kg/sq cm (4 lb/sq in.) until H_2O passing sieve is clear, with care to avoid loss of sample by splashing. Dry material remaining on sieve at 105° and transfer to No. 100 sieve in series with No. 200 sieve of same diam. and depth. Shake 8 min in mech. shaker. Det. % sample passing No. 100 sieve by subtracting wt of material retained on that sieve from 100. Det. % sample passing No. 200 sieve by subtracting sum of wts of material retained on that sieve and on No. 100 sieve from 100.

(**b**) *Soft phosphate with colloidal clay.*—Add 100 g sample to rapidly stirred soln of 50 mL dispersing agent and 450 mL tap H_2O, with care to avoid contact of unwetted material with shaft of stirrer and side of beaker. Stir 5 min after addn of sample is completed. Transfer slurry to No. 200 sieve and proceed as in (**a**).

2.012 Total Water—Official Final Action

(Not applicable to samples that yield volatile substances other than H_2O at drying temp.)

Heat 2 g sample, **2.007**, 5 hr in oven at 100±1°. In case of $NaNO_3$, $(NH_4)_2SO_4$, and K salts, heat to const wt at 130±1°. Report % loss in wt as H_2O at temp. used.

FREE WATER

Vacuum-Desiccation Methods (*7*)

2.013 ***Method I—Official Final Action***

Place 2 g prepd sample, **2.007**, in tared weighing dish. (Weigh extremely hygroscopic or damp materials by difference in covered dishes.) Dry sample at 25–30° (precise results depend on as const a temp. as possible) in vac. desiccator over anhyd. $Mg(ClO_4)_2$, P_2O_5, or BaO, under ≥50 cm (20") or ≤55 cm (22") vac. (20–25 cm (8–10") absolute pressure) 16–18 hr. Reweigh, and report % loss in wt as free H_2O.

2.014 ***Method II—Official Final Action***

(Not applicable to samples which yield volatile substances other than H_2O)

Weigh 2 g prepd sample, **2.007**, into tared glass weighing dish. Dry sample 2 hr ±10 min at 50±1.5° in oven under vac. of 48–53 cm (19–21") (23–28 cm (9–11") absolute pressure). (Temp. control within specified limits thruout oven chamber is essential.) Maintain vac. by passing desiccated air thru chamber. Cool dried sample in desiccator and reweigh. Report % loss in wt as free H_2O.

Alternative Extraction Method (*8*)
Official Final Action

2.015 ***Principle***

Free H_2O is extd with dioxane and detd by titrn with Karl Fischer reagent.

2.016 ***Reagents***

(Keep exposure of org. reagents to air at min.)

(**a**) *Karl Fischer reagent.*—Stabilized single soln (Fisher Scientific Co., So-K-3, or equiv.) dild ca 1 + 1 with stabilized diluent (Fisher, So-K-5, or equiv.), or soln equiv. to 2.5 mg H_2O/mL. Stdze daily with ca 0.2 g Na tartrate.$2H_2O$. 1 mg Na tartrate.$2H_2O$ = 0.1566 mg H_2O.

(**b**) *Methanol.*—Low in H_2O.

2.017 ***Determination***

Accurately weigh 2.5 g prepd sample, **2.007**, into 125 mL erlenmeyer, add 50.0 mL *1,4-dioxane,* stopper, mix by swirling, and let stand 15 min. Mix thoroly by swirling, and centrf. in closed tube. (*Caution: See* **51.005**.)

Transfer 10 mL aliquot to titrn vessel contg pretitrd MeOH and titr. with Karl Fischer reagent. (Discard contents of titrn vessel after 3 titrns, replace with enough MeOH to cover electrodes, and pretitr. before proceeding with next sample.) Det. blank on 10 mL dioxane as above and subtract from sample detns. Calc. and report as free H_2O.

2.018 ★ Acid-Insoluble Ash (*9*) ★
Official Final Action

HCl (1+4) digestion at 100°, ignition at 800°, and redigestion. *See* **2.015**, 11th ed.

PHOSPHORUS

Total Phosphorus

2.019 ***Reagent***

Magnesium nitrate soln.—Dissolve 950 g P-free $Mg(NO_3)_2 \cdot 6H_2O$ in H_2O and dil. to 1 L.

2.020 ***Preparation of Solution—Official Final Action***

(*Caution: See* **51.019**, **51.026**, **51.028**, **51.030**, and **51.069**.)

Treat 1 g sample by (**a**), (**b**), (**c**), (**d**), or (**e**), as indicated. Cool soln, transfer to 200 or 250 mL vol. flask, dil. to vol., mix, and filter thru dry filter.

★ Surplus method—*see* inside front cover.

(**a**) *Materials containing small quantities of organic matter.*—Dissolve in 30 mL HNO_3 and 3–5 mL HCl, and boil until org. matter is destroyed (30 min for liqs and suspensions).

★(**b**) *Fertilizers containing much Fe or Al phosphate, and basic slag.*★—Dissolve in 15–30 mL HCl and 3–10 mL HNO_3.

(**c**) *Organic material like cottonseed meal alone or in mixtures.*—Evap. with 5 mL $Mg(NO_3)_2$ soln, **2.019**, ignite, and dissolve in HCl.

★(**d**) *Materials or mixtures containing large amounts of organic matter.*★—Digestion with H_2SO_4 and $NaNO_3$ or KNO_3. *See* **2.017(d)**, 11th ed.

(**e**) *All fertilizers.*—Boil gently 30–45 min with 20–30 mL HNO_3 in suitable flask (preferably Kjeldahl for samples contg large amts of org. matter) to oxidize all easily oxidizable matter. Cool. Add 10–20 mL 70–72% $HClO_4$. Boil very gently until soln is colorless or nearly so and dense white fumes appear in flask. Do not boil to dryness at any time (Danger!). (With samples contg large amts of org. matter, raise temp. to fuming point, ca 170°, over period of ≥1 hr.) Cool slightly, add 50 mL H_2O, and boil few min.

Spectrophotometric Molybdovanadophosphate Method (10)—Official Final Action

(Not applicable to materials yielding colored solns or solns contg ions other than orthophosphate which form colored complexes with molybdovanadate. Not recommended for basic slag.)

2.021 ***Apparatus***

Photometer.—Beckman Instruments, Inc. Model DU (current models 24/25) spectrophtr with stray light filter and matched 1 cm cells. With other photometers analyst must det. suitability for use and conditions for satisfactory performance. Means for dispelling heat from light source is desirable.

2.022 ***Reagents***

(**a**) *Molybdovanadate reagent.*—Dissolve 40 g NH_4 molybdate.$4H_2O$ in 400 mL hot H_2O and cool. Dissolve 2 g NH_4 metavanadate in 250 mL hot H_2O, cool, and add 450 mL 70% $HClO_4$. (*Caution: See* **51.028(a)** and (**d**).) Gradually add molybdate soln to vanadate soln with stirring, and dil. to 2 L.

(**b**) *Phosphate std soln.*—Dry pure KH_2PO_4 (52.15% P_2O_5) 2 hr at 105°. Prep. solns contg 0.4–1.0 mg P_2O_5/mL in 0.1 mg increments by weighing 0.0767, 0.0959, 0.1151, 0.1342, 0.1534, 0.1726, and 0.1918 g KH_2PO_4 and dilg each to 100 mL with H_2O. Prep. fresh solns contg 0.4 and 0.7 mg P_2O_5/mL weekly.

2.023 ***Preparation of Standard Curve***

Pipet 5 mL aliquots of 7 std phosphate solns (2–5 mg P_2O_5/aliquot) into 100 mL vol. flasks and add 45 mL H_2O. Then, within 5 min for entire series, add 20 mL molybdovanadate reagent by buret or pipet, dil. to vol. and mix. Let stand 10 min.

Select 2 absorption cells (std and sample cells) and fill both with 2 mg std. Set spectrophtr to 400 nm and adjust to zero *A* with std cell. Sample cell must check zero *A* within 0.001 unit; otherwise read *A* for sample cell and correct subsequent readings. (Choose cell showing pos. *A* against other as sample cell so that this pos. *A* is always subtracted.) Using sample cell, det. *A* of other stds with instrument adjusted to zero *A* for 2 mg std. After each detn empty and refill cell contg 2 mg std, and readjust zero to avoid error that might arise from temp. changes. Plot *A* against concn in mg P_2O_5/mL std soln.

★ Surplus method—*see* inside front cover.

2.024 ***Preparation of Solution***

Treat 1 g sample as in **2.020**, preferably (**e**), when these acids are suitable solv. (Soln should be free of N oxides and NOCl.)

(**a**) For P_2O_5 content ≤5%, dil. to 250 mL.

(**b**) For P_2O_5 content >5%, dil. to such vol. that 5 or 10 mL aliquot contains 2–5 mg P_2O_5.

2.025 ***Determination***

Pipet, into 100 mL vol. flasks, 5 mL aliquots of std phosphate solns contg 2 and 3.5 mg P_2O_5/aliquot, resp., and develop color as in **2.023**. Adjust instrument to zero *A* for 2 mg std, and det. *A* of 3.5 mg std. (It is essential that *A* of latter std be practically identical with corresponding value on std curve.)

(**a**) *Samples containing up to 5% P_2O_5.*—Pipet, into 100 mL vol. flask, 5 mL sample soln, **2.024(a)**, and 5 mL std phosphate soln contg 2 mg P_2O_5. Develop color and det. *A* concurrently with and in same manner as for std phosphate solns in preceding par., with instrument adjusted to zero *A* for 2 mg std. Read P_2O_5 concn from std curve. With series of sample solns, empty and refill cell contg 2 mg std after each detn.

% P_2O_5 in sample = 100 × [(mg P_2O_5 from std curve − 2)/20].

(**b**) *Samples containing more than 5% P_2O_5.*—Pipet 5 or 10 mL sample soln, **2.024(b)**, into 100 mL vol. flask. Without adding std phosphate soln, proceed as in (**a**).

% P_2O_5 in sample = 100 × (mg P_2O_5 from std curve/mg sample in aliquot).

Gravimetric Quinolinium Molybdophosphate Method (11)—Official Final Action

2.026 ***Reagents***

(Store solns in polyethylene bottles.)

(**a**) *Citric-molybdic acid reagent.*—Dissolve 54 g 100% molybdic anhydride (MoO_3) and 12 g NaOH with stirring in 400 mL hot H_2O, and cool. Dissolve 60 g citric acid in mixt. of 140 mL HCl and 200 mL H_2O, and cool. Gradually add molybdic soln to citric acid soln with stirring. Cool, filter, and dil. to 1 L. (Soln may be green or blue; color deepens on exposure to light.) If necessary, add 0.5% $KBrO_3$ soln dropwise until green color pales. Store in dark.

(**b**) *Quinoline soln.*—Dissolve 50 mL *synthetic* quinoline, with stirring, in mixt. of 60 mL HCl and 300 mL H_2O. Cool, dil. to 1 L, and filter.

(**c**) *Quimociac reagent.*—Dissolve 70 g Na molybdate.$2H_2O$ in 150 mL H_2O. Dissolve 60 g citric acid in mixt. of 85 mL HNO_3 and 150 mL H_2O, and cool. Gradually add molybdate soln to citric acid-HNO_3 mixt. with stirring. Dissolve 5 mL *synthetic* quinoline in mixt. of 35 mL HNO_3 and 100 mL H_2O. Gradually add this soln to molybdate-citric acid-HNO_3 soln, mix, and let stand 24 hr. Filter, add 280 mL acetone, dil. to 1 L with H_2O, and mix.

2.027 ***Preparation of Solution***

Treat 1 g sample as in **2.020**, dilg to 200 mL.

2.028 ***Determination***

Pipet, into 500 mL erlenmeyer, aliquot contg ≤25 mg P_2O_5 and dil. to ca 100 mL with H_2O. Continue by one of the following methods:

(**a**) Add 30 mL citric-molybdic acid reagent and boil gently 3 min. (Soln must be ppt-free at this time.) Remove from heat and swirl carefully. Immediately add 10 mL quinoline soln from buret with continuous swirling. (Add first 3–4 mL dropwise and remainder in steady stream.) Or:

(**b**) Add 50 mL quimociac reagent, cover with watch glass, place on hot plate in well-ventilated hood, and boil 1 min.

After treatment by (**a**) or (**b**), cool to room temp., swirl carefully 3–4 times during cooling, filter into gooch with glass fiber filter paper previously dried at 250° and weighed, and wash with five 25 mL portions of H_2O. Dry crucible and contents 30 min at 250°, cool in desiccator to room temp., and weigh as $(C_9H_7N)_3H_3[PO_4.12MoO_3]$. Subtract wt reagent blank. Multiply by 0.03207 to obtain wt P_2O_5 (or by 0.01400 for P). Report as % P_2O_5 (or % P).

Alkalimetric Quinolinium Molybdophosphate Method (12)—Official Final Action

2.029 ***Reagents***

(**a**) *Quimociac reagent.—See* **2.026**(**c**).

(**b**) *Sodium hydroxide std soln.*—(1 mL = 1 mg P_2O_5.) Dil. 366.32 mL 1*N* NaOH, **50.032–50.036**, to 1 L with H_2O.

(**c**) *Nitric acid std soln.*—Prep. HNO_3 soln equiv. to concn of (**b**) and stdze by titrg against (**b**), using phthln. (For greater precision, use HNO_3 soln corresponding to 1/5 concn of (**b**).)

(**d**) *Citric acid.*—10% (w/v).

(**e**) *Indicators.*—*(1) Thymol blue soln.*—0.1%. Add 2.2 mL 0.1*N* NaOH to 0.1 g thymol blue and dil. to 100 mL with 50% alcohol. *(2) Phenolphthalein.*—0.1%. Dissolve 0.1 g phthln in 100 mL 50% alcohol. *(3) Mixed indicator.*—Mix 3 vols *(1)* and 2 vols *(2)*.

2.030 ***Preparation of Sample Solution***

Treat 1 g sample as in **2.020**, first par. and (**a**) or (**e**).

2.031 ***Determination***

(**a**) *Precipitation.*—Transfer aliquot contg ≤30 mg P_2O_5 and ≤5 mL concd acid to 500 mL erlenmeyer, add 20 mL citric acid soln, and adjust to ca 100 mL. Add 60 mL quimociac reagent, immediately cover with watch glass, and place on medium temp. hot plate. After soln comes to bp, move to cooler portion of hot plate and boil gently 1 min. Let cool until flask can be handled comfortably with bare hand.

(**b**) *Filtration and washing.*—Prep. pulped-paper pad ca 6 mm thick on perforated porcelain disk in funnel by adding ≥2 approx. equal increments of H_2O suspension of pulped paper and sucking dry with vac. between addns. Swirl flask, pour contents onto filter, and wash flask with five ca 15 mL portions H_2O, adding washings to funnel. Immediately after funnel has emptied, wash down sides with ca 15 mL H_2O to remove residual acetone, which causes excessively fast drying and later lump formation if allowed to evap. Wash with 3 addnl 15 mL portions H_2O, letting funnel empty between addns. Keep drying of ppt to min. Using only jet of H_2O, transfer ppt and pad to pptn flask and break up pad with jet of H_2O. Do not smear ppt against funnel or flask.

(**c**) *Titration.*—Titr. with std NaOH soln and add 3–5 mL excess. Add 1 mL mixed indicator and titr. with std HNO_3 soln to grey-blue end point. If overtitrd (greenish-yellow), add addnl excess std NaOH soln and titr. to grey-blue.

(**d**) *Blank.*—Det. blank on all reagents, adding known amt (1–2 mg) of P_2O_5. Use 1 + 9 dilns of std NaOH and HNO_3 for titrn and subtract theoretical titer equiv. to P_2O_5 added from experimental titer. Calc. difference equiv. to 0.3663*N* NaOH and subtract this blank from all sample detns.

Calc. and report as % P_2O_5.

Automated Method (13)—Official First Action

2.032 ***Principle***

Samples are extd for direct available P_2O_5 or for total P_2O_5 detns. Destruction of coloring matter, hydrolysis of nonorthophosphates, and elimination of citrate effect are accomplished by digestion with 4*N* $HClO_4$ at 95°. Digested samples are reacted with molybdovanadate reagent, and *A* of resulting complex is read in flowcell at 420 nm in range 0.15–0.35 mg P_2O_5/mL.

2.033 ***Apparatus and Reagents***

(*Caution: See* **51.028**.)

(**a**) *Automatic analyzer.*—AutoAnalyzer with following modules (Technicon Instruments Corp., or equiv.): Sampler II or IV with 40/hr (4:1) cam; proportioning pump III; P_2O_5 anal. cartridge (with 2 heating baths, each contg 10.6 mL coil held at 95±1°; or AAI type heating bath contg one 40′ × 1.6 mm id coil and holding constant temp. of 95±1°); AAII single channel colorimeter with 15 × 1.5 or 2.0 mm id flowcell and 420 nm interference filters; voltage stabilizer; and recorder. Construct manifold as in flow diagram, Fig. **2:06**.

(**b**) *Molybdovanadate reagent.*—Dissolve 16.5 g NH_4 molybdate.$4H_2O$ in 400 mL hot H_2O, and cool. Dissolve 0.6 g NH_4 metavanadate in 250 mL hot H_2O, cool, and add 60 mL 70% $HClO_4$. Gradually add molybdate soln to vanadate soln with stirring. Add 2 mL wetting agent, (**e**), and dil. to 2 L.

(**c**) *Perchloric acid.*—4*N*. Add 342 mL 70% $HClO_4$ to 500 mL H_2O in 1 L vol. flask. Add 1 mL wetting agent, and dil. to vol.

(**d**) *Sampler wash soln.*—Add 1 mL wetting agent to 1 L H_2O, and mix well.

(**e**) *Wetting agent.*—Ultrawet 60 L (Technicon No. T01-0214), or equiv.

(**f**) *Phosphorus std solns.*—*(1) Stock soln.*—10 mg P_2O_5/mL. Dissolve 9.5880 g dried (2 hr at 105°) KH_2PO_4 primary std (52.15% P_2O_5) in H_2O, and dil. to 500 mL with H_2O. *(2) Working solns.*—0.15, 0.19, 0.23, 0.27, 0.31, and 0.35 mg P_2O_5/mL. Using 25 mL buret, accurately measure 7.5, 9.5, 11.5, 13.5, 15.5, and 17.5 mL stock soln into six 500 mL vol. flasks. Dil. each to vol. with H_2O, and mix. *(3) Working soln for samples ≤7% P_2O_5.*—2 mg P_2O_5/mL. Pipet 100 mL stock soln into 500 mL vol. flask, dil. to vol. with H_2O, and mix.

2.034 ***Preparation of Samples***

Prep. samples for direct available P_2O_5 detn as in **2.050**(**a**). Prep. samples for total P_2O_5 detn as in **2.020**(**a**) or (*e*), and dil. to 250 mL.

2.035 ***Analytical System***

(Technicon part numbers are given to aid in construction of manifold; equiv. coils, fittings, etc., are satisfactory.)

Sample, air, and 4*N* $HClO_4$ are combined thru injection fitting (No. 116–0489) and mixed in 20T coil (No. 157–0248). Stream proceeds to heating bath(s) before resample thru modified AO fitting. Resample, air, and molybdovanadate reagent are combined thru injection fitting (No. 116–0489). Mixing and color development takes place in two 20T coils (No. 157–0248) before measurement at 420 nm. If only total P_2O_5 samples are to be analyzed, heating bath can be removed and 4*N* $HClO_4$ soln replaced by sampler wash soln, (**d**). Heating bath(s) and acid soln are necessary only when analyzing samples for direct available P_2O_5 or combination of direct available and total P_2O_5 detns.

If manifold is to be constructed following flow diagram, use clear std pump tubes for all air and soln flows. All fittings, coils, and glass transmission lines are AAII type and size. Use 1.6 mm glass transmission tubing for all connections after pump to colorimeter. Construct modified AO fitting, following heating bath, by using AO fitting, N13 stainless steel nipple connector,

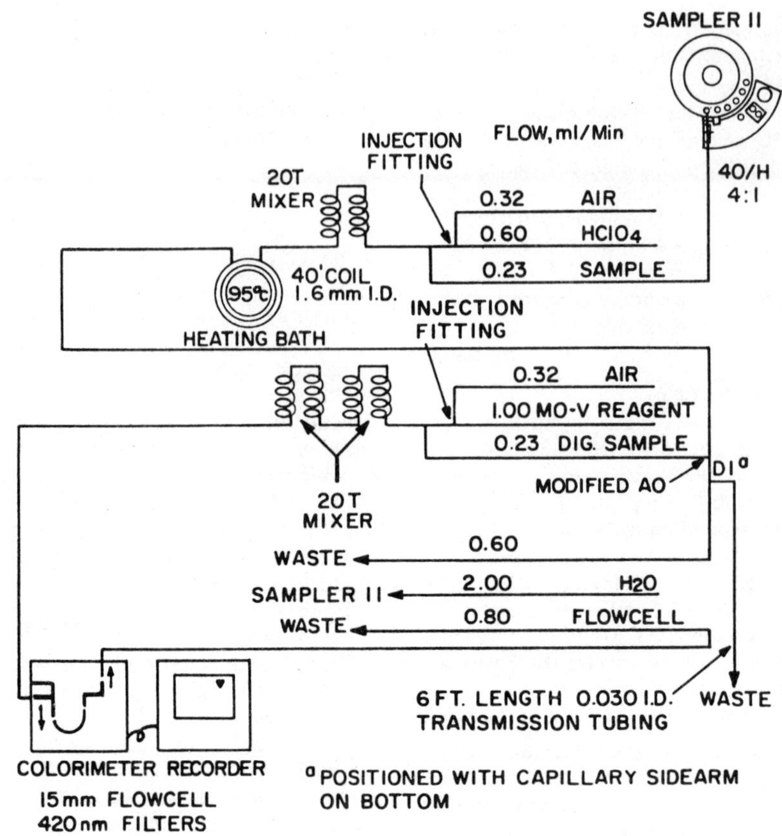

FIG. 2:06—Flow diagram for automated analysis for phosphorus

and 1.3 cm length of 0.035" id Tygon tubing. Insert N13 nipple approx. halfway into 0.035" Tygon tubing. Insert tubing into side arm of AO fitting far enough so resample line will not pump any air. Connect D1 fitting directly to waste side of AO fitting; position D1 fitting with capillary side arm on bottom. Attach 0.6 mL/min pump tube to top arm of D1 fitting, and attach 1.8 m (6') of 0.030" id transmission tubing to bottom arm. All air segments must pass thru 0.6 mL/min tube, leaving continuous column of liq. in 1.8 m length of tubing to provide for constant back pressure on heating bath coil. Length of resample pump tube should be ≤2.5 cm from shoulder at entrance end.

2.036 ***Start-Up***

Start automatic system, place all lines in resp. solns, and let equilibrate ≥30 min. Proceed as in **2.038**.

2.037 ***Shut-Down***

Pump water thru reagent lines ≥30 min. Do not remove $HClO_4$ lines from reagent until 20 min after last sample is run.

2.038 ***Check and Calibration***

After equilibration, set colorimeter to damp 1 position and pump 0.15 mg P_2O_5/mL working std soln continuously thru system. Adjust colorimeter baseline to read 10% of full scale. Pump 0.35 mg P_2O_5/mL std and adjust std calibration to read 90% of full scale. Range of 0.15–0.35 mg P_2O_5/mL will expand to read 10–90% of full scale. Check of bubble flow pattern will give indication of performance of system. Perfect bubble pattern is required to obtain optimum peak shapes. Check for air bubble in flowcell if noisy conditions exist. To check system carryover, place three 0.35 mg/mL stds, followed by three 0.15 mg/mL stds thru system. If first 0.15 mg/mL std following 0.35 mg/mL std is ≥1 chart division higher than other 2, carryover is indicated. If carryover occurs, check entire system for poor connections.

2.039 ***Determination***

Pipet aliquot of sample soln (*see* Table **2:02**) into 100 mL vol. flask, dil. to vol. with H_2O, and mix by inversion 20 times. For sample contg ≤7% P_2O_5, pipet 10 mL working soln, (**f**)(*3*), into flask before diln. Place 0.15–0.35 mg P_2O_5/mL working std solns in tray in increasing order of concn, followed by group of samples. Analyze lowest concn std in duplicate, discarding first peak. Precede and follow each group of samples with std ref. curve to correct for possible drift. If drift between first and last set of stds is ≥2 chart divisions, repeat sample analysis. Prep. std curve by averaging peak hts of first and second set of stds. Plot av. peak ht of stds against mg P_2O_5/mL contained in each std. Read mg P_2O_5/mL for each sample from graph.

% P_2O_5 = mg P_2O_5/mL from graph (−0.20, if spiked) × F × 100, where F = factor from Table **2.02**.

Table 2:02 Standard Dilutions

% P_2O_5 Expected	Aliquot (mL) Direct Available	Total	Factor
1–7	50 + "spike"	25 + "spike"	1
8–16	no diln	50	0.5
17–34	50	25	2 for direct available
≥35	25	15	1.667 for total

Water-Soluble Phosphorus

2.040 ***Preparation of Solution—Official Final Action***

Place 1 g sample on 9 cm filter and wash with small portions H_2O until filtrate measures ca 250 mL. Add H_2O in fine stream directed around entire periphery of filter paper in circular path, ensuring that H_2O and solids are thoroly mixed with each addn. Let each portion pass thru filter before adding more and use suction if washing would not otherwise be complete within 1 hr. If filtrate is turbid, add 1–2 mL HNO_3, dil. to 250 mL, and mix.

2.041 ***Gravimetric Quinolinium Molybdophosphate Method—Official Final Action***

Pipet aliquot contg ≤25 mg P_2O_5 into 500 mL erlenmeyer. Dil., if necessary, to 50 mL, add 10 mL HNO_3 (1+1), and boil gently 10 min. Cool, dil. to 100 mL, and proceed as in **2.028(b)**.

2.042 ***Alkalimetric Quinolinium Molybdophosphate Method—Official Final Action***

Pipet aliquot contg ≤30 mg P_2O_5 into 500 mL erlenmeyer. Dil., if necessary, to 50 mL, add 10 mL HNO_3 (1+1), boil gently 10 min, cool, and proceed as in **2.031(a)**, beginning ". . . add 20 mL citric acid soln . . ."

2.043 ***Spectrophotometric Molybdovanadophosphate Method—Official Final Action***

Adjust concn according to **2.024(a)** or **(b)** and proceed as in **2.025**.

Citrate-Insoluble Phosphorus (*14*) Official Final Action

2.044 ***Reagents***

(a) *Ammonium citrate soln.*—Should have sp gr of 1.09 at 20° and pH of 7.0 as detd potentiometrically.

Dissolve 370 g cryst. citric acid in 1.5 L H_2O and nearly neutze by adding 345 mL NH_4OH (28–29% NH_3). If concn of NH_3 is <28%, add correspondingly larger vol. and dissolve citric acid in correspondingly smaller vol. H_2O. Cool, and check pH. Adjust with NH_4OH (1+7) or citric acid soln to pH 7. Dil. soln, if necessary, to sp gr of 1.09 at 20°. (Vol. will be ca 2 L.) Keep in tightly stoppered bottles and check pH from time to time. If pH has changed from 7.0, readjust.

(b) *Other reagents and solns.—See* **2.019**, **2.022**, or **2.026**.

2.045 ***Preparation of Extract***

(a) *Acidulated samples, mixed fertilizers, and materials containing water-soluble compounds.*—After removing H_2O-sol. P_2O_5, **2.040**, transfer filter and residue, within 1 hr, to 200 or 250 mL flask contg 100 mL NH_4 citrate soln previously heated to 65°. Close flask tightly with smooth rubber stopper, shake vigorously until paper is reduced to pulp, and relieve pressure by removing stopper momentarily. Continuously agitate stoppered flask in const temp. app. at exactly 65°. (Action of app. should be such that dispersion of sample in citrate soln is continually maintained and entire inner surface of flask and stopper is continually bathed with soln.)

Exactly 1 hr after adding filter and residue, remove flask from app. and immediately filter by suction as rapidly as possible thru Whatman No. 5 paper, or equiv., using buchner or ordinary funnel with Pt or other cone. Wash with H_2O at 65° until vol. filtrate is ca 350 mL, allowing time for thoro draining before adding more H_2O. If material yields cloudy filtrate, wash with 5% *NH_4NO_3 soln*. Prep. citrate-insol. residue for analysis by one of following methods:

(*1*) Dry paper and contents, transfer to crucible, ignite until all org. matter is destroyed, and digest with 10–15 mL HCl until all phosphate dissolves; or (*2*) treat wet filter and contents as in **2.020(a)**, **(c)**, **(d)**, or **(e)**. Dil. soln to 250 mL, or other suitable vol., mix well, and filter thru dry paper.

(b) *Nonacidulated samples.*—Place 1 g sample (ground to pass No. 40 sieve in case of Ca metaphosphate) on dry 9 cm paper. Without previous washing with H_2O, proceed as in **(a)**. If sample contains much org. matter (bone, fish, etc.), dissolve residue insol. in NH_4 citrate as in **2.020(c)**, **(d)**, or **(e)**.

2.046 ***Determination***

(a) *Gravimetric quinolinium molybdophosphate method* (*11*).—Treat 1 g sample as in **2.045(a)** or **(b)**. Transfer aliquot of citrate-insol. P_2O_5 contg ≤25 mg P_2O_5 and proceed as in **2.028**.

(b) *Spectrophotometric molybdovanadophosphate method* (*15*).—Treat 1 g sample as in **2.045(a)** or **(b)**. Adjust concn of citrate-insol. P_2O_5 soln as in **2.024(a)** or **(b)** and proceed as in **2.025**.

(c) *Alkalimetric quinolinium molybdophosphate method* (*16*).—Treat 1 g sample by **2.045(a)** or **(b)**. Transfer aliquot of citrate-insol. P_2O_5 contg ≤5 mL concd acid to 500 mL erlenmeyer. Add 20 mL 10% citric acid soln and dil. to 100 mL with H_2O. Continue as in **2.031(a)**, beginning "Add 60 mL quimociac reagent, . . ."

2.047 **Citrate-Soluble Phosphorus—Official Final Action**

Subtract sum of H_2O-sol. and citrate-insol. P_2O_5 from total P_2O_5 to obtain citrate-sol. P_2O_5.

Available Phosphorus

2.048 ***Indirect Method—Official Final Action***

Subtract citrate-insol. P_2O_5 from total P_2O_5 to obtain available P_2O_5.

Direct Method (17)—Official Final Action

2.049 ***Reagents***

(*Caution: See* **51.026**, **51.028**, **51.030**, and **Acids**, Chap. **51**.)

(a) *Nitric-perchloric acid mixture.*—Add 300 mL 70% $HClO_4$ to 700 mL HNO_3.

(b) *Ternary acid mixture.*—Add 20 mL H_2SO_4 to 100 mL HNO_3, mix, and add 40 mL 70% $HClO_4$.

(c) *Modified molybdovanadate reagent.*—Prep. as in **2.022(a)** except use 250 mL 70% $HClO_4$ instead of 450 mL.

2.050 ***Preparation of Solution***

(a) *Acidulated samples, mixed fertilizers, and materials containing water-soluble compounds.*—(*1*) *Without filtration of citrate digest.*—Remove H_2O-sol. P_2O_5 as in **2.040**,collecting filtrate in 500 ml vol. flask, but do not add HNO_3 to filtrate. Treat H_2O-insol. residue with NH_4 citrate soln as in **2.045(a)**. Exactly 1 hr after adding filter and residue, remove flask from app. and transfer contents to flask contg H_2O-sol. fraction. Cool to room temp. immediately, dil. to vol., mix thoroly, and let stand ≥2 hr before removing aliquot.

(*2*) *With filtration of citrate digest.*—If desired, wash by gravity into 500 mL Kohlrausch flask contg 5 mL HNO_3 (1+1), catching filtrate from insol. residue, **2.045(a)**, in the Kohlrausch flask contg H_2O-sol. fraction, and wash residue until vol. soln in flask is ca 500 mL. Cool, dil. to 500 mL, and mix.

(**b**) *Nonacidulated samples.*—Place 1 g sample (ground to pass No. 40 sieve in case of Ca metaphosphate) on dry 9 cm paper. Without previous washing with H_2O, proceed as in (**a**)(*1*) or (*2*). If (*2*) is used, wash residue until vol. soln is ca 350 mL. Cool, dil. to 500 mL, and mix.

2.051 *Alkalimetric Quinolinium Molybdophosphate Method (16)—Official Final Action*

Treat 1 g sample by appropriate modification of **2.050**. Transfer aliquot contg ≤30 mg P_2O_5 and ≤10 mL NH_4 citrate soln, **2.044**(**a**), to 500 mL erlenmeyer. Dil., if necessary, to 50 mL, add 10 mL HNO_3 (1+1), and boil gently 10 min. Cool, dil. to 100 mL, and continue as in **2.031**(**a**), beginning "Add 60 mL quimociac reagent, . . ."

2.052 *Spectrophotometric Molybdovanadophosphate Method (18)—Official Final Action*

(Not applicable to materials yielding colored solns or solns contg ions other than orthophosphate which form colored complexes with molybdovanadate. Not recommended for basic slag.)

Prep. std curve as in **2.023**, using photometer, **2.021**.

Pipet, into 100 mL vol. flasks, 5 mL aliquots std phosphate solns contg 2 and 3.5 mg P_2O_5/aliquot, **2.022**(**b**), resp., add 2 mL 70% $HClO_4$, and develop color as in **2.023**. Adjust instrument to zero *A* for 2 mg std and det. *A* of 3.5 mg std. (*A* of latter must be practically identical with corresponding value on std curve.)

Prep. sample as in **2.050**.

(**a**) *Samples containing up to 5% P_2O_5.*—Pipet 10 mL sample soln into 125 mL erlenmeyer, and treat by one of following methods (*Caution: See* **51.019**, **51.026**, and **51.028**):

(*1*) Add 5 mL 20% $NaClO_3$ soln and 10 mL HNO_3-$HClO_4$ mixt., **2.049**(**a**). Boil gently until greenish-yellow color disappears (ca 20 min), cool, and add 2 mL HCl. After vigorous reaction subsides, evap. to fumes of $HClO_4$, and fume 2 min.

(*2*) Add 5 mL ternary acid mixt., **2.049**(**b**), swirl, boil gently 15 min, and digest at 150–200° until clear white salt or colorless soln remains. Evap. to white fumes and continue heating 5 min.

Cool, add 15 mL H_2O, and boil 5 min. Transfer to 100 mL vol. flask, dil. to 50 ml, swirl, and cool to room temp. Add 5 mL std phosphate soln contg 2 mg P_2O_5 and 20 mL modified molybdovanadate soln, **2.049**(**c**). Dil. to 100 mL, and continue as in **2.025**(**a**).

(**b**) *Samples containing more than 5% P_2O_5.*—Dil. soln to such vol. that 5–10 mL aliquot contains 2–5 mg P_2O_5. Digest as in (**a**)(*1*) or (*2*). Without adding std phosphate soln, continue as in (**a**).

2.053 *Gravimetric Quinolinium Molybdophosphate Method (19)—Official Final Action*

(**a**) *Solns containing no organic phosphorus.*—Prep. sample as in **2.050**. Pipet, into 500 mL erlenmeyer, aliquot contg ≤25 mg P_2O_5 and ≤10 mL original NH_4 citrate soln. Dil., if necessary, to ca 50 mL, add 10 mL HNO_3 (1+1), and boil gently 10 min. Cool, dil. to 150 mL, and proceed as in **2.028**(**a**) or (**b**).

(**b**) *Solns containing organic phosphorus.*—(*Caution: See* **51.019**, **51.026**, and **51.028**.) Select aliquot as in (**a**). Add 10 mL 20% $NaClO_3$ and 10 mL HNO_3-$HClO_4$ mixt., **2.049**(**a**). Boil vigorously until greenish-yellow color disappears (usually ca 30 min), cool, and add 2 mL HCl. After vigorous reaction subsides, evap. to white fumes, and continue heating 5 min. Cool, and proceed as in **2.028**(**a**) or (**b**).

NITROGEN

2.054 Detection of Nitrates—Official Final Action

Mix 5 g sample with 25 mL hot H_2O, and filter. To 1 vol. of this soln add 2 vols H_2SO_4, free from HNO_3 and oxides of N, and let cool. Add few drops *concd $FeSO_4$ soln* in such manner that fluids do not mix. If nitrates are present, junction at first shows purple, afterwards brown, or if only minute amt is present, reddish color. To another portion of soln add 1 mL *1% $NaNO_3$ soln* and test as before to det. whether enough H_2SO_4 was added in first test.

Total Nitrogen

(Provide adequate ventilation in laboratory and do not permit accumulation of exposed Hg.)

2.055 *Reagents—Official Final Action*

(**a**) *Sulfuric acid.*—93–98% H_2SO_4, N-free.

(**b**) *Mercuric oxide or metallic mercury.*—HgO or Hg, reagent grade, N-free.

(**c**) *Potassium sulfate (or anhydrous sodium sulfate).*—Reagent grade, N-free.

(**d**) *Salicylic acid.*—Reagent grade, N-free.

(**e**) *Sulfide or thiosulfate soln.*—Dissolve 40 g com. K_2S in 1 L H_2O. (Soln of 40 g Na_2S or 80 g $Na_2S_2O_3.5H_2O$ in 1 L may be used.)

(**f**) *Sodium hydroxide.*—Pellets or soln, nitrate-free. For soln, dissolve ca 450 g solid NaOH in H_2O, cool, and dil. to 1 L. (Sp gr of soln should be ≥1.36.)

(**g**) *Zinc granules.*—Reagent grade.

(**h**) *Zinc dust.*—Impalpable powder.

(**i**) *Methyl red indicator.*—Dissolve 1 g Me red in 200 mL alcohol.

(**j**) *Hydrochloric or sulfuric acid std soln.*—0.5*N*, or 0.1*N* when amt of N is small. Prep. as in **50.011** or **50.039**.

(**k**) *Sodium hydroxide std soln.*—0.1*N* (or other specified concn). Prep. as in **50.032–50.034**.

Stdze each std soln with primary std, Chap. **50**, and check one against the other. Test reagents before use by blank detn with 2 g sugar, which ensures partial reduction of any nitrates present.

Caution: Use freshly opened H_2SO_4 or add dry P_2O_5 to avoid hydrolysis of nitriles and cyanates. Ratio of salt to acid (wt:vol.) should be ca 1:1 at end of digestion for proper temp. control. Digestion may be incomplete at lower ratio; N may be lost at higher ratio. Each g fat consumes 10 mL H_2SO_4, and each g carbohydrate 4 mL H_2SO_4 during digestion.

2.056 *Apparatus—Official Final Action*

(**a**) *For digestion.*—Use Kjeldahl flasks of hard, moderately thick, well-annealed glass with total capacity ca 500–800 mL. Conduct digestion over heating device adjusted to bring 250 mL H_2O at 25° to rolling boil in ca 5 min or other time as specified in method. To test heaters, preheat 10 min if gas or 30 min if elec. Add 3–4 boiling chips to prevent superheating.

(**b**) *For distillation.*—Use 500–800 mL Kjeldahl or other suitable flask, fitted with rubber stopper thru which passes lower end of efficient scrubber bulb or trap to prevent mech. carryover of NaOH during distn. Connect upper end of bulb tube to condenser tube by rubber tubing. Trap outlet of condenser in such way as to ensure complete absorption of NH_3 distd over into acid in receiver.

2.057 ***Improved Kjeldahl Method for Nitrate-Free Samples (20)—Official Final Action***

(*Caution: See* **51.030** and **51.065**.)

Place weighed sample (0.7–2.2 g) in digestion flask. Add 0.7 g HgO or 0.65 g metallic Hg, 15 g powd K_2SO_4 or anhyd. Na_2SO_4, and 25 mL H_2SO_4. If sample >2.2 g is used, increase H_2SO_4 by 10 mL for each g sample. Place flask in inclined position and heat gently until frothing ceases (if necessary, add small amt of paraffin to reduce frothing); boil briskly until soln clears and then ≥30 min longer (2 hr for samples contg org. material).

Cool, add ca 200 mL H_2O, cool <25°, add 25 mL of the sulfide or thiosulfate soln, and mix to ppt Hg. Add few Zn granules to prevent bumping, tilt flask, and add layer of NaOH without agitation. (For each 10 mL H_2SO_4 used, or its equiv. in dild H_2SO_4, add 15 g solid NaOH or enough soln to make contents strongly alk.) (Thiosulfate or sulfide soln may be mixed with the NaOH soln before addn to flask.) Immediately connect flask to distg bulb on condenser, and, with tip of condenser immersed in std acid and 5–7 drops indicator in receiver, rotate flask to mix contents thoroly; then heat until all NH_3 has distd (≥150 mL distillate). Remove receiver, wash tip of condenser, and titr. excess std acid in distillate with std NaOH soln. Correct for blank detn on reagents.

$$\% \text{ N} = [(\text{mL std acid} \times \text{normality acid}) - (\text{mL std NaOH} \times \text{normality NaOH})] \times 1.4007/\text{g sample}$$

2.058 ***Improved Kjeldahl Method for Nitrate-Containing Samples—Official Final Action***

(Not applicable to liqs or to materials with high $Cl:NO_3$ ratio. *Caution: See* **51.030** and **51.065**.)

Place weighed sample (0.7–2.2 g) in digestion flask. Add 40 mL H_2SO_4 contg 2 g salicylic acid. Shake until thoroly mixed and let stand, with occasional shaking, ≥30 min; then add (*1*) 5 g $Na_2S_2O_3.5H_2O$ or (*2*) 2 g Zn dust (as impalpable powder, not granulated Zn or filings). Shake and let stand 5 min; then heat over low flame until frothing ceases. Turn off heat, add 0.7 g HgO (or 0.65 g metallic Hg) and 15 g powd K_2SO_4 (or anhyd. Na_2SO_4), and boil briskly until soln clears, then ≥30 min longer (2 hr for samples contg org. material).

Proceed as in second par. of **2.057**.

Comprehensive Nitrogen Method (21) Official Final Action

(Applicable to all fertilizer samples. *Caution: See* **51.030** and **51.079**.)

2.059 ***Reagents***

(**a**) *Chromium metal.*—100 mesh, low N (Fisher Scientific Co. No. C-318 or Sargent-Welch Scientific Co. No. SC11432 is satisfactory).

(**b**) *Alundum.*—Boiling stones. 8–14 mesh (Arthur H. Thomas Co. No. 1590–D18, or equiv.).

(**c**) *Dilute sulfuric acid.*—Slowly add 625 mL H_2SO_4 to 300 mL H_2O. Dil. to ca 1 L and mix. After cooling, dil. to 1 L with H_2O and mix. Avoid absorption of NH_3 from air during prepn, particularly if stream of air is used for mixing.

(**d**) *Sodium thiosulfate or potassium sulfide soln.*—160 g $Na_2S_2O_3.5H_2O$/L or 80 g K_2S/L.

For other reagents, *see* **2.055**.

2.060 ***Determination***

Place 0.2–2.0 g sample contg ≤60 mg nitrate N in 500–800 mL Kjeldahl flask and add 1.2 g Cr powder. Add 35 mL H_2O or, with liqs, amt to make total vol. 35 ml. Let stand 10 min with occasional gentle swirling to dissolve all nitrate salts. Add 7 mL HCl and let stand ≥30 sec but ≤10 min.

Place flask on preheated burner with heat input set at 7.0–7.5 min boil test, **2.056(a)**. After heating 3.5 min, remove from heat and let cool.

Add 22 g K_2SO_4, 1.0 g HgO, and few granules Alundum. Add 40 mL dil. H_2SO_4, (**c**). (If adequate ventilation is available, 25 mL H_2SO_4 may be added instead of dil. H_2SO_4. If org. matter which consumes large amt of acid exceeds 1.0 g, add addnl 1.0 mL H_2SO_4 for each 0.1 g org. matter in excess of 1.0 g.)

Place flask on burners set at 5 min boil test. (Pre-heated burners reduce foaming with most samples. Reduce heat input if foam fills ≥⅔ of bulb of flask. Use variable heat input until this phase is past.) Heat at 5 min boil test until dense white fumes of H_2SO_4 clear bulb of flask. Digestion is now complete for samples contg ammoniacal, nitrate, and urea N. For other samples, swirl flask gently and continue digestion 60 min more.

Proceed as in **2.057**, second par., substituting **2.059(d)** for **2.055(e)**.

Modified Comprehensive Nitrogen Method (22) Official First Action

(Applicable to all fertilizer samples)

2.061 ***Reagents***

See **2.055(a)**, (**c**), (**f**), (**i**), (**j**), (**k**), **2.059(a)**, (**b**), and in addn:

Copper sulfate pentahydrate (*or anhydrous copper sulfate*).—Reagent grade, N-free.

2.062 ***Determination***

(*Caution: See* **51.019** and **51.030**.)

Proceed as in **2.060**, par. 1 and 2, using 0.2–1.6 g sample. For samples contg orgs other than urea or urea-form, use ≥0.5 g sample.

Add 15 g K_2SO_4 or 12 g anhyd. Na_2SO_4, 0.4 g anhyd. $CuSO_4$ or 0.6 g $CuSO_4.5H_2O$, and ca 0.8 g Alundum granules. Add 37 mL H_2SO_4 (1+1). (If adequate ventilation is available, 20 mL H_2SO_4 may be added instead of H_2SO_4 (1+1). If org. matter other than urea exceeds 1.0 g, add addnl 1.0 mL H_2SO_4 for each 0.1 g fat or 0.2 g other org. matter in excess of 1.0 g.)

Proceed as in **2.060**, par. 4, substituting 75 min for 60 min in last sentence.

Cool flask until it can be handled without gloves, and add ca 250 mL H_2O. Swirl to dissolve contents, and cool <25°. Add ca 0.8 g Alundum granules to minimize bumping, tilt flask, and add layer of NaOH without agitation. (For each 10 ml H_2SO_4 used, or its equiv. in H_2SO_4 (1+1), add 15 g solid NaOH or enough soln to make contents strongly alk.) Proceed as in **2.057**, par. 2, beginning "Immediately connect flask to distg bulb . . ."

Raney Powder Method (21) Official Final Action

(Applicable to all fertilizer samples except "nitric phosphates" contg nonsulfate S. *Caution: See* **51.030** and **51.079**.)

2.063 ***Reagents***

(**a**) *Raney catalyst powder No. 2813.*—50% Ni, 50% Al (W. R. Grace & Co., Davison Chemical Division, 10 E Baltimore St, Baltimore, MD 21203). *Caution:* Raney catalyst powders react slowly in H_2O or moist air to form alumina; avoid prolonged contact with air or moisture during storage or use.

(**b**) *Sulfuric acid-potassium sulfate soln.*—Slowly add 200 mL H_2SO_4 to 625 mL H_2O and mix. Without cooling, add 106.7 g

K_2SO_4 and continue stirring until all salt dissolves. Dil. to ca 1 L and mix. Cool, dil. to 1 L with H_2O, and mix. Avoid absorption of NH_3 from air during prepn particularly if stream of air is used for mixing.

For other reagents, see **2.055**.

2.064 ***Determination***

Place 0.2–2.0 g sample contg ≤42 mg nitrate N in 500–800 mL Kjeldahl flask (800 mL flask is preferred with samples which foam considerably, especially orgs). Add 1.7 g Raney catalyst powder, 3 drops *tributyl citrate,* and 150 mL H_2SO_4-K_2SO_4 soln. If org. matter exceeds 0.6 g, add addnl 2.5 mL of this soln for each 0.1 g org. matter in excess of 0.6 g.

Swirl to mix sample with acid and place flask on cold burner. If burner has been in use, turn off completely ≥10 min before placing flask on burner. After flask is on burner, set heat input to 5 min boil test. When sample starts boiling, reduce heat to pass 10 min boil test. After 10 min, raise flask to vertical position and add 0.7 g HgO and 15 g K_2SO_4. (Contents of Kel-Pak No. 5 (Curtin Matheson Scientific, Inc.) without plastic container may be used.) Replace flask in inclined position and increase heat to 4–5 min boil test. (Reduce heat input if foam fills ≥⅔ of bulb of flask. Use variable heat input until this phase is past.) Heat at 4–5 min boil test until dense white fumes of H_2SO_4 clear bulb of flask. Digestion is now complete for samples contg only ammoniacal, nitrate, and urea N. For other samples, swirl flask gently and continue digestion addnl 30 min.

Proceed as in **2.057**, second par. If 800 mL Kjeldahl flasks have been used, add 300 instead of 200 mL H_2O.

Ammoniacal Nitrogen

2.065 ***Magnesium Oxide Method—Official Final Action***

(Not applicable in presence of urea)

Place 0.7–3.5 g, according to NH_3 content of sample, in distn flask with ca 200 mL H_2O and ≥2 g *carbonate-free MgO.* Connect flask to condenser by Kjeldahl connecting bulb, distil 100 mL liq. into measured amt std acid, **2.055(j)**, and titr. with std NaOH soln, **2.055(k)**, using Me red, **2.055(i)**.

2.066 ★ ***Formaldehyde Titration Method*** ★
Official Final Action

(Applicable to NH_4NO_3 and $(NH_4)_2SO_4$)

See **2.058**, 11th ed.

Nitrate and Ammoniacal Nitrogen

2.067 ★ ***Ferrous Sulfate-Zinc-Soda Method*** ★
Official Final Action

(Not applicable in presence of org. matter, Ca cyanamide, and urea)

See **2.059**, 11th ed.

2.068 ***Devarda Method (23)—Official Final Action***

(Not applicable in presence of org. matter, Ca cyanamide, and urea)

Place 0.35 or 0.5 g sample in 600–700 mL flask and add 300 mL H_2O, 3 g *Devarda alloy* (Cu 50, Al 45, Zn 5), and 5 mL NaOH soln (42% by wt), pouring latter down side of flask so that it does not mix at once with contents. By means of Davisson (J. Ind. Eng. Chem. **11**, 465(1919)) or other suitable scrubbing bulb that will prevent passing over of any spray, connect with condenser, tip of which always extends beneath surface of std acid in receiving flask. Mix contents of distg flask by rotating. Heat slowly at first and then at rate to yield 250 mL distillate in 1 hr. Collect distillate in measured amt std acid, **2.055(j)**, and titr. with std NaOH soln, **2.055(k)**, using Me red, **2.055(i)**.

Nitrate Nitrogen

2.069 ***Robertson Method (24)—Official Final Action***

(Applicable in presence of Ca cyanamide and urea. *Caution: See* **51.030** and **51.065**.)

(a) Det. total N as in **2.058**, **2.060**, or **2.064**.

(b) Det. H_2O-insol. N as in **2.072**, but use 2.5 g sample. Dil. filtrate to 250 mL.

(c) Place 50 mL portion filtrate in 500 mL Kjeldahl flask and add 2 g $FeSO_4.7H_2O$ and 20 mL H_2SO_4. (If total N is >5%, use 5 g $FeSO_4.7H_2O$.) Digest over hot flame until all H_2O is evapd and white fumes appear, and continue digestion at least 10 min to drive off nitrate N. If severe bumping occurs, add 10–15 glass beads. Add 0.65 g Hg, or 0.7 g HgO, and digest until all org. matter is oxidized. Cool, dil., add the K_2S soln, and complete detn as in **2.057**. Before distn, add pinch of mixt. of Zn dust and granular "20-mesh" Zn to each flask to prevent bumping.

Total N **(a)** − H_2O-insol. N **(b)** = H_2O-sol. N.

H_2O-sol. N − N obtained in **(c)** = nitrate N.

2.070 ***Jones Modification of Robertson Method (24)***
Official Final Action

(Applicable when H_2O-sol. N need not be detd. *Caution: See* **51.030** and **51.065**.)

Weigh 0.5 g sample into Kjeldahl flask, add 50 mL H_2O, and rotate gently. Add 2 g $FeSO_4.7H_2O$ and rotate. Add 20 mL H_2SO_4. Digest over hot flame. When H_2O evaps and white fumes appear, add 0.65 g Hg and proceed as in **2.057**.

Total N − N thus found = nitrate N.

2.071 ★ **Water-Insoluble Nitrogen in Cyanamide (25)** ★
Official Final Action

See **2.063**, 11th ed.

Water-Insoluble Nitrogen

(*See* **2.079(a)** and **(b)** for urea-formaldehyde or mixts contg such compds.)

2.072 ***Method I—Official Final Action***

Place 1 or 1.4 g sample in 50 mL beaker, wet with alcohol, add 20 mL H_2O, and let stand 15 min, stirring occasionally. Transfer supernate to 11 cm Whatman No. 2 paper in 60° long-stem funnel 60 mm diam., and wash residue 4 or 5 times by decanting with H_2O at room temp. (20–25°). Finally transfer all residue to filter and complete washing until filtrate measures 250 mL. Det. N in residue as in **2.057**.

Method II (26)—Official First Action

2.073 ***Apparatus***

Extraction tube.—Glass, 250 × 10 mm id, 12 mm od, constricted to 3–4 mm at one end.

2.074 ***Determination***

Weigh 3.0 g unground mixed sample and place in extn tube contg small glass wool plug. Place addnl glass wool pad on top

★ Surplus method—*see* inside front cover.

of sample. Connect 250 or 500 mL separator to column with 75 mm piece of rubber tubing. Close stopcock of separator and add 250 mL deionized H_2O. Open stopcock and let quick rush of H_2O pass thru column. After initial rush of H_2O, close stopcock. Adjust flow thru stopcock to ca 2 mL/min. Squeeze rubber connection to bring level of H_2O ca 25 mm above column bed. System then operates as constant-head feeder.

After H_2O wash is complete, disconnect column from rubber tubing. Invert column over Kjeldahl flask and force contents into flask with aid of pressure bulb. Wash traces of sample from tube into Kjeldahl flask and wash sample from walls of digestion flask with min. H_2O. Det. N in residue as in **2.059–2.060** or **2.063–2.064**.

★ Nitrogen Activity ★

2.075 ***Removal of Water-Soluble Nitrogen***
Official Final Action

(**a**) *Mixed fertilizers.—See* **2.058**, 10th ed.
(**b**) *Raw materials.—See* **2.058**, 10th ed.

2.076 ***Water-Insoluble Organic Nitrogen Soluble in Neutral Permanganate***
Official Final Action

See **2.059**, 10th ed.

2.077 ***Water-Insoluble Organic Nitrogen Distilled from Alkaline Permanganate (27)***
Official Final Action

See **2.060–2.061**, 10th ed.

Nitrogen Activity Index (AI) of Urea-Formaldehyde Compounds (*28*)
Official Final Action

(Applicable to urea-formaldehyde compds and mixts contg such compds)

2.078 ***Reagent***

Phosphate buffer soln.—pH 7.5. Dissolve 14.3 g KH_2PO_4 and 91.0 g K_2HPO_4 in H_2O and dil. to 1 L. Dil. 100 mL of this soln to 1 L.

2.079 ***Determination***

(**a**) Crush sample (do not grind) to pass No. 20 sieve.

(**b**) Det. cold H_2O-insol. N (*WIN*) as in **2.072**, keeping temp. at 25±2°. Stir at 5 min intervals during 15 min standing.

(**c**) Det. hot H_2O-insol. N (*HWIN*) in phosphate buffer soln as follows: Place accurately weighed sample contg 0.1200 g *WIN* in 200 mL tall-form beaker. Add ca 0.5 g $CaCO_3$ to mixed fertilizers contg urea-HCHO compds. From supply of boiling buffer soln, add 100 mL from graduate to sample, stir, cover, and immerse *promptly* in boiling H_2O bath so that liq. in beaker is below H_2O level in bath. Maintain bath at 98–100°, checked with thermometer, and stir at 10 min intervals. After exactly 30 min, remove beaker from bath and filter promptly thru 15 cm Whatman No. 12 fluted paper. If filtration takes >4 min, discard detn. Repeat detn, stirring in 1 g Celite filter-aid just before removing beaker from bath, and filter.

Wash insol. residue completely onto paper with boiling H_2O and continue washing until total vol. used is 100 mL. Complete washing before filtrate becomes cloudy or its temp. drops to <60°. Det. total N (*HWIN*) in wet paper and residue as in **2.057**, using 35 mL H_2SO_4 when $CaCO_3$ has been added.

Activity index (AI) = (%*WIN* − %*HWIN*) × 100/%*WIN*

Urea (*29*)—Official Final Action

2.080 ***Reagent***

Neutral urease soln.—Use fresh com. 1% urease soln, or dissolve 1 g urease powder in 100 mL H_2O, or shake 1 g jack bean meal with 100 mL H_2O 5 min. Transfer 10 mL soln to 250 mL erlenmeyer, dil. with 50 mL H_2O, and add 4 drops Me purple (available from Fisher Scientific Co.; No. So-I-9). Titr. with 0.1*N* HCl to reddish purple; then back-titr. to green with 0.1*N* NaOH. From difference in mL, calc. vol. 0.1*N* HCl required to neutze remainder of soln (usually ca 2.5 mL/100 mL), add this amount of acid, and shake well.

Verify enzyme activity of urease source periodically. Discard any source which does not produce soln capable of hydrolyzing 0.1 g urea/20 mL soln.

2.081 ***Determination***

Weigh 10±0.01 g sample and transfer to 15 cm Whatman No. 12 fluted filter paper. Leach with ca 300 mL H_2O into 500 mL vol. flask. Add 75–100 mL satd $Ba(OH)_2$ soln to ppt phosphates. Let settle and test for complete pptn with few drops satd $Ba(OH)_2$ soln. Add 20 mL 10% Na_2CO_3 soln to ppt excess Ba and any sol. Ca salts. Let settle and test for complete pptn. Dil. to vol., mix, and filter thru 15 cm Whatman No. 12 fluted paper. Transfer 50 mL aliquot (equiv. to 1 g sample) to 200 or 250 mL erlenmeyer and add 1–2 drops of Me purple. Acidify with 2*N* HCl and add 2–3 drops excess. Neutze soln with 0.1*N* NaOH to first change in color of indicator. Add 20 mL neutral urease soln, close flask with rubber stopper, and let stand 1 hr at 20–25°. Cool flask in ice-H_2O slurry and titr. at once with 0.1*N* HCl to full purple; then add ca 5 mL excess. Record total vol. added. Back-titr. excess HCl with 0.1*N* NaOH to neut. end point.

% Urea = (mL 0.1*N* HCl − mL 0.1*N* NaOH) × 0.3003.

Biuret
Spectrophotometric Method (30)
Official First Action

(Applicable to urea only. Do not use for mixed fertilizers)

2.082 ***Reagents***

(**a**) *Alkaline tartrate soln.*—Dissolve 40 g NaOH in 500 mL H_2O, cool, add 50 g $NaKC_4H_4O_6.4H_2O$, and dil. to 1 L. Let stand 1 day before use.

(**b**) *Copper sulfate soln.*—Dissolve 15 g $CuSO_4.5H_2O$ in CO_2-free H_2O and dil. to 1 L.

(**c**) *Biuret std soln.*—1 mg/mL. Dissolve 100 mg reagent grade biuret in CO_2-free H_2O and dil. to 100 mL. Biuret may be purified as follows: Dissolve 10 g in 1 L absolute alcohol and conc. by gentle heating to ca 250 mL. Cool at 5° and filter thru gooch (60% recovery). Repeat crystn and dry final product in vac. oven at 80°.

2.083 ***Preparation of Standard Curve***

Transfer series of aliquots, 2–50 mL, of std biuret soln to 100 mL vol. flasks. Adjust vol. to ca 50 mL with CO_2-free H_2O, add 1 drop Me red, and neutze with 0.1*N* H_2SO_4 to pink color. Add, with swirling, 20 mL alk. tartrate soln and then 20 mL $CuSO_4$ soln. Dil. to vol., shake 10 sec, and place in H_2O bath 15 min at 30±5°. Also prep. reagent blank. Det. *A* of each soln against blank at 555 nm (instrument with 500–570 nm filter is also satisfactory) with 2–4 cm cell. Plot std curve.

★ Surplus method—*see* inside front cover.

2.084 ***Determination***

Continuously stir ≤10 g sample contg 30–125 mg biuret in 150 mL ca 50° H_2O 30 min. Filter and wash into 250 mL vol. flask, and dil. to vol. Transfer 50 mL aliquot to 100 mL vol. flask and proceed as in **2.083**.

Atomic Absorption Spectrophotometric Method (31)
Official Final Action

2.085 ***Apparatus and Reagents***

(**a**) *Atomic absorption spectrophotometer.*—IL Model 353 (Instrumentation Laboratory, Inc., 113 Hartwell Ave, Lexington, MA 02173), or equiv., with Cu hollow cathode lamp.

(**b**) *Copper sulfate soln.*—Dissolve 15 g $CuSO_4.5H_2O$ in H_2O and dil. to 1 L.

(**c**) *Buffer soln.*—pH 13.4. Dissolve 24.6 g KOH and 30 g KCl in H_2O and dil. to 1 L.

(**d**) *Starch soln.*—Treat 1 g sol. starch with 10 mL cold H_2O, triturate to thin paste, and pour gradually into 150 mL boiling H_2O contg 1 g oxalic acid. Boil until soln clears, cool, and dil. to 200 mL. Prep. fresh weekly.

(**e**) *Bromocresol purple indicator.*—Dissolve 0.1 g bromocresol purple in 19 mL 0.1*N* NaOH and dil. to 250 mL with H_2O.

(**f**) *Biuret.*—To recrystallize, weigh ca 10 g reagent grade biuret, transfer to 800 mL beaker, add 500 mL H_2O, and heat on hot plate with occasional stirring until dissolved. Boil until vol. decreases to ca 250 mL. Remove, and let cool gradually to room temp. Filter thru fritted-glass funnel, transfer to evapg dish, and dry 1 hr in 105–110° oven. Remove from oven, place in desiccator, and cool to room temp.

(**g**) *Biuret std soln.*—0.4 mg/mL. Dissolve 0.4000 g recrystd biuret in warm H_2O, cool, transfer to 1 L flask, and dil. to vol.

(**h**) *Copper std solns.*—Dil. aliquots of Cu stock soln, **2.110(b)**, with H_2O to obtain ≥4 std solns within range of detn, 1–4 μg Cu/mL final soln.

2.086 ***Determination of Calibration Factor***

Transfer aliquots of biuret std soln contg 4, 8, and 12 mg biuret to sep. 100 mL vol. flasks, dil. to ca 30 mL with H_2O, and add 25 mL alcohol to each. While stirring with mag. stirrer, add 2 mL starch soln, 10 mL $CuSO_4$ soln, and 20 mL buffer soln. Remove stirring bar, rinse, dil. to vol., mix thoroly, and let stand 10 min. With vac., filter ca 50 mL thru dry 150 mL medium porosity fritted glass funnel into dry flask. Transfer 25 mL aliquots of each filtrate to 250 mL vol. flasks, acidify with 5 mL 1*N* HCl, and dil. to vol. with H_2O. Proceed as in **2.109–2.113**, using std solns, **2.085(h)**, to det. complexed Cu in soln by AA spectrophotometry after adding equiv. amts of alcohol, KOH soln, buffer soln, and 1*N* HCl. Take ≥3 readings of each soln. From mean value of Cu concn, calc. factor relating mg Cu found to mg biuret added. Redet. daily.

2.087 ***Determination***

(**a**) *In urea.*—Accurately weigh sample contg <10 mg biuret, dissolve in H_2O, transfer to 100 mL vol. flask, add 25 mL alcohol, and proceed as in **2.086**, beginning "While stirring with mag. stirrer, . . ." From Cu found, calc. biuret concn, using factor.

(**b**) *In mixed fertilizers.*—Transfer accurately weighed sample contg <40 mg biuret to 250 mL beaker and add 1 mL H_2O for each g of sample (5 g max.). Warm, add 65 mL alcohol and 7 drops bromocresol purple, and adjust pH to first blue color (pH 6–7) with 20% KOH. Place on hot plate, heat to bp, cool, and, if pH has changed, make final adjustment to first blue. Vac.-filter thru alcohol-washed paper pulp pad into 100 mL vol. flask. (If filtrate is not clear, improper pH adjustment has been made. Add HCl and readjust to pH 6–7.) Wash pad and ppt with alcohol and dil. to vol. with alcohol. Transfer 25 mL aliquot to 100 mL vol. flask, and proceed as in **2.086**, beginning "While stirring with mag stirrer, . . ." From Cu found, calc. biuret concn, using factor and appropriate diln factors. (Final aliquot can be varied to give Cu concn between 1 and 4 μg/mL.)

POTASSIUM

2.088 ★ ***Lindo-Gladding Method (32)*** ★
Official Final Action

Gravimetric detn as K_2PtCl_6. *See* **2.076–2.078**, 11th ed.

2.089 ★ ***Wet-Digestion Method (33)*** ★
Official Final Action

Pptn as K_2PtCl_6 after digestion with HNO_3 and HCl. *See* **2.079–2.080**, 11th ed.

2.090 ★ ***Recovery of Platinum (34)*** ★
Procedure

See **2.081–2.083**, 11th ed.

Flame Photometric Method (35)
Official Final Action

(*Caution: See* **51.007**.)

2.091 ***Reagents and Apparatus***

(**a**) *Ammonium oxalate soln.*—Dissolve 40 g $(NH_4)_2C_2O_4$ in 1 L H_2O.

(**b**) *Methyl red indicator.*—Dissolve 0.2 g Me red in 100 mL alcohol.

(**c**) *Dilute nitric acid.*—(1+10).

(**d**) *Anion exchange resin.*—REXYN 203(OH) (Fisher Scientific Co.); Duolite A-7 or Duolite A-41 (Diamond Shamrock, 1100 Superior Ave, Cleveland, OH 44114); Permutit S-100 (Permutit Co., E49 Midland Ave, Paramus, NJ 07652); or equiv.

(**e**) *Potassium nitrate or potassium chloride.*—Recrystallize reagent grade salt twice from H_2O and dry 5 hr at 105°.

(**f**) *Ion exchange column.*—Made from 30 cm length of std wall glass tubing, 2.5 cm od; one end closed by 1-hole No. 4 rubber stopper thru which is inserted 2-way stopcock or glass tubing connected to rubber tubing and compressor clamp. Do not let stopcock tubing protrude above stopper. Choose stopper large enough so that there is no space between stopper vertex and column wall. Alternatively use glass chromatgc tube 300 × 19 mm id with stopcock or valve at bottom to control flow rate (such as SGA Scientific Inc. No. C-4225).

Place glass wool plug in bottom of tube, close valve, and add H_2O to ht of 10 cm. Transfer portion of resin to 200 mL beaker and suspend in H_2O. Transfer slurry to column and adjust ht of packed resin to 20 cm, draining excess H_2O until 2.5 cm head remains. Regenerate resin after 10 successive aliquots have passed thru. For Na, regenerate after 5 aliquots have passed thru.

2.092 ***Preparation of Resin***

Place ca 450 g resin in 4 L beaker and add 2 L 5% *NaOH.* Stir 30 min with elec. stirrer. Let resin settle, and decant NaOH soln. Repeat treatment with 5% NaOH twice, decanting NaOH soln after final treatment. Add 2 L H_2O to resin, stir few min, let resin settle, and decant wash H_2O. Repeat 3–4 times. Resin is now in

★ Surplus method—*see* inside front cover.

free base form. Regenerate to nitrate form by treating 3 times with HNO_3 (1+19), in same manner as with NaOH soln. Wash resin with H_2O until pH of washings is ≥2 by backwashing in column or by stirring and decanting in large beaker. Store resin under H_2O in stoppered bottle.

2.093 ***Preparation of Solution***

(a) *Mixed fertilizers and potassium-magnesium sulfate.*—Weigh 1.5058 g sample into 250 mL vol. flask (500 mL flask if sample contains >30% K_2O), add 125 mL H_2O and 50 mL $(NH_4)_2C_2O_4$ soln, and boil 30 min. Cool, dil. to vol., mix, and pass thru dry filter.

(b) *Potassium chloride and sulfate.*—Dissolve 1.5058 g in H_2O and dil. to 500 mL.

2.094 ***Preparation of Standard Curve***

Dissolve 1.2931 g KNO_3 (or 0.9535 g KCl) in H_2O and dil. to 500 mL (1000 ppm K). Prep. std solns by diln to cover range 0–80 ppm K at intervals ≤10 ppm, adding appropriate amt $LiNO_3$ if internal std instrument is to be used. Prep. std curve of emission against concn, adjusting instrument so that 50 ppm K gives reading near mid-scale. Atomize portions of std solns until readings for series are reproducible.

2.095 ***Determination***

(a) *Mixed fertilizers, potassium sulfate, and potassium-magnesium sulfate.*—Transfer 10 mL aliquot of sample soln to 250 mL beaker. Add 1 drop Me red and neutze with HNO_3 (1+10). Adjust H_2O level in column to top of resin and quant. transfer aliquot to column. Open stopcock to give flow rate of 2 drops/sec, collecting effluent in 250 mL vol. flask. Wash aliquot into resin with 2–3 small portions H_2O. Collect 50–75 mL effluent; then open stopcock and collect addnl 100 mL by pouring H_2O onto column, making certain that H_2O level does not fall below top of resin bed. Dil. to vol. and mix (if internal std instrument is used, add required amt $LiNO_3$ before dilg to vol.). Atomize portions of sample several times to obtain reliable av. reading for each soln. Det. ppm K from std curve. (Temp. of std and sample solns must not differ by >2°.) Calc. % K_2O as follows:

0–30%: ppm K/2 = %K_2O
>30%: ppm K/1 = %K_2O

(b) *Potassium chloride.*—Proceed as in **(a)** but omit neutzn and resin treatment.

2.096 ***Instrument and Procedure Performance Test***

Weigh 1.5058 g K acid phthalate (primary std; %K_2O = 23.0) and transfer to 250 mL vol. flask. Add ca 0.5 g $(NH_4)_2HPO_4$ and proceed as in **2.093(a)**, beginning "... add 125 mL H_2O ..."

Table 2:03 Aliquots and factors for potassium determination

% K_2O Expected	Aliquot	Factor
2	no diln	0.0500
3–4	150	0.08333
5–6	100	0.1250
7–8	75	0.1667
9–13	50	0.2500
14–16	40	0.3125
17–20	30	0.4167
21–25	25	0.5000
26–30	20	0.6250
31–43	15	0.8333
44–65	10	1.250

Automated Flame Photometric Method (36)
Official Final Action

(*Caution: See* **51.007**.)

2.097 ***Apparatus***

Automatic analyzer.—AutoAnalyzer with following modules (available from Technicon Corp.): Sampler II, proportioning pump, flame photometer, range expander, and recorder. Assemble app. as in Fig. **2:07**.

2.098 ***Reagents***

(a) *Ammonium oxalate soln.*—4%. *See* **2.091(a)**.

(b) *Ammonium citrate soln.*—Prep. as in **2.044(a)**.

(c) *Lithium nitrate soln.*—Dissolve 0.6894 g dried (2 hr at 105°) $LiNO_3$ in 1 L H_2O.

(d) *Potassium std solns.*—*(1) Stock soln.*—0.5 mg K_2O/mL. Dissolve 1.4447 g dried (2 hr at 105°) KH_2PO_4 in H_2O and dil. to 1 L. *(2) Working solns.*—35, 38, 41, 44, 47, 50, and 55 μg K_2O/mL. Accurately measure 35–55 mL stock soln into 500 mL vol. flasks contg 0.2 g $(NH_4)_2C_2O_4$ if samples are prepd by **2.099(a)**, or 12 mL NH_4 citrate soln, **(b)**, if by **2.099(b)**. Dil. to vol. with H_2O and mix. (If std solns contg citrate must be held overnight, add 3–4 drops $CHCl_3$.)

2.099 ***Preparation of Samples***

(a) *Ammonium oxalate extraction.*—Weigh 1 g sample into 500 mL vol. flask, add 50 mL 4% $(NH_4)_2C_2O_4$ and 125 mL H_2O, boil 30 min, and cool. Dil. to vol. with H_2O, mix, and filter or let stand until clear.

(b) *Ammonium citrate extraction from direct available phosphorus extract.*—Prep. as in **2.050**. (If solns must be held overnight, add 3–4 drops $CHCl_3$.)

2.100 ***Calibration***

Pump 55 μg K_2O/mL std working soln continuously thru system. Set range expander to 1× position and adjust calibration control on flame photometer to read 85% *T* on recorder. Pump 35 μg/mL soln continuously and set range expander to 2× position. Turn adjustable range positioner or range expander to obtain 23% *T* on recorder. Range of 35–55 μg K_2O/mL will read ca 20–80% *T* on recorder with expander set at 2×. (Expansion from Model II flame photometers may be <20–80% *T*.)

2.101 ***Determination***

Pipet aliquot sample soln as indicated in Table **2:03** into 250 mL vol. flask. Dil. to vol. with H_2O and mix. Place 35–55 μg/mL working std solns in sampler tray before samples. Place 44 μg/mL std soln at end of series to check for drift. Read samples and stds at rate of 40/hr (2:1 sample-to-wash ratio). Prep. std curve of emission against K_2O concn and read μg K_2O/mL from graph.

% K_2O = (μg K_2O/mL from graph) × factor from Table **2:03**.

Volumetric Sodium Tetraphenylboron Methods

Method I (37)—Official Final Action

2.102 ***Reagents***

(a) *Formaldehyde soln.*—37%.

(b) *Sodium hydroxide soln.*—20%. Dissolve 20 g NaOH in 100 mL H_2O.

(c) *Sodium tetraphenylboron (STPB) soln.*—Approx. 1.2%. Dissolve 12 g $NaB(C_6H_5)_4$ in ca 800 mL H_2O. Add 20–25 g $Al(OH)_3$,

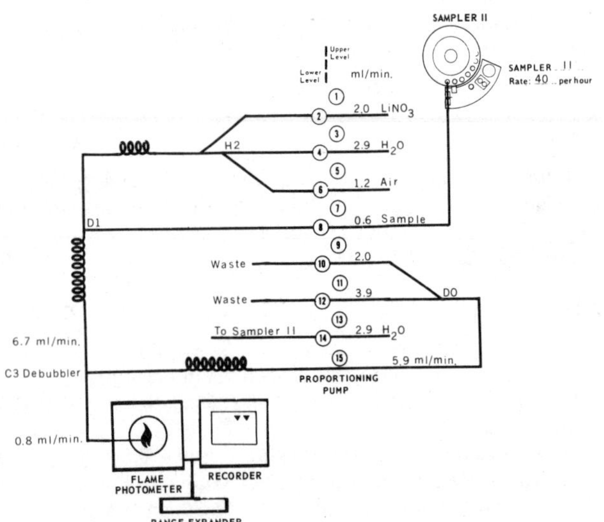

FIG. 2:07—Flow schematic for K_2O in fertilizers

stir 5 min, and filter (Whatman No. 42 paper, or equiv.) into 1 L vol. flask. Rinse beaker sparingly with H_2O and add to filter. Collect entire filtrate, add 2 mL 20% NaOH, dil. to vol. with H_2O, and mix. Let stand 48 hr and stdze. Adjust so that 1 mL STPB = 1% K_2O. Store at room temp.

(**d**) *Benzalkonium chloride (BAC) soln.*—Approx. 0.625%. Dil. 38 mL 17% Zephiran chloride (Winthrop Laboratories; also available at local pharmacies as benzalkonium chloride) to 1 L with H_2O, mix, and stdze. Cetyltrimethylammonium bromide may be substituted for Zephiran chloride. If other concn is used, adjust vol.

(**e**) *Clayton Yellow (Titan Yellow; Colour Index No. 19540).*—0.04%. Dissolve 40 mg in 100 mL H_2O.

2.103 ***Standardization of Solutions***

(**a**) *BAC soln.*—To 1.00 mL STPB soln in 125 mL erlenmeyer, add 20–25 mL H_2O, 1 mL 20% NaOH, 2.5 mL HCHO, 1.5 mL *4% $(NH_4)_2C_2O_4$*, and 6–8 drops indicator, (**e**). Titr. to pink end point with BAC soln, using 10 mL semimicro buret. Adjust BAC soln so that 2.00 mL = 1.00 mL STPB soln.

(**b**) *Sodium tetraphenylboron soln.*—Dissolve 2.500 g KH_2PO_4 in H_2O in 250 mL vol. flask, add 50 mL 4% $(NH_4)_2C_2O_4$ soln, dil. to vol. with H_2O, and mix. (It is not necessary to bring to boil.) Transfer 15 mL aliquot (51.92 mg K_2O, 43.10 mg K) to 100 mL vol. flask; add 2 mL 20% NaOH, 5 mL HCHO, and 43 mL STPB reagent. Dil. to vol. with H_2O, mix *thoroly,* let stand 5–10 min, and pass thru dry filter. Transfer 50 mL aliquot of filtrate to 125 mL erlenmeyer, add 6–8 drops indicator, (**e**), and titr. excess reagent with BAC soln. Calc. titer as follows:

F = 34.61/(43 mL − mL BAC) = % K_2O/mL STPB reagent. Factor F applies to all fertilizers if 2.5 g sample is dild to 250 mL and 15 mL aliquot is taken for analysis. If results are to be expressed as K rather than as K_2O, substitute 28.73 for 34.61 in calcg F.

2.104 ***Determination***

Place 2.5 g sample (1.25 g if K_2O >50%) in 250 mL vol. flask, add 50 mL 4% $(NH_4)_2C_2O_4$ and 125 mL H_2O, and boil 30 min. (If org. matter is present, add 2 g *K-free C* before boiling.) Cool, dil. to vol. with H_2O, mix, and pass thru dry filter or let stand until clear. Transfer 15 mL aliquot sample soln to 100 mL vol. flask and add 2 mL 20% NaOH and 5 mL HCHO. Add 1 mL std STPB soln for each 1% K_2O expected in sample plus addnl 8 mL excess to ensure complete pptn. Dil. to vol. with H_2O, mix *thoroly,* let stand 5–10 min, and filter thru dry paper (Whatman No. 12 or equiv.). Transfer 50 mL filtrate to 125 mL erlenmeyer, add 6–8 drops indicator, (**e**), and titr. excess reagent with std BAC soln.

% K_2O in sample = (mL STPB added − mL BAC) × F,

where F = % K_2O/mL STPB reagent. (Multiply by 2 if 1.25 g sample was used.)

Method II (38)—Official Final Action

(For use with sample prepd for available P detn)

2.105 ***Reagents***

See **2.102**(**a**), (**b**), (**c**), (**d**), and (**e**).

2.106 ***Standardization of Solutions***

(**a**) *Benzalkonium chloride.*—In 125 mL erlenmeyer, add 2.5 mL neut. NH_4 citrate soln, **2.044**(**a**), 15–20 mL H_2O, 4 mL HCHO, and 2.5 mL 20% NaOH soln. Swirl; then add 4.00 mL STPB soln and 6–8 drops indicator, **2.102**(**e**). Titr. to pink end point with BAC soln, using 10 mL semimicro buret. Adjust BAC soln so that 2.00 mL = 1.00 mL STPB soln.

(**b**) *Sodium tetraphenylboron soln.*—Dissolve 1.4447 g primary std KH_2PO_4 in H_2O in 500 mL vol. flask, add 100 mL neut. NH_4 citrate soln, **2.044**(**a**), dil. to vol. with H_2O, and mix. Transfer 25 mL aliquot (25.00 mg K_2O, 20.75 mg K) to 100 mL vol. flask; add 8 mL HCHO and 5 mL 20% NaOH, swirl, and add 25 mL STPB reagent. Dil. to vol. with H_2O, mix *thoroly,* let stand 5–10 min, and pass thru dry filter. Transfer 50 mL aliquot of filtrate to 125 mL erlenmeyer, add 6–8 drops indicator, **2.102**(**e**), and titr. excess reagent with BAC soln. Calc. titer as follows:

F = 25 mg K_2O/(25 mL STPB − mL BAC)
= mg K_2O/mL STPB reagent.

If results are to be expressed as K rather than K_2O, substitute 20.75 for 25 in calcg F.

2.107 ***Preparation of Sample***

Prep. as in **2.050**.

2.108 ***Determination***

Transfer 25 mL aliquot of sample soln to 100 mL vol. flask. (If org. matter is present, treat 100 mL portion with 1 g K-free C and filter before transferring aliquot.) Add 8 mL HCHO *first* and then 5 mL 20% NaOH soln, and wash down sides of flask with H_2O. Swirl and add 1 mL STPB for each 1.5 mg K_2O expected in sample aliquot plus addnl 8 mL excess to ensure complete pptn. Dil. to vol. with H_2O, mix *thoroly,* let stand 5–10 min, and pass thru dry filter (Whatman No. 12, or equiv.). Transfer 50 mL aliquot filtrate to 125 mL erlenmeyer, add 6–8 drops indicator, **2.102**(**e**), and titr. excess reagent with std BAC soln.

% K_2O in sample = (mL STPB added − mL BAC) × F × 2.

Calcn applies to all fertilizers if 1 g sample is dild to 500 mL and 25 mL aliquot is taken for analysis.

OTHER ELEMENTS

Minor Nutrients by Atomic Absorption Spectrophotometry (39)—Official Final Action

(*Caution: See* **51.006**.)

2.109 ***Apparatus and Reagent***

(**a**) *Atomic absorption spectrophotometer.*—Several com. models are available. Since each design is somewhat different, with varying requirements of light source, burner flow rate, and detector sensitivity, only general outline of operating parameters is given in Table **2:04**. Operator must become familiar with settings and procedures adapted to his own app. and use table only as guide to concn ranges and flame conditions.

(b) *Disodium EDTA soln.*—2.5%. Dissolve 25 g Na_2H_2EDTA in 1 L H_2O and adjust to pH 7.0 with 5*N* NaOH, using pH meter.

Table 2:04 Operating Parameters

Element	Wave-length, Å	Flame	Range µg/mL	Remarks
Ca	4227	Rich Air-C_2H_2	2–20	1% La, 1% HCl
	4227	Rich N_2O-C_2H_2	2–20	Requires special burner
Cu	3247	Air-C_2H_2	2–20	
Fe	2483	Rich Air-C_2H_2	2–20	
Mg	2852	Rich Air-C_2H_2	0.2–2	May need La
Mn	2795	Air-C_2H_2	2–20	
Zn	2138	Air-C_2H_2	0.5–5	

2.110 ***Standard Solutions***

(Do not use <2 mL pipets or <25 mL vol. flasks. Automatic diln app. may be used. Prep. std solns in 0–20 µg range fresh daily.)

(a) *Calcium solns.*—*(1) Stock soln.*—25 µg Ca/mL. Dissolve 1.249 g $CaCO_3$ in min. amt 3*N* HCl. Dil. to 1 L. Dil. 50 mL to 1 L. *(2) Working std solns.*—0, 5, 10, 15, and 20 µg Ca/mL contg 1% La. To 25 mL vol. flasks add 0, 5, 10, 15, and 20 mL Ca stock soln. Add 5 mL La stock soln and dil. to 25 mL.

(b) *Copper stock soln.*—1000 µg Cu/mL. Dissolve 1.000 g pure Cu metal in min. amt HNO_3 and add 5 mL HCl. Evap. almost to dryness and dil. to 1 L with 0.1*N* HCl.

(c) *Iron stock soln.*—1000 µg Fe/mL. Dissolve 1.000 g pure Fe wire in ca 30 mL 6*N* HCl with boiling. Dil. to 1 L.

(d) *Lanthanum stock soln.*—50 g La/L. Dissolve 58.65 g La_2O_3 (99.99%, Ventron Corp., Alfa Products, 8 Congress St, Beverly, MA 01915, or equiv.) in 250 mL HCl, adding acid slowly. Dil. to 1 L.

(e) *Magnesium stock soln.*—1000 µg Mg/mL. Place 1.000 g pure Mg metal in 50 mL H_2O and slowly add 10 mL HCl. Dil. to 1 L.

(f) *Manganese stock soln.*—1000 µg Mn/mL. Dissolve 1.582 g MnO_2 in ca 30 mL 6*N* HCl. Boil to remove Cl and dil. to 1 L.

(g) *Zinc stock soln.*—1000 µg Zn/mL. Dissolve 1.000 g pure Zn metal in ca 10 mL 6*N* HCl. Dil. to 1 L.

(h) *Other std solns.*—Dil. aliquots of solns **(b)**, **(c)**, **(e)**, **(f)**, and **(g)** with 0.5*N* HCl to make ≥4 std solns of each element within range of detn.

2.111 ***Preparation of Sample Solutions***

(*Caution: See* **51.019**, **51.025**, and **51.028**.)

(a) *Inorganic materials and mixed fertilizers.*—Dissolve 1.00 g well ground sample in 10 mL HCl in 150 mL beaker. Boil and evap. soln nearly to dryness on hot plate. *Do not bake residue.* Redissolve residue in 20 mL 2*N* HCl, boiling gently if necessary. Filter thru fast paper into 100 mL vol. flask, washing paper and residue thoroly with H_2O. Measure absorption of soln directly, or dil. with 0.5*N* HCl to obtain solns within ranges of instrument. If Ca is to be detd, add enough La stock soln to make final diln 1% La (i.e., 5 mL La to 25 mL flask, 20 mL to 100 mL flask, etc.).

(b) *Fertilizers containing organic matter (tankage, corncobs, cottonseed hulls, etc.).*—Place 1.00 g sample in 150 mL beaker (Pyrex, or equiv.). Char on hot plate and ignite 1 hr at 500° with muffle door propped open to allow free access of air. Break up cake with stirring rod and dissolve in 10 mL HCl as in **(a)**.

(c) *Fertilizers containing fritted trace elements.*— Dissolve ≤1.00 g well ground sample in 5 mL $HClO_4$ and 5 mL HF. Boil and evap. to dense $HClO_4$ fumes. Dil. carefully with H_2O, filter, and proceed as in **(a)**. Alternatively, dissolve sample in 10 mL HCl, 5 mL HF, and 10 mL MeOH. Evap. to dryness. Add 5 mL HCl and evap. Repeat HCl addn and evapn. Dissolve residue as in **(a)**. (Normally Pt ware should be used; Pyrex or other glassware may be used if Na, K, Ca, and Fe are not to be detd.)

(d) *For manganese.*—*(1) Acid-soluble, for both* Mn^{+2} *and* Mn^{+4}.—*See* **(a)**, **(b)**, and **(c)**, and **2.139(b)**. *(2) Acid-soluble, for* Mn^{+2} *only.*—*See* **2.139(a)**, **2.140**, and **2.141★**. *(3) Water-soluble, for* Mn^{+2} *only.*—*See* **2.142**.

(e) *For iron and zinc.*—*(1) Aqueous extraction.*—Place 1.00 g sample in 250 mL beaker, add 75 mL H_2O, and boil 30 min. Filter into 100 mL vol. flask, washing paper with H_2O. Dil. to vol. and redil. if necessary. *(2) Chelation extraction.*—Place 1.00 g sample in 250 mL beaker, and add 5 cm (2") mag. stirrer bar and 100 mL 2.5% EDTA soln. Stir exactly 5 min, and filter thru Whatman No. 41 paper, or equiv. If filtrate is cloudy, refilter immediately thru fine paper (Whatman No. 5, or equiv.). Redil., if necessary, with 0.5*N* HCl.

2.112 ***Determination***

(P interferes in Ca and may interfere in Mg detn with air-C_2H_2 burners. Eliminate interference by adding La stock soln to std and sample solns so that final dilns contain 1% La. P does not interfere with Ca detn when N_2O-C_2H_2 flame is used.)

Set up instrument as in Table **2:04**, or previously established optimum settings for app. to be used. Less sensitive secondary lines (Gatehouse and Willis, Spectrochim. Acta **17**, 710(1961)) may be used to reduce necessary diln, if desired. Read ≥4 std solns within anal. range before and after each group of 6–12 samples. Flush burner with H_2O between samples, and re-establish 0 absorption point each time. Prep. calibration curve from av. of each std before and after sample group. Read concn of samples from plot of absorption against µg/mL.

2.113 ***Calculations***

% Element = (µg/mL) × (*F*/sample wt) × 10^{-4},
F = mL original diln × mL final diln/mL aliquot, if original 100 mL vol. is dild.

Acid-Soluble Boron (*40*)—Official Final Action

2.114 ***Apparatus***

Use high sensitivity glass electrode pH meter for titrn. Use assembly with burets, electrodes, and mech. stirrer, arranged for convenient use with 250 mL beaker. Use ordinary 50 mL burets for the 0.025*N* NaOH and 0.02*N* HCl.

2.115 ***Reagents***

(a) *Boric acid std soln.*—Dissolve 1 g H_3BO_3 in H_2O and dil. to 1 L. 1 mL = 0.1748 mg B.

(b) *Sodium hydroxide std soln.*—CO_2-free, ca 0.025*N*. Stdze as follows: Pipet 25 mL std H_3BO_3 soln into 250 mL beaker, add 3.0 g NaCl, acidify to Me red, dil. to 150 mL, boil to expel CO_2, cool, and titr. potentiometrically as in **2.116**. Det. blank by repeating titrn, substituting 25 mL H_2O for H_3BO_3 soln. Calc. B equivalence as follows:

mg B/mL = 4.369/[(mL NaOH soln) − (mL blank)].

Protect from atm. CO_2 by soda-lime tubes or other suitable means.

(c) *Methyl red indicator.*—Dissolve 0.1 g Me red in 50 mL alcohol, dil. to 100 mL with H_2O, and filter if necessary.

2.116 ***Determination***

Weigh sample within 1 mg (1.0 g for up to 0.45% B, smaller samples for above that content) and place in 250 mL beaker. Add ca 50 mL H_2O and 3 mL HCl. Heat to bp and keep hot until carbonates are decomposed. Keep soln hot but do not boil during following phosphate removal:

Add *10% $Pb(NO_3)_2$ soln,* usually 10 mL, or 1 mL for each 1.2% P_2O_5 if P_2O_5 content is known to be >12%. Add $NaHCO_3$, little at time, until soln approaches neutrality (often observed by formation of white ppt in addn to insol. matter already present). Add few drops Me red and continue adding $NaHCO_3$ gradually until *just* alk. to Me red (yellow or very slightly orange). Keep mixt. hot but not boiling (H_2O bath or steam bath is best) 30 min, adding addnl small amts of $NaHCO_3$ if needed to keep same indicator color. (If indicator is bleached by nitrate present, add more; if color is obscured by org. matter, use external spot tests to follow neutzn.) After neutzn and heating, 40–50 mL soln should remain.

Filter hot soln into 250 mL beaker and wash solids thoroly with hot H_2O. Acidify filtrate with few drops HCl and boil briefly to expel most of CO_2. Neutze hot soln with 0.5*N* NaOH, and reacidify with 0.5*N* HCl, using 0.3–0.5 mL excess. Dil. to ca 150 mL and boil gently few min to expel remaining CO_2. Cool to room temp. in running H_2O. Roughly neutze mixt., using CO_2-free 0.5*N* NaOH, and place beaker in titrn assembly with electrodes and stirrer immersed. Start stirrer and adjust pH to exactly 6.30 by adding 0.025*N* NaOH or 0.02*N* HCl as required. (When properly adjusted, pH should be steady; drifting usually is due to incomplete removal of CO_2.) When reading of pH 6.30 is steady, read 0.025*N* NaOH buret, add 20 g *mannitol* or cryst. *D-sorbitol,* and titr. with 0.025*N* NaOH to pH 6.30. (Conveniently done with slidewire type instrument by opening pH meter circuit when mannitol is added, leaving scale setting at 6.30, closing circuit again when indicator color shows that end point is being approached, and carefully adding std NaOH soln until galvanometer needle returns to zero. With practice, somewhat slow approach to equilibrium, characteristic of glass electrode, can be anticipated so as not to overrun end point.) When end point is reached, read buret again. Obtain reagent blank by repeating detn with all reagents but without sample.

% B = (mL NaOH soln in detn − mL blank)
× (mg B/mL NaOH soln)/(10 × g sample)

2.117 Water-Soluble Boron (*40*)—Official Final Action

(Not applicable in presence of >5% urea or urea-formaldehyde resins)

Weigh 2.5 g sample into 250 mL beaker. Add 125 mL H_2O, boil gently ca 10 min, and filter hot thru Whatman No. 40 paper, or equiv., into 400 mL beaker. Wash solids well with 6 portions hot H_2O and dil. to ≥200 mL with H_2O. Heat filtrate just to bp. Add 15 mL *10% $BaCl_2$ soln* to ppt sulfates and phosphates, and add *powd $Ba(OH)_2$,* cautiously with stirring, until just alk. to phthln, avoiding large excess. Boil in open beaker ≥60 min to expel NH_3. (Samples colored by org. matter should be boiled longer.) If necessary, add H_2O to keep vol. to ≥150 mL. Add and stir 1–2 teaspoonfuls Filter-Cel or other inert filtering aid, and filter with suction thru packed paper pads into 500 mL Pyrex erlenmeyer. Wash ppt 6 times with hot boiled H_2O. (Avoid too large wash vols which increase vol. in flask to point of dangerous bumping in next step.)

Make filtrate just colorless to phthln with HCl (1+5), add Me red, and make just pink with the acid. Add 5 or 6 boiling stones and stirring rod, cover with watch glass, and boil 5 min to remove CO_2. Cool in cold H_2O while covered. Wash cover glass, stirrer, and sides of flask. Titr. to yellow of Me red with *std 0.05N NaOH,* **50.032–50.036**. Add 20 g *D-mannitol* and 1 mL or more phthln, shake, and wash down sides of flask. Titr. to pink end point. Det. blank in exactly same manner as sample.

1 mL 0.05*N* NaOH = 0.000540 g B or 0.00477 g $Na_2B_4O_7.10H_2O$. Or, (Titer − blank) × factor = lb $Na_2B_4O_7.10H_2O$/ton (factor = 3.807 for 0.05*N* NaOH).

2.118 ★ Carbonate Carbon (*41*)—Official Final Action ★

Proceed as in **1.010–1.011**, using 2 g sample. Report % CO_2 by wt.

Water-Soluble Chlorine (*42*)
Official Final Action

2.119 ***Reagents***

(a) *Silver nitrate std soln.*—Dissolve ca 5 g recrystd $AgNO_3$ in H_2O and dil. to 1 L. Stdze against pure, dry NaCl and adjust so that 1 mL soln = 0.001 g Cl.

(b) *Potassium chromate indicator.—See* **50.028(b)**.

2.120 ***Determination***

Place 2.5 g sample on 11 cm filter paper and wash with successive portions boiling H_2O until washings total nearly 250 mL, collecting filtrate in 250 mL vol. flask. Cool, dil. to vol. with H_2O, and mix well. Pipet 50 mL into 150 mL beaker, add 1 mL K_2CrO_4 indicator, and titr. with std $AgNO_3$ soln to permanent red of Ag_2CrO_4.

Acid-Soluble Calcium (*43*)—Official Final Action

2.121 ***Method I***

Weigh 2.5 g sample into 250 mL vol. flask, add 30 mL HNO_3 and 10 mL HCl, and boil 30 min. Cool, dil. to vol., mix, and filter if necessary. Transfer 25 mL aliquot to beaker and dil. to 100 mL. Add 2 drops bromophenol blue, **6.019(f)**. Add NH_4OH (1+4) until indicator changes from yellow to green (not blue). If overrun, bring back with HCl (1+4). (This gives pH of 3.5–4.0.) Dil. to 150 mL, bring to bp, and add 30 mL satd hot $(NH_4)_2C_2O_4$ soln slowly, stirring constantly. If color changes from green to blue or yellow again, adjust to green with HCl (1+4). If yellow, adjust with NH_4OH to green. Digest on steam bath 1 hr, or let stand overnight, and cool to room temp. Filter supernate thru quant. paper, gooch, or fritted glass filter, and wash ppt thoroly with NH_4OH (1+50). Place paper or crucible with ppt in original beaker and add mixt. of 125 mL H_2O and 5 mL H_2SO_4. Heat to ≥70° and titr. with 0.1*N* $KMnO_4$ until first slight pink appears. Correct for blank and calc. to Ca.

2.122 ***Method II (Atomic Absorption Method)***

See **2.109–2.113**.

2.123 ★ ***Method III*** **★**

Place CaC_2O_4 and filter paper from **2.136** in beaker in which pptn was made and dissolve and titr. as in **2.121**.

Cobalt (*44*)—Official Final Action

(*Caution: See* **51.026**, **51.028**, and **Acids**, Chap. **51**.)

2.124 ***Reagents***

(Use H_2O free of interfering elements. Check by shaking 2 drops 0.01% dithizone in CCl_4 with 10 mL H_2O. CCl_4 phase should remain green.)

(a) *Ternary acid mixture.—See* **2.049(b)**.

★ Surplus method—*see* inside front cover.

(b) *Ammonium hydroxide.*—Use fresh stock. (Reagent becomes contaminated with heavy metals on prolonged storage in glass.)

(c) *Isoamyl acetate.*—Distd.

(d) *2-Nitroso-1-naphthol soln.*—0.05%. Dissolve 0.05 g 2-nitroso-1-naphthol in 8 drops 1*N* NaOH and 1 mL H_2O. Add 50–60 mL H_2O and 6.5–7 mL NH_4OH, and dil. to 100 mL with H_2O. Divide into 2 ca equal parts and wash each part twice in 100 mL centrf. tube with 20 mL isoamyl acetate. Shake 30 sec and centrf. after each addn. (It may be necessary to remove part of aq. phase to ensure complete removal of foreign matter at interface.)

(e) *Cobalt std solns.*—*(1) Stock soln.*—200 μg Co/mL. Dissolve 0.0808 g $CoCl_2.6H_2O$ in H_2O and dil. to 100 mL. *(2) Working soln.*—2 μg Co/mL. Dil. 1 mL stock soln to 100 mL with H_2O.

2.125 ***Determination***

Slowly add 20 mL ternary acid mixt. to 2.00 g pulverized, mixed fertilizer in 150 mL beaker. Cover with watch glass and digest on steam bath overnight. Transfer to hot plate and heat covered until dense white fumes appear. (At this point HNO_3 will have been expelled. Take care not to lose significant amts of $HClO_4$.) Dil. sample contg undissolved residue with H_2O, transfer to 50 mL vol. flask, and dil. to vol. Transfer to 100 mL centrf. tube and centrf. 5 min at 2000 rpm. Transfer aliquot, contg 2–5 μg Co, to 50 mL g-s centrf. tube. Add 10 mL *20% diammonium citrate soln* and 2 drops phthln. Adjust pH carefully to distinct pink with NH_4OH (1+1) and add successively 1 mL *10% $Na_2S_2O_3$ soln,* 2 mL 2-nitroso-1-naphthol soln, and 5 mL isoamyl acetate. (Only isoamyl acetate addn requires high degree of precision.) Shake mixt. 5 min and let sep. Centrf., if necessary. Draw off and discard aq. phase thru glass capillary tube attached to vac. Wash isoamyl acetate phase with two 5 mL portions 1*N* NaOH and one 5 mL portion 1*N* HCl. Shake 5 min after each addn, let layers sep., and draw off and discard aq. phase. Centrf. 2 min at 1500 rpm and measure *A* or %*T* at 530 nm against isoamyl acetate. Det. Co from calibration curve relating *A* or log %*T* to Co content of std solns contg 0, 2, 4, and 5 μg Co.

Iron (*45*)—Official Final Action

(*Note:* Diphenylamine may be harmful.
Caution: See **51.079** and **51.084**.)

2.126 ***Reagents***

(a) *Diphenylamine soln.*—Dissolve 1 g in 100 mL H_2SO_4.

(b) *Diphenylamine sulfonate soln.*—Dissolve 0.5 g in H_2O in 100 mL vol. flask and dil. to vol.

(c) *Potassium dichromate std solns.*—0.1*N* and 0.01*N*. Prep. 0.1*N* $K_2Cr_2O_7$ as in **50.024**. Prep. 0.01*N* soln by dilg 100 mL 0.1*N* soln to 1 L.

(d) *Mercuric chloride saturated soln.*—Shake $HgCl_2$ with H_2O and let settle.

(e) *Stannous chloride soln.*—Dissolve 20 g $SnCl_2.2H_2O$ in 20 mL HCl, warming gently. Add 20 mL H_2O and dil. to 100 mL with HCl (1+1). Keep warm until clear; then add few granules Sn. Dispense from dropping bottle.

2.127 ***Preparation of Sample Solution***

(a) *Suitable for all fertilizers.*—Treat 1 g as in **2.020(e)**, using 15 mL $HClO_4$. Hold ≥1 hr at ca 170° to remove HNO_3 completely. Dil. to 200 mL.

(b) *Suitable for soluble salts and oxides.*—Dissolve 1 g in 10 mL HCl, warming gently. Dil. to 200 mL.

2.128 ***Reduction***

Heat aliquot of sample soln (100 mL and 50 mL, resp., for samples contg <0.5 and 0.5–4.0% Fe) to bp. Add few drops diphenylamine sulfonate soln; then $SnCl_2$ soln dropwise until violet color is discharged and 2 drops excess. (Usually 1–6 drops are required. Larger amt may be used with samples contg large amt of Fe.) If reduction does not occur, discard and proceed as follows with second aliquot:

Add few granules Zn, boil few min, and either filter off excess Zn, washing with hot H_2O, or let Zn dissolve. Heat to bp and finish reduction with $SnCl_2$ and diphenylamine sulfonate indicator as before. Add 10 mL HCl (1+1). Adjust vol. to 75–110 mL with H_2O. Cool rapidly in cold H_2O. Add 10 mL satd $HgCl_2$ soln, swirl gently, add 5 mL H_3PO_4, and titr. immediately. (Small amt of HgCl must ppt to ensure complete reduction.)

2.129 ***Titration***

Add 1 drop diphenylamine indicator by pipet (no more; excess will interfere with end point if amt of Fe is small). Titr. with 0.01*N* $K_2Cr_2O_7$ soln. Since end point may be difficult to see with very small amt Fe, approach end point slowly, allowing few sec for color to develop. Titr. to permanent blue (sometimes green with very small amt Fe). For samples contg >4% Fe, use 0.1*N* $K_2Cr_2O_7$ for titrn. 1 mL 0.1*N* $K_2Cr_2O_7$ = 0.00558 g Fe; 1 mL 0.01*N* = 0.000558 g Fe.

2.130 ***Atomic Absorption Method***

See **2.109–2.113**.

Acid-Soluble Magnesium—Official Final Action

2.131 ***Atomic Absorption Method***

See **2.109–2.113**.

EDTA Titration Method (*46*)

(Applicable to samples contg ≤0.25% Mn or Zn)

2.132 ***Reagents***

Use reagents **1.022(a)**, **(b)**, **(c)**, **(d)**, **(f)** (1 mL = 1 mg Ca, equiv. to 0.6064 mg Mg), **(g)**, **(h)** (stdzd as in **2.133**), and in addn:

(a) *Triethanolamine soln.*—(1+1).

(b) *Potassium ferrocyanide soln.*—Dissolve 4 g $K_4Fe(CN)_6.3H_2O$ in 100 mL H_2O.

(c) *Ferric ammonium sulfate soln.*—Dissolve 136 g $FeNH_4(SO_4)_2.12H_2O$ in H_2O contg 5 mL H_2SO_4, and dil. to 1 L. Filter if not clear.

2.133 ***Standardization***

Pipet 10 mL Ca std soln into 300 mL erlenmeyer. Add 100 mL H_2O, 10 mL KOH-KCN soln, 2 drops triethanolamine soln, 5 drops $K_4Fe(CN)_6$ soln, and 15±1 mg calcein indicator. Immediately place flask on mag. or other mech. stirrer in front of daylight fluorescent light and white background. While stirring, titr. with EDTA soln to disappearance of all fluorescent green and until soln remains pink. Titr. ≥3 aliquots. From av., calc. Ca titer in mg/mL EDTA soln. Ca titer × 0.6064 = Mg titer in mg/mL.

2.134 ***Preparation of Solution***

(*Caution: See* **51.019** and **51.028**.)

(a) *Organic materials.*—Weigh 1 g sample into 250 mL boiling flask or erlenmeyer. Add 5 mL HCl and 10 mL HNO_3, and boil on hot plate or over low flame until easily oxidized org. matter is destroyed (ca 15 min). Cool, add 5 mL 70–72% $HClO_4$, and heat to appearance of copious fumes and momentary cessation of boiling, but not to dryness. Cool, and transfer to 250 mL beaker with ca 100 mL H_2O. Continue with pH adjustment, as in **2.135**.

(**b**) *Inorganic materials and mixed fertilizers.*—Weigh 1 g sample into 250 mL beaker. Add 5 mL HCl and 10 mL HNO_3. Cover with watch glass and heat on asbestos mat on hot plate nearly to dryness (ca 30 min). If soln remains colored from org. residues, cool, add 5 mL $HClO_4$ (70–72%), and continue heating to copious fumes and momentary cessation of boiling, but not to dryness.

2.135 ***Determination***

Cool prepd soln to room temp. Wash watch glass and inside of beaker to ca 100 mL with H_2O. Using pH meter with glass electrode and mech. stirring, adjust to ca pH 3 with 30% KOH soln and finally to pH 4.0 with 10% KOH soln. Add $FeNH_4(SO_4)_2$ soln, 5 mL for sample <7% P_2O_5, 10 mL for sample 7–15% P_2O_5, 15 mL for sample 16–30% P_2O_5, and proportionate amts for samples >30% P_2O_5. Adjust to pH 5.0 with KOH solns as above, or with HCl (1+4) if pH is >5.0. Cool to room temp. and transfer to 250 mL vol. flask with H_2O. Dil. to vol. with H_2O and mix. Let stand until ppt settles. Disturbing ppt as little as possible, filter enough soln for aliquots required for titrn thru dry 11 cm fluted paper, Whatman No. 1, or equiv.

Pipet two equal aliquots contg <15 mg Ca + Mg (usually 25 mL) into two 300 mL erlenmeyers and dil. each to 100 mL with H_2O. To one (titrn *1* for Ca + Mg) add 5 mL pH 10 buffer soln, 2 mL KCN soln, 2 drops triethanolamine soln, 5 drops $K_4Fe(CN)_6$ soln, and 8 drops eriochrome black T indicator. Titr. immediately with EDTA soln, stirring and lighting as in stdzn. Color changes are wine red, purple, dark blue, to clear pure blue end point, becoming green if overtitrd.

To second aliquot (titrn *2* for Ca) add 10 mL KOH-KCN soln, 2 drops triethanolamine soln, 5 drops $K_4Fe(CN)_6$ soln, and 15±1 mg calcein indicator. Titr. immediately with EDTA soln as in stdzn.

(Titrn *1* − Titrn *2*) × Mg titer EDTA × 100/mg sample in aliquot = % Mg.

Titrn *2* × Ca titer EDTA × 10/mg sample in aliquot = % Ca.

2.136 ★ ***Gravimetric Method (47)*** ★ ***Official Final Action***

Removal of Ca as oxalate, pptn as $MgNH_4PO_4$, and ignition to $Mg_2P_2O_7$. *See* **2.123**, 11th ed.

2.137 ★ ***Volumetric Method—Official*** ★ ***Final Action***

Titrn of pptd $MgNH_4PO_4$ with acid. *See* **2.124**, 11th ed.

2.138 Water-Soluble Magnesium (47) Official Final Action

(**a**) *In potassium-magnesium sulfate, magnesium sulfate, and kieserite.*—Weigh 1 g sample into 250 mL vol. flask, add 200 mL H_2O, and boil 30 min. Cool, dil. to vol. with H_2O, and mix. If detn is to be conducted gravimetrically, **2.136★**, or volumetrically, **2.137★**, *see* **2.125**, 11th ed.

(**b**) *In other materials, including mixed fertilizers.*—Weigh 1 g sample into 500 mL vol. flask, add 350 mL H_2O, and boil 1 hr. Cool, dil to vol., mix, and filter if necessary. If detn is to be conducted gravimetrically, **2.136★**, or volumetrically, **2.137★**, *see* **2.125**, 11th ed.

(**c**) *By EDTA method.*—Transfer aliquot soln prepd as in (**a**) or (**b**) to beaker and det. Mg as in **2.135**, using HCl or KOH to adjust pH.

★ Surplus method—*see* inside front cover.

Acid-Soluble Manganese—Official Final Action

Atomic Absorption Spectrophotometric Method (48)

2.139 ***Preparation of Sample***

(**a**) *Applicable to* Mn^{+2} *only.*—Prep. sample soln as in **2.140**, omitting the 50 mL H_3PO_4 (1+9). Proceed as in **2.112**, using std solns prepd as in **2.110(f)** and (**h**), substituting 0.5*N* H_2SO_4 for 0.5*N* HCl in **2.110(h)**.

(**b**) *Applicable to total* Mn^{+2} *and* Mn^{+4}.—Prep. sample soln as in **2.111**. Proceed as in **2.112**, using std solns prepd as in **2.110(f)** and (**h**).

2.140 ***Colorimetric Method (49)***

(Applicable to samples contg Mn^{+2} only and with ≤5% Mn)

Place 1 g sample in 200 mL wide-neck vol. flask or 250 mL beaker. Add 10 mL H_2SO_4 and 30 mL HNO_3. Heat gently until brown fumes diminish; then boil 30 min. If org. matter is not destroyed, cool, add 5 mL HNO_3, and boil. Repeat process until no org. matter remains, and boil until white fumes appear. Cool slightly, and add 50 mL H_3PO_4 (1+9). Boil few min. Cool, dil. to 200 mL in vol. flask, mix, and let stand to allow pptn of $CaSO_4$.

Pipet 50 mL clear soln into beaker. Heat nearly to bp. With stirring or swirling, add 0.3 g KIO_4 for each 15 mg Mn present, and hold 30–60 min at 90–100°, or until color development is complete. Cool, and dil. to measured vol. that will provide satisfactory concn for colorimetric measurement by instrument chosen (usually <20 ppm Mn). Compare in colorimeter against std $KMnO_4$ soln, **7.116**, or in spectrophtr at 530 nm. Calc. to Mn.

2.141 ★ ***Bismuthate Method (50)*** ★

(Applicable to Mn^{+2} only)

See **2.127–2.128**, 11th ed.

Water-Soluble Manganese

2.142 ***Atomic Absorption Spectrophotometric Method (48)—Official Final Action***

(Applicable to Mn^{+2} only)

Place 1 g sample in 50 mL beaker, wet with alcohol, add 20 mL H_2O, and let stand 15 min, stirring occasionally. Transfer to 9 cm Whatman No. 5 paper, and wash with small portions H_2O until filtrate measures ca 230 mL. Let each portion pass thru paper before adding more. Add 3–4 mL H_2SO_4 to filtrate. Proceed as in **2.112**, using std solns prepd as in **2.110(f)** and (**h**), substituting 0.5*N* H_2SO_4 for 0.5*N* HCl in **2.110(h)**.

Copper—Official Final Action

2.143 ★ ***Long Volumetric Method (51)*** ★

See **2.129–2.130**, 11th ed.

Short Volumetric Method (52)

2.144 ***Reagents***

(**a**) *Sodium thiosulfate std soln.*—0.03*N*. Prep. daily by dilg 0.1*N* soln, **50.037–50.038**. 1 mL 0.03*N* $Na_2S_2O_3$ = 1.906 mg Cu.

(**b**) *Starch soln.*—Mix ca 1 g sol. starch with enough cold H_2O to make thin paste, add 100 mL boiling H_2O, and boil ca 1 min while stirring.

(**c**) *Bromocresol green indicator.*—Dissolve 0.1 g tetrabromo-*m*-cresolsulfonphthalein in 1.5 mL 0.1*N* NaOH, and dil. to 100 mL with H_2O.

2.145 ***Determination***

Place 2 g sample in 300 mL erlenmeyer and add 10 mL HNO_3 and 5 mL H_2SO_4. Digest on hot plate to white fumes. If soln darkens, owing to org. matter, cool slightly, add little more HNO_3, and digest again to white fumes, repeating operation if necessary until org. matter appears to be destroyed. Cool, add 50 mL H_2O, boil ca 1 min, and cool to room temp.

Add bromocresol green, then NH_4OH until indicator changes to light green (pH 4). Cool again to room temp., and if indicator changes back to more acid color, add NH_4OH dropwise until indicator becomes light green again, avoiding excess. Add 2 g *NH_4HF_2* (Toxic. *Caution: See* **51.084**), mix well, and let stand ca 5 min. Add 8–10 g KI, mix well, and titr. with std $Na_2S_2O_3$ soln to light yellow. Add ca 1 mL starch soln and continue titrg slowly until color is nearly same as just before addn of the KI and becomes no darker on standing 20 sec. Report as % Cu.

2.146 ***Atomic Absorption Method***

See **2.109–2.113**.

Sodium—Official First Action

Flame Photometric Method (53)—Official First Action

2.147 ***Reagents***

See **2.091(a)–(c)**, and in addn:
Sodium chloride.—Dry 2 hr at 105°.

2.148 ***Preparation of Solution***

Prep. soln as in **2.093(a)**, using 2.5 g sample (<4% Na) or 1.25 g (4–20% Na).

2.149 ***Preparation of Standard Curve***

(a) *Samples containing 1% or more sodium.*—Proceed as in **2.094**, using 1.2716 g NaCl, range of diln 0–40 ppm Na, intervals ≤5 ppm, and full scale for 40 ppm Na.

(b) *Samples containing less than 1% sodium.*—Proceed as in **2.094**, using 1.2716 g NaCl, range of diln 0–10 ppm Na, intervals 2 ppm, and full scale for 10 ppm Na.

2.150 ***Determination***

(*Caution: See* **51.007**.)

Transfer 25 mL (<4% Na) or 10 mL (4–20% Na) sample soln to 250 mL vol. flask, dil. to vol. with H_2O, and mix (if internal std instrument is used, add required amt $LiNO_3$ before dilg to vol.). Atomize portions of sample several times to obtain reliable av. readings for each soln. Det. ppm Na from std curve **(a)** or **(b)**. Calc. % Na as follows:

0–4%: ppm Na/10 = % Na
4–20%: ppm Na/2 = % Na

Zinc—Official Final Action

2.151 ★ ***Gravimetric Method (54)*** ★

(For samples contg ≥0.1% Zn)

Digestion with HNO_3 and H_2SO_4, sepn of interfering sulfides from acid soln with H_2S, pptn of ZnS at pH 3 with H_2S, and ignition to ZnO. *See* **2.138**, 12th ed.

2.152 ★ ***Colorimetric Method (55)*** ★

(For samples contg <4% Zn)

Digestion with HNO_3 and H_2SO_4, and detn with dithizone. *See* **2.139**, 12th ed.

Zincon Ion Exchange Method (56)

(Clean all glassware with hot chromic acid or HNO_3 (1+1). Rinse thoroly with H_2O. *Caution: See* **51.023**, **51.026**, and **51.030**.)

2.153 ***Reagents***

(a) *Anion exchange resin.*—100–200 mesh, strong base, polystyrene alkyl quaternary amine, 7% cross linkage, CGA-540 (J. T. Baker Chemical Co., No. 4602, or equiv.).

(b) *Zincon indicator.*—Dissolve 0.12 g zincon (*o*-[[α-[(2-hydroxy-5-sulfophenyl)azo]benzylidene]hydrazino]benzoic acid, Na salt) (J. T. Baker Chemical Co., No. X690) in 5 mL 0.3*N* NaOH and dil. to 100 mL with H_2O. Prep. fresh weekly.

(c) *Hydrochloric acid solns.*—*(1) 0.5N.*—Dil. 20 mL HCl to 500 mL with H_2O. *(2) 0.25N.*—Dil. 2 mL HCl to 100 mL with H_2O. *(3) 0.005N.*—Dil. 2.5 mL HCl to 6 L with H_2O.

(d) *Borate buffer soln.*—pH 9.8. Dissolve 4 g H_3BO_3 in 140 mL H_2O. Add 5 mL NH_4OH by pipet and then dropwise to pH 9.8. Check daily.

(e) *Ammonium thiocyanate.*—1*M*. Dissolve 0.76 g NH_4CNS in 10 mL H_2O.

(f) *Zinc std solns.*—*(1) Stock soln.*—1000 ppm. Dissolve 1.000 g pure Zn metal in small amt HCl-HNO_3 (1+1). Evap. to small vol., add 3 mL HCl, and heat. Dil. to 1 L with H_2O. *(2) Working soln.*—10 ppm. Dil. 10 mL stock soln to 1 L with H_2O.

(g) *Sodium hydroxide soln.*—0.3*N*. Dissolve ca 1.25 g NaOH in 100 mL H_2O.

2.154 ***Preparation of Resin Column***

Wash 12 g new resin in 250 mL beaker with H_2O until washings are neut. Introduce resin as slurry into 25 × 2.2 cm chromatgc tube with fritted glass disk and stopcock at bottom. Mark vol. levels on column at 10, 40, and 50 mL above packed resin and on 250 mL separator at 90 mL. (Keep resin wet and store under liq. when not in use.) Connect separator to top of column thru stopper. Attach inverted U-shaped glass dispensing tube to 250 mL vol. flask thru vented stopper or cork and connect with Zn-free plastic tubing to stopcock of column with stopcock grease. *See* Fig. **2:08**.

Mount reservoir (aspirator bottle or carboy) contg ≥1 L 0.005*N* HCl high enough to effect backwashing. Attach Zn-free tubing and pinch clamp.

2.155 ***Flow Calibration***

Use sweep sec hand of watch or stopwatch to establish flow rates. Det. number drops/mL leaving dispensing tube. Remove separator and vol. flask; drain and then backwash resin (*see* **2.157**). Remove reservoir tubing, open stopcock, elute 40 drops from dispensing tube, and measure vol. Use this factor to convert 0.5 mL/min (required in Zn elution, **2.157**) to drops/sec.

2.156 ***Preparation of Sample***

Remove separator and elution tubing from column. Activate resin by draining column and adding 50 mL 0.5*N* HCl. Drain column to 40 mL mark.

(a) *Samples containing 0.14% or more zinc.*—Dissolve 1.000 g well-ground sample in 10 mL HCl and 5 mL HNO_3 in 250 mL beaker. Evap. to near dryness on hot plate. (*Caution:* Do *not* bake.) Redissolve residue in ca 40 mL 0.5*N* HCl, boiling gently if necessary. Filter thru Whatman No. 41 paper into 100 mL vol. flask. Thoroly wash residue and dil. filtrate to vol. with 0.5*N* HCl. Drain column to 10 mL mark. Tap column to pack resin. Pipet aliquot contg 0.7–0.8 mg Zn onto column. Elute sample soln at ca 5 sec/drop.

★ Surplus method—*see* inside front cover.

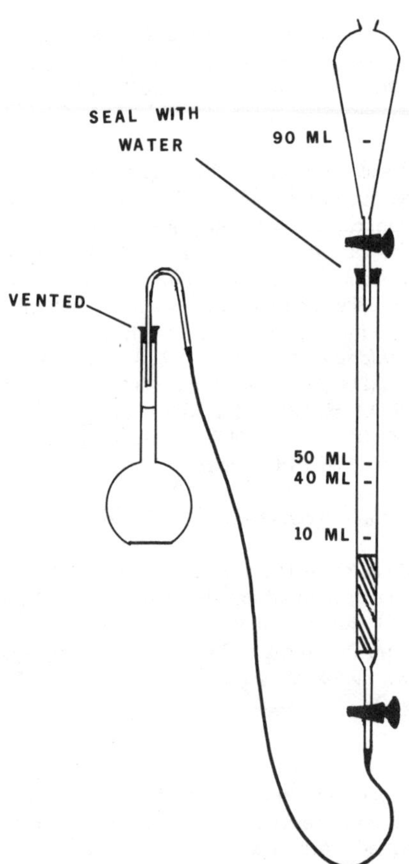

FIG. 2:08—Apparatus for elution of resin column.

(**b**) *Samples containing less than 0.14% zinc.*—Weigh, to nearest mg, sample contg 0.7–0.8 mg Zn into 250 mL beaker. Digest and filter sample and prep. column as in (**a**). Tightly attach open separator to column. Close stopcock. Transfer entire sample soln to separator, rinsing with two 10 mL portions 0.5*N* HCl. Open stopcock. Elute sample soln at ca 5 sec/drop. Remove empty separator, rinse twice with 20 mL 0.5*N* HCl, and add rinses to remaining soln in column.

2.157 ***Elution of Zinc***

After sample soln passes thru resin, immediately rinse column with 0.5*N* HCl at ca 1.5 sec/drop until 1 mL eluate gives clear, colorless soln with 1*M* NH_4SCN. If Fe^{+3} is present, soln will turn brown. Drain resin and backwash with 0.005*N* HCl from reservoir thru elution tubing, forcing out air bubbles from tubing and column. Simultaneously, tap resin into suspension as it is forced up. Close column stopcock when liq. reaches 50 mL mark on column. Attach dispensing tube to vol. flask. Reopen stopcock, and raise flask until flow just stops. Continue ht adjustment until a drop remains in equilibrium at tip of dispensing tube and neither rises nor falls. Secure flask. Attach open separator with H_2O seal to column and close stopcock. Add 240 mL 0.005*N* HCl to separator and reopen stopcock. Open column stopcock until rate of ca 0.5 mL/min is sustained 10 min. If rate decreases, increase rate slightly until nearly const. Let elution continue overnight. Then, if >90 mL remains in separator, readjust rate as above and continue elution to 90 mL mark. Finally, lower flask, fill to 250 mL mark at convenient rate from dispensing tip, and mix. Detach hose and separator from column, and drain all 3. Reactivate resin, and stopper column as in **2.156**.

2.158 ***Determination***

Pipet 20 mL eluate into 50 mL vol. flask contg small piece litmus paper. Make alk. with 0.3*N* NaOH, then just acidic with 0.25*N* HCl. Pipet in 2 mL more acid, 5 mL buffer, and 3 mL zincon soln. Dil. to vol. with H_2O. Similarly prep. 0, 1, 2, and 3 ppm std solns, using 0, 5, 10, and 15 mL std Zn working soln, resp. Using 0 ppm std soln as blank, det. *A* at 620 nm 15–45 min after zincon addn. Plot std curve of ppm against *A*.

$$\% \text{ Zn} = (C \times F)/W,$$

where C = ppm from std curve; W = g sample; and F = 0.0625 for samples contg <0.14% Zn or 6.25/mL aliquot pipetted onto resin for samples contg ≥0.14% Zn.

2.159 ***Atomic Absorption Method***

See **2.109–2.113**.

Total Sulfur (*57*)—Official Final Action

2.160 ***Reagents***

(**a**) *Barium chloride soln.*—10%. Dissolve 100 g $BaCl_2.2H_2O$ in 900 mL H_2O and filter thru Whatman No. 42 paper, or equiv. 1 mL = 14 mg S.

(**b**) *Bromine in carbon tetrachloride.*—10%. Add 10 g Br to 90 g reagent grade CCl_4. Stir until homogeneous. Store in g-s bottle. (*Caution: See* **51.047** and **51.049**.)

2.161 ***Determination***

Weigh sample contg 50–150 mg S into 250 mL beaker, and add 20 mL 10% Br in CCl_4, (**b**). Mix by swirling beaker at 5 min intervals during 30 min. Add 15 mL HNO_3 and mix as before. Evap. to 1–2 mL on warm hot plate. Add 15 mL HCl and 10 mL H_2O. Evap. just to dryness on warm hot plate or steam bath. Add 10 mL HCl and 50 mL H_2O, heat to boiling, boil 5 min, and filter thru Whatman No. 42 paper, or equiv. Wash paper with ten 20 mL portions hot H_2O.

Heat filtrate to boiling. Add 5–6 drops 10% $BaCl_2$ soln, (**a**). After 1 min, add dropwise amt $BaCl_2$ soln equiv. to expected S content plus 5 mL excess. Digest at gentle boil 1 hr. Remove from hot plate and let ppt settle 15–20 min. Filter immediately thru previously ignited and weighed gooch. Wash with hot H_2O until 10 mL wash H_2O shows no ppt with 3 mL 1% $AgNO_3$. Dry and ignite at 800° to const wt. Cool in desiccator over $MgClO_4$ and weigh.

$$\% \text{ S} = \text{g } BaSO_4 \times 0.1374 \times 100/\text{g sample}.$$

2.162 Free Sulfur (*58*)—Official Final Action

(*Caution: See* **51.011**, **51.047**, **51.048**, and **51.049**.)

Ext 1 g sample with CS_2 in Soxhlet app., letting extn thimble drain ≥12 times. Transfer ext to 250 mL beaker. Evap. CS_2 in draft at room temp. Heat in oven 20 min at 60–70°; then cool to room temp. Add 10 mL *satd soln of Br in* CCl_4, cover, and let stand ca 30 min, stirring several times. Add 15 mL HNO_3, cover, and let stand ca 30 min, stirring several times. Evap. on hot plate to ca 5 mL. Add 20 mL HCl and evap. to ca 5 mL. Add ca 50 mL H_2O, filter, and wash with HCl (1+49). Add 2 drops bromophenol blue, **6.019(f)**, and then NH_4OH to first color change. Add HCl dropwise until distinctly acid, then 5 drops excess; dil. to 150 mL, heat to bp, and add 10% $BaCl_2$ soln, **2.160(a)**, dropwise until ca 50% excess is present. Cover beaker and digest on steam bath ≥1 hr. Cool to room temp. and filter thru asbestos on gooch previously ignited at 800° and weighed. Wash 10 times with hot H_2O. Ignite in furnace at 800° ≥20 min. Cool in desiccator and weigh as $BaSO_4$. Calc. as S as in **2.161**.

2.163 ★ Acid-Forming or Nonacid-Forming ★ Quality (*59*)—Official Final Action

Fusion with std amt Na_2CO_3 followed by neutzn of melt with excess acid and back-titrn with std NaOH. *See* **2.141–2.142**, 11th ed.

PEAT

(Moss, humus, and reed-sedge types)

2.164 Sampling (*60*)—Procedure

Use slotted single or double tube or slotted tube and rod, all with pointed ends and min. 1" diam. for loose materials. Use cutting type core sampler, with plunger, for compressed materials. Pennsylvania State Forage Sampler (NASCO, 901 Janesville Ave, Fort Atkinson, WI 53538) is satisfactory core sampler.

Take representative sample from lot or shipment as follows: (**a**) *Packaged or baled peats.*—Lay bag or bale horizontally and remove core diagonally from end to end. From lots of 1–10 bags, sample all bags; from lots of ≥11, sample 10 bags. Take 1 core from each bag sampled; except for lots of 1–4 bags, take diagonal cores from each bag and addnl cores to total ≥5 cores.

(**b**) *Bulk samples.*—Draw ≥10 cores from different regions.

(**c**) *Small containers* (*10 lb or less*).—Take entire package. Working rapidly to prevent moisture losses, reduce composite sample to ≤500 g (by wt) or 2 L (by vol.) by mixing on clean plastic or paper and quartering. Place sample in air-tight container.

Sampling by random "grab" procedure is necessary if particle size range is to be detd or if representative sample cannot be taken with core sampler as above.

2.165 Preparation of Sample (*61*)—Official Final Action

Place representative field sample on square rubber sheet, paper, or plastic. Reduce sample to amt required by quartering and place in moisture-proof container. *Work rapidly to prevent moisture losses.*

Moisture (*61*)—Official Final Action

2.166 *Method I*

Mix sample thoroly and place 10–12 g in ignited and weighed (with fitted heavy-duty Al foil cover) Vycor or porcelain evapg dish, ≥75 mL capacity. Crush soft lumps with spoon or spatula. Cover immediately with Al foil cover and weigh to nearest mg. Dry, uncovered, 16 hr at 105°. Remove from oven, cover tightly, cool, and weigh.

% Moisture (report to nearest 0.1%) = (g as-received sample − g oven-dried sample) × 100/g as-received sample.

2.167 *Method II*

(Use when pH, N, fiber, etc., are to be detd.)

Mix thoroly and weigh 100–300 g representative sample, **2.165**, and spread evenly on large flat pan. Crush soft lumps with spoon or spatula and let come to moisture equilibrium with room air ≥24 hr. Stir occasionally to maintain max. air exposure of entire sample. When wt is const, calc. loss in wt as % moisture removed by air drying. Grind representative portion air-dried sample 1–2 min in high-speed blender; use for moisture, ash, and N detns.

Mix air-dried, ground sample and weigh, to nearest mg, equiv. of 10 g sample on as-received basis (g air-dried sample equiv. to 10.0 g as-received sample = 10.0 − [(10.0 × % moisture removed)/100]). Place weighed sample in ignited and weighed (with fitted heavy duty Al foil cover) Vycor or porcelain evapg dish and proceed as in **2.166**.

% Moisture (report to nearest 0.1%) = (10.0 − g oven-dried sample) × 10.0.

★ Surplus method—*see* inside front cover.

Mechanical Analysis for Determination of Particle Size Range (*60*)—Procedure

2.168 ***Apparatus***

Mechanical sieve shaker.—With 8" diam., Nos. 8 and 20 sieves equipped with cover and bottom pan.

2.169 ***Preparation of Sample***

Air-dry as in **2.167**.

2.170 ***Determination***

Mix thoroly and place 20.0 g air-dried sample on No. 8 sieve nested on No. 20 sieve. Secure sieves and shake at suitable speed 10 min. Remove and weigh foreign matter, such as sticks, stones, and glass, from No. 8 fraction. Weigh fractions of peat retained on Nos. 8 and 20 sieves and portion collected in bottom pan. Convert fraction and sample wts to as-received basis and calc. in terms of %. (If foreign matter is absent, conversion to as-received basis is not necessary.)

% Foreign matter = fraction removed from No. 8 sieve × 100;
% Coarse fiber = fraction retained on No. 8 sieve × 100;
% Medium fiber = fraction retained on No. 20 sieve × 100;
% Fine = fraction collected in pan × 100.

If mech. sieve shaker is not available, use hand sieving. Conduct sieving by appropriate lateral and vertical motions accompanied by jarring action. Continue until no appreciable change is noted in sieve fraction.

pH (*60*)—Procedure

2.171 ***Apparatus and Reagents***

(**a**) *pH meter.*—Battery-operated or on elec. line with voltage regulator.

(**b**) *Carbon dioxide-free water.*—*See* **50.007**.

(**c**) *Acid potassium phthalate buffer soln.*—0.05*m*. *See* **50.007(c)**.

(**d**) *Phosphate buffer soln.*—0.025*m*. *See* **50.007(d)**.

(**e**) *Calcium chloride solns* (*Method II only*).—(*1*) *Stock soln.*—1.0*M*. Dissolve 147 g $CaCl_2.2H_2O$ in H_2O in 1 L vol. flask, cool, dil. to vol., and mix. Dil. 15 mL of this soln to 200 mL with H_2O in vol. flask and stdze by titrg 25 mL aliquot dild soln. with std 0.1*N* $AgNO_3$, **50.029**, using 1 mL 5% K_2CrO_4 as indicator. (*2*) *Working soln.*—0.01*M* (pH 5.0–6.5). Dil. 20 mL stock soln. to 2 L with H_2O.

2.172 ***Determination***

(**a**) *Method I* (*in distilled water*).—Weigh ca 3.0 g air-dried peat or equiv. amt moist material into 100 mL beaker. Add 50 mL H_2O. (Addnl H_2O may be needed for very fibrous materials such as sphagnum moss peat.) Let soak 30 min, with occasional stirring. Read on pH meter.

(**b**) *Method II* (*in 0.01M calcium chloride soln*).— Weigh ca 3.0 g air-dried peat or equiv. amt moist material into 100 mL beaker. Add 50 mL 0.01*M* $CaCl_2$. Let soak 30 min, with occasional stirring. Read on pH meter. Report results as pH in 0.01*M* $CaCl_2$ soln. (pH values in $CaCl_2$ soln. are usually ca 0.5–0.8 units lower than those in H_2O. Observed pH in $CaCl_2$ soln is virtually independent of initial amt salt present in soil, whereas pH readings in H_2O can be modified by salts such as fertilizer material.)

2.173 Ash (*61*)—Official Final Action

Place uncovered (retain cover for weighing) Vycor or porcelain dish contg dried sample from moisture detn in furnace. Gradually bring to 550° and hold until completely ashed. Cover with retained Al foil cover, cool, and weigh.

% Ash (report to nearest 0.1%) = g ash × 100/g as-received sample taken for moisture detn. (If moisture Method II was used, g as-received sample = 10.0.)

Sand (*60*)—Procedure

2.174 ***Preparation of Sample***

Air-dry as in **2.167**.

2.175 ***Determination***

(*Caution: See* **51.056**.)

Place 25 g air-dried, ground sample into 125 mL tall-form beaker, or equiv. Nearly fill beaker with $CHCl_3$, stir briefly, and let settle ca 1 min. With spoon, discard most floating org. material, decant remaining org. material and $CHCl_3$, taking care not to disturb settled portion (sand), and air-dry to remove residual $CHCl_3$. (Stirring aids drying.)

When dry, weigh settled portion and calc. as % sand (includes other minerals present such as limestone, etc.).

% Sand = (g air-dried settled residue × 100)/g air-dried sample

2.176 Organic Matter (*61*)—Official Final Action

% Org. matter = 100.0 − (% moisture + % ash).

2.177 Total Nitrogen (*60*)—Procedure

Det. N as in **2.057**, using well mixed, air-dried, ground sample equiv. to 10.0 g sample on as-received basis.

Det. g air-dried sample equiv. to 10.0 g as-received sample as in **2.167**.

Water Capacity and Volumes (*62*)
Official Final Action

2.178 ***Apparatus***

Dispensing apparatus.—2 dispensing burets, 250 mL in 1 mL subdivisions, ±2 mL tolerance, pinchcock type; 1-hole No. 6 rubber stopper; straight polyethylene drying tube with serrated rubber tubing fittings, 15 cm long, ¾" od, ⅝" id (Cenco Instrument Corp. No. 14782–2); and stainless steel screen circle, ca 16 mesh and 28.7 mm diam.

Assemble dispensing app. as follows: Discard serrated rubber tubing fittings from polyethylene drying tube and use tube only. Center stainless steel screen on one end of tube and seal. (Soldering iron is useful.) Adjust length of tube to match convenient graduation of buret; then scallop end without screen to allow for H_2O drainage, and insert into dispensing buret with screen side up.

2.179 ***Preparation of Sample***

See **2.165**.

2.180 ***Determination***

Det. moisture content on sep. sample by **2.166** or **2.167**.

Weigh buret fitted with plastic tube and screen. Working rapidly to prevent moisture losses, mix sample thoroly, place on top of No. 4 screen, and shake until sieving is complete. Use only portion that has passed thru sieve for detn. Firmly pack buret with 25 cm (10") of 4 mesh sample as follows: Attach rubber stopper to delivery end of buret. Add ca 20 mL portions, *firmly* tapping 3 times vertically from ht of 15 cm (6") on rubber stopper, for final ht of 25 cm. (This will ensure that ht of final wet vol. is 19–25 cm.) Remove stopper; weigh buret to nearest g. Position buret to use sink as drain. Place H_2O source (19 L (5 gal.) bottle) equipped with siphon device above level of buret. Connect clamped rubber tubing of siphon device to buret with glass tubing (ca 13 cm (5") long, constricted at one end) inserted into one-hole rubber stopper *fitting tightly* into top of buret. Attach rubber tubing with pinch clamp to delivery end of buret. Open both clamps and pass H_2O thru sample ≥24 hr, maintaining water reservoir over sample at all times. (Moss-type samples may float but gradually settle as sample becomes wet.) After initial soaking, regulate H_2O flow thru column by adjusting screw clamp at delivery end of buret. (In-flow of H_2O should be ca equal to out-flow; flow of ca 1 drop/sec is suitable.) When sample is *supersatd,* close both clamps and let sample settle in H_2O ca 5 min. Top surface of sample should be as level as possible.

Raise buret and replace rubber tubing on delivery end of buret with 250 mL dispensing buret filled with H_2O, using rubber stopper for connection. Connect two burets tightly, *with no air leaks.* Remove siphon device and open outlet clamps of both burets to empty. (Suction created is equiv. to ca 38 cm (15") H_2O. Check for air leaks to ensure that std suction is exerted on sample. It is important to remove excess H_2O as described.) Measure ht of wet peat. Ht should be 19–25 cm. Record vol. in mL and weigh buret, plastic tube with screen, and wet peat to nearest g.

Wet sample again as above ≥1 hr, drain by suction, record vol., and weigh. Repeat until consistent results are obtained.

2.181 ***Calculations***

(**a**) *Saturated Volume Weights, g/mL*

As-recd = g as-recd sample/mL wet vol.

Oven-dried = g dried sample/mL wet vol., where g dried sample = g as-recd sample × [(100 − % moisture)/100].

Wet = g wet sample/mL wet vol.

(**b**) *Water-Holding Capacity, %*

(*1*) *Weight basis:*

As-recd = [(g wet sample − g as-recd sample) × 100]/g as-recd sample

Oven-dried = [(g wet sample − g dried sample) × 100]/g dried sample

(*2*) *Volume basis:*

Water vol. = [(g wet sample − g dried sample) × 100]/(mL wet vol. × 1.0)

(**c**) *Dry Peat Volume, %*

Dry peat vol. = (g dried sample × 100)/(mL wet vol. ×1.5)

(**d**) *Air Volume, %*

Air vol. = 100 − (% water vol. + % dry peat vol.)

Alternative Methods (60)

Volume—Procedure

2.182 ***Principle***

Method consists of dividing particles of peat from original container by passing them thru 12.7 mm (0.5") sieve and allowing them to fall into vol.-measuring container.

2.183 ***Apparatus***

(**a**) *Sieve*.—No. ½" (12.7 mm).

(**b**) *Measuring box*.—Steel or wood, bound with metal having one of the following sets of inner dimensions: (*1*) ½ cu. ft. = 12 × 12 × 12" with line scribed 6" from bottom; (*2*) ¾ cu. ft. = 12 × 12 × 12" with line scribed 9" from bottom; (*3*) 1 cu. ft. = 12 × 12 × 12" box, 2 cu. ft. = 16 × 16 base × 13.5" ht, 5 cu. ft = 16 × 16 base × 33.75" ht.

2.184 ***Determination***

(**a**) *Loose peat*.—Remove material from bag or container, pass it thru ½" sieve, and place directly into measuring box. Pour contents from ca 60 cm (2') into measuring box. Det. contents of bag or container only once. Fill corners of measuring box by shaking with rotary motion, 1 rotation/sec for 5 sec, without lifting box from floor or surface. When filled, level off by straightedge. Use ht of box to calc. vol. in cu. ft.

(**b**) *Baled peat*.—Vol. baled material = ht × area of base. Correct measurements for outside wrappers. Det. amt loose peat in bale by passing thru ½" sieve and measuring amt loose peat, using 12 × 12 × 12" box as in (**a**). Report vol. of peat in cu. ft.

Report total vol. of sieved peat from original container.

Volume Weight, Water-Holding Capacity, and Air Capacity of Water-Saturated Peat Materials—Procedure

2.185 ***Apparatus***

(**a**) *Hollow spray nozzle*.—Monarch F-97-W, nozzle No. 4.6160 (Monarch Mfg. Works Inc., 2501 E Ontario St, Philadelphia, PA 19134), or equiv.

(**b**) *Pipe connection*.—For installation of nozzle on H_2O faucet in sink.

(**c**) *Containers*.—Approx. 2 L (2 lb coffee cans are suitable) fitted with plastic covers. Replace metal bottom of one with No. 20 Cu screen (test container).

(**d**) *Aluminum pie pans*.—20 cm (8") diam. Drill holes in side walls of pan so that H_2O depth in pan remains ca 1.3 cm (0.5").

2.186 ***Preparation of Sample***

See **2.165**.

2.187 ***Determination***

Det. moisture content on sep. sample by **2.166** or **2.167**.

Weigh test container fitted with plastic cover, screen, and circle of filter paper (12.5 cm Whatman No. 4, or equiv.) which is placed on screen. Thoroly mix equal wts of H_2O and peat and place in container without pressure to ht of 10 cm (4"); record wt in g. (If peat is dried out, mix 1 part peat with 2 parts H_2O. If wet, mix 2 parts peat with 1 part H_2O.)

Place test container in Al pan filled with H_2O in sink ≥30 cm (12") directly under spray nozzle. Water ca 24 hr as mist to prevent compression of peat. Place cover on container, seal (tape is suitable) to prevent evapn, and let stand in Al pan, maintaining 1.3 cm H_2O head 2 days. Remove from pan and drain 2 hr with container at 45° angle. Remove seal on cover, and record wt and vol. Vol. can be detd by using container identical to test container not fitted with screen, filling H_2O to same ht as sample in test container, and transferring to graduate with mL markings.

2.188 ***Calculations***

(**a**) *Saturated Volume Weights, g/mL*

(*1*) *As-recd* = g as-recd sample/mL wet vol., where g as-recd sample = g total sample/2; or g total sample/3 if 2 parts H_2O used; or (g total sample × 2)/3 if 2 parts peat used.

(*2*) *Oven-dried*.—*See* **2.181**.

(*3*) *Wet*.—*See* **2.181**.

(**b**) *Water-Holding Capacity, %*

See **2.181**.

(**c**) *Dry Peat Volume, %*

See **2.181**.

(**d**) *Air Volume, %*

See **2.181**.

Cation Exchange Capacity (*63*)
Official Final Action

AOAC-ASTM Method

2.189 ***Principle***

Cation exchange capacity is measure of total amt exchangeable cations that can be held by peat, expressed as mequiv./100 g air-dried peat. Peat sample is shaken with 0.5*N* HCl to remove bases and to sat. sorption complex with H^+. Excess acid is removed; absorbed H^+ is replaced with Ba^{+2}, titrd with 0.1*N* NaOH, using phthln indicator, and calcd to mequiv./100 g air-dried peat.

2.190 ***Reagents***

(**a**) *Dilute hydrochloric acid*.—0.5*N*. Dil. 42 mL HCl to 1 L with H_2O.

(**b**) *Barium acetate soln*.—0.5*N*. Dissolve 64 g $Ba(OAc)_2$ in H_2O and dil. to 1 L.

(**c**) *Silver nitrate soln*.—1%. Dissolve 1 g $AgNO_3$ in 100 mL H_2O.

(**d**) *Sodium hydroxide std soln*.—0.1*N*. Prep. and stdze as in **50.032–50.035**.

2.191 ***Preparation of Sample***

See **2.165**.

2.192 ***Determination***

Thoroly mix air-dried ground peat sample and place 2.00 g in 300 mL erlenmeyer. Add ca 100 mL 0.5*N* HCl; stopper flask and shake vigorously periodically during 2 hr (or shake mech. 30 min). Filter thru rapid paper (24 cm fluted, or equiv.) in large powder funnel. Wash with 100 mL portions H_2O until 10 mL wash shows no ppt with ca 3 mL 1% $AgNO_3$. Discard filtrate. Immediately transfer moist peat to 300 mL erlenmeyer, by puncturing apex of paper and forcing moist peat thru funnel stem into erlenmeyer, using spray from wash bottle contg ca 100 mL 0.5*N* $Ba(OAc)_2$. Stopper flask and shake vigorously periodically during 1 hr (or shake mech. 15 min). Filter, and wash with three 100 mL portions H_2O. Discard peat, and titr. washings with 0.1*N* NaOH, using 5 drops phthln, to first pink.

Calc. mequiv./100 g air-dried peat = (mL × normality NaOH × 100)/g sample.

SELECTED REFERENCES

(*1*) JAOAC **12**, 97(1929); **33**, 424(1950); **38**, 108, 541(1955); **50**, 190, 382(1967); **51**, 859(1968); **55**, 709(1972).

(*2*) JAOAC **52**, 592(1969).

(*3*) JAOAC **42**, 500 (1959).

(*4*) JAOAC **12**, 98(1929); **24**, 253(1941).

(*5*) JAOAC **3**, 95(1917).

(*6*) JAOAC **40**, 711(1957).

(*7*) JAOAC **46**, 582(1963); **47**, 32, 1040(1964).
(*8*) JAOAC **52**, 1127(1969); **55**, 699(1972).
(*9*) JAOAC **38**, 413(1955).
(*10*) JAOAC **41**, 517(1958); **42**, 503(1959).
(*11*) Z. Anal. Chem. **189**, 243(1962); JAOAC **45**, 40, 201, 999(1962); **46**, 579(1963); **47**, 420(1964).
(*12*) Z. Anal. Chem. **189**, 243(1962); JAOAC **45**, 40, 999(1962); **49**, 1201(1966); **52**, 587(1969).
(*13*) JAOAC **61**, 533(1978).
(*14*) JAOAC **5**, 443, 460(1922); **6**, 384(1923); **14**, 182(1931); **19**, 269(1936); **22**, 254(1939); **42**, 512(1959).
(*15*) JAOAC **42**, 503(1959).
(*16*) JAOAC **52**, 587(1969).
(*17*) JAOAC **43**, 478(1960); **46**, 570(1963); **60**, 702(1977).
(*18*) JAOAC **44**, 233(1961).
(*19*) JAOAC **46**, 570(1963); **47**, 420(1964).
(*20*) JAOAC **38**, 56(1955).
(*21*) JAOAC **53**, 450(1970); **57**, 10(1974).
(*22*) JAOAC **61**, 299(1978).
(*23*) Chem. Ztg. **16**, 1952(1892); JAOAC **6**, 391(1923); **15**, 267(1932).
(*24*) JAOAC **13**, 208(1930); **15**, 267(1932).
(*25*) JAOAC **18**, 62, 218(1935); **19**, 68, 279(1936).
(*26*) JAOAC **53**, 808(1970); **56**, 853(1973).
(*27*) JAOAC **13**, 215(1930).
(*28*) JAOAC **38**, 436(1955); **44**, 245(1961).
(*29*) Ind. Eng. Chem., Anal. Ed. **7**, 259(1935); JAOAC **41**, 637(1958); **42**, 494(1959).
(*30*) JAOAC **43**, 499(1960); **57**, 1360(1974); **59**, 22(1976); **60**, 323(1977).
(*31*) JAOAC **59**, 22(1976).
(*32*) JAOAC **18**, 237, 260, 281(1935); **19**, 302(1936).
(*33*) Anal. Chem. **21**, 984(1949); JAOAC **35**, 674(1952); **36**, 649(1953).
(*34*) JAOAC **28**, 782(1945).
(*35*) J. Agric. Food Chem. **3**, 48(1955); JAOAC **41**, 533(1958); **51**, 857(1968).
(*36*) JAOAC **53**, 456(1970); **54**, 646(1971).
(*37*) Anal. Chem. **29**, 1044(1957); **30**, 1882(1958); JAOAC **41**, 533(1958); **43**, 472(1960).
(*38*) JAOAC **52**, 566(1969).
(*39*) JAOAC **48**, 406, 1100(1965); **50**, 401(1967); **51**, 847(1968); **58**, 928(1975).
(*40*) JAOAC **32**, 422(1949); **33**, 132(1950); **36**, 623(1953); **38**, 407(1955).
(*41*) JAOAC **38**, 413(1955).
(*42*) JAOAC **11**, 34, 201(1928); **16**, 69(1933).
(*43*) JAOAC **24**, 302(1941).
(*44*) Anal. Chem. **30**, 1153(1958); JAOAC **48**, 412(1965).
(*45*) JAOAC **50**, 397(1967).
(*46*) JAOAC **47**, 450(1964).
(*47*) JAOAC **20**, 252(1937); **22**, 270(1939); **23**, 249(1940); **24**, 268(1941); **25**, 326(1942).
(*48*) JAOAC **55**, 695(1972).
(*49*) JAOAC **23**, 249(1940).
(*50*) JAOAC **24**, 268(1941).
(*51*) JAOAC **24**, 305(1941).
(*52*) JAOAC **25**, 77, 352(1942).
(*53*) JAOAC **55**, 986(1972); **56**, 859(1973); **57**, 1402(1974).
(*54*) JAOAC **25**, 77, 361(1942).
(*55*) JAOAC **25**, 78(1942).
(*56*) JAOAC **56**, 846(1973).
(*57*) JAOAC **47**, 436(1964).
(*58*) JAOAC **25**, 348(1942).
(*59*) JAOAC **19**, 284(1936); **22**, 289(1939).
(*60*) Book of ASTM Stds (1971) Pts 11, 22, and 30, ASTM D2973-D2978, D2980, and D2944; JAOAC **56**, 154(1973).
(*61*) JAOAC **50**, 394(1967).
(*62*) JAOAC **51**, 1296(1968); **52**, 384(1969).
(*63*) JAOAC **56**, 154(1973).

3. Plants

3.001 Sampling (*1*)—Official Final Action

When more than one plant is sampled, include enough plants in sample to ensure that it adequately represents av. composition of entire lot of plants sampled. (This number depends upon variability in composition of the plants.) Det. details of sampling by purpose for which sample is taken.

3.002 Preparation of Sample (*1*)—Official Final Action

(**a**) *For mineral constituents.*—Thoroly remove all foreign matter from material, especially adhering soil or sand, but to prevent leaching, avoid excessive washing. Air- or oven-dry as rapidly as possible to prevent decomposition or wt loss by respiration, grind, and store in tightly stoppered bottles. If results are to be expressed on fresh wt basis, record sample wts before and after drying. When Cu, Mn, Zn, Fe, Al, etc. are to be detd, avoid contaminating sample by dust during drying and from grinding and sieving machinery.

(**b**) *For carbohydrates.*—Thoroly remove all foreign matter and rapidly grind or chop material into fine pieces. Add weighed sample to hot redistd alcohol to which enough pptd $CaCO_3$ has been added to neutze acidity, using enough alcohol so that final concn, allowing for H_2O content of sample, is ca 80%. Heat nearly to bp on steam or H_2O bath 30 min, stirring frequently. (Samples may be stored until needed for analysis.)

3.003 Moisture—Official Final Action

See **7.003**, **7.006★**, or **7.007**.

3.004 Ash—Official Final Action

See **31.012**, **31.013**, or **7.009**.

3.005 Sand and Silica—Official Final Action

Ignite 10–50 g sample in flat-bottom Pt dish in furnace, at 500–550°, until residue is white or nearly so. (Use Pt dishes with caution in ashing plant materials high in Fe; for such materials, use well-glazed porcelain crucibles and include blank detn.) Moisten with 5–10 mL HCl, boil ca 2 min, evap. to dryness, and heat on steam bath 3 hr to render SiO_2 insol. Moisten residue with 5 mL HCl, boil 2 min, add ca 50 mL H_2O, heat on H_2O bath few min, filter thru hardened paper, and wash thoroly. To this filtrate add filtrate and washings from alkali-sol. SiO_2 detn (**b**) and dil. to 200 mL. Designate as *Soln I.*

(**a**) *Sand.*—Wash residue from filter into Pt dish and boil ca 5 min with ca 20 mL satd Na_2CO_3 soln; add few drops 10% NaOH soln, let settle, and decant thru ignited and weighed gooch. Boil residue in dish with another 20 mL portion Na_2CO_3 soln and decant as before. Repeat process. Transfer residue to gooch and wash thoroly, first with hot H_2O, then with little HCl (1+4), and finally with hot H_2O until Cl-free. Dry filter and contents, ignite at 500–550°, and weigh as sand. Confirm by microscopic examination.

(**b**) *Alkali-soluble SiO_2.*—Combine alk. filtrate and washings from (**a**), acidify with HCl, evap. to dryness, add 5 mL HCl, again evap., and dehydrate by heating 2 hr at 110–120°. Moisten residue with 5–10 mL HCl, boil ca 2 min, add ca 50 mL H_2O, and heat on H_2O bath 10–15 min. Filter thru ashless filter or ignited and weighed gooch, wash with hot H_2O, ignite at 500–550°, and weigh as SiO_2. Add filtrate to *Soln I.*

METALS

Calcium, Copper, Iron, Magnesium, Manganese, Potassium, and Zinc

Atomic Absorption Method (*2*)—Official First Action

3.006 ***Apparatus and Reagents***

Deionized H_2O may be used. *See* **2.109–2.110**, and following:

(**a**) *Potassium stock soln.*—1000 μg K/mL. Dissolve 1.9068 g dried (2 hr at 105°) KCl in H_2O and dil. to 1 L. Use following parameters for Table **2:04**: 7665 A, air-C_2H_2 flame, and 0.04–2 μg/mL range.

3.007 ***Preparation of Sample***

(**a**) *Dry ashing.*—Accurately weigh 1 g sample, dried and ground as in **3.002(a)**, into glazed, high-form porcelain crucible. Ash 2 hr at 500°, and let cool. Wet ash with 10 drops H_2O, and carefully add 3–4 mL HNO_3 (1+1). Evap. excess HNO_3 on hot plate set at 100–120°. Return crucible to furnace and ash addnl 1 hr at 500°. Cool crucible, dissolve ash in 10 mL HCl (1+1), and transfer quant. to 50 mL vol. flask.

(**b**) *Wet ashing.*—Accurately weigh 1 g sample, dried and ground as in **3.002(a)**, into 150 mL Pyrex beaker. Add 10 mL HNO_3 and let soak thoroly. Add 3 mL 60% $HClO_4$ and heat on hot plate, slowly at first, until frothing ceases. (*Caution: See* **51.019.**) Heat until HNO_3 is almost evapd. If charring occurs, cool, add 10 mL HNO_3, and continue heating. Heat to white fumes of $HClO_4$. Cool, add 10 mL HCl (1+1), and transfer quant. to 50 mL vol. flask.

3.008 ***Determination***

To soln in 50 mL vol. flask, add 10 mL 5% La soln, and dil. to vol. Let silica settle, decant supernate, and proceed as in **2.112**.

3.009 ***Calculations***

$$\text{ppm Element} = (\mu g/mL) \times F/g \text{ sample},$$
$$\% \text{ Element} = \text{ppm} \times 10^{-4}.$$

where F = (mL original diln × mL final diln)/mL aliquot if original 50 mL is dild.

3.010 Iron and Aluminum (*3*)—Official Final Action

(*Caution: See* **51.030.**)

Take aliquot of *Soln I,* **3.005**, contg enough Fe and Al to form ca 40 mg Fe- and $AlPO_4$. Add few drops HNO_3, Br-H_2O, or H_2O_2 to oxidize Fe. If soln does not already contain excess phosphate, add 0.5 g $(NH_4)_2HPO_4$, stir until dissolved, and dil. to 50 mL with H_2O. Add few drops thymol blue soln, **22.040(e)**, and then add NH_4OH until soln just turns yellow. Add 0.5 mL HCl and 25 mL 25% NH_4OAc soln, and stir. Let stand at room temp. until ppt settles (ca 1 hr). Filter, and wash 10 times with hot 5% NH_4NO_3 soln. Ignite at 500–550° and weigh as $FePO_4$ and $AlPO_4$.

Fuse ignited residue in Pt crucible with ca 4 g Na_2CO_3-K_2CO_3 (1+1) mixt. When fusion is complete, let crucible cool, add 5 mL H_2SO_4, and heat until copious fumes of SO_3 are evolved. Cool, transfer to flask, add H_2O, and digest until soln is clear. Reduce Fe with Zn, cool, and titr. with 0.1*N* $KMnO_4$. Correct for blank and calc. as % Fe or % Fe_2O_3. Calc. to $FePO_4$ and subtract from total Fe- and $AlPO_4$ to obtain $AlPO_4$. Correct for blank and report as Al_2O_3.

Methods for Iron Only

Colorimetric Method (4)—Official Final Action

3.011 ***Reagents***

(**a**) *Acetic acid.—2M*. Dil. 120 g HOAc to 1 L with H_2O.

(**b**) *Ammonium citrate soln.*—1%. Dissolve 1 g NH_4 citrate in H_2O and dil. to 100 mL.

(**c**) *Bromophenol blue indicator.*—0.04%. Grind 0.1 g bromophenol blue in mortar with 3 mL 0.05*N* NaOH, transfer to vol. flask, and dil. to 250 mL with H_2O.

(**d**) *Buffer solns.—(1) pH 3.5.*—Mix 6.4 mL 2*M* NaOAc with 93.6 mL 2*M* HOAc and dil. to 1 L. (*2*) *pH 4.5.*—Mix 43 mL 2*M* NaOAc with 57 mL 2*M* HOAc and dil. to 1 L.

(**e**) *Hydroquinone soln.*—Dissolve 1 g hydroquinone in 100 mL pH 4.5 buffer, (**d**)(*2*). Keep in refrigerator, and discard when any color develops.

(**f**) *o-Phenanthroline soln.*—Dissolve 1 g *o*-phenanthroline H_2O in H_2O, warming if necessary, and dil. to 400 mL.

(**g**) *Sodium acetate soln.—2M*. Dissolve 272 g NaOAc.$3H_2O$ in H_2O and dil. to 1 L.

(**h**) *Iron std soln.*—1 mg/mL. Dissolve 1 g electrolytic Fe in 50 mL H_2SO_4 (1+9), warming if necessary to hasten reaction. Cool, and dil. to 1 L with H_2O.

3.012 ***Preparation of Sample***

(*Caution: See* **51.011**, **51.025**, and **51.030**.)

Use *Soln I*, **3.005**, or if *Soln I* is not available, weigh samples of finely ground plant material (1–5 g, depending on Fe content) into porcelain crucibles with smooth inner surfaces, and ash overnight at 500–550° in furnace. Cool, add 5 mL HCl (1+1), and heat on steam bath 15 min to dissolve Fe and to hydrolyze pyrophosphate. Filter into 100 mL vol. flask. Transfer insol. residue to filter and wash 5 times with 3 mL portions hot HCl (1+100), then with hot H_2O until washings are Cl-free. Ignite paper and any remaining C in Fe-free Pt crucible. Cool, add 2 drops H_2SO_4 and 1 mL HF, and carefully evap. to SO_3 fumes. Cool, add few drops HCl (1+1), and warm. Filter and wash as before into same vol. flask, dil. to vol., and mix.

3.013 ***Determination***

Pipet identical aliquots of *Soln I*, **3.005**, or sample soln, **3.012**, into 25 mL vol. flask and into test tube or small erlenmeyer. Add 5 drops bromophenol blue indicator to aliquot in test tube, and titr. with 2*M* NaOAc soln until color matches that of equal vol. of pH 3.5 buffer contg same amt of indicator. Add 1 mL hydroquinone soln and 2 mL *o*-phenanthroline soln to aliquot in vol. flask, and adjust pH to 3.5 by adding same vol. NaOAc soln found necessary for aliquot in test tube. If turbidity develops upon adjusting pH of aliquot in test tube, add 1 mL NH_4 citrate soln to vol. flask before adding the NaOAc soln. Dil. to vol., mix, and let stand 1 hr for complete color development, and measure *A* at max., ca 510 nm.

Prep. curve relating *A* to mg Fe in 25 mL by treating series of solns contg amts of Fe that cover usable range of instrument exactly as described for unknowns, detg their respective readings at max. *A*, ca 510 nm, and plotting these against corresponding concns of Fe. H_2O may be used as ref., and blanks detd to correct for amt Fe in reagents used, or blank soln itself may be made basis of comparison.

3.014 ***Titrimetric Method (5)—Official Final Action***

Take appropriate aliquot of *Soln I* or of soln prepd as in **3.012**, and oxidize Fe by adding soln of $KMnO_4$ (1+1000) dropwise until very faint permanganate color persists. Add 5 mL 10% NH_4SCN and titr. with *dil. $TiCl_3$ soln* until red color disappears. (To prep. appropriate $TiCl_3$ soln, boil 5–10 mL 20% $TiCl_3$ with 50 mL HCl few min, cool, and dil. to 1 L. Stdze against std Fe soln, keep in dark in well-filled container, and restdze each time it is used, or every few hr when many detns are being made. Discard when decomposition is indicated by loss of color and increased titer against std.)

Calcium—Official Final Action

3.015 ***Macro Method (6)***

Transfer aliquot of *Soln I*, **3.005**, to 200 mL beaker, add H_2O if necessary to vol. of 50 mL, heat to bp, and add 10 mL satd $(NH_4)_2C_2O_4$ soln and drop Me red, **2.055(i)**. Almost neutze with NH_4OH and boil until ppt is coarsely granular. Cool, add NH_4OH (1+4) until color is faint pink (pH 5.0), and let stand ≥4 hr. Filter, and wash with H_2O at room temp. until filtrate is oxalate-free. (Reserve filtrate and washings for Mg detn, **3.017**.)

Break point of filter with Pt wire, and wash ppt into beaker in which Ca was pptd, using stream of hot H_2O. Add ca 10 mL H_2SO_4 (1+4), heat to ca 90°, add ca 50 mL hot H_2O, and titr. with 0.05*N* $KMnO_4$. Finally add filter paper to soln and complete titrn.

3.016 ***Micro Method (7)***

Weigh 2 g sample into small crucible and ignite in furnace at 500–550°. Dissolve ash in HCl (1+4) and transfer to 100 mL beaker. Add 5 mL HCl and evap. to dryness on steam bath to dehydrate SiO_2. Moisten residue with 5 mL HCl, add ca 50 mL H_2O, heat few min on steam bath, transfer to 100 mL vol. flask, cool quickly to room temp., dil. to vol., shake, and filter, discarding first portion of filtrate.

Pipet 15 mL aliquot into conical-tip centrf. tube contg 2 mL satd $(NH_4)_2C_2O_4$ soln and 2 drops Me red, **2.055(i)**. Add 2 mL HOAc (1+4), rotating tube to mix contents thoroly. Add NH_4OH (1+4), while intermittently rotating tube, until soln is faintly alk.; then add few drops of the HOAc until color is faint pink (pH 5.0). (It is important at this point to rotate tube so that last bit of liq. in conical tip has required color.) Let stand ≥4 hr; then centrf. 15 min. (Ppt should be in firm lump in tip of tube.) Remove supernate, using suction device, Fig. **3:01**, taking care not to disturb ppt. Wash ppt by adding 2 mL NH_4OH (1+49), rotating tube to break up ppt. (It may be necessary to jar tube sharply.) Centrf. 10 min, again remove supernate, and wash with reagent as before. Repeat washing of ppt 3 times.

After removing last supernate, add 2 mL H_2SO_4 (1+4) to tube, break up ppt as before, heat on steam bath to 80–90°, and titr.

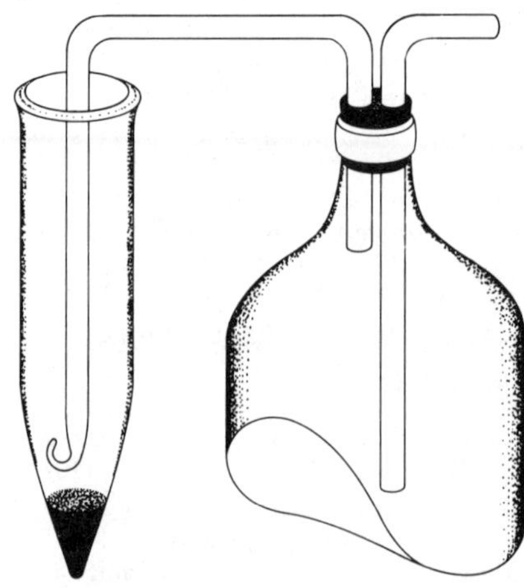

FIG. 3:01—Suction device used in micro method for determining calcium

in tube with $0.02N$ $KMnO_4$, rotating liq. during titrn to attain proper end point. If tube cools to <60° during titrn, as indicated by slow reduction of $KMnO_4$, reheat in steam bath few min and complete titrn. Perform blank on identical vol. H_2SO_4 in similar tube heated to same temp. to det. vol. $KMnO_4$ soln necessary to give end point color. Subtract this value from buret reading. 1 mL $0.02N$ $KMnO_4$ = 0.000400 g Ca. Report as % Ca.

3.017 Magnesium (*8*)—Official Final Action

(*Caution: See* **51.026**.)

To combined filtrate and washings from Ca detn, **3.015**, add 30 mL HNO_3 and evap. to dryness to decompose NH_4 salts. Take up with 5 mL HCl and dil. to ca 100 mL with H_2O. Add 5 mL *10% Na citrate soln* and 10 mL *10%* $(NH_4)_2HPO_4$ *soln,* or enough to ppt all the Mg. Add NH_4OH (1+4) with const stirring (using policeman) until soln is faintly alk. and ppt forms; then add 25 mL NH_4OH, stir vigorously until ppt is granular, and keep in cool place overnight. Filter, and wash Cl-free with cold NH_4OH (1+10). Incinerate in furnace at 500–550° until all C is oxidized, then at 900–950° ca 4 hr to form $Mg_2P_2O_7$. Cool, and weigh as $Mg_2P_2O_7$. (If sample is excessively high in Mn, dissolve residue in HNO_3, det. Mn as in **3.018**, and correct $Mg_2P_2O_7$ for $Mn_2P_2O_7$.) Report as % Mg.

3.018 Manganese (*9*)—Official Final Action

To aliquot of *Soln I,* **3.005**, contg 0.2–0.5 g ash, add 15 mL H_2SO_4 and evap. to ca 30 mL. Add 5–10 mL HNO_3 and continue evapn. (Do not evap. until dense fumes appear, because $Fe_2(SO_4)_3$ then dissolves with difficulty. HNO_3 may be present, but not HCl.) Add H_2O, little at time, heat until Fe salts dissolve, and dil. to ca 150 mL. Add 0.3 g KIO_4, or its equiv. in HIO_4, in small portions, boil few min or until color of $KMnO_4$ shows no further increase in intensity, and let cool.

Prep. std as follows: To vol. H_2O equal to sample add 15 mL H_2SO_4 and enough pure $Fe(NO_3)_3$, free from Mn, to equal approx. amt of Fe in sample. Add measured vol. $0.1N$ $KMnO_4$ until color is slightly darker than sample, then add 0.3 g KIO_4, and boil few min. When cool, transfer sample and std to 250 mL vol. flasks and dil. to vol. with H_2O. (If color is weak, it may be necessary to dil. to <250 mL.) Measure *A* with photometer or spectrophtr set at max., ca 530 nm. Report as % Mn.

3.019 ★ Potassium and Sodium ★ Official Final Action

Ignition, removal of Fe, Al, and P with NH_4OH, sulfate as $BaSO_4$, Ca as oxalate, NH_3 by ignition, and final weighing as NaCl + KCl. *See* **3.015**, 11th ed.

Potassium and/or Sodium

Flame Photometric Method (10) Official Final Action

3.020 ***Reagents***

(**a**) *Potassium stock soln.*—1000 ppm K. Dissolve 1.907 g dry KCl in H_2O and dil. to 1 L.

(**b**) *Sodium stock soln.*—1000 ppm Na. Dissolve 2.542 g dry NaCl in H_2O and dil. to 1 L.

(**c**) *Lithium stock soln.*—1000 ppm Li. Dissolve 6.108 g LiCl in H_2O and dil. to 1 L. (Needed only if internal std method of evaluation is to be used.)

(**d**) *Ammonium oxalate stock soln.*—$0.24N$. Dissolve 17.0 g $(NH_4)_2C_2O_4.H_2O$ in H_2O and dil. to 1 L.

★ Surplus method—*see* inside front cover.

(**e**) *Extracting solns.*—(*1*) *For potassium.*—For internal std method, dil. required vol. LiCl stock soln to 1 L; otherwise use H_2O. (*2*) *For sodium.*—To 250 mL NH_4 oxalate stock soln add required vol. LiCl stock soln (if internal std method is used) and dil. to 1 L. If internal std requirements are same for both Na and K detns, this reagent may be used as common extg soln.

3.021 ***Preparation of Standard Solutions***

Dil. appropriate aliquots of stock solns to prep. series of stds contg K and/or Na in stepped amts (including 0) to cover instrument range, and Li and NH_4 oxalate (if required) in same concns as in corresponding extg solns. (If common extg soln is used, 1 set of stds contg both K and Na suffices.)

3.022 ***Sample Extraction***

Transfer weighed portion of finely ground and well mixed sample to erlenmeyer of at least twice capacity of vol. of extg soln to be used. Add measured vol. extg soln, stopper flask, and shake vigorously at frequent intervals during ≥15 min. Filter thru dry, fast paper. If paper clogs, pour contents onto addnl fresh paper and combine filtrates. Use filtrate for detn.

Note: Do not make exts more concd than required for instrument because there is tendency toward incomplete extn as ratio of sample wt to vol. extg soln increases. Prep. sep. exts for K and Na when their concns in sample differ greatly. For K, use wt sample ≤0.1 g/50 mL extg soln; for low Na concns use ≥1.0 g/50 mL extg soln; and for higher concns, prep. weaker exts by reducing ratio of sample to extg soln rather than by dilg stronger exts.

3.023 ***Determination***

(*Caution: See* **51.007**.)

Rinse all glassware used in Na detn with dil. HNO_3, followed by several portions H_2O. Protect solns from air-borne Na contamination.

Operate instrument according to manufacturer's instructions. Permit instrument to reach operating equilibrium before use. Aspirate portions of std solns toward end of warm-up period until reproducible readings for series are obtained.

Run stds, covering concn range of samples involved, at frequent intervals within series of sample soln detns. Repeat this operation with both std and sample solns enough times to result in reliable av. reading for each soln. Plot curves from readings of stds, and calc. % K and/or Na in samples.

★ Potassium—Official Final Action ★

3.024 *Platinic Chloride Method*

See **3.020**, 11th ed.

3.025 *Perchloric Acid Method (11)*

See **3.021**, 11th ed.

3.026 *Rapid Method for Potassium Only*

See **3.022**, 11th ed.

Sodium Only

Uranyl Acetate Method (12)—Official Final Action

3.027 ***Reagent***

Magnesium uranyl acetate soln:

(**a**) *Uranyl acetate soln.*—To 85 g $UO_2(OAc)_2.2H_2O$ in 1 L vol. flask add 60 g HOAc and H_2O to ca 900 mL. Heat to dissolve, cool, and dil. to vol. with H_2O. (*Caution: See* **51.083**.)

(**b**) *Magnesium acetate soln.*—To 500 g $Mg(OAc)_2.4H_2O$ in 1 L vol. flask add 60 g HOAc and H_2O to ca 900 mL. Heat to dissolve, cool, and dil. to vol. with H_2O.

Reheat (**a**) and (**b**) sep. to ca 70° until all salts dissolve. Mix the solns at this temp. and let cool to ca 30°. Place vessel contg mixed reagent in H_2O bath at 20°, and hold 1–2 hr at 20°, or until slight excess of salts has crystd out. Filter thru dry filter into dry bottle.

3.028 ***Determination***

Moisten 1–10 g sample with H_2SO_4 (1+10), dry in oven, and ignite in furnace at 500–550° to destroy org. matter. Heat residue on steam bath with 2–5 mL HCl, add ca 40 mL H_2O, and heat to bp. Add enough *5% $CaCl_2$ soln* to ensure pptn of all phosphates. Ppt phosphates by making slightly alk. with NH_4OH. Filter, and evap. to ≤5 mL if no salts sep. Cool, add 100 mL Mg uranyl acetate soln, place mixt. in H_2O bath at 20°, and either stir vigorously 45 min or let stand 24 hr at this temp. Filter with suction, and wash with *alcohol satd with Na-Mg-uranyl acetate.* Dry 30 min at 105–110°, cool, and weigh. Wt Na-Mg-uranyl acetate × 0.0153 =wt Na.

Cobalt—Official Final Action

(*Caution: See* **51.011**, **51.040**, **51.049**, and **51.068**.)

Nitrosocresol Method (13)

3.029 ***Reagents***

(Make all distns in Pyrex stills with ₮ joints. Store reagents in g-s Pyrex bottles.)

(**a**) *Redistilled water.*—Distil twice, or pass thru column of ion exchange resin (IR-100A, H-form, or equiv.) to remove heavy metals.

(**b**) *Hydrofluoric acid.*—48%. Procurement in vinyl plastic bottles is advantageous.

(**c**) *Perchloric acid.*—60%. No further purification necessary.

(**d**) *Hydrochloric acid.*—(1+1). Add equal vol. HCl to distd H_2O and distil.

(**e**) *Ammonium hydroxide.*—(1+1). Distil concd NH_4OH into equal vol. redistd H_2O.

(**f**) *Ammonium hydroxide.*—0.02*N*. Add 7 mL of the NH_4OH (1+1) to 2.5 L redistd H_2O.

(**g**) *Carbon tetrachloride.*—Distil over CaO, passing distillate thru dry, acid-washed filter paper. Used CCl_4 may be recovered as in **3.044**(**a**).

(**h**) *Dithizone.*—Dissolve 0.5 g dithizone in 600–700 mL CCl_4 (tech. grade is satisfactory). Filter into 5 L separator contg 2.5–3.0 L 0.02*N* NH_4OH, shake well, and discard CCl_4 layer. Shake with 50 mL portions redistd CCl_4 until CCl_4 phase as it seps is pure green. Add 1 L redistd CCl_4 and acidify slightly with the HCl (1+1). Shake the dithizone into CCl_4 layer and discard aq. layer. Store in cool, dark place, preferably in refrigerator.

(**i**) *Ammonium citrate soln.*—40%. Dissolve 800 g citric acid in 600 mL distd H_2O, and, while stirring, slowly add 900 mL NH_4OH. Reaction is exothermic; take care to prevent spattering. Adjust pH to 8.5, if necessary. Dil. to 2 L and ext with 25 mL portions dithizone soln until aq. phase stays orange and CCl_4 remains predominantly green. Then ext soln with CCl_4 until all orange is removed.

(**j**) *Hydrochloric acid.*—0.1*N*. Dil. 16.6 mL of the HCl (1+1) to 1 L with redistd H_2O.

(**k**) *Hydrochloric acid.*—0.01*N*. Dil. 100 mL of the 0.1*N* HCl to 1 L with redistd H_2O.

(**l**) *Sodium hydroxide soln.*—1*N*. Dissolve 40 g NaOH in 1 L redistd H_2O.

(**m**) *Borate buffer.*—pH 7.8. Dissolve 20 g H_3BO_3 in 1 L redistd H_2O. Add 50 mL 1*N* NaOH and adjust pH, if necessary. Equal vols borate buffer and 0.01*N* HCl should give soln of pH 7.9.

(**n**) *Borate buffer.*—pH 9.1. To 1 L borate buffer, pH 7.8, add 120 mL 1*N* NaOH and adjust pH, if necessary.

(**o**) *Skellysolve B.*—Essentially *n*-hexane. Purify by adding 20–30 g silica gel/L, let stand several days, and distil. Available from Getty Refining and Marketing Co., PO Box 1650, Tulsa, OK 74102.

(**p**) *Cupric acetate soln.*—Dissolve 10 g $Cu(OAc)_2.H_2O$ in 1 L redistd H_2O.

(**q**) *o-Nitrosocresol soln.*—Dissolve 8.4 g anhyd. $CuCl_2$ and 8.4 g $NH_2OH.HCl$ in 900 mL H_2O. Add 8 mL *m*-cresol (Eastman Kodak Co., practical grade) and stir vigorously while slowly adding 24 mL 30% H_2O_2. Stir mech. 2 hr at room temp. (Standing for longer periods results in excessive decomposition.) Add 25 mL HCl and ext *o*-nitrosocresol with four 150 mL portions Skellysolve B, (**o**), in large separator. Then add addnl 25 mL HCl and again ext with four 150 mL portions Skellysolve B. Wash combined Skellysolve B exts twice with 50–100 mL portions 0.1*N* HCl and twice with 50–100 mL portions redistd H_2O. Shake *o*-nitrosocresol soln with successive 50–100 mL portions 1% $Cu(OAc)_2$ soln until aq. phase is no longer deep blood-red. When light purple is evident, extn is complete. Discard Skellysolve B phase, acidify aq. soln of Cu salt with 25 mL HCl, and ext reagent with two 500 mL portions Skellysolve B; wash twice with 150–200 mL portions 0.1*N* HCl and several times with 150–200 mL portions redistd H_2O. Store *o*-nitrosocresol soln in refrigerator at ca 4°. Reagent is stable ≥6 months.

(**r**) *Sodium o-nitrosocresol soln.*—Ext 100 mL *o*-nitrosocresol by shaking with two 50 mL portions borate buffer, pH 9.1, in separator. (If this is carried out as 2 extns, resulting reagent is more concd. It is important that total vol. *o*-nitrosocresol soln equal total vol. buffer.)

(**s**) *Cobalt std solns.*—(*1*) *Stock soln.*—Heat $CoSO_4.7H_2O$ in oven at 250–300° to const wt (6–8 hr). Weigh exactly 0.263 g of the $CoSO_4$ and dissolve in 50 mL redistd H_2O and 1 mL H_2SO_4. Dil. to 1 L. (*2*) *Working soln.*—0.5 μg/mL. Transfer 5 mL stock soln to 1 L vol. flask and dil. to vol. with redistd H_2O.

(**t**) *Hydroxylamine acetate buffer.*—pH 5.1±0.1. Dissolve 10 g $NH_2OH.HCl$ and 9.5 g anhyd. NaOAc in 500 mL redistd H_2O.

3.030 ***Apparatus***

(**a**) *Platinum dishes.*—Approx. 70 mL; for ashing.

(**b**) *Automatic dispensing burets.*—100 mL; type that can be fitted to ordinary 5 lb reagent bottle and filled by means of aspirator bulb is most convenient.

(**c**) *Wooden separator rack.*—Twelve-unit 125 mL separator size is convenient for dithizone extns. Rack is fitted across top with removable bar padded with sponge rubber so all 12 separators can be shaken as unit.

(**d**) *Racks.*—Consisting of 5 × 5 × 65 cm (2 × 2 × 25") wooden bars with holes drilled at close intervals to take 50 mL centrf. tubes fitted with No. 13 ₮ glass stoppers. To make these tubes, ream out necks of heavy-wall Pyrex centrf. tubes (Rockefeller Institute type) with ₮ C rod and grind to take ₮ stopper. Place tubes upright in one section, and place other section (fitted with sponge rubber disks 13 mm thick in bottom of holes) across their tops. Fasten 2 sections at ends with removable rubber connectors made from ordinary tubing of convenient size, so that any number of tubes can be shaken as unit. Use these tubes for reaction of Co with nitrosocresol, extn of complex into Skellysolve B, and washing of Skellysolve B soln.

(**e**) *Shaking machine.*—Mech. shaker giving longitudinal stroke of 5 cm at ca 180 strokes/min; use to make dithizone extns and to ext Co complex, or shake by hand.

3.031 ***Cleaning of Glassware***

Clean 120 mL Pyrex separators for dithizone extns by initially soaking 30 min in hot HNO_3 and rinsing several times with H_2O. As added precaution, shake with several portions dithizone in CCl_4. After use, clean by rinsing with H_2O, drain, and stopper to avoid contamination. It is not necessary to clean every time with acid. Repeat HNO_3 cleaning if blanks are unusually high.

Clean 50 mL g-s Pyrex centrf. tubes by soaking 30 min in HNO_3 followed by several rinsings in H_2O.

Completely submerge pipets in cylinder of chromic acid cleaning soln overnight, rinse several times with H_2O, and suspend upright in rack to dry.

Wash all other glassware thoroly in detergent and rinse well with tap H_2O followed by dip in chromic acid cleaning soln. Rinse off cleaning soln with tap H_2O followed by several distd H_2O rinses.

Clean Pt by scrubbing with sea sand followed by boiling in HCl (1+2) 30 min, and rinse several times with H_2O.

3.032 ***Preparation of Sample***

See **3.002(a)**. Oven-dry all plant material 48 hr and prep. for ashing by either of following methods:

(a) Grind material in Wiley mill equipped with stainless steel sieve, mix thoroly by rolling, and sample by quartering.

(b) Using stainless steel shears, cut material by hand fine enough for convenient sampling.

3.033 ***Ashing of Samples***

(*Caution: See* **51.011**, **51.025**, and **51.028**.)

Weigh 6 g dry plant tissue into clean Pt dish. Cover with Pyrex watch glass and place in cool furnace; heat slowly to 500° and hold at this temp. overnight. Remove sample and cool. Wet down ash carefully with fine stream redistd H_2O. From dispensing buret, slowly add 2–5 mL $HClO_4$, dropwise at first to prevent spattering. Add ca 5 mL HF, evap. on steam bath, transfer to sand bath, and keep at medium heat until fuming ceases.

Cover with Pyrex watch glass, return to partially cooled furnace, heat gradually to 600°, and keep at this temp. 1 hr. Remove sample and cool. Add 5 mL HCl (1+1) and ca 10 mL redistd H_2O. Replace cover glass and warm on steam bath to dissolve. (Usually clear soln essentially free of insol. material is obtained.) Transfer sample to 50 mL vol. flask, washing dish several times with redistd H_2O, dil. to vol., and mix thoroly. (Pt dishes can ordinarily be used several times between sand and acid cleanings.)

3.034 ***Dithizone Extraction***

(*Caution: See* **51.011(b)**, **51.028(a)** and **(d)**, and **51.049**.)

Transfer suitable aliquot (2–3 g dry material) to 120 mL separator (use petroleum jelly as stopcock lubricant). Add 5 mL NH_4 citrate soln and 1 drop phthln; adjust to pH 8.5 with NH_4OH (1+1). If ppt forms, add addnl NH_4 citrate. Add 10 mL dithizone in CCl_4 and shake 5 min. Drain CCl_4 phase into 100 mL beaker. Repeat as many times as necessary, using 5 mL dithizone soln and shaking 5 min each time. Extn is complete when aq. phase remains orange and CCl_4 phase remains predominantly green. Then add 10 mL CCl_4, shake 5 min, and combine with CCl_4 ext. Final 10 mL CCl_4 should be pure green. If not, extn was incomplete and must be repeated.

Add 2 mL $HClO_4$ to combined CCl_4 exts, cover beaker with Pyrex watch glass, and digest on hot plate until colorless. Remove cover glass and evap. slowly to dryness. (If sample is heated any length of time at high temp. when dry, losses of Co may occur. Heat only enough to evap. completely to dryness. If free acid remains, it interferes with next step where pH control is important.)

Add 5 mL 0.01*N* HCl to residue. Heat slightly to assure soln. If Cu is to be detd, transfer with redistd H_2O to 25 mL vol. flask, and dil. to vol. Transfer 20 mL aliquot to 50 mL g-s centrf. tube or 60 mL separator and reserve remainder for Cu detn, **3.043**. If Cu is not to be detd, transfer entire acid soln with redistd H_2O to centrf. tube or separator.

3.035 ***Determination***

Add 5 mL borate buffer, pH 7.8, and 2 mL freshly prepd Na *o*-nitrosocresol soln to sample soln. Add exactly 5 mL Skellysolve B and shake 10 min. Remove aq. phase by moderate suction thru finely-drawn glass tube. To Skellysolve B layer add 5 mL $Cu(OAc)_2$ soln and shake 1 min to remove excess reagent. Again remove and discard aq. phase. Wash Skellysolve B by shaking 1 min with 5 mL redistd H_2O, removing aq. layer as before; finally shake Skellysolve B 1 min with 5 mL NH_2OH-NaOAc buffer to reduce Fe. Transfer Skellysolve B soln of the Co complex to 5 cm cell and read in spectrophtr as close as possible to point of max. *A*, 360 nm.

3.036 ***Blanks and Standards***

With each set of detns include ashing blank and Co stds of 0.0, 0.5, and 1.0 μg. Beer's law holds for this range. *A* of 0.0 μg point should be <0.05. If above, repurify *o*-nitrosocresol by transferring alternately to aq. phase as Cu salt and to Skellysolve B phase as free compd after acidifying aq. phase.

It is also advisable to include std sample with each set of samples to detect contamination or unusual losses of Co in method. Com. buckwheat flour contg 0.05 ppm Co has proved satisfactory for this purpose.

3.037 ***Calculations***

Express results in terms of ppm Co, based upon dry wt of sample.

$$\text{ppm Co} = (\mu\text{g Co/mL dithizone aliquot}) \times (\text{mL total soln/g dry sample})$$

Value for μg Co is obtained from curve minus ashing blank.

Nitroso-R-Salt Method (14)

3.038 ***Reagents***

Those listed in **3.029** and following:

(a) *Nitroso-R-salt soln.*—0.2%. Dissolve 2 g powd nitroso-R-salt (Eastman Kodak Co., No. 1124) in redistd H_2O, **3.029(a)**, and dil. to 1 L.

(b) *Dilute nitric acid.*—(1+1). Dil. HNO_3 with equal vol. H_2O and redistil in Pyrex app. Store in Pyrex bottles.

(c) *Bromine water.*—Satd soln of Br in redistd H_2O, **3.029(a)**.

(d) *Citric acid soln.*—0.2*N*. Use special reagent grade Pb-free citric acid.

3.039 ***Preparation and Ashing of Samples***

Proceed as in nitrosocresol method, **3.032–3.033**, thru "(Usually clear soln essentially free of insol. material is obtained.)" except use 10 g instead of 6 g dry plant tissue.

3.040 ***Dithizone Extraction***

Transfer entire soln to 120 mL separator, and proceed as in **3.034**, thru "If free acid remains . . . pH control is important.)" Dissolve in 1 mL citric acid soln, **(d)**, transfer to 25 mL vol. flask, and dil. to vol. with redistd H_2O, **3.029(a)**.

3.041 ***Determination***

Transfer suitable aliquot (ca 8 g dry material) of citric acid soln, **3.040**, to 50 mL beaker. Evap. to 1–2 mL. Add 3 mL borate buffer, **3.029(n)**, and adjust pH to 8.0–8.5 with NaOH (check externally with *phenol red*). (Vol. ≤5 mL.) Add 1 mL nitroso-R-salt soln *slowly with mixing.* Boil 1–2 min and add 2 mL dil. HNO_3. Boil 1–2 min, add 0.5–1.0 mL Br-H_2O, cover with watch glass, and let stand warm 5 min. Boil 2–3 min to remove excess Br (use effective fume removal device). Cool, and dil. to 10 or 25 mL (depending on length of light path in absorption cell). Transfer to cell and read at 500 nm within 1 hr. Prep. stds contg 0.5, 1, 2, 3, and 4 μg Co and add 1 mL citric acid soln, **3.038(d)**, to each. Proceed as for unknowns, beginning "Evap. to 1–2 mL."

Copper (*14*)—Official Final Action

3.042 ***Reagents***

Those listed in **3.029** and following:

(**a**) *Sodium diethyldithiocarbamate soln.*—0.1%. Freshly prepd in redistd H_2O, **3.029(a)**.

(**b**) *Copper std soln.*—1 μg/mL. Dissolve 0.3929 g $CuSO_4.5H_2O$ in redistd H_2O, **3.029(a)**, add 5 mL H_2SO_4, dil. to 1 L, and mix. Take 10 mL aliquot, add 5 mL H_2SO_4, dil to 1 L, and mix.

3.043 ***Determination***

Transfer aliquot (0.5–1 g dry material) from soln obtained from **3.034** or **3.040** to 125 mL separator. Add 2 mL NH_4 citrate soln, 1 drop phthln, 5 mL Na diethyldithiocarbamate soln, and NH_4OH (1+1), **3.029(e)**, until pink. Add 10 mL CCl_4 and shake 5 min. Drain CCl_4, centrf. 5 min, transfer to absorption cell, and read at max. *A*, ca 430 nm.

Prep. std curve with 0, 1, 5, 10, 15, and 20 μg Cu treated as above.

Zinc—Official Final Action

Mixed Color Method (*15*)

3.044 ***Reagents***

(Redistil all H_2O from Pyrex. Treat all glassware with HNO_3 (1+1) or fresh chromic acid cleaning soln. Rinse repeatedly with ordinary distd H_2O and finally with Zn-free H_2O.)

(**a**) *Carbon tetrachloride.*—Use ACS grade without purification. If tech. grade is used, dry with anhyd. $CaCl_2$ and redistil in presence of small amt CaO. (Used CCl_4 may be reclaimed by distn in presence of NaOH (1+100) contg small amts of $Na_2S_2O_3$, followed by drying with anhyd. $CaCl_2$ and fractional distn in presence of small amts of CaO.) (*Caution: See* **51.011(b)** and **51.049**.)

(**b**) *Zinc std solns.*—(*1*) *Stock soln.*—1 mg/mL. Place 0.25 g pure Zn in 250 mL vol. flask. Add ca 50 mL H_2O and 1 mL H_2SO_4; heat on steam bath until all Zn dissolves. Dil. to vol. and store in Pyrex vessel. (*2*) *Working soln.*—10 μg/mL. Dil. 10 mL stock soln to 1 L. Store in Pyrex vessel.

(**c**) *Ammonium hydroxide soln.*—1*N*. With all-Pyrex app. distil NH_4OH into H_2O, stopping distn when half has distd. Dil. distillate to proper concn. Store in g-s Pyrex vessel.

(**d**) *Hydrochloric acid.*—1*N*. Displace HCl gas from HCl in glass flask by slowly adding equal vol. H_2SO_4 from dropping funnel that extends below surface of the HCl. Conduct displaced HCl gas thru delivery tube to surface of H_2O in receiving flask (no heat is necessary). Dil. to proper concn. Use of 150 mL each of HCl and H_2SO_4 will yield 1 L purified HCl soln of concn >1*N*.

(**e**) *Diphenylthiocarbazone* (*dithizone*) *soln.*— Dissolve 0.20 g dithizone in 500 mL CCl_4, and filter to remove insol. matter. Place soln in g-s bottle or large separator, add 2 L 0.02*N* NH_4OH (40 mL 1*N* NH_4OH dild to 2 L), and shake to ext dithizone into aq. phase. Sep. phases, discard CCl_4, and ext ammoniacal soln of dithizone with 100 mL portions CCl_4 until CCl_4 ext is pure green. Discard CCl_4 after each extn. Add 500 mL CCl_4 and 45 mL 1*N* HCl, and shake to ext dithizone into CCl_4. Sep. phases and discard aq. phase. Dil. CCl_4 soln of dithizone to 2 L with CCl_4. Store in brown bottle in dark, cool place.

(**f**) *Ammonium citrate soln.*—0.5*M*. Dissolve 226 g $(NH_4)_2HC_6H_5O_7$ in 2 L H_2O. Add NH_4OH (80–85 mL) to pH of 8.5–8.7. Add excess dithizone soln (aq. phase is orange-yellow after phases have been shaken and sepd), and ext with 100 mL portions CCl_4 until ext is full green. Add more dithizone if necessary. Sep. aq. phase from CCl_4 and store in Pyrex vessel.

(**g**) *Carbamate soln.*—Dissolve 0.25 g Na diethyldithiocarbamate in H_2O and dil. to 100 mL with H_2O. Store in refrigerator in Pyrex bottle. Prep. fresh after 2 weeks.

(**h**) *Dilute hydrochloric acid.*—0.02*N*. Dil. 100 mL 1*N* HCl to 5 L.

3.045 ***Preparation of Solutions***

To reduce measuring out reagents and minimize errors due to variations in composition, prep. 3 solns in appropriate amts from reagents and store in Pyrex vessels, taking care to avoid loss of NH_3 from *Solns 1* and *2*. Discard solns after 6–8 weeks because Zn increases slowly with storage. Det. std curve for each new set of reagents. Following amts of *Solns 1* and *2* and 2 L dithizone soln are enough for 100 detns:

(1) *Soln 1.*—Dil. 1 L 0.5*M* NH_4 citrate and 140 mL 1*N* NH_4OH to 4 L.

(2) *Soln 2.*—Dil. 1 L 0.5*M* NH_4 citrate and 300 mL 1*N* NH_4OH to 4.5 L. Just before using, add 1 vol. carbamate soln to 9 vols NH_3-NH_4 citrate soln to obtain vol. of *Soln 2* immediately required.

Note: If Zn-free reagents have been prepd, they can be used to test chemicals for Zn. Certain lots of NH_4OH and HCl are sufficiently free of Zn to be used without purification.

3.046 ***Ashing***

Ash 5 g finely ground, air-dried plant material in Pt dish in furnace at 500–550°. Include blank detn. Moisten ash with little H_2O; then add 10 mL 1*N* HCl (more if necessary) and heat on steam bath until all substances sol. in HCl are dissolved. Add 5–10 mL hot H_2O. Filter off insol. matter on 7 cm paper (Whatman No. 42, or equiv., previously washed with two 5 mL portions hot 1*N* HCl, then washed with hot H_2O until HCl-free), and collect filtrate in 100 mL vol. flask. Wash filter with hot H_2O until washings are not acid to Me red. Add 1 drop Me red, **2.055(i)**, to filtrate in 100 mL flask; neutze with 1*N* NH_4OH and add 4 mL 1*N* HCl. Cool, and dil. to vol. with H_2O.

3.047 ***First Extraction***

(Sepn of dithizone complex-forming metals from ash soln)

Pipet aliquot of ash soln contg ≤30 μg Zn into 125 mL Squibb separator. Add 1 mL 0.2*N* HCl for each 5 mL ash soln <10 mL taken, or 1 mL 0.2*N* NH_4OH for each 5 mL >10 mL taken. (10 mL aliquot is usually satisfactory in analysis of plant materials.) Add 40 mL *Soln 1* and 10 mL dithizone reagent. Shake vigorously 30 sec to ext from aq. phase the Zn and other dithizone complex-forming metals that may be present; then let layers sep. At this point excess dithizone (indicated by orange or yellow-orange aq. phase) must be present. If excess dithizone is not present, add more reagent until, after shaking, excess is indicated. Shake down the drop of CCl_4 ext from surface, and drain CCl_4 ext into second separator as completely as possible without letting any aq. layer enter stopcock bore. Rinse down CCl_4 ext from surface of aq. layer with 1–2 mL clear CCl_4; then drain this CCl_4 into second separator without letting aq. phase enter stopcock bore. Repeat rinsing process as often as necessary to flush ext completely into second separator. Add 5 mL clear CCl_4 to first separator, shake 30 sec, and let layers sep. (CCl_4 layer at this point will appear clear green if metals that form dithizone complexes have been completely extd from aq. phase by previous extn.) Drain CCl_4 layer into second separator and flush ext down from surface and out of separator as directed previously. If last ext does not possess distinct clear color, repeat extn with 5 mL clear CCl_4 and flushing-out process until complete extn of dithizone complex-forming metals is assured; then discard aq. phase.

3.048 ***Second Extraction***

(Sepn of Cu by extn of Zn into 0.02*N* HCl)

Pipet 50 mL 0.02*N* HCl into separator contg CCl_4 soln of metal dithizonates. Shake vigorously 1.5 min, and let layers sep. Shake down drop from surface of aq. phase, and as completely as possible drain CCl_4 phase contg all Cu as dithizonate, without letting any aq. phase, which contains all the Zn, enter stopcock bore. Rinse down CCl_4 ext from surface of aq. phase, and rinse out stopcock bore with 1–2 mL portions clear CCl_4 (same as in first extn) until all traces of green dithizone have been washed out of separator. Shake down drop of CCl_4 from surface of aq. phase, and drain CCl_4 as completely as possible without letting any aq. phase enter stopcock bore. Remove stopper from separator and lay it across neck until small amt of CCl_4 on surface of aq. phase evaps.

3.049 ***Final Extraction***

(Extn of Zn in presence of carbamate reagent)

Pipet 50 mL *Soln 2* and 10 mL dithizone soln into 50 mL 0.02*N* HCl soln contg the Zn. Shake 1 min and let phases sep. Flush out stopcock and stem of separator with ca 1 mL CCl_4 ext; then collect remainder in test tube. Pipet 5 mL ext into 25 mL vol. flask, dil. to vol. with clear CCl_4, and measure *A* with spectrophtr set at absorption max., ca 525 nm. (*Caution:* Protect final ext from sunlight as much as possible and read within 2 hr.)

Det. Zn present in aliquot from curve relating *A* and concn, correct for Zn in blank, and calc. % Zn in sample.

3.050 ***Standard Curve***

Place 0, 5, 10, 15, 20, 25, 30, and 35 mL Zn working std soln in 100 mL vol. flasks. To each flask add 1 drop Me red and neutze with 1*N* NH_4OH; then add 4 mL 1*N* HCl and dil. to vol. Proceed exactly as for ash solns, beginning with first extn, and using 10 mL aliquots of each of the Zn solns (0, 5, 10, 15, 20, 25, 30, and 35 μg Zn, resp.). Construct std curve by plotting μg Zn against *A*.

Single Color Method (16)

3.051 ***Reagents***

See **3.044–3.045** plus following:

(a) *Dilute dithizone soln.*—Dil. 1 vol. dithizone soln, **3.044(e)**, with 4 vols CCl_4.

(b) *Carbamate soln.*—Dissolve 1.25 g Na diethyldithiocarbamate in H_2O and dil. to 1 L. Store in refrigerator and prep. fresh after long periods of storage.

(c) *Dilute ammonium hydroxide.*—Dil. 20 mL 1*N* NH_4OH, **3.044(c)**, to 2 L.

3.052 ***Ashing***

Weigh 2 g sample finely ground plant material into well-glazed porcelain, Vycor, or Pt crucible, include crucible for blank detn, and heat in furnace at 500–550° until ashing is complete. Cool, moisten ash with little H_2O, add 10 mL 1*N* HCl (more if necessary to ensure excess of acid), and heat on steam bath until all sol. material dissolves. Add few mL hot H_2O and filter thru quant. paper into 200 mL vol. flask. Wash paper with hot H_2O until washings are not acid to Me red. Add 2 drops Me red soln to filtrate, neutze with 1*N* NH_4OH, add exactly 3.2 mL 1*N* HCl, dil. to vol. with H_2O, and mix.

3.053 ***Formation of Zinc Dithizonate***

(Removal of interferences and sepn of excess dithizone)

Pipet aliquot of ash soln contg $\leqslant$15 μg Zn into 125 mL amber glass separator. (25 mL aliquot is usually satisfactory.) If necessary to use different vol., add 0.4 mL 0.2*N* HCl for each 5 mL less, or 0.4 mL 0.2*N* NH_4OH for each 5 mL more, than 25 mL taken. If <25 mL of the soln is taken, add H_2O to 25 mL.

Add 10 mL dithizone reagent, **3.044(e)**, to aliquot in separator and shake vigorously 1 min. Let layers sep. and discard CCl_4 layer. Add 2 mL CCl_4 to aq. soln, let layers sep., and discard CCl_4. Repeat this rinsing once. Then add 5 mL CCl_4, shake vigorously 15 sec, let layers sep., and discard CCl_4. Rinse once more with 2 mL CCl_4 as above. Discard CCl_4 layer and let CCl_4 remaining on surface of soln in funnel evap. before proceeding.

Add 40 mL NH_4 citrate *Soln 1,* **3.045**(1), 5 mL carbamate soln, **3.051(b)**, and 25 mL dil. dithizone reagent, **3.051(a)**. Accurately add carbamate and dithizone reagents from pipet or buret. Shake vigorously 1 min. Let layers sep. and draw off aq. layer thru fine tip glass tube connected to aspirator with rubber tubing. To remove excess dithizone from CCl_4 layer, add 50 mL 0.01*N* NH_4OH and shake vigorously 30 sec.

3.054 ***Determination***

Dry funnel stem with pipestem cleaner and flush out with ca 2 mL of the Zn dithizonate soln. Collect adequate portion of remaining soln in 25 mL erlenmeyer, or other suitable container, and stopper tightly. (Amber glass containers are convenient, but colorless glassware will suffice if solns are kept in dark until *A* readings are made.)

Measure *A* of each soln against CCl_4 with spectrophtr set at absorption max., ca 535 nm. Correct for Zn in blank detns. Calc. amt Zn present in soln from curve relating concn and *A*.

3.055 ***Standard Curve***

Into 200 mL vol. flasks place 0, 2, 4, 6, 8, 10, 12, and 14 mL, resp., Zn working std soln. To each flask add 2 drops Me red soln, neutze with 1*N* NH_4OH, add 3.2 mL 1*N* HCl, and dil. to vol. with H_2O. Pipet 25 mL aliquots of each of these solns, contg 0, 2.5, 5, 7.5, 10, 12.5, 15, and 17.5 μg Zn, resp., into amber glass separators, and proceed as for ash solns, **3.053**, beginning with second par. Det. *A* of each soln and plot values against corresponding amts Zn.

Molybdenum (*17*)—Official Final Action

3.056 ***Apparatus***

Photoelectric colorimeter or spectrophotometer.— Capable of isolating band at ca 465 nm. (Photometer equipped with filter with max. *T* at 440–460 nm and 1 cm cells of 10 mL capacity is suitable.)

3.057 ***Reagents***

(**a**) *Isoamyl alcohol.*—Reagent grade 3-methyl-1-butanol, bp 128–132°.

(**b**) *Dilute hydrochloric acid.*—(*1*) *20% soln.*—Dil. concd HCl to ca 20% HCl (1+1.85). (*2*) *6N soln.*—Stdze to second decimal place.

(**c**) *Iron std soln.*—100 $\mu g/mL$. Dissolve 0.7022 g $Fe(NH_4)_2(SO_4)_2.6H_2O$ in H_2O, add 1 mL H_2SO_4, and dil. to 1 L.

(**d**) *Molybdenum std solns.*—(*1*) *Stock soln.*—100 $\mu g/mL$. Dissolve 0.0920 g $(NH_4)_6Mo_7O_{24}.4H_2O$ in H_2O and dil. to 500 mL. (*2*) *Working soln.*—5 $\mu g/mL$. Dil. 25 mL stock soln to 500 mL.

(**e**) *Potassium thiocyanate soln.*—20%. Dissolve 50 g KSCN in H_2O and dil. to 250 mL.

(**f**) *Sodium fluoride saturated soln.*—Add 200 mL H_2O to ca 10 g NaF. Stir until satd and filter.

(**g**) *Stannous chloride solns.*—(*1*) *20% soln.*— Weigh 10 g $SnCl_2.2H_2O$ into beaker, add 10 mL 20% HCl, (**b**)(*1*), and heat until completely dissolved. Cool, add granule of metallic Sn, dil. to 50 mL with H_2O, and store in g-s bottle. (*2*) *0.8% wash soln.*—Dil. 4 mL 20% soln to 100 mL with H_2O.

3.058 ***Determination***

(*Caution: See* **51.019**, **51.026**, and **51.028**.)

Weigh 1–5 g finely ground sample, contg ≤35 μg Mo, into 200 mL tall-form Pyrex beaker. To 1, 2, or 5 g samples add 10, 15, or 35 mL HNO_3, resp. Include 2 beakers for blanks. Cover beaker with cover glass, and let stand ca 15 min; then heat cautiously on steam bath or hot plate at ca 100°, avoiding frothing over top. If froth approaches cover glass, remove beaker from heat until frothing subsides; then continue heating. Digest, usually ca 2 hr, until most of solids disappear.

Cool to room temp. If contents should go to dryness, add few mL HNO_3. Add 6 mL 70–72% $HClO_4$, cover beaker, place on hot plate, and gradually raise temp. so that contents boil vigorously but do not bump. Continue heating until digestion is complete as indicated by liq. becoming colorless or pale yellow. If necessary, make repeated addns of HNO_3 and $HClO_4$ and continue to digest until C is completely oxidized.

After digestion is complete, place cover glass slightly to one side of top of beaker, or replace it with elevated watch glass, and evap. just to dryness or until residue appears only slightly moist. Remove beaker from hot plate, and cool. Wash down sides of beaker and underside of cover glass with few mL H_2O, return to hot plate, and boil few min. Remove from hot plate, cool, and again rinse sides of beaker and cover glass with small amt H_2O.

Add 2 drops Me orange and neutze with NH_4OH. Add 6*N* HCl, dropwise with stirring, until soln is just acid; then add 8.2 mL excess to give final concn of ca 3% HCl. Add 2 mL satd NaF soln, and 1 mL Fe soln, if sample contains <100 μg Fe.

Transfer soln to 125 mL separator and dil. to 50 mL with H_2O. Add 4 mL 20% KSCN soln, mix thoroly, and add 1.5 mL 20% $SnCl_2$ soln. Mix again, and from buret or pipet, add exactly 15 mL isoamyl alcohol. Stopper separator and shake vigorously 1 min, let phases sep., and drain and discard aq. layer. Ext into alcohol without delay, since colored complex is somewhat unstable in aq. soln.

Add 25 mL freshly prepd 0.8% $SnCl_2$ wash soln, and shake gently 15 sec. Let phases sep., and drain and discard aq. layer. Transfer isoamyl alcohol soln to centrf. tube, and centrf. 5 min at ca 2000 rpm to remove H_2O droplets. If alcohol layer is not clear, recentrf. Stopper tubes to prevent evapn, if *A* readings cannot be made immediately.

Compare unknown solns with isoamyl alcohol at ca 465 nm in spectrophtr, and make appropriate corrections in *A* readings for Mo in blanks. Obtain Mo concn from calibration curve relating *A* readings to concns of series of solns of known Mo content.

Prep. calibration curve for instrument used, as follows: Place aliquots of working std soln contg 0, 5, 10, 15, 20, 25, 30, and 35 μg Mo, resp., into 200 mL tall-form beakers and carry them thru entire detn, beginning with digestion with HNO_3 and $HClO_4$. Plot *A* against corresponding Mo concns.

NONMETALS

Arsenic—Official Final Action

3.059 ***Preparation of Solution***

See **25.008**.

3.060 ***Determination***

Proceed as in **25.009**, or take aliquot and det. as in **6.013**, beginning "... add 3 mL H_2SO_4, ..."

Sulfur—Official Final Action

Sodium Peroxide Method (18)

(*Caution: See* **51.035**.)

3.061 ***Preparation of Solution***

Place 1.5–2.5 g sample in ca 100 mL Ni crucible and add 5 g anhyd. Na_2CO_3. Mix thoroly, using Ni or Pt rod, and moisten with ca 2 mL H_2O. Add Na_2O_2, ca 0.5 g at time, mixing thoroly after each addn, and continue until mixt. becomes nearly dry and quite granular (ca 5 g Na_2O_2). Place crucible over S-free flame or elec. hot plate and heat carefully, stirring occasionally, until contents are fused. (If material ignites, detn is worthless.)

After fusion, remove crucible, let cool somewhat, and cover hardened mass with more Na_2O_2 to depth of ca 5 mm. Heat gradually and finally with full flame until fusion again takes place, rotating crucible occasionally to bring any particles adhering to sides into contact with oxidizing material. Continue heating 10 min after fusion is complete. Cool somewhat, place warm crucible and contents in 600 mL beaker, and carefully add ca 100 mL H_2O. After initial violent action ceases, wash material out of crucible, make slightly acid with HCl (adding small portions at time), transfer to 500 mL vol. flask, cool, dil. to vol., and filter.

3.062 ***Determination***

Dil. aliquot of prepd soln to ca 200 mL with H_2O and add HCl until ca 0.5 mL free acid is present. Heat to bp and add 10 mL 10% $BaCl_2$ soln dropwise with constant stirring. Continue boiling ca 5 min, and let stand ≥5 hr in warm place. Decant thru ashless paper or ignited and weighed gooch. Add 15–20 mL boiling H_2O to ppt, transfer to filter, and wash with boiling H_2O until filtrate is Cl-free. Dry ppt and filter, ignite, and weigh as $BaSO_4$. Wt ppt $\times$ 0.1374 = S.

Magnesium Nitrate Method (19)

3.063 ***Preparation of Solution***

Weigh 1 g sample into large porcelain crucible. Add 7.5 mL $Mg(NO_3)_2$ soln, **2.019**, so that all material comes in contact with soln. (It is important that enough $Mg(NO_3)_2$ soln be added to ensure complete oxidn and fixation of the S present. For larger samples and for samples with high S content, proportionally larger vol. of this soln must be used.) Heat on elec. hot plate

(180°) until no further action occurs. Transfer crucible while hot to furnace (≤500°) and let it remain until sample is thoroly oxidized. (No black particles should remain. If necessary, break up sample and return to furnace.) Remove crucible and let cool. Add H_2O; then HCl in excess. Bring soln to boil, filter, and wash thoroly. If preferred, transfer soln to 250 mL vol. flask before filtering and dil. to vol. with H_2O.

3.064 ***Determination***

Dil. entire filtered soln, **3.063**, to 200 mL, or take 100 mL aliquot of the measured vol., dil. to 200 mL, and proceed as in **3.062**.

Phosphorus (*20*)—Official Final Action

3.065 ★ Macro Method ★

(**a**) *For samples exceedingly high in P and low in Ca and Mg (certain seeds, grains, etc.)*—Prep. soln as in **3.063**, or evap. filtrate and washings from S detn, **3.062**, to 50 mL, and proceed as in **8.033**.

(**b**) *For other samples.*—Take 50 mL aliquot of Soln *I*, **3.005**, and proceed as in **8.033**.

Micro Method (21)

3.066 ***Reagents***

(**a**) *Phosphorus std soln.*—0.025 mg P/mL. Dissolve 0.4394 g pure dry KH_2PO_4 in H_2O and dil. to 1 L. Dil. 50 mL of this soln to 200 mL.

(**b**) *Ammonium molybdate soln.*—Dissolve 25 g NH_4 molybdate in 300 mL H_2O. Dil. 75 mL H_2SO_4 to 200 mL and add to NH_4 molybdate soln.

(**c**) *Hydroquinone soln.*—Dissolve 0.5 g hydroquinone in 100 mL H_2O, and add 1 drop H_2SO_4 to retard oxidn.

(**d**) *Sodium sulfite soln.*—Dissolve 200 g Na_2SO_3 in H_2O, dil. to 1 L, and filter. Either keep this soln well stoppered or prep. fresh each time.

3.067 ***Preparation of Solution***

To 1 or 2 g sample in small porcelain crucible add 1 mL $Mg(NO_3)_2$ soln, **2.019**, and place on steam bath. After few min, cautiously add few drops HCl, taking care that gas evolution does not push portions of sample over edge of crucible. Make 2 or 3 further addns of few drops HCl while sample is on bath so that as it approaches dryness it tends to char. If contents become too viscous for further drying on bath, complete drying on hot plate. Cover crucible, transfer to cold furnace, and ignite 6 hr at 500°, or until even gray ash is obtained. (If necessary, cool crucible, dissolve ash in little H_2O or alc.-glycerol, evap. to dryness, and return uncovered to furnace 4–5 hr longer.) Cool, take up with HCl (1+4), and transfer to 100 mL beaker. Add 5 mL HCl and evap. to dryness on steam bath to dehydrate SiO_2. Moisten residue with 2 mL HCl, add ca 50 mL H_2O, and heat few min on bath. Transfer to 100 mL vol. flask, cool immediately, dil. to vol., mix, and filter, discarding first portion of filtrate.

3.068 ***Determination***

To 5 mL aliquot filtrate in 10 mL vol. flask add 1 mL NH_4 molybdate soln, rotate flask to mix, and let stand few sec. Add 1 mL hydroquinone soln, again rotate flask, and add 1 mL Na_2SO_3 soln. (Last 3 addns may be made with Mohr pipet.) Dil. to vol. with H_2O, stopper flask with thumb or forefinger, and shake to mix thoroly. Let stand 30 min, and measure *A* with spectrophtr set at 650 nm. Report as % P.

Gravimetric Quinolinium Molybdophosphate Method (22)—Official Final Action

3.069 ***Preparation of Solution***

Accurately weigh ca 2 g plant sample in porcelain dish, and add 7.5 mL $Mg(NO_3)_2$ soln, **2.019**. Dry in oven 2 hr at 110–115° (or until dry). Ignite carefully over Fisher burner, or equiv., until bubbling and smoking cease. Complete ashing in furnace 4 hr at 550–600°. Dissolve ash in few mL HCl (2+1) and evap. to dryness on steam bath. Take up residue in 10–15 mL HCl (1+9) and filter thru coarse paper into 200 mL vol. flask. Wash paper thoroly with H_2O and let filtrate cool to room temp. Dil. to vol. with H_2O.

3.070 ***Determination***

Pipet 40 mL aliquot into 300 or 500 mL erlenmeyer and proceed as in **2.028**.

Chlorine (*23*)—Official Final Action

(If bromides or iodides are present in significant amts, correct results accordingly.)

3.071 ***Preparation of Solution***

Verify complete retention of Cl in each kind of material by trial, since losses can occur, especially with samples high in carbohydrates, if insufficient Na_2CO_3 is present during ignition, or in any case if excessive temp. is used.

Moisten 5 g sample in Pt dish with 20 mL 5% Na_2CO_3 soln, evap. to dryness, and ignite as thoroly as possible at ≤500°. Ext with hot H_2O, filter, and wash. Return residue to Pt dish and ignite to ash; dissolve in HNO_3 (1+4), filter, wash thoroly, and add this soln to H_2O ext.

3.072 ***Gravimetric Method***

To prepd soln, add 10% $AgNO_3$, avoiding more than slight excess. Heat to bp, protect from light, and let stand until ppt coagulates. Filter on weighed gooch, previously heated to 140–150°, and wash with hot H_2O, testing filtrate to prove excess of $AgNO_3$. Dry AgCl at 140–150°, cool, and weigh. Report as % Cl.

Volumetric Method I (24)

(Since precision of this titrn is considered to be ±0.2 mg Cl, accuracy of 1.0% requires samples contg ≥20 mg.)

3.073 ***Reagents***

(**a**) *Silver nitrate std soln.*—1 mL = 0.00355 g Cl. Prep. soln slightly stronger than 0.1*N*, stdze as in **50.031**, and adjust to exactly 0.1*N*.

(**b**) *Ammonium or potassium thiocyanate std soln.*—0.1*N*. Prep. soln slightly stronger than 0.1*N*, stdze as in **50.030(b)**, and adjust to exactly 0.1*N*.

(**c**) *Ferric indicator.*—Satd soln of $FeNH_4(SO_4)_2 .12H_2O$.

(**d**) *Nitric acid.*—Free from lower oxides of N by dilg HNO_3 with ca ¼ vol. H_2O, and boiling until perfectly colorless.

3.074 ***Determination***

To prepd soln, **3.071**, add known vol. std $AgNO_3$ soln in slight excess. Stir well, filter, and wash AgCl ppt thoroly. To combined filtrate and washings add 5 mL ferric indicator and few mL HNO_3, and titr. excess Ag with thiocyanate std soln to permanent light brown. From mL $AgNO_3$ used, calc. % Cl.

★ Surplus method—*see* inside front cover.

Volumetric Method II (25)

3.075 ***Reagents***

(**a**) *Potassium iodide std soln.*—1 mL = 1 mg Cl. Weigh 4.6824 g pure (ACS) KI, dried to const wt at 105–150°, dissolve in H_2O, and dil. to 1 L.

(**b**) *Silver nitrate stock soln.*—Approx. 0.3*N*. 1 mL = ca 10 mg Cl. Dissolve 48 g $AgNO_3$ in H_2O, filter, and dil. to 1 L.

(**c**) *Silver nitrate std soln.*—Dil. 100 mL reagent (**b**) to ca 900 mL and adjust by stdzg against reagent (**a**) so that 1 mL = 1 mg Cl.

(**d**) *Chloride-free starch indicator.*—For each 100 mL final soln take 2.5 g sol. starch and make to paste with cold H_2O. Stir out lumps, add 25–50 mL more cold H_2O, and stir or shake 5 min. Centrf., decant, and discard liq. Repeat extn 3 times and finally transfer residue to flask contg proper amt of boiling H_2O. Stir again, heat to bp, cover with small beaker, and cool under tap, shaking occasionally.

(**e**) *Dilute sulfuric acid.*—Add 35 mL H_2SO_4 to each 1 L H_2O, boil 5–10 min, and cool to room temp.

(**f**) *Iodine indicator.*—To ca 20 g I in 500 mL g-s bottle add 400 mL dil. H_2SO_4, (**e**), and shake 10 min. Decant and discard first soln, since it may contain iodides. Repeat process and store soln in small g-s bottles.

(**g**) *Potassium permanganate soln.*—Dissolve 60 g $KMnO_4$ in 400 mL warm H_2O (ca 50°) and dil. to 1 L.

(**h**) *Potassium sulfate-copper sulfate mixture.*— Thoroly mix 16 parts K_2SO_4 and 1 part $CuSO_4.5H_2O$.

(**i**) *Wash soln.*—Mix 980 mL H_2O and 20 mL HNO_3.

3.076 ***Determination***

(*Caution: See* **51.019**, **51.026**, and **51.080**.)

Weigh sample contg 10–40 mg Cl into beaker. (If >4 g is taken, use proportionately more HNO_3 and $KMnO_4$ soln.) Add 10 mL 0.3*N* $AgNO_3$ and stir until sample is thoroly soaked, adding little H_2O or warming if necessary. Add 25 mL HNO_3, stir, add 5 mL $KMnO_4$ soln, and stir until frothing stops. Place mixt. in H_2O bath or on hot plate and keep just below bp. Stir, and wash down sides of beaker at intervals with min. H_2O. After 20 min, or when reaction stops, add addnl $KMnO_4$ soln, little at time, until color begins to fade slowly. Dil. to ca 125 mL with boiling H_2O and heat 10 min longer. (Beaker may stand in bath or on hot plate until ready to filter.)

Filter while hot thru Whatman No. 5, or equiv. paper, with suction as follows: Place disk of 30-mesh stainless steel wire gauze or No. 40 filter cloth in bottom of 3" (7.6 cm) Hirsch funnel. Fold 9 cm paper over bottom of No. 11 rubber stopper, shaping it to funnel by making 9–10 folds up side of stopper. Place paper in funnel and apply strong suction. Wet paper and keep wet while fitting into funnel so as to avoid double thicknesses of paper. Wash paper thoroly, first with H_2O and then with wash soln. Discard washings and rinse out flask. Decant thru filter and transfer ppt and sample residue to filter. If filtrate is not turbid, or if it is only slightly opalescent, wash ppt thoroly, applying wash soln very gently, but keeping strong suction on filter. If combined filtrate and washings are clear, test for Ag. If turbid, reheat and pass thru filter, repeating until clear, and finally wash as above. If filtrate does not give definite test for Ag, repeat detn on smaller sample.

Place paper and contents in Kjeldahl flask and add such amts of K_2SO_4-$CuSO_4$ mixt. and H_2SO_4 as would be appropriate for protein detn on same kind and amt of sample, and digest similarly. (For 2 g grass, 8 g sulfate mixt. and 20 mL acid are enough.) When digest is cool, add 175 mL H_2O, boil 5–10 min, and cool to room temp. Titr. the Ag_2SO_4 in Kjeldahl flask with KI std soln, using 5 mL starch indicator and 30 mL I indicator. (Add latter just before titrn.) Rinse neck of flask after each addn of KI when near end point and titr. until soln stays blue after shaking. If <30 mg Cl is present, add starch and I solns at beginning. If larger but unknown amt is present, add 2 mL starch and 10 mL I indicator at beginning and titr. until end point approaches. Shake vigorously to coagulate ppt, add rest of starch and I solns, and proceed to end point. If known large amt is present, titr. to within 2 mL of end point, shake as above, add indicator reagents, and continue titrn. If end point is overrun, add 5 mL std $AgNO_3$ soln and titr. again.

Blank detns are not necessary after testing reagents. If blank made by using pure sugar as sample is >0.05 mg, examine filter paper, distd H_2O, and various reagents for Cl.

Fluoride

Potentiometric Method (26)—Official First Action

(Rinse all plastic and glass containers with HCl (1+3) and H_2O before use. Perform analyses in laboratory free from F; prep. samples in another laboratory.)

3.077 ***Principle***

F is extd from dry, pulverized foliage with HNO_3 followed by aq. KOH. Slurry is adjusted to pH 5.5, and complexing agent and background F are added. Potential is measured with ion selective electrode and compared against calibration curve. Method is applicable to 10–2000 μg F/g dry wt leaf tissue not exposed to unusual amts of Al or other F-binding agents; it is not applicable to insol. inorg. F or F in org. combinations. Between-laboratory precision of individual analyses is ±20% at 30 ppm F; ±10%, ⩾100 ppm F. Accuracy is 90–100%.

3.078 ***Apparatus***

Electrometer.—Range ±200 mv with readability of 0.1 mv (Model 701 or 701A digital pH/mv meter, Orion Research Inc., or equiv.) or expanded scale pH meter with mv mode of operation, with F ion selective electrode (No. 94–09 single electrode, Orion Research Inc., or equiv.) and reference electrode (No. 90–01 single junction, Orion Research Inc., or equiv.). Check system at intervals to assure adherence to following performance criteria: Using technic of **3.080**, system should reach equilibrium (ΔE <0.2 mv/min) within 5 min with each F working std soln, checked in following sequence: 0.1, 0.2, 0.5, 2.0, and 10.0 ppm F. Replicate std solns should differ by ⩽1 mv. Calibration curve should be linear between 0.2 and 10.0 ppm and slope should be 57±2 mv per 10-fold change in F concn. If any parameter is not obtained, check electrodes, reagents, and electrometer. Maintain temp. control to ±1°.

3.079 ***Reagents***

(Store all solns in tightly closed, plastic bottles.)

(**a**) *Nitric acid.*—(*1*) *10N.*—Add 63 mL HNO_3 to H_2O, cool, and dil. to 100 mL. (*2*) *0.2N.*—Dil. 5.0 mL 10*N* to 250 mL. (*3*) *0.05N.*—Dil. 5.0 mL 10*N* to 1 L.

(**b**) *Potassium nitrate soln.*—0.4*M*. Dissolve 4.0 g KNO_3 in H_2O and dil. to 100 mL.

(**c**) *Sodium citrate soln.*—0.8*M*. Dissolve 58.8 g Na citrate.$2H_2O$ in 200 mL H_2O, adjust to pH 5.5 by dropwise addn of 10*N* HNO_3, using pH meter, and dil. to 250 mL with H_2O.

(**d**) *Sodium citrate with fluoride soln.*—0.4*M* citrate with 1 ppm F. Dil. 125 mL 0.8*M* Na citrate soln and 25.0 mL 10 ppm F std soln to 250 mL with H_2O.

(**e**) *Fluoride std solns.*—(*1*) *Stock soln.*—100 ppm F. Dry ca 1 g NaF 2 hr at 110°. Accurately weigh 0.221 g NaF, dissolve in

Table 3:01 Preparation of Working Standard Solutions

	mL soln to be dild to 100 mL			
Concn, ppm	0.4*M* KNO_3	0.8*M* Na citrate	100 ppm F soln	10 ppm F soln
10	10.0	5.0	10.0	0.0
2	10.0	5.0	2.0	0.0
0.5	10.0	5.0	0.0	5.0
0.2	10.0	5.0	0.0	2.0
0.1	10.0	10.0 mL Na citrate soln contg 1 ppm F		

H_2O, and dil. to 1 L. (*2*) *Intermediate soln.*—10 ppm F. Dil. 10.0 mL stock soln to 100 mL with H_2O. (*3*) *Working solns.*—Prep. as in Table **3:01** in 100 mL vol. flasks. Prep. 0.2 and 0.1 ppm solns fresh as needed.

3.080 ***Preparation of Calibration Curve***

Place 25.0 mL 0.1 ppm F working std soln into plastic container contg stirring bar. Insert electrodes ca 12 mm into soln and stir mag. Record mv readings at 1 min intervals until change is <0.2 mv/min. Remove electrodes, blot lightly with absorbent paper, and repeat reading with 0.2, 0.5, 2.0, and 10.0 ppm std solns. Place electrodes in 0.2 ppm std soln until samples are analyzed. (10 ppm std soln may be omitted if samples are known to contain <400 ppm F.)

Plot potential (mv) on vertical arithmetic axis and F concn (μg/mL; ppm) on horizontal (logarithmic) axis of 2-cycle semilog graph paper.

3.081 ***Preparation of Sample***

Dry foliage 48 hr at 80°. Grind to pass No. 40 sieve and store in clean, dry, tightly closed plastic bottle. Rotate bottle to mix sample thoroly before removing aliquots.

3.082 ***Determination***

Accurately weigh ca 0.25 g powd sample, and place in 75–100 mL wide-mouth plastic container. Add 20 mL 0.05*N* HNO_3 and place on rotating shaker or stir mag. 20 min. Add 20 mL 0.1*N* KOH (5.6 g/L) and agitate addnl 20 min. Add 5.0 mL Na citrate soln contg 1 ppm F, adjusted to pH 5.5, and 5.0 mL 0.2*N* HNO_3. (Samples may be stored covered ≤4 hr at this point.) Det. mv readings as in **3.080** and prep. calibration curve before and after each series of samples.

If sample series contains mixt. of high and low samples, make preliminary estn of F content after 2 min. Then det. F concn in samples contg <40 ppm first and in higher ones last.

$$\text{ppm F } (\mu g/g) = (C - 0.10) \times 50/w,$$

where C = ppm F from curve; 0.10 = ppm background F in final soln; 50 = mL final soln; and w = g sample.

ASTM-Intersociety Committee-AOAC Semiautomated Method (27)

Official First Action

3.083 ***Principle***

Dried and ground plant material is ashed, fused with alkali, and dild to vol. In case of leaf samples, F on external surfaces may be washed off sep. Digest and H_2SO_4 are pumped into microdistn app. maintained at 170°. Stream of air carries acidified sample to fractionation column where F and H_2O are distd into condenser, and condensate passes into small collector. Distillate is mixed continuously with alizarin F blue-lanthanum reagent, colored stream passes thru tubular flowcell of colorimeter, and A is measured at 624 nm.

Interfering metal cations and inorg. phosphate are not distd, and org. substances are destroyed by ashing. Interference from remaining volatile inorg. anions is reduced with high concn acetate buffer with some reduction in sensitivity. Very large amts solid matter, particularly silicates, retard distn. Therefore, smallest sample consistent with obtaining suitable amt F should be used. Conditions must be carefully controlled, since accurate results depend upon obtaining same degree of efficiency of distn from samples as from std F solns used for calibration.

Acid concn during distn is maintained at const value by using specific amts CaO and NaOH for ashing and fusion and $HClO_4$ for transfer of fused samples. Any marked change in vac. (>0.2" Hg or 5 torr) over short time indicates either leak or block in system. Distil at same vac. each day and maintain proper ratio between air flow on line drawing liq. and solid wastes from distn coil and on line drawing HF and H_2O vapor from distn unit

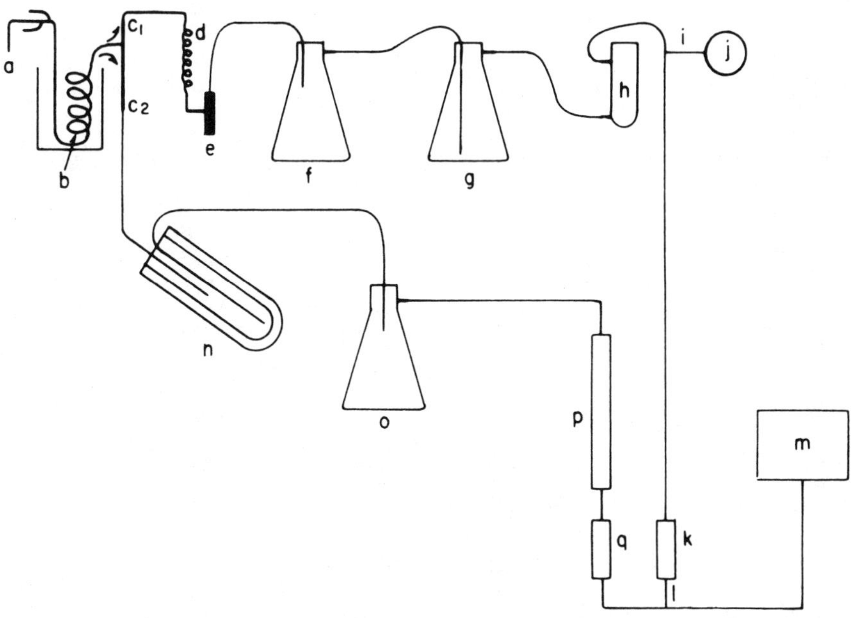

FIG. 3:02—Schematic drawing of air flow system used in semiautomated analysis for fluoride

(Fig. **3:02**). Adjust flowmeters to keep this ratio const and to maintain higher vac. on HF line, C_1, so that min. is diverted to waste line.

Method can detect 0.1 μg F/mL. Normal range is 0.1–4.0 μg F/mL. Dil. higher concns with NaOH-$HClO_4$ soln, (**k**). If digested samples routinely exceed 4.0 μg/mL, modify anal. portion of pump manifold to reduce sensitivity, or use smaller sample aliquot (preferred). Most accurate results are obtained in middle or upper part of calibration curve. For example, to decrease sensitivity, pump sample thru 0.081" tube (2.5 mL/min) and dil. with H_2O pumped thru 0.065" tube (1.6 mL/min) before sample enters distn app. Total vol. sample and diluent should approx. original vol. used (4.1 mL/min).

If air-borne contaminants are present in laboratory, attach small drying bulb contg $CaCO_3$ granules to air inlet tube of microdistn unit. Teflon distn coil of microdistn unit must be cleaned periodically to avoid accumulation of solids which reduce sensitivity.

Coefficient of variation of 20–100 ppm F is generally ≤10%. Samples with large amt of Si (orchard grass) or Al may present special difficulties. There should be no significant deviation from linearity with different amts sample and with different amts added F.

3.084 *Apparatus*

(Cat. Nos refer to current Technicon equipment, except where indicated. Corresponding equipment under previous Cat. Nos is satisfactory.)

(**a**) *Automatic analyzer.*—(Fig. **3:03**) AutoAnalyzer, Technicon Instruments Corp., or equiv. (*1*) *Sampler.*—Sampler IV with rotary stirrer and 8.5 mL plastic sample cups. Use 10 or 20/hr cam with 1:3 sample-to-wash ratio (No. 171-A015-07). (*2*) *Colorimeter.*—With 15 mm tubular flowcell and 624 nm interference filter (199-A001-05). (*3*) *Recorder.*—Ratio type with 2–100 mv full scale range (011-A115-01). (*4*) *Multichannel proportioning pump and manifold cartridge.*—With assorted pump tubes, nipple connectors, and glass connectors (pump III 113-A014-08; cartridge 116-8340-01).

(**b**) *Pulse suppressors.*—For sample and color reagent streams. Coil 10' length of 0.035" id Teflon std tubing around 2.5" diam. tube. Force outlet end into short length of 0.045" id Tygon tubing which is then sleeved with piece of 0.081" Tygon tubing. Slip sleeved end over "h" fitting which joins sample and reagent streams. (Pulse suppressor included with manifold cartridge.)

(**c**) *Voltage stabilizer.*—161-A007-01 (also part of 199-A001-05).

(**d**) *Rotary vacuum and pressure pump.*—With continuous oiler (Gast No. 0211-V45F-G8CX pump, available from SGA Scientific, Inc.).

(**e**) *Microdistillation apparatus.*—(Fig. **3:04**) Major components are (Cat. Nos. are those of SGA Scientific, Inc., except as noted): (*1*) Bottom only of jacketed 1 L resin reaction flask with conical flange (JR-5130), modified by evacuating space between inner and outer walls and sealing off port (*a*); (*2*) resin reaction flask top with conical flange (JR-7935) modified to have one ₮ 29/42 center joint and four ₮ 24/40 side joints; (*3*) resin reaction flask clamp (JR-9210); (*4*) variable high-speed stirrer (S-6362) (*d*); (*5*) stainless steel, heavy duty stirrer stuffing box with ₮ 29/42 and shredded Teflon packing (JS-1160 and JS-3050); (*6*) 10 mm diam. stainless steel stirrer rod with propeller to fit stuffing box; (*7*) thermometer-thermoregulator, range 0–200° (T-5715) (*c*); (*8*) electronic relay control box (T-5905); (*9*) low drift immersion heater, 750 watts (H-1265) (*b*); (*10*) 30' length coil of flexible Teflon TFE tubing, ⅛" id, 3/16" od, 0.030" wall, on rigid support of such diam. that completed coil will fit into resin reaction flask (avoid kinking of tubing) (*e*); (*11*) 2 flowmeters with ranges 0–1 and 0–5 L/min, both with needle valve controls (Dwyer Instrument, Inc., PO Box 373, Michigan City, IN 46360); (*12*) vac. gage with range 0–10" Hg or 0–254 torr (mm Hg); (*13*) fractionation column of borosilicate glass (*g*; *see also* Fig. **3:05**; 116-0635); (*14*) distillate collector (B2 fitting; 116-011-01); (*15*) H_2O-jacketed condenser (116-0156-01) (*h*); (*16*) Dow-Corning 200 fluid (100 centistokes at 25°) (*f*); and (*17*) condenser (116-0181-01) (*j*).

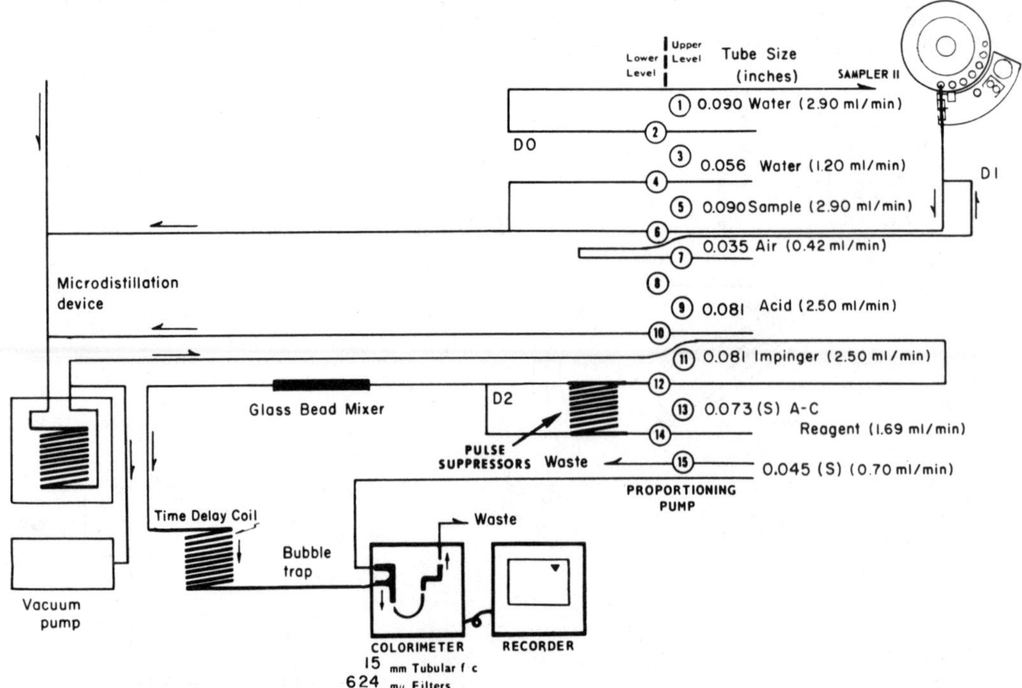

FIG. 3:03—Flow diagram for semiautomated analysis for fluoride

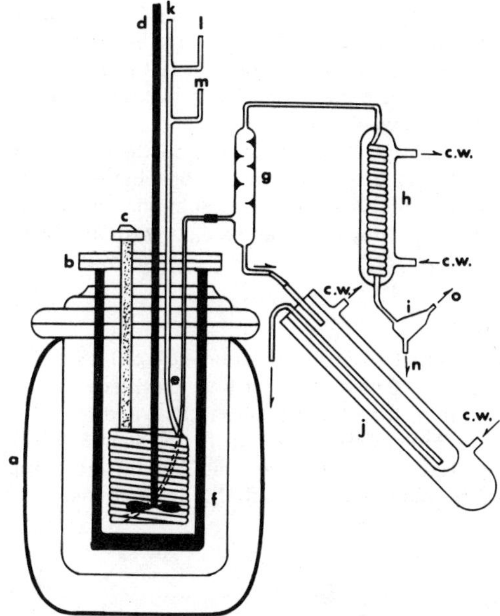

FIG. 3:04—Schematic drawing of microdistillation apparatus

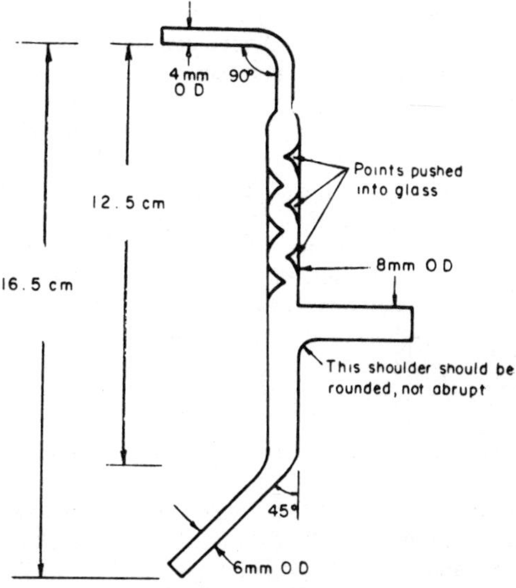

FIG. 3:05—Microdistillation column

(**f**) *Crucibles.*—Inconel, Ni, or Pt, 40–50 mL.

(**g**) *Air flow system.*—(Fig. **3:02**) Draw air thru air inlet tube, (*a*), before Teflon microdistn coil, (*b*). Air sweeps thru (*b*) to fractionation column, and is diverted into 2 channels. In channel c_1, air passes thru H_2O-jacketed condenser, (*d*), sample trap, (*e*), to waste bottle, (*f*). Air then passes thru ⅛" id glass tube directed against surface of H_2SO_4 in waste bottle, (*g*). Partially dehydrated air passes thru gas drying tower, (*h*), contg 450 g indicating silica gel. Emerging air passes thru T-tube, (*i*), connected to vac. gage, (*j*) (0–10" Hg or 0–254 torr), thru flowmeter, (*k*) (0–5 L/min), thru T-tube, (*l*), and then to vac. pump, (*m*).

In channel c_2, air passes thru H_2O-jacketed waste trap, (*n*), to waste bottle, (*o*). Air leaving waste bottle flows thru drying bulb, (*p*), filled with indicating silica gel, and the dry air then passes thru flowmeter, (*q*) (0–1 L/min). Air stream then connects thru T-tube, (*l*), with air from first channel.

3.085 *Reagents*

(*Caution: See* **51.028** and **51.030**.)

(Deionized H_2O may be used. CaO for ashing and NaOH for fusion must be low in F.)

(**a**) *Sulfuric acid.*—(1+1). Mix 500 mL H_2SO_4 with 500 mL H_2O and cool before use.

(**b**) *Acetate buffer.*—2.14*M* (pH 4.0). Dissolve 60 g $NaOAc.3H_2O$ in 500 mL H_2O, add 100 mL HOAc, and dil. to 1 L with H_2O. Stable at 25°.

(**c**) *Alizarin fluorine blue color reagent stock soln.*—0.01*M*. Suspend 0.9634 g reagent (alizarin complexone, alizarin complexan; 3-amino-ethylalizarin-*N,N*-diacetic acid; Burdick & Jackson Laboratories, Inc.) in ca 100 mL H_2O in 250 mL vol. flask. Add 2 mL NH_4OH and shake until completely dissolved. Add 2 mL HOAc and dil. to vol. with H_2O. Stable indefinitely at 4°.

(**d**) *Lanthanum nitrate stock soln.*—0.02*M*. Dissolve 8.6608 g $La(NO_3)_3.6H_2O$ in H_2O and dil. to 1 L in vol. flask.

(**e**) *Wetting soln.*—30% soln (w/v) polyoxyethylene lauryl ether in H_2O (Brij-35, Technicon No. T21-0110). Soln is stable at 25°.

(**f**) *Working reagent.*—Mix, in order listed, 300 mL acetate buffer, 244 mL H_2O, 300 mL acetone, 100 mL *tert*-butanol, 36 mL alizarin fluorine blue stock soln, 20 mL La $(NO_3)_3$ stock soln, and 2 mL wetting soln. Unused reagent is stable 7 days at 4°. Before using reagent, place under vac. 10 min to remove air bubbles from soln.

(**g**) *Fluoride std solns.*—(*1*) *Stock soln.*—100 μg F/mL. Dissolve 0.2207 g NaF in H_2O and dil. to 1 L. (*2*) *Working solns.*—Prep. 7 solns contg 0.2, 0.4, 0.8, 1.6, 2.4, 3.2, and 4.0 μg F/mL. Before dilg to vol., add 6 g NaOH and 20 mL 70% $HClO_4$ for each 100 mL final working soln so that stds have same composition as sample solns. Dil. with H_2O only for analysis of H_2O samples or air samples absorbed in H_2O. Store working solns at 4° in polyethylene bottles; stable in presence of NaOH.

(**h**) *EDTA solns.*—1%. Dissolve 1 g Na_4EDTA in 99 mL H_2O. Prep. 0.05% and 0.01% solns by mixing 5 mL 1% soln with 95 mL H_2O and 1 mL 1% soln with 99 mL H_2O, resp.

(**i**) *Phenolphthalein soln.*—Dissolve 1 g phthln in 50 mL absolute alcohol or isopropanol and add 50 mL H_2O.

(**j**) *Detergent.*—Alconox (Alconox, Inc., 215 Park Ave S, New York, NY 10003); available from laboratory supply firms.

(**k**) *Sodium hydroxide-perchloric acid soln.*—Dissolve 6 g NaOH in H_2O, add 40 mL 70% $HClO_4$ (1+1), and dil. to 100 mL with H_2O. Use to dil. samples when F in unknown sample exceeds std curve.

3.086 *Preparation of Sample*

(**a**) *Leaves.*—If it is necessary to remove surface F, wash sample with aq. soln contg 0.05% detergent and 0.05% Na_4EDTA in polyethylene container 30 sec with gentle agitation. Remove, drain 3–4 sec, and rinse 10 sec in each of 3 beakers of H_2O. Discard solns after use.

(**b**) *Fresh plant tissues.*—Dry 24–48 hr in 80° forced-draft oven, and grind as in (**c**).

(**c**) *Dry plant tissues.*—Grind in semimicro Wiley mill to pass No. 40 sieve, and store in plastic container.

3.087 *Ashing and Fusion*

Accurately weigh 0.1–2.0 g well mixed dried plant tissue into crucible. Add 100±10 mg low-F CaO, enough H_2O to make loose slurry, and 4 drops phthln soln. Mix thoroly with polyethylene policeman. Final mixt. should be purple and remain purple during evapn to dryness.

Place crucible on cold hot plate and under IR lamp. Evap. under lamp to dryness, turn on hot plate, and char 1 hr. Transfer crucible to furnace at 600° and ash 2 hr. (*Caution:* To avoid flaming, place crucibles at front of furnace with door open ca 5 min to further char samples; then reposition in furnace.)

Remove crucibles, add 3.0±0.1 g NaOH pellets, and replace in furnace with door closed to melt NaOH. (*Caution:* Avoid creeping of molten NaOH.) Remove crucibles individually and swirl to suspend particulate matter until melt is partially solidified. Let cool until addn of small amt H_2O does not cause spattering. Wash down inner walls with 10–15 mL H_2O. Suspend melt with polyethylene policeman and transfer with H_2O to plastic tube graduated at 50 mL. Rinse crucible with 20.0 mL 70% $HClO_4$ (1+1), add rinse to tube, and dil. to 50 mL with H_2O. Solns can be stored at this point if tightly capped.

Analyze blank contg all reagents with each set of ca 10 samples.

Clean crucibles as soon as possible after each use. Boil Inconel crucibles 1 hr in 10% NaOH soln. Rinse with hot tap H_2O, detergent, and then distd H_2O. Immerse crucibles which held samples contg >100 μg F in 4*N* HCl 45 min before boiling in NaOH soln. Perform blank analyses on these crucibles before addnl use to check for contamination. Scrub Ni and Pt crucibles with detergent and hot H_2O and rinse thoroly with H_2O. Briefly rinse crucibles which held samples contg >100 μg F in 4*N* HCl before rinsing with H_2O.

3.088 ***Analytical System***

Place F std solns, ashed and fused samples, or impinged air samples in 8.5 mL plastic cups in sample module. Actuate sampler and pump from cup at net rate of 2.48 mL/min with air segmentation of 0.42 mL/min after sampler crook, and pump into microdistn device thru sample inlet (*l*, Fig. **3:04**), using 0.051" id Teflon tubing. Pump H_2SO_4 at 2.5 mL/min thru acid inlet (*m*, Fig. **3:04**). Cool and discard acid and solids. Pump distillate from sample trap at 2.0 mL/min thru 0.051" Teflon tubing, add color reagent at 1.69 mL/min, and mix in 4" length of ⅛" id glass tubing packed with pieces of 20 mesh broken Pyrex glass. Pass colored stream thru time delay coil of 15' of 0.035" Teflon spaghetti tubing, thru debubbler fitting where small portion of stream and bubbles are removed to waste bottle at rate of 0.70 mL/min, and thru 15 mm tubular flowcell of colorimeter. *A* is measured at 624 nm and plotted on recorder. Lag time from sampling to appearance of peak is ca 5 min. Time between samples is 6 min with sampling rate of 10/hr and 3 min at 20/hr.

3.089 ***Start-Up***

Turn on H_2O to condenser and cooling jacket. Turn on colorimeter. Engage manifold on proportioning pump and start pump. Turn on stirring motor of microdistn unit, vac. pump adjusted for full vac., and heater of microdistn unit. Connect lines to H_2SO_4, color reagent, and H_2O bottles. Sampling tube of sampler unit should be in H_2O reservoir. Equilibrate app. until silicone oil in microdistn unit reaches 170±2°. Check that all connections are secure. Adjust distn flowmeter (*k*, Fig. **3:02**) to 2.5–3 L/min; adjust waste flowmeter (*q*) to 0.3 L/min. Distillate should now fill sample trap. Readjust flowmeter (*k*) to give reading on vac. gage of 5–6" Hg (127–150 torr). (Satisfactory setting for app. must be detd by trial and error. Once detd, use each day.) No air bubbles should be in anal. system beyond point where color reagent and distillate streams are joined. Turn on recorder, adjust baseline to desired level, and run several min to assure that all components are operating properly. Baseline should be reasonably smooth and straight.

Transfer F std solns to 8.5 mL plastic cups and place in sampler. Sep. last std soln from sample solns with cup of H_2O. Program sampler for 10 samples/hr (90 sec sampling period, 270 sec washout period) or 20 samples/hr (45 sec sampling period, 135 sec washout period).

Prep. std curve, **3.092**, before and after each day's set of samples. Net *A* of 0.7–0.9 should be obtained with std soln contg 4 μg F/mL. *A* of each std soln should be reproducible within 10% from day to day and std curve should be linear from 0.2 to ≥3.2 μg/mL.

3.090 ***Shut-Down***

Turn off chart recorder. Disconnect H_2SO_4 line and place in H_2O. Disconnect color reagent line and place in 0.01% EDTA soln ca 1 min; then transfer line to H_2O and let H_2O pass thru system ca 5 min. Clean Teflon distn coil as in **3.091(a)**. Turn off heater and stirrer of microdistn unit. Turn off vac. pump. Release pump tube manifold. Turn off H_2O to condenser and cooling trap.

3.091 ***Maintenance***

(**a**) *Cleaning of Teflon distillation coil.*—(After use with samples contg particulate matter.) Briefly insert Tygon tube connected to air inlet line of microdistn unit into 0.01% EDTA soln. After all deposited material has been removed, wash with 3–4 five mL portions distd H_2O.

(**b**) *Pump tubes.*—Replace after 200 working hr or earlier if hard and inflexible or flattened. Always leave in relaxed position when not in use. Remove dirt and grease from pump plates and rollers after each day of use.

(**c**) *Indicating silica gel.*—Regenerate when ca ⅔ has lost normal blue color.

(**d**) *Cleaning tubing.*—Clean tubing contg reagent after each daily run with 0.01% EDTA soln followed by distd H_2O.

(**e**) *Monthly checks.*—Oil proportioning pumps monthly. Check gain on recorder monthly and adjust.

3.092 ***Calibration and Standards***

Before and after each day's set of samples, prep. std curve by transferring aliquots of each working std soln to 8.5 mL sample cups and proceed with analysis. Draw straight line connecting baseline before and after analysis. Record *A* of each peak and subtract *A* of baseline at peak. Plot net *A* against μg F/mL.

3.093 ***Calculations***

ppm F in sample = $(F \times V \times D)/W$,

where F = μg F/mL sample from std curve; V = mL sample, usually 50; D = diln factor used only when F of sample exceeds std curve = mL final vol. to which original aliquot was dild with NaOH-$HClO_4$ soln, (**k**)/mL original aliquot taken; and W = g sample taken for analysis.

3.094 ***Check Procedure***

(**a**) *Contamination.*—Perform reagent and equipment blank with crucibles and reagents but without sample to detect contamination from previous samples, contaminated furnace, and reagents. Blank values >5 μg F are evidence of contamination. Perform 2 blank detns with each set of 20–40 samples. Usual blanks are 1–3 μg.

(**b**) *Recoveries.*—Occasionally add known amts F std soln from microburet to aliquots of low F tissue. Recovery of added F should be 100±10%. Low values indicate loss of F, possibly during pretreatment; high values indicate contamination.

(c) *Linearity.*—Occasionally analyze different amts (0.1–2.0 g) plant sample contg 50–65 ppm F. Linear relationship should exist between F found and amt tissue taken. Nonlinearity may indicate that some component of tissue is retarding distn or interfering with color development.

(d) *Calibration curves.*—Prep. at least twice daily.

3.095 ***Trouble Shooting***

(a) *Irregular baseline.*—May result from: (*1*) excessive pulse pressures—check for faulty pump tubes, absence of surge suppressors, or improperly made or placed suppressors; (*2*) air bubbles in flowcell—check for absence of debubbler bypass, blockage in reagent pump tube, or periodic emptying of sample trap (latter results if air flow to distn trap becomes too great); (*3*) excessive H_2SO_4 carryover—check for too high temp. in oil bath, improper H_2SO_4 concn, or too high vac. on system; (*4*) air flow imbalances—check flowmeter settings, trapped air in tubing, or leak or block in system; (*5*) high F content in samples (baseline may not return to normal between samples)—dil. or check sampling speed and sample-to-wash ratio.

(b) *Irregular peaks.*—Asymmetrical or double peaks or peaks with shoulders may result from: (*1*) baseline irregularities; (*2*) interfering substances from sample or impure reagents; (*3*) inadequate buffer concn; or (*4*) excessive amts solids in distn coil. Presence or accumulation of solids may be due to insufficient flow of H_2SO_4, too large sample, excess CaO or NaOH in sample, inadequate suspension of particles in samples, or lack of proper air segmentation in sample tubing.

(c) *Poor reproducibility.*—Check for: improper sample pickup; faulty pump tubes; inadequate washing of distn coil between samples; large deviations in acid concn, temp., or air flow in distn coil; or changes in vac. on waste system.

Selenium

3.096 ★ *Gravimetric Method (28)—Official Final Action* ★

(Applicable to materials contg >2 ppm Se)

See **3.073**, 11th ed.

Fluorometric Method (29)—Official Final Action

(*Caution: See* **51.008**, **51.019**, **51.026**, and **51.028**.)

3.097 ***Apparatus***

(a) *Micro-Kjeldahl flasks.*—30 mL Pyrex, ca 170 mm total length with ₮ 12/18 outer joint at mouth.

(b) *Air condensers.*—10 × 140 mm Pyrex tubes with ₮ 12/18 inner joint.

(c) *Micro-Kjeldahl digestion unit with glass fume duct.*—Fit rack to hold flasks and attached air condensers in nearly upright position during early stages of digestion. Use in fume hood.

(d) *Fluorometer.*—Capable of illuminating sample at 369 nm and measuring fluoresced light at 525 nm. Turner Associates, 2524 Pulgas Ave, Palo Alto, CA 94303, Model 110 or 111 filter fluorometer equipped with std lamp No. 110-850, primary filter No. 7-60, and secondary filter No. 58 is satisfactory. Model 430 spectrofluorometer set to above wavelengths is also satisfactory.

3.098 ***Reagents***

(Use deionized H_2O distd in glass for prepg solns and dilns.)

(a) *Nitric acid.*—Redistd in glass.

(b) *Hydroxylamine-ethylenediaminetetraacetic acid soln.*—Add ca 20 mL H_2O to 1.9 g EDTA (acid form). Slowly add ca 5*N* NH_4OH with stirring until EDTA just dissolves. Some excess NH_4OH is not harmful. Dissolve 6 g $NH_2OH.HCl$ in 100 mL H_2O. Combine solns and dil. to 250 mL with H_2O.

(c) *Cresol red indicator.*—Dissolve 0.1 g cresol red in 10 mL H_2O and 1 drop 50% NaOH soln. Dil. to 50 mL with H_2O.

(d) *Selenium std soln.*—0.3 μg Se/mL. Add 10 mL HNO_3 to 30.0 mg Se (purity ≥99%) and warm to dissolve. Dil. to 100 mL with H_2O, mix well, and transfer exactly 1 mL to micro-Kjeldahl flask. Add 2 mL 70% $HClO_4$ and 1 glass bead. Boil gently to $HClO_4$ fumes and cool. Add 1 mL H_2O and 1 mL HCl (1+4); heat 30 min in boiling H_2O bath. Transfer to 1 L vol. flask and dil. to vol. with ca 1*N* HCl. Store in all-glass container. Soln is stable several months at room temp.

(e) *Decalin.*—Eastman Kodak No. 1905 decahydronaphthalene, or equiv.

(f) *2,3-Diaminonaphthalene (DAN) soln.*—Prep. soln in semi-darkened room or in room with only yellow light at time of detn. Protect from light and prep. fresh for each set of detns. Add 50 mL ca 0.1*N* HCl to 0.05 g DAN (available from ICN-K&K Laboratories, Inc.). Place in 50° H_2O bath in dark 15 min. Cool to approx. room temp. and ext twice with 10 mL decalin, shaking vigorously each time and discarding decalin. Filter thru paper satd with H_2O. For >8 detns, prep. larger amt.

3.099 ***Preparation of Samples***

Grind air-dried samples to pass No. 18 or finer sieve. Cut fresh or wet samples finely with scissors or knife, or grind in food chopper to assure representative sample.

Some plants (e.g., *Astragalus bisulcatus, A. racemosus, Stanleya bipinnata,* and *Oonopsis condensata*) contain Se in volatile form that is lost during drying. Analyze these plants without drying. With usual agricultural crops, this is not a problem if drying is performed at 60–70°.

3.100 ***Preparation of Fluorometric Blanks and Standard***

(a) *Blank.*—Place 1 mL H_2O in micro-Kjeldahl flask. (For samples contg <0.1 ppm, carry 10 mL HNO_3 as blank thru entire detn.)

(b) *Std.*—Place 1.0 mL std Se soln in micro-Kjeldahl flask.

Add 2 mL 70% $HClO_4$ to each flask and continue as in detn, beginning "Mix contents of flasks . . ."

3.101 ***Determination***

(a) *Samples containing 4 or more ppm selenium.*—Weigh ≤1 g sample (air-dried wt basis) contg ≤0.4 μg Se into micro-Kjeldahl flask. Add 1 glass bead, previously cleaned with HNO_3. Add 10 mL HNO_3 and let stand at room temp. ≥4 hr. (Use 5 mL HNO_3 for samples <0.5 g.) Affix air condenser and place flask in nearly upright position on micro-Kjeldahl digestion unit. Heat ca 15 min with low flame and then increase heat until HNO_3 condenses in lower part of condenser. Heat 10 min longer, turn off burner, and let cool 5 min. Wash down sides of flask with 2 mL 70% $HClO_4$ thru air condenser. Swirl flask and continue refluxing 15 min. Remove condenser and continue heating, drawing off fumes in fume duct, until $HClO_4$ fumes appear and then 15 min longer. Cool, add 1 mL H_2O, and again heat to $HClO_4$ fumes and 1–2 min longer. Cool, and add 1 mL H_2O.

Mix contents of flasks and add 1 mL HCl (1+4) to each. Place in boiling H_2O bath 30 min. Cool to ca room temp.

To each flask add 5 mL NH_2OH-EDTA soln and 2 drops cresol red indicator. Neutze to yellow with ca 5*N* NH_4OH and add HCl (1+4) to orange-pink. *From this point, perform all operations in semidarkened room or room with yellow light only.* Prep. DAN soln, add 5 mL to each flask, and dil. to neck with ca 0.1*N* HCl. Mix and place in 50° H_2O bath in dark 25 min.

★ Surplus method—*see* inside front cover.

Remove flasks from H_2O bath and cool to ca room temp. in pan of H_2O. Pour solns into 125 mL separators with Teflon stopcocks and contg 10.0 mL decalin. Shake vigorously ≥30 sec, let stand ca 1 min, and drain and discard lower layer. Wash decalin twice by shaking vigorously ≥15 sec with 25 mL ca 0.1*N* HCl. (VirTis, Rt 208, Gardiner, NY 12525, Extractomatic shaker with 100 mL separators may be substituted. When used, shake ext 5 min and wash 1 min periods.) Transfer decalin layer to 12 mL centrf. tubes and centrf. 2 min at moderate speed. Pour decalin soln into fluorometer tubes, zero fluorometer against decalin, and read all tubes at 525 nm within 5 min. Correct std and unknown readings for blank.

ppm Se = 0.3 × sample reading/std reading × g sample.

(**b**) *Samples containing less than 4 ppm selenium.*—Proceed as in (**a**) thru second par. Dil. digest to adequate vol. and take aliquot contg ca 0.3 μg Se for detn. Alternatively, digest sample in 10 vols HNO_3 2 hr on steam bath. Dil. to definite vol., and carry appropriate aliquot thru detn. Latter method is especially applicable when proper sampling requires large sample. Do not dil. decalin soln contg piazselenol, as this introduces errors.

Boron (*30*)—Official Final Action

Quinalizarin Method

3.102 ***Reagents***

(**a**) *Dilute sulfuric acid.*—0.36*N*. Dil. 10 mL H_2SO_4 to 1 L.

(**b**) *Calcium hydroxide saturated soln.*—Filter before use.

(**c**) *Quinalizarin soln.*—Dissolve 45 mg quinalizarin in 1 L 95–96% H_2SO_4.

(**d**) *Boron std soln.*—0.5 mg B/mL. Dissolve 2.860 g H_3BO_3 and dil. to 1 L with H_2O. Prep. working stds by further diln with H_2O.

3.103 ***Determination***

Place 1.00–2.00 g dry, ground plant material in Pt or SiO_2 dish. Add 5 mL satd $Ca(OH)_2$ soln and dry at 105°. Carefully volatilize over burner, ash in furnace 1 hr at 600°, and cool. Add exactly 10 or 15 mL 0.36*N* H_2SO_4, break up ash with glass rod, stir gently, and filter. Transfer 2 mL filtrate to colorimeter tube, add an exact amt (e.g., 15 mL) quinalizarin reagent, stopper, and mix by swirling gently. Let stand at room temp. 24 hr (or until both unknowns and stds have cooled to same temp.). Shake tube again immediately before reading in photoelec. colorimeter (620 nm filter).

Adjust colorimeter to 100% *T* with blank soln prepd as above but using 2 mL H_2O in place of sample soln. Prep. std curve with series of stds contg 0.5–10 μg B/mL.

OTHER CONSTITUENTS

Sugars (*31*)—Official Final Action

3.104 ***Preparation of Solution***

(**a**) *General method.*—Prep. fresh sample as in **3.002(b)**. Pour alc. soln thru filter paper or extn thimble, catching filtrate in vol. flask. Transfer insol. material to beaker, cover with 80% alcohol, warm on steam bath 1 hr, let cool, and again pour alc. soln thru same filter. If second filtrate is highly colored, repeat extn. Transfer residue to filter, let drain, and dry. Grind residue so that all particles will pass thru 1 mm sieve, transfer to extn thimble, and ext 12 hr in Soxhlet app. with 80% alcohol. Dry residue and save for starch detn. Combine alc. filtrates and dil. to vol. at definite temp. with 80% alcohol.

For dried materials, grind samples finely, and mix well. Weigh sample into beaker, and continue as above, beginning "... cover with 80% alcohol, ..."

(**b**) *Applicable when starch is not to be determined.*— Prep. fresh sample as in **3.002(b)**, but boil on steam bath 1 hr. Decant soln into vol. flask, and comminute solids in high-speed blender with 80% alcohol. Boil blended material on steam bath 0.5 hr, cool, transfer to vol. flask, dil. to mark with 80% alcohol at room temp., filter, and take aliquot for analysis.

Grind dry material to pass No. 20 sieve or finer, transfer weighed sample to vol. flask, and add 80% alcohol and enough $CaCO_3$ to neutze any acidity. Boil 1 hr on steam bath, cool, adjust vol. at room temp. with 80% alcohol, filter, and take aliquot for analysis.

3.105 ***Clarification with Lead***

Place aliquot alc. ext in beaker on steam bath and evap. off alcohol. Avoid evapn to dryness by adding H_2O if necessary. When odor of alcohol disappears, add ca 100 mL H_2O and heat to 80° to soften gummy ppts and break up insol. masses. Cool to room temp. and proceed as in (**a**) or (**b**):

(**a**) Transfer soln to vol. flask, rinse beaker thoroly with H_2O, and add rinsings to flask. Add enough *satd neut. $Pb(OAc)_2$ soln* to produce flocculent ppt, shake thoroly, and let stand 15 min. Test supernate with few drops of the $Pb(OAc)_2$ soln. If more ppt forms, shake and let stand again; if no further ppt forms, dil. to vol. with H_2O, mix thoroly, and filter thru dry paper. Add enough solid Na oxalate to filtrate to ppt all the Pb, and refilter thru dry paper. Test filtrate for presence of Pb with little solid Na oxalate.

(**b**) Add twice min. amt of satd neut. $Pb(OAc)_2$ soln required to cause complete pptn, as found by testing portion of supernate with few drops dil. Na oxalate soln. Let mixt. stand only few min; then filter into beaker contg estd excess of Na oxalate crystals. Let Pb ppt drain on filter and wash with cold H_2O until filtrate no longer gives ppt in oxalate soln. Assure excess of oxalate by testing with 1 drop $Pb(OAc)_2$. Filter and wash pptd Pb oxalate, catching filtrate and washings in vol. flask. Dil. to vol. with H_2O and mix.

3.106 ***Clarification with Ion-Exchange Resins (32)***

Place aliquot alc. ext, **3.104**, in beaker and heat on steam bath to evap. alcohol. Avoid evapn to dryness by adding H_2O. When odor of alcohol disappears, add ca 15–25 mL H_2O and heat to 80° to soften gummy ppts and break up insol. masses. Cool to room temp. Prep. thin mat of Celite on filter paper in buchner or on fritted glass filter and wash until H_2O comes thru clear. Filter sample thru Celite mat, wash mat with H_2O, dil. filtrate and washings to appropriate vol. in vol. flask, and mix well.

Place 50.0 mL aliquot in 250 mL erlenmeyer; add 2 g *Amberlite IR-120(H)* analytical grade cation (replaced by REXYN 101(H) resin, Fisher Scientific Co.) and 3 g *Duolite A-4(OH)* anion ion exchange resins. Let stand 2 hr with occasional swirling. Take 5 mL aliquot deionized soln and det. reducing sugars as glucose as in **31.053**.

Glucose

3.107 ***Micro Method—Official Final Action***

See **31.053**.

Fructose (*33*)—Official Final Action

3.108 ***Reagents***

(**a**) *Glucose oxidase preparation.*—Add slowly, stirring constantly, 100 mL H_2O to 5 g glucose oxidase prepn ("DeeO L-750" code 4633000, Miles Laboratories, Inc., 1127 Myrtle St,

Elkhart, IN 46514). Stir ca 1 min and centrf. or filter to obtain clear soln. Add ca 1 mL $CHCl_3$ and refrigerate. Soln is stable ≥1 month.

(b) *McIlvaine's citrate-phosphate buffer.*—Dissolve 214.902 g $Na_2HPO_4.12H_2O$ and 42.020 g citric acid in H_2O and dil. to 1 L.

3.109 ***Determination***

To suitable aliquot add ¼ its vol. of buffer to give pH ca 5.8. Add 30% as much glucose oxidase prepn as estd glucose content (for 500 mg glucose add 150 mg glucose oxidase, *i.e.,* 3 mL soln), and few drops 30% H_2O_2 (omit if Somogyi method is to be used in detn). Let stand overnight at room temp.

Det. fructose by Somogyi micro method, **31.053**, or by Munson-Walker method, **31.038–31.039**, using Table **3:02**. Check equivs in range of interest, using pure fructose as std, and correct as necessary.

Table 3:02 Abbreviated Munson and Walker Table for Calculating Fructose

(*From Official and Tentative Methods of Analysis, AOAC, 5th Ed., 1940*)

Cuprous Oxide mg	Fructose mg	Cuprous Oxide mg	Fructose mg
10	4.5	300	148.6
50	23.5	350	174.9
100	47.7	400	201.8
150	72.2	450	229.2
200	97.2	490	253.9
250	122.7	—	—

Reducing Sugars—Official Final Action

3.110 ***Munson-Walker General Method***

See **31.038.**

3.111 ★ ***Quisumbing-Thomas Method*** ★

See **31.048–31.049,**11th ed.

Sucrose—Official Final Action

3.112 ***Hydrochloric Acid Inversion***

Using aliquot of cleared soln, **3.105**, proceed as in **7.079.**

3.113 ***Invertase Inversion***

(a) *For plants giving hydrolysis end point within 2 hours.*—Pipet aliquot of cleared soln, **3.105**, into 400 mL Pyrex beaker and make slightly acid to Me red with HOAc. Add 3 drops 1% soln of *Wallerstein invertase scales.* Let mixt. stand at room temp. 2 hr. Add reagents as in **31.035**, and det. reducing power. Calc. results as invert sugar. Deduct reducing power of original soln, also expressed as invert sugar, and multiply difference by 0.95.

(b) *For plants giving slower hydrolysis end point.*— Place aliquot of soln, **3.105**, in small vol. flask. Make slightly acid to Me red with HOAc. Add 3 drops 1% soln of *Wallerstein invertase scales* and few drops toluene. Stopper flask and let stand overnight or longer at room temp. Dil. to vol. with H_2O and use aliquot for reducing power as above.

3.114 Ether Extract—Official Final Action

See **7.056.**

3.115 Crude Fiber—Official Final Action

See **7.061–7.065.**

Total Nitrogen (Crude Protein)—Official Final Action

3.116 Kjeldahl Method for Nitrate-free Samples

See **2.057.**

3.117 Kjeldahl Method for Nitrate-Containing Samples

See **2.058.**

3.118 Automated Method

See **7.021–7.024.**

3.119 Semiautomated Method

See **7.025–7.032.**

Starch (*34*)—Official Final Action

3.120 ***Reagents***

(a) *Iodine-potassium iodide soln.*—Grind 7.5 g I and 7.5 g KI with 150 mL H_2O, dil. to 250 mL, and filter.

(b) *Alcoholic sodium chloride soln.*—Mix 350 mL alcohol, 80 mL H_2O, and 50 mL 20% NaCl soln, and dil. to 500 mL with H_2O.

(c) *Alcoholic sodium hydroxide soln.*—0.25*N*. Mix 350 mL alcohol, 100 mL H_2O, and 25 mL 5*N* NaOH, and dil. to 500 mL with H_2O.

(d) *Dilute hydrochloric acid.*—0.7*N*. Dil. 60 mL HCl to 1 L with H_2O.

(e) *Somogyi phosphate sugar reagent.*—Dissolve 56 g anhyd. Na_2HPO_4 and 80 g Rochelle salt in ca 1 L H_2O, and add 200 mL 1.00*N* NaOH. Then slowly add, with stirring, 160 mL 10% $CuSO_4.5H_2O$ soln. Dissolve 360 g anhyd. Na_2SO_4 in this soln, transfer to 2 L vol. flask, and add exactly 200 mL 0.1*N* KIO_3 soln (3.5667 g/L). Dil. to vol., mix well, let stand several days, and filter thru dry paper into dry flask, discarding first 50 mL filtrate. Store reagent at 20–25°. It is 0.01*N* with respect to KIO_3; 5.00 mL is equiv. to 10 mL 0.005*N* $Na_2S_2O_3$.

Det. glucose factor of reagent as follows: Accurately weigh 150 mg NBS glucose SRM into 1 L vol. flask, dissolve in H_2O, dil. to vol., and mix well. Transfer 5 mL aliquot to 25 × 200 mm Pyrex test tube, add exactly 5 mL Somogyi reagent, stopper with size 00 crucible, and heat (together with several blanks contg 5 mL H_2O and 5 mL reagent) exactly 15 min in boiling H_2O bath. Titr. as in detn. From difference between blank and std titrns, calc. mg glucose equiv. to 1 mL exactly 0.005*N* $Na_2S_2O_3$. Effective range for detn is 0.05–1.0 mg glucose in 5 mL aliquot.

(f) *Sodium thiosulfate std soln.*—0.005*N*. Dissolve 2.73 g $Na_2S_2O_3.5H_2O$ in H_2O and dil. to 2 L. Stdze daily as follows: Add 1 mL KI soln, **(g)**, and 3 mL 1.5*N* H_2SO_4 to 5 mL Somogyi sugar reagent. Let stand 5 min, and titr. with $Na_2S_2O_3$ soln, adding starch indicator, **(h)**, just before end point.

(g) *Potassium iodide soln.*—2.5%. Stabilize with little Na_2CO_3.

(h) *Starch indicator.*—Make 1.5 g sol. starch into paste with few mL H_2O, and add slowly, with stirring, to 300 mL boiling H_2O.

3.121 ***Determination***

Select sample as in **3.001**, remove all foreign matter, dry, and grind to pass No. 80 sieve. Accurately weigh 0.1–1.0 g powd sample contg ca 20 mg starch into 25 × 150 mm Pyrex test tube. Add ca 200 mg fine sand and 5 mL H_2O, and mix well with stirring rod to wet sample. Heat tube in boiling H_2O bath 15 min to gelatinize starch. Cool to room temp., and place in 22–25° bath. Add 5 mL 60% $HClO_4$ rapidly with const agitation. Grind tissue against lower wall of tube with stirring rod for approx.

★ Surplus method—*see* inside front cover.

min at time. Repeat grinding frequently during 30 min; then without delay, transfer quant. to 100 mL vol. flask with H_2O. Add 3 mL 5% *uranyl acetate soln* to ppt protein, dil. to vol. with H_2O, mix well, and centrf. portion of mixt. Pipet 10 mL clear supernate into 25 × 150 mm test tube. Add ca 100 mg Celite, 5 mL 20% NaCl soln, and 2 mL I-KI reagent, and mix well. Let stand overnight, centrf., and decant.

Wash starch-I ppt by suspending it in 5 mL alc. NaCl soln, centrf., and decant. Add 2 mL alc. NaOH soln to packed ppt. Gently shake and tap tube until ppt is no longer blue. (Do not use stirring rod; allow ample time for complex to decompose.) Wash walls of tube with 5 mL alc. NaCl soln, centrf. liberated starch, and wash with 5 mL alc. NaCl soln as before. Add 2 mL 0.7*N* HCl to ppt. Stopper tube loosely with size 00 crucible, and heat 2.5 hr in boiling H_2O bath. (Bath should have cover with holes to accommodate tubes; holes not occupied by tubes must be covered.) Cool, and transfer quant. to 25 mL vol. flask. Add drop phenol red, **50.008**, and neutze with 1*N* NaOH. Discharge color with *0.1N oxalic acid,* dil. to vol., and mix well. Transfer 5 mL aliquot to 25 × 200 mL Pyrex test tube, add exactly 5 mL Somogyi reagent, and stopper tube with size 00 crucible. Heat together with several blanks contg 5 mL H_2O and 5 mL Somogyi reagent in vigorously boiling H_2O bath exactly 15 min. Remove tube from bath and cool to 25–30°. Add 1 mL 2.5% KI soln down wall of tube without agitation and then add 3 mL 1.5*N* H_2SO_4 rapidly with agitation. After all Cu_2O dissolves, titr. soln with 0.005*N* $Na_2S_2O_3$, adding starch indicator, (**h**), just before end point is reached. Treat blank solns similarly.

$$\% \text{ Starch} = [50(\text{mL blank} - \text{mL sample}) \times 0.90/\text{mg sample}] \times (N/0.005) \times G \times 100,$$

where 50 = diln factor, 0.90 = factor glucose to starch, N = actual normality $Na_2S_2O_3$ soln, and G = mg glucose equiv. to 1 mL 0.005*N* $Na_2S_2O_3$.

Lignin (*35*)—Official Final Action

Direct Method

3.122 ***Preparation of Sample***

Grind sample in mill to pass No. 80 sieve and dry at 105°. Ext weighed sample (5–10 g) 30 hr in Soxhlet app. with alcohol-benzene soln (32 parts alcohol and 68 parts benzene by wt). Dry material in oven to free it from solvs and place in flask of suitable size. Add 150 mL H_2O/g sample, and reflux 3 hr. Filter mixt. while still hot, preferably thru weighed fritted glass crucible, and transfer extd material to flask. Add 1% HCl (111 g concd HCl + 3890 mL H_2O) in proportion of 150 mL acid soln/g plant material, and reflux 3 hr. Filter mixt. while still hot thru fritted glass crucible previously used, wash with H_2O until acid-free, dry at 105°, and weigh. Calc. % total loss due to successive extn with alcohol-benzene soln, hot H_2O, and 1% HCl. (With samples not especially rich in carbohydrates and proteins, extn with hot H_2O may be omitted.)

3.123 ***Apparatus***

App., Fig. **3:06**, consists of: (1) 1.5 L bottle, *A*, to which is attached by 2-hole rubber stopper 250 mL dropping funnel, *C*, having lower end of stem bent as illustrated and placed close to bottom of *A*; (2) Drechsel gas-washing bottle, *D*; (3) 3 Pyrex test tubes, 38 × 300 mm diam., *G, G', G"*, connected in parallel by device, *O*, and immersed in wooden box, *L*, filled with crushed ice, *H*; and (4) bottle contg H_2O for absorption of excess HCl, *K. G, G'*, and *G"* are provided with 2-hole rubber stoppers; glass tube with right angle bend extends thru 1 hole nearly to bottom of test tube, and similar tube extending ca 10 mm into test tube passes thru other hole. Rubber connections and stopcocks for regulating flow of gas are provided as indicated in diagram. *A* is filled with ca 500 mL H_2SO_4 and *C* with HCl; HCl flowing thru stoptock *B* into *A* generates HCl gas, which is dried by H_2SO_4 in *D*, and flows into *G, G'*, and *G"* contg samples and fuming HCl reagent.

3.124 ***Reagent***

Fuming hydrochloric acid.—(*Caution: See* **51.031**.) Density 1.212–1.223 at 15°. To 500 g NaCl in 1 L g-s Pyrex distg flask, add cold soln of 250 mL H_2O in 450 mL H_2SO_4. Connect side tube of distg flask to glass tube passing thru H_2SO_4 wash bottle, and connect outlet tube of H_2SO_4 wash bottle to another glass tube, immersed in flask contg 3 L HCl. Surround flask contg HCl with crushed ice. Heat distg flask with small flame and pass HCl gas into acid soln until it attains sp gr of 1.212–1.223 at 15°. Keep

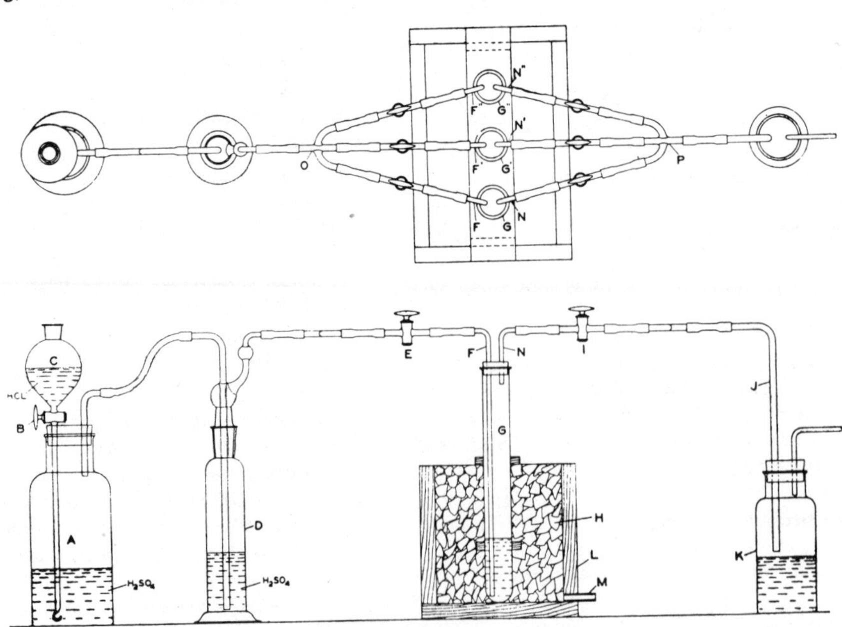

FIG. 3:06—Apparatus for determining lignin

reagent refrigerated at ≤0°. If only few detns are to be made, prep. correspondingly smaller amt.

3.125 ***Determination***

Weigh three 1 g samples of extd and dried sample in weighing bottle and place in 3 large test tubes, *G, G'*, and *G"*. Add 20 mL of the reagent to each tube, using this acid to wash down any particles clinging to sides. When all material is wet with reagent, add addnl 30 mL reagent. Add ca 3 drops *capryl alcohol* to minimize foaming. Place test tubes, *G, G'*, and *G"*, in wooden box, *L*, and surround with crushed ice. Lubricate tubes *F, F'*, and *F"* with drop of glycerol so that they move easily thru holes in rubber stoppers. Lead dry HCl gas from generator into reaction mixts thru tubes *F, F'*, and *F"* (*F'* and *F"* are shown in top view), which reach nearly to bottom of tubes *G, G'*, and *G"*. Regulate flow of gas thru reaction mixts in *G, G'*, and *G"* by stopcocks shown in top view, continuing passage of gas 2 hr. (At first rather slow stream of gas passes in, but during last 15 min, flow is fairly rapid.)

After reaction period, discontinue flow of gas, and disconnect long tubes *F, F'*, and *F"* and outlet tubes of test tubes *G, G'*, and *G"* from *O* and *P*. Pull tubes *F, F'*, and *F"* just above surface of reaction mixt., and close with short pieces of rubber tubing having one end plugged with short piece of glass rod. Similarly close off outlet tubes, *N, N'*, and *N"*. Place tubes contg reaction mixt. in cold room or refrigerator (8–10°) 24 hr.

Transfer contents of *G, G'*, and *G"* to 1 L erlenmeyers, taking care to remove any material adhering either to inside or outside of tubes *F, F'*, and *F"*. Dil. reaction mixts to 500 mL with H_2O. Connect flasks to reflux condensers and boil 1 hr. Prep. 3 gooches in usual manner, dry at 105°, and weigh. Ignite one of weighed crucibles, *X*, over Bunsen burner, cool in desiccator, and reweigh. Let contents of flasks cool to room temp. and filter thru weighed gooches. Wash ppts collected in gooches with hot H_2O, dry at 105°, and weigh in weighing bottles. Ignite crude lignin in crucible *X* over Bunsen flame and det. wt ash. Place one of other 2 gooches in wide-neck Kjeldahl flask and det. % N in crude lignin as in **2.057**. If methoxyl in lignin is to be detd, collect ppt from one of flasks in dried (105°) fritted glass crucible and proceed as in **47.050**.

Wt lignin = wt crude lignin − wt ash − wt crude protein (N × 6.25).

Calc. % lignin in original dry unextd material.

3.126 ***Indirect Method (36)***

(*Caution: See* **51.086**.)

Ext 1 g sample with alcohol-benzene (1+2) 4 hr in Soxhlet or comparable app. (extn vessel may be either coarse porosity Alundum or paper thimble, closed at top with filter paper or plug of cotton). Wash sample in thimble with suction, using 2 small portions alcohol followed by 2 small portions ether. Heat at 45° in nonsparking oven to drive off ether, and transfer sample to 250 mL wide-mouth erlenmeyer. Add 40 mL *1% soln of pepsin in 0.1N HCl*, wetting sample well by adding small portion reagent, stirring or shaking thoroly, and finally washing down sides of flask with remaining soln. Incubate at 40° overnight.

Add 20–30 mL hot H_2O and filter, using filter stick. (Filter sticks are made with Pyrex fritted glass disk, 30 mm diam., medium porosity. Thin layer of pre-ashed diat. earth (Hyflo Super-Cel, or similar filter-aid) is sucked onto disk from H_2O suspension. This is usually enough for easy filtration; if not, add extra Super-Cel to material being filtered. Some sticks filter slowly with some samples. It is advisable to obtain more than needed and discard slow-filtering ones. It is convenient to arrange filter sticks in set of 12 attached to vac. manifold by rubber tubing.)

Repeat washing twice and then wash residue into flask by forcing 7–8 mL 5% (w/w) H_2SO_4 downward thru filter stick, using air pressure. Wash stick further with the H_2SO_4, finally adding enough to bring total vol. to ca 150 mL. Reflux vigorously on hot plate 1 hr, adding H_2O occasionally to maintain original vol. Filter off acid. Wash residue with three 20–30 mL portions hot H_2O, two 15–20 mL portions alcohol, and two 15 mL portions ether. Leave vac. on few min to dry residue, and transfer from stick to flask by tapping and brushing. Heat to drive off any residual ether. If disk formed upon drying is difficult to break up into finely divided state (sometimes in case of immature plant samples), disperse residue in ether in flask and then boil off ether on steam bath. Add 20 mL 72% (w/w) H_2SO_4 at 20° to residue and hold 2 hr at 20°, stirring occasionally. Add 125 mL H_2O, filter, wash once with 20 mL hot H_2O, and filter again. Wash residue from filter stick and reflux as before 2 hr, using 150 mL 3% (w/w) H_2SO_4. Filter residue onto gooch with asbestos pad and wash with hot H_2O until acid-free. Dry at 105–110° and det. lignin by loss in wt on ignition at 600°.

PIGMENTS

Chlorophyll—Official Final Action

Photoelectric Colorimetric Method for Total Chlorophyll Only (37)

3.127 ***Apparatus***

(**a**) *Mortar and pestle.*—Deep glass mortar ca 10 cm id with well-defined lip.

(**b**) *Photoelectric colorimeter.*—Calibrate for chlorophyll, using plant ext as in **3.129** and light filters with max. *T* near 660 nm. (Combination of Corning Glass Works filters CS No. 2-60 and 1-58 (Glass No. 2408 and 3965, resp.) is suitable.)

(**c**) *Wash bottles.*—Type fitted with rubber bulb, permitting operation with one hand.

(**d**) *High-speed blender.*—Waring Blendor, or equiv.

3.128 ***Reagents***

(**a**) *Acetone.*—(*1*) Undild acetone and (*2*) 85% aq. soln by vol. Com. acetone, tech. grade, is satisfactory.

(**b**) *Quartz sand.*—Acid-washed and dried.

3.129 ***Determination***

(*Caution: See* **51.004**, **51.040**, and **51.046**.)

Select field material carefully to ensure representative sample. Remove representative portion from field sample, and if fresh, cut finely with hand shears and mix as thoroly as possible. Grind dried material in mill and mix thoroly.

Weigh 1–5 g into mortar and add ca 0.1 g $CaCO_3$ or Na_2CO_3. Macerate tissue with pestle, add quartz sand, and grind short time; then add 85% acetone, little at time, and continue grinding until tissue is finely ground. Transfer mixt. to funnel, filter with suction, and wash residue with 85% acetone. Return residue to mortar with more 85% acetone and grind again. Filter and wash as before. Repeat procedure until tissue is devoid of any green, and washings are colorless. (It is advisable to grind residue at least once with undild acetone and then to add enough H_2O at end to bring acetone concn to 85%. High-speed blender may be used instead of mortar to macerate and ext tissue (*see* **3.132**), but each investigator should satisfy himself that device used exts tissue completely.) When extn is complete, transfer filtered ext to vol. flask of appropriate size and dil. to vol.

Measure *T* of soln with photoelec. colorimeter, and read amt of chlorophyll present from curve relating *T* and concn. Express chlorophyll values as mg/g tissue, or in other convenient manner.

Calibrate photoelec. colorimeter as follows: Ext sample of fresh, green leaf material with 85% acetone, filter, wash residue, and dil. ext to vol. as above. Make series of dilns of ext and measure T of original and of each of dild solns with instrument in same manner as when chlorophyll prepn is being used as calibration std. Transfer aliquot of original ext to ether and evaluate total chlorophyll spectrophtric as in **3.132(b)** and **(c)**. From value thus obtained, calc. chlorophyll content of original ext and that of each of dild solns, and construct curve relating concn of chlorophyll with T or A.

Spectrophotometric Method for Total Chlorophyll and the a and b Components (38, 39)

3.130 ***Apparatus***

Use app. in **3.127** (except photoelec. colorimeter), plus following:

(a) *Scrubbing tubes for washing ether solns.*—Open tubes ca 20 mm diam. to one end of each of which is sealed tube of smaller diam. drawn to fine jet at lower end.

(b) *Spectrophotometer.*—Capable of isolating spectral region of ca 3 nm near 660 nm with negligible stray radiation. Tubulated cells with tightly fitting glass stoppers are recommended for work with ether.

3.131 ***Reagents***

Those listed in **3.128** and following:

Ether.—Com. grade is satisfactory without further purification.

3.132 ***Determination***

(Wash glassware with concd Na_3PO_4 soln to remove traces of acid that may decompose chlorophyll.)

(a) *Extraction of chlorophyll from tissue.*—Select and prep. sample as in **3.129**. Disintegrate weighed portion (2–10 g, depending on chlorophyll content) of fresh plant tissue in blender cup that contains ca 0.1 g $CaCO_3$, or by use of mortar as in **3.129**. After tissue is thoroly disintegrated, filter ext thru buchner fitted with quant. paper. Wash residue with 85% acetone, **3.128(a)**, and if necessary, use little ether to remove last traces of pigment. If extn is incomplete, return residue and paper to blender container with more 85% acetone and repeat extn. Filter and wash, as before, into flask contg first filtrate. Transfer filtrate to vol. flask of appropriate size and dil. to vol. with 85% acetone.

Pipet aliquot of 25–50 mL into separator contg ca 50 mL ether. Add H_2O carefully until it is apparent that all fat-sol. pigments have entered ether layer. Drain and discard H_2O layer. Place separator contg ether soln in upper rack of support. Add ca 100 mL H_2O to second separator placed in rack below first. Set scrubbing tube in place, and let ether soln run thru it to bottom of lower separator and rise in small droplets thru the H_2O. When all soln has left upper separator, rinse it and scrubbing tube with little ether added from medicine dropper. Place scrubbing tube in upper separator and exchange its place in support with separator now contg ether soln. Drain and discard H_2O in upper separator, add similar portion of fresh H_2O to lower separator, and repeat washing process. Continue washing ether soln until all acetone is removed (5–10 washings). Then transfer ether soln to 100 mL vol. flask, dil. to vol., and mix.

(b) *Spectrophotometric measurements.*—Add ca teaspoonful (ca 5 mL) anhyd. Na_2SO_4 to 60 mL reagent bottle, and fill it with ether soln of pigment. When this soln is optically clear, pipet aliquot into another dry bottle and dil. with enough dry ether to give A value of 0.2–0.8 at wavelength to be used. (Most favorable value is near 0.6 at 660 nm, since such soln yields satisfactory value at 642.5 nm.)

Fill 2 clean g-s absorption cells with dry ether from pipet and polish outside surfaces of each, first with cotton wet with alcohol and then with dry cotton. Place cells in instrument, and det. whether each gives same galvanometer deflection. If not, clean again or select cells that do, and do this daily. Empty one cell, fill it with the dried ether soln, and place in instrument. Adjust entrance and exit slits until spectral region isolated is 3–4 nm at 660.0 nm.

Det. whether instrument is in proper adjustment for wavelength by taking A readings thru soln against solv. at 1 nm intervals from 658 to 665 nm. Highest value should be at 660.0 nm; if not, adjust instrument until it is, or make 660.0 nm readings at wavelength setting that gave highest A. With grating instrument, apply same correction at 642.5 nm; however, with prism instrument, correction at 642.5 nm must be obtained from wavelength calibration curve for particular instrument in use. Calibrate instrument for wavelength in this way often enough to ensure that it remains in proper adjustment. Det. A at 660.0 and 642.5 nm (or corrected settings) for each unknown soln.

(c) *Calculation of chlorophyll concentration.*— Calc. total chlorophyll and each of a and b components (mg/L) as follows:

(1) Total chlorophyll $= 7.12\,A_{660.0} + 16.8\,A_{642.5}$.

(2) Chlorophyll $a = 9.93\,A_{660.0} - 0.777\,A_{642.5}$.

(3) Chlorophyll $b = 17.6\,A_{642.5} - 2.81\,A_{660.0}$.

3.133 Supplementary Information

Factors involved in spectrophtric analysis of chlorophyll system have been discussed in detail by Comar and Zscheile (*39*). These authors used Beer's law in form:

$$c = (\log_{10} I_0/I)/a \times t\ [= A/a \times t],$$

where I_0 is intensity of light transmitted by solv.-filled cell; I is intensity of light transmitted by soln-filled cell; c is concn of chlorophyll (g/L); a is absorptivity; t is thickness of soln layer in cm, and A is absorbance.

Since, at given wavelength, observed A value of soln having 2 components represents sum of A values of each of components, following equation holds in case of chlorophylls a and b at given wavelength:

(4) $$A_{observed} = A_a + A_b$$

If 1 cm cell is used, this equation may be expressed as:

(5) $$A_{observed} = a_a c_a + a_b c_b.$$

Concns of chlorophylls a and b in given ether soln can now be calcd by equation (5) as follows:

(a) Det. A for soln at 2 different wavelengths (660.0 and 642.5 nm have been found advantageous for this purpose).

(b) From table select proper absorptivities corresponding to wavelengths used.

(c) Substitute observed A value and absorptivities in equation (5) for each of the 2 wavelengths used as illustrated for 660.0 and 642.5 nm in equations (6) and (7). Solve these 2 equations simultaneously for 2 unknowns, the concns of chlorophylls a and b.

(6) $$A_{660.0} = 102\,c_a + 4.50\,c_b.$$

(7) $$A_{642.5} = 16.3\,c_a + 57.5\,c_b.$$

Equations (1), (2), and (3) were derived this way.

Criterion for accuracy of chlorophyll values detd by spectrophtric method is agreement between analytical results detd from measurements at different wavelengths. Comar and Zscheile (*39*) demonstrated that measurements at 660.0 and

642.5 nm are convenient for routine analysis; however, readings may be made at other wavelengths to check these values. Absorptivities for chlorophylls *a* and *b* in ether soln that may be used for this purpose are presented in Table **3:03**.

These values may be used for calcns as follows:

(**a**) Values for total chlorophyll and % composition may be calcd from *A* at 660.0 and 642.5 nm as described.

(**b**) Check values for total chlorophyll may be calcd from *A* at intersection points 600.0, 581.0, and 568.0 nm.

(**c**) Check values for % composition may be calcd from *A* for each of points 613.0 and 589.0 nm in combination with value of total concn obtained from (**a**) or (**b**).

Table 3:03 Absorption constants used in analysis (after Comar and Zscheile (*39*))

Wavelength nm	Absorptivities (for Ether Solns)	
	Chlorophyll a	Chlorophyll b
660.0	102	4.50
642.5	16.3	57.5
600.0	9.95	9.95
581.0	8.05	8.05
568.0	7.11	7.11
613.0	15.6	8.05
589.0	5.90	10.3

3.134 Carotenes—Official Final Action

See **43.014–43.023.**

TOBACCO

Moisture (*40*)—Official Final Action

3.135 ***Apparatus***

(**a**) *Drying oven.*—Forced-draft, regulated to 99.5±0.5°. Suggested dimensions: 19 × 19 × 19" (48 cm). Approx. oven settings: fresh air intake vent 1/5 open; air control damper ¼ open; air exhaust vent ⅓ open.

(**b**) *Moisture dish.*—Al, diam. 45–65 mm, depth 20–45 mm, with tight-fitting cover.

3.136 ***Determination***

Accurately weigh ca 5 g sample (ground to pass ≤1 mm screen) into weighed moisture dish and place uncovered dish in oven.

Do not exceed 1 sample/10 sq in. (650 sq cm) shelf space, and use only 1 shelf. Dry 3 hr at 99.5±0.5°. Remove from oven, cover, and cool in desiccator to room temp. (ca 30 min). Reweigh to nearest 1 mg and calc. % moisture.

Chlorides (*41*)—Official Final Action

Potentiometric Method

3.137 ***Reagent***

Silver nitrate std soln.—0.1*N*. Stdze against KCl as in detn.

3.138 ***Apparatus***

(**a**) *pH meter.*—Leeds and Northrup, Sumneytown Pike, N Wales, PA 19454, Beckman Instruments, or equiv., equipped with Ag and glass electrodes.

(**b**) *Buret.*—10 mL, graduated in 0.05 or 0.02 mL, preferably reservoir-type.

3.139 ***Determination***

Accurately weigh ca 2 g sample, ground to pass No. 40 sieve, into 250 mL electrolytic beaker. Add 100 mL H_2O, small amt at first to thoroly wet sample; then remainder. Let stand ≥5 min at room temp., stirring intermittently. Pipet 5 mL HNO_3 (1+9) into mixt. and insert clean electrodes. Start mag. stirrer and continue stirring thruout titrn at rate that produces vigorous agitation without spattering. Titr. with std 0.1*N* $AgNO_3$ soln to potential previously established as equivalence point. Det. equivalence point potential graphically by making several titrns on one or more tobacco samples. Recheck occasionally, and redet. when either electrode is replaced. Record vol. of titrant and calc.:

% Cl = mL $AgNO_3$ × normality × 3.5453/g sample.

Nitrogen (*42*)—Official Final Action

Kjeldahl Method for Samples Containing Nitrates

(For nitrate-free samples, omit salicylic acid and thiosulfate treatment.)

3.140 ***Reagents***

See **2.055** and the following:

(**a**) *Sodium hydroxide-thiosulfate soln.*—Dissolve 500 g NaOH pellets and 40 g $Na_2S_2O_3.5H_2O$ in H_2O and dil. to 1 L.

(**b**) *Indicators.*—(*1*) Dissolve 1 g Me red in 200 mL alcohol; or (*2*) prep. mixed indicator by dissolving 0.8 g Me red and 0.2 g methylene blue in 500 mL alcohol.

3.141 ***Apparatus***

See **2.056.**

3.142 ***Determination***

Place weighed sample (1–2 g) in digestion flask. Add vol. H_2SO_4 (contg 2 g salicylic acid/40 mL) corresponding to wt sample (35 mL for 1 g, 40 mL for 2 g for NO_3-contg samples; 20 and 25 mL, resp., for NO_3-free samples). Shake until thoroly mixed; let stand ≥30 min with occasional shaking; then add 5 g $Na_2S_2O_3.5H_2O$. Shake, let stand 5 min, and heat carefully until frothing ceases. Turn off heat, add 0.7 g HgO (or metallic Hg) and 15 g K_2SO_4, and boil briskly 1–1.5 hr after soln clears.

Cool, add ca 200 mL H_2O, cool to ca room temp., and add few Zn granules. Tilt flask and carefully add 50 mL NaOH-thiosulfate soln without agitation. Immediately connect flask to distn bulb on condenser whose tip is immersed in 50 mL std 0.1*N* acid in receiving flask. Then rotate digestion flask carefully to mix contents. Heat until ≥150 mL distillate collects, and titr. excess acid with std base, using Me red or mixed indicator. Correct for blank detn on reagents.

Potassium (*43*)—Official Final Action

3.143 ***Reagents***

(**a**) *Potassium std solns.*—(*1*) *Stock soln.*—1000 ppm K. *See* **3.020(a)**. (*2*) *Working solns.*—Place 0, 5, 10, 15, 20, 25, and 30 mL stock soln in seven 1 L vol. flasks, add 40 mL 3*N* HCl to each, and dil. to vol. with H_2O.

(**b**) *Diatomaceous earth.*—Celite 545, acid-washed.

3.144 ***Apparatus***

(**a**) *Flame photometer.*—Natural gas-air fuel, or equiv., ade quate for K analysis.

(**b**) *Chromatographic tube.*—20 × 150 mm with coarse fritted disk.

3.145 ***Preparation of Sample Solution***

Accurately weigh ca 0.5 g tobacco dust into ca 40 mL weighing dish. Add ca 1 g Celite and mix intimately with spatula. Transfer quant. thru powder funnel into chromatgc tube. Add addnl Celite thru funnel into tube until 2.5 cm layer accumulates on top of sample-Celite mixt. Compact sample and Celite by tapping tip of tube on table top, and insert tip of tube into neck of 1 L vol. flask. Add 40 mL 3*N* HCl into tube by pipet or dispenser, washing down sides, and let elute into vol. flask. When liq. level reaches top of Celite, add 25 mL H_2O and let elute. Add second 25 mL portion H_2O, let elute by gravity, or force thru rapidly with compressed air. Rinse tip of tube into vol. flask, dil. to vol. with H_2O, and mix well.

3.146 ***Determination***

Det % *T* for sample eluate and K stds as specified in instruction manual of instrument. *See* also **3.023**.

Prep. calibration curve and det. ppm K of sample from curve.

% K = ppm K × 0.1/g sample.

% K_2O = ppm K × 0.1205/g sample.

Glycerol, Propylene Glycol, and Triethylene Glycol in Cased Cigarette Cut Filler and Ground Tobacco (*44*)—Official First Action

(*Caution: See* **51.018** and **51.066.**)

3.147 ***Apparatus***

(a) *Gas chromatograph.*—With programmed temp. oven and W hot wire detector; F&M Model 720 (current models 5700 series; Hewlett-Packard, Inc.), or equiv. Conditions: Detector bridge 140 ma; temps (°): injection 265, detector 280, column 90–240 at 15°/min; He 60 mL/min adjusted, if necessary, to facilitate sepns; attenuation 4, adjusted according to sensitivity to yield peaks of sufficient size for accurate measurement (use same attenuation for all stds and samples); chart speed, 12"/hr.

(b) *Column.*—42 (105 cm) × 3/16" Cu tubing packed with 5% Carbowax 20M-terephthalic acid (TPA) on 60–80 mesh Chromosorb G AW-DMCS (Hewlett-Packard, Inc., No. 8501-6223 or Applied Science Laboratories, Inc., No. 04388). Prep. packing by placing 30.0 g Chromosorb in 500 mL ₮ r-b flask. Add soln of 1.50 g Carbowax 20M-TPA in 150 mL $CHCl_3$, and slurry. Remove $CHCl_3$ under vac. in rotary evaporator and air dry overnight at room temp. Condition new column 2 hr at 240°; then inject three 30 μL samples tobacco ext before analyzing samples. Recondition columns removed from app. before use.

3.148 ***Reagents***

(a) *Extracting soln.*—Dil. 20.0 mL 1,3-butylene glycol stock std soln, **(b)**, to 2 L with anhyd. MeOH.

(b) *1,3-Butylene glycol stock std soln.*—Accurately weigh 20.00 g USP 1,3-butanediol into 100 mL vol. flask and dil. to vol. with anhyd. MeOH.

(c) *Glycerol stock std soln.*—Accurately weigh 10.00 g USP glycerol into 100 mL vol. flask and dil. to vol. with extg soln.

(d) *Propylene glycol stock std soln.*—Accurately weigh 5.00 g USP propylene glycol into 100 mL vol. flask and dil. to vol. with extg soln.

(e) *Triethylene glycol stock std soln.*—Accurately weigh 5.00 g triethylene glycol into 100 mL vol. flask and dil. to vol. with extg soln.

(f) *Humectant std solns.*—Into each of four 100 mL vol. flasks, pipet 1.0, 2.0, 3.0, and 4.0 mL, resp., glycerol, propylene glycol, and triethylene glycol stock std solns. Dil. to vol. with extg soln. Each soln contains (in mg/100 mL):

Soln	Propylene Glycol	Glycerol	Triethylene Glycol
1	50	100	50
2	100	200	100
3	150	300	150
4	200	400	200

3.149 ***Extraction***

Place 10.00 g sample in 250 mL ₮ erlenmeyer. Pipet 100 mL extg soln into flask and stopper. Shake mech. 1 hr and let settle few min until supernate is clear. Alternatively, shake mech. 30 min and let stand overnight.

3.150 ***Determination***

Prime column by injecting two 30 μL aliquots supernate ext. Then alternately inject 30 μL supernate exts and a humectant std soln until all samples and stds have been run, repeating ext injections, if necessary. (Sequence is ext_1, ext_1, std_1, ext_1, std_2, ext_2, std_3, ext_3, std_4, ext_4, std_1, ext_5, std_2, etc. If <4 exts are available, distribute ext injections among those available so that sequence thru std_4 is run.) Det. peak hts and calc. ratios of propylene glycol, glycerol, and triethylene glycol to butylene glycol for each std and sample soln. Plot peak ht ratios against polyol concn for std solns and construct std curve for each humectant. Det. concn in mg/100 mL for propylene glycol, glycerol, and triethylene glycol in sample soln from resp. std curves.

% Humectant = (mg/100 mL) × 0.01.

Total Alkaloids (As Nicotine)

Distillation Method (45)—Official Final Action

3.151 ***Apparatus***

(a) *Distillation apparatus.*—500 mL Kjeldahl flask fitted with inlet tube for steam, trap bulb, and condenser; Griffith still (Tobacco Sci. **1**, 130(1957), available from Lab Glass, Inc., PO Box 5067, Kingsport, TN 37663); or other suitable steam distn app.

(b) *Spectrophotometer.*—Beckman Instruments Model DU (replaced by Models 24/25) or other instrument capable of accurately measuring *A* in 200–300 nm range, equipped with 1 cm quartz cells.

3.152 ***Reagents***

(a) *Alkali-salt soln.*—Dissolve 300 g NaOH in 700 mL H_2O and sat. with NaCl.

(b) *Silicotungstic acid soln (for gravimetric determination).*—Dissolve 120 g $SiO_2.12WO_3.26H_2O$ in H_2O and dil. to 1 L. (Soln should be clear and free from green color.)

3.153 ***Standardization***

(*Caution:* Nicotine is very toxic. Avoid contact with skin and eyes. *See* **51.011** and **51.015.**)

Purify best grade of nicotine com. available by successive vac. distns until center cuts from 2 successive distns have same *a* at 259 nm (ca 34.3). Accurately weigh ca 0.2 g purified nicotine; dissolve in and dil. to 1 L with ca 0.05*N* HCl. Dil. 10 mL aliquot of this soln to 100 mL with ca 0.05*N* HCl. Det. *A* at 259 nm and calc. $a = A/(c \times b)$, where *c* is concn of nicotine in g/L and *b* is cell length in cm.

3.154 ***Distillation***

Accurately weigh 2–5 g tobacco sample and transfer to distn flask or app. (If final detn of nicotine is gravimetric, use sample contg ⩾0.1 g alkaloids; if spectrophtric, use ⩾2 g sample.) (If Griffith still is used, use 0.05–0.2 g sample.) Place 25 mL HCl (1+4) in receiver (1 L vol. flask is desirable) and place receiver so that condenser tube dips into acid. (With Griffith still, use 10 mL HCl (1+4) in 250 mL vol. flask.) Add 50 mL alkali-salt soln to distn flask so that sample is rinsed into bottom of flask. (With Griffith still, use 5 mL alkali-salt soln.) If large vol. of liq. is required for proper function of still, add more alkali-salt soln; do not dil. Connect flask to app. immediately and steam distil with as rapid current of steam as can be condensed efficiently. Effluent condensate should not be above room temp. Apply heat to distn flask from burner, mantle, or other heat source to keep vol. in flask approx. const. Collect ca 900 mL condensate (or distil addnl 100 mL after condensate shows no nicotine by silicotungstic acid test). (With Griffith still, collect 225 mL.) Dil. distillate to vol.

3.155 ***Determination***

(**a**) *Spectrophotometric.*—Dil. aliquots of distillate (if necessary) with 0.05*N* HCl so that *A* at 259 nm is 0.5–0.8 and read *A* at 236, 259, and 282 nm. Calc. corrected $A'_{259} = 1.059 \times [\text{observed } A_{259} - \frac{1}{2}(A_{236} + A_{282})]$ after correcting all observed *A* values to original distillate vol. basis. Concn, *c*, of alkaloids as nicotine in g/L is given by $c = A'_{259}/(a \times b)$, where *a* is absorptivity at 259 nm, and *b* is cell length in cm.

% alkaloid (as nicotine) $= c \times$ vol. distillate (L) $\times$ 100/g sample.

(**b**) *Gravimetric.*—Det. alkaloids in distillate as in **6.176**, but double amt of silicotungstic acid specified, i.e., 2 mL/each 10 mg alkaloids expected.

Cundiff-Markunas Method (45)—Official Final Action

(Total alkaloids (as nicotine), tertiary alkaloids (as nicotine), and secondary alkaloids (as nornicotine))

3.156 ***Reagents***

(**a**) *Benzene-chloroform soln.*—Mix equal parts by vol. of benzene and $CHCl_3$ and sat. with H_2O.

(**b**) *Sodium hydroxide soln.*—36%. Dissolve 500 g NaOH in H_2O and dil. to 1 L.

(**c**) *Dilute acetic acid.*—5%. Dil. 50 mL HOAc to 1 L with H_2O.

(**d**) *Crystal violet indicator.*—Dissolve 0.5 g crystal violet in 100 mL HOAc.

(**e**) *Perchloric acid std soln.*—0.025*N*. Add 4.7 mL 72% $HClO_4$ to freshly opened 5 lb bottle HOAc and mix. (*Caution: See* **51.022** and **51.028**(**a**) and (**d**).) Stdze as follows: Accurately weigh 0.1 g KH phthalate (NBS) into 125 mL erlenmeyer, add 50 mL HOAc, and heat to dissolve. Cool, add 2 drops indicator, and titr. to blue-green end point. Perform blank titrn on 50 mL HOAc and 2 drops indicator soln, and correct vol. of titrant.

N = wt KH phthalate × 4.896/mL $HClO_4$ soln.

3.157 ***Determination***

Accurately weigh 2.5 g finely ground tobacco into 250 mL erlenmeyer. Add 15 mL 5% HOAc and swirl until tobacco is thoroly wetted. Pipet 100 mL benzene-$CHCl_3$ soln into flask, and then 10 mL 36% NaOH soln. Stopper flask tightly and shake 20 min, using wrist-action shaker. Add 4.5–5 g (2 teaspoonfuls) Filter-Cel, mix, and filter most of benzene layer thru Whatman No. 2 paper into second flask. If filtrate has any turbidity, add 2–2.5 g (1 teaspoonful) addnl Filter-Cel and refilter thru Whatman No. 2 paper. Filtrate must be clear.

Pipet 25 mL aliquots of filtrate into each of two 125 mL erlenmeyers. Pass stream of air over surface of soln in first flask 5 min, add 2 drops indicator, and titr. to green end point with 0.025*N* $HClO_4$. Add 1.0 mL Ac_2O to second flask and let stand ⩾15 min. Add 25 mL HOAc and 2 drops indicator, and titr. to blue-green end point with 0.025*N* $HClO_4$. Take first appearance of blue-green thruout soln as end point. For each series of analyses perform blank titrns and correct respective vols of titrant.

Calc. % alkaloids as follows: % total alkaloids (as nicotine) = $V_1 \times N \times 32.45$/wt sample; % tertiary alkaloids (as nicotine) = $(2V_2 - V_1) \times N \times 32.45$/wt sample; % secondary alkaloids (as nornicotine) = $2(V_1 - V_2) \times N \times 29.64$/wt sample; where V_1 = vol. titrant for nonacetylated aliquot; V_2 = vol. titrant for acetylated aliquot; and N = normality $HClO_4$.

Nicotine on Cambridge Filter Pads

Gas-Liquid Chromatographic Method (46)
Official First Action

3.158 ***Apparatus and Reagents***

(**a**) *Gas chromatograph.*—With flame ionization detector, heated injection port, and thermostated column oven. Following conditions have been found satisfactory: Column, 1.8 m (6′) × ⅛″ stainless steel; packing, 2% KOH and 10% Carbowax 20M (based on final packing wt) on 45–60 mesh calcined diat. earth (such as Chromosorb W, or equiv.), resieved before use to mesh range to remove fines and lumps; temps (°): column 165, detector and injection port 200–250; carrier gas flow, ca 40 mL/min. Adjust H and air flows for max. sensitivity and stability. Under these conditions, column should have ht equiv. to theoretical plate (HETP) <1 mm and resolution of >2, calcd with nicotine and anethole.

(**b**) *Measuring system.*—Measure peak areas with electronic integrator or other system with resolution of ⩾1 count/mv-sec.

(**c**) *Mechanical shaker.*—Capable of extg ⩾99% nicotine. Burrell Wrist-Action shaker has been found satisfactory.

(**d**) *Extracting soln.*—2-Propanol contg 1 mg anethole/mL as internal std for nicotine. If H_2O is also to be detd, add 20 mg EtOH/mL 2-propanol as addnl internal std.

(**e**) *Nicotine std solns.*—(*1*) *Stock soln.*—Weigh 2.500 g nicotine, **3.153**, or equiv. amt of nicotine salt. Transfer quant. into 100 mL vol. flask, and dil. to vol. with extg soln. (*2*) *Working std solns.*—Pipet 1, 2, 3, 4, and 5 mL stock soln into five 100 mL vol. flasks, and dil. to vol. with extg soln (0.25, 0.50, 0.75, 1.00, and 1.25 mg nicotine/mL). (*Caution: See* precaution in **3.153**.)

3.159 ***Extraction***

Place Cambridge filter material in flask or serum bottle accomodated by shaker used, add 10.00 mL extg soln, stopper, and shake until ⩾99% of nicotine is extd (usually ca 15 min).

3.160 ***Standardization***

Prime column with aliquots of 1.25 mg/mL std soln. Let baseline stabilize, inject 1 µL each std soln in succession, and repeat sequence 3 times. Det. area ratio (nicotine:anethole) for each injection, and calc. slope and intercept of response curve, preferably by method of least squares (*See Definition of Terms and Explanatory Notes No. (24)*). Correlation coefficient should be ⩾0.99 and intercept ⩽0.05 mg/mL.

3.161 ***Determination***

Prime column with aliquots of ext, **3.159**. Let baseline stabilize, and inject 1 µL of each sample soln. Calc. nicotine concn in soln (C, mg/mL) = $mx + b$, where m = slope of stdzn curve, b = intercept, and x = area ratio of nicotine to anethole.

Nicotine yield/cigaret = (C × 10.00)/(No. cigarets/pad)

Menthol (47)—Official Final Action

Colorimetric Method

3.162 ***Apparatus and Reagents***

(**a**) *Distillation apparatus.*—*See* Fig. **3:07**.
(**b**) *Spectrophotometer.*—With matched cells; capable of measuring *A* at 550 nm.
(**c**) *Menthol std soln.*—1 mg/mL. Accurately weigh 100 mg USP *l*-menthol into 100 mL vol. flask, add alcohol to dissolve, and dil. to vol. with alcohol.
(**d**) *DMAB color reagent.*—Dissolve 0.5 g *p*-dimethylaminobenzaldehyde (Eastman Kodak, white label) in 100 mL H_2SO_4 (1.6+1).

3.163 ***Preparation of Calibration Curve***

Prep. dil. stds by pipeting aliquots contg 0, 3, 4, 6, 8, and 10 mg menthol into 100 mL vol. flasks and dilg to vol. with alcohol (1+1). Pipet 1 mL each dil. std into 10 mL test tube, add 5 mL color reagent, mix, and place in boiling H_2O bath *exactly* 2 min. Cool in tap H_2O, and within 15 min det. *A* at 550 nm against 0 std. Prep. calibration curve by plotting *A* against menthol concn (mg/100 mL).

3.164 ***Determination***

Accurately weigh 2.00–2.15 g cigaret filler and transfer to distn flask, **A**. Add 80 mL H_2O and few boiling stones, connect flask to condenser with tube, **B**, attach adapter, **C**, to condenser, and immerse tip in 20 mL alcohol in 100 mL vol. receiving flask.

Gently heat distn flask until distn begins; then increase heat and lower receiving flask, **D**, so tip of adapter is no longer immersed. Distil until 20 mL distillate collects. Disconnect condenser from tube, and wash down condenser with alcohol. Remove receiving flask, dil. distillate to ca 70 mL with alcohol, and add H_2O almost to vol. Mix, add alcohol to vol., and mix again.

Pipet 1 mL distillate into 10 mL test tube, add 5 mL color reagent, mix, and place in boiling H_2O bath *exactly* 2 min. Cool in tap H_2O, and within 15 min det. *A* at 550 nm, using "color" soln from nonmentholated tobacco carried thru detn as blank. (If nonmentholated sample corresponding to mentholated sample is not available, use reagent blank.) Use nonmentholated tobacco blank within 15 min after color development step. Fresh nonmentholated tobacco blank soln may be required during multiple sample runs. Det. mg menthol from calibration curve.

% Menthol = mg menthol/(g original sample × 10).

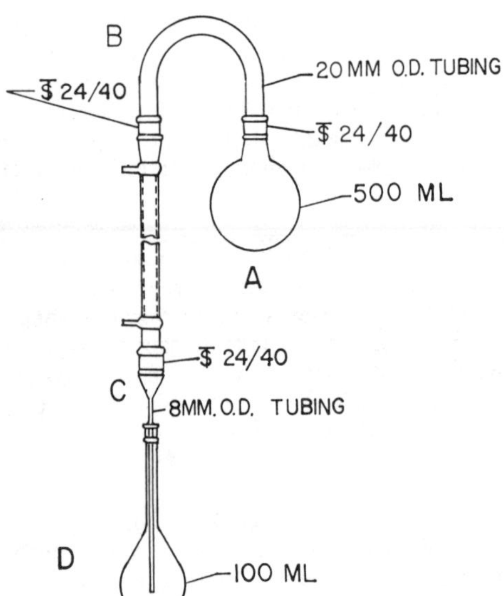

FIG. 3:07—Distillation apparatus; *see* 3.164 for explanation of symbols

Gas Chromatographic Method

3.165 ***Apparatus and Reagents***

(**a**) *Gas chromatograph.*—Equipped with flame ionization detector and thermostated injection port and column oven. Use following conditions for analysis: Column, 1.5 m (5′) × ⅛″ od stainless steel packed with 10% (w/w) silicone oil DC-550 on 60–80 mesh Chromosorb W; temps (°): column 150, detector 150, injection port 175; N carrier gas flow ca 35 mL/min. Adjust H and air flows for max. sensitivity and reasonable stability.
(**b**) *Mechanical shaker.*—Wrist action.
(**c**) *Menthol-anethole std soln.*—0.250 mg menthol and 0.50 mg anethole/mL. Weigh exactly 0.5000 g tech. grade anethole and wash into 1 L vol. flask with 200 mL alcohol. Transfer 0.2500 g USP *l*-menthol to the vol. flask with enough alcohol to bring to vol. Store soln in dark g-s bottle. Do not use >6 weeks.
(**d**) *Extracting soln.*—0.50 mg anethole/mL. Dissolve 1.000 g anethole in alcohol in 2 L vol. flask, dil. to vol. with alcohol, and store in dark.

3.166 ***Determination of Ratio Factor***

Weigh ca 3 g nonmentholated control filler, contg all usual humectants but no menthol or anethole, into 125 mL rubber-stoppered flask. Pipet 50 mL std menthol-anethole soln into flask, stopper, and shake 1 hr on mech. shaker. Let solids settle 15 min and chromatograph 2 μL aliquot of supernate. Repeat twice more to obtain total of 3 replicates of std chromatogram. For quant. results, inject both std and unknown samples by inserting 2″ (5 cm) needle to hilt, injecting 2 μL rapidly, and withdrawing needle at once. (Menthol elutes in ca 3 min, anethole in ca 5 min.) After ca 10 min, all other compds are eluted and new injection can be made.

Draw baselines under menthol and anethole peaks and measure peak hts in mm. Using mean peak ht of menthol and anethole from 3 std chromatograms, calc. std ratio factor of menthol to anethole as follows:

Std ratio factor = peak ht for menthol (0.25 mg/mL)/peak ht for anethole (0.50 mg/mL).

3.167 ***Determination***

Accurately weigh 8–8.5 g mentholated cigarette filler and place in 250 mL rubber-stoppered erlenmeyer. Pipet 100 mL extg soln into flask, stopper, and mech. shake 2 hr. Let solids settle 15 min and chromatograph 2 μL aliquot of supernate. Draw baselines under menthol and anethole peaks and measure peak hts in mm. Calc. ratio factor of unknown menthol as follows:

Ratio factor for unknown = peak ht for unknown menthol/peak ht for anethole (0.50 mg/mL).

% Menthol = (unknown ratio factor × 0.25 × 10)/(std ratio factor × g sample).

SELECTED REFERENCES

(*1*) Botan. Gaz. **73,** 44(1922); Proc. Am. Soc. Hort. Sci. 1927, p. 191; JAOAC **13,** 224(1930); **16,** 71(1933); **19,** 70(1936).
(*2*) JAOAC **58,** 436(1975).
(*3*) JAOAC **11,** 203(1928); **16,** 70(1933); **19,** 70(1936).
(*4*) Ind. Eng. Chem., Anal. Ed. **9,** 67(1937); **10,** 13(1938); JAOAC **25,** 555(1942); **27,** 526(1944).
(*5*) JAOAC **19,** 359(1936); **27,** 526(1944).

(*6*) J. Biol. Chem. **7**, 83(1910); JAOAC **4**, 392(1921); **16**, 70(1933).
(*7*) J. Biol. Chem. **47**, 475(1921); **50**, 527, 537(1922); JAOAC **14**, 216(1931); **16**, 71(1933); **19**, 71(1936).
(*8*) JAOAC **3**, 329(1920); **4**, 393(1921); **16**, 71(1933); **19**, 71 (1936).
(*9*) JAOAC **4**, 393(1921).
(*10*) JAOAC **39**, 419(1956).
(*11*) JAOAC **19**, 71(1936).
(*12*) J. Am. Chem. Soc. **51**, 1664(1929); JAOAC **19**, 71(1936).
(*13*) JAOAC **34**, 710(1951); **36**, 405(1953).
(*14*) JAOAC **36**, 405(1953).
(*15*) Ind. Eng. Chem., Anal. Ed. **13**, 145(1941); JAOAC **24**, 520(1941).
(*16*) JAOAC **36**, 397(1953).
(*17*) JAOAC **36**, 412(1956); **41**, 309(1958); **43**, 511(1960).
(*18*) USDA Bur. Chem. Bull. **105**, p. 151; **116**, p. 92; **137**, p. 30.
(*19*) JAOAC **6**, 415(1923).
(*20*) JAOAC **16**, 71(1933).
(*21*) JAOAC **14**, 216(1931); J. Biol. Chem. **59**, 255(1924).
(*22*) JAOAC **49**, 284(1966).
(*23*) JAOAC **11**, 209(1928); **12**, 195(1929); **21**, 107(1938).
(*24*) Sutton, "Systematic Handbook of Volumetric Analysis," 11th ed., 1924, p. 146; J. Am. Chem. Soc. **37**, 1128(1915).
(*25*) JAOAC **18**, 379(1935); **19**, 72(1936).
(*26*) JAOAC **58**, 1129(1975).
(*27*) JAOAC **55**, 991(1972); **61**, 150(1978).
(*28*) JAOAC **19**, 236(1936).
(*29*) JAOAC **52**, 627(1969).
(*30*) JAOAC **41**, 304(1958).
(*31*) JAOAC **14**, 73, 225(1931); **15**, 71(1932).
(*32*) JAOAC **36**, 402(1953).
(*33*) JAOAC **41**, 307, 681(1958); **42**, 650(1959); **43**, 512(1960); **44**, 267(1961).
(*34*) Anal. Chem. **20**, 850(1948); JAOAC **39**, 423(1956).
(*35*) JAOAC **15**, 124(1932); **18**, 386(1935); **19**, 107 (1936).
(*36*) JAOAC **32**, 288(1949).
(*37*) Ind. Eng. Chem., Anal. Ed. **12**, 148(1940); **15**, 524(1943).
(*38*) Ind. Eng. Chem., Anal. Ed. **14**, 877(1942); JAOAC **27**, 517(1944).
(*39*) Plant Physiol. **17**, 198(1942).
(*40*) JAOAC **49**, 525(1966).
(*41*) JAOAC **46**, 415(1963).
(*42*) JAOAC **42**, 302(1959).
(*43*) JAOAC **49**, 521(1966).
(*44*) JAOAC **54**, 560(1971).
(*45*) JAOAC **43**, 524(1960).
(*46*) JAOAC **62**, 229(1979).
(*47*) JAOAC **51**, 650(1968).

4. Disinfectants

Phenol Coefficient (*1*)—Official Final Action

(Applicable to testing disinfectants miscible with H_2O that do not exert bacteriostatic effects that cannot be neutzd by one of subculture media specified, or overcome by suitable subtransfer procedures. The 95% confidence limits are ±12%.)

1. Using Salmonella typhi

4.001 ***Culture Media***

(**a**) *Nutrient broth.*—Boil 5 g beef ext (Difco), 5 g NaCl, and 10 g peptone (Anatone, peptic hydrolysate of pork tissues, manufactured by American Laboratories, Inc., 4410 S 102nd St, Omaha, NB 68127) in 1 L H_2O 20 min, and dil. to vol. with H_2O; adjust to pH 6.8. (If colorimetric method is used, adjust broth to give dark green with bromothymol blue.) Filter thru paper, place 10 mL portions in 20 × 150 mm test tubes, and autoclave 20 min at 121°. Use this broth for daily transfers of test cultures.

(**b**) *Synthetic broth.*—*Soln A:* Dissolve 0.05 g L-cystine, 0.37 g DL-methionine, 0.4 g L-arginine.HCl, 0.3 g DL-histidine.HCl, 0.85 g L-lysine.HCl, 0.21 g L-tyrosine, 0.5 g DL-threonine, 1.0 g DL-valine, 0.8 g L-leucine, 0.44 g DL-isoleucine, 0.06 g glycine, 0.61 g DL-serine, 0.43 g DL-alanine, 1.3 g L-glutamic acid.HCl, 0.45 g L-aspartic acid, 0.26 g DL-phenylalanine, 0.05 g DL-tryptophan, and 0.05 g L-proline in 500 mL H_2O contg 18 mL 1*N* NaOH.

Soln B: Dissolve 3.0 g NaCl, 0.2 g KCl, 0.1 g $MgSO_4.7H_2O$, 1.5 g KH_2PO_4, 4.0 g Na_2HPO_4, 0.01 g thiamine.HCl, and 0.01 g niacinamide in 500 mL H_2O.

Mix *Solns A* and *B*, dispense in 10 mL portions in 20 × 150 mm tubes, and autoclave 20 min at 121°. Before using for daily transfers of test cultures, aseptically add 0.1 mL sterile 10% glucose soln per tube. Grow cultures with tube slanted 8° from horizontal.

(**c**) *Nutrient agar.*—Dissolve 1.5% Bacto agar (Difco) in nutrient broth and adjust to pH 7.2–7.4 (blue-green with bromothymol blue) or in synthetic broth, tube, autoclave, and slant.

(**d**) *Subculture media.*—Use (*1*), (*2*), or (*3*), whichever gives lowest result. (Com. dehydrated brands made to conform with preceding specifications may be used.) With oxidizing products and products formulated with toxic compds contg certain heavy metals like Hg, (*2*) will usually give lowest result. With products contg cationic surface active materials, (*3*) will usually give lowest result. *See* also **4.009**, par. 5.

(*1*) *Nutrient broth* described in (**a**);

(*2*) *Fluid thioglycolate medium USP XX:* Mix 0.5 g L-cystine, 0.75 g agar, 2.5 g NaCl, 5.5 g glucose.H_2O, 5.0 g H_2O-sol. yeast ext, and 15.0 g pancreatic digest of casein with 1 L H_2O. Heat on H_2O bath to dissolve, add 0.5 g Na thioglycolate or 0.3 g thioglycolic acid, and adjust with 1*N* NaOH to pH 7.1±0.2. If filtration is necessary, reheat without boiling and filter hot thru moistened filter paper. Add 1.0 mL freshly prepd 0.1% Na resazurin soln, transfer 10 mL portions to 20 × 150 mm tubes, and autoclave 20 min at 121°. Cool at once to 25° and store at 20–30°, protected from light.

(*3*) *"Letheen broth":* Dissolve 0.7 g lecithin (Azolectin, Associated Concentrates, 32–30 61st St, Woodside, NY 11377) and 5.0 g polysorbate 80 (Tween 80, or equiv.) in 400 mL hot H_2O and boil until clear. Add 600 mL soln of 5.0 g beef ext (Difco), 10.0 g peptone (Anatone, (**a**)), and 5 g NaCl in H_2O, and boil 10 min. Adjust with 1*N* NaOH and/or 1*N* HCl to pH 7.0 ±0.2 and filter thru coarse paper; transfer 10 mL portions to 20 × 150 mm tubes, and autoclave 20 min at 121°.

(*4*) *Cystine trypticase agar* (*BBL*): Suspend 29.5 g in 1 L H_2O. Heat gently with frequent agitation and boil ca 1 min or until soln is complete. Transfer 10 mL portions to 20 × 150 mm tubes, and autoclave 15 min at 12 lb pressure. Cool in upright position and store ≤25 days at 20–30°. Use for monthly transfer of stab stock cultures of *Ps. aeruginosa* PRD 10 (ATCC 15442).

(*5*) *Other subculture media:* Use **4.001**(**d**)(*2*) with 0.7 g lecithin (Azolectin, Associated Concentrates, Inc., 32–30 61st St, Woodside, NY 11377) and 5.0 g polysorbate 80 (Tween 80, or equiv.) added; or suspend 29.8 g prepd fluid thioglycolate medium (Difco), 0.7 g lecithin, and 5.0 g polysorbate 80 in 1 L H_2O, and boil until soln is clear. Cool, dispense in 10 mL portions in 20 × 150 mm tubes, and autoclave 20 min at 121°. Store at 20–30°. Protect from light.

4.002 ***Apparatus and Reagents***

(**a**) *Glassware.*—1, 5, and 10 mL vol. pipets; 1, 5, and 10 mL Mohr pipets graduated to 0.1 mL or less; 100 mL g-s cylinders graduated in 1 mL divisions; Pyrex lipped test tubes, 25 × 150 mm (medication tubes); bacteriological culture tubes, 20 × 150 mm (test culture and subculture tubes). Plug medication tubes with cotton wrapped in 1 layer of cheese cloth. Sterilize all glassware 2 hr in hot air oven at 180°. Loosely plug pipets with cotton at mouth and place in closed metal containers before sterilizing.

(**b**) *Water bath.*—Insulated, relatively deep H_2O bath, with cover having ≥10 well-spaced holes which admit medication tubes but not their lips.

(**c**) *Racks.*—Any convenient style. Blocks of wood (size depending on space in incubator) with deep holes are satisfactory. Have holes well spaced to ensure quick manipulation of tubes. It is convenient to have them large enough to admit medication tubes while dilns are being made.

(**d**) *Transfer loop.*—Make 4 mm id single loop at end of 50–75 mm (2–3") Pt or Pt alloy wire No. 23 B&S gage or 4 mm loop fused on 75 mm (3") shaft (available from Matthey-Bishop, Inc., Malvern, PA 19355). Fit other end in suitable holder (glass or Al rod). Bend loop at 30° angle with stem, Fig. **4:01**.

(**e**) *Test organism.*—Hopkins strain 26 of *Salmonella typhi* (Schroeter) Warren and Scott, ATCC No. 6539 (formerly called *Bac. typhosus* and *Eberthella typhosa*). Maintain stock culture on nutrient agar slants by monthly transfers. Incubate new stock transfer 2 days at 37°; then store at 2–5°. From stock culture inoculate tube of nutrient broth and make at least 4 consecutive daily transfers (≤30) in nutrient broth, incubating at 37°, before using culture for testing. (If only 1 daily transfer has been missed, it is not necessary to repeat the 4 consecutive transfers.) Use 22–26 hr culture of organism grown in nutrient broth at 37° in test. Shake, and let settle 15 min before using.

With *Ps. aeruginosa* PRD 10, proceed as in **4.011**.

(**f**) *Phenol stock soln.*—5% (w/v). Weigh 50 g USP phenol, which congeals at ≥40°, in beaker. Dissolve in H_2O, rinse soln into 1 L vol. flask, and dil. to vol. Stdze with 0.1*N* KBr-$KBrO_3$ soln, (**g**), as follows: Transfer 25 mL stock soln to 500 mL vol. flask and dil. to vol. with H_2O. Transfer 15 mL aliquot of dild soln to 500 mL I flask and add 30 mL std KBr-$KBrO_3$ soln. Add 5 mL HCl and immediately insert stopper. Shake frequently during 30 min and let stand 15 min. Remove stopper just enough to quickly add 5 mL 20% KI soln, taking care that no Br vapors escape, and immediately stopper flask. Shake thoroly, remove

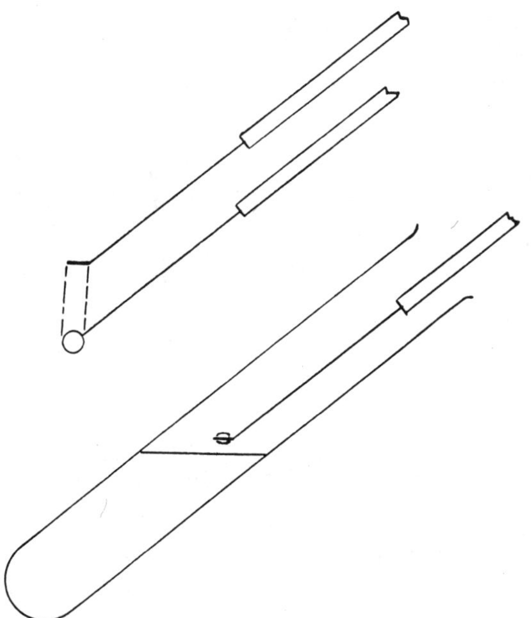

FIG. 4:01—Transfer loop and manner of using in phenol coefficient technic

stopper, and rinse it and neck of flask with little H_2O so that washings flow into flask. Titr. with 0.1*N* $Na_2S_2O_3$, using starch indicator, **6.005(f)**. 1 mL 0.1*N* KBr-$KBrO_3$ = 0.001569 g phenol.

% phenol in stock soln = (30 − mL 0.1*N* $Na_2S_2O_3$ soln from titrn) × 0.001569 × 1333 × 100/1000;

where 30 = mL 0.1*N* KBr-$KBrO_3$ soln added, 0.001569 = g phenol equiv. to 1 mL 0.1*N* KBr-$KBrO_3$ soln, 1333 = diln factor, and 1000 = original vol. phenol stock soln.

If necessary, adjust stock soln to 5.00±0.05% phenol by adding H_2O or phenol. Keep in well stoppered amber bottles in cool place, protected from light.

(g) *Potassium bromide-bromate soln.*—0.1*N*. Prep. as in **50.020**. Stdze as follows: Transfer 30 mL to I flask, and add 25 mL H_2O, 5 mL 20% KI soln, and 5 mL HCl. Shake thoroly and titr. with 0.1*N* $Na_2S_2O_3$, using starch indicator, **6.005(f)**.

4.003 ***Operating Technic***

Make 1% stock diln of substance to be tested (or any other convenient diln, depending on anticipated concn) in g-s cylinder. Make final dilns, from 1% stock diln, directly into medication tubes and remove all excess >5 mL. (Range of dilns should cover killing limits of disinfectant in 5–15 min and should at same time be close enough for accuracy.) From 5% stock phenol soln (1–20) dil. further to make 1–90 and 1–100 dilns, and place in medication tubes. Place these tubes, contg 5 mL each of final dilns of disinfectant and of phenol, and tube contg test culture in H_2O bath at 20° and leave 5 min. Add 0.5 mL test culture to each of dilns at time intervals corresponding to intervals at which transfers are to be made. (Thus, by time 10 tubes have been seeded at 30 sec intervals, 4.5 min has elapsed, and 30 sec interval intervenes before transference to subculture begins.) Add culture from graduated pipet large enough to seed all tubes in any one set. In using *Ps. aeruginosa* PRD 10 (ATCC 15442), proceed as in **4.011**.

In inoculating medication tubes, hold them in slanting position after removal from bath, insert pipet to just above surface of disinfectant, and run in culture without letting tip touch disinfectant. After adding culture, agitate tubes gently but thoroly to insure even distribution of bacteria, and replace in bath; 5 min after seeding first medication tube, transfer 1 loopful of mixt. of culture and dild disinfectant from medication tube to corresponding subculture tube. To facilitate transfer of uniform drops of medication mixt., hold tube at 60° angle, and withdraw loop so that plane of loop is parallel with surface of liq. (Fig. **4:01**). After 30 sec, transfer loopful from second medication tube to second subculture tube and continue process for each successive diln; 5 min after making first transfer, begin second set of transfers for 10 min period, and finally repeat for 15 min period.

Gently agitate medication tubes before taking each interval loop subsample for transfer to subculture medium. Before each transfer, heat loop to redness in flame and flame mouth of every tube. Sterilize loop immediately after each transfer (before replugging tubes) to allow time for cooling. Use care in transferring and seeding to prevent pipet or needle from touching sides or mouth of medication tube, and see that no cotton threads adhere to inner sides or mouths of tubes. Incubate subculture 48 hr at 37° and read results. Thoroly agitate individual subculture tubes before incubation. Macroscopic examination is usually sufficient. Occasionally 3-day incubation period, agar streak, microscopic examination, or agglutination with antityphoid serum may be necessary to det. feeble growth or suspected contamination.

4.004 ***Calculation***

Express results in terms of phenol coefficient number, or highest diln killing test organism in 10 min but not in 5 min, whichever most accurately reflects germicidal value of disinfectant. Phenol coefficient is number obtained by dividing numerical value of greatest diln (denominator of fraction expressing diln) of disinfectant capable of killing *S. typhi* in 10 min but not in 5 min by greatest diln of phenol showing same results.

Example:

Diln	5 Min	10 Min	15 Min
	Disinfectant (X):		
1–300	0	0	0
1–325	+	0	0
1–350	+	0	0
1–375	+	+	0
1–400	+	+	+
	Phenol:		
1– 90	+	0	0
1–100	+	+	+

Phenol coefficient would be $\frac{350}{90}$ =3.89.

Test is satisfactory only when phenol control gives one of following readings:

Phenol	5 Min	10 Min	15 Min
1– 90	+ or 0	+ or 0	0
1–100	+	+	+ or 0

If none of dilns of disinfectant shows growth in 5 min and killing in 10 min, est. hypothetical diln only when any 3 consecutive dilns show following results: first, no growth in 5 min; second, growth in 5 and 10 min but not in 15 min; and third, growth in 5, 10, and 15 min.

Example:

Diln	5 Min	10 Min	15 Min
	Disinfectant (X):		
1–300	0	0	0
1–350	+	+	0
1–400	+	+	+
	Phenol:		
1– 90	0	0	0
1–100	+	+	0

Phenol coefficient would be $\frac{325}{95}$ =3.42.

To avoid giving impression of fictitious accuracy, calc. phenol coefficient to nearest 0.1. Thus, in examples cited above, phenol coefficients would be reported as 3.9 and 3.4, instead of 3.89 and 3.42.

Note: Although it is commonly accepted criterion that disinfectants be at diln equiv. in germicidal efficiency to phenol against *S. typhi* by calcg 20 × *S. typhi* coefficient to det. number of parts H_2O in which 1 part disinfectant may be mixed, this should be regarded as presumptive and is subject to confirmation by Use-Diln Method.

4.005 ***2. Using Staphylococcus aureus (1)***

Proceed as in **4.001–4.004**, except change phenol dilns and test organisms. Use 22–26 hr culture of *Staph. aureus* FDA 209, ATCC No. 6538, having at 20° at least resistance indicated by following:

Phenol	5 Min	10 Min	15 Min
1–60	+ or 0	+ or 0	0
1–70	+	+	+

Note: Calc. results as in **4.004**. If conversion 20 × *Staph. aureus* coefficient is used to det. number of parts H_2O in which 1 part germicide may be incorporated to disinfect where pyogenic organisms are objective, this diln is subject to confirmation by Use-Diln Method.

4.006 ***3. Using Pseudomonas aeruginosa***
Official First Action

Proceed as in **4.001–4.004**. Use 22–26 hr culture of *Ps. aeruginosa* PRD 10 (ATCC 15442), having resistance to phenol at 20° at least as follows:

Phenol	5 Min	10 Min	15 Min
1–80	+ or 0	+ or 0	0
1–90	+	+	+

Use-Dilution Method (2)—Official Final Action

(Applicable to testing disinfectants miscible with H_2O to confirm phenol coefficient results and to det. max. dilns effective for practical disinfection)

1. Using Salmonella choleraesuis

4.007 ***Reagents***

(**a**) *Culture media.—See* **4.001**.

(**b**) *Test organism, Salmonella choleraesuis.*— (ATCC 10708). Maintain stock culture on nutrient agar slants by monthly transfers. Incubate new stock transfer 2 days at 37°; then store at 2–5°. From stock culture inoculate tube of nutrient broth and incubate at 37°. Make 3 consecutive 24 hr transfers; then inoculate tubes of nutrient broth (2 for each 10 carriers to be tested), using one loop of inoculum with each tube; incubate 48–54 hr at 37°.

(**c**) *Phenol.—See* **4.002(f)**.

(**d**) *Sterile distilled water.*—Prep. stock supply of H_2O in 1 L flasks, plug with cotton, sterilize 20 min at 121°, and use to prep. dilns of medicants.

(**e**) *Asparagine soln.*—Make stock supply of 0.1% asparagine ("Bacto") soln in H_2O in erlenmeyer of convenient size, plug with cotton, and sterilize 20 min at 121°. Use to cover metal carriers for sterilization and storage.

(**f**) *Sodium hydroxide soln.*—Approx. 1*N* (4%). (For cleaning metal carriers before use.)

4.008 ***Apparatus***

(**a**) *Glassware.*—As in **4.002(a)**. Also: straight side Pyrex test tubes, 20 × 150 mm; 15 × 110 mm petri dishes; 100 mL, 300 mL, and 1 L erlenmeyers. Sterilize petri dishes in closed metal containers.

(**b**) *Water bath and racks.—See* **4.002(b)** and (**c**).

(**c**) *Transfer loops and needles.*—(*1*) *See* **4.002(d)**. (*2*) Make 3 mm right angle bend at end of 50–75 mm nichrome wire No. 18 B&S gage. Have other end in suitable holder (glass or Al rod).

(**d**) *Carriers.*—Polished stainless steel cylinders (penicillin cups), 8±1 mm od, 6±1 mm id, length 10±1 mm, of type 304 stainless steel, SS 18–8. (Obtainable from S. & L. Metal Products Corp., 58–29 57 Drive, Maspeth, NY 11378.)

(**e**) *Petri dishes.*—Have available ca 6 sterile petri dishes matted with 2 layers of S&S No. 597 or Whatman No. 2, 9 cm filter paper.

4.009 ***Operating Technic***

Soak ring carriers overnight in 1*N* NaOH, rinse with tap H_2O until rinse H_2O is neut. to phthln, then rinse twice with distd H_2O; place cleaned ring carriers in multiples of 10 in cotton-plugged erlenmeyers or 25 × 150 mm cotton plugged Pyrex test tubes, cover with asparagine soln, **4.007(e)**, sterilize 20 min at 121°, cool, and hold at room temp. Transfer 20 sterile ring carriers, using flamed nichrome wire hook, into 20 mL 48–54 hr nutrient broth test culture in sterile 25 × 150 mm medication tube. After 15 min contact period remove cylinders, using flamed nichrome wire hook, and place on end in vertical position in sterile petri dish matted with filter paper, **4.008(e)**. Cover and place in incubator at 37° and let dry ≥20 min but ≤60 min. Hold broth culture for detn of its resistance to phenol by phenol coefficient method, **4.003**.

From 5% stock phenol soln (1–20) make 1–90 and 1–100 dilns directly into medication tubes. Place tube for each diln in H_2O bath and let come to 20°. Make stock soln of germicide to be tested in sterile g-s cylinder. From this soln make 10 mL dilns to be tested, depending upon phenol coefficient found and/or claimed against *S. typhi* at 20°, directly into each of ten 25 × 150 mm medication tubes; place the 10 tubes in H_2O bath at 20° and let come to temp. Det. diln to be tested by multiplying phenol coefficient number found and/or claimed by 20 to det. number of parts H_2O in which 1 part germicide is to be incorporated. This detn is not required when disinfectant under test yields phenol coefficient that cannot be converted validly to presumptive use-diln, or when analyst dets that use-diln range can be found without resort to phenol coefficient test.

Add 0.5 mL of test culture suspension to 1–90 diln of phenol control; after 30 sec interval, add 0.5 mL to 1–100 diln of control, using sterile cotton-plugged pipets. After adding culture, agitate tubes gently but thoroly to distribute bacteria evenly, and replace in bath; 5 min after seeding first medication tube, transfer 1 loopful of mixt. of culture and dild phenol from medication tube to corresponding subculture tube. After 30 sec, transfer loopful from second medication tube; 5 min after making first set of transfers begin second set of transfers for 10 min period; and finally repeat for 15 min period. Use technic of loop sampling, flaming loop and mouths of tubes, and agitating medication and subculture tubes as in phenol coefficient method, **4.003**. Incubate subcultures 48 hr at 37° and read results. Resistance in 48–54 hr culture of *S. choleraesuis* should fall within range specified for 24 hr culture of *S. typhi* in phenol coefficient method.

Add 1 contaminated dried cylinder carrier at 1 min intervals to each of the 10 tubes of use-diln of germicide to be tested. Thus, by time 10 tubes have been seeded, 9 min will have elapsed, plus 1 min interval before transfer of first carrier in series to individual tube of subculture broth. This interval is const for each tube with prescribed exposure period of 10 min.

The 1 min interval between transfers allows adequate time for flaming and cooling nichrome wire hook and making transfer in manner so as to drain all excess medication from carrier. Flame lips of medication and subculture tubes in conventional manner. Immediately after placing carrier in medication tube, swirl tube 3 times before placing it back in bath. Thoroly shake subculture tubes, incubate 48 hr at 37°, and report results as + (growth) or − (no growth) values.

Where there is reason to suspect that lack of growth at conclusion of incubation period may be due to bacteriostatic action of medicant adsorbed on carrier that has not been neutzd by subculture medium used, transfer each ring to new tube of sterile medium and reincubate for addnl 48 hr at 37°. Where soln under test is such that material adsorbed on ring carriers and transferred into subculture medium makes it unsuitable for growth of test organism, as may be case with concd acids and alkalies, products carrying antibiotics, and wax emulsions, transfer each ring to new tube of sterile medium 30 min after initial transfer and incubate both primary and secondary subculture tubes 48 hr at 37°. Results showing no growth on all 10 carriers will confirm phenol coefficient number found. Results showing growth on any of the 10 carriers indicate phenol coefficient number to be unsafe guide to diln for use. In latter case, repeat test, using lower dilns (higher concns) of germicide under study. Max. diln of germicide which kills test organism on 10 carriers in 10 min interval represents presumed max. safe use-diln for practical disinfection.

4.010 ***2. Using Staphylococcus aureus***

Proceed as in **4.009** except change phenol dilns and test organism to those specified in **4.005**. Use 48–54 hr culture of *Staph. aureus* FDA 209, ATCC No. 6538, having at least resistance specified for 24 hr culture at 20° in phenol coefficient method, **4.005**. Results showing growth on any of 10 carriers indicate that diln is too high for use in disinfecting where pyogenic bacteria must be killed. In such cases repeat test, using lower dilns (higher concns). Max. diln of germicide which kills both this test organism and *S. choleraesuis* on 10 carriers in 10 min interval represents max. presumed safe use-diln for disinfecting in hospitals, clinics, and other places where pyogenic bacteria have special significance.

Note: While killing in 10 of 10 replicates specified provides reasonably reliable index in most cases, killing in 59 out of 60 replicates is necessary for confidence level of 95%.

4.011 ***3. Using Pseudomonas aeruginosa***
Official First Action

Proceed as in **4.009**. Use 48–54 hr nutrient broth culture *Ps. aeruginosa* PRD 10 (ATCC 15442). Carry stock culture on BBL CTA (cystine trypticase agar) in stab culture incubated 48 hr at 37° and stored at 5° with transfer every 30 days. Transfer nutrient broth test cultures daily for 30-day intervals with incubation at 37°. Make fresh transfer from stock culture every 30 days. Do not shake 48–54 hr test culture but decant liq. culture aseptically, leaving pellicle behind, to obtain 20 mL culture for inoculating 20 carriers in medication tube.

Available Chlorine Germicidal Equivalent Concentration (3)—Official Final Action

(Applicable to H_2O-miscible disinfectants for detg available Cl germicidal equiv. concns with products offered for use as sanitizing rinses for previously cleaned nonporous surfaces, especially where speed of action and capacity are essential considerations)

4.012 ***Reagents***

Use reagents specified in **4.001** and **4.002(e)** and **(f)**, and in addn:

(a) *Sterile distilled H_2O.—See* **4.007(d)**.

(b) *Sterile phosphate buffer soln.*—pH 8.0. Add 97.5 mL soln contg 11.61 g anhyd. K_2HPO_4 in 1 L H_2O to 2.5 mL soln contg 9.08 g anhyd. KH_2PO_4 in 1 L H_2O and autoclave 20 min at 121° in cotton-plugged erlenmeyer.

(c) *NaOCl std stock soln.*—Approx. 5%. Store NaOCl stock soln in tightly closed bottle in refrigerator, and det. exact available Cl concn at frequent intervals by As_2O_3 titrn, **6.112**.

(d) *Test organisms.*—Use *S. typhi* ATCC No. 6539 or *Staph. aureus* ATCC No. 6538 or both.

4.013 ***Apparatus***

See **4.002**.

4.014 ***Operating Technic***

Det. resistance of test culture to phenol as in **4.001–4.005**, and use cultures with resistance specified. Prep., in sterile g-s cylinders, NaOCl solns contg 200, 100, and 50 ppm available Cl in sterile buffer soln, **4.012(b)**. Transfer 10 mL of each soln to 25 × 150 mm medication tubes, place tubes in 20° H_2O bath, and let come to temp.

Starting with tube contg 200 ppm available Cl, add 0.05 mL test culture prepd as in **4.002(e)**, shake, and return to H_2O bath. After 1 min, make transfer to tube of appropriate subculture medium, **4.001(d)**, using flamed 4 mm loop. At 1.5 min, add another 0.05 mL culture to the 200 ppm Cl soln, shake, and return to bath. After addnl 1 min interval (2.5 min in test), make second subculture in same manner, and in 30 sec, or at 3 min time in test, add another 0.05 mL culture, shaking and returning to H_2O bath. After another 1 min interval (4 min in test), make another transfer to tube of subculture medium.

Repeat operation to give total of 10 added increments. This requires total time of 14.5 min for each soln and addn of 0.5 mL total culture with subculture at std 1 min intervals after addn of culture aliquots. At conclusion of test shake all subculture tubes and incubate 48 hr at 37°.

Repeat operation with solns contg 100 and 50 ppm available Cl. Prep. soln of germicide to be tested at concn recommended

Table 4:01 Example for Determination of Chlorine Germicidal Equivalent Concentration

Germicide	Concn, ppm Avail. Cl	Subculture Series									
		1	2	3	4	5	6	7	8	9	10
NaOCl control	200	−	−	−	−	−	+	+	+	+	+
	100	−	−	−	+	+	+	+	+	+	+
	50	−	−	+	+	+	+	+	+	+	+
Unknown (X)	25	−	−	−	−	−	+	+	+	+	+
	20	−	−	−	−	+	+	+	+	+	+
	10	−	+	+	+	+	+	+	+	+	+

− = No growth + = growth

or selected for study in sterile H_2O in g-s graduate. Transfer 10 mL to 25 × 150 mm medication tubes, place in H_2O bath, and let come to temp. Repeat operation with this soln.

To be considered equiv. in disinfecting activity to 200 ppm available Cl, unknown germicide must show absence of growth in as many consecutive tubes of subculture tube series as 200 ppm available Cl std. Det. activity equiv. to 100 and 50 ppm available Cl in same manner. *See* example, Table **4:01**.

In this example, 25 ppm soln of germicide X could be considered equiv. to 200 ppm soln of available Cl, and 20 ppm soln equiv. to 100 ppm of available Cl, but 10 ppm soln of germicide X would not be considered equiv. in germicidal activity to 50 ppm of available Cl.

Draw conclusions relative to germicidal equiv. concns only when resistance of test culture to NaOCl control is such that ⩾1 neg. increment is obtained at 50 ppm concn and 1 pos. increment is obtained at 200 ppm level.

Sporicidal Test (*4*)—Official Final Action

(Suitable for detg sporicidal activity of liq. and gaseous chems. Applicable to germicides for detg presence or absence of sporicidal activity against specified spore-forming bacteria in various situations and potential efficacy as sterilizing agent.)

4.015 *Reagents*

(a) *Culture media.—(1) Soil extract nutrient broth.*—Ext 1 lb garden soil in 1 L H_2O, filter several times thru S&S No. 588 paper, and dil. to vol. (pH should be ⩾5.2). Add 5 g beef ext. (Difco), 5 g NaCl, and 10 g peptone (Anatone, **4.001(a)**). Boil 20 min, dil. to vol., adjust with 1*N* NaOH to pH 6.9, and filter thru paper. Dispense in 10 mL portions into 25 × 150 mm tubes, and autoclave 20 min at 121°. Use this broth to propagate test culture of *Bacilli*.

(*2*) *Nutrient agar.—See* **4.001(c)**. Use slants of this medium to maintain stock culture of *Bacilli.*

(*3*) *Modified fluid thioglycolate medium USP XX.*—Prep. as in **4.001(d)**(*2*), except add 20 mL 1*N* NaOH to each L before dispensing for sterilization. Use this medium to subculture spores exposed to 2.5*N* HCl. For spores exposed to unknown germicides, use fluid thioglycolate medium, **4.001(d)**(*2*).

(*4*) *Soil extract-egg-meat medium.*—Add 1.5 g Bacto Egg-Meat Medium dehydrated (Difco) to 25 × 150 mm tube; then add 15 mL garden soil ext, (*1*), and sterilize 20 min at 121°. Use this medium to propagate test cultures of *Clostridia* and maintain stock cultures of species of this genus.

(b) *Test organisms.*—Use *Bacillus subtilis,* ATCC No. 19659, or *Clostridium sporogenes,* ATCC No. 3584, for routine evaluation. Method is also applicable for use with strains of *B. anthracis, Cl. tetani,* or other spore forming species.

(c) *Dilute hydrochloric acid.*—2.5*N*. Use to det. resistance of dried spores. Stdze and adjust to 2.5*N* as in **50.012**.

4.016 *Apparatus*

(a) *Glassware.*—Bacteriological culture tubes, unflared, 25 × 150 mm; 100 mL g-s cylinders graduated in 1 mL divisions; 65 mm id funnels; supply of 15 × 110 mm petri dishes matted with 2 sheets 9 cm S&S No. 597 or Whatman No. 2 filter paper. Sterilize all glassware and matted petri dishes 2 hr in air oven at 180°.

(b) *Water bath.—See* **4.002(b)**.

(c) *Racks.—See* **4.002(c)**.

(d) *Transfer loop, hook, and forceps.—See* **4.008(c)**.

(e) *Tissue grinder.*—Arthur H. Thomas Co., No. 3431-E20, Size B, or equiv.

(f) *Suture loop carrier.*—From spool of size 3 surgical silk suture, prep. std loops by wrapping the silk around ordinary pencil 3 times, slipping coil so formed off end of pencil, and holding it firmly with thumb and index finger of left hand while passing another piece of suture through coil, knotting, and tying securely. Then shear off end of coil and knotted suture to within 2 mm. This should provide overall length of ca 65 mm of suture in 2-loop coil that can be conveniently handled in ordinary aseptic transfer procedure.

Ext loops in groups of 20 by immersion in 10 mL pet ether in stoppered, unflared test tube, shaking frequently during 30 min at room temp., and hold overnight (18–24 hr) at 2–5°. Shake, remove loops, drain, and dry.

(g) *Cylinder carriers.*—"Penicylinders," porcelain, 8±1 mm od, 6±1 mm id, 10±1 mm long. (Available from Fisher Scientific Co., No. 7-907.) Sterilize 2 hr in 180° air oven. Wash used Penicylinders with Triton X-100 and rinse with H_2O 4 times.

4.017 *Operating Technic*

Grow all *Bacilli* in soil ext nutrient broth and all *Clostridia* in soil ext-meat-egg medium. Inoculate 3 tubes, using 1 loop stock culture, and incubate 72 hr at 37°. Place supply of suture loops and cylinder carriers in sep. petri dishes matted with filter paper, and sterilize 20 min at 121°. Use new loops for each test. Penicylinders must be free from chips or cracks. Filter *Cl. sporogenes* thru funnel contg 2 × 5 × 5 cm sq piece of moist cotton or glass wool into sterile 25 × 150 mm test tubes, using same funnel. In prepg *B. subtilis* culture, pour tube of 72 hr culture into tissue grinder and macerate to break up pellicle. Filter thru sterile funnel contg moist cotton or glass wool into sterile 25 × 150 mm tube, repeating operation for other 2 tubes. Place 10 sterile suture loops or Penicylinders into each of 3 tubes contg 10 mL filtrate from 72 hr culture of *Cl. sporogenes,* agitate, and let stand 10–15 min. Using this technic, contaminate 35 loops or cylinders. Place contaminated suture loops and/or cylinders into petri dish matted with 2 layers of filter paper. Drain. Proceed similarly for *B. subtilis.*

Place the 35 suture loops or cylinders contaminated with *Cl. sporogenes* or *B. subtilis* in vac. desiccator contg $CaCl_2$ and draw vac. of 69 cm (27") Hg for 20 min. Dry 24 hr under vac. (Spores dried and held under these conditions will retain resistance ⩾7 days.)

Transfer 10 mL 2.5*N* HCl, **4.015(c)**, into sterile 25 × 150 mm tube. Place tube in 20° const temp. H_2O bath and let come to temp. Rapidly transfer 4 dried, contaminated loop or cylinder carriers to acid tube. Transfer remaining dried, contaminated suture loop or cylinder carriers to tube of thioglycolate subculture medium, **4.015(a)**(*3*), as viability control. After 2, 5, 10, and 20 min, withdraw individual loops or cylinders from acid and transfer to individual tubes of subculture medium. Rotate each tube vigorously 20 sec and resubtransfer. Incubate 21 days at 37°. Test spores should resist HCl ⩾2 min, and many may resist HCl for full 20 min.

When testing sporicidal or sterilizing activity of gas, place carriers in polyethylene bags or in petri dishes with lids ajar. Certain gases may require rehydration of spores before exposure to gas. Rehydrate spores on carriers by 1 hr immersion in H_2O, using ⩽20 mL H_2O/6 carriers. Drain carriers 20 min on petri dishes matted with filter paper. After exposure to gas, remove carriers, using aseptic technic to subculture media as specified in next par.

For aq. sporicides and sterilizers, place 10 mL product at diln recommended for use or under investigation into each of six 25 × 150 mm tubes. Place tubes in 20° H_2O bath and let come to temp. Using flamed forceps, place 5 suture loops or cylinders, contaminated with *Cl. sporogenes* or *B. subtilis* and dried 24 hr under vac., into each of the 6 tubes contg disinfectant, using 2-min intervals for seeding each tube. Five suture loops or cylinders can be placed into each tube within 5 sec. This seeding operation will take 10 min. After contact period specified for disinfectant has been achieved, remove suture loops or cylinders, using sterilized needle hook, from each tube of disinfectant to subculture medium or other subculture medium specified in **4.001(d)** (select medium contg most suitable neutralizer), placing 1 suture loop or cylinder per tube. Five cylinders can be removed within each 2 min interval. Flame transfer needle hook after each carrier has been transferred to subculture medium. After completing transfer, resubtransfer each suture loop or cylinder to fresh tube of thioglycolate medium and incubate 21 days at 37°. If no growth is observed after 21 days, heat-shock tubes 20 min at 80° and reincubate 72 hr at 37°. Report results as + (growth) or − (no growth) values.

Killing in 59 of 60 replicates on 1 carrier at diln and time specified is considered evidence of sporicidal efficacy against 1 test spore and for confidence level of 95%. Tests with both *B. subtilis* and *Cl. sporogenes,* using 30 replicates with each of 2 carriers specified to provide min. of 120 carriers, are required to presumptively support unqualified sporicidal claim or for presumptive evidence of sterilizing activity at concn, time, and conditions specified. For sporicidal claims, no more than 2 failures can be tolerated in this 120 carrier trial. For sterilizing claims, no failures can be tolerated.

Fungicidal Test (*5*)—Official Final Action

(Applicable for use with H_2O-miscible type fungicides used to disinfect inanimate objects)

Using Trichophyton mentagrophytes

4.018 ***Test Organism***

Use as test fungus typical strain of *Trichophyton mentagrophytes* isolated from dermatophytosis of foot. Strain must sporulate freely on artificial media, presence of abundant conidia being manifested by powdery appearance on surface of 10-day culture, particularly at top of agar slant, and confirmed by microscopic examination. Conidia-bearing mycelium should peel easily from surface of glucose agar. Conidia of required resistance survive 10 min exposure at 20° to phenol diln of 1:70, but not to one of 1:60. Strain No. 640, ATCC No. 9533, is suitable.

4.019 ***Culture Medium***

Carry fungus on agar slants of following composition: Glucose 2%, Neopeptone (Difco) 1%, agar 2%, adjusted to pH 6.1–6.3. Use same culture medium to prep. cultures for obtaining conidial suspension, and use fluid medium of same nutrient composition (without agar) to test viability of conidia after exposure to fungicide.

4.020 ***Care of Fungus Strain***

Store stock culture of fungus on glucose agar slants at 2–5°. At intervals ≤3 months, transfer to fresh agar slants, incubate 10 days at 25–30°, and store at 2–5° until next transfer period. Do not use culture that has been kept at or above room temp. >10 days as source of inoculum for culture. (Cultures may be kept at room temp. to preserve strain and to inoculate cultures if transferred at intervals ≤10 days.)

4.021 ***Preparation of Conidial Suspension***

Prep. petri dish cultures by planting inoculum at center of agar plate and incubating culture at 25–30° for ≥10, but ≤15 days. Remove mycelial mats from surface of 5 agar plate cultures, using sterile spatula or heavy flattened wire. Transfer to heat-sterilized glass tissue grinder, **4.016(e)**, and macerate with 25 mL sterile physiological NaCl soln (0.85% NaCl), or to heat-sterilized erlenmeyer contg 25 mL sterile saline with glass beads, and shake thoroly. Filter suspension thru sterile absorbent cotton to remove hyphal elements. Est. density of conidial suspension by counting in hemacytometer and store at 2–10° as stock spore suspension (125–155 × 10^6 conidia/mL) for ≤4 weeks for use in prepg test suspensions of conidia. Stdze test conidial suspensions as needed by dilg stock spore suspension with physiological NaCl soln so that it contains 5 × 10^6 conidia/mL.

4.022 ***Operating Technic***

Prep. dilns of fungicide. (Tests are similar to those described in **4.003**.) Place 5 mL of each fungicide soln and of phenol control solns in 25 × 150 mm test-culture tubes, arrange in order of ascending dilns, place tubes in 20° H_2O bath, and let come to temp. With graduated pipet, place 0.5 mL spore suspension in first tube of fungicidal soln, shake, and immediately replace in H_2O bath; 30 sec later add 0.5 mL conidial suspension to second tube. Repeat at 30 sec intervals for each fungicidal diln. If more convenient, run test at 20 sec intervals. After 5, 10, and 15 min exposure to fungicide, remove sample from each conidia-fungicide mixt. with 4 mm loop and place in 10 mL glucose broth, **4.019**. To eliminate risk of faulty results due to possible fungistatic action, make subtransfers from the initial glucose broth subculture tubes to fresh tubes of glucose broth, using the 4 mm loop before incubation, or make initial subcultures in glucose broth contg either 0.05% Na thioglycolate, 1.5% isooctylphenoxy-polyethoxy-ethanol, or mixt. of 0.07% lecithin (Azolectin, Associated Concentrates, Inc., 32–30 61st St, Woodside, NY 11377) and 0.5% polysorbate 80 (Tween 80), whichever gives lowest result. Incubate inoculated tubes at 25–30°. Read final results after 10 days, altho indicative reading can be made in 4 days.

Note: Highest diln that kills spores within 10 min is commonly considered as highest diln that could be expected to disinfect inanimate surfaces contaminated with pathogenic fungi.

Germicidal and Detergent Sanitizers (*6*) Official Final Action

(Suitable for detg min. concn of chem. that can be permitted for use in sanitizing precleaned, nonporous food contact surfaces. Min. recommended starting concn is 2–4× this concn. Test also dets max. water hardness for claimed concns. As control, check accuracy of hard-water tolerance results with pure C_{14} alkyl dimethyl benzyl NH_4 chloride (Onyx Chemical Co. 190 Warren St, Jersey City, NJ 07302) at 700 and 900 ppm hardness, and pure C_{16} alkyl dimethyl benzyl NH_4 chloride (Cetalkonium Chloride, Sterling Chemical Co.), at 400 and 550 ppm hardness, expressed as $CaCO_3$.)

4.023 ***Reagents***

(a) *Culture media.—(1) Nutrient agar A.*—Boil 3 g beef ext, 5 g peptone (Bacto or equiv.; special grades must not be used), and 15 g salt-free agar in 1 L H_2O. Do not use premixed, dehydrated media. Tube, and autoclave 20 min at 121°. Use for daily transfer of test culture. *(2) Nutrient agar B.*—Prep. as above but use 30 g agar. Use for growing test cultures in French square bottles. *(3) Nutrient agar (AOAC).—See* **4.001(c)**. Use for prepg stock culture slants.

(b) *Subculture media.—(1)* Use tryptone glucose ext agar (Difco), adding 25 mL stock neutralizer, **(c)**/L. *(2)* Tryptone glucose ext agar (Difco).

(c) *Neutralizer stock soln.*—Mix 40 g Azolectin (Associated Concentrates, 32–30 61st St, Woodside, NY 11377), 280 mL polysorbate 80, and 1.25 mL phosphate buffer, (**e**); dil. with H_2O to 1 L and adjust to pH 7.2. Dispense in 100 mL portions and autoclave 20 min at 121°.

(**d**) *Neutralizer blanks.*—For use with ≤200 ppm quaternary NH_4 compd. Mix 100 mL neutralizer stock soln, (**c**), 25 mL 0.25*M* phosphate buffer stock soln, (**e**), and 1675 mL H_2O. Dispense 9 mL portions into 20 × 150 mm tubes. Autoclave 20 min at 121°.

(**e**) *Phosphate buffer stock soln.*—0.25*M*. Dissolve 34.0 g KH_2PO_4 in 500 mL H_2O, adjust to pH 7.2 with 1*N* NaOH, and dil. to 1 L.

(**f**) *Phosphate buffer dilution water.*—Add 1.25 mL 0.25*M* phosphate buffer stock soln, (**e**), to 1 L H_2O and dispense in 99 mL portions. Autoclave 20 min at 121°.

(**g**) *Test organisms.*—Use *Escherichia coli* ATCC No. 11229 or *Staphylococcus aureus* ATCC 6538. Incubate 24 and 48 hr, resp. Maintain stock cultures on nutrient agar (AOAC), (**a**)(*3*), at refrigerator temp.

4.024 ***Resistance to Phenol of Test Cultures***

Det. resistance to phenol at least every 3 months by **4.001–4.005**. Resistance of *E. coli* should be equiv. to that specified for *S. typhi* in **4.004** and that for *Staph. aureus* equiv. to that specified for this organism in **4.005**.

4.025 ***Apparatus***

(**a**) *Glassware.*—250 mL wide-mouth erlenmeyers; 100 mL graduate; Mohr, serological, and/or bacteriological (APHA specification) pipets; 20 × 150 mm test tubes. Sterilize at 180° in hot air oven ≥2 hr.

(**b**) *Petri dishes.*—Sterile.

(**c**) *French square bottles.*—175 mL, borosilicate. Use of other containers will give variable results.

(**d**) *Water bath.*—Controlled at 25°.

4.026 ***Preparation of Culture Suspension***

From stock culture inoculate tube of nutrient agar *A*, **4.023(a)**(*1*), and make ≥3 consecutive daily transfers (≤30), incubating transfers 20–24 hr at 35–37°. Do not use transfers >30 days. If only 1 daily transfer has been missed, no special procedures are required; if 2 daily transfers are missed, repeat with 3 daily transfers.

Prep. 175 mL French square culture bottles contg 20 mL nutrient agar *B*, **4.023(a)**(*2*), autoclave 20 min at 121°, and let solidify with bottle in horizontal position. Inoculate culture bottles by washing growth from slant with 5 mL phosphate buffer diln H_2O, **4.023(f)**, into 99 mL phosphate buffer diln H_2O, and adding 2 mL of this suspension to each culture bottle, tilting back and forth to distribute suspension; then drain excess liq. Incubate 18–24 hr at 35–37°, agar side down. Remove culture from agar surface of 4 or more bottles, using 3 mL phosphate buffer diln H_2O and glass beads in each bottle to suspend growth. Filter suspension thru Whatman No. 2 paper prewet with 1 mL sterile phosphate buffer, and collect in sterile tube. (To hasten filtration, rub paper gently with sterile policeman.) Stdze suspension to give av. of 10 × 10^9 organisms/mL by diln with sterile phosphate buffer diln H_2O, **4.023(f)**.

If Lumetron colorimeter is used, dil. suspension in sterile Lumetron tube to give % *T* according to Table **4:02**.

If McFarland nephelometer and $BaSO_4$ stds are used, select 7 tubes of same id as that contg test culture suspension. Place 10 mL of each suspension of $BaSO_4$, prepd as indicated in Table **4:03**, in each tube and seal tube. Stdze suspension to correspond to No. 4 std.

Table 4:03 Preparation of $BaSO_4$ Suspensions Corresponding to Bacterial Concentrations

Std No.	mL 2% $BaCl_2$ Soln	mL 1% H_2SO_4 (v/v) Soln	Av. Bacterial Count/mL
1	4.0	96.0	5.0 × 10^9
2	5.0	95.0	7.5
3	6.0	94.0	8.5
4	7.0	93.0	10.0
5	8.0	92.0	12.0
6	10.0	90.0	13.5
7	12.0	88.0	15.0

4.027 ***Synthetic Hard Water***

Prep. *Soln 1* by dissolving 31.74 g $MgCl_2$ (or equiv. of hydrates) and 73.99 g $CaCl_2$ in boiled distd H_2O and dilg to 1 L. Prep. *Soln 2* by dissolving 56.03 g $NaHCO_3$ in boiled distd H_2O and dilg to 1 L. *Soln 1* may be heat sterilized; *Soln 2* must be sterilized by filtration. Place required amt *Soln 1* in sterile 1 L flask and add ≥600 mL sterile distd H_2O; then add 4 mL *Soln 2* and dil. to 1 L with sterile distd H_2O. Each mL *Soln 1* will give a water equiv. to ca 100 ppm of hardness calcd as $CaCO_3$ by formula:

$$\text{Total hardness as ppm } CaCO_3 = 2.495 \times \text{ppm Ca} + 4.115 \times \text{ppm Mg}.$$

pH of all test waters ≤2000 ppm hardness should be 7.6–8.0. Check prepd synthetic waters chemically for hardness at time of tests, using following method or other methods described in 14th Ed. of *Standard Methods for the Examination of Water, Sewage, and Industrial Wastes.*

4.028 ***Hardness Method***

(**a**) *EDTA std soln.*—Dissolve 4.0 g $Na_2H_2EDTA.2H_2O$ and 0.10 g $MgCl_2.6H_2O$ in 800 mL H_2O and adjust by subsequent diln so that 1 mL of soln is equiv. to 1 mg $CaCO_3$ when titrd as in (**c**). Check EDTA soln after prepn or, if com. purchased, against $CaCO_3$ std at least every 2 months.

(**b**) *Calcium std soln.*—1 mL = 1 mg $CaCO_3$. Weigh 1.00 g $CaCO_3$, dried overnight or longer at 105°, into 500 mL erlenmeyer and add dil. HCl thru funnel until $CaCO_3$ is dissolved. Add 200 mL H_2O, boil to expel CO_2, and cool. Add few drops Me red indicator and adjust color to intermediate orange with dil. NH_4OH or HCl as required. Transfer quant. to 1 L vol. flask and dil. to vol.

Table 4:02 Per Cent Light Transmission at Various Wavelengths Corresponding to Bacterial Concentrations

% Light Transmission with Filters, nm							Av. Bacterial Count/mL
370	420	490	530	550	580	650	
7.0	4.0	6.0	6.0	6.0	7.0	8.0	13.0 × 10^9
8.0	5.0	7.0	7.0	7.0	8.0	9.0	11.5
9.0	6.0	8.0	8.0	8.0	9.0	10.0	10.2
10.0	7.0	9.0	9.0	9.0	11.0	11.0	8.6
11.0	8.0	10.0	10.0	10.0	12.0	13.0	7.7
13.0	9.0	12.0	12.0	12.0	13.0	15.0	6.7

(c) *Determination.*—Dil. 5–25 mL sample (depending on hardness) to 50 mL with H_2O in erlenmeyer or casserole. Add 1 mL *buffer soln* (67.5 g NH_4Cl and 570 mL NH_4OH dild to 1 L with H_2O), 1 mL *inhibitor* (5.0 g $Na_2S.9H_2O$ or 3.7 g $Na_2S.5H_2O$ dissolved in 100 mL H_2O), and 1 or 2 drops *indicator soln* (0.5 g Chrome Black T in 100 mL 60–80% alcohol). Titr. with EDTA std soln slowly, stirring continuously, until last reddish tinge disappears from soln, adding last few drops at 3–5 sec intervals. Hardness as mg $CaCO_3$/L = (mL std soln × 1000)/mL sample.

4.029 ***Preparation of Samples***

Use composition declared or detd as guide to sample wt required for vol. sterile H_2O used to prep. 20,000 ppm soln. From this stock diln, transfer 1 mL into 99 mL of the water to be used in test to give concn of 200 ppm. In making transfer, fill 1 mL pipet and drain back into stock soln; then refill, to correct for adsorption on glass. After mixing, discard 1 mL to provide 99 mL of the test water in **4.030**.

4.030 ***Operating Technic***

Measure 99 mL water to be used in test, contg bactericide at concn to be tested, into chem. clean, sterile, 250 mL wide-mouth erlenmeyer and place in const temp. bath until it reaches 25°, or ≥20 min. Prep. duplicate flasks for each germicide to be tested. Also prep. similar flask contg 99 mL sterile phosphate buffer diln H_2O, **4.023(f)**, as "initial numbers" control.

Add 1 mL culture suspension to each test flask as follows: Whirl flask, stopping just before suspension is added, creating enough residual motion of liq. to prevent pooling of suspension at point of contact with test water. Add suspension midway between center and edge of surface with tip of pipet slightly immersed in test soln. Avoid touching pipet to neck or side of flask during addn. Transfer 1 mL portions of this exposed culture to neutralizer blanks exactly 30 and 60 sec after addn of suspension. Mix well immediately after transfer.

For "numbers control" transfer, add 1 mL culture suspension to 99 mL sterile phosphate diln H_2O in same manner. In case of numbers control, plants need be made only immediately after adding and mixing thoroly ≤30 sec. (It is advantageous to use milk pipets to add culture and withdraw samples.)

Plate from neutralizer tube to agar, using subculture medium **4.023(b)**(*1*) for quaternary NH_4 compds and **4.023(b)**(*2*) with numbers control. Where 0.1 mL portions are planted, use 1 mL pipet graduated in 0.1 mL intervals. For dilns to give countable plates, use phosphate buffer diln H_2O, **4.023(f)**. For numbers control, use following diln procedure: Transfer 1 mL exposed culture (1 mL culture suspension transferred to 99 mL phosphate buffer diln H_2O in H_2O bath) to 99 mL phosphate buffer diln H_2O, **4.023(f)**, (*diln 1*). Shake thoroly and transfer 1 mL *diln 1* to 99 mL phosphate buffer diln H_2O, **4.023(f)**, (*diln 2*). Shake thoroly and transfer 1 mL *diln 2* to 99 mL phosphate buffer diln H_2O (*diln 3*). Shake thoroly and transfer four 1 mL and four 0.1 mL aliquots from *diln 3* to individual sterile petri dishes.

For test samples, use following diln procedure: Transfer 1 mL exposed culture into 9 mL neutralizer, **4.023(d)**. Shake and transfer four 1 mL and four 0.1 mL aliquots to individual sterile petri dishes. For numbers control, use subculture medium **4.023(b)**(*2*); for tests with quaternary NH_4 compds, use medium **4.023(b)**(*1*). Cool agar to solidify, and then invert and incubate 48 hr at 35° before counting.

4.031 ***Results***

To be considered valid, results must meet std effectiveness: 99.999% reduction in count of number of organisms within 30 sec. Report results according to actual count and % reduction over numbers control. Counts on numbers control for germicide test mixt. should fall between 75 and 125 × 10^6/mL for % reductions to be considered valid.

4.032 ***Sterility Controls***

(a) *Neutralizer.*—Plate 1 mL from previously unopened tube.
(b) *Water.*—Plate 1 mL from each type of water used.
(c) *Sterile distilled water.*—Plate 1 mL.

After counting plates, confirm that surviving organisms are *E. coli* by transfer to brilliant green bile broth fermentation tubes or lactose broth and EMB agar; confirm *Staph. aureus* by microscopic examination.

Germicidal Spray Products (7)—Official Final Action

(Suitable for detg effectiveness of sprays and pressurized spray products as spot disinfectants for contaminated surfaces)

4.033 ***Reagents***

Use culture media and reagents specified in **4.001**, **4.002(e)** and **(f)**, and **4.007** except that test organism *Salmonella typhi* is not used.

Use as test organisms *Trichophyton mentagrophytes* ATCC No. 9533, prepd as in **4.021**, to which has been added 0.02 mL octylphenoxy-polyethoxy-ethanol (Triton X100, Rohm & Haas)/10 mL suspension to facilitate spreading, *Salmonella choleraesuis* ATCC No. 10708, **4.007(b)**, *Staphylococcus aureus* ATCC No. 6538, maintained as in **4.007(b)**, and *Pseudomonas aeruginosa* ATCC No. 15442, maintained as in **4.011**.

4.034 ***Apparatus***

Use app. specified in **4.002** and **4.008**, and in addn:
(a) *Capillary pipets.*—0.1 mL, graduated to deliver 0.01 mL. Sterilize in air oven 2 hr at 180°.
(b) *Microscope slides.*—Non-corrosive, 25 × 25 mm (1 × 1"), or 18 × 36 mm glass slide. Sterilize by placing individual slides in petri dish matted with 2 pieces 9 cm filter paper (Whatman No. 2, or equiv.) in air oven 2 hr at 180°.
(c) *Bacteriological culture tubes.*—Pyrex, 32 × 200 mm.
(d) *Metal forceps.*—Sharp points, straight, 115 mm long.

4.035 ***Operating Technic***

Thoroly shake 48 hr nutrient broth cultures of *S. choleraesuis* and *Staph. aureus* and let settle 10 min. With sterile capillary pipet or sterile 4.0 mm loop, transfer 0.01 mL culture onto 1 sq in. sterile test slide in petri dish and immediately spread uniformly over entire area. Cover dish immediately and repeat operation until 12 slides have been prepd for each organism. (Use 2 slides as control.) Dry all slides 30–40 min at 37°.

Spray 10 slides for specified time and distance. Hold each slide 10 min, drain off excess liq., and transfer slide to individual 32 × 200 mm tube contg 20 mL appropriate subculture medium, **4.001(d)**, with flamed forceps. Shake culture thoroly. If broth appears cloudy after 30 min, make subculture to fresh individual tubes of subculture broth. Transfer 2 unsprayed slides, as viability controls, to individual subculture tubes in same manner.

Incubate all tubes used for primary and secondary transfers 48 hr at 37°. Read as + (growth) or − (no growth). Killing of test organisms in 10 of 10 trials is presumptive evidence of disinfecting action.

Det. resistance of *S. choleraesuis* as in **4.003**; with *S. aureus* as in **4.005**; with *Ps. aeruginosa* as in **4.006**; and with *T. mentagrophytes* as in **4.018**.

If there is reason to believe that lack of growth in subtransfer tubes is due to bacteriostasis, inoculate all incubated subculture tubes with loop needle inoculation of respective test culture and reincubate. Growth of these inocula eliminates bacteriostasis as cause of lack of growth. If there is question as to possibility of contamination as source of growth in subculture tubes, make gram stains and/or subculture for identification, according to respective test culture.

If fungicidal activity as well as germicidal activity is involved, use test suspension of *T. mentagrophytes* spores, **4.021**, and prep. 12 slides, using 0.01 mL std spore suspension, spraying and subculturing exactly as above. Make subcultures in glucose broth, **4.019**, incubating 7 days at 25–30°.

Water Disinfectants for Swimming Pools (*8*)
Official Final Action

(Suitable for presumptive evidence of acceptability of products for disinfecting swimming pool water)

4.036 ***Test Culture Media***

(**a**) *Nutrient Agar A.—See* **4.023(a)**(*1*).

(**b**) *Nutrient Agar B* (Trypticase Soy Agar, BBL). *—See* **4.037(b)**.

(**c**) *Nutrient Agar C.*—Prep. as in **4.001(c)**.

4.037 ***Subculture Media***

(**a**) *Tryptone glucose extract agar (Difco)*.— Dissolve 24 g in 1 L freshly distd H_2O and heat to bp to dissolve completely. Autoclave 15 min at 121°. Use for plate counts of *E. coli* survivors.

(**b**) *Trypticase soy agar (BBL)*.—Suspend 40 g powder in 1 L H_2O. Let stand 5 min and mix thoroly. Heat gently with occasional agitation and boil ca 1 min or until soln is complete. Autoclave 15 min at 121°. Let cool and reautoclave 15 min at 121°. Use for plate counts of *S. faecalis* survivors.

(**c**) *Fluid thioglycolate medium (Difco)*.—*See* **4.001(d)**(*2*).

(**d**) *Lactose broth (Difco)*.—Dissolve 19 g in 1 L H_2O. Dispense 10 mL portions into tubes with fermentation vials. Autoclave 15 min at 121°. Use for detg presence of *E. coli* survivors.

(**e**) *Eosin methylene blue agar (Difco)*.—Suspend 36 g in 1 L H_2O and heat to bp to dissolve completely. Autoclave 15 min at 121°. Use for confirming *E. coli* survivors.

(**f**) *S-F agar (Difco)*.—Dissolve 36 g in 1 L H_2O. Add 15 g agar and heat to bp to dissolve completely. Autoclave 15 min at 121°. Use for confirming *S. faecalis* survivors.

4.038 ***Neutralizer Stock Solns***

(**a**) *Sodium thiosulfate soln.*—Dissolve 1 g $Na_2S_2O_3$ in 1 L H_2O. Dispense in 100 mL portions and autoclave 20 min at 15 lb.

(**b**) *Azolectin soln.—See* **4.023(c)**.

(**c**) *Other preparations.*—Prepns found to be suitable and necessary, depending upon nature of germicidal prepns to be tested.

4.039 ***Neutralizer Blanks***

(**a**) *With 0.6 ppm residual chlorine or less.*—Dil. 10 mL neutralizer stock soln, **4.038(a)**, with 90 mL sterile H_2O. Dispense aseptically in 9 mL portions into sterile 25 × 150 mm tubes.

(**b**) *With quaternary ammonium compounds and phenolic derivatives.*—Mix 10 mL neutralizer stock soln, **4.038(b)**, 2.5 mL 0.25*M* phosphate buffer stock soln, **4.040(a)**, and 167.5 mL H_2O. Dispense in 9 mL portions into 20 × 150 mm tubes. Autoclave 20 min at 121°.

(**c**) *Other preparations.*—Use dilns of **4.038(c)** as suitable.

4.040 ***Reagents***

(**a**) *Phosphate buffer stock soln.*—0.25*M. See* **4.023(e)**.

(**b**) *Phosphate buffer dilution water.*—See **4.023(f)**.

(**c**) *Sodium thiosulfate std solns.*—(*1*) *0.1N*. Dissolve exactly 24.820 g $Na_2S_2O_3.5H_2O$ in H_2O and dil. to 1 L. Stdze as in **50.038**.

(*2*) *0.001N.*—Dil. 10 mL soln (*1*) to 1 L with H_2O.

(**d**) *Starch indicator soln.—See* **6.005(f)**, except use few drops $CHCl_3$ instead of Hg as preservative.

(**e**) *Sterile phosphate buffer stock solns.*—(*1*) Dissolve 11.61 g anhyd. K_2HPO_4 in 1 L H_2O and autoclave 20 min at 121°. (*2*) Dissolve 9.08 g anhyd. KH_2PO_4 in 1 L H_2O and autoclave 20 min at 121°.

(**f**) *NaOCl stock soln.*—Approx. 5%. Store NaOCl stock soln in tightly closed bottle in refrigerator and det. exact available Cl at frequent intervals by As_2O_3 titrn, **6.112**.

(**g**) *Test organism.*—Use *Escherichia coli* ATCC 11229 and *Streptococcus faecalis* PRD (Microbiology Lab., Benefits and Field Services Div., EPA, Beltsville, MD 20705). Maintain, by monthly transfer, stock cultures of *E. coli* on *Nutrient Agar C,* **4.001(c)**, and *S. faecalis* on *Nutrient Agar B,* **4.037(b)**; store at 4–5°.

4.041 ***Apparatus***

(**a**) *Glassware.*—500 mL wide-mouth erlenmeyers; 100 mL graduates; Mohr pipets; milk pipets; 20 × 150 mm tubes; Board of Health tubes; 200, 500, and 1000 mL vol. flasks. Wash in strong, fresh chromic acid cleaning soln, and fill and drain with H_2O ≥3 times. Heat ≥2 hr at 180° in hot air oven.

(**b**) *Petri dishes.*—Sterile.

(**c**) *Water bath.*—Controlled at 20 or 25°.

4.042 ***Preparation of Culture Suspension***

From stock culture, inoculate tube Nutrient Agar A for *E. coli* and Nutrient Agar B for *S. faecalis;* make ≥3 consecutive daily transfers (≤30), incubating transfer 20–24 hr at 35–37°. Do not transfer >30 days. If only 1 daily transfer has been missed, no special procedures are required; if 2 daily transfers are missed, repeat with 3 daily transfers. Remove culture from agar surface, using 5 mL phosphate buffer diln H_2O, **4.040(b)**. Transfer culture suspension to sterile centrf. tube and centrf. 1–2 min at speed necessary to settle agar particles. Transfer supernate to another sterile centrf. tube and centrf. to obtain complete sepn of cells. Discard supernate and resuspend cells in 5 mL buffer diln H_2O. With *S. faecalis,* centrf., discard supernate, and resuspend cells in 5 mL buffer diln H_2O 2 addnl times. Finally, stdze suspension to give av. of 2.0×10^8 organisms/mL by diln with sterile phosphate diln H_2O.

If Lumetron is used, dil. suspension in sterile Lumetron tube to give % *T* according to Table **4:04**. Make serial diln plate count of each culture suspension before use, using phosphate buffer diln H_2O, **4.040(b)**, and subculture medium, **4.037(a)**, with *E. coli*, and (**b**) with *S. faecalis.* Incubate diln plates in inverted position 48 hr at 35–37°. Use Quebec Colony Counting Chamber and report results in terms of number of bacteria/mL suspension.

Table 4:04 Per Cent Light Transmission at Various Wavelengths Corresponding to Bacterial Concentrations

	% Light Transmission with Filter, nm						Av. Bacterial Count /mL
	370	420	490	530	580	650	
E. coli	90	88	89	88	91	92	2.0×10^8
S. faecalis	86	82	85	85	87	89	2.0×10^8

Count of 2.0×10^8 is desired so that 1 mL test culture suspension + 199 mL test soln will provide soln contg 1×10^6 organisms/mL. Permitted variation in test culture suspension is +500,000 and −100,000/mL of 200 mL test soln. Use actual count for calcg zero time count in later tests.

4.043 ***Determining Chlorine Demand of Freshly Distilled Test Water***

Place 200 mL H_2O in each of five 500 mL erlenmeyers. To flasks 1–5, resp., add 0.025, 0.05, 0.075, 0.1, and 0.15 mL of 200 ppm available Cl prepd from NaOCl soln, **4.040(f)**. Shake each flask, and let stand several min. Add crystal KI and 1 mL HOAc, and swirl. Add 1 mL starch soln, **4.040(d)**. Flask showing perceptible blue indicates Cl demand has been satisfied.

4.044 ***Operating Technic***

Place ca 600 mL freshly sterilized distd H_2O in 1 L vol. flask. Add ca 1.5–3.0 mL K_2HPO_4 buffer, **4.040(e)**(*1*), and 0.5 mL KH_2PO_4, **4.040(e)**(*2*), and dil. to 900 mL. Add enough NaOCl from suitable diluent of std stock soln, **4.040(f)**, to satisfy Cl demand of 1 L test H_2O, **4.043**, and to provide ca 0.6 ppm residual available Cl. Dil. to vol. (Example: If Cl demand of H_2O is 0.1 ppm, add 3.5 mL of 200 ppm soln of available Cl made from std stock NaOCl soln, **4.040(f)**, and dil. to vol. This should provide soln with ca 0.6 ppm residual available Cl at pH 7.5 ± 0.1.) Transfer 199 mL of this test soln to each of three 500 mL erlenmeyers and place in H_2O bath at either 20 or 25°. Let come to temp.

To first flask, add 1 mL boiled distd H_2O and det. residual available Cl as follows: Add small crystal KI and 1 mL HOAc; then add 1 mL starch soln, **4.040(d)**. Blue soln indicates presence of Cl. Titr. with 0.001*N* $Na_2S_2O_3$, **4.040(c)**(*2*), until color disappears; mL 0.001*N* $Na_2S_2O_3 \times 0.1773$ = ppm residual available Cl. This represents available Cl at 0 time in test. Result should be $\geq$0.58 but $\leq$0.62.

To each of remaining flasks add 1 mL test culture suspension, **4.042**, as follows: Swirl flask, stopping just before suspension is added, to create enough centrifugal motion to prevent pooling of suspension at point of contact with test H_2O. Add suspension midway between center and edge of liq. surface, immersing tip of pipet slightly below surface of H_2O. Avoid touching pipet to neck or side of test flask during operation.

From one of these 2 flasks transfer 1 mL aliquots to neutralizer blanks, **4.039(a)**, after intervals of 0.5, 1, 2, 3, 4, 5, and 10 min. Shake neutralizer blank thoroly immediately after adding sample. Prep. serial diln plate counts from neutralizer blanks, using phosphate buffer diln H_2O, **4.040(b)**, and subculture medium, **4.037(a)** for *E. coli*, and **(b)** for *S. faecalis*.

After prepg diln plate counts, inoculate 5 lactose broth tubes, **4.037(d)**, with 1.0 mL aliquots from each neutralizer blank tube for each time interval when *E. coli* is used as the test organism, and 5 thioglycolate broth tubes, **4.037(c)**, with 1.0 mL aliquots from each neutralizer blank tube for each time interval when *S. faecalis* is test organism.

Incubate all diln plates in inverted position and subculture tubes 48 hr at 37°. Use Quebec Colony Counting Chamber in reading diln plates and report results in terms of number of surviving bacteria/mL test H_2O. Absence of colony growth on diln plates and absence of growth in all 5 lactose or thioglycolate tubes, as case may be, is necessary to show complete kill of test organism.

Immediately after transferring 10 min interval sample from second flask to neutralizer blank tube, remove third flask from H_2O bath and det. residual available Cl exactly as specified for first flask. Results should represent residual available Cl present at 10 min exposure interval. To be acceptable, concn of available Cl in this flask should be >0.4 ppm. Results in Cl control test described above should show complete kill of *E. coli* and *S. faecalis* within 0.5 min.

With unknown sample, prep. 2 flasks contg 199 mL each of soln at concn recommended or to be studied, using Cl demand-free, unbuffered, freshly distd H_2O previously prepd in 1 L vol. flask where Cl demand, as detd above, has been satisfied by addn of NaOCl soln. Place flasks in H_2O bath at 20 or 25°; let come to temp. Inoculate 1 flask with 1 mL std test culture suspension of *E. coli* and other with 1 mL std test culture suspension of *S. faecalis*. Subculture at exactly same time intervals and in same manner used with NaOCl control except vary composition of neutralizer blank depending upon nature of chem. or mixt. of chems under investigation. For example, mixt. of Cl-contg chem. and quaternary NH_4 compd would require special neutralizer blank prepd by using both neutralizer stock solns, **4.038(a)** and **(b)**.

Where no concn of chem. under study has been recommended and objective of study is to det. concn of unknown necessary to provide result equiv. to that obtained with Cl control std, use series of three or four 500 mL flasks contg 199 mL of various concns of chem. and 1 mL stdzd culture suspension with each test organism. Report results as log (number of survivors) at each time interval both for Cl controls and various concns of unknown under test.

Lowest concn of unknown germicide or germicidal mixt. providing results equiv. to those obtained with NaOCl as Cl std is considered lowest concn which could be expected to provide acceptable disinfecting activity in swimming pool water.

Tuberculocidal Activity (*9*)—Official Final Action

(Suitable for detg max. tuberculocidal diln of disinfectants used on inanimate surfaces)

I. Presumptive In Vitro Screening Test Using Mycobacterium smegmatis

4.045 ***Reagents***

(a) *Test organism.—Mycobacterium smegmatis* (PRD No. 1) (available from Microbiology Lab., Benefits and Field Services Div., EPA, Beltsville, MD 20705). Maintain on nutrient agar slants by monthly transfers. Incubate new stock transfer 2 days at 37°; then store at 2–5°. From stock culture inoculate tubes of Proskauer-Beck broth, **(b)**(*1*), incubate 48 hr in slanting position, carry 30 days, using 48 hr transfers, and use these 48 hr cultures to start test cultures. Inoculate 1 or 2 tubes of Proskauer-Beck broth. Incubate 6–7 days at 37°. Incubate tubes 48 hr in slanting position to provide max. surface aeration and then in upright position 4–5 days. Add 1.5 mL sterile 2.0% Bacto-Gelatin soln and homogenize culture with sterilized glass tissue grinder, **4.016(e)**. Adjust to 20% *T* at 650 nm with sterile Proskauer-Beck broth for use in testing.

(b) *Culture media.—*(*1*) *Modified Proskauer-Beck broth.*—Dissolve 2.5 g KH_2PO_4, 5.0 g asparagine, 0.6 g $MgSO_4.7H_2O$, 2.5 g Mg citrate, 20.0 mL glycerol, 0.0046 g $FeCl_3$, and 0.001 g $ZnSO_4.7H_2O$ in 1 L H_2O. Adjust to pH 7.2–7.4 with 1*N* NaOH. Filter thru paper, place 10 mL portions in sep. 20 × 150 mm tubes, and sterilize 20 min at 121°. Use for propagating 48 hr test starter cultures and 6–7 day test cultures.

(*2*) *Subculture media.*—Use (*1*) with addn of suitable neutzg agents such as purified lecithin (Azolectin) or Na thioglycolate, where necessary.

(*3*) *Nutrient agar.*—Prep. as in **4.001(c)**. Use to maintain stock culture.

(*4*) *Sterile distilled water.*—See **4.007(d)**.

4.046 ***Apparatus***

(**a**) *Glassware, water bath, transfer loops and needles, and petri dishes.—See* **4.008(a)**, (**b**), (**c**), and (**e**).

(**b**) *Carriers.—See* **4.016(g)**.

4.047 ***Operating Technic***

Transfer 20 sterile Penicylinder carriers, using flamed nichrome wire hook, into 20 mL 6–7 day homogenized stdzd broth culture, **4.045(a)**, in sterile 25 × 150 mm medicant tube. After 15 min contact, remove cylinders and place on end in vertical position in sterile petri dish matted with filter paper, **4.008(e)**. Cover and place in incubator at 37° and let dry ≥20 min but ≤60 min. This will provide dried test carriers in groups of 20 in individual petri dishes. With each group of 20 carriers, add 1 dried cylinder at 30 sec intervals to each of 20 tubes contg 10 mL diln of germicide to be tested (at 20° in H_2O bath). Flame lips of medicant and subculture tubes. Immediately after placing carrier in medicant tube, swirl tube 3 times before placing it back in H_2O bath. (Thus, by time 20 tubes have been seeded, 9 min and 30 sec have elapsed, leaving 30 sec interval prior to subculturing series at 10 min exposure for each carrier. The 30 sec interval between transfers allows adequate time for flaming and cooling transfer hook and making transfer in manner so as to drain all excess medicant from carrier.) Transfer carrier to 10 mL subculture media, **4.045(b)**(*2*). Shake all subculture tubes thoroly and incubate 12 days at 37°. Report results as + (growth) or − (no growth). Where there is reason to suspect that results may be affected by bacteriostatic action of medicant carried over in subculture tubes, use suitable neutralizer in subculture media.

Make ≥30 carrier exposures at each of 3 relatively widely spaced dilns of germicide under test between no response and total response diln levels. Calc. % of carriers on which organism is killed at each diln. Using log % probit paper (3 cycle logarithmic normal No. 32.376, Codex Book Co., Inc., Norwood, MA 02062), locate % kill points on diln lines employed (log scale). Draw best fitting straight line thru these 3 points and extend to intercept 99% kill line. Read diln line (log scale) at point of intercept. This is presumed 95% confidence end point for product. (Do not use presumptive test organism for checking validity of this presumptive end point.)

II. Confirmative In Vitro Test for Determining Tuberculocidal Activity

4.048 ***Reagents***

(**a**) *Culture media.*—(*1*) *Modified Proskauer-Beck medium.*—Prep. as in **4.045(b)**(*1*), and in addn, place 20 mL portions in 25 × 150 mm tubes. Use 10 mL portions for daily transfers of test cultures and 20 mL portions for subculturing porcelain cylinders.

(*2*) *Middlebrook 7H9 Broth Difco A.*—Dissolve 4.7 g in 900 mL H_2O contg 2 mL glycerol and 15.0 g agar. Heat to bp to dissolve completely. Distribute in 180 mL portions and autoclave 15 min at 121°. To each 180 mL sterile medium at 45°, add 20 mL Middlebrook ADC Enrichment (Difco) under aseptic conditions and distribute in 10 mL portions in sterile 20 × 150 mm tubes. Slant. Use to maintain test culture.

(*3*) *Middlebrook 7H9 Broth Difco B.*—Dissolve 4.7 g in 900 mL H_2O contg 2 mL glycerol and 1.0 g agar. Heat to bp to dissolve completely. Distribute in 18 mL portions in 25 × 150 mm tubes, and autoclave 15 min at 121°. To each 18 mL sterile medium at 45° add 2 mL Middlebrook ADC Enrichment under aseptic conditions. Use to subculture for survival.

(*4*) *Kirchners Medium Difco.*—Dissolve 13.1 g in 1 L H_2O contg 20 mL glycerol and heat to bp to dissolve completely. Distribute in 18 mL portions in 25 × 150 mm tubes and autoclave 15 min at 121°. To each 18 mL sterile medium at 50–55° add 2 mL Middlebrook ADC Enrichment under aseptic conditions. Use to subculture for survival.

(*5*) *TB Broth Base Difco* (*without polysorbate 80*). —Dissolve 11.6 g in 1 L H_2O contg 50 mL glycerol and 1.0 g agar. Heat to bp to dissolve completely. Distribute in 18 mL portions in 25 × 150 mm tubes, and autoclave 15 min at 121°. To each 18 mL sterile medium at 50° add 2 mL Dubos Medium Serum (Difco) under aseptic conditions. Use to subculture for survival.

(**b**) *Test organism.—Mycobacterium bovis* (BCG) (available from ITR Biomedical Research, University of Illinois Medical Center, 904 W Adams St, Chicago, IL 60607). Maintain stock cultures on culture medium (**a**)(*2*) by monthly or 6 weeks transfer. Incubate new stock transfer 15–20 days at 37° until sufficient growth is indicated; then store at 2–5°. From stock culture, inoculate tube of culture medium (**a**)(*1*) and incubate 21–25 days at 37°. Shake gently once daily for 9 days; then allow to remain quiescent until 21–25th day. Make daily transfers from 21 day cultures. Transfer culture to heat-sterilized glass tissue grinder, add 1.5 mL sterile 2% Bacto-gelatin soln (Difco), grind, and dil. with culture medium (**a**)(*1*) to give 20% *T* at 650 nm. Use to inoculate porcelain cylinders used in test. Tests will be satisfactory only when organism is killed on all 10 carriers by aq. phenol (1+50) and shows survival after exposure to aq. phenol (1+75) control. Prep. dilns from 5% std phenol soln, **4.002(f)**.

(**c**) *Sterile distilled water.—See* **4.007(d)**.

(**d**) *Sterile normal horse serum without preservative.*—Difco Laboratories or Microbiological Associates, 4733 Bethesda Ave, Bethesda, MD 20014.

4.049 ***Apparatus***

(**a**) *Glassware, water bath, transfer loops and needles, and petri dishes.—See* **4.008(a)**, (**b**), (**c**), and (**e**).

(**b**) *Carriers.—See* **4.016(g)**.

4.050 ***Operating Technic***

Soak ring carriers overnight in 1*N* NaOH; rinse with tap H_2O and then with distd H_2O until distd H_2O is neut. to phthln; then rinse twice with distd H_2O. Place clean ring carriers in multiple of 10 or 20 in capped erlenmeyer or 20 × 150 mm tubes. Autoclave 20 min at 121°, cool, and hold at room temp. Transfer 10 sterile ring carriers, using flamed wire hook, into enough (ca 15–20 mL) 21–25 day stdzd test culture, **4.048(b)**, in 25 × 150 mm medication tube. After 15 min contact period, remove cylinders, using flamed wire hook, and place on end in vertical position in sterile petri dish matted with filter paper, **4.008(e)**. Cover, place in incubator at 37°, and let dry ≥20 min but ≤60 min.

Let 10 tubes contg 10 mL use-diln germicide sample to be tested come to 20° in H_2O bath and add 1 contaminated cylinder carrier at either 30 sec or 1 min intervals to each tube. Immediately after placing carrier in medication tube, swirl 3 or 4 times before placing tube back in bath. (Thus, by time 10 tubes have been seeded, 9 min will have elapsed, plus 1 min interval before transfer of first carrier in series to individual tube of 10 mL serum, **4.048(d)**, or 10 mL neutralizer blank, **4.023(d)**, if 1 min intervals are used. This interval is constant for each tube with prescribed exposure period of 10 min. Interval between transfers allows adequate time for flaming and cooling wire hook and making transfer in manner so as to drain all excess medication from carrier.) Transfer carrier to 10 mL serum, **4.048(d)**, after exactly 10 min contact. Shake tube contg carrier in serum thoroly and place carrier in tube contg 20 mL broth, **4.048(a)**(*1*). From same tube, take 2 mL portions serum and place in any 2 of the subculture media, **4.048(a)**(*3*), (*4*), (*5*). Repeat this with each of the 10 carriers. Incubate 1 tube of each subculture medium with 2 mL sterile serum as control. Where there is reason to suspect that germicide to be tested may possess bacteriostatic action, use suitable neutralizer in lieu of serum. Shake each subculture tube thoroly, incubate 60 days at 37°, and report results as + (growth) or − (no growth). If no growth or only occasional growth is observed in subculture, incubate addnl 30 days before making final reading. Max. diln of germicide which kills test organism on the 10 carriers, and no growth in each of the 2 mL aliquots for 2 extra media, represents max. safe use-diln for practical tuberculocidal disinfection.

Bacteriostatic Activity of Laundry Additives (*10*)
Official First Action

(Applicable to antimicrobial products, recommended for use during laundering operations, which are intended to provide residual bacteriostatic treatment to laundered fabric. Method includes treatment of fabric with product and subsequent bacteriostatic testing of treated fabric.)

4.051 ***Reagents***

(**a**) *Culture media.*—(*1*) *Nutrient broth.*—*See* **4.001**(**a**).

(*2*) *Nutrient agar A.*—*See* **4.001**(**c**). Use for monthly transfer of stock cultures.

(*3*) *Nutrient agar B.*—Boil 3 g beef ext, 5 g peptone (Anatone), 8 g NaCl, and 10 g agar (Difco) in 1 L H_2O. Transfer 100 mL portions to erlenmeyers, and autoclave 20 min at 121°. Use for agar plate tests to evaluate bacteriostatic activity of treated fabric. *See also* (**c**).

(**b**) *Test organisms.*—Use *Staphylococcus aureus* ATCC No. 6538 and *Klebsiella pneumoniae,* aberrant ATCC No. 4352 (formerly *Escherichia coli*), and maintain as in **4.002**(**e**).

(**c**) *2,3,5-Triphenyl tetrazolium chloride.*—Use as optional biological indicator. With *S. aureus,* use 0.15% soln; with *K. pneumoniae,* aberrant, use 0.25% soln. Autoclave each 20 min at 121°. Apply as in **4.054**.

(**d**) *Alkaline nonionic wetting agent.*—Prep. aq. soln contg 0.5% alkyl phenol polyglycol ether wetting agent and 0.5% Na_2CO_3. Use to scour test fabric.

4.052 ***Apparatus***

(**a**) *Test fabric.*—80 × 80 threads/sq in. plain weave cotton print cloth, completely desized, bleached, and without bluing or optical brighteners (available from Test Fabrics, Inc., 55 Van Dam St, New York, NY 10013). Scour before use by boiling ca 300 g 1 hr in 3 L H_2O contg 1.5 g nonionic wetting agent and 1.5 g Na_2CO_3. Then rinse fabric, first in boiling H_2O and then in cold H_2O, until all visual traces of wetting agent are removed. Air-dry and cut into long strip 5 cm (2″) wide and weighing exactly 15 g.

(**b**) *Stainless steel spindle.*—Fabricate from single continuous piece of stainless steel wire 1/16″ diam. and bent to contain 3 horizontal extensions 5 cm (2″) long connected by 2 vertical sections ca 5 cm (2″) long. Shape so that vertical sections form 150° angle, and sharpen free ends of 2 outer horizontal extensions to point (*see* Fig. **4:02**). Use as carrier for test fabric. Primary objective of spindle is to prevent wadding or lodging of test fabric during agitation in exposures to test chem. solns.

(**c**) *Exposure chamber.*—Clean, dry 1 pt Mason jar with rubber washer or gasket and metal screw cap.

(**d**) *Agitator.*—Device to rotate Mason jar thru 360° vertical orbit of 10–20 cm (4–8″) diam. at 45–60 rpm for 5 min. Launder-ometer or Tumble Jar described in AATCC70 B-1967, 43, B154, B155, or ASTM D583-63 is adequate.

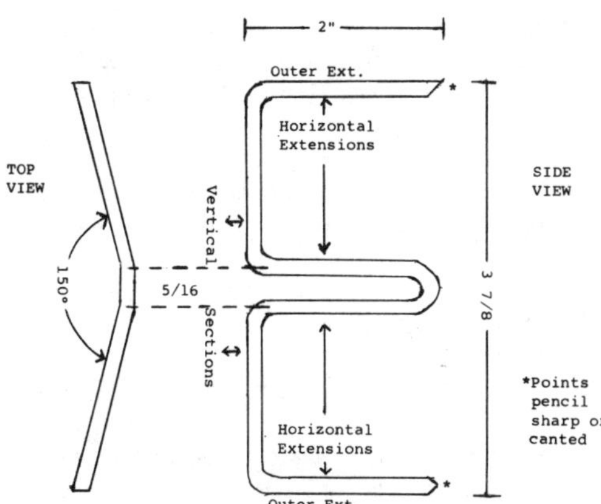

FIG. 4:02—Stainless steel spindle for winding test fabric

(**e**) *Water bath.*—Thermostatically controlled at 25°.

(**f**) *Petri dishes.*—Sterile, 100 × 15 mm.

(**g**) *Glassware.*—*See* **4.002**(**a**).

(**h**) *Transfer loops and needles.*—*See* **4.002**(**d**).

4.053 ***Preparation of Fabric***

(**a**) *Fabric mounting.*—Pierce one end of prescoured, 15 g test fabric strip and secure onto an outer horizontal extension of test spindle; then wind strip around 3 horizontal extensions with enough tension to obtain 12 (but not 13) entire laps. Secure final end of test fabric strip to previous laps with stainless steel safety pin.

(**b**) *Fabric treatment with product.*—Dil. product as directed to 75 mL (most frequently, use directions are based on dry wt of laundry fabric equiv. to 15 g test fabric), add to Mason jar (exposure chamber), and maintain in H_2O bath at 25°. Add addnl materials to Mason jar as required by use directions for product. These are:

(*1*) *Product recommended as final rinse additive in industrial laundering operation.*—Add no addnl materials; 5:1 (v/w) treatment product soln to dry fabric ratio is representative of industrial laundering operations.

(*2*) *Product recommended as final rinse additive in home or coin-operated laundering operations.*—Add 150 mL H_2O to Mason jar. Resultant 10:1 (v/w) treatment product soln to dry fabric ratio is representative of home and coin-operated laundering operations.

(*3*) *Product recommended as final rinse additive in both industrial and home laundering operations.*— Prep. 2 jars contg product soln according to (*1*) and (*2*) so that 2 test fabric strips may be treated at different treatment product soln to dry fabric ratios (5:1 and 10:1 (v/w)).

(*4*) *Product recommended as final rinse additive and described as compatible with adjunct chemicals which may be used in this cycle (sours, bleaches, optical brighteners, softeners, etc).*—Prep. so that required vol. of product treatment soln contains adjunct chemicals according to description and amts specified on product label or advertising literature.

4.054 ***Operating Technic***

Place test spindle with test fabric in Mason jar contg product soln. Secure rubber gasket and Mason jar cap, remove from H_2O bath, place jar in agitator, and rotate 5 min. Addnl manipulation with test spindle is required if use directions do not specify addn of product in final rinse phase of laundry cycle. In this instance, to det. durability of antimicrobial agent in fabric, execute 3 rinse operations as follows: Immediately after end of initial 5 min agitation, drain treatment soln from Mason jar and replace with 100 mL H_2O. Secure Mason jar contg test spindle, return to agitator, and rotate 2 min. Repeat operation twice more.

Following all required fabric treatment operations, remove test spindle from Mason jar and unwind test fabric strip from spindle. Let test fabric strip air dry with long axis of strip in horizontal position.

When test strip is dry, remove 1 sq in. bacteriological test samples. Five test samples are required for single bacteriostatic test against 1 test organism. In each such instance, at least 2 test samples must be removed from middle 20% of length of test strip.

Perform bacteriostatic agar plate tests as follows: Prep. 5 replicate plates in each test for each organism. Sep. inoculate flasks contg 100 mL sterile, liq. ($\leq 40°$) nutrient agar B with 1 mL 24 hr nutrient broth culture of *S. aureus* and *K. pneumoniae*, aberrant. Immediately thereafter, if desired, add 1 mL appropriate soln of 2,3,5-triphenyl tetrazolium chloride to inoculated nutrient agar B. Vigorously swirl contents of erlenmeyers to ensure complete mixing. Add 10 mL portions of inoculated agar to 100 mm sterile petri dishes, distribute evenly, and let cool and harden. As soon as plates harden, implant single 1 sq in. treated fabric test sample on center of 1 test agar plate surface. Using blunt forceps, press each fabric test sample onto agar surface to ensure complete and uniform contact. Incubate test plates 48 hr at 37°. If desired, test plates may be refrigerated 18–20 hr before incubation. Following incubation, examine test plates to det. presence or absence of zones of inhibition along each side of test fabric sample.

4.055 ***Interpretation***

Use clear zone of inhibition adjacent to each side of test fabric sample as index of bacteriostatic activity. Size of zone is not considered important, but zone is required to extend along entire edge to be acceptable. Score zone of inhibition along single side of sq test fabric samples as 1, so that for 5-replicate plate test, a score of 20 shows that bacteriostasis occurs along all 4 sides of each sample. Total score of 18/20 sides demonstrating bacteriostasis is required for effective demonstration of residual bacteriostatic activity of laundry fabric treated with antimicrobial laundry additive product during laundering operation. Unless qualified residual bacteriostatic claim is made, residual treatment must be bacteriostatic against both *S. aureus* and *K. pneumoniae*, aberrant.

SELECTED REFERENCES

(*1*) J. Roy. Sanit. Inst. **24**, 424(1903); Am. J. Public Health **3**, 575(1913); U.S. Dept. Agr. Circ. **198** (1931); JAOAC **32**, 408(1949); **38**, 465(1955); Soap Chem. Spec. **34**, No. 10, 79(1958).

(*2*) J. Bacteriol. **49**, 526(1945); Am. J. Vet. Res. **9**, 104(1948); JAOAC **36**, 466(1953).

(*3*) Soap Sanit. Chem. **27**, No. 2, 133(1951); JAOAC **38**, 274(1955); **40**, 755(1957).

(*4*) JAOAC **36**, 480(1953); **39**, 480(1956); **40**, 759(1957); **49**, 721(1966).

(*5*) Arch. Dermatol. Syphilol. **28**, 15(1933); J. Bacteriol. **42**, 225(1941); **47**, 102(1944); JAOAC **37**, 616(1954); **38**, 274(1955).

(*6*) Am. J. Public Health **38**, 1405(1948); J. Milk Food Technol. **19**, 183(1956); Fed. Regist. **21**, 7020(1956); JAOAC **41**, 541(1958).

(*7*) JAOAC **44**, 422(1961); **50**, 763(1967); Soap Chem. Spec. **38**(2), 69(1962).

(*8*) JAOAC **47**, 540(1964); **48**, 640(1965).

(*9*) JAOAC **48**, 635(1965); **50**, 767(1967).

(*10*) JAOAC **52**, 836(1969).

5. Hazardous Substances

PAINT

Lead (*1*)—Official Final Action

5.001 ***Reagents and Apparatus***

(**a**) *Lead std solns.*—(*1*) *Stock soln.*—1 mg Pb/mL 1% HNO_3. Dissolve 159.9 mg $Pb(NO_3)_2$ in HNO_3 (1+99) and dil. to 100 mL with HNO_3 (1+99). (*2*) *Intermediate soln.*—300 μg/mL dil. HNO_3. Dil. 15 mL stock soln to 50 mL with 0.5 mL HNO_3 and H_2O. (*3*) *Working solns.*—To each of seven 100 mL vol. flasks contg 1 mL HNO_3, add resp. 0, 1, 2, 3, 4, 5, and 6 mL intermediate soln and dil. to vol. with H_2O (0, 3, 6, 9, 12, 15, and 18 μg Pb/mL).

(**b**) *Atomic absorption spectrophotometer.*—With Pb hollow cathode lamp and 4″ single slot or 3 slot Boling burner head, capable of detecting 0.5 μg Pb/mL, such as Perkin-Elmer Model 403. Operating conditions: 283.3 nm, 0.7 nm band width slit, recorder response (if used) 0.25–1 sec time constant, air-C_2H_2 flame, with gas flows adjusted according to directions of manufacturer.

(**c**) *Heater for digestion.*—Drill 7.5 cm Al block to hold $\geq$16 test tubes, 16 $\times$ 150 mm. Place on hot plate capable of maintaining medium at 160–170° (Corning PC 35, or equiv.). Sand bath may be used instead of Al block.

(**d**) *Boiling chips.*—Unglazed boiling chips, 1.5 mm diam., Pb-free.

5.002 ***Determination of Solids***

Thoroly mix samples manually for 10 min or mech. for 5 min. Accurately weigh 0.3–0.4 g into weighed Al dish, 63 mm diam. Add 3–5 mL hexane or pet ether to oil-based paints or H_2O to latex paints and swirl to disperse. Warm on hot plate while swirling until solv. has evapd and film is formed. Heat in oven 4 hr at 105°, cool, and weigh.

% Solids = g dried sample $\times$ 100/g sample.

5.003 ***Determination of Lead***

Introduce ca 0.6 g (0.3 mL) thoroly mixed sample near bottom of 16 $\times$ 150 mm test tube with syringe and weigh accurately. Add 5$\pm$0.2 mL HNO_3 and 2 boiling chips to each, including blanks. Place in block or bath at 90–100° so that liq. surface is slightly above heated surface. (Use hood.) After initial fuming has subsided, increase temp. until vapors are condensing in top 1–2 cm of tube (bath temp., 160–170°) and maintain at this temp. 3 hr. Cool to 50–60°, transfer to 25 mL vol. flask, including chips and any ppt, and rinse with four 4 mL portions H_2O, transferring as much residue as possible. Dil. to vol. with H_2O and let settle 0.5–1 hr. Floating residue may be removed by aspiration thru disposable pipet.

Aspirate solns and stds into AA spectrophotometer, avoiding introduction of ppt. If *A* of sample is greater than highest std, dil. sample and re-aspirate. Det. μg Pb/mL from std curve.

$$\%\ \text{Pb in paint solids} = (\mu\text{g Pb/mL}) \times F \times 10^{-2}/(\text{g sample} \times \%\ \text{solids in sample})$$

$$F\ (\text{diln factor}) = 1/[(1/25)\ (b/c)\ (d/e) \ldots],$$

where 25 = vol. original sample digest, *b* = aliquot of original 25 mL dild to *c* mL; *d* = aliquot of *c* (mL) dild to *e* mL; etc. For dry paint films, % solids in sample = 100.

PREPARATIONS CONTAINING FLUORIDES

Fluoride (*2*)—Official Final Action

5.004 ***Apparatus***

(**a**) *pH meter.*—With expanded mv scale (digital Model 110, Corning Scientific Instruments, Medfield, MA 02052, or equiv.), fluoride ion-selective electrode (Model 94-09, Orion Research Inc., 11 Blackstone St, Cambridge, MA 02139, or equiv.), and single junction ref. electrode, plastic sleeve-type (Model 90-01, Orion Research Inc., or equiv.).

(**b**) *Magnetic stirrer.*—With Teflon-coated stirring bar. Use asbestos or foam mat to insulate sample from motor heat.

(**c**) *Beakers.*—4.5 oz (135 mL), polypropylene, or equiv.

(**d**) *Graph paper.*—Linear or semi-antilog, vol. corrected No. 90-00-90 Gran's plot paper (Orion Research Inc., or equiv.).

5.005 ***Reagents***

(**a**) *Buffer soln.*—pH 6.0. Add 77.0 g NH_4OAc and 0.452 g NH_4 citrate to 1 L H_2O. Adjust to pH 6.0 with HOAc.

(**b**) *Fluoride std soln.*—1 mg F/mL. Prep. 2.2108 g NaF (reagent grade, dried 4 hr at 105°)/L buffer soln. (*Caution: See* **51.084**.) Store in leakproof plastic bottles. Compare with 1 mg F/mL soln prepd from USP Ref. Std; equiv. reading of $\pm$1 mv is satisfactory.

5.006 ***Determination***

(Stir all solns constantly at same rate thruout titrns. Let electrodes equilibrate $\geq$2 min before addn of F std soln and 30 sec after each addn of F std soln.)

(**a**) *Blank.*—Record mv values (E') of 100 mL buffer soln after addn of 4 mL std F soln from 10 mL buret and after each addnl mL up to 10 mL. (Preliminary mv values will not fall on linear range of response curve.) Vol. std soln added = V'.

(**b**) *Samples.*—Est. molarity of samples from direct reading. Dil. samples, if necessary, to ca 0.001*M* F. Transfer 50 mL sample soln to beaker and add 50 mL buffer soln. Record initial mv reading, using expanded scale (E_0). If initial reading is <-50 mv, soln is too concd. Dil. sample to avoid asymptotic slope. Record mv values (E) after each mL F std soln is added up to 10 mL. Rinse electrodes with H_2O between samples. Vol. std soln added = V.

5.007 ***Calculations***

(**a**) *Linear graph paper.*—For each addn of F std soln and corresponding *E* value, calc. for blank:

$$Z' = \text{antilog}\ [\log(V_0 + V') - 0.017(E')],$$

where V_0 is original vol. soln to which F std soln was added (100mL) and E' is treated algebraically (+ or − as read). Plot Z' against mL (mg) F std soln added and extrapolate to intersection of mL (mg) F axis to obtain mL (mg) F in blank, V_e'. In graph, assign horizontal axis to mL (mg) F, with 0 at center and mL (mg) F increasing in both directions to left and right. Assign *Z* values to vertical axis. Plot actual readings of mL (mg) F on right portion of horizontal axis so that extrapolation will fall on left portion of axis.

Similarly, for original readings and each addn of F std soln and corresponding E value, calc. for sample:

$$Z = \text{antilog}\,[\log(V_0 + V) - 0.017(E)],$$

where V_0 is original vol. soln to which F std soln was added (100 mL). Plot Z against mL (mg) F std soln on same graph as blank and extrapolate to intersection of mL (mg) F axis to obtain mL (mg) F in sample, V_e.

(b) *Semi-antilog paper.*—Plot E directly for both blank and sample, descending 5 mv for each major line crossing vertical axis. At top of vertical axis place most neg. E reading which still allows extrapolation of V_e on left portion of mL (mg) side of horizontal axis. Obtain V_e and V_e' by extrapolation to left side of 0 mL (mg) F.

$$\%\ \text{F} = (V_e - V_e') \times (B \times 100)/[W \times C \times 1000\ (\text{mg/g})],$$

where B = vol. of diln, W = mL or g sample, and C = aliquot (50 mL max.) buffered to 100 mL.

PREPARATIONS CONTAINING METHANOL

Methanol (*3*)—Official Final Action

(Applicable in presence of acetone, BuOAc, EtOH, isopropanol, hexane, MeEt ketone, CH_2Cl_2, Me Cellosolve, paraffin, toluene, and H_2O. This includes many paint removers, fuels, liq. sanders, antifreezes, and paint products.)

5.008 ***Apparatus and Reagents***

(a) *Gas chromatograph.*—With flame ionization detector and oven capable of temp. changes ≥5°/min near 160° or preferably temp. programmer. *Column.*—1.8 m (6') × 4 mm id packed with 120–150 mesh Porapak R (Waters Associates, Inc., PO Box 246, Milford, MA 01757); condition 2 hr at 235°. *Conditions:* Temps (°): injection ca 200, column ca 160, detector ca 210; N flow ca 25 mL/min; set electrometer so that 8 μL std soln provides at least half scale peak. Adjust column temp. and N flow so that MeOH retention time is ca 5–7 min.

(b) *Methanol std soln.*—0.4% (v/v). Dil. 4.00 mL MeOH to 100 mL with dioxane; dil. 10.0 mL of this soln to 100 mL with dioxane. Rinse pipet into flask before dilg to vol. with dioxane. Prep. fresh daily.

5.009 ***Preparation of Sample***

(a) *For asphalt-base tar compounds and viscous adhesives.*—Refrigerate unopened sample container ≥3 hr (longer for larger containers) at 1–10°, open container, and mix well; close container and refrigerate 30 min more. Transfer 1.5–3 g sample to tared, 250 mL, wide-mouth g-s erlenmeyer (tared with stopper in place). Let sample reach room temp. in stoppered erlenmeyer and weigh. Refrigerate 30 min and quickly add 100.0 mL dioxane. Stopper and shake mech. 1 hr. Refrigerate 30 min and filter thru rapid paper (S&S sharkskin, or equiv.). Filter as quickly as possible, covering funnel with watch glass and placing funnel against neck of narrow-mouth g-s receiver. Proceed as in **5.010**, dilg with dioxane, if necessary.

(b) *For other less viscous products.*—Prep. soln with pipets and vol. flasks to contain ca 0.4% (v/v) MeOH, dilg with dioxane. Avoid excessive shaking of semiviscous products and do *not* fill pipet above mark. (Use safety pipet filler to draw liq. to mark and hold until transfer.) Wash pipet with dioxane and add washings to soln.

If MeOH concn is unknown, prep. 2% soln. Prep. addnl dilns as needed.

5.010 ***Determination***

Inject portion std soln with 10 μL syringe. Note vol. At R_{MA} (retention time relative to MeOH) ca 0.5, inject portion sample soln. Note vol. At R_{MA} ca 2 (from second injection), repeat injection of std soln. At R_{MA} ca 0.5 (from third injection), repeat injection of sample soln. After MeOH from fourth injection elutes, increase column temp. to 235° as rapidly as possible for time ca 4 × R_{MA} until all dioxane (R_{MA} ca 5) is removed from column. Cool column to 160° and repeat sequence for subsequent sample. Modify injection time if necessary to sep. MeOH from other peaks. (*Note:* Injection sequence is used only to save time; it need not be used if desired.)

5.011 ***Calculation***

Det. retention areas for each MeOH peak by multiplying peak ht by retention distance. Average retention areas for sample (RA) and for std (RA'). Presence of solv. in column changes retention times, requiring use of retention areas in calcn.

$$\%\ \text{MeOH (w/v) in sample soln} = F \times (RA/RA') \times (V'/V) \times C \times 0.79,$$

where F = diln factor, C = % (v/v) std soln, V and V' = vol. sample and std soln injected, resp., and 0.79 = density of MeOH.

Volatile Denaturants in Alcoholic Products (*4*) Official First Action

5.012 ***Apparatus and Reagents***

(a) *Gas chromatograph and integrator.*—See **19.001(a)** and **(b)**.

(b) *Std solns.*—6% (v/v). Dil. 6.00 mL of each denaturant of interest to 100 mL with anhyd. alcohol in sep. vol. flasks. Approx. slopes and retention times relative to *n*-PrOH are given in Table **5:01**.

Table 5:01 Approximate Slopes and Retention Times Relative to *n*-Propyl Alcohol (RT) for Denaturants

Compound	Slope	RT
Acetone	0.207	0.694
Benzene	0.464	2.309
n-Butyl alcohol	0.269	2.283
sec-Butyl alcohol	0.246	1.621
Chloroform	0.058	1.543
Ethyl acetate	0.192	1.640
Ethylene glycol monoethyl ether	0.187	3.868
Ethylene glycol monomethyl ether	0.151	2.071
Isopropanol	0.210	0.727
Methanol	0.130	0.266
Methyl isobutyl ketone	0.275	5.436
Toluene	0.454	5.302

5.013 ***Determination***

Pipet 25 mL of each expected denaturant std soln into sep. flasks and add 1.00 mL *n*-PrOH as internal std. Proceed as in **19.002**, starting with "Cap immediately . . .", except inject 0.3 μL portions. Det. peak areas and calc. slope for each compd as:

$$S_X = (PA_X/PA_I)/6.00,$$

where PA_X and PA_I = peak areas of compd X in std soln and of *n*-PrOH internal std, resp., and 6.00 = % compd X in std soln. Slopes and retention times should approximate those of Table **5:01**.

$$\%\ \text{Compd X in sample} = (PA/PA_I) = (1/S_X),$$

where PA = peak area of compd X in sample.

PREPARATIONS CONTAINING PHENOL

Phenol

Method I (5)—Official Final Action

(Applicable to com. cresols, saponified cresol solns, coal tar dips, and disinfectants, and to kerosene solns of phenols in absence of salicylates or β-naphthol)

5.014 ***Reagents***

(*Caution: See* **51.026** and **51.065**.)

(**a**) *Dilute nitric acid.*—Aerate HNO_3 until colorless and dil. 1 vol. with 4 vols H_2O.

(**b**) *Millon reagent.*—To 2 mL Hg in 200 mL erlenmeyer under hood, add 20 mL HNO_3. After first violent reaction, shake as needed to disperse Hg and maintain action. After ca 10 min, when action practically ceases even in presence of undissolved Hg, add 35 mL H_2O, and if basic salt seps, add enough dil. HNO_3 to dissolve it. Add 10% NaOH soln dropwise with thoro mixing until curdy ppt that forms after adding each drop no longer redissolves but disperses as permanent turbidity. Add 5 mL dil. HNO_3 and mix well. Prep. fresh daily. Millon reagent is dangerously poisonous and should not be transferred with ordinary pipet and mouth suction unless protective trap is used.

(**c**) *Phenol std soln.*—Dissolve weighed amt pure phenol (congealing point $\geqslant 40°$) in enough H_2O to make $\geqslant 1\%$ soln. On day it is to be used, dil. to make 0.025% aq. soln (final std).

(**d**) *Formaldehyde soln.*—Dil. 2 mL 37% HCHO soln to 100 mL with H_2O.

(**e**) *Methyl orange indicator.*—0.5% aq. soln.

5.015 ***Apparatus***

(**a**) *Nessler cylinders.*—50 mL tall-form, matched.

(**b**) *Test tubes.*—Approx. 180 × 20 mm, with rubber stoppers, marked at 25 mL.

(**c**) *Water bath for heating test tubes.*—Beaker contg disk of wire gauze raised ca 2.5 cm from bottom may be used.

5.016 ***Preparation of Sample***

(**a**) *Commercial cresol.*—Weigh by difference ca 2.5 g sample into 250 mL vol. flask, dissolve in 10 mL 10% NaOH soln, and dil. to vol. with H_2O.

(**b**) *Saponified cresol solns, coal tar dips and disinfectants, kerosene solns of phenols, etc.*—Weigh by difference ca 5 g sample (or use 5 mL and calc. wt from density) into 250 mL vol. flask and dil. to vol. with H_2O. With products consisting largely of kerosene, bring H_2O level to mark and take aliquots from aq. portion only.

5.017 ***Determination***

Transfer 5 mL aliquot prepd soln to 200 mL vol. flask and promptly dil. to ca 50 mL. Add 1 drop Me orange, (**e**), and then dil. HNO_3 until soln is practically neut. Dil. to vol. and shake well.

Place 5 mL dild soln in each of 2 marked test tubes; in each of 2 addnl test tubes place 5 mL std phenol soln. Flow 5 mL Millon reagent down side of each tube, mix, and place tubes in boiling H_2O bath; continue boiling exactly 30 min, cool immediately and thoroly by immersion in bath of cold H_2O $\geqslant 10$ min, and add 5 mL dil. HNO_3 to each tube.

Mix well and add 3 mL HCHO soln to one of each pair of tubes. Dil. all tubes to 25 mL mark with H_2O, stopper, shake well, and let stand overnight. (Tubes contg HCHO fade to yellow; others show orange or red color.)

Pipet 20 mL from each of the 2 phenol tubes to 100 mL vol. flasks; add 5 mL dil. HNO_3 to each, dil. to vol., and mix. (Red flask contains "phenol std," yellow flask "phenol blank.") Transfer these solns to burets. Pipet 10 mL of each sample soln into Nessler tubes. (The orange or red constitutes the "unknown" and the yellow the "sample blank." Mark each Nessler tube distinctly to avoid confusion.) To "sample blank" tube add measured amt of "phenol std" and add same vol. "phenol blank" to "unknown." Agitate thoroly (aided by insertion of rubber stoppers, if necessary), and compare colors. When tubes are brought to match, each mL phenol std used = 1% phenol if sample weighing exactly 5 g was used, or 2% if exactly 2.5 g was used.

Note.—Take following precautions: Pair of phenol tubes provides enough final solns to assay several unknowns, but all the latter must have accompanied phenol solns thruout entire process with identical reagents and treatment. If end point is inadvertently overrun it is possible to work back to it, but since mistakes may be made in this operation it is better to repeat comparison on fresh portions from original tubes. Too much delay in matching tubes must be avoided after titrn is started, otherwise excess HCHO present in blanks may have time after mixing to affect intensity of red color.

5.018 ***Method II (6)—Official Final Action***

(Applicable to detn of phenol in presence of salicylates)

Weigh by difference 10 g sample into separator (or use 10 mL and calc. wt from density of sample). Add 50 mL kerosene and ext with three 100 mL portions H_2O. Filter aq. exts thru wet filter into 500 mL vol. flask, dil. to vol. with H_2O, and proceed as in **5.017**.

When tubes are brought to match, each mL phenol std used = 1% phenol if sample weighing exactly 10 g was used.

SODA LYE

Carbonate and Hydroxide (7)—Official Final Action

5.019 ***Determination***

Weigh ca 10 g sample from weighing bottle, dissolve in CO_2-free H_2O, and dil. to definite vol. Titr. aliquot with 0.5*N* HCl, **50.011—50.012**, using Me orange, **5.014(e)**, and note total alky found. Transfer equal aliquot to vol. flask and add enough 10% $BaCl_2$ soln to ppt all carbonate, avoiding any unnecessary excess. Dil. to vol. with CO_2-free H_2O, stopper, shake, and let stand. When liq. clears, pipet off one-half and titr. with the 0.5*N* HCl, using phthln; mL 0.5*N* acid required for this titrn × 2 = mL 0.5*N* acid equiv. to NaOH present in original aliquot. Difference between this figure and mL 0.5*N* HCl required for total alky = mL 0.5*N* acid equiv. to Na_2CO_3 present in aliquot. Calc. % Na_2CO_3 and NaOH.

EARTHENWARE

5.020 Cadmium and Lead

See **25.031—25.037**.

SELECTED REFERENCES

(*1*) JAOAC **57**, 614(1974).
(*2*) JAOAC **56**, 798(1973).
(*3*) JAOAC **54**, 558(1971); **55**, 242(1972).
(*4*) JAOAC **57**, 148(1974).
(*5*) USDA Bull. **1308**, p. 17; JAOAC **13**, 160(1930).
(*6*) Ind. Eng. Chem., Anal. Ed. **1**, 232(1929).
(*7*) Sutton "Systematic Handbook of Volumetric Analysis," 10th ed., p. 61(1911).

6. Pesticide Formulations

(Pesticide ref. stds may be available from the following: Alltech Associates, 202 Campus Dr, Arlington Hts, IL 60004; Analabs, Inc.; Applied Science Laboratories; Chem Service Inc., Westchester, PA 19380; ICN-K&K Laboratories, Inc.; RFR Corp., 1 Main St, Hope, RI 02831; and Supelco.)

GENERAL METHODS

6.001 Sampling—Procedure

(*Caution:* See **51.041**.)

Examine shipping cases closely for code numbers, different labels, and other pertinent information. Give special attention to products subject to deterioration.

Caution: Use care in sampling and transporting toxic materials to avoid personal injury and contamination of transportation facilities in case of breakage. When dealing with rodenticides and weed-killers, avoid mutual contamination with other products during transportation.

Mark each sample container according to laboratory requirements.

(**a**) *Small package retail units.*—Take one unopened unit (1 lb if dry, 1 pt if liq.), except take min. of 2 units of small baits in cake form. Size of sample is governed by composition of material and anal. methods.

(**b**) *Large package dry products* (*25 lb or more*).— Sample unopened containers, using trier long enough to reach bottom of container by inserting into container at one edge or corner and probing diagonally toward opposite edge or corner. Take cores by code or batch number. Analyze cores from same code or batch number as composite or individually. Clean trier thoroly after sampling each batch.

Store samples in air-tight glass, metal, plastic, or cardboard containers.

(**c**) *Large package liquid products* (*5 gallons or more*).—Use glass, plastic tubing, or stainless steel trier with plunger, or rubber tubing for certain materials. Store samples in glass or containers of other noncorrosive material with screw top caps lined with Teflon or other inert material. Plastic containers may be used only for carefully selected products.

6.002 Sampling of Pressurized Containers (*1*) Official First Action

Delivery assembly.—Construct U-shaped stainless steel assembly from ⅛" od tubing, with 1 arm 70 mm long with front and back ferrules (Swagelok No. SS-204-1 and SS-203-1, Crawford Fitting Co., 29500 Solon Rd, Solon, OH 44139) permanently swaged 3 mm from end, and other arm 135 mm longer (205 mm total length) sepd by 75 mm bend. Remove spray head from can. For male-type outlet, attach assembly from above ferrule to outlet with short piece of Tygon tubing. For female-type outlet, insert ferrule directly into outlet. Sample is released from can by carefully applying firm hand pressure to shoulder of assembly. *See* Fig. **6:01**.

Sampling.—Remove cover and spray head from can. Place can and delivery assembly in 800 mL beaker and weigh (W_o). Shake can vigorously 5 min. Immediately after shaking attach delivery assembly to spray outlet. Immerse long end into 250 mL separator contg 100 mL $CHCl_3$. Press shoulder to deliver ca 9 g sample (ca 10 sec) into $CHCl_3$. Return can and delivery assembly to beaker and weigh. Shake can vigorously 3 min and repeat delivery of sample until total of 10–15 g is obtained in $CHCl_3$. Reweigh can and delivery assembly in beaker (W). Calc. sample wt as ($W_o - W$).

6.003 Preparation of Sample—Official Final Action

Thoroly mix all samples before analysis. Det. H_2O-sol. As on samples as received, without further pulverization or drying. In case of lye, NaCN, or KCN, weigh large amts in weighing bottles and analyze aliquots of their aq. solns.

6.004 Moisture—Official Final Action

(Applicable to Paris green, powd Pb arsenate, Ca arsenate, Mg arsenate, Zn arsenite, powd Bordeaux mixt., and Bordeaux mixt. with arsenicals)

Dry 2 g to const wt at 105–110° and report loss in wt as moisture.

ARSENIC

Total Arsenic—Official Final Action

Hydrazine Sulfate Distillation Method (*2*)

(Nitrates do not interfere. Applicable to detn of total As in Paris green, Pb arsenate, Ca arsenate, Zn arsenite, Mg arsenate, and Bordeaux mixt. with arsenicals)

6.005 *Reagents*

(**a**) *Arsenious oxide std soln.*—0.1 or 0.05*N*. *See* **50.005–50.006**.

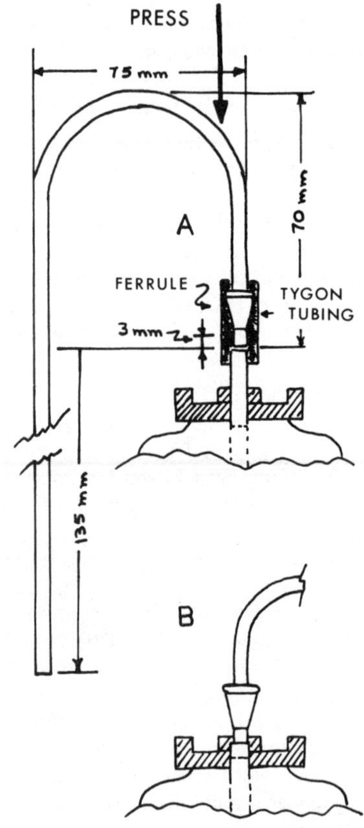

FIG. 6:01—Delivery assembly for sampling pressurized containers

(**b**) *Iodine std soln.*—0.1 or 0.05*N*. *See* **50.018–50.019**.

(**c**) *Bromate std soln.*—0.1 or 0.05*N*. Dissolve ca 2.8 or 1.4 g $KBrO_3$ in boiled H_2O and dil. to 1 L. Stdze as follows: Pipet 25 mL aliquots As_2O_3 soln, (**a**), into 500 mL erlenmeyers. Add 15 mL HCl, dil. to 100 mL, heat to 90°, and titr. with the $KBrO_3$ soln, using 10 drops Me orange, (**g**). Do not add indicator until near end of titrn, and agitate soln continuously to avoid local excess of $KBrO_3$ soln. Add $KBrO_3$ soln very slowly near end point; at end point soln changes from red to colorless.

(**d**) *Hydrazine sulfate-sodium bromide soln.*—Dissolve 20 g $N_2H_4.H_2SO_4$ and 20 g NaBr in 1 L HCl (1+4).

(**e**) *Sodium hydroxide soln.*—Dissolve 400 g NaOH in H_2O and dil. to 1 L.

(**f**) *Starch indicator.*—Mix ca 2 g finely powd. potato starch with cold H_2O to thin paste; add ca 200 mL boiling H_2O, stirring constantly, and immediately discontinue heating. Add ca 1 mL Hg, shake, and let soln stand over the Hg.

(**g**) *Methyl orange indicator.*—0.05%. Dissolve 0.5 g Me orange in H_2O and dil. to 1 L.

6.006 ***Apparatus***

See Fig. **6:02**. Set 500 mL distn flask on metal gauze that fits over circular hole in heavy sheet of asbestos board, which in turn extends out far enough to protect sides of flask from direct flame of burner. First receiving flask holds 500 mL and contains 40 mL H_2O; second holds 500 mL and contains 100 mL H_2O. Vol. in first flask should be $\leq$40 mL, otherwise compd of As may sep. that is difficult to dissolve without danger of loss of $AsCl_3$. Keep both flasks cool by placing in pan of circulating H_2O, or contg H_2O and ice.

6.007 ***Determination***

(*Caution: See* **51.041** and **51.078**.)

Weigh sample contg $\leq$0.4 g As and transfer to distg flask. Add 50 mL $N_2H_4.H_2SO_4$-NaBr soln, close flask with stopper that carries funnel tube, and connect side tube with condenser. Boil 2–3 min, add 100 mL HCl from dropping funnel, and distil until vol. in distg flask is reduced to ca 40 mL; add 50 mL more HCl and continue distn until vol. is again reduced to ca 40 mL. Wash down condenser, transfer contents of receiving flasks to 1 L vol. flask, dil. to vol., mix thoroly, and proceed as in (**a**) or (**b**):

(**a**) Pipet 200 mL aliquot into erlenmeyer and nearly neutze with NaOH soln, using few drops phthln, and keeping soln well cooled. If neut. point is passed, add HCl until again slightly acid. Neutze with $NaHCO_3$, add 4–5 g excess, and add std I soln from buret, shaking flask continuously until yellow color disappears slowly from soln. Add 5 mL starch indicator and keep adding std I soln dropwise to permanent blue.

(**b**) Pipet 200 mL aliquot into erlenmeyer and titr. with $KBrO_3$ soln, (**c**), beginning "... heat to 90° ..."

Calc. % As. Report as As_2O_3 or As_2O_5, according to whether As is present in trivalent or pentavalent form. If condition of arsenic is unknown, report as As.

***Iodimetric Method* (3)**

(Applicable in presence of sulfides, sulfites, thiosulfates, and large amts of S or org. matter)

6.008 ***Reagent***

Sodium thiosulfate soln.—Dissolve 13 g crystd $Na_2S_2O_3.5H_2O$ in H_2O and dil. to 1 L.

See **6.005** for other reagents and solns and **6.006** for app.

6.009 ***Determination***

(*Caution: See* **51.041** and **51.078**.)

Weigh sample contg $\leq$0.4 g As and transfer to distg flask. Add 50 mL $N_2H_4.H_2SO_4$-NaBr soln, **6.005(d)**, and distil as in **6.007**. Dil. distillate to vol. in 1 L vol. flask, mix thoroly, and transfer 200 mL aliquot to 400 mL Pyrex beaker or porcelain casserole. Add 10 mL HNO_3 and 5 mL H_2SO_4, evap. to sirupy consistency on steam bath, and then heat on hot plate to white fumes of H_2SO_4. Cool, and wash into 500 mL erlenmeyer. If vol. H_2SO_4 is appreciably lessened by fuming, add enough H_2SO_4 to make total vol. ca 5 mL. Dil. to 100–150 mL, add 1.5 g KI, and boil until vol. is reduced to ca 40 mL. Cool under running H_2O, dil. to 100–150 mL, and add $Na_2S_2O_3$ soln, **6.008**, dropwise until I color just disappears. Nearly neutze H_2SO_4 with NaOH soln, **6.005(e)**, finish neutzn with $NaHCO_3$, add 4–5 g excess, and titr. with std I soln as in **6.007(a)**. From mL std soln used, calc. % As in sample. Report as As_2O_3, As_2O_5, or As as in **6.007**.

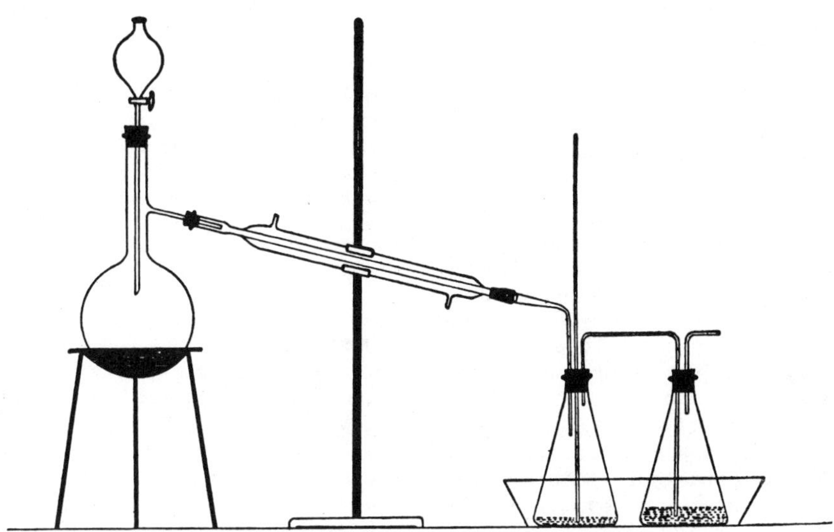

FIG. 6:02—Apparatus for distilling arsenious chloride

Ion Exchange Method (4)—Official Final Action

(Applicable to inorg. arsenates and arsenites)

6.010 ***Apparatus***

Ion exchange column.—Use Allihn filter tube 10 × 2.7 cm od with coarse filter disk. Attach piece of rubber tubing to bottom of filter tube and regulate flow with Hoffman clamp. To tube add aq. slurry of Dowex 50W-X8, 50–100 mesh, using resin bed vol. of 12 mL, and place 500 mL separator above tube.

Regenerate resin bed before each run by first back-washing column few min with H_2O; then elute with 350 mL 2*N* HCl followed by 200 mL H_2O at 20 mL/min.

6.011 ***Preparation of Sample***

(*Caution: See* **51.041**.)

Weigh 200 mg sample (100 mg if As content is >30%) into 150 mL beaker, add 7 mL HNO_3, and bring to bp. Add 3 mL 2*N* $KBrO_3$ and evap. to dryness, avoiding spattering. Backwash and regenerate resin during this evapn. Dissolve cooled residue in 2 mL 6*N* HCl without heat and add 8 mL H_2O. Filter into separator, and wash filter with three 10 mL portions H_2O. (If residue dissolves completely in 2 mL 6*N* HCl, omit filtration, and dil. directly to 40 mL.) Pass soln thru resin column at 20 mL/min and collect eluate in 250 mL erlenmeyer. Wash separator and column with 20 and 40 mL portions H_2O into same erlenmeyer.

6.012 ***Determination***

Add 50 mL HCl to eluate to make 4*N*. Add 1 g $NaHCO_3$, 0.2 g at time, swirling constantly. Add 1 g KI, stopper, and swirl until all KI dissolves. After 5 min, titr., without starch indicator, with 0.05*N* $Na_2S_2O_3$, **50.037—50.038**, to disappearance of I. (Recognition of end point is facilitated by titrg on porcelain stand. In presence of starch, reaction between I and $Na_2S_2O_3$ is retarded, so appreciable amt of $Na_2S_2O_3$ reacts with acid. End point becomes indistinct if >30 mL $Na_2S_2O_3$ is used in titrn.) 1 mL 0.05*N* $Na_2S_2O_3$ = 1.873 mg As.

Water-Soluble Arsenic—Official Final Action

(Applicable to detn of H_2O-sol. arsenic in Pb arsenate, Ca arsenate, Zn arsenite, Mg arsenate, and Bordeaux mixt. with arsenicals)

6.013 ***Determination***

(*Caution: See* **51.041**.)

To 2 g original sample if powder, or 4 g if paste, in 1 L Florence flask, add 1 L recently boiled H_2O that has been cooled to 32°. Stopper flask and place in constant temp. H_2O bath at 32°. Digest 24 hr, shaking hourly 8 hr during this period. Filter thru dry filter. If filtrate is not clear, refilter thru buchner contg paper and enough Filter-Cel coating to give clear soln. Discard first 50 mL.

Transfer 250–500 mL *clear* filtrate to erlenmeyer, add 3 mL H_2SO_4, and evap. to ca 100 mL on hot plate. Add 1 g KI, and continue boiling until vol. is ca 40 mL. Cool, dil. to ca 200 mL, and add $Na_2S_2O_3$ soln, **6.008**, dropwise, until I color is exactly removed. (Avoid use of starch indicator at this point.) Neutze with $NaHCO_3$, add 4–5 g excess, titr. with std I soln, shaking flask continuously, until yellow disappears slowly, add 5 mL starch indicator, **6.005(f)**, and continue titrn to permanent blue. Correct for amt std I soln necessary to produce same color, using same reagents and vol. From mL std I soln used, calc. % H_2O-sol. As in sample.

LEAD (5)—OFFICIAL FINAL ACTION

(Applicable to such prepns as Bordeaux-Pb arsenate, Bordeaux-Zn arsenite, Bordeaux-Paris green, and Bordeaux-Ca arsenate)

(*Caution: See* **51.026**, **51.031**, **51.041**, **51.059**, and **51.078**.)

6.014 ***Determination***

Weigh 1 g powd sample and transfer to beaker. Add 5 mL *HBr* (ca 1.38 sp gr) and 15 mL HCl, and evap. to dryness to remove As. Repeat treatment; add 20 mL HCl, and again evap. to dryness. Add 25 mL 2*N* HCl to residue, heat to bp, filter immediately to remove SiO_2, and wash with boiling H_2O to vol. of 125 mL. See that all $PbCl_2$ is in soln before filtering; if it will not dissolve completely in 25 mL 2*N* acid, add 25 mL more and dil. filtrate to 250 mL. Pass in H_2S until pptn is complete. Filter, and wash ppt thoroly with 0.5*N* HCl satd with H_2S. Save filtrate and washings for Zn detn.

Transfer paper with sulfides of Pb and Cu to 400 mL Pyrex beaker and completely oxidize all org. matter by heating on steam bath with 4 mL H_2SO_4 and ca 20 mL *fuming* HNO_3 in covered beaker. Evap. on steam bath, and then completely remove HNO_3 by heating on hot plate to copious white fumes of H_2SO_4. Cool, add 2–3 mL H_2O, and again heat to fuming. Cool, add 50 mL H_2O and 100 mL alcohol, and let stand several hr (preferably overnight). Filter thru gooch, previously washed with H_2O, then with *acidified alcohol* (100 parts H_2O, 200 parts alcohol, and 3 parts H_2SO_4), and finally with alcohol, and dried at 200°. Wash ppt of $PbSO_4$ in crucible ca 10 times with acidified alcohol, and then with alcohol, to remove H_2SO_4. Retain filtrate and washings for Cu detn, if desired.

Dry at 200° to const wt, keeping crucible covered to prevent loss from spattering. From wt $PbSO_4$, calc. % Pb in sample, using factor 0.6832.

COPPER (5)—OFFICIAL FINAL ACTION

(Applicable to such prepns as Bordeaux-Pb arsenate, Bordeaux-Zn arsenite, Bordeaux-Paris green, and Bordeaux-Ca arsenate)

6.015 ***Electrolytic Method***

Evap. filtrate and washings from $PbSO_4$ pptn, **6.014**, to fuming; add few mL *fuming* HNO_3 to destroy org. matter, and continue evapn to ca 3 mL. Take up with ca 150 mL H_2O, add 5 mL HNO_3, and filter if necessary. Wash into 250 mL beaker, adjust vol. to 200 mL, and electrolyze, using rotating anode and weighed gauze cathode with current of 2–3 amp. After all Cu has apparently deposited (ca 30 min), add 15–20 mL H_2O to electrolyte and continue electrolysis few min. If no further deposition occurs on newly exposed surface of electrode, wash with H_2O without breaking current either by siphoning or quickly replacing beaker with electrolyte successively with 2 beakers of H_2O. Interrupt current, rinse cathode with alcohol, dry few moments in oven, and weigh. Calc. % Cu in sample.

6.016 ***Volumetric Thiosulfate Method***

Proceed as in **6.015** to point at which filtrate and washings from $PbSO_4$ pptn are treated with fuming HNO_3 and evapd to vol. of ca 3 mL. Take up in ca 50 mL H_2O, add NH_4OH in excess, and boil to expel excess NH_3, as shown by color change in liq. and partial pptn. Add 3–4 mL HOAc (4+1), boil 1–2 min, cool, add 10 mL 30% KI soln, and titr. with std $Na_2S_2O_3$ soln, **31.040**, until brown color becomes faint. Add starch indicator, **6.005(f)**, and continue titrn cautiously until blue color due to free I entirely disappears. From mL std $Na_2S_2O_3$ soln used, calc. % Cu in sample.

ZINC (6)—OFFICIAL FINAL ACTION

(Applicable to such prepns as Bordeaux-Pb arsenate, Zn arsenite, Bordeaux-Zn arsenite, Bordeaux-Paris green, and Bordeaux-Ca arsenate)

6.017 ***Reagent***

Mercury-thiocyanate soln.—(*Caution: See* **51.079.**) Dissolve 27 g $HgCl_2$ and 30 g NH_4SCN in H_2O and dil. to 1 L.

6.018 ***Determination***

Conc. filtrate and washings from sulfide pptn, **6.014**, by gentle boiling to ca 50 mL; then evap. on steam bath to dryness. Dissolve residue in 100 mL H_2O contg 5 mL HCl, and add 35–40 mL Hg-thiocyanate soln with vigorous stirring. Let stand ≥1 hr with occasional stirring. Filter thru weighed gooch, wash with H_2O contg 20 mL Hg-thiocyanate soln/L, and dry to const wt at 105°. Calc. to % Zn, using factor 0.1312.

Note: Some Fe is usually present and during Zn detn should be in ferrous condition. In pptg sulfides pass H_2S into soln long enough to reduce Fe as well as to ppt Cu and Pb. $ZnHg(SCN)_4$ ppt normally is white, and occluded $Fe(SCN)_3$ should not give more than faint pink color.

FLUORINE

Total Fluorine—Official Final Action

Lead Chlorofluoride Method (7)

6.019 ***Reagents***

(**a**) *Fusion mixture.*—Mix 30 g anhyd. Na_2CO_3 with 40 g anhyd. K_2CO_3.

(**b**) *Lead chlorofluoride wash soln.*—Dissolve 10 g $Pb(NO_3)_2$ in 200 mL H_2O, dissolve 1 g NaF in 100 mL H_2O and add 2 mL HCl, and mix these 2 solns. Let ppt settle and decant. Wash ppt 4 or 5 times with 200 mL H_2O by decanting; then add ca 1 L cold H_2O to ppt and let stand ≥1 hr, with occasional stirring. Filter and use clear filtrate. (Prep. more wash soln as needed by adding more H_2O to ppt of PbClF and stirring.)

(**c**) *Silver nitrate std soln.*—0.1 or 0.2*N*. Stdze as in **50.031**.

(**d**) *Potassium or ammonium thiocyanate std soln.*—0.1*N*. Stdze against std $AgNO_3$ soln under same conditions as in detn.

(**e**) *Ferric indicator.*—To cold satd Cl-free $FeNH_4(SO_4)_2 \cdot 12H_2O$ soln add enough colorless HNO_3 to bleach brown color.

(**f**) *Bromophenol blue indicator.*—Grind 0.1 g powder with 1.5 mL 0.1*N* NaOH and dil. to 25 mL.

6.020 ***Determination***

(**a**) *Samples difficult to decompose such as cryolite, and others that contain aluminum or appreciable amounts of siliceous material.*—Mix 0.5 g sample (or less if necessary to contain 0.01–0.10 g F) with 5 g fusion mixt. and 0.2–0.3 g *powd. SiO_2* in Pt dish, cover with 1 g fusion mixt., and heat to fusion over Bunsen burner. (Use of blast lamp is unnecessary since it is preferable not to heat much beyond melting temp. If much Al is present, uniform, clear, liq. melt cannot be obtained; particles of white solid will sep. in melt. Cooled melt should be colorless, or at least should not have more than gray color.)

Leach cooled melt with hot H_2O and when disintegration is complete, filter into 400 mL beaker. Return insol. residue to Pt dish with jet of H_2O, add 1 g Na_2CO_3, dil. to 30–50 mL, and boil few min, disintegrating any lumps with flat-end rod. Filter thru same paper, wash thoroly with hot H_2O, and adjust vol. of filtrate and washings to ca 200 mL. Add 1 g *ZnO* dissolved in 20 mL HNO_3 (1+9), boil 2 min, stirring constantly, filter, and wash thoroly with hot H_2O. During this washing return gelatinous mass to beaker 3 times and thoroly disintegrate in wash soln because proper washing of this ppt on filter is difficult. (Mass can easily be returned to beaker by rotating funnel above beaker while cutting ppt loose from paper with jet of wash soln.)

Add 2 drops bromophenol blue to filtrate, and with cover glass almost entirely over beaker, add HNO_3 (1+4) until color just changes to yellow. Make soln slightly alk. with 10% NaOH soln, and with cover glass on beaker, boil gently to expel CO_2. Remove from burner; add the HNO_3 until color just changes to yellow and then 10% NaOH until color just changes to blue; then add 3 mL *10% NaCl soln.* (Vol. of soln at this point should be ca 250 mL.)

Add 2 mL HCl (1+1) and 5 g *$Pb(NO_3)_2$* and heat on steam bath. As soon as $Pb(NO_3)_2$ is in soln, add 5 g NaOAc, stir vigorously, and digest on steam bath 30 min with occasional stirring. Let stand overnight, filter, and wash ppt, beaker, and paper once with cold H_2O, then 4 or 5 times with PbClF wash soln, and then once more with cold H_2O.

Transfer ppt and paper to beaker in which pptn was made, stir paper to pulp, add 100 mL HNO_3 (5+95), and heat on steam bath until ppt dissolves. (5 min is ample to dissolve ppt. If sample contains appreciable amt of sulfates, ppt will contain $PbSO_4$, which will not dissolve. In such case heat 5–10 min with stirring and consider PbClF to be dissolved.) Add slight excess 0.1*N* or 0.2*N* $AgNO_3$, digest on steam bath 30 min, and cool to room temp., protecting from light; filter, wash with cold H_2O, and det. $AgNO_3$ in filtrate by titrn with std thiocyanate soln, using 10 mL ferric indicator. Subtract amt of $AgNO_3$ found in filtrate from that originally added. Difference is amt required to combine with Cl in the PbClF; from this difference calc. % F in sample. 1 mL 0.1*N* $AgNO_3$ = 0.00190 g F.

(**b**) *Water-soluble fluorides in presence of organic matter.*—In presence of ≤50% org. matter such as flour, pyrethrum, tobacco powder, and derris or cubé powders, which readily decompose without addn of powd SiO_2 and contain little or no sulfates, Al, or siliceous compds, mix 0.5 g sample (or less if necessary to contain 0.01–0.1 g F) with 5 g fusion mixt., cover with 1 g fusion mixt., and heat to fusion over Bunsen burner. Leach cooled melt with hot H_2O, and when disintegration is complete, filter into 600 mL beaker. Wash thoroly with hot H_2O and proceed as in (**a**), third par.

In presence of >50% org. matter or org. matter that is impractical to free without preliminary ashing, such as apple peel and pulp, transfer enough sample to Pt crucible to be representative of mixt. and to contain 0.01–0.1 g F. Add 15 mL H_2O and enough *F-free CaO* (0.3–0.4 g) to make mixt. distinctly alk. to phthln, mix with glass rod, and evap. to dryness on steam bath and in oven at 105°. Ignite at low heat, preferably in furnace (≤600°), until org. matter is thoroly charred. Pulverize, with glass rod, any lumps present in charred ash, mix with 5 g of the fusion mixt., and proceed as in (**a**), first par., beginning ". . . cover with 1 g fusion mixt., . . ."

(**c**) *Water-soluble samples in absence of organic matter and appreciable quantities of sulfates or aluminum salts.*—In absence of org. matter or other interfering substances, fusion may be omitted and detn made on aliquot of aq. soln contg 0.01–0.1 g F, as in (**a**), third par.

In presence of Al, as in samples contg Na_2SiF_6 and $KAl(SO_4)_2 \cdot 12H_2O$, transfer sample to 400 mL beaker, dissolve in 150 mL hot H_2O, add 6 g fusion mixt., and boil. Add 1 g *ZnO* dissolved in 20 mL HNO_3 (1+9), boil 2 min with const stirring, filter into 500 mL vol. flask, and wash thoroly with hot H_2O. Cool to room temp. and dil. to vol. Transfer 200 mL aliquot contg 0.01–0.10 g F to 600 mL beaker and proceed as in (**a**), third par.

(**d**) *Sodium and magnesium fluosilicates, or samples containing more than 5% sulfates in absence of aluminum and* *boron, with or without moderate amounts of organic matter.*—With large amts of Na_2SiF_6 and some other more volatile fluosilicates, *e.g.,* $MgSiF_6$, where there is possibility of some F being evolved as SiF_4 before fusion is effected, or in samples contg appreciable amts of sulfates, distil F as in **6.024**, and det. F in distillate as follows: Add several drops bromophenol blue, make alk. with NaOH, and adjust vol. to ca 250 mL by gently boiling down vol. from 400 to 250 mL. Proceed as in (**a**), third par., beginning "Remove from burner; . . ."

Notes: These methods give accurate results for 0.01–0.10 g F. Below 0.01 g, results tend to be slightly low, and above 0.10 g, slightly high. Convenient sample to fuse is one contg 0.07–0.08 g F; too large sample may result in incomplete fusion. Large amts of B compds and alkali salts retard or prevent complete pptn of PbClF. B has greater effect when amt of F is large than when it is small. In methods described B has little effect, and it may be disregarded in analysis of insecticides if amt of F to be pptd is $\leq$0.03 g. With some prepns contg $Na_2B_4O_7$ or H_3BO_3, where it is difficult to obtain representative mixt. when extremely small sample (0.1 g) is used for analysis, take larger sample and ppt PbClF from aliquot of fusion soln. Amt of alkali carbonates specified in fusion and in washing of insol. residue is not large enough to cause low results. If sample contains S, remove it with CS_2 and det. F on air-dried residue, allowing in calcns for % S removed. (*Caution: See* **51.039**, **51.040**, and **51.048**.)

Modified Travers Method (8)

(Applicable in absence of B, Al, and large amts of pyrethrum powder)

6.021 ***Reagents***

(**a**) *Alcoholic potassium chloride soln.*—Dissolve 60 g KCl in 400 mL H_2O, add 400 mL alcohol, and test with phthln; if soln is not neut., adjust to exact neutrality with NaOH or HCl soln.

(**b**) *Sodium hydroxide std soln.*—0.2*N*. Prep. and stdze as in **50.032—50.035**.

6.022 ***Determination***

Treat 0.5 g sample in small beaker with 20–25 mL H_2O. Add 0.3 g finely divided *pptd SiO_2* and few drops Me orange. Add HCl dropwise until soln assumes apparently permanent pink; then add 2 mL excess, cover beaker with watch glass, and boil 1 min. Cool to room temp., add 4 g KCl, and stir until KCl dissolves. Add 25 mL alcohol and let stand 1 hr, stirring frequently. Filter thru gooch contg disk of filter paper covered with medium pad of asbestos. Wash ppt with alc. KCl soln until one washing does not destroy color made by 1 drop 0.2*N* NaOH and phthln (usually 3–4 washings). Transfer crucible and contents to 400 mL beaker, add 100 mL recently boiled H_2O and 1–2 mL phthln, heat, and titr. with std NaOH soln. Finish titrn with the F soln actively boiling. Calc. % F. 1 mL 0.2*N* NaOH = 0.0057 g F.

Distillation Method (9)

(Applicable to H_2O-sol. or H_2O-insol. insecticides in absence of gelatinous SiO_2, B, and Al)

6.023 ***Reagents***

(**a**) *Sodium alizarin sulfonate indicator.*—Dissolve 0.1 g Na alizarin sulfonate in 200 mL H_2O.

(**b**) *Thorium nitrate soln.*—Approx. 0.05*N*. Stdze in terms of g F/mL by titrg F obtained by distn from std NaF as in **6.024**. In stdzg for use with **6.024(b)**, add 5 mL satd $KMnO_4$ soln in addn to other reagents in distn flask.

6.024 ***Determination***

(**a**) *In absence of organic matter.*—Weigh sample contg ca 0.09 g F, and with aid of little H_2O transfer to 250 mL Claisen distn flask contg 12 glass beads. Adjust to ca 30 mL and close flask with 2-hole rubber stopper, thru which pass thermometer and 4 mm glass tube, both of which extend into soln. (The 4 mm glass tube extends ca 5 cm above rubber stopper and by means of rubber tube, *E*, connects still with 1 L Florence flask contg H_2O for steam generation. Flask is equipped with steam discharge, *H*, and pressure tube, *G*. *See* Fig. **6:03**.)

Bring H_2O in steam generating flask to boil with pinchcock, *F*, in release tube open. Connect distg flask to condenser, and add 25 mL H_2SO_4 thru top of 4 mm tube, using pipet or special funnel. With pinchcock, *F*, open, connect rubber tubing to 4 mm

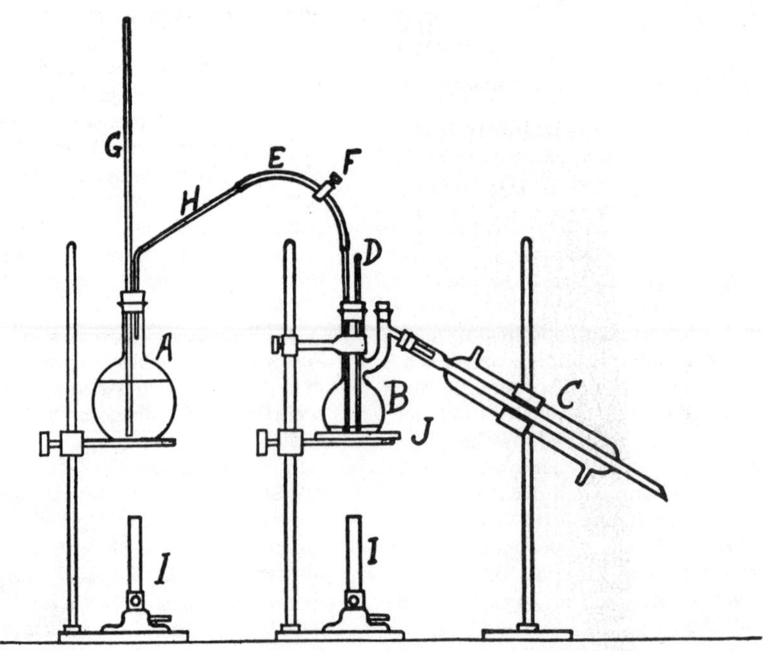

FIG. 6:03—Apparatus for determining fluorine

tube. Light burner under Claisen flask. Regulate flow of steam by adjusting burner flames and pinchcock, *F*, so that vol. of soln is held const and temp. in flask, *B*, is kept at 145–150°. Continue distn until 400 mL distillate collects. Dil. to 500 mL in vol. flask, transfer 50 mL aliquot to tall-form 150 mL beaker, and add 5 drops indicator, **6.023(a)**. Adjust acidity with 1% NaOH soln and HCl (1+249) until pink just disappears. Add 2 mL of the HCl, and titr. with 0.05*N* $Th(NO_3)_4$ to permanent pink, using buret graduated in 0.05 mL.

(**b**) *In presence of organic matter.*—(*Caution: See* **51.080**.) In presence of moderate amts of org. matter, transfer sample contg ca 0.09 g F and contg ≤0.2 g org. matter, with aid of little H_2O, to 250 mL Claisen distn flask contg 12 glass beads. Add 5 mL satd $KMnO_4$ soln, adjust to ca 30 mL, and proceed as in (**a**), beginning "... close flask with 2-hole rubber stopper, ..."

In presence of large amts of org. matter, transfer sample to medium-size Pt dish, add 15 mL H_2O and enough *F-free CaO* to make mixt. distinctly alk. to phthln, mix with glass rod, and evap. to dryness on steam bath and in oven at 105°. Ignite at low heat, preferably in furnace (≤600°), until org. matter is thoroly charred. Pulverize any lumps present in charred ash with glass rod, transfer to 250 mL Claisen distn flask by brushing, and finally wash out dish with 30 mL H_2SO_4 (1+9). Except to add 22 mL instead of 25 mL H_2SO_4, proceed as in (**a**), par. 2.

Note: If coating of pptd SiO_2 forms on inside of distn flask, remove by treatment with hot concd alkali soln, as it is capable of retaining F during distn of some samples and giving it up, at least in part, in later distns.

Fluorine Present as Sodium Fluosilicate
Official Final Action

(B, CaO, and alum absent)

6.025 ***Reagents***

Alcoholic potassium chloride and sodium carbonate soln.—Dissolve 1.0 g Na_2CO_3 in 100 mL alc. KCl reagent, **6.021(a)**.

For other reagent *see* **6.021**.

6.026 ***Determination***

Weigh 1 g sample into Pt dish, and add rapidly, with continuous stirring, 50 mL of the alc. KCl-Na_2CO_3 reagent. Do not let soln become acid, and if necessary, use more reagent to insure alky. Continue stirring until all sol. portions of sample dissolve. Proceed as in **6.022**, beginning: "Filter thru gooch ..." Calc. % Na_2SiF_6 (1 mL 0.2*N* NaOH = 0.009403 g Na_2SiF_6).

CONTAMINATION BY ORGANOCHLORINE PESTICIDES (*10*)—OFFICIAL FINAL ACTION

AOAC-CIPAC Method

(Applicable to detection of contamination by 0.01% chlorinated hydrocarbons such as aldrin, DDT, dieldrin, and endrin, and 0.05–0.10% of chlordane, Strobane, and toxaphene)

6.027 ***Apparatus***

(**a**) *Thin layer chromatographic apparatus.*—*See* **29.006**.

(**b**) *Ultraviolet apparatus.*—Sterilamp G-15T8 (Westinghouse Electric Corp., Lamp Divisions, One Westinghouse Plaza, Bloomfield, NJ 07003).

6.028 ***Reagents***

(**a**) *Adsorbent.*—Aluminum oxide G, Type E (Brinkmann Instruments, Inc.).

(**b**) *Mobile solvents.*—(*1*) *n*-Hexane, (*2*) *n*-hexane-acetone (98+2), and (*3*) *n*-hexane-alcohol (98+2).

(**c**) *Pesticide std solns.*—1 μg/μL EtOAc, acetone, or any convenient solv.

6.029 ***Preparation of Sample***

Ext 8 g sample with 20 mL acetone in 250 mL erlenmeyer by shaking intermittently 5 min. Let solids settle. If soln is turbid, filter or centrf. to obtain clear supernate for spotting. For samples contg large amts S, use 8 g sample and 20 mL pet ether.

6.030 ***Preparation of Plates***

Dissolve 0.1–0.15 g $AgNO_3$ in 1–2 mL H_2O in 100 mL beaker, add 58 mL MeOH, and mix. Weigh 40 g adsorbent, (**a**), in 250 mL flask, add $AgNO_3$-MeOH soln, and shake vigorously 20 sec. Apply slurry as 0.25 mm thick layer to five 20 × 20 cm (8 × 8") plates positioned on plastic mounting board. After plates appear dry, store in desiccator over desiccant. When plate is dry, scrape 1 cm strip from side edges to ensure even solv. front. Use plate immediately after removal from desiccator.

6.031 ***Detection***

Pour *n*-hexane into glass chromatgc tank to depth of 10–20 mm. Place 2 paper blotters (ca 7.5 × 22 cm) on each side of tank or large blotter covering back of tank and let equilibrate ≥2 hr before use.

Spot 10 μL sample ext on plate with 100 μL syringe. Do *not* disturb adsorbent layer. Also spot std solns of pesticides declared as part of formulation. Spots should be ≤6 mm diam. and placed <30 mm from bottom of plate. Place plate in chromatgc tank, and let plate develop ≥10 cm. Remove plate and expose to shortwave UV, **6.027(b)**. (*Caution: See* **51.016**.) Chlorinated org. pesticides should be visible as dark spots against white or light gray background. Expose plates ≥1 hr. Longer exposure will not harm plates.

To confirm identification of pesticide, repeat TLC step with different mobile solv., **6.028(b)**(*2*) or (*3*).

VOLATILITY OF ESTER FORMS OF HORMONE-TYPE HERBICIDES (*11*)—OFFICIAL FINAL ACTION

6.032 ***Material***

(**a**) *Paper bags.*—No. 20 to open with flat bottom. Close with paper clips.

(**b**) *Filter paper.*—7 cm diam.

(**c**) *Bacteriological loop.*—0.01 mL. Wash with acetone after each application or heat to cherry red in flame.

(**d**) *Test plants.*—Actively growing tomato seedlings 65–75 mm high in 3–4" pots.

(**e**) *Formulation to be tested.*—Use 0.01 mL aliquot of 4 lb/gal. formulation or equiv. vol. of other concns.

(**f**) *High and low volatile ester stds.*—Use Bu ester of 2,4-D as high volatile ester and tetrahydrofurfural ester of 2,4-D as low volatile ester with same wt of acid/gal. as formulations to be tested.

6.033 ***Operating Technic***

Open bags with flat bottom and place plant toward one side on bottom of bag. Apply 0.01 mL of formulation to middle of filter paper by means of bacteriological loop, and for controls, apply 0.01 mL solv. only. Place treated paper in bottom of bag. Do not touch treated part of paper against plant, sides of bag, or pot. Close bag by folding top, secure with clips, and let stand 24 hr at 85–110°F (29–43°C).

Use 3 plants per treatment and 3 for controls. Repeat test on another day.

Remove plants from bag, let stand 24 hr, and read curvature (stem bending, epinasty) response. (Fold and discard used bags to prevent contamination.) Rate plants according to scale as follows:

(1) Normal growth of untreated check–no apparent response.
(2) Epinasty 1–20° compared to normal–no curling.
(3) Epinasty 21–40° compared to normal–slight curling.
(4) Epinasty 41–60° compared to normal–moderate curling.
(5) Epinasty 61–80° compared to normal–moderate curling.
(6) Epinasty 81 to >90° compared to normal–severe formative effects.

Mean response of 1 to 2.4 for all tests indicates low volatility. Mean response of 2.5 to 6 indicates volatile formulation.

To detect small differences between low volatile esters, or differences between 2,4-D and 2,4,5-T types, hold plants 7 days after treatment to allow time for modified leaves or stem lesions to develop. Absence of such responses indicates that formulation was a low volatile 2,4,5-T ester.

INORGANIC AND ORGANOMETALLIC PESTICIDES AND ADJUVANTS

★ PARIS GREEN ★

(*Caution: See* **51.041**.)

6.034 Moisture—Official Final Action

See **6.004**.

6.035 Total Arsenic—Official Final Action

See **6.007**.

Total Arsenious Oxide—Official Final Action

(Following methods det. only As present in trivalent form (As_2O_3) and Sb present in trivalent form (Sb_2O_3) in absence of ferrous and cuprous salts.)

Method I (12)

6.036 ***Reagents***

See **4.028**, 10th ed.

6.037 ***Determination***

Iodometric titrn. *See* **4.029**, 10th ed.

6.038 ***Method II (13)***

Bromate titrn. *See* **4.030**, 10th ed.

6.039 Water-Soluble Arsenious Oxide Official Final Action

Iodometric titrn. *See* **4.031**, 10th ed.

Total Copper—Official Final Action

6.040 ***Electrolytic Method***

See **4.032**, 10th ed.

6.041 ***Volumetric Thiosulfate Method (14)***

See **4.033**, 10th ed.

★ Methods for this product are surplus—*see* inside front cover.

LEAD ARSENATE

(*Caution: See* **51.041** and **51.078**.)

6.042 Moisture—Official Final Action

(**a**) *Powder.*—Dry 2 g to const wt at 105–110°. Report loss in wt as H_2O.

(**b**) *Paste.*—Proceed as in (**a**), using 50 g. Grind dry sample to fine powder, mix well, transfer small portion to sample bottle, and again dry 1–2 hr at 105–110°. Use this anhyd. material to det. total Pb and total As.

Total Arsenic—Official Final Action

6.043 ***Method I***

See **6.007**.

6.044 ***Method II (15)***

(Not applicable in presence of Sb)

Dissolve 1 g powd sample with HNO_3 (1+4) in porcelain casserole or evapg dish, add 5 mL H_2SO_4, and heat on hot plate to copious evolution of white fumes. Cool, add little H_2O, and again evap. until white fumes appear, to assure removal of last trace of HNO_3. Wash into 200 mL vol. flask with H_2O, cool, dil. to vol., and filter thru dry filter. Transfer 100 mL filtrate to erlenmeyer and proceed as in **6.013**, beginning "... add 1 g KI, ..." From mL std I soln used, calc. % total As as As_2O_5.

6.045 Total Arsenious Oxide (*16*)—Official Final Action

Weigh 2 g powd sample and transfer to 200 mL vol. flask, add 100 mL H_2SO_4 (1+6), and boil 30 min. Cool, dil. to vol., shake thoroly, and filter thru dry filter. Nearly neutze 100 mL filtrate with NaOH soln, **6.005(e)**, using few drops phthln. If neut. point is passed, make acid again with the dil. H_2SO_4. Continue as in **6.013**, beginning "Neutze with $NaHCO_3$, ..." From mL std I soln used, calc. % As_2O_3.

Total Arsenic Oxide (*17*)—Official Final Action

6.046 ***Reagents***

(**a**) *Potassium iodide soln.*—Dissolve 20 g KI in H_2O and dil. to 100 mL.

(**b**) *Thiosulfate std soln.*—0.05*N*. Prep. daily by dilg 0.1*N* soln, **50.037–50.038**. 1 mL 0.05*N* $Na_2S_2O_3$ = 2.873 mg As_2O_5.

6.047 ***Determination***

Weigh 0.5 g powd sample and transfer to erlenmeyer. Add 25–30 mL HCl and evap. to dryness on steam bath. Add 50 mL HCl and if necessary to effect soln, heat on steam bath, keeping flask covered with watch glass to prevent evapn of acid. Cool to 20–25°, add 10 mL of the KI soln and 50 mL (or more if necessary to produce clear soln) 25% *NH_4Cl soln,* and immediately titr. liberated I with std $Na_2S_2O_3$ soln. When color becomes faint yellow, dil. with ca 150 mL H_2O and continue titrn carefully, dropwise, until colorless, using starch indicator, **6.005(f)**, near end point. From mL $Na_2S_2O_3$ soln used, calc. % As_2O_5.

6.048 Water-Soluble Arsenic—Official Final Action

Proceed as in **6.013**, and calc. results as As_2O_5.

6.049 Total Lead (*18*)—Official Final Action

In 600 mL beaker on hot plate heat 0.5 g powd sample and ca 25 mL HNO_3 (1+4). Filter to remove any insol. residue. Dil. to ⩾400 mL, heat nearly to bp, and add NH_4OH to slight pptn, then

HNO_3 (1+9) to redissolve ppt, adding 1–2 mL excess. Into this soln, kept almost boiling, pipet 50 mL hot *10% K_2CrO_4 soln,* stirring constantly. Decant while hot thru weighed gooch, previously heated to 140–150°, and wash ppt several times by decanting and then on filter with boiling H_2O until washings are colorless. Dry $PbCrO_4$ at 140–150° to const wt. From wt $PbCrO_4$, calc. % Pb, using factor 0.6411. ($PbCrO_4$ ppt may contain small amt $PbHAsO_4$, which will cause slightly high results, but this error rarely is >0.1–0.2%.)

CALCIUM ARSENATE

(*Caution: See* **51.041**.)

6.050 Moisture—Official Final Action

See **6.004**.

6.051 Total Arsenic—Official Final Action

See **6.007**.

6.052 Total Arsenious Oxide (*19*)—Official Final Action

(**a**) *Not applicable in presence of nitrates.*—Weigh 1 g sample, transfer to 500 mL erlenmeyer, and dissolve in 100 mL HCl (1+3). Heat to 90° and titr. with std $KBrO_3$ soln, **6.005(c)**, using 10 drops Me orange, **6.005(g)**. From mL std $KBrO_3$ soln used, calc. % As_2O_3.

(**b**) *Applicable in presence of small amounts of nitrates.*—Proceed as in (**a**) except to titr. at room temp.

6.053 Water-Soluble Arsenic—Official Final Action

Proceed as in **6.013**, and calc. results as As_2O_5. (In testing Ca arsenate by this method, low value for H_2O-sol. As is not assurance against plant injury when using this product.)

Total Calcium (*19*)—Official Final Action

6.054 ***Reagents***

(**a**) *Ammonium oxalate soln.*—Dissolve 40 g $(NH_4)_2C_2O_4.H_2O$ in 1 L H_2O.

(**b**) *Potassium permanganate std soln.*—0.1*N*. Prep. and stdze as in **50.025–50.026**.

6.055 ***Method I***

Dissolve 2 g sample in 80 mL HOAc (1+3), transfer to 200 mL vol. flask, dil. to vol., and filter thru dry filter. Transfer 50 mL aliquot to beaker, dil. to ca 200 mL, heat to bp, and ppt Ca with $(NH_4)_2C_2O_4$ soln. Let beaker stand 3 hr on steam bath, filter, and wash ppt with hot H_2O. Dissolve ppt in 200 mL H_2O contg 25 mL H_2SO_4 (1+4), heat to ca 70°, and titr. with std $KMnO_4$ soln. From mL $KMnO_4$ soln used, calc. % Ca.

6.056 ***Method II***

(Not applicable in presence of Pb. *Caution: See* **51.078**.)

Weigh 2 g sample, transfer to beaker, add 5 mL *HBr* (ca 1.38 sp gr) and 15 mL HCl, and evap. to dryness under hood to remove As. Repeat treatment, add 20 mL HCl, and again evap. to dryness. Take up with H_2O and little HCl, filter into 200 mL vol. flask, wash, and dil. to vol. Transfer 50 mL aliquot to beaker, add 10 mL HCl and few drops HNO_3, boil, and make slightly alk. with NH_4OH. Let stand few min and filter. Dissolve ppt in HCl (1+4), reppt, filter thru same paper, and wash with hot H_2O. To combined filtrates and washings add 20 mL HOAc (1+3) and adjust to ca 200 mL. Heat to bp, ppt with $(NH_4)_2C_2O_4$ soln, and let stand 3 hr on steam bath. Filter, and wash with hot H_2O. Ignite at 950°, and weigh as CaO; or dissolve and titr. as in **6.055**. From wt CaO or mL $KMnO_4$ soln used, calc. % Ca.

★ ZINC ARSENITE ★

(*Caution: See* **51.041**.)

6.057 Moisture—Official Final Action

See **6.004**.

6.058 Total Arsenic—Official Final Action

Proceed as in **6.007** and calc. as As_2O_3.

Total Arsenious Oxide—Official Final Action

6.059 ***Method I (19)***

Bromate titrn. *See* **4.051**, 10th ed.

6.060 ***Method II***

Iodometric titrn. *See* **4.052**, 10th ed.

6.061 Water-Soluble Arsenic—Official Final Action

Proceed as in **6.013**, and calc. results as As_2O_3.

6.062 Total Zinc (*19*)—Official Final Action

Gravimetric method. *See* **4.054**, 10th ed.

★ COPPER CARBONATE ★

Copper—Official Final Action

6.063 ***Electrolytic Method***

See **4.055**, 10th ed.

6.064 ***Volumetric Thiosulfate Method***

See **4.056**, 10th ed.

COPPER NAPHTHENATE

(*Caution: See* **51.041**.)

Copper (*20*)—Official First Action

6.065 ***Titrimetric Method***

Accurately weigh sample contg ca 0.2 g Cu into dry g-s flask. Add 5 mL pet ether to concd products. Add 100 mL H_2O, 1.5 g *NH_4HF_2*, and 5–10 g KI. Stopper and shake vigorously until reaction is complete (usually ca 2 min). Wash stopper and sides of flask with H_2O and titr. with std 0.1*N* $Na_2S_2O_3$ (stdzd against Cu) to light brown. Add starch indicator, **6.005(f)**, titr. almost to end point, add 2 g KSCN, shake to dissolve, and complete titrn to starch end point.

6.066 ***Electrolytic Method***

Accurately weigh sample contg ca 0.2 g Cu into 200 mL separator. Add 50 mL pet ether and 25 mL HNO_3 (1+4), and shake 2 min. Drain aq. phase into 250 mL beaker and save. Wash pet ether with 15 and 10 mL HNO_3 (1+4), and combine acid exts. Neutze with NH_4OH, acidify with 6 mL H_2SO_4 and 4 mL HNO_3, and proceed as in **6.015**, beginning ". . . adjust vol. to 200 mL, . . ." using ca 0.5 amp during first 10 min and 1.5–2.0 amp for ca 20 min.

★ Methods for this product are surplus—*see* inside front cover.

BORDEAUX MIXTURE

(*Caution: See* **51.041**.)

6.067 Moisture—Official Final Action

(**a**) *Powder.—See* **6.042**(**a**).

(**b**) *Paste.*—Heat ca 100 g in oven at 90–100° until dry enough to powder readily and note loss in wt. Powder this partially dried sample and det. remaining H_2O in 2 g as in (**a**). Det. CO_2 as in **6.069**, both in original paste and in partially dried sample. Calc. total H_2O by following formula:

$$M = a + \frac{(100 - a)(b + c)}{100} - d,$$

where M = % total H_2O in original paste; a = % loss in wt of original paste during first drying; b = % loss in wt of partially dried paste during second drying; c = % CO_2 remaining in partially dried paste after first drying; and d = % total CO_2 in original paste.

Carbon Dioxide (*21*)—Official Final Action

6.068 ***Apparatus***

Use 200 mL erlenmeyer with 2-hole stopper; in one hole fit dropping funnel with stem extending almost to bottom of flask, and thru other hole pass outlet of condenser that is inclined upward at 30° angle from horizontal. Connect upper end of condenser with $CaCl_2$ tube, which in turn connects with double U-tube filled in middle with pumice fragments, previously satd with *20% $CuSO_4.5H_2O$ soln* and subsequently dehydrated, and with $CaCl_2$ at either end. Connect 2 weighed U-tubes to absorb CO_2, first filled with porous soda-lime, and second, ⅓ with soda-lime and ⅔ with $CaCl_2$, placing the $CaCl_2$ at exit end of train. Attach Geissler bulb, partly filled with H_2SO_4, to last U-tube to show rate of gas flow, and connect aspirator with Geissler bulb to draw air thru app. Connect absorption tower filled with soda-lime to mouth of dropping funnel to remove CO_2 from air entering app.

6.069 ***Determination***

Weigh 2 g powder or 10 g paste into the erlenmeyer and add ca 20 mL H_2O. Attach flask to app., omitting the 2 weighed U-tubes, and draw CO_2-free air thru app. until it displaces original air. Attach weighed U-tubes as in **6.068**, close stopcock of dropping funnel, pour into it 50 mL HCl (1+4), reconnect with soda-lime tower, and let acid flow into erlenmeyer, slowly if there is much CO_2, rapidly if there is little. When effervescence diminishes, place low Bunsen flame under flask and start flow of H_2O thru condenser, letting slow current of air flow thru app. at same time. Maintain steady but quiet boil and slow air current thru app. Boil few min after H_2O begins to condense, remove flame, and continue air flow at ca 2 bubbles/sec until app. is cool. Disconnect weighed absorption tubes, cool in balance case, and weigh. Increase in wt = CO_2.

Copper—Official Final Action

6.070 ***Electrolytic Method***

(Also applicable to $CuCO_3$ and $CuSO_4$)

Dissolve powd sample contg 0.2–0.25 g Cu in 45 mL HNO_3 (1+4). Filter if necessary, dil. to 200 mL, and electrolyze as in **6.015**.

6.071 ***Volumetric Thiosulfate Method***

Dissolve 2 g powd sample in ca 25 mL HNO_3 (1+4), dil. to 50 mL, add NH_4OH in excess, and heat. Without removing ppt that has formed, boil off excess NH_3, add 3–4 mL HOAc, cool, add 10 mL 30% KI soln, and titr. as in **6.016**, beginning "... titr. with std $Na_2S_2O_3$ soln, ..."

★ BORDEAUX MIXTURE WITH PARIS GREEN ★

(*Caution: See* **51.041**.)

6.072 Moisture—Official Final Action

See **6.067**.

6.073 Carbon Dioxide—Official Final Action

See **6.069**.

6.074 Total Arsenic—Official Final Action

Proceed as in **6.007**, using 2 g sample, and calc. results as As_2O_3.

6.075 Total Arsenious Oxide—Official Final Action

Iodometric titrn. *See* **4.067**, 10th ed.

6.076 Water-Soluble Arsenious Oxide—Official Final Action

Iodometric titrn. *See* **4.068**, 10th ed.

Copper—Official Final Action

6.077 ***Electrolytic Method I***

See **6.015**.

6.078 ***Electrolytic Method II—(Short Method)***

See **4.070**, 10th ed.

6.079 ***Volumetric Thiosulfate Method***

See **6.016**.

★ BORDEAUX MIXTURE WITH LEAD ARSENATE ★

(*Caution: See* **51.041**.)

6.080 Moisture—Official Final Action

See **6.067**.

6.081 Carbon Dioxide—Official Final Action

See **6.069**.

6.082 Total Arsenic—Official Final Action

Proceed as in **6.007**, using 2 g sample, and calc. results as As_2O_5.

6.083 Water-Soluble Arsenic—Official Final Action

Proceed as in **6.013** and calc. results as As_2O_5.

Copper—Official Final Action

6.084 ***Electrolytic Method***

See **6.015**.

★ Methods for this product are surplus—*see* inside front cover.

6.085 ***Volumetric Thiosulfate Method***

See **6.016**.

6.086 Lead—Official Final Action

See **6.014**.

Lead and Copper—Official Final Action

6.087 ***Electrolytic Method (22)***

(*Caution: See* **51.026**, **51.047**, and **51.078**.)

See **4.079–4.080**, 10th ed.

★ BORDEAUX MIXTURE WITH CALCIUM ARSENATE ★

(*Caution: See* **51.041**.)

6.088 Moisture—Official Final Action

See **6.067**.

6.089 Carbon Dioxide—Official Final Action

See **6.069**.

6.090 Total Arsenic—Official Final Action

Proceed as in **6.007**, using 2 g sample, and calc. results as As_2O_5.

6.091 Water-Soluble Arsenic—Official Final Action

Proceed as in **6.013** and calc. results as As_2O_5.

Copper—Official Final Action

6.092 ***Electrolytic Method I***

See **6.015**.

6.093 ***Electrolytic Method II***

See **6.078**.

6.094 ***Volumetric Thiosulfate Method***

See **6.016**.

★ CALCIUM CYANIDE (*23*) ★

6.095 Cyanide—Official Final Action

$AgNO_3$ titrn. *See* **4.093–4.094**, 10th ed.

Chloride—Official Final Action

6.096 ***Method I***

See **4.095**, 10th ed.

6.097 ***Method II***

See **4.096**, 10th ed.

POTASSIUM CYANATE (*24*)—OFFICIAL FINAL ACTION

(*Caution: See* **51.041**.)

6.098 ***Reagent***

Wash soln.—Satd aq. soln of hydrazodicarbamide, NH_2CO-$NHNHCONH_2$. Prep. by mixing KOCN and semicarbazide.HCl, $NH_2CONHNH_2$.HCl, in H_2O, filter, and wash ppt with H_2O. Transfer ppt to flask, add small amt H_2O, shake vigorously, and filter. (Solubility of ppt in H_2O is ca 1 part in 6600.)

6.099 ***Determination***

Weigh sample contg 0.2–0.5 g KOCN into 100 mL beaker, add 20 mL wash soln and 1 g semicarbazide.HCl, and let stand 24 hr. Filter hydrazodicarbamide on gooch or fine fritted glass crucible, wash with 10 mL wash soln, and dry at 100° to const wt. KOCN = wt residue × 0.6868.

★ SODIUM AND POTASSIUM CYANIDES ★

(*Caution: See* **51.050**.)

6.100 Cyanide (*25*)—Official Final Action

$AgNO_3$ titrn. *See* **4.088–4.089**, 10th ed. (*Caution: See* **51.084**.)

Chloride (*26*)—Official Final Action

6.101 ***Method I***

Pptn with $AgNO_3$ and thiocyanate back-titrn. *See* **4.090–4.091**, 10th ed.

6.102 ***Method II***

Distn, pptn with $AgNO_3$, and thiocyanate back-titrn. *See* **4.092**, 10th ed.

LIME SULFUR SOLUTIONS AND DRY LIME SULFUR

Soluble Sulfur (*27*)—Official Final Action

(Use low S reagents.)

6.103 ***Preparation of Sample***

(**a**) *Solns.*—Accurately weigh ca 10 g soln, transfer to 250 mL vol. flask, and immediately dil. to vol. with recently boiled and cooled H_2O. Mix thoroly and either take necessary aliquots in individual pipets in min. time for detns or transfer to small bottles, filling them completely and avoiding contact of soln with air as much as possible. Stopper bottles, seal with paraffin, and store in dark, cool place.

(**b**) *Dry lime-sulfur.*—Thoroly stir 5 g sample with ca 50 mL H_2O in 250 mL beaker. Let settle and decant thru paper into 250 mL vol. flask. Repeat extn with H_2O until filtrate is colorless and ca 200 mL is obtained. Transfer residue to paper, wash with hot H_2O, cool to room temp., and dil. to vol. Dry residue 1.5 hr at 105°, and reserve for free S and sulfite S detns in residue, if desired. (Ext S from dry residue with CS_2 (*Caution: See* **51.039**, **51.040**, and **51.048**), evap. on steam bath or in air current, dry 15 min at 105°, weigh, and calc. % S.)

Prep. soln in min. time and keep beaker and funnel covered as much as possible.

6.104 ***Determination***

With clean, dry pipet transfer 10 mL prepd soln, **6.103(a)** or (**b**), to 250 mL beaker. Partially cover with cover glass and add 2–3 g *Na_2O_2* in small portions, with stirring, from tip of spatula. Continue adding Na_2O_2 until all S appears to be oxidized to sulfate (yellow color disappears). Add slight excess Na_2O_2, completely cover beaker with cover glass, and heat on steam bath, stirring occasionally, 15–20 min.

Wash off cover glass and sides of beaker, acidify with HCl (1+4), and filter if necessary. Dil. to 150–200 mL, heat to bp, and add *10% $BaCl_2$ soln* (11 mL/1 g $BaSO_4$), with const stirring, at such rate that ca 4 min is required to add necessary amt. Let stand until clear and cool, filter thru quant. paper, wash until Cl-free, ignite carefully, and heat to const wt over Bunsen burner. Calc. % S from wt $BaSO_4$, using factor 0.1374.

★ Methods for this product are surplus—*see* inside front cover.

Thiosulfate Sulfur (*27*)—Official Final Action

6.105 ***Reagent***

Ammoniacal zinc chloride soln.—Dissolve 50 g $ZnCl_2$ in ca 500 mL H_2O, add 125 mL NH_4OH and 50 g NH_4Cl, and dil. to 1 L.

6.106 ***Determination***

To 50 mL H_2O in 200 mL vol. flask add 50 mL prepd soln, **6.103(a)** or **(b)**. Add slight excess of the ammoniacal $ZnCl_2$ soln and dil. to vol. Complete detn as rapidly as possible. Shake thoroly and filter thru dry filter. To 100 mL filtrate add few drops Me orange, **6.005(g)**, or Me red, **2.055(i)**, and exactly neutze with 0.1*N* HCl. Titr. neut. soln with 0.05*N* I, **6.005(b)**, using few drops starch indicator, **6.005(f)**. From mL I soln used, calc. % thiosulfate S present. (Factor of I soln in terms of $As_2O_3 \times 1.296$ = equiv. in thiosulfate S.)

Sulfide Sulfur—Official Final Action

6.107 ***Zinc Chloride Method* (*27*)**

To 10–15 mL H_2O in small beaker add 10 mL aliquot prepd soln, **6.103(a)** or **(b)**. Calc. amt ammoniacal $ZnCl_2$ soln, **6.105**, necessary to ppt all S in aliquot and add slight excess. Stir thoroly, filter, wash ppt twice with cold H_2O, and transfer paper and ppt to beaker in which pptn was made. Cover with H_2O, disintegrate paper with glass rod, and add ca 3 g *Na_2O_2*, keeping beaker well covered with watch glass. Warm on steam bath with frequent shaking until all S is oxidized to sulfate, adding more Na_2O_2 if necessary. Acidify slightly with HCl (1+4), filter to remove shreds of paper, wash thoroly with hot H_2O, and det. S in filtrate as in **6.104**.

6.108 ***Indirect Method***

Difference between sol. S and sum of thiosulfate S and sulfate S = sulfide S.

6.109 Sulfate Sulfur—Official Final Action

Slightly acidify soln from **6.106** with HCl (1+4) and heat to bp. Add slowly, with const stirring, slight excess *10% $BaCl_2$ soln,* boil 30 min, let stand overnight, and filter. Calc. S from wt $BaSO_4$, and report as % sulfate S.

6.110 Total Calcium (*27*)—Official Final Action

To 25 mL prepd soln, **6.103(a)** or **(b)**, add 10 mL HCl, evap. to dryness on steam bath, and H_2O and few mL HCl (1+4), warm until all $CaCl_2$ dissolves, and filter to remove S and any SiO_2 present. Dil. filtrate to 200–250 mL, heat to bp, add few mL NH_4OH in excess, and then add excess *satd $(NH_4)_2C_2O_4$ soln.* Continue boiling until pptd CaC_2O_4 assumes well defined granular form, let stand 1 hr, filter, and wash few times with hot H_2O. Ignite at 950° in Pt crucible to const wt (CaO) and calc. % Ca. CaO × 0.7147 = Ca.

SODIUM HYPOCHLORITE SOLUTIONS (*28*)

Sodium Hypochlorite

Arsenious Oxide Titration Method—Official Final Action

6.111 ***Reagents***

(a) *Arsenious oxide std soln.*—0.1*N*. Prep. as in **50.005–50.006**.

(b) *Iodine std soln.*—Prep. as in **50.018**. Stdze against **(a)**.

6.112 ***Determination***

Transfer 20 mL sample to 1 L vol. flask and dil. to vol. Pipet 50 mL aliquot of mixt. into 200 mL erlenmeyer. Add excess As_2O_3 soln and then decided excess $NaHCO_3$. Titr. excess As_2O_3 with std I soln, using starch soln, **6.005(f)**, or the I as its own indicator. Subtract vol. I soln, corrected to 0.1*N*, from vol. As_2O_3 soln used, and from this value and sp gr of soln, calc. % NaOCl. 1 mL 0.1*N* As_2O_3 = 0.003722 g NaOCl.

6.113 Available Chlorine—Official Final Action

Calc. % available Cl from titrn, **6.112**. 1 mL 0.1*N* As_2O_3 = 0.003545 g available Cl.

6.114 Chloride Chlorine—Official Final Action

Pipet 50 mL aliquot prepd soln, **6.112**, into 200 mL erlenmeyer and add slight excess As_2O_3 soln, **6.111(a)**, calcd from NaOCl titrn; add slight excess HNO_3, neutze with *$CaCO_3$*, and titr. with 0.1*N* $AgNO_3$, **50.027–50.029**, using K_2CrO_4 soln, **50.028(b)**, or the Ag_3AsO_4 formed in soln, as indicator. Det. blank on reagents and correct for any Cl found. From this corrected titrn and sp gr of sample, calc. % Cl. From this value subtract ½ the % available Cl. Difference = % chloride Cl.

6.115 Sodium Hydroxide (*29*)—Official Final Action

Stdze pH meter equipped with calomel and glass electrodes, using std pH 6.9 buffer soln, **50.007(d)**.

Place 50 mL 10% $BaCl_2.2H_2O$ soln and 30 mL 3% H_2O_2 soln in 250 mL beaker. Neutze to pH 7.5 with ca 0.1*N* NaOH, using pH meter. Add 10 mL sample from pipet, stir vigorously 1 min, and titr. to pH 7.5 with stdzd 0.1*N* HCl, using pH meter.

% NaOH = (mL HCl × normality × 4.0)/(mL sample × sp gr)

6.116 ★ Carbon Dioxide—Official Final Action ★

Evolution into std $Ba(OH)_2$ soln. *See* **4.158–4.159**, 10th ed.

CALCIUM HYPOCHLORITE AND BLEACHING POWDER (*28*)

Available Chlorine

6.117 ***Arsenious Oxide Titration Method***
Official Final Action

Weigh 5–10 g thoroly mixed sample into porcelain mortar, add 30–40 mL H_2O, and triturate to smooth cream (high-test $Ca(OCl)_2$ will dissolve readily and not form a cream). Add more H_2O, stir well with pestle, and let insol. residue settle few moments. Pour mixt. off into 1 L vol. flask, add more H_2O, and thoroly triturate sample and pour off as before. Repeat operation until all material is transferred to flask. Rinse mortar and pestle, catch wash H_2O in flask, dil. to vol., and mix. Without letting material settle, pipet 25–50 mL aliquot into 200 mL erlenmeyer. Add excess std As_2O_3 soln, **6.111(a)**, and then decided excess of $NaHCO_3$. Titr. excess As_2O_3 with std I soln, **6.111(b)**, using starch soln, **6.005(f)**, or I as its own indicator. Subtract vol. I soln, corrected to 0.1*N*, from vol. As_2O_3 soln used, and calc. % available Cl. 1 mL 0.1*N* As_2O_3 = 0.003545 g available Cl.

★ Surplus method—*see* inside front cover.

CHLORAMINE T (*28*)

Active Chlorine

Arsenious Oxide Titration Method—Official Final Action

6.118 ***Determination***

Transfer 0.5 g sample to 300–500 mL erlenmeyer, dissolve in 50 mL H_2O, and add excess std As_2O_3 soln, **6.111(a)**, and 5 mL H_2SO_4 (1+4). Add decided excess $NaHCO_3$ and titr. excess As_2O_3 with std I soln, **6.111(b)**, using starch soln, **6.005(f)**, or I as its own indicator. From this titrn, calc. active Cl in sample. 1 mL 0.1*N* As_2O_3 = 0.001773 g active Cl. (To convert active Cl to available Cl, multiply active Cl by 2.)

6.119 Total Chlorine—Official Final Action

Dissolve 0.5 g sample in 50 mL H_2O in erlenmeyer and add slight excess std As_2O_3 soln as calcd from active Cl titrn, **6.118**. Add 5 mL HNO_3 (1+4), neutze with *$CaCO_3$*, and titr. with std $AgNO_3$, **50.027–50.029**, using K_2CrO_4, **50.028(b)**, as indicator. Det. blank on reagents and correct for any Cl found. From corrected titrn, calc. % total Cl in sample. 1 mL 0.1*N* $AgNO_3$ = 0.003545 g Cl. If total Cl exceeds active Cl, NaCl is indicated.

6.120 ★ Sodium—Official Final Action ★

From wt sulfated ash. *See* **6.183**, 11th ed.

MINERAL OILS

Unsulfonated Residue (*30*)—Official Final Action

6.121 ***Reagent***

(*Caution: See* **51.030** and **51.031**.)

Fuming 38N sulfuric acid.—In tared g-s bottle (2.5 L acid bottle is convenient) mix fuming H_2SO_4 (free from N oxides) (*x*) with H_2SO_4 (*y*) to obtain mixed acid (*z*), contg slightly >82.38% total SO_3. Depending on strength of fuming acid available, use following proportions of 2 acids: 100 parts *x* (15–20% free SO_3) to 50 parts *y*; 100 parts *x* (20–30% free SO_3) to 75 parts *y*; or 100 parts *x* (50% free SO_3) to 140 parts *y*. Mix thoroly (considerable heat is generated), let cool, and again weigh to det. amt mixed acid obtained. Det. exact strength of mixed acid (*z*) and also of reserve supply of acid (*y*) as follows:

Pour ca 50 mL into small beaker and fill ca 10 mL weighing bulb or pipet by slight suction, wiping off outside of bulb with moist, then with dry, cloth. Weigh on analytical balance and let acid flow slowly down sides of neck of 1 L vol. flask into ca 200 mL cold H_2O. (These sizes of bulb and flask give final soln ca 0.5*N*.) When bulb has drained, wash all traces of acid into flask, taking precautions against loss of SO_3 fumes. Dil. to vol. and titr. from buret with std alkali, using same indicator as used in stdzg. Calc. SO_3 content of both acids, and add calcd amt of reserve acid (*y*) to amt of mixed acid (*z*) on hand to bring *z* to 82.38% total SO_3 (equiv. to 100.92% H_2SO_4). After adding required amt of *y*, again analyze mixed acid to make certain it is of proper concn (±0.15% H_2SO_4). Keep acid in small bottles or in special dispenser bottle (*31*) to prevent absorption of H_2O from air.

6.122 ***Determination***

Pipet 5 mL sample into 6″ Babcock cream bottle, **16.157(a)**, either 9 g 50% or 18 g 30% type. To reduce viscosity of heavy oils, warm pipet after initial drainage by passing it several times thru flame; then drain thoroly. If greater accuracy is desired, weigh measured sample and calc. exact vol. from wt and sp gr. Slowly add 20 mL 38*N* H_2SO_4, gently shaking or rotating bottle and taking care that temp. does not rise above 60°. Cool in ice-H_2O if necessary. When mixt. no longer develops heat on shaking, agitate thoroly, place bottle in H_2O bath, and heat 10 min at 60–65°, keeping contents of bottle thoroly mixed by shaking vigorously 20 sec at 2 min intervals. Remove bottle from bath and add H_2SO_4 until oil is in graduated neck. Centrf. 5 min (or longer if necessary to obtain const vol. of oil) at 1200–1500 rpm. Read vol. of unsulfonated residue from graduations on neck of bottle and, to convert to mL, multiply reading from 9 g 50% bottle by 0.1 and reading from 18 g 30% bottle by 0.2. From result obtained, calc. % by vol. of unsulfonated residue.

★ Surplus method—*see* inside front cover.

SOAP

Moisture (*32*)

6.123 ***Toluene Distillation Method—Official Final Action***

Weigh ca 20 g sample into 300–500 mL flask; add 50 mL toluene (tech. grade is satisfactory); and, to prevent foaming, add ca 10 g lump rosin (do not use powd). Distil into Dean and Stark type distg tube receiver and continue distn until no more H_2O collects in receiver. Cool contents of tube to room temp., read vol. H_2O under toluene in tube, and calc. % H_2O.

6.124 ★ Sodium and Potassium (*33*)—Official Final Action ★

Removal of metal ions and P, and weighing as chlorides. *See* **6.094**, 11th ed.

MINERAL OIL-SOAP EMULSIONS

Water (*34*)

6.125 ***Toluene Distillation Method—Official Final Action***

Weigh ca 25 g sample and proceed as in **6.123**, except use less rosin.

6.126 Total Oil (*35*)—Official Final Action

Weigh ca 10 g sample into Babcock cream bottle, **16.157(a)**. Dil. with ca 10 mL hot H_2O and add 5–10 mL H_2SO_4 (1+1). Heat in hot H_2O bath ca 5 min to hasten sepn of oil, add enough satd NaCl soln to bring oil layer within graduated neck of bottle, centrf. 5 min at 1200 rpm, and let cool. Read vol. of oil layer, det. density, and from these values calc. wt and %. From this % value deduct % fatty acids (and phenols if present), detd sep., to obtain % oil.

6.127 Soap (*34*)—Official Final Action

(Error will result if apparent mol. wt of fatty acids varies appreciably from that of oleic acid.)

Weigh 20 g sample into separator, add 60 mL pet ether, and ext mixt. once with 20 mL and 4 times with 10 mL 50% alcohol. Break emulsion if necessary by letting 1 or 2 mL 20% NaOH soln run down wall of separator. Then gently swirl separator and let stand few min. Drain alc. layers and wash successively thru pet ether contained in 2 other separators. Combine alc. exts in beaker and evap. on steam bath to remove alcohol. Dissolve residue in ca 100 mL H_2O made alk. with NaOH. Transfer to separator, acidify with HCl or H_2SO_4, ext 3 times with Et ether, and wash ether exts twice with H_2O. Combine ether exts, evap. in weighed beaker on steam bath, and weigh as fatty acids. From wt fatty acids, calc. % soap in sample as Na or K oleate.

6.128 Unsulfonated Residues—Official Final Action

Using 5 mL of the recovered oil, **6.126**, proceed as in **6.122**.

6.129 Ash (*36*)—Official Final Action

Evap. 10 g sample, or more if necessary, in Pt dish. Ignite, and leach charred mass with H_2O. Ignite residue, add leachings, evap. to dryness, ignite, and weigh. From this wt, calc. % ash. Test ash for Cu, Ca, CaF_2, etc.

ORGANIC MERCURIAL SEED DISINFECTANTS

Mercury

6.130 ★ *Volatilization Method (37)* ★
Official Final Action

See **4.150–4.151**, 10th ed. (*Caution: See* **51.041** and **51.065.**)

6.131 ★ *Precipitation Method (37)* ★
Official Final Action

Digestion with H_2SO_4 and H_2O_2 and pptn as HgS. *See* **6.173**, 11th ed.

Titrimetric Method (38)—Official Final Action

6.132 ***Principle***

Sample is digested under H_2O-cooled condenser with fuming H_2SO_4-fuming HNO_3. Hg is detd by titrn with std SCN soln with ferric alum as indicator. Small amts of chloride are oxidized to Cl and expelled thru condenser. Not applicable in presence of large amts of Cl-contg materials.

6.133 ***Reagents***

(**a**) *Ferric indicator.*—Dissolve 8 g $FeNH_4(SO_4)_2.12H_2O$ in 80 mL H_2O. Add enough HNO_3 to destroy brown Fe color and dil. to 100 mL with H_2O.

(**b**) *Ferrous sulfate soln.*—Dissolve 1 g $FeSO_4.7H_2O$ in H_2O, add 1 mL H_2SO_4, and dil. to 100 mL with H_2O. Prep. fresh for each detn.

6.134 ***Preparation of Sample***

(**a**) *Solns.*—Mix thoroly and weigh, by difference, amt sample (max. 10 g) contg preferably 0.07 g Hg into 500 mL ₮ erlenmeyer.

(**b**) *Dusts.*—Mix thoroly and, using glass weighing dish, weigh amt sample as in (**a**). Transfer thru powder funnel into 500 mL ₮ erlenmeyer.

6.135 ***Determination***

(*Caution:* Conduct detn in well ventilated hood. Method is dangerous in presence of material which reacts violently with H_2SO_4 and/or HNO_3. *See* **51.019, 51.026, 51.030, 51.031**, and **51.079.**)

Connect straight-tube, H_2O-cooled condenser to erlenmeyer contg sample. Place flask in cold H_2O bath. Carefully add 10 mL H_2SO_4 thru top of condenser and mix by swirling. Add in small portions, swirling after each addn, 30–40 mL *fuming H_2SO_4* (20% free SO_3) thru top of condenser, followed by 10 mL red *fuming HNO_3* (98% HNO_3). Remove from bath and dry outside of flask. Heat with small flame to reflux at ca 30 drops/min with red fumes persisting in flask and condenser. Heat 30 min; if small amt chloride is present, heat 2 hr with occasional addn of fuming HNO_3 as required. Cool, and add 100 mL cold H_2O slowly thru top of condenser while cooling flask in cold H_2O bath. Add 2 or 3 glass beads or boiling chips and boil until N oxides have been expelled to top of condenser (ca 2 min). Wash condenser with 50 mL cold H_2O, disconnect flask, and add *satd $KMnO_4$ soln* until color remains purple. (If large amts insol. material are present, filter hot soln thru medium tight asbestos mat in gooch before addn of $KMnO_4$. Wash flask and filter 5 times with hot H_2O, and then add $KMnO_4$.) Cool flask, and destroy $KMnO_4$ with fresh 1% $FeSO_4$ soln. Add 10 mL ferric indicator and titr. with 0.1*N* NH_4SCN or KSCN, **50.003–50.004**, to appearance of first permanent faint orange. 1 mL 0.1*N* NH_4SCN or KSCN = 0.01003 g Hg.

★ Surplus method—*see* inside front cover.

AOAC-CIPAC Gravimetric Method (39)—Official Final Action

(Applicable in presence of large amts Cl-contg materials; not applicable to chloro- or nitrophenols nor to materials not decomposed by digestion mixt.)

6.136 ***Reagents***

(**a**) *Dilute sulfuric acid.*—Add 30 mL H_2SO_4 to H_2O in 100 mL vol. flask, cool, and dil. to vol. with H_2O.

(**b**) *Sodium sulfite soln.*—10%. Dissolve 10 g Na_2SO_3 in H_2O in 100 mL vol. flask and dil. to vol. with H_2O.

(**c**) *Ammonium citrate soln.*—pH 7.0. *See* **2.044**(**a**).

(**d**) *Precipitating reagent.*—Add 20 mL 1,2-propanediamine (Eastman Kodak Co., P3170) to 100 mL 1*M* $CuSO_4$ soln. Store in g-s container.

(**e**) *Wash soln.*—Add 1 g KI and 2 mL pptg reagent to 1 L H_2O.

6.137 ***Preparation of Sample***

(**a**) *Solns.*—Mix thoroly and weigh, by difference, sample (max. 5 g) contg 0.02–0.08 g Hg into 125 mL ₮ erlenmeyer.

(**b**) *Dusts.*—Mix thoroly and, using glass weighing dish, weigh sample as in (**a**). Transfer thru powder funnel into 125 mL ₮ erlenmeyer.

6.138 ***Determination***

(*Caution:* Conduct detn in well ventilated hood.)

Add to sample in following order: 5 mL *ethylene glycol*, swirling to thoroly suspend solids, 4 g KI, 10 mL dil. H_2SO_4, 0.4 g I, and 2 glass beads. After thoro mixing, connect straight-tube, H_2O-cooled condenser and, with low flame, heat to slight boil so that liq. condenses in lower portion of condenser. Swirl occasionally, avoiding excessive heat and crystn of large amt I in condenser. Reflux 1 hr and, while cooling flask in H_2O bath, immediately wash warm condenser with heavy stream of ca 25 mL H_2O. (If dye or I persists in condenser, loosen by reheating flask contents, without H_2O in condenser, until liq. refluxes slightly beyond adhering material. Wash condenser again with ca 25 mL H_2O, and cool flask.) Disconnect condenser and wash connections directly into flask. Add ca 2 mL 10% Na_2SO_3 dropwise, with swirling, until I color slightly lightens. (Excess I must be present.) Neutze soln with NH_4OH, using pH test paper, until very slightly alk. (pH 7.0–7.3). Cool, and filter with vac. thru retentive paper (S&S Blue Ribbon, or equiv.) in buchner into 400 mL beaker. Wash flask and paper thoroly, keeping total filtrate $<$150 mL. Add 50 mL NH_4 citrate soln, bring mixt. just to bp, and stir in 5 mL pptg reagent. Cool and let stand $\geqslant$2 hr (preferably overnight); filter thru medium porosity glass crucible, previously dried at 105° and weighed. Transfer ppt with wash soln, and wash with same soln several times. Rinse I from ppt with ca 25 mL alcohol in 5 mL portions (some samples may require up to 50 mL) until filtrate is colorless. (Let alcohol stand few min with occasional swirling after each addn before applying suction. Ppt should be suspended in liq. each time.) Wash ppt with three 5 mL portions $CHCl_3$, suspending ppt each time as above until dye and pesticides are completely removed. Finally wash with 5 mL alcohol, dry 30 min at 105°, cool, and weigh.

Wt Hg = wt ppt × 0.218.

ANT POISONS AND RODENTICIDES

6.139 ★ Alpha-Naphthylthiourea (*40*) ★
Official First Action

(*Caution: See* **51.039**, **51.041**, and **51.046**.)

N detn. *See* **4.132**, 10th ed.

6.140 Thallous Sulfate (*41*)—Official Final Action

(*Caution: See* **51.019**, **51.026**, **51.031**, and **51.041**.)

Weigh sample contg 0.1–0.15 g Tl_2SO_4 (usually 10 g), transfer to 800 mL Kjeldahl flask, and add 25 mL H_2SO_4 followed by 5–10 mL HNO_3. After first violent reaction ceases, heat until white fumes of H_2SO_4 appear. Add few drops *fuming* HNO_3 and continue heating and adding HNO_3 until org. matter is destroyed, as shown by colorless or light yellow soln. Cool, add 10–15 mL H_2O, again cool, and wash contents of flask into 400 mL beaker, continuing washing until vol. is 60–70 mL. Boil several min to remove all HNO_3, cool, and filter into 400 mL beaker. Wash with hot H_2O until vol. in beaker is 175 mL, neutze with NH_4OH, and then slightly acidify with H_2SO_4 (1+4). Add 1 g $NaHSO_3$ to ensure reduction of thallic to thallous state. Heat to bp, add 50 mL *10% KI soln,* stir, and let stand overnight. Filter thru tight gooch contg 2 disks S&S 589 white ribbon paper covered by medium pad of asbestos. Wash 4 or 5 times with 10 mL portions *1% KI soln,* and finally with absolute alcohol. Dry to const wt at 105° (1–1.5 hr), and weigh as TlI.

% Tl_2SO_4 = (g TlI × 0.7619 × 100)/g sample.

Warfarin (3-(α-Acetonylbenzyl)-4-hydroxycoumarin) (*42*)
Official Final Action

(Applicable to baits contg ca 0.025% and to concs contg ≥0.5% warfarin. Not applicable to pelleted baits or baits consisting of cracked corn treated with alc. warfarin soln and aq. sugar soln, and then dried.)

6.141 ***Reagents***

(**a**) *Sodium pyrophosphate soln.*—1%. Dissolve 5 g $Na_4P_2O_7.10H_2O$ in 500 mL H_2O.

(**b**) *Petroleum ether, purified.*—Ext 200 mL pet ether with three 20 mL portions 1% $Na_4P_2O_7$ soln.

(**c**) *Warfarin std soln.*—10 μg/mL. Dissolve 100 mg pure warfarin (Wisconsin Alumni Research Foundation, P.O. Box 7365, Madison, WI 53707) in 100 mL 1% $Na_4P_2O_7$ soln. Dil. 10 mL to 100 mL with 1% $Na_4P_2O_7$ soln, and dil. 10 mL of second soln to 100 mL with 1% $Na_4P_2O_7$ soln.

6.142 ***Determination***

Weigh 10 g sample (0.025%), 0.600 g (0.5%), or equiv. wt of higher concn, into 125 mL g-s flask or 100 mL centrf. tube and add 50 mL Et ether from pipet. Stopper tightly and shake mech. ca 30 min. Transfer 5 or 10 mL to centrf. tube (or centrf. directly), stopper, and centrf. 5 min at high speed or until clear. Take precautions to avoid evapn of ether.

Pipet 10 mL 1% $Na_4P_2O_7$ soln into g-s 16 × 150 mm test tube and add 2 mL centrfd ether ext from pipet. Stopper and shake vigorously 2 min. Centrf. at high speed until aq. layer is clear. Draw off ether layer, including any emulsion that remains, using fine-tip glass tube attached to aspirator. Add ca 2 mL Et ether, shake vigorously, centrf., and completely draw off ether layer. Repeat ether extn, and then ext twice with purified pet ether in same manner.

Prep. blank soln similarly, using 2 mL ether instead of 2 mL ether ext.

Det. *A* of aq. soln in 1 cm silica cell at 308 nm against blank soln in Beckman spectrophtr, model DU (replaced by models 24/25), or equiv. Det. *A'* (ca 0.46) of the std warfarin soln against 1% $Na_4P_2O_7$ soln.

$$\% \text{ Warfarin} = (A/A') \times (10^{-5} \text{ g std/mL}) \times [100/(\text{g sample} \times (2/50)(1/10))] = (A/A') \times (0.250/\text{g sample}).$$

FUMIGANTS

Fumigant Mixtures (*43*)—Official First Action

(Applicable to org. components of CS_2, CCl_4, $(CH_2)_2Cl_2$, and $(CH_2)_2Br_2$ mixts. *Precautions:* Handle with care in hood or well-ventilated area. Mixts are volatile, poisonous, and sometimes flammable and may be fatal if inhaled or swallowed. They cause skin and eye irritation. In case of contact, immediately remove contaminated clothing and flush affected area with copious amts of H_2O. Do not reuse clothing until free of contamination. Do not use containers or equipment of Al, Mg, or their alloys.)

6.143 ***Principle***

Components are detd by GLC. Peak area of each component is measured and compared to stds of same fumigant mixt. Precision of method is ±0.6% for each component.

6.144 ***Sampling***

Obtain representative 1 L sample from container. Sample bulk containers by means of weighted bottle, lowered toward bottom and raised at such rate that it is ¾ full when withdrawn. Sample drums or small containers with thief or thru tap or valve located so that sample comes from well below surface. Prevent contamination of product or sample.

Place sample in clean, dry, and solv. vapor-tight glass bottle of such size that it is nearly filled (not above shoulder) by sample. Vapor-tight g-s bottles or screw-cap bottles with Sn foil lined caps are satisfactory. Store samples at low temp.; cool to <18° before opening for analysis.

6.145 ***Apparatus***

(**a**) *Gas chromatograph.*—With flame ionization or thermal conductivity detector. Typical operating conditions: Column temp., 110°; injection port temp., 200°; flow rate, 80 mL He/min.

(**b**) *Recorder.*—0.05–1.05 mv, full scale response. Integrator may be used.

(**c**) *Syringe.*—Hamilton Co. 10 μL No. 701N, or equiv.

(**d**) *Column.*—1.2 m (4') stainless steel, ¼" od, 0.194" id, packed with reagent **6.146(a)**. Max. temp. is 160°. Other columns can be used but chromatgc conditions and sample size must be adjusted in accordance with column requirements. One such column is: 3 m (10') stainless, $^3/_{16}$" od, 0.12" id, packed with 20% by wt *N,N*-bis-(2-cyanoethyl) formamide on 80–100 mesh Chromosorb W, acid-washed. Columns are available from com. suppliers. Criterion for use is emergence of each component of mixt. of CS_2, CCl_4, $(CH_2)_2Cl_2$, and $(CH_2)_2Br_2$ as sep. peak.

6.146 ***Reagents***

(**a**) *Column packing.*—30% by wt tricresyl phosphate on Chromosorb P, 30–60 mesh.

(**b**) *Carbon disulfide std.*—ACS.

(**c**) *Carbon tetrachloride std.*—ACS.

(**d**) *Ethylene dichloride std.*—Purified 1,2-dichloroethane, available from laboratory supply houses, or use center cut of fractionation of com. product.

(**e**) *Ethylene dibromide (1,2-dibromoethane) std.*— Purified or distd as in (**d**).

6.147 ***Preparation of Standards***

Prep. fresh stds just before analysis which approximate expected composition, by wt, of fumigant mixt. Place proper wt of each component in 25 mL g-s vol. flask and mix well. Do not prep. by vol. Cool CS_2 to prevent loss. Adjust wt stds to detector response.

Carefully fill weighed 10 mL vol. flask to mark with prepd std and weigh. Use this wt to det. g/5 μL values for each component of std.

6.148 ***Determination***

Purge column thoroly at 110° before use. Establish 0 baseline at full sensitivity. Inject 5 μL std fumigant mixt. into chromatograph. Attenuate successively so that each peak is at max. % of chart scale, adjusting sample size and attenuation, if necessary. Repeat injection. Detd area for each component, corrected for any baseline drift, should differ by $\leqslant$1%. Order of elution from column is: CS_2, CCl_4, $(CH_2)_2Cl_2$, and $(CH_2)_2Br_2$. Total analysis time is ca 21 min.

Inject 5 μL sample into chromatograph. Det. corrected area of each component from chromatogram, or note integrator reading.

g Component = $S \times C/B$, where S = wt component in std, B = area for component in std, and C = area for component in sample. Perform calcn for each component in sample.

% Component = g component in sample × 100/ sum of g components in sample.

Last equation is not applicable in presence of unmeasured contaminants.

PESTICIDES RELATED TO NATURAL PRODUCTS AND THEIR SYNERGISTS

Technical Allethrin (*44*)—Official First Action

(*Caution: See* **51.041**.)

6.149 ***Principle***

Allethrin reacts quant. with ethylenediamine to form chrysanthemum monocarboxylic acid which is detd by titrn with std NaOMe in pyridine. Chrysanthemum monocarboxylic acid, anhydride, and acid chloride interfere quant. and are detd independently.

6.150 ***Reagents***

(**a**) *Absolute alcohol.*—SDF No. 2-B is satisfactory.

(**b**) *Methanolic hydrochloric acid std soln.*—0.1*N*. Dil. 17 mL HCl (1+1) to 1 L with anhyd. MeOH. Stdze against std 0.1*N* NaOH, using phthln. If used at temp., T, different from that at which stdzd, T_0, calc. corrected normality = $N[1–0.001(T - T_0)]$.

(**c**) *Sodium methylate std soln.*—0.1*N* in pyridine. Transfer 50 mL 2*N* NaOMe (*Caution: See* **51.038**) to 1 L bottle contg 75 mL anhyd. MeOH and dil. to 1 L with redistd pyridine. Stdze against NBS benzoic acid, using pyridine as solv. and thymolphthalein, (**i**), as indicator. Dispense from 50 mL automatic buret with vents connected to Ascarite tubes. Stdze daily against std methanolic HCl, (**b**).

(**d**) *Methanolic potassium hydroxide std soln.*— 0.02*N*. Dissolve 1.12 g KOH in 1 L MeOH. Stdze as in **50.035**.

(**e**) *Morpholine soln.*—Transfer 8.7 mL redistd morpholine to 1 L bottle and dil. to 1 L with anhyd. MeOH. Fit bottle with 2-hole rubber stopper; thru 1 hole insert 20 mL pipet so that tip extends below surface of liq., and thru other hole insert short piece of glass tubing to which is attached aspirator bulb.

(**f**) *Ethylenediamine.*—Redistd com. grade contg <3% H_2O. Dispense from automatic buret with vents connected to Ascarite tubes.

(**g**) *Dimethyl yellow-methylene blue mixed indicator.*—Dissolve 1 g dimethyl yellow (*p*-dimethylaminoazobenzene; *Caution: See* **51.085**) and 0.1 g methylene blue in 125 mL anhyd. MeOH.

(**h**) α-*Naphtholbenzein indicator.*—1% alc. soln.

(**i**) *Thymolphthalein indicator.*—1% pyridine soln.

6.151 ***Determination of Chrysanthemum Monocarboxylic Acid Chloride***

Add 8–10 drops mixed indicator, (**g**), to ca 150 mL anhyd. MeOH and add 0.1*N* HCl, (**b**), dropwise until soln appears reddish brown by transmitted light. Add 0.02*N* KOH, (**d**), dropwise until appearance of first green. Transfer 25 mL to each of three 125 mL g-s erlenmeyers, reserving 1 flask as ref. color for end point. Into each of other flasks add 1.5–2.5 g sample from weighing pipet, swirling flask while adding sample. Within 5 min, titr. with 0.02*N* KOH, (**d**), to first green end point, using blank as ref. color. Calc. milliequiv. chrysanthemum monocarboxylic acid chloride/g sample, $C = V \times N/\text{g}$ sample, where V= mL N normal KOH required;

% Chrysanthemum monocarboxylic acid chloride = C × 18.67.

6.152 ***Determination of Chrysanthemum Monocarboxylic Acid***

Transfer 25 mL anhyd. alcohol to each of two 125 mL g-s erlenmeyers, add 8–9 drops α-naphtholbenzein indicator, and cool to 0° in ice bath. Neutze by adding 0.02*N* NaOH dropwise to bright green end point. To each flask add 1.5–2.5 g sample from weighing pipet. Immediately titr. with 0.02*N* NaOH, **50.034**, to first bright green end point. Calc. milliequiv. chrysanthemum monocarboxylic acid and acid chloride/g sample: $D = X \times N/\text{g}$ sample, where X = mL N normal NaOH required; $(D - C) \times 16.82$ = % chrysanthemum monocarboxylic acid.

6.153 ***Determination of Chrysanthemum Monocarboxylic Anhydride***

Pipet 20 mL morpholine soln, (**e**), into each of four 250 mL erlenmeyers, using same pipet. Fill pipet by exerting pressure in bottle with aspirator bulb. Reserve 2 flasks for blanks; into each of other flasks add 1.5–2.5 g sample from weighing pipet. Swirl flasks and let samples and blanks stand 5 min at room temp. Add 4–5 drops mixed indicator, (**g**), to each flask and titr. with 0.1*N* HCl, (**b**), until color changes from green to faint red when viewed by transmitted light. Calc. milliequiv. chrysanthemum monocarboxylic anhydride/g sample: $E = (B - Y) \times N/\text{g}$ sample, where Y = mL N normal HCl required for sample, and B = mL N normal HCl required for blank; $(E - 2C) \times 31.84$ = % chrysanthemum monocarboxylic anhydride.

6.154 ***Determination of Allethrin***

Add sample contg 0.8–1.1 g allethrin to each of two 250 mL erlenmeyers from weighing pipet. To each of 2 flasks as blanks and to samples add 25 mL ethylenediamine, (**f**), with swirling. Let samples and blanks stand 2 hr at 25±2°. Wash down sides of flasks with 50 mL redistd pyridine. To each flask add 6–10 drops thymolphthalein indicator, (**i**), and titr. with 0.1*N* NaOMe, (**c**), to first permanent blue-green end point. (With colorless samples, first blue end point may be used.) Calc. milliequiv. allethrin/g sample: $F = (Z - B) \times N/\text{g}$ sample, where Z = mL N normal NaOMe required for sample, and B = av. mL N normal NaOMe required for blank; $(F + C - D - E) \times 30.24$ = % allethrin.

d-trans-Allethrin (*dl*-2-Allyl-4-hydroxy-3-methyl-2-cyclopentene-1 Ester of *d-trans*-2,2-Dimethyl-3-(2-methylpropenyl)cyclopropanecarboxylic Acid) (*45*) Official Final Action

Gas Chromatographic Method

(*Caution: See* **51.041**.)

6.155 ***Principle***

d-trans-Allethrin is dild in acetone contg dibutyl phthalate as internal std. Ratios of GLC peak hts of *d-trans*-allethrin and dibutyl phthalate in sample and std are compared for quant. detn. Method is applicable to both tech. *d-trans*-allethrin and various formulations of it. Not applicable to formulations contg large amt MGK Repellent 874 (2-hydroxyethyl-*n*-octyl sulfide).

6.156 ***Apparatus and Reagents***

(**a**) *Gas chromatograph.*—Equipped with flame ionization detector and 1.2 m (4′) × 4 mm id glass column packed with 5% OV-1 (Analabs, Inc.) on 80–100 mesh Chromosorb W (HP). Operating conditions: temps (°)—column 165, injection port 230, detector 230; gas flows (mL/min)—N carrier gas 125, air 350–400, H 40–50; sensitivity—10^{-9} amp full scale, attenuation 4× for tech. material, 10^{-9} amp full scale, attenuation 1 for formulations. Before use, condition column 2–3 hr at 275° with N flow 50 mL/min. If necessary, vary column temp. or gas flow to attain retention times of ca 4 and 7 min for internal std and *d-trans*-allethrin, resp. Also vary detector sensitivity or injection vol. to attain ≥100 mm peak ht for each compd (ca 16 μg *d-trans*-allethrin). Theoretical plates/ft must be >200.

Calc. theoretical plates/ft (N) as follows: $N = 16L^2/(M^2 \times F)$, where L = retention of GLC peak in mm; M = peak baseline produced by drawing tangents to points of inflection of peak; and F = length of column (ft).

(**b**) *Internal std soln.*—4.0 mg dibutyl phthalate/mL acetone.

(**c**) *d-trans-Allethrin std solns.*—(*1*) *Soln 1.*—Approx. 4 mg/mL. Accurately weigh ca 1.0 g *d-trans*-allethrin (available from McLaughlin Gormley King Co., 8810 Tenth Ave N, Minneapolis, MN 55427) into 50 mL vol. flask and dil. to vol. with acetone. Pipet 20 mL this soln into 100 mL vol. flask, add 50 mL internal std soln by pipet, and dil. to vol. with acetone. Use this soln for detn of tech. material. (*2*) *Soln 2.*—Approx. 1 mg/mL. Pipet 25 mL *Soln 1* into 100 mL vol. flask and dil. to vol. with acetone. Use this soln for detn of *d-trans*-allethrin in formulations.

6.157 ***Preparation of Sample***

(**a**) *Technical material.*—Accurately weigh sample contg ca 1.0 g *d-trans*-allethrin into 50 mL vol. flask and dil. to vol. with acetone. Pipet 20 mL aliquot into 100 mL vol. flask, add 50 mL internal std soln by pipet, and dil. to vol. with acetone.

(**b**) *Formulations.*—Accurately weigh sample contg ca 200 mg *d-trans*-allethrin into 50 mL vol. flask, add 25 mL internal std soln by pipet, and dil. to vol. with acetone. Pipet 25 mL aliquot into 100 mL vol. flask and dil. to vol. with acetone.

6.158 ***Gas Chromatography***

(**a**) *Technical material.*—Inject aliquots (ca 3 μL) std *Soln 1* until ratio of *d-trans*-allethrin:dibutyl phthalate peak hts varies <1% for successive injections. Repeat with sample soln, followed by duplicate injections of std soln. If peak ht ratios differ >±1% from previous std injections, repeat series of injections.

(**b**) *Formulations.*—Proceed as in (**a**), using std *Soln 2.* Repeat std injections after each series of 3 sample injections. If peak ht ratios differ >±1.5% from previous std injections, repeat injections.

6.159 ***Calculations***

(**a**) *Technical material.*—Calc. peak ht ratios for duplicate std injections before and after sample injections and average the 4 values. Calc. and average peak ht ratios for sample injections.

$$\% \textit{ d-trans}\text{-Allethrin} = (W' \times P \times R)/(W \times R'),$$

where W' and W = g std and sample, resp.; P = % purity of std; and R' and R = peak ht ratios of std and sample, resp.

(**b**) *Formulations.*—Calc. av. for all std peak ht ratios and for sample peak ht ratios.

$$\% \textit{ d-trans}\text{-Allethrin} = (W' \times P \times R \times 2)/(W \times R'),$$

where W' = g std in final diln.

DERRIS AND CUBE POWDER

Rotenone

Crystallization Method (46)—Official Final Action

(*Caution: See* **51.049** and **51.084**.)

6.160 ***Reagents***

(**a**) *Purified rotenone.*—Dissolve rotenone in boiling CCl_4; cool in refrigerator or ice bath at 0–10° until pptn of rotenone-CCl_4 solvate stops. Filter thru buchner and wash once or twice with ice-cold CCl_4. Conc. filtrate, crystallize, and filter as before. Transfer cryst. residue to beaker, add ca twice their vol. alcohol, and heat nearly to boiling. (Crystals need not dissolve completely.) Cool to room temp., filter thru buchner, and draw air thru cryst. residue until most alcohol is removed. Remove rotenone from funnel, dry in air, and finally heat 1 hr at 105°. Mp, detd in Pyrex, of purified material should be 163–164°. (Mother liquors may be concd and rotenone-CCl_4 solvate allowed to crystallize. Cryst. material may be used for further purification, or kept for prepn of wash solns or for seeding to induce crystn in detn.)

(**b**) *Rotenone-CCl_4 solvate.*—Ppt rotenone from CCl_4 soln, filter by suction, and dry in air.

(**c**) *Rotenone-CCl_4 wash soln.*—Sat. CCl_4 at 0°, and keep at 0° during use.

(**d**) *Alcohol saturated with rotenone at room temp.*

(**e**) *Charcoal, activated.*—Norit-A neutral, or equiv.

6.161 ***Preparation of Solution***

(**a**) Weigh 30 g (if sample contains >7% rotenone, use amt to give 1.0–1.5 g rotenone in 200 mL aliquot) finely powd root and 10 g of the C, (**e**), into 500 mL g-s erlenmeyer. Add 300 mL $CHCl_3$, measured at known room temp.; fasten stopper securely and place flask on shaking machine. Agitate vigorously ≥4 hr, preferably interrupting shaking with overnight rest (or flask may be shaken continuously overnight). Rapidly filter mixt. into suitable flask, using fluted paper without suction and keeping funnel covered with watch glass to avoid evapn loss. Stopper flask and adjust temp. of filtrate to that of original $CHCl_3$.

(**b**) *Alternative extraction method.*—If sample has ratio of rotenone to total ext of >0.4, use amt contg 1.0–1.5 g rotenone and successively ext 4 times with $CHCl_3$, using 300 mL $CHCl_3$ and 4 hr agitation for first extn as in (**a**) and 200 mL and 2 hr each for other extns. Filter after each extn and return marc to flask for extn with fresh solv. Finally combine exts, evap. almost to dryness, and use entire ext to det. rotenone.

(**c**) *Extraction method for formulations containing 0.75–1.0% rotenone with or without sulfur and/or pyrethrins.*—Weigh two 50 g portions sample into sep. 500 mL g-s erlenmeyers. Add 5 g of the C and 300 mL $CHCl_3$, measured at known room temp., to each. Stopper and continue as in (**a**).

6.162 ***Determination***

(*Caution: See* **51.011**, **51.018**, **51.046**, **51.049**, and **51.056**.)

Pipet 200 mL soln, **6.161** (or entire soln if alternative extn, (**b**), is used), into 500 mL Pyrex erlenmeyer and distil until ca 25 mL remains. (For formulations, **6.161(c)**: In absence of S, combine the 2 exts in one of the erlenmeyers. In presence of S, remove all $CHCl_3$ on steam bath in air current, avoiding prolonged heating. Add 35 mL acetone to each residue and boil gently on steam bath to dissolve all resins. Remove from steam bath, stopper tightly, and hold 2 hr at 0–5°. Filter both acetone solns thru same 15 mL, medium porosity, fritted glass buchner into single 500 mL erlenmeyer. Rinse and wash with acetone at 5°. Remove acetone as $CHCl_3$ was removed above.)

Evap. almost to dryness on steam bath in current of air. Remove remainder of solv. under reduced pressure, heating cautiously on steam bath when necessary to hasten evapn. (Suction may be applied directly to flask if stopper with vent is used to release pressure, so that excessive vac. may be avoided. Use flasks with slightly convex bottoms; do not use flasks below av. wt.) Dissolve ext in 15 mL hot CCl_4 and again, in similar manner, remove all solv. Repeat with another 10–15 mL portion hot CCl_4. (This treatment removes all $CHCl_3$ from resins. $CHCl_3$ ext is usually completely sol. in CCl_4; if small amts of insol. material are present, purification described later will eliminate them.)

Dissolve residue in ca 10 mL CCl_4 and transfer quant. with hot CCl_4 to 50 mL erlenmeyer marked at 25 mL. Adjust vol. to 25 mL by evapg on steam bath or by adding CCl_4. Cool flask in ice bath several min, stopper flask, and swirl until crystn is apparent. Seed with few crystals of rotenone-CCl_4 solvate if necessary to induce crystn. If at this stage only small amt of cryst. material seps, add accurately weighed amt of purified rotenone, **6.160(a)**, estd to be enough to assure that final result, expressed as pure rotenone, is $\geq$1 g. Then warm to dissolve completely, and again induce crystn. At same time prep. satd soln of rotenone in CCl_4, **6.160(c)**, for washing. Place flasks contg ext and washing soln in ice bath capable of holding temp. at 0°, and let stand overnight. (Store ice bath in refrigerator to keep ice from melting too rapidly.)

After 17–18 hr in ice bath, rapidly filter ext thru weighed gooch fitted with filter paper disk, removing flask from ice bath only long enough to pour each fraction of ext into crucible. Rinse cryst. residue from flask and wash under suction once with the ice-cold satd rotenone-CCl_4 wash soln. ($\leq$12–15 mL soln should be used for rinsing and washing.) Continue suction ca 5 min; then dry to const wt at 40° (ca 1 hr). Wt obtained is crude rotenone-CCl_4 solvate.

Break up contents of crucible with spatula, mix thoroly, and weigh 1.000 g into 50 mL erlenmeyer. Add 10 mL alcohol previously satd with rotenone at room temp., swirl flask few min, stopper tightly, and set aside $\geq$4 hr, preferably overnight, at same temp. Filter on weighed gooch fitted with filter paper disk. Rinse crystals from flask and wash under suction with alcohol satd with rotenone at temp. of recrystn (ca 10 mL usually required). Continue suction 3–5 min and then dry crucible at 105° to const wt (ca 1 hr).

Multiply g residue by g total crude rotenone-CCl_4 solvate, and add 0.07 g to product as correction for rotenone held in soln in the 25 mL CCl_4 used in crystn. If any pure rotenone was added, subtract its wt from value obtained. This gives wt pure rotenone contained in aliquot of ext.

Note: Most important precaution in using this method is to keep temp. of CCl_4-rotenone wash soln and crucibles as near 0° as possible. Keep wash soln surrounded by crushed ice except when actually being used. In warm weather keep crucibles in refrigerator until ready to use.

Infrared Method (47)—Official First Action

(Not applicable to derris products)

6.163 ***Standardization***

Prep. std solns of purified rotenone, **6.160(a)**, in $CHCl_3$ at concns of 5, 10, 15, and 20 mg/mL. Scan each std soln from 7.0 to 8.0 μm at speed of 6 min/μm and scale of 10 cm/μm, using 0.1 mm cell and accurately matching cell filled with $CHCl_3$ as ref. Scan each in duplicate. Obtain av. *A* of each concn, using 7.57 μm as base point and 7.65 μm as peak. Plot *A* against concn.

6.164 ***Determination***

Weigh sample contg 250–300 mg rotenone into 25 × 200 mm culture tube. Add 1–2 g anhyd. Na_2SO_4, 2 g activated charcoal, and 50 mL $CHCl_3$ by pipet. Close securely with Teflon-lined screw cap and tumble end over end 1 hr at ca 35 rpm. Filter thru medium paper, avoiding evapn losses. Transfer 20 mL aliquot to 50 mL erlenmeyer and evap. on steam bath with current of air. Transfer residue to 10 mL g-s vol. flask and dil. to vol. with $CHCl_3$. Stopper, and mix thoroly.

Scan from 7.0 to 8.0 μm, using 0.1 mm cell and matched cell filled with $CHCl_3$ as ref. Det. *A* by baseline method from 7.57 to 7.75 μm and peak at 7.65 μm, using same scanning speed and scale expansion as in stdzn.

Calc. % rotenone from std curve and wt sample in final diln.

6.165 Total Ether Extract—Official Final Action

(*Caution: See* **51.009**, **51.039**, **51.054**, and **51.070(b)**.)

Ext 5 g finely powd root with ether 48 hr in Soxhlet or other efficient extn app. Conc. ext and filter off any insol. material present. Receive filtrate in tared beaker, evap. ether on steam bath, and dry in oven at 105° to const wt.

Piperonyl Butoxide (*48*)—Official Final Action

6.166 ***Apparatus and Reagents***

(**a**) *Photoelectric colorimeter.*—Equipped with narrow band-pass interference type filter with central wavelength 630 nm. (Filter is available from: Baird-Atomic Inc.; Bausch and Lomb Optical Co., 10 Champeney Terrace, Rochester, NY 14602; and Photovolt Corp., 1115 Broadway, New York, NY 10010.) Spectrophtr set at wavelength in range 625–635 nm may also be used.

(**b**) *Purified tannic acid.*—Purify as follows: To 20 g tannic acid (USP reagent grade) add 100 mL EtOAc (99%) and stir mech. ca 1 hr. Filter by suction thru fritted glass funnel, and wash residue with three 5 mL portions EtOAc. To combined filtrate and washings add 2 g finely powd Darco G-60 (or equiv. decolorizing C), and stir mech. ca 0.5 hr. Filter by gravity thru double thickness Whatman No. 1, or equiv., paper into graduated dropping funnel. Wash residue several times with EtOAc until vol. filtrate and washings is ca 125 mL. Place dropping funnel over 1 L, 3-neck, r-b flask, equipped with mech. stirrer, and with vigorous agitation in flask, add filtrate dropwise to 5 times its vol. of toluene. Purified tannic acid is pptd immediately.

Filter by suction thru fritted glass funnel, and wash product thoroly with toluene, stirring solids with toluene to assure complete removal of EtOAc. Continue suction until practically all toluene is removed. Dry purified tannic acid in vac. oven at ca 40°, and place in tightly stoppered bottle.

(**c**) *Tannic acid reagent.*—Completely dissolve exactly 0.025 g purified tannic acid in 20 mL HOAc by shaking at room temp. Add 80 mL H_3PO_4 and mix thoroly. Prep. fresh daily. Store tightly stoppered, as it is hygroscopic.

(**d**) *Purified piperonyl butoxide.*—Purify by low pressure fractional distn of tech. product. (*Caution: See* **51.015**.) Also available from Fairfield American Corp., 3932 Salt Rd, Medina, NY 14103.

(**e**) *Piperonyl butoxide std soln.*—50 μg/0.1 mL. Weigh exactly 1.000 g purified piperonyl butoxide into 100 mL vol. flask. (Hypodermic syringe and needle are convenient for adding compd to flask.) Dil. to vol. with deodorized kerosene and mix well. Pipet 10 mL of this soln into 200 mL vol. flask. Dil. to vol. with deodorized kerosene and mix well. This soln is stable for several months. If std is to be used with sample contg pyrethrum, add enough pyrethrum ext to std before initial diln to give ratio piperonyl butoxide to pyrethrins similar to sample.

6.167 ***Preparation of Sample***

Accurately weigh sample contg 0.5–1.5 g piperonyl butoxide into tared 100 mL vol. flask, dil. to vol. with deodorized kerosene, and mix well. Pipet 10 mL into 200 mL vol. flask, dil. to vol. with deodorized kerosene, and mix well.

6.168 ***Determination***

Pipet 0.1 mL (from 1 mL pipet graduated in 0.1 mL) sample soln into 18 × 150 mm test tube. Add exactly 5 mL tannic acid reagent and shake vigorously 1 min. Treat std and blank, consisting of 0.1 mL deodorized kerosene, simultaneously in same manner.

Place test tubes in test-tube basket and place in vigorously boiling H_2O bath 5 min. Remove basket and let tubes cool to room temp. Transfer solns to colorimeter tubes and read, against H_2O, using 625–635 nm filter or setting. (After cooling to room temp. there is no appreciable change in *A* for several hr.)

Subtract A_0 of deodorized kerosene from readings of both sample, *A*, and std, *A'*.

$$\text{mg Piperonyl butoxide} = A \times 0.05/A'.$$

PYRETHRINS

Mercury Reduction Method (49)—Official Final Action

(*Caution: See* **51.039**, **51.054**, **51.070**, and **51.073**.)

6.169 ***Reagents***

(**a**) *Deniges reagent.*—Mix 5 g yellow HgO with 40 mL H_2O, and, while stirring, slowly add 20 mL H_2SO_4; then add addnl 40 mL H_2O and stir until all dissolves. Test for absence of mercurous Hg by adding few drops of (**b**) to 10 mL and titrg with (**c**) as in **6.171**, par. 2, beginning "Add 50 mL previously prepd and cooled dil. HCl . . ."

(**b**) *Iodine monochloride soln.*—Dissolve 10 g KI and 6.44 g KIO_3 in 75 mL H_2O in g-s bottle; add 75 mL HCl and 5 mL $CHCl_3$, and adjust to faint I color (in $CHCl_3$) by adding dil. KI or KIO_3 soln. If much I is liberated, use stronger soln of KIO_3 than 0.01*M* at first, making final adjustment with 0.01*M* soln. Keep in dark and readjust when necessary. Do not store in refrigerator.

(**c**) *Potassium iodate std soln.*—0.01*M*. Dissolve 2.14 g pure KIO_3, previously dried at 105°, in H_2O and dil. to 1 L. 1 mL = 0.0057 g pyrethrin I and needs no further stdzn.

(**d**) *Alcoholic sodium hydroxide soln.*—(*1*) *1.0N.*—Dissolve 40 g NaOH in alcohol and dil. to 1 L with alcohol. (*2*) *0.5N*—Dil. 1.0*N* with alcohol (1+1).

(**e**) *Petroleum ether.*—Aromatic-free, bp range 30–60°.

(**f**) *Ethyl ether.*—Peroxide-free, reagent grade.

6.170 ***Preparation of Sample***

(**a**) *Pyrethrum powder.*—Ext sample contg 40–150 mg total pyrethrins in Soxhlet or other efficient extn app. 7 hr with pet ether. After extn is complete, evap. pet ether to ca 40 mL, stopper flask, and place in refrigerator at 0±0.5° overnight. Filter cold ext thru cotton plug satd with cold pet ether, in stem of funnel, collecting filtrate in 250 mL erlenmeyer. Wash with three 15 mL portions cold pet ether. Evap. filtrate and washings on H_2O bath, using air current, until <1 mL solv. remains.

Add 15–20 mL 0.5*N* alc. NaOH to evapd ext, connect to reflux condenser, and boil gently 1–1.5 hr. Transfer to 600 mL beaker and add enough H_2O to bring vol. to 200 mL. Add few glass beads, or preferably use boiling tube, and boil down to 150 mL. Transfer to 250 mL vol. flask and add 1 g Filter-Cel and 10 mL *10% $BaCl_2$ soln.* Do not shake before dilg to vol. Dil. to vol., mix thoroly, filter off 200 mL, neutze with H_2SO_4 (1+4), using 1 drop phthln, and add 1 mL excess. (If necessary to hold soln overnight at this point, leave in alk. condition.)

(**b**) *Pyrethrum extracts in mineral oil.*—Weigh or measure sample contg 40–150 mg total pyrethrins, add 50 mL pet ether and 1 g Filter-Cel, and place in refrigerator at 0±0.5° overnight. Filter thru gooch into 300 mL erlenmeyer and wash with three 15 mL portions cold pet ether. Evap. filtrate and washings on H_2O bath, using air current, until <1 mL solv. remains.

Add 20 mL 1*N* alc. NaOH, or more if necessary, to ext, connect to reflux condenser, and boil gently 1–1.5 hr. Transfer to 600 mL beaker and add enough H_2O to make aq. layer 200 mL. If >20 mL alc. NaOH soln was used, add enough H_2O so that all alcohol is removed when vol. is reduced to 150 mL. Add few glass beads, or preferably use boiling tube, and boil aq. layer down to 150 mL. Transfer to 500 mL separator and drain aq. layer into 250 mL vol. flask. Wash oil layer once with H_2O and add wash H_2O to aq. portion. If slight emulsion still persists after draining aq. layer and washings, add 2–3 mL 10% $BaCl_2$ soln, but do not shake vigorously after adding $BaCl_2$ because reversed emulsion difficult to sep. may form. To aq. soln in 250 mL flask add 1 g Filter-Cel and ≥10 mL of the $BaCl_2$ soln. Swirl gently and let stand 30 min. Dil. to vol., mix thoroly, and filter off 200 mL. Test filtrate with $BaCl_2$ soln to see if enough has been added to obtain clear soln. Neutze with H_2SO_4 (1+4), using 1 drop phthln, and add 1 mL excess. (If necessary to hold soln overnight at this point, leave in alk. condition.)

6.171 ***Determination of Pyrethrin I***

Filter acid soln from **6.170**(**a**) or (**b**) thru 7 cm paper, coated lightly with suspension of Filter-Cel in H_2O, on buchner, and wash with three 15 mL portions H_2O. Transfer to 500 mL g-s separator and ext with two 50 mL portions pet ether. Shake each ext ≥1 min, releasing pressure if necessary by inverting separator and carefully venting thru stopcock. Let layers sep. ≥5 min or until aq. layer is clear before draining and re-extn. Reserve aq. layer for pyrethrin II detn. Do not combine pet ether exts but wash each in sequence with same three 10 mL portions H_2O, and filter pet ether exts thru small cotton plug into clean 250 mL separator. Wash separators and cotton in sequence with 5 mL pet ether. Ext combined pet ether solns with 5 mL 0.1*N* NaOH, shaking vigorously ≥1 min. Let layers sep. ≥5 min before draining aq. layer into 100 mL beaker. Wash pet ether with addnl 5 mL portion 0.1*N* NaOH and with 5 mL H_2O, adding washings to beaker. Add 10 mL Deniges reagent and let stand in complete darkness 1 hr at 25±2°.

Add 20 mL alcohol and ppt HgCl with 3 mL *satd NaCl soln.* Warm to ca 60° and let stand several min until ppt coagulates and settles. Filter thru small paper, transferring all ppt to paper, and wash with ≥10 mL hot alcohol. Wash with 2 or more 10 mL portions hot $CHCl_3$ and place paper and contents in 250 mL g-s erlenmeyer. Add 50 mL previously prepd and cooled dil. HCl (3+2). Add 5 mL $CHCl_3$ or CCl_4 and 1 mL freshly adjusted ICl soln, and titr. with 0.1*M* KIO_3 soln, shaking vigorously ≥30 sec after each addn, until no I color remains in $CHCl_3$ or CCl_4 layer. Take as end point when red color disappears from solv. layer and does not return within 1–3 min. From mL std KIO_3 soln used in titrn and blank on Deniges reagent, calc. % pyrethrin I.

(Reactions:

$$2Hg_2Cl_2 + 4ICl = 4HgCl_2 + 2I_2$$
$$2I_2 + KIO_3 + 6HCl = KCl + 5ICl + 3H_2O$$

Addn of ICl does not change vol. relationship between mercurous Hg and KIO_3 soln, and aids in detg end point in titrn of small amts of Hg.)

Note: Chrysanthemum monocarboxylic acid reacts with Deniges reagent to form series of colors beginning with phthln red, which gradually changes to purple, then to blue, and finally to bluish green. Color reaction is very distinct with 5 mg monocarboxylic acid, and amts as low as 1 mg can usually be detected. Therefore no pyrethrin I should be reported if color reaction is neg.

With samples contg much perfume or other saponifiable ingredients, it may be necessary to use as much as 50 mL 1*N* alc. NaOH. When lethanes are present, after washing HgCl ppt with alcohol and $CHCl_3$, wash once more with alcohol and then several times with hot H_2O.

6.172 ***Determination of Pyrethrin II (50)***

If necessary, filter aq. residue from pet ether extn thru gooch. Conc. filtrate to ca 50 mL and transfer to 500 mL g-s separator. Wash beaker with three 15 mL portions H_2O. Acidify with 10 mL HCl and sat. with NaCl. (Acidified aq. layer must contain visible NaCl crystals thruout following extns.)

Ext with 50 mL ether, drain aq. layer into second separator, and ext again with 50 mL ether. Continue extg and draining aq. layer, using 35 mL for third and fourth extns. Shake each ext ≥1 min, releasing pressure, if necessary, by inverting separator and carefully venting thru stopcock. Let layers sep. ≥5 min or until aq. layer is clear before subsequent draining and extn. Combine ether exts, drain, and wash with three 10 mL portions satd NaCl soln. Filter ether exts thru cotton plug into 500 mL erlenmeyer and wash separator and cotton with addnl 10 mL ether. Evap. ether on H_2O bath, and remove any fumes of HCl with air current and continued heating ≤5 min. Dry 10 min at 100°.

(a) *For crude pyrethrum exts.*—Treat residue with 75 mL boiling H_2O and filter thru 9–11 cm Whatman No. 1, or equiv., paper. Wash flask and paper with five 20 mL portions boiling H_2O or until filtrate from final wash is neut. to litmus. Add 1–2 drops phthln and rapidly titr. with 0.02*N* NaOH (1 mL = 0.00374 g pyrethrin II). Check normality of 0.02*N* NaOH same day sample is titrd.

(b) *For refined pyrethrum exts.*—Add 2 mL neut. alcohol and 20 mL H_2O, and heat to dissolve acid. Cool, filter thru gooch if necessary, add 1–2 drops phthln, and titr. with 0.02*N* NaOH (1 mL = 0.00374 g pyrethrin II). Check normality of 0.02*N* NaOH same day as sample is titrd.

Sabadilla Alkaloids (*51*)—Official Final Action

(In dust formulations)

6.173 ***Determination***

(*Caution: See* **51.011**, **51.040**, and **51.056**.)

Weigh 10 g mixed 50% sabadilla dust (or corresponding amt of lesser concn) into 500 mL g-s erlenmeyer. Add exactly 300 mL ether-$CHCl_3$ (3+1), and shake 5 min. Make alk. with 10 mL NH_4OH and shake mech. 2 hr. Let stand overnight; then shake 1 hr.

Filter, avoiding evapn. Place 200 mL aliquot in 500 mL separator, acidify with H_2SO_4 (3+97), and shake; withdraw small amt aq. layer and test with litmus paper, returning soln to separator. Add 50 mL of the dil. H_2SO_4 and shake. Let sep. and transfer acid ext to second 500 mL separator. Add 50 mL pet ether to acid ext and shake. Let layers sep. and transfer acid ext to third separator. Repeat extn of soln in first separator with two 50 mL portions of the dil. H_2SO_4, using same 50 mL pet ether in second separator for washing. Collect acid exts in third separator.

Make acid exts alk. to phthln with NH_4OH. Ext with three 50 mL portions $CHCl_3$. Wash each $CHCl_3$ ext by shaking gently with same 100 mL portion H_2O in fourth separator. (If emulsion forms, add small amt anhyd. Na_2SO_4.)

Filter each $CHCl_3$ ext thru cotton into weighed 250 mL flask. Evap. $CHCl_3$ on steam bath. Add few mL alcohol, and evap. again. Dry 1 hr at 100° and weigh sabadilla alkaloids. Calc. % total alkaloids.

6.174 ***Qualitative Test***

Add 1–2 mL H_2SO_4 to few mg of residue, **6.173**. Presence of sabadilla alkaloids is indicated by yellow that gradually becomes intensely red with greenish fluorescence.

TOBACCO AND TOBACCO PRODUCTS

Nicotine

(*Note:* Nicotine is very toxic. Avoid contact with skin.)

Silicotungstic Acid Method (52)—Official Final Action

(Includes nornicotine)

6.175 ***Reagent***

Silicotungstic acid soln.—Dissolve 120 g silicotungstic acid ($4H_2O.SiO_2.12WO_3.22H_2O$ or $SiO_2.12WO_3.26H_2O$) in H_2O and dil. to 1 L. (Acid should be white or pale yellow crystals, free from green color; soln should be free from cloudiness and green color. Of the several silicotungstic acids, $4H_2O.SiO_2.10WO_3.3H_2O$ and $4H_2O.SiO_2.12WO_3.20H_2O$ do not give cryst. ppts with nicotine and should not be used.)

6.176 ***Determination***

Weigh sample contg preferably 0.1–1.0 g nicotine. If sample contains very little nicotine (ca 0.1%), do not increase amt to point where it interferes with distn. Wash with H_2O into 500 mL Kjeldahl flask, and if necessary add little paraffin to prevent frothing and few small pieces pumice to prevent bumping. Add 10 g NaCl and 10 mL *NaOH soln (30% by wt)*, and close flask with rubber stopper thru which passes stem of trap bulb and inlet tube for steam. Connect trap bulb to well-cooled condenser, lower end of which dips below surface of 10 mL HCl (1+4) in suitable receiving flask. Steam distil rapidly. When distn is well under way, heat flask to reduce vol. of liq. as far as practicable without bumping or excessive sepn of insol. matter. Distil until few mL distillate shows no cloud or opalescence when treated with drop silicotungstic acid soln and drop HCl (1+4). Confirm alky of residue in distn flask with phthln.

Adjust distillate, which may total 1.0–1.5 L, to convenient exact vol. (soln may be concd on steam bath without loss of nicotine), mix well, and pass thru dry filter if not clear. Test distillate with Me orange to confirm acidity. Pipet aliquot contg ca 0.1 g nicotine into beaker. (If samples contain very small amts of nicotine, aliquot contg as little as 0.01 g nicotine may be used.) To each 100 mL liq., add 3 mL HCl (1+4) and 1 mL silicotungstic acid for each 0.01 g nicotine supposed to be present. Stir thoroly and let stand overnight at room temp. Before filtering, stir ppt to see that it settles quickly and is in cryst. form. Filter on either ashless paper or gooch and wash with HCl (1+1000) at room temp. Continue washing for 2 or 3 fillings of filter after no more opalescence appears when few mL fresh filtrate is tested with few drops nicotine distillate. With paper, transfer paper and ppt to weighed Pt crucible, dry carefully, and ignite until all C is destroyed. Finally heat over Meker burner ≤10 min. Wt residue × 0.1141 = wt nicotine in aliquot. With gooch, dry in oven 3 hr at 105° and weigh. Wt residue × 0.1012 = wt nicotine in aliquot.

HALOGENATED PESTICIDES

Aldrin, Dieldrin, and Endrin—Official Final Action

★ *Total Chlorine by Sodium Biphenyl* ★ *Reduction Method* (53)

6.177 ***Principle***

Org. halogen compds are decomposed by Na biphenyl and liberated halide ion is titrd by Volhard method or potentiometrically after extn with H_2O from reaction medium. Applicable to detn of aldrin, dieldrin, or endrin in dusts, granules, wettable powders, emulsifiable concs, and solns in absence of other org. Cl-contg compds. More than trace amts of H_2O and appreciable amts of org. compds contg labile H cause excessive consumption of Na biphenyl. Interference of S is avoided, when present, by special treatment.

6.178 ***Reagents***

(**a**) *Dilute nitric acid.*—6% by wt. Add 60 mL HNO_3 to 945 mL H_2O.

(**b**) *Sodium biphenyl reagent.*—30% w/w. (*Caution: See* **51.034** and **51.038**.) Place 300 mL dry toluene and 58 g Na in dry 2 L 3-neck flask equipped with adjustable speed sealed stirrer, inlet for N, and reflux condenser. With stirrer off, and with slow stream of N passing thru flask, warm until refluxing begins and Na is entirely melted. Agitate vigorously until Na is finely dispersed; then cool to <10°. Remove reflux condenser and add 1.25 L anhyd. ethylene glycol dimethyl ether. Add 390 g biphenyl with moderate stirring and with slow stream of N passing thru flask. Reaction should begin within few min, indicated by blue or green color which gradually darkens to black. Maintain temp. at <30° with oil bath or other cooling medium not involving hazard should flask contg Na break. Reaction should be complete in 1 hr. Reagent protected from moisture and air has useful life of 1–2 months at 25°.

(Premixed reagent, packed in 15 mL vials, each enough for 1 detn, is available from Southwestern Analytical Chemicals, Inc., PO Box 485, Austin, TX 78767.)

(**c**) *Toluene.*—Nitration grade, Cl-free.

6.179 ***Preparation of Sample***

(*Caution: See* **51.041** and **51.084**.)

(**a**) *Technical products.*—Accurately weigh ca 0.1 g sample into 125 mL separator contg 25–30 mL toluene. Cautiously add 10–14 g Na biphenyl reagent, mix by swirling, and let stand 5 min. If soln is not dark green, add addnl 10–14 g reagent. (Dieldrin and endrin require 15 min reaction time after final addn of reagent.)

Destroy excess reagent by dropwise addn of H_2O, shaking frequently between addns, until green color is completely removed. Then slowly add 25 mL dil. HNO_3, with intermittent swirling. Stopper separator, and mix with gentle rocking motion, venting occasionally. Avoid vigorous shaking during this first extn.

Let sep., rinse stopper and walls of separator with H_2O, and drain aq. phase into 250 mL g-s erlenmeyer. Re-ext reaction mixt. with two 25 mL portions dil. HNO_3, shaking vigorously. Add aq. exts to erlenmeyer and det. Cl.

(**b**) *Emulsifiable concentrates and oil spray solns.*— Mix thoroly and weigh sample contg 0.05–0.08 g Cl into 250 mL separator contg 25–30 mL toluene. Proceed as in (**a**), beginning "Cautiously add . . ."

(**c**) *Dusts, granules, and wettable powders.*—Weigh sample contg 0.1–0.15 g active ingredient in paper Soxhlet extn thimble, place in extn app., and ext with ca 150 mL acetone in 300 mL flask 3 hr. Evap. ext to dryness on steam bath, dissolve residue in few mL toluene, and quant. transfer to 250 mL separator, using 25–30 mL toluene. Continue as in (**a**), beginning "Cautiously add . . ."

If S is brought into soln by decomposition of emulsifiers or other compds such as org. thiophosphates, remove as follows: Add 30% NaOH soln to acid soln in erlenmeyer until alk. to phthln, and add 1 mL excess. Add 5 mL 30% H_2O_2, heat to bp on hot plate, and boil ca 10 min. Let cool slightly, cautiously add 5 mL more 30% H_2O_2, and boil again ca 10 min. Cool, and add small flake (ca 0.05 g) *hydrazine sulfate* to remove last traces of H_2O_2. Neutze with dil. HNO_3 to phthln and add 2–3 mL excess.

6.180 ***Determination***

(**a**) *Colorless solns.*—To acid aq. soln add 30 mL H_2O, 10 mL nitrobenzene, 3 mL ferric indicator, **6.019(e)**, and, from buret, 0.4–0.6 mL 0.05*N* KSCN. Swirling constantly, titr. with 0.1*N* $AgNO_3$ until red is discharged, and add 2–5 mL excess. Stopper flask tightly and shake vigorously 15 sec. Without refilling buret, titr. slowly with the 0.05*N* KSCN until end point approaches. Stopper flask, shake vigorously 20–30 sec, and continue titrn until 1 drop produces distinct reddish color which does not fade on swirling or vigorous shaking.

(**b**) *Colored solns or chloride in presence of bromide and/or iodide.*—To acid aq. soln add 30 mL H_2O, transfer to 400 mL beaker, adjust vol. to 200–250 mL, and add 0.5 g *$Ba(NO_3)_2$*. Titr. with 0.1*N* $AgNO_3$ potentiometrically, with stirring, using cell system of either glass ref. electrode and Ag indicating electrode or Ag-AgCl electrode system, electronic voltmeter, and 10 mL buret.

(**c**) *Blank determination.*—Det. blank on all reagents by adding 10–14 g Na biphenyl reagent to 25 mL toluene and continuing as in **6.179(a)**.

6.181 ***Calculations***

% Aldrin, dieldrin, or endrin = (net mL $AgNO_3$ − mL blank) × normality × 35.45 × $F/(10 \times$ g sample), where F is 1.61 for aldrin, 1.81 for dieldrin, and 1.74 for endrin. Net mL $AgNO_3$ = [mL 0.1*N* $AgNO_3$ − (mL 0.05*N* KSCN/2)].

(For most accurate results, det. factor F for specific batch of tech. pesticide used in formulation. Toxicant content is stenciled on drum. Calc. $F = P/C$, where P = % purity (toxicant content as stenciled on drum), and C = % Cl by wt.)

Infrared Method (53)

6.182 ***Principle***

Dieldrin and endrin in dusts, granules, wettable powders, emulsifiable concs, and solns are purified on adsorbent columns. Hexachloro-epoxy-octahydro-endo,exo-dimethanonaphthalene

★ Surplus method—*see* inside front cover.

(HEOD) content of the purified dieldrin or of tech. dieldrin is detd by IR, using baseline technic, and dieldrin is calcd assuming 85% HEOD content. Endrin content of purified or tech. endrin is detd as hexachloro-epoxy-octa-hydro-endo,endo-dimethanonaphthalene similarly.

Aldrin is extd from dusts, wettable powders, and inorg. fertilizers on adsorbent column. Hexachloro-hexahydro-endo,exo-dimethanonaphthalene (HHDN) content of the ext or of tech. aldrin is detd by IR, using baseline technic, and aldrin is calcd assuming 95% HHDN content. Method is not applicable to emulsifiable concs or granules contg petroleum hydrocarbon solvs or to mixts contg other common pesticides or adjuvants that absorb in same wavelength region as HHDN.

6.183 ***Reagents and Apparatus***

(**a**) *Chromatographic solvent A.*—Mix 1 vol. $CHCl_3$ with 19 vols hexane.

(**b**) *Chromatographic solvent B.*—Mix 1.5 vols acetone with 98.5 vols chromtgc solvent A.

(**c**) *Extraction solvent.*—Mix 1 vol. acetone with 19 vols CS_2.

(**d**) *Infrared spectrophotometer.*—With sealed liq. cells with NaCl windows, having optical path length of ca 0.1 mm (dieldrin and endrin) and 0.2 mm (aldrin).

6.184 ***Preparation of Standard Solutions***

(**a**) *HEOD std soln for dieldrin.*—Accurately weigh ca 100, 200, 300, 400, 500, and 600 mg std hexachloro-epoxy-octahydro-endo,exo-dimethanonaphthalene (HEOD) into 10 mL vol. flasks, dissolve in CS_2, and dil. to vol. Concns will be 1, 2, 3, 4, 5, and 6 g/100 mL, resp.

(**b**) *Std soln for endrin.*—Accurately weigh ca 50, 100, 150, 200, 300, and 400 mg std hexachloro-epoxy-octahydro-endo,endo-dimethanonaphthalene (endrin) into 10 mL vol. flasks, dissolve in CS_2, and dil. to vol. Concns will be 0.5, 1.0, 1.5, 2.0, 3.0, and 4.0 g/100 mL, resp.

(**c**) *HHDN std soln for aldrin.*—Accurately weigh ca 100, 150, 200, 250, 300, and 350 mg std hexachloro-hexahydro-endo,exo-dimethanonaphthalene (HHDN) into 10 mL vol. flasks, dissolve in CS_2, and dil. to vol. Concns will be 1.0, 1.5, 2.0, 2.5, 3.0, and 3.5 g/100 mL, resp.

6.185 ***Preparation of Standard Curve***

Fill 0.1 mm cell (0.2 mm for aldrin) with most dil. of stds solns, using hypodermic syringe. Adjust spectrophtr to optimum settings for gain, slit width, response, speed, and drum drive. Make duplicate scans of CS_2 soln over scanning range indicated in Table **6:01** and repeat with each of other std solns at same instrument settings.

For each of scans of the 6 std solns of each compd, draw line between baseline points indicated in table. Draw perpendicular from zero radiation line thru absorption peak to baseline and measure distance from 0 line to peak, P, and to baseline P_0. Calc. A (= $\log P_0/P$) and plot as ordinate against concn in g/100 mL as abscissa.

Since std curve intersects abscissa at pos. concn value, method is not applicable to concns below this value.

Peak wavelengths given in table are characteristic for low concns and they shift at higher concns. P is always detd as distance from 0 line to point of max. absorption.

Table 6:01 Characteristic Wavelength Points for Infrared Determination of Dieldrin, Endrin, and Aldrin, μm

Compound	Scanning Range	Baseline Points	Peak at Low Concn
HEOD	11.59–12.18	11.64, 12.18	11.80
Endrin	11.43–12.04	11.50, 11.97	11.76
HHDN	11.79–12.24	11.85, 12.24	12.01

6.186 ***Preparation of Sample***

(*Caution: See* **51.011, 51.041, 51.046, 51.056,** and **51.061.**)

(**a**) *Dusts and wettable powders.*—Transfer 3–20 g sample, depending on concn (75–0.5%), weighed to nearest 0.01 g, to chromatgc tube contg 25–50 mm (ca 5.5 g) Hyflo Super-Cel. (For finely divided dieldrin or endrin powder, use 3 g activated C instead of Super-Cel.) Tamp or vibrate column slightly to settle contents. Place 250 mL wide-mouth erlenmeyer or 500 mL evapg dish under tip of column.

Working in well ventilated hood, add 50 mL portions extn solv. to column (if S is present, ext with acetone instead of extn solv.), letting solv. percolate thru column between addns, until 150 mL ext collects. Rinse tip of column with addnl 10 mL extn solv.

Evap. solv. almost to dryness on steam bath under N. Dry HEOD or HHDN residues 15 min at 75°; dry endrin in vac. oven 15 min at 30° and 10 mm pressure. (Extd endrin may no longer be associated with its inhibitors. Residue must not be exposed to elevated temps and must be dissolved promptly to avoid decomposition.)

Cool residue and dissolve in few mL CS_2. Quant. transfer to vol. flask of such size (5–100 mL) as to give optimum concn of 3 g HEOD, 2 g endrin, or 2 g HHDN/100 mL, dil. to vol. with CS_2, and mix thoroly. If soln is cloudy from H_2O, add little NaCl, shake, and let settle.

(**b**) *Granules containing dieldrin or endrin.*—Slurry 40 g Florisil in 200 mL beaker with 100 mL hexane. Transfer to chromatgc column with stream of hexane from wash bottle. Eliminate any bubbles or voids by vibration or agitation. Let hexane drain until only 2–3 mm layer remains above surface of column. Add small layer of Na_2SO_4 to top of column.

Transfer 2–10 g finely ground sample, depending on concn (10–1%), to prepd column. Rinse down column walls with three 10 mL portions chromatgc solv. A, letting each portion enter column before adding next. Add 170 mL chromatgc solv. A, let percolate thru column, and discard.

Gently flow 10 mL chromatgc solv. B down walls of tube, avoiding disturbing surface of adsorbent. After solv. sinks into column, repeat washing with 2 addnl 10 mL portions. Add 220 mL chromatgc solv. B and let flow at rate of 2–5 mL/min, collecting eluate in 500 mL wide-mouth erlenmeyer or evapg dish. Evap. solv. to dryness on steam bath, avoiding spattering, and proceed as in (**a**), using 5–10 mL vol. flask.

(**c**) *Emulsifiable concentrates and solns.*—Weigh 1.5 g dieldrin conc. (1.5 lb/gal.), 1.0 g endrin conc. (1.6 lb/gal.), or 30.0 g 0.5% dieldrin soln, and add 5 mL hexane. Transfer to prepd column and proceed as in (**b**).

(**d**) *Technical materials.*—Transfer sample contg 1.75–4.00 g dieldrin, 1.50–3.00 g endrin, or 1.00–2.00 g aldrin, weighed to 0.01 g, to 100 mL vol. flask. Dissolve in CS_2 and dil. to vol. with CS_2.

6.187 ***Determination***

Fill same 0.1 mm cell (0.2 mm for aldrin) used for prepn of std curve with sample soln. Make duplicate scans, and calc. A and mean A as in prepn of std curve. From appropriate std curve, obtain g HEOD, endrin, or HHDN/100 mL sample soln, W.

% dieldrin = $W \times V \times 1.175/S$;
% endrin = $W \times V/S$;
% aldrin = $W \times V \times 1.053/S$;

where V = mL sample soln; S = g sample; 1.175 and 1.053 = conversion factors HEOD to dieldrin and HHDN to aldrin, resp.

Amiben (3-Amino-2,5-dichlorobenzoic Acid) (*54*)—Official Final Action

AOAC-CIPAC Method

6.188 ***Principle***

Amiben contains conjugated π electron system of benzene which absorbs strongly in UV. Absorption is measured quant. at 297 nm. (*Caution: See* **51.018** and **51.041**.)

6.189 ***Apparatus and Reagents***

(**a**) *Spectrophotometer.*—For use in UV, with 1 cm cells.

(**b**) *Shake-out flask.*—250 mL erlenmeyer, with screw cap.

(**c**) *Amiben std solns.*—(*1*) *Stock soln.*—0.38 mg/mL. Accurately weigh 19±2 mg amiben (Amchem Products, Inc., Ambler, PA 19002) into 50 mL vol. flask, add 25 mL 1% NaOH, agitate until dissolved, dil. to vol., and mix. (*2*) *Working soln.*—0.038 mg/mL. Pipet 5 mL stock soln into 50 mL vol. flask, dil. to vol. with 1% NaOH soln, and mix.

6.190 ***Preparation of Sample***

Mix 10 g granular sample on 12 × 12" paper by lifting alternate corners.

6.191 ***Determination***

(**a**) *Dry granular formulations.*—Add amt solid material and 1% NaOH soln specified in Table **6:02** to 250 mL shake-out flask and shake 30 min. Filter, and transfer stated aliquot to vol. flask. Dil. to vol. with 1% NaOH soln and mix. Det. *A* at 360 and 297 nm against 1% NaOH. Calc. $\Delta A = A_{297} - A_{360}$. Det. $\Delta A'$ of working std soln similarly.

% Amiben = (ΔA × (mg std/mL) × F)/($\Delta A'$ × g sample × 10), where F = factor in Table **6:02**.

(**b**) *Liquid formulations.*—Weigh amt liq. indicated in Table **6:02** into 100 mL vol. flask, dil. to vol. with 1% NaOH soln, and mix. Transfer 1 mL aliquot to 100 mL vol. flask, dil. to vol. with 1% NaOH, and mix. Proceed as in (**a**).

Benzene Hexachloride (BHC) (Hexachlorocyclohexane) Gamma Isomer (Lindane)

Partition Chromatographic Method (55) *Official Final Action*

(*Caution: See* **51.009, 51.011, 51.039, 51.040, 51.041**, and **51.054**.)

6.192 ***Apparatus***

(**a**) *Partition column.*—Column and O type reduction valve are shown in Fig. **6:04**. Construct column of heavy-wall Pyrex tubing ca 3.5 mm thick, 90 cm long × 2.5 cm diam. Seal coarse porosity fritted glass disk in place and attach No. 18/9 $ joint 5 cm below disk. Supply pressure from laboratory supply line. (Column available from SGA Scientific, Inc.; specify Cat. No. JC 1800 constructed from heavy rather than std wall tubing.)

(**b**) *Solvent evaporator.*—Fig. **6:04**. Evap. fractions to dryness under reduced pressure at 60°, with aid of H_2O pump. Recover solv. in trap consisting of Kjeldahl flask immersed in mixt. of NaCl and ice.

(**c**) *Melting point apparatus.*—Use Thiele mp app. equipped with mech. stirrer. App. shown in Fig. **6:05**, or Hershberg modification (*56*) (available from Ace Glass, Inc., Cat. No. 7686) is suitable.

(**d**) *Thermometer.*—Precision grade, meeting NBS specifications: partial immersion; range 90–120° in 0.2° subdivisions. Calibrated by NBS or against thermometer checked by NBS.

(**e**) *Melting point tubes.*—1–2 mm capillary tubes of uniform wall thickness and diam.

6.193 ***Reagents***

(**a**) *n-Hexane.*—Com. grade, distd before use.

(**b**) *Nitromethane.*—Reflux com. grade material 4 hr and distil. No visible residue is left after evapn of 10 mL purified material.

(**c**) *Silicic acid.*—Use Mallinckrodt reagent grade (for chromatgy) which meets following requirements: When column prepd as in **6.195** is used for detn on sample contg known amt of γ-isomer, flow rate and packing characteristics should be similar to those of an H_2SiO_3 known to be satisfactory, and recovery of γ-BHC should be within ±3% of the γ-BHC content.

(**d**) *Dye soln.*—Dissolve 25 mg D&C Violet No. 2 (1-hydroxy-4-*p*-toluidino-anthraquinone) in 50 mL mobile solv. and store in g-s bottle. (Available from Aldrich Chemical Co.)

(**e**) *Mobile solvent.*—Satd soln nitromethane in *n*-hexane. Vigorously shake 2 L *n*-hexane with excess nitromethane in g-s bottle. Decant mobile solvent from nitromethane as needed.

6.194 ***Preparation of Sample***

(**a**) *Powders containing more than 10% γ-BHC.*—Crush and thoroly mix sample with mortar and pestle. Weigh enough sample into tared 125 mL erlenmeyer to provide ca 0.2 g γ-isomer after extg and aliquoting. Add 25 mL mobile solv., heat just to bp on steam bath, and cool to room temp., shaking occasionally. Decant ext thru buchner with ca 34 mm medium porosity fritted disk into 100 mL Kohlrausch flask, with gentle suction. Re-ext residue in flask, using 10 mL mobile solv. Wash residue and flask with five 10 mL portions cold mobile solv., decanting each wash thru buchner. Add 2 mL dye soln and dil. to vol. with mobile solv.

(**b**) *Dusts containing less than 10% γ-BHC.*—Weigh enough sample to provide 1.75–2.00 g γ-isomer. Transfer to Soxhlet extractor and ext overnight with ether. Evap. most of ether on steam bath and evap. remainder at room temp. under vac. Ext γ-isomer from residue with mobile solv. as in (**a**).

6.195 ***Preparation of Column***

(*Caution: See* **51.004** and **51.061**.)

Transfer 100±0.5 g H_2SiO_3 to high-speed blender, add 300 mL mobile solv., and with mixing, add 55 mL nitromethane. Mix 15–30 sec; then pour into column thru glass funnel. Stir slurry with long glass stirring rod to displace air bubbles. Wash down

Table 6:02 Parameters for sample analysis

Sample	Amiben, %	Sample Wt, g±0.1	1% NaOH, mL	Aliquot, mL	Final Diln	Factor (*F*)
Dry granular	1.2	3.0	50	2	50	1,250
Dry granular	4	7.5	100	1	100	10,000
Dry granular	10	3.0	100	1	100	10,000
Liquid	21.6	1.8	100	1	100	10,000

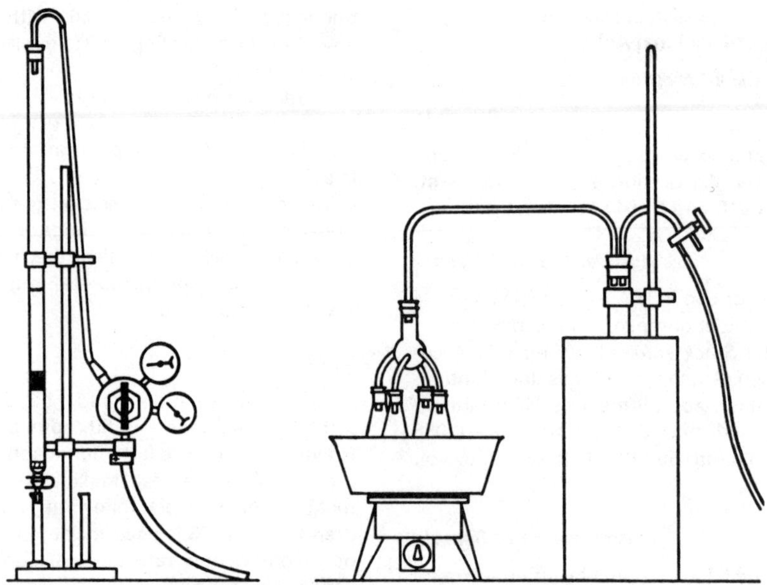

FIG. 6:04—Partition column and solvent evaporator

sides of column with few mL mobile solv. and apply 5 lb pressure to pack column and force out excess solv.; tap column gently to aid packing. When boundary between solv. and H_2SiO_3 remains stationary, release pressure cautiously, pipet out most of excess solv., and reapply pressure until ca 3 mm solv. remains above adsorbent.

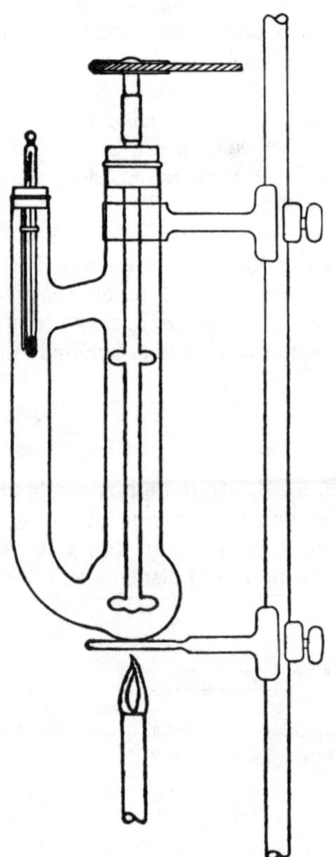

FIG. 6:05—Melting point apparatus

6.196 ***Determination***

(*Caution: See* **51.015** and **51.018**.)

Pipet 10 mL aliquot of sample soln onto column by letting it flow slowly down inside of column without disturbing H_2SiO_3 surface. Wash down side of column with 2 mL mobile solv. and force soln into column by applying 2–3 lb pressure, releasing pressure when all solv. has entered column. Add 10 mL mobile solv. and force into column. Release pressure and slowly add mobile solv. to within 7–12 cm from top of column. Apply enough pressure to force solv. thru column at 3–4 mL/min. Just before last trace of dye leaves column, begin to collect 10 mL fractions, alternately using two 10 mL graduates. Transfer each fraction to 125 mL erlenmeyer and evap. to dryness, using solv. evaporator. (Evap. fractions without boiling; if boiling begins, raise flask momentarily from H_2O bath.)

Appearance of γ-isomer upon evapn is recognized by its tendency to cover bottom of flask as white residual film with typical crystal formation. When first residue of γ-isomer is recognized, begin to collect 10 mL fractions until all γ-isomer is obtained (usually $\leq$8 fractions). Dissolve residue in each flask with 5 mL *n*-hexane and transfer to weighed flask, rinsing flasks successively with 5 mL portions *n*-hexane. Evap. solv., using solv. evaporator. Evacuate flask ca 20 min at room temp. with vac. pump. (There is little danger in evacuating 125 mL erlenmeyer; larger size erlenmeyer, however, is likely to collapse under vac.) Release vac., wipe with clean, moist towel, and let stand 5 min. Weigh, and calc. % γ-benzene hexachloride in original sample.

6.197 ***Melting Point Determination of the Gamma Fraction***

Dissolve residue in min. amt acetone and transfer quant. to 10 mL beaker. Evap. acetone at 40°, using filtered air stream. Scrape residue from beaker for mp detn. (Beaker may be set on piece of solid CO_2 to ensure prepn of finely powd product.) Place material in agate mortar and mix thoroly with pestle.

Select 2 clean, dry capillary tubes and fill with sample. Be sure material is well packed into bottom of tube to ensure max. contact between sample and wall of tube. Insert tubes and thermometer bulb in Thiele tube so that samples and thermometer bulb touch. Start stirrer and heater, and adjust heating rate to 1°/min at 90°. Continue heating until sample melts or reaches 106°. Reduce heating rate to 0.5°/min and continue heating until sample melts.

Sample mp is corrected temp. of bath when last solid disappears into the clear melt. If mp is <108°, check result by IR method, **6.198–6.201**.

Infrared Spectrophotometric Method (57)
Official Final Action

(Applicable to tech. BHC. *Caution: See* **51.018**, **51.041**, and **51.048**.)

6.198 ***Apparatus***

Infrared spectrometer.—With matched pair of liq. absorption cells, 0.5–1.1 mm thick.

6.199 ***Calibration of Cells***

Det., in spectrometer, difference between deflections of the 2 cells filled with CS_2. Plainly mark one cell to be used as sample cell for reading I. Correct values of I_0 obtained with other cell by adding or subtracting difference between cells and refer to this as cell factor F. Check factor every 10–14 days.

6.200 ***Preparation of Standards and Working Curves***

Obtain α, β, γ, and δ isomers of BHC, either by fractional crystn from tech. material or as sepd materials, and recrystallize several times from solvs that have been redistd from all-glass app. Recrystallize from following solvs until mps by capillary tube method become const: α isomer from benzene followed by MeOH (mp ca 158°); β isomer from toluene (mp ca 210.5°, sealed capillary); γ isomer from MeOH (mp ca 113°); and δ isomer from CCl_4 followed by $CHCl_3$ (mp ca 138.5°).

Confirm purity of each isomer as follows: Evap. to dryness enough mother liquor from last crystn to yield ≥1 g dissolved solids, grind residue, and dry overnight in evacuated desiccator. Weigh and dissolve in enough CS_2 to make 4 g/100 mL soln. Prep. corresponding soln of recrystd isomer as std. Compare solns of residue and std in spectrometer at wavelength points used for analysis of other isomers. Consider purity of isomer satisfactory if A of residue soln is not significantly greater than that of std at these points.

Prep. working curves of the isomers by detg T of their solns in CS_2 at various concns as in **6.201**. Calc. A and plot against concn in g/L.

6.201 ***Determination***

Reduce sample of tech. BHC to ca 2 g by grinding and quartering, and dry 24 hr *in vacuo* at room temp. Weigh 1.5000 g dried material into 50 mL vol. flask and dil. to vol. with CS_2 (equiv. to 30 g/L). Shake vigorously to dissolve (β isomer is not completely sol. and will settle out). Pipet 25 mL of this sample soln into another 50 mL vol. flask and again dil. to vol. with CS_2 (equiv. to 15 g/L). Fill sample cell with the concd soln for reading I, and fill blank cell with CS_2, place in spectrometer, and read T in duplicate at following wavelengths:

	Wavelength, μm
Alpha	12.58
Beta	13.46
Gamma	14.53
Delta	13.22
Epsilon	13.96

Average duplicates for calcns. Repeat readings with dil. soln (15 g/L) at α and γ wavelengths. Calc. A of each of isomers at the various wavelengths from T measurements by equation:

$$\text{Log}\,\frac{(F \times I_b) - (F \times I_b \times \%\,Sct)}{I_s - (F \times I_b \times \%\,\text{Sct})} = A,$$

where F = cell factor, I_b = reading of blank cell, % Sct = % scatter, I_s = reading of sample cell, and A = absorbance.

Obtain approx. concns from working curves, **6.200**. Correct A at each wavelength for absorption of interfering components. (Altho β isomer has low solubility in CS_2, this isomer interferes with δ analytical point; therefore det. A of β isomer in CS_2 at this point and apply as correction.) Since these new values are overcorrected, make repeated evaluations until successive values are const, within desired precision.

6.202 ★ ***Radioactive Tracer Method (58)*** ★
Official First Action

See **6.257–6.260**, 11th ed.

N-Butyl-N-ethyl-α,α,α-trifluoro-2,6-dinitro-p-toluidine (Balan®) or Trifluralin (α,α,α-Trifluoro-2,6-dinitro-N,N-dipropyl-p-toluidine (59)—Official Final Action

Ultraviolet Method

6.203 ***Principle***

Trifluralin or Balan is extd from solid carrier or dissolved in *n*-hexane if liq., purified by chromatgy on Florisil, and detd by UV spectrometry at 376 nm.

6.204 ***Reagents***

(a) *Florisil.*—100–200 mesh. Test elution characteristics of Florisil by adding 5 mL std soln to prepd column. Proceed as in **6.207**. Elution vol. should be ≥80 mL but <100 mL. If elution vol. does not fall within this range, adjust H_2O content of Florisil by trial and error to obtain proper elution (add H_2O to decrease elution time; dry at 130° to increase it).

(b) *Std soln.*—1.25 mg/mL. Weigh 0.125 g trifluralin or Balan Ref. Std (Elanco Products Co.), into 100 mL vol. flask, dil. to vol. with *n*-hexane, and mix.

6.205 ***Preparation of Column***

Insert glass wool plug in bottom of 25 × 400 mm glass tube with Teflon stopcock. Add, with const tapping of column, 5 g anhyd. Na_2SO_4, stdzd Florisil, (**a**), to ht of 50 mm, and 5 g anhyd. Na_2SO_4. With stopcock open, add 50 mL *n*-hexane and let drain to top of column. Close stopcock.

6.206 ***Preparation of Sample***

(a) *Dry formulations (containing more than 1% trifluralin or Balan).*—Weigh sample contg 0.25 g trifluralin or Balan into Soxhlet extn thimble (33 × 80 mm), cover with glass wool, and ext with $CHCl_3$ 1 hr beyond time when no further color is extd. Quant. transfer ext to 200 mL vol. flask with $CHCl_3$, dil. to vol. with $CHCl_3$, and mix. Transfer 5 mL to r-b flask and evap. *just* to dryness on rotary evaporator.

(b) *Dry formulations (containing 1% or less trifluralin or Balan).*—Weigh sample contg 0.05 g trifluralin or Balan, ext, transfer to 200 mL vol. flask, and dil. as in (**a**). Transfer 25 mL to r-b flask and evap. *just* to dryness on rotary evaporator.

(c) *Liquid formulations.*—Weigh sample contg 0.12 g trifluralin or Balan into 100 mL vol. flask. Dil. to vol. with *n*-hexane and mix vigorously. Proceed as in **6.207**.

★ Surplus method—*see* inside front cover.

6.207 ***Determination***

Transfer 5 mL soln from (**c**) or residue from (**a**) or (**b**), with aid of *n*-hexane, to Florisil column. Transfer 5 mL std soln to second Florisil column. Wash sample into column with small portions *n*-hexane. Let each portion drain to top of column before adding next. Fill column with *n*-hexane, discarding eluate until band has moved ca ¾ length of column. Collect eluate contg trifluralin or Balan band (first yellow-orange band to elute) in 100 mL vol. flask. (If band requires >100 mL vol. to elute, replace vol. flask with r-b flask, evap., and transfer quant. to 100 mL vol. flask.) (*Caution: See* **51.011**(**a**) and **51.061**.) Dil. to vol. with *n*-hexane and mix. Det. *A* of sample and std solns in 1 cm cells at 376 nm against *n*-hexane as ref.

6.208 ***Calculations***

% Trifluralin or Balan = $(A \times \text{g std} \times F \times P)/(A' \times \text{g sample})$,

where *A* and *A'* refer to sample and std solns, resp.; *P* = % purity of std; and *F* = 2, 0.4, or 1 for sample prepns (**a**), (**b**), or (**c**), resp.

Gas-Liquid Chromatographic Method

6.209 ***Principle***

Trifluralin or Balan is extd from solid carrier, or dissolved in acetone if liq., and detd by GLC.

6.210 ***Reagents***

(**a**) *Diisobutyl phthalate internal std soln.*—Weigh 0.625 g diisobutyl phthalate (ICN-K&K Laboratories, Inc.) into 250 mL vol. flask, dil. to vol. with acetone, and mix.

(**b**) *Std soln.*—1.6 mg/mL. Weigh 0.16 g trifluralin or Balan Ref. Std into 100 mL vol. flask, dil. to vol. with acetone, and mix.

6.211 ***Apparatus***

(**a**) *Gas chromatograph.*—Equipped with flame ionization detector; capable of programmed column temp. from 135 to 190° at 8°/min. Approx. instrumental conditions: inlet 205°, detector 275°, N carrier gas 60 mL/min.

(**b**) *Column.*—1.5 m (5') × ⅛ or ¼" od, stainless steel or Pyrex glass tube packed with 5% DC 200, 12,500 cstokes (Analabs, Inc.) on 80–100 mesh Chromosorb W (HP). Condition newly prepd column at 230° overnight with N carrier gas.

6.212 ***Preparation of Sample***

(**a**) *Dry formulations (containing more than 1% trifluralin or Balan).*—Weigh sample contg 0.16 g trifluralin or Balan into Soxhlet extn thimble (33 × 80 mm), cover with glass wool, and ext with acetone 1 hr beyond time when no further color is extd. (*Caution: See* **51.011**(**a**) and **51.046**.) Evap. to ca 60 mL on steam bath with stream of air directed into flask. Transfer quant. to 100 mL vol. flask with acetone. Dil. to vol. with acetone and mix.

(**b**) *Dry formulations (containing 1% or less trifluralin or Balan).*—Weigh sample contg 0.04 g trifluralin or Balan, ext, and evap. as in (**a**). Transfer quant. to 100 mL vol. flask with acetone and proceed as in **6.213** without dilg, beginning, ". . . add 10 mL internal std soln, . . ."

(**c**) *Liquid formulations.*—Weigh sample contg 0.16 g trifluralin or Balan into 100 mL vol. flask, dil. to vol. with acetone, and mix.

6.213 ***Determination***

Pipet 25 mL acetone soln, **6.212**(**a**) or (**c**), and 25 mL std soln, (**b**), into sep. 100 mL vol. flasks, add 10 mL internal std soln, dil. to vol. with acetone, and mix.

Inject 2.5 μL trifluralin or Balan std soln and start temp. program to give symmetrical peak ca 70% scale deflection and retention time 5.5 min. Diisobutyl phthalate internal std peak appears ca 2 min after std peak. Repeat injection of std soln until ratio of trifluralin or Balan peak area to internal std peak area is reproducible.

Without changing conditions inject 2.5 μL sample soln.

6.214 ***Calculations***

Calc. areas of trifluralin or Balan and diisobutyl phthalate peaks. Divide area of trifluralin or Balan peak by area of diisobutyl phthalate internal std peak to det. ratio, *R*.

% Trifluralin or Balan = $(R \times W' \times P)/(R' \times W \times F)$,

where *R* and *R'* = ratio for sample and std solns, resp.; *W* and *W'* = g sample and std, resp.; P = % purity of std; and *F* = 1, 1, or 4 for sample prepns (**a**), (**c**), *or* (**b**), resp.

Captan (N-(Trichloromethylthio)-4-cyclohexene-1,2-dicarboximide) (*60*)—Official First Action

AOAC-CIPAC Method

(*Caution: See* **51.039** and **51.041**.)

6.215 ***Principle***

Captan is extd from inerts with soln contg dieldrin in dioxane. Ratio of captan peak ht to dieldrin peak ht in gas chromatgy is measured and compared to ratio from std captan prepd similarly. Method applies to tech. and dry formulated products contg captan as only active ingredient.

6.216 ***Reagents***

(**a**) *Extracting soln.*—Weigh ca 5.0 g dieldrin (ca 85% HEOD) into 500 mL vol. flask, add ca 300 mL 1,4-dioxane, shake to dissolve dieldrin, and dil. to vol. with dioxane.

(**b**) *Captan std soln.*—Accurately weigh, by difference, 0.25 g captan ref. std into glass vial. Pipet 25 mL extg soln into vial, stopper, and shake until dissolved. Prep. fresh after 24 hr.

6.217 ***Gas Chromatography***

Use any app. that will completely sep. captan from HEOD and with following conditions: Sample inlet port 10–30° higher than column; thermal conductivity or H flame detector maintained ⩾20° higher than column (typical column temp. 220°); 1.5 m (5') × ¼" od glass column packed with 3% XE-60 silicone nitrile gum rubber on Chromosorb G, acid-washed and dimethyl dichlorosilane-treated (allowable variations are 0.6–1.8 m (2–6'), ⅛–¼" od, 2–10% liq. loading, Chromosorb W). Condition newly prepd column at 230° overnight while purging with carrier gas (He for thermal conductivity or N for H flame detectors).

6.218 ***Preparation of Sample***

Accurately weigh, by difference, well mixed portion of sample contg ca 0.25 g captan into 30 mL glass vial with plastic-lined screw cap. Into vial pipet 25 mL same extg soln used for prepn of std soln. Stopper and shake mech. 15 min. Centrf. if necessary to ppt inerts. Sample supernate with syringe for captan detn. Prep. fresh after 24 hr.

6.219 ***Determination***

Adjust column temp., carrier gas flow, injection size, and recorder attenuation so that captan and HEOD peaks are completely sepd in <10 min and so that ht of HEOD peak, which elutes first, is ca ¾ full scale. Repeat injections of std soln until peak ht ratio captan:HEOD of 2 consecutive injections varies

<2%. Without changing conditions, inject supernate from sample. If sample ratio differs by >±10% from std ratio, reweigh sample. For detn, inject std, sample in duplicate, and std.

Measure HEOD and captan peak hts. When solv. peak tailing extends into region of HEOD and captan peaks, draw curved extension as baseline. Det. peak ht ratio captan:HEOD and average the 2 values (R_S) for std injections just before and after sample injections. Calc. and average peak ht ratio of the 2 samples (R_X).

$$\% \text{ Captan} = (R_X/W_X) \times (W_S \times P/R_S),$$

where W_S = g std, W_X = g sample, and P = % purity of captan std.

Technical Chlordane

Total Chlorine Method (61)—Official Final Action

(*Caution: See* **51.011, 51.018, 51.038, 51.039, 51.040, 51.041,** and **51.045.**)

6.220 ***Standardization of Standard Solutions***

(**a**) *Sodium chloride std soln.*—0.1*N*. Dissolve 5.845 g NaCl, previously dried 2 hr at 105°, in H_2O, and dil. to 1 L in vol. flask.

(**b**) *Silver nitrate std soln.*—0.1*N*. Prep. as in **50.027**. To 250 mL g-s erlenmeyer add 15.00 mL 0.1*N* NaCl, (**a**), 50 mL H_2O, 10 mL HNO_3 (1+1), boiled to expel oxides of N, and 25.00 mL of the $AgNO_3$ soln. Add 3 mL nitrobenzene, stopper, and shake vigorously 15 sec. Add 5 mL ferric indicator, **6.019(e)**, and back-titr. with 0.1*N* KSCN, (**c**), to reddish-brown end point. (Potentiometric titrn using Ag indicator electrode and Ag-AgCl or glass ref. electrode may be substituted for indicator method, but must be used in both stdzn and detn.)

(**c**) *Potassium thiocyanate std soln.*—0.1*N*. Prep. and titr. against $AgNO_3$ soln, (**b**), as in **50.030(b)**. Calc. F = mL $AgNO_3$ soln/mL KSCN soln.

Normality $AgNO_3$ soln = mL NaCl soln × 0.1000/(mL $AgNO_3$ soln − mL KSCN soln × F).

6.221 ***Preparation of Sample***

(**a**) *Emulsifiable concentrate formulations.*—Accurately weigh sample contg 0.5±0.05 g tech. chlordane into 50 mL vol. flask, dissolve, and dil. to vol. with toluene. Transfer 5 mL aliquot to 125 mL separator, add 15 mL or g Na biphenyl reagent, **6.178(b)**, and swirl. If soln is not dark green, add more reagent. Let stand 3 min and add 3–5 mL H_2O dropwise. With stopper removed, swirl soln gently to decompose excess reagent. Add 25 mL H_2O, stopper, and mix with gentle rocking motion. (Do not shake vigorously.) Let layers sep. and drain lower aq. layer into 250 mL erlenmeyer. Re-ext solv. layer with two 25 mL portions 3*N* HNO_3 and combine aq. solns in erlenmeyer.

(**b**) *Dusts, granular impregnates, and wettable powders.*—Accurately weigh sample contg 0.5±0.05 g tech. chlordane into Soxhlet extn thimble. Ext with 80 mL benzene in Soxhlet app. 1 hr. Transfer to 100 mL vol. flask, washing with several 3 mL portions benzene. Dil. to vol. with benzene and transfer 10 mL aliquot to 125 mL separator. Proceed as in (**a**).

6.222 ***Determination***

Add 15.00 mL 0.1*N* $AgNO_3$ and 3 mL nitrobenzene to erlenmeyer, stopper, and shake vigorously 15 sec. Rinse stopper, add 5 mL ferric indicator, **6.019(e)**, and back-titr. with 0.1*N* KSCN to reddish-brown end point. (Designate mL KSCN as *D*.)

Det. blank on reagents by pipetting 5 mL toluene into 125 mL separator, add 15 mL or g Na biphenyl reagent, and proceed as in **6.221(a)**, thru combining aq. solns in erlenmeyer. Add 15.00 mL 0.1*N* NaCl, 25.00 mL 0.1*N* $AgNO_3$, and 3 mL nitrobenzene, and proceed as above. Calc. blank correction factor, C = mL KSCN used in stdzn of $AgNO_3$ − mL KSCN used in blank detn.

% Chlorine = [15 − (C + D) × F] × normality $AgNO_3$ × 3.545/g sample.

% Tech. chlordane = % Cl × 1.56.

Colorimetric Method (62)—Official Final Action

(Method is empirical; all conditions must be reproduced exactly to attain good precision. Temp., reaction time, and vol. of reagents affect color intensity.)

6.223 ***Apparatus***

(**a**) *Constant temperature bath.*—Capable of maintaining 100±1° and holding twelve 20 × 150 mm test tubes.

(**b**) *Cuvets.*—10 or 2 mm light path (available from Pyrocell Mfg. Co., 91 Carver Ave, PO Box 176, Westwood, NJ 07675).

(**c**) *Spectrophotometer.*—Capable of accepting cuvets, (**b**).

6.224 ***Reagents***

(**a**) *Methanol.*—90% (by vol.).

(**b**) *Methanol-benzene.*—Mix 7 vols MeOH with 3 vols benzene.

(**c**) *Diethanolamine.*—Purify by vac. distn at ca 20 mm Hg and take middle fraction. (*Caution: See* **51.011** and **51.015**.)

(**d**) *Diethanolamine-KOH soln* (*Davidow reagent*).—Mix 1 vol. reagent (**c**) with 2 vols 1.0*N* KOH in MeOH.

(**e**) *Chlordane std solns.*—1.5, 2.5, and 3.5 mg/mL. Ref. grade (available from Velsicol Chemical Corp.). Dissolve tech. chlordane in reagent (**b**). Discard stds after 2 weeks.

6.225 ***Preparation of Sample***

(**a**) *Liquid formulations.*—Transfer weighed sample contg 200–300 mg tech. chlordane to 100 mL graduate and dil. to 100 mL with MeOH-benzene.

(**b**) *High concentration solid formulations* (*10% chlordane or more*).—Treat as in (**a**) and shake vigorously several min. Let settle 1 hr.

(**c**) *Low concentration solid formulations* (*less than 10% chlordane*).—Transfer weighed sample contg 200–300 mg tech. chlordane to Soxhlet and ext 1 hr with pentane. (*Caution: See* **51.039** and **51.074.**) Evap. pentane on steam bath and transfer ext to 100 mL g-s graduate. Dil. to 100 mL with MeOH-benzene.

6.226 ***Determination***

Pipet 2 mL aliquot prepd sample to 20 × 150 mm test tube. Add No. 8 grit SiC boiling chip and 2 mL Davidow reagent, and place in 100° const temp. bath. Remove after exactly 45 min and cool immediately in beaker of cold H_2O. Transfer to 10 mL vol. flask and dil. to vol. with 90% MeOH. Transfer aliquot of soln to 2 mm cell and read A at 550 nm within 15 min with 90% MeOH as ref. (Comparable results are obtained by dilg soln to 50 mL and using 1 cm cell.)

Treat 2 mL each std soln with each set of samples. (Read 1 std soln before samples, 1 after half the samples are read, and 1 after last sample is read.)

6.227 ***Calculations***

Calc. absorptivity (a) for each of 3 stds, and use av. in subsequent calcns (expected a is ca 0.25): $a = A'/W$, where A' = A std soln and W = mg tech. chlordane (2 × concn std soln in mg/mL).

% Tech. chlordane in sample = A × 5000/(a × mg sample).

Hexachlorocyclopentadiene (HEX) (*63*)—Official Final Action

(Applicable to tech. chlordane, but not to formulations)

6.228 ***Reagent***

Hexachlorocyclopentadiene (HEX) std solns.— Stock soln.—0.1 g/100 mL. Weigh 0.1000 g hexachlorocyclopentadiene Ref. Std (available from Velsicol Chemical Corp.) in 100 mL vol. flask, dil. to vol. with MeOH, and shake to dissolve. *Std soln 1.*—0.005 g/100 mL. Dil. 5 mL stock soln to 100 mL with MeOH. *Std soln 2.*—0.002 g/100 mL. Dil. 2 mL stock soln to 100 mL with MeOH.

Method I

6.229 ***Calibration***

With MeOH in both ref. and sample cells (matched 1 cm silica), adjust 0 and 100% settings on UV spectrophtr at 324 nm. Empty sample cell, rinse several times with, and then fill with, *std soln 1,* and read *A*. Empty sample cell, rinse with MeOH, then rinse and fill with *std soln 2,* and read *A*. Calc. *A* factor, *K*, for each std soln = (g std HEX/100 mL)/*A*. Average the two *K* values.

6.230 ***Determination***

Weigh 0.5 g sample in 100 mL vol. flask, dil. to vol. with MeOH, and shake to dissolve. Proceed as in **6.229**, treating sample soln in same manner as stds.

% HEX in sample = (*A* of sample soln × 100 × *K*)/(g sample/100 mL).

6.231 ***Method II***

(Includes corrections for other components of chlordane which absorb at 324 nm)

Proceed as in **6.229–6.230**, except det. *A* of all solns at 300, 324, and 350 nm. Settings of 0 and 100% must be repeated at 300, 324, and 350 nm for *A* readings at those points. Calc. K = (g std HEX/100 mL)/ $[A_{324} - 0.5(A_{300} + A_{350})]$.

% HEX in sample = $[A_{324} - 0.5(A_{300} + A_{350})] \times 100 \times K$/(g sample/100 mL).

AG Chlordane (Octachloro-4,7-methanotetrahydroindane) (*64*)—Official Final Action

α- and γ-Isomers in Technical Products—Infrared Method

(Not applicable to tech. chlordane or its formulations)

6.232 ***Apparatus and Reagent***

(**a**) *Infrared spectrophotometer.*—Double beam, with matched NaCl cells, 0.1 and 0.2 mm.

(**b**) *Std soln.*—Into tared 10 mL vol. flask, weigh 1.00±0.05 g ref. std α-chlordane and 0.38±0.02 g ref. std γ-chlordane (Velsicol Chemical Corp.), dissolve in CS_2, and dil. to vol. with CS_2.

6.233 ***Preparation of Sample***

Melt entire sample in 100° oven and mix. Weigh 1.5±0.02 g into tared 10 mL vol. flask, dissolve in CS_2, and dil. to vol. with CS_2.

6.234 ***Determination***

(**a**) *α-Chlordane.*—Fill ref. cell with CS_2. Scan std and sample solns from 750 to 710 cm^{-1} (13.3 to 14.1 μm), using 0.1 mm NaCl cells. Construct baseline from 738 to 715 cm^{-1} (13.6 to 14.0 μm) and draw line from point of max. *A,* ca 725 cm^{-1} (13.8 μm), to intersect baseline.

(**b**) *γ-Chlordane.*—Fill ref. cell with CS_2. Scan std and sample solns from 1390 to 1290 cm^{-1} (7.19 to 7.75 μm), using 0.2 mm NaCl celis. Proceed as in (**a**), using min. at 1370 and 1310 cm^{-1} (7.30 and 7.63 μm), and det. *A* at max. 1320 cm^{-1} (7.58 μm).

6.235 ***Calculations***

Wt % α(α-chlordane) or γ(γ-chlordane) = $(A \times F \times 100)/W_S$

F = [W(α or γ in std) × % purity in std]/A'(α or γ of std),

where W = wt (g), and A and A' refer to sample and std, resp.

(Wts given are for cell thicknesses specified. For other cells, adjust wts to yield peak *A* between 0.2 and 0.5 (30–65% *T*).)

AG Chlordane in Granular Formulations—Infrared Method

(Not applicable to tech. chlordane or its formulations. *Caution: See* **51.011**, **51.041**, **51.046**, and **51.048**.)

6.236 ***Apparatus***

(**a**) *Infrared spectrophotometer.*—*See* **6.232**.

(**b**) *Soxhlet extraction apparatus.*—With 25 × 80 mm Whatman cellulose thimble.

(**c**) *Vigreux distilling tube.*—15 mm long.

(**d**) *Vials.*—5 dram, with plastic-lined screw caps.

6.237 ***Reagents***

(**a**) *Acetone.*—Spectral grade.

(**b**) *Std soln.*—Into tared 5 dram vial, weigh 1.00±0.05 g Ref. Std α-Chlordane and 0.38±0.02 g Ref. Std γ-Chlordane (Velsicol Chemical Corp.) and pipet in 10 mL CS_2.

6.238 ***Preparation of Sample***

Into tared thimble, weigh sample equiv. to wt of std and cover with glass wool. Insert into extn app. and attach to 250 mL flat-bottom ₮ flask contg boiling chips. Add 125 mL acetone, attach extractor to condenser, and ext 1 hr.

Rinse extn app. with acetone. Sep. flask from extractor and condenser, attach distg tube to flask, and evap. acetone on steam bath. Remove tube, add 5 mL CS_2, and evap. carefully. Repeat addn and evapn of CS_2 4 more times. (All residual acetone must be removed because acetone interferes with IR measurement.) Dry residue further, using forced air, until cryst. solid appears. Pipet 10 mL CS_2 into flask, and swirl carefully to dissolve solid. Release stopper pressure.

6.239 ***Determination***

Proceed as in **6.234**.

6.240 ***Calculation***

Proceed as in **6.235** for calcn of wt %.

% Total AG chlordane = % α-chlordane + % γ-chlordane.

Generally, factor representing specification grade of 95% AG chlordane may be used. Then,

% AG chlordane = % total (α + γ) × 1.053.

Heptachlor in AG Chlordane—Gas Chromatographic Method

(Not applicable to tech. chlordane or its formulations)

6.241 ***Apparatus and Reagents***

(**a**) *Gas chromatograph.*—Equipped with flame ionization detector and 1.5 m (5′) × ⅛″ id glass column packed with 5% silicone DC 200 (Viscosity 12500, Analabs, Inc.) on 130–140 mesh

Anakrom ABS. Operating conditions: temps (°)—column 165, injector 215, detector 220; N carrier gas 30 mL/min (ca 80 psig at inlet); and chart speed 0.5"/min.

(b) *Stds.*—Ref. Std α-Chlordane, γ-Chlordane, and Heptachlor (Velsicol Chemical Corp.) and hexachlorobenzene (C_6Cl_6) internal std (Eastman Kodak Co.), recrystd from benzene.

(c) *Std soln.*—Accurately weigh following components into 10 mL vol. flask, dissolve in CS_2, and dil. to vol.: 0.48 g α-chlordane, 0.18 g γ-chlordane, 0.010 g C_6Cl_6, and 0.010 g heptachlor.

6.242 ***Preparation of Sample***

Melt entire sample in 100° oven and mix. Accurately weigh 0.73 g sample and 0.010 g C_6Cl_6 into 10 mL vol. flask, and dil. to vol. with CS_2.

6.243 ***Determination***

Inject 1.5 μL sample soln into gas chromatograph; retention times for C_6Cl_6 and heptachlor are ca 2 and 4 min, resp. Also inject 1.5 μL std soln to det. response factor (*RF*).

Use attenuation (ca 2×) to keep internal std peak on scale and include in calcns.

6.244 ***Calculations***

Calc. each peak area by any convenient means. Built-in integrators or planimeters provide most accurate method of detg areas where peaks are not perfectly symmetrical.

$$\% \text{ Heptachlor} = (PH \times RF \times WI \times 100)/(PI \times W)$$
$$RF = (PI \times W')/(PH' \times WI),$$

where *PH, PH'*, and *PI* = peak areas of sample, std heptachlor, and internal std, resp.; *W, W'*, and *WI* = g sample, std heptachlor, and internal std, resp.

Chlorotoluron [3-(3-Chloro-4-methylphenyl)-1,1-dimethylurea], Chloroxuron [3-[4-(4-chlorophenoxy)phenyl]-1,1-dimethylurea], or Metoxuron (Dosanex®)[3-(3-Chloro-4-methoxyphenyl)-1,1-dimethylurea] *(65)*—Official Final Action

CIPAC-AOAC Method

6.245 ***Principle***

Pesticide is extd from formulations with CH_2Cl_2, free amines are removed with acid, and ext is hydrolyzed by alkali to Me_2NH which is distd and titrd. Related byproducts, 3-(3-chloro-4-methylphenyl)-1-methylurea (I), 3-(4-methylphenyl)-1,1-dimethylurea (II) (from chlorotoluron), 3-[4-(4-chlorophenoxy)phenyl]-1-methylurea (III) and 3-(4-chlorophenyl)-1,1-dimethylurea (IV) (from chloroxuron), and 3-(3,4-dichlorophenyl)-1,1-dimethylurea (V), 3-(3-chloro-4-hydroxyphenyl)-1,1-dimethylurea (VI), and 3-(4-methoxyphenyl)-1,1-dimethylurea (VII) (from metoxuron), which may interfere, are detd by semiquant. TLC. Limit of detection for TLC is 0.1% for each byproduct. On same TLC plate for chloroxuron, free amine 4-(4-chlorophenoxy)aniline (VIII) is detd by sep. detection technic. Other byproducts, 1,3-bis(3-chloro-4-methylphenyl) urea (IX), 1,3-bis[4-(chlorophenoxy)-phenyl]urea (X), and 1,3-bis(3-chloro-4-methoxyphenyl) urea (XI), do not interfere with chlorotoluron, chloroxuron, and metoxuron detns, resp.

6.246 ***Preparation of Sample***

(a) *Technical formulation.*—Accurately weigh ca 3 g sample (4 g for chloroxuron) and transfer, using 100 mL CH_2Cl_2, into 250 mL separator, dissolve, and add 50 mL 1*N* HCl.

(b) *Wettable powder.*—Accurately weigh ca 3.5–4.0 g sample (for 80%) or 6.0–6.5 g (for 50%) into 200 mL beaker. Add 100 mL CH_2Cl_2 and stir mag. 5 min. Filter thru fritted glass crucible contg paper and 0.5 g layer of Celite, and rinse beaker and crucible with portions of CH_2Cl_2 to total vol. of ca 200 mL. Use only slight vac. to prevent crystn of pesticide on walls of crucible. Transfer quant. to 500 mL separator, and add 50 mL 1*N* HCl.

6.247 ***Determination***

Vigorously shake mixt. 1 min and drain lower org. layer into second separator. Add 25 mL (50 mL for chloroxuron) 1*N* HCl, shake 30 sec, and drain lower layer into 500 mL r-b flask. Wash the 2 acid layers successively with same 100 mL portion CH_2Cl_2 (with two 50 mL portions for chloroxuron) and drain lower layer into the 500 r-b flask. Discard acid.

Vac.-evap. CH_2Cl_2 in rotary evaporator to dryness at max. of 40°. Remove all solv. to prevent interference in subsequent titrn. Add 100 mL propylene glycol, 40 g KOH, and some boiling stones to residue. Immediately connect flask securely to distn app. (Fig. **6:06**) whose joints are lubricated with thin film of silicone grease. Place end of condenser delivery tube (≥10 mm id) in 400 mL beaker below level of absorbing soln of 0.2 g H_3BO_3 and 1 mL mixed indicator soln (40 mg methylene blue and 60 mg Me red dissolved in 100 mL alcohol) in 150 mL H_2O. (To enhance end point, use 150 mL MeOH (2+1).)

Gently warm flask until all particles dissolve; then boil 10 min or until propylene glycol distils into condenser. Titr. distd Me_2NH continuously with stdzd 1*N* HCl, **50.011–50.017**. Complete distn by carefully adding H_2O dropwise from dropping funnel at rate of 1 drop/sec. Continue titrn until end point persists 2 min (*V* mL). Perform blank detn (*B* mL) with each series.

$$\% \text{ Pesticide} = [(V - B) \times N \times F/\text{g sample}] - \% \text{ byproducts (from } \mathbf{6.248}),$$

where *F* = 21.27 for chlorotoluron, 29.07 for chloroxuron, or 22.87 for metoxuron, and *N* = normality of stdzd HCl.

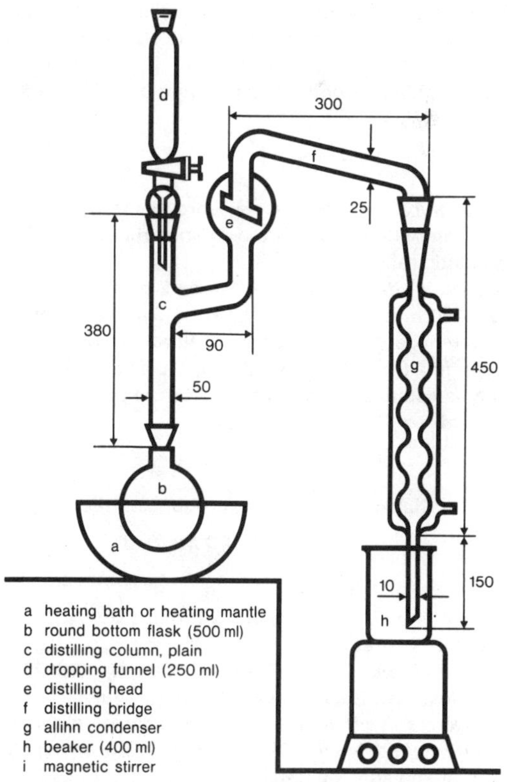

FIG. 6:06—Distillation apparatus (all dimensions in mm)

6.248 ***Determination of Byproducts***

(a) *For chlorotoluron.*—Dissolve 100 mg each of byproducts I and II (**6.245**) (available from Ciba-Geigy Ltd, Analytical Department, CH-4002 Basel, Switzerland) together in tetrahydrofuran and dil. to 50 mL in vol. flask. Dil. aliquots of 1, 2, 3, 4, and 5 mL to 20 mL with tetrahydrofuran, equiv. to 0.2, 0.4, 0.6, 0.8, and 1.0%, resp., of each byproduct.

Dissolve 1.0 g sample in tetrahydrofuran, and dil. to 20 mL with same solv.

Spot 5 μL each of sample and std solns on 20 × 20 cm glass plates precoated with 0.25 mm layer of silica gel 60 F-254 (No. 5715, E. Merck, Darmstadt, Germany, or equiv.), and develop by ascending technic in tank, presatd 30 min with developing solv. $CHCl_3$-EtOAc (4+1), without filter paper linings, for ca 70 min (13 cm migration). Expose plate to 254 nm UV light and compare spots of samples with those of stds to est. concn of byproducts. Approx R_f values: chlorotoluron, 0.50; byproduct I, 0.25; byproduct II, 0.35; and byproduct VI (does not interfere), 0.82.

(b) *For chloroxuron.*—Dissolve 100 mg each of byproducts III, IV, and VIII (available from Ciba-Geigy Ltd) together in acetone and dil. to 100 mL in vol. flask. Dil. aliquots of 1, 3, 5, 8, and 10 mL to 50 mL with acetone, equiv. to 0.1, 0.3, 0.5, 0.8, and 1% resp., of each byproduct.

Dissolve 1.0 g sample in acetone, and dil. to 50 mL with same solv. Proceed as in (**a**), but use $CHCl_3$-dioxane (9+2) as developing solv. for ca 80 min (14 cm). Approx R_f values: chloroxuron 0.75; byproduct III, 0.40; byproduct IV, 0.65; and byproduct X (does not interfere), 0.90.

Det. byproduct VIII on same TLC plate. Place beaker contg ca 2 g $NaNO_2$ in empty developing tank and pour ca 3 ml HCl over salt. After 2 min, insert plate into tank 3 min, remove, and dry 5 min at room temp. with hair dryer. Spray with 1% soln of *N*-(1-naphthyl)ethylenediamine.2HCl in 0.1*N* HCl and compare violet sample spots with those of stds (R_f, 0.85).

(c) *For metoxuron.*—Proceed as in (**a**), except use 100 mg each of byproducts V, VI, and VII (available from Sandoz Ltd, Agrochemical Division, Research, CH-4002 Basel, Switzerland). Approx. R_f values: metoxuron, 0.25; byproduct III, 0.34; byproduct IV, 0.08; byproduct V, 0.13; and byproduct VII (does not interfere), 0.46.

6.249 ***Identification***

(a) *Technical chloroxuron.*—Record IR spectrum of 1% CH_2Cl_2 soln of sample and compare with spectrum of 1% CH_2Cl_2 soln of authentic ref. std.

(b) *50% Wettable powder.*—Stir ca 2 g sample and 2 g silica gel (70–230 mesh) with 100 mL CH_2Cl_2 5 min and percolate thru fluted filter. Record IR spectrum of filtrate in NaCl cell (0.5 mm path length) from 3000 to 650 cm^{-1}, using blank solv. as ref. Identity is established if sample spectrum corresponds qual. to that of std.

Dichlobenil (2,6-Dichlorobenzonitrile) *(66)*

CIPAC—AOAC Method

6.250 ***Reagents and Apparatus***

(a) *Dichlobenil.*—⩾99.5% purity (Philips-Duphar B.V., Weesp, Netherlands), or equiv.

(b) *Methyl myristate.*—Fluka AG Cat. No. 70129, ⩾99.5% purity (Fluka AG, Buchs, Switzerland), or equiv.

(c) *Mixed solvent soln.*—1,2-Dichloroethane-ether (1 + 1).

(d) *Internal std soln.*—Dissolve 0.80 g Me myristate, (**b**), in 100 mL mixed solv. soln, (**c**).

(e) *Calibration soln.*—Accurately weigh ca 0.10 g dichlobenil, (**a**), into conical flask, pipet in 5 mL internal std soln, (**d**), and add 45 mL solv. soln, (**c**).

(f) *Gas chromatograph.*—With on-column injection, flame ionization detector, injection port heating, and, preferably, detector heating. Pyrex column 1.83 m × 3 mm id, packed with 10% Carbowax 20M on 100–120 mesh Chromosorb P, acid washed, dimethyldichlorosilane treated (available from Analabs, Cat. No. GCP-009D). Operating temps (°): oven 200, injection port 210, detector 210. Carrier gas (N) flow rate 25 mL/min. Approx. retention times 7 and 12 min for Me myristate and dichlobenil, resp.

6.251 ***Preparation of Sample***

(a) *Technical dichlobenil.*—Accurately weigh ca 2.0 g dichlobenil into 100 mL vol. flask. Dissolve in mixed solv. soln, (**c**), and dil. to vol. Pipet 5 mL aliquot into 100 mL conical flask, add 5.00 mL internal std soln, (**d**), and dil. to 50 mL with mixed solv., (**c**).

(b) *Wettable powders.*—Accurately weigh sample contg ca 1.0 g dichlobenil into 100 mL vol. flask, add few mL mixed solv., (**c**), swirl, and dil. to vol. with mixed solv. Let settle, pipet 10 mL clear supernate into 100 mL conical flask, and continue as in (**a**).

(c) *Granules.*—Accurately weigh ca 6.0 g sample into 100 mL conical flask. Add 20 mL dichloroethane and stir 10 min on mag. stirrer. Filter with vac. thru glass filter paper (Whatman GF 82, or equiv.), supported on fritted glass filter. Wash granules 5 times with 5 mL dichloroethane, collect filtrate in 100 mL vol. flask, and dil. to vol. with ether. Pipet aliquot of this soln, contg ca 0.1 g dichlobenil (10 mL for 20% granules, 25 mL for 7% granules), into 100 mL conical flask, add 5.00 mL internal std soln, (**d**), and dil. to 50 mL with mixed solv., (**c**).

6.252 ***Determination***

Inject 2 μL portions of calibration soln, (**e**), until response factor varies <1% for successive injections. Inject duplicate 2 μL portions of sample soln, followed by 2 μL portions of calibration soln, (**e**). Measure peak areas of dichlobenil and Me myristate, either by multiplying peak ht by retention time, or by digital integration. Use av. of duplicate values.

6.253 ***Calculation***

$$p = (I_q \times r \times 20)/(I_r \times q),$$

where p = response factor, I_q and I_r = peak areas of internal std and dichlobenil, resp., q = g internal std, r = g dichlobenil in calibration soln. (Response factor is ca 1.5.)

$$\% \text{ Dichlobenil} = (I_d \times q \times p \times F \times 100)/(I_m \times W \times 20),$$

where I_d and I_m = peak areas of dichlobenil and internal std, resp., p = response factor, F = diln factor for sample (100/x, where x = mL taken to obtain final soln), and W = g sample.

Dichlorodiphenyltrichloroethane (1,1,1-Trichloro-2,2-bis(p-chlorophenyl) Ethane) (DDT)—Official Final Action

★ *Total Benzene-Soluble Chlorine Method (67)* ★

(Applicable in absence of other org. Cl compds. Use H_2O_2 and isoamyl alcohol-ether extn method on dispersible powders or sprays that contain surface active agents or other ingredients that react with $AgNO_3$. *Caution: See* **51.034**, **51.039**, **51.040**, **51.041**, and **51.045**.)

6.254 ***Reagents***

(a) *Benzene.*—Thiophene- and Cl-free.

(b) *Metallic sodium.*—Ribbons or small pieces.

★ Surplus method—*see* inside front cover.

(**c**) *Decolorizing carbon.*—Test for presence of Cl by heating with HNO_3 (1+4), filtering, and adding $AgNO_3$ soln to filtrate. If Cl is present, wash with the HNO_3 until washings are Cl-free.

Note: Det. blank on all reagents, limiting 0.1*N* $AgNO_3$ to 5 mL.

6.255 *Preparation of Solution*

(**a**) *Technical grade DDT.*—Weigh sample contg ca 1 g DDT and transfer to 250 mL vol. flask. Dissolve sample in 10 mL benzene; then dil. to vol. with *99% isopropanol.* Transfer 25 mL aliquot to 250–500 mL Ŧ erlenmeyer. (Direct weighing of sample may be substituted, provided it does not introduce error >0.1%.)

Add 2.5 g Na and shake to mix sample with isopropanol. Do not add Na thru top of condenser or get Na on ground glass joints. Connect flask to reflux condenser and boil gently ≥30 min, shaking occasionally. Eliminate excess Na by cautiously adding 10 mL 50% isopropanol thru condenser at rate of 1–2 drops/sec. Disconnect condenser, add 60 mL H_2O, boil soln ca 30 min to expel isopropanol, and proceed as in **6.256**(**a**), (**b**), (**c**), or (**d**).

(**b**) *Dusting mixtures containing DDT in absence of organic matter.*—Weigh sample contg ca 0.75 g DDT, transfer to 100–200 mL vol. flask, and add exactly 100 mL benzene. Shake until DDT dissolves and soln is well mixed. Let settle and transfer 10 mL aliquot to 250–500 mL Ŧ erlenmeyer.

Evap. on steam bath to remove most of benzene. (Do not evap. to dryness, as DDT may decompose with loss of HCl.) Add 25 mL *99% isopropanol* and proceed as in (**a**), second par.

If free S is present, proceed as in (**f**), beginning "Then add 5 mL *30% H_2O_2, . . .*"

(**c**) *Dusting mixtures in presence of organic matter* (*coloring matter, plant resins, etc.*).—Weigh sample contg ca 0.75 g DDT, transfer to 100–200 mL vol. flask, and add 0.5–1.0 g decolorizing C and exactly 100 mL benzene. Shake until DDT dissolves and soln is well mixed. Filter into narrow-neck flask thru fast qual. paper without suction, keeping funnel covered with watch glass to avoid evapn loss. Transfer 10 mL aliquot to 250–500 mL Ŧ erlenmeyer. Proceed as in (**b**), second par. Before detg Cl remove org. matter as follows:

Cool, add 2–3 drops phthln, and neutze by adding HNO_3 (1+1) dropwise; then 10 mL excess. Cool, if necessary, to room temp., transfer contents of flask and aq. washings to small separator, and shake with 15 mL *isoamyl alcohol-ether* (1+1). Drain aq. layer into second separator and ext again with 15 mL isoamyl alcohol-ether (1+1). Drain aq. layer into 250 mL beaker. Wash the 2 exts successively with two 10 mL portions H_2O. Combine aq. wash solns with aq. soln in beaker. Det. Cl by one of following methods:

(*1*) Proceed as in **6.256**(**a**), beginning "Add slight excess 0.1*N* $AgNO_3$, . . ."

(*2*) Proceed as in **6.256**(**b**), beginning "Add 0.1*N* $AgNO_3$ . . ."

(*3*) Proceed as in **6.256**(**c**), beginning "Cool flask to room temp. . . ."

(*4*) Add 2–3 drops phthln to sample, make alk. by adding 1*N* NaOH, and proceed as in **6.256**(**d**), beginning ". . . transfer contents to Pt dish."

(**d**) *Mineral oil sprays in absence of organic matter* (*plant extractive material, organic thiocyanates*).— Transfer weighed sample contg 0.065–0.075 g DDT to 250–500 mL Ŧ flask. Add 25 mL *99% isopropanol* and proceed as in (**a**), second par.

Note: If DDT content is <2%, use isoamyl alcohol-ether extn, (**c**), second par., to remove excess oil.

Proceed as in **6.256**(**a**), (**b**), (**c**), or (**d**).

(**e**) *Mineral oil sprays in presence of organic matter* (*plant extractive material from pyrethrum or derris and/or cubé.*)—Proceed as in (**d**), using isoamyl alcohol-ether extn, (**c**), to remove excess oil.

(**f**) *Mineral oil sprays in presence of organic thiocyanates with or without plant extractive material.*—Transfer sample contg 0.065–0.075 g DDT to 250–500 mL Ŧ erlenmeyer. Add 25 mL *99% isopropanol* and proceed as in (**a**), second par., thru ". . . add 60 mL H_2O, . . ." Then add 5 mL *30% H_2O_2,* few drops at time, thru top of condenser, heat mixt. in flask to bp, and boil 15 min. Add addnl 5 mL H_2O_2 and again boil 15 min. Add 15 mL more H_2O_2, disconnect reflux condenser, and boil 15–30 min to expel isopropanol. Proceed as in (**c**), second par.

(**g**) Emulsions (*solvent, emulsifier, and water*).— Weigh well mixed sample contg ca 0.75 g DDT in weighing bottle. Wash into 100 mL vol. flask and dil. to vol. with *isopropanol.* Transfer 10 mL aliquot to 250–500 mL Ŧ erlenmeyer. Expel isopropanol and H_2O on steam bath in air current. If drops of H_2O still remain, add 10 mL isopropanol and repeat evapn. Add 25 mL 99% isopropanol and proceed as in (**a**), second par.

Note: If S is brought into the soln as by decomposition of emulsifier, proceed as in (**f**), beginning "Then add 5 mL *30% H_2O_2, . . .*"

6.256 *Determination*

(**a**) Cool flask and transfer contents to 250 mL beaker. Add 2–3 drops phthln and neutze with HNO_3 (1+1); then add 10 mL excess. Add slight excess 0.1*N* $AgNO_3$, **50.031**, and coagulate pptd AgCl by digesting on steam bath 30 min, stirring frequently. Cool, filter thru fast qual. paper, and wash thoroly with H_2O. Add 5 mL satd ferric indicator, **6.019**(**e**), and det. excess $AgNO_3$ in filtrate by titrn with 0.1*N* KSCN, **50.030**(**b**). Subtract amt $AgNO_3$ found in filtrate from that originally added. Difference is that required to combine with Cl in the DDT. 1 mL 0.1*N* $AgNO_3$ = 0.003545 g Cl. Cl × 2 = DDT.

(**b**) Cool flask, add 2–3 drops phthln soln, and neutze with HNO_3 (1+1); then add 10 mL excess. Add 0.1*N* $AgNO_3$ from buret in excess of amt necessary to ppt all Cl; then add 5 mL *nitrobenzene* and 0.5 g *$Fe_2(SO_4)_3$* and swirl flask to coagulate ppt. Back-titr. excess $AgNO_3$ with 0.1*N* KSCN to faint pink. Cross-titr. with both std solns, crossing end point in each direction to assure results. From vol. $AgNO_3$, calc. % DDT as in (**a**).

(**c**) Cool flask, add 2–3 drops phthln, neutze with HNO_3 (1+1), and add 6 mL excess. Cool flask to room temp. and transfer contents to 400 mL beaker. (Vol. should be 200–250 mL.) Titr. Cl with 0.1*N* $AgNO_3$ potentiometrically, using Ag-AgCl electrodes (Fisher Titrimeter, or equiv.). Calc. % DDT as in (**a**).

Note: When this method is used, decolorizing C step in **6.255**(**c**), and isoamyl alcohol-ether extn in **6.255**(**c**), (**d**), and (**e**), may be omitted.

(**d**) Cool flask and transfer contents to Pt dish. Evap. to dryness and ignite as thoroly as possible at ≤525°. Ext with hot H_2O, filter, and wash. Return residue to Pt dish and ignite to ash; dissolve in HNO_3 (1+4), filter from any insol. residue, wash thoroly, and add this soln to aq. ext. Add 0.1*N* $AgNO_3$, avoiding more than slight excess. Heat to bp, protect from light, and let stand until ppt coagulates. Filter on weighed gooch, previously heated to 140–150°, and wash with hot H_2O, testing filtrate to prove excess of $AgNO_3$. Dry AgCl at 140–150°, cool, and weigh. Calc. % Cl and DDT as in (**a**).

Infrared Method (68)

(*Caution: See* **51.041**.)

6.257 *Reagent*

DDT std soln.—Weigh 0.250 g tech. DDT into 50 mL vol. flask or g-s container and add exactly 25 mL CS_2. If sample to be analyzed contains S, add wt of S expected in portion of sample to be taken for analysis. Shake to dissolve and add small amt anhyd. Na_2SO_4. Centrf. portion of soln if it is not clear.

6.258 ***Determination***

Weigh sample contg ca 0.25 g DDT into 50 mL vol. flask and add exactly 25 mL CS_2 and small amt anhyd. Na_2SO_4. Let stand ≥30 min with occasional shaking. Transfer portion to g-s test tube and centrf. short time. Transfer to NaCl cell and scan with infrared spectrophtr, using 0.5 mm cell in region, 8.5–10.5 μm.

Scan std soln in same manner.

Measure *A* of DDT peak at 9.83 μm with baseline from 9.4 to 10.2 μm, and calc. % DDT.

Dimethyl 2,3,5,6-Tetrachloroterephthalate (Dacthal) (*69*)—Official Final Action

(*Caution: See* **51.011**, **51.018**, **51.039**, **51.040**, **51.041**, **51.045**, **51.046**, and **51.048**.)

Gas Chromatographic Method

(Under conditions specified, other pesticides or ingredients may interfere with GLC analysis, e.g., aldrin has same retention time as Dacthal. Aldrin and Dacthal may be sepd at 170° column temp.)

6.259 ***Apparatus***

Gas chromatograph.—1.8 m (6′) × ⅛″ id stainless steel column contg 10% silicone UC-98 (Applied Science Laboratories, Inc.) on 80–100 mesh silanized Diatoport S (Hewlett-Packard Co., Rt 41, Avondale, PA 19311). Conditions (applicable to Hewlett-Packard F&M Model 5750)—temps(°): column 200, injection port 240, flame ionization detector 260; H, air, and He carrier flows, 115, 600, and 25 mL/min, resp.; chart speed 0.25″/min; attenuation 4×; range setting 10^2 (10^{-10} amp full scale).

6.260 ***Preparation of Standard Curve***

(**a**) *Dacthal std solns.*—Weigh 0.5 g Dacthal (available from Diamond Shamrock Corp., PO Box 348, Painesville, OH 44077) into 100 mL vol. flask, add ca 90 mL acetone (soln is rapid), and dil. to vol. Pipet 5, 10, and 15 mL into sep. 25 mL vol. flasks and dil. to vol. with acetone.

(**b**) *Hexachlorobenzene* (*HCB*) *std solns.*—Weigh 0.5 g ref. grade HCB into 100 mL vol. flask, add 90 mL benzene, and dil. to vol. with benzene. Pipet 1, 2, and 3 mL into sep. 25 mL vol. flasks and evap. to dryness with current of dry air. Add 20 mL acetone to each flask and dil. to vol. with acetone.

Inject 5 μL each dild HCB and Dacthal std at least twice. Prep. curve of peak area or ht against concn for Dacthal and peak ht against concn for HCB.

6.261 ***Determination***

(**a**) *Benzene extraction.*—Grind granular product. Weigh portion contg ca 300–400 mg Dacthal into Whatman extn thimble (33 × 88 mm). Cover with glass wool. Place thimble in medium Soxhlet extractor; add 150–175 mL benzene and 3 glass beads. Ext 6 hr. Quant. transfer ext to 400 mL beaker and evap. to ca 5 mL on steam bath with dry air current; remove and evap. to dryness with air current. Add ca 150 mL acetone and let stand until soln is complete (white, flaky crystals may indicate incomplete soln; soln may be hastened by placing flask in ultrasonic cleaner). Filter soln thru glass wool into 200 mL vol. flask. Wash beaker with acetone, transfer washings to vol. flask, and dil. to vol.

(**b**) *Alternative acetone extraction.*—Substitute acetone for benzene in extn. Proceed as in (**a**) thru "Ext 6 hr." Continue with "Filter soln thru glass wool . . ."

Inject duplicate 5 μL sample soln into gas chromatograph. Compare peak ht or peak area to std curve to det. % hexachlorobenzene (HCB) and Dacthal.

Infrared Method

6.262 ***Preparation of Sample***

Grind granular product. Weigh sample contg 200–500 mg Dacthal into Whatman extn thimble. Proceed as in **6.261**(**a**) thru ". . . evap. to dryness with air current." Add 25 mL CS_2, allow ca 30 min for complete soln, and transfer quant. to 50 mL vol. flask with CS_2, filtering sample thru glass wool. Dil. to vol.

6.263 ***Preparation of Standard Solution***

Weigh 1.25 g Dacthal into 100 mL vol. flask. Add ca 90 mL CS_2 (soln may be hastened by placing flask in ultrasonic cleaner) and dil. to vol. Pipet 10, 15, and 20 mL into sep. 25 mL vol. flasks and dil. to vol.

6.264 ***Determination***

Set spectrophtr at optimum operating condition. Use 0.5 mm KBr (or NaCl) matched cells. Fill ref. cell with CS_2. Transfer dild stds to other cell and scan slowly from 1100 to 900 cm^{-1}. Repeat with samples. Construct baseline from 1030 to 925 cm^{-1} and draw line from midpoint of max. *A* at ca 964 cm^{-1} to intersect baseline. Compute ΔA at 964 cm^{-1} at point of intersection of stds and sample.

Prep. ΔA-concn curve for std; Beer's law is obeyed over concn range 2–15 mg Dacthal/mL. Calc. % Dacthal from std curve.

Dicamba (3,6-Dichloro-*o*-anisic Acid; 2-Methoxy-3,6-dichlorobenzoic Acid) (*70*)—Official Final Action

6.265 ***Reagents and Apparatus***

(**a**) *Acetone.*—Spectral grade.

(**b**) *Dimethylamine* (*DMA*) *soln.*—60% (w/w).

(**c**) *Dicamba std.*—Ref. grade (Velsicol Chemical Corp.).

(**d**) *Infrared spectrophotometer.*—With BaF_2 cells, 0.025 mm, and matched NaCl cells, 0.2 mm.

6.266 ***Preparation of Sample***

(Sample wts are for cell thicknesses specified. For other cells, adjust wts to yield peak between 30 and 60% *T*.)

(**a**) *Aqueous solns of DMA salt* (*4 lb/gal.*).—Pipet, using same pipet as for std, 5.00 mL sample into tared 25 mL vol. flask and weigh. Dil. to vol. with acetone. (Use this soln directly in 0.025 mm BaF_2 cell.)

(**b**) *Solns of DMA salt* (*other concentrations*).— Prep. as in (**a**), adjusting sample size to yield 2.4 g dicamba/25 mL.

(**c**) *Technical dicamba.*—Weigh 0.2±0.005 g sample into tared 25 mL vol. flask and dil. to vol. with CS_2.

6.267 ***Preparation of Standard***

(**a**) *Liquid formulations.*—(*1*) *Aqueous solns of DMA salt* (*4 lb/gal.*)*:* Weigh 11.98±0.02 g dicamba std into tared 50 mL beaker. Add 5 mL H_2O and 4 mL 60% DMA. Adjust pH to 7.0 by titrg with 60% DMA soln, using mag. stirrer and pH meter. (All solids should be dissolved at this time.) Rinse each pH electrode with two 1 mL H_2O rinses (4 mL total), collecting rinses in the 50 mL beaker. Cool soln to room temp. and transfer to tared 25 mL vol. flask. Rinse beaker twice with H_2O, collecting rinses in flask. Dil. to vol. with H_2O and mix thoroly. Weigh flask and contents to det. total wt of soln. Pipet 5.0 mL std formulation into tared 25 mL vol. flask, weigh, and dil. to vol. with acetone.

(*2*) *Aqueous solns of DMA salt* (*other concentrations*): Prep. as in (**a**)(*1*), adjusting dicamba content to required concn.

(**b**) *Technical dicamba*.—Weigh 0.2±0.005 g dicamba std into tared 25 mL vol. flask and dil. to vol. with CS_2.

6.268 ***Determination***

(**a**) *Liquid formulations*.—Record spectra of std and sample between 1070 and 930 cm^{-1} (9.3–10.7 μm), using BaF_2 cell. Use air in ref. beam. Obtain ΔA and $\Delta A'$ for sample and std, resp., at 1012 cm^{-1} (9.89 μm) from horizontal baseline tangent to min. between 1020 and 1070 cm^{-1} (9.4–9.7 μm).

(**b**) *Technical dicamba*.—Record spectra of std and sample from 1100 to 930 cm^{-1} (9.1–10.7 μm), using NaCl cells. Use CS_2 in ref. cell. Obtain ΔA and $\Delta A'$ for sample and std, resp., at 1012 cm^{-1} (9.89 μm) from horizontal baseline tangent to min. between 1075 and 1035 cm^{-1} (9.3–9.66 μm).

6.269 ***Calculations***

(**a**) *Liquid formulations*.—Dicamba, lb/gal. = $\Delta A \times C/\Delta A'$, where C = lb std/gal. = (g std × % purity of std × 8.35)/25.

% Dicamba by wt = ($\Delta A \times F$)/(g sample/25 mL), where F = [(g std/25 mL) × % purity of std]/$\Delta A'$.

(**b**) *Technical dicamba*.—% Dicamba by wt = $\Delta A \times F$/g sample, where F = (g std × % purity of std)/$\Delta A'$.

Dicamba–2-Methyl-4-chlorophenoxyacetic Acid (MCPA) and Dicamba–2,4-D (*71*)—Official Final Action

AOAC-CIPAC Method

(*Caution: See* **51.041**.)

6.270 ***Principle***

Method is applicable to aq. dimethylamine (DMA) salt formulations of dicamba and 2-methyl- 4-chlorophenoxyacetic acid (MCPA) or 2,4-D (2,4-dichlorophenoxyacetic acid). Active ingredients are pptd by HCl and extd with $CHCl_3$. Solv. is evapd, residue dissolved in acetone, and A measured at characteristic IR wavelengths.

6.271 ***Preparation of Standard Solutions***

(**a**) *Dicamba–MCPA*.—Accurately weigh 0.20±0.02 g dicamba and 0.60±0.02 g MCPA into tared weighing bottle. Pipet in 25 mL acetone and swirl until completely dissolved. If cells other than 0.2 mm are used, adjust wts to give A of 0.2–0.5 (30–65% T) for both std and sample solns.

(**b**) *Dicamba–2,4-D*.—Prep. as in (**a**), using 0.20±0.02 g dicamba and 0.40±0.02 g 2,4-D.

6.272 ***Preparation of Sample***

(**a**) *Dicamba–MCPA*.—Accurately weigh sample contg 0.20±0.02 g dicamba and 0.60±0.02 g MCPA into tared weighing bottle. Add 5 mL H_2O and transfer quant. to 125 mL separator with 5–10 mL H_2O.

(**b**) *Dicamba–2,4-D*.—Prep. as in (**a**), using 0.20±0.02 g dicamba and 0.40±0.02 g 2,4-D.

6.273 ***Determination***

To soln add HCl dropwise with const swirling to pH 1; then add 5 drops excess. Pipet in 25 mL $CHCl_3$ and shake to dissolve ppt. Drain $CHCl_3$ ext into 125 mL erlenmeyer and re-ext with two 15 mL portions $CHCl_3$. Add boiling chips to combined ext and evap. on steam bath to dryness. Let dry in hood overnight at room temp. (Do not dry in air or vac. oven.) Pipet in 25 mL acetone and swirl to completely dissolve residue. Add few g granular anhyd. Na_2SO_4 if any H_2O is present.

Record IR spectrum and measure ΔA in matched 0.2 mm NaCl cells with acetone in ref. cell at following wavelengths:

(**a**) *Dicamba–MCPA*.—Range, 1135–930 cm^{-1} (8.8–10.75 μm); dicamba peak, 1012 cm^{-1} (9.89 μm); MCPA peak, 1070 cm^{-1} (9.35 μm); baseline, horizontal tangent to min. at 970–965 cm^{-1} (10.3–10.4 μm) for both constituents.

(**b**) *Dicamba–2,4-D*.—Range, 1130–945 cm^{-1} (8.85–10.6 μm); dicamba peak, 1012 cm^{-1} (9.89 μm); 2,4-D peak, 1080 cm^{-1} (9.26 μm); baseline, horizontal tangent to min. at 970–960 cm^{-1} (10.3–10.4 μm) for both constituents.

6.274 ***Calculations***

% by wt of constituent = ($\Delta A/W$)($W' \times P/\Delta A'$), where ΔA and $\Delta A'$ = absorbance of constituent in sample and std solns, resp.; W and W' = g constituent in sample and std solns, resp.; and P = % purity of constituent in ref. std.

lb/gal. = % by wt × sp gr × 8.345.

2,4-D (2,4-Dichlorophenoxyacetic Acid)

Automated High Pressure Liquid Chromatographic Method (72)—Official First Action

6.275 ***Principle***

Esters of 2,4-D are saponified *in situ*; amine salts are converted to H_2O-sol. K salt of 2,4-D. Ionic 2,4-D is protonated by pH 2.95 CH_3CN-H_2O (1+4) eluant, and sepd from all known impurities and *p*-bromophenol internal std on reversed phase bonded microparticulate column. 2,4-D elutes between impurities 2,4- and 2,6-dichlorophenol.

6.276 ***Apparatus***

(**a**) *Liquid chromatograph*.—Fitted with 5000 psi pressure gage, 280 nm UV detector, line filter in eluant reservoir, and 10 mv full scale deflection strip chart recorder. Automated sampling system and computing integrator are optional. Typical operating conditions: chart speed, 0.2 cm/min; eluant flow rate, 0.9–3.0 mL/min depending upon psi range of pump; detector sensitivity, 0.64 A unit full scale; temp., ambient; injection valve vol., 10 μL.

(**b**) *Liquid chromatographic column*.—No. 316 stainless steel, 250 × 4.6 (id) mm, Partisil® 10 μm ODS column with 50 × 4.6 (id) mm Co:Pell ODS pellicular guard column (Nos. 6526-124 and 6561-404, resp., Whatman Inc., 9 Bridewell Pl, Clifton, NJ 07014). Regenerate, if necessary, by pumping CH_3CN thru column until baseline is stable. Repack first 5 mm of guard and main columns with Co:Pell ODS if peaks begin to "tail".

6.277 ***Reagents***

(**a**) *Eluant*.—pH 2.95. CH_3CN (distd-in-glass)-H_2O (deionized, 0.4 μm filtered) (1+4) contg NaOH added from (1+1) aq. soln of known normality, **50.033**(**b**), at final vol. concn of 0.3*M*. Add H_3PO_4 to adjust pH to 2.95.

(**b**) *Saponification-internal std soln*.—4 g *p*-Bromophenol/L 0.2*N* KOH in isopropanol-H_2O (2+1). Add KOH from (1+1) aq. soln of known normality.

(**c**) *2,4-D std soln*.—300 mg/25 mL. Accurately weigh ca 300 mg 2,4-D anal. ref. std (99+% isomer pure; available from Dow Chemical Co., Sample Coordinator, 9001 Bldg, Midland, MI 48640), previously dried 15 min at 100°, into 1 or 2 oz glass vial with polyethylene-lined screw cap. Pipet in 25 mL saponification-internal std soln, and shake to dissolve. Prep. 2,4-D std soln and sample soln, **6.278**, at same time, using same pipet.

6.278 ***Preparation of Sample***

Accurately weigh sample contg ca 300 mg 2,4-D acid equiv. into 1 or 2 oz glass vial with polyethylene-lined screw cap. Pipet in 25 mL saponification-internal std soln, and shake 15 min, warming ester formulations to 50° several min before shaking. Filter prepd sample thru 9 cm Whatman glass microfiber filter GF/A, or equiv., collecting major portion of aq. phase for chromatography. Adjust isopropanol-H_2O ratio, if necessary, to obtain complete dissoln of sample; e.g., amine formulations are best prepd with isopropanol-H_2O (1+1).

6.279 ***Determination***

Transfer ca 1 mL portions of samples and stds to automated sampler vials, and cap. Place samples and stds in position, and start automatic sampler. With programmed integrator use following calcn program automatically:

$$\% \text{ 2,4-D} = (R/R') \times (W'/W) \times P,$$

where R and R' = peak ht or area ratios of 2,4-D to internal std for sample and std, resp.; W' = mg 2,4-D in std; W = mg sample; and P = % purity of std. If automated sampler and computing integrator are unavailable, inject 10 μL samples and stds and perform calcns manually. As check on calibration, place stds in sample sequence at beginning, middle, and end. Periodically confirm linearity by analyzing stds contg 200, 300, and 400 mg 99+% 2,4-D/25 mL saponification-internal std soln. Continuously recycle and mag. stir eluant. Replace eluant after ca 200 injections/L.

Sodium Salt of Dalapon (2,2-Dichloropropionic Acid) (*73*)—Official Final Action

(*Caution: See* **51.041**.)

6.280 ***Apparatus***

(**a**) *Reflux apparatus*.—250 mL erlenmeyer connected thru § 35/25 ball joint to reflux condenser.

(**b**) *Filtering apparatus*.—60 mL, medium porosity fritted glass funnel attached to glass filter bell, 11 cm od, 18 cm high, with bottom gasket and slide valve.

6.281 ***Reagents***

(**a**) *Mercuric-cupric nitrate soln*.—(*Caution: See* **51.065**.) Dissolve 100.0 g yellow HgO and 60 g $Cu(NO_3)_2.3H_2O$ in 500 mL 3.100±0.003*N* HNO_3, measured from vol. flask, in 1 L vol. flask, dil. to vol. with H_2O, and filter.

(**b**) *Potassium iodide soln*.—Dissolve 150 g KI in H_2O, dil. to 1 L, and neutze to phthln.

6.282 ***Determination***

Accurately weigh sample contg 0.11–0.22 g Na salt of 2,2-dichloropropionic acid, transfer to erlenmeyer of reflux app., and add 100 mL Hg-Cu nitrate soln. Add some boiling chips, attach condenser, and reflux 15 min. Cool in H_2O bath. Filter thru filtering app., washing flask and ppt acid-free with H_2O from wash bottle. Discard filtrate and washings, and place 250 mL narrow-mouth erlenmeyer in filtering bell.

Add 50 mL KI soln to erlenmeyer to dissolve any remaining ppt, transfer to funnel, and stir until ppt dissolves. Draw soln into narrow-mouth erlenmeyer with vac. Wash flask and funnel with ≤50 mL KI soln from wash bottle, adding washings to filtrate. Add few boiling chips to filtrate and boil 1 min. Cool in H_2O bath. Titr. immediately with 0.1*N* HCl, using phthln.

% Na salt 2,2-dichloropropionic acid = mL 0.1*N* HCl × 0.004499 × 100/g sample.

Dicofol (Kelthane®, 4,4′-Dichloro-α-(trichloromethyl)-benzhydrol)

Potentiometric Method (74)—Official First Action

6.283 ***Principle***

Dicofol is hydrolyzed in alc. KOH under reflux, and hydrolyzable org. Cl is converted to ionizable Cl which is titrd potentiometrically with std $AgNO_3$.

6.284 ***Apparatus***

(**a**) *Condenser*.—₮ 24/40 Pyrex condenser, water cooled, 400 mm long with drip tip.

(**b**) *Potentiometer*.—Fisher Accumet Model 320 (new model 325) expanded scale pH meter, or equiv., with 50 mL buret graduated in 0.1 mL, Ag billet indicating electrode (Fisher No. 13-639-122), and Ag-AgCl ref. electrode (Fisher No. 13-639-53). Keep Ag electrode free from tarnish by polishing with aq. $NaHCO_3$-$CaCO_3$ (1+1) paste. Before each analysis, rinse Ag electrode with NH_4OH (1+1) followed by H_2O.

6.285 ***Reagents***

(Use deionized H_2O thruout.)

(**a**) *Alcoholic potassium hydroxide soln*.—0.5*N*. Dissolve 28.1 g KOH pellets in ca 600 mL alcohol and dil. to 1 L with alcohol.

(**b**) *Potassium chloride std soln*.—0.1*N*. Dissolve 7.456 g KCl in H_2O and dil. to 1 L with H_2O.

(**c**) *Silver nitrate std soln*.—0.1*N*. Dissolve 17.00 g $AgNO_3$ in 100 mL H_2O, add 1.7 mL HNO_3, and dil. to 1 L with H_2O. To stdze, dil. 25 mL 0.1*N* KCl to 200 mL with H_2O in 400 mL beaker. Adjust pH to 2.0±0.2, using NH_4OH (1+4) and/or HNO_3 (1+4), and dil. to 300 mL. Titr., using potentiometer as in **6.288**. Plot mv against vol. 0.1*N* KCl and det. mL 0.1*N* $AgNO_3$ at end point. Calc. normality of $AgNO_3$ std soln. Stdze $AgNO_3$ std soln daily. (Equiv. wt dicofol = 370.5/3 = 123.5.)

(**d**) *Thymol blue indicator soln*.—0.1%. Dissolve 100 mg thymol blue in 100 mL alcohol (1+1).

6.286 ***Preparation of Sample***

(**a**) *Kelthane technical*.—Fuse sample in loosely capped jar in 100° oven and mix thoroly with glass rod. Accurately weigh ca 4–6 g molten sample into 150 mL beaker. Add 50–75 mL isopropanol and heat with occasional swirling until sample dissolves. Transfer quant. to 500 mL vol. flask, let cool to 25°, and dil. to vol. with isopropanol. Pipet 25 mL sample soln into 300 mL ₮ 24/40 Pyrex erlenmeyer. (*Caution: See* **51.018**.)

(**b**) *Kelthane formulations*.—(*1*) *Kelthane MF and Kelthane 35*.—Accurately weigh ca 1 g sample into 300 mL ₮ 24/40 Pyrex erlenmeyer. (*2*) *Kelthane EC*.—Proceed as in (*1*), using ca 2 g sample.

6.287 ***Hydrolysis***

Transfer 50 mL alc. KOH soln to erlenmeyer contg sample. Attach condenser, seal with 2–3 drops alcohol, and reflux gently on hot plate 1.5 hr. Let cool, and rinse condenser and tip with 25 mL alcohol. Quant. transfer soln to 400 mL beaker, using 50 mL alcohol and 100 mL H_2O. Rinse erlenmeyer with addnl portions H_2O to total vol. of 250 mL.

Add 10 drops thymol blue indicator soln to beaker and, with

stirring, add HNO_3 (1+1) dropwise to first pink color of indicator. Adjust pH to 2±0.2, using NH_4OH (1+4) and/or HNO_3 (1+4). Adjust total vol. to 300 mL with H_2O.

6.288 ***Determination***

Place sample beaker on mag. stirrer, and adjust to rapid stirring. Titr. with $AgNO_3$ std soln to same mv end point used for stdzg $AgNO_3$ std soln. Titr. blank (unhydrolyzed sample).

% Active ingredient in tech. Kelthane =

$$\{[(V_s/S_a) - (V_b/S_b)] \times N \times V_t \times 0.1235 \times 100\}/V;$$

% Active ingredient in Kelthane formulations =

$$[(V_s/S_a) - (V_b/S_b)] \times N \times 0.1235 \times 100,$$

where V_s and V_b = mL $AgNO_3$ std soln required to titr. sample and blank, resp.; N = normality of $AgNO_3$ std soln; S_a *and* S_b = g sample taken for hydrolysis and blank, resp.; V_t = total vol. sample soln = 500 mL; and V = aliquot vol. sample soln = 25 mL.

Fluometuron (1,1-Dimethyl-3-(α,α,α-trifluoro-*m*-tolyl)urea)

Gas Chromatographic Method (75)—Official Final Action

6.289 ***Standard Solutions***

(**a**) *Diethyl phthalate internal std soln.*—Weigh 1.5±0.1 g tech. diethyl phthalate, dissolve in ca 100 mL alcohol-free $CHCl_3$, dil. to 250.0 mL with $CHCl_3$, and mix well. Std should be >98% pure and contain no impurities eluting at retention time of fluometuron.

(**b**) *Fluometuron std soln.*—Accurately weigh ca 125 mg tech. fluometuron of known purity (available from Ciba-Geigy Corp., PO Box 11422, Greensboro, NC 27409) into 2 oz round bottle with Teflon-lined or Poly-Seal screw cap. Pipet in 25 mL diethyl phthalate internal std soln and shake to dissolve. Pipet in 3 mL trifluoroacetic anhydride and shake mech. 15 min; then place bottle in 55° H_2O bath 30 min. Let cool to room temp.

6.290 ***Preparation of Sample***

Accurately weigh sample contg ca 125 mg fluometuron into 2 oz round bottle with Teflon-lined or Poly-Seal screw cap. Pipet in 25 mL diethyl phthalate internal std soln and shake well. Pipet in 3 mL trifluoroacetic anhydride and shake mech. 15 min; then place bottle in 55° H_2O bath 30 min. Let cool to room temp. Let insol. materials settle or centrf. portion of ext to obtain clear soln.

6.291 ***Gas Chromatography***

Use instrument equipped with flame ionization detector and 1.83 m × 2 (id) mm glass column packed with 2% OV-3 (Applied Science Laboratories, Inc.) on 80–100 mesh Gas-Chrom Q. Condition 24 hr at 240° with N or He at ca 40 mL/min. Column should have ≥1500 theoretical plates. Use on-column injection to prevent decomposition of derivative.

Typical operating conditions: temps (°)—inlet 150, column 115±10, detector 250; N or He carrier gas, 20–22 mL/min; air and H as specified by manufacturer; attenuation varied so that peak hts of pesticide and internal std are 60–80% full scale. Retention times for fluometuron derivative and diethyl phthalate are 3–5 and 8–10 min, resp.

6.292 ***Determination***

Proceed as in **6.433–6.434**, except inject 1 μL aliquots.

6.293 ***Calculations***

See **6.435**.

Folpet (*N*-(Trichloromethylthio)phthalimide)

High Pressure Liquid Chromatographic Method (76)
AOAC-CIPAC Method—Official Final Action

(Applicable to dry formulations contg folpet as only active ingredient and to folpet combination formulations except those contg propargite or Me parathion. Compds insol. in CH_2Cl_2, e.g., maneb or inorg. salts, do not interfere.)

6.294 ***Apparatus***

(**a**) *Liquid chromatograph.*—Equipped with 254 nm UV detector. Typical operating conditions: chart speed, 0.2″/min; eluant flow rate, 2 mL/min (ca 800 psi); detector sensitivity, 0.16 *A* unit full scale; temp., ambient; valve injection vol., 20 μL. Adjust operating conditions to elute folpet peak in 4±1 min. Factors such as different H_2O content in CH_2Cl_2 eluant can change retention times. Folpet peak must be completely resolved from dibutyl phthalate peak which normally elutes in ca 7 min.

(**b**) *Liquid chromatographic column.*—Stainless steel, 300 × 4 (id) mm, packed with 10 μm diam. silica gel particles (Waters Associates, Inc., No. 27477, or equiv.).

6.295 ***Reagents***

(**a**) *Eluant.*—Degassed CH_2Cl_2.

(**b**) *Internal std soln.*—Accurately weigh ca 0.5 g dibutyl phthalate (MC/B Manufacturing Chemists) into 200 mL vol. flask. Dil. to vol. with CH_2Cl_2 and mix.

(**c**) *Folpet std soln.*—(100 μg folpet + 250 μg dibutyl phthalate)/mL. Accurately weigh ca 20 mg folpet ref. std, 99+% pure (Chevron Chemical Co., 940 Hensley St, Richmond, CA 94804) into glass vial, pipet 20 mL internal std soln into vial, and shake to dissolve. Pipet 1 mL into 10 mL vol. flask. Dil. to vol. with CH_2Cl_2.

6.296 ***Preparation of Sample***

Accurately weigh sample contg 20 mg folpet into vial. Pipet 20 mL internal std soln into vial and shake 30 min. Centrf. to ppt solids. Pipet 1 mL supernate into 10 mL vol. flask, dil. to vol. with CH_2Cl_2, and mix. Sample contains ca (100 μg folpet + 250 μg dibutyl phthalate)/mL.

6.297 ***Determination***

Inject 20 μL folpet std soln onto column thru sampling valve and adjust operating conditions to give largest possible on-scale peaks with retention time of 4±1 min for folpet. Repeat injections until ratio of folpet to dibutyl phthalate peak hts is within ±1% of previous injection. Without changing conditions, inject sample soln until its ratio is within ±1% of previous ratio for sample. Average last 2 peak ht ratios for sample and for std, resp., and calc. % folpet.

$$\% \text{ Folpet} = (R/R') \times (W'/W) \times P,$$

where R and R' = av. peak ht ratios for sample and std, resp.; W' = mg folpet in std soln (ca 20 mg); W = mg sample extd for analysis; and P = % purity of std.

Heptachlor—Official Final Action

Active Chlorine Method (61)

6.298 ***Reagents***

(**a**) *Dilute acetic acid.*—80%. Dil. 800 mL HOAc to 1 L with H_2O.

(**b**) *Silver nitrate-acetic acid std soln.*—Dissolve 17 g $AgNO_3$ in 200 mL H_2O, add 56 mL HNO_3 (1+1), and dil. to 1 L with HOAc. Stdze potentiometrically by adding 25 mL of this soln to

600 mL beaker contg 250 mL 80% HOAc. Immerse glass and Ag electrodes in soln and stir with mag. stirrer. Titr. with 0.1*N* NaCl soln, **6.220(a)**, to end point (max. change in mv/mL NaCl soln). Normality $AgNO_3$ = mL NaCl × normality NaCl/mL $AgNO_3$.

6.299 ***Preparation of Sample***

(**a**) *Emulsifiable concentrate formulations.*—Accurately weigh sample contg 0.3±0.05 g heptachlor in 250 mL erlenmeyer. Dissolve in 50 mL HOAc, and pipet in 25 mL 0.1*N* $AgNO_3$, (**b**). Attach reflux condenser and reflux 1 hr.

(**b**) *Granular and dust formulations.*—(*Caution: See* **51.039, 51.041**, and **51.074**.) Accurately weigh sample contg 0.3±0.05 g heptachlor into 80 × 25 mm Soxhlet extn thimble. Ext 2 hr with *pentane* and transfer ext to 250 mL erlenmeyer. Attach short reflux column such as 3-ball Snyder or 12″ (30 cm) Vigreux to flask and evap. to dryness on steam bath. (Results will be low if reflux column is not used.) Rinse down column with 50 mL HOAc, pipet in 25 mL 0.1*N* $AgNO_3$, (**b**), attach reflux condenser, and reflux 1 hr.

(**c**) *Technical.*—Accurately weigh 0.40±0.05 g heptachlor and proceed as in (**a**).

6.300 ***Determination***

Rinse tip of condenser or column with H_2O and cool soln to room temp. Transfer quant. to 600 mL beaker, rinsing with four 10 mL portions 80% HOAc. Immerse glass and Ag electrodes in soln and stir with mag. stirrer. Titr. with 0.1*N* NaCl soln, **6.220(a)**, to end point.

% Heptachlor = 37.33 × (25 × normality $AgNO_3$ soln − mL NaCl soln × normality NaCl soln)/g sample.

Gas Chromatographic Method (77)

6.301 ***Apparatus***

(**a**) *Gas chromatograph.*—Equipped with H flame ionization detector; capable of accepting glass column and glass-lined sample introduction system or on-column injection. Use following conditions: Temps (°): column 175, detector 175–190, sample inlet 190; N carrier gas pressure 30 psig; recorder chart speed 2.5 cm/min.

(**b**) *Glass-stoppered tubes.*—Approx. 25 and 75 mL capacity.

(**c**) *Microliter syringe.*—10 μL, Hamilton Co., 701-N.

6.302 ***Reagents***

(**a**) *Heptachlor.*—Ref. grade (Velsicol Chemical Corp.).

(**b**) *Aldrin.*—Ref. grade (Velsicol Chemical Corp.).

6.303 ***Preparation of Column***

To 9.5 g 100–120 mesh Gas Chrom Q in vac. flask add 0.50 g silicone GE Versilube F-50 (available from Applied Science Labs) dissolved in 50 mL CH_2Cl_2. Shake slurry well to wet solid thoroly. Connect flask to H_2O aspirator and evap. solv. with frequent shaking. When solids appear dry, complete drying by placing flask in steam bath and connecting to vac. pump until ca 4 mm pressure is attained. Remove flask from steam bath and let cool under vac.

Fill 1.5 m (5′) × ⅛″ od (0.067″ id) Pyrex glass tube with this packing, using vac. pump and gentle tapping. Plug ends of column with glass wool. Condition column 24 hr in 190° oven while purging with N. Let column cool while still purging with N; then install in chromatograph.

6.304 ***Preparation of Sample***

(**a**) *Liquids.*—Weigh sample contg ca 750 mg heptachlor into 75 mL g-s vial and add 500 mg ref. grade aldrin. Add 75 mL fresh CS_2, stopper, and shake vigorously 2 min.

(**b**) *Solids.*—Transfer weighed sample contg ca 750 mg heptachlor to Soxhlet and ext 2 hr with 75 mL pentane. Let cool, add 500 mg ref. grade aldrin to soln, and swirl.

6.305 ***Calibration***

Weigh 0.2500 g ref. grade heptachlor and 0.1670 g ref. grade aldrin into 25 mL g-s flask. Dissolve in 25 mL CS_2. Chromatograph this soln under conditions given in **6.301(a)** 5 times to obtain accurate response correction factor. (On new column, it is sometimes desirable to inject several 5 μL aliquots of std soln to condition column before use.)

6.306 ***Determination***

Let instrument equilibrate as in **6.301(a)**. Inject ca 1 μL sample soln at sensitivity setting such that ht of heptachlor peak is ca ¾ full scale. For each analysis, allow 10–12 min for heptachlor related components to elute. Components and approx. retention times in min are: heptachlor 4.5, aldrin 5.9, chlordene 3.1, and γ-chlordane 9.9.

6.307 ***Calculations***

Calc. area of heptachlor and aldrin peaks by multiplying peak ht in mm by width of peak at half ht in mm. Alternatively, use integrator. Calc. response correction factor (*f*, ca 0.82) for each of the 5 std injections as follows:

f = (area of heptachlor peak × mg aldrin × purity of aldrin)/(area of aldrin peak × mg heptachlor × purity of heptachlor).

Average 5 replicates and use av. to calc. % heptachlor in samples.

% Heptachlor = (area of heptachlor peak × mg aldrin × purity of aldrin × 100)/(area of aldrin peak × mg sample × *f*).

Picloram (4-Amino-3,5,6-Trichloropicolinic Acid) and 2,4-D (2,4-Dichlorophenoxyacetic Acid)

High Pressure Liquid Chromatographic Method (78) *Official Final Action*

6.308 ***Apparatus***

(**a**) *Liquid chromatograph.*—Equipped with 280 nm UV detector and injection valve. Alternatively, septum injection head may be used; however, stop-flow injection is recommended. Operating conditions: eluant flow rate, 0.7 mL/min (ca 1000 psi); detector sensitivity, 0.08 *A* unit full scale; temp., ambient, but within ±2.5°.

(**b**) *Liquid chromatographic column.*—No. 316 stainless steel, 1000 × 2.1 mm id, with Varian No. 96-000075-00 reducing union (⅛″ × 1/16″) contg 2 μm frit (regular reducing union packed with glass wool may be used instead) packed with DuPont No. 820960005 Zipax® SAX (strong anion exchange) resin. Preclean column with few mL each of $CHCl_3$, acetone, and MeOH, and vac.-dry. Pack in small increments over 40 min period while tapping column on hard surface.

6.309 ***Reagents***

(**a**) *Eluants.*—Prep. sep. solns of 0.01*M* $Na_2B_4O_7.10H_2O$ (3.8 g/L) and 0.002*M* $NaClO_4.H_2O$ (0.28 g/L) in previously boiled and cooled deionized H_2O.

(**b**) *Salicylic acid internal std soln.*—Accurately weigh ca 3.6 g USP Ref. Std Salicylic Acid into 1 L vol. flask, dil. to vol. with 0.05*N* NaOH in isopropanol-H_2O (1+1), and mix.

(c) *Picloram-2,4-D std soln.*—(4 mg picloram + 12 mg 2,4-D + 3.6 mg salicylic acid)/mL. Accurately weigh ca 100 mg picloram ref. std, 99+% pure (Dow Chemical Co.), and ca 300 mg 2,4-D ref. std, 99+% pure (Dow Chemical Co.), into glass vial, pipet in 25 mL salicylic acid internal std soln, and shake to dissolve.

6.310 ***Preparation of Sample***

Accurately weigh ca 1.6 g sample into ca 10 dram glass vial, pipet in 25 mL salicyclic acid internal std soln, and shake to dissolve.

6.311 ***Determination***

Inject 2 μL picloram-2,4-D std soln onto column and adjust attenuation to give largest possible on-scale peaks. Repeat injections until peak ht ratios of herbicide:internal std vary $\leq$1% for successive injections. Without changing conditions, inject 2 μL aliquots sample soln until peak ht ratios vary $\leq$1%. Average last 2 peak ht ratios for picloram and 2,4-D and calc. % herbicide.

$$\% \text{ Herbicide} = (R_x/R_s) \times (W_s/W_x) \times P,$$

where R_x and R_s = av. peak ht ratios of each herbicide to the internal std for sample and std, resp.; W_s = mg herbicide in std; W_x = mg sample; and P = % purity of std.

Sodium Trichloroacetate (*79*)—Official Final Action

(*Caution: See* **51.011**, **51.039**, **51.041**, and **51.070**.)

6.312 ***Apparatus and Reagent***

(a) *Reflux apparatus.*—250 mL erlenmeyer attached thru ₮ 24/40 joint to 50 cm water-cooled condenser.

(b) *Dioxane.*—Freshly distd.

6.313 ***Determination***

Dissolve 25 g sample in H_2O and dil. to 100.0 mL. Pipet aliquot (usually 10 mL), titrg ca half that of blank, into 250 mL refluxing flask, add 1 drop Me red, and neutze with ca 1*N* H_2SO_4 to distinct orange-pink. pH is 5.3–5.5; usually <0.15 mL is required. If soln is acid, titr. with ca 1*N* NaOH. Add 25.00 mL 1*N* H_2SO_4, 35 mL dioxane, and few glass beads. Boil vigorously under reflux $\geq$60 min. Cool, add 2 drops Me red, and titr. with std 1*N* NaOH to sharp change from orange to yellow end point. Perform blank detn, omitting sample.

% Na trichloroacetate = Net mL 1*N* acid × 0.1854 × 100/g sample in aliquot.

6.314 Trifluralin—Official First Action

See **6.203–6.214**.

NONHALOGENATED PESTICIDES

Aldicarb (2-Methyl-2-(methylthio)propionaldehyde-*O*-(methylcarbamoyl) Oxime) (*80*)—Official Final Action

(*Caution: See* **51.041**.)

6.315 ***Apparatus and Reagents***

(a) *Infrared spectrophotometer.*—Perkin-Elmer Model 337, or equiv. Adjust conditions as required by specific instrument.

(b) *Soxhlet extractor.*—With 125 mL flask and 25 × 80 mm cellulose thimble.

(c) *Aldicarb std soln.*—0.18 g/100 mL. Accurately weigh (to 0.1 mg) 0.18±0.01 g anal. grade aldicarb (available from Union Carbide Corp., Agricultural Products and Services) into 100 mL g-s vol. flask, add ca 80 mL CH_2Cl_2, mix to dissolve, and dil. to vol. with CH_2Cl_2.

6.316 ***Determination***

Transfer accurately weighed sample contg 0.18±0.01 g aldicarb to extn thimble, cover with wad of surgical grade cotton, and place thimble in extractor. Add 2–3 Alundum boiling stones and ca 80 mL CH_2Cl_2 to flask, and ext at rate to provide 5 extns within 60 min. Let cool to room temp., transfer quant. to 100 mL g-s vol. flask with CH_2Cl_2, and dil. to vol.

Using matched 0.5 mm NaCl cells, scan sample and std solns from 5.2 to 6.0 μm (1900 to 1600 cm^{-1}) against CH_2Cl_2. Calc. A of sample and A' of std at 5.75 μm (1740 cm^{-1}), using corresponding A at 5.4 μm (1850 cm^{-1}) as I_0. (A and A' should both be ca 0.45.)

6.317 ***Determination of Binder Correction***

Pipet 50 mL sample soln into 100 mL beaker and place in room temp. H_2O bath in hood. Evap. to dryness, using gentle stream of clean, dry air. Add 25 mL MeOH, stir well, and filter thru 30 mL coarse fritted glass gooch. Rinse beaker and gooch with 25 mL MeOH, applying vac. until all liq. is in filter flask. Place gooch and contents in original beaker, place 20 mL CH_2Cl_2 in gooch, and swirl to dissolve binder, letting solv. drip into beaker. Repeat with addnl 20 mL CH_2Cl_2. Quant. transfer solv. to 50 mL g-s vol. flask and dil. to vol. with CH_2Cl_2. Scan soln as in detn and subtract A of binder soln (should be <0.005) from that of sample (=ΔA).

% Aldicarb by wt = (ΔA/g sample) × (g std/A') × P, where P is % purity of ref. std.

Amitrole (3-Amino-s-triazole) (*81*)—Official Final Action

(*Caution: See* **51.018** and **51.041**.)

6.318 ***Preparation of Sample Solution***

(a) *50% Dry powder formulation.*—Transfer 10.00 g sample to 100 mL g-s vol. flask, using powder funnel. Add 50 mL DMF. Shake 2–3 min to dissolve amitrole. (Undissolved amitrole is powder and can be differentiated visually from inerts which are usually crystals.) Let settle and carefully decant supernate into 100 mL vol. flask. Repeat extn of residue with three 15 mL portions DMF, letting settle each time before decanting into vol. flask. Dil. combined exts to vol. with DMF and shake well. Filter 40–50 mL thru fritted glass filter of medium porosity. Pipet 25 mL into 400 mL beaker contg 50 mL H_2O.

(b) *90% Dry powder formulation.*—Dissolve 1.0000 g sample in 100 mL H_2O in 400 mL beaker.

(c) *Aqueous amitrole.*—Pipet 5 mL sample into 400 mL beaker contg 50 mL H_2O.

6.319 ***Determination***

Adjust sample soln or dild aliquot to pH 1.8 with 0.5*N* HCl. Stir mech. and titr. with 0.5 mL increments 0.5*N* NaOH to pH 3.5–4.0. (Use Beckman Model G pH meter, or equiv., equipped with glass-calomel electrode system, and stdzd at pH 4.0 and 7.0 with buffers, **50.007(c)** and **(d)**.) Add 0.5*N* NaOH rapidly to pH 6.5 and then dropwise to pH 7.5 (second inflection point). Plot pH against mL 0.5*N* NaOH and det. first inflection point (occurs at pH 2.5–2.9).

% Amitrole by wt = $(B - C) \times 0.5 \times 8.408/F$,

where C = mL 0.5*N* NaOH required to titr. to first inflection point; B = mL 0.5*N* NaOH required to titr. to pH 7.5; and F = 2.5 for 50% dry powder formulation, **(a)**, g sample for 90% dry powder formulation, **(b)**, and 5.0 × sp gr sample for aq. amitrole, **(c)**.

lb Amitrole in aq. amitrole/U.S. gal. = % amitrole × sp gr × 8.32/100.

Carbaryl (1-Naphthyl Methylcarbamate) (*82*)
Official Final Action

(*Caution: See* **51.018**, **51.040**, **51.041**, and **51.056**.)

6.320 ***Apparatus***

(a) *Centrifuge.*—Clinical model, 8 place, or equiv.

(b) *Hypodermic syringe.*—1 mL, glass barrel with rubber-tipped plastic plunger (1 mL B-D Glaspak Tuberculin disposable syringe supplied by Becton, Dickinson, and Co. is suitable). Disposable syringe may be used repeatedly. Wash with H_2O and acetone or MeOH, air-dry, and lubricate rubber plunger tip with silicone stopcock grease.

(c) *Infrared spectrophotometer.*—Perkin-Elmer Corp., Model 337, or equiv. Operator must adapt conditions to instrument.

(d) *Rotator.*—Tube type, BBL, or equiv.

(e) *Shaking machine.*—Wrist-action shaker (Burrell Corp., or equiv.).

(f) *Tubes.*—Culture tubes, borosilicate glass, 16 × 150 mm with screw caps and Teflon liners (Corning Glass Works No. 9826, or equiv.).

6.321 ***Reagents***

(a) *Methanol-chloroform soln.*—10% (v/v) MeOH in $CHCl_3$.

(b) *Carbaryl std solns.*—(*1*) *8 mg/mL.*—Transfer 0.12±0.01 g carbaryl (anal. grade, available from Union Carbide Corp., Agricultural Products and Services), weighed to nearest 0.1 mg, to culture tube. Pipet 15 mL MeOH-$CHCl_3$ soln into tube, cap securely, and rotate or shake mech. 30 min. (*2*) *2.5 mg/mL.*—Transfer 0.25±0.01 g carbaryl, weighed to nearest 0.1 mg, to 250 mL g-s erlenmeyer. Pipet 100 mL $CHCl_3$ into flask, stopper, and swirl to dissolve.

6.322 ***Preparation of Sample***

(a) *Carbaryl dust and powder formulations.*— Transfer weighed sample (≤2.4 g) contg 0.12±0.01 g carbaryl to culture tube. Pipet 15 mL MeOH-$CHCl_3$ soln into tube and cap securely. Rotate or shake mech. 30 min and centrf. 10 min.

(b) *Liquid suspensions.*—Following steps must be performed in order described, as any deviation can cause erroneous results due to faulty sample transfer and incomplete extn: Place ca 20 g Na_2SO_4 in 250 mL g-s erlenmeyer. Pipet 100 mL $CHCl_3$ into flask. Vigorously shake sample bottle. Draw appropriate vol. sample into hypodermic syringe without needle. Use ca 0.5 mL sample for carbaryl 4 lb/gal. and ca 1.0 mL for carbaryl 2 lb/gal. Wipe outside of syringe with paper towel and weigh syringe and contents to nearest 0.1 mg. Add sample to erlenmeyer by slowly depressing syringe plunger. Do not let syringe or sample touch sides of flask. Sample must drop into $CHCl_3$. Reweigh syringe and calc. sample wt by difference. Stopper flask and shake vigorously 30 min on mech. shaker.

6.323 ***Determination***

(a) *Carbaryl dust and powder formulations.*—Using matched 0.2 mm NaCl cells, scan sample soln against MeOH-$CHCl_3$ soln from 5.2 to 6.0 μm (1900–1600 cm^{-1}). Repeat scan with std soln. Measure A of carbaryl peak at 5.75 μm (1740 cm^{-1}), using A at 5.40 μm (1850 cm^{-1}) as 0 point. A = ca 0.4 for both std and sample.

$$\% \text{ Carbaryl by wt} = (A \times B' \times P)/(A' \times B),$$

where A and A' = absorbance of sample and std, resp., at 5.75 μm; B and B' = mg sample and mg std/mL, resp.; and P = % purity of carbaryl std.

(b) *Liquid suspensions.*—Proceed as in **(a)**, except use matched 0.5 mm NaCl cells and scan sample soln against $CHCl_3$.

2,2-Dichlorovinyl Dimethyl Phosphate
(DDVP) (*83*)—Official First Action

Method I

(Applicable to sand/sugar base fly bait contg ca 0.5% and 4 lb/gal. DDVP emulsifiable concs. *Caution: See* **51.041**.)

6.324 ***Apparatus and Reagent***

(a) *Infrared spectrophotometer.*—Capable of recording in region 2–15 μm. Slit width must be adjustable to give signal-to-noise ratio of ca 100:1; with sealed liq. absorption cell, NaCl windows, and 0.2 mm path length.

(b) *Hypodermic syringe.*—Luer type, glass, 1.0 mL. Use 18 gage (Stubbs), 2″ slip-on needle.

(c) *2,2-Dichlorovinyl dimethyl phosphate.*—Use std DDVP of known purity. (Available from Shell Chemical Co.)

6.325 ***Calibration of Apparatus***

Into each of five 10 mL vol. flasks, weigh, to nearest 0.1 mg, 25, 75, 100, 150, and 200 mg DDVP std, and dil. to vol. with $CHCl_3$. Calibration solns contain ca 2.5, 7.5, 10, 15, and 20 g DDVP/L.

Fill sealed liq. absorption cell with $CHCl_3$, adjust spectrophtr to optimum settings, and scan over 10.7–9.9 μm. Without changing settings, fill cell in turn with each of prepd calibration solns, starting with most dil., and scan each soln over 10.7–9.9 μm.

For each scan, construct baseline thru absorption min. at ca 10.0 μm parallel to 0 radiation line. Draw perpendicular to 0 radiation line thru absorption max. of calibration soln at ca 10.2 μm and measure radiant power P_0 (at 10.0 μm) and P (at 10.2 μm), in any convenient units but keeping same units thruout. Calc. A as log (P_0/P). Repeat calcns, using absorption min. at ca 10.5 μm as ref. point.

Subtract A of cell and $CHCl_3$ obtained above from A of cell and calibration solns. Plot ΔA of DDVP as ordinate against g/L DDVP as abscissa for each ref. point (10.0 and 10.5 μm).

6.326 ***Preparation of Sample Solution***

(a) *Sand/sugar base fly baits.*—Prep. 25 × 400 mm extn column by adding enough diat. earth (Hyflo Super-Cel) to make layer 5 cm high when gently packed. Place 250 mL vol. flask under outlet. Accurately weigh sample contg 0.2–1.0 g DDVP. Transfer sample to extn column with $CHCl_3$, and rinse sample container with $CHCl_3$.

Working in well-ventilated hood, add 50 mL $CHCl_3$ to column. Using stirring device, vigorously agitate sample and top half of adsorbent layer to form slurry with solv. Withdraw stirring device, and rinse it and column with addnl $CHCl_3$ from wash bottle. Let solv. percolate thru column until level is few mm above diat. earth-sample layer.

Add ca 50 mL $CHCl_3$ to column, agitate sample and diat. earth with stirrer as above, and let solv. percolate thru column until upper level approaches sample layer. Repeat with two addnl 50 mL portions $CHCl_3$. When solv. ht has diminished to 2–3 mm, rinse column with three 10 mL portions $CHCl_3$, letting each portion enter diat. earth layer before adding next. Let column drain and rinse outlet tip with $CHCl_3$, collecting rinse in 250 mL vol. flask.

Transfer $CHCl_3$ eluate to evapg dish (125 mm diam.) marked at 40–50 mL. Evap. on steam bath to 40–50 mL. Remove dish and continue evapn at room temp. to 10–15 mL. Using $CHCl_3$, quant. transfer to vol. flask of such size to give DDVP concn of 0.5–1.0 g/100 mL when soln is dild to vol.

(b) *Emulsifiable concentrates.*—Weigh enough sample, to nearest 0.2 mg, to give ca 1 g DDVP/100 mL $CHCl_3$ when dild to vol. in 10, 25, or 50 mL vol. flask.

6.327 ***Determination***

Dil. $CHCl_3$ soln of DDVP to vol. with $CHCl_3$, mix thoroly, and fill calibrated liq. absorption cell with sample soln. Using same instrument settings as for calibration, scan sample soln over 10.7–9.9 μm.

Examine spectra for possible interference and use appropriate absorption min. as ref. point. (If solvs or other ingredients interfere at one of ref. points, use alternative ref. point.) For example, β-naphthol, often used as stabilizer in fly baits, exts with $CHCl_3$ and absorbs at ca 10.5 μm, requiring use of 10.0 μm ref. point.

Calc. *A* of sample soln as in **6.325**.

From calcd *A*, read g DDVP/L from calibration curve.

% DDVP by wt = [(g DDVP/L) × mL sample soln]/(10 × g sample).

Method II (84)

(Applicable to ca 0.5% (w/w) spray soln and ca 1.0% (w/w) cattle spray in hydrocarbon solvs)

6.328 ***Apparatus and Reagent***

(a) *Infrared spectrophotometer.*—Double beam instrument with specifications as in **6.324(a)**.

(b) *2,2-Dichlorovinyl dimethyl phosphate.—See* **6.324(c)**.

6.329 ***Preparation of Compensating Solvent***

Transfer ca 30 mL sample to 125 mL separator and ext (2–3 min per extn) with 4 ca 30 mL portions 0.5*N* NaOH. Dry DDVP-free hydrocarbon phase by passing it thru 2–3 g anhyd. Na_2SO_4. Reserve dried solv. for prepn of DDVP std soln and as compensating solv. in ref. cell.

6.330 ***Determination***

Prep. std DDVP soln in compensating solv. that approximates (on wt basis) DDVP content of sample. Calc. DDVP content of std soln to nearest 0.01% by wt.

After detg optimum instrument parameters for compensation technic, scan std soln over 9.9–10.7 μm (1010–935 cm^{-1}) region with ref. cell contg compensating solv. in ref. beam of spectrophtr. Scan sample against compensating solv. in same manner.

From differential spectra, det. *A* of DDVP at 10.2 μm (980 cm^{-1}) of std, *A'*, and sample, *A*, measured from baseline drawn between minima near 10.0 and 10.6 μm. Calc. DDVP as follows:

% DDVP by wt = % DDVP in std × A/A'.

6.331 Diazinon—Official First Action

See **6.431–6.435**.

Diquat (6,7-Dihydrodipyrido (1,2-*a*:2′,1′-*c*) Pyrazinediium Ion) (*85*)—Official Final Action

AOAC-CIPAC Method

6.332 ***Reagents***

(a) *Acetate buffer soln.*—pH 4.05. Dissolve 10.88 g NaOAc $.3H_2O$ in H_2O, add 19 mL HOAc, dil. to 2 L with H_2O, and mix.

(b) *Diquat std solns.*—*(1) Stock soln.*—0.2 mg diquat/mL. Prep. stock soln by dissolving 0.1968 g pure diquat dibromide monohydrate ($C_{12}H_{12}N_2Br_2.H_2O$, MW 362.1; 50.87% cation; available from Chevron Chemical Co., 940 Hensley St, Richmond, CA 94804) in buffer soln, dil. to 500 mL with buffer soln, and mix. *(2) Working soln.*—0.02 mg diquat/mL. Dil. 10.0 mL stock soln to 100 mL with buffer soln. Prep. dild stds fresh as required.

6.333 ***Determination***

Using buret, transfer 10.0, 20.0, and 30.0 mL std diquat soln, contg 0.2, 0.4, and 0.6 mg diquat, resp., to three 100 mL vol. flasks, dil. each soln to vol. with buffer soln, and mix. Measure *A* of stds at 310 nm in 1 cm silica cell, with buffer soln as ref., and draw std curve relating *A* to mg diquat.

Accurately weigh portion (*w* g) of well mixed sample contg ca 0.5 g diquat, transfer to 250 mL vol. flask, dil. to vol. with buffer soln, and mix (*Soln 1*). Transfer 10.0 mL *Soln 1* to 200 mL vol. flask, dil. to vol. with buffer soln, and mix (*Soln 2*). Transfer 5.0 mL *Soln 2* to 100 mL vol. flask, dil. to vol. with buffer soln, and mix (*Soln 3*).

Measure *A* of *Soln 3* at 310 nm in 1 cm silica cell, with buffer soln as ref. Read diquat content of *Soln 3* (*y* mg) directly from std curve or calc. diquat content by interpolation.

% Diquat, w/w = 100 y/w.

Paraquat (1,1′-Dimethyl-4,4′-bipyridinium Ion) (*85*)—Official Final Action

6.334 ***Reagents***

(a) *Sodium dithionite.*—1% soln in 0.1*N* NaOH. (Sodium dithionite, $Na_2S_2O_4.2H_2O$, is also called sodium hydrosulfite and sodium hyposulfite.) Do *not* keep soln >3 hr; solid is unstable in presence of moisture. Store solid in small air-tight bottles in vac. desiccator.

(b) *Paraquat std soln.*—0.25 mg paraquat/mL. Dry anal. std (available from Chevron Chemical Co., 940 Hensley St, Richmond, CA 94804) to const wt at 100–120° before weighing (paraquat salts are hygroscopic). Dissolve 0.1728 g paraquat dichloride (72.40% cation) in H_2O, dil. to 500 mL with H_2O, and mix. Prep. soln fresh as required.

(c) *Extracting soln.*—Dissolve 11 g $Na_2SO_4.10H_2O$ in 500 mL H_2O, add 500 mL alcohol, and mix.

6.335 ***Preparation of Standard Curve***

Pipet 50 mL std soln into 250 mL vol. flask, dil. to vol. with H_2O, and mix. Pipet 5, 10, 15, and 20 mL aliquots of this dild std soln into sep. 100 mL vol. flasks. (When dild to vol. these solns contain 2.5, 5.0, 7.5, and 10.0 μg paraquat/mL, resp.) Proceed as in **6.337**. Plot *A* against μg paraquat/mL at final diln.

6.336 ***Preparation of Sample***

(*Caution:* Open aerosol can behind safety shield.)

(a) *Formulations not containing oil base.*—Accurately weigh portion well mixed sample contg ca 0.25 g paraquat. Transfer to 500 mL vol. flask, dil. to vol. with H_2O, and mix well (*Soln 1*). Pipet 10 mL *Soln 1* into 100 mL vol. flask, dil. to vol. with H_2O, and mix well (*Soln 2*). Pipet 10 mL *Soln 2* into 100 mL vol. flask and proceed as in **6.337**.

(**b**) *Aerosol formulations containing oil base.*—Weigh aerosol can to nearest 0.1 g (*C*). Clamp can with bottom up and puncture smallest possible hole with punch and hammer. After hiss of escaping propellent is no longer heard, cut bottom ⅞ open with hand can opener. Push nearly detached lid into can. Immerse can 15 min in 50–70° H_2O bath or in hot tap H_2O running into 1 L beaker.

Add 50 mL extg soln, (**c**), and 50 mL *pentane* to 250 mL separator. Remove can from H_2O bath, dry well (especially inside cap and around valve), and weigh (*D*). Place pipet with capacity to deliver ca 20 mg paraquat in can, and weigh both (*E*). Withdraw liq., transfer contents to separator, replace pipet in can, and weigh (*F*). (Disregard material left in and on pipet.) Empty can, rinse completely with acetone, air dry, and weigh (*G*).

Stopper separator and shake 30 sec, venting frequently. Let layers sep, and drain lower layer into 200 mL vol. flask. Add 25 mL extg soln to separator, repeat extn, and drain lower layer into same vol. flask. Dil. to vol. with extg soln and mix well. Pipet 5 mL into 100 mL vol. flask and proceed as in **6.337**.

6.337 ***Determination***

(Complete analysis of one soln before adding dithionite to next soln.)

Add 10 mL Na dithionite soln to one 100 mL vol. flask and dil. to vol. with H_2O. Mix by inverting end-over-end 3 times at such speed that air bubble travels from one end to other; do *not* shake flask vigorously, as this tends to cause fading of color due to oxidn. Immediately measure *A* of soln at 600 nm, using reagent blank (no paraquat) to set the 100% *T* or for ref. side for dual beam instruments. Similarly, treat each flask in turn, completing color measurement without delay before adding dithionite to next soln.

% Paraquat = (μg/mL from std curve) × 5/g sample.

% Paraquat (in aerosol formulations) = [(μg/mL from std curve) × $(D - G)$ × 0.4]/[$(C - G) \times (E - F)$].

Dithiocarbamates (Ferbam, Maneb, Nabam, Zineb, and Ziram)

(*Caution: See* **51.041**.)

Carbon Disulfide Evolution Method (86) *Official Final Action*

(Applicable only to concs or formulations free from interfering substances)

6.338 ***Principle***

Dithiocarbamates decompose on heating in acid medium. Evolved CS_2 is passed thru $Pb(OAc)_2$ soln traps to remove H_2S and SO_2 formed from sample impurities. Washed CS_2 is reacted with methanolic KOH, and xanthate formed is titrd with I soln.

6.339 ***Apparatus***

Carbon disulfide evolution apparatus.—See Fig. **6:07**. Available from Scientific Glass Apparatus Co., No. JE-1000.

6.340 ***Reagent***

Methanolic potassium hydroxide.—2*N*. Dissolve 112 g KOH pellets in 500 mL anhyd. MeOH, filter thru cotton, and add addnl 500 mL anhyd. MeOH.

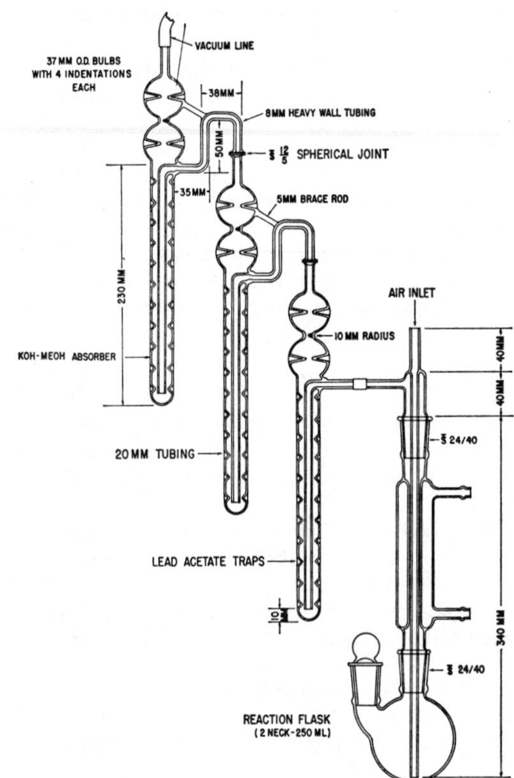

FIG. 6:07—Carbon disulfide evolution apparatus

6.341 ***Determination***

Add 20 mL 10% $Pb(OAc)_2$ soln to each $Pb(OAc)_2$ trap and pipet 50 mL 2*N* MeOH-KOH soln into MeOH-KOH absorber (Fig. **6:07**). (Absorber must be dry at time of addn and kept at 25±1°.) Add 50 mL H_2SO_4 (1+4) to reaction flask and heat acid to boiling. Adjust aspiration rate to ≤1 bubble/sec thru MeOH-KOH soln, using stopper in reaction flask.

Weigh ≤5 g sample (contg 0.1–0.3 g dithiocarbamates) into small filter paper cone and fold cone to prevent sample loss. Remove stopper from reaction flask, insert wrapped sample, and immediately stopper flask. Adjust air flow if necessary and maintain steady, moderate boil. Do not let acid soln enter air inlet tube. Some dust formulations react vigorously and require special care to prevent ejection of hot acid. As reaction proceeds, adjust system so that rates of boiling and aspiration are almost in equilibrium, producing only very slow rate of bubbling thru MeOH-KOH soln. Continue boiling 1.5 hr. Disconnect MeOH-KOH absorber and rinse contents into 500 mL erlenmeyer, using ca 250 mL H_2O. (To remove absorber contents, apply slight air pressure to top of absorber and force soln thru side arm. Rinse with 4 ca 25 mL portions H_2O, forcing out rinse H_2O in same manner with air pressure.)

Add 3 drops phthln, and titr. with 30% HOAc until red just disappears. Immediately titr. with 0.1*N* I; near end point, add 5 mL starch indicator soln, **6.005(f)**, and titr. to faint but definite color change.

Det. blank (usually 0.1–0.2 mL 0.1*N* I) by dilg 50 mL MeOH-KOH soln with 250 mL H_2O, neutzg with 30% HOAc, and titrg as above.

Calc. % dithiocarbamate = (Sample titrn − blank) × (I normality) × (equiv. wt dithiocarbamate)/(g sample × 10).

Equiv. wts (½ MW) of zineb, maneb, ziram, nabam, and (⅓ MW) ferbam are 137.87, 132.65, 152.91,128.18, and 138.82, resp.

Thiram (Bis(dimethylthiocarbamoyl)disulfide) (Tetramethylthiuram Disulfide)

CIPAC Method (87)—Official Final Action

6.342 ***Principle***

Thiram is decomposed by boiling with HOAc and $Zn(OAc)_2$ to Me_2NH, CS_2, and carbonyl sulfide. The gaseous mixt. is carried by air stream thru $CdSO_4$ scrubber to remove H_2S, and then into absorption system contg MeOH-KOH soln. Mixed xanthate-monothiocarbamate soln is neutzd and titrd with std aq. I.

Method is not specific for thiram. Sep. characterization test, **29.171**, must be made.

6.343 ***Apparatus***

Assembly and operating conditions.—Assemble app. as shown in Fig. **6:08** with 30 mL $CdSO_4$ soln in first absorber, 25 mL KOH soln in second absorber, and 5 mL in each bubbler. Turn on condenser H_2O and maintain H_2O bath surrounding $CdSO_4$ scrubber at 70–80° thruout test. Keep main KOH absorber at <25° by immersion in beaker of cold H_2O. Absorber must be dry or rinsed with MeOH before adding KOH soln. Air bleed must reach nearly to bottom of digestion flask. Make all joints gas-tight, using small amts H_3PO_4, petrolatum, or silicone grease.

Check app. for absorber leaks and efficiency periodically, using pure Na diethyldithiocarbamate. Recoveries should be 99–101%. Check purity of Na diethyldithiocarbamate by dissolving ca 0.5 g, accurately weighed, in 100 mL H_2O and titrg directly with 0.1*N* I, using ca 2% starch soln as indicator. 1 mL 0.1*N* I = 0.02253 g Na diethyldithiocarbamate. % Na diethyldithiocarbamate = 2.253 × mL 0.1*N* I/g sample.

6.344 ***Reagents***

(**a**) *Acid mixture.*—Dissolve 2.5 g ZnO in 100 mL HOAc (1+1).

(**b**) *Cadmium sulfate soln.*—Dissolve 18.5 g $3CdSO_4.8H_2O$ in 100 mL H_2O.

(**c**) *Potassium hydroxide soln.*—2*N* in MeOH and contg <1 ppm Cu or Fe.

(**d**) *Iodine std soln.*—0.1*N*. Stdze as in **50.019**.

6.345 ***Determination***

Accurately weigh and transfer sample contg ca 0.3 g thiram to digestion flask, using small amt H_2O, if necessary. Assemble air bleed and dropping funnel, Fig. **6:08**, and add 20 mL acid mixt. thru funnel. Connect app. to controlled aspiration (vac. or compressed air) so that ca 3 bubbles/sec pass thru absorbers. After sample is evenly dispersed, heat and reflux 30 min at moderate rate. Turn off cooling H_2O and flush condenser and first absorber with steam from flask ≤1 min. Remove burner and disconnect train. Wash contents of KOH absorber and bubblers into 600 mL beaker with 300–400 mL H_2O, add 1–2 drops phthln, just neutze with HOAc (1+9) from buret, and add 3 drops excess. With continual stirring, titr. immediately (preferably within 1 min, as decomposition of mixed xanthate/monothiocarbamate soln is extremely rapid under acidic conditions) with 0.1*N* I (*t* mL), using ca 2% starch soln as indicator. Det. blank in same manner, omitting sample (*b* mL). 1 mL 0.1*N* I = 0.01202 g thiram.

% Thiram = 1.202 $(t - b)$/g sample.

Dodine (n-Dodecylguanidine acetate) (*88*) Official Final Action

(*Caution: See* **51.022**, **51.028**(**a**) and (**d**), and **51.041**.)

6.346 ***Reagents***

(**a**) *Perchloric acid.*—0.05*N*. Dissolve 4.2 mL 72% $HClO_4$ in HOAc and dil. to 1 L with HOAc. Stdze as follows: Accurately weigh 0.200 g $KHC_8H_4O_4$ into 250 mL erlenmeyer. Dissolve in 20 mL HOAc by gently heating flask on hot plate. Add 80 mL Ac_2O and 8 drops metanil yellow indicator, (**b**). Place erlenmeyer contg bar on mag. stirrer and titr. with $HClO_4$ to first definite red (magenta). Titr. reagent blank and correct sample titer.

Normality = 0.200/(0.20422 × net mL $HClO_4$)

(**b**) *Metanil yellow.*—0.20%. Dissolve 0.200 g metanil yellow powder in 100 mL MeOH.

(**c**) *Potassium acid phthalate.*—NBS SRM $KHC_8H_4O_4$.

6.347 ***Determination***

Accurately weigh sample contg ca 0.600 g dodine into 250 mL erlenmeyer. Add 10 mL HOAc followed by 90 mL Ac_2O. Mix by swirling 5 min. Filter slurry with vac. thru large, medium porosity fritted glass buchner into 250 mL vac. flask. Wash erlenmeyer and residue in funnel with two 10 mL portions HOAc-Ac_2O (10+90). Place vac. flask contg bar on mag. stirrer, add 8 drops metanil yellow indicator, and titr. with stdzd ca 0.05*N* $HClO_4$ to first definite red (magenta). Titr. reagent blank and correct sample titer.

% Dodecylguanidine acetate
= (net mL $HClO_4$ × normality × 28.75)/g sample

Formaldehyde in Solutions—Official Final Action

Hydrogen Peroxide Method (89)

6.348 ***Reagents***

(**a**) *Sulfuric acid std soln.*—1*N*. Prep. and stdze as in **50.039–50.041**.

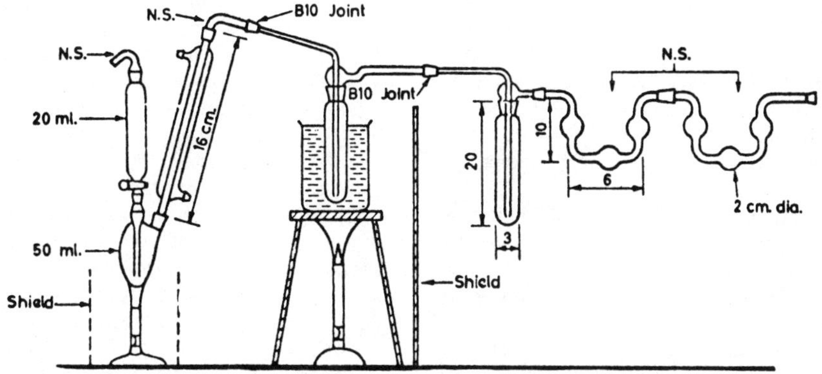

FIG. 6:08—Absorption system for thiram. Dimensions in cm; N.S. = nonstandard; B10 = $\overline{\mathrm{T}}$ 10/30

(**b**) *Sodium hydroxide std soln.*—1*N*. Stdze against (**a**), using litmus or bromothymol blue indicator. 1 mL = 30.03 mg HCHO.

(**c**) *Hydrogen peroxide soln.*—Com., contg ca 3% H_2O_2. If acid, neutze with NaOH, (**b**), using litmus or bromothymol blue indicator.

(**d**) *Litmus indicator.*—Soln. of purified litmus of such concn that 3 drops gives distinct blue color to 50 mL H_2O.

(**e**) *Bromothymol blue indicator.*—Dissolve 1 g bromothymol blue in 500 mL alcohol, 50% by vol.

6.349 ***Determination***

Pipet 50 mL 1*N* NaOH soln into 500 mL erlenmeyer and add 50 mL H_2O_2, (**c**). Add weighed amt sample (ca 3 g) from weighing pipet, letting point of pipet reach nearly to liq. in flask. Place funnel in neck of flask and heat on steam bath 5 min, shaking occasionally. Remove from bath, wash funnel with H_2O, cool to room temp., and titr. excess NaOH with std acid, using bromothymol blue or litmus. (Cool flask before titrn to obtain sharp end point with litmus.) From mL 1*N* NaOH used and wt sample, calc. % HCHO according to following equation

$$NaOH + HCHO + H_2O_2 = HCOONa + 2H_2O.$$

If HCHO soln contains appreciable free acid, titr. sep. portion and calc. acidity as % HCOOH. Correct for this acidity in calcg % HCHO.

6.350 ***Cyanide Method (90)***

(Applicable only to dil. solns)

Treat 15 mL 0.1*N* $AgNO_3$, **50.027–50.029**, with 6 drops HNO_3 (1+1) in 50 mL vol. flask, add 10 mL *KCN soln* (3.1 g in 500 mL H_2O), dil. to vol., shake well, filter thru dry filter, and titr. 25 mL filtrate with 0.1*N* NH_4SCN, **50.003–50.004**, as in **3.074**. Acidify another 15 mL portion 0.1 *N* $AgNO_3$ with 6 drops HNO_3 (1+1) and treat with 10 mL of the KCN soln to which has been added measured amt of sample (wt calcd from sp gr) contg ≤25 mg HCHO. Dil. to 50 mL, filter, and titr. 25 mL aliquot with the 0.1*N* NH_4SCN as before. Difference between mL NH_4SCN used in these 2 titrns × 2 = mL 0.1*N* NH_4SCN corresponding to KCN used by the HCHO. Calc. % HCHO present. 1 mL 0.1*N* NH_4SCN = 3.003 mg HCHO.

6.351 **Formaldehyde in Seed Disinfectants (*91*)**
Official Final Action

(Applicable to detn of HCHO absorbed in inert carrier, e.g., bentonite, talc, charcoal, sawdust)

Weigh ca 5 g sample contg 0.3–0.5 g HCHO in weighing bottle and transfer to 800 mL Kjeldahl flask. Add 25 mL H_2O and 12 mL H_2SO_4 (1+4). Steam distil rapidly, passing vapors thru condenser with delivery end dipping into 25 mL H_2O in 500 mL vol. flask. Collect ca 450 mL distillate, keeping vol. in distg flask nearly const with aid of small flame. After distn, wash delivery tube, and dil. distillate to vol. with H_2O.

Into each of two 200 mL vol. flasks measure 20 mL 0.1*N* $AgNO_3$. To each flask add 12 drops HNO_3 (1+1) and 30 mL H_2O. To one flask add slowly, with const shaking, 30 mL *KCN soln* (3.1 g in 1 L H_2O). Dil. to vol., shake well, and filter thru dry filter. To 100 mL filtrate add 3 mL HNO_3 and 5 mL ferric indicator, **6.019**(**e**), and titr. with 0.1*N* KSCN.

Pipet 25 mL HCHO distillate into small beaker contg 30 mL of the KCN soln, mix well, and add slowly, with const shaking, to second flask contg the acidified $AgNO_3$ soln. Dil. to vol. with H_2O, filter, acidify 100 mL filtrate with 3 mL HNO_3, and titr. with the KSCN soln, using $FeNH_4(SO_4)_2$ indicator.

Difference between mL KSCN soln used in these 2 titrns × 2 = mL 0.1*N* KSCN equiv. to HCHO. Calc. % HCHO present. 1 mL 0.1*N* KSCN = 3.003 mg HCHO.

Ethion (*O,O,O′,O′*-Tetraethyl *S,S′*-methylene bis-phosphorodithioate)

High Performance Liquid Chromatographic Method (92)
Official First Action

(Applicable to dry and liquid formulations contg ethion as only active ingredient.)

6.352 ***Apparatus***

(**a**) *Liquid chromatograph.*—Waters Associates with Model 6000A pump, or equiv., with 254 nm UV detector (Waters Associates, Inc). Typical operating conditions: eluant flow rate 1 mL/min (ca 1100 psi), chart speed 0.25 in./min, detector sensitivity 0.2 *A* unit full scale, ambient temp, injection vol. 10 μL. Adjust operating conditions to elute ethion peak in 6±2 min. Column condition and H_2O content of MeOH eluant can change retention times. Ethion peak must be sepd completely from internal std peak which normally elutes in ca 7 min (Waters C_{18} column).

(**b**) *Liquid chromatographic column.*—Either (*1*) Waters μBondapak C_{18}, 300 × 3.9 mm id; or (*2*) DuPont ODS Permaphase, 0.5 m × 2.1 mm id.

6.353 ***Reagents***

(**a**) *Eluant.*—Either (*1*) *degassed MeOH-H_2O* (90+10), UV cutoff <230 nm, or (*2*) *degassed acetonitrile-H_2O* (40+60), UV cutoff <230 nm.

(**b**) *Light mineral oil.*—USP, viscosity 38.1 centistokes at 37.8°.

(**c**) *Internal std soln.*—(*1*) *For Waters column.*—Accurately weigh ca 0.24 g pentachloronitrobenzene (PCNB), ref. grade, with no interfering peaks on HPLC, into 200 mL vol. flask. Dil. to vol. with MeOH and mix. (*2*) *For DuPont column.*—Using CH_3CN as solv., vary amt PCNB in internal std to give peak ht approx. same as ethion peak.

(**d**) *Ethion std solns.*—(*1*) *For Waters column.*—*Stock soln.*—Accurately weigh amt of std equiv. to 250 mg ethion, 95+% pure (available from Chemical and Biological Investigations, Environmental Protection Agency, Beltsville, MD 20705) into 25 mL vol. flask, dil. to vol. with MeOH, and mix. *Working soln.*—Pipet 10 mL stock soln into 50 mL vol flask, pipet 10 mL internal std soln, (**c**)(*1*), into flask, dil. to vol. with MeOH, and mix. Prep. std and samples daily. (*2*) *For DuPont column.*—Prep. as above, using CH_3CN instead of MeOH. (*3*) *For oil formulations.*—Pipet 10 mL 1% stock soln (*1*) or (*2*) into 50 mL vol. flask contg ca same wt of light mineral oil as sample. Add 20 mL MeOH (or CH_3CN) and proceed as in **6.354**(**c**) beginning with "Stopper and agitate . . ."

6.354 ***Preparation of Sample***

(**a**) *Dry powder.*—Accurately weigh sample contg ca 100 mg ethion into 250 mL g-s flask. Pipet in 40 mL MeOH (or CH_3CN) and 10 mL internal std soln. Shake 30 min on mech. shaker and centrf. to sep. phases.

(**b**) *Liquid concentrates.*—Prep. sample as in **6.353**(**d**).

(**c**) *Oil formulations.*—Accurately weigh sample contg ca 100 mg ethion into 50 mL vol. flask. Add 30 mL MeOH (or CH_3CN). Stopper and agitate vigorously 1 min, with side to side action, keeping mixt. in main body of flask. Pipet in 4 mL H_2O and repeat vigorous mixing 1 min. Dil. to approx. vol. with MeOH (or CH_3CN). Cool to ambient temp and dil. to vol. Mix thoroly by inverting 10 times and swirling vigorously each time. Centrf. to sep. phases.

6.355 ***Determination***

Use high-pressure liq. syringe or sample injection loop to inject 10 μL portions of std until 2 peak ht ratios agree within ±1%. Alternately inject two 10 μL portions each of sample and std solns. Measure peak hts and calc. av. peak ht ratios for both std and sample. Adjust attenuation or amt injected for convenient size peaks (60–80% full scale). Measure peak hts from baseline between ethion and internal std peaks.

$$\% \text{ Ethion} = (R/R') \times (W'/W) \times P,$$

where R and R' = av. peak ht ratios for sample and std, resp.; W' = mg ethion in working std soln (ca 100 mg); W = mg sample in final diln; and P = % purity of std.

Formothion [*S*-[2-(Formyl methylamino)-2-oxoethyl] *O,O*-dimethyl phosphorodithioate; *O,O*-Dimethyl *S*-(*N*-formyl-2-mercapto-*N*-methylacetamide) phosphorodithioate] (*93*)—Official Final Action

CIPAC-AOAC Method

6.356 ***Reagents***

(**a**) *Solvent I.*—Toluene contg 2% Ac_2O.

(**b**) *Solvent II.*—Hexane-acetone (2+1) plus 2% Ac_2O.

(**c**) *Internal std soln.*—Prep. soln contg ca 100 mg, accurately weighed, of ethion/mL solv. I. Ethion must be >95% pure and contain no impurities interfering at formothion retention time.

(**d**) *Reference std soln.*—Accurately weigh ca 500 mg Formothion Ref. Std (Sandoz Ltd, Agrochemical Division, CH4002 Basel, Switzerland) into 50 mL vol. flask, add 5.0 mL internal std soln, and dil. to vol. with solv. I.

6.357 ***Apparatus***

(**a**) *Gas chromatograph.*—(Varian Aerograph 1520, or equiv.) With flame photometric detector (Tracor, FPD 100AT, or equiv.), automatic injector (Hewlett-Packard 7600 A, or equiv.), integrator (Infotronics CRS 104, or equiv.), and effluent splitter at column end with ratio 1:100–1:1000 in favor of outlet. Use glass spiral column, 1.0 m × 3.6 mm id, packed with 3% OV 225 on 80–100 mesh Chromosorb W-HP. Operating conditions: temps (°)—oven 210, injector and detector 220; N carrier gas 60 mL/min; no. theoretical plates for ethion is ca 2000. Alternatively, flame ionization may be used. Conditions are same, except effluent splitter is not necessary.

(**b**) *Bottles.*—50 mL with Mininert valve, or equiv. inert system for closure (Pierce Chemical Co.).

6.358 ***Determination***

Accurately weigh well mixed sample contg ca 500 mg formothion into bottle, (**b**). Add 5.0 g internal std soln, (**c**), and dil. to 50 mL with solv. I. Close tightly and shake. Transfer 6 μL soln to vial contg 1 mL solv. II. Seal vial with inert valve system. (For automatic injections with Hewlett-Packard sampler, dil. in Al foil-sealed vials and use Teflon rubber laminated disks as septa.) Keep tightly closed. Inject 1.0 μL dild mixt. into column, bypassing solv. around detector by using splitter to avoid contamination and deterioration. Det. appropriate time for splitting by test chromatogram. Compds may be identified by retention times relative to ethion as 1.00 (ca 4.4 min): formothion 0.50, dimethoate (by-product) 0.36.

Inject 1 μL aliquots of reference std soln, (**d**), until ht or area ratio of formothion to ethion varies <2% for successive injections. Precede and follow each sample by reference std soln and make 3 sep. detns with all peak area ratios of reference std solns within ±2% of first accepted values.

$$\% \text{ Formothion} = W' \times H \times f \times P/W \times H',$$

where W and W' = mg sample and internal std, resp.; H and H' = peak hts or areas of formothion and internal std, resp.; P = % formothion in reference compd;

$$f = \text{correction factor} = w \times h'/w' \times h;$$

where w and w' = mg formothion ref. std and internal std, resp., and h and h' = peak hts or areas of formothion and internal std, resp.

Malathion (*O,O*-Dimethyl Dithiophosphate of Diethyl Mercaptosuccinate)

(*Caution: See* **51.011** and **51.061**.)

Argentimetric Method (94)—Official First Action

6.359 ***Principle***

Malathion is cleaved in alk. soln to dimethyl phosphorodithioate ion which forms insol. ppt with Ag ion. Pos. bias may be encountered.

6.360 ***Reagents***

(**a**) *Potassium hydroxide soln.*—1*N*. Dissolve 28 g KOH in 500 mL alcohol.

(**b**) *Silver nitrate soln.*—0.1*N*. Prep. as in **50.027** and stdze against primary NaCl as in **6.363**.

(**c**) *Cellulose powder.*—Reeve Angel No. CF-11.

6.361 ***Apparatus***

(**a**) *Potentiometer.*—Recording potentiometric titrator, operated in derivative mode (Metrohm Models E336 thru E576, or equiv.; available from Brinkman Instruments), or pH meter with mv scale.

(**b**) *Glass reference electrode with Ag/AgCl internal element.*—Corning Glass Works, No. 476022.

(**c**) *Silver billet electrode.*—Beckman Instruments, No. 39261.

(**d**) *Chromatographic tube.*—30 cm × 13.5 mm id.

6.362 ***Preparation of Samples***

(**a**) *Technical grade malathion or malathion emulsifiable concentrates.*—Place 2 g cellulose powder in 50 mL beaker, add 0.6 g H_2O dropwise, and mix thoroly. Place plug of glass wool in bottom of chromatgc tube and pack with the wetted cellulose powder. Compress column to 5 cm with glass rod. Wet column with 5 mL hexane.

Accurately weigh sample contg 0.5±0.1 g malathion into 250 mL beaker, add 50 mL hexane, and stir 10 min, using mag. stirrer. Transfer to column and collect eluate in another 250 mL beaker. Rinse original beaker with three 20 mL portions hexane and pour each thru column. Carefully evap. eluate just to dryness. Add 50 mL alcohol or isopropanol and stir mag.; add 20 mL 1*N* KOH and stir 1 min more. Add 50 mL H_2O and 20 mL 2*N* HNO_3, and stir.

(**b**) *Powder formulations.*—Accurately weigh sample contg 0.5±0.1 g malathion into 250 mL beaker, add 50 mL hexane, cover with watch glass, and stir mag. 20 min at high speed without splashing. Filter thru fiber glass paper in 4.25 cm buchner and quant. recover filtrate. Thoroly wash beaker and funnel with two 20 mL portions hexane. Quant. transfer filtrate to 250 mL beaker and evap. hexane just to dryness. Add 50 mL alcohol or isopropanol and stir mag.; add 20 mL 1*N* KOH and stir 1 min more. Add 50 mL H_2O and 20 mL 2*N* HNO_3, and stir.

6.363 ***Determination***

(**a**) *pH meter.*—Immerse electrodes in soln and set pH meter to read absolute mv. Titr. with 0.1*N* $AgNO_3$ soln until meter reads ca 520 mv (within 1–2 mL of end point). Continue titrn by dropwise addn of titrant to end point, 425 mv.

(**b**) *Recording potentiometric titrator.*—Set instrument in derivative mode and titr. at 2.0±0.2 mL 0.1*N* $AgNO_3$ soln/min to within ca 2 mL of expected end point. Decrease rate to 0.7±0.1 mL/min and continue titrn. Take first inflection in titrn curve as end point.

$$\% \text{ Malathion} = (V \times N \times 33.04)/W,$$

where V = mL $AgNO_3$ soln, N = normality of $AgNO_3$ soln, and W = g sample.

Colorimetric Method (95)—Official First Action

(Caution: See **51.018**, **51.040**, **51.041**, **51.043**, and **51.051**.)

6.364 ***Principle***

Malathion, *S*-(1,2-dicarbethoxyethyl) *O,O*-dimethyl phosphorodithioate, is decomposed by alkali in alcohol to Na *O,O*-dimethyl phosphorodithioate (NaDMTA), Na fumarate, and alcohol. NaDMTA is converted to Cu^{+2} complex sol. in cyclohexane with formation of intense yellow compd whose intensity is proportional to concn of *O,O*-dimethyl phosphorodithioic acid and which is measured colorimetrically at 420 nm. Pos. bias may be encountered.

6.365 ***Precautions***

Vol. of nonaq. solns is highly temp. dependent. Maintain all reagents at uniform temp.

All glassware must be clean and dry. Rinse tubes and pipets with MeOH and oven dry before use. After use, rinse all glassware in contact with Cu reagent with acetone before washing to prevent contamination in future analyses. If difficulties are still encountered, use 1% HCl in MeOH as wash prior to oven drying.

Det. *A* of blank against H_2O whenever new reagents are prepd. Deviation from range 0.010–0.020 *A* units, using 1 cm cells, indicates either contamination of glassware or reagents, or reagents of improper concn.

6.366 ***Reagents***

(**a**) *Cyclohexane.*—Pass thru column of activated silica gel or Al_2O_3, activity grade I. Accuracy of assay depends on stability of Cu complex which undergoes oxidn-reduction reaction catalyzed by strong proton donors. Net result is fading of developed color. Polar impurities in cyclohexane contribute to this problem and quality of solv. must be checked as follows before continuing with analysis: Perform detn, **6.368**, with std soln (**b**)(*1*) or (*2*) and det. *A* at 2 min and again at 12 min. Calc. fade rate (*FR*) as follows:

$$FR = [(A_{2\ min} - A_{12\ min}) \times 100]/(A_{2\ min} \times 10)$$

Fade rate should be ≤0.5%/min for std or samples. If fade rate exceeds that limit, pass cyclohexane thru silica gel or Al_2O_3 column contg ca 100 g adsorbent/2 L cyclohexane to be treated. Ratio of ht of adsorbent bed to its diam. should be >5 and flow should be ≤3 mL/min. Retest cyclohexane after treatment to det. its acceptability. Vol. of cyclohexane that can be treated in this manner will depend on extent of contamination. Check purity periodically.

(**b**) *Analytical stds.*—Use either malathion or KDMTA, anal. grade of known purity (available from American Cyanamid Co.), for std soln. Use of malathion will provide assurance that quant. elimination reaction is taking place. Store malathion in refrigerator, warming to room temp. before use. Store KDMTA in desiccator, avoiding elevated temp.

(*1*) *Malathion std solns.*—Accurately weigh 130–170 mg malathion into tared 50 mL vol. flask. Dissolve in and dil. to vol. with cyclohexane. Store in refrigerator; use at room temp. (*2*) *Potassium O,O-dimethyl phosphorodithioate (KDMTA) std solns.*—Accurately weigh 80–120 mg KDMTA into tared 50 mL vol. flask. Dissolve in and dil. to vol. with acetone. Mix. Store in tightly stoppered flask.

(**c**) *Copper reagent.*—Dissolve 410–430 mg cupric naphthenate (ICN–K&K Laboratories, Inc., No. 8172) or 8% Cu Nap-All liq. (Mooney Chemicals Inc., 2301 Scranton Rd, Cleveland, OH 44113) in 100 mL cyclohexane.

(**d**) *Ethyl acetate.*—Contg ≤0.2% H_2O and with acidity ≤0.005% expressed as HOAc.

(**e**) *Sodium hydroxide soln.*—1*N*. Dissolve 4 g carbonate-free NaOH in 100 mL absolute alcohol or absolute ethanol denatured with 0.5% benzene.

(**f**) *Acetonitrile.*—Bp 80–82°. Pass thru column of silica gel, discarding yellow first portions of eluate and collecting colorless eluate. pH of 10% aq. soln should be 5–7.

6.367 ***Preparation of Sample***

(**a**) *Technical materials and emulsifiable concentrates.*—Accurately weigh sample contg 130–170 mg malathion into tared 50 mL vol. flask. Dissolve in and dil. to vol. with cyclohexane. Stopper flask and mix well.

(**b**) *Wettable powders and dusts.*—Accurately weigh sample contg 130–170 mg malathion on tared weighing paper. Transfer to 8 oz narrow-mouth bottle fitted with Vinylite-lined screw caps. Add 100 mL cyclohexane or acetone, using vol. flask. Place sample 10 min on reciprocating shaker set for moderate agitation. Let solids settle or centrf. if necessary. Alternatively, use 150 mL g-s erlenmeyer and mag. stirrer.

Cyclohexane will not quant. ext malathion from powders formulated with bentonite (montmorillonite, $Al_2(Si_4O_{10})(OH)_2$), and possibly with other carriers. In these cases, ext malathion with CH_3CN or tetrahydrofuran. If CH_3CN is used, evap. ext to dryness in rotary evaporator under vac. at ≤50°. Similarly evap. appropriate vol. CH_3CN for reagent blank. Carefully dissolve residue in cyclohexane and proceed with detn. If tetrahydrofuran is used, proceed as directed, incorporating tetrahydrofuran reagent blank. Use alternative extn technics whenever it is not known whether method will give adequate extn.

6.368 ***Determination***

Pipet 5 mL aliquots from (**a**) or 10 mL aliquots from (**b**) and appropriate dild stds to sep. 50 mL vol. flasks. Prep. reagent blanks by transferring 5 or 10 mL aliquots cyclohexane to 50 mL vol. flask. Use acetone in reagent blank if KDMTA is std.

At 1 min intervals, add 2 mL 1*N* alc. NaOH to each flask in sequence, rinsing any sample adhering to neck or sides of flask into liq. in flask. Mix well by swirling. Stopper flasks and let stand 10 min. Do *not* have >9 flasks in a series. After 10 min, slowly dil. each to vol. with EtOAc, gently swirling flask during addn. (Voluminous ppt will form at this time.) Stopper flask and mix well. Complete this process for each flask before adding EtOAc to next. Let stand 10–20 min with occasional mixing.

Remix contents of flask and pour portion into centrf. tube. Stopper tube and centrf. 5 min. (Supernate should be clear; recentrf. if necessary.) Transfer 5 mL to 50 mL vol. flask, taking care not to transfer any pptd NaOAc which may remain on surface of soln after centrfg.

Add 35–40 mL cyclohexane to reagent blank followed by 2 mL Cu reagent and immediately dil. to vol. with cyclohexane. Stopper flask and mix. Use this soln to zero spectrophtr, using 1 cm cells at max. *A*, ca 420 nm. Proceed as above for sample. Det. *A* against reagent blank exactly *2 min* after adding Cu reagent. Slight haze may appear on initial diln with cyclohexane. If it does not clear after adding Cu reagent, check for presence of excessive H_2O in analysis.

Water can be introduced by EtOAc, acetone, CH_3CN, alcohol, tetrahydrofuran, or contaminated glassware. Correct this condition before proceeding with analysis.

6.369 ***Calculations***

(**a**) *Absorptivity of samples* (*a*).—

(1) Tech. malathion and emulsifiable concs

$a = (A \times 50 \times 50 \times 50)/(\text{mg sample} \times 5 \times 5)$
$= (A \times 5000)/\text{mg sample}$

(2) Wettable powders and dusts

$a = (A \times 100 \times 50 \times 50)/(\text{mg sample} \times 10 \times 5)$
$= (A \times 5000)/\text{mg sample}$

(**b**) *Absorptivity of stds* (*a'*).—

(1) Malathion: Use formula in (**a**)(*1*).

(2) Potassium *O,O*-dimethyl phosphorodithioate

$a' = [(A \times 50 \times 50 \times 50)/(\text{mg sample} \times 5 \times 5)] \times 0.5939$
$= (A \times 2969)/\text{mg sample},$

where 0.5939 is factor to convert K salt to equiv. wt malathion. (In general, *a* of stds are in range 17.2–17.6, corrected for quality of std, at concn 1 mg/mL in 1 cm cell.)

(3) % Malathion = ($a \times$ % purity of std)/a'

6.370 ***Preparation of Standard Curve (Optional)***

Transfer 3, 4, 5, and 6 mL aliquots centrfgd EtOAc soln of std, **6.368**, par. 3, into sep. 50 mL vol. flasks. Proceed with color development, and plot *A* against wt malathion in aliquot. Use std curve with considerable caution, since fade rate may vary from day to day, depending on solvs used for analysis. Std curve is not appropriate where fluctuations in temp. occur in laboratory environment.

6.371 ***Interferences***

Test for free *O,O*-dimethyl phosphorodithioic acid or other interfering components in sample ext as follows: Transfer 2 drops ext to test tube, dil. with ca 10 mL cyclohexane, add 8 drops Cu reagent, and mix. Development of discernible yellow in soln indicates necessity of obtaining sample-blank correction.

Obtain sample-blank correction as follows: Transfer 5 or 10 mL aliquot sample to 50 mL vol. flask and dil. to vol. with EtOAc. (Do *not* add alc. NaOH soln.) For color development, transfer 5 mL dild sample soln and continue as in **6.368**. Correct *A* for base-treated sample and proceed with calcn.

Gas Chromatographic Method (96)—Official First Action

6.372 ***Apparatus***

(**a**) *Gas chromatograph.*—With glass column, on-column injection system, flame ionization detector, and electrometer with sensitivity of $\geqslant 10^{-11}$ amp driving 1 mv recorder. Drift should be <1%/hr. Totally solid state amplifier with FET input is recommended. Electronic digital integrator or computer calcd area measurements must be used. Integrator should have independent controls for selection of up and down slope sensitivities so that start and stop integration points can be selected. Automated sample injection system contributes significantly to precision. Hewlett-Packard Model 7600 is suitable when equipped as described. Equiv. instrumentation may be used but may require modification of operating conditions to obtain good peak shape, adequate resolution, and appropriate retention times.

Typical conditions for Hewlett-Packard Model 7600 (instrument may have to be adjusted to give complete resolution of well shaped peaks): Cycle timers (min): analysis and stop integrate, 16; range, 10^3; temps (°): oven 180, injection port 200, flame detector 300; gas flow rotameters (mL/min): H 35, air 425, He carrier gas 30; integrator settings (adjusted so that deflections on slope meter do not exceed ±50% before injection): noise suppression max., slope sensitivity up and down 0.1, BL reset delay 0.15, area threshold 1000; retention times (min): malathion 10, internal std 6, min. time between malathion and internal std 3.5.

(**b**) *Column.*—Borosilicate glass tube 1.22 m (6') × 4 mm id, 6 mm od, bent to fit chromatograph and packed with 5% SP-2401 or OV-210 on Gas-Chrom Q or Supelcoport (100/120 mesh). Can be purchased as prepd packing from Supelco, Inc., (specify "Pesticide Grade"); Alltech Associates, 202 Campus Dr, Arlington Heights, IL 60006; and Applied Science Laboratories, Inc. Use exclusively for malathion analysis.

(**c**) *Glass wool.*—Silane treated. (No. 14502, Applied Science Laboratories, Inc.)

(**d**) *Syringes.*—10 μL, Series 700, Hamilton Co.

(**e**) *HI-EFF Fluidizer.*—Applied Science Laboratories, Inc.

6.373 ***Reagents***

(**a**) *Internal std soln.*—1.2% *m*-Diphenoxybenzene in $CHCl_3$. Must not contain any impurities which elute at or near malathion peak. Bring soln to consistent temp. above ambient (e.g. 25°) before taking aliquots.

(**b**) *Malathion std solns.*—Accurately weigh ca 170, 200, and 230 mg malathion std (anal. grade, available from American Cyanamid Co.) into sep. preweighed 25 mL vol. flasks. Add by pipet 5 mL internal std soln and dil. to vol. with $CHCl_3$. Label A, B, and C. Soln B is working std soln for detn; solns A and C are used for linearity check and to guard against weighing error in prepn of working std soln. Solns are stable ca 4 weeks if kept tightly sealed in refrigerator. Warm to room temp. before use. Soln B can be prepd independently of solns A and C, if conditions of linearity check are met.

6.374 ***Preparation and Conditioning of Column***

Weigh 6.25 g of trifluoropropylsilicone (SP-2401 or OV-210) in 250 mL beaker and dissolve in 125 mL EtOAc. Stir to obtain vortex and add 25 g solid support (Gas-Chrom Q or Supelcoport, 100/120 mesh) with continued agitation. Filter slurry thru Whatman No. 1 paper, or equiv., on buchner, using gentle vac. to minimize evapn of solv. Continue filtration until drop rate is ca 1/sec. Transfer packing to HI-EFF Fluidizer, connect source of N thru pressure reducer to base, and place fluidizer on controlled temp. hot plate set for 75°. Continue gas flow until solv. vapors can no longer be detected by odor, taking care that packing is not blown out top of fluidizer.

To pack column, attach 75 mm funnel to exit end of prebent glass tube. Tap tube with pencil or small wooden rod, and add prepd packing in small amts until exit end is filled to ca 15 mm from end. Move funnel to entrance end of column. Insert pledget of silane-treated glass wool in exit end and attach source of moderate vac. to this end. Continue to add packing slowly with tapping until tube is filled to ca 20 mm from entrance end. Insert pledget of silane-treated glass wool in entrance end, compressing it only enough to hold it in place.

Condition column with He carrier gas flowing at 30 mL/min

≥15 hr (overnight) at 255° or ca 20° below max. temp. recommended for liq. phase. Exit end of column should not be connected to detector during this conditioning.

Connect exit end of column to detector, adjust controls to conditions given in **6.372(a)**, and let instrument come to equilibrium. Inject 3 μL aliquots std soln C until ≥3 consecutive injections give response ratios agreeing within 2%.

6.375 ***Linearity Check***

Check gas chromatograph for linearity at least weekly, whenever new std solns are prepd, and whenever column, new or used, is newly installed in instrument.

Using digital integration for peak area measurements, det. appropriate attenuation setting and injection aliquot (2–4 μL) of std soln B to give area count of ≥100,000 counts (optimum electrometer output with acceptable noise level). Use conditions so detd for all samples and stds in series.

Inject triplicate aliquots of detd vol. of std solns A, B, and C into chromatograph, det. response ratio for each, and average ratios for each soln. Divide av. ratio for each soln by corresponding malathion content in mg. Ratio/mg should agree within 2%. Failure to meet this specification indicates either weighing error in prepn of a std soln or instrumental difficulties which must be corrected before proceeding with analysis of samples.

6.376 ***Preparation of Sample***

(Analyze samples at least in duplicate)

(**a**) *Liquid formulations and technical materials.*—Accurately weigh sample contg ca 200 mg malathion into preweighed 25 mL vol. flask. Pipet in 5 mL internal std soln, dil. to vol. with $CHCl_3$, and mix well.

(**b**) *Solid formulations containing 10% or more of malathion.*—Accurately weigh sample contg ca 1.0 g malathion and transfer to 200–250 mL (8 oz) bottle. Pipet in 50 mL $CHCl_3$, stopper tightly, and shake on reciprocating shaker 30 min. Let settle ca 15 min; if not clear, centrf. Layer of solids will float at interface. Avoid entrainment of particles by exerting pos. pressure from bulb on pipet while it is carefully inserted into soln for removal of aliquot. Particles in final soln can clog syringe needle. Transfer 10 mL aliquot clear soln to 25 mL vol. flask, pipet in 5 mL internal std soln, dil. to vol. with $CHCl_3$, and mix well.

(**c**) *Solid formulations containing less than 10% malathion.*—Accurately weigh sample contg ca 400 mg malathion and transfer to 500 mL (16 oz) bottle. Add exactly 200 mL $CHCl_3$ and shake 30 min on reciprocal shaker. Let settle, observing precautions given in (**b**). Pipet 100 mL aliquot to 500 mL r-b flask and evap. to dryness. Pipet in 5 mL internal std soln and 20 mL $CHCl_3$, swirl to dissolve residue, and mix well.

6.377 ***Determination***

Inject duplicate aliquots of appropriate vol. of std soln B as detd in linearity check, **6.375**. Response ratios should agree within 2%; if not, repeat with 2 more injections. Failure to meet specification with second pair of injections indicates instrumental difficulties which must be resolved before proceeding with analysis.

Inject duplicate aliquots of each sample soln of same vol. as std soln. Average response ratios for each sample. Precision considerations stated for std soln also apply to sample soln injection response.

Inject duplicate aliquots std soln B after every 2 sample solns. Average response ratios of stds immediately before and after sample solns. Use this av. to calc. malathion content of the 2 sample solns.

Each detn of av. response ratio for std soln B should yield value within 2% of previously detd value. Failure to meet this specification indicates instrumental drift which must either be corrected or compensated for by more frequent measurements of response of std soln B. In extreme cases, follow each sample injection with std injection but this would indicate an instability which should be corrected at once.

6.378 ***Calculations***

For each sample injection, calc. response ratio:

$$R = \text{area of malathion peak/area of internal std peak}$$

$$\% \text{ Malathion} = (R/R') \times (W'/W) \times P \times D$$

where R′ and R = av. response ratio for std soln B and sample soln, resp; W′ and W = g malathion std and sample, resp.; P = % purity of malathion std; and D = diln factor (1 for liqs; (50/10)(25/25) = 5 for solids ≥10% malathion; and (200/100)(25/25) = 2 for solids <10% malathion).

Parathion

Gas Chromatographic Method (97)—Official First Action

(Not applicable to dusts and powders)

6.379 ***Standard Solutions***

(**a**) *Dipentyl phthalate internal std soln.*—Dissolve 2.0±0.1 g dipentyl phthalate (Eastman Kodak Co., No. P2473, or equiv.) in CS_2 and dil. to 500 mL with CS_2.

(**b**) *Parathion std soln.*—Accurately weigh ca 125 mg parathion (Monsanto Chemical Co., or equiv.) into 50 mL g-s erlenmeyer, pipet in 25 mL internal std soln, and mix thoroly.

6.380 ***Preparation of Sample***

Accurately weigh sample contg ca 125 mg parathion into 50 mL g-s erlenmeyer. Pipet in 25 mL internal std soln and mix thoroly.

6.381 ***Gas Chromatograph***

See **6.402**. Column should have ≥1200 theoretical plates for parathion. Vary attenuation and injection vol. (1–2 μL) so that peak hts of parathion and dipentyl phthalate are 60–80% full scale on 1 mv recorder. Retention times for parathion and dipentyl phthalate are 6–8 and 8–10.5 min, resp.

6.382 ***Determination***

Proceed as in **6.403**, except substitute parathion for Me parathion and dipentyl phthalate for *p,p′*-DDE.

6.383 ***Calculations***

Proceed as in **6.404**, except substitute parathion for Me parathion and delete *F* from equation.

High Pressure Liquid Chromatographic Method (97)
Official First Action

(Not applicable to dusts and powders)

6.384 ***Apparatus***

(**a**) *Liquid chromatograph.*—*See* **6.405(a)**, except use eluant flow rate of 1.5 mL/min (ca 800 psi).

(**b**) *Liquid chromatographic column.*—*See* **6.294(b)**.

6.385 ***Reagents***

(**a**) *Choroform.—See* **6.406**(**a**).

(**b**) *Eluant.*—Stir 500 mL $CHCl_3$ on mag. stirrer 3–4 min under moderate vac. (ca 350 mm Hg).

(**c**) *Internal std soln.*—Accurately weigh ca 110 mg benzophenone (MC/B Manufacturing Chemists, No. BX0410, or equiv.) into 250 mL vol. flask, and dissolve and dil. to vol. with $CHCl_3$.

(**d**) *Parathion std solns.—(1) Stock soln.*—1500 μg/mL. Accurately weigh ca 75 mg anal. grade parathion (Monsanto Chemical Co., or equiv.) into 50 mL vol. flask, and dissolve and dil. to vol. with $CHCl_3$. *(2) Working soln.*—(150 μg parathion + 44 μg benzophenone)/mL. Pipet 5 mL stock soln and 5 mL internal std soln into 50 mL vol. flask, and dil. to vol. with $CHCl_3$.

6.386 ***Preparation of Sample***

Accurately weigh sample contg ca 75 mg parathion into 50 mL vol. flask, and dissolve and dil. to vol. with $CHCl_3$. Pipet 5 mL sample soln and 5 mL internal std soln into 50 mL vol. flask, and dil. to vol. with $CHCl_3$.

6.387 ***Determination***

Proceed as in **6.408**, except substitute parathion for Me parathion and benzophenone for acetophenone, and delete *F* from equation. Retention times for parathion and benzophenone are 4.0–5.5 and 7–9 min, resp.

Volumetric Method (98)—Official First Action

(Applicable to dusts and powders only. *Caution: See* **51.041**.)

6.388 ***Apparatus***

(**a**) *Photoelectric colorimeter.*—With filter to give max. *T* between 400 and 450 nm. Spectrophtr set at 405 nm may also be used.

(**b**) *Potentiometer.*—With adapter for outside Pt and calomel electrodes. Dead-stop end point equipment may also be used.

6.389 ***Reagents***

(**a**) *Zinc dust.*—Low in Fe.

(**b**) *Sulfanilic acid.*—Anhyd. recrystd material. Check purity by N detn.

(**c**) *p-Nitrophenol.*—Mp 112–113°.

(**d**) *Sodium nitrite std soln.*—0.1*N*. Stdze weekly. Accurately weigh 0.4–0.45 g of the sulfanilic acid into 400 mL tall beaker. Add 80 mL H_2O, 10 mL HCl, 30 mL HOAc, and 5 g NaBr. Place electrodes and mech. stirrer in reaction mixt. and titr. with the 0.1*N* $NaNO_2$. Add in 5 mL portions until within 1 mL of calcd end point; then add $NaNO_2$ soln in 0.1 mL portions until max. rise in potential is obtained. At first, 3–5 min is required for potential to become const; as end point approaches, especially after 0.1 mL addns, reaction should be complete within 1 min. As alternative, dead-stop end point technic may be used (**98**), or following spot test, adding $NaNO_2$ soln in 4 drop portions near end point: Dip glass rod into soln being titrd and touch rod quickly to piece of KI-starch paper, (**e**). End point is reached when intense blue-black color appears immediately and can be obtained repeatedly during 1 min period without further addn of $NaNO_2$.

Normality $NaNO_2$ soln = g sulfanilic acid × 1000/(mL $NaNO_2$ × 173.2).

(**e**) *Starch iodide paper.*—Triturate 10 parts starch with 200 parts H_2O, bring to bp, and add 1 part KI. Impregnate strips of filter paper with this soln, dry, and preserve in g-s bottles.

6.390 ***Preparation of Standard Curve of p-Nitrophenol***

Accurately weigh 100 mg *p*-nitrophenol, transfer to 1 L vol. flask, and dil. to vol. with 0.1*N* NaOH. Transfer 2, 4, 6, 8, 10, and 20 mL aliquots of this soln to 100 mL vol. flasks and dil. each soln to vol. with 0.1*N* NaOH. Read *A* of each soln in photoelec. colorimeter (400–450 nm) or spectrophtr (405 nm) against H_2O as ref. Plot *A* against concn in mg/mL.

6.391 ***Preparation of Sample***

Dust preparations and wettable powders.—Transfer weighed sample to thimble and ext with 150 mL ether in Soxhlet app. 1 hr. Transfer ether ext to 250 mL separator, and sep. *p*-nitrophenol and parathion as in **6.392**. Det. sample size by parathion concn as follows: 10%, 6.75 g; 15% 4–5 g; 25%, 2.5–3.5 g.

6.392 ***Separation of Parathion and p-Nitrophenol***

Ext ether soln with four (or until ext is colorless) 20 mL portions *chilled 1% Na_2CO_3 soln*, collecting combined aq. layers in 200 mL vol. flask. Transfer ether layer to 400 mL tall beaker, rinsing separator with small portions ether.

6.393 ***Determination of p-Nitrophenol***

Add 20 mL 1*N* NaOH to combined aq. exts and dil. to vol. with H_2O. Measure *A* of soln as in **6.390** and read concn *p*-nitrophenol in mg/mL from std curve.

% *p*-Nitrophenol = (mg/mL) × 200 × 100/(1000 × g sample).

6.394 ***Determination of Parathion***

(*Caution: See* **51.011**, **51.039**, and **51.054**.)

Add 35 mL HOAc-HCl mixt. (9+1) to ether soln, **6.392**. Add 2 g Zn dust, cover beaker with watch glass, and gently heat soln on steam bath 45 min, or until most of ether evaps and soln is colorless. Add 30 mL HCl and heat 10 min longer to complete soln of Zn dust. Wash down beaker and watch glass with H_2O. Filter reduced mixt. thru paper and rinse beaker thoroly with H_2O. Dil. to 125 mL and cool to room temp. Add 5 g NaBr (or KBr) and titr. with 0.1*N* $NaNO_2$ as in **6.389**(**d**).

% Parathion = mL $NaNO_2$ × normality × 29.13/g sample.

Colorimetric Method (99)—Official First Action

(Applicable to dusts and powders only)

6.395 ***Principle***

Parathion is extd with alcohol and hydrolyzed with KOH to form K *p*-nitrophenate, which is detd colorimetrically.

6.396 ***Preparation of Standard Curve***

Weigh 60 mg reagent grade *p*-nitrophenol into 100 mL vol. flask, dissolve in alcohol, and dil. to vol. with alcohol. Pipet 10 mL into 100 mL vol. flask and dil. to vol. with alcohol. Prep. *p*-nitrophenol stds contg 0.3, 0.18, and 0.06 mg/100 mL by pipetting 5, 3, and 1 mL aliquots, resp., of second diln into sep. 100 mL vol. flasks, adding from pipet 5 mL *1N KOH in 50% alcohol*, and dilg to vol. with 50% alcohol. Measure *A* at 405 nm in 1 cm Corex cells against 50% alcohol and plot *A* against concn.

6.397 ***Preparation of Sample***

Weigh sample contg ca 10 mg parathion into 250 mL g-s flask. Pipet in 100 mL alcohol and shake occasionally during 10 min. Filter ca 25 mL into g-s container.

6.398 ***Determination of Free p-Nitrophenol***

Pipet 10 mL aliquot of above soln into 100 mL vol. flask and dil. to vol. with 50% alcohol. Add 5 drops 1*N* KOH in 50% alcohol, and measure *A* at 405 nm within 2 min against 50% alcohol. Calc. free *p*-nitrophenol.

6.399 ***Determination of Parathion***

Pipet 5 mL filtered soln into 125 mL g-s flask, pipet in 5 mL 1*N* KOH in 50% alcohol, and add glass beads to prevent bumping. Reflux ≥30 min. Cool, and transfer to 100 mL vol. flask with 50% alcohol. Dil. to vol. with 50% alcohol and measure *A* as in **6.396**. Calc. parathion, using std curve, dilns, and factor: Parathion = *p*-nitrophenol/0.478. Correct for free *p*-nitrophenol.

Methyl Parathion

Gas Chromatographic Method (100)—Official First Action

6.400 ***Standard Solutions***

(**a**) *p,p'-DDE internal std soln.*—Dissolve 5.0±0.1 g 2,2-bis(*p*-chlorophenyl)-1,1-dichloroethylene (*p,p'*-DDE, No. 12.389-7, Aldrich Chemical Co., Inc., or equiv.) in CS_2 and dil. to 1 L with CS_2.

(**b**) *Methyl parathion std soln.*—Accurately weigh ca 125 mg Me parathion (Monsanto Chemical Co., 800 N Lindbergh Blvd, St. Louis, MO 63166, or equiv.) into 50 mL g-s erlenmeyer, pipet in 25 mL internal std soln, and mix thoroly.

6.401 ***Preparation of Sample***

(**a**) *Liquid.*—Accurately weigh into 50 mL g-s erlenmeyer sample contg ca 125 mg Me parathion. Pipet in 25 mL internal std soln and mix thoroly.

(**b**) *Wettable powder.*—Accurately weigh into 100–150 mL (4 oz) round bottle sample contg ca 625 mg Me parathion. Pipet in 50 mL $CHCl_3$-acetone (9+1), cap, and shake mech. 30 min. Let settle and pipet 10 mL supernate into 50 mL g-s erlenmeyer. Place erlenmeyer in 55° H_2O bath and evap. solv. under stream of dry air or N. Pipet in 25 mL internal std soln and mix thoroly.

6.402 ***Gas Chromatograph***

Use instrument equipped with flame ionization detector and 1.2 m × 4 (id) mm glass column packed with 1.5% SE-30 plus 1.5% OV-210 on 80–100 mesh Gas-Chrom Q.

Prep. column by accurately weighing ca 0.12 g SE-30 and ca 0.12 g OV-210 into 250 mL beaker. Add 50 mL $CHCl_3$-acetone (3+2), cover with watch glass, and heat on steam bath until stationary phases are dissolved. Speed dissoln of SE-30 by spreading material on walls of beaker with small spatula or stirring rod. Add enough 80–100 mesh Gas-Chrom Q to yield 1.5% of each phase on solid support. Heat on steam bath, stirring frequently until all solv. is removed. Air dry 2–3 hr. Pack in column and condition 24 hr at 245° with N or He at 30 mL/min. Column should have ≥1200 theoretical plates for *p,p'*-DDE.

Typical operating conditions: temps (°)—inlet 210, column 180±10, detector 250; N or He carrier gas, 55–75 mL/min; air and H as specified by manufacturer; attenuation and injection vol. (1–2 μL) varied so that peak hts of Me parathion and *p,p'*-DDE are 60–80% full scale on 1 mv recorder. Retention times for Me parathion and *p,p'*-DDE are 3.5–5.5 and 6–8 min, resp.

6.403 ***Determination***

Inject aliquots of std soln until peak ht ratio of Me parathion : *p,p'*-DDE varies ≤1% for successive injections. Then make duplicate injections of sample followed by duplicate injections of std. Peak ht ratios of stds must be within ±1% of first accepted std values or repeat series of injections. Repeat for addnl samples.

6.404 ***Calculations***

Calc. peak ht ratios for both duplicate std injections preceding and following samples. Average the 4 values (*R'*). Calc. and average peak ht ratios of the 2 samples (*R*).

$$\% \text{ Me parathion} = (R/R') \times (W'/W) \times F \times P,$$

where *W* and *W'* = mg sample and std, resp., *F* = 1 for liq. and 5 for wettable powder samples; and *P* = % purity of std.

High Pressure Liquid Chromatographic Method (101)
Official First Action

6.405 ***Apparatus***

(**a**) *Liquid chromatograph.*—Waters Model ALC 202/GPC 204 (Waters Associates, Inc.), or equiv., with 254 nm UV detector and 10 mv recorder. Typical operating conditions: eluant flow rate, 1.2 mL/min (ca 700 psi); detector sensitivity, 0.16 *A* unit full scale; temp., ambient; valve injection vol., 10 μL.

(**b**) *Liquid chromatographic column.*—See **6.294**(**b**).

(**c**) *Chromatographic tubes.*—Glass, 900 × 25 (id) mm, with coarse porosity frit in bottom (SGA Scientific, Inc., No. JC-2650, or equiv.).

6.406 ***Reagents***

(**a**) *Chloroform.*—Alcohol-free with <0.01% H_2O (Burdick & Jackson Laboratories, Inc., distd in glass, or equiv.).

(**b**) *Silicic acid-water.*—75% (w/v). Add 25 mL H_2O to 75 g silicic acid (Mallinckrodt Chemical Works, Code 2847, or equiv.), and shake until lumps disappear.

(**c**) *Water-saturated chloroform.*—Shake 700 mL $CHCl_3$ with 150 mL H_2O 2–3 min, and pass thru 900 × 25 mm glass tube packed with 100 g silicic acid-H_2O.

(**d**) *Eluant.*—Blend 200 mL H_2O-satd $CHCl_3$ with 300 mL $CHCl_3$ on mag. stirrer 2–3 min under moderate vac. (ca 350 mm Hg).

(**e**) *Internal std soln.*—Accurately weigh ca 115 mg acetophenone (MC/B Manufacturing Chemists, No. AX0164, or equiv.) into 250 mL vol. flask, and dissolve and dil. to vol. with $CHCl_3$.

(**f**) *Methyl parathion std solns.*—(*1*) *Stock soln.*— 700 μg/mL. Accurately weigh ca 70 mg anal. grade Me parathion (Monsanto Chemical Co., or equiv.) into 100 mL vol. flask, and dissolve and dil. to vol. with $CHCl_3$. (2) *Working soln.*—(70 μg Me parathion + 46 μg acetophenone)/mL. Pipet 5 mL stock soln and 5 mL internal std soln into 50 mL vol. flask, and dil. to vol. with $CHCl_3$.

6.407 ***Preparation of Sample***

Accurately weigh ca 95 mg tech. Me parathion into 100 mL vol. flask, or accurately weigh emulsifiable sample contg ca 35 mg Me parathion into 50 mL vol. flask, and dil. to vol. with $CHCl_3$. Pipet 5 mL sample soln and 5 mL internal std soln into 50 mL vol. flask, and dil. to vol. with $CHCl_3$.

6.408 ***Determination***

Pump sufficient eluant thru column to equilibrate system. Inject 10 μL working std soln onto column thru sampling valve, and adjust operating conditions to give peak hts 60–80% full scale and retention times of 3.5–5.0 and 5.5–8.0 min for Me parathion and acetophenone, resp. Repeat injections until ratio of Me parathion to acetophenone peak hts is within ±1% of previous injection. Without changing conditions, alternately inject 10 μL aliquots of working std soln and duplicate 10 μL aliquots of sample soln until peak ht ratios for sample soln vary

≤1% for successive injections. Average last 2 peak ht ratios for sample and for std, resp., and calc. % Me parathion.

$$\% \text{ Me parathion} = (R/R') \times (W'/W) \times (P/F),$$

where R and R' = av. peak ht ratios of Me parathion to acetophenone for sample and std, resp.; W and W' = mg sample and std, resp.; P = % purity of std; and F = 1 for tech. and 2 for emulsifiable samples.

Methyl Parathion in Water-based Microencapsulated Formulations

Gas Chromatographic Method (102)—Official First Action

6.409 ***Principle***

Me parathion is released from microcapsules by grinding, and is extd into CH_3CN. Dimethoate is added as internal std and concn of Me parathion is detd by flame ionization GLC.

6.410 ***Apparatus***

(**a**) *Gas chromatograph.*—Perkin-Elmer Model 900, or equiv., with flame ionization detector, glass lined injection port, 1 mv strip chart recorder, and 1.8 m × 2 (id) mm glass column packed with 3% OV-17 on 80–100 mesh Supelcoport (Supelco, Inc.). Typical operating conditions: temps (°): column 200, injection port 225, detector 250; flow rates (mL/min): He carrier gas 35, air 400, H optimize for max. sensitivity; sample: 1 μL CH_3CN contg dimethoate and Me parathion with retention times of ca 3 min and 4 min, resp. Injection vol. may be varied to give peak hts 50–90% of full scale.

(**b**) *Sample grinder.*—Spex Industries Mixer/Mill No. 8000 (Spex Industries, Inc., PO Box 798, Metuchen, NJ 08840) or 40 mL Corning 7726 glass tissue grinder (No. 441969, Corning Glass Works).

(**c**) *Weighing dishes.*—With natural Al surface to which sample does not stick (Fisher Scientific Co., No. 8-732, or equiv.).

6.411 ***Reagents***

(**a**) *Dimethoate.*—Cygon® insecticide, anal. grade (obtainable from American Cyanamid Co.).

(**b**) *Methyl parathion.*—Anal. grade (obtainable from Monsanto Chemical Co.).

6.412 ***Determination of Correction Factor***

Prep. 2 duplicate std solns by accurately weighing ca 0.1 g Me parathion and ca 0.1 g dimethoate directly into same 50 mL vol. flask, and dilg to vol. with CH_3CN. Shake thoroly to dissolve. Inject ca 1 μL each soln into gas chromatograph. Repeat injections until ratio of peak hts is reproducible; then record peak hts and attenuations for dimethoate and Me parathion.

$$CF = (P_d \times W_{mp})/(P_{mp} \times W_d),$$

where CF = correction factor, P_d = peak ht × attenuation for dimethoate, W_{mp} = g Me parathion, P_{mp} = peak ht × attenuation for Me parathion, and W_d = g dimethoate.

Average results for the 2 solns.

6.413 ***Preparation of Sample***

Prep. duplicate samples as follows: Thoroly shake sample container to assure that slurry of microcapsules is homogeneous. Withdraw ca 1 g sample using medicine dropper while stirring. Immediately discharge contents into tared Al weighing dish, and record exact wt. Transfer to Mixer/Mill or glass tissue grinder, using small amt of CH_3CN. (If anal. balance can accommodate grinder, sample may be weighed directly in it.) Add ca 30 mL CH_3CN and grind ca 4 min. Quant. transfer ground sample to 100 mL vol. flask, using CH_3CN. Accurately weigh ca 0.2 g dimethoate in tared Al weighing dish, transfer quant. to vol. flask, and dil. to vol. with CH_3CN.

6.414 ***Determination***

Inject ca 1 μL soln contg sample and internal std into gas chromatograph. Record peak hts and attenuations for dimethoate and Me parathion.

$$\text{wt \% Me parathion} = (P_{mp} \times W_d \times CF \times 100)/(P_d \times W),$$

where P_{mp} = peak ht × attenuation for Me parathion, W_d = g dimethoate, CF = correction factor, P_d = peak ht × attenuation for dimethoate, and W = g sample.

Analyze duplicate samples and av. results.

Phorate (Thimet®) (*O,O*-Diethyl *S*-(Ethylthio)methyl Phosphorodithioate) (*103*)—Official Final Action

(Applicable to analysis of 5 and 10% granules. Presence of other pesticides and extractable org. materials such as dispersing agents, emulsifiers, and solvs requires testing for interference.)

6.415 ***Apparatus***

(**a**) *Infrared spectrophotometer.*—Capable of measurement in 7.9–8.6 μm range; with 0.5 mm cell.

(**b**) *Chromatographic tube.*—15 × 450 mm with stopcock or Ultramax valve (Fischer & Porter Co., Lab Crest Scientific Div., Cat. No. 274–019 or 274–100).

6.416 ***Reagents***

(**a**) *Phorate reference std.*—Purified (obtainable from American Cyanamid Co.).

(**b**) *Phorate std soln.*—Accurately weigh by difference from Smith or Lunge pipet 1.0–1.1 g Phorate Ref. Std into 250 mL beaker contg 45 mL CH_3CN.

(**c**) *Cyclohexane.*—Practical grade.

(**d**) *Acetonitrile.*—Practical grade, bp 82–84°.

6.417 ***Preparation of Sample Solution***

(*Caution: See* **51.011**, **51.040**, and **51.043**.)

Accurately weigh 20±0.01 g sample of 5% granular material (10±0.01 g for 10%). Place small glass wool plug in bottom of chromatgc tube, transfer sample to tube, and gently tap sides with spatula or rod to settle contents. Place 250 mL beaker under column. Add 50 mL CH_3CN to column and let percolate thru at rate of 40–50 drops/min until flow stops. Place beakers contg std (from **6.416(b)**) and sample solns in shallow H_2O bath at 30–35° and evap. under gentle stream of air until odor of CH_3CN is no longer detectable. (Sample solns on evapn will change from clear to cloudy and then to residue of 2 layers.) Treat residue with four 5 mL portions and one 4 mL portion cyclohexane, quant. transferring cyclohexane layers to 25 mL vol. flask. (Keep cyclohexane-immiscible layer in beaker during each extn.) Dil. to vol. with cyclohexane.

6.418 ***Determination***

Using hypodermic syringe, fill 0.5 mm cell with prepd std soln, and obtain IR spectrum from 7.9 to 8.6 μm. (With single beam instrument, adjust to give 75% T at 8.2 μm with cell contg std soln in position.) Using same instrument settings, treat prepd sample solns similarly.

Draw baseline from inflection points 8.10 to 8.48 μm. Draw perpendicular from 0 radiation line thru absorption peak, and measure distance from 0 to baseline (Y) and from 0 to absorption peak (*X*) in same units. Calc. *A* = *log* (*Y*/*X*) for sample (*A*) and std (*A'*).

% Phorate = (*A*/*A'*) × (wt std/wt sample) × % purity of std.

6.419 ★ Sulfoxide (n-Octyl Sulfoxide of ★ Isosafrole) (*104*)—Official First Action

Sulfoxide is sepd from solvs, emulsifiers, pyrethrins, and other insecticides by silicic acid column chromatgy with successive eluting solns: $CHCl_3$, 2% acetone in $CHCl_3$, and 10% acetone in $CHCl_3$. Sulfoxide is removed in last eluate and is detd by UV spectrophotometry. *See* **6.296–6.302**, 11th ed.

Tetraethylpyrophosphate (TEPP) (*105*)—Official Final Action

(*Caution: See* **51.041**.)

6.420 ***Reagents***

(**a**) *Indicator*.—0.1% aq. soln Me red or chlorophenol red.

(**b**) *Amberlite IR-4B(OH) (free base form) resin*.—Anal. grade. Amberlite IR-45, Dowex 3, or equiv., are satisfactory.

6.421 ***Preparation of Resin Column***

Screen resin to remove particles <30 mesh. Slurry 30 g screened resin with H_2O, and pour into 100 mL buret contg small plug of glass wool at bottom. Wash resin column with 150 mL 3% NaOH soln at flow rate of ca 5 mL/min and then rinse with H_2O until effluent is acid to phthln, adjusting stopcock of buret so flow rate is ca 25 mL/min. Wash with aq. acetone (1+3) to displace H_2O. Column is now ready for use.

Notes: Because channeling may result if column runs dry, keep liq. level ca 2.5 cm above resin bed at all times. Because resin tends to pack in column as it adsorbs acidic material, expand resin bed after each detn before adding new sample by back-washing with acetone (1+3) as follows: Connect large funnel to tip of buret with rubber hose, and add the dil. acetone from funnel until liq. level reaches top of buret; let resin settle, and then let soln flow from buret until surface is 2.5 cm above resin bed. Column is now ready to receive next sample.

After 8–10 samples have passed thru column, regenerate resin by repeating original treatment with 3% NaOH soln, H_2O, and acetone (1+3). Washing with dil. acetone must be continued until effluent is colorless.

6.422 ***Determination***

(**a**) *In purified or technical grades of tetraethylpyrophosphate not mixed with solvent, emulsifying agent, etc*.—From 5–10 mL weighing buret, weigh by difference, to nearest mg, 2.5 g sample (1.0 g if tetraethylpyrophosphate content is >50%) into 50 mL acetone (1+3) in 125 mL separator. Mix by swirling, and let soln stand 15 min at 25±2°. Let soln flow thru resin column by gravity at ca 25 mL/min, and catch effluent in 250 mL vol. flask. Wash separator and column with three 50 mL portions acetone (1+3), collecting washings in same flask. Dil. combined effluent to vol. with H_2O, mix, and transfer 100 mL aliquot to 250 mL beaker. Add 50 mL 0.1*N* NaOH to beaker, stir well, let stand 30 min at room temp., and back-titr. with 0.1*N* HCl, using pH meter (or indicator, **6.420(a)**, if pH meter is not available). Calc. % tetraethylpyrophosphate = net mL 0.1*N* NaOH × 3.67/wt sample taken.

(**b**) *In formulations of tetraethylpyrophosphate containing organic solvent and emulsifying agent*.—Proceed as in (**a**), except filter acetone soln thru 25 mm cotton plug in cylindrical funnel (25 mm diam., 75 mm long) before adding it to column if oil seps from soln. Pass acetone washings successively thru separator, cylindrical funnel, and resin column as in (**a**). (Cotton plug absorbs oil.)

★ Surplus method—*see* inside front cover.

Organic Thiocyanates

Thiocyanate Nitrogen in Livestock or Fly Sprays (106)—Official Final Action

(*Caution: See* **51.041**.)

6.423 ***Reagents***

(**a**) *Strong potassium polysulfide soln*.—Dissolve 180 g KOH in 120 mL H_2O. Sat. 100 mL of this soln with H_2S (ca 42 g) (*Caution: See* **51.059**) while cooling. Add remaining 100 mL KOH soln and 80 g S. Shake until dissolved.

(**b**) *Mixed sulfide soln*.—To 100 mL (**a**) add 50 g $Na_2S.9H_2O$, 30 g KOH, and 200 mL H_2O.

(**c**) *Sodium bisulfite*.—$Na_2S_2O_5$ or $NaHSO_3$.

(**d**) *Copper sulfate soln*.—20% aq. soln $CuSO_4.5H_2O$.

(**e**) *Wash soln*.—To 300 mL H_2O add 1 mL H_2SO_4 (1+4), 1 g (**c**), 10 mL (**d**), and 12 g Na_2SO_4, and pass SO_2 into soln 10 min.

6.424 ***Preparation of Sample***

Weigh sample preferably contg ca 0.03 g thiocyanate N into 250 mL g-s erlenmeyer. (If SCN content is very low, do not unduly increase amt sample without correspondingly increasing amt mixed sulfide soln used; 20–25 g fly spray is usually enough.) Add 35 mL mixed sulfide soln and shake vigorously at room temp. 10 min, during which time reaction is nearly completed. Heat to 70° on steam bath, carefully releasing pressure resulting from heating, shake 15 min at 70°, and cool.

Removal of petroleum oil.—Transfer mixt. to separator with ca 200 mL H_2O. Add 50 mL pet ether, shake, and drain aq. layer into 600 mL beaker. Wash pet ether layer with two 10 mL portions H_2O, adding washings to main soln. (If emulsions form during washing, break by acidifying with H_2SO_4 (1+4).) Drain aq. layer and wash pet ether layer with H_2O as above. Discard pet ether layer.

6.425 ***Determination***

Dil. combined aq. soln to ca 300 mL and neutze with H_2SO_4 (1+4), using litmus paper as outside indicator. Add 2 mL H_2SO_4 (1+4), quickly bring mixt. to bp, and boil 8 min to remove H_2S. Cool. If fatty acids or oils are present, transfer to separator, ext with pet ether, and return aq. phase to original beaker. Filter thru small buchner and transfer filtrate to beaker. Neutze to litmus paper with 10% KOH soln and add 1 mL H_2SO_4 (1+4). Add 1 g Na bisulfite and stir until dissolved. Add excess (ca 15 mL) $CuSO_4$ soln and pass SO_2 into soln 10 min.

Let pptd CuSCN settle 2 hr, and filter with suction thru 56 mm buchner coated with layer of asbestos (*Caution: See* **51.086**), upon which is placed No. 42 Whatman paper, or equiv., second layer of asbestos, layer of diatomite, and finally third layer of asbestos. If filtrate is not clear, centrf. soln at 2000 rpm 10–15 min, and pour thru filter again. Wash filter and ppt once or twice with wash soln, continue suction until filter pad is dry, and transfer to 800 mL Kjeldahl flask. (Filter pad may be folded in filter paper together with bits of moist filter paper used to wipe out buchner, and whole placed in Kjeldahl flask.) Add few glass beads, 35 mL H_2SO_4, 10 g K_2SO_4, and ca 0.7 g HgO or 0.65 g Hg. (*Caution: See* **51.030** and **51.065**.) Digest until colorless; then 15 min more. Det. N as in **2.057**, second par. Perform blank analysis on paper, filter pad, and reagents.

Thiocarbamate Herbicides (*107*)—Official First Action

(*S*-Ethyl Dipropylthiocarbamate (EPTC, Eptam®), *S*-Ethyl Hexahydro-1H-azepine-1-carbothioate (Molinate, Ordram®), *S*-Ethyl Cyclohexylethylthiocarbamate (Cycloate, Ro-Neet®), *S*-Ethyl Diisobutylthiocarbamate (Butylate, Sutan®), *S*-Propyl Butylethylthiocarbamate (Pebulate, Tillam®), *S*-Propyl Dipropylthiocarbamate (Vernolate, Vernam®))

Gas Chromatographic Method

(Applicable to liq. and granular formulations. *Caution: See* **51.041**.)

6.426 ***Apparatus***

(**a**) *Gas chromatograph*.—With flame ionization detector. Operating conditions: temps (°)—injection port 225, column 130 (EPTC and butylate), 170 (molinate), 140 (cycloate, vernolate), 150 (pebulate), detector 250; gas flows (mL/min)—N carrier 30–35, H 25–30, air 200–300 (or as specified by manufacturer).

(**b**) *Recorder*.—1 mv full scale sensitivity and 1 sec response.

(**c**) *Columns*.—6′ (1.8 m) × 0.25″ od, Pyrex, Al, or stainless steel, packed with 3% OV-17 on 60–80 Gas-Chrom Q, or equiv. (for molinate), and 3% SE-30 or OV-1 on 60–80 mesh Gas-Chrom Q, or equiv. (for other 5 compds). Condition columns 12 hr at 250° under N flow of 30 mL/min.

6.427 ***Preparation of Standards***

(**a**) *Internal std solns*.—Accurately weigh ca 400 mg each ref. grade thiocarbamate (EPTC, cycloate, butylate, or pebulate; Stauffer Chemical Co., 1200 S 47th St, Richmond, CA 94804) and transfer to sep. 100 mL vol. flasks. Dil. to vol. with CS_2-$CHCl_3$-MeOH (80+15+5), and mix thoroly.

(**b**) *Std solns*.—Accurately weigh ca 100 mg each ref. grade thiocarbamate into sep. 2 oz (50 mL) polyethylene-lined screw-cap, conical bottles. Add 25 mL internal std soln indicated below, and mix thoroly.

Std soln	Approx. retention time, min	Internal std soln added	Approx. retention time, min
EPTC	2.0	Butylate	2.4
Molinate	4.3	Cycloate	4.8
Cycloate	5.4	Pebulate	2.6
Butylate	2.4	EPTC	2.0
Pebulate	4.0	Cycloate	8.0
Vernolate	3.5	Cycloate	5.5

6.428 ***Preparation of Sample***

Accurately weigh sample contg ca 100 mg thiocarbamate into 2 oz (50 mL) polyethylene-lined screw-cap, conical bottle. Add 25 mL appropriate internal std soln, (**a**), as indicated in (**b**), and shake thoroly. Vigorously shake granular formulations 30 min on wrist-action shaker.

6.429 ***Determination***

Inject 2 μL clear supernate or soln into chromatograph preadjusted to appropriate conditions. Make triplicate injections of sample and appropriate std soln in random order. Det. peak areas, preferably with digital integrator.

Adjust sensitivity of gas chromatograph so that larger component or internal std peak is ca ¾ full scale.

6.430 ***Calculations***

Response Factor (RF) = $(I' \times$ g compd in std soln $\times$ % purity$)/S'$

Wt % compd = $(RF \times S)/I \times$ g sample),

where I and I' = areas of internal std peak in sample and std solns, resp.; and S and S' = areas of compd peak in sample and std solns, resp.

Triazines and Other Pesticides (*108*)—Official Final Action

(*See* Table **6:03** for applicability to and official status of specific compds.)

AOAC-CIPAC Method

6.431 ***Standard Solutions***

(*Caution: See* **51.041**.)

(**a**) *Dieldrin internal std soln*.—Std should be ≥90% pure and contain no impurities eluting at retention time for pesticide being detd. (*1*) *For propazine*.—Weigh 14.0±0.1 g tech. dieldrin, dissolve in ca 300 mL $CHCl_3$, and dil. to 1 L with $CHCl_3$. (*2*) *For other compounds*.—Weigh 2.00±0.02 g tech. dieldrin, dissolve in ca 200 mL $CHCl_3$, and dil. to 250 mL with $CHCl_3$.

(**b**) *Aldrin internal std soln*.—(For Diazinon®.) Weigh 4.0±0.1 g tech. aldrin into 600 mL beaker. Slurry with 400 mL acetone to dissolve, filter thru paper into 1 L vol. flask, washing with several 100 mL portions acetone, and dil. to vol. Std should be ≥90% pure and contain no impurities eluting at retention time of Diazinon.

(**c**) *Dibenzyl succinate internal std soln*.—(For chlorobenzilate and chloropropylate.) Weigh 5.0±0.1 g dibenzyl succinate, dissolve in ca 300 mL acetone, and dil. to 1 L with acetone. Std should be >98% pure and contain no impurities eluting at retention time for pesticide being detd.

(**d**) *Pesticide std solns*.—Accurately weigh 250 mg (125 mg for Diazinon and 150 mg for simazine) of ref. std of pesticide being detd (available from Ciba-Geigy Corp., PO Box 11422, Greensboro, NC 27409) into 4 oz (125 mL) round bottle with Al-lined screw cap. Pipet in 50 mL internal std soln (*see* Table **6:03**) and shake mech. 30 min.

(**e**) *Dioctyl phthalate internal std soln.*—(For simazine.) Weigh 3.0±0.1 g tech. dioctyl phthalate, dissolve in ca 200 mL DMF, and dil. to 1 L with DMF. (*Caution: See* **51.053**.) Std should be >98% pure and contain no impurities eluting at retention time of simazine.

6.432 ***Preparation of Sample***

Accurately weigh amt sample specified in Table **6:03** into 4 oz (125 mL) round bottle with Al-lined screw cap. Pipet in same vol. internal std used for prepn of std soln, (**d**), and shake mech. 30 min. Let insol. materials settle or centrf. portion of ext to obtain clear soln.

6.433 ***Gas Chromatography***

Use instrument equipped with flame ionization detector and 4 mm id glass column (length specified in Table **6:03**) packed with 3% Carbowax 20M (Applied Science Laboratories, Inc.) on 80–100 mesh Gas-Chrom Q. (For Diazinon, use 10% silicone DC-200 viscosity 12500.) Condition 24 hr at 240° with N or He at ca 40 mL/min. Column should have ≥2000 (≥1500 for chlorobenzilate, chloropropylate, propazine, and simazine) theoretical plates (*see* **6.156**(**a**)).

Operate at following conditions: temps—as specified in Table **6:03**; N or He carrier gas, 80–100 mL/min; air and H, 80–100 mL/min; attenuation varied so that peak hts of pesticide and internal std are 60–80% full scale. Retention times are specified

Table 6:03 Chemical and Gas Chromatographic Parameters for Triazines and Other Pesticides

Chemical Name	Common or Trade Name	CA Registry No.	Internal Std Soln **6.431**	Wt Sample	Length Column m	Temperature (°)			Retention Times (min)	
						Inlet	Column	Detector	Pesticide	Internal Std
2-(Ethylamino)-4-(isopropylamino)-6-(methylthio)-*s*-triazine	Ametryn	834-12-8	(**a**)(*2*)	300 mg 80% wettable powder	1.8	240	215±15	240	8–12	9–15
2-Chloro-4-(ethylamino)-6-(isopropylamino)-*s*-triazine	Atrazine	1912-24-9	(**a**)(*2*)	300 mg 80% wettable powder	1.8	240	200±10	240	5–7	9–15
Ethyl-4,4′-dichlorobenzilate	Chlorobenzilate	510-15-6	(**c**)	500 mg liq. formulation	1.2	260	230±10	260	5–8	8–10
Isopropyl-4,4′-dichlorobenzilate	Chloropropylate	5836-10-2	(**c**)	1 g liq. formulation	1.2	260	230±10	260	4–6	8–10
O,O-Diethyl-*O*-(2-isopropyl-6-methyl-4-pyrimidinyl) phosphorothioate	Diazinon	333-41-5	(**b**)	Sample contg 110 mg	1.8	240	190±10	240	5–6	10–12
2,4-Bis(isopropylamino)-6-methoxy-*s*-triazine	Prometon	1610-18-0	(**a**)(*2*)	1 g liq. formulation	1.8	240	200±20	240	3–5	9–15
2,4-Bis(isopropylamino)-6-(methylthio)-*s*-triazine	Prometryn	7287-19-6	(**a**)(*2*)	300 mg 80% wettable powder	1.8	240	200±10	240	6–8	9–15
2-Chloro-4,6-bis(isopropylamino)-*s*-triazine	Propazine	139-40-2	(**a**)(*1*)	300 mg 80% wettable powder	1.2	250	210±10	240	3–5	7–9
2-Chloro-4,6-bis(ethylamino)-*s*-triazine	Simazine	122-34-9	(**e**)	190 mg 80% wettable powder	1.8	250	210±5	250	6–8	10–14
2-(*tert*-Butylamino)-4-(ethylamino)-6-(methylthio)-*s*-triazine	Terbutryn	886-50-0	(**a**)(*2*)	300 mg 80% wettable powder	1.8	240	200±20	240	8–10	9–15

in Table **6:03**. (Ametryn and dieldrin peaks must be resolved. Prep. new column if variation of flow rate or temp. does not resolve peaks. Resolution may be improved by increasing column temp.)

6.434 ***Determination***

Inject 3 μL aliquots std soln until peak ht ratio of pesticide: internal std varies ≤1% for successive injections. Then make duplicate injections of sample followed by duplicate injections of std. Peak ht ratios of stds must be within ±1% of first accepted std values or repeat series of injections. Repeat for addnl samples.

6.435 ***Calculations***

Calc. peak ht ratios for both duplicate std injections preceding and following samples. Average the 4 values (R'). Calc. and average peak ht ratios of the 2 samples (R).

$$\% \text{ Pesticide} = (R/W) \times (W' \times P/R'),$$

where W and W' = mg sample and std, resp.; and P = % purity of std.

Triphenyltin Compounds (Fentin)

Potentiometric Titration Method (109)—Official First Action (CIPAC Method)

6.436 ***Principle***

Org. Sn compds are extd with acetone, diphenyltin compds are quant. converted to insol. oxide with alk. alumina and filtered, and acetone soln is titrd potentiometrically.

6.437 ***Apparatus***

(**a**) *Filtration apparatus.*—Glass bell with neck and removable plate to permit glass buchner with fine porosity fritted disk and long stem to drain into beaker under vac. (Fig. **6:09**).

(**b**) *Potentiometric titration apparatus.*—pH meter with glass and satd calomel electrodes is satisfactory.

6.438 ***Reagents***

(**a**) *Alkaline alumina.*—Mix 150 g neutral Al_2O_3 (Woelm 4649, or equiv.) with 150 mL alcohol contg 15 g KOH in 1 L r-b flask. Reflux 30 min, cool, and filter with suction thru buchner. Dry powder in vac. 1 hr at 100° and 3-3.5 hr at 130°. Pour warm powder into bottle and stopper tightly. Com. alk. Al_2O_3 is not satisfactory.

(**b**) *Cellulose powder.*—Whatman CF 11, or equiv.

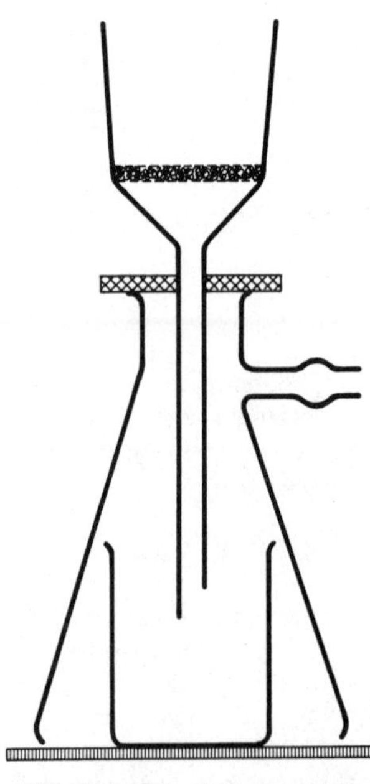

FIG. 6:09—Filtration apparatus

6.439 ***Determination***

Accurately weigh into 100 mL glass beaker sample contg ca 0.30 g triphenyltin compd. Add 2 g alk. Al_2O_3 and 25 mL acetone and stir with mag. stirrer 10 min. Prep. and process blank of 2 g alk. Al_2O_3 and 25 mL acetone in same manner. Place 1 g cellulose powder and 1 g alk. Al_2O_3 in funnel and mix thoroly. Assemble filtration app. contg 250 mL beaker and filter suspension thru funnel. Wash beaker and funnel with four 20 mL portions acetone. Titr. filtrate potentiometrically with stdzd 0.1*N* HCl.

$$\% \text{ Triphenyltin compd} = (S - B) \times N \times (M/W) \times 10$$

where S = mL HCl used for sample, B = mL HCl used for blank, N = normality of HCl, M = mol. wt of compd (367.0 for triphenyltin hydroxide and 409.0 for the acetate), and W = g sample.

QUATERNARY AMMONIUM COMPOUNDS

Chloride (*110*)—Official Final Action

6.440 ***Potentiometric Titration Method***

Transfer sample contg 30–35 mg Cl to 600 mL beaker, dil. to 200 mL with H_2O, and add 5 mL HNO_3 (1+1). Add just enough acetone to dissolve ppt that forms and titr. with 0.1*N* $AgNO_3$, using app. for potentiometric titrn. Calc. % Cl (1 mL 0.1*N* $AgNO_3$ = 3.545 mg Cl) and equiv. % quaternary NH_4 salt.

Adsorption Indicator Method

6.441 ***Reagents***

(**a**) *Bromothymol blue indicator*.—Dissolve 1 g indicator in 500 mL 50% alcohol.

(**b**) *Dichlorofluorescein soln*.—0.1%. Dissolve 100 mg indicator in 100 mL 70% alcohol.

6.442 ***Determination***

Transfer sample contg 30–140 mg Cl (usually ca 1 g quaternary NH_4 salt) into 300 mL erlenmeyer, dil. to 75 mL with H_2O, and add 25 mL isopropanol. Neutze if necessary with HOAc (1+9), using 1 drop bromothymol blue (pH 4–6). Add 10 drops dichlorofluorescein, and titr. with 0.1*N* $AgNO_3$, avoiding direct sunlight. Ppt becomes red at end point and may flocculate just before end point. Calc. % Cl and equiv. % quaternary NH_4 salt.

SELECTED REFERENCES

(*1*) JAOAC **62,** 494(1979)
(*2*) Ind. Eng. Chem. **14,** 207(1922); JAOAC **5,** 33, 402(1922); **6,** 313(1923).
(*3*) JAOAC **7,** 313(1924).
(*4*) Anal. Chem. **22,** 1066(1950); JAOAC **46,** 672 (1963).
(*5*) JAOAC **5,** 398(1922).
(*6*) J. Am. Chem. Soc. **40,** 1036(1918); JAOAC **5,** 398(1922).
(*7*) J. Res. Natl. Bur. Standards **3,** 581(1929); JAOAC **25,** 670 (1942); **27,** 74(1944); **28,** 72(1945).
(*8*) Compt. rend. **173,** 714, 836(1921); JAOAC **14,** 253(1931).
(*9*) J. Am. Chem. Soc. **55,** 1741(1933); Ind. Eng. Chem., Anal. Ed. **5,** 7(1933); **9,** 551(1937); **11,** 21(1939); JAOAC **21,** 459(1938).
(*10*) JAOAC **55,** 851(1972).
(*11*) JAOAC **43,** 367(1960).
(*12*) Ind. Eng. Chem. **1,** 208(1909); JAOAC **3,** 158(1917).
(*13*) JAOAC **5,** 34(1922).
(*14*) J. Am. Chem. Soc. **24,** 1082(1902).
(*15*) USDA Bur. Chem. Bull. **105,** p. 167.
(*16*) JAOAC **3,** 332(1920).
(*17*) JAOAC **3,** 333(1920).
(*18*) USDA Bur. Chem. Bull. **137,** p. 40; **152,** p. 68.
(*19*) JAOAC **5,** 33(1921); 392(1922).
(*20*) JAOAC **47,** 253(1964).
(*21*) Fresenius, "Quantitative Chemical Analysis," Trans. 6th German Ed., 1906, amplified and revised, Vol. **2,** 1180; U.S. Geol. Survey Bull. **700,** p. 218.
(*22*) JAOAC **15,** 289(1932); **17,** 62(1934).
(*23*) JAOAC **10,** 29(1927).
(*24*) JAOAC **35,** 377(1952).
(*25*) JAOAC **10,** 27(1927)
(*26*) JAOAC **10,** 28(1927).
(*27*) JAOAC **3,** 353(1920).
(*28*) JAOAC **18,** 63, 65(1935); **43,** 346(1960).
(*29*) JAOAC **43,** 346(1960).
(*30*) JAOAC **10,** 30, 124(1927); **11,** 35(1928).
(*31*) USDA Bull. **898,** p. 48.
(*32*) JAOAC **9,** 27(1926).
(*33*) USDA Bur. Chem. Circ. **10,** p. 7.
(*34*) JAOAC **9,** 28(1926).
(*35*) USDA Bur. Chem. Bull. **105,** p. 165.
(*36*) JAOAC **9,** 29(1926).
(*37*) Whitmore, "Organic Compounds of Mercury," p. 365; JAOAC **13,** 156(1930).
(*38*) JAOAC **54,** 685(1971).
(*39*) JAOAC **56,** 572(1973).
(*40*) JAOAC **31,** 366(1948).
(*41*) JAOAC **22,** 411(1939); **25,** 79(1942); **28,** 72(1945).
(*42*) JAOAC **43,** 365(1960).
(*43*) JAOAC **48,** 576(1965); **49,** 207(1966).
(*44*) Anal. Chem. **25,** 1207(1953); JAOAC **40,** 732 (1957).
(*45*) JAOAC **55,** 907(1972).
(*46*) Ind. Eng. Chem., Anal. Ed. **10,** 19(1938); JAOAC **21,** 148(1938); **22,** 408(1939); **24,** 70(1941); **43,** 376(1960).
(*47*) JAOAC **44,** 580(1961); **46,** 668(1963).
(*48*) JAOAC **35,** 771(1952); **43,** 350(1960).
(*49*) Contrib. Boyce Thompson Inst. **8,** No. 3, 175(1936); Ind. Eng. Chem., Anal. Ed. **10,** 5(1938); JAOAC **43,** 358(1960).
(*50*) Soap **10,** No. 5, 89(1934); JAOAC **43,** 354(1960); **46,** 664(1963).
(*51*) JAOAC **43,** 374(1960).
(*52*) USDA Bur. Animal Ind. Bull. **133.**
(*53*) JAOAC **44,** 595(1961).
(*54*) JAOAC **53,** 1155(1970).
(*55*) JAOAC **32,** 684(1949); **39,** 373(1956).
(*56*) Ind. Eng. Chem. **8,** 312(1936).
(*57*) Anal. Chem. **19,** 779(1947); Report No. 4760, May 15, 1949, Phys. Chem. Lab., Hooker Electrochemical Co., Niagara Falls, NY.
(*58*) Anal. Chem. **25,** 1661(1953); JAOAC **40,** 737(1957).
(*59*) JAOAC **56,** 567(1973).
(*60*) JAOAC **54,** 688(1971).
(*61*) JAOAC **45,** 513(1962).
(*62*) JAOAC **48,** 573(1965).
(*63*) JAOAC **49,** 254(1966).
(*64*) JAOAC **55,** 942(1972).
(*65*) JAOAC **59,** 716(1976); **61,** 1499(1978).
(*66*) JAOAC **62,** 8(1979).
(*67*) JAOAC **30,** 319(1947); **31,** 368(1948).
(*68*) JAOAC **40,** 286(1957); **43,** 342(1960).
(*69*) JAOAC **52,** 1284(1969).
(*70*) JAOAC **51,** 1301(1968).

(*71*) JAOAC **54,** 706(1971).
(*72*) JAOAC **61,** 1163(1978).
(*73*) Anal. Chem. **31,** 418(1959); JAOAC **43,** 382 (1960); **45,** 522(1962).
(*74*) JAOAC **59,** 1109(1976).
(*75*) JAOAC **60,** 716(1977).
(*76*) JAOAC **60,** 1157(1977).
(*77*) JAOAC **51,** 565(1968).
(*78*) JAOAC **59,** 748(1976).
(*79*) Anal. Chem. **27,** 1774(1955); JAOAC **43,** 382(1960); **45,** 522(1962).
(*80*) JAOAC **57,** 642(1974).
(*81*) JAOAC **50,** 568(1967).
(*82*) JAOAC **50,** 566(1967); **56,** 576(1973); **59,** 753, 1196(1976).
(*83*) JAOAC **47,** 268(1964).
(*84*) JAOAC **49,** 251(1966).
(*85*) Analyst **92,** 375(1967); JAOAC **51,** 1304, 1306 (1968); **55,** 857(1972).
(*86*) JAOAC **48,** 562(1965).
(*87*) J. Sci. Food Agric. **15,** 509(1964); JAOAC **49,** 40(1966); **51,** 447(1968).
(*88*) JAOAC **52,** 1292(1969).
(*89*) Ber. **31,** 2979(1898); J. Am. Chem. Soc. **27,** 1183(1905); USDA Bur. Chem. Bull. **99,** p. 30; **132,** p. 49; **137,** p. 47.
(*90*) Z. anal. Chem. **36,** 18(1897); USDA Bur. Chem. Bull. **132,** p. 49.
(*91*) Ind. Eng. Chem., Anal. Ed. **3,** 357(1931); JAOAC **25,** 80, 668(1942).
(*92*) JAOAC **62,** 11(1979).
(*93*) JAOAC **57,** 771(1974).
(*94*) JAOAC **55,** 1133(1972).
(*95*) JAOAC **55,** 926(1972).
(*96*) JAOAC **62,** 272(1979).
(*97*) JAOAC **61,** 495(1978).
(*98*) Anal. Chem. **23,** 1167(1951); JAOAC **35,** 381(1952); **36,** 384(1953).
(*99*) JAOAC **43,** 344(1960); **47,** 242(1964).
(*100*) JAOAC **60,** 720(1977).
(*101*) JAOAC **60,** 724(1977).
(*102*) JAOAC **60,** 862(1977).
(*103*) JAOAC **47,** 245(1964).
(*104*) JAOAC **51,** 562(1968).
(*105*) Anal. Chem. **21,** 808(1949).
(*106*) JAOAC **34,** 677(1951).
(*107*) JAOAC **57,** 53(1974).
(*108*) JAOAC **56,** 586(1973); **58,** 513, 516(1975); **59,** 758(1976).
(*109*) JAOAC **61,** 1504(1978).
(*110*) JAOAC **43,** 352(1960).

7. Animal Feed

7.001 Sampling (*1*)—Procedure

Use slotted single or double tube, or slotted tube and rod, all with pointed ends.

Take ≥500 g sample, 1 kg preferred, as follows: Lay bag horizontally and remove core diagonally from end to end. Det. number of cores as follows: From lots of 1–10 bags, sample all bags; from lot of ≥11, sample 10 bags. Take 1 core from each bag sampled, except that for lots of 1–4 bags take enough diagonal cores from each bag to total ≥5 cores. For bulk feeds draw ≥10 cores from different regions; in sampling small containers (≤10 lb) 1 package is enough. Reduce composite sample to amt required, preferably by riffling, or by mixing thoroly on clean oil-cloth or paper and quartering. Place sample in air-tight container.

A sample from less than these numbers of bags may be declared an official sample if guarantor agrees. For samples that cannot be representatively taken with probe described, use other sampling means.

7.002 Preparation of Sample—Official Final Action

Grind sample to pass sieve with circular openings 1 mm (1/25") diam. and mix thoroly. If sample cannot be ground, reduce to as fine condition as possible. Do not grind molasses feeds.

Moisture—Official Final Action

I. Drying in Vacuo at 95–100° (*2*)

7.003 ***Determination***

Dry amt sample contg ca 2 g dry material to const wt at 95–100° under pressure ≤100 mm Hg (ca 5 hr). For feeds with high molasses content, use temp. ≤70° and pressure ≤50 mm Hg. Use covered Al dish ≥50 mm diam. and ≤40 mm deep. Report loss in wt as moisture.

II. By Distillation with Toluene (*3*)

7.004 ***Apparatus***

Connect 250 mL flask of Pyrex or other resistant glass by means of Bidwell-Sterling moisture receiver to 500 mm Liebig condenser. Calibrate receiver, 5 mL capacity, by distg known amts H_2O into graduated column, and estg column of H_2O to 0.01 mL. Clean tube and condenser with chromic acid cleaning mixt., rinse thoroly with H_2O, then alcohol, and dry in oven to prevent undue amt H_2O from adhering to inner surfaces during detn.

7.005 ***Determination***

If sample is likely to bump, add dry sand to cover bottom of flask. Add enough toluene to cover sample completely (ca 75 mL). Weigh and introduce enough sample into toluene to give 2–5 mL H_2O and connect app. Fill receiving tube with toluene, pouring it thru top of condenser. Bring to boil and distil slowly, ca 2 drops/sec, until most of the H_2O passes over; then increase rate of distn to ca 4 drops/sec.

When all H_2O is apparently over, wash down condenser by pouring toluene in at top, continuing distn short time to see whether any more H_2O distils over; if it does, repeat washing-down process. If any H_2O remains in condenser, remove by brushing down with tube brush attached to Cu wire and satd with toluene, washing down condenser at same time. (Entire process is usually completed within 1 hr.) Let receiving tube come to room temp. If any drops adhere to sides of tube, force them down, using Cu wire with end wrapped with rubber band. Read vol. H_2O and calc. to %.

7.006 ★ *III. Drying without Heat over Sulfuric Acid* (*4*) ★

See **7.006–7.007**, 12th ed.

7.007 *IV. Drying at 135°* (*5*)

(Not to be used when fat detn is to be made on same sample)

Regulate air oven to 135±2°. Using low, covered Al dishes, **7.003**, weigh ca 2 g sample into each dish and shake until contents are evenly distributed. With covers removed, place dishes and covers in oven as quickly as possible and dry samples 2 hr. Place covers on dishes and transfer to desiccator to cool. Weigh, and calc. loss in wt as H_2O.

7.008 *V. In Highly Acid Milk By-products* (*6*)

Add ca 2 g ZnO, freshly ignited or oven dried, to flat-bottom dish ≥5 cm diam. and weigh. Add ca 1 g sample and weigh quickly. Add ca 5 mL H_2O and distribute sample evenly on bottom of dish. Heat on steam bath, exposing max. surface of dish bottom to live steam until apparently dry. Heat at 98–100° in air oven 3 hr or to const wt. Cool in desiccator; then weigh quickly. Det. wt residue. Titr. acidity of sample and calc. as lactic acid, **16.023**. To compensate for H_2O formed when acid is neutzd by ZnO, add 0.1 g to residue wt for each g acid (as lactic) in weighed sample. Report % residue (corrected) as total solids.

7.009 Ash (*7*)—Official Final Action

Weigh 2 g sample into porcelain crucible and place in temp. controlled furnace preheated to 600°. Hold at this temp. 2 hr. Transfer crucible directly to desiccator, cool, and weigh immediately, reporting % ash to first decimal place.

NITROGEN

Qualitative Tests for Proteins (*8*)—Official Final Action

7.010 ★ *Biuret Test* ★

See **22.012–22.013**, 10th ed.

7.011 ★ *Millon Test* ★

See **22.014–22.015**, 10th ed. (*Caution: See* **51.018**, **51.026**, and **51.065**.)

7.012 ★ *Glyoxylic Acid Test (Hopkins-Cole)* ★

See **22.016–22.017**, 10th ed. (*Caution:* Wear face shield and heavy rubber gloves as protection against reagent bump. *See also* **51.018** and **51.063**.)

★ Surplus method—*see* inside front cover.

7.013 ★ *Adamkiewicz Test* ★

See **22.018**, 10th ed.

7.014 ★ *Xanthoproteic Test* ★

See **22.019**, 10th ed.

Crude Protein—Official Final Action

7.015 *Kjeldahl Method (9)*

Det. N as in **2.057**. Multiply result by 6.25, or in case of wheat grains by 5.70.

Dumas Method (10)

7.016 ***Principle***

N, freed by pyrolysis and subsequent combustions, is swept by CO_2 carrier into nitrometer. CO_2 is absorbed in KOH and vol. residual N is measured and converted to equiv. protein by numerical factor.

7.017 ***Apparatus and Reagents***

(**a**) *Nitrogen analyzer and accessories*.—Consists of combustion and collection and measuring systems. Suitable instrument, Model 29A, with following accessories and reagents is available from Coleman Instruments Div., 2000 York Rd, Oak Brook, IL 60521: Al combustion boats, No. 29–412; Vycor combustion tubes, No. 29–328; CuO-Pt catalyst (CuO wire form with 2.5% Pt reforming catalyst), No. 29–160; reduced Cu wire, No. 29–120; Co_3O_4, No. 29–170; CuO powder, fines, No. 29–140; 45% KOH, No. 29–110.

(**b**) *Balance*.—Accurate to 0.01 mg.

(**c**) *Barometer*.—Hg type, readable to 0.1 mm.

7.018 ***Preparation of Samples***

Grind to pass No. 30 sieve. Store in capped bottles.

7.019 ***Determination***

Operate instrument in accordance with instructions of manufacturer. (Following directions apply to Coleman Model 29A Nitrogen Analyzer. Consult Operating Directions D-360B, Coleman Cat. No. 29–904, for addnl details.)

After combustion furnaces have come to thermal equilibrium, turn combustion cycle control to START and let proceed normally thru cycle. Observe indicated temp. on pyrometer of both upper and lower combustion furnaces at end of combustion portion of cycle. Furnace temps should be 850–900°. If not, adjust.

Prep. combustion tube by inserting stainless steel screen in lower end of combustion tube (end farthest from trademark). In upper end, place enough glass wool to form 6 mm plug when packed. With 11 mm glass rod, drive glass wool down to stainless steel plug. Holding tube vertically, pour CuO-Pt catalyst directly from dispenser bottle into combustion tube until it reaches upper end of trademark. Tap or vibrate tube on bench until reagent settles to approx. center of trademark.

Weigh and record wt of empty Al combustion boat. Place sample in boat. Weigh and record wt of sample and combustion boat. Difference between wts is sample wt. Use following sample wts (mg) as guides to suitable sample sizes: bermuda grass 150–300; rice bran, wheat shorts, dehydrated alfalfa 150–250; range feed 100–200; cottonseed meal 75–150; edible soy protein 50–150. Weigh sample to nearest 0.01 mg. To avoid wt changes,

★ Surplus method—*see* inside front cover.

Table 7:01 Volume correction for temperature correction factor (C_f) (μL/°K)[a]

Final Counter Reading (μL)	(C_f) (Nitrometers with Check Value)
0	12
5000	29
10000	45
15000	62
20000	79
25000	95
30000	112
35000	129
40000	145
45000	162
50000	179

[a] Vol. correction, $V_t = C_f(t_2 - t_1)$

record wt within 1 min after sample and boat are placed on balance. If this is impossible, weigh sample inside weighing bottle, such as Kimble No. 15165 or 15166.

Turn combustion tube to horizontal, and carefully insert loaded sample boat into open end of tube. Slide or push boat, without spilling contents, until it reaches trademark. Raise open end until tube forms 60–70° angle to horizontal. Tap or vibrate combustion tube on bench top while rotating tube between thumb and forefinger. Raise open end of tube and add vol. Co_3O_4 and vol. CuO fines equal to vol. sample. For convenient means of adding above reagents to samples, place vol. CuO fines and vol. Co_3O_4, each equal to vol. sample, in addnl combustion boat; add contents of boat, but not boat itself, to combustion tube; and rotate partially filled combustion tube between thumb and forefinger while varying angle of tube 20–45° from horizontal. Continue rotating, tapping, and vibrating until sample is dispelled from boat and is thoroly mixed with oxidizing agents. Raise open end until tube forms 60–70° angle to horizontal; add CuO-Pt catalyst ca 12 mm above sample boat. Tap or vibrate gently to eliminate voids. Add CuO-Pt catalyst to within 20 mm of top of tube, again tapping or vibrating gently to eliminate voids.

Install prepd combustion tube in N analyzer. Adjust 45% KOH soln meniscus to calibrating mark in nitrometer with digital readout meter. Record counter reading, R_1. (Counter reading should preferably lie between 500 and 1000 μL at this point. Vent control may be used to assist in arriving at this counter setting, if necessary.) Record syringe temp., t_1, indicated on special scale thermometer. Add 2 min more to combustion portion of cycle by turning auxiliary timer to setting 3. (Once this is done, addnl 2 min will be automatically programmed into each subsequent cycle.) Turn combustion cycle control to START. Let analyzer proceed thru its cycle. After cycle is complete and combustion cycle control has entered STAND-BY section, readjust KOH meniscus to calibration mark with digital readout counter. Record new counter reading, R_2, and syringe temp., t_2. Det. blank for instrument under same conditions as actual analysis except omit sample.

Table 7:02 Barometric temperature correction (P_b)

	P_o (mm Hg)	
Temperature, °C	700–749	750–780
10	1.2	1.3
15	1.8	1.9
20	2.3	2.5
25	2.9	3.1
30	3.5	3.7
35	4.1	4.3

7.020 ***Calculations***

(**a**) Record observed N vol., $V_o = R_2 - R_1$, where V_o = observed N vol. (μL), R_1 = initial counter reading, and R_2 = final counter reading.

(**b**) Det. corrected N vol. (in μL), $V_c = V_o - (V_b + V_t)$, where V_b = vol. blank (μL), V_t = vol. correction for temp. (μL) = $C_f(t_2 - t_1)$. C_f is obtained from Table **7:01** (based on final counter reading); t_2 and t_1 are in °K.

(**c**) Det. corrected barometric pressure, $P_c = P_o - (P_b + P_v)$, where P_o = observed barometric pressure (mm Hg), P_b = barometric temp. correction (from Table **7:02**), and P_v = pressure correction for vapor pressure of KOH soln (from Table **7:03**).

(*Note:* Empirical approximation of $(P_b + P_v) = 11.0$ will be satisfactorily accurate for P_o between 740 and 780 mm Hg and syringe temp. between 298 and 305°K.)

(**d**) Calc. % N = $(P_c \times V_c \times 0.0449)/(T \times W)$, where T = final syringe temp. in °K and W = sample wt in mg.

Example:

P_o = 750.1 mm Hg at 25°C; W = 148.91 mg

	Start	*Finish*
Counter readings, blank	500 μL	524 μL
Counter readings, sample	524	6955

$t_1 = 302.7$°K, $t_2 = 303.0$°K, $V_o = 6955 - 524 = 6431$ μL

$V_c = 6431 - [24 + C_f(t_2 - t_1)] = 6431 - (24 + 35 \times 0.3) = 6396$ μL

$P_c = 750.1 - (3.1 \times 9.6) = 737.4$

% N = $(737.4 \times 6396 \times 0.04493)/(303.0 \times 148.91) = 4.69\%$

(**e**) Calc. % protein = % N × 6.25, or % N × 5.70 in case of wheat grains.

Table 7:03 Pressure correction (P_v) for vapor pressure of KOH (for practical purposes, temp. of KOH is same as syringe)

Temperature, °K	P_v (mm Hg)
288	4.1
293	5.7
298	7.4
303	9.6
308	12.5
313	16.5

Automated Method (11)—Official Final Action

7.021 ***Principle***

Automation of macro Kjeldahl method is in 6 steps: sample and reagent addn, initial and final digestion, cooling and diln, NaOH addn, steam distn and titrn, and automatic pumping of flask contents to waste. Chemistry is carried out in macro Kjeldahl flasks equipped with side arms which are rotated at 3 min intervals thru each successive step.

7.022 ***Apparatus***

(**a**) *Kjeldahl (protein/nitrogen) analyzer.*—Kjel-Foss Automatic, Model 16210 (Foss America, Inc., PO Box 504, Rt 82, Fishkill, NY 12524), or equiv.

(**b**) *Weighing papers.*—120 × 120 mm N-free tissues, Foss America, Inc., or equiv.

7.023 ***Reagents***

(**a**) *Kjel-tabs.*—Contg 5 g K_2SO_4 and 0.25 g HgO (Foss America, Inc.).

(**b**) *Kjeldahl (protein/nitrogen) analyzer reagents.*—Prep. following according to manufacturer's instructions: (*1*) *Sulfuric acid.*—96–98%. (*2*) *Hydrogen peroxide.*—30–35%. (*3*) *Ammonium sulfate std solns.*—(*a*) *Std soln I.*—Dissolve 30.000±0.030 g $(NH_4)_2SO_4$ in H_2O and dil. to 1 L with H_2O. (*b*) *Std soln II.*—Dissolve 0.750±0.001 g $(NH_4)_2SO_4$ in H_2O and dil. to 1 L with H_2O. (*4*) *Mixed indicator soln.*—Dissolve 1.000 g Me red and 0.250 g methylene blue in alcohol and dil. to 1 L with alcohol. Dil. 10 mL this soln to 1 L with H_2O. (*5*) *Sodium hydroxide-sodium thiosulfate soln.*—40% NaOH-8% $Na_2S_2O_3.5H_2O$. (*6*) *Dilute sulfuric acid soln.*—0.6%. Dil. 30 mL 96–98% H_2SO_4 to 5 L with H_2O.

7.024 ***Determination***

(*Caution: See* **51.019, 51.030, 51.065,** and **51.070.**)

Place 3 Kjel-tabs in special flask (500 mL of design compatible to Foss instrument) in position 1. Shift dispenser arm over flask and depress H_2SO_4 lever, initiating simultaneous addn of 10 mL 30–35% H_2O_2 and 12–15 mL 96–98% H_2SO_4 (depending on fat content of sample). To flask, add accurately weighed sample (ca 1.0 g if <45% protein, and ca 0.5 g if >45% protein) wrapped in weighing paper and close lid. Flask automatically rotates to position 2 where sample digests 3 min, and then to position 3 for 3 min addnl digestion. In position 4, flask is cooled by centrifugal blower, lid opens automatically, and 140 mL H_2O is added automatically. Flask rotates to position 5, where NaOH-$Na_2S_2O_3$ soln is automatically introduced in excess. Released NH_3 is steam distd quant. into 200 mL tall-form titrn beaker contg 50 mL mixed indicator soln, and is simultaneously titrd automatically with dil. H_2SO_4 soln delivered by photometrically regulated syringe. Final position of syringe is measured by potentiometer, output of which feeds electronic circuitry for conversion to visual display and/or printout in % N or % protein with appropriate conversion factors. In position 6, flask is emptied. Calibrate instrument initially each day with aliquots of $(NH_4)_2SO_4$ std solns and check periodically as stated in operating manual.

Semiautomated Method (12)—Official Final Action

7.025 ***Principle***

Samples are digested in 250 mL calibrated tubes, using block digestor. *A* of NH_3-salicylate complex is read in flowcell at 660 nm, or NH_3, is distd into std acid and back-titrd with std alkali.

7.026 ***Apparatus***

(**a**) *Block digestor.*—Model BD-20 (Technicon Instruments Corp.) or Model DS-20 (Tecator, Inc., 1898 S Flatiron Ct, Boulder, CO 80301). Capable of maintaining 410° and digesting 20 samples at a time in 250 mL calibrated volumetric tubes constricted at top. Block must be equipped with removable shields to enclose exposed area of tubes completely at or above ht of constriction.

(**b**) *Automatic analyzer.*—AutoAnalyzer with following modules (Technicon Instruments Corp.), or equiv.: Sampler II or IV with 40/hr (2:1) cam (higher ratio cams result in carry-over and poorer peak sepn); proportioning pump III; NH_3 anal. cartridge No. 116-D531-01 (or construct equiv. manifold from flow diagram); AAII single channel colorimeter with 15 × 1.5–2.0 mm id tubular flowcell, matched 660 nm interference filters, and voltage stabilizer; and recorder of appropriate span. (*See* Fig. **7:01.**)

7.027 ***Reagents***

(**a**) *Phosphate-tartrate buffer soln.*—pH 14.0. Dissolve 50 g NaK tartrate and 26.8 g $Na_2HPO_4.7H_2O$ in 600 mL H_2O. Add 54 g NaOH and dissolve. Add 1 mL Brij-35 (Technicon Instruments Corp.), dil. to 1 L with H_2O, and mix.

(**b**) *Sodium chloride-sulfuric acid soln.*—Dissolve 200 g NaCl in H_2O in 2 L vol. flask. Add 15 mL H_2SO_4 and 2 mL Brij-35. Dil. to vol. with H_2O and mix.

(**c**) *Sodium hypochlorite soln.*—Dil. 6 mL com. bleach soln contg 5.25% available Cl (Clorox, or equiv.) to 100 mL with H_2O and mix. Prep. fresh daily.

(**d**) *Sodium nitroprusside-sodium salicylate soln.*— Dissolve 150 g $NaC_7H_5O_3$ and 0.3 g $Na_2Fe(CN)_5.NO.2H_2O$ in 600 mL H_2O. Add 1 mL Brij-35, dil. to 1 L with H_2O, and mix.

(**e**) *Nitrogen std solns.*—Prep. 6 stds by accurately weighing ($\pm$10 mg) 59, 118, 177, 236, 295, and 354 mg $(NH_4)_2SO_4$ primary std (Fisher Scientific Co. No. A-938, or equiv.; dry 2 hr at 105° before use and assume theoretical value of 21.20% N after drying) into individual 250 mL digestion tubes. Proceed as in **7.031**, beginning "Add 9 g K_2SO_4, 0.42 g HgO, and 15 mL H_2SO_4 . . ." Stds may be stored and reused until exhausted.

(**f**) *Sodium hydroxide-potassium sulfide soln:*—Dissolve 400 g NaOH in H_2O. While still warm, dissolve 30 g K_2S in soln, and dil. to 1 L.

7.028 ***Analytical System***

If manifold is to be constructed, use clear std pump tubes for all air and soln flows. All fittings, coils, and glass transmission lines are AAII type and size. Use glass transmission tubing for all connections after pump to colorimeter. Construct modified AO fitting on sample diln loop using AO fitting, N13 stainless steel nipple connector, and ½" length of 0.035" id Tygon tubing. Insert N13 nipple approx. halfway into 0.035" Tygon tubing. Insert tubing into side arm of AO fitting far enough so resample line will not pump any air. Space pump tubes equally across pump rollers. Cut 0.16 mL/min resample pump tube $\leqslant$1" at entrance before connecting to side arm of AO fitting. In operation, add buffer and hypochlorite solns thru metal side arms of A10 type fittings; add salicylate soln, (**d**), thru metal insert to 20T coil. Air, reagents, and sample are combined immediately after pump thru injection fittings.

7.029 ***Start-Up***

Start automatic system and place all lines except salicylate line in resp. solns. After $\geqslant$5 min, place salicylate line in resp. soln and let system equilibrate. If ppt forms after addn of salicylate, pH is too low. Immediately stop proportioning pump and flush coils with H_2O, using syringe. Before restarting system, check concns of $NaCl$-H_2SO_4 soln and phosphate-tartrate buffer soln.

Pump lowest concn N std soln continuously thru system $\geqslant$5 min and adjust baseline control on colorimeter to read 10% full scale. Pump highest concn N std soln continuously thru system until no drift exists (usually $\geqslant$10 min) and adjust "std. cal." control to read 85% full scale. Recorder tracings must be stable and show <0.3 division noise. If noisy conditions exist, replace dialyzer membrane. When recorder tracing indicates stable condition, immediately start sampling.

7.030 ***Shut-Down***

Place reagent lines in H_2O, removing salicylate line first. Let system wash out $\geqslant$20 min.

7.031 ***Colorimetric Determination***

(*Caution: See* **51.065**.)

Weigh samples (*See* Table **7:04**) into dry digestion tubes. Add 9 g K_2SO_4, 0.42 g HgO, and 15 mL H_2SO_4 to each tube. (Calibrated metal scoops may be used for solids.) Insert tubes into digestor block preheated to 410°, place shields around tubes, and digest 45 min.

After digestion, remove rack of tubes from block, place in hood, and let cool 8–10 min. (Time depends upon air flow around tubes.) Direct rapid spray of H_2O (kitchen sink dish rinsing sprayer works well) to bottom of each tube to dissolve acid digest completely. If ppt forms, place tube in ultrasonic bath to aid in redissolving salt. Let cool, dil. to vol., and mix thoroly. Transfer portion of each sample soln to AutoAnalyzer beaker.

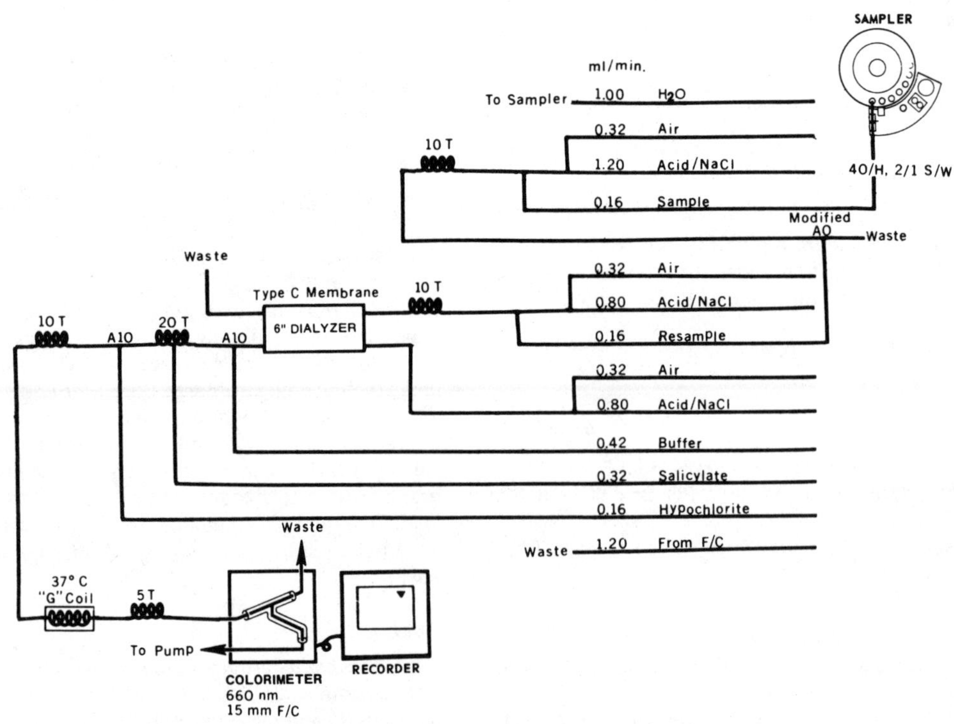

FIG. 7:01—Flow diagram for semiautomated analysis for crude protein

Table 7:04 Sample Weight

Protein, %	Sample, g
6–24	1.5±0.1
25–40	1.0±0.1
41–50	0.8±0.1
51–60	0.7±0.1
61–90	0.5±0.01
>90	Weigh sample equiv. to 50 mg N

Place stds in tray in increasing order of concn, followed by group of samples. Analyze lowest concn std in duplicate, discarding first peak. Precede and follow each group of samples with std ref. curve to correct for possible drift. Analyze stds and samples at rate of 40/hr, 2/1 sample-to-wash ratio. Prep. std curve by averaging peak hts of first and second set of stds. Plot av. peak ht stds against N concn contained in each 250 mL tube.

$$\% \text{ Protein} = [(\text{mg N}/250 \text{ mL from graph}) \times 6.25 \times 100]/\text{mg sample}$$

7.032 ***Titrimetric Determination***

Digest as in **7.031.** Cool 5 min and add only enough H_2O to dissolve salts (70–75 mL). Cool and attach digestion tube to distn head according to manufacturer's directions. Place receiver flask contg 25 mL std acid, **2.055(j)**, and 5–7 drops Me red indicator on platform. Condenser tip must be below surface of std acid soln. Add 50 mL NaOH-K_2S soln to tube and steam distil vigorously until 125 mL distillate collects. Titr. excess acid with std 0.1*N* NaOH soln, **2.055(k)**. Correct for reagent blank.

$$\% \text{ N} = [(\text{mL std acid} \times \text{normality acid}) - (\text{mL std NaOH} \times \text{normality NaOH})] \times 1.4007/\text{g sample}$$

$$\% \text{ crude protein} = \% \text{ N} \times 6.25$$

Urea and Ammoniacal Nitrogen (*13*) Official Final Action

7.033 ***Reagents***

(**a**) *Defoaming soln.*—Dow Corning Corp. Antifoam B Emulsion.

(**b**) *Urease soln.*—Prep. fresh soln by dissolving stdzd urease in H_2O so that each 10 mL neutzd soln will convert N of ≥0.1 g pure urea.

Standardization.—To det. alky of com. urease prepn dissolve 0.1 g in 50 mL H_2O and titr. with 0.1*N* HCl, using Me red, **2.055**(i). Add same vol. 0.1*N* HCl to each 0.1 g urease in prepg urease soln. To det. enzyme activity, prep. ca 50 mL neutzd 1% soln. Add different amts of soln to 0.1 g samples pure urea and follow with enzyme digestion and distn as in detn. Calc. activity of urease prepn from amt of this urease soln that completely converted urea, as detd by complete recovery of N by distn.

(**c**) *Calcium chloride soln.*—Dissolve 25 g $CaCl_2$ in 100 mL H_2O.

7.034 ***Determination***

Place 2 g sample in Kjeldahl flask with ca 250 mL H_2O. Add 10 mL urease soln, stopper tightly, and let stand 1 hr at room temp. or 20 min at 40°. Cool to room temp. if necessary. Use addnl urease soln if feed contains >5% urea (ca 12% protein equiv.). Rinse stopper and neck with few mL H_2O. Add ≥2 g MgO (heavy type), 5 mL $CaCl_2$ soln, and 3 mL defoaming soln, and connect flask with condenser by Kjeldahl connecting bulb. Distil 100 mL into measured vol. std acid, **2.055(j)**, and titr. with std alkali, **2.055(k)**, using Me red, **2.055(i)**.

★ Surplus method—*see* inside front cover.

Urea (*14*)—Official Final Action

(Applicable to animal feeds and their ingredients)

7.035 ***Apparatus***

Spectrophotometer.—Instrument with max. band width 2.4 nm at 420 nm, with 1 cm cells.

7.036 ***Reagents***

(**a**) *p-Dimethylaminobenzaldehyde (DMAB) soln.*—Dissolve 16.00 g (Eastman Kodak Co. No. 95 only) in 1 L alcohol and add 100 mL HCl. Stable 1 month. Prep. new std curve with each new batch of reagent.

(**b**) *Zinc acetate soln.*—Dissolve 22.0 g $Zn(OAc)_2.2H_2O$ in H_2O, add 3 mL HOAc, and dil. to 100 mL.

(**c**) *Potassium ferrocyanide soln.*—Dissolve 10.6 g $K_4Fe(CN)_6.3H_2O$ in H_2O and dil. to 100 mL.

(**d**) *Vegetable charcoal.*—Darco G-60.

(**e**) *Phosphate buffer soln.*—pH 7.0. Dissolve 3.403 g anhyd. KH_2PO_4 and 4.355 g anhyd. K_2HPO_4 sep. in ca 100 mL portions freshly distd H_2O. Combine solns and dil. to 1 L with H_2O.

(**f**) *Urea std solns.*—(*1*) *Stock soln.*—5 mg/mL. Dissolve 5.000±0.001 g reagent grade urea in H_2O and dil. to 1 L with H_2O. (*2*) *Working solns.*—0.2, 0.4, 0.6, 0.8, 1.0, 1.2, 1.4, 1.6, 1.8, and 2.0 mg urea/5 mL. Pipet 2, 4, 6, 8, 10, 12, 14, 16, 18, and 20 mL stock soln into 250 mL vol. flasks and dil. to vol. with phosphate buffer. (*3*) *Reference soln.*—Use std soln contg 1.0 mg urea/5 mL as ref. std. Store at <24°. Stable 1 week.

7.037 ***Preparation of Standard Curve***

Pipet 5 mL aliquots of working std solns into 20 × 150 mm (25 mL) test tubes and add 5 mL DMAB soln to each. Prep. reagent blank of 5 mL buffer soln and 5 mL DMAB soln. Shake tubes thoroly and let stand 10 min in H_2O bath at 25°. Read *A* in 1 cm cell at 420 nm with reagent blank at zero *A*. Plot *A* against concn urea. Plot should be straight line; if not, repeat, using new lot of DMAB.

7.038 ***Determination***

Weigh 1.00 g ground sample into 500 mL vol. flask. Add 1 g charcoal, ca 250 mL H_2O, 5 mL $Zn(OAc)_2$ soln, and 5 mL $K_4Fe(CN)_6$ soln. Shake mech. 30 min and dil. to vol. with H_2O. Let stand until ppt settles. Decant thru Whatman No. 40 paper and collect clear filtrate. Pipet 5 mL filtrate into test tube, add 5 mL DMAB soln, and shake thoroly. Include reference std (5 mL soln (**f**)(*3*) and 5 mL DMAB soln) and reagent blank with each group of samples. Let stand 10 min in H_2O bath at 25°. Read *A* at 420 nm against reagent blank.

$$\% \text{ Urea} = (1.0 \times A_{sample} \times 100)/(A_{std} \times \text{mg sample in aliquot}).$$

7.039 ★ **Albuminoid Nitrogen—Official Final Action** ★

Pptn with $Cu(OH)_2$ and N detn. *See* **22.020–22.021,** 10th ed.

7.040 ★ **Amido Nitrogen—Official Final Action** ★

% total N − % albuminoid N = % amido N.

Nitrate and Nitrite Nitrogen (*15*)—Official Final Action

7.041 ***Principle***

Nitrate and nitrite are extd with Cd and Ba chloride soln. Bulk of sol. proteins are pptd in alk. soln and clarified soln is passed thru metallic Cd column, reducing nitrate to nitrite. Nitrite is measured colorimetrically. (*Caution:* Cd salts are toxic. *See* **51.084.**)

7.042 ***Reagents and Apparatus***

(**a**) *Nitrate nitrogen std solns*.—(*1*) *Stock soln*.—12 μg nitrate N/mL. Dissolve 0.867 g KNO_3 in 1 L H_2O. Dil. 25 mL to 250 mL with H_2O. (*2*) *Working solns*.—0.6, 1.2, 1.8, 2.4, 3.0 μg N/mL. Dil. 5, 10, 15, 20, and 25 mL stock soln to 100 mL with H_2O.

(**b**) *Extracting soln*.—Dissolve and dil. 50 g $CdCl_2$ and 50 g $BaCl_2$ to 1 L with H_2O. Adjust to pH 1 with HCl.

(**c**) *Ammonium chloride buffer soln*.—pH 9.6. Dissolve 50 g NH_4Cl in 500 mL H_2O and adjust pH with NH_4OH. Dil. to 1 L with H_2O.

(**d**) *Sodium hydroxide soln*.—2.5*N*. Dissolve 50 g NaOH in 500 mL H_2O.

(**e**) *Sulfanilamide soln*.—0.5%. Dissolve 1.25 g sulfanilamide in 250 mL HCl (1+1). Soln is stable 1–2 months.

(**f**) *Coupling reagent*.—Dissolve 0.5 g N(1-naphthyl)ethylenediamine.HCl in 100 mL H_2O. Store in g-s dark bottle in refrigerator. Soln is stable several weeks.

(**g**) *Salt soln*.—Dissolve 100 g NaCl in 500 mL H_2O. Add 50 mL buffer soln, (**c**), and dil. to 1 L with H_2O.

(**h**) *Reduction tube*.—25 mL buret or equiv. id chromatgc tube with stopcock and reservoir (Kontes Glass Co. Cat. No. K-420280 or SGA Scientific Inc. Cat. No. JC-1506).

7.043 ***Preparation of Columns***

Prep. supply of metallic Cd by placing Zn rods into 500 mL 20% $CdSO_4$ soln. After reaction for 3 hr, discard soln and scrape moss-like Cd growth from Zn rods. Place Cd in high-speed blender, add 500 mL H_2O, and blend 2 sec. Wash fine metal particles with H_2O onto sieves, collecting only 20–40 mesh size. Fill reduction tube with H_2O and add 2 cm plug of glass wool. Press any trapped air from glass wool as it is pushed to bottom of column with glass rod. Add Cd to depth of 10 cm, using min. of very gentle tapping. Wash column with 25 mL 0.10*N* HCl, two 25 mL portions H_2O, and finally 25 mL buffer, (**c**), dild 1 + 9. Keep column covered with salt soln, (**g**), when not in use.

Normally columns can be used repeatedly if kept under salt soln between analyses. When succession of highly proteinaceous or other sol. org. contg samples are treated, flow rate may decrease gradually. Repeating 25 mL 0.10*N* HCl treatment may restore original flow rate; if not, prep. new column. Reproducible flow rate is important. Actual rate can be 3–5 mL/min but once established, it must be identical ($\pm$0.1 mL) for samples and stds.

7.044 ***Preparation of Standard Curve***

Prep. std curve of 3, 6, 9, 12, and 15 μg nitrate-nitrite N by pipetting 5.0 mL aliquots of working std solns into 30 mL beakers. Add 5 mL buffer soln, (**c**), and 15 mL H_2O, mix well, and transfer quant. to reduction column, using min. H_2O. Adjust flow rate thru column to 3–5 mL/min. Just as reservoir empties, add 15 mL salt soln, (**g**). Collect eluate, including salt wash, in 50 mL vol. flask (total vol. of eluate should be ca 40 mL). Add 5 mL sulfanilamide soln, (**e**), mix, and let stand 3 min. Add 2 mL coupling reagent, (**f**), mix, dil. to vol. with H_2O, mix, and let stand 20 min for max. color development. Color is stable $\geq$2 hr. Det. *A* in 1 cm cells at 540 nm against reagent blank. Plot *A* against μg nitrate-nitrite N.

7.045 ***Extraction***

(**a**) *Low level nitrate samples* (*grains, meals, supplements, etc.*).—Wash 5.0 g finely ground sample into 250 mL vol. flask. Add 100 mL extg soln, (**b**), and 100 mL H_2O, and mix. Let stand 1 hr with occasional swirling. Add 20 mL 2.5*N* NaOH, dil. to vol. with H_2O, mix, and filter immediately thru rapid paper. Pipet 10 mL buffer soln, (**c**), into 100 mL vol. flask, dil. to vol. with clear filtrate, and mix.

(**b**) *Dry, high level nitrate products* (*dried plants, hays, meals, etc.*).—Weigh 5.0 g finely ground sample into 500 mL vol. flask. Add 100 mL extg soln, (**b**), and 300 mL H_2O, and mix. Let stand 1 hr with occasional swirling, add 40 mL 2.5*N* NaOH, dil. to vol. with H_2O, mix, and filter immediately thru rapid paper. Pipet 10 mL buffer soln, (**c**), into 100 mL vol. flask, dil. to vol. with clear filtrate, and mix.

(**c**) *Grasses, silages, and other wet materials*.— Weigh 100 g sample into 1 gal. capacity high-speed blender. Add 100 mL extg soln, (**b**), and 800 mL H_2O, including vol. H_2O contributed by sample as detd in **7.003** or **7.005**. Homogenize 1 min, pour into 2 L beaker, and let stand 1 hr. Add 100 mL buffer soln, (**c**) (total vol. 1 L), mix well, and filter thru Whatman No. 42 paper, collecting portion of clear filtrate.

7.046 ***Determination***

(**a**) *Nitrate plus nitrite nitrogen*.—Pipet 25 mL buffered sample exts, **7.045**(**a**) or (**b**), or 5 mL ext, (**c**), into reduction column and treat as in **7.044**, beginning, "Adjust flow rate thru column . . ." Rinse column with 30 mL H_2O between samples to remove NaCl. Use portion of buffered sample exts with equiv. diln and pH as ref. soln in detg *A* at 540 nm. Also det. nitrate-nitrite in reagents and correct for this blank value. Calc. total nitrate-nitrite N from std curve.

(**b**) *Nitrite nitrogen*.—Pipet aliquot clear sample filtrate (contg $<$15 μg nitrite) into 50 mL vol. flask and dil. with H_2O to ca 40 mL. Mix well, add 5 mL sulfanilamide soln, (**e**), mix, and let stand 3 min. Add 2 mL coupling reagent, (**f**), and dil. to vol. with H_2O. Mix well and let stand 20 min for max. color development. Measure *A* in 1 cm cells against sample ext with equiv. diln at 540 nm. Correct for nitrite reagent blank.

(**c**) *Nitrate nitrogen*.—Calc. by difference between (**a**) and (**b**) above.

7.047 ***Calculation***

$$\text{ppm } NO_2 \text{ and/or } NO_3\text{-N} = \mu g\ NO_3\text{-N found} \times \text{diln factor/g sample.}$$

Diln factors for exts: **7.045**(**a**), 11.1; (**b**), 22.2; (**c**), 200.

Pepsin Digestibility of Animal Protein Feeds (*16*)
Official Final Action

7.048 ***Principle***

Defatted sample is digested 16 hr with warm soln of pepsin under const agitation. Insol. residue is isolated by filtering, washed, dried, and weighed to det. % residue. Residue is examined microscopically and analyzed for protein. Filtration method is applicable to all animal proteins. Methods are not applicable to vegetable proteins or mixed feeds because of presence of complex carbohydrates and other compds not digested by pepsin.

7.049 ***Apparatus***

(**a**) *Agitator*.—*See* Fig. **7:02**. Continuous, slow speed (15 rpm), end-over-end type, to operate inside incubator at 45$\pm$2° and carry 8 oz screw-cap prescription bottles, or equiv. Agitator and bottles available from D. E. Sims, 716 Forrest Ave, Quincy, IL 62301. Stirring or reciprocating (shaking) type agitator cannot be used because solid particles collect on sides of bottle and do not contact pepsin soln. If heat from agitator motor raises incubator temp. to $>$45°, mount motor outside incubator by drilling hole thru side of incubator and connecting motor to

FIG. 7:02—Agitator

agitator with extension shaft and coupling (available from agitator supplier). (*Caution: See* **51.012**.)

(**b**) *Settling rack.*—Wood or metal to hold digestion bottles at 45° angle. May be made from 2 boards nailed horizontally into "V" cut into vertical end pieces. Also available from agitator supplier, (**a**).

(**c**) *Filtering device.*—Modified California buchner, **7.063**(**d**), available from Labconco Corp., 8811 Prospect Ave, Kansas City, MO 64132, No. 55100. (If edge of screen is rough, smooth with small-tip soldering iron.) Use with retainer sleeve, 2 × 2.75" od stainless steel tube, available from agitator supplier, (**a**).

(**d**) *Glass fiber filter.*—7 cm, Reeve Angel No. 934-AH, or equiv.

(**e**) *Moisture dishes.*—Al, 78 mm od × 20 mm, with outside cover and vertical sides (Curtin Matheson Scientific, Inc., No. 19370-30, or equiv.).

7.050 ***Reagent***

Pepsin soln.—0.2% pepsin (activity 1:10,000) in 0.075*N* HCl; do *not* use pepsin of activity other than 1:10,000. *Prep. just before use* by dilg 6.1 mL HCl to 1 L and heating to 42–45°. Add pepsin and stir gently until dissolved. Do not heat pepsin soln on hot plate or overheat.

7.051 ***Preparation of Sample***

Sieve sample, **7.001**, thru No. 20 sieve. Grind portion retained on sieve to pass No. 20 sieve. Combine both portions and blend by stirring and shaking in pt (500 mL) jar. Thoro blending is essential. Because of high fat content of many animal products, grinding without sieving may cause sticking in mill, loss of moisture or fat, or poorly blended sample.

7.052 ***Extraction***

(*Caution: See* **51.011**, **51.039**, and **51.054**.)

Prep. extn thimble from 11 cm Whatman No. 2 paper, or equiv., as follows: Fold paper in half; straighten paper and refold at right angles to first fold; turn paper over and repeat process with folds at 45° to original fold; while holding creased paper in one hand, place short test tube (6–8 mm smaller in diam. than extractor sample holder or cup in which thimble is to be used) at its center; fold along natural crease lines to form 4-pointed star around tube; and wrap points in same direction around tube to complete thimble.

Weigh 1.000 g ground sample (0.500 g of poultry byproducts or hydrolyzed feathers because of gummy nature and amt of residue) into thimble and ext 1 hr with ether at condensation rate of 3–4 drops/sec. (If Soxhlet is used, top of thimble should extend above siphon tube to avoid loss of solid particles. If paper contg sample is totally submerged in siphon cup, sample must be completely wrapped in paper.) Observe ether ext to det. that no solid particles were carried into solv. For approx. fat content detn, evap. ether, and dry and weigh residue. Remove paper from sample container or cup and let dry at room temp. Unfold, and quant. brush defatted sample into digestion bottle, avoiding contamination by brush bristles or filter paper fibers. Use of powder funnel is helpful to avoid loss.

7.053 ***Pepsin Digestion***

To defatted sample in agitator bottle add 150 mL freshly prepd pepsin soln prewarmed to 42–45°. Be sure sample is completely wetted by pepsin soln. Stopper bottle, clamp in agitator, and incubate with const agitation 16 hr at 45°.

7.054 ***Treatment of Residue***

Dry individual sheets of glass fiber filter, (**d**), 30 min at 110° in moisture dishes with cover open. Cool in desiccator 30 min with cover closed, and weigh (W_1).

Remove bottles from agitator. Place in 45° angle settling rack and loosen caps. Let residue settle ≥15 min. Place weighed filter in California buchner, (**c**), apply suction, and moisten with H_2O. Place retainer sleeve on filter and press down gently. Rinse particles of residue on cap onto filter with small amt H_2O. Carry bottle from rack to filter at same angle as settled and slowly pour contents thru filter as continuous small stream, avoiding all unnecessary agitation. Liq. passes thru paper as rapidly as poured, with residue spreading over surface of filter but not covering it completely until all or pratically all of liq. has passed thru. If filtration rate becomes slow, it may be accelerated by adding acetone washes described below, but only if no significant amt of digestion mixt. remains on funnel when acetone is added. (Filtration (passage of aq. mixt. thru filter) should be complete within 1 min with most proteins.) After supernate has passed thru filter, quant. transfer residue onto filter as follows:

Add 15 mL acetone to bottle. Hold thumb over bottle neck and shake vigorously. Release pressure, replace thumb over bottle neck, and shake bottle in inverted position over filter. Remove thumb, letting acetone and residue discharge onto filter. Repeat rinse with second 15 mL portion acetone, shaking and releasing pressure as above. Inspect bottle, and rinse further with acetone, using policeman, if necessary. If >3 mm liq. remains on paper when acetone washes are started, it may be necessary to use three 15 mL acetone washes instead of 2 to increase filtration rate.

After all liq. passes thru funnel, wash residue and inside surface of retainer sleeve with 2 small portions acetone from wash bottle or hypodermic syringe, and suck dry. Remove retainer sleeve from funnel. Transfer filter to original moisture dish. Scrape or brush any residue particles or filter clinging to retainer sleeve or funnel onto filter in moisture dish. Dry in oven, cool, and weigh as before (W_2). Calc. % indigestible residue = $(W_2 - W_1) \times 100$/g sample.

Det. indigestible protein by transferring filter contg residue directly to Kjeldahl flask. Proceed as in **7.015**. (*Caution:* Violent reaction may take place when NaOH is mixed with dild digestion mixt., caused by large excess H_2SO_4 due to small amt org. material from residue and none from glass filter. Avoid by thoroly mixing and cooling digestion mixt. before addn of NaOH or by using 20 mL H_2SO_4 in Kjeldahl digestion instead of 25 mL.) Make blank detn on 1 sheet of glass filter and subtract from each sample detn, if necessary. Calc. % protein based on original sample wt. Result represents % indigestible protein in *sample*. Convert to % crude protein content of sample not digested, "protein indigestible" = % indigestible protein in sample × 100/% total crude protein in sample.

OTHER CONSTITUENTS

Crude Fat or Ether Extract

Use method **7.056** or **7.057** for mixed feeds other than (*1*) entirely baked and/or expanded, (*2*) entirely dried milk products, or (*3*) contg urea.

Direct Method—Official Final Action

7.055 ***Reagent***

Anhydrous ether.—Wash com. ether with 2 or 3 portions H_2O, add solid NaOH or KOH, and let stand until most of H_2O is abstracted from the ether. Decant into dry bottle, add small pieces of carefully cleaned metallic Na, and let stand until H evolution ceases. Keep ether, thus dehydrated, over metallic Na in loosely stoppered bottles. (*Caution: See* **51.034** and **51.054**.)

7.056 ***Determination***

(Large amts H_2O-sol. components such as carbohydrates, urea, lactic acid, glycerol, and others may interfere with extn of fat; if present, ext 2 g sample on small paper in funnel with five 20 mL portions H_2O prior to drying for ether extn. *Caution: See* **51.009**, **51.011**, and **51.054**.)

Ext ca 2 g sample, dried as in **7.003** or **7.006★**, with anhyd. ether. Use thimble with porosity permitting rapid passage of ether. Extn period may vary from 4 hr at condensation rate of 5–6 drops/sec to 16 hr at 2–3 drops/sec. Dry ext 30 min at 100°, cool, and weigh.

7.057 ***Indirect Method—Official Final Action***

Det. moisture as in **7.003** or **7.006★**; then ext dried substance as in **7.056**, and dry again. Report loss in wt as ether ext.

7.058 ***In Baked or Expanded and Intermediate Moisture (Semimoist or Soft-Moist) Pet Foods (17) Official Final Action***

(To be used only on products which have been baked and/or expanded, and on intermediate moisture pet foods. Not applicable to canned, fresh, or frozen pet food. Such products should be dried at 70–110°, then ground, and drying completed by **7.003** or **7.006★** followed by **7.056** or **7.057**. *Caution: See* **51.011**, **51.054**, and **51.073**.)

Place ca 2 g, accurately weighed, ground, well mixed sample in Mojonnier fat-extn tube, add 2 mL alcohol to prevent lumping on addn of acid, and shake to moisten all particles. Add 10 mL HCl (25+11), mix well, and set tube 30–40 min in H_2O bath at 70–80°, shaking frequently. Cool to room temp. and add alcohol until liq. level rises into constricted portion of Mojonnier tube.

Add 25 mL ether, stopper with glass, Neoprene, or good quality rubber stopper thoroly cleaned with alcohol, and shake vigorously 1 min. Carefully release pressure so that no solv. is lost. Wash adhering solv. and fat from stopper back into extn tube with few mL redistd pet ether (bp <60°). Add 25 mL redistd pet ether, stopper, and shake vigorously 1 min. Let stand until upper liq. is practically clear or centrf. 20 min at ca 600 rpm. Pour as much of ether-fat soln as possible thru filter consisting of cotton pledget packed just firmly enough in funnel stem to let ether pass freely into 150 mL beaker contg several glass beads. Rinse lip of tube with few mL pet ether. Re-ext liq. remaining in tube twice, each time with only 15 mL of each ether, shaking 1 min after addn of each ether. Pour clear ether soln thru filter into same beaker as before, and wash tip of tube, stopper, funnel, and end of funnel stem with few mL of mixt. of 2 ethers (1+1). Evap. slowly on steam bath under gentle stream of air or N. Continue heating on steam bath 15 min after solv. has evapd; then cool to room temp.

Redissolve dried fat residue in four 10 mL portions Et ether, filtering each portion thru small pledget of cotton into 100 mL beaker, contg few glass beads, that has been predried 30 min at 100°, cooled to room temp. in desiccator, and weighed immediately. Use fifth 10 mL portion ether for rinsing cotton and funnel. Evap. ether on steam bath, dry 90 min at 100°, cool to room temp. in desiccator, and weigh immediately. Correct this wt by blank detn on reagents used.

7.059 ***In Dried Milk Products (18)—Official Final Action***

Proceed as in **16.199(b)** and **16.200**, using 8.5 mL H_2O and 1.5 mL NH_4OH.

7.060 ***In Fish Meal***

See **18.046** and **18.047–18.049**.

Crude Fiber (*19*)—Official Final Action

AOCS-AOAC Method

(*Caution: See* **51.086**.)

7.061 ***Principle***

Crude fiber is loss on ignition of dried residue remaining after digestion of sample with 1.25% H_2SO_4 and 1.25% NaOH solns under specific conditions. Method is applicable to grains, meals, flours, feeds, and fiber-bearing material from which fat can be extd to leave workable residue.

7.062 ***Reagents***

(a) *Sulfuric acid soln.*—0.255±0.005*N*. 1.25 g H_2SO_4/100 mL. Concn must be checked by titrn.

(b) *Sodium hydroxide soln.*—0.313±0.005*N*. 1.25 g NaOH/100 mL, free, or nearly so, from Na_2CO_3. Concn must be checked by titrn.

(c) *Prepared asbestos.*—Spread thin layer acid-washed, medium or long fiber asbestos in evapg dish and heat 16 hr at 600° in furnace. Boil 30 min with 1.25% H_2SO_4, filter, wash thoroly with H_2O, and boil 30 min with 1.25% NaOH. Filter, wash once with 1.25% H_2SO_4, wash thoroly with H_2O, dry, and ignite 2 hr at 600°.

Det. blank by treating 1.0 g prepd asbestos with acid and alkali as in detn. Correct crude fiber results for any blank, which should be negligible (ca 1 mg). Asbestos recovered from detn may be used in subsequent detns.

(d) *Alcohol.*—95% or reagent alcohol, MeOH, or isopropanol.

(e) *Antifoam.*—Dow Corning Corp. Antifoam A compd dild 1+4 with mineral spirits or pet ether, or H_2O-dild Antifoam B Emulsion (1+4). Do not use Antifoam Spray.

(f) *Bumping chips or granules.*—Broken Alundum crucibles or equiv. granules (RR Alundum 90 mesh, Norton Co., 1 New Bond St, Worcester, MA 01606) are satisfactory.

7.063 ***Apparatus***

(a) *Digestion apparatus.*—With condenser to fit 600 mL beaker, and hot plate adjustable to temp. that will bring 200 mL

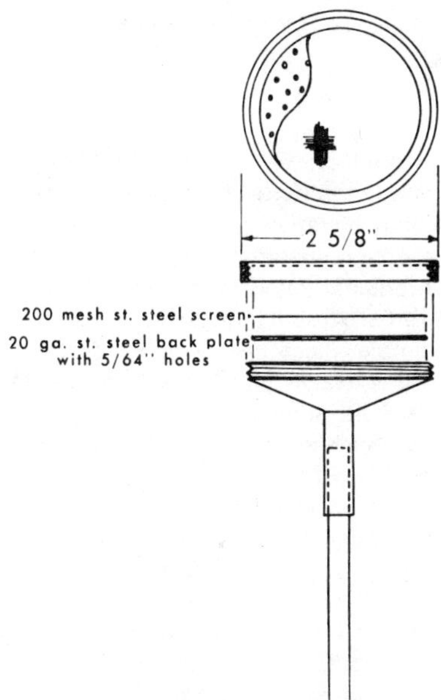

FIG. 7:03—Oklahoma State filter screen

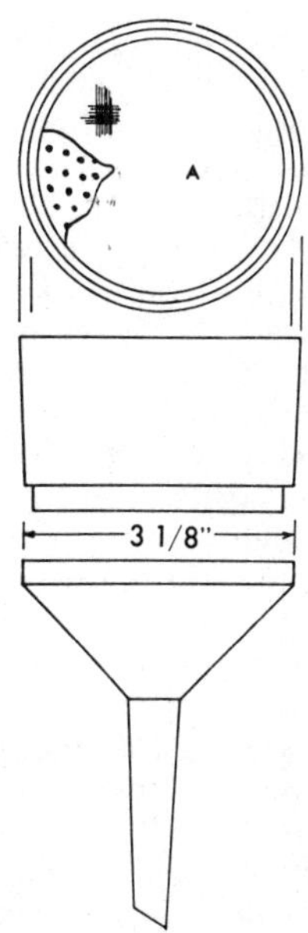

FIG. 7:04—Modified California State buchner funnel, 2-piece polypropylene plastic, covered with 200-mesh screen, A, heat-sealed to edge of filtering surface

H_2O at 25° to rolling boil in 15±2 min. (Available from Labconco Corp., 8811 Prospect Ave, Kansas City, MO 64132.)

(**b**) *Ashing dishes*.—Silica, Vitreosil 70 × 15 mm; or porcelain, Coors, No. 450, size 1, or equiv.

(**c**) *Desiccator*.—With efficient desiccant such as 4–8 mesh Drierite ($CaCl_2$ is not satisfactory).

(**d**) *Filtering device*.—With No. 200 type 304 or 316 stainless steel screen (W. S. Tyler Co., 8200 Tyler Blvd, Mentor, OH 44060), easily washed free of digested residue. Either Oklahoma State filter screen (*see* Fig. **7:03**; available from Labconco Corp.) or modified California plastic buchner (*see* Fig. **7:04**; consists of 2 piece polypropylene plastic funnel manufactured by Nalge Co., 75 Panorama Creek Drive, Rochester, NY 14602, Cat. No. 4280, 70 mm (without No. 200 screen), or equiv. (also available from Labconco Corp.). Seal screen to filtering surface of funnel, using small-tip soldering iron).

(**e**) *Suction filter*.—To accommodate filtering devices. Attach suction flask to trap in line with aspirator or other source of vac. with valve to break vac.

(**f**) *Liquid preheater*.—For preheating H_2O, 1.25% H_2SO_4, and 1.25% NaOH solns to bp of H_2O. Convenient system, shown in Fig. **7:05**, consists of sheet Cu tank with 3 coils of ⅜" (10 mm) od Cu tubing, 12.5′ (3.8 m) long. Solder inlets and outlets where tubing passes thru tank walls. Connect to reflux condenser and fill with H_2O. Keep H_2O boiling with two 750 watt thermostatically controlled hot plates. Use Tygon for inlet leads to reservoirs of H_2O, acid, and alkali; use gum rubber tubing for outlets. Capacity of preheater is adequate for 60 analyses in 8 hr.

7.064 ***Preparation of Sample***

Reduce sample (riffle is suitable) to 100 g and place portion in sealed container for H_2O detn. Immediately det. H_2O. Grind remainder to uniform fineness. (Weber mill (Sargent-Welch Scientific Co. S-60870) with screen 0.033–0.040" (No. 18 or 20), Micro mill (Pulverizing Machinery, Div. Mikropul Corp., 10 Chatham Rd, Summit, NJ 07901) with screen 1/25–1/16" (No. 18–No. 12), and Wiley mill with 1 mm (No. 18) screen give comparable fineness.) Since most materials lose moisture during grinding, det. H_2O on ground sample at same time sample is taken for crude fiber detn.

7.065 ***Determination***

Ext 2 g ground material with ether or pet ether, **14.088**. If fat is <1%, extn may be omitted. Transfer to 600 mL beaker, avoiding fiber contamination from paper or brush. Add ca 1 g prepd asbestos, 200 mL boiling 1.25% H_2SO_4, and 1 drop dild antifoam. (Excess antifoam may give high results; use only if necessary to control foaming.) Bumping chips or granules may also be added. Place beaker on digestion app. with preadjusted hot plate and boil exactly 30 min, rotating beaker periodically to keep solids from adhering to sides. Remove beaker, and filter as in (**a**) or (**b**).

(**a**) *Using Oklahoma filter screen*.—Turn on suction and insert screen (precoated with asbestos if extremely fine materials are analyzed) into beaker, keeping face of screen just under surface of liq. until all liq. is removed. Without breaking suction or raising filter, add 50–75 mL boiling H_2O. After wash is removed,

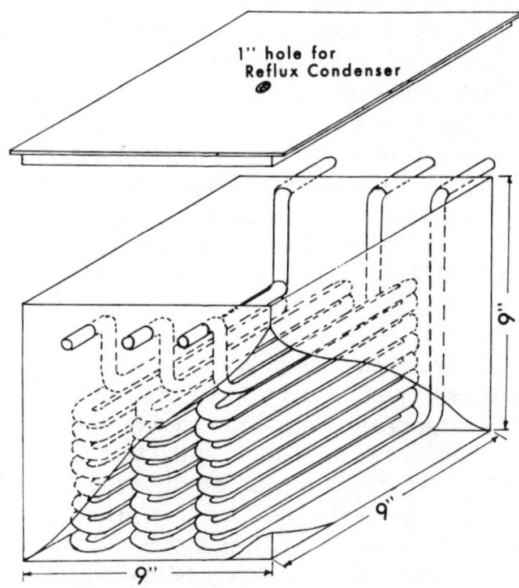

FIG. 7:05—Continuous heater for distilled water, 1.25% alkali, and 1.25% acid

repeat with three 50 mL washings. (Work rapidly to keep mat from becoming dry.) Remove filter from beaker and drain all H_2O from line by raising above trap level. Return mat and residue to beaker by breaking suction and blowing back. Add 200 mL boiling 1.25% NaOH and boil exactly 30 min. Remove beaker, and filter as above. Without breaking suction, wash with 25 mL boiling 1.25% H_2SO_4 and three 50 mL portions boiling H_2O. Drain free of excess H_2O by raising filter. Lower filter into beaker and wash with 25 mL alcohol. Drain line, break suction, and remove mat by blowing back thru filter screen into ashing dish. Proceed as in **(c)**.

(b) *Using California buchner*.—Filter contents of beaker thru buchner (precoated with asbestos if extremely fine materials are being analyzed), rinse beaker with 50–75 mL boiling H_2O, and wash thru buchner. Repeat with three 50 mL portions H_2O, and suck dry. Remove mat and residue by snapping bottom of buchner against top while covering stem with thumb or forefinger and replace in beaker. Add 200 mL boiling 1.25% NaOH and boil exactly 30 min. Remove beaker, and filter as above. Wash with 25 mL boiling 1.25% H_2SO_4, three 50 mL portions H_2O, and 25 mL alcohol. Remove mat and residue; transfer to ashing dish.

(c) *Treatment of residue*.—Dry mat and residue 2 hr at 130±2°. Cool in desiccator and weigh. Ignite 30 min at 600±15°. Cool in desiccator and reweigh.

% Crude fiber in ground sample = C = (Loss in wt on ignition − loss in wt of asbestos blank) × 100/wt sample.

% Crude fiber on desired moisture basis = C × (100 − % moisture desired)/(100 − % moisture in ground sample).

Report results to 0.1%.

Asbestos-Free (AF) Method (20)
Official Final Action

7.066 ***Principle***

Principle is same as in **7.061**, except sample is exposed to min. vac. needed to regulate filtration, and heating of sample solns prevents gelling or pptn of possible satd solns.

7.067 ***Apparatus and Reagents***

See reagents **7.062(a)**, **(b)**, and **(f)**; app. **7.063(a)**, **(c)**, **(d)**, and **(f)**, and **14.088**; and in addn:

(a) *Filtration apparatus*.—System to permit application of min. vac. necessary for filtration and washing of each sample within 3–5 min. Each unit consists of reservoir manifold connected to *(1)* H_2O aspirator thru 120° stopcock, *(2)* atm. thru second stopcock with metering device, and *(3)* receptacle contg cone-shaped hard rubber gasket which provides vac. seal with crucible. Vac. gage attached to manifold indicates vac. applied to crucible. Crucible can be heated before and during filtration by flow of hot H_2O in surrounding jacket. (For photograph of app., *see* JAOAC **56**, 1353(1973). Filtration unit is available as Model 150 from Analytical BioChemistry Laboratories, Inc., PO Box 1097, Columbia, MO 65201.)

(b) *Crucible*.—Fritted glass, 50 mL, coarse porosity. Clean as follows: Brush, and flow hot tap H_2O into crucible to remove as much ash as possible. Submerge crucible in base soln, **(c)***(2)*, ≥5 min, remove, and rinse with hot tap H_2O. Submerge in HCl (1+1), **(c)** *(1)*, ≥5 min, remove, and rinse thoroly with hot tap H_2O followed by distd H_2O. After 3–4 uses, back wash by inverting crucible on hard rubber gasket in filtration app., and flowing near-boiling H_2O thru crucible under partial vac.

(c) *Cleaning solns*.—*(1) Acid soln*.—HCl (1+1). *(2) Base soln*.—Dissolve 5 g Na_2H_2EDTA, 50 g Na_2HPO_4 (tech. grade), and 200 g KOH in H_2O, and dil. to 1 L. Storage in sep. wide mouth containers holding 2–3 L soln into which crucibles can be placed is convenient.

7.068 ***Determination***

(*Caution: See* **51.011** and **51.073**.)

Ext 2 g ground material with ether or pet ether, **14.088**. If fat is <1%, extn may be omitted. Transfer to 600 mL reflux beaker, avoiding fiber contamination from paper or brush. Add 0.25–0.5 g bumping granules, followed by 200 mL near-boiling 1.25% H_2SO_4 soln in small stream directly on sample to aid in complete wetting of sample. Place beakers on digestion app. at 5 min intervals and boil exactly 30 min, rotating beakers periodically to keep solids from adhering to sides. Near end of refluxing place California buchner, **7.063(d)**, previously fitted with No. 9 rubber stopper to provide vac. seal, into filtration app., and adjust vac. to ca 25 mm Hg (735 mm pressure). At end of refluxing, flow near-boiling H_2O thru funnel to warm it; then decant liq. thru funnel, washing solids into funnel with min. of near-boiling H_2O. Filter to dryness, using 25 mm vac., and wash residue with four 40–50 mL portions near-boiling H_2O, filtering after each washing. Do not add wash to funnel under vac.; lift funnel from app. when adding wash.

Wash residue from funnel into reflux beaker with near-boiling 1.25% NaOH soln. Place beakers on reflux app. at 5 min intervals and reflux 30 min. Near end of refluxing, turn on filtration app., place crucible, **(b)**, in app., and adjust vac. to ca 25 mm. Flow near-boiling H_2O thru crucible to warm it. (Keep near-boiling H_2O flowing thru jacket during filtration and washing.) At end of refluxing, decant liq. thru crucible and wash solids into crucible with min. of near-boiling H_2O. Increase vac. as needed to maintain filtration rate. Wash residue once with 25–30 mL near-boiling 1.25% H_2SO_4 soln, and then with two 25–30 mL portions near-boiling H_2O, filtering after each washing. (Filtering and washing takes ca 3–5 min/sample.) Do not add wash to crucible under vac.

Dry crucible with residue 2 hr at 130±2° or overnight at 110°, cool in desiccator, and weigh. Ash 2 hr at 550±10°, cool in desiccator, and weigh. Do not remove crucibles from furnace until temp. is ≤250°, as fritted disk may be damaged if cooled too rapidly.

% Crude fiber = Loss in wt on ignition × 100/wt sample.

Acid-Detergent Fiber and Lignin (*21*)
Official Final Action

(*Caution: See* **51.086**.)

7.069 ***Reagents***

(a) *Sulfuric acid*.—72% by wt. Stdze reagent grade H_2SO_4 to sp gr 1.634 at 20° or 24.00*N*: Add 1200 g H_2SO_4 to 440 mL H_2O in 1 L MCA vol. flask with cooling. Stdze to 1634 g/L at 20° by removing soln and adding H_2O or H_2SO_4 as required. (*Caution: See* **51.030**.)

(b) *Acid-detergent soln*.—Add 20 g cetyl trimethylammonium bromide (tech. grade) to 1 L 1.00*N* H_2SO_4, previously stdzd. Agitate to aid soln.

(c) *Asbestos*.—Place 100 g asbestos in 3 L flask contg 850 mL H_2O. Add 1.4 L H_2SO_4 (tech. grade), mix, and let cool 2 hr at room temp. Filter on large buchner and wash with H_2O. Resuspend mat in H_2O and pour into bag sewn from rectangle of fiberglass window screening, 14 × 18 mesh (bag should be ≥45 cm wide × 30 cm deep). Wash by immersion and agitation in partly filled sink to remove fine particles. Ash recovered asbestos 16 hr in 800° furnace. Store in dry form until use. Used asbestos may be rewashed, reashed, and reused. Com. prepd acid-washed asbestos is unsatisfactory unless treated with 72% H_2SO_4 and ashed at 800°.

7.070 ***Apparatus***

(**a**) *Refluxing apparatus.*—Any conventional app. suitable for crude fiber detns. Berzelius beakers (600 mL) and condensers made from 500 mL r-b flasks are also satisfactory.

(**b**) *Fritted glass crucibles.*—Use coarse porosity, 40–50 mL Pyrex crucible. Wash new crucibles and ash at 500°. Remove while still hot and place in 100° forced-draft oven ≥1 hr. Cool 15 min in desiccator over P_2O_5 or $Mg(ClO_4)_2$ and weigh in same order samples are to be weighed. Check balance 0 after each weighing if crucibles are still warm. Hold length of time from oven to balance pan as const as possible and always weigh crucibles in same order.

7.071 ***Determination of Acid-Detergent Fiber***

Weigh 1 g air-dried sample ground to pass 1 mm screen, or approx. equiv. amt wet material, into refluxing container. Add 100 mL acid-detergent soln at room temp.

Heat to boiling in 5–10 min; reduce heat to avoid foaming as boiling begins. Reflux 60 min from onset of boiling, adjusting boiling to slow, even level. Remove container, swirl, and filter thru weighed (W_1) fritted glass crucible, using min. suction. Increase vac. only as needed. Shut off vac. Break up filtered mat with rod and fill crucible ⅔ full with hot (90–100°) H_2O. Stir and let soak 15–30 sec. Dry with vac. and repeat H_2O washing, rinsing sides of crucible. Wash twice similarly with acetone.

Repeat acetone washings until no more color is removed, breaking up all lumps so that solv. wets all particles of fiber. Remove residual acetone with vac. Dry 3 hr or overnight in 100° forced-draft oven and weigh (W_2). Calc. % acid-detergent fiber $= 100\ (W_2 - W_1)/S$, where S = g sample × g oven-dried matter/g air-dried or wet matter, detd on sep. sample.

7.072 ***Determination of Lignin***

To crucible contg fiber, **7.071**, add 1 g asbestos. Place crucible in 50 mL beaker for support or arrange crucibles in shallow enamel pan. Cover contents of crucible with cooled (15°) 72% H_2SO_4 and stir with glass rod to smooth paste, breaking all lumps. Fill crucible about half-way with acid and stir. Leave glass rod in crucible; refill with 72% H_2SO_4 and stir hourly as acid drains, keeping crucible at 20–23° (cool if necessary). After 3 hr, filter as completely as possible with vac., and wash with hot H_2O until acid-free to pH paper. Rinse sides of crucible and remove stirring rod. Dry crucible in 100° forced-draft oven, cool in desiccator over P_2O_5 or $Mg(ClO_4)_2$, and weigh (W_3). Ignite crucible in 500° furnace 2 hr or until C-free. Place crucible while still hot into 100° forced-draft oven 1 hr. Transfer to desiccator, cool, and weigh (W_4).

Det. asbestos blank by weighing 1 g asbestos into tared crucible. Proceed as above, beginning "Cover contents of crucible . . ." Record any loss in wt on ashing (W_5). Discontinue detn of blank if asbestos blank is <0.0020 g/g asbestos. Calc. % acid-insol. lignin $= (W_3 - W_4 - W_5)/S$.

Total Sugars (*22*)—Official Final Action

7.073 ***Reagents***

(**a**) *Soxhlet modification of Fehling soln.*—Prep. as in **31.034(a)** and (**b**).

(**b**) *Invert sugar std soln.*—1.0%. Prep. as in **31.034(c)**, but do not neutze. Dil. to 0.5% just before use for analysis of most products.

(**c**) *Lactose std soln.*—1.0%. Dissolve 5.000 g lactose in H_2O and dil. to 500 mL. Prep. daily.

7.074 ***Apparatus***

(**a**) *Lamp.*—Fluorescent desk lamp or 150 watt reflector spot lamp, to illuminate boiling soln.

(**b**) *Heater.*—Glas-Col mantle, 250 mL, placed over mag. stirrer. Adjust heat so that 50 mL H_2O contg stirring bar will boil in 3 min. Mag. stirring hot plate is also satisfactory.

7.075 ***Preparation of Sample and Inversion***

(**a**) *Feeds containing molasses.*—Weigh appropriate size sample, prepd as in **7.002** but not ground, to provide final soln ca 0.5% invert sugar but ≥5 g, into 250 mL P flask (Corning Glass Works No. 5840, or equiv.). Add 150 mL H_2O, swirl to wet and mix, and heat just to bp. Let stand to cool, dil. to vol., mix, and let stand to settle coarse particles. Transfer 50 mL supernate to 100 mL vol. flask and add 2.5 mL HCl (sp gr 1.18 at 20/4°). Let stand overnight at ≥25°, dil. to vol., and mix. (If aliquot to be used in detn is >25 mL, it is necessary to neutze inverted soln.)

(**b**) *Feeds containing milk products.*—Weigh appropriate size sample to provide final soln ca 1% lactose into 250 mL vol. flask. Thoroly moisten sample with H_2O, swirl to dissolve lactose, dil. to vol., mix, and let stand to settle coarse particles. Proceed as in **7.077(b)**.

7.076 ***Standardization***

Fill 50 mL buret, with offset tip, with std sugar soln (invert sugar for use with **7.077(a)** and lactose with **7.077(b)**). Proceed as in **31.080**, par. 2, except use same type flask as used in **7.077**, do not add H_2O, and start stirring after addn of indicator.

7.077 ***Determination***

(**a**) *Difference method.*—Add reagents and stirring bar to 250 mL extn flask (Corning Glass Works No. 5160, or equiv.) or to erlenmeyer, as in **7.076**. Transfer aliquot inverted soln, (**a**), to flask so that >1 but <5 mL std soln will be required to reach end point, place on preheated mantle or hot plate, heat to bp, boil 2 min, add ca 1 mL indicator, and begin stirring. Complete detn by titrg with std sugar soln to same end point used in stdzn. Color change is not so sharp as in stdzn, but under suitable light it is definite, discernible, and repeatable.

(**b**) *Alternative method.*—Fill buret with sample soln, (**b**), or inverted sample soln, (**a**). As in **7.076**, place reagents in flask, place on heater, add sample soln to within 2 mL of final titrn (detd by trial), bring to bp, boil 2 min, and complete titrn as in (**a**).

7.078 ***Calculations***

% Total sugar (as invert or lactose)

$$= [(F - M) \times I \times 100]/[V \times (W/250) \times D)],$$

where F = mL std sugar required to reduce mixed Soxhlet reagent in stdzn; M = mL std soln required to complete detn (omit in alternative method); I = concn std soln; V = mL sample soln in aliquot used; W = g sample; and D = diln factor.

Report total sugars, expressed as invert or as lactose.

7.079 Sucrose (*23*)—Official Final Action

Place 10 g sample in 250 mL vol. flask. If material is acid, neutze by adding 1–3 g $CaCO_3$. Add 125 mL 50% alcohol by vol., mix thoroly, and boil on steam bath or by partially immersing flask in H_2O bath 1 hr at 83–87°, using small funnel in neck of flask to condense vapor. Cool and let mixt. stand several hr, preferably overnight. Dil. to vol. with neut. 95% alcohol, mix thoroly, let settle or centrf. 15 min at 1500 rpm, and decant closely. Pipet 200 mL supernate into beaker and evap. on steam bath to 20–30 mL. Do not evap. to dryness. Little alcohol in residue does no harm.

Transfer to 100 mL vol. flask and rinse beaker thoroly with H_2O, adding rinsings to flask. Add enough *satd neut. $Pb(OAc)_2$ soln* (ca 2 mL) to produce flocculent ppt, shake thoroly, and let stand 15 min. Dil. to vol. with H_2O, mix thoroly, and filter thru dry paper. Add enough anhyd. Na_2CO_3 or K oxalate to filtrate to ppt all Pb, again filter thru dry paper, and test filtrate with little anhyd. Na_2CO_3 or K oxalate to make sure that all Pb has been removed.

Place 50 mL prepd soln in 100 mL vol. flask, add piece of litmus paper, neutze with HCl, add 5 mL HCl, and let inversion proceed at room temp. as in **31.026(c)**. When inversion is complete, transfer soln to beaker, neutze with Na_2CO_3, return soln to 100 mL flask, dil. to vol. with H_2O, filter if necessary, and det. reducing sugars in 50 mL soln (representing 2 g sample) as in **31.038**. Calc. results as invert sugar.

% Sucrose = [% total sugar after inversion − % reducing sugars before inversion (both calcd as invert sugar)] × 0.95.

Because insol. material of grain or cattle food occupies some space in flask as originally made up, correct by multiplying all results by factor 0.97, as results of large number of detns on various materials show av. vol. of 10 g material to be 7.5 mL.

★ Starch—Official Final Action ★

7.080 ***Direct Acid Hydrolysis***

See **8.019**. Use sample contg 2.5–3 g dry material.

7.081 ***Diastase Method with Subsequent Acid Hydrolysis***

See **7.067**, 12th ed.

7.082 ***Extraction with Subsequent Enzyme Hydrolysis***

See **14.075–14.080.**

7.083 ***In Presence of Interfering Polysaccharides (24)***

See **22.048**, 10th ed.

7.084 ***In Condensed or Dried Milk Products—Qualitative Test (25)***

See **22.049**, 10th ed.

7.085 ★ Pentosans (*26*)—Official Final Action ★

See **22.050–22.051**, 10th ed.

7.086 ★ Galactan—Official Final Action ★

See **22.052**, 10th ed. (*Caution: See* **51.011** and **51.026.**)

7.087 ★ Water-Soluble Acidity (*27*) ★ Official Final Action

See **22.053**, 10th ed.

7.088 ★ Ferrous Salts (*28*)—Official Final Action ★

$K_3Fe(CN)_6$ spot test. *See* **7.074**, 12th ed.

7.089 ★ Copper Salts (*28*)—Official Final Action ★

$K_4Fe(CN)_6$ spot test. See **7.075**, 12th ed.

★ Surplus method—*see* inside front cover.

7.090 ★ Potassium Iodide (*28*)—Official Final Action ★

Starch-iodine spot test. *See* **7.076**, 12th ed.

Minerals in Feeds by Atomic Absorption Spectrophotometry (*29*)—Official Final Action

(*Caution: See* **51.006**.)

7.091 ***Apparatus***

Atomic absorption spectrophotometer.—See **2.109**.

7.092 ***Operating Parameters***

See Table **2:04**, except use fuel-rich air-C_2H_2 flame for Ca and Mg, and ranges of operation for μg element/mL soln are: Ca 5–20, Cu 2–20, Fe 5–20, Mg 0.5–2.5, Mn 5–20, and Zn 1–5.

7.093 ***Reagents***

(*See* introduction to **2.110**. Com. prepd std solns may be used.)

(**a**) *Calcium std solns*.—Prep. as in **2.110(a)**.

(**b**) *Copper, iron, magnesium, manganese, and zinc std solns*.—Prep. stock solns as in **2.110(b)**, (**c**), (**e**), (**f**), and (**g**), and dil. aliquots with 0.1–0.5*N* HCl to make ≥4 std solns of each element within range of detn.

7.094 ***Preparation of Sample Solution***

(**a**) *Dry ashing* (*not applicable to mineral-mix feeds*).—Ash 2–10 g sample in well-glazed porcelain dish. Start in cold furnace, bring to 550°, and hold 4 hr. Cool, add 10 mL 3*N* HCl, cover with watch glass, and boil gently 10 min. Cool, filter into 100 mL vol. flask, and dil. to vol. with H_2O. Subsequent dilns with 0.1–0.5*N* HCl may be necessary to bring sample solns into anal. range, except for Ca. Final Ca diln must contain enough La soln, **2.110(d)**, to provide 1% La concn after diln to vol. with H_2O.

(**b**) *Wet digestion*.—Proceed as in **7.097(a)**, adding 25 mL HNO_3 for each 2.5 g sample and dilg to 100 mL with H_2O. Digestion can be made at low heat on hot plate, using 600 mL beaker covered with watch glass. Subsequent dilns with 0.1–0.5*N* HCl may be necessary to bring sample solns into anal. range, as in (**a**).

7.095 ***Determination and Calculation***

See **2.112–2.113**.

Calcium—Official Final Action

7.096 ***Method I (30)***

(Applicable to mineral feeds only)

Weigh 2 g finely ground sample into SiO_2 or porcelain dish and ignite in furnace to C-free ash, but avoid fusing. Boil residue in 40 mL HCl (1+3) and few drops HNO_3. Transfer to 250 mL vol. flask, cool, dil. to vol., and mix thoroly. Pipet 25 mL clear liq. into beaker, dil. to ca 100 mL, and add 2 drops Me red, **2.055(i)**. Add NH_4OH (1+1) dropwise to pH 5.6, as shown by intermediate brownish-orange. If overstepped, add HCl (1+3) with dropper to orange. Add 2 more drops HCl (1+3). Color should now be pink (pH 2.5–3.0), not orange. Dil. to ca 150 mL, bring to boil, and slowly add, with const stirring, 10 mL hot satd (4.2%) soln of $(NH_4)_2C_2O_4$. If red changes to orange or yellow, add HCl (1+3) dropwise until color again changes to pink. Let stand overnight for ppt to settle. Filter supernate thru quant. paper, gooch, or fritted glass filter (fine Pyrex is preferable), and wash ppt thoroly with NH_4OH (1+50). Place paper or crucible with ppt in original beaker, and add mixt. of 125 mL H_2O and 5 mL H_2SO_4.

Heat to ⩾70° and titr. with 0.1*N* $KMnO_4$, **50.025–50.026**, to first slight pink. Presence of paper may cause color to fade in few sec. Correct for blank and calc. % Ca.

Method II (31)

7.097 ***Preparation of Solution***

(*Caution: See* **51.026** and **51.028**.)

(**a**) Weigh 2.5 g sample into 500 or 800 mL Kjeldahl flask. Add 20–30 mL HNO_3 and boil gently 30–45 min to oxidize all easily oxidizable matter. Cool soln somewhat and add 10 mL 70–72% $HClO_4$. Boil very gently, adjusting flame as necessary, until soln is colorless or nearly so and dense white fumes appear. Use particular care not to boil to dryness (Danger!) at any time. Cool slightly, add 50 mL H_2O, and boil to drive out any remaining NO_2 fumes. Cool, dil., filter into 250 mL vol. flask, dil. to vol., and mix thoroly.

(**b**) Weigh 2.5 g finely ground sample into SiO_2 or porcelain dish and ignite as in **7.009**. Add 40 mL HCl (1+3) and few drops HNO_3 to residue, boil, transfer to 250 mL vol. flask, cool, dil. to vol., and mix thoroly.

7.098 ***Determination***

Pipet suitable aliquot of clear soln, **7.097(a)** or (**b**), into beaker, dil. to 100 mL, and add 2 drops Me red, **2.055(i)**. Continue as in **7.096**, beginning "Add NH_4OH (1+1) dropwise . . ." except use 0.05*N* $KMnO_4$ for titrn.

(100 mL is suitable aliquot of sample soln for grain feeds; for mineral feeds, 25 mL aliquot may be taken and titrd with 0.1*N* $KMnO_4$. For suitable precision, size of sample, aliquot, and concn of $KMnO_4$ must be so adjusted that ⩾20 mL std $KMnO_4$ soln is used.)

Soluble Chlorine

Titration Method (32)—Official Final Action

7.099 ***Reagents***

(**a**) *Potassium chloride std soln.*—0.001 g Cl/mL. Recrystallize reagent KCl 3 times from H_2O, dry at 110°, and heat at ca 500° to const wt. Dissolve 2.1028 g in H_2O and dil. to 1 L.

(**b**) *Silver nitrate soln.*—Dissolve 5 g $AgNO_3$ in 1 L H_2O and adjust soln so that 1 mL = 1 mL std KCl soln.

(**c**) *Potassium thiocyanate soln.*—Dissolve 2.5 g KSCN in 1 L H_2O and adjust so that 1 mL = 1 mL std $AgNO_3$ soln. Stdze as in **50.004**.

(**d**) *Ferric sulfate soln.*—Dissolve 60 g $Fe_2(SO_4)_3$ + Aq. in H_2O and dil. to 1 L.

(**e**) *Ferric sulfate indicator.*—To filtered 25% soln of $Fe_2(SO_4)_3$ + Aq. add equal vol. HNO_3.

7.100 ***Determination***

Transfer 3 g sample to 300 mL erlenmeyer. Add 50 mL $Fe_2(SO_4)_3$ soln (accurately measured), swirling flask to prevent caking of sample and to facilitate soln of Cl. Add 100 mL (also accurately measured) NH_4OH (1+19). Swirl flask just enough to ensure soln of Cl and thoro mixing of soln. (Very little swirling is necessary. If soln is agitated by vigorous vertical shaking, filtration will be difficult.) Let mixt. settle 10 min. Filter thru dry 11 cm Whatman No. 41 paper, or equiv. Use 50 mL aliquots (⅓ of total) on samples low in Cl (0–2% Cl) and 25 mL aliquots (1/6 of total) on samples high in Cl (>2%). For mineral and other feeds contg ⩾10% Cl, weigh 1 g and use 15 mL (1/10 of total).

If approx. % Cl in sample is not known, take 10 mL aliquot for trial titrn. To this add 10 mL HNO_3 and 10 mL $Fe_2(SO_4)_3$ indicator. Dil. to ca 50 mL. Add 0.5 mL KSCN soln and immediately add, with stirring, enough $AgNO_3$ soln to entirely eliminate any reddish color. From this titrn calc. vol. $AgNO_3$ soln necessary to ppt all Cl in aliquot to be used, adding excess equal to ca 10% total vol. necessary, altho somewhat greater excess will not affect results. Use min. total of 10 mL.

To sample aliquot in 250 mL beaker add 10 mL HNO_3 and 10 mL $Fe_2(SO_4)_3$ indicator (or 20 mL soln contg equal vols of these solns). Add, with stirring, calcd vol. $AgNO_3$ soln. Heat to boiling and cool to room temp., stirring enough to coagulate ppt. (Cooling may be hastened by immersion of beakers in cold H_2O.) Titr. excess $AgNO_3$ with KSCN. End point is indicated by first appearance of reddish tint that persists 15 sec. For accurate work, use ref. soln contg all ingredients except KSCN. End point is first change in color.

Potentiometric Method (33)
Official Final Action

7.101 ***Apparatus***

Potentiometer.—With Ag-AgCl reference electrode and Ag-indicating electrode (Fisher Scientific Co. No. 9–313–216 and 13–639–122, or equiv.).

7.102 ***Standardization***

Weigh 125 mg dry NaCl into 400 mL beaker. Add 200 mL H_2O and 1 mL HNO_3.

Null potentiometer and titr. NaCl soln with 0.1*N* $AgNO_3$ soln. Plot mL $AgNO_3$ soln against mv or scale readings. Add titrant in small enough increments so that voltage end point is obvious. Use same end point for samples.

7.103 ***Determination***

(**a**) *Samples containing less than 5% sodium chloride.*—Weigh 5.844 g sample into 400 mL beaker. Add ca 200 mL H_2O and 1 mL HNO_3. Swirl mixt. gently and let stand 10 min for complete soln of chlorides. Titr., while stirring, to same voltage end point as in stdzn.

% NaCl = mL 0.1*N* $AgNO_3$/10.

(**b**) *Samples containing more than 5% sodium chloride.*—Weigh 5.844 g sample into 200 mL vol. flask. Add ca 190 mL H_2O and 1 mL HNO_3, dil. to vol. with H_2O, mix, and let stand 10 min. Transfer aliquot contg equiv. of ca 125 mg NaCl to 400 mL beaker, dil. to ca 200 mL, add 1 mL HNO_3, and titr. as in (**a**).

% NaCl = diln factor × mL 0.1*N* $AgNO_3$/10.

Cobalt (*34*)—Official Final Action

7.104 ***Reagents***

(**a**) *Cobalt std soln.*—0.05 mg Co/mL. Dissolve 0.2385 g $CoSO_4.7H_2O$ (do not dry; use as received) in H_2O and dil. to 1 L. Dil., if necessary, to suitable concn to prep. std curve.

(**b**) *Nitroso-R salt soln.*—Dissolve 1 g $C_{10}H_4OH.NO(SO_3Na)_2$ in H_2O and dil. to 500 mL.

(**c**) *Spekker acid.*—Mix 150 mL 85% H_3PO_4 and 150 mL H_2SO_4, and dil. to 1 L with H_2O.

(**d**) *Sodium acetate soln.*—Dissolve 500 g $NaOAc.3H_2O$ in H_2O and dil. to 1 L with H_2O.

7.105 ***Preparation of Standard Curve***

To 1, 2, etc., up to 11 mL portions std Co soln in 100 mL vol. flasks add 2 mL Spekker acid, 10 mL nitroso-R salt soln, and 10 mL NaOAc soln. Prep. blank by using 2 mL Spekker acid and 10 mL NaOAc soln, but omitting nitroso-R salt soln. Bring solns to bp on hot plate. Add 5 mL HNO_3 and boil ⩾1, but ⩽2 min. Cool, and dil. to 100 mL.

7.106 ***Determination***

(*Caution: See* **51.026** and **51.059**.)

Ash 2 g sample 2 hr at 600°, transfer to 200 mL vol. flask with 20 mL HCl and 50 mL H_2O, boil 5 min, cool, and dil. to vol. Let soln settle. Pipet suitable aliquot into small flask. For samples contg 0.01–0.2% Co use equiv. of 0.25 g sample. Adjust amt to ≤0.5 mg Co. Soln no longer appears to follow Beer's law above this amt.

Pass brisk current of H_2S thru soln 10 min. Filter directly into 100 mL vol. flask thru Whatman No. 40 paper. Wash with ca 50 mL *1% H_2SO_4 satd with H_2S*. Add 2 small glass beads and boil off H_2S. (Flasks must be given individual attention, as violent bumping may occur.) Shake flasks often. Add 5 mL HNO_3 and boil until nitrous fumes no longer appear. (Take care, as vol. of soln will be low and bumping and spattering may occur. At first indication of this, remove immediately from hot plate.) Small amt HNO_3 remaining will not affect result. Cool, add 2 drops phthln, and adjust to first faint pink with ca 30% NaOH soln. Immediately add 2 mL Spekker acid followed by 10 mL nitroso-R salt soln and 10 mL NaOAc soln. Bring to vigorous boil, carefully add 5 mL HNO_3, and boil ≥1 but ≤2 min. Cool, and dil. to vol.

Compare color with std Co solns in photoelec. colorimeter, using green or No. 54 filter, or in spectrophtr at 540 nm. Read color within 2 hr. Report % Co to third decimal place.

Copper (*35*)—Official Final Action

7.107 ***Preparation of Standard Curve***

Dissolve 1.9645 g $CuSO_4.5H_2O$ in H_2O and dil. to 500 mL. (1 mL = 1 mg Cu.) Use from 1 to 10 mL of this soln to prep. set of stds in 100 mL Pyrex g-s vol. flasks. Add 4 mL HCl, dil. to 50 mL, add 5 mL *tetraethylenepentamine*, dil. to vol. with H_2O, stopper, and mix thoroly. Prep. blank, using all reagents except Cu. Filter blank and stds before reading color as in **7.108**.

7.108 ***Determination***

Prep. sample soln as in **7.106**, using 8 g sample. Pipet 50 mL aliquot into 100 mL Pyrex g-s vol. flask, add 5 mL tetraethylenepentamine, dil. to vol. with H_2O, and mix thoroly. Filter, and compare colors within 30 min in photoelec. colorimeter (red or No. 66 filter) or read in spectrophtr at 620 nm. Report % Cu to third decimal place.

Fluorine—Official Final Action

7.109 ***Colorimetric Method***

See **25.049–25.055**, especially **25.053**.

Ion Selective Electrode Method (*36*)

7.110 ***Apparatus***

(**a**) *Electrodes*.—Fluoride ion selective electrode (Model 94-09, Orion Research Inc., or equiv.) and single junction calomel ref. electrode, plastic sleeve-type (Model 90-01, Orion Research Inc., or equiv.).

(**b**) *Magnetic stirrer*.—With 4 cm (1½") Teflon-coated stirring bar. Use mat to insulate sample from motor heat.

(**c**) *pH meter*.—Corning digital Model 112 (Corning Scientific Instruments, Medfield, MA 02052, or equiv.).

7.111 ***Reagents***

(Deionized H_2O may be used.)

(**a**) *Sodium acetate soln*.—*3M*. Dissolve 408 g $NaOAc.3H_2O$ with H_2O in 1 L vol. flask. When soln warms to room temp., dil. to vol. with H_2O. Adjust to pH 7.0 with few drops HOAc.

(**b**) *Sodium citrate soln*.—1.32*M*. Dissolve 222 g Na citrate.$2H_2O$ with ca 250 mL H_2O in 1 L vol. flask. Add 28 mL $HClO_4$, dil. to vol., and mix.

(**c**) *Fluoride std solns*.—(*1*) *Stock soln*.—500 ppm. Accurately weigh 1.105 g NaF (reagent grade, dried 4 hr at 100°) into 1 L vol. flask. Dissolve and dil. to vol. with H_2O, and mix. Store in plastic bottle. (*2*) *Intermediate soln I*.—100 ppm. Pipet 20 mL stock soln into 100 mL vol. flask, dil. to vol. with H_2O, and mix. (*3*) *Intermediate soln II*.—10 ppm. Pipet 2 mL stock soln into 100 mL vol. flask, dil. to vol. with H_2O, and mix. (*4*) *Working solns*.—Pipet 3, 5, and 10 mL intermediate soln II and 5 and 10 mL intermediate soln I into five 100 mL vol. flasks to prep. 0.3, 0.5, 1.0, 5.0, and 10 ppm F working solns, resp. To each add 10.0 mL 1*N* HCl, 25.0 mL $NaOAc.3H_2O$ soln, (**a**), and 25.0 mL Na citrate soln, (**b**). Dil. to vol. with H_2O and mix.

7.112 ***Preparation of Sample***

Accurately weigh well mixed sample contg ca 400 μg F into 200 mL vol. flask. Pipet in 20 mL 1*N* HCl and stir 20 min at high speed on mag. stirrer. Add 50.0 mL NaOAc soln, (**a**), and 50.0 mL Na citrate soln, (**b**), to dissolved sample. Dil. to vol. with H_2O and mix.

7.113 ***Determination***

Connect F and ref. electrodes to pH meter, place electrodes in low concn F soln, and warm up pH meter. Pour 50–70 mL std and corresponding sample solns into sep. 100 mL beakers. Place electrodes in each soln and while stirring with mag. stirrer at const rate, read mv of std and unknown solns. Rinse and blot off electrodes and stirring bar between solns. Construct std curve on 3 cycle semilogarithmic paper. Read ppm F of sample soln from std curve.

$$\% \text{ F} = \text{ppm F} \times \text{mL sample soln} \times 10^{-6} \times 100/\text{g sample}$$

Iodine in Mineral Mixed Feeds—Official Final Action

7.114 ★ ***Knapheide-Lamb Method*** (*37*) ★

See **22.084–22.086**, 10th ed.

7.115 ***Elmslie-Caldwell Method*** (*38*)

(Not applicable to iodized mineral feeds contg little or no org. matter. *Caution: See* **51.047**.)

Place sample contg 3–4 mg I in 200–300 mL Ni dish. Add ca 5 g Na_2CO_3, 5 mL NaOH soln (1+1), and 10 mL alcohol, taking care that entire sample is moist. Dry at ca 100° to prevent spattering upon subsequent heating (30 min is usually enough).

Place dish and contents in furnace heated to 500° and keep at that temp. 15 min. (Ignition of sample at 500° appears to be necessary only to carbonize any sol. org. matter that would be oxidized by Br-H_2O if not so treated. Temp. >500° may be used if necessary.) Cool, add 25 mL H_2O, cover dish with watch glass, and boil gently 10 min. Filter thru 18 cm paper and wash with boiling H_2O, catching filtrate and washings in 600 mL beaker (soln should total ca 300 mL). Neutze to Me orange with 85% H_3PO_4 and add 1 mL excess.

★ Surplus method—*see* inside front cover.

Add excess Br-H_2O and boil soln gently until colorless, and then 5 min longer. Add few crystals *salicylic acid* and cool soln to ca 20°. Add 1 mL 85% H_3PO_4 and ca 0.5 g KI, and titr. I with 0.005*N* $Na_2S_2O_3$, adding starch soln when liberated I color is nearly gone. 1 mL 0.005*N* $Na_2S_2O_3$ = 0.1058 mg I.

Acid-Soluble Manganese (*39*)
Official Final Action

7.116 ***Reagent***

Potassium permanganate std soln.—500 ppm Mn. Prep. and stdze as in **50.025–50.026**, except use 1.4383 g $KMnO_4$ and 0.12 g Na oxalate. Transfer aliquot contg 20 mg Mn to beaker. Add 100 mL H_2O, 15 mL H_3PO_4, and 0.3 g KIO_4, and heat to bp. Cool, and dil. to 1 L. Protect from light. Dil. this soln contg 20 ppm Mn with H_2O (previously boiled with 0.3 g KIO_4/L) to make convenient working stds in range of concns to be compared.

7.117 ***Determination***

(*Caution: See* **51.026** and **51.030**.)

Ash weighed sample, 5–15 g, at dull red heat (ca 600°) in porcelain dish. Cool, and add 5 mL H_2SO_4 and 5 mL HNO_3 to ash in dish or to ash transferred to beaker with 20–30 mL H_2O. Evap. to white fumes. If C is not completely destroyed, add addnl portions HNO_3, boiling after each addn. Cool slightly, transfer to 50 or 100 mL vol. flask, and add vol. dil. H_3PO_4 soln (8+92) equal to ½ vol. of flask (25 or 50 mL). Cool, dil. to vol., mix, and filter or let stand until clear.

If 50 mL flask was used, pipet 25 mL clear soln into beaker or 50 or 100 mL vol. flask and add 15 mL H_2O. If 100 mL flask was used, pipet 50 mL into beaker or 100 mL flask and add 30 mL H_2O. Heat nearly to bp, and with stirring or swirling add 0.3 g KIO_4 for each 15 mg Mn present. Keep 30–60 min at 90–100°, or until color development is complete. Cool, dil. to measured vol. of 50 or 100 mL, and mix. Compare with std $KMnO_4$ soln in photoelec. colorimeter or in spectrophtr at 530 nm. Calc. ppm Mn.

Phosphorus

Alkalimetric Ammonium Molybdophosphate Method (40)—Official Final Action

7.118 ***Reagents***

(**a**) *Molybdate soln.*—Dissolve 100 g MoO_3 in mixt. of 144 mL NH_4OH and 271 mL H_2O. Cool, and slowly pour soln, stirring constantly, into cool mixt. of 489 mL HNO_3 and 1148 mL H_2O. Keep final mixt. in warm place several days or until portion heated to 40° deposits no yellow ppt. Decant soln from any sediment and keep in g-s vessels.

(**b**) *Acidified molybdate soln.*—To 100 mL molybdate soln, (**a**), add 5 mL HNO_3. Filter immediately before use.

(**c**) *Sodium hydroxide std soln.*—Dil. 324.03 mL 1*N* alkali, carbonate-free, **50.032–50.036**, to 1 L. (100 mL of this soln should neutze 32.40 mL 1*N* acid; 1 mL = 1 mg or 1% P_2O_5 on basis of 0.1 g sample.) (Since burets in const use may become so corroded as to increase their capacity, test them at least annually.)

(**d**) *Std acid soln.*—Prep. soln of HCl or of HNO_3, corresponding to concn of (**c**) or to ½ this concn, and stdze by titrn against (**c**), using phthln.

7.119 ***Determination***

Prep. sample soln as in **7.097**(**a**). Pipet, into beaker or flask, aliquot corresponding to 0.4 g sample for P_2O_5 content of sample <5%; 0.2 g for 5–20%; 0.1 g for >20%. Add 5–10 mL HNO_3, depending on method of soln (or equiv. in NH_4NO_3); then add NH_4OH until ppt that forms dissolves only slowly on vigorous stirring, dil. to 75–100 mL, and adjust to 25–30°. If sample does not give ppt with NH_4OH as test of neutzn, make soln slightly alk. to litmus paper with NH_4OH and then slightly acid with HNO_3 (1+3). Add 20–25 mL acidified molybdate soln for P_2O_5 content <5%; 30–35 mL for 5–20%; and enough acidified molybdate soln to ensure complete pptn for >20%. Shake or stir mech. 30 min at room temp.; decant *at once* thru filter and wash ppt twice by decanting with 25–30 mL portions H_2O, agitating thoroly and allowing to settle. Transfer ppt to filter and wash with cold H_2O until filtrate from 2 fillings of filter yields pink color on adding phthln and 1 drop of the std alkali. Transfer ppt and filter to beaker or pptg vessel, dissolve ppt in small excess of the std alkali, add few drops of phthln, and titr. with std acid. Report as % P.

Photometric Method (41)—Official Final Action

7.120 ***Apparatus***

Spectrophotometer.—Capable of isolating 400 nm band and accepting ≤15 mm diam. cells.

7.121 ***Reagents***

(**a**) *Molybdovanadate reagent.*—Prep. as in **2.022**(**a**), except add only 250 mL 70% $HClO_4$ to NH_4VO_3 soln.

(**b**) *Phosphorus std solns.*—(*1*) *Stock soln.*—2 mg P/mL. Dissolve 8.788 g KH_2PO_4 in H_2O and dil. to 1 L. (*2*) *Working soln.*—0.1 mg P/mL. Dil. 50 mL stock soln to 1 L.

7.122 ***Preparation of Standard Curve***

Transfer aliquots of working std soln contg 0.5, 0.8, 1.0, and 1.5 mg P to 100 mL vol. flasks. Treat as in **7.123**, beginning "Add 20 mL molybdovanadate reagent, . . ." Prep. std curve by plotting mg P against %*T* on semilog paper.

7.123 ***Determination***

Ash 2 g sample, in 150 mL beaker, 4 hr at 600°. Cool, add 40 mL HCl (1+3) and several drops HNO_3, and bring to bp. Cool, transfer to 200 mL vol. flask, and dil. to vol. with H_2O. Filter, and place aliquot contg 0.5–1.5 mg P in 100 mL vol. flask. Add 20 mL molybdovanadate reagent, dil. to vol. with H_2O, and mix well. Let stand 10 min; then read %*T* at 400 nm against 0.5 mg std set at 100% *T*. (Use ≤15 mm diam. cells.) Det. mg P from std curve.

% P = mg P in aliquot/(g sample in aliquot × 10).

Basic Feed Microscopy (*42*)—*Official Final Action*

7.124 ***Apparatus***

(**a**) *Magnifier-fluorescent illuminator with desk base, 3×, or reading glass.*

(**b**) *Microscopes and illuminator.—See* **44.002**(**n**) and (**q**). Following are preferred:

(*1*) *Widefield stereoscopic microscope.*—With arm rests, flat stage (remove spring holders), optional substage illumination, inclined eyepiece, and lenses to magnify ca 7–30×, 15× optimum.

(*2*) *Compound microscope.*—With mech. stage, substage condenser, inclined binocular eyepiece, 3 position rotating nosepiece, lenses to magnify ca 36–400×, 120× optimum.

(3) *Microscope illuminator*.—With iris diaphragm; movable stand holder with rod to permit adjusting light source as to ht and angle for substage or direct over-stage lighting; able to hold 2 blue glass filters or 1 blue and 1 ground glass; 60–100 watt bulb.

(**c**) *Sieves*.—Nest of 5" No. 10, 20, 40, 60, 80, and bottom pan.

(**d**) *Stages*.—Dark Co glass plates 4 × 4" (Fisher Scientific Co. No. 13-735); or blue paper and microscope slides.

(**e**) *Spot plates*.—Black and white.

(**f**) *Forceps*.—Fine pointed, curved. If necessary, bend and grind on emery wheel for good contact of points.

(**g**) *Dropping bottles*.—Amber, 30 mL, as reagent dispensers.

(**h**) *Micro-spatula; micro-stirring rods made by drawing out glass rods; spoon.*

7.125 ***Reagents***

(**a**) *Chloroform*.—Tech. Recover by filtration and distn.

(**b**) *Acetone*.—Tech.

(**c**) *Acetone, dilute*.—Dil. 75 mL acetone with 25 mL H_2O.

(**d**) *Dilute hydrochloric acid*.—Dil. 1 vol. HCl with 1 vol. H_2O.

(**e**) *Dilute sulfuric acid*.—Dil. 1 vol. H_2SO_4 with 1 vol. H_2O.

(**f**) *Iodine soln*.—Dissolve 0.75 g KI and 0.1 g I in 30 mL H_2O and add 0.5 mL HCl. Store in amber dropping bottle.

(**g**) *Millon reagent*.—Dissolve, by gently warming, 1 part by wt Hg in 2 parts by wt HNO_3. Dil. with 2 vols H_2O. Let mixt. stand overnight and decant supernate. Soln contains $Hg(NO_3)_2$, $HgNO_3$, HNO_3, and some HNO_2. Store in g-s bottle. (*Caution: See* **51.079**.)

(**h**) *Molybdate soln*.—Add 100 mL 10% NH_4NO_3 soln to 400 mL molybdate soln, **7.118**(**a**). Use only clear supernate to fill 30 mL amber dropping bottle. Discard and refill when crystn occurs.

(**i**) *Mountant I*.—Dissolve 10 g chloral hydrate in 10 mL H_2O and add 10 mL glycerol. Store in amber dropping bottle.

(**j**) *Mountant II*.—Dissolve 160 g chloral hydrate in 100 mL H_2O and add 10 mL HCl.

(**k**) *Silver nitrate soln*.—10%. Dissolve 10 g $AgNO_3$ in 100 mL H_2O.

7.126 **Standards**

(**a**) *Feed ingredients*.—Collect ingredients used in grain and stock feeds known to conform to definitions of Association of American Feed Control Officials as stds. Store in 4 oz bottles. To control insects, add ca 1 mL CS_2, and stopper. Become thoroly familiar with structural appearance of stds before and after treatment with org. solvs.

(**b**) *Weed seeds*.—Collect common weed seeds occurring in grains. Most may be found in foreign material obtained after sieving com. whole grains with U.S. Grain Testing Sieve having 5/64" (2.5 mm) triangular holes. Identify from illustration in "Identification of Crop and Weed Seeds" (USDA Handbook 219 (1963), Government Printing Office, Washington, DC 20402). Store in numbered vials. Become familiar with those weed seeds designated as prohibited and restricted noxious under state laws of individual concern. (*See* "State Noxious-Weed Seed Requirements Recognized in the Administration of the Federal Seed Act" (USDA, Agricultural Marketing Service, Grain Div., Hyattsville, MD 20782).)

Identification of Vegetable Tissues

7.127 ***Principle***

Feeds are fractionated according to particle size and cleared where necessary for clear observation; conglomerates are disintegrated into constituents and fractions arranged on stage suitable for microscopic examination at lowest magnification that permits identification of components when compared to std feed ingredients.

7.128 ***General Methods***

(**a**) *Scratch feeds*.—Spread representative portion of sample on white paper and examine under magnifier-fluorescent illuminator at 3× or with reading glass. Identify grains and weed seeds; note other foreign material, heat- and insect-damaged particles, live insects, and rodent excreta; examine for smut, ergot, and mold ("Grain Inspection Manual," USDA).

(**b**) *Mashes comparatively free from adhering fine particles*.—(*1*) *Low power microscopy*.—Arrange in nest form 3 sieves that will adequately fractionate feed according to particle size. Generally, for cattle feeds use No. 10, 20, and 40; for poultry feeds, No. 20, 40, and 60. Include bottom pan. Add ca 10 g unground feed (plastic tablespoon makes convenient scoop) to nest, and sieve thoroly. With spatula, spread portion from each sieve on 4 × 4" Co glass stage and place under stereoscopic microscope. (Blue paper may also be used as stage.) Arrange illuminator above and near stage so light strikes sample at angle of ca 45° for shadow contrast. Adjust magnification (ca 15× optimum), illumination, and light filters to individual preference for clear observation. Blue light or northern daylight is preferred. Examine each fraction on stage sep. and systematically. Observe feed particles, continually probing, turning, and testing resistance to pressure with forceps. Note particle size, shape, color, resistance to pressure, texture, odor, and major structural features. Compare with stds. If desired, transfer individual particles with forceps to second glass plate for direct comparison with corresponding tissues from stds. Likewise transfer and break up conglomerates by gentle pressure with flat end of forceps. Make list of observed ingredients. Neglect trace grains which may be normal inpurities in major grains. (Consult "Official Grain Standards of the United States," USDA, for amts of "other grains" permissible as impurities in whole grains.)

(*2*) *High power microscopy*.—Lower illuminator and select filters so adequate blue light is reflected thru substage condenser of high power microscope. With microspatula, transfer little of fine sievings from bottom sieve and pan to slide, add 2 drops mountant I, stir, and disperse with microstirring rod. Examine microscopically (120× optimum). Compare histologically with stds. Remove slide, add 1 drop I soln, stir, and re-examine. Starch cells are stained pale blue to black; yeasts and other protein cells, pale yellow to brown. If further tissue clarification is desired, boil little of same fine sievings 1 min with ca 5 mL mountant II. Cool, transfer drop or 2 of bottom settlings to slide, cover, and examine microscopically.

(**c**) *Oily feeds or those containing large particles obscured by adhering fine particles*.—(Most poultry feeds and unknowns are best examined by this technic.) Place ca 10 g unground feed in 100 mL tall-form beaker and nearly fill with $CHCl_3$ (hood). Stir briefly and let settle ca 1 min. With spoon, transfer floating (org.) material to 3.5" (9 cm) cover glass, drain, and dry on steam bath. Sieve, and proceed as in (**b**). If desired, filter, dry, suspend fine particles in $CHCl_3$, and examine microscopically (rarely necessary).

(**d**) *Feeds in which molasses has caused lumpiness and otherwise obscured vision*.—Place ca 10 g unground feed in 100 mL tall-form beaker. Add 75 mL 75% acetone, stir few min to dissolve molasses, and let settle. Carefully decant and repeat extn. Wash residue twice with acetone by decantation, dry on steam bath, sieve, and proceed as in (**b**).

(**e**) *Pellets or crumbles*.—Gently grind few pellets at time in mortar with pestle with enough pressure to sep. pellet into its constituents, but not to break up constituents themselves. Sieve first grind thru No. 20 sieve and return particles remaining on sieve to mortar for further grinding. Depending on nature of pellet, proceed with ground material as in **(b)**, **(c)**, or **(d)**.

Identification of Animal Tissues and Major Mineral Constituents

7.129 ***Principle***

Feeds contg animal tissues and minerals when suspended in $CHCl_3$ readily sep. into 2 fractions: *(1)* Org. fraction which floats, consisting of muscle fibers, connective tissue, dried ground organs, feather remains, hoof and horn particles, etc. from either animal or marine products, plus all vegetable tissues. *(2)* Mineral fraction which sinks, consisting of bones, fish scales, teeth, and minerals.

7.130 ***Preparation of Sample***

Perform $CHCl_3$ flotation sepn as in **7.128(c)**. Collect floating material and dry on steam bath. Decant $CHCl_3$, collect mineral fraction, and dry on steam bath.

7.131 ***Identification of Animal Tissue***

Examine dried floating material as in **7.128(b)**.

7.132 ***Identification of Major Mineral Constituents***

Place dried mineral fraction on nest of No. 40, 60, and 80 sieves and bottom pan. Sieve and place the 4 fractions in sep. groups on same Co glass plate or blue paper stage. Examine under stereoscopic microscope at ca 15×. Animal and fish bones, fish scales, and mollusc shells are generally recognizable. Salt usually occurs in cubes which may be dyed. Calcite form of limestone occurs as rhombohedrons.

7.133 ***Confirmatory Tests***

With forceps, place unknown particle on glass plate and break up by applying gentle pressure with flat surface. Working under stereoscopic microscope, sep. particles ca 2.5 cm and place beside each a fractional drop of reagent solns listed by touching end of dropper to plate. Push particle into liq. with microstirring rod and observe what occurs at interface. Follow order given until pos. identification is obtained. If preferred, perform tests in black spot plate.

(a) *Silver nitrate soln.*—*(1)* Crystal immediately turns chalk white and slowly expands: chloride, probably salt. *(2)* Crystal turns yellow and yellow needles begin to grow: mono- or dibasic phosphate, generally dicalcium phosphate. *(3)* Sparingly sol. white needles form (Ag_2SO_4): sulfate, Mn-$MgSO_4$. *(4)* Particles slowly darken: bone.

(b) *Dilute hydrochloric acid.*—*(1)* Vigorous effervescence: $CaCO_3$. *(2)* Mild effervescence or none: make following tests.

(c) *Molybdate soln.*—Formation of minute yellow crystals at some distance from particle: tricalcium phosphate, either bone or rock phosphate. (All phosphates react, but mono- and dibasic phosphates have been identified with $AgNO_3$.)

(d) *Millon reagent.*—*(1)* Disintegrated particles mostly float, turn pink to red (protein), and fade in ca 5 min: bone phosphate. *(2)* Particles appear to swell and disintegrate but remain on bottom: defluorinated rock phosphate. *(3)* Particles merely disintegrate slowly: rock phosphate.

(e) *Dilute sulfuric acid.*—Long, thin white needles slowly form on addn of drop of H_2SO_4 (1+1) to HCl (1+1) soln of particle: confirms Ca.

7.134 ***Identification of Furazolidone, Tylosin, and Zoalene***

See **42.001–42.004**.

PRESERVATIVES

Ethoxyquin (1,2-Dihydro-6-ethoxy-2,2,4-trimethylquinoline) *(43)*—Official Final Action

7.135 ***Reagents and Apparatus***

(a) *Quinine sulfate reference soln.*—1 μg/mL 0.1*N* H_2SO_4. Dissolve 0.100 g quinine sulfate USP in 1 L 0.1*N* H_2SO_4. Dil. 10 mL aliquot of this soln to 1 L with 0.1*N* H_2SO_4. Use to calibrate photofluorometer.

(b) *Ethoxyquin std solns.*—Add 100.0 mg liq. ethoxyquin to 100 mL vol. flask and dil. to vol. with pet ether (*Soln A*). Dil. 5 mL *Soln A* to 100 mL with pet ether (*Soln B*, 50 μg/mL). Dil. 5 mL *Soln B* to 100 mL with pet ether (*Soln C*, 2.5 μg/mL). Dil. 10 mL *Soln C* to 20 mL with pet ether (1.25 μg/mL) and 5 mL to 25 mL (0.50 μg/mL).

(c) *Photofluorometer.*—Equipped with primary filter passing 365 nm Hg line (Corning Glass Works No. 5874 (CS7-39), or equiv.) and secondary filter passing 420–500 nm (Corning Glass Works 3389 + 5543 + 4784, half stock thickness, or equiv.).

7.136 ***Preparation of Standard Curve***

Adjust photofluorometer to read 0 with pet ether and 100 with quinine sulfate ref. soln. Obtain fluorescence readings for ethoxyquin std solns contg 0–2.5 μg/mL. Plot readings against μg ethoxyquin/mL on linear paper.

7.137 ***Determination***

Place 10±0.1 g finely ground sample in 100 mL beaker and slurry with 50 mL MeOH. Stir and let stand 10 min. Decant thru plug of glass wool into 250 mL vol. flask. Reslurry residue with two 50 mL portions MeOH, decant, and filter, combining all filtrates. Dil. to vol. with MeOH. Transfer 25 mL aliquot to 250 mL separator, add 100 mL H_2O, and mix well. Add 50 mL pet ether, stopper, and shake moderately 1 min. Let stand few min to sep. (If emulsion forms, add ca 100 mg NaCl crystals. After emulsion breaks, drain aq. lower layer into 250 mL beaker.) Transfer pet ether layer to second 250 mL separator, return aq. layer to first separator, and re-ext with two 25 mL portions pet ether.

Add 50 mL H_2O to combined pet ether exts in separator, stopper, and shake moderately. Let sep., drain lower aq. layer, and discard. Transfer pet ether layer to 100 mL vol. flask, and dil. to vol. with pet ether. Adjust photofluorometer as above and det. fluorescence readings. Obtain μg ethoxyquin/mL from std curve. Ppm ethoxyquin = 100 × μg/mL.

If untreated feed is available, prep. std curve from series of samples contg 0–250 μg ethoxyquin/10 g and carried thru detn.

7.138 Drugs in Feeds

See Chapter **42**.

7.139 Molasses and Molasses Products

See Chapter **31**.

7.140 Cyanogenetic Glucosides

See **26.134**.

7.141 Hydrocyanic Acid Formed by Hydrolysis of Glucosides in Beans

See **26.135–26.136**.

SELECTED REFERENCES

(*1*) JAOAC **33**, 424(1950); **41**, 223(1958); **48**, 658(1965).
(*2*) JAOAC **17**, 68(1934).
(*3*) JAOAC **8**, 295(1925); **9**, 30(1926).
(*4*) USDA Bur. Chem. Bull. **122**, p. 219; **132**, p. 150.
(*5*) JAOAC **13**, 173(1930); **14**, 152(1931); **17**, 178(1934); **18**, 80(1935).
(*6*) JAOAC **36**, 213(1953); **37**, 253(1954).
(*7*) JAOAC **25**, 857(1942); **26**, 220(1943).
(*8*) JAOAC **18**, 81, 369(1935).
(*9*) JAOAC **37**, 241(1954); **38**, 56(1955).
(*10*) JAOAC **51**, 766(1968).
(*11*) JAOAC **59**, 141(1976).
(*12*) JAOAC **59**, 134(1976); **62**, 290(1979).
(*13*) JAOAC **24**, 867(1941); **25**, 874(1942); **27**, 494(1944).
(*14*) JAOAC **50**, 56(1967).
(*15*) JAOAC **51**, 763(1968).
(*16*) J. Agric. Food Chem. **3**, 159(1955); JAOAC **40**, 606(1957); **41**, 233(1958); **42**, 231(1959); **43**, 320(1960); **54**, 669(1971); **55**, 702(1972).
(*17*) JAOAC **37**, 250(1954); **38**, 225(1955); **59**, 1218(1976).
(*18*) JAOAC **15**, 524(1932); **17**, 190(1934); **18**, 351(1935); **28**, 80(1945).
(*19*) JAOAC **42**, 222(1959); **43**, 335(1960); **44**, 567(1961); **45**, 578(1962).
(*20*) JAOAC **61**, 154(1978).
(*21*) JAOAC **46**, 829(1963); **56**, 781(1973).
(*22*) JAOAC **57**, 382(1974).
(*23*) USDA Bur. Chem. Circ. **71**; JAOAC **41**, 276(1958); **42**, 39(1959).
(*24*) J. Agr. Research **23**, 995(1923); JAOAC **9**, 31 (1926).
(*25*) JAOAC **21**, 595(1938); **23**, 656(1940).
(*26*) J. Landw. **48**, 357(1900); **49**, 7(1901).
(*27*) USDA Bur. Chem. Bull. **137**, p. 152; JAOAC **30**, 594(1947).
(*28*) JAOAC **14**, 142(1931); **15**, 77(1932); **23**, 86(1940); **28**, 80(1945).
(*29*) JAOAC **51**, 776(1968); **59**, 937(1976).
(*30*) JAOAC **10**, 177(1927); **19**, 93, 574(1936); **28**, 80(1945).
(*31*) Ind. Eng. Chem., Anal. Ed. **7**, 116, 167(1935); JAOAC **30**, 606(1947); **31**, 98(1948); **32**, 650(1949); **33**, 162(1950); **34**, 563(1951).
(*32*) JAOAC **26**, 87(1943); **28**, 80(1945).
(*33*) JAOAC **52**, 607(1969)
(*34*) JAOAC **35**, 559(1952).
(*35*) Anal. Chem. **19**, 325(1947); JAOAC **37**, 246 (1954); **38**, 222(1955).
(*36*) JAOAC **58**, 477(1975).
(*37*) JAOAC **17**, 67, 173(1934); **18**, 335(1935); **38**, 96(1955).
(*38*) JAOAC **18**, 338(1935); **21**, 596(1938); **23**, 688(1940); **33**, 83(1950).
(*39*) J. Am. Chem. Soc. **39**, 2366(1917); G. Frederick Smith Chemical Co. Pub. 209, 5th ed. (1950); JAOAC **22**, 78, 673(1939); **24**, 865(1941); **25**, 892(1942).
(*40*) USDA Div. Chem. Bull. **56**, 36(1898); JAOAC **47**, 420(1964).
(*41*) JAOAC **48**, 654(1965).
(*42*) JAOAC **47**, 504(1964).
(*43*) JAOAC **44**, 560(1961); **46**, 306(1963); **47**, 512 (1964).

8. Baking Powders and Baking Chemicals

8.001 Preparation of Sample—Official Final Action

Remove entire sample from package, pass thru No. 20 sieve, and mix thoroly.

Total Carbon Dioxide (*1*)—Official Final Action

(Applicable to baking powders contg added $CaCO_3$)

8.002 ***Reagent***

Displacement soln.—Dissolve 100 g NaCl or $Na_2SO_4.10H_2O$ in 350 mL H_2O. Add ca 1 g $NaHCO_3$ and 2 mL Me orange, **5.014(e)**, and then enough H_2SO_4 (1+5) or HCl (1+2) to make just acid (decided pink). Stir until all CO_2 is removed. This soln is used in gas-measuring tube and leveling bulb and seldom needs replacement.

8.003 ***Apparatus***

Chittick apparatus.—Fig. **8:01**. Connect decomposition flask, *A*, by glass T-tube, *B*, provided with stopcock, *C*, to graduated gas-measuring tube, *D*, connected in turn with leveling bulb, *E*. For *A* always use 250 mL wide-mouth extn flask of Pyrex or other resistant glass fitted with 2-hole rubber stopper, thru one hole of which passes extended tip of 25 mL buret, *F*, and thru other, glass tube of same diam. as connecting T-tube. Use buret graduated in mL at 20°, numbered at 5 mL intervals, and fitted with extra-long tip bent to pass thru rubber stopper. Connect glass tube leading from decomposition flask to T-tube with rubber tubing to permit rotation of flask. Use gas-measuring tube graduated in mL at 20° with 0 mark at point 25 mL below top marking to allow for graduating upward from 0 to 25 mL and downward from 0 to 200 mL. Connect gas-measuring tube to ca 300 mL leveling bulb with long rubber tube.

(Available from Sargent-Welch Scientific Co.)

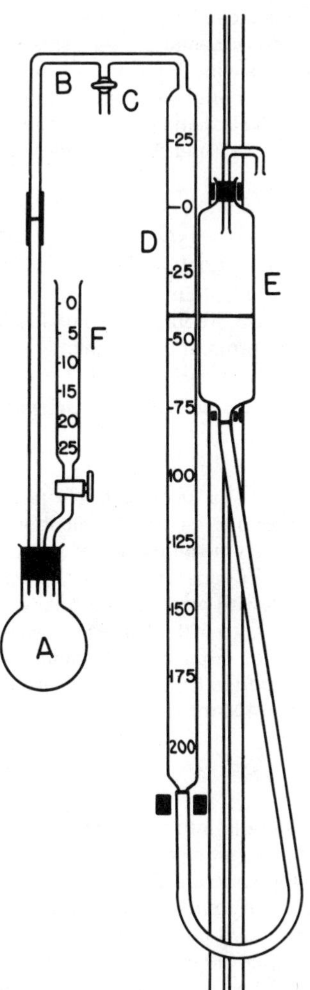

FIG. 8:01—Chittick apparatus for gasometric determination of carbon dioxide

8.004 ***Determination (2)***

Weigh 1.7 g prepd sample, **8.001**, into flask *A*, and connect flask with app., Fig. **8:01**. Open stopcock *C*, and using leveling bulb *E*, bring displacement soln to 10 mL graduation above 0 mark. (This 10 mL is practically equal to vol. of acid to be used in decomposition.) Let app. stand 1–2 min for temp. and pressure within app. to come to room conditions.

Close stopcock, lower leveling bulb somewhat to reduce pressure within app., and slowly add 10 mL H_2SO_4 (1+5) or HCl (1+2) to decomposition flask from buret *F*. To prevent escape of liberated CO_2 thru acid buret into air, at all times during decomposition keep displacement soln at level lower in leveling bulb than that in gas-measuring tube. Rotate and then vigorously agitate flask to mix contents intimately. Let stand 5 min to secure equilibrium. Equalize pressure in measuring tube, using leveling bulb, and read vol. of gas in tube. Observe temp. of air surrounding app. and also barometric pressure, and multiply mL gas evolved by factor given in table, **52.007**, for this temp. and pressure.

% CO_2 by wt = corrected reading/10.

8.005 Residual Carbon Dioxide (*3*)—Official Final Action

(a) *After drying on water bath.*—Place 1.7 g baking powder in clean, dry, 250 mL wide-mouth Soxhlet extn flask, *A*, Fig. **8:01**. Add 20 mL H_2O. Put flask *on cover* of H_2O bath (single or multiple) in which boiling H_2O is kept at const level of 5 cm below top of bath. (H_2O in bath must boil vigorously all thru detn. Opening in cover of bath must be 7.5 cm diam. to prevent flask from touching H_2O.) Evap. contents of flask until no moisture is visible in residue or inside surface of flask. (Sample should be completely dry in 1.5–2 hr.) Leave flask on H_2O bath 2 hr more. Add 10 mL H_2O, and let stand until flask is at room temp. (ca 1 hr).

Det. CO_2 with Chittick app. as in **8.004**, using correction factors in **52.007**. Shake flask vigorously until further shaking produces no increase in reading.

(b) *After drying in oven.*—Place 1.7 g sample in clean, dry, 250 mL wide-mouth Soxhlet extn flask, *A*, Fig. **8:01**. Tap flask to spread sample evenly on bottom. Add 10 mL H_2O with pipet. Stir with glass rod to break up powder that may have caked on bottom of flask. Wash down stirring rod and sides of flask with 10 mL H_2O. Place flask on shelf near center of air oven set at 100±2°, and evap. to dryness. After 5 hr, remove from oven, add 10 mL H_2O, and cool to same temp. as air surrounding Chittick app., **8.003**. Det. CO_2 in residue with Chittick app., using correction factors in **52.007**. Shake flask vigorously until further shaking produces no increase in reading.

8.006 Available Carbon Dioxide—Official Final Action

(Applicable to baking powders contg added $CaCO_3$)

Subtract residual CO_2, **8.005**, from total CO_2, **8.004**.

Neutralizing Value—Official Final Action

8.007 ***Of Acid-Reacting Materials Other Than Phosphates***

Dissolve 1 g sample in hot H_2O and titr. with 0.2*N* NaOH, using phthln. Express result as parts $NaHCO_3$ equiv. to 100 parts of the acid-reacting material.

8.008 ***Of Monocalcium Phosphate (4)***

Weigh 0.84 g sample into 375 mL casserole. Add 24 mL cold H_2O and, after stirring for moment, add 90.0 mL 0.1*N* NaOH. Bring suspension to bp in exactly 2 min, and boil 1 min. While soln is still boiling hot, add 1 drop phthln, and back-titr. with 0.2*N* HCl until all pink disappears. Boil soln 1 min, and again add 0.2*N* HCl until pink just disappears.

90 − (mL 0.2*N* HCl × 2) = neutzg value, parts $NaHCO_3$ equiv. to 100 parts of the phosphate.

8.009 ***Of Anhydrous Monocalcium Phosphate (4)***

Use 100 mL 0.1*N* NaOH and stir intermittently 5 min before bringing to bp. Proceed as in **8.008**.

8.010 ***Of Sodium Acid Pyrophosphate (4)***

Weigh 0.84 g sample and 20 g NaCl into 375 mL casserole, and slowly add 25 mL H_2O while stirring. Stir and crush with flat-end rod 3–5 min. Add 90.0 mL 0.1*N* NaOH and 1 drop phthln, and titr. with 0.2*N* HCl until pink disappears. If "starch filled" or 50% neutzg strength pyrophosphate is being titrd, use 70.0 mL 0.1*N* NaOH.

Vol. (mL) 0.1*N* NaOH − (mL 0.2*N* HCl × 2) = neutzg value, parts $NaHCO_3$ equiv. to 100 parts Na acid pyrophosphate.

Of Sodium Aluminum Phosphate (5)

AOAC-Food Chemicals Codex Method

8.011 ***Apparatus***

Magnetic stirrer-hot plate.—Must be capable of bringing assay soln to bp within 5 min. Alternatively, use ordinary hot plate and manual stirring.

8.012 ***Determination***

Accurately weigh ca 0.84 g sample, transfer to 250 mL beaker, and add 20 g NaCl, 5 mL 10% Na citrate.$2H_2O$ soln, and 25 mL H_2O. Pipet (or deliver from buret) 120 mL stdzd 0.1*N* NaOH, **50.032–50.034**, swirling during addn. Stir on mag. stirrer-hot plate at slow to medium speed; avoid spattering. Bring to bp in 3–5 min, and boil *exactly* 5 min. Remove from hot plate, and immediately cool to 25°. Titr. immediately with mag. stirring to pH 8.5 with stdzd 0.2*N* HCl, **50.011–50.012**, using pH meter previously stdzd with pH 7.0 buffer. Stir addnl 5 min and add 0.2*N* HCl to obtain pH 8.5.

$$\text{Neutzg value} = (V_1N_1 - V_2N_2) \times (0.84 \times 10)/W,$$

where V_1 and N_1 = vol. and normality of NaOH, resp.; V_2 and N_2 = vol. and normality of HCl, resp.; and W = g sample.

8.013 Tartaric Acid, Free or Combined (Qualitative Test) (6)—Official Final Action

(Applicable in presence of phosphates)

Shake ca 5 g sample repeatedly with ca 250 mL cold H_2O in flask, and let insol. portion settle. Decant soln thru filter, and evap. filtrate to dryness. Powder residue, add few drops 1% resorcinol soln, **31.146**, and ca 3 mL H_2SO_4, and heat slowly. Tartaric acid is indicated by rose-red, discharged on diln with H_2O.

Cream of Tartar and Free Tartaric Acid in Tartrate Powders (7)—Official Final Action

Total, Combined, and Free Tartaric Acid

8.014 ***Determination***

To 2.5 g sample in 250 mL vol. flask add 100 mL H_2O at ca 50°, and hold at room temp. ca 30 min, shaking occasionally. Cool, dil. to vol. with H_2O, shake vigorously, and filter thru large fluted paper. Pipet 2 portions of 100 mL each of *clear* filtrate into 250 mL beakers, and evap. to ca 20 mL. To 1 portion add 3.5 mL ca 1*N* KOH. Mix well, and add 2 mL HOAc. Again mix well and add 100 mL alcohol, stirring constantly. Treat other portion similarly, but use 1*N* NaOH instead of KOH. Then treat each mixt. sep. as follows: Cool to ca 15°, stir vigorously ca 1 min, and leave in refrigerator overnight. Collect ppt in gooch on thin, tightly tamped pad of asbestos. Rinse beaker with ca 75 mL ice-cold 80% alcohol, carefully washing down sides of beaker. Finally wash sides of crucible with 25 mL alcohol and suck dry. Transfer contents of crucible to original beaker with ca 100 mL hot H_2O, and titr. with 0.1*N* alkali, using phthln. Designate titer of portion treated with KOH as "x" and that treated with NaOH as "y."

8.015 ***Calculations***

% Total tartaric acid = $1.5(x + 0.6)$.
% Cream of tartar = $1.88(y + 0.6)$.
% Free tartaric acid = $1.5(x - y)$.

In above formulas "0.6" represents solubility of cream of tartar in reaction mixt. in terms of 0.1*N* alkali.

Free Tartaric Acid (Direct Determination)

8.016 ***Reagent***

Saturated alcohol.—To ca 50 g finely powd pure cream of tartar in erlenmeyer add ca 100 mL alcohol and 100 mL H_2O, shake vigorously several min, and let stand 15 min, shaking occasionally. Filter on paper in buchner; wash with ca 200 mL alcohol (1+1), then with alcohol, and finally with ether. Dry at temp. of boiling H_2O. To 500 mL *absolute* alcohol add ca 5 g of the purified cream of tartar and let stand 2 hr, shaking occasionally. Properly purified cream of tartar requires ≤0.15 mL 0.1*N* alkali to neutze 100 mL of mixt. of 50 mL $CHCl_3$ and 150 mL of the satd alcohol.

8.017 ***Determination***

Weigh 1.25 g sample into *absolutely dry* 200 mL vol. flask, add 50 mL $CHCl_3$, and let stand ca 5 min, shaking occasionally. (Discard detn if upon addn of $CHCl_3$, powder sticks to bottom of flask, indicating moisture.) Add 100 mL satd alcohol, shake ca 5 min, and let stand 30 min, shaking at frequent intervals. (It is not necessary to filter the alcohol reagent.) Dil. to vol. with the satd alcohol, shake few min, and filter thru large fluted paper. Titr. 100 mL clear filtrate with 0.1*N* alkali, using phthln. Vol. (mL) alkali used × 1.2 = % free tartaric acid.

8.018 ***Free Tartaric Acid (Qualitative Test)***

Ext 5 g sample with absolute alcohol and evap. alcohol from ext. Dissolve residue in NH_4OH (1+10), transfer to test tube, add good-size crystal of $AgNO_3$, and heat gently. Tartaric acid is indicated by formation of Ag mirror. (If desired, alc. ext may be tested as in **8.013**.)

Starch—Official Final Action

8.019 ***Direct Acid Hydrolysis Method***

(For baking powders and baking chemicals free from Ca)

Stir 5 g sample 1 hr in 250 mL beaker with 50 mL cold H_2O. Transfer to filter and wash with 250 mL cold H_2O. Heat insol. residue 2.5 hr with 200 mL H_2O and 20 mL HCl (sp gr 1.125, **52.002(c)**) in flask provided with reflux condenser. Cool, and nearly neutze with NaOH. Transfer to 250 mL vol. flask, dil. to vol., filter, and det. glucose in aliquot of filtrate as in **31.038**. Wt glucose obtained × 0.925 = wt starch.

8.020 ***Indirect Method (8)***

(For baking powders and baking chemicals contg Ca)

Mix 5 g sample with 200 mL HCl (1+11) in 500 mL vol. flask and let mixt. stand 1 hr, shaking frequently. Filter on 11 cm hardened paper, taking care to obtain clear filtrate. Rinse flask once without attempting to remove all starch, and wash paper twice with cold H_2O. Carefully wash starch from paper back into flask with 200 mL H_2O. Add 20 mL HCl (sp gr 1.125) and proceed as in **8.019**. (Treatment with HCl, without dissolving starch, effectively removes Ca, which otherwise would be pptd as tartrate by alk. Cu soln.)

Aluminum

Qualitative Test (9)—Official Final Action

(In presence of phosphates)

8.021 ***Reagents***

(**a**) *Ammonium acetate soln.*—50%. Dissolve 50 g NH_4OAc in 50 mL H_2O.

(**b**) *Aurintricarboxylic acid soln.*—0.1%. Dissolve 0.1 g aurintricarboxylic acid in H_2O and dil. to 100 mL.

8.022 ***Detection***

Place 1 g sample in 250 mL beaker, add 5 mL ca 1*N* HCl and 20 mL H_2O, and heat until starch hydrolyzes. Add 100 mL cold H_2O, 5 mL *10% $NaNH_4HPO_4.4H_2O$ soln*, and 3 drops Me orange. Add NH_4OH dropwise until ppt forms or color changes; then add 1*N* HCl dropwise until ppt dissolves or color changes plus 2 or 3 drops excess. Add 5 mL aurintricarboxylic acid soln and let stand 1 min. Add 50% NH_4OAc soln dropwise until ppt forms or color changes and then 1 mL excess. Let stand 5 min, stirring occasionally, and filter. Bright red ppt on filter paper indicates presence of Al.

Atomic Absorption Spectrophotometric Method (*10*)—Official First Action

8.023 ***Apparatus***

Atomic absorption spectrophotometer.—Perkin-Elmer Model 303, or equiv. Typical operating parameters for this app. are given in Table **8:01**. Operator must become familiar with optimum settings for his own app. and use table only as guide. (*Caution: See* **51.006**.)

Table 8:01 Operating Parameters

Wavelength, nm	309.3
Slit width, mm	1
Source, ma	30
N_2O, aspirating	4.5 (scale divisions)
N_2O, auxiliary and aspirating	5.5 (scale divisions)
C_2H_2 fuel	6 (metal ball scale division)
Flame	reducing
Ht, burner to light path, in.	⅛
Sample uptake, mL/min	4
Optimum concn range, μg/mL	50–150

8.024 ***Reagents***

(Do *not* use <2 mL pipets or <25 mL vol. flasks. Stock solns and (1+10) dilns may be stored indefinitely.)

(**a**) *Diluting soln.*—To 500 mL H_2O add 20 mL H_2SO_4 and 2.5 g NaCl; dil. to 1 L with H_2O.

(**b**) *Aluminum std solns.*—(*1*) *Stock soln.*—1 mg Al/mL. Dissolve 1.000 g pure Al wire in min. amt HCl. Evap. almost to dryness, add 500 mL H_2O, 20 mL H_2SO_4, and 2.5 g NaCl, and dil. to 1 L with H_2O. (*2*) *Working solns.*—Dil. aliquots of stock soln with dilg soln, (**a**), to make ≥4 std solns within concn range of instrument.

8.025 ***Preparation of Sample***

(*Caution: See* **51.019**.)

Accurately weigh ca 1 g sample into 250 mL Kjeldahl flask, add 2.0 mL H_2SO_4, and then slowly add 3 mL *30% H_2O_2*. When initial vigorous reaction subsides, apply heat from Bunsen flame until sample begins to char. Add addnl 1 mL increments H_2O_2 and heat until soln no longer chars; finally heat to fumes of SO_3. Cool, add 50 mL H_2O and 1 Pyrex glass chip, and boil 3–5 min. Cool and filter, if necessary, thru Whatman No. 2 paper into 100 mL vol. flask, washing paper thoroly with H_2O, and dil. to vol. Prep. reagent blank of 2.0 mL H_2SO_4 and same total amt 30% H_2O_2 used for sample. Measure *A* directly or dil. with dilg soln, (**a**), within range of instrument.

8.026 ***Determination***

Set up app. as in Table **8:01**, or use previously established optimum settings for app. Zero app. while aspirating dilg soln, (**a**). Det. *A* of ≥4 std solns within anal. range, alternating with sample soln readings. Flush burner with dilg soln, (**a**), and check 0 point between readings. Correct for reagent blank reading if significant, and det. Al content from std curve of *A* against μg Al/mL:

$$\% \text{ Al} = (\mu\text{g Al/mL}) \times (F/\text{g sample}) \times 10^{-4},$$

where F = 100 or 100 × mL final diln/mL aliquot, if original 100 mL is dild.

8.027 **Insoluble Ash and Preparation of Solution (*11*) Official Final Action**

Char 5 g sample in Pt dish at heat below redness (ca 500°). Boil carbonaceous mass with HCl (1+2.5), filter into 500 mL vol. flask, and wash with hot H_2O. Return residue, together with paper, to Pt dish, and burn to white ash. Boil again with the dil. HCl, filter, wash, combine filtrates, and dil. to 500 mL. Incinerate residue after last filtration and weigh ash insol. in acid.

8.028 **Iron and Aluminum (*11*)—Official Final Action**

Sep. SiO_2, if necessary, from 100 mL aliquot prepd soln, **8.027**. Mix soln with excess *10% $Na_2HPO_4.12H_2O$ soln*. Add NH_4OH until permanent ppt is obtained, then HCl dropwise until ppt dissolves. Bring soln to bp and boil 2–3 min; mix with considerable excess 50% NH_4OAc soln, **8.021(a)**, and 4 mL HOAc (4+1). As soon as ppt of $AlPO_4$, mixed with $FePO_4$, settles, collect on filter, wash with hot H_2O, ignite, and weigh. Fuse mixed phosphates with 10 parts Na_2CO_3, dissolve in H_2SO_4 (1+6), reduce with Zn, and det. Fe by titrn with std $KMnO_4$ soln (1 mL = 1 mg Fe). Det. P_2O_5 in aliquot from **8.027** as in **8.033** or **7.119**.

Wt Al_2O_3 = wt mixed phosphates − wt (Fe_2O_3 + P_2O_5).

8.029 Calcium (*11*)—Official Final Action

Heat combined filtrate and washings obtained in **8.028** to 50°, and add excess *satd NH_4 oxalate soln*. Let stand in warm place until ppt settles, filter, wash ppt with hot H_2O, dry, and ignite over Bunsen burner and finally over blast lamp at ≥950°. Cool in desiccator and weigh as CaO.

8.030 Potassium and Sodium (*11*)—Official Final Action

Evap. aliquot prepd soln, **8.027**, nearly to dryness to remove excess HCl, dil., and heat to bp. While soln is still boiling add *10% $BaCl_2.2H_2O$ soln* as long as ppt forms, and then enough *satd $Ba(OH)_2$ soln* to make liq. strongly alk. After ppt settles, filter, and wash with hot H_2O; heat filtrate to bp, add enough *$(NH_4)_2CO_3$ soln* (1 part $(NH_4)_2CO_3$ in 5 parts NH_4OH soln (1+12)) to ppt all the Ba, filter, and wash with hot H_2O. Evap. filtrate to dryness and ignite residue below redness to remove NH_4 salts. Add little H_2O and few drops $(NH_4)_2CO_3$ soln to residue. Filter into weighed Pt dish, evap., ignite below redness, and weigh mixed K and Na chlorides.

Digest residue with hot H_2O, filter thru small filter, and dil. filtrate, if necessary, to provide ≥20 mL liq. for each 100 mg K_2O. Acidify with few drops HCl and add excess Pt soln (10.5 g H_2PtCl_6/100 mL). Evap. on H_2O bath to thick paste; treat residue repeatedly with 80% alcohol, decanting thru weighed gooch or other filter; transfer ppt to filter, and wash thoroly with 80% alcohol. Dry 30 min at 100° and weigh. Calc. K found to its equiv. of KCl and subtract result from wt mixed chlorides to obtain wt NaCl.

Phosphorus—Official Final Action

8.031 ***Reagents***

(**a**) *Ammonium nitrate soln.*—Dissolve 100 g P-free NH_4NO_3 in H_2O and dil. to 1 L.

(**b**) *Magnesia mixture.*—(*1*) Dissolve 55 g crystd $MgCl_2.6H_2O$ in H_2O, add 140 g NH_4Cl and 130.5 mL NH_4OH, and dil. to 1 L. Or, (*2*) dissolve 55 g crystd $MgCl_2.6H_2O$ in H_2O, add 140 g NH_4Cl, dil. to 870 mL, and add NH_4OH to each required portion of soln just before using, at rate of 15 mL/100 mL soln.

(**c**) *Ammonium hydroxide soln for washing.*—(1+9). Should contain ≥2.5% NH_3 by wt.

8.032 ***Preparation of Solution***

Mix 5 g sample with little $Mg(NO_3)_2$ soln, **2.019**, dry, ignite, dissolve in HCl (1+2.5), and dil. to definite vol. In aliquot of soln det. P as in **8.033** or **7.119**.

8.033 ***Determination***

Pipet aliquot of prepd soln into 250 mL beaker; add NH_4OH in slight excess and barely dissolve ppt formed with few drops HNO_3, stirring vigorously. If HCl or H_2SO_4 has been used as solv., add ca 15 g cryst. NH_4NO_3 or soln contg that amt. To hot soln add 70 mL molybdate soln, **7.118(a)**, for every 100 mg P_2O_5 present. Digest 1 hr at ca 65° and test for complete pptn of P_2O_5 by adding more molybdate soln to clear supernate. Filter, and wash with cold H_2O or preferably with the NH_4NO_3 soln. Dissolve ppt on filter with NH_4OH (1+1) and hot H_2O, and wash into beaker to vol. ≤100 mL. Neutze with HCl, using litmus paper or *bromothymol blue* as indicator; cool, and from buret slowly add (ca 1 drop/sec), stirring vigorously, 15 mL magnesia mixt./100 mg P_2O_5 present. After 15 min add 12 mL NH_4OH and let stand until supernate is clear (usually 2 hr); filter, wash ppt with NH_4OH (1+9) until washings are practically Cl-free, dry, burn at low heat, and ignite to const wt, preferably in furnace at 950–1000°; cool in desiccator, and weigh as $Mg_2P_2O_7$. Report as % P_2O_5.

8.034 *Qualitative Test—Official Final Action*

Add 10 mL H_2O to 1–2 g sample in 150 mL beaker. Make just acid with HNO_3, filter, take equal vols filtrate and molybdate soln, **7.118(a)**, and warm at 40–50°. Yellow ppt indicates presence of phosphate.

8.035 Sulfate (*12*)—Official Final Action

Boil 5 g sample 1.5 hr with mixt. of 300 mL H_2O and 15 mL HCl. Filter, wash filter thoroly with hot H_2O, cool combined filtrate and washings, and dil. to 500 mL with H_2O. Det. sulfate in 100 mL aliquot as in **3.062**.

8.036 Ammonia—Official Final Action

To 2 g sample in distn flask add 300–400 mL H_2O and excess of NaOH soln (1+1), connect with condenser, and distil into measured vol. std acid. Titr. excess acid in distillate with std alkali, using Me red.

8.037 Arsenic—Official Final Action

Place 5 g sample directly in generator, **25.007(a)**; add 10 mL H_2O, little at time to prevent foaming over, and then 15 mL As-free HCl, adding it dropwise until foaming ceases. Heat on steam bath until drop of mixt., when dild and treated with I soln, does not show blue. Then dil. to ca 30 mL with H_2O and continue as in **25.010** or **25.012**, beginning with addn of KI reagent. Prep. blank and stds for comparison, using As-free HCl of same concn as that used in detn.

8.038 Fluorine—Official Final Action

See **25.049–25.055**.

8.039 Lead—Official Final Action

See **25.061–25.062** and **25.095–25.105**.

SELECTED REFERENCES

(*1*) JAOAC **6**, 453(1923).
(*2*) JAOAC **10**, 36(1927).
(*3*) JAOAC **31**, 278(1948); **32**, 83, 269(1949); **33**, 77(1950).
(*4*) JAOAC **33**, 77(1950); **34**, 296(1951).
(*5*) JAOAC **59**, 26(1976).
(*6*) Ann. chim. anal. **4**, 263(1899).
(*7*) JAOAC **13**, 385(1930); **22**, 599(1939).
(*8*) Conn. Agr. Expt. Sta. Rpt. 1900 (II), p. 174.
(*9*) J. Am. Chem. Soc. **47**, 142(1925); JAOAC **34**, 61(1951); **35**, 57(1952).
(*10*) JAOAC **55**, 684(1972).
(*11*) Conn. Agr. Expt. Sta. Rpt. 1900, p. 178.
(*12*) USDA Bur. Chem. Bull. **13** (V), p. 596; Conn. Agr. Exp. Sta. Rpt. 1900, p. 179.

9. Beverages: Distilled Liquors

SPIRITS

9.001 Physical Examination—Procedure

Note and record following: (**a**) Color and depth of color; (**b**) odor—whisky, brandy, rum, etc., or foreign; (**c**) taste—whisky, brandy, rum, etc., or foreign.

Color (*1*)—Official Final Action

9.002 ***Definition***

Whisky color units are defined as $10 \times A$ at 430 nm, measured in monochromatic light, of sample ½" thick which has spectral color characteristics of an av. whisky free of turbidity.

This definition applies only to A values obtained with precise spectrophtr with band width of $\leqslant 1$ nm at 430 nm, and whose wavelength and photometer scales have been checked and corrected by methods recommended by NBS, in LC-1017, Jan. 1967, and in SP260–41.

Potassium Dichromate Calibration Method

9.003 ***Preparation of Standard Curve***

Prep. solns of $K_2Cr_2O_7$ in 0.01N H_2SO_4 as follows:

Color Unit	g/L	Color Unit	g/L
1	0.0500	6	0.3000
2	0.1000	7	0.3500
3	0.1500	8	0.4000
4	0.2000	9	0.4500
5	0.2500	10	0.5000

Read A of these solns in spectrophtr at 430 nm against H_2O, using same size cell as used in detns. If other than ½" cell is used, convert reading to this size. Plot color units against A or calc. av. factor for converting instrument reading to color units if straight line is obtained.

9.004 ***Determination***

Place sample, or sample dild with 50% alcohol, in cell and det. A against H_2O. Calc. color units, using factor or std curve.

Natural and Artificial Coloring Matter (Organic and Water-Soluble Color) (*2*)—Official Final Action

Spectrophotometric Method

9.005 ***Apparatus***

(**a**) *Spectrophotometer.—See* **9.002**.

(**b**) *Graduated cylinder.*—Cylindrical type of uniform diam., with pressed or molded base and ₮ stopper. Distance from base to top is 285–295 mm. To contain 50 mL at 20°, graduated in 0.2 mL with each fifth mark distinguished by longer line; numbered from bottom upward at 2 mL intervals; error of graduations $\leqslant 0.2$ mL at any point. (Available from SGA Scientific Inc., No. JC-9675.)

9.006 ***Reagents***

(**a**) *n-Methyl propyl ketone.*—2-Pentanone, practical.

(**b**) *Saturated sodium chloride soln.*—Use USP or ACS NaCl.

(**c**) *Alcohol.*—MeOH, reagent grade, or alcohol, USP.

9.007 ***Determination***

Pipet 20 mL whisky into cylinder, **9.005**(**b**). Add by pipet, in order, 10 mL satd NaCl soln, 0.5 mL HCl, and 10 mL Me Pr ketone. Immediately invert 10–15 times and let layers sep. Color in lower layer indicates presence of caramel, vegetable extractives, or synthetic dye. Read vol. of org. layer within 1 hr and det. its A at 430 nm. If A is too great or if solv. layer is cloudy, dil. aliquot to known vol. with either 50% MeOH or 50% alcohol and read A.

9.008 ***Calculation***

Example: If from 20 mL sample, org. layer of 16.1 mL was obtained which had A of 0.420 in 1 cm cell after diln 1+1 with 50% alcohol: $(16.1 \times 0.420 \times 12.7 \times 2)/20 = 8.59$ color units (Lovibond number), where 12.7 is conversion factor to color units.

Specific Gravity (Apparent)—Official Final Action

9.009 ***Apparatus***

(**a**) *Constant temperature water bath.*

(**b**) *Pycnometers.*—100 and 50 mL (Fig. **9:01**).

9.010 ***Calibration***

Fill thoroly cleaned pycnometer with recently distd H_2O, stopper, and immerse in const temp. H_2O bath with bath level above graduation mark on pycnometer. After 30 min, remove stopper and with capillary tube adjust until bottom of meniscus is tangent to graduation mark. With small roll of filter paper, dry inside neck of pycnometer, stopper, and immerse in H_2O at room temp. 15 min. Remove pycnometer, dry, let stand 15 min, and weigh. Empty pycnometer, rinse with acetone, and dry thoroly in air with suction. Let empty flask come to room temp., stopper, and weigh. Wt in air of contained H_2O = wt filled pycnometer − wt empty pycnometer.

9.011 ***Determination***

Obtain wt sample as in **9.010**.

Sp gr in air = S/W, where S = wt sample, and W = wt H_2O.

Alcohol by Volume

From Specific Gravity by Pycnometer (3) *Official Final Action*

9.012 ***Apparatus***

Distillation apparatus.—500 mL flask, connected thru bulb (Iowa State type is convenient) to vertically assembled Liebig condenser with jacket $\geqslant 400$ mm long, inner tube 9 ± 1 mm id, with adapter. Joints may be live rubber or ₮. Heat with elec.- or gas-operated unit.

9.013 ***Determination***

(Some samples do not require distn prior to detn, e.g., straight bourbon whisky; alcohol-H_2O mixts contg traces of volatile ingredients.)

(**a**) *Samples containing 60% or less alcohol by volume.*—Calibrate 100 mL pycnometer, Fig. **9:01**, as in **9.010**, at one of

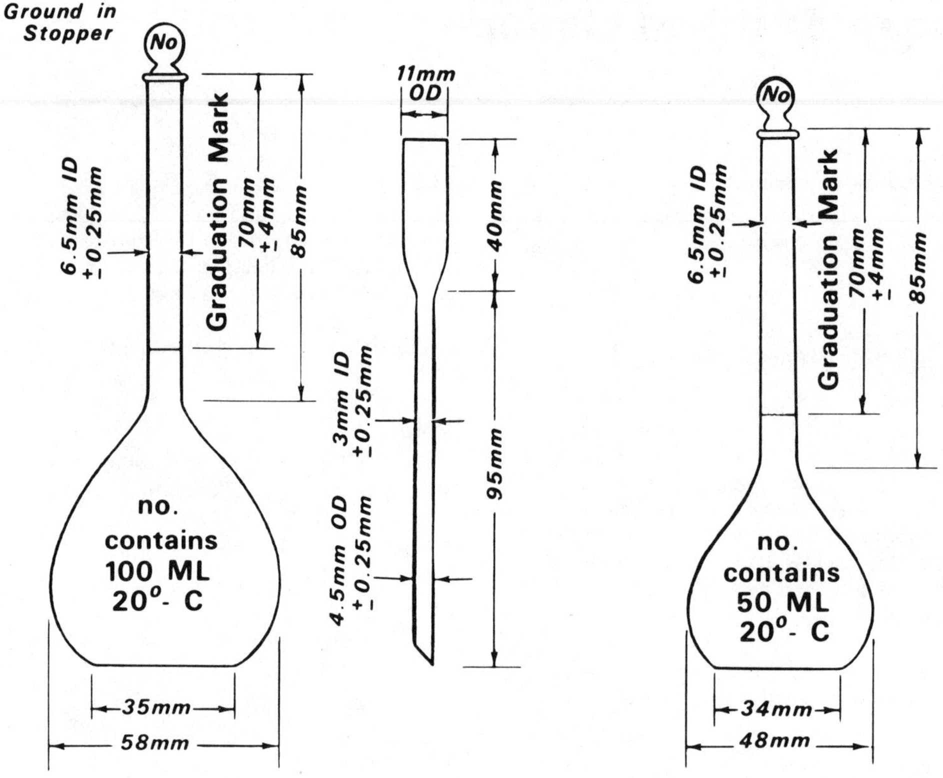

FIG. 9:01—100 mL and 50 mL pycnometers

temps specified in **52.003**. Fill clean, dry pycnometer with sample and adjust to vol. at calibration temp. as in **9.010**.

Transfer contents of pycnometer to distg flask, just previously rinsed with cold H_2O and contg few glass beads, or equiv. Rinse pycnometer 3 times, using total of 25 mL cold H_2O (40 mL for cordials or wines), and add rinse H_2O to flask. Place wet pycnometer so that adapter extends just into bulb. Surround pycnometer with ice or ice-H_2O. Complete connections and pass thru condenser rapid stream of H_2O kept at ≤25° at outlet. Distil ca 96 mL at uniform rate in ≥30 but ≤60 min, using longer times for higher percentages of alcohol. Remove and stopper pycnometer, mix distillate by swirling, and wash down with H_2O any drops that may be above graduation mark. Immerse in const temp. bath at calibration temp. and after 30 min carefully dil. to vol., with aid of capillary tube, by adding H_2O previously boiled and cooled to same temp. Det. sp gr of distillate as in **9.011**. Obtain corresponding % alcohol by vol. from **52.003**. (This result is % alcohol by vol. at 15.56° (60°F).)

(b) *Samples containing more than 60% alcohol by volume.*—Proceed as in **(a)** with following changes: Calibrate 100 mL and 50 mL pycnometers, Fig. **9:01**, at 15.56°, fill 50 mL pycnometer with sample, and adjust to vol. at 15.56°. Add 50 mL cold H_2O to distg flask before transfer of sample and collect distillate in 100 mL pycnometer. Adjust to vol. at 15.56°. Obtain sp gr of distillate, and from table, **52.003**, obtain % alcohol by vol. in distillate. Calc. as follows:

$$\text{\% alcohol by vol. in sample at } 15.56° = D \times W/W';$$

where D = % alcohol by vol. in distillate at 15.56°; W = wt H_2O at 15.56° in 100 mL pycnometer; and W' = wt H_2O at 15.56° in 50 mL pycnometer.

From Specific Gravity by Hydrometer (4)
Official Final Action

(Applicable to spirits contg ≤600 mg ext/100 mL)

9.014 ***Apparatus***

(a) *Hydrometer.*—Graduated to 0.1 or 0.2° proof, with calibration corrections.
(b) *Thermometer.*—Graduated to 0.25 or 0.5°F, with calibration corrections.
(c) *Cylinder.*—Clear glass, 2.5" diam., 14" high.
(d) *Metal clips.*—To hold thermometer in cylinder.

9.015 ***Determination***

Clean and dry hydrometer before use. Let hydrometer, thermometer, cylinder, and sample come to room temp. Rinse cylinder, contg thermometer held in place by spring frame clip, 2 or 3 times with portion of sample. Fill cylinder to desired level with sample, holding cylinder at ca 45° angle to reduce agitation and air bubbles. (After hydrometer is inserted, liq. level should be slightly below rim of cylinder.) Place palm of hand over top of cylinder and slowly invert 3 or 4 times to equalize temps of liq. and cylinder. Wipe off any liq. on outside of cylinder. (Do not place hands on cylinder in such way as to warm liq. inside.) Insert hydrometer in liq.; then raise and lower hydrometer bulb from top to bottom 5 or 6 times to temper and distribute slight temp. changes thruout liq. Keep hydrometer bulb in liq., dry stem, and let hydrometer come to rest without wetting more than few tenths degrees of exposed stem.

Read hydrometer, then thermometer. To read hydrometer

scale, place eye slightly below plane of surface of liq., and then slowly raise head, keeping eye perpendicular to hydrometer, until surface flattens from ellipse into straight line. Take point where this line intersects hydrometer scale as reading of hydrometer.

Raise hydrometer slightly above its point of rest and again let it come to rest in liq. Read hydrometer and thermometer again to verify original readings. Read hydrometer to nearest 0.02° and thermometer to nearest 0.1°. Remove and dry hydrometer. Reinvert cylinder and contents several times (with thermometer left in place) to thermally equilibrate system. Retemper hydrometer, dry stem, and again read hydrometer and thermometer. Apply calibration corrections for both hydrometer and thermometer. Calc. true % of proof from Table No. 1 of the U.S. Treasury Department Gauging Manual, 1970. Average calcd values if they agree within 0.1° proof; otherwise take addnl readings and average.

Det. ext as in **9.022**, and for every 100 mg ext/100 mL add 0.4° proof to apparent proof.

9.016 *From Refraction—Official Final Action*

Measure 25 mL sample into distn flask, noting temp.; dil. with 100 mL H_2O, distil nearly 100 mL, dil. to vol. at same temp., and det. immersion refractometer reading. Obtain corresponding % alcohol from **52.004**.

When vol. measurements are made at temp. other than 15.56°, multiply % alcohol from **52.004** by appropriate factor from Table **9:01**.

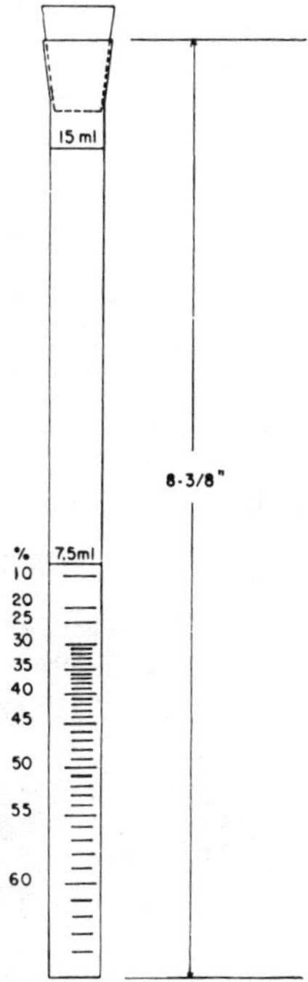

FIG. 9:02—Williams tube

Williams Field Test (5)—Procedure

9.017 *Apparatus*

Williams tube.—See Fig. **9:02**. Available from Kontes Glass Co., No. K-899400. Clean frequently and dry.

9.018 *Reagents*

(**a**) *Dilute hydrochloric acid.*—Dil. 10 mL HCl to 100 mL with H_2O.

(**b**) *Solvent.*—Mix 70 mL Pentasol or isoamyl alcohol, 28 mL toluene, and 2 mL dil. HCl. Shake well until acid completely dissolves.

9.019 *Determination*

Place sample in tube, accurately adjusting bottom of meniscus to coincide with 7.5 mL mark. Remove any excess sample on sides of tube above 7.5 mL mark with swab or roll of filter paper. Add solv. to 15 mL mark. Stopper tube and invert number of times to mix intimately. Stand tube upright and let sep. When sepn is complete, rotate tube to shake down globules of lower soln that adhere to sides, and stopper. When settling and drainage are complete, read % alcohol (by vol.) where meniscus between the 2 layers falls on calibration mark. Repeat mixing and settling, and read again.

9.020 *Temperature Correction*

Correct for temp. and alcohol concn according to Table **9:02**.

Example: % alcohol from tube: 48.0% at 90°F. Correction factor from table: −1.1; 48.0 − 1.1 = 46.9%.

9.021 Alcohol by Weight—Official Final Action

Accurately weigh 40–50 g sample in clean, dry 50 mL pycnometer, Fig. **9:01**, or other closed vessel. (If alcohol is ≤60% by vol., the 100 mL sample of **9.013(a)** may be weighed and used.) Transfer to 500 mL distn flask contg 50 mL H_2O and few

Table 9:01 Factors for calculating original alcohol content for 25 and 50 mL samples distilled to 100 mL when refractometer measurements are made at 20, 25, 30, or 35°

Alc. % by Vol. in Distillate at 15.56°	25 mL Sample				50 mL Sample			
	Temp. of Measurement				Temp. of Measurement			
	20°	25°	30°	35°	20°	25°	30°	35°
	Multiply Alcohol in Distillate by:				Multiply Alcohol in Distillate by:			
0–3.99	4.001	4.002	4.003	4.004	2.000	2.000	2.000	2.000
4–5.99	4.003	4.006	4.009	4.013	2.000	2.001	2.001	2.001
6–7.99	4.005	4.011	4.016	4.021	2.001	2.001	2.002	2.002
8–9.99	4.007	4.015	4.023	4.030	2.001	2.002	2.003	2.004
10–11.99	4.009	4.019	4.028	4.037	2.001	2.003	2.004	2.006
12–13.99	4.010	4.021	4.031	4.041	2.002	2.004	2.006	2.007
14–15.99	4.011	4.022	4.032	4.043	2.002	2.005	2.007	2.009
16–19.99	4.011	4.023	4.034	4.045	2.003	2.006	2.008	2.011
20–more	4.011	4.024	4.036	4.047	2.003	2.006	2.009	2.012

Table 9:02. Temperature (°F) correction factors

%	60°	62°	64°	66°	68°	70°	72°	74°	76°	78°
43	+0.5	+0.3	+0.2	0.0	−0.1	−0.2	−0.4	−0.5	−0.7	−0.8
43.4	+0.5	+0.4	+0.2	+0.1	0.0	−0.2	−0.3	−0.5	−0.6	−0.7
44	+0.6	+0.4	+0.3	+0.2	0.0	−0.1	−0.3	−0.4	−0.5	−0.7
45	+0.7	+0.5	+0.4	+0.3	+0.1	0.0	−0.2	−0.3	−0.4	−0.6
46	+0.8	+0.7	+0.5	+0.4	+0.2	+0.1	0.0	−0.2	−0.3	−0.5
47	+0.9	+0.8	+0.6	+0.5	+0.3	+0.2	+0.1	−0.1	−0.2	−0.4
47.5	+1.0	+0.8	+0.7	+0.5	+0.4	+0.3	+0.1	0.0	−0.2	−0.3
48	+1.1	+0.9	+0.7	+0.6	+0.4	+0.3	+0.2	0.0	−0.1	−0.2
49	+1.1	+1.0	+0.8	+0.7	+0.6	+0.4	+0.3	+0.1	0.0	−0.1
50	+1.2	+1.1	+0.9	+0.8	+0.7	+0.5	+0.4	+0.3	+0.1	0.0

%	80°	82°	84°	86°	88°	90°	92°	94°	96°	98°
43	−0.9	−1.1	−1.2	−1.4	−1.5	−1.6	−1.8	−1.9	−2.0	−2.2
43.4	−0.9	−1.0	−1.2	−1.3	−1.4	−1.6	−1.7	−1.9	−2.0	−2.2
44	−0.8	−0.9	−1.1	−1.2	−1.4	−1.5	−1.6	−1.8	−1.9	−2.1
45	−0.7	−0.8	−1.0	−1.1	−1.3	−1.4	−1.5	−1.7	−1.8	−2.0
46	−0.6	−0.7	−0.9	−1.0	−1.2	−1.3	−1.4	−1.6	−1.7	−1.8
47	−0.5	−0.6	−0.8	−0.9	−1.0	−1.2	−1.3	−1.5	−1.6	−1.7
47.5	−0.4	−0.6	−0.7	−0.8	−1.0	−1.1	−1.3	−1.4	−1.5	−1.7
48	−0.4	−0.5	−0.6	−0.8	−0.9	−1.1	−1.2	−1.3	−1.5	−1.6
49	−0.3	−0.4	−0.5	−0.7	−0.8	−1.0	−1.1	−1.2	−1.4	−1.5
50	−0.2	−0.3	−0.4	−0.6	−0.7	−0.9	−1.0	−1.1	−1.3	−1.4

clean glass beads, or equiv. Rinse pycnometer 3 times, bringing contents of distn flask to ca 125 mL. Distil, and det. % alcohol by vol. in distillate as in **9.013(a)**. Det. corresponding % alcohol by wt in distillate from table, **52.005**. Multiply result by wt distillate and divide by wt sample.

9.022 Extract—Official Final Action

Weigh, or measure at 20°, 25–100 mL sample, evap. to dryness on steam bath, dry 30 min at 100°, cool in desiccator 30 min, and weigh.

9.023 Ash—Official Final Action

Proceed as in **31.012** or **31.013**, using residue from **9.022**.

Potassium

Flame Photometric Method (6)—Official Final Action

9.024 ***Reagent and Apparatus***

(**a**) *Std solns.*—Prep. as in **11.024(a)**, except make final dilns, i.e., 1–10 ppm K, with 50% alcohol.
(**b**) *Flame spectrophotometer.*—*See* **11.024(b)**.

9.025 ***Determination***

(*Caution: See* **51.007**.)

Proceed as in **11.025**, except burn sample undild, or, if necessary, dild with 50% alcohol (usually 2.5–5.0 times). Calc. ppm K as in **11.025**.

Sodium

Flame Photometric Method (6)—Official Final Action

9.026 ***Reagent and Apparatus***

(**a**) *Std solns.*—Prep. as in **11.026**, except make final dilns, i.e., 1–10 ppm Na, with 50% alcohol.
(**b**) *Flame spectrophotometer.*—*See* **11.024(b)**.

9.027 ***Determination***

(*Caution: See* **51.007**.)

Proceed as in **11.025**, except burn sample undild, or, if necessary, dild with 50% alcohol until %*T* falls within %*T* range of stds. Calc. ppm Na as in **11.025**.

9.028 Phosphorus—Official Final Action

See **11.034**.

Copper—Official Final Action

Atomic Absorption Method (7)

9.029 ***Reagent***

(Distil H_2O and alcohol from all-Pyrex stills into Cu-free receiver.)

Copper std solns.—(*1*) *Stock soln.*—0.2 mg/mL. Dissolve 0.393 g $CuSO_4.5H_2O$ (free from any whitish deposit) in 500 mL vol. flask contg H_2O and 2 mL H_2SO_4. Dil. to vol. and mix. (*2*) *Working soln.*—0.004 mg/mL. Prep. daily by dilg 2.00 mL stock soln to 100 mL.

9.030 ***Preparation of Standard Curve***

To series of 50 mL vol. flasks each contg 25 mL alcohol, add 0, 2, 4, 6, 10, and 12 mL Cu working std soln. Dil. nearly to mark with H_2O, mix, and cool to room temp. before dilg to vol. Stds contain 0.0, 0.16, 0.32, 0.48, 0.80, and 0.96 ppm Cu (μg/mL), resp.

9.031 ***Determination***

(*Caution: See* **51.006**.)

Follow operating instructions supplied by manufacturer or previously established optimum settings for AA spectrophtr used. Adjust instrument to 0 *A* while aspirating blank. Read at 324.7 nm $\geq$4 std solns within anal. range before and after each 6–10 samples. Prep. calibration curve from av. of each std before and after sample group. Use std curve to convert *A* values for samples to ppm Cu.

ZDBT Colorimetric Method (8)

9.032 ***Reagents***

Prep. H_2O, alcohol, and Cu stds as in **9.029**, and in addn:

Zinc dibenzyldithiocarbamate (ZDBT)-carbon tetrachloride soln.—0.2%. Dissolve 2 g ZDBT (Uniroyal Chemical or ICN–K&K Laboratories) in 1 L CCl_4 by warming in H_2O bath at $<77°$. Filter thru Whatman No. 41, or equiv. acid-washed paper, into dark bottle. Store in refrigerator.

9.033 ***Apparatus***

Separators.—60 or 125 mL pear-shaped separators with Teflon stopcocks. Clean separators with hot chromic acid cleaning soln and rinse with H_2O. Before each analysis, shake mixt. of 10 mL H_2O, 0.5 mL 6*N* H_2SO_4, and 10 mL ZDBT-CCl_4 soln in each separator 1 min. Clean inside of stems with cotton swab soaked in ZDBT-CCl_4 soln. Drain and rinse separators with H_2O.

9.034 ***Preparation of Standard Curves***

(**a**) *80–135° proof alcoholic samples.* — To separators contg 5 mL alcohol, add 0, 0.50, 1.00, 2.00, and 3.00 mL Cu working std soln and 5, 4.5, 4, 3, and 2 mL H_2O, resp. Solns in separators contain 0.0, 0.20, 0.40, 0.80, and 1.20 μg Cu/mL (ppm), resp. Treat as in **9.035**. Plot ppm Cu against *A*.

(**b**) *Aqueous samples, wines, and other low proof samples.*—Prep. as in (**a**) except use 5 mL H_2O instead of alcohol.

9.035 ***Determination***

To separator contg 10 mL sample (dil. sample $>135°$ proof to 80–135° proof) or std, add 0.5 mL 6*N* H_2SO_4 and 10.0 mL ZDBT-CCl_4 soln. Stopper and shake briefly; release pressure by removing stopper. Replace stopper and shake vigorously 100 times. If funnel stems are not dry, remove drops of liq. with small roll acid-washed paper (e.g., Whatman 41) to prevent draining H_2O drops into cell. Insert plug of fibre glass (Corning Glass Works No. 3950) or cotton into each stem to filter out possible haze materials. Within 10–60 min, det. *A* of CCl_4 layer at 438 nm. Let few mL CCl_4 layer pass thru filtering medium before collecting sample in cell. Use CCl_4 layer from appropriate 0 ppm Cu soln (prepd as for std curve (**a**) or (**b**)) as ref. Det. Cu concn from appropriate std curve. Multiply by diln factor if sample was dild.

Iron (*9*)—Official Final Action

Atomic Absorption Method

9.036 ***Apparatus***

Spectrophotometer.—Perkin-Elmer Corp. 303 (or later double beam model), or equiv., with 3-slot Boling burner head, or equiv.

9.037 ***Reagent***

(Use Fe-free H_2O and reagents; rinse glassware with HCl and H_2O before use.)

Iron std solns.—(*1*) *Stock soln.*—10 μg/mL. Dissolve 0.0684 g ferrous ethylenediammonium sulfate ($FeC_2H_4(NH_3)_2SO_4.4H_2O$, G. Frederick Smith Chemical Co.) in H_2O, add 2.5 mL H_2SO_4, dil. to 1 L with H_2O, and mix thoroly. (*2*) *Working solns.*—0.0, 0.1, 0.2, 0.3, and 0.4 ppm. To 100 mL vol. flask contg 50 mL 43% alcohol, add 0, 1, 2, 3, and 4 mL stock soln and dil. each soln nearly to vol. with 43% alcohol. Mix thoroly, let cool to room temp., and adjust to 100 mL with 43% alcohol.

9.038 ***Determination***

(*Caution: See* **51.006**.)

Follow manufacturer's operating instructions, using lean air-C_2H_2 flame and single element Fe lamp. Set wavelength at 248.3 nm and adjust spectrophtr to 0 *A* while aspirating blank (0.0 ppm Fe). Analyze stds before and after duplicate series of samples. Det. av. *A* values. Aspirate H_2O between each detn to flush burner, and reset *A* to 0 with blank. Plot std curve of *A* against ppm Fe. Read ppm Fe in sample from this curve.

TPTZ Colorimetric Method

(Not applicable to brandy)

9.039 ***Apparatus***

(**a**) *Spectrophotometer.*—Beckman Instruments Model DU, or equiv., or photoelec. colorimeter with suitable filter, e.g., Klett colorimeter with No. 60 filter.

(**b**) *Water bath.*—To maintain const temp. at ca 60°.

9.040 ***Reagents***

(Use Fe-free H_2O and reagents; rinse glassware with HCl and H_2O before use.)

(**a**) *Hydroxylamine hydrochloride soln.*—40%. Dissolve 10 g $NH_2OH.HCl$ in 25 mL H_2O.

(**b**) *Ammonium perchlorate soln.*—10%. Dissolve 10 g NH_4ClO_4 in 100 mL H_2O.

(**c**) *1,2-Propanediol cyclic carbonate (propylene carbonate).*—Reagent grade (MC/B Manufacturing Chemists).

(**d**) *2,4,6-Tripyridyl-s-triazine (TPTZ) soln.*—0.001*M*. Add 0.0781 g TPTZ (G. Frederick Smith Chemical Co.) to 100 mL H_2O contg 5 drops HCl in 250 mL vol. flask. Dil. to vol. with H_2O and filter thru coarse fritted glass funnel. Store in Fe-free glassware.

(**e**) *Sodium acetate soln.*—40%. Dissolve 48.2 g anhyd. NaOAc in 75.7 mL H_2O and 24.3 mL HCl. Add 5 mL 0.001*M* TPTZ, 5 mL 40% $NH_2OH.HCl$, 2 mL 10% NH_4ClO_4, and 10 mL propylene carbonate. Add 5 mL $CHCl_3$, shake, and discard lower layer. After 2 $CHCl_3$ extns, add 5 mL 0.001*M* TPTZ and repeat $CHCl_3$ extn. (Four extns are necessary to obtain colorless soln.) Store in Fe-free glassware.

(**f**) *Ascorbic acid solns.*—(*1*) *5%.*—Dissolve 2.5 g ascorbic acid in 25 mL H_2O and dil. to 50 mL with alcohol. Prep. fresh daily. (*2*) *5% Ascorbic acid in sodium acetate buffer.*—Dissolve 2.5 g ascorbic acid in 20 mL H_2O, add 5 mL 40% NaOAc, and dil. to 50 mL with alcohol. Prep. fresh daily.

(**g**) *Iron std solns.*—Prep. same concns as in **9.037**, but prep. 200 mL each working soln.

9.041 ***Preparation of Standard Curve***

Pipet 50 mL 43% alcohol contg known amts Fe (i.e., 0 (reagent color blank), 0.1, 0.2, 0.3, and 0.4 ppm) into 5 sep. 100 mL vol. flasks. Add 2 mL 5% ascorbic acid in NaOAc buffer and 2 mL TPTZ, and heat 15 min in ca 60° H_2O bath.

Cool solns to room temp. and det. *A* on spectrophtr at 593 nm or photoelec. colorimeter with appropriate filter. Use 43% alcohol to zero colorimeter. Subtract *A* of reagent color blank from *A* of samples. Plot corrected *A* readings against ppm Fe to obtain std curve. (Straight line should be obtained with Fe concns used.)

9.042 ***Determination***

Pipet 50 mL sample into each of 2 sep. 100 mL vol. flasks and add 2 mL 5% ascorbic acid to each. Add 2 mL TPTZ to one flask and 2 mL H_2O to other (product blank). Heat 15 min in ca 60° H_2O bath. Cool solns and measure *A* of each soln as for std curve. Subtract *A* of reagent color blank, **9.041**, and also *A* of product color blank from *A* of samples. Det. Fe concn from std curve.

Chloride (*10*)—Official Final Action

9.043 ***Apparatus***

See **11.029**.

9.044 ***Reagents***

See **11.030** and in addn:

(a) *Dilute chloride std soln.*—Dil. 50 mL chloride std soln, **11.030(c)**, to 500 mL with H_2O. Alternatively, dissolve 0.2103 g KCl in H_2O and dil. to 1 L. 1 mL = 0.1 mg Cl.

(b) *Dilute silver nitrate std soln.*—Dil. 50 mL std soln, **11.030(d)**, to 500 mL with H_2O. Alternatively, dissolve 0.4791 g $AgNO_3$ in H_2O and dil. to 1 L. 1 mL = 0.1 mg Cl.

(c) *Alcohol soln.*—Place 500 mL alcohol in 1 L vol. flask, add ca 475 mL H_2O, mix, cool to room temp., and dil. to 1 L with H_2O.

9.045 ***Determination***

Det. equivalence point voltage as in **11.031** except use alcohol soln instead of H_2O to adjust vol. to 100 mL. Use std solns **11.030(c)** and **(d)**.

Pipet 5 mL dil. std Cl soln into 250 mL beaker, and add 95 mL alcohol soln and 1.0 mL HNO_3. Titr. with dil. std $AgNO_3$ soln to predetd equivalence voltage as in **11.031**.

Pipet 100 mL distd spirits sample into 250 mL beaker, add 1.0 mL HNO_3, and titr. with dil. std $AgNO_3$ soln as above.

Ppm Cl in sample = $(V_w/V_s) \times C \times 10$,

where V_w = mL std $AgNO_3$ used by sample, V_s = mL std $AgNO_3$ used by std Cl soln, and C = 0.5 mg Cl in 5 mL std Cl soln used.

9.046 Total Acids—Official Final Action

Neutze ca 250 mL boiled H_2O in porcelain evapg dish (185 mm dish is convenient). Add 25 mL sample and titr. with 0.1*N* NaOH, using ca 2 mL phthln.

9.047 Fixed Acids—Official Final Action

Evap. 25–50 mL sample to dryness in Pt dish on steam bath and dry 30 min in oven at 100°. Dissolve and transfer residue with several portions of neut. alcohol of ca same proof as sample, using 25–50 mL in all, to porcelain dish contg ca 250 mL neutzd boiled H_2O. Titr. with 0.1*N* NaOH, using 10 mL buret graduated in 0.05 mL, and ca 2 mL phthln.

9.048 Volatile Acids—Official Final Action

Volatile acids = total acids from **9.046** − fixed acids from **9.047**.

Esters and Aldehydes—Official Final Action

9.049 ***Reagents***

(a) *Sodium thiosulfate std soln.*—0.05*N*. Prep. by dilg 0.1*N* soln, **50.037**.

(b) *Iodine soln.*—Approx. 0.05*N*.

(c) *Sodium bisulfite soln.*—Approx. 0.05*N*. (Deterioration is retarded if soln contains ca 10% alcohol; do not use after ca 1 week.)

9.050 ***Preparation of Sample***

To 200 mL sample in 500 mL erlenmeyer, add ca 35 mL H_2O and few grains SiC (Carborundum). Distil slowly into 200 mL vol. flask until distillate is nearly at mark. Dil. to vol. and mix.

9.051 ***Determination of Esters (11)***

Transfer 100 mL distillate to 500 mL flask, neutze free acid, add measured excess 0.1*N* NaOH, connect flask with air-cooled condenser ca 60 cm long, heat 2 hr on steam bath, let cool, and titr. excess alkali. Reject detns in which excess 0.1*N* alkali is <2 mL, or is >10 mL. Calc. esters as EtOAc. Correct for blank detn performed on 100 mL 50% alcohol (absolute alcohol-H_2O, 1+1).

9.052 ***Determination of Aldehyde***

(*Indirect Method*)

Place remainder of distillate from **9.050** in 500 mL flask, add ca 100 mL H_2O and excess $NaHSO_3$ soln, and let stand ca 30 min, shaking occasionally. (Excess $NaHSO_3$ should be equiv. of ca 25 mL I soln.) Add excess I soln, and titr. this excess with std $Na_2S_2O_3$ soln. Run blank contg same vols of I soln and bisulfite soln as used in sample. Difference between titrns in mL $Na_2S_2O_3$ soln $\times$ 1.1 = mg acetaldehyde in sample.

Esters

Spectrophotometric Method (12)—Official Final Action

9.053 ***Principle***

Esters react quant. with H_2NOH in alk. soln to form a hydroxamic acid which, after acidification, forms colored complex with ferric ions. Ester concn is proportional to *A* at 525 nm at const alcohol concn and can be calcd from either of 2 std curves: (*1*) *At constant proof.*—Plot *A* against known EtOAc concn in 100° proof spirits (or any other convenient const proof); or (*2*) *At any actual proof.*—Plot *A* of EtOAc/g against proof and calc. concn from this proof factor.

9.054 ***Reagents***

(a) *Hydrochloric acid.*—4*N*. Dil. 333 mL HCl to 1 L with H_2O.

(b) *Ferric chloride soln.*—0.37*M*. Dissolve 50 g $FeCl_3.6H_2O$ in ca 400 mL H_2O in 500 mL vol. flask. Add 12.5 mL 4*N* HCl and dil. to vol. with H_2O.

(c) *Hydroxylamine hydrochloride soln.*—2*M*. Dissolve 69.6 g $H_2NOH.HCl$ in H_2O in 500 mL vol. flask and dil. to vol. with H_2O. Store in refrigerator.

(d) *Sodium hydroxide soln.*—3.5*N*. Dissolve 70 g NaOH in ca 400 mL H_2O in 500 mL vol. flask. Cool, and dil. to vol. with H_2O.

9.055 ***Preparation of Ethyl Acetate Standard Solutions***

(a) *Stock soln No. 1 for std curve.*—0.333 g EtOAc/L in 100° proof spirits. Weigh 0.1667 g EtOAc in weighing bottle and transfer quant. to 500 mL vol. flask with 100° proof spirits. Dil. to vol. with 100° proof spirits at room temp.

(b) *Std solns for std curve.*—To series of five 100 mL vol. flasks add, from pipet or buret, 0.0, 15.0, 30.0, 45.0, and 60.0 mL stock soln No. 1. Dil. to vol. with 100° proof spirits and mix. Stds contain 0.0, 5.0, 10.0, 15.0, and 20.0 g EtOAc/100 L, resp.

(c) *Stock soln No. 2 for proof factor determination.*—0.500 g EtOAc/L H_2O. Weigh 0.2500 g EtOAc in weighing bottle and transfer quant. to 500 mL vol. flask with H_2O. Dil. to vol. with H_2O and mix.

(**d**) *Stock soln No. 3 for proof factor determination.*—0.500 g EtOAc/L 192° proof spirits. Prep. as in (**c**), using 192° proof spirits for transfer and diln.

(**e**) *Proof factor std solns.*—*(1) 0–50° stds.*—To 6 sep. 250 mL vol. flasks add 50.0 mL EtOAc stock soln No. 2. Using graduate, add 0, 13, 20, 39, 53, and 66 mL 192° proof spirits. Dil. each nearly to vol. with H_2O, mix, and cool to room temp. before dilg to vol. with H_2O. Std solns contain 10 g EtOAc/100 L in ca 0, 10, 20, 30, 40, and 50° proof spirits. *(2) 60–192° stds.*—To 9 sep. 250 mL vol. flasks, add 50.0 mL EtOAc stock soln No. 3. Using appropriate graduate, add 29, 55, 81, 108, 134, 161, 174, 187, and 200 mL 192° proof spirits, resp. Dil. nearly to vol. with H_2O, mix, and cool to room temp. before dilg to vol. with H_2O. Std solns contain 10 g EtOAc/100 L in ca 60, 80, 100, 120, 140, 160, 170, 180, and 192° proof spirits, resp.

Det. exact proof of solns by std method, e.g. hydrometer.

9.056 ***Preparation of Samples***

Analyze whisky distillates, spirits, and colorless gin samples directly. Distil colored or turbid samples as in **9.050**. If sample contains >20 g ester/100 L, dil. with H_2O to ester concn of 5–20 g/100 L.

9.057 ***Determination***

(Mix all solns by swirling to avoid formation of bubbles.)

Just before use, prep. stock soln of reaction mixt. by combining 5.0 mL $H_2NOH.HCl$ and 5.0 mL 3.5*N* NaOH for each std and sample soln. Discard after 6 hr.

Prep. ref. soln by pipetting 4 mL reaction mixt. and 2 mL 4*N* HCl into 25 × 200 mm test tube. Mix and add 2.0 mL sample. Same ref. soln may be used for series of samples of different ester content, but they must have same proof.

Pipet 2 mL sample and 4 mL reaction mixt. into another 25 × 200 mm test tube. Mix and let react 1–20 min. Pipet in 2 mL 4*N* HCl and mix.

To ref. soln, pipet in 2 mL $FeCl_3$ soln. Rinse ref. cell twice with this soln, fill cell, and place in cell holder. This ref. soln may be used for 1 day if tightly capped; otherwise refill periodically to avoid evapn error.

To sample soln, pipet in 2 mL $FeCl_3$ soln and mix. Complete reading of each sample before proceeding to next. Rinse sample cell twice, fill cell, and place in cell holder. Read *A* at 525 nm immediately, since color of sample fades rapidly. If instrument has single cell or tube, use same cell or tube for both ref. and sample. Calc. or obtain $\Delta A = A_{sample} - A_{ref}$.

9.058 ***Preparation of Standard Curve***

Analyze std solns, **9.055(b)**, as in **9.057**. Plot ΔA against EtOAc concn (g/100 L at 100° proof). (*Note:* Std curve need not be repeated for each analysis. Check periodically and repeat if new instrument or reagents are used.)

9.059 ***Preparation of Proof Factor Curve***

Analyze std solns, **9.055(e)**, as in **9.057**. Plot ΔA/g EtOAc against proof in the 15 solns (0–192° proof). *See Note*, **9.058**.

To calc. ester content of samples, read *A*/g value from proof factor curve at sample proof. If sample was dild, use dild proof in calcn. Divide observed *A* by *A*/g to obtain g EtOAc/100 L. Correct for sample diln, if necessary. To express as g/100 L at 100° proof, multiply above ester value by ratio: 100/sample proof.

Aldehydes—Official Final Action

Method I (13)

(Applicable to ext-free spirits—brandy and wine spirits)

9.060 ***Reagents***

(**a**) *Potassium metabisulfite soln.*—Dissolve 15 g $K_2S_2O_5$ in H_2O, add 70 mL HCl, and dil. to 1 L with H_2O. Bisulfite titer of 10 mL soln should be ≥24 mL 0.1*N* I soln.

(**b**) *Phosphate-EDTA soln.*—Dissolve 200 g $Na_3PO_4.12H_2O$ (or 188 g $Na_2HPO_4.12H_2O$ + 21 g NaOH; or 72.6 g $NaH_2PO_4.H_2O$ + 42 g NaOH; or 71.7 g KH_2PO_4 + 42 g NaOH) and 4.5 g Na_2H_2EDTA in H_2O and dil. to 1 L.

(**c**) *Dilute hydrochloric acid.*—Dil. 250 mL HCl to 1 L with H_2O.

(**d**) *Sodium borate soln.*—Mix 100 g H_3BO_3 with 170 g NaOH and dil. to 1 L with H_2O.

9.061 ***Total Aldehydes***

Pipet 50 mL sample (contg ≤30 mg acetaldehyde), reduced to ca 100° proof, or 25 mL high proof sample and 25 mL H_2O, into 750 mL or 1 L erlenmeyer contg 300 mL boiled or deaerated H_2O and 10 mL $K_2S_2O_5$ soln. Stopper flask, swirl to mix, and let stand 15 min. Add 10 mL phosphate-EDTA soln. (pH should be 7.0–7.2. If not, adjust pH by adding HCl or NaOH soln to $K_2S_2O_5$ soln and start with new sample.) Stopper flask, swirl, and let stand addnl 15 min. Add 10 mL HCl, (**c**) (when analyzing series, make complete detn on first sample before adding acid to next), and ca 10 mL fresh *0.2% starch indicator*. Swirl to mix. Add enough ca 0.1*N* I soln to just destroy excess bisulfite and bring soln to light blue end point.

Add 10 mL Na borate soln, and rapidly titr. liberated bisulfite with 0.05*N* I soln from 10 mL buret (or 0.02*N* I soln from 25 mL buret) to same light blue end point as above, swirling gently and continuously, avoiding direct sunlight. (pH should be 8.8–9.5. If necessary, adjust by adding HCl or NaOH soln to Na borate soln and start with fresh sample.)

mg CH_3CHO/100 mL = mL I soln × normality I soln × 22.0 × 100/mL sample.

9.062 ***Free Aldehydes***

Pipet identical sample as in **9.061** into 750 mL or 1 L erlenmeyer contg 300 mL boiled or deaerated H_2O and 10 mL each $K_2S_2O_5$ and phosphate-EDTA solns. Stopper flask, swirl, and let stand 15 min. Proceed as in **9.061**, beginning "Add 10 mL HCl, (**c**) . . ."

Method II

(Applicable to spirits contg ext—aged in wood)

9.063 ***Free Aldehydes***

Pipet 50 mL sample (contg ≤30 mg acetaldehyde), reduced to 80–100° proof, if necessary, into 500 mL distg flask, add 50 mL *satd borax soln*, and distil ca 50 mL into 750 mL or 1 L erlenmeyer contg 300 mL H_2O and 10 mL each $K_2S_2O_5$ and phosphate-EDTA solns. (pH should be 7.0–7.2. If necessary, adjust by adding HCl or NaOH soln to $K_2S_2O_5$ soln and start with fresh sample.) Proceed as in **9.061**, beginning "Add 10 mL HCl, (**c**) . . ."

9.064 ***Aldehydes as Acetal***

Transfer 200 mL sample measured at std temp. in vol. flask to 500 mL distg flask, and rinse vol. flask 2–3 times with small amts H_2O into distg flask. Add 50 mL *satd borax soln* and distil, slowly at first, nearly 200 mL into same vol. flask contg 2–3 mL H_2O and immersed in ice bath. Bring distillate to vol. at same temp. used for measuring sample.

Det. total aldehydes (including acetal) as in **9.061**. Det. free aldehydes as in **9.062**. Total aldehydes − free aldehydes = combined aldehydes equiv. to acetal as mg CH_3CHO/100 mL. Alternatively, combined aldehydes as acetal/100 mL = (combined aldehydes equiv. to acetal as mg CH_3CHO/100 mL) × 2.68.

9.065 ***Total Aldehydes***

Report total aldehydes as sum of free aldehydes, **9.063**, and combined aldehydes equiv. to acetal, **9.064**.

Fusel Oil—Official Final Action

Method I (14)

9.066 ***Reagents***

(**a**) *p-Dimethylaminobenzaldehyde (DMAB) soln.*— In 100 mL vol. flask dissolve 1 g DMAB in mixt. of 5 mL H_2SO_4 and 90 mL H_2O, and dil. to vol. with H_2O.

(**b**) *Isobutyl alcohol.*—Eastman Kodak Co. 303 (highest purity for fusel oil assay).

(**c**) *Isoamyl alcohol.*—Eastman Kodak Co. X-18, isopentyl alcohol (highest purity for fusel oil assay).

(**d**) *Ethyl alcohol.*—Redistd middle 50% fraction.

(**e**) *Synthetic std fusel oil.*—Weigh 2 g std isobutyl alcohol and 8 g std isoamyl alcohol into 1 L vol. flask and dil. to vol. with H_2O. Pipet two 10 mL portions into 100 mL vol. flasks and dil. to vol., one with H_2O and other with alcohol. Prep. working stds for products in range of 0–170 proof contg 1.0–6.0 g synthetic fusel oil/100 L by dilg 1.0–6.0 mL aliquots of aq. std soln to 100 mL with alc. soln of proof expected for dild sample when pipetted into analysis tube. Prep. similar working stds for products in range of 170–190 proof by dilg 1.0–6.0 mL aliquots of alc. std soln to 100 mL with alc. soln of proof of sample or its diln.

When 6 mL synthetic std dild with 190 proof alcohol is analyzed, *A* should be 0.83±0.03 at 530 nm.

9.067 ***Preparation of Samples***

(Aged, blended and rectified products, whiskies, brandies, rums, vodka, and liqueurs require distn prior to analysis.)

Determination of true proof of sample.—Det. alcohol as in **9.013**.

For samples contg >6 g fusel oil/100 L, dil. distd sample with H_2O to concn of 2.0–5.0 g fusel oil/100 L. Dil. 5 mL brandy, rum, or blended whisky to 100 mL; dil. 5 mL heavy brandy, rum, or straight whisky to 250 mL.

9.068 ***Determination***

Pipet 2 mL aliquots of sample or dild sample, distd, if necessary, 2 mL H_2O (for reagent blank), and 2 mL aliquots of stds into 15 × 150 mm g-s or covered test tubes. Stopper or cover tubes, and place in rack, then in ice bath. Pipet 1 mL DMAB soln into each tube, shake, and replace in ice bath for 3 min. With tubes still in ice bath, add 10 mL chilled H_2SO_4 from buret down side of tubes. Shake tubes individually and replace in ice bath for 3 min. Transfer rack of tubes from ice bath to boiling H_2O bath and boil 20 min. Transfer tubes to ice bath for 3–5 min, then to room temp. bath. Read %*T* of developed color of samples and stds on spectrophtr at 538–543 nm against reagent blank as ref. (Use same wavelength for both stds and unknowns.)

Plot g fusel oil in std samples/100 L on linear scale as abscissa against %*T* as ordinate on log scale of semilog paper. Convert %*T* of samples to g fusel oil/100 L from std curve. If diln was used, multiply g fusel oil/100 L found by diln factor to obtain g fusel oil/100 L in original sample. Analyze 2 levels of stds with each series of unknowns.

Precision expected: Whisky and brandy, ±5%; rum, ±8%; gin, vodka, and spirits, ±0.4 g/100 L.

Method II (15)

9.069 ***Reagents***

(**a**) *Color reagent.*—Dissolve 1 g Na salt of 4-hydroxybenzaldehyde-3-sulfonic acid in H_2O, dil. to vol. in 25 mL vol. flask with H_2O, and filter.

(**b**) *Fusel oil std solns.*—Weigh 2 g isobutyl alcohol, **9.066(b)**, and 8 g isoamyl alcohol, **9.066(c)**, into 1 L vol. flask and dil. to vol. with 50% alcohol. Dil. 0, 1, 2, 3, 5, 10, and 15 mL portions to vol. with 50% alcohol in 100 mL vol. flasks (0.0, 0.1, 0.2, 0.3, 0.5, 1.0, and 1.5 g fusel oil/L). Std soln contg 1.0 g fusel oil/L should give *A* of ca 0.4 at 445 nm in **9.071**.

(**c**) *Alcohol.*—50%. Free of fusel oil (ACS).

9.070 ***Preliminary Distillation***

Add 20 mL H_2O to 50 mL sample and distil, slowly at first, collecting ca 50 mL in 50 mL vol. flask. Dil. to vol. with H_2O. (For samples known to contain >150 g fusel oil/100 L, use 25 mL sample plus 45 mL H_2O.)

9.071 ***Determination***

To dry 10 mL vol. flask, add 0.1 mL distillate from serological blow-out pipet. (Pipet should have pointed tip and should be thoroly cleaned (chromic acid plus H_2O rinse) before use. Rinse pipet several times with distillate, and wipe end dry. Bring liq. to line while holding tip to outside surface of vol. flask. Then insert end to bottom of vol. flask and release sample. After draining pipet, hold flask at 45° angle and blow out pipet.)

Add 0.1 mL color reagent from 1 mL buret graduated in 0.01 mL; then add 2 mL H_2SO_4 from 50 mL buret. Mix, and place unstoppered flask in H_2O bath at room temp. (250 mL beaker is convenient). Bring to bp and boil 30 min. Let cool, dil. to vol. with H_2SO_4, and det. *A* at 445 nm against H_2O on Beckman DU spectrophtr, or equiv. instrument.

9.072 ***Blank and Standards***

Develop color of 0.1 mL 50% alcohol and 0.1 mL portions of std solns. Use same 0.1 mL pipet for blank, stds, and sample. Subtract *A* of 50% alcohol blank from *A* of sample and stds.

9.073 ***Calibration Curve or Factor***

Plot corrected *A* of stds against concn. (Straight line is obtained up to ca 150 g fusel oil/100 L; above this value, curve flattens. Concn of color reagent may be increased, but it is best to dil. distd sample so that *A* is <0.6.) Calc. or obtain *A′* (*A* of 1.0 g fusel oil/L) from curve.

9.074 ***Calculations***

$$\text{g fusel oil/100 L} = 100\,A \times D/A'$$

where 100 = diln of 0.1 mL sample to 10 mL in color development, *A* = corrected *A* of sample, *A′* = factor, **9.073**, and *D* = diln of sample before distn.

Higher Alcohols (*n*-Propyl Alcohol, Isobutyl Alcohol, and Isoamyl Alcohol) and Ethyl Acetate—Official Final Action

Gas Chromatographic Method (16)

9.075 ***Apparatus***

(**a**) *Gas chromatograph.*—Equipped with flame ionization detector. (*1*) *Column.*—23% Carbowax 1500 (w/w) on Chromosorb W (60–80 mesh, acid-washed). Weigh 9 g Carbowax 1500 into 250 mL beaker and mix with H_2O on steam bath. Weigh 30 g Chromosorb W in 250 mL beaker and combine with Carbowax soln in large flat-bottom Pyrex glass baking dish or flat-bottom polyethylene container (ca 20 × 25 cm). Add H_2O to just cover solid support and mix thoroly. Evap. H_2O with frequent stirring in hood. (Gentle steam may be applied to hasten evapn.) After evapn of H_2O, heat coated support ca 2 hr in 100° oven.

Pack 2.4 m (8′) × ¼″ od Cu tubing tightly and evenly by repeated tapping, and condition in column oven at 150° with He flow rate of 150 mL/min until steady baseline is observed at attenuation 1× at operating parameters (ca 24 hr).

(*2*) *Approximate parameters.*—Column temp. 70° (isothermal); detector and inlet temp. 150°; He carrier flow 150 mL/min.

Optimum operating conditions vary with column and instrument, and must be detd by using std solns. Adjust parameters for max. peak sharpness and optimum sepn. With high level std, *n*-PrOH should give almost complete baseline sepn from EtOH.

(**b**) *Syringe.*—10 μL, Hamilton Co. No. 701, or equiv.

9.076 ***Reagents***

(**a**) *Isobutyl alcohol.*—*see* **9.066**(**b**).
(**b**) *Isoamyl alcohol.*—*See* **9.066**(**c**).
(**c**) *n-Propyl alcohol.*—Redistd, reagent grade.
(**d**) *Ethyl acetate.*—Redistd, reagent grade.
(**e**) *n-Butyl alcohol.*—Redistd, reagent grade.

(**f**) *n-Butyl alcohol internal std solns.*—(*1*) *High level.*—Dil. 10 mL *n*-BuOH to 100 mL with 40% alcohol. (1 mL added to 100 mL sample or std is equiv. to ca 81 g *n*-BuOH/100 L.) (*2*) *Low level.*—Dil. 1 mL *n*-BuOH to 200 mL with 95% alcohol. (1 mL added to 100 mL sample or std is equiv. to ca 4.1 g/100 L.)

(**g**) *n-Propyl alcohol, isobutyl alcohol, isoamyl alcohol, and ethyl acetate high level std solns.*—(*1*) *Stock soln.*—Accurately weigh 1 mL *n*-PrOH, 1 mL isobutyl alcohol, 2 mL isoamyl alcohol, and 1 mL EtOAc into 100 mL vol. flask and dil. to vol. with 40% alcohol. (*2*) *Intermediate soln.*—Dil. 10 mL stock soln to 200 mL with 40% alcohol. (*3*) *Working soln.*— (Approx. 40.2, 41.1, 81.2, and 45.1 g/100 L *n*-PrOH, isobutyl alcohol, isoamyl alcohol, and EtOAc, resp.) Dil. 5 mL stock soln to 100 mL with 40% alcohol. Add 1 mL high level *n*-BuOH internal std soln, (**f**)(*1*), and mix. Prep. fresh weekly.

(**h**) *n-Propyl alcohol, isobutyl alcohol, isoamyl alcohol, and ethyl acetate low level working solns.*— (Approx. 2.0, 2.1, 4.1, and 2.3 g/100 L *n*-PrOH, isobutyl alcohol, isoamyl alcohol, and EtOAc, resp.) Dil. 5 mL high level intermediate soln, (**g**)(*2*), to 100 mL with 95% alcohol. Add 1 mL low level internal std soln, (**f**)(*2*), and mix. Prep. fresh weekly.

Prep. std soln of ca same concn as sample if latter differs grossly from appropriate (high or low level) std.

9.077 ***Determination***

Make preliminary injection of 10 μL sample to det. absence of *n*-BuOH. (If present, subtract its amt from total *n*-BuOH (original and internal std) content.) Add 1 mL internal std soln, (**f**) (high or low level, depending on higher alcohol and EtOAc concn), to 100 mL sample in vol. flask, and chromatograph 10 μL aliquots of sample and std solns in triplicate.

Measure peak hts of *n*-PrOH, isobutyl alcohol, isoamyl alcohol, and EtOAc to nearest 0.05 cm and calc. peak ht ratio of each to *n*-BuOH (internal std) in sample and std solns. (For more accurate detn of isoamyl alcohol, use peak areas.)

$X = H \times S/H'$, where X = concn of higher alcohol or EtOAc in sample (g/100 L); H = peak ht (or area for isoamyl alcohol) ratio of higher alcohol or EtOAc to *n*-BuOH in sample; H' = peak ht (or area for isoamyl alcohol) ratio of higher alcohol or EtOAc to *n*-BuOH in std; S = concn of higher alcohol or EtOAc in std (g/100 L).

Sum of isoamyl and isobutyl alcohol concns is ca equiv. to fusel oil concn as detd in **9.069–9.074**.

Alternative Method (17)

9.078 ***Apparatus***

Gas chromatograph.—Equipped with flame ionization detector. (*1*) *Column.*—2% glycerol and 2% 1,2,6-hexanetriol (Aldrich Chemical Co.) (w/w) on Gas-Chrom R (100–120 mesh, non-acid-washed) (Applied Science Laboratories, Inc.). Weigh 0.2 g each of glycerol and 1,2,6-hexanetriol into 50 or 100 mL beaker and dissolve by stirring with MeOH. Weigh 9.6 g Gas-Chrom R in evapg dish (top diam. ca 100–125 mm), moisten with MeOH, and add soln of stationary phases. Mix thoroly, and gently heat mixt. on steam bath, stirring continuously. When material appears to be dry (light pink), continue heating and occasional stirring to ensure complete removal of solv. Store in capped jar. Pack 3 m (10′) × ⅛″ od Cu or stainless steel tube (0.030″ wall; if steel is used, rinse inside several times with acetone to remove manufacturing oils, and air dry) with prepd support, using vibrator to ensure complete packing of column. Condition overnight in 80° column oven with He flow rate of 10–25 mL/min and detector end of column disconnected.

(*2*) *Approximate parameters.*—Column, injector, and detector temps (°)—80, 100, and 125, resp.; gas flows (mL/min)—He carrier and H 25, air 250–400; attenuation 64×.

Optimum operating conditions vary with column and instrument and must be detd by using std solns. Adjust parameters for max. peak sharpness and optimum sepn. Analysis is complete in ca 11 min.

9.079 ***Reagents***

(Use absolute alcohol thruout when alcohol is specified.)

(**a**) *n-Propyl alcohol.*—Reagent grade.

(**b**) *Isobutyl alcohol.*—(Fisher Scientific Co., Certified Reagent No. A-379.)

(**c**) *Amyl alcohol.*—(Gallard-Schlesinger Chemical Manufacturing Co., 584 Mineola Ave., Carle Place, NY 11514, AnalaR No. 10038.) Mixt. of active-amyl and isoamyl alcohols, ca 22 and 78%, resp. Concn of 2 isomers varies from batch to batch. Det. composition of reagent by **9.080**. Measure areas of 2 peaks by triangulation (ht × width at half-ht), and obtain concn of each by dividing area of each peak by sum of both peak areas.

(**d**) *3-Pentanol internal std soln.*—40.76 mg/mL (Aldrich Chemical Co., Inc., No. P802-5). Prep. soln contg 10 mL reagent in 200 mL alcohol-H_2O (1+1).

(**e**) *Ethyl acetate.*—(Fisher Scientific Co., Certified Reagent No. E-145.)

(**f**) *n-Propyl alcohol, isobutyl alcohol, and amyl alcohol std solns.*—Prep. 3 or 4 std solns contg varying amts alcohols as follows: Into tared 100 mL vol. flasks contg alcohol-H_2O (1+1), pipet fusel alcohols and weigh after addn of each component.

Proportions of fusel alcohols in each std soln should vary so that desired concn range of each is represented in random manner in series of std solns. Suggested amts: 0.25–1.5 mL *n*-PrOH, 1.0–2.5 mL isobutyl alcohol, and 2.0–5.0 mL amyl alcohol. Dil. each to vol. with alcohol-H_2O (1+1).

(**g**) *n-Propyl alcohol, isobutyl alcohol, and amyl alcohol working std solns.*—Dil. 10 mL each std soln and 2.0 mL 3-pentanol internal std soln to 200 mL with alcohol-H_2O (1+1) (1:20 diln).

(**h**) *Ethyl acetate std solns.*—Prep. 3 or 4 std solns contg 0–0.5 g/L (0–50 g/100 L) in H_2O or alcohol-H_2O (1+1). Use for prepg direct std curve by plotting peak ht (mm) against concn in g/100 L.

9.080 ***Determination***

Pipet 10 mL sample into convenient vessel (e.g., 1 oz French sq glass bottle with screw cap), add, by pipet (0.2 mL pipet graduated in 0.01 mL), 0.1 mL 3-pentanol internal std soln, and mix. Inject 2 μL sample and working std solns. Measure peak ht of each component in working std soln and calc. peak ht ratio of each to internal std. Calc. concn ratio of each by dividing wt of component by that of internal std. (Proportion of active-amyl and isoamyl alcohols in mixt. must be taken into consideration in calcns of actual wts of each isomer in working std solns.)

Plot concn ratios (horizontal axis) against peak ht ratios (vertical axis) for each higher alcohol in all working stds to obtain family of curves. For EtOAc, plot peak ht directly against concn.

Similarly, measure peak ht of each component in sample and calc. peak ht ratios. Read concn ratios of all alcohols, using proper std curve. Multiply concn ratio of each fusel alcohol in sample by 40.76 to obtain g/100 L. New std curves need be prepd only when new instruments, parameters, or stds are used.

Furfural (*18*)—Official Final Action

9.081 ***Reagent***

Furfural std soln.—Redistil furfural thru short packed fractionating column at atm. pressure, and collect fraction boiling at 161.2° (uncorrected). Weigh 1 mL redistd furfural into 100 mL vol. flask and dil. to vol. with alcohol. Pipet 5 mL of this soln into 500 mL vol. flask and dil. to vol. with 50% alcohol (concn, ca 116 mg/L). Concd soln retains strength, but dil. soln does not.

9.082 ***Determination***

Pipet 25 mL distd spirits into volatile acid distn flask, Fig. **9:03**, with Ŧ joints and steam distil until 200 mL collects. If haze is present in distillate, dil. with known vol. alcohol. Det. *A* at 277 nm.

Det. *A* of std solns of furfural contg 0, 1, 2, 3, 4, and 5 mg furfural/L. Plot std curve or calc. av. *A* of 1 mg furfural/L, *A'* (ca 0.15).

$$\text{mg Furfural/L} = (A/A') \times F,$$

where *F* is diln factor (vol. final soln on which *A* is detd/vol. sample).

Detection of Acetone, Other Ketones, Isopropanol, and Tertiary Butyl Alcohol Official Final Action

9.083 ***Reagent***

Mercuric sulfate soln.—Mix 5 g yellow HgO with 40 mL H_2O and add, with stirring, 20 mL H_2SO_4 and 40 mL H_2O. Stir until completely dissolved. (*Caution: See* **51.079**.)

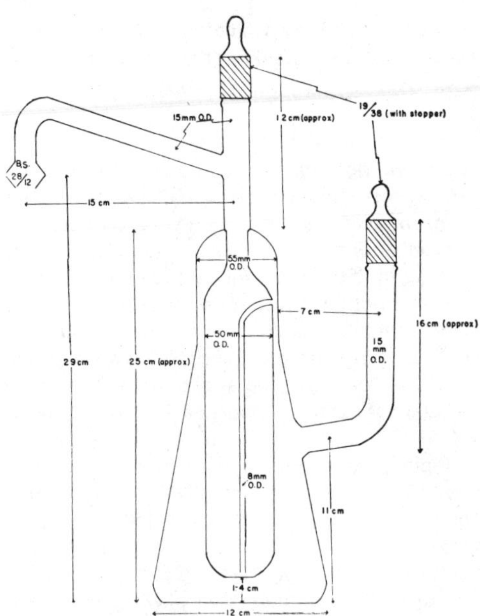

FIG. 9:03—Steam distillation flask

9.084 ***Determination***

To 2 mL distillate, **9.050**, add 3 mL H_2O and 10 mL $HgSO_4$ soln. Heat on boiling H_2O bath 3 min. White or yellow ppt forming within 3 min indicates presence of acetone, other ketones, or *tert*-BuOH. Disregard any ppt forming after 3 min on boiling H_2O bath.

If no ppt forms, test for isopropanol as follows: Place 8 g CrO_3 in 100 mL Kohlrausch flask, and add 15 mL H_2O and 2 mL H_2SO_4. Connect flask with reflux condenser and add 5 mL sample very slowly thru condenser. Reflux 30 min; then cool and distil 2 mL, collecting distillate in 10 mL graduate. Add 3 mL H_2O and 10 mL $HgSO_4$ soln, and proceed as above.

9.085 Sugars—Official Final Action

See Chapter **31**.

Methanol—Official Final Action

Chromotropic Acid Colorimetric Method (*19*)

9.086 ***Reagents***

(**a**) *Potassium permanganate soln.*—Dissolve 3.0 g $KMnO_4$ and 15.0 mL H_3PO_4 in 100 mL H_2O. Prep. monthly.

(**b**) *Sodium salt of chromotropic acid* (*sodium 1,8-dihydroxynaphthalene-3,6-disulfonate*) *soln.*—5% aq. soln. Filter if not clear. Prep. weekly. Either acid or salt may be used.

9.087 ***Purification of Chromotropic Acid***

If *A* of blank is >ca 0.05, purify reagent as follows:

Dissolve 10 g chromotropic acid or its salt in 25 mL H_2O. (Add 2 mL H_2SO_4 to aq. soln of salt to convert it to free acid.) Add 50 mL MeOH, heat just to bp, and filter. Add 100 mL isopropanol to ppt free chromotropic acid. (Add more isopropanol to increase yield of purified acid.)

9.088 ***Preparation of Sample***

Dil. or adjust sample to total alc. concn of 5–6%. Using 50 mL sample, distil thru simple still, collecting 40 mL distillate. Dil. to 50 mL with H_2O. (If alcohol has been detd previously, distillate may be adjusted to 5–6% alc. concn and used for this test.) If

>0.05% MeOH by vol. is present, dil. to ca that concn with 5.5% alcohol. For samples contg <0.05% MeOH, measure 200 mL into efficient fractionating still, place system under total reflux 15 min, and then slowly distil at high rate of reflux (≥20:1). Collect 10 mL distillate and dil. to 160 mL with H_2O.

9.089 ***Determination***

Pipet 2 mL $KMnO_4$ soln into 50 mL vol. flask. Chill in ice bath, add 1 mL chilled dild sample, and let stand 30 min in ice bath. Decolorize with little dry $NaHSO_3$ and add 1 mL chromotropic acid soln. Add 15 mL H_2SO_4 slowly with swirling and place in hot (60–75°) H_2O bath 15 min. Cool, add enough H_2O to bring approx. to 50 mL mark, mix, and dil. to vol. with H_2O at room temp. Read A at 575 nm against reagent blank of 5.5% alcohol treated similarly. Treat *std MeOH soln* contg 0.025% by vol. MeOH in 5.5% alcohol simultaneously in same manner, and read A'. (Temp. of std and sample should be within 1° since temp. affects A.)

$$\% \text{ MeOH in sample} = (A/A') \times 0.025 \times F,$$

where F = diln factor of sample.

Example: Sample was dild 25×; A of sample = 0.421; A of std MeOH = 0.368. Then (0.421/0.368) × 0.025 × 25 = 0.715%

(If color of sample is too intense, dil. with H_2SO_4-alcohol blank prepd as above. Not more than 3-fold diln is permitted, as ratio of chromotropic acid to HCHO is too low if diln is greater.)

9.090 ***Immersion Refractometer Method (20)***

Det. Zeiss immersion refractometer reading at 17.5° of distillate obtained in detn of alcohol. If, on ref. to table, **9:03**, refractometer reading shows sp gr agreeing with that obtained in alcohol detn, **9.013**, it may be assumed that MeOH is absent. Low refractometer reading indicates presence of appreciable amt of MeOH. If absence from the soln of refractive substances other than H_2O and the alcohols is assured, this difference in refraction is conclusive evidence of presence of MeOH.

Addn of MeOH to alcohol decreases refractive index in direct proportion to amt added; hence, quant. calcn is made by interpolation in Table **9:03** of figures for pure alcohol and MeOH of same sp gr as sample.

Example.—Distillate has sp gr at 15.56° of 0.9625 and refractometer reading at 17.5° of 43.1. By interpolation in Table **9:03**, readings for alcohol and MeOH at this gravity are 65.2 and 31.7, resp., and difference is 33.5; 65.2 − 43.1 = 22.1; (22.1 ÷ 33.5) × 100 = 66.0, showing 66.0% of total alcohol present is MeOH.

Gas Chromatographic Method (*21*)

9.091 ***Apparatus***

See **9.075**.

9.092 ***Reagents***

(**a**) *Alcohol.*—USP, MeOH-free.

(**b**) *Methanol stock soln.*—Dil. 10 mL MeOH, 99.9 mol % (Fisher Scientific Co., A-936, or equiv.) to 100 mL with 40% alcohol.

(**c**) *n-Butyl alcohol internal std stock soln.*—Dil. 10 mL *n*-BuOH, 99.9 mol % (Fisher Scientific Co., A-384, or equiv.) to 100 mL with 40% alcohol.

(**d**) *Methanol std soln.*—0.050% MeOH plus 0.030% *n*-BuOH internal std. Fill 100 mL vol. flask to ca 99 mL with 40% alcohol and add, by syringe, 500 μL MeOH stock soln, (**b**), and 300 μL *n*-BuOH stock soln, (**c**). Mix and dil. to vol. with 40% alcohol. Mix again.

Table 9:03 Scale readings on Zeiss immersion refractometer at 17.5°, corresponding to specific gravities of ethyl and methyl alcohol solutions

Sp. Gr. 15.56°/15.56°	Scale Readings: Ethyl Alcohol	Scale Readings: Methyl Alcohol	Differences	Sp. Gr. 15.56°/15.56	Scale Readings: Ethyl Alcohol	Scale Readings: Methyl Alcohol	Differences
1.0000	15.0	15.0	0.0	0.9720	51.5	27.0	24.5
.9990	15.8	15.3	0.5	.9710	53.0	27.5	25.5
.9980	16.6	15.6	1.0	.9700	54.6	28.1	26.5
.9970	17.5	15.9	1.6	.9690	56.1	28.7	27.4
.9960	18.5	16.2	2.3	.9680	57.6	29.2	28.4
.9950	19.4	16.5	2.9	.9670	59.1	29.6	29.5
.9940	20.4	16.9	3.5	.9660	60.6	30.1	30.5
.9930	21.4	17.2	4.2	.9650	62.0	30.6	31.4
.9920	22.5	17.5	5.0	.9640	63.3	31.0	32.3
.9910	23.6	17.9	5.7	.9630	64.6	31.5	33.1
.9900	24.7	18.2	6.5	.9620	65.8	31.9	33.9
.9890	25.9	18.6	7.3	.9610	67.0	32.4	34.6
.9880	27.1	19.0	8.1	.9600	68.1	32.8	35.3
.9870	28.4	19.5	8.9	.9590	69.2	33.3	35.9
.9860	29.6	19.9	9.7	.9580	70.2	33.7	36.5
.9850	31.0	20.4	10.6	.9570	71.2	34.1	37.1
.9840	32.4	20.8	11.6	.9560	72.1	34.5	37.6
.9830	33.8	21.3	12.5	.9550	73.0	34.9	38.1
.9820	35.2	21.8	13.4	.9540	73.8	35.3	38.5
.9810	36.7	22.3	14.4	.9530	74.6	35.6	39.0
.9800	38.3	22.8	15.5	.9520	75.4	35.9	39.5
.9790	39.9	23.4	16.5	.9510	76.2	36.2	40.0
.9780	41.5	24.0	17.5	.9500	76.9	36.5	40.4
.9770	43.1	24.5	18.6	.9490	77.6	36.8	40.8
.9760	44.8	25.0	19.8	.9480	78.3	37.0	41.3
.9750	46.5	25.5	21.0	.9470	79.0	37.3	41.7
.9740	48.2	26.0	22.2	.9460	79.7	37.6	42.1
.9730	49.8	26.5	23.3				

Scale readings are applicable only to instruments calibrated in arbitrary scale units proposed by Pulfrich, *Z. angew. Chem.*, 1899, p. 1168. According to this scale, 14.5 = 1.33300, 50.0 = 1.34650, and 100.0 = 1.36464. If instrument used is calibrated in other arbitrary units, refractive index corresponding to observed reading can be converted into equivalent Zeiss reading by referring to **52.004**.

9.093 ***Determination***

Inject 10 μL MeOH std soln. Adjust operating parameters and attenuation to obtain measurable peak ht (ca ¼ full scale deflection). Det. retention time of MeOH and *n*-BuOH (ca 3 and 12 min, resp.). Inject 10 μL sample to est. MeOH, using attenuation if necessary, and to check for absence of *n*-BuOH. On basis of presence or absence of *n*-BuOH in sample, det. MeOH content from std curve prepd according to (**a**) or (**b**):

(**a**) *n-Butyl alcohol absent*.—On basis of est. of MeOH, prep. series of stds (4 or 5) in which range of concn includes MeOH concn in sample. Add internal std to both sample and std solns at concn similar to that of MeOH in sample. Calc. peak ht ratios of MeOH:*n*-butyl alcohol, using av. of duplicate injections, and plot ratios against MeOH concn.

(**b**) *n-Butyl alcohol present*.—Prep. series of MeOH stds as in (**a**), but do *not* add *n*-BuOH to sample or stds. Plot actual peak ht of MeOH against concn.

Artificial Colors

(*See* also **9.005–9.008**)

9.094 ***Marsh Test—Official First Action***

To 10 mL sample in 20 mL test tube add enough freshly shaken *Marsh reagent* (100 mL amyl alcohol, 3 mL H_3PO_4, and 3 mL H_2O) to nearly fill tube, and shake several times. Let layers sep. Color in lower layer indicates that sample has been colored with caramel, synthetic dye, or extractive material from uncharred white oak chips.

In absence of any color, test 10 mL in same manner, using enough fusel oil, amyl alcohol, or Pentasol to nearly fill tube and shaking several times. Deeply colored lower layer indicates synthetic dye. Det. its identity as in Chapter **34**. To confirm caramel apply one or more of following tests:

9.095 ***Mathers Test—Official Final Action***

See **11.055**.

9.096 ★ ***Cyclohexanol Test—Official Final Action*** ★

See **9.059**, 10th ed.

9.097 **Coal-Tar Colors**

See Chapter **34**.

Tannin (*22*)—Official Final Action

9.098 ***Reagents***

(**a**) *Folin-Denis reagent*.—To 750 mL H_2O add 100 g $Na_2WO_4.2H_2O$, 20 g phosphomolybdic acid, and 50 mL H_3PO_4. Reflux 2 hr, cool, and dil. to 1 L.

(**b**) *Sodium carbonate saturated soln*.—To each 100 mL H_2O add 35 g anhyd. Na_2CO_3, dissolve at 70–80°, and let cool overnight. Seed supersatd soln with crystal of $Na_2CO_3.10H_2O$, and after crystn filter thru glass wool.

(**c**) *Tannic acid std soln*.—0.1 mg/mL. Dissolve 100 mg tannic acid in 1 L H_2O. Prep. fresh soln for each detn.

9.099 ***Preparation of Standard Curve***

Pipet 0–10 mL aliquots std tannic acid soln into 100 mL vol. flasks contg 75 mL H_2O. Add 5 mL Folin-Denis reagent and 10 mL Na_2CO_3 soln, and dil. to vol. with H_2O. Mix well and det. *A* after 30 min at 760 nm. Plot *A* against mg tannic acid/100 mL.

9.100 ***Determination***

Using 1 mL sample, det. *A* as in **9.099** and obtain mg tannic acid/100 mL from std curve. If *A* is too great, repeat detn on 1+4 diln of sample. Samples treated as above may be compared in Nessler tubes against freshly prepd tannic acid stds treated in same manner.

Cyanide (*23*)—Official First Action

9.101 ***Apparatus***

(Letters refer to Fig. **9:04**.)

(**a**) *Distilling flask*.—500 mL, r-b, 3-neck with ₮ joints, angle-type (Fisher Scientific Co., No. 10-165B, or equiv.) (A).

(**b**) *Thermometer*.—Range −10 to 110°, with ₮ screw-cap adapter to fit one ₮ side neck of distg flask (B).

(**c**) *Air inlet tube*.—With ₮ cone to fit side neck of distg flask (C).

(**d**) *Condenser*.—Graham coil-type, with inner and outer ₮ joints, ₮ cone to fit center neck of distg flask (Fisher Scientific Co., No. 7-728B, 400 mm jacket length, or equiv.) (D).

(**e**) *Flange assembly*.—Consisting of 2 sep. ground-glass flanges at one end of sep. glass tubing, 7 mm diam. Lower tube (E) is ca 14 mm long and is also fitted with ₮ cone to fit ₮ socket at top of condenser; ₮ cone has 2 glass hooks. Upper tube (F) is ca 5 mm long.

(**f**) *Clip*.—To connect 2 ground-glass flanges together (G).

(**g**) *Springs*.—To connect (D) and (F) securely together (H).

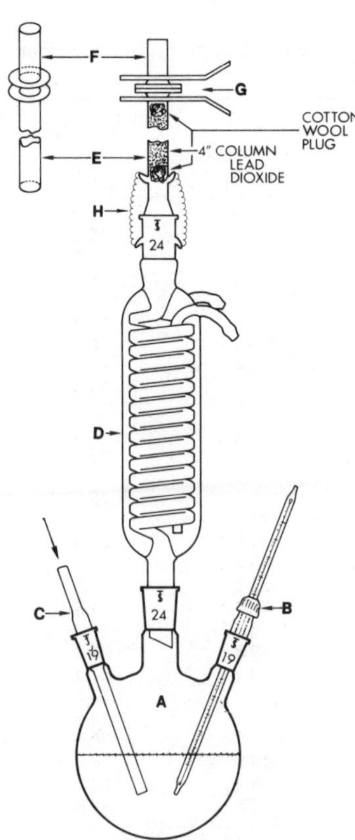

FIG. 9:04—Apparatus for determining hydrogen cyanide in distilled spirits.

★ Surplus method—*see* inside front cover.

9.102 ***Reagents***

(**a**) *Potassium ferrocyanide soln.*—(*1*) *Stock soln.*— 0.01% $K_4Fe(CN)_6.3H_2O$ in 0.2% Na_2CO_3. Store in amber bottle. Na_2CO_3 stabilizes this soln. (*2*) *Working soln.*—0.0001% $K_4Fe(CN)_6.3H_2O$; 27 mL equiv. to 10 μg CN. Prep. fresh daily by dilg 1.0 mL stock soln to 100 mL with H_2O.

(**b**) *4,4'-Methylenebis(N,N-dimethylaniline)* (*tetrabase*).—Eastman Kodak Co., No. 244; or equiv.

(**c**) *Bis(ethyl acetoacetato) copper* (*copper ethyl acetoacetate*).—Fisher Scientific Co., No. 10057; or equiv.

(**d**) *Color reagent.*—Dissolve 50 mg tetrabase and 50 mg Cu Et acetoacetate in 10 mL $CHCl_3$. Store in closed bottle; prep. fresh weekly.

(**e**) *Test papers.*—Whatman No. 44 paper, or equiv., cut to size in strips to fit between flanges of ground-glass flange assembly. Impregnate with several drops color reagent immediately before use; let $CHCl_3$ evap. completely before inserting test paper between flanges of assembly.

(**f**) *Lead dioxide.*—Dissolve ca 40 g $Pb(OAc)_2$ in 200 mL H_2O by heating on H_2O bath in hood. Add NaOCl (13% available Cl) until there appears to be no further darkening in color (ca 100 mL). Ppt should be dark brown at this stage. Let stand ca 15 min. Filter thru double thickness Whatman No. 42 papers in buchner. Wash with H_2O, discard filtrate, and wash ppt with ca 200 mL HNO_3 (1+9). Finally wash with H_2O and dry overnight in 105° oven. PbO_2 produced by this method is granular and should be broken into pieces ca 20 mesh, but must not be ground any finer. Check each batch by applying control test for ferrocyanide std, **11.057(a)**, on 100 mL aliquots of H_2O contg 10 μg CN and 500 ppm SO_2 (as $NaHSO_3$) and comparing stain produced with std stain. Anal. grade PbO_2 is not suitable because it is too fine and prevents free flow of N to test papers.

9.103 ***Distilled Spirits Free of Sulfur Dioxide***

(For products contg SO_2, *see* **11.057**.)

(**a**) *Control test.*—Add 27 mL $K_4Fe(CN)_6.3H_2O$ working soln (equiv. to 10 μg CN) to 100 mL alcohol and 100 mL H_2O in 500 mL 3-neck flask with stopper in 1 side neck and gas inlet tube connected to N (or CO_2) in other. (Use of gas to flush HCN thru test papers is preferred, but vac. may be used.) Connect center neck of flask to condenser and place ground-glass flange assembly in top of condenser; then connect hooks with springs. Insert test paper between 2 glass flanges and clip together. Remove stopper momentarily, add 10 mL H_2SO_4 (1+9), and immediately replace stopper.

Assure rapid flow of *cold* H_2O thru condenser and then heat contents of flask just to bp. When boiling temp. is reached, pass N thru liq. at rate such that individual bubbles just cease to be visible as sep. bubbles, but form continuous stream. Check that all joints are tight. Let distn proceed 15 min; then remove test paper and examine for blue stain which indicates cyanide. (Alcohol vapors must *not* reach test paper.) Intense, well defined blue circle should be obtained with 10 μg CN. Blank detn performed concurrently must show no color. (1 μg CN, equiv. to 0.01 ppm CN in 100 mL sample, can be readily detected.)

(**b**) *Samples.*—Add 100 mL sample to 100 mL H_2O in 500 mL 3-neck distg flask, and test as in (**a**). For pos. results, confirm test papers showing faint or questionable stains by 2 addnl analyses. Blue stains are stable ca 1 week if kept out of direct light.

(**c**) *Confirmation.*—To confirm that pos. reactions from samples of unknown origin are due to CN, expose blue test paper to NH_3 vapors. Colorless carbinol base is formed. With addn of HOAc, blue reappears.

CORDIALS AND LIQUEURS

9.104 Physical Examination—Procedure

Note and record following: (*a*) Appearance, whether bright or turbid and presence of sediment; (*b*) color and depth of color; (*c*) odor; (*d*) taste.

9.105 Specific Gravity—Official Final Action

See **9.011**.

9.106 Alcohol—Official Final Action

(**a**) *By weight.*—*See* **9.021**.

(**b**) *By volume.*—*See* **9.013**. Use pycnometer calibrated at 15.56°.

Methanol—Official Final Action

9.107 ***Preparation of Sample***

Measure sample contg 20–25 mL absolute alcohol into distg flask, add enough H_2O to make total ca 100 mL, and distil, collecting ca 50 mL distillate. To distillate add 4 g NaCl for each 10 mL H_2O and let stand several hr for complete satn.

Transfer to separator, using ca 10 mL satd NaCl soln to wash out container, and shake with 25 mL pet ether. When sepn is complete, transfer aq. soln to second separator contg 25 mL pet ether; shake, and transfer aq. soln to third separator, also contg 25 mL pet ether; shake, and when sepn is complete, drain aq. soln into 200 mL distg flask. Meanwhile add 25 mL satd NaCl soln to first separator and follow sample thru with this soln, finally adding washings to sample soln in distg flask. Repeat this operation with second 25 mL portion satd NaCl soln, finally adding this also to distg flask. Distil mixt. into 50 mL vol. flask, using suitable adapter. After 48–49 mL distils, disconnect app., fill flask to mark with H_2O, mix, and det. MeOH as in **9.089** or **9.090**.

9.108 Aldehydes—Official Final Action

Measure 100–200 mL sample into distn flask. If solid content is $\leq$25 g/100 mL, add 12.5–25 mL H_2O; if >25 g/100 mL, add 5 mL H_2O for each 10 g solids present; distil slowly, collecting vol. distillate equal to that of sample, and proceed as in **9.052**.

9.109 Fusel Oil—Official Final Action

Using 50 mL prepd distillate, **9.108**, proceed as in **9.068**, **9.071–9.074**, or **9.077**.

9.110 Total Solids—Official Final Action

(**a**) *From specific gravity of dealcoholized sample.*—Transfer residue from alcohol detn, **9.106(b)**, to original pycnometer with H_2O, dil. to mark with H_2O at 15.56°, and mix. Adjust temp. of pycnometer and contents to 20°; adjust meniscus to mark, using capillary tube or narrow strips of filter paper to remove any excess liq. while in 20° bath. Weigh, and calc. sp gr of liq. From **52.008** det. % dry substance and corresponding sp gr at 20°/4°. Sp gr at 20°/4° $\times$ % dry substance = total solids (g/100 mL).

(**b**) *By evaporation.*—Fill 25 mL vol. flask with sample at 20°, and adjust meniscus, using capillary tube or narrow strips of filter paper, while flask is immersed in bath held at same temp. ca 30 min. Quant. transfer contents of flask to 100 mL vol. flask with H_2O and dil. to vol. with H_2O at convenient temp. At same temp., pipet 10 mL dild sample into dish contg sand and dry as in **31.008**. Wt residue $\times$ 40 = total solids (g/100 mL).

(c) *From refractive index of dealcoholized sample.*—Restore residue from alcohol detn to original vol. by evapg or dilg as necessary. Det. refractometer reading of soln at 20° and obtain corresponding % dry substance. From **52.008** det. sp gr corresponding to % dry substance found and multiply by % dry substance to obtain g total solids/100 mL sample. To obtain % total solids, divide total solids/100 mL by sp gr, **9.011**.

9.111 ★ Glycerol—Official Final Action ★

By direct weighing, or by oxidn with $K_2Cr_2O_7$ soln. *See* **9.111**,12th ed.

9.112 Sucrose—Official Final Action

(a) *By polarization.*—Pipet, into evapg dish, vol. sample equiv. to 52 g as calcd from sp gr, **9.011**, and exactly neutze with 1*N* NaOH, calcg amt required from acidity, **9.119**. Evap. on steam bath to remove alcohol, transfer to 200 mL vol. flask, and proceed as in **31.025** or **31.026**, beginning "... add necessary clarifying agent, ..." in **31.025(a)**.

(b) *By reducing sugars before and after inversion.*—Approximate sugar content of sample from total solids, **9.110**, and pipet sample contg 5–7 g sugars into porcelain dish; exactly neutze with 1*N* NaOH soln, calcg amt required from acidity, **9.119**, and evap. on steam bath to remove alcohol. Transfer to 200 mL vol. flask, clarify with neut. $Pb(OAc)_2$ soln, **31.021(d)**, remove excess Pb with K oxalate, and proceed as in **31.031**, using **31.038** for detn of reducing sugars.

9.113 Ash—Official Final Action

Proceed as in **31.012** or **31.013**, using 25 mL sample.

9.114 Soluble and Insoluble Ash—Official Final Action

Using ash from **9.113**, proceed as in **31.015**.

9.115 Alkalinity of Soluble Ash—Official Final Action

Using sol. ash from **9.114**, proceed as in **31.016**.

9.116 Alkalinity of Insoluble Ash—Official Final Action

Using insol. ash from **9.114**, proceed as in **31.017**.

9.117 Phosphorus—Official Final Action

Using ash obtained in **9.113**, det. P_2O_5 as in **11.034**.

9.118 Caramel—Official Final Action

See **11.055**.

9.119 Total Acidity—Official First Action

Place ca 600 mL H_2O in 800 mL beaker, add ca 1 mL phthln, and titr. to pink soln with 0.1*N* NaOH. Add 10–20 mL sample (unless this vol. gives soln such deep color that it will obscure end point, in which case 5 mL may be used) and titr. to pink comparable to that of soln before sample was added. Calc. acidity as g/100 mL sample in terms of predominating acid present in sample.

9.120 Characteristic Acids—Preparation of Sample—Procedure

Use sample contg ≤30 g solids and ≤200 mg acid to be detd, as calcd from acidity; evap. to ca 30 mL and treat as in **9.121–9.124**.

★ Surplus method—*see* inside front cover.

9.121 ★ Tartaric Acid—Official Final Action ★

See **9.121**, 12th ed.

9.122 ★ Citric Acid—Official Final Action ★

See **9.122**, 12th ed.

9.123 ★ Total Malic Acid (Laevo and Inactive) ★ Official First Action

See **9.123**, 12th ed.

9.124 ★ Laevo-Malic Acid—Official First Action ★

See **9.124**, 12th ed.

9.125 Volatile Esters—Official Final Action

Measure 100–500 mL sample into distg flask and steam distil as in **12.026**, collecting vol. distillate at least twice as great as vol. alcohol contained in sample. (If detn **9.126** is to be made, use 500 mL sample.) Disconnect app. and wash out condenser with little H_2O. Add ca 1 mL phthln, and titr. to pink that persists >1 min, using 0.1*N* NaOH or KOH. Add measured excess of 25–50 mL 0.1*N* alkali to soln, reflux 1 hr, cool, and titr. excess alkali with 0.1*N* H_2SO_4. Calc. number of mL 0.1*N* alkali used in saponification of esters as EtOAc. 1 mL 0.1*N* alkali = 8.8 mg EtOAc.

9.126 ★ Gamma Undecalactone ★ (Qualitative Test) (*24*) Official Final Action

(Peach and apricot cordials)

See **9.087**, 10th ed.

9.127 ★ Optical-Crystallographic Properties ★ of Hydrazino-γ-Undecalactone Official Final Action

See **9.088**, 10th ed.

9.128 Benzaldehyde—Official Final Action

See **19.100–19.101**.

9.129 Thujone (*25*)—Official First Action

To 500 mL sample add 1 mL *freshly distd aniline* and 1 mL H_3PO_4, and reflux 30 min on steam bath. Distil two 100 mL portions; reject first and test second for thujone as follows:

Add 0.5 g *semicarbazide hydrochloride* and 0.6 g anhyd. NaOAc (or 1.0 g crystd salt) and let mixt. stand overnight. Distil off alcohol at min. pressure. Steam distil to remove essential oils and other volatile material; collect and reject first ca 15 mL distillate. Wash down condenser with little alcohol and with H_2O. Cool sample, add 1 mL H_2SO_4 (1+1), and again steam distil, collecting 20 mL distillate in cylinder. Pour distillate into small separator, and add 20 mL ether, using receiver as measure. Shake and sep. ether soln. Add 10 mL 65% alcohol and let ether evap. spontaneously. After all ether evaps, note odor of residue. Odor of thujone will be apparent if ≥2 mg is present in soln, provided it is not masked by presence of other odoriferous substances. Make modified Legal test as follows:

To soln obtained as above, add 1 mL *10% $ZnSO_4$ soln* and 0.25 mL freshly prepd *aq. Na nitroprusside soln* (0.1 g/mL). Slowly, with const stirring, add 2 mL 5% NaOH soln. Let stand 1–2 min. Add 1.5 mL HOAc and mix. Ppt of raspberry red color (resembling alcohol ppt of red fruit juice) shows presence of thujone. Neg. test is shown by similar ppt having appearance similar to that of alcohol ppt from apple jelly or other light colored fruit.

SELECTED REFERENCES

(*1*) JAOAC **39,** 723(1956); **41,** 118(1958).
(*2*) JAOAC **38,** 821(1955); **39,** 730(1956); **40,** 440(1957).
(*3*) Ind. Eng. Chem., Anal. Ed. **14,** 237(1942); JAOAC **28,** 88(1945); **41,** 118(1958); **42,** 329(1959).
(*4*) JAOAC **40,** 436(1957); **42,** 327(1959); **43,** 657(1960).
(*5*) Ind. Eng. Chem. **18,** 841(1926); JAOAC **35,** 239(1952).
(*6*) JAOAC **37,** 945(1954); **46,** 299(1963); **47,** 720(1964).
(*7*) JAOAC **50,** 338(1967).
(*8*) JAOAC **50,** 334(1967).
(*9*) JAOAC **53,** 12(1970).
(*10*) JAOAC **49,** 498(1966).
(*11*) JAOAC **37,** 921(1954).
(*12*) JAOAC **55,** 559(1972).
(*13*) JAOAC **55,** 566(1972).
(*14*) JAOAC **42,** 331(1959); **43,** 655(1960); **44,** 383(1961).
(*15*) JAOAC **46,** 285(1963).
(*16*) JAOAC **51,** 915(1968).
(*17*) JAOAC **55,** 549(1972).
(*18*) JAOAC **43,** 659(1960); **44,** 392(1961).
(*19*) JAOAC **41,** 121(1958); **42,** 336(1959).
(*20*) J. Am. Chem. Soc. **27,** 964(1905); Ind. Eng. Chem. **19,** 844(1927); JAOAC **28,** 800(1945).
(*21*) JAOAC **55,** 564(1972).
(*22*) JAOAC **35,** 255(1952); **37,** 665(1954).
(*23*) JAOAC **53,** 777(1970).
(*24*) JAOAC **16,** 420(1933); **19,** 75, 183(1936).
(*25*) Ann. chim. anal. **13,** 227(1908); Schweiz. Wochschr. **49,** 337, 507(1911); JAOAC **19,** 120(1936); **20,** 69(1937).

10. Beverages: Malt Beverages and Brewing Materials*

BEER

(Unless otherwise directed, express results as % by wt.)

10.001 Preparation of Sample
Official Final Action

Remove CO_2 by transferring sample to large flask and shaking, gently at first and then vigorously, keeping temp. of beer at 20–25°. If necessary, remove suspended material by passing the CO_2-free beer thru dry filter paper.

Color

Spectrophotometric Method (Standard Reference Color Method) (1)
Official Final Action

10.002 ***Apparatus***

Spectrophotometer.—Capable of isolating band width of ≤1 nm at 430 nm with wavelength and photometer scales checked and corrected for inaccuracies in accordance with instructions contained in NBS Letter Circular LC-1017 of Jan. 1967.

10.003 ***Preparation of Sample***

Partially degas sample by opening bottle at room temp., pouring contents into 1 L erlenmeyer, and swirling gently. Avoid formation of turbidity, and conduct partial degassing and readings as rapidly as possible.

10.004 ***Determination***

Place prepd sample in suitable cell and det. *A* at 430 nm and at 700 nm.

10.005 ***Calculations***

Calc. *A* from thickness at which read to ½" (1.27 cm) ($A_{½}$). If ($A_{½\ \text{at 430 nm}}$) × 0.039 > ($A_{½\ \text{at 700 nm}}$), sample is assumed "free of turbidity" and color is calcd as follows:

Beer color intensity = 10 × ($A_{½\ \text{at 430 nm}}$). If ($A_{½\ \text{at 700 nm}}$) > 0.039 × ($A_{½\ \text{at 430 nm}}$), clarify sample by centrfg or filtering, and redet. *A*.

Report color intensity values to nearest 0.1 unit.

Photometric Method—Official Final Action

10.006 ***Apparatus***

Use any com. available filter photometer or abridged spectrophtr utilizing moderately broad spectral band and having adequate sensitivity. Use light filter with peak *T* in range 420–450 nm (blue-violet) for max. sensitivity and precision. (Filters for wavelengths in blue or blue-green range may also be used, but result in reduced precision.) Cell should be of such size, if possible, as to give *A* values between 0.187 and 0.699 (20–65% T), where max. precision is achieved. Use same size cell for both color measurement and calibration.

10.007 ***Calibration of Photometers***

Beer calibration method.—For each color intensity value for which measurements are to be made, obtain 6–8 replicate bottles of beer which are low in air content and have been pasteurized.

Det. color intensity value of the beer by averaging readings obtained for ≥2 bottles by *Standard Reference Color (SRC) Method,* **10.004**. If these values must be obtained from another laboratory, ship bottles of beer by the fastest available method, marked to avoid rough handling.

Det. photometer reading of the beer by averaging readings obtained for ≥2 bottles with wavelength and cell as in **10.006**. Calc. calibration factor in accordance with photometer instructions or prep. calibration curve by plotting *A* or photometer scale reading against the *SRC* value for sample, assuming that curve passes thru origin. This calibration will be accurate only for readings in immediate vicinity of calibration point. If it is desired to accurately measure color intensity of >1 sample or colors over range of values, calibrate photometer for each sample or use beers having colors which cover desired range. Calc. av. calibration factor or prep. av. calibration curve.

10.008 ***Preparation of Sample***

See **10.003**.

10.009 ***Determination***

Place sample in cell and det. photometer reading. Calc. color intensity value, using calibration factor or calibration curve. Report color to nearest 0.1 unit.

Total Haze after Chilling (*2*)—Official Final Action

10.010 ***Reagents***

(Use turbidity-free distd H_2O thruout.)

(**a**) *Hydrazine sulfate soln.*—1%. Dissolve 1.000 g $H_4N_2.H_2SO_4$ in H_2O (may require 4–6 hr) and dil. to 100 mL.

(**b**) *Stock formazin suspension.*—Dissolve 2.500 g hexamethylenetetramine (formin) in 25 mL H_2O in 125 mL erlenmeyer, pipet in 25 mL 1% hydrazine sulfate soln, and stopper flask. Formazin begins to ppt in 6–8 hr and pptn is complete within 24 hr. Prep. every 3 months.

(**c**) *1000 Turbidity std.*—Dil. 14.5 mL well mixed stock suspension, (**b**), to 1 L with H_2O in vol. flask. Prep. weekly. (1000 formazin turbidity units (FTU) on empirical formazin turbidity scale represents reflectance of insol. reaction products of 0.0725 g hydrazine sulfate with 0.7250 g hexamethylenetetramine dild to 1 L.)

(**d**) *Working stds for visual method.*—Prep. suitable dilns, daily, of 1000 turbidity std with H_2O. FTU stds <100 are suitable for fresh beers; higher stds may be required for older samples. Use increments of 10 FTU for stds <100 FTU; in 20 FTU increments for 100–200; and in 50 FTU increments for >200 FTU.

Visual Method

10.011 ***Apparatus***

(**a**) *Clark Turbidimeter, Model CLT.*—Code 648. Available from Cargille Scientific Inc., 55 Commerce Rd, Cedar Grove, NJ 07009.

---

* Many methods in this chapter have been tested by both American Society of Brewing Chemists and Association of Official Analytical Chemists and have been adopted by both Associations. *See* "Methods of Analysis, A.S.B.C.," 7th rev. ed., 1976.

Viewing box of same dimensions and lighting is also suitable.

(b) *Red Plexiglas sheet.*—¼" thick, ca 1 sq ft (930 sq cm).

(c) *Constant temperature bath.*—0±0.2°.

(d) *Ice-water bath.*—Contg few drops wetting agent.

(e) *Flint glass bottles.*—Of same dimensions as flint glass bottles contg beer test samples; or clear drinking glasses (shells), 10 oz (300 mL), od ca 66 mm at bottom and 67 mm at top.

10.012 ***Determination***

(Make comparisons with samples at 0°. Keep test samples in 0° bath when not matching turbidities.)

Place container of beer to be tested in upright position in 0° bath and hold 24 hr.

Prep. series of formazin turbidity working stds covering range of expected turbidities of test samples. Fill into flint glass bottles of same dimensions as those holding beer test samples.

If beer is in flint glass bottles, carefully remove bottle from const temp. bath without disturbing sediment. Dip bottle into ice-H_2O bath contg few drops wetting agent to prevent fogging or accumulation of H_2O droplets on bottle while in viewing box. Place bottle of beer in viewing box between 2 bottles of formazin turbidity working stds. Compare turbidities by viewing thru red Plexiglas sheet placed 5 cm (2") in front of bottles. Change formazin stds until that working std is found which most closely matches turbidity of test sample.

If beer is not in flint glass bottles, carefully remove container from const temp. bath and, without disturbing sediment, pour beer into clear 10 oz drinking glass (shell) which has been prechilled by standing (external contact only) in ice-H_2O bath contg wetting agent. Degassing is not necessary. Use formazin turbidity working stds in identical 10 oz glasses to match turbidities as above for bottles.

Report as total haze of the beer after chilling, formazin turbidity units (FTU) of working std giving closest match. In range 0–100 FTU, report to nearest 10 FTU; 100–200, 20; >200, 50.

Nephelometric Method

10.013 ***Calibration***

Nephelometer.—Prep. calibration curve at 580 nm or other suitable wavelength for instrument employed by use of series of working stds or dilns of 1000 turbidity std. If readout device of nephelometer is 0–100 scale of arbitrary units, set needle to indicate 0 units when cell is filled with turbidity-free distd H_2O and 100 units when it is filled with selected formazin turbidity std.

10.014 ***Determination***

Place containers of beer to be tested in upright position in 0° bath and hold 24 hr.

Prechill nephelometer cell in small ice-H_2O bath contg wetting agent (external contact only). Carefully remove container of beer from bath and, without disturbing sediment, rinse and fill cell with test sample. Place cell in ice-H_2O bath contg wetting agent, and degas beer by stirring with thermometer. When beer temp. is 0°, place cell in sample chamber of nephelometer and det. reading. (Beer must be at 0° when taking reading.)

10.015 ***Calculations***

Calc. FTU total haze from calibration curve or by formula: FTU = $R \times S/100$, where R = nephelometer (galvanometer scale) reading; S = FTU of formazin turbidity std used for calibration of nephelometer.

10.016 Specific Gravity—Official Final Action

Det. sp gr of prepd sample, **10.001**, at 20/20° (in air) as in **9.011**, but use pycnometers described in **10.106(i)** and **10.107(b)** or **(c)**.

Viscosity of Beer (*3*)—Official Final Action

10.017 ***Apparatus***

(a) *Constant temperature bath.*—Adjusted to 20.00±0.05°.

(b) *Viscometer.*—Ostwald or Cannon-Fenske; H_2O time range 50–150 sec.

10.018 ***Determination***

Prep. sample as in **10.001**, ensuring complete decarbonation but avoiding loss of surface active components. Det. sp. gr. as in **10.016**.

Clean viscometer with chromic acid cleaning soln, rinse with H_2O, and drain. Attemperate viscometer, H_2O, and beer to 20° in H_2O bath. Add appropriate vol. H_2O (usually 5 or 10 mL) at 20° to viscometer. Using suction, draw H_2O above upper mark. Let liq. level fall, and start timing with stopwatch as meniscus passes upper mark. Stop timing when meniscus passes lower mark.

Rinse viscometer with beer sample, and det. time required for passage of beer between menisci as above.

10.019 ***Calculations***

(a) *Absolute or dynamic viscosity (Centipoise).*—(*1*)

Viscosity (cP) = flow time of beer at 20° × sp gr of beer × 1.002/flow time of H_2O at 20°,

where 1.002 = viscosity of H_2O in cP at 20°. Report to second decimal place.

(*2*) *Example.*—Flow time of H_2O = 89.8 sec; flow time of beer = 130.2 sec; sp gr of beer = 1.03425;

Viscosity, cP = 130.2 × 1.03425 × 1.002/89.8 = 1.503 = 1.50 cP

(b) *Kinematic viscosity (Centistoke).*—(*1*)

Viscosity (cS) = flow time of beer at 20° × 1.0038/flow time of H_2O at 20°,

where 1.0038 is viscosity of H_2O at 20° in cS. Report to second decimal place.

(*2*) *Example.*—Flow time of H_2O = 89.8 sec; flow time of beer = 130.2 sec;

Viscosity, cS = 130.2 × 1.0038/89.8 = 1.455 = 1.46 cS

(c) *SI system.*—(*1*) SI unit for dynamic viscosity is Pascal-second (Pa·sec). 1 cP = 0.001 Pa·sec = 1 mPa·sec.

Example.—1.503 cP = 0.001503 Pa·sec, or 1.503 milliPascal-sec, or 1.50 mPa·sec.

(*2*) SI unit for kinetic viscosity is meter²/second (m^2/sec). 1cS = 0.000001 m^2/sec = 1 μ^2/sec.

10.020 Apparent Extract—Official Final Action

Find apparent ext corresponding to sp gr detd at 20/20° from **52.009**, reporting to second decimal place.

10.021 Real Extract—Official Final Action

(a) Evap. 75–100 mL sample (accurately weighed to 0.1 g) on H_2O bath or asbestos plate, at temp. ≤80°, to ca ⅓ original vol. Cool, dil. to original wt with H_2O, and det. sp gr with pycnometer at 20/20°. Det. real ext directly from **52.009**.

(b) If no antifoam material was used in detn of alcohol, **10.023**, quant. transfer residue with hot H_2O to 100 mL vol. flask. Cool, and dil. to 100 mL at 20°. Det. sp gr at 20/20°, **10.016**, and find ext directly from **52.009**. If 100 mL beer was taken, correct as follows:

Ext found × sp gr of dealcoholized beer /sp gr of beer = g ext/100 g beer.

10.022 Extract of Original Wort—Official Final Action

Calc. from following formula and report to first decimal place:

$$O = [(P \times 2.0665) + E] \times 100/[100 + (P \times 1.0665)],$$

where O = ext of original wort; P = % alcohol by wt (g/100 g beer); and E = % real ext, **10.021(a)** or **(b)**.

10.023 Alcohol by Volume—Official Final Action

See **11.005**, but use pycnometers described in **10.106(i)** and **10.107(b)** or **(c)**.

Alcohol by Weight

10.024 *Specific Gravity Method—Official Final Action*

See **9.021**, but use pycnometers described in **10.106(i)** and **10.107(b)** or **(c)**.

Refractometer Method (4) *Official Final Action*

10.025 *Apparatus*

(**a**) *Immersion refractometer.*—Bausch & Lomb, Carl Zeiss, Inc., 444 Fifth Ave, New York, NY 10018, or equiv., with prisms covering range 1.32–1.37 *n*.

(**b**) *Water bath.—See* **10.106(k)**.

(**c**) *Pycnometer.—See* **10.106(i)** and **10.107(b)** or **(c)**.

10.026 *Calibration*

Adjust refractometer light to give max. contrast between light and dark fields. Adjust color compensator and focus for sharp, color-free dividing line. H_2O, double-distd from glass, should read ca 14.50 at 20°. Read H_2O before each sample series. Rinse prism with H_2O after each sample and dry with soft tissue.

Prep. calibration curve to convert refractometer readings and sp gr detns to % alcohol by wt by analyzing beers covering alcohol range of interest by **10.024** and **10.027**. Plot results, using ordinates $(R - N)$, where R = refractometer reading $(R_{beer} - R_{water})$, N = 1000 × (sp gr − 1.00000), and abscissa = % alcohol by wt, **10.024**. Fit least squares line to adequate number of points to get accuracy desired. Det. equation of line and slope. (*See* Definitions of Terms and Explanatory Notes, Item (24).) Calc. % alcohol by wt by formula or read from calibration curve. % alcohol by wt = $F \times (R - N) + C$, where F = slope of calibration line, and C = const of calibration curve equation.

10.027 *Determination*

Det. sp gr of decarbonated beer by **10.016**. Place refractometer cuvet contg distd H_2O and clear decarbonated beer samples in 20° H_2O bath. Place prism of refractometer in H_2O cuvet and check temp. after 15 min. Make 5 readings to nearest 0.1 scale division and average results (R_{water}). Transfer dry prism to beer sample cuvet, wait ≥1 min, make 5 readings to nearest 0.1 scale division, and average results (R_{beer}). Calc. % alcohol by wt by formula or read from calibration curve.

10.028 Real Degree of Fermentation or Real Attenuation—Official Final Action

Calc. as follows and report to first decimal place:

(orig. ext − real ext) × 100/orig. ext.

10.029 Apparent Degree of Fermentation or Apparent Attenuation—Official Final Action

Calc. as follows and report to first decimal place:

(orig. ext − apparent ext) × 100/orig. ext.

10.030 End Fermentation (Yeast Fermentable Extract) (Fermentable Sugars)—Official Final Action

Det. real ext, **10.021**, or apparent ext, **10.020**. Ferment 250 mL beer with 1 g active compressed brewers yeast 24–48 hr at 15–25°, or until fermentation is complete, providing fermentation flask with H_2O or Hg seal. Filter; det. real ext, **10.021**, or apparent ext, **10.020**. Fermentable sugars = difference in real ext before and after fermentation; or fermentable sugars = 0.82 × difference in apparent ext before and after fermentation.

10.031 Caloric Content—Official First Action

Det. sp gr (= density), **10.016**, % alcohol by wt, **10.024** or **10.027**, real ext, **10.021**, and ash, **10.047**, of beer sample.

Calories/100 g = (g real ext − % ash) × 4 + (% EtOH by wt × 6.9);

Calories in vol. = (Calories/100g) × (beer vol.$_{20°}$ × density)/100, where vol. is expressed in units required by test.

10.032 ★ Glycerol—Official Final Action ★

Dichromate oxdn method. *See* **11.010(b)**, 12th ed.

Total Acidity (5)—Official Final Action

10.033 *Indicator Titration Method*

Bring 250 mL H_2O to bp and continue boiling 2 min. From fast-flowing pipet add 25 mL beer previously decarbonated by shaking and filtering, **10.001**. After emptying pipet, continue heating 60 sec, regulating heat so that soln resumes boiling during final 30 sec. Remove from heat, stir 5 sec, and cool rapidly to room temp.

Add 0.5 mL 0.5% phthln. Titr. with 0.1*N* NaOH against white background. Make frequent color comparisons with sample of equal vol. and diln to which has been added approx. anticipated amt of alkali but no indicator. Titr. to first appearance of faint pink. Read buret. Add 0.2 mL more alkali; color should then be permanent, definite pinkish red, indicative of overtitrn. Take first buret reading as end point.

Observe strictly all details of method. However, 100 mL H_2O, 10 mL beer, and 0.2 mL indicator may be used in place of amts specified above. (Use potentiometric titrn method, **10.034**, for beers of dark color which, even when dild, may not permit judging phthln end point with necessary precision.)

Report results: (**a**) as lactic acid, to nearest 0.01% (1 mL 0.1*N* alkali = 0.0090 g lactic acid); or (**b**) as mL 1*N* alkali, to nearest 0.1 mL, necessary for neutzn of 100 g beer.

10.034 *Potentiometric Titration Method*

Use glass-calomel electrode system. Decarbonate beer completely by shaking, **10.001**. Using 50 mL undild sample (or such amt as best suits titrn assembly), titr. potentiometrically with 0.1*N* NaOH to pH 8.2. Add alkali in 1.5 mL portions to ca pH 7.6, and in 0.15 mL portions from there to pH 8.2. Make sure that complete equilibrium and good convergence are attained before reading buret at exactly pH 8.2. Report results as in **10.033**.

★ Surplus method—*see* inside front cover.

Precautions: Observe all details of good potentiometric technic, including following: Stdze potentiometer against fresh 0.05*M* K acid phthalate, **50.007(c)**, before and after any set of titrns; read potentiometer to nearest 0.02 unit; use flexible shielding around electrode leads and motor cords; ground motor and motor cords, preferably to H_2O pipes; avoid contact between electrodes and glass beaker; use proper stirring speed to ensure quick mixing but to avoid foaming which may temporarily trap some of alkali added; stop titrn at ≤pH 8.6 to minimize alkali contamination of glass electrode; check batteries frequently. Follow manufacturer's instructions for potentiometer used.

Hydrogen-Ion Activity (pH)
Official Final Action

10.035 ***Potentiometric Method***

Det. pH of undild sample, **10.001**, using glass-calomel electrode system. Follow manufacturer's instructions for potentiometer used. Check pH meter before and after use against std K acid phthalate buffer, **50.007(c)**. Observe precautions in **10.034**. Report results to nearest 0.05 pH.

10.036 Volatile Acids—Official Final Action

Using 100 mL beer, proceed as in **11.040**. Express result as HOAc, g/100 mL. 1 mL 0.1*N* alkali = 0.0060 g HOAc.

10.037 Carbohydrate Content—Official First Action

Det. sp gr (=density), **10.016**, real ext, **10.021**, ash, **10.047**, and protein, **10.045**, of beer sample.

g Carbohydrate/100 g
= (g real ext/100g) − (% protein + % ash)

g Carbohydrate in vol.
= (g carbohydrate/100 g) × (beer $vol._{20°}$ × density)/100,

where vol. is expressed in units required by test.

10.038 Reducing Sugars—Official Final Action

Dil. 25 mL prepd sample, **10.001**, measured at 20°, to 100 mL with H_2O at same temp. Det. reducing sugars in 25 mL of this soln by Munson-Walker method, **31.060**, or dil. 50 mL beer with H_2O to 100 mL and use Lane-Eynon method, **31.059**. Express result as g maltose/100 mL beer. For conversion to % by wt, divide results by sp gr of beer.

10.039 Dextrin—Official Final Action

To 25 mL prepd sample, **10.001**, measured at 20° in 500 mL boiling flask, add 15 mL HCl (sp gr 1.125) and dil. to 200 mL. Attach flask to reflux condenser, and keep in boiling H_2O bath 2 hr. Cool, nearly neutze with NaOH soln (1+1), dil. to 250 mL in vol. flask, filter, and det. glucose as in **31.051**.

g Dextrin/100 mL beer = [glucose (g/100 mL)
− (1.053 × maltose, **10.038**)] × 0.9.

Diacetyl (*6*)—Official Final Action
ASBC Colorimetric Method

10.040 ***Apparatus***

(**a**) *Compressed carbon dioxide gas.*—In steel cylinder with reducing valve connected thru 1-hole rubber stopper into 1 neck of boiling flask, (**b**), ending high up in flask.

(**b**) *Glass distillation apparatus.*—With following parts: boiling flask, 2-neck, 500 mL; distg tube, mounted vertically on boiling flask; condenser, H_2O-cooled, connected by 75° adapter, if necessary, to distg tube so that condenser slopes downward; curved, tapered tube adapter, connected to condenser delivery tip to dip below liq. level in receiver; and receiver, such as 50 mL beaker, marked at 15 and 35 mL.

(**c**) *Heating mantle.*—For boiling flask, (**b**), or burner.

(**d**) *Spectrophotometer or colorimeter.*—Capable of measuring *A* at 520 nm; with matched 1 cm cells.

10.041 ***Reagents***

(**a**) *Dimethylglyoxime std soln.*—0.0674 mg/mL. Dissolve 0.1348 g dimethylglyoxime in 3–5 mL alcohol, dil. to 2 L with H_2O, and mix well.

(**b**) *Dipotassium hydrogen phosphate in aqueous acetone soln.*—0.827*M*. Dissolve 14.4 g K_2HPO_4 (or 19.9 g $K_2HPO_4.3H_2O$) in H_2O, add 20 mL acetone, dil. to 100 mL with H_2O, and mix well. Store in refrigerator.

(**c**) *Ferrous sulfate soln.*—5%. Dissolve 5 g $FeSO_4.7H_2O$ in 100 mL H_2SO_4 (1+99), and mix well. Discard when soln turns yellow due to oxidn of Fe.

(**d**) *Hydroxylamine hydrochloride soln.*—6% aq. soln of $NH_2OH.HCl$.

(**e**) *Potassium dihydrogen phosphate alkaline soln.*—0.30*M*. Dissolve 1.0 g KH_2PO_4 in 25 mL 0.1*N* NaOH, and mix well.

(**f**) *Potassium sodium tartrate, saturated soln.*—Shake 90 g K Na tartrate well with 50 mL H_2O, and let settle.

(**g**) *Silicone antifoam.*—Dow Corning Antifoam A, or equiv.

10.042 ***Preparation of Standard Curve***

In 20 mL vol. flasks, prep. series of dimethylglyoxime std solns contg, in increments of 0.025 mg, 0.025–0.200 mg diacetyl by mixing appropriate vols dimethylglyoxime std soln, (**a**) (0.741 × mg dimethylglyoxime/mL = mg diacetyl/mL), with 0.75 mL 6% $NH_2OH.HCl$ soln and sufficient H_2O to yield 15 mL. Heat each soln 15 min in ca 80° H_2O bath, cool to room temp., add 1.0 mL 0.827*M* K_2HPO_4, and let stand 5 min. Successively add 0.6 mL NH_4OH, 2.5 mL satd K Na tartrate soln, and 0.2 mL 5% $FeSO_4$ soln. Dil. to 20 mL with H_2O, and mix by inversion.

Prep. blank contg all reagents, except dimethylglyoxime, in sufficient H_2O to yield 20 mL.

Set spectrophtr to read 0 *A* at 520 nm with blank in cell. Obtain *A* readings at 520 nm for dimethylglyoxime std solns contg 0.025–0.200 mg diacetyl equiv. Plot *A* at 520 nm against mg diacetyl/20 mL. Std curve should be straight line passing thru origin.

10.043 ***Determination***

Place 25 mL 0.30*M* KH_2PO_4 in 500 mL boiling flask. Add 250 mL cold beer, not decarbonated, and 1 drop antifoam. Fit 1 neck of boiling flask to lower joint of vertical distg tube of distn app. Place tip of adapter into 0.75 mL 6% $NH_2OH.HCl$ soln and 2–3 mL H_2O to seal adapter. Cool receiver during distn. If sample is expected to have high diacetyl concn, e.g., if diacetyl can be smelled or tasted readily, use 1.50 mL $NH_2OH.HCl$ soln and divide distillate into 2 equal portions. Use only 1 portion for distn, and multiply result by 2.

Connect CO_2 line to feed into boiling flask well above liq. level, and adjust CO_2 gas flow to maintain CO_2 atm. in entire system. Heat, and distil at ca 1 drop/sec. Collect 30 mL distillate.

Place receiver in ca 80° H_2O bath 15 min. Raise temp. of H_2O bath to 100° or transfer receiver to boiling H_2O bath. Let distillate evap. to 15 mL. Cool to room temp., and transfer quant. to 20 mL vol. flask.

Add 1.0 mL 0.827*M* K_2HPO_4 and let stand 5 min. Successively add 0.6 mL NH_4OH, 2.5 mL satd K Na tartrate soln, and 0.2 mL $FeSO_4$ soln. Dil. to 20 mL with H_2O and mix. Within 20 min, read *A* of colored soln at 520 nm against blank.

From calibration curve, det. mg diacetyl in 250 mL sample. Multiply by 4 to obtain mg diacetyl/L beer. Report result to 2 decimal places.

10.044 Iodine Reaction for Unconverted Starch—Procedure

(**a**) *For light beer.*—Fill 15 mm diam. test tube to within 2.5 cm from rim with beer, **10.001**. Carefully add 0.02*N* I from dropper to form distinct layer on top of beer. Observe at once, by transmitted light, color developed at interface. Report blue as indicating presence of starch; purple, amylodextrin; and reddish tinge, erythrodextrin. Qualify results by using terms faint trace, trace, and plain trace according to whether the color developed is faint, distinct, or strong.

(**b**) *For dark beer, but applicable also to a light beer.*—To 5 mL beer in test tube add 25 mL alcohol, shake thoroly, and let stand. Decant, pouring off last trace of beer-alcohol mixt. Dissolve ppt (dextrin) in 5 mL H_2O and to this soln add 0.02*N* I soln dropwise. Interpret as in (**a**).

10.045 Protein—Official Final Action

To 25 mL prepd sample, **10.001**, at 20° in Kjeldahl flask, add 2–3 mL H_2SO_4 and conc. to sirupy consistency. Det N as in **2.057**. %N × 6.25 = % protein.

$$\% \text{ protein} = [(\text{mL } 0.1N \text{ acid} - \text{mL } 0.1N \text{ base}) \times 1.4 \times 6.25 \times 100]/(\text{sp gr} \times \text{mL sample} \times 1000).$$

10.046 Free Amino Nitrogen in Beer (*26*) Official Final Action

Prep. sample as in **10.001**. Dil. 1.0 mL prepd sample to 50 mL with H_2O. Transfer 2.0 mL to each of three 16 × 150 mm test tubes and proceed as in **10.180**.

10.047 Ash—Official Final Action

Evap. to dryness 50 mL prepd sample, **10.001**, measured at 20°. Proceed as in **31.012** or **31.013**.

10.048 Phosphorus—Official Final Action

To 50 mL prepd sample, **10.001**, measured at 20°, add 20 mL *2% Ca(OAc)₂ soln,* evap. to dryness, and ignite at low redness to white ash. Add 10–15 mL boiling HNO_3 (1+9) and det. P_2O_5 as in **7.119**. (Washing phosphomolybdate ppt with 1% KNO_3 soln instead of H_2O prevents creeping.)

Carbon Dioxide—Official Final Action

Manometric Method (*7*)

10.049 ***Apparatus***

(**a**) *Piercing apparatus*—(*1*) *For bottles.*—Consists of gas-tight packing box and fastening for adjustment over container, and hollow spike connected to accurate pressure gage and outlet valve. Check gages frequently. (*2*) *For cans.*—Consists of metal frame in which can is placed. Top of app., which is pressed or screwed down and locked over can top, contains hollow spike surrounded by compressible rubber sealing plug; hollow spike leads to accurate pressure gage and outlet valve. (One app., adjustable for use with both bottles and cans, may be employed.)

Notes: Piercing devices can be obtained from Zahm and Nagel Co., Inc., 74 Jewett Ave, Buffalo, NY 14214; and Micromat, 185 Rt 17, North Mahwah, NJ 07430.

For suitable manometer for calibrating gages, *see* Gray and Stone, Ind. Eng. Chem., Anal. Ed., **10**, 15 (1938). Dead wt testing unit suitable for calibration can be obtained from AMETEK/-Mansfield & Green Division, 6185 Cochran Rd, Solon, OH 44139; Amthor Testing Instrument Co., Inc., 45–53 Van Sinderen Ave., Brooklyn, NY 11207; Dresser Industries, Inc., 250 E Main St, Stratford, CT 06497, and other companies.

(**b**) *Absorption buret.*—(Fig. **10:01**). Consists of graduated tube (one type has 0–5 mL graduated in 0.05 mL divisions, 5–15 mL in 0.1 mL, and 15–25 mL in 0.5 mL) with bulb marked at 40 mL, and closed at each end by stopcocks. Connect buret to valve of piercing app. and to leveling bulb by transparent alkali-resistant plastic or rubber tubing. (Burets are available from Zahm and Nagel Co. and Micromat Co., (**a**), and from New York Laboratory Supply Co.)

(**c**) *Leveling bulb.*—Approx. 300 mL, with support.

10.050 ***Determination***

Bring samples to 25° by immersion in H_2O bath at 25°. If sample is bottle, make scratch on bottle at beer level. If sample is can, weigh unopened can.

Fill leveling bulb and then absorption buret with 15% NaOH soln. Completely displace air in tubing connecting it to piercing app. with H_2O or NaOH soln and attach piercing device to bottle or can. Take care that no air is trapped in system that will be carried into buret during detn.

With valve of piercing device closed, pierce bottle crown or can by depressing hollow steel spike. Shake bottle or can until pressure reaches const max. value; then stop, and record pressure reading. Open valve on piercing app. cautiously and let gas-foam mixt. flow into absorption buret until pressure gage reads zero. Close valve and shake or tip buret (depending on its construction) until CO_2 is absorbed and gas vol. in buret reaches min. value. Adjust leveling bottle to equalize hydrostatic pressure and read vol. of "headspace air" contained in buret.

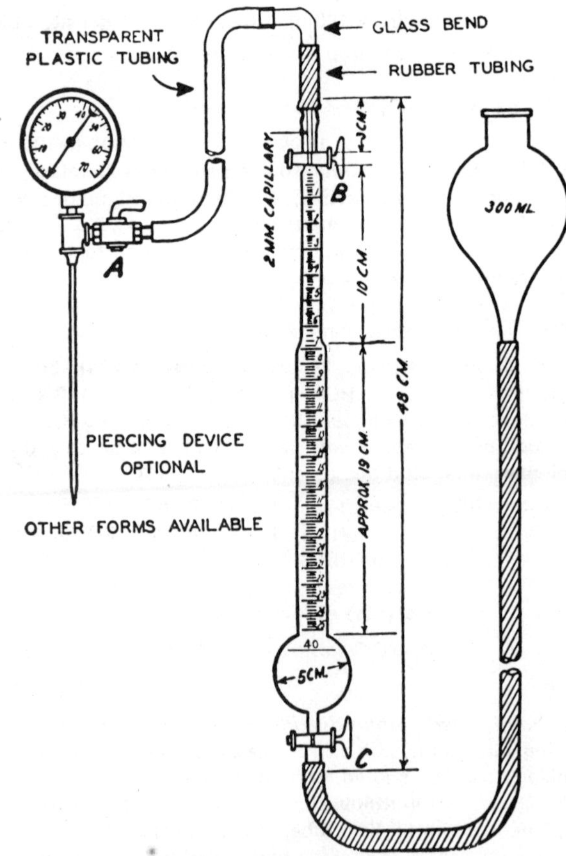

FIG. 10:01—Absorption buret (other forms available)

If detn of "total air" is also desired, continue evolution of gas from bottle or can by shaking it. Absorb evolved CO_2 by swirling and shaking buret. Continue shaking and CO_2 absorption until there is no further increase in vol. of unabsorbed gas in buret. Final vol. of unabsorbed gas may be considered the "air content" or "total air" of container.

Disconnect piercing device from package and insert thermometer to be sure that temp. is 25°. Det. headspace vol. as follows:

(**a**) *Bottles.*—Fill bottle to top with H_2O and pour from it into 100 mL graduate until liq. level in bottle corresponds to scratch mark placed on it. Vol. in mL of liq. poured off is headspace vol.

(**b**) *Cans.*—Empty beer from weighed can and let it drain completely. Weigh empty can. Fill empty can with H_2O and weigh. Subtract wt empty can from wt unopened can of beer to obtain wt of beer before opening can. Divide beer wt by sp gr of beer to obtain vol. beer in can in mL. Subtract wt empty can from wt can filled with H_2O. Difference is wt H_2O, equiv. to vol. in mL required to fill can completely. Subtract vol. beer from vol. can to obtain headspace in can before opening. (This detn of headspace in cans is only approx. correct, due to unknown degree of bulging of cans under pressure, distortion of end on opening or puncturing can, and difficulty of accurately defining when can is completely filled with H_2O.)

Calc. % CO_2 by wt and vol. as follows:

$$\% \ CO_2 \text{ by wt} = [P - (\text{mL ``head-space air''} \times 14.7/\text{mL headspace})] \times 0.00965,$$

where P = absolute pressure in psi = gage pressure + 14.7.

$$\text{Vol } CO_2 = \% \ CO_2 \text{ by wt} \times \text{sp gr of beer}/0.1976 = \% \ CO_2 \text{ by wt} \times 5.0607 \times \text{sp gr of beer}.$$

Report % by wt to second decimal, and vol CO_2 to first decimal.

Foam Collapse Rate (*8*)—Official Final Action

Sigma Value Method

10.051 ***Apparatus***

(**a**) *Special foam funnel.*—Marked at 800 mL. Kontes Glass Co. drawing No. 9357B or CGW drawing No. XA-7396 (Science Products Div., Corning Glass Works).

(**b**) *Stopwatch.*—Or clock that indicates sec.

10.052 ***Determination***

Perform detn at room temp. (22–27°).

Attemperate beer in container to 25±0.5° in H_2O bath or const temp. room.

Clean foam funnel thoroly with warm detergent soln; rinse well, first with warm H_2O and then with H_2O at ca 25°. Clamp funnel at suitable ht to ringstand and let drain 1 min.

Make foam detns immediately after draining.

Open beer container, rest side of container on funnel edge, and direct stream of beer into center of funnel, pouring smoothly to avoid entrapping air in beer. Pour until foam reaches 800 mL mark, start stopwatch, and cover funnel with ≥100 mm watch glass. After 30 sec, open stopcock to let all beer flow out in 25–30 sec at as uniform rate as possible; open stopcock wide for last 1–2 sec until small amt of foam drains out. Immediately close stopcock, reset stopwatch to 0, and start it again. Discard drained beer.

After exactly 200 sec, let beer formed from collapsed foam flow out into 100 mL graduate at such rate that all beer drains off in 25–30 sec (total time 225–230 sec). Just as last drop of beer drains off, close stopcock and stop stopwatch. Record time in sec as "t" and mL drained beer as "b."

To collapse remaining foam, wash down inside of funnel with 2 mL isopropanol or n-BuOH delivered from fine-point pipet. Open stopcock wide and let liq. drain into 25 mL graduate 1 min.

Record mL drained beer as "c" (mL liq. drained − 2 mL defoaming agent).

10.053 ***Calculations***

$$\text{Sigma value} = t/(2.303 \log[(b + c)/c]),$$

where t = time of foam collapse (225–230 sec), b = mL beer collapsed from foam in time t, c = mL beer from residual foam at time t. Report to nearest whole number.

Foam Flashing Method

10.054 ***Apparatus***

(**a**) *Compressed carbon dioxide gas.*—Contained in steel cylinder with reducing valve.

(**b**) *Pressure surge tank.*—Approx. 7.6 L (2 gal.), fitted with inlet and outlet gas connections, bleeder valve, and pressure gage. (Or use ¼" Type 10 Pressure Regulator, 2–60 psi, Lexington Control, Inc., PO Box 132, Burlington, MA 01803.)

(**c**) *Orifice foam flashing apparatus.*—Foam flashing orifice tube connected to stainless steel Master Volume Gage Bottle attachment seated pressure-tight on open bottle. Permits application of gas pressure to expel beer from bottle as foam. Furnished with inlet valve (No. 1) and outlet valve (No. 2), and adjustable ht sample tube (Micromat Co., 185 Rt 17, North Mahwah, NJ 07430).

(**d**) *Graduated cylinder.*—200 mL, 4.6 cm id × 12 cm deep, graduated in 5 mL intervals to brim (Labtician Products Co., 190–99th Ave, Hollis, NY 11423) (500 mL graduate truncated smoothly at 200 mL mark may be used).

(**e**) *Stopwatch.*—Or clock that indicates sec.

10.055 ***Determination***

Perform detns at room temp. (22–27°).

Clean grease from equipment, and connect CO_2 cylinder, pressure surge tank, and orifice foam flashing app. in that order, with Tygon tubing. Be sure all connections are gas-tight. Set CO_2 cylinder reducing valve to 31 lb gage pressure (1600 mm Hg, 214 KPa). Replace air in pressure surge tank with CO_2. Close inlet valve (No. 1) and adjust pressure on surge tank to 29 lb (1500 mm Hg, 200 KPa), using bleeder valve to reduce excess pressure.

Attemperate bottles of beer to 25±0.5° in H_2O bath or const temp. room.

Clean 200 mL graduate with detergent soln, rinse well with H_2O, and fill with H_2O. Let graduate drain free of H_2O 1 min; then secure graduate beneath foam flashing orifice tube in upright position with clamp and ringstand so placed that they do not interfere with reading graduations.

Open attemperated beer bottle; fit its neck to bottle attachment of orifice foam flashing app. to secure bottle in place. Raise sample tube so that it is above liq. level in headspace. Open inlet and outlet valves (No. 1 and No. 2) to flush headspace and connecting Tygon tubing with CO_2. Close valves. Bring sample tube to ca 1 cm from bottom of bottle and secure tube in this position by tightening gasket sealing nut at top of bottle attachment portion of app. Open inlet valve (No. 1). If pressure on surge tank drops, readjust to 29 lb (1500 mm Hg, 200 KPa).

With orifice tube diverted from foam receiving cylinder, open outlet valve (No. 2) and let outflowing foam go to waste for 10 sec. Then direct stream of foam into measuring cylinder by placing orifice tube at oblique angle below (tip ca 6 mm away from) rim of inside wall of cylinder. Fill cylinder just to overflowing. Just as overflow begins, divert stream of foam out of cylinder, start stopwatch, and close outlet valve (No. 2) to stop flow of foam. After exactly 90 sec, read mL liq. beer formed from collapsed foam. Wash down cylinder walls with 2 mL isopropanol from pipet and carefully swirl liq. in cylinder so all foam collapses. Read mL liq. at rest; this reading − 2 mL (added isopropanol) = total mL beer formed by collapse of 200 mL foam.

10.056 ***Calculations***

Foam Value Units (FVU) = 200 × $(B_2 - B_1)/B_2$, where 200 = arbitrary factor chosen to give FVU generally near 100, B_2 = total mL beer from collapse of 200 mL foam, B_1 = mL beer formed from foam collapsed in 90 sec. Report mL to nearest whole number.

Calcium (*9*)—Official Final Action

ASBC Method I

10.057 ***Reagents***

(**a**) *Ammonium oxalate soln.*—Satd soln (ca 6%) of $(NH_4)_2C_2O_4.H_2O$ in H_2O.

(**b**) *Buffer soln.*—pH 10.0. Dissolve 67.5 g NH_4Cl in 200 mL H_2O. Measure pH, and add NH_4OH (ca 200 mL) to pH 10.0. Dil. to 1 L.

(**c**) *Eriochrome black T indicator soln.*—Dissolve 0.1 g indicator (Eastman Kodak Co., No. P6361, or equiv.) in 25 mL MeOH contg 1 g $H_2NOH.HCl$. Store <2 months.

(**d**) *Sodium sulfide soln.*—2%. Dissolve 2 g Na_2S in 100 mL H_2O.

(**e**) *Magnesium std soln.*—1.00 mg/mL. Dissolve 1.00 g Mg turnings in 100 mL 0.1*N* HCl and dil. to 1 L with double distd H_2O.

(**f**) *Disodium dihydrogen EDTA std soln.*—0.1%. Dissolve 1 g Na_2H_2EDTA in 1 L H_2O. Stdze against Mg std soln.

10.058 ***Standardization***

Pipet 5 mL Mg std soln into 250 mL erlenmeyer and add 50 mL H_2O and 1 mL Na_2S soln. Prep. blank soln with 50 mL H_2O and 1 mL Na_2S soln. Add 5 mL buffer soln and 10 drops indicator soln to each erlenmeyer. Titr. flask contg Mg with EDTA std soln until permanent blue color exactly matches blank. Titr. 3 aliquots and use av. to calc. titer Mg soln, M = 5/mL EDTA std soln.

Calc. Ca factor, C = (40.08/24.32) × M.

10.059 ***Determination***

(**a**) *Total calcium and magnesium.*—Pipet 5 mL prepd sample, **10.001**, into 250 mL erlenmeyer and add 40 mL H_2O, 1 mL Na_2S soln, 5 mL buffer soln, and 10 drops indicator soln. Titr. immediately with EDTA std soln. mL EDTA std soln = X.

(**b**) *Magnesium.*—Pipet 25 mL prepd sample, **10.001**, into 125 mL erlenmeyer and add 0.5 mL $(NH_4)_2C_2O_4.H_2O$ soln and 2 drops buffer soln. Refrigerate 2 hr at 0–2°. Filter thru Whatman No. 40, or equiv., paper. Add 1 drop HCl to filtrate. Pipet 5 mL filtrate into 250 mL erlenmeyer and add 40 mL H_2O, 1 mL Na_2S soln, 5 mL buffer soln, and 10 drops indicator soln. Titr. immediately with EDTA std soln. mL EDTA std soln = Y.

$$\text{ppm Ca} = [X - (25.5Y/25)] \times C \times 200$$

ASBC Method II

10.060 ***Reagents***

(**a**) *Calcein indicator soln.*—Dissolve 0.2 g indicator (G. Frederick Smith Chemical Co., Eastman Kodak Co., or equiv.) in 100 mL H_2O contg 1 mL 5*N* NaOH.

(**b**) *EDTA std soln.*—1 mL = 1 mg $CaCO_3$. Available from Hach Chemical Co., PO Box 389, Loveland, CO 80537; Betz Laboratories, Inc., 4636 Somerton Rd, Trevose, PA 19047; or equiv.

10.061 ***Determination***

Pipet 20 mL prepd sample, **10.001**, into 250 mL erlenmeyer. Add 100 mL H_2O, 3 mL 5*N* NaOH, and 0.5 mL calcein indicator soln. Swirl to mix. Titr. with EDTA soln at 1 drop/sec, using overhead light and black background until yellow-green fluorescence is replaced by orange-brown color. mg Ca/L = mL EDTA std soln × 20.

Copper

Direct, Nonashing Method (10)
Official Final Action

10.062 ***Reagents***

(**a**) *Zinc dibenzyldithiocarbamate (ZDBT) soln.*— 0.5%. Dissolve 5 g ZDBT (available from Uniroyal Chemical under trade name "Arazate") in toluene and dil. to 1 L with toluene. Filter, if necessary, thru Whatman No. 42 paper, and store in brown bottle in cool, dark place. CCl_4 may be used instead of toluene.

(**b**) *Copper std solns.*—(*1*) *Stock soln.*—1 mg/mL. Dissolve 3.93 g $CuSO_4.5H_2O$ (free of whitish deposit of lower hydrates) and dil. to 1 L with H_2O. Or dissolve 1.000 g pure Cu wire or foil in 75 mL HNO_3 (1+4) by warming. Boil to expel fumes, cool, and dil. to 1 L with H_2O. (*2*) *Working soln.*—10 μg/mL. Prep. immediately before use by dilg 5 mL stock soln with Cu-free distd H_2O to 500 mL in vol. flask.

(**c**) *Copper-free distilled water.*—Ext distd H_2O with ZDBT soln in separator.

10.063 ***Apparatus***

(**a**) *Photometer.*—Any com. instrument with blue filter (430–460 nm) or spectrophtr set at 435 nm.

(**b**) *Copper-free centrifuge tubes.*—Clean and rinse 50 mL centrf. tubes; add 15 mL H_2O, 3 mL H_2SO_4 (1+3), and 5 mL ZDBT soln. Stopper with corks or glass stoppers and shake thoroly. Discard soln and let tube drain.

10.064 ***Preparation of Standard Curve***

Into series of cleaned, corked or g-s, 50 mL centrf. tubes add 0.0, 1.0, 2.0, 3.0, 4.0, and 5.0 mL Cu working std soln, contg 0.0, 0.4, 0.8, 1.2, 1.6, and 2.0 ppm Cu, resp. Add 25 mL beer, degassed as in **10.065**, and 1 drop *n-hexyl alcohol;* mix, and proceed as in **10.066**.

Color over this range follows Beer's law. Calc. factor, F, to convert A to ppm Cu after subtracting A of std contg 0.0 ppm Cu from those contg added Cu. If instrument response is not linear, use calibration curve.

10.065 ***Preparation of Sample***

Cool bottle or can and shake thoroly immediately before opening. Let gas bubbles leave liq. before removing cap or puncturing can. Discard ca ⅓ of sample and degas by swirling. Remove sample directly from container.

10.066 ***Determination***

To cleaned 50 mL centrf. tube, add 25 mL cold sample, measured in graduate, 3 mL H_2SO_4 (1+3), and 1 mL 30% H_2O_2. If foam interferes with sample measurement, add 1 drop hexyl alcohol. Mix, and place tube in boiling H_2O bath 0.5 hr. If excessive foaming occurs, add 1 drop hexyl alcohol. Remove tube and cool to 25°. Add 5 or 10 mL, accurately measured, ZDBT soln, depending upon size of photometer cell, and stopper tube. Ext at 25° by shaking vigorously 60 times. Re-ext again 4 times, giving 60 snapping shakes each time to obtain fine emulsion, allowing partial sepn between extns. Digested sample must be shaken vigorously with the ZDBT soln; thoro and complete emulsification must be obtained during each series of extns or results may be low.

Centrf. tube 2–3 min and draw off clear, colored layer to photometer cell of same size used in calibration, and det. *A*. If droplets of aq. layer are carried into pipet, remove by flowing solv. from pipet down wall of clean, dry test tube. H_2O droplets will adhere to test tube and clear solv. can be poured off into cell.

Prep. reagent blank by extg, in clean 50 mL centrf. tube, 25 mL Cu-free H_2O at 25° and 3 mL H_2SO_4 (1+3) with 5 (or 10) mL ZDBT soln and det. A_1. To correct for *A* of color extd by solv., perform entire detn, omitting ZDBT soln, but shaking with toluene (or CCl_4) and det. A_2. Do not give tubes used for this solv.-extractable beer color blank preliminary cleaning with ZDBT soln, since carryover of ZDBT may give high readings.

$$\text{ppm Cu} = [A - (A_1 + A_2)] \times F,$$

where *F* is factor for converting *A* to ppm Cu.

Cuprethol Method (*11*)—Official Final Action

10.067 ***Apparatus***

(**a**) *Photometer.*—Any com. instrument with blue-green or green filter, or spectrophtr set at 445 nm and with 40–50 mm cells.

(**b**) *Copper-free glassware.*—Clean all glassware with 0.1*N* HNO_3 and rinse thoroly with Cu-free distd H_2O.

10.068 ***Reagents***

(**a**) *Diethanolamine soln.*—Dissolve 4.0 mL $(HOCH_2CH_2)_2NH$ (Eastman Kodak Co., No. 1598) in 200 mL MeOH.

(**b**) *Carbon disulfide soln.*—Add 1.0 mL CS_2 (free of pptd S) to 200 mL MeOH.

(**c**) *Cuprethol soln.*—Mix 3 vols soln (**a**) and 1 vol. soln (**b**). Prep. fresh daily. Also mix equal vols soln (**a**) and MeOH for blank.

(**d**) *Copper std solns.*—Prep. as in **10.062(b)**.

(**e**) *Buffer soln.*—pH 4.4. Dissolve 63.3 g anhyd. NaOAc in ca 800 mL H_2O contg 65 mL HOAc. Dil. to 1 L with H_2O.

(**f**) *Copper-free distilled water.*—Use distd H_2O redistd from all-glass app. thruout method.

10.069 ***Preparation of Standard Curve***

Into series of g-s 100 mL vol. flasks add 0.0, 1.0, 2.0, 4.0, 8.0, and 12.0 mL Cu working std soln contg 0.0, 0.4, 0.8, 1.6, 3.2, and 4.8 ppm Cu, resp. Add H_2O to 12 mL in each flask. Dil. to vol. with degassed low-Cu beer, **10.065**, mix, and proceed as in **10.070**. Use 0.0 sample to zero instrument, and obtain *A* or scale readings for 0.1, 0.2, 0.4, 0.8, and 1.2 ppm added Cu. *A* over this range follow Beer's law. Calc. av. factor, *F*, converting *A* or scale readings to ppm Cu. If instrument response is not linear, draw and use smooth curve for calcg ppm Cu.

10.070 ***Determination***

Slowly pour 50 mL cold beer into 50 mL graduate; avoid foaming. Transfer to 125 mL flask, add 25 mL buffer soln, (**e**), and mix. Measure two 30 mL aliquots in 50 mL graduate and transfer to sep. 50 mL flasks. Add 3 mL cuprethol soln, (**c**), to one flask and 3 mL blank soln to other. Mix each and let stand 10 min. Zero instrument with blank. Det. *A* in same size cell and at same wavelength used in calibration. Calc. ppm Cu by multiplying *A* or scale reading by *F*, or use curve.

Iron (*12*)—Official Final Action

10.071 ***Apparatus***

Photometer.—Spectrophtr set at ca 505 nm or photometer with filter in blue-green region, 500–550 nm, or preferably, 505–520 nm.

10.072 ***Reagents***

(**a**) *Color reagent:* (*1*) *2,2'-Bipyridine.*—0.2%. Dissolve 1 g 2,2'-bipyridine in 20 mL HOAc (1+2) and dil. to 500 mL with H_2O; or—

(*2*) *o-Phenanthroline.*—0.3%. Dissolve 1.5 g *o*-phenanthroline in 500 mL H_2O at 70°.

(**b**) *Iron std soln.*—0.1 mg/mL. (*1*) *From iron wire.*—Dissolve 0.500 g reagent grade Fe wire, wiped free of oxide, in 5 mL HCl (1+4) and 1 mL HNO_3. Cover with watch glass, heat, and evap. to dryness; add H_2O and evap. to dryness again. Dissolve residue in 3–5 mL HCl, cool, and transfer quant. to 500 mL vol. flask. Add 2 drops satd Br-H_2O, dil. to vol. with H_2O, and mix. Transfer 50 mL of this soln to 500 mL vol. flask, add 2 drops Br-H_2O, dil. to vol. with H_2O, and mix.

(*2*) *From ferrous ammonium sulfate.*—Dissolve 3.512 g $Fe(NH_4)_2(SO_4)_2.6H_2O$ in H_2O, add 5 mL HCl, transfer quant. to 500 mL vol. flask, dil. to vol. with H_2O, and mix. Transfer 50 mL of this soln to 500 mL vol. flask, dil. to vol. with H_2O, and mix.

(**c**) *Ascorbic acid.*—USP, ground to fine powder.

10.073 ***Preparation of Standard Curve***

Prep. series of *beer stds* contg 0.0, 0.25, 0.50, 1.00, 2.00, and 3.00 ppm Fe as follows: Pipet 0.0, 0.25, 0.50, 1.00, 2.00, and 3.00 mL Fe std soln to series of 100 mL vol. flasks, add, from pipet, enough H_2O to total 3.00 mL, and dil. to vol. with decarbonated beer, **10.074**. Depending upon size cell to be used, develop color in 25 or 50 mL aliquots of each of the beer stds as in **10.075(a)** or (**b**).

If *T* values are obtained, convert to $A = -\log T$, and plot *A* against ppm Fe. If straight line results, calc. factor, *m*, for converting *A* to ppm Fe, *y*, by use of equation $y = mA + b$ ($b = 0$ if line passes thru origin). If instrument response is such that curve is obtained, use this curve to calc. results.

10.074 ***Preparation of Sample***

Adjust temp. of beer to 20–25°. Decarbonate by transferring sample to large erlenmeyer and shaking, first gently and then vigorously, until all gas is released. Do not filter unless necessary. If filtration is required, make sure filter paper is Fe-free by spotting sample of paper with drop of reagent prepd by dissolving 25 mg ascorbic acid in 2 mL color reagent, **10.072(a)**.

If beer sample is suspected of high Fe content, degas by shaking only, and permit foam to subside before sampling.

10.075 ***Determination***

Pipet 2 aliquots of degassed beer (25 or 50 mL as used in prepn of std curve) into 50 mL or 125 mL erlenmeyers; add 25 mg ascorbic acid to each aliquot, and add 2 mL color reagent, **(a)**, to one and 2 mL H_2O to other.

(a) Stopper and heat both aliquots 15 min at 60°, or

(b) let stand 30 min at room temp.

Cool, and read both solns in photometer against H_2O as ref., or read colored aliquot against beer blank as ref. Use same size cell and wavelength as used in prepn of std curve.

10.076 ***Calculations***

If H_2O is used as ref. and factor is used, ppm Fe = $(A_{sample} - A_{blank}) \times$ factor. If values are taken from std curve, ppm Fe = ppm Fe in sample − ppm Fe in blank.

If beer blank is used as ref. and factor is used, ppm Fe = $A_{sample} \times$ factor. If values are taken from std curve, ppm Fe = ppm Fe directly.

10.077 Other Metals

See Chapter **25**.

10.078 Chlorides—Official Final Action

Place 50 mL sample in Pt dish, add 20 mL 5% Na_2CO_3 soln, and proceed as in **3.071**. Det Cl as in **3.072** or **3.074**.

Sulfur Dioxide (*13*)—Official Final Action

10.079 ***Reagents***

(a) *Color reagent.*—Weigh 100 mg *p*-rosaniline.HCl into 250 mL vol. flask and dissolve in ca 200 mL H_2O. Add 40 mL HCl (1+1), mix, and dil. to vol. with H_2O. Let stand ca 15 min before use. Store in brown, g-s bottle in refrigerator.

(b) *Formaldehyde soln.*—Dil. 5 mL 40% HCHO soln to 1 L with H_2O and store in brown, g-s bottle in refrigerator.

(c) *Mercury stabilizing soln.*—Dissolve 27.2 g $HgCl_2$ and 11.7 g NaCl in H_2O, and dil. to 1 L with H_2O. (*Caution: See* **51.079**.)

10.080 ***Calibration***

Accurately weigh ca 250 mg $NaHSO_3$ into exactly 50 mL 0.1*N* I soln in g-s flask. Let stand at room temp. 5 min. Add 1 mL HCl, and titr. excess I with 0.1*N* $Na_2S_2O_3$, using 1% aq. starch soln as indicator (1 mL 0.1*N* I consumed = 3.203 mg SO_2 or 5.20 mg $NaHSO_3$). From results of $NaHSO_3$ assay, prep. soln contg 10 mg SO_2/mL (ca 8.6–9.0 g $NaHSO_3$/500 mL) (*Soln I*).

Transfer 100 mL Hg stabilizing soln to 500 mL g-s vol. flask. Add 1.00 mL *Soln I*, and dil. to vol. with H_2O (1 mL = 20 μg SO_2) (*Soln II*).

Using 10 mL graduate contg 1 drop *n-hexyl alcohol* as antifoam, transfer 10 mL portions of cold, undegassed beer (preferably of low SO_2 content) into series of eight 100 mL vol. flasks. To series add 0.0, 1.0, 2.0, 3.0, 4.0, 5.0, 6.0, and 8.0 mL *Soln II* (0–160 μg SO_2). Dil. to vol. with H_2O, and mix. Transfer 25 mL aliquots of each soln to sep. 50 mL vol. flasks. To each flask, add 5 mL color reagent. Mix, and add 5 mL HCHO soln. Mix, dil. to vol. with H_2O, mix, and hold in 25° H_2O bath 30 min. Read color in spectrophtr at 550 nm or in photometer with green filter. Plot *A* as ordinates against μg SO_2 added to beer as abscissas (color follows Beer's law over range). Calc. calibration factor *F*, converting readings to μg SO_2 in 25 mL aliquot used, or convert directly to ppm SO_2.

10.081 ***Preparation of Sample***

Using pipets, add 2 mL Hg stabilizing soln and 5 mL 0.1*N* H_2SO_4 to 100 mL vol. flask. Measure 10 mL cold, undegassed beer into 10 mL graduate contg 1 drop *n*-hexyl alcohol, and add to vol. flask. Swirl gently, and add 15 mL 0.1*N* NaOH. Swirl, and hold 15 sec. Add 10 mL 0.1*N* H_2SO_4, then H_2O to vol., and mix thoroly. Transfer 25 mL aliquot to 50 mL vol. flask.

10.082 ***Determination***

To soln in 50 mL vol. flask, add 5 mL color reagent, swirl, add 5 mL HCHO soln, swirl, and dil. to vol. with H_2O. Mix, and hold in 25° bath 30 min. Read color as in **10.080**, using cells of same size and same instrument settings.

Correct for blank as follows: Measure 10 mL cold, undegassed beer into 100 mL vol. flask. Add 0.5 mL 1% aq. starch soln, then 0.05*N* I soln, dropwise until permanent bluish tinge persists. Add 1 drop more, dil. to vol., and mix thoroly. When blue fades, develop color in 25 mL aliquot as above.

(Color readings for I blanks are usually low and uniform; when test is performed on series of similar beers, blank tests on all may be unnecessary.)

$$\text{ppm } SO_2 = (A_s - A_b) \times F,$$

where A_s = *A* of sample (or photometric reading with green filter equiv. to *A*), A_b = *A* of I blank, and *F* = factor derived from **10.080** for converting *A* to μg SO_2 in aliquot, or directly to ppm SO_2.

10.083 Caramel—Official Final Action

See **11.055**.

Beer Bitterness (*14*)—Official Final Action

(Certain preservatives, such as heptyl-*p*-hydroxybenzoate and sorbates and possibly some brewing adjuncts or coloring agents, may contribute to *A* at wavelengths specified. Interference from UV-absorbing material is greater for Bitterness Units method than for Iso-Alpha Acids.)

Bitterness Units

10.084 ***Reagents***

(a) *2,2,4-Trimethylpentane (isooctane).*—Spectral grade or equiv. (ASTM certified ref. fuel grade isooctane may be used after 1 distn or use practical grade isooctane, purified by passage thru silica gel column (12–28 mesh, Fisher Scientific Co. No. S-156, grade 408).) *A* at 275 nm in 1 cm cell should be equiv. to that of H_2O ($A \leq 0.005$).

(b) *Octyl alcohol.*—Reagent grade or redistd equiv. One drop added to 20 mL isooctane increases *A* at 275 nm ≤0.005 in 1 cm cell.

10.085 ***Apparatus***

(a) *Mechanical shaker.*—Platform or wrist-action type with extending arm adjusted vertically so that tube is held horizontally.

(b) *Spectrophotometer.*—For use in UV range.

(c) *Centrifuge tubes.*—50 mL, g-s or screw-cap with Teflon lining.

10.086 ***Determination***

Transfer 10.0 mL chilled (10°C, 50°F) carbonated beer to 50 mL centrf. tube, using pipet which has minute amt octyl alcohol in tip. Add 1 mL 3*N* HCl and 20 mL isooctane. Tightly stopper centrf. tube and shake vigorously 15 min on mech. shaker. If required, centrf. long enough to sep. phases. Immediately transfer portion clear upper (isooctane) layer to cell. Set instrument to read 0 *A* at 275 nm for isooctane-octyl alcohol blank (20 mL isooctane + 1 drop octyl alcohol). Record *A* in 1 cm cell at 275 nm.

$$\text{Calc. bitterness units (BU)} = A_{275} \times 50.$$

Report BU to nearest 0.5 unit.

Iso-Alpha Acids

10.087 ***Reagents***

(**a**) *2,2,4-Trimethylpentane (isooctane).—See* **10.084(a)**. *A* at 255 nm in 1 cm cell should be equiv. to that of freshly redistd H_2O from all-glass still.

(**b**) *Methanol.*—Reagent grade, with *A* ≤0.04 at 260 nm in 1 cm cell compared with freshly redistd H_2O from all-glass still.

(**c**) *Acid methanol.*—Mix 6.8 parts MeOH with 3.2 parts 4*N* HCl.

(**d**) *Alkaline methanol.*—Just before use, mix 1.0 mL 1.5*N* NaOH with 500 mL MeOH.

(**e**) *Octyl alcohol.—See* **10.084(b)**.

10.088 ***Apparatus***

See **10.085**.

10.089 ***Determination***

Transfer 15.0 mL chilled carbonated beer to 50 mL centrf. tube, using pipet with minute amt octyl alcohol in tip. Add 2.0 mL 6*N* HCl and 15.0 mL isooctane. Close tube tightly and shake vigorously on mech. shaker ≥30 min until completely extd. Place tube in centrf. set to run at highest permissible speed. Centrf. long enough to sep. phases. Break difficult emulsions by adding 1 drop detergent to centrf. tube. Verify that detergent does not contribute to *A* at 255 nm. (Union Carbide Corp. "Tergitol Anionic 7" (Na heptadecyl sulfate) is satisfactory.)

Transfer 10.0 mL clear upper layer to 50 mL g-s graduate contg 10.0 mL acid MeOH. Stopper and invert 100 times at rate causing contents to pass from end to end. Let phases sep.

Transfer 5.0 mL upper layer to 25 mL vol. flask and dil. to vol. with alk. MeOH. Read *A* in 1 cm cell at 255 nm in spectrophtr set to read 0 *A* for reagent blank consisting of 5 mL isooctane dild to 25 mL with alk. MeOH.

$$\text{ppm Iso-alpha acids of beer} = 96.15\, A_{255} + 0.4.$$

Report to nearest 0.5 ppm.

Proteolytic Chillproofing Enzymes (*15*) Official Final Action

Casein Coagulation Method

10.090 ***Reagent***

Substrate mixture.—Thoroly mix by grinding in large mortar and pestle 50 g com. skim milk powder (do not use special casein powder prepd for microbiological or other uses), 5.0 g L(+)-cysteine.HCl.H_2O, 4.4 g Na_2HPO_4, 2.5 g NaCl, and 1.8 g citric acid.H_2O. Store at 0–4° and let warm to room temp. before use.

10.091 ***Test***

Place ca 100 mL degassed beer into 150 mL beaker and adjust pH to 6.4±0.1 with 1*N* NaOH. Transfer 50 mL aliquot to 25 × 200 mm test tube contg 250±30 mg substrate mixt. Suspend substrate mixt. with rubber-tipped glass stirring rod. Invert tube twice to mix uniformly, and place in 60° H_2O bath.

Progressive change in appearance of suspension, initially clouding, then formation of "pebbles," followed by coagulation and settling of casein indicates pos. test. Control beers, without chill-proofing enzymes, should remain unchanged. If semi-quant. data are desired, record time required to reach first stage of "pebbling."

MALT

10.092 Sampling—Official Final Action

For complete descriptions of trier, divider, sampler, and bushel weight tester, see "Grain Inspection Manual" GR Instruction 918-6 (latest edition available from Federal Grain Inspection Service, Standardization Div., US Dept. of Agriculture, 1400 Independence Ave SW, Washington, DC 20250).

(**a**) *Bulk malt in cars or bins.*—Using 60" (1.5 m) trier, take ≥6 probes from different parts of car, preferably 2 from center and 2 from each end.

(**b**) *Bulk malt during discharge thru spouts or openings.*—At different times during filling or unloading of car, take, with trier or Pelican sampler, ≥6 samples, each representing complete cross section of grain stream from spout.

(**c**) *Bagged malt.*—Sample lengthwise thru center of open bags, ≥2% of bags selected from different parts of car or storage room. Use 36" (0.9 m) trier.

Indicate approx. proportion of inferior grain and take representative samples from each portion as outlined above. Immediately place each portion of sample in suitable large dry container and keep tightly closed.

10.093 Preparation of Sample—Official Final Action

Divide samples, either by quartering or by using sample divider, until ca 1.4 kg (3 lb) remains. Place reduced sample in air-tight container (preferably tin with screw or friction-type cover); do not use cartons, bags, wooden boxes, glass Mason jars, or wrapping paper. Remove foreign particles, such as stone, wood, and twine. Do not remove foreign seeds or dust particles.

Bushel Weight (*16*)—Official Final Action

10.094 ***Method I***

Place sample in filling hopper of Winchester tester, open slide underneath, and let malt fill measuring cylinder to overflowing. Without jarring, level off with straight-edge longer than diam. of measuring cylinder, making one forward stroke consisting of 3 distinct zigzag motions. Weigh and report to nearest 100 g (¼ lb).

10.095 ***Method II***

Weigh 110 g sample to nearest 0.1 g and pour evenly into metal funnel provided with plunger discharge and placed on top of 250 mL cylinder graduated to meet NBS specifications. (Funnel must fit snugly into graduate and be large enough to hold the grain without danger of spilling when plunger is raised.) Then drop material into cylinder by pulling plunger up. Do not jar or tap cylinder during operation or before reading vol., and do not read uppermost grain level, as compensation must be made for ends of few kernels that protrude. If grain surface has slant, repeat test.

Calc. bushel wt of malt (lb) as = 8545/vol. in mL of 110 g.

Const 8545 is derived from *W*, wt in lb of US (Winchester) bushel of 2150.42 cu in. (35,239 mL). If *V* = vol. in mL of 110 g malt,

$$110/453.6W = V/35{,}239.$$
$$W = 8545/V.$$

10.096 Length of Acrospire—Procedure

For methods (**a**) and (**b**), quarter sample until ca 200 kernels remain in 2 opposite quarters, and count out 100 kernels, rejecting those that are broken or those in which growth is not ascertainable.

(**a**) *Cutting.*—Hold each kernel, furrow downward, on flat surface with pair of tweezers, cut thru kernel longitudinally with razor blade or other sharp instrument, and examine cut acrospire in both halves, comparing its length with that of kernel. Tally according to classifications below.

(**b**) *Peeling.*—Remove husk covering acrospire with sharp instrument and examine acrospire length in comparison with kernel length. Tally according to classifications below.

(**c**) *Boiling.*—Boil 10–15 g av. sample with 100–150 mL H_2O 20–30 min. After boiling, add cold H_2O to cool contents of beaker. Decant, and pour grain on glass plate. Select 100 kernels at random, inspect acrospire, and tally according to classifications below.

Classify kernels as follows and report % in each group:

0–¼: those kernels without apparent growth, or having acrospire development up to, but not including, ¼ length of grain.

¼–½: those kernels having acrospire development from ¼ up to, but not including, ½ length of grain.

½–¾: those kernels having acrospire development from ½ up to, but not including, ¾ length of grain.

¾–1: those kernels having acrospire development of ¾ but not greater than entire length of grain.

Overgrown: those kernels having acrospire development in excess of length of grain.

If it is apparent that overgrown acrospire has been broken off during processing, include kernel in overgrown classification regardless of length of remaining stub.

10.097 Mealiness—Procedure

Count out 100 kernels remaining from preceding test if method **10.096(a)** or (**b**) was used. Otherwise select 100 kernels as in **10.096** and cut kernels in longitudinal halves. Det. % mealy, half glassy, and glassy kernels. In case of uncertainty, pierce starch body with sharp point; if mealy, it will break away and crumble from point.

Classify kernels as follows:

Mealy kernels—those kernels in which ≤¼ of the endosperm body is glassy.

Half glassy—those kernels in which >¼ but <¾ of the endosperm body is glassy.

Glassy—those kernels in which ≥¾ of the entire endosperm body is glassy.

10.098 1,000 Kernel Weight—Procedure

Quarter sample until ca 500 kernels remain in 2 opposite quarters. Count out 500 kernels and weigh to nearest 0.1 g. Calc. results to 1,000 kernels on as-is and dry basis.

10.099 Assortment—Procedure

Weigh 100 g from quartered sample to nearest 0.1 g. Place in top compartment of grader (frame and screens available from S. Howes Co. Inc., Silver Creek, NY 14136) and shake 3 min. Weigh portions remaining on various screens and in catch pan to nearest 0.1 g, and report % on each of the following screens: 7/64", 6/64", 5/64", and thru 5/64", in percentages totaling 100%. (When testing large berried malts (2 row, California, etc.), addn of 8/64" screen is optional.)

10.100 Mold—Procedure

Det. presence or absence of mold by visual inspection and report as "none," "trace," etc.

10.101 Foreign Seeds and Broken Kernels—Procedure

Weigh 50 g sample. Pick out foreign seeds and broken kernels, classify, and report sep. in %.

Moisture—Official Final Action

10.102 ***Apparatus***

(**a**) *Weighing dish.*—Use glass bottle or Al dish, with tight-fitting cover, ca 40 mm diam. for 5 g sample, or 55 mm for 10 g sample.

(**b**) *Oven.*—With automatic control holding temp. within ±0.5°, and large enough to hold all samples on 1 shelf in such manner that no sample is outside area indicated by test to give comparable results in duplicate samples. Stdze oven as follows: Place weighed duplicate samples in oven at 103–104° and dry 3 hr. Weigh, and redry 1 hr longer. If loss of moisture is >0.1%, raise temp. 1° and again test with new duplicate samples. Take, as std, lowest temp. <106° giving moisture content that, after 3 hr of drying, is within 0.1% of value attainable at same temp. within 4 hr. Keep ventilators of oven open during entire drying period, and do not open door during the 3 hr of drying.

10.103 ***Preparation of Sample***

(**a**) *If extract determination is to be made.*—Grind sample as in **10.108**, and transfer in one continuous operation. When many samples are to be analyzed, grind first sample, remove beaker, and grind second sample while adjusting wt of first sample. Remove second sample, insert third sample, and repeat operation.

(**b**) *If extract determination is not to be made.*— Have sample of same fineness as finely ground malt used to det. ext. Weigh ca 5 g whole malt (or 10 g if 55 mm diam. weighing bottle is used) and grind thru clean dry mill directly into weighing bottle. Brush all malt from mill into weighing bottle and cover immediately.

10.104 ***Determination***

Weigh sample to 1 mg and place in oven previously heated to std temp. Remove cover of weighing bottle and heat exactly 3 hr at std temp. Replace cover, transfer to desiccator, cool to room temp., and weigh to 1 mg. Report moisture to nearest 0.1%.

Extract—Official Final Action

10.105 ***Reagent***

Iodine std solns.—(**a**) 0.01*N*. Dissolve 0.63 g I and 1.25 g KI in H_2O, and dil. to 500 mL. (**b**) 0.02*N*. Dissolve 1.27 g I and 2.50 g KI in H_2O, and dil. to 500 mL. Prep. fresh solns monthly and store in dark. For daily use, keep portion of soln in small brown dropper bottle.

10.106 ***Apparatus***

(**a**) *Mills.*—Miag-Seck (available from Buhler-Miag, Inc., PO Box 9497, Minneapolis, MN 55440). For fine grinding use cone-type, 300 rpm, and for coarse grinding, roller-type, 150 rpm.

(**b**) *Sieves.*—Half-ht, 8" std sieve No. 30 (with pan and cover). For classification of laboratory and brewery grindings use addnl std sieves Nos. 10, 14, 18, 60, and 100.

(**c**) *Mash beakers and counter weights.*—Made of either pure Ni, stainless steel, or brass, not Cu, and of such dimensions as to ensure tight connection between beakers and Miag-Seck mill while grinding.

If counter wts are used for the mash beakers, check tare wts frequently.

(**d**) *Mashing apparatus.*—Use beakers, stirrers, and solder made of same metal. Provide each stirrer with blade that in operation has clearance of ca 2 mm from bottom and 5 mm from wall of mash beaker. Blade is ca 8 mm wide, and each side has 45° pitch, arranged as in a propeller, to force mash upward. Speed of mash stirrer must be 80–100 rpm, each stirrer of each beaker having same speed. Mech. stir H_2O in bath thoroly to assure uniformity of temp. and have level of H_2O above max. mash level.

(**e**) *Gypsum plate.*—Thoroly mix 100 mL H_2O with 135 g plaster of Paris. Pour mixt., while still free-flowing, into suitable flat molds (cigar boxes, etc.). Porcelain plate for color reactions, Coors No. 550, size 00, may be used.

(**f**) *Filter paper.*—Use S&S 32 cm fluted paper No. 560 (or No. 597, 32 cm, fluted by analyst) or Eaton-Dikeman Co., Mt. Holly Springs, PA 17065, 32 cm fluted paper No. 509 (or No. 609, 32 cm, fluted by analyst).

(**g**) *Funnels.*—Use short-stem glass funnels ca 20 cm diam. and do not let paper project above rim. Stem must extend 3–5 cm into receiving flask.

(**h**) *Flasks.*—Use dry 500 mL erlenmeyers marked at 100 mL level.

(**i**) *Pycnometers.*—Use any suitable pycnometer, but preferably Reischauer or Boot (vac.) type. Reischauer type is ca 15 cm high with neck ca 9 cm long and 2.5–3.5 mm id. Fine, well-defined mark is found 55–70 mm below upper rim of neck. When filled with H_2O at 20° its capacity must be 48–50 g. Use ca 15 mL glass funnels to fill pycnometers.

Boot type is cylindrical and holds ca 50 g H_2O at 20°. Vac. seal must be well rounded off and not pointed. Pycnometer opening is wide enough to permit easy filling and emptying, and stopper has fine capillary opening. Walls of bottle meet stopper in rising acute angle of ca 45° so that no depression or groove retaining moisture is formed at this point. (Available from Rascher and Betzold, Inc., 5410 N Damon Ave, Chicago, IL 60625.)

(**j**) *Emptying device for Reischauer pycnometer.*— Bend piece of metal capillary tubing (brass, stainless steel), $<$2 mm od, to ca 45° angle. End to be inserted into pycnometer must reach within 2–3 mm of bottom. Connect other end either to rubber aspirator bulb or to compressed air supply ≤5 psi.

(**k**) *Water bath.*—Automatically controlled. If automatic control is not available, use following app. Have H_2O level of bath (5–15 L) reach above neck marks of pycnometer, keep H_2O bath temp. at 20±0.05°, and read on accurate thermometer, calibrated to 0.1°. Maintain temp. of H_2O bath by very slow but continuous flow of ice-H_2O from container (2–4 L, contg ice and H_2O). Regulate flow of ice-H_2O by hand. Stir H_2O in bath mech. and continuously without splashing.

10.107 ***Standardization***

(**a**) *Setting of mill.*—Use malt of following characteristics:

Variety: Malt made from 6-rowed midwestern variety of barley

Moisture	4.2–4.8%
Ext in finely ground malt, dry basis	74.0–77.0%
Color of laboratory wort, **10.112** or **10.113**	≤1.8
Diastatic Power, dry basis	≥100°
Ratio sol. protein to total protein	36–42
Mealiness: Glassy	≤5%
Mealy	≥90%
Acrospire development: 0–¼ grown	≤5%
¾ to full grown	≥80%
Overgrown	≤5%

Assortment: From malt meeting above specifications, take that portion passing thru 7/64″ screen and remaining on 6/64″ screen for actual stdzg operation.

Fine grinding.—Weigh 50 g specified malt into mash beaker, grind, and collect in same beaker. Mill must not be in motion when sample is introduced. Transfer to No. 30 sieve placed on receiving pan and shake in horizontal plane on flat surface 3 min, pausing every 15 sec long enough to give screen and pan 2 sharp taps on surface over which it is sliding. Transfer and weigh particles remaining on and adhering to screen. Consider mill as having stdzd setting when wt of ground malt remaining on No. 30 sieve is between 4.5 and 5.5 g (9–11%). Stdze mill at least twice yearly. Suitable mech. shaking device, giving equiv. results, may be used to stdze mill.

Coarse grinding.—Proceed as for *fine grinding.* Consider mill as having stdzd setting when portion of ground malt remaining on No. 30 sieve is between 37 and 38 g (74–76%).

(**b**) *Reischauer type pycnometer.*—Clean interior and exterior of pycnometer with chromic acid soln, discharge carefully with air, and wash several times with H_2O, then alcohol, and finally ether. To remove last traces of ether vapor and to replace with laboratory air, connect dry metal capillary tubing to vac. and insert into pycnometer 1–2 min. Carefully wipe pycnometer, let stand few min, and det. wt to 0.2 mg.

Fill with freshly distd H_2O and place in H_2O bath held at 20±0.05°. Tap gently to force out air bubbles. After 25 min, remove liq. above mark with capillary pipet provided with small rubber bulb. To make final adjustment of meniscus, absorb last portion of liq. with thin strips of blotting paper; also remove any liq. adhering to inner surface of neck. Adjust H_2O level so that lower part of meniscus rests on mark. Make all adjustments of liq. level within pycnometer neck while holding by neck, without touching body of pycnometer with hands. Keep body of pycnometer submerged during entire period of meniscus adjustment.

Raise pycnometer to room temp. by insertion into H_2O bath kept at exactly that temp., and hold 10 min. Remove pycnometer, carefully dry exterior, and weigh to 0.2 mg. Subtract wt empty pycnometer. Difference in wts represents H_2O capacity of pycnometer at 20°. Redet. tare wt and H_2O capacity at frequent intervals.

(**c**) *Boot type pycnometer.*—Clean pycnometer and det. its wt in same way as for Reischauer type. Cool H_2O in ice bath to temp. slightly $<$20°. Rinse pycnometer once with the cool H_2O, fill, stopper, and dry exterior. Remove stopper, insert thermometer adjusted to 20° in H_2O, and note temp., which should be 20±0.1°. If it is not, choose different "filling" temp., which may vary with analyst and season from 19.4° to 19.7° or more. Make subsequent detns, using predetd filling temp. Place cap over stopper and weigh.

Redet. wt, H_2O capacity, and filling temp. at least weekly.

10.108 ***Determination***

Fine grinding.—Weigh ca 55 g sample (at room temp.) into tared mash beaker and grind thru mill set for stdzd fineness of grind. Collect finely ground malt in same mash beaker, carefully brushing malt particles remaining in mill into mash beaker. Mix, and without delay, place mash beaker with contents on balance accurate to within ±0.05 g under 750 g load and adjust wt malt to 50±0.05 g by removing excess into tared dish for moisture detn.

Coarse grinding.—Weigh 50.5 g sample (at room temp.) into tared mash beaker and grind thru mill set for stdzd coarseness of grind. Collect coarsely ground malt in same mash beaker, carefully brushing particles remaining in mill into mash beaker. Without delay, place mash beaker with contents on balance accurate to within ±0.05 g under 750 g load and adjust wt malt to 50±0.05 g by removing excess.

(**a**) *Mashing procedure.*—"Mash in" ground malt with 200 mL H_2O at 46° and mix well with glass rod to prevent formation of lumps. Carefully rinse glass rod and wall of beaker with small amt H_2O. Note odor of mash and report as aromatic, slightly aromatic, musty, green, stale, etc. Promptly place mash beakers in mashing app. contg H_2O previously heated to 46°, and set stirrers in motion. Place thermometer in each mash beaker. Keep temp. at 45° exactly 30 min from time beakers were placed in mashing app. Raise mash temp. 1°/min to 70°. Add 100 mL H_2O, previously heated to 70–71°, and hold mash 60 min at 70°. (Temp. deviations during mashing procedures should not exceed 0.5°.)

(**b**) *Conversion.*—Transfer drop of mash with thin glass rod (ca 3 mm diam.) onto absorbent gypsum plate, **10.106(e)**, or into one cavity of porcelain plate, and test with drop of 0.01*N* I soln on gypsum plate, or with drop of 0.02*N* I soln, **10.105(b)**, on porcelain plate. Make tests 5, 7, and 10 min after 70° is reached, and thereafter if necessary, at 5 min intervals. Conversion is complete when test drop and I soln produce only yellow stain on gypsum or porcelain plate. Report time of conversion in periods: $<$5 min, 5–7 min, etc. Time of conversion is not detd on coarsely ground malt.

(**c**) *Cooling and filtration.*—After 60 min, cool mash promptly (within 10–15 min) to prevailing room temp. Stop stirrers. Remove thermometers after adhering mash particles are rinsed into beaker with H_2O. Remove each beaker with its stirrer from mashing app. Rinse mash particles adhering to stirrer into beaker with H_2O. Dry outside of each beaker, taking care to remove moisture adhering to rim. Without delay, adjust wt of contents of mash beaker to 450.0±0.05 g by adding H_2O.

Stir mash thoroly with glass rod, once when removing beakers from balance pan and again immediately before pouring mash onto filter. (Stirrings must be ≥5 min but $<$15 min apart.) While stirring cooled mash, take care to prevent splashing or spilling. Mix drops adhering to beaker wall into mash by rotary stirring with glass rod.

Pour entire contents of beaker into funnel provided with specified filter paper. Cover funnel with ca 20 cm diam. watch glass during entire filtration. Return first 100 mL filtrate to filter. When no more liq. is present above filter cake, discontinue filtration and remove receiving flask contg wort for later observations and tests. In case of slow running worts, stop filtration after 2 hr. In case of coarse ground malt mash, collect exactly 200±2 mL wort. When filtration is complete, mix wort in receiving flask thoroly by rotary motion. Speed of filtration is normal if filtration is complete (as defined above) within 1 hr after returning the 100 mL filtrate to filter bed; slow, if filtration takes longer. Observe degree of clarity and report as clear, slightly hazy, or hazy.

Remove ca 100 mL wort for detn of color. (Color is not detd on wort from coarsely ground malt.)

(**d**) *Specific gravity.*—Rinse empty pycnometer twice with ca 10 mL wort, and if Reischauer pycnometer is used, remove rinsings each time with emptying device. Fill with wort, place in H_2O bath, and proceed as in **10.107(b)** or (**c**). Weigh filled pycnometer within 3 hr of completed filtration. Difference between this wt and that of empty pycnometer represents wort capacity of pycnometer at 20°. Calc. sp gr of wort to fifth decimal place, rounding off to 0.00005 or 0.00010, by dividing wt wort by wt H_2O.

No calcn is made of sp gr *in vacuo.* If duplicate detns made by same analyst in different beakers differ by $>$2 units in fourth decimal place, repeat entire detn.

(**e**) *Extract.*—Det. ext yield of wort by ref. to sp gr values given in **52.009**, and calc. ext yield of malt by following formulas:

Ext as-is basis $= P(800 + M)/(100 - P)$,

where P = g ext in 100 g wort (Plato, **52.009**); and M = % H_2O in the malt.

Ext dry basis $= (E \times 100)/(100 - M)$,

where E = ext as-is basis; and M = % H_2O in the malt.

Report ext as-is basis and dry basis to nearest 0.1%.

10.109 Extract in Caramel Malt—Official Final Action

Use mill for fine grinding, **10.106(a)**. Weigh ca 30.5 g caramel malt, grind, and adjust to 25±0.05 g, removing excess for moisture detn. Weigh ca 25.5 g malt of known moisture, ext, and color, and having Diastatic Power ≥100°; grind, and adjust to 25±0.05 g. Quant. transfer the 2 portions to mash beaker, mash, and det. sp gr as in **10.108(d)**. Det. moisture as in **10.103(b)** and **10.104**.

Calc. by following formulas:

Total ext $= P \times (800 + M$ in 50 g malt $+ M$ in 50 g caramel malt$)/(100 - P)$,

where P = g ext in 100 g wort (Plato, **52.009**), and M = moisture (g).

Ext in caramel malt = (total ext − ext in 50 g malt) × 100/50.

10.110 Color in Caramel Malt—Official Final Action

Use mixed wort obtained for ext detn, dilg wort enough to make color reading ca 4.0 units. Det. color on dild wort as in **10.113** or **10.114**.

Calc. by following formula:

Color of carmel malt $= 2[C \times (D + 1)]$ − color of malt used for conversion,

where C = color reading on dild wort, and D = parts of H_2O to dil. one part of wort.

Report diln used for making color reading. Report color to nearest whole number.

10.111 Color in Black Malt—Official Final Action

Use mill for fine grinding, **10.106(a)**. As precautionary measure grind small amt of sample to be analyzed and clean out mill. For detn weigh 5.5 g, grind, and collect all particles by careful brushing of mill.

Weigh 5.00 g on anal. balance, transfer to 600 mL beaker, add 400 mL H_2O at room temp., and heat to bp in ≥15 but $<$20 min. Boil gently exactly 5 min, cool to room temp., and without delay transfer to 500 mL vol. flask; dil. to vol. with H_2O, mix, and filter thru 32 cm fluted paper. Pipet 10 mL filtrate into 100 mL vol. flask, dil. to vol. with H_2O, and mix.

Det. color of dild wort as in **10.113** or **10.114**. Calc. color found for this filtrate to same concn of materials used for regular malt mash (12.5 g malt to 100 mL H_2O) by formula:

$$\text{Color of black malt} = L \times 10 \times 12.5,$$

where L = color reading on dild filtrate. Report color to nearest whole number.

Color of Laboratory Wort (*17*)
Official Final Action

10.112 *Preparation of Sample*

Add 5 g Celite (anal. grade) to 100 mL filtered wort, **10.108(c)**, and mix. Let stand 5 min. Filter thru S&S No. 597 paper, or equiv. Return first 40 mL filtrate to filter. Det *A* on clear total filtrate.

10.113 *Spectrophotometric Method*

Fill cell with clear filtrate and det. *A* of wort at 430 nm with spectrophtr, **10.002**.

Wort color = 10 × A_{430} × correction to ½" cell size.
Report color to nearest 0.05 unit.

10.114 ***Photometric Method***

Calibrate photometer, **10.006**, against spectrophtr as in **10.007**. Read clear filtrate in same size cell and at same wavelength as used in calibration. Multiply scale reading by av. calibration factor to give wort color. Report to nearest 0.05 unit.

10.115 Protein—Official Final Action

Weigh 1.4 g finely ground malt, **10.108**, and proceed as in **2.057**. %N × 6.25 = % protein.

10.116 Wort Nitrogen—Official Final Action

Using 25 mL laboratory wort, **10.108(c)**, det. N as in **10.045**. Calc. as wort N in terms of % malt (dry basis) as follows:

Wort N (% malt, dry basis) = (mL 0.1*N* H_2SO_4 − mL 0.1*N* NaOH) × 0.0056 × % malt ext (dry basis)/(°Plato of wort × sp gr of wort).

Report to second decimal place.

Diastatic Power (*18*)—Official Final Action

10.117 ***Preparation of Glassware***

Wash all glassware with chromic acid cleaning soln, rinse with tap H_2O ≥4 times, and finally rinse with H_2O at least twice. Thoroly dry digestion flasks. (*Caution:* $Na_2Cr_2O_7$-H_2SO_4 can cause severe burns. *See* **51.023** and **51.030**.)

10.118 ***Reagents***

(**a**) *Acetate buffer soln.*—Dissolve 68 g $NaOAc.3H_2O$ in 500 mL 1*N* HOAc and dil. to 1 L with H_2O.

(**b**) *Fehling soln.*—Stdze as in **31.035–31.036**. Check soln from time to time by detg its oxidizing value against std soln of invert sugar, **31.034(c)**, as in **31.035**.

(**c**) *Alkaline ferricyanide soln.*—0.05*N*. Dissolve 16.5 g dry $K_3Fe(CN)_6$ and 22 g anhyd. Na_2CO_3 in H_2O, and dil. to 1 L with H_2O. Soln keeps its strength for long period if stored in dark glass bottle in dark.

(**d**) *Sodium thiosulfate std soln.*—0.05*N*. Prep. daily by dilg 0.1*N* soln, **50.037–50.038**. Check $Na_2S_2O_3$ against $K_3Fe(CN)_6$ soln as follows: To 10 mL $K_3Fe(CN)_6$ soln add 25 mL HOAc reagent, 1 mL 50% KI soln, and 2 mL sol. starch indicator. Titr. with the $Na_2S_2O_3$. (Exactly 10 mL $Na_2S_2O_3$ soln should completely discharge blue starch-I color. Adjust if necessary.)

(**e**) *Acetic acid reagent.*—200 mL HOAc, 70 g KCl, and 20 g $ZnSO_4.7H_2O$/L.

(**f**) *Potassium iodide soln.*—50%. Dissolve 50 g KI in H_2O, add 1 drop NaOH soln (1+1), and dil. to 100 mL with H_2O. (Adding NaOH soln substantially delays deterioration of soln, with liberation of I, on standing; soln must be colorless.)

(**g**) *Starch soln.*—Have final concn of 2 g sol. starch (weighed on dry basis) in 100 mL soln. Use sol. starch, according to Lintner, special for diastatic power detn, with solubility at least 1:50 in hot H_2O, that contains no dextrins, contains <0.75% reducing substances calcd as maltose, and has moisture content of 10–12%. Freshly made 2% soln must have pH of 4.5–5.5 without adjustment with buffer. Subsequent batches of starch, when tested on a malt of ca 100° Diastatic Power (dry basis) having other characteristics as specified under detn of ext in malt, must show variation ≤±3° Diastatic Power from value obtained by using original starch in parallel detn. Test addnl batches of starch, when purchased, in parallel with starch in use. Permit no variation >±3° Diastatic Power. In no case may cumulative correction as referred to original starch, approved above, amt to >5° Diastatic Power. (Starch meeting these specifications is available from ASBC, 3340 Pilot Knob Rd, St. Paul, MN 55121.)

Macerate starch with just enough cold freshly distd H_2O to form smooth, thin paste (≤5% of final vol.). Pour, with const stirring, into boiling freshly distd H_2O representing ≥ ca 75% of final vol. of starch soln, at such rate that boiling does not cease. Continue boiling 2 min after thin paste is completely added. Quickly add to beaker addnl 10% of final vol. of cold, freshly distd H_2O and quant. transfer mixt. to g-s vol. flask; mix by inverting flask, wash down neck of flask, and cool to 20° before adding buffer soln. Add 2 mL buffer soln for each 100 mL of final vol. of starch soln and dil. to vol. Mix again by inverting flask and keep tightly stoppered at 20° until used.

(**h**) *Soluble starch indicator.*—1% sol. starch in 30% NaCl soln. Prep. sol. starch suspension and pour slowly into boiling H_2O. Add NaCl and dil. to vol. (Soln should be transparent and colorless.)

10.119 ***Determination***

Grind sep. ≤25.5 g malt as in **10.108**. Collect finely ground malt in mash beaker, carefully brushing in malt particles remaining in mill. Without delay, adjust wt contents to 25±0.05 g. Transfer quant. to container (ca 1 L) in which infusion is to be made. Add 500 mL 0.5% NaCl soln at 20° and close container. Let infusion stand 2.5 hr at 20±0.2° and agitate by rotating at 20 min intervals. Take care that in agitation of malt suspension min. amt of grist is left adhering to inner surface of flask above level of the H_2O. (Do *not* invert flask to mix; gentle whirling of contents without splashing on sides of container is sufficient.) Filter infusion by transferring entire charge to 30–32 cm fluted filter (S&S 588, or equiv.) in 185 mm funnel. Return first 50 mL filtrate to filter. Collect filtrate for 3 hr after H_2O and ground malt were first mixed. Prevent evapn during filtration as far as possible by placing watch glass over funnel and some suitable cover around stem of funnel, resting on neck of receiver.

Immediately dil. 20 mL of this infusion to 100 mL with 0.5% NaCl soln at 20°, transfer 10 mL dild infusion to 250 mL vol. flask, and bring to 20°. Add 200 mL buffered starch soln from fast-flowing pipet, all at 20°. Mix soln by rotating flask during addn. Keep "starch infusion" mixt. at 20±0.1° exactly 30 min, timed on stop-watch from time addn of starch was begun. Rapidly add 20 mL 0.5*N* NaOH and mix well by whirling flask. Dil. to vol. at 20° and mix thoroly.

Det. reducing power by (**a**) Fehling soln modification, or (**b**) ferricyanide modification:

(**a**) *Fehling soln modification.*—Boil 10 mL Fehling soln and 10 mL H_2O in 200 mL erlenmeyer. (For heating soln, elec. plate is preferable to gas flame.) Add, from buret, ca ⅔ of amt of above digested starch soln probably required and boil 15–20 sec, rotating constantly. Remove from heat. If still decidedly blue, add more soln, boil ca 10 sec, and again observe color. When blue is almost discharged, and after soln boils gently ca 2 min, add 3 drops *1% aq. methylene blue soln.* Continue boiling and add more soln until 0.1 mL, or even 1 drop, upon boiling, discharges blue. (Color becomes violet-lavender as end point nears.)

Repeat titrn, adding at once almost whole amt of digested starch required, and proceed to end point as directed. Designate vol. of digested starch soln required to reach end point in this second titrn as *V*. Interrupt boiling as little as possible after indicator is added, so that flask remains filled with steam, preventing much access of air. (Upon cooling, blue usually returns.)

Prep. blank by processing exactly as in par. 2, except add the 0.5N NaOH to malt infusion before adding starch soln. To 10 mL Fehling soln and 10 mL H_2O add a vol. of this blank soln equal to final vol. of digested starch soln required in above detn. Boil and again det. end point as in detn. Designate vol. of digested starch soln used as B.

(b) *Ferricyanide modification.*—Pipet 5 mL dild digested starch soln into 125 mL erlenmeyer. Pipet exactly 10 mL $K_3Fe(CN)_6$ soln into soln, and immerse flask in vigorously boiling H_2O bath. Have surface of liq. in flask 3–4 cm below surface of boiling H_2O. Let flask remain in boiling H_2O bath *exactly* 20 min; then cool under running H_2O, and add 25 mL HOAc reagent with thoro mixing. Add 1 mL KI soln, followed by 2 mL sol. starch indicator, **10.118(h)**, and mix thoroly. Titr. with 0.05N $Na_2S_2O_3$ to complete disappearance of blue (10 mL buret is recommended). Designate mL 0.05N $Na_2S_2O_3$ used as V.

Prep. blank by proceeding exactly as in par. 2, except add the 0.5N NaOH to malt infusion before adding starch soln. Det. reducing power of blank as in preceding par. Designate mL 0.05N $Na_2S_2O_3$ used for blank as B.

10.120 *Calculation of Diastatic Power*

(a) *Fehling soln modification.*—Degrees Diastatic Power as-is basis = $(5000/V) \times (B/V)$;

°Diastatic Power dry basis = (°Diastatic Power as-is basis × 100)/(100 − M),

where V and B have same meaning as in **10.119(a)**, and M = % moisture.

In above formula, $5000/V$ is apparent °Diastatic Power, which must be modified by fraction representing ratio of blank titrn to original titrn, which measures influence of starch in detn.

Report °Diastatic Power as-is and dry basis to nearest whole number.

(b) *Ferricyanide modification.*—°Diastatic Power, as-is = $(B - V) \times 23$, where V and B have same meaning as in **10.119(b)**. Calc. dry basis from this as in **(a)** and report to nearest whole number.

When conditions given in method are followed, net vol. of ferricyanide, after correcting for blank, × 23 = °Diastatic Power as-is basis.

Alpha-Amylase (*19*)—Official Final Action

10.121 *Reagents*

(a) *Special starch.*—Use sol. Lintner starch, special for Diastatic Power detn, **10.118(g)**.

(b) *Beta-amylase.*—Use special β-amylase powder free from α-amylase, made by Wallerstein Co. (Travenol Laboratories, Inc., Morton Grove, IL 60053). This prepn has been stdzd to 2000° and should comply with following specifications: At addn level used, variation is ≤5% in dextrinization of std malt infusion when 1 and 3 day old substrates are compared. Further, substrate prepd by adding twice the level of β-amylase indicated must deviate by ≤5% from that prepd with recommended level after 24 hr standing. Store powder in tightly closed bottle in refrigerator. To avoid moisture condensation on cold enzyme prepn, let bottle warm to room temp. before opening.

(c) *Stock iodine soln.*—Dissolve 5.50 g I crystals (ACS) and 11.0 g KI in H_2O, and dil. to 250 mL with H_2O. Store in dark bottle and make fresh soln monthly.

(d) *Dilute iodine soln.*—Dissolve 20.0 g KI in H_2O, add 2.00 mL of the stock I soln, and dil. to 500 mL with H_2O. Series of 13 × 100 mm test tubes contg 5 mL dil. I soln must be made up beforehand and adjusted to 20° in readiness for testing. All-glass automatic pipet such as the Machlett type is recommended for rapidly dispensing this soln.

(e) *Buffer soln.*—Dissolve 120 mL HOAc and 164 g anhyd. NaOAc in H_2O, and dil. to 1 L.

(f) *Sodium chloride soln.*—0.5%. Dissolve 5 g reagent NaCl in 1 L H_2O. This soln need not be made up in vol. flask.

(g) *Buffered limit-dextrin (alpha-amylodextrin) substrate.*—Prep. suspension of 10.00 g (dry wt) sol. starch, **10.118(g)**, in cold H_2O and pour slowly into boiling H_2O. Boil with stirring 1–2 min, cool, and add 25 mL buffer soln and 250 mg β-amylase dissolved in small amt H_2O. Dil. to 500 mL with H_2O, sat. with toluene, and store at ca 20° for ≥18 hr but ≤72 hr before use.

10.122 *Apparatus*

(a) *Constant temperature bath.*—Set at 20±0.05°.

(b) *Reference color std.*—Use special Alpha- Amylase Color Disk (Cat. No. 620S-5) made by Hellige Inc., 877 Stewart Ave, Garden City, NY 11530.

(c) *Comparator.*—Use either std Hellige comparator (Cat. No. 607-A13) or pocket comparator (Cat. No. 605-HT) with prism attachment (Cat. No. 605-AHT). Illuminate comparator with 100 watt frosted lamp mounted in such manner that direct rays from lamp do not shine in operator's eyes. Place lamp 15 cm (6") from rear opal glass of comparator. Slight differences in color discrimination between different operators are minimized by use of prism attachment, by maintaining 15–25 cm (6–10") reading distance between eye and comparator, and by experience gained with continued practice.

(d) *Comparison tubes.*—Use precision bore sq tubes with 13 mm viewing depth. Place tube filled with distd H_2O behind color disk.

The α-amylase color disk is correct only when used with specified 13 mm viewing depth. Precision bore sq tubes are specified to obviate need for individual calibration of test tubes and to ensure use of std viewing depth. The 13 mm precision sq tubes are supplied as std equipment with Hellige comparator and are also used with Coleman Universal spectrophtr. They may be secured from either Hellige Inc., distributors of Coleman instrument, or Fischer & Porter Co.

10.123 *Determination*

(a) *Preparation of malt infusion.*—Ext 25±0.05 g finely ground malt exactly as in **10.119**, par. 1, using 500 mL 0.5% NaCl soln. Dil. 20 mL malt infusion to 100 mL with 0.5% NaCl soln at 20°.

(b) *Dextrinization.*—Transfer 20.0 mL substrate soln at 20° to 50 mL erlenmeyer, add 5 mL 0.5% NaCl soln, and again adjust to 20°. Add 5 mL dild malt infusion at 20°, blowing it in and counting time from instant first of the dild malt infusion reaches starch substrate in flask. After 10 min reaction time, add 1 mL hydrolyzing mixt. to 5 mL dil. I soln at 20°, shake, pour into 13 mm sq tube, and compare with α-amylase color disk in comparator. At appropriate intervals remove addnl 1 mL aliquots hydrolyzing mixt., add to dil. I soln, mix, and compare with color disk until α-amylase color is reached. Take care to keep tubes contg reaction mixt. plus I from changing temp. while comparing colors. If color comparisons are made immediately after addn of reaction mixt. to I, there will be essentially no temp. change and no change in color.

During initial stages of reaction, 1 mL sample need not be measured precisely before addn to dil. I soln. As end point approaches, make addn accurately with 1 mL pipet. (Use fast-flowing pipet such as 1 mL bacteriological pipet for withdrawing 1 mL aliquot.) Blow contents of pipet into I soln. Near end point, take readings every 0.5 min on the min or half min. In case two readings 0.5 min apart show that one is darker than α-amylase color disk and other is lighter, record end point at nearest 15 sec. Shake out 13 mm sq tube used for color comparison between successive readings.

For accuracy and convenience, it is desirable that dextrinization times fall between 10 and 30 min. With malts of low α-amylase activity it may be necessary to use 10 mL dild infusion. In this case, do not add 5 mL NaCl soln. Final vol. of reaction mixt. should always be 30 mL.

10.124 ***Calculation of Alpha-Amylase Activity***

From time interval in min necessary for dextrinization, T, and wt malt in g represented by infusion aliquot taken, W, calc. α-amylase dextrinizing units (DU). An α-amylase unit is defined as amt of α-amylase which will dextrinize sol. starch in presence of excess of β-amylase at rate of 1 g/hr at 20°.

$$20°\ DU\ \text{(as-is basis)} = 24/(W \times T);$$
$$20°\ DU\ \text{(dry basis)} = DU\ \text{(as-is)} \times 100/(100 - M);$$

where M = % moisture in sample, and 24 = wt starch used (0.4 g) multiplied by 1 hr (60 min).

Example: $W = 0.05$ g; $T = 20$ min; 20° DU (as-is) = 24/(0.05 × 20) = 24.

Report dextrinizing units to nearest 0.1 unit.

CEREAL ADJUNCTS

10.125 Sampling—Official Final Action

See **10.092**.

10.126 Preparation of Sample—Official Final Action

See **10.093**.

10.127 Physical Characteristics—Procedure

(**a**) *Accidental foreign particles.*—Before proceeding with laboratory detns remove any accidental foreign particles from sample. Report presence and amt.

(**b**) *Color.*—Spread suitable portion of sample evenly and observe against white background. Report as white, cream, yellow, buff, gray, brown.

(**c**) *Odor.*—Det. after shaking sample in closed container. Report as clean and normal, moldy, musty, rancid, or other foreign odor.

(**d**) *Husks, germs, and foreign seeds.*—Classify and report in %.

(**e**) *Mold.*—Det. by visual inspection and report as none, trace, considerable.

(**f**) *Weevils, larvae, etc.*—Det. presence or absence by visual inspection. Report as none, very few, few, considerable; indicate if alive or dead.

Assortment of Corn Grits (*20*)
Official Final Action

10.128 ***Apparatus***

(**a**) *Sieve shaker.*—Such as Ro-Tap testing sieve shaker (W. S. Tyler Co., 8200 Tyler Blvd, Mentor, OH 44060).

(**b**) *Nested set of sieves and pans.*—8" sieve diam., Nos. 20, 30, 40, 60, 100, or other similar series.

10.129 ***Determination***

Accurately weigh ca 50±0.1 g of well mixed, representative sample of grits, **10.125–10.126**. (To obtain representative sample <100 g, pass successively thru sample divider.) Transfer sample to top sieve of set of sieves with pan, assembled and fixed in shaker, and shake 5 min. Weigh, to 0.1 g, grits particles remaining on and adhering to each of sieves, or caught in pan.

Calc. wt of each sieve fraction and pan fraction as % of sample wt. Report % of each fraction to 1 decimal place.

Moisture—Official Final Action
Air Oven Method (103–104°)

10.130 ***Apparatus***

See **10.102**.

10.131 ***Determination***

Grind as in **10.108**, fine grinding, and proceed as in **10.104**.

Oil or Petroleum Ether Extract
Official Final Action

10.132 ***Reagent***

Petroleum ether.—AOCS. Initial boiling temp., 35–38°; dry-flask end point, 52–60°; ≥95% distg at <54°, and ≤60% distg at <40°; sp gr at 60°F, 0.630–0.660; appearance, colorless; evapn residue, ≤0.0011 g/100 mL; doctor test, sweet; Cu strip corrosion test, noncorrosive; only trace of unsatd compds permitted; residue in distg flask, neut. to Me orange; blotter strip odor test, odorless within 12 min; aromatic compds, no nitrobenzene odor; saponification value, <1.0 mg KOH/100 mL.

Make distn test according to ASTM method D216-54 and make blank detn by evapg 250 mL with ca 0.25 g stearin or other hard fat (previously brought to const wt by heating) and drying as in actual detn. Blank must be ≤3 mg.

10.133 ***Determination***

(*Caution: See* **51.011**, **51.039**, and **51.073**.)

Accurately weigh 5–10 g sample ground as in **10.108**. Without previous drying, ext in Soxhlet or other suitable extractor with pet ether for ≤6 hr. Filter ext thru small, hardened paper into weighed vessel, washing paper finally with small portion of hot fresh solv. Distil or evap. solv. at temp. ≤100° and dry vessel contg residue in air oven 1 hr at 100–105°. Report as % oil to second decimal place.

Extract—Official Final Action

10.134 ***Apparatus***

Same as in **10.106** except that mill may be of any suitable type.

10.135 ***Standardization***

Setting of mill.—Use sample of rice or grits with moisture content ≤12%. Grind enough sample to obtain ≥51 g ground portion. Det. fineness of grinding as in **10.107(a)**. Fine grinding of rice should show 40±2.5 g (= 80±5%) and grits 35±2.5 g (= 70±5%) of ground portion passing thru std sieve.

10.136 ***Determination***

Grind enough sample to obtain ≥21 g. Grind ca 31 g malt made mainly from 6-rowed barley of Manchurian type, conversion time ≤7 min, Diastatic Power 100–120°. Det. ext of malt simultaneously with that of the cereal.

Mash in 20±0.05 g sample (with exception of flaked corn and flaked rice) and 5±0.05 g ground malt with 200 mL H_2O at 46°. Mix well with glass rod, place on wire gauze over flame, and bring to bp in ≥10 min but <15 min, stirring constantly. Boil grits and rice gently 30 min, and refined grits 10 min, avoiding burning, spattering, and excessive frothing. During boiling, stir mash and keep vol. const by adding boiling H_2O every 15 min. After boiling, cool to 46° and add 25±0.05 g remaining ground malt. When ext is detd on flaked corn or flaked rice, do not boil, but mash in 20 g unground sample and 30 g ground malt with 200 mL H_2O at 46°. Mix well to prevent formation of lumps, rinse inner walls of beaker, promptly place mash beakers in mashing app. contg H_2O previously heated to 46°, and set stirrers in motion. Hold 30 min at 45° from time mash beakers were placed in app. Raise mash temp. 1°/min until 70° is reached. Add 100 mL H_2O, previously heated to 70–71°, and hold mash 60 min at 70°. (All temps refer to mash, not H_2O bath temp. Temp. deviation during mashing should be ≤0.5°.)

To test conversion, transfer drop mash to one cavity of porcelain plate and add drop 0.02*N* I soln, **10.105(b)**; conversion is complete when test drop and I soln give yellow soln. Report time of conversion in periods: <15 min, 15–30, 30–45, 45–60, incomplete at 60 min. Cool, filter as in **10.108(c)**, and det. sp gr and corresponding ext as in **10.108(d)** and **(e)**.

10.137 ***Calculation***

Total ext = $P \times (800 + M$ in 60 g malt $+ M$ in 40 g sample$)/(100 - P)$,

where P = ext from Plato's table, **52.009**, and M = % moisture.

Ext in sample = (total ext − ext in 60 g malt) × 100/40.

Enzyme Method for Corn Grits (21)
Official Final Action

10.138 ***Reagents***

(a) *Enzyme mixture.*—Alpha-amylase and malt diastase, "Special for Analytical Purposes" (Wallerstein Co., Travenol Laboratories, Inc., Morton Grove, IL 60053). Mix in proportions 1+4.

(b) *Iodine soln.*—0.02*N*. *See* **10.105(b)**.

10.139 ***Apparatus***

(a) *Wiley or other mill.*—For fine grinding, equipped with 1 mm (openings) sieve (No. 18 or similar).

(b) *Other apparatus.*—Same as for **10.106**, except **(a)**, **(b)**, and **(e)**.

10.140 ***Determination***

Preparation of corn grits for mashing.—Grind enough grits to yield 36 g grist passing thru 1 mm sieve openings (collect 72 g if detn is to be made in duplicate). Prep. addnl 24 g if single detns of moisture, oil, protein, and ash are to be made.

Mashing procedure.—Weigh, into mash beaker, 35 ±0.05 g ground corn grits and 0.5±0.05 g enzyme mixt. Mix dry ingredients, add 200 mL H_2O at 46°, and mix well with glass rod. Mark liq. level on beaker wall. Place mash beaker on wire gauze over flame. With const stirring, bring contents to bp within 15 min and boil gently 30 min, avoiding burning, spattering, and excessive frothing. During boiling, dil. contents to original vol. every 15 min with boiling H_2O.

Cool to 46° and add 2.5±0.05 g enzyme mixt. Mix well to disperse mixt. thoroly and to prevent formation of lumps. Wash down inside walls of beaker with rubber policeman and little H_2O.

Promptly place mash beaker in mashing app. contg H_2O previously heated to 46°, insert thermometer in beaker, and start stirrers. Starting at 45°, raise mash temp. 1°/min to 70°. Add 100 mL H_2O previously heated to 70–71°. Hold mash 30 min at 70°. Do not let temp. deviations during mashing exceed 0.5°. (All temps are *mash* temps, not H_2O bath temps.)

Conversion.—Using ca 3 mm diam. glass rod, transfer 1 drop mash to cavity of porcelain spot test plate and test with 1 drop 0.02*N* I. Judge color exactly 2 min after addn. Make spot test every 15 min after mash temp. has reached 70°. Conversion is complete when I produces only yellow color with mash. Report conversion time in periods of <15 min, 15–30, or incomplete in 30 min.

Cooling and filtration.—After 30 min at 70°, cool and filter mash as in **10.108(c)**.

Determination of specific gravity.—*See* **10.108(d)**. Obtain Plato value of ext corresponding to its sp gr from **52.009**.

Enzyme extract blank.—Det. ext value of enzyme reagent by carrying 3.0 g enzyme mixt., without ground corn grits, thru mashing operation as above. Omit conversion tests. Cool, filter, and det. Plato value of filtrate from its sp gr as above.

Make single ext detn for each lot of enzyme mixt.

10.141 ***Calculations***

% Ext in corn grits, as-is,

$$= \left[\frac{Pg(830 + 0.7M - 2D)}{100 - Pe} - EE\right] \times \frac{100}{70}$$

GE, dry basis, % = GE, as-is × 100/(100 − M),

where M = % moisture in grits sample, D = g enzyme reagent mixt. used, Pe = g ext in 100 g enzyme blank filtrate (°Plato), Pg = g ext in 100 g grits mash filtrate (°Plato), and EE = ext added with enzyme reagents mixt. = $Pe(900 - 2D)/(100 - Pe)$.

Report % ext in corn grits to nearest 0.1%.

10.142 Crude Fat or Ether Extract—Official Final Action

See **7.056**.

10.143 Protein—Official Final Action

See **2.057**. Multiply results by 6.25.

10.144 Ash—Official Final Action

See **14.006**.

10.145 Crude Fiber—Official Final Action

See **7.061–7.065**.

HOPS

10.146 Sampling—Official Final Action

(Oregon sampler, Bates divider, and sampling procedure are described in "Hop Inspection Manual Covering the Determination of Leaves and Stems and Seeds in Hops," Instruction No. 918(GR)-1, available from Federal Grain Inspection Service, Standardization Div., US Dept. of Agriculture, 1400 Independence Ave SW, Washington, DC 20250.)

(a) *Unpressed hops.*—Draw equal portions from 5 or 10 different parts of heap, from surface as well as from different depths, until ca 200 g is obtained. Place sample in suitable container such as tin can having screw- or friction-type cover, moisture-proof plastic bags, or jars.

(b) *Baled hops.*—Use Oregon sampling device or sharp knife to cut 200 g samples from ≥10% of bales in shipment <100 bales and sq root of number of bales if >100, avoiding sampling at press seam. Place each bale sample in sep. container. (If chem. tests are to be made, store in tin cans having friction or screw tops, not cartons, paper bags, wrapping paper, or wooden boxes.) Take sufficient equal amt from each bale sample so that total of 100 g is combined in one composite sample. (Use of Bates divider gives most accurate results.)

10.147 Physical Examination (*22*)—Official Final Action

(**a**) *Leaves and stems.*—With tweezers or forceps, pick out stems and leaves from 20±0.01 g sample. Det. wt leaves and stems to 1 decimal place. Use remainder of sample for seed detn, if required.

(**b**) *Size and condition of cones.*—Report size according to following classification:

	Length, Inches
Large	2¼–3
Medium	1¼–2
Small	¾–1

Report condition of cones as unbroken, partly broken, much broken.

(**c**) *Lupulin.*—Break 10 cones into longitudinal halves and examine lupulin grains thereby exposed in good light, preferably daylight, as to amt, color, and condition. Report amt as plentiful, fairly plentiful, scarce. Report color as lemon-yellow, orange-yellow, brownish. Report condition as sticky, fairly sticky, not sticky.

(**d**) *Seeds.*—Dry portion remaining from leaf and stem detn, or sep. 20 g sample, in oven 3–6 hr at >100° or 2 hr at 114–116° (long enough to eliminate stickiness). (If rapid drying is necessary, place sample in 60 cm (2′) sq muslin cloth, immerse in bowl of MeOH or trichloroethylene 1 min, press out excess liq. by hand, using rubber gloves for protection, and spread cloth contg hops on screen to dry in air or over steam radiator. *Caution: See* **51.040**.)

Fold portions of the dried hops in dry sq of muslin and rub between hands to crush petals completely; then empty finely pulverized material onto 4 × 20 wire mesh screen to sep. petal substance. Continue this process until portion left on screen consists mainly of seeds and rachillae; sep. these by rolling seeds off large sheet of sandpaper into tared dish, weigh, and report % by wt to 1 decimal place.

(**e**) *Color and luster.*—Det. color and luster on whole cones and refer findings to predominating character of sample. Report color as greenish-yellow, yellowish-green, pale green, olive-green, dark green. Describe presence of amts of differently colored cones as: small, medium, or large amt of ______ cones present, using appropriate color terminology, such as brownish, reddish, etc.

(**f**) *Aroma.*—Rub several cones between hands. Report odor as aromatic, mildly aromatic, abnormal. Use term flowery to describe exceptionally fine aroma. Use proper designations, such as musty, cheesy, etc., to describe abnormal odors.

10.148 Aphids—Official First Action

See **44.009–44.011**.

10.149 Preparation of Sample for Chemical Analysis Official Final Action

Grind hop samples immediately before analysis. Let samples stored in refrigerator come to room temp. before grinding.

Grind 50–75 g sample in No. 2 or 72 Universal food chopper, using 12-tooth cutter. Discard first 5 or 10 g. Place polyethylene bag over discharge of chopper so that hops pass directly into bag. Pass hops evenly and slowly thru grinder, taking care to avoid choking orifices so as to prevent undue heating of hops. Thoroly mix ground portion into homogeneous mass and store in air-tight container in cool, dark place. (In some cases definite amts of ground portions from several samples may be mixed together, and analyses made, in duplicate, on mixed portion.)

For accurate results in analysis for resins, detn must be completed on same day as grinding, since resins are subject to oxidn.

10.150 Moisture—Official Final Action

Use one of following methods which are listed in order of accuracy:

(1) Me cyclohexane or *n*-heptane distn method with 10.00 g sample, **7.004–7.005**.

(2) Vac. drying 3 hr at 60° at 560–580 mm (22–23″) Hg, **7.003**.

(3) Drying 1 hr at 103–104°, **10.102–10.104**.

For (2) and (3) use 2.5 g ground sample in 55 mm weighing bottle or Al dish, or 5 g ground sample in 70 mm dish. (Amt of hops and dimensions of dish used are important for accurate results.) Report results in % to 1 decimal place, and state method used.

Alpha and Beta Acids (*23*)—Official Final Action

10.151 ***Reagents***

(**a**) *Methanol.*—Reagent grade. *A* in 1 cm cell <0.060 at 275 nm against H_2O.

(**b**) *Alkaline methanol.*—Add 0.2 mL 6*N* NaOH to 100 mL MeOH, (**a**). Soln must be fresh.

(**c**) *Benzene.*—Reagent grade. *A* in 1 cm cell <0.110 against H_2O at 275 nm when 1 mL is dild to 100 mL with reagent (**b**). (*Caution: See* **51.018**, **51.040**, and **51.045**.)

10.152 ***Apparatus***

Spectrophotometer.—For UV use with 1 cm cells. Calibrate with soln contg 0.0400 g K_2CrO_4/L of 0.05*N* KOH. *See* Definitions of Terms and Explanatory Notes, item (23).

10.153 ***Determination***

Weigh 5±0.001 g ground hops into 250 mL g-s bottle or flat-bottom flask. With pipet, add 100 mL benzene, (**c**). Grease stopper with *Dow Corning high vac. silicone stopcock grease* and stopper tightly. Weigh bottle or flask to nearest 0.1 g and record. Shake vigorously 30 min on mech. shaker and reweigh. If wt loss is >0.2–0.3 g, start new detn. Let flask stand until supernate clears.

Dil. appropriate aliquot of benzene ext with alk. MeOH, (**b**), so that *A* falls within most accurate range of instrument used. For hops contg ca 8% total *alpha* and *beta* acids, pipet 5 mL benzene ext into 50 mL vol. flask and dil. to vol. with alk. MeOH (*Diln I*); then dil. 4.00 mL *Diln I* to 50 mL with alk. MeOH (*Diln II*). For hops of high *alpha* and *beta* acid content, dil. 4.00 mL *Diln I* to 100 mL for *Diln II*.

Det. *A* of *Diln II* at 275, 325, and 355 nm, first setting instrument to 0 *A* with blank prepd by dilg 5 mL benzene, (**c**), with alk. MeOH in same sequence used for samples.

10.154 ***Calculations***

(**a**) % alpha acids $= d \times (-51.56A_{355} + 73.79A_{325} - 19.07A_{275})$, where d = diln factor, and A_{355}, A_{325}, and A_{275} = *A* of *Diln II* at resp. wavelengths. For diln sequence 5 to 50 mL, followed by second diln of 4 to 50 mL,

$$d = (50 \times 50 \times 100 \times 20)/(1000 \times 4 \times 5 \times 1000) = 0.25$$

(**b**) % beta acids $= d \times (55.57A_{355} - 47.59A_{325} + 5.10A_{275})$, where d and A_{355}, A_{325}, and A_{275} have same values as in (**a**).

Report both *alpha* and *beta* acids to 1 decimal place.

BREWING SUGARS AND SIRUPS

10.155 Color and Clarity—Official Final Action

(a) *Clarity.*—Observe degree of clarity of unfiltered "10% soln," **10.156(a)**. Report as clear, slightly hazy, or hazy.

(b) *Color.*—Free "10% soln," **10.156(a)**, from suspended matter and, if possible, from haze by filtration thru dry paper. Det. color as in **10.004**, **10.113**, or **10.114**. Report as color of "10% soln" to nearest 0.1 unit.

10.156 Extract—Official Final Action

(a) *Preparation of "10% soln."*—Accurately weigh ca 50 g well mixed representative sample, dissolve in warm H_2O, transfer quant. to 500 mL vol. flask, and dil. to vol. at 20°. Mix thoroly.

(b) *Determination.*—With suitable pycnometer, det. sp gr of soln at 20/20°, as in **10.107(b)** or **(c)**. Obtain corresponding ext from **52.009**. Calc. % ext in original sample, *E*, from following formula:

$$E = P \times B \times 500/W,$$

where P = ext of dild sample; B = sp gr of dild sample; and W = actual wt (ca 50 g) of sample taken. Report to 1 decimal place.

(c) *Degrees Baumé.*—Obtain degrees Baumé (Modulus 145) equiv. to ext of original sample, **(b)**, from **52.009**.

10.157 Nonextract (Apparent Water) Official Final Action

Obtain by subtracting ext of original sample, **10.156(b)**, from 100.

10.158 Fermentable Extract (*24*)—Official Final Action

(a) *Regular fermentation method.*—Ferment 250 mL "10% soln" of sample, **10.156(a)**, with equiv. of 5 g washed, active brewers compressed yeast 48 hr at 15–25° or until fermentation is complete. In case of refined sugars and sirups, such as corn sirup, add to soln, before fermenting, 0.8 g K_2HPO_4 crystals, 1 g $NH_4H_2PO_4$, and 0.5 g dried yeast ext, stdzd for bacteriological culture media purposes, as nutrients. If such nutrient material needs to be added, redet. ext of the "10% soln" after adding nutrient material, but before adding yeast. Use fermentation flasks equipped with either H_2O, Hg, or acid seals, and shake flasks several times a day during fermentation. When fermentation is complete, filter soln thru dry paper, refiltering first 20–30 mL filtrate. (Filtrate should be clear, but not necessarily brilliant.) Det. real ext in filtrate as in **10.021(a)**, after removal of alcohol.

Use following formulas for calcn:

$$\text{Fermentable ext (ext basis)} = (p - n) \times 100/P;$$
$$\text{Fermentable ext (as-is basis)} = (p - n) \times E/P;$$

where P = ext of "10% soln" before addn of any nutrients; p = ext of "10% soln" before fermentation; n = real ext of "10% soln" after fermentation; and E = ext of original sample, **10.156(b)**.

If nutrients have not been used (as in case of malt sirups), $p = P$, and will have been detd in **10.156(b)**, and no redetn before fermentation is required. Report to 1 decimal place.

(b) *Rapid fermentation method.*—Proceed as in **(a)**, but for 250 mL "10% soln" of sample, **10.156(a)**, use equiv. of 32 g fresh compressed brewers yeast or liq. yeast that has been dewatered by suction on buchner (more precise results are obtained by washing yeast with "10% soln" of sample before final suction filtration). For refined sugars and sirups, use nutrients as in **(a)**. Ferment mixt. at room temp. (20–23°) and stir continuously with 4-blade glass stirrer (ca 5 cm diam.) at 100–120 rpm until fermentation is complete (4–5 hr). Keep stirring and time at min., as evapn can be important variable. Filter, det. real ext, and calc. as in **(a)**.

Yeast autolysis can affect results by contributing solids to fermented liq. Effect may be checked by detg pH of fermented liq., its alcohol content, and calcd original gravity, **10.022**. If pH is high and original gravity is appreciably higher than ext of "10% soln" originally detd, yeast autolysis has probably occurred and detn should be repeated with fresh yeast.

10.159 Protein—Official Final Action

(a) Transfer 25 mL "10% soln," **10.156(a)**, to Kjeldahl digestion flask, and proceed as in **10.045**.

$$\% \text{ protein } (N \times 6.25) \text{ in original as-is sample} = 100 \times (\text{mL } 0.1N\ H_2SO_4 - \text{mL } 0.1N\ \text{NaOH}) \times 0.0014 \times 6.25 \times 500/(25 \times W),$$

where W = actual wt sample used in prepg "10% soln." Report to 2 decimal places.

(b) Det. N as in **31.019**, and calc. protein, using factor N × 6.25.

10.160 Diastatic Power—Official Final Action

(Malt sirups only)

Transfer 10 mL "10% soln," **10.156(a)**, to 100 mL vol. flask and dil. to vol. at 20° with H_2O. Transfer 10 mL "1% soln" so prepd to 250 mL vol. flask, bring to 20°, add 200 mL buffered starch soln at 20°, **10.118(g)**, and proceed as in **10.119**, last 4 sentences in second par., beginning "Mix soln . . ." and ending ". . . mix thoroly." Follow Fehling soln modification, **10.119(a)**.

Calc. on as-is basis according to formula:

$$°\text{Diastatic Power (as-is basis)} = (5000 \times B \times 50)/(V \times V \times W),$$

where V = mL digested starch soln required to reach end point in detn; B = mL digested starch soln required to reach end point in blank; and W = wt sirup used to prep. "10% soln."

10.161 Iodine Reaction for Unconverted Starch Official Final Action

Use "10% soln," **10.156(a)**, and proceed as in **10.044**.

10.162 Acidity—Official Final Action

Transfer 100 mL "10% soln," **10.156(a)**, to suitable beaker or flask and proceed as in **10.033**, second par., or **10.034**, beginning ". . . titr. potentiometrically . . ." Calc. and report results as follows (W = actual wt sample, in g, used to prep. "10% soln"):

(a) In terms of mL 1*N* NaOH/100 g original sample, as-is basis:

$$\text{Acidity} = \text{mL } 0.1N\ \text{NaOH consumed} \times 500/(10 \times W).$$

Report to 1 decimal place.

(b) In terms of "lactic acid" as % original sample, as-is basis:

$$\text{Acidity} = \text{mL } 0.1N\ \text{NaOH consumed} \times 0.009 \times 500/W.$$

Report to 2 decimal places.

10.163 Hydrogen-Ion Activity (pH)—Official Final Action

Using "10% soln," **10.156(a)**, proceed as in **10.035**.

10.164 Ash—Official Final Action

Proceed as in **31.012** or **31.013**.

Total Reducing Sugars (*25*)—Official Final Action

10.165 ***Munson-Walker General Method***

Transfer 50 mL "10% soln," **10.156(a)**, to 250 mL vol. flask. Clarify, if necessary, with alumina cream or neut. $Pb(OAc)_2$ soln only (never basic $Pb(OAc)_2$), and dil. to vol. at 20° with H_2O. Mix thoroly and either centrf. or filter until clear. If $Pb(OAc)_2$ soln was used for clarification, remove excess Pb with dry $Na_2C_2O_4$. Filter, and det. reducing sugars on 10 mL aliquot as in **31.038–31.039**, **31.051**, or **31.060**. Calc. results in terms of invert sugar for invert sirups and sugars; glucose for corn sugars and sirups; and maltose for malt sirups. If character of sample is in doubt, express reducing sugars as glucose.

$$\% \text{ Reducing sugar, as-is} = 25M/W,$$

where M is mg sugar from appropriate column of **52.019**, and W is g sample used to prep. "10% soln."

10.166 ***Lane-Eynon General Volumetric Method***

Dil. 50 mL soln, clarified as in **10.165**, to 100 mL and proceed as in **31.035–31.036**, **31.050**, or **31.059**, referring titer to **52.017** or **52.018**. Calc. results as in **10.165**.

10.167 Glucose—Official Final Action

To 5 mL aliquot of soln prepd as in **10.165**, add 15 mL H_2O and proceed as in **13.052** or **13.055**.

10.168 Other Determinations

See Chapter **31**.

WORT—OFFICIAL FINAL ACTION

10.169 Preparation of Sample

Store 1 gal. wort 12–15 hr at 4–7°; then filter all but last portion of this sample at 4–7° thru paper of types specified in **10.106(f)**. If filtrate is not brilliant after first filtration, return to filter, but do not use filter-aid. (Some worts cannot be filtered brilliantly clear.) To prevent spoiling, keep sample in refrigerator, and if necessary, place in beer bottles and pasteurize. Mix sample well to insure uniformity before removing portion for analysis.

10.170 Specific Gravity

Proceed as in **10.016** or **10.108(d)**. Report to 5 decimal places.

10.171 Viscosity (*3*)

Det. sp gr as in **10.170**. Proceed as in **10.017–10.019**, beginning, "Clean viscometer . . ." and substituting "wort" for "beer."

10.172 Original Extract or Original Gravity

From **52.009**, find ext corresponding to sp gr detd at 20/20°, **10.170**. Report as °Plato (g/100 g) to 2 decimal places.

10.173 Fermentable Extract

(**a**) *Regular method.*—Ferment 250 mL wort with equiv. of 5 g washed, active brewers compressed yeast 48 hr at 15–25°, or until fermentation is complete. Use either H_2O, Hg, or acid seal to prevent evapn. Filter soln and det. real ext in filtrate as in **10.021(a)**, after removal of alcohol.

Calc. % by wt of fermentable ext as in **10.158**. Report to 2 decimal places.

Calc. also real degree of fermentation as in **10.028**. Report to 1 decimal place.

(**b**) *Rapid method.*—(Dets fermentability of worts contg up to ca 14% ext in 4–5 hr within 0.3–0.1% of attenuation limit.)

To 200 mL wort in 400–600 mL glass beaker add 32 g fresh, compressed, washed brewers lager yeast or liq. yeast that has been dewatered by suction on buchner (more precise results are obtained by washing yeast with wort to be pitched before final suction filtration). Keep mixt. at room temp. (20–23°) and stir continuously with glass stirrer until fermentation is complete (4–5 hr). Filter mixt. thru ordinary filter paper, refiltering first 20–30 mL filtrate. (Filtrate should be clear, but not necessarily brilliant.) As evapn can be important variable, keep stirring and time at min. Four-blade glass stirrer (ca 5 cm diam.) operating at 100–120 rpm is satisfactory. Abnormal effects due to autolysis are likely to be indicated by too high pH of final beer and high calcd original gravity compared to actual original gravity. *See* **10.158(b)**.) Det. real ext and calc. as in (**a**).

10.174 Iodine Reaction

See **10.044**.

10.175 Total Acidity

See **10.033** or **10.034**.

10.176 Hydrogen-Ion Activity (pH)

See **10.035**.

10.177 Color

Prep. sample as in **10.169**. If prepd wort has developed haze or sediment that would interfere with detn, clarify by centrfg or filtering without use of filter-aid. Indicate such clarification in report. Det. depth of color of prepd sample as in **10.113** or **10.114**.

10.178 Protein

Prep. sample as in **10.169**. If prepd sample shows sediment, mix thoroly to ensure uniform distribution of sediment before removing portion for analysis. To det. protein in the brilliant wort (free from any haze or sediment), reclarify prepd sample by centrfg or filtering without use of filter-aid. Indicate such clarification in report.

Pipet 25 mL prepd sample, measured at 20°, into 800 mL Kjeldahl flask and proceed as in **10.045**.

Free Amino Nitrogen in Wort (*26*)

10.179 ***Reagents***

(**a**) *Ninhydrin color reagent.*—Dissolve 10.0 g $Na_2HPO_4.12H_2O$, 6.0 g KH_2PO_4, 0.5 g 1,2,3-indantrione.H_2O, and 0.3 g fructose in H_2O, and dil. to 100 mL. pH should be 6.6–6.8. Reagent is stable 2 weeks if kept cold in amber bottle.

(**b**) *Dilution soln.*—Dissolve 2 g KIO_3 in 600 mL H_2O, and add 400 mL alcohol. Store at 5°.

(**c**) *Glycine std solns.*—(*1*) *Stock soln.*—Dissolve 107.2 mg glycine in H_2O, and dil. to 100 mL. Store at 0°. (*2*) *Working soln.*—2 mg amino N/L. Dil. 1.0 mL stock soln to 100 mL with H_2O.

10.180 ***Determination***

(**a**) *Wort.*—Prep. sample as in **10.169**. Dil. 1.0 mL to 100 mL with H_2O. Transfer 2.0 mL dild sample to each of three 16 × 150 mm test tubes. Other dilns may be necessary to obtain 1–3 mg free amino N/L in dild soln.

(**b**) *Calibration std.*—Transfer 2.0 mL glycine working std soln to each of 3 test tubes.

(c) *Blank.*—Transfer 2.0 mL H_2O to each of 3 test tubes.

(d) *Reaction.*—Add 1.0 mL ninhydrin color reagent to each test tube. Place tubes in rack, and stopper all tubes with 15–20 mm glass marbles to reduce evapn. Heat exactly 16 min in boiling H_2O bath, cool 20 min in 20±1° bath, and add 5 mL diln soln. Mix thoroly and det. *A* at 570 nm against H_2O within 30 min.

(e) *Calculations.*—Average *A* readings for each set of triplicates. Subtract av. blank *A* from *A* of samples and of std.

mg Free amino N/L = net *A* of sample soln × 2 × diln/net *A* of std soln

(f) *Example.*—Av. *A* of blank = 0.050; av. *A* of std = 0.490; av. *A* of wort dild 1 to 100 = 0.380.

mg Free amino N/L = (0.380 − 0.050) × 2 × 100/(0.490 − 0.050) = 150.0

Report in whole numbers, i.e., 150 mg free amino N/L.

10.181 Total Reducing Sugars

Prep. sample as in **10.169**. If prepd wort contains appreciable amts of suspended matter, remove by centrfg or filtering. Transfer 50 mL sample to 250 mL vol. flask, dil. to vol. at 20°, and mix thoroly. In general, worts do not require clarification for detn of reducing sugars, but if clarification is necessary, proceed as in **10.165**. Det. reducing sugars in 10 mL of this soln by Munson-Walker method as in **31.060**. Or dil. 50 mL of this soln with H_2O to 100 mL and use Lane-Eynon method as in **31.059**. Express results as % maltose.

YEAST

LIQUID AND PRESSED YEAST

Sampling (27)—Procedure

10.182 ***Apparatus***

Dry, wide-mouth 1 L containers with suitable cover or dry Mason jars with covers are satisfactory for collecting samples. Jar should hold ca twice vol. of original sample.

10.183 ***Collecting Primary Sample***

(a) *Bottom fermenting yeast.*—(*1*) From small fermenters from which the yeast is collected in cans or tubs, collect at least five 100 mL portions of the yeast slurry at intervals as it is forced out thru bung hole into brink. (*2*) From large tanks from which the yeast is removed by pump, collect 5–10 100 mL portions of the yeast slurry from sampling cock at regular intervals on discharge side of yeast pump.

(b) *Top fermenting yeast.*—Push aside upper fluffy layer of yeast and take portion from under layer. Collect at least five 100 mL portions from various parts of tank. (For routine work, top fermenting yeast is usually sampled after it has been skimmed into yeast buggy. Mix thoroly before sampling.)

(c) *Any liquid yeast from small tanks or tubs.*—Mix contents of tub thoroly to uniform consistency, taking care to blend in heavier deposits on bottom of vessel and to remove gases. Take ≥500 mL sample from this mixt.

(d) *Pressed yeast.*—Remove portions from different parts of cake—from surface as well as from center— and collect ca 150 g in 1 L beaker. Weigh to nearest 0.1 g. Prep. slurry by adding H_2O at rate of ca 3 parts H_2O to 1 part pressed yeast. Again weigh to nearest 0.1 g. With stirring rod, break up yeast portions and stir until liq. suspension is completely uniform.

10.184 ***Preservation of Samples***

To prevent changes in analytical results due to autolysis and fermentation, proceed with examination immediately after sampling. Keep sample at 2° or below.

10.185 ***Preparation of Laboratory Sample***

Mix primary composite sample thoroly and transfer working amt to sep. container. If lumps or particles of trub are present, pass thru sieve entire bulk sample of liq. yeast, which should amt to ≥500 mL if yeast requires screening, or slurry prepd from ca 150 g pressed yeast. Make sure all lumps and particles are broken up and forced thru sieve. Recover, by scraping, any liq. or solids adhering to sieve, and reincorporate them with sieved sample. Mix well by stirring.

Total Solids

(When reporting total solids, state whether alcohol method, **10.188**, or 16 hr drying method, **10.191**, was used.)

Alcohol Method—Official Final Action

10.186 ***Apparatus***

(a) *Sieve.*—Approx. 100-mesh.

(b) *Moisture oven.*—*See* **10.102(b)**.

(c) *Weighing dish.*—Glass or Al, ≥65 mm id, with cover, and glass stirring rod of such length that it fits within covered dish.

10.187 ***Reagents***

(a) *Alcohol.*—Pure alcohol or MeOH, or alcohol denatured with completely volatile liq., such as SDF Nos. 1, 2-B, 3-A, 12-A, 13-A, 23-A.

(b) *Sand.*—Use clean, sharp sand. Wash with H_2O and dry overnight at 105°. Cool in desiccator. Keep in closed container. Loss of wt of 5 g of this sand when dried 3 hr at 105° must be ≤0.005 g.

10.188 ***Determination***

Place ca 5 g dry sand in weighing dish. Weigh dish together with sand, cover, and stirring rod. Transfer to weighing dish ca 10 g well mixed liq. yeast or yeast slurry from pressed yeast, cover, and weigh to nearest mg. Remove cover and add 5 mL alcohol. Mix thoroly with stirring rod. Drop rod into weighing dish. Dry 3 hr (±2 min) at 105°. Cover, cool in desiccator, and weigh.

For liq. yeast, calc. drying loss of aliquot used as % and report total solids to 1 decimal place. For pressed yeast calc. according to following formula:

$$\% \text{ total solids} = D \times S \times 100/(W \times P),$$

where P = wt (g) pressed yeast used for prepg slurry; S = total wt (g) yeast slurry; W = wt (g) slurry aliquot before drying; and D = wt (g) slurry aliquot after drying.

16 Hour Drying Method (28)—Official First Action

10.189 ***Apparatus***

(a) *Drying oven.*—Forced-draft or convection type, regulated at 100±2°.

(b) *Moisture dish.*—Diam. 50–65 mm, depth 20 mm, Al, with tight-fitting cover.

(c) *Glass rods.*—3 mm diam. and of such length to fit into covered moisture dish. Fire-polish both ends.

10.190 ***Standardization of Oven***

Adjust oven to 98–102° after operation ≥30 min with door closed. Then note and record temp. at 10 min intervals for 2 hr. If temp. at any time is <98° or >102°, replace thermostat.

Accurately weigh (to 0.1 mg) ca 5 g dried yeast into weighed moisture dish previously dried 1 hr at 100±2° and cooled in desiccator, **10.192(b)**. Dry in oven 16 hr at 100±2°, cover, transfer to desiccator, and weigh soon after it reaches room temp. Redry 2 hr, cool, and weigh. If moisture has increased by 0.1%, oven is not operating properly and should be serviced.

10.191 ***Determination***

Dry moisture dish and stirring rod in oven 1 hr at 100±2°. Cover, transfer to desiccator, and weigh to 1 mg soon after it reaches room temp. Remove cover, transfer to dish ca 10 g well mixed liq. yeast or yeast slurry from pressed yeast, cover, and reweigh. Spread evenly with stirring rod and place rod in dish. Transfer dish, with cover loose, to oven and dry 16 hr at 100±2°. Cover, transfer to desiccator, and weigh soon after attaining room temp. Calc. drying loss and report total solids as in **10.188**.

DRIED YEAST

Total Solids—Official Final Action

Vacuum Oven Method (29)

10.192 ***Apparatus***

(**a**) *Metal dish.*—Diam. ca 55 mm, ht ca 15 mm, provided with inverted slip-in cover fitting tightly on inside. Or, diam. ca 65 mm, ht ca 20 mm, provided with slip-over cover fitting tightly on outside.

(**b**) *Air-tight desiccator.*—$CaCl_2$, reignited CaO, and Drierite are satisfactory drying agents.

(**c**) *Vacuum oven.*—Connected with pump or vac. system capable of maintaining pressure ≤50 mm Hg, and provided with thermometer passing into oven with bulb near samples. Connect H_2SO_4 gas-drying bottle to oven to admit dry air when releasing vac.

10.193 ***Determination***

Accurately weigh ca 2 g well mixed sample in covered dish, previously dried at 98–100°, cooled in desiccator, and weighed soon after attaining room temp. Loosen cover (do not remove) and heat 5 hr at 98–100° at pressure ≤50 mm Hg. Admit dry air into oven to bring to atm. pressure. Immediately tighten cover on dish, transfer to desiccator, and weigh soon after it reaches room temp.

Air Oven Method (30)

10.194 ***Determination***

Accurately weigh ca 2 g well mixed sample in covered dish, **10.192(a)**, previously dried at 100±1°, cooled in desiccator, and weighed soon after it reaches room temp. Loosen cover (do not remove) and heat 16 hr at 100±1°. Tighten cover, transfer to desiccator, and weigh soon after it reaches room temp.

10.195 Protein—Official Final Action

Proceed as in **2.057**, using 0.5 g sample. Digest 30 min after soln clears. % Protein = %N × 6.25.

BREWERS' GRAINS* (*31*)
OFFICIAL FINAL ACTION

10.196 Sampling

(**a**) *Wet brewers' grains.*—Using scoop, collect numerous small samples at uniform intervals during emptying of tub, so that at end of operation composite sample of 25–30 lb (11–14 kg) is obtained in clean, dry bucket. From mash filters, collect numerous small samples in similar manner at equal time intervals from grain conveyor. Mix thoroly and quarter grains carefully so as to obtain representative sample of 3–4 lb (1.4–1.8 kg). Place reduced sample in suitable container with screw- or friction-type cover, add few drops of toluene as preservative, close tightly, and refrigerate.

(**b**) *Dry brewers' grains.*—*See* **10.092**. Take great care in sampling dry brewers' grains for analysis, particularly for feed, as it is very difficult to obtain truly representative sample. Because brewers' grains are composed of large husks and small, heavy particles, there is usually difference in composition at different levels of container.

If brewers' grains are in sacks, sample ≥2% of the sacks, using trier as long as ht of sacks. Quarter sample down to ca 250 g (0.5 lb) for laboratory sample.

If brewers' grains are in car, unsacked, it is practically impossible to obtain representative sample because of segregation at bottom of fine heavy material, which is higher in protein than lighter material at top.

Store sample in refrigerator pending laboratory analysis. On each sample container show date of sampling; name of company owning grains at time of sampling; and brew, lot, car, or ref. number or letter for identification. Before making analysis, mix grains thoroly.

10.197 Preliminary Drying (Wet Brewers' Grains)

Accurately weigh (±0.1 g) ca 1 kg quartered wet brewers' grains on weighed, shallow, galvanized Fe or Al tray so that layer is ≤6 mm thick. After spreading, moisten grains with little toluene to inhibit fermentation during drying. Dry in oven at 55–60°, or overnight in air by means of fan and heater, until grains appear air-dry. Note accurately (±0.1 g) wt dried grains and store in moisture-proof container. Thoroly mix dried sample and finely grind 100 g, as in **10.108**. Keep ground portion in moisture-tight container.

10.198 Moisture

(**a**) *On sample after preliminary drying (when available and soluble extracts are determined).*—Use 5–10 g accurately weighed and ground sample and proceed as in **10.104**. Calc. % moisture in dried grains (W). Calc. % moisture, M, in original wet grains by following formula:

$$M = [(W \times D) + 100(G - D)]/G,$$

where G = wt wet grains before preliminary drying, D = wt wet grains after preliminary drying, and W = % moisture in grains after preliminary drying.

(**b**) *On sample in wet condition (when only soluble extract is determined).*—Use ca 15 g sample, accurately weighed into 70 mm Al dish, and dry first at temp. <60° until air-dry; then dry addnl 3 hr as in **10.104**.

(**c**) *On dry brewers' grains.*—Proceed as in (**a**) and calc. % moisture.

* For examination of brewers' grains for feeding purposes *see* Chap. **7**.

Available Extract

10.199 *Wet Brewers' Grains*

(**a**) *Apparatus.*—Mash beakers and counter wts, mashing app., filter paper, funnels, flasks, pycnometers, emptying device, and H_2O bath. *See* **10.106**.

(**b**) *Preparation of sample.—See* **10.197**. *Preparation of finely ground malt.—See* **10.108**.

(**c**) *Mashing procedure.—See* **10.136**. Proceed as for flaked corn and flaked rice.

(**d**) *Cooling and filtration.—See* **10.108**(**c**).

(**e**) *Specific gravity.—See* **10.108**(**d**). Det. corresponding Plato values from **52.009**.

(**f**) *Calculation.*—Use following formulas:

Total ext = $P \times$ (800 + W in 60 g malt + W in 40 g dried grains)/(100 − P),

where P = g ext in 100 g wort (Plato), and W = moisture (g).

% Available ext in wet grains, dry basis = [(E in mixt. − E in 60 g malt) × 10,000]/40(100 − M of dried grains),

where E = g ext, and M = % moisture.

% Available ext in wet grains, as-is basis = (available E, dry basis) × (100 − M of wet grains)/100,

where E = % ext, and M = % moisture.

10.200 *Dry Brewers' Grains*

Preparation of sample.—Grind finely 100 g sample and proceed as in **10.199**. Calc. ext as in **10.137**.

Soluble Extract (Wet Brewers' Grains)

10.201 *On Sample After Preliminary Drying*

(**a**) *Mashing procedure.*—"Mash in" 25±0.05 g unground sample with 350 mL H_2O at 70° in mash beaker. Place mash beakers in mashing app., **10.106**(**c**) and (**d**), contg H_2O previously heated to 70–71°, and set stirrers in motion. Hold mash 60 min at mash temp. of 70±0.5°.

(**b**) *Cooling and filtering.—See* **10.108**(**c**). Dil. mash to 425 g.

(**c**) *Specific gravity.—See* **10.108**(**d**). Det. corresponding Plato values from **52.009**.

(**d**) *Calculation.*—Use following formulas:

% Sol. ext in wet grain, dry basis = P(M of dried grains + 1600) × 100/(100 − P)(100 − M of dried grains).

% Sol. ext in wet grains, as-is basis = (E, dry basis)(100 − M of wet grains)/100,

where P = g ext in 100 g wort (Plato, **52.009**), E = % ext, and M = % moisture.

10.202 *On Sample in Wet Condition*

Mashing method.—Using 100±0.05 g well mixed and quartered brewers' grains and 300 mL H_2O at 71°, proceed as in **10.201**. Dil. mash to 450 g.

Calculation.—Use following formulas:

% Sol. ext, as-is basis = $P(M + 350)/(100 - P)$;

% Sol. ext, dry basis = $E \times 100/(100 - M)$;

where P = g ext in 100 g wort (Plato, **52.009**), M = % moisture content, and E = % sol. ext, as-is.

Report sol. ext on as-is and dry basis in %, to 1 decimal place.

10.203 Soluble Extract (Dry Brewers' Grains)

Proceed as in **10.201**, but use following formulas:

% Sol. ext, as-is basis = $P(1600 + M)/(100 - P)$;

% Sol. ext, dry basis = $E \times 100/(100 - M)$;

where P = g ext in 100 g wort (Plato, **52.009**), E = % sol. ext, as-is, and M = % H_2O in dry brewers' grains.

SELECTED REFERENCES

(*1*) ASBC, Methods of Analysis, 7th Ed., 1976, The Society, 3340 Pilot Knob Rd, St. Paul, MN 55121: Beer 10-A and B.
(*2*) ASBC: Beer 27-I; JAOAC **49**, 502(1966).
(*3*) ASBC: Proceedings 29(1974); 86(1975).
(*4*) ASBC: Beer 4C.
(*5*) ASBC: Beer 8.
(*6*) ASBC: Proceedings 183(1962); 205(1963); 269(1964).
(*7*) ASBC: Beer 13B.
(*8*) ASBC: Beer 22.
(*9*) ASBC: Proceedings 225(1970); 324(1971); 135(1972); JAOAC **59**, 678(1976).
(*10*) ASBC: Beer 19A.
(*11*) ASBC: Beer 19B.
(*12*) ASBC: Beer 18.
(*13*) ASBC: Beer 21.
(*14*) ASBC: Beer 23.
(*15*) ASBC: Beer 28.
(*16*) ASBC: Malt 2A.
(*17*) ASBC: Malt 5.
(*18*) ASBC: Malt 6.
(*19*) ASBC: Malt 7.
(*20*) ASBC: Adjunct Materials; Cereals 2.
(*21*) ASBC: Adjunct Materials; Cereals 5B.
(*22*) ASBC: Hops 2.
(*23*) ASBC: Hops 6A.
(*24*) ASBC: Adjunct Materials; Sugars and Syrups 7.
(*25*) ASBC: Adjunct Materials; Sugars and Syrups 14.
(*26*) ASBC: Proceedings 34(1974); 88(1975).
(*27*) ASBC: Yeast 1.
(*28*) JAOAC **44**, 394(1961).
(*29*) JAOAC **39**, 738(1956).
(*30*) JAOAC **40**, 446(1957).
(*31*) ASBC: Brewers' Grains 1–6.

11. Beverages: Wines

11.001 Physical Examination—Procedure

Note and record following: (*a*) Whether container is "bottle full"; (*b*) appearance, whether bright or turbid and presence of sediment; (*c*) condition when opened, whether still, gaseous, or carbonated; (*d*) color and depth of color; (*e*) odor, whether vinous, foreign, or acetous; and (*f*) taste, whether dry, sweet, vinous, foreign, or acetous.

Immediately det. sp gr and those ingredients that are subject to change, such as alcohol, sugars, and acids.

11.002 Specific Gravity—Official Final Action

Det. sp gr at 20/20° by pycnometer as in **9.011**, or by small, accurately graduated hydrometer.

Color in White Wines (*1*)
Official Final Action

11.003 ***Apparatus and Reagents***

(a) *White wine colorimeter.*—Double beam filter photometer utilizing W incandescent lamp with Corning 5-61 high pass filter, Se photocells, 1" path test and ref. cells, and zero set cell for calibration. Combination of responses of photocell and filter approximates monochromatic peak at 430 nm. Available from Huggins Engineering Co., 2070 Walsh Ave, Santa Clara, CA 95050.

(b) *Potassium chromate std soln.*—0.0002059*M*. Dissolve 0.0400 g K_2CrO_4 primary std (J. T. Baker Chemical Co., No. 3058) in 0.05*N* KOH and dil. to 1 L with 0.05*N* KOH.

11.004 ***Determination***

Let instrument warm up 2 hr. Stdze with K_2CrO_4 soln according to manufacturer's instructions. %*T* should be reproducible to ±0.1%.

Fill ref. and test cells with H_2O, and place both in colorimeter. Set indicator knob to zero, and null colorimeter by adjusting zero set knob. Remove test cell and replace with zero set cell. Null meter by adjusting indicator. Indicator should read ca 98.5 on duplicate tests. Repeat each hr or after every 10–15 samples.

With zero set cell in place, set indicator to value (ca 98.5) detd above. Null meter with zero set knob. Replace zero set cell with test cell contg wine sample. Null meter by adjusting indicator. Read %*T* on indicator.

Alcohol

11.005 ***By Volume from Specific Gravity***
Official Final Action

Measure 100 mL sample into 300–500 mL distn flask, noting temp., and add 50 mL H_2O. Attach flask to vertical condenser by means of bent tube, distil almost 100 mL, and dil. to 100 mL at same temp. (Foaming, which sometimes occurs, especially with young wines, may be prevented by adding small amt of antifoam material.) For wines that contain abnormal amt of HOAc, neutze exactly with 1*N* NaOH soln (calcd from acidity, **11.037**) before proceeding with distn (unnecessary for wines of normal taste and odor). Proceed as in **9.011**, at room temp. if desired, and obtain corresponding % alcohol by vol. from **52.003**.

11.006 ***By Volume from Refraction (Rapid Method)***
Official Final Action

Det. immersion refractometer reading of distillate obtained in **11.005** and find corresponding % alcohol from **52.004**.

11.007 ***By Weight—Official Final Action***

From **52.005**, obtain % alcohol by wt in distillate corresponding to % alcohol by vol., multiply by sp gr of distillate, and divide by sp gr of sample.

By Dichromate Oxidation (2)
Official Final Action

11.008 ***Principle***

Sample is steam distd into acidified $K_2Cr_2O_7$ soln of known vol. and concn. Oxidn of EtOH to HOAc is completed by heating. Unreacted dichromate is detd by titrn with std $Fe(NH_4)_2(SO_4)_2$ soln, using *o*-phenanthroline as indicator.

11.009 ***Apparatus***

Micro Kjeldahl apparatus.—With gas micro-burner. *See* Fig. **11:01**. (Glassware available from Scott Laboratories, Inc., PO Box 3576, San Rafael, CA 94901.)

11.010 ***Reagents***

(a) *Potassium dichromate soln.*—Add 325 mL H_2SO_4 to ca 400 mL H_2O in 1 L vol. flask. Mix and cool to 80–90°. Add 33.768 g $K_2Cr_2O_7$ (primary std). Dissolve, cool, and dil. to vol. with H_2O at 20°.

(b) *Ferrous ammonium sulfate soln.*—Dissolve 135.5 g $FeSO_4(NH_4)_2SO_4.6H_2O$ in ca 500 mL H_2O in 1 L vol. flask. Add 30 mL H_2SO_4. Dil. to vol. with H_2O at 20°.

(c) *1,10-Phenanthroline ferrous sulfate indicator.*— Dissolve 0.695 g $FeSO_4.7H_2O$ in ca 50 mL H_2O, add 1.485 g *o*-phenanthroline.H_2O, and dil. to 100 mL with H_2O. (Prepd soln available from G. Frederick Smith Chemical Co.)

11.011 ***Determination***

See Fig. **11:01**. To begin distn, boil H_2O in steam generator. Open steam trap discharge. Turn 3-way stopcock so that steam from trap vents thru side tube and distg bulb is closed. Place 25 mL $K_2Cr_2O_7$ soln in 50 mL erlenmeyer under condenser with tip below surface of soln. Close sample stopcock and place small amt H_2O in sample funnel. Distg bulb is empty and micro-burner is not lighted.

Transfer 1 mL samples as follows: Fill 1 mL pipet (class A) slightly over mark, and wipe excess wine from exterior. Hold pipet vertical; with tip touching inside neck of sample bottle, drain to mark. Drain pipet completely into sample funnel. Open sample stopcock to drain sample into still; then reclose. Add small amt H_2O to funnel, drain into still, and rinse with H_2O until distg bulb is half filled. Place H_2O in funnel to ensure seal.

Close steam trap discharge with pinch clamp. Open 3-way stopcock, permitting steam to enter bulb while vent is closed. Light micro-burner. Distil until receiving flask contains ca 40 mL, lower flask, and rinse outside of condenser outlet into flask with H_2O. Stopper flask and immerse to shoulder in 60±2° H_2O.

Admit cold H_2O into steam generator to flush contents of distg bulb into steam trap. Refill bulb with H_2O, flush again, open trap

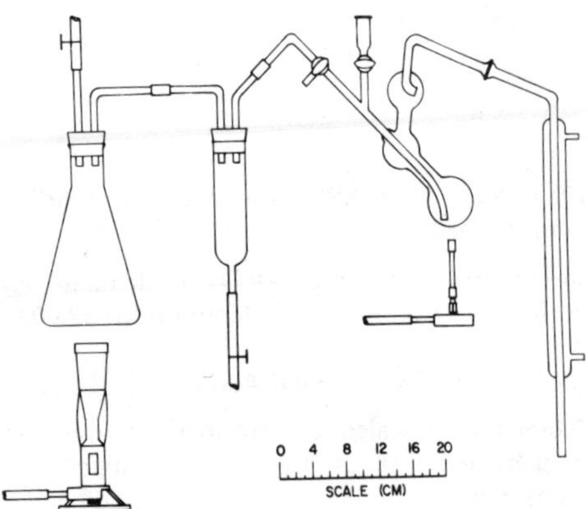

FIG. 11:01—Distillation apparatus for chemical determination of alcohol in wine

discharge, and vent 3-way stopcock. App. is now ready for next sample.

Remove flask from bath after 20–25 min. Rinse contents into 500 mL flask with H_2O. Titr. with $FeSO_4(NH_4)_2SO_4$ soln to almost clear green in front of daylight fluorescent light, add 3 drops indicator, and titr. to end point (change is from blue-green to brown) (V mL).

Since $FeSO_4(NH_4)_2SO_4$ soln is slowly oxidized by air, perform blank detn daily by titrg 25 mL $K_2Cr_2O_7$ (V' mL). Discard $FeSO_4(NH_4)_2SO_4$ soln that has been standing in buret >30 min.

Calc. % alcohol by vol. = 25.00 − (25 × V/V').

11.012 ★ Glycerol in Dry Wines ★ Official Final Action

Glycerol is isolated from other org. material and detd by oxdn with $K_2Cr_2O_7$ or by direct weighing. *See* **11.010**, 12th ed.

11.013 ★ Glycerol in Sweet Wines ★ Official Final Action

Glycerol is isolated from other org. material and detd by oxdn with $K_2Cr_2O_7$ or by direct weighing. *See* **11.011**, 12th ed.

11.014 Extract—Official Final Action

(**a**) *By specific gravity of dealcoholized wine.*—Calc. sp gr of dealcoholized wine, $D = S + 1 - S'$, where S = sp gr of sample, **11.002**, and S' = sp gr of alc. distillate, **11.005**.

From **52.008**, det. % by wt of ext in dealcoholized wine corresponding to value of D. This figure × value of D = g ext/100 mL wine.

(**b**) *By evaporation.*—(*1*) *In dry wines, extract content less than 3 g/100 mL.*—In 75 mL flat-bottom Pt dish, ca 85 mm diam., evap. 50 mL sample on H_2O bath to sirupy consistency. Heat residue 2–5 hr in drying oven at 100°, cool in desiccator, and weigh as soon as room temp. is reached.

(*2*) *In sweet wines.*—If ext content is 3–6 g/100 mL, treat 25 mL sample as in (*1*). If ext is >6 g/100 mL, accept result obtained as in (**a**), and attempt no gravimetric detn because of inaccurate results obtained by drying fructose at high temp.

11.015 Nonsugar Solids (Sugar-Free Extract)—Official Final Action

Subtract amt of reducing sugars before inversion, **11.016**, plus sucrose, if present, from ext, **11.014**.

★ Surplus method—*see* inside front cover.

11.016 Reducing Sugars—Official Final Action

(**a**) *Dry wines.*—Place 200 mL sample in porcelain dish, exactly neutze with 1*N* NaOH, calcg amt required from acidity, **11.037**, and evap. to ca 50 mL. Transfer to 200 mL vol. flask, add enough neut. $Pb(OAc)_2$ soln, **31.021(d)**, to clarify, dil. to vol. with H_2O, shake, and filter thru folded paper. Remove Pb with dry K oxalate and det. reducing sugars as in **31.038**.

(**b**) *Sweet wines.*—Approximate sugar content by subtracting 2 from ext, **11.014**, and use such amt of sample that aliquot taken for Cu reduction contains ≤240 mg invert sugar. Proceed as in (**a**).

11.017 Sucrose—Official Final Action

(**a**) *By reducing sugars before and after inversion.*—Proceed as in **9.112(b)**.

(**b**) ★ *By polarization.*★—*See* **11.015(b)**, 12th ed.

11.018 ★ Commercial Glucose—Procedure ★

By polarization. *See* **11.016**, 12th ed.

11.019 Ash—Official Final Action

Proceed as in **31.012** or **31.013**, using residue from 50 mL sample. Char carefully (decrepitation), and ash at ≤550°.

11.020 Alkalinity of Ash—Official Final Action

Evap. 10 mL sample to dryness in Pt dish and ash at 550°. If solid content of sample is high, it may be necessary to moisten ext with ether and to burn off carefully over flame to prevent spattering. If any C remains, add few mL H_2O, dry, and again heat to 550°. To ash add 10 mL 0.1*N* H_2SO_4, bring acid in contact with all of the ash, and fill dish ca ¾ full of boiling H_2O. Cool, add 4 drops *Me purple* (available from Fisher Scientific Co., Cat. No. SO-I-9) or Me orange, and immediately titr. excess acid with 0.1*N* NaOH. Express alky as mL 0.1*N* H_2SO_4 required to neutze ash from 100 mL sample.

11.021 Copper—Official Final Action

See **9.029–9.035**.

Iron—Official Final Action

11.022 *Atomic Absorption Method*

Pipet 20 mL 40° proof wine into 200 mL vol. flask, add 88 mL 95% alcohol from graduate, and mix well. Dil. almost to vol. with H_2O and mix well. Let soln reach room temp., dil. to 200 mL with H_2O, and mix well. Proceed as in **9.038**. Multiply results by 10 to obtain ppm Fe in original wine sample.

11.023 *TPTZ Colorimetric Method*

Prep. sample as in **11.022**, and proceed as in **9.042**.

Potassium (*3*)—Official Final Action

11.024 *Reagents and Apparatus*

(**a**) *Potassium std solns.*—Dry reagent grade KCl at 100° overnight and dil. 1.9068 g to 1 L with H_2O. Dil. 10 mL of this soln to 100 mL and further dil. 1, 2, 4, 6, 8, and 10 mL of dild soln to 100 mL to make std solns contg, resp., 1, 2, 4, 6, 8, and 10 ppm K in H_2O. Store std solns in clean, dry polyethylene bottles.

(**b**) *Flame spectrophotometer.*—Beckman Model DU with oxy-hydrogen flame and photomultiplier accessory, or equiv. instrument.

11.025 ***Determination***

Dil. 10 mL sample 50–200 times with H_2O if necessary to fall within $\%T$ range of stds. Set instrument, fill sample cup, and burn. Read $\%T$ 3–5 times at 740 nm (T_b), 768 nm ($T_{max.}$), and 790 nm (T_a). ($T_{max.}$ = T at max. emission, T_b = T before max., T_a = T after max.) Det. $\%T$ for 1–10 ppm K std solns immediately after sample under same conditions, and plot "unit rise" against ppm K to obtain "semipermanent" calibration curve:

For stds: $T_{max.} - [(T_a + T_b)/2]$ = "Unit Rise X"

For sample: $T_{max.} - [(T_a + T_b)/2]$ = "Unit Rise Y"

Jet correction: Check "semipermanent" calibration curve frequently with stds. Calc. % deviation, if any, and apply correction to sample, as:

Theoretical Unit Rise from Calibration Curve/Unit Rise X = corr. factor. Then, Unit Rise Y × corr. factor = corrected Unit Rise Y.

ppm K in sample = Diln factor × ppm equiv. to Unit Rise Y taken from calibration curve.

Sodium (*3*)—Official Final Action

11.026 ***Reagents and Apparatus***

Prep. std solns as in **11.024(a)**, except use 2.5421 g reagent grade NaCl. Use flame spectrophtr, **11.024(b)**.

11.027 ***Determination***

Proceed as in **11.025**, except dil. sample 50–100 times as necessary to fall within $\%T$ range of stds. For Na, (T_b) = 570, ($T_{max.}$) = 589, and (T_a) = 610. Calc. ppm Na in sample as in **11.025**.

11.028 Chlorides—Official Final Action

Method I

To 100 mL dry wine or 50 mL sweet wine add enough Na_2CO_3 to make distinctly alk. Evap. to dryness, ignite at ≤500°, cool, ext residue with hot H_2O, acidify H_2O ext with HNO_3 (1+4), and det. Cl as in **3.072** or **3.074**.

Method II (4)

11.029 ***Apparatus***

(**a**) *pH meter.*—With millivolt scale, Beckman Zeromatic, or equiv.

(**b**) *Electrodes.*—Beckman Instruments general purpose glass electrode No. 41263 as ref. electrode and Beckman No. 19151 Ag-AgCl pressed billet electrode with 30" lead and pin connector as indicating electrode. Other electrode combinations such as Beckman No. 39187 Ag billet combination electrode may be used.

(**c**) *Magnetic stirrer.*—With glass or plastic coated stirring bar.

(**d**) *Buret.*—10 mL with 0.05 mL subdivisions.

11.030 ***Reagents***

(**a**) *Potassium chloride.*—Reagent grade contg ≤0.005% Br. Dry in desiccator several days before use.

(**b**) *Distilled water.*—Cl-free. Use wherever H_2O is specified.

(**c**) *Chloride std soln.*—1 mg Cl/mL. Weigh 2.1028 g KCl, transfer to 1 L vol. flask, and dil. to vol. with H_2O.

(**d**) *Silver nitrate std soln.*—1 mL = 1 mg Cl. Weigh 4.7914 g reagent grade $AgNO_3$, transfer to 1 L vol. flask, and dil. to vol. with H_2O.

11.031 ***Determination***

Connect glass electrode to input terminal and indicating electrode to ref. terminal of pH meter set to read on ±700 millivolt (mv) scale. Warm up ≥30 min. Pipet 5.0 mL std Cl soln into 250 mL beaker. Adjust vol. to ca 100 mL with H_2O and add 1.0 mL HNO_3 by pipet. Insert electrodes so that billet is completely covered, add stirring bar, and titr. with std $AgNO_3$ soln, stirring moderately. Add in 1.00 mL increments until 4.0 mL have been added, then 0.20 mL increments until 2.0 mL more have been added, then 1.00 mL increments to total of 10.00 mL. Read buret to 0.01 mL and mv scale to 1 mv after addn of each increment. Record readings. Let pH meter stabilize ≥30 sec before each reading. Plot observed mv against mL soln added and det. equivalence point (inflection) voltage from resulting curve. This value will vary with electrode system used.

Use of glass electrode as ref. electrode is reverse of usual function; hence curve obtained will be reverse of those produced by other electrode combinations. Rinse electrodes before each use.

Pipet 5.0 mL std Cl soln into 250 mL beaker, and add 95 mL H_2O and 1.0 mL HNO_3. Insert electrodes, stir, and titr. with std $AgNO_3$ soln to predetd equivalence voltage, adding titrant dropwise as end point is reached. Repeat until results are in close agreement. Conduct all titrations within 5° of temp. of equivalence point detn. Repeat this detn at least daily or before each group of samples.

Pipet 50 mL wine into 250 mL beaker, add 50 mL H_2O and 1.0 mL HNO_3, and titr. as above.

$$\text{ppm Cl} = (V_w/V_s) \times C \times 2 \times 10,$$

where V_w = mL std $AgNO_3$ used by sample, V_s = mL std $AgNO_3$ used by std Cl soln, and C = 5.0 = mg Cl in 5 mL std Cl soln used.

Phosphorus (*5*)—Official Final Action

(*Caution: See* **51.018**, **51.019**, **51.026**, and **51.028**.)

11.032 ***Reagents***

(**a**) *Molybdovanadate reagent.*—Prep. as in **2.022(a)**, except use 200 mL 70% $HClO_4$.

(**b**) *Phosphate std soln.*—1 mg P_2O_5/mL. Dissolve 1.9174 g pure, dry (2 hr at 105°) KH_2PO_4 in 1 L H_2O. Prep. fresh weekly.

11.033 ***Preparation of Standard Curve***

Prep. series of std solns contg 0.0, 0.1, 0.2, 0.3, and 0.4 mg P_2O_5/mL. Perform following operations within 5 min: Pipet 5 mL aliquots into 100 mL vol. flasks, and add 50 mL H_2O and 4 mL 70% $HClO_4$. Pipet 20 mL molybdovanadate reagent into each flask, dil. to vol. with H_2O, and shake thoroly. Let stand 15 min.

Det. A of blank and stds in set of matched cells against H_2O as ref. at 400 nm. Correct stds for A of blank and plot corrected A against concn in mg P_2O_5/100 mL soln.

11.034 ***Determination***

(**a**) *Wet ash method.*—Pipet 5 mL sample into 100 mL Pyrex beaker and evap. to dryness on steam bath. Add 15 mL HNO_3 and few SiC boiling chips, cover with watch glass, and heat gently until residue dissolves. Boil gently 10–15 min to oxidize easily oxidizable org. matter, cool, add 4 mL 70% $HClO_4$, and boil gently until soln fumes copiously and is nearly colorless. (Remove watch glass when soln starts to fume. Do not evap. to dryness.) If soln is brown, add 2 mL HNO_3 and boil again. Cool slightly, add ca 25 mL H_2O, boil few min, and transfer to 100 mL vol. flask. Rinse beaker with H_2O, adding washings to flask to total vol. of 50–60 mL.

Within 5 min for series, add 20 mL molybdovanadate reagent to each flask, dil. to 100 mL, mix thoroly, and read A at 400 nm after 15 min. Carry blank and std thru entire detn. Subtract A of blank from that of sample.

(**b**) *Dry ash method.*—Pipet 5 mL sample into Pt dish and evap. to dryness on steam bath. Carefully char over low flame and ash in furnace at ≤550°. Pipet in 4 mL 70% $HClO_4$, add ca 20 mL H_2O, and warm to dissolve ash. Transfer quant. to 100 mL vol. flask, cool to room temp., and proceed as in (**a**).

mg P_2O_5/100 mL = $A_{sample} \times 20/A_{1\ mg\ std.}$

11.035 Sulfates—Official Final Action

See **30.083**.

11.036 pH—Official Final Action

Let pH meter with glass and calomel electrodes warm up before use according to manufacturer's instructions. Check meter with freshly prepd, satd, aq. soln of K bitartrate, **50.007(b)**. Adjust meter to read 3.55 at 20°, 3.56 at 25°, or 3.55 at 30°.

Rinse electrodes free of bitartrate by dipping in H_2O and then in sample. Place electrodes in fresh sample, det. temp., and read pH to nearest 0.01 unit.

11.037 Total Acidity—Official Final Action

American Society of Enologists Method (6)

Remove CO_2, if present, by either of following methods: (*1*) Place ca 25 mL sample in small erlenmeyer and connect to H_2O aspirator. Agitate 1 min under vac. (*2*) Place ca 25 mL sample in small erlenmeyer, heat to incipient boiling and hold 30 sec, swirl, and cool.

Add 1 mL phthln indicator soln to 200 mL hot, boiled H_2O in 500 mL wide-mouth erlenmeyer. Neutze to distinct pink. Add 5.00 mL degassed sample and titr. with 0.1*N* (or 0.0667*N*) stdzd NaOH to same end point, using well-illuminated white background.

Calc. g tartaric acid/100 mL wine = mL NaOH × normality × 0.075 × 100/5. If 0.0667*N* alkali is used, g tartaric acid/100 mL = mL NaOH/10.

Total Volatile Acidity (7)—Official Final Action

11.038 ***Apparatus***

(**a**) *Steam distillation apparatus.—See* Fig. **9:03**.

(**b**) *Cash electric still.—See* Fig. **11:02**. Consists of outer chamber, inner chamber, trap, 2-way stopcock, elec. coil heater, and glass "T" inlet-outlet for H_2O. All parts are of Pyrex. Residue in inner chamber after distn is flushed out automatically by vac. action when current is shut off. Addn of H_2O thru funnel above stopcock gives automatic spray bath to inner chamber, and waste drains thru outlet in glass "T." Two-way stopcock permits introduction of sample, serves as escape vent for CO_2, and allows introduction of wash H_2O. (Available from VWR Scientific, Inc., PO Box 3200, San Francisco, CA 94119, Cat. No. 26308 001.)

11.039 ***Preparation of Sample***

Remove dissolved CO_2 from ca 50 mL sample by either: Placing under low vac. (H_2O aspirator) 2 min with continuous stirring; or bringing to incipient boiling under air condenser and cooling immediately.

11.040 ***Determination***

(**a**) *Steam distillation apparatus.*—Add ca 600 mL boiled H_2O to outer chamber of still. Pipet 25 mL freshly prepd sample into inner chamber and stopper. Boil H_2O 3 min with sidearm open. Close and distil ca 300 mL into erlenmeyer. Add 0.5 mL phthln

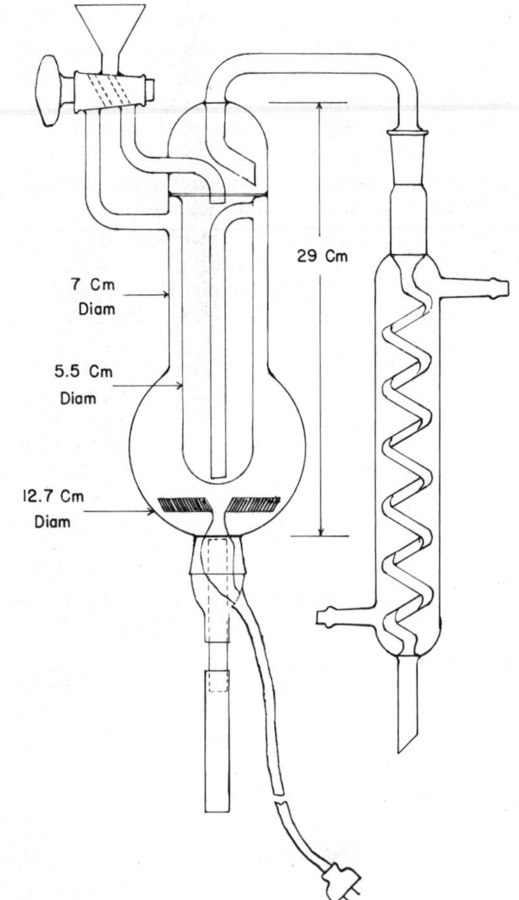

FIG. 11:02—Volatile acid still (Cash still)

to distillate and titr. rapidly with 0.1*N* NaOH until pink persists 15 sec. Express results as g HOAc/100 mL = mL 0.1*N* NaOH × 0.006 × 4.

(**b**) *Cash electric still.*—Add H_2O and pipet sample as in (**a**). Rinse funnel with ca 5 mL H_2O. Distil ca 300 mL into erlenmeyer. Titr. and express results as in (**a**). (Disconnect heating coil immediately and empty still by opening drain tube and stopcock to inner tube. Rinse still with two 10–15 mL portions H_2O by adding thru funnel; evacuate each portion thru drain tube.)

Volatile Acidity—Exclusive of SO_2

11.041 By Barium Hydroxide Treatment (*8*) Official First Action

Pipet 50 mL sample into 100 mL vol. flask. If white, add 2–3 drops phthln, and neutze to decided pink with clear *satd* $Ba(OH)_2$ *soln*; if red, add enough $Ba(OH)_2$ soln to bring mixt. to ca pH 8, using phthln as external indicator. Let mixt. stand 30 min and keep at phthln end point by adding more $Ba(OH)_2$ if necessary. Dil. to 100 mL, mix, and filter rapidly thru fluted, rapid paper (such as Whatman No. 2). Pipet 50 mL prepd sample and 1 mL H_2SO_4 (1+3) into inner chamber of still, **11.038(a)** or (**b**), and stopper. Proceed as in **11.040**. Express results as g HOAc/100 mL as in **11.040(a)**.

By Mercuric Oxide Treatment (9)—Official Final Action

11.042 ***Apparatus and Reagents***

(**a**) *Cash electric still.—See* **11.038(b)** and Fig. **11:02**.

(**b**) *Antifoam soln.*—Dil. 1 mL Antifoam C Emulsion to 50 mL with H_2O.

(**c**) *Mercuric oxide soln.*—Dissolve 1 g red HgO in 100 mL H_2SO_4 (1+9).

(**d**) *Phenolphthalein indicator soln.*—Dissolve 1 g phthln in 70 mL alcohol, add 30 mL H_2O, and mix.

(**e**) *Sodium hydroxide std soln.*—0.0167*N*. Prep. as in **50.032–50.034**. Stdze as in **50.035** or **50.036**, using phthln indicator, (**d**).

11.043 ***Determination***

(*Caution: See* **51.065**.)

Pipet 10 mL sample into funnel of still, (**a**), letting it flow into inner tube. When analyzing young wines, add 2–3 drops antifoam soln, (**b**), to funnel. Rinse sample and antifoam soln into inner tube with ca 5 mL H_2O. Add 2 mL HgO soln, (**c**), to funnel (to form nonvolatile mercuric bisulfite complex with SO_2), and rinse into inner tube with ca 5 mL H_2O. Turn stopcock so that outer chamber of still is open to atm., and heat ca 600 mL H_2O in outer chamber until steam escapes. After 15 sec, close stopcock and collect 100 mL distillate in 250 mL erlenmeyer. Disconnect heating coil immediately and empty still by opening drain tube to outer chamber and stopcock to inner tube. Rinse inner tube with two 10–15 mL portions H_2O by adding thru funnel; evacuate each portion thru drain tube. Bring distillate to bp on hot plate and boil ≤30 sec. Add 3 drops phthln indicator soln, (**d**), and titr. while still hot with NaOH std soln, (**e**), to pink end point that lasts 15–30 sec.

$$\text{g HOAc/100 mL} = \text{mL NaOH} \times N \times 0.60,$$

where N = normality of NaOH soln.

11.044 Fixed Acidity—Official Final Action

Calc. fixed acidity by multiplying total volatile acidity by 1.25 for tartaric, 1.12 for malic, or 1.17 for citric acid (hydrate), and subtracting product from total acidity.

Total Tartaric Acid (*10*)—Official Final Action

11.045 *Titration Method*

Neutze 100 mL sample with 1*N* NaOH, calcg from acidity, **11.037**, mL 1*N* alkali necessary. If >10 mL alkali is added, evap. to ca 100 mL. Add, to neutzd soln, 0.075 g tartaric acid for each mL 1*N* alkali added. It is essential that the tartaric acid be pure; recrystallize from H_2O, if necessary. After tartaric acid dissolves, add 2 mL HOAc and 15 g KCl. After KCl dissolves, add 15 mL alcohol, stir vigorously until $KHC_4H_4O_6$ begins to ppt, and refrigerate ≥15 hr at 15–18°.

Decant onto gooch prepd with very thin film of asbestos, or onto filter paper in buchner. Wash ppt from beaker with filtrate (keep cold) and finally rinse beaker and filter 3 times with few mL mixt. of 15 g KCl, 20 mL alcohol, and 100 mL H_2O, using ≤20 mL wash soln in all. Transfer asbestos or paper and ppt to beaker in which pptn was made; wash gooch or buchner with hot H_2O, using ca 50 mL in all; heat to bp, and titr. hot soln with 0.1*N* NaOH, using phthln. Increase number of mL 0.1*N* alkali required by 1.5 mL to allow for solubility of ppt. Under these conditions 1 mL 0.1*N* alkali = 0.015 g tartaric acid. To obtain g total tartaric acid/100 mL wine, subtract wt tartaric acid added from this result.

11.046 ★ *Bitartrate Method* ★

See **22.063★**.

★ Surplus method—*see* inside front cover.

11.047 ★ Citric and Malic Acids—Official First Action ★

For citric and malic acids occurring in normal wines in small amts only, use 100 mL sample and evap. to 45 mL. After saponification, **22.063★**, proceed as in **22.064★**, **22.067★**, or **22.075**.

11.048 Lactic Acid (*11*)—Official Final Action

Transfer 25 mL sample to 250 mL vol. flask, add ca 25 mL H_2O and 100 mL alcohol, and shake vigorously. Dil. to vol. with alcohol and filter thru folded paper. Transfer 200 mL filtrate to 400 mL beaker and evap. to ca 25 mL. Add 50 mL H_2O and again evap. to 25 mL. Transfer material to continuous extractor with 25 mL H_2O and proceed as in **16.030–16.031**.

11.049 Tannin—Official Final Action

See **9.100**.

11.050 Total Nitrogen—Official Final Action

Det. N in 50 mL sample as in **2.057**. Crude protein = N × 6.25.

11.051 ★ Pentosans—Official Final Action ★

(Applicable to dry wines only)

See **11.044**, 10th ed.

Free Aldehydes (*12*)—Official Final Action

Direct Method

11.052 ***Reagents***

See **9.060**.

11.053 ***Determination***

Pipet 50 mL sample, contg ≤30 mg acetaldehyde, into 500 mL distg flask and proceed as in **9.063**, beginning "... add 50 mL *satd borax soln*, ..."

Caramel—Official Final Action

Mathers Test (13)

11.054 ***Reagents***

(**a**) *Pectin soln.*—Dissolve 1 g pectin in 75 mL H_2O, add 25 mL alcohol to preserve, and shake well before using.

(**b**) *2,4-DNPH soln.*—Dissolve 1 g 2,4-dinitrophenylhydrazine in 7.5 mL H_2SO_4 and dil. to 75 mL with alcohol. (If kept in g-s bottle, soln will remain clear and stable several months.)

11.055 ***Preliminary Test***

Place 10 mL filtered sample in Babcock cream bottle, **16.157(a)**, or other centrf. tube. Add 1 mL pectin soln and mix; add 3–5 drops HCl and mix; fill bottle with alcohol (ca 50 mL), mix, centrf., and decant. Dissolve ppt in 10 mL H_2O, and add HCl and alcohol as above; shake well, centrf., and decant. Repeat operation until alc. liq. is colorless. Finally, dissolve gelatinous residue in 10 mL hot H_2O. If soln is colorless, caramel is absent; if soln is clear brown, caramel may be present. Confirm as follows: Add 1 mL 2,4-DNPH soln, mix, and heat 30 min in boiling H_2O. Ppt forms if caramel is present.

11.056 **★ *Confirmatory Test* ★**

See **11.047**, 10th ed.

Cyanide (*14*)—Official First Action

11.057 ***Wines, Other Nondistilled Products, and Products Containing Sulfur Dioxide***

(**a**) *Control test.*—Add 27 mL $K_4Fe(CN)_6.3H_2O$ working soln (equiv. to 10 μg CN), **9.102(a)**(*2*), to 100 mL H_2O in 500 mL 3-neck flask which has thermometer in screw-cap adaptor in one side neck and gas inlet tube connected to N (or CO_2) in other. Pack lower tube of flange assembly (E), which fits into top of condenser, with 10 cm column of PbO_2 (ca 7 g), which is held in position by cotton wool plugs at each end. Connect center neck of flask to condenser, place ground-glass flange assembly in top of condenser, and connect hooks with springs. Insert test paper as in **9.103(a)**. Remove thermometer momentarily, add 10 mL H_2SO_4 (1+9) and 10 mg *powd* Cu_2Cl_2, and immediately replace thermometer. Proceed as in **9.103(a)**, except maintain contents of flask at 90° for duration of test and heat 30 min. (It may be necessary to turn on N before 90° is reached to avoid "blow back.")

(**b**) *Samples.*—Use 100 mL sample (or other suitable aliquot) and evaluate results as for distd spirits, **9.103**. Similary, analyze blank of 100 mL H_2O.

Carbon Dioxide—Official First Action

Manometric Method (*15*)

11.058 ***Reagents***

(**a**) *Sodium bicarbonate std solns.*—Dry 150–200 g $NaHCO_3$ over H_2SO_4 24 hr. Weigh designated amts of dried $NaHCO_3$, transfer to 1 L vol. flasks with ca 700 mL recently boiled H_2O, and add 15 mL NaOH soln, (**c**). Add 200 mL absolute alcohol, mix, cool, and dil. to vol. with boiled H_2O. Use 4.2955 g for 225 mg CO_2/100 mL std; 4.7727 g for 250; and 5.2500 g for 275.

(**b**) *Hydrogen peroxide soln.*—10%. Dil. 20 mL 30% H_2O_2 with 40 mL recently boiled H_2O.

(**c**) *Sodium hydroxide soln.*—50%. Transfer 763 g reagent grade NaOH pellets to 1 L Pyrex graduate, add recently boiled H_2O, cool, and dil. to 1 L. Mix until soln is complete and set aside ≥5 days until Na_2CO_3 settles, leaving clear soln.

11.059 ***Apparatus***

(**a**) *Carbon dioxide apparatus.*—*See* Fig. **11:03**. Vol. of system is ca 350 mL. (Available from New York Laboratory Supply Co. and Scott Laboratories, Inc., PO Box 3576, San Rafael, CA 94901.) Test all glass joints with vac. tester.

(**b**) *Vacuum tester.*—High frequency self-contained generator operated from 115 v ac outlet. Consists of adjustable interrupter, vibrating spark gap, condenser, resonator coil, and gap tip.

(**c**) *Magnetic stirrer with Teflon stirring bar.*— Fisher Flexa-Mix, or equiv., with stirring bars 1–1³/₁₆" long.

(**d**) *Vacuum pump.*—Sargent-Welch pump, No. 1399B, or equiv., with motor, single stage, vented exhaust; to be operated with vented exhaust valve open for pumping condensable vapors. Insert 3-way stopcock between pump and app. to allow air to enter system. Ordinary high vac. pump can be used if H_2SO_4 trap with 3-way stopcock is inserted between pump and app. Change acid frequently.

(**e**) *Silicone grease, high vacuum type.*—Stable to heat and contains no carbon-to-carbon linkages. Grease may be removed from glassware with Varsol or hot kerosene.

11.060 ***Calibration of Vacuum System***

(*Caution: See* **51.015**.)

Pipet 50 mL std $NaHCO_3$ soln and 3 mL 10% H_2O_2 soln into reaction flask, and carefully grease joints. Start mag. stirrer and evacuate system ca 1 min. Close system to pump at 3-way

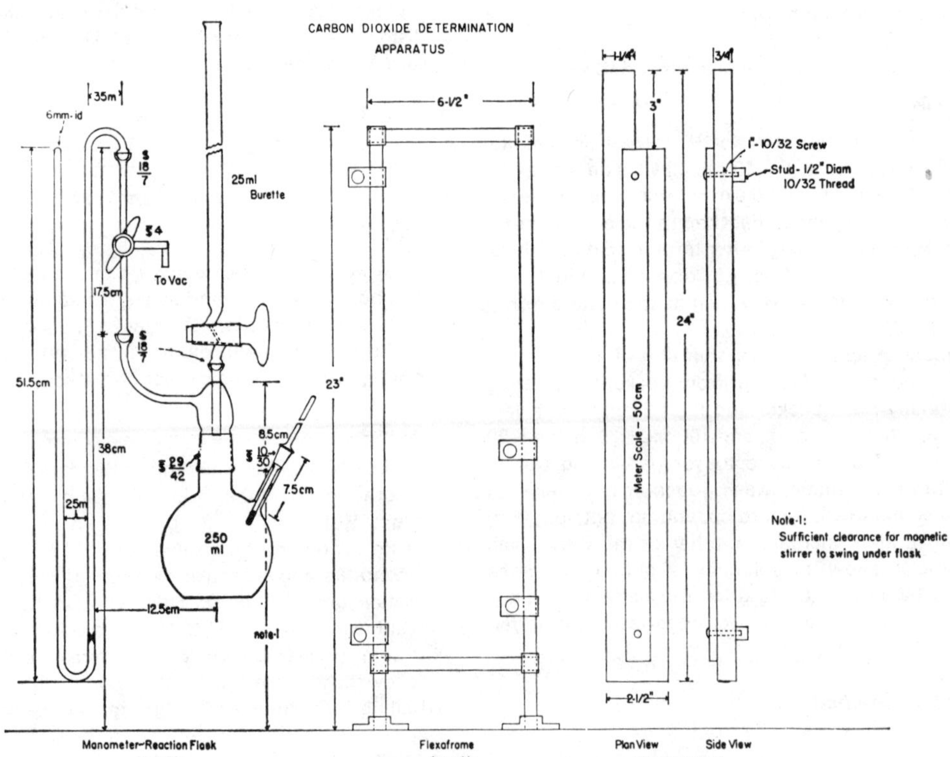

FIG. 11:03—Carbon dioxide apparatus; manometric method

stopcock, gently tap Hg columns, and read manometer to nearest 0.5 mm to obtain initial reading. Hg levels should remain const; changes indicate leak, probably caused by insufficient grease at joints.

Add 10 mL H_3PO_4 and continue rapid stirring 5 min. Gently tap Hg columns and read total pressure in cm Hg to nearest 0.5 mm to obtain final reading. Record gas temp. in °C.

Open 3-way stopcock on app. to pump. Then slowly open 3-way stopcock between pump and app. to let air flow into system. Disconnect app. and thoroly wash inner portion of acid dispensing unit and reaction flask. Rinse with acetone and dry with suction.

Det. total pressure from each $NaHCO_3$ std soln in triplicate and calc. av. vol. of system as follows:

From final pressure reading in cm Hg, subtract initial reading and vapor pressure increase due to H_3PO_4 effect as given in table:

% Alcohol	Vapor Pressure, cm, Increase Due to H_3PO_4
0	0.67
5	0.68
10	0.69
15	0.75
20	0.77
25	0.77
50	1.00
75	1.53
100	2.80

Then $V = 76RTg/MP$, where V is system vol. in L; R is gas const in L-atm./degree/mole, 0.08205; T is absolute temp., 273 + room temp. in °C; g is g CO_2 in 50 mL sample; M is MW of CO_2 in g; and P is corrected pressure of CO_2 in cm Hg.

Calc. correction for Hg displaced in manometer tubing, $V_m = \pi r^2 L/2$, where L is difference in ht of Hg column in cm and r is internal radius of manometer tubing.

Calibrated vol. of system, $V_o = V - V_m$.

In calcg wt CO_2 in sample, Hg displaced in manometer tubing, V_m, is added to calibrated vol. of system, V_o. ($V = V_o + V_m$)

11.061 ***Preparation of Sample***

Chill unopened bottle of wine in ice-salt bath to slightly <32°F (30 min for ⅒ gal. bottle and 1 hr for ⅕). Open bottle and rapidly add 1.5 mL 50% NaOH soln for each 100 mL wine. Quickly close bottle with rubber stopper, remove from bath, and shake several min. Let contents come to room temp.

11.062 ***Determination***

Pipet 50 mL sample and 3 mL 10% H_2O_2 into reaction flask, carefully grease joints, and proceed as in **11.060**.

From total pressure in cm Hg, subtract vapor pressure of alcohol-H_2O and pressure due to H_3PO_4 effect. Calc. g CO_2/100 mL wine = $14.327PV/T$.

To correct for anomalous results which occur with certain fruit wines (e.g., apple), place duplicate sample in 500 mL heavy-wall flask at room temp., shake 1–2 min under ca 69 cm (27″) vac., and proceed as above. Subtract value obtained from apparent CO_2 concn of carbonated wine.

Volumetric Method (16)

11.063 ***Reagents***

(**a**) *Sodium hydroxide std soln.*—0.25*N*. Prep. as in **50.032–50.034**. Stdze as in **50.035** or **50.036**, using phthln-thymolphthalein indicator, (**e**). Restdze daily against std HCl, (**b**), in presence of 5 mL $BaCl_2$ soln, (**c**), and indicator, (**e**).

(**b**) *Hydrochloric acid std soln.*—0.25*N*. Stdze against std NaOH, (**a**), using indicator (**e**).

(**c**) *Barium chloride soln.*—Dissolve 60–65 g $BaCl_2.2H_2O$ in 1 L H_2O and neutze to phthln.

(**d**) *Acid phosphate soln.*—Dissolve 20 g $NaH_2PO_4.H_2O$ in H_2O, add 3 mL H_3PO_4, and dil. to 100 mL.

(**e**) *Phenolphthalein-thymolphthalein mixed indicator.*—Dissolve 1 g phthln and 0.5 g thymolphthalein in 100 mL alcohol.

11.064 ***Apparatus***

See Fig. **11:04**. Connect 500 mL special distg flask (rubber stopper and ordinary distg flask may be used) thru ca 8 mm glass tubing to series of 3 Pyrex test tubes, 25 × 200 mm, each fitted at inlet with gas dispersion tube with 12 mm fritted end of coarse porosity and 8 mm stem (Fisher No. 11–138, or equiv.). Connect final exit tube to trapped vac. line or filter pump.

11.065 ***Determination***

Connect app. and place test tube receivers in beaker of H_2O at <27°. Pipet 20 mL std 0.25*N* NaOH into first 2 receivers and 10 mL 0.25*N* NaOH and 10 mL $BaCl_2$ soln into third.

Pipet 50 mL alk. wine, **11.061**, into distg flask and add 3 mL 10% H_2O_2, **11.058(b)**. Add boiling chips (not marble). Attach vac. line to last receiver and slowly increase vac. until bubbling practically stops; then open vac. line fully. (This keeps system under partial vac. so that stoppers will not be blown out on heating by sudden surge of steam or CO_2.) Add ca 35 mL acid phosphate soln to dropping funnel and carefully admit ca 30 mL into distg flask. Agitate flask gently to mix acid and sample.

Heat gently and when CO_2 evolution slows, heat vigorously. After few mL of liq. distils and top of first receiver is warm, all CO_2 will have been driven into receivers. Close vac. line between trap and receivers and slowly admit air thru dropping funnel until pressure equilibrium is reached.

Transfer contents and rinsings of first 2 receivers and dispersion tubes into titrn flask. (Also add contents of third if $BaCO_3$ has pptd.) Add 50 mL $BaCl_2$ soln and titr. with std HCl to phthln end point.

Wt CO_2 in g/100 mL = [(mL NaOH × normality) − (mL HCl × normality)] × 0.022 × (100/50) × 1.015.

Enzymatic Method (17)—Official Final Action

11.066 ***Reagent***

Carbonic anhydrase soln.—Prep. aq. soln contg ca 1 mg enzyme/mL. Soln is stable ca 2 weeks in refrigerator.

11.067 ***Determination***

Cool sample to ≤0°, so that it can be pipetted without loss of CO_2. With automatic 25 or 30 mL pipet with Teflon stopcock, dispense aliquot of 0.1*N* NaOH into beaker. Rinse 20 mL pipet with sample to prevent warming sample with possible loss of CO_2. Pipet sample with tip submerged just below surface of NaOH in beaker. Add 3–4 drops enzyme, and place beaker under glass and calomel electrodes. Titr. to pH 8.45 with 0.1*N* H_2SO_4 from 5 mL buret graduated in 0.01 mL.

To correct for presence of acids other than H_2CO_3, place 50 mL wine in 500 mL heavy-wall flask at room temp. and agitate 1 min under vac. of ca 27″ (69 cm). Titr. 20 mL to pH 7.75 with 0.1*N* NaOH as above. Subtract mL used from that used in first titrn. Calc. as follows: (Net mL NaOH × normality − mL H_2SO_4 × normality) × 100 × 44/mL sample = mg CO_2/100 mL wine.

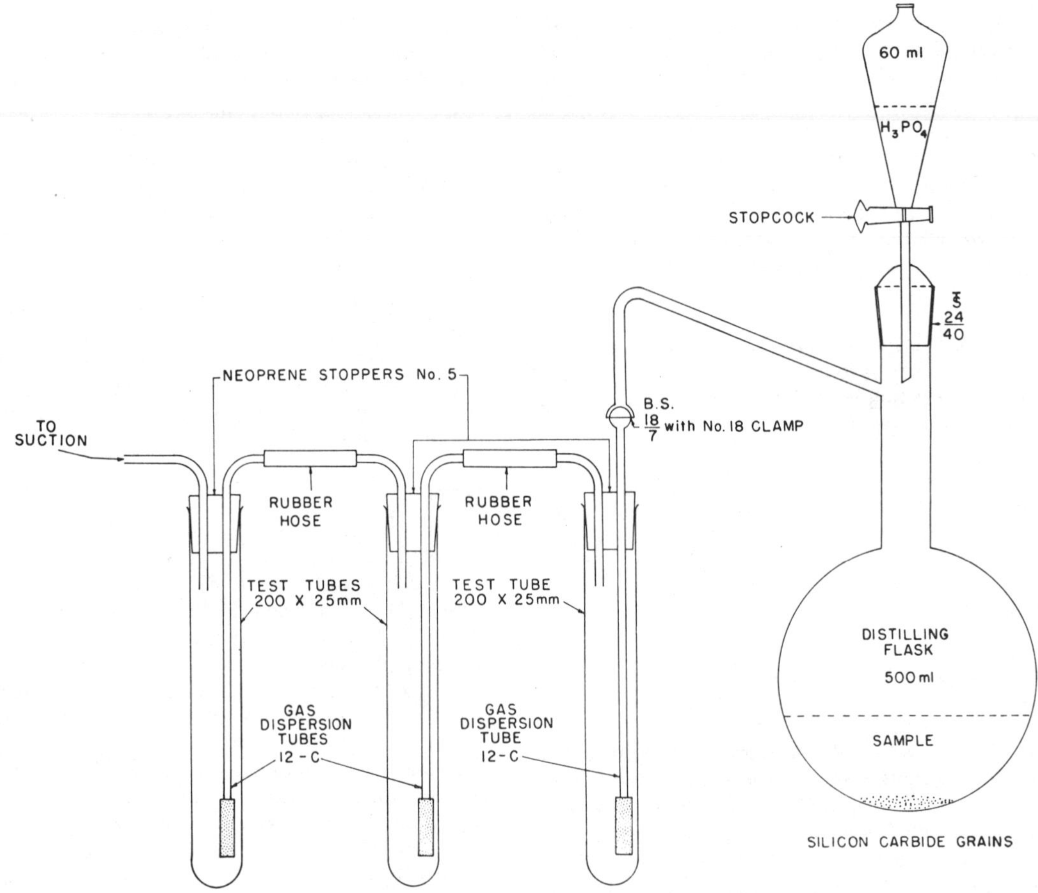

FIG. 11:04—Carbon dioxide apparatus; volumetric method

PRESERVATIVES

11.068 Preservatives—Official Final Action

See also Chap. **20**.

11.069 Sulfurous Acid (*18*)—Official Final Action

Proceed as in **20.108**, using 100–300 mL sample. Report results as mg SO_2/L. (As SO_2 in wine is unstable, give sample no preparatory degassing treatment and expose to air for min. time prior to detn.)

Sorbic Acid—Official Final Action (*19*)

Ultraviolet Method

11.070 ***Apparatus***

(**a**) *Cash electric still.—See* **11.038(b)** and Fig. **11:02**.
(**b**) *Ultraviolet spectrophotometer.*

11.071 ***Reagents***

(**a**) *Hydrochloric acid.*—0.1*N*. Dil. 8.2 mL HCl to 1 L with H_2O.

(**b**) *Sorbic acid std soln.*—1.0 mg/mL. Accurately weigh 1.340 g K sorbate (equiv. to 1.000 g sorbic acid) in 1 L vol. flask, and dissolve and dil. to vol. with H_2O. Soln is stable several days when refrigerated.

11.072 ***Preparation of Standard Curve***

Pipet 0, 10, 20, 30, and 40 mL sorbic acid std soln into sep. 100 mL vol. flasks, and dil. to vol. with H_2O. Pipet 2 mL of each soln into sep. 200 mL vol. flasks, add 0.5 mL 0.1*N* HCl, and dil. to vol. with H_2O. Read *A* at 260 nm in 1 cm cell and plot *A* against concn.

11.073 ***Determination***

Pipet 2 mL wine sample into Cash still. Rinse in with 2–3 mL H_2O. Steam distil into 200 mL vol. flask contg 0.5 mL 0.1*N* HCl. Collect ca 190 mL distillate; dil. to vol. with H_2O. Read *A* at 260 nm in 1 cm cell. Det. concn from std curve.

Colorimetric Method

11.074 ***Reagents and Standard Curve***

See **20.099(a)**(*2*)–(**d**) and **20.100**.

11.075 ***Determination***

Pipet 2 mL wine sample into Cash still, **11.038(b)**. Rinse in with 2–3 mL H_2O. Steam distil ca 190 mL into 200 mL vol. flask. Dil. to vol. with H_2O. Proceed as in **20.100**, beginning "Pipet 2 mL each soln . . ." Det. concn sorbic acid from std curve.

Diethylcarbonate (*20*)—Official Final Action

11.076 ***Reagents***

(**a**) *Carbon disulfide.*—Treat 200 mL CS_2 with 20 mL fuming HNO_3; then wash with 20 mL portions H_2O until wash is neut. to pH paper. (*Caution: See* **51.026**, **51.031**, and **51.048**.)

(**b**) *Diethylcarbonate std soln.*—0.5 mg/mL. Dissolve 50 mg diethylcarbonate in 100 mL alcohol. (If sample contains <1 or >10 mg diethylcarbonate/L, change concn appropriately.)

11.077 ***Apparatus***

Use gas chromatograph with H flame ionization detector. Column: 1.8 m (6′) × ⅛″ od stainless steel packed with 15% trimethylolpropantripelargonate (Analabs, Inc.) on 60–100 mesh Celite 545 (10–20% Carbowax 20M (Analabs, Inc.) on 60 mesh Firebrick C-22 (Analabs, Inc.) may be used, but yields poorer sepn). GLC conditions: temps (°)—column 80, injection port 180, detector 200; flow rates (mL/min)—N carrier gas 35, H 35, air 400; recorder 1–2.5 mv. Diethylcarbonate retention time is ca 15 min.

11.078 ***Determination***

Measure 100 mL sample in graduate and transfer to 250 mL separator. Add 1 mL alcohol and 20 mL CS_2, and shake ≥1 min. Let sep., transfer portion of lower layer to small test tube, and centrf. 2–3 min at 2000 rpm to clarify.

Slowly (5 sec) inject 5 μL clear soln from 10 μL syringe. Designate peak area obtained as PA. Likewise, inject 5 μL wine prepd by adding 1 mL diethylcarbonate std soln to 100 mL wine. Proceed with detn, beginning "... transfer to 250 mL separator." Designate peak area obtained as PA′.

$$\text{mg Diethylcarbonate/L} = (C \times PA \times 10)/(PA' - PA),$$

where C = mg diethylcarbonate/mL std soln.

After each detn increase column temp. to 200° for ≥20 min to purge other extd compds from column.

FLAVORS

Coumarin (1,2-Benzopyrone) *(21)*

Gas Chromatographic Method
Official First Action

11.079 ***Reagents and Apparatus***

(**a**) *Coumarin std soln*.—0.5 mg/mL alcohol. Accurately weigh 100 mg coumarin (Eastman Kodak No. 79, or equiv.), dissolve in alcohol in 200 mL vol. flask, and dil. to vol.

(**b**) *Gas chromatograph*.—With flame ionization detector and 1.8 m (6′) × 2 mm id *glass* column packed with 10% SP-1000 (Carbowax 20 M-TPA) on 100–120 mesh Chromosorb W AW (No. 01-1962, Supelco, Inc.). Operating conditions: He (use gas purifier filter) carrier gas flow rate—30 mL/min; temps (°)—column 180, injector and detector 200. Adjust GLC operating parameters to obtain optimum sepn and efficiency, with coumarin retention time of ca 15 min.

11.080 ***Determination***

Add 100 mL sample to each of two 250 mL separators. Add 1.0 mL coumarin std soln to one (spiked sample) and 1.0 mL alcohol to other (unspiked sample). Mix thoroly and ext with 20 mL $CHCl_3$, shaking vigorously 2 min. Let layers sep. and drain ca 10–12 mL $CHCl_3$ layer into centrf. tube. Swirl stirring rod in tube to aid in breaking emulsion and freeing $CHCl_3$. Centrf., if necessary, to clarify. Inject 5 μL clear $CHCl_3$ ext onto GLC column. Average 3 values for calcn.

$$\text{mg Coumarin/L} = [U/(S - U)] \times 0.5 \times (1000/100),$$

where U = peak ht of unspiked sample, S = peak ht of spiked sample, and 0.5 = mg coumarin added to 100 mL spiked sample.

β-Asarone (*cis*-2,4,5-Trimethoxy-1-propenylbenzene)

Gas Chromatographic Method (22)
Official First Action

11.081 ***Apparatus and Reagents***

(**a**) *Gas chromatograph.*—With flame ionization detector and 1.8 m × 2 (id) mm glass or stainless steel column packed with 10% SP-1000 (No. 01-1872, Supelco, Inc.) on Chromosorb W HP 80/100. Typical operating conditions—temps (°): column 180, detector and injection port 200; He carrier gas (with purifier filter) flow rate 40 mL/min. Retention times of Et palmitate and β-asarone are ca 5 min and 6 min, resp.

(**b**) *Ethyl palmitate internal std soln.*—Prep. 1 mg/mL soln in hexane.

(**c**) *β-Asarone std soln.*—Prep. 1 mg/mL soln in alcohol. (β-asarone is available on special order as No. TT150 from Fritzsche, Dodge, & Olcott, Inc., 76 Ninth Ave, New York, NY 10011.)

11.082 ***Preparation of Standard Curve***

Prep. std solns contg 1, 2, 3, 4, and 5 mg β-asarone/L by adding 100, 200, 300, 400, and 500 μL std soln to sep. 100 mL vol. flasks contg ca 90 mL 20% alcohol. Mix, dil. to vol. with 20% alcohol, and remix.

Transfer entire soln, rinsing with 50 mL H_2O, to simple distg app. and distil ca 100 mL. Transfer distillate to 250 mL separator, add 100 mL satd soln of NaCl, and mix. Add 10 mL hexane, shake vigorously 2 min, and let sep. Drain and discard aq. soln. Dry inside of drain tube of separator with tissue or pipe cleaner. Collect hexane in calibrated centrf. tube (10±0.5 mL should be recovered). Add 200 μL Et palmitate internal std soln and mix well. Chromatograph 5 μL of each ext and plot std curve of original concn of mg β-asarone/L against peak ht ratio of β-asarone:Et palmitate.

11.083 ***Determination***

Distil 100 mL sample and 50 mL H_2O, collecting 100 mL distillate. Transfer distillate, ext with 10 mL hexane, and chromatograph 5 μL as in **11.082**. Check for presence of β-asarone and Et palmitate. If there is no β-asarone peak, β-asarone is not present at 0.5 mg/L level. If β-asarone is present in range of std curve and no Et palmitate is present, add 200 μL Et palmitate internal std soln to hexane ext, mix, and rechromatograph. Use ratio of peak hts to det. β-asarone concn from std curve. If β-asarone peak is off scale, dil. hexane ext with hexane to 1–5 mg β-asarone/L, add internal std soln, mix, and rechromatograph. If peak is present in ext with same retention time as Et palmitate, use peak hts directly to det. β-asarone concn from std curve prepd from peak hts.

SELECTED REFERENCES

(*1*) JAOAC **59,** 777(1976); **60,** 739(1977).
(*2*) Wines and Vines **30,** 65(1949); JAOAC **52,** 85(1969).
(*3*) JAOAC **37,** 945(1954); **46,** 299(1963).
(*4*) JAOAC **49,** 498(1966).
(*5*) JAOAC **45,** 624(1962).
(*6*) Am. J. Enol. Viticult. **13,** 40(1962); JAOAC **46,** 293(1963).
(*7*) JAOAC **47,** 722(1964).
(*8*) JAOAC **23,** 183(1940).
(*9*) JAOAC **61,** 292(1978).
(*10*) USDA Bur. Chem. Bull. **162,** p. 72.
(*11*) JAOAC **20,** 605(1937).
(*12*) JAOAC **55,** 566(1972).
(*13*) JAOAC **31,** 178(1948).
(*14*) JAOAC **53,** 777(1970).
(*15*) JAOAC **42,** 679(1959); **56,** 286(1973).
(*16*) JAOAC **43,** 652(1960).
(*17*) JAOAC **47,** 711(1964).
(*18*) JAOAC **23,** 189(1940); **25,** 70, 82, 296(1942); **27,** 85(1944).
(*19*) JAOAC **57,** 951(1974); **58,** 133(1975).
(*20*) JAOAC **55,** 557(1972).
(*21*) JAOAC **58,** 140(1975).
(*22*) JAOAC **59,** 675(1976).

12. Beverages: Nonalcoholic and Concentrates

12.001 Preliminary Examination—Procedure

Note and record (*a*) appearance, whether bright or turbid, or any sediment; (*b*) color and depth of color; (*c*) odor, whether fruity, foreign, or artificial; (*d*) taste, whether tart or sweet, fruity, artificial, or foreign, and whether any synthetic substance can be identified by odor or taste.

12.002 Specific Gravity—Official Final Action

See **9.011**.

12.003 Alcohol

(**a**) *From specific gravity (Official Final Action).—See* **9.012–9.013**.
(**b**) *From refractive index (Official Final Action).—See* **9.016**.
(**c**) *By weight (Official Final Action).—See* **9.021**.
(**d**) *From gas chromatography (Official First Action).—See* **19.001–19.002**.

12.004 Total Solids—Official Final Action

See **31.007** or **31.008**.

Sucrose—Official Final Action

12.005 *By Polarization*

Det. by polarizing before and after inversion as in **31.025** or **31.026**.

12.006 *By Reducing Sugars Before and After Inversion*

See **31.031**.

12.007 Reducing Sugars—Official Final Action

Use value obtained for reducing sugars before inversion, **12.006**.

12.008 Commercial Glucose—Procedure

See **31.033**.

12.009 Ash—Official Final Action

Proceed as in **31.012** or **31.013**, using sample contg ≤10 g solids.

12.010 Soluble and Insoluble Ash—Official Final Action

Proceed as in **31.015**, using ash of **12.009**.

12.011 Alkalinity of Soluble Ash—Official Final Action

Proceed as in **31.016**, using sol. ash of **12.010**.

12.012 Alkalinity of Insoluble Ash—Official Final Action

Proceed as in **31.017**, using insol. ash of **12.010**.

12.013 Analysis of the Ash—Official Final Action

See Chapter **22**.

12.014 Monochloroacetic Acid—Official Final Action

See **20.068(b)**, **20.069(b)**, and **20.072**.

12.015 Quaternary Ammonium Compounds Official Final Action

See **20.088–20.089**.

12.016 Total Acidity—Official Final Action

See **9.119**.

12.017 Preparation of Sample for Determination of Dibasic Acids—Official First Action

(**a**) *Alcoholic products.—See* **9.120**.
(**b**) *Nonalcoholic products*.—Use sample contg ≤30 g solids and ≤200 mg acid to be detd, as calcd from acidity. Evap. to 30 mL, if necessary, and treat as in **12.018–12.021**.

12.018 ★ Tartaric Acid—Official Final Action ★

See **12.018**, 12th ed.

12.019 ★ Citric Acid—Official First Action ★

See **12.019**, 12th ed.

12.020 ★ Total Malic Acid (Laevo and Inactive) ★ Official First Action

See **12.020**, 12th ed.

12.021 ★ Laevo Malic Acid—Official First Action ★

See **12.021**, 12th ed.

12.022 Volatile Acidity—Official Final Action

See **11.041**.

12.023 Esters—Official Final Action

Proceed as in **9.125**, collecting ca 300 mL distillate.

Methyl Anthranilate—Official Final Action

Colorimetric Method (1)

(Applicable to samples contg <500 mg/L)

12.024 ***Reagents***

(**a**) *Dilute hydrochloric acid*.—Dil. 83 mL HCl to 1 L with H_2O.
(**b**) *Sodium nitrite soln*.—Dissolve 2 g $NaNO_2$ in 100 mL H_2O.
(**c**) *Hydrazine sulfate soln*.—Dissolve ca 3 g $N_2H_4.H_2SO_4$ in 100 mL H_2O.
(**d**) *Sodium-α-naphthol-2-sulfonate soln*.—Dissolve 5 g of the sulfonate in 100 mL H_2O.
(**e**) *Sodium carbonate soln*.—Dissolve 25 g Na_2CO_3 in 75 mL H_2O.
(**f**) *Methyl anthranilate std soln*.—1 mg/mL. Dissolve 0.25 g Me anthranilate in 60 mL alcohol and dil. to 250 mL with H_2O.

12.025 ***Apparatus***

(**a**) *Steam generator filled with H_2O*.—Oil can holding 1 gal. (ca 4 L) serves purpose.
(**b**) *Distillation flask*.—Kjeldahl flask, ca 750 mL, with shortened neck, ca 25 cm over-all ht.

★ Surplus method—*see* inside front cover.

(**c**) *Spray tube*.—Glass tube with small perforated bulb at end, passing thru rubber stopper and reaching to bottom of distn flask.

(**d**) *Connecting bulb*.—Kjeldahl bulb with bent connecting tube.

(**e**) *Worm condenser*.—With H_2O jacket 25–30 cm long, and outlet tube reaching bottom of 500 mL erlenmeyer receiving flask.

12.026 ***Determination***

Place just enough H_2O in receiving flask to seal end of extended condenser tube. Place 10–100 mL sample in distn flask and add, if necessary, H_2O to make 100 mL. Insert stopper carrying spray tube and connecting bulb, and connect with condenser and receiving flask. Immerse distn flask in H_2O bath near bp to level of contents. When sample reaches temp. of bath, connect to steam generator with H_2O boiling and rapidly pass steam thru sample until ca 300 mL distillate collects.

Disconnect app. and wash out condenser with little H_2O. Add 25 mL dil. HCl and 2 mL $NaNO_2$ soln to distillate, mix well, and let stand exactly 2 min. Add 6 mL $N_2H_4.H_2SO_4$ soln and mix well 1 min, so that liq. comes in contact with all parts of flask that soln may have touched when it contained free HNO_2. Keep liq. in flask in rapid motion, quickly add 5 mL Na α-naphthol-2-sulfonate soln, and then immediately add 15 mL Na_2CO_3 soln. Dil. colored soln to 500 mL with H_2O, mix, and compare color of portion with color of std, or set of stds, prepd as nearly as possible at same time. Calc. results as mg Me anthranilate/L.

Gravimetric Method (2)

(Applicable to samples contg $\geqslant$500 mg/L)

12.027 ***Reagents and Apparatus***

(**a**) *α-Naphthol soln*.—Dissolve 0.2 g α-naphthol in 100 mL 30% alcohol.

(**b**) *Sodium bicarbonate soln*.—Dissolve 8.4 g $NaHCO_3$ in 100 mL H_2O.

(*See* **12.024** for reagents and **12.025** for app.)

12.028 ***Determination***

Place sample contg 50–125 mg Me anthranilate in distn flask and dil., if necessary, to 100 mL with H_2O. Steam distil as in **12.026**, collecting ca 400 mL distillate.

Wash out condenser with little H_2O and dil. distillate to 500 mL. Mix, and to 200 mL aliquot add 5 mL dil. HCl and 5 mL $NaNO_2$ soln. Mix well and let stand 1 min. Mix 25 mL α-naphthol soln and 6 mL $NaHCO_3$ soln, pour diazotized soln into mixt., and let stand 10 min. Fold 2 Whatman 1 or S&S 595 papers, 12.5 cm diam., and det. difference in their wts by placing one on each pan of balance and counterpoising with added wts. Place heavier inside lighter paper, fit into funnel, and moisten. Pour mixt. thru this filter and wash ppt 7 or 8 times, using total of ca 100 mL H_2O. Fill filter only to ca 1 cm from top. Place funnel carrying filter and washed ppt in oven, and dry ca 10 min at 100°. Sep. and dry filter papers ca 1 hr at same temp. Det. difference in wts, dry again, weigh again, and repeat until difference in wts remains const. (Const difference in wts − original difference in wts of 2 papers) $\times$ 0.4935 = wt anthranilic acid ester, as Me anthranilate. Report as g/L.

12.029 Benzaldehyde (*3*)—Official Final Action

Measure 500 mL beverage, 100 mL flavoring sirup, or 10–25 mL flavor into distg flask. Add 32 mL alcohol, and in case of sirup or flavor, ca 300 mL H_2O, and proceed as in **19.101**.

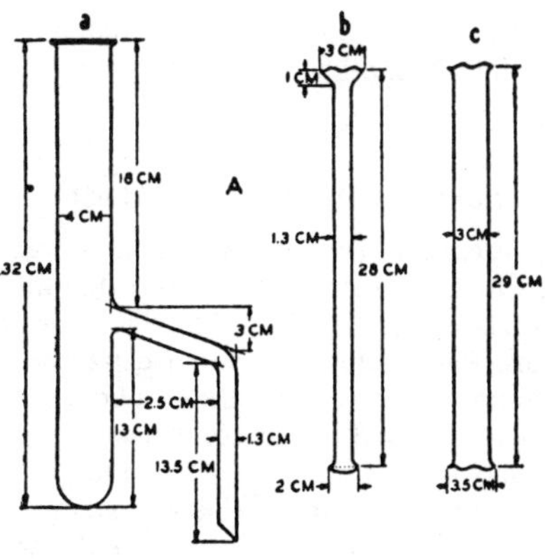

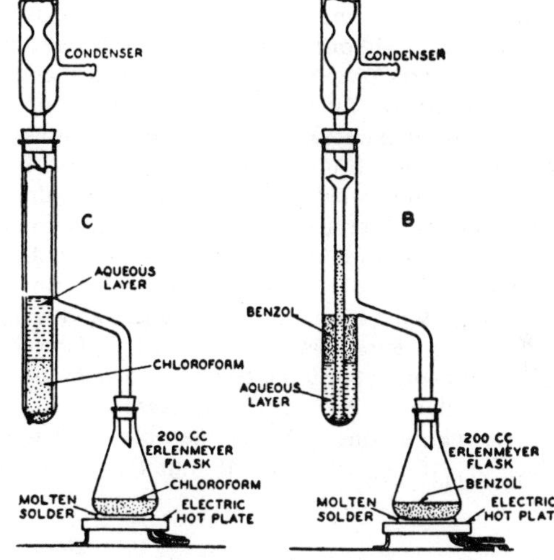

FIG. 12:01—Continuous extraction apparatus

12.030 ★ Gamma Undecalactone ★ (*4*)—Official Final Action

See **8.030**, 10th ed.

12.031 Essential Oils—Official First Action

See **19.128**.

Caffeine (*5*)—Official First Action

12.032 ***Apparatus***

(**a**) *Continuous extractor*.—Similar to Fig. **12:01**, with outer part of 43 mm od tubing, 45 cm long, with side tube 25 cm above bottom, fitted with drip tip ₮ 24/40 joint; inner tube of 30 mm od tubing, 39–40 cm long; receiver is 250 mL erlenmeyer with ₮ 24/40 joint.

(**b**) *Filtering device*.—Glass buchner with 30 mm fine fritted disk and 45 mm high side wall, fitted with 2 interchangeable rubber stoppers, one to fit suction flask, other to fit 20 $\times$ 150 mm side arm test tube.

12.033 ***Reagents***

(**a**) *Phosphomolybdic acid soln*.—Dissolve 10 g phosphomolybdic acid in ca 25 mL warm H_2O, cool to room temp., and dil. to 50 mL with H_2O. Let stand overnight and filter thru S&S 589 blue ribbon paper. Store in dark.

★ Surplus method—*see* inside front cover.

(b) *Caffeine std soln.*—1 mg/mL. Weigh 100 mg caffeine alkaloid, dissolve in H_2O, and dil. to 100 mL.

12.034 ***Extraction***

(*Caution: See* **51.011**, **51.040**, and **51.056**.)

Place few glass beads in receiver, assemble extractor, and add 210–220 mL $CHCl_3$ to inner tube. Measure 150 mL sample in graduate and make alk. with ca 2 mL 10*N* NaOH, using litmus paper as indicator. Place funnel in top of extractor and add sample to inner tube, letting $CHCl_3$ in outer tube overflow into receiver. Remove funnel and attach condenser. If tip of condenser is >2 cm above inner tube, place small funnel with 2–3 cm stem in top of inner tube to prevent splashing. Ext 2 hr, keeping steady stream of solv. flowing from condenser.

Remove hot plate and let receiver cool somewhat. Disconnect condenser and tilt extractor to permit as much $CHCl_3$ as possible to flow into receiver without letting any aq. phase rise into space between the 2 parts of extractor. Transfer entire contents of extractor to separator. Rinse extractor with H_2O and discard. Attach outer part of extractor to receiver and to condenser, and heat carefully until vol. $CHCl_3$ in receiver is 30–40 mL. Do not let soln bump or foam into extractor. Cool somewhat, drain $CHCl_3$ ext from separator into receiver, and distil $CHCl_3$ into extractor as before until 10–15 mL remains in receiver. Cool $CHCl_3$ in receiver and transfer to weighed 50 mL beaker, rinsing with several small portions $CHCl_3$. Evap. to dryness and weigh.

If residue wt is ≤5 mg, dissolve in 5 mL H_2O, filter thru very small circle of paper into 50 mL beaker, and wash beaker and paper with 5 mL H_2O; if wt is >5 mg, dissolve, using several successive 5 mL portions H_2O, and filter into vol. flask (25 mL for residue of ≤15 mg; 50 mL if >15 mg). Dil. to vol. with H_2O and mix.

12.035 ***Determination***

Place soln or aliquot contg 2–5 mg residue in 50 mL beaker; add 1 mL HCl (1+1) and enough H_2O to make 11 mL. Cover with watch glass and warm on steam bath. Add 2 mL phosphomolybdic acid soln dropwise with stirring, re-cover, and continue heating 20 min. Filter hot soln thru buchner into suction flask, and wash ppt and funnel with three 5 mL portions HCl (1+9), using policeman to scrub down walls of beaker. Aspirate dry. Wipe away any aq. soln at tip of buchner, change stopper to fit side arm test tube, and assemble. Dissolve ppt in three 5 mL portions acetone. Wash tip of buchner with few drops acetone, transfer to 25 mL vol. flask, and dil. to vol. with acetone. Det. *A* at 440 nm against acetone, and det. mg caffeine from std curve. Calc. to g/100 mL.

12.036 ***Preparation of Standard Curve***

Pipet 0, 1, 2, 3, 4, and 5 mL portions std caffeine soln into 50 mL beakers and proceed as in **12.035**, beginning ". . . add 1 mL HCl (1+1) . . ." Plot *A* against mg caffeine.

Alternative Method (6)—Official First Action

12.037 ***Reagents***

(a) *Reducing soln.*—Dissolve 5 g Na_2SO_3 and 5 g KSCN in H_2O and dil. to 100 mL.

(b) *Dilute phosphoric acid soln.*—Dil. 15 mL H_3PO_4 to 85 mL with H_2O.

(c) *Sodium hydroxide soln.*—Dissolve 25 g NaOH in 75 mL H_2O.

(d) *Caffeine std soln.*—1 mg/mL $CHCl_3$. Purify caffeine, if necessary, by recrystn and/or sublimation. Dissolve 100 mg in $CHCl_3$ and dil. to 100 mL with $CHCl_3$.

12.038 ***Preparation of Standard Curve***

Prep. dild std solns contg 0.10, 0.25, 0.50, 1.00, 1.50, and 2.00 mg caffeine/100 mL $CHCl_3$. Det. wavelength of max. *A* of 1 mg/100 mL soln at ca 276.5 nm and det. *A* of all solns at this wavelength against $CHCl_3$ in 1 cm matched cells. Plot *A* against concn or calc. factor = 10/av. reading for 1 mg/100 mL std calcd from all readings.

12.039 ***Determination***

Remove any gas by pouring sample back and forth in beakers. Pipet 10 mL sample into 125 mL separator, add 5 mL *1.5% $KMnO_4$ soln,* and mix. After exactly 5 min, add 10 mL reducing soln and mix. Add 1 mL dil. H_3PO_4 soln, mix, add 1 mL NaOH soln, mix, and ext with 50 mL $CHCl_3$ 1 min. After sepn, drain lower layer thru 7 cm paper into 100 mL g-s vol. flask. Add 2–3 mL $CHCl_3$ to separator and drain thru paper to rinse separator stem. Wash paper with 2–3 mL $CHCl_3$. Re-ext soln with 40 mL $CHCl_3$ and wash stem and paper as before. Dil. to vol. with $CHCl_3$. Det. *A* of this soln at wavelength of max. *A* against $CHCl_3$. Det. amt caffeine from std curve or from factor and calc. mg/100 mL beverage.

Spectrophotometric Method (7)—Official First Action

(Method is preferable to **12.037–12.039** when only few samples are to be analyzed. Use **12.032–12.036** for complex mixts requiring extensive cleanup.)

12.040 ***Apparatus***

Chromatographic tubes.—Glass, ca 25 × 250 mm.

12.041 ***Reagents***

(Use $CHCl_3$ and ether washed with ½ vol. H_2O thruout.)

Caffeine std solns.—*(1) Stock soln.*—*See* **12.037(d)**. *(2) Working solns.*—Prep. dilns of stock soln contg 0.25, 0.50, and 0.75 mg caffeine/50 mL $CHCl_3$. Check factor, **12.045**, frequently to minimize instrument variations.

12.042 ***Preparation of Sample***

Remove any gas by pouring sample back and forth in beakers. Pipet appropriate amt sample (5 or 10 mL) into 250 mL beaker. Evap. to near dryness on steam bath. Dissolve residue in 5 mL NH_4OH (1+2) and heat 2 min on steam bath. Remove from heat, add 6 g Celite 545, and mix carefully to homogeneity before prepg column.

12.043 ***Preparation of Columns***

(a) *Column I.*—Carefully mix 2 mL 4*N* H_2SO_4 with 2 g Celite 545, place in chromatgc tube over glass wool plug, and tamp to uniform mass with moderate pressure. Top with glass wool plug to minimize damage to column surface.

(b) *Column II.*—*(1) Layer 1.*—Carefully mix 3 g Celite 545 with 2 mL 2*N* NaOH, transfer to tube over glass wool plug, and tamp to uniform mass. *(2) Layer 2.*—Transfer prepd sample and Celite mixt. to column directly over layer *1* and tamp. Dry-wash beaker with 1–2 g dry Celite and transfer to column. Tamp to uniform mass and top column with glass wool pad.

12.044 ***Determination***

Mount column II over column I. Pass 150 mL ether thru column II and into column I, using initial portion of ether to rinse sample beaker. Drain well and remove column II. Pass addnl 50 mL ether thru column I and drain well. Pass 50 mL $CHCl_3$ thru column I, using initial portion to wash tip of column II. Collect eluate in 50 mL vol. flask and adjust vol. to 50 mL. Read A of $CHCl_3$ soln at 276 nm against $CHCl_3$ ref., using Beckman Model DU, or equiv., spectrophtr, with 1 cm silica cells. If necessary, adjust concns to acceptable levels by dilg with $CHCl_3$.

12.045 ***Calculations***

Factor F = mg caffeine in 50 mL std soln/A.
mg Caffeine in sample = F × A.
Express results as mg caffeine/100 mL beverage.

Dihydroanethole, Dihydrosafrole, Isosafrole, Methyl Salicylate, and Safrole (8)
Official Final Action

(Quant. for Me salicylate; semiquant. for other compds)

12.046 ***Reagents***

All solvs must be chromatographically pure and meet following test: Conc. 500 mL solv. to 10 mL in evaporative concentrator and chromatograph on prepd column with instrument set at max. sensitivity to be used during analysis; 5 μL concd solv. must not show any trace of peaks beyond solv. front. (Distd-in-glass solvs generally conform to test stds.) Purify solvs not passing test as in (**a**) and (**b**).

(**a**) *Methanol*.—Anhyd. Reflux 1 L with 10 g KOH and 25 g Zn dust 3 hr. Distil, discarding first 100 mL. (*Caution: See* **51.011**, **51.037**, and **51.066**.)

(**b**) *Chloroform*.—Redistil at bp. Add 1% MeOH if stored. (*Caution: See* **51.056**.)

(**c**) *Flavor std soln*.—(*1*) *Stock soln*.—79 mg/mL (10,000 ppm). Dil. 7.90 g compd to 100 mL with MeOH. (*2*) *Working soln*.—7.9 mg/mL (1000 ppm). Dil. 1 mL stock soln to 10 mL with MeOH.

(**d**) *Internal std solns*.—Use *n*-decyl alcohol for Me salicylate detn and *m*-tolyl acetate for detn of other compds. Prep. stock and working std solns as in (**c**).

(**e**) *Defoaming agent*.—Dow Corning Antifoam A, or equiv.

12.047 ***Apparatus***

(**a**) *Steam distillation apparatus*.—500 mL r-b flask with long neck, ₮ 24/40 joint; adapter, ₮ 24/40 inner joint at bottom and at side at 75° angle and with ₮ 24/40 joint at top; gas inlet tube, 30 cm, ₮ 24/40 inner joint and perforated 8 mm bulb at dispersion tip; condenser, 200 mm ₮ 24/40 joint; and adapter, vac. takeoff type with extended lower tube, straight joint ₮ 24/40.

(**b**) *Concentrator*.—Evaporative concentrator, Kuderna-Danish type, 500 mL, with 10 mL receiving flask.

(**c**) *Gas chromatograph*.—With flame ionization detector, and operating parameters as follows: 1.8 m (6′) × 4 mm id glass column, coiled or U-shaped, packed with 15% polypropylene glycol adipate (Reoplex 400) on 60–80 mesh Gas-Chrom P (w/w); temps (°)—column 130 (isothermal), detector 220, injection port 180; N carrier gas 40 psi at ca 90 mL/min. Column may be programmed over range 90–150° at 2°/min.

12.048 ***Determination of Relative Retention Time (RT)***

(**a**) *Methyl salicylate*.—Pipet 1 mL working std soln and 1 mL *n*-decyl alcohol working internal std soln into 10 mL vol. flask, and dil. to vol. with MeOH.

(**b**) *Other flavor compounds*.—Pipet 1 mL appropriate working std soln and 5 mL *m*-tolyl acetate working internal std soln into 10 mL vol. flask, and dil. to vol. with MeOH.

Inject 3–5 μL into gas chromatograph. Set sensitivity and attenuation controls to provide peak ht ≤80% of chart scale.

Calc. RT = time for std component peak to emerge/time for internal std peak to emerge. (Time is measured from emergence of solv. front.) Use RT to identify component peak in sample. Calc. peak area (PA).

12.049 ***Determination***

(Analyze samples on same day and under same conditions used for detn of RT. *Caution: See* **51.011** and **51.056**.)

(**a**) *Methyl salicylate*.—Place 200 mL sample, degassed if necessary, in 500 mL r-b flask; add 10 mL MeOH, few SiC chips, and small amt defoamer. Add 1 mL *n*-decyl alcohol working internal std, (**d**), and attach to distg app. not connected to steam generator. Bring sample to incipient boil, connect steam generator, and collect 90 mL distillate at ca 2 mL/min in 100 mL Nessler tube or graduate contg 10 mL MeOH to cover delivery tube outlet. Rinse condenser and delivery tube into distillate twice with 5 mL MeOH. Quant. transfer distillate to 250 mL separator. Add 50 mL satd NaCl soln and ext with 25, 25, and 10 mL $CHCl_3$ by carefully shaking 5 min for each extn. Filter $CHCl_3$ thru 12.5 cm Whatman No. 30 paper contg 3–5 g Na_2SO_4 into 500 mL evaporative concentrator. Wash separator and paper with 10–15 mL $CHCl_3$ into concentrator. Add few SiC chips and evap. on steam bath to ca 7 mL. Cool, and dil. to 10.0 mL with $CHCl_3$. Det. Me salicylate by GLC as in **12.048**.

mg Me salicylate/mL or ppm = $(PA/PA')(PA_I'/PA_I) \times C \times F$,

where PA and PA' are peak areas of sample and std solns, resp., PA_I' and PA_I are peak areas of internal std in std and sample solns, resp., C = concn Me salicylate in working std soln (7.9 mg/mL or 1000 ppm), and F = diln factor (1/20).

(**b**) *Other flavor compounds*.—Proceed as in (**a**) except use 5.0 mL *m*-tolyl acetate working internal std soln, (**d**), and collect 150 mL distillate at 5 mL/min.

Benzoate, Caffeine, and Saccharin in Soda Beverages
High Performance Liquid Chromatographic Method (9)
Official First Action

12.050 ***Principle***

Saccharin, benzoate, and caffeine are simultaneously quantitated in soda beverages by HPLC, using HOAc soln as mobile phase. Artificial colors and sorbates may interfere. Beverage blanks contg color or sorbate should be run to assure noninterference by these compds. In absence of beverage blanks, analyze samples with 2 different mobile phases with different amts of isopropanol and/or HOAc or by method of std additions. Adjustment of mobile phase (% acid and/or % isopropanol) can resolve interfering peaks.

12.051 ***Apparatus and Reagents***

(**a**) *Liquid chromatograph*.—Waters Associates ALC/GPC with 6000A solv. delivery system and model U6K injector, or equiv., UV 254 nm detector, 10 mv strip chart recorder (Houston Omni Scribe, or equiv.), and μ Bondapak C_{18} column, 300 × 4 (id) mm, or equiv., with flow rate of 2 mL/min. Detector sensitivity: adjustable from 0.02–0.05 aufs.

(**b**) *Mobile phase*.—20% HOAc (v/v) buffered to pH 3.0 with satd NaOAc soln. Modify with 0–2% isopropanol to obtain baseline resolution and retention times of stds from mixed std soln in ca 10 min. Soln is stable 2–3 days. Degas prior to use. (Alternatively, lower HOAc concn may be used, and, for some columns, may be necessary to obtain retention and/or resolution. Lower HOAc concn solns give longer retention times, e.g. 5% HOAc elutes compds in 35 min.)

(**c**) *Std solns*.—Prep. individual std solns from compds of known purity to give following concns: Na saccharin, 0.50 mg/mL; caffeine, 0.050 mg/mL; and Na benzoate, 0.50 mg/mL. Use these solns to det. sensitivity for detector response and retention times of individual stds.

(**d**) *Mixed std solns*.—Prep. soln contg 0.50 mg/mL Na saccharin, 0.50 mg/mL Na benzoate, and 0.050 mg/mL caffeine. Use this soln to optimize HPLC conditions for complete resolution of the 3 compds and to quantitate.

12.052 ***Preparation of Sample***

(**a**) *Carbonated beverages*.—Decarbonate by agitation or ultrasonic treatment. If free of particulate matter, inject directly.

(**b**) *Beverages containing particulate matter*.—Filter thru Millipore filter (0.45 μ), discarding first few mL filtrate. If large amt of particulate matter is present, centrf. prior to filtering. Inject filtered soln directly.

12.053 ***Determination***

Inject known vol. (ca 10 μL) of mixed std soln in duplicate. Peak hts should agree within $\leqslant$2.5%. Inject known vol. (ca 10 μL) of prepd sample in duplicate. Measure peak hts of std and sample components.

$$\% \text{ Compd} = C' \times (H/H') \times (V'/V) \times 0.1,$$

where C' = concn of std in mg/mL; H and H' = av. peak ht of sample and std, resp.; V and V' = vol. injected in μL of sample and std, resp.

12.054 Alginates in Chocolate Beverage Products
Official Final Action

See **13.058**.

SELECTED REFERENCES

(*1*) J. Agr. Research **33,** 301(1926); JAOAC **11,** 46, 505(1928).
(*2*) Ind. Eng. Chem. **15,** 732(1923); JAOAC **11,** 47, 505(1928).
(*3*) JAOAC **19,** 408(1936).
(*4*) JAOAC **16,** 420(1933); **19,** 75(1936).
(*5*) JAOAC **39,** 712(1956); **40,** 433(1957).
(*6*) JAOAC **41,** 617(1958); **45,** 252(1962).
(*7*) JAOAC **50,** 857(1967).
(*8*) JAOAC **52,** 481(1969); **54,** 900(1971).
(*9*) JAOAC **62,** 1011(1979).

13. Cacao Bean and Its Products

13.001 Preparation of Sample—Procedure

(**a**) *Powdered products.*—Mix thoroly and preserve in tightly stoppered bottles.

(**b**) *Chocolate products.*—(*1*) Chill ca 200 g sweet or bitter chocolate until hard, and grate or shave to fine granular condition. Mix thoroly and preserve in tightly stoppered bottle in cool place. Alternatively—

(*2*) Melt ca 200 g bitter, sweet, or milk chocolate by placing in suitable container and partly immersing container in bath at ca 50°. Stir frequently until sample melts and reaches temp. of 45–50°. Remove from bath, stir thoroly, and while still liq., remove portion for analysis, using glass or metal tube, 4–10 mm diam., provided with close-fitting plunger to expel sample from tube, or disposable plastic syringe.

13.002 Moisture (*1*)—Official First Action

Dry 2 g prepd sample, **13.001**, to const wt in Pt dish in air oven at 100°. (Al dish may be used when ash is not detd on same sample.) Report loss in wt as H_2O.

Karl Fischer Method (2)—Official Final Action

(Applicable to milk chocolate and confectionary coatings)

13.003 ***Apparatus and Reagents***

(**a**) *Karl Fischer titration assembly.*—Manual or automatic, with stirrer.

(**b**) *Syringes.*—1 mL with needle end cap (0–40 unit insulin type is satisfactory) and 10 mL without needle (disposable plastic type is satisfactory).

(**c**) *Karl Fischer reagent.*—*See* **32.048(a)**.

(**d**) *Karl Fischer solvent.*—Mix equal vols anhyd. MeOH and $CHCl_3$.

13.004 ***Determination***

Stdze reagent, (**c**), by accurately weighing ca 125 mg H_2O from 1 mL syringe (5 units) into 30–50 mL pretitrd solv. (Keep needle capped except while delivering H_2O, to eliminate evapn.) Titr. with reagent, (**c**), until near end point; then add in 0.1 mL increments until end point remains 1 min (usually >50 μamp.). Calc. C = g H_2O/mL reagent. Duplicates must agree within 0.1 mg H_2O/mL reagent.

Melt sample in closed Whirl-Pak bag supported in 400 mL beaker ≤2 hr in oven at 40±2°. Mix thoroly by first gently squeezing bag and then stirring ca 1 min with glass rod or spatula. Remove portion with 10 mL syringe, weigh, add portion contg ca 100 mg H_2O to 30–50 mL pretitrd reagent, and reweigh. Titr. as in stdzn.

$$\% \, H_2O = \text{mL reagent} \times C \times 100/\text{g sample}$$

13.005 Ash (*3*)—Official Final Action

AOAC-Office International du Cacao et du Chocolat Method

Accurately weigh 2–5 g prepd sample, **13.001**, into 25–50 mL Pt, quartz, or Vycor dish previously heated to 600°, covered with watch glass, cooled in desiccator, and weighed. Carbonize by either (*1*) slowly bringing temp. of furnace to 600° in hood with exhaust vent open or door not completely closed; or (*2*) heating under IR lamps until smoking ceases and then transferring to 600° furnace. Heat 2 hr, moisten cooled ash with alcohol, dry under IR lamps or on steam bath, and re-ash at 1 hr intervals until change in wt is <1 mg, or overnight. Cover with watch glass, cool in desiccator, and weigh as soon as room temp. is attained.

13.006 Soluble and Insoluble Ash
Official Final Action

Proceed as in **31.015**, using ash from **13.005**.

Alkalinity of Insoluble and Soluble Ash (*4*)
Official First Action

AOAC-Office International du Cacao et du Chocolat Method

13.007 ***Reagents***

(**a**) *Bromocresol green indicator soln.*—Dissolve 0.75 g indicator in 100 mL alcohol.

(**b**) *Citrate buffer soln.*—pH 4.50 at 20°. Dissolve 21.008 g citric acid.H_2O in 200 mL 1*N* NaOH and dil. to 1 L with freshly boiled H_2O. Mix 719 mL of this soln with 281 mL 0.1*N* HCl, **50.011–50.012**, and add 10 mg HgI_2 as preservative.

13.008 ***Determination***

(**a**) *Insoluble ash.*—Ash sample as in **13.005**. Add 10 mL H_2O to ash, heat nearly to bp, filter thru ashless paper into 300 mL erlenmeyer, and wash with hot H_2O to total vol. of ca 60 mL. Cool and reserve for (**b**). Return paper and contents to ashing dish, burn off paper, and reignite 30 min at 600°. Cover with watch glass, cool in desiccator, and weigh as soon as room temp. is attained (insol. ash). Add 10 mL hot H_2O and 10.0 mL 0.5*N* HCl, **50.011–50.012**, heat to incipient boiling, and cool. Transfer quant. to 300 mL erlenmeyer. Wash ashing dish with H_2O to total vol. of ca 60 mL. Heat in boiling H_2O bath 15 min, with repeated swirling. Cool, add 2 drops bromocresol green, (**a**), and titr. excess HCl with 0.1*N* NaOH, **50.032–50.035**, using citrate buffer soln with 2 drops bromocresol green as end point color ref. Titr. blank similarly. Express alky in terms of mL 1*N* alkali/100 g sample.

(**b**) *Soluble ash.*—Titr. reserved filtrate from (**a**) with 0.1*N* HCl, **50.011–50.012**, using Me orange, **6.004(g)**. Express alky in terms of mL 1*N* acid/100 g sample.

13.009 Ash Insoluble in Acid—Official Final Action

Proceed as in **30.008**, using total ash obtained in **13.005**, or H_2O-insol. residue obtained in **13.006**.

13.010 pH (*5*)—Official Final Action

Office International du Cacao et du Chocolate-AOAC Method

(**a**) *For products other than cacao butter.*—Weigh 10 g sample into 150 mL beaker and slowly add, with stirring, 90 mL boiling H_2O. Suspension must be free from lumps. Filter, cool filtrate to 20–25°, and immediately det. pH, using electrodes and potentiometer stdzd with buffers at pH 4.00, **50.007(c)**, and 6.86, **50.007(d)**. Report to nearest 0.1 pH unit.

(**b**) *For cacao butter.*—Melt sample and mech. stir 5 min with equal wt of H_2O at 50°. Sep. aq. layer, cool to 20–25°, filter, and det. pH as in (**a**).

13.011 Total Nitrogen—Official Final Action

AOAC-Office International du Cacao et du Chocolat Method

Proceed as in **2.057**, using 0.7–2.2 g sample. Small amt of paraffin or silicone antifoam may be added to reduce foaming. Digest 1–2 hr after soln is clear. Protein = N × 6.25 (includes N from purines and other N-contg compds). Report % N to nearest 0.01%; protein, 0.05%. Duplicate detns should agree within 0.30% protein.

SHELL (*6*)

13.012 ★ *In Cacao Nibs—Official Final Action* ★

Sample is reduced and sieved, and shell is picked out by hand. *See* **13.010–13.014**, 12th ed.

In Cacao Products Other Than Cacao Nibs

(Following methods include detns the results of which can be used to est. amt of shell when compared with corresponding values obtained on authentic samples of cacao shell.)

13.013 Crude Fiber (*7*)—Official Final Action

(**a**) *In cacao products not containing dairy ingredients*.—Treat 7 g liquor (or amt of sweet chocolate or cocoa equiv. to 7 g liquor) in centrf. bottle with two 100 mL portions ether, centrfg and decanting after each addn. Dry residue on steam bath and then in oven at ca 100° and crush to powder in bottle with flat-end rod. If necessary, grind material in mortar and ext third time with ether. Wash mixt. in bottle with three 100 mL portions H_2O at room temp., shaking well each time, until no cacao material adheres to bottle. Centrf. 10–15 min after each washing, and decant aq. layer. Wash residue in same fashion with two 100 mL portions alcohol and one 100 mL portion ether. Transfer residue to Pt dish, dry to const wt, and grind in mortar. Weigh 2 g dried material and det. % crude fiber (D) as in **7.065**. Calc. % crude fiber on H_2O-, fat-, and sugar-free basis (E) by formula $E = 0.7D$.

(**b**) *In cacao products containing dairy ingredients*.—Treat 50 g milk chocolate with three 100 mL portions ether in centrf. bottle, centrfg and decanting after each addn. Dry residue in bottle and crush to powder with flat-end glass rod as in (**a**). Shake with 100 mL *1% $Na_2C_2O_4$ soln*, and let stand 30 min. Centrf. and decant. Wash in bottle with three 100 mL portions H_2O at room temp., shaking well each time, until no cacao material adheres to bottle. Centrf. 10–15 min after each washing and decant. Wash residue in same fashion with two 100 mL portions alcohol and one 100 mL portion ether. Transfer residue to Pt dish, dry to const wt at 100°, and grind in mortar. Weigh 2 g dried material and det. % crude fiber as in **7.065**. % Crude fiber found × 0.7 = % crude fiber on fat-, sugar-, H_2O-, and milk-free basis.

13.014 Pectic Acid (*8*)—Official Final Action

(Sweet chocolate, usually characterized by its color, may contain small amts of milk solids. When in doubt, use method for milk chocolate, (**c**). *Caution: See* **51.086**.)

(**a**) *In sweet chocolate containing no milk solids.*—(*1*) *Extraction of fat*.—Weigh, within ±0.15 g, amt (14–60 g) of well mixed grated sample contg 4.7–5.2 g dry, fat-free cacao, and place in one or two 250 mL centrf. bottles. (If sample is >50 g, distribute it ca equally between 2 bottles.) (Make detns in duplicate.) Add 120 mL pet ether (bp 30–65°), or ether, at ca 30°, to each bottle, shake thoroly, centrf., and decant. Repeat extn with another 100 mL solv.; then ext with 100 mL alcohol, decant, and discard exts.

(*2*) *Extraction of color, tannins, etc.*—To each bottle add (from graduate) 150 mL *acidified 82% alcohol* (10 mL HCl + 432 mL alcohol dild to 500 mL with H_2O) that has been warmed so that temp. of liq. in centrf. bottle is 55°. Stopper, shake vigorously 2 min, centrf. 6–8 min, decant, and discard supernate. Add 100 mL alcohol to residue in each bottle, shake, centrf. as before, decant, and discard exts.

(*3*) *Extraction of pectin*.—Measure 150 mL H_2O in graduate, add ca 75 mL to 1 bottle, stopper, shake vigorously to disperse residue thoroly, decant into other bottle contg remainder of sample, and again shake vigorously until residue is thoroly dispersed. Decant mixt. into 500 mL wide-mouth erlenmeyer, rinse mouth of bottle with ca 1 mL H_2O from wash bottle, and complete transfer of residue from bottles with ca 45 and 30 mL successive portions of H_2O remaining in graduate. Make mixt. in flask just alk. to litmus with NH_4OH (1+1) (ca 0.7 mL; note vol. used; *See Note*). Acidify with HOAc, add 0.5 mL excess, and then add 50 mL *2% $(NH_4)_2C_2O_4 \cdot H_2O$ soln*, using soln to wash down sides of flask.

Pass glass stirrer, with 2.5–3 cm (1–1¼") diam. loop (perpendicular to shaft on end), loosely thru hole in rubber stopper or thru glass tube of slightly larger diam. held in rubber stopper placed in mouth of flask. Attach shaft of stirrer to motor, or air rotor, to stir contents of flask continuously, immerse flask below level of contents in H_2O bath held at 90–92°, and stir moderately 3 hr. If level of liq. in flask is appreciably reduced, add enough hot H_2O to bring back to original level.

Remove flask, cool to 45°, quant. transfer contents to 250 mL vol. flask, dil. to vol. with H_2O at 45°, and add 1.5 mL excess to correct for vol. of cacao solids. Mix contents well, pour into centrf. bottle, and centrf. at 1800 rpm ca 15 min. Decant supernate ext, which may be turbid or opalescent, into 400 mL beaker. Rinse any residue in flask into centrf. bottle with alcohol and reserve this cacao residue for further treatment to est. fat-free cacao in the sample. Warm ext to 45°, pour into graduate, note vol., and return to beaker. Rinse graduate with two 5 mL portions H_2O, and add to beaker. Cool in bath to 15–17°, make alk. to phthln (internal indicator) with *15% NaOH soln*, and add 11 mL excess. (*See Note*.) Stir, and let stand in bath 20 min at 15–17°. Decant alk. liq. into two 250 mL centrf. bottles, distributing vol. ca equally. Let drain, and rinse twice with 5–8 mL cold H_2O, adding 1 rinsing to each bottle. Add 10 mL HCl to each bottle, with stirring, and then gradually add, with continued stirring, 40 mL alcohol. Add to each bottle 0.8–1.0 g *mixt. of Filter-Cel and Celite 545* (1+1). Stir, rinse rod, stopper bottles, shake well, and centrf. 10–12 min. Decant and discard supernates without disturbing sediment, and wash residues once by shaking contents of each bottle with 100 mL alcohol, centrfg, and decanting.

Add 75 mL H_2O to 1 bottle, stopper, and shake well. Make slightly alk. with few drops NH_4OH (1+1) and shake again. Decant liq. into second bottle, stopper, shake again, make alk. to litmus with NH_4OH (1+1), and add 0.5 mL excess. Stopper, and shake thoroly 1–1.5 min to dissolve pectic acid ppt. (Drops of liq. clinging to lip of bottle may be washed into second bottle with small squirt of H_2O from wash bottle; otherwise do not rinse at this point.) Filter, with suction, thru hardened paper (Whatman 41-H or 54, or equiv.) on 11 cm buchner. Let bottle drain well; then rinse bottle twice with 25 mL portions H_2O, each contg 1–2 drops NH_4OH (1+1), pour rinsings on filter, and wait for each rinse to drain thru filter before adding another.

Pour filtrate into 250 mL centrf. bottle, let flask drain, and rinse twice with 5 mL H_2O. (Use of bell jar permits filtration directly into centrf. bottle.) Add 5 mL HCl to contents of centrf. bottle, stir in 90–100 mL alcohol, rinse rod with alcohol (do not add

★ Surplus method—*see* inside front cover.

filter-aid), stopper, shake, and centrf. 8 min at 1500–1800 rpm. Decant into beaker, retaining most of ppt in bottle, and filter liq. thru 15 cm Whatman 41-H paper, or equiv., on fluted funnel. Pour ppt and liq. remaining in centrf. bottle onto filter paper and drain thoroly. (Do not rinse.)

Quant. transfer ppt in bottle and on filter to 250 mL beaker, using total of 75 mL 60–75° H_2O. Cool beaker and contents in bath at 15–17° and add, with stirring, 15% NaOH soln (also cooled) until mixt. is alk. to phthln (internal indicator). Add 3 mL excess and let stand in bath 15 min at 15–17°. During this time, heat on steam bath 2 wash bottles, contg, resp., *wash solns: A,* mixt. of 200 mL H_2O, 50 mL alcohol, and 20 mL HCl (1+2.5); *B,* 400 mL alcohol dild to 950 mL with H_2O.

Remove beaker from bath, acidify contents with 10 mL HCl (1+2.5) while stirring, and dil. to 100 mL with H_2O. (Est. vol. by comparison with 100 mL in similar beaker.) Add few glass beads, cover, bring contents to bp, and boil 5 min. Remove from heat; add 10 mL HCl, with stirring, and then 400 mg *prepd asbestos* (previously alkali- and acid-washed and ignited, and free of coarse particles). Stir 40 sec, and immediately filter thru Whatman 41-H paper, or equiv., on 7–11 cm buchner with very gentle suction. (Suction should be so gentle that it can hardly be felt when thumb is placed on rubber tube before attaching tube to flask; sample should filter in small steady stream, and filtrate should be clear or only slightly opalescent, with no immediate sepn of ppt.) Wash beaker and filter with three ca 25 mL portions wash soln *A*, and then with four or five ca 25 mL portions wash soln *B* to remove acid. (Washings should be clear and pass thru filter readily. Ignore any appearance of ppt in flask at this stage.)

Place filter and ppt on fairly large, short-stem funnel, and wash pectic acid ppt and asbestos into Pt dish with hot H_2O. Det. blank on 400 mg asbestos by adding it to hot acid soln, filtering, and drying in same manner as sample. Heat dishes on steam bath until asbestos and ppt appear thoroly dry. Dry sample and blank in oven at 100° to const wt (±0.2 mg; ca 1 hr), cool in desiccator, weigh, ignite, cool, and reweigh. Loss in wt of sample − loss in wt of blank = wt of pectic acid in aliquot taken.

This wt × 250/vol. ext taken = wt pectic acid in sample.

To obtain dry, fat-free cacao in sample, add 100 mL alcohol to cacao residue reserved in centrf. bottle, stopper, shake well, centrf., and decant. Again shake with 100 mL alcohol, rinse stopper, and wash down sides of bottle with alcohol from wash bottle; centrf. and decant. Repeat extn, using 100 mL ether, washing down sides, centrfg, and decanting. Let residual ether evap. Using brush and spatula, quant. transfer residue to tared Al dish with cover; dry dish and contents 1–2 hr in oven at 100°; cover dish, cool in desiccator, and weigh. Wt residue × 1.9 = wt dry, fat-free cacao in sample,

Wt pectic acid × 100/wt dry, fat-free cacao = % pectic acid.

(b) *In chocolate liquor, breakfast cocoa, cocoa, and low-fat cocoa.*—Place ca 15 g cocoa or 25 g chocolate liquor, prepd as in **13.001**, in centrf. bottle. To remove most of fat, shake thoroly with 100 mL pet ether (bp 30–65°) or ether; centrf., decant, and repeat extn with another 100 mL pet ether or ether. Shake residue with third portion solv., and filter thru Whatman 41-H or 54 paper, or equiv., on 11 cm buchner with gentle to moderate suction. (Apply vac. and wet filter with solv. before starting filtration.) Let residue suck dry, transfer to porcelain dish or casserole, grind gently with pestle to pulverize and mix, and transfer to Al dish with cover. Dry ca 45 min in oven at 100°, cover dish, and cool in desiccator. Weigh 5 g of the dry, fat-free residue into 250 mL centrf. bottle, and proceed as in **(a)**(*1*), last sentence, beginning ". . . then ext with 100 mL alcohol, . . ." and continue as in (*2*) and (*3*) thru next-to-last par. (directions for calcg wt pectic acid in sample).

(Wt pectic acid found/5) × 100
= % pectic acid in dry, fat-free cacao.

(No estn of dry, fat-free cacao is necessary, since weighed amt of dry, fat-free cacao is used for pectic acid detn.)

(c) *In products containing milk solids.*—(*1*) *Removal of fat.*—Weigh (±0.2 g) sample contg ca 5 g dry, fat-free liquor (60–110 g milk chocolate, etc.), and distribute ca equally between two 250 mL centrf. bottles. Add 120 mL pet ether or ether at 25–30°, shake thoroly, centrf., and decant. Add another 120 mL portion tepid solv. to each bottle, shake thoroly, centrf., and decant. In same manner ext contents of each bottle with 100–110 mL acetone.

(*2*) *Extraction of milk protein.*—Add enough acetone (ca 90 mL) to make total of ca 110 mL with acetone remaining in residue. (Est. on basis that ½ original sample of 75 g retains ca 20 mL acetone in residue of each bottle.) Stopper, and shake vigorously to disperse residue thoroly. Quickly add 100 mL *triethanolamine soln* (90 mL triethanolamine dild to 500 mL with H_2O) to each bottle, stopper immediately, and shake well 2 min. Let stand ca 1 min for foam to rise; then centrf. 12–14 min at 1500–1800 rpm. Carefully decant and discard supernate without disturbing residue, and ext residue with 100–120 mL mixt. of acetone and the triethanolamine soln (110+100), centrfg and decanting as before. Then add 100 mL 85% alcohol to each bottle, shake, centrf., decant, and discard ext.

To residue in each bottle add 15–20 mL acidified 82% alcohol, **(a)**(*2*), stir, and add enough HCl to make residue acid to litmus. Continue as for sweet chocolate, beginning with **(a)**(*2*).

Note: Vol. of NH_4OH used should be noted, excess avoided, and approx. concn of NH_3 detd. (Soln becomes much less concd on standing from loss of NH_3 around stopper.) This is necessary because in first hydrolysis (saponification) of pectin, part of NaOH soln added (after soln of sample has been made alk. to phthln) is used up in replacing with Na the NH_4 in NH_4 salts present. The 11 mL 15% NaOH soln added furnishes excess of 4–5 mL of this soln over amt required to neutze acid and replace NH_4 with Na, provided ≤1.15 mL 7.5*N* NH_4OH (= 2.3 mL 15% NaOH soln) is added to neutze residual HCl. (Approx. 3.75 mL 15% NaOH soln is needed to replace with Na the NH_4 in $(NH_4)_2C_2O_4$ soln used in extn of pectin.) If >1.15 mL of the NH_4OH soln is needed to neutze HCl in **(a)**(*3*), correspondingly increase vol. of 15% NaOH soln used for saponification, but avoid excess of >5–6 mL.

Spiral Vessel Count (*9*)—Official Final Action

13.015 ***Apparatus***

(a) *Sieve.*—No. 230, 5" (13 cm) diam., stainless steel.

(b) *Grinding equipment.*—(*1*) *Coarse grinding* (*cutting action*).—Labconco mill No. 900 (discontinued), Hobart Food Cutter No. 84181-D (Hobart Manufacturing Co., Troy, OH 45374), or equiv. (*2*) *Fine grinding.*—13 cm (5") glass mortar and pestle or Torsion Balance Co. elec. mortar grinders MG1 or MG2 (Torsion Balance Co., 35 Monhegan St, Clifton, NJ 07013). Adjust MG2 so that pestle and shaft are not under tension by loosening top knob and lock nut by 3 turns and adjust closing spring control to ½ tension.

(c) *Aluminum dish.*—Diam. ca 77 mm, ht ca 33 mm; with cover.

(d) *Brush.*—No 10, nylon, rubber set, oval sash paint brush with bristles cut to 4–4.5 cm (available from Sherwin-Williams Co., Prospect Ave, Cleveland, OH 44101, or distributors).

13.016 ***Preparation of Sample***

(a) *Chocolate liquor, chocolate.*—Prep. as in **13.001(b)**.

(b) *Expeller cake.*—Crush with mortar and pestle and grind to pass No. 30 sieve in mill, (**b**)(*1*), ca ½ teaspoonful at time. Mix well and store in tightly stoppered jar.

(**c**) *Cocoa press cake*.—Prep. and store as in (**b**). (Many samples can be easily pulverized after drying 2–3 hr at 60–70°.)

(**d**) *Cocoa*.—Use as is. Store as in (**b**).

13.017 ***Defatting and Grinding***

(*Caution: See* **51.054**.)

Set up in hood No. 230, 5" (12.7 cm) sieve in 15 cm (6") glass funnel with tip dipping ca 2 cm into 500 mL flat-bottom Pyrex centrf. bottle.

Place 15 g cocoa, coarsely ground (30–40 mesh) cocoa press cake, or expeller cake, or 25–30 g chocolate or chocolate liquor in 250 mL centrf. bottle. Add 100 mL ether, stopper, shake thoroly to dissolve fat, and pour onto sieve. Wash material on sieve well with ether. Wash lower rim and both sides of sieve and inside of funnel with ether. Let material on sieve stand until dry (ca 15 min).

Centrf. mixt. in 500 mL centrf. bottle 10 min at 2000 rpm. Decant and discard supernate. Replace centrf. bottle under funnel.

Place sieve with dried cocoa material in receiver (sieve bottom pan). Brush material thru sieve with No. 10 sash paint brush. Transfer retains, using brush, to 12.7 cm glass mortar and grind ca 45 sec with glass pestle, or grind 2 min in motor-driven mortar grinder. Transfer to sieve and rebrush. Repeat grindings and brushings until virtually all material passes thru sieve. Quant. transfer material, including small amt on sieve (<20 mg), thru funnel to the 500 mL centrf. bottle. Clean with brush, and clean brush against rim of sieve. Wash screen, receiver, mortar and pestle, and funnel (but not brush) with ether, letting washings run into centrf. bottle. Rub off coated material on funnel and other app. with policeman, rinsing with ether thru funnel into centrf. bottle. Stopper bottle and shake thoroly. Remove stopper and rinse with ether. Centrf. 10 min at 2000 rpm. Decant and discard supernate. Add 100 mL ether and repeat extn. Add 100 mL ether, stopper, and shake. Immediately pour into fritted glass crucible (disk diam. 60 mm; medium porosity) under vac. Wash material from bottle into crucible with ether. Wash twice with ca 35 mL ether and continue vac. until dry (ca 20 min).

Quant. transfer material from crucible to glass mortar and grind gently until fine. (Spoon may be used in transfer but use rubber policeman to scrape disk.) Quant. transfer ground material to Al dish. With cover in place, rotate dish until contents are well mixed. Dry on steam bath 10–15 min to remove traces of ether, and then in oven 1 hr at 100°.

13.018 ***Determination***

Make duplicate detns. Accurately weigh 0.350 g extd and dried material and transfer to 150 mL beaker. Gradually stir in 25 mL *4% NaOH soln* until smooth. Bring to initial boil, using asbestos mat over flame. Immediately reduce to weak flame and boil gently 2 min with frequent stirring. Cool somewhat and transfer to 25 × 100 mm Pyrex culture tube with small portions H_2O. Centrf. until clear (3 min) at full speed of International Clinical Centrifuge, using No. 571 curved rubber cushion in No. 320 shield, or equiv. Decant carefully and discard supernate. Add H_2O to tube until ca ¾ full, stopper, and shake until residue is well dispersed. Centrf. and decant as before.

Add H_2O to tube until ca ½ full, stopper, and shake until product is well dispersed. Transfer soln to 50 mL g-s graduate contg 25 mL glycerol. Wash remaining material from tube to graduate with small portions H_2O, stoppering and shaking tube to aid transfer. Stopper graduate, shake, dil. to 50 mL with H_2O, and shake. Transfer to 100 mL beaker. Stir well with vertical rotary motion. While stirring, withdraw small drop to Howard mold counting chamber, and make slide as in **44.096**. Fisher Scientific Co. Scoopula (Cat. No. 14–357) bent at right angles ca 2 cm from broad end is useful for stirring; metal prong strip of Acco paper fastener ca 6 mm wide bent ca 135°, 6 mm from end, is useful for withdrawing drop.

With microscope adjusted for mold counting (field of view 1.382 mm at 100×), count fields pos. for spiral vessels, at varying depths, at 200× in 25 fields of each of 8 slides of each of the 2 detns (total of 400 fields). Report as pos. field one that contains any portion of section of spiral vessels, but none smaller than well developed "S" or "Z" either sep. or attached to piece of shell. (*See* **13.020**.) Average results and report as % pos. fields present. This is spiral vessel count.

Det. % shell in chocolate component by comparison with std curve prepd from spiral vessel count values listed in Table **13:01** plotted against % shell in chocolate component. Use column for counts listed under "≤15% shell."

Table 13:01. Standard Spiral Vessel Count Values

% Shell in Chocolate component	Spiral Vessel Counts ≤ 15% Shell (0.350 g/50 mL)	>15% Shell (0.200 g/100 mL)
0	4.5	1.5
1	15	5.8
2	24.4	9.7
3	32.8	13.2
4	40	16.6
5	47	19.7
8	62.2	27.7
11	72.9	34.8
15	83.4	42.4
20	91.1	50.1
30	98.2	62.1
60		80.0
100		86.8

13.019 ***Spiral Vessel Count Values***

For 1–15% shell (spiral vessel counts of 15–83.4), following formula gives values comparable to Table **13:01**:

$$S = (538P - 1777)/(7043 - 50P),$$

where S = shell in chocolate component and P = spiral vessel count.

For samples contg >15% shell (spiral vessel count >83.4) repeat detn thruout, but weigh 0.200 g sample and dil. to 100 mL with H_2O in 100 mL g-s graduate contg 50 mL glycerol. Count at 200×. Use column for counts listed under ">15% shell" for prepg std curve.

13.020 ***Counting Instructions***

Spiral vessels vary greatly in size. No distinction is made in counting because of size differentiation. In appearance spiral vessels have parallel walls of even intensity with clear centers. On occasional piece, walls may be frayed due to grinding. Walls of very small vessels do not appear as sharp as those of the larger ones at 200×. Some spirals are closely knit together. Photomicrographs of spiral vessels and pos. sections of them are shown in Fig. **13:01**.

In counting spiral vessels, most pos. fields counted will have easily recognized pos. spiral vessel figures such as long or short mass of spiral vessels, large broken sections of these, or sometimes tangled mass of spiral vessels. Some sine wave-like figures and some full "S"- or "Z"-like figures will be found.

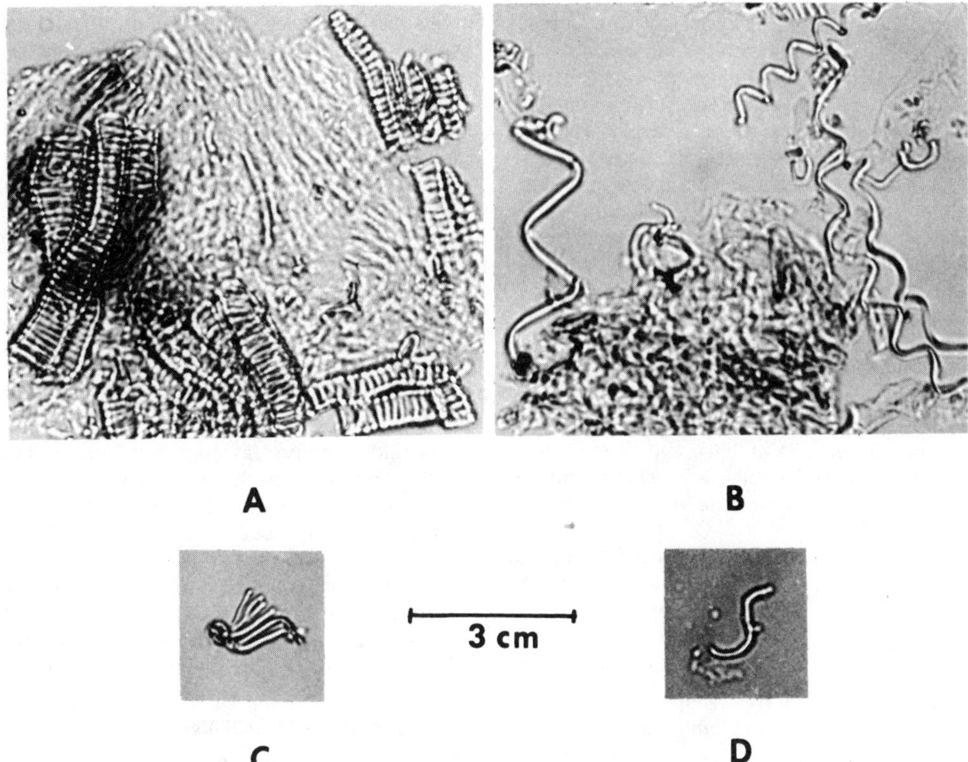

FIG. 13:01—Spiral vessel sections ca 340×. A, Mass of spiral vessels; note size differential and narrowing effects. B, Spiral vessels stretched out; note difference in size. C, Broken section; count pos. if three joined rods are present. D, Pos. "S"-shaped section.

There will, however, be some smaller figures and some poorly formed "S"- or "Z"-like figures present in some fields. For these figures, the following applies:

"S"- or "Z"-like figures or mirror images of these should have ⅓ or more of top and bottom normal linear distance for such figure and not just stubs. One-third of center section is est. of this distance. If "2"-like figure is found, lower portion or "V" part of figure should be well extended and sufficient top curve should be present so that figure does not appear essentially like a "V." Figures may be stretched out. Spiral vessels in breaking sometimes break so that there will be joined sections of half circles or less. Count as pos. any such section consisting of ≥3 nearly ½ circles joined. Two spiral circles joined together are counted pos. Circles showing no spiraling are not counted. A "W" figure is pos.; a "V" or "C" is not. In viewing small section of spirals perpendicular to axis, 2nd and 3rd spiral, etc., may be just faintly seen, but the section should be counted as pos.

There is some fine cell wall structure present which when broken may fracture into "Z"-like characters similar in appearance to "Z" formed from small thin spiral vessels. Care should be exercised in discriminating between the two.

Stone Cell and Group Count Method (*10*)
Official Final Action

13.021 ***Apparatus and Reagents***

(**a**) *Slide and cover glass.*—75 × 38 mm slide with lines 0.5 mm apart, nearly across slide, parallel to 75 mm side, and ruled from top to bottom; 33 × 33 × 0.2 mm cover glass.

(**b**) *Scoop.*—Thin (ca 0.01–0.02 mm thick) stainless steel strip ca 4.8 mm wide with 90° bend extending outward 3 mm.

(**c**) *Magnetic stirrer.*—With stirring bar ca 16 mm long × 6 mm diam. Stirring bar 13 × 8 mm with ridge in center will circle walls of 1 oz ointment jar (ca 36 mm diam × 40 mm high internal measurements) with distinct convex bottom, giving both vortex mixing and stirring.

(**d**) *Bellucci's reagent.*—HOAc-H_2O-HNO_3 (36 + 9 + 5).

13.022 ***Defatting and Grinding***

See **13.017**.

13.023 ***Determination***

Mix dried (1 hr at 100°) product by tumbling in covered dish. Make duplicate detns. Accurately weigh 0.500 g extd and dried material and transfer to 150 mL beaker. Gradually stir in 20 mL portion Bellucci's reagent until smooth; rinse walls of beaker and stirring rod with remainder. Stir gently. Fill short-neck, 100 mL, r-b flask with cold H_2O to neck and place on top of beaker; let rod rest in spout of beaker. Bring soln to initial boil, using asbestos mat over small flame. Immediately reduce to very weak flame and boil gently 10 min with frequent gentle swirling, keeping beaker and flask together. Cool ca 5 min.

Accurately weigh 25 × 100 mm Pyrex, rimless culture tube in 30 mL beaker (holder). Quant. transfer sample to culture tube with small portions H_2O, scrubbing beaker and rod with rubber policeman. Centrf. ≥3 min at full speed in International Clinical centrf., using IEC No. 571 curved rubber cushion in IEC No. 320 shield, or equiv. Decant carefully and discard supernate (some flocculent material may be present). Add H_2O to tube to ca ¾ full, stopper, and shake until residue is well dispersed. Remove stopper, rinse, centrf., and decant as before.

Add aq. glycerol (3+2) to culture tube until tube and holder weigh 20±0.03 g more than original wt. Stopper, shake vigorously until well mixed, and transfer immediately to 1 oz ointment jar contg small mag. bar. Stopper jar and let stand until bubbles disappear (ca 5–10 min).

Accurately weigh together ruled glass slide and cover glass. Stir liq. in jar 1 min on mag. stirrer at max. speed at which small bubbles do not form. Stop. In rapid sequence, push jar (to put mag. bar next to wall of jar) and, using scoop, immediately transfer drop liq. (ca 0.04±0.01 g) to center of tared slide, rulings up. Tap slide gently with scoop several times to remove as much liq. as possible. Place cover slip so that one edge rests just above and parallel to lower edge of slide. Lower cover slip carefully until it touches liq. and then let it drop. Liq. will ooze to edges. Do not press cover slip. Weigh prepd slide to 0.1 mg. Place rubber stopper in jar to prevent evapn.

Place slide on compd microscope with or without upper half of condenser and with transmitted day-light-type filtered and diffused light. Count 2 slides from each of 2 detns as in (**a**) or (**b**):

(**a**) *Stone cell count.*—For cocoa, cocoa press cake, chocolate liquor, and expeller cake. Scan slide at 100× and count stone cells at ≥200×. Count whole stone cells, both single and in groups, and all broken stone cells which are ≥0.5 cell. Do not count smaller fragments.

(**b**) *Stone cell group count.*—For other chocolate products. Proceed as in (**a**), counting only stone cell groups contg ≥2 stone cells.

13.024 ***Description of Stone Cells***

Stone cells vary considerably in size, shape, and general appearance. Some are very distinct and others are relatively indistinct. Their size varies from ca 10 to 38 μm; the longest are very slender. Some very coarse stone cells up to ca 40 μm with thick, beaded-appearing outside wall ca 7 μm wide are occasionally found. Stone shapes are polygonal, generally irregular, and may contain curved areas. On well developed stone cells outside walls are 2–3.5 μm wide. On less distinct stone cells, outside walls are narrower and thinner; such cells are immature or not fully developed. Several near-parallel thin walls or lines, viewed microscopically, are easily visible in many stone cells. They are generally more distinct in those where outside wall is thin. *See* Fig. **13:02** for photomicrographs of stone cells. Stone cells usually are in group formation, consisting of ≥2 stone cells.

13.025 ***Calculations***

For either method, average four S values from one of formulas below and report as % shell in chocolate component:

(**a**) *Stone cell count.*—$S_1 = 84C/(17200M - C)$

(**b**) *Stone cell group count.*—$S_2 = 84G/(1700M - G)$,

where W = g sample; L = g dild sample; D = g of drop counted; C = stone cell count of drop; M = mg dry, fat-free sample in drop counted (= 1000 WD/L); S = % shell in chocolate component; G = stone cell groups in drop; and 9340 = number stone cells in 1 mg dry, fat-free, 250 mesh shell.

(*Example:* for 0.5 g sample dild to 20 g, $S_1 = 84C/(430000D - C)$ and $S_2 = 84G/(42500D - G)$.)

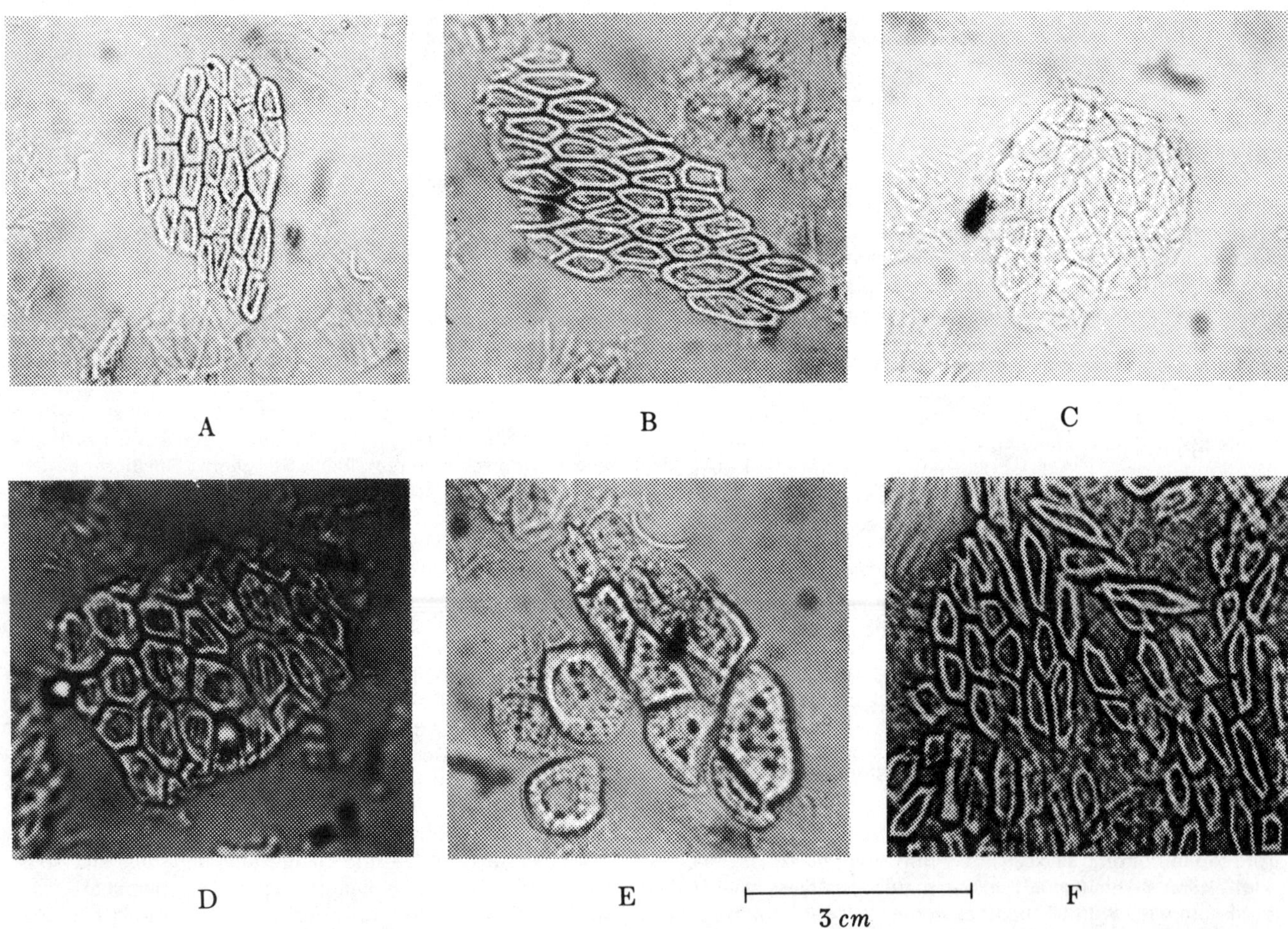

FIG. 13:02—Stone cells ca 330×: A and B, distinct stone cells; C, indistinct stone cells; D, stone cells showing distinct parallel lines in central area; E, very large stone cells infrequently found; F, long stone cells attached to a large piece of shell, showing separations between stone cells on shell

13.026 Ash Insoluble in Acid—Official Final Action

See **13.009**.

CACAO PRODUCTS PROCESSED WITH ALKALIES

13.027 Ash—Official Final Action

See **13.005**.

13.028 Soluble and Insoluble Ash—Official Final Action

See **13.006**.

13.029 Alkalinity of Insoluble and Soluble Ash Official First Action

See **13.007–13.008**.

13.030 CHOCOLATE LIQUOR (*11*) OFFICIAL FINAL ACTION

(*Caution: See* **51.011**, **51.039**, and **51.054**.)

Ext 25–50 g sample (50 g if light color, indicating low liquor) as in **13.013**, except in first aq. extn use 200 mL H_2O for products referred to in (**a**) and 200 mL *1% $Na_2C_2O_4$ soln* for products referred to in (**b**). Follow method thru aq., alcohol, and ether extns only.

With aid of small portions ether (45, 20, 15 mL, etc.) transfer residue resulting from ether, alcohol, and aq. extns to tared Al dish provided with tight-fit cover. Use small amt of acetone and policeman to transfer any material that sticks to bottle. Evap. liq. carefully on steam bath or hot plate, and dry residue in oven at 100°. Cover dish, cool in desiccator, and weigh.

To obtain wt dry, fat-free cacao mass, multiply wt residue by factor 1.43. To obtain wt chocolate liquor, multiply wt dry, fat-free cacao mass by factor 2.2. (This factor is based on fat content of 54% in chocolate liquors.)

FAT

(*Caution: See* **51.011**, **51.039**, and **51.073**.)

13.031 ***Method I (12)—Official Final Action***

(Not applicable to cacao products contg milk ingredients or to products prepd by cooking with sugar and water, and drying; cacao nibs must be finely ground. *All* pet ether used in this detn must be redistd at <60°.)

Prep. in Knorr extn tube, **17.021(d)**, first par., 6 mm tightly packed mat of asbestos, purified as for detn of crude fiber, **7.062(c)**, and carefully freed from coarse pieces. (Allihn type filter tube with coarse fritted disk such as Ace Glass Inc. No. 7195 is also satisfactory.) Wash filter with alcohol, ether, and little pet ether. Weigh 2–3 g prepd sample, **13.001**, into tube and insert tube into rubber stopper in filtering bell jar connected to suction thru 2-way stopcock, taking care that no rubber particles adhere to tip of stem. Place weighed 200 mL erlenmeyer at such ht that tube stem passes thru neck into flask. (Lengthen stem of tube if necessary.) Fill tube to ca ⅔ capacity with pet ether, and stir sample thoroly with flat-end rod, crushing all lumps. Let stand 1 min and drain by suction. Regulate suction so that collected solv. will not boil violently. Release vac. after each draining before adding more solv. Add solv. from wash bottle while turning tube between thumb and finger so that sides of tube are washed down by each addn. Repeat extns, with stirring, until fat is removed (usually 10 extns). Remove tube with stopper from bell jar, wash traces of fat from end of stem with pet ether, evap. solv., and dry to const wt at 100°.

Method II (13)—Official Final Action (Office International du Cacao et du Chocolat-AOAC Method)

(Applicable to cacao products with or without milk ingredients or to products prepd by cooking with sugar and H_2O, and drying)

13.032 ***Apparatus and Reagents***

(**a**) *Soxhlet apparatus*.—With ₮ joints, siphon capacity ca 100 mL (33 × 80 mm thimble), 250 mL erlenmeyer, and regulated heating mantle.

(**b**) *Petroleum ether*.—Distd in glass, bp 30–60°.

13.033 ***Determination***

Prep. sample as in **13.001(b)**(*1*). Accurately weigh 3–4 g chocolate liquor, 4–5 g cocoas, 4–5 g sweet chocolate, or 9–10 g milk chocolate into 300–500 mL beaker. Add slowly, while stirring, 45 mL boiling H_2O to give homogeneous suspension. Add 55 mL ca 8*N* HCl (2+1) and few defatted SiC chips or other antibumping agent, and stir. Cover with watch glass, bring slowly to boil, and boil gently 15 min. Rinse watch glass with 100 mL H_2O. Filter digest thru 15 cm S&S 589 medium fluted paper, or equiv., rinsing beaker 3 times with H_2O. Continue washing until last portion of filtrate is Cl-free as detd by addn of 0.1*N* $AgNO_3$. Transfer wet paper and sample to defatted extn thimble and dry 6–18 hr in small beaker at 100°. Place glass wool plug over paper.

Add few defatted antibumping chips to 250 mL erlenmeyer and dry 1 hr at 100°. Cool to room temp. in desiccator and weigh. Place thimble contg dried sample in soxhlet, supporting it with spiral or glass beads. Rinse digestion beaker, drying beaker, and watch glass with three 50 mL portions pet ether, and add washings to thimble. Reflux digested sample 4 hr, adjusting heat so that extractor siphons ≥30 times. Remove flask, and evap. solv. on steam bath. Dry flask at 100–101° to const wt (1.5–2 hr). Cool in desiccator to room temp. and weigh. Const wt is attained when successive 1 hr drying periods show addnl loss of <0.05% fat. % Fat = g fat × 100/g sample. Duplicate detns should agree within 0.1% fat.

13.034 Separation and Preparation of Fat for Determination of Constants—Procedure

(*Caution: See* **51.011**, **51.039**, and **51.054**.)

(**a**) *Not applicable to cacao products containing milk ingredients or to products prepared by cooking with sugar and H_2O, and drying*.—Sep. fat from 10–40 g sample (depending upon fat content) by shaking with two or three 100 mL portions ether. Centrf. and decant. Combine exts in beaker and evap. most of ether on steam bath. Filter ether exts thru dry, folded paper and dry at 100°.

(**b**) *Applicable to cacao products containing milk ingredients or to products prepared by cooking with sugar and H_2O, and drying*.—Proceed as in **13.033**, using 20 g sample in case of milk chocolate and combining fat obtained in duplicate detns for examination.

13.035 Iodine Absorption Number—Official Final Action

See **28.019** or **28.021**.

13.036 Melting Point—Official Final Action

Proceed as in **28.011**. Keep fat ≥24 hr in cool place before making detn.

13.037 Index of Refraction—Official Final Action

See **28.007** or **28.008**.

13.038 Reichert-Meissl and Polenske Values (*14*) Official Final Action

See **28.037**.

13.039 ★ Milk Fat in Milk Chocolate ★ Official Final Action

Calcn. from Reichert-Meissl value. *See* **13.042**, 12th ed.

Unsaponifiable Matter in Cocoa Butter (*15*) Official First Action

(If unsaponifiable matter is to be used for examination of sterols, use ethyl ether extn method, **28.081**. *Caution: See* **51.039** and **51.073**.)

13.040 ***Determination***

(All ₮ joints must be free of lubricants; clean with pet ether before starting. Use tools to handle flasks contg fat.)

Melt fat in 50–55° oven and filter. Accurately weigh ca 5 g filtered fat into 250 mL g-s flask. Add 50 mL alcohol and 10 mL KOH soln (60 g KOH dissolved in 40 mL H_2O). Attach reflux condenser and heat 60 min on boiling H_2O bath. Add 50 mL H_2O thru top of condenser, shake, and cool to room temp. Run blank with all reagents.

Transfer soln to 250 mL separator with Teflon stopcock and stopper. Rinse condenser and flask with five 10 mL portions pet ether and add to separator. Shake vigorously 1 min, periodically releasing pressure by inverting separator and opening stopcock. Let stand until sepn is nearly complete. Drain soap soln as completely as possible into second 250 mL separator (do not include any pet ether). (If emulsion forms, add few mL alcohol.) Repeat extn twice with two 50 mL portions pet ether, and combine pet ether exts. Wash combined pet ether ext 3 times with 50 mL portions dil. alcohol (1+1). Drain wash solns to ca 2 mL (do not include any pet ether); then gently rotate separator and let layers sep. 5–10 min. Drain remaining wash soln. Close stopcock when pet ether starts to pass bore of stopcock. Check last wash with phthln; if alkali is present, rewash and recheck.

Transfer pet ether into 250 mL flask thru top of separator. Rinse separator and pouring edge twice with 10 mL pet ether and add rinsings to main soln. Evap. to ca 5 mL on steam bath. Transfer quant. to 50 mL flask, previously dried ≥1 hr at 100° and cooled ≥1 hr in desiccator.

Evap. to dryness on steam bath. Add 2–3 mL *acetone* and reheat on boiling H_2O bath with gentle flow of air (or N) thru flask. Dry residue 30 min in 100° oven, placing flask horizontally. Cool ≥1 hr in desiccator and weigh. Repeat drying, cooling, and weighing after each drying period, until change of wt is <1.5 mg. Discard sample if wt after third weighing varies by >1.5 mg from second.

% Unsaponifiable matter = 100 × (g residue − g blank residue)/g sample

13.041 Saponification Number—Official Final Action

See **28.026**.

★ Surplus method—*see* inside front cover.

13.042 ★ Detection of Coconut and Palm ★ Kernel Oils in Cocoa Butter and Fat Extracted from Milk Chocolate (*16*) Official First Action

Saponification and observing turbidity of fatty acids from coconut and palm kernel oils on acidification. *See* **13.044**, 12th ed.

13.043 ★ Silver Number for Detection of Coconut ★ and Palm Kernel Oils (*17*) Official Final Action

Saponification, removal of Mg soaps, and pptn of Ag soaps. Ag no. is mg Ag used/g fat. *See* **13.045–13.046**, 12th ed.

13.044 ★ Critical Temperature of Dissolution of Fat ★ in Acetic Acid (*18*)—Official Final Action

Turbidity temp. of HOAc soln. *See* **13.047–13.048**, 12th ed.

13.045 Lecithin (*19*)—Official First Action

(*Caution: See* **51.011**, **51.040**, and **51.056**.)

Weigh 5 g prepd sample, **13.001**, into 200 mL vol. flask, add ca 150 mL $CHCl_3$-absolute alcohol (1+1), and shake occasionally during day. At end of day dil. to vol. with same solv., pour into 250 mL centrf. bottle, stopper, and let stand overnight. Next day centrf. stoppered bottle until clear (ca 15 min at 1800 rpm). Pipet 100 mL clear liq. into 500 mL Kjeldahl flask. Place Kjeldahl flask on steam bath, remove solv. with air current and det. P_2O_5 as in **22.044** and **22.045**. $P_2O_5 \times 11.19$ = lecithin.

P_2O_5 may be detd by **3.068**, in which case conc. the 100 mL clear liq. in 250 mL beaker, wash into small crucible with solv., evap., and proceed as in **3.067**. After digestion on steam bath, crucible must be heated cautiously on gauze until dry, and heating continued until frothing ceases and most of fat has smoked off before ashing in furnace. Ashing may be done in beaker in which ext is evapd.

DAIRY INGREDIENT CONSTITUENTS

13.046 Milk Fat in Milk Chocolate—Official Final Action

See **28.037** and **13.039**.

13.047 Milk Protein (*20*)—Official Final Action

(Not applicable to chocolate products contg milk protein which has been subjected to high heat treatment)

Weigh 10.0 g finely divided milk chocolate into 250 mL or larger centrf. bottle and ext twice with ca 100 mL ether by shaking until uniform, centrfg, and decanting ether layer each time. Place in bottle 2-hole stopper carrying bent glass tube, and straight glass tube that extends into bottle ca ⅓ of way to bottom. Expel ether by applying suction to bent tube and drawing moderate air current thru bottle while it is in moderately warm (not hot) place. When ether is expelled, pipet 100 mL H_2O into bottle. Stopper, and shake vigorously 4 min. Pipet in 100 mL *1% $Na_2C_2O_4$ soln*. Stopper, and shake vigorously 3 min. Let stand ca 10 min and again shake 1–2 min. Centrf. ca 15 min at high speed (ca 1800 rpm).

Decant supernate into beaker. Pipet 100 mL into dry 250 mL beaker and add 1 mL HOAc while stirring gently. Let stand few min so ppt can partly sep., and add, with stirring, 4 mL *10% tannic acid soln* (soln should be ≤1 week old). Let ppt settle few min; then filter on 7 cm buchner with moderate suction. Filtrate should be clear. Use as filter S&S 589 white ribbon paper, or equiv., overlaid with medium layer of paper pulp, prepd by shaking one 15 cm No. 1 Whatman paper, torn to bits, with H_2O. Using *wash soln* (add 1 mL HOAc and 2 mL 10% tannic acid soln to 100 mL 1% $Na_2C_2O_4$ soln), transfer all ppt to funnel with aid of policeman. Wash on filter 1 or 2 times. Loosen filter around edge with spatula. Carefully roll up and remove filter and ppt to Kjeldahl flask. Transfer to flask any particles of ppt clinging to funnel or spatula with small pieces of damp filter paper. Det. N as in **2.057**. N × 2 × 6.38 = total casein and albumin in the 10 g taken for analysis. Casein and albumin × 1.07 = total milk protein.

13.048 Lactose (*21*)—Official Final Action

(In absence of other reducing sugars)

Det. reducing sugars before inversion as in **31.038** in aliquot (usually 20 mL) of the Pb-free filtrate obtained in **13.049**. Det. reduced Cu as Cu_2O by volumetric thiosulfate method, **31.041**. Correct for Cu_2O due to sucrose as follows: Obtain approx. % lactose, using data obtained in **13.049**, as follows:

$$\text{Approx. lactose} = [P(1.1 + X/100) - S]/0.79.$$

From calcd polarimetric sucrose/lactose ratio and total Cu_2O obtained as above, det. amt of Cu_2O to be subtracted from total Cu_2O found, using graph, Fig. **13:03**. Convert corrected Cu_2O to g lactose (L), using table, **52.019**. Then obtain % lactose from following relationship:

$$\%\ \text{lactose} = L(110 + X)/0.26C,$$

where X = value obtained in polarimetric sucrose detn and C = vol. soln (mL) used in above lactose detn.

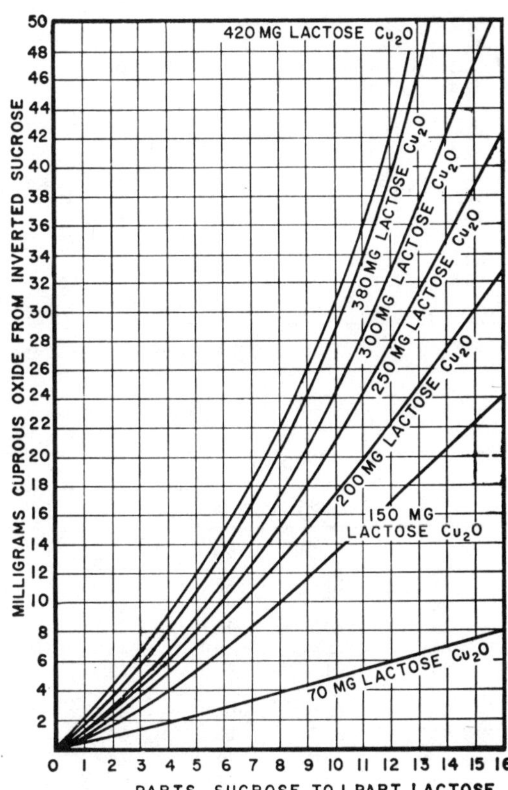

FIG. 13:03—Graph used in correcting cuprous oxide for effect of sucrose

SACCHARINE INGREDIENTS OTHER THAN LACTOSE

13.049 Sucrose (*21*)—Official Final Action

Transfer 26 g prepd sample, **13.001**, to 250 mL centrf. bottle, add ca 100 mL pet ether, shake 5 min, and centrf. Decant clear solv. carefully and repeat extn with pet ether. Place bottle contg defatted residue in warm place until pet ether is expelled. Add 100 mL H_2O and shake until most of chocolate is detached from sides and bottom of bottle. Loosen stopper and carefully immerse bottle 15 min in H_2O bath kept at 85–90°, shaking occasionally to remove all chocolate from sides of bottle. Remove from bath, cool, and add *basic Pb(OAc)₂ soln* (sp gr 1.25) to complete pptn (5 mL is usually enough). Add H_2O to make total of 110 mL added liq. Mix thoroly, centrf., and decant supernate thru small filter. Ppt excess Pb with powd dry $K_2C_2O_4$ and filter. Dil. 10 or 20 mL filtrate with equal vol. H_2O, mix, and polarize in 200 mm tube at 20°. Obtain invert reading as in **31.026(b)**. Multiply both readings by 2 to obtain direct and invert polarizations "P" and "I." From data obtained, calc. % sucrose (S) from following formulas:

$$S = \frac{(P - I)(110 + X)}{143.0 - t/2},$$

where

$$X = \frac{0.2244(P - 21d)}{1 - 0.00204(P - 21d)},$$

where

$$d = \frac{P - I}{143.0 - t/2}.$$

13.050 Glucose (*22*)—Official First Action

Prep. clarified and deleaded sample soln as in **13.049**, except use only 10 g. Proceed as in **13.051** or **13.055**.

Glucose by Steinhoff Methods—Official First Action

***Zerban-Sattler Modification* (*23*)**

13.051 ***Reagents***

(**a**) *Soxhlet modification of Fehling copper soln.*—See **31.034(a)**.

(**b**) *Sodium acetate soln.*—Dissolve 500 g NaOAc.3H_2O in ca 800 mL hot H_2O, cool, and dil. to 1 L.

(**c**) *Potassium iodide-iodate soln.*—Dissolve 5.4 g KIO_3 and 60 g KI in H_2O, add 0.25 g NaOH dissolved in little H_2O, and dil. to 1 L.

(**d**) *Sulfuric acid.*—Approx. 2*N*. Dil. 57 mL H_2SO_4 to 1 L.

(**e**) *Saturated potassium oxalate soln.*—Dissolve 165 g $K_2C_2O_4.H_2O$ in 500 mL hot H_2O, and cool.

(**f**) *Sodium thiosulfate std sol.*—0.1*N* Use std soln, **50.037–50.038.** 1 mL 0.1*N* $Na_2S_2O_3$ = 6.354 mg Cu.

(**g**) *Sugar soln.*—Dissolve amt of sample contg ca 10 g solids in H_2O and dil. to 1 L.

13.052 ***Determination***

Transfer 10 mL Soxhlet soln, 20 mL NaOAc soln, 10 mL sugar soln, and 10 mL H_2O to 250 mL erlenmeyer. Mix, close flask with rubber stopper provided with Bunsen valve, and immerse in briskly boiling H_2O bath exactly 20 min. Immerse in cold running H_2O, venting valve to prevent boiling caused by vac. Cool, add 25 mL KI-KIO_3 soln by pipet, and mix by gentle shaking. Rapidly add 40 mL 2*N* H_2SO_4 from graduate; then add 20 mL $K_2C_2O_4$ soln from graduate. Shake until ppt completely dissolves, and titr. excess I with 0.1*N* $Na_2S_2O_3$.

Det. blank, substituting H_2O for sugar soln. Difference between titer of blank and that of sample is direct measure of Cu_2O pptd. From Table **13:02** obtain glucose equiv. corresponding to titer of 0.1*N* $Na_2S_2O_3$.

Correction for reducing effect of maltose.—If maltose is present, correct observed titer of 0.1*N* $Na_2S_2O_3$ for reducing effect of maltose by subtracting correction obtained from Table **13:02** by interpolation.

Sichert-Bleyer Modification (24)

13.053 ***Reagents***

(**a**) *Ferric ammonium sulfate soln.*—Dissolve 120 g $Fe_2(SO_4)_3.(NH_4)_2SO_4.24H_2O$ and 100 mL H_2SO_4 in H_2O and dil. to 1 L.

(**b**) *Potassium permanganate soln.*—0.1*N*. Prep as in **50.025**.

13.054 ***Standardization***

To obtain factor for 0.1*N* $KMnO_4$ make analysis as in **13.055** on 10 mL soln contg 50 mg pure glucose. From Table **13:03**, titer of 15.38 mL corresponds to 50 mg glucose; 15.38 divided by titer obtained gives correction factor for $KMnO_4$ soln. Multiply all titers by this factor before referring to Table **13:03**. Redet. factor each day analyses are made.

13.055 ***Determination***

Proceed and in **13.052** thru "... immerse in briskly boiling H_2O bath exactly 20 min." Filter Cu_2O ppt thru gooch prepd as in **31.037**, and wash flask and crucible 3 times with hot H_2O. (It is not necessary to remove all ppt from flask.)

Transfer asbestos mat and crucible to 150 mL beaker marked at 60 mL. Wash flask with exactly 20 mL $FeNH_4(SO_4)_2$ soln in 3 portions and transfer quant. to beaker contg crucible. (All ppt must be dissolved.) Finally wash flask and crucible with hot H_2O and remove crucible. Add hot H_2O to 60 mL mark. Heat to bp on hot plate, let stand 3 min, and titr. with 0.1*N* $KMnO_4$. Addn of 1 mL H_3PO_4 toward end of titrn facilitates reading of end point. Pink-gray end point persists ca 20 sec. Multiply titer by factor and obtain mg glucose from Table **13:03**.

STARCH—OFFICIAL FINAL ACTION

13.056 ***Direct Acid Hydrolysis Method***

(*Caution: See* **51.039**, **51.054**, and **51.070**.)

Weigh 4 g sample if unsweetened, or 10 g if sweetened, into small porcelain mortar; add 25 mL ether and grind. After coarser material settles, decant ether, together with fine suspended matter, on 11 cm paper of fine enough texture to retain crude

Table 13:02 Zerban-Sattler Table for Determination of Glucose with Copper Acetate Reagent*

	Glucose (mg)										Maltose Corrections (Subtracted from Observed Titer) Maltose Present (mg)		
Titer	0.0	0.1	0.2	0.3	0.4	0.5	0.6	0.7	0.8	0.9	200	100	50
10	25.7	26.0	26.3	26.6	26.9	27.2	27.5	27.8	28.1	28.4	2.5	1.4	0.6
11	28.7	29.0	29.3	29.6	29.9	30.3	30.6	30.9	31.2	31.5	2.3	1.2	.4
12	31.8	32.2	32.5	32.9	33.2	33.6	34.0	34.3	34.7	35.0	2.2	1.1	.4
13	35.4	35.8	36.1	36.5	36.8	37.2	37.6	37.9	38.3	38.6	2.0	1.0	.3
14	39.0	39.4	39.9	40.3	40.7	41.2	41.6	42.0	42.4	42.9	1.9	1.0	.3
15	43.3	43.8	44.2	44.7	45.1	45.6	46.1	46.5	47.0	47.4	1.8	1.0	.3
16	47.9	48.4	49.0	49.5	50.1	50.6	51.1	51.7	52.2	52.8	1.7	1.0	.3
17	53.3	53.9	54.5	55.2	55.8	56.4	57.0	57.6	58.3	58.9	1.6	0.9	.3
18	59.5	60.2	60.9	61.6	62.3	63.1	63.8	64.5	65.2	65.9	1.4	.8	.3
19	66.6	67.4	68.2	69.0	69.8	70.6	71.4	72.2	73.0	73.8	1.2	.7	.3
20	74.6	75.6	76.5	77.5	78.4	79.4	80.3	81.3	82.2	83.2	1.0	.6	.2
21	84.1	85.2	86.3	87.4	88.5	89.6	90.6	91.7	92.8	93.9	0.6	.4	.2
22	95.0										.4	.3	.1

* Table may be interpolated for each 0.01 mL, but should not be extrapolated.

Table 13:03 Sichert-Bleyer Table for Determination of Glucose*

Titer, 0.1*N* Permanganate	Glucose (mg) 0	0.1	0.2	0.3	0.4	0.5	0.6	0.7	0.8	0.9
mL										
10	26.5	26.8	27.1	27.4	27.8	28.1	28.4	28.7	29.0	29.3
11	29.7	30.0	30.4	30.7	31.1	31.5	31.8	32.2	32.6	32.9
12	33.3	33.7	34.1	34.5	34.9	35.4	35.8	36.2	36.6	37.0
13	37.4	37.9	38.4	38.8	39.3	39.8	40.3	40.7	41.2	41.7
14	42.2	42.7	43.2	43.8	44.3	44.9	45.4	46.0	46.5	47.0
15	47.6	48.2	48.8	49.4	50.1	50.7	51.3	51.9	52.5	53.2
16	53.8	54.5	55.2	55.9	56.6	57.3	58.0	58.7	59.4	60.2
17	60.9	61.7	62.5	63.3	64.1	64.9	65.7	66.5	67.4	68.2
18	69.0	69.9	70.9	71.9	72.8	73.8	74.8	75.7	76.7	77.6
19	78.6	79.6	80.7	81.7	82.7	83.7	84.8	85.8	86.8	87.8
20	88.9	90.0	91.2	92.3	93.5	94.7	96.0	97.2	98.5	99.7

* Table may be interpolated for each 0.01 mL, but should not be extrapolated

starch. Repeat treatment until no more coarse material remains. After ether has evapd from filter, transfer fat-free residue to mortar by means of jet of cold H_2O and rub to smooth paste, filtering on paper previously used. Repeat this process until all sugar is removed. (In case of sweetened products filtrate should measure ≥500 mL.) Det. crude starch in extd residue as in **8.019**.

13.057 ★ *Diastase Method* ★

See **12.043**, 10th ed.

CHOCOLATE PRODUCTS

Alginates (*25*)—Official Final Action

13.058 ***Reagent***

Ferric hydroxide-sulfuric acid reagent.—Dissolve 10 g $FeCl_3.6H_2O$ in ca 100 mL H_2O in each of 2 centrf. bottles, and ppt $Fe(OH)_3$ by adding excess NH_4OH (by odor). Wash ppt with ca 5 portions H_2O, centrfg and decanting until little odor of NH_3 remains. Break up centrfd ppt each time before washing. Dry ppt on steam bath or in oven overnight, break up, and dry again. Mix with spatula or grind in mortar to obtain moderately fine powder. Keep in closed container.

Ferric hydroxide (moist) (ICN–K&K Laboratories, Inc.) may be used instead of pptg $Fe(OH)_3$ as above. Transfer this product to centrf. bottles, shake, centrf., decant, wash, and dry as above. Place 0.5 g dry powder in 50 mL g-s graduate, add 50 mL H_2SO_4, shake vigorously, and let settle until clear (usually 4–7 days). Some ferric sulfate appears to stick to sides, but reagent is ready for use after 7 days. Prep. fresh after 3 weeks. Check as follows before use:

Dissolve small amt (1–5 mg) of com. alginate in H_2O contg 5 drops 0.1*N* NaOH, add 4 vols alcohol to ppt alginate, centrf., decant, and dry on steam bath until no odor of alcohol remains, using air current to remove last traces of alcohol. Add 3 drops 0.1*N* NaOH, dissolve with aid of glass rod, and add 2 mL Fe-H_2SO_4 reagent. Soln turns purple slowly, usually within 1 hr, depending on amt of algin present, but may take longer. If soln appears to be turning brown, add addnl 2 mL reagent, mix with glass rod, and let stand.

13.059 ***Test***

Weigh sample contg 10–20 mg alginate into 250 mL centrf. bottle, add H_2O to vol. of 40–50 mL, and dissolve by swirling. Adjust pH to 8–9 with *satd* Na_3PO_4 *soln;* usually 5 drops is enough. Add ca 0.5 g *pancreatin* and 3 drops HCHO, and shake vigorously 1 min. Let stand 2–16 hr.

Centrf. at 1200 rpm 2–3 min, decant into 250 mL centrf. bottle, and discard residue. Add 3–4 vols alcohol, shake, and let stand ≥1 hr, shaking several times. Centrf. as before and discard liq. Add 50 mL H_2O and 1 drop 10% NaOH to residue and shake vigorously until no more residue appears to dissolve. Add 3 g decolorizing C (Nuchar) and shake vigorously 1 hr, preferably on shaking machine. Do not centrf. but pour directly into folded filter paper, collecting filtrate in 250 mL centrf. bottle. If filtrate is not clear, pour back thru paper several times. If filtration is slow, let filter overnight. Since C retains some alginate, for recovery of very small amts (ca 1 mg) re-ext C by shaking with another 50 mL portion H_2O and 5 drops 0.1*N* NaOH, and add this filtrate to first extn.

To filtrate add 4 vols alcohol, shake, and let stand ≥1 hr, or overnight if convenient. Centrf. and decant, saving residue. Residue contains alginates, gums, and gelatin. Dry residue on steam bath, using air current, if desired, until no odor of alcohol can be detected. Cool, add 3 drops 0.1*N* NaOH, and dissolve residue, using glass rod, as completely as possible. Add 2 mL Fe-H_2SO_4 reagent, mixing with glass rod. If soln turns purple very soon, enough reagent was added; if brown appears, add addnl 2 mL reagent. Let stand overnight, since color develops slowly. Deep purple is pos. test for alginates. If test is neg., repeat detn, using twice the size sample, increasing Nuchar to 4 g, and shaking 1.5 hr, for confirmation.

★ Surplus method—*see* inside front cover.

13.060 THEOBROMINE (*26*)—OFFICIAL FINAL ACTION

(*Caution: See* **51.011** and **51.040**.)

(Not applicable to materials contg >ca 12% sweetening ingredients)

Ext materials contg considerable fat, such as chocolate liquor or cacao nibs, with pet ether (bp <65°) to remove fat. (This preliminary extn is unnecessary with samples of cocoas or cacao shell.)

Place 10 g sample or prepd sample in small porcelain dish. Add 2–3 g freshly *calcined MgO* and mix well with flat-end glass rod. Add H_2O, few mL at time, and triturate carefully and thoroly until every particle is damp (9–20 mL, usually 14 mL; material should be compressible to firm cake). Place dish contg damp mixt. on steam bath 30 min, mixing at intervals to prevent any part from becoming dry, during which time material should granulate.

After 30 min, remove dish and triturate mixt. well so that every particle is damp; then transfer to 250 mL flask. Add 150 mL *tetrachloroethane*, attach air condenser, and boil 30 min. Filter nearly boiling hot liq. into second ca 200 mL flask, preferably with ₮ joint. (Filtrate should be clear and almost colorless.)

Transfer residue and filter to first flask with 120 mL addnl solv. and again reflux 20–30 min. Meanwhile, distil most of liq. in second flask from first extn thru air condenser. Filter hot liq. (second extn) into second flask and repeat process of refluxing and distn twice more, using 120 mL portions tetrachloroethane. Receive filtrates from all extns in flask 2, intermittently distg off portions as above. Distil liq. after last extn until reduced to 3–5 mL.

Cool flask and residue, and add 65 mL ether with rotation; mix well, stopper, and let stand ≥1 hr (until supernate is clear). Collect ppt on tared filter paper, using several 5–7 mL portions ether to transfer and wash. Dry filter and ppt at 100°, and weigh. Add 0.004 g to wt found to compensate for theobromine dissolved in the ether. Calc. % theobromine in original material.

SELECTED REFERENCES

(*1*) JAOAC **14**, 529(1931).
(*2*) JAOAC **60**, 654(1977).
(*3*) JAOAC **55**, 1027(1972).
(*4*) JAOAC **58**, 150(1975).
(*5*) Analytical Methods of the Office International du Cacao et du Chocolat, Niklausstrasse 4, Zurich, Switzerland, page 9-E/1963; JAOAC **53**, 474 (1970).
(*6*) Fed. Regist., October 19, 1940, p. 4152; JAOAC **23**, 593 (1940).
(*7*) JAOAC **13**, 482(1930); **14**, 526, 530(1931); **16**, 66 (1933).
(*8*) JAOAC **35**, 650(1952).
(*9*) JAOAC **51**, 725(1968).
(*10*) JAOAC **53**, 476(1970).
(*11*) JAOAC **14**, 526, 530(1931); **24**, 720(1941).

(*12*) JAOAC **8,** 705(1925); **9,** 469(1926).
(*13*) JAOAC **28,** 482(1945); **33,** 342(1950); **34,** 442(1951); **53,** 490(1970); Analytical Methods of the OICC (Ref. *2*), page 8a-E/1963.
(*14*) JAOAC **13,** 43, 255(1930).
(*15*) JAOAC **57,** 284(1974).
(*16*) JAOAC **11,** 45, 517(1928); **13,** 45, 78, 486(1930).
(*17*) JAOAC **15,** 548(1932); **17,** 64, 375(1934).
(*18*) JAOAC **5,** 263(1921); **7,** 150(1923).
(*19*) JAOAC **32,** 167(1949); **35,** 656(1952); **36,** 263 (1953).
(*20*) JAOAC **22,** 603(1939); **24,** 715(1941); **25,** 716(1942); Analyst **93,** 116(1968).
(*21*) JAOAC **16,** 564(1933); **17,** 377(1934).
(*22*) Ind. Eng. Chem., Anal. Ed. **10,** 669(1938); JAOAC **28,** 531(1945).
(*23*) Ind. Eng. Chem., Anal. Ed. **10,** 669(1938); Z. Spiritusind. **56,** 64(1933).
(*24*) Z. Anal. Chem. **107,** 328(1936); Z. Spiritusind. **56,** 64(1933).
(*25*) JAOAC **40,** 478(1957); **42,** 370(1959).
(*26*) Analyst **46,** 35(1921).

14. Cereal Foods

WHEAT FLOUR (*1*)

14.001 Sampling—Official Final Action

Sample number of sacks equiv. to sq root of number in lot, but $\geq$10, *i.e.*, 10 from $\leq$100, 15 from 225, 20 from 400 sacks, etc.

Select sacks to be sampled according to their exposure in ratio of 4 from most exposed, 3 from next less exposed, 2 from next, and 1 from least exposed portion of lot.

From each sack to be sampled, draw core from one corner of top diagonally to center of sack by means of cylindrical, pointed, polished metal trier, ½″ (13 mm) diam., with slit $\geq$⅓ of circumference. Draw second core from other top corner to ½ distance to center of sack.

Deliver the 2 cores at once to clean, dry, air-tight container that has stood open for few min near lot of flour to be sampled, and seal immediately. Use sep. container for each sack sampled. Use one of following containers: (*1*) pt (500 mL) fruit jar provided with rubber gasket; (*2*) rubber or plastic pouch that can be tied or sealed to exclude moisture or air; (*3*) tin can or box with moisture- and air-tight friction top.

Before opening sample for analysis, alternately invert and roll each container $\geq$25 times to secure homogeneous mixt. Avoid extreme temps and humidities when opening containers for analysis. Keep sample tightly sealed at all other times.

Total Solids (Moisture, Indirect Method)

(Also applicable to flour mixes contg $NaHCO_3$ as ingredient)

Vacuum Oven Method (2)—Official Final Action

14.002 ***Apparatus***

(**a**) *Metal dish*.—Diam. ca 55 mm, ht ca 15 mm, with inverted slip-in cover fitting tightly on inside.

(**b**) *Air-tight desiccator*.—Reignited CaO is satisfactory drying agent.

(**c**) *Vacuum oven*.—Connect with pump capable of maintaining partial vac. in oven with pressure equiv. to $\leq$25 mm Hg (3.3 kPa) and provided with thermometer passing into oven in such way that bulb is near samples. Connect H_2SO_4 gas-drying bottle with oven to admit dry air when releasing vac.

14.003 ***Determination***

Accurately weigh ca 2 g well mixed sample in covered dish previously dried at 98–100°, cooled in desiccator, and weighed soon after reaching room temp. Loosen cover (do not remove) and heat at 98–100° to const wt (ca 5 hr) in partial vac. having pressure equiv. to $\leq$25 mm Hg (3.3 kPa). Admit dry air into oven to bring to atm. pressure. Immediately tighten cover on dish, transfer to desiccator, and weigh soon after reaching room temp. Report flour residue as total solids and loss in wt as moisture (indirect method).

14.004 *Air Oven Method (3)—Official Final Action*

(Results closely approximate those obtained by **14.003**.)

In cooled and weighed dish (provided with cover), **14.002(a)**, previously heated to 130±3°, accurately weigh ca 2 g well mixed sample. Uncover sample, and dry dish, cover, and contents 1 hr in oven provided with opening for ventilation and maintained at 130±3°. (1 hr drying period begins when oven temp. is actually 130°.) Cover dish while still in oven, transfer to desiccator, and weigh soon after reaching room temp. Report flour residue as total solids and loss in wt as moisture (indirect method).

14.005 Extract Soluble in Cold Water (*4*) Official Final Action

Weigh 20 g flour into 500 mL erlenmeyer and gradually add 200 mL H_2O at ca 0°. Shake vigorously after ca 50 mL H_2O is added and continue shaking while adding remaining H_2O. Let mixt. stand 40 min at 0°, shaking occasionally. Filter rapidly, returning filtrate to filter until clear. Pipet 20 mL clear filtrate into weighed dish, evap. to dryness on steam bath, and dry in vac. oven at ca 100° for 30 min periods to const wt.

Ash (*5*)

14.006 *Direct Method—Official Final Action*

Weigh 3–5 g well mixed sample into shallow, relatively broad ashing dish that has been ignited, cooled in desiccator, and weighed soon after reaching room temp. Ignite in furnace at ca 550° (dull red) until light gray ash results, or to const wt. Cool in desiccator and weigh soon after reaching room temp. Reignited CaO is satisfactory drying agent for desiccator.

Magnesium Acetate Method (6)—Official Final Action

14.007 ***Reagent***

Magnesium acetate soln.—Dissolve 4.054 g $Mg(OAc)_2.4H_2O$ in 50 mL H_2O and dil. to 1 L with alcohol.

14.008 ***Determination***

From buret add 5 mL of the reagent to 3–5 g flour, bread, etc., or 10 mL to 1 g bran, wheat germ, etc. Let stand 1–2 min, evap. excess alcohol, and place in furnace at 700°, closing door after flaming ceases. When incineration is complete, place dish in desiccator until cool; then weigh. Det. blank on soln and deduct blank from wt ash. Evap. blank cautiously.

Original Ash of Flour in Phosphated and Self-Rising Flour (*7*)

(*Caution: See* **51.040** and **51.049**.)

14.009 *Gustafson Method—Official Final Action*

To 20–25 g sample in metal centrf. tube (cup 2″ diam., 6″ deep), add enough CCl_4 to fill tube to within 25 mm of top (ca 250 mL). Centrf. 5–7 min at 1600 rpm and let centrf. come to rest slowly. With large tablespoon, carefully skim off flour, which is in compact layer on surface of CCl_4, recovering as much flour as possible in 1 spoonful. (With care, ca 90% of original flour may be recovered.) Let wet flour dry overnight and proceed as in **14.006**. (CCl_4 may be filtered, distd, and used again.)

14.010 Added Inorganic Material in Phosphated Flour (*8*)—Official Final Action

Transfer 20 g flour to dry 250 mL separator, add ca 200 mL CCl_4, shake well, and let stand until soln at bottom is nearly clear, usually ca 15 min. Draw off sediment with min. of soln, by turning stopcock quickly from side to side, into 100 mL CCl_4 in dry 125 mL separator. Again shake 250 mL separator and let stand, with occasional gentle swirling if necessary to dislodge sediment from sides, until lower portion of soln clears. Draw off sediment from 125 mL separator into prepd and weighed gooch, using suction. Draw off sediment from 250 mL separator into 125 mL separator as before, and let stand with occasional gentle swirling to dislodge sediment from sides of separator. After lower portion of liq. clears, draw off into gooch as before, taking care that no sediment remains on ledge in separator. Wash crucible and contents with 25 mL fresh CCl_4, continue aspirating 2 or 3 min, weigh at once, and report as % added phosphate. Ignite crucible at 700°, cool, and weigh as $Ca(PO_3)_2$.

Wt $Ca(PO_3)_2 \times 1.27 \times 5 = \% \; Ca(H_2PO_4)_2.H_2O$ in flour.

Iron (*9*)—Official Final Action

(Applicable to enriched, enriched self-rising, and phosphated flours. Rinse all flasks, beakers, funnels, etc., with H_2O before use, and filter all reagents to remove suspended matter.)

14.011 ***Reagents***

(**a**) *Orthophenanthroline soln*.—Dissolve 0.1 g *o*-phenanthroline in ca 80 mL H_2O at 80°, cool, and dil. to 100 mL.

(**b**) *Alpha,alpha-dipyridyl soln*.—Dissolve 0.1 g α,α-dipyridyl in H_2O and dil. to 100 mL.

(Reagents (**a**) and (**b**) kept in cool, dark place will remain stable several weeks.)

(**c**) *Iron std soln*.—0.01 mg Fe/mL. (*1*) Dissolve 0.1 g anal. grade Fe wire in 20 mL HCl and 50 mL H_2O, and dil. to 1 L. Dil. 100 mL of this soln to 1 L. Or—(*2*) Dissolve 3.512 g $Fe(NH_4)_2(SO_4)_2.6H_2O$ in H_2O, add 2 drops HCl, and dil. to 500 mL. Dil. 10 mL of this soln to 1 L.

(**d**) *Hydroxylamine hydrochloride soln*.—Dissolve 10 g $H_2NOH.HCl$ in H_2O and dil. to 100 mL.

(**e**) *Magnesium nitrate soln*.—Dissolve 50 g $Mg(NO_3)_2.6H_2O$ in H_2O and dil. to 100 mL.

(**f**) *Acetate buffer soln*.—Dissolve 8.3 g anhyd. NaOAc (previously dried at 100°) in H_2O, add 12 mL HOAc, and dil. to 100 mL. (It may be necessary to redistil the HOAc and recrystallize the NaOAc from H_2O, depending on amt of Fe present.)

(**g**) *Sodium acetate soln*.—*2M*. Dissolve 272 g $NaOAc.3H_2O$ in H_2O and dil. to 1 L.

(**h**) *Buffer soln, pH 3.5*.—Dil. 6.4 mL *2M* NaOAc soln, (**g**), and 93.6 mL *2M* HOAc (120 g/L) to 1 L with H_2O.

14.012 ***Preparation of Standard Curve***

Prep. 11 solns contg 0.0, 2.0, 5.0, 10.0, 15.0, 20.0, 25.0, 30.0, 35.0, 40.0, and 45.0 mL, resp., of the final dild Fe std soln, plus 2.0 mL HCl, in 100 mL. Using 10 mL of each of these solns, proceed as in **14.013**, beginning "... add 1 mL $H_2NOH.HCl$ ..." Plot concn against scale reading.

14.013 ***Determination***

(**a**) *By dry ashing*.—Ash 10.0 g flour in Pt, SiO_2, or porcelain dish (ca 60 mm diam., 35 mL capacity) as in **14.006**. (Porcelain evapg dishes of ca 25 mL capacity are satisfactory. Do not use flat-bottom dishes of diam. >60 mm.) Cool, and weigh if % ash is desired. Continue ashing until practically C-free. To diminish ashing time, or for samples that do not burn practically C-free, use one of following ash aids:

Moisten ash with 0.5–1.0 mL $Mg(NO_3)_2$ soln or with redistd HNO_3. Dry and carefully ignite in furnace, avoiding spattering. (White ash with no C results in most cases.) Do not add these ash aids to self-rising flour (products contg NaCl) in Pt dish because of vigorous action on dish. Cool, add 5 mL HCl, letting acid rinse upper portion of dish, and evap. to dryness on steam bath. Dissolve residue by adding 2.0 mL HCl, accurately measured, and heat 5 min on steam bath with watch glass on dish. Rinse watch glass with H_2O, filter into 100 mL vol. flask, cool, and dil. to vol.

Pipet 10 mL aliquot into 25 mL vol. flask, and add 1 mL $H_2NOH.HCl$ soln; in few min add 5 mL buffer soln, (**f**), and 1 mL *o*-phenanthroline or 2 mL dipyridyl soln, and dil. to vol. Det. *A* in spectrophtr or photometer at ca 510 nm. From reading, det. Fe concn from equation of line representing std points or by ref. to std curve for known Fe concn. Det. blank on reagents and make correction. Calc. Fe in flour as mg/lb.

(**b**) *By wet digestion*.—(*Caution: See* **51.011**, **51.019**, **51.026**, and **51.030**.) Transfer 10.00 g flour to 800 mL Kjeldahl flask, previously rinsed with dil. acid, then with H_2O; add 20 mL H_2O and mix; pipet 5 mL H_2SO_4 into flask and mix; add 25 mL HNO_3 and mix well. After few min, heat flask very gently at brief intervals (to avoid foaming out of flask) until heavy evolution of NO_2 fumes ceases. Continue to heat gently until material begins to char; then add few mL HNO_3 cautiously at intervals until SO_3 fumes evolve and colorless or very pale yellow liq. is obtained (60–65 mL HNO_3 total in ca 2 hr). Cool, add 50 mL H_2O and 1 Pyrex glass bead, and heat to SO_3 fumes; cool, add 25 mL H_2O, and filter quant. thru 11 cm paper into 100 mL vol. flask; cool, and dil. to vol.

Pipet 10 mL into 25 mL vol. flask, add 1 mL $H_2NOH.HCl$ soln, rotate flask, and let stand few min. Add 9.5 mL *2M* NaOAc soln, (**g**), and 1 mL *o*-phenanthroline soln, dil. to vol., and mix. Let stand ≥5 min and det. *A* in spectrophtr or photometer at ca 510 nm.

With self-rising flour, the 9.5 mL *2M* NaOAc soln, (**g**), may be reduced to 8.0 mL. To det. exact amt of buffer soln, (**g**), needed to adjust each digest to most desirable pH range, mix 10 mL aliquot of sample with measured amt of buffer soln, (**g**), dil. with H_2O to 25 mL, and det. pH either potentiometrically or colorimetrically.

For colorimetric detn, add 5 drops bromophenol blue indicator, **6.019(f)**, to soln and compare color with that of equal vol. of pH 3.5 buffer soln, (**h**), also treated with 5 drops indicator. Altho color develops from pH 2–9, avoid pH <3.0 and preferably work at pH 3.5–4.5. With cereal products, 9.5 mL buffer soln, (**g**), is satisfactory. With samples high in Fe, aliquot of 5 mL instead of 10 mL may be used with 4.8 mL buffer soln, (**g**).

Conduct digestion so as to avoid contamination with Fe, and det. blank. After correction for blank, calc. as mg Fe/lb.

14.014 Calcium (*10*)—Official Final Action

(Applicable to enriched, enriched self-rising, and phosphated flours)

Ash 10 g flour or air-dried bread as in **14.006**, and proceed as in **14.013(a)** thru "Rinse watch glass with H_2O, . . .", then filter into 400 mL beaker; or transfer 50 mL soln from Fe detn to 400 mL beaker. Dil. to ca 150 mL.

Add 8–10 drops bromocresol green indicator, **50.008**, and enough *20% NaOAc soln* to change pH to 4.8–5.0 (blue). Cover with watch glass and heat to bp. Ppt Ca slowly by adding *3% oxalic acid soln*, 1 drop every 3–5 sec, until pH is 4.4–4.6 (optimum for Ca oxalate pptn) as indicated by distinct green shade. (Avoid excess of oxalic acid indicated by yellow tints, showing undesirable displacement of pH.) Boil 1–2 min and let mixt. settle until clear or overnight. Filter supernate thru quant. paper, gooch, or fine fritted glass filter, and wash beaker and ppt with ca 50 mL NH_4OH (1+50) in small portions, using wash bottle delivering very small stream. Break point of filter and wash filter or crucible with mixt. of 125 mL H_2O and 5 mL H_2SO_4 at 80–90°. Titr. at 70–90° with 0.05*N* $KMnO_4$ until slight pink is obtained, add filter paper, and continue titrn if necessary. Correct for blank and calc. Ca as mg/lb. 1 mL 0.05*N* $KMnO_4$ = 1 mg Ca.

Phosphorus (11)—Official Final Action

14.015 ***Reagent***

(**a**) *Magnesium nitrate soln.*—Dissolve 8 g MgO in HNO_3 (1+1), avoiding excess acid; add little MgO in excess, boil, filter from excess MgO, Fe_2O_3, etc., and dil. to 100 mL.

(**b**) *Molybdate soln.—See* **7.118**(**a**).

14.016 ***Determination***

(**a**) Transfer 1.00 g sample to ca 140 mL porcelain casserole, add 3 mL $Mg(NO_3)_2$ soln, and mix well, using small glass rod. Clean rod with small piece filter paper and place in casserole. Dry in oven at 100° ca 2 hr, transfer to cold furnace, and ignite at 550° to white or gray ash (6–8 hr). Cool, cover with watch glass, take up with 10 mL HCl (1+4), and add 5 mL HCl. Rinse watch glass and evap. to dryness on steam bath. Add 5 mL HCl and 50 mL H_2O, heat 15 min on steam bath, filter into 100 mL vol. flask, cool, and dil. to vol. Pipet 50 mL into 300 mL erlenmeyer, neutze to litmus paper with NH_4OH, make just faintly acid with HNO_3, dil. to 75–100 mL, add ca 15 g NH_4NO_3, and proceed as in **7.119**, beginning "Add . . . enough acidified molybdate soln to ensure complete pptn . . ." Or—

(**b**) Transfer 5.00 g sample to 35 mL porcelain evapg dish, mix well with 0.5 g Na_2CO_3, and ignite at 550° to gray ash. Cool, cover with watch glass, take up with 2 mL HCl (1+4), and add 5 mL HCl. Rinse watch glass, evap. to dryness, add 5 mL HCl and 10 mL H_2O, heat ca 10 min on steam bath, filter into 100 mL vol. flask, cool, and dil. to vol. Pipet 10 mL aliquot into 300 mL erlenmeyer and proceed as in (**a**), beginning ". . . neutze to litmus paper with NH_4OH, . . ."

Report results as % P.

14.017 Total Carbon Dioxide in Self-Rising Flour (*12*)
Official Final Action

(Not applicable to flours contg added $CaCO_3$)

Use 17 g flour, 15–20 glass beads (4–6 mm diam.), and 45 mL H_2SO_4 (1+5). Proceed as in **8.002–8.004**, as far as calcn, except agitate flask vigorously 3 min and let stand 10 min to attain equilibrium.

Calc. as follows: Subtract vol. acid used from total buret reading and correct for temp. and pressure. Divide reading by 100 to obtain % CO_2 (by wt). Correct apparent % CO_2 to compensate for varying atm. conditions by immediately assaying synthetic sample of known composition and like ingredients by same method in same app. Divide wt CO_2 recovered from synthetic sample by wt CO_2 contained in $NaHCO_3$ used and record quotient. Apparent % total CO_2 in official sample ÷ this quotient = corrected % total CO_2 in sample.

14.018 Crude Fat or Ether Extract—Official Final Action

Proceed as in **7.056**; with fine flour, addn of equal wt clean, dry sand may be necessary.

14.019 Fat (Acid Hydrolysis Method) (*13*)
Official Final Action

(*Caution: See* **51.011**(**a**), **51.054**, and **51.073**.)

Place 2 g sample in 50 mL beaker, add 2 mL alcohol, and stir to moisten all particles to prevent lumping on addn of acid. Add 10 mL HCl (25+11), mix well, set beaker in H_2O bath held at 70–80°, and stir at frequent intervals during 30–40 min. Add 10 mL alcohol and cool.

Transfer mixt. to Mojonnier fat-extn app. Rinse beaker into extn tube with 25 mL ether, added in 3 portions; stopper flask (with glass, cork, Neoprene, or other synthetic rubber stopper not affected by solvs) and shake vigorously 1 min. Add 25 mL redistd pet ether (bp $<60°$) and again shake vigorously 1 min. Let stand until upper liq. is practically clear, or centrf. 20 min at ca 600 rpm.

Draw off as much as possible of ether-fat soln thru filter consisting of cotton pledget packed just firmly enough in funnel stem to let ether pass freely into weighed 125 mL beaker-flask contg porcelain chips or broken glass. Before weighing beaker-flask, dry it and similar flask as counterpoise in oven at 100°; then let stand in air to const wt.

Re-ext liq. remaining in tube twice, each time with only 15 mL of each ether. Shake well on addn of each ether. Draw off clear ether solns thru filter into same flask as before and wash tip of spigot, funnel, and end of funnel stem with few mL of mixt. of the 2 ethers in equal vols, free from suspended H_2O. Evap. ethers slowly on steam bath; then dry fat in oven at 100° to const wt (ca 90 min). Remove flask and counterpoise from oven, let stand in air to const wt (ca 30 min), and weigh. (Owing to size of flask and nature of material, there is less error by cooling in air than by cooling in desiccator.) Correct this wt by blank detn on reagents used. Report as % fat by acid hydrolysis.

14.020 Crude Fiber—Official Final Action

See **7.065**.

14.021 Fat Acidity (*14*)—Official Final Action

See **14.072**.

Hydrogen-Ion Activity (pH)—Official Final Action

14.022 ***Potentiometric Method* (*15*)**

Weigh 10.0 g sample into clean, dry erlenmeyer and add 100 mL recently boiled H_2O at 25°. Shake until particles are evenly suspended and mixt. is free of lumps. Digest 30 min, shaking frequently. Let stand 10 min more, decant supernate into the H-ion vessel, and immediately det. pH, using electrode and potentiometer stdzd by buffer solns of pH 4.01, **50.007**(**c**), and of pH 9.18, **50.007**(**f**), both at 25°.

Reducing and Nonreducing Sugars (*16*)
Official Final Action

14.023 ***Reagents***

(**a**) *Acetate buffer soln.*—Dil. 3 mL HOAc, 4.1 g anhyd. NaOAc, and 4.5 mL H_2SO_4 to 1 L with H_2O.

(**b**) *Sodium tungstate soln.*—12%. Dil. 12.0 g $Na_2WO_4.2H_2O$ to 100 mL with H_2O.

(**c**) *Alkaline ferricyanide soln.*—0.1*N*. 33.0 g pure dry $K_3Fe(CN)_6$ and 44.0 g Na_2CO_3/L.

(**d**) *Acetic acid-salts soln.*—Dil. 200 mL HOAc, 70 g KCl, and 40 g $ZnSO_4.7H_2O$ to 1 L with H_2O.

(**e**) *Soluble starch-potassium iodide soln.*—Add 2 g sol. starch to small amt cold H_2O and pour slowly into boiling H_2O with const stirring. Cool thoroly (or resulting mixt. will be dark colored), add 50 g KI, and dil. to 100 mL with H_2O. Add 1 drop NaOH soln (1+1). Use 1 mL.

(**f**) *Thiosulfate std soln.*—0.1*N*. 24.82 g $Na_2S_2O_3.5H_2O$ and 3.8 g $Na_2B_4O_7.10H_2O$/L.

Make blank detn with each day's series of sugar detns to guard against changes in the $K_3Fe(CN)_6$ soln and correct for any reducing impurities in reagents as follows:

Combine 5 mL alcohol, 50.0 mL acetate buffer soln, and 2 mL Na tungstate soln. To 5 mL of this mixt. (used in place of 5 mL flour ext) add 10.0 mL $K_3Fe(CN)_6$ soln and proceed as in **14.025(a)**. (10.0 mL $Na_2S_2O_3$ soln should disharge the blue starch-I color.) If titrn falls within 10±0.05 mL do not discard reagents but correct in subsequent sugar calcns by using $Na_2S_2O_3$ equiv. of 10 mL $K_3Fe(CN)_6$ soln (*i.e.*, mL $Na_2S_2O_3$ soln required in above titrn) instead of 10.0 as basis for subtraction.

14.024 ***Preparation of Extract***

Place 5.675 g flour in 100 or 125 mL erlenmeyer. Tip flask so that all flour is at one side; then wet flour with 5 mL alcohol. Tip flask so that wet flour is at upper side and add 50.0 mL acetate buffer soln, keeping soln from coming in contact with flour until all is added to flask. Then shake flask to bring flour into suspension. Immediately add 2 mL Na tungstate soln and again mix thoroly. Filter at once (Whatman No. 4, or equiv.), discarding first 8–10 drops filtrate.

14.025 ***Determination***

(**a**) *Reducing sugars.*—Pipet 5 mL flour ext into ca 75 mL test tube (Pyrex 25 × 200 mm). Add exactly 10 mL $K_3Fe(CN)_6$ soln to test tube, mix, and immerse in vigorously boiling H_2O bath so that liq. in tube is 3–4 cm below surface of boiling H_2O.

After exactly 20 min in boiling H_2O bath, cool tube under running H_2O, and pour at once into 100 or 125 mL erlenmeyer. Rinse test tube with 25 mL HOAc-salts soln, (**d**), add to erlenmeyer, and mix thoroly. Then add 1 mL starch-KI soln. Titr. with 0.1*N* $Na_2S_2O_3$ soln until blue completely disappears (10 mL micro buret recommended). Subtract mL 0.1*N* $Na_2S_2O_3$ used in titrn from 10.00. In case of slight blank in $K_3Fe(CN)_6$-$Na_2S_2O_3$ titrn, correct by subtracting from $Na_2S_2O_3$ equiv. of $K_3Fe(CN)_6$ soln. This difference represents definite amt of reducing sugar/10 g flour, calcd as maltose from Table **14:01**.

(**b**) *Nonreducing sugars.*—Pipet 5 mL flour ext into 20 cm test tube and immerse in vigorously boiling H_2O bath. After boiling 15 min, cool under running H_2O and add exactly 10 mL $K_3Fe(CN)_6$ soln. Proceed as in (**a**). $K_3Fe(CN)_6$ reduced after hydrolysis − $K_3Fe(CN)_6$ reduced by maltose in flour = nonreducing sugars calcd as sucrose and detd from Table **14:01**.

14.026 Total Protein—Official Final Action

Det N as in **2.057**, and multiply % N by 5.7 to obtain % protein.

Table 14:01. 0.1*N* Ferricyanide Maltose-Sucrose Conversion Table[a]

0.1*N* Ferricyanide Reduced mL	Maltose per 10 g Flour mg	Sucrose per 10 g Flour mg	0.1*N* Ferricyanide Reduced mL	Maltose per 10 g Flour mg	Sucrose per 10 g Flour mg
0.10	5	5	4.50	237	214
0.20	10	10	4.60	244	218
0.30	15	15	4.70	251	223
0.40	20	19	4.80	257	228
0.50	25	24	4.90	264	233
0.60	31	29	5.00	270	238
0.70	36	34	5.10	276	242
0.80	41	38	5.20	282	247
0.90	46	43	5.30	288	251
1.00	51	48	5.40	295	256
1.10	56	52	5.50	302	261
1.20	60	57	5.60	308	266
1.30	65	62	5.70	315	270
1.40	71	67	5.80	322	275
1.50	76	71	5.90	328	280
1.60	80	76	6.00	334	285
1.70	85	81	6.10	341	290
1.80	90	86	6.20	347	294
1.90	96	91	6.30	353	299
2.00	101	95	6.40	360	304
2.10	106	100	6.50	367	309
2.20	111	104	6.60	373	313
2.30	116	109	6.70	379	318
2.40	121	114	6.80	385	323
2.50	126	119	6.90	392	328
2.60	130	123	7.00	398	333
2.70	135	128	7.10	406	337
2.80	140	133	7.20	412	342
2.90	145	138	7.30	418	347
3.00	151	143	7.40	425	352
3.10	156	148	7.50	431	357
3.20	161	152	7.60	438	362
3.30	166	157	7.70	445	367
3.40	171	161	7.80	451	372
3.50	176	166	7.90	458	377
3.60	182	171	8.00	465	382
3.70	188	176	8.10	472	387
3.80	195	181	8.20	478	392
3.90	201	185	8.30	485	397
4.00	207	190	8.40	492	402
4.10	213	195	8.50	499	407
4.20	218	200	8.60	505	—
4.30	225	204	8.70	512	—
4.40	231	209	8.80	519	—

[a] These values are arbitrarily given for 10 g flour altho detn is made on only 0.5 g flour.

14.027 Water-Soluble Protein-Nitrogen Precipitable by 40 Per Cent Alcohol (*17*)—Official Final Action

Weigh 20 g sample (20-mesh or finer) into 250 mL centrf. bottle. Pipet in 100 mL H_2O, shaking bottle to prevent lumping of sample. Add 100 mL more H_2O from pipet. Stopper bottle and shake 1 hr in shaking machine or by hand. (Preferably use horizontal shaker with bottle lengthwise. If vertical wrist-type motion machine is used, shake by hand 5 min after the 1 hr shaking.) Temp. of H_2O should be $\leq 30°$. Centrf. at 1200 rpm ca 15 min and filter into 500 mL suction flask thru pad of fine asbestos on buchner (51 mm diam.), using suction. Det. N in 50 mL filtrate as in **2.057** with glass bead in each flask, distg NH_3 into 20 mL 0.1*N* acid. Digest 1 hr after clear. Correct for blank on reagents used in digestion.

Pipet 100 mL of above filtrate into 200 mL vol. flask, add 15 mL *NaCl soln* (28 g dild to 300 mL), fill nearly to mark with alcohol, mix well, cool to room temp., dil. to vol., mix, and let stand overnight. Pipet off supernate and filter thru 18.5 cm fluted paper (S&S 588, or equiv.). Det. N in 100 mL filtrate as above, using glass bead to avoid bumping. Add H_2SO_4, mix, and carefully boil off alcohol before adding Na_2SO_4-HgO mixt. Rinse Na_2SO_4-HgO mixt. down neck of flask. Digest 1 hr after clear. (Watch for foaming before clearing and keep contents out of neck of flask.) Distil into 20 mL 0.1*N* acid as before. Correct for blank on reagents used in digestion. Subtract this number of mL acid used from number of mL acid used for H_2O-sol. N detn and convert to % H_2O-sol. N precipitable by 40% alcohol.

14.028 Lipids (*18*)—Official Final Action

(*Caution: See* **51.005**, **51.011**, **51.054**, and **51.055**.)

Add 15 mL alcohol, 70% by vol., to 5 g sample (20-mesh or finer) in 250 mL centrf. bottle. Give bottle gentle rotary motion so as to moisten all particles, stopper firmly (to keep in place during heating), and set in H_2O bath kept at 75–80°. (Consider that temp. of bath may drop when bottles are introduced.) Heat 15 min, mixing frequently with same rotary motion. Immediately add 27 mL alcohol, stopper bottle, and *shake vigorously* 2 min. Cool, add 45 mL ether, and shake vigorously 5 min. (Sample should now be finely divided.) Centrf. at ca 1000 rpm few min and decant into 250 mL beaker contg some bits of broken porcelain or glass; rinse bottle neck with ether. Re-ext sample with three 20 mL portions ether, shaking ca 2 min each time, centrfg, and decanting into beaker contg first ext. Break up sample each time with glass stirring rod, rinsing with ether on removal.

Evap. combined ether-alcohol exts just to dryness on steam bath. Drive off any remaining moisture on sides of beaker by placing in oven 5 min at 100°. Dissolve dry ext in ca 15 mL $CHCl_3$ and filter soln into previously dried and weighed 100 mL Pt dish thru asbestos mat 3–4 mm thick, covered with ca 10 mm layer of sand in Knorr-type extn tube (20 mm diam. × 11 cm long; stem 10 cm long). Wash sides of dish and tube with 10 mL and two 5 mL portions $CHCl_3$. With glass rod, free any solid ext adhering to dish to be sure all lipids dissolve. Finally wash tube and tip with 5 mL $CHCl_3$. Evap. $CHCl_3$ on steam bath and dry in oven at 100° to const wt (ca 90 min). Weigh. Report ext as lipids.

14.029 Lipid Phosphorus (*18*)—Official Final Action

Wash sides of Pt dish with 10 mL $CHCl_3$ to dissolve lipids, **14.028**; likewise wash sides of dish with 10 mL *4% alc. KOH soln*. Cautiously evap. to dryness on steam bath and ash 1 hr at 500°. Cover dish with watch glass, add 15 mL HNO_3 (1+9) to make soln definitely acid, heat on steam bath ca 5 min, and filter into 300 mL erlenmeyer. Wash residue and filter with ca 25 mL hot H_2O. Make soln slightly alk. to litmus paper with NH_4OH from Mohr pipet and then slightly acid with HNO_3 (1+9). Keep vol. <ca 60 mL. Add 20 mL NH_4NO_3 soln (500 g dild to 1 L), and heat in H_2O bath to 45–50°. Add 20 mL freshly prepd and filtered molybdate soln, **7.118(a)**, and let flasks remain in bath 30 min at 40–45°, swirling contents at ca 5 min intervals. To prevent tipping, weight flask with lead rings or by other means.

For filtration, use filter tube (so-called carbon filter), ca 28 mm id, fitted with removable, perforated porcelain disk from Caldwell crucible. (Caldwell crucible or gooch may also be used.) Prep. quick filtering pad 3–4 mm thick, using short-fiber asbestos. For convenience in washing and in transferring filter tubes, provide suction flask with rubber stopper having hole somewhat larger than stem of filter tube.

With full suction, filter ppt and wash flask and then filter tube with ca 6 portions cold H_2O, using 150–200 mL total. Test for complete washing by passing 25 mL CO_2-free H_2O thru flask and filter tube into clean suction flask. Immediately disconnect suction and add 1 drop each of 0.1*N* NaOH and phthln, which should yield strong pink color.

Loosen pad and porcelain disk with wire or narrow rod inserted in stem end, and transfer to flask. Place filter tube in neck of flask, dissolve any ppt on walls with measured vol. std alkali, and rinse down filter tube with ca 25 mL CO_2-free H_2O. (Enough std alkali must have been added to dissolve ppt.) Stopper flask, swirl, and let stand, mixing occasionally, until yellow ppt completely dissolves. Dil. to ca 75 mL with CO_2-free H_2O, add 10 drops phthln, and titr. with std acid to complete disappearance of pink, matching end point with another flask contg H_2O and asbestos only. If alkali adheres to fragments of asbestos, making end point uncertain, add slight excess of std acid and complete titrn with std alkali. 1 mL 0.1*N* NaOH = 0.3086 mg P_2O_5. Subtract alkali consumed in blank detn.

14.030 Unsaponifiable Residue—Official Final Action

See **14.147**.

Starch (*19*)—Official First Action

14.031 ***Reagent***

Calcium chloride soln.—Dissolve 2 parts $CaCl_2.6H_2O$ in 1 part H_2O and adjust to density of 1.30 at 20° (soln contains ca 33% $CaCl_2$). Make faintly pink to phthln by adding 0.1*N* NaOH. (Anhyd. $CaCl_2$ may be used, but it is usually alk. and requires addn of acid to bring it to correct pH.)

14.032 ***Determination***

Grind sample finely (100-mesh if possible) and weigh 2.0–2.5 g into 50 mL r-b centrf. tube with lip. Wash with ether to remove fat, then with 10 mL ca 65% by wt alcohol (d_{20} = 0.88), and stir thoroly with glass rod. Centrf. (if no centrf. is available, wash samples on filter paper, using Pt cone and slight suction) and pour off soln. Repeat washing until 60 mL wash liq. has been used, stirring each time with same rod.

Stir residue with 10 mL H_2O and pour into 200–250 mL erlenmeyer. Complete transfer by washing with total of 60 mL $CaCl_2$ soln contg 2 mL 0.8% HOAc. Transfer rod to flask and bring mixt. to bp quickly over wire gauze, stirring frequently. Boil briskly 15–17 min, taking precautions to prevent burning and foaming. Rub down particles on sides of flask with rod from time to time.

Cool soln quickly in running H_2O and pour into 100 mL vol. flask, rinsing thoroly with $CaCl_2$ soln from wash bottle with medium jet. In dilg to vol., add 1 drop alcohol, if necessary to destroy froth.

After thoroly mixing sample, pour ca 10 mL soln onto fluted filter (Whatman 42 or 44), wetting paper completely. Let filter run dry and discard filtrate. Resume filtration, using dry receiver, and collect 40–50 mL. As filtering aids, use Celite with Pyrex glass filters and asbestos with Hirsch-type funnel and suction.

Polarize liq. in 10 cm tube, taking 2 sets of 10 readings each. (Av. of 2 sets should agree within 0.006°.)

$$\% \text{ Starch} = 100 \times R \times 100/1 \times 203 \times W = 49 \times R/W,$$

where R is observed angular rotation and W is wt sample; 203 is arbitrarily taken as specific rotation for all starches. If 200 mm tube and saccharimeter are used, 2 g sample weighed, and mixt. dild to 100 mL; °S × 4.2586 = % starch.

14.033 Vitamins in Enriched Flours

See Chapter **43**.

Chlorine in Fat of Flour

14.034 *Qualitative Test (Chlorine-Bleached Flours)* *Official Final Action*

Ext 30 g flour with 50 mL pet ether and let solv. evap. (Small amt of oil remains.) Heat piece of Cu wire in colorless gas flame until it is black and no longer colors flame green. Dip hot end of wire into oil and again bring into flame. If Cl or Br has been used as bleaching agent, green or blue coloration is produced.

Quantitative Method (20)—Official Final Action

14.035 *Extraction of Fat*

(*Caution: See* **51.011(a)** and **51.073**.)

Weigh 500 g flour into 2 L flask. Add 700 mL pet ether and shake at 5 min intervals 30 min. Filter thru buchner, pressing flour to obtain as much solv. as practicable. Transfer pet ether ext to large beaker and evap. on steam bath to ca 10 mL. Filter into container thru small funnel contg pledget of cotton packed firmly in stem. (Filtrate must be clear and free from flour.)

14.036 *Determination*

Heat ca 90 mL porcelain crucible contg 10 g *fusion mixt.* (138 g K_2CO_3, 106 g Na_2CO_3, and 75 g powd KNO_3) 30 min in 100° oven; dry in desiccator and weigh. Transfer filtered 10 mL pet ether ext to crucible, using pet ether for rinsing. Evap. pet ether on steam bath and dry fat in 100° oven 30 min. Cool, and det. wt fat by difference. Add 5 g more fusion mixt. to crucible and spread evenly. Ignite to white ash in furnace at 525° (ca 1 hr) and cool.

Add 25 mL hot H_2O to mixt. and transfer with small amt of hot H_2O to 200 mL tall beaker or beaker-flask. Cautiously add HNO_3 until soln is slightly acid to litmus paper. Add 25 mL more HNO_3. Add 5 mL 0.3*N* $AgNO_3$. Boil 5 min in hood and cool to room temp. Filter thru 9 cm Whatman No. 1 paper, or similar Cl-free paper. Use 1% HNO_3 soln for rinsing. Digest as in **3.076**, par 3, beginning "Place paper and contents in Kjeldahl flask . . ." After digestion use 175 mL H_2O. Det. blank on reagents. Report Cl as mg/g fat.

Nitrite Nitrogen (*21*)—Official Final Action

14.037 *Reagents*

(**a**) *Sulfanilic acid soln.*—Dissolve 0.5 g sulfanilic acid in 150 mL HOAc (1+4), warming slightly if necessary.

(**b**) *Alpha-naphthylamine hydrochloride soln.*— Dissolve, by heating, 0.2 g of the salt in 150 mL HOAc (1+4). (*Caution: See* **51.085**.)

(**c**) *Nitrite std soln.*—Dissolve 0.1097 g dry $AgNO_2$ in ca 20 mL hot H_2O, add 0.10 g NaCl, shake until AgCl flocculates, and dil. to 1 L. Draw off 10 mL clear soln and dil. to 1 L; 1 mL = 0.0001 mg N. Prep. just before use.

Prep. $AgNO_2$ as follows: To cold soln of ca 2 g $NaNO_2$ or KNO_2 in 50 mL H_2O, add soln of $AgNO_3$ as long as ppt forms. Decant liq. and thoroly wash ppt with cold H_2O. Crystallize from boiling H_2O and dry crystals in dark at room temp. (preferably in vac.).

14.038 *Determination*

Select series of 100 mL vol. flasks of uniform dimensions and color (125 mL erlenmeyers can be used). Place 2 g untreated (nitrite-free) flour in each flask. To flasks add 0, 5, 10, 15, 20, 25, 30, and 35 mL std nitrite soln, resp., and dil. with H_2O to make 80 mL. Shake while adding std soln and H_2O to moisten and disperse flour before mixt. becomes too dil.

Add 2 g flour sample to similar flask, and add 80 mL H_2O. Place flasks in H_2O bath at 40° and digest ≥15 min. Add 2 mL sulfanilic acid soln from Mohr pipet to each flask in succession, mix well, and add 2 mL α-naphthylamine.HCl soln. Continue digestion at 40° for 20 min from time of addn to last flask. Shake samples occasionally during first 10 min and let flour settle during last 10 min.

Remove from bath without disturbing settled flour. Compare unknown with series of stds and est. closest match. Multiply mL std nitrite soln in flask by 0.05 to obtain ppm N (*e.g.*, unknown may be between 30 and 35 mL, ca 32 mL; or 32 × 0.05 = 1.6 ppm N).

14.039 Benzoyl Peroxide Bleach (Benzoic Acid) (*22*) Official Final Action

(*Caution: See* **51.018**.)

Place 50 g flour in (preferably) 500 mL g-s erlenmeyer, and add 30–40 glass beads (ca 6 mm diam.), 0.1 g *powd Fe*, and 100 mL ether. Let stand few min, shake with rotary motion, and slowly (preferably dropwise) add 2.5 mL HCl from Mohr pipet. Let stand ca 30 min, rinse down sides with small amt of ether, and let stand overnight. Shake well with rotary motion, let flour settle few min, and decant thru 100 mm buchner, fitted with paper moistened with ether, into 500 mL suction flask. Add 50 mL ether, shake, and let settle few min. Decant as before, repeat twice more, and after last addn, transfer whole contents to filter.

Transfer ether thru large funnel into 250 mL separator, add 20 mL *5% $NaHCO_3$ soln*, mix without too much vigorous shaking, and drain clear lower layer into 125 mL erlenmeyer. Repeat with one more 20 mL portion and two 10 mL portions $NaHCO_3$ soln. To this soln add 0.3 g *Nuchar W*, shake, and filter (11 cm S&S 589 white ribbon, or equiv.) into 200 mL erlenmeyer. Wash flask and filter with 20–25 mL H_2O, using fine stream from wash bottle. Add 2.0 mL H_2SO_4 (1+1) dropwise to avoid foaming out of flask and gently swirl contents to reduce foaming. (Soln should be definitely acid to litmus paper.)

Transfer to 125 mL separator, rinse flask with 12 mL ether, and add to separator. Shake gently, frequently releasing pressure. (During first extn with ether, it is preferable to release pressure after each shake to avoid possible loss.) Repeat with 2 more 12 mL ether extns. Rinse flask each time with ether. After each extn drain aq. soln into same 200 mL erlenmeyer and transfer ether to ca 50 mL Pyrex test tube (25 × 150 mm). Add 2 mL 10% NaOH soln, hold top of tube firmly against palm of hand, and shake vigorously. Insert piece of *Cu wire* (1 mm diam.

$\times$ 200 mm) into tube, and evap. ether very slowly on steam bath. Remove wire, place tubes in beaker of boiling H_2O, and evap. nearly to dryness. Slowly add up to 0.5 mL *30% H_2O_2*, followed by another 0.5 mL as soon as foam permits. (Min. frothing is desirable to permit better contact for nitration.) Break crust or film that forms before complete dryness by tapping tube against hands as evapn proceeds. Continue evapn to absolute dryness. (Introduction of gentle air current into tube hastens evapn.)

From Mohr pipet, add 4 mL mixt. of H_2SO_4 and *fuming HNO_3* (1+1), taking care that it washes down sides of tube, and heat 20 min in gently boiling H_2O bath. Place slender glass rod in test tube, and occasionally rotate or rub rod against sides of tube to ensure contact with nitrating mixt. Immediately cool under tap to below room temp. and add 6 mL H_2O while keeping tube cool. Then *slowly* add 5 mL NH_4OH from Mohr pipet with continuous shaking under tap to keep soln cool. Add 10 mL addnl NH_4OH, keeping soln cool. Add 2 mL *6% $H_2NOH.HCl$ soln*, stir, and place in 65° H_2O bath 5–6 min, stirring occasionally. (Initially temp. of bath should be few degrees above 65° to compensate for cold tubes.) Cool to room temp. under tap, filter immediately thru folded paper into similar tube, and observe color of filtrate. Red or definite pink indicates presence of benzoic acid.

Transfer this soln (within 30 min) to 5 cm (2") glass cell and read in photometer, using No. 51 filter, or spectrophtr set at 510 nm. Prep. std curve by placing in test tubes 0.0, 0.4, 0.8, 1.0, and 1.2 mg *benzoic acid in acetone soln* (0.5 mg/mL). Add 2 mL 10% NaOH soln, shake to mix well, and proceed as in par. 3, beginning ". . . place tubes in beaker of boiling H_2O, . . ." Report as ppm benzoic acid.

Bromates and Iodates in White and Whole Wheat Flour (23)—Official Final Action

14.040 *Qualitative Test for Bromates and Iodates*

Cover bottom of white pan (ca 150 sq in.) with reagent prepd by mixing equal vols HCl (1+7) and *1% KI soln*. Distribute ca 4 g flour evenly over liq. by sifting thru No. 60 sieve. Alternatively, sift flour over surface of dry pan and spray mixed reagent onto flour from glass atomizer until all particles are wetted. Black specks or purple spots not observed before the reagent was added indicate presence of bromate or iodate.

14.041 *Qualitative Test for Iodates*

(a) *Applicable to 10 ppm or more.*—Distribute ca 1 g flour evenly over bottom of petri dish and completely cover with freshly prepd mixt. of 1 vol. *1% KSCN* to 4 vols HCl (1+32). Break up any lumps with stirring rod and observe with dish on white surface. Interpret results as in **14.040**.

(b) *Applicable to 1 ppm or more.*—Proceed as in **14.040** but use acid-KSCN reagent, **(a)**.

Quantitative Method for Bromates (23)

(Applicable in absence of iodates)

14.042 *Reagents*

(a) *Zinc sulfate soln.*—Dissolve 20 g $ZnSO_4.7H_2O$ in 800 mL H_2O and dil. to 1 L.

(b) *Sodium hydroxide std soln.*—0.4*N*. Dissolve 17 g NaOH in 1 L H_2O. Titr. against std acid and adjust to 0.4±0.01*N*.

(c) *Sodium hydroxide std soln.*—0.5*N*. Dissolve 21 g NaOH in 1 L H_2O. Titr. against std acid and adjust to 0.5±0.01*N*.

(d) *Dilute sulfuric acid.*—Approx. 4*N*. Add 112 mL H_2SO_4 to 800 mL H_2O. Cool, and dil. to 1 L.

(e) *Potassium iodide soln.*—Dissolve 25 g KI in 30 mL H_2O and dil. to 50 mL. Store in amber bottle in cool place. Discard soln showing yellow (free I).

(f) *Ammonium molybdate soln.*—Dissolve 3 g $(NH_4)_6Mo_7O_{24}.4H_2O$ in 80 mL H_2O and dil. to 100 mL.

(g) *Potassium bromate std solns.*—*(1) Stock soln.*—5 mg/mL. Dissolve 5.000 g $KBrO_3$ (dried 1 hr at 110°) in ca 800 mL H_2O and dil. to 1 L. *(2) Working soln.*—0.25 mg/mL. Dil. 25 mL stock soln to 500 mL.

(h) *Potassium iodate std solns.*—*(1) Stock soln.*—0.0898*N*. Dissolve 3.204 g KIO_3 (dried 1 hr at 110°) in ca 800 mL H_2O and dil. to 1 L. *(2) Working soln.*—0.00359*N*. Dil. 10 mL stock soln to 250 mL. Prep. fresh daily.

(i) *Sodium thiosulfate std solns.*—*(1) Stock soln.*—Dissolve 22.5 g $Na_2S_2O_3.5H_2O$ and 0.06 g anhyd. Na_2CO_3 in 800 mL H_2O, and dil. to 1 L. Dil. 10 mL to 250 mL. Transfer 5 mL dild soln to 200 mL erlenmeyer. Add 100 mL H_2O, 10 mL dil. H_2SO_4, and 1 mL KI soln. Add 5 mL freshly prepd starch soln, **2.144(b)**, and titr. with 0.00359*N* KIO_3 from 10 mL buret graduated in 0.05 mL. Adjust stock $Na_2S_2O_3$ soln so that 10 to 250 diln is 0.00359*N*. Store stock soln in amber bottle in cool place.

(2) Sodium thiosulfate working soln.—0.00359*N*. Dil. 10 mL stock soln to 250 mL. Prep. fresh daily and check titer at least monthly. 1 mL = 0.1 mg $KBrO_3$.

14.043 *Determination*

Quant. transfer 200 mL $ZnSO_4$ soln to 600 or 800 mL beaker and stir with speed-controlled, motor-driven glass stirrer. (Enough agitation to disperse flour is provided by vortex ca 40 mm deep which does not extend to bottom of beaker.) Transfer 50±0.1 g sample to stirred soln in 2–5 g portions. Continue stirring ca 5 min, or until all dry flour on surface is uniformly dispersed in liq. While stirring, add 50 mL 0.4*N* NaOH from pipet. Decrease speed of stirrer and stir ca 5 min. Filter or centrf., clarifying supernate by filtration, if necessary (24 cm Whatman No. 12 folded paper, or equiv., is satisfactory).

Transfer 50 mL of this sample soln to 200 mL erlenmeyer. If smaller aliquot is taken, dil. to ca 50 mL with H_2O. Add 10 mL 4*N* H_2SO_4, 1 mL KI soln, 1 drop NH_4 molybdate soln, and 50 mL H_2O. While stirring, add 5–10 mL 0.00359*N* $Na_2S_2O_3$ (an excess). Add 5 mL freshly prepd starch soln, **2.144(b)**, and titr. excess $Na_2S_2O_3$ with 0.00359*N* KIO_3. (Use 10 mL buret graduated in 0.05 mL for std solns. End point is best observed straight down.) As end point approaches, add KIO_3 soln slowly, 1 or 2 drops at time, swirling and viewing flask after placing it on white surface after each addn. Take first reddish or purple tinge as end point; then add several more drops to confirm. Add addnl 1 mL $Na_2S_2O_3$ soln, and again titr. to addnl end point. Average the 2 differences between amts of $Na_2S_2O_3$ soln added and KIO_3 used in titrns; ppm $KBrO_3$ = 10 $\times$ (mL 0.00359*N* $Na_2S_2O_3$ − mL 0.00359*N* KIO_3). Correct results by recovery factor detd as below.

14.044 *Recovery Factor*

Dil. known vol. (*x* mL), >3 mL but <10 mL, of std $KBrO_3$ soln to 250 mL. Using 50 mL aliquot, proceed as in second par. of detn.

"Added bromate" in ppm = 10 $\times$ (mL 0.00359*N* $Na_2S_2O_3$ − mL 0.00359*N* KIO_3).

Suspend 50 g portions nonbromated flour in 2 sep. 200 mL portions $ZnSO_4$ soln by stirring as above. To 1 (blank) suspension, add 10 mL H_2O; to other (recovery) suspension, add *x* mL std $KBrO_3$ soln and (10 − *x*) mL H_2O. Continue as above, except add 40 mL 0.5*N* NaOH from pipet with continuous stirring. Use 5 mL std $Na_2S_2O_3$ for "blank" and 10 mL for "recovery." Deduct blank value, if any, from value of $KBrO_3$ found in "recovery" detn and multiply result by 10 to obtain ppm "recovered bromate."

Recovery factor = added bromate/recovered bromate.

14.045 Pigments in Flour (*24*)—Official Final Action

Place 10 g flour in 125 mL g-s flask and from pipet add 50 mL *H_2O-satd n-BuOH*. Stopper flask tightly, shake well 1 min, and let stand 15 min protected from sunlight. Again shake well and filter thru 12.5 cm folded Whatman No.1 paper, collecting filtrate in 50 mL erlenmeyer or suitable container. Fill 1 cm cell with flour ext and duplicate cell with corresponding solv. Read A at 435.8 nm with spectrophtr. From av. of 3 readings, calc. pigment as carotene in ppm from std curve, or in absence of std carotene, from following formula:

$$C = 5.0 \times A/bK = 30.1 \times A,$$

where C = pigment as carotene in ppm; b = cell thickness (cm); and K = 0.16632 (a (mg/L) for carotene at 435.8 nm in H_2O-satd n-BuOH in 1 cm cell).

Caution: Use strictly clean cells and filter thru paper the H_2O-satd n-BuOH used as blank.

Diastatic Activity of Flour (*25*)—Official Final Action

14.046 ***Reagent***

Acetate buffer soln.—pH 4.6–4.8. Dil. 3 mL HOAc and 4.1 g *anhyd.* NaOAc to 1 L with H_2O.

14.047 ***Determination***

(Total maltose after diastasis 1 hr)

Place 5 g flour and teaspoonful ignited *quartz sand* in 100 or 125 mL erlenmeyer, and mix by rotating flask. Add 46 mL acetate buffer soln, and again mix by rotating flask until all flour is suspended. Bring flask and all ingredients *individually* to 30° before mixing. Digest 1 hr at 30°, preferably in temp.-controlled H_2O bath, rotating flask every 15 min. After 1 hr add 2 mL H_2SO_4 (3.58±0.05*N*, ca 1+9), and mix thoroly. Add 2 mL *12% $Na_2WO_4.2H_2O$ soln*, mix, and let stand 1–2 min. Filter thru paper (Whatman No. 4, or equiv.), discarding first 8 or 10 drops. Proceed as in **14.025(a)**.

These operations may be used with all ordinary flours whose values for mg maltose produced by 10 g flour in 1 hr seldom, if ever, exceed 350. For material giving higher values, such as products from malted or sprouted grain, use smaller portions of ext, *i.e.*, 1, 2, or 3 mL instead of 5 mL. In such cases, however, add enough H_2O to make up difference, and use appropriate factor to convert results into mg maltose/10 g flour. If material in test tubes is colorless instead of yellow after treatment in boiling H_2O bath and does not turn blue upon addn of KI, there is too much maltose to reduce all $K_3Fe(CN)_6$, and detn must be repeated with smaller amt of ext.

14.048 ***Blank Determination***

Blank detn to indicate amt of reducing sugar originally present in the flour—value for which presumably should be deducted from total maltose value after 1 hr diastasis—has been generally regarded as essential step in estn of flour diastatic activity. This operation ordinarily is unnecessary when dealing with flour milled from *sound* wheat, because amt of reducing sugars originally present as such is so small and so nearly const that it may be disregarded for all practical purposes. Blank detn may therefore be omitted in routine testing. It need be used only when there is doubt as to soundness of the wheat, or where there is known to have been appreciable amt of frosted, sprouted, heat-damaged, or otherwise unsound kernels in wheat from which flour was milled.

If blank detn is desired, proceed as in **14.024**.

Alpha-Amylase

AACC Falling Number (FN) Determination Method (26)
Official First Action

(Applicable to both meal and flour of wheat, rye, barley, and other grains, and malted cereals. Not applicable to detn of α-amylase activity from fungal sources.)

14.049 ***Principle***

α-Amylase liquefies starch gel. Activity of enzyme is measured by falling number (FN), defined as time in sec required to stir and let stirrer fall measured distance thru hot aq. flour gel undergoing liquefaction.

14.050 ***Apparatus***

(a) *FN apparatus.*—Available from Falling Number AB, Box 32072, S-12611, Stockholm, Sweden. Specify test tube tolerances: id ±0.2 mm, od ±0.3 mm, length ±0.3 mm. Check wt of tubes, and use those that agree most closely with mean value.

(b) *Mill.*—Must produce meal with particle size distribution as follows: >500 μm, 0–10%; >210 but <500 μm, 25–40%; <210 μm, 75–50%. Use either of following: Weber Pulverizer with 0.5 mm sieve (Pulverizing Machinery, Division of MikroPul Corp., 10 Chatham Rd, Summit, NJ 07901); Udy Cyclone with 0.024" sieve (UD Corporation, 1898 S Flatiron Ct, Boulder, CO 80301); or equiv.

(c) *Automatic pipet.*—Calibrated to deliver 25±0.3 mL.

(d) *Thermometer.*—NBS or equiv., calibrated in 0.1° and certified accurate to ±0.3°.

14.051 ***Preparation of Sample***

Grind ca 250 g grain sample in mill. Moisture content of grain should be within range of ca 8–16%. Add H_2O to grain with <8% moisture, and air- or vac.-dry grain with >16% moisture.

14.052 ***Temperature Adjustment of FN Apparatus***

Const temperature H_2O bath of FN apparatus must be maintained at 100.0°. Prep. as follows: Fill reservoir with H_2O to H_2O-level control fixed at 2.5 cm below cover. Place rubber stopper contg thermometer in tube well and let remain until temp. is const. If bath temp. is between 98.0° and 99.8°, adjust it to 100.0° with amt ethylene glycol or glycerol indicated in Table **14:02**.

If bath temp. is <98.0°, do not attempt temp. readjustment because of danger of boiling out contents of FN tube. Instead,

Table 14:02 Ethylene Glycol or Glycerol Required to Adjust Constant Temperature Water Bath to 100.0°

Temp Elevation, °C	Amt to be Added, % by Vol.	
	Ethylene Glycol	Glycerol
0.2	1.9	2.5
0.4	3.9	4.9
0.6	5.8	7.4
0.8	7.8	9.8
1.0	9.7	12.3
1.2	11.3	14.2
1.4	12.9	16.1
1.6	14.4	18.1
1.8	16.0	20.0
2.0	17.6	21.9

det. FN at observed bp, e.g., 96.0°, as in **14.053**. Then adjust temp. to 97.5° by adding 13.6% ethylene glycol and det. FN again. Plot both values against temp. on graph paper and extrapolate to 100.0°. Read FN from graph at this point.

If bath temp. is >100.2°, add 0.1% isopropanol to H_2O for each 0.1° of excess temp. above 100.0°. Observe thermometer-immersion point, and if stem correction is applicable, use following formula:

$$\text{Stem correction} = K \times n \times (T - t),$$

where K = 0.00016 for Hg, n = no. of degrees Hg column above stoppered H_2O bath, T = bath temp., and t = Hg temp. above stopper (room temp.).

14.053 ***Determination***

Weigh 7.00 g (or appropriate wt sample calcd to 14% H_2O basis = 7.00(100 − 14)/(100 − x), where x = actual % H_2O) flour or ground meal into dry FN tube and tip to 45° angle. Add 25 mL H_2O with automatic pipet. Insert rubber stopper and shake in upright position 10 times (up and down), making sure all flour is suspended by upending. Scrape down upper part of tube with viscometer-stirrer. Remove stopper from bath well. Simultaneously start timer; place tube in bath and lock into position, taking ≤5 sec. Stir sample with viscometer-stirrer at rate of 2 strokes/sec (down and up is 1 stroke) until clock reaches 60 sec, for total of 110 strokes. Stop with stirrer in up position. If automatic timer is used, set wire against stirrer so that buzzer and shut-off mechanism will be activated at conclusion of test. Let stirrer drop by its own wt. Stop buzzer by pushing small top knob, which controls contact wire, counterclockwise. Record time in sec (stirring plus dropping time). Quickly remove test tube from bath and insert stopper or another empty test tube to prevent H_2O evapn. Hold tube under running H_2O and remove viscometer-stirrer. Remove starch gel from tube by means of spatula with extended handle. Clean viscometer-stirrer with test-tube brush. Use air jet to remove any remaining gel and H_2O from orifice.

$$\text{FN (14\% moisture basis)} = FN_{\text{as is}} \times (100 - 14)/(100 - M),$$

where M = % moisture in sample.

Proteolytic Activity of Flour and Malted Wheat Flour (*27*)—Official Final Action

(Applicable to slightly active materials such as patent flour or to dild exts of active proteolytic prepns)

14.054 ***Reagents***

(**a**) *Buffer stock soln.*—pH 4.7. Dil. 120 mL HOAc and 164 g anhyd. NaOAc to 1 L with H_2O. Dil. with 20 vols H_2O before using.

(**b**) *Bacto-hemoglobin substrate.*—Obtainable from Difco Laboratories.

(**c**) *Trichloroacetic acid (TCA) soln.*—Dissolve 180 g trichloroacetic acid in 320 mL H_2O. (*Caution: See* **51.082**.)

14.055 ***Determination***

(**a**) *Preparation of enzyme solns.*—For slightly active materials such as flour, weigh as much as 10 g directly into digestion flasks. For active enzyme prepns, prep. ext or suspension in dild buffer, **14.054(a)**, immediately before digestion. (Amt of ext or dilns thereof used in digestion mixt. may vary up to 2 mL; appropriate activation technics may be applied to enzyme exts.)

(**b**) *Digestion procedure.*—Weigh 2.50 g (H_2O-free basis) Bacto-hemoglobin into each of two 125 mL erlenmeyers, add ca 5 g or 1 teaspoon fine pumice and flour sample, (**a**), to each flask, and agitate mixt. by rotation until flour and substrate are intimately mixed. Then to each flask add 50 mL dild acetate buffer soln, previously warmed to 40±0.1° in temp.-controlled bath, and agitate mixt. to suspend uniformly. Place tightly stoppered flasks in 40° bath and agitate either continuously or at 1 hr intervals.

Add 10 mL portion TCA soln, (**c**), to one flask after 15 min digestion and to second flask after 5.25 hr digestion. Shake each flask, using 25 vigorous horizontal movements, and keep flasks in bath at 40° exactly 30 min. Centrf. suspension 5 min at 1800 rpm and filter. (Some materials such as flour may remain turbid after final filtration; clear by boiling centrfd digestion mixt. few sec before final filtration. Replace liq. lost thru evapn by adding H_2O.) Pipet duplicate 10 mL aliquots directly into Kjeldahl flasks and det. sol. N.

Follow essentially same operations in detg enzyme activity of an ext. In place of solid material, use total of 2 mL ext or ext plus dild buffer soln. After 0 time and 5 hr digestion periods, add 10 mL aliquot of TCA soln, (**c**), to each flask. Mix thoroly, keep in H_2O bath exactly 30 min, and filter without centrfg. Analyze 10 mL aliquots for sol. N.

(**c**) *Determination of soluble nitrogen.*—Proceed as in **2.057**. Use definite vol. H_2O (350 mL) to dil. cooled digest and add in such way as to wash down all TCA that has condensed in neck of flask during digestion. Also add NaOH soln, **2.055(f)** (1.5 times usual amt), so as to rinse neck of flask. After distn, back-titr. unneutzd std acid with stdzd ca 0.07*N* NaOH.

(**d**) *Expression of proteolytic activity.*—Proteolytic activity is measured by difference in back-titrn vols for 15 min or 0 time digestions and corresponding long-time digestion, calcd as mL 0.0714*N* NaOH. Transform proteolytic activity detd for 10 mL aliquot to 3/2 power. Multiply this value by 6 (total final vol. of digest/10 mL aliquot) and by 1000/mL enzyme source. This value is activity expressed in hemoglobin units (HU)/g enzyme prepn (Arch. Biochem. **32,** 200(1951)).

(**e**) *Curve method.*—Use 3 to 5 levels of flour or dilns of active enzyme prepns, and digest and det. sol. N as in (**b**) and (**c**). Plot mg sample (for 60 mL final vols of digest) against mL 0.0714*N* NaOH titrn difference (= mg increase in sol. N) for the 10 mL aliquots. From smooth curve obtained, read mg sample equiv. to titrn difference of 5.00 mL. Raise 5.00 to 3/2 power (= 11.18). Multiply this value by 6 and by 1000/mg enzyme source to obtain activity as HU/g.

(**f**) *Std curve method.*—Use 5 dilns of active enzyme prepn to be used as std, and digest and det. sol. N as in (**b**) and (**c**). Plot curve and calc. HU/g as in (**e**) for this std sample. For each unknown sample, using single sample size, digest and det. sol. N as in (**b**) and (**c**). From std curve, det. mg std sample to give titrn difference found for unknown sample. Multiply proteolytic value HU/g for std by ratio obtained by dividing wt std sample by wt unknown sample. Result is activity of unknown as HU/g.

Notes: (1) Careful washing down of TCA from neck of digestion flasks is mandatory. If not neutzd, TCA steam distils.

(2) More reproducible results will be obtained if Kjeldahl detns are completed without delay between digestion and distn.

(3) If other than 10 mL aliquots are analyzed for sol. N, convert results to 10 mL aliquot basis before transforming to 3/2 power. If titrn difference, using 10 mL aliquot, is >10 mL 0.0714*N* NaOH, reanalyze, using smaller amt of enzyme. For most precise results, titrn difference should be 4.0–6.0 mL 0.0714*N* NaOH.

(4) For each lot of hemoglobin, adjust pH of stock buffer, if necessary, so that pH of mixt. of 50 mL dild buffer, 2.5 g hemoglobin, and ca 5 g pumice will be 4.70±0.05. This pH for buffer substrate mixt. is critical for accuracy of method.

(5) Accurate results are obtainable only when titrn difference for detn is close to 5.00 mL 0.0714*N* NaOH. For single point method, restricted range of titrn difference between 4.0 and 6.0 is recommended, but even within extremes of this range,

variations in sol. N for different wt enzyme samples will cause differences of several % in calcd HU/g values.

(6) Curve methods for detn of proteolytic activity have advantage of using exactly 5.00 mL titrn difference (5.00 mg increase in sol. N) as ideal ref. point. They permit working in range 3.0–8.0 mL titrn difference.

(7) Std curve method using std sample and unknowns each at 1 level is especially useful where routine assays on large number of samples are required. Advantage of using std sample is that it affords automatic check on minor day-to-day variations in technic.

(8) It is convenient for routine analyses to use 0.0714*N* NaOH for back-titrn, since 1 mL titrn difference = 1 mL increase in sol. N.

Apparent Viscosity of Acidulated Flour-Water Suspension Official Final Action

By MacMichael Viscosimeter (28)

14.056 ***Adjustment of Machine***

(**a**) Use No. 30 MacMichael viscosimeter wire.

(**b**) Have diam. of disk plunger 2.375±0.01".

(**c**) Adjust clearance between bottom of disk and inner surface of bottom of bowl to 0.25±0.005". Carefully check clearance with depth gage reading in 0.001".

(**d**) Use viscosimeter bowl with ca 7 cm diam. (depth of bowl will vary according to age of machine).

(**e**) Adjust regulating device to permit speed of exactly 12 rpm and check carefully and frequently with stop-watch, because as motor warms up, machine tends to increase its speed.

(**f**) Adjust machine and keep it level, and when bob is placed see that it is riding freely and not touching sides of guide.

(**g**) Adjust dial so that when it comes to rest, pointer is on 0 mark.

14.057 ***Preparation of Lactic Acid***

To concd lactic acid add ca proportion of H_2O to give slightly >1*N* soln. Reflux 3 hr, cool, and adjust to 1*N* by adding H_2O. Or proceed as follows: Use enough concd lactic acid to prep. soln ca 0.85*N* when stdzd with 0.1*N* NaOH. Transfer to erlenmeyer fitted with air condenser to prevent undue evapn of H_2O, and heat 24 hr at 80° (soln will have increased in strength to ca 1.18*N*). Adjust to exactly 1*N* with H_2O.

14.058 ***Preparation of Flour-Water Suspension***

In clean, dry, 500 mL erlenmeyer, place 20 g flour (15% moisture basis) and add 100 mL H_2O at 30°. Close with rubber stopper and shake vigorously 1 min. Place flask in const temp. cabinet or H_2O bath 1 hr at 30°, shaking ca 10 times every 15 min. Remove flask, add 3 or 4 drops *capryl alcohol*, shake 10 times to remove any foam that may be present, and pour suspension into bowl of viscosimeter.

14.059 ***Determination***

After pouring suspension into viscosimeter bowl, make sure bowl is flush on its supports. Start machine, but before placing bob or disk in place, stir soln with bob 25 times to ensure uniform suspension. Place wire of bob in holder and take reading after damping swing of dial by placing a finger on indicator pointer and then gradually touching swinging dial. Make second reading after adding 1 mL 1*N* lactic acid, and likewise third and following readings after adding 2 mL increments 1*N* lactic acid. Do not stop motor between readings. After or during addn of lactic acid, stir suspension 25 times by up-and-down motion of bob. Suspend bob by the wire and take reading. Det. max. apparent viscosity of the acidulated flour-H_2O suspension by plotting apparent viscosity readings against vol. acid added. Usually total of 7 mL 1*N* lactic acid is enough for max. reading, but 2 mL increments should be added continuously until apparent viscosity no longer increases.

Soybean Flour in Uncooked Cereal Products (*29*)

14.060 ***Qualitative Test—Official Final Action***

Place ca 0.5 g sample in small test tube contg strip of red litmus paper partly immersed in 5 mL *2% urea soln*. Mix, stopper tube, and heat 3 hr at 40°. If soybean flour is present in more than traces, litmus paper turns blue. (Bromothymol blue may also be used as indicator; it likewise turns blue if soybean flour is present.)

14.061 Uric Acid in Flour—Official Final Action

See **44.178–44.182**.

WHEAT, RYE, OATS, CORN, BUCKWHEAT, RICE, AND BARLEY AND THEIR PRODUCTS EXCEPT CEREAL ADJUNCTS (*30*)—OFFICIAL FINAL ACTION*

14.062 ***Preparation of Sample***

Grind sample to pass No. 20 sieve, or sieve having circular openings 1 mm (1/25") diam., and mix thoroly.

14.063 Moisture

See **14.003**.

14.064 Ash

See **14.006**.

14.065 Crude Fiber

See **7.065**.

14.066 Iron in Degerminated, Bolted, Whole Corn Meal

See **14.013**.

14.067 Crude Fat or Ether Extract

See **7.056**.

Protein (*31*)

14.068 Kjeldahl Method

See **2.057**. Protein = N × *F*, where *F* = 5.83 for barley, millet, oats, rye, and whole kernel wheat; 6.25, corn and sorghum; 5.95, rice; 6.31, wheat bran; 5.80, wheat embryo; 5.70, wheat endosperm; 5.71, soybeans; 6.25, beans (adzuki, jack, lima, mung, navy, and velvet); 5.30, castor beans; 5.30, seeds (cantaloupe, cotton, flax, hemp, pumpkin, sesame, and sunflower).

14.069 Automated Method—Official First Action

See **7.021–7.024**.

Fat Acidity

14.070 ***Reagents***

(**a**) *Benzene-alcohol-phenolphthalein soln*.—0.02%. To 1 L benzene add 1 L alcohol and 0.4 g phthln.

(**b**) *Alcohol-phenolphthalein soln*.—0.04%. To 1 L alcohol add 0.4 g phthln.

* Unless otherwise indicated.

(**c**) *Potassium hydroxide std soln.*—0.0178*N*, carbonate-free. 1 mL = 1 mg KOH.

14.071 ***Apparatus***

(**a**) *Grain mill.*—Suitable for grinding small samples.

(**b**) *Fat extraction device.*—Soxhlet or other suitable type. (Durable paper thimbles or Alundum RA-360 thimbles are suitable for extn.)

14.072 ***Method I (14)***

(*Caution: See* **51.009**, **51.011**(**a**), and **51.073**.)

Obtain representative sample of ca 50 g grain (corn, 200 g) by hand quartering or by use of mech. sampling device. Preferably grind sample so that ≥90% will pass No. 40 sieve (somewhat coarser grind will not materially affect results). If sample is too moist to grind readily, dry at temp. of ca 100° just long enough to remove excess moisture.

Ext 10±0.01 g ground sample with pet ether ca 16 hr in extractor. Start extn as soon as possible after grinding and never let ground sample remain overnight. Completely evap. solv. from ext on steam bath. Dissolve residue in extn flask with 50 mL benzene-alcohol-phthln soln and titr. with std KOH soln to distinct pink, or in case of yellow soln to orange-pink. If emulsion forms during titrn, dispel by adding second 50 mL portion of benzene-alcohol-phthln soln. End point should match color of soln made by adding 2.5 mL *0.01% $KMnO_4$ soln* to 50 mL *$K_2Cr_2O_7$ soln* of proper strength to match color of original soln being titrd. (Add 0.5% $K_2Cr_2O_7$ soln dropwise to 50 mL H_2O until color matches. Then add 2.5 mL 0.01% $KMnO_4$ soln.)

Make blank titrn on 50 mL benzene-alcohol-phthln soln and subtract this value from titrn value of sample. If addnl 50 mL portion benzene-alcohol-phthln soln was added, double blank titrn. Report fat acidity as mg KOH required to neutze free fatty acids from 100 g grain (dry basis). Fat acidity = 10 × (titrn − blank).

14.073 ***Method II. Rapid Method for Corn***

(Result may be obtained in <1 hr)

Prep. sample as in **14.072**. Weigh 20±0.01 g into 100 mL g-s flask or bottle. Add exactly 50 mL benzene, insert stopper, shake few sec to sat. air in flask with benzene vapor, momentarily loosen stopper to release pressure, and replace stopper. Shake flask 30 min in mech. shaker, or periodically by hand 45 min. Tilt flask and let meal settle at an angle ≥3 min. Carefully decant as much liq. as possible into 15 cm folded paper inserted in 8 cm glass funnel, and cover funnel with cover glass to reduce evapn. Collect exactly 25 mL filtrate in 25 mL vol. flask. Transfer this filtrate to 250 mL Florence flask. Refill vol. flask to 25 mL mark with alcohol-phthln soln and transfer to flask contg benzene ext.

Using color std prepd as in **14.072**, titr. ext with std KOH soln to distinct pink in case of white corn, and to orange-pink for yellow corn. If emulsion forms during titrn, dispel by adding 25 mL each of benzene and of alcohol-phthln soln. Det. blank titrn on mixt. of 25 mL benzene and 25 mL alcohol-phthln soln. If addnl benzene and alcohol were added, double blank titrn. Report fat acidity as mg KOH required to neutze free fatty acids from 100 g corn (dry basis).

Fat acidity = 10 × (titrn − blank), calcd on dry basis.

14.074 Vitamins in Enriched Grains

See Chapter **43**.

Starch (*32*)—Official First Action

(Applicable to grains, stock feeds, and cereals)

14.075 ***Reagents***

(**a**) 80% *Isopropanol-salt soln.*—Dissolve 10 g NaCl in ca 150 mL H_2O, add 800 mL isopropanol (USP or reagent grade) on basis of 100% purity, and dil. to 1 L at ca 20°.

(**b**) *Acetate buffer, 4M.*—Dissolve 330 g anhyd. NaOAc in 1 L H_2O, add 240 mL (or 251 g) HOAc, cool, and dil. to 2 L.

(**c**) *Acetate buffer, 0.4M.*—pH 4.7–4.8. Dil. 4*M* acetate buffer to 0.4*M*. Check pH with pH meter.

(**d**) *Enzyme prepn.*—Rhozyme-S, high potency conc., low reducing sugar content (Rohm and Haas Co.). Prep. daily required vol. of 2% aq. soln.

Note: 25 mg enzyme prepn, Factor 4 (manufacturer's activity factor based on maltose hydrolysis), yields 99% calcd glucose from 200 mg ash-free dry matter of USP Reference Potato Starch at pH 4.7 after 6 hr at 50°. Use 100 mg enzyme to hydrolyze ≤400 mg total available carbohydrate. Thus at least twice necessary amt is used. This amt will completely hydrolyze sucrose, maltose, lactose, and cellobiose, if present.

(**e**) *2-Octanol (capryl alcohol).*—Ketone-free, bp 178–180° (Eastman Kodak Co.).

(**f**) *Zinc sulfate soln.*—10% $ZnSO_4.7H_2O$.

(**g**) *Ferricyanide (FeCy) reagent.*—0.04*N*. Dissolve 100 g anhyd. Na_2CO_3 and 26.40 g anhyd. $K_3Fe(CN)_6$ in H_2O and dil. to 2 L at 20°. Protect from strong light during prepn. Store in bottle completely covered with heavy Al foil or black paint. Soln is stable indefinitely at 25° when protected from light; however, prep. fresh soln every 6 months. 5 mL FeCy soln with 5 mL H_2O, 1 mL KI soln, and 5 mL $ZnSO_4$-HOAc soln should yield I equiv. to 20.0 mL 0.01*N* thiosulfate.

(**h**) *Potassium iodide soln.*—20 g/100 mL. Protect from strong light; keep cold when not in use. Prep. fresh after 1–2 months.

(**i**) *Zinc sulfate-acetic acid soln.*—60 mL HOAc and 60 g $ZnSO_4.7H_2O$/L.

(**j**) *Sodium thiosulfate std solns.*—(*1*) Approx. 0.1*N*. Prep. and stdze as in **50.037–50.038**. Normality decreases rapidly during first week, but thereafter remains virtually const, decreasing ca 0.0001*N*/ month under usual laboratory conditions. (*2*) *Working soln.*—Prep. daily from (*1*) exactly 0.01*N* soln. Protect 0.01*N* soln from heat and strong light.

(**k**) *Starch soln.*—Suspend 10 g sol. starch in cold H_2O. Add to ca 500 mL boiling H_2O, dil. to ca 1 L with boiling H_2O, and boil several min. Keep in refrigerator. Prep. fresh soln after 1–2 months. Decant supernate as needed in titrns.

(**l**) *Glucose std solns.*—(*1*) *Stock soln.*—10 mg/mL. To 500 vol. flask transfer 5.0025 g (assume 99.95% purity) NBS Dextrose SRM No. 41, dried in vac. at 25–40°, add 5 mL 0.1*N* HCl, and dil. to vol. at 20°. Store in refrigerator. (*2*) *Working solns.*—0.5–5.0 mg glucose/5 or 10 mL. Dil. 1–10 mL aliquots stock soln to 100 or 200 mL.

14.076 ***Apparatus***

(**a**) *Weighing funnels.*—Glass, 15 × 45 mm (similar to No. 30287-029, VWR Scientific, Inc., PO Box 3200, San Francisco, CA 94119, or No. 12803, New York Laboratory Supply Co.).

(**b**) *J-rods.*—Glass rods, 3 mm diam. and 300 mm long, bent and shaped at one end to fit round bottom of 25 mm diam. test tube.

(**c**) *Test tubes.*—Pyrex, 32 × 200 mm, calibrated at 50 and 75 mL for starch detn. Pyrex, thin-wall, 29 × 200 mm, for reducing sugars detn.

(**d**) *Water baths.*—Electrically heated, thermostatically controlled to ±1°, fitted with elec. stirrer, 36 × 60 cm (14 × 24") od.

(**e**) *Cooling bath*.—With running H_2O at ca 20°, 36 × 60 × 13 cm (14 × 24 × 5").

(**f**) *Spectrophotometer*.—Prism or grating, with Corex 1 cm sq cells, or equiv.

14.077 ***Extraction***

(Conduct blanks thru entire detn.)

Transfer 250–1000 mg sample, contg ≤400 mg starch and sol. sugars, to test tube. Use weighing funnel for <500 mg samples, letting tared funnel and sample slide to bottom of tube. Add ca 500 mg NaCl. Pipet in 35 mL isopropanol (on basis of 100% purity). Insert J-rod, mix thoroly, and let stand ca 10 min, mixing frequently to ext lipids. Add H_2O to 50 mL, plus 1.5 mL to allow for vol. of weighing funnel. Let stand 60 min in H_2O bath at ca 20°, mixing frequently to assure soln of sol. carbohydrates. Add ca 200 mg Celite and continue extn 30 min (total of 90 min) at ca 20°, mixing frequently.

Decant thru 15 cm Whatman No. 54 paper; let liq. drain completely from paper. Transfer remaining solids in tube, using 80% isopropanol-NaCl soln cooled to 15–20°. Save tube and J-rod. Wash paper and contents with small vols cooled isopropanol-NaCl soln, letting contents drain after each washing. Use ca 150 mL cooled isopropanol-NaCl soln for transfer and washings. Keep funnel covered thruout. Discard filtrate and washings.

With cool H_2O, transfer residue from paper to original test tube. (Quant. removal requires care and previous practice.) Remove last traces of sample by rubbing entire surface of paper several times with rubber policeman, followed by washing with fine jets of cool H_2O. Finally, wash entire surface and funnel. Vol. in test tube should be ≤75 mL. (At this point analysis may be delayed 24–48 hr without significant loss of enzymatic digestibility of starch.) Store in refrigerator.

14.078 ***Enzymatic Hydrolysis***

Add 1–2 drops octanol; heat 60 min in H_2O bath at ≥90°, mixing frequently with J-rod, especially during first 10 min. (Residues of some samples, especially those which contain much starch, may "explode" and foam over when heated >90°.) Cool and, *without delay, perform enzymatic hydrolysis*. (Storage in refrigerator overnight or longer may significantly decrease yield of reducing sugar.) Add 5 mL 0.4*M* acetate buffer and 5 mL enzyme soln. Incubate 6 hr at 50°, mixing frequently, especially during first 10 min.

14.079 ***Clarification***

Quant. transfer contents to 250 mL vol. flask. Add 10 mL $ZnSO_4$ soln, 2–3 drops phthln, and 1–2 drops octanol. While rotating flask, rapidly add 0.5*N* NaOH until $Zn(OH)_2$ begins to ppt, and carefully add alkali until contents are faint pink. Add 0.5*N* HCl drop by drop until colorless, and dil. to vol. Let stand ca 10 min, mixing frequently, and filter.

Store filtrate in refrigerator; analyze within 24 hr.

14.080 ***Ferricyanide Reduction and Determination of Starch***

(**a**) *Titrimetric method*.—Transfer 2, 3, 4, or 5 mL sample and reagent blank, from **14.079**, to bottom of 29 × 200 mm test tubes, covered with small beakers or, preferably, with large glass bulbs; add H_2O to *exactly* 5 mL. Add *exactly* 5 mL FeCy reagent, and mix immediately by gently rotating tube. Incubate *exactly* 30 min in H_2O bath at 80±1°; cool rapidly in running H_2O bath at 20–25°. (Greatest accuracy is obtained with vol. of sample soln contg 3–3.5 mg glucose and resulting in ca 50% reduction of FeCy. Accuracy in measurement of 5 mL FeCy reagent is important, since errors are increased in detn of residual FeCy.)

If 5 mL sample soln contains <1 mg glucose, use 10 mL sample and blank soln, add 5 mL FeCy reagent, mix immediately, and proceed as before.

Add 1 mL KI soln and 5 mL $ZnSO_4$-HOAc soln, mixing by gentle rotation after each addn. To prevent I loss, cover tubes immediately and keep covered until titrn. Let stand ≥20 min, mixing contents twice. Titr. with 0.01*N* $Na_2S_2O_3$ until almost colorless, adding first few mL around sides of tube to prevent loss of I vapors. Add ca 0.5 mL starch soln; wash sides of tubes and continue titrn drop by drop until color is pure white.

(**b**) *Spectrophotometric method*.—To enzymatic digest, in 250 mL vol. flask, add 10 mL $ZnSO_4$ soln and 0.5*N* NaOH to ca pH 7.5. (Phthln interferes in detn. Det. vol. 0.5*N* NaOH required by titrg blank contg 5 mL 0.4*M* acetate buffer and 10 mL $ZnSO_4$ soln, using pH meter or titrg until red to phenol red and colorless to phthln.) Dil. to vol., mix, filter, and check pH. Transfer 2, 3, 4, 5, or 10 mL to 29 × 200 mm test tube and conduct ferricyanide reduction as in (**a**).

Dil. FeCy reaction mixt. to 250 mL, and det. %*T* at 418 nm, using 1 cm sq Corex cells.

(**c**) *Standardization*.—Stdze detn, using 5 mL std glucose soln contg 1–5 mg glucose or 10 mL std soln contg 1–5 mg glucose. Use 5 mL FeCy reagent in all stdzns. Using 4 detns, calc. av. mg glucose/mL FeCy reagent reduced.

(**d**) *Calculations*.—Calc. % reducing sugar, RS, expressed as glucose. Assume 97.5% recovery of RS, due to incomplete mobilization of starch from sample tissues, recovery from paper, hydrolysis to RS, and loss during pptn and filtration.

% Starch = 0.923 × % RS.

AACC Glucoamylase Method with Subsequent Measurement of Glucose with Glucose Oxidase (*33*) Official First Action

(Applicable to raw and cooked cereals)

14.081 ***Reagents***

(**a**) *Glucoamylase soln*.—10 mg (30 IU)/mL H_2O. Purity of enzyme is critical; should be prepd from *Rhizopus delemar*. Prepn Sumizyme 3000 from Shin Nihon Chemical Co., 19-10 Showa-cho, Anjyo-city, Aichi, Japan has been found satisfactory.

(**b**) D-*Glucose std soln*.—400 mg anhyd./L. Let stand 4 hr to complete mutarotation before use.

(**c**) *Acetate buffer*.—4*M*, pH 4.8. Dil. 120 mL HOAc and 164 g anhyd. NaOAc to 1 L with H_2O.

(**d**) *Tris-phosphate buffer*.—pH 7.0. Dissolve 36.3 g trihydroxymethlyaminomethane and 50.0 g $NaH_2PO_4.H_2O$ (or 45.5 g anhyd.) in 500 mL H_2O. Adjust pH to 7.0 with H_3PO_4 *at 37°* and dil to 1 L with H_2O at 37°.

(**e**) *Enzyme-buffer-chromogen mixture*.—Dissolve in 100 mL tris-phosphate buffer: 30 mg glucose oxidase (Type II from *Aspergillus niger*, Sigma Chemical Co.), 3 mg peroxidase (Type I from horseradish, Sigma Chemical Co.), and 10 mg *o*-dianisidine.2HCl. Disperse *o*-dianisidine completely in small amt of buffer before adding it to enzyme-buffer mixt. Store ≤10 days at 4°. Available in prepd form from Worthington Biochemical Corp. Freehold, NJ 07728, as Glucostat special, Sigma Chemical Co., and Calbiochem.

14.082 ***Determination***

(For products cont D-glucose and polysacharides derived from starch with dextrose equiv. <14, ext with 2 portions boiling 80% alcohol and 2 portions 80% alcohol at 25°. Remove alcohol completely by evapn, since alcohol inhibits glucoamylase activity.)

Grind sample to <0.5 mm (No. 40 sieve). Det. moisture. Weigh 0.5 g sample (≤1.0 g contg ≤0.5 g starch) into dried, weighed erlenmeyer. Add 25 mL H_2O with stirring and adjust pH to 5–7, if necessary. Boil with gentle stirring 3 min and then autoclave 1 hr at 135°. (Lower autoclave pressure and temp. but ≥1 hr may be used with some starches to achieve complete gelatinization.) Remove from autoclave, cool to ca 55°, and add 2.5 mL acetate buffer and sufficient H_2O to total wt of soln of 45±1 g. Immerse flask in H_2O bath with shaker at optimal temp. of glucoamylase used (usually 55±1°) and add 5 mL glucoamylase soln. Hydrolyze 2 hr with continuous shaking, filter thru folded paper into 250 mL vol. flask, wash quant., and dil. to vol.

Transfer 1 mL aliquots contg 20–60 μg D-glucose to test tubes. Dil. filtrate, if necessary, to obtain this concn. Add 2 mL enzyme-buffer-chromogen mixt., shake tubes, and place in dark at 37±1° exactly 30 min to develop color. Stop reaction by adding 2 mL H_2SO_4 (1+1) and measure A at 540 nm.

Prep. std curve from, 0–60 μg D-glucose/mL and blank. Include control of sample contg starch of known purity from source similar to material being examined.

$$\% \text{ starch} = 0.9 \times (M/10^6) \times (V_1/1) \times (250/V_0) \times (100/E) \times (100/MS) = 2.25 \times (M \times V_1/V_0 \times E \times MS),$$

where E = g sample, M = μg D-glucose from std curve, V_0 = mL aliquot from 250 mL vol., MS = % solids in sample, and V_1 = final mL if 250 mL is further dild (V_1 = 1 if no further diln).

14.083 ***Antioxidants***

(Applicable to corn and rice breakfast cereals)

See **20.009–20.012**.

SOYBEAN FLOUR (*34*)—OFFICIAL FINAL ACTION

14.084 ***Moisture***

Proceed as in **14.004**, except use 5 g sample and dry 2 hr.

14.085 Ash

See **7.009**.

14.086 Nitrogen

See **2.057**.

14.087 Crude Fiber

See **7.065**.

Petroleum Ether Extract or Oil

14.088 ***Reagent***

Petroleum ether.—Initial boiling temp., 35–38°; dry-flask end point, 52–60°; ≥95% distg <54°, and ≤60% distg <40°; sp gr at 60°F, 0.630–0.660; evapn residue ≤0.002% by wt.

14.089 ***Determination***

Accurately weigh duplicate samples of 2 g full-fat or 5 g low-fat soy flour and wrap each portion in 150 mm filter paper (S&S 597, or equiv.); rewrap in second paper or papers so as to prevent escape of sample, leaving top of second paper open like thimble. Place piece of absorbent cotton in top of thimble to distribute the dropping ether. Place 25 mL pet ether in 125 mL tared flask, and ext sample 5 hr in Butt-type or similar extractor. (Ether should drop on center of thimble at rate of ≥150 drops/min, and vol. solv. should be kept ca const.) Evap. solv. until no trace remains, cool sample to room temp., and weigh. As last traces of ether are sometimes difficult to detect by odor, heat ≥1 hr to const wt.

BREAD

14.090 Preparation of Sample—Official Final Action

(When total solids of original loaf are not desired)

(**a**) *All types of bread not containing fruit* (*35*).—Cut loaf, or ½ loaf, of bread into slices 2–3 mm thick. Spread slices on paper and let dry in warm room until sufficiently crisp and brittle to grind well in mill. Grind entire sample to pass No. 20 sieve, mix well, and keep in air-tight container.

(**b**) *Raisin bread*.—Proceed as in (**a**), except comminute by passing twice thru food chopper instead of grinder.

14.091 Total Solids in Entire Loaf of Bread Official Final Action

(**a**) *All types of bread not containing fruit* (*35*).—Accurately weigh loaf of bread immediately upon receipt (X), using scales sensitive to at least 0.2 g. If impossible to weigh accurately at this time, seal sample in air-tight container and weigh accurately as soon thereafter as is practicable (X). Preserve sample in such manner that no loss of bread solids can occur whereby loss would be calcd as moisture.

Cut bread into slices 2–3 mm thick (½ loaf may be used). Spread slices on paper, let dry in warm room (15–20 hr), and when apparently dry, break into fragments. If bread is not entirely crisp and brittle, let it dry longer—until it is in equilibrium with moisture of air—so that no moisture changes occur during grinding. Quant. transfer air-dried bread to scale pan and weigh accurately (Y). Grind sample to pass No. 20 sieve, mix well, and keep in air-tight container. Det. % total solids (Z) of ground sample as in **14.003** or **14.004**. Calc. total solids (TS) of bread:

$$TS = (100 \times Y \times Z/100)/X, \text{ or } Y \times Z/X,$$

where X = wt loaf (or ½ loaf) at time of receipt; Y = wt air-dried sliced bread; and Z = % total solids in prepd ground sample.

(**b**) *Raisin bread and bread containing raisins and fruit*.—Proceed as in (**a**), except comminute by passing twice thru food chopper instead of grinder and dry air-dried sample in uncovered dish ca 16 hr at 70° under pressure ≤50 mm Hg (6.7 kPa).

14.092 Total Solids of Air-Dried Ground Sample (*35*) Official Final Action

Use 2 g prepd sample, **14.090**, and proceed as in **14.003** or **14.004**.

14.093 Fat and Fat Number (*36*)—Official Final Action

(*Caution: See* **51.011**, **51.054**, **51.073**, and **51.086**.)

Slice one loaf of bread, and let dry overnight, or until dry enough to grind. Grind bread to ca size of openings on No. 20 sieve, mix, and transfer 50 g to 600 mL beaker. Add 100 mL H_2O and mix. Add 100 mL HCl, mix, cover, and heat on steam bath 1 hr, stirring well 6 or 7 times. Cool in cold H_2O bath (≤15°) and stir. Add 10 g Filter-Cel, or similar absorbent, stir, and mix completely. Prep. 90 mm buchner as follows:

Place two 9 cm S&S 589 Blue Ribbon, or equiv., filter papers in funnel and apply suction. Mix 10 g Filter-Cel with 50 mL H_2O and rapidly pour mixt. into funnel. (This should make smooth, even layer of Filter-Cel over paper, without cracks or openings.) Immediately filter sample. Rinse beaker several times with ice-cold H_2O. Just before filtration is complete, wash sides of buchner with ca 100 mL ice-cold H_2O (or until clear filtrate comes thru). Up to this point do not let pad suck dry. Continue with suction until Filter-Cel pad seems dry. Transfer this mass, without paper, from buchner to original beaker. Break up mass with rod, dry overnight on steam bath, and then heat in oven at 100° ca 30 min to remove all moisture (material must be dry or fat results will be low). Break up any lumps. Cool.

Prep. large Knorr extn tube of ca 200 mL capacity (glass tubing 5 cm diam., 12 cm high from shoulder to top of tube). Pack tube with asbestos tamped tightly to form ca 1 cm pad. Insert stem of tube into 2-hole rubber stopper in filtering bell jar connected to suction thru 2-way stopcock. Place 500 mL erlenmeyer within bell jar so that stem of tube passes thru neck of flask.

To beaker and contents, add 100 mL ether-pet ether (1+1) and macerate 3–4 min against sides of beaker with medium-size, stiff metal spatula. Decant into extn tube. Suck dry. Add 80 mL mixed ethers to beaker. Work as before 2 min. Transfer contents of beaker to extn tube, suck dry, and tamp with flat-end stirring rod until all ether is removed. To material in tube add 80 mL mixed ethers used just previously to rinse out beaker, mix thoroly with stirring rod few min, let stand 1 min, then suck dry, and tamp material as before. Make 2 addnl extns, turning suction on and off carefully to avoid loss of sample in erlenmeyer. Transfer to 1 L beaker. Evap. on steam bath, completely transfer fat with small amts of pet ether to weighed 150 mL beaker, carefully evap. pet ether on steam bath, dry at 100° to const wt (ca 30 min), cool, and weigh. Calc. % total fat on H_2O-free basis.

Weigh duplicate samples of 1±0.03 g fat into 300 mL Florence flasks and add 4 mL glycerol-soda soln, **28.036(b)**. Heat flask carefully over asbestos gauze until bubbles start to appear; then hold flask ca 2–3 cm over the heated gauze until cloudiness or turbidity disappears and mixt. is perfectly clear. After mixt. first becomes clear, 30–60 sec addnl gentle heating ensures complete saponification. Cool; add few pieces of previously ignited pumice stone, 138 mL CO_2-free H_2O, and 3 mL H_2SO_4 (1+4); and proceed as in **28.037**, using same app. Use 0.02*N* NaOH for titrn. Multiply mL 0.02*N* NaOH used by 1.1 and divide by wt fat used. Perform blank detn and make correction. Report number of mL 0.02*N* NaOH/g fat as "fat number."

Acetic and Propionic Acids (*37*)—Official Final Action

14.094 ***Preparation of Sample***

(a) *Air-dried bread.*—Prep. sample as in **14.090–14.091**.

(b) *Fresh bread.*—For analysis of fresh product, which may be difficult to air-dry without spoilage or loss of volatile acids, pass sample thru meat grinder equipped with ⅛" (3 mm) hole plate, and divide finely by rubbing thru No. 8 sieve. Proceed with analysis promptly (24–48 hr) or preserve with $CHCl_3$ as follows:

To prepd bread in Mason jar filled to ¾ capacity, add washed $CHCl_3$ absorbed in ca 1 g cotton (ca 5 mL $CHCl_3$/500 mL (1 pt) container). Close jar tightly (self-sealing lids are recommended) and roll to mix contents thoroly. Store samples at ca 25° or refrigerate where higher temps occur.

14.095 ***Reagents***

See **18.051**.

14.096 ***Apparatus***

(a) *Distillation apparatus.*—Use steam distn app. **18.050(a)**, or gas-fired steam generator.

(b) *Chromatographic tubes.*—Approx. 15 × 250 mm or ca 15 × 450 mm, constricted at lower end to ca 4 mm id.

(c) *Test tubes.*—Approx. 16 × 150 mm, g-s.

(d) *Eyedropper pipet.*—Approx. 180 mm long.

14.097 ***Distillation***

Transfer 10 g air-dried bread or 15 g prepd fresh bread to 150 mL distg flask. Add 50 mL H_2O and 10 mL ca 1*N* H_2SO_4. Mix thoroly and add 10 mL *20% phosphotungstic acid soln*. Mix by swirling and add 40 g $MgSO_4.7H_2O$. Swirl again to partially dissolve salt. Mixt. should now be acid to *congo red paper;* if not, acidify with H_2SO_4 (1+1). Connect to condenser and steam generator, heat contents of distg flask to bp, and distil 200 mL in 35–40 min. (Connect steam source just before heating bread solids suspension to prevent clogging of steam tube and to agitate bread solids.) Keep vol. in distg flask at ca 60–80 mL by means of small burner.

Transfer distillate to 400–600 mL beaker, add ca 10 mL *ca 0.01N formic acid*, make alk. to phthln with ca 1*N* NaOH, and evap. to ca 5 mL. Transfer to 25–30 mL g-s test tube, rinsing beaker with 3 portions H_2O. If insol. material adheres, add few drops of ca 1*N* H_2SO_4 with 1 rinse. Make alk. to phthln and evap. just to dryness by inserting tube in steam bath or in boiling H_2O. (Air current hastens evapn.) Det. acetic and propionic acids in evapd distillate by the sepn technic, **18.057(d)**, after prepg, testing, and stdzg column as in **14.098**.

14.098 ***Chromatographic Separation***

(a) *Preparation of partition column.—See* **18.056**. (Where amt of propionic acid approaches 20 mg in column and definite band is observed below propionic acid band, use long chromatgc tube (450 mm) and ca 10 g silicic acid. Then take twice amts of H_2O, indicator, and NH_4OH as used for 5 g silicic acid.)

(b) *Test of silicic acid for suitability and standardization of column.*—Prep. stock solns of formic, acetic, and propionic acids (reagent grade) by dilg 5 mL acid to 250 mL and stdze acetic and propionic acids by titrg 1.0 mL aliquots with 0.01*N* NaOH, using cresol red indicator, to pink persisting ca 45 sec.

Prep. following dil. stock solns from stock solns and boiled H_2O: Formic acid, 10 mL to 50 mL; acetic acid, 20 mL to 50 mL.

Prep. following trial mixts of formic acid and known amts of acetic and propionic acids:

Acids and Water	Mixture A; Stock Solns	Mixture B; Stock Solns	Mixture C
	mL	mL	
Formic	10	10	1 mL dil. stock soln
Acetic	10	10	1 mL dil. stock soln
Propionic	10	30	1 mL stock soln
Water	20	None	None
Total vol.	50	50	3 mL
Test aliquot	1	1	3 mL

(Above mixts cover range of acetic and propionic acids usually present when 15 g fresh bread preserved with propionate is used as initial sample.)

Pipet indicated test aliquots from mixts *A* and *B* and entire mixt. *C* into bottom of g-s test tubes (16 × 150 mm), neutze with ca 1*N* NaOH, using phthln, and add 1 drop excess.

Proceed with evapn, sepn, and titrn as in **18.057(c)** and **(d)**. Calc. results for acetic and propionic acids to mg/100 g sample. Following factors are based on 15 g fresh bread or 10 g air-dried bread:

Fresh bread (mg/100 g):

Acetic acid = 4.00 × mL 0.01*N* $Ba(OH)_2$

Propionic acid = 4.93 × mL 0.01*N* $Ba(OH)_2$

Air-dried bread (mg/100 g):

Acetic acid = 6.00 × mL 0.01*N* $Ba(OH)_2$

Propionic acid = 7.40 × mL 0.01*N* $Ba(OH)_2$

(c) *Identification of acids.—See also* **18.058** and **14.101**. With trial mixts *A, B,* and *C* and with most breads to which propionate has been added, only 3 definite bands appear on column and they elute in this order: propionic, acetic, and formic acids. Method provides for addn of enough formic acid to supply definite following band to ensure that acetic acid is completely eluted. Amt of mobile solv. required to move each acid from top of column to point of emergence is function of concn of that acid. For amt of acetic acid normally present in bread, differences in threshold vol. are not critical. To identify propionic acid by threshold vol., however, it is necessary to check threshold vol. for the concn indicated by titrn. Sepn of mixts *A, B,* and *C* supply enough data for amt normally found. Threshold vols may be predicted for intervening concns by plotting concn against detd threshold vols.

Due to differences in propionic threshold vol., make change in mobile solv. from 1% BuOH-$CHCl_3$ to 10% BuOH-$CHCl_3$ at a const vol. of 1% BuOH-$CHCl_3$ rather than at propionic acid threshold, preferably when greater part of propionic acid has been eluted. Then acetic acid threshold vol. will not be affected by changes in propionic acid threshold vol.

Acids as sepd in BuOH-$CHCl_3$ solns may be further identified by formation of mercurous acetate or mercurous propionate crystals (JAOAC **28,** 644(1945)) or by paper chromatgy, **14.101**.

Identification of Volatile Acids by Paper Chromatography (*38*)—Official Final Action

(Also applicable to confirming identity of acids sepd by **18.054–18.058** and as qual. test for propionates in bread)

14.099 ***Apparatus***

Chromatographic tank and accessories.—See **29.007**.

14.100 ***Reagents***

(a) *Mobile solvent.*—Mix acetone, *tert*-BuOH, *n*-BuOH, and NH_4OH (2 + 1 + 1 + 1). Prep. fresh daily.

(b) *Chromogenic reagent.*—Add 200 mg each Me red and bromothymol blue to mixt. of 100 mL formalin and 400 mL alcohol. Adjust to pH 5.2 with 0.1*N* NaOH.

(c) *Acids std solns.*—Pipet 1 mL each acetic, propionic, butyric, and valeric acids into sep. 100 mL vol. flasks and dil. to vol. with H_2O to prep. stock solns. Pipet 1 mL each of these stock solns into sep. 25 mL beakers; pipet 1 mL each of the 4 stock solns into single 25 mL beaker to prep. known mixt. Neutze acids and mixt. with 0.1*N* NaOH, using cresol red indicator, **16.222(f)**, avoiding excess alkali. Evap. to ca 0.5 mL, or evap. just to dryness and take up in 0.5 mL H_2O.

14.101 ***Technic***

Steam distil 20 g well mixed sample as in **14.097**, collecting 200 mL distillate. Immediately neutze distillate, using cresol red, **16.222(f)**, and 0.1*N* NaOH. Evap. to 0.5 mL, or evap. just to dryness and then take up in 0.5 mL H_2O. (To save time, place distillate in large porcelain evapg dish, and evap. to 5–10 mL; transfer to 25 mL beaker and evap. to 0.5 mL.)

With hard pencil, rule starting line 2.5 cm from bottom edge of 8 × 8″ Whatman No. 1 unwashed chromatgc paper. Spot seven 1 μL spots with 1 μL pipet on paper, 2.5 cm apart, leaving 2.5 cm margin, to permit 1 spot for each acid, 1 for mixt., and 2 for unknowns. Spot in following order: acetic, propionic, unknown, mixt. of 4, unknown, butyric, valeric. Let dry. Clip paper to glass rod and suspend in tank with 50 mL mobile solv. in trough. (Since mobile solv. is heavy liq., use 3 clips to fasten paper to glass rod to prevent sagging and to give more uniform solv. front. Do not sat. tank with mobile solv. before inserting paper.) Seal glass cover with cellophane or other suitable tape and let develop until solv. is ca 2.5 cm from top of paper. Remove paper from tank, let air dry, and spray on front side with chromogenic reagent. (Spraying should be uniform and rather heavy but not to extent that chromogenic reagent runs or drips.) Faint yellow spots indicate presence of acids; heavier blue spots are due to Na ion. To intensify acid spots, place paper in atm. of NH_3 fumes momentarily (e.g., by placing ca 50 mL NH_4OH in 2 L beaker, rolling paper, and exposing to fumes by placing each end in beaker momentarily); entire paper immediately turns green. Remove paper from NH_3 fumes. Acids gradually appear as red spots, and presence of specific acids in sample may be detd by comparing their R_f values with those of mixt. and individual acids.

Since color of acids is not stable, mark spots with pencil as soon as they are completely developed.

14.102 ★ Citric Acid (*39*)—Official First Action ★

See **13.088**, 10th ed. (*Caution: See* **51.059**.)

14.103 Ash (*40*)—Official Final Action

Use 3–5 g prepd sample, **14.090**, and proceed as in **14.006** or **14.008**.

14.104 Chlorides in Ash as Sodium Chloride Official Final Action

See **32.025–32.030**.

Iron—Official Final Action

14.105 ***Preparation of Sample***

Slice bread, let air dry until in equilibrium with air, and crush to ca 20-mesh size on wooden surface with wooden rolling pin. (Grinding may be done in mill if tests show no increase in Fe due to grinding of particular material under examination. In general, grinding in mills increases Fe content.)

Proceed as in **14.013**.

14.106 Calcium—Official Final Action

See **14.014**.

Vitamins in Enriched Bread—Official Final Action

14.107 ***Preparation of Sample***

Det. fresh wt of entire sample taken for drying, usually 6 loaves of 1 lb size or alternate slices from 6 loaves of 1.5 lb size. Slice unsliced bread into slices ca 1 oz each. Spread slices on coarse screens, elevated to provide good air circulation, and let air dry until crisp enough for efficient grinding. (If riboflavin is also to be detd, drying should be done in absence of light.) Weigh air-dried bread and grind entire amt to pass No. 20 sieve. Mix well, and store in air-tight glass jars at ca 10°. Det. air-dry wt:fresh wt ratio for subsequent use in calcn of results to fresh basis.

Proceed as in Chapter **43**.

14.108 Protein—Official Final Action

Det. N as in **2.057**, using 2 g prepd air-dried ground sample, **14.090**. Multiply % N by factor 5.7 to obtain % protein.

14.109 Fat (Acid Hydrolysis Method) Official Final Action

See **14.019**.

★ Surplus method—*see* inside front cover.

14.110 Sterols (As Cholesterol)—Official Final Action

Weigh 5 g air-dried, ground sample and proceed as in **14.149**.

14.111 Crude Fiber—Official Final Action

(For bread and other baked products not contg fruit)

Proceed as in **7.065**.

14.112 Sugars—Official Final Action

(a) *Reducing sugars*.—Prep. sample as in **7.079**, par. 1 and 2. Proceed as in **31.038**, using 25 mL aliquot (representing 2 g sample). Express results as glucose or invert sugar.

(b) *Sucrose*.—Proceed as in **7.079**.

Lactose (*41*)—Official First Action

14.113 ***Apparatus***

(a) *Rack*.—Metal rack so constructed as to prevent agitation of tubes while in boiling H_2O bath.

(b) *Titration stirrer*.—For stirring soln during titrn; rod made from glass tubing, sealed and flared at lower end to form button-like foot, is convenient. Make side arm consisting of several layers adhesive tape attached near enough to top of tube to prevent breaking bottom of titrn tube.

14.114 ***Reagents***

(a) *Yeast suspension*.—Wash 25 g fresh com. bakers yeast with five 100 mL portions H_2O or until last washings are clear. Centrf. and decant after each wash. Suspend in 100 mL H_2O and store 24 hr at 0–4° before use. Discard after 1 week.

(b) *Yeast nutrient soln*.—Dissolve 1.7 g Bacto peptone (Difco Laboratories), 0.50 g K_2HPO_4, and 0.33 g $MgSO_4.7H_2O$ in H_2O, and dil. to 100 mL with H_2O.

(c) *Protein precipitant*.—Dissolve 50 g Na tungstate and 6 g Na_2HPO_4 in 200 mL H_2O. Slowly add 220 mL 2*N* HCl, mix, and dil. to 500 mL with H_2O.

(d) *Somogyi reagent*.—Dissolve 12 g Rochelle salt, 20 g Na_2CO_3, and 25 g $NaHCO_3$ in ca 500 mL H_2O and pour into soln, with stirring, 6.5 g $CuSO_4.5H_2O$ dissolved in ca 100 mL H_2O; add soln of 10 g KI, 0.80 g KIO_3, and 18 g $K_2C_2O_4.H_2O$, and dil. to 1 L. (Only KIO_3 need be weighed accurately.) Let stand few days; then filter off any small amt of ppt.

(e) *Sodium thiosulfate soln*.—0.005*N*. Prep. daily by dilg 0.1*N* soln, **50.037–50.038**.

14.115 ***Determination***

Weigh 10 g air-dried bread, add 5 g Filter-Cel, and mix well. Transfer mixt. to extn thimble (ca 30 × 77 mm), cover with cotton pad, place in Soxhlet extractor, add 150 mL alcohol-H_2O mixt. (126 mL alcohol + 61 mL H_2O), and ext overnight on hot plate set at medium heat. Transfer ext to 250 mL beaker (previously marked at 40 mL), evap. on steam bath with aid of weak air current to ca 40 mL, and transfer to 100 mL vol. flask, rinsing well. Cool, dil. to vol., and mix well. Pipet 10 mL aliquot into 50 mL erlenmeyer; add 6 mL yeast suspension and 5 mL yeast nutrient soln. Prep. blank test, using 10 mL H_2O in place of sample ext. Stopper flask with 1-hole rubber stopper fitted with piece of 6 mm (not smaller) glass tubing ca 10 cm long. Shake at moderate rate 2.5 hr in const temp. H_2O bath at 30°.

Transfer to 50 mL centrf. tube and centrf. ca 10 min at ca 1000 rpm. Decant supernate into 50 mL vol. flask. Rinse erlenmeyer with 10 mL H_2O, decanting onto residue in centrf. tube. Mix residue and H_2O with glass rod. Centrf., and combine washing with previous supernate in 50 mL vol. flask. Repeat washing, using 10 mL H_2O. Add, with shaking, 2.5 mL protein precipitant. Dil. to vol., mix well, and filter, discarding first few mL filtrate. (This is convenient stopping point; stopper flask for continuation next day.)

Pipet 5.0 mL clear filtrate into Pyrex test tube (22 × 175 mm) and neutze to phenol red end point with 0.5*N* NaOH. Add 5.0 mL Somogyi reagent, mix by rotary motion, and add 2 drops benzene. Cap tube with glass bulb and place in metal rack. Immerse rack contg tubes in vigorously boiling H_2O bath exactly 15 min. Cool, avoiding agitation, to ca 35° in H_2O bath. Add 2.5 mL 2*N* H_2SO_4, shake with rotary motion, let stand 1–2 min, and titr. excess I with 0.005*N* $Na_2S_2O_3$, adding 6 drops 1% starch indicator near end of titrn. (Titrns should be finished in 30 min.) From difference between titrn value of blank (H_2O, yeast suspension, and yeast nutrient) and that of sample, det. wt lactose present from std curve. This value in mg lactose represents amt in 100 mg air-dry bread or % lactose.

Prep. std curve, using 0–4.5 mg pure *lactose hydrate* (0, 0.2, 0.5, 1.0, 2.0, 3.0, 4.0, and 4.5 mg from portions of soln contg 1.0 mg/mL) in enough H_2O to make 5 mL. Add 5.0 mL Somogyi reagent, mix by rotary motion, and add 2 drops benzene. Proceed as above from "Cap tube . . ." Plot difference between titrn value for 0 mg lactose and that for each lactose soln against corresponding lactose concn in mg.

14.116 Hydrogen-Ion Activity (pH)—Official Final Action

See **14.022**.

BAKED PRODUCTS

Mineral Oil (*42*)—Official First Action

(*Caution: See* **51.004**, **51.011**, **51.056**, and **51.073**.)

14.117 ***Reagents and Apparatus***

(a) *Chromatographic tube*.—250 mL dispensing burets or tube 30 × 450 mm, with stopcock at lower constricted end.

(b) *Alumina*.—Adsorption, Brockmann I, basic, or equiv., 80–200 mesh, suitable for chromatgy, pH 9–11 in aq. slurry (Fisher Scientific Co. No. A-540, A-941, or equiv.).

14.118 ***Preparation of Sample and Oil Separation***

Dry weighed sample in oven at 50° or in air on nonabsorbent surface until crisp and brittle enough to crush and grind (do not char). Grind, mix thoroly, weigh, and store in air-tight container. Det. dry wt:fresh wt ratio for use in calcg results to fresh basis and detg sample wt to be used, calcd to fresh basis.

Weigh dried sample equiv. to 225 g, fresh basis, into large mortar. Add, with stirring, 50 mL HCl (1+1) until thoroly mixed and uniformly wet. Let stand ca 1 hr. Break up lumps with pestle or spatula, transfer to 800 mL beaker, add 450 mL $CHCl_3$, and heat on steam bath until $CHCl_3$ boils, stirring constantly. Transfer to large size high-speed blender, blend, and decant $CHCl_3$ thru buchner fitted with rapid paper, using suction. Repeat blending, decanting, and filtering with 2 addnl 300 mL portions $CHCl_3$. Dry combined $CHCl_3$ exts by passing thru 8 cm Na_2SO_4 in 3 cm diam. column. If filter or Na_2SO_4 column becomes clogged, loosen surface enough to permit free flow. Wash Na_2SO_4 with ca 50 mL $CHCl_3$. Evap. combined $CHCl_3$ to small vol. on steam bath under dry air stream. Transfer quant. to weighed beaker, evap. remainder of solv., dry oil overnight in convection oven at 100°, and weigh.

14.119 ***Preparation of Alumina Column***

Pack pledget of glass wool into constricted end of glass tube. Add, thru powder funnel, 175 g alumina, tapping tube to ensure uniform packing. Cover surface with disk cut from rapid filter paper of slightly smaller diam. than inside of tube. Prewash column with 200 mL pet ether. Just before last of pet ether settles into alumina, stop flow.

14.120 ***Determination***

Accurately weigh 5 g warmed, well mixed, extd oil into small beaker. Mix well with 5–10 mL pet ether. Pour carefully onto alumina column, open stopcock, and collect eluate at rate <5 mL/min. Close stopcock when ether-oil mixt. has settled to just above surface of alumina. Rinse sample beaker with two 5 mL portions pet ether, rinsing sides of column with each rinse. Open stopcock and let ether settle almost to surface of alumina. Fill column with pet ether. Continue adding pet ether to column until total of 400 mL collects. Evap. pet ether to small vol. on steam bath, using gentle stream of dry air to aid solv. removal. Stirring rod placed in flask will help prevent superheating and possible boiling over. Transfer quant. to small weighed beaker. Evap. to dryness on warm surface, using gentle stream of dry air. Dry in convection oven 1 hr at 100°. Calc. % by wt of this unsaponifiable oil to fresh basis of product.

Transfer ca 2 drops residue oil to face of NaCl or Irtran plate. Cover with another plate and prep. IR spectrum. Prep. similar curve, using USP mineral oil. If vol. of residue oil is too small to transfer to plate directly, transfer with aid of CS_2. Evap. solv. completely before covering plate with second plate. Peaks occur at 3.4, 6.82, and 7.25 μm.

Obtain refractive index on another drop or two of residue oil and compare with refractive index of USP mineral oil read at same temp.

BAKED PRODUCTS OTHER THAN BREAD (NOT CONTAINING FRUIT) *(43)*

14.121 Solids—Official Final Action

See **14.091**.

14.122 Ash—Official Final Action

See **14.006**.

14.123 Protein—Official Final Action

See **14.108**.

14.124 Fat—Official Final Action

See **14.019**.

14.125 Sterols (As Cholesterol)—Official First Action

Weigh 5 g air-dried, ground sample and proceed as in **14.149**.

14.126 Crude Fiber—Official Final Action

See **7.065**.

14.127 Sugars—Official Final Action

See **14.112**.

14.128 Hydrogen-Ion Activity (pH)—Official Final Action

See **14.022**.

14.129 Acetic and Propionic Acids in Cake *(37)* Official Final Action

Proceed as in **14.097**, using 15 g sample prepd as for fresh bread or fresh bread preserved with $CHCl_3$.

FIG BARS AND RAISIN-FILLED CRACKERS *(44)* OFFICIAL FINAL ACTION

14.130 Moisture

Place 25–30 g prepd sand and short stirring rod in dish ca 55 mm diam. and 40 mm deep, fitted with cover. Dry thoroly, cover dish, cool in desiccator, and weigh immediately. Remove cover, place 3–5 g prepd sample, **14.090(b)**, in dish, and weigh accurately. Remove dish contg sand, stirring rod, and weighed sample from balance. Add 5–10 mL H_2O and mix with the sand. Heat carefully on H_2O bath, stirring at 2–3 min intervals, until excess H_2O is removed and contents of dish are consistency of heavy paste. Place uncovered dish in vac. oven and dry ca 16 hr at 70° under pressure ≤ 50 mm Hg (6.7 kPa). After drying, cover dish, transfer to desiccator, cool to room temp., and weigh immediately.

Notes: Quartz sand that passes No. 40 sieve but is retained on No. 60 sieve, has been digested with HCl, washed free of acid, and ignited, is recommended. Al dishes with fit-over covers are most convenient. Dish can be set in cover during heating on H_2O bath and during oven-drying period. After drying, cover can be easily and quickly refitted on dish as it is transferred to desiccator.

14.131 Fat

(*Caution: See* **51.011**, **51.054**, and **51.073**.)

Accurately weigh ca 2 g well mixed sample, prepd by grinding twice thru food chopper, and transfer to Mojonnier tube. Add 2 mL alcohol, warm to 60–70°, and shake gently until sample is thoroly disintegrated and mixed with alcohol. Add 10 mL HCl (25+11). Place tube in H_2O bath held at 70–80° and shake frequently until sample is thoroly digested (40–80 min).

If weighed sample cannot be transferred to tube directly, digest in 50 mL beaker. Transfer digested mixt. to tube as completely as possible by draining from lip of beaker down small stirring rod. Rinse beaker thoroly with 10 mL alcohol, transfer to tube, mix thoroly, and cool. Rinse beaker with portions of first 25 mL ether added for first extn. Repeat rinsing with portions of pet ether (bp $<60°$) as it is added for first extn. Rinse thoroly so that all fat is transferred to extn tube. (After digestion, all particles should be completely disintegrated, except hard seeds (in fig fillers) and strong fibers. Very small amt of fat may be retained by such particles after digestion, but in analysis of biscuits and crackers this loss will be within experimental error.)

When digesting in extn tube, add 10 mL alcohol to digested charge and cool. (Level of liq. should be in neck of Mojonnier tube just below pour-off level.) Add 25 mL ether, stopper flask with cork, Neoprene, or other synthetic rubber stopper not affected by solvs, and shake thoroly ca 1 min. Carefully release pressure so that none of solv. contg fat is lost. Wash adhering solv. and fat from stopper into extn tube with few mL pet ether. (Glass wash bottle producing fine jet is convenient.) Let mixt. stand few min; then add 25 mL pet ether (bp $<60°$), stopper tube tightly, and again shake thoroly ca 1 min. Carefully release pressure, remove stopper, and again wash adhering solv. and fat into tube with few mL of pet ether. Let mixt. stand until ether layer is clear (10–20 min), or centrf. 20 min at ca 600 rpm.

Pour off as much as possible of clear ether-fat soln thru small, fast filter by tilting tube gradually. (Plug of ether-extd cotton packed just firmly enough in stem of funnel to let ether pass freely makes excellent filter for these extns.) Catch ether-fat solns from extns in clean 250 mL beaker or flask. Re-ext digested sample remaining in tube 3 times more as for first extn. (Vol. of ether may be reduced to 15 or 20 mL for last 3 extns.) Wash mouth of tube each time after draining ether-fat soln, and filter this ether thru funnel into receptacle.

Evap. combined ethers from extns with air current or suction. After ethers are practically off, heat ca 10 min on hot H_2O or steam bath to drive off most of alcohol and H_2O carried over with ethers. Transfer beaker to 100° oven, dry 1 hr, remove, and let cool. Redissolve dried fat in 15–20 mL mixt. of equal parts of ether and pet ether, and filter thru small fat-free paper into beaker or flask previously dried at 100°, cooled in desiccator, and weighed.

Wash all traces of fat from first receptacle, filter paper, and funnel into the tared beaker or flask with jet of pet ether from wash bottle. Evap. ethers from tared receptacle with air current or suction and dry purified fat to const wt in 100° oven (1–1.5 hr). Cool in desiccator and weigh as soon as room temp. is attained. Make blank detns on reagents.

Notes: Good quality rubber stoppers thoroly cleaned with alcohol are satisfactory for stoppering extn tubes. Remove stoppers from tubes after each shaking period and do not allow to remain in contact with solvs longer than necessary. Solv. may have some action on rubber. Very fine grain cork stoppers washed with alcohol and ether are also satisfactory for stoppering extn tubes, provided leakage of solvs can be prevented during shaking.

If trouble is experienced in releasing pressure after shaking extn tube contg ethers, cool tube slightly by holding it under stream of cold H_2O before removing stopper.

Al beakers are very satisfactory for weighing purified fat; they are light wt and cool to room temp. rapidly.

MACARONI, EGG NOODLES, AND SIMILAR PRODUCTS—OFFICIAL FINAL ACTION

14.132 Collection and Preparation of Sample (*45*)

Select from lot to be analyzed enough strips or pieces to assure representative sample, break these into small fragments with hands or in mill, and mix well. Grind 300–500 g in mill until all material passes thru No. 20 sieve. Keep ground sample in sealed container to prevent moisture changes.

Total Solids and Moisture

14.133 *Vacuum Oven Method* (*46*)

Use 2 g prepd sample, **14.132**, and proceed as in **14.003**.

14.134 *Air Oven Method*

Use 2 g prepd sample, **14.132**, and proceed as in **14.004**.

14.135 Ash

Use 3–5 g prepd sample, **14.132**, and proceed as in **14.006**.

14.136 Original Ash in Macaroni Products Containing Added Salt But Not Containing Added Eggs (*47*)

Proceed as in **14.006**. Dissolve ash in 25 mL HNO_3 (1+3), transfer to 150 mL beaker, dil. to 75 mL with H_2O, and boil 15 min, maintaining original vol. (necessary to convert all phosphate to ortho form). Det. P_2O_5 as in **7.119**. $P_2O_5 \times 2$ = NaCl-free ash.

14.137 Chlorides in Ash as Sodium Chloride (*48*) Official First Action

See **32.025–32.030**.

14.138 Iron

See **14.013**.

14.139 Vitamins in Enriched Macaroni and Noodle Products

See Chapter **43**.

14.140 Fat (Acid Hydrolysis Method) (*49*)

Place 2 g sample in Mojonnier or Roehrig extn tube, add 2 mL alcohol to prevent lumping on addn of acid, and shake to moisten all particles. Add 10 mL HCl (25+11), mix well, set tube in H_2O bath held at 70–80°, and shake at frequent intervals during 30–40 min. Fill to within 1–2 mL of mark with alcohol and cool. Add 25 mL ether and shake mixt. well. Then add 25 mL pet ether (bp <60°) and mix well. Let stand until upper liq. is practically clear and proceed as in **14.019**, beginning "Draw off as much as possible . . ."

14.141 Crude Fiber

See **7.065**.

14.142 Protein (*50*)

Det. N as in **2.057**, using 1 g prepd sample, **14.132**. % protein = % N × 5.7.

14.143 Water-Soluble Protein-Nitrogen Precipitable by 40 Per Cent Alcohol

See **14.027**.

14.144 Hydrogen-Ion Activity (pH)

See **14.022**.

14.145 Lipid and Lipid Phosphorus

Proceed as in **14.028** and **14.029**.

Unsaponifiable Residue (*51*)

14.146 *Reagents and Apparatus*

See **17.017** and **17.018**. (Concd KOH soln is not needed.)

14.147 *Determination*

Weigh 10 g sample, ground to pass No. 20 sieve, into 500 mL erlenmeyer and add, with shaking, 30 mL HCl (1+1). Heat on steam bath 30 min, shaking occasionally to break up any lumps. While cooling inclined flask under tap, carefully add, with shaking, 30 g KOH pellets at such rate that liq. may boil, but not so violently as to cause loss by spurting. Place flask on steam bath while still hot, cover with small watch glass, and heat 3 hr, swirling occasionally to carry down any material adhering to sides. Cool until just warm, add 30 mL alcohol and 50 mL H_2O, and mix well. Add 100 mL ether, swirl vigorously 1 min, and transfer to separator, washing flask with 50 and 25 mL portions ether. Wash flask with 50 mL KOH soln, pour washings into separator in slow stream while gently swirling liq., and continue gentle swirling 10–15 sec. Proceed as in **17.019**, beginning "Let liq. sep. (ca 10 min) . . ." but omitting first acid wash. If emulsion forms and does not break to give sharp interface in 10 min, pour 5 mL alcohol into separator and let stand until sharp interface appears.

Sterols (as Cholesterol)

14.148 *Bromination Method* (*51*)

Det. sterols in unsaponifiable matter as in **17.022**. However, to unsaponifiable matter from egg-free products or from any product contg <0.23% unsaponifiable matter (as-is basis), add

10 mg cholesterol before applying cholesterol method and correct result accordingly. (For the added cholesterol use highest quality obtainable (mp ≥147°) and test its purity by carrying 20 mg thru detn.)

14.149 ***Digitonin Method (52)***

(*Caution; See* **51.011(a)** and **51.054.**)

Weigh 5 g sample, ground to pass No. 20 or finer sieve, into 300 mL erlenmeyer and add, with shaking, 15 mL HCl (1+1) in such manner as to keep particles on sides at min. Heat on steam bath 30 min, shaking frequently to break up any lumps and ensure complete hydrolysis. While cooling inclined flask under tap, carefully add, with swirling, 15 g KOH pellets at such rate that liq. may boil, but not so violently as to cause loss by spurting. Cool, add 20 mL alcohol, rinsing down sides of flask, and heat on steam bath 45 min with air condenser, shaking frequently.

Add 25 mL H_2O, rinsing down sides of flask, mix well, and cool. Add 50 mL ether, vigorously swirl mixt. 1 min, and transfer to 500 mL separator. Wash flask with 25 and 10 mL portions ether and with 50 mL 1% KOH soln, pouring washings into separator in slow stream while gently swirling liq., and continue gentle swirling 10–15 sec. Let liq. sep. and slowly drain soap soln into 250 mL separator, but do not drain any small amt of emulsion or of insol. matter at interface. Rinse down sides of 500 mL separator with 5 mL 1% KOH soln and drain this into smaller separator. Add 25 mL ether to smaller separator and shake vigorously ca 1 min. After liqs sep., discard lower layer. Add ether layer to soln in larger separator, rinsing 250 mL separator with 10 mL ether. Wash ether soln as before with 3 addnl 50 mL portions 1% KOH, still keeping any insol. matter or emulsion in separator. Wash ether soln twice by swirling with 50 mL H_2O. Finally drain as much of aq. layer as possible without loss of ether soln. Add porcelain chip to 300 mL erlenmeyer, transfer ether to flask, rinse separator with three 5 mL portions ether, and rinse stem of separator with ether. Add rinsings to flask and evap. ether on steam bath.

Dissolve residue in 5 mL acetone; filter, with suction if necessary, thru Knorr-type (Allihn) extn tube contg medium porosity fritted glass disk (Ace Glass, Inc., No. 7195-08, or equiv.), covered with few g washed and ignited sand, into 100 mL centrf. tube or test tube under bell jar. Wash flask and tube with three 4 mL portions acetone, and rinse tube and stem with few mL acetone (total vol. ca 20 mL). Add 5 mL freshly prepd *digitonin soln in 80% alcohol* contg 40 mg digitonin. (Hasten soln of digitonin by warming to ca 40–50° under hot H_2O tap.) (Products contg >6% egg yolk solids or equiv. (moisture-free basis) require addnl digitonin soln or use of aliquot portion for pptn.) Rotate to mix. Place porcelain chip in the tube, suspend tube in steam bath with small amt of steam to avoid boiling or spattering, evap. nearly to dryness, add 50 mL hot H_2O (near bp), and stir well with glass rod to disperse ppt and dissolve excess digitonin. Place tube in boiling H_2O bath and hold several min with frequent stirring. Cool to ca 60°, add 25 mL acetone, mix well by stirring, and cool to room temp. in beaker of cold H_2O.

When ppt has nearly all settled (ca 15 min), remove glass rod, rinsing off any adhering ppt with acetone. Decant into previously dried and weighed gooch (preferably 10 mL capacity) contg asbestos pad covered with ca 1 g washed and ignited sand. Using wash bottle, wash tube several times with few mL portions acetone to transfer all ppt. (*Caution:* Avoid transfer of any particles of chips.) Finally rinse crucible with acetone to dissolve any fat-like material, rinse with 5 mL ether, dry 30 min at 100°, and weigh. Check wt after second 30 min of drying. Wt residue × 0.243 = wt sterol. Report as % sterol on moisture-free basis.

Fluorometric Method (53)—Official First Action

(*Caution: See* **51.008, 51.018, 51.022,** and **51.056.**)

14.150 ***Apparatus***

(a) *Soxhlet extractor.*—Medium-size, with 250 mL flask and 33 × 94 mm thimble.

(b) *Spectrophotofluorometer (Fluorescence spectrophotometer).*—With high intensity Xe source, and grating or prism excitation and emission monochromators, each with resolution ≤5 nm. Instrument should be able to detect ≤1 ng quinine sulfate/mL 0.1*N* H_2SO_4. Excitation wavelength, 546 nm; emission wavelength 577 nm. Cells must be scrupulously clean on all 4 sides. Rinse exterior of cells with alcohol and dry with lint-free absorbent tissue before placing in instrument.

14.151 ***Reagents***

(a) *Cholesterol std soln.*—Prep. soln contg 6.0 mg cholesterol/100 mL $CHCl_3$. Pipet duplicate 2 mL aliquots into 25 mL erlenmeyers and evap. to dryness on steam bath under gentle stream of air. Proceed as in **14.152**, beginning "Into each flask, . . ."

(b) *Chloroform-acetic anhydride soln.*—(5 + 1). Freshly prepd for each series of detns. Use Ac_2O from fresh or recently opened bottle.

14.152 ***Determination***

Ext ca 5 g noodles, ground to pass No. 40 or finer sieve, in Soxhlet 4 hr with ca 120 mL vigorously boiling $CHCl_3$ and boiling chip. Wash ext into 100 mL vol. flask with $CHCl_3$, cool, dil. to vol., and mix.

Pipet duplicate 2 mL aliquots into 25 mL erlenmeyers and evap. to dryness on steam bath under gentle stream of air. Into each flask, pipet 10 mL $CHCl_3$-Ac_2O; swirl to mix; let stand 15 min; then add exactly 0.4 mL H_2SO_4. Stopper, mix, and let stand 40 min. (Solns should contain no turbidity due to H_2O.) Read within 1 hr from end of fluorescence development step.

Adjust fluorometer to ca 60% *T* with cholesterol std soln. Transfer ca 4 mL sample soln to clean 10 × 10 mm cell and read. Use 5 mL $CHCl_3$-Ac_2O and 0.2 mL H_2SO_4 as blank.

14.153 ***Calculation***

% Cholesterol in sample = 100 (mL) × C × (F/F') × 100/W, where C is concn of ref. std in mg/mL (0.060); F and F' are, resp., av. fluorescence at 577 nm of sample duplicates and std duplicates, each corrected for blank; and W is mg sample.

14.154 Extraction, Separation, and Identification of Coloring Matter* (*54*)

Place ca 500 g coarsely ground sample (depending on amt of color present) in 1 L erlenmeyer, add ca 700 mL 80% alcohol, and shake at intervals for 24 hr, or until no more color is extd. Place in refrigerator overnight to permit dissolved protein to ppt. Filter, and evap. filtrate to 100 mL. Add ca ¼ vol. *25% NaCl soln* and slight excess of NH_4OH to filtrate; cool, and transfer to separator. Ext with equal vol. pet ether, bp <60°; sep. lower layer and repeat extns with addnl portions solv. until no more color is extd. Reserve lower layer, if colored, for further treatment; if colorless, discard.

Combine pet ether exts and wash with several small portions

* See **34.015(b)** for corresponding color numbers.

NH_4OH (1+50) to remove any material mech. adhering to solv. This ether soln contains fats; it also may contain oil-sol. synthetic dyes, which can be identified as in (**a**). If colored, immediately acidify alk. aq. soln, freed from fat and oil-sol. synthetic dyes, with HOAc and ext in 25 mL portions with two 50 mL portions ether. Solv., if colored, may contain turmeric, annatto, and trace of saffron, which may be identified as in (**b**).

If original aq. soln, freed from ether-sol. colors, is still colored and H_2O-sol. dyes are suspected, proceed as follows: Ext aq. soln with 50 mL portions *isoamyl alcohol* to remove balance of saffron, as well as common orange dyes and Martius yellow; to sep., proceed as in (**c**). Drain lower aq. layer, which, if colored, may contain naphthol yellow S, tartrazine, and sunset yellow. Ext these dyes with isoamyl alcohol after acidifying soln with HCl to ca 1*N*. Remove tartrazine from solv. with 0.25*N* HCl. Sunset yellow is also removed at this stage with slightly lower acid concn, and naphthol yellow S from nearly neut. soln. Proceed as in Chap. **34**.

(**a**) Ext original pet ether ext with two or three 10 mL portions of mixt. consisting of HCl and HOAc (1+5).

In presence of yellow OB or yellow AB, pink or red soln is obtained. Test small portion of this acid ext with few drops *40% $SnCl_2$ soln*, which in presence of these dyes causes either decoloration or decided fading. Dil. balance of acid ext with H_2O, make slightly alk., and ext color with pet ether. Wash solv. with two 5 mL portions H_2O to remove excess alkali. Proceed as in Chap. **34**. Remaining coloring matters in pet ether ext may be due to natural coloring matter of wheat or coloring matter of egg. Coloring principle of egg yolk, lutein, when heated with *alc. $FeCl_3$*, produces green soln. This test, however, is not specific for lutein; carotene and xanthophyll give similar reactions.

(**b**) Wash ether ext with 5 mL portions H_2O to remove excess acid. To remove annatto and traces of saffron, wash successively with 20 mL portions *5% $NaHCO_3$ soln*. Divide alk. soln into 2 portions. Heat one portion to 60° on steam bath, dye the color on unmordanted cotton, and compare spot tests with a std. Acidify remaining portion of the alk. annatto soln with HOAc and re-ext with ether. Divide ether ext into 2 small casseroles and evap. to dryness. Dissolve contents of one casserole in 10 mL NH_4OH (1+9) and impregnate on strip of cotton or filter paper. Orange-yellow to orange-red stain is obtained, depending on amt of dye present. Dry filter paper or cotton, add drop *40% $SnCl_2$ soln*, and again dry. In presence of annatto, purple stain is produced. Spot contents of other casserole with H_2SO_4 and HNO_3, which yield blue and greenish-blue colors, resp.

Transfer 2 portions (ca 10 mL each) of original ether ext, from which annatto has been removed, into test tubes and treat with equal vol. 10% NaOH soln and equal vol. HCl (1+1), resp. In presence of turmeric (curcuma), alk. soln is reddish brown; acid soln is red.

Turmeric can be further confirmed by its behavior with H_3BO_3. Test as follows: Shake portion of original ether ext with equal vol. 70% alcohol; add 1/10 vol. HCl, mix, and divide soln equally into 2 test tubes. To one tube add few crystals H_3BO_3 and shake. Use other tube as control. In presence of turmeric, red soln is produced after short time.

(**c**) To sep. and identify saffron and the orange synthetic dyes, dil. isoamyl alcohol ext with 2 vols pet ether and ext the mixed dyes with several 10 mL portions H_2O. To small portion of this aq. ext. add 1/10 vol. HOAc and few mg dry *Na hyposulfite* to reduce all the azo dyes. This treatment will not affect saffron, which can then be re-extd with isoamyl alcohol. After washing solv. repeatedly with small portions of H_2O (to remove decomposition products), evap. to dryness, and confirm presence of saffron by spot tests. Examine remainder of color soln as in Chap. **34**.

14.155 Rapid Method for Tartrazine (*55*)

Place 800 mL cold H_2O and 5 mL NH_4OH in 1 L erlenmeyer and add 200 g unground sample. Stopper flask and shake at intervals; 3–4 hr is usually enough time to disintegrate material. Use glass rod to dislodge material caking on bottom. Centrf. and decant clear supernate into 1 L flask. Add soln of 50 g $MgSO_4.7H_2O$ dissolved in 100 mL H_2O, 10 mL *12% silicotungstic acid soln*, and 10 mL HCl; shake well, and let stand 1 hr. (This treatment will ppt almost all protein.)

Centrf., decant clear soln into container, and examine as in Chap. **34**.

Carotenoids (*56*)

(Applicable only to detn of carotenoids added for coloring purposes)

14.156 ***Reagents***

(**a**) *Alcoholic potassium hydroxide soln.*—Dissolve 10 g KOH in 100 mL alcohol by warming on steam bath.

(**b**) *Methanol.*—92%. 8 mL H_2O + 92 mL absolute MeOH.

(**c**) *Adsorption mixture.*—Mix equal portions by vol. of activated magnesia (Micron brand No. 2641, 2642, or Adsorptive Magnesia No. S-120, Fisher Scientific Co.) and diat. earth (Hyflo Super-Cel, Johns-Manville Products Corp.).

(**d**) *Carotene std soln.*—20 mg/L. Dissolve 100 mg *natural mixt. of α- and β-carotene* in 5–6 mL CS_2, add 35–40 mL absolute alcohol, cool in refrigerator ca 1 hr to ensure max. crystn, and filter on *hard* paper. Dissolve carotene crystals in 5–6 mL CS_2, add 40 mL pet ether, refrigerate as before, filter on *hard* paper, and dry crystals in vac. desiccator 1 hr.

Accurately weigh 20 mg purified crystals and wash with 20 mL absolute ether into 1 L g-s vol. flask. Continue to wash with pet ether, and dil. to vol. by adding pet ether as soon as carotene dissolves completely.

14.157 ***Preparation of Standard Curve***

Dil. 0.0, 1.25, 2.50, 3.75, 5.00, 6.25, 7.5, 8.75, and 10.00 mL carotene std soln to 250 mL with pet ether. (Concns 0.0, 0.10, 0.20, 0.30, 0.40, 0.50, 0.60, 0.70, and 0.80 mg/L.) Read solns at 436 nm in spectrophtr or in photometer. Obtain line of best fit for data by method of least sqs, item (*24*), *Definitions of Terms and Explanatory Notes*. In applying this method, let *x* represent scale reading and *y*, concn in mg/L.

Stdze on same day stock soln is prepd.

14.158 ***Preparation of Sample***

Grind macaroni and noodles to as near flour fineness as possible in ordinary coffee-type mill. (Products contg egg give no difficulty, but plain macaroni products require several grindings.) Take care not to set mill too tight, as enough heat may be generated to damage pigments.

14.159 ***Determination of Total Carotenoids and Carotene***

Weigh 20 g flour, semolina, or macaroni, or 10 g egg noodles, or 2 g egg yolk into 125 mL erlenmeyer. Add 50 mL alc. KOH soln and boil on steam bath 30 min under reflux condenser. Occasionally rotate flask but be as careful as possible to keep sample from collecting on sides of flask. Remove flask and cool to room temp. Filter thru buchner-type medium fritted glass filter into 250 mL suction flask, using suction, transferring most of material with few mL alcohol from wash bottle. Turn off suction, rinse flask with 25 mL ether, pour rinsing onto glass filter, and stir material with rod to let ether come in contact with all portions. Filter, and repeat this operation twice.

Transfer filtrate to 250 mL g-s separator and rinse with ca 25 mL ether, disregarding soapy material in flask. Add 175 mL H_2O, carefully invert, and rotate several times. When layers sep., remove lower aq.-alcohol layer and ext this layer again with 25 mL ether. Discard lower layer and add the ether to original ether soln. Wash ether by pouring 50 mL H_2O thru it. After layers sep., withdraw aq. layer and discard. Add 50 mL pet ether to ether soln, and wash with five 50 mL portions H_2O, carefully inverting and rotating separator. Discard all aq. layers (slight emulsions usually clear in few min but may be discarded, especially if there is no significant yellow tinge).

Transfer ether-pet ether mixt. to 250 mL distn flask, rinsing separator with pet ether; place flask in beaker of H_2O at 45–50°. Stopper flask, connect side arm with vac., and conc. to ca 5 mL to remove ether. Filter thru Allihn-type adsorption tube with coarse fritted glass plate contg ca 3 mm layer anhyd. powd Na_2SO_4, or thru 5.5–7.0 cm paper half filled with the Na_2SO_4 (use small, long-stem funnel reaching thru neck of flask) into 25 mL vol. flask. Dil. to vol. with pet ether used to rinse distn flask and which has been passed portionwise thru the filter contg Na_2SO_4, and mix by inverting few times. Transfer to 1 cm absorption cell and read A at 436 nm in spectrophtr, making ≥3 readings. From av. reading, calc. total carotenoid pigment in ppm from std curve. If pure carotene is not available for stdzn, multiply A by 64.2 for yolk, 13.05 for noodles, or 6.52 for semolina and macaroni.

14.160 *Separation of Carotene from Xanthophylls*

(**a**) *Carotene by phase separation*.—Quant. transfer all soln from cell and vol. flask to 125 mL separator, rinse with pet ether, and dil. to ca 100 mL. Add 15 mL 92% MeOH, shake moderately ca 2 min by hand or 10 min on mech. shaker, and let separator stand in upright position ca 1 min until layers sep. Decant lower layer contg xanthophyll and repeat extns 5 more times or until aq. MeOH layer is nearly colorless for semolina. (Eight extns are generally enough for noodles but higher than normal egg content may require 10 extns.) Examine final MeOH layer recovered in test tube over white background to be sure soln is nearly colorless.

Wash pet ether with 25 mL H_2O, inverting separator several times; discard aq. layer and repeat twice more. Filter pet ether thru Allihn-type adsorption tube contg 6 mm layer of anhyd. powd Na_2SO_4, or thru 9 cm paper half filled with the Na_2SO_4, into 250 mL distn flask, washing color from filter with pet ether. Conc. to 5 mL by vac. as in **14.159** and transfer to 10 mL vol. flask, using very small portions of pet ether; dil. to vol., mix by inverting, and read A in spectrophtr as in **14.159**. Calc. carotene in ppm from std curve. If pure carotene is not available for stdzn, multiply A by 5.22 for noodles, or by 2.61 for semolina.

(**b**) *Carotene by chromatographic separation*.— Prep. column in adsorption tube ca 18 mm od × 240 mm with ca 5 cm tip inserted thru rubber stopper. Loosely plug with small pad of cotton, place in 250 mL suction flask, and turn on suction. Add adsorption mixt., **14.156(c)**, thru funnel in small amts from spatula to ht of ca 11 cm; pack column by pressing down (*only once after all this mixt. has been added*) with cork stopper, just fitting the tube, on end of rod. Place 1–2 cm anhyd. powd Na_2SO_4 on top.

Quant. transfer all soln from cell and vol. flask to 250 mL distn flask, and conc. as in **14.159** to ca 5 mL, continuously applying suction to flask. Transfer to prepd column and rinse with four ca 5 mL portions pet ether to remove all color. Finally rinse down sides of tube with few mL pet ether. After few drops have come thru column, change to another 250 mL suction flask. When nearly all pet ether is down to Na_2SO_4 layer, add 50 mL pet ether-acetone mixt. (9+1) to wash thru carotene. When all this solv. has passed thru Na_2SO_4, turn off suction. (Keep top of column covered with solv. during entire operation.) Transfer carotene soln (which should be only few mL) to 10 mL vol. flask, using very small portions of pet ether, dil. to vol. with pet ether, and mix by inverting. Read as in (**a**) and calc. in ppm. (These solns should be read on same day as extn.)

SELECTED REFERENCES

(*1*) JAOAC **8,** 424, 664(1925); **9,** 39, 88, 423(1926).
(*2*) JAOAC **8,** 665(1925); **9,** 39, 88(1926); **34,** 278(1951).
(*3*) JAOAC **8,** 665(1925); **9,** 40(1926).
(*4*) JAOAC **21,** 406(1938); **22,** 76, 548(1939).
(*5*) JAOAC **7,** 132(1923).
(*6*) JAOAC **19,** 85(1936); **20,** 69(1937); **22,** 522(1939).
(*7*) JAOAC **19,** 82(1936); "Cereal Laboratory Methods, A.A.C.C.," 1962.
(*8*) JAOAC **31,** 259(1948); **32,** 257(1949).
(*9*) JAOAC **27,** 86, 396(1944); **28,** 77(1945).
(*10*) JAOAC **27,** 402(1944); **28,** 77(1945).
(*11*) JAOAC **31,** 269(1948).
(*12*) JAOAC **15,** 588(1932); **20,** 365(1937); **21,** 398(1938); **23,** 502(1940); **25,** 71(1942).
(*13*) JAOAC **6,** 508(1922); **9,** 41, 429(1926).
(*14*) JAOAC **22,** 526(1939); **23,** 493(1940); **24,** 587(1941); **50,** 198(1967).
(*15*) JAOAC **26,** 109(1943); **27,** 87(1944); **28,** 66(1945).
(*16*) JAOAC **22,** 535(1939); Cereal Chem. **14,** 603(1937).
(*17*) JAOAC **7,** 84(1923); **12,** 40(1929); **14,** 500(1931); **35,** 701(1952).
(*18*) JAOAC **7,** 91(1923); **9,** 40, 88(1926); **35,** 693(1952); **36,** 760(1953).
(*19*) Z. Untersuch. Lebensm. **40,** 1(1920); Can. J. Res. **11,** 751(1934); JAOAC **24,** 113(1941); **27,** 87(1944).
(*20*) JAOAC **22,** 539(1939); **23,** 498(1940).
(*21*) JAOAC **34,** 273(1951).
(*22*) JAOAC **18,** 493(1935); **19,** 86(1936); **33,** 166(1950); Analyst **78,** 467(1953).
(*23*) JAOAC **39,** 664(1956).
(*24*) JAOAC **33,** 165(1950).
(*25*) JAOAC **15,** 572(1932); **16,** 497(1933); **17,** 397(1934); **18,** 76(1935); **19,** 86(1936); Cereal Chem. **9,** 378(1932); Am. Inst. Baking Bull. **8** (1932).
(*26*) AACC Method **56-81B.**
(*27*) JAOAC **30,** 659(1947); **32,** 261(1949); **43,** 560(1960); **44,** 344(1961); **49,** 219(1966).
(*28*) JAOAC **18,** 76(1935); **20,** 69, 380(1937); **22,** 76(1939); Cereal Chem. **11,** 121, 299(1934); Nebraska Agr. Expt. Sta. Bull. **8** (1916).
(*29*) JAOAC **17,** 329(1934).
(*30*) JAOAC **23,** 513, 520, 526(1940); **25,** 645(1942).
(*31*) USDA Handbook No. 8 (Revised Dec. 1963).
(*32*) JAOAC **50,** 944, 958(1967).
(*33*) AACC Method **76-11.**
(*34*) JAOAC **32,** 267(1949); **33,** 168(1950); **37,** 413(1954).
(*35*) JAOAC **9,** 42(1926); **15,** 72(1932); **17,** 65(1934).
(*36*) JAOAC **18,** 574(1935); **19,** 86(1936); **32,** 260(1949).
(*37*) JAOAC **33,** 677(1950); **34,** 284(1951); **36,** 769(1953).
(*38*) JAOAC **48,** 622(1965).
(*39*) JAOAC **16,** 427(1933); **19,** 86(1936).
(*40*) JAOAC **9,** 42(1936).
(*41*) JAOAC **35,** 56, 697(1952).
(*42*) JAOAC **49,** 820(1966).
(*43*) JAOAC **16,** 518(1933); **17,** 404(1934); **23,** 537(1940); **35,** 687(1952).

(*44*) JAOAC **26,** 305(1943); **28,** 497(1945).
(*45*) JAOAC **9,** 43, 396(1926).
(*46*) JAOAC **9,** 397(1926).
(*47*) JAOAC **25,** 618(1942).
(*48*) JAOAC **54,** 471(1971); **57,** 1209(1974).
(*49*) JAOAC **6,** 508(1923); **11,** 38(1928).
(*50*) JAOAC **9,** 43(1926).
(*51*) JAOAC **24,** 75, 143(1941); **25,** 83, 639(1942).
(*52*) JAOAC **37,** 408(1954); **50,** 851(1967); **51,** 590(1968); **52,** 319(1969).
(*53*) JAOAC **51,** 1220(1968).
(*54*) JAOAC **6,** 12(1922); **8,** 109(1924); **15,** 367(1932); **19,** 83(1936); USDA Bull. **448.**
(*55*) JAOAC **27,** 231(1944).
(*56*) JAOAC **21,** 339(1938); **34,** 275(1951).

15. Coffee and Tea

GREEN COFFEE

15.001 Macroscopic Examination—Procedure

Macroscopic examination usually shows presence of excessive amts of blank and blighted coffee beans, coffee hulls, stones, and other foreign matter. Sep. these by hand picking and det. % by wt.

15.002 Coloring Matters—Procedure

Vigorously shake ≥100 g sample with cold H_2O or 70% alcohol. Strain thru coarse sieve and let settle. Identify sol. colors in soln and insol. pigments in sediments as in Chap. **34**.

15.003 Caffeine (*1*)—Official First Action

Grind sample to pass No. 40 sieve. Use coffee grinder or large high-speed blender, and keep sample cold with solid CO_2 during grinding to avoid pastiness. Proceed as in **15.023** or **15.024**.

Chlorogenic Acid (*2*)—Official First Action

15.004 ***Reagents***

(**a**) *Basic lead acetate soln.*—Sp gr 1.25. Soln **31.178(a)** may be used, or prep. soln from dry powder or Horne's Dry Lead.
(**b**) *Chlorogenic acid.*—Prep. from green coffee as in JAOAC **40**, 350(1957). Available from ICN-K&K Laboratories, Cat. No. 2172. Mp after drying in vac. over efficient desiccant is 207–209°; *a* is ≥52.0.

15.005 ***Preparation of Sample Solution***

Weigh 0.7 g ground sample, **15.003**, into 50 mL centrf. tube. Add 25 mL pet ether, mix thoroly, centrf., and decant supernate. Repeat twice. Dry residue in gentle stream of air until odor can no longer be detected. Transfer to 750 mL erlenmeyer with small amt of H_2O. Add 400 mL boiling H_2O, reheat quickly to boiling, and continue to boil gently exactly 15 min; then cool quickly to room temp. under tap. During boiling, swirl frequently to keep coffee submerged in soln. Transfer to 500 mL vol. flask and dil. to vol. Filter thru retentive paper, discarding first 25–50 mL filtrate. If filtrate is more than faintly cloudy, refilter thru fine porosity fritted glass filter, using suction. Do not use filter aids.

15.006 ***Determination***

Transfer 10 mL filtrate to 100 mL vol. flask and dil. to vol. with H_2O. Det *A* at 324 nm against H_2O. Transfer 100 mL sample soln to 200 mL Pyrex vol. flask or Kohlrausch flask. Add 2 mL *satd KOAc* soln and 10 mL basic $Pb(OAc)_2$ soln with swirling. Place flask in boiling H_2O bath 5 min, swirling occasionally. Remove, cool under tap, and place in ice-H_2O bath. Stir mech. 1 hr, using glass rod with paddle-shaped blade at lower end reaching bottom of flask, with flask immersed in bath. Remove, wash down stirrer, warm to room temp., and dil. to vol. with H_2O. Filter thru fluted paper, discarding first 25–50 mL filtrate. Immediately det. *A* of soln at 324 nm. Clean cells carefully after each use of Pb-treated solns because $PbCO_3$ slowly accumulates on optical surfaces.

From std curve det. (1) apparent concn of chlorogenic acid in soln taken for *A* measurement without Pb treatment (C_0); (2) apparent concn in filtrate after Pb treatment (C_1). From latter value subtract 0.00045 mg/mL to correct for solubility of Pb chlorogenate.

Calc. corrected concn = $C_0 - [(C_1 - 0.00045)/5]$.

15.007 ***Preparation of Standard Curve***

Weigh 40.0 mg dried chlorogenic acid, transfer to 500 mL vol. flask, dissolve, and dil. to vol. with H_2O. Prep. series of stds by transferring 5, 10, 15, and 20 mL aliquots to 100 mL vol. flasks and dilg to vol. Det. *A* at 324 nm of each soln against H_2O. Plot concn of chlorogenic acid in mg/mL against *A*.

ROASTED COFFEE

15.008 Macroscopic Examination—Procedure

Pick out and microscopically identify artificial coffee beans, apparent from their regular form, and roasted legumes and lumps of chicory in whole roasted coffee. For ground coffee, sprinkle some of sample on cold H_2O and stir lightly. Fragments of pure coffee float, if not overroasted, while fragments of chicory, legumes, cereals, etc., sink immediately, chicory coloring the H_2O decidedly brown. In all cases use microscopic examination to identify particles that sink.

15.009 Preparation of Sample—Official First Action

Grind sample to pass No. 30 sieve and store in tightly stoppered bottle.

Loss on Drying (*3*)—Official Final Action

15.010 ***Apparatus***

(**a**) *Aluminum dish.*—Diam. ca 70 mm, ht ca 30 mm; with close-fitting cover.
(**b**) *Desiccator.*—*See* **14.002(b)**.
(**c**) *Vacuum oven.*—*See* **14.002(c)**.

15.011 ***Determination***

Sample directly without grinding. Accurately weigh ca 5 g well mixed sample in dish previously dried at 98–100°, cooled in desiccator, and weighed with cover soon after attaining room temp. Place in oven, lean cover against dish, and heat to const wt (ca 5.5 hr) at 98–100° at pressure ≤25 mm Hg. During heating admit slow current of air (ca 2 bubbles/sec thru H_2SO_4) into oven. Carefully admit dry air into oven to bring to atm. pressure. Cover dish, transfer to desiccator, and weigh soon after room temp. is attained. Report % loss in wt.

ISO Method (4)—Official First Action

(Applicable to instant coffees)

15.012 ***Apparatus***

(**a**) *Vacuum oven.*—Elec. heated with adjustable temp. so that temp. of *shelves* is maintained at 70±1°. During operation, vac. must be maintained at max. of 5000 N/m² (Pa) (37.5 mm Hg) by vac. pump, with air admitted thru drying train consisting of 2 gas washing bottles contg glycerol connected to 2 drying towers in series contg P_2O_5 or indicating silica gel connected to oven.

(**b**) *Drying dishes.*—Glass or Al with close fitting slip on lids, 50 mm diam. and 20–30 mm high.

15.013 ***Determination***

(Instant coffees are very hygroscopic. Work rapidly to minimize exposure to atmosphere.)

Dry empty dishes and lids in convection oven 1 hr at 100–105°. Cool in desiccator over indicating silica gel and weigh. Place ca 3 g sample in dish, spread uniformly over bottom, cover, and reweigh. If series of samples are to be run, replace in desiccator until all samples are weighed.

Remove lid and place dish and lid in oven. Close oven and reduce pressure slowly (≥2 min) to 5000±1000 N/m² (37.5 mm). Dry 16±0.5 hr at shelf temp. of 70±1° with air admitted at rate of 1 bubble/sec. Then close valve to pump and admit air slowly (≥2 min) into oven. Open oven, replace lid on dish, place in desiccator, cool, and weigh.

$$\text{Loss on drying}/100\ g = (M_1 - M_2) \times 100/(M_1 - M_0),$$

where M_0 = wt (g) empty dish and lid; M_1 = wt (g) dish, lid, and sample before drying; and M_2 = wt (g) dish, lid, and sample after drying.

15.014 Soluble Solids—Official Final Action
European Decaffeination Assocation Method (5)

Weigh 10 g sample, **15.009**, into 500 mL erlenmeyer. Place 20 cm glass stirring rod into flask, add 200 mL H_2O, and weigh. Bring to bp while stirring and boil exactly 5 min. Cool, reweigh, and add H_2O to bring wt back to original. Filter. Evap. 25 mL filtrate. Dry in 105° air oven, and weigh residue. Continue drying to const wt.

15.015 Ash—Official Final Action

Proceed as in **31.012** or **31.013**, using sample prepd as in **15.009**.

15.016 Soluble and Insoluble Ash—Official Final Action

Proceed as in **31.015**, using the ash obtained in **15.015**.

15.017 Alkalinity of Soluble Ash—Official Final Action

Proceed as in **31.016**, using the filtrate obtained in **15.016**.

15.018 Ash Insoluble in Acid—Official Final Action

Proceed as in **30.008**, using the ash obtained in **15.015** or H_2O-insol. ash obtained in **15.016**.

15.019 Soluble Phosphorus in Ash—Official Final Action

Proceed as in **7.121** or **8.033**, using soln obtained in **15.016**.

15.020 Insoluble Phosphorus in Ash—Official Final Action

Boil insol. ash, **15.016**, with 25 mL HCl (1+2), filter, wash thoroly with hot H_2O, and det. P_2O_5 in combined filtrate and washings as in **7.119** or **8.033**.

15.021 Chlorides—Official Final Action

See **3.071–3.072**.

Caffeine

15.022 ★ *Power-Chesnut Method (6)* ★
Official Final Action

(Not applicable to coffee exts. *Caution: See* **51.011** and **51.056**.)

See **14.019**, 10th ed.

15.023 *Bailey-Andrew Method—Official Final Action*

Proceed as in **15.051**, using 10 g regular coffee or 5 g regular sol. coffee.

15.024 *Micro Bailey-Andrew Method (7)*
Official Final Action

Weigh 2 g regular coffee or 1 g regular instant coffee, add 5 g powd MgO, and transfer to weighed 500 mL erlenmeyer. Add ca 150–200 mL H_2O, heat to boiling, and boil 45 min, shaking occasionally. Add H_2O, when necessary, to prevent frothing (final wt of H_2O must be 100 g). Cool to room temp. Make mixt. to tare wt + 105 g + sample wt.

Filter directly into 50 mL graduate until exactly 50 mL soln (equiv. to ½ sample wt) is obtained. Transfer soln to 125 mL separator. Wash graduate with 2 mL H_2O and add washing to separator. Add 4 mL H_2SO_4 (1+9). Ext with five 10 mL portions $CHCl_3$, shaking vigorously 1 min for each extn. Let emulsion break; then drain $CHCl_3$ into 125 mL separator. Add 5 mL 1% KOH soln. Shake vigorously 1 min, let emulsion break, and drain $CHCl_3$ thru cotton plug into 100 mL Kjeldahl flask. Ext KOH soln with 5 mL $CHCl_3$ and add to Kjeldahl flask. To digestion flasks add 1.9±0.1 g K_2SO_4, 40±10 mg HgO, and 2.0±0.1 mL H_2SO_4. Add boiling chips and rinse down neck of flask with 3 mL $CHCl_3$. Place flask on digestion rack and proceed as in **47.023**. 1 mL 0.02*N* acid = 0.971 mg caffeine.

Chromatographic-Spectrophotometric Method (*1*)
Official First Action

(Applicable to regular and decaffeinated coffee)

15.025 ***Reagents and Apparatus***

(**a**) *Caffeine std solns.*—10, 20, and 30 μg caffeine/mL. Accurately weigh 100 mg caffeine (USP, anhyd.) into 100 mL vol. flask, dissolve in $CHCl_3$, and dil. to vol. with $CHCl_3$. Dil. 10 mL aliquot of this soln to 100 mL with $CHCl_3$. Further dil. 10, 20, and 15 mL aliquots to 100, 100, and 50 mL, resp., with $CHCl_3$ to obtain std solns of 10, 20, and 30 μg/mL.

(**b**) *Recording spectrophotometer.*—To record 350–250 nm range, with matched 1 cm cells.

15.026 ***Preparation of Sample***

(**a**) *Green and roasted coffee.*—Accurately weigh ca 1 g ground sample, transfer to 100 mL beaker, add 5 mL NH_4OH (1+2), and warm on boiling H_2O bath 2 min. Cool, transfer to 100 mL vol. flask, and dil. to vol. with H_2O. To 5 mL aliquot of the turbid soln add 6 g Celite 545 and mix carefully.

(**b**) *Decaffeinated green and roasted coffee.*—Accurately weigh ca 1 g ground sample. Transfer to 100 mL beaker, add 5 mL NH_4OH (1+2), and warm on boiling H_2O bath 2 min. Add 6 g Celite 545 and mix carefully.

(**c**) *Soluble coffee.*—Proceed as in (**a**), except use 0.5 g sample and 3 mL aliquot.

(**d**) *Decaffeinated soluble coffee.*—Proceed as in (**b**), except use 0.5 g sample.

15.027 ***Preparation of Columns***

(**a**) *Acid column.*—Place fine glass wool plug in base of 25 × 250 mm tube. Add 3 mL 4*N* H_2SO_4 to 3.0 g Celite 545 and mix well by kneading with spatula blade. Transfer to tube and tamp, using gentle pressure, to uniform mass. Place small glass wool wad above surface.

(**b**) *Basic column.*—*Layer I.*—Mix 3 g Celite 545 and 2 mL 2*N*

★ Surplus method—*see* inside front cover.

NaOH, and place in 25 × 250 mm tube over glass wool plug as in (**a**). *Layer II.*—Transfer sample plus Celite mixt. from **15.026**, in ca 2 g portions, to tube directly over Layer *I*, tamping before adding next portion of sample, until homogeneous and compact layer is obtained. Dry-wash beaker with ca 1 g Celite 545, transfer to tube, and tamp to uniform mass. Dry-wash beaker with wad of glass wool and transfer to top of basic column.

15.028 ***Determination***

Mount basic column above acid column. Pass 150 mL H_2O-satd ether sequentially thru basic column to acid column and discard ether. Then pass 50 mL H_2O-satd ether thru acid column and discard ether. Place 50 mL vol. flask under acid column. Pass 48 mL H_2O-satd $CHCl_3$ thru acid column, washing tip of basic column with first portions. Dil. contents of vol. flask to vol. with H_2O-satd $CHCl_3$, mix, and read *A* at 276 against H_2O-satd $CHCl_3$ blank, by scanning from 350 to 250 nm.

Det. *A* of stds and calc. *a* (*see* Definitions of Terms and Explanatory Notes, Item 23(**c**)) at 276 nm for spectrophtr used, and check occasionally. Calc. caffeine content of samples from av. *a*.

15.029 Chlorogenic Acid (*2*)—Official First Action

(**a**) *Roasted coffee.*—Weigh 1 g ground sample, **15.009**, transfer to 750 mL erlenmeyer, and proceed as in **15.005**, beginning "Add 400 mL boiling H_2O, . . ."

(**b**) *Instant coffee.*—Weigh 0.35 g sample, transfer to 500 mL vol. flask, dil. to vol., and proceed as in **15.006**.

15.030 Crude Fiber—Official Final Action

Proceed as in **7.065**, using sample prepd as in **15.009**.

15.031 Starch—Official Final Action

Ext 5 g prepd sample, **15.009**, on hardened filter with five 10 mL portions ether, and wash with small portions alcohol until total of 200 mL has passed thru. Transfer residue from paper to beaker with 50 mL H_2O and proceed as in **31.101**, beginning with third par.

15.032 Sugars (*8*)—Official Final Action

Weigh 10 g prepd sample, **15.009**, into 250 mL vol. flask, add 1 g powd NH_4NaHPO_4, and proceed as in **7.079**, par. 1 and 2, beginning with addn of 50% alcohol, and **31.038**. Det. Cu in Cu_2O ppt either volumetrically, **31.041**, or electrolytically, **31.044**.

15.033 Petroleum Ether Extract—Official Final Action

(*Caution: See* **51.011**, **51.039**, and **51.073**.)

Dry 2 g prepd sample, **15.009**, at 100°, ext with pet ether (bp 30–60°) 16 hr, evap. solv., dry residue at 100°, cool, and weigh.

15.034 Total Acidity—Official Final Action

Treat 10 g prepd sample, **15.003** or **15.009**, in erlenmeyer with 75 mL 80% alcohol, stopper, and let stand 16 hr, shaking occasionally. Filter, transfer aliquot of filtrate (25 mL for green coffee, 10 mL for roasted coffee) to beaker, dil. to ca 100 mL with H_2O, and titr. with 0.1*N* alkali, using phthln. Express result as mL 0.1*N* alkali required to neutze acidity of 100 g sample.

15.035 Coating and Glazing Substances Procedure

(*Caution: See* **51.011**, **51.039**, and **51.073**.)

(**a**) *Sugar and dextrin.*—To 100 g whole coffee in beaker, add exactly 300 mL H_2O, stir, and let stand 5 min, stirring frequently. Filter thru dry paper and carefully add dry $Pb(OAc)_2$ to filtrate until pptn is complete, avoiding excess reagent. Filter thru dry filter and remove Pb from filtrate by adding slight excess of dry, powd $K_2C_2O_4$. Filter thru dry filter and det. reducing sugars as invert sugar in 50 mL of the filtrate as in **31.038**.

Invert 75 mL aliquot filtrate as in **31.026(b)**. Cool, nearly neutze with NaOH soln (1+1), dil. to 100 mL, and det. reducing sugars as invert sugar in resulting soln as in **31.038**.

Measure 100 mL aliquot filtrate into 200 mL vol. flask, add 10 mL HCl (sp gr 1.125), and hydrolyze as in **8.019**. Cool, neutze with NaOH soln (1+1), dil. to vol., filter thru dry filter, and det. reducing sugars as invert sugar in 50 mL filtrate as in **31.038**.

Calc. reducing sugars in each instance to % by wt original coffee. Calc. sucrose from reducing sugars before and after inversion as in **31.031**, and calc. dextrin as follows: Subtract reducing sugars after inversion from reducing sugars after hydrolysis and multiply difference by factor 0.86.

In some instances presence of sucrose in H_2O ext may be verified by polarization. Presence of dextrin in H_2O ext may be verified by polarization as in **31.033**, and by erythrodextrin test, (**b**).

(**b**) *Erythrodextrin test for commercial glucose.*— To aq. ext, (**a**), prior to clarification with $Pb(OAc)_2$, add few mL I soln (1 g I, 3 g KI, 50 mL H_2O). In presence of com. glucose, soln turns red or violet, depth and character of color depending upon quality and nature of glucose used. If amt of glucose is very small, ppt dextrin that may be present by adding several vols alcohol. Let ppt settle (do not filter), decant liq., dissolve residue of dextrins in hot H_2O, cool, and apply I test. Neg. result does not prove absence of com. glucose, because some glucose, especially of high conversion, does not give reaction with I.

(**c**) *Egg albumen and gelatin.*—Add 500 mL H_2O to 100 g whole coffee and let stand 5 min, stirring frequently. Filter and treat sep. portions of filtrate with (*1*) *5% soln of tannic acid,* and (*2*) Millon reagent, **7.125(g)**. Boil third portion of filtrate. In presence of egg albumen more or less heavy ppt will form in each case.

As confirmatory test, treat aliquot of filtrate with excess tannic acid soln, add little NaCl if necessary to flocculate ppt, filter, and without washing, insert paper and contents into Kjeldahl flask, and det. N. By this method coffee not coated with albumen or gelatin yields <10 mg N/100 g sample.

(**d**) *Fats and waxes.*—Treat 100–200 g coffee beans 10 min with low-boiling pet ether, pour off pet ether, and repeat process. Filter combined ext, evap., and det. refractive index and saponification number of the residue as in **28.007** and **28.026**.

15.036 Chicory Infusion—Procedure

Cover 100–150 g whole coffee with H_2O, let soak 2–3 min, stirring frequently, and drain aq. washings thru coarse sieve. Wash coffee on sieve with ca 100 mL H_2O and centrf. combined washings. Decant clear liq. from sediment, drain sediment almost dry on filter paper, mount in chloral hydrate soln, **30.029(b)**, and examine microscopically for chicory.

TEA

15.037 Preparation of Sample—Official Final Action

Grind sample to pass No. 30 sieve.

15.038 Moisture—Official Final Action

See **7.003**.

15.039 Water Extract (*9*)—Official Final Action

To 2 g ground sample in 500 mL vol. flask, add 200 mL hot H_2O and boil over low flame 1 hr, rotating occasionally. Close flask with rubber stopper thru which passes tube 75 cm long for condenser. Boil very slowly so that no steam escapes from top of air condenser. Cool, dil. to vol., mix thoroly, and filter thru dry paper. Transfer 50 mL aliquot to weighed dish, and evap. to dryness on steam bath. Place in oven, heat 1 hr at 100°, cool, and weigh.

15.040 Ash—Official Final Action

See **31.012** or **31.013**.

15.041 Soluble and Insoluble Ash—Official Final Action

Proceed as in **31.015**, using the ash obtained in **15.040**.

15.042 Alkalinity of Soluble Ash—Official Final Action

Proceed as in **31.016**, using the filtrate obtained in **15.041**.

15.043 Alkalinity of Insoluble Ash—Official Final Action

Proceed as in **31.017**, using insol. ash obtained in **15.041**.

15.044 Ash Insoluble in Acid—Official Final Action

Proceed as in **30.008**, using total ash obtained in **15.040**, or insol. residue obtained in **15.041**.

15.045 Soluble Phosphorus in Ash—Official Final Action

Proceed as in **7.119** or **8.033**, using soln of sol. ash obtained in **15.042**.

15.046 Insoluble Phosphorus in Ash—Official Final Action

Proceed as in **7.119** or **8.033**, using soln obtained in **15.043**.

15.047 Petroleum Ether Extract—Official Final Action

See **15.033**.

15.048 Protein—Official Final Action

Det. N as in **2.057**. Protein = (% total N − % N present as caffeine) × 6.25.

15.049 Crude Fiber—Official Final Action

See **7.065**.

Caffeine

15.050 ★ Power-Chesnut Method (10) ★ Official Final Action

See **15.022**.

15.051 *Modified Bailey-Andrew Method (11) Official Final Action*

Weigh 5 g prepd sample, **15.037**, into weighed 1 L erlenmeyer. Add ca 500 mL H_2O, swirl, and heat to bp. Add 10 g *heavy MgO*. Boil gently over low flame 2 hr with occasional shaking. Add H_2O to prevent frothing and to wash down sides of flask. Cool, and make to wt with H_2O (tare wt + 510 g + wt sample). Filter, collect 200 mL clear filtrate (equiv. to 0.4 sample wt), add 20 mL H_2SO_4 (1+9), and transfer to 500 mL separator. Shake 6 times with $CHCl_3$, using 25, 20, 15, 10, 10, and 10 mL portions. Treat combined exts with 5 mL 1% KOH soln; when liqs sep. completely, drain $CHCl_3$ layer into Kjeldahl flask. Wash alk. soln in separator with two 10 mL portions $CHCl_3$ and combine washings with remaining bulk of ext. Evap. or distil off the $CHCl_3$ to <25 mL, and proceed as in **2.057**. 1 mL 0.1*N* H_2SO_4 = 4.85 mg anhyd. caffeine.

★ Surplus method—*see* inside front cover.

Ultraviolet Spectrophotometric and Gas-Liquid Chromatographic Methods for "Instant Tea" (12)—Official Final Action

(First action for leaf tea)

15.052 ***Reagents***

(**a**) *Caffeine std solns.*—(*1*) *Soln No. 1.*—500 μg/mL. Accurately weigh ca 100 mg caffeine, USP; dissolve and dil. to 200 mL with $CHCl_3$ in vol. flask. (*2*) *Soln No. 2.*—10 μg/mL. Pipet 20 mL *Soln No. 1* into 100 mL vol. flask and dil. to vol. with $CHCl_3$; dil. 10.0 mL of this soln to 100 mL with $CHCl_3$.

(**b**) *Pentobarbital internal std soln.*—2 mg/mL. Accurately weigh ca 200 mg pentobarbital; dissolve and dil. to 100 mL with alcohol in vol. flask.

(**c**) *GLC working std soln.*—250 μg caffeine and 1 mg pentobarbital/mL. Pipet equal vols caffeine std *Soln No. 1* and pentobarbital internal std into g-s flask and mix thoroly. Prep. fresh daily.

15.053 ***Apparatus***

(**a**) *Gas chromatograph.*—Equipped with thermionic KCl detector. Typical operating conditions: Temps (°): column 190, detector 220, and injector 220; N carrier gas. Inject 5 μL GLC working std soln and record chromatogram. Adjust attenuation and sensitivity (1 × 10^{-8} AFS), if necessary, to bring peaks to ca half-scale deflection. Adjust flow rate of N so that caffeine is eluted in ca 7 min.

(**b**) *Gas chromatographic column.*—Glass, 1.8 m (6′) × 4 mm id packed with 10% DC-200 oil on 80–100 mesh Gas-Chrom Q (Applied Science Laboratories, Inc., precoated, or equiv.). Condition column >24 hr at 250–260° (with N flow of 100±20 mL/min).

(**c**) *Recording spectrophotometer.*—350–250 nm range with matched 1 cm cells.

(**d**) *Chromatographic tubes.*—Glass, 25 × 250 mm.

15.054 ***Preparation of Sample***

(**a**) *Leaf tea.*—Grind sample in high-speed blender or other suitable device to pass No. 30 or 40 sieve. Accurately weigh ca 1 g tea into 100 mL beaker, add ca 40 mL NH_4OH (1+2), and heat 5 min on steam bath. Transfer quant. to 100 mL vol. flask, cool, and dil. to vol. with NH_4OH (1+2). Transfer 5.0 mL aliquot to 6 g Celite 545 (acid-washed) in 100 mL beaker and proceed as in **15.027**.

(**b**) *Instant tea.*—Place 0.5 g sample in 100 mL beaker and continue as in **15.027**.

15.055 ***Preparation of Columns and Sample Solution***

Prep columns as in **15.027(a)** and **(b)**. Isolate caffeine as in **15.028**, dil. to 50 mL, and proceed as in **15.056**.

15.056 ***Spectrophotometric Determination***

Transfer 10.0 mL aliquot leaf tea sample soln to 50 mL vol. flask and dil. to vol. with $CHCl_3$. Transfer 10.0 mL aliquot instant tea sample soln to 100 mL vol. flask, dil. to vol. with $CHCl_3$, and further dil. 20.0 mL aliquot to 100 mL with $CHCl_3$. Det. *A* at 276 nm on recording spectrophtr against $CHCl_3$ as ref. Compare with A of std caffeine *Soln No. 2* (10 μg/mL).

$$\% \text{ Caffeine} = (A/A') \times (C'/C) \times 100$$

where A and A' refer to sample and std, resp., and C and C' refer to sample and std concns, resp.

15.057 ***Gas Chromatographic Determination***

Complete detn within 1 day. Pipet equal vols pentobarbital internal std soln and concd sample soln into g-s flask and mix (assay soln). Inject 5 μL working std soln and record chromatogram. Inject 5 μL assay soln and record chromatogram. Measure ht of each peak. Let P_s = ht of std peak of GLC working std soln; P_u = ht of sample peak of assay soln; I_s = ht of internal std peak of std; I_u = ht of internal std peak of assay soln; C_s = mg caffeine/mL in GLC working std soln; C_u = mg sample/mL.

$$\% \text{ Caffeine in sample} = (P_u \times I_s \times C_s \times 100)/(P_s \times I_u \times C_u).$$

15.058 Copper and Nickel—Official First Action

See **25.044–25.048.**

SELECTED REFERENCES

(*1*) JAOAC **48,** 705(1965); **62,** 705(1979).
(*2*) JAOAC **40,** 350(1957).
(*3*) JAOAC **51,** 577(1968).
(*4*) ISO/DIS 3726(1975).
(*5*) Z. Unters. Nahr. und Genusm. Gebrauchsgegenstände 7/8. bd. 41(1921), 145.
(*6*) J. Amer. Chem. Soc. **41,** 1298(1919); JAOAC **5,** 267(1921); **13,** 265(1930); **14,** 533(1931); **16,** 567(1933); **17,** 380(1934); **27,** 168(1944); **29,** 37(1946); **30,** 416(1947).
(*7*) JAOAC **40,** 346(1957); **43,** 620(1960); **49,** 219 (1966).
(*8*) JAOAC **3,** 498(1920).
(*9*) JAOAC **7,** 154(1923).
(*10*) J. Amer. Chem. Soc. **41,** 1298(1919); JAOAC **5,** 288(1921); **6,** 107(1922).
(*11*) JAOAC **5,** 288(1921); **6,** 107(1922); **43,** 620 (1960).
(*12*) JAOAC **52,** 653, 1133(1969).

16. Dairy Products

SAMPLING (*1*)—OFFICIAL FINAL ACTION

(Prepd by a joint committee of International Dairy Federation, International Organization for Standardization, and AOAC, 1965, for the Joint FAO/WHO *Code of Principles Concerning Milk and Milk Products and Associated Standards.* Methods are intended to obtain from unit (e.g., bulk container, small retail container, individual cheese, etc.) portion (subsample) which is as representative as possible of that unit.)

General Instructions

16.001 ***Instructions of Administrative Character***

(This section is usually prescribed by specific regulatory agency. It is included for completeness.)

Sampling should be performed by authorized or sworn independent agent, properly trained in appropriate technic. Agent should be free from any infectious disease. If possible, representatives of parties concerned should be given opportunity to be present when sampling is performed.

Samples should be accompanied by report, signed by sworn or authorized sampling agent and countersigned by any witnesses present. Report should give particulars of place, date, and time of sampling; name and designation of agent and of any witnesses; precise method of sampling which is followed if this deviates from prescribed std method; nature and number of units constituting consignment together with their batch code markings, where available; number of samples duly identified as to batches from which they are drawn; and place to which the samples will be sent.

When appropriate, report should also include any relevant conditions or circumstances, e.g., condition of packages and their surroundings, temp. and humidity of atm., method of sterilization of sampling equipment, whether preservative has been added to samples, and any other special information relating to material being sampled.

Each sample should be sealed and labeled to give nature of product, identification number, and any code markings of batch from which sample has been taken, date of sampling, and name and signature of sampling agent. When necessary, addnl information may be required, for example, wt of sample and unit from which it was taken.

All samples should be taken at least in duplicate, one set being held, if necessary, in cold storage and put at disposal of second party as soon as possible. Precise method of sampling and wt or vol. of product to be taken as sample vary with nature of product and purpose for which sampling is required and are defined for each particular case.

When previously agreed between parties, take addnl sets of samples and retain for independent arbitration, if necessary. Send samples to testing laboratory immediately after sampling.

16.002 ***Technical Instructions***

(*See* sampling equipment specifications laid down for each product to be sampled.)

(**a**) *Sampling for chemical purposes.*—Clean and dry all equipment.

(**b**) *Sampling for bacteriological purposes.*—Clean and treat equipment by one of following methods: (*1*) Expose to hot air 2 hr at 170° (may be stored if kept under sterile conditions). (*2*) Autoclave 15–20 min at 120° (may be stored if kept under sterile conditions). (*3*) Expose to steam 1 hr at 100° (use equipment same day). (*4*) Immerse in H_2O 1 min at 100° (use equipment immediately). (*5*) Immerse in 70% alcohol and flame to burn off alcohol immediately before use. (*6*) Expose to hydrocarbon (propane, butane) torch flame so that all working surfaces contact flame immediately before use.

Choice of treatment depends on nature, shape, and size of equipment and on conditions of sampling. Sterilize wherever possible by method (*1*) or (*2*).

Methods (*3*), (*4*), (*5*), and (*6*) are regarded as secondary methods only.

(**c**) *Sampling for organoleptic purposes.*—Use equipment as in (**a**) or (**b**), or as specified for specific product. Equipment should not impart any flavor or odor to product.

16.003 ***Sample Containers***

(**a**) *For liquids.*—Use clean and dry containers of suitable waterproof, greaseproof material (glass, stainless metal, suitable plastic material) of quality suitable for sterilization by **16.002(b)**, if necessary, and of suitable shape and capacity for material to be sampled (as defined in each particular case).

Securely close containers either with suitable rubber or plastic stopper or by screw cap of metal or plastic having, if necessary, liq.-tight plastic liner which is insol., nonabsorbent, and greaseproof, and which will not influence odor, flavor, or composition of milk products.

If rubber stoppers are used, cover with nonabsorbent, flavorless material (such as suitable plastic) before pressing into sample container. Suitable plastic bags may also be used.

(**b**) *For solids or semisolids.*—Use clean and dry wide-mouth, cylindrical receptacles of suitable waterproof, greaseproof material (glass, stainless metal, suitable plastic material) of quality suitable for sterilization by **16.002(b)**, if necessary, and of capacity suited to size of sample to be taken (as defined in each particular case). Make air-tight as in (**a**). Suitable plastic bags may also be used.

(**c**) *Small retail containers.*—Contents of intact and unopened containers constitute samples.

16.004 ***Preservation of Samples***

To samples of liq. products or cheese intended for chem. analysis, suitable preservative may be added. Such preservative should not interfere with subsequent analysis. Indicate nature and amt of addn on label and in any reports.

Do not add preservatives to samples of semisolid, solid (except cheese), or dried products intended for chem. analysis. Rapidly cool and store samples in refrigerator at 0–5°. Dried milks may be kept at room temp.

Do not add preservatives to samples intended for bacteriological or organoleptic examination. Hold at 0–5°, except for condensed (conserved) milk products when sample comprises unopened hermetically sealed containers in which products are sold. Keep liq. products and butter cold. Start bacteriological examination of liq. products as soon as possible and never >24 hr after sampling.

16.005 ***Transport of Samples***

Transport samples to laboratory as quickly as possible after sampling. Take precautions to prevent, during transit, exposure to direct sunlight, or to temps $<0°$ or $>10°$ in case of perishable products. For samples intended for bacteriological examination, use insulated transport container capable of maintaining temp.

at 0–5°, except for samples of condensed (conserved) milk products in unopened containers, or in case of very short journeys.

Maintain samples of cheese under such conditions as to avoid sepn of fat or moisture. Maintain soft cheese at 0–5°.

Sampling of Milk and Liquid Milk Products (Except Evaporated and Sweetened Condensed Milk)

16.006 ***Sampling Equipment***

(**a**) *Plungers or agitators, necessary for mixing liquids in bulk.*—Use equipment, **16.008(a)**, of sufficient area to produce adequate agitation of product and light enough in wt for operator to be able to move it rapidly thru liq. Mix contents of large vessels by mech. stirring.

(**b**) *Dipper of suitable size, for collecting sample.*— When sample is required for bacteriological examination, sterilize sampling equipment as in **16.002(b)**.

16.007 ***Sampling Technic***

Thoroly mix all liqs by pouring from one vessel to another, by plunging, or by mech. stirring. With large containers, continue agitation until liq. is thoroly mixed. In case of cream, plunge sufficient number of times to ensure thoro mixing. Move submerged plunger from place to place with special care to avoid foaming, whipping, and churning. Take sample with dipper immediately after mixing. If obtaining perfect homogeneity presents difficulties, take sample from different positions of container totaling ≥200 mL.

(For addnl instructions, *see* **16.019** for milk and **16.144** for cream.)

Sampling of Condensed Milk and Evaporated Milk

16.008 ***Bulk Containers (Barrels, Drums, Etc.)***

(**a**) *Sampling equipment.*—Broad-bladed metal stirrer fitted with wide perforated disk at bottom and long enough to reach bottom of container.

(**b**) *Sampling technic.*—Use stirrer to mix contents very carefully and to scrape adhering material from sides and bottom of container. Remove 2–3 L well mixed contents to smaller receptacle, repeat stirring, and take sample ≥200 mL.

(**c**) *Sample containers.*—Use wide-mouth sample jars with air-tight lids.

16.009 ***Small Retail Containers***

Sample unit is one intact, unopened container that, whenever possible, bears manufacturer's code markings. Do not open container until just before analysis.

(For prepn of sample, *see* **16.167** for evapd milk and **16.181** for sweetened condensed milk.)

Sampling of Dried Milk and Dried Milk Products

(Perform sampling for bacteriological examination first, independent of other sampling, from same bulk container, whenever possible.)

16.010 ***Sampling for Chemical Analysis and Organoleptic Examination***

(**a**) *Sampling equipment.*—Use suitable clean, dry borer tube or trier of stainless steel, Al, or Al alloy.

(**b**) *Sampling technic.*—Pass tube steadily thru powder at even rate of penetration. When tube reaches bottom of container withdraw contents and discharge immediately into sample container. Do not touch powder with fingers. Take ≥1 bores to make up 300–500 g samples.

(**c**) *Sample containers.*—Place samples in clean, dry containers, air-tight and, if required for examination, opaque. Use sample container large enough to allow mixing by shaking.

(**d**) Submit unopened original container of gas-packed dried milk if gas analysis is required.

16.011 ***Sampling for Bacteriological Examination***

Take samples for bacteriological examination, whenever possible, from same package as for chem. and organoleptic examination. Take sample for bacteriological examination first.

(**a**) *Sampling equipment.*—Sterilize suitable stainless steel or Al spoon or trier as in **16.002(b)**(*1*), (*2*), (*5*), or (*6*).

(**b**) *Sampling technic.*—Using sterile metal implement (e.g., broad-bladed knife or spoon), remove surface layer of powder from sampling area. With another sterile spoon or trier, take sample of 50–200 g, if possible, from point near center of container. Place sample as quickly as possible into sample container, and close immediately, using aseptic precautions. In case of dispute concerning bacteriological conditions of top layer of powder in packing, take special sample from this top layer.

(**c**) *Sample containers.*—Place samples in clean, dry, sterile containers, preferably brown if transparent, capable of air-tight closure.

(For addnl instructions, *see* **16.190**.)

Sampling of Butter

16.012 ***Sampling Equipment***

Use butter triers long enough to pass diagonally to base of container. Use stainless steel spatulas or knives for removing portions of sample from trier. Clean and dry triers, spatulas, and knives before use, and if sampling for bacteriological purposes is required, sterilize as in **16.002(b)**(*4*), (*5*), or (*6*).

16.013 ***Sampling Technic***

(**a**) *Butter in bulk.*—Take ≥2 cores of butter so that min. wt of total sample is ≥200 g. For butter in barrels, take 1 core by inserting trier diagonally thru butter from edge of barrel. Take others by inserting trier from arbitrary points of surface, vertically downward to bottom. For butter in cubes, take cores by inserting trier from top corners diagonally thru center to bottom. In both cases, make 1 complete turn and withdraw full core. Hold point of trier over mouth of sample container and immediately transfer core from trier in ca 75 mm pieces with spatula or knife. Leave plug ≥25 mm to place in hole from which core was removed. Do not include moisture adhering to outside of trier.

Clean and dry trier before each drawing. Soften butter, frozen so hard as to resist trier, by storing 24 hr at ca 10°.

(**b**) *Butter in pats or rolls of small size.*—Divide units weighing ≥250 g in 4, and take 2 opposite quarters. In sizes weighing <250 g take whole unit.

(For addnl instructions, *see* **16.203**.)

16.014 ***Sample Containers***

Use wide-mouth jars conforming to **16.003(b)**. Fill jar ≥½ full and hermetically seal. Immediately after closure, wrap jars in paper or store in dark, if examination so requires. Do not let butter come into contact with paper or any H_2O or fat absorbing or trapping surface.

1

Sampling of Cheese

16.015 ***Sampling Equipment***

(**a**) *Cheese triers of shape and size suited to cheese to be sampled.*
(**b**) *Stainless steel knife with pointed blade.*
(**c**) *Sealing compounds.*—(*1*) Mix by heating paraffin, beeswax, and white petrolatum (1+1+2); or (*2*) mix by heating white petrolatum and paraffin (1+1).

16.016 ***Sampling Technic***

Draw enough subsamples to give total sample of $\geq$50 g. Use one of following technics, depending on shape, wt, type, and maturity of cheese (when choice is necessary between (**a**) and (**b**), method (**a**) is preferable but (**b**) is acceptable, especially with hard cheese of large size).

(**a**) *Sampling by cutting.*—Using knife with pointed blade, make 2 cuts radiating from center of cheese, if cheese has circular base, or parallel to sides if base is rectangular. Size of piece thus obtained should be such that, after removal of inedible surface layer, remaining edible portion weighs $\geq$50 g.

(**b**) *Sampling by means of trier.*—According to shape, wt, and type of cheese, use one of following sampling technics: (*1*) Insert trier obliquely towards center of cheese once or several times into one of flat surfaces at point $\geq$10 cm from edge. (*2*) Insert trier perpendicularly into one face and pass thru center of cheese to reach opposite face. (*3*) Insert trier horizontally into vertical face of cheese, midway between 2 plane faces, toward center of cheese. (*4*) In case of cheese transported in barrels, boxes, or other bulk containers, or cheese which is formed into large compact blocks, perform sampling by passing trier obliquely thru contents of container from top to base. (*5*) For large cheeses, use outer 2 cm or more of plug contg rind for closing hole made in cheese. Remainder of plug constitutes sample. Close plug holes with great care and, if possible, seal over with sealing compd, **16.015**(**c**).

(**c**) *Sampling by taking entire cheese.*—Normally use for small cheese and for wrapped portions of cheese packaged in small containers. Take enough packages to have $\geq$50 g.

Weigh, at time of sampling, cheese sold by piece for which min. wt dry matter in unit is specified by national legislation, and state wt on label.

(**d**) *Sampling of cheese in brine.*—Take fragments of $\geq$200 g each and enough brine to cover cheese in sample container. Before analysis, place sample on filter paper 1–2 hr.

(For addnl instructions, *see* **16.231**.)

16.017 ***Sample Containers***

Use sample containers with air-tight closures. Immediately after sampling, place samples (plugs, sectors, entire small cheese, fragments of brine cheese) in container of suitable size and shape. Sample may be cut into pieces for insertion into container but do not compress or grind.

16.018 ***Treatment of Samples***

In prepn of sample, whatever method of sampling is used, carefully remove only inedible surface layer of cheese, if any, such as moldy and horny portions, unless prescribed otherwise. Do not remove outer rind or crust from soft cheese sold by piece, and for which min. wt of dry matter in unit is specified by national legislation.

(For addnl instructions, *see* **16.232**.)

MILK

16.019 ***Collection of Sample—Procedure***

(*See* also **16.001–16.007**.)

Sample size necessary varies with analyses required. For usual analysis collect 250–500 mL (½–1 pt) sample; for fat detn only, collect 50–60 mL (ca 2 fl oz).

For bottled milk, collect $\geq$1 container as prepd for sale. Thoroly mix bulk milk by pouring from one clean vessel into another 3 or 4 times or stir $\geq$30 sec with utensil reaching to bottom of container. If cream has formed, detach all of it from sides of vessel and stir until liq. is evenly emulsified or use hand homogenizer.

Place in nonabsorbent, air-tight containers and keep cold, but above freezing temp., until examined. When transporting samples, completely fill containers, stopper tightly, and identify. Tablets contg $HgCl_2$, $K_2Cr_2O_7$, or other suitable preservative, $\geq$0.5 g active ingredient per tablet for each 8 fl oz (250 mL) milk, but total wt of such tablet $\leq$1 g, or 36% soln of HCHO, 0.1 mL (2 drops) per fl oz (30 mL), may be used unless presence of preservative is objectionable in physical or chem. tests to be made in addn to detn of fat. If phosphatase test is to be made, only $CHCl_3$ can be used as preservative, and stoppers must be of phenol-free material such as red rubber.

16.020 ***Preparation of Sample—Procedure***

Bring sample to ca 20°, mix until homogeneous by pouring into clean receptacle and back repeatedly, and promptly weigh or measure test portion. If lumps of cream do not disperse, warm sample in H_2O bath to ca 38° and keep mixing until homogeneous, using policeman, if necessary, to reincorporate any cream adhering to container or stopper. Where practical and fat remains dispersed, cool warmed samples to ca 20° before transferring test portion.

When Babcock method, **16.061**, is used, adjust both fresh and composite samples to ca 38°, mix until homogeneous as above, and immediately pipet portions into test bottles.

16.021 Specific Gravity—Procedure

Det sp gr at 15.6/15.6° with pycnometer or std hydrometer.

16.022 Somatic Cell Count—Official First Action

See **46.086–46.109**.

16.023 Acidity (*2*)—Official Final Action

Measure or weigh suitable amt (ca 20 mL or 20 g) sample into suitable dish and dil. with twice its vol. CO_2-free H_2O. Add 2 mL phthln, and titr. with 0.1*N* NaOH to first persistent pink. If measured vol. sample was used, det. its wt from sp gr of sample. Report acidity as % lactic acid by wt. (1 mL 0.1*N* NaOH = 0.0090 g lactic acid.) If Babcock milk pipet, **16.060**(**b**), is used, mL 0.1*N* NaOH required ÷ 20 = % acid as lactic acid.

Results may also be expressed as mL 0.1*N* NaOH/100 g sample.

Citric Acid (*3*)—Official Final Action

16.024 ***Preparation of Sample***

To 50 g milk in 150 mL beaker, add ca 100 mg *tartaric acid* and 6 mL 1*N* H_2SO_4, and heat on steam bath 15 min. Immediately add 3 mL *20% phosphotungstic acid soln,* mix well, and return to steam bath for 5 min. Transfer to 250 mL vol. flask with alcohol, cool, dil. to vol. with alcohol, mix, and filter thru folded paper. Pipet 200 mL clear filtrate into centrf. bottle.

16.025 ***Reagents***

(**a**) *Potassium permanganate soln.*—Dissolve 5 g $KMnO_4$ in H_2O and dil. to 100 mL.

(**b**) *Ferrous sulfate soln.*—Dissolve 200 g $FeSO_4.7H_2O$ in H_2O, dil. to 500 mL with H_2O, and add 5 mL H_2SO_4.

(**c**) *Lead acetate soln.*—Dissolve 75 g $Pb(OAc)_2.3H_2O$ in H_2O, add 1 mL HOAc, and dil. to 250 mL.

16.026 ***Determination***

To soln in centrf. bottle add 10 mL $Pb(OAc)_2$ soln, shake vigorously ca 2 min, and centrf. 15 min at ca 1000 rpm. Carefully decant supernate from pptd Pb salts and test with little $Pb(OAc)_2$ soln. If ppt forms, return to centrf. bottle, add more Pb soln, shake, and again centrf. If sediment lifts, centrf. again, increasing speed and time, and decant. Invert bottle and drain thoroly several min. To Pb salts in centrf. bottle add ca 150 mL H_2O, shake thoroly, and sat. with H_2S. (*Caution: See* **51.059**.) Transfer to 250 mL vol. flask, dil. to vol. with H_2O, mix, and filter thru folded paper.

Evap. 200 mL filtrate to ca 20 mL, rinse into 250–300 mL tared, g-s erlenmeyer, and adjust with H_2O to net wt of ca 40 g. Add 2 g KBr and 5 mL H_2SO_4, and, if necessary, heat to ca 50° and let stand 5 min. Slowly (1–2 mL portions) add 20 mL $KMnO_4$ soln from pipet or buret, swirling flask few sec after each addn. Let stand undisturbed 5 min and cool to 15°. Slowly add $FeSO_4$ soln with const agitation until mixt. starts to clear. Shake 1 min, continue addn of $FeSO_4$ soln until MnO_2 is dissolved, and add few mL excess. Add 20 g anhyd. Na_2SO_4, with swirling to assure soln (if Na_2SO_4 remains substantially undissolved, repeat detn). Cool to 15° and shake vigorously 5 min.

Immediately, while still cold, collect pentabromacetone ppt on asbestos in gooch and wash residual ppt from flask with portion of filtrate. Wash crucible with 50 mL cold H_2O and leave under suction few min. Dry crucible overnight in H_2SO_4 desiccator and weigh, or place crucible in drying train and aerate until loss in wt does not exceed few tenths mg, making first weighing after 20 min.

Remove pentabromacetone from crucible with alcohol followed by ether, filling crucible 3 times with each solv. Dry crucible 10 min at 100°, cool in desiccator, and weigh. Difference in 2 wts = wt pentabromacetone. Calc. g anhyd. citric acid from formula: $X = 0.424P$, where X = g citric acid in aliquot; P = g pentabromacetone; and 0.424 = theoretical factor for converting pentabromacetone to anhyd. citric acid. Anhyd. citric acid in sample taken for analysis = $X/0.64$.

For drying pentabromacetone by aspiration, use app. shown in Fig. **16:01**, where *A* is gooch, 28 mm diam., loosely packed with cotton; *B* is gooch, 35 mm diam., for pentabromacetone; and *C* is 500 mL suction flask. Dry air by passing thru H_2SO_4 and soda-lime, and finally filter thru cotton. Cool air entering drying train by passing thru spiral condenser cooled with H_2O.

Let crucible, *B*, contg pentabromacetone, remain under suction ca 1 min to remove surface moisture before placing in app. If air does not pass thru freely, place crucible in desiccator short time. Maintain slow uniform flow of air by just "cracking" suction.

Lactic Acid (*4*)—Official Final Action

16.027 ***Reagents***

(**a**) *Barium lactate std soln.*—(*Caution: See* **51.011**, **51.039**, and **51.054**.) Dissolve in ca 10 mL H_2O amt of a pure lactate, such as Li, Zn, or Ca lactate, contg equiv. of ca 300 mg free lactic acid. Transfer material to extractor, Fig. **16:02**, add 0.5 mL H_2SO_4 (1+1), and adjust vol. to 50 mL. Ext with ether 3 hr. Add

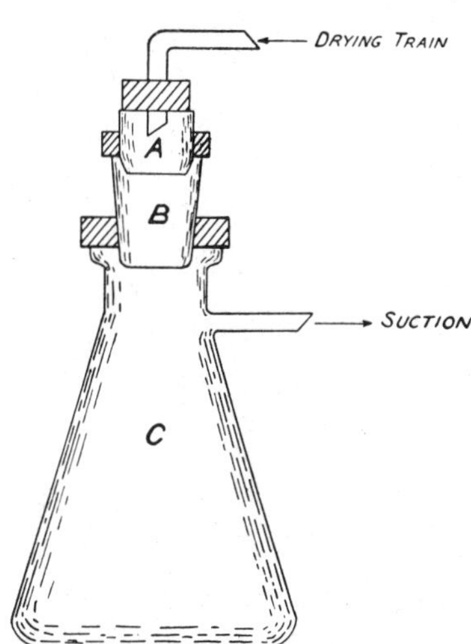

FIG. 16:01—Apparatus for drying pentabromacetone by aspiration

ca 20 mL H_2O to extn flask, evap. ether on steam bath, and carefully titr. with 0.1*N* $Ba(OH)_2$, using phthln. Transfer neutzd material to 200 mL vol. flask, dil. to vol., and mix. Pipet into 500 mL vol. flask amt of this Ba lactate soln contg equiv. of exactly 250 mg free lactic acid, dil. to vol., mix, and designate as *lactate std soln.* (2 mL equiv. to 1 mg lactic acid. To plot std curve, use freshly prepd soln.) Transfer 20 mL lactate std soln to 100 mL vol. flask, dil. to vol., and designate as *dil. lactate std soln* (10 mL equiv. to 1 mg lactic acid).

(**b**) *Carbon.*—To 10 g high-grade C (Nuchar C-190-N, Suchar, or Darco G60) in 600 mL beaker, add ca 200 mL H_2O and 30 mL 1*N* HCl, and keep on steam bath 20 min, agitating continuously with air passed thru cotton. Filter on buchner and suck as dry as possible, tamping with flat-end rod. Transfer cake to beaker, add ca 200 mL H_2O, mix thoroly, and refilter. Repeat washing and filtering twice, and dry at 100°.

(**c**) *Ferric chloride soln.*—Dissolve 2 g $FeCl_3.6H_2O$ in H_2O, add 5 mL 1*N* HCl, and dil. to 200 mL.

16.028 ***Preparation of Solution***

(**a**) *Liquid, whole and skim milks.*—Weigh 50 g into 100 mL vol. flask.

(**b**) *Dried, whole and skim milks.*—Weigh 5 g into 100 mL beaker, and using heavy stirring rod, make into smooth paste with H_2O. Transfer mixt. to 100 mL vol. flask with ca 50 mL H_2O.

(**c**) *Cream and ice cream.*—Weigh 20 g into 100 mL vol. flask and add ca 50 mL H_2O.

(**d**) *Sweetened condensed milk.*—Weigh 25 g into 100 mL beaker and transfer to 100 mL vol. flask with ca 50 mL H_2O.

(**e**) *Evaporated milk.*—Weigh 25 g into 100 mL vol. flask and add ca 50 mL H_2O.

To mixts add 6 mL 1*N* H_2SO_4 and mix, avoiding vigorous agitation. Add 5 mL *20% phosphotungstic acid soln* (1 mL for cream and 2 mL for ice cream) and dil. to vol. with H_2O. Mix, and filter thru folded paper.

(**f**) *Butter.*—Weigh 20 g into centrf. bottle, add 25 mL H_2O, and warm on steam bath. Neutze with 1*N* NaOH, using phthln. Cool, add 50 mL ether, and mix well, avoiding vigorous agitation. Add 50 mL pet ether, mix well, and centrf. Draw off ether layer as completely as possible by siphon with lower end bent upward. Repeat extn, using 25 mL of each ether. Place bottle on steam bath to remove most of remaining ethers. Transfer residue in bottle to 100 mL vol. flask, add 3 mL 1*N* H_2SO_4, and mix. Cool mixt., and ppt proteins with *20% phosphotungstic acid soln,*

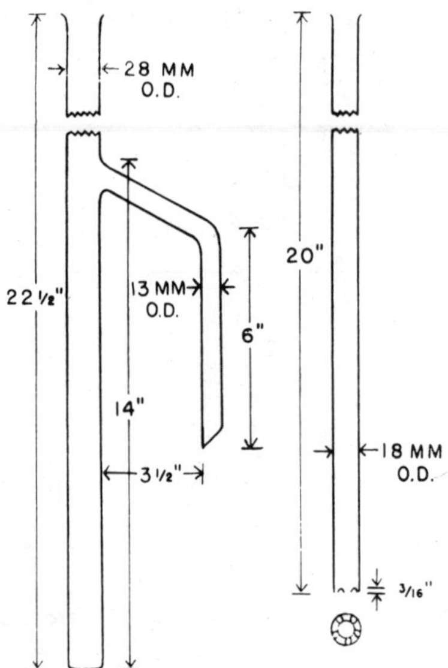

FIG. 16:02—Liquid extractor

adding reagent dropwise until pptn stops. Dil. to vol., mix by shaking, and filter thru folded paper.

16.029 *Preparation of Standard Curve*

Transfer from buret to vol. flasks, graduated at 50 and 55 mL, vols of std solns in left-hand column of Table **16:01**. Right-hand column gives mg of lactic acid in 40 mL filtrate from each sample after C treatment described below, and that will therefore be read in spectrophtr. Blank using 40 mL H_2O in place of lactate soln must be included in each series.

To each flask, including blank, add 6.6 mL 0.1*N* HCl and H_2O until vol. is ca 40 mL. Now add 200±1 mg prepd C, shake, and keep on steam bath 10 min, mixing frequently. Cool, dil. to 55 mL mark with H_2O at room temp., and promptly filter thru quant. paper, pouring back until clear.

Transfer 40 mL of each clear filtrate to 50 mL vol. flask, painted black or wrapped in black paper. As 40 mL filtrate used contains only 4.8 mL acid added during C treatment, add 1.2 mL 0.1*N* HCl. (Total of 6 mL 0.1*N* HCl is required in flask.) Pipet 5 mL $FeCl_3$ soln into one flask at time, dil. to vol., and mix. Pour soln into 1 cm quartz cell and det. wavelength of max. *A* on recording spectrophtr between 350 and 600 nm, using baseline correction at 600 nm. If recording spectrophtr is not available, manually

Table 16:01 Preparation of Dilutions for Standard Curve

Soln to be Transferred to 50–55 mL Vol. Flask, mL	Lactic Acid in 40 mL Aliquot, mg
dil. lactate std soln	
6.90	0.5
13.80	1.0
27.60	2.0
lactate std soln	
8.25	3.0
11.00	4.0
13.75	5.0
16.50	6.0
19.25	7.0
22.00	8.0
24.75	9.0
27.50	10.0
30.25	11.0
33.00	12.0

scan region around 365 nm to det. wavelength of max. *A*. Read all std solns at this wavelength against blank set at 0 *A*. (On exposure to direct light, color fades, but protected as provided it is stable for number of hr.) From readings obtained, prep. std curve, plotting mg lactic acid as abscissa and scale readings as ordinates. (Large-scale graph paper is recommended to permit more accurate interpolations.)

Recheck wavelength of max. *A* and std curve occasionally and whenever new batch of C or $FeCl_3$ is used. If different, adjust spectrophtr or prep. new std curve at new wavelength of max. *A*.

16.030 *Extraction*

(*Caution: See* **51.011**, **51.039**, and **51.054**.)

Place 50 mL prepd filtrate and 0.5 mL H_2SO_4 (1+1) in inner tube of extractor and connect to longest bulb-type condenser available, having outlet ≥13 mm id to minimize ether regurgitation. Run H_2O thru condenser at max. condensation efficiency. Connect extn flask contg 200 mL ether, and lower flask slowly onto preheated heating mantle or hot plate to prevent superheating the ether. Protect extractor from heat of hot plate by upright sheet of asbestos and ext all the lactic acid.

When ether in extn flask is kept at rapid boiling and condenser H_2O is cold enough to let condensed ether return to extn flask in steady stream, extn for 3 hr delivers all the lactic acid. When this rate of extn cannot be maintained because of high temp. of H_2O passing thru condenser, continue extn until equiv. of 7500 mL ether has passed thru soln. Time required, *T*, established for each set of new conditions, is calcd from 2 factors: *x*, vol. ether necessary to fill extractor to overflowing at side-arm, which is constant for each app.; and *y*, time in min required for vol. *x* to pass from extn flask and fill extractor.

To det. *x*, place 50 mL H_2O and 0.5 mL H_2SO_4 (1+1) in extractor. With extractor held upright, carefully pour ether from graduate into inner tube until it just starts passing out of side-arm. Det. *y* in ordinary course of starting each detn. With stopwatch, record interval from time ether first drops from condenser and falls into inner tube to time first drops return to extn flask from overflow into side-arm. Time, *T*, necessary for 7500 mL to pass thru app. = 7500 y/x. Calcd *T*. holds only if rate of boiling and condensing is const thruout extn period.

16.031 *Determination*

To flask contg ether ext add 20 mL H_2O and expel ether on steam bath. Do not let flask remain on steam bath after ether is expelled. Neutze with *satd* $Ba(OH)_2$ *soln*, using phthln. Wash into 110 mL vol. flask with alcohol until vol. is ca 90 mL. Heat almost to boiling on steam bath, cool, dil. to vol. with alcohol, and filter thru quant. paper. To expel alcohol, evap. 100 mL filtrate to ca 10 mL, add ca 50 mL H_2O, and again evap. to ca 10 mL (or evap. the 100 mL filtrate to dryness on steam bath).

Add, from buret, 6.6 mL 0.1*N* HCl and transfer contents of beaker with H_2O to 50–55 mL vol. flask until vol. is ca 40 mL. Prep. blank contg 6.6 mL 0.1*N* HCl dild to ca 40 mL with H_2O. Add 200 mg prepd C, mix immediately, and keep on steam bath 10 min, mixing frequently. Cool, dil. to 55 mL mark with H_2O at room temp., and filter thru quant. paper, pouring back until clear.

Transfer 10 mL filtrate to 50 mL *black vol. flask.* (Total of 6 mL 0.1*N* HCl must be in flask; 10 mL filtrate contains 1.2 mL 0.1*N* HCl from C treatment; therefore, add 4.8 mL addnl acid.) Add 5 mL $FeCl_3$ soln from buret or pipet, dil. to vol., and mix. (After color develops, dilg to reduce color intensity is not permissible.) Fill 1 cm quartz cell with soln and read in spectrophtr at wavelength of max. *A* against blank set at 0 *A*.

Det. amt lactic acid present in the 10 mL aliquot from std curve. If amt lactic acid in 10 mL portion is <2 mg, repeat detn on 40 mL portion of remaining filtrate. The 40 mL aliquot contains 4.8 mL 0.1*N* HCl; therefore, add 1.2 mL acid. Report lactic acid in mg/100 g.

mg Lactic acid in ether ext = *Z*
= mg read × (55/10 (or 40)) × (110/100).

mg Lactic acid/100 g = *Z*
× (mL sample diln/mL aliquot for extn) × (100/g sample).

Total Solids

16.032 ***Method I—Official Final Action***

Weigh 2.5–3 g prepd sample, **16.020**, into weighed flat-bottom dish ≥5 cm diam.; use ca 5 g and Pt dish if ash is to be detd on same portion. Heat on steam bath 10–15 min, exposing max. surface of dish bottom to live steam; then heat 3 hr in air oven at 98–100°. Cool in desiccator, weigh quickly, and report % residue as total solids.

16.033 ***Method II—(Approximate) Procedure***

Det. sp gr of milk with Quévenne lactometer (reading top of meniscus), observe temp., and correct reading *L* to 60°F by **52.023**. Calc. total solids either from formula 0.25 *L* + 1.2 *F*, in which *F* = % fat in milk, or from **52.022**.

16.034 ***Infrared Method—Official First Action***

See **16.087**.

16.035 Ash (*5*)—Official Final Action

Into suitable Pt dish weigh ca 5 g prepd sample, **16.020**, and evap. to dryness on steam bath. Ignite in furnace at ≤550° until ash is C-free. Cool in desiccator, weigh, and calc. % ash.

16.036 Total Nitrogen—Official Final Action

Transfer 5 g sample to Kjeldahl digestion flask and proceed as in **2.057**. % N × 6.38 = % "protein."

Dye Binding Method I (6)—Official Final Action

16.037 ***Reagents***

(**a**) *Purified Acid Orange 12.*—Dissolve 100 g dye in 400 mL boiling H_2O and stir in 400 mL boiling denatured alcohol. Let cool at 0–5° ca 15 hr. Filter thru buchner, wash once with cold alcohol, and continue suction until alcohol is removed. Dry at 125°. Repeat recrystn and dry in vac. oven at 100°.

(**b**) *Reagent dye soln.*—(*1*) *Formulation I.*—Dissolve 1.300 g (corrected for assay) twice recrystd Acid Orange 12 in 1 L 0.05*M* phosphate buffer, (**d**). (*2*) *Formulation II**.—Dissolve 1.250 g (corrected for assay) twice recrystd Acid Orange 12 in 1 L soln contg 60 mL HOAc and 10 g oxalic acid.

Make assay correction by calcg dye concn, *c*, in soln from *A*, using equation $c = A/(5.90 \times b)$, where *b* is mm path length of cell. Check soln further against either milk of known protein content or previous valid dye soln. (Same dye formulation must be used for assay and calibration.)

(**c**) *Reference dye soln.*—Dissolve 0.600 g twice recrystd Acid Orange 12 and 1 mL propionic acid in ca 900 mL H_2O. Dil. to 1 L with H_2O. Correct for assay as in (**b**) above.

(Recrystd dye and solns available from U D Corporation, 1898 Flatiron Ct, Boulder, CO 80301.)

* Official First Action as an alternative for, but not interchangable with, Formulation I.

(**d**) *0.05 M phosphate buffer.*—pH 1.8–1.9. Dissolve 3.4 g KH_2PO_4, 3.4 mL H_3PO_4 (1 (85%) + 1), 60 mL HOAc, 1 mL propionic acid, and 2 g oxalic acid in ca 800 mL H_2O. Dil. to 1 L with H_2O.

16.038 ***Apparatus***

(**a**) *Spectrophotometer.*—Photoelec. colorimeter or spectrophtr set at 480 nm. Use buffer dilns of reagent dye soln representing 0.350, 0.600, 0.750, and 0.850 g/L to calibrate spectrophtr. Plot *A* against concn to use as calibration chart.

(**b**) *Short-path cell.*—Cell with path length ca 0.3 mm; flow-thru type is convenient. Measure A_s at 370 nm of 0.0400 g/L K_2CrO_4 in 0.05*N* KOH. Calc. path length in mm, *b*, from $b = A_s/0.09914$. Arrange drain tube, and supply tube if any, according to manufacturer's instructions to ensure proper flow and liq. levels.

Suitable colorimeter with short-path, flow-thru cell, and calibration curve are available from U D Corporation.

(**c**) *Automatic pipet.*—Adjust to deliver 40.44 g reagent dye soln at 20° (equiv. to 39.887 g H_2O; 40 mL). Adjust so that 10 successive deliveries are all within 40.44±0.02 g by wt.

(**d**) *Syringe.*—Stdze sampling syringe to deliver 2.24 mL at 20° (equiv. to 2.2337 g H_2O).

(**e**) *Polyethylene plastic bag.*—6 oz, Whirlpak (available from Fisher Scientific Co.), or equiv.

16.039 ***Preparation of Samples***

(**a**) *Fluid milk, ice cream mix.*—Use as received.

(**b**) *Buttermilk, half-and-half, chocolate drink.*— Warm to 35–38° and agitate thoroly.

(**c**) *Nonfat dry milk* (*NFDM*).—Use as powder or reconstitute as follows: Weigh plastic bag to nearest 0.5 mg. Add 1 level tablespoon NFDM (ca 7.5 g) and reweigh. Add ca 75 mL (ca 60°) H_2O. Seal bag and shake vigorously 3 min. Let cool to room temp. Do not use H_2O bath. Reweigh. Refrigerate overnight. Reconstitute new portion of NFDM sample for each replicate.

16.040 ***Determination***

Zero spectrophtr. Adjust gain so that ref. dye soln, (**c**), reads 42%*T* at 480 nm. Place 2.24 mL milk, buttermilk, or half-and-half, 2.5–2.8 mL chocolate drink or reconstituted NFDM, from syringe, or 2.0–2.3 g ice cream mix or 0.22–0.24 g NFDM powder in 2 oz squeeze-type polyethylene dispenser bottle with fitted spun glass paper inside cap. Det. sample wt to 0.5 mg. Add 40.44 g reagent dye soln, (**b**), to bottle by automatic pipet. Shake vigorously 30 sec, except shake bottle contg NFDM powder 3 min. Reset ref. dye soln reading at 42%*T*, if necessary. Drop filtrate from dispenser bottle into cell funnel and draw into cell. When reading is const, record to nearest 0.1%, avoiding parallax. Check spectrophtr gain. If reading is not 42% with ref. dye soln, adjust instrument, and reread sample.

All solns must be 25±1° when placed in cell. Measure temp. before reading; soln warms while in instrument.

16.041 ***Calculations***

(**a**) *For formulation I.*—Using calibration chart prepd for instrument, det. dye concn (mg/mL) in sample filtrate from observed reading. Vol. = (1/1.012) × (g sample + 40.44); mg dye not bound = vol. × dye concn; mg bound dye = 52 mg dye available − mg dye not bound. Protein in mg = mg bound dye/0.312.

% Protein = mg protein/(g sample × 10).

% Protein in NFDM = % protein in reconstituted NFDM × g reconstituted NFDM prepd/g NFDM sample used.

(**b**) *For formulation II.*—Using calibration chart prepd for instrument, det. dye concn (mg/mL) in sample filtrate from observed reading.

% Protein = (1.250 − sample dye concn)/0.1824.

Dye Binding Method II (7)—Official First Action

16.042 Reagents and Apparatus

(**a**) *Reagent dye solns.*—(*1*) *Working soln.*—Dissolve 9.0–9.5 g Amido Black 10B (available from Merck and Co., Inc.) in ca 3 L H_2O by heating to ca 70°. Sep. dissolve 158.40 g citric acid.H_2O, 19.80 g $Na_2HPO_4.2H_2O$, and 3 g thymol in ca 2 L H_2O. Add resulting buffer soln to dye soln. Add exactly 10 kg H_2O. Let dye soln stand overnight before use. (*2*) *Reference std soln.*—Dil. 1 part working soln with 2.5 parts (w/w) H_2O.

(**b**) *Spectrophotometer.*—Photoelec. colorimeter or spectrophtr set at 620 nm with 0–100 scale and nonlinear protein scale from 2.5 to 5.5% (such as ProMilk Mark II app. or automatic Pro-Milk PMA manufactured by Foss Electric Co., Hillerod, Denmark); protein extremes correspond to ca 18 and 84, resp., on 0–100 scale.

(**c**) *Short path cell.*—Flow-thru, with ca 0.2 mm path length.

(**d**) *Automatic pipet.*—Adjustable to deliver ca 20 g reagent working soln at 20°. Adjust to maintain agreement of results with Kjeldahl method, **16.036**.

(**e**) *Syringe.*—Adjust to deliver 1.00 g H_2O at 20°.

(**f**) *Pneumatic pressure filter.*—App. for using slight air pressure to force sample-reagent mixt. thru Fiberglass filter and filtrate into cell.

(Suitable equipment ((**a**)–(**f**)) is available from Foss America, Inc., Rt 82, Fishkill, NY 12524.)

16.043 ***Start-Up***

Zero spectrophtr using 0–100 scale. Dispense reagent working soln thru filter into cell according to manufacturer's directions. If reading is not 0±0.25 scale division, adjust zero control. Dispense std ref. soln thru filter into cell according to manufacturer's instructions. Adjust gain control to obtain reading of 45 on 0–100 scale. Repeat every 50 samples.

(If either gain or zero control is adjusted, repeat above steps until both readings are correct without further adjustment. This constitutes double-scale expansion.)

16.044 ***Determination***

Install clean filter in mixing tube on filtration app. Place 1 mL prepd sample, **16.039**, in tube, using syringe. Dispense 20 mL ref. dye soln into mixing tube. Mix according to manufacturer's directions. Apply air pressure (*e.g.*, from squeeze bulb) to force filtrate thru filter and into cell. Release pressure and read protein content from 2.5–5.5 scale. Remove and clean mixing tube, and renew filter according to manufacturer's directions.

16.045 ***Calibration***

Det. protein content, **16.036**, of ca 10 milk samples of type to be analyzed contg as wide a range of protein contents as possible. Perform each detn in triplicate.

Analyze known milk samples by **16.042–16.044**. If mean difference between methods is >0.02%protein, adjust vol. of ref. dye soln delivered by dispenser. Increase dye vol. if values from **16.044** are high relative to **16.036** and decrease vol. if low. Test known milk daily as check on validity of calibration.

Complete recalibration is necessary in event of disassembly, replacement, or repair of either sample syringe or dye-dispensing syringe; adjustments or repair to any part of photometric system, other than zero and gain adjustments referred to in **16.043**; or use of new batch of reagent or ref. dye solns.

16.046 ***Infrared Method—Official First Action***

See **16.083–16.084**.

Casein—Official Final Action

(Make detn while milk is fresh or nearly so. If delayed >24 hr, add HCHO to milk (1:2500) and keep mixt. cool.)

16.047 ***Method I***

Place 10 g sample in beaker with 90 mL H_2O at 40–42° and immediately add 1.5 mL HOAc (1+9). Stir and let stand 3–5 min. Decant on acid-washed filter, wash by decanting 2 or 3 times with cold H_2O, and transfer ppt to filter. Wash once or twice on filter. (Filtrate should be clear, or nearly so.) If first portions of filtrate are not clear, refilter, and finish washing ppt. Retain filtrate for detn of albumin, **16.050**. Det. N in washed ppt and paper as in **2.057**, and multiply result by 6.38 to obtain equiv. of casein.

To preserved sample of milk, add HOAc (1+9) dropwise with stirring, and continue addn until liq. above ppt becomes clear, or very nearly so.

Method II (8)

16.048 ***Reagent***

Pipet 250 mL 1*N* HOAc into 1 L vol. flask. Add 125 mL CO_2-free 1*N* NaOH, dil. to vol. with CO_2-free H_2O, and mix thoroly.

16.049 ***Determination***

Pipet 20 mL sample into 100 mL vol. flask. Add 50 mL reagent, mix, dil. to vol. with H_2O, and shake well. Set flask in 50—60° H_2O (*not* >60°) for 15 min. Cool to room temp., add 0.5 g Celite analytical filter-aid, shake thoroly, and filter clear thru suitable folded paper, avoiding evapn during filtration. Det. N, *x*, in 50 mL clear filtrate, and det. total N, *y*, in 10 mL of the milk. $(y - x) \times 6.38$ = casein in 10 mL milk. Report g casein/100 mL milk, or divide g/100 mL by density of milk and report as % by wt.

16.050 Albumin—Official Final Action

Exactly neutze filtrate obtained in **16.047** with 10% NaOH soln, add 0.3 mL HOAc (1+9), and heat on steam bath until albumin is completely pptd. Collect ppt on acid-washed filter, wash with cold H_2O, and det. N as in **2.057**. N × 6.38 = albumin.

Protein-Reducing Substances (*9*)—Official Final Action

(Complete analyses same day they are begun. Do not permit tests to stand too long after cooling or after filtration. Oxidizing or reducing fumes (H_2S, Cl, HNO_3, etc.) must be absent from laboratory during detn.)

16.051 ***Reagents***

(**a**) *Phthalate buffer soln.*—pH 5.6. Dissolve 2.0 g NaOH in H_2O and dil. to 250 mL. Dissolve 10.2 g KH phthalate in H_2O and dil. to 250 mL. Mix 159 mL NaOH soln with 200 mL phthalate soln and dil. to 800 mL in graduate. Adjust to pH 5.6 by addn of NaOH or phthalate soln.

(**b**) *Potassium ferricyanide soln.*—1%. Dissolve 10 g $K_3Fe(CN)_6$ in H_2O and dil. to 1 L. Discard if soln appears green or contains blue ppt. Prep. new std curve with each new batch of reagent.

(**c**) *Ferric chloride soln.*—0.1%. Dissolve 0.1 g or 0.1 mL liquefied portion of $FeCl_3.6H_2O$ in 100 mL H_2O. Prep. fresh daily.

16.052 ***Apparatus***

(**a**) *Centrifuge tubes.*—50 mL graduated, Pyrex, conical red line, Corning No. 8100.

(**b**) *Spectrophotometer.*—For use in visible range, with matched set of 10 mm Corex cells.

16.053 ***Preparation of Standard Curve***

Weigh 0.1147 g $K_4Fe(CN)_6.3H_2O$ just before use and dil. to 1 L with H_2O. Dil. 50 mL to 100 mL in vol. flask (1 mL = 0.05 mg $K_4Fe(CN)_6$). Pipet 0, 0.5, 1.0, 1.5, 2.0, 2.5, 3.0, 3.5, and 4 mL of the dil. soln into series of clean, dry test tubes. Pipet in H_2O to give total vol. of 5.0 mL. To each tube add 5 mL of "blank soln" prepd as follows: Dil. 3 mL *satd urea soln* to 15 mL with H_2O; add 5 mL phthalate buffer soln, 5 mL $K_3Fe(CN)_6$ soln, (**b**), and 5 mL *10% trichloroacetic acid* soln. Mix with stirring rod.

At convenient intervals add 1 mL of the $FeCl_3$ soln to each tube, mix, and after exactly 10 min read in spectrophtr set to read 100%*T* at 610 nm with control soln (0.0 mL $K_4Fe(CN)_6$ soln). Plot %*T* against mg $K_4Fe(CN)_6$ on semilog paper.

16.054 ***Determination***

Store samples preferably at ca 3°. Frozen or preserved samples are unsuitable for test.

Mix sample thoroly by pouring into container and back until homogeneous. Pipet 15 mL sample into 50 mL graduated centrf. tube contg 15 mL H_2O. Add 3 mL 5% HOAc soln, stir thoroly, and centrf. 5 min at 1000–1500 rpm. Decant supernate. (Small amt of floating curd may be disregarded; if sample contains excessive cream, curd will float and supernate cannot be decanted. Discard test and remix sample thoroly.) Wash ppt twice with 15 mL portions H_2O, each time mixing ppt with rod, centrfg 5 min, and decanting.

To ppt and to clean centrf. tube as blank, add 3 mL satd urea soln and then dil. to 15 mL with H_2O. Stir thoroly, add 5 mL phthalate buffer soln and 5 mL 1% $K_3Fe(CN)_6$ soln, and stir. Place in 70° H_2O bath exactly 20 min and cool in ice-H_2O.

When cool, add 5 mL 10% trichloroacetic acid soln, stir, and filter thru 11 cm Whatman No. 40 paper, or equiv. Use first few mL filtrate to wash sides and bottom of receiver, and discard. Filter remainder of soln and let drain completely; then refilter if cloudy.

Add 5 mL H_2O to clean, dry test tube and add 5 mL clear filtrate. Add 1 mL 0.1% $FeCl_3$ soln to develop color. Stir, and let stand exactly 10 min. Read in spectrophtr set to read 100%*T* at 610 nm against blank. With series of samples, add $FeCl_3$ soln at convenient intervals to permit readings 10 min after addn. From std curve, det. amt of reducing substances as mg $K_4Fe(CN)_6$ and calc. to 100 mL milk basis by multiplying by 40 (100/2.5 mL equiv. aliquot).

Lactose

Polarimetric Method (10)—Official Final Action

16.055 ***Reagents***

(**a**) *Acid-mercuric nitrate soln.*—Dissolve Hg in twice its wt HNO_3 and dil. with 5 vols H_2O. Or—

(**b**) *Mercuric iodide soln.*—Dissolve 33.2 g KI and 13.5 g $HgCl_2$ in 200 mL HOAc and 640 mL H_2O.

16.056 ***Determination***

Weigh 65.8 g (2 normal wt) milk into each of 2 vol. flasks, 100 and 200 mL, resp. To each flask add 20 mL acid-$Hg(NO_3)_2$ soln or 30 mL HgI_2 soln. To 100 mL flask add *5% phosphotungstic acid soln* to mark, and to the 200 mL flask add 15 mL 5% phosphotungstic acid soln and dil. to mark with H_2O. Shake both flasks frequently during 15 min, filter thru dry filter, and polarize. (It is preferable to read soln from 200 mL flask in 400 mm tube to reduce error of reading; soln from 100 mL flask may be read in 200 mm tube.) Calc. % lactose in sample as follows: (1) Subtract reading of soln from 200 mL flask (using 400 mm tube) from reading of soln from 100 mL flask (using 200 mm tube); (2) multiply difference by 2; (3) subtract result from reading of soln from 100 mL flask; (4) divide result by 2.

16.057 ***Gravimetric Method—Official Final Action***

Dil. 25 g sample with 400 mL H_2O in 500 mL vol. flask. Add 10 mL $CuSO_4$ soln, **31.034(a)**, and ca 7.5 mL KOH soln of such concn that 1 vol. is just enough to completely ppt the Cu as hydroxide from 1 vol. of the $CuSO_4$ soln. (Instead, 8.8 mL 0.5*N* NaOH may be used. After addn of alkali soln, mixt. must still be acid and contain Cu in soln.) Dil. to vol., mix, filter thru dry filter, and det. lactose in aliquot of filtrate as in **31.038**. From **52.019** obtain wt lactose equiv. to wt Cu_2O.

16.058 ***Infrared Method—Official First Action***

See **16.085–16.086**.

Fat

16.059 ***Roese-Gottlieb Method (Reference Method) (11)—Official Final Action***

(Details of this method comply with method which has been agreed upon by International Dairy Federation, International Organization for Standardization, and AOAC for publication by each organization and which is published as international std in *FAO/WHO Code of Principles Concerning Milk and Milk Products and Associated Standards.*)

(*Caution: See* **51.011**, **51.039**, **51.054**, and **51.073**.)

Prep. as in **16.020** and weigh, to nearest mg, ca 10 g sample into fat-extn flask or tube. Add 1.25 mL NH_4OH (2 mL if sample is sour) and mix thoroly. Add 10 mL alcohol and mix well. Add 25 mL ether (all ether must be peroxide-free), stopper with cork or stopper (synthetic rubber) unaffected by usual fat solvs, and shake very vigorously 1 min. Cool, if necessary; add 25 mL pet ether (boiling range 30–60°) and repeat vigorous shaking. Centrf. flask at ca 600 rpm or let it stand until upper liq. is practically clear. Decant ether soln into suitable flask or metal dish. Wash lip and stopper of extn flask or tube with mixt. of equal parts of the 2 ethers and add washings to weighing flask or dish. Repeat extn of liq. remaining in flask or tube twice, using 15 mL of each solv. each time and adding H_2O if necessary, but omitting rinsing with mixed solvs after final extn. (Third extn is not necessary with skim milk.)

Evap. solvs completely on steam bath at temp. that does not cause spattering or bumping (boiling chips may be added). Dry fat to const wt in oven at $102 \pm 2°$ or vac. oven at 70–75° under pressure <50 mm Hg (6.7 kPa). Weigh cooled flask or dish, without wiping immediately before weighing. Remove fat completely from container with 15–25 mL warm pet ether, dry, and weigh as before. Loss in wt = wt fat. Correct wt fat by blank detn on reagents used. If blank is >0.5 mg, purify or replace reagents. Difference between duplicate detns obtained simultaneously by same analyst should be ≤0.03 g fat/100 g product.

Babcock Method (12)—Official Final Action

16.060 ***Apparatus***

(**a**) *Standard Babcock milk-test bottle.*—8%, 18 g, 6" milk-test bottle, total ht 150–165 mm (5.9–6.5"). Bottom of bottle is flat, and axis of neck is vertical when bottle stands on level surface. Quantity of milk for bottle is 18 g.

(*1*) *Bulb.*—Capacity of bulb to junction with neck must be ≥45 mL. Shape of bulb may be either cylindrical or conical. If cylindrical, od must be between 34 and 36 mm; if conical, od of base must be between 31 and 33 mm, and max. diam. between 35 and 37 mm.

(*2*) *Neck.*—Cylindrical and of uniform diam. from ≥5 mm below lowest graduation mark to ≥5 mm above highest mark. Top of neck is flared to diam. of ≥10 mm. Graduated portion of neck has length ≥63.5 mm and is graduated in whole %, 0.5%, and 0.1%, resp., from 0.0 to 8.0%. Tenths % graduations are ≥3 mm long; 0.5% graduations are ≥4 mm long and project 1 mm to left; and whole % graduations extend at least half-way around neck to right and project ≥2 mm to left of tenths % graduations. Each whole % graduation is numbered, with number placed to left of scale. Capacity of neck for each whole % on scale is 0.20 mL. Max. error of total graduation or any part thereof must not exceed vol. of smallest unit of graduation.

Each bottle must be constructed so as to withstand stress to which it will be subjected in centrf.

(*3*) *Testing.*—Hg and cork, alcohol and buret, and alcohol and brass plunger methods may be used for rapid testing of bottles, but accuracy of any questionable bottle must be detd by calibration with Hg (13.5471 g clean, dry Hg at 20° to be equal to 5% on scale of 18 g bottle and 10% on scale of 9 g bottle, **16.157(a)**), bottle having been previously filled to 0 with Hg.

(**b**) *Pipet.*—Std milk pipet conforms to following specifications:

	mm
Total length	≤330
Od of suction tube	6–8
Length of suction tube	130
Od of delivery tube (Must fit into bottle (**a**))	4.5–5.0
Length of delivery tube	100–120
Distance of graduation mark above bulb	15–45

Nozzle parallel with axis of pipet, but slightly constricted so as to discharge in 5–8 sec when filled with H_2O.

Graduation, to contain 17.6 mL H_2O at 20° when bottom of meniscus coincides with mark on suction tube.

Max. error in graduation, ≤0.05 mL. Pipet is to be marked "Holds 17.6 mL."

Test pipet by measuring from buret vol. H_2O (at 20°) which it holds up to graduation mark.

(**c**) *Acid measure.*— Device used to measure H_2SO_4, whether graduate or pipet attached to Swedish acid bottle, must be graduated to deliver 17.5 mL.

(**d**) *Centrifuge or "tester."*—Std centrf., however driven, must be constructed thruout and so mounted as to be capable, when filled to capacity, of rotating at necessary speed with min. vibration and without liability of causing injury or accident. It must be heated, elec. or otherwise, to temp. of ≥55° during centrfg. It must be provided with speed indicator, permanently attached, if possible. Proper rate of rotation may be detd by ref. to table below. By "diam. of wheel" is meant distance between inside bottoms of opposite cups measured thru center of rotation of centrf. wheel while cups are horizontally extended.

Diam of wheel, inches	*rpm*
14	909
16	848
18	800
20	759
22	724
24	693

(**e**) *Dividers or calipers.*—For measuring fat column.

(**f**) *Water bath for test bottles.*—Provided with thermometer and device to maintain temp. of 55–60°.

(**g**) *Reading light.*—As background when measuring fat columns. Light should be diffused (soft green color preferred) and provide illumination from angles above and below level of fat column. Attached magnification devices are suggested.

16.061 ***Determination***

With pipet, (**b**), transfer 18 g prepd sample, **16.020**, to milk-test bottle. Blow out milk in pipet tip ca 30 sec after free outflow ceases. Adjust milk to ca 22° and add portionwise ca 17.5 mL H_2SO_4 (sp gr 1.82–1.83 at 20°) tempered at 22±1°, washing all traces of milk into bulb. Immediately shake by rotation until all traces of curd disappear (reaction temp. should be 100–105°); place bottle in heated (ca 60°) centrf., counterbalance, and after proper speed is reached, centrf. 5 min. Add soft H_2O at 60°, or above, until bulb of bottle is filled. Centrf. 2 min. Add hot H_2O until liq. column approaches top graduation of scale. Centrf. 1 min longer at ca 60°. Transfer bottle to warm H_2O bath kept at 55–60° (preferably 57°), immerse it to level of top of fat column, and leave until column is in equilibrium and lower fat surface assumes final form (≥5 min). Remove bottle from bath, wipe it, and with aid of reading light, **16.060(g)**, use dividers or calipers to measure fat column, in terms of % by wt to nearest 0.05%, from lower surface to highest point of upper meniscus.

Fat column, at time of measurement, should be translucent, golden-yellow or amber, and free from visible suspended particles. Reject all tests in which fat column is milky or shows presence of curd or of charred matter, or in which reading is indistinct or uncertain; repeat test, adjusting vol. H_2SO_4 added.

16.062 ★ *Rapid Detergent Method for ★ Raw Milk (13)—Official Final Action*

See **16.055–16.057**, 11th ed.

AUTOMATED METHODS

(Following manufacturers have shown thru studies published in JAOAC that their instruments can meet indicated specifications:

Automated Method I: Mark III Industrial Model and Model UFM 100 with photometer and calibration units for each type of milk, manufactured by Foss Electric, Hillerod, Denmark and available from Foss America, Inc., PO Box 504, Fishkill, NY 12524; Anritsu milk-checker K373A, available from American Metering Systems, PO Box 129, Hopewell Junction, NY 12533.

Automated Method II: Technicon Instruments Corp.

Infrared Methods: "IRMA" Model Mark II, available from Accurate Metering Systems, Inc., 1731 Carmen Dr, Elk Grove Village, IL 60007; Milko-Scan Model 300 or 203, available from Foss America, Inc. and Foss Electric Canada, Ltd, 700 Campbell St, Cornwall, Ontario, Canada K6H 6C9; Multispec, available from Shields Instrument Ltd, Osbaldwick Industrial Estate, Osbaldwick, York YO1 3US, UK, and Berwind Instrument Group, Suite 378, 30100 Telegraph Rd, Birmingham, MI 48010.)

Automated Method I (14)—Official First Action

(All models applicable to raw, unhomogenized milk; Mark III Industrial Model and Anritsu Milk-Checker are also applicable to homogenized milk)

16.063 ***Principle***

Milk is homogenized to produce uniform-size fat globules, treated with EDTA soln to dil. sample and eliminate turbidity

★ Surplus method—*see* inside front cover.

caused by casein micelle, and passed thru photocell to measure light scattering of soln which is proportional to amt fat in milk. Amt of light passing thru photocell is registered on galvanometer calibrated to read % fat directly.

16.064 ***Apparatus and Reagents***

(**a**) *Instrument.*—Number of firms manufacture various model instruments based upon principle, **16.063**. It is imperative that individual instrument utilized meet performance requirements of **16.066** and is applicable to type of milk to be analyzed, i.e., raw unhomogenized or homogenized.

(**b**) *Sodium (tetra) ethylenediamine tetraacetate (EDTA) soln.*—Dissolve 45.0 g Na_4EDTA, 10.0 mL polysorbate 20 (Tween 20), and 7.6 g NaOH in 10 L H_2O, using container connected to tester with plastic hose.

16.065 ***Operation of Tester***

Sampling, homogenization, and heating are performed automatically, as may be mixing of EDTA. Most of mixt. purges instrument of previous sample. Mixt. flows into photometer where light at 600 nm passes thru mixt. and is automatically measured with galvanometer or digital readout in % fat when tester is calibrated by testing samples of milk by ref. method as in **16.066**.

16.066 ***Calibration of Tester***

(Sep. calibrations, using different calibration units and samples, are required for homogenized and unhomogenized milks.)

Test in triplicate 20 representative milks, ranging from 3 to 6% fat by **16.059** or **16.061** and tester. Calc. av. for each sample by each method to nearest 0.01%. Calc. std deviation of difference, S_D, as follows:

$$S_D = \sqrt{[\Sigma(D^2) - ((\Sigma D)^2/N)]/(N-1)}$$

where D = av. of results by **16.059** or **16.061** on sample minus av. of tester results on same sample, e.g.,

$$[(B_1 + B_2 + B_3)/3] - [(M_1 + M_2 + M_3)/3] = D;$$

where B = reading by **16.059** or **16.061** and M = reading by tester; and N = number of samples tested. If specification of 20 samples is exceeded, include all samples tested in calcns except for those for which an error in $\geqslant$1 detns can be proven.

Tester is properly calibrated when S_D so calcd is $\leqslant$0.10 for individual cow sample or $\leqslant$0.06 for herd or composite samples. Should S_D exceed these values, adjust vol. EDTA soln and/or elect. input to galvanometer of tester in accordance with manufacturer's instructions for calibration and operation.

During any calendar day of use, make performance check consisting of comparison of results obtained on 1 milk bulk sample, using both tester and **16.059** or **16.061**. If difference is $>$0.10% fat, repeat detn on 3 addnl samples. If av. differences of 3 addnl samples is $>$0.10% fat, recalibrate tester.

16.067 ***Collection and Preparation of Samples***

See **16.019–16.020**.

16.068 ***Determination***

Bring sample(s) in loosely stoppered bottle to 35–40° in H_2O bath. Mix by pouring gently from original container into another container. Repeat 4 times. Do *not* mix all samples at once and then let them stand before testing. *Immediately* after mixing sample, obtain readings as in **16.065**.

Automated Method II (15)—Official First Action

(Applicable to raw, whole, mixed herd milk)

16.069 ***Principle***

Raw whole milk is dild with H_2O contg surfactant, mixed with HOAc contg different surfactant, serially dild with H_2O contg surfactant, heated to 60°, and passed thru flowcell to measure light scattering of soln, which is proportional to amt dispersed fat in milk. T is measured at 600 nm on instrument calibrated to read % fat directly. Response is linear in range 2–6%. Presence of formalin results in slight pos. bias, $<$0.04% fat; $HgCl_2$ and $K_2Cr_2O_7$ have no effect.

16.070 ***Apparatus***

Automatic analyzer.—See Fig. **16:03**. AutoAnalyzer II with following modules (Technicon Instruments Corp.): Sampler IV with rotary mixer; proportioning pump; manifold cartridge with temp. controlled heating bath; colorimeter with flowcell and 600 nm filters; and recorder with chart paper calibrated 0–10% in 0.05%.

16.071 ***Reagents***

(**a**) *Milk fat reagent.*—Mix 1.6 mL dialkyl quaternary ammonium chloride (Arquad 2C-75; Armak Chem. Div., PO Box 1805, Chicago, IL 60690) and ca 500 mL HOAc in 1 L vol. flask, dil. to

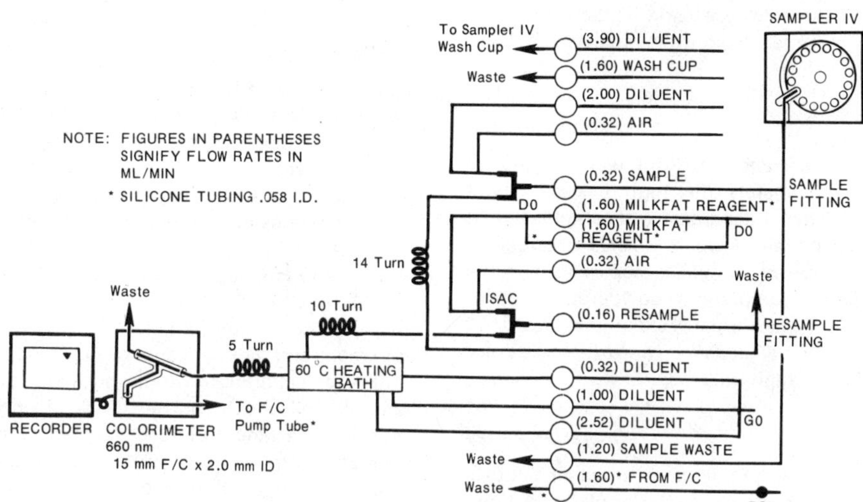

FIG. 16:03—Flow diagram for determination of fat in milk

vol. with HOAc, and mix. (Prepd reagent is available from Technicon Instruments Corp., No. Tol-5049.) Store at room temp. in glass bottles. Rate of consumption is 4.8 mL/sample. Do *not* let this reagent come in contact with Tygon tubing.

(b) *Stock diluent.*—Mix equal vols Triton X-100 (Rohm & Haas Co.) and absolute MeOH.

(c) *Milk diluent.*—Dil. 2 mL stock diluent, **(b)**, to 1 L with H_2O and mix. Prep. fresh just before use. Rate of consumption is 6.0 mL/sample.

16.072 ***Preparation of Standards***

(a) *High std milk.*—Approx. 4%. Det. fat content by **16.059** or **16.061**.

(b) *Low std milk.*—1.5–2.0% fat. Dil. high std milk with skim milk. Det. fat content by **16.059** or **16.061**.

16.073 ***Start-Up Procedure***

Turn on colorimeter and heating bath. (These may be left on when app. is used daily.) Place milk fat reagent line in milk fat reagent reservoir, and start proportioning pump. After 5 min, insert H_2O lines into milk diluent and let reagents pump 10 addnl min. During this period, invert PC1 valve, let fill ⅓ with liq., and reposition. Check bubble pattern for uniform segmentation; check for leaks; maintain heating bath at 60±1°. Turn on chart drive and pen recorder switches. Operate app. at max. energy for sample and ref. flowcells and adjust mech. aperture, if necessary, to obtain 90–95% deflection. Proceed as in **16.075**.

16.074 ***Shut-Down Procedure***

After last sample curve has appeared on recorder, turn off sampler and pump reagents thru system 10 min more. Turn recorder off. Remove H_2O lines and let milk fat reagent pump 1 min more. Remove milk fat reagent line and let system pump until lines are dry. Turn off pump and remove platen.

16.075 ***Calibration***

Place low std milk in first 2 positions of sampler tray and high std milk in next 2 positions. Turn on sampler. (Approx. 6 min is required for first sample to reach flowcell.) During this period, adjust elec. 0 to record same value as detd for low std milk. When first low std milk reaches recorder, use baseline control to adjust recorder to read predetd fat content. If necessary, adjust as second low milk std passes thru flowcell. When high milk std passes thru flowcell, use "std cal" control to adjust recorder to read predetd value. If necessary, adjust for second high fat sample. Proper recorder response is indicated by level peak for ca 15 sec.

16.076 ***Determination***

Prep. sample as in **16.020**. Transfer 6–7 mL warm aliquot to sampler tray test tube, immediately after high milk std. About 1.8 mL is aspirated into system. Pace transfer of samples to test tubes to avoid visible formation of cream layer. For duplicate analyses, transfer freshly mixed sample to sep. sample tube. Read result from chart paper. Sampler may be operated at 60/hr if fat content varies <0.5%. Place high milk std after every 10–12 samples to check calibration. *Use baseline control,* if necessary to adjust to predetd value of high milk std.

16.077 ***Operating Notes***

Drift of baseline caused by accumulation of small air bubbles in flowcell may be eliminated by momentarily pinching flow-thru line.

Erratic response may be due to accumulation of milk solids in sample line, resample line, and waste milk line just beyond roller contact. Pinching lines at point of accumulation will correct problem.

After prolonged use, fat may accumulate on sampler stirrer. Rinse stirrer with water from wash bottle.

Infrared Milk Analysis (*16*)
Interim Official First Action

16.078 ***Principle***

Analysis of milk by IR is based on absorption of IR energy at specific wavelengths by carbonyl groups in ester linkages of fat molecules (5.723 μm), by peptide linkages between amino acids of protein molecules (6.465 μm), and by OH groups in lactose molecules (9.610 μm). Total solids are detd by assigning experimentally detd factor to percentage of all other solid milk components, and by adding this amt to total % fat, protein, and lactose. Analysis by IR is dependent on calibration against suitable std method. *See* "Definition of Terms and Explanatory Notes" item (24), for calcn of regression lines.

16.079 ***Performance Specifications***

Number of firms manufacture various model instruments based upon principle, **16.078.** It is imperative that individual instrument utilized meet following performance specifications, based upon analysis of 8 samples:

Std deviation of difference between duplicate instrument estimates:

Fat, protein, and lactose	≤0.02%	Total solids	≤0.04%

Mean difference between duplicate instrument estimates:

Fat, protein, and lactose	≤0.02%	Total solids	≤0.03%

Std deviation of difference between instrument estimates and values by ref. methods:

Fat (**16.059**), protein (**16.036**), and lactose (**16.056** or **16.057**)	≤0.06%	Total solids (**16.032**)	≤0.12%

Mean difference between instrument estimates and values by ref. methods:

Fat, protein, and lactose	≤0.05%	Total solids	≤0.09%

Calc. std deviation of difference as in **16.066**, where S_D = algebraic difference either between duplicate instrument estimates or between instrument estimates and values by ref. methods.

16.080 ***Precautions***

Differences in fat readings for homogenized and unhomogenized samples of same milk should be <0.05% to assure accurate results at high fat levels. If larger differences occur and servicing homogenizer does not correct fault, consult manufacturer. Changes in moisture vapor content of instrument console will cause changes in optical 0 and shift in calibration level. Replace desiccant frequently, preferably at end of each day, as 3–4 hr are required to restore equilibrium conditions. For best accuracy, calibrate with type of milk to be analyzed (herd, individual cow, homogenized, unhomogenized, market, etc.). Do not use mixts of cream and milk for calibration. Avoid abnormal (low lactose) milks for calibration. Single pumping of milk thru instrument sample cell should purge ≥99% of previous sample. To test purging efficiency, perform fat detns on H_2O and single pasteurized, homogenized whole milk in sequence: H_2O, H_2O, milk, milk, H_2O, etc., until total of 20 detns have been obtained. Calc.

$$\text{purging efficiency} = (\Sigma M_1 - \Sigma W_2) \times 100/(\Sigma M_2 - \Sigma W_2),$$

where M_1 and M_2 are first and second values for milk and W_2 second value for H_2O.

I. Fat

16.081 ***Calibration***

Before first calibration, check linearity of output signals. Mix accurately measured vols of H_2O and homogenized cream to prep. ca 8 mixts of known relative fat contents covering required range. Prep. samples as in **16.020**, and pump each mixt. into instrument twice, using second readings to prep. plot against relative concns. If plot is not linear, adjust as indicated in operating manual. Repeat measurements and adjustments until plot is linear.

If analyzing unhomogenized milks, check linearity again with ca 4 dilns of unhomogenized cream or high fat milk. If these mixts deviate significantly from linearity, *see* **16.080** and check differences between readings for homogenized and unhomogenized milk samples.

Det. % fat for series of ≥8 preanalyzed (**16.059**) milk samples of type to be analyzed (*see* **16.080**). Prep. samples as in **16.020** and analyze in triplicate. Compare averages of second and third instrument readings with std values and follow instructions in operating manual for required changes to calibration.

16.082 ***Determination***

Prep. sample as in **16.020**. Operate instrument in accordance with manufacturer's instructions.

II. Protein

16.083 ***Calibration***

Proceed as in **16.081**, first and last par., substituting Ca propionate soln (dissolve 15.0 g pure Ca propionate.H_2O in H_2O and dil. to 1 L with H_2O at 20°) for homogenized cream to prep. mixts of known relative concns from 0 to required max. for protein. Det. % protein for series of ≥8 preanalyzed (**16.036**) milk samples having range of protein content approx. that of population of milks to be analyzed. Prep samples as in **16.020** and analyze in triplicate. Compare averages of second and third instrument readings with std values and follow directions in operating manual for making required adjustments to calibration.

16.084 ***Determination***

Prep. sample as in **16.020**. Operate instrument according to manufacturer's instructions.

III. Lactose

16.085 ***Calibration***

Proceed as in **16.081**, par. 1, substituting lactose soln (dissolve 50.00 g lactose.H_2O and 0.25 g $HgCl_2$ in H_2O and dil. to 1 L with H_2O at 20°) for homogenized cream to prep. mixts of known relative concns ranging from 0 to required max. for lactose. Det. lactose for series of ≥8 preanalyzed (**16.052** or **16.053**) milk samples having range of lactose content approx. that of population of milks to be analyzed.

Prep. samples as in **16.020** and analyze in triplicate. Use averages of second and third values for each sample in estg calibration requirements. Adjust instrument controls, as directed in operating manual, to make $\Sigma L = \Sigma L'$, where L = instrument readings for lactose and L' = values from ref. method.

16.086 ***Determination***

Prep. sample as in **16.020**. Operate instrument according to manufacturer's instructions.

IV. Total Solids

16.087 ***Calibration***

Use std method **16.032** to det. % total solids for series of ≥8 milks. Det. % fat, % protein, and % lactose. Calc. mean difference for total solids $(TS) - F - P - L = a$, where F, P, and L are ests of fat, protein, and lactose, resp. For routine control of calibration, analyze addnl series of milks and adjust value for mean difference in accordance with accumulated data.

$$\text{Calc. \% total solids} = a + F + P + L.$$

16.088–16.096 ***Reserved***

Added Water

16.097 ***Acetic Serum Method (18)—Official Final Action***

(**a**) *Zeiss immersion refractometer reading.*—To 100 mL sample, measured at 20° into beaker, add 2 mL 25% HOAc (sp gr 1.035). Cover beaker with watch glass, keep in H_2O bath 20 min at 70°, then in ice-H_2O 10 min, and sep. curd from serum by rapid filtration thru small filter. Transfer portion of clear serum to refractometer beaker, place in constant temp. bath, and take refractometer reading when temp. of serum is exactly 20°, as detd by thermometer graduated in 0.1°. (Scale readings are identical on Bausch & Lomb refractometers except those with serial Nos. 4000–10,000, for which readings of 38.6 and 39.6 correspond, resp., to 39 and 40 on Zeiss instrument. (Zeiss scale = B & L scale × 1.0092.))

(**b**) *Ash.*—Transfer 25 mL serum to weighed flat-bottom Pt dish and evap. to dryness on H_2O bath. Heat over low flame (to avoid spattering) until contents are thoroly charred, place dish in furnace, and ignite to white ash at ≤500°. Cool and weigh. Express result as g/100 mL.

16.098 ***Copper Serum Method (19)—Official Final Action***

To 1 vol. $CuSO_4$ soln (72.5 g $CuSO_4.5H_2O$/L, adjusted if necessary to read 36 at 20° on scale of Zeiss immersion refractometer, or to sp gr of 1.0443 at 20/4°), add 4 vols milk. Shake well and filter. Det. refractometer reading of clear serum at 20°. (Scale readings are identical on Bausch & Lomb immersion refractometers except those with serial Nos. 4000–10,000 for which reading of 35.6 corresponds to 36 on Zeiss instrument.)

CRYOSCOPIC METHODS

Temps used in Hortvet scale for detg fp of milk were initially thought to be equiv. to Celcius scale. Subsequently, it has been shown that fp of std salt soln at −0.422°H is actually −0.406°C and the one at −0.621°H is −0.598°C, producing >3.7% error between the 2 scales. Most cryoscopes are calibrated in terms of °H but results are reported in °C. Original error, which has since led to use of this unconventional temp. scale, was made at time when methods for detg fps were not as precise as at present. Data in methods **16.099–16.108** have now been converted to °C as should all similar data in future. Convert °H to °C by formula:

$$°C = [(0.1915 \times (-°H)) - 0.0004785]/0.199,$$
$$°H = [(0.199 \times (-°C)) + 0.0004785]/0.1915,$$

where °H is absolute °H reading below fp of H_2O.

16.099 ★ Hortvet Method (20) ★
Official Final Action

See **16.086–16.088**, 12th ed.

Thermistor Method (21)—Official Final Action

16.100 ***Cryoscope***

Consists of cooling bath, sample agitator, seeding rod, thermistor probe (elec. resistance thermometer), and Wheatstone bridge and galvanometer, or taut band meter measuring circuit. Bath may be cooled by mech. or elec. means or by insulated ice-salt mixt. Sample may be immersed in cooling bath or bath may be "brought up" to sample mech. Observed fp value is read from measuring dial, calibrated in millidegrees C (0.001°C; more correctly, degrees Hortvet or "H"), when galvanometer or meter is nulled by rotation of dial.

Fill cooling bath at room temp. to proper level each time instrument is used. Proper coolant level is detd by observing coolant issuing from bath overflow or by visually checking coolant level, depending on the make and model of cryoscope. Cooling bath temp. should be −7 or −8±0.5°, depending on make of cryoscope, and temp. is measured by placing thermometer in empty sample well.

Locate thermistor probe, both horizontally and vertically, at midpoint of sample. Check location visually, using 2.5 mL H_2O in sample tube.

Amplitude of stirring wire should be great enough to assure uniform temp. in sample thruout detn and may be checked visually, using 2.5 mL H_2O in sample tube to which small amt of dust, powder, or dye has been added.

(App. available as Advanced Cryoscope from Advanced Instruments, Inc., 1000 Highland Ave, Needham Hts, MA 02194; as Precision Cryoscope from Precision Systems, Inc., 60 Union Ave, Sudbury, MA 01776; and as Fiske Cryoscope from Fiske Associates, Inc., Quaker Hwy, Junction Rt 146, Uxbridge, MA 01569.)

16.101 ***Preparation of Standards***

(Use distd H_2O recently boiled and cooled to 20° for prepn of stds.)

Prep. following sucrose primary stds or salt secondary stds. Det. fp values of salt stds as in (**b**).

(**a**) *−0.406°C (−0.422°H) Standard.*—(*1*) Weigh 7.0000 g NBS std sucrose sample SRM 17 into 100 mL vol. flask and dil. to vol. with H_2O; or (*2*) weigh 100 g H_2O into 100 mL vol. flask and add 0.6892 g reagent grade NaCl (dried to constant wt just before weighing).

(**b**) *−0.598°C (−0.621°H) Standard.*—(*1*) Weigh 10.0000 g NBS sucrose into 100 mL vol. flask and dil. to vol. with H_2O; or (*2*) weigh 100 g H_2O into 100 mL vol. flask and add 1.0206 g reagent grade NaCl.

(Secondary salt stds with fp values equiv. to 7 and 10% sucrose primary stds may be purchased from cryoscope manufacturers.)

Microorganisms attack sucrose after limited storage at refrigerator temps, changing fp value of primary stds. Salt (sucrose equiv.) secondary stds, stored in polyethylene bottles with screw caps, have long shelf life at room temp.; use these each time fp value detns are made. If it is suspected that salt secondary stds are in error, check them against *freshly* prepd sucrose primary stds. It is responsibility of the analyst to be certain that fp values of salt secondary stds are same as fp values of *freshly* prepd sucrose primary stds.

★ Surplus method—*see* inside front cover.

16.102 ***Calibration of Cryoscope***

(*See* introduction to **16.099**.)

Using calibration controls and fp values of stds, calibrate cryoscope to obtain correct "span" (0.598 − 0.406 = 0.192°C) and reference values (−0.598°C and −0.406°C). Follow directions in manufacturer's operating manual. Calibration controls and procedures vary with make and model of cryoscope but with all instruments 2 calibration controls (A and B or I and II) are adjusted, individually or in combination, so that 7 and 10% sucrose primary stds and/or sucrose equiv. salt secondary stds yield fp values of −0.406°C and −0.598°C, resp., with 0.192°C span.

16.103 ***Determination***

(If titratable acidity, **16.023**, is >0.18%, results may underest. actual amt of added H_2O in sample.)

Apply following technic in exactly same manner for both stds and sample to obtain valid sample fp value.

Check cooling bath level, cooling bath temp., stirring efficiency, and probe position in sample tube as in **16.100**.

Check ref. fp values and "span," using salt secondary stds or sucrose primary stds. If "span" is other than 0.192°C, recalibrate cryoscope as in **16.102**. If "span" is correct but reference fp values differ from known values of stds, it is not necessary to recalibrate cryoscope; simple arithmetic correction will give correct observed fp value of sample.

Using clean, dry syringe or pipet, measure 2–3 mL sample and transfer to clean, dry sample tube supplied by manufacturer. Set measuring dial to expected fp value. Place sample tube in cooling bath sample well or in operating head and lower operating head to position sample in cryoscope cooling bath.

Cool sample if not already being cooled above. Proper cooling is indicated by rapid and uniform (steady) movement of light spot or needle from right to left over scale of galvanometer or meter.

If cryoscope raises cooling bath to sample level, begin slow cooling at −1.5 to −2.0°, depending on extent of supercooling desired. If cryoscope immerses sample in cooling bath, do *not* isolate sample in air above cooling bath.

Seed sample at −2.0 or −3.0°, depending on make of cryoscope. Galvanometer spot or meter needle will jump to right as temp. of supercooled sample rises toward fp. Extent of supercooling (seeding point) must be same for sucrose primary stds or salt secondary stds as for milk samples.

Adjust galvanometer spot or meter needle to 0 if necessary. Switch galvanometer or meter to high sensitivity position. With temp. dial, keep galvanometer or meter nulled (reading 0). Galvanometer spot or meter needle will cease to move to right, remain steady at 0, and finally begin to move to left. Read fp value from measuring dial to nearest millidegree, while spot or needle is steady just before movement to left begins. Do *not* read fp value from measuring dial at some predetd time after seeding sample; always wait for movement of galvanometer spot or meter needle to left before recording fp value. Spot or needle will become steady and begin to move to left sooner with stds than with milk samples. Check 0 point of galvanometer or meter.

16.104 ***Interpretation***

If fp is −0.508°C (−0.525°H) or below, milk *may* be presumed to be H_2O-free *or may* be confirmed as H_2O-free by tests specified below. If fp is above −0.508°C, milk *will* be designated "presumptive added H_2O" and *will* be confirmed as "added H_2O" or "H_2O-free" by tests specified below. Evaluate extreme daily fluctuations in fp of herd, pooled herd, or processed milk for presence of added H_2O.

To confirm herd milk as "added H_2O" or "H_2O- free," det. fp of authentic sample of herd milk obtained ≤72 hr after sample to be "confirmed." Authentic sample is sample of milk from 1 complete, supervised herd milking (either AM or PM but beginning not <11 or >13 hr after beginning of previous milking) obtained from bulk tank after entire herd has been milked thru approved, properly sanitized, and thoroly drained milking system into empty bulk tank but before rinsing or washing of system has begun. Compare fp of authentic sample and sample to be confirmed. If fps differ by ≤0.010°, sample is confirmed as H_2O-free.

To confirm pooled herd milk as "added H_2O" or "H_2O-free," det. fp of authentic samples of all herd milks composing pooled herd milk, calc. weighted av. fp for the authentic samples of herd milk, and compare values as above.

To confirm processed milk as "added H_2O" or "H_2O-free," det. fp of samples of all pooled herd milk received by processing plant, calc. weighted av. fp for milk received, and compare with fp value to be confirmed. If fps differ by ≤0.010°, processed sample is confirmed as H_2O-free during processing. If ≥1 sample of pooled herd milk is "presumptive added H_2O," proceed as above for pooled herd milk. Fp for pasteurized-homogenized milk should be same as that of pooled herd milk unless processing includes vac. pasteurization, which raises fp approx. 0.005°.

Vapor Pressure Osmometric (VPO) Method (22)
Official First Action

16.105 ***Principle***

Vapor pressure of milk sample is measured by osmometer as function of dewpoint depression. Thermocouple detector senses temp. of 5–7 μL sample at vapor pressure equilibrium in sample chamber headspace. Readout in milliosmols (mOs)/kg H_2O is converted to % added H_2O in milk by comparison with readout of authenticated ref. milk samples known to be free of added H_2O.

16.106 ***Apparatus and Reagents***

(**a**) *Vapor pressure osmometer.*—With either digital LED or taut band panel meter readout (Models 5100B or 5130B, Wescor, Inc., 459 S Main St, Logan, UT 84321, or equiv.). Install instrument in area relatively free from large ambient temp. changes, and adjust balance as specified in manufacturer's operating manual.

(**b**) *Reference milk samples.*—Authenticated to be free of added H_2O, **16.104**.

(**c**) *Thermocouple cleaning soln.*—NH_4OH (1+2). Rinse cleaning soln off sample chamber with ≥5 portions ≥1 megohm distd or deionized H_2O; then dry chamber using blow clean pressure vessel supplied by manufacturer or stream of filtered, compressed air. Cleaning accessory is also available from manufacturer.

(**d**) *Sodium chloride std soln.*—290 mOs, 0.1566*m*. Add 9.158 g NaCl to 1 L previously boiled and cooled H_2O.

16.107 ***Calibration***

Using clean, dry stainless steel forceps, sat. 6.4 mm diam. filter paper (Whatman No. 1, or equiv.) by immersing 2 sec in NaCl std soln, (**d**). Do not dip forceps into soln. Promptly transfer satd paper to concave depression in VPO sample chamber. If sample touches outer surface of chamber, wipe dry with lint-free paper tissue and resample. Gently push sample slide into instrument to initiate automatic time sequence. Seal sample chamber by rotating sealing knob clockwise. Adjust "Compensate 0–200" knob to 3 o'clock position and "Calibrate 1000" knob to 12 o'clock position. When tone sounds (after ca 90 sec), adjust "Calibrate 290" knob until panel meter reads 290 mOs. Repeat satn with NaCl std soln and reading in VPO with 3–4 sep. papers to assure that instrument repeatability is 290±3 mOs. Repeat using distd H_2O, which should read 20–40 mOs. Higher readings indicate thermocouple contamination. When distd H_2O reading reaches 70 mOs, clean thermocouple according to manufacturer's instructions, (**c**). Cleaning may be necessary after every 100–200 samples. (*Caution:* Thermocouple must be kept clean or large errors may result.)

16.108 ***Determination***

Introduce milk samples, including authenticated ref. milk samples, (**b**), into VPO sample chamber as in **16.107**, except allow 5–6 sec to sat. paper if churned fat interferes. Clean sample chamber between samples with lint-free paper tissue contg acetone.

$$\% \text{ Added } H_2O = [(R-S)/R] \times 100,$$

where R = mOs/kg authenticated ref. milk sample known to be free of added H_2O; and S = mOs/kg sample.

Gelatin (*23*)

16.109 ***Qualitative Test—Official Final Action***

(*Caution: See* **51.029** and **51.079**.)

To 10 mL sample add 10 mL *acid-$Hg(NO_3)_2$ soln* (Hg dissolved in twice its wt HNO_3 and this soln dild to 25 times its vol. with H_2O). Shake mixt., add 20 mL H_2O, shake again, let stand 5 min, and filter. If much gelatin is present, filtrate will be opalescent and cannot be obtained quite clear. To portion of filtrate in test tube add equal vol. *satd aq. picric acid soln.* Yellow ppt is produced in presence of any considerable amt of gelatin; smaller amts are indicated by cloudiness.

Note: In applying this test to sour, fermented, cultured, or very old samples of milk, cream, or buttermilk; to sterilized cream or evaporated milk; or to cottage cheese, use care to recognize ppts produced by picric acid when added to the $Hg(NO_3)_2$ filtrates from these materials in absence of gelatin. Such samples, with or without rennet and entirely free from gelatin, give, on standing, distinct ppts when treated as above. In every case, however, these ppts differ in character from those produced by picric acid with gelatin.

Gelatin-picric acid ppt is finely divided, more apt to remain in suspension, settles only slowly, and adheres tenaciously to sides and bottom of container, from which it is rinsed with difficulty. Ppts produced by picric acid in absence of gelatin are flocculent, sep. readily (leaving serum practically clear), do not adhere to walls of container, and are easily removed by rinsing with H_2O. When gelatin is present in sample, gelatin-picric acid ppt will remain in suspension long after flocculent ppt has settled, but on standing overnight the characteristic sticky deposit will be found adhering tenaciously to bottom and sides of test vessel. If gelatin is present in relatively high concn (1%), gelatin-picric acid ppt will be voluminous and will settle rather quickly.

16.110 Preservatives—Official Final Action

Proceed as in Chap. **20**. To test for benzoic acid or salicylic acid, acidify 100 mL milk with 5 mL HCl (1+3), shake until curdled, filter, and treat clear filtrate as in **20.020** and **20.094** or **20.095**.

To test for HCHO proceed as in **20.062–20.064**.

Table 16:02 Reactions with the Various Tests

Concentration of Available Cl	1:1,000	1:2,000	1:5,000	1:10,000	1:25,000	1:50,000
Test **a**	Yellowish brown	Deep yellow	Pale yellow, fades	—	—	—
Test **b**	Yellowish brown	Deep yellow	Light yellow	—	—	—
Test **c**	Yellowish brown	Deep yellow	Yellow	Yellow	Pale yellow	Yellowish
Test **d**	Blue-purple	Blue-purple	Blue-purple	Dark red-purple	Red-purple	Pale red-purple

Hypochlorites and Chloramines (*24*)—Procedure

(Unreliable in presence of >2.5 ppm Cu)

16.111 ***Reagents***

(**a**) *Potassium iodide soln.*—Dissolve 7 g KI in 100 mL H_2O. Prep. fresh.

(**b**) *Dilute hydrochloric acid.*—To 100 mL HCl add 200 mL H_2O.

(**c**) *Starch soln.*—Boil 1 g starch in 100 mL H_2O. Cool before using.

16.112 ***Tests***

(**a**) To 5 mL milk in test tube add 1.5 mL KI soln, mix thoroly by shaking, and note color of milk.

(**b**) If unaltered, add 4 mL dil. HCl, mix thoroly with flat-end stirring rod, and note color of curd.

(**c**) Next place tubes in large H_2O bath, previously heated to 85°, and let stand 10 min (during this interval curd rises to surface); then cool rapidly by placing in cold H_2O. Note color of curd and liq.

(**d**) Then add 0.5–1 mL starch soln to liq. below curd and note color.

16.113 Color Additives (*25*)—Official Final Action

Warm ca 150 mL milk in casserole over flame, add ca 5 mL HOAc (1+3), and continue to heat slowly nearly to bp while stirring. Gather curd, when possible, into one mass with stirring rod and pour off whey. If curd breaks up into small flecks, sep. from whey by straining thru sieve or colander. Press curd free from adhering liq., transfer to small flask, macerate with ca 50 mL ether, keeping flask tightly corked and shaking at intervals, and let stand several hr, preferably overnight. Decant ether ext into evapg dish, remove ether by evapn, and test fatty residue for annatto as follows:

Pour on moistened filter paper alk. soln of color obtained by shaking out oil or melted and filtered fat with warm 2% NaOH soln. If annatto is present, paper absorbs color, so that when washed with gentle stream of H_2O it remains dyed straw color. Dry paper, add drop of 40% $SnCl_2$ soln, and again dry carefully. If color turns purple, presence of annatto is confirmed.

Curd of uncolored milk and milk colored with annatto is perfectly white after complete extn with ether. If extd fat-free curd is distinctly orange or yellowish, synthetic dye is indicated. In many cases if lump of fat-free curd in test tube is treated with little HCl, color changes to pink, indicating presence of dye similar to aniline yellow or butter yellow or perhaps one of the acid azo yellows or oranges. In such cases, sep. and identify coloring matter present in curd as in Chap. **34**.

In some cases presence of synthetic dyes can be detected by directly treating ca 100 mL milk with equal vol. HCl in porcelain casserole, giving dish slight rotary motion. In presence of some dyes sepd curd becomes pink.

16.114 Sediment Test—Official Final Action

See **44.014–44.017**.

Residual Phosphatase

(All glassware, stoppers, and sampling tools must be scrupulously clean. It is desirable to soak them in hot running H_2O after cleaning and rinse with distd H_2O. Phenolic plastic closures on reagent bottles may cause phenolic contamination and their use should be avoided.)

16.115 ★ *Method I (26)—Official Final Action* ★

Colorimetric method using Folin-Ciocalteu phenol reagent. *See* **15.049–15.055**, 10th ed.

Method II (27)—Official Final Action

16.116 ***Reagents***

(**a**) *Buffers:*

(*1*) *Barium borate-hydroxide buffer.*—pH 10.6±0.15 at 25°. Dissolve 25.0 g $Ba(OH)_2.8H_2O$ (fresh, not deteriorated) in H_2O and dil. to 500 mL. Sep. dissolve 11.0 g H_3BO_3 and dil. to 500 mL. Warm each soln to 50°, mix solns, stir, cool to ca 20°, filter, and keep filtrate in tightly stoppered container.

(*2*) *Color development buffer.*—pH 9.8±0.15 at 25°. Dissolve 6.0 g Na metaborate ($NaBO_2$) and 20 g NaCl in H_2O, and dil. to 1 L with H_2O.

(*3*) *Color dilution buffer.*—Dil. 100 mL color development buffer, (*2*), to 1 L with H_2O.

(*4*) *Borax std buffer for checking pH meter.*—0.00996*M*, pH 9.183 at 25°, **50.007(f)**.

(**b**) *Buffer substrates:*

(*1*) *For evaluating pasteurization.*—Dissolve 0.10 g phenol-free cryst. disodium phenyl phosphate in 100 mL Ba borate-hydroxide buffer, (**a**)(*1*), dild (1+1). (Cryst. $Na_2C_6H_5PO_4$ should be stored in freezing compartment of refrigerator or in desiccator.) If $Na_2C_6H_5PO_4$ is not phenol-free, purify it as follows: Dissolve 0.5 g in 4.5 mL H_2O, add 0.5 mL buffer (**a**)(*1*) and 2 drops BQC reagent, (**d**), and let stand 30 min. Ext color with 2.5 mL BuOH, (**f**), and let stand until alcohol seps. Remove alcohol with dropper and discard. Dil. 1.0 mL aq. soln to 100 mL with dil. Ba borate-hydroxide buffer, (**a**)(*1*), for prepn of buffer substrate. Heat soln at 85° for 2 min, stopper immediately, and store in refrigerator. Soln is stable 1 year if portions are withdrawn with min. exposure to atm. Develop color, and re-ext before use, if necessary.

(*2*) *For quantitative results with raw milk.*—Prep. as in (*1*), except to use 0.20 g $Na_2C_6H_5PO_4$ or 2.0 mL purified soln.

(**c**) *Zinc-copper protein precipitant.*—Dissolve 3.0 g $ZnSO_4.7H_2O$ and 0.6 g $CuSO_4.5H_2O$ in H_2O and dil. to 100 mL with H_2O.

★ Surplus method—*see* inside front cover.

(**d**) *BQC (2,6-dibromoquinonechloroimide) soln (Gibbs reagent).*—Dissolve 40 mg BQC powder in 10 mL absolute alcohol or MeOH and transfer to dark color dropper bottle. (Reagent remains stable ≥1 month if kept in ice tray of refrigerator; do not use after it begins to turn brown. Store powd BQC in freezing compartment of refrigerator or in desiccator. (*Note:* Explosions of BQC reagent stored in bottles on reagent shelf have been reported.) Check new lots of BQC before use by prepg std curve with phenol and comparing curve obtained with that from lot of BQC known to be suitable. Repeat test at least semi-annually.)

(**e**) *Copper sulfate soln for stds.*—0.05%. Dissolve 0.05 g $CuSO_4.5H_2O$ in H_2O and dil. to 100 mL.

(**f**) *Butyl alcohol.*—Use *n*-BuOH, bp 116–118°. To adjust pH, mix 1 L with 50 mL color development buffer, (**a**)(*2*). Store in g-s container.

(**g**) *Phenol std solns:*

(*1*) *Stock soln.*—Accurately weigh 1.000 g pure phenol, transfer to 1 L vol. flask, dil. to vol. with H_2O, and mix (1 mL = 1 mg phenol). (Soln is stable several months in refrigerator.)

(*2*) *Working stds.*—Dil. 10.0 mL stock soln to 1 L with H_2O and mix (1 mL = 10 μg, 0.00001 g, or 10 units of phenol). Use this std soln to prep. more dil. std solns: *e.g.,* dil. 5, 10, 30, and 50 mL to 100 mL with H_2O to prep. std solns contg 0.5, 1.0, 3.0, and 5.0 μg or units of phenol/mL, resp. Keep these std solns in refrigerator ≤1 week.

In similar manner prep. from stock soln std solns contg 20, 30, and 40 units/mL.

Measure appropriate vols of working std solns into series of tubes (preferably graduated at 5.0 and 10.0 mL) to provide suitable range of stds as needed, contg 0 (control or blank), 0.5, 1.0, 3.0, 5.0, 10.0, 20.0, 30.0, and 40.0 units. To increase brightness of blue solns and improve stability of std, add 1.0 mL $CuSO_4$ soln, (**e**), to each tube. Then add 5.0 mL color diln buffer, (**a**)(*3*), and dil. to vol. of 10.0 mL with H_2O. Add 4 drops (0.08 mL) BQC soln, (**d**), mix, and let blue develop 30 min at room temp. If BuOH extn method is used, ext stds as in **16.118**, *Step 10*(*b*).

Read color intensities in photometer with 610 nm filter, subtract value of blank from value of each phenol std, and prep. std curve (should be straight line).

If stds are to be used for visual comparison, store in refrigerator. Prep. new set weekly.

16.117 *Sampling*

Mix product well, pour several mL into small tube, stopper, and keep in refrigerator. If preservative is necessary, add 1–3% $CHCl_3$, and label *"Poison, preservative added."*

16.118 *Determination*

Chem. principles involved in detection and measurement of milk phosphatase activity are same for all dairy products, but different dairy products require modifications of methods because of their different physical properties, compositions, and especially buffering capacities.

For milk and other fluid products, proceed as follows:

Step 1.—Pipet 1.0 mL portions of sample into 2 or 3 tubes (1 tube is needed for control or blank; it is preferable to have 2 more tubes for duplicate detns). (For goat's milk, use 3 mL portions.)

Step 2.—Heat *blank* ca 1 min in covered beaker of boiling H_2O (temp. of entire tube must be 85–90°) and cool to room temp. From this point on, treat blank and test identically.

Step 3.—Add 10.0 mL Ba buffer substrate, (**b**)(*1*) or (*2*), stopper tube, and mix (pH 10.0±0.15).

(This substrate is satisfactory for fresh milk, sweet buttermilk, or cheese whey. For old or slightly sour milk use substrate prepd from undild buffer, (**a**)(*1*); for chocolate drinks, prep. substrate from buffer dild with ¼ vol. H_2O; for very acid (pH <4.5) buttermilk, prep. substrate from 26-11 buffer, **16.275(a)**(*2*); and for goat's milk, prep. substrate from 27-11 buffer, **16.275(a)**(*2*).

For quant. results on unknown samples, adjust pH to 10.0–10.05.

Step 4.—Immediately after adding substrate, incubate in H_2O bath 1 hr at 37–38°, mixing or shaking contents occasionally.

Step 5.—Heat in beaker of boiling H_2O nearly 1 min. (Temp. of contents of tubes should reach 85–90°, as detd by thermometer in another tube of same size and shape contg same vol. liq.) Cool to room temp. in vessel of cold H_2O.

Step 6.—Pipet in 1.0 mL Zn-Cu protein precipitant, (**c**), for fresh milk, sweet buttermilk, or cheese whey. (For old or slightly sour milk or acid buttermilk, substitute 1.0 mL 6.0% $ZnSO_4.7H_2O$ soln; for chocolate drinks, use 1.0 mL of soln contg 4.5 g $ZnSO_4.7H_2O$ and 0.1 g $CuSO_4.5H_2O$/100 mL; and for goat's milk, use 1.0 mL of soln contg 7.5 g $ZnSO_4.7H_2O$ and 0.1 g $CuSO_4.5H_2O$/100 mL.) Mix thoroly (pH of mixt. should be 9.0–9.1).

Step 7.—Filter (5 cm funnel, 9 cm Whatman No. 42 or No. 2 paper, or equiv.) and collect 5.0 mL filtrate in tube, preferably graduated at 5.0 and 10.0 mL.

Step 8.—Add 5.0 mL color development buffer, (**a**)(*2*), (pH of mixt. should be 9.3–9.4).

Step 9.—Add 4 drops BQC soln, (**d**), mix, and let color develop 30 min at room temp. (For merely detecting underpasteurization, add only 2 drops of the BQC soln.)

Step 10.—Det. intensity of blue color by one of following methods:

(*a*) *With photometer.*—Read color intensities of blank and test solns (using filter with max. *T* ca 610 nm), subtract reading of blank from that of test, and convert result to phenol equivs by ref. to std curve, (**g**)(*2*). [Ordinarily BuOH extn is unnecessary when photometer is used; if BuOH extn is made as in (*b*), centrf. sample 5 min to break emulsion and remove H_2O suspended in alcohol layer. (Babcock centrf. can be adapted for this purpose by making special tube holders as follows: Slice section 6 mm thick from rubber stopper of suitable diam. to fit into bottom of centrf. cup. Glue together 2 cork stoppers of appropriate diam., bore thru center a hole of proper size to hold tube snugly, and insert double cork section into cup.) After centrfg, remove nearly all BuOH by pipet with rubber bulb on top end. Filter into photometer cell and read with filter with max. *T* ca 650 nm.]

(*b*) *With visual stds.*—With samples yielding >5 units, compare colors in tubes with those of aq. phenol stds, (**g**)(*2*). For quant. results in borderline instances, (*e.g.,* tests yielding 0.5–5 units of color), ext with BuOH, (**f**). Add 5.0 mL of BuOH and invert tube slowly several times; centrf. as in (*a*) if necessary to increase clearness of alcohol layer, and compare blue with colors of phenol stds, (**g**)(*2*), similarly treated.

Step 11.—In tests observed to be strongly pos. during color development (*e.g.*, ≥20 units), in which 4 drops of BQC soln may be insufficient to combine with all the phenol, pipet appropriate proportion of contents into another tube, dil. to 10.0 mL with color diln buffer, (**a**)(*3*), and add 2 addnl drops BQC soln. With each test, dil. and treat blank similarly. If test on dild sample is still very strongly pos., dil. again in same manner until final color is within range of visual stds or photometer std curve. Allow 30 min for color development after last addn of BQC soln before making final reading. To correct reading for diln, multiply by 2 for 5 + 5 diln, by 10 for 1 + 9 diln, and by 50 for 1 + 9 diln followed by 2 + 8 diln, etc.

Step 12.—When using 1.0 mL sample and adding 11.0 mL reagents (total liq. 12.0 mL, 5.0 mL filtrate used), multiply value of reading by 1.2 to convert to phenol equivs/0.5 mL sample.

(If desired, results may be converted to phenol equivs/1 mL by multiplying by 2.4.) Phenol equivs >2/0.5 mL indicate underpasteurization in cow's milk, chocolate drinks, buttermilk, and cheese whey; phenol equivs >1/1.5 mL indicate underpasteurization in goat's milk.

Notes: To test concd milk products, reconstitute product with H_2O to original concn of milk solids and test in manner specified for original product.

See also Notes in **16.277**.

16.119 ★ *Method III (28)—Official Final Action* ★

Residual phosphatase liberates free phenol within cellulose bag. Phenol diffused thru membrane is detd colorimetrically. *See* **16.104–16.107**, 12th ed.

Method IV (29)—Official Final Action

16.120 ***Principle***

Milk is incubated 3 hr with phthln monophosphate in carbonate buffer at pH 9.6. Free phthln is liberated by residual alk. phosphatase of milk and passes thru membrane along with buffer and other solutes into H_2O, resulting in clear dialysate which can be measured directly in spectrophtr.

16.121 ***Reagents***

(**a**) *Phenolphthalein monophosphate soln (substrate concentrate).*—pH 10.15 at 25°. Dissolve 3.9 g dicyclohexylamine salt of phthln monophosphate and 73.2 g 2-amino-2-methyl-1-propanol in 21.9 mL HCl. Soln is stable indefinitely under refrigeration. (Available as Phosphastrate® Alkaline from General Diagnostics Div., Warner-Chilcott Laboratories, 201 Tabor Rd, Morris Plains, NJ 07950.)

(**b**) *Sodium sesquicarbonate dihydrate buffer soln.*—Dissolve 10 g $NaHCO_3.Na_2CO_3.2H_2O$ in H_2O and dil. to 100 mL.

(**c**) *Dialyzing, seamless cellulose tubing.*—Available as "Dialysis Membrane" from Union Carbide Corp., Films-Packaging Div., 6733 W 65 St, Chicago, IL 60638. Order No. 27 DC; 0.0009" wall thickness, width flat 1.31", diam. round 21 mm, 100' random lengths. Cut enough 20 cm lengths of tubing and immerse in H_2O ≥30 sec. Remove, and wrinkle one end with fingers. Twist and tie this end tightly into leakproof knot, and cut off excess cellulose beyond knot with scissors. Store bags in H_2O until ready to use. Tubing may require several rinsings with H_2O to remove surface film. During use, take precautions against phenol or enzyme contamination from contact with fingers or phenol-contg substances, e.g., plastics.

(**d**) *Phenolphthalein stock std soln.*—100 μg/mL. Dissolve 100 mg fresh phthln in 1 L 50% alcohol.

16.122 ***Preparation of Standard Curve***

Pipet 0.0, 0.1, 0.2, 0.3, 0.5, 0.7, and 1.0 mL phthln stock soln into sep. 15 × 100 mm test tubes. Add amt buffer soln to bring vol. to 10 mL in each tube. (Final phthln concns are 0.0, 1.0, 2.0, 3.0, 5.0, 7.0, and 10.0 μg/mL, resp.) Mix, and det. *A* at 550 nm. Plot *A* against μg phthln/mL.

16.123 ***Determination***

Pipet 3 mL milk into 15 × 100 mm test tube and temper 3–5 min in 37° H_2O bath. Add 3 drops (0.04 mL/drop) substrate conc. to tube and mix thoroly, preferably with mech. mixer. Prep. and incubate blank similarly, using milk heated 2 min at 80°.

Insert short-stem funnel (35 × 75 mm), into presoaked, knotted dialysis bag, transfer sample mixt., press air out of bag, and knot top end tightly. Rinse outside with H_2O and dry lightly with paper towel. Immediately suspend bag in 20 × 100 mm test tube contg 5 mL H_2O, stopper (No. 3 rubber stopper), and incubate 3 hr in 37° H_2O bath. (Contents of bag *must* be completely immersed in H_2O but top knot must *not* contact soln to avoid possible contamination of dialysate with milk.)

Remove bag from tube and discard. Read *A* of dialysate at 550 nm, using dialysate from heated milk sample to set instrument at 100% *T*. Calc. phthln concn from std curve.

16.124 ***Interpretation***

Reading of >1.15 μg phthln/3 mL milk indicates underpasteurization or contamination of milk with raw milk.

Method V (30)—Official First Action

16.125 ***Reagents***

(**a**) *Carbonate buffer.*—Dissolve 46.89 g Na_2CO_3 and 37.17 g $NaHCO_3$ in H_2O and dil. to 1 L with H_2O.

(**b**) *Buffer substrate.*—Dissolve 0.5 g phenol-free cryst. disodium phenyl phosphate in H_2O, add 25 mL of buffer, (**a**), and dil. to 500 mL with H_2O. If $Na_2C_6H_5PO_4$ is not phenol-free, purify as follows: Place 0.5 g in separator and dissolve in 10 mL H_2O. Add 25 mL buffer, (**a**), and 2–3 drops CQC contg catalyst, (**d**). Mix, and let stand 5 min. Ext color with 5 mL BuOH, (**e**), and let stand until alcohol seps. Remove bottom aq. layer into 500 mL vol. flask and dil. to vol. with H_2O. *Prep. fresh daily.*

(**c**) *CQC soln.*—Dissolve 40 mg cryst. 2,6-dichloroquinonechloroimide in 10 mL absolute alcohol or MeOH and transfer to dark bottle. Or, prep. soln by dissolving 1 Indo-Phax tablet (contg catalyst) (available from Applied Research Institute, 90 Brighton Ave, Perth Amboy NJ 08861) in 5 mL alcohol or MeOH. Store soln in refrigerator. Discard after 1 week or when brown.

(**d**) *Catalyst.*—Dissolve 200 mg $CuSO_4.5H_2O$ in H_2O and dil. to 100 mL.

(**e**) Butyl alcohol.—Use *n*-BuOH, bp 116–118°. To adjust pH, mix 10 mL buffer, (**a**), and 40 mL H_2O with 1 gal. (3.8 L) BuOH. Store in refrigerator in dark bottle.

(**f**) *Phenol std solns.*—(*1*) *Stock soln.*—Accurately weigh 1.000 g pure phenol, transfer to 1 L vol. flask, dil. to vol. with 0.1*N* HCl, and mix (1 mL = 1 mg phenol. Soln is stable several months in refrigerator). (*2*) *Working stds.*—Dil. 5 mL stock soln to 500 mL with H_2O and mix (1 mL = 10 μg phenol). Dil. 0.0, 0.5, 1.0, 2.5, and 5.0 mL to 5.0 mL with H_2O to prep. std solns contg 0.0, 1.0, 2.0, 5.0, and 10.0 μg phenol equivs/mL, resp. Prep. fresh daily.

(**g**) *Color std solns.*—Prep. working std solns in series of tubes, add 0.1 mL CQC soln, (**c**), and 2 drops catalyst, (**d**), or use 0.1 mL Indo-Phax soln, (**c**). Mix well, and incubate 5 min at 40°. Remove from bath, cool, and ext with 3 mL BuOH as in **16.126**.

16.126 ***Determination***

Pipet 0.5 mL of well mixed sample into test tubes (1 tube needed for boiled control or blank). Add 5 mL buffer substrate soln and mix. Immediately incubate in H_2O bath 15 min at 40° (allow 1 min warm-up time for a total of 16 min), mixing samples at least once during warm-up time. Remove from H_2O bath, add 0.1 mL CQC soln, and 2 drops catalyst, or 0.1 mL Indo-Phax soln (contains catalyst). Mix, and immediately place in H_2O bath 5 min, mixing contents at least once. Remove from bath and cool in ice-H_2O bath 5 min. Add 3 mL BuOH and ext by inversion 6 full turns. Let stand in ice-H_2O bath 5 min. Centrif. 5 min. Remove BuOH layer into cuvets with Pasteur pipet. Det. *A* of BuOH layer against 0 phenol color std, and calc. phenol equivs.

★ Surplus method—*see* inside front cover.

Read A of BuOH exts of color std solns, using red filter in colorimeter or with spectrophtr set at 650 nm. Std curve of μg phenol against A should be straight line.

Qualitative (Screening) Method (31)—Official Final Action

(Applicable to skim and whole milk and light cream)

16.127 ***Reagents***

(**a**) *Phenolphthalein monophosphate soln (substrate concentrate).—See* **16.121**(**a**).

(**b**) *Phenolphthalein-tartrazine soln (std concentrate).*—0.01 and 0.04% by wt, resp.; pH 10.15 at 25°. Dissolve 10 mg phthln, 40 mg tartrazine, and 73.2 g 2-amino-2-methyl-1-propanol in 21.9 mL HCl. Soln is stable indefinitely under refrigeration.

(**c**) *Color developer.*—2.5*N* NaOH.

16.128 ***Determination***

Pipet 1 mL milk into each of two 15 × 100 mm test tubes and warm to 37°. To 1 tube add 1 drop (0.04 mL) substrate conc. (pH of incubation mixt. 10.0) and to other add 1 drop std conc. Mix and incubate 30 min at 37°. Add 1 drop 2.5*N* NaOH to each tube, mix, and compare visually. If sample soln (in tube contg substrate conc.) is less pink than std soln, milk has been pasteurized to extent equiv. to <0.1% raw milk.

Reactivated and Residual Phosphatase, Differential Test (*32*)—Official First Action

16.129 ***Reagent***

Magnesium acetate soln.—40.1 g Mg/mL. Dissolve 35.4 g $Mg(OAc)_2.4H_2O$ in 25 mL H_2O, warming slightly. Transfer quant. to 100 mL vol. flask with H_2O, cool, and dil. to 100 mL.

16.130 ***Reactivation***

Place 10 mL of each sample in boiling H_2O bath and hold 1 min after temp. of sample reaches 95°. Cool, and use portion of each for diln, as required, and for boiled control. Place 5 mL aliquot of sample in screw-cap (phenol-free) test tube. Add 0.1 mL H_2O. To second 5 mL aliquot in identical tube add 0.1 mL $Mg(OAc)_2$ soln. Incubate both tubes 1 hr at 34°. Remove samples from bath and cool in ice-H_2O bath. Dil. aliquot of 1 mL sample contg Mg with 5 mL of corresponding boiled control. Test undild sample contg no Mg and 1+5 diln contg Mg for phosphatase activity as in **16.118**, **16.123**, **16.126**, or **16.164**, keeping tubes cool until analysis.

If 1 + 5 diln contg Mg has equal or greater phosphatase activity than undild sample contg no Mg, sample is regarded as neg. for residual phosphatase and indicates that phosphatase originally measured is of reactivated origin. If dild sample contains less activity than undild sample, it is considered pos. for residual phosphatase provided that initial conventional phosphatase test was pos. False pos. test for residual phosphatase may be obtained if reactivatable sample stood at elevated temp. (21–24°; 70–75°F) for ≥2 hr.

PENICILLINS IN MILK

Bacillus Stearothermophilus Qualitative Disc Method (33) Official First Action

16.131 ***Culture Media***

(**a**) *Agar medium B.—See* **42.196**(**b**).

(**b**) *Agar medium M*—Dissolve 15.0 g pancreatic digest of casein, 5.0 g papaic digest of soybean, 5.0 g NaCl, and 15.0 g agar in H_2O and dil. to 1 L. Adjust if necessary so that after sterilization pH is 7.3±0.2. (BBL Trypticase Soy Agar has been found satisfactory.)

(**c**) *Broth medium C.*—Dissolve 17.0 g pancreatic digest of casein, 3.0 g papaic digest of soybean, 5.0 g NaCl, 2.5 g K_2HPO_4, and 2.5 g dextrose in H_2O, and dil. to 1 L. Adjust if necessary so that after sterilization pH is 7.3±0.2. (BBL Tripticase Soy Broth has been found satisfactory.)

16.132 ***Reagent and Apparatus***

(**a**) *Penicillin stock soln.*—Accurately weigh, in atm. of ≤50% relative humidity, ca 30 mg USP K (or Na) penicillin G Ref. Std. Dissolve in enough pH 6 buffer, **42.197(f)**, to give known concn of 100–1000 units/mL. Store in dark ≤2 days at 2–10°.

(**b**) *Penicillinase (beta-lactamase).*—Prepns are available from Difco Laboratories; BBL; ICN Nutritional Biochemicals, 26201 Miles Road, Cleveland, OH 44128; Schwarz/Mann, Orenbury, NY 10962; and Calbiochem. Penicillinase prepns are not stdzd. It is therefore important to choose prepn of sufficient strength to ensure complete inactivation of antibiotic soln under test.

(**c**) *Control disks.*—Prep. fresh daily from pos. control milks contg 0.008 and 0.005 unit/mL as in **16.138(b)**.

(**d**) *Petri dishes (plates).—See* **42.198(b)**.

16.133 ***Stock Culture of Test Organism***

Maintain *B. stearothermophilus* (ATCC 10149) on agar medium M, (**b**), transferring to fresh slant weekly. Inoculate slant of agar medium M with test organism and incubate overnight at 55°. Inoculate three 300 mL erlenmeyers, each cong 150 mL broth medium C, (**c**), with 1 loopful of test organism. Incubate at 55° and periodically make spore stains to det. extent of sporulation. When ca 80% sporulation has occurred (usually in 72 hr), centrf. cell suspension 15 min at 2000 rpm. Decant supernate, resuspend cells in saline soln, **42.197(r)**, and recentrf. Repeat saline washing. Resuspend washed cells in 30 mL saline and store at 4°. Spore suspension will remain viable 6–8 months. Check viability periodically by prepn of trial test plates.

16.134 ***Preparations of Plates***

Inoculate aliquot of liquified agar medium B, (**a**), cooled to 55° with previously prepd spore suspension (usually 1–2 mL/100 mL agar medium). Adjust inoculum level to provide clear, readable zones of inhibition from penicillin pos. control disks, (**c**), after 3–4 hr incubation. Pour 8 mL inoculated agar medium B into each plate, and let harden on flat, level surface.

16.135 ***Assay***

Thaw frozen milk samples at room temp. Subdivide each sample into 2 portions and add penicillinase, (**b**), to one portion (ca 0.1 mL/5 mL milk). Test both milk portions. Using forceps, touch paper disk to surface of milk and let milk be adsorbed by capillary action. Drain excess milk by touching disk to inside surface of sample vessel. Place 6 disks (one disk from penicillinase-treated sample and one from untreated portion of same sample for each of 2 samples) and 2 std penicillin pos. control disks (0.005 and 0.008 unit/mL). Prep. duplicate plates for each assay. Invert plates and incubate 3–4 hr at 55° or until visible zones of inhibition appear. Read by holding plates up to diffuse light source and measure diams of zones of inhibition.

16.136 ***Interpretation***

Penicillinase inactivation of test soln may produce following results:

(*1*) *Complete inactivation (positive test):* Loss of activity of treated versus untreated aliquot of sample soln indicates that *beta*-lactam residue was present.

(*2*) *Incomplete inactivation* (*presumptive test*): Significant reduction in activity of treated versus untreated aliquots of sample soln indicates that *beta*-lactam residue was present, but that other active agents or ingedients have caused interference problems.

(*3*) *No inactivation* (*false test*): No significant reduction in activity of treated versus untreated aliquots of sample soln indicates that interfering agents or ingredients may be masking presence of *beta*-lactam residue. No qual. analysis can be made of residue.

(*4*) *No activity* (*neg. test*): Absence of zones of inhibition from treated and untreated aliquots of sample soln indicates that no *beta*-lactam residue(s) has been detected (within limitations of test method).

Penicillin pos. control soln at 0.008 unit/mL level should produce clear, well-defined zones of inhibition. Penicillin pos. control at 0.005 unit/mL may or may not produce discernible zones of inhibition and degree of activity produced by this 0.005 unit/mL level may vary from one day to another. If no zones of inhibition are produced by either of penicillin pos. control solns, adequate test sensitivity has not been obtained and test should be repeated.

B. stearothermophilus disk method has been used successfully for qual. detection of residues of penicillin G, at 0.005–0.008 unit/mL, ampicillin and cephapirin at 0.005–0.008 μg/mL, and cloxacillin at 0.05–0.08 μg/mL.

Bacillus subtilis Qualitative Field Disk Assay (34)
Official Final Action

(Sensitive to ca 0.05 unit/mL)

16.137 ***Culture Media***

(**a**) *Agar medium A.*—For carrying test organism and for performing assay. *See* **42.196**(**a**).

(**b**) *Agar medium G.*—For prepg test suspension. *See* **42.196**(**g**).

16.138 ***Reagents***

(**a**) *Stock penicillin soln.*—Accurately weigh, in atm. of ≤50% relative humidity, ca 10 mg USP K (or Na) Penicillin G Ref. Std. Dissolve in enough pH 6 buffer, **42.197**(**f**), to give concn of exactly 100 units/mL. Store in dark at ca 5° ≤2 days.

(**b**) *Control disks.*—Dil. stock penicillin soln with antibiotic-free, whole, homogenized milk to final concns of 0.05 and 0.1 unit/mL. Use S&S 740E ¼" disks or prep. ¼" round, white disks from S&S 470W or 470 paper, of equiv. absorption performance qualities and purity. Dip disks into std penicillin-contg milks and shake off excess. Dry on rust-proof wire screening under fan. Stored in refrigerator in tightly stoppered vial with desiccant, disks are usable 1 month.

16.139 ***Stock Culture of Test Organism***

Maintain *Bacillus subtilis* on agar medium A, transferring to fresh slant monthly. Inoculate fresh slant of agar medium A with test organism and incubate 16–24 hr at 37°. Wash culture from slant with 2–3 mL *sterile 0.9% NaCl soln* with aid of sterile glass beads onto surface of Roux bottle contg 300 mL agar medium G. Incubate 5 days at 37°. Wash resulting growth from surface with aid of the beads and 50 mL sterile 0.9% NaCl soln into sterile centrf. tube, centrf., and decant supernate. Reconstitute sediment with ca 70 mL sterile 0.9% NaCl soln and heat-shock spore suspension by heating 30 min at 70°. Store in g-s flask in refrigerator. Suspension is stable several months.

With each new suspension, det. amt to be used as follows: Prep. plates as directed below with varying amts of inoculum, *i.e.*, 0.2, 0.5, 1.0, and 2.0 mL/100 mL medium. Refrigerate 3–5 days. Place control disks of 0.05 and 0.1 unit/mL on plates and incubate as in test. Use as concn of inoculum that concn showing best response, considering both sensitivity and discernibility of zones of inhibition.

16.140 ***Preparation of Plates***

Melt agar medium A, cool to 55–60°, and add 0.2– 2.0 mL spore suspension, **16.139**, to each 100 mL agar medium A. Mix well.

Add 10 mL inoculated agar to each 20 × 100 mm glass or plastic petri dish. Distribute agar evenly, cover with porcelain covers glazed only on outside, and let harden on level surface. Store in refrigerator ≥3 but ≤5 days. Remove each dish from refrigerator as needed and use within 15 min.

16.141 ***Assay***

With forceps place 0.05 and 0.1 unit/mL control disks on each plate.

Thoroly shake each milk sample to disperse fat evenly. Using forceps, dip blank disk completely into sample, withdraw, and shake off excess milk by vigorously waving in air several times. Place disk on surface of agar and touch gently with tip of forceps to assure proper contact. *Do not touch so heavily that milk is squeezed out of disk.* Place disks so that they are ≥20 mm apart, measured center to center, to avoid overlapping of zones. Flame tips of forceps to avoid carryover from contaminated samples. Place control and sample disks on plate within few min of one another.

Incubate plates 2.5–3 hr at 37°, and examine for zones of inhibition. Hold plates at various angles to light (either elec. bulb or daylight) to det. optimum conditions for observation. Zones around control disks indicate sensitivity of test.

To det. if zone of inhibition is due to penicillin, add 0.05 mL (ca 1 drop) *penicillinase conc.* (BBL or Difco penicillinase have been found satisfactory) to 5 mL aliquot milk sample and shake well. Prep. 3 disks from this treated sample and from untreated sample. Place all disks on same plate, incubate as before, and observe. Zone around untreated sample disks but no zone around treated sample disks is pos. test for penicillin. Zone of inhibition around both treated and untreated sample disks indicates antibacterial activity other than penicillin.

16.142 ***Quantitative Overnight Method***

Use method for penicillin in feed, **42.278–42.281**, prepg std solns for std curve with antibiotic-free, whole, homogenized milk instead of pH 6 buffer. Cylinders must be used for application of samples and stds for detection of as little as 0.01 unit penicillin/mL. Disk method of application, **16.141**, instead of cylinders may be used for concns >0.025 unit/mL. Milk sample is assay soln unless concn >0.2 unit/mL is anticipated, in which case dil. sample with antibiotic-free milk to estd concn of 0.05 unit/mL.

16.143 Vitamin D in Milk—Official Final Action

See **43.195–43.208**.

CREAM

16.144 Collection of Sample—Procedure

(*See* also **16.001–16.007**.)

Proceed as in **16.019**. Promptly analyze sample, preferably within 3 days after collection.

16.145 Preparation of Sample—Procedure

Immediately before withdrawing test portions, mix sample by shaking, pouring, or stirring (or use hand homogenizer) until it pours readily and uniform emulsion forms. If sample is very thick, warm to 30–35° and mix. In case lumps of butter have sepd, heat sample to ca 38° by placing in warm H_2O bath. (Temp. appreciably >38° may cause fat to "oil off," especially in case of thin cream.) Thoroly mix portions for analysis and weigh immediately. (In com. testing for fat by Babcock method, it may be advisable to warm all samples to ca 38° in H_2O bath previous to mixing.)

16.146 Preparation of Sample of Pressurized Cream (*35*)—Official Final Action

Place containers in freezer overnight to freeze contents. Release as much gas as possible from frozen contents thru nozzle, holding container upright. Refreeze if necessary. Open container, using can opener on nonreturnable type or wrench on heavier, returnable type. Empty contents into weighed 1 L jar of high-speed blender, and weigh to 0.1 g. Let thaw (complete thawing is not necessary). Beat to smooth, creamy liq., keeping blender covered. Beat intermittently to prevent overheating sample and blender. (Process may require 15 min. "Butter" stage is intermediate, and beating must be continued until this stage is passed.) When sufficiently mixed, weigh blender jar and contents again. Calc. % loss in wt and apply this correction to subsequent detns. Weigh samples for fat, solids, sucrose, or other analyses, beating few sec between withdrawals of samples.

16.147 Lactic Acid—Official Final Action

See **16.027–16.031**.

16.148 Water-Insoluble Fatty Acids (*36*) Official Final Action

Weigh 50 g prepd sample, **16.145**, into 250 mL centrf. bottle, add 20 mL alcohol, shake, and add 50 mL ether. Proceed as in **16.220**, par. 2, except use 10 mL Na_2WO_4 soln. (When Na_2WO_4-treated mixt. is shaken with ether, emulsions may form and not break completely on centrfg. These emulsions may be broken by adding 10–20 mL alcohol, mixing gently, and again centrfg.)

16.149 ★ *Rapid Method—Official First Action* ★

See **16.208–16.210**, 12th ed.

16.150 Volatile Acids (*37*)—Official Final Action

Weigh 100 g sample into 250 mL vol. flask, add 100 mL H_2O and 2 mL H_2SO_4 (1+1), and mix, avoiding violent shaking. Add 15 mL *10% $Na_2WO_4.2H_2O$ soln,* dil. to vol., mix, and filter thru rapid paper. Transfer 150 mL filtrate to distn flask and proceed with distn, chromatgc sepn, and detn as in **18.054–18.058** or **18.059**. Calc. to mg acids/100 g fat.

See **14.099–14.101** for identification of volatile acids.

16.151 Total Solids—Official Final Action

Proceed as in **16.032**, using 2–3 g sample.

16.152 ★ Added Water (*38*)—Official Final Action ★

Hortvet cryoscope method. *See* **16.086–16.088**, 12th ed.

16.153 Ash—Official Final Action

See **16.035**.

★ Surplus method—*see* inside front cover.

16.154 Total Nitrogen—Official Final Action

See **16.036**.

Lactose

16.155 *Gravimetric Method—Official Final Action*

See **16.057**.

Fat

16.156 *Roese-Gottlieb Method—Official Final Action*

Using 5 g sample and dilg with H_2O to ca 10.5 mL, proceed as in **16.059**, beginning "Add 1.25 mL NH_4OH . . ."

Babcock Method—Official Final Action

16.157 *Apparatus*

(**a**) *Test bottles.*—Std Babcock cream-test bottles are as follows:

(*1*) *50%, 9 g, short-neck, 6" cream-test bottle.*—Total ht 150–165 mm (5.9–6.5"). Bottom of bottle must be flat, and axis of neck vertical when bottle stands on level surface. Amt of cream for bottle is 9 g.

Bulb.—Capacity of bulb to junction with neck is ≥45 mL. Bulb may be either cylindrical or conical. If cylindrical, od must be 34–36 mm; if conical, od of base must be 31–33 mm, and max. diam., 35–37 mm.

Neck.—Cylindrical and of uniform diam. from ≥5 mm below lowest graduation mark to ≥5 mm above highest. Top of neck is flared to diam. of ≥15 mm. Graduated portion of neck is ≥63.5 mm long. Total % graduation is 50. Graduations shall represent 5, 1, and ½%, resp., from 0.0 to 50%. 5% graduations must extend at least half-way around neck to right; ½% graduations must be ≥3 mm long; and 1% graduations must be intermediate in length between 5% and ½% graduations and project 2 mm to left of ½% graduations. Each 5% graduation must be numbered (thus: 0, 5, 10, . . . 45, 50), number being placed to left of scale. Capacity of neck for each whole % on scale must be 0.1 mL. Max. error in total graduation or any part thereof must not exceed vol. of smallest unit of graduation.

(*2*) *50%, 9 g, long-neck, 9" cream-test bottle.*— Same specifications as in (*1*), except that total ht of this bottle is 210–229 mm (8.25–9.0") and graduated portion of neck has length of ≥120 mm.

(*3*) *50%, 18 g, long-neck, 9" cream-test bottle.*— Same specifications as in (*2*), except that amt of cream for this bottle is 18 g.

Each bottle must bear on top of neck above graduations, in plain legible characters, mark denoting wt sample to be used, *viz.,* "9 g" or "18 g," as case may be.

Each bottle must be constructed so as to withstand stress to which it will be subjected in centrf.

(*4*) *Testing.*—Proceed as in **16.060**(**a**)(*3*).

(**b**) *Water bath for cream samples.*—Provided with thermometer and control to maintain temp. of 38°.

(**c**) *Cream weighing scales.*—With sensibility reciprocal of 30 mg, *i.e.,* addn of 30 mg to either pan of scale, when loaded to capacity, causes deflection of ≥1 subdivision of graduation. Set scales level upon support and protect from drafts.

(**d**) *Weights.*—9 g and 18 g, resp., and plainly marked "9 g" or "18 g," as case may be. Must be made of material capable of resisting corrosion or other injury, and preferably of low squat shape, with rounded edges. Verify them at frequent intervals by comparison with stdzd wts.

(**e**) *Acid measure.*—*See* **16.060**(**c**).

(**f**) *Centrifuge or "tester."*—*See* **16.060**(**d**).
(**g**) *Dividers or calipers.*—*See* **16.060**(**e**).
(**h**) *Water bath for test bottles.*—*See* **16.060**(**f**).

16.158 ***Determination***

Weigh 9 g prepd sample, **16.145**, directly into 9 g cream-test bottle, or 18 g into 18 g bottle, and proceed by one of following methods.

(**a**) *Method 1.*—After weighing cream into test bottle, add 8–12 mL H_2SO_4 (sp gr 1.82–1.83 at 20°) to 9 g bottle; or 14–17 mL to 18 g bottle; or add acid until mixt. of cream and acid, after shaking, is chocolate-brown. Shake until all lumps completely disappear and add 5–10 mL soft H_2O at 60° or above. Transfer bottle to centrf., counterbalance it, and after proper speed is reached, centrf. 5 min. Add soft hot H_2O until liq. column approaches top graduation of scale; then centrf. 1 min longer at 55–60°. Adjust temp. as in **16.061**, and with aid of dividers or calipers measure fat column, in terms of % by wt, from lower surface to bottom of upper meniscus.

(**b**) *Method 2.*—*For 9 g bottle only.*—After weighing cream into test bottle, add 9 mL soft H_2O and mix thoroly; add ca 17.5 mL of the H_2SO_4 and shake until all lumps completely disappear. Transfer bottle to centrf., counterbalance it, and after proper speed is reached, centrf. 5 min. Fill bottle to neck with hot H_2O and centrf. 2 min. Add hot H_2O until liq. column approaches top graduation of scale, and centrf. 1 min longer at 55–60°. Adjust temp. and measure fat column as in (**a**).

Whichever method is followed, fat column, at time of reading, should be translucent, golden yellow to amber, and free from visible suspended particles. Reject all tests in which fat column is milky or shows presence of curd or of charred matter, or in which reading is indistinct or uncertain; repeat test, adjusting amt of H_2SO_4 added.

If desired, add glymol or pure white mineral oil (sp gr $\leq$0.85 at 20°). Introduce only few drops into bottle just before reading is made, letting it flow down inside of neck. For purpose of measurement, surface sepg glymol and fat is regarded as representing upper limit of column. Oil-sol. artificial color may be added to the white mineral oil.

16.159 Gelatin—Official Final Action

See **16.109**. Observe *Note*.

16.160 Preservatives—Official Final Action

See **16.110** and Chap. **20**.

16.161 Color Additives—Official Final Action

See **16.113** and Chap. **34**.

Residual Phosphatase—Official Final Action

16.162 ★ *Method I* ★

Folin-Ciocateu colorimetric method. *See* **15.049–15.055**, 10th ed.

***Method II* (*27*)**

16.163 ***Reagents and Sampling***

See **16.116** and **16.117**.

16.164 ***Determination***

Proceed as in **16.118**, except for following:

In *Step 1,* use 1.0 g instead of 1 mL sample if desired.

In *Step 3,* treat fresh cream in same manner as fresh milk; for old or slightly sour cream use 8 mL of the Ba borate-hydroxide buffer, **16.116**(**a**)(*1*), and 2 mL H_2O.

In *Step 6,* treat fresh cream in same manner as fresh milk; for old or slightly sour cream substitute 1.0 mL 4.5 g/100 mL soln $ZnSO_4.7H_2O$ for the Zn-Cu precipitant.

Phenol equivs >2/0.5 mL or 0.5 g indicate underpasteurization.

16.165 Reactivated and Residual Phosphatase Official First Action

See **16.129–16.130**.

EVAPORATED MILK (UNSWEETENED)

16.166 Sampling—Official Final Action

See **16.001–16.005** and **16.008–16.009**.

16.167 Preparation of Sample (*39*)—Procedure

(FAO/WHO method. *See Introduction,* **16.059**.)

(**a**) Temper unopened can in H_2O bath at ca 60°. Remove and vigorously shake can every 15 min. After 2 hr, remove can and let cool to room temp. Remove entire lid and thoroly mix by stirring contents in can with spoon or spatula. (If fat seps, sample is not properly prepd.)

(**b**) Dil. 40 g prepd mixt. (**a**) with 60 g H_2O and mix thoroly.

16.168 Lactic Acid—Official Final Action

See **16.027–16.031**.

16.169 Total Solids (*5*)—Official Final Action

Proceed as in **16.032**, using 4–5 g dild sample, **16.167**(**b**). Correct result for diln.

16.170 Ash (*5*)—Official Final Action

Ignite residue from total solids detn, **16.169**, at temp. $\leq$550° until ash is C-free. Correct result for diln.

16.171 Lead—Official First Action

See **25.068–25.082**.

16.172 Fat (*39*)—Official Final Action

(FAO/WHO method. *See Introduction,* **16.059**.)

Weigh, to nearest mg, 4–5 g undild sample, **16.167**(**a**), into fat-extn flask or tube; dil. with ca 7 mL H_2O to ca 10.5 mL and shake with slight warming (40–50°) until sample is completely dispersed. Proceed as in **16.059**, beginning "Add 1.25 mL NH_4OH . . ." Some evapd milks may require centrfg as long as 20 min at 600 rpm for complete sepn of emulsion. Difference between duplicate detns obtained simultaneously by same analyst should be $\leq$0.05 g fat/100 g product.

16.173 Total Nitrogen—Official Final Action

Weigh 5 g undild sample, **16.167**(**a**), transfer to Kjeldahl flask, and proceed as in **2.057**.

% N × 6.38 = % "protein."

16.174 Casein—Official Final Action

Weigh 10 g dild sample, **16.167**(**b**), into beaker, and proceed as in **16.047** or **16.049**. Correct result for diln.

★ Surplus method—*see* inside front cover.

16.175 Albumin—Official Final Action

Proceed as in **16.050**, using filtrate from casein detn, **16.174**. Correct result for diln.

16.176 Lactose—Official Final Action

Proceed as in **16.056** or **16.057**, using dild sample, **16.167(b)**, and correct result for diln.

16.177 Gelatin—Official Final Action

See **16.109**.

16.178 Preservatives—Official Final Action

See **16.110** and Chap. **20**.

16.179 Color Additives—Official Final Action

See **16.113** and Chap. **34**.

SWEETENED CONDENSED MILK

16.180 Sampling—Official Final Action

See **16.001–16.005** and **16.008–16.009**.

16.181 Preparation of Sample—Procedure

(**a**) Temper unopened can in H_2O bath at 30–35° until warm. Open, scrape out all milk adhering to interior of can, transfer to dish large enough to permit stirring thoroly, and mix until whole mass is homogeneous.

(**b**) Weigh 100 g thoroly mixed sample into 500 mL vol. flask, dil. to vol. with H_2O, and mix thoroly. If sample will not emulsify uniformly, weigh out sep. portion of (**a**) for each detn.

16.182 Lactic Acid—Official Final Action

See **16.027–16.031**.

16.183 Total Solids—Official Final Action

Transfer 10 mL prepd soln, **16.181(b)**, to weighed flat-bottom dish, ≥5 cm diam, contg 15–20 g previously dried sand or asbestos fiber. (*Caution: See* **51.086**.) Heat on steam bath 30 min and then in vac. oven at 100° to const wt. Cool in desiccator and weigh quickly to avoid absorption of H_2O. Correct result for diln.

16.184 Ash—Official Final Action

Evap. 10 mL prepd soln, **16.181(b)**, to dryness on H_2O bath and ignite residue as in **31.012** or **31.013**. Correct result for diln.

16.185 Fat (*39*)—Official Final Action

(FAO/WHO method. *See Introduction,* **16.059**.)

Accurately weigh 2–2.5 g prepd sample, **16.181(a)**, into fat-extn flask or tube; dil. with H_2O to ca 10.5 mL, and proceed as in **16.172**.

16.186 Protein—Official Final Action

Det. N as in **2.057**, using 10 mL prepd soln, **16.181(b)**, and correct result for diln.

% N × 6.38 = % total "protein."

16.187 Lactose—Official Final Action

Dil. 100 mL prepd soln, **16.181(b)**, in 250 mL vol. flask to ca 200 mL; add 6 mL $CuSO_4$ soln, **31.034(a)**, and alkali soln of concn and in proportion as in **16.057**. Dil. to vol. and mix thoroly. Filter thru dry filter and det. lactose as in **31.038**. Correct result for diln.

Sucrose—Official Final Action

16.188 ***Reagent***

(*Caution: See* **51.079** and **51.084**.)

Mercuric nitrate soln.—To 220 g yellow HgO, add 300–400 mL H_2O and enough (but with min. excess) HNO_3 to form clear soln (ca 140 mL), being careful to use least possible excess of acid. Dil. to 800–900 mL and slowly add 10% NaOH soln with const shaking until slight permanent ppt forms. Dil. to 1 L and filter. As soln tends to become acid with age owing to deposition of basic Hg salts, add dil. alkali occasionally until slight permanent ppt forms, and refilter.

16.189 ***Determination***

Place 50 mL prepd soln, **16.181(b)**, in 100 mL vol. flask; add 25 mL H_2O, mix, add 5 mL $Hg(NO_3)_2$ soln, and shake thoroly. Without delay and with const shaking, neutze to litmus paper with 0.5*N* NaOH, but avoid alk. reaction (12–13 mL). Dil. to 100 mL with H_2O, mix thoroly, and filter thru dry paper. Polarize filtrate in 200 mm tube; then invert at room temp. as in **31.026(c)** and polarize inverted soln. Correct both readings for vol. occupied by protein, **16.186**, and fat, **16.185**; 1 g protein occupies 0.8 mL and 1 g fat, 1.075 mL. Calc. % sucrose by following formula, using corrected direct and invert readings obtained above:

$$S = [100(a - b)/(142.35 - (t/2))] \times (26/W),$$

where S = % sucrose in sample; a = corrected direct polarization; b = corrected invert polarization; t = temp. of soln polarized; and W = wt sample taken (10 g).

DRIED MILK, NONFAT DRY MILK, AND MALTED MILK

16.190 Sampling Dried Milk (*40*)—Procedure

(*See* also **16.001–16.005** and **16.010–16.011**.)

Avoid sampling on rainy day or when humidity is high, so as to reduce moisture absorption from air to min.

On surface of milk at top of barrel locate point on each end of a diam. and on radius perpendicular to this diam., 2.5–5 cm (1–2") in from edge of barrel. Midway on each side of triangle between these points locate one point. At 6 points so located, using tubular trier long enough to extend full length of barrel, draw core parallel to vertical axis of barrel. Transfer cores to clean, dry, air-tight container and seal immediately.

Before opening sample for analysis, make homogeneous either by shaking or by alternately rolling and inverting container. Avoid excessive temp. and humidity when opening sample container.

16.191 Preparation of Sample—Procedure

Avoid absorption of moisture during prepn of sample. Mix sample by transferring to dry, air-tight container with capacity ca twice vol. of sample. Carefully mix by shaking and inverting repeatedly. When sampling, operate as rapidly as possible. If lumps are present, sift sample thru No. 20 sieve, rubbing material thru sieve and tapping vigorously, if necessary.

16.192 Moisture (*41*)—Official Final Action

Weigh 1–1.5 sample into round, flat-bottom metal dish (≥5 cm diam. and provided with tight-fitting slip-in cover). Loosen cover and place dish on metal shelf (dish resting directly on shelf) in vac. oven at 100°. Dry to const wt (ca 5 hr) under pressure ≤100 mm (4") of Hg. During drying, admit slow current of air into oven (ca 2 bubbles/sec), dried by passing thru H_2SO_4. Stop vac. pump and carefully admit dried air into oven. Press cover tightly into dish, remove from oven, cool, and weigh. Calc. % loss in wt as moisture.

Protein—Official Final Action

16.193 ***Kjeldahl Method***

Weigh 1 g sample into Kjeldahl digestion flask and det. N as in **2.057**.

% N × 6.38 = % "protein."

16.194 ***Dye Binding Method***

See **16.037–16.045**.

16.195 Casein in Malted Milk and Chocolate Malted Milk (*42*)—Official Final Action

Place 10 g sample in 250 mL (or larger) centrf. bottle and ext with two 100 mL portions pet ether by shaking until uniform, centrfg, and decanting. To dry residue add exactly 200 mL *3% $Na_2C_2O_4$ soln.* Shake occasionally over 4 hr period. Centrf. 15 min at high speed (1800 rpm if Size 1 type SB centrf. is used). Pipet 50 mL supernate (100 mL for chocolate malted milk product) into 250 mL beaker. Add 50 mL paper pulp suspension (1 filter paper) and 2 mL HOAc dropwise with const stirring. Set beaker in 45–50° H_2O 15 min. Cool to room temp. and filter with moderate suction thru 7 cm buchner, previously fitted with S&S 589 white ribbon paper, or equiv., and overlaid with layer of paper pulp. Wash ppt 2 or 3 times with cold H_2O. (Filtrate should be clear, or nearly so. If first portions of filtrate are not clear, repeat filtration and finish washing ppt.) Det. N in washed ppt and filter paper as in **2.057**, and multiply by 6.38 to obtain equiv. casein. Correct result for blank on reagents and paper pulp.

16.196 Ash—Official Final Action

Ignite 1 g sample at ≤550° until C-free. If suitable dish was used for moisture detn, **16.192**, ash may be detd on same portion. Cool in desiccator and weigh.

16.197 Alkalinity of Ash in Dry Skim Milk (*43*) Official Final Action

Ash 2 g dry skim milk 1 hr at ≤550°. Add few mL H_2O to ash, break up with flat-end stirring rod, evap. to dryness over steam bath, again ash 1 hr, and weigh. Again add few mL H_2O to ash, break up, and transfer to beaker with 50–75 mL H_2O. Add 50 mL 0.1*N* HCl, heat to boiling, and boil gently 5 min. Cool, add 30 mL *40% $CaCl_2$ soln* (neutzd with 0.1*N* HCl and filtered) and ca 10 drops phthln, and titr. excess acid with 0.1*N* NaOH.

Acid used (mL) × 50 = alky of ash.

16.198 Fat in Malted Milk (*44*)—Official Final Action

Quickly weigh ca 1 g well mixed sample into small, lipped beaker. Add 1 mL H_2O and rub to smooth paste. Add 10 mL more of H_2O, warm on steam bath, and transfer to fat-extn flask or tube with 10 mL alcohol. Mix thoroly, cool, and proceed as in **16.059**, beginning "Add 25 mL ether . . .", rinsing beaker with this ether.

Fat in Dried Milk (*45*)—Official Final Action

(FAO/WHO method. *See Introduction,* **16.059**.)

16.199 ***Preparation of Solution***

Proceed as in one of following methods:

(**a**) Quickly weigh to nearest mg ca 1 g well mixed sample into small beaker. Add 1 mL H_2O and rub to smooth paste. Add 9 mL addnl H_2O and 1–1.25 mL NH_4OH, and warm on steam bath. Transfer to fat-extn flask or tube. Cool, and proceed as in **16.200**, rinsing beaker successively with the alcohol and ethers used in first extn.

(**b**) Quickly weigh to nearest mg ca 1 g well mixed sample and transfer to fat-extn flask or tube. Add 10 mL H_2O and shake until homogeneous, warming if necessary. Add 1–1.25 mL NH_4OH and heat in H_2O bath 15 min at 60–70°, shaking occasionally. Cool, and proceed as in **16.200**.

16.200 ***Determination***

Add 10 mL alcohol to sample and mix. Ext with ether and pet ether as in **16.059**. For second extn add 4 mL alcohol, and again ext as in **16.059**. With whole milk and cream powders make third extn, using 15 mL of each solv. after adding, if necessary, enough H_2O to bring aq. layer in tube to original vol.

Difference between duplicate detns obtained simultaneously by same analyst should be ≤0.2 g fat/100 g product.

16.201 Citric Acid in Dried Milk (*3*) Official Final Action

Weigh 6 g well mixed sample, mix well with 44 mL H_2O, and proceed as in **16.024**, beginning ". . . add ca 100 mg *tartaric acid* . . ."

16.202 Lactic Acid (*4*)—Official Final Action

See **16.027–16.031**.

BUTTER

(Methods are also applicable to renovated or process butter and margarine)

16.203 Sampling (*46*)—Procedure

(*See also* **16.001–16.005** and **16.012–16.014**.)

(**a**) *Tub or cube butter.*—Sample lots as follows:

(*1*) *Tubs (or cubes) marked with churn numbers.*—Sample 1 tub of each churn of 1–9 tubs, 2 of each churn of 10–14 tubs, and 3 of each churn of >14 tubs. In no case sample <2 tubs in lot.

(*2*) *Tubs (or cubes) not marked with churn numbers.*—Sample number of tubs equiv. to sq root of number in lot, with min. of 3 and max. of 25. If sq root is not whole number, sample 1 extra tub.

(**b**) *Print butter.*—Withdraw 1 print from each of number of cases equiv. to sq root of number of cases in lot, with min. of 5 and max. of 25. When sq root is not whole number, sample 1 extra case. Select cases to include each churn or batch mark when so marked. With <5 cases, sample all, taking 5 prints as min. Remove wrapper and transfer each print to sep. sample container.

These directions provide min. sampling, to be increased if object of examination demands.

Preparation of Sample (*47*)

16.204 ***Shaking Method—Official Final Action***

Soften entire sample in sample container, **16.014**, by warming in H_2O bath kept at as low temp. as practicable, ≤39°. Avoid overheating, which causes visible sepn of curd. Shake frequently during softening process to reincorporate any sepd fat, and observe fluidity of sample. Optimum consistency is attained when emulsion is still intact but fluid enough to reveal sample level almost immediately. Remove from bath and frequently shake vigorously or place sample container in mech. shaking machine that simulates hand shaking, with arm 23 cm (9") long, set to oscillate at 425±25 times/min thru arc of 4.5 cm (1.75"). Continue shaking until sample cools to thick, creamy consistency and sample level can no longer readily be seen. Promptly weigh portion for analysis.

16.205 Moisture—Official Final Action

(FAO/WHO method. *See Introduction*, **16.059**.)

Weigh 1.5–2.5 g prepd sample of salted butter or 2–6 g unsalted butter, **16.204**, into weighed flat-bottom dish ≥5 cm diam. and dry to const wt in oven kept at temp. of boiling H_2O. Clean, dry sand may be used if fat is not to be detd in residue by **16.206**.

Fat (*47*)—Official Final Action

16.206 ***Indirect Method***

(FAO/WHO method. *See Introduction,* **16.059**.)

Take up dry butter obtained in moisture detn in which no absorbent was used, **16.205**, by macerating with 15 mL absolute ether or pet ether; transfer to weighed gooch or fritted glass crucible (16–40 μm) with aid of wash bottle filled with the solv.; and wash free from fat with 100 mL solv. (Pass last 25 mL solv. thru crucible without suction.) Dry crucible and contents at 100° to const wt. Repeat washing with 25 mL solv. and dry to const wt. Repeat operation until there is no loss in wt due to washing.

% Fat = 100 − (% moisture + % residue).

16.207 ***Direct Method***

From dry butter obtained in detn of moisture either with or without use of absorbent, ext fat with anhyd., alcohol-free ether or pet ether (bp <65°), receiving soln in weighed flask. Evap. solv. and dry ext to const wt at 100°.

16.208 Casein, Ash, and Salt—Official Final Action

Cover crucible contg residue from fat detn by indirect method, **16.206**; heat, gently at first, and gradually raise temp. to ≤500°. Remove cover and continue heating until residue is white. Loss in wt represents casein; residue in crucible represents mineral matter. Dissolve residue in H_2O slightly acidified with HNO_3 and det. Cl, either gravimetrically as in **3.072**, or volumetrically as in **3.074**, and calc. % NaCl.

16.209 Salt (*48*)—Official Final Action

(FAO/WHO method. *See Introduction,* **16.059**.)

Accurately weigh (±10 mg) ca 5 g sample into 250 mL erlenmeyer and add 100 mL boiling H_2O. Let stand, swirling occasionally, 5–10 min while cooling to 50–55°. Add 2 mL K_2CrO_4 indicator, **50.028(b)**, and titr. with 0.1*N* $AgNO_3$, stdzd as in **50.029**, until orange-brown color persists 30 sec.

mL 0.1*N* $AgNO_3$ × 0.585/g sample = % NaCl.

16.210 Examination of Fat—Official Final Action

Melt butter and keep 2–3 hr in dry place at ca 60°, or until H_2O and curd sep. completely. Filter clear supernatant fat thru dry paper in hot H_2O funnel or in oven at ca 60°. If filtered liq. fat is not perfectly clear, refilter. Det. physical and chem. consts as in Chap. **28**, particularly mole per cent butyric acid, **28.038–28.043**, cholesterol and phytosterol in mixts of animal and vegetable fats, **28.085–28.087**, **28.089–28.098**, and sol. and insol. volatile acids (Reichert-Meissl and Polenske values), **28.036–28.037**.

Acid Value of Fat (*49*)—Official Final Action

(Prepd by joint committee of International Dairy Federation, International Organization for Standardization, and AOAC for publication by each organization and published as an international standard in *FAO/WHO Code of Principles Concerning Milk and Milk Products and Associated Standards*.)

16.211 ***Definition and Principle***

Acid value of fat from butter = mg KOH required to neutze 1 g fat. Fat sepd by melting butter, is dissolved in alcohol-ether mixt., and titrd with std alkali.

16.212 ***Reagents***

(**a**) *Alcoholic potassium hydroxide std soln.*—0.1*N*. Use absolute alcohol or alcohol denatured with MeOH.

(**b**) *Alcohol-ether mixture.*—Equal vols alcohol (or alcohol denatured with MeOH) and ether. Add 0.3 mL phthln soln, (**c**)/100 mL mixt., and add alc. KOH soln, (**a**), to faint pink.

(**c**) *Phenolphthalein soln.*—1% in alcohol or alcohol denatured with MeOH.

16.213 ***Determination***

Weigh, to nearest mg, 5–10 g well mixed sample, **16.210**, into 250–300 mL erlenmeyer. Add 50–100 mL alcohol-ether mixt. and 0.1 mL phthln soln. Titr. with 0.1*N* alc. KOH until permanent faint pink appears and persists for ≥10 sec.

Acid value = mL alc. KOH soln × normality alc. KOH soln × 56.1/g sample. Difference between duplicate detns should be ≤0.1 mg KOH/g fat.

16.214 Refractive Index of Fat (*49*)
Official Final Action

(*See Introduction,* **16.211**.)

Prep. sample as in **16.210** and proceed as in **28.006**, adjusting circulating H_2O to 40±0.1°. Correct observed refractive index by adding 0.000045 for each unit of acid value if latter is ≥2 as detd in **16.213**, rounding off to fourth decimal.

Difference between duplicate detns should be ≤0.0002.

Critical Temperature of Dissolution (*50*)
Official Final Action

16.215 ***Reagent***

Alcohol-isoamyl alcohol reagent.—Mix 2 vols 95% (by vol.) alcohol (checked by sp gr) with 1 vol. redistd isoamyl alcohol (bp 128–132°), both measured with pipet or vol. flask. Keep well-stoppered.

16.216 ***Apparatus***

(**a**) *Test tubes.*—Pyrex, 18 × 150 mm, marked at 2 and 4 mL, measured by adding H_2O from buret.

(**b**) *Micro burner.*

(**c**) *Pipet*.—Glass tube, ca 2–3 mL capacity, drawn to fast-flowing tip.

(**d**) *Thermometer*.—Range 0–100°, graduated in degrees.

16.217 ***Determination***

Prep. oil from butter or margarine as in **16.210**. Oil must be clear. Fill test tube to 2 mL mark with oil, using pipet. Immediately add alcohol reagent to 4 mL mark (or add 2 mL with pipet). Using thermometer as stirring rod, mix the 2 layers and heat in flame of micro burner. Keep stirring and heating until mixt. becomes clear and homogeneous. *Do not boil*. Remove from heat and keep stirring until definite turbidity appears in *mixture proper*. Record temp. at first discernible turbidity. (Opalescence will immediately follow thruout entire mixt. with further drop in temp.)

16.218 Color Additives—Official Final Action

Pour ca 2 g filtered fat, dissolved in ether, into each of 2 test tubes. To one tube add 1–2 mL HCl (1+1) and to other ca same vol. 10% NaOH soln. Shake tubes well and let stand. In presence of some azo dyes, acid soln turns pink to wine-red, white alk. soln in other tube shows no color. If, on other hand, annatto or other vegetable color is present, alk. soln is yellow, while no color is apparent in acid soln. (Red changing to yellow, especially on warming, in alk. soln may be due to presence of gallate antioxidants.)

General test.—Proceed as in Chap. **34** for detection of oil-sol. synthetic dyes and as in **16.113** for annatto.

16.219 Lactic Acid—Official Final Action

See **16.027–16.031**.

Water-Insoluble Fatty Acids (WIA)

16.220 ***Gravimetric Method (36)—Official Final Action***

(*Caution: See* **51.011**, **51.039**, and **51.054**.)

Weigh 50 g prepd sample, **16.204**, into 250 mL centrf. bottle, and add 10 mL H_2O; if necessary, remelt in warm H_2O (not steam) bath and add 50 mL ether. Shake until fat dissolves.

Add 1*N* NaOH in ca 0.2 mL increments to mixt. in centrf. bottle until neutzd to decided pink, using 10 drops phthln, and shaking between addns of alkali. Then add 0.5 mL excess and shake again ≥2 min. During this and all subsequent shakings, carefully release pressure several times to avoid blowing out stopper and losing some of contents. (It is difficult to shake >1 bottle at a time because of greasy stoppers and pressure that develops.)

Remove stopper and add 50 mL pet ether, shake few times, and centrf. 5 min at ca 1200 rpm (longer if sepn is not sharp). Set bottle on horizontal surface and siphon off ether-fat layer. (If ether layer, after centrfg, is reddish, add 10 mL H_2O, shake, and again centrf. as before. If reddish tinge still persists in ether layer, add 25 mL ether, shake, and again centrf.) Wash aq. layer remaining in centrf. bottle by adding 25 mL ether; mix thoroly by shaking several sec, add 25 mL pet ether, and again mix by shaking. Centrf., siphon off ether layer as before, and repeat washing as above. If after any washing, basic red of phthln fades, add addnl phthln and alkali to give decided red (not pink).

Add 1 mL H_2SO_4 (1+1) to residue in centrf. bottle and shake vigorously few sec. Then add 5 mL *10% $Na_2WO_4.2H_2O$ soln* and again shake vigorously few sec. (Mixt. should be distinctly acid to *Congo red paper;* if it is not, add more H_2SO_4.) Now add 75 mL ether, shake violently ≥2 min, and centrf. Siphon off ether layer into 500 mL separator. Wash siphon inside and out with 75 mL ether so that washings drain into centrf. bottle. Shake bottle violently ≥2 min, centrf., and siphon off ether layer into the separator. (Disregard slight opalescence of ether layer.)

Add 100 mL alcohol (1+1) to combined exts in separator and neutze in same manner as before with 1*N* NaOH to decided pink. Add 0.5 mL excess and shake vigorously 2 min more. Immediately add 25 mL H_2O, mix by single inversion of separator, and let stand until aq. layer is clear. (Sepn usually occurs in few min; slow sepn may sometimes be hastened by playing fine stream of H_2O on ether surface. If vol. of emulsion at interface is only ca 10 mL it may be included in subsequent extn.) Drain aq. layer into 600 mL beaker. Add 50 mL alcohol (1+1) and ca 10 drops phthln to separator and neutze with 1*N* alkali, shaking vigorously ca 2 min. Add 50 mL H_2O, mix by single inversion of separator, and let stand until aq. layer is clear. Drain aq. layer into the beaker. Then add 10 mL H_2O to separator, mix by single inversion, let sep. until aq. layer is clear, and drain into beaker.

Place beaker contg combined exts and washings on steam bath (or carefully heat on hot plate) to expel any ether. Evap. to ca 25 mL (small fan is useful if foaming is serious). (Soln should remain decided red thru all these operations and up to point where soaps are acidified.) Transfer to 250 mL beaker with ca 25 mL H_2O. (As alternative, material may be evapd to dryness on steam bath and residue dissolved in ca 50 mL H_2O.)

Dissolve 5 g anhyd. Na_2SO_4 in warm soln (vol. must be ≥50 mL when Na_2SO_4 and H_2SO_4 are added), heating if necessary. Cool to ≤20°, stirring frequently to keep soaps from forming hard crust on surface. Make acid by adding H_2SO_4 (1+1) dropwise, using Congo red paper as indicator. Stir vigorously to effect thoro liberation of fatty acids, mashing all pink soap curds. Add ca 500 mg filter-aid and mix. Filter with suction on suitable filter crucible. Rinse beaker with three ca 15 mL portions H_2O at ≤20° and transfer rinsings to crucible. Maintain suction *several min after visible dripping ceases* to dry ppt. (Heavy ppts can be sucked drier if cracks are plastered up with some of ppt. Filtrate should be clear.)

Substitute tared beaker or flask (weighed with similar vessel as counterpoise), contg few glass beads or grains of sand, for receiving flask of filtering app. Ext acids with four ca 15 mL portions ether, breaking up ppt with stirring rod between extns and thoroly mixing with the ether. Let ether drip thru filter before applying suction. (Filter pad must not be disturbed.) Evap. ether ext, which should be no more than faintly opalescent, on steam bath, and dry acids 1 hr in 100° oven. Cool and weigh. Report results as mg H_2O-insol. acids (WIA)/100 g butterfat.

Dissolve weighed acids in 10 mL neut. benzene and titr. with 0.1*N* Na ethylate (prepd similarly to 0.05*N* Na ethylate, **17.035(b)**), using 10 drops phthln as indicator, until end point holds ≥1 min. (Neut. alcohol instead of benzene and 0.1*N* NaOH instead of Na ethylate may be used.) Compute mean mol. wt of fatty acids by dividing mg acids found by mL 0.1*N* alkali used for titrn and multiplying by 10. (Mean mol. wt should be ≤290. When amt acids is <150 mg/100 g butterfat, mean mol. wt is without significance.)

Notes: To siphon off ether, use tube similar to delivery tube of ordinary wash bottle but with intake end bent up into U shape in opposite direction to outlet end, with opening 6–12 mm higher than bottom of U, cut off horizontally. (Avoid excessive constriction when bending.) Set delivery tube loosely enough in stopper that it can be raised or lowered. In operating, adjust opening of U bend to ca 3 mm above surface of aq. layer and blow ether layer off by gently blowing thru mouthpiece tube inserted in adjacent hole in stopper.

Following setup is convenient for filtration of fatty acids: Bell jar and gooch with removable bottom charged with thin layer of asbestos overlaid with small amt of filter-aid (flux calcined diatomite "Speedex," Dicalite Div., Grefco, Inc., 3435 W Lomita Blvd, Torrance, CA 90505, added as suspension in H_2O). Use long fiber, amphibole variety, acid and alkali-washed asbestos for gooch, washed twice by decantation. (Coarse fritted glass crucibles overlaid with small amt of filter-aid are also satisfactory.)

Water-Insoluble Fatty Acids (WIA) and Butyric Acid

Chromatographic Method—Official Final Action

16.221 ***Apparatus***

Chromatographic tube.—Approx. 2 × 40–50 cm. Tube described in **28.038** is also satisfactory.

16.222 ***Reagents***

(**a**) *n-Hexane-butanol soln.*—*n*-Hexane contg 1% *n*-BuOH. *See* **28.039(d)**.

(**b**) *Silicic acid.*—Mallinckrodt's powder especially prepd for chromatgy. Dry 2 hr at 130° and keep in tightly stoppered bottles.

(**c**) *Ammoniacal glycol soln.*—Dissolve 500 mg bromocresol green in 500 mL ethylene glycol by warming on steam bath. Cool, add NH_4OH dropwise until soln is dark blue (1–3 drops), and then add 1 drop excess. This soln should turn olive-green when mixed with the silicic acid.

(**d**) *Alcoholic potassium hydroxide std soln.*— 0.05*N*. Dissolve 4 g KOH pellets in 100 mL isopropanol by warming and swirling on steam bath. Decant supernate from small amt of aq. KOH soln clinging to flask. Dil. to 1 L with 400 mL isopropanol and 500 mL alcohol. Stdze with NBS benzoic acid (SRM 350), using 2 drops thymol blue as indicator.

(**e**) *Thymol blue soln.*—Dissolve 300 mg thymol blue in 10 mL 0.05*N* alc. KOH and add 90 mL isopropanol. Soln should be blue; if not, add enough 0.05*N* alc. KOH to make soln dark blue.

(**f**) *Cresol red indicator.*—Dissolve 50 mg *o*-cresolsulfonphthalein in 20 mL alcohol. Add 1.3 mL 0.1*N* NaOH and dil. to 50 mL with H_2O.

16.223 ***Preparation of Sample***

(*Caution: See* **51.011**, **51.039**, **51.054**, and **51.073**.)

Weigh 100 g prepd sample, **16.204**, into 250 mL beaker. Melt on steam bath and transfer to 500 mL separator. Rinse beaker with 20 mL H_2O and then with 100 mL ether, and add rinsings to separator. Shake until fat dissolves.

Add 1*N* NaOH in ca 0.2 mL increments to mixt. in separator until neutzd to decided pink, using 10 drops phthln as indicator and shaking between addns of alkali. Then add 0.5 mL excess and shake again ⩾2 min. Add 100 mL pet ether, shake few times, and let layers sep. (5–10 min). Drain aq. layer and any emulsion into 250 mL centrf. bottle. Shake fat layer with 10 mL H_2O and add aq. layer to centrf. bottle after sepn. Wash soln in centrf. bottle by adding 50 mL ether, mixing thoroly by shaking; add 50 mL pet ether and again mix by shaking. Centrf. 5 min at ca 1200 rpm and siphon off ether-fat layer. If sepns have not been sharp and if much fat is still present, repeat washing with 50 mL ether and 50 mL pet ether. Continue as in **16.220**, beginning, 4th par., "Add 1 mL H_2SO_4 (1+1) . . .", except use 10 mL 10% $Na_2WO_4.2H_2O$ instead of 5 mL and two 100 mL portions ether instead of 75 mL. When material has evapd to 25 mL on hot plate or steam bath, transfer to 100 mL beaker and evap. to dryness on steam bath or, with extreme care, on hot plate.

16.224 ***Preparation of Chromatographic Column***

To 20.0 g silicic acid in mortar add 14 mL ammoniacal glycol soln. Mix thoroly with pestle until homogeneous. Add few mL hexane-BuOH soln and mix to form smooth paste; then add enough solv. to form slurry. Add slurry with spoon thru funnel to chromatgc tube contg small, loosely-packed cotton plug in constricted end, and ca 30 mL hexane-BuOH soln. Force excess solv. thru column, using pressure of 5–10 psi (34.5–69 kPa), **18.050(c)**. Remove pressure when all of solv. has passed into gel but before column "cracks." Keep small amt of solv. on top of column until ready for use. Do not use cracked column.

16.225 ***Separation of Fatty Acids***

To dry residue of Na salts in 100 mL beaker, **16.223**, add 0.50 mL H_2O and mix well. Add 0.50 mL H_2SO_4 (1+1) and mix well, being careful to break up and neutze all lumps. (Sharp needle or stirring rod is sometimes needed to scrape material from bottom of beaker.) Add 2.0 g silicic acid and stir to uniform powder.

Add enough solv. to top of column to make 5 mL. Dry sides of tube by stream of air from glass tube and rubber bulb. Transfer powder to liq. in tube. Mix powder and solv. on top of column with long stirring rod. Do not disturb surface of original gel. Force excess solv. into column with pressure. Rinse stirring rod, funnel, beaker, and sides of tube with two 10 mL portions solv., forcing excess solv. into column after each addn.

Fill tube with solv. and force solv. thru column dropwise (2–3 mL/min) with as much pressure as necessary. If column cracks or solv. flows thru column too rapidly, prep. new column, reducing amt of ammoniacal glycol soln added to silicic acid (use ca 1 mL less). If solv. flows too slowly even with pressure, use more ammoniacal glycol soln.

Collect first 125 mL eluate and titr. with std 0.05*N* alc. KOH, using 10 drops thymol blue soln as indicator. 1 mL 0.05*N* KOH = 13.5 mg WIA. Discard next 40–60 mL or until yellow band of butyric acid starts to elute. Collect next 75 mL eluate and titr. with 0.01*N* NaOH, using 25 mL *CO_2-free, neutzd H_2O* and 2–3 drops cresol red indicator. 1 mL 0.01*N* NaOH = 0.88 mg butyric acid. Calc. WIA and butyric acid to mg/100 g fat.

16.226 ★ ***Rapid Method (51)—Official Final Action*** ★

(Does not recover salts of WIA produced by neutzn)

Butterfat sepd from cream or butter is dissolved in ether and titrd with NaOEt, using phthln. *See* **16.208–16.210**, 12th ed.

16.227 Volatile Acids—Official Final Action

Weigh 50 g sample into each of 2 centrf. bottles and proceed as in **16.220**, beginning "Add 1*N* NaOH . . ." and continuing thru second washing with mixed ethers to remove fat. Then remove residual ethers from bottles by evapn on steam bath, transfer contents of both to single 200 mL vol. flask with H_2O, and add 1 mL H_2SO_4 (1+1) and 10 mL *10% $Na_2WO_4.2H_2O$ soln*. Dil. to vol., mix, and filter. Transfer 150 mL filtrate to distn flask and proceed with distn, chromatgc sepn, and detn as in **18.054–18.058** or **18.059**. Calc. to mg acids/100 g fat.

See **14.099–14.101** for identification of volatile acids.

16.228 Preservatives—Official Final Action

See **16.110** and Chap. **20**.

16.229 ★ **Microscopic Examination—Procedure** ★

See **15.153**, 10th ed.

16.230 Residual Phosphatase (*27*)—Official Final Action

See **16.118**. Take sample from beneath surface with clean knife or spatula and proceed as follows:

★ Surplus method—*see* inside front cover.

Step 1.—Weigh 1.0 g sample (preferably in duplicate) on piece of waxed paper ca 2.5 cm sq and insert paper with sample into tube. Similarly, weigh another sample and place in tube as control or blank.

Step 2.—Heat *blank* ca 1 min to 85–90° in beaker of boiling H_2O (covered so entire tube is heated to 85–90°), and cool to room temp. From this point treat blank and test alike.

Step 3.—Add 10.0 mL buffer substrate prepd as in **16.116(b)**, except dissolve $Na_2C_6H_5PO_4$ in 100 mL undild Ba borate-hydroxide buffer made from 18 g $Ba(OH)_2.8H_2O$ and 8 g H_3BO_3/L. Stopper tube and mix.

Step 4.—Immediately after adding substrate, incubate 1 hr in H_2O bath at 37–38°, mixing or shaking contents occasionally.

Step 5.—Heat in beaker of boiling H_2O nearly 1 min, heating to 85–90° (use thermometer in another tube of same size and shape contg same vol. of liq.), and cool to room temp. in vessel of cold H_2O.

Step 6.—Pipet in 1 mL 6.0% $ZnSO_4.7H_2O$ soln, and mix thoroly (pH of mixt. should be 9.0–9.1).

Step 7.—Filter (5 cm funnel, 9 cm Whatman No. 42 or No. 2 paper recommended), and collect 5.0 mL filtrate in tube, preferably graduated at 5.0 and 10.0 mL.

Steps 8—11.—Proceed as in **16.118**.

Step 12.—When using 1.0 g butter and adding 11.0 mL liq., multiply value of reading by 1.1 to convert result to phenol equivs/0.5 g butter. (Values >2 equivs/0.5 g indicate underpasteurization.)

See **16.129–16.130** for differential test for reactivated and residual phosphatase.

CHEESE

16.231 Collection of Sample—Procedure

(*See* also **16.001–16.005** and **16.015–16.018**.)

When cheese can be cut, take narrow wedge reaching from outer edge to center. When not permissible to cut cheese, take sample with cheese trier. If only one plug can be obtained, take it perpendicular to surface of cheese at point ⅓ distance from edge to center and extending either entirely or half-way thru. When >1 plug can be taken, draw 3 plugs, 1 from center, 1 near outer edge, and 1 midway between other two. Use ca 2 cm (¾") of rind portion of core to reseal hole.

Sample bulk containers of cottage and similar cheeses by stirring can thoroly for ≥5 min with dairy stirrer (ca 14 cm (5.5") perforated concave metal disk attached to ca 70 cm (27") metal rod as handle) so that all portions of container are reached. Remove portions from top surface with small spoon to fill 0.5 L (1 pt) jar, and cover.

16.232 Preparation of Sample—Procedure

Cut wedge sample into strips and pass 3 times thru food chopper. Grind plugs in food chopper (preferable method), or cut or shred very finely and mix thoroly.

With creamed cottage and similar cheeses, place 300–600 g sample at <15° in 1 L (1 qt) cup of high-speed blender and blend for min. time (2–5 min) required to obtain homogeneous mixt. Final temp. should be ≤25°. This may require stopping blender frequently after channeling and spooning cheese back into blades until blending action starts. (Use of variable transformer in line to permit slow speed at first minimizes channeling when speed is increased later.)

Moisture

16.233 *Method I (52)—Official Final Action*

Weigh 2–3 g prepd sample, **16.232**, into weighed round, flat-bottom metal dish, ≥5 cm diam. and provided with tight-fit, slip-in cover. In case of soft cheese and process cheese of high moisture content, weigh 1–2 g and partially dry on steam bath. Place loosely covered dish on metal shelf (dish resting directly on shelf) in vac. oven, kept at 100°. Dry to const wt (ca 4 hr) under pressure ≤100 mm Hg (13.3 kPa). During drying admit into oven slow current of air (ca 2 bubbles/sec) dried by passing thru H_2SO_4. Stop vac. pump and carefully admit air into oven. Press cover tightly into dish, remove dish from oven, cool, and weigh. Express loss in wt as moisture.

16.234 *Method II (Rapid Screening Method) (53) Official First Action*

Weigh 2–3 g prepd sample into moisture dish with tight-fit cover. Partially dry on steam bath with lid removed and then insert in forced-draft oven that has come to equilibrium at 130±1°. Dry 1.25 hr (with cover entirely off), cover tightly, remove from oven, cool, and weigh.

Method III (Distillation Method) (54)—Official Final Action

(Applicable to blue and other cheeses contg significant amts of substances other than H_2O volatile at 100°)

16.235 *Apparatus*

(**a**) *Receiver.*—Bidwell & Sterling, or modified Bidwell & Sterling, with 5 mL volumetric tube 146–156 mm long, graduated in 0.05 or 0.1 mL divisions, with ₸ or ⱻ joints, upper 24/40, lower 24/40 or 40/50 (SGA Scientific Inc., No. D8580 or JD7780, or equiv.).

(**b**) *Condenser.*—Cold-finger type, supported by smooth, uniform shoulder in uniformly and symmetrically flared glass tube connected to receiver by ₸ joint. Diam. of shoulder is 20–35 mm, and length below shoulder 75–100 mm. Powder funnel with ₸ or ⱻ joint is suitable support. Flare exceeds diam. of condenser shoulder, and makes close, uniform, but never tight, fit with condenser at entire ring of contact with shoulder. Maintain ring of solv. between shoulder and support during heating-up period, while allowing expanding air in system to bubble past. Portion of condenser below shoulder should hang free, and cooling H_2O entrance and exit tubes should be clear of condenser support. Lower tip should be well above the surface of solv. in receiver.

(**c**) *Boiling flask.*—250 mL, r-b, short neck, ₸ or ⱻ 40/50 joint with, if necessary, reducing adapter, ₸ 24/40–40/50, for receivers with lower joint ₸ 24/40.

(**d**) *Heating mantle connected to voltage controller.*

16.236 *Distillation Solvent*

Mix *n*-amyl alcohol and xylene, 1+2, and distil at temp. plateau, ca 129–134°. Add ≤5 mL H_2O to convenient vol. of distd solv. mixt., distil off H_2O as in stdzn of app., cool, and store solv. mixt. in g-s container. If in stdzn of app., using solv. mixt. without distg or equilibrating, no significant difference is found from value obtained with distg, these steps may be omitted. (Baker's Analyzed Reagent, or equiv., *n*-amyl alcohol and xylene have been found satisfactory as received.)

16.237 *Standardization of Apparatus*

Support app. adequately to maintain tight connections. Lubricate lower joints with USP White Petrolatum. Sep. insulate side arm of receiver and exposed portion of flask with Fiberglass, nonabsorbent cotton, or other suitable material. Thoroly clean and dry interior of app., rinse with anhyd. MeOH and then with distn solv., and fill volumetric tube of receiver with solv. Likewise rinse interior portion of condenser, wipe with clean, dry wiping tissue, and immediately insert condenser in app. Dry externally exposed portion of condenser with tissue wipes, and shield as needed to prevent accumulation of condensed atm. H_2O.

Add to clean, dry boiling flask enough SiC fragments, or similar sharp, nonporous boiling aids of mixed size, 6–25 mesh, mostly 10–20, to cover bottom to diam. ≥4 cm. Add ca 10 mL distn solv., and redry by distn, if necessary, at low heat. Cover flask loosely and cool; then cover flask tightly to exclude H_2O and weigh to 0.001 g. Add ca 4.5 g H_2O, quickly re-cover flask, and reweigh to obtain wt H_2O to ±0.001 g.

Immediately add ca 60 mL distn solv. to flask and connect to receiver. Heat slowly until refluxing starts; adjust heat to distil 20–30 min at ca 0.2–0.3 mL H_2O/min; then increase rate of refluxing gradually to rate attained by full voltage. When no more H_2O droplets fall from tip of condenser, lift condenser and rinse walls of receiver and that portion of condenser inside system with distn solv. from plastic squeeze-type bottle with fine tip. Continue distn few min and repeat rinsing. Repeat this operation at intervals of 1–2 min until no more H_2O droplets are seen to fall into volumetric tube. Remove condenser and support it in dry, clean flask, e.g., 125 mL ₮ 24/40 erlenmeyer. Remove boiling flask, first tilting receiver slightly to return some of solv. to flask, and place on supporting ring to cool.

Immerse volumetric tube in H_2O at convenient temp. (25° or room temp.) and when equilibrium is reached, read, and est. vol. distd H_2O to nearest 0.01 mL. Magnifier is helpful; avoid parallax.

Calc. distn factor at temp. selected = g H_2O added/mL H_2O distd.

Repeat stdzn until consecutively detd factors agree within ±0.002 of av. of 2. Use av. of the 2 detns as distn factor.

16.238 ***Determination***

Prep. app. and distn solv. as in **16.237**. Place in covered, dry, weighed boiling flask, contg boiling aids and ca 10 mL distn solv., portion of well mixed sample contg ca 4.5 g H_2O, e.g., 9–11 g soft cheeses (camembert, etc.), 11–13 g cheddar, blue, etc. (35–40% H_2O), and 13–15 g hard, dry cheeses. Immediately re-cover tightly and reweigh to ±0.005 g.

Add ca 60 mL distn solv. and connect to app. (or, after addn of solv., samples may be held in tightly closed flasks until ready to distil). Start heating slowly and distil H_2O in same manner as in **16.237**, but refluxing slowly at low heat for ca 40–50 min, then increasing heat gradually to full voltage for few min, using same criteria for completion of distn. Cheese will spread in thin layer over bottom of flask and will become tan to brownish yellow, depending on variety, but not dark brown or scorched in appearance. Complete distn in 1–1.25 hr. Read vol. distd H_2O under exactly same conditions as in **16.237**. Calc. % H_2O in sample = (distn factor × vol. H_2O distd × 100)/g sample.

Remove dried cheese from flask by digesting with dil. alkali soln on steam bath until dispersed, then washing with hot H_2O, reusing washed boiling aids. Used solv. may be distd for re-use.

Method IV (Microwave Oven Method) (55)
Official First Action

16.239 ***Apparatus***

Microwave tester.—App. consists of microwave oven operating at 2,450 megahertz and calibrated at factory to give direct readout in % moisture (vac. oven method, **16.233**) using specified power setting and time. Available from Apollo Microwave Products, 6204 Official Rd, Crystal Lake, IL 60014. Operate in accordance with instructions from manufacturer.

16.240 ***Determination***

Prep. sample as in **16.232**. Place 100 × 10 mm Petri dish contg 11 cm circle of glass fiber filter and Teflon ring on built-in weighing mechanism of oven and tare to zero. Evenly spread 10.00 g sample over surface of dish and cover with glass paper held in place with Teflon ring. Place dish on weighing platform within microwave cavity. Close door and set timer for 2.25 min and power for 74 units. Activate unit and when app. shuts off, read % moisture directly.

Check calibration periodically against samples analyzed by **16.233**. Adjust time and power setting to maintain correspondence in values. Adjustment is necessary only when several samples consistently give values outside 2 times std deviation of difference from **16.233**.

16.241 Ash *(56)*—Official Final Action

Weigh 3–5 g prepd sample, **16.232**, into Pt dish, place on steam bath, and dry ca 1 hr. (If cheese is high in fat, place small amt of absorbent cotton in dish.) Ignite cautiously to avoid spattering and remove burner while fat is burning. When flame ceases, complete ignition in furnace at ≤550°, cool, and weigh.

Total Chlorides *(57)*—Official Final Action
IDF-ISO-AOAC Method

(Applicable to all cheeses contg ≥0.5% Cl)

16.242 ***Principle***

Cheese is digested with $KMnO_4$ and HNO_3, and Cl is detd by titrn with $AgNO_3$ in presence of $NH_4Fe(SO_4)_2$ as indicator.

16.243 ***Determination***

(*Caution: See* **51.069**.)

Accurately weigh ca 2 g prepd sample, **16.015–16.018** and **16.231–16.232**, into 300 mL erlenmeyer. Pipet in 25 mL 0.1*N* $AgNO_3$, **50.027–50.031**, add 25 mL HNO_3, and mix thoroly. Heat to boiling, add ca 10 mL satd $KMnO_4$ soln, and maintain gentle boiling. After decolorization, add addnl 5–10 mL satd $KMnO_4$ soln until brown color indicates destruction of org. matter is complete. Remove excess $KMnO_4$ by adding small amt oxalic acid or glucose. Add 100 mL cold H_2O and 2 mL satd $NH_4Fe(SO_4)_2$ soln and mix thoroly. Immediately titr. excess $AgNO_3$ with 0.1*N* NH_4SCN or KSCN, **50.002–50.004**, until soln is red-brown 30 sec. Analyze blank, using 2 mL H_2O in place of 2 g cheese.

$$\% \text{ Cl} = [(V_1 - V_2) \times f \times N]/W,$$

where V_1 = mL SCN soln used for blank, V_2 = mL SCN soln used for sample, N = normality of SCN soln, W = g sample, and f = 3.55 for Cl (5.85 for NaCl).

16.244 Salt—Procedure

See **24.011–24.014**.

16.245 Nitrogen—Official Final Action

Det. N in weighed portion (ca 2 g) prepd sample, **16.232**, as in **2.057**.

$$\% \text{ N} \times 6.38 = \% \text{ "protein."}$$

16.246 Titanium *(58)*—Official Final Action

See **25.139–25.142**.

16.247 Acidity—Official Final Action

To 10 g prepd sample, **16.232**, add H_2O at 40° to vol. of 105 mL, shake vigorously, and filter. Titr. 25 mL portion filtrate, representing 2.5 g sample, with std NaOH, preferably 0.1*N*, using phthln. Express result as lactic acid. 1 mL 0.1*N* NaOH = 0.0090 g lactic acid. Results may also be expressed as mL 0.1*N* NaOH/100 g.

16.248 Color Additives—Official First Action

(*Caution: See* **51.011**, **51.039**, and **51.054**.)

Ext 25–50 g prepd sample, **16.232**, with ether, remove ether by evapn, and proceed as in Chap. **34**.

Nitrate and Nitrite (*59*)—Official Final Action

(Applicable to cheeses contg ≥1 ppm NO_3)

16.249 ***Apparatus and Reagents***

(**a**) *Modified Jones reductor*.—Glass tube, 300 × 10 mm id, with stopcock, and reservoir consisting of 200 mL addn funnel with ₮ 24/40 stopper (*see* Fig. **16:04**), or equiv. chromatgc column with stopcock.

(**b**) *Ammonia buffer soln*.—pH 9.6–9.7. Dil. 20 mL HCl to 500 mL with H_2O. Mix, and add 50 mL NH_4OH. Dil. to 1 L and mix. Check pH, and adjust if necessary.

(**c**) *Cadmium sulfate soln*.—0.14*M*. Dissolve 37 g $3CdSO_4.8H_2O$ in H_2O and dil. to 1 L.

(**d**) *Color reagent*.—Dissolve 2.10 g sulfanilic acid (Eastman Organic Chemicals, or equiv.) in 250 mL 15% (v/v) HOAc by heating on steam bath. Dissolve 0.521 g 1-naphthylamine.HCl (*Caution: See* **51.085**) (Eastman Organic Chemicals, or equiv.) in 30 mL H_2O by heating on steam bath. Pour while still hot into 250 mL 15% HOAc. Mix the 2 solns, filter if necessary, and store in g-s brown glass bottle in refrigerator. Prep. fresh weekly.

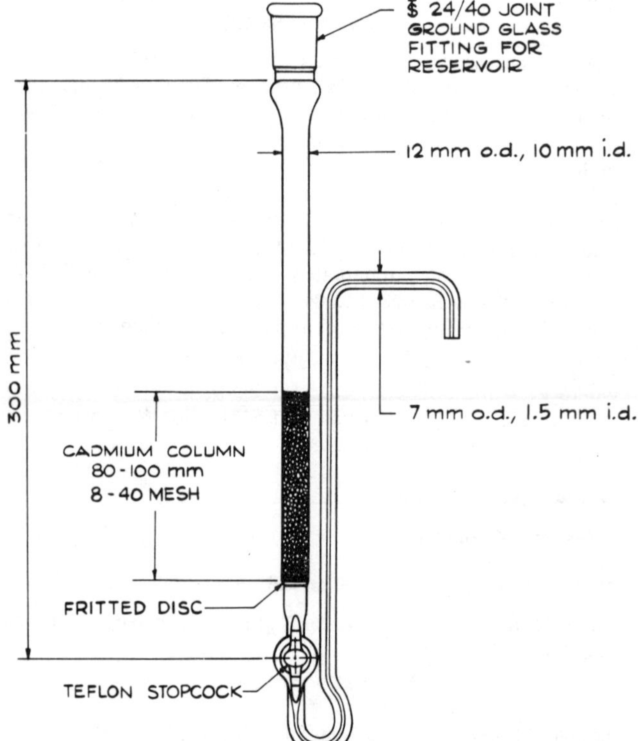

FIG. 16:04—Modified Jones reductor

(**e**) *Zinc*.—Approx. 10 cm sticks.

(**f**) *Zinc sulfate soln*.—0.42*M*. Dissolve 120 g $ZnSO_4.7H_2O$ in H_2O and dil. to 1 L.

(**g**) *Potassium nitrate std solns*.—(*1*) *Stock soln*.— 1 mg NO_3/mL. Dissolve ca 1.6308 g KNO_3 primary std (Fisher Scientific Co., or equiv.), previously dried 1 hr at 110° and accurately weighed, in H_2O, dil. to 1 L, and mix. (*2*) *Working soln*.—10 μg NO_3/mL. Transfer 10.0 mL stock soln to 1 L vol. flask, dil. to vol. with H_2O, and mix.

(**h**) *Sodium nitrite std solns*.—(*1*) *Stock soln*.—0.2 mg NO_2/mL. Dissolve ca 0.3000 g $NaNO_2$ primary std (Fisher Scientific Co., or equiv.), previously dried 1 hr at 110° and accurately weighed, in H_2O, dil. to 1 L, and mix. (*2*) *Working soln*.—2 μg NO_2/mL. Transfer 10 mL stock soln to 1 L vol. flask, dil. to vol. with H_2O, and mix.

16.250 ***Preparation of Samples***

Remove any wax coating and outer portion of cheese rind and any surface mold.

(**a**) *Very hard (less than 25% moisture) and hard and semisoft (less than 40% moisture) cheeses*.—Dice into ≤6 mm cubes and mix thoroly. Grind 3 times. Some hard varieties may be grated.

(**b**) *Soft (more than 40% moisture) cheeses*.—Composite and mix well.

Store all cheese in glass jars with tight-fitting lids. Prep. cheese-H_2O slurry (1+2) (cheese factor = ⅓, inverse of which appears in final equation). Blend in high-speed blender at high speed until smooth.

16.251 ***Extraction***

Accurately weigh ca 30±0.1 g slurry into 200 mL vol. flask. Add 70 mL H_2O and heat to ca 50°, swirling occasionally. Add 10 mL $ZnSO_4$ soln and 12 mL 2% NaOH soln, swirling after each addn. Maintain temp. at ca 50° for addnl 10 min, swirling occasionally. Cool to room temp. in H_2O bath. Dil. to vol. with H_2O and mix thoroly. Filter thru fluted paper, discarding first 20 mL filtrate, into 250 mL g-s flask. Refilter if ext is not clear. Sample exts are stable at this point. Reserve portion of this unreduced filtrate for **16.254**.

Prep. H_2O reagent blank by omitting cheese slurry. Reserve blank for use in **16.253** and **16.254**.

16.252 ***Preparation of Standard Curve***

Add 0, 1, 2, 3, 4, 5, 10, and 15 mL $NaNO_2$ working std soln to sep. 50 mL vol. flasks. Add 10.0 mL color reagent, dil. to vol. with H_2O, mix, and let stand in dark 25 min. Read spectrophtric in 1 cm cells at max. *A*, 522±2 nm, against blank (0 std addn). Scan from 640 to 440 nm with recording spectrophtr. Prep. calibration curve by plotting *A* at max. against μg NO_2/50 mL.

16.253 ***Preparation of Modified Jones Reductor***

Place 3–5 Zn sticks each in 2 sep. 800 mL beakers contg 500 mL $CdSO_4$ soln. Remove Zn sticks every 2–3 hr and scrape off spongy metallic Cd by rubbing sticks against each other. After 6–8 hr, decant and wash deposits with two 500 mL portions H_2O. (*Caution:* Cd must be kept covered with aq. soln.) Transfer Cd with H_2O to high-speed blender and blend 2–3 sec. Retain 8–40 mesh particles. Repeat to increase yield of particles. Wash particles with 0.1*N* HCl, stirring occasionally with glass rod. Leave overnight in acid. Stir once more to degas. Decant and wash with two 100 mL portions H_2O. Fill modified Jones reductor to depth of 8–10 cm with Cd, draining occasionally during filling but not letting liq. level fall below top of bed. Eliminate bubbles in bed by tapping sides of column.

With stopcock closed, add 10 mL NH_3 buffer soln to column. Add 40 mL KNO_3 working std soln to column with reservoir in place. Adjust flow rate initially to 3–5 mL/min, and do not readjust. Collect eluate in 100 mL vol. flask. Just as column empties, wash reservoir and column walls with ca 15 mL H_2O. Repeat with two 15 mL portions H_2O. After collecting nearly 100 mL eluate, remove flask and dil. to vol. with H_2O. Recondition column with 25 mL 0.1*N* HCl followed by two 25 mL portions H_2O and 25 mL NH_3 buffer soln, and repeat process, using 40 mL H_2O reagent blank from **16.251**. Mix, and add 5 mL of blank and std eluates to sep. 50 mL vol. flasks. Proceed as in **16.252**, beginning "Add 10.0 mL color reagent, . . ." Read spectrophtric as in **16.252** against blank similarly treated.

If NO_2 concn, as detd from calibration curve, is <13.4 μg/50 mL (<90% recovery), recondition column: Transfer Cd particles to beaker contg 2*N* HCl for 1 min. Decant and wash with two 100 mL portions H_2O. Proceed as in par. 1, beginning "Fill modified Jones reductor . . .".

Jones reductor may be stored under H_2O between analyses. Recondition column before each analysis with 25 mL 0.1*N* HCl followed by two 25 mL portions H_2O and 25 mL NH_3 buffer soln.

16.254 ***Determination***

Proceed as in **16.253**, par. 2, from beginning to ". . . remove flask and dil. to vol. with H_2O.", except add 40 mL sample filtrate from **16.251** to column instead of KNO_3 std.

Add 2.0 mL unreduced sample filtrate, 2.0 mL H_2O reagent blank from **16.251**, and 5.0 mL reduced eluate from **16.253** to sep. 50 mL vol. flasks, and proceed as in **16.252**, beginning "Add 10.0 mL color reagent, . . .", except read unreduced sample filtrate and reduced eluate against the blank. Alter dilns, if necessary, using 1–40 mL reduced eluate and unreduced filtrate, depending upon NO_3 concn of sample. Final dilns should give similar diln factors. For very high NO_3 concns, prior diln with H_2O may be necessary.

$$\text{ppm } NaNO_3 = [(R - U) \times D \times 3 \times 1.3478 \times 1.371]/W = [(R - U) \times D \times 5.544]/W,$$

where R = μg NO_2/50 mL reduced eluate (from std curve), U = μg NO_2/50 mL unreduced filtrate (from std curve), D = diln factor, $\frac{1}{3}$ = cheese factor, 1.3478 = NO_2 to NO_3 conversion factor, 1.371 = NO_3 to $NaNO_3$ conversion factor, and W = g sample slurry.

16.255 Fat (*60*)—Official Final Action

(FAO/WHO method. *See Introduction,* **16.059**.)

Weigh, to nearest mg, ca 1 g prepd sample, **16.232**, into small tall-form beaker; add 9 mL H_2O and, if desired, 1 mL NH_4OH. Mix until smooth; then warm mixt. at low heat until casein is well softened. If NH_4OH was used, neutze with HCl, using litmus as indicator. Add 10 mL HCl and few glass beads or other inert material, previously digested with HCl, to prevent bumping, cover with watch glass, and boil gently 5 min, or place beaker in boiling H_2O bath 20 min. Cool soln; transfer to fat-extn flask or tube; rinse beaker successively with 10 mL alcohol, 25 mL ether, and 25 mL pet ether (boiling range 30–60°); transfer rinsings to flask; and mix thoroly after adding each reagent. Proceed as in **16.059**, beginning "Centrf. flask . . ." Difference between duplicate detns obtained simultaneously by same analyst should be ≤0.2 g fat/100 g product.

16.256 Fat in Whey Cheese (*61*)—Official First Action

(FAO/WHO method. *See Introduction,* **16.059**.)

Weigh, to nearest mg, ca 3 g prepd sample, **16.232**, into extn flask and add 10 mL H_2O. Disperse by gentle agitation in boiling H_2O bath and continue heating 20 min in bath. Add 2 mL NH_4OH, mix, and cool. Continue as in **16.059**, beginning "Add 10 mL alcohol and mix well." Difference between duplicate detns obtained simultaneously by same analysts should be ≤0.2 g fat/100 g product.

16.257 Examination of Fat—Official Final Action

(**a**) *Alkaline extraction*.—In large, wide-mouth flask, treat ca 300 g sample, cut to ca pea-size, with 700 mL 5% KOH soln at 20°, shaking vigorously to dissolve casein. (In 5–10 min, casein dissolves, and fat rises to surface in lumps.) Collect lumps of fat into as large mass as possible by shaking gently. Pour cold H_2O into flask until fat is driven up into neck, and remove by suitable means. Wash fat thus obtained with just enough H_2O to remove residual alkali. Fat is not perceptibly attacked by alkali in this treatment, is practically all sepd in short time, and is then easily prepd for chem. analysis by filtering and drying as in **16.210**. Examine fat as in Chap. **28**.

(**b**) *Acid extraction*.—Pass cheese thru grinder, transfer to large flask, and cover with warm H_2O, using 1 mL/g cheese. Shake thoroly and add H_2SO_4 slowly and in small amts, shaking after each addn of acid. (Vol. H_2SO_4 should equal vol. H_2O used.) Transfer fat, which seps after standing few min, to separator; wash free from sulfate, filter, and dry as in **16.210**. Examine fat as in Chap. **28**.

Tartaric Acid (*62*)

16.258 ***Qualitative Test—Procedure***

To 5 g ground cheese, **16.232**, add 40 mL H_2O at ca 50° and shake until cheese is thoroly broken up. Add 3 mL 1% H_2SO_4 and shake vigorously. Add 2 mL *20% phosphotungstic acid soln* and again shake vigorously. Let stand 5 min and filter. To 25 mL filtrate add enough *satd* $Ba(OH)_2$ *soln* to make alk. and 25 mL alcohol, shake vigorously, and let settle. Filter thru buchner, using light suction, and wash residue on filter several times with H_2O. Transfer portion of paste to small evapg dish and dry on steam bath. Add few mL H_2SO_4 and few crystals of *resorcin*, and heat slowly. If tartaric acid is present, soln turns rose-red; color is slowly discharged on diln with H_2O.

Quantitative Method (62)—Official Final Action

16.259 ***Reagents***

(**a**) *Potassium chloride wash soln*.—Dissolve 15 g KCl in 100 mL H_2O and add 20 mL alcohol.

(**b**) *Tartaric acid soln*.—Dissolve 1.5 g pure tartaric acid in previously boiled and cooled H_2O and dil. to 100 mL at 20°. Titr. with 0.1*N* NaOH to det. wt tartaric acid in 10 mL soln.

(**c**) *Hydrochloric acid soln*.—2%. Dil. 47 mL HCl to 1 L with H_2O.

16.260 ***Determination***

Weigh 25 g prepd sample, **16.232**, into 500 mL wide-mouth bottle and add, 25 mL at time, 100 mL H_2O at 50–60°, shaking vigorously after each addn. Continue shaking until cheese is thoroly broken up. Add 25 mL *2%* $Na_2C_2O_4$ *soln* and shake vigorously 1 min. Add 100 mL 2% HCl, 25 mL at time, shaking vigorously after each addn. Add 50 g powd KCl and shake 5 min. To avoid churning, keep mixt. warm (ca 50°) during shaking. Transfer mixt., with aid of H_2O, to 300 mL vol. flask, cool to 20°, and dil. to vol. with H_2O. Mix thoroly; let stand 10 min, with occasional shaking, and filter thru dry folded paper, discarding first few mL filtrate. Disregard any opalescence and transfer 200 mL filtrate to 250 mL vol. flask. Neutze with 1*N* NaOH, using phthln, and add 5.2 mL in excess. Dil. to vol. with H_2O, mix thoroly, let stand few min, and filter thru dry folded paper, discarding first few mL filtrate.

To 100 mL filtrate in 250 mL beaker add, with constant stirring, 10 mL of the tartaric acid soln, 2 mL HOAc, and 23 mL alcohol. Cool in ice bath, stir vigorously until cream of tartar begins to crystallize, and let stand in refrigerator overnight. Prep. Caldwell crucible with pad of asbestos ca 10 mm thick. (*Caution: See* **51.086.**) Decant most of liq. thru this filter, wash ppt into crucible with KCl wash soln, and wash beaker and ppt 3 times, using total of 20–30 mL wash soln. Place asbestos and ppt in beaker in which pptn was made and wash crucible with ca 50 mL hot H_2O. Heat soln to bp and titr. while hot with 0.1*N* NaOH, using phthln. Calc. % tartaric acid in cheese by formula:

$$X = 14.26[0.015(B+1.5) - C],$$

where C = g tartaric acid in 10 mL of the tartaric acid reagent; and B = mL 0.1*N* NaOH required for titrn. In factor 14.26, concn caused by insol. solids of cheese of av. composition is taken into consideration.

Citric Acid (*63*)

16.261 ***Qualitative Test—Procedure***

To 10 g prepd sample, **16.232**, add 20 mL H_2O at ca 50° and shake vigorously until cheese is thoroly broken up. Add 20 mL H_2SO_4 (1+1) and 2 mL *20% phosphotungstic acid soln*, and shake vigorously. Let stand 5 min and filter. To 20 mL filtrate add 10 mL Br-H_2O (*Caution: See* **51.047**) and 5 mL KBr soln (15 g in 40 mL H_2O), and proceed with oxidn as in **16.262**. Add enough $FeSO_4$ soln (**16.262**, par. 3) to dissolve pptd MnO_2. If citric acid is present, heavy white ppt forms which settles rapidly.

16.262 ***Quantitative Gravimetric Method***
Official Final Action

Prep. suspension as in **16.260** thru addn of $Na_2C_2O_4$ soln. Shake vigorously 1 min and add 100 mL 1% H_2SO_4, 25 mL at time, shaking vigorously after each addn. Add 3 mL *20% phosphotungstic acid soln* and shake; then add 25 g powd anhyd. Na_2SO_4, and shake 5 min. To avoid churning, keep mixt. warm (ca 50°) during shaking. Transfer mixt. with aid of warm H_2O to 300 mL vol. flask, cool to 20°, and dil. to vol. with H_2O. Mix thoroly, shake occasionally during 10 min, and filter thru dry folded paper, discarding first few mL filtrate.

Heat 200 mL filtrate to bp and while still hot add 20 mL H_2SO_4 (1+1) and 2 mL phosphotungstic acid soln. Mix, and let stand 15 min. With aid of H_2O, transfer mixt. to 250 mL vol. flask, cool to 20°, dil. to vol. with H_2O, and filter thru dry folded paper.

Transfer 100 mL clear filtrate to 500 mL erlenmeyer (ca 0.3 g washed and dried asbestos may be added). Add 10 mL freshly prepd satd Br-H_2O (*Caution: See* **51.047**) and 5 mL *KBr soln* (15 g KBr in 40 mL H_2O), mix thoroly, and heat to 48–50°. Hold at this temp. 5 min, add 25 mL *5% $KMnO_4$ soln*, shake, and let stand ca 5 min. Cool flask and contents to ca 8°, add 40 mL cold *$FeSO_4$ soln* (20 g $FeSO_4.7H_2O$ in 100 mL H_2O and 1 mL H_2SO_4), shake continuously 5 min, and let mixt. stand overnight in refrigerator.

Decant supernate thru gooch, measure vol. filtrate (v), and wash ppt from erlenmeyer into crucible with this filtrate. Wash ppt with three 20 mL portions ice-cold H_2SO_4 (1+100), suck dry after each addn, and finally wash with three 20 mL portions ice-cold H_2O. Dry ppt to const wt over H_2SO_4 in vac. desiccator, protecting ppt from strong light or, to save time, dry in current of air passed thru H_2SO_4, and weigh.

Remove pentabromacetone by extg first with three 20 mL portions alcohol and then with three 20 mL portions ether. Dry and weigh crucible. To wt pentabromacetone add 0.004 g/100 mL filtrate (v) to compensate for solubility of pentabromacetone and multiply result by 6.06 to obtain % anhyd. citric acid in cheese. (In this factor, concn caused by insol. solids in 25 g cheese is taken into consideration. It is assumed that solids of cheese are almost insol. under conditions maintained and that av. process cheese contains ca 60% solids. No allowance is made for variation in salt or moisture content or for variation in specific vol. of solids, as such variations do not appreciably affect results.)

IDF-ISO-AOAC Colorimetric Method (57)
Official Final Action

16.263 ***Principle***

Cheese is dispersed in H_2O and protein is pptd by CCl_3COOH. Filtrate is treated with pyridine and Ac_2O and A of yellow color of citric acid complex is measured at 428 nm.

16.264 ***Apparatus and Reagents***

(**a**) *Test tubes.*—16 or 18 × 150 mm, with glass or plastic stoppers.

(**b**) *Trichloroacetic acid soln.*—1.836*M*. Dissolve 300 g CCl_3COOH in H_2O and dil. to 1 L. (*Caution: See* **51.082.**)

(**c**) *Citrate std soln.*—0.003252*M*. Dissolve 0.9565 g trisodium citrate ($C_6H_5O_7Na_3.2H_2O$) in H_2O and dil. to 1 L.

16.265 ***Preparation of Sample***

Accurately weigh ca 0.5 g prepd sample, **16.015–16.018** and **16.231–16.232**, and place in porcelain mortar. Disperse by crushing with pestle, adding small portions warm H_2O (60–70°). Transfer quant. to 100 mL vol. flask with $\leq$50 mL H_2O. Let cool to room temp. and add 40 mL CCl_3COOH soln, mix by swirling, dil. to vol. with H_2O, and remix again. Let stand 30 min at room temp. and filter thru dry, hard paper. Discard filtrate ($\geq$10 mL) until filtrate is clear.

16.266 ***Determination***

Pipet 1 mL clear filtrate into test tube. Add 1.3 mL pyridine, mix, and immediately add 5.7 mL Ac_2O. Stopper tube, mix thoroly, and place in 32° H_2O bath.

After 30 min, remove tube from H_2O bath, let cool to room temp., dry, and measure A against blank at 428 nm. Convert reading to μg anhyd. citric acid by ref. to std curve.

$$\% \text{ Anhyd. citric acid} = W'/(100 \times W),$$

where W' = μg anhyd. citric acid from std curve and W = g sample.

16.267 ***Preparation of Standard Curve***

Transfer 0, 4, 8, 12, 16, and 20 mL citrate std soln, (**c**), to sep. 50 mL vol. flasks and add H_2O to total vol. of ca 25 mL in each. Add 20 mL CCl_3COOH soln to each, mix by swirling, dil. to vol. with H_2O, and remix.

Pipet 1 mL from each flask into sep. test tubes to prep. stds contg 0, 50, 100, 150, 200, and 250 μg anhyd. citric acid, and proceed as in **16.266**.

Prep. std curve by plotting A against μg citric acid.

16.268 Lactose in Process Cheese (64)
Official Final Action

Prep. suspension as in **16.260** thru addn of $Na_2C_2O_4$ soln. Shake vigorously 1 min; add 25 g powd Na_2SO_4 and shake 2 min; add 10 mL H_2SO_4 (1+1) and shake; then add 25 mL *20% phosphotungstic acid soln* and shake vigorously. Transfer contents of bottle to 500 mL vol. flask, cool at once to 20°, and dil. to vol. with H_2O. Mix thoroly, let stand 10 min, and filter thru dry folded paper. Transfer 150 mL filtrate to each of two 250 mL vol. flasks, add 10% NaOH soln to one flask until mixt. is alk. to litmus, and then add 5 g solid KCl and mix thoroly. Cool to 20° and dil. to vol. with H_2O. Mix well, let stand 10 min, and filter thru dry folded paper.

Det. lactose in 50 mL aliquot as in **31.038**. Treat the 150 mL in second flask as in **31.026(c)**, using 10 mL HCl, etc. Add 10% NaOH soln until alk. to litmus, and add 5 g solid KCl. Mix thoroly, cool to 20°, and dil. to vol. with H_2O. Let stand 10 min. Filter if necessary thru dry paper. Det. lactose in 50 mL aliquot as before. Agreement between amts of Cu_2O reduced before and after inversion establishes absence of sucrose.

Since insol. material of cheese and phosphotungstic acid ppt occupy some space in flask as originally prepd, it is necessary to correct for this vol. From av. composition of cheese, vol. of ppt was calcd to be 14 mL. To obtain true amt lactose present, multiply all results by factor 0.97.

Gums in Soft Curd Cheese (*65*)—Official Final Action

(Not applicable to detection of alginates)

16.269 ***Reagents***

(**a**) *Benedict soln* (*qualitative*).—Dissolve 17.3 g Na citrate and 10 g anhyd. Na_2CO_3 in ca 80 mL hot H_2O; dissolve 1.73 g $CuSO_4.5H_2O$ in 10 mL H_2O. Filter alk. citrate soln, add $CuSO_4$ soln slowly with constant stirring, and dil. with H_2O to 100 mL.

(**b**) *Trichloroacetic acid* (*TCA*) *soln*.—(*1*) 50%. (*2*) 10%. Prep. just before use from nonhydrolyzed reagent. (*Caution: See* **51.082**.)

16.270 ***Preparation of Sample***

Weigh 100 g cheese into 250 mL centrf. bottle. Add hot H_2O to total vol. of 170 mL, heat in hot H_2O bath 30 min, and cool to room temp. Add 50 mL pet ether, shake, and centrf. Remove pet ether layer by decantation or by use of blow-off siphon, **16.220**, *Notes*. Repeat extn with pet ether at least twice. (Small amt of fat remaining is harmless.)

Warm bottle in hot H_2O bath to remove residual pet ether from cheese. Centrf., if necessary, to break any foam. Make vol. to ca 190 mL with H_2O and add 3.5 mL NH_4OH, few drops at time, while stirring. Keep in hot H_2O bath and stir until all curd dissolves. If curd fails to dissolve completely, add few more drops NH_4OH, stir, and macerate to dissolve. Add HOAc, few drops at time, with shaking, until pH is ca 4.75 (nitrazine test paper or pH meter). Use care in approaching pH point because isoelec. point for casein is ca pH 4.73. (If acid is added very slowly with const shaking and centrf. bottle is kept hot, marked sepn of casein and liq. will be noted at this point.) Stopper bottle, shake thoroly, and let stand overnight in the hot H_2O bath as H_2O cools. Check pH and centrf. at 1200 rpm 10 min. Decant supernate into 250 mL beaker with 40 mL graduation mark. Do not wash ppt.

16.271 ***Separation of Gum***

Evap. decanted liq. on steam bath to 40 mL mark of beaker. Remove beaker from bath and cool to room temp. Disregard ppt formed during concn and add 10 mL 50% TCA soln (note directions under **16.269(b)**). Replace on steam bath ≥15 min to coagulate protein. Remove beaker from steam bath, cool, transfer to 250 mL Pyrex centrf. bottle with 5 mL 10% TCA soln, and centrf. at 1200 rpm 10 min. Decant supernate into another 250 mL centrf. bottle and add alcohol with stirring until bottle is full. (Vol. before addn of alcohol should be ≤50 mL and ca 4 vols alcohol should be added.) Let mixt. stand 1 hr to coagulate gums. Centrf. at 1800 rpm, decant, and discard liq.

Add ca 50 mL 70% alcohol to residue in bottle, stopper, and shake to break up material thoroly. Wash down stopper and sides of bottle with little 70% alcohol, centrf. at 1800 rpm, decant, and drain. Add 40 mL hot H_2O to bottle and shake well to dissolve gum and disperse insol. material. Add 10 mL 50% TCA soln to bottle and heat on steam bath 15 min to coagulate any protein left after first treatment.

Remove bottle, cool, and centrf. at 1200 rpm 10 min. Decant supernate into another 250 mL Pyrex centrf. bottle, and fill bottle with alcohol while stirring contents. Add 0.5 mL 5% *$KAl(SO_4)_2$ soln*. Shake, and let stand ≥1 hr. Centrf. at 1800 rpm and decant. Add 50 mL 70% alcohol, shake to disperse material, and centrf. at 1800 rpm. Decant supernate and drain. Add 40 mL hot H_2O and shake well to dissolve gum. Transfer to 50 mL conical heavy-duty centrf. tube, keeping vol. to 40 mL. Centrf. at 1200 rpm 10 min to remove any undissolved material, and decant supernate back into 250 mL centrf. bottle. Reppt in bottle by filling with alcohol plus 1 drop HOAc. To ensure pptn of gum tragacanth and karaya, add 0.5 mL 5% $KAl(SO_4)_2$ soln.

Let stand ≥1 hr to coagulate ppt, centrf., and decant liq. If ppt is small and will not remain on bottom of 250 mL centrf. bottle, centrf. the alcohol and pptd gum, portion at time, at 1500 rpm 15 min in 50 mL conical heavy-duty centrf. tube, until all contents of 250 mL bottle are transferred to 50 mL tube. After decanting supernate from last portion centrfd, add 40 mL 70% alcohol to tube (or bottle if tube is not used), and shake until ppt is dispersed; centrf., decant, and drain.

16.272 ***Detection of Gum***

Add 10 mL hot H_2O to residue in tube or bottle, shake, and transfer to 50 mL beaker. Rinse tube or bottle with 10 mL hot H_2O and add rinse to beaker. Warm on elec. hot plate to dissolve gum and evap. to 10 mL. Add 2 mL HCl, cover beaker with watch glass, and boil gently 5 min. Cool, transfer to 10 mL graduate, adjust to 10 mL with H_2O, and mix. Place 1 mL aliquot in 30 mL beaker and neutze with 10% NaOH soln, using litmus paper as indicator. Remove litmus paper, add 5 mL Benedict soln, boil vigorously 2 min, and let cool spontaneously. Voluminous ppt appearing on cooling, which may be yellow, orange, or red, caused by reducing sugars formed by hydrolysis of the gums, indicates presence of gums.

Gelatin in Cottage Cheese

16.273 ***Qualitative Test—Official Final Action***

Thoroly mix 5 g sample with 10 mL H_2O at 50–60° and add 5 mL $Hg(NO_3)_2$ soln, **16.109**. Shake, let stand 5 min, and filter thru medium-fast retentive paper. To filtrate add addnl 5 mL $Hg(NO_3)_2$ soln and test as in **16.109**, using filtrate so obtained. *See also Note* in **16.109**.

16.274 Sorbic Acid—Official First Action

See **20.098–20.104**.

Residual Phosphatase (*27*)
Official Final Action

16.275 ***Reagents***

(**a**) *Buffers:*

(*1*) *25-11 Barium borate-hydroxide buffer*.—*See* **16.116(a)**(*1*).

(2) *26-11, 27-11, 28-11, and 29-11 Barium borate-hydroxide buffers.*—Prep. as in **16.116(a)**(*1*), except use 26.0, 27.0, 28.0, or 29.0 g $Ba(OH)_2.8H_2O$, resp., instead of 25.0 g.

(**b**) *Buffer substrates:*

Dissolve 0.10 g phenol-free cryst. $Na_2C_6H_5PO_4$ in 100 mL appropriate buffer, (**a**), specified in Table **16:03**. *See* **16.116(b)**(*1*) for prepn of phenol-free substrate.

(**c**) *Protein precipitants:*

(*1*) *6.0–0.1 Precipitant.*—Dissolve 6.0 g $ZnSO_4.7H_2O$ and 0.1 g $CuSO_4.5H_2O$ in H_2O and dil. to 100 mL.

(*2*) *6.0 Precipitant.*—Dissolve 6.0 g $ZnSO_4.7H_2O$ in H_2O and dil. to 100 mL.

For other reagents, *see* **16.116**.

16.276 ***Sampling***

(**a**) *Hard cheese.*—Take sample from interior with *clean* Roquefort trier, place in small tube, stopper, and keep in refrigerator.

(**b**) *Soft and semisoft ripened cheese.*—Harden cheese by chilling in freezing compartment of refrigerator. Take special precautions to avoid contaminating sample with phosphatase that may be present on surface. Sample by either of following methods:

(*1*) Cut portion from end of loaf or side of cheese, extending in ≥5 cm (2″) if possible, to point somewhat beyond center in case of small cheese. Cut slit 6–12 mm (¼–½″) deep at least half way around portion and midway between top and bottom. Break portion into 2 parts, pulling apart so that break occurs on line with slit and taking care not to contaminate freshly exposed broken surface. Remove sample from freshly exposed surface at or near center of cheese.

(*2*) Remove surface of area to be sampled (*e.g.*, end and adjacent sides), with clean knife or spatula, to depth of 6 mm (¼″). Clean instrument and hands with hot H_2O and phenol-free soap, and wipe dry. Remove freshly exposed surface to same or greater depth, and repeat cleaning. Take sample from center of freshly exposed area, preferably at or near center of cheese if cheese is small.

(**c**) *Process cheese and cheese spreads.*—Take sample from beneath surface with clean knife or spatula.

If preservative is necessary, put 1–3 mL $CHCl_3$ in container, cover with plug of cotton, insert sample, and stopper tightly. Label *"Poison, preservative added."*

16.277 ***Determination***

(*See* **16.118**.) Different kinds of cheese and cheeses of different ages have different buffering capacities and therefore require different concns of reagents. Modifications of the Ba buffer needed to produce optimal pH conditions during incubation (9.85–10.20) and of precipitant to yield uniformly clear filtrates and minimize interference during development of color under optimal pH conditions (9.3–9.4) are specified in Table **16:03**.

Proceed as follows:

Step 1.—Weigh, on clean balance pan or watch glass, 0.50 g sample (preferably in duplicate) and place in culture tube 16 or 18 × 150 mm. Similarly weigh another sample and place in tube as control or blank. If cheese is sticky, weigh sample on piece of wax paper ca 2.5 × 2.5 cm (1 × 1″) and insert paper with sample into tube. Macerate blank and test samples with glass rod ca 8 × 180 mm.

Step 2.—Add to *blank* 1.0 mL appropriate Ba buffer, Table **16:03** (without substrate), macerate with rod, leave rod in tube, and heat ca 1 min to 85–90° in beaker of boiling H_2O (covered, to ensure that entire tube will be heated to 85–90°); cool to room temp., and again macerate with rod.

Step 3.—*To each test sample* add 1.0 mL appropriate Ba buffer substrate, **16.275(b)**, and macerate.

From this point, treat blank and test alike.

Add 9.0 mL more Ba buffer substrate (total 10.0 mL), and mix. (Rod may be left in tube during incubation. If it is removed at this point, wrap piece of ca 2.5 cm sq filter paper tightly around it and wipe it clean by rotating while withdrawing from tube. Insert paper with adhering fat in tube.) Stopper tube.

For quant. results on unknown samples, adjust pH to 10.0–10.05 by dropwise addn of 1*N* or 0.5*N* Na_2CO_3 or HCl.

Table 16:03 Phosphatase Test Modifications for Different Kinds of Cheese and Cheese of Different Ages

Kind of Cheese	Age or Extent of Curing; Other Details	Buffer for Opt. pH[a] (9.85–10.20)	Precipitant	Criterion, Phenol Equivalent[b]
				μg/0.25 g
Cheddar, granular, stirred curd, hard cheese	<1 wk	25–11	6.0–0.1[c]	3
	1–6 wk	25–11	6.0[d]	3
	1.5–4 mo.	26–11	6.0[d]	3
	>4 mo.	27–11	6.0[d]	3
Washed curd, soaked curd, colby	<1 wk	25–11	6.0–0.1[c]	3
	1–8 wk	25–11	6.0[d]	3
	>2 mo.	26–11	6.0[d]	3
Swiss, gruyère	<1 wk	25–11	6.0–0.1[c]	3
	1–4 wk	25–11	6.0[d]	3
	1–3 mo.	26–11	6.0[d]	3
	>3 mo.	27–11	6.0[d]	3
Brick, muenster	<1 wk	25–11	6.0–0.1[c]	3
	1–4 wk	25–11	6.0[d]	3
	1–2 mo.	25–11	6.0[d]	3
	>2 mo.	26–11	6.0[d]	3

[a] $Ba(OH)_2.8H_2O$ and H_3BO_3, resp., g/L.
[b] Higher values indicate underpasteurization.
[c] $ZnSO_4.7H_2O$ and $CuSO_4.5H_2O$ resp., g/100 mL.
[d] $ZnSO_4.7H_2O$ g/100 mL.
[e] See also alternative, more sensitive modification in Notes, **16.277**.
[f] 8 parts 25–11 buffer + 2 parts H_2O.

(*Continued*)

Table 16:03 Phosphatase Test Modifications for Different Kinds of Cheese and Cheese of Different Ages—*Continued*

Kind of Cheese	Age or Extent of Curing; Other Details	Buffer for Opt. pH[a] (9.85–10.20)	Precipitant	Criterion, Phenol Equivalent[b]
				µg/0.25 g
Edam, gouda	<1 wk	25–11	6.0–0.1[c]	3
	1–8 wk	25–11	6.0[d]	3
	2–4 mo.	26–11	6.0[d]	3
	>4 mo.	27–11	6.0[d]	3
Blue mold, blue, gorgonzola	<1 wk	25–11	6.0–0.1[c]	3
	1–4 wk	26–11	6.0[d]	3
	1–4.5 mo.	27–11	6.0[d]	3
	>4.5 mo.	28–11	6.0[d]	3
Camembert, limburger	<1 wk	25–11	6.0–0.1[c]	4
	1–4 wk	25–11	6.0[d]	4
	1–2 mo.	26–11	6.0[d]	4
	>2 mo.	27–11	6.0[d]	4
Monterey	<1 wk	25–11	6.0–0.1[c]	3
	1–8 wk	25–11	6.0[d]	3
	>2 mo.	26–11	6.0[d]	3
High moisture Jack	<1 wk	25–11	6.0–0.1[c]	3
	1–10 wk	25–11	6.0[d]	3
	>2.5 mo.	26–11	6.0[d]	3
Provolone, paste filata	<1 wk	25–11	6.0–0.1[c]	3
	1–4 wk	25–11	6.0[d]	3
	1–3 mo.	26–11	6.0[d]	3
	>3 mo.	27–11	6.0[d]	3
Parmesan, reggiano, monte, modena, romano, asiago old	<1 wk	25–11	6.0–0.1[c]	3
	1–8 wk	26–11	6.0[d]	3
	2–6 mo.	27–11	6.0[d]	3
	6–12 mo.	28–11	6.0[d]	3
	>1 yr	29–11	6.0[d]	3
Asiago, fresh	Same as Cheddar			
Asiago, medium	<1 wk	25–11	6.0–0.1[c]	3
	1–4 wk	25–11	6.0[d]	3
	1–3 mo.	26–11	6.0[d]	3
	>3 mo.	27–11	6.0[d]	3
Cottage[e], cook cheese, koch kaese	Dry	25–11	6.0–0.1[c]	1
	Moist	25–11 (8+2)[f]	4.5–0.1[c]	1
Cream cheese		25–11 (7+3)	4.5–0.1[c]	3
Semisoft cheese	<1 wk	25–11	6.0–0.1[c]	3
	1–4 wk	25–11	6.0[d]	3
	>1 mo.	26–11	6.0[d]	3
Soft ripened cheese	<1 wk	25–11	6.0–0.1[c]	4
	1–4 wk	25–11	6.0[d]	4
	>1 mo.	26–11	6.0[d]	4
Nokkelost, kuminost, sage cheese	<1 wk	25–11	6.0–0.1[c]	3
	1–6 wk	25–11	6.0[d]	3
	1.5–4 mo.	26–11	6.0[d]	3
	>4 mo.	27–11	6.0[d]	3
Past. proc.; ditto, pimiento; ditto, with fruits, meats, etc.	Soft, mild	25–11	6.0[d]	3
	Med. firm	26–11	6.0[d]	3
	Firm, sharp (incl. Swiss, gruyère	27–11	6.0[d]	3
Past. proc. cheese foods; ditto, with fruits, meats, etc.	Same as past. proc.			
Past. proc. cheese spreads; ditto, with fruits, meats, etc.	Soft, high moisture, incl. cream spreads	25–11	6.0[d]	3
	Less soft, incl. blue	26–11	6.0[d]	3
Cold pack, club; cold pack cheese foods; ditto, with fruits, meats, etc.	Mild-med. flavored, soft	26–11	6.0[d]	3
	Sharp, firm	27–11	6.0[d]	3

Step 4.—Immediately incubate in H_2O bath 1 hr at 37–38°, mixing or shaking contents occasionally.

Step 5.—Heat in beaker of boiling H_2O nearly 1 min (temp. of contents of tube ca 85° as detd by thermometer in another tube of same size and shape contg same vol. liq.), and cool to room temp. in vessel of cold H_2O.

Step 6.—Pipet in 1.0 mL appropriate protein precipitant, Table **16:03**, and mix thoroly (pH of mixt., 9.0–9.1).

Steps 7—11.—Proceed as in **16.118**.

Step 12.—When using 0.5 g solid sample and adding total of 11.0 mL liq., multiply value of reading by 1.1 to convert to units of color or phenol equivs/0.25 g cheese. (If desired, multiply by 4.4 to convert result to phenol equivs/g.) Evaluate result by comparing with criteria of pasteurization in Table **16:03**.

Notes: With some cheese samples of unknown history, slight deviations from optimal pH range may occur, but such deviations do not materially affect results. For example, pH values as low as 9.6 or as high as 10.35 during incubation have been found to result in av. decrease of ≤20% in amt phenol liberated. Use of 25–11 buffer substrate with samples for which 27–11 buffer substrate is specified yields pH values ≥9.8.

Trace of cloudiness in filtrate, following use of prescribed precipitant, indicates concn of $Ba(OH)_2$ in buffer was insufficient (i.e., buffer substrate was not alk. enough). For example, the 25–11 buffer, for use with unripened cheese, may yield cloudy filtrate if used with ripened cheese. Increasing concn of $ZnSO_4$ in precipitant also eliminates turbidity of filtrate.

In testing cheese of unknown history or age, information as to % solids, especially nonfat solids, is useful as indication of correct buffer to use; cheese with relatively high % nonfat solids generally requires use of relatively concd buffer to adjust pH of mixt. correctly. Av. buffer within cheese group (generally 26–11) is usually satisfactory for cheese of uncertain age.

Cottage cheese curd is heated in presence of considerable acid during manufacture, and therefore its phosphatase values are comparatively low. To increase sensitivity of test on cottage cheese, apply following modifications: Use 1.0 g sample, 27–11 buffer substrate, 2 hr incubation, 6.0–0.1 precipitant, and pasteurization criterion of 2 units/0.5 g.

To test for presence of microbial phosphatase, e.g., in surface-ripened cheeses and their processed products, (*a*) indicated by blue tinge in blank of *Step 2*, repeat detn, adding 1 mL of the Ba buffer (without substrate) to blank and heating 5 min in boiling H_2O in covered beaker. If blank so treated is neg., blue tinge in original blank was due to microbial phosphatase. (*b*) In suspected instances in absence of blue tinge in blank of *Step 2*, heat sample itself 5 min at 70° to completely destroy milk phosphatase and then perform test. If pos., microbial phosphatase is present.

See also Notes under **16.118**.

Qualitative (Screening) Method (66)
Official First Action

16.278 ***Reagents***

(**a**) *Color developer.*—2.5*N* NaOH. Dissolve 10 g NaOH in 100 mL H_2O.

(**b**) *Phenolphthalein monophosphate soln (substrate concentrate).—See* **16.121(a)**.

(**c**) *Phenolphthalein-tartrazine solns (std concentrates).—See* **16.127(b)** (0.1% std). Also prep. addnl std concs contg 0.02% and 0.05% phthln by using 20 mg and 50 mg phthln, resp. Stds approximate milk contg 0.1, 0.2, and 0.5% raw milk.

(**d**) *Solvent.*—7.5% (v/v) *n*-butyl alcohol neutzd to pH 7.0.

16.279 ***Determination***

To 5.0 g cheese in 18 × 150 mm test tube add 20 mL solv. Grind with glass rod 2 min, and filter immediately thru Whatman No. 4 paper. Pipet 1 mL filtrate into each of two 15 × 100 mm test tubes and warm to 37°. To 1 tube add 1 drop (0.04 mL) substrate conc. (pH mixt. 10.0) and to other add 1 drop 0.1% std conc. Mix and incubate 30 min at 37°. Add 1 drop 2.5*N* NaOH to each tube, mix, and compare visually. If sample soln (in tube contg substrate conc.) is less pink than std soln, cheese has been manufactured from pasteurized milk. Use 0.2 and 0.5% std concs, (**c**), to semiquantitate pos. test.

ICE CREAM AND FROZEN DESSERTS

Weight per Unit Volume of Packaged Ice Cream—Official Final Action

16.280 ★ ***Method I (67)*** ★

Using kerosene and special overflow can. *See* **16.220–16.221**, 11th ed.

Method II (68)

16.281 ***Apparatus and Materials***

(**a**) *Container.—See* Fig. **16:05**. Plastic desiccator, ca 1–1.5 L (1–1.5 qt) capacity (Ace Glass Co., No. 1810, or equiv.) modified to include ca 6 mm (¼") hole in cover center for air escape and leak-free side arm tube. Clean with detergent before use and grease rims lightly.

(**b**) *Clamps.*—To secure desiccator lid (Hoge No. 25 binder clips (available from stationery stores), or equiv.); *see* Fig. **16:05**.

(**c**) *Balance.*—Approx. 4.5 kg (10 lb) capacity and 0.3 g (0.01 oz) sensitivity.

(**d**) *Ice chest.*—Approx. 15–20 L (4–5 gal.) capacity, packed with solid CO_2.

(**e**) *Immersion fluid.*—Approx. 0.001% aq. polysorbate 80 (Tween 80) soln. Prep. ca 4 L for each detn and cool to 4±4°.

16.282 ***Determination***

Pack and store samples overnight in solid CO_2. Unwrap hard frozen sample. If sample is 0.5 gal. or larger unit, break by scoring with chisel or other sharp instrument and driving knife or wedge into block along scored line. Quickly det. wt in air (W_a, oz) of piece selected for wt/vol. detn and return to ice chest.

Place container on level surface and secure lid in place with 4 clamps. Completely fill container thru inlet tube with chilled immersion fluid dispensed from separator with rubber tubing attached. Wipe outer surface dry and det. wt (W_p, oz).

Place container in sink or on drainboard and remove lid. Place previously weighed sample piece in container and secure lid with 4 clamps. Fill container completely with immersion fluid, letting all air bubbles escape thru air hole in lid. Wipe outer surface and det. wt (W_i, oz).

Wt per unit vol. (lb/gal.) = $(W_a \times 8.338)/[W_a + (W_p - W_i)]$, where 8.338 = density of H_2O at 0–8° (lb/gal.).

16.283 Preparation of Sample (*69*)—Procedure

Cut frozen blocks of product into ca ½ pt pieces. Select 2 or 3 pieces at random, place in cup of high-speed blender, and close tightly. Let soften at room temp. and mix (2 min for plain products and ≤7 min for those contg nuts or hard candy chips). Do not let temp. exceed 12° at any time during softening and mixing steps. If fat sepn or "churning" occurs, discard sample and repeat, using shorter mixing time. Immediately pour mixt. into wide-mouth jar and cap tightly. If allowed to stand, shake vigorously before removing samples.

16.284 Total Solids (*70*)—Official Final Action

Into round, flat-bottom dish ≥5 cm diam., quickly weigh 1–2 g sample. (Sample may be weighed by means of short, bent, 2

★ Surplus method—*see* inside front cover.

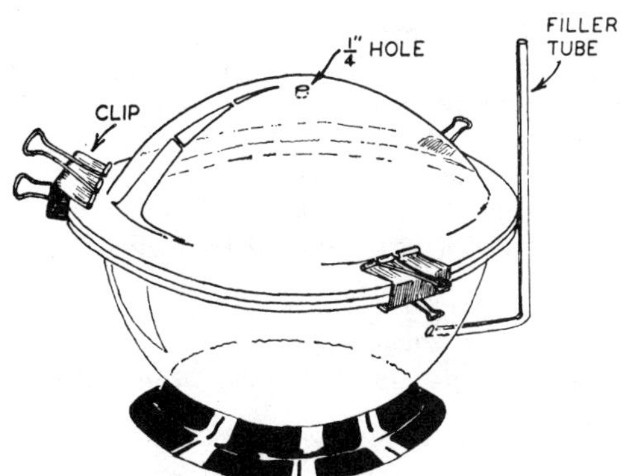

FIG. 16:05 Modified plastic desiccator

mL measuring pipet.) Heat on steam bath 30 min and then in air oven 3.5 hr at 100°. Cool in desiccator and weigh quickly to avoid absorption of moisture.

Nitrogen—Official Final Action

16.285 ***Kjeldahl Method***

Proceed as in **2.057**, using 4–5 g sample.
% N × 6.38 = % "protein."

16.286 ***Dye Binding Method***

See **16.037–16.041**.

Fat

16.287 ***Roese-Gottlieb Method (71)—Official Final Action***

Accurately weigh 4–5 g thoroly mixed sample directly into fat-extn flask or tube, using free-flowing pipet; dil. with H_2O to ca 10 mL, working sample into lower chamber and mix by shaking. Add 2 mL NH_4OH, mix thoroly, and heat in H_2O bath 20 min at 60° with occasional shaking. Cool, and proceed as in **16.059**, beginning "Add 10 mL alcohol and mix well."

16.288 **Separation of Fat from Ice Cream**
Official Final Action

(*Caution: See* **51.011**, **51.039**, and **51.054**.)

Melt sample and screen out any large pieces of fruit, nuts, etc. on No. 20 sieve. Place 300 mL melted sample in 1 L separator, add 100 mL H_2O and 50 mL NH_4OH, and shake well. Add 200 mL alcohol and shake 1 min. Add 200 mL ether and shake 1 min. Add 200 mL pet ether and shake 1 min. Let stand until emulsion breaks, and drain and discard lower layer. Add 25 g anhyd. Na_2SO_4, shake, and decant thru rapid folded paper. Evap. ether and alcohol, and dry fat overnight at 55°. Examine fat as in Chap. **28**.

16.289 **Lactic Acid—Official Final Action**

See **16.027–16.031**.

Gums

Infrared Method (72)—Official Final Action

(Guar flour gum and locust bean gum cannot be distinguished by this method. Karaya gum cannot be identified when isolated by this method.)

16.290 ***Reagents***

(**a**) *Dioxane*.—Tech. grade is satisfactory. (*Caution:* Vapors are obnoxious and harmful.)

(**b**) *Trichloroacetic acid* (*TCA*) *soln*.—50%. *See* **16.269**(**b**).

(**c**) *Organo-silicone compound*.—To prep. nonwettable surface. Desicote® (Beckman Instruments) has been found satisfactory.

16.291 ***Apparatus***

(**a**) *Infrared spectrophotometer*.—Recording, for operation in 2–15 μm region.

(**b**) *Water-repellent plate*.—Wash 7–10 cm (3–4") glass sq thoroly with detergent, rinse, and dry with towel. Dip glass rod in organo-silicone compd and streak adhering liq. across plate. Repeat streaking several times. Rub plate with lens paper to distribute evenly; then rub with clean lens paper to remove excess. Plate is now ready for use. Wash plate with cold H_2O and dry with towel after each use. Plate can be reused as long as it remains nonwettable.

16.292 ***Preparation of Sample***

Weigh 50 g sample of frozen dessert into 250 mL centrf. bottle and heat to 60° in H_2O bath. Add 150 mL dioxane, shake vigorously 2 min, and centrf. 10 min at 1800 rpm. Decant and discard supernate. Add 30 mL ether, and shake vigorously to break mass at bottom, using rod if necessary. Decant ether and repeat ether wash once. Heat in H_2O bath to remove residual ether. Add 30 mL 80° H_2O and shake vigorously 2 min to dissolve or disperse residue.

16.293 ***Separation of Gum***

Add 20 mL 50% TCA soln and heat to 60° in H_2O bath. Shake 1 min and centrf. 10 min at 1200 rpm. Decant soln thru fast folded paper into second centrf. bottle, and discard residue.

Fill centrf. bottle with alcohol, add 1 mL satd NaCl soln, mix, and let stand until coagulation occurs. If ppt does not form, gums are absent. (Let opalescent solns stand overnight to facilitate pptn. Centrf., and discard if no ppt is present.) Centrf. 10 min at 1800 rpm and immediately decant and discard supernate.

Purify pptd gum by adding 30 mL 80° H_2O and shake vigorously to dissolve or disperse ppt. Fill centrf. bottle with alcohol, add 1 mL satd NaCl soln and 1 drop HCl (1+1), mix, let ppt coagulate, centrf. 10 min at 1800 rpm, decant, and discard supernate. Repeat purification step twice.

16.294 ***Detection of Gum***

(**a**) *Chemical test for small amounts*.—Scrape small amt of pptd gum from centrf. bottle with spatula and transfer to 50 mL beaker with ca 10 mL hot H_2O. Add 2 mL HCl and boil 5 min. Neutze to multirange indicator paper, using 30% NaOH soln first and completing with 10% NaOH soln. Remove paper and continue as in **16.272**, beginning ". . . add 5 mL Benedict soln, . . ."

(**b**) *Chemical test for entire precipitate*.—If IR spectrum is not desired, spectrum indicates presence of ≥2 gums, or pptd gum will not form film (as with karaya), proceed as in **16.272**, beginning "Add 10 mL hot H_2O . . ."

(**c**) *Infrared method*.—(May not be applicable to mixts of gums.) Dissolve or disperse residue in 35 mL H_2O. Prep. film as in **16.295**, obtain IR spectrum against air, and compare with spectra of ref. gums.

16.295 ***Preparation of Gum Films***

Place H_2O-repellent glass plate over 5 cm (2") opening on steam bath. Pour enough of aq. gum soln on plate to form circle ca 5 cm diam. (Vol. required to produce film of sufficient area to cover light path of app. and of thickness to produce characteristic spectrum varies depending upon nature of gum and its concn.) Heat plate until film is dry and remove film with forceps. If film sticks to plate, remove with razor blade or tissue lifter. Transfer film to beaker and dry 15–30 min at 100°. (Excessive heating may char some gums.) Place piece of film between 2 salt plates and obtain IR spectrum against air.

16.296 ***Preparation of Reference Gum Films***

Disperse 0.2 g gum in 30 mL 80° H_2O and add 20 mL 50% TCA soln. Continue as in **16.293**, beginning "Shake 1 min and centrf. 10 min at 1200 rpm."

16.297 Alginates in Chocolate Frozen Desserts Official Final Action

See **13.058–13.059.**

16.298 Gelatin—Official Final Action

Using 10 g sample, proceed as in **16.109.**

16.299 Color Additives—Official Final Action

Curdle 150–200 g melted sample by adding equal vol. H_2O and 10–20 mL HOAc. Heat mixt. to 70–80°, with stirring, and let cool. Continue as in **16.113** and **16.218**, and in Chap. **34** for detection of oil-sol. synthetic dyes and annatto.

16.300 Residual Phosphatase (*27*)—Official Final Action

Melt portion of sample and let it remain melted ≥1 hr before testing. Then proceed as in **16.118** except as follows:

In *Step 3*, proceed as for milk in case of sherbets; for ice cream, substitute buffer substrate made by dissolving $Na_2C_6H_5PO_4$ in mixt. of 4 parts Ba buffer, **16.116(a)**(*1*), and 1 part H_2O.

In *Step 6*, proceed as for milk in case of sherbets; for ice cream, ppt with 1.0 mL soln contg 4.5 g $ZnSO_4.7H_2O$ and 0.1 g $CuSO_4.5H_2O$/100 mL.

Controls are essential since phenols may be present from flavors or plastic containers.

SELECTED REFERENCES

(*1*) JAOAC **49,** 58(1966); **50,** 531(1967).
(*2*) JAOAC **30,** 130(1947); **34,** 239(1951).
(*3*) JAOAC **15,** 643(1932); **16,** 427(1933).
(*4*) JAOAC **20,** 130(1937); **25,** 253(1942); **26,** 199(1943); J. Dairy Sci. **27,** 743(1944); **46,** 135(1963).
(*5*) JAOAC **23,** 453(1940); **28,** 211(1945); **34,** 239(1951).
(*6*) JAOAC **50,** 542, 557(1967); **51,** 811(1968); **52,** 138(1969); **58,** 773(1975).
(*7*) JAOAC **57,** 1338(1974); **58,** 770(1975).
(*8*) JAOAC **10,** 259(1927); **13,** 254(1930); **14,** 246(1931); **16,** 489(1933); **17,** 357(1934); **19,** 383(1936).
(*9*) J. Milk Food Technol. **16,** 241(1953); JAOAC **38,** 310(1955); **39,** 345(1956); **43,** 407(1960).
(*10*) Analyst **21,** 182(1896); JAOAC **25,** 603(1942); **27,** 232(1944).
(*11*) Z. Nahr. Genussm. **9,** 531(1905); JAOAC **34,** 237(1951); **52,** 235(1969).
(*12*) JAOAC **8,** 4(1924); **8,** 471(1925); **56,** 1401(1973); **58,** 949(1975).
(*13*) JAOAC **43,** 746(1960).
(*14*) JAOAC **52,** 131(1969); **58,** 572(1975).
(*15*) JAOAC **56,** 1401(1973).
(*16*) JAOAC **55,** 488(1972).
(*17*) JAOAC **61,** 1015(1978).
(*18*) J. Am. Chem. Soc. **26,** 1195(1904); JAOAC **31,** 124(1948); **32,** 309(1949); **34,** 248(1951).
(*19*) JAOAC **31,** 124(1948); **32,** 309(1949); **34,** 248(1951).
(*20*) J. Ind. Eng. Chem. **13,** 198(1921); JAOAC **5,** 172, 470, 484(1922); **6,** 424, 429(1923); **43,** 411(1960).
(*21*) JAOAC **44,** 438(1961); **51,** 816(1968); **53,** 539(1970); **55,** 504(1972).
(*22*) JAOAC **61,** 1038(1978).
(*23*) JAOAC **19,** 386, 476(1936).
(*24*) USDA Bull. **1114** (1922); JAOAC **28,** 417(1945); **30,** 655 (1947).
(*25*) J. Am. Chem. Soc. **22,** 207(1900).
(*26*) J. Dairy Res. **6,** 191(1935); J. Milk Technol. **1,** 18(1938); JAOAC **21,** 82(1938).
(*27*) J. Dairy Sci. **29,** 737(1946); **30,** 909(1947); JAOAC **31,** 306(1948).
(*28*) JAOAC **48,** 811(1965).
(*29*) JAOAC **55,** 498(1972); **57,** 710(1974).
(*30*) JAOAC **62,** 822(1979).
(*31*) JAOAC **51,** 802(1968).
(*32*) JAOAC **44,** 444(1961); **62,** 822(1979).
(*33*) JAOAC **62,** 000(1979).
(*34*) JAOAC **45,** 301, 307(1962).
(*35*) JAOAC **40,** 496(1957).
(*36*) JAOAC **30,** 575(1947); **31,** 739(1948); **32,** 731(1949).
(*37*) JAOAC **31,** 750(1948).
(*38*) JAOAC **10,** 281(1927).
(*39*) JAOAC **28,** 207(1945); **52,** 239(1969).
(*40*) JAOAC **18,** 402(1935).
(*41*) JAOAC **10,** 308(1927); **11,** 289(1928).
(*42*) JAOAC **24,** 546(1941).
(*43*) JAOAC **24,** 744(1941); **25,** 253, 610(1942); **28,** 205(1945).
(*44*) JAOAC **5,** 507(1922); **6,** 435(1923); **23,** 465(1940).
(*45*) JAOAC **15,** 524(1932); **52,** 240(1969).
(*46*) JAOAC **18,** 396(1935).
(*47*) JAOAC **21,** 361(1938); **35,** 194(1952).
(*48*) JAOAC **49,** 518(1966).
(*49*) JAOAC **52,** 235, 394(1969).
(*50*) JAOAC **33,** 492(1950).
(*51*) JAOAC **36,** 1077(1953).
(*52*) JAOAC **9,** 44(1926); **18,** 57(1935).
(*53*) JAOAC **31,** 300(1948); **32,** 303(1949).
(*54*) JAOAC **52,** 117(1969).
(*55*) JAOAC **60,** 1392(1977).
(*56*) JAOAC **18,** 401(1935); **20,** 339(1937).
(*57*) JAOAC **59,** 1142(1976).
(*58*) JAOAC **56,** 535(1973).
(*59*) JAOAC **59,** 284(1976).
(*60*) JAOAC **16,** 584(1933); **31,** 300(1948); **32,** 303(1949); **52,** 240(1969).
(*61*) JAOAC **57,** 264(1974).
(*62*) JAOAC **11,** 287(1928).
(*63*) JAOAC **3,** 402(1920); **10,** 264(1927); **11,** 288(1928); **15,** 520(1932); **59,** 1142(1976).
(*64*) JAOAC **13,** 243(1930); **16,** 484(1933).
(*65*) JAOAC **20,** 527(1937); **23,** 597(1940); **28,** 245(1945); **34,** 361(1951).
(*66*) JAOAC **61,** 1035(1978).
(*67*) JAOAC **28,** 601(1945).
(*68*) JAOAC **51,** 807(1968).
(*69*) JAOAC **52,** 236(1969).
(*70*) JAOAC **24,** 575(1941).
(*71*) JAOAC **35,** 212(1952).
(*72*) JAOAC **43,** 624(1960).

17. Eggs and Egg Products

17.001 Collection and Preparation of Sample (*1*)—Procedure

No simple rules can be made for collection of sample representative of av. of any particular lot of egg material, as conditions may differ widely. Experienced judgment must be used in each instance. For large lots, preferably draw several samples for sep. analyses rather than attempt to get one composite representative sample. Sampling for microbiological examination, if required, should be performed first; *see* **46.003–46.004**.

(**a**) *Liquid eggs.*—Obtain representative container or containers. Mix contents of container thoroly and draw ca 300 g. (Long-handle dipper or ladle serves well.) Keep sample in hermetically sealed jar in freezer or with solid CO_2. Report odor and appearance.

(**b**) *Frozen eggs.*—Obtain representative container or containers. Examine contents as to odor and appearance. (Condition of contents can be detd best by drilling to center of container with auger and noting odor as auger is withdrawn. If impossible to secure individual containers, samples may consist of composite of borings from contents of each container.) Take borings diagonally across can from $\geq$3 widely sepd parts, starting 2–5 cm in from edge and extending to opposite side as near to bottom as possible. Pack shavings tightly into sample jar and fill it completely to prevent partial dehydration of sample. Seal jar tightly and store in freezer or with solid CO_2. Before analyzing, warm sample in bath held at <50°, and mix well.

(**c**) *Dried eggs.*—Obtain representative container or containers. For small packages, take entire parcel or parcels for sample. For boxes and barrels, remove top layer to depth of ca 15 cm (6″) with scoop or other convenient instrument. Draw small amts of sample totaling 300–500 g from accessible parts of container and place in hermetically sealed jar. Report odor and appearance. Prep. sample for analysis by mixing 3 times thru domestic flour sifter to thoroly break up lumps. (Grind flake albumen samples to pass entirely thru No. 60 sieve. Mix well.) Keep in hermetically sealed jar in cool place.

Yolk Color (*2*)—Official Final Action

17.002 ***Preparation of Standard Carotene Solutions***

Carotene std solns.—(*1*) *Stock soln.*—Approx. 6 μg/mL. Accurately weigh ca 5 g 0.03% β-carotene soln (available in sealed 5 mL (in Et laurate) ampuls, stable ca 6 months under refrigeration, from Poultry and Egg Institute of America, 4350 Oakton St, Skokie, IL 60076; exact assay supplied with ampul). Transfer to 250 mL g-s vol. flask with acetone and dil. to vol. with acetone. (*2*) *Working solns.*—Dil. to 100 mL with acetone 10, 20, 30, 45, 60, and 75 mL stock soln to obtain solns contg ca 0.6, 1.2, 1.8, 2.7, 3.6, and 4.5 μg/mL, resp. Use acetone for blank.

Solns are stable ca 1 week in dark under refrigeration.

17.003 ***Preparation of Standard Curve***

Det. % *T* or *A* of dild std solns as soon as possible with spectrophtr at 450 nm or with instrument with suitable filter system such as Klett photometer with No. 44 filter, Evelyn photoelec. colorimeter with 440 filter, or with Cenco-Sanford-Sheard Photelometer, Industrial Type B-2 with 410 filter. Plot μg β-carotene against % *T*, omitting values >90% or <10%, on semilog paper or against *A* on plain coordinate paper.

17.004 ***Determination***

Weigh sample contg ca 1.0 g egg yolk solids (1 g dried yolk, 2.5 g liq. yolk, 5.0 g liq. whole egg, or equiv.) into 150 mL beaker. Add ca 1–2 mL acetone and stir to smooth paste. Add ca 50 mL acetone, mix, and filter. Add ca 2.5 mL H_2O before the acetone to products contg sugar or salt. Wash material onto Whatman No. 4 filter paper, or equiv., with successive small portions of acetone, catching filtrate in g-s 100 mL vol. flask. Dil. to vol. with acetone. Det. *A* or % *T* as soon as possible. Report yolk color equiv. to μg β-carotene/g sample.

17.005 Carotenoids—Official Final Action

See **14.156–14.160**.

Total Solids

Vacuum Method (3)—Official Final Action

17.006 ***Apparatus***

Vacuum oven.—Connected with pump to maintain pressure $\leq$25 mm Hg (3.3 kPa) and provided with thermometer passing into oven with bulb near samples. Connect H_2SO_4 gas-drying bottle to oven for admitting dry air to release vac.

17.007 ***Determination***

(**a**) *Liquid eggs.*—Accurately weigh by difference, using weighing buret, ca 5 g samples, **17.001**(**a**) or (**b**), in covered dish previously dried at 98–100°, cooled in desiccator, and weighed soon after coming to room temp. Remove cover and evap. most of H_2O by heating on steam bath. Replace cover loosely and complete drying in vac. oven as in (**b**).

(**b**) *Dried eggs.*—Weigh ca 2 g sample, **17.001**(**c**), in covered dish previously dried at 98–100°, cooled in desiccator, and weighed soon after coming to room temp. Loosen cover (do not remove) and heat at 98–100° to const wt (ca 5 hr) in vac. oven. Admit dry air into oven to bring to atm. pressure. Immediately tighten cover of dish, transfer to desiccator contg fresh efficient desiccant, and weigh soon after coming to room temp. Report as % total solids.

Nitrogen (*4*)—Official Final Action

17.008 ***Preparation of Sample***

(**a**) *Liquid eggs.*—Weigh 2–3 g well mixed sample,**17.001**(**a**) or (**b**), by difference into 500 mL Kjeldahl flask.

(**b**) *Dried eggs.*—Transfer ca 1 g prepd sample,**17.001**(**c**), accurately weighed, to 500 mL Kjeldahl flask.

17.009 ***Determination***

Det. N as in **2.057**. Distil NH_3 into 30–50 mL 0.1*N* std acid.

Water-Soluble Nitrogen and Crude Albumin Nitrogen in Liquid Eggs (*5*) Official Final Action

17.010 ***Preparation of Solution***

Accurately weigh, by difference, into 250 mL vol. flask contg 150 mL H_2O, ca 10 g well mixed sample **17.001**(**a**) or (**b**), and mix gently. Add 5 mL 0.01*N* HOAc for each g egg solids, dil. to vol. with H_2O, shake gently, and filter thru 18.5 cm folded paper, covering filter with watch glass during filtration. If filtrate is cloudy, let filtration continue until drops of filtrate are clear, change receiver, and return cloudy filtrate to filter.

17.011 ***Determination***

(**a**) *Water-soluble nitrogen.*—Transfer 50 mL clear filtrate to 500 mL Kjeldahl flask, and det. N as in **2.057**. Calc. N and report as % H_2O-sol. N.

(**b**) *Crude albumin nitrogen.*—Transfer 100 mL clear filtrate to 200 mL vol. flask, add 15 mL NaCl soln (28 g NaCl dild to 300 mL), fill nearly to vol. with alcohol, and mix. Cool to room temp., dil. to vol. with alcohol, mix, and let stand overnight. Filter, transfer 100 mL filtrate to 500 mL Kjeldahl flask, and det. N as in **2.057**. Calc. % N, subtract it from % H_2O-sol. N, and report difference as % crude albumin N.

Fat by Acid Hydrolysis (*6*)—Official Final Action

17.012 ***Preparation of Solution***

(**a**) *Liquid eggs.*—From well mixed sample, **17.001**(**a**) or (**b**), accurately weigh, by difference, into Mojonnier fat-extn tube ca 2 g yolks, 3 g whole eggs, or 5 g whites. Slowly, with vigorous shaking, add 10 mL HCl, set tube in H_2O bath heated to 70°, bring to boiling, and continue heating at bp 30 min, shaking tube carefully every 5 min. Remove tube, add H_2O to nearly fill lower bulb of tube, and cool to room temp.

(**b**) *Dried eggs.*—Transfer 1 g well mixed sample to fat-extn tube, slowly add 10 mL HCl (4+1), washing down any egg particles adhering to sides of tube, and proceed as in (**a**).

17.013 ***Determination***

To extn tube contg treated sample, **17.012**, add 25 mL ether and mix. Add 25 mL redistd pet ether (bp <60°), mix, and let stand until solv. layer is clear. Proceed as in **14.019**, beginning "Draw off as much as possible . . ." but omitting filtration.

Lipids and Lipid Phosphorus (P_2O_5) (*7*) Official Final Action

17.014 ***Reagents***

(**a**) *Mixed solvent.*—Equal vols $CHCl_3$ and absolute alcohol.

(**b**) *Alcoholic sodium hydroxide soln.*—Prep. CO_3-free soln by dissolving 100 g NaOH in 100 mL H_2O. Let stand until clear, or filter thru hardened paper previously soaked in alcohol. (5 mL NaOH soln contains ca 4 g NaOH.) Dissolve 50 mL of this soln in 900 mL alcohol and dil. with alcohol to 1 L.

17.015 ***Preparation of Solution***

(**a**) *Liquid eggs.*—Accurately weigh, by difference, ca 4 g well mixed sample, **17.001**(**a**) or (**b**), into 100 mL vol. flask, and add 25 mL mixed solv. very slowly (dropwise) from pipet, shaking constantly until proteins coagulate and are then thoroly broken up. Add 60–65 mL addnl solv. and let stand 1 hr, shaking every 5 min. Dil. to vol. with solv., mix, and let mixt. stand until clear.

(**b**) *Dried eggs.*—Transfer 2 g well mixed sample, **17.001**(**c**), to 100 mL vol. flask, add 85–90 mL mixed solv., and let stand 1 hr, mixing every 5 min. Proceed as in (**a**).

17.016 ***Determination***

(**a**) *Lipids.*—Transfer 50 mL aliquot to 150 mL beaker and evap. ext to dryness on steam bath. (Elec. fan or gentle blast of dry air may be used to hasten evapn.) Place beaker in oven 5–10 min at 100° to remove any remaining H_2O. Dissolve dry ext in 5–10 mL $CHCl_3$, and filter into weighed 100 mL Pyrex beaker thru pledget of cotton packed into stem of funnel, transferring all sol. ext from bottom and sides of beaker with $CHCl_3$. Finally wash funnel and stem tip. (Filtrate should be clear.) Evap. $CHCl_3$ on steam bath and dry beaker and contents in oven at 100° to const wt (ca 90 min). Let beaker stand in air to const wt (ca 30 min), weigh, and report % lipids.

(**b**) *Lipid phosphorus* (P_2O_5).—Dissolve dried lipids in 2–3 mL $CHCl_3$, add 10–20 mL alc. NaOH soln, evap. to dryness on steam bath, using care to avoid spattering, and place beaker in oven 30 min at 100° to remove any remaining H_2O. Transfer beaker while hot to furnace heated to 500° (faint red), and keep at this temp. 1 hr. Cool, add few drops H_2O, and break up residue with flat-end glass rod. Cover beaker with watch glass, slowly add 5 mL HNO_3 (1+3), mix, wash watch glass, and filter, collecting filtrate in 300 or 500 mL erlenmeyer. Thoroly wash charred material and filter paper with H_2O.

Det. P in filtrate as in **7.119**, using 20–50 mL molybdate soln. Report % lipid P_2O_5 in eggs.

Cholesterol (*8*)—Official Final Action

Separation of Unsaponifiable Matter

17.017 ***Reagents***

(**a**) *Concentrated potassium hydroxide soln.*—Dissolve 60 g KOH in 40 mL H_2O.

(**b**) *Dilute potassium hydroxide soln.*—Dissolve 10 g KOH in 1 L H_2O.

(**c**) *Ether.*—USP or ACS, peroxide-free. Test immediately before use.

(**d**) *Dried ether.*—Immediately before use, shake peroxide-free ether with anhyd. $CaCl_2$ equal to 10% of the vol. of the ether, and filter.

(**e**) *Anhydrous sodium sulfate.*—Powder to pass No. 60 sieve.

17.018 ***Apparatus***

(**a**) *Separators.*—One 250 mL and one 500 mL. *Wash separators free of grease*. Must be ether-tight when lubricated only with H_2O.

(**b**) *Filtration bell jar.*—Large enough to hold 300 mL erlenmeyer and provided with air-leak valve to control vac.

(**c**) *Fritted glass filter.*—Fine porosity.

17.019 ***Determination***

(*Caution: See* **51.011**, **51.039**, and **51.054**.)

Accurately weigh into 125 mL erlenmeyer ca 2.5 g whole egg, 1.5 g yolk, 1 g dried whole egg, or 0.7 g dried yolk, and add 10 mL concd KOH soln. Cover with small watch glass and heat 3 hr on steam bath, swirling occasionally to disintegrate any lumps. Cool until just warm, add 30 mL alcohol, and swirl until all insol. matter is *finely* dispersed. Add 50 mL ether, mix thoroly by swirling, and transfer to 500 mL separator. Wash flask with 2 addnl 50 mL portions ether and thoroly mix ether soln by swirling. Wash saponification flask with 100 mL dil. KOH soln, pour soln slowly into separator, while gently swirling liq., and continue gentle swirling 10–15 sec. Let liq. sep. (ca 10 min) and slowly drain soap soln into 250 mL separator, but do not drain any emulsion or insol. matter at interface. Rinse down sides of 500 mL separator with 10 mL dil. KOH soln and drain this into smaller separator. Add 50 mL ether to smaller separator and shake vigorously. After liq. seps, discard lower layer. Add ether layer to soln in large separator, rinsing 250 mL separator with 10 mL ether. Wash ether soln as before with 100 mL dil. KOH soln, keeping any insol. matter or emulsion in separator. Add 20 mL HCl (1+4) to ether, swirl, add 100 mL H_2O, and swirl again. Discard acid washings.

Wash ether soln as before with 2 addnl 100 mL portions dil. KOH soln. Test portion of last washings for soap by acidifying with HCl (1+4) (acidified washings should be clear or only faintly turbid). If necessary, repeat washing with dil. KOH soln until acidified washings are clear. Wash ether soln by successively swirling with 50 mL H_2O, 50 mL H_2O contg 0.5 mL 0.1*N* HCl, and 2 addnl 50 mL portions H_2O. Finally, drain as much H_2O as possible without loss of ether soln. Filter ether soln into dry 300 mL erlenmeyer thru 15 g layer Na_2SO_4 on fritted glass filter, using no suction for first few mL and then gentle suction for remainder. Rinse separator and filter successively with 10, 5, 5, and 5 mL ether. Rinse filter stem with ether, add porcelain chip to flask, and evap. ether on steam bath.

Dissolve residue in 20 mL dried ether, transfer thru small short-stem funnel to 50 mL erlenmeyer contg porcelain chip, and rinse with 10, 5, and 5 mL dried ether. Approx. unsaponifiable matter can be detd by collecting ether solns in previously dried and weighed flask as follows: Dry flask contg chip, and similar flask as counterpoise, 1 hr at 100–105°; remove from oven and place near balance 30 min; weigh flask, using counterpoise. Evap. ether on steam bath. Wipe flask with clean towel, dry, and weigh with counterpoise as before. From wt unsaponifiable matter, deduct blank obtained from reagents used, detd similarly.

Determination of Cholesterol

17.020 ***Reagents***

(**a**) *Ice.*—For 4 detns have available ca 12 L (3 gal.) crushed ice.

(**b**) *Bromine soln.*—(*Caution: See* **51.047**.) Weigh, to 0.1 g, narrow-mouth, g-s 25 mL flask contg 5 mL CCl_4. Add 0.6 mL Br from graduated 1.0 mL pipet, weigh again, and dil. with CCl_4 to calcd final concn of 0.22±0.02 g Br/mL. Use reagent within 48 hr after prepn.

(**c**) *Acetic acid soln.*—Pipet 200 mL HOAc into 250 mL g-s vol. flask; dil. to vol. with H_2O, mix cautiously, dil. to vol., and mix again.

(**d**) *Asbestos.*—Prep. asbestos as in **31.037**.

(**e**) *Sand.*—Pass clean sand thru No. 60 sieve and treat with warm HCl until exts are practically colorless. Wash, dry, and ignite.

(**f**) *Sodium hypochlorite soln.*—Dissolve 88 g NaOH (*Caution: See* **51.037** and **51.047**) in 200 mL H_2O in wide-mouth 3 L flask. Add ca 1.5 L crushed ice and pass in Cl until 71 g is absorbed; dil. to 2 L and store in dark bottles in refrigerator. (Soln should be alk. to phthln.) Before use, check concn of available Cl as follows: Pipet 5 mL into flask contg soln of 2 g KI in 100 mL H_2O, add 5 mL 6*N* HCl, and titr. with 0.1*N* $Na_2S_2O_3$. Soln should be equiv. in available Cl to 0.95–1.05*N* NaOCl. Reagent or com. NaOCl soln, 5%, checked for concn as above, is also satisfactory.

(**g**) *Sodium formate soln.*—Prep. aq. soln contg 0.5 g $NaCHO_2$/mL.

(**h**) *Hydrochloric acid.*—Approx. 6*N*; mix 520 mL HCl with H_2O and dil. to 1 L.

(**i**) *Methyl red indicator.*—Dissolve 0.5 g Me red in 50 mL alcohol, dil. to 100 mL with H_2O, and filter. Since soln must be free from insol. matter, refilter immediately before use, if necessary.

(**j**) *Potassium iodide soln.*—20%. (Soln must be colorless when acidified with HCl.)

(**k**) *Starch soln.*—1% soln of sol. starch.

(**l**) *Sodium thiosulfate soln.*—0.02*N*. Prep. daily by dilg 0.1*N* soln, **50.037–50.038**.

(**m**) *Potassium hydroxide soln.*—Dissolve 10 g KOH in 10 mL H_2O.

(**n**) *Ammonium molybdate soln.*—Dissolve 5 g $(NH_4)_6Mo_7O_{24}.4H_2O$ in 100 mL H_2O.

17.021 ***Apparatus***

(**a**) *Ice bath.*—Container holding ca 4 L, 10–15 cm deep, filled with crushed ice.

(**b**) *Mohr pipets.*—One graduated to 0.01 mL; one graduated to 0.1 mL.

(**c**) *Filtration bell jar.*—Size to hold 300 mL erlenmeyer, connected to vac. by 2-way stopcock.

(**d**) *Device for filtering at 0°.*—Filter tube of Knorr extn tube style, ca 20 mm id, with body ca 11 cm long and stem 6–8 mm od, ca 10 cm long, provided with removable, close fitting perforated Ni, monel metal, glass, or porcelain disk at bottom of larger tube. (Allihn fritted glass filter, coarse porosity, Ace Glass, Inc. No. 7195-06 with 10 cm stem is suitable.)

Remove stem at apex from 60° Bunsen funnel, 11 cm diam. Enlarge opening at apex to ca 1 cm diam. by grinding or grating off glass. Cut ca 1 cm from end of 1-hole rubber stopper of size that fits snugly in opening of funnel. Pass stem of filter tube thru stopper in funnel apex and then thru stopper in bell jar.

Prep. mat of asbestos, (**d**), 6–8 mm thick in filter tube and cover with ca 12 mm layer of sand, (**e**). (*Caution: See* **51.086**.)

17.022 ***Determination***

Pack Br soln and 25 mL graduate in ice. Pack ice around filter tubes, taking care none gets into filters. Cool HOAc soln to ca −5° in ice-NaCl mixt.

Wash down sides of 50 mL erlenmeyers contg unsaponifiable matter, while rotating, with 2.0 mL absolute ether delivered from Mohr pipet; stopper with cork, swirl until porcelain chips no longer stick to flasks, and pack flasks in ice bath up to necks ≥10 min. To one of flasks add, from Mohr pipet, 0.20 mL cold Br soln, mix by swirling, stopper, and replace in ice bath. Start this operation at 3 min intervals with other flasks (4 detns can be made at one time if bell jars are available).

After 10 min, rapidly add 15 mL HOAc soln from cold 25 mL graduate, swirl 3 min while holding in ice-H_2O, and replace in ice bath 10 min. With suction on, pour all mixt. down stirring rod into filter tube, leaving rod in filter. Wash down sides of flask with 5 mL cold HOAc soln and replace in ice bath. When liq. in filter just recedes below surface of sand, add HOAc from flask. Repeat washing similarly with 5 mL HOAc soln and suck filter free of excess liq. Wash flask and filter with cold H_2O, filling filter tube ca 3 times. Drain flask thoroly and apply suction to filter until drops of H_2O cease to fall from stem. Remove ice pack from around filter tube and discard filtrate and washings.

Place 300 mL erlenmeyer under filter so that stem projects well into neck of flask. Wash filter tube and filter with 10 mL alcohol; 10, 5, and 5 mL portions ether; and finally with 10 mL alcohol, gently stirring sand with each portion of solv. and letting mixt. stand ca 1 min before applying suction. Wash stem of filter with few mL ether, add 1 mL KOH soln, mix, and wash down sides of flask with 5 mL ether. Completely evap. ether and alcohol on steam bath, finally using stream of clean air to remove last of alcohol vapors.

Add 40 mL hot H_2O to residual alk. liq., mix, and neutze alkali with 6*N* HCl, using *1 drop* Me red. (This neutzn need be only approx.) Add 10 g NaCl, 3 g $NaH_2PO_4.H_2O$, and 20 mL NaOCl soln. Bring soln just to vigorous boiling, remove from heat, and immediately add, with care, 5 mL $NaCHO_2$ soln. Cool, and dil. to ca 150 mL with H_2O. Add 5 mL KI soln, 1 or 2 drops NH_4 molybdate soln, and 25 mL 6*N* HCl. Titr. rapidly at once with $Na_2S_2O_3$ soln, using starch soln as indicator. Correct titer for blank detn on reagents, starting at point where KOH soln is added to alcohol-ether soln.

mg Cholesterol = 0.55 + 0.688 × mL 0.02*N* $Na_2S_2O_3$

Total Phosphorus (P_2O_5) (*9*)—Official Final Action

17.023 ***Preparation of Solution***

(**a**) *Liquid eggs.*—From well mixed sample, **17.001**(**a**) or (**b**), accurately weigh, by difference, into 250 mL Pyrex beaker, ca 2 g yolks, 4 g whole eggs, or 10 g whites. Add 20 mL 10% Na_2CO_3 soln and evap. to dryness on hot plate or in oven overnight at 100–105°. Transfer beaker while hot to furnace at 500° (faint red), and keep at this temp. 1 hr. Cool, add few drops H_2O, break up residue with flat-end glass rod, and cover beaker with watch glass; slowly add 10 mL HNO_3 (1+3) while stirring, mix, wash watch glass, and filter, collecting filtrate in 300 or 500 mL erlenmeyer. Thoroly wash charred material and filter with H_2O.

(**b**) *Dried eggs.*—Transfer 1 g well mixed sample, **17.001**(**c**), to 150 mL Pyrex beaker, add 20 mL 10% Na_2CO_3 soln, and proceed as in (**a**).

17.024 ***Determination***

Det. P_2O_5 in prepd filtrate as in **7.119**, using 40–50 mL molybdate soln. Report as total P_2O_5.

Chloride (*10*)—Official Final Action

17.025 ***Method I***

(**a**) *Liquid eggs* (*in absence of added salt.*)—From well mixed sample, **17.001**(**a**) or (**b**), accurately weigh, by difference, into 150 mL Pyrex beaker, ca 4 g yolks, 7 g whole eggs, or 10 g whites; add 20 mL 10% Na_2CO_3 soln, mix, and evap. to dryness on hot plate or overnight in oven at 100°. Transfer beaker while hot to furnace at 500° (faint red), and keep 1 hr at 500°. Cool, add few drops H_2O, and break up residue with glass rod. Add 50 mL H_2O, cover beaker with watch glass, slowly add 20 mL HNO_3 (1+3), and wash watch glass. Mix, filter, and wash charred material and filter paper thoroly with H_2O. Proceed by one of following alternatives:

(*1*) To combined filtrate and washings add known vol. 0.1*N* $AgNO_3$ in slight excess and proceed as in **3.074**.

(*2*) Collect filtrate and washings in 250 mL vol. flask, keeping total vol. filtrate ≤180 mL. Add known vol. 0.1*N* $AgNO_3$ in slight excess and dil. to vol. Filter, and using aliquot of filtrate, proceed as in **3.074**, beginning ". . . add 5 mL ferric indicator . . ."

(**b**) *Liquid eggs* (*in presence of added salt*).—From well mixed sample, **17.001**(**a**) or (**b**), accurately weigh 1–2 g, by difference, into 150 mL Pyrex beaker, and proceed as in (**a**).

(**c**) *Dried eggs.*—From well mixed sample, **17.001**(**c**), transfer 2 g whole eggs or yolks or 1 g whites to 150 mL Pyrex beaker, and proceed as in (**a**).

17.026 ***Method II*** **(*11*)**

From well mixed sample, **17.001**(**a**), (**b**), or (**c**), accurately weigh, by difference, ca 4 g yolks, 7 g whole eggs, or 10 g whites; or transfer 2 g dried whole eggs or yolks or 1 g dried whites to 300 mL erlenmeyer. Add known vol. 0.1*N* $AgNO_3$ in slight excess and 20 mL HNO_3, and place on steam bath 15–30 min. Add 15 mL 5% $KMnO_4$ soln and let stand 60–90 min longer on steam bath. Cool to ≤25°; add 75 mL H_2O and 1 mL *nitrobenzene* (or 1 mL for each 50 mg NaCl present); stopper flask, and shake vigorously to coagulate ppt. Add 5 mL satd ferric alum indicator and titr. with 0.1*N* thiocyanate soln to end point that persists after soln stands 15 min. (Make titrn at ≤25°; soln is yellow-green before end point and yellow-orange at end point.) At first permanent color change, note buret reading and time; stopper flask, shake vigorously, and let stand 15 min. If soln fades, add thiocyanate soln in half-drop portions until end point color reappears. From mL $AgNO_3$ used, calc. NaCl after deducting blank detd on reagents, using ca 0.25 g sucrose instead of egg.

17.027 ***Potentiometric Method***

See **32.025–32.030**.

Glucose and Sucrose (*12*)—Official Final Action

17.028 ***Preparation of Solution***

(**a**) *Liquid eggs.*—Accurately weigh, by difference, ca 25 g well mixed sample, **17.001**(**a**) or (**b**), into 250 mL vol. flask contg 1 g $CaCO_3$ and 50 mL 5% NaCl soln. Add 130 mL alcohol with continuous mixing. Let stand few min for gas bubbles to rise to surface, cool to room temp., dil. to vol. with H_2O, mix, and filter (18.5 cm folded paper). Transfer 150 mL filtrate to 250 mL beaker and evap. to 20–30 mL to remove alcohol. Cool, and wash with H_2O into 100 mL vol. flask, holding vol. to 80–90 mL. Add dry powd *phosphotungstic acid* in small amts in slight excess to ppt any protein, mix, let stand few min for gas bubbles to rise to surface, dil. to vol. with H_2O, mix, and filter. To filtrate add, in very small portions, enough dry powd KCl to ppt any excess phosphotungstic acid, filter if necessary, and test filtrate for complete pptn.

To correct for error due to vol. occupied by ppt in samples contg added sucrose, repeat detn, weighing same amt of sample into 500 mL vol. flask contg 1 g $CaCO_3$ and 100 mL 5% NaCl soln. Add 260 mL alcohol with continuous mixing. Let stand few min for gas bubbles to rise to surface, cool to room temp., dil. to vol. with H_2O, mix, and filter thru 18.5 cm folded paper. Transfer 300 mL filtrate to 400 mL beaker, evap. to 20–30 mL, and proceed as above. To obtain amt of sucrose, subtract % sucrose obtained in 250 mL diln detn from twice the % obtained in 500 mL diln detn.

(**b**) *Dried eggs.*—From well mixed sample, **17.001**(**c**), transfer 2.5 g whites or 10 g yolks or whole eggs to 250 mL vol. flask contg 1 g $CaCO_3$ and 50 mL 5% NaCl soln, and let stand 1 hr, mixing every 5 min. Add 130 mL alcohol with continuous mixing, and proceed as in (**a**), beginning with third sentence.

17.029 ***Determination***

(**a**) *Reducing sugars direct.*—Transfer 25 mL prepd filtrate to 400 mL beaker, and proceed as in **31.038**. Report as % glucose.

(**b**) *Reducing sugars invert.*—Transfer 50 mL prepd filtrate to 100 mL vol. flask, and invert sucrose as in **31.026**(**b**) or (**c**). Neutze with NaOH soln, cool to room temp., and dil. to vol. with H_2O. Transfer ≤50 mL to 400 mL beaker, and proceed as in **31.038**. Deduct % invert sugar obtained before inversion from that obtained after inversion, multiply difference by 0.95, and report as % sucrose.

Glycerol (*13*)

Qualitative Test—Procedure

17.030 ***Reagent***

Fuchsin-bisulfite soln.—Dissolve 0.2 g basic fuchsin in 120 mL hot H_2O and cool; add soln of 2 g anhyd. Na_2SO_3 in 20 mL H_2O, and then 2 mL HCl. Dil. soln with H_2O to 200 mL and let stand 1 hr.

17.031 ***Detection***

Add 20 mL alcohol to ca 5 g sample in erlenmeyer or beaker-flask, shake vigorously, and filter thru 12.5 cm fluted paper. Evap. filtrate rapidly until no odor of alcohol is perceptible, cool, and add 3–4 drops H_2O and then 10–15 mL anhyd. ether. Carefully mix solns, let sep., and pour off as much of ether layer as possible, disregarding cloudiness in this layer. Shake well with two 10 mL portions anhyd. ether, pouring off ether carefully in each case. (Vol. aq. soln should be $\geqslant$0.4–0.5 mL.) Evap. remaining liq. on steam bath to 0.1–0.2 mL. Cool, and add 15 mL mixt. of equal vols absolute alcohol and $CHCl_3$. Cool, shake, and let stand 5 min.

Shake, and filter thru fluted paper into 25 × 150 mm Pyrex test tube. Evap. filtrate rapidly (small flame and current of air is convenient) until no odor of $CHCl_3$ or alcohol is perceptible. Add several g powd $KHSO_4$ and insert stopper with glass tube leading into 2 mL H_2O in test tube immersed in ice-H_2O. Heat with small flame until frothing ceases and contents of tube are liq. Remove receiver, immediately add 4–5 drops of fuchsin-bisulfite soln, and warm to room temp. In presence of glycerol, strong pink (due to acrolein) develops within 1 min and becomes deep violet within 5 min.

Quantitative Method (14)—Official Final Action

17.032 ***Reagents***

(a) *Sodium tungstate soln.*—Dissolve 10 g $Na_2WO_4.2H_2O$ and dil. to 100 mL.

(b) *Potassium periodate soln.*—0.02*M*. Dissolve 4.6 g KIO_4 in ca 500 mL hot H_2O, dil. to ca 900 mL with H_2O, cool to room temp., and dil. to 1 L. Test for alky by adding 0.02*N* H_2SO_4 to 25 mL of the soln contg bromocresol purple, (**c**). Do not use if >1 drop acid is required to give yellow acid color.

(c) *Bromocresol purple indicator.*—Dissolve 0.1 g bromocresol purple in 100 mL alcohol and filter if necessary.

(d) *Calcium oxide, powdered.*—Reagent grade.

17.033 ***Determination***

(a) *Eggs with no added sugars.*—Accurately weigh, by difference, ca 2 g well mixed sample, **17.001(a)** or **(b)**, into 100 mL vol. flask contg 50–75 mL H_2O. Mix and add 2.0 mL Na_2WO_4 soln. Slowly add 2.0 mL 1*N* H_2SO_4 with continuous mixing. Dil. to vol. with H_2O, mix well, and filter (18.5 cm folded paper). Transfer aliquot of filtrate contg $\leqslant$40 mg glycerol to 300 mL erlenmeyer, and dil. with H_2O to 20 mL if necessary. Add 2 mL 10% NaOH soln, heat to bp, and boil 30 sec. Cool slightly, add 3 drops bromocresol purple, neutze with 1*N* H_2SO_4 (use buret), and add 1–2 drops excess. Boil 1 min, cool to room temp., and neutze carefully with 0.02*N* NaOH, titrg to light purple.

Quant. transfer neut. soln to 100 mL vol. flask, restricting total vol. to <50 mL. (As aid, mark side of flask to indicate vol. of ca 45 mL.) If necessary, add more 0.02*N* NaOH to maintain light but definite purple. Continue as in **35.081(b)**, beginning ". . . add 50 mL KIO_4 soln." and using **35.082(a)** for detn.

Excess periodate must be present after oxidn. If periodate test is neg., repeat detn, using smaller aliquots.

(b) *Eggs containing added sugars.*—Prep. sample soln as in (**a**), using ca 2 g sample.

Transfer aliquot of filtrate contg $\leqslant$40 mg glycerol to 400 mL beaker. Adjust vol. to 20 mL by evapn on steam bath or by addn of H_2O. Add 0.5 g powd CaO, mix, and let stand 30 min at room temp. with occasional mixing. Add 25 mL alcohol, mix, and filter with suction, using buchner and 7 cm S&S 597 paper, or equiv. Rinse beaker, funnel, and paper with several portions alcohol. Transfer as much residue as possible to paper but do not attempt to remove film of lime salts adhering to beaker. Quant. transfer filtrate to original 400 mL beaker, rinsing flask with several portions H_2O. Evap. filtrate on steam bath to ca 10 mL. Filter thru 9 cm S&S 597 paper, or equiv., collecting filtrate in 300 mL erlenmeyer. Rinse beaker, funnel, and paper with small amts of H_2O, restricting total filtrate to $\leqslant$25 mL. Add 1 mL 10% NaOH soln to filtrate and complete detn as in (**a**), beginning ". . . heat to bp, and boil 30 sec."

Acidity of Ether Extract (*15*)—Official Final Action

(Not applicable to egg white)

17.034 ***Reagents***

(*Caution: See* **51.038**.)

(a) *Benzene.*—Use best quality available. If not neut., titr. 50 mL with 0.05*N* Na ethylate, (**b**), and correct subsequent results accordingly.

(b) *Sodium ethylate std soln.*—0.05*N*. Dissolve piece of metallic Na (*Caution: See* **51.034**), ca 1 mL in vol., in 800 mL absolute alcohol. Titr. 10 mL 0.1*N* HCl with this soln and add calcd vol. absolute alcohol to make soln 0.05*N*. Stdze against 0.1*N* HCl on day soln is used.

17.035 ***Determination***

(*Caution: See* **51.011**, **51.039**, and **51.054**.)

(a) *Dried eggs.*—Weigh 2 g dried eggs into small lipped erlenmeyer, add 30 mL ether, and mix well. After ether layer clears, decant thru small filter paper into weighed flask. Repeat extn with three 20 mL portions ether. Evap. ether on steam bath and dry ext 15 min at 100°. Cool, weigh, dissolve in 30 mL benzene, add 3–4 drops phthln, and titr. with NaOEt soln. (End point is reached when yellow changes to orange.) Report as mL 0.05*N* NaOEt required/g ether ext.

(b) *Liquid eggs.*—Weigh ca 8 g liq. eggs into 9 cm lipped evapg dish, and dry at 55° under pressure $\leqslant$125 mm Hg (16.7 kPa) until eggs are thoroly dry (ca 5 hr). Grind dried eggs in evapg dish with small pestle, and proceed as in (**a**), beginning ". . . add 30 mL ether, and mix well."

Lactic, Succinic, and Beta-Hydroxybutyric Acids (*16*) Official Final Action

17.036 ***Reagents***

(a) *Boron trifluoride-1-propanol soln.*—10%. Prep. as follows: In fume hood, assemble following or equiv. gas train. Connect two 500 mL all-glass gas washing bottles (Corning Glass Works No. 1760), with longer arms adjacent, in tandem to BF_3 cylinder (Matheson Gas Products, PO Box E, Lyndhurst, NJ 07071) with short lengths of Teflon tubing. Transfer 250 mL PrOH to end bottle, weigh, and cool in ice bath. Connect bottle in ice bath to gas train and bubble BF_3 slowly into PrOH until 22 g is taken up. (BF_3 must be passing thru glass tube before tube is placed in and until after it is removed from PrOH.) If >22 g BF_3 is added, dil. with PrOH until total mL PrOH is 11.4 × g BF_3. Store reagent in g-s bottle in refrigerator.

Com. reagent, 14% w/v (Applied Science Laboratories, Inc.), may be used undild or dild 1 vol. + 0.6 vol. PrOH. (*Note:* Remove BF_3 vapors with effective fume removal device. Avoid contact with skin, eyes, and respiratory tract. *See* **51.010**.)

(b) *Calcium lactate std solns.*—Prep. fresh daily. Dissolve 0.856 g USP Ca lactate.$5H_2O$ in H_2O and dil. to 100 mL (*Soln A:* 5.0 mg lactic acid equiv./mL). Dil. 25, 20, 15, and 5 mL *Soln A* to 50 mL with H_2O to prep. solns contg 2.5 (*B*), 2.0 (*C*), 1.5 (*D*), and 0.5 (*E*) mg lactic acid equiv./mL, resp.

(c) *Succinic acid std solns.*—Prep. fresh daily. Dissolve 1.000

g succinic acid (Fisher Certified, or equiv.) in H_2O and dil. to 100 mL (*Soln F:* 10.0 mg/mL). Dil. 25, 25, and 15 mL Soln *F* to 50, 100, and 100 mL with H_2O to prep. solns contg 5.0 (*G*), 2.5 (*H*), and 1.5 (*I*) mg/mL, resp.

(**d**) *Acetophenone (AP) solns.*—(*1*) Std soln.—Dissolve 0.800 g acetophenone (MC/B Manufacturing Chemists, C-Q AX0164) in PrOH and dil. to 100 mL in vol. flask. Store at room temp. (*2*) *Diluting soln.*—Prep. fresh daily. Pipet 20 mL PrOH, 10 mL AP std soln *1*, and 20 mL $CHCl_3$ into 125 mL separator. (If $CHCl_3$ cannot be used in GLC system, ether may be substituted. However, ether solns must be chromatographed ≤24 hr after esterification.) Add 40 mL satd $(NH_4)_2SO_4$ soln, stopper, shake separator ca 1 min, and let layers sep. Drain bottom aq. layer and discard. Transfer upper layer to g-s flask and add 5 g anhyd. Na_2SO_4.

(**e**) *Ether.*—Anhyd., contg ≤0.05% alcohol.

(**f**) *Sodium beta-hydroxybutyrate std soln.*—Dissolve 0.121 g Na β-hydroxybutyrate (Sigma Chemical Co.) in H_2O and dil. to 100 mL (1 mg β-hydroxybutyric acid equiv./mL).

17.037 *Apparatus*

(*Caution: See* **51.039** and **51.046**.)

(**a**) *Gas chromatograph.*—With flame ionization detector. Operating conditions: 3 m (10′) × 4 mm id glass tube packed with 10% stabilized diethyleneglycol succinate (DEGS) on 100–120 mesh Gas-Chrom Z. Temps (°): column 130, injection zone 200, detector 200; He 80 mL/min; H 37 mL/min; air 400 mL/min; electrometer sensitivity 9×10^{-10} amp full scale; 5 mv recorder; chart speed 50 cm (20″)/hr.

(**b**) *GLC column.*—Dissolve 1.2 g stabilized DEGS (Analabs, Inc., No. C6) in 100 mL acetone in 250 mL beaker. Add 10.8 g 100–120 mesh Gas-Chrom Z to DEGS-acetone soln. Evap. acetone on steam bath, stirring occasionally with glass rod, and complete evapn in 50–60° vac. oven 1 hr. Rinse GLC tube with acetone and dry with vac. line. Fill tube with 5% soln of dimethyldichlorosilane in toluene and let stand ca 5 min. Rinse tube with MeOH until washings are neut. to litmus (ca 300 mL) and dry with vac. line. Pack tube with coated support and condition 48 hr at 200° with N flow of ca 30 mL/min. Do *not* pack inlet portion of column that may be exposed to flash heater. (Any column giving equiv. sepn of Pr esters may be used.)

(**c**) *Filtering funnel.*—Glass, short stem, ca 35 mm diam. (Kimble Products No. 28950, or equiv.).

17.038 *Calibration*

(*Caution: See Note,* **17.035**(**a**), and **51.018**.)

(**a**) *Lactic and succinic acids.*—*See* Table **17:01** for std solns to be used for calibration. For each combination, pipet indicated vols Ca lactate and succinic acid std solns into 250 mL ₸ 24/40 r-b flask and evap. to dryness on steam bath or, more rapidly, in rotary evaporator at 100°. Remove only enough BF_3-PrOH for one day's use to 25 mL g-s erlenmeyer. Pipet 2 mL BF_3-PrOH into 250 mL r-b flask, insert short-stem filtering funnel, (**c**), into neck, and reflux 10 min on steam bath.

Remove from steam bath and let cool to room temp. Add 4 mL satd $(NH_4)_2SO_4$, pipet 1 mL AP std soln and 2 mL $CHCl_3$ into flask, and swirl to mix. (If $CHCl_3$ cannot be used in GLC system, ether may be substituted. However, ether solns must be chromatographed ≤24 hr after esterification.) Pour contents of flask into 30 mL separator. Stopper, shake 1 min, and let layers sep. Drain bottom aq. layer and discard. Transfer upper layer to screw-capped glass vial, add ca 3 g anhyd. Na_2SO_4, cover with Al foil, seal with cap, and shake briefly. Store in refrigerator if soln is to be used after day of prepn.

Table 17:01 Standard Solutions for Calibration of Gas Chromatograph

	Calcium Lactate (**b**)[a]			Succinic Acid (**c**)[a]		
Combi-nation	mg[b]	mL	Std Soln	mg	mL	Std Soln
1	1	2	E	3	2	I
2	3	2	D	5	2	H
3	4	2	C	7.5	3	H
4	5	2	B	10	2	G
5	6	4	D	15	3	G
6	8	4	C	20	2	F
7	10	2	A	25	5	G
8	12.5	5	B	30	3	F
9	15	3	A	40	4	F

[a] Letters refer to solutions under *Reagents*.
[b] Lactic acid equivalent.

Adjust sensitivity and attenuation of gas chromatograph to fit range of stds without addnl diln. (With gas chromatograph so adjusted, ht of internal std (AP) peak is ca ⅓ full scale.) Use same attenuation and sensitivity settings for calibration stds and sample solns.

When withdrawing soln for GLC, insert syringe needle thru Al foil. Make duplicate injections of 3±0.2 μL clear soln into gas chromatograph. For each run, measure peak hts and calc. peak ht ratio, *r*, for each acid. Make calibration charts by plotting values of *r* against *W*. For each acid, *r* = ht of acid ester peak/ht of internal std (AP) peak and *W* = total mg acid esterified with PrOH.

When solv. peak tails into region of Pr lactate peak, extend tail of solv. peak as if no other peak were present. Use this extension as baseline for measuring ht of Pr lactate peak.

(**b**) *Beta-hydroxybutyric acid.*—Pipet 1, 5, 10, and 15 mL Na β-hydroxybutyrate std soln into sep. 250 mL ₸ 24/40 r-b flasks and evap. to dryness in rotary evaporator at 50° and <4 kPa (30 mm Hg) pressure. Proceed as in (**a**).

17.039 *Determination*

(*Caution: See* **51.011**, **51.018**, **51.039**, and **51.054**.)

Use reagent grade anhyd. ether contg ≤0.05% alcohol. Otherwise, results may be low due to formation of Et lactate, di-Et succinate, and Et Pr succinate with retention times, relative to AP, of ca 0.27, 1.02, and 1.38, resp.

Prep. sample soln and ext acids with anhyd. ether in continuous extractor as in **17.048**(**a**), **17.050**, and **17.051**. In **17.050**, note that sample is made to 1 kg (by wt) before filtering; 24 cm fluted S&S 588 filter paper is satisfactory for filtration. Cover funnel and receiver with Al foil during filtration to prevent evapn. Gently evap. aliquot filtrate (usually 500 mL) to ca 100 mL on hot plate and then to ca 25 mL on steam bath. In **17.051**, make calibration mark on extractor at 40 mL. Use 250 mL ₸ 24/40 r-b extn flask. Add few SiC chips. Ext as long as necessary for complete extn, making sure that all ether from condenser returns to inner tube of extractor. (Det. time necessary for complete extn as follows: Ext mixt. of 0.342 g Ca lactate.$5H_2O$ (equiv. to 0.200 g lactic acid), 0.5 mL 18*N* H_2SO_4, 15 g $(NH_4)_2SO_4$, and 40 mL H_2O for time required for min. 98% recovery (ca 3–5 hr). Add 20 mL H_2O to flask and expel ether on steam bath. Do *not* let flask remain on steam bath after ether is expelled. Det. recovery by titrn with std alkali (1 mL 0.1*N* NaOH = 9.008 mg lactic acid).)

Do *not* add 5 mL H_2O to ether ext as specified in **17.051**, par. 3. Evap. ether with rotary evaporator at 30° to ≤1 mL, but *not* to dryness. Pipet 2 mL BF_3-PrOH reagent into flask and continue as in **17.038**.

(*Note:* It is necessary to pipet 2 mL BF_3-PrOH into flask within few min after removing ether because of tendency for polymerization between org. acids when β-hydroxybutyric acid is present. After adding BF_3-PrOH reagent, heating can be delayed until remaining samples are ready for esterification (applies when several extractors are operated simultaneously). Flasks should be stoppered during interval. If ether extns are completed near end of working day, do *not* evap. ether. Flasks contg ether exts should be left attached to extg tubes. Ether exts can then be left at room temp. overnight and ether removed next day just before esterification. (*Caution:* Use effective fume removal devices to prevent hazardous accumulation of flammable vapors.))

Measure peak hts and calc. *r* for each acid. Det. *W* from calibration chart. Make duplicate GLC analyses and calc. av. wt of acid, *W*.

If acid concns give responses greater than full scale, pipet 1 mL sample soln and ≥1 mL AP dilg soln into screw-capped glass vial, add ca 0.2 g anhyd. Na_2SO_4, cover with Al foil, seal with cap, and shake briefly. Record vols of sample and dilg solns used. Make duplicate injections of 3±0.2 μL dild soln into gas chromatograph. Store in refrigerator if soln is to be used after day of prepn.

If further dilns are required, pipet addnl AP dilg soln into dild sample soln and mix. Alternatively, pipet greater vol. of AP dilg soln into 1.0 mL undild sample soln, mix, and make duplicate injections of 3±0.2 μL into gas chromatograph.

For each acid, use max. peak ht (min. diln factor) consistent with range and response limitations of recording device used. (For example, if only lactic acid is concd enough to require diln, calc. lactic acid from chromatogram of dild soln and other acids from chromatogram of undild soln.) Multiply result by diln factor (*F*): *F* = vol. after diln/vol. before diln. For confirmatory test for succinic acid, *see* **17.053**.

Lactic Acid (*17*)—Official Final Action

Colorimetric Method

(If succinic acid is also to be detd, proceed as in **17.048–17.053**.)

17.040 ***Preparation of Solution***

(**a**) *Liquid or frozen eggs.*—Transfer 40 g sample to weighed 300 mL erlenmeyer, add ca 75 mL H_2O, and shake thoroly. Add 15 mL 1*N* H_2SO_4 and 25 mL *20% phosphotungstic acid soln*, dil. to 200 g with H_2O, shake ca 1 min, and filter thru folded paper.

(**b**) *Dried eggs.*—Mix 10 g sample and 100 mL H_2O into paste with stirring rod and add, with const stirring, 10 mL 1*N* H_2SO_4, followed by 15 mL *20% phosphotungstic acid soln*. Transfer mixt. with H_2O to weighed 300 mL erlenmeyer, dil. to 200 g with H_2O, shake ca 1 min, and filter thru folded paper.

Weigh 100 g filtrate obtained as in (**a**) or (**b**) into 250 mL beaker and evap. to ca 25 mL. Transfer material to liq. extractor with 25 mL H_2O and proceed as in **16.030–16.031**. Report lactic acid in terms of mg/100 g, making no correction for insol. solids in portion taken for analysis.

Volatile Fatty Acids (*18*)—Official Final Action

Column Chromatographic Method

17.041 ***Preparation of Solution***

(**a**) *Liquid or frozen eggs.*—Weigh 80 g sample, **17.001**(**a**) or (**b**), into weighed 500 mL erlenmeyer, add ca 150 mL H_2O, and shake vigorously.

(**b**) *Dried eggs.*—Weigh 25 g sample, **17.001**(**c**), into 250 mL beaker, and with heavy stirring rod make into smooth paste with H_2O. Transfer mixt. to weighed 500 mL erlenmeyer, using ca 200 mL H_2O.

Add 25 mL 1*N* H_2SO_4 to mixt. obtained as in (**a**) or (**b**) and shake ca 1 min. Add *20% phosphotungstic acid soln* (40 mL usually enough to give clear filtrate), dil. to 350 g with H_2O, and shake 1 min. Filter thru 24 cm folded paper.

17.042 ***Determination***

Pipet 150 mL filtrate, **17.041** (equiv. to 150 g; sp gr is ca 1.00), into distn flask of app. (Fig. **18:02**) and proceed as in **18.054–18.058**.

Fraction of each acid recovered in first 200 mL distillate is: Formic 0.405, acetic 0.57, propionic 0.81, and butyric 0.92; fraction of formic acid recovered in second 200 mL distillate is 0.24. To calc. mg of each acid in wt of sample used for distn, divide mg detd in distillate by fraction recovered. For liq. or frozen eggs, multiply by 2.92 and for dried eggs by 9.34 to obtain mg acid/100 g sample.

Gas Chromatographic Method (19)
Official Final Action

17.043 ***Reagents***

(**a**) *Acetone.*—Redistd.

(**b**) *Dichloroacetic acid (DCA) soln.*—0.5*N*. Redistil DCA, weigh 0.645 g into 10 mL vol. flask, and dil. to vol. with acetone. Prep. daily.

(**c**) *Methyl heptyl ketone (MHK) solns.*—(*1*) *Std soln.*—Dil. 280 mg MHK to 200 mL with acetone. (Concn may be adjusted, if required by sensitivity of gas chromatograph, provided that same concn is used for calibration and detn.) (*2*) *Diluting soln.*—Dil. 1 vol. std soln wtih 3 vols acetone.

(**d**) *Std acid solns.*—Check purity of formic, acetic, propionic, and butyric acid reagents initially by gas chromatgy. Prep. std soln of each acid by dissolving ca 0.834 g in acetone and dilg to 100 mL. Pipet 10 mL soln into erlenmeyer, add 10 mL H_2O and 2 drops phthln and det. acid content by titrg with 0.1*N* NaOH.

mg Acid/mL std soln = mL 0.1*N* NaOH × normality × *F*, where *F* = 4.60 for formic; 6.01 for acetic; 7.41 for propionic; and 8.81 for butyric acid.

17.044 ***Apparatus***

(Gas chromatgc equipment, column packings, and operating conditions other than those described below may be used if they provide at least equiv. peak sepn (*JAOAC* **46**, 486(1963)).)

(**a**) *Distillation apparatus.*—Stdze distn app. (Fig. **18:02**) as in **18.052**.

(**b**) *Gas chromatograph.*—Use gas chromatograph equipped with all-glass injection and column system. If HCOOH is among acids to be detd, use Ar ionization detection; otherwise, flame ionization detector can be used.

Typical operating conditions: temps (°)—injection zone 200, detector 170, and column 100; Ar flow 50 mL/min, and 1.8 m (6′) glass column. He may be used as carrier gas with flame ionization detector.

(**c**) *Preparation of column packing.*—Weigh 1.3 g ethylene glycol adipate (Applied Science Laboratories, Inc.) into 150 mL beaker and dissolve by stirring in 70 mL acetone. Weigh 0.26 g 85% H_3PO_4 into second beaker and dissolve in 30 mL acetone. Combine both solns. Weigh 12.5 g Anakrom ABS, 110–120 mesh (Analabs, Inc.), into 500 mL r-b flask, add combined acetone solns, and evap. in rotating evaporator at reduced pressure in H_2O bath at 35° (enough to pack one 1.8 m (6′) column).

Pack column evenly. Condition in column oven >12 hr at 150°

by passing Ar or N thru column at ca 20 mL/min. Direct effluent thru $\frac{1}{16}$" (1.6 mm) stainless steel tubing into small test tube shielded from heat of oven. Column is ready for use when bleeding of column substrate into test tube over 2 hr period has practically stopped.

17.045 ***Calibration***

Prep. std acid mixts as follows: Pipet 20 mL each std acid soln into same 100 mL vol. flask, dil. to vol. with acetone, and mix (*Soln I:* ca 5 mg each acid/3 mL). Dil. 15, 10, and 5 mL *Soln I* to 25 mL, and dil. 5 and 1 mL *Soln I* to 50 mL with acetone to prep. solns contg ca 3, 2, 1, 0.5 and 0.1 mg each acid/3 mL, resp. Pipet 3 mL each std acid mixt. into glass vial, add 1.0 mL MHK internal std, seal tightly with Sn foil- or Teflon-lined screw cap, and mix.

Adjust sensitivity and attenuation of gas chromatograph to fit range of stds without addnl diln. Use same instrument settings for calibration stds and sample solns. Make duplicate injections of 2±0.2 μL soln into gas chromatograph. Use smaller vol. (e.g., 1.5 μL) if necessary to keep stds on scale. Make calibration chart for each acid by plotting r against W (r = ht of acid peak/ht of internal std peak and W = mg acid in total vol. of acetone soln, 4 mL). Store solns in refrigerator if they are to be used after day of prepn.

When solv. peak tailing extends into other peaks, draw tail of solv. peak as it would normally appear if no other peaks were present. Use this curved extension as baseline for measuring hts of all peaks above it. Measure hts of remaining peaks to normal baseline.

17.046 ***Preparation of Solution***

(If less than specified sample is available, adjust all wts and vols proportionally.)

(a) *For volatile acids only.—(1) Liquid or frozen eggs.*—Weigh 80 g sample, **17.001(a)** or **(b)**, into weighed 500 mL erlenmeyer, add ca 150 mL H_2O, and shake vigorously. *(2) Dried eggs.*—Weigh 25 g sample, **17.001(c)**, into 250 mL beaker and, with heavy stirring rod, make into smooth paste with H_2O. Transfer mixt. to weighed 500 mL erlenmeyer, using ca 200 mL H_2O.

Add 25 mL 1*N* H_2SO_4 to mixt. obtained as in *(1)* or *(2)* and shake ca 1 min. Add *20% phosphotungstic acid soln* (40 mL usually enough to give clear filtrate), dil. to 350 g with H_2O, and shake 1 min. Centrf. in 250 mL bottles 10 min at 2000 rpm and filter (24 cm fluted S&S 588 paper is satisfactory).

(b) *For volatile acids and succinic or other nonvolatile acids.—(1) Liquid or frozen eggs.*—Weigh 200 g sample into 1 L erlenmeyer, add 500 mL H_2O, and mix well, avoiding violent shaking; add 75 mL 1*N* H_2SO_4 and mix well. Add 125 mL *20% phosphotungstic acid soln*, dil. to 1 kg with H_2O, and shake 1 min. Centrf. in 250 mL bottles 10 min at 2000 rpm and filter (24 cm fluted S&S 588 paper is satisfactory). Pipet 150 mL into distg flask and proceed as in **17.047**. Record vol. of remaining filtrate and use for detn of nonvolatile acids, **17.039**.

(2) Dried eggs.—Weigh 50 g sample into 400 mL beaker and, with heavy stirring rod, make into smooth paste with H_2O. Transfer to 1 L erlenmeyer and add enough H_2O to make total wt of 700 g. Add 50 mL 1*N* H_2SO_4 and mix well. Add 75 mL *20% phosphotungstic acid soln* and proceed as in *(1)*, beginning ". . . dil. to 1 kg with H_2O, . . ."

17.047 ***Determination***

Pipet 150 mL filtrate, **17.046** (sp gr is ca 1.00), into distn flask of app. (Fig. **18:02**). Make acid to *Congo red paper* with H_2SO_4 (1+1). Steam distil as in **18.052**. Collect 200 mL distillate, transfer distillate to 500 mL ₸ 24/40 r-b flask, and quant. neutze with 0.01*N* NaOH, using phthln. Add 1 mL 0.1*N* NaOH excess. If color is discharged, repeat addn. Conc. to 5–10 mL on rotary evaporator at 50–60°. If color is discharged, add 0.5 mL more 0.1*N* NaOH. Transfer to 50 mL ₸ 24/40 r-b flask and evap. to dryness on rotary evaporator at 50–60°. Prevent bumping by degassing with vac. before applying heat.

Alternatively, transfer steam distillate to 600 mL beaker, neutze with 0.01*N* NaOH, add 1 mL 0.1*N* NaOH as above, and conc. to ca 50 mL on steam bath under air stream. Transfer to 150 mL beaker, and conc. to 5–10 mL on steam bath in air stream. Transfer to 50 mL ₸ 24/40 r-b flask, and evap. to dryness on steam bath in air stream.

Add vol. 0.5*N* DCA equiv. to total NaOH added and slight excess. Red due to phthln disappears before acids are completely liberated. Add DCA soln until irregular, coarse particles of salts of volatile acids are completely replaced by fine flocculent Na dichloroacetate.

Add 1.0 mL MHK internal std soln and acetone to total vol. of 4.0 mL. (It is necessary to make total 4.0 mL only if dilns are required, as described in following par., when acid concns give greater than full scale response.) Stopper with ₸ 24/40 stopper and mix thoroly with vortex-type test tube mixer. If vortex mixer is not available, scrape walls of r-b flask with spatula and crush crystals. Stopper and shake thoroly. Mix or shake again after 5–10 min. Decant soln into Sn foil- or Teflon-lined screw-cap vial and seal tightly.

Inject 2±0.2 μL into gas chromatograph, or smaller vol. if such was used in calibration. If acid concns give greater than full scale response, dil. 1.0 mL soln with ≥1 mL MHK dilg soln in screw-cap vial. Record vols of sample and dilg solns used. If further dilns are required, pipet addnl MHK dilg soln into dild sample soln and mix. For each acid, use max. peak ht (min. diln factor) consistent with range and response limitations of recording device. (For example, if only HOAc is concd enough to require diln, calc. HOAc from chromatogram of dild soln and other acids from chromatogram of undild soln.) Det. mg each acid from calibration chart and multiply by diln factor, F = vol. after diln/vol. before diln. Make duplicate GLC detns and calc. av. wt of acid, W. Store solns in refrigerator if they are to be used after day of prepn. Run blank detn on 200 mL distillate obtained by steam distg 150 mL soln contg vols 1*N* H_2SO_4 and 20% phosphotungstic acid = (vol. each reagent used in **17.046** × 150)/(total wt sample mixt. before filtration (**17.046**) − wt solids in sample).

To calc. mg of each acid in wt sample used for distn, divide mg detd in distillate by fraction recovered in distn. Typical recoveries for first 200 mL distillate are: Formic acid 0.405, acetic acid 0.57, propionic acid 0.81, and butyric acid 0.92. To obtain mg acid/100 g sample, multiply result by appropriate factor. Factors for solns prepd by **17.046(a)**: 2.92 for liq. or frozen eggs, 9.34 for dried eggs; for solutions prepd by **17.046(b)**: 3.33 for liq. or frozen eggs, 13.33 for dried eggs. For confirmatory tests, *see* **14.098**, last par.

Succinic Acid (*20*)—Official Final Action

17.048 ***Apparatus***

(a) *Continuous extractor.—See* Fig. **16:01**.

(b) *Chromatographic tube.*—Approx. 17 mm od × 250 mm, plugged at constricted end with either cotton or glass wool.

17.049 ***Reagents***

(a) *Solvent.—Tert*-BuOH-$CHCl_3$ (1+4). Store over granular anhyd. Na_2SO_4.

(b) *Glycerol indicator soln.*—Dissolve 75 mg mono NH_4 salt of 3-(4-anilino-1-naphthylazo)-2,7-naphthalenedisulfonic acid (Alphamine Red R, Eastman Kodak Co. No. 6394) in 50 mL glycerol, warming on steam bath.

(**c**) *Phenol red indicator*.—Rub 100 mg phenolsulfonphthalein in mortar with 5.7 mL 0.05*N* NaOH until dissolved; then dil. to 100 mL with H_2O.

17.050 ***Preparation of Solution***

(**a**) *Liquid or frozen eggs*.—Weigh 200 g sample into 1 L erlenmeyer, add 500 mL H_2O, and mix well, avoiding violent shaking; add 75 mL 1*N* H_2SO_4 and mix well. Add 125 mL *20% phosphotungstic acid soln*, dil. to 1 kg with H_2O, and shake 1 min. Divide between two 24 cm rapid folded filter papers. Transfer 250 mL filtrate to 400 mL beaker, evap. to ca 50 mL, add another 250 mL to same beaker, and evap. to 10 mL. If material starts to bump when vol. becomes low, transfer to steam bath.

If <200 g sample is available, take 100 g sample and half quantities of reagents, and dil. to 500 g with H_2O. Filter ppt on buchner with suction, collecting as much filtrate as possible. Use total weighed filtrate for evapn.

(**b**) *Dried eggs*.—Weigh 50 g sample into 400 mL beaker, and with heavy stirring rod make into smooth paste with H_2O. Transfer to 1 L erlenmeyer and add enough H_2O to make total wt of 700 g. Add 50 mL 1*N* H_2SO_4 and mix well. Add 75 mL *20% phosphotungstic acid soln* and proceed as in (**a**), beginning ". . . dil. to 1 kg with H_2O, . . ."

17.051 ***Extraction***

(*Caution: See* **51.011**, **51.039**, and **51.054**.)

Place 15 g $(NH_4)_2SO_4$ in dry extractor. Transfer evapd material, **17.050**(**a**) or (**b**), to inner tube of extractor by washing thru small funnel with enough H_2O to make total vol. of 40 mL, add 0.5 mL H_2SO_4 (1+1), and mix by raising and lowering inner tube. Rinse beaker with 50 mL ether and pour rinsings into inner tube of extractor. Connect efficient condenser to extractor and proceed with extn as in **16.030**, placing 150 mL ether in extn flask and extg 3 hr or as long as necessary for complete extn.

(To det. time necessary for complete extn, transfer ca 20 mg *succinic acid*, accurately weighed, to extractor contg 20 g $(NH_4)_2SO_4$, add enough H_2O to give total vol. of 40 mL, and proceed with extn as above. After 3 hr, add 10 mL H_2O to extn flask, evap. ether on steam bath, and titr. If recovery is <95%, ext another 20 mg succinic acid for longer period and titr. Continue until 95% recovery is obtained, and use this period of extn for detn.)

To flask contg ether ext add 5 mL H_2O and evap. ether on steam bath. Using graduated 5 mL pipet, neutze contents of flask with satd $Ba(OH)_2$ soln, using phthln. Adjust vol. to 20 mL with H_2O, add 90 mL alcohol, heat almost to boiling on steam bath, and cool. Add ca 0.5 g filter-aid and filter with suction thru suitable filter, such as Caldwell crucible covered with thin layer of asbestos overlaid with small amt of filter-aid added from suspension in H_2O. Rinse flask with 3 portions of alcohol (9+2), transferring each rinsing to crucible and sucking dry before adding another portion. Reserve filtrate for detn of lactic acid, **16.031**, beginning line 6, "To expel alcohol, evap . . .", using entire filtrate and modifying calcns.

Transfer contents of crucible to 100 mL beaker with 15–20 mL H_2O, acidify to *Congo red paper* with 1–2 drops H_2SO_4 (1+1), warm on steam bath, and refilter with suction, rinsing beaker with three 10 mL portions H_2O, transferring each rinsing to crucible, and sucking dry before adding another. Evap. filtrate to ca 5 mL, neutze with 1*N* NaOH, transfer with H_2O to 50 mL beaker, and evap. to dryness on steam bath.

17.052 ***Preparation of Partition Column***

Place 5 g H_2SiO_3, **18.051**(**g**), in glazed porcelain evapg dish and add 0.5 mL freshly prepd glycerol indicator soln. (More soln may be necessary if it has stood several weeks.) Then add max. amt of glycerol (1+1) that gel will hold without becoming sticky (usually 1–3 mL) and 1 drop (ca 0.05 mL) ca 1*N* NH_4OH. Grind into uniform powder with pestle, make into slurry with ca 30 mL of solv., and transfer to chromatgc tube, which is clamped vertically. Apply 5–10 lb (34.5–68.9 kPa) air pressure to top of tube until solv. just disappears into top of gel; release pressure, add 1 mL $CHCl_3$ contg ca 5 mg HOAc, and again apply pressure until solv. just disappears into gel. Release pressure, add 5 mL solv., and once more apply pressure just long enough for solv. to disappear into gel. (Pressure should never be left on with no liq. above gel; gel would then dry and crack, becoming useless.)

17.053 ***Determination***

To dry residue of Na succinate, **17.051**, add 2 mL solv. and 3 drops H_2SO_4 (1+1), and stir with glass rod until all particles are moistened (material should be acid to Congo red paper). Add anhyd. Na_2SO_4 in 0.5 g portions until material is dry (not gummy), stir, and decant onto prepd partition column, pouring it slowly down side of tube in order to keep surface of gel level. Apply pressure until solv. just disappears into gel. Again wash beaker with 1 mL solv., pour onto column, and with stirring rod transfer residue in beaker to column. Wash beaker with another 1 mL solv., transfer to column, wash inside of tube with 1 mL solv., and apply pressure until solv. just disappears into gel. Fill tube with solv. and apply pressure. Let HOAc band pass out of tube. When front of succinic acid band reaches constricted portion of tube, start collecting eluate in 50 mL graduate. Continue collecting until band has passed entirely from column or until lower edge of any following band reaches 2–5 mm above narrowest portion of constriction of tube and until enough eluate collects to ensure removal of succinic acid from column. (Light placed adjacent to column, but not so close as to heat it, increases visibility of bands.)

(To ensure complete removal of succinic acid from column when there is no following band, det. total amt of eluate to be collected by prepg soln of known amt of Na succinate, transferring free acid to column, eluting, etc., as above, and titrg 25 mL and successive 10 mL fractions of eluate until last fraction requires <0.2 mL 0.01*N* alkali to neutze. Total amt of eluate required is amt to collect in detn.)

Add 10 mL H_2O to flask and titr. with 0.01*N* $Ba(OH)_2$, using phenol red indicator. As end point approaches, stopper flask and shake vigorously to ext acid completely from solv. phase. Correct titrn for blank detn on equal vol. of eluate from blank column. 1 mL 0.01*N* $Ba(OH)_2$ = 0.59 mg succinic acid. If crystallographic identification of Ba succinate (JAOAC **32**, 787(1949)) is not desired, 0.01*N* NaOH may be used for titrn.

Water-Insoluble Fatty Acids (*21*)—Official Final Action

17.054 ***Preparation of Solution***

(**a**) *Liquid or frozen eggs*.—Weigh 10 g prepd sample, **17.001**(**a**) or (**b**), into 250 mL centrf. bottle, add 25 mL H_2O, and mix. Add 20 mL alcohol, shake vigorously, and add 50 mL ether.

(**b**) *Dried eggs*.—Weigh 2 g prepd sample, **17.001**(**c**), into 100 mL beaker and stir to uniform paste with small amt H_2O, using heavy stirring rod. Transfer material to 250 mL centrf. bottle with total of 25 mL H_2O, and shake vigorously. Rinse beaker with 25 mL alcohol, transfer rinsings to centrf. bottle, shake vigorously, and add 50 mL ether.

17.055 ***Determination***

Proceed as in **16.220**.

Pyoverdine

Fluorometric Method (22)—Official Final Action

(Protect from daylight and other sources of UV light. Incandescent light and pink fluorescent light may be used. Avoid dissolved metals and contact with rubber.)

17.056 ***Reagents***

(**a**) *Alcohol.—95%* USP, redistd from glass.

(**b**) *Chloride buffer soln.*—pH 1. Dry ca 50 g KCl at 120° overnight. Weigh 37.28 g into 500 mL vol. flask, dissolve in H_2O, and dil. to vol. Add 50 mL of this 1*N* KCl to 97 mL stdzd 1*N* HCl in 200 mL vol. flask, and dil. to vol. with H_2O.

(**c**) *Potassium acid phthalate soln.*—0.1*M*. Dry ca 20 g at 120° overnight. Weigh 10.21 g into 500 mL vol. flask, dissolve in H_2O, and dil. to vol. with H_2O.

(**d**) *Riboflavin std soln.*—0.50 μg/mL, pH 4. Pipet 5 mL riboflavin intermediate soln, **43.040(a)**(*2*), into 100 mL vol. flask, add 50 mL 0.1*M* K acid phthalate, and dil. to vol. with H_2O. Prep. weekly and store in refrigerator.

17.057 ***Determination***

Weigh 50±0.1 g foam-free sample, thawed and warmed to 25° on day of analysis, into dry 250 mL centrf. bottle. Add 154 mL alcohol at ca 25°, using pipets, with continuous stirring. Insert polyethylene stopper and shake ca 50 strokes by hand. Centrf. ca 15 min at ca 1200 rpm. Pipet 100 mL supernate into 250 mL separator, add ca 125 mL $CHCl_3$, and shake ca 100 strokes by hand. Freeze by immersing separator to base of stopper 10 min in alcohol-solid CO_2 bath; remove from bath.

As soon as ice crystals in $CHCl_3$ layer thaw, but while outside of separator is still frosty, drain and discard $CHCl_3$. Wash sides of separator with 10 mL $CHCl_3$, added from pipet without disturbing aq. layer. Let stand 10 min, and drain and discard $CHCl_3$. Pass stream of air into emulsion in separator thru small glass tube until soln clears. Remove tube and rinse with small vol. H_2O. Pipet 10 mL pH 1 buffer into 50 mL vol. flask, quant. add contents of separator, and dil. to vol. with H_2O.

Measure fluorescence of test and std solns in photofluorometer, using Corning 5874 as primary filter, and Corning 3486 as secondary filter. Swirl std soln before each reading. Calc. concn of pyoverdine expressed as μg riboflavin/100 g egg = $2 \times C \times R/S$, where 2 is derived from concn sample in final ext, C = concn riboflavin std in μg/100 mL, R = reading of sample, and S = reading of std riboflavin soln.

17.058 Quaternary Ammonium Compounds (*23*)
Official Final Action

See **20.088(d)**.

SELECTED REFERENCES

(*1*) JAOAC **8**, 599(1925).
(*2*) JAOAC **41**, 274(1958); **56**, 272(1973).
(*3*) JAOAC **8**, 600(1925); **9**, 354(1926); **14**, 395(1931).
(*4*) JAOAC **8**, 601(1925).
(*5*) JAOAC **15**, 344(1932).
(*6*) JAOAC **8**, 601(1925); **16**, 298(1933).
(*7*) JAOAC **7**, 91(1923); **8**, 602(1925); **16**, 298(1933).
(*8*) JAOAC **24**, 119(1941); **25**, 365(1942).
(*9*) JAOAC **14**, 416(1931); **16**, 298(1933).
(*10*) JAOAC **16**, 298(1933); **22**, 302(1939).
(*11*) Ind. Eng. Chem., Anal. Ed. **7**, 38(1935); JAOAC **26**, 352(1943).
(*12*) JAOAC **14**, 397(1931); **16**, 305(1933); **22**, 302(1939).
(*13*) JAOAC **15**, 331(1932); **16**, 293(1933).
(*14*) JAOAC **31**, 498(1948); **32**, 506(1949).
(*15*) JAOAC **10**, 411(1927); **15**, 341(1932); **20**, 155(1937); **21**, 179(1938); **31**, 498(1948); **33**, 696(1950).
(*16*) J. Chromatogr. **51**, 423(1970); JAOAC **52**, 41, 471(1969); **53**, 28(1970); **54**, 773(1971); **55**, 888, 1142(1972).
(*17*) JAOAC **27**, 204(1944); **31**, 134(1948).
(*18*) JAOAC **21**, 684(1938); **27**, 204(1944); **28**, 644(1945); **33**, 848(1950); **54**, 720(1971).
(*19*) JAOAC **54**, 720(1971).
(*20*) JAOAC **31**, 134(1948); **32**, 787(1949).
(*21*) JAOAC **30**, 575(1947); **31**, 731(1948).
(*22*) JAOAC **42**, 289(1959); **44**, 493(1961).
(*23*) JAOAC **33**, 666(1950).

18. Fish and Other Marine Products

18.001 Net Contents of Frozen Seafoods (*1*) Procedure

Set scale, **32.050**, on firm support and level. Adjust 0 load indicator or rest point and check sensitivity.

(**a**) *Glazed seafoods.*—Remove package from low temp. storage, open immediately, and place contents under gentle spray of cold H_2O. Agitate carefully so product is not broken. Spray until all ice glaze that can be seen or felt is removed. Transfer product to circular No. 8 sieve, 20 cm (8") diam. for ≤0.9 kg (2 lb) and 30 cm (12") for >0.9 kg (2 lb). Without shifting product, incline sieve at angle of 17–20° to facilitate drainage and drain exactly 2 min (stop watch). Immediately transfer product to tared pan (*B*) and weigh (*A*). Wt product = $A - B$.

(**b**) *Unglazed seafoods.—See* **32.051**.

18.002 Fish Content of Frozen Breaded Fish Products (*2*)—Official Final Action

Weigh each unit while it is hard frozen. Using clip tongs, place each portion or stick individually in H_2O bath maintained at 17–49°C (63–120°F). Let remain until breading becomes soft (5–110 sec for portions held in storage at −18°C (0°F) and can easily be removed from the still frozen flesh with round tip, 10 cm (4") blade spatula or table knife. *Limit dip time in >100°F H_2O to 15 sec max.*

(*Note:* Several preliminary trials may be necessary to det. dip time required for debreading sample units. *For these trials only,* prep. satd soln of $CuSO_4.5H_2O$ (450 g (1 lb)/2 L tap H_2O). Correct dip time is min. time of immersion in $CuSO_4$ soln required before breading can be easily scraped off, provided that debreaded portions are still solidly frozen, and only slight trace of blue color is visible on surface of debreaded portions. As guide, use lower temps with raw and higher temps with precooked products.)

After immersion, remove portion and blot lightly with double thickness paper towel. Complete this step in ≤7 sec. Scrape and remove breading and batter from flesh with spatula, removing material from narrow sides and ends in initial movements followed by removal from wide flat surfaces. If breading is difficult to remove, redip partially debreaded portion in H_2O at room temp. (17–30°C; 63–86°F) ca 2 sec. Blot with towel and remove residual batter and breading material. Reweigh debreaded portion and record.

% flesh = (wt debreaded portion × 100)/wt original unit.

18.003 Cooking Seafood Products (*3*)—Procedure

Following procedures are based on heating product to internal temp. ≥70°C (160°F). Cooking times vary according to size of product and equipment used. If detg cooking time, cook extra sample, using temp. measuring device to det. internal temp.

For fish blocks or other unbreaded samples, cut ≥3 portions, each ca 10 × 7.5 × 1.2 cm (4 × 3 × 0.5") from sample.

(**a**) *Bake procedure.*—Wrap product in Al foil and distribute evenly on flat cookie sheet or shallow flat pan. Heat in ventilated oven, preheated to 204°C (400°F), until internal temp. of product reaches ≥70°C (160°F).

(**b**) *Boil-in-bag procedure.*—Place thawed, unseasoned product in boilable film-type pouch. Fold open end of pouch over suspension bar. Clamp to provide *loose* seal to let vapors escape during heating. Immerse pouch and contents in boiling H_2O and heat until internal temp. of product reaches ≥70°C (160°F).

(**c**) *Deep fat frying procedure.*—Place frozen, breaded product in wire mesh fry basket large enough to hold all items in single layer. Heat by immersing in 190°C (375°F) liq. or hydrogenated cooking oil 2–3 min or until items float to surface. After cooking, let items drain 15 sec and place on paper napkin or towel to absorb excess oil.

(**d**) *Steam procedure.*—Wrap product in Al foil and place on wire rack suspended over boiling H_2O in covered container. Heat until internal temp. of product reaches ≥70°C (160°F).

Detection of Frozen and Thawed Shucked Oysters (*4*) Official Final Action

18.004 *Principle*

Latent forms of malic enzyme (ME) activity, solubilized by freezing and thawing, are differentiated from normally sol. form by their differing rates of electrophoretic migration. Medium used to develop sites of ME activity on gels is derived from reaction mixt. used for spectrophtric assay of nicotinamide adenine dinucleotide phosphate (NADP) reduction by ME, together with tetrazolium dye and adjuvant. Sharply discontinuous (disc) buffer system during polyacrylamide gel electrophoresis and carefully timed incubation period for histochem. staining are essential. Gels and solns must be kept cold during electrophoresis. Full work-day is required for test. Do *not* use com. prepd gel solns; pH control is critical. All glassware must be meticulously cleaned, with final soak ≥6 hr in H_2O before rinsing and drying. Give glass columns final rinse with Kodak Photo-Flo soln (1+200) to ease removal of electrophoresed gels.

18.005 *Apparatus*

(**a**) *Articles used in making gel columns.*—(*1*) *Glass columns.*—62 mm long × 5 mm id soft glass tubing, with unpolished ends. (*2*) *Disposable syringes.*—5 mL without needle (Glaspak Discardit No. 705 S, Becton, Dickinson, and Co., or equiv.), used with 0.76 mm id, 1.22 mm od polypropylene tubing (Adams Intramedic PE No. 60, Clay-Adams, Inc., Webro Rd, Parsippany, NJ 07054), for loading gels. (Syringes may be washed and reused.) (*3*) *Water-layer applicator.*—2 mL syringe, without plunger, used with 25 gage 1" hypodermic needle bent slightly for ease of application. (*4*) *Disposable syringes.*—2.5 mL, with needle (Plastipak Discardit), for removing unpolymerized gel solns during rinse. (*5*) *Removing tool.*—Grind off flanges of 1 mL glass syringe; no plunger. Attach 22 gage 2" hypodermic needle to one end and short length of rubber tubing to other. Keep another short length of rubber tubing attached to faucet adapter; add ½ plastic tubing-connector to each piece of rubber tubing so that removing tool can be easily attached.

(**b**) *Apparatus for photopolymerization of gels.*— Convenient set-up for photopolymerizing large pore gels is open-ended wooden box with removable bottom panel. Glue row of small rubber-base caps to bottom panel; (use those supplied with app. or obtain rubber cushions for file tray feet from office supply house). Mount fluorescent light beneath top of box, positioned so that row of rubber caps will be directly under light when bottom panel is in place. Tops of glass columns, placed in rubber caps, should be ca 2.5 cm from light.

(**c**) *Electrophoresis apparatus.*—Disc electrophoresis bath assembly (Canalco models 12, 1200, or 1200L, Miles Laboratories) with regulated power source capable of maintaining *const current* over 0–50 milliamp range.

18.006 ***Preparation of Electrophoretic Reagents***

(**a**) *Running gel.*—(Small pore, chem. polymerized.) (*1*) *Soln A.*—Prep. by mixing equal vols *Solns A-1* and *A-2.* (*2*) *Soln A-1.*—Mix 91.5 g Tris (tris(hydroxymethyl) aminomethane), 0.575 mL TEMED (*N,N,N',N'*-tetramethylethylenediamine, Eastman Kodak Co. No. 8178, or equiv.), and ca 116 mL 1*N* HCl to pH 9.0, and dil. with H_2O to 250 mL. (*3*) *Soln A-2.*—Dissolve 70.0 g acrylamide (Eastman Kodak Co. No. X5521, or equiv.) and 1.8375 g BIS (*N,N'*-methylenebisacrylamide, Eastman Kodak Co. No. 8383, or equiv.) in H_2O and dil. to 250 mL. (*4*) *Soln B.*—0.14% NH_4 persulfate in H_2O. (*Caution:* Acrylamide monomers are neurotoxins. Wear impervious gloves, avoid pipetting solns by mouth, and when dry, handle only in effective fume removal device. Close medical supervision is advisable for persons exposed to this material.)

Solns A-1 and *A-2* are stable ca 6 months stored in brown bottles in refrigerator; *Solns A* and *B*, only 1 week in refrigerator. Prep. running gel by mixing equal vols *Solns A* and *B* just before use.

(**b**) *Stacker and sample gels.*—(Large pore, photopolymerized.) (*1*) *Soln C.*—Prep. by mixing *Solns C-1, C-2,* and *C-3* (1+2+1). (*2*) *Soln C-1.*—Mix 14.95 g Tris, 1.15 mL TEMED, and ca 120 mL 1*N* HCl to pH 5.1, and dil. with H_2O to 250 mL. (*3*) *Soln C-2.*—Dissolve 50.0 g acrylamide and 12.5 g BIS in H_2O and dil. to 500 mL. (*4*) *Soln C-3.*—4.0 mg riboflavin in 100 mL H_2O. (*5*) *Soln D.*—40% (w/v) sucrose in H_2O.

All solns are stable ca 6 months stored in brown bottles in refrigerator. Prep. stacker gel by mixing equal vols *Solns C* and *D* within 1 hr of use; store at room temp. away from light. Prep. sample gels by mixing 0.04 mL centrfgd tissue fluid with 1 mL stacker gel just before use.

(**c**) *Electrode buffer* (*10X*).—Dissolve 57.6 g glycine and 12.0 g Tris in H_2O and dil. to 2 L. Dil. 1+9 just before each run; pH should be 8.3. Add few drops ca 0.1% bromophenol blue aq. soln to cathode buffer to light blue tint. Discard both cathode and anode buffers after each run.

18.007 ***Preparation of Histochemical Reagent***

For incubating 12 columns, prep. mixt. of 20.0 mg NADP (nicotinamide adenine dinucleotide phosphate, ICN-Pharmaceuticals, Life Sciences Group), 15.0 mL 0.144*M* Tris buffer (17.44 g/L; store in refrigerator; pH 8.0), 9.0 mL 0.095*M* K malate (127 mg L-malic acid neutzd with KOH and dild to 10 mL), 2.4 mL 0.06*M* KCN (dissolve 0.40 g in H_2O, add 1*N* HCl to pH 8.0 (ca 6 mL) in hood, and dil. to 100 mL; refrigerate in g-s erlenmeyer) (to block electron flux to respiratory chain), and ca 1.0 g polyvinylpyrrolidone (type K30 (MW 40,000), GAF Corp.) (to help solubilize dye). Mixt. may be prepd several hr in advance and stored in refrigerator. Also prep. control medium with H_2O replacing K malate, if considered necessary.

Prep. 2.4 mg phenazine methosulfate/mL H_2O. This soln is stable several weeks in refrigerator in dark.

Within hr of use, prep. soln of 15.4 mg *p*-nitro blue tetrazolium chloride (NBT.Cl) in 7.0 mL 0.144*M* Tris buffer (1.74 g/100 mL). (Double amt if using control medium.)

Immediately before incubation of gels, add 0.4 mL phenazine methosulfate soln and the 7.0 mL NTB.Cl soln to main soln.

18.008 ***Preparation of Centrifuged Tissue Fluid***

Centrifuge 4 or 5 *whole* oyster meat samples 20 min at 20,000*g* in refrigerated centrifuge. (Never use minced or homogenized samples. Mech. disruption of tissue produces results similar to freezing.) Withdraw clear supernatant fluid (CTF) with disposable syringe and refrigerate until ready to prep. sample gels. Begin centrfg early in morning, before setting up running gel, so that CTF will be ready in ample time.

18.009 ***Electrophoresis***

(**a**) *Preparation of gel columns.*—Remove solns for prepg gels from refrigerator and warm slightly to 10–15° (50–60°F). It is not necessary to bring them to room temp., but the colder the solns, the slower the polymerization. Place glass columns in vertical position in small rubber base caps glued to bottom panel of photopolymerization box. (*Caution:* Protect eyes from direct rays of UV light.) If run is for 12 columns, set up 14 or 15, to have replacements available for any defective columns. Slowly pour equal vols *Soln A* and NH_4 persulfate successively into small beaker and swirl gently (10 mL each is enough for 16 columns). Avoid getting air bubbles in mixt. This running gel will polymerize ca 45 min after mixing.

Using 5 mL disposable syringe, **18.005**(**a**)(*2*), gently draw up running gel soln; wipe off tip of syringe and insert 7.5–10 cm length of small polypropylene tubing. Push gel soln thru tubing to remove any air; then fill columns to within 15 mm of top, refilling syringe and repeating as needed.

When running gel is in all columns, they must be H_2O-layered, both to keep gel from contact with air and to establish flat interface between running gel and subsequently added stacker gel. Add drop of 0.1% aq. bromophenol blue tracking dye to small flask of H_2O, enough to tint H_2O pale blue. Add ca 2 mL to 2 mL syringe, (**a**)(*3*). Perform H_2O-layering carefully; even small drop falling suddenly can violently disturb ("bomb") gel, and bombed gels must be discarded. Steady each column with one hand, holding H_2O-layering syringe in other. Wipe tip of needle (finger of hand steadying column is simplest), to keep any sizable drop from forming as it is brought to column. Place needle quickly and gently against inner side of column, sliding it rapidly down to gel surface. If gel is "bombed," remove disturbed gel with disposable syringe, (**a**)(*4*), and refill column with fresh running gel mixt.

When H_2O-layering is completed, set timer for 40 min polymerization period. Mix stacker gel soln at this point, pouring equal vols *Soln C* and 40% sucrose soln carefully into small beaker. Allow 5 or 6 mL for stacker gels and 2 mL each for sample gels. Swirl mixt. and store at room temp. away from light.

When running gels are polymerized, invert columns and gently remove H_2O layer. Use cotton swabs to draw off any large remaining drops, being careful not to disturb gel surface or to leave fibers on glass. Set columns upright again and add small amt stacker gel to each to rinse out last of H_2O, using another 5 mL disposable syringe with short length of polypropylene tubing attached. Remove rinse mixt. with disposable syringe, (**a**)(*4*). Add stacker gel to each column, to ca 6 mm above running gel surface, and H_2O-layer as before.

Push columns to within 7.5–10 cm of fluorescent light in box, turn on light, let gels stand 10 min, and then position columns directly under light for final 10 min. Light should be ca 2.5 cm from top of columns. Retrieve CTF from centrf. and refrigerate during this step.

When stacker gels are photopolymerized, turn off light, remove H_2O layer from columns as before, and prep. sample gels. Add 0.08 mL CTF of each sample to 2 mL stacker gel in 5 mL beaker, or any amt in proportion. Mix well; add to columns first as rinse, then as 6 mm sample gel, as in stacker gel procedure (use individual 5 mL disposable syringes and tubing), and H_2O-layer. Photopolymerize as for stacker gels.

(**b**) *Separation.*—Set up electrophoresis in cold room and chill electrode buffers before use. (Alternatively, place bath assembly in refrigerator, or circulate ice-H_2O thru cooling coils immersed in baths.) Prep. histochem. medium during run, reserving tetrazolium dye and adjuvant until just before gel incubation; keep solns refrigerated until use.

As soon as sample gels are polymerized, set up electrophoresis in cold room. Place columns in upper bath container with sample gel on top, toward cathode. (*Caution:* Cover for electrophoresis chamber should have switch to disconnect current to electrodes when chamber is open. Shield contacts and electrodes against body contact.) Add 1 L dild electrode buffer to lower (anode) bath, and bead ends of columns with buffer before setting upper (cathode) bath (from which columns extend) in place above lower bath. Add 1 L dild electrode buffer, tinted pale blue with bromophenol blue, to upper bath, first pipetting small amts into tops of columns, to avoid creating air bubbles. Bromophenol blue migrates more rapidly than proteins, which it will overtake and pass to form visible moving front.

Use const current and do not stop electrophoresis during run. Set at 1 ma/column for first 0.5 hr and then at 2 ma/column for 2 hr. Continue until tracking dye has left columns.

18.010 ***Incubation of Gels***

(**a**) *Removal of gel columns.*—When electrophoresis is finished, remove glass columns from bath assembly, discard buffers, and remove gels from glass columns. Connect rubber tubing on removal tool to suitable faucet adapter and use steady flow of H_2O while gently reaming gels from glass columns with needle. Loosen anode end of gel column first, then cathode end; gels will slip out easily under H_2O pressure. Discard sample and stacker gels and place running gels, cathode end up, in 10 × 75 mm test tubes.

(**b**) *Staining of gels.*—Add histochem. reagent immediately, cork tubes, and invert several times; then place in dark 25–30 min (but not >30 min) at room temp. Rinse gels immediately and thoroly with tap H_2O; then store in H_2O. No counterstaining is necessary.

18.011 ***Interpretation***

Use densitometer or Polaroid camera for permanent records, as formazan bands on gels will diffuse with time. Unfrozen oysters show, at most, single band, often faint or missing. Frozen and thawed oysters produce broad band at same place with or without 1 or 2 accessory bands and a thin cathodal band.

Freeze and thaw portion of questionable lot and test against portion of original sample. If patterns are alike, lot has been frozen and thawed; if different, lot has not been frozen and thawed.

18.012 Preliminary Treatment and Preparation of Sample (*5*)—Procedure

To prevent loss of H_2O during prepn and subsequent handling, use samples as large as practicable. Keep ground material in container with air-tight cover. Begin all detns as soon as practicable. If any delay occurs, chill sample to inhibit decomposition. In general, prep. sample of fish as it is usually prepd by consumer, by including skin and discarding bones, but subject to overall rule of edibility, e.g., inedible catfish skin is discarded; softened canned salmon bones are included; sardines are examined whole. Instructions may be modified in accordance with purpose of specific examination. Prep. samples for analysis as follows:

(**a**) *Fresh fish.*—Clean, scale, and eviscerate fish. In case of small fish ≤15 cm (6″), use 5–10 fish. In case of large fish, from each of ≥3 fish cut 3 cross-sectional slices 2.5 cm (1″) thick, 1 slice from just back of pectoral fins, 1 slice halfway between first slice and vent, and 1 slice just back of vent. Remove bone. For intermediate-size fish, remove and discard heads, scales, tails, fins, guts, and inedible bones; fillet fish to obtain all flesh and skin from head to tail and from top of back to belly on both sides. For detn of fat and fat-sol. components, skin must be included, since many fish store large amts of fat directly beneath skin.

Pass sample rapidly thru meat chopper 3 times. Remove unground material from chopper after each grinding and mix thoroly with ground material. Meat chopper should have holes as small as practicable (1.5–3 mm (1/16–1/8″) diam.) and should not leak around handle end. As alternative for soft fish, high-speed blender may be used. Blend several min, stopping blender frequently to scrape down sides of cup.

(**b**) *Canned fish, shellfish, and other canned marine products.*—Place entire contents of can (meat and liq.) in blender and blend until homogeneous or grind 3 times thru meat chopper. For large cans, drain meat 2 min on No. 8–12 sieve and collect all liq. Det. wt of meat and vol. of liq. Recombine portion of each in proportionate amts. Blend recombined portions in blender (or grind) until homogeneous.

(**c**) *Canned marine products packed in oil, sauce, broth, or water.*—Drain 2 min on No. 8 sieve. Prep. solid portion as in (**b**). Liq. may be analyzed sep., if desired, or reincorporated with solids. H_2O is usually discarded.

(**d**) *Fish packed in salt or brine.*—Drain and discard brine and rinse off adhering salt crystals with satd NaCl soln. Drain again 2 min and proceed as in (**a**).

(**e**) *Dried smoked or dried salt fish.*—Proceed as in (**a**).

(**f**) *Frozen fish.*—Let thaw at room temp., and discard draining. (*1*) *Fillet.*—Use entire piece. (*2*) *Whole fish.*—Proceed as in (**a**).

(**g**) *Shellfish other than oysters, clams, and scallops.*—If sample is received in shell, wash as in (**h**) and sep. edible portions in usual way. Prep. edible portion for analysis as in (**a**).

(**h**) *Shell oysters, shell clams, and scallops.*—Wash shells in potable H_2O to remove all loose silt and dirt, and drain well. Shuck enough oysters or clams into clean dry container to yield ≥500 mL (1 pt) drained meats. Transfer shellfish meats to skimmer, **18.014**, pick out pieces of shell, drain 2 min on skimmer, and proceed as in (**i**) or (**j**).

(**i**) *Shucked clams or scallops.*—Prep. as in (**b**).

(**j**) *Shucked oysters* (***6***).—Blend meats, including liq., 1–2 min in high-speed blender.

(**k**) *Breaded fish, raw or cooked.*—Do not remove breading or skin. Proceed as in (**a**).

18.013 Volume Determination (*5*)—Official Final Action

(Shucked oysters, clams, or scallops)

Fluff entire contents of com. container, or container in which sample is received (≤3.8 L; 1 gal.), by pouring into std measuring vessel thru distance of ≥30 cm (1′), then pouring back into container from same ht, and again pouring into measuring vessel. Use metal funnel (stainless steel preferable) 20–25 cm (8–10″) diam. at top, with stem 7.6 cm (3″) diam. and ca 7.6 cm long, to facilitate pouring from one vessel to another. Measures are straight-side, cylindrical, made of metal (stainless steel preferable), holding exactly 1 gal. or 1 qt, resp., and having smooth rims. Plane of rim must be level when measure is standing on level surface. Diam of top of gal. measure is 4.25–5.25″, and that of qt measure is 3.25–3.5″. Calibrate with std glass measures, and for estg vols less than level full, use graduated mechanic's depth gage to measure distance from rim to surface of contents. Tabulate depth gage readings against vols or % shortages as desired for each measuring vessel.

Measure head space with depth gage and det. vol. For ≤1 pt containers, calibrated glass cylinders may be used.

Drained Liquid (*7*)—Official Final Action

(Shucked oysters)

18.014 ***Apparatus***

Skimmer or strainer.—Flat-bottom metal pan or tray with ca 5 cm (2") sides, with area of ≥1900 cm² (300 sq in.) for each gal. of oysters to be poured on tray, and with perforations 0.6 cm (0.25") diam. and 3.2 cm (1.25") apart in sq pattern, or perforations of equiv. area and distribution. Support skimmer over slightly larger solid tray so that liq. drains into solid tray.

18.015 ***Determination***

Weigh tared container with shellfish meats, transfer contents to skimmer, and quickly distribute meats evenly over draining surface with min. of handling. Drain 2 min, return meats to container, and reweigh. Calc. loss of wt as % drained liq. Make detns at 7±1° (45±2°F). If further analysis is desired, proceed as in **18.012(j)**.

Drained Weight (*8*)—Official Final Action

(Applicable to frozen shrimp and Alaska king and snow crabmeat)

18.016 ***Apparatus***

(a) *Container.*—Wire mesh basket large enough to hold contents of 1 package and with openings small enough to retain all pieces. Expanded metal test-tube basket or equiv., fully lined with std 16 mesh per linear in. insect screen is satisfactory.

(b) *Balance.*—Sensitive to 0.25 g or 0.01 oz.

(c) *Sieves.*—U.S. No. 8, 20 cm (8") and 30 cm (12") diam.

18.017 ***Determination***

Place contents of individual package in wire mesh basket and immerse in ≥15 L (4 gal.) container of fresh H_2O at 26±3°C (80±5°F) so that top of basket extends above H_2O level. Introduce H_2O of same temp. at bottom of container at flow rate of 4–11 L (1–3 gal.)/min. As soon as product thaws, as detd by loss of rigidity, transfer all material to 30 cm (12") (for package >450 g (1 lb)) or 20 cm (8") (for package ≤1 lb) No. 8 sieve, distributing evenly. Without shifting material on sieve, incline sieve to ca 30° from horizontal to facilitate drainage. Two min from time placed on sieve, transfer product to previously weighed pan, and weigh. Wt so found minus wt of pan is drained wt of product.

***Alaska King Crab Marketing and Control Board Method* (*9*)**

(Applicable to Alaska king and snow crabmeat)

18.018 ***Apparatus***

(a) *Balance.*—Sensitive to 1 g or 0.01 lb.

(b) *Thermometer.*—Accurate in 0–30°C (30–80°F) range.

(c) *Plastic bowls.*—Marked at 48 oz (1440 mL), 64 oz (1920 mL), or 1 gal. (3840 mL) level for 6 oz, 8 oz, or 1 lb packages, resp.

18.019 ***Determination***

Weigh bare block free of all wrappings and record wt. Place block in bowl contg amt fresh potable water at 27°C (80°F) equal to 8× declared wt. Leave block in H_2O until all ice is melted. Turn block over several times during thawing. Point at which thawing is complete can be detd by probing block apart.

Pour entire thawed sample onto tared 20 cm (8") No. 8 sieve. Incline screen to aid drainage, drain exactly 2 min, and weigh. Subtract tare wt of sieve for thawed drained wt of sample.

% Drained wt = (thawed drained wt × 100)/declared net wt.

Shrimp in Shrimp Cocktail (*10*)—Official Final Action

18.020 ***Preparation of Sample***

Thaw unopened jars in 16±5° H_2O bath until product is defrosted to temp of 6±5°. Keep jar lids above H_2O level. Alternatively, place frozen jars in refrigerator until contents have thawed.

18.021 ***Determination***

Empty thawed contents of jar onto No. 8 sieve. Wash jar and lid with H_2O and pour washings onto sieve until jar is clean. Rinse shrimp on sieve with gentle stream or spray of cold tap H_2O. Use rubber spatula to remove adhering material. Cover sieve with metal cover or moisture barrier film, incline at 17–20° angle, and let drain exactly 2 min. Transfer shrimp to container previously tared with cover and weigh to ±0.1 g.

% Shrimp = wt shrimp × 100/*declared wt* total contents

18.022 Seafood in Seafood Cocktail other than Shrimp in Shrimp Cocktail (*11*)—Procedure

(a) *For seafood other than crabmeat.*—Proceed as in **18.020** and **18.021**, using rubber spatula gently to remove sauce from irregular surfaces without unduly fragmenting seafood.

(b) *For crabmeat.*—Prep. sample as in **18.020**. Empty thawed contents of jar onto No. 8 sieve nested on top of No. 20 sieve. Wash jar and lid with H_2O until jar is clean and pour washings onto sieves. Rinse crabmeat on No. 8 sieve with gentle stream or spray of cold tap H_2O. Use rubber spatula to remove adhering material. Cover sieves with metal cover or moisture barrier film, incline at 17–20° angle, and let drain exactly 2 min. Sep. sieves. Invert, dropping No. 8 sieve onto nonabsorbent surface (such as wax paper). Transfer crabmeat to container previously tared with cover. Transfer crabmeat from No. 20 sieve to same container and weigh to ±0.1 g.

% Crabmeat = wt crabmeat × 100/*declared wt* total contents

Total Solids

18.023 *For All Marine Products Except Raw Oysters* (*12*) *Official Final Action*

(*Caution:See* **51.086**.)

Cut into short lengths ca 2 g asbestos fibers of type used in prepg gooches. Place cut fibers and glass stirring rod ca 8 cm long with flat end into flat-bottom metal weighing dish, ca 9 cm diam., with cover. Dry dish, asbestos, and rod in oven 1 hr at 100°, cool, and weigh. Quickly weigh into dish, to nearest mg, 9.5–10.5 g prepd sample. Add 20 mL H_2O and mix sample thoroly with asbestos. Support end of rod on edge of dish and evap. just to dryness on steam bath, stirring once while still moist. Drop rod into dish and heat 4 hr in oven at 100°, or in preheated forced-draft oven set for full draft, 1 hr at 100°. Cover dish, cool in desiccator, and weigh promptly.

18.024 *For Raw Oysters Only* (*13*)—*Official Final Action*

Quickly weigh, to nearest mg, 9.5–10.5 g prepd sample into weighed, flat-bottom metal dish ca 9 cm diam. and 2 cm high with cover. Spread sample evenly over bottom of dish. Then:

(a) Evap. just to dryness on steam bath and dry 3 hr in oven at 100°; or—

(**b**) Insert directly into preheated forced-draft oven set at full draft and dry 1.5 hr at 100°.

Cover, cool in desiccator, and weigh promptly.

18.025 Ash (*14*)—Official Final Action

Dry sample contg ca 2 g dry material and proceed as in **31.012** or **31.013**, using temp. ≤550°. If material contains large amt of fat, make preliminary ashing at low enough temp. to allow smoking off of fat without burning.

18.026 Total Nitrogen (*14*)—Official Final Action

See **2.057**.

Ammonia (*15*)—Official First Action

(Applicable to crabmeat)

18.027 ***Reagents***

(Use NH_3-free H_2O thruout; ordinary distd H_2O is suitable.)

(**a**) *Bromine soln.*—Dil. 10 mL NaOH soln (1+1), **50.033(b)**, to ca 100 mL with H_2O, add 1.0 mL Br, shake, and dil. to 200 mL with H_2O. Prep. fresh daily.

(**b**) *Thymol soln.*—10% in alcohol. Prep. fresh daily.

(**c**) *Dilute sodium hydroxide soln.*—Dil. 25 mL NaOH soln (1+1), **50.033(b)**, to 100 mL with H_2O.

(**d**) *Ammonia std soln.*—40 μg/mL. Dissolve 0.314 g NH_4Cl, previously dried 1 hr at 100°, in H_2O, and dil. to 100 mL. Transfer 4.0 mL to 100 mL vol. flask, and dil. to vol. with H_2O.

18.028 ***Preparation of Samples***

Remove shell, if necessary, and grind meat 3 times thru food chopper, mixing after each grinding.

18.029 ***Determination***

Place 20 g prepd sample in 500 mL g-s erlenmeyer. Add 180 mL *2.5% phosphotungstic acid soln,* shake vigorously 2 min, and filter thru Whatman No. 1, or equiv., paper into 250 mL g-s erlenmeyer. Pipet 2 mL filtrate (equiv. to 0.2 g sample) into 125 mL separator. Save remainder of filtrate. To another separator, add 2.0 mL 2.5% phosphotungstic acid soln as blank.

To each separator add 8.0 mL H_2O. Then, in immediate succession, add 1.0 mL dil. NaOH soln, (**c**), swirl to mix, 2.0 mL thymol soln, (**b**), swirl to mix, and 5.0 mL Br soln, (**a**), in ca 30 small addns, swirling vigorously after each addn. Shake vigorously 1 min. With series of samples or stds, complete reagent addns in sequence on each separator before proceeding to next. Let stand ≥20 min.

To each separator add 20.0 mL *n*-BuOH and shake vigorously 1 min. Let stand 20 min. Drain aq. layer and pass *n*-BuOH thru ca 30 g anhyd. Na_2SO_4 in glass funnel plugged with glass wool into g-s erlenmeyer. Measure A of soln at max., ca 680 nm, in 1 cm cell against blank as ref.

If A is greater than that of highest NH_3 std, quant. dil. reserved filtrate with 2.5% phosphotungstic acid soln so that 2.0 mL dild soln will produce A below this level.

18.030 ***Preparation of Standard Curve***

Pipet 0, 1, 2, 3, 4, and 5 mL std NH_3 soln into 125 mL separators. Add 2.0 mL 2.5% phosphotungstic acid soln to each and dil. to 10.0 mL with H_2O. Proceed as in **18.029**, beginning "Then, in immediate succession, add 1.0 mL dil. NaOH soln, . . ." Using 0 soln as ref., measure A of each std at max. as above. Prep. std curve.

Trimethylamine Nitrogen (*16*)—Official Final Action

(Do *not* use stopcock grease; mixt. of sugar and glycerol ground together may be used if necessary. Do not wash tubes with soap or detergent; rinse with H_2O and occasionally clean thoroly with HNO_3.)

18.031 ***Reagents***

(**a**) *Trichloroacetic acid soln.*—7.5% aq. soln. (*Caution: See* **51.082**.)

(**b**) *Toluene.*—Dried over anhyd. Na_2SO_4. To remove interferences, shake 500 mL toluene with 100 mL 1*N* H_2SO_4, distil, and dry with anhyd. Na_2SO_4. (*Caution: See* **51.011** and **51.039**.)

(**c**) *Picric acid solns.*—(*1*) *Stock soln.*—Dissolve 2 g picric acid (*Caution: See* **51.029**) in 100 mL H_2O-free toluene. (*2*) *Working soln.*—Dil. 1 mL stock soln to 100 mL with H_2O-free toluene.

(**d**) *Potassium carbonate soln.*—Dissolve 100 g K_2CO_3 in 100 mL H_2O.

(**e**) *Formaldehyde.*—20%. Shake 1 L com. formalin (40%) with 100 g $MgCO_3$ until nearly colorless and filter. Dil. 100 mL to 200 mL with H_2O. (*Caution: See* **51.058**.)

(**f**) *Trimethylamine* (*TMA*) *std solns.*—(*1*) *Stock soln.*—Add 0.682 g $(CH_3)_3N.HCl$ to 1 mL HCl (1+3) and dil. to 100 mL with H_2O. Check basic N content of 5 mL aliquots by adding 6 mL 10% NaOH soln, distg into 10 mL 4% boric acid in micro-Kjeldahl distn app., **47.022**, and titrg with 0.1*N* H_2SO_4, using indicator, **47.021(f)**. This soln is stable. (*2*) *Working soln.*—0.01 mg TMA-N/mL. Add 1 mL stock soln to 1 mL HCl (1+3) and dil. to 100 mL with H_2O.

18.032 ***Preparation of Sample***

Weigh 100 g minced or chopped, well mixed sample. Add 200 mL 7.5% trichloroacetic acid and blend. Centrf. blended soln at 2000–3000 rpm until supernate is practically clear.

18.033 ***Determination***

Pipet aliquot (preferably contg 0.01–0.03 mg TMA-N) into 20 × 150 mm Pyrex g-s test tube and dil. to 4.0 mL with H_2O. For stds, use 1.0, 2.0, and 3.0 mL working std soln, dilg to 4.0 mL with H_2O; for blank, use 4.0 mL H_2O. Add 1 mL HCHO, (**e**), 10 mL toluene from automatic pipet, and 3 mL K_2CO_3 soln. Stopper tube and shake vigorously by hand ca 40 times. Pipet off 7–9 mL toluene layer into small test tube contg ca 0.1 g anhyd. Na_2SO_4. Avoid removing droplets of aq. layer. Stopper tube and shake well to dry toluene. Pipet 5 mL toluene layer into dry colorimeter tube. Add 5 mL picric acid soln and mix by swirling gently. Det. A at 410 nm against blank carried thru detn. Color is stable. If original aliquot contains >0.03 mg TMA-N, dil. ext with trichloroacetic acid soln and repeat detn.

mg TMA-N/100 g sample (based on 1 mL aliquot)
$= (A/A') \times$ (mg TMA-N/mL std soln) × mL std soln used × 300.
Use A' of std nearest to A of sample for calcn.

Salt (Chlorine as Sodium Chloride)

Volumetric Method (17)—Official Final Action

18.034 ***Reagents***

(**a**) *Silver nitrate std soln.*—0.1*N*. Prep. as in **50.027** and stdze against 0.1*N* NaCl contg 5.844 g of pure dry NaCl/L.

(**b**) *Ammonium thiocyanate std soln.*—0.1*N*. Prep. as in **50.030(b)** and stdze against 0.1*N* $AgNO_3$.

(**c**) *Ferric indicator.*—Satd soln of $FeNH_4(SO_4)_2.12H_2O$.

18.035 ***Determination***

(**a**) *Shellfish meats.*—Weigh 10 g meats, liq., or mixed meats and liq., into 250 mL erlenmeyer or beaker.

(**b**) *Other fish products*.—Use suitable size sample, depending on NaCl content.

Add known vol. 0.1*N* $AgNO_3$ soln, more than enough to ppt all Cl as AgCl, and then add 20 mL HNO_3. Boil gently on hot plate or sand bath until all solids except AgCl dissolve (usually 15 min). Cool, add 50 mL H_2O and 5 mL indicator, and titr. with 0.1*N* NH_4SCN soln until soln becomes permanent light brown. Subtract mL 0.1*N* NH_4SCN used from mL 0.1*N* $AgNO_3$ added and calc. difference as NaCl. With 10 g sample each mL 0.1*N* $AgNO_3$ = 0.058% NaCl.

18.036 ***Potentiometric Method—Official First Action***

Prep. sample as in **18.012** and proceed as in **32.025–32.030**.

18.037 ***Indicating Strip Method—Procedure***

See **24.011–24.014**.

Sodium and Potassium (*18*)—Official Final Action

18.038 ***Apparatus and Reagents***

(**a**) *Glassware*.—Borosilicate glassware and intact Vycor, Pt, or Si crucible precleaned with dil. HNO_3 and rinsed in distd H_2O immediately before use.

(**b**) *Distilled water*.—H_2O, free from Na and K; either double-distd or deionized. Use for prepg stds and dilns.

(**c**) *Sodium std solns*.—(*1*) *Stock soln*.—1 mg Na/mL. Dry reagent grade NaCl 2 hr at 110°; cool in desiccator. Weigh 2.5421 g into 1 L vol. flask and dil. to vol. with H_2O. (*2*) *Working solns for flame emission*.—0.01, 0.03, and 0.05 mg Na/mL. Pipet 1, 3, and 5 mL Na stock soln into sep. 100 mL vol. flasks; add 7 mL K stock soln and 2 mL HNO_3 to each flask; dil. to vol. with H_2O. (*3*) *Working solns for flame absorption*.—0.00003, 0.0001, 0.0003, and 0.0005 mg Na/mL. Pipet 1 mL Na stock soln into 100 mL vol. flask and dil. to vol. with H_2O. Pipet 0.3, 1.0, 3.0, and 5.0 mL dild stock soln into sep. 100 mL vol. flasks and dil. to vol. with H_2O.

(**d**) *Potassium std solns*.—(*1*) *Stock soln*.—1 mg K/mL. Dry and cool reagent grade KCl as in (**c**). Weigh 1.9068 g into 1 L vol. flask and dil. to vol. with H_2O. (*2*) *Working solns for flame emission*.—0.04, 0.07, and 0.10 mg K/mL. Pipet 4, 7, and 10 mL stock soln into sep. 100 mL vol. flasks; add 3 mL Na stock soln to each flask; dil. to vol. with H_2O. (*3*) *Working solns for flame absorption*.—0.0001, 0.0005, 0.0007, and 0.0010 mg K/mL. Pipet 1 mL K stock soln into 100 mL vol. flask and dil. to vol. with H_2O. Pipet 1, 5, 7, and 10 mL dild stock soln into sep. 100 mL vol. flasks and dil. to vol. with H_2O.

18.039 ***Wet Ashing***

(*Caution: See* **51.011**, **51.019**, and **51.026**.)

Prep. sample as in **18.012**.

Weigh 1 g sample into 50 mL Pyrex beaker. Dry 2.5 hr at 110°, cool, and weigh if % solids is to be detd.

(**a**) *Samples with unknown or known high oil content*.—Add ca 10 mL pet ether, and warm on steam bath or low temp. hot plate until oil is extd. Decant and repeat until sample is defatted. Proceed as in (**b**).

(**b**) *Samples with low oil content*.—Add 5 mL HNO_3 (if total Cl content is desired, add enough 0.1*N* $AgNO_3$ to ppt chlorides (3.0 mL)) to each beaker. Digest on steam bath or low temp. hot plate until sample dissolves; evap. to dryness. Add 5 mL HNO_3 and take to dryness. Repeat. Add 2 mL HNO_3 and warm to dissolve. Proceed as in (**c**) or (**d**).

(**c**) *For flame emission*.—Transfer digest to 25 mL vol. flask with hot H_2O, wash down sides of beaker 3 times with hot H_2O, and add washings to flask. Cool, and dil. to vol. with H_2O. If particles are too finely dispersed to settle, centrf. aliquot at 2000 rpm.

(**d**) *For flame absorption*.—Transfer digest to 100 mL vol. flask and proceed as above. Dil. for direct readout as follows: Place 1 mL aliquot in 25 mL vol. flask and dil. to vol. with H_2O for Na; place 2 mL aliquot in 10 mL vol. flask and dil. to vol. with H_2O for K.

Prep. blank soln by dilg 2 mL HNO_3 to 100 mL with H_2O.

18.040 ***Dry Ashing***

Prep. sample as in **18.012**.

Weigh 4 g sample into crucible, and char on elec. hot plate or over low flame. Place in cold furnace and bring to 525°. Ash 2 hr to white ash. Cool, and weigh if total ash is desired.

Add 15 mL dil. HNO_3 (1+4) to crucible, breaking up ash with stirring rod if necessary. Filter thru acid-washed quant. paper into 100 mL vol. flask. Wash residue and paper 3 times with H_2O. Dil. to vol. Proceed as in (**a**) or (**b**).

(**a**) *For flame emission*.—Read directly.

(**b**) *For flame absorption*.—Dil. for direct readout as follows: Place 1 mL aliquot in 100 mL vol. flask and dil. to vol. with H_2O for Na; place 1 mL aliquot in 25 mL vol. flask and dil. to vol. with H_2O for K.

Prep. blank soln by dilg 2 mL HNO_3 to 100 mL with H_2O.

18.041 ***Determination***

(*Caution; See* **51.006** and **51.007**.)

Follow manufacturer's directions for type of instrument available. Dil. samples if necessary to bring *T* readings within range of working stds. Read blank, stds, and samples at 589 nm for Na and 767 nm for K until results are reproducible; record % *T* or % absorption for each.

18.042 ***Calculations***

For flame emission photometers not equipped with direct readout:

$$\text{mg Na or K/100 g} = 100 \times F \times \left(\left[\frac{(E_x + E_1)}{(E_2 - E_1)} \times (C_2 - C_1)\right] + C_1\right)/\text{g sample},$$

where E_x = (% *T* of unknown) − (% *T* of blank); E_1 = (% *T* of std of lower concn than sample) − (% *T* of blank); E_2 = (% *T* of std of higher concn than sample) − (% *T* of blank); C_1 = mg Na or K/mL in std of lower concn than sample; C_2 = mg Na or K/mL in std of higher concn than sample; *F* = diln factor.

For flame absorption photometers: Convert % absorption to absorbance (*A*). Plot std curve of *A* against concn. Read unknown concns.

mg Na or K/100 g = (Concn unknown × *F* × 100)/g sample.

Crude Fat

By Acid Hydrolysis (19)—Official Final Action

18.043 ***Preparation of Sample***

Prep. sample according to type of pack as in **18.012** and keep ground material in sealed jar. If jar has been chilled, let sample come to room temp. and shake jar so that any sepd liq. is absorbed by fish. Open jar and stir contents with spatula, thoroly scraping sides and lid so as to incorporate any sepd liq. or fat.

18.044 ***Determination***

Weigh 8 g well mixed sample into 50 mL beaker and add 2 mL HCl. Using stirring rod with extra large flat end, break up coagulated lumps until mixt. is homogeneous. Add addnl 6 mL HCl, mix, cover with watch glass, and heat on steam bath 90 min, stirring occasionally with rod. Cool soln and transfer to Mojonnier fat-extn flask. Rinse beaker and rod with 7 mL alcohol, add to extn flask, and mix. Rinse beaker and rod with 25 mL ether, added in 3 portions; add rinsings to extn flask, stopper with cork or stopper of synthetic rubber unaffected by usual fat solvs, and shake vigorously 1 min. Add 25 mL pet ether (bp <60°) to extn flask and repeat vigorous shaking. Centrf. Mojonnier flask 20 min at ca 600 rpm and proceed as in **14.019**, beginning "Draw off as much as possible of ether-fat soln . . ."

Drying to const wt takes ca 40 min for fish. Long heating periods may increase wt of fat. If centrf. is not available, extn can generally be made by letting Mojonnier flask stand until upper liq. is practically clear, then swirling flask and again letting stand until clear. If troublesome emulsion forms, let stand, pour off as much of ether-fat soln as possible, add 1–2 mL alcohol to Mojonnier flask, swirl, and again let mixt. sep.

Rapid Modified Babcock Method (20)—Official First Action

(Applicable to raw, canned, and frozen fish)

18.045 ***Determination***

(*Caution: See* **51.022**, and **51.028(a)** and **(d)**.)

Weigh 9.0 g ground and mixed sample into Paley-type Babcock cheese bottle (Kimble Products No. 508, 20% size), stopper, and add ca 30 mL reagent prepd by mixing equal vols HOAc and 70–72% $HClO_4$. Place in H_2O bath (2 L stainless steel beaker is satisfactory) maintained at 92±2°, swirling occasionally until no lumps remain (usually ca 20 min). Remove from bath, add reagent until fat is well up in calibrated neck of bottle, centrf. 2 min at ca 600 rpm, and read % fat with dividers, using bottom of top meniscus. If fat falls below calibration, add more reagent, centrf. 1 min, and read again.

With very fat fish, it may be necessary to use <9 g sample. In this case, correct reading by multiplying % fat by factor 9/g sample.

18.046 ***In Fish Meal (21)—Official Final Action***

(*Caution: See* **51.009, 51.011, 51.039**, and **51.046**.)

Weigh 4–5 g sample to nearest 0.01 g into Alundum or paper extn thimble, cover with light layer of cotton, and ext with acetone in continuous extractor 16 hr. Distil off acetone until vol. in flask is 10–15 mL, transfer to 100 mL tared beaker, washing flask free of all oil with fresh acetone, and evap. with current of warm air. (Convenient method is to place flask on warm surface, *e.g.*, over steam radiator, in front of small elec. fan.) When no H_2O or acetone can be observed, place beaker in vac. oven at 80° and apply 610–640 mm (24–25"; 81.3–85.3 kPa) vac. 1 hr. Transfer to desiccator, cool, and weigh.

Transfer extd meal residue from thimble to 150 mL beaker. Remove any remaining solv. by heating on warm surface and then add 60 mL 4*N* HCl. Digest 1 hr at or near bp on hot plate, stirring occasionally with glass rod and adding H_2O as needed to maintain vol. in beaker. (Complete removal of acetone is necessary before this digestion, otherwise vaporization of solv. will carry meal particles over side of vessel onto hot plate.) Filter thru 12.5 cm fluted paper. Wash residue on filter until acid-free, using Me red on portions of filtrate to follow progress of washing. Place filter and meal in 150 mL beaker and dry 1 hr in air oven at 80–90°. Transfer filter and contents to thimble and ext 16 hr with acetone. Remove solv. and weigh ext as above. Sum of wts of exts = total fat.

Semimicro Method (22)—Official Final Action

18.047 ***Apparatus***

Extraction apparatus.—See Fig. **18:01**. (*1*) Reaction chamber (Corning Glass Works, No. 9820 tube (38 × 200 mm) sealed to ₮ 45/50 joint, No. 6560); (*2*) receiving chamber (₮ 45/50 joint, No. 6580); (*3*) No. 100–150 stainless steel screen. Add openings, Teflon stopcocks, and hooks as shown. Use Teflon ring to seal joint at screen. Opening in *1* lets atm. pressure be exerted on liq. surface when app. is inverted to filter sample. Flared opening in *2* is used to remove filtrate and to add solv. for second extn. Side outlet in *2* is used to apply rapid short gusts of vac. to remove max. amt solv. from samples or to aid in filtration.

18.048 ***Extraction***

Close all stopcocks of extn app. Place Teflon-coated mag. stirring bar and ca 2–4 g accurately weighed sample, ground to pass No. 40 sieve, in reaction chamber. Add 30 mL $CHCl_3$, 20 mL MeOH, and 7 mL H_2O. Attach receiving chamber with screen inserted, using springs or rubber bands. Fasten app. on stirring plate with std clamp and stir mag. 15 min. Remove app. and invert. Open stopcock of reaction chamber (now on top) to equalize air pressure.

Place opening of receiving chamber (now on bottom) in 100 mL graduate contg 10 mL H_2O, and open top stopcock. Close bottom stopcock. With top stopcock open, briefly apply vac. from aspirator to remove solvs more thoroly, and drain solv. into graduate. Invert app. to original position. Add 10 mL $CHCl_3$ thru top stopcock. Invert app. and drain solv. into same 100 mL graduate. Invert app. to original position and close bottom stopcock. Slowly add 40 mL $CHCl_3$ thru top stopcock so that sides of app. will be rinsed clean.

Close top stopcock, place app. on stirrer, and ext 2 min. Repeat rinsing of app. as above, beginning "Remove app. and invert." except use 2 rinses of 10 mL $CHCl_3$. Collect extn solv. and rinses in same graduate.

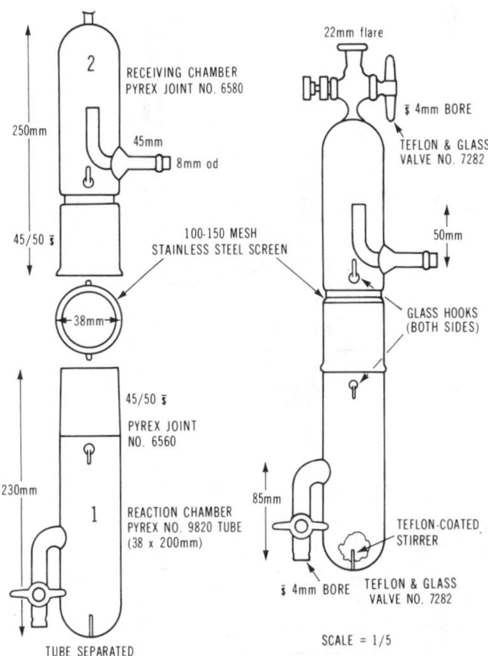

FIG. 18:01—Extraction apparatus

18.049 ***Determination***

Let filtrate stand overnight to clarify; then record vol. $CHCl_3$ layer. Remove most of MeOH layer by suction. Mix contents of graduate well; remove remaining MeOH layer and small amt $CHCl_3$ layer by suction. Pipet 25–50 mL $CHCl_3$ layer into 50 mL tared beaker, and dry under N in 50° H_2O bath. Place dried sample in vac. desiccator over P_2O_5 or silica gel ≥90 min before weighing.

$$\text{Wt lipid in sample} = (W \times V)/V',$$

where W = wt lipid in aliquot taken, V = vol. $CHCl_3$ layer, and V' = vol. $CHCl_3$ aliquot taken.

Volatile Fatty Acids

Column Chromatographic Method (23)—Official Final Action

18.050 ***Apparatus***

(**a**) *Steam distillation assembly*.—Fig. **18:02**. Assembly consists of boiler flask (3 L) giving steam at const rate so as to produce const rate of distn, distn flask, condenser, and 200 mL vol. flasks as receivers. Std distn flask with side arm (ca 9 mm od) attached near center of neck, and with steam inlet tube (ca 10 mm od), is satisfactory. Heating coil of steam generator is made by winding 1.5 m (5') 28 gage Chromel wire (or equiv.) around hollow pipe ca 6 mm (0.25") diam. and heating red hot to detemper wire. Leads into boiler flask are brass, Cu, or other nonferrous metal ca 3/32" (2 mm) diam. Insulate and shield elec. leads and contacts to avoid possible shorting and elec. shocks.

Any similar distn assembly may be used if it is of capacity to handle vols specified in method and gives 57±2% recovery of acetic acid on distn.

(**b**) *Chromatographic tube*.—Approx. 15 × 250 mm.

(**c**) *Source of air pressure or compressed N gas equipped with pressure regulator*.—If such source is not available, following system serves purpose: Fit 1 L side arm flask with 2-hole rubber stopper. Pass glass manometer tube 70 cm long thru one hole in stopper so that it reaches bottom of flask, and thru other hole pass glass tube ca 8 cm long, whose upper end is connected to top of chromatgc tube by rubber tubing. Connect rubber hand-aspirator bulb to side arm of flask. Fill flask with Hg to depth of 1.5 cm. (Ht of Hg column in manometer tube indicates pressure in system; 25 cm is equiv. to ca 5 lb.) To maintain reservoir pressure when chromatgc tube is disconnected, fit stopcock into line leading from flask to chromatgc tube; and to prevent valve in hand aspirator from leaking, insert second stopcock between side arm and bulb.

(**d**) *Rubber bulb*.—5 mL. (Type used on dropping bottles.)

(**e**) *Microfunnel*.—Buchner-type, 2 mL capacity with coarse fritted disk; Corning No. 36060.

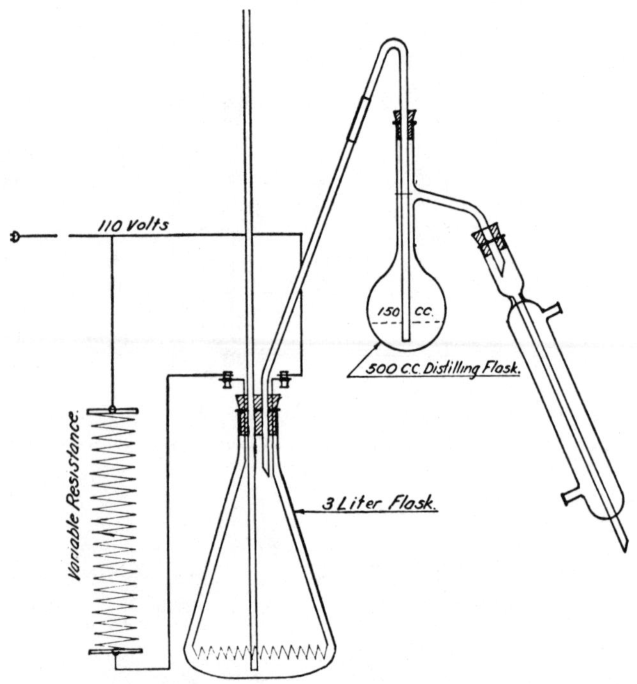

FIG. 18:02—Steam distillation assembly

18.051 ***Reagents***

(**a**) *Butanol in chloroform*.—1%. Remove alcohol from USP $CHCl_3$ by washing 3 times with ½ vol. H_2O. Add 10 mL *n*-BuOH to 1 L washed $CHCl_3$ in separator, shake vigorously, add 25 mL H_2O, and shake again. Let stand until lower layer clears, and drain. Discard upper aq. layer. Store in contact with granular anhyd. Na_2SO_4.

(**b**) *Butanol in chloroform*.—10%. To 900 mL USP $CHCl_3$ (*not* previously washed) in separator add 100 mL *n*-BuOH, shake vigorously, add 25 mL H_2O, and shake again. Let $CHCl_3$ stand until clear, and drain. Discard aq. layer. Store in contact with granular anhyd. Na_2SO_4.

(**c**) *Alphamine Red R indicator*.—Dissolve 50 mg mono-NH_4 salt 3-(4-anilino-1-naphthylazo)-2,7-naphthalene disulfonic acid (Eastman Kodak Co. No. 6410) in 25 mL H_2O. (Red soln produced by 1 drop indicator in 20 mL H_2O must be changed to violet by 1 drop 0.01*N* HCl.) Prep. fresh weekly.

(**d**) *Cresol red indicator*.—Dissolve 50 mL *o*-cresolsulfonphthalein in 20 mL alcohol, add 1.3 mL 0.1*N* NaOH, and dil. to 50 mL with H_2O. Use 2 drops for each 25 mL aq. soln.

(**e**) *Barium hydroxide std soln*.—0.01*N*. (Store in polyethylene or paraffin-lined bottle and protect from CO_2 of atm. with soda-lime or Ascarite; dispense from 10 mL buret.) (0.01*N* NaOH may be used instead of $Ba(OH)_2$ except in titrn of Soln *B*, **18.054**. NaOH soln must be used in titrn of Soln *A*, **18.054**, since Na salts are required for chromatgy.)

(**f**) *Sodium acetate-sodium chloride soln*.—Dissolve 12 g NaCl and 25 g $NaOAc.3H_2O$ in H_2O and dil. to 500 mL.

(**g**) *Silicic acid*.—Reagent grade "100-mesh" powder, suitable for chromatgy (Mallinckrodt Chemical Works No. 2847, or equiv.).

18.052 ***Standardization of Distillation Apparatus***

Place app., **18.050(a)**, in laboratory so that it is free from drafts and sudden changes in temp. Make mark on boiler flask at 1.5 L level, fill to this mark with H_2O, heat to boiling, and boil several min before starting distn. Transfer 150 mL H_2O to distn flask, add 1 drop H_2SO_4 (1+1), connect condenser, insert steam inlet tube into distn flask, and bring contents of flask to incipient boiling with burner. Connect steam inlet tube with steam supply from boiler and steam distil. Regulate rate of evolution of steam and ht of small flame of burner under distn flask so that vol. of liq. in distn flask is kept const at 150 mL and distillate collects at 200 mL/hr. (Period of collection may vary 5 min for 200 mL distillate. Keep vol. in distn flask at 150±10 mL. Stop boiling, if necessary, to permit test of constancy of 150 mL vol. by momentarily interrupting steam supply. Few trials will show conditions necessary to maintain const vol. in distn flask and const rate of distn.) Det. blank on 2 successive 200 mL portions of distillate by titrg with 0.01*N* alkali (phthln) in CO_2-free atm.

Transfer 50 mL ca 0.1*N* HOAc (concn must be accurately

known) to distn flask; add 1 drop H_2SO_4 (1+1) (avoid contact with neck of flask) and 100 mL H_2O. Collect 200 mL distillate and titr. with 0.1*N* alkali. Correct for titrn blanks and compute % acid distd. Distn technic and app. are satisfactory when recovery is 57±2%. App. so adjusted gives recoveries (±2%) of formic, propionic, and butyric acids of 40.5, 81, and 92%, resp. (JAOAC **21**, 684, 688(1938)), on 200 mL distillate.

18.053 ***Preparation of Solution***

Weigh 50 g comminuted material, **18.012**, into tared 500 mL wide-mouth erlenmeyer, add ca 150 mL H_2O, stopper flask, and shake vigorously ca 1 min to effect thoro suspension of material. Add 25 mL 1*N* H_2SO_4, mix, ppt proteins with *20% phosphotungstic acid soln* (40 mL is usually enough), make to 300 g with H_2O, shake vigorously ca 1 min, and filter thru 24 cm rapid folded paper.

18.054 ***Distillation and Computation of Volatile Acid Number***

Pipet 150 mL prepd soln into distn flask of app. and make acid to *Congo red paper* with H_2SO_4 (1+1). Steam distil as in **18.052**. Collect 200 mL distillate, titr. with 0.01*N* NaOH to phthln end point, and designate as *A*. Collect second 200 mL portion distillate, titr. with 0.01*N* $Ba(OH)_2$ soln to phthln end point, and designate as *B*. To calc. volatile acid number, multiply titrn obtained on distillate *A*, corrected for blank, by 4.

18.055 ***Determination of Formic Acid (24)***

(*Caution: See* **51.079**.)

Add 2 drops satd $Ba(OH)_2$ soln to distillate *B*, **18.054**, and evap. to dryness on steam bath. Add ca 5 mL H_2O to residue and 1 mL more of 1*N* HCl than necessary to liberate volatile acids. Filter thru small paper into 125 mL erlenmeyer with ₮ joint, and wash paper with H_2O in such manner that total filtrate equals 30–40 mL. Add 10 mL NaOAc-NaCl soln and 10 mL *5% $HgCl_2$ soln.* Connect flask with ₮ air condenser and place on steam bath 2.5 hr.

With suction thru glass siphon attached to funnel by rubber stopper, transfer ppt of Hg_2Cl_2 to previously weighed microfunnel, **18.050(e)**, provided with mat of asbestos ca 2 mm thick. Rinse flask with H_2O followed by alcohol. Dry 30 min at 100°, cool, and weigh. Weigh funnel with another funnel, prepd with asbestos and treated similarly to one contg ppt, as counterpoise.

Wt Hg_2Cl_2 (mg) × 0.0975 = mg formic acid in distillate. To calc. total formic acid originally present in aliquot of sample in distn flask before distn, divide mg formic acid found by 0.24 (fraction formic acid distd in second 200 mL distillate) and multiply by 4 to obtain formic acid in 100 g sample being analyzed. (*Note:* Factor 4 applies only to products prepd as in **18.053**. If other sample wts and aliquots are used as for eggs, **17.041**, appropriate factor must be used.)

Chromatographic Separation of C_2 to C_4 Saturated Fatty Acids (25)

18.056 ***Preparation of Partition Column***

To 5 g silicic acid in glazed porcelain evapg dish add 1 mL Alphamine Red R indicator soln and just enough 1*N* NH_4OH to give alk. color of the indicator (1 drop is usually enough). Add max. amt of H_2O that the silicic acid will hold without becoming sticky or agglomerating in the BuOH-$CHCl_3$ soln. (This amt must be detd for each batch of silicic acid and usually varies from 50 to 75% of wt of silicic acid.) Mix thoroly with pestle until homogeneous. Add ca 25 mL 1% BuOH in $CHCl_3$, and mix to form slurry that pours readily. Pour this slurry into chromatgc tube contg small cotton plug in neck of constricted end. To avoid air pockets, tilt tube slightly while pouring. If air bubbles form while pouring, eliminate by stirring suspension in tube with long glass rod.

Clamp tube vertically in ring stand. In top insert 1-hole rubber stopper fitted with glass tube bent to 90° angle and held in place by Bunsen clamp against pressure to be exerted. Connect bent glass tube to pressure source, **18.050(c)**. Adjust pressure to 5–10 psi (34.5–68.9 kPa) so that excess solv. is forced thru column dropwise.

During removal of excess solv., gel packs down. As column packs down, particles of gel adhere to wall of tube, but eventually gel leaves wall of tube relatively clean. This is point of optimum density of column, and column is ready for use. Apply pressure until solv. reaches surface of column. If solv. passes below surface, causing drying or "cracking" of column, or if air pockets are present, extrude packing from tube, reslurry with solv., and repack column.

18.057 ***Test of Silicic Acid for Suitability and Standardization of Column***

(a) *Preparation of std acid solns.*—Pipet 1 mL of each of following acids into sep. 1 L vol. flasks: Acetic, propionic, butyric, and valeric. Dil. to vol. with H_2O, and mix. Pipet 10 mL of each soln into sep. 125 mL erlenmeyers and titr. with 0.01*N* NaOH, using cresol red indicator, to pink persisting ca 45 sec.

$$\text{mL } 0.01N \text{ NaOH} \times \text{normality} \times F = \text{mg acid/mL std acid soln},$$

where *F* = 6.01 for HOAc; 7.41, propionic; 8.81, butyric; and 10.2, valeric acid.

(b) *Preparation of std acid mixture.*—Pipet 50 mL of each std acid soln into same 250 mL vol. flask and dil. to vol. with H_2O. Concn of each acid in std acid mixt. = 1/5 concn in std acid soln.

(c) *Preparation of known samples.*—Pipet 5 and 25 mL aliquots of std acid mixt. into sep. 50 mL beakers. Just neutze with 0.1*N* NaOH, using phthln, and add 10 drops excess. Evap. to dryness on steam bath. If desired, chromatograph acids individually by using 5 mL aliquots of each std soln and 5 mL aliquots of 5-fold dilns of each std acid soln. Combinations approximating compositions in samples may also be prepd.

(d) *Column separation.*—(Good sepn and yields depend upon transfer of sample to column with amt of solv. specified.) To dry residue of Na salts add 2 mL 1% BuOH in $CHCl_3$ soln and while stirring with glass rod add H_2SO_4 (1+1) dropwise until all Na salts are converted to free acids (acid to Congo red paper). Add 1 g anhyd. Na_2SO_4.

Acids elute in following order: valeric, butyric, propionic, and acetic. Place 50 mL graduate under column as receiver. Decant supernate onto column, pouring it slowly down side of tube without disturbing level surface of column. Apply pressure until solv. reaches surface of gel. Wash beaker with 1 mL solv., pour onto column, and with stirring rod transfer residue in beaker to column. Apply pressure until solv. just disappears into Na_2SO_4 layer. Wash beaker with another 1 mL solv., transfer to column, wash inside of tube with 1 mL solv., and apply pressure until solv. just disappears into Na_2SO_4 layer. Fill tube with solv. and apply pressure. Each time front (lower edge) of a band reaches point 2–5 mm above narrowest portion of constriction of tube, record vol. collected and change receiver. For each acid, total cumulative vol. is threshold vol. used for identifying bands in succeeding runs. After propionic acid (third band) has been eluted, fill tube with 10% BuOH in $CHCl_3$ and use this solv. to elute HOAc. (Propionic acid is eluted after ca 50 mL 1% BuOH in $CHCl_3$ has passed thru column. Observe vol. actually used. In succeeding runs, change to 10% BuOH in $CHCl_3$ at that vol. whether or not propionic acid is present.)

Transfer eluates to sep. 125 mL erlenmeyers, rinsing each graduate with three 5 mL portions H_2O. Add 1 drop cresol red indicator soln and titr. with 0.01*N* alkali. As end point approaches, stopper flask and shake vigorously to completely ext acids from solv. phase. Correct titrn of each eluted band for blank as follows: Collect 25 mL BuOH-$CHCl_3$ mixt. from column before any acids are transferred, add 15 mL boiled and cooled H_2O, and titr. as above with 0.01*N* alkali.

If bands are not clearly differentiated or recoveries are <90%, reject the silicic acid. (Addnl stdzn with respect to threshold vol. may be desirable for identification in some instances, **18.058**.)

18.058 ***Identification and Determination***

Add 1 drop 1*N* NaOH to neutzd distillate *A* obtained in **18.054** and evap. to small vol. Transfer to 50 mL beaker, evap. to dryness on steam bath, and proceed exactly as in **18.057(d)**.

Identify acids by comparing their threshold vols with those for approx. same amts and ratios of known acids found in stdzn operation. Threshold vol. of given amt of each fatty acid is characteristic and reproducible under similar conditions. However, if conditions change, such as use of different batch of silicic acid or different amt of same batch, or different amt of H_2O, threshold vol. for each acid must be redetd. (If present, isobutyric acid is measured as *n*-butyric acid.) For further identification as characteristic salts, *see* JAOAC **28**, 644(1945). Acids may also be identified by paper chromatgy, **14.101**.

mg Acid/100 g sample

= mL 0.01*N* NaOH (corrected for blank) × normality × *F*,

where *F* includes equiv. wts of acids, corrected for distn recoveries, and dilns. *F* = 421 for HOAc; 366, propionic; and 383, butyric acid.

(*Note:* Factors given apply only to products prepd as in **18.053**. If other sample wts and aliquots are used as for eggs, **17.041**, appropriate factors must be used.)

18.059 ***Gas Chromatographic Method (26)***
Official Final Action

Proceed as in **17.043–17.047**, except substitute **18.053** for **17.046**. To calc. volatile acid no., multiply mL 0.01*N* NaOH required to neutze 200 mL distillate, corrected for blank, by 4.

Histamine

Biological Method (27)—Official Final Action

18.060 ***Apparatus***

(**a**) *Kymograph.*—With horizontal muscle lever arm having friction or gravity writing point.

(**b**) *Muscle bath.*—At least 50 mL capacity, in 37° const temp. bath. *See* Fig. **18:03**. May be conveniently filled and emptied thru 3-way stopcock; 1 tube connected to reservoir of Ringer-Locke soln thru bulb or coil immersed in bath; other tube connected to vac. thru suction flask as waste receiver. Bubble air, filtered thru cotton, slowly and continuously around intestine from fine capillary tube.

18.061 ***Reagents***

(**a**) *Sodium chloride stock soln.*—180 g/L.
(**b**) *Potassium chloride stock soln.*—42 g/500 mL.
(**c**) *Sodium bicarbonate stock soln.*—15 g/500 mL.
(**d**) *Atropine sulfate stock soln.*—1.0 g/500 mL.
(**e**) *Calcium chloride stock soln.*—24 g anhyd. salt/500 mL.

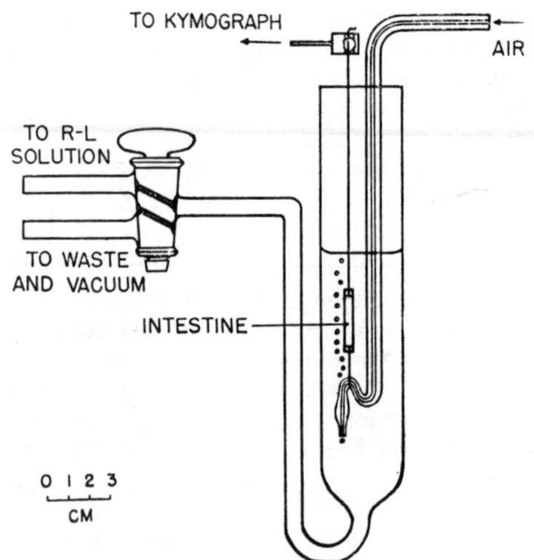

FIG. 18:03—Muscle bath

(**f**) *Ringer-Locke soln.*—NaCl, 0.9%; KCl, 0.042%; $CaCl_2$, 0.024%; $NaHCO_3$, 0.015%; glucose, 0.1%; and atropine sulfate, 0.001%. Add 100 mL (**a**) and 10 mL (**b**),(**c**), and (**d**) to 2 L vol. flask. Add H_2O to vol. of ca 1800 mL and then 10 mL (**e**) while swirling. Add 2 g anhyd. glucose before use. Dil. to vol. with H_2O. Keep soln contg glucose in refrigerator when not in use, discarding when it becomes moldy.

(**g**) *Histamine diphosphate std solns.*—0.1 mg histamine diphosphate/mL boiled H_2O. If stored in refrigerator when not in use, it will keep ≥3 months. Prep. dild stds of 0.01 mg/mL and 0.005 mg/mL as required. If bath <50 mL is used, prep. dilns of (**g**) with (**f**) to avoid diln of bath when stds are added.

(**h**) *Guinea pig intestine.*—Use guinea pigs weighing 300–400 g. Starve pig 24 hr, kill by blow on head, and remove intestine, severing at point proximal to ileocecal junction, retaining ca 12 cm of terminal ileum. Wash this section with soln (**f**) and use ca first 2 cm for first series of assays. Place remainder of intestine on cotton in petri dish, just covering with soln (**f**). Prop lid to admit air and store in refrigerator at ca 4–7° (40–45°F). (Below 4° intestine loses its activity.) Use addnl portions of intestine as required as long as material shows enough response to histamine stimulus (usually 8 days). These addnl portions of intestine are not as sensitive as ileum but give uniform response with barely noticeable pendulum movements after storage.

18.062 ***Preparation of Sample***

See **18.012**. Freeze ground sample for storage, if desired.

18.063 ***Assay***

Weigh 10 g prepd sample into small mortar. Add enough H_2O to make smooth paste while grinding with pestle. Transfer paste with little addnl H_2O to 100 mL Kohlrausch flask and add 1 mL HCl (1+1). Add H_2O to total vol. of ca 70 mL, mix well, and heat flask ca 20 min in boiling H_2O bath. Remove from bath, cool, dil. to vol. with H_2O, mix, and filter on Whatman No. 12 folded paper (or equiv.). (Ext filters slowly but only ca 5 mL need be collected for analysis.) Filtrate may be stored in refrigerator 10 days without diminished activity. Neutze 1 mL filtrate with 2 mL 1% $NaHCO_3$ soln. Dil. to 10 mL with Ringer-Locke soln (without glucose).

Attach intestine to muscle lever and let stand at least 0.5 hr in 50 mL Ringer-Locke soln, (**f**), in const temp. bath at 37°. With fresh ileum, contractions and relaxations may be nonrhythmic for ca 2–3 hr with extreme and not always uniform responses to histamine stimuli. Detns may be performed during this period, but it is necessary to add small and increasing amts of dild stds to stabilize intestine response, and to check responses several times until readings are reproducible.

Add known amt of dil. std soln, (**g**), to bath, record response, and remove writing lever from contact with drum. Drain inner bath, add fresh 37° soln (**f**) to wash chamber and intestine, remove, and refill with fresh soln. Let intestine rest 3 min. Est. amt and diln of neutzd fish ext that will give approx. equal response, and add to bath. Repeat recording of response, washing muscle chamber, and resting 3 min. During this interval, measure step hts with mm scale and calc. amt std necessary to match assay step ht. Alternately add ext and std as above until exact match is obtained.

Chemical Method (28)—Official Final Action

(Use H_2O redistd from glass for prepn of reagents and for detns. Do not clean glassware with soap; use fresh chromic acid cleaning soln, rinsing well with tap H_2O, then 3 times with distd H_2O, and 3 times with redistd H_2O. Alcohol may be used to soak or rinse glassware.)

18.064 ***Reagents***

(**a**) *Benzene-n-butanol mixture.*—(3+2) v/v.

(**b**) *Cotton acid succinate.*—Dissolve 5 g anhyd. NaOAc, fused just before use, and 40 g succinic anhydride in 300 mL HOAc in 500 mL erlenmeyer. Immerse 10 g absorbent cotton, cut into strips, in soln; attach drying tube contg drying agent, and heat 48 hr at 100°. (Flask may be immersed to neck in active steam bath.) Filter; wash well with H_2O, HCl (1+9), H_2O, and finally with alcohol. Dry in vac. oven at 100°.

(**c**) *Diazonium reagent.*—Dissolve 0.1 g *p*-nitroaniline, recrystd from hot H_2O, and dil. to 100 mL with 0.1*N* HCl. Store in refrigerator. Dissolve 4 g $NaNO_2$ in H_2O and dil. to 100 mL. Store in refrigerator. Just before use, place 10 mL *p*-nitroaniline soln in ice bath 5 min, add 1 mL $NaNO_2$ soln, mix, and let stand in bath $\geq$5 min before use.

(**d**) *Coupling buffer.*—Dissolve 7.15 g Na metaborate ($NaBO_2$) and 5.7 g Na_2CO_3 in H_2O, and dil. to 100 mL. Store in polyethylene bottle.

(**e**) *Barbital buffer.*—Dissolve 10 g Na barbital in 1 L H_2O and adjust to pH 7.7 with HOAc (1+15) (ca 25–30 mL), using pH meter. Store in refrigerator to prevent mold growth. Dissolve any ppt by warming before use. (50–250 mL bottle of the buffer may be kept at room temp. and replenished from main supply when mold growth is apparent.)

(**f**) *Histamine std solns.*—Dry histamine.2HCl (USP Ref. Std or material checked against Std as in **18.066**) 2 hr over H_2SO_4. Dissolve 0.1656 g dried histamine.2HCl in H_2O and dil. to 100 mL (1 mL = 1 mg histamine). Dil. 10 mL of this stock soln to 100 mL with H_2O (1 mL = 100 μg histamine). Dil. 5 mL of this dil. std soln and 5 mL MeOH to 100 mL with H_2O (1 mL = 5 μg histamine). Store in cold. Prep. fresh stds weekly.

(**g**) *4-Methyl-2-pentanone (methyl isobutyl ketone).*—Com. purified grade (Eastman Kodak Co. No. 416 has been found satisfactory). To recover used ketone, wash once with satd $NaHCO_3$ soln and 3 times with H_2O, distil, retaining fraction boiling at 115–118°, and check *A* at 475 nm.

(**h**) *Benzaldehyde.*—Cl-free.

(**i**) *Dilute sulfuric acid.*—0.40±0.02*N*, accurately stdzd.

18.065 ***Preparation of CAS Column***

Prep. column by firmly placing small plug of cotton acid succinate (CAS) (ca 50 mg) in column prepd by cutting off or blowing out bottom of 15 mL centrf. tube. Wash plug with three 15 mL portions H_2O and two 3 mL portions alcohol. Let solvs drip thru CAS, syringing out column by blowing out last portion of each solv., using 10 mL syringe with needle inserted thru rubber stopper. CAS plugs may be reused for months by washing shortly after use with H_2O and alcohol as above, and protecting from dust with inverted beaker.

18.066 ***Determination***

Transfer 10 g prepd sample, **18.062**, to semimicro container of high-speed blender, add ca 50 mL MeOH, and blend ca 2 min. Transfer to 100 mL g-s vol. flask, rinsing lid and blender jar with MeOH and adding rinsings to flask. Heat in H_2O bath to 60° and let stand 15 min at this temp. Cool to 25°, dil. to vol. with MeOH, and filter thru folded paper. Alcohol filtrate may be stored in refrigerator several weeks. (Light powdery ppt sepg on storage may be ignored.)

Dil. 5 mL filtrate to 100 mL with H_2O (disregard turbidity). Pipet 5 mL aliquot into 16 × 150 mm g-s test tube, and add 1 drop benzaldehyde (Cl-free) and 0.2 mL 20% NaOH. (pH after adding alkali should be ca 12.4–12.5.) Shake vigorously ca 25 times. Let stand 2 min and add 5 mL benzene-BuOH mixt. Shake vigorously ca 25 times and let stand 5 min to sep. If emulsion forms, centrf.

Transfer upper layer with fine-tip tube equipped with rubber bulb to previously prepd CAS column, avoiding transfer of any aq. phase. Re-ext aq. soln with 5 mL benzene-BuOH mixt. as before, shaking, letting stand 5 min, and transferring upper layer to column. Rinse lip and sides of column with fine stream of alcohol from wash bottle, syringing out CAS. Wash column with 3 mL alcohol; syringe out; wash with two 3 mL portions H_2O, and syringe out. Discard solvs and washings.

Elute histamine from CAS into 25 mL g-s erlenmeyer by washing down sides of tube with 2.0 mL 0.40±0.02*N* H_2SO_4 (vol. and concn of acid are critical) followed by 3 mL H_2O. Syringe out after dripping ceases.

Cool eluate in ice bath, weighting flask with lead ring or clamp to prevent tipping, and let stand 5–10 min. Add 0.5 mL cooled diazonium reagent and let stand 5 min in ice bath. Add 0.50 mL coupling buffer (vol. is critical; Ostwald pipet is convenient) with continuous shaking or swirling to avoid localized alky (pH after addn of coupling buffer, 5–6). Let stand 5 min in ice bath. Sat. soln with ca 0.25 g powd $Na_2B_4O_7.10H_2O$ added in one portion. Shake soln immediately and continuously ca 30 sec to ensure rapid and complete satn (final pH ca 8.6). Let stand 15 min in ice bath.

Pipet in 5.0 mL methyl isobutyl ketone and shake vigorously 25 times. Immediately transfer both layers to 16 × 150 mm test tube (do not rinse) and let stand 10 min at room temp. to sep. and to warm up. Transfer upper layer with fine-tip dropper to second 16 × 150 mm g-s test tube contg 5.0 mL barbital buffer. Avoid transferring aq. and solid phases (if present) (transfer need not be quant.). Shake vigorously ca 25 times (pH of barbital buffer after washing, ca 8.3–8.4). Let stand 10 min to sep.

Transfer upper layer with fine-tip dropper to 1 cm cell and det. *A* at 475 nm against methyl isobutyl ketone. Repeat detn on samples yielding *A* values >25 μg std by dilg 1 mL MeOH filtrate to 100 mL with H_2O. Alternatively, aq. diln may be dild 1+4 (or more) with H_2O.

Conduct std and blank thru detn as follows: Pipet 5 mL 5 μg/mL histamine std soln into 16 × 150 mm g-s test tube and pipet 5 mL 5% MeOH into similar tube for blank. Proceed as in detn, beginning, par. 2, line 2, "... add 1 drop benzaldehyde ..."

Subtract blank *A* from *A* of std (*A'*) and of sample (*A*) and calc. histamine in sample aliquot:

$$\mu g \text{ Histamine} = \Delta A \times 25/\Delta A'.$$

Fluorometric Method (29)—Official Final Action

(Rinse all plastic and glass containers with HCl (1+3) and H_2O before use.)

18.067 ***Apparatus***

(**a**) *Chromatographic tube.*—200 × 7 (id) mm polypropylene tube. (Chromaflex, Kontes Glass Co. No. K-420160, or equiv.) fitted with Kontes No. K-422372 Kel-F Hubs and ca 45 cm Teflon tubing. Control flow rate at >3 mL/min by adjusting ht of column relative to tubing outlet.

(**b**) *Photofluorometer.*—Perkin-Elmer Model 203 or 204 with medium pressure Hg lamp, American Instrument Co. No. 4-7125 with GEF4T4/BL lamp, or equiv. instrument with excitation at 350 nm and measuring emission at 444 nm.

(**c**) *Repipets.*—1 and 5 mL (Labindustries, 620 Hearst Ave, Berkeley, CA 94710, or equiv.).

18.068 ***Reagents***

(**a**) *Ion exchange resin.*—Bio-Rad AG 1-X8, 50–100 mesh (Bio-Rad Laboratories, 32nd & Griffin Ave, Richmond, CA 94804) or Dowex 1-X8, 50–100 mesh. Convert to -OH form by adding ca 15 mL 2*N* NaOH/g resin to beaker. Swirl mixt. and let stand <30 min. Decant liq. and repeat with addnl base. Thoroly wash resin with H_2O, slurry into fluted paper (S&S No. 588, or equiv.), and wash again with H_2O. Prep. resin fresh weekly and store under H_2O.

Place glass wool plug in base of tube, (**a**), and slurry in enough resin to form 8 cm bed. Maintain H_2O level above top of resin bed at all times. Do not regenerate resin in packed column; rather, use batch regeneration in beaker when necessary. Wash column with ca 10 mL H_2O before applying each ext.

(**b**) *Phosphoric acid.*—3.57*N*. Dil. 121.8 mL 85% H_3PO_4 to 1 L. For other concn H_3PO_4, vol. required for 1 L 3.57*N* acid = 17493/(density H_3PO_4 × % H_3PO_4). Stdze 5.00 mL by titrn with 1.00*N* NaOH to phthln end point, and adjust concn if necessary.

(**c**) *o-Phthalicdicarboxaldehyde (OPT) soln.*— 0.1%. Dissolve 100 mg OPT (Aldrich Chemical Co., Inc., No. P3,940-0, or equiv.) in 100 mL distd-in-glass MeOH (Burdick & Jackson Laboratories, Inc., or equiv.). Store in amber bottle in refrigerator. Prep. fresh weekly.

(**d**) *Histamine std solns.*—Store in refrigerator. (*1*) *Stock soln.*—1 mg/mL as free base. Accurately weigh ca 169.1 mg histamine.2HCl (98%, Aldrich Chemical Co., Inc., No. 11,260-7, or equiv.) into 100 mL vol. flask, and dissolve and dil. to vol. with 0.1*N* HCl. Prep. fresh weekly. (*2*) *Intermediate soln.*—10 μg/mL. Pipet 1 mL stock soln into 100 mL vol. flask, and dil. to vol. with 0.1*N* HCl. Prep. fresh weekly. (*3*) *Working solns.*—0.5, 1.0, and 1.5 μg/5 mL. Pipet 1, 2, and 3 mL intermediate soln into sep. 100 mL vol. flasks, and dil. each to vol. with 0.1*N* HCl. Prep. fresh daily.

18.069 ***Preparation of Standard Curve***

Pipet duplicate 5 mL aliquots of each working std soln into sep. 50 mL glass or polypropylene erlenmeyers. Pipet in 10 mL 0.1*N* HCl to each flask and mix. Pipet in 3 mL 1*N* NaOH and mix. Within 5 min, pipet in 1 mL OPT soln and mix immediately. After exactly 4 min, pipet in 3 mL 3.57*N* H_3PO_4 and mix immediately. It is important to mix thoroly after each addn and at least once during OPT reaction. (Run 6–10 OPT reactions simultaneously by adding reagents to erlenmeyers in set order.) Prep. blank by substituting 5 mL 0.1*N* HCl for histamine soln. Within 1.5 hr, record fluorescence intensity (I) of working std solns with H_2O in ref. cell, using excitation wavelength of 350 nm and emission wavelength of 444 nm. Plot I (corrected for blank) against μg histamine/5 mL aliquot.

18.070 ***Determination***

Ext prepd sample with MeOH as in **18.066**, par. 1. Pass 4–5 mL H_2O thru column, (**a**), and discard eluate. Pipet 1 mL ext onto column and add 4–5 mL H_2O. *Immediately* initiate column flow into 50 mL vol. flask contg 5.00 mL 1.00*N* HCl. When liq. level is ca 2 mm above resin, add ca 5 mL H_2O and let elute. Follow with H_2O in larger portions until ca 35 mL has eluted. Stop column flow, dil. to vol. with H_2O, stopper, and mix. Refrigerate eluate.

Pipet 5 mL eluate into 50 mL erlenmeyer, and pipet in 10 mL 0.1*N* HCl. Proceed as in **18.069**, beginning "Pipet in 3 mL 1*N* NaOH . . ."

If sample contains >15 mg histamine/100 g fish, pipet 1 mL sample-OPT mixt. into 10 mL beaker contg exactly 2 mL blank-OPT mixt., and mix thoroly. Read fluorescence of new soln. Dil. and mix aliquots with blank-OPT mixt. as needed to obtain measurable reading. This approximation indicates proper diln of eluate required prior to second OPT reaction needed for reliable quantitation of sample. Alternatively, use sensitivity range control of fluorometer (if instrument has one) to est. diln. Use these approximations to prep. appropriate diln of aliquot of eluate with 0.1*N* HCl, and proceed as in **18.069**, beginning "Pipet in 3 mL 1*N* NaOH . . ."

18.071 ***Calculations***

Plot of I (measured by meter deflection or recorder response and corrected for blank) against μg histamine/5 mL soln should be straight line passing thru origin with slope = $m = [(I_a/1.5) + I_b + 2I_c]/3$.

$$\text{mg Histamine/100 g fish} = (10)(F)(1/m)(I_s),$$

where I_s, I_a, I_b, and I_c = fluorescence from sample, 1.5, 1.0, and 0.5 μg histamine stds, resp.; and F = diln factor = (mL eluate + mL 0.1*N* HCl)/mL eluate. F = 1 for undild eluate.

If calibration plot is not linear, use std curve directly for quantitation. Each subdivision on absicca should be ≤0.1 μg histamine/5 mL soln. Read all values from curve to nearest 0.05 μg histamine/5 mL soln.

$$\text{mg Histamine/100 g fish} = (10)(F)(W),$$

where W = μg histamine/5 mL soln as detd from std curve.

Indole

Colorimetric Method (30)—Official Final Action

18.072 ***Apparatus and Reagents***

(**a**) *Color reagent.*—Dissolve 0.4 g *p*-dimethylaminobenzaldehyde in 5 mL HOAc and mix with 92 mL H_3PO_4 and 3 mL HCl. As purity of *p*-dimethylaminobenzaldehyde affects intensity of reagent blank, purify yellow com. reagent as follows:

Dissolve 100 g in 600 mL HCl (1+6). Add 300 mL H_2O and ppt aldehyde by slowly adding 10% NaOH soln with vigorous stirring. As soon as pptd aldehyde appears white, stop addn of NaOH soln, filter, and discard ppt. Continue neutzn until practically all aldehyde is pptd, but do not carry to completion, because last 4–5 g may be colored. Filter, and wash ppt with H_2O until washings are no longer acid. Dry aldehyde, which should be practically white, in desiccator.

(**b**) *Acetic acid, purified.*—If this reagent turns pink with color reagent, purify as follows: Add, in order specified, to ₮ 1 L r-b flask: 500 mL HOAc, 25 g $KMnO_4$, and 20 mL H_2SO_4. Distil in all-glass still *not* >400 mL.

(**c**) *Dilute hydrochloric acid.*—Dil. 5 mL HCl to 100 mL with H_2O.

(**d**) *Indole std soln.*—Accurately weigh 20 mg indole into 200 mL vol. flask and dil. to vol. with alcohol. Keep refrigerated and discard after 2 weeks.

(**e**) *Distillation apparatus*.—Use sep. steam generator for each unit. Steam generator may be made from 1 L erlenmeyer and connected to all-glass steam distn app. with min. use of rubber tubing. Distn flask (capacity ≥500 mL) is connected to straight bore condenser thru spray trap; 500 mL erlenmeyer is effective receiver. Foil-covered rubber stoppers may be used in absence of all-glass app. (Unprotected natural or synthetic rubber connections and stoppers cause variable distn blanks.)

Ensure absence of Cl in the H_2O which may partly or entirely inhibit development of indole color.

18.073 ***Preparation of Sample***

Crabmeat, oysters, and shrimp.—For oyster meats weigh 50 g; for drained crabmeat or peeled raw or cooked shrimp, weigh 25 or 50 g (depending upon amt of indole expected). Transfer weighed portion to high-speed blender, add 80 mL H_2O (if oysters or crabmeat) or 80 mL alcohol (if shrimp), and mix several min until homogeneous. Quant. transfer mixt. to distn flask, and rinse mixing chamber with min. amt of same solv. used for prepg mixt.

18.074 ***Determination***

Connect flask for steam distn and gently apply steam until distn is well started, using care not to pass in steam so vigorously as to cause excessive foaming. Apply enough heat to distn flask to maintain vol. of 80–90 mL. Collect 350 mL distillate in ca 45 min. (If alcohol was used in prepn of sample, collect 450 mL.) Wash condenser with small amt of alcohol and drain into receiving flask contg distillate.

Transfer distillate to 500 mL separator and add 5 mL dil. HCl and 5 mL satd Na_2SO_4 soln. Ext successively with 25, 20, and 15 mL portions $CHCl_3$, shaking vigorously ≥1 min each time. Combine the 25 and 20 mL exts in 500 mL separator and wash with 400 mL H_2O, 5 mL satd Na_2SO_4 soln, and 5 mL dil. HCl. Save wash H_2O. Filter combined exts thru cotton plug into dry 125 mL separator. Wash 15 mL portion, using same wash H_2O, and combine with other portions in same 125 mL separator.

Add 10 mL color reagent to combined exts, shake vigorously exactly 2 min, and let acid layer sep. as completely as possible. Transfer 9.0 mL acid layer to 50 mL vol. flask, dil. to vol. with HOAc, mix well, transfer soln to suitable photometer cell, and det. *A* at 560 nm. Color soln may be dild with HOAc contg 9.0 mL color reagent/50 mL of soln, provided blanks are detd at same dilns.

Prep. std curve as above by steam distg series of freshly prepd dilns of std indole soln. Det. distn blank similarly, omitting addn of indole.

Gas Chromatographic Method (31)—Official Final Action

(Use reagents and materials that will not contribute P-contg compds capable of giving GLC response. Avoid plastic app. and residues of detergents and oxidg cleaning agents on glassware. Carry reagent blank thru entire method.)

18.075 ***Reagents***

(**a**) *Carbonate buffer*.—pH ca 9.6; 0.2*N* each Na_2CO_3 and $NaHCO_3$. Dissolve 21.2 g Na_2CO_3 and 16.8 g $NaHCO_3$ in H_2O and dil. to 1 L.

(**b**) *Indole std solns*.—(*1*) *Stock soln*.—1.2 mg/mL. Dissolve 120 mg indole in 100 mL EtOAc. (*2*) *Indole std soln I*.—12.0 μg/mL. Pipet 1 mL stock soln into 100 mL vol. flask and dil. to vol. with EtOAc. (*3*) *Indole std soln II*.—6.0 μg/mL. Pipet 25 mL std soln I into 50 mL vol. flask and dil. to vol. with EtOAc. (*4*) *Indole std soln III*.—0.96 μg/mL. Pipet 2 mL std soln I into 25 mL vol. flask and dil. to vol. with EtOAc.

(**c**) *2-Methylindole solns*.—(*1*) *Stock soln*.—1.25 mg/mL. Dissolve 125 mg 2-methylindole in 100 mL alcohol. (*2*) *Working soln*.—25 μg/mL. Pipet 2 mL stock soln into 100 mL vol. flask and dil. to vol. with alcohol.

(**d**) *Solvents*.—Ether, anhyd., contg 0.05% alcohol, EtOAc and hexane, distd from glass.

(**e**) *Silica gel*.—E. Merck No. 7734 (Silica gel 60, particle size 0.063–0.20 mm).

18.076 ***Apparatus***

(**a**) *Gas chromatograph*.—With N-sensitive detector such as thermionic flame ionization detector or Coulson conductivity detector and 1.8 m (6′) × 4 mm id glass tube packed with 10% neopentyl glycol adipate (NPGA) coated on 80–100 mesh Chromosorb W (acid-washed). Operating conditions for flame detector: Temps (°): column 195, injection zone 220, detector 250; gas flows (mL/min): N 65 (use He for Coulson conductivity detector), air 350, H ca 25 (adjust to give standing current ca 5×10^{-10} amp or 30–40% recorder deflection on 5 mv recorder at electrometer sensitivity ca 1×10^{-9} amp full scale). Working electrometer sensitivity ca 4×10^{-10} amp full scale with 5 mv recorder.

(**b**) *GLC column*.—Dissolve 1.2 g NPGA (HI-EFF-3A, Applied Science Laboratories, Inc.) in 100 mL $CHCl_3$ in 400 mL beaker. Add 10.8 g 80–100 mesh acid-washed Chromosorb W with stirring. Evap. solv. on steam bath with stirring. Transfer powder to rotary evaporator and remove last of solv. at 40–50° with vac. Fill clean, dry tube, (**a**), with *5% soln of dimethyldichlorosilane in toluene* and let stand ca 5 min. Rinse column with ca 50 mL MeOH and dry under N. (*Caution: See* **36.019(d)**.) Pack column with coated support and purge ≥2 hr with N. Condition 24 hr at 220° with 10 mL N/min. Representative retention times are: (*1*) tri-*n*-butyl phosphate, 5.0 min; (*2*) indole, 6.8 min; (*3*) 3-methylindole, 8.5 min; and (*4*) 2-methylindole, 9.4 min. Peaks *1, 2,* and *3* should be resolved at baseline; peaks *3* and *4* may overlap, but peak valley should be <20% of peak ht.

(**c**) *Whatman 1PS phase separating filter paper*.

18.077 ***Calibration***

Prep. calibration solns contg vols as indicated in Table **18:01**. Pipet indicated vols into sep. screw-cap vials with Teflon-lined caps and mix. Store in refrigerator.

Adjust instrument to give ≥10% recorder deflection for 5 ng indole. Use min. injection vol. (ca 3 μL) that gives required sensitivity. Use same injection vol. for calibration stds and samples. Make duplicate injections of each soln. Measure peak hts and calc. peak ht ratio, *R* = ht indole peak/ht internal std peak. Prep. std curve by plotting *R* against μg indole in std soln.

18.078 ***Determination***

Weigh 25.0 g well mixed whole shrimp or 5.00 g dry shrimp and transfer to high-speed blender bowl. Add 100 mL buffer

Table 18:01 Solutions for Calibration of Gas Chromatograph

Calib. Soln	Indole			2-methyl-indole,[a] mL	Ethyl acetate, mL
	Std Soln	mL	μg		
1	III	2.00	1.92	1.00	0
2	II	1.00	6.00	1.00	1
3	II	2.00	12.00	1.00	0
4	I	2.00	24.00	1.00	0

[a] Internal std, 25 μg/mL.

and blend 2 min at high speed. Quant. transfer slurry to 500 mL separator. Rinse blender with 25 mL H_2O from squeeze bottle and add rinse to separator. Add exactly 200 mL EtOAc to separator and shake vigorously 2 min.

Let layers sep. and drain lower layer into beaker. If EtOAc (upper layer) is <150 mL, centrf. lower layer, sep., and combine resulting org. layers. Pass thru Whatman phase-sepg paper. Measure exactly 150 mL filtrate into g-s flask, and add 1.00 mL 2-methylindole working soln and 10 g anhyd. Na_2SO_4. Shake 1 min.

Decant ext and conc. to ca 5–10 mL, using rotary evaporator and ca 35–40° H_2O bath. *Do not evap. to dryness.* (Alternatively, conc. under stream of N in 50°H_2O bath.) Transfer ext to vial and conc. to ca 1–1.5 mL under N.

Prep. cleanup column by firmly placing plug of glass wool in bottom of 100 × 12 mm id glass chromatgc tube. Add 6 g silica gel and tamp firmly. Pipet ca 0.5 mL hexane on top of column. Immediately after hexane is absorbed, transfer ca 0.5 mL concd ext to column with min. disruption of packing. When level of liq. reaches top of bed, add 10 mL hexane. Similarly add 10 mL ether-hexane (1+9) and 40 mL ether-hexane (1+9). Collect all column effluent. Conc. to 0.8–1.2 mL at ≤50° under N. *Do not evap. to dryness.*

Make duplicate injections, measure peak hts, and calc. *R*. Det. *I* (μg indole isolated) from std curve and calc. amt indole in each sample:

μg indole/100 g shrimp = $I \times 100/[\text{g sample} \times (150/200)]$

Calc. av. amt indole from duplicate injections.

Paralytic Shellfish Poison

Biological Method (32)—Official Final Action

(*Caution:* Use rubber gloves when handling materials which may contain paralytic shellfish poison.)

18.079 ***Materials***

(**a**) *Paralytic shellfish poison std soln.*—100 μg/mL. Available from Division of Microbiology, Food and Drug Administration, 1090 Tusculum Ave, Cincinnati, OH 45226, as acidified 20% alc. soln. Std is stable indefinitely in cool place.

(**b**) *Paralytic shellfish poison working std soln.*—1 μg/mL. Dil. 1 mL std soln to 100 mL with H_2O. Soln is stable several weeks at 3–4°.

(**c**) *Mice.*—Healthy mice, 19–21 g, from stock colony used for routine assays. If <19 g or >21 g, apply correction factor to obtain true death time (see Table **18:02**). Do not use mice weighing >23 g and do not re-use mice.

18.080 ***Standardization of Bioassay***

Dil. 10 mL aliquots of 1 μg/mL std soln with 10, 15, 20, 25, and 30 mL H_2O, resp., until intraperitoneal injection of 1 mL doses into few test mice causes median death time of 5–7 min. pH of dilns should be 2–4 and must not be >4.5. Test addnl dilns in 1 mL increments of H_2O, e.g., if 10 mL dild with 25 mL H_2O kills mice in 5–7 min, test solns dild 10 + 24 and 10 + 26.

Inject group of 10 mice with each of 2 or preferably 3 dilns that fall within median death time of 5–7 min. Give 1 mL dose to each mouse by intraperitoneal injection and det. death time as time elapsed from completion of injection to last gasping breath of mouse.

Repeat assay 1 or 2 days later, using dilns prepd above which differed by 1 mL increments of H_2O. Then repeat entire test, starting with testing of dilns prepd from newly prepd working std soln.

Calc. median death time for each group of 10 mice used on each diln. If all groups of 10 mice injected with any 1 diln gave median death time <5 or >7 min, disregard results from this diln in subsequent calcns. On other hand, if any groups of 10 mice injected with 1 diln gave median death time falling between 5 and 7 min, include all groups of 10 mice used on that diln, even though some of median death times may be <5 or >7 min. From median death time for each group of 10 mice in each of selected dilns, det. number of mouse units/mL from Sommer's Table. Divide calcd μg poison/1 mL by mouse units/1 mL to obtain conversion factor (CF value) expressing μg poison equiv. to 1 mouse unit. Calc. av. of individual CF values, and use this av. value as ref. point to check routine assays. Individual CF values may vary significantly within laboratory if technics and mice are not rigidly controlled. This situation will require continued use of working std or secondary std, depending on vol. of assay work performed.

18.081 ***Use of Standard with Routine Assays of Shellfish***

Check CF value periodically as follows: If shellfish products are assayed less than once a week, det. CF value on each day assays are performed by injecting 5 mice with appropriate diln of working std. If assays are made on several days during week, only 1 check need be made each week on diln of std such that median death time falls within 5–7 min. CF value thus detd should check with av. CF value within ±20%. If it does not check within this range, complete group of 10 mice by adding 5 mice to the 5 mice already injected, and inject second group of 10 mice with same diln of std. Average CF value detd for second group with that of first group. Take resulting value as new CF value. Variation of >20% represents significant change in response of mice to poison, or in technic of assay. Changes of this type require change in CF value.

Repeated checks of CF value ordinarily produce consistent results within ±20%. If wider variations are found frequently, possibility of uncontrolled or unrecognized variables in method should be investigated before proceeding with routine assays.

18.082 ***Preparation of Sample***

(**a**) *Clams, oysters, and mussels.*—Thoroly clean outside of shellfish with fresh H_2O. Open by cutting adductor muscles. Rinse inside with fresh H_2O to remove sand or other foreign material. Remove meat from shell by sepg adductor muscles and tissue connecting at hinge. Do not use heat or anesthetics before opening shell, and do not cut or damage body of mollusk at this stage. Collect ca 100–150 g meats in glazed dish. As soon as possible, transfer meats to No. 10 sieve without layering, and let drain 5 min. Pick out pieces of shell and discard drainings. Grind in household-type grinder with ⅛–¼" (3–6 mm) holes or in blender until homogeneous.

(**b**) *Scallops.*—Sep. edible portion (adductor muscle) and apply test to this portion alone. Drain and grind as in (**a**).

(**c**) *Canned shellfish.*—Prep. by blending as in **18.012(b)**.

18.083 ***Extraction***

Weigh 100 g well mixed material into tared beaker. Add 100 mL 0.1*N* HCl, stir thoroly, and check pH. (pH should be <4.0, preferably ca 3.0. If necessary, adjust pH as indicated below.) Heat mixt., boil gently 5 min, and let cool to room temp. Adjust cooled mixt. to pH 2.0–4.0 (never >4.5) as detd by *BDH Universal Indicator, phenol blue, Congo red paper*, or pH meter. To lower pH, add 5*N* HCl dropwise with stirring; to raise pH, add 0.1*N* NaOH dropwise with const stirring to prevent local alkalinization and consequent destruction of poison. Transfer mixt. to graduate and dil. to 200 mL.

Return mixt. to beaker, stir to homogeneity, and let settle until portion of supernate is translucent and can be decanted free of solid particles large enough to block 26-gage hypodermic needle. If necessary, centrf. mixt. or supernate 5 min at 3000 rpm or filter thru paper. Only enough liq. to perform bioassay is necessary.

18.084 ***Mouse Test***

Intraperitoneally inoculate each test mouse with 1 mL acid ext. Note time of inoculation and observe mice carefully for time of death as indicated by last gasping breath. Record death time from stopwatch or clock with sweep second hand. One mouse may be used for initial detn, but 2 or 3 are preferred. If death time or median death time of several mice is <5 min, make diln to obtain death times of 5–7 min. If death time of 1 or 2 mice injected with undild sample is >7 min, total of ≥3 mice must be inoculated to establish toxicity of sample. If large dilns are necessary, adjust pH of diln by dropwise addn of dil. HCl (0.1 or 0.01*N*) to pH 2.0–4.0 (never >4.5). Inoculate 3 mice with diln that gives death times of 5–7 min.

Table 18:02 Sommer's Table

Death time:mouse unit relations for paralytic shellfish poison (acid)

Death Time[a]	Mouse Units	Death Time[a]	Mouse Units
1:00	100	5:00	1.92
10	66.2	05	1.89
15	38.3	10	1.86
20	26.4	15	1.83
25	20.7	20	1.80
30	16.5	30	1.74
35	13.9	40	1.69
40	11.9	45	1.67
45	10.4	50	1.64
50	9.33		
55	8.42	6:00	1.60
		15	1.54
2:00	7.67	30	1.48
05	7.04	45	1.43
10	6.52		
15	6.06	7:00	1.39
20	5.66	15	1.35
25	5.32	30	1.31
30	5.00	45	1.28
35	4.73		
40	4.48	8:00	1.25
45	4.26	15	1.22
50	4.06	30	1.20
55	3.88	45	1.18
3:00	3.70	9:00	1.16
05	3.57	30	1.13
10	3.43	10:00	1.11
15	3.31	30	1.09
20	3.19		
25	3.08	11:00	1.075
30	2.98	30	1.06
35	2.88		
40	2.79	12:00	1.05
45	2.71		
50	2.63	13	1.03
55	2.56	14	1.015
		15	1.000
4:00	2.50	16	0.99
05	2.44	17	0.98
10	2.38	18	0.972
15	2.32	19	0.965
20	2.26	20	0.96
25	2.21	21	0.954
30	2.16	22	0.948
35	2.12	23	0.942
40	2.08	24	0.937
45	2.04	25	0.934
50	2.00	30	0.917
55	1.96	40	0.898
		60	0.875

[a] Minutes:Seconds.

Correction table for weight of mice

Wt of Mice, g	Mouse Units
10	0.50
10.5	0.53
11	0.56
11.5	0.59
12	0.62
12.5	0.65
13	0.675
13.5	0.70
14	0.73
14.5	0.76
15	0.785
15.5	0.81
16	0.84
16.5	0.86
17	0.88
17.5	0.905
18	0.93
18.5	0.95
19	0.97
19.5	0.985
20	1.000
20.5	1.015
21	1.03
21.5	1.04
22	1.05
22.5	1.06
23	1.07

18.085 ***Calculation of Toxicity***

Det. median death times of mice, including survivors, and from Sommer's Table det. corresponding number of mouse units. If test animals weigh <19 g or >21 g, make correction for each mouse by multiplying mouse units corresponding to death time for that mouse by wt correction factor for that mouse from Sommer's Table; then det. median mouse unit for group. (Consider death time of survivors as >60 min or equiv. to <0.875 mouse unit in calcg median.) Convert mouse units to μg poison/mL by multiplying by CF value.

μg Poison/100 g meat = (μg/mL) × diln factor × 200.

Consider any value >80 μg/100 g as hazardous and unsafe for human consumption.

Identification of Fish Species

Starch Gel-Zone Electrophoresis Method (33)
Official Final Action

(*Caution:* Cover for electrophoresis chamber should have switch to disconnect current to electrodes when chamber is open. Shield contacts and electrodes against body contact.)

18.086 ***Apparatus***

(¼" Lucite or Plexiglas is suitable plastic for trays, cabinet, and containers; Fig. **18:04**.)

(a) *Trays.*—Plastic; 20 × 250 mm, 6 mm deep, to hold starch gel.

(b) *Cabinet.*—Plastic; 7.5 × 20 × 36 cm (3 × 8 × 14") with flat cover. Make slots in rear for inserting electrodes.

(c) *Buffer and electrode containers.*—Plastic; 5 × 5 × 18 cm (2 × 2 × 7") with electrode compartment 5 × 5 × 2.5 cm (2 × 2 × 1") at one end.

(d) *Electrodes.*—18 gage Ag wire. Make tight coil at one end and insert in electrode compartment; place other end thru glass tube and attach to power supply.

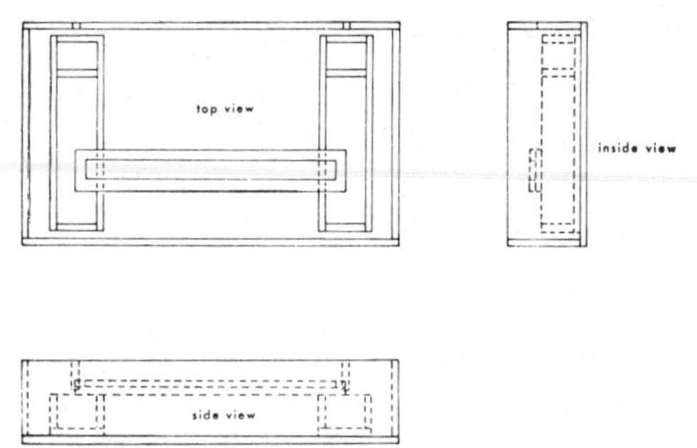

FIG. 18:04—Electrophoresis cabinet (Scale: 1" = 10")

(**e**) *Filter paper strips.*—Whatman No. 3; 6 × 19 mm for samples; 18 × 75 mm for connecting gel to buffer and buffer to electrode compartment.

(**f**) *Power supply.*—To supply const 15 ma at 190–210 volts, *e.g.*, Heathkit or Constat.

18.087 ***Reagents***

(**a**) *Borate buffer.*—pH 8.65. Dissolve 18.5 g H_3BO_3 and 4.8 g NaOH in H_2O and dil. to 1 L. Adjust with 10% NaOH soln, if necessary. Dil. 1 + 9 for prepg starch gel.

(**b**) *Sodium chloride soln.*—Prep. satd soln and dil. 1 + 2 for use in electrode compartment.

(**c**) *Hydrolyzed potato starch.*—Hydrolyze 300 g potato starch 1 hr at 40° in 600 mL acetone contg 6 mL HCl. Stop reaction by addn of 150 mL 1*M* NaOAc.$3H_2O$ (136 g/L) and filter with suction. Wash pptd starch with 2–3 L H_2O. Resuspend starch in 1.5 L H_2O and stir 1 hr. Refilter and wash with 2 L H_2O, and dry overnight at 50°. Grind to fine powder and test for correct gel consistency by prepg test lots contg 12, 13, 14%, etc. starch in pH 8.65 buffer, heat to just below bp, and pour into starch gel trays to cool and harden. Prep. night before use and store in refrigerator. Using known protein ext, det. starch concn giving best pattern sepn in detn. Use this concn for all detns with this batch of starch. (Prepd starch available from Fisher Scientific Co., S-676.)

(**d**) *5-5-1 solvent.*—Mix 5 parts H_2O, 5 parts MeOH, and 1 part HOAc.

(**e**) *Amido black 10B.*—1.0%. Dissolve 2 g dye in 200 mL 5-5-1 solv.

18.088 ***Determination***

Weigh 20–30 g minced sample into blender cup. Add 40–60 mL H_2O and blend 2 min at high speed. Pour mixt. into 50 mL centrf. tubes and centrf. at 1800 rpm until sepn is complete (10–15 min). Filter supernate thru folded Whatman No. 1 paper or on buchner with suction to obtain protein ext.

Dip small filter paper strips into protein ext and insert into starch strips by cutting starch crosswise at midpoint of length of strip. Place loaded trays in cabinet (Fig. **18:04**). Place one end of large paper strip satd with pH 8.65 buffer on each end of starch tray and dip other end into tray of pH 8.65 buffer. Connect buffer compartment to electrode compartment contg dild NaCl soln with similar strip satd with the NaCl soln. Immerse Ag electrodes in both electrode compartments. Pass const 15 ma current (190–210 volts) thru system 5 hr.

Remove trays and immerse starch strips 5 min in dye soln. Return excess dye to stock soln (may be used 6–9 times). Wash dyed strips with several portions 5-5-1 solv. to remove dye from unstained portions of starch, leaving protein fractions permanently stained as blue bands.

Compare pattern with patterns of authentic materials and stds run simultaneously.

Acrylamide Disc Electrophoresis Method (34)
Official Final Action

18.089 ***Apparatus***

(**a**) *Disc electrophoresis.*—Assemble app. shown in Fig. **18:05**, consisting of regulated power source (60 ma, 500 volts, DC); 2 plastic reservoirs, ca 13 cm (5") diam.; C or Pt electrodes; tube grommets (std elec. grommets); glass tubes, 65 × 5 mm id. "Top view" represents base of upper reservoir showing holes lined with rubber grommets. Gel tubes protrude from base of upper reservoir and dip into lower reservoir buffer. (*See Caution* above **18.086**.) (Available as Canalco models 6, 12, 1200, 1200L from Miles Laboratories.)

Polyacrylamide gel column is composed of 3 layers: upper, large-pore (stacking) gel contg sample ions in which electrophoretic concn of ions is initiated; middle, large-pore gel (spacer gel) in which electrophoretic concn of sample ions is completed; and lower, small-pore gel in which electrophoretic sepn occurs.

Thoroly clean and rinse app. after each detn. Wash sample tubes and soak in chromic acid cleaning soln followed by thoro rinsing with H_2O. When app. is not in use, remove buffer, **18.090(b)**(*7*), from upper and lower reservoirs and store in sep. containers in refrigerator. Upper buffer is usually good for ca 6 detns. Discard buffer when pH drops to <8.2.

(**b**) *Photopolymerizing light.*—15 watt fluorescent light, 15" long.

18.090 ***Reagents***

(**a**) *Relatively stable.*—Acrylamide monomer, *N,N'*-methylenebisacrylamide (Bis), 2-amino-2-hydroxymethyl-1,3-propanediol (Tris), *N,N,N',N'*-tetramethylethylenediamine (TEMED), ammonium persulfate, riboflavin, glycine (NH_3-free), aniline black.

(**b**) *Relatively unstable (solns).*—Stable ca 6 months; refrigerate solns *1–6*. (*1*) 48 mL 1*N* HCl, 36.3 g Tris, 0.23 mL TEMED, H_2O to 100 mL (pH 8.8–9.0). (*2*) 25.6 mL 1*M* H_3PO_4, 5.7 g Tris, 0.46 mL TEMED, H_2O to 100 mL (pH 6.6–6.9). (*3*) 30.0 g acrylamide, 0.8 g Bis, H_2O to 100 mL. (*4*) 10.0 g acrylamide, 2.5 g Bis, H_2O to 100 mL. (*5*) 4.0 mg riboflavin, H_2O to 100 mL. (*6*) *Catalyst.*—0.14 g $(NH_4)_2S_2O_8$, H_2O to 100 mL (mix fresh weekly).

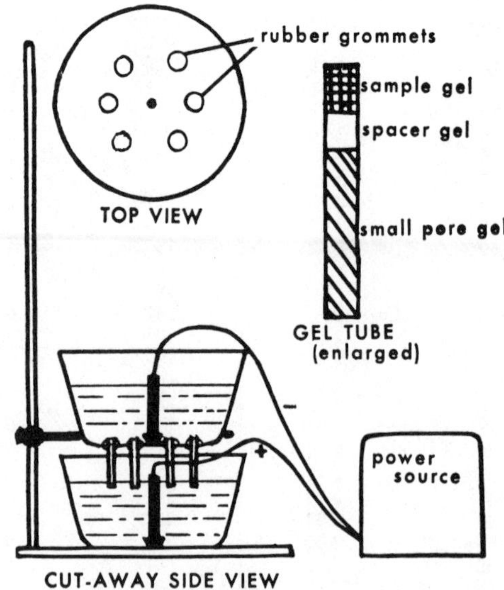

FIG. 18:05—Disc electrophoresis apparatus

(7) *Buffer*.—3.0 g Tris, 14.4 g glycine, H_2O to 1 L (pH 8.8–9.0). (8) *Specimen stain*.—1.0 g aniline black, 7.5% HOAc (v/v) to 200 mL. (9) *Tracking dye*.—0.005% aq. bromophenol blue.

(**c**) *Working solns*.—Prep. fresh for each detn. (1) *Lower gel (separating gel)*.—Mix solns (**b**)(1), (3), and H_2O (1+2+1), pH 8.8–9.0. To form gel, mix with catalyst soln, (6) (1+1). (2) *Upper gel (stacking gel)*.—Mix solns (**b**)(2), (4), and (5) (1+2+1), pH 6.6–6.8. To form gel, expose to fluorescent light, e.g., **18.005**(**b**).

18.091 ***Preparation of Column***

(**a**) *Lower and spacer gels*.—Cap base of glass tube and set tube in rack. Prep. sepg gel with catalyst soln, (**c**)(1), in 20 mL syringe and add mixt. to tube to ca 12 mm from top. Tap tube occasionally during filling to avoid trapping air bubbles under gel surface. Place few drops tracking dye in ca 20 mL H_2O and with eye dropper cautiously layer 6 mm dye soln on top of sepg gel without disturbing gel surface by touching dropper to tube edge (dye soln aids in differentiating H_2O and gel layers). Discard tubes in which distinct, sharp boundary line is not visible. Let gel polymerize 30 min. (Polymerization time is based on reaction at 24°. Let refrigerated reagents stand at room temp. ca 20 min before using.) Gently shake off H_2O layer and add ca 0.1 mL stacking gel soln, (**c**)(2), to top of column (functionally this is "spacer gel layer"). Cautiously layer 3 mm H_2O atop gel. Set photopolymerizing light 7–13 cm in front of gel column rack to polymerize spacer gel in 10–15 min. Polymerization is complete when spacer gel changes from light green to translucent white. Shake off top H_2O layer.

(**b**) *Sample gel*.—Prep. sample ext as in first par., **18.088**, and mix ext, H_2O, and solns, (**b**)(2), (4), and (5) (1+3+1+2+1) (sample stacking mixt.). If inadequate (no bands or only very faint band appears in detn), prep. new sample stacking mixt. (2+2+1+2+1).

Add 0.1 mL sample stacking mixt. to tube prepd in (**a**) and polymerize, using fluorescent light as in (**a**). Remove base cap from tube by pressing at bottom and peeling off edge to break vac. Avoid displacement of gel column from tube wall. Do not touch gel or sharp glass edge of column.

18.092 ***Determination***

Pour ca 500 mL buffer soln, (**b**)(7) (contg enough tracking dye soln to produce definite blue tinge), into lower bath or enough to cover lower electrode ≥6 mm. Insert sample end of column (top) into rubber holes in underside of upper bath until tops of glass tubes are flush with tops of rubber holes. Plug unused holes with stoppers to avoid top buffer leakage. Place upper bath over lower bath.

Slowly pour ca 250 mL buffer soln (contg tracking dye) into middle of upper bath. Fill slowly to avoid cross contamination of samples. Take extra caution to liberate all air entrapped between sample gel and buffer to permit elec. current to flow by gently introducing buffer soln into top of each sample tube, using syringe to drive out air. Set polarity of electrodes so that sample ions migrate to lower bath (pos. electrode). Turn on current and adjust power unit to give 5 ma/sample tube (5 ma × no. of sample columns = total ma adjustment of power supply). Turn off current when "front" band is within 5 mm of bottom of sample column (ca 30–40 min).

Transfer gel column ("sample end" or "top" first) to test tube, ⅔ full with specimen stain dild with H_2O (1+1), *immediately* after electrophoresis to stain and fix. Protein fractions in gel diffuse if not properly fixed or stained. Remove gel column from tube under H_2O in pan as follows: Fill 10 or 20 mL syringe with cold H_2O and insert gel-removing needle at sample end of column between glass and gel so that needle tip reaches sepg gel. Keeping needle flat against glass surface to avoid scratching gel, rotate needle completely around circumference of gel. Remove needle and insert it from other end to depth of ca 1 cm, holding it against inner surface of glass column and at same time forcing stream of H_2O thru needle. If these steps are carefully performed, entire intact gel will come free and can be slipped out of tube. If necessary, little air pressure from rubber bulb will assist in ejecting column.

While gel is being stained (above), prep. 75 × 7 mm id glass destain tube as follows: Place fire polished end of tube in large diam. base cap. Add ca 1 cm sepg gel with catalyst to bottom of column and let polymerize. When staining is complete (ca 15 min), decant stain by placing lip of test tube against inside lip of beaker to retain gel in tube. Rinse twice with 7.5% HOAc (v/v) to remove excess stain. Transfer gel bottom "front" first into destain tube in which bottom plug of gel has been cast and cap removed.

Place destaining tubes in rubber holes in underside of upper bath. Plug any vacant holes. Pour ca 500 mL 7.5% HOAc in lower bath and ca 250 mL into upper bath. As previously, use syringe contg 7.5% HOAc to ensure no air bubbles exist between gel and HOAc bath. Turn on current, adjusting to 5 ma/column (5 × no. of columns = total ma). Gels will be destained in ca 45–60 min. When gel part contg no protein is clear of stain, or has pale blue color, remove specimens, and place in small test tube contg 7.5% HOAc for viewing and storage. Visually compare finished tubes with patterns prepd from authentic samples and stds run simultaneously.

Cellulose Acetate Strip Method (35)—Official Final Action

18.093 ***Principle***

Fish protein is applied to cellulose acetate supporting medium and travels when fixed voltage is applied for definite length of time. Finished strips are stained, washed, and dried to fix patterns.

18.094 ***Apparatus and Reagents***

(**a**) *Electrophoresis cabinet*.—Divided into 2 compartments (Gelman Instrument Co., 600 S Wagner Rd, Ann Arbor, MI 48106) with adjustable const voltage power supply with 300 v min. output voltage; with voltammeter which permits reading and adjusting voltage to produce desired current (Beckman Instrument Duostat power supply, or equiv.). (*See Caution* above **18.086**.)

(**b**) *Gelman applicator.*

(**c**) *Cellulose acetate strips*.—6¾ × 1" (Gelman Instrument Co.).

(**d**) *Capillary tubes*.—1.6–1.8 × 100 mm.

(**e**) *Filter paper*.—Whatman No. 1 sheets cut to convenient size.

(**f**) *Veronal buffer*.—pH 8.6, ionic strength 0.04; Na diethylbarbiturate 8.64 g, diethylbarbituric acid 1.2 g, and H_2O to 1 L.

(**g**) *Stain*.—Dissolve 200 mg Ponceau S stain in 100 mL 5% trichloroacetic acid.

(**h**) *Wash soln*.—5% HOAc.

18.095 ***Preparation of Samples***

(**a**) *Fresh*.—Grind ca 3 g fish flesh in mortar with 3 mL H_2O and squeeze through several thicknesses of cheesecloth. If centrf. is available, place pieces of fish in centrf. tubes and express fluid by centrfg; no added H_2O is required.

(**b**) *Frozen*.—Thaw sample and use drip that forms undild.

(**c**) *Freeze-dried*.—Reconstitute samples with H_2O and treat as in (**a**).

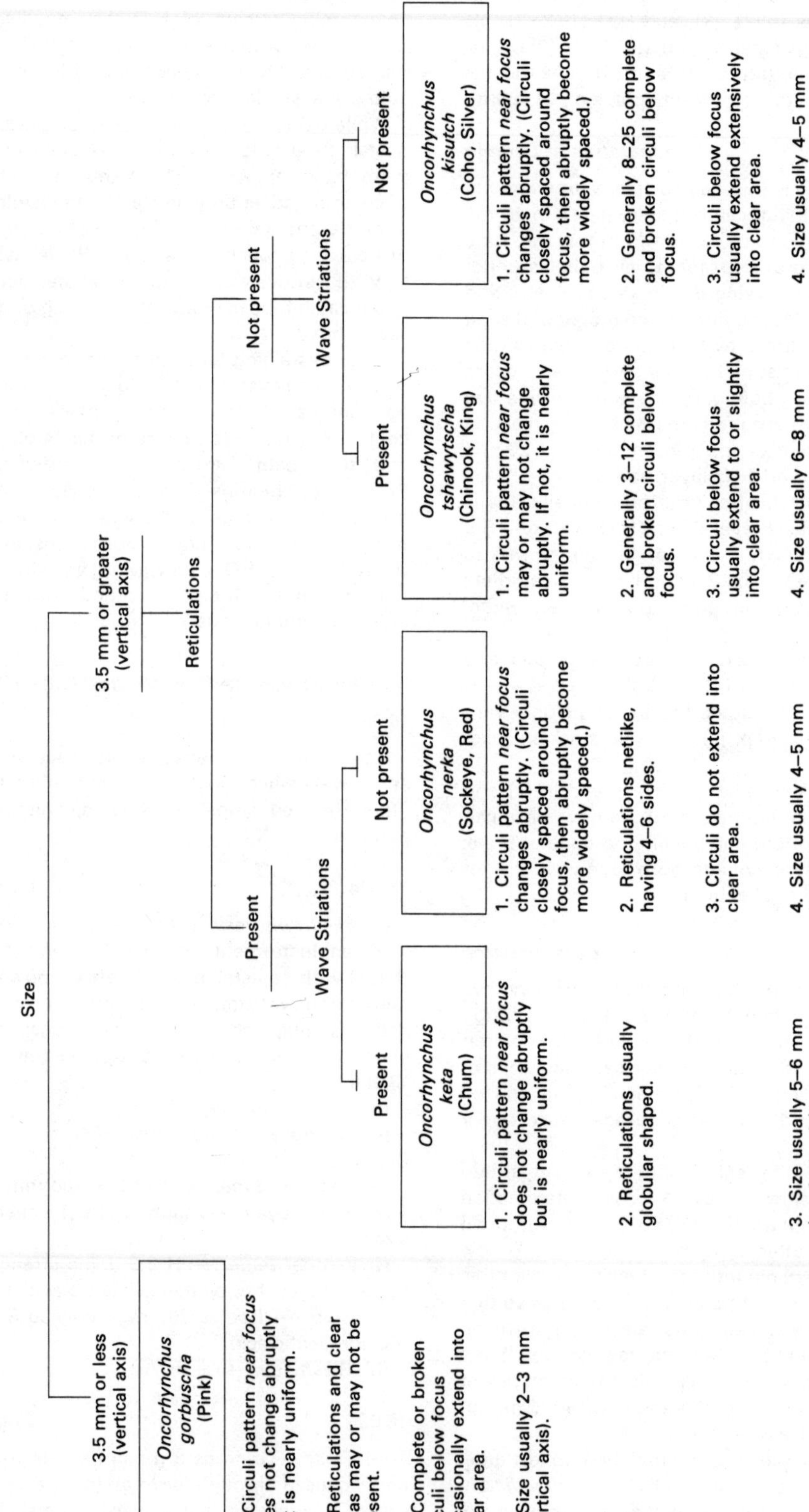

FIG. 18:06—Key to identification of canned salmon species by scale characteristics

(**d**) *Breaded raw sticks and portions*.—Remove breading by soaking for few sec in H_2O and scraping off breading with spatula. Treat in same manner as in (**b**) or (**a**).

(**e**) *Precooked sticks and portions*.—Trim breading and all surface meat until internal center section remains. Treat as in (**a**).

18.096 ***Determination***

Soak cellulose polyacetate strips 30 min in buffer (soaking is required to bring strips back to original gel structure). Use new buffer supply each time. Since 6 strips can be run simultaneously, each with different sample, identify each stip with pencil notation before soaking.

Add chilled (1°C; 34°F) buffer to each chamber of cabinet and level to point slightly below compartment dividers. Remove 1 strip from buffer and gently blot between sheets of filter paper to remove excess buffer.

Take up sample of tissue fluid into capillary tube and transfer to applicator. Draw capillary tube along applicator to within 6 mm of both ends. Then press applicator firmly against strip about 5 cm from one end. Place strip contg sample across cabinet dividers so that sample is on cathode side and both ends are immersed in buffer in the 2 outer chambers. Secure acetate strips at each end with magnets or glass wedges to prevent slippage. Keep taut. Repeat sample application with each strip, working quickly to prevent strips from drying out.

Put cabinet cover in place, connect electrodes, and set power supply to give const voltage. Adjust voltage (between 200 and 300 v) to produce initial current of 1.5 ma/strip. Maintain this voltage 30 min. Shut off power supply, remove strips from cabinet, and place in Ponceau S stain 5 min. Immerse strips in series of 3 rinsing solns of 5% HOAc to remove excess dye. Rinse strips until only protein bands are left stained and remainder of strip is free from dye. Finally, blot strips and dry between several sheets of filter paper. Compare protein patterns of samples with those of authentic flesh samples.

Identification of Canned Pacific Salmon (*36*)—Official First Action

18.097 ***Apparatus and Reagent***

(**a**) *Microscopes*.—(*1*) Wide-field; and (*2*) compd, with variable iris diaphragm.

(**b**) *Glycerol jelly*.—To 60 mL H_2O add 5 g gelatin and heat gently until completely dissolved. Add 40 mL glycerol and 0.5 g phenol, and mix. Cool and store in closed container at room temp.

18.098 ***Method***

Empty entire contents of can into pan. Remove as much skin as possible from meat with aid of spatula and place skin in petri dish. Keep skin surface moist with H_2O at all times; if skin is allowed to dry, scales will curl, become brittle, and be unsuitable for mounting. Examine skin under wide-field microscope, using ca 10× magnification. Scales generally will be inside folds of skin (scale pockets) with portion of one end of scale protruding from pocket. Scan entire surface of all skin, and select largest and most nearly intact scales available. This is very important; if size difference is seen on same piece of skin, larger scales will have the most intact clear areas, and also internal scale pattern will be more complete.

Gently insert thin-tipped spatula well underneath whole scale between bottom side of exposed portion of scale and skin. Completely fold back this entire portion to make whole scale visible. Again, gently insert spatula between scale and skin and remove scale with back-and-forth motion. While keeping scale moist with H_2O, rub very gently with small tool, such as artist's brush, to remove any adhering skin or foreign material. Place small amt glycerol jelly on microscope slide and melt by placing slide on heat source. Pick up scale with spatula and remove any excess H_2O by touching gently to towel. Place scale in jelly and cover with cover glass. If scale curls during mounting, invert, uncurl, and cover quickly. Examine under compd microscope at 25–50×, using transmitted light. Adjust light intensity for optimum contrast of scale patterns.

Examine whole scales with intact clear areas, avoiding undeveloped, distorted, or damaged scales. Intact clear area must be present for accurate identification (except pink salmon). Det. salmon species by using key in Fig. **18:06** and by comparing to scales in Figs. **18:07–11** with pertinent features noted. Examine sufficient no. of scales to ensure pos. identification.

Precautions.—Use only scales that contain distinct wave striations and reticulations for comparison with key and photographs.

Scale patterns of coho and chinook species are somewhat similar. Circuli extending into clear area (coho), and wave striations in clear area (chinook) can be mistaken for each other. Note differences in Fig. **18:08** and **18:09**. Chinook scales may have only few striations. Follow key (Fig. **18:06**) carefully.

Chum and sockeye scales are both reticulated, but sizes and shapes of this feature differ. Under low (30×) power, chum reticulations appear globular, or like small round air bubbles; in sockeye they are netlike, 4–6 sided, and larger.

When pink salmon scales occur with reticulations and intact clear area, they may be differentiated from sockeye by their length. Vertical axis of pink is ≤3.5 mm; of sockeye, >3.5.

Relative size of scales (as length of vertical axis) is important in identification of all 5 species: chinook and chum have largest scales (7 and 6 mm, resp.), coho and sockeye scales are 4–5 mm, and pink salmon scales (easily recognized by their small size) are ≤3.5 mm.

Disregard scales which are damaged, have hard rib-like structure, or are distorted (all circuli surrounding focus are completely missing with this void extending about half way to scale edge).

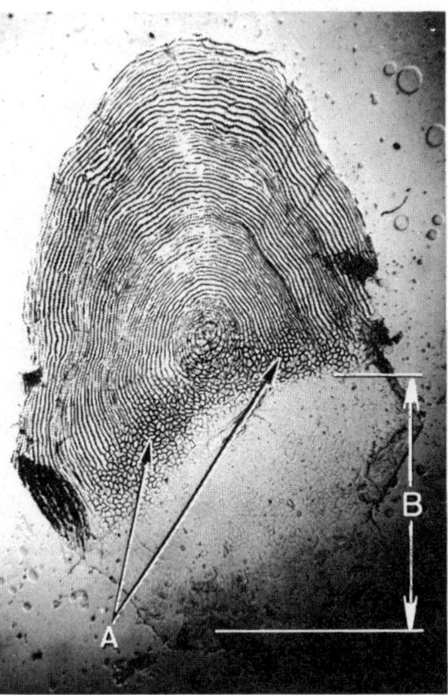

FIG. 18:07—Sockeye (red) salmon scale (*Oncorhynchus nerka*), 10×: A, Reticulations: Net-like divisions at junction of circuli and clear area; B, Clear area.

FIG. 18:08—Chinook (King) salmon scale (*Oncorhynchus tshawytscha*), 10×: A, focus (the area within first circulus). B, Wave striations (irregularly shaped nearly horizontal wavy lines in clear area).

FIG. 18:09—Coho (silver) salmon scale (*Oncorhynchus kisutch*), 10×: A, Circuli (concentric rings).

Note: For coho and pink as in above photo.
When circuli are present in clear area they extend from concentric pattern to form complete circle; if broken they are still in line of curvature of concentric ring.
For coho and sockeye as in above photo.
Circuli pattern (*near focus*) changes abruptly. Circuli closely spaced around focus, then abruptly become more widely spaced.

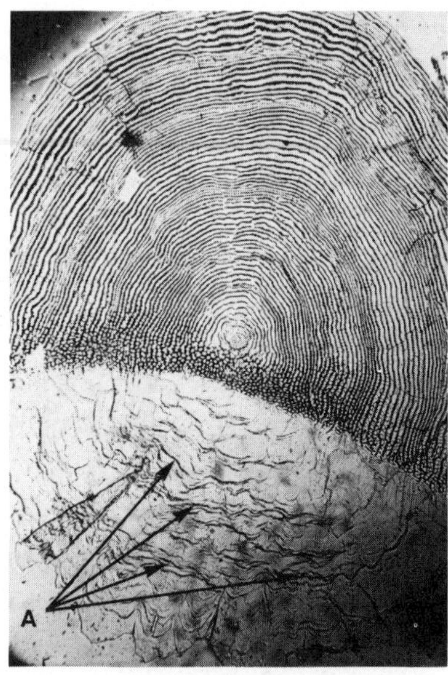

FIG. 18:10—Chum salmon scale (*Oncorhynchus keta*), 10×: A, wave striations (irregularly shaped nearly horizontal wavy lines in clear area).

Note: For chum and chinook as in above photo.
Wave striations are not connected to and are not in line with concentric rings of circuli and should not be confused with circuli.
For chum and pink as in above photo.
Circuli pattern (*near focus*) does not change abruptly but is nearly uniform.

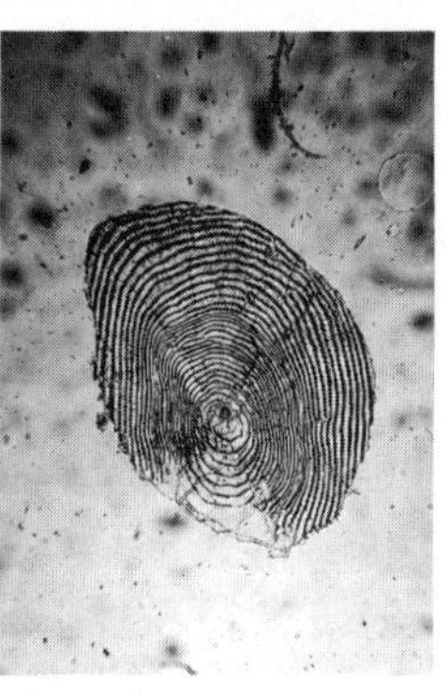

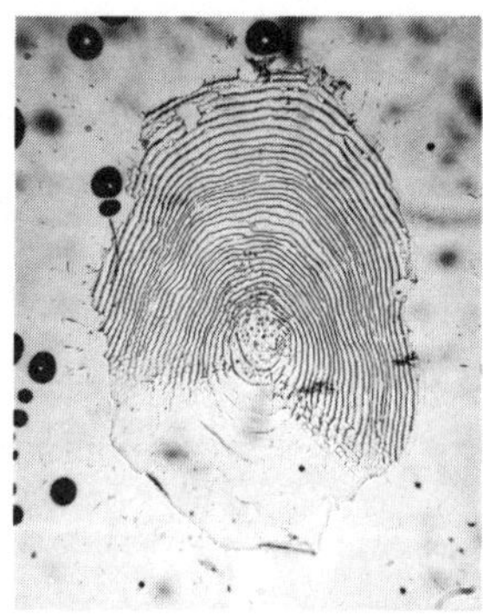

FIG. 18:11—Pink salmon scale (*Oncorhynchus gorbuscha*), 10×.

(Left) Pink scale with clear area mostly absent.

(Right) Pink scale with clear area present. Note broken circuli near focus extending into clear area.

SELECTED REFERENCES

(*1*) JAOAC **46,** 31(1963).
(*2*) JAOAC **54,** 640(1971).
(*3*) JAOAC **59,** 225(1976).
(*4*) JAOAC **53,** 1237(1970); **56,** 541(1973).
(*5*) JAOAC **20,** 70(1937); **21,** 85(1938); **35,** 218(1952); **36,** 608(1953); **38,** 194(1955); **59,** 312(1976).
(*6*) JAOAC **35,** 218(1952); **36,** 608(1953); **38,** 194(1955).
(*7*) CFR Title **21, 161.130**(c)(2)(i); JAOAC **36,** 947(1953); **38,** 194(1955).
(*8*) JAOAC **50,** 275(1967); **52,** 692(1969); **53,** 9(1970); **56,** 886(1973).
(*9*) JAOAC **53,** 9(1970); **56,** 886(1973).

(*10*) JAOAC **59**, 644(1976).
(*11*) JAOAC **60**, 963(1977).
(*12*) JAOAC **35**, 216(1952); **37**, 602(1954).
(*13*) JAOAC **20**, 71(1937); **35**, 218(1952); **36**, 608(1953); **37**, 607(1954); **44**, 276(1961); **46**, 744(1963).
(*14*) JAOAC **21**, 85(1938); **23**, 589(1940).
(*15*) JAOAC **56**, 598(1973).
(*16*) JAOAC **54**, 725(1971).
(*17*) JAOAC **20**, 410(1937); **23**, 589(1940).
(*18*) JAOAC **52**, 55(1969).
(*19*) JAOAC **31**, 334(1948).
(*20*) JAOAC **40**, 343(1957); **42**, 261(1959); **45**, 259(1962); **46**, 746(1963); **47**, 708(1964).
(*21*) JAOAC **31**, 98, 606(1948).
(*22*) JAOAC **52**, 688(1969); **54**, 1132(1971); **55**, 654(1972).
(*23*) JAOAC **21**, 684(1938); **25**, 176(1942); **28**, 644(1945); **33**, 848(1950).
(*24*) Biochem. Z. **51**, 253(1913); JAOAC **21**, 684, 688(1938).
(*25*) JAOAC **28**, 644(1945); **33**, 848(1950); **48**, 628(1965).
(*26*) JAOAC **56**, 271(1973).
(*27*) JAOAC **37**, 568(1954); **39**, 91, 609(1956).
(*28*) JAOAC **40**, 892(1957).
(*29*) JAOAC **60**,1125, 1131(1977).
(*30*) JAOAC **31**, 96, 507(1948).
(*31*) JAOAC **57**, 813(1974).
(*32*) JAOAC **42**, 263(1959).
(*33*) JAOAC **45**, 275(1962); **48**, 123(1965).
(*34*) JAOAC **50**, 282(1967).
(*35*) JAOAC **52**, 703(1969); **53**, 7(1970).
(*36*) JAOAC **52**, 696(1969); **55**, 648(1972); **62**, 722(1979).

19. Flavors

ALCOHOL

Gas Chromatographic Method (*1*)
Official First Action

19.001 ***Apparatus and Reagents***

(**a**) *Gas chromatograph.*—With flame ionization detector (F& M Model 400, 402, Hewlett-Packard 7600 series, or equiv.). Column 1.2 m (4′) × 2 mm id glass packed with 100–120 mesh Chromosorb 102; column temp. 160° (isothermal), detector and inlet 200°; He flow rate 50 mL/min; relative retention times: EtOH 1.00 (≤100 sec), *n*-PrOH 2.06, and tetrahydrofuran 3.04.

(**b**) *Integrator.*—Hewlett-Packard 3370A (new model 3370B), or equiv.

(**c**) *Alcohol std solns.*—Dil. 5, 10, 15, and 20 mL absolute alcohol at 60°F (15.56°C) to 100 mL with H_2O, adjusting final vol. at 60°F, to prep. 5, 10, 15, and 20% solns.

19.002 ***Determination***

Pipet 25 mL of each EtOH std soln into sep. flasks or bottles and add 1.00 mL *n*-PrOH internal std. Cap immediately with rubber stoppers, shake 3 min, and let stand 10 min at room temp. Inject 0.1 μL portions from 1 μL microsyringe. Det. peak areas with integrator, calc. ratio (*R*) of areas of EtOH to *n*-PrOH, and plot % EtOH as abscissa against *R* as ordinate. Slope should be 0.195±0.006.

Perform detn on sample as above but shake 10 min. If sample contains >20% EtOH, pipet 5 mL sample, 20 mL *tetrahydrofuran* (Fisher Scientific Co.), and 1 mL *n*-PrOH into flask or bottle. Analyze ≥1 std EtOH-*n*-PrOH soln daily as check on performance.

$$\%\ \text{EtOH} = (\text{EtOH peak area}/n\text{-PrOH peak area}) \times (1.00/\text{slope}) \times F,$$

where $F = 1$ for undild samples and 5 for dild samples.

VANILLA EXTRACT AND ITS SUBSTITUTES

19.003 Specific Gravity—Official Final Action

Det. sp gr at 20/20° with pycnometer as in **9.011**.

19.004 Alcohol—Official Final Action

Proceed as in **9.013** or **9.021**, but measure sample at 15.56° in pycnometer, Fig. **9:01**, calibrated at that temp.

19.005 ★ Glycerol—Official Final Action ★

Proceed as in **11.010★**, 12th ed., or **11.011★**, 12th ed., selecting method according to amt of sugar present. Use sample contg 0.1–0.4 g glycerol.

Propylene Glycol (*2*)—Official Final Action

19.006 ***Apparatus***

All-glass distn app. with ₮ 24/40 joints: 250 mL erlenmeyer, 20 mL Barrett H_2O trap with ₮ stopcock, and West condenser with drip tip.

19.007 ***Reagents***

(**a**) *Heptane.*—Eastman Kodak Co. practical grade, bp 96–100°, or equiv.

(**b**) *Potassium arsenite std soln.*—0.02*N*. (*Caution: See* **51.078** and **51.084**.) Dissolve 4.9460 g reagent As_2O_3, pulverized and dried to const wt at 100°, in 75 mL 1*N* KOH. Add 40 g $KHCO_3$, dissolved in ca 200 mL H_2O, and dil. with H_2O to 1 L at 25°. Dil. 200 mL of this soln to 1 L with H_2O.

(**c**) *Potassium periodate std soln.*—0.02*M*. Dissolve 4.6 g KIO_4 in ca 500 mL hot H_2O. Dil. to ca 900 mL with H_2O, cool to room temp., and dil. to 1 L. Stdze frequently, since this soln decomposes on standing.

(**d**) *Bromocresol purple indicator soln.*—Dissolve 0.1 g indicator in 100 mL alcohol and filter if necessary.

(**e**) *Propylene glycol.*—Reagent grade or com. product that meets following test: Dil. 0.5 mL to 25 mL with H_2O, add 25 mL 0.02*M* KIO_4 soln, and let stand 10 min. Titr. with 0.02*N* NaOH, using 3 drops bromocresol purple. Vol. NaOH soln consumed minus end point correction obtained by titrg 50 mL H_2O should be ≤0.1 mL.

19.008 ***Isolation of Propylene Glycol***

Place sample contg ca 1 g propylene glycol in 250 mL ₮ erlenmeyer; add enough H_2O, if necessary, to make total vol. 10 mL. Add 60 mL heptane, few glass beads, and/or SiC grains. Connect flask to receiver attached to condenser. Fill receiver with heptane, heat flask with variable heat hot plate, and reflux at such rate that rapid stream of distillate flows from tip. Reflux ca 8 hr and cool.

Open stopcock of receiver and transfer aq. layer to 250 mL (or other convenient size) vol. flask. Wash condenser, receiver, and solv. layer by pouring six 10 mL portions H_2O down condenser, collecting each portion in receiver, and draining it into vol. flask. Finally wash with enough H_2O (ca 25 mL) to completely fill receiver, causing solv. layer to return to distn flask. Dil. to vol. and mix well.

19.009 ***Determination***

(**a**) *Glycerol absent.*—Place aliquot of aq. soln contg ≤45 mg propylene glycol in g-s flask, add 35 mL 0.02*M* KIO_4 soln, dil. to ca 100 mL with H_2O, and let stand 1 hr. Add ca 1.0 g $NaHCO_3$, 0.5 g KI, and 2.5 mL starch indicator, **2.144(b)**. Titr. with 0.02*N* $KAsO_2$ soln to disappearance of blue. Stdze 25 mL 0.02*M* KIO_4 soln by same titrn, using H_2O for sample, and calc. amt of KIO_4 reduced by sample. 1 mL 0.02*N* $KAsO_2$ = 0.76 mg propylene glycol.

(**b**) *Glycerol present.*—Proceed as in (**a**). If I is not liberated on addn of $NaHCO_3$ and KI, insufficient KIO_4 was present. Repeat detn, using smaller aliquot or increasing vol. of KIO_4 soln.

To det. glycerol in the aq. soln, place same vol. aliquot used above in g-s flask, add 1 drop bromocresol purple, and add 0.02*N* NaOH until soln is light purple. Add same vol. KIO_4 soln used above, dil. to ca 100 mL, and let stand 1 hr. Add 10 drops propylene glycol (ca 0.5 mL), mix well, wash down sides of flask with H_2O, and let stand 10 min. Add 3 drops indicator and titr. with 0.02*N* NaOH to light purple end point. Titr. rapidly but do not shake flask vigorously in order to avoid excessive absorption of interfering CO_2 from air. Det. blank for this detn as above, using H_2O in place of sample and omitting 1 hr standing. Subtract blank from titrn obtained for sample aliquot. 1 mL 0.02*N* $KAsO_2$ = 0.46 mg glycerol; 1 mL 0.02*N* NaOH = 1.84 mg glycerol.

$$\text{mg Propylene glycol in aliquot} = [\text{mL } 0.02N\ KAsO_2 - (4 \times \text{mL } 0.02N\ \text{NaOH})] \times 0.76$$

★ Surplus method—*see* inside front cover.

Vanillin

19.010 ***Ultraviolet Screening Method* (3)**
Official Final Action

(*Caution: See* **51.016.**)

(In absence of coumarin and Et vanillin. Make all readings ≤2 hr of final diln.)

Pipet 5 mL sample (for imitations and concs, use 2 mL) into 100 mL vol. flask, dil. to vol. with H_2O, and mix well. Pipet 2 mL of this soln into second 100 mL vol. flask, add 2 mL 0.1*N* NaOH, and dil. to vol. with H_2O. Pour ca 20 mL of this soln into small beaker and place under UV lamp in dark room. If coumarin is present to extent of 0.01% in original ext, brilliant green fluorescence will develop in 5 min.

If no coumarin is observed, read *A* of remaining alk. soln at 270, 348, and 380 nm. Obtain background $A = 0.29A_{270} + 0.71A_{380}$. Subtract this value from A_{348} and divide by A' of 1 ppm vanillin (ca 0.150), detd from std soln of 3 ppm vanillin, and multiply by diln (1000) to give ppm vanillin in original sample.

Prep. 3 ppm std vanillin soln by dissolving 0.1000 g vanillin in 3 mL alcohol in 100 mL vol. flask, and dilg to vol. with H_2O (1 mL = 1 mg). Pipet 3 mL into 1 L vol. flask, add 2 mL 0.1*N* NaOH, and dil. to vol. with H_2O. Calc. corrected A' as above. Divide this value by 3 to obtain corrected A' of 1 ppm vanillin.

If background *A* is too high (>0.15), clarify with isopropanol as follows:

Pipet 5 mL sample into 50 mL vol. flask and dil. to vol. with isopropanol. Transfer to centrf. bottle and centrf. ca 10 min at high speed. Without disturbing sepd solids, carefully pipet 1 mL liq. into 100 mL vol. flask, add 2 mL 0.1*N* NaOH, dil. to vol. with H_2O, and proceed as above.

***Ultraviolet Spectrophotometric Method* (4)**
Official Final Action

19.011 ***Preparation of Standard Curve***

Dissolve 0.100 g vanillin in 5 mL alcohol and dil. to 100 mL with H_2O. Transfer 15, 10, and 5 mL, resp., to 250 mL vol. flask, dil. to vol. with H_2O, and mix (*Solns X*). Pipet 10 mL of each *Soln X* into 100 mL vol. flask, dil. to vol. with H_2O, and mix. Pipet another set of 10 mL *Solns X* into 100 mL vol. flasks, add ca 80 mL H_2O and 2 mL 0.1*N* NaOH, mix, dil. to vol. with H_2O, and mix again. Obtain *A* of alk. solns at 348 nm, using neut. solns as ref. blanks. Plot std curve.

19.012 ***Determination***

If sample contains >0.3 g vanillin/100 mL, dil. with 35% alcohol to below this level. Pipet 10 mL sample (or dild sample) into 100 mL vol. flask, dil. to vol. with H_2O, and mix. Pipet 2 mL dild soln into each of two 100 mL vol. flasks, dil. one to vol. with H_2O, and mix. To other flask add 80 mL H_2O and 2 mL 0.1*N* NaOH, mix, dil. to vol. with H_2O, and mix again. Det. *A* of alk. soln at 348 nm, using neut. soln as ref. blank. Obtain vanillin content from std curve.

Vanillin and Ethyl Vanillin (5)
Official Final Action

19.013 ***Reagents and Apparatus***

(**a**) *Mobile solvent.*—Cyclohexane (practical)-EtOAc-MeOH (100+30+20).

(**b**) *Immobile solvent.*—10% Dimethylformamide (DMF) in ether.

(**c**) *Sodium carbonate soln.*—Dissolve 4 g Na_2CO_3 in H_2O and dil. to 1 L.

(**d**) *Chromatographic paper.*—Whatman No. 3MM, 8 × 8″.

(**e**) *Chromatographic tank.*—Mitchell tank and equipment, **29.007**(**a**).

(**f**) *Spotting pipet.*—10 μL.

(**g**) *Longwave ultraviolet light.*—(*Caution: See* **51.016.**)

19.014 ***Preparation of Standard Curve***

Prep. solns of vanillin and Et vanillin in 35% alcohol contg 0.10, 0.15, 0.20, 0.30, and 0.40 g/100 mL. Draw parallel lines on chromatgc paper 2.5 and 3.7 cm above bottom edge, using hard pencil. Apply one 10 μL spot of each soln on the 2.5 cm line, keeping spots 2.5 cm apart and starting 5 cm from left side of paper. Use sep. papers for vanillin and Et vanillin curves. Use same micropipet for all spottings, rinsing thoroly before each application. Let spots air dry, without heat. Handle paper carefully near edges to avoid high blanks.

Meanwhile place 100 mL H_2O in bottom of chromatgc tank contg one trough. Fill trough with mobile soln., cover tank, and seal. Let stand 15 min. Dip paper into immobile solv. from top down to 3.7 cm line, leaving bottom 3.7 cm of paper free from immobile solv. Do not permit solv. to reach spots. (Dipping can readily be done by use of shallow pan contg solv.) Air dry paper few min, remove seal from tank, and place paper in tank with bottom edge dipping into mobile solv. Reseal tank and develop 2 hr, even tho solv. front reaches top before end of this period. Remove paper and air dry. Do not expose developed paper to air >1 hr. If delay is necessary, place paper in jar and store in refrigerator.

Expose paper to NH_3 fumes for few min by placing paper in wide-mouth half-gal. (2 L) jar contg small beaker with NH_3 on bottom, and capping jar. Examine paper under longwave UV light and outline dark blue areas with soft pencil. Et vanillin will show higher R_f value than vanillin. Remove marked areas with scissors and cut each into smaller pieces before placing them in 50 mL erlenmeyers. Cut out 2 blanks from side of paper, each approx. equal in area to developed spots. Use side area for these blanks, away from spotted areas and their developed rise.

Pipet 10 mL Na_2CO_3 soln into each flask, swirl, and let stand 10–15 min, with frequent swirling. Centrf. or filter thru rapid paper, discarding first portion of filtrate. Det. *A* at 348 nm, using Na_2CO_3 soln as ref. Also obtain av. *A* of the 2 blanks and subtract from std *A* before plotting std curve.

19.015 ***Determination***

If sample contains >0.4 g vanillin/100 mL, dil. below this level with 35% alcohol. Make one 10 μL spotting on the 2.5 cm line with same micropipet used to prep. std curves. Proceed as above and det. vanillin and Et vanillin by comparison with appropriate std curves.

Coumarin—Official Final Action

19.016 ★ ***Photometric Method* (6)** ★

See **19.009–19.011**, 10th ed. (*Caution: See* **51.068.**)

Vanillin, Ethyl Vanillin, and Coumarin (7)
Official Final Action

Chromatographic Separation Method

19.017 ***Apparatus***

(**a**) *Spectrophotometer.*—Capable of detg *A* at 270 and 325 nm. Adjust to high sensitivity to utilize slit width <10 nm.

(**b**) *Silica cells.*—1 cm. Match cells at 270 and 325 nm, using

★ Surplus method—*see* inside front cover.

isooctane-$CHCl_3$ solv., **19.018(c)**. (This solv. dets differences that other media do not.) Cells must be free of other solvs before adding isooctane-$CHCl_3$ solv., std, and sample solns. Drain each cell well between readings by inverting on towel. Fill cells for reading so that meniscus is >3 mm above light path.

(**c**) *Chromatographic tube.*—14 mm od × 450.

19.018 ***Reagents***

(Same batch of isooctane must be used to prep. solv. mixt. and all dilns for set of detns.)

(**a**) *Silicic acid.*—Reagent grade "100-mesh" powder, suitable for chromatgy (Mallinckrodt Chemical Works No. 2847, or equiv.). Det. SiO_2 content as follows: Accurately weigh ca 1 g silicic acid into weighed Pt crucible. Ignite in furnace 15 min at 615°, cool in desiccator, and reweigh. Calc. % SiO_2 (z) in silicic acid. Calc. wt silicic acid (x) required for 5.8 g column as: $x = 3.384 \times 100/z$. Vol. (mL) H_2O (y) required for column is $5.80 - x$.

(**b**) *Isooctane.*—Practical grade 2,2,4-trimethylpentane, 99.5+ %, bp 98–100°.

(**c**) *Isooctane-chloroform solvent mixture.*—Add 40 mL $CHCl_3$ to 1 L isooctane and mix. Store in airtight bottle. (Do not use rubber stopper.) Soln contains ca 3.85% $CHCl_3$.

(**d**) *Coumarin std soln.*—1 mg/mL. Accurately weigh 100 mg coumarin into 100 mL vol. flask, dissolve in 50 mL $CHCl_3$, and dil. to vol. with isooctane.

(**e**) *Ethyl vanillin std soln.*—Prep. as in (**d**), using Et vanillin.

(**f**) *Vanillin std soln.*—Prep. as in (**d**), using vanillin.

19.019 ***Determination of Absorptivities***

Pipet 1 mL vanillin std soln into 100 mL vol. flask, add 3.4 mL $CHCl_3$, dil. to vol. with isooctane, and mix. Det. A at 270 and 325 nm against solv., (**c**), as ref. in the 1 cm silica cells. Calc. a (g/L; 1 cm) for vanillin at 270 and at 325 nm as: $a = 100A$.

Det. a for Et vanillin and vanillin similarly.

19.020 ***Preparation of Chromatographic Column***

Pack small cotton wad in bottom of *dry* chromatgc tube. To x g silicic acid in mortar add y mL H_2O from buret, mix thoroly and quickly to uniform powdery consistency with pestle, and immediately add 25 mL solv., (**c**). Mix and rapidly pour slurry thru funnel into tube. Rinse mortar and funnel with small vol. solv. Remove any air bubbles formed by stirring with long thin glass rod. Pack column with ca 13.8 kPa (2 lb/sq in.; 10.4 cm Hg) air pressure until bottom of meniscus of free solv. just touches top surface of silicic acid but outer part of meniscus is still clearly visible. *Immediately release pressure*. (*Important:* If column channels or cracks, discard. During packing and thereafter, keep column vertical. Tipping ruins column for further use altho it may appear normal.) Carefully add 15 mL solv. down side of tube with aid of glass rod so column is not disturbed. Drive solv. thru column. Washed column is now ready for calibration.

19.021 ***Calibration of Column***

Pipet and combine 1 mL of each std soln, (**d**), (**e**), and (**f**), in 25 mL vol. flask. Dil. to vol. with isooctane and mix. Pipet 2 mL soln down one side of chromatgc tube onto top of column. Drive soln into column with ca 2 lb/sq in. (10.4 cm Hg) air pressure and collect eluate in 10 mL graduate. Release pressure when bottom of meniscus touches top of column and outer part of meniscus is still clearly visible. Pipet 1 mL solv., (**c**), down same side of tube onto column and drive into column. Repeat with 2 addnl 1 mL portions solv. Fill tube to within 2 cm of top with solv. Drive solv. thru column at rate of 5 mL/2–2.5 min, collecting 5 mL eluate fractions, alternating two 10 mL graduates during collection. Pour fractions into sep. test tubes in rack, numbering fractions consecutively. Drain graduate before reusing by inverting on towel. Collect 10 fractions and det. A at 270 and 325 nm against solv., (**c**), as ref. in 1 cm silica cells. Drain cells by inverting on towel before refilling; rinsing is not necessary. Permit column to elute by gravity while reading first 10 fractions, changing graduates for each 5 mL portion.

Coumarin elutes first, Et vanillin second, and vanillin third. In ideal column coumarin begins to elute in fraction 6–7, reaches max. in 8–9, and fades considerably in 10. Earlier elution does not sep. compds entirely; later elution takes more fractions and time but does give good recoveries. Somewhat slower elution does not matter. Et vanillin elutes in ca fraction 11–18, and vanillin in ca 19–30.

If column is satisfactory, collect 25 addnl fractions (35 in all) or until vanillin is completely eluted. Det. A of each fraction at 270 and 325 nm as above.

If coumarin begins to elute at fraction 5 or earlier, discard, prep. another column with less H_2O in the silicic acid, and recalibrate. If coumarin does not elute by fraction 9–10, prep. new column with more H_2O in the silicic acid.

Use calibrated column for identification, **19.023**

19.022 ***Preparation of Sample Solution***

If concn of none of the compds is >0.4 g/100 mL, pipet 25 mL sample into 250 mL centrf. bottle. If concn of any compd is >0.4 g/100 mL, dil. 25 mL sample with H_2O to vol. specified in Table **19:01**, and use 25 mL aliquot. Add 75 mL H_2O, 20 mL H_2SO_4 (1+4), and 50 mL $CHCl_3$. Stopper with rubber stopper and shake well 3 min. Centrf. 5 min at 1500 rpm. If emulsion persists, break with thin glass rod and recentrf. Pour contents slowly thru large-bore, short-stem funnel into 250 mL separator. Break emulsion with glass rod and drain $CHCl_3$ into 100 mL vol. flask. Pour aq. phase thru same funnel back into bottle.

Rinse separator with 15 mL $CHCl_3$, add to bottle thru funnel, and repeat extn by mixing phases thoroly with rocking motion. Do not shake vigorously as in first extn. Centrf., sep., and drain $CHCl_3$ into 100 mL vol. flask. Repeat extn with 15 mL portions $CHCl_3$ until flask is filled to mark. Pipet 2 mL aliquot into 25 mL vol. flask, dil. to vol. with isooctane, and mix.

19.023 ***Identification***

Pipet 2 mL sample soln (use 1 mL if concn of most abundant compd is >3.2 g/100 mL) onto prepd column, letting it flow down one side of tube without disturbing column. Drive soln into column with ca 2 lb/sq in. (10.4 cm Hg) air pressure and collect eluate in 10 mL graduate. Pipet 1 mL solv., (**c**), down same side of tube and drive into column. Repeat with 2 addnl 1 mL portions of solv. Fill tube with solv. and elute compds by same technic and conditions as for calibration. Collect 3 more fractions than indicated necessary by calibration. Det A of all fractions at 270 and 325 nm as in calibration.

Positions of absorbing fractions compared to those obtained during column calibration reveal compds present in sample.

Table 19:01 Dilutions and Dilution Factors for Flavorings

Concn of Most Abundant Constituent, g/100 mL	Dil. to: (mL)	Diln Factor (F)
<0.4	none	12.5
0.4–0.8	50	25.0
0.8–1.6	100	50.0
1.6–3.2	200	100
>3.2	400	200

Table 19:02 Spectrophotometric Characteristics of Coumarin, Ethyl Vanillin, and Vanillin

Coumarin	Ethyl Vanillin	Vanillin
	Maxima, nm	
271 (1.00)	270 (1.00)	269.5 (1.00)
282 (0.82)	297 (0.59)	296 (0.60)
313 (0.46)	—	—
	Minima, nm	
243 (0.30)	242.5 (0.24)	242.5 (0.24)
278.5 (0.81)	286 (0.46)	286 (0.48)
291.5 (0.31)	—	—

Coumarin is also identified by absorbing at 325 nm slightly >⅓ its A at 270 nm. Vanillin and Et vanillin absorb very little at 325 nm. If desired, confirm by obtaining UV spectrum of one high absorbing fraction of each compd. Compare with spectra prepd on same instrument. Spectra of compds exhibit approx. max. and min. given in Table **19:02**. Approx. ratio of A at given wavelength to that at highest max. for respective compd is given in parentheses after that wavelength. Ratio of 1.00 indicates highest max.

19.024 ***Determination***

Add A at 270 nm of all fractions contg coumarin and calc. coumarin concn in original sample:

$$c = F \times \Sigma A/a,$$

where ΣA is sum of A at 270 nm of fractions contg coumarin, a is absorptivity of coumarin at 270 nm, c is concn coumarin in g/100 mL original sample, and F is diln factor, given in Table **19:01**.

Calc. concns of Et vanillin and vanillin similarly.

If neg. A are obtained on fractions not contg the compds, correct A of fractions contg compds by adding to each A the av. of the neg. readings.

Lead Number (Wichmann) (*8*)
Official Final Action

19.025 ***Principle***

Org. acids from vanilla are pptd with neut. $Pb(OAc)_2$ under std conditions, insol. Pb salts are removed, and excess Pb is detd by chelometric titrn with Na_2EDTA. From this titrn and blank titrn, Wichmann lead number is calcd. Applicable to single-fold exts.

19.026 ***Reagents***

(**a**) *Disodium ethylenediamine tetraacetate* (*Na_2EDTA*) *std soln.*—0.025*N*. Dissolve 9.3061 g $Na_2EDTA.2H_2O$ in 1 L boiled, cooled CO_2-free H_2O.

(**b**) *Buffer soln.*—Mix 2 vols 0.1*N* NaOAc with 1 vol. 0.1*N* HOAc.

(**c**) *Xylenol orange soln.*—Dissolve 0.1 g xylenol orange in 100 mL 35% alcohol.

(**d**) *Lead acetate soln.*—Dissolve 8 g neut. $Pb(OAc)_2$ in 100 mL boiled H_2O, let stand 24 hr, and use clear supernate.

(**e**) *Phenolphthalein soln.*—Dissolve 0.1 g phthln in 100 mL alcohol.

19.027 ***Preparation of Sample Solution***

Place 175 mL boiled H_2O in 1 L r-b distn flask. From pipet add 25 mL clear $Pb(OAc)_2$ soln and 50 mL single-fold ext. Swirl to mix thoroly and ppt Pb salt. Support distg flask on asbestos or transite board, placing flask over 10 cm diam. hole cut in board to permit distn without overheating upper portion of flask. Fit with distn head and condenser, apply moderate heat, and distil 200 mL into vol. flask, reserving distillate for detn of alcohol. When vol. in distn flask is reduced to ca 50 mL, level of liq. should be approx. even with board. Quant. transfer residue to 100 mL vol. flask with small vols CO_2-free H_2O, using bent glass rod with rubber tip to loosen residue. Cool, and dil. to vol. with CO_2-free H_2O. Mix thoroly and filter thru dry paper. Filtrate (*Soln X*) contains excess Pb after forming Pb salt complex.

Prep. blank, using 5 drops HOAc in place of sample and distil 150 mL. Cool, dil. to 100 mL with boiled H_2O, and filter.

19.028 ***Determination of Lead***

(**a**) *As sulfate.*—Pipet 10 mL *Soln X* into 250 mL beaker and add 25 mL H_2O, 2 mL H_2SO_4 (1+1), and 100 mL alcohol; stir and let settle overnight. Filter on gooch, wash with alcohol, ignite at 525–550°, cool in desiccator, and weigh. (Wt $PbSO_4$ obtained from blank − wt obtained from sample) × 13.66 = Pb number.

(**b**) *As chromate.*—Pipet 10 mL *Soln X* into 400 mL beaker and add 2 mL HOAc, 25 mL H_2O, and 25 mL ca 0.1*N* $K_2Cr_2O_7$. Heat immediately with moderate flame until ppt changes from yellow to orange. Filter on gooch, and wash thoroly with hot H_2O, then with few mL each of alcohol and ether. Dry at 100°, cool in desiccator, and weigh. (Wt $PbCrO_4$ obtained from blank − wt obtained from sample) × 12.82 = Pb number.

(**c**) *By chelometric titration.*—Pipet 10 mL *Soln X* into 125 mL erlenmeyer. Add 1 drop phthln and make just alk. with 1.0*N* NaOH, pptg $Pb(OH)_2$. Add 10 mL buffer soln and 1 mL xylenol orange indicator. Titr. with 0.025*N* Na_2EDTA soln to end point, indicated by abrupt change from reddish pink to yellow or orange. Ten mL microburet is convenient for titrn, and fluorescent lamp should be arranged so indirect light illuminates flask.

Perform titrn on blank soln in same manner.

Lead number = 20 × (mL Na_2EDTA blank − mL Na_2EDTA sample) × 0.025 × (207.2/1000) = (mL Na_2EDTA blank − mL Na_2EDTA sample) × 0.1036.

19.029 Total Solids (*9*)—Official Final Action

Proceed as in **31.007** or **31.008**, using 10 mL sample.

19.030 Ash—Official Final Action

Evap. 10 mL ext and proceed as in **31.012** or **31.013**.

19.031 Sucrose (*10*)—Official Final Action

See **31.025**, **31.026**, or **31.031**.

Vanilla Resins

19.032 ***Quantitative Method (11)***
Official Final Action

Pipet 50 mL sample into 150 or 250 mL beaker and dil. to 100 mL with H_2O. Boil rapidly on hot plate or over flame to ca 50 mL. Cool, and add NH_4OH (1+3) dropwise until slightly alk. Add 3 drops excess and stir vigorously 2 min to ensure soln of resins. Add HCl (1+1) dropwise, with stirring, until acid to indicator paper and then 2 mL excess. Stir, and let stand at room temp. ≥1 hr but ≤24 hr. Add 0.5 g filter-aid (Celite, Hyflo Super-Cel) and filter with suction thru long stem, medium porosity, 30 mL, fritted glass buchner funnel contg pad prepd by pouring aq. suspension of 1 g filter-aid thru funnel and washing with H_2O. If filtration slows, gently scratch surface of pad to break resin film. Quant. transfer resins to funnel with aid of policeman, using six 20 mL portions 0.05*N* HCl to wash beaker and funnel. Let each portion of wash soln drain before adding next. Dry material as much as possible by suction, transfer funnel to dry suction flask, and dissolve resins from filter with boiling alcohol added in small portions, using some of alcohol to rinse beaker. Suck each portion thru funnel before adding next. Mix filter-aid in funnel with the hot alcohol, using small glass rod. Repeat extns until alcohol soln is colorless. Rinse tip of funnel stem with hot alcohol and quant. transfer soln to weighed beaker or Pt dish. Evap. to dryness on steam bath and dry 1 hr at 100°. Cool in desiccator and weigh. Report results to 2 decimal places only. Reserve resins for qual. tests.

19.033 ***Paper Chromatographic Qualitative Test (12)—Official First Action***

Sep. and dissolve resins in warm alcohol as in **19.032**, collecting alc. ext in 50 mL vol. flask. Cool, and dil. to vol. with alcohol. Evap. 40 mL aliquot to dryness on steam bath and dry to const wt at 100° to obtain mg resins/mL alc. ext. (Alternatively, use *value* obtained from **19.032**. Do not use dried resins obtained from **19.032** for this detn.) Evap. 5 mL aliquot of alc. ext nearly to dryness on steam bath and complete drying with aid of gentle heat such as warm air current from hair dryer. Dissolve residue in calcd vol. of 0.1*N* NaOH in 50% alcohol to give soln of 5 mg resins/mL.

Spot 6 μL alk. soln (using two 3 μL spottings with intervening drying) on 8 × 8" paper as in **19.039(a)**. Develop as in **19.040**, using solv. systems **19.037(a)** or **(b)**. On same paper spot alk. soln of alc. ext of resins from authentic vanilla ext, **19.038**, at same concn, 5 mg/mL. Compare developed patterns under longwave UV light.

19.034 Methanol—Official First Action

Proceed as in **9.089** or **9.090**, using distillate from alcohol detn, **19.004**.

19.035 Color Insoluble in Amyl Alcohol (*13*) Official First Action

Evap. 25 mL sample just to dryness on steam bath. Dissolve residue in H_2O and alcohol, and dil. to 50 mL, using total vol. of 26.3 mL alcohol. Place 25 mL of this soln in separator and add 25 mL freshly shaken Marsh reagent, **9.094**, shaking gently so as not to form emulsion. Let layers sep. completely, drain aq. lower layer (which contains any caramel present) into 25 mL graduate, and dil. to vol. with alcohol (50% by vol.). Compare this soln in colorimeter with 25 mL untreated sample. From this reading, calc. % color insol. in amyl alcohol.

Foreign Plant Material

Paper Chromatographic Method (14) *Official Final Action*

19.036 ***Apparatus***

(**a**) *Chromatographic chamber for small papers.—See* **29.007(a)**.

(**b**) *Chromatographic chamber for large papers.*—Use box suitable for this size paper chromatgy. A satisfactory box is ca 29.5 × 21.5 × 23.75" (75 × 55 × 60 cm) covered with Formica or other material resistant to org. solvs, acid, alkali, etc. Lid of box is hinged and plastic gasket is used to obtain tight seal to prevent escape of vapors. Front of box contains window 11 × 17" (28 × 43 cm) to observe progress of solv. front. Semicircular glass troughs ca 26.5 × 2" (67 × 5 cm) are supported by stainless steel clamps on metal strips ca 2" (5 cm) wide placed 2.5" (6 cm) from top and extending from front to back along sides. Clamps also support glass rods on both sides of trough and parallel to it.

(**c**) *Chromatographic papers.*—Whatman No. 1, 8 × 8"; Whatman No. 1, 22 × 18"; Whatman No. 3MM, 8 × 8".

(**d**) *Ultraviolet light.*—Long wavelength. Two 15 watt Black Light tubes, 18" long, preferably enclosed in glass filters (such as No. 5873 tubular glass filters, George W. Gates & Co., Hempstead Tnpk & Lucille Ave, Franklin Sq., NY 11010). (*Caution: See* **51.016**.)

19.037 ***Solvent Systems***

(**a**) Dissolve 20 g KOH and 50 g KBr in H_2O, add 200 mL alcohol, and dil. to 1 L with H_2O.

(**b**) Dissolve 20 g $KHCO_3$ and 50 g KBr in H_2O, add 200 mL alcohol, and dil. to 1 L with H_2O.

(**c**) Shake 20 parts isobutanol, 0.8 part HOAc, and 15 parts H_2O in separator, let sep., and drain and discard lower layer. Use upper layer.

(**d**) Mix 8 parts isopropanol, 5 parts NH_4OH, and 15 parts H_2O.

(**e**) Mix 30 parts HOAc, 3 parts HCl, and 10 parts H_2O.

(**f**) Dissolve 20 g $KHCO_3$ in H_2O, add 200 mL alcohol, and dil. to 1 L with H_2O.

(**g**) Mix 75 parts isopropanol with 25 parts H_2O.

19.038 ***Preparation of Authentic Vanilla Extract***

Prep. single-fold authentic vanilla ext with and without added sugar by either NF or Flavoring Extract Manufacturers Association (FEMA) method. Prep. concs by evapg single-fold ext under vac. in rotary evaporator and dilg with 50% alcohol to appropriate vol.

(**a**) *NF method.*—Cut 100 g vanilla beans in small pieces, add 200 mL H_2O, and macerate 12 hr in covered container, preferably in warm place. Add 200 mL alcohol, mix well, and macerate ca 3 days. Transfer mixt. to percolator contg 200 g coarse granular sucrose (omit sucrose for prepn without sucrose) and drain. Pack solids firmly and percolate slowly with alcohol (1+1) to obtain total vol. of 1 L.

(**b**) *FEMA method* (Proc. 40th Flavoring Extract Manufacturers Association Convention 1949, pp. 49–67 (as revised)).—(Boil all rubber stoppers in 5% NaOH soln and use Tygon tubing for connections.) Prep. laboratory continuous percolator as follows:

Fit 2-hole rubber stopper into neck of custom-made Pyrex gas washing bottle made from No. 2962 cylinder, 4.5 od × 12" long (11.4 × 30.5 cm), plain neck opening ca 3" (7.6 cm) diam., with coarse porosity fritted glass disk sealed in as close to bottom as possible but above side arm, 9 mm od, extending out from side wall between disk and base (available from Corning Glass Works or H. S. Martin Co., 1916 Greenleaf St, Evanston, IL 60204). Thru one hole place 0–220°F (−20–110°C) thermometer with bulb at ca center of bottle; thru other hole insert short piece of glass tubing so that end is 2.5 cm above level of chopped vanilla beans. Attach piece of 100 mesh stainless steel wire cloth tied with cord to end of tubing in bottle as strainer and attach other end to Fischer & Porter Co. Flowrator Meter, Model 10A 1017A (tube ¼" to meter liq., sp gr 0.96, 700 mL/min max., direct reading scale, stainless steel float). Attach upper end of flowmeter with right-angle bend tube to side arm of T-tube with upper end connected with Tygon tubing to glass tube in 1-gal. (3.8 L) jar fitted with 2-hole rubber stopper. Other hole of stopper holds glass tube fitted with Bunsen valve (rubber tube, closed at one end, with short longitudinal slit) as safety valve. Place gal. jar above rest of equipment (serves as overflow reservoir when percolator runs overnight).

Attach lower end of T-tube thru Y-tube and 1-hole rubber stoppers to 2 Pyrex buchners (connected in parallel) with coarse porosity fritted disks (80 mm diam., Corning No. 36060-C). Place circles of Whatman 41H paper on disks, and cover with 3 mm clean sand. Place stems of funnels thru rubber stoppers inserted in filter tubes (Corning No. 9480, 32 × 160 mm). Tubes are connected in parallel with Tygon tubing to Y-tube connected to menstruum reservoir (Corning No. 1220, 2 L aspirator bottle) with 45° bend glass tube thru 2-hole rubber stopper. Thru second hole, fit stem of thermoregulator (No. 17502–0, stainless steel, Fenwal, Inc., PO Box 309, Ashland, MA 01701) which controls 200 watt mantle fitted to reservoir. Connect mantle to thermoregulator thru relay. Connect outlet of bottle to inlet of stainless steel pump with nipple connections (Model B 1, 1/20 h.p., LFE Corp., Fluids Control Div., 100 Skiff St, Hamden, CT 06514, or equiv.). Control flow rate by pinch clamp on tubing from discharge side of pump to bean reservoir, to give flow rate of 575 mL/min. Set thermoregulator so thermometer reads 120°F (49°C).

Cut vanilla beans into 3 mm pieces with razor blade, or preferably shred in Model D Fitzpatrick Comminuter, or equiv., using No. 4 screen (The Fitzpatrick Co., 832 Industrial Dr, Elmhurst, IL 60126). Place 10 oz (280 g) dry wt cut beans (calcd from moisture detn) in extractor, and place several 8 cm, 90° bends of glass rod on surface to keep beans submerged. Place dild alcohol (1136 g alcohol plus 1090 g H_2O) in reservoir. Percolate ≥16 hr and remove 25 mL sample for alcohol detn, **19.004**. Calc. g H_2O to add to give 47.5% alcohol (= 2790 − 132414/% alcohol), add this amt to reservoir, and continue percolation at least addnl 24 hr.

Drain ext from both reservoirs and remove 25 mL sample for alcohol detn. Det. vol. remaining ext, and calc. vol. H_2O needed to adjust to 35% alcohol. If desired, add sugar equiv. to 10%, det. final vol., and dil. to 35% alcohol with H_2O.

19.039 ***Preparation of Papers***

(**a**) *For 8 × 8" papers, single dimension development.*—Use Whatman No. 1 for ext with little or no sugar, and No. 3MM for ext with considerable sugar. Apply no more than 7 samples, including authentics, to single paper. Spot samples equal distance apart. For single strength exts apply four 3 μL spots at same point, drying between applications with hair dryer, IR lamp, or other source of mild heat. Do not apply next spot until previous one is dry. For concd exts, dil. to 4-fold concn with 50% alcohol and apply one 3 μL spot.

For products contg large amts of sugar, ext 1 mL with 1 mL $CHCl_3$, centrf., and spot $CHCl_3$ ext as above. Compare with authentic ext treated similarly. (JAOAC **44**, 549(1961).)

(**b**) *For 22 × 18" papers, single dimension development.*—For single strength exts, apply four 10 μL spots at same point with intervening drying as in (**a**). For concd exts, dil. to 4-fold concn with 50% alcohol and apply one 10 μL spot.

(**c**) *For 8 × 8" papers, two dimension development.*—Use Whatman No. 3MM paper. Apply four 3 μL spots of single strength vanilla ext sample at lower right side of 8 × 8" paper and eight 3 μL spots at lower left side, locating each spot ca 2.5 cm from outer edges of paper. Apply each set of spots at same point, drying between applications with warm air dryer or other source of mild heat. Do not apply next spot until previous one is dry.

19.040 ***Development***

(**a**) *Single dimension.*—Use ascending technic with small papers and descending technic with large papers. Use solvs (**a**), (**b**), (**c**), (**d**), or (**e**), listed in approx. order of usefulness. Develop small papers 2–3 hr and large papers 12–16 hr until solv. approaches end of paper. Remove papers from tank and let air dry. Examine under transmitted UV light and compare fluorescent pattern of spots from samples with those from authentic material.

It is sometimes useful to return dry paper to original solv. and repeat development. Second development may cause greater sepn of some fluorescent constituents.

(**b**) *Two dimension.*—Transfer papers, prepd as in **19.039(c)**, to tank, and develop first dimension with solv. (**f**) and ascending technic. Remove paper when solv. front reaches upper edge, and air dry. Turn paper 90° so that 24 μL spot is at bottom; then develop second dimension in solv. (**g**). Remove paper before front reaches developed 12 μL spot, and air dry. Examine paper under longwave UV light, and compare chromatogram with one made from authentic vanilla ext. Foreign plant material is indicated by spots not found in authentic ext.

Flavoring Additives

Thin Layer Chromatographic Method (15)
Official Final Action

19.041 ***Apparatus***

(**a**) *Applicator.*—For depositing thin layer on glass plates.

(**b**) *Glass plates.*—8 × 8" or 2 × 8"; of uniform thickness.

(**c**) *Plastic board.*—22 × 113 cm, with retaining edges 1.8 cm wide along short and long sides.

(**d**) *Developing jars or tanks.*—Use equipment, **29.007(a)**, for 8 × 8" glass plates and glass cylinders for small plates. Cylinders can be covered with plastic caps.

19.042 ***Reagents***

(**a**) *Solvents.*—Hexane (99%)-EtOAc (4+1); benzene-MeOH (97+3).

(**b**) *Chromogenic agents.*—(*1*) Mix 90 mL 0.1*N* $KMnO_4$ and 10 mL 0.1*N* NaOH. (*2*) Sat. 1*N* HCl with $N_2H_4.H_2SO_4$. (*3*) 5% KOH in MeOH. (*4*) 10% phosphomolybdic acid in alcohol.

(**c**) *Silica Gel G.*—Fine grade silica gel with added plaster of Paris. Check ability to make satisfactory sepns by testing activated plates with known mixts of additives.

19.043 ***Test***

Place glass plates on plastic board held on laboratory bench so that long edge faces worker and short retaining ledge is on right. Mix 30 g Silica Gel G in beaker with 60 mL H_2O, stirring thoroly ca 1 min. Slurry must be uniform and free from air bubbles. Pour into applicator, which is on glass plate at left side of board. Make film 0.250 mm thick by slowly moving applicator across row of plates. Total time from addn of H_2O to silica gel until end of spreading operation must be ca 4 min. Air dry plates 10–20 min and then dry 2 hr at 110° to activate layers. Cool, wipe backs and edges of plates free from excess silica gel, and store plates in storage cabinet. Protect from laboratory fumes.

Scratch line across a plate 17 cm from bottom edge and apply 10 μL spot of single-fold sample 2 cm from bottom edge. Spots should be ca 0.5 cm in diam. (It may be necessary to apply small portion at time, drying between applications.) Different samples can be spotted 2 cm apart. Apply ref. stds similarly. Place plate in jar or tank so that bottom edge dips 1 cm into solv. and lean top of plate against side of jar or tank, so that plate has slight angle. Cover tank or jar and let develop to 17 cm scratch line. Remove from solv. and air dry.

All additives, if present in sufficient amt, can be detected by $KMnO_4$ spray. Tan spots appear on pink background, which soon turns brown. Second spraying helps bring out spots. Small amts of coumarin may not show up for several min, so that it is necessary to examine plate ca 10 min after spraying.

Yellow spots are shown by *p*-hydroxybenzaldehyde, vanillin, Et vanillin, veratraldehyde, and piperonal when plates are sprayed with $N_2H_4.H_2SO_4$ soln. Let air dry and examine under reflected UV light (longwave). *p*-Hydroxybenzaldehyde usually shows up as lemon-yellow spot, vanillin and Et vanillin appear orange to brown, veratraldehyde is bright orange, and piperonal is bluish-yellow. Shades depend on amts of additive present and amt of spray, and may vary somewhat.

To detect coumarin, spray with alc. KOH, and let air dry. Examine under reflected UV light; coumarin appears as bright blue-white spot.

Vanitrope can be detected by spraying with phosphomolybdic acid soln. Blue spot develops after plate is dried at 100° few min.

Approx. R_f values, with vanillin = 1, are: Hexane-EtOAc solv.: Et vanillin, 1.6; veratraldehyde, 1.7; coumarin, 2.3; piperonal, 3.0; and vanitrope, 4.0. Benzene-MeOH solv.: *p*-hydroxybenzaldehyde, 0.4; Et vanillin, 1.4; coumarin, 1.7; veratraldehyde, 1.9; piperonal, 2.4; and vanitrope, 2.4.

p-Hydroxybenzaldehyde is difficult to detect with hexane-EtOAc solv. since vanillin spot is near origin. With this solv., Et vanillin and veratraldehyde cannot usually be sepd. *p*-Hydroxybenzaldehyde can be detected with benzene-MeOH solv., and Et vanillin and veratraldehyde show good sepn, but piperonal and vanitrope appear at same R_f value. These can be distinguished by phosphomolybdic acid and $N_2H_4.H_2SO_4$ tests on sep. plates.

Organic Acids

Paper Chromatographic Sorting Method (16)

19.044 ***Apparatus***

(**a**) *Chromatographic tank*.—For ascending chromatgy with 12 × 12" sheets; cylindrical glass jar with ground top and glass plate cover, or rectangular jar with tight lid. Use smallest jar that will hold paper. (Neoprene gasket may be used to ensure tight fit.)

(**b**) *Chromatographic paper*.—Whatman No. 1, 12 × 12".

19.045 ***Reagents***

(**a**) *Developing soln*.—Ether-HCOOH-H_2O (20+4+3). If necessary, add HCOOH in small amts until soln is clear.

(**b**) *Chromogenic agents*.—(*1*) *Aniline-furfural*.—Dissolve 0.3 mL aniline and 0.3 mL furfural in 100 mL acetone. Use as dip. Hang paper in air until spots are fully developed (red spots on pink background). For spray use, replace acetone with MeOH. (*2*) *Aniline-xylose*.—Dissolve 1 g xylose in 3 mL H_2O, add 57 mL MeOH, and mix. Add 1.0 mL aniline and 40 mL acetone, and mix. (Dip or spray.) Hang paper in air 5 min to let excess solv. evap.; then place in oven 10 min at 105° (stable brown spots on tan background). (*3*) *pH indicators:* (*a*) Dissolve 0.02 g bromocresol purple in 10 mL alcohol and dil. to 100 mL with acetone. Add NH_4OH dropwise until soln is red by transmitted light. Use as dip, and air dry. Repeat until best contrast is obtained. If used as spray, replace acetone with alcohol. (*b*) Dissolve 0.02 g bromocresol green in 10 mL alcohol and dil. to 100 mL with acetone. Add 1*N* NaOH until soln is blue-green by transmitted light. Use as dip. For spray use, replace acetone with alcohol.

19.046 ***Determination***

(*Caution: See* **51.059**.)

Place 10 mL single strength vanilla ext, or equiv. of concd ext dild to 10 mL with 35% alcohol, in 50 mL centrf. tube and add 25 mL alcohol. Mix, add 2.5 mL $Pb(OAc)_2$ soln (8 g/100 mL), mix thoroly, and centrf. Decant clear supernate. Wash residue twice with 10 mL portions 80% alcohol, mixing well each time and discarding clear wash. Disperse ppt in 10 mL H_2O (no lumps) and pass in H_2S 5 min. Filter thru small rapid paper into beaker and wash ppt twice with small portions H_2O satd with H_2S. Mix ppt well with each wash to break up all large clumps. (Filtrate should be clear.) Evap. nearly to dryness on steam bath, using air jet if desired. Complete drying carefully and remove from heat as soon as dry. Cool, and take up with exactly 1 mL H_2O, warming gently if necessary.

Spot 12 μL soln on 12 × 12" paper, 2.5 cm from bottom and 4 cm from side edge, by applying four 3 μL portions at same place and drying between applications with warm air. Spot different samples 4 cm apart. Hang paper in rectangular jar with lower end dipping 1 cm into solv. If cylindrical jars are used, roll paper and connect edges slightly apart (use stainless steel clips or cotton thread to connect). If small jars are not available, equilibrate by adding large excess of solv. to larger jars and let stand overnight before inserting paper. (Line larger jars with blotting paper with lower edge immersed in solv.) Cover jars with weighted covers or seal with tape. Develop, preferably at 20–23°, until front is 2.5 cm from top (ca 6 hr; spottings can be made in afternoon and development started early next day).

Air dry overnight. To ensure complete removal of HCOOH, steam paper, without wetting, by rolling and inserting into 15 cm stove-pipe section with bottom over rapid source of steam (paper must not touch sides). Steam 15 min, remove, and air dry. Treat with one of chromogenic agents, (**b**), by dipping or spraying ((**b**)(*1*) preferred for initial tests). Mark spots with pencil, indicating weak and strong spots, and compare pattern with authentic vanilla org. acid sample treated simultaneously. Note position, size, and intensity of acid spots. Vanilla ext org. acid chromatogram will show 4 strong spots and several weak ones.

Derivative Gas-Liquid Chromatographic Method (17)—Official Final Action

19.047 ***Apparatus***

(**a**) *Vials*.—5 mL, with screw caps provided with Teflon liners. (Other plastic or metal liners are not satisfactory.)

(**b**) *Gas chromatograph*.—Varian Aerograph Model 1520, dual column, and thermal conductivity detectors, at 225° and 200 ma (or equiv.). Operating conditions: 1.8 m (6') × ¼" stainless steel column packed with 3.8% SE-30 on 60–80 mesh Diatoport S (silanized) (Varian Associates, 611 Hansen Way, Palo Alto, CA 94303), programmed at 6°/min, from 75 to 210°; injector temp. 225°; He gas flow 40 mL/min; sample injection 5 μL; attenuation, to give 50% chart width response to internal std.

Other equipment may be used with following conditions: thermal conductivity detector temp. 225–275°; injection port temp. 200–300°; programming rate 6–10°/min; He flow 40–60 mL/min; sample injection 5–25 μL. (Flame ionization detectors may also be used, with proper adjustment of sample size and sensitivity.)

19.048 ***Reagents***

(*Note:* Tri-Sil reagent and pyridine may be harmful. *Caution:* Protect skin and eyes when using. Use effective fume removal device.)

(**a**) *Neutral lead acetate soln*.—Dissolve 8 g $Pb(OAc)_2.3H_2O$ in H_2O and dil. to 100 mL with H_2O.

(**b**) *Internal std soln*.—Dissolve 0.100 g glutaric acid in 80% alcohol and dil. to 100 mL with 80% alcohol. Store in tightly closed bottle.

(**c**) *Tri-Sil reagent*.—Pyridine soln of trimethylchlorosilane (TMS) and hexamethyldisilazane (10+1+2) (available as Tri-Sil 48999, Pierce Chemical Co.). Use to prep. TMS derivatives.

19.049 ***Determination***

Transfer 2.0 mL single-strength vanilla ext to 15 mL screw-cap centrf. tube, and add ca 0.2 g Celite 545 and exactly 1.0 mL internal std soln. Mix, and add 0.7 mL $Pb(OAc)_2$ soln; mix again, and add 5.0 mL alcohol. Cap tube, mix, and centrf. at moderate speed until ppt is well packed and supernate is clear. Discard supernate, add 5.0 mL 80% alcohol to ppt, mix, and centrf. again. Discard clear supernate and repeat washings twice more, using 5.0 mL alcohol for first wash and 5.0 mL ether for second. Each time mix thoroly, cap, centrf., and discard clear supernate. Drain ether for few min; then place tube in 50–55° H_2O bath. Stir residue with stainless steel wire until most of ether is removed and solid material in tube appears dry and powdery. Brush any powder adhering to wire into tube and place open tube in 100° oven 1 hr. Remove tube from oven, cool somewhat, add 3 pieces of *Drierite*, and cap tightly. Inject 1.5 mL Tri-Sil reagent into cool tube from 2 mL syringe, recap, and mix thoroly, making sure that all residue in tube is wet with pyridine soln. Place tube in 37° oven 1 hr, with occasional mixing. Centrf. and decant clear supernate into dry 5 mL vial contg several pieces of Drierite. Cap tightly with Teflon-lined screw cap.

Inject sample into gas chromatograph and program as in **19.047(b)**. Compare sample curve with curves of authentic vanilla exts obtained under same conditions. Authentic vanilla exts show many peaks, with 8 major ones. Internal std appears between peaks 1 and 2. Peak 7 is always highest peak in pure vanilla samples. Sum of 8 peak hts, calcd on basis of internal std peak ht = 1.00, provides useful information on amt of vanilla acids present. Ratio peak 2:peak 7 also provides significant information. Note also presence or absence of foreign peaks. If some peaks are too high for measurement, repeat detn with greater attenuation.

(*Note:* TMS derivatives tend to break down with heat, and continued use may impair column efficiency. Also, artifacts occur sometimes, particularly on first run of day. Columns usually can be reconditioned by overnight heating at 250° with slow stream of He. Disconnect column from detector when performing such reconditioning. Special regenerating liqs (e.g., Silyl-8, Pierce Chemical Co.) are also available for injection into columns used for TMS work. Heating thermal conductivity detectors at higher temps, without current, helps keep them free from decomposition products.)

Direct Gas Chromatographic Method (18)
Official Final Action

19.050 ***Gas Chromatograph***

Use gas chromatograph with thermal conductivity or flame ionization detector. Temps: Program column from 70 to 250° at 4°/min, injector 240°, detector 240°. Columns: 6 m × ⅛" stainless steel or Cu, packed with 3% silicone oil (SE-30, SF-96, OV-1, or OV-101) on silanized 100–120 mesh Chromosorb W, acid-washed and dichlorodimethylsilane-treated, or Gas-Chrom Q; He carrier gas flow 30–35 mL/min. Alternatively, use 1.8 m × ¼" column with same packing material at flow rate of 60–80 mL/min.

19.051 ***Reagents***

(a) *2-Methyl butane (isopentane)*.—Bp 27.5–28.5° (less pure grades may be purified by passing thru silica gel and distg). Reagent blanks should show no peaks in test. (*Caution: See* **51.011** and **51.039**. Isopentane is very flammable. Evap. in fume hood away from sparks and open flame.)

(b) *Internal std*.—0.2% hexadecane in absolute alcohol.

19.052 ***Determination***

Place 100 mL single-fold vanilla ext (dil. stronger exts with 35% alcohol to single-fold) in 250 mL separator or g-s cylinder, add 0.5 mL internal std and 40 mL isopentane, and gently invert 10–15 times. Vigorous agitation may result in emulsions. Let layers sep. and transfer clear upper layer to dry flask. Remove upper layer by aspiration or by decantation from separator after draining lower colored layer. Repeat extn twice with 40 mL isopentane. Add 1 g anhyd. Na_2SO_4 to flask, shake, and decant soln thru small glass wool plug into beaker. Rinse flask with small amt solv.

Evap. carefully on warm H_2O bath under hood until solv. is reduced to ca 5 mL. (*Caution: See* **19.051(a)**.) Transfer to 15 mL graduated centrf. tube with small amts solv., add small boiling chip, and immerse tube in warm H_2O to remove solv. When solv. is reduced to 0.5 mL, transfer tube to beaker contg acetone and ice, and let vanillin ppt. When upper layer is clear, transfer this soln to small container with Teflon cap or liner, using syringe or glass tube drawn out to capillary tip at one end. If desired, this soln can be further concd to ca 0.2 mL. Chromatograph as soon as possible after concg. Do not let conc. remain overnight before chromatgy.

Inject into chromatograph, using cooled syringe to avoid premature volatilization of solv. Sample size depends on sensitivity of instrument; use ca 2 μL with flame ionization and 10–15 μL with thermal conductivity detector. Adjust instrument to obtain ca 50% deflection with internal std, which shows peak shortly after vanillin peak. Use pure vanilla ext samples as comparison stds. Added aromatics over 10 ppm will be detected as foreign peaks.

LEMON, ORANGE, AND LIME EXTRACTS AND FLAVORS

19.053 Specific Gravity—Official Final Action

Det. sp gr at 20/20° with pycnometer as in **9.011**.

Alcohol

19.054 ***Specific Gravity Method (19)***
Official Final Action

(Applicable to exts consisting only of oil, alcohol, and water)

Det. sp gr at 15.56/15.56° or at 20/20° as in **9.011** and oil content as in **19.065**, **19.066**, or **19.126**, and apply following formula: Let S represent sp gr of sample; O, sp gr of oil; and p, % oil found. Then $(100 - p)$ = % H_2O-alcohol soln, sp gr of which, represented by P, is:

$$S = [Op + P(100 - p)]/100;$$

therefore

$$P = (100S - Op)/(100 - p).$$

Det. E, alcohol equiv. of P, from **52.003**. It gives % alcohol in alcohol-H_2O soln. To find % alcohol in ext, apply following formula:

$$\% \text{ by vol. of alcohol in ext} = E[1 - (p/100)].$$

Value of O for lemon oil may be taken as 0.86 and for orange oil as 0.85.

19.055 ***Gas Chromatographic Method***
Official First Action

See **19.001–19.002**.

19.056 ★ Methanol—Official Final Action ★

See **19.047**, 10th ed.

Isopropanol—Official Final Action

Applicable to Lemon Extract in Absence of Acetone (20)

19.057 ***Preparation of Sample***

Place sample contg ≤8 g total alcohols (approximation of alc. content may be made from sp gr detn and ref. to **52.003**), into separator in stem of which is cotton pledget wet with H_2O. Add 25 mL 10% NaCl soln and 25 mL pet ether. Shake well, let layers sep., and drain lower layer into flask. Repeat extn with 3 addnl 25 mL portions NaCl soln or until alcohol is completely extd. Add H_2O to combined aq. exts until vol. is ca 150 mL. Connect flask to vertical condenser and distil into 100 mL vol. flask, removing flask when distillate is 2–3 mL below mark. Dil. to vol. and mix.

19.058 ***Qualitative Test for Acetone***

To 2 mL distillate add 0.5 mL *5% alc. o-nitrobenzaldehyde soln* and 1 mL 10% NaOH soln. Mix; then shake with small vol. $CHCl_3$. If $CHCl_3$ turns blue, acetone is present.

19.059 ***Determination***

Pipet 10 mL distillate into 500 mL erlenmeyer contg 50 mL ca 2*N* $K_2Cr_2O_7$ and add 100 mL H_2SO_4 (1+3). Stopper flask, swirl, and let stand 30 min. Add 100 mL *30% $FeSO_4.7H_2O$ soln*. Connect flask to vertical condenser thru foam trap. Slowly distil ca 100 mL into 500 mL vol. flask contg 200–300 mL cold H_2O. Dil. to vol., mix, and pipet 25 mL into g-s flask contg 25 mL 1*N* NaOH; add 50 mL stdzd 0.1*N* I with swirling. Let stand 15 min. Add 26 mL 1*N* HCl and at once titr. residual I with stdzd 0.1*N* $Na_2S_2O_3$, adding starch soln when I color is nearly discharged. Each mL 0.1*N* I consumed in reaction = 1.001 mg isopropanol.

Applicable to Lemon and Orange Flavors in Presence of Acetone (21)

19.060 ***Apparatus***

Glassware.—Use foil-wrapped stoppers or preferably all-glass still. Provide condenser with adapter which reaches several inches into vol. flask.

19.061 ***Preparation of Sample***

Proceed as in **19.057**, placing 100 mL vol. flask in ice-H_2O bath.

19.062 ***Determination of Acetone***

Pipet aliquot preferably contg 0.1–0.3 g acetone into 100 mL vol. flask and dil. to vol. with H_2O. Det. *A* at 265 nm with H_2O as ref. soln in Beckman Model DU (current model 24/25) spectrophtr, or equiv. Correct for *A* of H_2O in same cell as used for sample, if necessary. Det. amt of acetone in the 100 mL vol. flask by ref. to std curve prepd from redistd acetone.

In absence of purified acetone, g acetone/100 mL may be estd as $C = A/3.08$, where C = g acetone/100 mL, A = corrected *A* in 1 cm cell, and 3.08 = assumed *A* of 1 g/100 mL soln of acetone in 1 cm cell. Calc. to g acetone/100 mL sample.

19.063 ***Determination of Isopropanol***

Proceed as in **19.059**, distg ca 100 mL into 250 mL vol. flask contg ca 100 mL cold H_2O and held in ice-H_2O bath. Dil. to vol. with H_2O and det. corrected *A* as in **19.062**. Det. amt of acetone in 250 mL vol. flask by ref. to std curve prepd as in **19.062**.

In absence of purified acetone, g acetone/250 mL may be estd as $C' = 2.5A/3.08$, where C' = g acetone/250 mL, 2.5 = diln factor; *A* and 3.08 are defined in **19.062**. Calc. to g acetone/100 mL sample. Deduct amt of free acetone as detd in **19.062**, and multiply by 1.035 to obtain g isopropanol/100 mL sample.

19.064 ***Glycerol—Official Final Action***

Proceed as in **11.010★**, 12th ed., or **11.011★**,12th ed., selecting method according to amt of sugar present. Use sample contg 0.1–0.4 g glycerol.

Oils of Lemon and Orange in Extracts

19.065 ***By Polarization (22)—Official Final Action***

Without dilg, polarize sample at 20° in 200 mm tube. Divide reading in °S, **31.020(a)**, by 3.2 for lemon ext and by 5.2 for orange ext. In absence of other optically active substances, result will be % oil by vol. If sucrose is present, det. as in **19.077** and correct reading accordingly. To obtain % oil by wt from % by vol., multiply vol. % by 0.86 for lemon exts, and by 0.85 for orange exts, and divide results by sp gr of original ext.

19.066 ***By Precipitation (23)—Official Final Action***

Pipet 20 mL sample into Babcock milk bottle, **16.060(a)**. Add 1 mL HCl (1+1), then 25–28 mL H_2O previously warmed to 60°. Mix, and let stand 5 min in H_2O at 60°. Centrf. 5 min, fill bottle with warm H_2O to bring oil into graduated neck of flask, again centrf. 2 min, and place flask in H_2O at 60° few min. Note % oil by vol. If >2% oil is present, add 0.4% to % oil noted to correct for solubility of oil. If <2% but >1% is present, add 0.3% for this correction. To obtain % oil by wt from % by vol., multiply vol. % by 0.86 for lemon exts, and by 0.85 for orange exts, and divide result by sp gr of original ext.

19.067 ***By Precipitation in Presence of Mineral Oil—Official First Action***

Proceed as in **19.126**.

Oils of Lemon, Orange, or Lime in Oil Base Flavors

By Steam Distillation (24)—Official Final Action

19.068 ***Apparatus***

(a) *Steam generator filled with H_2O.*—Oil can holding 1 gal. (3.8 L) will serve purpose.

(b) *Distillation flask.*—750 mL Kjeldahl flask with short neck; total ht ca 25 cm.

(c) *Spray tube.*—Glass tube connected to steam generator; with small perforated bulb at end of tube passing thru rubber stopper and reaching bottom of distn flask.

(d) *Bent glass tube.*—Approx. 8 mm diam. Connects distn flask to upright condenser. Shape of this tube allows vapor condensing in tube to return to distn flask.

(e) *Liebig condenser.*—With 500 mm H_2O jacket.

(f) *Wilson receiving flask.*—(Fig. **19:01**.) Babcock test bottle shape with graduated neck but of 250 mL capacity and with vertical glass outlet tube sealed on near bottom. Upper end of outlet tube is turned down. Neck may consist of portion of buret graduated from 0 to 25 mL with flared top. Outlet tube is ca 3 mm diam.; end is at such ht that when flask is filled with H_2O, meniscus in neck will be between 0 and 1 mL marks.

★ Surplus method—*see* inside front cover.

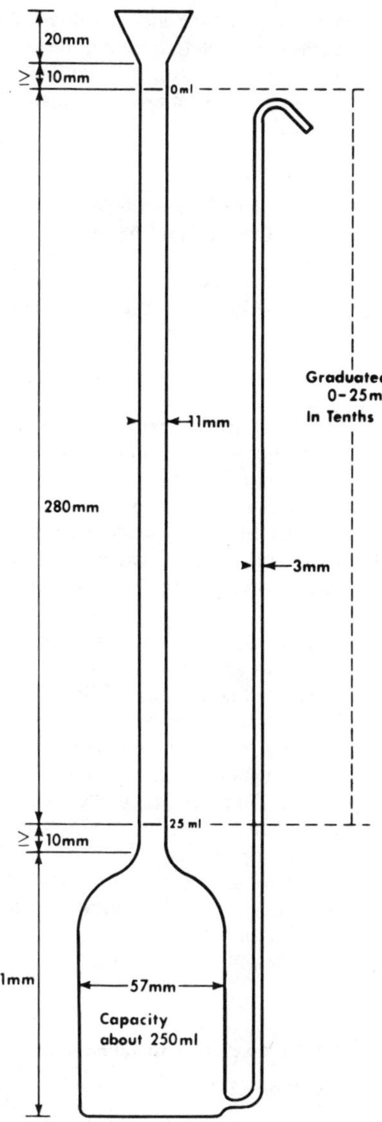

FIG. 19:01—Wilson flask

19.069 ***Determination***

Measure 100 mL sample in graduate and transfer to distn flask. Immerse flask in H_2O bath and connect to condenser with the bent glass tube. Fill receiving flask with H_2O and so place under condenser that end of condenser is ca 1 cm above level of H_2O in receiving flask. Place 200 mL graduate under end of outlet tube to catch displaced liq. Heat H_2O bath to bp and pass steam thru sample until 200 mL liq. collects in graduate.

Disconnect app., let receiving flask stand 15 min, or until sepn of oil is complete, and read vol. of oil in flask. Calc. % (by vol.) of essential oil in sample by dividing reading by 0.90 for lemon oil in corn and cottonseed oils, 0.95 for orange oil in corn and cottonseed oils, and 0.78 for distd or expressed lime oil in corn and cottonseed oils. Where menstruum is mineral oil, subtract 0.3 mL from reading before dividing by factors 0.90, 0.95, and 0.78 for lemon oil, orange oil, and lime oil, resp.

19.070 By Polarization (25)—Official First Action

Polarize sample at 20° in 200 mm tube, making 5 readings. From av. of readings in °S, **31.020(a)**, subtract: for corn oil +0.6°, for cottonseed oil −0.3°, for peanut oil +0.2°, and for mineral oil +5.5°, as correction for rotatory effect of menstruum. To obtain % by vol. of essential oil in mixt., divide corrected polariscopic reading so obtained by factor 3.4 for lemon oil in corn oil, 3.7 for lemon oil in cottonseed oil, 3.6 for lemon oil in peanut oil, 3.5 for lemon oil in mineral oil, 5.4 for orange oil in corn oil, 5.7 for orange oil in cottonseed oil, 5.6 for orange oil in mineral oil, 2.0 for lime oil in corn oil, 2.3 for lime oil in cottonseed oil, and 2.2 for lime oil in mineral oil.

Total Aldehydes (*26*)—Official Final Action

19.071 ***Reagents***

(**a**) *Aldehyde-free alcohol.*—Let alcohol, contg 5 g *m*-phenylenediamine.2HCl/L, stand ≥24 hr with frequent shaking. (Nothing is gained by previous treatment with KOH.) Reflux at least 8 hr, longer if necessary; let stand overnight, and distil, rejecting first 10 and last 5 mL distillate. Store in dark, cool place in well filled bottles. (25 mL of this alcohol, on standing 20 min at 14–16° with 20 mL of the fuchsin-bisulfite soln, should develop only faint pink tinge. If stronger color develops, repeat above *m*-phenylenediamine treatment.) (Avoid skin and eye contact and breathing *m*-phenylenediamine dust.)

(**b**) *Fuchsin-bisulfite soln.*—Dissolve 0.5 g fuchsin in 250 mL H_2O, add aq. soln contg 16 g SO_2, let stand until colorless or nearly so, and dil. to 1 L with H_2O. Let stand 12 hr before use and keep in refrigerator. (This soln may deteriorate and should be reasonably fresh when used.)

(**c**) *Citral std soln.*—1 mg/mL. Weigh 0.5 g citral into 50 mL vol. flask, dil. to vol. with aldehyde-free alcohol at room temp., stopper flask, and mix by shaking. Dil. 10 mL of this soln with aldehyde-free alcohol to 100 mL in vol. flask, stopper, and mix.

19.072 ***Determination***

Weigh ca 25 g sample in stoppered weighing flask, transfer to 50 mL vol. flask, and dil. to vol. at room temp. with aldehyde-free alcohol. Measure, at room temp., 2 mL (or other suitable vol.) of this soln into comparison tube. Add 25 mL aldehyde-free alcohol (previously cooled to 14–16°), then 20 mL fuchsin-bisulfite soln (also cooled), and dil. to 50 mL with aldehyde-free alcohol. Mix thoroly, stopper, and keep 15 min at 14–16°.

Prep. std for comparison at same time and in same manner, using 2 mL std citral soln, and compare colors developed. Calc. amt of citral present and repeat detn, using amt sufficient to give sample ca strength of the std. From this result calc. amt of citral in sample. If comparisons are made in Nessler tubes, stds contg 1, 1.5, 2, 2.5, 3, 3.5, and 4 mg citral may be prepd and trial comparison made against these, final comparison being made with stds lying between 1.5 and 2.5 mg with 0.25 mg increments.

It is absolutely essential to keep reagents and comparison tubes at required temp., 14–16°. If comparisons are made in a bath (possible only when bath is of glass), use stds within 25 min after adding fuchsin-bisulfite soln. Treat samples and stds identically.

Citral (*27*)—Official Final Action

(Lemon and orange exts)

19.073 ***Reagent***

Metaphenylenediamine hydrochloride-oxalic acid soln.—(*Caution:* Avoid skin and eye contact and breathing *m*-phenylenediamine dust.) Remove interfering colored impurities in *m*-phenylenediamine.2HCl by digesting 3–5 g ca 5 min with ca 25 mL alcohol, decanting, and repeating 3 times. Dry crystals short time on steam bath. Dissolve 1 g in ca 45 mL 85% alcohol, dissolve 1 g crystd oxalic acid in 45 mL 85% alcohol, and pour

2 solns into 100 mL vol. flask. Add 2 or 3 g fuller's earth, dil. to vol. with 85% alcohol, mix, and filter thru double folded paper.

19.074 ***Determination***

Weigh 25 g sample into 50 mL vol. flask, dil. to vol. with alcohol (95% by vol. for exts made with the oils; 50–95% by vol. for terpeneless exts), and mix. Pipet 2 mL or other suitable vol. of this soln into colorimeter tube, add 10 mL reagent, dil. to suitable vol., and compare resulting color with colors of set of stds contg known amts of citral std soln, **19.071(c)**.

19.075 Total Solids—Official Final Action

Proceed as in **9.022**, using 10 mL sample measured at 20°.

19.076 Ash—Official Final Action

Ignite residue from 10 mL sample as in **31.012** or **31.013**.

19.077 Sucrose—Official Final Action

Neutze normal wt of sample, evap. to dryness, wash several times with ether, dissolve in H_2O, and proceed as in **31.025**, **31.026**, or **31.031**.

LEMON AND ORANGE OILS

19.078 Specific Gravity—Official Final Action

Det. sp gr at 20/20° with pycnometer as in **9.011**.

19.079 Refractive Index—Official Final Action

Use any std instrument, making reading at 20°. *See* **28.008**.

19.080 Optical Rotation—Official Final Action

Det. rotation at 20° with any std instrument, 50 mm tube, and Na light. State results in angular degrees on 100 mm basis. If instruments having sugar scale are used, reading for orange oils is above range of scale, but readings may be obtained by use of std levorotatory quartz plates, or by 25 mm tube. (True rotation cannot be obtained by dilg oil with alcohol and correcting rotation in proportion to diln.)

19.081 Spectrophotometric Absorbance Characteristics (*28*) Official Final Action

Accurately weigh 1 g (to nearest mg) sample in g-s weighing bottle. Dissolve in alcohol and transfer quant. to 100 mL vol. flask. Dil. to vol., mix well, and pipet 25 mL aliquot into another 100 mL vol. flask, dil. to vol. with alcohol, and mix well.

Det. A of the prepd soln in UV region from 260 to 375 nm with recording or manual (5 nm intervals) spectrophtr against alcohol in matched cell. (Readings at closer intervals (ca 3 nm) are preferred between 305 and 320 nm. Above 325 nm readings can be made at intervals of 10 nm.)

If instrument does not read directly in A, calc. from % T from tables or as $A = 2 - \log \%T$. Plot A against wavelength and draw smooth curve thru points.

Correct for background A as follows: Draw straight (base) line tangent to curve at point of min. A near 285 nm (285–295 nm) and at inflection point where curve levels off at ca 365 nm (365–370 nm). Drop vertical line CD from absorption peak (ca 315 nm) to baseline. Obtain length of vertical line CD in A units and record as corrected A.

19.082 Physical Constants of 10 Per Cent Distillate (*29*) Official Final Action

Place 50 mL sample in 3-bulb, 120 mL Ladenburg flask having main bulb 6 cm diam. and condensing bulbs 3.5, 3, and 2.5 cm. Distance from bottom of flask to opening of side arm should be 20 cm. Distil oil at rate of 2 mL/min until 5 mL distils. Det. refractive index and optical rotation of this distillate as in **19.079** and **19.080**.

Residue after Steam Distillation (*30*) Official Final Action

19.083 ***Apparatus***

Use steam distn assembly, Fig. **18:02**, except use 250 mL distg flask.

19.084 ***Determination***

Add 50 mL H_2O and 15 mL sample to 250 mL distn flask. Weigh 15 mL oil delivered by same pipet to obtain wt sample. Place steam inlet tube in flask, heat contents of flask just to bp, and connect inlet tube to steam. Adjust flame so that H_2O level remains approx. const. Steam distil at const rate of ca 200 mL/hr until 100 mL H_2O collects. Discontinue distn and let flask partially cool; then decant contents into 125–250 mL separator, and drain.

Rinse flask twice with 15 and 8 mL portions alcohol, warming if necessary to dissolve any residue. Pour alcohol rinsings into tared 150 mL beaker. Ext cooled liq. in separator with 25 and 20 mL portions $CHCl_3$. (Add 1–2 drops HCl (1+2) to separator if there is any tendency for liqs to emulsify.) Add exts to tared beaker contg alcohol washings. Ext once with 25 mL ether and add this ext to others. Evap. exts carefully without spattering on cover of steam bath until ether and $CHCl_3$ are removed. Then evap. residual liq. on open steam bath. Let beaker remain on bath 15 min after odor of alcohol disappears. Remove, wipe outside of beaker with clean dry cloth, let cool, and weigh. Reheat, cool, and weigh until loss is <2 mg/5 min heating period. Calc. % residue by steam distn.

Total Aldehydes—Official Final Action

19.085 ***Hiltner Method (27)***

Accurately weigh ca 2 g lemon oil or 8 g orange oil into 100 mL vol. flask, dil. to vol. with alcohol, and proceed as in **19.074**, using 2 mL dild soln for comparison.

Kleber Method (31)

(For orange oil)

19.086 ***Reagent***

Phenylhydrazine soln.—Prep. 10% soln in absolute alcohol. Sufficiently pure phenylhydrazine can be obtained by distg com. product *in vacuo*, rejecting first portions coming over that contain NH_3. (*Caution: See* **51.015**.)

19.087 ***Determination***

Accurately weigh ca 15 g sample into small, g-s flask, and add 10 mL phenylhydrazine soln. Let stand 30 min at room temp. and titr. with 0.5*N* HCl, using Me or Et orange indicator. Similarly titr. 10 mL phenylhydrazine soln. Difference in mL 0.5*N* acid used in these 2 titrns × 0.076 = wt citral in sample. If end point is difficult to detect, titr. until soln is distinctly acid, transfer to separator, and drain alc. portion. Wash oil with H_2O, adding washings to alc. soln, back-titr. with 0.5*N* alkali, and make necessary corrections.

Kirsten Modification of the Kleber Method (32)

(For lemon oil)

19.088 ***Reagents***

(**a**) *p-Toluenesulfonic acid*.—0.5*N*. Dissolve 95 g *p*-toluenesulfonic acid ($CH_3C_6H_4SO_3H.H_2O$) in absolute alcohol and dil. to 1 L with absolute alcohol. Mix thoroly and filter. Stdze against 0.5*N* NaOH, using Me red.

(**b**) *Methyl yellow indicator*.—Dissolve 0.1 g *p*-dimethylaminoazobenzene in 100 mL absolute alcohol. (*Caution: See* **51.085**.)

19.089 ***Determination***

Accurately weigh ca 15 g sample into 125 mL g-s flask and pipet in 10 mL phenylhydrazine soln, **19.086**. Let stand 30 min at room temp. and add 25 mL benzene. Titr. with 0.5*N* *p*-toluenesulfonic acid, using 0.2 mL Me yellow. Similarly titr. 10 mL phenylhydrazine soln. Difference in mL 0.5*N* acid used in 2 titrns × 0.076 = g citral in sample.

Hydroxylamine Method (30)

(For lemon oil)

19.090 ***Reagents***

(**a**) *Bromophenol blue indicator*.—Dissolve 0.1 g bromophenol blue in 5 mL 0.05*N* NaOH and dil. to 100 mL with 60% alcohol.

(**b**) *Ethyl orange indicator*.—Dissolve 0.05 g Et orange in 60% alcohol and dil. to 50 mL.

(**c**) *Potassium hydroxide std soln*.—0.5*N*. Dissolve 28.06 g KOH in 60% alcohol and dil. to 1 L with same solv. Stdze against std HCl.

(**d**) *Hydroxylamine soln*.—Dissolve 7.0 g $H_2NOH.HCl$ in 175 mL 60% alcohol. Add either: (*1*) 0.3 mL bromophenol blue indicator and enough 0.5*N* KOH to give permanent blue soln, or (*2*) 0.3 mL Et orange and enough 0.5*N* KOH to give permanent yellow soln. In either case dil. resulting soln to 200 mL with 60% alcohol.

19.091 ***Determination***

Weigh, to nearest 10 mg, ca 10 g sample into g-s 50 mL graduate and add 7 mL hydroxylamine soln and 0.1 mL indicator. Shake and neutze liberated acid with 0.5*N* KOH to permanent full alk. color of indicator used. Continue shaking and neutzg until permanent alk. color remains in lower layer after shaking mixt. vigorously 2 min and letting sep. (Reaction is complete in ca 15 min.) 1 mL 0.5*N* KOH = 0.0761 g citral.

This titrn approximates citral in the oil. Repeat detn as above, using as color std for end point titrd liq. of first detn, and as vol. $H_2NOH.HCl$ soln 1–2 mL more than vol. 0.5*N* KOH used in first detn.

Esters (*32*)—Official Final Action

(For lemon oil)

19.092 ***Apparatus***

Expeller.—Prep. rubber stopper with glass inlet and outlet tubes similar to wash bottle. Adjust outlet tube to just reach bottom of centrf. bottle and place soda-lime tube between inlet tube and source of air.

19.093 ***Reagents***

(**a**) *Aldehyde-free isoamyl alcohol*.—Reflux ca 1 L reagent grade isoamyl alcohol over 35–40 g KOH 60–70 min. Distil in all-glass app., reject first 25 mL distillate, and collect next 850 mL. Store at ca 5°.

(**b**) *Sodium chloride soln*.—Dissolve 160 g NaCl in 500 mL H_2O.

(**c**) *Carbon dioxide-free water*.—Use freshly boiled and cooled H_2O thruout detn.

19.094 ***Determination***

Weigh 5 mL oil in beaker or bottle and transfer to 125 mL separator, using 25 mL alcohol to complete transfer. Add 1 mL *50% $H_2NOH.HCl$ soln* and few drops phthln, and mix. Add, from buret or graduated pipet, enough 4% KOH in 80% alcohol to make soln just pink and add drop or so excess. Add 1 drop 20% $H_2NOH.HCl$ soln and shake; pink should be discharged. Add 25 mL isoamyl alcohol and shake. Add 50 mL NaCl soln, shake vigorously, let layers sep. (line of division should be sharp), drain, and discard lower layer. Repeat extn with four 30 mL portions NaCl soln and once with 6 mL H_2O, draining and discarding exts each time. Drain remaining isoamyl alcohol-oil layer into 500 mL erlenmeyer. Wash separator once with 25 mL Et alcohol and combine with soln in flask. Add phthln, make liq. just pink with ca *0.2N stdzd KOH*, and then add from pipet exactly 20 mL std KOH in excess.

Reflux soln 45 min on hot plate; then cool with flask loosely stoppered. Add ca 150 mL H_2O and rotate ca 30 sec, but avoid violent shaking. Transfer liq. into 500 mL separator thru short-stem funnel, rinse flask with 20 mL H_2O, and add to separator. Stopper funnel and let layers sep. Drain lower layer into original flask. Add ca 60 mL H_2O to separator, invert, and rotate to mix; then let layers sep. until most of aq. layer seps. (Small layer of emulsion may remain between layers.)

Drain aq. layer into flask, retaining any emulsion in separator. Keep flask and separator stoppered between addns to avoid contact with air. Add ca 100 mL H_2O to separator, shake vigorously, and drain entire contents into 250 mL centrf. bottle. Stopper, and centrf. until 2 well sepd layers are obtained. Blow off lower layer in centrf. bottle, using expeller, into flask contg aq. fractions previously sepd, add ca 0.2 mL phthln, and titr., using *stdzd 0.2N HCl*. As end point approaches, repeat addn of indicator and titr. to disappearance of pink. (Liq. becomes white or grayish.)

Conduct blank detn similarly, using same amts of all reagents. Subtract titrn of sample from that of blank to obtain equiv. of 0.2*N* alkali consumed. 1 mL 0.2*N* alkali = 39.2 mg esters as linalyl acetate.

Pinene (*33*)—Official Final Action

19.095 ***Qualitative Test***

(*Caution:* Ethyl nitrite may be harmful. Avoid contact with skin and breathing vapor.)

Mix 10% distillate, **19.082**, with 5 mL HOAc, cool mixt. thoroly in freezing bath, and add 10 mL *Et nitrite*. Add 2 mL HCl (2+1) slowly with const stirring. Keep mixt. in freezing bath 15 min. Collect crystals formed on filter, using suction, and wash with alcohol. Return combined filtrate and washings to freezing bath 15 min. Collect addnl crystals formed on original filter. Wash combined crops of crystals thoroly with alcohol. Dry at room temp. and dissolve in min. vol. of $CHCl_3$. Add MeOH to $CHCl_3$ soln, little at time, until nitrosochlorides crystallize out. Mount sepd and dried crystals in olive oil and examine under microscope. Pinene nitrosochloride crystals have irregular pyramidal ends; limonene nitrosochloride crystallizes in needles.

ALMOND EXTRACT

Alcohol—Official First Action

19.096 ***Method I (34)***

Fill 50 mL pycnometer with sample at 15.56°, and empty into separator contg ca 10 g NaCl. Wash out pycnometer several times with satd NaCl, using total of ca 100 mL. Ext twice with 50 mL portions pet ether (bp 40–60°). Collect pet ether ext in second separator and wash with two 25 mL portions satd NaCl soln. Combine original NaCl soln with washings, add little *powd pumice*, and distil into 100 mL pycnometer (Fig. **9:01**). When almost 100 mL collects, dil. to vol. with H_2O at convenient temp. and det. alcohol from sp gr as in **9.013**, using table, **52.003**.

19.097 ***Method II (35)***

Det. sp gr of ext at 15.56/15.56° or at 20/20° as in **9.011** and benzaldehyde content as in **19.099**. Apply formula given in **19.054**, using benzaldehyde content as % oil found.

19.098 ***Method III (Gas Chromatographic Method)***
Official First Action

See **19.001–19.002**.

Benzaldehyde

19.099 ***Gravimetric Method (36)—Official First Action***

Measure 10 mL sample into each of two 300 mL erlenmeyers and add 10 mL *phenylhydrazine soln* (3 mL HOAc, 40 mL H_2O, 2 mL phenylhydrazine) to one flask and 15 mL to other. Let mixts stand overnight in dark place.

Add 200 mL H_2O and filter thru weighed gooch provided with thin layer of asbestos. Wash ppt first with cold H_2O and finally with 10 mL 10% alcohol. Dry 3 hr at 70° at pressure ≤100 mm Hg (13.3 kPa) or to const wt over H_2SO_4. Wt ppt × 5.408 = wt benzaldehyde in 100 mL sample. If the 2 detns do not agree, repeat operation, using larger vol. phenylhydrazine soln.

Alternative Gravimetric Method (37)
Official Final Action

19.100 ***Reagent***

2,4-Dinitrophenylhydrazine soln.—Add 50 mL alcohol to 3.0 g 2,4-dinitrophenylhydrazine. Slowly add 10.0 mL H_2SO_4 while stirring. After reagent dissolves, add addnl 40 mL alcohol and filter thru Whatman No. 12 paper.

19.101 ***Determination***

Measure sample contg ca 10–50 mg benzaldehyde (ca 5 mL flavors, 100–200 mL cordials) into distn flask. Add enough alcohol to ensure ≥10% by vol. in distillate and dil. to ca 150 mL for flavors and 250 mL for cordials with H_2O. Distil ca 100 mL flavors and 200 mL cordials and collect in vol. flask in ice bath. Transfer distillate to 600 mL beaker (also in ice bath) with 100 mL chilled alcohol. Add 25 mL H_2SO_4, mix thoroly, and immediately add 25 mL 2,4-dinitrophenylhydrazine soln, while stirring. Heat on steam bath or hot plate 30 min at ca 75°, stirring occasionally (avoid boiling).

Remove from heat, let ppt settle, and filter by decanting most of supernate thru weighed gooch prepd with thin asbestos mat before transferring bulk of ppt. Wash ppt with ca 25 mL H_2O at room temp. or below. Dry at 100° to const wt (ca 2 hr).

Wt benzaldehyde = wt ppt × 0.3707.

Ultraviolet Spectrophotometric Method (37)
Official Final Action

19.102 ***Reagents and Apparatus***

(**a**) *Spectrophotometer.*—Quartz spectrophtr, Beckman Model DU, or equiv., with UV sensitive phototube and H lamp.

(**b**) *Benzaldehyde.*—Redistd; sp gr 1.041–1.046.

(**c**) *Alcohol.*—Reagent grade alcohol or MeOH.

(**d**) *Benzaldehyde std soln.*—Weigh 1 g benzaldehyde into 100 mL vol. flask and dil. with alcohol. Transfer 1 mL of this soln to 100 mL vol. flask, using 10% alcohol. Dil. 1, 2, 4, 6, 8, 10 mL aliquots to 100 mL with 10% alcohol (1, 2, 4, 6, 8, 10 ppm benzaldehyde).

19.103 ***Determination***

Pipet sample (usually ca 5 mL flavor or 25 mL cordial) into distn flask. Add enough alcohol to ensure min. of 10% alcohol in distillate. Add ca 110 mL H_2O to flavor or 200 mL H_2O to cordial and distil, collecting 100 mL or 200 mL, resp. If necessary, dil. aliquot of distillate with 10% alcohol to produce A of ca 0.5 at 249 nm, using 10% alcohol blank.

Det. A of std benzaldehyde solns at 249 nm against blank of 10% alcohol, and plot std curve.

Det. benzaldehyde concn from A of sample at 249 nm and std curve, or calc. av. A of 1 ppm benzaldehyde (A').

Concn of benzaldehyde in ppm = $(A/A') \times F$,

where F is diln factor. (For most accurate work conduct 5 ppm std with each detn.)

For flavors giving higher A than std at 222 nm, subtract av. of A for minima at 222 and 350 nm from A for max. at 249 nm to calc. A.

19.104 **Benzoic Acid (*38*)—Official First Action**

Measure 10 mL sample into 100 mL flask and add 10 mL 10% NaOH soln and 20 mL 3% H_2O_2 soln; cover with watch glass and place in 100° oven. Oxidn of aldehyde to benzoic acid begins almost immediately; continue heating 5–10 min after all benzaldehyde odor disappears (20–30 min).

Remove flask from oven, transfer contents to separator, rinsing off watch glass, add 10 mL H_2SO_4 (1+5), and cool contents of funnel to room temp. under tap. Ext benzoic acid with 25, 25, 20, and 20 mL portions ether, and wash combined exts with 2 portions of 5–10 mL H_2O, or until all H_2SO_4 is removed. Filter into weighed dish, evap. at room temp., dry overnight in desiccator, and weigh the benzoic acid. Multiply result by 10.

Multiply g/100 mL benzaldehyde obtained in **19.099**, **19.101**, or **19.103** by 1.151 to obtain equiv. of benzoic acid and subtract this product from g/100 mL total benzoic acid obtained above. Difference = g benzoic acid/100 mL ext.

Hydrocyanic Acid

19.105 ***Qualitative Test—Procedure***

To several mL sample add several drops freshly prepd 3% $FeSO_4.7H_2O$ soln and single drop 1% $FeCl_3.6H_2O$ soln. Mix thoroly and add 10% NaOH soln, dropwise, until no further ppt forms and then H_2SO_4 (1+9) to dissolve ppt. In presence of even small amts of HCN, Prussian blue coloration or suspension develops.

19.106 ***Quantitative Method—Official Final Action***

(In absence of chlorides)

Measure 25 mL sample into small flask and add 5 mL *freshly pptd* $Mg(OH)_2$, Cl-free. Titr. with 0.1*N* $AgNO_3$, using K_2CrO_4 as indicator. 1 mL 0.1*N* $AgNO_3$ = 0.0027 g HCN.

Nitrobenzene

19.107 ★ *Qualitative Test—Procedure* ★

See **19.094**, 10th ed.

CASSIA, CINNAMON, AND CLOVE EXTRACTS

Alcohol—Official Final Action

19.108 *Method I*

See **19.096**.

19.109 *Method II* (*35*)

Det. sp gr of ext at 15.56/15.56° or 20/20° as in **9.011**, and oil as in **19.112**, and apply formula given in **19.054**. Use following values for sp gr of the oil: cassia, 1.05; cinnamon, 1.03; and clove, 1.055.

19.110 *Method III* (*Gas Chromatographic Method*) *Official First Action*

See **19.001–19.002**.

19.111 Isopropanol—Official Final Action

See **19.057–19.059**.

19.112 Oil (*39*)—Official First Action

Pipet 10 mL sample into Babcock milk test bottle. Remove nearly all alcohol by blowing air into bottle thru small glass tube 30 min, or longer if necessary. From 10 mL buret add 1 mL *solv.* (equal parts USP mineral oil and H_2O-free kerosene), shake well, and fill with satd $MgSO_4$ soln. Centrf. 10 min and read vol. of oil from extreme bottom to extreme top of column. To obtain % oil subtract 5 divisions and multiply remainder by 2.

GINGER EXTRACT

19.113 Alcohol—Official First Action

See **9.013**.

19.114 Solids (*40*)—Official First Action

Evap. 10 mL sample nearly to dryness on steam bath, dry 2 hr at 100°, and weigh.

19.115 Ginger (Qualitative Test) (*41*) Official First Action

Dil. 10 mL sample to 30 mL, evap. to 20 mL, decant into separator, and ext with equal vol. ether. Let ether evap. spontaneously in porcelain dish, and to residue add 5 mL 75% H_2SO_4 (by wt) and ca 5 mg *vanillin*. Let stand 15 min and add equal vol. H_2O. In presence of ginger ext, soln turns azure blue.

19.116 ★ Capsicum (Qualitative Test) ★ (*42*)—Official First Action

See **19.102**, 10th ed.

★ Surplus method—*see* inside front cover.

PEPPERMINT, SPEARMINT, AND WINTERGREEN EXTRACTS

Alcohol—Official First Action

19.117 *Method I*

See **19.096**.

19.118 *Method II* (*33*)

Det. sp gr at 15.56/15.56° or at 20/20° as in **9.011**, and oil content as in **19.112**, and apply formula in **19.054**. Use following values for sp gr of oil: peppermint, 0.90; spearmint, 0.93; and wintergreen, 1.18.

19.119 *Method III* (*Gas Chromatographic Method*) *Official First Action*

See **19.001–19.002**.

19.120 Isopropanol—Official Final Action

See **19.057–19.059**.

19.121 Oil—Official First Action

See **19.126**.

ANISE AND NUTMEG EXTRACTS

19.122 Alcohol—Official First Action

See **19.001–19.002**.

Oil (*43*)—Official First Action

19.123 *Method I*

To 10 mL sample in Babcock milk test bottle add 1 mL HCl (1+1), then enough half-satd NaCl soln, previously heated to 60°, to fill flask nearly to neck. Stopper and let stand in H_2O at 60° ca 15 min, rotate occasionally, and centrf. 10 min at ca 800 rpm. Fill bottle to neck with satd NaCl soln and again centrf. 10 min. If sepn is not satisfactory or liq. is not clear, cool to ca 10° and centrf. addnl 10 min. Reading × 2 = % oil by vol.

19.124 *Method II*

See **19.126**.

OTHER EXTRACTS AND TOILET PREPARATIONS

19.125 Alcohol—Official First Action

See **19.001–19.002**.

19.126 Essential Oil (*44*)—Official First Action

(Applicable to exts of allspice, anise, caraway, lemon, nutmeg, orange, peppermint, pimiento, rosemary, thyme, wintergreen, and Me salicylate)

Pipet 10 mL sample (5 mL when oil content is >5% by vol.) into Babcock milk test bottle, add 0.50 mL *solv.* (equal parts USP mineral oil and H_2O-free kerosene) and 1 mL HCl (1+1), and fill to shoulder with satd NaCl soln. Shake bottle 3 min; then add the NaCl soln to bring column of oil within graduations on neck. Centrf. 10 min at high speed and read vol. oil from extreme bottom to extreme top of column. (Read from extreme bottom to bottom of meniscus at top of column for allspice, peppermint, and pimiento exts.) To obtain % oil, subtract 2.5 divisions and multiply remainder by 2. (Multiply by 4 if 5 mL sample is used.)

Essential Oil in Emulsion (*45*)
Official First Action

19.127 ***Apparatus***

Use modified oil separator trap, Fig. **19:02**, connected to 500 mL r-b flask thru ₮ 24/40 joint, and equipped with tight fitting condenser having projection at bottom to facilitate return of oil to trap.

19.128 ***Determination***

Weigh 5–10 mL sample contg ≤2 mL essential oil in tared g-s graduate. Transfer to the 500 mL flask contg ca 200 mL H_2O, rinsing graduate by shaking with several 5 mL portions H_2O. Add rinsings to flask.

Fill oil trap with H_2O to overflowing, connect to flask and condenser, and carefully boil 1 hr. Remove heat and let stand several min. Remove enough H_2O from trap to bring oil layer within graduations, let stand 5 min to complete drainage, and measure amt of oil from bottom of lower meniscus to highest point of upper meniscus.

Citral—Official Final Action

Barbituric Acid Condensation Method (46)

19.129 ***Reagent***

Barbituric acid soln.—Transfer 1.0 g reagent grade barbituric acid to dry 100 mL vol. flask. Add 20 mL H_2O from pipet, rinsing down neck of flask. Stopper lightly and dissolve by warming gently on hot plate or immersing in beaker of hot H_2O. Dil. gradually to vol., with shaking, with alcohol (or, preferably, anhyd. alcohol). Temper soln in H_2O bath at 25° (soln will contract slightly). Dil. back to vol. and mix thoroly. If some barbituric acid ppts on prolonged standing, redissolve by warming soln gently; then adjust to 25°.

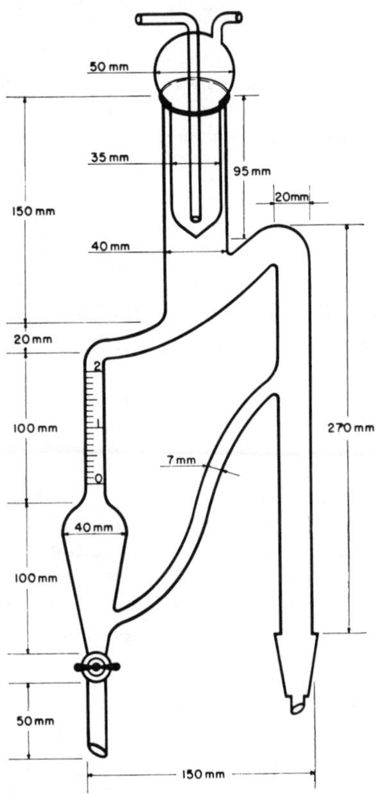

FIG. 19:02—Oil separator trap

Table 19:03 Weights and Volumes Used in Reaction

Oil	Sample Wt, mg	Reaction Vol., mL
Bergamot	70–80	10
Citronella	50–90	10
Grapefruit	100–150	10
Lemon	50–150	25
Lemongrass[a]	20–30	25
Lime		
expressed	30–60	25
distilled	100–600	5
Mandarin	100–250	10
Neroli	75–100	5
Orange		
sweet	150–400	10
bitter	150–400	10
Petitgrain	150–250	5
Tangerine	200–350	10

[a] Dil. 1 mL to 200 mL for *A* measurements.

19.130 ***Determination***

Weigh suitable amt of oil into vol. flask of appropriate size, dil. to vol. with reagent, and place in H_2O bath at 25°. After 40 min, withdraw aliquots into vol. flasks half-filled with alcohol, shake gently to quench reaction, dil. to vol. with alcohol, and det. *A* of soln at 336 nm. Use similarly dild aliquot of reagent as cell blank. From *A* of sample, subtract corresponding *A* of untreated oil when similarly dild.

Use Table **19:03** as guide for sample wts and dilns. Except as noted, weigh indicated amts of oil into vol. flask for reaction; then dil. 2 mL to 50 mL with alcohol for *A* measurements.

19.131 ***Calculations***

Convert *A* values to *a* at 336 nm of 1 g/L soln in 1 cm cell, and substitute in equation:

% Citral = 0.6153 × [*a* of sample after reaction
− *a* of unreacted, similarly dild sample]

Beta-Ionone (*47*)—Official Final Action

19.132 ***Method I***

(Applicable to pure solns contg ≤100 mg in 5 mL alcohol)

Place 5 mL alc. sample contg 10–100 mg β-ionone in 125 erlenmeyer. Add 95–100 mg solid *m-nitrobenzhydrazide* and dissolve by warming on steam bath, taking precautions to prevent loss of alcohol thru evapn. Add 5 mL H_2O, and if soln becomes cloudy, warm until clear. Remove from steam bath, add 0.2 mL HOAc, stopper flask lightly, and place on wooden surface to prevent too rapid cooling.

If ≥20 mg of β-ionone is present, crystals begin to form within 30 min after soln reaches room temp. Let stand in room ≥2 hr (overnight does no harm) and add 5 mL H_2O dropwise, mixing soln continuously during addn by rotating flask. Stopper, let stand in room ≥1 hr, and refrigerate overnight (≤48 hr). Filter thru fine fritted glass crucible, wash with 30 mL dil. alcohol (3+7), using wet policeman to remove ppt adhering to flask, and dry at 100°. Wt ppt × 0.541 = wt β-ionone. Identify crystals microscopically, **19.135**.

Method II (48)

(Applicable to raspberry concs)

19.133 ***Apparatus***

(**a**) *Steam generator filled with water.*—Oil can holding 1 gal. (3.8 L) is convenient.

(**b**) *Distillation flask.*—R-b boiling flask with Ŧ 24/40 joint, capacity ca twice vol. of sample to be used.

(**c**) *Still head.*—Adapter, 75° angle, with male connections Ŧ 24/40 at bottom and side, and female connection 14/35 at top, with side arm lengthened and bent to fit vertical condenser.

(**d**) *Spray tube.*—Adapter, for use with Woulff bottles with Ŧ joints; aeration tube with Ŧ 14/35, holes in bulb ca 2 mm diam., length of tubing such that when app. is set up, bulb is ≤20 mm above bottom of distg flask.

(**e**) *Condenser.*—Coil type with female connection Ŧ 24/40 at top with 250–300 mm jacket and outlet tube lengthened to ca 200 mm to reach bottom of 500 mL erlenmeyer receiving flask.

19.134 ***Determination***

(*Caution: See* **51.011**, **51.039**, and **51.054**.)

Place 250–1000 mL sample contg ≤100 mg β-ionone in distg flask and connect with app. Add enough H_2O to receiving flask to just cover outlet of condenser. Heat sample nearly to bp on asbestos mat with flame or by immersing it in boiling H_2O bath. As soon as sample reaches temp. of bath or just begins to boil, connect with steam generator and pass rapid current of steam thru sample until ca 500 mL distillate collects.

Add enough H_2O to distillate to reduce alcohol content to ≤10% and transfer to large separator. Add 150–200 mL ether, depending upon vol. of soln, so that ca 100 mL is obtained upon sepn. Shake thoroly ca 2 min. Let mixt. settle till clear and drain aq. layer till ca 25 mL remains in separator. Centrf. liq. and again let settle.

When clear, drain remainder of aq. layer; then drain ether soln into 125 mL erlenmeyer contg 95–100 mg *m-nitrobenzhydrazide*. After separator drains ca 1 min, close stopcock, pour 10–15 mL ether into separator to wash down sides, let soln settle 1 min, and add to main ether soln. Add 0.2 mL HOAc and dissolve solid reagent by stirring and breaking up lumps with glass rod, warming if necessary to complete soln. Let mixt. stand ca 1 hr and evap. on steam bath to ca 10 mL, passing current of air into flask to hasten evapn and keep down temp.

Meanwhile make second extn of distillate, using 100 mL ether. Add sepd ether soln to flask contg residue from first ether ext, follow with ether washings of separator, let stand ≥15 min, and evap. to 10 mL as before. Similarly make third extn, using 100 mL ether, add to flask, and evap. as before until 1–3 mL watery liq. and perhaps some oily residue remain.

While flask is still warm, add 5 mL alcohol from pipet, washing down sides of flask, and dissolve residue completely by warming on steam bath, protecting liq. against loss by evapn. Add 5 mL H_2O and warm if necessary to obtain clear soln. Add 0.2 mL HOAc, close with cork stopper, and place flask on wooden surface to prevent too rapid cooling.

After 2 hr, add 5 mL H_2O dropwise, mixing liq. by continuously rotating flask, stopper, and keep at room temp. ≥1 hr (overnight does no harm); then refrigerate overnight (≤48 hr).

Filter on fine fritted glass crucible and wash with ca 30 mL dil. alcohol (3+7). Dry in vac. oven at 70° and weigh. Wt ppt × 0.541 = wt β-ionone. Identify crystals microscopically, **19.135**.

If pptd material consists of oily matter mixed with cryst. matter, place fritted glass crucible in gooch holder attached to suction flask. Support test tube with wire within suction flask so as to catch any liq. that passes thru crucible. Add ca 5 mL pet ether, cover crucible, and let stand ca 5 min. Apply suction just long enough to carry thru any solv. that remains in crucible. Transfer pet ether soln to small beaker and let evap. spontaneously. Repeat several times until no more sol. matter is obtained by extn. Examine remaining contents of crucible and several residues microscopically for crystals of β-ionone-*m*-nitrobenzhydrazide.

19.135 Optical-Crystallographic Properties of Beta-Ionone-*m*-Nitrobenzhydrazide (*49*)—Procedure

This substance in mass is yellowish, but when examined in ordinary light under microscope it is essentially colorless and crystallizes in thin, rod-like plates, many having lath-like or frayed ends, some having 6-side outline. In parallel polarized light (crossed nicols), extinction is parallel and sign of elongation neg. Refractive indices are the min. value, n_α = 1.548, invariably shown on elongated fragments when their long dimension is parallel to vibration plane of lower nicol (lengthwise), and max. value, n_γ = 1.648, usually shown on elongated fragments when their long dimension is at right angles to vibration plane of lower nicol (crosswise).

Ammonium Glycyrrhizinate (*50*)—Official Final Action

(Applicable to liqs)

19.136 ***Principle***

NH_4 glycyrrhizinate is hydrolyzed to glycyrrhetic acid, active ingredient in licorice, and this compd is silylated for GLC detn, with cholesterol as internal std. Method is applicable to 30–400 ppm NH_4 glycyrrhizinate.

19.137 ***Apparatus***

Gas chromatograph.—With dual columns, H flame detector, and 1.2 m × 4 mm id glass or stainless steel columns packed with 1.5% OV-1 on 60–80 mesh Gas-Chrom Q (Applied Science Laboratories, Inc.). Operating conditions: temps (°)—detector 300, column 200–260, injection port 280; flow rates (mL/min)—N carrier gas and H 75, O 300; sensitivity 1000; or equiv. conditions so that 3–5 μL silylated glycyrrhetic acid (6–9 μg) and 3 μL cholesterol internal std (1.5 μg) will give ½ scale deflection. Retention times are ca 7 and 4 min, resp.

19.138 ***Reagents***

(**a**) *Silylating mixture.*—Mix, in order, following reagents: 5 vols anhyd. pyridine, 2 vols trimethylchlorosilane, and 3 vols *N,O*-bis(trimethylsilyl) acetamide (all available from Pierce Chemical Co.). (*Caution:* This mixt. is toxic; avoid contact with skin or eyes. Use effective fume removal device when prepg, using, or heating mixt.) Store mixt. under N in tightly stoppered bottle and refrigerate when not in use. Refrigerated mixt. is stable indefinitely. Reagent is satisfactory if color of grains of activated indicating type silica gel desiccant (Grace Davison Chemical Co., Charles & Baltimore Sts, Baltimore, MD 21203) added to mixt. remains deep blue. Store anhyd. pyridine over Molecular Sieve 13×.

(**b**) *Ammonium glycyrrhizinate std soln.*—1.0 mg/mL H_2O. Dissolve 100 mg purified NH_4 glycyrrhizinate (MacAndrews & Forbes Co., 3rd St & Jefferson Ave., Camden, NJ 08104) in H_2O in 100 mL vol. flask and dil. to vol. with H_2O.

(**c**) *Cholesterol internal std soln.*—0.5 mg/mL. Weigh 5 mg USP cholesterol into 100 mL vol. flask and dissolve and dil. to vol. with MeOH.

19.139 ***Determination***

(*Caution: See* **51.011**, **51.039**, and **51.056**.)

Pipet 25 mL sample, decarbonated if necessary, into 300 mL Ŧ 24/40 r-b boiling flask, add 25 mL *dioxane*, and swirl to mix. Slowly add 25 mL H_2SO_4 (1+3) and 2–3 SiC chips. Connect flask to H_2O-cooled condenser and reflux vigorously 1 hr. Add, thru top of condenser, 75 mL H_2O followed immediately by 100 mL $CHCl_3$ and reflux 15–20 min more. Let mixt. cool to room temp. and transfer to 500 mL separator. Add 100 mL ice-H_2O and shake vigorously ca 1 min. Let phases sep. completely. Drain $CHCl_3$ layer into 250 mL separator contg 100 mL *2% $NaHCO_3$ soln*. Shake and let layers sep. Filter $CHCl_3$ layer into 200 mL vol. flask thru 100 × 20 mm chromatgc tube or suitable glass funnel with glass wool plug and ca 25 g anhyd. Na_2SO_4. Repeat extns with 50 and 25 mL $CHCl_3$, swirling to prevent emulsions. Filter as before and dil. to vol. with $CHCl_3$ passed thru same Na_2SO_4.

Transfer all of 200 mL ext (or aliquot if concn of active ingredient is ≥400 ppm) to 250 mL beaker, add 2–3 SiC chips, and evap. to 10–15 mL on steam bath under gentle N flow. Transfer quant. to 30 mL screw-cap bottle with Teflon liner. Add 2 mL cholesterol internal std soln, (**c**). Evap. to dryness on steam bath with gentle N flow. Flush bottle until cool with N or cool in desiccator. Add 1 mL silylating mixt., (**a**), and stopper bottle tightly. Rotate bottle so that reagent comes in contact with all glass surfaces. Let stand ca 4 hr at 50° or overnight at room temp. Inject 2–5 μL into gas chromatograph operated as in **19.137**. Attenuate or inject larger amts for desired peak hts.

19.140 ***Calculations***

Det. relative response actor (*RF*) from chromatogram of 6 mL NH_4 glycyrrhizinate std soln, (**b**), and 19 mL H_2O pipetted into 300 mL ₮ 24/40 r-b boiling flask, hydrolyzed, and silylated as in **19.139**. Use peak areas obtained by triangulation.

$RF = [(PA_{AG} \times S_{AG})/(PA_C \times S_C)] \times (W_C/W_{AG})$, where subscripts AG and C refer to hydrolyzed std NH_4 glycyrrhizinate (glycyrrhetic acid) and cholesterol internal std, resp.; PA = peak area; S = attenuation; and W = mg std weighed.

$$\text{ppm AG } (\mu g/mL) = [(PA_{sample} \times S_{sample})/(PA_C \times S_C)] \times (W_C \times 10^3/RF) \times (1/V),$$

where V = mL sample.

SELECTED REFERENCES

(*1*) JAOAC **56**, 697(1973).
(*2*) JAOAC **30**, 651(1947); **33**, 103(1950); **38**, 726(1955).
(*3*) JAOAC **47**, 555(1964); **49**, 571(1966).
(*4*) JAOAC **48**, 509(1965); **49**, 566(1966); **50**, 859(1967).
(*5*) JAOAC **47**, 1161(1964); **49**, 566(1966).
(*6*) JAOAC **34**, 335(1951); **35**, 268(1952); **36**, 695(1953).
(*7*) JAOAC **38**, 730(1955); **39**, 715(1956).
(*8*) J. Ind. Eng. Chem. **13**, 414(1921); JAOAC **8**, 689, 691(1925); **9**, 456(1926); **51**, 822(1968).
(*9*) J. Am. Chem. Soc. **24**, 1132(1902).
(*10*) J. Am. Chem. Soc. **24**, 1133(1902).
(*11*) JAOAC **9**, 446, 456(1926).
(*12*) JAOAC **43**, 600(1960); **45**, 250(1962).
(*13*) USDA Bur. Chem. Bull. **152**, p. 149.
(*14*) JAOAC **42**, 638(1959); **43**, 596(1960); **46**, 626(1963).
(*15*) JAOAC **47**, 551(1964); **48**, 507(1965).
(*16*) JAOAC **46**, 626(1963).
(*17*) JAOAC **51**, 1224(1968).
(*18*) JAOAC **54**, 39(1971).
(*19*) J. Ind. Eng. Chem. **1**, 84(1909); JAOAC **4**, 472(1921); **5**, 308(1922); **8**, 695(1925); **33**, 302(1950).
(*20*) JAOAC **25**, 693(1942); **41**, 616(1958).
(*21*) JAOAC **35**, 78, 272(1952); **41**, 616(1958).
(*22*) JAOAC **4**, 472(1921); **8**, 692(1925).
(*23*) J. Ind. Eng. Chem. **1**, 84(1909); JAOAC **8**, 692(1925).
(*24*) JAOAC **9**, 450(1926); **11**, 45, 503(1928).
(*25*) JAOAC **9**, 453(1926); **10**, 495(1927).
(*26*) J. Am. Chem. Soc. **28**, 1472(1906).
(*27*) J. Ind. Eng. Chem. **10**, 608(1918); JAOAC **12**, 83, 405(1929); **13**, 475(1930).
(*28*) JAOAC **36**, 112(1953).
(*29*) Schimmel and Co., Semi-Annual Rpt., Oct. 1898, p. 41.
(*30*) JAOAC **36**, 119(1953).
(*31*) USDA Bur. Chem. Bull. **137**, p. 72; JAOAC **4**, 474(1921); **14**, 68, 519(1931).
(*32*) JAOAC **38**, 738(1955).
(*33*) USDA Bur. Chem. Circ. **46**, p. 9.
(*34*) JAOAC **33**, 307(1950).
(*35*) JAOAC **33**, 302(1950).
(*36*) JAOAC **19**, 408(1936); **24**, 665(1941).
(*37*) JAOAC **49**, 504(1966); **50**, 319(1967).
(*38*) J. Ind. Eng. Chem. **1**, 84(1909).
(*39*) JAOAC **15**, 539(1932); **19**, 407(1936).
(*40*) USDA Bur. Chem. Bull. **137**, p. 76.
(*41*) USDA Bur. Chem. Bull. **152**, p.137.
(*42*) USDA Bur. Chem. Bull. **152**, p. 145.
(*43*) J. Ind. Eng. Chem. **1**, 84(1909); JAOAC **2**, 212(1917).
(*44*) JAOAC **15**, 539(1932); **16**, 65, 541(1933); **17**, 364(1934); **19**, 407(1936).
(*45*) JAOAC **25**, 692(1942); **31**, 200(1948); **35**, 261(1952).
(*46*) JAOAC **45**, 475(1962).
(*47*) JAOAC **22**, 383(1939); **23**, 572(1940).
(*48*) JAOAC **22**, 386(1939); **24**, 663(1941).
(*49*) JAOAC **22**, 390(1939).
(*50*) JAOAC **55**, 570(1972).

20. Food Additives: Direct

ACIDULANTS

Fumaric Acid (*1*)—Official Final Action

20.001 ***Apparatus***

Polarograph.—Any voltammetric or polarographic instrument with necessary accessories (cells, electrodes, Hg, capillaries, etc.) capable of effectively scanning up to 3.0 volts in either pos. or neg. direction starting at selected initial potential.

20.002 ***Reagents***

(**a**) *Fumaric acid std solns.*—(*1*) *Stock soln.*—500 μg/mL. Transfer 50 mg fumaric acid to 100 mL vol. flask. Dissolve in and dil. to vol. with MeOH. (*2*) *Working std soln.*—25 μg/mL. Pipet 5 mL stock soln into 100 mL vol. flask, add 15 mL MeOH, and dil. to vol. with electrolyte soln.

(**b**) *Electrolyte soln.*—Dissolve 7.70 g $(CH_3)_4NBr$ and 0.210 g LiCl in H_2O and dil. to 500 mL. (LiCl is very hygroscopic; weigh rapidly with min. exposure to air.)

(**c**) *Nitrogen gas.*—Purified H_2O-pumped N in cylinder.

20.003 ***Preparation of Sample Solutions***

(**a**) *Sample soln A.*—(*1*) *Aqueous samples* (*fruit juice drinks, etc.*).—If insol. matter is present, shake with Celite and filter. Transfer 25.00 g clear soln to 100 mL vol. flask, using MeOH, and dil. to vol. with MeOH. (*2*) *Powders.*—Shake weighed sample with measured vol. MeOH. Filter, or use clear supernate.

(**b**) *Sample test soln B.*—Use in preliminary detn. Transfer $\leq$5 mL *sample soln A* to 25 mL vol. flask (if <5 mL is taken, add MeOH to make 5 mL) and dil. to vol. with electrolyte soln.

(**c**) *Sample test soln C.*—Use in final detn. After preliminary detn is performed on *sample test soln B*, adjust wt of sample to give final concn of *sample test soln C* of 25 μg fumaric acid/mL, prepg soln as in (**b**).

20.004 ***Preparation of Standard Curve***

Transfer 1, 3, and 5 mL fumaric acid stock soln to sep. 25 mL vol. flasks. To flasks contg 1 and 3 mL stock soln, add 4 and 2 mL MeOH, resp. Dil. all flasks to vol. with electrolyte soln. Polarograph solns as in detn. Plot numerical values of solns against μg fumaric acid/mL.

20.005 ***Determination***

Prep. polarograph cell and pass N thru *sample test soln B* 3 min at ca 3–5 bubbles/sec. Polarograph, using starting potential of -0.8 v. Peak potential of fumaric acid under these conditions is ca -1.15 v with Hg pool electrode. Wave ht $\times$ instrument scale factor gives "numerical value," which shows relative concn of fumaric acid in polarographed soln. From numerical value of *sample test soln B* and std curve, calc. approx. % fumaric acid in sample.

Make second detn, using calcd wt sample for *sample test soln C* contg 25 μg fumaric acid/mL and working std soln contg exactly 25 μg fumaric acid/mL. Polarographic values of sample and std should be very close. From second detn calc.:

(**a**) mg fumaric acid/mL in *sample test soln C* = (mg fumaric acid/mL in working std soln (= 0.025)) $\times$ (numerical value of *sample test soln C*)/(numerical value of working std soln).

(**b**) % fumaric acid in sample = (mg fumaric acid/mL in *sample test soln C*) $\times$ (mL *sample test soln C* (= 25)) $\times$ 100/(mg sample in aliquot *sample soln A* used in prepg *sample test soln C*).

ANTIOXIDANTS

Qualitative Tests (*2*)—Official Final Action

(*Caution:* *See* **51.011**, **51.039**, and **51.073**.)

20.006 ***Reagents***

(**a**) *Barium hydroxide.*—1% $Ba(OH)_2.H_2O$ in boiled distd H_2O. Keep in tightly stoppered bottle.

(**b**) *Ehrlich reagent.*—Diazobenzene sulfonic acid. Prep. 0.5% soln $NaNO_2$ in H_2O and 0.5% soln sulfanilic acid in HCl (1+19). Prep. $NaNO_2$ soln fresh every 3 weeks. Keep solns refrigerated. Mix $NaNO_2$ and sulfanilic acid solns (1+100) daily.

(**c**) *Dianisidine soln.*—(*Caution:* Dianisidine may be harmful. *See* **51.084**.) Dissolve 250 mg dianisidine (3,3′-dimethoxybenzidine) in 50 mL anhyd. MeOH. Add 100 mg activated charcoal, shake 5 min, and filter. Mix 40 mL clear filtrate with 60 mL 1*N* HCl. Prep. daily and protect from light.

(**d**) *Activated Florisil adsorbent.*—60–100 mesh. Activated by manufacturer at 260° or 650° (available from Floridin Co.).

Test Florisil for BHT retention as follows: Add 0.2 mg BHT in 25 mL pet ether to prepd column, **20.007**, elute with 150 mL pet ether, and apply BHT test after evapg ether just to dryness as in **20.008(d)**. If BHT is not eluted, activate remaining Florisil by heating 2 hr at 650°, cool, add 6.5% H_2O by wt, and homogenize by shaking 1 hr in closed container.

20.007 ***Preparation of Florisil Column for Cleanup of BHT Extract***

Insert small glass wool plug into chromatgc tube 20 (od) $\times$ 250 mm with Teflon stopcock, and add ca 12 g Florisil with gentle tapping. Wash with two 15 mL portions pet ether, adding second portion when liq. level drops to just above top of Florisil. When level of second portion is ca 1 cm above Florisil, close stopcock. Do not let column become dry.

20.008 ***Tests***

(**a**) *Propyl gallate* (*PG*).—Weigh ca 30 g fat (melted by gentle warming) or oil, dissolve in ca 60 mL pet ether, and transfer to 250 mL separator. Add 15 mL H_2O and shake gently 1 min. Let sep. and drain aq. phase into 125 mL separator, leaving any emulsion in org. phase. Repeat extn of pet ether with 2 addnl 15 mL portions H_2O and reserve pet ether soln for further extn with CH_3CN, (**b**). Add 15 mL ether to combined aq. exts and shake 1 min. Discard aq. phase and evap. ether just to dryness in small beaker. Add 4 mL 50% alcohol to residue, swirl, and add 1 mL NH_4OH. If soln turns rose, PG is present. (Color is unstable and fades after few min.)

(**b**) *Nordihydroguaiaretic acid* (*NDGA*).—Ext pet ether soln from (**a**) by shaking 2 min with 20 mL CH_3CN. Let layers sep. and drain CH_3CN into 1 L separator. Repeat extn with 2 addnl 30 mL portions CH_3CN and discard pet ether. Dil. combined CH_3CN exts with 400 mL H_2O, add 2–3 g NaCl, and shake 2 min with 20 mL pet ether. Let layers sep., and drain dild CH_3CN into second 1 L separator. Ext dil. CH_3CN with 2 addnl 20 mL portions pet ether and reserve dild CH_3CN soln for further extn. Combine pet ether exts in 100 mL beaker and set aside for BHA and BHT tests.

Add 50 mL ether-pet ether (1+1) to dild CH_3CN and shake 2 min. (*Caution:* Vent separator.) Let layers sep., discard CH_3CN, and evap. ether just to dryness in small beaker. Add 4 mL 50% alcohol, swirl, and then add 1 mL 1% $Ba(OH)_2$ soln and mix. If NDGA is present, soln turns blue and fades rapidly.

(**c**) *Butylated hydroxyanisole (BHA).*—Take ⅓ of combined pet ether soln reserved for BHA-BHT tests and evap. just to dryness in small beaker, using gentle heat, under air current. Add 2.5 mL alcohol to dissolve residue and dil. with 2.5 mL H_2O. Swirl, add 1 mL Ehrlich reagent, immediately add 1 mL 1*N* NaOH, and swirl again. If soln turns red-purple, BHA is present.

(**d**) *Butylated hydroxytoluene (BHT).*—Pass remaining ⅔ combined pet ether soln thru Florisil column and elute with 150 mL pet ether. Collect eluate in 200 mL beaker and evap. just to dryness. Add 2.5 mL alcohol, swirl, and dil. with 2.5 mL H_2O. Add 2 mL dianisidine soln and mix. Add 0.8 mL 0.3% $NaNO_2$ soln. Mix, and let stand 5 min; then transfer to small separator. Add 0.5 mL $CHCl_3$, shake vigorously 30 sec, and let sep. If $CHCl_3$ turns pink to red, BHT is present. Confirm BHT by comparing spectrophtric curve of colored $CHCl_3$ ext with control prepd from ref. std BHT as follows: Dissolve ca 15 mg BHT in 5 mL aq. alcohol (1+1), add 2 mL dianisidine soln, and proceed as above.

Butylated Hydroxyanisole (BHA) and Butylated Hydroxytoluene (BHT) (*3*)—Official Final Action

(*Caution: See* **51.011**, **51.039**, **51.040**, **51.048**, and **51.049**.)

20.009 *Principle*

BHA and BHT are extd from ready-to-eat breakfast cereals with CS_2 and detd by GLC, using flame ionization detection.

20.010 *Apparatus*

(**a**) *Gas chromatograph.*—With H flame ionization detector. *Operating conditions:* temps (°)—column 160, detector 210, flash heater 200; N flow rate, to elute BHT in 3–4 min from QF-1 column and elute BHA in 3–4 min from Apiezon column; H flow rate, ca 40 mL/min for Apiezon and ca 25 mL/min for QF-1; air flow rate, ca 340 mL/min; electrometer sensitivity, 500× (5 × 10^{-10} amp full scale deflection) with 1 mv recorder. Adjust H and air flow rates if necessary. Alternatively, adjust electrometer sensitivity so 0.1 μg BHA gives ca 50% deflection. Repeat injections until const peak hts are obtained on successive injections of identical vol. of std mixt.

Order of appearance from Apiezon column (1.2 m; 4′): BHA, BHT, di-BHA. Order of appearance from QF-1 column (1.8 m; 6′): BHT, BHA, di-BHA.

Use of 2 GLC columns serves to identify BHA and BHT. Use Apiezon L/Gas-Chrom Q, 1.2 m column to resolve 2- and 3-isomers of BHA. Adjust GLC parameters to obtain good sepn of BHA isomers, such as adjusting column temp. to 150° and electrometer sensitivity to 1000×. Adjust amt BHA std injected to give 50% deflection.

(**b**) *GLC columns.*—Glass, 1.2 m (4′) × 4 mm and 1.8 m (6′) × 4 mm, packed with Apiezon L and QF-1 silicone oil (Fluoro silicone fluid, FS 1265), resp., on 80–100 mesh Gas-Chrom Q (Applied Science Laboratories). Prep. columns and column material by carefully washing insides of tubes and small amt fine glass wool with dichlorodimethylsilane soln, rinsing with MeOH, and drying. (*Caution:* Dichlorodimethylsilane is toxic. Avoid contact with skin and eyes. Use effective fume removal device.)

Slowly sprinkle ca 50 g Gas-Chrom Q into 800 mL beaker almost filled with CCl_4. Remove fine particles that remain on surface with vac. line and trap. Decant solv. and dry GLC support.

Transfer 20.0 g dried Gas-Chrom Q to 500 mL r-b flask. Add 100 mL $CHCl_3$ or CH_2Cl_2 and mix gently. Dissolve 1.0 g Apiezon L or 2.0 g QF-1 in 50 mL $CHCl_3$ or CH_2Cl_2, add to flask, and mix gently. Evap. to dryness, using rotary vac. evaporator and H_2O bath (35° for CH_2Cl_2 and 70° for $CHCl_3$).

Carefully plug exit of column with small plug of fine glass wool and thru-hole septum. Apply vac. to exit port and slowly add coated support (Apiezon L/Gas-Chrom Q for 1.2 m column; QF-1/Gas-Chrom Q for 1.8 m column) thru injection port, tapping very gently to aid compaction. Pack to within 1 cm of area heated by flash heater. Plug with fine glass wool and condition ca 3 days at 200° with slow stream of N (ca 10 mL/min) or until steady baseline is obtained.

(**c**) *Chromatographic tube.*—25 × 200 mm glass tube with small drip tip (6 mm od × 50 long), with or without medium porosity fritted disk, with close-fitting tamping rod.

(**d**) *Fine glass wool.*—Wash with CS_2 and dry.

20.011 *Reagents*

(**a**) *Carbon disulfide.*—Reagent grade; nearly colorless. If distinctly yellow, distil before use.

(**b**) *BHA, BHT, and di-BHA std mixture.*—0.02 μg/μL each of BHA, BHT, and di-BHA in CS_2. Dissolve 1.00 mg each of BHA and BHT in small amt CS_2, add 10.0 mL internal std soln, and dil. to 50 mL with CS_2 or prep. by diln of more concd solns with CS_2. Prep. fresh and store in low-actinic glassware.

(**c**) *Internal std soln.*—0.1 μg di-BHA/μL CS_2. Prep. fresh and store in low-actinic glassware.

(**d**) *Dichlorodimethylsilane soln.*—Dil. 5 mL to 100 mL with toluene.

20.012 *Determination*

(Protect all solns from light; complete assay in 1 day. Use either GLC column for analysis.)

Grind sample to pass No. 20 sieve and mix well. (When necessary, ground sample may be stored frozen under N for few days.) Place, if necessary, small plug of fine glass wool at bottom of chromatgc tube, add 20.0 g sample to column, using tamping rod to pack it firmly without solv., and top column with another small glass wool plug, tamped down. Mark 100 mL beaker at 50 mL level and place under column to collect eluate. Add three 5 mL portions CS_2 to column, letting each portion sink into column before adding next. Elute CS_2 at ca 5 mL/min; use N, if necessary, to maintain flow rate.

Add several 10 mL portions CS_2, letting each portion sink into column until 50 mL eluate collects. Rinse tip of column with small amt CS_2. Accurately add di-BHA to eluate to obtain concn after evapn of 0.02 μg di-BHA/μL final soln. Evap. eluate under gentle stream of N in hood at room temp. to small vol. (<5.0 mL). Accurately dil. evapd sample to appropriate vol. (e.g., 5.0 mL) for GLC analysis. Inject 3.0–9.0 μL sample, using 10 μL syringe, into gas chromatograph. Before and after each series of sample chromatograms, inject 3.0–9.0 μL std mixt. and average std values for calcns. Measure each peak ht in mm. (Ht of BHA, BHT, and di-BHA peaks should be in range of 30–95% full scale deflection.)

Calc. ppm antioxidant present, correcting for internal std, as follows:

$$\text{ppm BHA or BHT} = (H/H') \times (C'/C) \times (H'_i/H_i) \times (C_i/C'_i),$$

where H and H' = ht (mm) of sample and std peaks, resp.; H_i and H'_i = ht (mm) of internal std peaks in sample and std, resp.; C and C' = concn of sample (g/μL) and std (μg/μL), resp.; and C_i and C'_i = concn (μg/μL) of internal std in sample and std solns, resp.

Propyl Gallate (PG) (*4*)—Official First Action

(*Caution: See* **51.011**, **51.039**, and **51.073**.)

20.013 ***Reagents***

(**a**) *Petroleum ether reagent*.—Mix 1 vol. 30–60° pet ether (**14.088**, or equiv.) with 3 vols 60–100° pet ether (Skellysolve B and H have been found satisfactory) and shake mixt. 5 min with 1/10 its vol. H_2SO_4. Discard acid layer, wash several times with H_2O, then once with 1% NaOH soln, and then again with H_2O until washings are substantially neut. Discard all washings and distil pet ether in all-glass app.

(**b**) *Ammonium acetate solns*.—1.25%, 1.67%, and 10% aq. solns. Soln contg 1.67% NH_4OAc in 5% alcohol may also be required.

(**c**) *Ferrous tartrate reagent*.—Dissolve 0.100 g $FeSO_4.7H_2O$ and 0.500 g Rochelle salt ($NaKC_4H_4O_6.4H_2O$) in H_2O and dil. to 100 mL. Reagent must be used within 3 hr of prepn.

(**d**) *Propyl gallate std soln*.—50 μg/mL. Dissolve 50 mg PG in H_2O and dil. to 1 L with H_2O.

20.014 ***Preparation of Standard Curve***

Place $\geqslant$7 aliquots of std soln, (**d**), covering range from 50 to 1000 μg, in 50 mL g-s erlenmeyers. Add exactly 2.5 mL 10% NH_4OAc to each flask, dil. to exactly 24 mL with H_2O, and pipet 1 mL ferrous tartrate reagent into each flask. Let solns stand $\geqslant$3 min. Measure A at 540 nm against soln contg 20 mL 1.25% NH_4OAc soln, 4 mL H_2O, and 1 mL ferrous tartrate soln. Plot μg PG against A.

20.015 ***Determination***

Dissolve 40 g fat or oil in the pet ether reagent and dil. to 250 mL with this reagent. (Gentle warming may be necessary to obtain complete soln.) Pipet 100 mL fat soln into 250 mL separator. Ext fat soln with 20 mL aq. 1.67% NH_4OAc soln by continuously inverting separator 2.5 min. After phases sep. completely, drain aq. layer into 100 mL vol. flask, being careful not to let any oil droplets fall into flask. (Some shortenings show strong tendency to emulsify during aq. extn. To prevent emulsification, add 2 mL *n-octanol* to fat soln aliquot before beginning extn and use 1.67% NH_4OAc soln in 5% alcohol for extn in place of aq. soln. This procedure need be used only when usual method fails.) Repeat extn twice with 20 mL portions 1.67% NH_4OAc soln, combining aq. layers in vol. flask. Finally, ext fat soln with 15 mL H_2O 30 sec and combine aq. layer with previous washings. Let layers sep. completely after each washing. Add exactly 2.5 mL 10% NH_4OAc soln to combined exts in vol. flask and dil. to vol. with H_2O. This soln now contains 1.25% NH_4OAc. Filter thru dry rapid paper to remove any turbidity. (Colors must be developed on same day ext is prepd. If combined exts stand more than several hr, yellow color may develop and solns must be discarded.)

Pipet aliquot of ext, $\leqslant$20 mL, into 50 mL g-s erlenmeyer. Dil. to 20 mL with 1.25% NH_4OAc soln. Add exactly 4 mL H_2O and pipet 1 mL ferrous tartrate reagent into flask. Mix well, and measure A at 540 nm against soln contg 20 mL 1.25% NH_4OAc soln, 4 mL H_2O, and 1 mL ferrous tartrate reagent. Calc. amt of PG from std curve.

CHEMICAL PRESERVATIVES

BENZOIC ACID

(*Caution: See* **51.011**, **51.039**, **51.040**, **51.054**, and **51.056**.)

Qualitative Tests—Official Final Action

20.016 ***Preliminary Test***

Ext benzoic acid as in **20.094** or **20.096**. If appreciable benzoic acid is present, it will crystallize from ether in shining leaflets having characteristic odor on warming. Dissolve cryst. deposit in hot H_2O, divide into 2 portions, and test as in **20.017** or **20.018**. Deposit may also be purified as in **20.094(c)** and mp detd.

20.017 ***Ferric Chloride Test***

Make soln, **20.016**, alk. with few drops NH_4OH, expel excess NH_3 by evapn, dissolve residue in few mL hot H_2O, filter if necessary, and add few drops *aq. 0.5% $FeCl_3$ soln*. Salmon color ppt of ferric benzoate indicates presence of benzoic acid.

20.018 ***Modified Mohler Test (5)***

(Presence of phthln interferes)

To aq. soln, **20.016**, add 1 or 2 drops ca 10% NaOH soln and evap. to dryness. To residue add 5–10 drops H_2SO_4 and small crystal KNO_3. Heat 10 min in glycerol bath at 120–130° (must be $\leqslant$130°). Cool, add 1 mL H_2O, and make distinctly ammoniacal. Boil soln to decompose any NH_4NO_2 that may form. Cool, and add drop of fresh, *colorless $(NH_4)_2S$ soln*, but do not let layers mix. Red-brown ring indicates benzoic acid. On mixing, color diffuses thruout liq., and on heating finally changes to greenish-yellow. This change differentiates benzoic acid from salicylic or cinnamic acids. Salicylic and cinnamic acids form colored compds that are not destroyed by heating.

Quantitative Methods—Official Final Action

(Presence of vanillin interferes (*6*))

Titrimetric Method

20.019 ***Preparation of Sample***

(**a**) *General method*.—Thoroly mix sample, grinding if solid or semisolid. Transfer 150 mL or 150 g to 500 mL vol. flask, add enough pulverized NaCl to sat. H_2O in sample, make alk. to litmus paper with 10% NaOH soln or with milk of lime (1 part powd recently slaked $Ca(OH)_2$ suspended in 3 parts H_2O), and dil. to vol. with satd NaCl soln. Shake thoroly, let stand $\geqslant$2 hr, shaking frequently, and filter. If sample contains large amts of fat, portions of which may contaminate filtrate, add few mL 10% NaOH soln to filtrate and ext with ether before proceeding as in **20.020**. If alcohol is present, proceed as in (**d**). If sample contains large amts of matter precipitable by NaCl soln, proceed as in (**e**).

(**b**) *Catsup*.—Add 15 g pulverized NaCl to 150 g sample, and transfer mixt. to 500 mL vol. flask, rinsing with ca 150 mL satd NaCl soln. Make slightly alk. to litmus paper with 10% NaOH soln and dil. to vol. with satd NaCl soln. Let stand $\geqslant$2 hr, shaking frequently. Squeeze thru heavy muslin bag, and filter.

(**c**) *Jellies, jams, preserves, and marmalades*.— Digest 150 g sample in ca 300 mL satd NaCl soln. Add 15 g pulverized NaCl. Make alk. to litmus paper with milk of lime. Transfer to 500 mL vol. flask and dil. to vol. with satd NaCl soln. Let stand $\geqslant$2 hr, shaking frequently; centrf. if necessary, and filter.

(**d**) *Cider containing alcohol, and similar products*.—Make 250 mL sample alk. to litmus paper with 10% NaOH soln and evap. on steam bath to ca 100 mL. Transfer to 250 mL vol. flask, add 30 g pulverized NaCl, and shake until dissolved. Dil. to original vol. of 250 mL with satd NaCl soln; let stand ≥2 hr, shaking frequently, and filter.

(**e**) *Salted or dried fish*.—Wash 50 g ground sample into 500 mL vol. flask with H_2O. Make slightly alk. to litmus paper with 10% NaOH soln and dil. to vol. with H_2O. Let stand ≥2 hr, shaking frequently, and filter. Pipet as large a measured portion of filtrate as possible (≥300 mL) into second 500 mL vol. flask, and add 30 g pulverized NaCl for each 100 mL soln. Shake until NaCl dissolves and dil. to vol. with satd NaCl soln. Mix thoroly, and filter off pptd protein and other extraneous matter.

20.020 ***Determination***

Pipet 100–200 mL filtrate, **20.019**, into separator. Neutze to litmus paper with HCl (1+3) and add 5 mL excess. With salted fish, protein usually ppts on acidifying, but ppt does not interfere with extn. Ext carefully with $CHCl_3$, using successive portions of 70, 50, 40, and 30 mL. To avoid formation of emulsion, shake cautiously each time, using rotary motion. $CHCl_3$ layer usually seps readily after standing few min. If emulsion forms, break it by stirring $CHCl_3$ layer with glass rod, by drawing off into second separator and giving 1 or 2 sharp shakes from one end of separator to other, or by centrfg few min. As this is progressive extn, carefully drain as much clear $CHCl_3$ soln as possible after each extn, but do not drain any of emulsion with $CHCl_3$ layer. If this precaution is taken, $CHCl_3$ ext need not be washed.

Transfer combined $CHCl_3$ exts to porcelain evapg dish, rinse container several times with few mL $CHCl_3$, and evap. to dryness at room temp. in current of dry air.

Ext may also be transferred from separator to 300 mL erlenmeyer and separator rinsed with three 5–10 mL portions $CHCl_3$. Distil very slowly at low temp. to ca ¼ original vol. Transfer residue to porcelain evapg dish, rinsing flask with three 5–10 mL portions $CHCl_3$, and evap. to dryness at room temp. in current of dry air.

Dry residue overnight (or until no odor of HOAc can be detected if product is catsup) in desiccator contg H_2SO_4. Dissolve residue of benzoic acid in 30–50 mL alcohol neut. to phthln; add ca ¼ this vol. of H_2O and 1 or 2 drops phthln; and titr. with 0.05*N* NaOH. 1 mL 0.05*N* NaOH = 0.0072 g anhyd. Na benzoate.

Spectrophotometric Method (7)

(Applicable to catsup, other tomato products, jams, jellies, beverages contg small amts of alcohol, soft drinks, and fruit juices. Not applicable to solids.)

20.021 ***Preparation of Standard Curve***

Prep. soln of benzoic acid in ether contg 50 mg/L. Det. *A* of this soln in tightly stoppered cell in Beckman DU or recording spectrophtr between 265 and 280 nm in 1 nm intervals. Plot *A* against wavelength and record wavelength of min. at ca 267.5 nm as point *B*, other min. at ca 276.5 nm as point *D*, and highest max. at ca 272 nm as point *C*.

Prep. solns of benzoic acid in ether contg 20, 40, 60, 80, 100, and 120 mg/L. Det. *A* of these solns in tightly stoppered cell in spectrophtr at points *B, C,* and *D*. For each concn, average *A* at *B* and *D* and subtract this value from *A* at *C*. Plot difference against concn.

20.022 ***Preparation of Sample***

Mix sample thoroly. Transfer 10 g or 10 mL to separator and dil. to 200 mL with satd NaCl soln. Make soln definitely acid to litmus with HCl and mix well.

20.023 ***Determination***

Ext prepd soln with 70, 50, 40, and 30 mL portions ether, shaking well to ensure complete extn. (Break emulsions by standing, stirring, or centrfg.) Drain and discard aq. phase. Wash combined ether exts with 50, 40, and 30 mL portions HCl (1+1000) and discard HCl washings. (If ext requires no purification, proceed to next par.) Ext ether soln with 50, 40, 30, and 20 mL portions 0.1% NH_4OH and discard ether. Neutze combined NH_4OH exts with HCl and add 1 mL excess. Ext acidified soln with 70, 50, 40, and 30 mL ether.

Dil. combined ether exts to 200 mL with ether and det. *A* in tightly stoppered cell in spectrophtr at wavelengths *B, C,* and *D*, dilg with ether if necessary to obtain optimum concn of 20–120 mg/L. Average *A* at *B* and *D* and subtract this value from *A* at *C*. Det. concn benzoic acid from std curve, correcting for dilns. Benzoic acid × 1.18 = Na benzoate.

Conduct detn similarly on benzoate-free sample of product and det. *A* in region 265–280 nm at 1 nm intervals. If curve is straight line in this region, method is applicable to this product.

Thin Layer Chromatographic Method (8)
Official First Action

20.024 ***Apparatus and Reagents***

(**a**) *Steam distillation apparatus*.—See Fig. **20:01**. (*1*) Connecting tube only, with flask joint ₮ 34/45 and condenser joint ₮ 24/40 (JD 1710); (*2*) Kjeldahl flask, 800 mL, with outer joint ₮ 34/45 (JF 6030); (*3*) condenser, 30 cm with outer joint ₮ 24/40 at top and drip tip at delivery end (JC 6400); (*4*) steam generator, *see* **18.050(a)**; (*5*) variable transformers, 10 amp; and (*6*) Glas-Col heating mantle, 500 mL (11-472-10F). (Items 1–3 cite SGA Scientific Inc. Nos; items 5 and 6 cite Fisher Scientific Co. Nos.)

(**b**) *Ultraviolet recording spectrophotometer and accessories*.—Recording between 250 and 350 nm; with 5 cm micro cells and cell adapter (Pyrocell Mfg. Inc., PO Box 176, Westwood, NJ 07675, Nos. 5009, 5009A).

(**c**) *Thin layer chromatographic equipment and adsorbents*.—*See* **29.006**; kieselguhr G and silica gel GF 254 (Brinkmann Instruments, Inc.).

20.025 ***Preparation of Plates***

In 250 mL erlenmeyer, mix 10 g each of kieselguhr G and silica gel GF 254. Add 45 mL H_2O and shake 30 sec. Set applicator

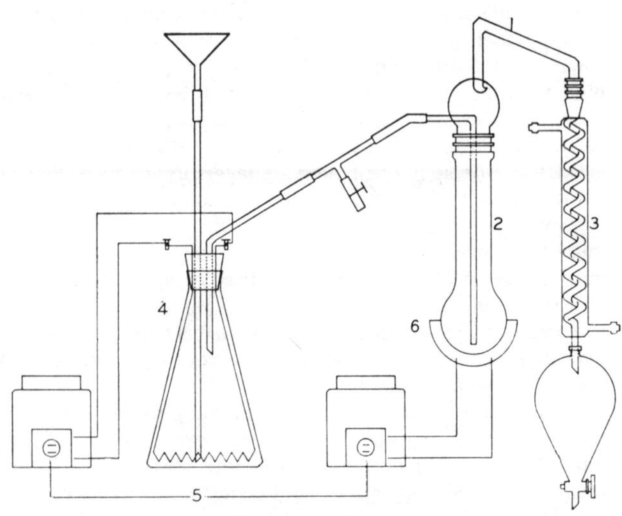

FIG. 20:01—Steam distillation apparatus

at 0.25 mm and apply mixt. to 5 glass plates. Air dry 10 min and dry in forced-draft oven 1 hr at 100°.

20.026 ***Preparation of Sample***

(**a**) *Liquids*.—Accurately weigh ca 50–60 g sample directly into 800 mL Kjeldahl flask. Continue as in (**c**), beginning "Add 200 g $MgSO_4.7H_2O$ . . ."

(**b**) *Solids*.—Accurately weigh ca 40 g sample into high-speed blender. Add 100 mL H_2O (or more if necessary) and blend until homogeneous. Quant. transfer to 800 mL Kjeldahl flask with small portions H_2O. Continue as in (**c**), beginning "Add 200 g $MgSO_4.7H_2O$ . . ."

(**c**) *Semisolids and solid-liquid mixtures*.—Blend entire unit sample in high-speed blender to homogeneous mixt. Quant. transfer ca 50–60 g blended sample (accurately weighed) to 800 mL Kjeldahl flask with small portions H_2O, if necessary. Add 200 g $MgSO_4.7H_2O$ and 25 mL H_3PO_4. Wash down neck of flask with H_2O until total vol. is 350–375 mL. Steam distil sample directly into 1 L separator contg 50 mL NaOH soln (4 g/100 mL); collect 725–750 mL distillate in ≥90 min by adjusting transformers. (Distn rate is very critical; typical drop time is 50 drops/20 sec.) Rinse condenser with ca 20 mL H_2O. Acidify distillate to litmus with ca 20 mL HCl. Ext with one 100 mL and four 50 mL portions $CHCl_3$-ether (2+1). Shake each ext vigorously ≥1 min and collect exts in 600 mL beaker. Evap. combined exts carefully on steam bath, using gentle air current, to ca 25 mL, washing down sides of beaker occasionally with $CHCl_3$-ether. (Do not let exts go to dryness.) Transfer to 50 mL vol. flask, wash beaker with small portions $CHCl_3$-ether, and transfer washings to vol. flask. Dil. to vol. with $CHCl_3$-ether for TLC analysis.

20.027 ***Determination***

Spot 100 μL sample soln, using 50 μL syringe twice, under gentle air draft on prepd plate. Also, spot 100 μL benzoic acid std soln (50 mg/50 mL alcohol). Spot sample(s) and std ca 2.5 cm from bottom edge of plate and 4 cm apart, beginning 2.5 cm in from side edge. Place plate in chromatgc tank contg 250–300 mL mobile solv., *n*-hexane-HOAc (96+4), and develop chromatogram for 10 cm. Remove and air dry 5 min. Observe under UV shortwave radiation (2540Å). Sample and std benzoic acid appear as dark blue-purple spots on light fluorescent background. With pencil, circle spots 1 cm out from edge of each spot. (This gives exact location of each acid when plate is removed from radiation.) Scrape encircled area with steel spatula onto piece of Glassine paper and carefully transfer to 10 mL vol. flask. From unused portion of plate, scrape off area ca equal to that used for sample into 10 mL vol. flask to serve as blank. To each, add 7 mL alcohol, stopper, and shake 30 sec. Dil. to vol. with alcohol, transfer to centrf. tube, and centrf. until clear (ca 5 min) at high speed. Decant clear supernate into 5 cm micro cell and scan on recording spectrophtr from 310 to 250 nm against blank. Det. A of sample and A' of std at max. absorbance, ca 272 nm.

% Benzoic acid
$= [(A/A') \times (\text{g std}/50\text{ mL})/(\text{g sample}/50\text{ mL})] \times 100,$

% Na benzoate = % benzoic acid × 1.180

20.028 ***Qualitative Tests***

Evap. 2 mL portions $CHCl_3$-ether ext to dryness. On this residue, perform test for benzoic acid, **14.039**, par. 4, beginning "From Mohr pipet, add . . ." and ending ". . . benzoic acid." Use 50 mL Pyrex test tube (25 × 150 mm).

Det. IR spectrum. Evap. 5 mL $CHCl_3$-ether exts to dryness and make KBr disk with residue.

BORIC ACID AND BORATES

20.029 Qualitative Test (*9*)—Official Final Action

(**a**) *Preliminary test*.—Acidify sample with HCl (7 mL acid to each 100 mL sample). Heat solid or pasty samples with enough H_2O to make sufficiently fluid before acidifying. Immerse strip of turmeric paper, **20.033(a)**, in acidified liq., and let paper dry spontaneously. If $Na_2B_4O_7$ or H_3BO_3 is present, paper turns characteristic red, changed by NH_4OH to dark blue-green, but restored by acid.

(**b**) *Confirmatory test*.—Make ca 25 g sample decidedly alk. with lime-H_2O or milk of lime and evap. to dryness on steam bath. Ignite dry residue at low red heat until org. matter is thoroly charred. Cool, digest with ca 15 mL H_2O, and add HCl dropwise until soln is distinctly acid. Immerse piece of turmeric paper in soln and dry without heat. In presence of $Na_2B_4O_7$ or H_3BO_3 color change will be same as in (**a**).

Qualitative Thin Layer Test for Boron in Caviar (Screening Technique)(*10*)—Official Final Action

20.030 ***Reagents***

(**a**) *TLC plates*.—3 × 1″ microscopic slides coated with 250 μm silica gel G (E. Merck).

(**b**) *Developing solvent*.—Anhyd. alcohol-benzene (1+10).

(**c**) *Spray reagents*.—(*1*) NH_4OH; (*2*) HOAc-H_2SO_4 (1+1).

(**d**) *Curcumin soln*.—0.125%. Dissolve 125 mg curcumin (available from Eastman Kodak Co.) in 100 mL HOAc. Prep. fresh daily.

20.031 ***Preparation of Silica Gel Slides***

Clean slides with soap and rinse thoroly until they drain cleanly (without beading). Place slides on template, as shown in Fig. **20:02**.

To make slides adhere to template, place 1 drop H_2O under each slide as it is set in place.

Weigh 30 g silica gel into 250 mL g-s erlenmeyer. Add 60 mL H_2O and agitate gently 45 sec. Pour quickly into Desaga-Brinkmann spreader set to give 250 μm thickness. Pull applicator evenly over slides. Air dry slides 30 min. Place slides in oven 30 min at 100°.

20.032 ***Determination***

(*Caution: See* **51.017**.)

Put 10 mL developing solv. into 250 mL lipless beaker or suitable jar. Place filter paper wick (2.5 × 8 cm) in solv., cover beaker with watch glass, and let equilibrate 5 min.

Place 100±20 mg caviar in mortar. Grind and ext with 20 mL H_2O. Transfer washings to g-s centrf. tube and centrf. 5 min. Decant supernate into 100 mL vol. flask. Add 10 mL H_2O to residue in tube, stopper, and shake vigorously 1 min. Centrf. and decant supernate into same vol. flask. Repeat with 10 mL H_2O, dil. to vol., and mix. Place 2 mL each of sample soln, std

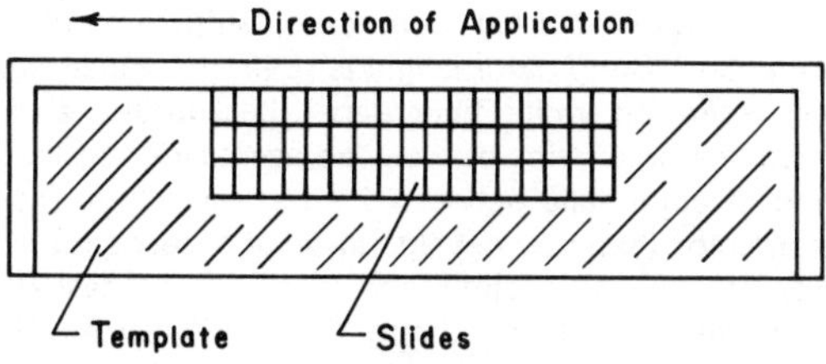

FIG. 20:02—Placement of slides on template for applying silica gel coating

soln, and H_2O for blank in sep. Pt dishes. Add ca 6 drops 10% NaOH to each dish and swirl to mix thoroly. Evap. to chalk white dryness on vigorous steam bath (expose directly to steam). (Hot plate may be used; avoid spattering.) Dissolve residue in ca 1.5 mL 0.125% curcumin soln, applying gentle heat if necessary to dissolve residue. Add ca 1.5 mL HOAc-H_2SO_4 soln (1+1), mix thoroly with stainless steel or plastic spatula, and let stand 15 min. Transfer solns to graduated beakers with absolute alcohol, dil. to 50 mL, and stir. Sep. spot 40 μL blank, std soln, **20.039(e)**(*2*), and sample soln on same slide. Place slide in beaker, cover, and let develop 10 min. Remove slide, air dry, and note red-purple spot at origin and excess curcumin dye above. Spray with spray reagent (*1*) and note blue color change in spot at origin. Respray with spray reagent (*2*) and note change to red-purple.

Semiquantitative Method (*11*)—Official Final Action

(Applicable to meat)

20.033 ***Reagents***

(**a**) *Turmeric paper.*—Add 100 mL 80% alcohol to 1.5–2.0 g turmeric powder in 250 mL g-s erlenmeyer. Shake 5 min and filter. Dip sheets of Whatman No. 2 paper into the clear filtrate in flat-bottom dish (petri dish). Hang paper to dry. After 1 hr cut into 6 × 1 cm strips and store in tightly stoppered container protected from light.

(**b**) *Boric acid std soln.*—10 mg H_3BO_3/mL. Dissolve 1.000 g H_3BO_3 in H_2O and dil. to 100 mL.

20.034 ***Preparation of Reference Standards***

Transfer 0.00, 0.10, 0.20, 0.50, 0.75, 1.00, 2.50, and 5.00 mL std H_3BO_3 soln to 15 mL test tubes. Dil. to 10 mL with H_2O and add 0.7 mL HCl. Keep tubes tightly stoppered to prevent evapn. These stds represent 0.00, 0.02, 0.04, 0.10, 0.15, 0.20, 0.50, and 1.00% H_3BO_3 in meat (based on 25 g sample extd with 50 mL H_2O and 10 mL aliquot used for test). Std solns may be stored in Pyrex test tubes >6 months. On long storage, borate is leached from Pyrex.

20.035 ***Determination***

Disperse 25 g ground meat in 50 mL H_2O in 125 mL erlenmeyer, using flat-end stirring rod. Cover with watch glass or small funnel. Bring to boil on hot plate (or over medium flame) with agitation. Do not overheat. Cool in ice bath or in beaker of H_2O in refrigerator until fat solidifies (ca 0.5 hr). Filter thru pledget of glass wool. Transfer 10 mL filtrate to 15 mL test tube, add 0.7 mL HCl, stopper, and mix.

Mark identification on end of piece of turmeric paper and dip unmarked end into unknown soln to ½ the length of paper. Quickly remove moistened paper and place on sheet of white filter paper. Flat-tipped forceps are useful in handling paper.

Place freshly prepd std strips of test paper (made by dipping turmeric papers in similar manner into series of std solns) alongside sample turmeric strips.

After ≥1 hr (but <2 hr) at room temp., strips are dry enough for comparison. Good natural light is preferred. Place std strips ca 1 cm apart on white filter paper background and bring "unknown" sample strips between adjacent stds for close color matching. If color falls between 2 stds, est. value. Disregard streaks of color that may develop at edge of test strip.

If color intensity is beyond range of stds, repeat test with diln of meat filtrate (e.g., 5 mL filtrate, 5 mL H_2O, 0.7 mL HCl and multiply final reading by 2). Use freshly prepd set of std papers with each series of samples tested.

Quantitative Methods

20.036 ***Titrimetric Method—Official Final Action***

Make 10–100 g sample (depending upon material and amt of H_3BO_3 present) distinctly alk. with 10% NaOH soln and evap. to dryness in Pt dish. Ignite until org. matter is thoroly charred, avoiding intense red heat; cool, digest with ca 20 mL hot H_2O, and add HCl dropwise until reaction is distinctly acid. Filter into 100 mL vol. flask and wash with little hot H_2O. (Vol. filtrate should be <50–60 mL.) Return filter contg any unoxidized C to Pt dish, make alk. by wetting thoroly with lime-H_2O, dry on steam bath, and ignite to white ash.

Dissolve ash in few mL HCl (1+3) and add to liq. in 100 mL vol. flask, rinsing dish with few mL H_2O. To combined solns add 0.5 g $CaCl_2$ and few drops phthln, then 10% NaOH soln until permanent light pink is produced. Finally dil. to vol. with lime-H_2O, mix, and filter thru dry filter. To 50 mL filtrate add 1*N* H_2SO_4 until pink disappears; then add Me orange, **6.005(g)**, and continue addn of acid until yellow changes to pink. Boil ca 1 min to expel CO_2. Cool, and carefully add 0.2*N* NaOH until liq. becomes yellow, avoiding excess alkali. (All H_3BO_3 is now in free state with no uncombined H_2SO_4 present.) Add 1–2 g neut. mannitol and few drops phthln, read buret, and again titr. soln with the std NaOH until pink. Add little more mannitol, and if pink disappears, continue addn of the std alkali until pink reappears. Repeat alternate addn of mannitol and std alkali until permanent end point is reached. Vol. glycerol (neut. to phthln) equal to vol. soln to be titrd may be substituted for mannitol. 1 mL 0.2*N* NaOH = 0.0124 g H_3BO_3.

Spectrophotometric Method (10)—Official Final Action

(Applicable to caviar. Rinse all glassware with H_2O before use. Carry reagent and caviar blanks thru detn with stds and samples. For caviar blank use caviar shown to be B-free by **20.032**.)

20.037 ***Principle***

B reacts with curcumin in nonaq. acid soln to form stable color complex. Intensity of color is measured spectrophtric at 555 nm.

20.038 ***Apparatus***

(**a**) *Spectrophotometer.*—Beckman DK-2A ratio recording spectrophtr (superceded by model 5240) (or DU spectrophtr), or equiv., with silica 1 cm cells with g-s stoppers.

(**b**) *Platinum dishes.*—3 cm deep × 7 cm diam.

20.039 ***Reagents***

(**a**) *Curcumin soln.*—0.125%. See **20.030(d)**.

(**b**) *Sodium hydroxide soln.*—10%. Keep in plastic bottle.

(**c**) *Sulfuric acid-acetic acid.*—(1+1). Use new bottles of acids.

(**d**) *Anhydrous alcohol* (*used thruout method*).—MeOH may be substituted. Let stand 24 hr over CaO, decant, and distil twice from KOH.

(**e**) *Boron std solns.*—(*1*) *Stock soln.*—100 μg B/mL. Accurately weigh 57±3 mg H_3BO_3, ACS crystal, into 100 mL vol. flask. Add 50 mL H_2O and shake mech. 20 min. Dil. to vol. and mix. (Prep. on day method is run.) (*2*) *Working soln.*—1 μg B/mL. Pipet 1 mL stock soln into 100 mL vol. flask, dil. to vol. with H_2O, and mix.

20.040 ***Preparation of Sample Solutions***

Weigh 270±25 mg caviar into 250 mL 2-neck, r-b flask; place sample in exact center of bottom of flask. Connect flask to straight-tube H_2O condenser to facilitate rinsing, and place condenser in center hole of flask and glass stopper in side hole.

(Do *not* use lubricating grease.) Add 1 mL H_2SO_4, close flask with glass stopper, apply small flame from Bunsen burner to circumference of acid soln, and heat until surface of liq. begins to move. Remove flame. Promote gentle evolution of bubbles with intermittent flame. Do not cause acid to spatter or to evolve copious fumes. Continue heating 5 min, or until solids are dissolved; soln will be black and smooth. Cool flask in ice-H_2O. If fumes are present, let settle. With syringe, quickly add 1 mL 30% H_2O_2 thru stoppered opening, close flask immediately, and gently heat soln with intermittent flame to initiate boiling. Heat ca 5 min, or until fumes start to evolve. (Soln should be generally clear with some minute particles.) Cool flask to room temp. in ice-H_2O. Rinse condenser directly into reaction flask with H_2O. Disconnect flask, quant. transfer soln, using glass funnel, with H_2O into 100 mL vol. flask, dil. to vol., and mix. (Solns should be pale yellow or colorless.)

20.041 ***Determination***

Pipet following into individual Pt dishes: 1 mL H_2O for reagent blank; 1, 2, 3, 4, and 5 mL working std soln; 1 mL caviar sample soln; 1 mL caviar blank soln (B-free). Add 1 mL 10% NaOH to each dish and swirl to mix thoroly. Place dishes on vigorous steam bath (expose directly to steam) and dry until chalk white (ca 2.5–3 hr). Transfer dishes to 100±5° oven and continue to dry residue 0.5 hr. (*Caution:* Higher temps will cause spattering.) Remove dishes and cool. Add 3 mL curcumin soln. Use individual spatula for each dish and stir residue with stainless steel or plastic spatula to dissolve. (All std residues will dissolve in 2–3 min, but sample soln does not dissolve completely and must be stirred 5 min. Very gentle heat may be applied to promote soln.) Cool dishes to room temp. and add 3 mL HOAc-H_2SO_4 soln. Stir with same spatula to mix completely until no visible yellow color remains in dish or on spatula; continue to stir and rotate dish for 2 min after yellow color disappears. Let soln stand 15 min. Transfer solns with ca 50 mL anhyd. alcohol (eye dropper works well) to 100 mL vol. flasks, using glass funnels. Thoroly rinse dishes into flasks with anhyd. alcohol and dil. to vol. within 5 mL of mark. Treat each soln sep. as follows: Dil. to vol. and mix. Filter thru dry paper and discard first 3 mL. Collect filtrate directly in spectrophtr cells and read A against anhyd. alcohol at 700 and 555 nm.

Calc. ΔA of std solns ($A_{555} - A_{700}$). Subtract reagent blank ΔA from std readings. Likewise, calc. ΔA of caviar solns. Subtract caviar blank ΔA from sample ΔA. Plot std curve on graph paper: μg B/100 mL as abscissa against ΔA as ordinate. Det. μg B/100 mL for caviar from graph.

$$g\ B = [\mu g\ B/100\ mL\ (from\ graph)]10^4$$

$$\%\ Boric\ acid = (g\ B \times 5.7142 \times 100)/g\ sample.$$

★ Atomic Absorption Spectrophotometric ★ Method (12)—Official First Action

20.042 ***Apparatus***

Atomic absorption spectrophotometer.—Perkin-Elmer Model 303, or equiv. Typical operating parameters for this app. are given in Table **20:01**. Operator must become familiar with optimum settings for his own app. and use table only as a guide. (*Caution: See* **51.006**.)

20.043 ***Reagents***

(**a**) *Extracting soln.*—20% (v/v) 2-ethyl-1,3-hexanediol in methyl isobutyl ketone. Sat. with H_2O by gently shaking soln with ½ its vol. H_2O ca 1 min, letting sep. completely, and discarding aq. phase.

(**b**) *Boron std solns.*—(*1*) *Stock soln.*—1 mg B/mL. In 1 L vol. flask dissolve 5.716 g H_3BO_3 in ca 500 mL H_2O, dil. to 1 L, and mix. (*2*) *Working solns.*—Pipet 10 mL stock soln into 100 mL vol. flask, dil. to vol., and mix. Pipet 5, 10, 15, and 20 mL portions this soln into sep. 50 mL g-s graduates, add 5 mL H_2SO_4 to each, mix, cool, and dil. to 30±3 mL with H_2O. Pipet 10 mL extg soln, (**a**), into each, mix ca 1 min, and let phases sep. completely. Org. layers now contain 50, 100, 150, and 200 μg B/mL, resp.

Table 20:01 Operating Parameters

Wavelength, Å	2497.7
Slit width, mm	1 (setting 3)
Source, ma	30
N_2O flow rate, L/min	12 (scale divisions −6)
C_2H_2 rate, L/min	7 (metal ball scale divisions − 5.5)
Aspiration rate, mL/min	4
Scale expansion	3× or 10×
Noise suppression setting	2 or 3
Concn range, μg/mL	0–200

20.044 ***Preparation of Sample***

(*Caution: See* **51.018** and **51.019**.)

Accurately weigh ca 1 g sample into 150 mL ₮ r-b flask. Add 5 mL H_2SO_4 and connect flask to H_2O-cooled condenser. Add 3 mL HNO_3 thru top of condenser and heat mixt. with Bunsen flame to start reaction. Apply heat as necessary to maintain moderate reaction rate until most org. matter is destroyed and no brown fumes are evolved. If sample chars, remove flame, add 1 mL HNO_3, and resume heating. Repeat addn of 1 mL HNO_3, if necessary. Digestion is completed when no brown fumes are being evolved. (Total digestion time is ca 30 min and usually requires 3–4 mL HNO_3. Some fat may remain.) Cool, and rinse condenser with H_2O to bring total vol. in flask to 30±3 mL. Disconnect flask, pipet 10 mL extg soln into flask, stopper, and mix ≥1 min. Pour mixt. into 50 mL graduate and let phases sep. completely.

20.045 ***Determination***

Set up app. as in Table **20:01**, or use previously established optimum settings. Zero app. while aspirating extg soln, (**a**). Det. A of sample and stds in org. layer. Flush burner with extg soln, and check 0 point between readings. Det. B content from std curve of A against μg B/mL.

$$\%\ H_3BO_3 = [(\mu g\ B/mL) \times 10 \times 5.714]/\ (g\ sample \times 10^4),$$

where 5.714 is factor to convert B to H_3BO_3.

Emission Spectroscopic Method (13) Official Final Action

(Before proceeding with sample analysis, analyze known H_3BO_3 soln until ≥90% recovery is obtained.)

20.046 ***Apparatus***

(**a**) *Atomic absorption spectrophotometer.*—Operated in emission mode, Perkin-Elmer Model 403, or equiv. Operating parameters: N_2O-H flame with N_2O single-slot burner head; flow rates ca 12 L/min; wavelength 518 nm; spectral slit width 5 nm; equipped with strip chart recorder. (*Caution: See* **51.006**.)

(**b**) *Digestion vessel.—See* **25.115**.

20.047 ***Reagents***

(**a**) *Chelating-extracting soln.*—15% (v/v) 2-Ethyl-1,3-hexanediol in methyl isobutyl ketone.

★ Surplus method—*see* inside front cover.

(**b**) *Boron std solns.*—(*1*) *Stock soln.*—500 μg B/mL. In 1 L vol. flask, dissolve 2.858 g H_3BO_3 in H_2O, dil. to vol., and mix. (*2*) *Working soln.*—150 μg B/mL. Dil. 15.0 mL stock soln to 50.0 mL with H_2O.

20.048 ***Preparation of Sample***

Accurately weigh ca 1 g well mixed sample into Teflon digestion vessel. Add 5.0 mL HNO_3 and close vessel, tightening metal screw cap contg Teflon sealing disk. Similarly prep. blank, using 5.0 mL HNO_3 only. Place vessel in 150° oven 1 hr. Remove vessel and let cool to room temp. Unscrew cap, snap on spout, and transfer digested sample with aid of 10 mL H_2O to Mojonnier flask (25 mL bulb capacity). (If Mojonnier flask is not available, 125 mL separator marked at 25 mL may be used.) Make soln just basic (litmus paper) by slowly adding NH_4OH; usually ca 5 mL is required. Acidify by dropwise addn of H_2SO_4 (1+1). For optimum extn, dil. contents of Mojonnier flask with H_2O to center of neck. Add 10 mL chelating-extg soln, stopper, and shake 1 min. Let phases sep. and decant upper org. layer into 25 mL vol. flask. Repeat chelation-extn with 10 and 5 mL chelating-extg soln, combining org. layers in vol. flask. Dil. to 25 mL with chelating-extg soln, stopper flask, and mix.

20.049 ***Preparation of Standards***

Pipet 0, 1, 2, and 3 mL portions of B working std soln into sep. Mojonnier flasks (or separators, as for sample). Add 1–2 drops H_2SO_4 (1+1) and dil. with H_2O to center of neck of flasks for optimum extns. Ext as for sample, beginning "Add 10 mL chelating-extg soln, . . ."

20.050 ***Determination***

Using N_2O burner head, N_2O-H flame, and ca 5 nm spectral slit width, measure boron oxide molecular emission at 518 nm. Record signals on strip chart recorder. Suppress background signal, given by 0 μg B std ext, to near 0 on chart, and control amplifier gain to give near full scale signal for highest B std. Aspirate 0 μg B std soln between each sample or std reading. Measure each std and sample peak using 0 μg B std as baseline. Plot std calibration curve and obtain amt B in sample from this curve.

20.051 DIETHYLCARBONATE—OFFICIAL FINAL ACTION

See **11.076–11.078**.

DEHYDROACETIC ACID

20.052 Qualitative Test (*14*)—Official Final Action

(*Caution: See* **51.011**, **51.039**, and **51.054**.)

(**a**) *Salicylaldehyde reagent.*—Dissolve 10 mL salicylaldehyde in alcohol and dil. to 50 mL.

(**b**) *Test.*—Transfer dehydroacetic acid soln remaining in 500 mL vol. flask after quant. detn, **20.053**, to 1 L separator. Add 100–125 mL ether and shake vigorously. Let sep., drain aq. layer, and discard. Drain ether into 125 mL erlenmeyer, taking care not to include any emulsion or H_2O. Evap. ether ext to dryness on steam bath and dissolve residue in 1 mL ca 0.5*N* NaOH. Pour alk. soln into test tube (do not rinse flask); add 0.5 mL of alc. salicylaldehyde soln and 1 mL NaOH (1+1). Mix, and place in boiling H_2O bath 5 min. Remove from bath, add 2 mL H_2O, and observe color. Include reagent blank and control contg 0.2 or 0.3 mg dehydroacetic acid for comparison. With $\leqslant$10 ppm dehydroacetic acid in cheese, red or orange soln is obtained. Intensity of color is approx. proportional to quantity of dehydroacetic acid present.

Quantitative Method (*14*)—Official Final Action

20.053 ***Determination***

Weigh 50–60 g cheese to nearest 0.1 g, place in high-speed blender, and comminute (covered) with 80 mL $CHCl_3$ 3 min, scraping down walls and cover once during operation. Place filter paper on 6–8 cm diam. fritted glass buchner (if fritted glass funnel is not available, use ordinary buchner), transfer mixt. to funnel with spatula, and filter with suction. Return cake and paper to blender, add 80 mL $CHCl_3$, blend 1 min, and refilter into same flask. Use fresh paper for each filtration. Repeat extn and filtration for third time with 80 mL $CHCl_3$. Wash sides of filter and cake once with 25 mL $CHCl_3$. Remove greater portion of $CHCl_3$ by compressing cheese cake.

Transfer combined $CHCl_3$ filtrates to 500 mL separator. Rinse filter flask with 2 small portions $CHCl_3$ and add to separator. Ext $CHCl_3$ soln with ca 33 mL ca 0.5*N* NaOH. Transfer $CHCl_3$ layer to 600 mL beaker and aq. layer to 300 mL erlenmeyer. Return $CHCl_3$ to separator and repeat above alk. extn twice. Emulsion may be formed during extn, but most of it will break on standing. Transfer emulsified layer to alk. soln only in final extn. Acidify alk. ext with 70 mL ca 1*N* HCl, and rapidly aerate for such time as required to remove dissolved $CHCl_3$ (5–10 min). To check complete removal of $CHCl_3$, smell top of flask while aerating. Be sure to remove all $CHCl_3$ by aeration, or low values will be obtained. Filter soln thru medium or fine porosity fritted glass funnel fitted with filter paper and dil. to vol. with H_2O in 500 mL vol. flask. If soln is turbid, clarify by refiltering thru fine filter or asbestos pad.

Prep. reagent blank by extg 250 mL $CHCl_3$ with alkali, adding acid to ext, aerating, and dilg to vol. with H_2O. Place portion of reagent blank in one cell and portion of sample soln in another. Det. *A* at 307 nm with Beckman DU spectrophtr, or equiv. Dil. sample soln if necessary to obtain readings in range of std curve. (Ordinary range of diln for *A* readings is from no diln to diln of 1 + 5.)

20.054 ***Preparation of Standard Curve***

To prep. std curve use fresh dehydroacetic acid soln, as low readings are obtained from older solns. Weigh exactly 100 mg dehydroacetic acid (Eastman, or equiv.) and transfer to 100 mL vol. flask. Dissolve in ca 50 mL H_2O and 4 mL ca 0.5*N* NaOH. Dil. to vol. with H_2O, and mix. Pipet 1.0, 3.0, and 5.0 mL (1.0, 3.0, and 5.0 mg dehydroacetic acid) aliquots of this stock soln into sep. 500 mL vol. flasks. To each add equiv. of ca 100 mL ca 0.5*N* NaOH and 70 mL ca 1*N* HCl, dil. to vol., and mix. Det. *A* at 307 nm, using reagent blank prepd as above. Plot *A* against mg dehydroacetic acid/500 mL prepd soln.

ppm Dehydroacetic acid = (mg/500 mL) × 1000/wt sample.

SOLUBLE FLUORIDES

Qualitative Tests

20.055 *Hydrofluoric Acid Test (15)*—*Official Final Action*

(**a**) *Not applicable in presence of silicates.*—After thoroly mixing sample, transfer to beaker 150 mL, or equiv. amt of aq. ext in case of solid foods, and boil, adding 5 mL *10% K_2SO_4 soln* and 10 mL *10% $Ba(OAc)_2$* soln. Collect ppt (BaF_2) in compact mass (centrf. may be used advantageously) and wash on small filter. Transfer to Pt crucible and ignite.

Carefully dip cleaned glass plate, while hot, in mixt. of equal parts of *carnauba wax* and *paraffin*, and let cool. Make distinctive mark thru wax with sharp instrument, taking care not to scratch surface of glass.

Add few drops H_2SO_4 to residue in crucible and cover crucible with waxed plate, having mark over center of crucible and making sure edge of crucible is in close contact with plate. Keep top surface of plate cool, and heat crucible 1 hr at as high temp. as practicable without melting wax (elec. stove gives most satisfactory form of heat). If fluorides are present, distinct etching is apparent on exposed glass.

(**b**) *Applicable in presence of silicates*.—Mix small amt of pptd SiO_2 with pptd BaF_2, (**a**), and proceed as in **20.059** or **20.060**. (This method is valuable for foods which contain considerable amt of SiO_2 in the ash. Under these circumstances H_2SO_4 liberates SiF_4, which would escape detection in (**a**).)

Quenching of Aluminum 8-Hydroxyquinolate Fluorescence (16)—Official First Action

20.056 ***Reagents***

(**a**) *Aluminum soln*.—Dissolve 2.22 g $AlNH_4(SO_4)_2.12H_2O$ in H_2O, add 3 drops HCl, and dil. to 250 mL with H_2O.

(**b**) *Oxine reagent*.—Dissolve enough 8-hydroxyquinoline in 2*N* HOAc to make 5% soln. 1 mL of this soln is equiv. to ca 5 mL Al soln.

(**c**) *Ammonium acetate soln*.—Dissolve 77 g NH_4OAc in H_2O and dil. to 500 mL with H_2O.

(**d**) *Aluminum 8-hydroxyquinolate*.—Warm 250 mL Al soln to 50–60° and add excess of oxine reagent. Slowly add NH_4OAc soln until permanent ppt forms. Then add 20–25 mL more to ensure complete pptn. Let ppt settle and filter thru fritted glass crucible. Wash ppt well with at least seven or eight 30 mL portions cold H_2O and dry at 120–140°. Store in desiccator.

(**e**) *Chloroform soln of aluminum 8-hydroxyquinolate*.—Dissolve Al oxine in $CHCl_3$ to prep. 0.5 mg/mL soln. Prep. daily.

(**f**) *Sulfuric acid*.—Concd. If blank detn reveals presence of F, purify as in **25.052(c)**, dilg and boiling 3 times.

20.057 ***Test***

Proceed as in **20.055(a)**, adding 3 mL HOAc to soln in addn to K_2SO_4 and $Ba(OAc)_2$ solns. Transfer ignited residue to small porcelain crucible ($\leq$5 mL).

Wet piece of filter paper with $CHCl_3$ soln of Al oxine in spot larger in diam. than top of crucible and let air dry. Add H_2SO_4 to cover ash, crimp paper over crucible edge, and put wt (e.g., beaker) on paper. Heat crucible covered with paper 5 min at 50–60°. Observe paper under UV light. In presence of F, fluorescence of the Al oxine is quenched in area of spot over crucible. Limit of identification is ca 0.05 mg F. Conduct blank detn on H_2SO_4.

INSOLUBLE FLUORIDES—OFFICIAL FINAL ACTION

(Fluoborates, fluosilicates, etc.)

20.058 Preparation of Sample

Make ca 200 g sample alk. with lime-H_2O, evap. to dryness, and ash. Ext crude ash with H_2O contg enough HOAc to decompose carbonates; filter, ignite insol. portion, ext with HOAc (1+2), and again filter. Insol. portion now contains $CaSiO_3$ and CaF_2, while filtrate contains all H_3BO_3 present.

20.059 Qualitative Test I (*17*)

Ash filter contg insol. portion from **20.058**, mix with little pptd SiO_2, transfer to short test tube attached to small U-tube contg few drops H_2O, and add 1–2 mL H_2SO_4. Keep test tube in beaker of H_2O on steam bath 30–40 min. If any F is present, SiF_4 generated is decomposed by H_2O in U-tube and forms gelatinous deposit on walls of tube.

Test filtrate for H_3BO_3 as in **20.029**. If both HF and H_3BO_3 are present, it is probable that they are combined as BF_3. If, however, SiF_4 is detected and H_3BO_3 is not, repeat test without adding SiO_2, in which case formation of SiO_2 skeleton is conclusive evidence of presence of fluosilicate. In ash contg appreciable amt of SiO_2, H_2SO_4 liberates SiF_4 rather than HF. Therefore presence of fluosilicate, not fluoride, is indicated.

20.060 Qualitative Test II

Ash filter contg insol. portion from **20.058** in Pt crucible, mix with little pptd SiO_2, and add 1 mL H_2SO_4. Cover crucible with watch glass from underside of which drop of H_2O is suspended, and heat 1 hr at 70–80°, keeping watch glass well cooled. The H_2O decomposes SiF_4 formed, leaving gelatinous deposit of SiO_2 and etching ring at periphery of drop of H_2O. Test filtrate for H_3BO_3 as in **20.029**.

20.061 Quantitative Method

See **25.049–25.055**.

FORMALDEHYDE

(*See also* **31.189–31.194**.)

20.062 Preparation of Sample—Official First Action

If sample is solid or semisolid, macerate 100 g with 100 mL H_2O in mortar. Transfer to 800 mL Kjeldahl flask, acidify with H_3PO_4, add 1 mL excess, connect with condenser thru trap, and slowly distil 50 mL. For milk, dil. 100 mL with 100 mL H_2O, and acidify and distil as for solids. With other liq. foods, acidify 200 mL and distil as for solids.

Qualitative Tests—Official First Action

20.063 ***Chromotropic Acid Test (18)***

(**a**) *Reagent*.—Prep. satd soln of 1,8-dihydroxynaphthalene-3,6-disulfonic acid (ca 500 mg/100 mL) in ca 72% H_2SO_4 (pour 150 mL H_2SO_4 into 100 mL H_2O and cool). Soln is light straw-colored.

(**b**) *Test*.—Place 5 mL reagent in test tube and add, with mixing, 1 mL distillate, **20.062**. Place in boiling H_2O bath 15 min, and observe during heating period. Presence of HCHO is indicated by appearance of light to deep purple (depth of color depending on amt of HCHO present).

20.064 ***Hehner-Fulton Test (19)***

(*Caution: See* **51.030** and **51.047**.)

(**a**) *Oxidizing soln*.—To cold H_2SO_4 add, in small portions, equal vol. satd Br-H_2O, cooling thruout operation.

(**b**) *Test*.—To 6 mL cold H_2SO_4 add 5 mL distillate, **20.062**, slowly and with cooling. Place 5 mL mixt. in test tube, and add, slowly and with cooling, 1 mL aldehyde-free milk, then 0.5 mL oxidizing soln. Mix. Purplish-pink indicates HCHO.

20.065 FORMIC ACID—OFFICIAL FINAL ACTION

See **18.050–18.055**; **17.043–17.047**.

HYDROGEN PEROXIDE

20.066 Qualitative Test (*20*)—Official Final Action

(Applicable to milk)

(**a**) *Reagent*.—Dissolve 1 g V_2O_5 in 100 mL H_2SO_4 (6+94).

(**b**) *Test*.—Add 10–20 drops reagent to ca 10 mL sample and mix. Pink or red indicates H_2O_2.

MONOCHLOROACETIC ACID (*21*)
OFFICIAL FINAL ACTION

Qualitative Tests

20.067 ***Optical-Crystallographic Properties of Barium Salt***

(Applicable to com. preservatives)

Dil. 4–5 mL sample to 100 mL, add 6 mL H_2SO_4 (1+1), and ext with equal vol. ether in separator. If emulsions form, ext in continuous extractor 1 hr. Transfer ether ext to separator, add few drops phthln and 5 mL 0.1*N* $Ba(OH)_2$, and shake 30 sec. If aq. layer takes on pink typical of phthln, filter thru paper into small beaker. Add ca 0.05*N* HOAc until colorless and evap. to 1–2 mL on steam bath. Let remaining liq. evap. spontaneously in air and finally in desiccator. If 5 mL 0.1*N* $Ba(OH)_2$ does not give pink aq. layer, add 5 mL more before sepg. Repeat extn with $Ba(OH)_2$ soln several times or until pink soln is obtained, evapg each Ba soln in sep. beaker. Examine crystals under polarizing microscope.

Barium monochloroacetate monohydrate crystallizes from H_2O in plates, many of which are hexagonal in habit and frequently form in overlapping layers. Even in material that has been finely powd for microscopic examination, pointed terminations of the plates, often in pairs, can be observed. In parallel polarized light (crossed nicols) extinction is parallel and sign of elongation is neg. on more elongated plates. Plates invariably extinguish sharply with crossed nicols and therefore interference figures are not observed in convergent polarized light (crossed nicols). Since plates persistently lie in one orientation, significant refractive indices are detd by statistical method, lowest and highest indices resp. being measured on plates showing max. double refraction. These 2 indices are therefore arbitrarily designated as $n\alpha$ (min. value) and $n\gamma$ (max. value). Two significant refractive indices are: $n\alpha = 1.582$ and $n\gamma = 1.611$, both ± 0.002, frequently shown on the platey fragments.

20.068 ***Indigo Test***

(*Caution: See* **51.011**, **51.039**, and **51.054**.)

(**a**) *Commercial preservatives*.—Dil. 2 mL sample to 100 mL, add 3 mL H_2SO_4, and shake with 100 mL ether. Add 3 mL *anthranilic acid reagent* (1 g + 0.3 g NaOH/50 mL) to ether ext, evap. at low temp., filter off any insol. matter, and proceed as in (**c**), beginning "Test with litmus paper."

(**b**) *Carbonated beverages, orange juice, and wine*.—Acidify 100 mL sample with 3 mL H_2SO_4 and ext, using either continuous extractor or separator. Add 3 mL anthranilic acid reagent, (**a**), to ether ext and evap. at low temp. If any insol. matter seps, filter thru small wet paper. To clear liq. in 50 mL beaker add 30 mg Na_2CO_3 and proceed as in (**c**), beginning "Test with litmus paper."

(**c**) *Barium monochloroacetate*.—Dissolve 0.17 g Ba salt, **20.067**, in 5 mL H_2O in 10 mL graduate, add 1.05 mL 0.1*N* H_2SO_4, dil. to 10 mL, and mix. Let stand until ppt settles, or filter. Pipet 3 mL clear liq. into small beaker; add 2 mL *anthranilic acid reagent*, (**a**), and 30 mg Na_2CO_3 (weighed). Test with litmus paper. If acid, add addnl 30 mg Na_2CO_3. Pour mixt. into test tube and heat 30 min in H_2O bath. Place tube in oven at 125±5° until only moist residue remains. Remove tube from oven, and drop 2 drops NaOH soln (1+1) directly upon residue. (If residue is entirely dry, add 1–2 drops H_2O and let stand until absorbed before adding NaOH soln.)

Return to oven until completely dry ($\geq$1 hr); then remove from oven and heat test tube at 310–320° until contents become orange. (This requires 15 sec to 2 min, but must be carefully watched and tube removed from heat as soon as reaction is complete.) Cool slightly; add 5–7 mL H_2O from wash bottle, splashing H_2O to incorporate air into it. Warm over flame and blow air thru soln 1–2 min, using pipet or glass tube. Heat to bp over flame and again blow air thru soln. (As oxidn progresses, soln turns red if monochloroacetic acid is present, then green or blue or combination of two, and finally solid particles of indigo sep. out. These tend to rise to surface at first.) Let mixt. stand ca 10 min; then acidify slightly with HCl (1+1). Let stand 30 min more, filter, and wash pptd indigo with H_2O to remove acid. Let paper dry in air and preserve as exhibit.

Note: For fusion at 310–320° use brass block having one well to contain test tube and second well to contain thermometer. Wrap block with coil of nichrome wire and control temp. by variable voltage transformer. Furnaces, microburners, Wood's metal, solder baths, etc., may be used for fusion with equal success.

20.069 ***Pyridine Test***

(*Caution: See* **51.011**, **51.039**, and **51.054**.)

(**a**) *Commercial preservatives*.—Ext 2 mL sample as in **20.068(a)**. Transfer ether ext to separator and add small piece of universal indicator paper and enough satd $NaHCO_3$ soln (ca 5 mL) to make aq. layer alk. (pH 7–8) after vigorous shaking. Add enough H_2O to make total vol. of aq. layer ca 10 mL, and shake again. Drain aq. layer into small separator, wash ether with two 5 mL portions H_2O, and add washings to original aq. layer. Wash combined aq. exts once with 5–10 mL ether and discard ether; then add ca 1 mL H_2SO_4 (1+1) in excess of vol. required to neutze alk. soln (ca 1.5 mL), and ext acidified soln with two 25 mL portions ether. Wash combined ether exts once with 1–2 mL H_2O and let ether soln stand few min after draining most of H_2O and swirling to get as complete sepn of H_2O from ether as possible. Pour ether thru folded paper into 200 mL flask, and wash separator and paper with two 10 mL portions ether.

To ether filtrate add 0.5 mL pyridine and small glass beads, mix, and evap. on steam bath to 2–3 mL. Transfer immediately with eye dropper to 15 mL centrf. tube, and wash flask successively with 2, 1, and 1 mL portions ether. Evap. liq. in tube to ca 0.3 mL, add enough pyridine to increase vol. to ca 0.5 mL, and place in const temp. bath at 60±2°.

If crystals appear, test is pos. If they do not appear, remove tube from bath and evap. excess pyridine under reduced pressure. (Placing tube in beaker of hot H_2O hastens evapn.) When all liq. has been removed, add 0.5 mL pyridine, mix well, centrf., and decant supernate. Add ca 5 mL ether to residue, shake well, centrf., and decant. To residue add 1–3 mL absolute alcohol, varying amt of alcohol with amt of ppt, place tube in holder, and heat in hot H_2O or steam bath until ppt dissolves, being careful to swirl tube gently to avoid superheating and to boil alcohol so slowly that no loss occurs. Cool in ice bath, add ca 10 mL ether, mix well, and let stand in ice bath ca 5 min. Centrf., decant supernate, and wash ppt once with ca 5 mL ether. If tube now contains crystals of pyridine betaine, test is pos.

(**b**) *Carbonated beverages, orange juice, and wine*.—Acidify 100 mL sample with 3 mL H_2SO_4 and ext with ether, using either continuous extractor or separator. Continue as in (**a**), beginning "Transfer ether ext . . ."

Quantitative Method

(Applicable to carbonated beverages, fruit juices, and wine)

20.070 ***Apparatus***

Continuous extractor similar to Fig. 12:01B.—Outer part is made from 43 mm tubing, 45 cm long, with side tube, 25 cm above bottom, fitted with drip tip, ₸ 24/40 joint. Inner tube is made from 12 mm tubing 40 cm long. Receiver is 250 mL conical flask with ₸ neck to fit side tube.

20.071 ***Reagents***

(**a**) *Silver nitrate soln.*—Dissolve 9 g $AgNO_3$ in H_2O and dil. to 1 L. 1 mL = ca 5 mg $CH_2ClCOOH$.

(**b**) *Ammonium thiocyanate std soln.*—1 mL = ca 5 mg $CH_2ClCOOH$. Dissolve 4.03 g NH_4SCN in H_2O and dil. to 1 L. Stdze against pure NaCl soln, 3.093 g/L, which contains 1.876 g Cl (equiv. to 5 g monochloroacetic acid)/L.

(**c**) *Ferric indicator.*—Satd soln of $FeNH_4(SO_4)_2.12H_2O$.

20.072 ***Determination***

(*Caution: See* **51.011**, **51.039**, and **51.054**.)

In outer part of continuous extractor place vol. sample (≤150 mL) contg 50–100 mg $CH_2ClCOOH$. (With com. preservatives, make preliminary diln to permit convenient measurement of proper size aliquot.) If necessary, dil. to 150 mL, add 3–5 mL H_2SO_4, mix, and ext with ether 2–3 hr. (Extn time for particular app. should be established by detg time required to ext ≥95% of known amt of $CH_2ClCOOH$.)

Tilt extractor so as to drain as much ether as possible into flask. Disconnect flask, add 25 mL 1*N* NaOH in excess of that required to make aq. layer alk. to litmus paper after shaking, shake, and evap. ether on steam bath to ca 25 mL, hastening process by passing air current into mouth of flask. Digest on steam bath 2 hr or boil under reflux condenser 30 min.

Add 50 mL H_2O, 15 mL HNO_3, and known vol. of the $AgNO_3$ soln in excess. Shake 0.5–1 min, add ferric indicator, and titr. excess Ag with the NH_4SCN soln. In titrn, carefully add NH_4SCN soln until pink formed fades slowly on mixing; shake soln ca 30 sec and filter thru folded paper into second flask. When first flask is empty, wash down walls with ca 50 mL H_2O and add this to filter after all soln has passed thru. When wash H_2O has passed thru, complete titrn. Similarly titr. vol. $AgNO_3$ soln equal to that added to sample. Difference between 2 titrns is measure of $CH_2ClCOOH$.

Instead of using the continuous extractor, $CH_2ClCOOH$ may be extd equally efficiently (except with orange juice) as follows: To 100 mL sample add 3 mL H_2SO_4 and shake in separator with three 100 mL portions ether. Combine ether exts and wash by shaking with two 30 mL portions 1*N* NaOH. Combine the two NaOH solns and digest as above.

NITRITES (*22*)—OFFICIAL FIRST ACTION

(Applicable to dry cure mix or curing pickle)

20.073 ***Apparatus***

Bend piece of glass tubing 250 mm long, 6 mm od, to form right angle ca 60–70 mm from one end. Connect short end with rubber tube to outlet of pressure regulator on CO_2 tank.

20.074 ***Preparation of Sample***

(**a**) *Dry cure mix.*—Weigh 50.0 g sample and dissolve in 1 L H_2O. Transfer 25 mL aliquot to 250 mL erlenmeyer.

(**b**) *Pickle soln.*—Filter thru dry paper. Weigh 50.0 g filtrate into 250 mL erlenmeyer.

20.075 ***Determination***

To soln in flask, add 20 mL colorless *15% KI soln* and ca 2 mL starch soln, **32.065(g)**. Insert long end of gas inlet tube and adjust flow of CO_2 to ca 5 bubbles/sec.

After ca 5 min, raise CO_2 delivery tube to just above surface of liq., add 20 mL H_2SO_4 (1+7) from buret, and mix thoroly. Titr. with std 0.0725*N* $Na_2S_2O_3$, with CO_2 flowing, to first complete disappearance of starch-I color. 1 mL 0.0725*N* $Na_2S_2O_3$ = 0.0050 g $NaNO_2$.

20.076 PROPIONATES (MOLD INHIBITORS)

See **14.094–14.101**.

QUATERNARY AMMONIUM COMPOUNDS (QAC)

Qualitative Tests

20.077 ***Bromophenol Blue Method (23)***
Official First Action

(Applicable to milk. Note precautions of **20.084–20.089**. *Caution: See* **51.011**, **51.039**, and **51.046**.)

Pipet 25 mL milk into 250 mL vol. flask contg 10 mg bromophenol blue, **20.085(d)**, and agitate until solid reagent dissolves. Gradually add 50 mL acetone with shaking; then add, dropwise, enough HCl (1+1) to produce bright yellow in mixt. (ca 1 mL); then add 0.2–0.3 mL excess. Gradually, with continuous mixing, dil. to vol. with acetone. Mix, let stand 30 min, and filter thru folded paper.

Measure 200 mL filtrate in graduate and pour into 500 mL separator; fill graduate to 200 mL with H_2O and add to separator. Wash aq. acetone mixt. by shaking with three 50 mL portions pet ether. When sepd, pour each portion of pet ether thru filter paper and reserve paper for filtration of ethylene chloride (CH_2ClCH_2Cl) ext later. Evap. aq. acetone soln on steam bath under air current until vol. is reduced to ≤100 mL and acetone odor is gone. Cool, transfer to 250 mL separator with H_2O (reserve beaker), and add 5 mL HCl (1+1).

Pipet 50 mL CH_2ClCH_2Cl into separator and shake 1–2 min. Drain lower layer into beaker used for evapn in such manner as to wash down sides and return this liq. to separator, washing beaker with little H_2O. Again shake 2–3 min, let stand until clear, and drain lower layer thru paper reserved above into 125 mL separator contg 10 mL *1% Na_2CO_3 soln.* Stopper, invert separator, and shake carefully 2–3 min, using rotary motion. Reverse funnel to normal position and let stand to sep. Top layer will be usual purple of alk. soln of strong bromophenol blue; blue lower layer is pos. test for QAC. To better observe color, drain lower layer into g-s flask contg 1–2 g anhyd. granular (not powd) Na_2SO_4 which will absorb on contact any drops of purple soln that may unavoidably enter flask. Decant CH_2ClCH_2Cl layer into another vessel, if necessary, to avoid any color reflected from colored salt in flask. Solv. layer must not be filtered, since most papers contain enough residual acid to change the bromophenol blue-QAC complex from blue to practically invisible yellow.

20.078 ***Optical-Crystallographic Properties of the Reineckates (24)*—Procedure**

Use reineckate salt obtained in **20.083** or proceed as follows: Add excess of NH_4 reineckate to aq. soln of QAC and stir. In most cases, if >20 mg QAC is present, ppt forms at once. With smaller amts, let soln stand at room temp. ≥30 min and then stir 1–2 min. Let mixt. stand several hr, filter thru fine porosity fritted glass crucible, and wash several times with H_2O. Dry ppt with suction, dissolve thru filter with acetone, and evap. off acetone. Dissolve dry residue by warming with min. amt alcohol. If considerable amt of ppt is used, crystals deposit on cooling. Filter thru fritted glass crucible and dry by suction. With <30 mg ppt, dissolve in 10 mL alcohol and let solv. evap. on warm, but not hot, surface with aid of gentle current of air.

Table 20:02 Optical-crystallographic properties of reineckates of quaternary ammonium compounds

Compound	Quant. Factor (Anhyd.)	Refractive Indices[a] α	β	γ	Optic Sign	Extinction[b]	Elongation	Habit
Cetyldimethylbenzylammonium Reineckate (Zettyn®)	0.5834	1.572	1.651	1.660	−	i, s		Rhomboid plates
Alkyldimethylbenzylammonium Reineckate	0.5579	1.576		1.651	−	s		Rhomboid plates
Lauryldimethylbenzylammonium Reineckate (DC-12)	0.5457	1.576	1.669[i]	1.678	−	p, s	−	Rhomboid plates
Di-isobutylphenoxyethoxyethyldimethylbenzylammonium Reineckate (Hyamine 1622®, Phemerol®)	0.6130	1.577	1.671	1.678	−	p, i	+	Rods, plates, fibrous
Cetylpyridinium Reineckate (Ceepyrn®)	0.5458	Unsatisfactory for optical study				p	−	Fibrous
Lauryldimethyldichlorobenzylammonium Reineckate (Dichloran)	0.5220	1.582	1.593[i]	1.677	−	p	−	Rods and plates
Di-isobutylcresoxyethoxyethyldimethylbenzylammonium Reineckate (Hyamine 10-X®)	0.6028	1.582	1.638	1.670	−	p	+	Plates
Dodecyldimethylacetamidobenzylammonium Reineckate (Dobenzyl chloride)	0.5911	1.582		1.664		p	−	Plates and rods
Cetyldimethylethylammonium Reineckate (Ethyl Cetab)	0.6135	1.587	1.599	1.626		p	+	Plates and rods
Cetyltrimethylammonium Reineckate (Cetab)	0.6045	1.591	1.609[i]	1.616		p	+	Rods
Triethylbenzylammonium Reineckate	0.4460	1.593	1.687	1.697 (ca)	−	s		Rhomboid plates
Laurylpyridinium Reineckate	0.5112	1.609	1.636[i]	1.651		p	+	Plates

[a] Refractive indices ±0.003, at 24–26°; [i] = intermediate index.
[b] Extinction: p = parallel; i = inclined; s = symmetrical.

Det. optical-crystallographic properties of the crystals as in **36.108** and compare with those listed in Table **20:02** or with those detd on crystals obtained from known QAC compds.

Quantitative Methods

Ferricyanide Method (23)—Official Final Action

(Applicable to com. preservatives)

20.079 ***Reagents***

(**a**) *Acetate buffer soln.*—Dissolve 130 g $NaOAc.3H_2O$ in H_2O, add 42 mL HOAc, and dil. to 500 mL.

(**b**) *Ferricyanide soln.*—Dissolve 6.6 g $K_3Fe(CN)_6$ in H_2O and dil. to 1 L.

(**c**) *Zinc sulfate soln.*—Dissolve 20 g $ZnSO_4.7H_2O$ in 180 mL H_2O.

(**d**) *Thiosulfate std soln.*—0.02*N*. Prep. daily by dilg 0.1*N* soln, **50.037–50.038**. 1 mL 0.02*N* soln = 0.02142 g alkyldimethylbenzylammonium chloride, MW 357.

20.080 ***Determination***

Det. approx. QAC concn as follows: Pipet 1 mL buffer soln, 2 mL $K_3Fe(CN)_6$ soln, and 20 mL H_2O into each of 4 small erlenmeyers. To these flasks add 0.5, 1.0, 2.0, and 4.0 mL, resp., of sample, mix, and filter. Add 2 mL addnl sample to each filtrate, mix, and compare results with table, **20.081**.

Into 100 mL Kohlrausch flask, pipet aliquot of sample contg ca 0.5 g QAC, as indicated by **20.081**, dil. if necessary to 50 mL, add 5 mL buffer soln, and mix. Add 30 mL $K_3Fe(CN)_6$ soln from pipet while swirling flask. Dil. to 100 mL with H_2O and mix. After 30 min, filter, discarding first 10–15 mL filtrate. Pipet 50 mL filtrate into 500 mL erlenmeyer, and add 100 mL H_2O and 1–2 g KI. Rotate flask until salt dissolves, add 10 mL HCl (1+1), mix, and let stand 2 min. Add 10 mL $ZnSO_4$ soln, mix, and titr. with 0.02*N* $Na_2S_2O_3$ soln, adding starch indicator, **6.005(f)**, when color fades to tinge of yellow. Make blank detn including all of above operations but substituting H_2O for sample. Calc. QAC content from difference in 2 titrns.

If sample contains ca 0.5 g QAC/100 mL, instead of proceeding as above, pipet 100 mL sample into 200 mL vol. flask, add 10 mL buffer soln and 30 mL $K_3Fe(CN)_6$ soln, dil. to vol. with H_2O, mix, let stand 30 min, filter, and titr. 100 or 150 mL aliquot filtrate as above.

20.081 ***Approximation of Content of Alkyldimethylbenzylammonium Chloride (MW 357)***

Quaternary Ammonium Chloride, %	Sample Added A 0.5 mL	B 1.0 mL	C 2.0 mL	D 4.0 mL
≥8.4	No ppt	No ppt	No ppt	No ppt
5	Ppt	No ppt	No ppt	No ppt
2.5	Ppt	Ppt	No ppt	No ppt
1.25	Ppt	Ppt	Ppt	No ppt
≤1	Ppt	Ppt	Ppt	Ppt

Reineckate Method (25)—Official Final Action

(Applicable to preservatives, tinctures, and isotonic solns)

20.082 ***Reagent***

Reineckate reagent.—Place 0.75 g NH_4 reineckate ($NH_4[Cr(NH_3)_2(SCN)_4].H_2O$; MW = 354.47) in 125 mL erlenmeyer, add 50 mL H_2O, stopper, shake ca 2 min, and filter.

20.083 ***Determination***

Place 100 mL sample contg 10–100 mg QAC in 250 mL beaker; add, with stirring, 5 mL portions reineckate reagent until liq. is bright pink. Let stand 30 min and add more reagent unless supernate is deep pink. Stir again 1–2 min. After several hr, filter thru fine porosity fritted glass crucible, and wash beaker and filter with at least three 15 mL portions H_2O. (It is unnecessary to transfer all ppt to crucible.) Wash down sides of crucible with H_2O and dry by suction. If ppt forms cake in filter, mix with the wash H_2O with stirring rod used before.

Dissolve reineckate salt in acetone as follows: Set up suction app. to fit glass crucible, using as receiver side-arm test tube for application of suction. With 5 mL pipet, wash down sides of beaker used for pptn and add this liq. to crucible. Rinse beaker second time and add to liq. in crucible. Stir to dissolve and draw liq. thru with suction. Wash out beaker third time and wash down sides of crucible several times with small portions of acetone. When liq. passing thru is colorless, disconnect, and wash into test tube with acetone any pink material which may have dried on bottom or outside of crucible or on inside of funnel. Discard small amt of greenish solid in crucible due to impurities and decomposition products of reagent.

Transfer acetone soln to tared beaker (50 mL beaker for ≤20 mg QAC and 100 mL beaker for >20 mg) and evap. on warm (but not hot) surface. If few drops of moisture remain, pass gentle air current into beaker until it appears dry. Dissolve residue by warming in 10 mL alcohol (or more, if needed); let solv. evap. spontaneously, dry in desiccator, and weigh. Wt QAC = factor (Table **20:02**) × wt ppt. Ppt may be used for detn of optical-crystallographic properties, Table **20:02**.

(To remove greenish solid from crucible, add 10–12 mL HCl (1+1) and stir to dissolve. Draw liq. thru by suction and wash several times with H_2O. Reverse crucible and wash by filling bottom cavity with solv. Use 2 fillings each of H_2O, alcohol, H_2O, acetone, and H_2O in order given.)

Bromophenol Blue Method (23)—Official Final Action

(*Precaution:* Have all glassware scrupulously clean, and especially avoid soap, since reaction occurs between soap and QAC. If soap is used in cleansing, rinse all glassware with H_2O, and as extra precaution, rinse all pipets with alcohol and dry by suction.)

20.084 *Apparatus*

Steam distillation apparatus.—See **18.050(a)** for generator. Use 500 mL or 1 L distn flask, fitted with spray tube, **12.025(c)**, reaching to within 1 or 2 cm of bottom of flask (all connections ₸ joints), and with stopper for steam inlet (to be used during early part of distn). Suitable app. is described in **19.133**.

20.085 *Reagents*

(**a**) *Sodium carbonate soln.*—Dissolve 5 g Na_2CO_3 in 500 mL H_2O.

(**b**) *Sodium sulfate.*—Anhyd. granular (not powd). (Mallinckrodt A.R. granular grade is satisfactory.)

(**c**) *D.C. 12.*—Lauryldimethylbenzylammonium chloride, or other solid QAC.

(**d**) *Bromophenol blue soln.*—Dissolve 40 mg tetrabromophenolsulfonphthalein in warm H_2O, cool, and dil. to 100 mL.

Bromophenol blue should pass following test for purity: Place 20 mg bromophenol blue in 125 mL separator; add 50 mL CH_2ClCH_2Cl and 5 mL 1% Na_2CO_3 soln, and shake until dissolved. Let stand until mixt. seps into 2 layers. Lower layer should be colorless; upper layer purple. Add 10 mL soln contg 0.1 mg D.C. 12 or other QAC, shake again, and let sep. Lower layer should be clear blue. Drain lower layer and examine in spectrophtr. Absorption peak should be at ca 608 nm. Compare absorption curve with that of sample purified as in **20.086**. If test gives yellow or green soln or if absorption curve is essentially different from that of purified sample, purify as in **20.086**.

20.086 *Purification of Bromophenol Blue*

Place 2 g bromophenol blue in 400 mL beaker and dissolve in 25 mL 1% Na_2CO_3 soln. Transfer to 1 L separator, using ca 300 mL H_2O. Add 500 mL CH_2ClCH_2Cl and shake. Add 1 mL soln contg 10 mg D.C. 12 or other QAC and shake until thoroly extd. If lower layer is yellow, repeat addn of D.C. 12 soln in 1 mL portions with shaking until upon sepn of the 2 layers, lower one has greenish tint. Drain lower layer and discard. Add 200 mL CH_2ClCH_2Cl and 1 mL D.C. 12 soln to separator and shake. This time lower layer should be clear blue. If layer is green, drain and repeat addn of CH_2ClCH_2Cl and D.C. 12 until blue soln is obtained. Wash aq. layer with 100 mL portions CH_2ClCH_2Cl until lower layer is colorless or only faint blue. Acidify aq. layer with HCl and ext yellow ppt with CH_2ClCH_2Cl until aq. soln is only faint yellow. Distil off most of CH_2ClCH_2Cl and permit remainder to evap. spontaneously in beaker. Grind residual powder. Test portion for purity as in **20.085(d)** and if suitable, use as reagent.

20.087 *Preparation of Standard Curve*

Stdze 1% soln QAC to be detd as in **20.080**. (If this compd is not available, use any solid QAC of known composition such as D.C. 12, lauryldimethylbenzylammonium chloride. If necessary, prep. std soln from com. soln stdzd by ferricyanide method, **20.080**.) By performing method below, det. max. and min. concns of this compd that produce, in 50 mL CH_2ClCH_2Cl, A at 610 nm suited to color-measuring instrument used. Prep. set of ≥3 stds contg, in 50 mL, amt of QAC covering range between these max. and min. concns, and plot curve as directed below. (If Beckman spectrophtr is used, 0.0, 0.1, 0.2, and 0.25 mg/50 mL are suitable stds.)

Pipet 50 mL of each std into separator; add 3 mL bromophenol blue soln, 1 mL HCl (1+1), and 50 mL CH_2ClCH_2Cl; and shake 2–3 min. When clear, drain lower layer into another separator contg 10 mL Na_2CO_3 soln, and shake 2–3 min. Let stand until clear, drain lower layer into g-s flask contg 1–2 g Na_2SO_4, and after 30 min read in instrument. (Use same or similar cell for all stds, and light filter centering at 610 nm.) Plot scale readings, if these are in terms of A or proportional to it, against concns used; if instrument reads in terms of T, convert readings to A before plotting.

20.088 *Preparation of Sample*

(**a**) *Bottled beverages containing fruit juices.*—Mix thoroly, and measure 50 mL sample into graduate. Filter on 7 cm buchner and dil. filtrate to 100 mL with H_2O (Soln *I*). Place filter paper in 400 mL beaker and ext with small portions of alcohol until no more color is extd and paper remains white. Transfer alc. ext to 500 mL distg flask; add 10 mg bromophenol blue, 2 mL HCl (1+1), and 100 mL H_2O. Steam distil and collect vol. distillate ≥100 mL greater than vol. alcohol in ext. Cool residue in distg flask, transfer to separator, wash with 40, 30, and 30 mL portions pet ether, and proceed as in **20.089**.

Also take suitable aliquot of Soln *I* (first try 5 mL), transfer to separator, add 3 mL bromophenol blue soln and 1 mL HCl (1+1), and proceed as in **20.089**.

(**b**) *Beer.*—Place 100 mL decarbonated beer, **10.001**, in steam distn flask and add 10 mL bromophenol blue and 2 mL HCl (1+1). Steam distil and collect ca 200 mL distillate. Cool residue, transfer to separator, wash with 100 and 50 mL portions pet ether, and proceed as in **20.089**.

(**c**) *Table sirup.*—Transfer 20 g sample to 100 mL vol. flask, dil. to vol. with H_2O, and mix thoroly. Pipet aliquot of soln into separator, add 5 mL bromophenol blue soln and 1 mL HCl (1+1), and proceed as in **20.089**.

(**d**) *Eggs.*—Weigh 12.5±0.25 g well mixed sample in tared 50 mL beaker. Add 10 mL H_2O, mix well with rod, pour carefully into 250 mL vol. flask, and wash beaker with 5–10 mL more H_2O, adding washings to flask. While swirling flask, gradually add acetone, little at time, mixing constantly, until flask is filled to mark; stopper and invert several times. Let stand 10–15 min and filter thru folded paper (Whatman No. 12, 18.5 cm) into 250 mL graduate until 200 mL filtrate is obtained. Pour filtrate into 1 L separator, wash down sides of graduate with 25 mL acetone, and add to separator; fill graduate to 250 mL with H_2O and add to separator. Add 25 mL HCl (1+1) to separator and mix. Ext liq. in separator with pet ether, using 300, 250, 150, and 100 mL, and shaking gently to prevent formation of emulsions. Transfer extd aq. layer to 600–800 mL beaker, add 2–3 glass beads, and evap. to 50–75 mL on steam bath.

After evapn, add 10 mg bromophenol blue and wash down sides of beaker with little H_2O. When soln is cool, pipet 50 mL CH_2ClCH_2Cl into beaker, letting solv. flow down sides of beaker. Pour contents of beaker into 250 mL separator, washing out beaker with little H_2O. Shake ca 1 min. Return liq. to beaker, letting it flow down sides of beaker. Again return liq. to separator and shake ca 2 min. Proceed as in **20.089**, beginning "Let stand until clear, . . ."

20.089 ***Determination***

Pipet 50 mL CH_2ClCH_2Cl into separator, **20.088(a)**, (**b**), or (**c**), and shake 3–4 min. Let stand until clear, drain lower layer into second separator contg 10 mL 1% Na_2CO_3 soln, and shake 3–4 min. Let sep. and observe lower layer. If blue, quaternary base is present. Judge from depth of color whether or not it is suitable for reading in photometer. If color is suitable for reading without diln, dry by draining lower layer into g-s flask contg 1–2 g of the Na_2SO_4, let stand 30 min, transfer to suitable cell, and read color in instrument at 610 nm. Det. amt QAC present from std curve, **20.087**, and calc. to mg/100 mL.

If color is too deep for direct reading, acidify contents of second separator with 1–2 mL HCl (1+1), shake until yellow, and return to first separator. Pipet second 50 mL portion CH_2ClCH_2Cl into first separator, shake 3–4 min, let stand until lower layer is clear, and drain lower layer into flask. (If sample is known to contain >1 mg QAC/100 mL, entire 100 mL CH_2ClCH_2Cl may be added at one time.)

Det. proper aliquot as follows: Pipet 5 mL into 125 mL separator, dil. with 25 mL CH_2ClCH_2Cl, add 10 mL 1% Na_2CO_3 soln, and carefully shake 2 min. Let sep. and observe lower layer. If depth of color is suitable for reading, dil. to 50 mL by adding 20 mL CH_2ClCH_2Cl from pipet, shake 1 min, let settle, drain lower layer, dry as above, and read. If color is not deep enough, add addnl soln in 5 mL increments until suitable color is obtained, add solv. if necessary to total vol. of 50 mL, shake, drain, dry, and read in instrument.

When proper aliquot has been detd, check as follows: Pipet aliquot of CH_2ClCH_2Cl soln into 50 mL vol. flask, dil. to vol. with CH_2ClCH_2Cl, and pour into 125 mL separator. Pipet 10 mL 1% Na_2CO_3 soln into vol. flask, swirl, pour into separator, and wash out vol. flask with 2–3 mL H_2O from wash bottle. Shake, settle, drain, dry, and read, adding ca 5 mg dry bromophenol blue to separator if aliquot used was ≤10 mL.

For bottled beverages contg fruit juices, add amt of QAC found in residue to amt found in Soln *I* to obtain total amt in sample.

Eosin Yellowish Method (26)—Official First Action

(Applicable to aq. solns and milk)

20.090 ***Apparatus***

(**a**) *Centrifuge.*—Clinical high-speed type fitted for 50 mL tubes. International No. 2 centrf. with head No. 241 at speed of 2500 rpm is also satisfactory.

(**b**) *Centrifuge tubes.*—Heavy-wall, 40 mL centrf. tubes, Pyrex, No. 8400, or equiv.

(**c**) *Test tubes.*—Pyrex, g-s, 15 × 150 mm.

20.091 ***Reagents***

(**a**) *Acetylene tetrachloride.*—$CHCl_2CHCl_2$. (*Caution:* Toxic reagent. *See* **51.040**.) Should give distinct pink lower layer after sepn, when 5 mL is shaken 1 min with 2 mL buffer soln, (**c**), 0.5 mL eosin yellowish soln, (**d**), and 5 mL aq. soln contg 1 ppm Cetab, Dobenzyl chloride, Et Cetab, Hyamine 10-X, or laurylpyridinium chloride, or 2 ppm lauryldimethylbenzylammonium chloride. If reagent does not meet this test, distil under reduced pressure, rejecting first 10% of distillate and collecting ca 80% of vol. placed in distn flask.

(**b**) *Aerosol OT std solns.*—(*1*) *Stock soln.*—Prep. soln of dioctyl Na sulfosuccinate to contain 100 mg/100 mL. Det. strength as follows: Pipet 2 mL soln contg, in 100 mL, 100 mg QAC to be detd, into g-s test tube contg 2 mL $CHCl_2CHCl_2$, 2 mL buffer soln, and 0.5 mL eosin yellowish soln. Carefully add Aerosol OT soln from buret in small amts, violently shaking mixt. ≥30 sec after each addn until, after sepn into 2 layers, only light pink is noticeable when test tube is placed against white background. Continue addns in 0.01 or 0.02 mL portions until lower layer is no longer pink. (*2*) *Working soln.*—Dil. to 100 mL such vol. stock soln as will produce soln 1 mL of which is equiv. to 0.1 mg QAC to be detd. Stdze against std soln (1 mL = 0.1 mg) of QAC to be detd.

(**c**) *Citrate buffer soln.*—pH 4.5. Dissolve 25 g citric acid in 75 mL H_2O and add enough 50% NaOH soln (ca 13 mL) to bring pH to 4.5.

(**d**) *Eosin yellowish soln.*—Dissolve 25 mg D&C Red No. 22 in H_2O and dil. to 50 mL.

(**e**) *Lactic acid soln.*—50%. Add 41 g H_2O to 59 g lactic acid, 85% reagent grade, and mix.

(**f**) *Sodium hydroxide soln.*—4*M*. Dissolve 32 g NaOH in H_2O and dil. to 200 mL.

20.092 ***Determination***

(**a**) *Milk.*—Pipet 15 mL $CHCl_2CHCl_2$ (*Caution: See* **51.018**) into centrf. tube, add 6 mL lactic acid soln and 15 mL milk to be tested, stopper, and shake ca 3 min. Add 6 mL 4*M* NaOH and mix carefully until curd seps thruout mixt.; then shake ≥30 sec. Centrf. at high speed (ca 3200 rpm) 7 min. Decant serum and discard; puncture layer of curd at 2 points and drain $CHCl_2CHCl_2$ ext into small beaker. Avoiding any drops of aq. soln, transfer 5 mL ext with pipet into g-s test tube contg 2 mL buffer soln and 0.5 mL eosin yellowish soln; stopper and shake ca 2 min. Let stand to sep. and observe color of lower layer. If color is faint, place against white background. If layer is pink, QAC is present. If deep pink or red, titr. with std Aerosol OT soln; after each addn of std soln, shake mixt. violently 0.5–1 min, let sep., and observe lower layer. Continue addns until no pink is observed in lower layer when placed against white background or compared with blank detn. Titrn found represents amt of QAC in 5 mL sample. Calc. to ppm.

(**b**) *Water solns.*—Pipet 5 mL sample into g-s test tube contg 2 mL $CHCl_2CHCl_2$, 2 mL buffer soln, and 0.5 mL eosin yellowish soln, and proceed as in (**a**), beginning ". . . stopper and shake ca 2 min."

SALICYLIC ACID

20.093 Preparation of Sample—Official Final Action

(**a**) *Nonalcoholic liquids.*—Many liqs may be extd directly as in **20.094** or **20.096** without further treatment. If troublesome emulsions form during extn, pipet 100 mL into 250 mL vol. flask and add ca 5 g NaCl, shaking until dissolved. Dil. to vol. with alcohol, shake vigorously, let stand 10 min, shaking occasionally, filter, and treat aliquot of filtrate as in (**b**).

(**b**) *Alcoholic liquids.*—Make 200 mL of sample alk. to litmus paper with ca 10% NaOH soln and evap. on steam bath to ca ⅓ its original vol. Dil. to original vol. with H_2O and filter if necessary.

(**c**) *Solid or semisolid substances.*—Grind sample and mix thoroly. Transfer convenient amt (50–200 g according to consistency of sample) to 500 mL vol. flask, add H_2O to make ca 400 mL, and shake until mixt. becomes uniform. Add 2–5 g $CaCl_2$ and shake until dissolved. Make distinctly alk. to litmus paper with ca 10% NaOH soln, dil. to vol. with H_2O, shake thoroly, let stand ≥2 hr, shaking frequently, and filter.

Qualitative Tests—Official Final Action

20.094 ***Ferric Chloride Test***

(*Caution: See* **51.011**, **51.039**, and **51.054**.)

Place 50 mL sample or equiv. vol. of aq. ext, prepd as in **20.093**, in separator; add $^1/_{10}$ its vol. HCl (1+3) and ext with 50 mL ether. If mixt. emulsifies, add 10–15 mL pet ether (bp <60°) and shake. If this treatment fails to break emulsion, centrf., or let stand until considerable portion of aq. layer seps; drain latter, shake vigorously, and again let sep. Wash ether layer with two 5 mL portions H_2O, evap. greater portion of ether in porcelain dish on steam bath, let remainder evap. spontaneously, and add 1 drop *0.5% neut. $FeCl_3$ soln*. Violet color indicates salicylic acid.

If coloring matter or other interfering substance is present in residue after evapn of ether, purify salicyclic acid by one of following methods:

(**a**) Dissolve original residue from ether ext, obtained as above, in ca 25 mL ether; transfer soln to separator and shake with equal vol. H_2O made distinctly alk. with several drops NH_4OH (1+9). Let sep., filter aq. layer thru wet paper into porcelain dish, evap. almost to dryness, and test residue with $FeCl_3$ as above.

(**b**) Dry original residue from ether ext, obtained as above, in desiccator over H_2SO_4 and ext with several 10 mL portions CS_2 (*Caution: See* **51.040** and **51.048**) or pet ether (bp <60°), rubbing contents of dish with glass rod and filtering successive portions of solv. thru dry paper into second porcelain dish. Evap. greater portion of solv. on steam bath, let remainder evap. spontaneously, and test residue with $FeCl_3$ as above.

(**c**) With few mL of ether, transfer original residue from ether ext obtained as above to small porcelain crucible, and let solv. evap. spontaneously. Cut hole in asbestos board large enough to admit ca ⅔ of crucible, cover crucible with small r-b flask filled with cold H_2O, and heat over small flame until any salicylic acid present sublimes and condenses upon bottom of flask. Test sublimate with $FeCl_3$ as above.

20.095 ***Jorissen Test (27)***

Dissolve residue from ether ext, **20.094**, or, if impurities are present, purified material obtained as in **20.094(a)**, (**b**), or (**c**), in little hot H_2O. Cool 10 mL soln in test tube and add 4 or 5 drops *10% KNO_2 soln*, 4 or 5 drops HOAc (ca 50%), and 1 drop *1% $CuSO_4$ soln*. Mix thoroly, boil liq. 0.5 min, and let stand 2 min. In presence of salicylic acid, Bordeaux-red color develops.

Quantitative Method—Official Final Action

20.096 ***Extraction***

(*Caution: See* **51.011**, **51.039**, and **51.054**.)

Transfer to separator 100 mL sample, or vol. soln prepd as in **20.093** that represents ≥20 g original material. If alk., neutze to litmus with HCl (1+3) and add excess of HCl equiv. to 2 mL acid for each 100 mL soln. Ext 4 times with ether, using for each extn vol. ether equiv. to ½ vol. aq. layer. If emulsion forms on shaking, this may usually be broken by adding little ($^1/_5$ vol. ether layer) pet ether (bp <60°) and shaking again, or by centrfg. If small amt of emulsion still persists, let remain with aq. layer, where frequently it is broken during next extn. If emulsion remains after fourth extn, sep. it from clear ether and clear aq. layer and ext sep. with 2 or 3 small portions ether.

Combine ether exts, wash with vol. H_2O equal to $^1/_{10}$ total vol. ether exts, let sep., and discard aq. layer. Wash in this way until aq. layer after sepn yields yellow soln upon addn of Me orange soln and 2 drops 0.1*N* NaOH. Slowly distil greater part of ether, transfer remainder to porcelain dish, and let evap. spontaneously. If no interfering substances are present, proceed as in **20.097**; if interfering substances are present, purify residue by one of following methods:

(**a**) Thoroly dry residue *in vacuo* over H_2SO_4. Ext 10 times with 10–15 mL portions CS_2 (*Caution: See* **51.040** and **51.048**) or pet ether (bp <60°), rubbing contents of dish with glass rod, and filter successive portions of solv. thru dry filter into porcelain dish. Test extd residue with drop *2% Fe alum soln*, and if it gives reaction for salicylic acid, dissolve in H_2O; acidify soln with HCl (1+3), ext with ether, evap., ext dry residue thus obtained with CS_2 or pet ether, and add to ext first obtained. Distil greater portion of the CS_2 or pet ether and let remainder evap. spontaneously. Proceed as in **20.097**.

(**b**) Dissolve residue in 40–50 mL ether. Transfer ether soln to separator and ext with three 15 mL portions 1% NH_4OH. (If fat is known to be present in original ether ext, ext latter directly with 4 portions 1% NH_4OH instead of 3.) Combine alk. aq. exts, acidify, again ext with ether, and wash combined ether exts as directed previously. Slowly distil greater portion of ether, and let remainder evap. spontaneously.

20.097 ***Determination***

Dissolve residue, **20.096**, in small amt of hot H_2O, and after cooling, dil. to definite vol. (usually 50 or 100 mL). If soln is not clear, filter thru dry paper. Dil. aliquots of the soln and treat with 0.5% $FeCl_3$ soln or 2% Fe alum soln until max. color is developed. Generally few drops will suffice.

(The Fe alum soln should be boiled until ppt appears, allowed to settle, and filtered. Acidity of soln is slightly increased in this manner, but soln remains clear for considerable time, and turbidity caused by its diln with H_2O is much less and does not appear so soon as when unboiled soln is used. This turbidity interferes with exact matching of color.)

Compare colors developed with color obtained when std *salicylic acid soln* (contg 1 mg salicylic acid in 50 mL H_2O) is similarly treated, using Nessler tubes or colorimeter. In either case, and especially with $FeCl_3$, avoid excess reagent, although excess of 0.5 mL 2% Fe alum soln may be added to 50 mL comparison soln of salicylic acid without negating results.

SORBIC ACID

Oxidation Method (*28*)—Official First Action

(Applicable to cheese)

20.098 ***Apparatus***

Steam distillation apparatus.—See Fig. **20:03**. Trap and distg tube available from SGA Scientific Inc. as Quote FDA No. 584696. Steam generator, Fig. **18:02**, may be substituted for 3-neck flask boiler.

20.099 ***Reagents***

(**a**) *Sulfuric acid solns.—(1) 2N.*—Dil. 14.2 mL H_2SO_4 with H_2O to 250 mL. *(2) 0.3N.*—Dil. 15 mL 2*N* H_2SO_4 to 100 mL.

(**b**) *Potassium dichromate soln.*—Dissolve 147 mg $K_2Cr_2O_7$ in H_2O and dil. to 100 mL with H_2O.

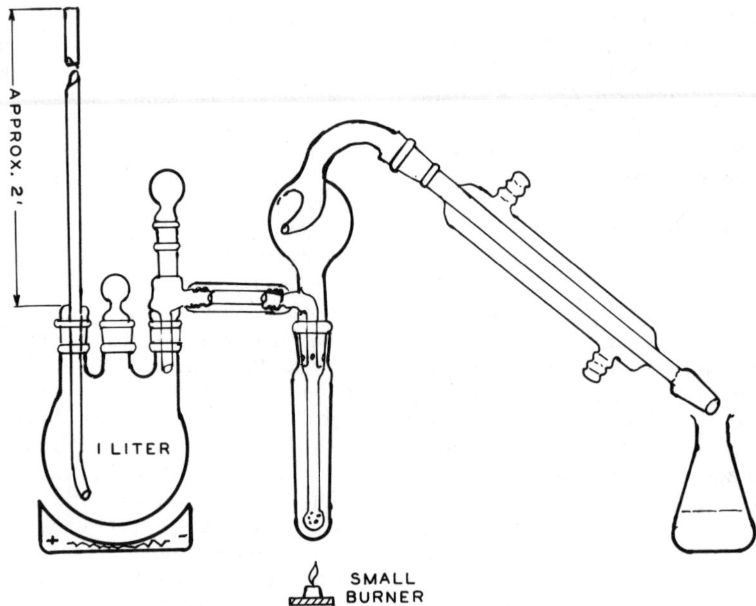

FIG. 20:03—Steam distillation apparatus

(**c**) *Thiobarbituric acid soln.*—0.5%. Dissolve 250 mg thiobarbituric acid (Eastman Kodak Co. No. 660, or equiv.) in 5 mL 0.5*N* NaOH in 50 mL vol. flask by swirling under hot H_2O. Add ca 20 mL H_2O, neutze with 3 mL 1*N* HCl, and dil. to vol. with H_2O. Prep. fresh daily.

(**d**) *Sorbic acid std soln.*—0.1 mg/mL. Accurately weigh 134 mg K sorbate (equiv. to 100 mg sorbic acid) and dil. to 1 L with H_2O. Soln is stable several days when refrigerated.

20.100 ***Preparation of Standard Curve***

Just before use, pipet 5, 10, and 15 mL sorbic acid std soln into sep. 500 mL vol. flasks. Dil. each to vol. and mix. Pipet 2 mL each soln and 2 mL H_2O (for blank) into sep. 15 mL test tubes. Add 1.0 mL 0.3*N* H_2SO_4 and 1.0 mL $K_2Cr_2O_7$ soln, and heat in boiling H_2O bath exactly 5 min. Immerse tubes in ice bath and add 2 mL thiobarbituric acid soln. Replace in boiling H_2O bath and heat addnl 10 min. Cool, and det. *A* of each soln at 532 nm against blank, using matched 1 cm cells. Plot *A* against μg sorbic acid/mL.

20.101 ***Determination***

Weigh 1.5–2.0 g prepd sample, **16.232**, into distg tube containing SiC chips. Add 10 mL 2*N* H_2SO_4 and 10 g $MgSO_4.7H_2O$. Steam distil, maintaining ca 20–30 mL vol. in distg tube with small burner. Avoid charring. Collect 100–125 mL distillate in 250 mL vol. flask within ca 45 min. Rinse condenser with H_2O, dil. distillate to vol., and mix. If sample contains >0.05% sorbic acid, dil. soln to equiv. concn.

Proceed as in **20.100**, beginning "Pipet 2 mL each soln . . ." Det. concn sorbic acid from std curve and calc. % in sample.

Spectrophotometric Method (*29*)—Official Final Action

(Applicable to fresh dairy products—cottage, ricotta, and mozzarella cheese, sour cream, and yogurt)

20.102 ***Reagents and Apparatus***

(**a**) *Metaphosphoric acid soln.*—Dissolve 5 g HPO_3 in 250 mL H_2O and dil. to 1 L with alcohol.

(**b**) *Mixed ethers.*—Pet ether-anhyd. ether (1+1).

(**c**) *Potassium permanganate soln.*—Dissolve 15 g $KMnO_4$ in H_2O, dil. to 100 mL, and filter thru glass wool.

(**d**) *Sorbic acid soln.*—(*1*) *Stock soln.*—1.0 mg/mL. Dissolve 200 mg sorbic acid in 200 mL mixed ethers, (**b**). (*2*) *Working soln.*—0.05 mg/mL. Dil. 10 mL stock soln to 200 mL with mixed ethers, (**b**).

(**e**) *Reference soln.*—Shake 100 mL mixed ethers, (**b**), with 10 mL HPO_3 soln, (**a**), and dry supernate ether soln with 5 g anhyd. granular Na_2SO_4.

(**f**) *Spectrophotometer.*—For use in UV, with matched 1 cm cells, transparent to UV.

20.103 ***Preparation of Standard Curve***

Add 1, 2, 4, and 6 mL working std soln, (**d**)(*2*), to sep. 100 mL vol. flasks and dil. to vol. with mixed ethers. Det. *A* of solns at 250 nm against mixed ethers. Plot *A* against mg sorbic acid/100 mL.

20.104 ***Determination***

Accurately weigh 10.0 g sample, prepd as in **16.232**, in high-speed blender cup; add enough HPO_3 soln to yield total of 100 mL liq. in mixt. (i.e., to 10.0 g cottage cheese contg 8 g H_2O, add 92 mL). Blend 1 min and immediately filter thru 18.5 cm Whatman No. 3 paper. Transfer 10 mL filtrate to 250 mL separator contg 100 mL mixed ethers and shake 1 min. Discard aq. layer and dry ether ext with 5 g anhyd. Na_2SO_4. Det. *A* at 250 nm against ref. soln, (**e**). Det. concn sorbic acid from std curve.

% Sorbic acid

$$= (\text{mg sorbic acid/g sample}) \times (1/1000\ \text{mg}) \times 100$$
$$= \text{mg sorbic acid}/10.$$

Confirm presence of sorbic acid as follows: Add 2 mL $KMnO_4$ soln to remaining ether soln and shake 1 min. Filter thru Whatman No. 3 paper, add 5 g anhyd. Na_2SO_4, shake, and scan spectrum between 300 and 220 nm. Absence of peak at 250 nm confirms presence of sorbic acid in sample.

SULFUROUS ACID

20.105 Qualitative Test (*30*)—Official Final Action

Add small amt of S-free Zn and several mL HCl to ca 25 g sample (with addn of H_2O, if necessary) in 200 mL erlenmeyer. H_2S generated in presence of sulfites may be detected with $Pb(OAc)_2$ paper. Traces of metallic sulfides occasionally present in vegetables give same reaction as sulfites under conditions of above test. Verify positive results obtained by this method by Monier-Williams method, **20.108**.

It is always advisable to make quant. detn of sulfites because of possibility of pos. test caused by traces of sulfides. Trace should not be considered sufficient indication of presence of SO_2 either as bleaching agent or as preservative.

Total Sulfurous Acid

Modified Monier-Williams Method (31)
Official Final Action

(Applicable in presence of other volatile S compds; not applicable to dried onions, leeks, and cabbage.)

20.106 ***Reagents***

(**a**) *Hydrogen peroxide soln.*—3%. Check 30% ACS reagent to ensure compliance with sulfate specification. Det. H_2O_2 content by $KMnO_4$ titrn, dil. to ca 6% H_2O_2, neutze to Me red, (**b**), and dil. to calcd vol. to give 3.0%.

(**b**) *Methyl red indicator.*—0.25% in alcohol. Adjust to transition color.

20.107 ***Apparatus***

See Fig. **20:04**. Connect 3 neck (₮ 24/40) 1 L distg flask at an outer neck to 30 cm Allihn condenser (Ful-Jak, SGA Scientific Inc. No. JC-5450, or equiv.) in reflux position. (Condenser must condense all HCl but none of SO_2.) Place inner joint adapter with right angle hose connection in condenser and connect thru piece of ¼ × 6″ silicone tubing (SGA Scientific Inc. No. R-8425) preboiled in HCl (1+20) and rinsed with H_2O, to set of 2 U-tubes of 20 mm tubing, ball joint 35/20, 55±5 mm center to center and 150±5 mm long, connected with cross-over tube, ball joint 35/20, 55±5 mm center to center and 115±5 mm long. To each U-tube add 2 ca 25 mm lengths of solid glass tube, 10 mL 3 mm glass beads at exit side, and 10 mL 3% H_2O_2 contg drop Me red.

Attach either curved gas inlet tube for outer neck or straight tube for center neck of distg flask with tip reaching nearly to bottom.

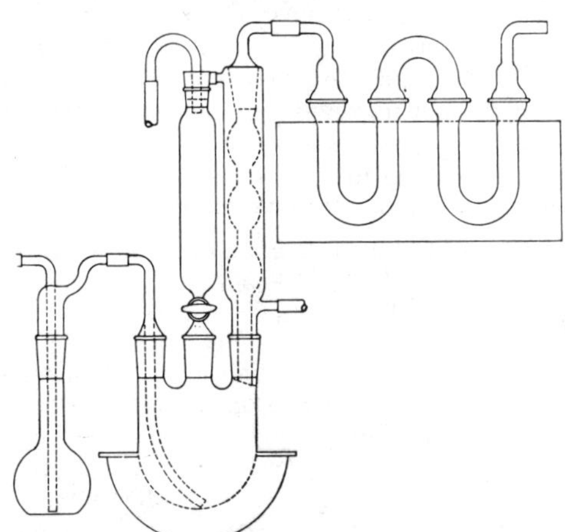

FIG. 20:04—Apparatus for modified Monier-Williams method for sulfur dioxide

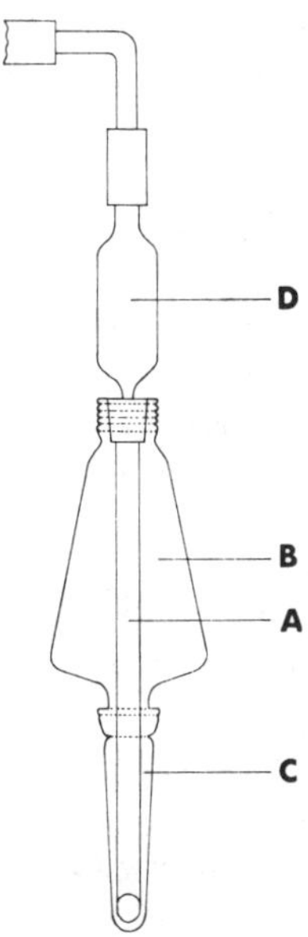

FIG. 20:05—Alternative SO_2 absorber

Alternatively substitute app. shown in Fig. **20:05** for U-tubes. Connect right angle hose connection to 30–50 mL bulb (*D*) and fritted cylindrical gas dispersion tube (*A*) (SGA Scientific Inc. No. G-5420, or equiv.). Suspend fritted end near bottom of Kuderna-Danish Evaporative Concentrator (*B, C*) (Kontes Glass Co. No. K-570000, part *B*, vol. 500 mL, ₮ 24/25 lower joint; part *C*, ca 15 mL, ₮ 24/25 joint) contg 10–12 mL 3% H_2O_2 and drop Me red. Diam. of *C* should provide min. gas scrubber path of 10 cm with 10 mL H_2O_2.

Grind 4.5 g *pyrogallol* with 5 mL H_2O in small mortar and transfer slurry to 250 mL ₮ 24/40 gas washing bottle. Repeat grinding and transfer with two 5 mL portions H_2O. Pass H_2O-pumped N from tank thru 2-stage regulator into gas washing bottle to flush out air and add to bottle, thru long stem funnel, cooled soln of 65 g KOH in ca 85 mL H_2O. (Prep. complete soln fresh daily.) Turn off N, and attach ¼ × 6″ silicone tubing, preboiled in HCl (1+20) and rinsed with H_2O, to exit end and to gas inlet tube of distg flask. Clamp off both ends of washing bottle.

Attach 125 mL separator thru ₮ 24/40 joint to third neck of distg flask. Attach piece of rubber tubing to short U-tube inserted thru rubber stopper in neck of separator. Blow into rubber tubing, and close separator stopcock. Let stand for few min to check for leaks shown by liqs leveling in U-tubes.

Place distg flask in heating mantle controlled by variable transformer.

20.108 ***Determination***

Place sample, contg ⩾45 mg SO_2, in distg flask, using H_2O for transferring, if necessary. Dil. to ca 400 mL with H_2O. Add 90 mL HCl (1+2) to separator and force HCl into flask with gentle pressure. Start N flow at slow steady stream of bubbles. Heat flask to cause refluxing in 20–25 min (ca 80 volts on 7 amp transformer). When steady refluxing is reached, apply line voltage and reflux 1.75 hr. Turn off H_2O in condenser and continue heating until inlet joint of first U-tube shows condensation and slight warming. Remove separator, and turn off heat. When joint at top of condenser cools, remove connecting assembly and rinse into second U-tube. Attach cross-over tube to exit joint of first U-tube, rotate until open ends touch, add drop Me red, and titr. with 0.1*N* NaOH just to clear yellow, mixing with gentle rocking. 1 mL 0.1*N* NaOH = 3.203 mg SO_2. Titr. second U-tube similarly. If alternative app. is used, disconnect, and rinse bulb *D* and tube *A* with few mL H_2O into Kuderna-Danish app. *B, C*. Add 2 drops Me red and titr. with 0.1*N* NaOH.

Gravimetric detn may be made after titrn by rinsing tubes into 400 mL beaker. Add 4 drops 1*N* HCl and excess of filtered *10% $BaCl_2$ soln*, and let stand overnight. Wash ppt by decantation 3 times with hot H_2O thru weighed gooch. Wash with 20 mL alcohol and 20 mL ether, and dry at 105–110°.

mg $BaSO_4$ × 274.46/g sample = ppm SO_2.

Det. blank on reagents, both by titrn and gravimetrically, and correct results accordingly.

Colorimetric Method (32)—Official Final Action

(Applicable to dried fruit)

20.109 ***Reagents***

(**a**) *Formaldehyde soln.*—0.015%. Prep. from 40% HCHO by dilg in 2 steps: 10 to 1000, and 75 to 2000.

(**b**) *Acid-bleached p-rosaniline hydrochloride.*—Place 100 mg *p*-rosaniline.HCl (Allied Chemical Corp.) and 200 mL H_2O in 1 L vol. flask. Add 160 mL HCl (1+1) and dil. to vol. Let stand 12 hr before use.

(**c**) *Sodium tetrachloromercurate.*—Place 23.4 g NaCl and 54.3 g $HgCl_2$ in 2 L vol. flask. Dissolve in ca 1900 mL H_2O and dil. to vol. (*Caution: See* **51.079**.)

(**d**) *Sulfur dioxide std soln.*—Dissolve ca 170 mg $NaHSO_3$ in H_2O and dil. to 1 L. Stdze with 0.01*N* I soln before use (ca 100 μg SO_2/mL).

20.110 ***Preparation of Standard Curve***

Add 5 mL mercurate reagent to series of 100 mL vol. flasks; then add 0, 1.0, 2.0, 3.0, etc., mL of SO_2 std soln. Dil. to vol. and mix. Transfer 5.0 mL portions to 200 mm test tubes contg 5 mL rosaniline reagent. Add 10 mL 0.015% HCHO soln, mix, and hold 30 min at 22°. Read *A* at 550 nm against 0 std and plot std curve.

20.111 ***Determination***

Weigh 10±0.02 g ground dried fruit and transfer to blender with 290 mL H_2O. Cover and blend 2 min. Withdraw 10 g aliquot from bottom of blender with 10 mL calibrated free-running pipet, and transfer to 100 mL vol. flask contg 4 mL 0.5*N* NaOH. (Use 2 mL for apples and 1 mL for golden raisins.) Swirl and mix ca 13–30 sec. Add 4 mL 0.5*N* H_2SO_4 (2 mL for apples and 1 mL for golden raisins) and 20 mL mercurate reagent, and dil. to vol. For blank, omit 10 mL fruit ext.

Transfer 2 mL sample soln to 200 mm test tube contg 5 mL rosaniline reagent. Add 10 mL 0.015% HCHO soln, mix, and hold 30 min at 22°. Read *A* at 550 nm against blank. Refer to std curve and convert results to ppm SO_2.

(If same colorimeter tube or cell is used for successive samples, clean between use with HCl (1+1) and H_2O.)

Sulfites in Meats (*33*)—Official Final Action

Qualitative Test

20.112 ***Reagent***

Malachite green soln.—Dissolve 200 mg malachite green, certified by Biological Stain Commission, in H_2O and dil. to 1 L. Soln is stable for several weeks if dispensed from polyethylene dropper bottle assembly with Neoprene bulb. Discard when visible deterioration occurs. (Tablets for prepn of 15 mL reagent are available from LaMotte Chemical Products Co., Chestertown, MD 21620.)

20.113 ***Test***

Transfer ca 3.5 g (½ teaspoonful) ground meat to 10 × 10 cm sq of waxed white freezer paper or other impervious white surface. Add 0.5 mL reagent and mix vigorously 2 min with hardwood tongue blade or spatula, turning mass frequently. Observe color after few min.

Dye is decolorized in presence of sulfites. Normal meat becomes blue-green. Verify pos. results by Monier-Williams method, **20.108**.

20.114 Free Sulfurous Acid (*34*)—Official Final Action

Treat 50 mL sample in 200 mL flask with ca 5 mL H_2SO_4 (1+3), add ca 0.5 g Na_2CO_3 to expel air, and titr. H_2SO_3 with 0.02*N* I, using few mL starch indicator, **6.005(f)**. Add I soln as rapidly as possible and continue addn until soln stays blue several min. 1 mL 0.02*N* I = 0.64 mg SO_2.

THIOUREA (*35*)

Qualitative Tests—Procedure

(Applicable to orange juice)

20.115 ***Pentacyanoammonioferroate Test***

(**a**) *Reagent.*—(*Caution: See* **51.050**.) Dissolve 10 g $Na_2Fe(CN)_5NO.2H_2O$ in 40 mL NH_4OH and let stand at ca 0° until all nitrosoferricyanide decomposes (shown when few drops mixt. no longer give red soln when added to soln of creatinine in 1*N* NaOH; decomposition is complete after 24 hr). Filter, and add absolute alcohol to filtrate until there is no further pptn of pentacyanoammonioferroate. Filter, wash with absolute alcohol until NH_3-free, dry *in vacuo* over H_2SO_4, and store in desiccator over $CaCl_2$ in dark. Reagent is 1% soln of this salt in H_2O, exposed to light and air 1 day and then stored in brown glass bottle in dark. It gains in potency for several weeks, and can be kept ca 6 months.

(**b**) *Test.*—Ext orange juice with ca ⅔ vol. ether, centrf., and sep. lower layer. Stir in some Filter-Cel and filter with suction. Keep vac. on short time and agitate soln to remove most of ether. To ca 5 mL filtered soln add 5 drops reagent and note color. If blue color does not develop, add I soln, ca 0.1*N*, dropwise, shaking after each drop. Blue-green soln indicates presence of $CS(NH_2)_2$. (Usually ca 5 drops I soln are necessary to develop max. color; excess I tends to reduce color.)

20.116 ***Grote Reagent Test***

To 5–10 mL orange juice, ether-extd and filtered as in **20.115(b)**, add 0.02*N* I dropwise until I color does not immediately disappear. Add few mL dil. Grote reagent, **20.118(b)**. Blue-green or blue color developing rather gradually indicates presence of $CS(NH_2)_2$.

Quantitative Methods

Rapid Oxidation Method for Orange Juice
Official Final Action

20.117 ***Apparatus***

Siphon.—Insert 2 bent glass tubes in 2-hole cork or stopper, one terminating just below stopper (blow tube) and other (siphon tube) long enough to reach bottom of centrf. bottle when cork with tubes is inserted in mouth of bottle. Attach another glass tube to outside end of siphon tube with flexible rubber tube so that end of outside tube is below end of inside tube. This assembly is used to siphon lower layer from centrf. bottle, and rate of flow is controlled by squeezing rubber connection. Prep. cap for inner siphon tube by boring hole of same diam. as tube part way thru small cork.

20.118 ***Reagents***

(**a**) *Modified Grote reagent*.—Dissolve 0.5 g $Na_2Fe(CN)_5NO.2H_2O$ in 10 mL H_2O in 50 mL erlenmeyer. Weigh 0.5 g $NH_2OH.HCl$ and 1 g $NaHCO_3$. Uniformly mix the 2 solids in small beaker or porcelain dish by gentle grinding with small pestle or flat-end glass rod, crushing any lumps in sample. Brush off rod or pestle and quant. transfer mixed solid to nitroprusside soln with aid of short-stem funnel and brush. Do not agitate flask but let it stand until CO_2 evolution nearly stops. Then swirl to dissolve any remaining $NaHCO_3$. When evolution of CO_2 practically ceases, add 0.10 mL Br (11 small drops). Second evolution of gas occurs. When agitation no longer produces effervescence, dil. to 25 mL with H_2O and filter. Test reagent as follows: Dil. 2 mL as in (**b**); add 1 mL dild reagent to 10 mL soln composed of 5 mL thiourea stock soln, (**c**), (dild 10×), 5 mL H_2O, and 1 drop HOAc. Strong blue color should develop in 5 min. If it does not, prep. new reagent and repeat test. Store at room temp. 5–10 hr to age soln. (Soln should be mahogany brown. If it has greenish cast, it is not as effective and soon loses its value.) This stock soln keeps several weeks when stored in refrigerator.

(**b**) *Dilute Grote reagent*.—Dil. 1 vol. reagent (**a**) with 4 vols H_2O. Use 1 mL dild reagent for each detn. Dild reagent keeps 1 day.

(**c**) *Thiourea stock soln*.—Dissolve 100 mg $CS(NH_2)_2$ in H_2O and dil. to 200 mL.

(**d**) *Citrate soln*.—Dissolve 0.84 g $K_3C_6H_5O_7.H_2O$ and 1 g citric acid in H_2O, and dil. to 100 mL.

(**e**) *Sulfuric acid*.—1.00±0.02*N*.

20.119 ***Preparation of Sample***

Juice oranges in ordinary reamer, strain out seeds and pulp, and mix well. Measure 125 mL into 250 mL centrf. bottle, add 70 mL ether, and shake well 1–2 min. Centrf. ca 10 min at 1800 rpm. Cap short end of siphon tube (inside bottle), insert into bottle, and lower thru top layer into lower aq. layer. Push off cork cap with glass rod. Lower tube to bottom of bottle, push cork (which carries both tubes) into mouth of bottle, and blow in short tube to start flow of liq. Carefully siphon into beaker as much of lower layer as possible, controlling rate of flow by squeezing on rubber connection. Stop flow when material from center emulsion layer begins to enter tube.

Add teaspoonful of Filter-Cel to siphoned liq. in beaker, stir well, and filter on buchner (7–11 cm) with suction, using Whatman 54 or 41-H paper. Measure filtrate with graduate, pour into separator, and add ca ½ its vol. ether. Shake well, let sep., drain lower layer into beaker, add pinch of Filter-Cel, stir well, and filter thru Whatman No. 12 folded filter. Place filtrate in clean, dry suction flask, warm on steam bath to 36°, and apply suction to remove ether.

Pipet 25 mL filtrate (clear or nearly so) into clean 50 mL vol. flask. In 2 similar flasks place 25 mL aliquots citrate soln. To one flask add 2 mL thiourea stock soln; use other as a blank. To each of the 3 flasks add 5 mL 1*N* H_2SO_4. Slowly add 0.1*N* I, **50.018**, with rotation, to each flask until I color does not disappear; then add 1 mL excess. Let flasks (samples, std, and blank) stand 10 min at room temp. Now add *soln of* $NaHSO_3$ (2.5 g/L) to contents of flasks until I color disappears; add 3 or 4 drops excess. Add 4 mL 25% NaOAc soln gradually and slowly to each flask, with swirling, dil. to vol. with H_2O, and mix. Filter if cloudy. Designate oxidized dild sample as Soln X.

20.120 ***Determination***

Prep. 2 stds by placing 5 and 10 mL portions of soln from the std flask in test tubes. Dil. first tube to 10 mL by adding 5 mL liq. from blank soln (no thiourea). Place 10 mL portions blank soln and sample Soln X in 2 other test tubes. Pipet 1 mL dild Grote reagent (*Caution: See* **51.018** and **51.050**) into each tube with shaking or stirring. Let tubes stand 1 hr at ca 25°, or 10–15 min in bath at 45–50°, to develop blue color. Read developed color of solns from each tube (sample, blank, and stds) in spectrophtr at 610 nm. From readings of blank and stds construct curve (linear), plotting *A* against ppm $CS(NH_2)_2$. Oxidized std in flask represents 20 ppm (1 mg/50 mL); 10 mL aliquot therefore represents 20 ppm, and 5 mL, 10 ppm.

Slight correction on sample color reading obtained is necessary because of natural color present in Soln X before addn of Grote reagent. Obtain readings on blank soln and sample Soln X contained in vol. flask, without added reagent, using same photometer cell. Subtract difference between these readings (X − blank) from sample reading with Grote reagent. Obtain from graph ppm $CS(NH_2)_2$ corresponding to corrected reading. This value × 2 = $CS(NH_2)_2$ concn in original orange juice.

Method for Frozen Peaches—Official First Action

20.121 ***Preparation of Sample***

(*Caution: See* **51.011**, **51.039**, and **51.046**.)

Weigh 200–400 g frozen sample on rough balance (0.1–0.2 g sensitivity) into tared 800 mL beaker. Cut contents of 1 lb (450 g) package into quarter or eighth portions, select alternate portions for detn, and keep remainder as reserve sample. (Several packages can be composited in this manner if desired.)

Immediately add to sample, vol. *$NaHSO_3$ soln* (2.5 g/L) equal to ½ wt sample (*See Note*). Mix and pour into high-speed blender (or other mixing machine), drain well, and blend 20–30 sec. Return dild comminuted sample to beaker.

Weigh 150±0.2 g blended sample, transfer to 250 mL vol. flask, and dil. to ca 200 mL with H_2O. Add ca 4 drops *hexyl alcohol* and attach to flask 2-hole stopper (No. 0), carrying small bent glass tube and another straight tube, extending ca 8 cm into flask, end of which is drawn to small bore (near capillary). Remove most of air by applying gentle suction to bent tube and shaking flask with rotation. (Bore of small tube should be large enough so that reduction of pressure is not too great.) If froth rises in neck, release vac. for moment. Continue with suction and rotation until most of air is removed, add 20 mL addnl $NaHSO_3$ soln, and dil. to vol. with H_2O. Mix well and pour ca 165 mL into 250 mL centrf. bottle. Add 50 mL ether to bottle, rotate few times, stopper, and shake; open once to release pressure; then shake vigorously 1–1.5 min. (If preferred, divide liq. in vol. flask between 2 centrf. bottles and ext each with ca 30 mL ether, etc.)

Centrf. ca 10 min at ca 1800 rpm. Carefully pour off little of top ether layer into beaker; then inclining bottle, push sludge cake toward bottom of bottle with glass rod and pour liq. contents on cotton filter in funnel. To prep. filter, place small cotton pledget in apex of 85–100 mm funnel, and insert piece of absorbent cotton of half thickness (split sheet), ca 9 cm diam.

Pipet 100 mL lower aq. filtrate into 200 mL vol. flask, squeezing cotton on side of funnel with rod if necessary to obtain enough filtrate. Gradually add enough acetone to contents of flask (from separator), with const shaking, to bring contents to 200 mL mark. As surface of liq. enters neck of flask, stopper, and mix by inverting few times before dilg to mark. Mix, cool to room temp. (in bath if desired), dil. to mark again, and mix well.

(Acetone causes some rise in temp.) Let ppt sep. and pour contents of flask into 250 mL centrf. bottle. Add 1 spoonful of Filter-Cel, stopper, and shake well. Centrf. ca 8 min at ca 1800 rpm. Decant supernate and filter if turbid. Measure 125 mL clear liq. into 250 mL beaker, add several glass beads, and boil off acetone on steam bath. Then boil down to ca 35 mL on hot plate, remove, and cool to room temp. Add 15% NaOH soln dropwise until alk. and ca 2 drops excess. Add HOAc (1+5) with stirring until just acid and add 2 drops excess.

Quant. transfer liq. to 50 mL vol. flask, dil. to vol. with H_2O, and mix. Pour contents of flask into small beaker or flask (100–125 mL), add 1 spoonful Filter-Cel, and mix well by stirring or stoppering and shaking. Filter liq. on 12.5 cm folded paper (Eaton-Dikeman 195 is suitable). Pour thru filter again if not clear. Filtrate or final sample soln is designated *FS.*

20.122 ***Determination***

Pipet 10 mL Soln *FS* into 150 mm test tube. For ≤50 ppm $CS(NH_2)_2$, prep stds contg 0, 1, 2, and 4 mL portions of 1 + 9 diln $CS(NH_2)_2$ stock soln, **20.118(c)** (5 mg $CS(NH_2)_2$/100 mL). Add *0.6% Na citrate soln* to tubes to make stds to 10 mL; then add 1 drop HOAc (1+5) to each tube (samples and stds). Place stirring rod in each tube and stir up and down to mix, leaving rod in tube. Place tubes in bath or room held at 20–25°.

Add to each tube, with stirring, 1 mL dil. Grote reagent, (**b**) (recently dild). Let tubes stand 60 min at 20–25° and det. *A* of each soln in spectrophtr at ca 610 nm. Designate reading of sample as *X*. Construct linear curve from std readings, plotting ppm $CS(NH_2)_2$ (1 mL std soln = 10 ppm $CS(NH_2)_2$ in sample) against *A*. Extrapolate std curve up to 50 ppm.

To correct reading *X* for natural color present in soln before reagent is added, make readings of Soln *FS* with no added reagent in same cell and also that of H_2O. *FS* reading − H_2O reading = *d*; *X* − *d* = *R* (corrected reading). From reading *R* obtain ppm $CS(NH_2)_2$ in Soln *FS*, using curve. Multiply $CS(NH_2)_2$ thus found by factor 1.065 to correct for vol. increase due to solubility of ether and obtain true $CS(NH_2)_2$ content of original sample. Repeat detn (color development) on smaller aliquot (1–5 mL) for amts >50 ppm.

Note: Sample of 200 g is enough to be representative and should be used where portion is to be reserved. Keep unused portion of sample frozen. It is necessary to add the $NaHSO_3$ soln to frozen sample immediately before blending to prevent losses of $CS(NH_2)_2$ due to attack by enzyme systems present. Blender whips air thruout the material, and if enzymes are not inactivated, large losses of $CS(NH_2)_2$ may occur. Enzymes can also be inactivated by plunging frozen sample into boiling H_2O and boiling 3 or 4 min. Action of enzymes is slow in frozen condition if material is unbroken cakes or chunks.

Method for Orange Peel—Official Final Action

20.123 ***Reagents***

(**a**) *Thiourea std soln.*—0.5 mg/mL. *See* **20.118(c)**.

(**b**) *Diluted modified Grote reagent.*—Dil. modified Grote reagent, **20.118(a)**, with 2 vols H_2O just before use.

(**c**) *Extraction solvent.*—Mix EtOAc with acetone (2+1).

(**d**) *Dilute phosphoric acid.*—0.9±0.1*N*, stdzd to phthln end point.

20.124 ***Preparation of Sample***

(*Caution: See* **51.004**, **51.039**, and **51.054**.)

Bisect 6–8 fruit and ream firmly to remove all possible juice without removing peel. Pass peel thru food chopper or grinder and mix thoroly in bottle.

Weigh 75 g sample into high-speed blender cup. Add 250 mL ether and blend 2 min in hood with draft operating. Filter on 11 cm buchner with moderate suction and rinse blender and filter with ether, pressing down cake with bottom of 100–150 mL beaker. Remove ether from suction flask, discard ether, and continue suction on cake to remove ether.

Remove buchner from flask and transfer cake to 750 mL (135 mm diam.) casserole. Strip off paper, and transfer any remaining peel on paper or in funnel to casserole with spatula. Add 100 g anhyd. Na_2SO_4 and mix well with spatula and spoon. Transfer mixt. to blender, dry-wash casserole with little more Na_2SO_4, and add to blender. Add ca 275 mL extn solv., blend at low speed, and gradually increase to full speed, using variable transformer. Blend at full speed 3 min, and filter into 11 cm buchner, using Whatman 41-H paper with moderate suction, transferring most of residue with policeman and few small spurts of extn solv. from wash bottle. Distribute residue over filter, press down cake with bottom of 100–150 mL beaker, and suck dry. Remove cake and return to blender, stripping off paper. Add 150 mL extn solv., and blend ca 2 min. Filter on buchner, rinse blender and filter with ca 50 mL extn solv., and suck dry. Combine extn solv. filtrates, add 1.2 mL 0.9*N* H_3PO_4, dil. to convenient vol. in flask or graduate, and mix.

Accurately measure 2 aliquots of solv. ext, each equiv. to 10 g sample, into 150 mL beakers, and evap. on steam bath sep. to ca 12 mL. Cool, add small amt of Celite, and stir. Filter each soln into sep. side arm test tube thru fritted filter tube or crucible overlaid with fine, firm asbestos mat or thru small buchner and S&S 589 Blue Ribbon paper, using moderate suction. Rinse beaker and filter with 3 mL EtOAc.

Quant. transfer filtrates to small separators with aid of eye-dropper pipet and bulb, rinsing with ca 1 mL EtOAc. Ext with two 5 mL portions H_2O, shaking well and letting sep. each time. Combine aq. exts of each detn in small beaker and boil ca 20 sec to remove most of org. solv. Cool, dil. each to 10 mL with H_2O in vol. flask, and mix well.

20.125 ***Determination***

Pipet 5 mL aliquots of final aq. solns from each detn into 25 mm diam. test tubes. Add 0.5 mL dild modified Grote reagent, **20.123(b)**, mix, and det. *A* after 75 min against blank as in **20.126**. Det. mg thiourea from std curve.

To correct for loss of thiourea, if any, during evapn of org. solv., place same vol. extn solv. as contained equiv. of 10 g sample in 150 mL beaker, add 0.6 mL thiourea std soln (0.3 mg) and 0.12 mL 0.9*N* H_3PO_4, and evap. to ca 12 mL on steam bath. Proceed as in **20.124**, par. 4, beginning "Cool, add small amt of Celite, and stir."

Correct thiourea found in sample aliquot, if necessary, for loss on evapn. Calc. to original sample basis.

20.126 ***Preparation of Standard Curve***

Prep. blank soln contg 1.20 mL 0.9*N* H_3PO_4 dild to 100 mL with H_2O. Pipet 6 mL thiourea std soln into 100 mL vol. flask, add 1.20 mL 0.9*N* H_3PO_4, and dil. to vol. with H_2O. Place 1.0, 2.5, and 5.0 mL aliquots of this std soln in 25 mm diam. test tubes and add 4.0, 2.5, and 0 mL blank soln. Place 5.0 mL blank soln in similar tube. To all solns add 0.5 mL dild modified Grote reagent, mix, and let stand 1 hr. Read *A* of stds against blank at 610 nm. Plot mg thiourea against *A*. Check std curve occasionally and prep. new curve with each new lot of modified Grote reagent.

EMULSIFYING AGENTS

Polysorbate 60 (Polyoxyethylene (20) Sorbitan Monostearate) (*36*)—Official First Action

(Applicable to shortening, food oils, and nonstdzd dressings)

20.127 ***Principle***

Polysorbate 60 is extd from dressing with $CHCl_3$-absolute alcohol (93+7). Shortening or dressing ext is saponified with alc. KOH and acidified; fatty acids are extd with hexane. Aq. polyol soln is desalted by mixed-bed ion exchange and Ba phosphomolybdate is used to ppt polyoxyethylated polyols as insol. heteropoly acid complex. Ppt is dried to const wt and polysorbate 60 content is calcd using gravimetric factor obtained by analyzing known amts polysorbate 60. Method is applicable in range 0.1–1.0% polysorbate 60.

20.128 ***Apparatus***

(**a**) *Reflux apparatus.*—(*1*) Alkali-resistant erlenmeyers, ₸ 24/40 g-s joint, 300 mL; with (*2*) enlarging adapter tubes, g-s joint, ₸ 29/42 top outer, ₸ 24/40 bottom inner; (*3*) H_2O-cooled condensers, ₸ 29/42 g-s joint.

(**b**) *Ion exchange tube.*—400 × 28 mm id, ₸ 29/42 top outer g-s and Teflon stopcock, coarse fritted glass disk; 250 mL addn funnel, ₸ 29/42 g-s joint fitted with glass drip tip.

(**c**) *Extraction apparatus.*—Soxhlet extn tube, 40 mm id; Whatman extn thimbles, 8 × 33 mm; and 250 mL extn flasks with caps.

20.129 ***Reagents***

(**a**) *Alcoholic potassium hydroxide soln.*—1*N* in absolute alcohol.

(**b**) *Mixed-bed ion exchange resin.*—Illco exchange resin, research grade TMD-8 (anion-dyed) (Illinois Water Treatment Co., 4669 Shepherd Trail, Rockford, IL 61105).

(**c**) *Asbestos.*—Medium fiber, gooch grade. (*Caution: See* **51.086**.)

(**d**) *Absorbing filter aid.*—Hyflo Super-Cel, or equiv.

20.130 ***Determination***

(**a**) *For shortening and food oils.*—Weigh sample contg 10–40 mg polysorbate 60 (total wt ≤9 g) into 300 mL alkali-resistant flask. Add 50 mL 1*N* alc. KOH, and attach adapter tube and reflux condenser. Reflux 45 min on hot plate. Add 10 mL H_2O and continue refluxing addnl 45 min. Transfer quant. to 250 mL separator with ca 50 mL ca 60° H_2O. Add 4.5 mL HCl and mix by swirling. Cool so that separator may be held comfortably in hand. Add 50 mL redistd hexane, shake vigorously, and let sep. Drain lower layer into second separator and ext with another 50 mL portion hexane. Drain lower layer into 250 mL addn funnel. Combine hexane exts and wash with two 20 mL portions alcohol (1+1). Combine aq. alc. exts in addn funnel and cool to room temp.

Pour aq. suspension of mixed-bed resins, **20.129(b)**, into tube, to bed ht ca 30 cm. Add polyol soln to column from addn funnel, and adjust flow to ca 2 mL/min. Collect eluate in 600 mL beaker. Rinse sides of tube and wash resin bed with 200 mL H_2O. (Rate may be increased to 3–4 mL/min during washing step.) Evap. combined eluates in steam bath to 300 mL (support lip of beaker on edge of bath opening.) Remove hot soln and immediately add 2.0 mL 3*N* HCl, 4.0 mL *10% $BaCl_2$ soln*, and 4.0 mL *10% phosphomolybdic acid soln* to ppt Ba phosphomolybdic-polyol complex. Stir soln and let stand overnight.

Filter thru 40 mL size gooch provided with asbestos mat, previously dried at 110° and weighed. Quant. transfer ppt with rubber policeman and H_2O wash. Wash ppt in gooch with 50 mL H_2O. Dry 1 hr in 110° oven. Cool in desiccator, and weigh.

Det. gravimetric factor by analyzing known amt (ca 25 mg) polysorbate 60.

$$\% \text{ Polysorbate } 60 = (C \times 100)/(F \times W),$$

where C = g dry ppt, W = g sample, F = gravimetric factor = wt complex/unit wt polysorbate 60 (ca 2.8).

(**b**) *For nonstandardized dressings.*—Weigh sample contg 10–40 mg polysorbate 60 (total wt ≤9 g) into 150 mL beaker and mix thoroly with 7 g Hyflo Super-Cel. Transfer mixt. to Soxhlet thimble, and ext 16 hr in Soxhlet app. with 150–200 mL $CHCl_3$-absolute alcohol (93+7). Quant. transfer ext to 300 mL alkali-resistant flask, and evap. solv. on steam bath using boiling rod. (*Caution: See* **51.056**.) To ensure complete removal of $CHCl_3$ from residue, add 50 mL absolute alcohol and evap. to dryness again. Proceed as in (**a**), par. 1, line 3, beginning "Add 50 mL 1*N* alc. KOH, . . ."

Sodium Lauryl Sulfate (*37*)—Official Final Action

20.131 ***Reagents***

(*Caution: See* **51.022**, **51.028(a)** and **(d)**, and **51.079**.)

(**a**) *Crystal violet indicator.*—*See* **3.156(d)**.

(**b**) *Methyl yellow indicator.*—Dissolve 40 mg *p*-dimethylaminoazobenzene in 100 mL MeOH. (*Caution: See* **51.085**.)

(**c**) *Standard acetous perchloric acid.*—0.1*N*. Mix 8.5 mL 72% $HClO_4$ with 500 mL HOAc and add 30 mL Ac_2O. Cool, and dil. to 1 L with HOAc. Let stand 24 hr before using. Stdze as follows: Accurately weigh 400–500 mg KH phthalate, previously dried 2 hr at 105°, into 250 mL erlenmeyer and dissolve in 80 mL HOAc. Add 3 drops crystal violet indicator and titr. with acetous $HClO_4$ to blue-green end point, which is stable 60 sec. Perform blank titrn on 80 mL HOAc and 3 drops indicator soln, and correct vol. of titrant.

$$N = \text{mg } KHC_8H_4O_4/(204.23 \times \text{mL } HClO_4)$$

(**d**) *Mercuric acetate soln.*—6%. Dissolve 6.0 g $Hg(OAc)_2$ crystals in 100 mL HOAc, heating gently, if necessary, to dissolve.

(**e**) *Azure A soln.*—Dissolve 40 mg dye (CI No. 52005) in H_2O, add 10 mL 0.1*N* H_2SO_4, and dil. to 100 mL.

(**f**) *Benzethonium chloride.*—Approx. 99% pure (available from Aldrich Chemical Co., Inc.). Det. purity as follows: Accurately weigh ca 1 g benzethonium chloride, previously dried 2 hr under vac. at 80°, into 250 mL erlenmeyer. Dissolve in 80 mL HOAc and add 10 mL 6% $Hg(OAc)_2$ in HOAc. Add 3 drops crystal violet indicator and titr. with 0.1*N* $HClO_4$ to same blue-green end point used in stdzn of $HClO_4$. Perform blank detn on 80 mL HOAc and 10 mL $Hg(OAc)_2$, and correct vol. of titrant.

% Purity = (corrected titrant vol. × N × 44.81)/g benzethonium chloride

(**g**) *Benzethonium chloride std soln.*—0.005*N*. Accurately weigh ca 2.25 g dried benzethonium chloride and dil. to 1 L with H_2O. N = (g benzethonium chloride × % purity)/448.1

(**h**) *Sodium lauryl sulfate* (*SLS*).—Approx. 95% pure. Det. purity as follows: Accurately weigh ca 500 mg SLS, transfer to 250 mL vol. flask with H_2O, and dil. to vol. Pipet 25 mL into 250 mL g-s erlenmeyer. Add 50 mL $CHCl_3$, 10 mL 1*N* H_2SO_4, and 1 mL Me yellow indicator. Titr. with 0.005*N* benzethonium chloride as follows: Add 20 mL titrant, shake vigorously, and let layers sep. Add titrant in 1 mL increments, shaking vigorously after each addn until pink in $CHCl_3$ layer begins to change to orange. (Emulsion will begin to break rapidly at this time.) Add titrant in 2 drop increments until $CHCl_3$ layer changes to definite yellow. Make detn in duplicate. 1 mL 0.005*N* benzethonium chloride = 1.442 mg SLS.

(i) *Sodium lauryl sulfate (SLS) std soln.*—5 μg/mL. Transfer SLS equiv. to 100 mg pure SLS to 1 L vol. flask with H_2O and dil. to vol. Transfer 5.0 mL to 100 mL vol. flask, dil. to vol. with H_2O, and mix.

20.132 ***Preparation of Standard Curve***

Pipet 0, 1, 3, 5, 10, and 15 mL aliquot SLS std soln into 125 mL separators. Dil. each to ca 25 mL with H_2O. Add 10 mL 0.1*N* H_2SO_4 and 1.0 mL Azure A. Ext with two 20 mL portions H_2O-satd $CHCl_3$. Drain each $CHCl_3$ ext thru pledget of glass wool into 50 mL vol. flask. Dil. to vol., read *A* at 637 nm against H_2O-satd $CHCl_3$, and prep. std curve.

20.133 ***Determination***

(Rinse all glassware several times with H_2O to eliminate all traces of detergent.)

(a) *Liquid and frozen egg white.*—Let frozen egg white thaw at room temp. Accurately weigh ca 20 g liq. egg white into beaker and transfer to 500 mL g-s erlenmeyer with 400 mL H_2O. Swirl gently ca 1 min and let stand 1 hr with occasional swirling. Add 400 mL alcohol and mix by gentle shaking. Heat mixt. on steam bath 15 min and shake at 3 min intervals to promote complete pptn. Let cool 45 min and filter thru Whatman No. 30 paper, using 11 cm buchner. Wash ppt in flask and on filter with three 50 mL portions alcohol. Transfer filtrate to 1 L vol. flask and dil. to vol. with alcohol. Pipet 2 aliquots, each contg 50 μg SLS, into sep. 100 mL beakers and evap. to dryness on steam bath with current of air. Take up residues with H_2O and transfer each to 125 mL separator with several small portions H_2O to make total of ca 25 mL. To one add 1.0 mL 0.005*N* benzethonium chloride to serve as blank. Continue with each as in **20.132**, beginning "Add 10 mL 0.1*N* H_2SO_4 . . ." Read *A* of sample and blank against H_2O-satd $CHCl_3$. Subtract blank *A* from sample *A*. Det. SLS from std curve.

(b) *Powdered egg white.*—Accurately weigh ca 2.5 g powd egg white into 300 mL g-s erlenmeyer and add 40 mL H_2O. Let stand 2 hr with occasional swirling. If egg white is not completely suspended after 1 hr, break up lumps with stirring rod and swirl at 5 min intervals until all egg white is suspended. After 2 hr, add 20 mL alcohol and shake gently 1 min. Heat mixt. on steam bath 0.5 hr, remove, and let cool 0.5 hr. Continue as in (a), beginning ". . . filter thru Whatman No. 30 . . ."

(c) *Flake dried egg white.*—Grind flakes in mortar to pass No. 20 sieve. Proceed as in (b).

ENZYMES

Proteolytic Activity of Papain (*38*)—Official First Action

20.134 ***Reagents***

(a) *Casein soln.*—Make 6% soln of Hammersten casein (US Biochemical Corp, PO Box 22400, Cleveland, OH 44122) by rubbing 60 g with little H_2O in mortar and gradually adding 60 mL 1*N* NaOH and H_2O until vol. totals 1 L. Heat viscous soln 30 min in boiling H_2O bath, cool, and filter thru glass wool if necessary.

(b) *Citrate buffer soln.*—Prep. 0.2*M* monosodium citrate soln by partial neutzn of citric acid with NaOH.

(c) *Titrating soln.*—Stdzd 0.1*N* alc. KOH.

(d) *Indicator.*—1% alc. thymolphthalein soln.

20.135 ***Preparation of Sample***

(a) *Unactivated.*—If enzyme prepn is solid, grind to smooth paste in small mortar with little freshly boiled, cold H_2O. Suspend in cold boiled H_2O in proportion of 10 mg original prepn/mL H_2O. After 5–10 min centrf. suspension and discard sediment.

(b) *Activated.*—Proceed as in (a), but use half-satd H_2S-H_2O (*Caution: See* **51.059**) instead of boiled H_2O. After centrfg, incubate enzyme soln 1 hr at 40° to complete activation.

20.136 ***Determination***

Place 10 mL casein soln and small charge of 4 mm diam. glass beads in each of several 125 mL g-s bottles, and bring bottles and contents to 40°. Add desired vol. of prepd enzyme soln, but ≤4 mL. If this amt is insufficient (*see* **20.137**), prep. more concd soln of enzyme. Immediately add exactly 3 mL buffer soln (pH of system should be 5.0±0.1). Vigorously shake bottle few sec and place in const temp. H_2O bath at 40°.

Incubate 20 min at 40°, counting time from addn of buffer. Add 1 mL indicator and begin titrg with alc. KOH soln. As soon as deep blue appears, shake bottle until color is discharged or ppt is completely dissolved. (It is usually best to add alkali in ca 0.5 mL portions.) When all pptd casein dissolves, transfer soln to 400–500 mL flask and rinse bottle 2 or 3 times with alcohol, using total of 25 mL. Add enough KOH soln to restore blue; then add 175 mL boiling alcohol. Carefully add more KOH soln until pale but distinct blue persists in soln.

Make control titrn exactly as described, but do it immediately after addn of buffer, without any incubation time. Difference between titrn of undigested sample and that of digested sample is measure of proteolytic activity of enzyme.

20.137 ***Calculation of Proteinase Unit***

For smaller amts of enzyme, extent of hydrolysis detd by above titrn is straight line function of amts of papain used. For accurate work, det. this straight line by making several titrns with different amts of enzyme. If amts of papain used are too large, straight-line relationship no longer holds; if they are too small, detn is inaccurate. Amts of enzymes giving titrn differences of 0.6–1.2 mL 0.1*N* KOH are recommended.

Unit of papain is amt of enzyme that produces, under conditions outlined, titrn difference of 1 mL 0.1*N* KOH, detd either graphically or arithmetically. Value of original prepn is then expressed in units/mg, or as mg papain prepn necessary to make one unit.

Pharmaceutical Manufacturers Association–Food Chemicals Codex–AOAC Method (*39*) Official First Action

20.138 ***Reagents***

(a) *Sodium phosphate soln.*—0.05*M*. Dissolve 7.1 g anhyd. Na_2HPO_4 in enough H_2O to make 1 L. Add drop of toluene as preservative.

(b) *Citric acid soln.*—0.05*M*. Dissolve 10.5 g citric acid.H_2O in enough H_2O to make 1 L. Add drop of toluene as preservative.

(c) *Casein substrate.*—Disperse 5 g Hammersten-type casein in 250 mL 0.05*M* Na_2HPO_4. Place in boiling H_2O bath 30 min with occasional stirring. Cool to room temp. and add 0.05*M* citric acid to pH 6.0±0.1. Stir soln rapidly and continuously during addn of citric acid to prevent pptn of casein. Dil. to 500 mL with H_2O. Prep. fresh daily.

(d) *Phosphate-cysteine disodium ethylenedinitrilotetraacetate buffer soln.*—Dissolve 3.55 g Na_2HPO_4 in 400 mL H_2O in 500 mL vol. flask. Add 7.0 g Na_2H_2EDTA and 3.05 g cysteine.HCl.H_2O. Adjust to pH 6.0±0.1 with 1*N* HCl or 1*N* NaOH and dil. to vol. with H_2O. Prep. fresh daily.

(e) *Trichloroacetic acid (TCA) soln.*—30%. Dissolve 60 g trichloroacetic acid in H_2O and dil. to 200 mL with H_2O. (*Caution: See* **51.082**.)

(f) *Papain std soln.*—Accurately weigh 100 mg USP Papain Ref. Std in 100 mL vol. flask and add buffer soln, (**d**), to dissolve. Dil. to vol. with buffer soln, (**d**). Further dil. 4 mL of this soln to 100 mL with buffer soln. Use within 30 min of prepn.

20.139 ***Preparation of Sample***

Accurately weigh amt sample contg activity equiv. to 100 mg ref. std and proceed exactly as in prepn of papain std soln.

20.140 ***Determination***

Into each of 12 g-s 100 mL vol. flasks, pipet 25 mL casein substrate. Label flasks in duplicate (tests are run in duplicate except for blanks) S_1, S_2, and S_3 for papain std soln and U_2 for sample soln. Label remaining 4 flasks (blanks) S_{1B}, S_{2B}, S_{3B}, and U_{2B}.

Add 5, 2.5, and 0 mL buffer soln, resp., to flasks S_1, S_2, and S_3 and also to their resp. blanks S_{1B}, S_{2B}, and S_{3B}. To U_2 and U_{2B} add 2.5 mL buffer soln. Place all flasks in 40° H_2O bath and allow 10 min to reach bath temp.

Into each of duplicate flasks S_1, pipet 5 mL papain std soln, noting 0 time upon release of pipet with simultaneous swirling of flask to mix. Stopper and replace in bath. Into 2 flasks labeled S_2, pipet 7.5 mL papain std soln and proceed as before. Repeat for 2 flasks S_3 to which 10 mL papain std soln is added and for 2 flasks U_2 to which 7.5 mL sample soln is added.

After exactly 60 min add 15 mL 30% TCA to all 12 flasks and shake vigorously. With 4 flasks to which no std or unknown solns were added, prep. blanks by pipetting, resp., 5 mL (S_{1B}), 7.5 mL (S_{2B}), and 10 mL (S_{3B}) papain std soln, and 7.5 mL (U_{2B}) sample soln. Replace all flasks in 40° bath 30–40 min and let pptd protein fully coagulate. Filter thru Whatman No. 42, or equiv., paper, refiltering ca first half of filtrate thru same filter (filtrates must be completely clear).

Read A of filtrates at 280 nm against respective blanks. Plot readings for S_1, S_2, and S_3 against enzyme concn of each corresponding level in terms of mg/mL of 50 mL total test mixt. By interpolation from this curve, taking into consideration diln factors, calc. potency of sample in USP Units of Papain Activity/mg = $C \times (100/W) \times (100/4) \times (50/7.5) \times U$, where C = mg/mL obtained from std curve, W = mg sample, and U = activity of ref. std in units/mg.

20.141 ***Definition of Unit***

One unit of papain activity represents activity which releases equiv. of 1 μg tyrosine from specified casein substrate, under conditions of assay and at enzyme concn which liberates 40 μg tyrosine/mL test soln. USP Papain contains ≥6000 papain units/mg.

MISCELLANEOUS

Acetone Peroxides (*40*)—Official Final Action

20.142 ***In Baking Premixes***

Accurately weigh ca 8 g sample into flat-bottom centrf. bottle, pipet in 100 mL H_2O, and stir 10 min after making sure no lumps remain. Centrf. at ca 1500 rpm ca 10 min. Pipet 25 mL supernate into erlenmeyer, add 25 mL H_2SO_4 (1+4), and let stand ≥3 min, swirling occasionally. Ttitr. to light pink that lasts >20 sec with std 0.1*N* $KMnO_4$ soln, **50.025–50.026**.

Total peroxides in g H_2O_2 equiv./100 g premix
= mL $KMnO_4$ × normality × 0.0170 × 100/0.25 × g sample.

20.143 **In Milling Premixes**

Accurately weigh ca 200 mg sample into erlenmeyer, add 50 mL H_2SO_4 (1+9), let stand >3 min, stirring occasionally, and titr. with std 0.1*N* $KMnO_4$, **50.025–50.026**, to light pink that persists >20 sec.

Total peroxides in g H_2O_2 equiv./100 g premix = mL $KMnO_4$ × normality × 0.0170 × 100/g sample.

Qualitative Test

(Acetone peroxides are extremely explosive. Do not ext more org. peroxides from adsorbents than necessary for test. *Caution: See* **51.070(b)**.)

20.144 ***Apparatus***

(**a**) *Recording infrared spectrophotometer.*—Suitable for work from 2 to 16 μm.

(**b**) *Rock salt plate.*—Or other support stable to acetone and acetone peroxides and transparent in 2–16 μm region.

20.145 ***Test***

Weigh sample contg ca 10 mg H_2O_2 equiv. of acetone peroxides into g-s flask. Add ca 1 g anhyd. Na_2SO_4 and 10 mL acetone for every g adsorbate. Shake 3 min, filter (Whatman No. 12 paper has been found satisfactory) or centrf. (for baking premix), and carefully evap. clear soln to ca 1 mL under vac. at room temp.

Under warm light and gentle current of dry warm air, add concd acetone ext dropwise to rock salt plate. When film of viscous liq. is visible on plate, place it in IR light path and, without recording, check T of peak at ca 12.1 μm. If necessary, add addnl portions of ext to give 20–25% T. Set spectrophtr at acetone peak at ca 9.2 μm. Let radiation pass thru sample on plate until raised pen reaches max. T (acetone has evapd). Then record spectrum of film on salt plate from 2 to 16 μm.

Compare curve to one obtained from ref. acetone peroxides treated in same manner.

Brominated Vegetable Oils

Gas Chromatographic Method (41)—Official Final Action

(*Caution: See* **51.011**, **51.018**, **51.034**, **51.039**, **51.040**, **51.045**, **51.054**, and **51.066**.)

20.146 ***Principle***

Extd brominated oil is methylated and detd by GLC, using internal std.

20.147 ***Apparatus and Reagents***

(**a**) *Gas chromatograph.*—Varian Model 1740-10, or equiv., with flame ionization detector, strip chart recorder fitted with disk integrator, 0.9 m (3′) × ⅛″ od stainless steel column packed with 3% JXR or SE-30 (Supelco, Inc.) on 80–90 mesh Anakrom ABS. Operating conditions: temps (°)—injector 260, detector 270, column programmed from 150 to 270 at 10°/min; He carrier gas 40 mL/min.

(**b**) *Solvents.*—Ether, distil before use; anhyd. benzene, distil from Na wire; anhyd. MeOH, prep. as follows: Place 5 g clean, dry Mg turnings and 0.5 g resublimed I in 2 L r-b Pyrex flask fitted with double surface reflux condenser. Add 50–75 mL com. anhyd. MeOH thru condenser and warm mixt. on 100° H_2O bath until I disappears. As H is vigorously evolved, remove flask from H_2O bath. If vigorous evolution of H does not take place, add 0.5 g more I and heat mixt. until all Mg is converted to methoxide. Add 900 mL MeOH and boil 30 min under reflux. Distil mixt., with exclusion of moisture, discarding first 25 mL distillate.

(c) *Sodium in anhydrous methanol.*—Clean ca 1 g Na metal in hexane, dry with filter paper, and dissolve in 100 mL anhyd. MeOH in 250 mL conical flask fitted with silica gel drying tube.

(d) *Methyl 9,10-dibromostearate (DBS) std soln.*—2.0 mg/mL. Prep. DBS by dissolving 500 mg Me oleate (Applied Science Laboratories, Inc.) in 15 mL distd ether in 100 mL erlenmeyer held at 0°. Stir mag. and add 0.15 mL Br dropwise over 20 min. Stir addnl 10 min at 0°. Transfer soln with addnl 30 mL ether to 250 mL separator contg 50 mL 10% aq. $Na_2S_2O_5$, shake, let layers sep., and discard aq. layer. Wash ether layer successively with two 10 mL portions 2% aq. $Na_2S_2O_3$ and two 10 mL portions H_2O. Dry ether layer over anhyd. Na_2SO_4 and evap. on rotary evaporator at 40°.

Dissolve 200 mg DBS in anhyd. benzene in 100 mL vol. flask and dil. to vol. with anhyd. benzene.

(e) *Methyl 9,10,12,13-tetrabromostearate (TBS) std soln.*—2.0 mg/mL. Prep. TBS as in (d), except use Me linoleate (Applied Science Laboratories, Inc.) and 0.30 mL Br. Prep. std soln as in (d).

(f) *Brominated vegetable oil (BVO) std soln.*—1.0 mg/mL. Dissolve 50 mg BVO (Dominion Products, Inc., 882 3rd Ave, Brooklyn, NY 11232) in acetone in 50 mL vol. flask and dil. to vol. with acetone.

(g) *Methyl pentadecanoate (MPD) internal std soln.*—1.0 mg/mL. Dissolve 100 mg MPD (Applied Science Laboratories, Inc.) in anhyd. benzene in 100 mL vol. flask and dil. to vol. with anhyd. benzene.

20.148 *Preparation of Standards*

(a) *Methyl 9,10-dibromostearate and methyl 9,10,12,13-tetrabromostearate std solns.*—Pipet 3, 5, and 10 mL (6, 10, and 20 mg) DBS std solns into 3 sep. dry conical flasks and add 3, 5, and 10 mL (3, 5, and 10 mg) MPD std soln to each. Similarly prep. TBS-MPD solns. Treat each soln as follows: Evap. solv. with N at 40°. Add 25 mL 1% Na in MeOH and 12 mL anhyd. benzene, and reflux 1 hr. Cool, and transfer to 125 mL separator contg 50 mL H_2O. Acidify with 2*N* H_2SO_4 and ext with three 30 mL portions ether, using first 30 mL to rinse flask. Combine ether exts in second separator, wash with two 10 mL portions H_2O, dry over anhyd. Na_2SO_4, filter, and evap. solv. on rotary evaporator at 40°. Dissolve residue in 3 mL ether.

(b) *Brominated vegetable oil.*—Pipet 5 and 10 mL BVO std soln (5 and 10 mg) into sep. dry conical flasks, add 1 and 2 mL MPD std soln (1 and 2 mg), resp., and evap. solv. with N at 40°. Proceed as in (a), beginning "Add 25 mL 1% Na in MeOH . . ."

20.149 *Preparation of Sample*

Decarbonate and mix by transferring several times from 1 beaker to another. Transfer 280 mL sample to 500 mL separator, sat. thoroly with NaCl, and add 1 mL MPD std soln (1 mg). Ext with three 100 mL portions ether. Combine exts in second separator and wash successively with 50 mL 2*N* NaOH, 50 mL 2*N* HCl, and two 25 mL portions H_2O. Dry ether layer over anhyd. Na_2SO_4, filter, and evap. on rotary evaporator at 40°. Quant. transfer residue with ether to clean, dry conical flask, and evap. ether with N at 40°. Proceed as in **20.148(a)**, beginning "Add 25 mL 1% Na in MeOH . . ."

20.150 *Determination*

Inject duplicate portions methylated DBS, TBS, BVO std, and sample solns. Det. peak area (*PA*) with disk integrator. Correct apparent areas of both TBS and DBS for area of common peak *a* (Fig. **20:06**) as follows: Assume PA_a in TBS chromatograms is

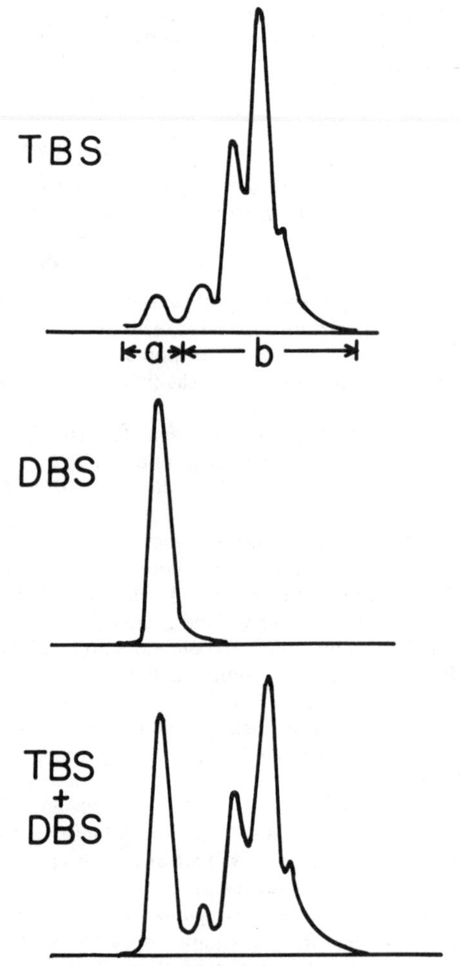

FIG. 20:06—Gas chromatograms of TBS, DBS, and TBS + DBS

5% of PA_b and apparent PA_{DBS} and PA_{TBS} are 100 and 200 units, resp.

True DBS PA = 100 − 1/20 (200) = 90 units

True TBS PA = 200 + 1/20 (200) = 210 units

Det. av. response factors (*RF*) for each soln.

$$RF_{DBS\ or\ TBS} = (\text{mg DBS or TBS} \times PA_{MPD})/(\text{mg MPD} \times \text{true } PA_{DBS\ or\ TBS})$$

(a) *Brominated vegetable oil (no sample) calculated from total peak areas.*—(Use for checking response factors, recoveries, and *B*, required for (b).)

$$\text{mg BVO} = ([PA_{16} + PA_{18} + (\text{true } PA \times RF)_{DBS} + (\text{true } PA \times RF)_{TBS}] \times \text{mg MPD})/PA_{MPD},$$

where PA_{16} and PA_{18} = areas of C_{16} and C_{18} Me esters, resp.

(b) *Brominated vegetable oil in sample calculated from brominated derivatives only.*—

$$\text{mg BVO} = [(\text{true } PA \times RF)_{DBS} + (\text{true } PA \times RF)_{TBS} \times \text{mg MPD}]/(PA_{MPD} \times B),$$

where B = % (DBS + TBS) in BVO found by direct analysis (a).

Sorbitol (*42*)—Official Final Action

(Apple and apple by-products contain naturally occurring sorbitol.) (*Caution: See* **51.011**, **51.022**, and **51.066**.)

20.151 *Principle*

Sorbitol is extd with MeOH, and acetate derivative is formed in presence of pyridine, extd with $CHCl_3$, and detd by GLC.

20.152 ***Apparatus***

(**a**) *Soxhlet extractor.*—Medium size (Corning No. 3740, Kimble No. 24071, or equiv.), with 33 × 80 mm extn thimble.

(**b**) *Gas chromatograph.*—Equipped with flame ionization detector, 1 mv strip chart recorder, and 1.8 m (6′) × 4 mm id U-shaped glass column packed with 10% DC-200 on 100–120 mesh Gas-Chrom Q (Applied Science Laboratories, Inc.). Operating conditions: temps (°)—column 200 (or such that retention time of sorbitol acetate is 9–10 min), injector 230, detector 210; flow rates (mL/min)—N carrier gas 120, air 350–400, H optimal; sensitivity 0.4 × 10^{-9} amp for full scale deflection; or equiv. conditions so that acetate equiv. to 2.5 μg sorbitol will give ½ scale deflection.

20.153 ***Reagents***

(**a**) *Diatomaceous earth.*—Celite 545, acid-washed.

(**b**) *Sorbitol.*—Reagent grade, or equiv. (Fisher Scientific Co. S-459).

20.154 ***Extraction***

Place moist products in 60° forced-draft oven until dry (overnight drying is convenient). Chop dry sample in Hobart mixer. Weigh sample contg ca 400 mg sorbitol (usually ca 10 g), mix with 5 g Celite, and place in extn thimble. Place piece of glass wool on top of sample. Add 125 mL anhyd. MeOH to extn flask, and ext 2 hr at rapid boil. Quant. transfer MeOH ext to 200 mL vol. flask with MeOH and dil. to vol. with MeOH.

20.155 ***Preparation of Standard Curve***

Accurately weigh ca 20, 40, 60, and 80 mg sorbitol into sep. 125 mL ₸ 24/40 erlenmeyer. Add 3 mL pyridine and 10 mL Ac_2O. Fit flask with air condenser and reflux 1 hr on steam bath. Add 60–80 mL H_2O, mix, and cool. Ext with four 20 mL and one 15 mL portion $CHCl_3$. Dil to 100 mL with $CHCl_3$ in vol. flask. Inject ca 5 μL into gas chromatograph.

Prep. std curve by plotting response (sq mm/μL injected) against mg sorbitol initially weighed.

20.156 ***Determination***

Pipet 25 mL MeOH ext into 125 mL ₸ 24/40 erlenmeyer. Evap. ext to dryness on steam bath with current of air. Proceed as in **20.155**, beginning "Add 3 mL pyridine . . .", dissolving residue as completely as possible. Calc. % sorbitol as follows:

% Sorbitol = (mg from std curve × 0.8)/g sample

NONNUTRITIVE SWEETENERS

Identification (*43*)—Official First Action

(Applicable to nonalcoholic beverages)

20.157 ***Apparatus***

(**a**) *Thin layer apparatus.—See* **19.041**.

(**b**) *Ultraviolet light.*—Capable of providing shortwave (254 nm) radiation (Spectronics Corp., 956 Brush Hollow Rd, Westbury, NY 11590, or equiv.).

20.158 ***Reagents***

Prep. solns fresh on day of use.

(**a**) *Developing solv.*—*n*-BuOH-alcohol-NH_4OH-H_2O (40+4+1+9, by vol.).

(**b**) *Chromogenic agents.*—(*1*) Br in CCl_4, 5% by vol. (*Caution: See* **51.047** and **51.049**); (*2*) 0.25% fluorescein in dimethylformamide-alcohol (1+1); and (*3*) 2% *N*-1-naphthylethylenediamine.2HCl in alcohol.

(**c**) *Std mixture.*—50 mg Ca cyclamate, 10 mg Na saccharin, 4 mg dulcin, and 4 mg 5-nitro-2-propoxyaniline (P-4000) in 10 mL dil. alcohol (1+1). (5 μL = 25μg cyclamate, 5 μg saccharin, 2 μg dulcin, and 2 μg P-4000.) Warm soln to dissolve dulcin, if necessary. Avoid contact with P-4000.

(**d**) *Silica gel.*—Adsorbosil-1 (Applied Science Laboratories, Inc.) or silica gel H (E. Merck, distributed by Brinkmann Instruments, Inc.).

20.159 ***Preparation of Sample***

(*Caution: See* **51.011**, **51.040**, and **51.057**.)

Decarbonate beverage by repeated shaking and pouring. To 50 mL sample in 125 mL separator, cautiously add 10 mL H_2SO_4 (1+1). Cool, ext with two 50 mL portions pet ether (shake *gently* but thoroly), and discard pet ether. To aq. layer, cautiously add 5 mL 50% NaOH soln (w/w), cool, and ext with two 50 mL portions EtOAc. (Use 60 mL for cola samples to prevent emulsions.) Filter EtOAc exts thru EtOAc-washed cotton into beaker or flask with pouring lip. Evap. to 5–10 mL on steam bath, using air current, and transfer to graduated tube. (Do *not* let soln evap. to dryness before transfer. Compds may be difficult to redissolve.) Evap. soln in graduated tube to dryness on steam bath with air current. Dil. to 2.5 mL with NH_4OH-H_2O-alcohol (5+5+10) and mix thoroly. (Insol. residue in tube will not interfere with detn.)

20.160 ***Preparation of Plates and Tank***

Slurry 35 g Adsorbosil-1 with 50 mL H_2O or 30 g silica gel H with 75–80 mL H_2O, and apply as 0.25 mm layer to five 8× 8″ (20 × 20 cm) plates. Dry plates >1 hr at room temp. Do *not* dry in oven. Do *not* store in desiccator cabinet. Score layer 5 mm from each side edge and remove 5 mm band of adsorbent from bottom edge of layer. Use plates within 36 hr after prepn.

Line developing tank with absorbent paper. Pour 25 mL developing solv. into tank, wetting paper. Place V-shaped trough in tank and add 25 mL developing solv. to trough. (Alternatively, put developing solv. in tank to ca 1 cm.) Place lid on tank, seal, and let stand ca ½ hr to sat. tank atm.

20.161 ***Determination***

(*Caution: See* **51.016** and **51.017**.)

Mark TLC plate at side edges only, 2.5 cm from bottom to designate spotting line. Mark dotted line 10 cm above spotting line. Spot total of 5 μL each of std mixt. and sample (*Level 1*). Dil. sample to 5 mL with NH_4OH-H_2O-alcohol (5+5+10) and spot 5 μL (*Level 2*). Place spots ⩾2 cm apart and 2 cm from edges. Spot 1 μL at a time and use warm-air blower to dry spot between applications to confine spot diam. Use same technic to spot sample and std. (Total vol. spotted should be ⩽5 μL. Use mixed std rather than superimposed single stds.)

Place plate in tank and develop to 10 cm line (ca 1 hr). Dry plate in hood until layer is no longer translucent (ca 10 min). View under shortwave (254 nm) UV. Outline fluorescent saccharin spot at R_f ca 0.5. (Spot may be crescent-shaped if large amt of cyclamate is present.) In hood, spray chromogenic agents (*1*) and (*2*), lightly to moderately, in immediate succession, on plate until cyclamate std appears as pink spot at R_f ca 0.3–0.4. P-4000 is brown-pink spot at R_f ca 0.85. Spray chromogenic agent (*3*) on plate until background pink fades to light yellow; contrast of cyclamate and P-4000 improves and at R_f ca 0.7 dulcin appears. Dulcin spot may be brownish-pink or blue, depending on condition of spray reagents and concn of sweetener. Plate may be resprayed with chromogenic agent (*3*) to restore contrast if pink background reappears.

CYCLOHEXYLSULFAMATE (CYCLAMATE) SALTS

Qualitative Test—Official First Action

(SO_2 will interfere with test. Verify absence by **20.105**.)

20.162 ***Sodium Nitrite Test***

Add 2 g $BaCl_2$ to 100 mL sample or aq. ext, prepd as in **20.093(c)**. Let stand 5 min and filter. Acidify with 10 mL HCl and add 0.2 g $NaNO_2$. White ppt of $BaSO_4$ indicates presence of cyclohexylsulfamate.

20.163 Quantitative Method (*44*)—Official Final Action

(Applicable to aq. solns and clear carbonated beverages; if caramel is present, confirm cyclamates by **20.157–20.161**. SO_2 will interfere; verify absence by **20.105**.)

To 100 mL soln contg 10–300 mg Na or Ca cyclohexylsulfamate add 10 mL HCl and 10 mL *10% $BaCl_2$ soln*. Stir and let stand 30 min. If ppt forms, filter and wash with H_2O. To filtrate or clear soln, add 10 mL *10% $NaNO_2$ soln*, stir, cover with watch glass, and heat on steam bath ≥2 hr. Stir up ppt 3 times at 0.5 hr intervals. Remove from steam bath and leave in warm place overnight. Collect ppt on tared gooch, wash, and dry on asbestos mat over flame ≥10 min. Ignite, cool in desiccator, and weigh.

Wt $BaSO_4$ × 0.8621 = Na cyclohexylsulfamate;
Wt $BaSO_4$ × 0.9266 = Ca cyclohexylsulfamate.$2H_2O$.

Cyclohexylamine (CHA) in Cyclamates and Artificially Sweetened Products (*46*)
Official First Action

(*Caution:* Use effective fume removal device when evapg or distg CH_2Cl_2.)

20.168 ***Apparatus***

(Glassware Cat. numbers refer to Kontes Glass Co., unless otherwise noted.)

(**a**) *Evaporative concentrator*.—Kuderna-Danish, 250 mL, with ₮ 24/40 column connection and ₮ 19/22 lower joint (K-570000).
(**b**) *Concentrator tube*.—Size 425, ₮ 19/22 joint, 4 mL; from 0 to 2 mL subdivided in 0.1 mL (K-570050), with ₮ 19/22 pennyhead stopper (K-850500).
(**c**) *Distilling column*.—Snyder, size 121, column length 150 mm with ₮ 24/40 joint (K-503000).
(**d**) *Funnel*.—Buchner, 60 mL, coarse porosity disk (K-955000).
(**e**) *Separator*.—250 mL, with Teflon stopcocks (K-636030).
(**f**) *Microliter syringes*.—10 and 100 μL (Hamilton Co., or equiv.).
(**g**) *Distillation apparatus*.—(*1*) 1 and 2 L r-b boiling flasks with ₮ 24/40 joint (K-601000); (*2*) connecting adapter with ₮ 24/40 and 10/30 joints (K-167000); (*3*) Liebig condenser, 200 mm jacket length with ₮ 24/40 joints (K-447000); (*4*) adapter, bent 105° with ₮ 24/40 joint (K-157000); (*5*) thermometer with ₮ 10/30 joint, range −10 to 110°, 3″ immersion (K-871000).
(**h**) *Heating mantles*.—Hemispherical, for 1 and 2 L r-b flasks. (Use with variable transformer heat control.)
(**i**) *Gas chromatographs*.—For convenience, 2 instruments may be used, one for actual detns and second for trapping: (*1*) Perkin-Elmer Corp., Model 881 (current equiv. model is 3920B), with dual flame ionization detectors, or equiv., with following column and conditions: 12′ (3.7 m) × ⅛″ stainless steel column packed with 10% Carbowax 20M (solid polyethylene glycols) plus 2.5% NaOH on 90–100 mesh Anakrom SD support. Condition columns 16 hr at 200° while maintaining carrier gas (N) flow of 40 mL/min. Maintain following parameters thruout analyses: temps (°)—column 100, injector 180, detector 175; carrier gas flow 72 mL/min, H flow 35 mL/min, air flow 550 mL/min and attenuation range 5–50× at 1 × 10^{-11} amp into 1 mv full scale recorder. (*2*) Hewlett-Packard Model 5750B research chromatograph (or 5800 series), with dual flame ionization detectors and effluent splitters (Hewlett-Packard, Rt 41, Avondale, PA 19311, or equiv.), and with same column and conditions used with Perkin-Elmer Model 881 above, with following exceptions: Carrier gas flow 75 mL/min thru column and 62 mL/min thru splitter, and attenuation range 640× at 2 × 10^{-14} amp into 1 mv full scale recorder.
(**j**) *Infrared spectrophotometer and accessories*.—Perkin-Elmer Corp., Model 621 with 6× beam condenser and micro KBr attachment, or equiv.
(**k**) *Septum*.—Silicone rubber, diam. 19 mm (K-774150).
(**l**) *Aluminum foil*.—Ordinary household foil.
(**m**) *Microsampling die and accessories*.—KBr Ultra Micro Die, Perkin-Elmer Corp., or equiv. *See* Fig. **20:07**. (*1*) *Metal funnel*.—Perkin-Elmer Corp., No. 186–1044, consisting of metal disk ca 2 cm diam. × 5 mm thick, with hole 1.5 mm diam. bored thru center of disk. Upper part of hole is flared out to width of 5–7 mm to form funnel. (*2*) *Plunger*.—Perkin-Elmer Corp., No. 186–1041, consisting of metal rod, one end of which has been turned down to 1.5 mm diam. to fit into funnel. (*3*) *Two polished stainless steel blocks*.—Approx. 5 cm diam. and 20–25 mm thick. (*4*) *Micro syringe*.—With end of needle cut off flat. (*5*) *Punch*.—Made from syringe needle 2 mm od with end cut off flat. (*6*) *Press*.—Capable of delivering 25,000 psi.

20.169 ***Reagents***

(**a**) *Methylene chloride*.—Certified reagent (D-37, Fisher Scientific Co.), or equiv. Redistil and check purity before use as follows:

Purify by distg in all-glass app. with air-cooled reflux condenser (ca 30 cm long) between distg flask and H_2O-cooled condenser. Provide collection flask with drying tube to protect distd solv. from moisture. Distil solv. in 2 L lots, discard first 200 mL distillate, and collect next 1.5 L for use.

Purity test.—Place 80 mL (vol. used in actual extn) into 250 mL Kuderna-Danish concentrator fitted with 4 mL concentrator tube and conc. to 0.5 mL as in **20.170(a)**. Inject 1 μL into gas chromatograph. Solv. must be free of interfering peaks.

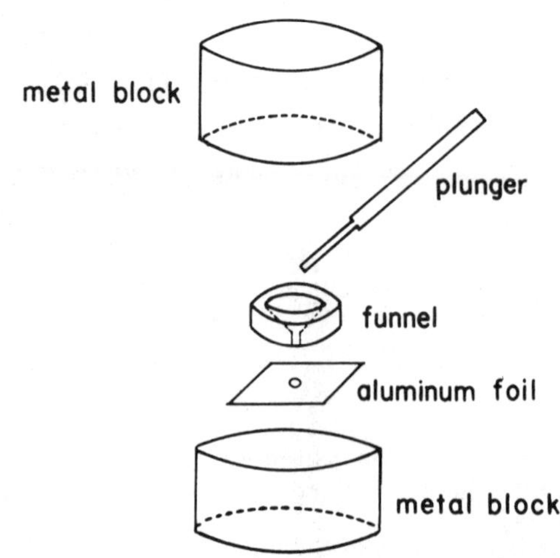

FIG. 20:07—Microsampling die

In addn to purity test, test solv. before use by concg 80 mL CH_2Cl_2 contg 120 μg CHA to 1.0 mL in Kuderna-Danish concentrator. If recovery of CHA is <90%, purify solv. by following alkali treatment and retest as above, after passage thru 30 g anhyd. Na_2SO_4 prewetted with 25 mL alkali-treated solv. prepd as follows: Dissolve 40 g NaOH in 200 mL H_2O in 500 mL erlenmeyer and cool under tap water. Transfer soln to 500 mL separator and add 105 mL CH_2Cl_2 (80 mL for extn and 25 mL for Na_2SO_4 wash). Shake 3 min, let layers sep., and drain CH_2Cl_2 (lower layer) for use.

(b) *Carbon disulfide.*—Spectral grade (MC/B Manufacturing Chemists CX393, or equiv.).

(c) *Hydrochloric acid.*—6*N* (approx.). Transfer 50 mL HCl to 100 mL vol. flask and dil. to vol. with H_2O.

(d) *Sodium hydroxide.*—10*N* (approx.). Add 60 mL H_2O to 40 g NaOH.

(e) *Cyclohexylamine (CHA).*—99.6%, bp 132–134° (Eastman Kodak Co., or equiv.). Prep. std solns as follows: (*1*) *For cyclohexylamine analysis of dietetic beverage and food products.*—Weigh 60 mg CHA into 50 mL vol. flask and dil. to vol. with redistd CH_2Cl_2 (1.2 mg/mL). Transfer 20 mL of this soln to 200 mL vol. flask and dil. to vol. with redistd CH_2Cl_2 (120 μg/mL). Also, prep. 1.0 and 1.2 mg/mL CHA stds in H_2O. Transfer 8 and 10 mL of these solns, resp., to 200 mL vol. flasks and dil. to vol. with H_2O (40 and 60 μg/mL, resp.). (*2*) *For cyclohexylamine analysis of artificial sweetener concentrates (liquid and dry) and cyclamates.*—Weigh 50 mg CHA into 50 mL vol. flask and dil. to vol. with redistd CH_2Cl_2. Transfer 10 and 20 mL aliquots to 200 mL vol. flasks and dil. to vol. with redistd CH_2Cl_2 (50 and 100 μg/mL, resp.). Also, prep. CHA std contg 1.0 mg/mL in H_2O. Transfer 5 and 10 mL of this soln to 200 mL vol. flasks and dil. to vol. with H_2O (25 and 50 μg/mL, resp.).

(f) *pH test papers.*—Ranges 9–14 (No. 708) and 0–11 (No. DJ905, Micro Essential Laboratory, Inc., 4224 Ave H, Brooklyn, NY 11210).

(g) *Disodium dihydrogen ethylenedinitrilotetraacetate* (*Na_2H_2EDTA*).—ACS.

20.170 *Isolation by Distillation*

(Applicable to following artificially sweetened products: carbonated beverages and fruit juice drinks, dry beverage bases, canned fruits, and liq. and dry wt control formulations)

(a) *Carbonated beverages and fruit juice drinks.*—Transfer 300 mL aliquot of well mixed sample to 1 L boiling flask. Add boiling chips and enough 10*N* NaOH to obtain pH 14 as detd with test paper. Connect distn app. to boiling flask. Set up as receiver 250 mL beaker contg 2 mL 6*N* HCl and 2 boiling chips, and place under 105° adapter so that adapter tip is 5 cm above acid. Collect ca 35 mL distillate (ca 20 min). Mix by swirling and set beaker on hot plate; evap. to ca 3–5 mL at temp. just below bp.

Remove beaker from hot plate and cool under tap H_2O. Quant. transfer sample to 250 mL separator with four 25 mL portions H_2O. Add enough NaOH to obtain pH 14 as detd with test paper. Add 20 mL CH_2Cl_2 and shake 2 min. Let layers sep. Filter CH_2Cl_2 layer thru 30 g anhyd. granular Na_2SO_4 (prewetted with 25 mL CH_2Cl_2) into Kuderna-Danish evaporator with 4 mL concentrator attached. Immediately pass 20 mL CH_2Cl_2 wash thru the Na_2SO_4. Repeat extn with two 10 mL portions CH_2Cl_2. Follow passage of each ext thru Na_2SO_4 immediately with 10 mL portions CH_2Cl_2. Place SiC grains in concentrator tube, insert distg column into fitting of Kuderna-Danish concentrator, and carefully conc. solv. to ca 4 mL in steam bath. Remove app. from bath, let cool, and drain any remaining solv. in distg column and concentrator into concentrator tube. Conc. solv. in tube to 1.0 mL under stream of ultra high purity N and reserve for injection into gas chromatograph.

(b) *Dry beverage bases.*—Dissolve content of each package according to directions. Transfer 300 mL well mixed sample to 1 L boiling flask and proceed as in (**a**).

(c) *Canned fruits.*—Place sample (fruit and sirup) in high-speed blender and blend ca 5 min. Transfer 300 g sample to 1 L boiling flask. Add 200 mL H_2O and enough 10*N* NaOH to obtain pH 14 as detd with test paper. Then add 10 drops Dow Corning *Antifoam Emulsion H-10* and distil as in (**a**), but collect 100 mL distillate in 400 mL beaker contg 2 mL 6*N* HCl and 2 boiling chips. Evap. acid soln to 3–5 mL, ext with CH_2Cl_2, and conc. combined exts as in (**a**).

(d) *Liquid weight control formulations.*—Transfer 200 g well mixed sample to 2 L boiling flask with 400 mL H_2O. Add enough 10*N* NaOH to obtain pH 14 as detd with test paper. Then add 7–8 drops *Antifoam Emulsion H-10* and mix. Distil as in (**a**). Collect 100 mL distillate in 400 mL beaker contg 2 mL 6*N* HCl and 2 boiling chips. Evap. on hot plate to 3–5 mL at temp. just below bp and, after cooling, quant. transfer to 250 mL separator with 100 mL H_2O. Adjust pH of soln to ca 1.0 with 6*N* HCl (test paper). Add 20 mL CH_2Cl_2 and shake 2 min. Let layers sep. and discard CH_2Cl_2 layer. Repeat extn with two 10 mL portions CH_2Cl_2. After discarding final CH_2Cl_2 wash, adjust pH to 14 with 10*N* NaOH as detd with test paper. Ext with CH_2Cl_2 and conc. combined exts as in (**a**).

(e) *Dry weight control formulations.*—Transfer content of packet (ca 20 g) to 1 L boiling flask. Add 300 mL H_2O and dissolve by swirling. Then add boiling chips, adjust pH to 14 with 10*N* NaOH as detd with test paper, and add 7–8 drops *Antifoam Emulsion H-10*. Proceed as in (**d**).

20.171 *Isolation by Extraction*

(Applicable to cyclamate salts and food sweetener prepns (dry bases and liq. concs))

(a) *Sodium cyclamate.*—Weigh 25 g well mixed sample in 100 mL beaker. Using powder funnel, transfer to 250 mL separator. Wash beaker with two 25 mL portions hot H_2O (ca 90°) and transfer each portion to separator. Add 50 mL more hot H_2O and shake to dissolve cyclamate completely. Cool under tap H_2O to ca 30°. Add enough 10*N* NaOH to obtain pH 14 as detd with test paper. Ext with CH_2Cl_2 and conc. combined exts as in **20.170(a)**.

(b) *Food sweetener preparations (liquid concentrates containing sodium cyclamate).*—Weigh 25 g well mixed sample in 100 mL beaker and transfer to 250 mL separator. Wash beaker with four 25 mL portions H_2O and transfer each portion to separator. Shake to dissolve cyclamate completely. Add enough 10*N* NaOH to obtain pH 14 as detd with test paper. Ext with CH_2Cl_2 and conc. combined exts as in **20.170(a)**.

(c) *Calcium cyclamate.*—Weigh 25 g well mixed sample in 100 mL beaker. Using powder funnel, transfer to 250 mL separator. Wash beaker with three 25 mL portions hot H_2O (ca 90°) and transfer each portion to separator. Shake to dissolve cyclamate completely. Dissolve 25 g Na_2H_2EDTA in 65 mL H_2O and 10 mL 10*N* NaOH on steam bath. Pour this soln into separator and mix. Add enough 10*N* NaOH to obtain pH 14 as detd by test paper. Cool under tap H_2O to ca 30°. Ext with CH_2Cl_2 and conc. combined exts as in **20.170(a)**.

(d) *Food sweetener preparations (liquid concentrates and dry bases containing calcium cyclamate).*—Weigh 25 g well mixed sample in 100 mL beaker and transfer to 250 mL separator. Wash beaker with four 25 mL portions H_2O and transfer each portion to separator. For dry bases, use 25 mL portions hot H_2O (ca 90°) for transfer and shake funnel to dissolve dry base completely. Dissolve 2.5 g Na_2H_2EDTA in 20 mL H_2O on steam bath, pour soln into separator, and mix. Add enough 10*N* NaOH to obtain pH 14 as detd by test paper. (For dry bases, cool separator under tap H_2O to ca 30°.) Ext with CH_2Cl_2 and conc. combined exts as in **20.170(a)**.

20.172 ***Gas Chromatography and Confirmation by Infrared Spectrophotometry***

Inject 1 μL CH_2Cl_2 soln of sample ext into column. Det. presence and amt of CHA by comparing with appropriate aliquots of std solns injected directly into gas chromatograph. To confirm identity, install effluent splitters (use 5:1, vent: detector) and special triple laminated septa, and assemble collection trap as shown in Fig. **20:08**. (*Note:* All glassware and associated equipment must be scrupulously clean.) Conc. CH_2Cl_2 ext, **20.170(a)**, under N stream without heat to 0.1 mL (100 μL) and det. total CHA content. When <50 μg is present, inject 80 μL into column. Collect peak effluent corresponding to retention time for CHA in 60 μL CS_2 (previously cooled in solid CO_2). Rinse connection tube with two 10 μL portions CS_2 into collection trap, stopper, and place in desiccator 10 min. Remove collection trap, add 3 mg anhyd. KBr, and remove excess CS_2 under vac. at 64 cm.

For samples contg $\geqslant 50$ μg CHA, inject 50 μL CH_2Cl_2 soln into column, collect appropriate effluent in 100 μL CS_2, and continue as above.

To prep. KBr disk (*see* Fig. **20:07**), fold Al foil to provide 16 thicknesses and punch 2 mm hole thru it with punch. Place folded foil on steel block and place funnel, centered on hole, on foil. Firmly pack small portion KBr from collection trap into foil by use of plunger and funnel. Rub walls of collection tube with 2 mg powd KBr to ensure complete removal of the dithiocarbamate. Transfer this KBr loosely on top of thin layer of KBr in hole, tamp lightly, and carefully lift off funnel. Place second steel block on top of Al foil, and apply pressure of 6.89×10^7 Pa (10,000 psi) for 30 sec. This produces transparent KBr disk suitable for IR spectroscopy.

Record IR spectrum and compare with ref. curve detd under identical conditions.

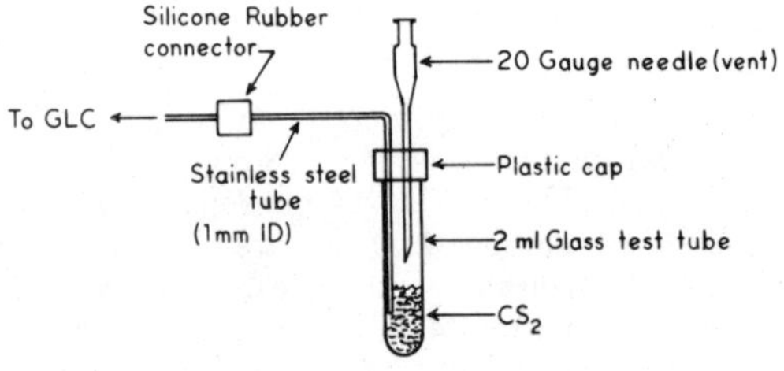

FIG. 20:08—GLC effluent collection trap for determination of cyclohexylamine

DULCIN

20.173 Preparation of Sample—Official First Action

(*Caution: See* **51.011** and **51.054**.)

Ext 100 mL sample (made alk. with 10% NaOH soln, if necessary), or alk. aq. ext, prepd as in **20.093(c)**, with two or three 50 mL portions ether. Divide ether ext equally between 2 porcelain dishes, let ether evap. at room temp., and dry residues in oven at 110°.

Qualitative Tests

20.174 ***Deniges-Tourrou Test (47)—Official First Action***

Moisten dry residue, **20.173**, with HNO_3 and add 1 drop H_2O. Presence of dulcin is indicated by formation of orange or brick-red ppt.

20.175 ***Modified LaParola-Mariani Test (48) Official Final Action***

Expose dry residue, **20.173**, to HCl gas for 5 min and add 1 drop *anisaldehyde*. Presence of dulcin is indicated by orange-red to blood-red color. Presence of 25 mg/L or kg original sample can usually be detected by this test.

20.176 Quantitative Method (*49*)—Official First Action

(Applicable to nonalcoholic beverages. *Caution: See* **51.011**, **51.039**, and **51.054**.)

Pipet 50 mL sample into separator. If 5-nitro-2-propoxyaniline (P-4000) is present, ext with four 50 mL portions pet ether, shaking 2 min each time, and discard pet ether. Make aq. phase alk. to litmus with 10% NaOH soln and ext with four 100 mL portions ether, shaking 2 min each time. Combine exts, wash with 10 mL H_2O, and discard H_2O. Evap. ether in 400 mL beaker and dry residue 30 min at 110°.

Dissolve residue in ca 50 mL EtOAc, transfer to 100 mL vol. flask, dil. to vol. with 4 or 5 washings of the EtOAc, and mix. Read *A* in spectrophtr at 294 nm against redistd EtOAc. Det. amt of dulcin in final soln from previously prepd std curve and calc. to mg/L.

5-NITRO-2-PROPOXYANILINE (P-4000)

Qualitative Tests

20.177 ***Organoleptic Test (50)—Official First Action***

(Caution: See **51.011**, **51.039**, and **51.073**.)

Make alk. (pH 7.5–8.0) with 10% NaOH 200 mL liq. food or aq. ext of 200 g solid food or semisolid product, **20.185(c)**, and ext with three 25 mL portions pet ether. Wash combined exts once with 5 mL H_2O, transfer pet ether to small beaker or empty dish, let evap. spontaneously, and taste residue. Presence of 5 mg P-4000/L or kg original material may be detected by intensely sweet taste; or 12.5 mg/L or kg original material may be detected by its strong anesthetic effect.

20.178 ***Diamine Test (51)—Official Final Action***

(*Caution: See* **51.011**, **51.039**, **51.047**, and **51.073**.)

Pipet 50 mL sample or aq. ext, **20.185(c)**, into separator, make alk. with 10% NaOH, and ext ca 1 min with 50 mL pet ether. Repeat extn with two 50 mL portions pet ether. Combine exts, wash with 10 mL H_2O, and discard H_2O. Transfer ext to small beaker and add 4 mL HCl (1+1). Evap. pet ether on steam bath. Add small piece mossy Sn and keep 5 min longer on steam bath. Decant soln into test tube; add, dropwise, *satd Br-H_2O*. Rose-red to deep burgundy-red soln is formed if P-4000 is present; this color is destroyed by excess Br.

Quantitative Method (*51*)—Official Final Action

(Applicable to nonalcoholic beverages)

20.179 ***Reagent***

1-Naphthol soln.—Dissolve 50 mg 1-naphthol in 500 mL 1% Na_2CO_3 soln. Prep. fresh daily and store in brown glass bottle.

20.180 ***Preparation of Standard Curve***

Dissolve 100 mg 5-nitro-2-propoxyaniline in ca 150 mL 60% alcohol. Transfer to 250 mL vol. flask, dil. to vol. with 60% alcohol, and mix. Transfer 1.00, 2.00, 3.00, and 4.00 mL aliquots to 250 mL vol. flasks, dil. to vol. with H_2O, and mix. Using 25 mL aliquots from each flask, proceed as in **20.181**, beginning "Ext with three 25 mL portions pet ether, . . ." Plot *A* against concn (0 to 0.16 mg/25 mL) final soln.

20.181 ***Determination***

(*Caution: See* **51.011**, **51.039**, and **51.073**.)

Pipet 20 mL sample into 250 mL vol. flask, dil. to vol. with H_2O, and mix. Transfer 25 mL aliquot to small separator, and add 10% NaOH soln, dropwise, until just alk. Ext with three 25 mL portions pet ether, shaking 1–2 min each time. Combine exts, wash with 5 mL H_2O, and discard wash H_2O. Transfer ext to small beaker, and add ca 10 mL H_2O and 0.5 mL 0.1*N* HCl. Evap. pet ether on steam bath. Remove when few mL pet ether remain; let remaining pet ether evap. spontaneously. Cool soln to ca 20°, add 1.0 mL 0.125% $NaNO_2$ soln, and stir. After 1 min, add 5.0 mL 1-naphthol soln, mix, and dil. to 25 mL. Det. *A* at 515 nm within 1 hr against blank carried thru detn.

(mg P-4000/25 mL, from std curve) × 500 = mg/L.

SACCHARIN

Qualitative Tests—Official Final Action

20.182 ***Organoleptic Test***

(*Caution: See* **51.011**, **51.039**, and **51.054**.)

Acidify with HCl 50 mL nonalc. liq. food or aq. ext of 50 g solid or semisolid product, **20.185(c)**, and ext with three 25 mL portions ether. Wash combined ether exts once with 5 mL H_2O, transfer to small beaker or evapg dish, let ether evap. spontaneously, and taste residue. (Presence of 20 mg saccharin/L or kg of original sample can usually be detected by its sweet taste.) Confirm by heating with NaOH and detecting salicylic acid formed thereby as in **20.183**.

20.183 ***By Conversion to Salicylic Acid***

(*Caution: See* **51.011**, **51.039**, and **51.054**.)

Acidify with HCl 50 mL nonalc. liq. food, or equiv. vol. aq. ext, **20.185**, and ext with 3 portions ether as in **20.182**. Dissolve residue remaining after evapn of ether in little hot H_2O and test small portion of soln for salicylic acid as in **20.094** or **20.095**.

Dil. remainder of soln to ca 10 mL and add 2 mL H_2SO_4 (1+3). Heat to boiling and add slight excess of *5% $KMnO_4$ soln* dropwise; partly cool soln, dissolve ca 1 g NaOH in it, and filter mixt. into Ag dish (Ag crucible lids are suitable). Evap. to dryness and heat 20 min at 210–215°. Dissolve residue in H_2O, acidify with HCl, and test ether ext for salicylic acid as in **20.094** or **20.095**. By this method all so-called "false saccharin" (J. Amer. Chem. Soc. **26**, 1627(1904)) and any salicylic acid naturally present (also added salicylic acid when not present in too large amt) are destroyed, whereas 5 mg saccharin/L is detected with certainty.

20.184 ***Phenol-Sulfuric Acid Test (52)***

(Applicable to nonalc. beverages, semisolid prepns, and baked goods. *Caution: See* **51.011**, **51.039**, **51.054**, and **51.073**.)

Prep. ether ext of sample as follows:

(**a**) *Nonalcoholic beverages*.—Add 3 mL HCl to 25 mL sample in separator. If vanillin is present, remove by extg with several portions pet ether. Discard pet ether. Ext with 50, 25, and 25 mL ether-pet ether (1+1). Wash combined ether exts once with 5 mL H_2O, remove major portion of solv., transfer to 30 mL beaker, and evap. at room temp.

(**b**) *Semisolid preparations*.—Transfer 25 g sample to 100 mL vol. flask with small amt hot H_2O and add enough boiling H_2O to make ca 75 mL. Let mixt. stand 1 hr, shaking occasionally. Then add 3 mL HOAc, mix thoroly, add slight excess (5 mL) of *20% neut. $Pb(OAc)_2$ soln*, dil. to vol. with cold H_2O, mix, let stand 20 min, and filter. Transfer ≥60 mL filtrate to separator and proceed as in (**a**).

(**c**) *Baked goods*.—Grind 25 g sample, mix thoroly with 50 g washed and ignited sea sand, and ext with pet ether in Soxhlet app. until essentially fat-free (1–2 hr). Transfer extd mass to 300 mL erlenmeyer, add 100 mL alcohol, and reflux on boiling H_2O bath 30 min, shaking frequently. Filter thru buchner contg 7 cm Whatman No. 2 paper wet with alcohol. Transfer alc. filtrate to 100 mL beaker, evap. to ½ vol., add 50 mL H_2O and enough 10% Na_2CO_3 soln to make alk., and evap. to 50 mL. Transfer aq. soln to separator and proceed as in (**a**).

To residue remaining after evapn of solv. add 5 mL *phenol-H_2SO_4 reagent* (pure colorless cryst. phenol dissolved in equal wt H_2SO_4) and heat 2 hr at 135–140°. Cool, dissolve in small amt of hot H_2O, and pour into ca 250 mL H_2O. Add small amt of Filter-Cel, let stand 3 hr or overnight, and filter. Make alk. with 10% NaOH soln and dil. to 500 mL. Magenta or reddish-purple color develops if saccharin is present. Yellow, buff, or pale salmon shade is not significant.

Quantitative Methods

General Method I (53)—Official Final Action

20.185 ***Preparation of Sample***

(**a**) *Fruit juices and sirups*.—Transfer 100–200 g sample to 250 mL vol. flask with little H_2O and dil. to ca 200 mL with H_2O. Add 5 mL HOAc and mix. Add slight excess of *20% neut. $Pb(OAc)_2$ soln*, mix thoroly, dil. to vol. with H_2O, again mix thoroly, and filter.

(**b**) *Alcoholic liquids*.—Heat 100–200 mL liq. on steam bath to remove alcohol (usually done by evapg to ½ original vol.). With heavy sirups, dil. liq. with equal vol. H_2O before beginning evapn. After removal of alcohol, transfer liq. to 250 mL vol. flask and proceed as in (**a**).

(**c**) *Solid or semisolid preparations*.—Transfer 50–75 g sample to 250 mL vol. flask with little hot H_2O and add enough boiling H_2O to make ca 200 mL. Let stand 2 hr, shaking occasionally. Add 5 mL HOAc, mix thoroly, add slight excess *20% neut. $Pb(OAc)_2$ soln*, dil. to vol. with cold H_2O, mix, let stand 20 min, and filter.

20.186 ***Determination***

(*Caution: See* **51.011**, **51.039**, and **51.054**.)

Transfer 150 mL filtrate, **20.185**, to separator, add 15 mL HCl, and ext with three 80 mL portions ether, shaking separator 2 min each time. Wash combined ether exts once with 5 mL H_2O, remove ether by distn, and transfer residue to Pt crucible with little ether; or, if substances difficultly sol. in ether are present, use alternately small portions of H_2O and ether. Evap. ether on steam bath, add to residue 2–3 mL 10% Na_2CO_3 soln (or enough to make mixt. strongly alk.), rotate so that all saccharin is brought in contact with soln, and evap. to dryness on steam bath.

To dry residue add 4 g mixt, of equal parts of anhyd. Na_2CO_3 and K_2CO_3. Heat gently at first and then to complete fusion 30 min. (Fusion may be conducted by closely fitting crucible into hole cut into piece of heavy asbestos board so that ⅓ of crucible projects above asbestos, and heating lower portion of crucible by large Bunsen, Meker, or similar burner.) Cool, dissolve melt in H_2O, add ca 5 mL Br-H_2O, acidify with HCl, filter, wash paper with little H_2O, dil. filtrate and washings to ca 200 mL, heat to bp, and slowly add excess of *10% $BaCl_2$ soln*. Let mixt. stand overnight, collect $BaSO_4$ on filter or on gooch, wash until Cl-free, dry, ignite, cool, and weigh. Correct results thus obtained for any S present in fusion mixt. as found by blank detn. Saccharin = corrected wt $BaSO_4 \times 0.7848$.

Instead of mixed Na and K carbonates, 3–4 g Na_2O_2 may be used for fusion. In this case Ni crucible must be used, and time of fusion may be reduced to 5 min. Sepn of little $PbCl_2$ during extns does not interfere with accuracy of method.

20.187 ***General Method II (By Sublimation) (54)***
Official First Action

(*Caution: See* **51.011**, **51.039**, **51.040**, **51.049**, and **51.054**.)

Acidify 200 mL sample with 15 mL HCl and ext with three 50 mL portions CCl_4. Discard CCl_4, and ext aq. layer with three 80 mL portions ether. Let ether ext evap. to small vol. and transfer to sublimator with small amt of ether or alcohol. Evap. to dryness at room temp. or on H_2O bath, depending on whether ether or alcohol was used to transfer residue. Sublime residue 1 hr at 1–2 mm pressure and 140–160°. (Raise temp. so slowly that ca ½ hr is required to reach 140°.) Wash saccharin from condenser bulb of sublimator with warm alcohol into weighed beaker, and repeat sublimation until no further residue appears on condensing bulb. Evap. alcohol on H_2O bath, heat residue 2 hr at 100°, cool, and reweigh beaker.

20.188 ***Special Method for Nonalcoholic Beverages (55)***
Official Final Action

(*Caution: See* **51.011**, **51.039**, and **51.054**.)

Add 2 mL HCl to 50 mL sample in separator. Ext with two 50 mL portions ether. Filter ether exts thru cotton, and wash combined filtrates with ca 5 mL H_2O contg 1 drop HCl.

Sep. ether layer and evap. to dryness on H_2O bath. Add 5 mL NH_3-free H_2O and 6 mL HCl to residue, and evap. soln to ca 1 mL on hot plate, stirring constantly. Again add 5 mL NH_3-free H_2O and 6 mL HCl, and evap. to ca 1 mL. Dil. to 50 mL with NH_3-free H_2O and dil. 2 mL of this soln to 25 mL with NH_3-free H_2O. Add 1 mL Nessler reagent, **33.053(j)**, and compare with NH_4Cl stds in usual manner; 0.2921 g NH_4Cl = 1 g saccharin, insol. form ($C_7H_5NO_3S$), and 1.317 g Na salt ($C_7H_4NNaO_3S.2H_2O$). For convenience prep. NH_4Cl std equiv. to 200 ppm insol. form of saccharin.

NUTRIENTS

Monosodium Glutamate (*56*)—Official First Action

20.189 ***Apparatus and Reagents***

(**a**) *Chromatographic column*.—500 × 22 mm od tube, 30 mL bed vol., with Dowex 50W-X8 (H^+ form), 100–200 mesh.

(**b**) *Activated carbon*.—Darco G-60.

20.190 ***Preparation of Sample***

For products in dry form, reduce ca 40 g to powder in mortar and weigh 10 g sample into 250 mL beaker. For undild, concd soups or canned green beans, homogenize entire undild content of can in blender and weigh 20 g sample into 250 mL beaker. For consommé-type (clear, condensed) soup, weigh 20 g into 250 mL beaker.

Dil. sample to ca 70 mL with H_2O at room temp., and mix until all H_2O-sol. substances are in soln (ca 15 min). Add 6 g C and mix thoroly. (For products contg starch, also add 60 mL acetone to ppt starch and to aid sample soln.) Let stand 30 min. Filter with vac. thru 60 mL coarse fritted glass funnel contg asbestos pad. Wash flask and residue with six 25 mL portions H_2O or, if acetone was added, with six 25 mL portions acetone-H_2O (1+1). Collect filtrate and washings in 400 mL beaker, add 2 drops HCl (1+2.5), and evap. on steam bath to ca 40 mL. (HCl prevents conversion of glutamic acid to pyrrolidone carboxylic acid.) Quant. transfer to 50 mL vol. flask, dil. to vol. with H_2O, and mix.

20.191 ***Determination***

Transfer 25 mL aliquot to prepd column and adjust flow to ca 0.5 mL/min. After all soln enters resin, wash column wall with ca 10 mL H_2O; let wash pass into resin. Add 120 mL 0.8*N* HCl and maintain flow rate (0.8*N* HCl will elute any serine, threonine, and aspartic acid). After all 0.8*N* HCl passes into resin, add 170 mL 1*N* HCl and adjust flow to between 25 and 30 drops/min to elute glutamic acid; collect eluate in 400 mL beaker. (Any glycine present will elute after 200 mL 1*N* HCl.) Nearly neutze eluate with 50% NaOH and adjust potentiometrically to pH 7 with 0.1*N* NaOH.

Neutze 25 mL 37% HCHO to pH 7 with 0.1*N* NaOH and add to prepd neut. sample. Mix 10 min on mag. stirrer and titr. potentiometrically to pH 8.9 with 0.1*N* NaOH.

Det. blank by titrg to pH 8.9 mixt. of 25 mL neutzd HCHO and 170 mL 1*N* HCl neutzd to pH 7.

$$\% \text{ Glutamic acid} = [(S - B) \times N \times 0.147 \times 100]/W,$$

where S = mL NaOH used to titr. sample, B = mL NaOH used to titr. blank, N = normality of NaOH, and W = g sample in aliquot.

$$\% \text{ MSG} = \% \text{ glutamic acid} \times 1.15$$

Before using resin column again, remove any remaining amino acids by passing 150 mL 4*N* HCl thru column. Wash column with H_2O until $AgNO_3$ soln gives neg. test for Cl.

SOLVENTS

Ethylene Dichloride and Trichloroethylene (*57*)
Official Final Action

(Applicable to spice oleoresins)

20.192 ***Apparatus***

(All glassware must be $CHCl_3$-free; rinse with alcohol if necessary. Rinse pipets with alcohol after each use.)

(**a**) *Column*.—Porapak Q (50–80 mesh), available from Waters Associates, Inc. Pack 1.8 m × 6 mm od Al tube plugged at one end with glass wool, using slight vac. and light tapping to settle polymer beads. Add plug of glass wool to open end of column. Condition column 2 hr at 230°, passing N thru at 20 mL/min.

(**b**) *Gas chromatograph*.—Micro-Tek GC2503R or MT 220 gas chromatograph (Tracor Inc., 6500 Tracor Ln, Austin, TX 78721; current Models 550 or 222) or equiv., equipped with column, (**a**), Dohrmann Model C-200, C-200-A, or C-200-B microcoulometer (Dohrmann Division of Envirotech Corp.) connected to 1 mv (full-scale) strip chart recorder, combustion furnace, and Dohrmann T-200 titrn cell sensitive to halogens. Prep. Vycor tube in injection port with Pt gauze wrapped around loose plug of glass wool. Do not plug tube too tightly.

Operating parameters are as follows:

Coulometer, Mode II (low gain) and ca 200 ohms range, or range that provides ca half-scale deflection for 40 μL injection of $C_2H_4Cl_2$ std; removable inlet temp. 200°; column temp. 160°;

furnace temp. ca 825°; N flow 100 mL/min (measure with soap bubble flow meter); sweep 10–20 mL/min; O ca 25 mL/min.

20.193 ***Reagents***

(Densities $C_2H_4Cl_2$ and C_2HCl_3 for converting from vol. to wt are 1.25 and 1.46, resp. Use absolute alcohol for all dilns.)

(**a**) *Internal std.*—(*1*) *Stock soln.*—Pipet 2.0 mL 1,2-dichloropropane into 200 mL vol. flask half filled with alcohol, immersing tip of pipet below surface of alcohol and then releasing contents. Wash pipet exterior with alcohol before withdrawing it from flask. Dil. to vol. and mix. (*2*) *Working std soln.*—Pipet 1.0 mL stock soln into 200 mL vol. flask half filled with alcohol, immersing pipet tip, as above, before releasing contents. Wash pipet exterior into flask, dil. to vol., and mix. Soln contains 0.05 μL or 57.95 μg 1,2-dichloropropane/mL alcohol.

(**b**) *Reference std.*—Prep. sep. $C_2H_4Cl_2$ and C_2HCl_3 stds as follows:

Pipet 2.0 mL chlorinated solv. into 200 mL vol. flask half filled with alcohol, immersing tip of pipet below surface of alcohol and then releasing contents. Wash pipet exterior with alcohol before withdrawing it from flask. Dil. to vol. and mix. Pipet 2.0 mL soln into 200 mL vol. flask as above, dil. to vol., and mix. Pipet 2.0 mL into 100 mL vol. flask as before, add 8.0 mL working internal std soln, and dil. to vol. Concn of stds:

Ethylene dichloride std = 2.50 ng $C_2H_4Cl_2$/μL and 4.64 ng 1,2-dichloropropane/μL.

Trichloroethylene std = 2.92 ng C_2HCl_3/μL and 4.64 ng 1,2-dichloropropane/μL.

20.194 ***Determination***

Weigh 2.5 g well mixed oleoresin into 25 mL vol. flask, add 2.0 mL working internal std soln, and dil. to vol. with absolute alcohol. Shake vigorously ca 5 min.

Chromatograph duplicate portions, ca 30 μL, in microcoulometric gas chromatograph set at prescribed conditions. Chromatograph duplicate portions of appropriate stds required to identify and quantitate. Vent ca 2 min after each injection and clean Vycor tube and contents after every 4 sample injections. (Det. venting time experimentally to release all alcohol.)

Approx. relative retention ratios relative to $C_2H_4Cl_2$ = 1: C_2HCl_3, 1.6; 1,2-dichloropropane, 2.0.

Use relative retention ratios to identify chlorinated solv. residues found in samples. Inject 30 μL absolute alcohol as solv. blank.

20.195 ***Calculations***

Det. area of each peak and calc. as follows:

ppm chlorinated solv. residue = $[(D \times I')/(I \times D')] \times C' \times (V/W)$, where D = area of sample peak; D' = area of std peak; I = area of internal std peak from sample soln; I' = area of internal std from ref. std soln; C' = concn, μg/mL, of std chromatgd; V = mL to which sample is dild; W = g sample weighed.

SELECTED REFERENCES

(*1*) JAOAC **49,** 701(1966); **51,** 533(1968).
(*2*) JAOAC **48,** 489(1965).
(*3*) JAOAC **50,** 880(1967); **51,** 943(1968); **53,** 39(1970).
(*4*) JAOAC **35,** 186(1952).
(*5*) Z. Nahr. Genussm. **19,** 137(1910); Chem. Abstr. **4,** 1523(1910).
(*6*) JAOAC **46,** 767(1963); **47,** 68(1964).
(*7*) JAOAC **42,** 486(1959); **43,** 587(1960).
(*8*) JAOAC **50,** 985(1967); **51,** 876(1968).
(*9*) USDA Div. Chem. Bull. **51,** p. 113.
(*10*) JAOAC **51,** 987(1968); **52,** 485(1969).
(*11*) JAOAC **42,** 487(1959).
(*12*) JAOAC **54,** 1138(1971); **55,** 890(1972).
(*13*) JAOAC **58,** 293(1975).
(*14*) JAOAC **36,** 744(1953).
(*15*) Chem. News **91,** 39(1905); Ann. Rept. Mass. State Bd. Health 1905, p. 498.
(*16*) JAOAC **37,** 381(1954).
(*17*) Mon. Sci. (4th Ser.) **9,** Part 1, 324(1895).
(*18*) Z. Anal. Chem. **110,** 22(1937).
(*19*) Ind. Eng. Chem., Anal. Ed. **3,** 199(1931).
(*20*) JAOAC **40,** 789(1957).
(*21*) JAOAC **25,** 145(1942); **27,** 195, 339, 446(1944); **28,** 302 (1945); **29,** 100(1946); **31,** 484(1948); **32,** 489(1949).
(*22*) JAOAC **47,** 395(1964).
(*23*) J. Am. Med. Ass. **120,** 289(1942); Ind. Eng. Chem., Anal. Ed. **15,** 492(1943); **16,** 739(1944); JAOAC **29,** 310, 311(1946); **31,** 480(1948).
(*24*) JAOAC **35,** 459(1952).
(*25*) JAOAC **35,** 455(1952).
(*26*) JAOAC **37,** 374(1954).
(*27*) J. Ind. Eng. Chem. **2,** 24(1910); **3,** 492(1911); JAOAC **14,** 76(1931); **16,** 77(1933).
(*28*) JAOAC **54,** 663(1971); **60,**1044(1977).
(*29*) JAOAC **57,** 675(1974).
(*30*) USDA Div. Chem. Bull. **13**(8), p. 1032.
(*31*) Monier-Williams, Repts on Public Health and Med. Subject No. 43 (London, Ministry of Health, 1927); JAOAC **12,** 120(1929); **16,** 77(1933); **17,** 70(1934); **18,** 82(1935); **45,** 905(1962); **46,** 618(1963); **48,** 796(1965); **49,** 834(1966).
(*32*) JAOAC **44,** 641(1961); **46,** 618(1963); **48,** 796(1965).
(*33*) JAOAC **44,** 485(1961).
(*34*) J. prakt. Chem. **46,** 428(1892); Repts on Public Health and Med. Subject No. 43 (London, Ministry of Health, p. 12).
(*35*) JAOAC **31,** 476(1948); **44,** 476(1961).
(*36*) JAOAC **57,** 62(1974); **61,** 506(1978).
(*37*) JAOAC **51,** 540(1968).
(*38*) JAOAC **18,** 140(1935); **19,** 373(1936); **21,** 97(1938).
(*39*) JAOAC **54,** 978(1971).
(*40*) JAOAC **47,** 363(1964).
(*41*) JAOAC **56,** 602(1973).
(*42*) JAOAC **56,** 66(1973).
(*43*) JAOAC **52,** 487(1969).
(*44*) JAOAC **38,** 559(1955); **43,** 583(1960); **54,** 1449(1971).
(*45*) JAOAC **51,** 1274(1968).
(*46*) JAOAC **52,** 492(1969); **53,** 701(1970).
(*47*) Compt. Rend. **173,** 1184(1921).
(*48*) Ann. Chim. Applicata **36,** 134(1946).
(*49*) JAOAC **40,** 785(1957).
(*50*) JAOAC **35,** 321(1952).
(*51*) JAOAC **39,** 652(1956).
(*52*) Z. Nahr. Genussm. **31,** 67(1915); JAOAC **24,** 326(1941).
(*53*) JAOAC **56,** 162(1973).
(*54*) JAOAC **30,** 492(1947).
(*55*) Z. Nahr. Genussm. **18,** 577(1909); JAOAC **17,** 193(1934); **18,** 56(1935); **21,** 184(1938).
(*56*) JAOAC **52,** 744, 1131(1969).
(*57*) JAOAC **52,** 477(1969).

21. Food Additives: Indirect

Polycyclic Aromatic Hydrocarbons and Benzo[*a*]pyrene (*1*)
Official Final Action

(*Caution: See* **51.011, 51.016, 51.039, 51.040, 51.045, 51.062,** and **51.066.**)

21.001 ***Principle***

Polycyclic aromatic hydrocarbons are extd from comminuted food sample after saponification with alc. KOH, purified by solv. partition and column chromatgy, sepd by TLC, detd by UV spectrophotometry, and confirmed by spectrophotofluorometry.

21.002 ***General Instructions***

Because of sensitivity of method, possibility of errors from contamination is great. All glassware must be thoroly cleaned to remove all org. matter such as oil, grease, detergent residues, etc. Do not use grease on stopcocks or joints. Rinse all glassware with purified solvs immediately before use. Because these compds are somewhat susceptible to photooxidn, perform detn as far as possible under subdued light and store std solns in low actinic flasks. Use care in prepg stds and handling exts, since some of these compds are carcinogenic.

21.003 ***Apparatus***

(**a**) *Separators.*—125, 500, 1000, and 2000 mL, with Teflon stopcocks.

(**b**) *Evaporation flasks.*—125, 250, and 1000 mL all-glass flasks (Kontes Glass Co., No. K-617250, or equiv.) with ₮ 24/40 wash bottle stopper (No. K-331751, or equiv.) having inlet and outlet tubes to permit passage of N across surface of liq. to be evapd. Inlet tube of stopper used to convey N is cut off 2 cm below joint, and outlet tube connected to vac. is bent downward at 45° angle to prevent backflow of condensate into flask.

(**c**) *Boiling flask.*—1 L r-b, with ₮ 24/40 joint and pouring lip.

(**d**) *Condenser.*—Friedrich-type with ₮ 24/40 joint.

(**e**) *Chromatographic tube.*—230 × 38 mm id, with coarse porosity fritted glass filter.

(**f**) *Pressure filter.*—30 mL, fine porosity, with ₮ 24/40 outer joint (Kontes Glass Co., No. K-953100, or equiv.) and adapter with ₮ 24/40 inner joint (Kontes Glass Co., No. K-183000, or equiv.) for connection to N cylinder.

(**g**) *Nitrogen cylinder.*—H_2O-pumped purity N, or equiv., in cylinder with regulator and valve to control flow at 5 psig.

(**h**) *Heating mantle.*—Elec., hemispherical, for 1 L, r-b flask with variable transformer heat control.

(**i**) *Ultraviolet equipment.*—(*1*) *Lamps.*—Longwave, 3660Å; shortwave, 2537Å. (*2*) *Chromato-Vue cabinet.*—Available from Ultra-Violet Products, Inc.

(**j**) *Recording spectrophotometer and accessories.*—Cary 11 (current Models Cary 14 and 17, Varian Instrument Division), or equiv., with fused rectangular quartz cells, optical path 10±0.005 mm, 1.5 mL (Optical Cell Co., Inc., 10792 Tucker St, Beltsville, MD 20705, No. 2-203 Q-QUV (Tol. A), or equiv.).

(**k**) *Spectrophotofluorometer and accessories.*—Aminco-Bowman with 1P28 photomultiplier tube and slit arrangement No. 2 (American Instrument Co., No. 4-8202, or equiv.); fused rectangular quartz cells (Optical Cell Co., Inc., No. 5-501 QS-QUV, or equiv.).

(**l**) *Thin layer chromatographic apparatus.*—(Available from Brinkmann Instruments, Inc.). (*1*) Glass plates, 10 × 20 cm (No. 25-10-110-3); (*2*) applicator, adjustable, Model S-II (No. 25-09-050-1); (*3*) mounting board, Plexiglas, std size for plate up to 20 cm wide (No. 04-10-000-0); (*4*) drying rack (No. 25-09-150-7); (*5*) developing tank, std, rectangular, 22 deep × 8.5 wide × 20.5 cm long (No. 04-10-080-8); (*6*) desiccating storage cabinet, stainless steel, 30 wide × 25 cm deep (No. 04-11-500-7).

(**m**) *Dipping tank.*—Type 302 stainless steel, capacity 370 mL; inside dimensions 8⅜ × 3/16 × 8⅜″, with cover (Arthur H. Thomas Co., No. 2749-H50, or equiv.).

(**n**) *Syringe.*—50 μL (Hamilton Co., Inc., Type 705N, or equiv.).

21.004 ***Reagents***

Distil all reagents, where specified, with use of air-cooled, 30 cm reflux condenser between distg flask and H_2O-cooled condenser. Use 2 L lots, discarding first 200 mL distillate and collecting next 1600 mL for use.

Purify isooctane, benzene, and MeOH to meet following test: To specified vol. solv. in 250 mL evapn flask, add 1 mL purified *n*-hexadecane and place container on steam bath. Insert tube assembly, and connect inlet tube to N supply and outlet tube to solv. trap and vac. line. Discontinue evapn when ≤1 mL residue remains. (To residue from benzene, add 10 mL purified isooctane, reevap., and repeat once to ensure complete removal of benzene.) Add 4.0 mL isooctane to 1.0 mL *n*-hexadecane residue. Det. *A* in 1 cm path length cell (1.5 mL) against isooctane as ref.; *A* of soln of solv. residue (except for MeOH) must be ≤0.01/cm path length between 250 and 400 nm. For MeOH, *A* must be ≤0.03/cm path length between 250 and 275 nm; ≤0.015 between 275 and 300 nm; ≤0.010 between 300 and 350 nm; and 0.00 between 350 and 400 nm.

(**a**) *Isooctane* (*2,2,4-Trimethylpentane*).—Purify by distn or by passing thru column of activated silica gel, (**k**)(*2*), ca 90 long × 5–8 cm id. Use 180 mL for test.

(**b**) *Benzene.*—ACS. Purify by distn. Use 150 mL for test.

(**c**) *Hexadecane.*—99%, olefin-free. Purify by percolation thru column of activated silica gel, (**k**)(*2*). Det. *A* of 1 mL in 1 cm cell against isooctane as ref.; *A* must be 0.00/cm path length between 250 and 400 nm.

(**d**) *Methanol.*—ACS. Purify as follows: Reflux 2 L MeOH with 10 g KOH and 25 g Zn dust 3 hr. Distil thru air-cooled reflux condenser connected to H_2O-cooled condenser. Provide collection flask with drying tube to protect distd solv. from moisture. Use 50.0 mL for test.

(**e**) *Alcohol.*—USP. Redistil before use.

(**f**) *Toluene.*—ACS. Redistil before use. (*Caution:* Flammable liq.)

(**g**) *Dimethyl sulfoxide* (*DMSO*).—Spectroquality (MC/B Manufacturing Chemists, MX1457, or equiv.). (*Caution: See* **42.124**(**c**).)

(**h**) *Acetylated linters powder.*—21% acetylated (S&S No. 124/21 ac, or equiv.).

(**i**) *Florisil.*—60–100 mesh (available from Fisher Scientific Co., No. F-100, or equiv.). Place 300 g Florisil in 1 L g-s erlenmeyer. Add 700 mL redistd MeOH, stopper, and shake 1 min, removing stopper periodically to release pressure. Transfer slurry to 600 mL coarse porosity fritted buchner and let drain by gravity. Wash flask with three 35 mL portions redistd MeOH and pass thru buchner. Wash adsorbent in funnel with addnl 100 mL redistd MeOH and let drain. Apply vac. to remove most of MeOH. Transfer treated Florisil to tray lined with Al foil (free of rolling oil). Dry in vac. oven (66–71 cm; 26–28"; 88–94 kPa) at 50° overnight. Store adsorbent in amber bottle.

Test prepd adsorbent before use as follows: Pour 10 g treated Florisil into clean 30 mL coarse porosity fritted glass funnel (30 mm diam.). Place 15 g anhyd. Na_2SO_4 on adsorbent and wash with 50 mL purified isooctane. Prep. 1.0 μg/mL soln of benzo[*a*]pyrene in isooctane. Pipet 1 mL soln onto anhyd. Na_2SO_4, let filter into 125 mL evapn flask, and wash adsorbent with four 20 mL portions isooctane, letting column drain completely between washes. Remove and retain first evapn flask and replace with second 125 mL evapn flask. Elute benzo[*a*]pyrene from column, using four 25 mL portions redistd benzene; let column drain completely between washes. Add 1.0 mL hexadecane to each eluate in the 2 evapn flasks. Evap. under stream of N on steam bath to residue of 1 mL hexadecane. Add 5 mL isooctane to residue from benzene eluate in second evapn flask and re-evap. Repeat once to ensure complete removal of benzene. Transfer the 1.0 mL residue to 1.0 cm path length cell (1.5 mL capacity) and record *A* with recording spectrophtr from 350 to 400 nm, against isooctane in ref. cell. No benzo[*a*]pyrene should be present in first (isooctane) eluate, and 95–100% of added benzo[*a*]pyrene should be found in benzene eluate as calcd from *A* at 386 nm max. Concn of 1 μg benzo[*a*]pyrene/mL isooctane gives *A* of 0.12/cm path length at 386 nm max. (Reading in hexadecane results in bathochromic shift of max.)

(j) *Sodium sulfate.*—Anhyd., granular.

(k) *Silica gel.*—Activated (available from Fisher Scientific Co.). (*1*) *Desiccant.*—Grade 42, 6–16 mesh (No. S-160). (*2*) *Adsorbent.*—Grade 12, 28–200 mesh (No. S-157).

(l) *Polycyclic aromatic hydrocarbons.*—Prep. sep. std solns contg 0.5 and 1.0 μg hydrocarbon/mL isooctane. Check purity by TLC, using cellulose and cellulose acetate plates. No fluorescent impurities should be observed after chromatgy of 2–3 μg hydrocarbon stds. If impurities are noted, purify by recrystn from benzene.

To prep. std curve for benzo[*a*]pyrene and other polycyclic hydrocarbon compds (e.g., benzo[*e*]pyrene, benzo[*a*]anthracene, benzo[*ghi*]perylene, etc.), transfer 1 mL hexadecane to 2 sep. 50 mL erlenmeyers and add 1 mL std soln contg 0.5 μg std/mL to 1 flask and 1 mL std soln contg 1.0 μg std/mL to other flask. Place flasks on steam bath and evap. under N to 1 mL hexadecane. For benzo[*a*]pyrene in hexadecane, observed max. are 255, 267, 285, 297, 363, 382, and 386 nm. *A* of 1 μg benzo[*a*]pyrene/mL hexadecane is 0.12/cm path length at 386 nm (major max. in 350–400 nm region), using isooctane as ref.

(m) *Cellulose.*—Purified (Brinkmann Instruments, Inc., No. MN 300-HR; 66 00 110-5).

(n) *N,N-Dimethylformamide* (*DMF*).—Redistil before use.

21.005 *Extraction*

Grind sample in meat grinder. Place 100 g in 1 L boiling flask and add 400 mL alcohol, 15 g KOH (10 g for cheese), and boiling chips. Insert Friedrich condenser and reflux 2 hr at rapid rate. (To prevent foaming, gradually increase heat to rapid reflux rate only after refluxing at relatively slow rate ca 5–10 min.)

21.006 *Purification*

Remove condenser and transfer material while warm to 2 L separator. Wash flask twice with 125 mL H_2O and then twice with 100 mL alcohol and transfer washes to separator. Wash flask with 150 mL isooctane and pour into separator. Shake separator 3 min. Let layers sep. and drain lower layer into second 2 L separator. Let residual solids in first separator settle addnl min and carefully drain completely into second separator. Repeat extn with 100 mL isooctane. Let sep., drain aq. layer and residual solids as before into third separator, and again ext with 100 mL isooctane. Drain aq. layer, let solids settle, and carefully remove. Discard aq. layer and solids. Wash each isooctane ext 4 times with 250 mL warm (ca 50°) H_2O by gentle swirling. (Avoid vigorous shaking; it may cause emulsions.) Discard aq. layer after each wash.

Pour 60 g treated and tested Florisil into chromatgc tube, with gentle tapping to settle contents. Place 50 g anhyd. Na_2SO_4 on top of adsorbent, tapping to level surface. Prewet column with ca 75 mL isooctane, let drain by gravity, and discard eluate. Place 1 L evapn flask under column. Pass isooctane ext in first separator thru column. Let column drain by gravity. Wash first separator with ext contained in second separator and filter thru column by gravity. Wash second and first separators successively with ext in third separator, filter thru column, and again let drain. Wash third, second, and first separators in that order with 50 mL isooctane and pass wash thru column as before. Pass 125 mL benzene thru column into 1 L evapn flask. Let column drain completely. (If only benzo[*a*]pyrene is desired, discard all isooctane eluates and collect benzene eluate in 250 mL evapn flask.)

Add 2 mL hexadecane to eluate. Fit tube assembly into evapn flask and evap. solv. under N on steam bath as in purity test, **21.004**, but evap. only to 2 mL residual hexadecane (loose Al foil jacket around flask speeds evapn). To ensure complete removal of benzene, add 10 mL isooctane, re-evap., and repeat once.

Quant. transfer the 2 mL hexadecane conc. to 500 mL separator, using total of 198 mL isooctane. Wash soln twice with 100 mL portions H_3PO_4, shaking 1 min each time. After each wash, let layers sep. (ca 10 min) and discard lower (acid) layer. After draining acid in final wash, swirl separator and let stand few min. Carefully drain any residual acid which settles out. Add 50 mL DMSO, pre-equilibrated with isooctane, and shake 2 min. Set up three 125 mL separators contg 25 mL isooctane pre-equilibrated with DMSO. After sepn of phases in 500 mL separator, drain lower (DMSO) layer into first 125 mL separator, and wash in tandem with isooctane in the three 125 mL separators, shaking each wash 1 min. Repeat extn with 2 addnl 50 mL portions DMSO, washing each ext in tandem thru same 3 portions isooctane.

Collect successive DMSO exts (150 mL total) in 1 L separator contg 300 mL H_2O and 50 mL isooctane. Let mixt. cool few min after addn of last ext, as some heat of diln is generated. Shake vigorously 2 min and let sep. Drain lower aq. phase into second 1 L separator, and repeat extn with 50 mL isooctane. Drain and discard aq. phase. Wash each 50 mL ext twice with 75 mL portions H_2O, shaking each wash ca 15 sec. Let sep. and discard aq. layer after each wash. Filter isooctane ext in first separator thru anhyd. Na_2SO_4 (ca 35 g in 30 mL coarse fritted glass funnel or in 65 mL funnel with glass wool plug, and previously washed with isooctane) into 250 mL evapn flask. Rinse first separator with ext from second separator, and pass thru filter. Wash second and first separators successively in tandem with two 25 mL portions isooctane and pass individual portions thru filter. Evap. combined filtrate on steam bath under N as before to ca 10 mL. Quant. transfer soln with benzene to 50 mL g-s erlenmeyer and conc. on steam bath under N to $\leq$0.5 mL. (Do not evap. to dryness, since prolonged heating of polycyclic hydrocarbons in dry state will cause losses.) Reserve concd soln for TLC.

21.007 *Thin Layer Chromatography*

To det. individual polycyclic aromatic hydrocarbons, use cellulose reverse phase technic in conjunction with cellulose acetate multiphase technic. To det. only benzo[*a*]pyrene, apply conc. directly to cellulose acetate plate.

Place 20 g cellulose, (**m**), and 100 mL H_2O in high-speed blender and homogenize 3 min at rapid speed. With thin layer applicator, apply adsorbent to five 20 × 20 cm plates at thickness of 500 μm. Let plates air dry completely. Wash plates before use in chromatgc tank by allowing mobile solv., isooctane, to migrate to top of plate in same direction as in development of chromatogram and 90° angle to application of adsorbent. Remove plate and let excess isooctane evap. Scrape off 1 cm band across top of plate to remove interfering background material which has migrated during wash. Store plates in desiccator until needed.

Pour 50 mL mobile solv., isooctane, in developing tank and equilibrate ≥30 min. In partially darkened room, apply entire benzene ext conc. to plate with micropipet or 50 μL syringe in streak ca 0.5 cm wide, 10 cm long, 2 cm from bottom of plate. (For complete sepns it is essential to maintain narrow band in application of conc. This is best achieved by applying conc. in 50 μL increments and letting solv. evap. after each application without prolonged drying.) Wash sides of flask with three 0.2 mL portions benzene from graduated pipet and transfer solv. from each wash to plate as before. Complete application of conc. with 3 washings in ca 10 min. To aid identification, spot mixt. of std solns of polycyclic hydrocarbons adjacent to unknown.

Invert plate 180° and wet it to within 0.5 cm of starting line by immersion in dipping tank contg immobile solv., DMF-ether (20+80). Remove plate and let excess immobile solv. drain ca 15–20 sec. Return plate to original position (starting line on bottom), place in tank satd with isooctane, and develop in dark until mobile solv. reaches top of plate (ca 1 hr at 25°).

When development is complete, remove plate from tank and observe positions of polycyclic compds on *wet* plate under both longwave and shortwave UV light. Outline fluorescent bands.

Remove plate from cabinet, scrape off excess adsorbent around bands with spatula, and discard. Transfer each outlined band of adsorbent to sep. 125 mL beakers, and immediately elute polycyclic hydrocarbon by extg with 5–10 mL portions hot MeOH until fluorescence under UV light can no longer be seen in last portion of solv. Swirl flask repeatedly during extn and successively decant individual exts thru 30 mL pressure filter, **21.003(f)**, under N into 50 mL flask. (Pulverize collected adsorbent in beaker with spatula prior to hot MeOH extn to aid complete recovery of compds. Three or 4 extns are usually enough to remove compds from adsorbent.) After extn, evap. each ext to ca 0.5 mL, add 5 mL benzene, and re-evap. to ca 0.2–0.3 mL. Do *not* evap. to dryness. Reserve concs for TLC on cellulose acetate plates.

Place 50 g cellulose acetate and 275 mL alcohol in high-speed blender and homogenize 3 min at rapid speed. (Ten plates can be prepd with this amt slurry.) With thin layer applicator, apply adsorbent to plates (10 × 20 cm) at thickness of 1000 μm. Let plates air dry 4 hr and store in desiccator over silica gel, (**k**)(*1*), until needed.

Pour 50 mL mobile solv. (alcohol-toluene-H_2O, 17+4+4) in

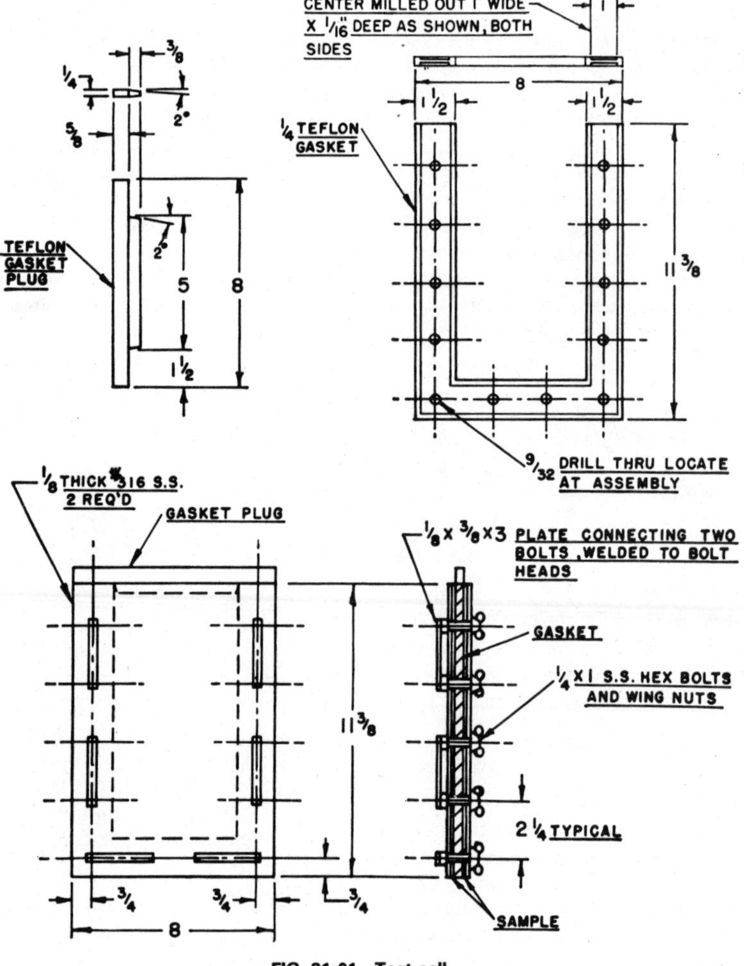

FIG. 21:01—Test cell

developing tank and equilibrate ≥1 hr. In partially darkened room, apply exts obtained from cellulose plate in streak as above. Wash sides of flask with four 0.2 mL portions benzene from graduated pipet and transfer solv. from each wash to plate as before. Complete transfer of each ext in ca 10 min. After solv. evaps, place plate in tank and let chromatogram develop in dark until solv. front reaches top of plate (ca 1.5 hr at 25°).

When development is complete, remove plate from tank and observe positions on *wet* plate under both longwave and shortwave UV light in Chromato-Vue cabinet. Outline fluorescent bands.

21.008 ***Ultraviolet Spectrophotometry***

Remove plate from cabinet, scrape off adsorbent around bands with spatula, and discard. Transfer each outlined band of adsorbent to sep. 50 mL pressure filters; elute hydrocarbons from adsorbent by extg with 5–10 mL portions hot MeOH, and filter thru 30 mL pressure filter, **21.003(f)**, under N into 50 mL flask. Repeat this operation 3 addnl times with 5–10 mL portions hot MeOH. After extn, add 1 mL hexadecane to combined ext and evap. MeOH on steam bath under N. Remove any residual MeOH in flask by adding two 5 mL portions isooctane and re-evapg under N.

Carefully transfer 1.0 mL hexadecane soln to 1 cm path length cell (total capacity 1.5 mL) and record UV spectrum in 250–400 nm range against isooctane in ref. cell. Compare any max. observed with those in spectra obtained for std solns of polycyclic aromatic hydrocarbons. Est. amt of identified hydrocarbons by using baseline technic.

21.009 ***Spectrophotofluorometry***

Carefully transfer soln from spectrophtr cell into fluorometer cell and record excitation and emission spectra. Compare fluorescence spectra obtained with those of 0.5 and 1.0 μg/mL std solns of compds and calc. amt present.

Exposing Flexible Barrier Materials for Extraction

ASTM-AOAC Method (2)—Official Final Action

21.010 ***Principle***

Method provides std liq. extn method for flexible barrier materials, singly, coated, or combined, including extns thru flexible barrier materials of surface coating ingredients, by food-simulating solvs. Specimens of flexible barrier materials are exposed to extg liqs in test cell and amt of nonvolatile extractives remaining after exposure is measured.

21.011 ***Apparatus***

(**a**) *Test cell.*—See Fig. **21:01**. Consists of two 8 × 11¾ × ⅛" No. 316 stainless steel plates, degreased; one ¼ × 1½" U-shaped virgin TFE-fluorocarbon (Teflon) gasket, grooved on both sides as shown; twelve ¼ × 1" stainless steel bolts with wing nuts; one ¼ × 1 × 8" TFE-fluorocarbon gasket plug tapered to provide tight fit. (Available from Scientific Products, No. E6200.) To prep. app. for use, wash plates and gaskets in aq. detergent soln. Rinse with H_2O and dry at 100°. Wash with *n*-heptane and redistd acetone. Immerse new gaskets in *n*-heptane overnight. Rinse gaskets with fresh *n*-heptane and dry at 100°.

(**b**) *Oven rack.—See* Fig. **21:02**. To hold extn test cells.

(**c**) *Hot air oven.*—With safety provisions for flammable solvs. Vac. oven or autoclave is suitable.

21.012 ***Reagents***

Use solvs (usually H_2O, dil. alcohol, and *n*-heptane) specified in regulations (Code of Federal Regulations, Title 21, Sec. 175.300(d) Table 2; 176.170(c) Table 2). Solv. for blanks and detn should be from same container.

21.013 ***Preparation of Cells***

Select samples of flexible barrier material and protect from exposure to liqs or contamination by migration from contact

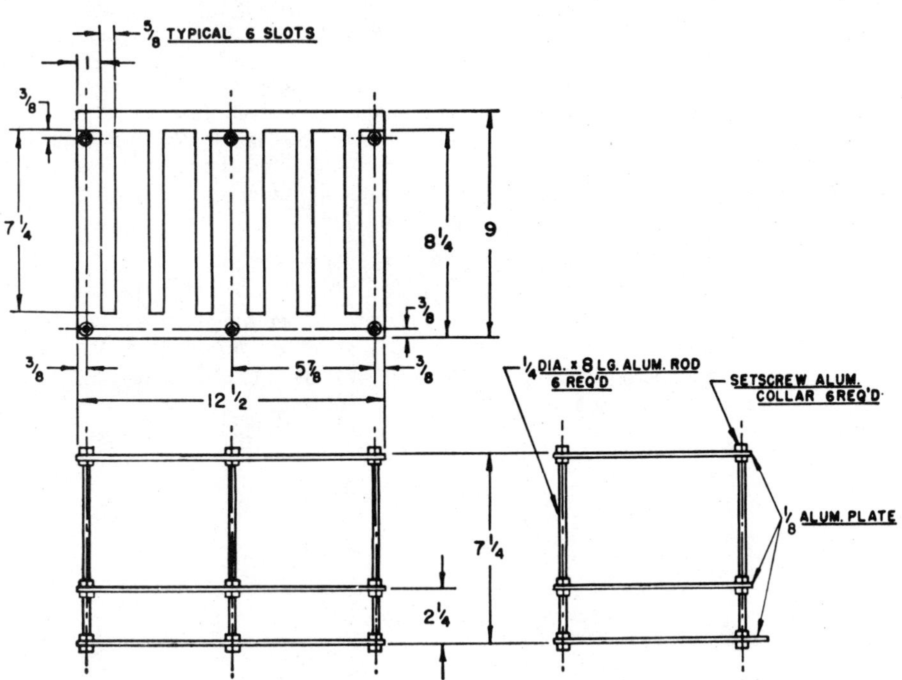

FIG. 21:02—Oven rack

with other materials, and from wrinkling or abrasion. Samples shall equal or exceed cell dimensions (8 × 11¾").

Place 1 stainless steel plate of cell on flat surface with bolts protruding up thru holes in plate. Place prepunched specimen (side to contact liq. up) on plate with 1 edge aligned with bottom of plate, 2 edges aligned with sides of plate, and bolts passing thru prepunched holes. Place gasket on specimen with outer edges of gasket aligned with cell bottom and sides. If desired, place second prepunched specimen (side to contact liq. down) on top of gasket. If only 1 sheet is used for test, place inert barrier sheet such as Teflon or electrolytically cleaned Sn foil in place of second sheet. Place second stainless steel plate on top of assembly. Place wing nuts on bolts and tighten.

Preheat assembly (including TFE-fluorocarbon gasket plug) to test temp. and retighten nuts so that assembly is liq.-tight.

21.014 ***Determination***

Place measured vol. of extg liq., preheated to test temp., into assembly. Use vol. of liq. such that top of liq. is 0.5" below top of specimen. In no case should vol. of extg liq. be >200 mL. Insert gasket plug in top of cell. Expose cell in rack in oven to conditions of time and temp. specified by regulations. If vac. oven is used, operate it at atm. pressure. Align cells in rack in oven parallel with air flow.

After exposure, remove cell from rack, remove gasket plug, and immediately pour out extg liq. into graduate. (If solids flake from specimen and it is desired to det. only sol. materials, filter thru fritted glass filter from cell into graduate.) If vol. of extg liq. is <90% of original vol., investigate cause.

Det. total nonvolatile extractives by evapg total vol. extg liq. to apparent dryness in weighed Pt evapg dish on steam bath. Dry in oven 30 min at 100°. Cool 30 min in desiccator and weigh.

Perform ≥2 blank detns with 200 mL extg liq. each and glassware that will be used in detn. Preclean glassware with chromic acid soln followed by H_2O rinse. Place equal vol. extg liq. into each of blank-receiving containers. If filter is used on extg liq. from exposed samples, include contact of solv. of blank with filter. Wt blank must be <2.0 mg/200 mL and <30% of wt extractives.

21.015 ***Calculation***

With 2 sheets in cell, ratio of exposure area to vol. extg liq. used to fill cell is 2 mL/sq in. Calc. mg extractives/sq in. exposed sample = (mg extractives − mg blank)/sq in. exposed sample.

Extractives from Rubber Articles (*3*)—Official Final Action

21.016 ***Apparatus***

(**a**) *Extraction flasks.*—500 mL wide-mouth erlenmeyer, neck id ca 35 mm (500 mL Pyrex g-s ₮ 40/50 flasks are satisfactory).

(**b**) *Reflux condenser.*—Block Sn coil (Sargent-Welch Scientific Co., No. S-31555, or equiv.).

(**c**) *Measuring tools.*—Micrometer and precision ruler.

(**d**) *Punch.*—1-, 2-, or 3-hole conventional paper punch with punch of ≥⅜" diam.

21.017 ***Preparation of Sample***

Punch out disks of ca ⅜" diam. from test material. Wash disks by hand in dil. soap soln at ca 40°; rinse with 40° H_2O and then distd H_2O and blot dry with paper towel.

21.018 ***Measurement of Surface Area***

Measure thickness of 20 disks with micrometer (±0.001") and calc. av. thickness. Measure diam. to nearest 1/32" and verify measurements of ≥10 disks. If deviations of ±1/32" are noted, then det. av. diams for ≥20 disks. Calc. total surface area for disks tested as follows:

$$\text{Total surface area} = N[2 \times (22/7) \times (d^2/4) + (22/7) \times d \times t],$$

where N = no. of disks, d = av. diam. in in., and t = av. thickness in in.

21.019 ***Determination***

(*Caution: See* **51.011**, **51.039**, and **51.061**.)

Place counted number of disks into extn flask; add few SiC chips and measured vol. of solv. (*n*-hexane or H_2O). (Total surface area of disks should be 10–20 sq in. and vol. of solv., in mL, is 20 times number of sq in. surface area.) Mark level of solv. and add fresh solv. if losses occur during extn. Attach thoroly cleaned and acetone-rinsed condenser to flask and reflux 7 hr on hot plate. Adjust temp. of hot plate to give boiling rate that keeps disks in motion without excessive foaming. If disks tend to stick together, agitate them 5–6 times during extn. Rinse condenser with small amt solv. and remove flask from hot plate. Decant ext into beaker and rinse flask and disks with three small portions hot solv. Discard disks.

Weigh 125 mL fat flask, or 100 mL beaker, contg few SiC chips, after heating 1 hr at 100° and cooling 1 hr in desiccator. Transfer ext and rinses, in 50–80 mL portions, to tared flask or beaker. For blank, transfer vol. solv. equal to ext plus rinses to similar weighed beaker or flask. Evap. each portion to ca 20 mL before adding more ext. Swirl flask or beaker frequently while heating until soln begins to boil. Hexane ext can be evapd to dryness entirely on steam bath with stream of filtered air; H_2O ext can be concd to ca 10 mL on hot plate before evapg to dryness on steam bath.

Wipe outside of flask with damp paper towel and place flask on its side in oven. Dry hexane ext at 70° and H_2O ext at 105° 1 hr. Cool in desiccator 1 hr and weigh on anal. balance. Subtract wt of solv. blank from wt of residue. Divide corrected wt of residue in mg by total surface area of test disks and report as mg/sq in.

SELECTED REFERENCES

(*1*) JAOAC **49**, 611(1966); **51**, 122, 544(1968); **56**, 68 (1973).

(*2*) JAOAC **45**, 70(1962); **47**, 386(1964); **51**, 449(1968); ASTM F34-63T, 1963 Sup. to Book of ASTM Stds, Part 6, pp. 105–109.

(*3*) JAOAC **50**, 840(1967); **53**, 43(1970).

22. Fruits and Fruit Products

22.001 Sampling (*1*)—Procedure

(**a**) *Boxed dried fruit.*—Remove cover, bottom, or one side of box, as convenient. Remove block comprising ⅛ of contents of box taken from one corner as follows: With sharp knife make vertical cut midway between *ends* of box to center of top surface, extending cut half way to bottom. Make another vertical cut midway between *sides* of box, extending half way to bottom, and continue it until it meets first cut. Remove all fruit included in angle formed by the 2 cuts. Working rapidly, break up lumps, mix thoroly, and take enough sample to fill qt (1 L) Mason jar, replacing remainder in box. Seal jar and send to laboratory. Sample enough boxes from different parts of pile to constitute at least sq root of lot.

(**b**) *Frozen pack fruit in barrels.*—Use stainless steel or corrosion-resistant tube ca 3 cm (1.25") diam. and 90 cm (36") long, one end serrated and set to run freely, other end with removable cap and arrangement for use of elec. motor in drilling. To aid in removal of core samples use wooden ram smaller in diam. but longer than tube.

Remove bottom of barrel and take 3 cores evenly spaced around its circumference near chime, parallel to and thru full length of barrel. Take fourth core at approx. center of barrel.

(**c**) *Frozen pack fruit in small containers (30–50 lb).*—Use modified corrosion-resistant auger 2.5–3.0 cm (1–1.5") diam. and 50 cm (19") long that can be operated by elec. motor. (Auger should have no lead screw or cutters and angle of face should not be flat but 170–175°.) Collect borings in corrosion-resistant sampling can ca 15 cm (6") diam. and 10 cm (4") high, open at one end, with outlet at other end ca 2.5 cm (1") long and of diam. slightly larger than that of auger. Place sampling can on surface of frozen fruit and operate auger thru small opening at bottom. Take 3 vertical cores evenly spaced around circumference and ca 1.3 cm (0.5") from edge of container and take 1 core at or near center. Remove both sampling can and auger simultaneously to prevent borings from falling thru delivery outlet.

22.002 Net Contents of Frozen Fruits—Procedure

See **32.050–32.051**.

Fill of Container of Frozen Fruits (*2*)—Official First Action

22.003 ***Apparatus***

(**a**) *Overflow can.*—With device for lowering frozen fruit into liq. and for removing it, Fig. **22:01**. Can is ca 20 cm (8") diam. and ca 23 cm (9") high with overflow spout of 0.5 cm (3/16" id) (¼" od) Cu tubing. Solder tubing to opening on side of can ca 1.3 cm (0.5") from bottom and bend upward parallel to side of can to ca 5 cm (2") below top where it is bent away and downward to form inverted U. Form spout by cutting tubing on outer side of U where it makes ca 45° angle with can, making cut parallel to bottom of can. Opening of spout is ca 0.3 cm (⅛") below lower surface of U-bend. Bend end of spout up or down until overflow, caused by adding excess of liq. to can, will end abruptly. (Proper adjustment of tube and addn of enough liq. will secure this effect.) Lowering device consists of 1.3 cm (0.5") metal frame 14.6 cm (5.75") square contg 1.3 cm (0.5") mesh screening attached on one side to perpendicular handle 30 cm (12") long bent outward at top.

(**b**) *Plastic bags.*—Polyethylene; pliable at 0°F; capable of holding vac.; ca 8 × 10" when flat.

(**c**) *Freezer or cold room.*—At or near 0°F.

(**d**) *Refined light mineral oil such as odorless kerosene.*

22.004 ***Determination***

Transfer frozen sample from container and inner wrapper, if any, to plastic bag. Remove excess air from bag by inserting glass tube attached to vac. line. Twist bag top to close, hold twist with pinch clamp, and trim off loose end. Pretest bags to be certain they will not leak.

Place overflow can in freezing compartment and fill can, in which lifting device is inserted, with light mineral oil at temp. of freezing compartment (ca 0°F). Add enough excess mineral oil (ca 300 mL) to produce siphon effect in overflow, collecting overflow in beaker. Place empty, calibrated graduate under overflow tube and immerse frozen fruit sample completely in the mineral oil, using lifting device. Record vol. of overflow in graduate to nearest mL. Correct this vol. for displacement of empty plastic bag and pinch clamp (ca 7 mL) to obtain net displacement of frozen fruit. Redet. displacement of sample to check reproducibility of operation.

For packages with square corners, calc. H_2O capacity of outer container by multiplying inside length, width, and ht in cm. For packages with curved edges or irregular shape, det. H_2O capacity as follows: Place empty container in beaker or pan contg enough H_2O to reach to within 1 cm of top of container when it is resting on bottom of beaker or pan. Note that no air is trapped by bottom of container. Add H_2O from calibrated 500 mL buret to fill container to capacity, or to measured headspace if indented top has been removed. Read H_2O capacity directly from buret.

Det. % fill of container by dividing net displacement of frozen fruit by H_2O capacity of outer container and multiply by 100.

22.005 Drained Weight of Frozen Fruits (*3*)
Official First Action

After obtaining gross wts, immerse packages in H_2O agitated and maintained at 20±1°. (If packages are not H_2O-tight, place in suitable plastic bag, remove excess air by use of vac., and tie off.) Avoid agitation of packages during thawing by using clamps

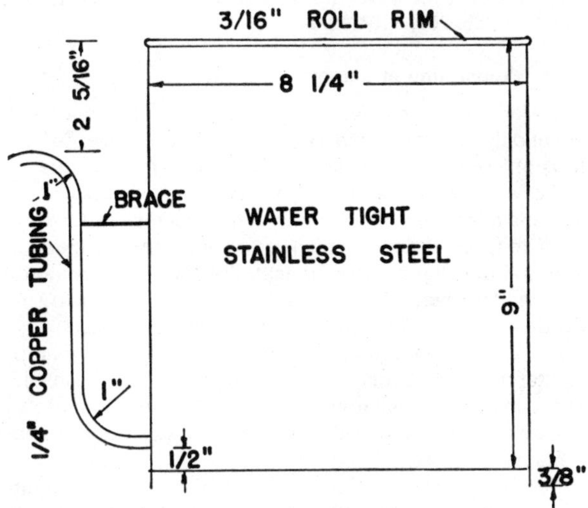

FIG. 22:01—Apparatus for determining volume of frozen fruits by displacement

or weights if necessary. When center of packages reaches bath temp. as detd by preliminary experiments (ca 2–3 hr for 10.5–16 oz (300–450 g) containers), remove from bath, blot off adhering H_2O, and open with min. agitation.

Tare No. 8 sieve with light-wt drip pan. Use 8″ (20 cm) diam. sieve if container holds ≤3 lb (1.4 kg), 12″ (30 cm) if more. With screen tilted and supported for drainage, distribute contents of package evenly over screen in one sweeping motion. After 2 min from time drainage begins, transfer sieve with fruit to drip pan and weigh. Obtain net wt of packages by subtracting wt empty containers from their gross wts.

22.006 Thawing Frozen Fruit (*4*)—Procedure

(FAO/WHO Method)

Use entire package or intact sample unit; for bulk products, use 1–2 kg representative sample. Apply 1 of following technics appropriate to product, e.g., for corn, use air thawing or indirect contact to avoid leaching solids. Use method which will provide most rapid thawing without altering or degrading product characteristics. Proceed until product is sufficiently free from ice crystals to permit easy sepn and handling of individual units. Light-colored fruits (apricots, peaches) and red cherries oxidize readily and should be examined for color while some ice crystals remain in product.

(**a**) *Air thawing.*—Thaw in unopened container at room temp. To hasten thawing, apply forced air from fan and sep. packages.

(**b**) *Indirect water thawing.*—Place sample in plastic bag capable of being sealed H_2O-tight. Remove most of air, seal, and apply wts or clamps if necessary to avoid agitation of sample. Immerse in stationary or flowing H_2O at ≤30°.

22.007 Approximate Fruit Content of Fruit-Sugar Mixtures (*5*)—Procedure

Let sample thaw and come to room temp. in original container. Mix sample thoroly in high-speed blender. Filter portion of sample thru strong lens paper or other suitable medium. Det. refractometer reading, **31.011**, correct to 20°, and report as % sol. solids (sucrose). Calc. % fruit, X, from equation:

$$X = (100 - M)\ 100/(100 - F),$$

where M is sol. solids (as sucrose) of fruit-sugar mixt. and F is sol. solids of fruit ingredient in mixt. if known; otherwise use av. sol. solids of authentic fruits (JAOAC **21**, 502(1938); **47**, 1068(1964); **48**, 523(1965); **51**, 1203(1968); **52**, 643, 1047, 1150(1969); **55**, 200, 1104(1972).

22.008 Preparation of Sample—Procedure

Transfer samples received in open packages (*i.e.,* not sterile) without delay to g-s containers and keep in cool place. To avoid effects of fermentation, make prompt detns of alcohol, total and volatile acids, solids, and sugars, particularly in case of fruit juices and fresh fruits. (Portions for detn of sucrose and reducing sugars may be weighed and kept several days without fermenting if the slight excess of neut. $Pb(OAc)_2$ soln required in detn is added. *Note:* $Pb(OAc)_2$ is toxic. Label samples to show its addn.) Prep. various products for analysis as follows:

(**a**) *Juices.*—Mix thoroly by shaking to ensure uniform sample, and filter thru absorbent cotton or rapid paper. Prep. fresh juices by pressing well pulped fruit and filtering. Express juice of citrus fruits by one of common devices used for squeezing oranges or lemons, and filter.

(**b**) *Jellies and sirups.*—Mix thoroly to ensure uniform sample. Prep. soln by weighing 300 g thoroly mixed sample into 2 L flask and dissolve in H_2O, heating on steam bath if necessary. Apply as little heat as possible to minimize inversion of sucrose. Cool, dil. to vol., mix thoroly by shaking, and use aliquots for the various detns. If insol. material is present, mix thoroly and filter before taking aliquots.

(**c**) *Fresh fruits, dried fruits, preserves, jams, and marmalades.*—Pulp by passing thru food chopper, or by use of soil dispersion mixer, Hobart mixer, or other suitable mech. mixing app., or by grinding in large mortar, and mixing thoroly, completing operation as quickly as possible to avoid loss of moisture. With dried fruits, pass sample thru food chopper 3 times, mixing thoroly after each grinding. Set burrs or blades of food chopper as close as possible without crushing seeds. Grind entire contents of No. 10 or smaller container. Mix contents of larger containers thoroly by stirring and remove portion for grinding. With stone fruits, remove pits and det. their proportion in weighed sample.

Prep. soln by weighing into 1.5–2 L beaker 300 g fresh fruit, or equiv. of dried fruit, preserves, jams, and marmalades, well pulped and mixed in blender or other suitable type of mech. grinder; add ca 800 mL H_2O; and boil 1 hr, replacing at intervals H_2O lost by evapn. Transfer to 2 L vol. flask, cool, dil. to vol., and filter. With unsweetened fruit, ashing is facilitated by addn of sugar before boiling; therefore weigh 150 g fruit, add 150 g sugar and 800 mL H_2O, and proceed as above.

(**d**) *Canned fruits.—See* **32.001–32.002**. Carefully invert by hand all fruits having cups or cavities if they fall on sieve with cups or cavities up. Cups or cavities in soft products may be drained by tilting sieve, but no other handling of these products while draining is permissible. Examination of sirup in which fruits are preserved is often enough. Sep. liquor by draining, **32.002**, and treat as in (**a**).

Apparent Viscosity (Consistency) (*6*)—Official Final Action

(Applicable to fruit nectars and fruit juice products)

22.009 ***Apparatus***

Capillary viscometer.—See Fig. **22:02**. *A*, Lucite tube chamber; *B*, inner tube, ground 120° included angle; *C*, Lucite plug, 60° included angle; *D* Tygon packing gland, turned 60° included angle (both ends); *E*, brass outer tube, ground 60° for packing gland nut; *F*, brass tube, chrome plated; *G*, inner tube, precision Pyrex glass, id 3±0.01 mm; *H*, Tygon sleeve. Scribe calibration line around outside of reservoir at level reached by H_2O in 13 sec under conditions specified in **22.010**. (Available from S. M. I. Inc., 800 University Ave, Berkeley, CA 94710, Cat. No. 8500.)

22.010 ***Calibration***

Add H_2O to tube at 24±2° and establish steady flow. Stop flow by placing finger over end of capillary tube. Completely fill tube to overflow point and level off with spatula or by sighting across top of tube. Remove finger from tube and immediately begin timing. Time required for top of meniscus to reach calibration line must be 13.0±0.2 sec.

22.011 ***Determination***

Clean and dry app. and maintain at 24±0.5° during detn. Adjust sample to 24±0.5° and mix thoroly without incorporating air bubbles. Add sample to tube and let flow until steady flow is obtained. Place finger over end of capillary tube to stop flow. Fill tube almost full and check for air bubbles; if air bubbles occur, remove by gently stirring with stirring rod or thermometer (check temp. at this point). Fill to overflow point and level off as in **22.010**. Remove finger from tube and immediately begin timing. Record time to nearest 0.1 sec for top of meniscus to reach calibration line.

Obtain ≥2 readings on each sample, mixing sample before

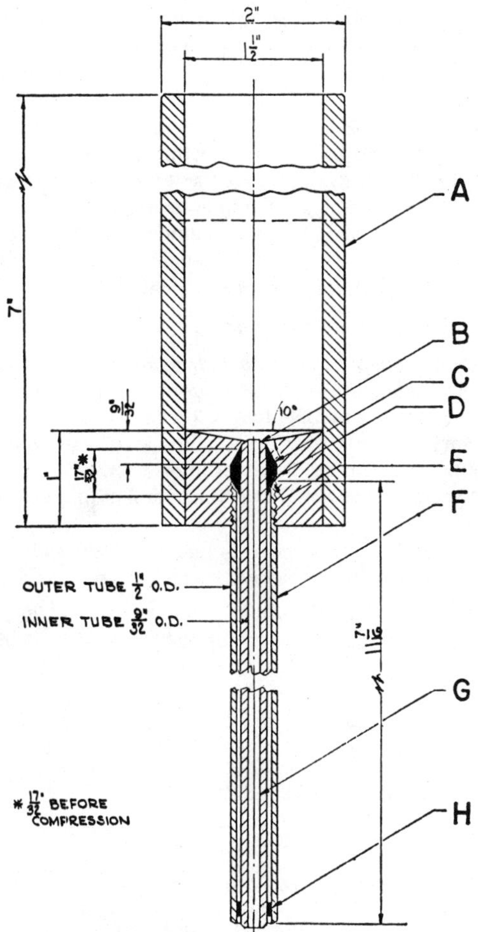

FIG. 22:02—Capillary viscometer

each detn. Rinse viscometer with H_2O between each reading of viscous samples (>30 sec flow time). (Do not let product dry in app. or let app. become greasy or develop air leak at packing seal of capillary tube.) Remove H_2O in capillary tube by letting sample flow thru before making detn. Check calibration at frequent intervals.

22.012 Alcohol—Official Final Action

Det. alcohol in 50 g original material as in **11.005**.

22.013 Moisture in Dried Fruits (7)—Official Final Action

Spread 5–10 g prepd sample, **22.008(c)**, as evenly as possible over bottom of metal dish ca 8.5 cm diam. provided with tight-fit cover, weigh, and dry 6 hr at 70±1° under pressure ≤100 mm Hg (13.3 kPa). (Metal dish must be in direct contact with metal shelf of oven.) During drying, admit to oven slow current of air (ca 2 bubbles/sec) dried by passing thru H_2SO_4. Replace cover, cool dish in desiccator, and weigh. Disregard any temporary drop in oven temp. during early part of drying period owing to rapid evapn of H_2O.

With raisins, and other fruit rich in sugar, use ca 5 g sample and dry and weigh in dish with ca 2 g finely divided asbestos. (*Caution: See* **51.086**.) Moisten with hot H_2O, mix sample and asbestos thoroly, evap. barely to dryness on steam bath, and complete drying as above.

Duplicate detns should agree within 0.2%.

Moisture in Prunes and Raisins—Official First Action

Alternative Method (8)

22.014 ***Apparatus***

Dried fruit moisture tester meter.—Type A series (DFA of California, PO Box 270A, Santa Clara, CA 95052); *see* Fig. **22:03** for elec. circuit.

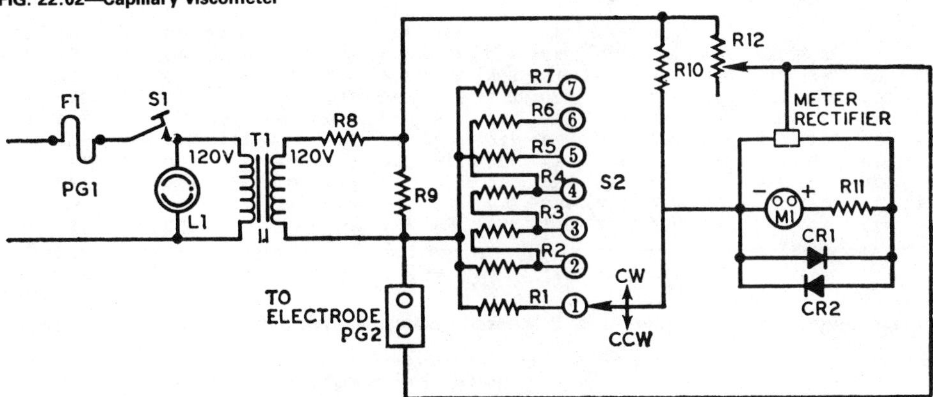

FIG. 22:03—Electrical circuit diagram for dried fruit moisture tester

Explanation:

Item	Item	Value	Toler-ance, %	Power Rating, w
F1—Fuse 3AG 2A, 125 v	R1	10K	1	1
S1—Push-button switch	R2	200K	1	½
L1—Neon light	R3	1K	1	1
T1—Isolating transformer 1–1, 120 v, 50 ma	R4	100K	1	½
PG1—Plug, 120 v	R5	40K	1	½
PG2—Plug to electrode	R6	20K	1	½
M1—Microammeter rectifier, type 0–100 ma meter rectifier	R7, R10	3K	1	1
CR1—Rectifier F4 (5M2483)	R8	2.5K	—	10
CR2—Rectifier F4 (5M2483)	R9	5K	—	10
S2—2 Wafer 7-point tap switch	R11	1.5K	10	½
	R12	10K	±5	(wire-wound)

22.015 ***Determination***

Grind sample 3 times thru food chopper, using cutter with 16 teeth. If testing hot fruit from processor, cool fruit as follows: Mix ca 60 g chopped solid CO_2 with fruit and then grind mixt. 3 times before taking moisture reading. Pack ground sample into Bakelite cylinder with fingers, making certain that it is packed tightly around bottom electrode. Fill cylinder completely with tightly packed sample, and level.

Lower top electrode and press it into sample until top electrode lever is against stop. Insert thermometer into ground sample until thermometer bulb is ca halfway between electrodes.

Select correct table for type and condition of fruit being tested (Table **22:01**: natural or low moisture, tap 6 setting; Table **22:02**: processed, tap 3 setting). Set switch (S2) to number given on table selected.

Plug tester into 110 v ac outlet and put switch to "on". (Red light indicates current.) Keep push button down and turn dial so that meter needle moves toward 0. Adjust dial so that needle is at its lowest, or turning, point. After making fine adjustment of dial to meter 0 or turning point, read dial and then read thermometer.

22.016 ***Use of Tables***

Choose temp. column of appropriate table nearest to sample temp. Read down this column to figure closest to dial reading, then read across to "% Moisture" column.

22.017 ***Example***

Examination of processed raisin sample gave following data: dial setting 76 and temp. 74°F, on tap 3. Looking down 74° column (Table **22:02**), obtain 75.2 at 18.5% moisture and 78.4 at 19.0% moisture. Since reading is nearer to 18.5 than 19.0%, report sample as contg 18.5% moisture, or interpolate.

Total Solids—Official Final Action

22.018 ***Insoluble Matter Present***

Fresh and canned fruits, jams, marmalades, and preserves.—Accurately weigh, into large flat-bottom dish, 20 g pulped fresh fruit, or wt of fruit products that will give ≤3–4 g dry material. If necessary to secure thin layer of material, add few mL H_2O and mix thoroly. Dry at 70° under pressure ≤100 mm Hg (13.3 kPa) until consecutive weighings made at 2 hr intervals vary ≤3 mg.

22.019 ***Insoluble Matter Absent***

Fruit juices, jellies, and sirups.—Proceed as in **31.007**, **31.008**, **31.009**, **31.010**, or **31.011**, using sample prepd as in **22.008(a)** or **(b)**.

Table 22:01. Conductance-temperature Correlation for Natural or Low Moisture Raisins; Switch Setting, Tap 6

% Moisture	Conductance readings at temperature (°F):																							
	56	58	60	62	64	66	68	70	72	74	76	78	80	82	84	86	88	90	92	94	96	98	100	102
9.0																9.0	15.0	21.0	25.0	29.0	33.0	36.0	39.0	42.0
9.5													4.0	11.0	17.5	22.5	27.0	32.5	37.0	40.5	44.0	47.0	49.0	51.5
10.0									1.0	7.0	13.5	17.5	23.0	28.5	34.0	38.0	41.5	45.5	49.0	52.0	54.5	57.0	59.0	61.5
10.5							7.5	13.0	18.0	24.0	29.5	35.0	40.0	44.5	49.0	51.5	54.0	57.0	60.0	62.0	64.0	66.0	68.0	70.0
11.0					8.5	16.0	22.5	28.0	34.0	39.0	44.0	48.5	53.0	56.0	59.0	61.5	64.0	66.0	68.5	70.5	72.5	73.8	75.3	76.8
11.5			9.0	18.0	26.0	31.0	36.0	42.0	47.5	51.5	55.5	58.7	62.5	64.7	67.5	69.5	71.0	73.0	75.0	76.5	78.3	79.6	81.0	82.5
12.0			23.5	30.5	37.5	42.5	47.0	52.0	56.5	60.0	63.3	66.5	69.0	71.0	73.0	74.5	76.0	78.0	79.7	81.0	82.0	83.8	85.2	86.5
12.5	16.5	27.0	34.5	40.0	46.0	50.5	55.0	59.0	63.0	65.8	68.6	71.0	73.3	75.0	76.6	78.0	79.7	81.3	82.6	84.0	85.4	86.7	88.0	89.3
13.0	30.5	37.2	42.5	48.0	52.3	56.5	60.5	64.3	67.7	70.0	72.5	74.8	76.7	78.3	79.7	81.2	82.6	83.8	85.2	86.5	87.8	89.2	90.5	91.3
13.5	40.0	45.0	49.7	54.0	58.0	61.5	65.0	68.5	71.3	73.4	75.4	77.5	79.4	80.7	82.0	83.5	85.0	86.2	87.3	88.5	89.8	91.0	92.2	93.0
14.0	48.3	52.5	56.5	60.0	63.0	66.0	69.2	72.0	74.5	76.4	78.0	80.0	81.7	83.0	84.4	85.6	87.0	88.0	89.3	90.3	91.5	92.6	93.8	94.6
14.5	55.3	59.0	62.3	65.0	67.6	70.4	72.7	75.0	77.0	78.7	80.4	82.0	83.7	85.0	86.2	87.3	88.7	89.7	90.8	91.8	93.0	94.0	95.0	95.8
15.0	61.6	64.5	67.7	70.8	72.4	74.3	76.0	78.0	79.7	81.1	82.6	84.0	85.6	86.7	87.9	89.1	90.3	91.4	92.5	93.5	94.5	95.5	96.4	97.0

Table 22:02. Conductance-temperature Correlation for Processed Raisins; Switch Setting, Tap 3

% Moisture	Conductance readings at temperature (°F):																							
	56	58	60	62	64	66	68	70	72	74	76	78	80	82	84	86	88	90	92	94	96	98	100	102
13.0											0.0	6.7	12.8	18.0	22.2	26.8	31.4	35.4	39.5	43.7	48.0	52.2	55.8	59.0
13.5										2.5	9.0	15.4	21.0	25.2	29.4	34.0	38.3	42.7	46.5	50.5	54.3	58.0	61.5	64.8
14.0									5.7	11.7	17.0	23.0	27.5	32.4	36.6	40.8	44.2	48.3	52.6	56.2	59.6	62.8	66.3	69.2
14.5							1.0	7.5	14.0	19.0	24.3	29.4	34.2	39.0	42.8	46.7	50.9	54.4	57.5	60.8	64.2	67.2	70.3	73.0
15.0						2.5	9.3	15.5	21.7	27.0	31.6	36.3	40.9	45.5	49.2	53.0	56.8	59.7	62.7	65.4	68.2	70.9	73.6	76.1
15.5					4.0	11.0	17.7	23.1	29.7	34.0	38.2	42.7	47.3	51.6	55.2	58.5	62.1	64.9	67.2	69.7	72.0	74.2	76.6	78.7
16.0					13.5	20.0	25.3	31.0	36.0	41.0	45.5	50.0	54.0	58.0	61.6	64.5	67.4	69.6	72.0	73.7	75.5	77.3	79.3	81.0
16.5			13.0	20.5	26.5	32.0	36.6	42.0	46.5	50.7	54.8	58.5	62.0	65.5	68.8	71.0	73.0	75.2	77.0	78.4	79.7	81.3	82.8	84.3
17.0	13.5	22.0	28.4	34.0	39.0	43.5	47.2	51.7	55.7	59.4	62.6	66.0	68.8	71.5	74.1	76.0	77.8	79.4	80.9	82.0	83.2	84.2	85.5	86.7
17.5	31.0	36.0	41.0	45.0	49.0	52.5	56.0	59.5	63.0	66.0	69.0	71.6	74.0	76.2	78.4	80.0	81.5	82.6	83.9	84.8	85.8	86.8	87.8	88.7
18.0	43.0	47.0	50.0	53.5	57.0	59.7	62.7	64.8	69.0	71.5	73.8	76.0	78.0	79.8	81.6	82.7	84.0	85.0	86.0	86.8	87.7	88.5	89.5	90.2
18.5	50.5	53.3	56.0	59.4	62.5	65.0	67.7	70.4	73.0	75.2	77.3	79.2	81.0	82.4	83.8	84.8	85.8	86.7	87.7	88.4	89.0	89.9	90.7	91.3
19.0	56.0	58.5	61.2	64.0	66.8	69.2	71.6	74.0	76.4	78.4	80.2	81.7	83.3	84.5	85.7	86.7	87.6	88.5	89.3	89.8	90.4	91.0	91.7	92.3
19.5	60.7	63.0	65.5	68.3	70.5	72.7	74.7	77.2	79.2	80.8	82.5	83.9	85.2	86.2	87.2	88.0	88.8	89.5	90.3	90.9	91.4	91.9	92.5	93.0
20.0	65.0	67.5	69.6	71.8	74.0	76.0	77.9	79.8	81.7	83.1	84.6	85.7	87.0	87.8	88.7	89.5	90.1	90.7	91.4	91.8	92.3	92.8	93.4	93.9
20.5	69.2	71.3	73.3	75.2	77.2	78.6	80.6	82.4	83.9	85.3	86.4	87.4	88.4	89.3	90.0	90.6	91.2	91.8	92.5	92.9	93.3	93.8	94.3	94.7

Water-Insoluble Solids (*9*)—Official First Action

22.020 ***Method I***

For use with buchner, prep. filtering medium consisting of either circular disk of absorbent cotton ca 80 mm diam., weighing ca 1.5 g, or coarse, qual. filter paper (7–15 cm diam., Whatman No. 4 or 41-H, or equiv.). For use with 60° funnel, prep. absorbent cotton circle ca 12.5 cm diam. weighing ca 2 g, or 12.5 cm filter paper. Wash filtering medium with hot H_2O, and dry overnight at 100–110° in open, flat-bottom Al dish of suitable size provided with tight-fit cover. Cool closed dish and contents 1 hr in desiccator and weigh to nearest mg.

Weigh 25 or 50 g well mixed sample, **22.008(c)**, to nearest 10 mg, transfer to 400 mL beaker, dil. to ca 200 mL mark with hot H_2O, mix, and boil gently 15–20 min, occasionally replacing H_2O lost by evapn. Filter by gravity thru the prepd cotton or paper, and keep H_2O-insol. solids from forming closely adhering mat on surface of filtering medium by frequent addns of portions of sample. Wash with ca 800 mL hot H_2O, loosening H_2O-insol. solids from filter with each addn. Remove excess H_2O from cotton by gently squeezing it on 60° funnel, or by application of suction on buchner. Transfer to original weighing dish, and wipe off any remaining portions of H_2O-insol. solids on filter or funnel with previously weighed portion of prepd filtering medium. Dry overnight at 100–110°, cool 1 hr in desiccator, and weigh.

Method II (Rapid Method)

22.021 ***Apparatus***

(**a**) *Weighing dishes.*—Al or tinned Fe, 13 cm (5.25") diam. × 1.9 cm (0.75") high, with tight-fit cover (16 mm film holders obtainable from camera stores; Al dishes weigh ca 40 g, tinned Fe ca 85–90 g).

(**b**) *Rapid drying device.*—Moisture Teller, model 276, manufactured by Harry W. Dietert Co., 9330 Roselawn Ave, Detroit, MI 48204, or forced-draft drying oven set at 100°.

22.022 ***Determination***

Fit 15 cm filter paper (Whatman No. 4 or 41-H, or equiv.) into 12.5 cm buchner, add half of 7 cm paper (used to wipe any insol. solids from buchner after filtering and washing sample), wash with boiling H_2O, apply suction, and dry, using Moisture Teller and pan or forced-draft oven. Transfer to weighing dish, cool, and weigh, using tare consisting of weighing dish and paper. (Approx. time of drying, 5 min at 102±3°.)

Weigh 25 or 50 g well mixed sample (high-speed blender) to nearest 10 mg, transfer with hot H_2O to 400 mL beaker, adjust to ca 200 mL with hot H_2O, stir, and boil gently few min. Place prepd filter in buchner; attach to suction flask, but do not attach flask to suction line. Pour 50–100 mL boiling H_2O on filter, and when steady flow of H_2O passes thru filter, transfer sample to filter, portionwise if necessary. Wash insol. solids with boiling H_2O and collect 850–900 mL filtrate. During washings, keep solids from forming tight mat on surface by portionwise addns of boiling H_2O. When washing is finished, apply suction and aspirate thoroly. Transfer paper and H_2O-insol. solids to Moisture Teller pan, using extra piece of weighed filter paper to complete transfer, and dry at 102±3° ca 15 min, depending on amt of H_2O-insol. solids. After drying, transfer sample to weighing dish, cool in desiccator, and weigh. (Wt H_2O-insol. solids/wt sample) × 100 = % H_2O-insol. solids.

22.023 Seeds in Berry Fruits (*10*)—Official First Action

Prep. sample by mixing with blender, **22.008(c)**. Transfer 50±0.01 g with ca 500 mL hot H_2O to blender and mix 1–2 min. Transfer mixt. to No. 20 screen and use addnl hot H_2O to transfer and wash bare seeds (hot H_2O from tap is suitable). Transfer seeds on screen to Al dish, previously weighed, with tight-fit cover (readily accomplished by transferring to 7 cm Whatman No. 4 paper previously dried and weighed with the dish, in 12.5 cm buchner). Dry at 100° in forced-draft oven 30 min and weigh. To det. av. wt of one seed, count out and weigh sep. several 100-unit lots. Report av. wt of one seed in mg and number of seeds/100 g sample. After detn of H_2O-insol. solids of sample, calc. and report % of total due to bare seeds and % due to nonseed H_2O-insol. solids.

Soluble Solids by Refractometer—Official First Action

22.024 Fresh and Canned Fruits, Fruit Jellies, Marmalades, and Preserves (*11*)

(Insol. matter present)

Proceed as in **31.011**. % sol. solids = % solids detd by refractometer × (100 − b)/100, where b = % H_2O-insol. solids.

Note: U.S. Federal stds for frozen fruits, canned fruits, fruit jellies, and preserves make no correction for H_2O-insol. solids, invert sugar, or other substances.

22.025 Frozen Concentrate for Lemonade (*12*)

Proceed as in **22.024**. Correct values for sucrose by refractometer for acidity by adding (− 0.027 + 0.125 x) to sucrose value, where x = % anhyd. citric acid in sample as detd in **22.060** or **22.061**.

22.026 Ash (*13*)—Official Final Action

Proceed as in **31.012** or **31.013**, ashing at ≤525°, using 25 g juices, fresh fruits, or canned fruits, and 10 g jellies, sirups, preserves, jams, marmalades, or dried fruits.

If ash of H_2O-sol. portion only is desired, evap. 100 mL prepd soln, **22.008(b)** or (**c**), to dryness on steam bath. Proceed as in **31.012** or **31.013**.

22.027 Alkalinity of Ash—Official Final Action

Introduce measured excess of 0.1*N* HCl into Pt dish contg ash obtained in **22.026**, warm on steam bath, cool, add few drops Me orange, and titr. excess acid with 0.1*N* NaOH. Report as alky, number of mL 0.1*N* acid required to neutze ash from 100 g sample, and as alky number, number of mL 1*N* acid required to neutze 1 g ash. Reserve soln for detn of S in ash.

Potassium (*14*)—Official Final Action

22.028 ***Ashing of Sample***

(**a**) *Slow ashing.*—Ash 15–30 g sample (representing ca 15 g fruit) as in **22.026**.

★(**b**) *Rapid ashing.*★—*See* **20.019(b)**, 10th ed.

★ *Chloroplatinate Methods* ★

22.029 ***Reagents***

(**a**) *Ammonium chloride soln.*—Dissolve 100 g NH_4Cl in 500 mL H_2O, add 5–10 g pulverized K_2PtCl_6, and shake at intervals 6–8 hr. Let mixt. settle overnight and filter. (Residue may be used to prep. fresh supply.)

(**b**) *Chloroplatinic acid soln.*—Dissolve 4.4 g H_2PtCl_6 (contains 2.1 g Pt) in H_2O and dil. to 100 mL. 1 mL of this soln ppts ca 10 mg K_2O. Use ca 20% excess.

★ Surplus method—*see* inside front cover.

22.030 ***Preparation of Ash Solution***

Wet down ash, **22.028**, with 5–10 mL H_2O, cover dish with watch glass, and acidify with slight excess of HCl (1+4) (2–3 mL).

22.031 ***Determination***

(**a**) *Gravimetric chloroplatinate method.*—Rinse watch glass into dish and evap. ash soln to dryness on steam bath. Add 5 drops HCl (1+1) to residue. Add 5–10 mL hot H_2O and rub sides and bottom of container with policeman. Transfer ash soln to 250 mL beaker with 50–75 mL hot H_2O, add few glass beads, and heat to bp. Make distinctly alk. with NH_4OH and add enough satd $(NH_4)_2C_2O_4$ soln for complete pptn (usually $\leq$1 mL), cover beaker, and heat until ppt becomes granular enough to filter readily (incipient boiling 30 min usually suffices). Filter thru 5 or 7 cm fine texture paper into large Pt dish and wash thoroly with hot H_2O (5–6 fillings of filter usually suffice).

Evap. soln nearly to dryness on steam bath and add 1 mL H_2SO_4 (1+1). Rotate dish so that H_2SO_4 comes in contact with all residue, adding little H_2O if necessary. Return dish to steam bath and evap. all H_2O possible at that temp. Heat dish, preferably on hot plate, at ca 150° until bubbling caused by decomposition of oxalates ceases, and gradually increase temp. until H_2SO_4 evaps. (When properly controlled, this treatment takes 45–90 min.) Cautiously heat sample over burner, being careful to avoid loss due to sputtering during decomposition of NH_4 compds. Finally heat dish to redness to remove traces of NH_4 compds and complete ignition. Cool, and add 5 drops HCl (1+1) to residue.

Transfer ash soln to 100–200 mL r-b porcelain dish, using ca 50 mL hot H_2O. Add small excess H_2PtCl_6 soln. Place mixt. on steam bath and rotate dish from time to time to prevent ppt from baking on side of dish, and evap. to paste. (It is advisable to start evapn with several steam bath rings removed, and as concn progresses, to replace rings so that heat is applied only to surface of dish covered by liq.) Avoid exposure to NH_3 fumes at all times.

Add ca 50 mL 90% alcohol to dish and transfer to gooch with asbestos mat, or 30 mL gooch with medium porosity fritted disk. Wash 8 or 10 times with 20 mL portions 90% alcohol; then 5 or 6 times with 10 mL portions NH_4Cl soln, (**a**). Again wash thoroly 6 or 8 times with 20 mL portions 90% alcohol.

Dry ca 30 min in 100° oven, cool, and weigh. Wash the K_2PtCl_6 thru gooch with hot H_2O, using slight suction; then wash gooch with alcohol, dry, cool, and weigh. Difference in wt × 0.1938 = K_2O. Report results as mg/100 g original sample.

(**b**) *Short gravimetric chloroplatinate method.*— Proceed as in (**a**), pars. 3–5, using ash soln, **22.030**, from ash, **22.028**(**a**).

★(**c**) *Short volumetric chloroplatinate method.*★—*See* **22.022**(**c**), 10th ed.

★(**d**) *Long volumetric chloroplatinate method.*★—*See* **22.022**(**d**), 10th ed.

22.032 ★ Gravimetric Cobaltinitrite Method ★

See **22.026–22.027**, 11th ed.

22.033 ***Rapid Flame Photometric Method(15)***
Official Final Action

(*Caution: See* **51.007**.)

Prep. sample soln as in **22.008**. Dil., if necessary, to reduce K concn to range covered by flame photometer (preferably 40–80 ppm). Aspirate sample soln (dild or undild) directly into flame.

Prep. stds as in **11.024**(**a**) except cover range 10–100 ppm K in 10 ppm steps. Det. %*T* for stds or follow instructions of manufacturer, making check detns as necessary. If internal std instrument is used, add appropriate amt of LiCl to both std and sample solns.

From %*T* of sample and std curve, det. ppm K. Report as mg K_2O/100 g sample. K × 1.2046 = K_2O.

Sodium (*16*)—Official Final Action

(*Caution: See* **51.007**.)

22.034 ***Reagents and Apparatus***

(**a**) *Sodium std solns.*—Dry reagent grade NaCl at 100° overnight and dil. 2.5422 g to 1 L with H_2O. (Soln contains 1000 ppm Na.) Dil. 10 mL to 100 mL, and further dil. 1, 2, 4, 6, 8, and 10 mL dild soln to 100 mL to make std solns contg, resp., 1, 2, 4, 6, 8, and 10 ppm Na. Store in clean, dry polyethylene bottles.

(**b**) *Flame spectrophotometer.*—*See* **11.024**(**b**).

22.035 ***Determination***

Prep. sample soln as in **22.008**. Dil., if necessary, to reduce Na concn to range covered by flame photometer (preferably 4–10 ppm Na). Aspirate sample soln (dild or undild) directly into flame.

Det. %*T* for stds and plot curve of %*T* against ppm Na. Det. %*T* for sample and use std curve to det. ppm Na in sample or follow instructions of manufacturer, making check detns as necessary. If internal std instrument is used, add appropriate amt of LiCl to both std and sample solns.

Report as mg Na_2O/100 g sample. Na × 1.3480 = Na_2O.

22.036 ★ Manganese (*17*)—Official First Action ★

(*Caution: See* **51.047** and **51.081**.)

See **20.026–20.027**, 10th ed.

★ Calcium (*18*)—Official First Action ★

22.037 ***Double Precipitation Method***

See **20.028**, 10th ed.

22.038 ***Single Precipitation Method***

See **20.029**, 10th ed.

22.039 ★ Magnesium (*19*)—Official First Action ★

See **20.030**, 10th ed.

Phosphorus

22.040 ★ *Volumetric Method (20)* ★
Official Final Action

(Not applicable to acid fruit products stored for appreciable time in tin cans)

Pptn as phosphomolybdate, soln in excess std NaOH, and back titrn of excess alkali (*see* **14.029**). *See* **22.039–22.040**, 12th ed.

22.041 ★ *Colorimetric Method (21)* ★

See **22.037–22.039**, 11th ed.

★ Surplus method—*see* inside front cover.

Spectrophotometric Molybdovanadate Method (22)
Official First Action

(Do not clean glassware with P-contg detergents.)

22.042 ***Apparatus and Reagents***

(**a**) *Spectrophotometer.*—Prism or grating, with matched 1 cm cells.

(**b**) *Molybdovanadate reagent.*—Dissolve 60 g NH_4 molybdate.$4H_2O$ in 900 mL hot H_2O, cool, and dil. to 1 L. Dissolve 1.5 g NH_4 metavanadate in 690 mL hot H_2O, add 300 mL HNO_3, cool, and dil. to 1 L. Gradually add molybdate soln to vanadate soln with stirring. Store at room temp. in polyethylene or g-s Pyrex bottle. (Reagent is stable indefinitely in polyethylene, but in Pyrex, ppt gradually forms after several months. Discard reagent if ppt forms.)

(**c**) *Phosphate std solns.*—(*1*) *Stock soln.*—0.5 mg P_2O_5/mL. Dissolve 0.2397 g pure (if assay <100% KH_2PO_4, 0.2397 g × 100/% KH_2PO_4 = correct wt) and dried (2 hr at 105°) primary std KH_2PO_4 in H_2O and dil. to 250 mL. (*2*) *Working solns.*—Dil. 0, 5, 10, 15, 20, 25, 30, and 35 mL stock soln to 500 mL to obtain 0.00, 0.05, 0.10, 0.15, 0.20, 0.25, 0.30, and 0.35 mg P_2O_5/10 mL, resp.

22.043 ***Preparation of Standard Curve***

(*Caution: See* **51.018** and **51.026**.)

Pipet 10 mL of each working std soln into 25 mL erlenmeyers and stopper immediately to prevent evapn. As rapidly as possible for entire series, pipet 5 mL molybdovanadate reagent into each, stopper, and mix. Let stand 10 min for color development and read *A* of each soln within 1 hr.

Fill 4 matched cells with 0.00 mg std. Set spectrophtr at 400 nm and adjust to 0 *A* with 1 cell. Read each cell *A* against this cell. Use cell with lowest *A* with 0.00 mg std in future measurements. If *A* of 0.00 mg std in other cells are >0.001 against this std in ref. cell, subtract these *A* from subsequent readings. Det. *A* of each std with instrument adjusted to 0 *A* for 0.00 mg std. After every 3 detns, refill cell contg 0.00 mg std to avoid error due to evapn and temp. changes. Plot *A* against mg P_2O_5/10 mL (vol. working std soln).

(*Note:* Use Pyrex dropper to fill and empty cells. Do not remove cells from holder. Use dropper tube with greater capacity than cell to prevent liq. from entering bulb. Bulb should be just large enough that cell can be filled or emptied in one operation. Rinse cell with succeeding std or sample soln. Use different dropper to fill and empty ref. cell.)

22.044 ***Preparation of Sample***

Proceed as in **22.026**. (Add 1 teaspoon sucrose to samples low in sugar to speed ashing.) Dissolve ash in 10 mL HCl (1+3) and evap. to dryness on steam bath. Dissolve residue in 10 mL HCl (1+9) on steam bath and transfer to 100 mL vol. flask. Cool, dil. to vol., and mix. Filter thru dry paper if any insol. matter is present. If ash has >3.5 mg P_2O_5, dil. to >100 mL or make secondary dilns so 10 mL aliquot contains <0.35 mg P_2O_5. (*See* Watt, B. K., and Merrill, A. L., *Composition of Foods,* USDA Handbook No. 8, p. 6–67, Superintendent of Documents, U.S. Government Printing Office, Washington, DC 20402, rev. Dec. 1963, for data on P content of fruit products and other foods.) If ash wt is not desired, use smaller sample aliquot to reduce drying and ashing time.

22.045 ***Determination***

Into sep. 25 mL erlenmeyers pipet 10 mL aliquots std solns contg 0.00 and 0.20 mg P_2O_5/10 mL. Develop color as for std curve. Adjust instrument to 0 *A* for 0.00 mg std and det. *A* of 0.20 mg std. (*A* of this std should be within ±1% of *A* of std curve; if not, prep. new std curve.) Develop color and det. *A* of sample ash solns concurrently with and in same manner as for std solns. Calc. as follows:

(**a**) *From std curve.*—mg P_2O_5/100 g sample = 100 × (mg P_2O_5/10 mL from std curve)/g sample in 10 mL ash soln.

(**b**) *From formula.*—mg P_2O_5/100 g sample = $A \times S \times 100/W$, where *A* refers to sample soln at 400 nm, *S* = slope of std curve = $(\Sigma r)/n$; Σr = sum of ratios of mg P_2O_5/10 mL to *A* of each std, and *n* = number of std solns used in calcns; and *W* = g sample in 10 mL ash soln.

Gravimetric Quinoline Molybdate Method
(22)—Official First Action

22.046 ***Reagent***

See **2.026**(**c**).

22.047 ***Preparation of Sample***

Prep. as in **22.044**, but transfer HCl (1+9) soln of residue to 500 mL erlenmeyer, filtering if any insol. matter is present. If sample ash has >25 mg P_2O_5 (*see* Watt and Merrill, **22.044**), dil. to 100 mL or other definite vol. and use aliquot contg <25 mg P_2O_5. Dil. soln to ca 100 mL with H_2O.

22.048 ***Determination***

Proceed as in **2.028**(**b**), except boil 3 min. Report results as mg P_2O_5/100 g.

22.049 ★ Sulfur in Ash (*23*)—Official Final Action ★

(For products contg a basic ash)

Gravimetric detn of pptd $BaSO_4$. *See* **22.050**, 12th ed.

22.050 ★ Total Sulfur (*24*)—Official First Action ★

(For sulfured products and for samples contg little ash or acidic ash)

Gravimetric detn of pptd $BaSO_4$. *See* **22.050**, 12th ed.

22.051 Total Chlorine (*25*)—Official First Action

See **3.071–3.074**.

22.052 ★ Alcohol Precipitate (*26*) ★ Official First Action

Gravimetric detn of alcohol ppt. *See* **22.052**, 12th ed.

22.053 ★ Pectic Acid (*27*)—Official First Action ★

Pptn of pectin with alcohol, soln in alkali, repptn with acid, and weighing. *See* **22.053**, 12th ed.

22.054 Protein—Official Final Action

Proceed as in **2.057**, using 5 g jelly or other fruit product contg large amt of sugar, or 10 g juice or fresh fruit, and larger amt of H_2SO_4 if necessary for complete digestion. % N × 6.25 = % protein.

Betaine (*28*)—Official First Action

(Applicable to orange juice)

22.055 ***Reagents***

(**a**) *Ammonia soln.*—2%. Dil. 140 mL NH_4OH to 2 L with H_2O.

(**b**) *Ammonium reineckate soln.*—2.5%. Shake 2.5 g in 75 mL

★ Surplus method—*see* inside front cover.

H_2O 30 min. Filter thru paper and dil. to 100.0 mL. Adjust pH to 1.0 with HCl and filter thru fine porosity glass crucible. Prep. fresh before betaine pptn. Do not use reagent contg ppt.

(**c**) *Acetone soln.*—70%. Dil. 70 mL to 100 mL with H_2O.

(**d**) *Aqueous ether.*—Add 1 mL H_2O to 140 mL ether.

(**e**) *Ion exchange resins.*—(*1*) *Amberlite IR-120 medium porosity* (*20–50 mesh, wet*).—Prep. 250 g in H form by treating with 2 bed vols 2*N* HCl (ca 500 mL). Soak 2 hr. Drain resin and wash with H_2O until neut. and Cl-free. (*2*) *Amberlite IRA-400* (*20–50 mesh, wet*). —Prep. 250 g in OH form by treating with 2 bed vols 2*N* NaOH (ca 500 mL). Drain and wash NaOH-free with H_2O. Mix with IRC-50 immediately for column II prepn. (*3*) *Amberlite IRC-50.*—Prep. 125 g in H form by treating with 2 bed vols 2*N* HCl. Drain and wash Cl-free with H_2O.

(**f**) *Betaine std soln.*—1 mg anhyd. betaine/mL. Weigh 0.2623 g betaine.HCl in 200 mL vol. flask and dil. to vol. with H_2O.

22.056 ***Preparation of Columns***

(**a**) *Column I.*—Use 18 mm id chromatgc tube with medium or coarse porosity fritted glass and with stopcock. Add aq. slurry Amberlite IR-120(H) to 12.5 cm bed depth (wet resin). To regenerate resin, pour thru 100–200 mL 1*N* HCl and wash Cl-free with H_2O.

(**b**) *Column II.*—Intimately mix 2 vols Amberlite IRA-400(OH) with 1 vol IRC-50(H) and transfer to column as above to 7.5 cm bed depth. Resins have different densities, and excess H_2O causes undesirable sepn. Bed must be intimate mixt. Resin mixt. cannot be regenerated. Use for 2 detns only.

22.057 ***Preparation of Sample***

Prep. juice as in **22.008**(**a**).

22.058 ***Determination***

Add accurately measured amt prepd juice (10–20 mL) contg 5–7 mg betaine to small beaker. Dil. to ca 30 mL with H_2O and adjust to pH 3.0 with 0.1*N* HCl, using pH meter. Transfer to column I. Collect eluate at ca 3 mL/min. When liq. reaches top of resin, wash column with 200 mL H_2O or until carbohydrate-free. Discard eluate and wash soln. Elute betaine by washing column with ≥150 mL 2% NH_4OH, ensuring eluate is alk. Follow with 100 mL H_2O. Reduce eluate to ca 25 mL by boiling. Cool, adjust to pH 7.0 with 0.1*N* HCl, and transfer to Column II. (Reduce vol. in erlenmeyer and then transfer to small beaker for pH adjustment.)

Collect eluate at 1 mL/min. When liq. reaches top of resin bed, wash with 50 mL H_2O. Conc. combined eluates and washings to 15–20 mL, cool, and adjust to pH 1.0 with 1*N* HCl. Cool to 0±3° and gradually add, with stirring, 20 mL 2.5% NH_4 reineckate, adjusted to pH 1.0 and cooled to 0±3°. Let stand 3 hr at 0±3°. Filter while cold thru medium porosity 60 mL fritted glass crucible with vac. Transfer ppt with small amts cold filtrate. Wash ppt with three 5 mL portions aq. ether. Dissolve ppt in 10 mL 70% acetone and transfer to 25 mL vol. flask. Dil. to vol. with 70% acetone. Det. *A* at 525 nm on spectrophtr, using 1 cm cell, against 70% acetone as ref. (Make readings within 4 hr.) Det. amt betaine from std curve.

22.059 ***Preparation of Standard Curve***

Transfer 2.5, 5.0, 7.5, 10.0, 12.5, and 15.0 mL betaine std soln to beakers, using 10 mL buret. Add H_2O to ca 20 mL and proceed as in **22.058**, beginning, ". . . adjust to pH 1.0 with 1*N* HCl."

Plot of mg anhyd. betaine/mL against *A* should be straight line.

Titratable Acidity (*29*)—Official Final Action

22.060 ***Indicator Method***

(**a**) *Colorless or slightly colored solns.*—Dil. to ca 250 mL, with neutzd or recently boiled H_2O, 10 g prepd juice, **22.008**(**a**), or 25 mL prepd soln, **22.008**(**b**) or (**c**). Titr. with 0.1*N* alkali, using 0.3 mL phthln for each 100 mL soln being titrd, to pink persisting 30 sec. Report as mL 0.1*N* alkali/100 g or 100 mL original material.

(**b**) *Highly colored solns.*—Dil. sample of known wt with neutzd H_2O and titr. to just before end point with 0.1*N* alkali, using 0.3 mL phthln for each 100 mL soln being titrd. Transfer measured vol. (2 or 3 mL) of soln into ca 20 mL neut. H_2O in small beaker. (In this extra diln, color of fruit juice becomes so pale that phthln color is easily seen.) If test shows that end point is not reached, pour extra dild portion back into original soln, add more alkali, and continue titrn to end point. By comparing dilns in small beakers, differences produced by few drops 0.1*N* alkali can be easily observed.

Glass Electrode Method—Official First Action

22.061 ***Determination***

Before use, check app. with std buffer solns, **50.007** and Table **50:02**. Rinse glass electrode in H_2O several times until reading is ca pH 6. Immerse electrodes in sample contained in beaker. (Sample should titr. 10–50 mL 0.1*N* NaOH and be contained in initial vol. of 100–200 mL.) Stir moderately. Add alkali quite rapidly until near pH 6. Then add alkali slowly to pH 7. After pH 7 is reached, finish titrn by adding 0.1*N* alkali 4 drops at time, and record total vol. and pH reading after each addn. (Add whole drops, so that fraction of drop does not remain on buret tip.) Continue titrn ≥4 drops beyond pH 8.1, and interpolate data for titrn corresponding to pH 8.1. pH values used for interpolation should lie in range 8.10±0.2.

Notes: (1) Always keep glass electrode covered with H_2O when not in use.

(2) If strongly acid cleaning solns are used, electrode requires several hr to come to equilibrium on standing in H_2O.

(3) If electrode and stirrer are wiped lightly with piece of filter paper before insertion into std buffer, same soln may be used for several checks on instrument.

22.062 Volatile Acidity—Official Final Action

Dissolve 10 g sample, dil. to 25 mL, and steam distil as in **11.040**. 1 mL 0.1*N* alkali = 0.0060 g HOAc.

Total Tartaric Acid (*30*)

22.063 ★ Bitartrate Method—Official Final Action ★

Removal of pectin with alcohol, pptn of org. acids as Pb salts, removal of Pb with H_2S, and pptn of K bitartrate which is titrd with alkali. *See* **22.063–22.065**, 12th ed.

Citric Acid

22.064 ★ *Pentabromacetone Method* (*31*) ★ Official Final Action

Removal of pectin with alcohol, pptn of org. acids as Pb salts, removal of Pb with H_2S, and oxidn of citric acid with $KMnO_4$ in presence of bromide to insol. pentabromacetone which is detd gravimetrically. *See* **22.066–22.069**, 12th ed.

★ Surplus method—*see* inside front cover.

22.065 ★ Total Malic Acid (Laevo- and Inactive) (*32*) ★ Official First Action

(Either isocitric acid or tartaric acid or both may be present.)

Removal of pectin with alcohol, pptn of org. acids as Pb salts, removal of Pb with H_2S, sepn of liberated acids by silica gel chromatography, and titrn of malic acid fraction with alkali. *See* **22.070–22.073**, 12th ed.

Citric and Isocitric Acids

22.066 ★ *Chromatographic Method (33)* ★ *Official First Action*

Org. acids pptd as Pb salts, liberated with H_2SO_4, and incorporated into silica gel column. Citric acid fraction is titrd to det. total citric acid. Normal citric acid is detd by volumetric pentabromacetone method and isocitric acid is detd by difference. *See* **22.074–22.077**, 12th ed.

Laevo-Malic Acid

22.067 ★ *Method I (34)—Official First Action* ★

Removal of pectin with alcohol, pptn of org. acids as Pb salts, removal of Pb with H_2S and tartaric acid as K bitartrate, repptn or org. acids as Pb salts, removal of Pb with H_2S, and detn of laevo-malic acid polariscopically as the uranyl complex. *See* **22.078–22.080**, 12th ed.

22.068 ★ *Method II (35)—Official First Action* ★

(Not applicable in presence of isocitric acid—blackberry)

Caution: See **51.083** and **51.084**.)

Laevo-malic acid is detd polariscopically as uranyl complex in filtrate from tartaric detn, **22.063★**, after decolorization with C. *See* **22.081**, 12th ed.

Method III (36)—Official First Action

(*Caution: See* **51.083** and **51.084**.)

22.069 ***Apparatus and Reagents***

(**a**) *Polarimeter.*—Accurate to 0.01°, with Na lamp.

(**b**) *Carbon.*—Activated, acid-washed (Darco G-60, or equiv.).

(**c**) *l-Malic acid.*—Calbiochem A Grade, or equiv. Must meet following purity test: Dissolve 0.5 g (−)malic acid in ca 50 mL H_2O, adjust pH to 5.5 with 1*N* NaOH, and dil. to 100 mL with H_2O. To ca 35 mL, add 1.5 g uranyl acetate.$2H_2O$ and let stand in dark 30 min. Filter, and read optical rotation in 200 mm tube. Optical rotation of $\alpha = -4.88°$ to $-4.84°$ should be obtained.

(**d**) *l-Malic acid std solns.*—(*1*) *Stock soln.*—10 mg/ mL. Place 1.0 g *l*-malic acid and 4.0 g citric acid in 150 mL beaker, add ca 50 mL H_2O, and adjust to pH 5.5 with 50% NaOH soln, using pH meter and mag. stirrer. Quant. transfer to 100 mL vol. flask and dil. to vol. with H_2O. (*2*) *Working solns.*—1, 2, and 3 mg/mL. Pipet 10, 20, and 30 mL stock soln to sep. 100 mL vol. flasks and dil. to vol. with H_2O.

22.070 ***Preparation of Standard Curve***

Det. optical rotation (α_1) of each std soln in 200 mm polarimeter tube. To ca 35 mL of each std soln in 50 mL erlenmeyer, add 1.5 g uranyl acetate.$2H_2O$. Keep in dark 30 min and swirl occasionally. Filter and det. optical rotation (α_u) of clear uranyl malate complex in 200 mm polarimeter tube. Plot mg *l*-malic acid/100 mL against difference in rotation ($\alpha = \alpha_u - \alpha_1$).

★ Surplus method—*see* inside front cover.

22.071 ***Preparation of Sample***

(**a**) *Fruit juices.*—Weigh 62.5 g into 250 mL vol. flask. Add 0.1 g KOAc and 100 mL alcohol, and mix. Dil. to vol. with alcohol, mix, and let stand 1 hr. Filter thru rapid paper.

(**b**) *Preserves and high-sugar content products containing pieces of fruit.*—Comminute, and weigh 62.5 g into 250 mL beaker. Add 0.1 g KOAc, 30 mL H_2O, and 100 mL alcohol, mix, and transfer quant. to 250 mL vol. flask, using alcohol. Dil. to vol. with alcohol, mix, and let stand 1 hr. Filter thru rapid paper.

(**c**) *Fruit.*—Comminute, and weigh 62.5 g into 250 mL beaker. Proceed as in (**b**) except omit addn of 30 mL H_2O.

(**d**) *Grape juice.*—Weigh 125 g into 500 mL vol. flask, add 1.0 mL satd KOAc soln and 200 mL alcohol, and mix. Dil. to vol. with alcohol, mix, and let stand overnight. Filter thru Whatman No. 40 paper, or equiv.

(**e**) *Grape preserves and other high-sugar content grape products.*—Comminute, and weigh 125 g into 500 mL beaker. Add 1.0 mL satd KOAc soln, 50 mL H_2O, and 200 mL alcohol. Mix and transfer quant. to 500 mL vol. flask with alcohol. Dil. to vol. with alcohol, mix, and let stand overnight. Filter thru Whatman No. 40 paper, or equiv.

(**f**) *Grapes.*—Comminute, and weigh 125 g into 500 mL beaker. Proceed as in (**e**) except omit addn of 50 mL H_2O.

22.072 ***Determination***

Transfer 200 mL aliquot filtrate to 250 mL (8 oz) wide mouth bottle, 5.7 cm od × 13 cm high (2.25 × 5″). Add mag. stirring bar and 30 mL absolute alcohol. Potentiometrically titr. 10 mL remaining filtrate to pH 8.4, using 0.1*N* NaOH. Calc. mL NaOH necessary to neutze the 200 mL aliquot. Add to bottle 0.6 mL satd $Pb(OAc)_2$ soln for each mL 1*N* NaOH calcd to neutze 200 mL aliquot. Stir 10 min with mag. stirrer and centrf. 6 min at 1500 rpm. Test supernate for complete pptn with few drops satd $Pb(OAc)_2$ soln. Decant and wash ppt by stirring 5 min with 200 mL alcohol. (Use 85% alcohol with grapes and grape products.) Centrf. 5 min, decant, add 25 mL H_2O to ppt, and mix well to slurry. Use pH meter and adjust pH to 1.5 with H_2SO_4 (1+9). Remove $PbSO_4$ by vac. filtration on coarse porosity 60 mL fritted glass crucible contg asbestos pad. Wash ppt with 10 mL portions H_2O and combine washings with filtrate in 150 mL graduated beaker. Total vol. should be <90 mL. Adjust pH to 5.5 with 50% NaOH, using pH meter. Transfer quant. to 100 mL vol. flask and dil. to vol. with H_2O. Add ca 6 g C and mix thoroly. Let stand 30 min and filter thru fine paper. Filtrate must be colorless. Det. optical rotation (α_1) on this filtrate, using 200 mm tube. To ca 35 mL filtrate in 50 mL erlenmeyer add 1.5 g uranyl acetate.$2H_2O$ and keep in dark 30 min with occasional swirling. Filter and det. optical rotation (α_u) of clear soln of uranyl malate complex. Calc. mg *l*-malic acid/100 g sample by one of following:

(**a**) $(\alpha_x \times C \times 100)/(\alpha_s \times W)$, where α_x = difference in rotation of sample $= \alpha_{ux} - \alpha_{1x}$; α_s = difference in rotation of std $= \alpha_{us} - \alpha_{1s}$; C = mg *l*-malic acid in 100 mL std soln; and W = g sample in 100 mL final soln.

(**b**) $\alpha_x \times 2 \times$ (sum of mg *l*-malic acid in std curve solns)/(sum of number degrees in std curve solns).

(**c**) (mg *l*-malic acid/100 mL) (from std curve) × 2.

Inactive Malic Acid (*37*)—Official First Action

(As method is empirical, all directions must be rigidly followed, particularly with respect to dilns. Substitution of vol. flasks of capacities different from those specified is not permissible.)

22.073 ***Reagents***

(**a**) *Lead acetate soln.*—Dissolve 40 g $Pb(OAc)_2.3H_2O$ in H_2O, add 0.5 mL HOAc, and dil. to 100 mL.

(b) *Tribasic lead acetate std soln.*—Prep. soln from tribasic $Pb(OAc)_2$, **(c)**. To 5 g of the salt in 500 mL erlenmeyer add 200 mL H_2O and shake vigorously. Neutze 3 mL 1*N* H_2SO_4, dild with 200 mL H_2O, with the soln, using Me red as indicator. Note vol. Pb soln required. In detn use 2 mL in excess of this vol. (Soln should be freshly prepd.)

(c) *Tribasic lead acetate.*—Dissolve 82 g $Pb(OAc)_2.3H_2O$ in 170 mL H_2O. Prep 100 mL dil. NH_4OH soln contg 5.8 g NH_3 as detd by titrn (Me red). Heat solns to 60°, mix thoroly, and let stand overnight. Shake vigorously to break up ppt, and filter on buchner. Wash once with H_2O and suck dry, then twice with alcohol, and finally with ether. Let dry in air.

(d) *Potassium permanganate std soln.*—Dissolve 14.5214 g purest $KMnO_4$ in H_2O and dil. to 1 L. Stdze as follows: Pipet 50 mL oxalic acid soln, **(e)**, into 600 mL beaker and add 70 mL H_2O and 10 mL H_2SO_4 (1+1). Heat to 80°, immediately add $KMnO_4$ soln to faint pink, again heat to 80°, and finish titrn. 50 mL $KMnO_4$ soln should be equiv. to 50 mL oxalic acid soln.

(e) *Oxalic acid std soln.*—Dissolve 28.7556 g purest $H_2C_2O_4.2H_2O$ in H_2O and dil. to 1 L (1 mL = 5 mg malic acid (laevo or inactive)).

22.074 ***Preparation of Sample***

Subject 2 portions of sample to isolation, **22.075(a)**; use one portion for detn of laevo-malic acid (polarization), **22.075(b)**, and other for total malic acid, laevo + inactive (oxidn), **22.075(c)**. Choose amt of sample with titratable acidity ≤150 mg acid calcd as malic acid. Designate as *x* mL 1*N* alkali required to neutze amt of sample chosen. In no case should solids content be >20 g (200 mL sample soln of jam or jelly).

Adjust sample soln to ca 35 mL by evapn or addn of H_2O, pour into 250 mL vol. flask, rinse with 10 mL hot H_2O and then with alcohol, and dil. to vol. with alcohol. Shake, let stand until pectin seps, leaving clear liq. (overnight if necessary), and filter thru folded paper, draining thoroly and covering funnel with watch glass. Pipet 225 mL filtrate into centrf. bottle.

22.075 ***Determination***

(*Caution: See* **51.059.**)

(a) *Isolation of total malic acid.*—To soln in centrf. bottle add ca 25 mg *citric acid* and vol. of $Pb(OAc)_2$ soln, **(a)**, equal to *x* (*x* + 3 mL if saponification was made), shake vigorously 2 min, and centrf. Carefully decant supernate from pptd Pb salts and test with small amt of $Pb(OAc)_2$ soln. If ppt forms, return to centrf. bottle, add more $Pb(OAc)_2$, shake, and again centrf. If sediment lifts, repeat centrfg, increasing speed and time. Let ppt drain thoroly by inverting bottle several min.

Add 200 mL 80% alcohol, shake vigorously, and again centrf., decant, and drain. To Pb salts add ca 150 mL H_2O, shake vigorously, and pass in rapid stream of *H_2S to saturation.* Stopper bottle and shake ca 1 min. Transfer mixt. to 250 mL vol. flask with H_2O, dil. to vol., shake, and filter thru folded paper.

Pipet 225 mL filtrate into 600 mL beaker, and evap. to ca 100 mL to expel H_2S. Transfer to 250 mL vol. flask with H_2O. (Vol. in flask should be ca 200 mL.) Add 5 mL HOAc (1+9) and same amt of $Pb(OAc)_2$ soln previously used. Shake vigorously, dil. to vol. with H_2O, and filter.

Pass rapid stream of H_2S into *clear* filtrate *to saturation,* stopper flask, shake vigorously, and filter. Pipet 225 mL filtrate into 600 mL beaker, add ca 75 mg *tartaric acid,* and evap. over burner and gauze to ca 50 mL. Cool, neutze with 1*N potassium hydroxide* (phthln), and add 5 drops excess. Add 2 mL HOAc and transfer mixt. to 250 mL vol. flask with alcohol. Dil. to vol. with alcohol, shake, and pour into 500 mL erlenmeyer. Add small handful of glass beads and cool to 15°. Stopper flask, shake vigorously 10 min, and place in refrigerator 30 min. Again shake 10 min and filter thru folded paper.

Adjust *clear* filtrate to 20° and pipet 225 mL into centrf. bottle. Add $Pb(OAc)_2$ soln equal to *x* (*x* + 3 mL if saponification was made), shake vigorously ca 2 min, centrf., decant, and drain. Add 200 mL 80% alcohol, shake, centrf., decant, and drain.

Transfer Pb salts to 500 mL erlenmeyer with ca 175 mL H_2O. Add 3 mL 1*N* H_2SO_4 and heat to bp; add 1 mL HOAc (5+95) and vol. std tribasic $Pb(OAc)_2$ soln previously detd in **22.073(b)**. Boil mixt. 5 min, cool to room temp., transfer to 250 mL vol. flask with H_2O, dil. to vol., shake, and pour into 500 mL erlenmeyer. Add small handful of glass beads, cool to ca 15°, shake vigorously 5 min, and place in refrigerator 30 min. Again shake 5 min and filter thru folded paper. Sat. *clear* filtrate with H_2S, shake vigorously, and filter. Use one of the two portions for polarization and other for oxidn.

(b) *Polarization.*—Evap. 225 mL clear filtrate over burner and gauze to ca 10 mL, neutze with 1*N* KOH (phthln), make slightly acid with HOAc (5+95), and evap. to ca 5 mL. Transfer to 25–27.5 mL Giles flask with H_2O, dil. to 27.5 mL mark, shake, and pour into small g-s erlenmeyer. If Giles flask is not available, use 25 mL graduate, dil. to vol., and add 2.5 mL H_2O from buret. Add small handful of glass beads and 4 g powd *uranyl acetate,* shake vigorously 10 min, and filter. (As U-malic complex is light sensitive, wrap flask in towel while shaking and protect from light as much as possible during filtration and polarization.) Polarize in 200 mm tube at 20°, using white light. After filling tube, release tension on glass disks by slightly loosening caps, and let stand ≥30 min at 20° before making readings. °S (**31.020(a)**) × 10.2 = mg laevo-malic acid contained in aliquot (*l* in formula, **(d)**).

If control for adjusting to std temp. of 20° is lacking, det. temp. of polariscope and at this temp. prep. soln of U-complex as above. Make readings after letting tube remain in trough of instrument 30 min.

(c) *Oxidation.*—Evap. 225 mL clear soln to ca 10 mL to expel all alcohol, dil. to ca 120 mL with H_2O, and add 10 mL 30% NaOH soln and 25 mL $KMnO_4$ soln. Heat to ca 80° and keep in boiling H_2O bath 30 min. Add 25 mL oxalic acid soln and 10 mL H_2SO_4 (1+1), stirring vigorously. Adjust to 80°, and titr. to faint pink with $KMnO_4$ soln. Again heat to 80° and finish titrn. mL $KMnO_4$ soln used × 5 = total oxidizable material (as malic acid) present in aliquot (*t* in formula, **(d)**).

(d) *Calculation.*—Calc. mg inactive malic acid, *X*, in portion taken for analysis = $4(t - 5 - l)$, where *t* = mg oxidizable as malic acid; *l* = mg laevo-malic acid; 5 = correction factor for mg nonmalic material as malic acid; and 4 = factor for reverting inactive malic acid in aliquot back to amt of inactive acid in sample taken for analysis.

22.076 ★ Lactic Acid (38)—Official Final Action ★

Removal of pectin wih alcohol, extn of lactic acid with ether, and spectrophtric detn as ferric lactate. *See* **22.089**, 12th ed.

Foreign Organic Acids (*39*)—Official First Action

(*Caution: See* **51.059.**)

22.077 ***Apparatus***

See **19.044.**

★ Surplus method—*see* inside front cover.

22.078 ***Reagents***

(**a**) *Sodium acetate soln.*—Dissolve 15 g anhyd. NaOAc in H_2O and dil. to 100 mL.

(**b**) *Lead acetate soln.*—Dissolve 8 g $Pb(OAc)_2.3H_2O$ in H_2O and dil. to 100 mL.

(**c**) *Std acid soln.*—Dissolve 1.5 g DL-malic acid, 0.85 g anhyd. citric acid, and 0.25 g tartaric acid in H_2O, and dil. to 100 mL.

(**d**) *Aniline-furfural chromogenic agent.—See* **19.045(b)**(*1*).

22.079 ***Determination***

Place 10 mL single-strength juice in 50 mL capped centrf. tube, add 1 mL 1*N* HNO_3 and 25 mL alcohol, and mix. Centrf. and filter supernate thru small cotton plug into second 50 mL capped centrf. tube. Discard material in first tube. Add 1 mL NaOAc soln and 2.5 mL $Pb(OAc)_2$ soln to second tube and mix. Centrf. and discard supernate. Wash ppt with 25 mL portions 80% alcohol, 95% alcohol, and ether, successively mixing, centrfg, and discarding supernate each time. Let ether evap. spontaneously ca 10 min, add 2.0 mL H_2O, and break up any lumps with narrow end of glass tube. Pass *H_2S* thru this tube 5 min and then pass air thru same tube 5 min to remove excess H_2S. Centrf. and decant clear supernate into small vial. In some cases it may be necessary to transfer material to 15 mL conical centrf. tube and centrf. until clear supernate is obtained.

Spot 20 μL liq. on 12 × 12" Whatman No. 1 chromatgc paper, using two 10 μL portions and drying each spotting with warm air jet. Also spot 20 μL std acid soln in same way. Develop paper as in **19.046**, beginning ". . . roll paper and connect edges slightly apart . . ." except use ether-HCOOH-H_2O (20+5+3) developing solv.

After development, let paper air dry overnight. Treat portion of air-dried paper with aniline-furfural chromogenic agent by dipping and note color of background. If not pink, steam and dry paper as in **19.046**, last par., to ensure complete removal of HCOOH.

If paper is pink, it need not be treated with steam. If background is dark, redistil furfural and prep. new chromogenic agent. Dip paper in chromogenic agent and let spots form by air drying. Note position and intensity of spots and compare with std acid soln. Top std spot (malic acid) has intensity value of I (intense); center spot (citric acid) has intensity value of D (dense); lowest spot (tartaric acid) has intensity value of F (faint). Classify acid spots obtained from juices as VI (very intense), I, D, F, or VF (very faint). Compare with chromatograms made simultaneously from pure fruit juices.

Carbohydrates in Juices (*40*)—Official First Action

22.080 ***Apparatus***

Gas chromatograph.—Varian Aerograph Model 1520 (replaced by model 3720), with dual column and thermal detectors operated at 250° and 200 ma. GLC conditions: 1.8 m × 6 mm (6' × ¼") stainless steel column packed with 3.8% SE-30 on 60–80 mesh silanized Diatoport S (replaced by Supelcoport, Supelco, Inc., or Chromosorb W-HP, Analabs, Inc.), programmed at 4°/min from 190 to 275° (for sharper sepn of sorbitol and glucose peaks, program at 2°/min until complete invert sugar pattern appears, and then at 4°/min); injector temp. 225°; He gas flow 40 mL/min; sample size and attenuation adjusted to give 50% full scale deflection for fructose peak.

22.081 ***Reagents***

(**a**) *Neutral lead acetate soln.—See* **19.048(a)**.

(**b**) *Tri-Sil reagent.—See* **19.048(c)**.

22.082 ***Determination***

Place 2.0 mL single-strength fruit juice in 15 mL capped centrf. tube, add 0.5 mL $Pb(OAc)_2$ soln and 10 mL alcohol, mix, and centrf. Decant clear supernate into small porcelain dish. Wash residue once with 5 mL 80% alcohol, mix, centrf., and add clear supernate to porcelain dish. Evap. to dryness on steam bath and keep on bath 15 min after apparent dryness. Ext sugars with five 2 mL portions hot pyridine, thoroly mixing each portion with residue and heating on steam bath during mixing. Filter each hot ext thru small glass wool plug into small flask. Cool combined exts and transfer 0.5 mL to 5 mL vial with Teflon-lined cap. Add few pieces of Drierite to vial; then add 2.0 mL Tri-Sil reagent. Let stand 1 hr at 37° and inject vol. soln such that fructose peak is ca half scale. (Turbidity in final soln does not affect GLC detn.) Compare curve with authentic sample prepd in same way. Order of appearance is fructose, α-glucose, sorbitol, β-glucose, and sucrose.

Sucrose—Official Final Action

22.083 ***By Polarization***

Det. by polarizing before and after inversion. *See* **31.025**, **31.026**, or **31.030**.

22.084 ***By Reducing Sugars Before and After Inversion***

Transfer sample representing (if possible) ca 2.5 g total sugars to 200 mL vol. flask; dil. to ca 100 mL and add excess of satd neut. $Pb(OAc)_2$ soln, **31.021(d)** (ca 2 mL is usually enough). Mix, dil. to vol., and filter, discarding first few mL filtrate. Add dry K or Na oxalate to ppt excess Pb used in clarification, mix, and filter, discarding first few mL filtrate. Take 25 mL filtrate or aliquot contg (if possible) 50–200 mg reducing sugars and proceed as in **31.038–31.039**.

For inversion at room temp. transfer 50 mL aliquot clarified and deleaded soln to 100 mL vol. flask, add 10 mL HCl (1+1), and let stand at room temp. ($\geq$20°) 24 hr; exactly neutze with concd NaOH soln, using phthln, and dil. to 100 mL. Take aliquot and det. total sugars as invert as in **31.038–31.039**. Calc. sucrose as in **31.031**.

22.085 Reducing Sugars—Official Final Action

Proceed as in **22.084**, par. 1. Express results as invert sugar.

22.086 Commercial Glucose—Procedure

See **31.033**.

Starch

22.087 ***Qualitative Test—Official Final Action***

Dil. portion of sample with H_2O, heat nearly to bp, add several mL H_2SO_4 (1+9), and then 10% $KMnO_4$ soln until all color is destroyed. Cool, and test with I soln, **30.029(d)**. (Presence of starch is not necessarily indication of its addn as adulterant. It is usually present in small amt in apples and occasionally in other fruits, and unless it is found in the fruit product in considerable amt its presence may be due to these natural sources.)

Essential Oil (*41*)—Official First Action

22.088 ***Apparatus***

Use app. of **19.127**, substituting 2 L flask with ₮ 24/40 joint.

22.089 ***Determination***

Place 1 L sample in boiling flask and add few glass beads. Fill oil separatory trap with H_2O, connect with boiling flask and condenser, and boil 1 hr. Remove heat and let stand several min. Drain enough H_2O to bring oily layer within graduated portion of trap, let stand ≥5 min to complete drainage, and measure vol. of oil from bottom of lower meniscus to highest point of upper meniscus.

Recoverable Oil (*42*)—Official Final Action

22.090 ***Principle***

Oil recoverable by distn from orange, tangerine, and grapefruit juices is ≥98% *d*-limonene, which, after co-distn with isopropanol, is detd after acidification by titrn with std KBr-$KBrO_3$ soln. Reaction involves release of Br *in situ* and subsequent formation of limonene tetrabromide. Oil from lemon juice contains up to 5% α-pinene and 4% citral. Since α-pinene consumes Br at same rate, and citral at ½ rate, as *d*-limonene, method is only slightly less accurate with lemon juice.

22.091 ***Reagents***

(**a**) *Potassium bromide-bromate std solns.*—(*1*) *Stock soln.*—0.099*N*. Prep. and stdze as in **50.020–50.021**. (*2*) *Titrating soln.*—*0.0247N*. Dil. stock soln 1+3. 1 mL 0.0247*N* KBr-$KBrO_3$ = 0.0010 mL (equiv. to 0.00084 g) *d*-limonene. Solns are stable 6 months.

(**b**) *Methyl orange indicator.*—0.1% in H_2O. Use 1 drop per titrn, or add 5 mL to 1 L HCl (1+2).

22.092 ***Apparatus***

(**a**) *Electric heater.*—With recessed refractory top, 500–750 watts.

(**b**) *Still, all-glass.*—500 mL distn flask with ₸ 24/40 neck; 200 mm Graham condenser with 28/15 receiving socket and drip tip; connecting bulb and adapter. *See* Fig. **22:04**.

(**c**) *Buret.*—10 mL, 0.05 mL subdivisions; suitable for rapid and dropwise titrn.

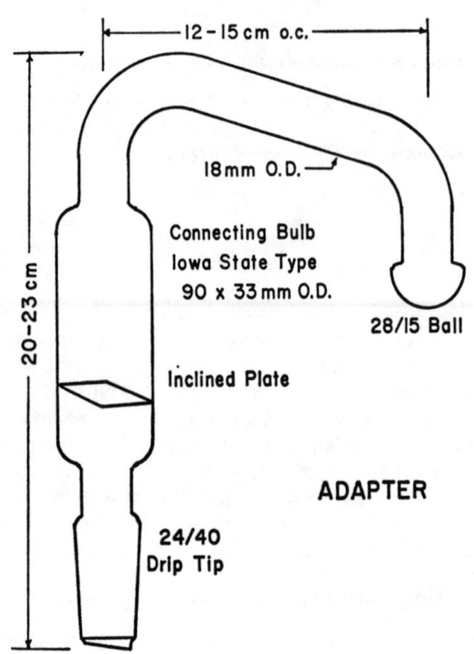

FIG. 22:04—Connecting tube adapter for direct distillation

22.093 ***Determination***

Preheat elec. heater. Pipet 25 mL well mixed sample into distn flask contg SiC chips or glass beads, and add 25 mL isopropanol. Distil into 150 mL beaker. Continue distn until solv. ceases to reflux, and remove flask, leaving heater on for next detn. Place short mag. bar in beaker, and add 10 mL HCl (1+2) and indicator. Titr. with std KBr-$KBrO_3$ while stirring. Major portion of titrant may be added rapidly, but end point (disappearance of color) must be approached at ca 1 drop/ sec.

Det. reagent blank by titrg 3 sep. mixts of 25 mL isopropanol, 10 mL HCl (1+2), and indicator without refilling buret. Total mL titrant/3 = av. blank.

% recoverable oil by vol. = (mL KBr-$KBrO_4$ soln used in titrn − mL av. blank) × 0.001 × 100/25.

Anthocyanins (*43*)—Official Final Action

(Applicable to grape and dark colored fruit juices. *Caution: See* **51.017**.)

22.094 ***Apparatus***

(**a**) *Chromatographic tank or cylinder.*—To hold cylinder made from 12 × 12" Whatman No. 1 chromatgc paper. (18 × 6" (46 × 15 cm) glass cylindrical tank, with ground top and glass cover, is convenient.)

(**b**) *Spectrophotometer.* — Beckman Model DU, Bausch & Lomb Spectronic 20, or equiv.

22.095 ***Reagents***

(**a**) *Lead acetate soln.*—*See* **22.078**(**b**).

(**b**) *Developing solvent.*—*n*-BuOH-HOAc-H_2O (6+1+2).

(**c**) *Modified Forestal solvent.*—Dissolve 0.5 g oxalic acid in 60 mL H_2O, add 30 mL HCl and 150 mL HOAc, and mix.

(**d**) *Chromogenic spray.*—2% phosphomolybdic acid in H_2O.

(**e**) *Eluting solvent.*—Dissolve 0.2 g oxalic acid in 100 mL alcohol, add 0.2 mL HCl, and mix.

22.096 ***Extraction of Anthocyanins***

Add 10 mL $Pb(OAc)_2$ soln to 10 mL single-strength juice in 50 mL screw-cap centrf. tube and mix. Add 0.5 mL NH_4OH and mix. Centrf. until ppt is well packed and discard clear supernate. (If supernate is not clear, add more $Pb(OAc)_2$ soln and recentrf.) Wash ppt twice with 25 mL portions 80% alcohol, mixing well each time before centrfg; discard washings. After second wash, invert tube 5 min to drain liq. Add 10 mL *n*-BuOH and 1 mL HCl, shake vigorously until all colored ppt has been transformed into $PbCl_2$, and centrf. Decant clear liq. into 125 mL separator. Wash ppt with 5 mL *n*-BuOH, mix well, and centrf. to obtain clear upper liq. Add washings to first ext in separator. Add 100 mL pet ether to separator, shake well, and swirl to bring down colored aq. soln. (If no aq. liq. seps, add 0.5 mL H_2O, shake, and swirl.) Let liqs sep. completely and drain lower aq. layer (usually ca 2 mL) into 15 mL conical graduated centrf. tube. Add 0.2–0.5 mL portions H_2O to separator, shaking each time and draining lower layers, until total of 2.5 mL is collected. (Occasionally, ≥2.5 mL will be collected in first sepn of liqs; make no addnl H_2O extns in this case.) Mix soln and use 0.5 mL for chromatgc test for anthocyanin. Retain anthocyanin soln in refrigerator until used.

22.097 ***Preparation of Anthocyanidins***

Add equal vol. 2*N* HCl to liq. in centrf. tube contg small boiling chip. Fit tube with air condenser made from glass tubing and cork. Place tube in boiling H_2O bath and heat 30 min. Remove from bath and cool in H_2O. Add 1 mL isoamyl alcohol, shake vigorously, and centrf. With glass tube drawn out to capillary tip at one end and small bulb, transfer clear, upper layer to small bottle. (Do not remove any turbid aq. liq. in tube.) Keep anthocyanidin soln in refrigerator until used.

22.098 ***Chromatography***

Use 12 × 12" Whatman No. 1 papers for tests (**a**) and (**b**). Papers require overnight development; prep. in late afternoon to permit 16 hr development.

(**a**) *Qualitative anthocyanin ascending paper chromatography.*—(Definitive for fruit juices other than grape juice; not definitive for grape juice where pattern is extremely complicated, but may be useful as guide.) Prep. streaks of soln, **22.096**, 2.5 cm above bottom of paper and ca 2.5 cm apart. Make streaks 3 cm long and 0.3–0.6 cm wide, using capillary mp tube, **22.101(c)**. Concord grape juice requires 5–7 applications to obtain satisfactory intensity; other juices usually require more; some may require fewer. Make 2 sep. streakings from same soln, using different intensities, one of which may yield better chromatgc pattern. Dry between each application with cold air blast only. After streakings are completed, dry streaks, and make cylinder of paper by sewing ends with cotton, leaving ca 1 cm space between ends. (Do not use metal clips to make cylinder.) Place developing solv., (**b**), to ca 1 cm depth in tank and place cylinder in tank. Let develop overnight at room temp., remove paper, and air dry.

Simultaneously test authentic fruit juice anthocyanins and compare patterns. Note differences in daylight and under long-wave UV light. Spray with phosphomolybdic acid soln and observe changes in pattern. Foreign natural coloring material is indicated by significant differences from authentic pattern.

(**b**) *Quantitative anthocyanidin ascending paper chromatography.*—(Definitive for grape juice but optional for other fruit juices.) Pipet 0.10 mL anthocyanidin soln, **22.097**, into small flask, add 10.0 mL eluting solv., and mix. Read *A* at 545 nm in 1 cm cell. Calc. vol. anthocyanidin soln to give *A* of 0.400 under these conditions; use this vol. for transfer to chromatgc paper.

Place calcd vol. anthocyanidin soln in small test tube. Using capillary tube, make successive applications on paper, each ca 3 cm long and 0.5 cm wide. Keep different sample streaks ca 2.5 cm apart. Dry each application with cold air blast before applying next streak. Prep. streaked paper as in (**a**).

Develop overnight (16 hr) at room temp., using Forestal solv. Air dry and examine under longwave UV light. (3 distinct orange to red spots should be present. For juices other than grape, compare pattern with authentic pattern. If no differences in intensities of the 3 spots are noted, it is not necessary to make quant. measurements of the anthocyanidin colors.) Alternatively, measure intensity of colors in spots with densitometer, using green filter. (Expose paper to HCl fumes few min before using densitometer.)

Elute colors and measure in spectrophtr as follows: Outline top spot and bottom 2 spots with soft pencil under longwave UV light. Cut out top spot, and cut it into several small pieces before transferring to screwcap test tube or small g-s erlenmeyer. Cut out each of 2 lower spots, starting ca 0.6 cm above origin line for lowest spot. Combine these 2 spots for grape juice, but keep sep. for other juices. Cut strips into several smaller pieces and place in test tube(s) or flask(s). Pipet 10 mL eluting solv., (**e**), into each tube or flask, and agitate 1 hr. (Rotating device can be used with test tubes and agitator with flasks. In absence of agitating device, let eluting soln remain in contact with paper 3 hr in dark, with occasional swirling.) Centrf. alc. exts in 15 mL conical centrf. tube and decant clear, upper liq. for color measurements. Cover cells while reading to avoid evapn. Read *A* at 445, 545, and 645 nm. Correct 545 nm (max.) readings for background by subtracting ½ algebraic sum of 445 and 645 nm readings.

Designate the 3 spots as S1 (lowest), S2 (central), and S3 (top) spots. Calc. % color in each spot of total color (S1 + S2 + S3), using corresponding corrected *A*. Significant differences from authentic % indicate presence of foreign coloring.

Concord anthocyanidins show deeply colored S1 and S2 spots while S3 spot is faint. Significant increase in S3 color % indicates addn of other grape juice to Concord. Use qual. anthocyanin chromatograms to confirm presence of non-Concord grape juice.

Malvidin Glucosides (*44*)—Official First Action

22.099 ***Principle***

Anthocyanin components are sepd by paper chromatgy, pigments are converted to oxychlorides with HCl vapor, and chromatogram is scanned for presence of malvidin mono- or diglucosides, which are present in minimal concns in Concord grape juice.

22.100 ***Reagent***

Citric acid soln.—0.1*M* (MacIlvaine's buffer soln B). Dissolve 45 g citric acid.H_2O and dil. to 2 L with H_2O. Titr. 10 mL with 0.1*N* NaOH, **50.034–50.035**, using phthln. Adjust with H_2O or citric acid to require 30.00 mL 0.1*N* NaOH in repeat titrn.

22.101 ***Apparatus***

(**a**) *Densitometer.*—Beckman Analytrol Model RB, 550 nm interference filter, or equiv.

(**b**) *Spectrophotometer.* — Beckman Model B (replaced by model 25), or equiv.

(**c**) *Melting point capillary tubes.*—1.5–2.0 × 100 mm. Heat and draw out to form application tubes, 1 mm id, open at both ends, and drawn out to ca ½ diam. at one end. Diam. should be such that streak 3 mm wide is deposited.

22.102 ***Preparation of Sample***

Mix 5 mL grape juice sample with 5 mL MeOH. Filter thru glass wool.

Det. streaking vol. so amt of pigment in each streak is comparable. Mix sep. 1 mL Concord grape juice std and 1 mL of each sample filtrate with 25 mL citric acid buffer. Det. *A* at 525 nm with spectrophtr.

Calc. mL of filtrate to be streaked = (*A* Concord grape juice std × 0.6 mL)/*A* sample.

0.6 mL Concord grape juice std with *A* = 0.54 gives optimum sepn and color intensity of bands.

Acidify filtrates with 4 drops HCl/5 mL filtrate. Transfer samples to small capped vials to prevent evapn of MeOH.

22.103 ***Chromatography***

Draw line 4 cm from bottom of paper, 46 × 57 cm, Whatman 3MM, or equiv., along length of paper to locate five 8 cm streaks. Apply filtrates 8–12 times with application tubes to form 8 cm streaks, 3 mm wide. Let dry between applications. Apply one streak of Concord grape juice std and others of samples. Dry thoroly and acidify by exposing both sides of paper to HCl vapor.

Form streaked paper lengthwise into cylinder and staple both ends, making sure edges of paper do not touch. Fasten 2–3 addnl staples by hand thru holes made with needle.

Add 250 mL H_2O to cylindrical chromatgy jar, Pyrex or equiv.,

10⅛" diam., 18" high. Carefully lower paper cylinder into jar (cylinder should not touch sides of jar), cover jar with plastic bag, 12 × 6 × 24", Kordite Turkey Bag, or equiv., and seal bag with masking tape. Remove bag when H_2O has risen to top of cylinder. Fold filter paper (46 × 57 cm Whatman 3 MM, or equiv.) lengthwise, cut semi-circle at folded edge with diam. ca that of cylindrical chromatogram, open, and place as collar around paper cylinder, resting on top edge of jar. Place cardboard over exposed top edge of cylinder which is just above top of jar and continue developing 10 hr. Pigments should be resolved into well-defined bands. Air dry at room temp. Expose both sides of chromatogram to HCl vapor to convert pigments to red oxychlorides.

22.104 ***Determination***

Cut 4 cm strip from center of each streak, mark origin and point 25 cm from origin, and use second mark to position strip in densitometer with 550 nm filter. Obtain densitometer traces and compare std with samples.

Pigments sep. by classes. Sequence of classes from origin is: acylated monoglucosides, monoglucosides, acylated diglucosides, diglucosides, sugars, and more H_2O-sol. compds. Within classes from origin are: delphinidin, petunidin, cyanidin, peonidin, and malvidin. Malvidin compds, very intense purple or violet, travel at front edge of each class.

Concord grape juice contains min. concns of malvidin mono- and diglucosides while California red grape concs and Italian grape juice color (Enocianina) contain relatively high concns of malvidin mono- or diglucoside. Comparison of malvidin peak of Concord control with malvidin peak of sample will indicate presence of malvidin-contg products (JAOAC **50**, 299(1967); *J. Agr. Food Chem.* **11**, 263(1963)).

LEMON JUICE (*45*)—OFFICIAL FIRST ACTION

22.105 Preparation of Sample

Mix ca 5–6 g Celite analytical filter aid with 175 mL lemon juice (ca 80–100 milliequiv. acid/100 mL juice). Filter with suction (if not completely clear, refilter thru fresh Celite pad) and store in g-s flask.

22.106 Total Amino Acids

Pipet 25 mL prepd sample into 150 mL beaker. (If sample is suspected of contg SO_2, boil exactly 1 min and cool.) Add NaOH (1+1) dropwise to pH 6–7. Titr. potentiometrically with 0.1*N* NaOH to pH 8.4. Add 10 mL neutzd 37% HCHO (titrd potentiometrically with 0.1*N* NaOH to pH 8.4 ≤1 hr before use) and titr. resulting acidity back to pH 8.4 with 0.1*N* NaOH. Total amino acids (milliequiv./100 mL juice) = 0.4 × mL 0.1*N* NaOH for second titrn.

22.107 Total Polyphenolics

(**a**) *Calibration of spectrophotometer.*—Accurately weigh two 1.4–1.5 g portions KNO_3. Transfer to 250 mL vol. flasks, dissolve in H_2O, and dil. to vol. Zero instrument at 302 nm and measure A of each soln in 1 cm cell. Calc. std A for each soln, $A' = a \times$ molarity $KNO_3 = (6.99 \times \text{g } KNO_3)/(101.11 \times 0.25) = 0.2765 \times$ g KNO_3. Divide av. A' by av. measured A at 302 nm to obtain correction factor.

(**b**) *Determination.*—Pipet 0.5 mL prepd sample into 10 mL vol. flask, and dil. to vol. with alcohol. Transfer to centrf. tube, cover with Al foil to prevent evapn, and centrf. Measure UV spectrum of supernate with recording spectrophtr from 300 to 400 nm or with manual spectrophtr at 2 nm intervals from 325 to 335 nm. Multiply A of 325–335 nm peak by correction factor, (**a**), and report as A of total polyphenolics.

l-Malic Acid (*46*)

22.108 ***Standard Rotation for l-Malic Acid***

Accurately weigh ca 15, 25, and 35 mg *l*-malic acid (Calbiochem) into 25 mL vol. flasks. Add ca 0.4 g citric acid to each flask. Dissolve in 5 mL H_2O, add 1 drop phthln, and neutze with NaOH (1+1). Add HOAc until phthln color disappears, then 2 drops excess. Dil. to vol. with H_2O. Measure initial optical rotation (α_1) of each std soln. (Exercise great care in measuring optical rotation, since small uncertainty in measurement will cause large error in final result.) Sat. 10 mL of each std soln with 1.3 g uranyl acetate.$2H_2O$. Keep in dark 30 min with occasional shaking. (Exposure of uranyl complex to strong light causes it to become insol.; therefore conduct operations in semidarkness.) Filter off excess uranyl acetate and measure optical rotation (α_u) within 5 min after filtering. Calc. std rotation (R_{std}) for each soln as follows:

$$C_{malic} = (\text{mg malic acid}/67.04) \times 4$$
$$= \text{milliequiv. malic acid}/100 \text{ mL}$$
$$\Delta\alpha = \alpha_1 - \alpha_u$$
$$R_{std} = C_{malic}/\Delta\alpha$$

Use av. std rotation for subsequent calcns.

22.109 ***Determination***

In graduate mix 15 mL sample, **22.105**, with 45 mL alcohol and let stand 10 min. Centrf. pectin ppt. Evap. alc. juice to thick sirup (ca 1–2 mL) in rotary vac. evaporator (≤50°). Add 13–14 mL H_2O to sirup and mix thoroly. Pipet 2 mL pectin-free sample into 100 mL beaker, and add 25 mL H_2O. Titr. potentiometrically to pH 8.4 with stdzd 0.1*N* NaOH. Acidity (milliequiv./100 mL pectin-free sample) = 5 × (mL alkali). Pipet 10 mL pectin-free sample into 25 mL vol. flask, add 1 drop phthln, and proceed as in detn of std rotation. *l*-Malic acid concn in dild, neutzd sample, $[MA]_D = R_{std} \times (\alpha_1 - \alpha_u)$. Calc. citric acid:malic acid ratio by dividing 0.4 times acidity of pectin-free sample by $[MA]_D$.

22.110 Recoverable Oil—Official Final Action

See **22.090–22.093.**

SELECTED REFERENCES

(*1*) JAOAC **17**, 66(1934); **30**, 274(1947).
(*2*) JAOAC **36**, 860(1953); **38**, 609(1955).
(*3*) JAOAC **36**, 270(1953); **37**, 309(1954); **38**, 611(1955).
(*4*) FAO/WHO Food Standards Program CAC/RM 32–1970.
(*5*) JAOAC **36**, 270(1953); **37**, 309(1954); **38**, 611(1955); **47**, 902(1964).
(*6*) JAOAC **42**, 411(1959); **50**, 288(1967).
(*7*) JAOAC **17**, 215(1934); **18**, 80(1935).
(*8*) JAOAC **52**, 858(1969); **54**, 219(1971); **55**, 202(1972).
(*9*) JAOAC **6**, 34(1922); **21**, 504(1938); **30**, 260(1947); **32**, 177(1949); **33**, 349(1950).
(*10*) JAOAC **32**, 179(1949); **33**, 349(1950).
(*11*) JAOAC **15**, 384(1932).
(*12*) JAOAC **59**, 386(1976).
(*13*) JAOAC **23**, 314(1940).
(*14*) JAOAC **12**, 366(1929); **24**, 391, 454(1941); **25**, 90, 232, 429, 433(1942); **26**, 324(1943); Ind. Eng. Chem., Anal. Ed. **9**, 136(1937).
(*15*) JAOAC **48**, 521(1965).
(*16*) JAOAC **49**, 617(1966).

(*17*) JAOAC **14,** 465(1931).
(*18*) JAOAC **12,** 366(1929); **14,** 465(1931).
(*19*) JAOAC **14,** 473(1931).
(*20*) JAOAC **25,** 441(1942); **27,** 88(1944).
(*21*) Ind. Eng. Chem., Anal. Ed. **7,** 116, 227(1935); JAOAC **22,** 133, 167(1939); **23,** 321(1940); **24,** 393(1941); **25,** 443(1942).
(*22*) JAOAC **52,** 865(1969); **53,** 575(1970).
(*23*) JAOAC **8,** 125(1924).
(*24*) JAOAC **8,** 126(1924).
(*25*) JAOAC **11,** 209(1928); **26,** 437(1943).
(*26*) JAOAC **8,** 127(1924); **21,** 505(1938).
(*27*) JAOAC **8,** 129(1924); **21,** 502(1938); **35,** 872(1952).
(*28*) J. Sci Food Agr. **17,** 316(1966); JAOAC **53,** 568(1970).
(*29*) JAOAC **25,** 412(1942); **28,** 507(1945).
(*30*) Bull. soc. chim. **7,** 567(1910); **11,** 886(1912); JAOAC **8,** 637(1925); **13,** 103(1930); **36,** 266(1953).
(*31*) JAOAC **26,** 444(1943); **34,** 445(1951).
(*32*) JAOAC **37,** 305(1954).
(*33*) Anal. Chem. **23,** 467(1951); JAOAC **40,** 333(1957).
(*34*) JAOAC **15,** 648(1932); **17,** 214(1934); **18,** 198(1935).
(*35*) JAOAC **36,** 268(1953).
(*36*) JAOAC **51,** 934(1968); **52,** 1153(1969).
(*37*) JAOAC **16,** 281(1933).
(*38*) JAOAC **20,** 605(1937); **26,** 199(1943).
(*39*) JAOAC **52,** 646(1969).
(*40*) JAOAC **53,** 1193(1970).
(*41*) JAOAC **27,** 201(1944).
(*42*) JAOAC **49,** 628(1966); **51,** 928(1968).
(*43*) JAOAC **50,** 293(1967); **51,** 464, 937(1968); **52,** 649(1969).
(*44*) JAOAC **51,** 931(1968).
(*45*) JAOAC **46,** 353, 359(1963); **48,** 530(1965); **51,** 6, 464(1968).
(*46*) JAOAC **46,** 353(1963); **48,** 530(1965); **49,** 621(1966).

23. Gelatin, Dessert Preparations, and Mixes

GELATIN

23.001 Preparation of Sample—Procedure

Mix ground gelatin thoroly. Break sheet gelatin into small pieces by hand. Further comminution is unnecessary in either case.

23.002 Moisture—Official Final Action

Proceed as in **14.003**, using 2 g sample prepd as in **23.001**.

23.003 Ash—Official Final Action

See **31.012** or **31.013**.

Total Phosphorus

Gravimetric Quinolinium Molybdophosphate Method (1)—Official Final Action

23.004 ***Reagents***

(**a**) *Magnesium oxide-magnesium nitrate slurry.*— See **42.005(b)**.
(**b**) *Citric-molybdic acid reagent.—See* **2.026(a)**.
(**c**) *Quinoline soln.—See* **2.026(b)**.

23.005 ***Determination***

Weigh ca 3 g sample into Pt dish and mix with 10 mL MgO-$Mg(NO_3)_2$ slurry, (**a**). Evap. mixt. to dryness under IR lamp or on steam bath. Ash 1 hr at 500°.

Moisten cooled ash with H_2O, partially cover dish with watch glass, and cautiously add 10 mL HCl (1+1). Heat sample 30 min on steam bath with occasional stirring. Filter into 500 mL erlenmeyer thru S&S white ribbon paper, or equiv. Wash dish and residue on filter with hot H_2O until filtrate vol. is ca 100 mL. Det. P as in **2.028(a)**. Report as % P_2O_5.

23.006 Nitrogen—Official Final Action

Proceed as in **2.057**, using 1 g sample. To convert to ash-free, anhyd. gelatin multiply by factor 5.55 (USDA Circ. **183**, August 1931).

23.007 Jelly Strength (*2*)—Official Final Action

(*Caution:* Check shot hopper on Bloom Gelometer to assure it is grounded electrically.)

Pipet 105 mL H_2O at 10–15° into std Bloom bottle, add 7.5 g sample, and stir. Let stand 1 hr and then bring to 62° in 15 min by placing in H_2O bath regulated at 65° (sample may be swirled several times to aid soln). Finally mix by inversion, let stand 15 min, and place in H_2O bath at 10±0.1°. Chill 17 hr. Det. jelly strength in Bloom Gelometer (Ind. Eng. Chem., Anal. Ed. **2**, 348(1930)), adjusted for 4 mm depression and to deliver 200±5 g shot/5 sec, using 0.5″ plunger, Fig. **23:01**.

GELATIN DESSERT POWDERS

23.008 Preparation of Sample—Procedure

Sift sample thru No. 30 sieve onto large sheet of paper, rubbing material thru sieve and tapping vigorously, if necessary. Sift sample 2 more times, mixing thoroly each time. To avoid absorption of moisture, work as rapidly as possible, and store sample in air-tight container.

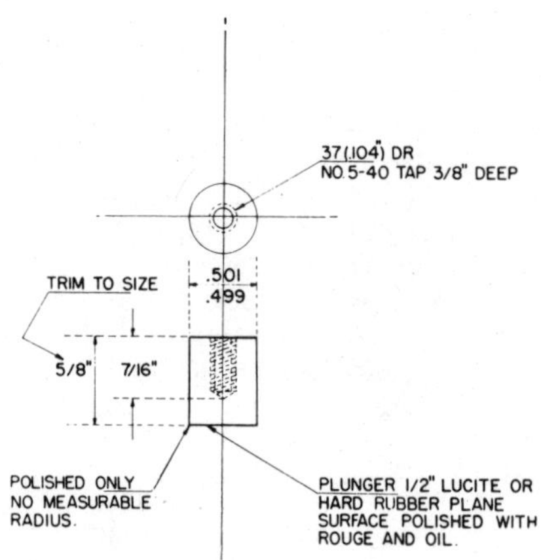

FIG. 23:01—0.5 Inch Bloom Gelometer plunger

23.009 Moisture—Official Final Action

Proceed as in **31.005**, using 2 g sample prepd as in **23.008**.

23.010 Ash—Official Final Action

See **31.012** or **31.013**.

23.011 Nitrogen—Official Final Action

See **23.006**.

23.012 Total Acidity—Official Final Action

Dissolve 20 g sample in 2 L recently boiled H_2O. Titr. 100 mL with 0.1*N* NaOH, using 0.3 mL phthln. Report as % by wt citric acid.

23.013 Jelly Strength—Official Final Action

(*Caution:* Check shot hopper on Bloom Gelometer to assure it is grounded electrically.)

To 20 g sample in std Bloom bottle, add from pipet, with stirring, 100 mL H_2O at 10–15°. Let stand 15 min and then bring to 62° in 15 min in H_2O bath regulated at 65° (sample may be swirled several times to aid soln). Mix by inversion, let stand 15 min, place in H_2O bath controlled at 10±0.1°, and let stand 17 hr. Det. jelly strength in Bloom Gelometer (Ind. Eng. Chem., Anal. Ed. **2**, 348(1930)), adjusted for 4 mm depression and to deliver 200±5 g shot/5 sec, using 1.0″ plunger, Fig. **23:02**, and light wt shot receiver (paper or plastic).

Sucrose (*3*)—Official Final Action

23.014 ***Reagents***

(**a**) *Tannin soln.*—Dissolve 5 g tannin in 100 mL cold H_2O.
(**b**) *Lead acetate soln.*—Dissolve 100 g $Pb(OAc)_2.3H_2O$ in 200 mL H_2O. (This makes 30° Bé. soln.)

23.015 ***Determination***

Place 13 g sample in 300 or 400 mL beaker, add 2 g $CaCO_3$ and 2 g Filter-Cel, and mix well with glass rod. Add 175 mL boiling H_2O, creaming mixt. with little of the H_2O at first. Stir thoroly and let stand few min to ensure soln. Cool under cold

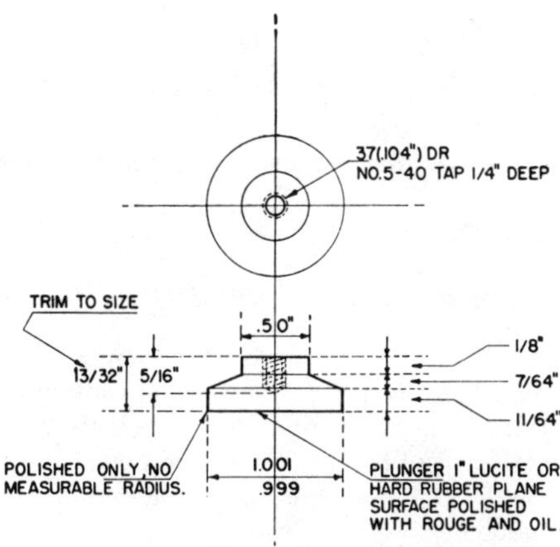

FIG. 23:02—1.0 Inch Bloom Gelometer plunger

H_2O to 30°, slowly add 25 mL tannin soln with stirring, and let stand 5 min. (This vol. tannin soln is enough for most powders; if 30 mL is required, use 170 mL H_2O instead of 175 mL.) Slowly add 10 mL $Pb(OAc)_2$ soln with stirring, and filter on 18.5 cm Whatman No. 2 paper. (Total vol. liq. used in each case is 210 mL, which yields 200 mL after evapn and concn. If pptn has been conducted properly, soln will filter readily and filtrate will be clear.) Read optical rotation of this soln in 200 mm tube at 20°.

If sample contains reducing sugar, delead with $K_2C_2O_4$, add Filter-Cel, and filter. Invert by placing 50 mL filtrate in 100 mL vol. flask with 5 mL HCl and letting stand overnight. After inversion, neutze with concd NaOH soln, using phthln. Discharge color of indicator with 0.1*N* HCl. Cool to 20°, dil. to vol., and read optical rotation in 200 mm tube. Use following Clerget formula modified for % sucrose in gelatin dessert powders:

$$S = \frac{100(4P - 8I)}{142.66 + 0.0676(m - 13) - t/2},$$

where S = % sucrose; P = direct reading; I = invert reading; t = temp. at which readings are made (20°); and m = g total solids from original sample/100 mL invert soln (3.25 g). Simplified:

$$S = 100(4P - 8I)/132.$$

23.016 Glucose—Official Final Action

Det. polarization due to glucose (D) by subtracting % sucrose (S) as found in **23.015** from direct reading of polariscope in circular degrees (P) multiplied by 4: $D = 4P - S$.

$$\% \text{ Glucose} = D \times 66.5/52.5 = 1.267D,$$

where D = polarization due to glucose; 66.5 = specific rotation of sucrose; and 52.5 = specific rotation of glucose.

STARCH DESSERT POWDERS

23.017 Preparation of Sample—Procedure

See **23.008**.

23.018 Moisture—Official Final Action

Proceed as in **31.005** or **31.006**, using 2 g prepd sample, **23.008**.

23.019 Ash—Official Final Action

See **31.012** or **31.013**.

23.020 Nitrogen—Official Final Action

Proceed as in **2.057**, using 1 g sample. To convert to protein, multiply by factor 6.25.

23.021 Sucrose and Glucose—Official Final Action

See **23.015** and **23.016**.

23.022 Starch—Official Final Action

(**a**) *By direct acid hydrolysis.—See* **8.019**.
(**b**) *Polarimetric method.—See* **14.032**.

SELECTED REFERENCES

(*1*) JAOAC **55**, 581(1972).
(*2*) JAOAC **31**, 511(1948).
(*3*) Annual Report Dept. Farms and Markets, New York, 1926, Legislative Document No. 15, p. 78 (1927).

24. Meat and Meat Products

MEAT

24.001 Preparation of Sample—Procedure

To prevent H_2O loss during prepn and subsequent handling, do not use small samples. Keep ground material in glass or similar containers with air- and H_2O-tight covers. Prep. samples for analysis as follows:

(**a**) *Fresh meats, dried meats, cured meats, smoked meats, etc.*—Sep. as completely as possible from any bone; pass rapidly 3 times thru food chopper with plate openings $\leq 1/8''$ (3 mm), mixing thoroly after each grinding; and begin all detns promptly. If any delay occurs, chill sample to inhibit decomposition.

(**b**) *Canned meats.*—Pass entire contents of can thru food chopper, as in (**a**).

(**c**) *Sausages.*—Remove from casings and pass thru food chopper, as in (**a**).

Dry portions of samples of (**a**), (**b**), and (**c**) not needed for immediate analysis, either *in vacuo* $<60°$ or by evapg on steam bath 2 or 3 times with alcohol. Ext fat from dried product with pet ether (bp $<60°$) and let pet ether evap. spontaneously, finally expelling last traces by heating short time on steam bath. Do not heat sample or sepd fat longer than necessary because of tendency to decompose. Reserve fat in cool place for examination as in Chap. **28**, and complete examination before it becomes rancid.

Moisture

24.002 *Drying in Vacuo at 95–100°—Official Final Action*

Proceed as in **7.003**. (Not suitable for high fat products sucl as pork sausage.)

24.003 *Air Drying (1)—Official First Action*

(**a**) With lids removed, dry sample contg ca 2 g dry material 16–18 hr at 100–102° in air oven (mech. convection preferred). Use covered Al dish ≥ 50 mm diam. and ≤ 40 mm deep. Cool in desiccator and weigh. Report loss in wt as moisture.

(**b**) With lids removed, dry sample contg ca 2 g dry material to const wt (2–4 hr depending on product) in mech. convection oven or in gravity oven with single shelf at ca 125°. Use covered Al dish ≥ 50 mm diam. and ≤ 40 mm deep. Avoid excessive drying. Cover, cool in desiccator, and weigh. Report loss in wt as moisture. (Dried sample is not satisfactory for subsequent fat detn.)

24.004 Added Water in Sausage (*2*)—Procedure

$$\text{Per cent } H_2O \text{ added} = (W - 4P)/(1 - 0.01W + 0.04P);$$

where $W = \%\ H_2O$, and P (% protein) $= 6.25 \times \%$ N (corrected if necessary for protein in added substances such as nonfat dry milk, cereal, soybean flour).

24.005 Crude Fat or Ether Extract—Official Final Action

(**a**) Weigh 3–4 g sample by difference into thimble contg small amt of sand. Mix with glass rod, place thimble and rod in 50 mL beaker, and dry in oven 6 hr at 100–102° or 1.5 hr at 125°. Proceed as in **7.056**. Pet ether, **10.132**, may be used instead of anhyd. ether, if desired.

(**b**) Weigh 3–4 g sample by difference into small disposable Al dish, add sand, and mix, spreading mixt. on bottom of dish with glass or Al paddle. Dry with paddle as in (**a**). Roll edges of dish and insert with paddle into thimble. Proceed as in **7.056**. Pet ether, **10.132**, may be used in place of anhyd. ether, if desired.

Rapid Method (3)—Official Final Action

24.006 *Principle*

Fat is extd from sample with C_2Cl_4 in motor-driven, orbital shaker in presence of drying agent to absorb moisture. Ext is filtered and sp gr of filtrate is measured at 37° by mag. driven hydrometer. Digital reading is converted into fat content, using precalibrated chart.

24.007 *Apparatus and Reagents*

(**a**) *Foss-let fat analyzer.*—Includes orbital shaker, sp gr readout unit, solv. dispenser, ref. std oil (sp gr at 23° = 0.915; for periodic check of potentiometer calibration), stainless steel cup with cover and 8 mm bore brass hammer, pressure filtration device, and conversion chart (Foss America, Inc., PO Box 504, Rt 82, Fishkill, NY 12524).

(**b**) *Drying agent.*—Plaster of Paris (available locally thru paint, hardware, or building supply dealers), 8 mesh Drierite, or anhyd. $CaSO_4$.

(**c**) *Tetrachloroethylene.*—Tech. grade C_2Cl_4 (distributed locally thru dry cleaning suppliers or Fisher Scientific Co., No. C-182).

24.008 *Determination*

Prep. samples as in **24.001**. Check calibration of Foss-let potentiometer daily by using C_2Cl_4 alone to set zero point and mixt. of 22.5 g ref. std oil and 120 mL C_2Cl_4 (sp gr of mixt. at 37° = 1.4763) to set 50% fat point at 850.0.

Using either top-load or triple-beam balance with 0.1 g sensitivity, tare Foss-let cup after setting brass hammer on its spindle. To analyze products contg $\leq 60\%$ fat, weigh 45.0 g sample into cup; for products contg $>60\%$ fat, weigh 22.5 g. Add ca 80 g Plaster of Paris (or ca 60 g anhyd. $CaSO_4$). Dispense 120 mL C_2Cl_4 into cup. Press cover onto cup and install in orbital shaker. Set shaker timer for 2 min and turn unit on. While extn proceeds, assemble pressure filtration device by placing first 7 cm circle of Whatman No. 50 paper and then 7 cm circle of Whatman No. 1 PS phase sepg paper into perforated base. After 2 min extn, remove cup from shaker, lift cover, and remove brass hammer from cup. Immerse cup in ice-H_2O bath ca 0.4 min while stirring contents with thermometer to cool contents from 47–52° to ca 40°. Wipe H_2O from outer surface of cup and pour contents into assembled filter. Place piston at top of filtration device and slowly press ext thru measuring system. Depress drain valve button when ext appears in overflow tube and let chamber drain; then release valve button. Repeat filling and draining 2 more times until 40–50 mL ext has flowed thru, retaining final 10 mL ext in measuring chamber. Remove filtration device, slide viewing lens into position, rotate control of readout potentiometer clockwise until hydrometer rises, and record reading. Establish that ext is at chamber temp. by repeating reading 3–4 times. Average readings and convert into % fat by means of conversion chart. (Multiply chart % fat by 2 if 22.5 g portion of high-fat sample was taken.)

24.009 Ash—Official Final Action

See **31.012** or **31.013**.

Salt (Chlorine as Sodium Chloride)

24.010 ***Volumetric Method—Official First Action***

Moisten 2.5–3 g sample in 300 mL flask with excess 0.5*N* $AgNO_3$ soln, **50.027** (≥5 mL, depending on NaCl content of sample). Add 15 mL HNO_3 and boil until meat dissolves (10 min usually enough). Add concd aq. $KMnO_4$ soln in small portions, boiling after each addn until $KMnO_4$ color disappears and soln becomes colorless or nearly so. Add 25 mL H_2O and boil 5 min. Cool, dil. to ca 150 mL, add 25 mL ether, and shake. Det. Cl. as in **18.035**.

Indicating Strip Method (4)—Procedure

(Applicable to meat, fish, and cheese)

24.011 ***Principle***

QUANTAB Chloride Titrator is thin, chem. inert plastic strip, ca 13 × 90 mm, laminated with absorbent paper capillary column impregnated with brown $Ag_2Cr_2O_7$. When strip is placed in aq. soln, fluid rises in column by capillary action and continues to rise as long as Cl soln enters column. Cl in soln reacts with Ag impregnated in column to produce white color change of insol. AgCl. When capillary column is completely satd, moisture-sensitive signal across top of column turns dark blue to indicate completion of titrn. Length of white color change in column is proportional to Cl concn in test soln. Numbered scale is read at tip of white color change and converted to % salt by use of calibration table in package.

24.012 ***Apparatus***

QUANTAB Chloride Titrator.—No. 1176 (Ames Co., Div. Miles Laboratories, Inc.); range: 0.3–10% NaCl in food product; precision: ca ±10%.

24.013 ***Preparation of Sample***

(**a**) *Meat.—See* **24.001**.
(**b**) *Fish.—See* **18.012**.
(**c**) *Cheese.—See* **16.232**.

24.014 ***Determination***

Follow directions on package insert. Place 10 g prepd sample in suitable container, add 90 mL hot H_2O, and stir thoroly to ext NaCl. (If meat coagulates on adding hot H_2O, take new sample, add H_2O at room temp., heat to bp, cool, and proceed.) Cool. Place filter paper folded into cone-shaped cup directly into ext. Place QUANTAB into filtrate collected in bottom of cup and let reaction go to completion. After test signal is completely blue, read Titrator and convert reading to % NaCl with calibration table. Multiply by diln factor of 10.

Total Phosphorus

24.015 ***Method I—Official Final Action***

Destroy org. matter as in **2.020(c)** or (**d**), and proceed as in **7.119** or **8.033**.

24.016 ***Method II (5)—Official First Action***

Weigh, to nearest mg, 2.5±0.1 g sample, prepd as in **24.001**, into ashing dish (Pt, Vycor, or other suitable material) and dry 30 min at 125° in forced-draft oven. Ash in furnace at 550° to whiteness or near whiteness. Cool, add 25 mL HNO_3 (1+4), and heat on steam bath ca 30 min. Quant. filter into 400 mL beaker, using H_2O in transfer. Adjust vol. to ca 100 mL and proceed as in **2.028(b)**.

Automated Method (6)—Official First Action

24.017 ***Principle***

Phosphate and Mo^{+6} react in acid soln to produce 12-molybdophosphoric acid, which is reduced with 1-amino-2-naphthol-4-sulfonic acid to phosphomolybdenum blue. Max. *A* at 660 nm is proportional to amt P present. Method is applicable to 0.05–0.4% P.

24.018 ***Apparatus***

(**a**) *Automatic analyzer.*—AutoAnalyzer with following modules (Technicon Instruments Corp.): Sampler II; proportioning pump I; continuous digestor; proportioning pump II; current stabilizer; constant temp. bath equipped with variable temp. regulator (set at 70°); colorimeter with 15 mm tubular flowcell, 660 nm filters, and No. 9 aperture; voltage stabilizer; recorder with transmittance paper; vac. pump; 2 manifolds (Figs. **24:01** and **24:02**); and 8.5 mL sample cups.

(**b**) *Pipet.*—Automatic zeroing, 50 mL (Kontes Glass Co., K-763280).

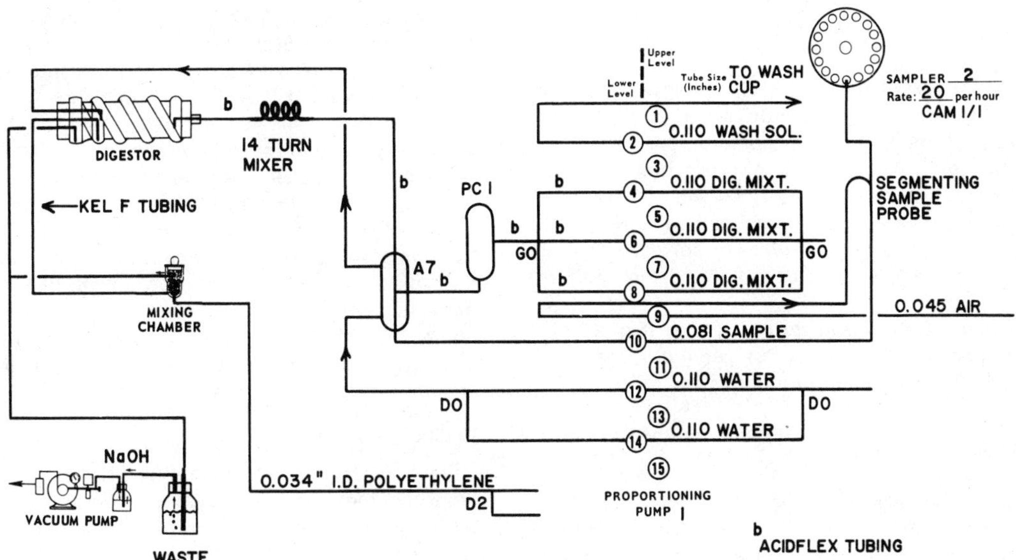

FIG. 24:01—Helix inlet manifold

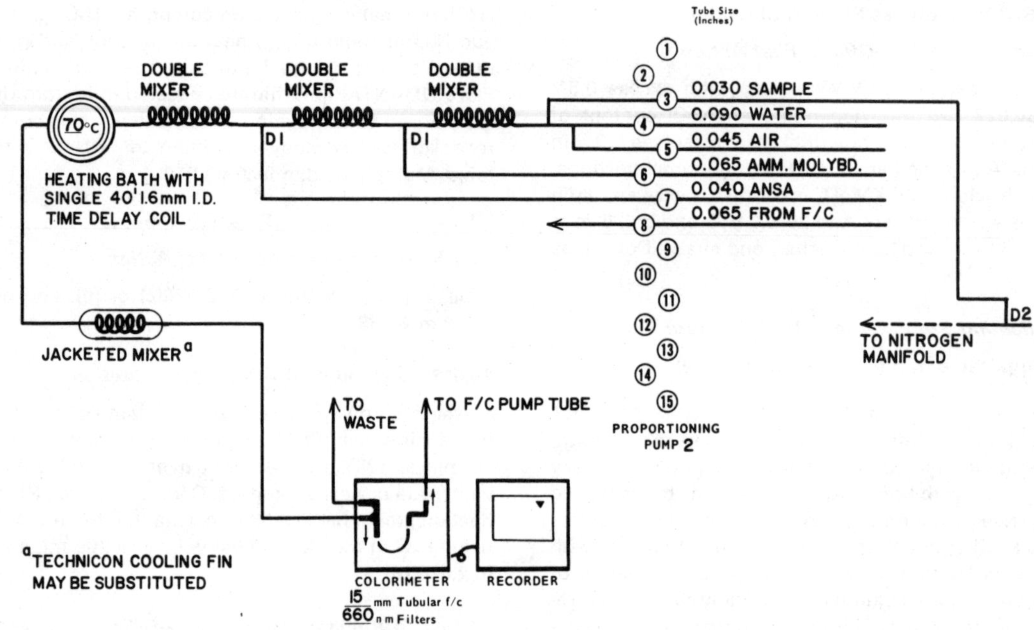

FIG. 24:02—Phosphorus analytical manifold

(**c**) *Tubing.*—Fluran F-5000, 0.125" id, or Teflon, 0.133" id.

(**d**) *Pipetting machine.*—Automatic Model 60453, with Model 70327 valve syringe (Sepco, 2201 Aisquith St., Baltimore, MD 21218).

24.019 ***Reagents***

(**a**) *Vanadium pentoxide soln.*—Weigh 40.0 g NaOH pellets and transfer to 1 L vol. flask. Add 500 mL H_2O, dissolve, and cool. Add 12.5 g V_2O_5 to flask, dissolve, dil. to vol., and mix.

(**b**) *Digestion mixture.*—Mix in order: 150 mL V_2O_5 soln, 90 mL 60–62% $HClO_4$, and 3460 mL H_2SO_4. (*Caution: See* **51.028** and **51.030**.) Rate of consumption is 495 mL/hr.

(**c**) *Wash soln.*—H_2SO_4 (1+1). To 1 L H_2O in 2 L vol. flask, add 1 L H_2SO_4 slowly with swirling. (*Caution: See* **51.030**.) Cool to room temp., dil. to vol. with H_2O, and mix. Rate of consumption is 234 mL/hr.

(**d**) *1-Amino-2-naphthol-4-sulfonic acid (ANSA).*— (*1*) *Soln A.*—Add 2.0 g Na_2SO_3 and 60 g $NaHSO_3$ to 320 mL H_2O in 500 mL vol. flask. Heat to 50° and add 1 g ANSA. Dissolve, cool, dil. to vol., and mix. Store in amber bottle; discard when ppt forms. (*2*) *Soln B.*— Dil. 100 mL Soln *A* to 1 L with H_2O. Add 0.5 mL Levor IV wetting agent (slurry contg 40% Na nonylbenzene sulfonate, Technicon Instruments Corp.). Store in amber bottle. Refrigerate when not in use. Rate of consumption is 36 mL/hr.

(**e**) *Ammonium molybdate soln.*—Dissolve 30 g $(NH_4)_6Mo_7O_{24}.4H_2O$ in ca 1 L H_2O. Dil. to 2 L and mix. Rate of consumption is 96 mL/hr.

(**f**) *Dilution water.*—(*1*) Pumped thru A7 fitting (Fig. **24:01**). Rate of consumption is 468 mL/hr. (*2*) Pumped thru P analytical manifold (Fig. **24:02**). Rate of consumption is 174 mL/hr.

24.020 ***Preparation of Standards***

Weigh 10.9839 g KH_2PO_4 into 250 mL vol. flask, add H_2O to dissolve, and dil. to vol. Transfer 5.0, 7.5, 10.0, 15.0, 20.0, 25.0, 30.0, and 40.0 mL to 8 sep. 1 L vol. flasks. Add H_2O to 500 mL. Place flasks in ice bath and slowly add 500 mL H_2SO_4 to each. Cool, dil. to vol. with H_2O, and store in 1 L polyethylene bottles. Based on 10 g sample, as prepd in **24.021**, % P = 0.050, 0.075, 0.100, 0.150, 0.200, 0.250, 0.300, and 0.400.

24.021 ***Preparation of Sample***

Accurately weigh 10.00 g sample into 200 mL tall-form beaker. Pipet 53 mL H_2O into beaker with pipetting machine, (**d**). Add 1" (2.5 cm) Teflon-coated stirring bar, cover with 60 mm watch glass, and disperse sample, using mag. stirrer. With stirring, add 50 mL H_2SO_4, using automatic pipet, (**b**), and continue stirring until sample is dissolved. Cool to room temp. in cooling bath.

24.022 ***Analytical System***

Use std 0.0625" id transmission tubing thruout system unless otherwise specified. Pump sample at 2.5 mL/min and segment with air pumped at 0.8 mL/min. Pump digestion mixt. at 8.28 mL/min thru PC1 fitting and add to sample at A7 fitting. Pass sample stream thru 14-turn mixing coil into inlet of digestor helix. Pump diln H_2O at 7.80 mL/min thru A7 fitting to outlet end of digestor helix. Aspirate dild sample into bubble chamber and remove aliquot for analysis at 0.35 mL/min. Dil. aliquot with H_2O pumped at 2.90 mL/min and segment with air at 0.80 mL/min. Pass stream thru 28-turn mixer, and add NH_4 molybdate at 1.60 mL/min. Pass stream thru second 28-turn mixer followed by addn of ANSA Soln *B* pumped at 0.60 mL/min. After final 28-turn mixer, pass stream into 70° heating bath for color development, cool in jacketed mixer, and pass into colorimeter equipped with 660 nm filters and 15 mm tubular flowcell. Measure *A* at 660 nm. Pump stream from flowcell at 1.60 mL/min.

24.023 ***Start-Up Procedure***

Place all reagent lines, except Acidflex, in water; turn on both proportioning pumps and digestor power. Turn on vac. pump, setting gage at 12–15 psi. Pump digestion mixt. and all anal. reagents thru their respective lines after detg that system is operating properly. After 5 min, turn on heat switch and adjust amperage to proper settings. Amperage should be adjusted to give temp. readout in range of 280–400° in first stage and 250–380° in second and third stages. Warm-up time is ca 20 min (older digestor units may require longer). Set recorder baseline at 99% *T* or 0.01 *A*.

24.024 ***Shut-Down Procedure***

Turn off heat switch and let first stage temp. reach 200°. Remove helix cover and place all reagent lines except digestion mixt. in H_2O after first stage temp. is $<150°$. Place digestion mixt. line in empty erlenmeyer and let Acidflex pump tubes "air-wash." Rinse entire system for 15 min. Shut off proportioning pumps and break vac. in liq. waste bottle. Turn off digestor power switch and replace helix cover.

24.025 ***Determination***

Pour std and prepd samples into 8.5 mL cups and place in Sampler II turntable. Adjust sampling rate to 20/hr, with 1:1 sample-to-wash ratio to provide 1.5 min sampling and 1.5 min wash. Press reset button and activate sampler turntable, thus passing stds and samples into anal. system. Place stop bar in turntable. (Formation of excessive fat deposits in sample line between segmenting sample probe and input manifold can be retarded by passing wash soln thru double mixer wrapped with heating tape and covered with layer of Al foil and layer of asbestos; adjust temp. to 60° with variable transformer connected to heating tape.)

Read % *T* of samples from recorder strip chart and compare with std curves of % *T* against % P on 1 cycle, 70 division semilog paper. *A* strip chart paper may also be used. Include std curve with every 30 samples. (% P can be converted to % Na tripolyphosphate, using gravimetric factor 3.96, after % P naturally occurring in meat is deducted.) Diln error caused by variation in moisture content of samples does not significantly affect P detn. Std curve is linear thru range of stds.

24.026 Arsenic—Official Final Action

See **25.014–25.019**.

Nitrogen

24.027 ***Kjeldahl Method (7)—Official Final Action***

Proceed as in **2.057**, using ca 2 g fresh sample and 40 mL H_2SO_4 for digestion.

Automated Method I (8)—Official First Action

24.028 ***Principle***

NH_3 reacts with hypochlorite and phenate ion in alk. soln to produce quinonechloroamine which reacts with addnl phenate ion, producing blue dissociated form of indophenol with max. *A* at 630 nm in alk. soln.

24.029 ***Apparatus***

See **24.018(b)**, **(c)**, and **(d)**, and in addn:

(a) *Automatic analyzer.—See* **24.018(a)**. N input manifold is same as for P, Fig. **24:01**. N anal. manifold is shown in Fig. **24:03**.

24.030 ***Reagents***

See **24.019(a)**, **(b)** (consumption rate, 497 mL/hr), and **(c)**, and in addn:

(a) *Alkaline tartrate soln.*—Dissolve 150 g K Na tartrate.$4H_2O$ in 1950 mL H_2O and add 1050 mL 50% NaOH soln. Consumption rate is 174 mL/hr.

(b) *Sodium hypochlorite soln.*—4–6% NaOCl (Fisher Scientific Co.). Consumption rate is 25 mL/hr.

(c) *Alkaline phenol soln.*—Prep. 15*N* NaOH soln by adding 2400 mL 50% NaOH (w/w) to 600 mL H_2O, cooling, and storing in polyethylene bottle. To 500 mL 15*N* NaOH in vessel cooled by circulating cold H_2O, slowly add 276 mL 90% liq. phenol. Cool to room temp. and dil. to 1 L. Store in dark in polyethylene bottle. Consumption rate is 48 mL/hr.

(d) *Dilution water.*—(*1*) *Input manifold.*—Consumption rate is 468 mL/hr. (*2*) *Analytical manifold.* —Consumption rate is 234 mL/hr.

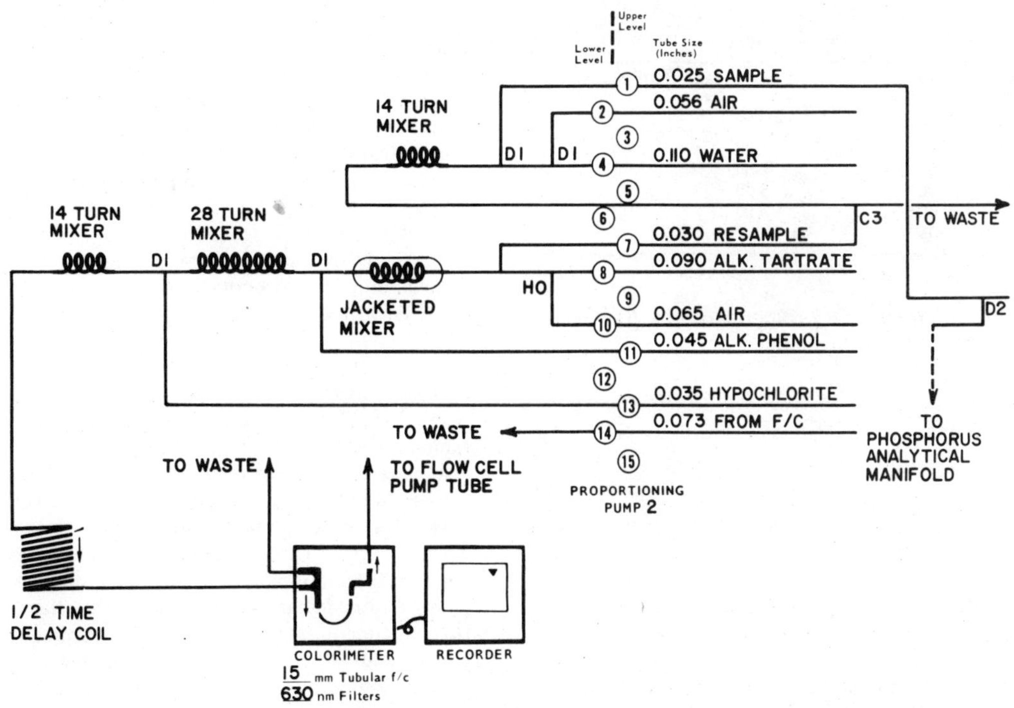

FIG. 24:03—Nitrogen analytical manifold

24.031 ***Preparation of Standard***

Grind freeze-dried beef (available from camping supply stores) 4 times in std laboratory mill (Straub Co., Croydon, PA 19020), Model 4-E, or equiv.). Store ground material in freezer to prevent deterioration. Det. Kjeldahl N by **24.027**, using 0.3–0.5 g. Based on N content, prep. stds contg 0.8, 1.2, 1.6, 2.0, 2.4, 2.8, 3.2, 3.6, and 4.0 mg N/mL as follows: Into 9 sep. 1.5 L beakers, transfer weighed amt freeze dried beef. Add 400 mL H_2O and disperse thoroly, using mag. stirrer. Slowly add, with stirring, 500 mL H_2SO_4 and continue stirring 15 min. Cool in ice bath until fat solidifies. With aid of stirring rod and funnel, transfer soln thru glass wool pad into 1 L vol. flask. Let warm to room temp., dil. to vol., and mix. Store in polyethylene bottle. Soln is stable ≥75 days.

24.032 ***Preparation of Sample***

Proceed as in **24.021**.

24.033 ***Analytical System***

Proceed as in **24.022** thru ". . . digestor helix." Aspirate dild sample into bubble chamber and remove aliquot for analysis at rate of 0.23 mL/min. Dil. aliquot with H_2O pumped at 3.90 mL/min and segment with air at 1.20 mL/min. Pass stream thru 14 turn mixer and C3 debubbler, and resample at 0.32 mL/min. Add alk. tartrate soln at 2.90 mL/min and air at 1.60 mL/min. Then pass stream thru jacketed mixer, add alk. phenol soln at 0.80 mL/min, and pass thru double mixer. Add NaOCl soln at 0.42 mL/min and pass stream thru 14 turn mixer and ½ time-delay coil for color development. Finally pass stream into colorimeter with 630 nm filter and 15 mm tubular flowcell into waste at 2.00 mL/min.

24.034 ***Start-Up Procedure***

Prior to routine use, optimize digestor unit as follows: Using 2.0 mg N/mL std in duplicate, vary amperage setting according to following table, and record *A*. Allow 20 min interval after changing setting to stabilize helix temp. before std is analyzed. Use settings giving highest *A*.

Amperage Settings		Amperage Settings	
Stage 1	Stages 2 & 3	Stage 1	Stages 2 & 3
2.50	3.00	4.20	6.40
3.00	4.00	4.50	7.00
3.50	5.00	5.00	8.00
3.80	5.60	5.50	9.00
4.00	6.00		

Set digestor helix to rotate at 6.7 rpm, referring to Technicon Manual T-69-123 (1970) for instructions.

24.035 ***Shut-Down Procedure***

Proceed as in **24.024**.

24.036 ***Determination***

Proceed as in **24.025**. Read *A* of samples from recorder chart and compare with std curve of *A* against mg N/mL. Include std curve with every 30 samples.

As 53 mL H_2O + 50 mL H_2SO_4 added to samples gives 95 mL (8 mL contraction), it may be assumed that 10 g samples contg 50% H_2O give final vol. of 100 mL. However, certain dry products (e.g., pepperoni) or wet products (e.g., corned beef brisket) may contain considerably more or less than 50%, causing an error by as much as 0.6% protein. Close approximation may be obtained by adding H_2O content of sample, **24.003(a)** or **(b)**, to 95 mL to obtain final total vol. Using this assumption,

% N = [(% H_2O in sample/10) + 95] × (mg N/mL) × 0.01.

% Protein = % N × 6.25.

24.037 Automated Method II (*9*)—Official First Action

See **7.021–7.024**.

Nitrates and Nitrites

Xylenol Method (10)—Official First Action

24.038 ***Apparatus***

Use simple distn app., including distn bulb. Type of glass condenser utilizing thin, rapidly moving H_2O film as cooling medium (West type) is recommended.

24.039 ***Reagents***

(a) *m-Xylenol*.—2,4-Dimethylphenol. Eastman Kodak Co. No. 1150, or equiv.

(b) *Silver-ammonium hydroxide soln*.—Dissolve 5 g *nitrate-free* Ag_2SO_4 in 60 mL NH_4OH. Heat to bp, conc. to ca 30 mL, cool, and dil. to 100 mL with H_2O.

(c) *Bromocresol green indicator*.—Dissolve 0.1 g bromocresol green in 1.5 mL 0.1*N* NaOH, and dil. to 100 mL with H_2O.

(d) *Nitrate std soln*.—Dissolve 0.1805 g recrystd KNO_3 in H_2O and dil. to 1 L, or dil. 17.85 mL 0.1*N* HNO_3 to 1 L; 10 mL contains 0.25 mg nitrate N.

24.040 ***Determination***

Mix 5–10 g finely comminuted and thoroly mixed sample with 80 mL warm H_2O. Break up all lumps and heat on steam bath 1 hr, stirring occasionally. Transfer to 100 mL vol. flask, cool, dil. to vol., and mix. Filter, or let settle, and pipet 40 mL filtrate, or supernate, into 50 mL vol. flask. (No correction for vol. occupied by meat is necessary.) Add 3 drops bromocresol green indicator. Add H_2SO_4 (1+10) dropwise until color changes to yellow. Oxidize nitrites to nitrates by adding 0.2*N* $KMnO_4$ soln dropwise with shaking until faint pink remains ca 1 min. Add 1 mL H_2SO_4 (1+10) and 1 mL *phosphotungstic acid soln* (20 g/100 mL). Dil. to vol., mix, and filter.

Into 500 mL flask (erlenmeyer is satisfactory) measure aliquot (≤20 mL) contg 0.025–0.25 mg nitrate N. (If >20 mL is required, make slightly alk. and conc. by evapn.) Add enough Ag-NH_4OH soln to ppt all chlorides and most of excess phosphotungstic acid. (Slight excess of Ag reagent is not harmful; 1 or 2 mL is usually enough.) Without decanting or filtering, add vol. H_2SO_4 (3+1) ca 3 times vol. liq. in flask. Stopper flask, mix, cool to ca 35°, add 0.05 mL (1–2 drops) of the *m*-xylenol, stopper, shake, and hold 30 min at 30–40°.

(Yellow to brownish yellow color, indicative of nitrates, appears. Bright red ppt, due to incomplete removal of phosphotungstic acid, may also appear. Slight excess of phosphotungstic acid causes no interference but large excess may.)

After nitration is complete, add 150 mL H_2O, taking care to wash off stopper, and distil 40–50 mL into receiver contg 5 mL NaOH (10 g/L). Quickly remove any nitroxylenol solidifying in condenser by stopping H_2O flow and letting condenser become warm. Transfer distillate to 100 mL vol. flask, dil. to vol. with H_2O, and det. nitrate N by comparing reading of color of suitable aliquot with std curve prepd at ca 450 nm.

Prep. color std from 10 mL nitrate std soln, using 0.05 mL *m*-xylenol and 30 mL H_2SO_4 (3+1), and dilg distillate to 500 mL.

Nitrites (*11*)—Official First Action

(Applicable to cured meats)

24.041 ***Reagents and Apparatus***

(**a**) *NED reagent.*—Dissolve 0.2 g *N*-(1-naphthyl) ethylenediamine.2HCl in 150 mL 15% (v/v) HOAc. Filter, if necessary, and store in g-s brown glass bottle.

(**b**) *Sulfanilamide reagent.*—Dissolve 0.5 g sulfanilamide in 150 mL 15% HOAc. Filter, if necessary, and store in g-s brown glass bottle.

(**c**) *Nitrite std solns.*—(*1*) *Stock soln.*—1000 ppm $NaNO_2$. Dissolve 1.000 g $NaNO_2$ in H_2O and dil. to 1 L. (*2*) *Intermediate soln.*—100 ppm $NaNO_2$. Dil. 100 mL stock soln to 1 L with H_2O. (*3*) *Working soln.*— 1 ppm $NaNO_2$. Dil. 10 mL intermediate soln to 1 L with H_2O.

(**d**) *Filter paper.*—Test for nitrite contamination by analyzing 3–4 sheets, at random, thruout box. Filter ca 40 mL H_2O thru each sheet. Add 4 mL sulfanilamide reagent, mix, let stand 5 min, add 4 mL NED reagent, mix, and wait 15 min. If any sheets are positive, discard entire box.

24.042 ***Determination***

Weigh 5 g finely comminuted and thoroly mixed sample into 50 mL beaker. Add ca 40 mL H_2O heated to 80°. Mix thoroly with glass rod, taking care to break up all lumps, and transfer to 500 mL vol. flask. Thoroly wash beaker and rod with successive portions of the hot H_2O, adding all washings to flask. Add enough hot H_2O to bring vol. to ca 300 mL, transfer flask to steam bath, and let stand 2 hr, shaking occasionally. Cool to room temp., dil. to vol. with H_2O, and remix. Filter, add 2.5 mL sulfanilamide reagent to aliquot contg 5–50 μg $NaNO_2$ in 50 mL vol. flask, and mix. After 5 min, add 2.5 mL NED reagent, mix, dil. to vol., mix, and let color develop 15 min. Transfer portion of soln to photometer cell and det. *A* at 540 nm against blank of 45 mL H_2O, 2.5 mL sulfanilamide reagent, and 2.5 mL NED reagent.

Det. nitrite present by comparison with std curve prepd as follows: Add 10, 20, 30, and 40 mL nitrite working std soln to 50 mL vol. flasks, add 2.5 mL sulfanilamide reagent, mix, and proceed as above, beginning "After 5 min, . . ." Std curve is straight line to 1 ppm $NaNO_2$ in final soln.

★ Creatine—Official Final Action ★

24.043 ***Preparation of Solution***

Exhaust 7–25 g sample (depending upon H_2O content) as follows: Weigh into 150 mL beaker, add 5–10 mL cold (15°) NH_3-free H_2O, and stir to homogeneous paste. Add 50 mL cold H_2O, stir at 3 min intervals during 15 min, let stand 2–3 min, and decant liq. thru quant. filter, collecting filtrate in 500 mL vol. flask. Drain beaker, pressing out liq. from meat residue with glass rod. Add 50 mL cold H_2O to residue in beaker, stir 5 min, let stand 2–3 min, and decant as before. If much meat is transferred to filter, return it to beaker with glass rod. Repeat extns, using two 50 mL portions and four 25 mL portions cold H_2O. After last extn, transfer entire insol. portion to filter and wash with three 10 mL portions H_2O, letting material drain thoroly after each addn. Dil. to vol. and mix thoroly.

Measure 150 mL ext into 250 mL beaker and evap. to 40 mL on steam bath, stirring occasionally. Neutze to phthln, using indicator outside the soln. Add 1 mL 0.1*N* HOAc and boil gently 5 min. (Coagulum should sep. at once, leaving clear liq.) Filter thru quant. paper, wash beaker thoroly 4 times with hot H_2O, wash coagulum on filter 3 times, and discard coagulum.

24.044 ***Determination***

(*Caution: See* **51.029** and **51.068**.)

Evap. filtrate and washings, **24.043**, to 5–10 mL, transfer with min. amt hot H_2O to 50 mL vol. flask, keeping vol. $<$30 mL, add 10 mL 2*N* HCl, and mix. Hydrolyze 20 min in autoclave at 117–120°, let cool somewhat, and chill under running H_2O. Partially neutze excess acid by adding 7.5 mL 10% NaOH soln (CO_3-free), dil. to vol., and mix.

Make preliminary reading after carrying thru reaction on 20 mL with Duboscq colorimeter to det. vol. needed to obtain reading of ca 8 mm. Transfer such vol. to 500 mL vol. flask and add 10 mL 10% NaOH soln and 30 mL *satd* (*1.2%*) *picric acid soln*. Mix, rotate 30 sec, and let stand exactly 4.5 min. Dil. to vol. at once with H_2O, shake thoroly, and compare, preferably in Duboscq colorimeter, with std soln prepd by treating with NaOH and picric acid, and dilg to 500 mL as above, 50 mL of soln contg 1.603 g *creatinine Zn chloride* in 1 L 0.1*N* HCl (1 mL = 0.001 g creatinine; g creatinine $\times$ 1.16 = g creatine.

Amino Nitrogen

24.045 ★ ***Van Slyke Method (12)—Official First Action*** ★

Reaction of amino group with HNO_2 to form N which is measured gasometrically. *See* **24.041–24.042**, 12th ed.

24.046 ★ ***Sorensen Method (13)—Official First Action*** ★

To 20 mL filtrate, **24.043**, second par., neutzd to phthln with $Ba(OH)_2$ or NaOH, or to 20 mL of equiv. ext of meat (sometimes larger vol. may be necessary) add 10 mL freshly prepd *phthln-formol mixt.* (50 mL 40% HCHO soln contg 1 mL 0.05% phthln soln in 50% alcohol, exactly neutzd with 0.2*N* $Ba(OH)_2$ or NaOH). Titr. mixt. with 0.2*N* $Ba(OH)_2$ to distinct red, add small but known excess 0.2*N* $Ba(OH)_2$, and back-titr. to neutrality with 0.2*N* HCl.

Conduct blank titrn with same reagents, using 20 mL H_2O in place of soln to be tested. From vol. 0.2*N* $Ba(OH)_2$ required to neutze mixt., corrected for vol. used in blank titrn, calc. amt amino N present (including NH_3 if this has not been removed).

1 mL 0.2*N* $Ba(OH)_2$ soln = 2.8 mg amino N.

24.047 Starchy Flour—Qualitative Tests—Procedure

(In chopped meat, sausage, deviled meat, etc.)

(**a**) Treat 5–6 g sample with boiling H_2O 2–3 min, cool mixt., and test supernate with I soln, **30.029(d)**. (In interpreting test, note that small amt of starch may be present from use of spices. If strong reaction is given, cereal products are present. This qual. test may be replaced by microscopic examination, which discloses not only presence of added starch but also variety used.)

(**b**) *Not applicable in presence of cellulosic material other than that from starchy flour and spice.*—To 10 g sample in 100 mL graduated oil tube (ASTM conical form with stem graduated from 0 to 3 mL in 0.1 mL), add 50 mL *8% alc. KOH soln* and digest on steam bath 1 hr, stirring occasionally. Dil. to 100 mL with alcohol and mix. Let stand 1 hr, gently rotating once or twice during this period to loosen particles on sides of tube. After 1 hr, read vol. of sediment in tube. Vol. $>$1 mL, if sample contains spices, or $>$0.5 mL if only spice oils are present, indicates presence of added starchy flour. Vol. $<$3 mL indicates that $<$3% flour is present, and vol. $>$3.5 mL indicates presence of $>$3.5% flour. (If sample contains dried skim milk or dried corn sirup, before proceeding with test remove lactose or

★ Surplus method—*see* inside front cover.

maltose by shaking 10 g in 100 mL centrf. tube with two 50 mL portions warm H_2O and centrfg and decanting after each shaking.)

24.048 Soybean Flour—Qualitative Test (*14*)—Procedure

Mix 10 g finely divided sample in 250 mL beaker with 75 mL *8% alc. KOH soln*, and heat on steam bath until all meat is dissolved (30–45 min). Transfer liq. and residue to 100 mL graduated sedimentation tube, dil. to 100 mL with alcohol, and let settle. Decant as completely as possible, and cover residue with ca 50 mL warm H_2O. Stopper tube and shake vigorously; let stand few min until foam subsides; then transfer to 50 mL centrf. tube, and centrf. Pour off and discard supernate, and add 10 mL HCl to centrf. tube. Stopper and shake, or mix contents thoroly with glass rod. Add ca 15 mL 25% alcohol, mix, and centrf. Decant supernate and examine residue under microscope for characteristic "hour-glass" or I-shaped cells (sometimes called "bearer cells"), preferably with polarized light.

24.049 Preservatives—Official Final Action

See Chap. **20**.

Qualitative Test for Agar—Official Final Action

24.050 ***Reagents***

(**a**) *Trichloroacetic acid soln.*—25 g acid in 50 mL H_2O. (*Caution: See* **51.082**.)

(**b**) *Iodine soln.*—Approx. 0.033*N*.

(**c**) *Benedict qualitative soln.*—*See* **16.269**(**a**).

24.051 ***Preparation of Sample***

(**a**) *Boned chicken or meat.*—Refrigerate overnight to jell broth. With thin-blade spatula, sep. as much jell as possible, and warm on steam bath until completely liquefied.

(**b**) *Consommé or broth.*—No prepn necessary.

24.052 ***Detection of Gum***

Transfer up to 40 mL liquefied jell from meat, or 40 mL consommé, to 100 mL beaker. Add 5 mL trichloroacetic acid soln, stir, and let stand 15–30 min. Transfer to 50 mL conical centrf. tube and centrf. 15–20 min at ca 1200 rpm. Decant clear supernate into 250 mL (8 oz) centrf. bottle or nursing bottle, add 4–5 vols alcohol, and let stand until ppt coagulates, or overnight. (No ppt indicates absence of gums.) Centrf. at 1200 rpm 15–30 min until ppt packs to bottom of centrf. bottle. Carefully decant alcohol, taking care not to disturb packed gum ppt. Remove few remaining drops of alcohol by spontaneous drying or by gentle air current. Add 1 drop 0.033*N* I soln. Evanescent violet or black color indicates presence of agar. (Neg. test does not necessarily mean agar is absent.)

Add 3 mL hot H_2O and warm on steam bath until gum ppt dissolves. Chill gum soln in ice and H_2O mixt. Thickening, or stiff jell, indicates agar. Warm cooled mixt. on steam bath, transfer to 50 mL beaker, rinse centrf. bottle with 3–4 mL H_2O, and add rinsings to jell soln. Add 1 mL HCl and boil 30 sec. Transfer 1 mL hydrolyzed gum soln to test tube, neutze with 10% NaOH soln, using litmus paper as indicator (ca 2 mL required), remove litmus paper, add 5 mL Benedict soln, and boil cautiously over free flame 30–60 sec. Green, yellow, or brick-colored ppt after spontaneous cooling indicates agar (or other hydrolyzable gum).

24.053 Nonfat Dry Milk (Qualitative Test) (*15*)—Procedure

(In absence of maltose)

To 10 g comminuted sample in small beaker add 20 mL hot (70–90°) H_2O. Mix thoroly and filter. Transfer 4 mL filtrate to test tube, add 3–4 drops *5% $MeNH_2.HCl$ soln*, and boil 30 sec. Remove from flame, add 3–5 drops 20% NaOH soln, and shake 10 sec. Soln turns yellow immediately, then slowly changes to carmine if lactose is present, indicating presence of nonfat dry milk.

Lactose (*16*)—Official First Action

24.054 ***Reagents***

(**a**) *Acclimated yeast suspension (for use in presence or absence of maltose).*—Macerate 2 cakes (0.6 oz (17 g) each) bakers yeast and wash with 3 ca 50 mL portions H_2O, centrfg between washings. Prep. medium contg 1.0 g anhyd. $MgSO_4$, 2.0 g NH_4Cl, 1.0 g anhyd. K_2HPO_4, 0.5 g KCl, 0.02 g $FeSO_4.7H_2O$, 0.7 g peptone, and 20.0 g tech. maltose. Dissolve each ingredient in small amt H_2O and add, in order given, to flask contg ca 500 mL H_2O. Dil. to 1 L. Warm, filter, bring filtrate to rolling boil, and let cool to room temp. Add washed yeast to 1 L medium and incubate ca 24 hr at 30°, stirring frequently first few hr. Sep. yeast by decanting and centrfg, wash twice with H_2O, add to 1 L fresh medium, and incubate addnl 24 hr with agitation first few hr. Sep. yeast from medium, wash thoroly ≥4 times with H_2O, dil. to 100 mL, and refrigerate. Yeast remains active 2–3 weeks. (Yeast may remain active longer if frozen.)

(**b**) *Washed yeast suspension (for use in absence of maltose).*—Mix 2 cakes bakers yeast to smooth suspension with ca 150 mL H_2O. Centrf. 5 min and discard aq. layer. Repeat mixing with H_2O and centrfg 4 more times, or until supernate after centrfg is practically clear. Again suspend yeast in H_2O and dil. with H_2O to 100 mL. Store in refrigerator at ca 4° and shake well before using. Discard after 2 weeks.

(**c**) *Benedict soln.*—Dissolve 16 g $CuSO_4.5H_2O$ in 125–150 mL H_2O. Dissolve 150 g Na citrate.$2H_2O$, 130 g anhyd. Na_2CO_3, and 10 g $NaHCO_3$ in ca 650 mL hot H_2O. Combine the 2 solns, cool, dil. to 1 L, and filter.

(**d**) *Lactose std soln.*—1.5 mg anhyd. lactose/mL. Dissolve 1.5789 g lactose.H_2O in H_2O and dil. to 1 L.

(**e**) *Iodine std soln.*—Mix 5.08 g I with 10.2 g KI, dissolve in small vol. of H_2O, filter, and dil. to 1 L.

(**f**) *Sodium thiosulfate std soln.*—Dissolve 9.92 g $Na_2S_2O_3.5H_2O$ in H_2O and dil. to 1 L.

(**g**) *Dilute acetic acid.*—Dil. 240 mL HOAc to 1 L with H_2O.

(**h**) *Dilute phosphoric acid.*—Dil. 240 mL H_3PO_4 to 1 L with H_2O.

(**i**) *Citric acid-phosphate buffer.*—pH 4.8. Mix solns in proportions of 10.14 mL 0.1*M* citric acid (19.21 g/L) and 9.86 mL 0.2*M* Na_2HPO_4 (28.4 g anhyd./L), and adjust to pH 4.8, using pH meter. Store in refrigerator and discard if soln becomes turbid.

(**j**) *Starch soln.*—Rub 2.5 g sol. starch and ca 10 mg HgI_2 in little H_2O. Dissolve in ca 500 mL boiling H_2O.

24.055 ***Determination (in Presence of Maltose)***

Place 10 g sample in 100 mL vol. sugar flask, add small vol. of H_2O, and break up sample by agitation. Add ca 50 mL H_2O and warm on steam bath ca 30 min. Cool to room temp., add 2 mL HCl, and dil. to vol., using bottom of fat layer as meniscus. Add 5.0 mL *20% phosphotungstic acid soln*, mix well, let stand few min, and filter thru moist paper. Pipet 40 mL filtrate into 50 mL vol. flask and neutze just to acid side of chlorophenol red or other indicator which shows change at ca pH 4.8. Add 5 mL pH 4.8 buffer soln, dil. to vol., and mix.

Transfer ca 40 mL of this soln to centrf. tube to which 5 mL yeast suspension, (**a**), has been added and from which H_2O has been sepd. Mix yeast and sample well and incubate 3 hr at 30°, stirring frequently. Centrf. and det. reducing sugars:

Pipet 10 mL clear soln into 300 mL erlenmeyer, add 20 mL Benedict soln, (**c**), bring to bp in 3–5 min, and boil slowly exactly 3 min. Remove from heat, cool, and add 100 mL H_2O and 10 mL dil. HOAc, (**g**), slowly while swirling. Add ca 30% excess std I, (**e**) (15 mL for ca 1.5% lactose), and agitate to dissolve Cu_2O. Let flask stand ≥5 min, add 20 mL dil. H_3PO_4, (**h**), and titr. excess I with std $Na_2S_2O_3$ soln, (**f**), using starch indicator.

Det. lactose:I ratio by using 10 mL std lactose soln and carrying thru detn as above, beginning "... add 20 mL Benedict soln, ..." Det. I:$Na_2S_2O_3$ ratio by using 10 mL H_2O and carrying thru detn as above, beginning "... add 20 mL Benedict soln, ..."

% Lactose = $100\,KV/W$, where K = g lactose/mL I soln, V = vol. I soln consumed, and W = g sample in aliquot, considering vol. original sample soln as 100 mL rather than 105 mL, to correct for vol. occupied by meat.

24.056 ***Determination (in Absence of Maltose)***

Prep. soln as in **24.055**, first par. Place 5 mL washed yeast suspension, (**a**) or (**b**), in lipless centrf., tube, centrf., and drain and discard supernate. Add 40 mL prepd soln to yeast residue in centrf. tube, stopper, and shake vigorously to dislodge and suspend yeast. Let stand with occasional shaking 1 hr. Centrf. and det. lactose in clear soln as in **24.055**, third par.

Starch (*17*)—Official Final Action

(Not applicable to liver products)

24.057 ***Reagents***

(**a**) *Zinc acetate soln.*—Dissolve 12 g $Zn(OAc)_2.2H_2O$ in H_2O and dil. to 100 mL.

(**b**) *Potassium ferrocyanide soln.*—Dissolve 6 g $K_4Fe(CN)_6.3H_2O$ in H_2O and dil. to 100 mL.

(**c**) *Copper sulfate soln.*—Dissolve 40.0 g $CuSO_4.5H_2O$ in H_2O and dil. to 1 L.

(**d**) *Alkaline tartrate soln.*—Dissolve 200 g Rochelle salt and 150 g NaOH in hot H_2O, filter, and dil. to 1 L.

(**e**) *Glucose std soln.*—Dissolve 0.40 g pure glucose in H_2O and dil. to 200 mL.

(**f**) *Starch indicator soln.*—Mix 1 g powd sol. starch with 20 mL cold H_2O. Pour mixt. into 500 mL boiling H_2O and boil 10 min. Cool, and add few drops $CHCl_3$.

(**g**) *Phosphotungstic acid soln.*—Dissolve 20 g phosphotungstic acid in H_2O, dil. to 100 mL, and filter.

24.058 ***Extraction and Hydrolysis***

Weigh 10 g finely ground and thoroly mixed sample into 250 mL heat-resistant centrf. bottle. If fat content is so high as to interfere with subsequent filtering, add 25 mL pet ether, mix thoroly with glass rod, decant, and repeat with 2 addnl 25 mL portions pet ether. Add 100 mL H_2O, 5 mL freshly prepd $Zn(OAc)_2$ soln, and 5 mL freshly prepd $K_4Fe(CN)_6$ soln. Stopper tightly and let stand 15 min, shaking vigorously several times during this period. Centrf. 15 min at 1500 rpm. Decant supernate into 12.5 cm Whatman No. 3 filter paper in conical funnel, using light suction. To residue in centrf. bottle add 25 mL freshly prepd soln contg 1 mL $Zn(OAc)_2$ plus 1 mL $K_4Fe(CN)_6$ solns/200 mL soln. Let stand 10 min, shaking several times during this period; then centrf. 10 min at 1500 rpm and decant thru same paper. Repeat last extn with addnl 25 mL $Zn(OAc)_2$-$K_4Fe(CN)_6$ washing soln. Rinse stopper with H_2O.

Transfer funnel contg filter paper to centrf. bottle. From graduate contg 90 mL hot (ca 70°) 1.5*N* HCl pour 40 mL into paper to melt adhering fat and to free starch. Poke hole in tip of paper and let acid run into centrf. bottle. Wash paper with remainder of acid soln. Suspend bottle in open boiling H_2O bath so that level of H_2O in bath is at approx. level of soln within bottle. Do not reflux. Hydrolyze exactly 1.5 hr, keeping H_2O level of bath at original position, stirring contents of bottle occasionally. Do not transfer paper to centrf. bottle, as it will hydrolyze and give high values.

Cool immediately. (If necessary, sample may stand overnight at this point.) Make just alk. to litmus with 20% NaOH (ca 27 mL) and then add 10 mL HCl (1+2). Transfer to 200 mL phosphoric acid flask or 200 mL erlenmeyer marked at 200 mL. Rinse centrf. bottle with 15 mL phosphotungstic acid soln, followed by several 10 mL portions H_2O. Dil. to vol. with fat layer, if any, just above mark. Stopper, shake, let stand ca 30 min, and filter soln thru Whatman No. 1 paper.

24.059 ***Determination of Reducing Sugars***

Pipet 20 mL filtrate into 200 mL erlenmeyer. Pipet in 20 mL $CuSO_4$ soln and 20 mL alk. Rochelle salt soln. Bring to boil within 2 min, swirling occasionally, and continue boiling 1 min. Cool immediately under running H_2O, transfer to 200 mL vol. flask, dil. to vol. with H_2O, stopper, and shake.

Pipet 50 mL soln into 200 mL erlenmeyer. Add 25 mL 10% KI and 5 mL H_2SO_4 (1+3). Titr. with ca 0.025*N* $Na_2S_2O_3$ soln, adding 2 mL starch indicator and ca 2.0 g solid KSCN when yellow has almost disappeared. (1 drop $Na_2S_2O_3$ soln should change color from blue to white or faint lilac shade.) Det. blank, using 20 mL H_2O instead of filtrate, starting at first par. Conduct detn on 20 mL std glucose soln similarly.

% Starch = $4 \times 0.9 \times (B - S)/(B - D)$,

where B = blank titrn in mL; S = sample titrn in mL; D = std glucose titrn in mL; 0.9 = factor to convert glucose to starch.

MEAT EXTRACTS AND SIMILAR PRODUCTS

24.060 Preparation of Sample—Procedure

Remove liq. and semiliq. meat exts and similar prepns from container, and mix thoroly. (Slight heating expedites mixing of pasty exts.) Carefully remove from bottom of container sediment that forms in many liq. prepns and include in sample. If sample is in form of cubes, grind 10–12 cubes in mortar.

24.061 Moisture—Official Final Action

(*Caution: See* **51.015.**)

Boil H_2SO_4 in large Kjeldahl flask 4 hr, close flask with stopper carrying $CaCl_2$ tube, and cool. (Only needed if glycerol is present.)

Proceed as in **7.003**, using ca 2 g powd prepns, ca 3 g pasty prepns, and 5–10 g liq. exts, according to solid content. Dry powd prepns directly without admixture. Dissolve pasty prepns in H_2O and dry with enough ignited sand or pumice stone to absorb soln. When glycerol is present, proceed as follows:

Weigh 2–5 g sample into 5–10 cm diam. metal dish with tight-fit cover. (If subsequent fat detns are to be made, fat extn cones may be used.) Mix substances that dry down to horn-like material with fat-free cotton or other suitable material. Place 200 mL of the fresh H_2SO_4 in strong, tight vac. desiccator. Place uncovered dish in desiccator and exhaust with vac. pump to pressure ≤10 mm Hg (1.33 kPa).

If pump is not available, place 10 mL ether in small beaker in desiccator and exhaust with H_2O filter pump. Between pump and desiccator interpose empty bottle next to desiccator and bottle of H_2O next to pump. Draw air from desiccator thru the H_2O and turn desiccator stopcock the instant H_2O begins to rise in tube leading from empty bottle.

Gently rotate desiccator 4 or 5 times during first 12 hr. After 24 hr, open desiccator, bubbling incoming air thru H_2SO_4. Place cover on dish and make first weighing. After weighing, place sample in desiccator contg fresh H_2SO_4 and exhaust as before. Rotate desiccator several times during interval and weigh again after suitable drying period. Repeat process to const wt.

24.062 Ash—Official Final Action

Proceed as in **31.012** or **31.013**. Add enough H_2O to pasty prepns to effect soln and evap. to dryness so as to distribute solids evenly over bottom of dish.

24.063 Total Phosphorus—Official Final Action

Destroy org. matter as in **2.020(c)** or **(d)**, and proceed as in **7.119** or **8.033**.

24.064 Chlorides—Official Final Action

Dissolve ca 1 g prepd sample, **24.060**, in 20 mL 5% Na_2CO_3 soln and proceed as in **3.071–3.072**.

24.065 Total Nitrogen—Official Final Action

See **2.057**.

24.066 Creatine—Official Final Action

Dissolve ca 7 g sample in cool (20°) NH_3-free H_2O in 150 mL beaker, transfer soln to 250 mL vol. flask, dil. to vol., and mix thoroly. Transfer 20 mL aliquot to 50 mL vol. flask and proceed as in **24.044**. From total creatinine value subtract equiv. of preformed creatinine, **24.067**, and multiply difference by 1.16 to convert to creatine. Express result as % creatine.

24.067 Creatinine—Official Final Action

(*Caution: See* **51.029** and **51.068**.)

Measure ca 5 mL soln used in **24.066** into 500 mL vol. flask, add 10 mL 10% NaOH soln and 30 mL *satd (1.2%) picric acid soln*, mix, and rotate 30 sec. Let stand exactly 4.5 min and dil. to vol. at once with H_2O. Shake thoroly and read color in colorimeter after standing. If reading is <7 or >9.5 mm, repeat, calcg vol. of soln necessary to obtain reading of ca 8 mm. Express result as % creatinine, making calcns as in **24.044**.

24.068 Preservatives—Official Final Action

See Chap. **20**.

Sulfur Dioxide

24.069 Qualitative Test

See **20.113**.

24.070 Distillation Method

See **20.108**.

24.071 Pesticide Residues

See Chap. **29**.

SELECTED REFERENCES

(*1*) JAOAC **33**, 749(1950); **36**, 279(1953).
(*2*) JAOAC **11**, 112(1928); **12**, 407(1929); **33**, 749(1950).
(*3*) JAOAC **58**, 1182(1975); **59**, 225(1976).
(*4*) JAOAC **54**, 587(1971).
(*5*) JAOAC **52**, 634(1969).
(*6*) JAOAC **55**, 123(1972).
(*7*) JAOAC **11**, 408(1928).
(*8*) JAOAC **56**, 31(1973).
(*9*) JAOAC **59**, 141(1976); **60**, 345(1977).
(*10*) JAOAC **18**, 459(1935); **22**, 596(1939).
(*11*) JAOAC **56**, 922(1973); **60**, 594(1977).
(*12*) J. Biol. Chem. **9**, 185(1911); **12**, 275(1912); **16**, 121(1913); **23**, 407(1915).
(*13*) Biochem. Z. **7**, 45(1907).
(*14*) Winton, "Microscopy of Vegetable Foods," 2nd ed., p. 248; "British Yearbook of Pharmacy," 1913, pp. 467–468.
(*15*) Analyst **67**, 130(1942).
(*16*) J. Biol. Chem. **75**, 33(1927); **79**, 649(1928); J. Dairy Research **7**, 41(1936); Conn. Agr. Expt. Sta. Bull. **401**, 869(1937); **415**, 695(1938); **426**, 14(1939); JAOAC **23**, 811(1940); **40**, 770(1957); **41**, 293(1958).
(*17*) JAOAC **41**, 288(1958).

25. Metals and Other Elements as Residues in Foods

ANTIMONY

American Conference of Governmental Industrial Hygienists-AOAC Method (*1*)—Official Final Action

25.001 ***Principle***

Pentavalent Sb in aq. HCl soln reacts with Rhodamine B to form colored complex extractable with org. solvs. Intensity of extd color is measured spectrophtric at 565 nm.

25.002 ***Reagents***

(H_2O for aq. reagents should be double distd; final distn from glass.)

(**a**) *Hydrochloric acid soln.*—6*N*. Dil. concd acid with H_2O (1+1).
(**b**) *Dilute phosphoric acid.*—3*N*. Dil. 70 mL H_3PO_4 (85%) to 1 L with H_2O.
(**c**) *Rhodamine B soln.*—0.02% in H_2O.
(**d**) *Antimony std solns.*—(*1*) *Stock soln.*—100 μg Sb/mL. Dissolve 0.1000 g pure Sb in 25 mL H_2SO_4 with heat; cool, and cautiously dil. to 1 L with H_2O. (*2*) *Working soln.*—1 μg/mL. Dil. 2.0 mL stock soln to 200 mL with H_2O.

(Cool reagents (**a**), (**b**), (**c**), ca 100 mL benzene, and eight 125 mL separators with Teflon stopcocks in refrigerator before use; maintain temp. of 5–10° during extn and color development. Work in subdued light.)

25.003 ***Preparation of Sample***

Digest sample as in **25.008**. Oxidizing conditions must be maintained.

25.004 ***Determination***

(*Caution: See* **51.019**, **51.028**, and **51.030**.)

Transfer digest or aliquot to 125 mL g-s erlenmeyer, add enough H_2SO_4 to make total of 5 mL H_2SO_4, and evap. to fumes of SO_3. Cool flask, add 10 drops 70% $HClO_4$, and again evap. to white fumes. Cool digest in ice bath ≥30 min; then *slowly* add 5 mL precooled 6*N* HCl by pipet. Let stand in ice bath 15 min; then add 8 mL precooled 3*N* H_3PO_4. (Until color is extd into benzene, perform subsequent operations as quickly as possible. Color is stable in benzene several hr.) Immediately add 5 mL precooled Rhodamine B soln, stopper, and shake vigorously. Transfer to precooled 125 mL separator. Pipet 10 mL precooled benzene into separator, shake vigorously 1 min, and discard aq. layer. Transfer benzene layer (red if Sb is present) into test tube and let H_2O settle. Rinse 1 cm cell with ext, fill cell, and read at 565 nm against benzene blank taken thru entire detn. Refer readings to std curve.

25.005 ***Preparation of Standard Curve***

Pipet 0, 2, 4, 6, 8, and 10 mL Sb working std soln into 125 mL g-s erlenmeyers, add 5 mL H_2SO_4 to each, and proceed as in detn. Plot *A* against μg Sb.

ARSENIC

25.006 ***Reagents***

(**a**) *Bromine water.*—Half satd. Dil. 75 mL satd Br-H_2O with equal vol. H_2O.
(**b**) *Sodium hypobromite soln.*—Place 50 mL 0.5*N* NaOH in 200 mL vol. flask, and dil. to vol. with half-satd Br-H_2O, (**a**).
(**c**) *Ammonium molybdate-sulfuric acid soln.*—Dissolve 5.000 g $(NH_4)_6Mo_7O_{24}.4H_2O$ in H_2O and slowly add 42.8 mL H_2SO_4. Dil. to 100 mL with H_2O.
(**d**) *Arsenious oxide std solns.*—(*1*) *Stock soln.*—1 mg/mL. Dissolve 1.000 g As_2O_3 (*Caution: See* **51.078** and **51.084**) in 25 mL 20% NaOH soln and dil. to 1 L. (*2*) *Intermediate soln.*—10 μg/mL. Dil. 10 mL stock soln to 1 L. (*3*) *Working soln.*—1 μg/mL. Dil. 100 mL intermediate soln to 1 L.
(**e**) *Hydrazine sulfate soln.*—1.5% $N_2H_4.H_2SO_4$ in H_2O.
(**f**) *Potassium iodide soln.*—15%. Keep in dark. Discard when soln turns yellow.
(**g**) *Stannous chloride soln.*—Dissolve 40 g As-free $SnCl_2.2H_2O$ in HCl and dil. to 100 mL with HCl.
(**h**) *Dilute hydrochloric acid soln.*—Dil. 144 mL HCl to 200 mL with H_2O.
(**i**) *Lead acetate soln.*—10% $Pb(OAc)_2.3H_2O$ in H_2O.
(**j**) *Zinc metal.*—30 mesh.
(**k**) *Sea sand.*—To clean sand ("30 mesh") before use and between detns, mount piece of 3 mm id glass tubing thru rubber stopper in suction flask. Fit piece of rubber or Tygon tubing over top to take bottom of sulfide absorption tube easily and to maintain it upright. Add, in turn, with suction, aqua regia, H_2O, HNO_3, and H_2O to remove all traces of acid (≥5 washings). Wet sand with $Pb(OAc)_2$ soln and remove excess with suction.
(**l**) *Silver diethyldithiocarbamate.*—Chill 200 mL 0.1*M* $AgNO_3$ soln (3.4 g/200 mL) and 200 mL 0.1*M* Na diethyldithiocarbamate soln (4.5 g/200 mL) to 10° or lower. Add carbamate soln to $AgNO_3$ soln slowly with stirring. Filter thru buchner, wash with chilled H_2O, and dry under reduced pressure at room temp. Dissolve salt in pyridine (reagent grade) with stirring, chill, and add cold H_2O slowly until completely pptd. Filter thru buchner, and wash with H_2O to remove all pyridine. Dry pale yellow crystals under reduced pressure (mp 185–187°; recovery 85–90%). Store in amber bottle in refrigerator. (Second recrystn may be necessary to obtain correct mp.)
(**m**) *Silver diethyldithiocarbamate soln.*—Dissolve 0.5000 g salt, (**l**), in colorless pyridine in 100 mL vol. flask, and dil. to vol. with pyridine. Mix, and store in amber bottle. Reagent is stable several months at room temp.

25.007 ***Generators and Absorption Tubes***

See Fig. **25:01**. Use 2 oz (60 mL) wide-mouth bottles of uniform capacity and design as generators, and fit each by means of perforated stopper with glass tube 1 cm diam. and 6–7 cm long, with addnl constricted end to facilitate connection. Place small wad of glass wool in constricted bottom end of tube and add 3.5–4 g sand, taking care to have same amt in each tube. Moisten sand with 10% $Pb(OAc)_2$ soln and remove excess by light suction. Clean sand when necessary by treatment (do not remove sand from tube) with HNO_3 followed by H_2O rinse and suction. Treat with $Pb(OAc)_2$ soln. If sand has dried thru disuse, clean and remoisten it as directed. Connect tube by means of rubber stopper, glass tube, and rubber sleeve to bent capillary tubing (7 mm od, 2 mm id) tapered at end to slide easily into connecting tube and later into neck of 25 mL vol. flask. Other end of capillary is sealed to Pyrex ₮ 19/38 female joint. To transfer contents of trap, attach bulb aspirator to male ₮ 19/38 joint and place in top of trap.

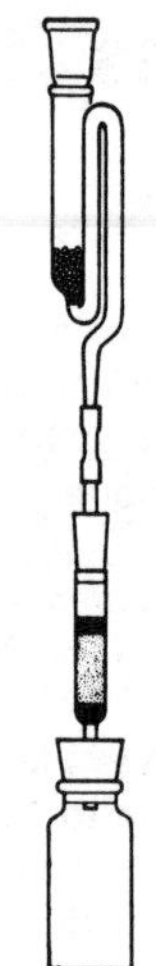

FIG. 25:01—Arsenic apparatus

Clean traps between detns without removing beads by flushing with H_2O, followed by HNO_3, soaking for 30 min or until HNO_3 becomes colorless. Remove all traces of acid with H_2O, rinse with acetone, and dry with air current applied by suction to tip of trap.

25.008 ***Preparation of Sample***

(*Caution: See* **51.019**, **51.026**, and **51.030**.)

(For details of convenient churn-type washer that will remove arsenical spray residues from firm fruits or vegetables with an aq. NH_4NO_3-HNO_3 soln, *see* JAOAC **26**, 150(1943). Digest aliquot of "strip" soln and proceed as in (**a**).

All digestions can be greatly facilitated by following optional method, *JAOAC* **47**, 629(1964): Proceed as in (**a**) until mixt. no longer turns brown or darkens. Cool, add 0.5 mL 70% $HClO_4$ (*Caution: See* **51.028**), and heat until fuming occurs and digest is clear. Cool, and add 2 addnl 0.5 mL portions $HClO_4$, heating each time as above. Finish digestion with H_2O and satd NH_4 oxalate as in (**a**).

Conduct ≥1 blank detn with samples. Blanks should not show >1 μg As.)

(**a**) *For fresh fruits (apples, pears, or similar products)*.—Weigh and peel representative sample (1–5 lb; 0.5–2 kg). At blossom and stem ends cut out all flesh thought to be contaminated with As compds and include with peelings, if desired. Place peelings in 1 or more 800 mL Kjeldahl flasks. (As-free Pyrex glassware and "wet ashing" app. of Duriron are available.) Add 25–50 mL HNO_3; then cautiously add 40 mL H_2SO_4 (20 mL if Gutzeit method is used). Place each flask on asbestos mat with 5 cm hole. Warm slightly and discontinue heating if foaming becomes excessive.

When reaction has quieted, heat flask cautiously and rotate occasionally to prevent caking of sample upon glass exposed to flame. Maintain oxidizing conditions in flask at all times during digestion by cautiously adding small amts of HNO_3 whenever mixt. turns brown or darkens. Continue digestion until org. matter is destroyed and SO_3 fumes are copiously evolved. (Final soln should be colorless, or at most light straw color.) Cool slightly, and add 75 mL H_2O and 25 mL satd NH_4 oxalate soln to assist in expelling oxides of N from soln. Evap. again to point where fumes of SO_3 appear in neck of flask. Cool, and dil. with H_2O to 500 or 1000 mL in vol. flask.

(**b**) *For dried fruit products*.—Prep. sample by alternately grinding and mixing 4–5 times in food chopper. Place 35–70 g portions in 800 mL Kjeldahl flasks, and add 10–25 mL H_2O, 25–50 mL HNO_3, and 20 mL H_2SO_4. Continue digestion as in (**a**). Dil. digested soln to 250 mL.

(**c**) *For small fruits, vegetables, etc.*—Use 70–140 g sample and digest as in (**a**) or (**b**).

(**d**) *For materials other than* (**a**), (**b**), *or* (**c**).—Digest 5–50 g, according to moisture content and amt of As expected, as in (**a**) or (**b**). Dil. to definite vol. detd by As concn expected.

(**e**) *For products containing stable organic As compounds, products liable to yield incompletely oxidized organic derivatives that inhibit arsine evolution, or products that are difficult to digest*.—Shrimp, tobacco, oils, and some other products require special treatment to complete oxidn of org. As to inorg. As_2O_5, or to destroy org. interferences previous to As detn. For details consult:

Ind. Eng. Chem., Anal. Ed. **5**, 58(1933); **6**, 280, 327(1934); JAOAC **20**, 171(1937); **47**, 629(1964).

Dil. As solns obtained by these special methods of prepn to definite vol.

(**f**) *For ultra-micro quantities of As, very labile forms of As, and vacuum-accelerated Gutzeit reduction system for mercuric bromide spot filtration.*— Consult Ind. Eng. Chem., Anal. Ed. **16**, 400(1944).

25.009 ***Isolation of Arsenic***

Before making detns, isolate As, when interfering substances are present in digests (*e.g.*, pyridine from tobacco), or when samples contain excessive amts of salts, or H_2SO_4 from digestions. Consult first ref. of **25.008(e)** for method of isolating As after digestion, or isolate As by $AsCl_3$ distn (JAOAC **16**, 75, 325(1933); **17**, 202(1934) or **36.036**, par. 2). Gelatin may be hydrolyzed with HCl and As isolated as in first ref. of **25.008(e)**.

Molybdenum Blue Method (2)—Official Final Action

25.010 ***Determination***

Transfer 20 mL aliquots of sample and blank digest solns to generator bottles. Add, swirling after each addn, 10 mL H_2O, 5 mL dil. HCl, (**h**), 5 mL KI soln, (**f**), and 4 drops $SnCl_2$ soln, (**g**). Let stand ≥15 min.

Place 4 g sea sand over small glass wool wad in sulfide absorption tube and cap with glass wool. Place 3 mm diam. solid glass beads in trap over small glass wool pad until ¼ full and add 3.0 mL NaOBr soln, (**b**). Assemble app. except for generator bottle. Add 4 g Zn, (**j**), to generator bottle, attach immediately, and let react 30 min.

Disconnect trap and transfer contents to 25 mL vol. flask with aspirator assembly. Rinse trap with six 2 mL portions H_2O and aspirate into flask. Add, with swirling, 0.5 mL NH_4 molybdate-H_2SO_4 soln, (**c**), and 1.0 mL $N_2H_4.H_2SO_4$ soln, (**e**). Dil. to vol., mix, and let stand 75 min. Mix, and read in spectrophtr or colorimeter at 845 nm against blank prepd similarly. Alternatively, heat vol. flask and contents 10 min at 50° and cool in tap H_2O to room temp. before reading. Det. As_2O_3 (or As) in aliquot from std curve.

25.011 ***Preparation of Standard Curve***

Place 0.0, 1.0, 2.0, 3.0, 5.0, 6.0 mL std soln contg 10 μg As_2O_3/mL in 25 mL vol. flasks. Add 3.0 mL NaOBr soln, (**b**), and H_2O to 15 mL. Add, with swirling, 0.5 mL NH_4 molybdate-H_2SO_4 soln, (**c**), and 1.0 mL $N_2H_4.H_2SO_4$ soln, (**e**). Dil. to vol., mix, and let stand 75 min or heat 10 min at 50° as for samples. Mix, and read at 845 nm. Plot *A* against μg As_2O_3 (or As).

Silver Diethyldithiocarbamate Method (*3*)
Official Final Action

25.012 ***Determination***

Transfer aliquot of sample digest, **25.008** (usually 2–5 mL), and same vol. blank to generator bottles. Add H_2O to 35 mL; then add, with swirling, 5 mL HCl, 2 mL KI soln, (**f**), and 8 drops $SnCl_2$ soln, (**g**), and let stand ≥15 min. Evolve AsH_3 as in **25.010**, except add 4.0 mL Ag diethyldithiocarbamate soln, (**m**), to trap.

Disconnect trap and mix trapping soln by gently drawing back and forth 5 times with aspirator assembly. Transfer soln directly to spectrophtr cell (g-s preferred) and read at 522 nm. Det As_2O_3 (or As) in aliquot from std curve.

25.013 ***Preparation of Standard Curve***

Place 0.0, 1.0, 3.0, 6.0, 10.0, and 15.0 mL std soln contg 1.00 μg As_2O_3/mL in generator bottles. Add H_2O to 35 mL and proceed as in **25.012**. Read at 522 nm and plot *A* against μg As_2O_3 (or As).

Molybdenum Blue Method for Meat and Poultry (*4*)
Official Final Action

25.014 ***Principle***

Sample is ashed in presence of $Mg(NO_3)_2$ at 600°. Ash is dissolved in dil. HCl; Zn is added to generate AsH_3, which is trapped with I soln in cell. Heteropoly blue compd is developed and read at 840 nm in same cell. Chief source of error is often contamination. Always perform reagent blank and, when possible, std sample.

25.015 ***Reagents***

(Glassware should not be subjected to routine washing with soap or detergents, which are often source of As contamination. When soap or detergent is used, clean with aqua regia before use. Rinse delivery tubes by holding in slanted position with crook up and squirting jet of H_2O up and over inside crook until tube is filled; then rinse outside while tube drains. Repeat rinsing 3 times. Rinse funnels in each direction alternately by filling end that is up and placing funnel on 1-hole rubber stopper in mouth of vac. flask to pull H_2O thru frit by vac.)

(**a**) *Tissue solvent*.—$CHCl_3$ (or benzene)-acetone-absolute alcohol (1+1+2).

(**b**) *Dilute hydrochloric acid*.—Mix 175 mL HCl and 280 mL H_2O.

(**c**) *Potassium iodide soln*.—15%. *See* **25.006**(**f**).

(**d**) *Stannous chloride soln*.—40% in dil. HCl, (**b**). Store in contact with metallic Sn.

(**e**) *Zinc*.—Shot of uniform size and shape, ca 0.5 g each.

(**f**) *Lead acetate soln*.—Prep. satd aq. $Pb(OAc)_2.3H_2O$ soln in dropping bottle. Prep. fresh weekly or when soln becomes cloudy.

(**g**) *Iodine solns*.—(*1*) *0.02N*.—Dissolve 8 g KI and 2.54 g I in small amt H_2O and dil. to 1 L with H_2O. Store in dark bottle. (*2*) *0.001N*.—Dil. 5 mL 0.02*N* I to 100 mL with H_2O. Prep. fresh daily.

(**h**) *Ammonium molybdate soln*.—Dissolve 7.0 g $(NH_4)_6Mo_7O_{24}.4H_2O$ in warm mixt. of 70 mL H_2SO_4 and 300 mL H_2O, cool, and dil. to 500 mL with H_2O.

(**i**) *Hydrazine sulfate soln*.—Dissolve 0.3 g $N_2H_4.H_2SO_4$ in H_2O and dil. to 200 mL.

(**j**) *Arsenious oxide std solns*.—(*1*) *Stock soln*.—1 mg As/mL. Dissolve 0.1320 g As_2O_3 in 50 mL H_2O contg 0.7 mL 50% NaOH. Neutze with 50% H_2SO_4 and dil. to 100 mL. (*2*) *Working solns*.—Dil. sep. 1.0 mL portions stock soln to 100, 200, and 500 mL with H_2O (10, 5, and 2 μg As/mL, resp.).

(**k**) *Arsanilic acid std solns*.—(*1*) *Stock soln*.—1 mg As/mL. Dissolve 0.2897 g arsanilic acid (based on label assay) in H_2O and dil. to 100 mL with H_2O. (*2*) *Working solns*.—Prep. in same concns as in (**j**).

25.016 ***Apparatus***

(**a**) *Cell rack*.—Metal rack capable of holding eight 19 × 105 mm cells in 600 mL beaker.

(**b**) *Distilling apparatus*.—Kingsley-Schaffert As distg app. (Corning Glass Works, No. 33680), consisting of 125 mL flask, funnel trap, and bent dispersion tube.

(**c**) *Absorbent cotton.—See* **25.022**(**i**).

25.017 ***Preparation of Sample***

Assure absence of interferences arising from laboratory and reagent contamination. Recoveries thru method of added compds should be ≥90%. Conduct one or more reagent blanks and std samples along with samples.

To obtain representative aliquot of large sample (≥100 g), grind entire sample ≥2 times, using fine plate (grind liver sample only once or blend). Mix thoroly and weigh calcd amt into 50 mL Vycor crucible. Add 4 g $Mg(NO_3)_2.6H_2O$/10 g sample and mix, using stainless steel spatula or glass rod, until all $Mg(NO_3)_2$ is dissolved. Spread mixt. in even layer around sides of crucible.

For smaller samples (<100 g), weigh known amt or entire sample into homogenizer or blender, add 4 g $Mg(NO_3)_2.6H_2O$/10 g sample and enough tissue solv. to aid blending, weigh, and blend 1 min. (*Caution:* Use explosion-proof blender when benzene-acetone-alcohol is used as tissue solv.) Weigh aliquot equiv. to desired amt sample into 50 mL Vycor crucible and carefully evap. excess solv. and H_2O from tissue on steam bath or in 95° oven.

25.018 ***Determination***

Place crucible in cool furnace, gradually increase temp. to 600°, and ash sample at 600° until most visible C is burned. Cool crucible and cool furnace. Dampen ash with H_2O and add 3 mL HNO_3 (1+4). Place in cooled furnace (100°) and heat gradually to 600°. Hold at 600° ca 1 hr until all HNO_3 fumes are evolved. Repeat dil. HNO_3 treatment if necessary to obtain white ash.

Remove crucibles and let cool. Dampen ash with H_2O and dissolve in 10 mL dil. HCl, (**b**), delivered from all-glass hypodermic syringe without needle. Quant. transfer to 125 mL flask, **25.016**(**b**), with aid of two 10 mL portions dil. HCl and wash sides of flask with fourth 10 mL portion. (Use same vol. liq. for each sample because vol. of air space above liq. affects efficiency of distn of H and AsH_3.) Cool to room temp. Add 2.0 mL 15% KI soln and mix thoroly by swirling. Add 1.0 mL 40% $SnCl_2$ soln and mix thoroly by swirling. Let stand ≥15 min (but <30 min). Place 7.0 mL 0.001*N* I soln in cell. Place small ball absorbent cotton in top of funnel and dampen with satd $Pb(OAc)_2$ soln. Lubricate ground glass joint with H_2O and join delivery tube to funnel firmly. This union must be firm enough to hold together under wt of funnel, flask, and contents. Union must not be so firm as to prevent disassembly. Do not dry parts by heating before use. Teflon sleeves are not satisfactory.

Fill 600 mL beaker with finely crushed ice layered between levels of cell holder. Add ice-H_2O to ca ⅔ ht of beaker and place cell in holder. (It may be necessary to make path thru ice for cell.) Lubricate lower ground glass joint of funnel with H_2O, add ca 12.5 g Zn to flask, join flask and funnel firmly, and place delivery tube in cell as quickly as possible. Let distn continue 1 hr (without added heat).

Carefully and slowly remove delivery tube from cell, letting liq. drain as tube is removed. Add 0.5 mL NH_4 molybdate soln and mix thoroly. Add 0.3 mL $N_2H_4.H_2SO_4$ soln and mix thoroly. Place cell (in cell holder) in moderately boiling H_2O bath or on medium (not vigorous) steam bath 10 min. Remove from bath, wipe cell dry with soft lintless material, and place in cool, dark place ca 1 hr (to ensure that samples reach same temp. and full color development). Read in precalibrated spectrophtr or colorimeter at 840 nm against CO_2-free H_2O. Correct for blanks.

25.019 ***Preparation of Standard Curve***

Prepare stds of 10 g As-free liver, 4 g $Mg(NO_3)_2$, and suitable amts arsanilic acid working solns in definite progression, such as 2, 4, 6, 8, and 10 μg As. Repeat analysis of stds $\geqslant$3 times. Det. mean for each level and prep. curve; or fit line by method of least sqs, in *Definitions of Terms and Explanatory Notes,* Item (24), if desired.

25.020 ★ Gutzeit Method (*5*)—Official Final Action ★

Sample is wet ashed, and As is reduced with Zn to AsH_3, which reacts with $HgBr_2$-impregnated paper strips to form a darkened area whose length is proportional to amt As. *See* **25.006–25.009**, 11th ed.

CADMIUM

Dithizone Method (*6*)—Official Final Action

25.021 ***Principle***

Sample is digested with H_2SO_4 and HNO_3. All reactive metals are extd from soln (after adjustment to pH ca 9) with dithizone-$CHCl_3$. Cu, Hg, and most of any Ni or Co present are removed by stripping $CHCl_3$ soln with dil. HCl. Aq. layer, adjusted to 5% NaOH, is extd with dithizone-CCl_4. At this alky, Zn, Pb, and Bi do not ext, whereas Cd dithizonate is relatively stable. Stripping with dil. HCl and development of Cd dithizonate in 5% NaOH are repeated. Cd is finally estd photometrically as dithizonate. Zn constitutes chief interference.

25.022 ***Reagents***

(**a**) *Citrate.*—Diammonium salt or citric acid.

(**b**) *Chloroform.*—Distil from hot H_2O bath, collecting distillate in absolute alcohol in proportion of 10 mL alcohol to 1 L distillate. Intermittently shake receiver during distn.

(**c**) *Diphenylthiocarbazone* (*dithizone*), *twice purified.*—Purify as in **25.095**(**e**), but make only 3 dil. NH_4OH extns of $CHCl_3$ soln. Carry thru, including H_2O-washing steps, and then repeat purification with 3 NH_4OH extns, pptn with dil. acid, etc. Instead of heating ext to dryness, evap. spontaneously, and complete drying under vac. in bell jar overnight.

(**d**) *Carbon tetrachloride.*—(*Caution: See* **51.011**(**b**) and **51.049**.) Reflux vigorously on steam bath 1 hr with 1/20 vol. 20% KOH in MeOH. Cool, add H_2O, drain off CCl_4 layer, and wash $\geqslant$3 times with copious vols of H_2O until alkali-free. Dry over $CaCl_2$, filter, and distil on hot H_2O bath. (Unless reagent is so purified, erratic Cd results may be obtained with some lots of CCl_4.)

(**e**) *Dithizone in carbon tetrachloride.*—20 mg/L CCl_4, (**d**). Prep. daily, as dil. solns of dithizone are unstable. (When many detns are to be made, dithizone reagent may be prepd by diln from 300 mg/L soln. Store concd reagent under 0.1*M* SO_2 soln in refrigerator.)

(**f**) *Dithizone in chloroform.*—1000 mg/L $CHCl_3$, (**b**), prepd as needed.

★ Surplus method—*see* inside front cover.

(**g**) *Sodium hydroxide soln.*—28%. Dissolve 28 g NaOH pellets in H_2O and dil. to 100 mL.

(**h**) *Thymol blue indicator.*—Triturate 0.1 g indicator in agate mortar with 4.3 mL 0.05*N* NaOH. Dil. to 200 mL in g-s flask with H_2O.

(**i**) *Absorbent cotton.*—Metal-free. If traces of metal are present, remove by digesting cotton several hr with 0.2*N* HCl, filtering on buchner, and finally washing with copious vols of redistd H_2O until acid-free.

(**j**) *Cadmium std solns.*—(*1*) *Stock soln.*—1 mg/mL. Dissolve 1 g Cd (Fisher Chemical Co., certified 99.9% pure, C-565, or equiv.) in 20–25 mL HNO_3 (1+9), evap. to dryness, add 5 mL HCl (1+1), evap. to dryness, and then add several mL H_2O and again evap. to dryness. Dil. to 1 L. (*2*) *Intermediate soln.*—100 μg/mL. Dil. 10 mL stock soln to 100 mL. (*3*) *Working soln.*—2 μg/mL. Transfer 20 mL intermediate soln to 1 L vol. flask, add 15 mL HCl, and dil. to vol. to give final acidity of ca 0.2*N*.

25.023 ***Preparation of Standard Curve***

Prep. in duplicate 6 stds contg 0, 5, 10, 15, 20, and 25 μg Cd as follows: Add appropriate vols std soln to Squibb-type separators (125 mL size is convenient), adjust to 40 mL with 0.2*N* HCl, add 10 mL NaOH soln (soln is then 5% with respect to NaOH) and 25 mL dithizone soln, (**e**), shake vigorously exactly 1 min, let stand exactly 3 min, and filter org. layer thru pledget of absorbent cotton, discarding first 5 mL. Fill absorption cell (1 cm length is convenient) and det. *A* at 510 nm. Plot std curve or calc. ref. equation by method of least squares, *Definitions of Terms and Explanatory Notes*, Item (24).

25.024 ***Preparation of Sample***

Use sample equiv. to 5–10 g of product, calcd to dry basis. (Sample size is of concern only when comparatively large amts of Mg and P are present.) Digest with 10 mL H_2SO_4 (1+1) and HNO_3 as needed. If sample tends to char rather than to oxidize evenly, add 5 or 10 mL addnl H_2SO_4. Continue digestion, adding HNO_3 as required, until digestion is complete and SO_3 is evolved. Cool, add 15 mL satd NH_4 oxalate soln, and again heat to fumes.

Fat in biological materials, such as liver and kidney, may cause bumping and frothing during digestion. If comparatively large samples of such materials are available, make partial digestion with warm HNO_3 until only fat remains undissolved. Cool, filter free of solid fat, wash residue with H_2O, make combined filtrate to suitable vol., and digest appropriate aliquots as above.

25.025 ***Determination***

Dil. digest, **25.024**, with 25 mL H_2O, filter free from excessive insol. matter (sulfates or silica) if present, and transfer to separator marked at 125 mL, using addnl 10 mL portions H_2O for rinsing and completing transfer. Add 1–2 g citrate reagent, (**a**), and 1 mL thymol blue indicator, (**h**), and adjust to ca pH 8.8 by adding NH_4OH slowly, while cooling intermittently, until soln changes from yellowish green to greenish blue. Dil. to 125 mL mark with H_2O. Ext vigorously with 5 mL portions dithizone soln, (**f**), until $CHCl_3$ layer remains green. Then ext with 3 mL $CHCl_3$.

Transfer all $CHCl_3$ exts to second separator previously wetted with 2–3 mL $CHCl_3$. Add 40 mL 0.2*N* HCl to combined dithizone exts, shake vigorously $\geqslant$1 min, and after layers sep., carefully drain $CHCl_3$ phase contg any Cu, Ni, Co, or Hg that may be present, and discard. Remove remaining droplets of dithizone by extg with 1–2 mL CCl_4, (**d**), carefully conducting draining operation so that no acid enters bore or stem of separator, as its presence there would in part decompose Cd dithizonate subsequently formed and extd in next step.

Adjust aq. phase to 5% alky by adding 10 mL NaOH soln, (**g**). Ext Cd with 25 mL dithizone soln, (**e**), shaking vigorously ≥1 min, and transfer to third separator previously wetted with 2–3 mL same dithizone soln. Repeat extn with addnl 10 mL portions dithizone soln until CCl_4 layer becomes colorless. Amts of Cd usually found in foods or biological materials (ca 100 μg) are completely removed by third extn.

To verify assumption that pale pink persisting after third extn is due to Zn, transfer questionable ext to fourth separator contg 5% NaOH soln, add several mL dithizone soln, (**e**), and shake vigorously. If CCl_4 layer becomes colorless, original pink was due to Zn and no further extns are necessary. If, however, pink persists, indicating presence of Cd, add ext to contents of third separator, and continue extn.

Convert Cd and Zn dithizonates in third separator to chlorides by adding 40 mL 0.2*N* HCl and shaking vigorously ≥1 min. Carefully drain CCl_4 layer, which may contain traces of Co and Ni not removed in second step, and discard. Remove droplets of dithizone from aq. phase by rinsing with 1–2 mL CCl_4 and drain off as completely as possible, but do not permit any acid to pass bore of separator. Again adjust alky to 5% by adding 10 mL NaOH soln, (**g**). Wipe separator stems dry with cotton, (**i**). Det. Cd present by adding exactly 25 mL dithizone soln, (**e**), shaking vigorously exactly 1 min, permitting layers to sep. exactly 3 min, and continuing as in **25.023**, beginning ". . . filter org. layer . . ." Calc. Cd in μg by substituting *A* in linear equation or from std curve.

Note: If photometric measurement indicates >25 μg Cd, make first approximation by dilg dithizonate soln with CCl_4 and evaluating *A*. For best results repeat analysis with wts or aliquots of samples contg ≤25 μg Cd; 30 μg is upper limit of solubility of Cd dithizonate in 25 mL CCl_4. Therefore amts >30 μg are incompletely extd.

Atomic Absorption Spectrophotometric Method (7)
Official Final Action

(*Caution: See* **51.006**, **51.019**, **51.026**, and **51.030**.)

25.026 *Principle*

Sample is digested with HNO_3, H_2SO_4, and H_2O_2. All reactive metals are extd from soln, after adjustment to ca pH 9, with dithizone-$CHCl_3$. Cd is removed by stripping $CHCl_3$ soln with dil. HCl and detd by AA spectrophotometry at 228.8 nm.

25.027 *Reagents and Apparatus*

(Thoroly wash all new glassware and glassware which has contained high Cd concn with 8*N* HNO_3, and rinse with H_2O. Cover beakers with watch glasses during all operations.)

(**a**) *Nitric acid.*—Low in Pb and Cd (G. Frederick Smith Chemical Co., No. 63).

(**b**) *Hydrogen peroxide.*—50% (Fisher Scientific Co., No. H-341).

(**c**) *Citric acid.*—Monohydrate, fine crystal.

(**d**) *Thymol blue indicator.*—*See* **25.022(h)**.

(**e**) *Dithizone solns.*—(*1*) *Concentrated soln.*—1 mg/mL. Prep. 200 mL in $CHCl_3$. (*2*) *Dilute soln.*—0.2 mg/mL. Dil. concd soln 1+4 with $CHCl_3$. Prep. fresh daily.

(**f**) *Cadmium std solns.*—(*1*) *Stock soln.*—1.0 mg/mL. Dissolve 1.000 g Cd, **25.022(j)**, in 165 mL HCl in 1 L vol. flask. Dil. to vol. with H_2O. (*2*) *Intermediate soln.* —10 μg/mL. Dil. 10 mL stock soln with 2*N* HCl to 1 L. Prep. just before use. (*3*) *Working solns.*—Dil. 0, 1, 5, 10, and 20 mL intermediate soln to 100 mL with 2*N* HCl (0, 0.1, 0.5, 1.0, and 2.0 μg Cd/mL, resp.).

(**g**) *Atomic absorption spectrophotometer.*—With hollow-cathode Cd lamp and 10 cm burner head for air-C_2H_2 flame; wavelength 228.8 nm, range 0–2.0 μg/mL.

25.028 *Digestion*

Weigh 50.0 g sample into 1.5 L beaker. Add several boiling chips or beads, and cover. Carefully add 25 mL HNO_3, cover, and warm gently with flame to initiate reaction. (Meker-type burners are preferred thruout for their versatility and speed.) When reaction subsides, add 25 mL HNO_3, warm again, and continue until 100 mL HNO_3 has been added. (Alternatively, add 100 mL HNO_3 all at once, with caution, and let stand at room temp. overnight.) Heat until most NO fumes have evolved; control excessive frothing by cooling or quenching with H_2O from wash bottle. Only some cellulose and fatty materials, if any, remain undissolved.

To remove any fat visible in hot soln, proceed as follows: Cool beaker in ice, and decant clear, aq. soln from coagulated oils and solids thru glass wool pad into 1 L beaker. Add 100 mL H_2O to 1.5 L beaker with fat, heat, swirl vigorously to rinse fat, chill, and filter as before. Wash funnel and glass wool pad with ca 20 mL H_2O.

Add 20 mL H_2SO_4 to sample, dil. to ca 300 mL with H_2O, and evap. over flame until charring begins. When charring becomes extensive, cautiously add 50% H_2O_2, 1 mL at time. Let reaction subside before adding next portion of oxidant, and never add >1 mL at a time. Continue addns of H_2O_2 until soln is colorless. Heat vigorously to SO_3 fumes, adding more H_2O_2 as required to remove char. Heat vigorously to expel excess H_2O_2. Cool colorless digest to room temp.

Prep. reagent blank of 100 mL HNO_3, 20 mL H_2SO_4, and *same amts* of H_2O as added to sample. Cautiously add *same amts* 50% H_2O_2, as above, and remove all HNO_3 from blank. Carry blank thru same operations as sample.

25.029 *Extraction*

Add 2 g citric acid to cooled digest and cautiously dil. to ca 25 mL with H_2O. Add 1 mL thymol blue indicator and adjust to ca pH 8.8 by slowly adding NH_4OH while cooling in ice bath, until soln changes from yellowish green to greenish blue. Transfer quant. to 250 mL separator, using H_2O, and dil. to ca 150 mL.

Cool soln, and ext with two 5 mL portions concd dithizone soln, shaking 1–2 min each time. Continue extn with 5 mL portions dil. dithizone soln until last 5 mL portion dithizone ext shows no change in color. Combine dithizone exts in 125 mL separator; wash with 50 mL H_2O, and transfer solv. to another 125 mL separator. Ext H_2O wash with 5 mL $CHCl_3$ and add this to dithizone exts. Add 50 mL 0.2*N* HCl to combined dithizone exts, shake vigorously 1 min, and let layers sep.; discard dithizone layer. Wash aq. soln with 5 mL $CHCl_3$ and discard $CHCl_3$. Quant. transfer aq. soln to 400 mL beaker, add boiling chips, and evap. carefully to dryness. Carefully rinse down sides of beaker with 10–20 mL H_2O and again evap. to dryness.

25.030 *Determination*

Set instrument to previously established optimum conditions, using air-C_2H_2 oxidizing flame and 228.8 nm resonant wavelength. Dissolve dry residue in 5.0 mL 2*N* HCl and det. *A* of sample and std solns against 2*N* HCl as blank. Flush burner with H_2O between readings. Use scale expansion controls to obtain 4–10× expansion, as convenient. Det. Cd from curve of *A* against μg Cd/mL:

$$\text{ppm Cd} = (\mu g\ Cd/mL) \times (mL\ 2N\ HCl/g\ sample).$$

For concn >2.0 μg Cd/mL, dil. soln with 2*N* HCl.

Cadmium and Lead in Earthenware (8)
Official Final Action

AOAC-ASTM Method

25.031 ***Apparatus***

Atomic absorption spectrophotometer.—Equipped with 4" single slot or Boling-type burner head and operated as follows: Pb hollow cathode lamp, 283.3 or 217.0 nm; Cd hollow cathode lamp, 228.8 nm; flame, air-C_2H_2. (*Caution: See* **51.006**.) App. should have sensitivity of ca 0.5 µg Pb/mL and 0.25 µg Cd/mL for 1% absorption. Use operating conditions specified by manufacturer.

25.032 ***Reagents***

(Use glassware of chemically resistant borosilicate glass.)

(**a**) *Acetic acid.*—4%. Mix HOAc and H_2O (1+24). Analyze each new batch of reagent for Pb and Cd.

(**b**) *Detergent wash.*—Add 15 g alk. detergent (e.g., Calgonite, Calgon Corp., PO Box 1346, Pittsburgh, PA 15230, or equiv.) to 1 gal. (3.8 L) lukewarm tap H_2O.

(**c**) *Lead std solns.*—(*1*) *Stock soln.*—1000 µg/mL. Dissolve 1.5985 g $Pb(NO_3)_2$ in 4% HOAc and dil. to 1 L with same soln. (*2*) *Working solns.*—Dil. 0.0, 5.0, 10.0, 15.0, and 20.0 mL stock soln to 1 L with 4% HOAc (0, 5, 10, 15, and 20 µg/mL).

(**d**) *Cadmium std solns.*—(*1*) *Stock soln.*—1000 µg/mL. Dissolve 0.9273 g anhyd. $CdSO_4$ in 250 mL HCl (1+37), and dil. to 500 mL with HCl (1+37). (*2*) *Intermediate soln.*—10 µg/mL. Dil. 10 mL stock soln to 1 L with 4% HOAc. (*3*) *Working solns.*— Dil. 0.0, 3.0, 5.0, 10.0, 15.0, and 20.0 mL intermediate soln to 100 mL with 4% HOAc (0.0, 0.3, 0.5, 1.0, 1.5, and 2.0 µg/mL).

25.033 ***Extraction***

Take, at random, 6 identical units of product and cleanse each with detergent wash. Rinse with tap H_2O followed by distd H_2O, and dry. Fill each unit with 4% HOAc from graduate to within 6–7 mm of overflowing. (Measure distance along surface of test unit, not vertical distance.) Record vol. acid required for each unit in sample. Cover each unit with clear, colorless glass plate to prevent evapn of soln, avoiding contact between cover and surface of leaching soln, and expose to normal laboratory light for 8–10 hr during leaching period. Let stand 24 hr at room temp. (22±2°).

If test unit is extremely shallow or has scalloped brim, evapn losses should be anticipated. In those cases, record headspace after filling. After 24 hr leaching period, adjust soln vol. to same recorded headspace, using 4% HOAc.

25.034 ***Determination***

(**a**) *Lead.*—Set instrument for max. signal at 283.3 or 217.0 nm, using Pb hollow cathode lamp and air and C_2H_2 flow rates recommended by manufacturer. Stir sample soln and decant portion into clean flask. Det. *A* of sample and Pb working std solns. Flush burner with H_2O and check 0 point between readings. Det. Pb from std curve of *A* against µg Pb/mL or calibrate DCR unit in concn mode with Pb working solns, and read and record sample concn directly. Bracket sample soln with next higher and lower working solns.

Dil. samples contg >20 µg Pb/mL with 4% HOAc. Conc. samples contg <1 µg Pb/mL by accurately transferring min. of 50.0 mL of soln to 250 mL beaker and evapg to dryness on steam bath. Dissolve residue in 4% HOAc by adding exactly 0.1 vol. of soln taken for concn (i.e., for 50.0 mL soln, add exactly 5.0 mL 4% HOAc), cover with watch glass, and swirl to complete dissoln. Det. Pb as above, except substitute "3.0 mL" and "3 µg/mL" for "20.0 mL" and "20 µg/mL", resp., in **25.032**(**c**)(*2*).

(**b**) *Cadmium.*—Proceed as for Pb, setting instrument for max. signal at 228.8 nm, using Cd hollow cathode lamp. Dil. samples contg >2 µg Cd/mL with 4% HOAc. Conc. samples contg <0.1 µg/mL as in (**a**)

Report type of units tested and for each, vol. acid used and Pb and Cd leached in µg/mL.

Rapid Screening Method (9)—Official First Action

(Detects 0.3 µg Pb and 0.05 µg Cd/mL 4% HOAc)

25.035 ***Reagents***

(**a**) *Buffer soln I.*—Dissolve 1 g $NH_2OH.HCl$ and 10 g NH_4 citrate in 150 mL H_2O, make soln alk. to phenol red indicator by adding NH_4OH, and add 5 g KCN, 975 mL NH_4OH, and 1315 mL H_2O. Mix well. Add 16 mL this buffer soln to 8 dram screw-cap vial for field test. (*Caution: See* **51.050**.) (Buffer is good for 16 tests.)

(**b**) *Sodium hydroxide soln.*—40% (w/v). (*Caution: See* **51.037**.)

(**c**) *Potassium sodium tartrate soln.*—Dissolve 25 g $C_4H_4O_6KNa.4H_2O$ in 100 mL H_2O; mix well.

(**d**) *Sodium hydroxide-potassium cyanide soln.*—Dissolve 40 g NaOH and 1 g KCN in 100 mL H_2O; mix well.

(**e**) *Hydroxylamine . hydrochloride soln.*—Dissolve 20 g $NH_2OH.HCl$ in 100 mL H_2O. Transfer soln to 250 mL separator and ext with 5 mL portions 0.01% (w/v) dithizone in $CHCl_3$ until last ext remains green; then wash soln free from excess dithizone with 10 mL portions $CHCl_3$. Transfer soln to 250 mL beaker, warm to remove excess $CHCl_3$, cool, and filter into 100 mL flask.

(**f**) *Buffer soln II.*—Mix reagents (**b**) : (**c**) : (**d**) : (**e**) in ratio of 1:1:5:1, and add 8 mL prepd buffer to 8 dram screw-cap vial for field test. (Buffer is good for 16 tests.)

(**g**) *Conditioned chloroform.*—Redistd $CHCl_3$, stabilized with 20 mL absolute alcohol/L. (*Caution: See* **51.056**.)

(**h**) *Dithizone reagent.*—Add 75 mg diphenylthiocarbazone to 250 mL vol. flask, dissolve in conditioned $CHCl_3$, (**g**), and dil. to vol. Add 0.5 mL this soln to 1 dram screw-cap vial and evap. to dryness without heat. (Dithizone reagent, when reconstituted with 2 mL $CHCl_3$, is good for 16 tests.)

(**i**) *Acetic acid soln.*—(4%) HOAc-H_2O (1+24). Analyze each new batch of reagent for Pb and Cd as in **25.034**(**a**) and (**b**).

25.036 ***Extraction***

Take, at random, 2 identical units of product, wipe clean to remove surface contaminants, and designate as *Y* and *Z*. Add 150 mL 4% HOAc soln, (**i**), to each unit and let stand 30 min. If 150 mL does not completely cover decoration, if present, add 4% HOAc until it does. (Note: If test is conducted in cold weather, warm HOAc to >65°F.)

25.037 ***Determination***

(**a**) *Test for lead.*—Using pipet or calibrated dropper, add 1 mL buffer soln I, (**a**), to each of three 10 × 75 mm test tubes. Add 0.25 mL 4% HOAc soln (equiv. to 7 drops using 2 mL Pasteur pipet; hold pipet almost horizontal to obtain proper size drop) to 1 test tube; add 0.25 mL leach soln from unit *Y* to second tube and 0.25 mL from unit *Z* to third tube. Reconstitute dithizone reagent in vial, (**h**), by adding 2 mL $CHCl_3$, (**g**). Add 0.125 mL reconstituted dithizone reagent to each test tube (due to surface tension and density of $CHCl_3$, 13 drops = 0.125 mL when disposable Pasteur pipet is used). Close end of tube with inverted hollow stopper (9 × 15 mm, Mallinckrodt P310-001, or equiv.) and shake ca 10 sec. Let layers sep. and observe color of lower $CHCl_3$ layer. Definite change from reagent blank color indicates possible presence of Pb. Verify pos. results by **25.033–25.034(a)**.

(**b**) *Test for cadmium.*—Using pipet or calibrated dropper, add 0.5 mL buffer soln II, (**f**), to each of three 10 × 75 mm test tubes. Add 0.6 mL (17 drops using 2 mL disposable Pasteur pipet) 4% HOAc soln (reagent blank) to 1 test tube, add 0.6 mL leach soln from unit *Y* to second tube, and 0.6 mL from unit *Z* to third tube. Continue as in (**a**), beginning "Reconstitute dithizone reagent in vial, (**h**), by adding 2 mL $CHCl_3$, . . ." Definite change from reagent blank color indicates possible presence of Cd. Verify pos. results by **25.033–25.034(b)**.

COPPER

International Union of Pure and Applied Chemistry Carbamate Method (*10*)—Official Final Action

25.038 ***Principle***

Sample is digested with HNO_3 and H_2SO_4. Cu is isolated and detd colorimetrically at pH 8.5 as diethyldithiocarbamate in presence of chelating agent, EDTA. Bi and Te also give colored carbamates at pH 8.5 but are decomposed to colorless compds with 1*N* NaOH. Cu complex is stable. Range of color development is 0–50 μg. Blank is ca 1 μg Cu.

25.039 ***Precautions***

Clean glassware with hot HNO_3. Use white petrolatum to lubricate stopcocks of separators, and do not use brass chains. Purify H_2O and HNO_3 by distn in Pyrex.

25.040 ***Reagents***

(**a**) *Sodium diethyldithiocarbamate* (*carbamate soln*).—Dissolve 1 g of the salt in H_2O, dil. to 100 mL, and filter. Store in refrigerator and prep. weekly.

(**b**) *Citrate-EDTA soln.*—Dissolve 20 g dibasic NH_4 citrate and 5 g Na_2EDTA (Eastman Kodak Co.) in H_2O and dil. to 100 mL. Remove traces of Cu by adding 0.1 mL carbamate soln and extg with 10 mL CCl_4. Repeat extn until CCl_4 ext is colorless.

(**c**) *Copper std solns.*—(*1*) *Stock soln.*—1 mg/mL. Place 0.2000 g Cu wire or foil into 125 mL erlenmeyer. Add 15 mL HNO_3 (1+4), cover flask with watch glass, and let Cu dissolve, warming to complete soln. Boil to expel fumes, cool, and dil. to 200 mL. (*2*) *Intermediate soln.*—100 μg/mL. Dil. 20 mL stock soln to 200 mL. (*3*) *Working soln.*—2 μg/mL. Prep. daily by dilg 5 mL intermediate std soln to 250 mL with 2.0*N* H_2SO_4.

(**d**) *Ammonium hydroxide.*—6*N*. Purify as in (**b**).

(**e**) *Thymol blue indicator.*—0.1%. Dissolve 0.1 g thymol blue in H_2O, add enough 0.1*N* NaOH to change color to blue, and dil. to 100 mL.

25.041 ***Preparation of Sample***

(*Caution: See* **51.026** and **51.030**.)

Weigh sample contg ≤20 g solids, depending upon expected Cu content. If sample contains <75% H_2O, add H_2O to obtain this diln. Add initial vol. HNO_3 to equal ca 2 times dry sample wt and 5 mL H_2SO_4, or as many mL H_2SO_4 as g dry sample, but ≥5 mL. Digest as in **25.008**.

When sample contains large amt of fat, make partial digestion with HNO_3 until only fat is undissolved. Cool, filter free of solid fat, wash residue with H_2O, add H_2SO_4 to filtrate, and complete digestion as above. After digestion, cool, add 25 mL H_2O, and remove nitrosylsulfuric acid by heating to fumes. Repeat addn of 25 mL H_2O and fuming. If after cooling and dilg, insol. matter is present, filter thru acid-washed paper, rinse paper with H_2O, and dil. to 100 mL.

Prep. reagent blank similarly.

25.042 ***Isolation and Determination of Copper***

Pipet 25 mL sample soln into 100 or 250 mL short-stem separator and add 10 mL citrate-EDTA reagent. Add 2 drops thymol blue indicator, (**e**), and 6*N* NH_4OH dropwise until soln turns green or blue-green. Cool, and add 1 mL carbamate soln and 15 mL CCl_4. Shake vigorously 2 min. Let layers sep. and drain CCl_4 through cotton pledget into g-s tube or flask. Det *A* or *T* in suitable instrument at ca 400 nm.

If >50 μg Cu is present in 25 mL aliquot, use smaller aliquot and dil. to 25 mL with 2.0*N* H_2SO_4. Highest accuracy is obtained at ca 25 μg Cu level (*A* ca 0.3 in 1 cm cell).

To test for Bi and Te, return CCl_4 soln to separator, add 10 mL 5% KCN soln, and shake 1 min. If CCl_4 layer becomes colorless, Bi and Te are absent.

If test is pos., develop color in another 25 mL aliquot as above (without KCN). Drain CCl_4 layer into second separator, add 10 mL 1*N* NaOH, and shake 1 min. Let layers sep. and drain CCl_4 into third separator. Again wash CCl_4 ext with 10 mL 1*N* NaOH. Det. *A* or *T* of CCl_4 layer and convert to μg Cu.

25.043 ***Preparation of Standards and Calibration Curves***

Transfer 0, 1, 2.5, 5, 10, 15, 20, and 25 mL of Cu std soln (2 μg/mL) to separators and add 2.0*N* H_2SO_4 to make total vol. of 25 mL.

Add 10 mL citrate-EDTA reagent and proceed as in **25.042**, beginning "Add 2 drops thymol blue indicator, . . ."

Plot *A* against μg Cu on ordinary graph paper. If readings are in % *T*, use semilog paper, and plot *T* on log scale. Since there is usually some deviation from linearity, read sample values from smoothed curve.

Atomic Absorption Method (*11*)—Official Final Action

(Applicable to copper and nickel in tea)

25.044 ***Principle***

Samples are wet ashed and after diln are detd by AA at 232.0 nm (Ni) and 324.7 nm (Cu). Matrix of std solns is matched to that of sample to avoid interference from Na and K.

25.045 ***Apparatus***

Atomic absorption spectrophotometer.—Capable of measuring content or change of content of 0.05 μg Ni or Cu/mL in aq. soln.

25.046 ***Preparation of Standard Solutions***

(**a**) *Copper std soln.*—1000 μg/mL. Dissolve 1.000 g 99.99% Cu in 20 mL HNO_3, cool, and dil. to 1 L with H_2O.

(**b**) *Nickel std soln.*—1000 μg/mL. Dissolve 1.000 g 99.99% Ni in 20 mL HNO_3, cool, and dil. to 1 L with H_2O.

(**c**) *Matrix std solns.*—Prep. solns contg 0, 0.2, 0.4, 0.8, 1.6, 2.0, 4.0, 8.0, and 10 μg Ni and Cu/mL and major metal matrix components: (*1*) *For 3 g sample tea.*—To contain 180 μg Ca, 100 μg Mg, and 40 μg Al/mL with final concn of 8% (v/v) $HClO_4$. (*2*) *For 6 g sample instant tea.*—To contain 7000 μg K, 70 μg Na, 700 μg Mg, and 130 μg Ca/mL with final HNO_3 concn of (1+9).

25.047 ***Preparation of Calibration Curve***

(*Caution: See* **51.006** and **51.026**.)

Let instrument stabilize. Optimize conditions for Cu or Ni according to manufacturer's instructions.

Aspirate 10 μg/mL std enough times to establish that *A* reading is not drifting. Record 6 readings and calc. std deviation $(\sigma) = (x - y) \times 0.40$, where *x* and *y* are max. and min. readings, resp., and 0.40 is factor to convert range of 6 values to σ.

Beginning with soln contg 0 Cu, aspirate each matrix std soln and record *A*. If value for 10 μg/mL soln differs from av. of the 6 values used to calc. σ by $>0.01 \times$ (av. of the 6 values), repeat measurements. If these detns indicate drift, det. cause (e.g., deposits in burner or clogged capillary), correct it, and repeat calibration. Repeat for Ni solns. Plot *A* against μg metal/mL.

25.048 ***Determination***

Select sample wt to give soln contg $\geqslant 0.05$ but $\leqslant 10$ μg Ni/mL, usually 3 g for teas and 6 g for instant teas.

(a) *Wet ashing.*—Accurately weigh sample into 400 mL beaker, add 100 mL HNO_3, and swirl. Cover, and let react 10 min; then place on hot plate. Evap. to near dryness and cool. Add 50 mL HNO_3, and for tea, add 10 mL $HClO_4$. Continue evapn to obtain clear soln. (*Caution: See* **51.019**, **51.026**, and **51.028**.)

Transfer to 50 mL vol. flask and dil. to vol. with H_2O. (Insol. $KClO_4$ which settles to bottom of flask does not interfere.)

Prep. reagent blank contg same amts of acids taken from same lots, evapd as above.

(b) *Photometry.*—Aspirate sample and blank solns, and record *A*. Measure *A* of matrix std soln contg 10 μg/mL. If this value differs from value of av. of the 6 values used to calc. σ by $>2\sigma$, repeat measurement. If these values indicate drift, det. cause, correct it, and repeat calibration and sample and blank readings.

(c) *Calculations.*—Correct readings of sample soln for blank. Convert corrected *A* to μg/mL from calibration curve.

$$\text{ppm Ni (or Cu)} = (C \times V)/W,$$

where C = μg metal/mL from curve, V = final vol. sample soln (50), and W = g sample.

FLUORINE (*12*)—OFFICIAL FINAL ACTION

25.049 ***Principle***

Sample is ashed with $Ca(OH)_2$ as F fixative; F is isolated by Willard-Winter distn (Ind. Eng. Chem., Anal. Ed. **5,** 7(1933)) from $HClO_4$, and estd in distillate by $Th(NO_3)_4$ back-titrn method (JAOAC **27,** 246(1944)). Technic and reagent concns are designed to handle $\leqslant 10.0$ mg F conveniently. Modifications applicable to specific products are described.

25.050 ***Precautions and Interferences***

Control magnitude of detn blank by careful choice and purification of reagents (*see* **25.052**). With care, blank will be low (1–3 μg F), but with low-F foods it may represent considerable part of total F detd; hence, it must be stable. Large part of it will be "distn blank" apparently resulting from F leached from glassware of still during distn. This blank can be minimized by preliminary treatment of stills, **25.054**, and av. distn blank detd if stills of same material and design are routinely used; otherwise, each still must bear its special blank. New, unused stills will usually be found to exhibit high blank, which will diminish to const low figure after several detns. They should not be used until several consecutive blank detns yield const, low amt of F.

Check ashing utensils by blank detns with fixative soln to det. if they contribute appreciable F. Even Pt vessels may become contaminated (owing presumably to slight Ca content) if they have been used recently for HF volatilization of SiO_2. In addn, such blank detns are useful for testing reagents and app. used in method and also evaporators, hoods, furnaces, and laboratory atm. for presence of F fumes and dust. If HF bottles are permitted in same laboratory, seal immediately after use; avoid contamination from roach powders.

Ordinary tap H_2O may be source of F contamination, since 1 mL H_2O contg 2 ppm F will contribute 2 μg F if allowed to remain or to dry in still. Therefore, routinely rinse all glassware (stills, flasks, burets, etc.) with H_2O, preferably redistd from alk. $KMnO_4$. Filter papers may contribute μg amts of F, and glass filters are preferred if filtration is required in micro detns.

Interferences are gelatinous SiO_2, Al, and B compds, which repress evolution of F as H_2SiF_6 in distn; materials such as nitrates, nitrites, peroxides, Cl, SO_2, and H_2S, which act upon indicator in titrn or otherwise interfere; halides (Cl), which distil to give excessive acidity in distillate; and phosphates and sulfates, which react with Th in titrn to give high results. Method is so designed that most of these interferences are automatically eliminated, but analyst should be on guard against their possible occurrence under unusual circumstances.

General Method

25.051 ***Apparatus***

(a) *Fluorine still.*—Claisen 100–125 mL distg flask is most practical for general work. It must be of Pyrex glass with auxiliary neck sealed off immediately above side arm to prevent pocketing and refluxing of distillate. Still should be as small and simply designed as practicable; ordinary distg flasks can be used for some work and they are slightly more efficient than Claisen type, except that danger of spraying over of distg acid is greater.

Equip still with dropping funnel and 0–150° thermometer, latter extending to within 6 mm of bottom of flask, so that bulb is immersed in boiling acid mixt. Acid-alkali washed beads, preferably Pyrex, should be on hand. Clean rubber stoppers by boiling in 10% NaOH soln. All-glass app. with ₮ accessories is convenient, especially in routine work, and eliminates need for rubber stoppers.

While not entirely necessary for heating still, use of Wood metal (50 Bi, 25 Pb, 12.5 Sn, 12.5 Cd) bath, adequately shielded, will prevent undue decomposition of $HClO_4$ and aid materially in securing low blank and low-acid distillate; hence, its use is strongly urged. If metal bath is used, do not immerse flask so deeply that bath level is above that of liq. in flask; if bath is not used, transite or asbestos shielding boards are essential, and flask should be heated thru small hole in such shield by low "clean" flame. (Bath and shielding boards prevent over-heating of upper still walls.)

At analyst's option, distg H_2O may be added as steam instead of thru dropping funnel; elec. boiler, Fig. **18:02,** is convenient steam generator. If steam is used, inlet tube should dip below surface of liq. in still. One advantage in adding distg H_2O thru funnel is that last portions of rinse H_2O used in transferring an ash can be used in distn. If funnel plug is thinly notched with sharp file on either side of bore, dropping rate can be more easily controlled, and end of funnel stem need not extend into liq. in still. Still is used in conjunction with clean straight-tube condenser no longer than necessary for adequate cooling. (Vertical arrangement of condenser will conserve bench space.)

(b) *Nessler tubes.*—Tall-form, 100 and 50 mL, g-s type preferred. Matched in sets of $\geqslant 6$. (100 mL size is used most frequently in general method.)

(c) *Additional apparatus.*—(*See* **25.050**.) Carefully cleaned and tested Pt, or well-glazed porcelain, dishes of ⩾100 mL size; 150 mL vol. flasks, or if these are not available, 200 mL size; and 10 mL burets (conveniently automatic) to deliver various solns required in distn and titrn. Overhead radiant heater will be found invaluable for drying and preliminary charring of samples, especially those of high-sugar type.

25.052 ***Reagents***

(*Caution: See* **51.011**, **51.025**, **51.028**, and **51.030**.)

(a) *Lime suspension.*—Carefully slake ca 56 g (1 mole) low-F CaO (ca 2 ppm F) with ca 250 mL H_2O, and *slowly* add 250 mL 60% $HClO_4$ with stirring. Add few glass beads and boil down to copious fumes of acid; cool, add 200 mL H_2O, and boil down again. Repeat diln and boiling down once more; cool, dil. considerably, and filter thru fritted glass filter, if pptd SiO_2 appears. Pour clear soln, with stirring, into 1 L NaOH soln (100 g/L), let ppt settle, and siphon off supernate. Remove Na salts from ppt by washing 5 times in large centrf. bottles, shaking mass thoroly each time. Finally, shake ppt into suspension and dil. to 2 L. Store in paraffined bottles. (100 mL of this suspension should give no appreciable F blank when evapd, distd, and carried thru titrn, (**l**).) Always shake suspension well before use.

(b) *Perchloric acid soln.*—60%. Dil. $HClO_4$ with 3–4 vols H_2O and boil down to original vol. Do not fume strongly. Repeat, and store in Pyrex. (Prepd acid should be Cl-free by test.)

(c) *Sulfuric acid soln.*—Carefully mix equal vols H_2SO_4 and H_2O, boil down to fumes, cool, dil. *carefully*, boil down once more, and dil. to 1+1 vol.

(d) *Silver perchlorate soln.*—50 g/100 mL.

(e) *p-Nitrophenol indicator.*—0.5% alc. soln.

(f) *Potassium hydroxide soln.*—Exactly 0.05*N*.

(g) *Potassium chloride soln.*—0.05*N*. 3.728 g/L.

(h) *Hydroxylamine hydrochloride soln.*—1.0%.

(i) *Hydrochloric acid soln.*—Exactly 0.05*N*.

(j) *Alizarin indicator.*—0.01% aq. soln of sodium alizarin sulfonate (Alizarin Red S).

(k) *Potassium fluosilicate std solns.*—(*1*) *Stock soln.*—0.5 mg F/mL. Dissolve and dil. 0.9661 g (corrected for purity as indicated below) K_2SiF_6 to 1 L (much more will not dissolve). Soln keeps indefinitely in paraffined bottle. (*2*) *Working soln.*—10 μg F/mL. Prep soln used in titrn, **25.055**, by dilg 20 mL stock soln to 1 L. Soln is stable several weeks in ordinary volumetric ware.

If pure K_2SiF_6 is not obtainable, prep. as follows: Add, thru dropping funnel, satd soln of NaF, or suspension of crude K_2SiF_6, into 500 mL Claisen distg app. contg 60 mL H_2SO_4 (1+1), some glass beads, and 10–20 g powd SiO_2 (or glass) kept at boiling temp. of 120–125°. Distil into 25% soln of KCl, held at simmering temp. on hot plate so that vol. of distillate does not become excessive. If necessary, add more H_2O to mixt. from dropping funnel in side-neck of still. Regulate rate of addn of NaF to still and temp. of condensing H_2O so that side arm and condenser do not become clogged with evolved H_2SiF_6, which tends to lodge as gelatinous mass. K_2SiF_6 is formed in receiver, and altho entirely cryst. it assumes appearance of gelatinous mass.

When substantial amt collects, pour contents of receiver into large centrf. bottle and wash repeatedly by centrfg (shaking up ppt thoroly each time), until washings are Cl-free by test. Collect on buchner and either air dry or bring to const wt *in vacuo* at 50–70°.

Det. purity by Travers titrn, **6.022**, at boiling temp. with 0.2*N* NaOH (1 mL = 0.01101 g K_2SiF_6); also by conversion to K_2SO_4 by treating 0.3–0.4 g in deep Pt dish with little H_2O, then H_2SO_4 plus little HF, fuming off excess acid *carefully* (if overheated, mixt. has tendency to spatter), and heating to const wt of K_2SO_4 at 650°. With glass app., entirely pure product is not usually obtained, as some contamination with SiO_2 results from leaching effect of vapors on condenser. Pure product can be obtained by use of Pt still. Prep. stock soln, correcting wt of 0.9662 by purity factor of the K_2SiF_6 (figure for purity obtained from av. of 2 above methods of assay).

(l) *Thorium nitrate soln.*—0.25 g $Th(NO_3)_4.12H_2O$ or 0.20 g $Th(NO_3)_4.4H_2O$/L. Check titer against std (10 μg/mL) F soln as follows: Measure 10, 20, 30, etc., up to 80 μg F into 100 mL Nessler tubes, and add 4.00 mL 0.05*N* HCl (2.00 mL if 50 mL Nessler tubes are used, and limiting range to only 50 μg F) (JAOAC **24**, 350(1941)). Dil. mixt. to ca 80 (or 40) mL mark and add 1.00 mL 1.0% $NH_2OH.HCl$ soln. Mix; then add exactly 2.00 mL alizarin indicator (or 1.00 mL for smaller tube) and add Th soln from buret, mixing frequently until, when sighting down tube toward white reflecting surface, incipient pink or salmon pink color is observed. Add little H_2O occasionally so that soln is nearly to mark as end point is approached. Finally, dil. exactly to mark and mix thoroly before checking final end point. Do not shake tube vigorously (5–6 gentle inversions are enough).

Make effort to secure end point shade intermediate between yellowish green of acid indicator and reddish purple of fully developed Th lake. Complete series and plot mL Th soln against mL std fluoride to obtain rough equivalence curve for 2 solns. Depending upon amt of F known to be present, add Th soln in 1–2 mL portions at first, with final addns of 0.25 mL.

25.053 ***Preparation of Sample***

(*Caution: See* **51.011** and **51.028**.)

Methods of sample prepn are designed to furnish representative sample in workable amt of material and to obtain sample in condition for final distn. Mineralization by ashing is usually involved. Some mineral food products can be dissolved in and distd from $HClO_4$, **25.054**, provided no interferences appear in final distillate.

In general, ⩾20 g dry material, 50–100 mL liq. samples, and 50–100 g undried food products or plant material can be taken for analysis, depending upon expected F content and interferences, such as excessive Cl, which use of large samples may introduce. For reasonable precision in analysis of low-F foods, sample should be sufficient to yield titer of ⩾0.5 mL for aliquot taken in final titrn. However, it may not always be possible to handle this amt of material. If adequate grinding and mixing equipment is available, it is often feasible to prep. large amts of material (vegetables, mixed foods) and to take aliquot portions for analysis (Ind. Eng. Chem., Anal. Ed. **13**, 93(1941)).

Dry plant materials, feeds, bone meal, etc., can be ground to convenient size in Wiley mill and thoroly mixed before sample is taken. Following special methods for certain products are indicated:

(a) *Direct ashing.*—Applicable to fibrous (not highly fatty) foods, liq. samples and, in general, to all foods that can be thoroly wet with aq. fixative soln. This method will apply to majority of food products.

Weigh suitable portion of prepd sample into clean Pt dish and add 25 mL $Ca(OH)_2$ suspension. (Porcelain casseroles or dishes are second choice because they may contribute small amts of F and Al_2O_3 to sample.) Mix in $Ca(OH)_2$ suspension with glass rod, adding addnl H_2O if necessary; rinse and remove rod. Dry *thoroly* on steam bath or in hot air oven; then slowly char sample by heating over low flame or elec. plate with thermostat. Overhead radiant heater is convenient for both drying and charring sample. Control excessive swelling of high sugar foods by playing small flame over surface of sample from time to time, and char these products *slowly* so that excessive acidity is not generated. When sample is charred past danger of catching fire, ash in furnace at 600°. (For very small samples and min. blanks, it may be advisable to cover ashing vessel with inverted Pyrex petri dish while ashing.)

For plants high in silica, fusion with NaOH may be necessary (Anal. Chem. **25**, 450, 1061(1953)).

When clean ash is obtained, cool dish and wet ash with ca 10 mL H_2O. (Small amt of unburned C does not interfere but if much is apparent, dry down and repeat ashing.) Cover dish with watch glass and cautiously introduce under cover just enough $HClO_4$ soln to dissolve ash. Rinse down cover with little H_2O and transfer soln to freshly prepd F still, **25.054**, thru long-stem funnel. Rinse dish with remainder of distg acid, using ca 20 mL in all, and adding and transferring in several small portions. *Do not prolong transferring operation*. Finally rinse funnel and stirring rod into dish, assemble still, and complete rinsing of dish with several small portions H_2O, pouring these into dropping funnel of still. If distg H_2O is added as steam, **25.051(a)**, rinse dish with little addnl H_2O and add directly to acid mixt. in still, but avoid excessive initial vol. Add ca 6 Pyrex beads and enough $AgClO_4$ soln, **25.052(d)**, to ppt all Cl. (Reasonable excess of $AgClO_4$ does no harm; enough solid Ag_2SO_4 may also be used.) Proceed as in **25.054**.

(**b**) *Preliminary distillation*.—(Necessary with certain products high in phosphate, such as Ca phosphate and bone meal, in order to eliminate distd H_3PO_4 that may be present in appreciable amts in first distillates. Also advisable with certain excessively fatty materials that may not be thoroly wet with $Ca(OH)_2$ fixative, thus causing F loss in direct ashing method.)

(*1*) *For inorganic phosphatic materials, such as Ca phosphate*.—Weigh sample, usually 10 g, into still; add few glass beads, enough $AgClO_4$ to ppt possible Cl, and ca 20 mL $HClO_4$ soln. (If inorg. phosphatic material does not contain excessive Ca (enough to cause heavy ppt of $CaSO_4$ in still), use similar amt of 1+1 H_2SO_4.) Distil at 135–140°, collecting ca 200 mL distillate. (For this preliminary distn, extreme care in securing low-acid distillate is not essential.) Evap. distillate to dryness in Pt dish after addn of excess $Ca(OH)_2$ suspension, assuring alk. conditions by testing with drop of phthln. (If H_2SO_4 is used in this preliminary distn, add few drops *F-free 30% H_2O_2* to distillate to oxidize possible sulfites.) Heat dried residue at 600° few min to destroy indicator residues and possible Cl-contg compds. Transfer contents of dish to freshly prepd still, **25.054**, with 20 mL distg $HClO_4$ soln as in (**a**), and proceed with final distn as in **25.054**.

Take 20 mL samples of sirupy H_3PO_4 and collect ≥300 mL first distillate at 135°, letting H_3PO_4 function as its own distg acid. (More distillate is necessary because H_3PO_4 is less effective as F distg acid.) Neutze with $Ca(OH)_2$ suspension, evap. to dryness, transfer to prepd still as above, and proceed as in **25.054**.

(*2*) *For organic phosphatic materials, such as bone meal, feed supplements, etc*.—As preliminary ashing treatment to destroy most org. matter, moisten sample with enough $Ca(OH)_2$ suspension, dry, char, and heat 2–3 hr at 600°. Transfer ashed material to still, which contains several beads and enough $AgClO_4$ to ppt Cl, with 20 mL distg acid ($HClO_4$ or H_2SO_4, depending on Ca content of sample) as in (**a**), and continue as in (**b**)(*1*), beginning, "Distil at 135–140°, . . ."

Certain org. phosphatic materials (small samples of bone, 2–5 g, such as entire bones of small test animals) *in which amt of org. matter is not excessive*, may be distd directly as in (**b**)(*1*) without preliminary ashing. If sample contains appreciable Ca (bone samples), use $HClO_4$ with reasonable precaution; if org. phosphatic material does not contain excessive Ca, use 1+1 H_2SO_4. In either case, add more $Ca(OH)_2$ to first distillates and ash for longer periods to completely destroy distd org. matter (fatty acids). Transfer contents of dish to freshly prepd still, **25.054**, with 20 mL $HClO_4$ soln as in (**a**) and proceed with final distn, **25.054**.

Baking powders (Ca phosphate and combination types): Place 10 g sample in deep, covered Pt dish or casserole and slake cautiously with ca 20 mL $Ca(OH)_2$ suspension. After action subsides, rinse cover, dry contents of dish *thoroly*, and ash 2–3 hr at 600°. Cool dish and, because of excess of carbonate in ash, treat it with several small portions of warm H_2O, breaking up with flat-end stirring rod, and transfer leachings to still. Transfer remaining contents of dish with 20 mL $HClO_4$ soln, avoiding excessive effervescence when acid is added to carbonate soln in still. Add several glass beads and enough $AgClO_4$ soln, and proceed as in (**b**)(*1*), beginning, "Distil at 135–140°, . . ." With *combination* or *Na Al sulfate* baking powders, collect ≥400 mL preliminary distillate, (**b**)(*4*).

Use of special still trap makes possible analysis of highly phosphatic *inorg. or thoroly ashed* materials, and phosphoric acids, with single distn. Special trap, or scrubber, consists of 12–15 g small, hollow glass beads supported in side-neck of the 125 mL Claisen flask by several indentations punched in side wall, and capped by glass disk or inverted bottom of 15 mm test tube. After construction of glass-bead scrubber, side-neck is sealed off immediately above outlet tube. (Beads in scrubber must be wet with little H_3PO_4 (by tipping flask) before distn to furnish liq. acid phase.) Take 20 mL sirupy H_3PO_4, by itself, and 10 g samples Ca phosphate with 20 mL $HClO_4$ soln, for distn, and collect ≥400 mL distillate at 135°. With single distn, observe precautions in **25.051(a)**, and also in **25.054**, regarding neutzn of final distillates. (Distillates should show practically no acidity.) Presence of only *traces* of distd H_3PO_4 will vitiate titrn; as little as 20 μg P_2O_5 will definitely interfere. Accordingly, if single distn procedure is to be applied with confidence, it is necessary to test distillates obtained from phosphatic materials, by means of the special still, for presence of this interference.

For convenient test utilizing Schricker reagent (JAOAC **22**, 167(1939)), add 5 mL of 1+9 diln of this reagent to 45 mL distillate in 50 mL graduate or Nessler tube, mix, and immerse in steam bath 5–10 min. Compare against blank by sighting down tube. Blue or blue-green color indicates phosphate, and as little as 5 μg (as P_2O_5) is readily detected. If distillate shows traces, make sure that such amts are below interference level of 15 μg in titrn aliquot before titrg addnl portions of distillate. (Test with Schricker reagent is also useful in usual double distn where phosphate interference is possible. Use of special trap will save time where highly phosphatic materials are handled routinely, but it is not justified in ordinary work because of poor efficiency owing to excessive refluxing in distn.)

(*3*) *For excessively fatty and oily food materials* (*oil-packed foods, certain meats, etc.; also entire undried and unground organs of test animals*).—If there is danger of F loss thru incomplete wetting with $Ca(OH)_2$ fixation soln, handle as follows: Weigh appropriate amt of sample, usually 10–25 g, into still, and add Ag (preferably 0.1–0.2 g solid Ag_2SO_4), several glass beads, and 20–25 mL H_2SO_4 (1+1). Distil at 130–135° and collect 200–250 mL distillate in beaker or open vessel. If foaming is excessive, increase vol. of distg acid, and where necessary, use larger (250–300 mL) still. If larger still or more acid is used, collect proportionately more of first distillate. (Oil or fat of many of these products will tend to prevent foaming, and, in some instances, use of ca pea-size piece of pure paraffin is addnl aid.)

Oxidize distillate in cold by cautious addn of 2–3 mL *F-free 30% H_2O_2* to remove sulfites, let stand few min, and evap. portionwise in Pt dish contg excess (10–15 mL) $Ca(OH)_2$ suspension. Ash residue at 600° until clean. Proceed as in (**b**)(*1*), beginning "Transfer contents of dish to freshly prepd still, . . ."

Handle pure oils by similar procedure: Use 10 g sample with 25 mL H_2SO_4 (1+1) and carry temp. at first to ca 170° to saponify; then carefully bring temp. down to 140° with distg H_2O and collect ≥250 mL distillate. (It will probably be necessary to use higher reading thermometer for this procedure.) Oxidize distillate with 30% H_2O_2 and evap. to dryness after adding excess $Ca(OH)_2$ suspension. Ash at 600° and after brief preliminary ash period remove dish, add little H_2O plus addnl 1–2 mL of the H_2O_2 to remove sulfides, dry, and complete ashing. Proceed as in (**b**)(*1*), beginning "Transfer contents of dish to freshly prepd still, . . ."

(*4*) *For aluminum and boron compounds*.—Al and B repress evolution of F. Isolate F by preliminary distn at elevated temp. For this purpose, weigh sample, usually 5–10 g, into still, add 25 mL H_2SO_4 (1+1), and conduct first distn at 160–165° (special thermometer), collecting 300 mL distillate. Oxidize distillate with 30% H_2O_2 as above, evap. in Pt dish with excess $Ca(OH)_2$ suspension, ash briefly at 600°, and proceed as in (**b**)(*1*), beginning, "Transfer contents of dish to freshly prepd still, . . ."

25.054 ***Final Distillation***

(*Caution: See* **51.011** and **51.028**.)

Always make final distn from $HClO_4$, and take precautions to secure low-acid distillate, **25.051(a)**. Since interferences, such as org. matter, phosphate, sulfate, etc., must be absent from distillate, make distn with careful temp. control in presence of enough Ag salt to repress HCl evolution (**25.050**). It is well to check distillates for presence of possible phosphate as in **25.053(b)**(*2*), and where advisable, as in (**b**)(*4*), to test for sulfate with little dil. $BaCl_2$ soln. $HClO_4$ used in final distn is usually used in transferring ash to still, **25.053(a)**. Few acid-alkali washed beads are used to control bumping. (Use of powd SiO_2 does not appear necessary for microdetn.)

To promote better recoveries, and to minimize and render const distn blank discussed in **25.050** and **25.055**, prep. still by special cleaning process before this transfer by treating it with *hot* 10% NaOH soln after each detn, flushing out with tap H_2O, and then rinsing with distd H_2O. Occasionally (at least once daily, and especially after it has stood idle for any length of time), give still addnl treatment by boiling down 15–20 mL H_2SO_4 (1+1) until still is filled with fumes. Cool, pour off acid, treat with the 10% NaOH soln, and *thoroly* rinse out. (Cleaning should be especially meticulous after high-F or high-SiO_2 samples have been distd, and in such cases condenser should also be cleaned.)

At this stage, prepd sample has been transferred to specially treated still, as directed above, for final isolation of F. Begin distn, and when temp. reaches 137°, keep at this point (±2°) by adding H_2O from dropping funnel, **25.051(a)**. Heat still at such rate that all distns require ca same time. (Time promotes uniformity in blank correction.) Collect distillate in 150 or 200 mL vol. flask. After few mL distillate collects, add 1–2 drops *p*-nitrophenol indicator, (**e**), and keep distillate alk. to this indicator (faintest perceptible yellow) by occasionally adding 1–2 drops 0.05*N* KOH from 10 mL buret during distn while swirling receiver. So regulate this addn of alkali that distillate is neutzd (within 1 drop of alkali) as it approaches mark. Carefully note vol. alkali used. Dil. distillate to vol. and mix thoroly. Do not let F distillate stand more than few min before neutzg.

If sample contains such large amts of Cl that bumping in still cannot be controlled, dissolve ash of another sample, and acidify *slightly* with $HClO_4$. Dil. considerably and ppt Cl in dish with $AgClO_4$ soln, avoiding large excess. Filter thru glass filter, wash ppt *thoroly* with hot H_2O, and evap. filtrate and washings to dryness after adding excess (to alky) of $Ca(OH)_2$ suspension. Transfer residue to still with $HClO_4$ soln and repeat distn as above.

25.055 ***Titration***

(*Caution: See* **51.011** and **51.028**.)

Place aliquot of final distillate in Nessler tube and mark "S" (sample). (Optimum F content for titrn is 60–70 μg for 100 mL Nessler tubes and 30–40 μg for 50 mL size, and it is well to make exploratory titrn on small aliquot to check approx. F content of distillate. Larger tubes are necessary for precise results on low-F foods.)

Add 0.05*N* HCl, 4.00 mL for 100 mL tubes and 2.00 mL for 50 mL size, and 1.00 mL $H_2NOH.HCl$ soln. (For routine work *with 100 mL tubes*, dissolve 1.0 g $H_2NOH.HCl$ in 500 mL 0.04*N* HCl and dil. to 500 mL. Then proper amt of both reagents can be added in single operation with 5 mL pipet.) Dil. to ca 90 (or 40) mL, mix well, then add alizarin indicator (2.00 or 1.00 mL), and mix again. Always add and mix in $H_2NOH.HCl$ before adding indicator.

Prep. blank tube "B" by adding proper amt HCl and $H_2NOH.HCl$, and amt 0.05*N* KCl soln representing same proportion of total vol. of 0.05*N* KOH used to neutze distillate as aliquot vol. taken for sample tube represents of total distillate vol. (Thus, if 1.50 mL 0.05*N* KOH was used to neutze distillate of 150 mL and aliquot taken for tube "S" was 75 mL, add 0.75 mL 0.05*N* KCl to tube "B.") Dil. and mix, allowing slightly more headspace than in sample tube. Then add proper vol. alizarin indicator and mix.

Measure Th soln into tube "S," mixing between addns, until end point of about proper shade is reached. Dil. to mark, mix, and check this end point shade. Note from curve, **25.052(l)**, approx. vol. std F soln corresponding to this vol. Th soln, and add ca 0.5 mL *less* than this amt of std F soln to "B." Mix; then add exactly same vol. Th soln as was added to "S," duplicating approx. increments in which it was added and number of mixings. Dil. nearly to mark and compare colors of "S" and "B." (If vol. std F soln added to "B" was properly chosen, this tube should be only slightly pinker in shade than sample tube.)

Bleach "B" tube to exact match with tube "S" by adding more std F soln to "B" in increments of 1–2 drops, mixing gently between addns. Dil. to mark for final comparison and observe usual precautions of letting bubbles subside and of transposing tubes when final comparisons are made. (At match-point, F content of tube "S" equals amt added to tube "B.") Check this end point by adding 1–2 drops excess std F soln to tube "B." Distinct overbleach should develop.

Repeat titrn on aliquots of different size to obtain total amt of F distd. If time is available, repeat entire detn with different wt sample.

For precise work, evaluation of reagent and of distn blank is necessary, **25.050**. Det. distn blank by making several distns with prescribed amts $HClO_4$ and $AgClO_4$ solns from freshly cleaned still, titrg distillate as above with as large aliquot as practicable. Av. of values found should be ≤3 μg F. If amts found by individual blank detns are too small to be detd accurately, make ≥5 sep. distns and evap. distillates, 150 mL each time, successively in same Pt dish for final distn and average blank figure. Distn and total detn blanks can usually be *combined* by carrying run (with same amts of reagents and similar evapn and ashing treatment) thru entire detn. Reagents and manipulations should increase distn blank but little.

Calc. total amt F distd from amt found in aliquot titrd, subtract proper blank, and refer net figure to wt sample taken. If double distn procedure was used, make appropriate blank correction.

Rapid Method Restricted to Fluoride Residues on Apples and Pears

25.056 ***Principle***

Add filtrate from strip soln of apples and pears prepd with HCl rinse and acidification, **25.106**, is used. Aliquot of filtrate is oxidized colorless with $KMnO_4$, soln is then reduced with H_2NOH, and subaliquot is backtitrd in Nessler tubes; $Zr(NO_3)_4$ is used in titrn, with purpurin (1,2,4-trihydroxyanthraquinone) as indicator (Ind. Eng. Chem., Anal. Ed. **6**, 118(1934)). Principle of back-titrn, as applied here, is similar to that used in general method where $Th(NO_3)_4$ and alizarin occupy similar roles. Provision is made for removal of interfering anions, and high acidity used in titrn minimizes interference of metals that would otherwise lake with indicator.

25.057 ***Apparatus***

Nessler tubes.—50 mL g-s, tall-form, matched for ht and color (*see* **25.060**).

25.058 ***Reagents***

(**a**) *Mixed nitrate soln*.—Dissolve 3.0 g $Ba(NO_3)_2$ and 2.0 g $Th(NO_3)_4.4H_2O$ in H_2O, and dil. to 100 mL.

(**b**) *Potassium permanganate soln*.—Satd; ca 6%.

(**c**) *Hydroxylamine hydrochloride soln*.—5%.

(**d**) *Ferrous chloride soln*.—Dissolve ca 1.0 g Fe powder or wire in 50 mL HCl (1+1), dil., and filter into 500 mL vol. flask. Add few mL 5% $H_2NOH.HCl$ soln and dil. to vol. Dil. still further before use, if desired.

(**e**) *Purpurin indicator*.—0.01% in alcohol. Dissolve 25 mg pure 1,2,4-trihydroxyanthraquinone in alcohol, heating if necessary, and dil. to 250 mL with same solv. Prep. fresh weekly.

(**f**) *Zirconium nitrate soln*.—Dissolve 1.50 g $Zr(NO_3)_4.5H_2O$ in H_2O, acidify with 20 mL HCl, and dil. to 1 L. Filter if not clear.

(**g**) *Fluoride std soln*.—54.5 μg F/mL. Dissolve 0.1464 g NaF in H_2O and dil. to 1 L.

25.059 ***Determination***

Place 20 mL well mixed acid strip filtrate, **25.106**, in 50 mL vol. flask. Add 2.0 mL mixed nitrate soln, then 4.0 mL $KMnO_4$ soln. Rinse down neck of flask with little H_2O and place on active steam bath 5 min. Remove flask, and while still hot, add 5% $H_2NOH.HCl$ soln from buret, slowly and with swirling, until MnO_2 is dissolved and soln is colorless; then add ca 0.5 mL in excess. (Appreciable phosphate is revealed as flocculent $Th_3(PO_4)_4$, and sulfate as ppt with Ba. Sometimes $KMnO_4$ is occluded in sulfate and/or phosphate ppt, and pink color tends to persist but does not interfere.) Cool, dil. to vol., and filter. (Filtrate must be clear. If there is perceptible turbidity, return filtrate thru filter several times if necessary, until filtrate is *brilliant*.) Pipet 25 mL clear filtrate into Nessler tube and mark "S."

For blank or comparison tube use 25 mL "blank" soln, contg reagents used in method, prepd as follows:

Dil. 50 mL 10% Na oleate soln, **25.095(k)**, 50 mL 30 g/100 mL NaOH soln, and 15 mL HCl to 1 L. Acidify portions with 1/10 vol. HCl as if soln were an actual "strip," and filter, refiltering until filtrate is perfectly clear. (Chilling soln and shaking vigorously will "churn" pptd oleic acid and aid in obtaining clear filtrate.) Carry 20 mL portions of acidified filtrate thru method exactly as above. (In order more closely to duplicate conditions of actual detn, use 50 mL vol. flasks and 20 mL aliquots in preference to using larger aliquots with correspondingly larger amts of reagents. After being dild to vol. and filtered, blank soln may be combined to form supply of "blank"; 10 portions worked up as above yield ca 500 mL "blank," or enough for ca 20 detns.)

Add 25 mL of this "blank" to second Nessler tube, "B," and to both tubes "S" and "B" add 15.0 mL HCl measured as carefully as possible from graduate. (Always add acid to soln instead of vice versa.) Mix, and match tubes for color. "S" tube will usually be found to have slight greenish tint in comparison with "B" tube, due presumably to traces of Fe. Balance both tubes to same shade by adding $FeCl_2$ soln dropwise to appropriate tube and mixing. *This operation must be done carefully*. When tints are indistinguishable, add exactly 1.00 mL purpurin indicator to each tube. Mix; then add 1.50 mL Zr soln to each tube from 10 mL buret, and mix. Do not shake tubes violently when mixing in reagents; 4 or 5 gentle inversions are enough. Observe color difference, if any, between tubes when looking down their length toward white reflecting surface. If there is no appreciable difference *after 5 min*, F content of sample is negligible. If color of tube "S" is yellower, presence of F is indicated. In this case, add addnl amts of $Zr(NO_3)_4$ soln to tube "S" until its color about matches that of tube "B" (to nearest 0.5 mL Zr soln). Dil. "S" to mark and mix.

Now add to "B" exactly same total vol. Zr soln as was added to tube "S," mix, and let tube stand 2 min for lake to develop fully. Back-titr. std F soln into "B" from 10 mL buret until tubes match, mixing frequently, and dilg nearly to vol. as end point approaches. Add NaF soln in increments of ca 0.1 mL at this stage, and observe usual precautions of transposing and letting bubbles subside when making comparisons. Dil. to mark for final comparison. Check end point by adding 0.1–0.2 mL std F soln in excess. Distinct overbleach should develop.

For sample wt of 1 kg and aliquots specified above, each mL std F soln consumed in back-titrn is equiv. to F content on fruit sample, *removable by solv. treatment*, of 3.0 ppm. Correct result obtained in titrn by sample wt ratio. (Thus, titer of 3.27 mL std F soln, with 1.40 kg sample (ca 10 fruit), represents F content of 7.0 ppm. Vol. restrictions of 50 mL Nessler tube will allow estn of spray residue content up to ca 11 ppm F.) If calibration mark is exceeded in back-titrn, use 10 mL aliquot of acid filtrate in tube "S," and dil. to 25 mL with "blank" soln, correcting titer of std F soln by appropriate factor.

25.060 ***Notes on Rapid Method***

G-s Nessler tubes are almost essential with concd acid prescribed in this detn. Analysts familiar with Th-alizarin back-titrn method should have no difficulty with Zr-purpurin titrn. With latter, however, color changes are not so apparent and titrn is less sensitive. However, with careful work, results accurate to ≥0.5 ppm may be expected.

Indicator color at prescribed acidity is yellow, and fully laked indicator is orange-red. This contrasts with Th titrn where corresponding range is from yellowish green to reddish purple. Hence, in rapid method, choice of end point involves discrimination between varying shades of orange. Addn of 1.50 mL Zr soln to tube "B" at start is merely to provide intermediate shade of orange to guide analyst in amt of Zr to be added to tube "S." Analysts may prefer to work with redder or yellower end point shade. In any event, make number of titrns by adding varying amts of std F soln as unknowns to Nessler tubes and carrying thru back-titrn as above, for purpose of learning color changes involved. Pure aq. solns instead of "blank" may be used, with acidities of 20 mL HCl/50 mL.

Accuracy of results with rapid method presupposes complete removal of spray residue F by solv. process and good accuracy (not necessarily precision) in titrn. These conditions may not always hold; unless carefully done, solv. method may not be entirely effective, and result on strip solns contg known amts of F have tended to be slightly low. Hence accuracy >95% is not to be expected with this method.

LEAD

25.061 ***Principle***

Instrumental methods, polarography and atomic absorption (AA) spectrophotometry, are generally more reliable than colorimetric method at lower concns. Method **25.063–25.067** is particularly applicable to samples contg high Ca concn. Special instrumental methods optimized for evapd milk and fish are given in **25.068–25.092**.

General colorimetric method calls for ashing, **25.096**, sepn of Pb, either as dithizone complex, **25.098**, or as sulfide, **25.099**, followed by colorimetric dithizone detn, **25.100**, in comparator tubes, or with spectrophtr. Interference is treated sep., **25.101–25.103**, and analyst should familiarize himself with details of these sections before applying method. Special methods of sample prepn are given in **25.104–25.105**.

25.062 ***Precautions***

Analyst should decide whether nature of detn requires unusual care in purification of reagents, or whether blank detn will suffice. Smaller the amt of Pb to be detd, greater the care required in reduction of blank (*see also* **25.100**).

To test suitability of reagents, place 10–15 g solid reagents dissolved in redistd H_2O or 15–20 mL concd acids previously neutzd with redistd NH_4OH in separator and add enough Pb-free citric acid to prevent pptn by NH_4OH of Fe, Al, alk. earth phosphates, or other substances. Make soln ammoniacal and add 2–3 mL 10% KCN soln. Shake soln with ca 5 mL dithizone soln, **25.095(e)** (5–10 mg/L). If lower layer is green, transfer it to another separator and ext excess dithizone with NH_4OH (1+99) to which has been added drop of KCN soln. If $CHCl_3$ layer is colorless, consider test neg. for use with dithizone methods.

When special purification becomes necessary, redistil H_2O (distd H_2O stored in Sn-lined tanks usually contains Pb and Sn), HNO_3, HCl, HBr, Br, and $CHCl_3$ in all-glass stills (preferably Pyrex). Prep. NH_4OH by distg ordinary reagent into ice-cold redistd H_2O. If stills are new, steam them out with hot HCl or HNO_3 vapors to remove "surface" Pb. (Subsequent distillates may not be totally Pb-free.)

$Pb(NO_3)_2$ may be purified as follows: Dissolve 20–50 g in min. of hot H_2O and cool with stirring. Filter crystals with suction on small buchner, redissolve, and recrystallize. Dry crystals at 100–110° to const wt. Cool in desiccator and store in tightly stoppered bottle. (Product has no H_2O of crystn and is not appreciably hygroscopic.)

Purify citric acid, NaOAc or NH_4OAc, $Al(NO_3)_3$, $Ca(NO_3)_2$, and Na_2SO_4 by pptg Pb from their aq. solns with H_2S (*Caution: See* **51.059**), using 5–10 mg $CuSO_4$ as coprecipitant (citric acid and $Al(NO_3)_3$ solns require adjustment with NH_4OH to pH 3.0–3.5, bromophenol blue indicator). Filter (fritted glass filter is most convenient), boil filtrates 20 min to expel excess H_2S, and refilter if necessary to obtain brilliantly clear solns. Purify other reagents by recrystn.

Store redistd acids or purified solns of reagents in resistant glass containers of min. Pb content (Pyrex is suitable), carefully cleaned of surface Pb with hot HNO_3. Paraffin-lined bottles may be used for alk. reagents.

Carefully clean new glass and chemical ware with hot 10% NaOH soln followed by hot HNO_3, and use only for Pb detns.

In prepn of samples for analysis, avoid Pb contamination. If mixing or grinding is necessary, use porcelain mortar if possible. Avoid use of metal food grinders unless previous experiment has shown that no contamination of sample with Pb or Sn results. If product to be analyzed cannot be thoroly mixed in its own container, or if composite sample of number of containers is desired, empty into large glass jar or porcelain dish and mix thoroly with wooden spoon or porcelain spatula. If liq. portion of sample cannot be incorporated into ground solid material to obtain homogeneous mixt., analyze sep. If food is packed in tins having soldered seams (sardines and meats), open tins from bottom to avoid contaminating sample with bits of solder. Avoid sifting in prepn of samples to prevent metallic contamination or segregation of Pb.

Atomic Absorption Spectrophotometric Method (*13*)
Official Final Action

25.063 ***Principle***

(*Caution: See* **51.006**, **51.019**, **51.026**, **51.028**, and **51.030**.)

Org. matter is digested and Pb released coppts with $SrSO_4$. Sol. sulfate salts are decanted, and ppt is converted to carbonate salt, dissolved in acid, and detd by AA at 217 or 283.3 nm.

25.064 ***Apparatus***

(**a**) *Atomic absorption spectrophotometer*.—Operated at 217 or 283.3 nm. (*Caution: See* **51.006**.)

(**b**) *Stirring motor*.—With eccentric coupling for stirring centrf. tubes (Sargent-Welch Scientific Co. Model S-76509 (Vortex, Jr.), or equiv.).

25.065 ***Reagents***

(Age all new glassware and all glassware which has contained high Pb concn in boiling HNO_3 before washing. *Never* let used glassware dry before washing, and *always* include final HNO_3 rinse followed by deionized H_2O rinse.)

(**a**) *Strontium soln*.—2%. Dissolve 6 g $SrCl_2.6H_2O$ in 100 mL H_2O.

(**b**) *Ternary acid mixture*.—Add 20 mL H_2SO_4 to 100 mL H_2O, mix, add 100 mL HNO_3 and 40 mL 70% $HClO_4$, and mix.

(**c**) *Nitric acid*.—Add 128 mL redistd HNO_3 to 500–800 mL distd or deionized H_2O and dil. to 2 L. Redistd HNO_3 (G. Frederick Smith Chemical Co., No. 53) may be dild and used without redistn.

(**d**) *Lead std solns*.—(*1*) *Stock soln*.—1000 μg/mL. Dissolve 1.5985 g $Pb(NO_3)_2$, recrystd as in **25.062**, in ca 500 mL 1*N* HNO_3 in 1 L vol. flask and dil. to vol. with 1*N* HNO_3. (*2*) *Working solns*.—Prep. 100 μg Pb/mL by dilg 10 mL stock soln to 100 mL with 1*N* HNO_3. Dil. 1, 3, 5, 10, 15, and 25 mL aliquots of this soln to 100 mL with 1*N* HNO_3 (1, 3, 5, 10, 15, and 25 μg Pb/mL, resp.).

25.066 ***Separation of Lead***

Accurately weigh sample contg $\leq$10 g dry matter and $\geq$3 μg Pb. Place in 500 mL boiling or Kjeldahl flask and add 1 mL 2% Sr soln, (**a**), and several glass beads. Prep. reagent blank and carry thru same operations as sample. Add 15 mL ternary acid mixt., (**b**), for each g dry matter and let stand $\geq$2 hr. Heat under hood or H_2O vac. manifold system until flask contains only H_2SO_4 and inorg. salts. (*Note:* Take care to avoid sample loss from foaming when heat is first applied, and when foaming occurs soon after sample chars. Remove heat and swirl flask before continuing digestion. Add HNO_3, if necessary.)

Cool digest few min. (Digest should be cool enough to add ca 15 mL H_2O safely, but hot enough to boil when H_2O is added.) Wash while still hot into 40–50 mL tapered-bottom centrf. tube and swirl. Let cool, centrf. 10 min at 350×*g*, and decant liq. into waste beaker. (Film-like ppt on surface may be discarded.) Dislodge ppt by vigorously stirring with eccentric-coupled stirring motor. To complete transfer, add 20 mL H_2O and 1 mL 1*N*

H_2SO_4 to original flask and heat. *Do not omit this step* even though it appears transfer was complete in first wash. Wash hot contents of original digestion flask into centrf. tube contg ppt. Swirl to mix, cool, centrf., and decant liq. into waste beaker.

Dislodge ppt by stirring vigorously, add 25 mL *satd* $(NH_4)_2CO_3$ *soln* (ca 20%), and stir until all ppt is dispersed. Let stand 1 hr, centrf., and decant liq. into waste beaker. Repeat $(NH_4)_2CO_3$ treatment.

After decanting, invert centrf. tube on paper towel and drain all liq. Add 5 mL 1*N* HNO_3 (use larger vol. 1*N* HNO_3 in both sample and blank if >25 μg Pb is expected), stir vigorously to expel CO_2 or use ultrasonic bath 2–3 min, let stand 30 min, and centrf. if ppt remains. (Use same technic for all samples.)

25.067 ***Determination***

Set instrument to previously established optimum conditions, using air-C_2H_2 oxidizing flame and 217 or 283.3 nm resonant wavelength. Det. *A* of sample and blank solns and ≥5 stds within optimum working range (10–80% *T*) before and after sample readings. Flush burner with 1*N* HNO_3 and check 0 point between readings. Det. Pb from std curve of *A* against μg Pb/mL:

$$\text{ppm Pb} = [(\mu\text{g Pb/mL}) \times (\text{mL } 1N \text{ HNO}_3)]/\text{g sample}.$$

Atomic Absorption Method for Evaporated Milk (*14*)
Official Final Action

25.068 ***Principle***

Sample is dry-ashed; Pb is extd as the 1-pyrrolidinecarbodithioate into BuOAc, and detd by AA spectrophotometry at 283.3 nm.

25.069 ***Apparatus***

(**a**) *Atomic absorption spectrophotometer*.—Equipped with 4" single slot burner head. (*Caution: See* **51.006**.)

(**b**) *Ashing vessels*.—Approx. 100 mL, flat-bottom Pt crucible or dish, Vycor or quartz tall-form beaker, or evapg dish (Corning Glass Works, No. 13180, or equiv.). Discard Vycor vessels when inner surfaces become etched.

(**c**) *Centrifuge*.—Capable of holding 15 mL conical tubes and centrfg at 2000 rpm.

(**d**) *Furnace*.—With pyrometer to control range of 250–600° with variation ≤10°.

25.070 ***Reagents***

(**a**) *Nitric acid*.—1*N. See* **25.065**(**c**).

(**b**) *Butyl acetate*.—Spectral grade, H_2O-satd.

(**c**) *Ammonium 1-pyrrolidinecarbodithioate* (*APDC*).—2%. Dissolve 2.00 g APDC in 100 mL distd or deionized H_2O. Remove insol. free acid and other impurities normally present by 2–3 extns with 10 mL portions BuOAc.

(**d**) *Lead std solns*.—(*1*) *Stock soln*.—1 mg Pb/mL 1*N* HNO_3. *See* **25.065**(**d**)(*1*). (*2*) *Intermediate soln*.— 5.0 μg Pb/mL. Pipet 5 mL stock soln into 1 L vol. flask, add 1 mL HNO_3, and dil. to vol. with H_2O. (Soln is stable several months if stored in polyethylene bottle.) (*3*) *Working solns*.—Pipet 20, 10, 5, and 2 mL intermediate soln into sep. 100 mL vol. flasks, and dil. to vol. with 1*N* HNO_3 (1.0, 0.50, 0.25, and 0.10 μg Pb/ mL, resp.). Pipet 10 and 5 mL soln contg 0.50 μg Pb/mL into sep. 100 mL vol. flasks, and dil. to vol. with 1*N* HNO_3 (0.05 and 0.025 μg Pb/mL, resp.).

(**e**) *Citric acid soln*.—10%. Weigh 10.0 g Pb-free citric acid into 100 mL vol. flask, dissolve in H_2O, and dil. to vol. Stopper flask and shake thoroly. If necessary, remove Pb impurity as in **25.062**.

(**f**) *Bromocresol green*.—0.1%. pH range, 3.8 (yellow) to 5.4 (blue). Transfer 0.100 g bromocresol green, Na salt, to 100 mL vol. flask, and dil. to vol. with H_2O. Use 1 drop/10 mL anal. soln.

25.071 ***Ashing***

(Clean all glassware thoroly in HNO_3 (1+1).)

Weigh ca 25 g (to nearest 0.1 g) sample into ashing vessel. Dry samples overnight in 120° forced-draft oven. (Sample must be absolutely dry to prevent flowing or spattering in furnace.) Place sample in furnace set at 250°. *Slowly* (50° increments) raise temp. to 350° and hold at this temp. until smoking ceases. Increase temp. to 500° in ca 75° increments (sample must not ignite). Ash 16 hr (overnight) at 500°. Remove from furnace and let cool. Ash should be white and essentially C-free. If ash still contains excess C particles (i.e., ash is gray rather than white), proceed as follows: Wet with min. amt H_2O followed by dropwise addn of HNO_3 (0.5–3 mL). Dry on hot plate. Transfer to furnace at 250°, slowly increase temp. to 500°, and continue heating 1–2 hr. Repeat HNO_3 treatment and ashing if necessary to obtain C-free residue. (*Note:* Local overheating or deflagration may result if sample still contains much intermingled C and especially if much K is present in ash (*see* **25.096**).)

Dissolve residue in 5 mL 1*N* HNO_3, warming on steam bath or hot plate 2–3 min to aid soln. Filter, if necessary, by decantation through S&S 589 black paper into 50 mL vol. flask. Repeat with two 5 mL portions 1*N* HNO_3, filter, and add washings to original filtrate. Dil. to vol. with 1*N* HNO_3.

Prep. duplicate reagent blanks for stds and samples, including any addnl H_2O and HNO_3, if used for sample ashing. *Note:* Do *not* "ash" HNO_3 in furnace, since Pb contaminant will be lost. Dry HNO_3 in ashing vessel on steam bath or hot plate, and then proceed as above.

25.072 ***Extraction***

(Complete analysis on same day.)

Pipet 20 mL each working soln, reagent blank for stds (if different from that used for samples), sample soln, and appropriate reagent blank(s) for samples into sep. 60 mL separators. Treat each soln as follows: Add 4 mL citric acid soln, (**e**), and 2–3 drops bromocresol green indicator, (**f**). (Color of soln should be yellow.) Adjust pH to ca 5.4, using NH_4OH initially and then (1+4) in vicinity of color change (first permanent appearance of light blue). Add 4 mL APDC soln, (**c**), stopper, and shake 30–60 sec. Pipet in 5 mL BuOAc, (**b**). Stopper separator and shake vigorously ca 30–60 sec. Let stand until layers sep. cleanly; drain and discard lower aq. phase. If emulsion forms or solv. layer is cloudy, drain solv. layer into 15 mL centrf. tube, cover with Al foil or Parafilm, and centrf. ca 1 min at 2000 rpm.

25.073 ***Determination***

Set instrument to previously detd optimum conditions for org. solv. aspiration (3–5 mL/min), using 283.3 nm Pb line and air-C_2H_2 flame adjusted for max. Pb absorption. Flame will be somewhat fuel-lean. Optimum position in flame for max. absorption should be just above burner top. If using recorder, DCR, etc., adjust to manufacturer's specifications. Depending upon signal-to-noise ratio, scale expansion up to 10× may be used. Check 0 point while aspirating H_2O-satd BuOAc. Aspirate sample and std solns, flushing with H_2O and then BuOAc between measurements. Record *A* of each soln.

Prep. std curve by plotting *A* of each std corrected for blank against concn of that std in μg Pb/mL BuOAc. Concn of std in BuOAc is 4 times that in aq. std. Det. Pb concn from std curve, using *A* corrected for sample reagent blank, if used.

ppm Pb = [(μg Pb/mL from curve) × 5 (mL BuOAc)]/(g sample × 20/50)

Anodic Stripping Voltammetric Method for Evaporated Milk (*14*)—Official Final Action

25.074 ***Principle***

Evapd milk is dry-ashed and residue is dissolved in dil. HNO_3. Pb is electroanal. concd on hanging Hg drop or Hg film electrode, and detd by reversing potential sweep and measuring anodic current peak.

25.075 ***Apparatus***

See **25.069(b)** and (**d**), plus following:

Polarograph.—Capable of anodic stripping voltammetric measurements at ≥0.05 ppm Pb.

25.076 ***Ashing***

Proceed as in **25.071**.

25.077 ***Preparation of Standard Curve***

Prep. stds as in **25.070(d)** and 1*N* HNO_3 reagent blank. Transfer 10–20 mL std soln to cell, depending on cell capacity. Adjust to 25±1°, and bubble N thru soln 5 min. Adjust gas inlet tube to let N flow gently above and across soln surface. If hanging drop Hg electrode is used, add fresh drop Hg to capillary tip with micrometer (Hg drop must be reproducible for each measurement), turn on stirrer motor, and electrolyze soln 1–10 min at −0.6 v against satd calomel electrode (time depends on manufacturer's instructions). Stop stirring and let soln stand 30 sec. Linearly increase applied voltage (pos. voltage scan). Use manufacturer's instructions for rate of scan, e.g., 2–6 mv/sec. Measure wave ht at half-wave potential (−0.45±0.05 v against satd calomel electrode). Plot μg Pb/mL std soln against wave ht × sensitivity factor (*SF*). Repeat for each std soln and reagent blank soln. Prep. new curve with each batch of samples.

25.078 ***Determination***

Transfer to cell same vol. sample soln as used in stdzn. Bubble N, add Hg drop, and apply voltage as in stdzn. Measure wave ht at appropriate potential and det. Pb concn by comparing wave ht of sample soln with that of std curve or analyze std soln immediately before or after sample soln (preferable when instrument scale factor must be changed).

Prep. reagent blank soln as in **25.071**, last par., and analyze as above.

25.079 ***Calculations***

Calc. μg Pb/mL as follows:

$$C = C'\{[(WH \times SF) - (WH_B \times SF_B)]/[(WH' \times SF') - (WH'_B \times SF'_B)]\}$$

where C and C' = μg Pb/ml sample and std, resp.; SF, SF', SF_B, and SF'_B = sensitivity factor settings of sample, std, and reagent blank (may be different for sample (SF_B) and std (SF'_B)) solns, resp.; and WH, WH', WH_B, and WH'_B = wave hts.

$$\text{ppm Pb} = (C \times 50)/\text{g sample}$$

Direct Determination by Anodic Stripping Voltammetry (*15*) Official First Action

(Applicable to milk and fruit juices only)

25.080 ***Apparatus***

(**a**) *Voltammetric analyzer.*—With staircase anodic stripping ramp and graphite electrode coated with thin film of Hg. Capable of measuring 5 ng Pb in presence of dissolved O. (Solns cannot be deaerated). Peak area integration desirable. ESA Model 3010A Trace Metals Analyzer (Environmental Sciences Associates, Inc., 45 Wiggins Ave, Bedford MA 01730), or equiv.

(**b**) *Micropipets.*—50, 100, 200, and 300 μL, pos. displacement type. (SMI or Drummond, available from supply houses, or equiv.).

25.081 ***Reagents***

(Use deionized H_2O to prep. std solns. Prep. and store solns in same Pyrex vol. flasks. Do not wash flasks with strong acids between use; just rinse 3 times with deionized H_2O. Always prep. same soln in same flask.)

(**a**) *Lead releasing reagent.*—Contg <1 ppb Pb. Acid soln of cation able to displace Pb from sample. Metexchange Reagent (Environmental Sciences Associates, Inc.), or equiv.

(**b**) *Lead std solns.*—(*1*) *Stock soln.*—1 mg/mL. Prep. as in **25.065(d)**(*1*). (*2*) *Intermediate soln.*—10 μg/mL. Pipet 1 mL stock soln into 100 mL vol. flask contg 1.0 mL HNO_3 and ca 50 mL H_2O. Mix, and dil. to vol. Prep. each week. After soln is prepd 6 times in same flask, it is stable 1 month. (*3*) *Working soln for fruit juice detn.*—3 μg/mL. Pipet 30 mL soln (*2*) into 100 mL vol. flask contg 0.7 mL HNO_3 and ca 50 mL H_2O. Mix, and dil. to vol. (*4*) *Working soln for evaporated milk detn.*—1 μg/mL. Prep. as in (*3*), using 10 mL soln (*2*) and 1.0 mL HNO_3. Working solns are stable 3 days. After being prepd 5 times in same flask, they are stable 2 weeks. (*5*) *Calibration solns.*—Evapd milk or fruit juice of type being detd, and contg ≥ 0.5 ppm added Pb.

25.082 ***Determination***

Calibrate instrument according to manufacturer's directions. Mix aliquot of sample with releasing reagent, (**a**), and perform detn according to manufacturer's instructions. Data for ESA analyzer are as follows:

	Juice	Milk
Initial potential, v	−1.025±0.005	−1.090±0.005
Final potential, v	−0.100±0.005	−0.100±0.005
Sweep rate, mv/step	14.0±0.05	10.50±0.05
Integration set points, v	−0.490±0.005	−0.490±0.005
Sample size, μL	300	200

Run control or spiked sample with each 15–20 analyses in a series.

Atomic Absorption Method for Fish (*16*) Official Final Action

25.083 ***Apparatus***

(**a**) *Atomic absorption spectrophotometer.*—*See* **25.069(a)**; range 0–10 μg/mL.

(**b**) *Lead lamp.*—Hollow cathode Pb lamp.

(**c**) *Crucible.*—Porcelain, ca 50 mL capacity and 5 cm deep; or tall-form Vycor or quartz beaker, 100 mL (Kontes Glass Co., K319000).

25.084 ***Reagents***

(**a**) *Hydrochloric acid.*—1*N*. Dil. 82 mL HCl to 1 L with H_2O.

(**b**) *Lead std solns.*—(*1*) *Stock soln.*—1 mg Pb/mL 1*N* HNO_3. *See* **25.065(d)**. (*2*) *Working soln.*—10 μg Pb/mL. Pipet 10 mL stock soln into 1 L vol. flask, add 82 mL HCl, and dil. to vol. with H_2O.

(**c**) *Buffer soln.*—Disperse 163 g EDTA in 200 mL H_2O in 2 L vol. flask and add enough NH_4OH to dissolve. Dil. 60 mL 70.5% $HClO_4$ (*Caution: See* **51.028**) by pouring carefully into ca 500 mL H_2O and cool. Dissolve 5.0 g La_2O_3 in soln as follows: Add 8 drops Me orange indicator to ammoniacal EDTA soln and add La_2O_3 to EDTA soln while stirring vigorously. If necessary, add NH_4OH to maintain alky of above soln to Me orange. Dil. to 2 L.

25.085 ***Reagent Blank***

(*Caution: See* **51.026**.)

Before proceeding with analysis, test purity of reagents as follows: Evap. 4 mL HNO_3 in crucible to dryness on hot plate or steam bath, dissolve residue in 1*N* HCl, and transfer to 25 mL vol. flask. Heat residue again successively with two 5 mL portions 1*N* HCl and add to flask. Cool, dil. to vol. with 1*N* HCl, and mix. Proceed with detn. Total reagent blank should be $\leqslant$10 μg Pb (equiv. to 0.4 ppm in sample) for detns at levels $\geqslant$1 ppm. For detns at <1 ppm, purify reagents as in **25.062** to attain blank <50% of limiting level of concern.

25.086 ***Preparation of Sample***

Weigh ca 25 g (to nearest 0.1 g) sample into crucible, (**c**), and dry 2 hr at 135–150°. Transfer to cold, temp.-controlled furnace and slowly raise temp. to 500°. Set control and check for maintenance of 500°. (Temp. as low as 550° may cause loss of Pb.) Ash overnight (16 hr). Remove sample, let cool to room temp., cautiously add 2 mL HNO_3, and swirl. Evap. carefully *just* to dryness on *warm* hot plate or steam bath. Transfer to cooled furnace, slowly raise temp. to 500°, and hold at this temp. 1 hr. Remove dish and cool. Repeat HNO_3 ashing, if necessary, to obtain clean, practically C-free ash. Add 10 mL 1*N* HCl and dissolve ash by heating cautiously on hot plate. Transfer to 25 mL vol. flask. Heat ash residue again successively with two 5 mL portions 1*N* HCl and add to flask. Cool, dil. to vol. with 1*N* HCl, and mix.

25.087 ***Preparation of Standard Curve***

Transfer 0, 1, 3, 5, 15, 25, and 50 mL Pb working soln, **25.084**(**b**)(*2*), to sep. 50 mL vol. flasks and dil. to vol. with 1*N* HCl (0, 0.2, 0.6, 1.0, 3.0, 5.0, and 10.0 μg Pb/mL, resp.). Set spectrophtr to previously established optimum conditions for max. signal at 283.3 nm. Use air-C_2H_2 flow rates recommended by manufacturer for std conditions for Pb. For digital concn readout, calibrate in concn mode with solns contg 0.2 and 10.0 μg Pb/mL. Record concn directly after calibration of instrument. For strip chart readout, set amplification to give $\geqslant$1% absorption reading for 0.2 μg/ mL working soln and prep. std curve of *A* against μg Pb/mL.

25.088 ***Determination***

Use aliquot of sample soln, **25.086**, and proceed as in (**a**) or (**b**). Treat reagent blank, **25.085**, as sample and subtract reading from *A* of samples.

(**a**) *Clear solns*.—Det. *A* of sample and std solns as in **25.087**, using following sequence 3 times: Read std soln first, then sample soln, alternating until all sample and std solns have been read. When many samples are to be analyzed, std solns may be read after series of 3 samples instead of after each.

ppm Pb = [(μg Pb/mL sample soln) × 25]/g sample.

(**b**) *Cloudy solns*.—Proceed as in (**a**), but add 1 mL buffer soln, (**c**), to aliquots of sample and std solns before reading.

If addnl dilns are necessary or if buffer is added:

ppm Pb = (μg Pb/mL dild sample) × (ml dild sample/mL original aliquot) × (25/g sample).

Polarographic Method for Fish (*16*)
Official Final Action

25.089 ***Apparatus***

Polarograph.—Any voltammetric or polarographic instrument with necessary accessories (cells, electrodes, Hg, capillaries, etc.) capable of effectively scanning up to 3.0 volts in either pos. or neg. direction, starting at selected initial potential, and of measuring $\geqslant$1.0 ppm Pb.

25.090 ***Preparation of Standard Curve***

Transfer 0, 1, 3, 5, 15, 25, and 50 mL Pb std working soln, **25.084**(**b**)(*2*), to sep. 50 mL vol. flasks and dil. to vol. with 1*N* HCl (0, 0.2, 0.6, 1.0, 3.0, 5.0, and 10.0 μg Pb/mL, resp.). Transfer 5 mL soln to polarographic cell, adjust to 25±1°, and bubble N thru soln 5 min. Polarograph between −0.2 and −0.7 v against Hg pool ref. electrode.

Peak potential for Pb at 25° is −0.45±0.05 v. Plot μg Pb/mL cell soln against wave ht × sensitivity factor.

25.091 ***Determination***

Transfer 5 mL sample soln to polarographic cell, adjust to 25±1°, bubble N thru soln 5 min, and polarograph as in **25.090**. Measure ht of wave whose potential corresponds to that of Pb and det. concn from newly prepd std curve or, preferably, by comparing wave ht of sample soln with that of std soln polarographed immediately before or after sample. Use latter method for greater accuracy, particularly when it is necessary to change instrument scale factor.

C_u (μg Pb/mL) = $(C_s \times WH_u \times SF_u)/(WH_s \times SF_s)$,
where subscripts s and u refer to std and sample, resp.; *C* = μg Pb/mL cell soln; *WH* = wave ht; and *SF* = sensitivity factor setting.

ppm Pb = (C_u × 25)/g sample.

25.092 ***Interference from Tin***

Sn polarographs at same peak potential as Pb. If presence of Sn is suspected, add 1 mL NH_4OH and 0.4 g *tartaric acid* to cell soln, bubble N thru soln, and polarograph as in **25.090**. Treat std in same manner. Peak potential for Pb is 0.54 v. Sn does not polarograph at this peak potential.

25.093 Atomic Absorption Spectrophotometric Methods for Earthenware—Official Final Action

See **25.031–25.034**.

25.094 Rapid Screening Method for Earthenware Official First Action

See **25.035–25.037**.

General Dithizone Method (*17*)
Official Final Action

Sn and Bi Absent

(Applicable to such materials as carbohydrates, cereals and cereal products, cacao and dairy products, feeds, meats, fish, plant material, fruit and fruit products, fresh vegetables, etc., and in general to all org. materials (except fats) in which no Sn and Bi are encountered. For products contg Sn (canned foods) or Bi, proceed as in **25.101–25.103**.)

25.095 ***Reagents***

(*Caution: See* **51.047**.)

(**a**) *Lead std solns*.—(*1*) *Stock soln*.—2 mg Pb (3.197 mg $Pb(NO_3)_2$)/mL in 1% HNO_3. Prep. from $Pb(NO_3)_2$ purified as in

25.062. (*2*) *Working solns.*—Prep. as needed by dilg stock soln with 1% HNO_3.

(**b**) *Nitric acid.*—1%. Dil. 10 mL fresh, colorless HNO_3 (sp gr 1.40) to 1 L with redistd H_2O. If acid has been redistd, boil off nitrous fumes before dilg.

(**c**) *"Ash-aid" soln.*—Dissolve 40 g $Al(NO_3)_3.9H_2O$ and 20 g $Ca(NO_3)_2.4H_2O$ in 100 mL H_2O.

(**d**) *Citric acid soln.*—Concd Pb-free soln. 1 mL = 0.5 g citric acid (reagent partially neutzd with NH_4OH during purification, **25.062**, fifth par.).

(**e**) *Diphenylthiocarbazone* (*dithizone*).—Dissolve ca 1 g com. reagent in 50–75 mL $CHCl_3$ and filter if insol. material remains. Ext in separator with four 100 mL portions metal-free (redistd) NH_4OH (1+99). (Dithizone passes into aq. phase to give orange soln.) Filter aq. exts into large separator thru cotton pledget inserted in stem of funnel. Acidify slightly with dil. HCl and ext pptd dithizone with two or three 20 mL portions $CHCl_3$. Combine exts in separator and wash 2 or 3 times with H_2O. Drain $CHCl_3$ into beaker and evap. with gentle heat on steam bath, avoiding spattering as soln goes to dryness. Remove last traces of moisture by heating 1 hr at ≤50° *in vacuo*. Store dry reagent in dark in tightly stoppered bottle. Prep. reagent solns for extn to contain 100, 50, and 10 mg/L in freshly redistd $CHCl_3$ (JAOAC **21**, 695(1938); **26**, 26(1943)) and store in dark at 5–10°. (Stock soln of dithizone in $CHCl_3$ contg 1 mg/mL will keep long time and is convenient for use in making dilns.) Soln of 30 mg/L $CHCl_3$ stored in dispensing app. is required for use in rapid method, **25.107**.

(**f**) *Ammonia-cyanide mixture.*—To 100 mL 10% recrystd, PO_4-free KCN (JAOAC **20**, 191(1937)) in 500 mL vol. flask, add enough redistd NH_4OH to introduce 19.1 g NH_3, and dil. to vol. with redistd H_2O. (Concn of redistd NH_4OH can be detd by sp gr or titrn.)

(**g**) *Pure metallic tin.*—Purest obtainable, such as NBS Sample No. 42. Granulate Sn as finely as possible by melting and pouring very slowly into H_2O. Det. Pb content as follows: Dissolve 1–2 g sample in HBr or HCl and volatilize Sn by evapg soln to dryness and treating with several 5 mL portions of the HBr-Br mixt., (**h**), evapg to dryness on steam bath after each treatment. Take up with 2–3 mL HNO_3, evap. to dryness to expel Br, and take up with ca 50 mL hot H_2O. Filter, and proceed as in **25.098** and **25.100**.

(**h**) *Hydrobromic acid-bromine mixture.*—To 250 mL 40% redistd HBr add 35 mL redistd liq. Br.

(**i**) *Sodium polysulfide soln.*—Dissolve 480 g $Na_2S.9H_2O$ and 40 g NaOH in H_2O, add 16 g powd S, shake until S dissolves, filter, and dil. to 1 L.

(**j**) *Hydrochloric-citric acid soln.*—Add vol. reagent (**d**) equiv. to 50 g citric acid to 50 mL HCl and dil. to 250 mL.

(**k**) *Sodium oleate soln.*—10%. To 45 mL 30% NaOH soln and 400 mL H_2O in 1.5 L beaker, add slowly, while heating and stirring, 90 g (by difference from separator) oleic acid. Heat mixt. on steam bath until soap is entirely dissolved. (Small flocculent ppt of impurities may remain.) Cool, dil. to 1 L, mix, and filter.

(**l**) *Ammonia-cyanide-citrate soln.*—Dissolve 10 g phosphate-free KCN and 10 g citric acid in 250 mL NH_4OH (sp gr 0.90) and dil. to 1 L. Reagent is conveniently preserved in dispensing app. that causes min. volatilization of NH_3.

(**m**) *Washed filter paper.*—Soak 9 cm quant. papers overnight in 1% HNO_3. Wash with large vols H_2O on buchner to remove acid and any traces of Pb.

25.096 *Preparation of Sample (Ashing)*

(*Caution: See* **51.025** and **51.028**.)

Accurately weigh representative sample of 5–200 g, depending upon amt sample available and expected Pb content, into suitable porcelain dish or casserole. Dry wet samples on steam bath or in oven. Add 2–5 mL "ash-aid" soln, (**c**), to products difficult to ash (meats), or to furnish ash bulk to low-ash products (candies, and jellies low in fruit content); mix well, and dry.

Char gelatin, carbohydrate foods such as jam, and other products that tend to swell excessively by carefully heating over burner. (Swelling can be controlled by playing small flame from glass jet over surface of material in dish, but metallic burner must not be used because of possible metallic contamination.) Do not let material ignite. Milk, candies, etc., may be charred without ignition by adding sample little at time to casserole heated over burner or hot plate. (Overhead radiant heater is often very convenient.) When samples are dry or charred, place in temp.-controlled furnace and raise temp. *slowly* to 500° without ignition.

If sample contains fat, "smoke" it away by heating long enough at ca 350°. Cover floor of furnace with piece of asbestos board or SiO_2 plate so that sample receives most of its heat by radiation from sides and roof and not by conduction from hotter floor of furnace.

If furnace has automatic control, ash overnight at ≤500°. If sample is not completely ashed next morning or if day-time ashings at 500° are not proceeding satisfactorily, remove casserole, cool, and moisten char with 2–5 mL ash-aid. Dry contents of casserole past danger of spattering (no free liq.) and replace in furnace. If ashing is not complete or proceeding rapidly after 30 min, remove casserole, cool, and cautiously add 2–3 mL HNO_3. Dry, place in furnace, and continue ashing until practically C-free. Avoid excessive use of ash-aid, and particularly HNO_3, if sample still contains much intermixed C, because local overheating or deflagration may result, especially if much K is present in ash.

When clean ash is obtained, cool, cover casserole with watch glass, and cautiously add 15–20 mL HCl. Rinse down watch glass with H_2O and heat on steam bath. If *clear* soln is not obtained, evap. again to dryness and repeat addn of HCl. If insol. matter persists, evap. HCl and dehydrate SiO_2 by heating to fumes with 5–10 mL 60% $HClO_4$ (double distd preferred). If $HClO_4$ is used, considerable H_2O (200 mL) may be necessary to completely dissolve $KClO_4$ later, as when KCN is used in dithizone extn of Pb, **25.098**.

Dil. with H_2O and filter soln when necessary with suction thru fine fritted glass filter. Catch filtrate in 500 mL g-s erlenmeyer under bell jar. Leach insol. material on filter successively with few mL hot HCl, hot HCl-citric acid soln, and hot 40% NH_4OAc soln.

In certain instances take following special precautions:

(*1*) If amt of insol. material (SiO_2) remaining on filter is abnormal, flush it into Pt dish with H_2O, evap., and treat residue with one or two 5 mL portions HF. Evap. to dryness, take up residue with H_2O and few drops of HCl or $HClO_4$, and add to bulk of ash filtrate.

(*2*) When ashing is of long duration, no ash-aid has been used, or natural ash is low with little ash bulk, Pb may be baked on dish. To remove this Pb, add few pellets (2–3 g) of NaOH and dissolve in few mL hot H_2O. Tilt dish so that sirupy soln completely wets that portion of interior originally occupied by sample; then heat short time on steam bath, but do not bring to dryness. (Overheating with concd NaOH may result in extg few μg Pb from casserole. Porcelain retains Pb to less extent than does SiO_2 but may contain very small amts of Pb.) Take up residue with H_2O and add directly to filtrate. Finally rinse dish with few mL hot HCl followed by hot H_2O.

25.097 ***Isolation of Lead: Principle***

Method **25.098**, while rapid and convenient, is limited to those materials that, with aid of citric acid, yield clear ammoniacal soln required for quant. extn of Pb with dithizone. Pb is readily occluded by many alk. ppts (Mg and Ca phosphates, Al and Fe hydroxides and silicates). Many food materials may be handled in this way because the naturally occurring amts of these substances are not excessive. However, some materials contain more of these substances than can be kept in soln under alk. conditions with any reasonable amt of citric acid (JAOAC **26**, 26(1943)). In these cases proceed as in **25.099**. Difficulty of ammoniacal pptn may sometimes be overcome by limiting sample size in cases where sampling is no problem.

25.098 ***Dithizone Extraction***

(Applicable to most carbohydrates and cereal foods, fruit and fruit products, milk, fresh vegetables, plant materials, etc.)

Transfer ash soln to 300 mL short-stem separator and add citric acid reagent, (**d**), equiv. to 10 g citric acid. Make slightly alk. to litmus with NH_4OH, keeping soln cool, and let stand 1–2 min. If ppt forms, redissolve with HCl and isolate Pb as in **25.099**. If no ppt forms, add 5 mL 10% KCN soln (more may be necessary if large amts of Zn, Cu, Cd, etc., are present), and check pH of soln by adding drop of *thymol blue soln* and observing color of drop (pH should be ≥8.5, blue-green to blue with thymol blue).

If ash was highly colored with Fe, keep pH of soln comparatively low, because pH of ≥10 in presence of Fe may cause oxidn of dithizone. Immediately ext with 20 mL portions dithizone reagent, using more dil. solns unless exceptionally large amts of Pb are present. Shake 20–30 sec, let layers sep., and note color of $CHCl_3$ phase. (Pb dithizone complex is red, but color may be masked by excess green dithizone, giving intermediate hues of purple and crimson. Color of $CHCl_3$ ext gives first indication of amt of Pb present, and progress of extn can be followed by noting color of successive exts.)

Drain exts directly into small separator contg 25 mL 1% HNO_3, (**b**). When extn is complete, shake combined exts in smaller separator and drain green dithizone layer into another separator contg addnl 25 mL portion 1% HNO_3. Shake, let layers sep., and discard $CHCl_3$ fraction. Filter acid exts contg Pb in succession thru small pledget of wet cotton inserted in stem of small funnel, into 50 mL flask or g-s graduate, using second acid ext to rinse separator in which first acid extn was made. (This procedure removes $CHCl_3$ globules.) Make up any slight deficiency in vol. with 1% HNO_3 and mix. Proceed as in **25.100**.

25.099 ***Sulfide Separation***

(Applicable to all products and usually necessary in case of cacao products, tea, sardines, and all food products contg high proportion of alk. earth phosphates, especially those of Mg, which promote formation of ppts in ammoniacal citrate solns.)

Cool acid soln of ash, add citric acid soln, (**d**), equiv. to 10 g citric acid, and adjust to pH 3.0–3.4 (bromophenol blue) with NH_4OH. If enough Fe is present to color soln strongly, make final adjustment with help of spot plate. (Phosphates pptd by local action of NH_4OH may usually be redissolved by shaking and cooling.) If amt of Pb is small, add 5–10 mg pure $CuSO_4.5H_2O$ to soln to act as coprecipitant. Ppt sulfides by passing in H_2S until soln is satd (3–5 min). (*Caution: See* **51.059**.) Immediately filter with suction into flask in bell jar (fine fritted glass filter is preferred).

Dissolve sulfides, without previous washing, with 5 mL hot HNO_3, drawing soln thru into original flask; wash with hot H_2O, stopper, shake, and boil to remove H_2S. Transfer to 200 mL separator, add citric acid soln equiv. to 5 g citric acid, make ammoniacal, ext, and det. Pb as in **25.098** and **25.100**(**a**) or (**b**).

25.100 ***Colorimetric Dithizone Determination (18)***

(Pb 0.001–0.200 mg)

Limiting factor in detn of minute amts of Pb by colorimetric dithizone method is size of reagent blank, particularly when amts of Pb of order of 1–5 μg are being detd. With special care in purification of reagents and by use of carefully cleaned Pyrex ware, including separators, it is possible to reduce reagent blank to ≤1 μg. Owing to Pb-bearing dust, vapors, etc., it is necessary to expose blank detn in furnace or on steam bath for same length of time as sample is exposed, and to use exactly same amts of reagents (even H_2O) for blank and actual detns.

Pb is extd from aq. soln, under std conditions of vol. and pH, with definite vol. of $CHCl_3$ soln of dithizone of std concn. Optimum pH of operation is 9.5–10.0. Dithizone strengths are so chosen that excess dithizone is always present in reaction mixt. Pb is brought into $CHCl_3$ phase in form of red complex, and uncombined green dithizone partitions between aq. and $CHCl_3$ phases and modifies color of ext according to relative amts of Pb and dithizone. Thus, series of colors from red to green may be arranged with intermediate crimsons, purples, and blues. Vols and strengths of $CHCl_3$ solns depend upon Pb range it is desired to cover and are so chosen as to give same general color progression from red to green for each range. Limiting range increases accuracy at expense of flexibility. Colors produced with std amts of Pb furnish basis for quant. estn by comparison. Vols and concns of std dithizone for various ranges are as follows when 1 cm cell is used:

Pb Ranges μg	Concn mg/L	Volume mL
1–10	8	5
0–50	10	25
0–200	20	40

See Anal. Chem. **19**, 684(1947), for modification operated at pH 11.5.

(**a**) *Simple color matching*.—Prep. 10 stds covering in equal steps the desired concn range, as follows: Use std Pb soln, **25.095**(**a**), in 1% HNO_3, 1 mL of which equals some simple fraction or multiple of 1 μg Pb. Measure vols representing various steps of range into series of separators and add 1% HNO_3 so that total vol. is always 50 mL. (Add acid first so that Pb soln is not lost around stopcock of separator.) Add 10 mL NH_3-cyanide mixt., (**f**), and mix. Resultant pH will be ca 9.7. Immediately add appropriate vol. std dithizone soln, which depends on range to be covered (*see* table), and shake 1 min. Drain lower layers into series of tubes or vials and arrange in order. For lower ranges, i.e., <20 μg Pb, matching is best done by viewing longitudinally in small flat-bottom vials ca 75 mm long. For higher ranges, 20–50 μg and above, depth of column must be reduced, and matching is conveniently done by viewing transversely in Nessler tubes of matched diam., because even pure dithizone solns appear red by transmitted light if concn or depth of column is increased beyond certain point. If stds are kept covered when not in use, they should last ≥1 day.

For detn, place aliquot part, or entire amt, of the 50 mL 1% HNO_3 in which Pb has been isolated, **25.098** or **25.099**, in separator, and if aliquot is taken, dil. to 50 mL with 1% HNO_3. Add 10 mL NH_3-cyanide mixt., (**f**), and mix. Immediately develop color by shaking 1 min with proper amt std dithizone soln. Drain lower layer into tube or vial similar to those used with stds and compare. If range is exceeded, repeat with smaller aliquot or re-ext with excess dithizone before draining from separator, isolate once more in 50 mL 1% HNO_3 reagent, and compare with stds covering higher range. Interpolation between steps of various ranges should be easily made.

If aliquot of the 50 mL 1% HNO_3 in which Pb has been isolated is taken, subtract only corresponding amt of total reagent blank from amt of Pb found.

(**b**) *Photometric methods*.—Absorption spectra of the 2 components in dithizone ext (Pb dithizone complex and free dithizone) show marked difference in ability to absorb 510 nm light, red Pb complex absorbing stongly and green dithizone transmitting freely. Thus, when absorption of light of this wavelength is detd photometrically, linear relationship is observed between amt of Pb and *A*. In making measurements, spectrophtr set at this wavelength or photometer equipped with blue-green filter centered at about this point can be used.

Stdze dithizone solns as follows: Using appropriate vols and concns of solns specified for various ranges (*see* above) in separators, prep. std colors as in visual color-matching procedure, satg std Pb and 1% HNO_3 solns with clear $CHCl_3$ before use, and thereby eliminating differences in vol. of ext between stds and unknowns. (It is unnecessary to prep. full 10 steps of the range, and number of stds may be limited to 5 or 6.) Develop colors by shaking separators 1 min, let stand few min, and filter exts thru specially prepd papers, (**m**). (Fitting 9 cm paper directly into mouth of 50 mL Pyrex beaker eliminates need of funnel in filtering operation.) Fill cell with filtered exts and det. *A* for various steps of range.

Plot against amt of Pb to obtain std curve for particular lot of dithizone. Preferably calc. slope of line connecting std points and intercept of line on *A* axis, making calcn by least squares method as in *Definitions of Terms and Explanatory Notes*, Item (24).

Det. Pb content of unknown falling within the range of detg *A*, using std dithizone and same cell with which std readings were made, and calc. Pb from equation $X = (Y/b) - (a/b)$, using values of *a* and *b* detd previously. If protected from evapn and direct sunlight, std factors of dithizone solns should not change appreciably for $\geq$1 month (JAOAC **21**, 695(1938); **26**, 26(1943)).

For actual detn proceed as in (**a**), except to filter ext thru prepd papers before photometric measurement. Det. *A*, using stdzd dithizone with same cell used in making std curve, and read amt of Pb from this std curve or calc. from factor of dithizone soln. If range is exceeded, repeat with smaller aliquot, or re-ext and repeat with dithizone stdzd to cover higher range. If aliquot of the 50 mL 1% HNO_3 in which Pb has been isolated is taken, subtract only corresponding amt of total reagent blank from amt of Pb found.

25.101 *Interferences*

Interferences in colorimetric dithizone method are limited by use of KCN to Sn^{+2}, Bi, and Tl. Rarity of Tl makes its interference unlikely in ordinary work, and no method of removal is given (JAOAC **26**, 26(1943)). Dithizone itself is destroyed by strong oxidizing agents, such as free halogens and large amts of ferric Fe, under conditions of dithizone extn of Pb.

25.102 *Removal of Tin*

(*Caution: See* **51.028**, **51.047**, and **51.059**.)

Sn becomes problem in analysis of canned foods; in amts >150 ppm it will usually appear in ash soln as milky suspension of SnO_2. It must be dissolved to facilitate filtration and to release occluded Pb. Quantities of Sn of this order may cause trouble by pptg under conditions of dithizone extn of Pb, **25.098**.

Two methods for elimination of larger amts of Sn are given: (**a**) Volatilization as $SnBr_4$ from acid soln of ash, and (**b**) leaching mixed sulfides with warm Na polysulfide soln, when sulfide method of isolation, **25.099**, has been applied. These methods may not eliminate Sn completely. Stannic Sn is not extd with dithizone, and as small amts of residual Sn will be in Sn^{+4} form after application of either (**a**) or (**b**), final isolation of Pb by dithizone extn will eliminate Sn completely.

In general, amts <100 mg should not interfere in colorimetric dithizone methods of Pb detn provided Sn is in Sn^{+4} form and preliminary isolation with dithizone is made; hence, this method of isolation should be applied wherever possible.

(**a**) *Volatilization as $SnBr_4$ from acid soln of ash*.—After almost C-free ash is obtained, **25.096**, add 15–20 mL 40% redistd HBr. If nitrates were used as ash aids, cover casserole with watch glass and heat on steam bath until Br evolution diminishes; then rinse watch glass with H_2O and bring to boil to complete expulsion of Br. (This process destroys undecomposed nitrates.) Add more HBr if necessary to dissolve ash, and examine solns for clearness. If there is insol. residue of SnO_2, add 50–100 mg pure Sn, (**g**), to simmering HBr soln of ash and let it dissolve. (Metallic Sn is best agent to bring ignited SnO_2 into soln. To be effective, ash soln must be in reduced state. Fe_2O_3 sometimes becomes "noble" during ashing and dissolves with difficulty, but treatment with metallic Sn also brings it into soln. Treatment with Sn is necessary only with contents of badly corroded cans.)

When soln of ash is free from milkiness due to SnO_2, add 20 mL 60% $HClO_4$ (double distd preferred), oxidize mixt. with few mL HBr-Br mixt., (**h**), and then add addnl 15 mL of the reagent portionwise, while soln is evapd to incipient fumes of $HClO_4$ (ca 150°) on hot plate. Repeat with addnl 10 mL portion HBr-Br mixt. if >100 mg Sn was used to dissolve ash. (Hot $HClO_4$ helps keep ash salts in soln and with Br holds Sn as volatile $SnBr_4$.) When HBr and Br are completely volatilized, cool, and take up with hot H_2O (200 mL may be necessary if much $KClO_4$ is present). Filter off any small amts of dehydrated SiO_2, ext residue twice with 5 mL hot HCl-citric acid reagent, (**j**), and hot H_2O, treat dish if necessary with NaOH as in **25.096**(*2*), and isolate Pb by dithizone extn as in **25.098**, or by sulfide sepn, **25.099**, finally detg Pb as in **25.100** (**a**) or (**b**).

(**b**) *With sodium polysulfide*.—(Recommended for routine work on canned foods.)

Isolate Pb by sulfide pptn, **25.099**, filter, and wash flask and filter with 3–6 portions of ca 5 mL each of warm Na polysulfide soln, (**i**). (Sn, As, and Sb sulfides are dissolved; CuS may be partially dissolved and repptd in filtrate.) Wash flask and residual sulfides several times with 3% Na_2SO_4 soln adjusted to pH 3.0–3.4 and satd with H_2S, and proceed as in **25.099**, beginning "Dissolve sulfides, without previous washing, . . ." When ash contains much Sn, as when metallic Sn has been added to dissolve insol. metallic oxides, sulfide ppt will be so bulky as to be difficult to handle, and it will be necessary to use volatilization method (**a**) before sulfiding. For colorimetric dithizone detn of Pb, ext HNO_3 soln of dissolved sulfides and proceed as in **25.099** and **25.100**(**a**) or (**b**).

25.103 *Detection and Removal of Bismuth*

(*Caution: See* **51.026**, **51.047**, **51.050**, and **51.078**.)

(**a**) *By dithizone at pH 2.0 after preliminary dithizone extraction at pH 8–11* (*19*).—(This method completely removes small amts of Bi.)

Ext metals from $CHCl_3$ dithizone ext with 50 mL 1% HNO_3 as in **25.098**. Adjust acid ext to pH 2.0 (metacresol purple indicator) with 5% NH_4OH soln and shake vigorously ca 1 min with 10 mL $CHCl_3$ soln of dithizone (200–250 mg/L). Let layers sep., and if $CHCl_3$ ext is orange red to red (Bi), drain off and ext with addnl 10 mL dithizone soln. If shades of green or purple are visible, indicating excess dithizone, drain $CHCl_3$ ext and ext aq. phase once more with 5 mL dithizone soln (shaking should be prolonged (3–5 min) to ensure complete extn of Bi). Continue extns until dithizone ext remains pure green. Adjust aq. soln to pH 8.5 with NH_4OH, add KCN, and ext with dithizone as in **25.098**. Det. Pb colorimetrically as in **25.100(a)** or (**b**).

(Method of Bambach and Burkey (Ind. Eng. Chem., Anal. Ed. **14**, 904(1942)) seps small amts of Bi from Pb by shaking out $CHCl_3$ soln of their mixed dithizonates with aq. soln buffered at pH 3.4; Bi remains as dithizonate in $CHCl_3$ phase, while Pb enters aq. phase and can be sepd Bi-free. Only *slight* excess of free dithizone should be present in $CHCl_3$ mixt. of dithizonates, otherwise Pb does not strip out completely. System of photometric detection and evaluation of Bi interference has also been outlined (JAOAC **26**, 26(1943)).

(**b**) *From acid soln of sulfides*.—(Intended for small amts of Bi, particularly when sulfide sepns may be necessary.) Dissolve mixed sulfides, **25.099**, with hot HNO_3 and sep. Bi and Pb as in (**a**).

Special conditions.—(Intended for products contg large amts of Bi.) Dissolve inorg. Bi compds directly in HBr-Br, (**h**). Prep. org. Bi compds or Bi prepns mixed with org. matter contg little ash, as in **25.096**, and dissolve residue in HBr-Br. If sample contains org. matter with appreciable ash material other than Bi compds, proceed as in **25.096** or **25.105**, apply sulfide sepn, **25.099**, and dissolve mixed sulfides in HNO_3. Evap. HNO_3 soln of sulfides to dryness in porcelain dish and treat with small portions HBr-Br mixt. Evap. contents of dish contg Bi dissolved in HBr-Br, after any of above methods of prepn, on steam bath to volatilize Sn and to convert other metals to bromides. Evap. to dryness, place in furnace with temp. control, and raise temp. gradually to 300°. ($AsBr_3$ and $SbBr_3$ volatilize first at 100° or above; $BiBr_3$ volatilizes as dense orange fumes at 300°.) After 5 min, or when fumes cease, remove dish, cool and treat again with small portions HBr-Br. Again evap. to dryness and heat addnl 5 min at 300–325° ($PbBr_2$ does not volatilize appreciably at $<$350°). Remove dish, cool, and dissolve residue in hot HNO_3. Proceed with removal of last traces of Bi at pH 2.0 and det. Pb as in (**a**).

Special Methods of Sample Preparation

25.104 ***Solution in Acids***

(Applicable to chemicals sol. in H_2O or acid, e.g., phosphates, sulfates, etc., and org. products of type of tartrates and citrates; *Caution: See* **51.059**.)

Dissolve 5–100 g sample, according to its nature and amt of Pb expected, in HCl in 400 mL beaker. With Ca phosphates, use 10–50 g. Dissolve in smallest practicable vol. of soln by warming and adding alternately small amts of hot H_2O and HCl. Filter soln with suction (fritted glass preferred) into beaker or flask under bell jar and leach any residue with 10–25 mL hot HCl-citric acid, (**j**), followed by 10–25 mL hot 40% NH_4OAc soln. Rinse beaker and filter with hot H_2O and cool soln.

Proceed as in **25.098**. If interfering ppt forms, again acidify and isolate Pb by sulfide pptn, **25.099**. If it is difficult to obtain clear soln with Ca phosphates at pH 3.0–3.4 (sulfide ppt may be contaminated with excessive phosphates), redissolve ppt, add more citric acid soln, (**d**), readjust pH, and reppt sulfides; or make one sulfide pptn, dissolve sulfides in hot HNO_3, boil off H_2S, and ext Pb with dithizone, **25.098**. Sometimes difficulty due to ppt formation in **25.098** can be avoided by using smaller sample for extn and colorimetric detn. If Sn or Bi is suspected, remove by methods described in **25.102** and **25.103**. Finally det. isolated Pb colorimetrically, **25.100**.

25.105 ***Complete Digestion***

(Applicable to most food or biological products; with difficulty to fats and oils, oily products, etc. *Caution: See* **51.011** and **51.078**.)

Digest representative sample in Kjeldahl flask as in **25.008**. Distil As, if desired, as $AsCl_3$, **25.009**. If As is not to be distd, add 100 mL H_2O and enough HCl to flask to dissolve any $CaSO_4$ in residue. Filter on fritted glass filter, pulverizing any insol. residue (anhyd. SiO_2 or $BaSO_4$) with flat-end stirring rod. Dissolve any $PbSO_4$ in flask and leach residue on filter with 10–20 mL hot HCl-citric acid soln, (**j**), followed by 10–20 mL hot 40% NH_4OAc. Finally rinse both flask and filter with hot H_2O. Isolate Pb by dithizone, **25.098**, or sulfide pptn, **25.099**, methods. (In general, sulfide method is preferable, especially when $BaSO_4$ or excessive $CaSO_4$ is present, as insol. sulfates readily occlude Pb.) If Bi and Sn are present, remove them as in **25.102** or **25.103**. After isolation, det. Pb by colorimetric method, **25.100**.

Rapid Method Restricted to Apples and Pears
Official Final Action

(Efficiency of 95% expected)

(For rapid detn of Pb spray residue on apples and pears; ppm $\times$ 0.007 = grains/lb; (grains/lb) $\times$ 143 = ppm)

25.106 ***Preparation of Sample***

Weigh $\geqslant$10 units and pull or cut out stems with narrow-blade knife, cutting no more of flesh than necessary. Trim off sepals (dried residue of blossom) and discard sepals and stems. To 25 mL 30% NaOH soln in 600 mL beaker, add 175 mL H_2O and 25 mL Na oleate soln, (**k**), and bring to gentle boil. Have ready in wash bottle 250 mL hot HNO_3 (2+98) or hot HCl (3+97). (Reasonably accurate figure for As_2O_3 can be obtained by using the HCl rinse and applying Gutzeit As detn, **25.020★**, to portion of filtrate, after acidifying part of the 500 mL alk. strip soln with $^1/_{10}$ vol. HCl instead of HNO_3 (*see* later in this section). Rapid method for F, **25.059**, likewise specifies HCl rinse and acidification.)

Impale each fruit in turn upon pointed glass rod; immerse in the alk. soln, with occasional rotation, until skin begins to check; then remove to large funnel inserted in 500 mL vol. flask and rinse with stream of the hot acid, being careful to flush out stem and calyx ends thoroly. When all fruit has been so treated, cool alk. soln and add it thru funnel to acid soln in flask. Rinse beaker and funnel with any remaining acid and with H_2O, using entire 250 mL rinse acid. Cool, and dil. to vol.

In dry 200 mL erlenmeyer place exactly 10 mL HNO_3 (10 mL HCl for As or F). Thoroly mix contents of vol. flask and immediately add 100 mL to acid in erlenmeyer while swirling vigorously. Filter on rapid paper. If first portion of filtrate is cloudy, refilter until clear. Det. Pb as in **25.107** or **25.108**.

(*See* JAOAC **26**, 150(1943)) for details of churn-type washer for removing Pb spray residues from apples and pears.)

25.107 ***Determination with Nessler Tubes***

(At least 15 tall-form tubes matched for uniformity in color *and diam*. are necessary. *Caution: See* **51.050**.)

(**a**) *Stds*.—To each of two 1 L vol. flasks add 47.5 mL 30% NaOH soln. If HNO_3 was used in rinsing and acidification, **25.106**, add 100 mL HNO_3 to each flask. If HCl (3+97) was used in rinsing, add 91 mL HNO_3 and 13.6 mL HCl to each flask. Do not mix in the acids unless solns are cold and dil. To one flask add stock reagent, (**a**), equiv. to 25.45 mg Pb. Mark this flask "std" and other "blank." Dil. both solns to vol. at room temp. and mix. These 2 solns contain reagents as they occur in acidified and filtered sample soln. The "std" is equiv. in Pb content to acidified soln from sample of 1400 g carrying Pb load (removable by "stripping" operation) of 10 ppm. By combination of the 2 solns in suitable proportions, equiv. of any Pb load from 0 to 10 ppm may be obtained.

Std tubes made up in intervals corresponding to 1.0 ppm may be interpolated to 0.5 ppm. Following table gives vols of "std" and "blank" to be added to Nessler tubes for each interval; measure into tube by burets:

Pb ppm	"Standard" mL	"Blank" mL
0.0	0.0	10.0
1.0	1.0	9.0
2.0	2.0	8.0
3.0	3.0	7.0
4.0	4.0	6.0
5.0	5.0	5.0
6.0	6.0	4.0
7.0	7.0	3.0
8.0	8.0	2.0
9.0	9.0	1.0
10.0	10.0	0.0

Working with 1 tube at time, add 10 mL NH_3-cyanide-citrate soln, **(l)**, to each tube followed by 30 mL std dithizone soln, 30 mg/L, **25.095(e)**. Shake vigorously 1 min and let sep. The pH of aq. phase should be ca 9.4 regardless of whether HCl or HNO_3 is used in rinsing. Stopper each std tube securely with new cork stopper. It is unnecessary to make up entire series of stds if only portion of range, e.g. 5.0–10.0 ppm, is of quant. interest.

(b) *Comparison.*—Transfer 10 mL portions of clear filtrate from **25.106** to each of 3 Nessler tubes. First add 10 mL NH_3-cyanide-citrate soln, **(l)**, to each tube; to one tube add 30 mL std dithizone soln, 30 mg/L, **25.095(e)**, and to other 2 tubes 30 mL clear $CHCl_3$. Shake vigorously 1 min and let sep. With tube of clear $CHCl_3$ backing sample tube (contg the dithizone) and 1 sample tube contg $CHCl_3$ backing each of 2 std tubes, compare color in lower layer of sample with that of stds, looking thru tubes at right angles to their lengths toward strong diffused light. (Comparator box similar to boxes used in colorimetric pH measurements but of larger size is convenient. When working with apple strip solns, slight turbidity is produced in sample tube, which slightly changes color observed. To compensate for this effect, same turbidity is introduced in field of view of std tubes made up exactly as sample, except that $CHCl_3$ is substituted for the dithizone soln.)

If color produced by sample is redder than 10 ppm std, repeat with smaller aliquot of filtrate, dilg to 10 mL with "blank" soln. If, for example, 5 mL aliquot is taken, indicated reading must be doubled. After match is obtained, calc. result to basis of 10 mL aliquot and 1400 g sample.

25.108 ***Determination with Photometer***

(This method is suitable for photometric measurement of "mixed color," **25.100(b)**. Changes in **25.107** are introduced here to prevent formation of colors too dense for measurements. Use 5 mL instead of 10 mL aliquots of acidified wash soln, **25.106**. *Caution: See* **51.050**.)

(a) *Stds.*—Measure following proportions of "std" and "blank" solns, **25.107(a)**, into separators:

Pb ppm	"Standard" mL	"Blank" mL
0.0	0.0	10.0
2.0	1.0	9.0
4.0	2.0	8.0
6.0	3.0	7.0
8.0	4.0	6.0
10.0	5.0	5.0

Add 10 mL NH_3-cyanide-citrate soln, **(l)**, and working with 1 separator at time, immediately develop color by shaking 1 min with 50 mL pure dithizone soln of 10 mg/L strength. Let stand few min to cool, filter $CHCl_3$ layers thru specially washed papers, **(m)**, and fill cell of appropriate length (1 cm is convenient). Det. *A* and plot against ppm Pb to obtain std curve.

(b) *Comparison.*—Place appropriate size aliquot of acidified strip soln in separator and dil. to 10 mL with "blank" soln. Add 10 mL NH_3-cyanide-citrate soln, **(l)**, and ext with 50 mL 10 mg/L std dithizone soln. Let stand few min to cool, filter, and read as above. Det. amt of Pb from std curve prepd as in **(a)** and calc. to basis of 5 mL aliquot and 1400 g sample.

25.109 MANGANESE—OFFICIAL FINAL ACTION

See **3.018** or **22.036★**.

MERCURY

Flameless Atomic Absorption Method *(20)*
Official Final Action

(Rinse all glassware before use with HNO_3 (1+9). *Caution: See* **51.019, 51.026, 51.028, 51.030**, and **51.079**.)

25.110 ***Apparatus***

(a) *Atomic absorption spectrophotometer.*—Instrumentation Laboratory, Inc., 113 Hartwell Ave, Lexington, MA 02173, Model 153 (or successors), or equiv. Equipped with Hg hollow cathode lamp and gas flow-thru cell (Fig. **25:02**), 25 (id) × 115 mm with quartz windows cemented in place. *Operating conditions:* Wavelength 253.7 nm, slit width 160 μm, lamp current 3 ma, and sensitivity scale 2.5.

(b) *Diaphragm pump.*—Neptune Dyna-Pump, or equiv. Coat diaphragm and internal parts of pump with acrylic-type plastic spray. Use 16 gage Teflon tubing for all connections.

(c) *Water condenser.*—12–18 (id) × 400 mm borosilicate, 24/40 ₮ joint, modified to hold 6 mm Raschig rings. Fill condenser with Raschig rings to ht of 100 mm; then place 20 mm layer of 4 mm diam. glass beads on top of rings.

(d) *Gas inlet adapter.*—24/40 ₮ (Kontes Glass Co. No. K-181000).

(e) *Digestion flask.*—250 mL flat-bottom boiling flask with 24/40 ₮ joint.

25.111 ***Reagents***

(a) *Reducing soln.*—Mix 50 mL H_2SO_4 with ca 300 mL H_2O. Cool to room temp. and dissolve 15 g NaCl, 15 g hydroxylamine sulfate, and 25 g $SnCl_2$ in soln. Dil. to 500 mL.

(b) *Diluting soln.*—To 1 L vol. flask contg 300–500 mL H_2O, add 58 mL HNO_3 and 67 mL H_2SO_4. Dil. to vol. with H_2O.

(c) *Magnesium perchlorate.*—Drying agent placed in filter flask (Fig. **25:02**). Replace as needed. (*Caution:* $Mg(ClO_4)_2$ is explosive when in contact with org. substances.)

(d) *Mercury std solns.*—*(1) Stock soln.*—1000 μg/mL. Dissolve 0.1354 g $HgCl_2$ in 100.0 mL H_2O. *(2) Working soln.*—1 μg/mL. Dil. 1 mL stock soln to 1 L with 1*N* H_2SO_4. Prep. fresh daily.

25.112 ***Determination***

Weigh 5.0 g sample into digestion flask; add 25 mL 18*N* H_2SO_4, 20 mL 7*N* HNO_3, 1 mL 2% *Na molybdate soln*, and 5–6 boiling chips. Connect condenser (with H_2O circulating thru it) and apply gentle heat ca 1 hr. Remove heat and let stand 15 min. Add 20 mL HNO_3-$HClO_4$ (1+1) thru condenser. Turn off H_2O circulating thru condenser and boil vigorously until white fumes appear in flask. Continue heating 10 min.

★ Surplus method—*see* inside front cover.

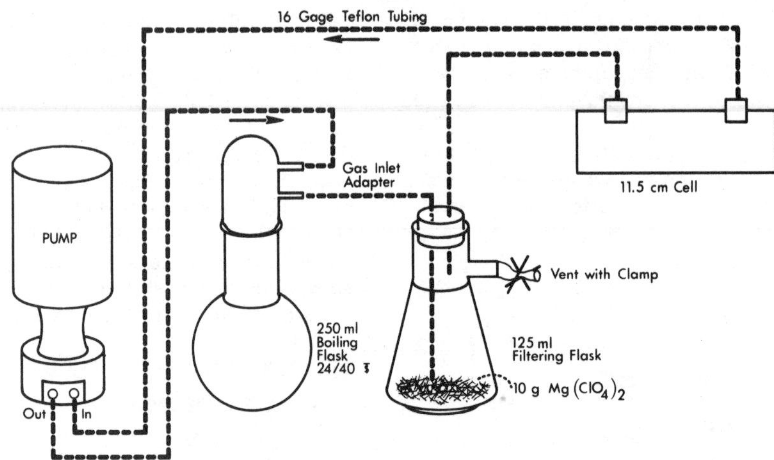

FIG. 25:02—Apparatus for flameless atomic absorption analysis

Cool. Cautiously add 10 mL H_2O thru condenser while swirling liq. in flask. Again boil soln 10 min. Remove heat and wash condenser with three 15 mL portions H_2O.

Cool soln to room temp. Completely transfer digested sample with H_2O to 100 mL vol. flask and dil. to vol. with H_2O. Transfer 25.0 mL aliquot from each sample to another digestion flask. Adjust vol. to ca 100 mL with dilg soln, (**b**).

Adjust output of pump to ca 2 L air/min by regulating speed of pump with variable transformer. Connect app. as in Fig. **25:02**, except for gas inlet adapter. With pump working and spectrophtr zeroed, add 20 mL reducing soln to dild aliquot. Immediately connect gas inlet adapter and aerate ca 3 min. (Adjust aeration time to obtain max. *A*.) Record *A*, disconnect pressure on "out" side of pump, and open vent on filter flask to flush system.

Prep. reagent blank and std curve by adding 0, 0.2, 0.4, 0.6, 0.8, and 1.0 μg Hg to series of digestion flasks. To each flask add 100 mL dilg soln. Finally, add reducing soln and areate stds as for sample.

Plot std curve from least squares linear regression of *A* against μg Hg. (*See* "Definitions of Terms and Explanatory Notes," item (24), or use calculator which performs linear regression.) Det. μg Hg in aliquot from curve. If μg Hg detd falls outside range of calibration, repeat detn with smaller aliquot of sample soln to bring μg Hg into region of std curve. From size of aliquot used, det. total μg Hg in original sample.

$$\text{ppm Hg} = \mu\text{g Hg/g sample.}$$

Alternative Method for Fish (21)—Official Final Action

(Rinse all glassware before use with HNO_3 (1+9). *Caution: See* **51.019**, **51.026**, **51.030**, and **51.079**.)

25.113 ***Apparatus***

See **25.110**(**a**), (**b**), (**e**), and in addn:

(**a**) *Boiling stones.*—6–8 mesh (SGA Scientific Inc., No. D-7325).

(**b**) *Gas inlet adapter.*—₮ 24/40 (Kontes Glass Co., No. K-181000). Cut off end of glass tube which extends downward from adapter and affix gas dispersion tube with fritted cylinder (Corning Glass Works, No. 39533, porosity 12C).

(**c**) *Trap.*—Construct from cut off bulb of 15 mL pipet and place between digestion flask and cell, replacing flask of Fig. **25:02**, to trap overflow.

(**d**) *Water condenser.*—12–18 (id) × 300 mm Liebeg condenser with ₮ 24/40 joint. Modify by making indentations in glass between lower std taper and H_2O jacket with pointed C rod. Indent glass to hold 6 mm Raschig rings. Add 8–10 rings to condenser and cover with ⅛" (3.17 mm) id glass helices (SGA Scientific Inc., No. JD-5360) to ht of 90 mm.

25.114 ***Determination***

Weigh 5.0 g (wet wt) thoroly mixed fish sample into digestion flask, **25.110(e)**. Rinse neck of flask with <5 mL H_2O, if necessary. Add ca 20 boiling stones, (**a**), 10–20 mg V_2O_5, and 20 mL H_2SO_4-HNO_3 (1+1). Quickly connect flask to condenser, (**d**), and swirl to mix. Circulate cold H_2O thru condenser during digestion. Apply sufficient heat (luminous flame is suitable) to produce low initial boil (ca 6 min) and finish digestion with strong boil (ca 10 min). Swirl flask intermittently during digestion. No solid material should be apparent except for globules of fat after ca 4 min.

Remove flask from heat and wash condenser with 15 mL H_2O. Add 2 drops 30% H_2O_2 thru condenser and wash into flask with 15 mL H_2O. Cool digested fish soln to room temp. by placing flask, still connected to condenser, in beaker of H_2O. Disconnect flask, rinse ground joint with H_2O, and quant. transfer digest to 100 mL vol. flask. Ignore solidified fat; it does not interfere. Carefully rinse digestion flask with several portions H_2O and dil. to vol. with rinse H_2O.

Pipet 25 mL soln into original digestion flask and add ca 75 mL dilg soln, **25.111(b)**. Proceed as in **25.112**, beginning "Adjust output of pump . . .", except aerate ca 1 min. 1 μg std should give $A \geqslant 0.400$.

Alternative Digestion Method for Seafood (22)

(Do not change sample wt or acid vol. substantially; otherwise excessive pressure during heating may damage vessel.)

25.115 ***Apparatus***

Digestion vessel.—*See* Fig. **25:03**. Stainless steel body supporting Teflon crucible and screw-on cap with Teflon liner to provide Teflon sealing surface. Teflon spout is snapped on outside rim to permit quant. transfer of contents without contact with metal parts. (Available from Uni-Seal Decomposition Vessels, PO Box 9463, Haifa, Israel.)

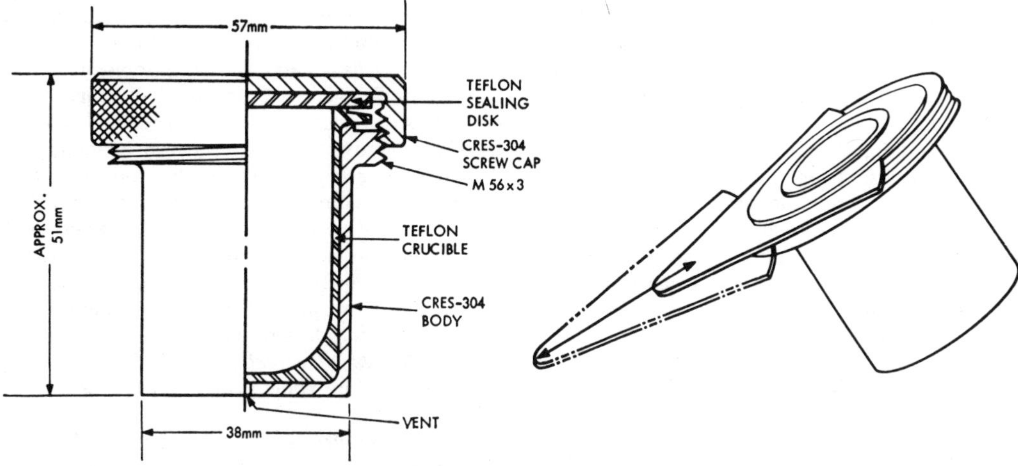

FIG. 25:03—Digestion vessel

25.116 ***Digestion***

Accurately weigh 1±0.1 g sample (*Caution:* Do not use >300 mg dry wt.) into digestion vessel, add 5.0 mL HNO_3, and close vessel by tightening screw cap. Place vessel, without tilting, into preheated 150° oven 30–60 min or until clear. Remove vessel and let cool to room temp. Unscrew cap, snap on spout, and transfer with aid of 95 mL dilg soln, **25.111(b)**, to 250 mL flask, **25.110(e)**. Proceed as in **25.112**, beginning "Adjust output of pump . . ."

Colorimetric Dithizone Method (*23*)—Official Final Action

25.117 ***Principle***

Sample is digested with HNO_3 and H_2SO_4 under reflux in special app., Hg is isolated by dithizone extn, Cu is removed, and Hg is estd by photometric measurement of Hg dithizonate.

25.118 ***Precautions***

Critical step is digestion of sample, which must be almost complete, otherwise residual org. matter may combine with Hg and prevent or hinder extn with dithizone. Oxidizing material in digest must also be destroyed or dithizone reagent is decomposed and Hg is not quant. extd. Because of volatility of Hg compds, careful heating of digest during sample prepn is required. Acidity of final sample soln (after partial neutzn with NH_4OH) before extn should be ca 1*N* and not >1.2*N*. Do not use silicone grease in stopcocks.

25.119 ***Apparatus***

(As Hg compds tend to adsorb on glassware, app. and particularly separators should be rinsed with dil. HNO_3 and then with H_2O.)

Special digestion apparatus.—See Fig. **25:04**. App. is made from Pyrex with ₸ joints thruout. Unit *A* is modified Soxhlet extractor, 5 cm od, 200 mL capacity to overflow, without inner siphon tube but equipped with stopcock on tube leading to digestion flask, *D*. With stopcock open, app. is in reflux position; when closed, unit serves as trap for condensed H_2O and acids. Top of *A* is attached to Friedrichs condenser, 35 cm long. Bottom of *A* is attached thru center neck of 2 neck ₸ 24/40 r-b 500 mL flask, *D*. Necks are 3 cm apart to provide clearance. Second neck is used for attaching 75 mL dropping funnel, *B*.

25.120 ***Reagents***

(**a**) *Mercury std solns.—*(*1*) *Stock soln.—*1 mg/mL. Prep. from dry, recrystd $HgCl_2$ (67.7 mg/50 mL). (*2*) *Working soln.—*2 μg/mL is convenient. Prep. from stock soln and store in Pyrex bottles. Add HCl in proportion of 8 mL/L to all stds before dilg to final vol.

(**b**) *Chloroform.—See* **25.022(b)**.

(**c**) *Dithizone soln.—See* **25.095(e)**. Reagent as now distributed needs no purification for this method. Prep. stock soln in redistd $CHCl_3$ (100 mg/L is convenient) and store in refrigerator. Prep. dilns as needed.

(**d**) *Sodium thiosulfate soln.—*1.5%. Prep. daily.

(**e**) *Sodium hypochlorite soln.—*Preferably 5% available Cl reagent. As distributed, reagent varies in available Cl content. Det. strength by **6.112**. Store in refrigerator when not in use and det. titer monthly. (Certain prepns of hypochlorite intended for household use contain traces of Hg. If these prepns are used, det. blank. Reagent with >0.1 μg Hg/mL should not be used.)

(**f**) *Dilute acetic acid.—*30% by vol.

(**g**) *Hydroxylamine hydrochloride soln.—*20% w/v. Ext with dil. dithizone until $CHCl_3$ layer remains green, remove excess dithizone with $CHCl_3$, and filter.

25.121 ***Preparation of Sample***

(Conduct acid digestion in hood.)

In all detns use wt sample equiv. to ≤10 g dry wt.

(**a**) *Fresh fruits or vegetables and beverages.—*Place weighed sample in digestion flask with 6 glass beads, connect assembly, and add, thru dropping funnel, 20 mL HNO_3. Pass rapid stream of H_2O thru condenser, adjust stopcock of Soxhlet unit to reflux position, and apply small flame to flask. Use asbestos board with 2–5 cm diam. hole between flask and flame. (Original reaction must not proceed violently or evolved NO_2 will carry vapors of digest mech. thru condenser and cause loss of Hg.) After initial reaction is complete, apply heat so that digest just refluxes. If mixt. darkens, add HNO_3 dropwise thru funnel as needed. Continue refluxing 0.5 hr, or until digest does not change consistency, and cool.

Slowly add 20 mL cold HNO_3-H_2SO_4 mixt. (1+1). (Use 10 mL acid mixt. for ≤5 g (dry wt) of sample.) Heat with small flame, subsequently adding HNO_3 dropwise as needed to dispel darkening of digest. Continue heating until fibrous material (fruit skin, cellulose, etc.) is apparently digested. Turn stopcock of

Soxhlet unit to trap H_2O and acids, and continue heating. Let digest become dark brown (not black) before adding further increments of HNO_3. (Fats and waxes cannot be totally digested by the hot acids under reflux. Therefore no attempt should be made to effect complete digestion in this step.) When all except fat and wax is in soln, let digest cool, and cautiously drain H_2O and acids into main digest. Cool, and pour two 25 mL portions H_2O thru condenser and intermediate unit. Remove reaction flask, chill under cold H_2O or by surrounding with ice to solidify fats and waxes, and filter off insol. matter on small pledget of glass wool. Rinse reaction flask and filter pad successively with two 10 mL portions H_2O. Remove Soxhlet unit, and wash it and flask with hot H_2O to remove insol. material. Pour hot H_2O thru condenser to remove volatile fats and oils. Discard all washings.

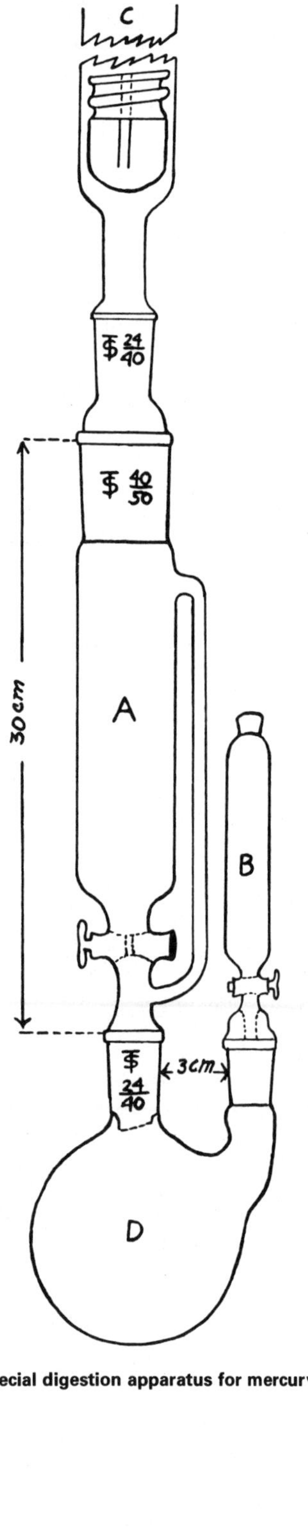

Connect flask contg filtered sample soln to assembled app., heat, and collect H_2O and acids in trap. Complete digestion, using small addns of HNO_3 as needed. In final stage of digestion, adjust flame until digest reaches incipient boiling (soln simmers) and acid vapors do not rise beyond lower half of condenser. Continue heating 15 min after last addn of HNO_3. Digest should now be colorless or pale yellow. Let digest cool, drain trapped liqs carefully into reaction flask, and add two 50 mL portions H_2O thru condenser. Reflux soln until all NO_2 is expelled from app. Add 5 mL *40% w/v urea soln* and reflux 15 min. (Digest should be colorless or pale yellow.)

(**b**) *Dried fruit, cereal, seeds, and grains.*—Dil. sample with 50 mL H_2O before adding HNO_3, and proceed with sample prepn as in (**a**).

(**c**) *Meats, fish, and biological material.*—Because of high fat and protein content of these materials, conduct initial digestion carefully to avoid foaming of digest into condenser. Add 20 mL HNO_3 to sample, swirl flask, and let stand 0.5 hr in digestion assembly before heating. Add 25 mL H_2O and heat cautiously with small rotating flame until initial vigorous reaction is over and foaming ceases. Proceed as in (**a**).

FIG. 25:04—Special digestion apparatus for mercury residues

25.122 ***Isolation of Mercury***

Titr. 1 mL prepd sample soln, **25.121**, with std alkali. Add calcd amt of concd NH_4OH to reduce acidity to 1.0*N*: swirl flask during addn of the NH_4OH to avoid local excess. (Soln should never be ammoniacal to avoid formation of Hg complexes.)

Transfer sample soln to 500 mL separator. Add 10 mL 4 mg/L dithizone and shake vigorously 1 min. (If characteristic green of dithizone is visible in $CHCl_3$ layer, indicating excess of dithizone, amt of Hg is within 0–5 μg.) Let layers sep., and drain $CHCl_3$ layer quickly to second separator contg 25 mL 0.1*N* HCl and 5 mL $H_2NOH.HCl$ soln. (Small amt of oxidizing material may still be present. On long contact with dithizone soln, oxidizing substances may destroy dithizone reagent and prevent extn of Hg.)

Repeat extn of sample soln with two 5 mL portions dithizone soln, transferring $CHCl_3$ layer successively to second separator. If first extn indicates >5 μg Hg, add stronger concns of dithizone, as indicated by table, **25.124**, until, after 1 min vigorous shaking, $CHCl_3$ layer contains dithizone in marked excess. Drain $CHCl_3$ layer into second separator contg 0.1*N* HCl and again ext sample soln with two 10 mL portions 4 mg/L dithizone soln, draining each successive ext into second separator.

Shake contents of second separator vigorously 1 min, and drain $CHCl_3$ layer into third separator contg 50 mL 0.1*N* HCl. (Shaking dithizone ext with dil. acid in second separator removes entrained org. matter. With biological materials or those of high protein content, aq. layer is usually light yellow because of nitrated org. compds. Small amts are carried into third separator where they are destroyed by Cl.) Ext soln in second separator with 1–2 mL $CHCl_3$ and transfer org. layer to third separator.

To contents of third separator add 2 mL $Na_2S_2O_3$ soln, shake vigorously 1 min, let layers sep., drain off $CHCl_3$ as completely as possible, and discard. (Cu if present is removed as dithizonate.) Ext again with 1–2 mL $CHCl_3$, drain carefully, and discard. Add 3.5 mL NaOCl reagent (or enough soln of different titer to furnish 175 mg available Cl) to decompose Hg thiosulfate complex and to oxidize excess thiosulfate, and shake vigorously 1 min. Add 5 mL $H_2NOH.HCl$ reagent from pipet, taking care to wet both stopper and neck of separator. Shake vigorously 1 min. Hold mouth of separator in front of air vent and blow out any remaining gaseous Cl. Stopper separator and shake vigorously

1 min. (It is imperative that all hypochlorite be reduced. Trace amts remaining would oxidize dithizone, subsequently added, to yellow oxidized form which would be measured in photometer as Hg.) Ext soln with 2–3 mL $CHCl_3$, drain off org. layer carefully, and discard. Final aq. soln should now be colorless.

25.123 ***Determination***

To third separator add 3 mL 30% HOAc and appropriate vol. and concn of dithizone soln as indicated by table, **25.124**, and proceed with colorimetric detn of Hg as in **25.124**, converting *A*, measured at 490 nm, to μg Hg from working curve.

25.124 ***Preparation of Standard Curve***

Following table is useful in prepg std curve and for establishing approx. Hg range in sample soln when 1 cm cells are used:

Hg Range, μg	Dithizone Concn, mg/L	Volume Dithizone, mL
0–10	6	5
0–50	10	25
0–100	10	40

Prep. working curve of required range, starting with blank and extending to final std of range, with 4 intermediate increments. Add appropriate amts of Hg to 50 mL 0.1*N* HCl in separator. Add 5 mL $H_2NOH.HCl$ reagent and 5 mL $CHCl_3$, and shake vigorously 1 min. Let layers sep., drain off $CHCl_3$, and discard, being careful to remove as completely as possible all droplets of $CHCl_3$. Add 3 mL 30% HOAc and appropriate vol. dithizone soln, shake vigorously 1 min, and let layers sep. (HOAc aids in stabilizing mercuric dithizonate.) Insert cotton pledget into stem of separator and collect dithizone ext (discarding first mL) in test tube for transfer to appropriate cell. Make photometer readings at 490 nm. (Since both dil. dithizone and mercuric dithizonate are somewhat unstable, read immediately.) Plot *A* against μg Hg.

NICKEL

25.125 Atomic Absorption Method for Tea
Official Final Action

See **25.044–25.048**.

SELENIUM

Fluorometric Method (*24*)—Official Final Action

25.126 ***Apparatus***

(**a**) *Fluorometer*.—Filter fluorometer or spectrophotofluorometer capable of excitation at 366 nm and detection of fluorescence at 525 nm. (*Caution: See* **51.008**.)

(**b**) *Cuvets or tubes*.—Pyrex culture tubes, 12 × 75 mm, selected by matching, are suitable for fluorometer.

(**c**) *Wrist-action shaker*.—Model BB (Burrell Corp.), or equiv., set at max. speed.

(**d**) *Separators*.—Glass, 250 and 125 mL, with Teflon stopcocks.

25.127 ***Reagents***

(Use anal. grade reagents and glass-distd H_2O thruout except as noted.)

(**a**) *Nitric acid*.—Distil from glass, discarding first and final 10%.

(**b**) *Dilute sulfuric acid*.—5*N*. Dil. 140 mL H_2SO_4 to 1 L with H_2O.

(**c**) *Ammonium hydroxide soln*.—Approx. 6*N*. Dil. 400 mL NH_4OH to 1 L with H_2O.

(**d**) *Disodium EDTA soln*.—0.02*M*. Dissolve 7.445 g Na_2H_2-EDTA.$2H_2O$ and dil. to 1 L with H_2O.

(**e**) *2,3-Diaminonaphthalene* (*DAN*) *soln*.—1 mg/mL. Pulverize DAN (purest grade available; product from Aldrich Chemical Co. has been found satisfactory) in clean mortar to fine powder. Insert glass wool plug in stem of 250 mL separator and add 150 mL 5*N* H_2SO_4. Transfer 0.150 g DAN to separator and place on shaker 15 min to dissolve. Add 50 mL cyclohexane and shake 5 min. Let phases sep. 5 min, drain lower phase into another separator, and discard cyclohexane (upper) phase. Repeat cyclohexane extn twice more; after third extn, drain lower phase into low-actinic g-s flask, add 1 cm layer hexane, and store in cold. Soln is stable several weeks.

(**f**) *Selenium std soln*.—(*1*) *Stock soln*.—100 μg/mL. Dissolve 0.1000 g black Se (purity ≥99.9%) in ca 5 mL HNO_3, (**a**), and warm to dissolve. Dil. with H_2O and 20 mL 5*N* H_2SO_4 to 1 L. (*2*) *Working soln*.—Dil. stock soln with H_2O and 5*N* H_2SO_4 to give Se concns in 0.1*N* H_2SO_4 appropriate for level of Se expected in sample. Store all solns in all-glass containers. Solns are stable indefinitely.

25.128 ***Preparation of Standard Curve and Fluorometric Blank***

Conduct appropriate vols of Se std solns (≤10 mL contg ≤800 ng Se) and 10 mL H_2O each thru entire detn, including digestion, along with samples. Zero fluorometer against blank soln and read fluorescence at 525 nm or subtract blank fluorescence from that of stds. Plot reading against ng Se/6 mL cyclohexane soln. Prepare new std curve daily.

25.129 ***Determination***

(To ensure adequate cleanliness for fluorometry, acid-wash all glassware except cells. In particular, clean Kjeldahl flasks and erlenmeyers, separators, centrf. tubes, and glass beads before each detn. Rinse glassware with hot H_2O, dry in oven, and wash with hot HNO_3-H_2SO_4 (1+1). Rinse with hot tap H_2O followed by distd H_2O and dry in oven or let air dry. Rinse cells with alcohol followed by acetone. Do not use plastic ware other than that mentioned. *Caution: See* **51.019**, **51.026**, **51.028**, and **51.030**.)

Place accurately weighed sample contg ≤1.0 g dry matter and ≤0.8 μg Se with 3 glass beads into 100 mL Kjeldahl flask contg 10 mL H_2O, and swirl to wet sample. Add 10 mL HNO_3, (**a**). (Alternatively, omit the 10 mL H_2O, add 10 mL HNO_3, or more if all HNO_3 is absorbed by sample, and let digest overnight at room temp.) Heat cautiously to reduce vol. to ca 5 mL, taking care to prevent severe foaming or bumping, and cool. Add 6.0 mL 70% $HClO_4$ and 5.0 mL H_2SO_4, return to cool heater, and heat until soln first turns yellow and then becomes colorless. Avoid charring of sample during digestion which may result in loss of Se. If charring occurs, repeat analysis with new sample, using higher HNO_3-$HClO_4$/sample wt ratio. If this fails, add small amts of HNO_3 at first signs of darkening.

Remove flask from heat, swirl to wet entire bulb area and lower neck of flask, replace flask on heater, and continue heating until soln becomes colorless and white fumes appear.

Remove flask from heat, swirl, add 1.0 mL 30% H_2O_2, rinsing walls of flask, and swirl until fuming ceases. Resume heating until contents boil briskly and white fumes are again evolved. Repeat addn of H_2O_2 and heating twice more, and continue final heating 5 min after appearance of white fumes. Let flask cool, add 30 mL H_2O, rinsing walls of flask, and mix thoroly. Transfer quant. to 250 mL g-s erlenmeyer, using two 10 mL and one 5 mL H_2O rinses. Add, successively with mixing, 10.0 mL EDTA soln, 25.0 mL 6*N* NH_4OH, and 5.0 mL DAN soln. Bring quickly to brisk boil and boil exactly 2 min.

Let reaction mixt. stand at room temp. for definite interval between 1 and 2 hr. Use *same* interval for all samples, stds, and blank in set. Accurately add 6.0 mL cyclohexane, stopper flask, and place on shaker 5 min. Transfer to 125 mL separator, and let phases sep. ca 5 min. Discard lower aq. phase and drain cyclohexane soln into 15 mL centrf. tube. Centrf. 5 min to further sep. H_2O and transfer ca 5 mL to fluorometer cell.

Zero fluorometer against reagent blank and read fluorescence of sample at 525 nm. Alternatively, subtract fluorescence of blank from that of sample. Det. Se content from std curve. Altho fluorescence readings for both samples and blanks increase with time, net readings (sample − blank) remain constant with 1–2 hr complexing period.

25.130 ★ Titrimetric Method *(25)*—Official Final Action ★

Sample is digested with HNO_3 and H_2SO_4 in presence of HgO fixative. Se is sepd by distn as volatile bromide, reduced to elementary Se with SO_2, isolated, and estd as H_2SeO_3 by titrn with std $Na_2S_2O_3$ and I. *See* **25.121–25.126**, 12th ed.

TIN—OFFICIAL FINAL ACTION

25.131 ***Preparation of Sample***

Digest 50–100 g sample as in **25.008**.

★ Gravimetric Method *(26)* ★

25.132 ***Reagents***

(a) *Wash soln.*—Mix 100 mL satd NH_4OAc soln with 50 mL HOAc and 850 mL H_2O.

(b) *Ammonium polysulfide soln.*—(*Caution: See* **51.059**.) Pass H_2S into 200 mL NH_4OH in bottle immersed in running H_2O or in ice-H_2O until gas is no longer absorbed; add 200 mL NH_4OH and dil. with H_2O to 1 L. Digest this soln with 25 g flowers of S several hr and filter.

25.133 ***Determination***

(*Caution: See* **51.059**.)

Add 200 mL H_2O to digested sample and transfer to 600 mL beaker. Rinse Kjeldahl flask with 3 portions boiling H_2O, making total ca 400 mL. Cool, and add NH_4OH until just alk.; then add 5 mL HCl or 5 mL H_2SO_4 (1+3) for each 100 mL soln. Place beaker, covered, on hot plate; heat to ca 95° and pass in slow stream of H_2S 1 hr. Digest 1 hr at 95° and let stand 30 min longer.

Filter, and wash ppt of SnS alternately with 3 portions each of wash soln and hot H_2O. Transfer filter and ppt to 50 mL beaker, add 10–20 mL $(NH_4)_2S_x$ soln, heat to bp, and filter. Treat contents of beaker with 2 addnl portions hot $(NH_4)_2S_x$ soln and wash filter with hot H_2O. Acidify combined filtrate and washings with HOAc (1+9), digest on hot plate 1 hr, let stand overnight, and filter thru double 11 cm paper. Wash alternately with 2 portions each of wash soln and hot H_2O and dry thoroly in weighed porcelain crucible. Ignite over Bunsen flame, very gently at first to burn off paper and to convert sulfide to oxide; then partly cover crucible and heat strongly over large Bunsen or Meker burner. (SnS must be roasted gently to SnO_2, which then may be heated to high temp. without loss by volatilization.) Weigh as SnO_2 and calc. to metallic Sn, using factor 0.7877.

★ Volumetric Method (27) ★

25.134 ***Reagents***

(a) *Air-free wash soln.*—Dissolve 20 g $NaHCO_3$ in 2 L boiled H_2O and add 40 mL HCL. Prep. fresh.

(b) *Iodine std soln.*—0.01*N*. Stdze soln frequently against **(c)**, adding asbestos mat and proceeding as in **25.135**, omitting pptn with H_2S and boiling with HCl and $KClO_3$. Amt of Sn in soln used for stdzn should equal ca that contained in sample under examination.

(c) *Tin std soln.*—1 mg/mL. Dissolve 1 g Sn in ca 500 mL HCl and dil. to 1 L with H_2O.

(d) *Sheet aluminum.*—About 30 gage, Sn-free.

(e) *Starch indicator.*—Dil. 1 g sol. starch to 200 mL.

25.135 ***Determination***

(*Caution: See* **51.047** and **51.086**.)

Proceed as in **25.133** thru "Digest 1 hr at 95° and let stand 30 min longer."

Filter thru asbestos in Caldwell crucible, using suction. Wash ppt of SnS few times with H_2O and transfer detachable bottom and asbestos pad to 300 mL erlenmeyer. Remove all traces of ppt from inside of crucible, using jet of hot H_2O and policeman, and using min. amt of H_2O for washing.

Add 100 mL HCl and 0.5 g $KClO_3$ to flask. Boil ca 15 min, making ca 4 more addns of smaller amts of $KClO_3$ as Cl is boiled out of soln. Wash particles of $KClO_3$ down from neck of flask with H_2O and finally boil to remove Cl. Add ca 1 g sheet Al to dispel last traces of Cl.

Fit 2-hole rubber stopper to flask. Thru 1 hole pass bulbed glass tube that reaches nearly to surface of liq. Attach this tube to large CO_2 generator thru scrubber contg H_2O. The CO_2 passes out of flask thru short, bulbed tube inserted in second hole of stopper and ending slightly below it. With rubber tube connect this second glass tube to another glass tube, ca 25 cm long, immersed in cylinder of H_2O to depth of ca 20 cm. (This connection acts as seal to restrain any strong flow of gas when not desired and to permit pressure in flask.)

Raise delivery tube nearly out of H_2O seal, allowing rapid flow of CO_2 for few min to dispel air from system. Then lower delivery tube into H_2O seal, slightly raise stopper, and quickly drop into flask 1–2 g sheet Al, folded into narrow bent strip to prevent breaking flask. After Al dissolves completely, raise tube in H_2O seal, letting CO_2 pass thru rapidly; place flask on hot plate and boil few min. Remove flask from heat and cool with tap or ice-H_2O, continuing flow of CO_2. Lower delivery tube into cylinder, disconnect flask, and, with glass plug, close rubber tube thru which CO_2 enters flask. Wash glass tubes, rubber stopper, and sides of flask with air-free wash soln, **(a)**, add starch indicator, **(e)**, and titr. immediately with 0.01*N* I.

If desired, make titrn by slightly raising rubber stopper after cooling and adding excess 0.01*N* I. Then disconnect flask; wash tubes, rubber stopper, and sides of flask with air-free wash soln; and titr. excess I with 0.01*N* $Na_2S_2O_3$.

Atomic Absorption Method *(28)*
Interim Official First Action

25.136 ***Reagents and Apparatus***

(a) *Atomic absorption spectrophotometer.*—With N_2O-C_2H_2 burner head, and reading device capable of 10× scale expansion. Sn hollow cathode and electrodeless discharge lamps are both suitable.

(b) *Digestion apparatus.*—Macro Kjeldahl; with 800 mL flasks carefully checked to be free of minute stress cracks.

(c) *Tin std soln.*—1000 μg/mL. Dissolve 1.000 g pure Sn in 150 mL HCl. Dil. to 1 L with H_2O.

25.137 ***Preparation of Sample***

Weigh 20 g sample into 800 mL Kjeldahl flask. Wash down

★ Surplus method—*see* inside front cover.

inside neck of flask with small amt H_2O, add 3–4 boiling chips or glass beads, 60 mL HNO_3, and 20 mL H_2SO_4. Bring to bp at medium heat and continue boiling to dense white fumes. If soln turns dark, add 10 mL HNO_3 and reheat to white fumes. Repeat as necessary until soln is clear and colorless or straw colored. Turn off heat. Let sample cool partially; then add ca 60 mL H_2O rapidly enough to cause boiling, but not so rapidly that soln is lost by spurting. Boil off H_2O until dense white fumes reappear. Remove from heat, let cool partially, and repeat H_2O addn and boiling to fumes. Turn off heat and let cool. Transfer quant. to 100 mL vol. flask with two 10 mL portions H_2O. Add 5 mL *satd NH_4Cl soln*, let sample cool completely, and carefully add 50 mL MeOH. (*Caution:* Do not let soln become too hot during MeOH addn. Cool under H_2O if necessary.) After soln has cooled to room temp., dil. to vol with H_2O. Small amt of finely divided cryst. ppt, usually $CaSO_4$, does not interfere. Conduct 1–2 reagent blanks with each series. For each sample and blank, add 1.00 mL H_2O to 25 mL vol. flask; to second 25 mL vol. flask add 1.00 mL std Sn soln, (**c**). Dil. both to vol. with sample soln (or blank soln).

25.138 ***Determination***

Set up AA spectrophtr according to manufacturer's specifications for org. solvs. Use 235.5 nm Sn line and N_2O-C_2H_2 flame. Optimize for max. Sn absorption. Depending on signal to noise ratio, scale expansion up to 10× may be used. Set nonabsorbing conditions with H_2O. Read blanks, samples, and spiked soln in turn, aspirating H_2O between readings. Record A for all solns. Calculate:

$$X = (A' - A)/C, \text{ and}$$
$$\text{ppm Sn} = [25 \times F \times (A - A_0]/24X,$$

where: A, A', and A_0 refer to sample, spiked sample, and blank, resp.; C = spiking soln concn (40 ppm); and F = sample diln. factor (5).

TITANIUM (*29*)—OFFICIAL FINAL ACTION

(Applicable to cheese. *Caution: See* **51.030**.)

25.139 ***Standard Solution***

Titanium dioxide std soln.—0.1 mg/mL. Accurately weigh 50 mg TiO_2 and transfer to 250 mL beaker; add 15 g anhyd. Na_2SO_4 and 50 mL H_2SO_4. Add boiling chips, cover with watch glass, and heat to bp on hot plate to dissolve. Cool, and cautiously add 100 mL H_2O with stirring. (Warm on steam bath if soln becomes cloudy.) Cool, transfer soln to 500 mL vol. flask contg 200 mL H_2O, and dil. to vol. with H_2O.

25.140 ***Preparation of Sample***

Weigh, to nearest 0.1 g, 10 g prepd sample, **16.232**, into 100 mL Pt dish and char under IR lamp. Place in cold furnace and ignite at 850° to white ash.

Cool, add ca 1.5 g anhyd. Na_2SO_4 and 10 mL H_2SO_4, cover with watch glass, and bring to bp on hot plate to dissolve. Turn heat off and let cool on hot plate. Cautiously rinse cover, carefully add ca 30 mL H_2O, and mix with stirring rod to disperse any insol. salts. Heat on steam bath if insol. material forms cake on bottom of dish.

Transfer quant. to 100 mL vol. flask with aid of ca 40 mL H_2O. If soln is cloudy, heat on steam bath or in boiling H_2O bath to clarify. Cool, and dil. to vol. with H_2O.

25.141 ***Preparation of Standard Curve***

Transfer 0, 1, 2, 3, 4, and 5 mL TiO_2 std soln to sep. 5 mL g-s graduates (or vol. flasks) and dil. to vol. with H_2SO_4 (1+9). Add 0.2 mL 30% H_2O_2, mix, and det. A on recording spectrophtr in 1.0 cm cells from 650 to 325 nm against 0.2 mL 30% H_2O_2 in 5.0 mL H_2SO_4 (1+9). Det. A at max., ca 408 nm, and prep. std curve.

25.142 ***Determination***

Transfer 3.0 mL sample soln to 5 mL g-s graduate (or vol. flask), dil. to vol. with H_2SO_4 (1+9), and continue as in **25.141**, beginning "Add 0.2 mL 30% H_2O_2, . . ."

Det. mg TiO_2 in sample from std curve, and calc. as % TiO_2.

ZINC—OFFICIAL FINAL ACTION

Colorimetric Method (*30*)

25.143 ***Principle***

Method involves wet oxidn of sample; elimination of Pb, Cu, Cd, Bi, Sb, Sn, Hg, and Ag as sulfides with added Cu as scavenger agent; simultaneous elimination of Co and Ni by extg metal complexes of α-nitroso-β-naphthol and dimethylglyoxime, resp., with $CHCl_3$; extn of Zn dithizonate with CCl_4; transfer of Zn to dil. HCl; and final extn of Zn dithizonate for color measurement.

25.144 ***Reagents***

(All H_2O must be redistd from glass. Pyrex glassware should be used exclusively and must be scrupulously cleaned with hot HNO_3. Purify HNO_3 (usually unnecessary) and NH_4OH by distn in Pyrex if appreciably contaminated. Test H_2SO_4 if Zn contamination is suspected.)

(**a**) *Copper sulfate soln.*—2 mg Cu/mL. Dissolve 8 g $CuSO_4.5H_2O$ in H_2O and dil. to 1 L.

(**b**) *Ammonium citrate soln.*—Dissolve 225 g $(NH_4)_2HC_6H_5O_7$ in H_2O, make alk. to phenol red with NH_4OH (pH 7.4, first distinct color change), and add 75 mL in excess. Dil. to 2 L. Ext this soln immediately before use as follows: Add slight excess of dithizone and ext with CCl_4 until solv. layer is clear bright green. Remove excess dithizone by repeated extn with $CHCl_3$, and finally ext once more with CCl_4. (It is essential that excess dithizone be entirely removed, otherwise Zn will be lost during elimination of Co and Ni.)

(**c**) *Dimethylglyoxime soln.*—Dissolve 2 g reagent in 10 mL NH_4OH and 200–300 mL H_2O, filter, and dil. to 1 L.

(**d**) *Alpha-nitroso-beta-naphthol soln.*—Dissolve 0.25 g in $CHCl_3$ and dil. to 500 mL.

(**e**) *Chloroform.*—Redistd.

(**f**) *Diphenylthiocarbazone (dithizone) soln.*—Dissolve 0.05 g dithizone in 2 mL NH_4OH and 100 mL H_2O, and ext repeatedly with CCl_4 until solv. layer is clear bright green. Discard solv. layer and filter aq. portion thru washed ashless paper. (This soln is best prepd as needed, since it is only moderately stable, even when kept in dark and under refrigeration.)

(**g**) *Carbon tetrachloride.*—Redistd.

(**h**) *Dilute hydrochloric acid.*—0.04*N*. Dil. required amt of HCl with H_2O (redistd acid may be used altho usually unnecessary).

(**i**) *Zinc std solns.*—(*1*) *Stock soln.*—500 μg/mL. Dissolve 0.500 g pure granulated Zn in slight excess of dil. HCl and dil. to 1 L. (*2*) *Working soln.*—5 μg/mL. Dil. 10 mL stock soln to 1 L with 0.04*N* HCl.

25.145 ***Preparation of Sample***

(*Caution: See* **51.019**, **51.026**, **51.028**, and **51.030**.)

Weigh, into suitable size erlenmeyer, representative sample ≤25 g, estd to contain 25–100 μg Zn. If sample is liq., evap. to small vol. Add HNO_3 and heat cautiously until first vigorous reaction subsides somewhat; then add 2–5 mL H_2SO_4. Continue heating, adding more HNO_3 in small portions as needed to prevent charring, until fumes of SO_3 evolve and soln remains clear and almost colorless. Add 0.5 mL $HClO_4$ and continue heating until it is almost completely removed. Cool, and dil. to ca 40 mL. (Wet digestion and subsequent sulfide sepn may also be advantageously performed in small Kjeldahl flask.)

25.146 ***Separation of Sulfide Group***

(*Caution: See* **51.047** and **51.059**.)

To H_2SO_4 soln add 2 drops Me red and 1 mL $CuSO_4$ soln, and neutze with NH_4OH. Add enough HCl to make soln ca 0.15*N* with respect to this acid (ca 0.5 mL excess in 50 mL soln is satisfactory); pH of soln as measured with glass electrode is 1.9–2.1. Pass stream of H_2S into soln until pptn is complete. Filter thru fine paper (Whatman No. 42, or equiv., previously fitted to funnel and washed with HCl (1+6), then with redistd H_2O). Receive filtrate in 250 mL beaker, and wash flask and filter with 3 or 4 small portions H_2O. Gently boil filtrate until odor of H_2S can no longer be detected; then add 5 mL satd Br-H_2O and continue boiling until Br-free. Cool, neutze to phenol red with NH_4OH, and make slightly acid with HCl (excess of 0.2 mL 1+1 HCl). Dil. resultant soln to definite vol. For optimum conditions of measurement, soln should contain 0.2–1.0 μg Zn/mL.

25.147 ***Elimination of Nickel and Cobalt***

Transfer 20 mL aliquot of prepd soln to 125 mL separator; add 5 mL NH_4 citrate soln, 2 mL dimethylglyoxime soln, and 10 mL α-nitroso-β-naphthol soln; and shake 2 min. Discard solv. layer and ext with 10 mL $CHCl_3$ to remove residual α-nitroso-β-naphthol. Discard solv. layer.

25.148 ***Isolation and Estimation of Zinc***

To aq. phase following removal of Ni and Co, which at this point has pH of 8.0–8.2, add 2.0 mL dithizone soln and 10 mL CCl_4, and shake 2 min. Let phases sep. and remove aq. layer as completely as possible, withdrawing liq. with pipet attached to vac. line. Wash down sides of separator with ca 25 mL H_2O and without shaking again draw off aq. layer. Add 25 mL 0.04*N* HCl and shake 1 min to transfer Zn to acid-aq. layer. Drain and discard solv., being careful to dislodge and remove drop that usually floats on surface. To acid soln add 5.0 mL NH_4 citrate soln and 10.0 mL CCl_4 (pH of soln at this point is 8.8–9.0).

Det. vol. dithizone to be added as follows: To separator contg 4.0 mL working Zn std (20 μg), dild to 25 mL with 0.04*N* HCl, 5.0 mL citrate buffer, and 10.0 mL CCl_4, add dithizone reagent in 0.1 mL increments, shaking briefly after each addn until faint yellow in aq. phase indicates bare excess of reagent. Multiply vol. dithizone soln required by 1.5 and add this vol. (to nearest 0.05 mL) to all samples. Shake 2 min. Pipet exactly 5.0 mL solv. layer into clean, dry test tube, dil. with 10.0 mL CCl_4, mix, and det. *T* (or *A*) at 540 nm.

25.149 ***Preparation of Standard Curves***

Prep. series of separators contg 0, 5, 10, 15, and 20 μg Zn dild to 25 mL with 0.04*N* HCl; add 5.0 mL citrate buffer, and proceed as with final extn of Zn, **25.148**.

Plot *T* in logarithmic scale (or *A* on linear scale) against concn and draw smooth curve thru points. (Intercept of this curve may vary slightly from day to day, depending on actual concn of dithizone used in final extn, but slope should remain essentially same.)

Atomic Absorption Method (*31*)—Official Final Action

25.150 ***Principle***

Representative sample is dry or wet ashed. Residue is taken up in acid and dild to optimum working range. *A* of this soln as detd by AA spectrophotometry at 213.8 nm is converted to Zn concn thru calibration curve.

25.151 ***Reagents***

(Use Pyrex glassware exclusively; clean thoroly before use with hot HNO_3. If glass beads are used to prevent bumping, clean first with strong alkali followed by hot HNO_3. Since Pt used in laboratory may contain significant traces of metals, clean Pt dishes by $KHSO_4$ fusion followed by 10% HCl leach.)

(**a**) *Zinc std solns.*—(*1*) *Stock soln.*—500 μg/mL. Dissolve 0.500 g pure Zn metal in 5–10 mL HCl. Evap. almost to dryness and dil. to 1 L with H_2O. Soln is stable indefinitely. (*2*) *Working soln.*—Dil. aliquots of stock soln with H_2SO_4 (1+49) or 0.1*N* HCl (depending on method of ashing) to obtain $\geqslant$5 solns within range of instrument. Prep. stds in 0–10 μg/mL range daily. (Do not use $<$2 mL pipets or $<$25 mL vol. flasks.)

(**b**) *Acids.*—Reagent grade HNO_3, HCl, and H_2SO_4. Test acids for freedom from Zn by AA measurement of appropriately dild sample. If contaminated, purify HNO_3 and HCl by distn. Further test purity of reagents and efficiency of cleaning by conducting blank detns by appropriate ashing method.

25.152 ***Preparation of Sample Solution***

Prep. representative sample by mixing, blending, or grinding.

(**a**) *Wet ashing.*—Accurately weigh, into 300 or 500 mL Kjeldahl flask, representative sample $\leqslant$10 g, estd to contain 25–100 μg Zn. (If sample is liq., evap. to small vol.) Add ca 5 mL HNO_3 and cautiously heat until first vigorous reaction subsides. Add 2.0 mL H_2SO_4 and continue heating, maintaining oxidizing conditions by adding HNO_3 in *small* increments (large amts may introduce Zn) until soln is colorless. Continue heating until dense fumes of H_2SO_4 are evolved and all HNO_3 has been removed. Cool, dil. with ca 20 mL H_2O, filter thru fast paper (pre-washed) into 100 mL vol. flask, and dil. to vol. with H_2O. Dil. further, if necessary, with H_2SO_4 (1+49) to attain working range of spectrophtr.

(**b**) *Dry ashing.*—Accurately weigh, into clean Pt dish, representative sample estd to contain 25–100 μg Zn. Char under IR lamp and ash at temp. $\leqslant$525° until C-free. (Raise temp. of furnace slowly to 525° to avoid ignition.) Dissolve ash under watch glass in min. vol. HCl (1+1). Add ca 20 mL H_2O and evap. to near dryness on steam bath. Add 20 mL 0.1*N* HCl and continue heating ca 5 min. Filter thru fast paper into 100 mL vol. flask. Wash dish and filter with several 5–10 mL portions of 0.1*N* HCl, cool, and dil. to vol. with 0.1*N* HCl. Dil. further, if necessary, with 0.1*N* HCl to attain working range of instrument.

25.153 ***Determination***

Set instrument to previously established optimum conditions or according to manufacturer's instructions. Det. *A* of ashed soln or diln, and $\geqslant$5 stds within optimum working range, taking $\geqslant$2 readings (before and after sample readings). Flush burner with H_2O and check 0 point between readings. Det. Zn content from std curve obtained by plotting *A* against μg Zn/mL:

ppm Zn = [(μg Zn/mL from curve) × (diln factor, mL)]/g sample.

SELECTED REFERENCES

(*1*) Manual of Analytical Methods ACGIH, May 1963; JAOAC **47**, 191, 630(1964).

(*2*) Ind. Eng. Chem., Anal. Ed. **14,** 442(1942); JAOAC **46,** 246(1963).
(*3*) Chem. Listy **46,** 341(1952); Anal. Chem. **31,** 1589(1959); JAOAC **46,** 246(1963).
(*4*) JAOAC **56,** 1144(1973).
(*5*) USDA Bur. Chem. Circ. **102** (1912); JAOAC **7,** 48(1923); **16,** 398(1933); **18,** 189, 506(1935); **19,** 95(1936).
(*6*) JAOAC **28,** 257(1945); **32,** 349(1949); Anal. Chem. **21,** 300(1949).
(*7*) JAOAC **56,** 876(1973).
(*8*) JAOAC **56,** 869(1973); **59,** 158(1976); ASTM C 738–72.
(*9*) JAOAC **61,** 1124(1978).
(*10*) JAOAC **43,** 695(1960).
(*11*) JAOAC **53,** 531(1970); **54,** 658(1971).
(*12*) JAOAC **27,** 90, 246(1944); **28,** 277(1945); **33,** 587(1950).
(*13*) JAOAC **55,** 737(1972).
(*14*) JAOAC **56,** 1246(1973).
(*15*) JAOAC **61,** 653(1978).
(*16*) JAOAC **55,** 727, 733(1972).
(*17*) JAOAC **17,** 108(1934); **18,** 315(1935); **19,** 130(1936).
(*18*) JAOAC **19,** 130(1936); Ind. Eng. Chem., Anal. Ed. **11,** 400(1939).
(*19*) Ind. Eng. Chem., Anal. Ed. **7,** 285(1935).
(*20*) JAOAC **54,** 202(1971).
(*21*) JAOAC **60,** 833(1977).
(*22*) JAOAC **55,** 741(1972); **57,** 568(1974); Anal. Chem. **40,** 1682(1968).
(*23*) JAOAC **35,** 537(1952).
(*24*) JAOAC **57,** 368, 373(1974).
(*25*) JAOAC **22,** 346(1939); **26,** 346(1943).
(*26*) JAOAC **1,** 257(1915).
(*27*) Original communications, VIII Intern. Cong. Appl. Chem. **18,** 35(1912).
(*28*) JAOAC **62,** 1050(1979).
(*29*) JAOAC **56,** 535(1973).
(*30*) JAOAC **27,** 325(1944); **28,** 271(1945).
(*31*) JAOAC **51,** 1042(1968); **52,** 404(1969).

26. Natural Poisons

MYCOTOXINS

Mycotoxins should be handled as very toxic substances. Perform manipulations under hood whenever possible, and take particular precautions, such as use of glove box, when toxins are in dry form because of electrostatic nature and resulting tendency to disperse in working areas. Swab accidental spills of toxin with 5% NaOCl bleach. Rinse all glassware exposed to aflatoxins with 1% NaOCl soln and then wash thoroly. *See* JAOAC **48,** 681(1965) for more detail on decontamination.

(*Caution: See* **51.005, 51.011, 51.018, 51.039, 51.040, 51.046, 51.055, 51.056, 51.061, 51.066,** and **51.073.**)

In following mycotoxin methods, TLC is critical sepn and detn step. Batch-to-batch variation in particle size and site activity of adsorbents, and variations such as temp. and humidity to which plates are exposed during handling and spotting require adjustments of layer thickness and solv. polarity. Reactive vapors, e.g., O_3, SO_2, and HCl, can affect adsorbents as well as stability of adsorbed spots. Perform TLC only in laboratory free of volatile reagents. If necessary to protect adsorbent layer and developed spots, handle TLC plates in box with inert atm. or place clean glass plate over adsorbent layer while spotting (with only spotting area exposed) and after development and drying.

Always dry plates thoroly before exposure to UV light. UV light from sunlight or fluorescent lamps can catalyze changes in compds being examined when exposed on adsorbent surface, particularly in presence of solv. Avoid exposure to UV light of undeveloped spots (use incandescent light) and expose developed spots to UV light for min. time needed for visualization.

26.001 ***General Apparatus***

(**a**) *Apparatus for sample size reduction.*—Hobart Vertical Cutter/Mixer (VCM); Wiley mill, Std Model No. 3; hammer mill, e.g., Fitzpatrick, Micropulverizer; disk mill, e.g., Straub, Bauer; Waring Blendor; food cutter, e.g., Hobart Model 84181-D; meat chopper; Polytron; or equivs. Effective device for prepg subsample is Dickens-Satterwhite mill (available from Federal-State Inspection Service, PO Box 3050, Albany, GA 31706).

(**b**) *Centrifuge.*—International Size 2, or equiv.

(**c**) *Centrifuge bottles.*—250 mL.

(**d**) *Chromatographic tubes.*—22 × 300 mm with Teflon stopcock, reservoir type (250 mL) (for 50 g samples); and 45 × 600 mm (for 1 kg samples).

(**e**) *Densitometer.*—Schoeffel SD 3000 (Schoeffel Instrument Div., 24 Booker St, Westwood, NJ 07675); Aminco-Bowman Spectrophotofluorometer 4-8202 with TLC scanner 4-8247 (American Instrument Co.); Perkin-Elmer fluorospectrometer MPF-2A or successors with TLC accessory 018-0057 (Perkin-Elmer Corp.); Zeiss chromatogram spectrophotometer (Carl Zeiss, Oberkochen, West Germany or 444-5th Ave, New York, NY 10018); or equivs. Follow instructions of manufacturer. Following refs contain supplementary information: J. Am. Oil Chem. Soc. **43,** 665(1966), **45,** 694(1968); JAOAC **51,** 602(1968), **52,** 61(1969), **54,** 870(1971).

(**f**) *Funnel.*—150 mm with fluted S&S 588, or equiv., paper to fit; or buchner, 32 cm diam., with Whatman No. 1 paper, or equiv., to fit.

(**g**) *Heating block.*—Al or brass, 254 mm thick × 254 mm wide. Drilled 190 mm deep on 762 mm centers to accommodate vials.

(**h**) *High-speed blender.*—Explosion-proof, with 1 L (qt) jar. Drill 32 mm (⅛") hole ca 1 cm from center of lid to permit escape of vapors.

(**i**) *Hollow polyethylene stoppers.*—13 mm top diam., 7 mm bottom diam.

(**j**) *Rotary evaporator.*—With continuous feed.

(**k**) *Thin layer chromatographic apparatus.*—Glass plates, 20 × 20 cm (ca 8 × 8"); Desaga/Brinkmann applicator; mounting board; spotting template; micro-syringe, 10 μL; desiccating storage cabinet, Fisher 8-645-6; storage rack, SGA Scientific Inc., C-4116-3; Thomas-Mitchell tank, Arthur H. Thomas Co. 2749-F05; longwave 15 watt UV lamp (use with UV-absorbing eyeglasses) or Chromato-Vue cabinet equipped with one or two 15 watt lamps (Ultra-Violet Products, Inc.); or equivs.

(**l**) *Tube shaking machine.*—Vortex, or equiv.

(**m**) *Vials.*—1, 2, amd 4 dram, screw-cap (Kimble Products No. 60910-L, but foil-lined).

(**n**) *Microflex tube.*—1 mL, (Kontes K-749000) fitted with Microflex valve (Kontes K-749100).

(**o**) *Wrist-action shaker.*—Burrell, or equiv.

(**p**) *Stirrer.*—Motor, 1/30 hp, 1400–1600 rpm, with stainless steel shaft and propeller blade.

26.002 ***General Reagents***

(**a**) *Benzene-acetonitrile mixt.*—98+2; prep. from ACS solvs stored in glass.

(**b**) *Boiling chips.*—SiC (Carborundum Co.). Float off fines and extraneous matter with H_2O, wash with acetone, and dry.

(**c**) *Diatomaceous earth.*—Hyflo Super-Cel.

(**d**) *Silica gel for thin layer chromatography.*—Any silica gel that meets following test may be used (test each shipment). (Macherey-Nagel GHR (Macherey, Nagel & Co., PO Box 307, D-516 Duren, Germany, distributed by Brinkmann Instruments, Inc.), Applied Science Adsorbosils-1 or -5, and Mallinckrodt Silic AR 4G or 7G have been found satisfactory.) Prep. TLC plates, spot, develop, and observe as in **26.031(a)** and (**b**).

Place on same origin spot, from solns of stds, 10 ng each of aflatoxins B_1, M_1, and G_1, 2 ng each of aflatoxins B_2 and G_2, 1 μg sterigmatocystin, and 50 ng each of ochratoxins A and B. Repeat application of test spots to give ≥3 test spots evenly spaced across plate. Place origin spots of individual mycotoxins adjacent to spots of multiple mycotoxins. Develop plate and examine. Individual mycotoxins of interest must be sepd from each other and appear in the following R_f sequence: Aflatoxins M_1, G_2, G_1, B_2 and B_1, ochratoxins B and A, and sterigmatocystin. Time for solv. front to travel 12 cm must be ≤1.5 hr.

On second plate, place number of origin spots contg amt of each mycotoxin which is barely visible under UV illumination employed, plus adjacent spots contg twice these amts to serve as guide. Develop and observe. Store in dark in clean air for ≥18 hr. Observe again. Disappearance of one or both spots after storage is evidence of excessive fading, and silica gel fails tests.

Note special requirement for silica gel to be used in aflatoxin methods for proper background sepn.

(**e**) *Sodium sulfate.*—Anhyd. granular ACS grade.

(**f**) *Solvents.*—ACS grade in glass: Acetonitrile, acetone, alcohol, benzene, $CHCl_3$, hexane, HOAc, MeOH, and pet ether. Ether (anhyd., ≤0.01% alcohol).

AFLATOXINS

Aflatoxins are extremely potent carcinogens to many animals. Neither effects of aflatoxins on man nor possible routes of entry are presently known. Observe precautions given in introductory statement of this chapter.

26.003 *Sampling and Preparation of Sample (1)—Procedure*

(*Caution:* Grinding of dry samples may result in airborne dust. Even if no toxin is present, there is potential harm from inhalations of mold spores or from allergic response to inhaled dust. Use protective mask and/or dust collector. Prep. samples in area sepd from anal. laboratory.)

(**a**) *Preparation of lot sample.*—Mycotoxin contamination of particulate products, such as grains and nuts, is likely to occur in pockets of high concn which may not be randomly distributed. Perform sampling and sample prepn with this factor in mind. Because of possibility of pockets of contamination, include total laboratory sample in sample prepn. Aim at max. practical size reduction and thoroness of mixing to achieve effective distribution of contaminated portions. One contaminated peanut (ca 0.5 g) can contain enough aflatoxins to result in significant level when mixed with 10,000 peanuts (ca 5 kg or 10 lb). To obtain ≥1 piece of contaminated nut in each 50 g portion, the single bad nut must be reduced to 100 pieces, and these 100 pieces must be uniformly blended thru entire mass. To achieve this degree of size reduction, nut must be ground to pass No. 20 sieve. Altho further size reduction may not be needed with flours, liqs, or pastes, thoro mixing is still needed before removal of anal. sample. Adsorption of aflatoxins on sediments in liq. commodities is possible.

Batch-type size reduction equipment, **26.001(a)**, like Hobart VCM, Waring Blendor, Polytron, and food cutter reduce particle size and mix in one operation. With other types of size reduction equipment and when product is received in finely ground state, mixing is needed. Free flowing dry materials can be mixed in double cone or twin shell blender such as Twin Shell Blender. (Available from Patterson-Kelley Co., Inc., 100 Burson St, East Stroudsburg, PA 18301.) Grains are most easily ground in disk mill such as Bauer or Staub; soft materials are best handled with meat chopper. Pastes and powders can be mixed in food cutter or with flat beater in planetary mixer, e.g., Hobart Model A-120.

Greatest homogeneity of nut meats is achieved by reducing to paste with disk mill, liquefying the paste with *n*-heptane and mixing, and further grinding slurry with Polytron. Practical homogeneity of hard, in-shell nuts is achieved by size reduction in hammer mill, followed by mixing in planetary mixer or by simultaneous size reduction and mixing in Hobart VCM. Nut meats can be handled in Hobart VCM in same manner as in-shell nuts, if mixed with equal wt of grinding aid such as coarse-ground oyster shells.

When handling large samples, coarse-grind and mix entire sample, remove ca 1/20, and regrind this portion to finer size for drawing anal. sample.

(**b**) *Drawing of analytical sample.*—Draw with same precautions as apply to lot sample. Wherever practical, divide by riffling or similar random dividing procedure until subdivision is close to desired sample wt. Where such subdivision is not practical, composite number of small randomly taken portions. With liqs. suspend any particulate matter before drawing anal. sample.

Preparation of Standards—Official Final Action

26.004 *Apparatus*

(Rinse all containers which contact aflatoxin solns with dil. acid, H_2O, and acetone, and dry.)

See **26.001(k)**, and(**l**), and in addn:

a) *Spectrophotometer.*—Capable of measurements from 200 to 400 nm, with 1 cm quartz-face cells.

Calibrate as follows: Det. *A* of the 3 solns of $K_2Cr_2O_7$ in H_2SO_4 (0.25, 0.125, and 0.0625*mM*), **26.005(b)**, at max. absorption near 350 nm, against 0.018*N* H_2SO_4 as solv. blank. Calc. molar absorptivity (ϵ) at each concn: $\epsilon = (A \times 1000)$/concn in *mM*. If the 3 values vary by more than guaranteed accuracy of *A* scale, check either technic or instrument. Average the 3 ϵ values to obtain ϵ. Det. correction factor (*CF*) for particular instrument and cells by substituting in equation: $CF = 3160/\epsilon$, where 3160 is value for ϵ of $K_2Cr_2O_7$ solns. If *CF* is <0.95 or >1.05, check either technic or instrument to det. and eliminate cause. (Use same set of cells in calibration and detn of purity.)

(**b**) *Analytical microbalance.*—With sensitivity of 0.001 mg.

26.005 *Reagents*

See **26.002(a)**, (**d**), (**f**), and in addn:

(**a**) *Sulfuric acid.*—Approx. 0.018*N*; dissolve 1 mL H_2SO_4 in 2 L H_2O.

(**b**) *Potassium dichromate std solns.*—(*1*) *Approx. 0.25 millimolar (mM).*—Accurately weigh ca 78 mg $K_2Cr_2O_7$ (primary std) and dissolve in 1.0 L 0.018*N* H_2SO_4; calc. molarity to 3 significant figs (MW $K_2Cr_2O_7$ = 294.2). (*2*) *Approx. 0.125mM.*—Dil. 25 mL 0.25*mM* $K_2Cr_2O_7$ to 50 mL with 0.018*N* H_2SO_4 in vol. flask. (*3*) *Approx. 0.0625mM.*—Dil. 25 mL 0.125*mM* $K_2Cr_2O_7$ to 50 mL with 0.018*N* H_2SO_4 in vol. flask.

Primary Standards (*2*)

(Mycotoxin stds are available from: Calbiochem; Rijksinstitut voor de Volksgezondheid, PO Box 1, 3720 BA Bilthoven, The Netherlands; Makor Chemicals Ltd., Box 6570, Jerusalem, 91060 Israel; Applied Science Laboratories, Inc.; Senn Chemicals, Laboratorium Guido A. Senn, Postfach 2, CH-8157 Dielsdorf, Switzerland; Aldrich Chemical Co.; ICN K&K Laboratories, Inc.; Myco Lab Co., P.O. Box 321, Chesterfield MO 63017; RFR Corp., 1 Main St, Hope, RI 02831, C. Roth, Postfach 1387, 7500 Karlsruhe 1, FDR; Sigma Chemical Co., Supelco Inc; TCI Tridom Chemical Inc, Hauppauge, NY 11787.)

26.006 *Criteria of Purity*

Aflatoxins B_1, B_2, G_1, and G_2 to be used as primary stds must meet following criteria of purity: (*1*) chromatgc purity as detd by **26.010**, (*2*) molar absorptivities within confidence limits given in Table **26:01**, (*3*) absorption peak ratios within confidence limits given in Table **26:02**.

Table 26:01 Molar Absorptivities of Aflatoxins in Methanol and 95% Confidence Limits Expected from Single Determination of Molar Absorptivity

Aflatoxin	λ, nm	Molar Absorptivity in MeOH	95% Confidence Limits (±)
B_1	223	22,100	1,600
	265	12,400	800
	360	21,800	1,100
B_2	222	18,600	1,000
	265	12,100	600
	362	24,000	500
G_1	216	27,400	2,500
	242	9,600	300
	265	9,600	1,200
	362	17,700	700
G_2	214	25,300	2,300
	244	10,500	300
	265	9,000	1,100
	362	19,300	800

Table 26:02 Ratios of Major Peaks of UV Absorption Spectra of Aflatoxins in Methanol and 95% Confidence Limits Expected from Single Spectra

Major Peaks Compared, nm	Parameter	Aflatoxins B_1	B_2	G_1	G_2
223/265	Ratio	1.77	1.54		
	95% Conf. limits	±0.04	±0.05		
214/265	Ratio			2.86	2.83
	95% Conf. limits			±0.15	±0.13
242/265	Ratio			1.00	1.20
	95% Conf. limits			±0.02	±0.07
362/265	Ratio	1.76	1.98	1.84	2.09
	95% Conf. limits	±0.04	±0.08	±0.06	±0.18

26.007 ***Preparation of Solutions in Methanol and UV Measurements***

Weigh ca 1 mg aflatoxin std to nearest 0.001 mg and transfer quant. to 100 mL vol. flask. Dissolve in and dil. to vol. with MeOH. Calc. concn of soln in μg/mL. Measure A of soln at max. absorption, Table **26:01**. Calc. molar absorptivities:

$$\epsilon = (A \times MW \times 1000)/(\mu g \text{ aflatoxin/mL}),$$

where MW = molecular wt of aflatoxin (B_1, 312; B_2, 314; G_1, 328; G_2, 330).

Calc. ratios of A for each aflatoxin at wavelengths given in Table **26:02**.

Standards for Thin Layer Chromatography (2)

26.008 ***Preparation of Solutions***

(**a**) *For aflatoxin stds received as dry films or crystals.*—To container of dry aflatoxins B_1, B_2, G_1, or G_2, add vol. benzene-CH_3CN, **26.002(a)**, calcd to give concn of 8–10 μg/mL. For aflatoxin M_1, use CH_3CN. Use label statement of aflatoxin wt as guide. Vigorously agitate soln 1 min on Vortex shaker and transfer without rinsing to convenient size g-s flask. (Dry films on glass are not completely recoverable because of adsorption. Continued contact with solv. may result in slow dissoln.) Do not transfer dry aflatoxin for weighing or other purposes unless facilities are available to prevent dissemination of aflatoxins to surroundings due to electrostatic charge on particles.

(**b**) *For aflatoxin stds received as solns.*—Transfer soln to convenient size g-s flask. Dil., if necessary, to adjust concn to 8–10 μg/mL.

26.009 ***Determination of Aflatoxin Concentration***

Record UV spectrum of aflatoxin soln from 330 to 370 nm against benzene-CH_3CN, **26.002(a)**, or CH_3CN (for aflatoxin M_1), in ref. cell. Det. concn of aflatoxin soln by measuring A at wavelength of max. absorption close to 350 nm and using following equation:

$$\mu g \text{ aflatoxin/mL} = (A \times MW \times 1000 \times CF)/\epsilon,$$

where CF = correction factor obtained in **26.004(a)** and MW and ϵ are as follows:

Aflatoxin	MW	ϵ
B_1	312	19,800
B_2	314	20,900
G_1	328	17,100
G_2	330	18,200
M_1	328	19,850

Return aflatoxin soln to original g-s flask. (Normal exposure to UV light during A measurement results in no observable conversion to photoproducts.)

26.010 ***Determination of Chromatographic Purity***

Follow TLC technic described in **26.031(a)** and (**b**). Spot successively, at 2 cm intervals, 5 μL resolution ref. std, **26.012**, 5 μL aflatoxin soln, **26.008**, 5 μL this aflatoxin soln + 5 μL resolution ref. std, and 5 μL resolution ref. std. After development, spot of individual aflatoxin std should reveal no other aflatoxins and at most only faint fluorescent spots near origin.

26.011 ***Preparation and Storage of TLC Standards***

After concn and purity of each std soln are established, dil. portion of each to spotting concn (0.5 μg aflatoxin B_1, G_1, or M_1/mL, and 1/5 this concn for B_2 or G_2). Use benzene-CH_3CN, **26.002(a)**, to dil. solns of aflatoxins B_1, B_2, G_1, and G_2; to dil. soln of aflatoxin M_1, use appropriate ratios of benzene and CH_3CN to obtain solv. composition of (9+1). Prep. 1 mL of each at a time in g-s vol. flask. Transfer this working soln to Microflex tube, **26.001(n)**, for convenience in storage and dispensing.

Before storage, after aliquots have been removed for diln or spotting, weigh flasks contg std solns to nearest mg and record wts for future ref. Wrap flasks tightly in Al foil and store at 0°. When soln is to be used after storage, reweigh flask and record any change. To avoid incorporation of H_2O by condensation, bring all stds to room temp. before use; do not remove Al foil from flask until contents have reached room temp.

Recheck concn stored std soln by UV detn and recheck purity each time portion is taken for diln to spotting concn. When vol. of original soln becomes less than can be employed in std photometer cell, use microcells (accurately positioned). Instrument must be recalibrated with each set of cells, since calibration includes cell pathlength. Any observed change in concn should correspond with observed loss in wt due to solv. evapn.

Std solns of B_1, B_2, G_1, and G_2 are stable $\geq$1 year.

26.012 ***Preparation of Resolution Reference Standard***

Prep. resolution ref. std by mixing aflatoxin B_1, B_2, G_1, and G_2 solns, **26.008**, to give concn at final diln with benzene-CH_3CN (98+2) the same as those prepd individually in **26.011**.

Identification of Mycotoxins by Thin Layer Chromatography

26.013 ***Alternative Developing Solvents***

Samples or laboratory conditions may be encountered which result in inadequate sepns with specified TLC developing solv. Following are alternative solvs which may be useful in such situations (systems are unequilibrated unless otherwise specified):

For aflatoxins B_1, B_2, G_1, G_2

Benzene-MeOH-HOAc	(90+5+5)
Ether-MeOH-H_2O	(96+3+1)
CH_2Cl_2-C_2HCl_3-*n*-amyl alcohol-HCOOH (order of R_f changed to B_1, G_1, B_2, G_2)	(80+15+4+1)
$CHCl_3$-C_2HCl_3-*n*-amyl alcohol-HCOOH	(80+15+4+1) (equilibrated tank)
$CHCl_3$-acetone-H_2O	(88+12+1.5)
$CHCl_3$-acetone-isopropanol-H_2O	(88+12+1.5+1)
$CHCl_3$-isopropanol	(99+1)

For aflatoxin M_1

Ether-MeOH-H_2O	(95+4+1)
Ether-hexane-MeOH-H_2O	(85+10+4+1)

For aflatoxin B_{2a}

$CHCl_3$-acetone-isopropanol	(85+12.5+2.5)

For aflatoxin M_1 derivative

$CHCl_3$-MeOH-acetone-H_2O (46+4+1+0.4)

See also **26.027(c)**.

Proportions of solvs may be varied to compensate for changes in silica gels and laboratory conditions. Increase in polar component will increase R_f.

Questionable identity of spots may sometimes be resolved by development of samples with number of different solvs. Different R_f of sample spot with reference to std spot in even 1 solv. is pos. proof of difference in identity. Coincidence of migration does not prove identity; for such proof *see* **26.076–26.082**.

MINICOLUMN DETECTION METHODS

Romer All Purpose Method (*3*)—Official First Action

(Applicable to detection of ≥5 ppb total aflatoxins ($B_1+B_2+G_1+G_2$) in almonds; ≥10 ppb total aflatoxins in white and yellow corn, peanut and cottonseed meals, peanuts, peanut butter, and pistachio nuts; and ≥15 ppb total aflatoxins in mixed feeds)

(Other adoptions: American Association of Cereal Chemists Method 45-10: 1975 revisions to AACC Approved Methods.)

26.014 ***Apparatus***

(**a**) *High-speed blender.—See* **26.001(h)** (explosion-proof feature not required), or **26.001(o)**.

(**b**) *Ultraviolet light.*—Longwave UV with intensity of 430 μwatt/cm² at 15 cm at 365 nm, or Chromatovue cabinet, **26,001(k)**.

(**c**) *Minicolumn.*—Borosilicate std wall tubing, ca 6 (id) × 190 mm, tapered at 1 end to ca 2 mm.

(**d**) *Minicolumn support rack.*—To hold minicolumns upright. Test tube rack may be used.

(**e**) *Rubber bulb.*—2 oz, with 7 mm hole in 1 end.

26.015 ***Reagents***

(Deionized H_2O may be used thruout.)

(**a**) *Solvents.*—$CHCl_3$ and acetone; tech. grade in glass may be used, except ACS grade is required for elution solv.

(**b**) *Potassium hydroxide wash soln.*—0.02*N* KOH with 1% KCl. Dissolve 1.12 g KOH pellets and 10 g KCl in 1 L H_2O.

(**c**) *Sodium hydroxide soln.*—0.2*N*. 8.00 g NaOH/ L.

(**d**) *Sulfuric acid soln.*—0.03%. Dil. 0.3 mL H_2SO_4 to 1 L.

(**e**) *Precipitating reagents.*—(*1*) *Copper carbonate, basic.* (*2*) *Ferric chloride slurry.*—Mix 20 g anhyd. $FeCl_3$ (Fisher Scientific Co. No. I-89, or equiv.) with 300 mL H_2O.

(**f**) *Diatomaceous earth.*—Hyflo Super-Cel, or equiv.

(**g**) *Column packings.*—(*1*) *Florisil.*—Fisher Scientific Co. No. F-101, 100–200 mesh. (*2*) *Silica gel.*—E. Merck No. 7734 (Silica Gel 60) for column chromatgy. (*3*) *Alumina neutral.*—Woelm, activity V, or E. Merck 100–200 mesh, Brockman activity *I*. (*4*) *Calcium sulfate, anhydrous.*—Drierite, nonindicating, 20–40 mesh (W. A. Hammond Drierite Co., Xenia, OH 45385, or equiv.). If this mesh size is not available, grind coarser mesh with mortar and pestle so that enough fines are obtained to prevent mixing of Florisil layer into Drierite layer when column is packed.

Dry packing materials 1–2 hr at ca 110°. Store all conditioned packing materials and packed columns in vapor-tight containers.

(**h**) *Std soln.—See* **26.006–26.011**. Dil. solns of aflatoxins B_1 and G_1, **26.008(a)** or (**b**), with $CHCl_3$ to common soln contg final concn of 2 mg each⁄mL.

26.016 ***Preparation of Minicolumns***

Tamp small plug of glass wool into tapered end of column. To column, add to ht indicated in following order: 8–10 mm Drierite, 8–10 mm Florisil, 16–20 mm silica gel, 8–10 mm neutral alumina, and 8–10 mm Drierite. Tamp small plug of glass wool on top of column. Tap column after each addn and apply pressure to the glass wool at top of column with thin rod after completion. (Packed minicolumns are available from The Myco-Lab Co., PO Box 321, St. Louis, MO 63017.)

26.017 ***Extraction***

Weigh 50 g sample into blender jar, add 250 mL acetone-H_2O (85+15), and blend 3 min. Alternatively, use 500 mL g-s erlenmeyer and shake 45 min on mech. shaker at fast speed. Filter thru 24 cm Whatman No. 4 paper in 160 mm funnel into 250 mL graduate. Collect 150 mL filtrate and transfer to 400 mL beaker.

26.018 ***Purification***

To 600 mL beaker, quant. add 170 mL 0.2*N* NaOH and 30 mL $FeCl_3$ slurry, and mix well. Add ca 3 g basic $CuCO_3$ to sample ext in the 400 mL beaker, mix well, and add to mixt. in 600 mL beaker. Add 150 mL diat. earth (150 mL beaker used as scoop is convenient) and mix well. Filter, using 160 mm funnel or 10 cm (id) buchner with Whatman No. 4 paper, or equiv.

Quant. transfer 150 mL filtrate to 500 mL separator; add 150 mL 0.03% H_2SO_4 and 10 mL $CHCl_3$. Shake vigorously ca 2 min and let sep. Transfer lower $CHCl_3$ layer (13–14 mL) to 125 mL separator. Add 100 mL KOH wash soln, (**b**), swirl gently 30 sec, and let sep. (If emulsion occurs, drain emulsion into 10 mL g-s graduate, add ca 1 g anhyd. Na_2SO_4, stopper, shake 30 sec, and let sep. ($CHCl_3$ phase need not be completely clear.) If emulsion is not broken, transfer emulsion to 125 mL separator and wash with 50 mL 0.03% H_2SO_4. Collect 3 mL $CHCl_3$ layer in 10 mL g-s graduate.

26.019 ***Chromatography***

Transfer 2 mL $CHCl_3$ soln to minicolumn, using 5 mL syringe with 5″, 15 gage needle. Let drain by gravity (15–30 min); or for faster elution, place top of column in hole of rubber bulb, hold column vertically, and apply slight air pressure to force solv. thru column at rate ≤10 cm/min until solv. appears at tip. Let rest of solv. drain by gravity. Remove bulb, if used. When solv. reaches top of adsorbent, add 3 mL elution solv., $CHCl_3$-acetone (9+1). Let drain by gravity until solv. again reaches top of adsorbent. Do not let columns run dry during detn; aflatoxin losses may occur.

Examine columns in darkened room under UV lamp or in Chromatovue cabinet. Look for blue fluorescent band at top of Florisil layer (ca 2.5 cm from bottom of column) indicative of aflatoxin. Perform analysis with "clean" sample, and with sample "spiked" with known amt of aflatoxin (above detection limit) to obtain comparison std. Some uncontaminated samples show faint white, yellow, or brown fluorescent band at top of Florisil in sample column. If band has no definite bluish tint, sample is neg.

Holaday-Velasco Method for Corn (*4*)—Official First Action

(Applicable to detection of ≥10 ppb of total aflatoxins in white and yellow corn)

26.020 ***Preparation of Sample***

See **26.049**.

26.021 ***Apparatus***

(**a**) *See* **26.014(a)**, (**b**), (**c**), and (**d**).

(**b**) *Disposable items.*—Culture tubes (20×150 mm) with plastic tube closures, pipets (1 mL), and plastic funnels (57 mm (2.25″) top diam.).

26.022 ***Reagents***

(**a**) *Benzene*.—Reagent grade.

(**b**) *Methanol-water.*—Mix 800 mL MeOH with 200 mL H_2O.

(**c**) *Salt soln.*—Dissolve 600 g NaCl, 600 g $Zn(OAc)_2$, and 15 mL HOAc in 4 L H_2O.

(**d**) *Chloroform-acetone.*—Mix 900 mL $CHCl_3$ with 100 mL acetone.

(**e**) *Column packing.*—*See* **26.015(g)**.

26.023 ***Preparation of Column***

Plug one end of chromatgc column with pad of glass wool ca 5 mm deep. Add, in order, 5–7 mm $CaSO_4$ (granular, anhyd.), 5–7 mm Florisil, 20 mm silica gel, 10–15 mm Al_2O_3, and 5–7 mm $CaSO_4$. Do not compress packing. Tap lightly between each addn to settle adsorbent and keep interfaces as level as possible. Store in vapor tight container.

26.024 ***Extraction***

Blend 50 g ground and blended corn sample with 100 mL MeOH-H_2O soln 1 min at high speed in blender. Filter 15 mL extract into culture tube, Add 15 mL salt soln. Close tube with plastic closure and shake vigorously 10 sec. (Small separator may be substituted for culture tube). Filter 15 mL of contents into second culture tube, add 3 mL benzene, close, and shake gently 10 sec. Let layers separate.

26.025 ***Chromatography***

Pipet 1 mL benzene (upper) layer onto top of minicolumn. Let extract drain into column; then add 3 mL $CHCl_3$-acetone, (**d**), and let drain. Examine column for blue fluorescent band at top of Florisil layer as in **26.019**.

QUANTITATIVE METHODS

Peanuts and Peanut Products—Official First Action

Method I (*CB Method*) (*5*)

(Other endorsements: International Union of Pure and Applied Chemistry in IUPAC Inform. Bull. No 31, March 1968.)

26.026 ***Apparatus***

See **26.001(a)**, **(d)–(o)**, and in addn:

Extractors.—500 mL g-s erlenmeyers, or 11 L (12 qt) stainless steel pail.

26.027 ***Reagents***

See **26.002**, **26.008–26.012**, and in addn:

(**a**) *Silica gel for column chromatography.*—E. Merck (Darmstadt) Silica Gel 60, 0.063–0.2 mm for 50 g samples, or 0.2–0.5 mm for 1 kg samples. Activate by drying 1 hr at 105°. Add H_2O, 1 mL/100 g, seal, shake until thoroly mixed, and store ≥15 hr in air-tight container.

(**b**) *Silica gel for thin layer chromatography.*—Silica gel, **26.002(d)**, should also meet following test: Prep. aflatoxin-free ext of commodity being tested as in **26.030(a)**. Dissolve in 500 μL benzene-CH_3CN (98+2). Place 10 μL on origin spot. To this spot, add, from solns of stds, 10 ng each of aflatoxins B_1 and G_1 and 2 ng each of aflatoxins B_2 and G_2. Repeat application of test spots to give ≥3 test spots evenly spaced across plate. Develop plate and examine. The 4 aflatoxins must be sepd from each other in clearly defined spots and sepd from non-aflatoxin fluorescent material in ext of commodity being examined.

(**c**) *Benzene-alcohol-water developing solvent.*—Prep. enough for several analyses. Shake benzene-alcohol-H_2O (46+35+19) in separator and let stand overnight at ≤22°. Then store the 2 layers that sep. in sep. g-s containers. Warm gently before use if they appear cloudy. Alternatively, use benzene-alcohol-H_2O (40+6+3) for top layer and (40+27+20) for bottom layer (J. Amer. Oil Chem. Soc. **50,** 1424(1973)).

26.028 ***Preparation of Sample***

Peanut butter and peanut meal need no prepn for extn unless they contain large particles, in which case reduce by milling. Use hammer mill, rotary cutter, or disk (burr) type mill for meals. Grind raw and roasted peanuts and peanut butter with pieces of peanuts to paste with disk (burr) type mill before extn. *See* **26.003**.

26.029 ***Extraction***

(**a**) *Fifty gram sample.*—Weigh 50 g prepd sample into 500 mL g-s erlenmeyer. Add 25 mL H_2O, 25 g diat. earth, and 250 mL $CHCl_3$, and secure stopper with masking tape. Shake 30 min on wrist action shaker and filter thru fluted paper. If filtration is slow, transfer to buchner precoated with ca 5 mm layer diat. earth, **26.002(c)**, and use light vac. (Use vac. filtration only for slow filtering samples since evapn of $CHCl_3$ is rapid, resulting in concn of ext.) Collect first 50 mL portion $CHCl_3$ filtrate and proceed as in **26.030(a)**.

(**b**) *One kilogram sample.*—Weigh 1 kg prepd sample into 12 qt stainless steel pail. Add 500 mL H_2O and mix with spatula until visually uniform. Add 5 L $CHCl_3$ and cover pail, leaving small opening for stirrer shaft. Position stirrer to achieve max. agitation without splashing. Stir 30 min; mix in 500 g diat. earth, **26.002 (c)**. For quant. analysis, remove enough mixt. to give 50 mL $CHCl_3$ filtrate and filter as in (**a**). Filter remainder thru buchner. Wash solids on funnel with 2 L $CHCl_3$; conc. combined $CHCl_3$ filtrate and washing in rotary evaporator to ca 800 mL when sample contains fat and to ca 200 mL for low-fat meals. Add 1 L hexane-$CHCl_3$ (1+1) to concd ext. If ppt appears, filter thru layer of filter-aid in buchner, washing with 1 L hexane-$CHCl_3$ (1+1).

26.030 ***Column Chromatography***

(**a**) *Fifty gram sample.*—Place ball of glass wool loosely in bottom of 22 × 300 mm chromatgc tube and add ca 5 g anhyd. Na_2SO_4 to give base for silica gel. Add $CHCl_3$ until tube is ca ½ full; then add 10 g silica gel, **26.027(a)**. Wash sides of tube with ca 20 mL $CHCl_3$ and stir to disperse silica gel. When rate of settling slows, drain some $CHCl_3$ to aid settling, leaving 5–7 cm above silica gel. Slowly add 15 g anhyd. Na_2SO_4. Drain $CHCl_3$ to top of Na_2SO_4. Add 50 mL sample ext to column, elute at max. flow rate with 150 mL hexane followed by 150 mL anhyd. ether, and discard. Elute aflatoxins with 150 mL MeOH-$CHCl_3$ (3+97), collecting this fraction from time of addn until flow stops.

Add few boiling chips to eluate, evap. nearly to dryness on steam bath, and quant. transfer residue to vial with $CHCl_3$. Add 2–3 boiling chips and evap., preferably under gentle stream of N. Seal vial with hollow polyethylene stopper and cap. Save for TLC.

(**b**) *One kilogram sample.*—Prep. column as in (**a**), using 45 × 600 mm chromatgc tube, 20 g Na_2SO_4 on glass wool ball, 100 g silica gel, **26.027(a)**, and 150 g Na_2SO_4 on top of silica gel. Add sample ext to column and elute at 40–60 mL/min with 500 mL $CHCl_3$-hexane (1+1), 1.5 L anhyd. ether, and 1 L MeOH-$CHCl_3$ (3+97). Evap. MeOH-$CHCl_3$ eluate as in (**a**). Retain final conc. for optional quantitation, **26.031(c)**, and/or preparatory sepn of aflatoxin B_1 for confirmation of identity by **26.076–26.082**.

If cleaner ext is required for preparatory TLC, direct bioassay, or quant. assay of sample contg low levels of aflatoxin, conc. MeOH-$CHCl_3$ eluate to ca 50 mL. Transfer to 10 g silica gel (0.063–0.2 mm) column and proceed as for 50 g samples, omitting hexane elution.

Alternatively, use acid Al_2O_3 chromatgy (JAOAC **54**, 1310(1971)).

26.031 *Thin Layer Chromatography*

(**a**) *Preparation of plates.*—Weigh 30 g silica gel, **26.027(b)**, into 300 mL g-s erlenmeyer, add amt of H_2O recommended by manufacturer, shake vigorously $\leqslant$1 min, and pour into applicator. Adjust amt of H_2O to obtain best consistency of slurry for spreading, as required by batch-to-batch variation in silica gel. Immediately coat five 20 $\times$ 20 cm glass plates with 0.25 mm thickness of silica gel suspension, and let plates rest undisturbed until gelled (ca 10 min). Adjust thickness of spread (and wt gel) to 0.5 mm, if necessary, to provide good resolution of aflatoxins and tightness of spots. Dry coated plates $\geqslant$2 hr at 80° or $\geqslant$1 hr at 110°, and store in desiccating cabinet with active silica gel desiccant until just before use. To prep. plate for chromatgy, scribe line 16 cm from bottom edge as solv. stop; scribe lines ca 0.5 cm in from each side or remove 0.5 cm gel from each side to prevent edge effects.

(**b**) *Preliminary thin layer chromatography.*—(This step may be omitted when approx. aflatoxin content is known.) Uncap vial contg sample ext, add 200 μL benzene-CH_3CN (98+2), and reseal with polyethylene stopper. Shake vigorously to dissolve, preferably with Vortex shaking machine. Puncture polyethylene stopper to accommodate needle of 10 μL syringe. In subdued incandescent light and as rapidly as possible, spot 2, 5, and two 10 μL spots on imaginary line 4 cm from bottom edge of TLC plate. Keep vial for quant. analysis. On same plate, spot 2, 5, and 10 μL aflatoxin stds, **26.011**. Spot 5 μL std used on top of one of the two 10 μL sample origin spots as internal std. Spot at least one 5 μL resolution ref. std, **26.012**, to show whether adequate resolution is attained.

Place 50 mL acetone-$CHCl_3$ (1+9) in trough of unlined developing tank. If tank is other than Thomas-Mitchell, use vol. to provide solv. depth of ca 2 cm. Composition of acetone-$CHCl_3$ can be varied from (5+95) to (15+85) to compensate for variations in silica gel and developing conditions. Use only one plate per tank, placing trough near one side to permit max. exposure of coated surface to tank vol. Immediately insert plate into tank and seal tank.

Develop plate 40 min at 23–25° or until aflatoxins reach R_f 0.4–0.7. Adjust development time to compensate if different developing temp. is used. Adjust developing solv. if developing time is >90 min. Remove from tank, evap. solv. at room temp., and illuminate plate from below by placing it flat, coated side up, on longwave UV lamp in darkened room, or view plate in Chromato-Vue cabinet, or illuminate from above. (If illumination requires looking directly at lamps, protect eyes with UV-absorbing filter, such as Eastman Kodak Co. 2A.) Observe pattern of 4 fluorescent spots of resolution ref. std. In order of decreasing R_f, they are B_1, B_2, G_1, and G_2. Note small color difference (bluish fluorescence of "B" contrasted with slightly green "G" aflatoxins). Examine patterns from sample for fluorescent spots having R_f close to those of stds and similar appearances. From this preliminary plate, est. suitable diln for quant. TLC analysis. In final calcns, take into account amt of ext used for preliminary TLC.

(**c**) *Quantitative thin layer chromatography.*—If preliminary plate shows that new concn of sample ext is required, evap. to dryness on steam bath and redissolve in calcd vol. benzene-CH_3CN (98+2).

Spot successively 3.5, 5.0, and two 6.5 μL portions of sample ext. All spots should be approx. same size and $\leqslant$0.5 cm diam. On same plate, spot 3.5, 5.0, and 6.5 μL aflatoxin stds, **26.011**, corresponding to aflatoxins observed on preliminary plate. Spot 5.0 μL of each std used on top of one of the two 6.5 μL sample origin spots as internal std. Spot at least one 5 μL resolution ref. std, **26.012**, to show whether adequate resolution is attained. Proceed as in (**b**).

(**d**) *Interpretation of the chromatogram.*—Four clearly identifiable spots should be visible in resolution ref. std.

Examine pattern from sample spot contg internal std for aflatoxin spots. R_f values of aflatoxins used as internal stds should be same as or only slightly different from those of resp. std aflatoxin spots. (Since spots from sample ext are compared directly with std aflatoxins on same plate, magnitude of R_f is unimportant. These may vary from plate to plate.)

Compare sample patterns with pattern contg internal std. Fluorescent spots in sample thought to be aflatoxins must have R_f values identical to and color similar to aflatoxin std spots when unknown spot and internal std spot are superimposed. Spot from sample and internal std combined should be more intense than either sample or std alone.

Compare fluorescent intensities of B_1 spots of sample with those of std spots and det. which sample portion matches one of stds. To aid in detn, move plate away from lamp to attenuate UV light so any particular pair of spots can be compared at extinction. Interpolate if intensity of sample spot is between those of 2 of std spots. If spots of smallest portion of sample are too intense to match stds, dil. sample and rechromatograph. Compare B_2, G_1, and G_2 spots in same manner.

Calc. concn of aflatoxin B_1 in μg/kg from formula:

$$\mu g/kg = (S \times Y \times V)/(X \times W),$$

where S = μL aflatoxin B_1 std equal to unknown; Y = concn of aflatoxin B_1 std, μg/mL; V = μL of final diln of sample ext; X = μL sample ext spotted giving fluorescent intensity equal to S (B_1 std); W = g sample applied to column (10 g if 50 mL $CHCl_3$ ext is used). If final ext diln does not represent 10 g, calc. correct sample wt and substitute. The 50 mL aliquot of $CHCl_3$ ext of peanut butter or whole nuts removed for analysis in **26.029(a)** or (**b**) usually contains 5–6 mL fat which adds to vol. Thus, 45 mL aliquot of $CHCl_3$ has been removed and ext actually represents 9 g starting material, instead of 10 g as for low-fat materials.

Calc. aflatoxins B_2, G_1, and G_2 similarly.

(**e**) *Thin layer chromatographic confirmation of aflatoxin G_1 and/or G_2.*—(Applicable only when commodity, such as peanut butter, contains interferences that tend to migrate in aflatoxin G area.) If G_1 plus G_2 is $\geqslant$20% of total aflatoxins, confirm amt and identity of G_1 and G_2 by chromatgy, using solv. system, **26.027(c)**.

Respot sample and stds on silica gel plate as in (**c**). Put 50 mL lower phase in bottom of insulated, unlined developing tank, and 50 mL upper phase in trough. Use only 1 plate per tank, placing trough near one side to permit max. exposure of coated surface to tank vol. Without equilibrating, insert plate in trough and seal. Let solv. rise to stop line 12–14 cm above origin (30–50 min) and remove plate. In order of decreasing R_f values, resolution ref. std gives B_1, B_2, G_1, G_2 as before, but many extraneous fluorescent substances found in samples will have completely different R_f values relative to those of aflatoxins in the 2 solv. systems. G_1 and G_2 aflatoxins of sample should have same R_f as those of resp. stds. Make quant. estn for G_1 and G_2 as in (**c**) and (**d**).

Method II (BF Method) (6)

(Other adoptions: American Oil Chemists' Society Tentative Method Ab 6-68 (revised 1973).)

26.032 ***Apparatus***

See **26.001(b)**, **(c)**, **(g)**, **(h)**, **(i)**, **(k)**, **(l)**, **(m)**, and in addn:
Beakers.—Stainless steel, 600 mL.

26.033 ***Reagents***

See **26.002(a)**, **(b)**, **(d)**, **(f)**, **26.008–26.012**.

26.034 ***Preparation of Sample***

See **26.028**.

26.035 ***Extraction***

Weigh 100 g prepd sample of peanuts or meal or 50 g peanut butter into blender jar. Add 250 mL MeOH-H_2O (55+45) and 100 mL hexane to peanut butter, and 500 mL MeOH-H_2O (55+45), 200 mL hexane, and ca 4 g NaCl to peanuts or meal.

Blend 1 min at high speed. Transfer to 250 mL centrf. bottle and centrf. 5 min at 2000 rpm. (If time is unimportant or centrifuge is not available, let mixt. stand undisturbed in blender jar, as sepn will occur within 30 min for peanut butter and raw or roasted peanuts.)

Pipet 25 mL aq. MeOH phase into 125 or 250 mL separator, add 25 mL $CHCl_3$, stopper, and shake 30–60 sec. Let layers sep. and drain bottom $CHCl_3$ layer into 600 mL stainless steel beaker (if available). Do not include any meal with ext. Place beaker on steam plate under stream of N and add small amt of H_2O under beaker to improve heat transfer. (100 mL glass beaker is satisfactory, but more time is required for evapn.) Evap. solv. to between 2 mL and just dryness or as soon as condensing vapor is no longer visible on beaker lip. Do not leave beaker on hot plate after solv. has evapd. (Alternatively, evapn may be performed using erlenmeyers and steam bath.) Transfer ext. with careful washing, to 4 dram vial and evap. to dryness under gentle stream of N in hot H_2O bath or in heating block. Dissolve ext in 200 μL benzene-CH_3CN (98+2) for spotting on TLC plate.

26.036 ***Thin Layer Chromatography and Calculations***

Proceed as in **26.031**, except that no correction is required for fat carried by extg solv.

Cocoa Beans (7)—Official Final Action

(Other endorsements: International Union of Pure and Applied Chemistry in IUPAC Inform. Bull. Tech. Rep. No 8, August, 1973.)

26.037 ***Principle***

Method I for peanuts, **26.026–26.031**, is modified by preliminary hexane defatting step and by treatment of $CHCl_3$ ext with $AgNO_3$ to reduce theobromine concn.

26.038 ***Apparatus***

See **26.001(a)**, **(d)**, **(e)**, **(f)**, **(g)**, **(h)**, **(j)**, **(k)**, **(l)**, **(m)**, **26.004**, and in addn:
Soxhlet apparatus.—To take 43 × 123 mm Whatman extn thimble.

26.039 ***Reagents***

See **26.002(a)**, **(b)**, **(d)**, **(e)**, **(f)**, **26.005–26.012**, **26.027(a)**, and in addn:
Silver nitrate soln.—25 g/100 mL H_2O.

26.040 ***Preparation of Sample***

Freeze cocoa beans with liq. N. (*Caution:* Perform under good ventilation and wear insulated rubber gloves and face shield to protect against liq. N splashes.) Powder anal. sample in high-speed blender or grind lot samples directly in suitable app. and mix well before removing anal. sample.

26.041 ***Extraction***

(*Caution: See* **51.011**, **51.039**, **51.040**, **51.056**, and **51.061**.)

Weigh 50 g powd cocoa beans into extn thimble and defat with *n*-hexane in Soxhlet app. at siphon rate of 4–5 cycles/hr for 12–15 cycles, but ≤3 hr. (Excess extn may result in loss of aflatoxin.) Invert thimble and contents into 400 mL beaker and let dry overnight at room temp. Transfer, using powder funnel, to 500 mL g-s erlenmeyer. Scrape as much residual powder as possible from thimble with spatula. Add 25 mL $AgNO_3$ soln to sample and mix until uniform. Add 250 mL $CHCl_3$, using portion to rinse extn thimble. Tape stopper in place. Shake 30 min on mech. shaker (low-speed setting). Filter $CHCl_3$ (lower) layer thru fluted paper and collect first 75 mL $CHCl_3$ ext. Transfer to 250 mL g-s erlenmeyer, add 7.5 mL $AgNO_3$ soln, and shake 15 min on mech. shaker. Pour mixt. into 250 mL separator and collect 50 mL $CHCl_3$ layer.

26.042 ***Column Chromatography***

Prep. column and chromatograph 50 mL $CHCl_3$ layer as in **26.030(a)**, using flow rate of ca 10 mL/min.

26.043 ***Thin Layer Chromatography***

Proceed as in **26.031(a)–(d)**. Note that no correction is needed for fat carried by extg solv. Sample will not be completely sol. in benzene-CH_3CN spotting solv. Centrf. vials to compact sediment, if needed, to avoid clogging syringe needle.

Coconut, Copra, and Copra Meal (8)—Official First Action

(Other endorsements or adoptions: International Union of Pure and Applied Chemistry in IUPAC Inform. Bull. Tech. Rep. No 9, August 1974; American Oil Chemists' Society Official Method Ah 1-72.)

26.044 ***Apparatus***

See **26.001(a)**, **(d)**, **(f)**, **(g)**, **(h)**, **(j)**, **(k)** **(l)**, **26.004**, and in addn:
Funnel.—185 mm with Eaton-Dikeman No. 617 or Whatman No. 2 paper, and Whatman GF/A glass filter to fit.

26.045 ***Reagents***

See **26.002(a)**, **(b)**, **(d)**, **(e)**, **(f)**, **26.005–26.012**, and **26.027(a)**.

26.046 ***Preparation of Sample***

Freeze copra or coconut at ≤−27.8° (−18°F). Feed continuously into hammermill at ca 450 g (1 lb)/min. Grind meal pellets in high-speed blender without freezing.

26.047 ***Extraction***

Weigh 50 g sample into blender jar. Add 4 g NaCl, 100 mL H_2O, and 250 mL $CHCl_3$, and blend 3 min at high speed. Decant into 400 mL beaker. Prep. funnel by first folding paper and then placing glass filter inside folded paper. Decant ext from beaker thru funnel into 250 mL erlenmeyer. Collect 60–70 mL filtrate.

26.048 ***Column and Thin Layer Chromatography***

Proceed as in **26.030(a)** and **26.031(a)–(d)**.

Corn (*9*)—Official First Action

(Other adoptions: American Association of Cereal Chemists Method 45-05: 1972 revisions to AACC Approved Methods, pp. 1–9.)

26.049 ***Preparation of Sample***

Grind entire lot sample thru hammer, Wiley, or disk mill to pass No. 14 sieve. Split sample sequentially in sample splitter, such as "riffle," until 1–2 kg portion is obtained for analysis. Retain remainder. Regrind 1–2 kg portion to completely pass No. 20 sieve. Mix reground portion thoroly in tumble blender or planetary mixer. Take anal. samples from this mix, using sample splitter. Prep. addnl portions from lot sample in same way, if needed.

26.050 ***Rapid Screening***

Proceed as in **26.026–26.029(a)**, but collect second 50 mL portion $CHCl_3$. Evap. ext in steam bath to leave residue of corn oil. Immediately spot 5, 10, and 10 μL warm corn oil on origin line 1.5 cm from bottom edge of plate, **26.031(a)**. Silica gel will absorb oil most readily if both oil and plate are warm and if oil is spotted immediately on completion of evapn of solv. On same plate, spot 5 μL resolution ref. std, **26.012**. Spot 5 μL std used on top of one 10 μL sample ext spot as internal std. Scribe horizontal line across center of plate with pencil or other sharp object for half-plate development. (Plate can be reused after development by redrying and turning 180° for next spotting.) Develop plate with anhyd. ether, **26.002(f)**, in unequilibrated developing tank to scored line (<30 min). Let plate dry. Redevelop in same direction in unequilibrated tank with acetone-$CHCl_3$ (1+9) (<20 min). Adjust acetone-$CHCl_3$ ratio as needed to modify R_f of aflatoxins as in **26.031(b)**, par. 2. Observe developed plate for presence or absence of spot originating from sample and with same R_f and appearance as authentic aflatoxin B_1. Observe internal std for any change in R_f or appearance of aflatoxin caused by the ext. Observe only for presence or absence of aflatoxin B_1 in sample spot.

26.051 ***Determination***

Proceed as in **26.026–26.031**.

Cottonseed Products

Rapid Modification (10)—Official First Action

26.052 ***Apparatus***

See **26.001(k)**, **(l)**, **(m)**, **(n)**, and in addn:

(a) *Butt tube.*—32 × 125 mm. (Similar to chromatgc tube but without stopcock.)

(b) *Chromatographic tubes.*—22 (id) × 500 mm, with Teflon valve (Corning Glass Works No. 2145 or Kimble Products No. 17800, or equiv.).

(c) *Densitometer.*—*See* **26.001(e)**.

26.053 ***Reagents***

See **26.002(a)**, **(b)**, **(c)**, **(d)**, **(e)**, **(f)**, and in addn:

(a) *Solvents.*—Reagent grade CH_2Cl_2, anhyd. ether (≤0.01% EtOH), and hexane (bp 68–69°).

(b) *Lead acetate soln.*—Dissolve 200 g $Pb(OAc)_2.3H_2O$ in H_2O with warming, add 3 mL HOAc, and dil. to 1 L.

(c) *For column chromatography.*—*(1) Silica gel.*—*See* **26.027(a)**. *(2) Wash solvents.*—Benzene-HOAc (9+1); ether-hexane (3+1). *(3) Aflatoxin elution solvent.*—$CHCl_3$-acetone (4+1).

(d) *Acidic alumina.*—Fisher A-948, 80–200 mesh. Add 3% H_2O by wt, shake well, and equilibrate overnight.

(e) *Aflatoxin stds.*—*See* **26.006–26.012**.

26.054 ***Preparation of Sample***

Grind whole seed or kernels in Wiley mill, or equiv., to pass No. 10 sieve. For seed contg lint, screen ground sample on 4/64" screen to remove coarse lint. Grind meals to pass No. 18 sieve. Quarter or riffle ground sample to obtain 50–100 g anal. sample.

26.055 ***Extraction***

(a) *Meats (kernels) and conventional meals.*—Weigh 25 g sample into 500 mL erlenmeyer, add 250 mL acetone-H_2O (85+15), and stopper with leakproof glass or polyethylene stopper. Shake vigorously 30 min on mech. shaker. Alternatively, weigh 25 g sample into 1 L blender jar, add 250 mL acetone-H_2O (85+15), and blend 2 min at low speed and 3 min at high speed.

Filter thru folded 18.5 cm Whatman No. 4 paper, or equiv., collecting ≥100 mL filtrate.

(b) *Ammoniated meals.*—Weigh 25 g sample, add 40 mL 0.1*N* HCl, and let soak 5 min. Add 210 mL anhyd. acetone, and ext and filter as in **(a)**.

26.056 ***Purification***

Measure 100 mL filtrate into 250 mL beaker, add 80 mL H_2O and 20 mL 20% $Pb(OAc)_2$ soln, **(b)**, stir well, and let stand ca 5 min to coagulate ppt. Add ca 5 g filter-aid, **26.002(c)**, stir well, and filter thru folded 18.5 cm Whatman No. 4 paper, or equiv., collecting ≥100 mL filtrate.

Ext 100 mL filtrate with 50 mL CH_2Cl_2 in 250 mL separator, shaking vigorously 1 min, and let sep. Prep. Butt tube with loose plug of glass wool in constriction, cover with ca 2 cm anhyd. granular Na_2SO_4, and add 5 g acidic alumina (5 mL beaker filled to top), 5 g silica gel 60 for column chromatgy (10 mL beaker filled to top), and ca 2 cm Na_2SO_4. Drain CH_2Cl_2 (lower) layer thru tube, collecting filtrate in clean 250 mL beaker. Repeat with addnl 50 mL CH_2Cl_2, and finally wash tube with 50 mL CH_2Cl_2-acetone (9+1). Evap. combined eluates to dryness on steam bath. Do not overheat dry ext.

(a) *Meats and conventional meals.*—Transfer quant. with CH_2Cl_2 to 2 dram vial, evap. to dryness under N, and reserve for preliminary TLC. If desired, ext may be cleaned up further by **26.057**, but omit benzene-HOAc (9+1) wash with nonammoniated cottonseed products.

(b) *Ammoniated meals.*—Dissolve dry ext in ca 3 mL CH_2Cl_2 and proceed as in **26.057**.

26.057 ***Column Chromatography***

Place small wad of glass wool in constriction of chromatgc tube, and add ca 2 cm Na_2SO_4. Slurry 10 g silica gel for column chromatgy with ca 40 mL ether-hexane (3+1) in 50 mL beaker, and pour into tube. Wash beaker with ca 25 mL ether-hexane (3+1), and add to tube. When gel settles, carefully top with ca 2 cm layer of Na_2SO_4. Drain solv. to top of Na_2SO_4 layer.

Add CH_2Cl_2 soln of ext to column, washing beaker with 2 ca 3 mL portions CH_2Cl_2; add to column. When solv. level reaches top of Na_2SO_4, add 100 mL benzene-HOAc (9+1) and drain to top of Na_2SO_4. Add 150 mL ether-hexane (3+1) and drain to top of Na_2SO_4. Discard washes. Elute aflatoxins with 200 mL $CHCl_3$-acetone (4+1), collecting eluate in clean 250 mL beaker. Evap. to dryness on steam bath, transfer quant. with CH_2Cl_2 to 2 dram vial, evap. to dryness under N, and reserve for preliminary TLC.

26.058 ***Preliminary Thin Layer Chromatography***

See **26.031(a)** and **(b)**.

Dissolve dry ext from **26.056** or **26.057** in exactly 0.5 mL benzene-CH_3CN (98+2), and proceed as in **26.031(b)**, except that plate is developed 20 min and sample wt, *W*, is 5 g. After quantitation, confirm identity as follows:

Spray plate with fine mist of H_2SO_4 (1+3) and view under longwave UV. Aflatoxins B_1 and B_2 should now have yellow fluorescence, and G_1 and G_2, yellow-blue fluorescence. While G aflatoxins are rarely found in cottonseed, blue fluorescent spots sometimes found in cottonseed exts at or near R_f of G_1 or G_2 will not exhibit characteristic color change. Test is not confirmatory, but will rule out presumptive aflatoxins which do not show color change.

26.059 ***Quantitative Thin Layer Chromatography***

Evap. remaining ext from **26.058** and dissolve in appropriate vol. benzene-CH_3CN (98+2) as in (**a**), for either visual or densitometric analysis.

(**a**) *Sample dilution and aliquots for visual and densitometric analysis.—See* Table **26:03**.

Table 26:03 Aliquots for visual and densitometric analysis

Approx. B_1 Content from Prelim. TLC, μg/kg	Visual Analysis: Diln of Ext, mL	Visual Analysis: Aliquots on Plate, μL	Densitometric Analysis: Diln of Ext, mL	Densitometric Analysis: Aliquots on Plate, μL
0–10	0.125	3–5–7	0.125	10–10
10–25	0.125	3–5–7	0.125	5–5
25–50	0.50	3–5–7	0.25	6–6
50–75	0.75	3–5–7	0.50	6–6
75–125	1.00	3–5–7	0.50	5–5
125–150	1.25	3–5–7	0.75	5–5
150–175	1.50	3–5–7	1.00	6–6
175–200	2.00	3–5–7	1.25	6–6

(**b**) *Visual analysis.*—Spot 3, 5, and 7 μL sample ext on plate, along with 2, 3, 4, and 5 μL aflatoxin std, **26.011**. Spot and develop plates as in **26.031(b)**. Interpret chromatogram as in **26.031(d)**.

(**c**) *Densitometric analysis.*—Spot suggested sample aliquots, (**a**), on plate, along with duplicate aliquots of mixed aflatoxin std to provide 5 ng aflatoxin B_1 and G_1 and 1 ng B_2 and G_2/spot. Also adjust sep. sample aliquots to these values for B_2, G_1, and G_2 by dilg, and spot sep. Place spots along imaginary line ca 4 cm from bottom of plate. Develop as in **26.031(b)**. Do not damage gel layer during spotting, as significant errors may be introduced. If plate is visually inspected before densitometry, use low wattage UV source and min. exposure time.

Scan plate with densitometer according to instructions of manufacturer. Irradiate with 365 nm source: observe for emission at 420–460 nm.

Calc. concn of aflatoxin B_1 in μg/kg as follows:

$$\mu g/kg = (B \times Y \times S \times V)/(Z \times X \times W),$$

where B = av. area aflatoxin B_1 peaks in sample aliquots; Y = concn aflatoxin B_1 std, μg/mL; S = μL aflatoxin B_1 std spotted; V = final diln of sample ext, μL; Z = av. area aflatoxin B_1 peaks in std aliquots; X = μL sample ext spotted; W = g sample represented by final ext (10 g if 25 g sample used for analysis).

Repeat calcn for each of other aflatoxins observed.

Correct aflatoxin concn values from densitometric measurement for amt of sample ext removed for either *Preliminary TLC*, **26.058**, or *Visual analysis*, (**b**), if used before densitometric measurements, as follows:

$$\text{Corrected } \mu g/kg = \frac{\text{apparent } \mu g/kg}{1 - [(p/P) + (q/Q)]},$$

where p = total μL sample ext spotted in **26.058**; P = μL sample ext prepd in **26.058**; q = total μL sample ext spotted in (**b**) (if done prior to densitometric analysis); Q = μL sample ext prepd for (**b**) (if done prior to densitometric analysis).

26.060 ***TLC Confirmation of Aflatoxin G_1 and/or G_2***

Aflatoxins G_1 and G_2 are rarely observed in cottonseed products, but some exts may contain bluish fluorescent non-aflatoxin spot at or near R_f of G_1 or G_2, depending on TLC conditions. If G_1 or G_2 is judged to be present, confirm by respotting two 5 μL aliquots of sample ext on new plate. Spot 5 μL aflatoxin std on top of one sample aliquot and develop plate in 150 mL $CHCl_3$-MeOH (95+5). Although aflatoxins are not well resolved in this solv., bluish fluorescent nonaflatoxin component will be resolved from aflatoxins G_1 and G_2 as indicated by comparison of sample aliquots with and without internal std.

Green Coffee (*11*)—Official First Action

26.061 ***Apparatus***

See **26.001(b)**, (**c**), (**d**), (**h**), (**i**), (**k**), (**m**), and (**n**).

26.062 ***Reagents***

See **26.002(a)**, (**b**), (**d**), (**e**), (**f**), **26.008–26.012**, and in addn:

(**a**) *Tetrahydrofuran (THF).—(Caution: See* **51.070**.) Purify by passing 250 mL THF thru 25 g Woelm neut. alumina to remove peroxides. Adjust proportionately for larger vols of THF.

(**b**) *Deactivated Florisil.*—60–100 mesh, preactivated at 1200° (Fisher Scientific Co. No. F-100), washed and deactivated as follows: Wash 500 g Florisil in chromatgc tube with 1 L *n*-hexane-HOAc (99+1) and rinse with 500 mL *n*-hexane to remove excess HOAc. Place in flat tray and dry in fume hood to remove solvs; then dry overnight in oven at 120–135°. Remove from oven, place in desiccator, and cool to room temp. Use proportionate amts of solv. to prep. less Florisil. (Acid-washed Florisil can be stored indefinitely.) Place ca 100 g washed Florisil in airtight, g-s reagent bottle ca ⅔ full, add 10% (w/w) H_2O, and shake vigorously by hand ca 5 min and then on mech. shaker 1 hr; let Florisil-H_2O equilibrate overnight. Prep. deactivated Florisil only in 100 g amts and use within 1 week.

(**c**) *Neutral alumina.*—Woelm (ICN Pharmaceuticals, Inc., Life Sciences Group).

26.063 ***Preparation of Sample***

Freeze green coffee beans with solid CO_2 or liq. N and grind to fine powder in high-speed blender.

26.064 ***Extraction***

Weigh 25 g powd green coffee beans in 500 mL g-s erlenmeyer, add 12.5 mL H_2O and 125 mL $CHCl_3$, and shake 30 min on mech. shaker. Transfer to centrf. bottle and centrf. 10 min at 2000 rpm. Use 50 mL aliquot of $CHCl_3$ layer for Florisil column cleanup.

26.065 ***Florisil Chromatography***

Place glass wool plug loosely in bottom of 22 × 300 mm chromatgc tube, add ca 5 g anhyd. Na_2SO_4 to form even base, and add 100 mL $CHCl_3$; then add 5 g washed and deactivated Florisil with stirring to disperse Florisil and prevent air entrapment. Let Florisil settle and drain $CHCl_3$, leaving ca 7.5 cm above Florisil; then slowly add 15 g anhyd. Na_2SO_4. Rinse sides of column and drain $CHCl_3$ to top of Na_2SO_4; then add 50 mL sample ext. Wash column with 150 mL purified THF at ca 10 mL/min and discard wash. Elute aflatoxins with 300 mL acetone-MeOH (9+1) at ≤10 mL/min into 500 mL erlenmeyer. Transfer acetone-MeOH fraction to r-b flask and evap. to dryness on steam bath under N. Quant. transfer residue to small vial with $CHCl_3$, evap. to dryness on steam bath under N, and reserve for TLC.

26.066 ***Thin Layer Chromatography***

Proceed as in **26.031(a)**, **(b)**, **(c)**, and **(d)**, except use benzene-alcohol-H_2O developing solv., **26.027(c)**.

Pistachio Nuts (*12*)—Official First Action

26.067 ***Method I***

Weigh 50 g nutmeats or equiv. from **26.003** (100 g in-shell or 100 g nutmeats and oyster shell) into 1 L g-s erlenmeyer, add 50 mL H_2O, 50 g diat. earth, and 500 mL $CHCl_3$, and secure stopper with tape. Proceed as in **26.029(a)**, beginning "Shake 30 min . . .", **26.030(a)**, and **26.031**.

26.068 ***Method II***

Weigh 50 g nutmeats or equiv. from **26.003** (100 g in-shell or 100 g nutmeats and oyster shell) into blender jar and add 500 mL MeOH-H_2O (55+45), 200 mL hexane, and ca 4 g NaCl. Proceed as in **26.035**, par. 2, using 50 mL aq. MeOH phase, 250 mL separator, and 50 mL $CHCl_3$ in par. 3.

Soybeans (*9*)—Official First Action

26.069 ***Determination***

Prep. sample as in **26.049** and proceed as in **26.026–26.031** for detn. Because of oil in original $CHCl_3$ ext, *W* (g original soybean sample represented by final purified ext) = 9.6 g.

Eggs (*13*)—Official First Action

(*Caution: See* **51.046**, **51.054**, **51.056**, and **51.073**.)

26.070 ***Apparatus***

See **26.001(e)** and in addn:

(a) *Explosion-proof blender.*—Waring Model EP-1, or equiv., with 1 L jar and cover. (See **26.001(h)**.) Control speed with variable transformer.

(b) *Butt tube.*—32 × 200 mm (Corning Glass Works No. 92195, or equiv.).

(c) *Thin layer plates.*—10 × 10 or 20 × 20 cm plates coated with 0.25–0.5 mm (wet thickness) layer of Macherey-Nagel GHR silica gel for TLC (Macherey, Nagel & Co., 516 Duren, Germany, distributed by Brinkmann Instruments, Inc.) dried 1 hr at 105° or Adsorbosil-1 silica gel for TLC (Applied Science Laboratories, Inc.), or equiv.

(d) *Development tank.*—Glass tank with ground-to-fit cover and metal trough, or equiv. Use silicone grease seal.

(e) *Viewing cabinet.*—Chromato-Vue Model C-6 (Ultra-Violet Products, Inc.), or equiv., fitted with 15 watt longwave UV lamp.

(f) *Sample vial.*—2 dram, with foil-lined screw cap. *See* **26.001(m)**.

26.071 ***Reagents***

See **26.002(c)**, **(e)**, **(f)**, **26.053(b)**, and in addn:

(a) *Sodium chloride soln.*—ACS grade, satd soln (ca 40 g/100 mL H_2O).

(b) *Silica gel.*—E. Merck silica gel 60 (No. 7734), 0.063–0.200 mm (70–230 mesh), or equiv. Activate by drying 1 hr at 105°, add 3 mL H_2O/100 g, seal in jar, shake until mixed thoroly, and store overnight before use.

(c) *Aflatoxin reference std.*—Prep. as in **26.004–26.011** to contain 0.50 μg aflatoxin B_1/mL benzene-CH_3CN (98+2). Store dild stds in refrigerator in leak-proof container.

26.072 ***Extraction and Lipid Removal***

Weigh amt liq. or powd egg and add H_2O into blender jar, as indicated in Table **26:04**. Add 42 mL satd NaCl soln, and blend 1 min at moderate speed (variable transformer set at 40 v). Add 300 mL acetone and blend addnl 3 min. Filter thru folded paper into 250 mL graduate.

Table 26:04 Preparation of Sample of Egg Products

Egg Product	% H_2O	Sample Wt, g	H_2O Added before Extn, mL	Sample Equiv. in Final Ext, g
Whole egg	74	100	0	45
Egg white	88	100	0	44
Egg yolk	51	100	20	46
Dried whole egg	5	27	73	12.2
Dried egg yolk	4	27	73	12.2
Dried egg white	9	28	72	12.7

Transfer 235 mL filtrate to 500 mL erlenmeyer. Add 20 mL $Pb(OAc)_2$ soln and 150 mL H_2O. Stir and let stand ca 5 min. Add 10 g diat. earth, stir, and filter thru paper into clean 500 mL graduate. If first filtrate is cloudy, refilter thru same paper.

Transfer 325 mL filtrate to 500 mL separator with Teflon plug and stopper; add 100 mL pet ether, and shake vigorously ca 1 min. Let layers sep., drain lower aq. layer into another 500 mL separator, and discard upper pet ether layer. Add 50 mL $CHCl_3$ to aq. layer, shake separator vigorously ca 1 min, and let layers sep.

26.073 ***Column Chromatography***

Prep. Butt tube column by inserting loose plug of glass wool in constriction; add ca 2 cm bed of anhyd. Na_2SO_4 followed by 10 g silica gel slurried in 50 mL $CHCl_3$. Drain $CHCl_3$ and add another 2 cm bed of anhyd. Na_2SO_4 on top of drained silica gel.

Filter lower $CHCl_3$ layer from separator thru Butt tube, collecting filtrate in clean 300 mL erlenmeyer. Add 20 mL acetone to aq. layer, and ext with second 50 mL portion of $CHCl_3$. Filter lower $CHCl_3$ layer thru same Butt tube; follow with 20 mL $CHCl_3$-acetone (9+1).

Evap. combined filtrate and washings to near dryness on steam bath, quant. transfer ext to 2 dram vial, and evap. to dryness on steam bath under N stream. Avoid overheating of dry ext. Reserve for TLC. Final ext represents wt egg product indicated in Table **26:04**.

Example: Whole egg (74% H_2O)

$$\text{Wt egg} = 100 \text{ g} \times [235/(300+42+74)] \times [325/(235+20+150)] = 45 \text{ g}$$

26.074 ***Thin Layer Chromatography***

(Perform TLC analysis without delay. Aflatoxins are unstable on silica gel when exposed to air, light, and moisture.)

Add 100 μL benzene-CH_3CN (98+2) to dry sample residue in vial, cap, and shake vigorously ca 1 min on vortex shaker. For screening analysis, use 10 × 10 cm TLC plate scored and spotted as shown in Fig. **26:01**, using 20 μL ext soln and 2 μL aflatoxin B_1 std soln. If sample is pos., respot ext for quantitation on 20 × 20 cm plate as shown in Fig. **26:01**. Take precaution to avoid loss of solv. from ext during spotting, i.e., hold vial at top to reduce heating from hands; immediately close vial upon removing each 10 μL portion. Spot second plate as above and overspot sample spot with 1 ng aflatoxin B_1 as internal std.

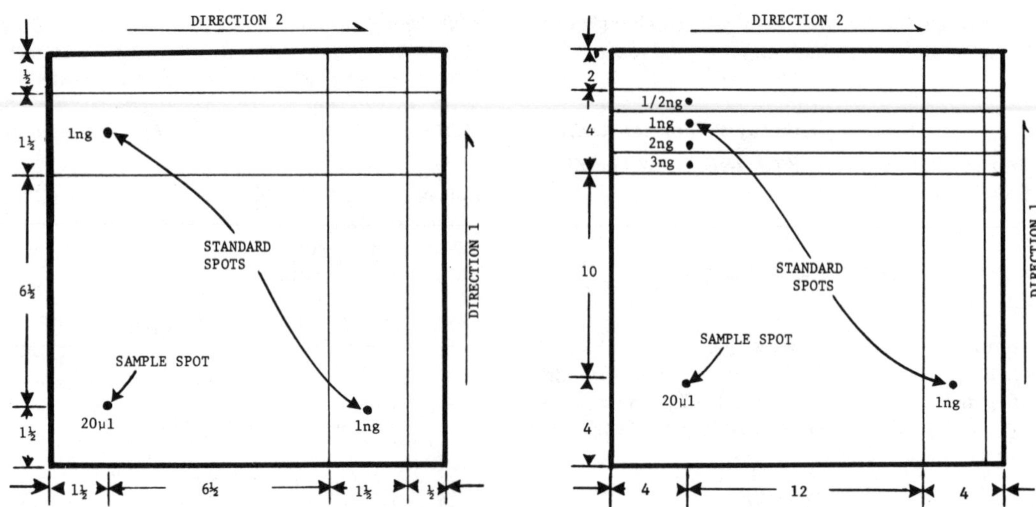

Fig. 26:01—Spotting and scoring patterns for 2-dimensional TLC plates: left, miniplates 10 × 10 cm; right, full plates 20 × 20 cm (all dimensions in cm)

(Internal std plate may be omitted if aflatoxin B_1 R_f area is free of artifact spots.) Reserve remaining ext in freezer for confirmation of aflatoxin identity, if detected.

Develop plates in first direction with anhyd. Et ether-MeOH-H_2O (96+3+1) in sep., well-sealed, unequilibrated tanks. Remove plates from tanks and dry in forced-draft oven 1 min at 50°. Cool ca 1 min and immediately develop in second direction with acetone-$CHCl_3$ (1+9). Evap solv. at room temp. and observe in dark under longwave UV light. Look for aflatoxin B_1 at intersection of projected imaginary lines from std aflatoxin B_1 spots in side channels across each direction of development. If aflatoxin B_1 is thought to be present, compare plates with and without internal std. For pos. samples, aflatoxin B_1 from sample plus added internal std are perfectly superimposed, combination spot fluorescence is more intense than that of sample or 1 ng ref. std alone, and no. of spots on both plates is same.

If aflatoxin B_1 is present, quantitate visually as in **26.031** or by densitometry as follows: Carefully cover sample plate with clean glass plate to avoid damage to silica gel layer. Sep. the 2 plates, if necessary, with narrow strips of masking tape placed along plate edges. Mark aflatoxin B_1 spot from sample by placing small piece of masking tape with lines 1 cm apart parallel to direction to be scanned and ca 1 cm removed from aflatoxin B_1 spot. Select direction of scan to coincide with long dimension of aflatoxin B_1 spot. Scan stds as in **26.059**; then position aflatoxin B_1 sample spot, guided by markings on masking tape, and scan. Alternative methods for locating aflatoxin B_1 spots, some of which obviate need to cover plate, may also be used. Check instrumental response of the 3 std spots for linearity by plotting response against concn or by performing ratio calcn. Calc. μg aflatoxin B_1/kg as in **26.059(*c*)**.

26.075 ***Confirmation of Identity***

Occasionally, blue fluorescent spots appear which can easily be mistaken for aflatoxin B_1. Therefore, chem. confirmation of identity of toxin from all pos. samples is essential. Spot ext equiv. to 9 g eggs for 2-dimensional chromatgy as in **26.074** (*see* Fig. **26:01**). Spot 3 μL aflatoxin B_1 std soln in each of 2 ref. channels, 1 for each direction of development. Add 2 μL trifluoroacetic acid (TFA) to each sample and std aflatoxin B_1 spot on plate, using glass capillary pipet, and let stand in dark 5 min at room temp. Dry in forced-draft oven 10 min at ca 45° or blow warm air (temp. of air at plate surface, 35–40°) 10 min from 30 cm above plate. (Hot air blower, Master Appliance Corp., 2512-18th St, Racine, WI 53403, or hair dryer, is convenient.) Let plate cool, and develop in first direction with anhyd. Et ether-MeOH-H_2O (96+3+1). Dry in forced-draft oven 1 min at 50°, cool, and develop in second direction with $CHCl_3$-acetone-isopropanol (85+12.5+2.5). Examine chromatogram. For pos. confirmation of identity of aflatoxin B_1, look for formation of new blue fluorescent spot, aflatoxin B_{2a}, in sample at R_f ca 0.3 positioned at intersection of imaginary lines projected from ref. stds perpendicularly across direction of each development. For most eggs, yellow fluorescent spot is present with R_f only slightly different from that of aflatoxin B_{2a} and should not be confused with aflatoxin B_{2a} spot to give erroneous pos. confirmation.

Identification of Aflatoxin B_1 by Derivative Formation (*14*)
Official First Action

26.076 ***Apparatus***

(**a**) *Chromatographic tubes.—See* **26.001(d)**, 22 × 300 mm.

(**b**) *Thin layer plate scraper.*—(Fig. **26:02**.) Adapt from sealing tube with fritted disk (Corning Glass Works No. 39580, 30 M, or equiv.).

(**c**) *Vials.*—½, 1, and 4 dram, screw cap (Kimble Products No. 60910-L, but foil-lined, or equiv.).

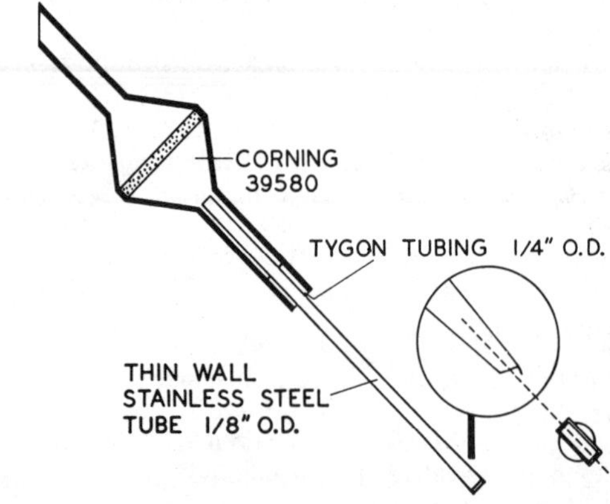

FIG. 26:02—Plate scraper for removing adsorbent from TLC plates

(**d**) *Micro bell jar with suction side arm.*—Corning Glass Works 6880, or equiv.

(**e**) *Thin layer chromatographic apparatus.*—*See* **26.001(k)**.

(**f**) *Pipets.*—Pasteur disposable.

(**g**) *Distilling apparatus.*—All-glass ₮ 24/40 joints, with one 250 mL r-b flask; two 100 mL r-b flasks; Claisen distilling head-condenser; and flask adapter with side arm for drying tube attachment.

26.077 ***Extraction***

See **26.029(a)** and (**b**). Sample ext should contain ≥2 μg aflatoxin B_1. If preparatory TLC is being used to obtain material for bioassay, **26.084–26.089**, aflatoxin B_1 in ext should be ≥30 μg.

26.078 ***Column Cleanup***

Proceed as in **26.030(a)** and (**b**), if addnl cleanup is needed for preparatory TLC.

26.079 ***Preparative TLC***

Prep. plates and use TLC technic as in **26.031**.

Dissolve residue from column cleanup in 250 μL $CHCl_3$. Transfer $CHCl_3$ soln to origin line of TLC plate, using 10 μL per spot at 5 mm spot intervals. About 1 cm beyond each spot at either end, place 5 μL spot of resolution ref. std which will also serve for locating line of aflatoxin B_1 spots.

Develop plate and examine. Expose plate to lowest intensity UV light required to see fluorescent spots. Keep time and intensity of irradiation by UV light at min. With needle, mark off area contg aflatoxin B_1. Collect silica gel from marked off area, using suction to pull coating loosened by plate scraper into filter portion of device. Elute aflatoxin from silica gel by swirling with six 5 mL portions MeOH-$CHCl_3$ (1+2). Use filter bell to pull MeOH-$CHCl_3$ thru fritted glass into 50 mL erlenmeyer by suction. Evap. solv. to dryness on steam bath under N stream. Dissolve residue in enough benzene-CH_3CN (98+2) to give estd aflatoxin B_1 concn of 1 μg/mL.

Det. purity and amt of aflatoxin B_1 in residue as in **26.031(c)** and (**d**). If spots other than aflatoxin B_1 are present, repeat preparative TLC until aflatoxin B_1 is chromatgc pure. Est. amt of aflatoxin B_1 collected by comparison with spots of TLC std. Calc. aflatoxin B_1 from equation:

$$\mu g = (S \times Y \times V)/(X \times 1000),$$

where symbols are same as in **26.031(d)**.

Use residue soln for prepn of derivatives by **26.080**.

26.080 ***Preparation of Derivatives***

Transfer ext contg 1 μg aflatoxin B_1 to 1 dram vial, remove $CHCl_3$ by evapn under N on steam bath, and dissolve residue in 1.0 mL benzene-CH_3CN (98+2). Transfer vol. benzene-CH_3CN soln calcd to contain 0.25 μg aflatoxin B_1 to 2 sep. 0.5 dram vials. Add 100 μL H_2O and 1 drop HCl to vial 1 and 250 μL Ac_2O and 1 drop HCl to vial 2. Use disposable pipets for adding drops. Close vials with Teflon or Al foil-lined caps, shake both vials vigorously, and heat 10 min on steam bath with occasional agitation. Evap. to dryness on steam bath under N.

For controls, prep. 2 derivatives, as above, using 0.1 μg portions aflatoxin B_1 from std soln, **26.011**.

26.081 ***Thin Layer Chromatography***

Dissolve each derivative in the 4 vials in 20 μL benzene-CH_3CN (98+2). Using 10 μL syringe, transfer 10 μL of each derivative soln to origin spots at ca 2 cm intervals on activated TLC plate in following sequence: vial 1 reaction product, vial 1 control, vial 2 reaction product, vial 2 control, 20 ng presumptive aflatoxin from original ext, 20 ng unmodified std aflatoxin B_1, and resolution ref. std.

Develop plate as in **26.031(b)**.

Reactions should produce *dominant* characteristic fluorescent spots. R_f values for these spots fluctuate; compare with derivatives prepd from std B_1.

Acid-catalyzed reaction with H_2O produces single, characteristic spot at R_f ca 10% of that of unreacted aflatoxin.

Acid-catalyzed reaction with Ac_2O produces 2 characteristic spots of ca equal size but of different intensity, migrating close to or slightly behind aflatoxin B_1–G_2 area. Lower R_f spot is brighter of the two.

26.082 ***Record***

Illuminate developed plate with longwave UV lamp used for viewing. Photograph plate, using 200 (ASA) speed Polaroid black and white film. Operate camera with Kodak 3A lens filter, or equiv., cutting off all light below 380 nm, and lens opening of *f*/4.6 and shutter speed of 5 sec, or other combination of lens opening and shutter speed which produces proper exposure (e.g., 2000 (ASA) speed Polaroid film, 0.5 sec exposure, *f*/4.6). Cover developed area of plate with black mask, add legend strip to identify each spot, and superimpose legend on original picture by double exposure, using white light for second exposure.

26.083 ***Identification of Aflatoxin by Derivative Formation on TLC Plate (15)—Official First Action***

Divide silica gel plate, **26.031(a)**, in 2 equal vertical sections by scoring thick line down plate. Cover one section with clean glass plate. On uncovered side, spot two 1–10 μL aliquots of sample ext prepd for TLC contg 0.5–5 ng aflatoxin B_1 and/or G_1. On 1 of these spots add same amts B_1 and G_1 stds as in sample spot; also place on plate sep. spot contg same amts of these stds. To ext, ext plus stds, and stds spot, add 1 μL trifluoroacetic acid (TFA), and let react 5 min. Blow warm air (temp. of air at plate surface 35–40°) over plate ≥10 min. (Hot air blower, Master Appliance Corp., 2420–18th St, Racine, WI 53403, or hair dryer, is convenient.) All TFA must be removed; otherwise second front forms in TLC. Uncover second section of plate and spot same as first, but do not add TFA.

Develop plate in $CHCl_3$-acetone (85+15) or EtOAc satd with H_2O. Pour 50 mL solv. directly into tank. Place trough or 3 small beakers with H_2O in front of plate. Do not equilibrate.

After development, examine plate under longwave UV light. Unreacted aflatoxin appears near top of plate on section without TFA. Blue fluorescent derivatives (B_{2a} and G_{2a}) appear at R_f ca ¼ that of B_1 and G_1. If R_f of anticipated derivative spots is <0.25, increase polarity of developing solv. and repeat with fresh plate. Presence of aflatoxins B_{2a} and/or G_{2a} in reacted sample ext channel, established by comigration with superimposed stds, is proof of identity of aflatoxin B_1 and/or G_1 in sample ext. Also examine plate under shortwave UV light, which often discloses spurious spots in aflatoxins areas, especially in G areas. Any spot which shows increase in fluorescent intensity under shortwave UV light over that under longwave UV light is not aflatoxin.

Spray plate with H_2SO_4 (1+3), which changes aflatoxin fluorescence from blue or blue-green to yellow. This test only confirms absence of aflatoxins; *i.e.*, spots which do not turn yellow are positively not aflatoxin, whereas many materials other than aflatoxin may give yellow spot with H_2SO_4.

Chicken Embryo Bioassay for Aflatoxin B_1 Toxicity (*16*)
Official Final Action

26.084 ***Apparatus***

(Decontaminate all syringes, needles, vials, and other app. which have been in contact with aflatoxin B_1 by soaking in 5% NaOCl soln before disposal or cleaning.)

(**a**) *Egg candling light*.—60 watt candler (Speed King; Schlueter Co., 112 E Centerway, Janesville, WI 53545, or equiv.).

(**b**) *Drill*.—Dremel Moto-Tool, Model 270 (30,000 rpm) with steel cutter No. 178 (Dremel Mfg. Co., 4915–21st St, Racine, WI 53406). Any drill with comparable speed may be used, but cutter *must* deflect removed shell outwards.

(**c**) *Forceps*.—Dissecting, medium-fine point, curved, 115 mm long (No. 079-392, Curtin Matheson Scientific Co., or equiv.).

(**d**) *Syringe*.—Microburet syringe, equipped to deliver 1–100 μL (Micro-Metric Instrument Co., PO Box 22226, Cleveland, OH 44122, or equiv.).

(**e**) *Needles*.—B-D Yale, 1–1.5" long, 22 to 27 gage (Becton, Dickinson, and Co., or equiv.).

(**f**) *Sealing tape*.—Adhesive-cellophane tape, ½" wide. Scotch brand, or equiv.

(**g**) *Incubator/hatcher*.—Forced-draft, controlled temp. and humidity, with automatic turning (Humidaire Hatchette, 450 egg capacity; Humidaire Incubator Co., 217 W Wayne St, New Madison, OH 45346, or equiv.).

26.085 ***Reagents***

(**a**) *Aflatoxin B_1 std soln*.—10 μg/mL absolute alcohol. *See* **26.004–26.011**. ϵ in absolute alcohol is same as in MeOH.

(**b**) *Hypochlorite soln*.—5% com. soln of NaOCl.

26.086 ***Egg Supply***

Eggs, fertile, from inbred Single-Comb White Leghorn flock (or other strain suitable for research or bioassay). Min. specifications are: (*1*) Nest clean (not dipped); (*2*) candled by supplier to eliminate misplaced and tremulous air cells, blood spots, hair-line cracks or other shell imperfections, and other abnormalities; (*3*) delivered in new cartons and filler flats; (*4*) Pullorum typhoid clean and *Mycoplasma gallisepticum* neg.; (*5*) av. wt $\leqslant$26 but $\geqslant$23 oz/dozen; (*6*) $\leqslant$48 hr laid; (*7*) stored at 60°F and 80% relative humidity prior to delivery; (*8*) fertility $\geqslant$85%; (*9*) feed of supplying flock must not contain any antibiotics, arsenicals, or nitrofurazones, but must be fully fortified to produce strong healthy chicks. Samples of feed must be supplied upon request for check analyses.

26.087 ***General Technic***

Candle eggs and outline clearly with pencil location of air cell. Reject any eggs with imperfections such as those listed under **26.086**(*2*).

Using random selection, divide eggs into groups of required number for each level of samples to be injected. Date and label each egg of all groups with identifying code. Use pencil with No. 3 hardness lead to avoid smearing of markings when handling.

In center of air cell of each egg, drill hole ca 5 mm diam. Remove visible *shell* membrane with forceps (*see* Fig. **26:03**) so that no fragments remain to interfere with introduction of needle.

Using syringe, and needle bent to form 90° angle (*see* Fig. **26: 03**), dispense required amt of sample onto *egg membrane*, being careful not to penetrate membrane. Immediately seal hole with piece of cellophane-adhesive tape large enough to cover hole, but covering as little as possible of remaining air cell. Let eggs remain undisturbed in vertical position (air cell up) ca 1 hr to let material disperse.

Place eggs in incubator trays and load incubator set to maintain temp. and relative humidity (rh) recommended by manufacturer. Optima are 37.4° (99.75°F) and 60% rh. Fumigate incubator immediately after loading, using fumigant and technics recommended by manufacturer of incubator. If automatic

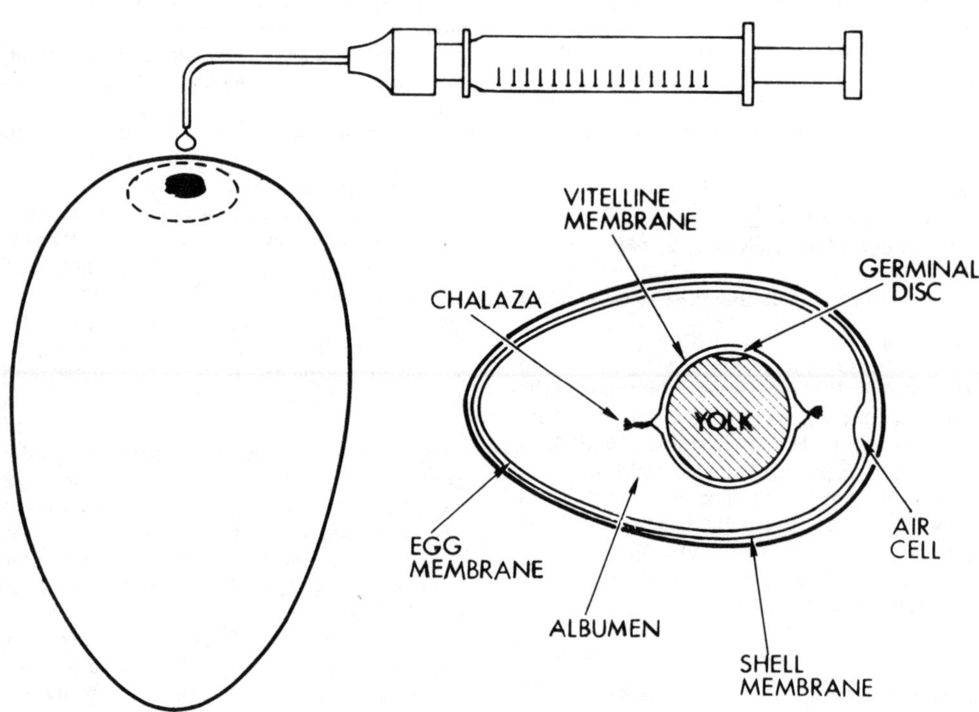

FIG. 26:03—Schematic showing parts of egg and modes of test material introduction

turning is provided, set for turning every 2 hr; if no automatic turning is provided, turn by hand at least twice daily thru 17th day of incubation.

Candle eggs on fourth day, and daily thereafter. Remove clear eggs and dead embryos for opening and examination. Keep record of age at death and appearance of all embryos for all test solns and controls thruout incubation period. On 17th day, place eggs in hatching tray (no further turning necessary), place in hatcher, set at recommended temp. and rh, and fumigate. Let eggs continue hatching and remove after all have hatched and dried (22nd or 23rd day).

Open and examine all unhatched eggs, examine chicks that hatch, and record observations.

26.088 ***Standard Aflatoxin B_1 Dose Response***

Using aflatoxin B_1 std soln, det. dose response for egg supply under experimental conditions that will prevail in future assays:

Using ≥100 eggs/dose level, treat eggs as in **26.087**, at ≥5 dose levels ranging from no effect to 100% mortality. (Altho this may be done as single experiment, it is preferable to do it over period of time, e.g., 25 eggs/level repeated 4 times, or any combination until total of ≥100 eggs/level has been reached.)

Construct dose-response curve (μg–log % mortality), using method of Litchfield and Wilcoxon, *J. Pharmacol. Exp. Therap.* **96**, 99–113(1949). Per cent mortality for each treatment is total of nonviable embryos and unhatched chicks divided by total eggs treated. (Precise LD_{50} and slope may vary depending upon sensitivity of embryos and environmental factors, but no-effect level to 100% mortality may be expected to fall between 0.01 and 0.20 μg/egg; *see* JAOAC **47**, 1003(1964).)

26.089 ***Assay***

(**a**) *Complete protocol*.—For initial assay of system or when new std, new supply of solv., or eggs from new flock are employed. Include ≥30 noninjected controls in all assays to check fertility and hatchability of eggs used, and to monitor incubation conditions.

Prep. ext as in **26.077–26.079**. Dissolve material to be assayed in absolute alcohol to obtain final aflatoxin B_1 concn of 10 μL/mL (test soln), based on chem. analysis. Set up protocol, based on dose response obtained in **26.088**, according to Table **26:05**.

(**b**) *Routine protocol*.—After complete protocol is performed several times to assure system is functioning properly, levels of std and solv. indicated by [b] in Table **26:05** may be omitted. Complete protocol must be performed when there is any change in experimental conditions.

(**c**) *Lower level protocol*.—If insufficient material is available for complete protocol, reduce number of eggs per level and number of levels. Use min. of 2 levels: highest level, to assure some toxic response even if chem. analysis is higher than true value, and 1 of 2 lowest levels. Besides mortality, presence of aflatoxin B_1 is also demonstrated by teratogenic effects occurring in Single Comb White Leghorn embryo after 12 days, severe growth retardation (e.g., 21-day embryo may be as small as normal 12-day embryo), short feet, edema, and hemorrhaging.

Table 26:05 Complete protocol

No. of Eggs	Quantity Injected[a] mL	μg	Expected Mortality, %	Material Injected
≥20	0.020	0.20	100	Test soln
≥20	0.010	0.10	100	Test soln
≥20	0.005	0.05	90	Test soln
≥20	0.0025	0.025	50	Test soln
≥20	0.020	0.20	100	B_1 std soln, 10 μg/mL
≥20[b]	0.010	0.10	100	B_1 std soln, 10 μg/mL
≥20[b]	0.005	0.05	90	B_1 std soln, 10 μg/mL
≥20	0.02		≤20	Absolute alcohol
≥20[b]	0.01		≤10	Absolute alcohol
≥20[b]	0.005		≤10	Absolute alcohol
≥30			≤20	Non-injected controls

[a] Figures given are examples, based on *JAOAC* **47**, 1003(1964).
[b] *See* **26.089(b)**.

AFLATOXIN M_1

(Aflatoxin M_1 is hydroxylated metabolite of aflatoxin B_1, secreted in milk of mammals receiving aflatoxin B_1. It is potential hepatocarcinogen. Handle with same care as other aflatoxins.)

Aflatoxin M_1 in Dairy Products (*17*)—Official Final Action

(*Caution: See* **51.011, 51.039, 51.040, 51.045, 51.046, 51,054, 51.056**, and **51.061**.)

26.090 ***Apparatus***

(**a**) *Explosion-proof blender*.—Waring Model EP-1, or equiv., with 1 L jar and cover.

(**b**) *Chromatographic tubes*.—500 × 22 (id) mm, with Teflon stopcock and glass tip (Kimble 17800 or Corning 2145).

(**c**) *Densitometer*.—*See* **26.001**(**e**).

26.091 ***Reagents***

(**a**) *Solvents*.—Distd-in-glass acetone, benzene, $CHCl_3$, ether (0.01% EtOH), hexane (bp 68–69°), MeOH, and isopropanol.

(**b**) *Lead acetate soln*.—*See* **26.053**(**b**).

(**c**) *Sodium sulfate soln*.—Satd. Dissolve ≥150 g anhyd. Na_2SO_4 in 500 mL H_2O at room temp. Prep. 2–3 days before use to ensure satn.

(**d**) *Diatomaceous earth*.—Hyflo Super-Cel.

(**e**) *Cellulose*.—Whatman CF-11 or CF-1 cellulose powder for column chromatgy. Soak ca 4 hr in hot $CHCl_3$, filter, wash with $CHCl_3$, and air dry. Check each lot for M_1 recovery by adding 1 μg to neg. milk ext and treating as in **26.093–26.094**.

(**f**) *Aflatoxin M_1 std solns*.—Approx. 0.50 μg/mL for visual analysis and 0.10 μg/mL for densitometric analysis. *See* **26.004–26.011**.

26.092 ***Preliminary Purification***

Weigh or measure fluid or powd milk or butter into blender jar and add H_2O as indicated in Table **26:06**. Add ca 10 g diat. earth and 300 mL acetone, and blend 3 min. With cheese, cut into small cubes and add individually to mixt. of acetone, H_2O, and diat. earth. Filter thru folded 32 cm Whatman No. 2V paper, or equiv., into 500 mL graduate.

Transfer 275 mL filtrate to 600 mL beaker contg 20 mL $Pb(OAc)_2$ soln. Rinse graduate with 200 mL H_2O and add rinse to beaker. Stir and let stand ca 5 min for pptn. Add 10 mL satd Na_2SO_4 soln and 10 g diat. earth, stir, and filter thru paper into same 500 mL graduate used above.

Transfer 350 mL filtrate to 500 mL separator, add 100 mL hexane (with annato-colored cheese or butter use ether), and shake vigorously ca 1 min. Let phases sep., and drain lower aq. phase into clean 600 mL beaker. Discard upper ether phase and pour aq. phase back into same separator. Retain beaker for $CHCl_3$ ext. Rinse beaker with 50 mL 5% *NaCl soln*, transfer rinse to separator, and add 100 mL $CHCl_3$. Shake funnel ca 1 min and let phases sep. 2–3 min. Drain lower $CHCl_3$ layer into the 600 mL beaker and re-ext aq. mixt. with addnl 50 mL $CHCl_3$. Combine $CHCl_3$ exts; discard aq. layer, and transfer combined $CHCl_3$ ext back to separator. Rinse beaker with 100 mL 5% NaCl soln, transfer rinse to separator, and wash $CHCl_3$ ext by vigorously shaking 1 min. Drain lower ($CHCl_3$) phase thru ca 5 cm anhyd.

granular Na_2SO_4 in Butt tube or ca 45 g in folded Whatman No. 2V paper into clean 400 mL beaker. Discard aq. phase. Rinse 600 mL beaker twice with $CHCl_3$ and filter rinse thru the Na_2SO_4. Evap. $CHCl_3$ on steam bath under gentle stream of N; do not overheat dry ext (vac. evapn may be used).

26.093 ***Column Chromatography***

Place small glass wool pad in bottom of chromatgc tube, and tamp firmly. Slurry 10 g cellulose powder in ca 70 mL MeOH-H_2O (7+3), pour into column, and wash walls with the aq. MeOH. Drain solv. to top of cellulose, add ca 100 mL hexane, and let ca 50 mL drain thru column. Place small glass wool pad on top of cellulose, and tamp firmly to pack cellulose and prevent channeling. Drain remaining hexane to top of glass wool pad.

Dissolve dry ext, **26.092**, in 1 mL $CHCl_3$, and add 2 mL benzene and 10 mL hexane. Transfer to prepd column, wash sample beaker with ca 5 mL hexane-benzene (3+1), and add wash to column. When sample soln reaches top of glass wool pad, wash column with 150 mL hexane-benzene (3+1) and then 150 mL hexane-ether (2+1), letting first soln drain to top of glass wool pad before adding second. Discard column washes. Elute aflatoxin M_1 (B_1 also, if present) with 200 mL hexane-$CHCl_3$ (1+1), and collect eluate in clean 250 mL beaker. Evap. solv. to near dryness on steam bath (vac. evapn may be used), transfer quant. with $CHCl_3$ to small vial (ca 1–2 drams), **26.001(m)**, and evap. to dryness on steam bath under stream of N.

26.094 ***Thin Layer Chromatography***

Add 100 μL $CHCl_3$ to dry sample residue in vial, cap, and shake vigorously ca 1 min, preferably on Vortex shaker. Sample vol. is sufficient for *either* visual or densitometric analysis, but not both.

a) *Visual analysis.*—Proceed as in **26.031(a)**, **(b)** (except spot two 20 μL sample spots and 2, 4, 6, 8, and 10 μL M_1 std, 0.5 μg/mL; spot 4 μL M_1 std on top of one sample spot as internal std; and develop ca 12 cm (ca 50 min) with isopropanol-acetone-$CHCl_3$ (5+10+85)), and **26.031(d)**, where W = vol. or wt milk product represented by final ext for TLC, Table **26:06**.

(b) *Densitometric analysis.*—Spot three 20 μL sample spots and two 20 μL M_1 std spots, 0.1 μg/mL. Spot third 20 μL std spot on top of one 20 μL sample spot as internal std. Develop plate as in **(a)**. Examine plate under longwave UV light to confirm presence or absence of M_1 in sample. If M_1 is present, scan plate as in **26.059(c)**. W = vol. or wt milk product represented by final ext for TLC, Table **26:06**.

Table 26:06 Data for Preparation of Sample of Milk Products

Milk Product	Sample Vol. or Wt	H_2O Added Before Extn,[a] mL	Sample Equiv. in Final Ext[b]
Fluid milk	100 mL	10	47.6 mL
Powdered milk	10 g	100	4.8 g
Blue cheese	50 g	80	23.8 g
Ricotta cheese	50 g	65	23.8 g
Cheddar cheese	50 g	80	23.8 g
Butter	50 g	90	23.8 g

[a] H_2O calcd to provide const vol. of 100 mL per sample; mL H_2O added = [100 − (W' × M/100)], where W' = wt or vol. sample extd and M = % H_2O from values obtained from USDA Handbook No. 8, 1963.

[b] Values represent sample wt, W, in calcns, based on aliquot factors used in method, (275/400) × (350/505) × sample size.

26.095 Confirmation of Aflatoxin M_1 Identity by Derivative Formation and TLC (*17*)—Official First Action

Place ca 30 ng aflatoxin M_1, obtained by either preparative TLC, **26.079**, or by column chromatgy, **26.093**, and 30 ng M_1 std in 1 dram vials with Teflon liners, and evap. to dryness under slow stream of N. Add 100 μL freshly prepd pyridine-Ac_2O (1+1), cap vial, and mix vigorously. Let stand 15 min at room temp. Evap. to dryness on steam bath under N. Dissolve in 60 μL $CHCl_3$ by mixing vigorously.

Spot 20 μL acetate derivative from sample and from std and 1–2 ng aflatoxin M_1 on TLC plate. Reserve remainder for hemiacetal formation. Develop plate ca 1 hr at 25° with acetone-$CHCl_3$ (1+9) in unlined, unequilibrated tank. Examine plate under longwave UV light (365 nm). Aflatoxin M_1 appears at R_f = ca 0.11 and the acetate at ca 0.55.

Evap. reserved soln under N. Add 100 μL H_2O and 1–2 drops HCl. Cap vial, shake vigorously, heat 10 min on steam bath, and evap. to dryness on steam bath under N. Dissolve residue in 40 μL $CHCl_3$. Spot 20 μL sample hemiacetal derivative, 20 μL std derivative prepd similarly, and 1–2 ng aflatoxin M_1. Develop plate in isopropanol-acetone-$CHCl_3$ (1+1+8) and examine for hemiacetal derivative. Aflatoxin M_1 appears at R_f = ca 0.70 and the hemiacetal at ca 0.15.

OCHRATOXINS

(Ochratoxin A causes kidney and liver damage in some animals. Observe precautions given in introductory statement of this chapter.)

Barley (*18*)—Official First Action

(Quant. for ochratoxin A, qual. for B and for esters of A and B. *Caution: See* **51.011**, **51.016**, **51.045**, **51.056**, and **51.061**.)

26.096 ***Principle***

Ochratoxin acids and esters are extd from barley by $CHCl_3$-aq. H_3PO_4. Acids are entrapped on aq. $NaHCO_3$-diat. earth column, esters and fat are removed with hexane and $CHCl_3$, and acids are eluted with HCOOH-$CHCl_3$. Esters are isolated by entrapment on MeOH-aq. $NaHCO_3$-diat. earth column, fats are removed with hexane-benzene, and esters are eluted with HCOOH-hexane-benzene. Compds are detd from fluorescence intensity on thin layer chromatograms.

All glassware must be free of alk. soap or detergent residues to avoid loss of the toxins from neut. solv. by salt formation, pptn, and/or adsorption onto glassware.

26.097 ***Apparatus***

(a) *Chromatographic tubes.*—700 × 17 (od) mm and 350 × 25 mm, with stopcocks.

(b) *Buchner funnels.*—Glass, 9 cm diam. fitted with Whatman GF/B glass fiber paper, or equiv.; 24 cm diam. fitted with Whatman No. 1 paper, or equiv.

(c) *Thin layer chromatographic apparatus.—See* **26.001(k)**.

(d) *Densitometer.—See* **26.001(e)**.

26.098 ***Reagents***

See **26.002(b)**, plus the following:

(a) *Diatomaceous earth.*—Soak ca 900 g acid-washed Celite 545 overnight in MeOH. Filter thru double thickness Whatman No. 1 paper in 24 cm buchner, wash with 8 L H_2O, and dry 12 hr at 150°.

(b) *Silica gel for thin layer chromatography.—See* **26.002(d)**. Test adsorbent for resolution and fading of ochratoxins as in **26.002(d)**, using ochratoxins A and B and their Et esters as in **26.102**. Develop with benzene-MeOH-HOAc, **(h)**(*1*). TLC spots should be round or slightly elliptical, well sepd, in R_f range 0.4–0.9, and located away from primary and secondary solv. fronts. Ochratoxins on occasion fade rapidly on some silica gel plates, especially when exposed to ≥60% humidity. Protect plate from humidity during spotting by placing in chamber under N or under stream of warm air from hair dryer, or by covering with clean glass plate, using tape on sides as spacers. After development, dry plate 15 min at 50° and immediately cover with clean glass plate, using tape on sides as spacers, for protection during scanning densitometry.

(**c**) *Solvents*.—ACS, in glass: $CHCl_3$, hexane, HOAc, MeOH, HCOOH (90%), and H_3PO_4 (85%).

(**d**) *Methanolic sodium bicarbonate soln*.—Dissolve 0.3 g $NaHCO_3$ in 30 mL H_2O and add 70 mL MeOH.

(**e**) *Alcoholic sodium bicarbonate soln*.—Dissolve 6.0 g $NaHCO_3$ in 100 mL H_2O and add 20 mL alcohol.

(**f**) *Formic acid-benzene-hexane soln*.—Shake 100 mL benzene-hexane (20+80) with 10 mL H_2O-MeOH (30+70), let layers sep., and discard lower layer. Shake upper layer with 5 mL HCOOH, let sep., and discard lower layer.

(**g**) *Boron trifluoride*.—14% (w/w). Bubble gaseous BF_3 into chilled alcohol. (*Caution:* Perform in hood. Avoid contact with skin, eyes, and respiratory tract.)

(**h**) *Developing solvents*.—(*1*) *Benzene-methanol-acetic acid (18+1+1)*.—Combine 2 vols MeOH-HOAc (1+1) with 18 vols benzene. Adjust benzene:(MeOH-HOAc) ratio, if necessary, to produce development described in **26.102**. Decrease benzene to increase R_f. (*2*) *Hexane-acetone-acetic acid (18+2+1)*.—Combine 3 vols acetone-HOAc (2+1) with 18 vols hexane. Adjust hexane:(acetone-HOAc) ratio, if necessary, to produce development described in **26.102**. Decrease hexane to increase R_f.

(**i**) *Ochratoxin std solns*.—*See* **26.004–26.011**. Prep. original solns, each ca 40 μg/mL, in HOAc-benzene (1+99). Det. concn as in **26.004–26.010**, using following information:

Ochratoxin	λ max., nm	MW	ε
A	333	403	5550
B	320	369	6000
A Et ester	333	431	6200
B Et ester	320	397	6500

Combine portions of ochratoxin solns and dil. with benzene to give concn in range 1–5 μg/mL for each ochratoxin.

(**j**) *Purified cotton*.—Wash 50 g absorbent cotton in beaker with 1 L $CHCl_3$. Decant soln., evap. residual $CHCl_3$, and store cotton in closed container.

26.099 ***Preparation and Extraction of Sample***

Prep. entire sample as in **26.003**.

Weigh 50 g into 500 mL g-s erlenmeyer. Add 25 mL 0.1*M* H_3PO_4 and 250 mL $CHCl_3$, and secure stopper with masking tape. Shake 30 min on wrist-action shaker, **26.001(o)**, and filter thru glass fiber paper, covered with ca 10 g diat. earth, on 9 cm buchner.

26.100 ***Separation of Ochratoxin Acids***

(**a**) *Removal of esters*.—Place plug of purified cotton, (**j**), in bottom of 700 × 17 mm chromatgc tube. Mix 2.0 g diat. earth with 1 mL *1.25% $NaHCO_3$ soln* in 50 mL beaker. Add to chromatgc tube and tamp firmly. Mix 50 mL sample ext with 40 mL hexane, and add to column. Reserve remainder of $CHCl_3$ sample ext for confirmation of identity, **26.103**. Elute at max. flow rate; then elute with 75 mL $CHCl_3$. Combine eluates, evap. to dryness on steam bath, and reserve for ochratoxin ester sepn, **26.101**.

(**b**) *Removal of acids*.—Elute ochratoxins A and B with 75 mL freshly prepd HCOOH-$CHCl_3$ (1+99), and collect in 250 mL erlenmeyer. Immediately add 2 boiling chips, **26.002(b)**, evap. nearly to dryness on steam bath, and quant. transfer residue to 15 mL conical centrf. tube with $CHCl_3$. Evap. to dryness under gentle stream of N on steam bath. (*Note:* Delay in evapn of HCOOH-$CHCl_3$ may result in loss of ochratoxins.) Reserve ext for TLC, **26.102**.

26.101 ***Separation of Ochratoxin Esters***

Prep. column as in **26.100(a)**, using 350 × 25 mm chromatgc tube, 2.5 mL methanolic $NaHCO_3$ soln, (**d**), and 4 g diat. earth. Dissolve residue, **26.100(a)**, in 50 mL hexane and add to column. Rinse extn vessel with each subsequent solv. in turn; add rinses to column. Force eluting solvs thru column at convenient rate with compressed gas at 1–2 psi (6.9–13.8 kPa). Do *not* let liq. fall below top of column. Elute with 50 mL benzene-hexane (1+9) previously equilibrated with 2.5 mL methanolic $NaHCO_3$ soln (discard). Then elute with 100 mL HCOOH-benzene-hexane mixt. Immediately evap. eluate to dryness, quant. transfer to conical centrf. tube with $CHCl_3$, evap. to dryness under gentle stream of N on steam bath, and reserve for TLC, **26.102**.

26.102 ***Thin Layer Chromatography***

(**a**) *Visual analysis*.—Proceed as in **26.031**, with following modifications: Use silica gel, **26.098(b)**, and dissolve ext from **26.100(b)** in 750 μL HOAc-benzene (1+99). Spot 3, 5, 7.5, and 10 μL. On same plate, spot 10 μL ext superimposed with 10 ng each ochratoxin A and B std solns as internal std. Also spot 5, 7.5, and 10 μL ochratoxin A and B std solns. Develop plate to solv. stop line, but <90 min, with benzene-MeOH-HOAc (18+1+1) in unlined, unequilibrated tank. Remove plate, let solv. evap. at room temp., and view in dark under long- and shortwave UV lamps. Ochratoxins A and B should be found in R_f range 0.4–0.8 with ochratoxin A above B, typically at 0.65 and 0.5, resp. Ochratoxin A fluoresces most intensely under longwave UV light, while ochratoxin B is brightest under shortwave light. Examine pattern from sample for fluorescent spots having R_f values close to those of stds and with similar appearance. Compare fluorescence intensities of ochratoxin A spots in sample with those of std spots, and det. std and sample which match most closely, interpolating, if necessary. If sample concn is outside range of stds, conc. or dil. sample ext and rechromatograph. Calc. concn of ochratoxin A in μg/kg. Spray plate with alc. $NaHCO_3$ soln, (**e**), dry at room temp., and view in dark under longwave UV light. Fluorescence should have changed from greenish blue to blue and increased in intensity. Again est. ochratoxin A in sample. In case of disagreement, use est. obtained before spraying.

Proceed with TLC of ochratoxin A and B esters from **26.101** on sep. plate in same manner as above for acids, and develop plate with hexane-acetone-HOAc (18+2+1). R_f value of ochratoxin A ester is ca 0.5, above ochratoxin B ester.

(**b**) *Densitometric analysis*.—Prep. and develop TLC plate as in **26.098(b)** and **26.102(a)**. In sep. channels, spot ≥4 spots with increasing amts std ochratoxin A in range 3–10 ng/spot. Scan TLC plate with densitometer according to instructions of manufacturer. Optimum spectral settings for ochratoxin A are excitation 310–340 nm; emission, 440–475.

Plot std curve from instrument response, drawing line thru origin to check for linearity and system performance. Dissolve sample ext in 0.5 mL HOAc-benzene (1+99) and spot ≥2 replicates of ≥3 μL sample ext and std solns. Amt sample spotted must contain amt ochratoxin close to or within range of std curve.

26.103 ***Confirmation of Identity of Ochratoxins A and B by Formation of Ethyl Esters***

Purify reserved $CHCl_3$ ext as in **26.100(a)** and **(b)**. Dissolve portion of ext, **26.100(b)**, contg equiv. of ≥10 g sample, in 5 mL $CHCl_3$ in 25 mL erlenmeyer. Into sep. 25 mL erlenmeyer, add 250 ng ochratoxin A and B std soln. (This step may be omitted when ester stds are available.) Add 10 mL 14% BF_3 in alcohol. Heat to bp and hold on steam bath 5 min. Transfer to 125 mL separator contg 30 mL H_2O. Ext with three 10 mL portions $CHCl_3$. Combine $CHCl_3$ exts, wash with three 10 mL portions H_2O, evap. to dryness, quant. transfer to 15 mL centrf. tube with $CHCl_3$, and evap. to dryness under gentle stream of N. Dissolve residue in 250 µL HOAc-benzene (1+99) and proceed as in **26.102(a)**, modified as follows:

Spot 10 µL unmodified ext, 10 µL esterified sample ext, 10 µL std ochratoxin esters, and 10 µL esterified sample ext plus 10 µL std ochratoxin esters. Develop plate with benzene-MeOH-HOAc, **26.098(h)**(*1*). Examine plate under long- and shortwave UV light. R_f of ochratoxin A ester is greater than that of ochratoxin B ester, typically 0.8 and 0.7, resp. Et esters have much higher R_f values than ochratoxins A and B, but approx. same fluorescence. For pos. confirmation, presumptive ochratoxin A or B spots should be absent after esterfication and spots at R_f values of esters should be present.

Photograph TLC plate as in **26.082**, using long- and shortwave UV light, *f*/8, and 5 sec exposure.

Green Coffee (*19*)—Official First Action

26.104 ***Principle***

Toxin is extd from ground, green coffee beans with $CHCl_3$. Ochratoxin A is entrapped on basic diat. earth, interferences are removed with hexane and $CHCl_3$, and ochratoxin A is eluted with benzene-HOAc. Ochratoxin A is detd from fluorescent intensity on thin layer chromatograms.

Observe precautions of **26.096**.

26.105 ***Apparatus***

(**a**) *Chromatographic tubes*.—*See* **26.001(d)**.
(**b**) *Thin layer chromatographic apparatus*.—*See* **26.001(k)**.
(**c**) *Vials*.—*See* **26.001(m)**.
(**d**) *Buchner funnel*.—Glass, 90 mm, fitted with Reeve Angel glass fiber filter paper, or equiv.

26.106 ***Reagents***

(**a**) *Solvents*.—ACS grade in glass: HOAc, benzene, $CHCl_3$, MeOH.
(**b**) *Alcoholic sodium bicarbonate soln*.—*See* **26.098(e)**.
(**c**) *Bicarbonate-diatomaceous earth mixture*.—Add 25 mL 5% aq. $NaHCO_3$ soln to 50 g acid-washed diat. earth, **26.098(a)**, and mix well. Can be stored 2–3 weeks in tightly closed container.
(**d**) *Ochratoxin A std soln*.—1 µg/mL. *See* **26.098(i)**.
(**e**) *Silica gel for thin layer chromatography*.—*See* **26.098(b)**.

26.107 ***Preparation and Extraction of Sample***

Prep. entire sample as in **26.003**.

Weigh 25 g sample into 500 mL g-s erlenmeyer. Add 12.5 mL H_2O, mix to wet sample, and add 125 mL $CHCl_3$. Shake 30 min on mech. shaker, **26.001(o)**, and filter thru 18.5 cm glass fiber paper in powder funnel or thru 9 cm glass fiber paper, using buchner.

26.108 ***Column Chromatography***

Place glass wool plug in bottom of chromatgc tube. Weigh 6 g $NaHCO_3$-diat. earth mixt., transfer to tube, and tamp firmly. Add 50 mL $CHCl_3$ ext to column, and elute until meniscus reaches top of column. Wash with 70 mL hexane followed by 70 mL $CHCl_3$, discarding washings. Elute with 100 mL HOAc-benzene (2+98), collecting eluate in 125 mL erlenmeyer. Evap. to near dryness on steam bath under N, and transfer quant. with $CHCl_3$ to 4 dram vial. Evap. under N, and add 500 µL HOAc-benzene (1+99). Shake vigorously to dissolve, preferably with Vortex shaker.

26.109 ***Thin Layer Chromatography***

Proceed as in **26.102(a)** except that toluene-EtOAc-formic acid (5+4+1) is preferred developing solv. Alternatively, use benzene-MeOH-HOAc (18+1+1), but 2 sequential developments with this solv. may be necessary to obtain adequate sepn from background.

26.110 ***Confirmation***

Spray plate with alc. $NaHCO_3$ soln or alc. $AlCl_3$ soln (20 g $AlCl_3.6H_2O$ in 100 mL alcohol) or expose plate to NH_3 vapor. Fluorescence of ochratoxin under longwave UV light changes to bright blue and increases in intensity.

See also **26.103**.

PATULIN

(*Caution:* Patulin is antibiotic with demonstrated mutagenicity and unknown toxicity to man. Handle with caution as possibly deleterious substance)

Apple Juice (*20*)—Official First Action

26.111 ***Principle***

Apple juice is extd with EtOAc and ext is cleaned up on silica gel column. Patulin is detected in eluate, after concn, by TLC, by spraying with 3-methyl-2-benzothiazolinone hydrazone.HCl soln. Limit of determination is ca 20 µg/L.

26.112 ***Apparatus***

See **26.001(d)**, **(g)**, **(i)**, **(l)**, and **(m)** plus following:
(**a**) *Beakers*.—Glass, 250 mL with 25 mL graduations.
(**b**) *Thin layer chromatographic apparatus*.—*See* **26.001(k)**, plus the following: spray bottle, 125 mL flask, to produce fine, even spray (Kontes Glass Co., No. K-422500); sample streaker for preparative TLC (Applied Science Laboratories, Inc., No. 17700, or equiv.).
(**c**) *Analytical microbalance*.—*See* **26.004(b)**.

26.113 ***Reagents***

(**a**) *Solvents*.—Benzene, EtOAc; redistil and discard forerun.
(**b**) *Sodium sulfate*.—*See* **26.002(e)**.
(**c**) *Silica gel*.—(*1*) *For column chromatography*.—E. Merck silica gel 60, 0.063–0.2 mm, **26.027(a)**. (*2*) *For thin layer chromatography*.—Adsorbosil-5, **26.002(d)**; E. Merck silica gel G precoated Uniplate (Analtech, Inc., 75 Blue Hen Dr, Newark, DE 19711); or equiv.
(**d**) *Patulin std soln*.—(*1*) *From crystals*.—Weigh ca 0.5 mg pure cryst. patulin (available from Makor Chemicals Ltd., POB 6570, Jerusalem, Israel) to nearest 0.001 mg and dissolve in $CHCl_3$ to 10 µg/mL. (*2*) *From stock soln in* $CHCl_3$.—Withdraw vol., using precision syringe, and dil. with $CHCl_3$ to prep. concn of 10 µg/mL.

Using precison syringe, withdraw 5.0 mL std soln (10 μg/mL) into 4 dram vial and evap. to dryness under N. Immediately add 5.0 mL absolute alcohol. Record UV spectrum of patulin soln from 350 to 250 nm against absolute alcohol in ref. cell. Det. concn of patulin soln from A at wavelength of max. absorption, ca 275 nm, using following equation (1 cm cell pathlength): μg patulin/mL = $(A \times MW \times 1000 \times CF)/\epsilon$, where CF = correction factor obtained in **26.004(a)**, MW = 154, and ϵ = 14,600.

Store std and stock solns at 0° in g-s vol. flasks, wrapped tightly in Al foil. Bring std to room temp. before use; do not remove Al foil from flask until contents have reached room temp. Do not store std as thin film from evapd soln because of decomposition of patulin.

(**e**) *3-Methyl-2-benzothiazolinone hydrazone (MBTH) hydrochloride soln.*—Dissolve 0.5 g MBTH.HCl.H_2O (Aldrich Chemical Co., Inc., No. 12,973-9) in 100 mL H_2O. Store in refrigerator and prep. fresh every 3 days.

26.114 ***Extraction***

Analyze sample immediately after opening can or bottle. Vigorously ext 50 mL sample with three 50 mL portions EtOAc in 250 mL separator. Dry combined exts (upper phase) ca 30 min over 20 g anhyd. Na_2SO_4; break up initially formed lumps with glass rod. Decant into graduated 250 mL beaker. Wash Na_2SO_4 with two 25 mL portions EtOAc and add to ext. Evap. to <25 mL (*Caution:* Do not evap. to dryness) on steam bath under gentle stream of N. Let cool to room temp., adjust vol. to 25 mL mark, if necessary, with EtOAc, and dil. to 100 mL with benzene.

26.115 ***Column Chromatography***

Place glass wool plug firmly in bottom of chromatgc tube contg ca 10 mL benzene and add slurry of 15 g silica gel in benzene. Wash sides of tube with benzene, let silica gel settle, and drain solv. to top of adsorbent. Carefully add sample ext to column, drain to top of silica gel, and discard eluate. Elute patulin with 200 mL benzene-EtOAc (75+25) at ca 10 mL/min. Evap. eluate to near dryness under N on steam bath.

Quant. transfer residue to 4 dram vial with $CHCl_3$ and evap. to dryness under N on steam bath. Immediately dissolve residue in 500 μL $CHCl_3$ with aid of Vortex mixer. Seal with polyethylene stopper. If TLC is not performed on same day, store soln in freezer to avoid evapn of solv.

26.116 ***Thin Layer Chromatography***

(**a**) *Preparation of plates.—See* **26.031(a)**.

(**b**) *Preliminary thin layer chromatography.*—Puncture polyethylene stopper to accommodate needle of 10 μL syringe. Spot two 5 μL spots and one 10 μL spot of ext soln and 1, 3, 5, 7, and 10 μL spots of std soln on imaginary line 4 cm from bottom edge of TLC plate. Spot 5 μL std soln on top of one 5 μL ext spot. Develop plate with toluene-EtOAc-90% formic acid (5+4+1) contained in V-shaped metal trough inside unlined but equilibrated tank, with silica gel layer facing max. tank vol. When solv. front reaches 4 cm from top of plate, remove plate from tank and dry in air, preferably in hood.

Spray plate with 0.5% MBTH soln until layer appears wet; then heat ca 15 min in 130° oven. Examine plate in transmitted and reflected longwave UV light. Patulin appears as yellow-brown fluorescent spot at R_f ca 0.5. One μL std soln (10 μg/mL) should be just detectable. Patulin may also be seen as yellow spot under visible light if ≥0.05 μg.

Compare sample chromatogram patterns with that contg internal std. Fluorescent spot in sample thought to be patulin must have R_f value and color identical to patulin std spot when unknown spot and internal std spot are superimposed. Spot from sample and internal std combined should be more intense than either sample or std alone. Visually compare fluorescence intensity of patulin spots in sample and std. To aid in detn, move plate away from lamp to attenuate UV light so that any particular pair of spots can be compared at extinction. If intensity of sample spot is between those of 2 std spots, interpolate or rechromatograph, spotting appropriate vols of sample and std soln to obtain closer est. If weakest sample spot is too intense to match stds, dil. sample ext and rechromatograph.

$$\mu g\ Patulin/L = (S \times Y \times V)/50 \times X,$$

where S = μL std equal to unknown, Y = concn of std in μg/mL, V = μL of final diln of sample ext, and X = μL sample ext spotted giving fluorescent intensity equal to S (std).

Sprayed TLC plate will slowly turn blue on standing in air for few hr, unless covered by second glass plate.

(**c**) *Preparative thin layer chromatography.*—Streak ext on TLC plate. Spot patulin std and 10 μL ext plus internal std at side of plate. Scribe line between std and sample area to prevent cross contamination of sample area. Develop plate as in (**b**). Dry in air. Cover most of plate with second glass plate and spray stds and streak ca 1 cm wide with 0.5% MBTH soln; then heat 15 min at 130°. Det. position of patulin under longwave UV light. Remove unsprayed patulin band with suction and filter device, **26.076(b)**. Elute patulin from silica gel with ca 10 mL $CHCl_3$-acetone (2+1), using slight air or N pressure. Evap. eluate to dryness in 4 dram vial and immediately dissolve residue in 100 μL $CHCl_3$.

(**d**) *Confirmatory thin layer chromatography.*—Spot 10–20 μL soln from (**c**) and 5 μL patulin std for confirmatory TLC in each of following 3 solv. systems, using unlined, unequilibrated developing tank: hexane-anhyd. ether (1+3), $CHCl_3$-MeOH (95+5), and $CHCl_3$-acetone (90+10). Approx. R_f values of patulin are 0.4, 0.4, and 0.5, resp.

STERIGMATOCYSTIN

(Sterigmatocystin is carcinogen. Observe precautions given in introductory statement of this chapter.)

Barley and Wheat (*21*)—Official First Action

26.117 ***Apparatus***

(**a**) *Thin layer chromatographic apparatus.—See* **26.001(k)** and **26.076(b)**.

(**b**) *Chromatographic tubes.*—22× 300 mm, **26.001(d)**.

26.118 ***Reagents***

(**a**) *Solvents.*—ACS, in glass: CH_3CN, hexane, benzene, alcohol, MeOH, HOAc, EtOAc, cyclohexane, acetone, pyridine, and Ac_2O.

(**b**) *Potassium hydroxide soln.*—20%. Dissolve 20 g KOH pellets in 100 mL MeOH.

(**c**) *Aluminum chloride soln.*—20%. Dissolve 20 g $AlCl_3.6H_2O$ in 100 mL alcohol.

(**d**) *Silica gel.*—(*1*) *For column chromatography.*— 0.063–0.2 mm (E. Merck, thru Brinkmann Instruments, Inc., or equiv.). (*2*) *For thin layer chromatography.*—Adsorbosil-1 (Applied Science Laboratories, Inc.), or equiv.

(**e**) *Sterigmatocystin std solns.*—Det. chromatgc purity of cryst. sterigmatocystin as in **26.010**. (*1*) *Qualitative R_f reference std soln.*—Approx. 100 μg/mL benzene. (*2*) *Quantitative reference std soln.*—Approx. 5 μg/mL benzene. Prep. soln ca 10 μg/mL, and det. concn as in **26.009**, using for sterigmatocystin: max. A 325 nm, MW 324, ϵ 15,200. Dil. quant. to ca 5 μg/mL.

26.119 ***Sample Preparation and Extraction***

(*Caution: See* **51.011, 51.039, 51.040, 51.043, 51.056,** and **51.061.**)

Grind total sample as in **26.003**. Weigh 50 g finely ground sample into 500 mL g-s erlenmeyer, add 180 mL CH_3CN and 20 mL 4% KCl soln, and secure stopper with masking tape. Agitate 30 min on wrist-action, **26.001(o)**, or oscillating shaker, and decant thru Whatman No. 1, or equiv., fluted paper in 150 mm short-stem funnel. Transfer 100 mL filtrate to 250 mL separator, add 50 mL hexane, shake, and let layers sep. Discard upper (hexane) layer. Repeat with addnl 50 mL hexane and discard. Add 25 mL H_2O and 50 mL $CHCl_3$ to CH_3CN-H_2O and shake. Collect clear lower layer in 250 mL erlenmeyer. Add 25 mL $CHCl_3$ to H_2O layer and shake. Add clear lower layer to erlenmeyer. Add few SiC boiling chips, **26.002(b)**, evap. to incipient dryness in steam bath, and quant. transfer residue with $CHCl_3$ thru filter paper into 4 dram vial, **26.001(m)**. Evap. to dryness on steam bath under gentle stream of N. Seal vial with hollow polyethylene stopper, **26.001(i)**, and cap. Reserve for TLC, **26.120**.

26.120 ***Preliminary Thin Layer Chromatography***

Prep. plates as in **26.031(a)** and proceed as in **26.031(b)**, except use 1 mL benzene as solv. and spot 1 μL, two 5 μL, and one 10 μL spots of sample. On same plate, spot 1, 2, 5, and 10 μL quant. ref. std sterigmatocystin, **26.118(e)**(*2*). Spot 5 μL std on top of one 5 μL sample spot.

Develop plate with benzene-HOAc-MeOH (90+5+5) in lined tank, equilibrated with same solv. When solv. front reaches line 4 cm from top of plate, remove plate from tank and dry. Spray plate evenly with $AlCl_3$ soln. Heat plate 10 min at 80°. Examine under shortwave UV light for bright yellow fluorescent sterigmatocystin std spots. (*Caution: See* **51.016.**) Examine sample pattern for similar yellow fluorescent spots at same R_f. If similar spots are not seen in sample channel, sample contains <100 μg sterigmatocystin/kg. If yellow fluorescent spots are seen, compare fluorescent intensity of sample spots with those of std spots and det. which sample portion matches one of stds. Interpolate, if necessary. If weakest sample spot is stronger than most concd std spot, adjust sample ext vol. and rechromatograph.

$$\mu g\ \text{Sterigmatocystin/kg} = (S \times Y \times V)/25 \times X,$$

where S = μL std equiv. to unknown, Y = μg std/mL, V = μL final sample ext diln, and X = μL sample ext spotted giving fluorescent intensity equal to std S.

If no fluorescent yellow spot is seen at proper R_f or there is too much interference for proper quantitation, proceed as in **26.121**.

26.121 ***Column Chromatography***

(*Caution: See* **51.011, 51.039, 51.051,** and **51.057.**)

Place glass wool plug loosely in bottom of chromatgc tube and add ca 5 g *anhyd. Na_2SO_4* to give even base for silica gel. Add cyclohexane until column is ca ½ full; add 10 g silica gel, **(d)**(*1*). Wash sides of column with ca 20 mL cyclohexane and stir to disperse silica gel. When settling of silica gel slows, drain cyclohexane to aid settling, leaving 5–8 cm solv. above silica gel. Slowly add ca 15 g anhyd. Na_2SO_4. Drain cyclohexane to top of Na_2SO_4.

Quant. transfer remaining ext, **26.119**, to column with smallest vol. benzene necessary to effect transfer. Elute column with 200 mL cyclohexane-EtOAc (4+1). Collect entire eluate in 300 mL erlenmeyer.

Add few SiC boiling chips, evap. solv. nearly to dryness on steam bath, and quant. transfer residue to 4 dram vial with $CHCl_3$. Evap. solv. to dryness on steam bath under N.

26.122 ***Final Thin Layer Chromatography***

Dissolve ext, **26.121**, in vol. benzene to give sterigmatocystin concn of ca 5 μg/mL based on preliminary est., **26.120**. Stopper vial and shake, preferably with Vortex mixer.

Proceed as in preliminary TLC, **26.120**, and spot successively 3.5, 5.0, and two 6.5 μL portions ext. On sample plate, spot 3.5, 5.0, and 6.5 μL quant. ref. std soln. Spot 5 μL std on top of one 6.5 μL sample spot. Develop, make comparisons, and calc. sterigmatocystin concn as in **26.120**, correcting for vol. used in preliminary TLC.

26.123 ***Confirmation of Sterigmatocystin Identity by Derivative Formation***

On silica gel plate prepd as in **26.031(a)**, spot twelve 10 μL spots of sample ext, **26.119** or **26.121**, successively at 0.5 cm intervals. Approx. 1 cm beyond spot at each end, place 10 μL spots of qual. ref. std soln. Scribe lines between std and sample spots to prevent sample contamination during development.

Develop plates as in **26.120**, and examine under longware UV light. Sterigmatocystin marker spots in end channels fluoresce brick red. Mark band ca 1 cm wide in sample area of plate at same R_f as sterigmatocystin std spots, being careful not to include any std sterigmatocystin. Collect silica gel from marked area, using suction to pull coating loosened by plate scraper, **26.076(b)**, into filter portion of device. Pipet 3 mL MeOH into device and swirl with silica gel. Use filter bell to draw MeOH through fritted disk into small flask.

Pipet 1 mL aliquots MeOH soln into 2 sep. 0.5 dram vials. Dispense 5 μL qual. std soln into 2 other sep. 0.5 dram vials. Evap. solv. on steam bath. Treat std-sample pairs as follows: *Pair 1:* To each vial add 500 μL 0.1*N* HCl; cap vial, shake, and heat 30 min on steam bath. Evap. solv. to dryness on steam bath under N. *Pair 2:* To each vial add 500 μL pyridine and 100 μL Ac_2O. Cap vial, shake, and heat 30 min on steam bath. Evap. solv. to dryness on steam bath under N.

Add 20 μL $CHCl_3$ to each vial. Spot 10 μL from each vial on silica gel TLC plate. Spot derivatives in following sequence: Vial 1 reaction product of std, Vial 1 reaction product of sample, Vial 2 reaction product of std, Vial 2 reaction product of sample, and qual. ref. std. Develop plate with acetone-$CHCl_3$ (5+95) in lined tank equilibrated with same solv.

Examine developed plate under longware UV light. Compare sample and std spots. Acetate derivative appears as blue fluorescent spot at R_f ca ½ that of brick red sterigmatocystin spot. Remove plate, spray with KOH soln, and re-examine under UV light. Sterigmatocystin derivative formed by treatment with aq. HCl is seen as yellow fluorescent spot at R_f ca ¼ that of sterigmatocystin, which also fluoresces yellow after exposure to KOH. Some unreacted sterigmatocystin may also appear above derivatives. If spots occur from reaction products of sample similar to and at same R_f as derivatives of std, sterigmatocystin identify is confirmed.

ZEARALENONE

(*Caution:* Zearalenone is estrogen with less potency than DES. Handle with due regard to its biological activity.)

Corn (*22*)—Official First Action

(Other adoptions: American Association of Cereal Chemists Method 45-20: 1976 revisions to AACC Approved Methods, pp. 1–6.)

26.124 ***Apparatus***

See **26.026.**

26.125 ***Reagents***

See **26.002**, **26.027(a)** and **(b)**, and in addn:

(a) *Alcohol-chloroform mixt.*—5+95.

(b) *Aluminum chloride soln.*—Dissolve 20 g $AlCl_3.6H_2O$ in 100 mL alcohol.

(c) *Zearalenone std soln.*—Det. chromatgc purity of cryst. zearalenone (available from Commercial Solvents Corp., Terre Haute, IN 47808) as in **26.010**. UV absorption in benzene: max. *A* 317 nm; ϵ 6060±5%. UV absorption spectrum in MeOH: max. *A* 314, 274, and 236 nm; MW 318; ϵ 6000±5%, 13,900±5%, 30,000±5%, resp.; GLC purity of trimethylsilyl derivative >98%. Prep. soln contg 50 μg/mL benzene.

26.126 ***Preparation of Sample***

Proceed as in **26.049**.

26.127 ***Extraction***

Proceed as in **26.029(a)**.

26.128 ***Column Chromatography***

(*Caution: See* **51.011**, **51.043**, **51.045**, **51.046**, and **51.061**.)

Prep. column, and add 50 mL $CHCl_3$ ext and 150 mL hexane wash as in **26.030(a)**. Wash column with 150 mL hexane and elute zearalenone with 250 mL acetone-benzene (5+95).

26.129 ***Liquid-Liquid Partition***

Add few SiC chips to eluate contg zearalenone and evap. to near dryness on steam bath, preferably under gentle stream of N. Transfer residue to 60 mL separator with four 10 mL hexane washes. Finally, rinse with 10 mL CH_3CN and transfer to separator. Shake, and let phases sep. Sep. CH_3CN (lower) phase and ext hexane layer with 5 mL CH_3CN. Combine CH_3CN fractions and evap. to dryness in rotary vac. evaporator. Transfer to vial with $CHCl_3$. Evap., preferably under gentle stream of N. Seal with polyethylene stopper and cap. Save for TLC.

26.130 ***Preparation of Plates for Thin Layer Chromatography***

Proceed as in **26.031(a)**, except that zearalenone replaces aflatoxin as test mycotoxin.

26.131 ***Thin Layer Chromatography***

To residue, **26.129**, add 500 μL benzene, seal with stopper, and shake vigorously on tube shaking machine to dissolve. For preliminary plate, apply 10 μL benzene soln to 2 spots. On one spot superimpose 5 μL zearalenone std soln, **26.125(c)**, for internal std, and apply 5 μL zearalenone std soln to third spot.

Develop plate with alcohol-$CHCl_3$ (5+95), alcohol-$CHCl_3$ (3.5+96.5), HOAc-benzene (5+95), or HOAc-benzene (10+90), in lined, equilibrated tank ca 40 min. Compare spots presumed to be zearalenone with std. Zearalenone has greenish-blue fluorescence under shortwave UV (256 nm) at R_f ca 0.5 and is not visible under longwave UV light except at high concns. Examine sample spot contg internal std to verify identity of zearalenone. When presence of zearalenone is suspected, spray plates with $AlCl_3$ soln, heat 5 min at 130°, and examine under longwave UV light (365 nm). Zearalenone fluoresces blue under longwave UV light after spraying with $AlCl_3$ soln.

If zearalenone is detected in sample soln, perform quant. TLC. Spot 3, 5, and 7 μL zearalenone std soln and 4, 6, and 8 μL sample soln, and develop plate with alcohol-$CHCl_3$ (5+95) or other appropriate solvs as in par. 2. Compare fluorescent intensities of zearalenone spots of sample with those of std and det. which sample spot matches that of std. If spots of smallest portion of sample are too intense to match stds, dil. sample soln and rechromatograph.

26.132 ***Calculations***

Calc. concn of zearalenone in μg/kg corn:

$$\mu g/kg = (S \times Y \times V)/(X \times W),$$

where S = μL zearalenone std soln equal to unknown; Y = concn of zearalenone std soln, μg/mL; V = μL of final diln of sample ext; X = μL sample ext spotted giving fluorescent intensity equal to S (zearalenone std soln); and W = g sample applied to column (10 g). If final ext diln does not represent 10 g, calc. correct sample wt and substitute.

MARINE TOXINS

26.133 Paralytic Shellfish Poison

See **18.079–18.085**.

PHYTOTOXINS

Cyanogenetic Glycosides in Feeds and Similar Materials (*23*)

26.134 ***Qualitative Test—Official Final Action***

Prep. Na picrate paper by dipping strips of filter paper into 1% picric acid acid soln and drying, then dipping into 10% Na_2CO_3 soln and drying. Store these papers in stoppered bottle.

Finely chop small amt of plant material and place in test tube. Insert piece of moistened Na picrate paper in tube, taking care that it does not come in contact with sample. Add few drops $CHCl_3$ and stopper tube tightly. The Na picrate paper gradually turns orange, then brick red, if plant tissue contains cyanogenetic glycosides. (Test is delicate, and rapidity of change in color depends upon amt of free HCN present. This test works well with fresh plant materials, but relatively dry substances, particularly seeds of various plants, should be ground and moistened with H_2O and allowed to hydrolyze in stoppered test tube contg Na picrate paper. If necessary, small amt of *emulsin* may be added.)

Hydrocyanic Acid Formed by Hydrolysis of Glycosides in Beans (*24*)—Official Final Action

26.135 ***Acid Titration Method***

Place 10–20 g sample, ground to pass No. 20 sieve, in 800 mL Kjeldahl flask, add 100 mL H_2O, and macerate at room temp. 2 hr. Add 100 mL H_2O and steam distil, collecting distillate in 20 mL 0.01*N* $AgNO_3$ acidified with 1 mL HNO_3. Before distg, adjust app. so that tip of condenser dips below surface of liq. in receiver. When 150 mL has passed over, filter distillate thru gooch, wash receiver and gooch with little H_2O, and titr. excess $AgNO_3$ in combined filtrate and washings with 0.02*N* KSCN, using Fe alum indicator.

1 mL 0.02*N* $AgNO_3$ = 0.54 mg HCN.

26.136 ***Alkaline Titration Method***

Place 10–20 g sample, ground to pass No. 20 sieve, in 800 mL Kjeldahl flask, add ca 200 mL H_2O and let stand 2–4 hr. (Autolysis should be conducted with app. completely connected for distn.) Steam distil, collect 150–160 mL distillate in NaOH soln (0.5 g in 20 mL H_2O), and dil. to definite vol.

To 100 mL distillate (it is preferable to dil. to 250 mL and titr.

100 mL aliquot) add 8 mL 6*N* NH_4OH and 2 mL 5% KI soln and titr. with 0.02*N* $AgNO_3$, using microburet. End point is faint but permanent turbidity and may be easily recognized, especially against black background.

1 mL 0.02*N* $AgNO_3$ = 1.08 mg HCN. (Ag equiv. to 2 CN.)

SELECTED REFERENCES

(*1*) Pure Appl. Chem. **49,** 1709(1977).
(*2*) JAOAC **53,** 92, 96(1970); IUPAC Infor. Bull. Tech. Report No. 1, June 1971.
(*3*) JAOAC **58,** 500(1975); **59,**110(1976); **62,** 136(1979).
(*4*) JAOAC **62,** 1070(1979).
(*5*) JAOAC **51,** 67(1968).
(*6*) JAOAC **53,** 104(1970).
(*7*) JAOAC **52,** 72(1969); **54,** 540(1971).
(*8*) JAOAC **54,** 874(1971).
(*9*) JAOAC **55,** 781(1972).
(*10*) JAOAC **58,** 746(1975).
(*11*) JAOAC **52,** 1300(1969).
(*12*) JAOAC **57,** 1114(1974).
(*13*) JAOAC **60,** 795(1977).
(*14*) JAOAC **53,** 101, 102(1970).
(*15*) JAOAC **58,** 110(1975).
(*16*) JAOAC **47,** 1003(1964); **56,** 901(1973).
(*17*) JAOAC **56,** 1431(1973); **57,** 847, 852(1974).
(*18*) JAOAC **56,** 486(1973).
(*19*) JAOAC **58,** 258(1975).
(*20*) JAOAC **57,** 621(1974).
(*21*) JAOAC **54,** 86(1971); **56,** 1123(1973).
(*22*) JAOAC **59,** 666(1976).
(*23*) JAOAC **19,** 94, 589(1936); **20,** 444(1937); **21,** 614(1938).
(*24*) J. Am. Chem. Soc. **37,** 601(1915); JAOAC **4,** 151(1920); **17,** 182(1934); **18,** 347(1935); **19,** 589(1936); **33,** 83(1950); **38,** 96(1955).

SPECIAL REFERENCE

Mycotoxin Mass Spectral Data Bank (1978) AOAC, Box 540 Benjamin Franklin Station, Washington, DC 20044.

27. Nuts and Nut Products (*1*)

Volume of Packaged Nuts (*2*)—Official Final Action

27.001 ***Apparatus***

(**a**) *Graduated cylinders.—(1) For less than 500 mL nuts.*—Use 500 mL cylinder with ca 4.7 cm id. *(2) For 500 mL or greater volume of nuts.*—Use 1 L cylinder with ca 5.7 cm id.

(**b**) *Balance.*—Accurate to 0.01 oz or 0.25 g.

(**c**) *Funnel.*—With min. opening of 3.8 cm diam. (suitable funnel may be shaped from smooth cardboard).

27.002 ***Determination***

Open container and pour nuts loosely into vertical graduate (do not tilt) fitted with funnel. Without shaking, est. location of horizontal plane representing av. ht of product, read vol. nuts, and record max. vol.

Raise graduate 5 cm and drop vertically onto level, firm, resilient surface (do not tamp). Repeat total of 5 times and observe vol. as above. Repeat in successive 5-drop increments until nuts have so settled that vol. decreases ≤2% in last 5-drop increment. Read vol. as above and record as "min. vol." Arithmetical av. of "max," and "min." vol. = mean vol.

27.003 Preservation of Sample—Procedure

Store sample in air-tight container at 5–10°. Store meats in glass containers only.

27.004 Preparation of Sample—Procedure

(**a**) *Nuts in shell.*—Remove meats from shells, and sep. all shell particles from meats. Skin or spermoderm should be included with meat in all nuts, including peanuts and coconuts unless specifically excluded by description. Prep. sepd meats as in (**b**).

(**b**) *Nut meats, shredded coconut, or small pieces.*—Grind ≥250 g twice thru Enterprise No. 5 food chopper, equipped with revolving knife blade and plate with holes ca 3 mm diam. (Other types of food choppers, graters, or comminuting devices that give smooth homogeneous paste without loss of oil may be used.) Mix sample well and store in air-tight glass container.

(**c**) *Nut butters and pastes.*—Transfer sample to container of convenient size and shape, warming semi-solid products, and mix carefully with stiff-blade spatula or knife. (Elec. mixers or stirrers may be used instead if sample is of consistency to give uniform mixt.) Store sample in air-tight glass container.

27.005 Moisture (*3*)—Official First Action

(Not applicable to high sugar products or products contg glycerol or propylene glycol)

Dry sample representing ca 2 g dry material to const wt (ca 5 hr) at 95–100° under pressure ≤100 mm Hg (13.3 kPa). Report loss in wt as moisture.

27.006 Crude Fat (*4*)—Official First Action

(*Caution: See* **51.011, 51.039,** and **51.054.**)

(**a**) *Direct method.*—If large amts of sol. carbohydrates interfere with complete extn of fat, ext with H_2O before making detn. Ext ca 2 g sample with ether, dried as in **7.055,** 16 hr in Soxhlet-type extractor. Evap. ether, dry residue 30 min at 95–100°, cool in desiccator, and weigh; continue this alternate drying and weighing at 30 min intervals to const wt (1–1.5 hr is usually required).

(**b**) *Indirect method.*—Proceed as in **27.005**; then ext dried substance 16 hr as in (**a**), and dry as in (**a**). Report loss in wt as ether ext.

27.007 Crude Protein (*5*)—Official First Action

Det. N as in **2.057,** and multiply result by 5.46 for peanuts and brazil nuts, 5.18 for almonds, and 5.30 for other tree nuts and coconut. (It may be desirable to defat with pet ether.)

27.008 Crude Fiber—Official First Action

See **7.065.**

27.009 Ash (*6*)—Official First Action

See **31.012,** or **31.013** if added chlorides are present.

27.010 Reducing Sugars (*6*)—Official Final Action

Prep. sample as in 1st and 2nd par. of **7.079.** Proceed as in **31.038,** using 25 mL aliquot (representing 2 g sample). Express results as glucose or invert sugar.

27.011 Sucrose (*6*)—Official Final Action

See **7.079.**

27.012 Sodium Chloride (*6*)—Official Final Action

To 2 g prepd sample, **27.004,** in Pt dish, add and thoroly incorporate 10 mL *10% $Ca(OAc)_2$ soln.* For nut butters and pastes, disperse sample in 10 mL acetone before adding $Ca(OAc)_2$, and remove acetone at room temp. with air current. Dry on steam bath, and ash in furnace at lowest visible red heat (550°). (Complete ashing is not necessary.)

Dissolve ash in 25 mL HNO_3 (1+3), add known vol. 0.1*N* $AgNO_3$, more than enough to ppt all Cl, heat to bp, cool, add 5 mL ferric indicator, **6.019(e),** and titr. excess Ag with 0.1*N* NH_4SCN, **50.030(b)** until soln turns permanent light brown. Calc. Cl as NaCl, after correcting for any Cl in the $Ca(OAc)_2$ soln.

27.013 Water-Insoluble Inorganic Residue Official First Action

See **44.032★.**

27.014 Mycotoxins

See Chap. **26.**

PEANUT BUTTER

27.015 Preliminary Examination—Procedure

Make microscopic examination to detect addn of starch or any off-grade material not identifiable chem.

27.016 Starch (*7*)—Official First Action

Weigh 4–5 g sample by difference into 250 mL centrf. bottle and ext twice with 50 mL portions pet ether, shaking 5 min each time. Wash down sides of bottle with pet ether, centrf., and pour off solv., disregarding opalescence. Warm bottle to drive off remaining solv., transfer residue to mortar, and grind. Return fine powder to bottle with aid of 100 mL 10% NaCl soln. Shake bottle 15 min, wash down sides NaCl soln, centrf. well, and pour off supernate, disregarding opalescence. Repeat washing twice.

Ext in same manner, once with 70% alcohol and once with H_2O, shaking 1–2 min each time. Drain bottle several min., chill, and from pipet add 100 mL HCl (20.5–21.0 g HCl/100 mL) at temp. $\leq 15°$. Shake vigorously 3 min, centrf. well, and pour off soln thru cotton pledget in funnel stem. Cool soln to temp. at which the HCl was added, and pipet off 50 mL into nursing bottle contg 115 mL alcohol. Shake with whirling motion 1 min, let stand 2 min, centrf. 2 min, pour off thru weighed gooch contg thin asbestos pad, and add 50 mL 70% (v/v) alcohol to ppt. Stopper bottle, shake vigorously, wash down sides with the 70% alcohol, centrf. lightly, and pour off thru crucible. Repeat once with 70% alcohol and once with alcohol. Dry crucible and contents 1.5 hr at 130° in air, or 5 hr at 98–100° *in vacuo*. Cover crucible, place in desiccator contg efficient desiccant, and weigh when crucible reaches room temp.

SHREDDED COCONUT

27.017 ★ Glycerol—Official First Action ★

Ext. 4 times, with suction, 4 g shredded coconut (dried 5–6 hr *in vacuo* at 70°) on filter (fritted glass buchner is most convenient), using 50 mL pet ether (bp <65°) for each extn, and allowing 3 min intervals between extns. Use flat-end glass rod for stirring. After removing fat, ext residue on filter with four 50 mL portions absolute alcohol, allowing 3 min intervals with stirring, as before. Dil. ext to 250 mL with absolute alcohol at room temp.

Pipet 100 mL into 500 mL erlenmeyer, and add 5 mL H_2O and paste made by adding hot H_2O to 2 or 3 g $Ba(OH)_2$ in small mortar. Heat mixt. on steam bath to bp and boil ca 1 min; transfer to 250 mL centrf. bottle and centrf. at 2000 rpm ca 5 min. Transfer clear liq. to large porcelain dish and wash residue in centrf. bottle with 50–75 mL absolute alcohol, stirring with glass rod and centrfg as before. Evap. on steam bath at temp. <70° to few drops, or almost dryness.

Transfer to 50 mL g-s graduate with 10 mL absolute alcohol and wash dish with two 5 mL portions absolute alcohol. Further wash dish with three 10 mL portions anhyd. ether, shaking g-s graduate thoroly after each addn of anhyd. ether. Transfer to sediment tube and centrf. 10 min at 3200 rpm. Transfer clear soln in sediment tube to evapg dish, preferably Pt, and wash sediment tube with 25 mL of mixt. of absolute alcohol and anhyd. ether (2+3), stirring with glass rod and centrfg as before. Evap. on steam bath at 85–90° to ca 5 mL, add 20 mL H_2O, and evap. to ca 5 mL; repeat this operation twice. Transfer residue with hot H_2O to 50 mL vol. flask and proceed as in **30.080** ★.

SELECTED REFERENCES

(*1*) JAOAC **18,** 418(1935).

(*2*) JAOAC **54,** 584(1971).

(*3*) JAOAC **8,** 295(1925); **31,** 521(1948); **32,** 527(1949); **33,** 753(1950); **34,** 357(1951); **37,** 845(1954).

(*4*) JAOAC **31,** 521(1948); **33,** 753(1950); **34,** 357(1951); **37,** 845(1954).

(*5*) JAOAC **33,** 753(1950); **34,** 357(1951); **37,** 845(1954).

(*6*) JAOAC **33,** 753(1950); **34,** 357(1951).

(*7*) JAOAC **37,** 845(1954).

28. Oils and Fats

28.001 Preparation of Sample—Procedure

Melt solid fats and filter, using hot H_2O funnel or similar app. Make detns on samples of this melted, homogeneous mass. Filter oils that are not clear. To retard rancidity, keep oils and fats in cool place and protect from light and air.

Moisture and Volatile Matter (*1*)

28.002 *Vacuum Oven Method—Official Final Action*

Soften sample, if necessary, by gentle heat, taking care not to melt it. When soft enough, mix thoroly with effective mech. mixer.

Weigh 5±0.2 g prepd sample into Al moisture dish ca 5 cm diam. and 2 cm deep with tight-fit slip-over cover. Dry to const wt in vac. oven at uniform temp. 20–25° above bp of H_2O at working pressure, which should be ≤100 mm Hg (13.3 kPa). Cool in efficient desiccator 30 min and weigh. Const wt is attained when successive 1 hr drying periods show addnl loss of ≤0.05%. Report % loss in wt as moisture and volatile matter.

Specific Gravity (Apparent) at 25/25°
Official Final Action

28.003 *Standardization of Pycnometer*

(*Caution: See* **51.023** and **51.030**.)

Carefully clean pycnometer (ca 50 mL capacity, Kimble Products No. 15123, or equiv.) by filling with chromic acid cleaning soln and letting stand several hr. Empty pycnometer and rinse thoroly with H_2O; fill with recently boiled H_2O previously cooled to ca 20°, and place in const temp. bath at 25°. After 30 min, adjust H_2O level to proper point on pycnometer and stopper; remove from bath, wipe dry with clean cloth or towel, and weigh. Empty pycnometer, rinse several times with alcohol and then ether, let dry completely, remove ether vapor, and weigh. Det. wt of contained H_2O at 25° by subtracting wt pycnometer from its wt when filled with H_2O.

28.004 *Determination*

Fill clean, dry pycnometer with sample previously cooled to ca 20°, place in const temp. bath 30 min at 25°, adjust oil level to proper point on pycnometer, and stopper. Remove from bath, wipe dry, and weigh as in **28.003**. Subtract wt empty pycnometer from its wt when filled with oil and divide difference by wt H_2O at 25°, as detd in **28.003**. Quotient is sp gr at 25/25° (apparent).

If sp gr at 20/20° is required, proceed as above and as in **28.003** but subtract 5° from each temp. specified.

28.005 Temperature Correction for Specific Gravity of Oils (*2*)—Official Final Action

If sp gr of oil is detd at other than std temp., approx. sp gr at 25/25° may be calcd as follows:

$$G = G' + 0.00064(T - 25°),$$

where G = sp gr at 25/25°, G' = sp gr at T/25°, T = temp. at which sp gr was detd, and 0.00064 = mean correction for 1°.

Index of Refraction—Official Final Action

28.006 *General Directions*

Det. index of refraction (n) with any std instrument, reading oils at 20 or 25° and fats at 40°. Place instrument so that diffused daylight or some form of artificial light such as Na vapor lamp can be used for illumination. Circulate stream of const temp. (±0.2°) H_2O thru prisms. Approx. temp. corrections of butyrorefractometer readings may be made by following formula:

$$R = R' + K(T' - T),$$

where R = reading reduced to std temp., R' = reading obtained at temp. T', T = std temp., and K = 0.55 for fats and 0.58 for oils.

Readings of instruments that give n directly can be reduced to std temp. by substituting factor 0.000365 for 0.55 and 0.000385 for 0.58 in formula. As temp. rises, n falls. Instrument used may be stdzd with H_2O at 20°, theoretical n of H_2O at that temp. being 1.3330. Any correction found should be made on all readings. Index of refraction varies with density and in same direction.

28.007 *By Means of Abbé Refractometer*

To charge instrument, open double prism by means of screw head and place few drops sample on prism or, if preferred, open prisms slightly by turning screw head and pour few drops sample into funnel-shape aperture between prisms. Close prisms firmly by tightening screw head. Let instrument stand few min before reading, so that temp. of sample and instrument will be same. Clean prisms between readings by wiping off oil with soft cloth, then with cotton pad moistened with solv. (e.g., trichloroethylene, toluene, or pet ether), and let dry.

Method of measurement is based upon observation of position of *border line of total reflection* in relation to faces of flint glass prism. Bring this border line into field of vision of telescope by rotating double prism by means of alidade in following manner: Hold sector firmly and move alidade backward or forward until field of vision is divided into light and dark portion. Line dividing these portions is "border line," and, as a rule, will not be sharp line but band of color. Colors are eliminated by rotating screw head of compensator until sharp, colorless line is obtained. Adjust border line so that it falls on point of intersection of cross hairs. Read n of substance directly on scale of sector, estg 4th decimal place. Take ≥3 readings, approaching intersection alternately from one field to other, and average. Range of readings should be ≤0.0002. Check correctness of instrument as in **28.006**, or with quartz plate that accompanies it, using monobromonaphthalene, ($n_{20°}$ = 1.6587), and make necessary correction in reading.

28.008 *By Means of Zeiss Butyrorefractometer*

Place 2 or 3 drops filtered sample on surface of lower prism. Close prisms and adjust mirror until it gives sharpest reading. If reading is indistinct after running const temp. H_2O thru instrument for some time, sample is unevenly distributed on prism surfaces. As n is greatly affected by temp., use care to keep temp. const. Carefully adjust instrument, using std fluid supplied with it. Convert instrument reading to n from Table **28:01**.

Table 28:01 Butyrorefractometer Readings and Indices of Refraction

Reading	Index of Refraction	Reading	Index of Refraction
40.0	1.4524	60.0	1.4659
40.5	1.4527	60.5	1.4662
41.0	1.4531	61.0	1.4665
41.5	1.4534	61.5	1.4668
42.0	1.4538	62.0	1.4672
42.5	1.4541	62.5	1.4675
43.0	1.4545	63.0	1.4678
43.5	1.4548	63.5	1.4681
44.0	1.4552	64.0	1.4685
44.5	1.4555	64.5	1.4688
45.0	1.4558	65.0	1.4691
45.5	1.4562	65.5	1.4694
46.0	1.4565	66.0	1.4697
46.5	1.4569	66.5	1.4700
47.0	1.4572	67.0	1.4704
47.5	1.4576	67.5	1.4707
48.0	1.4579	68.0	1.4710
48.5	1.4583	68.5	1.4713
49.0	1.4586	69.0	1.4717
49.5	1.4590	69.5	1.4720
50.0	1.4593	70.0	1.4723
50.5	1.4596	70.5	1.4726
51.0	1.4600	71.0	1.4729
51.5	1.4603	71.5	1.4732
52.0	1.4607	72.0	1.4735
52.5	1.4610	72.5	1.4738
53.0	1.4613	73.0	1.4741
53.5	1.4616	73.5	1.4744
54.0	1.4619	74.0	1.4747
54.5	1.4623	74.5	1.4750
55.0	1.4626	75.0	1.4753
55.5	1.4629	75.5	1.4756
56.0	1.4633	76.0	1.4759
56.5	1.4636	76.5	1.4762
57.0	1.4639	77.0	1.4765
57.5	1.4642	77.5	1.4768
58.0	1.4646	78.0	1.4771
58.5	1.4649	78.5	1.4774
59.0	1.4652	79.0	1.4777
59.5	1.4656	79.5	1.4780

Melting Point of Fats and Fatty Acids—Official Final Action

Wiley Method

28.009 ***Reagent***

Alcohol-water mixture.—Sp gr should be same as that of fat to be examined. Prep. by sep. boiling H_2O and alcohol 10 min to remove dissolved gases. While still hot, pour H_2O into test tube until it is almost half full. Nearly fill test tube with hot alcohol, pouring it down side of inclined tube to avoid too much mixing. If alcohol is added after the H_2O has cooled, air bubbles will make mixt. unfit for use.

28.010 ***Determination***

Let melted and filtered fat fall 15–20 cm from dropping tube upon piece of ice or upon surface of cold Hg. Disks thus formed should be 1–1.5 cm diam. and weigh ca 200 mg. Remove disks when solid, and let stand 2–3 hr to obtain normal mp.

Alternatively, disks may be prepd using app. consisting of Al plate ca 3 mm thick and 100 mm sq with perforations ca 10 mm diam. and steel plate ca 10 mm thick and 150 mm sq. Thoroly chill steel plate in refrigerator and place Al plate on top (surfaces should be flush). Pour melted and filtered fat into holes of Al plate and let stand in refrigerator ≥2 hr. Remove fat above surface of Al plate and remove disks.

Place 30 × 3.5 cm test tube, contg alcohol-H_2O mixt., in tall 35 × 10 cm beaker contg ice and H_2O, and leave until mixt. is cold. Drop disk of fat into tube. It will sink immediately to point where density of alcohol-H_2O mixt. is exactly equiv. to its own. Lower accurate thermometer, that can be read to 0.1°, into test tube until bulb is just above disk. To secure even temp. in all parts of alcohol-H_2O mixt. around disk, stir gently with thermometer. Slowly heat H_2O in beaker, constantly stirring with air stream or other suitable device.

When temp. of alcohol-H_2O mixt. rises to ca 6° below mp of fat, disk of fat begins to shrivel and gradually rolls up into irregular mass. Lower thermometer until fat particle is even with center of bulb. Rotate thermometer bulb gently and so regulate heat that ca 10 min is required for last 2° increase in temp. As soon as fat mass becomes spherical, read thermometer. This is Wiley mp. At this point, temp. of bath must be ≤1.5° above mp of sample. Conduct 2 addnl detns exactly as above. Second and third results should agree closely.

If edge of disk touches side of tube, make new detn.

28.011 ***Capillary Tube Method (3)***

Draw ca 10 mm melted and filtered fat into thin-wall capillary tube, 1 mm id. Seal end of tube with sample in small flame. Do not burn fat. Hold tubes contg fat overnight (ca 16 hr) in refrigerator at 4–10°. Attach tube to accurate thermometer graduated to 0.2°, so that lower end is even with bottom of Hg bulb. Suspend in 600 mL beaker half filled with H_2O so that thermometer is immersed ca 30 mm. Starting 8–10° below mp of sample, apply heat so as to increase bath temp. ca 0.5°/min, agitating H_2O in bath by small stream of air or with slow stirrer. Take as mp temp. at which substance becomes transparent. (Magnifying glass is useful to detect complete melting.) Report av. of 3 detns (should agree within 0.5°).

Titer Test (*4*)—Official Final Action

28.012 ***Specifications for Titer Test Thermometers***

Type.—Etched stem, glass.

Liquid.—Mercury.

Range and subdivision.—Minus 2 to +68° in 0.2°.

Total length.—385–390 mm.

Stem.—Constructed of suitable thermometer tubing of either plain or lens front type. Diam., plain front type: 6–7 mm; diam., lens front type: cross section of stem must be such that it will pass thru 8 mm ring gage but not enter 5 mm slot gage.

Bulb.—Corning normal or equally suitable thermometric glass. Length, 15–25 mm; diam., 5.5 mm to not greater than that of stem.

Distance from bottom of bulb to −2° mark.—50–60 mm.

Distance to 68° mark from top of thermometer.— 20–35 mm.

Length of unchanged capillary.—Between highest graduation and expansion chamber, 10 mm.

Expansion chamber.—To permit heating to ≥85°. Space above Hg to be evacuated or filled with N or other suitable gas.

Top finish.—Glass ring.

Graduation.—All lines, figures, and letters to be clear-cut and distinct. Each degree mark to be longer than remaining lines. Graduations to be numbered at 0 and at each multiple of 2°.

Immersion.—45 mm.

Marking.—"A.O.A.C. Titer Test," serial number, and manufacturer's name or trademark must be etched on stem. Words "45 mm immersion" must also be etched on stem, as well as line extending around stem 45 mm above bottom of bulb.

Scale error.—Error at any point on scale must be ≤0.2°.

Standardization.—Thermometer must be stdzd at ice point

and at intervals of ca 20°, for condition of 45 mm immersion, and for av. stem temp. of emergent Hg column of 25°.

Case.—Thermometer must be supplied in suitable case on which appears markings "A.O.A.C. Titer Test," "−2° to +68° in 0.2°."

Note: For interpreting these specifications, following definitions apply:

Total length is over-all length of finished instrument. Diam. is that measured with ring gage or micrometer. Length of bulb is distance from bottom to beginning of enamel backing. Top of thermometer is top of finished instrument.

ASTM 36C titer test thermometer is satisfactory (Fisher Scientific Co. or Scientific Products, Inc.).

28.013 ***Apparatus***

Stirring titer assembly, as shown in Fig. **28:01**, consisting of 2 L beaker, 450 mL wide-mouth bottle (ht 190 mm, id of neck, 38 mm), titer test tube (25 × 100 mm), and stirrer (2–3 mm od, one end bent in form of loop, 19 mm diam.).

28.014 ***Determination***

Heat 110 g *glycerol-KOH soln* (25 g KOH in 125 g glycerol) to 150° in 800 mL beaker and add 50 mL oil or melted fat, previously filtered if necessary to remove foreign substances. (Altho saponification often takes place almost immediately, continue heating and frequent stirring 15 min. Do not heat >150°.)

When saponification is complete, usually indicated by perfectly homogeneous soln, cool slightly and add 200–300 mL H_2O. After complete soln of the soap, add with stirring 50 mL dil. H_2SO_4 (16 mL H_2SO_4 in 70 mL H_2O). Heat soln, with frequent stirring and addn of H_2O if necessary, until layer of fatty acids is completely melted and clear. Siphon off aq. acid layer, add H_2O to fatty acids, boil 2–3 min, and again siphon off aq. layer. Repeat treatment with H_2O until wash H_2O is neut. to Me orange. Remove fatty acids so as not to include H_2O, and filter while melted thru rapid paper. Heat to 130° on hot plate to remove traces of H_2O and pour fatty acids into titer tube to ht of 57 mm from bottom. If H_2O is present in fatty acids, decant, refilter, and reheat.

Fill H_2O bath and adjust to 20° for all samples with titers ≥35°, and to 15–20° below titer for samples with titers <35°. (H_2O level should be 1 cm above sample level.) Place test tube contg fatty acids in app., Fig. **28:01**. Insert thermometer to immersion mark and equidistant from sides of tube. Stir vertically with stirring rod at rate of 100 complete up-and-down motions/min, starting agitation while temp. is ≥10° above titer point. (Stirrer should move thru vertical distance of ca 3.8 cm. If preferred, stirring may be performed mech.) Continue stirring until temp. remains const 30 sec or begins to rise in <30 sec interval. Immediately discontinue stirring and observe rise in temp. Report as titer highest point reached by thermometer. Duplicate detns should normally agree within 0.2°.

28.015 ★ Acetyl Value (*5*)—Official Final Action ★

See **26.016–26.017**, 10th ed.

Hydroxyl Value (*6*)—Official Final Action

American Oil Chemists' Society Method

(Hydroxyl value is number of mg KOH equiv. to hydroxyl content of 1 g sample. Applicable to fatty oils and derivatives such as fatty alcohols, mono- and diglycerides, and hydroxystearic acid.)

28.016 ***Reagents***

(**a**) *Pyridine.*—Reagent grade, redistd at 114–115°.

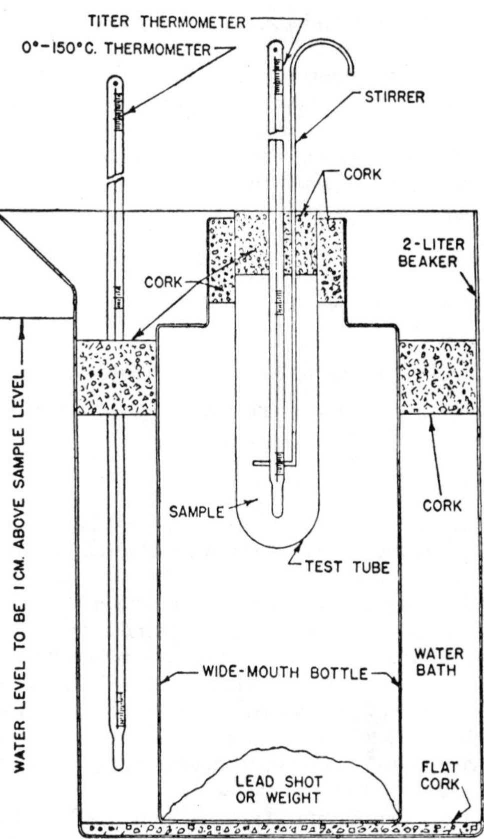

FIG. 28:01—Titer stirring assembly

(**b**) *Acetic anhydride.*—ACS, fresh.

(**c**) *Pyridine-acetic anhydride reagent.*—Mix 3 vols reagent (**a**) with 1 vol. (**b**) just before use.

(**d**) *n-Butyl alcohol.*—Reagent grade. Neutze with 0.5*N* KOH to faint pink phthln end point.

(**e**) *Alcoholic potassium hydroxide std soln.*—0.5*N*. (Should be ≥0.5*N* so that blank titers do not require refilling of 50 mL buret.)

28.017 ***Determination***

(*Caution: See* **51.018** and **51.022**.)

According to expected hydroxyl value, weigh following amts of sample into 250 mL ₮ g-s erlenmeyers to nearest mg for acetylation:

Hydroxyl Value	*Weight, g*
0– 20	10±0.1
20– 50	5
50–100	3
100–200	2

Weigh 9.0–11.0 g sample into another flask for acidity detn. (For fatty acids such as hydroxystearic acid, take 0.9–1.1 g.)

Pipet 5.0 mL reagent (**c**) into flask contg acetylation sample. For samples with 0–20 hydroxyl value, add addnl 5 mL pyridine. Mix thoroly by gentle swirling. Pipet 5 mL reagent (**c**) (and 5 mL pyridine, if used in acetylation) into another flask for reagent blank. Place flasks on steam bath under ₮ reflux condenser and heat 1 hr. (Do not use hot plate or mantle.) Add 10 mL H_2O thru

★ Surplus method—*see* inside front cover.

condenser and heat addnl 10 min. Let flasks cool with condenser attached. Add 25 mL *n*-BuOH, ca half thru condenser, remove condenser, and use rest to wash down sides of flask. Add 1 mL phthln and titr. to faint pink end point with 0.5*N* alc. KOH.

Add 10 mL pyridine, neutzd to phthln, to sample for acidity detn. Swirl gently to mix, add 1 mL phthln, and titr. to faint pink end point with 0.5*N* alc. KOH.

Hydroxyl value = $[B + (W \times V/C) - S] \times$ normality $\times$ 56.1/W, where V = mL KOH for acidity titrn, B = mL KOH for reagent blank, C = g sample for acidity titrn, S = mL KOH for acetylated sample, W = g sample used for acetylation.

Iodine Absorption Number—Official Final Action

(All reports should specify method used)

Hanus Method

28.018 ***Reagent***

Hanus iodine soln.—Dissolve 13.2 g pure I in 1 L HOAc that shows no reduction with dichromate and H_2SO_4. Add enough Br to double halogen content as detd by titrn (ca 3 mL). The I may be dissolved by heating, but soln should be cold when Br is added. Hanus I soln may also be prepd as follows: Measure 825 mL HOAc and dissolve 13.615 g I in it with aid of heat. Cool, and titr. 25 mL with 0.1*N* $Na_2S_2O_3$, **50.037–50.038**. Measure another portion of 200 mL HOAc and add 3 mL Br. To 5 mL of this soln add 10 mL 15% KI soln, and titr. with the 0.1*N* $Na_2S_2O_3$. Calc. vol. Br soln required to double halogen content of remaining 800 mL I soln as follows:

$X = B/C$, where X = mL Br soln required; B = 800 × thiosulfate equiv. of 1 mL I soln; and C = thiosulfate equiv. of 1 mL Br soln. If necessary, reduce mixed soln to proper concn by diln with HOAc.

28.019 ***Determination***

Weigh ca 0.5000 g fat, or 0.2500 g oil (0.1000–0.2000 g of oils that have high absorbent power), into 500 mL g-s flask or bottle and dissolve in 10 mL $CHCl_3$. With pipet, add 25 mL Hanus I soln, draining pipet definite time, and let stand 30 min in dark, shaking occasionally. (For accurate results use exact time. Excess I should be $\geqslant$60% of amt added.)

Add 10 mL 15% KI soln, shake thoroly, and add 100 mL freshly boiled and cooled H_2O, washing down any free I on stopper. Titr. I with std 0.1*N* $Na_2S_2O_3$, adding it gradually, with const shaking, until yellow soln turns almost colorless. Add few drops starch indicator, **2.144(b)**, and continue titrn until blue entirely disappears. Toward end of titrn, stopper bottle and shake violently, so that any I remaining in soln in $CHCl_3$ may be taken up by KI soln.

Conduct 2 blank detns along with detn on sample. Number of mL 0.1*N* $Na_2S_2O_3$ required by blank (B) minus mL used in detn (S) gives $Na_2S_2O_3$ equiv. of I absorbed by the fat or oil. Calc. % by wt of I absorbed (I number, Hanus method).

$$\text{I number} = [(B - S) \times N \times 12.69]/\text{g sample},$$

where N is normality of $Na_2S_2O_3$ soln.

Wijs Method (7)

28.020 ***Reagents***

(*Caution: See* **51.018**, **51.022**, and **51.047**.)

Wijs iodine soln.—(*1*) Dissolve 13 g resublimed I in 1 L HOAc, and pass in dried (thru H_2SO_4) Cl until original $Na_2S_2O_3$ titrn of soln is not quite doubled. (Characteristic color change at end point indicates proper amt of Cl. Convenient method is to reserve some of original I soln, add slight excess of Cl to bulk of soln, and bring to desired titer by readdns of reserved portion.) Or: (*2*) Dissolve 16.5 g ICl in 1 L HOAc.

Store in amber bottle sealed with paraffin until ready for use. Wijs solns are sensitive to temp., moisture, and light. Store in dark at <30°. Det. I/Cl ratio as follows:

Iodine content.—Pipet 5 mL Wijs soln into 500 mL erlenmeyer contg 150 mL satd Cl-H_2O and some glass beads. Shake, heat to bp, and boil briskly 10 min. Cool, add 30 mL H_2SO_4 (1+49) and 15 mL 15% KI soln, and titr. immediately with 0.1*N* $Na_2S_2O_3$.

Total halogen content.—Pipet 20 mL Wijs soln into 500 mL erlenmeyer contg 150 mL recently boiled and cooled H_2O and 15 mL 15% KI soln. Titr. immediately with 0.1*N* $Na_2S_2O_3$.

$$I/Cl = 2X/(3B - 2X),$$

where X = mL 0.1*N* $Na_2S_2O_3$ required for I content and B = mL required for total halogen content. I/Cl ratio must be 1.10±0.1.

28.021 ***Determination***

Use sample wt calcd as 26/expected I value, or from following table:

I Value	g Sample[a]	Accuracy, mg
3	10.58—8.46	±5.
10	3.17—2.54	0.2
20	1.59—1.27	0.2
40	0.79—0.63	0.2
80	0.40—0.32	0.2
120	0.26—0.21	0.2
160	0.20—0.16	0.2
200	0.16—0.13	0.2

[a] For 100 and 150% excess, resp.

Weigh melted and filtered sample into clean, dry, 500 mL g-s flask contg 20 mL CCl_4. With pipet, add 25 mL I soln, draining pipet definite time. Excess of I should be 50–60% of amt added, that is, 100–150% of amt absorbed. Swirl, and let bottle stand in dark 30 min at 25±5°. Let samples with I values >150 (linseed and perilla) stand 1 hr.

Add 20 mL 15% KI soln and 100 mL recently boiled and cooled H_2O. Titr. the I with 0.1*N* $Na_2S_2O_3$, **50.037–50.038**, added gradually, shaking constantly until yellow soln turns almost colorless. (Vigorous mag. stirring is convenient.) Add few drops starch indicator, **2.144(b)**, and continue titrn until blue entirely disappears. Toward end of reaction, stopper bottle and shake violently so that any I remaining in soln in CCl_4 may be taken up by KI soln.

Conduct 2 detns on blanks in same manner as sample, but without fat. Slight variations in temp. appreciably affect titer of I soln, as HOAc has high coefficient of expansion. It is essential, therefore, that blanks and detns on sample be made at same time. $Na_2S_2O_3$ equiv. of I absorbed by sample taken = mL std $Na_2S_2O_3$ soln required by blank (B) − mL used in detn (S). Calc. % by wt of I absorbed as in **28.019** and report as I number, Wijs method.

Peroxide Value—Official Final Action

American Oil Chemists' Society Method (8)

28.022 ***Reagents***

(**a**) *Acetic acid-chloroform soln.*—Mix 3 vols HOAc with 2 vols $CHCl_3$, USP.

(**b**) *Potassium iodide soln, saturated.*—Dissolve excess KI in freshly boiled H_2O. Excess solid must remain. Store in dark. Test daily by adding 0.5 mL to 30 mL HOAc-$CHCl_3$, (**a**); then add 2 drops 1% starch soln, **2.144(b)**. If soln turns blue, requiring >1 drop 0.1*N* $Na_2S_2O_3$ to discharge color, prep. fresh soln.

(c) *Sodium thiosulfate std solns.*—0.1 and 0.01*N*. Prep. and stdze as in **50.037–50.038**. For 0.01*N*, dil. 0.1*N* with freshly boiled and cooled H_2O.

28.023 ***Determination***

(a) *Fats and oils.*—Weigh 5.00±0.05 g sample into 250 mL g-s erlenmeyer. Add 30 mL HOAc-$CHCl_3$, (a), and swirl to dissolve. Add 0.5 mL satd KI soln, (b), from Mohr pipet, let stand with occasional shaking 1 min, and add 30 mL H_2O. Slowly titr. with 0.1*N* $Na_2S_2O_3$ with vigorous shaking until yellow is almost gone. Add ca 0.5 mL 1% starch soln, **2.144(b)**, and continue titrn, shaking vigorously to release all I from $CHCl_3$ layer, until blue just disappears. If <0.5 mL 0.1*N* $Na_2S_2O_3$ is used, repeat detn with 0.01*N* $Na_2S_2O_3$.

Conduct blank detn daily (must be ≤0.1 mL 0.1*N* $Na_2S_2O_3$). Subtract from sample titrn.

Peroxide value (milliequiv. peroxide/kg sample) = $S \times N \times 1000$/g sample, where S = mL $Na_2S_2O_3$ (blank corrected) and N = normality $Na_2S_2O_3$ soln.

(b) *Margarine.*—Melt sample by heating with const stirring on hot plate at low heat, or heat in air oven at 60–70°. (Avoid excessive heat and long exposure >40°.) When completely melted, hold in warm place until aq. portion and most of solids have settled. Decant oil into clean beaker and filter thru Whatman No. 4, or equiv. paper. Do not reheat unless necessary to obtain clear filtrate. Proceed as in (a).

28.024 ★ Thiocyanogen Number ★
Official First Action

(*Caution:* Thiocyanogen is toxic. *See* **51.018, 51.022, 51.047**, and **51.050**.)

See **26.026–26.027**, 10th ed.

Saponification Number (Koettstorfer Number)
Official Final Action

28.025 ***Reagent***

Alcoholic potassium hydroxide soln (JAOAC **19**, 427(1936)).—(*1*) Reflux 1.2 L alcohol 30 min in distg flask with 10 g KOH and 6 g granulated Al (or Al foil). Distil and collect 1 L after discarding first 50 mL. Dissolve 40 g KOH in this 1 L alcohol, keeping temp. <15° while dissolving alkali. Keep soln in g-s bottle. Or, (*2*) crush 40 g KOH in 185 mm mortar. Add 45 g granulated CaO and grind mixt. to powder. From 1 L alcohol add 100 mL to mortar and transfer to flask, rinsing mortar with several more portions. Add remainder of alcohol to flask, shake mixt. ≥5 min, and invert beaker over neck of flask. Repeat shaking several times during day. Next morning filter soln into clean, dry, g-s bottle.

28.026 ***Determination***

Accurately weigh ca 5 g filtered sample into 250–300 mL erlenmeyer. Pipet 50 mL alc. KOH soln into flask, draining pipet definite time. Connect flask with air condenser and boil until fat is completely saponified (ca 30 min). Cool, and titr. with 0.5*N* HCl, **50.011–50.012**, using phthln. Conduct blank detn along with that on sample, using same pipet for measuring KOH soln and draining same time.

Calc. saponification no. (mg KOH required to saponify 1 g fat) = 28.05 $(B - S)$/g sample,

where B = mL 0.5*N* HCl required by blank and S = mL 0.5*N* HCl required for sample.

★ Surplus method—*see* inside front cover.

28.027 ★ Soluble Acids—Official Final Action ★

See **26.030**, 10th ed.

28.028 ★ Insoluble Acids (Hehner Number) ★
Official Final Action

See **26.031**, 10th ed.

Free Fatty Acids in Crude and Refined Oils

28.029 ***National Cottonseed Products Association Method—Official Final Action***

(a) *In crude oils.*—Weigh 7.05 g well mixed oil into 250 mL flask or 4 oz bottle. Add 50 mL alcohol, previously neutzd by adding 2 mL phthln soln and enough 0.1*N* NaOH to produce faint permanent pink. Titr. with 0.25*N* NaOH, **50.034–50.035**, with vigorous shaking until permanent faint pink appears and persists ≥1 min. Report as % free fatty acids expressed as oleic acid; mL 0.25*N* NaOH used in titrn corresponds to this %.

(b) *In refined oils.*—To ca 50 mL alcohol in clean, dry 150 mL flask, add few drops of the oil and 2 mL phthln. Place flask in H_2O at 60–65° until warm, and add enough 0.1*N* NaOH to produce faint permanent pink. Weigh 56.4 g oil into the neutzd alcohol and titr. with 0.1*N* NaOH, **50.034–50.035**, occasionally warming and violently shaking mixt. until same faint permanent pink appears in supernate alcohol. Multiply mL 0.1*N* NaOH by 0.05 and report as % free fatty acids expressed as oleic acid.

Free fatty acids may also be expressed in terms of acid value (mg KOH necessary to neutze 1 g sample). Acid value = % free fatty acids (as oleic) × 1.99.

Crude Fatty Acids (*9*)—Official First Action

AOAC-American Oil Chemists' Society Method

28.030 ***Principle***

Sample is saponified and, after acidification, fatty acids and unsaponifiable matter are removed by continuous extn with hexane. Extn of second sample without acidification yields unsaponifiable matter. Fatty acids are detd by difference.

28.031 ***Apparatus***

(a) *Liquid-liquid extractor.*—*See* Fig. **28.02**. With mag. stirring disk, condenser, and refluxing flask (available as No. 4112A-E, Glencoe Scientific, Inc., 2802 White Oak Dr, Houston, TX 77007).

(b) *Combination hot plate-magnetic stirrer.*—Sargent-Welch Model H, or equiv., to provide mag. stirring at 25 and 80°.

(c) *Heating mantle or other device for refluxing hexane.*

(d) *Rotary evaporator.*—Sargent-Welch No. S-31210, or equiv., which releases vac. with N or He.

28.032 ***Reagents***

(a) *Potassium hydroxide soln.*—50%. Dissolve 50 g KOH in H_2O and dil. to 100 mL with H_2O.

(b) *Hexane.*—Redistd or residue-free when 200 mL is evapd (Phillips Chemical Co. *n*-hexane has been found satisfactory).

(c) *Nitrogen* (*low oxygen content*) *or helium.*

28.033 ***Preparation of Sample***

Warm sample to liq., mix thoroly, transfer ca 5 g to 50 mL beaker, and cool. Weigh, with dropper, warm to liq., transfer 2–2.5 g by dropper to reaction vessel contg mag. stirring disk, cool beaker and dropper, and reweigh. Add 50 mL alcohol and 3 mL KOH soln, cover with watch glass, and heat just at bp, with

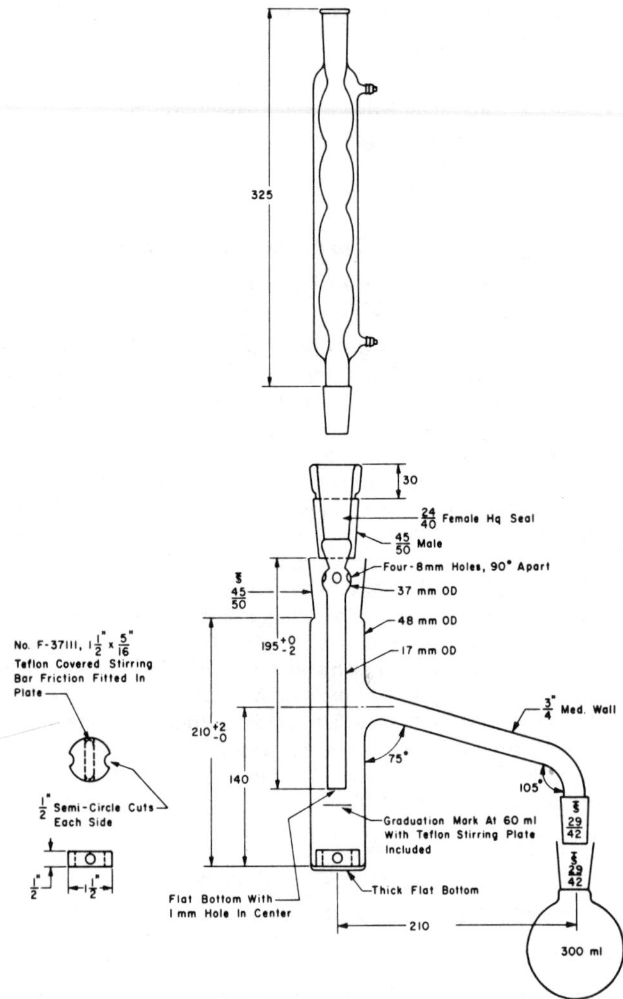

FIG. 28:02—Liquid-liquid extractor

gentle stirring, 30 min. Add alcohol to original vol., add 50 mL H_2O, and warm if necessary to dissolve soap.

28.034 ***Total Fatty Acids and Unsaponifiable Matter***

Acidify freshly saponified sample by slowly adding 6*N* HCl (ca 5 mL) to reaction vessel. Test with Me orange indicator to assure that soln is strongly acid. Fill inner tube of extractor with hexane, immediately insert into position in reaction vessel to prevent backflow of aq. soln, and attach condenser. Add 100 mL hexane to r-b flask, add No. 20 SiC boiling chip or inverted mp tube, attach to side arm, and begin refluxing with mag. stirrer rotating at min. speed. While checking to see that emulsions do not rise in reaction vessel, gradually increase rotation to ca 500 rpm and reflux rate to 200–250 drops/min. Continue refluxing with stirring 2.0 hr. Cool r-b flask and filter soln, if cloudy, thru 2–3 cm paper on fritted disk. Remove solv. either on steam bath with stream of N or in rotary evaporator, applying vac. cautiously 1 min, then full vac. with flask immersed in 80° bath addnl 20 min. Cool, release vac. with N, dry outer surface of r-b flask, and weigh. Repeat 80° vac. step, if necessary, to assure const wt. Calc. % total fatty acids plus unsaponifiable matter (crude fatty acids). Subtract value for unsaponifiable matter, **28.035**, to obtain total fatty acids.

28.035 ***Unsaponifiable Matter***

Starting with freshly saponified sample, **28.033**, ext (without acidification) as in **28.034**. Cool r-b flask and transfer hexane soln to 250 mL separator, rinsing gently with 10 mL hexane.

Det. unsaponifiable matter as in **28.081**, par. 1, beginning "Shake vigorously, . . ." but use hexane instead of ether.

Soluble and Insoluble Volatile Acids (Reichert-Meissl and Polenske Values) (*10*)—Official Final Action

28.036 ***Reagents***

(**a**) *Sodium hydroxide soln.*—(1+1). Prep. as in **50.033(b)**.

(**b**) *Glycerol-soda soln.*—Add 20 mL 1 + 1 NaOH soln to 180 mL pure glycerol.

(**c**) *Silicon carbide.*—Grit No. 6, Carborundum Co.

28.037 ***Determination***

Accurately weigh 5±0.1 g sample into clean, dry 300 mL r-b flask. Add 20 mL glycerol-soda soln and heat with swirling over flame or asbestos-covered hot plate until completely saponified, as shown by mixt. becoming perfectly clear. No oil should remain on surface; walls of flask are wet by soln. Let flask cool to ca 100° (ca 5 min) and *dissolve* contents in 135±1 mL recently boiled H_2O with min. loss of H_2O vapor. (135 mL H_2O is conveniently measured from 125 mL erlenmeyer previously calibrated to deliver 134.6±1.0 g H_2O at 25°.) Add 6 mL H_2SO_4 (1+4) and 15 pieces of SiC. Distil, using app. with dimensions given in Fig. **28:03**. (Adapter may be used for distg into 110 mL vol. flask.) Rest flask on piece of asbestos board with center hole 5 cm diam., and regulate flame so as to collect 110 mL distillate in 30±2 min (measure time from passage of first drop of distillate from condenser to receiving flask), letting distillate drip into receiving flask at temp. of ca 20°.

When 110 mL has distd, substitute 25 mL graduate for receiving flask, remove flame, and disconnect distn head from condenser. Mix without violent shaking, immerse flask contg distillate almost completely in 15° H_2O 15 min, filter thru dry 9 cm moderately retentive paper (S&S 589 White Ribbon is satisfactory), and titr. 100 mL filtrate with 0.1*N* NaOH, **50.034–50.035**, using phthln. Soln should remain pink 2–3 min. Reichert-Meissl value is mL 0.1*N* NaOH used, corrected for titrn of blank detn, ×1.1, calcd to 5.00 g sample.

Remove remainder of sol. acids from insol. acids on filter by washing with three 15 mL portions 15° H_2O, each previously passed thru condenser, 25 mL graduate, and 110 mL receiving flask. Dissolve insol. acids by passing three 15 mL portions neut. alcohol thru filter paper, each portion having previously passed thru condenser, 25 mL graduate, and 110 mL receiving flask. Titr. combined alc. washings with 0.1*N* NaOH, using phthln. Polenske value is mL 0.1*N* NaOH required for titrn, corrected for titrn obtained in blank detn, and calcd to 5.00 g sample.

Note: Unless these directions are followed in every detail, reproducible results cannot be obtained.

Mole Per Cent Butyric Acid in Fat

Chromatographic Method (11)—Official Final Action

28.038 ***Apparatus***

Chromatographic tube.—Fuse 15 cm section of 38 mm od tubing to 20 cm of 22 mm tubing, which in turn is fused to 5 cm of 7 mm tubing, with drip tip.

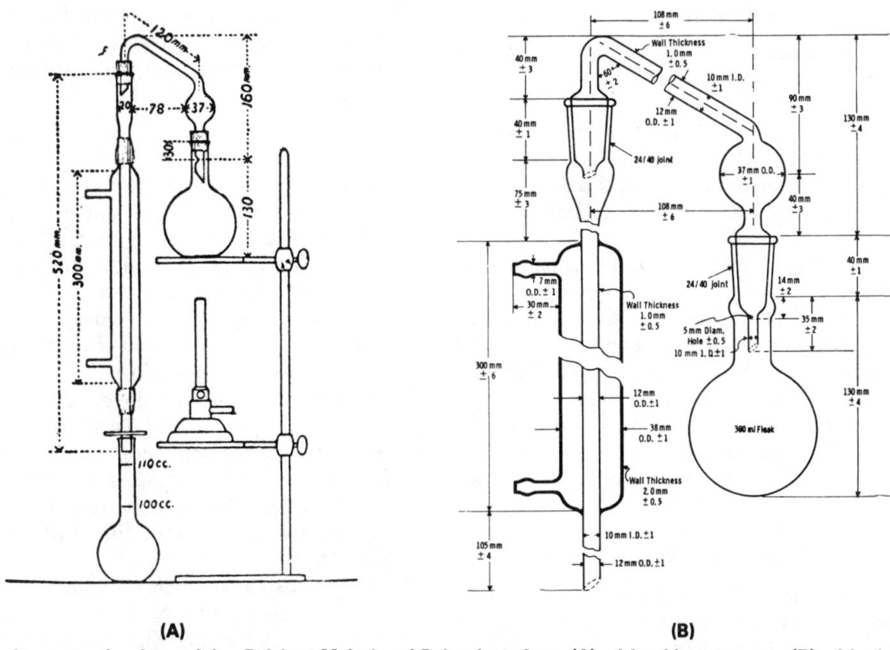

FIG. 28:03—Apparatus for determining Reichert-Meissl and Polenske values; (A) with rubber stoppers, (B) with glass joints

28.039 ***Reagents***

(**a**) *Silicic acid.*—Mallinckrodt Chemical Works No. 2847. Heat in shallow pan or evapg dish 18 hr at 175°. Store in desiccator or tightly sealed container.

(**b**) *Bromocresol green-glycol soln.*—Dissolve 700 mg bromocresol green in 700 mL ethylene glycol by warming on steam bath. Cool, and add ca 200 mL H_2O. Prep. 0.1*N* NH_4OH by dilg ca 6.6 mL NH_4OH to 1 L with H_2O. Add 40 mL of this soln to indicator soln and addnl H_2O to make 1 L. Store this ink-blue soln in stoppered bottle.

(**c**) *Packing material.*—Mix H_2SiO_3, (**a**), in ratio of 100 g to ca 95 mL bromocresol green-glycol soln, (**b**), until homogeneous olive-green powder is obtained. Small batches may be mixed in mortar; larger batches, in mech. mixer. Prepd packing material may be stored in tightly stoppered container several months.

(**d**) *Hexane-butanol mixture.*—Add 1 vol. *n*-BuOH to 100 mL vols *n*-hexane (com. grade; Phillips Chemical Co., or equiv.).

(**e**) *Isopropanol-KOH soln.*—Dissolve 25 g KOH pellets in 400 mL isopropanol by warming and swirling on steam bath. Decant supernate alc. soln from the small amt of aq. soln clinging to bottom of flask. Cool and decant supernate isopropanol-KOH soln, which contains ca 50 mg KOH/mL. Store in refrigerator.

(**f**) *Potassium hydroxide soln.*—Approx. 0.05*N*. Dil. 60 mL isopropanol-KOH soln, (**e**), with 440 mL isopropanol and 500 mL MeOH. Store in amber or "Lifetime Red" Pyrex bottle.

(**g**) *Thymol blue soln.*—Dissolve 300 mg thymol blue in 25 mL 0.05*N* alc. KOH soln, (**f**), and add 75 mL isopropanol.

28.040 ***Preparation of Fatty Acid Solution***

(**a**) *Saponification.*—Transfer 0.5–0.7 g well mixed, melted fat to 20 × 150 mm test tube with lip, and add 5 mL isopropanol-KOH soln, (**e**), and boiling chip. Place tube to depth of 5 cm in boiling H_2O bath 20 min to saponify fat, and evap. isopropanol, leaving solid soap. Stopper, and analyze within 48 hr.

(**b**) *Determination of quantity of acid required to hydrolyze soap.*—Add 5 mL isopropanol-KOH soln, (**e**), to 10 mL H_2O and 2 drops thymol blue soln, (**g**), in small beaker or flask. Add H_2SO_4 (2+1) dropwise, with const stirring, until initial blue color turns to yellow, orange, and finally red. This vol. H_2SO_4, measured with same dropper, is subsequently used to hydrolyze the soap. (If top of chromatgc column turns blue on addn of fatty acid soln, use of more H_2SO_4 to hydrolyze soap is indicated; top of chromatgc column should be yellow.)

(**c**) *Hydrolysis of soap and extraction of fatty acids.*—Add to soap, while cooling tube in cold H_2O, number of drops H_2SO_4 (2+1) indicated in (**b**). Break up lumps in bottom of tube with glass stirring rod. After mass in tube is thoroly mixed, yellow mixt. of fatty acids clinging to viscous aq. layer of K_2SO_4 should be obtained. Add 10 mL hexane-BuOH soln to tube and thoroly mix with glass rod. Aq. phase should cling to white ppt of K_2SO_4, allowing easy decantation of solv. soln of fatty acids. This soln of acids is ready for chromatgy.

28.041 ***Preparation of Chromatographic Column***

Overlay 35 g packing material with hexane-BuOH soln in mortar. Mix with pestle to form slurry. Place small glass wool plug loosely in constricted end of column and gently tamp into place with glass rod. Place finger over constricted end of column and add hexane-BuOH soln until reservoir is half full. Using teaspoon, underlay prepd slurry beneath solv. Jiggle spoon up and down along side of reservoir, and let flocculent slurry settle to bottom of column.

After adding all packing material, remove finger and let solv. flow out and packing material settle. Apply 5–10 lb (34.5–68.9 kPa) air pressure to top of column to speed up flow of solv. and facilitate uniform packing of slurry. Release pressure just before last portion of solv. sinks into column. If column looks uniformly packed, it is ready for use; if not, add more hexane-BuOH soln to reservoir and again apply pressure as before. Prepd column should have flow rate of ca 3.5 mL/min without use of pressure. If flow rate is <3 mL/min, add more bromocresol green-glycol soln to packing material, and remix. If flow rate is >4 mL/min, add more H_2SiO_3 to packing material, and remix. Hexane-BuOH soln, recovered during prepn of column, may be used subsequently to prep. other columns or for chromatgy.

28.042 ***Chromatography of Fatty Acids***

Decant solv. soln of fatty acids onto top of packed column and immediately start collecting eluate in 250 mL erlenmeyer. As soon as fatty acid soln completely settles into packing, wash down inside of reservoir with three 5 mL portions hexane-BuOH soln. Let each washing sink into packing before refilling reservoir. Yellow band should always be observed at very top of column; this band contains inorg. acids (H_2SO_4 and acid sulfate) and will not move.

If sample contains butterfat, second distinct yellow band due to butyric acid appears and slowly migrates down column, breaking away from top band. Long-chain fatty acids, $\geq C_6$, pass rapidly thru column and do not form yellow bands. Eluate vol. between elution of last traces of long-chain acids and first traces of butyric acid will be 20–30 mL. When lower edge of yellow butyric acid zone is 1 cm from lower end of chromatgc column, change fraction collector. First fraction contains long-chain acids and is usually 100±10 mL. Next 120 mL fraction contains butyric acid.

28.043 ***Titration of Fatty Acid Fractions***

Add 1 drop thymol blue soln for each 10 mL eluate being titrd. Titr. each fraction to first permanent appearance of purple-blue end point, using ca 0.05*N* KOH, **(f)**, dispensed from 50 mL buret for first fraction and from 5 mL buret, graduated in 0.01 mL, for second fraction. End point for each fraction is sharp but is subject to fading because of CO_2 absorption. The CO_2 effect is negligible if titrn is conducted rapidly with little agitation. If necessary, titrn may be carried out in CO_2-free atm. which tends to make titrn values more reproducible. (Pass air thru 20% aq. KOH soln, then thru H_2O, and finally into titrn flask.)

Blank corrections are not required. Alkali added to thymol blue soln takes care of blank.

Express butyric acid titrn as % of sum of the 2 titrns, calcd to nearest 0.1%. *Example:* Long-chain acid titrn = 26.1 mL; butyric acid titrn = 2.83 mL; sum = 28.93. Mole % butyric acid = 2.83 × 100/28.9 = 9.8.

★ Saturated and Unsaturated Fatty Acids ★

28.044 ***Lead Salt-Ether Method (12)—Official Final Action***

See **28.039**, 11th ed.

Polyunsaturated Acids (*13*)—Official Final Action

American Oil Chemists' Society Method

28.045 ***Principle***

Natural conjugated constituents are detd by measuring UV absorption at specified wavelengths in purified solv. Nonconjugated polyunsatd constituents are partially conjugated by heating in KOH-glycol soln, and absorptions of conjugated constituents are redetd. The % conjugated diene, triene, tetraene, and pentaene acids are calcd from predetd *a* by simultaneous equations.

Method is applicable to detn of polyunsatd acids, dienoic thru pentaenoic, in animal and vegetable fats contg only natural or *cis* isomers, only small amts of preformed conjugated material, and only small amts of pigments whose absorption may undergo considerable change during the alkali isomerization. Method is not applicable, or is applicable only with specific precautions, to hydrogenated oils or other fats contg *trans* isomers of unsatd fatty acids, to fish oils or similar fats contg acids more highly unsatd than pentaenoic, to crude oils or samples contg pigments whose absorption undergoes changes during alkali isomerization, or to fats and oils contg large amts of preformed conjugated fatty acids.

★ Surplus method—*see* inside front cover.

28.046 ***Apparatus***

(a) *Isomerization apparatus.*—(*See* Fig. **28:04.**) (*1*) *Constant temperature bath.*—180±1°. Capacity sufficient to immerse 25 × 250 mm Pyrex test tubes to depth of 114 mm (4.5"). (Westinghouse, or equiv. household deepfat fryer has been found satisfactory.) For bath liq. use Fisher Scientific Co. No. B-219 bath wax or DC 550 Fluid, Dow Corning Corp. Place bath in insulated box with insulated cover having holes for stirrer and cork supports for test tubes.

(*2*) *Test tubes.*—Pyrex, lipped, 25 × 250 mm.

(*3*) *Distributing heads.*—To fit test tubes snugly. Tubing in center of head has both ends open and 2 small holes 25 and 38 mm, resp., from bottom. (*See* Fig. **28:05**, right.)

(*4*) *Manifold.*—With 10 outlets, each connected to 50 mm long capillary tube, 1 mm bore. Cap unused outlets. (*See* Fig. **28:05**, left.)

(*5*) *Nitrogen manometer.*—Construct from 6 mm od tubing bent in shape of U-tube, ht ca 380 mm, width ca 30 mm. Fill manometer ca half full with H_2O contg 1 drop Me orange and 1 drop H_2SO_4. To adjust flow of N, attach ca 90 cm rubber tubing to one of N outlets on distributing head. Fill 100 mL graduate with H_2O and invert in container of H_2O. Insert end of rubber tubing under graduate. Turn on N supply and measure rate of displacement of H_2O in graduate. Rate of flow should be 50–100 mL/min. Mark level of liq. in manometer at this flow rate.

(b) *Spectrophotometer.*—Covering range of 220–360 nm with wavelength scale readable to 0.1 nm. Beckman Model DU is satisfactory. Adjust H lamp with no cell in beam so meter balances at lowest possible wavelength (usually ≤211 nm). Slit widths are critical for absorption measurements at 262, 268, and 274 nm where, at final balancing, adjustments must be 0.8–0.9 mm.

(c) *Absorption cells.*—Quartz, matched pairs in lengths 1.000±0.005 cm. When filled with H_2O or isooctane, must match within 0.01 *A* unit.

28.047 ***Reagents***

(a) *Methanol, absolute.*—Check *A* of 1 cm layer of MeOH against H_2O at 220 nm and thru range of wavelengths used in

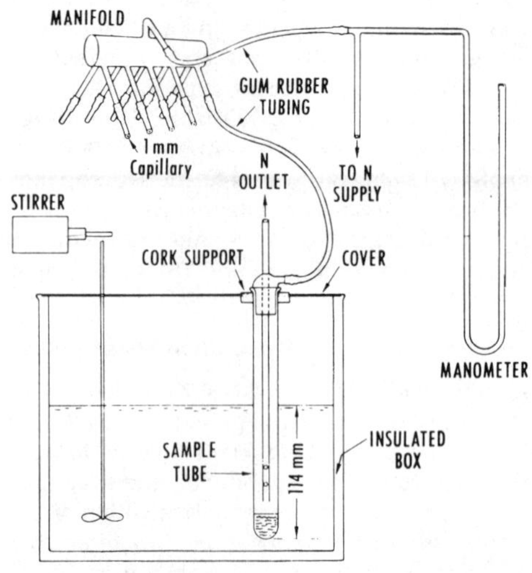

FIG. 28:04—Constant temperature bath and accessories

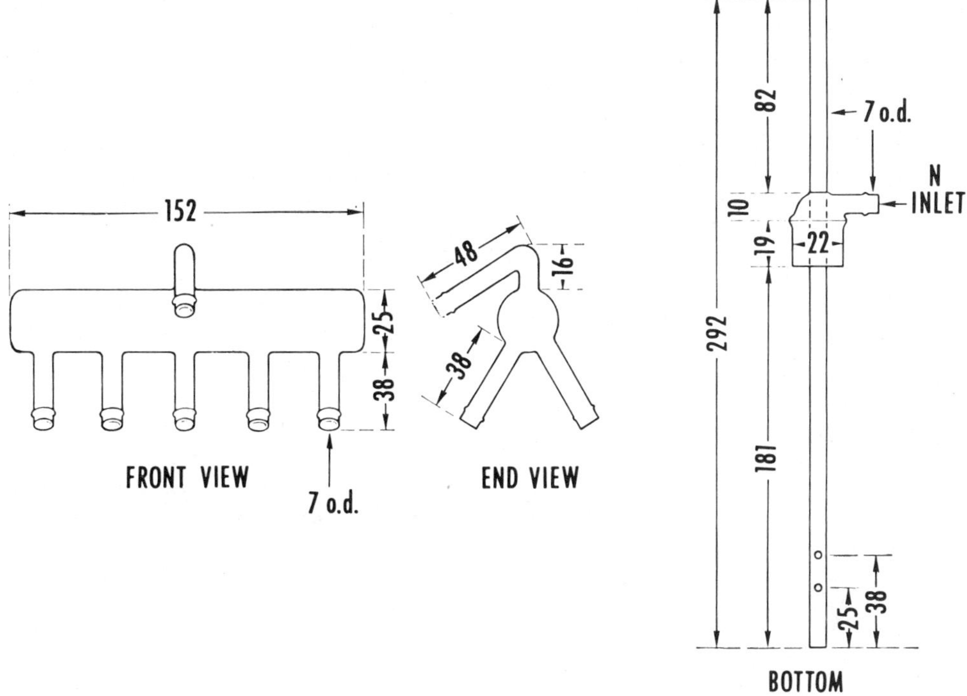

FIG. 28:05—Right, distribution heads. Left, manifold. All dimensions are in mm

analysis. *A* at 220 nm must be <0.4 and curve should be smooth in range 262–322 nm. Otherwise purify as follows, and recheck *A*:

Place 2 L MeOH from new drum or glass bottles into 3 L double-neck ₮ distg flask; add 10 g KOH and 25 g Zn dust. Stopper one outlet and place reflux condenser in other, and reflux on steam bath 3 hr. Remove from steam bath; replace reflux tube with distg trap, 75° connecting tube, and condenser. Place flask in H_2O bath or elec. heating mantle and distil, collecting distillate in 2 L erlenmeyer. Store in g-s bottle. Absolute alcohol is satisfactory if of comparable purity (as obtained or purified).

(b) *Isooctane (2,2,4-trimethylpentane).*—NBS certified grade or spectral grade, Phillips Chemical Co. Hexane or cyclohexane is satisfactory if *A* requirements are met. Purify as follows: Place ca 9 cm glass wool above stopcock at lower end of 80 × 4.5 cm filter tube. Add ca 30 cm silica gel (Grade 12, 28–200 mesh, Fisher No. S-157, or equiv.). Pour isooctane slowly into tube, filling ca ¾ full. Insert cork stopper covered with Al foil loosely in top of tube and let isooctane filter thru silica gel, collecting in 2 L erlenmeyer. Renew silica gel as often as necessary to yield isooctane conforming to *A* limit. Check *A* of 1 cm layer of the isooctane against H_2O thru range of wavelengths used in analysis. *A* compared with H_2O set at 0 must be ≤0.070 at all wavelengths, and the resultant *A* versus wavelength curve must be smooth. Otherwise refilter and recheck *A*.

(c) *Potassium hydroxide-glycol soln.*—6.6% KOH for 25 min isomerization. Weigh ca 750 g ethylene glycol into 1 L r-b Pyrex flask. Close with hollow stopper contg short outlet tube and inlet tube reaching to bottom of flask. Connect inlet tube to O-free N supply (<0.01 % O) and bubble N thru liq. during all stages of prepn to exclude all air and to agitate liq. slightly. Place in oil bath at 100–150°; raise bath temp. to 190° and hold 10 min to dry glycol. Remove bath and let bath temp. drop to 120°. Slowly and carefully add 60 g 85% KOH, keeping soln under N. Return to oil bath; reheat bath to 190° and hold at this temp. 10 min. Remove from bath, and cool. Remove hollow stopper and close with solid stopper. Store in refrigerator at ca 4° (40°F) under N.

Check KOH content by adding 10.00 g KOH-glycol soln to ca 90 mL MeOH, neutzd with 1*N* HCl to phthln end point. Titr. with stdzd 1*N* HCl until pink just disappears. % KOH = mL × normality × 5.61/wt soln. If % KOH is not 6.5–6.6, dry some glycol by heating under N at 190° as above, and adjust to 6.6% KOH.

(d) *Potassium hydroxide-glycol soln.*—21% KOH for 15 min isomerization. Prep. as in (**c**), except use 210 g 85% KOH. Titr., and adjust to 21±0.1% KOH, if necessary.

(e) *Nitrogen gas.*—Pre-purified grade, <0.01% O.

28.048 ***Preparation of Sample***

Melt sample carefully on steam bath, stir thoroly, and filter if not clear.

28.049 ***Determination***

(The 6.6% KOH method is preferred when samples contain only linoleic and linolenic acids; the 21% KOH method is preferred when samples contain linoleic, linolenic, and arachidonic acids. When pentaenoic acids are present, 21% KOH method must be used.)

(a) *For conjugated polyunsaturated acids.*—Into 1 mL Pyrex cup (diam. 14 mm, ht 10 mm) weigh enough sample to give *A* reading of ≥0.2 (ca 200 mg). Drop cup into 75 mL isooctane in 150 mL beaker, and rotate beaker to dissolve sample, warming if necessary. Cool to room temp., transfer to 100 mL g-s vol. flask, dil. to vol. with solv., and mix thoroly. Measure *A* in UV region against matched cell contg solv., dilg soln (and/or using other cell lengths if necessary so that observed *A* is 0.2–0.8). Also take readings on both sides of specified wavelengths to det. that max. is present. Component is considered absent if max. is not found in characteristic region and no further calcns are made in this region. Measure at: Dienoic, *233* nm; trienoic, 262, *268,* 274 nm; tetraenoic, 308, *315,* 322 nm; pentaenoic, *346* nm.

(**b**) *For nonconjugated polyunsaturated acids, 6.6% KOH, 25 min isomerization.*—Weigh 100 mg (to nearest 0.5 mg) sample into 1 mL Pyrex glass cup. Weigh 11.0±0.1 g of the 6.6% KOH-glycol soln into 25 × 250 mm Pyrex test tube. Conduct ≥2 blank detns with sample. Cover tube with distributing head and connect to a capillary tube on manifold. Adjust flow of N to permit ≥50–100 mL N to pass thru tube/min. Let N sweep thru tube 1 min to remove air; then immerse to depth of 114 mm in bath at 180±1°. Check temp. frequently and stdze thermometer at frequent intervals.

After 20 min remove distributing head and drop 1 mL cup contg weighed sample into tube, note exact time, and replace head. Drop clean 1 mL cup into blanks. Keeping distributing head in place, remove tube from bath, swirl vigorously few sec, and return to bath; after 1 min, examine soln. If clear, return to bath; if not clear, indicating incomplete saponification, swirl tube 2–3 times and return to bath. At 1 min intervals, repeat swirling until saponification is complete. Keep bath temp. at 180±1°.

Exactly 25 min after dropping sample into tube, remove from bath, wipe clean, and place in 3 L beaker to cool, continuing to pass N over soln. Cold H_2O bath may also be used. After cooling, remove head, and wash lower tubing with 20 mL purified MeOH, collecting washings in test tube. Wash with MeOH from beaker; do not use wash bottle.

Insert glass stirring rod 30 cm long with curved end at bottom into test tube and move cup up and down to mix soln. Transfer soln to 100 mL g-s vol. flask, dil. to vol. with purified MeOH, and mix thoroly. Measure *A* as in (**a**), using KOH-glycol blank as ref. If diln of sample soln is required, make similar dilns of blank. If blanks do not check, repeat tests, increasing flow of N.

(**c**) *For nonconjugated polyunsaturated acids, 21% KOH, 15 min isomerization.*—Proceed as in (**b**), except use 80 mg sample and 21±0.1% KOH-glycol soln, and isomerize exactly 15 min.

28.050 ***Spectrophotometric Readings***

If polyunsatd fatty acid constituent is known to be absent, or its absence is confirmed during analysis (no max. detected at its anal. wavelength), no spectrophtric reading is required in region of its absorption and no *a* at that region need be included in equations. For example, cottonseed oil is known to contain no polyunsatd constituents more highly unsatd than dienoic (linoleic acid). Hence, in analysis of this oil, measurements are required only at 233 nm, and equation to calc. linoleic acid content requires *a* only at this wavelength.

Correction for background absorption is used only when measuring very small traces of fatty acids. When fatty acid is present in more than trace, background corrections are not required and their use may lead to erroneous results. When *a* of any polyunsatd constituent after isomerization, at its analytical wavelength, is >1.0, no background correction should be made. No background corrections are to be made after isomerization with 21% KOH.

28.051 ***Calculations***

(**a**) *Absorptivity for conjugated constituents.*—Calc. *a* for each wavelength recorded in detn, **28.049(a)**, using subscripts, 233, 268, 315, 346, to designate each individual *a*.

Absorptivity, $a = A/bc$, where A = observed absorbance, b = cell length in cm, and c = g sample/L final diln used for A measurement.

In following equations, subscripts 2, 3, 4, and 5 refer to diene, triene, tetraene, and pentaene constituents, resp.

Absorptivity at 233 nm corrected for absorption by acid or ester groups $= a_2 = a_{233} - a_0$, where $a_0 = 0.07$ for esters and 0.03 for soaps and fatty acids.

Absorptivity at 268 nm corrected for background absorption $= a_3 = 2.8\,[a_{268} - \frac{1}{2}(a_{262} + a_{274})]$.

Absorptivity at 315 nm corrected for background absorption $= a_4 = 2.5\,[a_{315} - \frac{1}{2}(a_{308} + a_{322})]$.

Absorptivity at 346 nm $= a_5 = a_{346}$.

(**b**) *Conjugated acids.*—If quantities within brackets of a_3 or a_4 are 0 or neg., no characteristic absorption maxima are present and corresponding constituent is reported as absent. As preformed constituents are usually present in small amts, background absorption corrections are usually required. If large amts of preformed constituents are present, this method is not applicable. However, no background corrections are to be applied to readings in pentaenoic region, 346 nm.

% Conjugated diene $= C_2 = 0.91a_2$.
% Conjugated triene $= C_3 = 0.47a_3$.
% Conjugated tetraene $= C_4 = 0.45a_4$.
% Conjugated pentaene $= C_5 = 0.39a_5$.

(**c**) *Absorptivities for nonconjugated constituents, 6.6% KOH, 25 min isomerization.*—Calc. a' for each wavelength in detn, (**b**). $a' = A/bc$.

Absorptivity at 233 nm corrected for conjugated diene acids originally present $= a'_2 = a'_{233} - a_2 - 0.03$.

Absorptivity at 268 nm corrected for background absorption and for undestroyed conjugated triene $= a'_3 = 4.03[a'_{268} - \frac{1}{2}(a'_{262} + a'_{274})] - a_3$.

Absorptivity at 315 nm corrected for background absorption and for undestroyed conjugated tetraene $= a'_4 = 2.06[a'_{315} - \frac{1}{2}(a'_{308} + a'_{322})] - a_4$.

(**d**) *Nonconjugated acids, 6.6% KOH, 25 min isomerization.*—
(*1*) Without background corrections:
% Linoleic acid $= X = 1.086a'_2 - 1.324(a'_{268} - a_{268}) + 0.40(a'_{315} - a_{315})$.
% Linolenic acid $= Y = 1.980(a'_{268} - a_{268}) - 4.92\,(a'_{315} - a_{315})$.
% Arachidonic acid $= Z = 4.69(a'_{315} - a_{315})$.
(*2*) When background corrections are required:
% Linoleic acid $= X = 1.086a'_2 - 1.324a'_3 + 0.40a'_4$.
% Linolenic acid $= Y = 1.980a'_3 - 4.92a'_4$.
% Arachidonic acid $= Z = 4.69a'_4$.

(**e**) *Absorptivities for nonconjugated constituents, 21% KOH, 15 min isomerization.*—Calc. a' for each wavelength 233, 268, 315, and 346 nm. (If no max. is found, report component as 0 without further measurement or calcn.)

Absorptivity at 233 nm $= a'_2 = a'_{233} - a_2$.
Absorptivity at 268 nm $= a'_3 = a'_{268} - a_{268}$.
Absorptivity at 315 nm $= a'_4 = a'_{315} - a_{315}$.
Absorptivity at 346 nm $= a'_5 = a'_{346} - a_{346}$.

(**f**) *Nonconjugated acids, 21% KOH, 15 min isomerization.*—(Spectrophtric method will not differentiate between acids with same number of double bonds but different chain length, e.g., between C_{20} and C_{22} pentaenes. First 2 sets of equations below are for samples contg C_{20} pentaene acid and for samples contg C_{22} pentaene acid, resp. If chain length is unknown, assume that these pentaene acids are present in equal amts, and apply third set of equations.)

(*1*) *Samples contg C_{20} pentaene acid:*
% Linoleic acid $= X = 1.09a'_2 - 0.57a'_3 - 0.26a'_4 + 0.002a'_5$.
% Linolenic acid $= Y = 1.10a'_3 - 0.88a'_4 + 0.31a'_5$.
% Arachidonic acid $= Z = 1.65a'_4 - 1.55a'_5$.
% Pentaenoic acids $= P = 1.14a'_5$.

(*2*) *Samples contg C_{22} pentaene acid:*
% Linoleic acid $= X = 1.09a'_2 - 0.57a'_3 - 0.26a'_4 - 0.12a'_5$.
% Linolenic acid $= Y = 1.10a'_3 - 0.88a'_4 - 0.02a'_5$.

% Arachidonic acid = Z = $1.65a'_4 - 1.86a'_5$.
% Pentaenoic acids = P = $1.98a'_5$.

(3) Samples contg pentaene acids of unknown chain length (calcd as 50% C_{20}–50% C_{22} pentaenoic acids):

% Linoleic acid = X = $1.09a'_2 - 0.57a'_3 - 0.26a'_4 - 0.03a'_5$.
% Linolenic acid = Y = $1.10a'_3 - 0.88a'_4 + 0.19a'_5$.
% Arachidonic acid = Z = $1.65a'_4 - 1.67a'_5$.
% Pentaenoic acids = P = $1.45a'_5$.

(g) *Total composition:*

% Total conjugated polyunsatd acids = $C_2 + C_3 + C_4 + C_5$.
% Total nonconjugated polyunsatd acids = $X + Y + Z + P$.
% Oleic acid = {I value (Wijs) of sample − [1.811 ($C_2 + X$) + 2.737($C_3 + Y$) + 3.337($C_4 + Z$) + 4.014* ($C_5 + P$)]}/0.899.
% Satd acids = % total fatty acid − (% oleic acid + % conjugated acid + % nonconjugated acid).

(% total fatty acid of most naturally occurring oils is 95.6. To calc. to fatty acid basis, multiply the % value by 100/% total fatty acid.)

Preparation of Methyl Esters

28.052 ★ *Esterification in Presence of Sulfuric Acid* ★ *Official First Action*

See **26.052**, 10th ed.

Boron Trifluoride Method (14)—Official First Action AOAC-IUPAC Method

28.053 ***Principle***

Glycerides and phospholipids are saponified, and fatty acids are liberated and esterified in presence of BF_3 catalyst for further analysis by IR, **28.079**, or GLC, **28.062**.

Method is applicable to common animal and vegetable oils and fats, and fatty acids. Unsaponifiables are not removed, and if present in large amts, may interfere with subsequent analyses.

Method is not suitable for prepn of methyl esters of fatty acids contg major amts of epoxy, hydroperoxy, aldehyde, ketone, cyclopropyl, and cyclopropenyl groups, and conjugated polyunsatd and acetylenic compds because of partial or complete destruction of these groups.

28.054 ***Apparatus***

(a) *Reaction flasks.*—50 and 125 mL flasks with outer ₸ joints.
(b) *Condenser.*—Water-cooled, reflux, with 20–30 cm jacket and ₸ inner joint.

28.055 ***Reagents***

(a) *Boron trifluoride reagent.*—125 g BF_3/L MeOH. Available com. or prep. as follows: Weigh 2 L flask contg 1 L MeOH. Cool in ice bath and with flask still in bath, bubble BF_3 from cylinder thru glass tube into MeOH until 125 g is absorbed. Work in hood. BF_3 must be flowing thru glass tube before it is placed in and until it is removed from MeOH to prevent liq. from being drawn into cylinder valve system. Gas should not flow so fast that white fumes emerge from flask. Reagent is stable 2 years. (*Caution:* Remove BF_3 vapors with effective fume removal device. Avoid contact with skin, eyes, and respiratory tract. *See* **51.010.**)

(b) *Methanolic sodium hydroxide soln.*—0.5*N*. Dissolve 2 g NaOH in 100 mL MeOH contg ≤0.5% H_2O. White ppt of Na_2CO_3 forming on long standing may be ignored.

(c) *Heptane.*—Pure, as detd by GLC. If fatty acids contg ≥20 C atoms are absent in sample, hexane may be substituted.
(d) *Methyl red soln.*—0.1% in 60% alcohol.
(e) *Nitrogen.*—Contg <5 mg O/kg.

Check new batches of reagents, particularly BF_3, by prepg and chromatographing Me esters of pure oleic acid. If extraneous peaks appear (in C_{20}-C_{22} region with BF_3), reject reagent.

28.056 ***Preparation***

(*Caution: See* **51.011** and **51.073.**)

(Work in hood. Wash all glassware immediately after use. If fatty acids contg >2 double bonds are present, remove air from MeOH and flask by passing in stream of N few min. Me esters should be analyzed as soon as possible. If necessary, heptane soln may be kept under N in refrigerator. For prolonged storage, seal in ampule and store in freezer or add equiv. of 0.005% 2,6-di-*tert*-butyl-4-methylphenol (BHT). For IR analysis, solv. removal must be as complete as possible; for GLC, 5–10% soln is suitable.)

Precise weighing is not required. Sample size need be known only to det. size of flask and amts of reagents, according to following table:

Sample mg	Flask mL	0.5*N* NaOH mL	BF_3 Reagent mL
100–250	50	4	5
250–500	50	6	7
500–750	100	8	9
750–1000	100	10	12

Sample ca 350 mg is preferred for GLC.

(a) *For fats and oils.*—Add sample to flask and then add methanolic NaOH soln and boiling chip. Attach condenser, and reflux until fat globules disappear (usually 5–10 min). Add BF_3 soln from bulb or automatic pipet thru condenser and continue boiling 2 min. Add 2–5 mL heptane thru condener and boil 1 min longer. Remove heat, then condenser, and add several mL *satd NaCl soln.* Rotate flask gently several times. Add addnl satd NaCl soln to float heptane soln into neck of flask. Transfer ca 1 mL upper heptane soln into g-s test tube and add small amt anhyd. Na_2SO_4 to remove H_2O. If necessary, dil. soln to concn of 5–10% for GLC.

To recover dry esters, transfer aq. and heptane phases to 250 mL separator. Ext with two 50 mL portions pet ether (bp 30–60°) or hexane. Wash combined exts with 20 mL portions H_2O until acid-free to Me red indicator. Dry over anhyd. Na_2SO_4, filter, and evap. solv. under stream of N on steam bath. If sample is <500 mg, reduce vols of solv. and H_2O.

More volatile esters may be lost if evapn is prolonged or if stream of N is too vigorous. For IR spectroscopy, terminate evapn as soon as solv. is removed. For GLC, method is applicable to fatty acids with ≥8 C atoms, if solv. is not completely removed.

(b) *For fatty acids.*—Add fatty acid sample to flask, then add BF_3 soln, and continue as in (a) with 2 min boiling under reflux.

Methyl Esters of Fatty Acids

AOAC-IUPAC Gas Chromatograpic Method (15) Official First Action

28.057 ***Principle***

Me esters of fatty acids from animal and vegetable fats having 8–24 C atoms are sepd and detd by gas chromatogy. Method is not applicable to epoxy, oxidized, or polymerized fatty acids.

* Corresponding constant for sample contg all C_{20} pentaene acids is 4.197; for all C_{22} pentaene acids it is 3.841.

★ Surplus method—*see* inside front cover.

28.058 ***Apparatus***

Following conditions are for use with flame ionization detector:

(**a**) *Gas chromatograph.*—With min. dead space in injection system, which is maintained at 20–50° higher than column temp. Maintain column temp. within ±1° to at least 220°. If programmed heated, dual columns are recommended.

(**b**) *Columns.*—1–3 m × 2–4 mm (id) glass or stainless steel (do not use stainless steel with polyunsatd components with >3 double bonds). Use short column when long-chain (>20 C atoms) acids are present.

(**c**) *Packing.*—Acid-washed and silanized diat. earth, with narrow range (25 μm) grain size between 125–250 μm (No. 60–120). Av. grain size is inversely related to id and directly related to column length. Coat with 5–20% polyester type polar liq. stationary phase (diethylene glycol polysuccinate, butanediol polysuccinate, ethylene glycol polyadipate, etc.) or other liq. (e.g., cyanosilicones) meeting efficiency and resolution specifications. Nonpolar phase can be used for certain sepns.

Condition column while disconnected from detector at 185° with current of inert gas at 20–60 mL/min for ≥16 hr and for addnl 2 hr at 195°. Conditioning temp. may vary with specific liq. phase.

(**d**) *Syringe.*—Max. vol. 10 μL, graduated to 0.1 μL.

(**e**) *Recorder.*—0–2.5 or 5.0 mv range, <1.5 sec response rate (time for pen to pass from 0 to 90% following momentary introduction of 100% signal), 25 cm min. paper width, and 25–100 cm/hr paper speed, with attenuator switch to change range. If integrator is used, it must have linear response with adequate sensitivity and satisfactory baseline correction.

If thermal conductivity detector is used, conditions must be modified as follows: Column, 2–4 m × 4 mm id; support, grain size 150–250 μm (No. 60–100); stationary phase, 15–25%; carrier gas, He or H; no auxiliary gas; temps (°): column 180–200, injector 40–60° above that of column; carrier gas flow, 60–80 mL/min; recorder, 0–1 mv range; and amt sample injected, 0.5–2 μL. Correction factors must be used.

28.059 ***Reagents***

(**a**) *Carrier gas.*—N, He, Ar dried and contg <10 mg O/kg.

(**b**) *Other gases.*—H, 99.9+%, free from org. impurities. Air or O, free from org. impurities (<2 ppm hydrocarbons equiv. to CH_4).

(**c**) *Reference stds.*—Known mixts of Me esters or Me esters of oil of known composition, preferably similar to that of material to be analyzed.

28.060 ***Operating Conditions***

Following variables are involved in selecting appropriate test conditions: length and id of column, temp. of column, carrier gas flow, resolution required, size of sample, and time of analysis. Size of sample should be such that linear response of detector and electrometer is obtained. In general, following conditions will elute Me stearate within ca 15 min at ≥2000 theoretical plates:

Column id, mm	Carrier gas flow, mL/min	Concn of stationary phase, %	Column temp., °C
2	15–25	5	175
3	20–40	10	180
4	40–60	15	185
		20	185

If app. permits, injector should be at ca 200° and detector at temp. above that of column. Flow of H to detector should be ca half that of carrier gas (H flow may be equal to carrier gas flow with N and 2 mm (id) column); flow of O ca 5–10 times that of H.

28.061 ***Performance Specifications***

Perform analysis on mixt. of Me stearate and Me oleate in ca equal proportions (e.g., Me esters from cocoa butter). Adjust sample size, column temp., and carrier gas flow so that Me stearate peak is recorded ca 15 min after solv. peak, ca ¾ full scale. Measure base widths in mm of Me stearate (w_1) and Me oleate (w_2) between points of intersection with baseline of tangents drawn to inflection points of curves. Also measure retention distance in mm (S) from start to peak max. for Me stearate and distance in mm between peak max. for Me stearate and Me oleate, Y. Calc. theoretical plates, n (efficiency), and resolution, R:

$$n = 16(S/w_1)^2,$$
$$R = 2Y/(w_1 + w_2).$$

Select conditions to obtain $n \geq 2000$ and $R \geq 1.25$. In addn, linolenic acid (18:3) Me ester should be sepd from arachidic acid (20:0) and gadoleic acid (20:1) esters. Columns will show gradual loss in R with use; when value becomes ≤1.25, replace.

28.062 ***Determination***

With app. showing stable baseline, inject 0.1–2 μL 5–10% heptane soln of Me esters, **28.053**. If trace components are desired, sample may be increased ≤10×. Pierce septum of inlet port and quickly discharge sample. Withdraw needle and note on chart small peak due to air or solv., marking start ref. point. Adjust sample size so major peak is not attenuated >8×, preferably less. Change setting of attenuator as necessary to keep peaks on chart paper. Mark attenuator setting on chart.

For detn of acids $<C_{12}$, lower column temp. is needed; for $>C_{20}$, higher. Temp. programming is useful in such cases, e.g., with acids $<C_{12}$, inject at 100° and raise temp. 4–8°/min to optimum, or program up to a fixed temp. and continue at const temp. until all components are eluted. If app. does not use programmed heating, operate at 2 fixed temps between 100° and 195°.

28.063 ***Identification***

Analyze ref. std mixts under same operating conditions as for sample. Measure retention distances (S) for known esters. Plot log S as function of no. of C atoms of acids. Under isothermal conditions, graphs of straight chain esters of same degree of unsatn should be straight lines, approx. parallel. Identify peaks from sample from these graphs, interpolating if necessary. Avoid conditions which permit "masked peaks," i.e., which are not sufficiently resolved.

Esters appear in order of increasing no. of C atoms and of increasing unsatn for same no. of C atoms. C_{16} is ahead of C_{18}, and C_{18} Me esters appear in order: stearate (18:0), oleate (18:1), linoleate (18:2), and linolenate (18:3). C_{20} satd ester (arachidic, 20:0) usually appears before 18:3 ester, but may be reversed on some columns, or positions may change with column use.

28.064 ***Calculations***

Use method of normalization, which assumes all components of sample are represented on chromatogram, so that sum of areas under peaks represents 100% of constituents (total elution).

If instrument is equipped with integrator, use figures shown. If not, use triangulation: Draw lines for each peak tangent to sides and intersecting baseline. Calc. area of resulting triangle by multiplying ht (corrected for any change in attenuation) by ½ base. For automatically attenuated peak, obtain peak width by drawing tangents to outer sides of peak (these must be full chart span, and upper ⅔ of peak must be used) and intersecting baseline. Calc. area by multiplying ht (corrected for attenuation) by ½ base.

If significant amts of components with <12 C atoms are absent, calc. % by wt of each component, expressed as Me ester,

$$C_i = G_i \times 100/\Sigma G_i,$$

where G_i = area of peak corresponding to component i, and ΣG_i = sum of areas under all peaks.

In certain cases, e.g., in presence of components with <12 C atoms, large differences in mol. wts, and presence of secondary groups, correction factors must be used to convert peak areas into wt %. Det. correction factors by analyzing known ref. stds of Me esters of composition similar to that of sample under identical operating conditions. For ref. std,

$$\% \text{ by wt component i} = B_i \times 100/\Sigma B_i,$$

where B_i = wt of component i in ref. std, and ΣB_i = total wt of all components in ref. std. Calc. from chromatogram:

$$\% \text{ (area/area) of component i} = G_i \times 100/\Sigma G_i,$$

from which calc. correction factor for each component

$$K_i = (B_i/\Sigma B_i) \times (\Sigma C_i/C_i)$$

Det. correction factors relative to palmitic acid, $K_{16} = 1$, so that

$$K' = K_i/K_{16}.$$

Then to calc. % of each component (as Me esters), multiply its area by appropriate correction factor, and sum corrected areas:

$$\% \text{ by wt component i} = (K'_i \times G_i) \times 100/\Sigma(K'_i \times G_i).$$

In certain cases, e.g., when all components are not eluted, use internal std, S, such as C_{15} or C_{17} Me ester, and det. its correction factor. Then,

% by wt of component i as Me ester

$$= (w_S/w) \times (K'_i/K'_S) \times (G_i/G_S) \times 100,$$

where w_S = mg internal std and w = total mg sample, and subscript S refers to internal std component.

Report results to following significant figures, with 1 figure beyond decimal point in all cases: 3 for >10%, 2 for 1–10%, and 1 for <1%.

28.065 ***Precision***

(**a**) *Repeatability.*—Two single detns performed on same day by same operator with same app. on same sample for major components (>5%) should not differ by >3% relative, with an absolute value of 1%.

(**b**) *Reproducibility.*—Two single detns performed in different laboratories for major components should not differ by >10% relative, with an absolute value of 3%.

Docosenoic Acid

Gas Chromatographic Method (*16*)—Official First Action

28.066 ***Principle***

Erucic acid, an isomer of docosenoic acid, is characteristic acid of rapeseed. Oil or fat is converted to Me esters, which are detd by GLC, with Me tetracosanoate as internal std.

28.067 ***Apparatus***

(**a**) *Gas chromatograph.*—Varian Model 1740-10, Hewlett-Packard 5700 series, or equiv., with flame ionization detector and 0.9 m (3′) × ⅛″ od stainless steel column contg 15% diethylene glycol succinate (DEGS) on 80–100 mesh Chromosorb W, acid washed. Operating conditions: temps (°)—injector 250, detector 290, column 190; He carrier gas flow rate adjusted to give retention time of ca 17 min for Me tetracosanoate. Measure peak areas by electronic integrator, disk integrator, or triangulation.

(**b**) *Transesterification flask.*—125 mL conical flask with ₮ 24/40 joint and neck elongated and constricted to 8–10 mm id.

28.068 ***Reagents***

(*Caution: See* **51.011(a)**, **51.034**, **51.061**, **51.063**, and **51.066**.)

(**a**) *Hexane.*—Distil reagent grade hexane and dry over anhyd. Na_2SO_4 before use.

(**b**) *Methanol, anhydrous.*—Distil with Mg turnings.

(**c**) *Sodium methoxide soln.*—Approx. 1% in anhyd. MeOH. Clean ca 1 g Na metal in hexane, dry with filter paper, and dissolve in 100 mL anhyd. MeOH in 250 mL conical flask fitted with silica gel drying tube.

(**d**) *Methyl erucate std soln.*—2 mg/mL hexane. Dissolve 100 mg Me erucate (Applied Science Laboratories, Inc., 99.5% $C_{22:1}$) in hexane in 50 mL vol. flask and dil. to vol. with hexane.

(**e**) *Methyl tetracosanoate std soln.*—2 mg/mL hexane. Dissolve 100 mg Me tetracosanoate (Sigma Chemical Co., 99% C_{24}; No. L 1126) in hexane in 50 mL vol. flask and dil. to vol. with hexane.

28.069 ***Determination***

(**a**) *Weight response factor for methyl docosenoate, $R_{22:1}$.*—Pipet 1, 2, and 3 mL Me erucate std soln into sep. 25 mL conical flasks. Pipet in 3 mL Me tetracosanoate std soln into each flask and hexane to make 8.0 mL total vol. Inject 2 μL of each soln into gas chromatograph.

$$R_{22:1} = (W_{22:1}/W_{24}) \times (P_{24}/P_{22:1}),$$

where $R_{22:1}$ = wt response factor for erucate relative to tetracosanoate; $W_{22:1}$ = mg docosenoate (erucate); W_{24} = mg tetracosanoate; P_{24} = peak area tetracosanoate; and $P_{22:1}$ = peak area docosenoate.

(**b**) *Docosenoic acids in fats and oils.*—Accurately weigh ca 50 mg oil into dry transesterification flask, add 3 mL Me tetracosanoate std soln and 10 mL NaOMe soln, and reflux 1 hr. Cool, add 5 mL hexane, swirl, add 7 mL 1*N* HCl, stopper, and shake vigorously 1 min. Add H_2O until hexane reaches constricted neck and inject 2 μL hexane layer into gas chromatograph.

$$\% \text{ Docosenoic acids} = (P_{22:1}/P_{24}) \times (W_{24}/W_{oil}) \times R_{22:1} \times 100,$$

where W_{oil} = mg oil.

Polymers and Oxidation Products of Heated Vegetable Oils

28.070 Gas Chromatographic Method for Non-Elution Materials (*17*)—Official First Action

Accurately weigh ca 40 mg oil and 10 mg triheptadecanoin internal std (Applied Science Laboratories, Inc., No. 21322) into 50 mL erlenmeyer. For ease of handling, empty entire vial internal std supplied (100 mg) into tared 100 mL vol. flask, weigh accurately, dissolve triglyceride in hexane, and dil. to vol. To avoid vol. changes, immediately transfer 10 mL aliquots to nine 50 mL erlenmeyers and carefully evap. solv. under N stream.

Flasks may be stoppered and stored at 0° if desired. Weigh sample directly into flask after temp. equilibrium. Add 4 mL 0.5*N* alc. NaOH soln and boiling chip, and reflux 10 min with H_2O condenser. Add 5 mL BF_3-MeOH, prepd as in **28.056(a)**, thru condenser and boil 2 min. Add 2–5 mL pet ether (bp 30–60°) and boil 1 min more. Cool mixt. and transfer to 30 mL separator, washing flask several times with total of 10 mL pet ether. Shake 1 min to ext methyl esters into pet ether. Drain methanolic (lower) phase into second separator and ext again with 10 mL pet ether. Combine pet ether exts, and wash with 5 mL portions H_2O until washings are acid-free when tested with Me red. Dry with anhyd. Na_2SO_4, preferably by pouring sample thru narrow glass column contg Na_2SO_4; wash column with 5 mL dry pet ether. Evap. solv. under N with aid of steam bath. Because of small vol. of esters, transfer dry esters to 1 mL test tube-shaped vol. flask or cone-shaped vial to facilitate removal with syringe for injection onto GLC column.

Analyze sample with flame ionization detector as in **28.058–28.063**. Measure peak areas of chromatogram by either planimeter or electronic integrator.

$$\%\text{ Non-elution material} = \frac{\left[PA' + \left(\frac{W' + W}{W'}\right) - PA\right] \times 100}{PA' \times \left[\left(\frac{W' + W}{W'}\right) - 1\right]},$$

where PA′ = peak area of internal std; W′ and W = wts internal std and sample, resp.; and PA = total area of chromatogram.

cis, cis-Methylene Interrupted Polyunsaturated Fatty Acids (*18*)—Official First Action

28.071 ***Reagents***

(**a**) *Potassium borate buffer.*—1.0*M*, pH 9.0. Dissolve 61.9 g H_3BO_3 and 25.0 g KOH in ca 800 mL H_2O by stirring and heating. Cool to room temp. and adjust to pH 9.0 with 1.0*N* HCl or 1.0*N* KOH, as required. Dil. to 1 L with H_2O and mix.

(**b**) *Dilute potassium borate buffer.*—0.2*M*, pH 9.0. Dil 200 mL 1.0*M* buffer, (**a**), to 1 L with H_2O and mix.

(**c**) *Lipoxidase solns.*—(*1*) *Stock soln.*—Dissolve 10 mg lipoxidase, from soybean, 50,000 units/mg (ICN Life Sciences Group, Nutritional Biochemicals Division, or equiv.), in 10 mL ice-cold dil. borate buffer, (**b**). Refrigerated soln is stable 30 days. (*2*) *Working soln.*—Mix 2.0 mL stock soln with 8.0 mL ice-cold dil. borate buffer, (**b**). If large no. of analyses are to be performed, dil. 5.0 mL stock soln to 25 mL with ice-cold dil. borate buffer, (**b**). (*3*) *Inactivated soln.*—Pipet 4 mL working enzyme soln, (*2*), to 10 mL vol. flask and hold 5 min in boiling H_2O.

(**d**) *Alcoholic potassium hydroxide soln.*—0.5*N*. Dissolve 1.40 g KOH in alcohol and dil. to 50 mL with alcohol. Prep. fresh daily.

28.072 ***Preparation of Sample***

Accurately weigh ca 100 mg vegetable oil and transfer with *n*-hexane into 100 mL vol. flask, which has just been flushed with N. Dil. to vol. with *n*-hexane or acetone. Pipet 1 mL dild soln into 100 mL vol. flask and completely evap. solv. under N.

28.073 ***Determination***

Add 1 mL alc. KOH, (**d**), soln to solv.-free residue in vol. flask. Heat gently on steam bath to dissolve. Flush with N and hold stoppered, in dark, min. of 5 hr to overnight. After saponification is complete, add 20 mL 1.0*M* borate buffer, (**a**), and 50 mL H_2O, and mix. Add 1 mL 0.5*N* HCl, dil. to vol. with H_2O, and mix.

Pipet 3 mL saponified soln into each of four 13 × 100 mm test tubes. To 2 tubes (blanks) add 0.10 mL inactivated enzyme soln, (**c**)(*3*), and mix well. To remaining duplicate tubes, add 0.10 mL working enzyme soln, (**c**)(*2*). Mix by shaking vigorously 30 sec immediately after adding enzyme soln, and let all tubes stand exposed to air at room temp. 30 min. Zero spectrophtr at 234 nm with blank tubes and measure *A* of reacted samples.

For sample, calc. g polyunsatd fatty acid (PUFA) as trilinolein/100 g sample = $W \times DF \times 10^{-4}$, where W = μg trilinolein/mL final soln from std curve, and DF = diln factor.

28.074 ***Preparation of Standard Curve***

Weigh 100 mg *cis,cis*-trilinolein, 99% (NuCheck Prep, PO Box 172, Elysian, MN 56028, or equiv.), transfer quant. to 100 mL vol. flask, and dil. to vol. with *n*-hexane or acetone. Pipet 10 mL aliquot into 100 mL vol. flask and dil. to vol. with same solv. Pipet 2, 4, 6, 8, 10 and 12 mL aliquots into sep. 100 mL vol. flasks, and evap. each to dryness in stream of N. Pipet 1 mL alc. KOH, (**d**), into each flask, flush with N, and store stoppered in dark 5 hr or overnight.

Add 20 mL 1.0*M* borate buffer, (**a**), 50 mL H_2O, and 1 mL 0.5*N* HCl to each, dil. to vol. with H_2O, and mix. Pipet four 3 mL aliquots of each std soln into test tubes, incubate, and proceed as in detn, beginning "To 2 tubes (blanks) . . ." Plot av. *A* at each level against μg trilinolein/mL.

Two single detns in 1 laboratory should not differ by >1.6%; 2 single detns performed in 2 laboratories should not differ by >2.2%.

Isolated Trans Isomers (*19*)—Official First Action

American Oil Chemists' Society Method

(Applicable to margarines and shortenings contg <5% total conjugates)

28.075 ***Principle***

Unsatd constituents of most vegetable fats and oils contain only nonconjugated (isolated) double bonds in *cis* configuration; these may isomerize to *trans* form during extn and processing due to oxidn or partial hydrogenation. Animal and marine fats may naturally contain some *trans* isomers. In long-chain fatty acids, esters, and glycerides, isolated *trans* bonds show absorption at ca 10.3 μm that can be measured with IR spectrophtr. *Cis* double bonds and satd compds do not show this band.

Long-chain fatty acids also show band at ca 10.6 μm (carboxyl). Correction for this band and any background is made by baseline technic. But if isolated *trans* content is small, correction may greatly affect absorption at 10.3 μm. Therefore, long-chain fatty acids contg <15% isolated *trans* isomers must be converted to their Me esters before making IR measurements.

Triglycerides give isolated *trans* values which are ca 2–3% high and Me esters give isolated *trans* values which are ca 1.5–3% low. Factors are applied to correct for these errors.

Do not apply method to samples contg >5% conjugated unsatn (e.g., tung oil), materials contg functional groups which modify absorption of C-H deformation around *trans* bond (e.g., castor oil contg ricinoleic or ricinelaidic acids), mixed glycerides with long- and short-chain moieties (e.g., diacetostearin), or any materials where specific groups may absorb close to 10.3 μm.

28.076 ***Apparatus***

Infrared spectrophotometer and accessories.—Covering region ca 9–11 μm, wavelength readable to 0.01 μm, holding fixed thickness cells 0.2–2.0 mm with NaCl or KBr windows. Most convenient are split-beam automatic recording instruments such as Perkin-Elmer Models 21, 221, 567, 621, Beckman Models IR-18A, IR-20A or their successors. All instruments must be checked for accuracy of wavelength and photometric scales by manufacturer's instructions. Absorptivities of stds (reagents **28.077(b)**) must be established for each instrument, and rechecked periodically. With split-beam instruments, cells filled with CS_2 solv. must balance to 0.01 *A*. With null type instruments, matched pairs of cells must balance to this figure. Chart paper must be linear in either wavelength or wave no. (depending upon instrument) and calibrated in either *T* or *A*.

28.077 ***Reagents***

(**a**) *Carbon disulfide.*—Dry, ACS grade. Use with adequate ventilation.

(**b**) *Primary stds.*—Elaidic acid, Me elaidate, and trielaidin, highest possible purity, >99% (Nu-Chek Prep, Inc., PO Box 172, Elysian, MN 56028).

28.078 ***Preparation of Samples and Standards***

Melt solid fats on steam bath and mix; filter if cloudy. If *dild* sample is cloudy due to H_2O, add little anhyd. Na_2SO_4 to melted sample, mix, and let settle before taking portion for analysis.

Accurately weigh (±0.2 mg) ca 0.2000 g std or sample into 10 mL vol. flask, dil. to vol. with CS_2, and mix thoroly. *T* at *trans* absorption max. should be 20–70%; if not, use different sample wt or cell thickness.

28.079 ***Infrared Determination***

Fill cell with CS_2 solv. and matching cell with prepd sample or std soln, **28.078**. Use hypodermic syringe with blunted needle, and with cell upright, inject from bottom so bubbles pass up thru cell. Measure *T* or *A* from 9 to 11 μm.

(Programming of instruments depends upon type, but once basic curve for primary std is derived, all samples must be read on same instrument with controls at identical positions. Proper technics of slit width, scanning speed, etc., must be used (*see* "Recommended Practices for General Techniques of Infrared Quantitative Analysis," ASTM, 1916 Race St, Philadelphia, PA 19103). If instrument requires adjustment or replacements (glower, detector, etc.) and exact settings cannot be duplicated, calibration curve of std *must* be rerun and new values used in calcns.)

28.080 ***Calculations***

Acids, methyl esters, and triglycerides.—Compare curve of sample (acid, ester, triglyceride) with its appropriate std, **28.077(b)**. Note *A* at 10.36 μm peak or convert *T* at this point to *A*, and calc. *a*. On charts, draw baseline from 10.10 to 10.65 μm for acids, from 10.02 to 10.59 μm for Me esters, or from 10.05 to 10.67 μm for triglycerides. For charts registering *T*, draw vertical line at peak (ca 10.3 μm) connecting 0 line of chart, *x*; peak, *b*; and baseline, *c*. Fractional $T = xb/xc$. Convert this value to *A* and then to background-corrected *a* as below. For charts registering *A*, subtract *A* at baseline from *A* at peak to obtain *A* of sample.

Absorptivity, $a = A/bc$, where A = corrected absorbance, b = cell thickness in cm, and c = concn of soln (g/L).

% *Trans* as elaidic acid, Me elaidate, or trielaidin = [*a* (sample, background corrected)/*a* (appropriate std, background corrected)] × 100.

Corrected trans values.—Triglycerides with 0 or low *trans* content read ca 2–3% high; their derived Me esters, **28.056**, read 1.5–3% low or neg. Oils similar to test samples but contg no *trans* isomers may be analyzed to det. suitable correction factors to be used, or following equations may be used to correct approx. for pos. triglyceride or neg. Me ester errors:

For fats and oils contg primarily long-chain fatty acids (peanut oil, cottonseed oil, etc.):

Triglycerides, % *trans* (corrected) = (% *trans* (calcd) − 2.5)/0.975.

Me esters, % *trans* (corrected) = (% *trans* (calcd) + 1.5)/1.015.

For fats and oils contg large proportions of lower and medium-chain fatty acids (coconut oil, etc.):

Triglycerides, % *trans* (corrected) = (% *trans* (calcd) − 3.0)/0.970.

Me esters, % *trans* (corrected) = (% *trans* (calcd) + 3.0)/1.030.

Absence of peak at 10.3 μm, regardless of baseline *A*, indicates no *trans* isomers in sample.

28.081 Unsaponifiable Residue (*20*)—Official Final Action

(*Caution: See* **51.011**, **51.039**, and **51.054**.)

Accurately weigh 2–2.5 g fat into saponification flask (200 mL erlenmeyer with ₸ 24/40 outer joint is recommended). Add 25 mL alcohol and 1.5 mL KOH soln (3+2). Saponify by boiling, with occasional swirling, on steam bath 30 min under reflux air condenser. (No loss of alcohol should occur during saponification.) Transfer alc. soap soln while still warm to 250 mL separator, using total of 50 mL H_2O. Rinse saponification flask with 50 mL ether and add ether to separator. Shake vigorously, and let layers sep. and clarify. Drain lower layer and pour ether layer thru top into second separator contg 20 mL H_2O. Rinse pouring edge with ether, adding rinsings to second separator. Ext soap soln with two 50 mL portions ether in same manner. Make total of 4 extns for marine oils or other oils of high unsaponifiable content.

Rotate combined ether exts gently with the 20 mL H_2O (violent shaking at this stage may cause troublesome emulsions). Let layers sep. and drain aq. layer. Wash with two addnl 20 mL portions H_2O, shaking vigorously. Then wash ether soln 3 times with alternate 20 mL portions ca 0.5*N* aq. KOH and H_2O, shaking vigorously each time. If emulsion forms during washing, drain as much aq. layer as possible, leaving emulsion in separator with ether layer, and proceed with next washing. After third KOH treatment, wash ether soln successively with 20 mL portions H_2O until washings are no longer alk. to phthln.

Transfer ether soln to 250 mL lipped, conical beaker, rinse separator and its pouring edge with ether, and add rinsings to main soln. Evap. to ca 5 mL and transfer quant., using several small portions ether, to 50 mL fat flask or erlenmeyer previously dried and weighed with similar flask as tare. Evap. ether. When nearly all ether has been removed, add 2–3 mL acetone, and while heating on steam or H_2O bath, completely remove solv. in gentle air current. Dry at 100° for 30 min periods to const wt.

Dissolve contents of flask in 2 mL ether, add 10 mL neutzd (phthln) alcohol, and titr. with 0.1*N* alc. NaOH (or KOH). (≤0.10 mL is usually required.) Correct wt residue for free fatty acid present (1 mL 0.1*N* alkali = 0.0282 g oleic acid).

Correct wt residue for reagent blank obtained by conducting detn similarly but omitting fat.

Squalene (*21*)—Official Final Action

28.082 ***Reagents***

(**a**) *Concentrated potassium hydroxide soln.*—Dissolve 60 g KOH in 40 mL H_2O.

(**b**) *Dilute potassium hydroxide soln.*—Dissolve 28 g KOH in H_2O and dil. to 1 L.

(**c**) *Petroleum ether.*—Skellysolve B (bp 63–70°), or equiv.

(**d**) *Aluminum oxide adsorbent, 80–200 mesh.*—Adsorption alumina for chromatgc analysis, Fisher A-540, or equiv. Keep in tightly closed container, away from moisture.

(e) *Pyridine sulfate bromide soln.*—0.1*N*. (*Caution: See* **51.047**, **51.072**, and **51.081**.) Dissolve 8 g Br in 20 mL HOAc. Prep. another soln by gradually adding, with cooling, 5.45 mL H_2SO_4 to mixt. of 20 mL HOAc and 8.15 mL pyridine. Mix 2 solns, cool, and dil. to 1 L with HOAc.

(f) *Sodium thiosulfate std soln.*—0.05*N*. Prep. daily by dilg 0.1*N* soln, **50.037–50.038**.

28.083 ***Apparatus***

Adsorption column.—Prep. fresh column for each detn immediately before use. Place small wad of cotton in constricted end of glass tube, 8 mm id and 30 cm long. (For convenience, column may have Teflon stopcock in stem and top reservoir of ≥40 mL capacity.) Add alumina adsorbent in ca 10 small portions until column is ca 10 cm high. Apply gentle suction and tamp each portion alumina lightly with flattened end of heavy glass rod. Place small wad of cotton on top of column and tamp lightly. Wash column with ca 15 mL pet ether, remove suction, and keep top of column covered with shallow layer of pet ether until ready for use.

28.084 ***Determination***

(*Caution: See* **51.011**, **51.039**, and **51.073**.)

Accurately weigh (±20 mg) ca 5 g sample into 125 mL erlenmeyer with ₮ joint, add 3 mL concd KOH soln and 20 mL alcohol, and boil under air condenser 30 min, shaking occasionally. Cool somewhat, and while still warm, add 50 mL pet ether; mix, and transfer to separator. Rinse flask with 20 mL alcohol and then with 40 mL H_2O, adding rinsings to soln in separator. Shake vigorously, let sep. completely, and slowly drain soap soln. Pour pet ether ext from top of separator into another separator contg 20 mL H_2O. Repeat extn of soap soln with 50 mL pet ether. Rotate combined exts gently with the 20 mL H_2O and, after letting layers sep., discard wash H_2O. Repeat washing by shaking vigorously with 20 mL H_2O and again discard lower layer after sepn. Wash pet ether soln with 20 mL dil. KOH soln and then with 20 mL portions H_2O until wash liq. is alkali-free, shaking vigorously each time. After final washing, drain last drops of H_2O brought down by swirling separator. Pour pet ether soln from top of separator into lipped conical beaker. Rinse separator with pet ether and add rinsings to beaker. Add few pieces of broken porcelain or SiC and evap. almost all of solv. on steam bath. Remove last traces of solv. in current of CO_2 or other inert gas while warming beaker. To avoid oxidn of residue, do not expose to air while still warm.

Dissolve unsaponifiable matter in 5 mL pet ether and transfer to adsorption column. (Eluate, which is caught in 250 mL g-s I flask, should emerge dropwise, ca 1 mL/min but no faster, gentle pressure being used if necessary.) When soln has been nearly drawn into column, add ca 5 mL pet ether previously used to rinse beaker. Continue adding solv., previously used to rinse beaker, in 5–10 mL portions, always keeping surface of column covered with liq., until total of 50 mL has eluted. (If column with Teflon stopcock and top reservoir is used, proceed as above thru addn of 5 mL rinse; then rinse beaker with remaining 40 mL pet ether, add to reservoir, and let pass thru column.)

Add few pieces of broken porcelain or SiC and remove most of solv. on steam bath. Finally pass current of CO_2 or other inert gas thru heated flask until last traces of solv. are expelled. Cool residue to room temp. under inert atm. (All traces of solv. must be removed before detn is continued.)

Dissolve unadsorbed residue in 5 mL $CHCl_3$ and add enough pyridine sulfate bromide soln to provide ≥50% excess (10 mL is usually adequate). Let mixt. remain in dark 5 min and then add 5 mL 10% KI soln, together with 40 mL H_2O. Mix thoroly, wash down any free I on stopper, and titr. with 0.05*N* $Na_2S_2O_3$. Toward end of titrn add starch indicator, **2.144(b)**, shake vigorously, and continue titrn to disappearance of blue. Conduct blank detn on pyridine sulfate bromide soln similarly and calc. mL 0.05*N* $Na_2S_2O_3$ equiv. to absorbed halogen. Blank detn on all reagents used should show practically no halogen consumption. 1 mL 0.05*N* $Na_2S_2O_3$ = 1.71 mg squalene. Report results as mg squalene/100 g sample.

Vegetable Fats in Butterfat

Sterol Acetate Melting Point Method (22)
Official Final Action

28.085 ***Apparatus***

(a) *Special micro filter.*—*See* Fig. **28:06**.

(b) *Platinum spatula.*—Heavy Pt wire, hammered flat, to ca 3 mm wide × 15 mm long, on one end. Mount in dissecting needle holder.

28.086 ***Determination***

To 15 g filtered fat in 150 mL beaker add 4 g KOH dissolved in 4 mL H_2O. Add 20 mL 95% alcohol, cover with watch glass, and heat 0.5 hr on steam bath, stirring occasionally.

Add 60 mL H_2O, mix, and pour into 400 mL beaker contg 180 mL 95% alcohol. Warm to ca 40° and add 40 mL *1% digitonin in alcohol.* (Heat may be necessary to dissolve digitonin.) Stir and let stand overnight in refrigerator.

Filter cold mixt. with strong suction on rapid qual. 11 cm paper in buchner. When liq. has passed thru, pour 50 mL H_2O over paper without stopping suction. Swirl occasionally. Continue to apply strong suction (H_2O filters rather slowly) until all H_2O has passed thru paper to wash out most of soaps. Pour 50 mL alcohol over paper and continue suction until all liq. has passed thru. Finally wash paper with four 50 mL portions ether, letting each portion pass thru completely before adding next.

Dry paper and ppt 15 min at 100°. Sep. ppt from paper. Crush or crumble ppt, and place it in 18 × 150 mm test tube. Add 2 mL Ac_2O and heat in 130° glycerol bath 15 min. (Ppt should dissolve

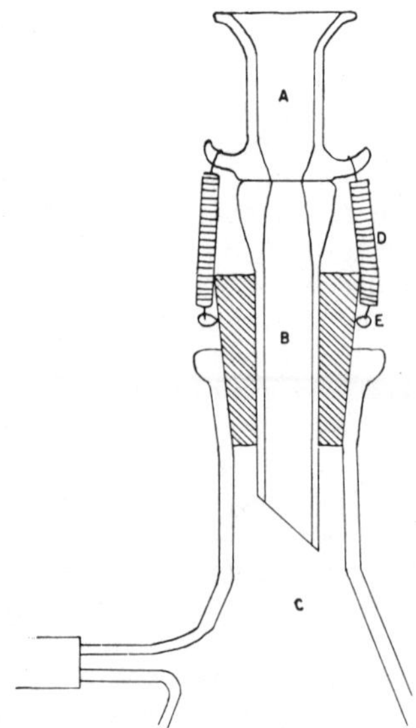

FIG. 28:06—Glass micro filter for sterol acetate precipitates
A: Top portion of filter, capacity 1 mL. **B**: Lower portion of filter. Ground surfaces between **A** and **B** hold filter pad. **A** and **B** are held together by springs, **D**. **C**, filter flask. **E**, wire twisted around stopper to hold lower end of springs.

in ca 5 min; do not use direct heat, since spattering may occur and material may be lost.) Cool to ca 70°.

Carefully add 4 mL alcohol and mix. Filter hot soln by gravity thru pledget of cotton in micro filtering tube (Pregl type), receiving filtrate in 20 mL beaker. Place beaker on small hot plate and carefully bring liq. to gentle boil. Add H_2O drop by drop until sterol acetate is just about to ppt but still remains in soln at bp.

Let cool, stirring occasionally with Pt spatula, for 15–20 min or longer. Filter on small disk of paper in micro buchner (ca 15 mm diam.). Suck dry and sep. ppt from paper. Place ppt in 5 mL beaker and heat with 1 mL 95% alcohol to dissolve completely. Cool beaker by setting in petri dish of ice-H_2O. When thoroly chilled, material usually sets to semisolid cryst. slurry.

Transfer slurry to special microfilter, using Pt spatula, and apply suction. As liq. is drawn thru filter, compact ppt by tamping with flat end of glass rod of suitable size. (Ppt can then be cleanly and completely removed from paper in form of small button or tablet.) Redissolve ppt in same 5 mL beaker with addnl 1 mL hot alcohol (or 0.5 mL if ppt is very small), and after chilling to recrystallize, filter second time on microfilter. Repeat recrystn and filtration third and fourth time; then dry ppt 1 hr at 100°.

Det. mp of recrystd, dried sterol acetates (temp. at which liq. first starts to run, detd when heated at rate of 0.5–1.0°/min). If mp is ≥2° higher than that of pure butter similarly treated, vegetable fat is indicated.

28.087 ***Microcrystal Test***

Dissolve sterol acetate remaining from mp detn in 2 mL alcohol in 20 mL beaker and add 3 drops 40% aq. KOH. Heat on steam bath 5 min. Add 10 mL H_2O and transfer liq. to 125 mL separator. Add 25 mL ether and shake. Let layers sep.; then drain and discard aq. layer. Wash ether with three 5 mL portions H_2O and evap. ether to dryness in 50 mL beaker.

Add 10 mL 70% alcohol to residue and heat to dissolve. Cool, place drop of clear soln on slide, and examine drop microscopically at 100–200× for typical crystals of phytosterol or phytosterol-cholesterol mixt. (*see* Fig. **28:07**).

28.088 Digitonin Recovery—Procedure

Combine filtrates from digitonide pptns and add enough *cholesterol* dissolved in alcohol to combine with all digitonin present. Let mixt. stand 3 hr or overnight. Filter off ppt and wash with H_2O, alcohol, and ether; then suck dry. Crush ppt and tamp it lightly into paper extn thimble. Suspend thimble in ₮ erlenmeyer closed by reflux condenser and contg small amt of *xylene*. Heat xylene to bp and let thimble and contents hang in hot vapors of boiling xylene 16 hr.

Remove thimble and dry at 100° until xylene has evapd. Remove digitonin residue, weigh, and transfer to beaker. Dissolve residue in enough H_2O to make ca 2% digitonin soln. Add ca ½ vol. alcohol and heat on steam bath. Add 1 mL *n-amyl alcohol* (reagent grade), cool, and filter off digitonin compd on buchner of suitable size. Suck dry and transfer ppt to watch glass. Dry at 100° until all amyl alcohol is volatilized. Digitonin may then be pulverized and is ready for reuse.

Gas Chromatographic Method (Sterol Acetates) (23)
Official Final Action

28.089 ***Preparation of Sample***

Obtain fat from butter by **16.210**. Weigh 5–10 g filtered fat into 150 mL beaker and proceed as in **28.086**, beginning "... add 4 g KOH ..." (Sterol acetate need not be recrystd unless mp is also desired.)

28.090 ***Reagents***

(**a**) *GLC column packing.*—(*1*) *Stationary phase.*—JXR, or OV–1, or OV–101 dimethylpolysiloxane, or OV–17, or OV–22 methylphenylpolysiloxane. (*2*) *Support.*—100–120 mesh Gas-Chrom Q. Com. prepd packing of 1 or 3% stationary phase available from Applied Science Laboratories, Inc., or Supelco, Inc.

(**b**) *Ethyl acetate.*—Distd in glass (Burdick and Jackson Laboratories, Inc., or equiv.).

(**c**) *Cholestane std soln.*—0.4 μg/μL. Weigh 40.0 mg cholestane std (Applied Science Laboratories, Inc.) into 100 mL vol. flask and dil. to vol. with EtOAc.

(**d**) *Cholestane internal std soln.*—0.2 μg/μL. Dil. 10.0 mL std soln, (**c**), to 20.0 mL with EtOAc.

(**e**) *β-Sitosterol acetate std soln.*—2.0 μg/μL. Weigh 22.2 mg β-sitosterol acetate std (ICN Pharmaceuticals, Inc., Life Sciences Group, ca 90% pure) into 10 mL vol. flask and dil. to vol. with EtOAc. Com. β-sitosterol acetate is mixt. of campesterol acetate (earlier eluting minor component) and β-sitosterol acetate. Det. concn of β-sitosterol acetate in std by chromatographing 2–3 μL std soln. Det. area of campesterol acetate and β-sitosterol acetate peaks by drawing lines tangent to sides of peak and intersecting baseline. Det. areas of resulting triangles by multiplying ht by ½ base.

$$\text{Concn } \beta\text{-sitosterol acetate} = (C_s \times P_s)/(P_s + P_c),$$

where C_s = mg sterol acetate std/mL, P_s = area β-sitosterol acetate peak, and P_c = area campesterol acetate peak.

(**f**) Cholestane-β-sitosterol acetate std mixture.—0.2 μg cholestane and 1.0 μg β-sitosterol acetate/μL. Mix equal vols (**c**) and (**e**).

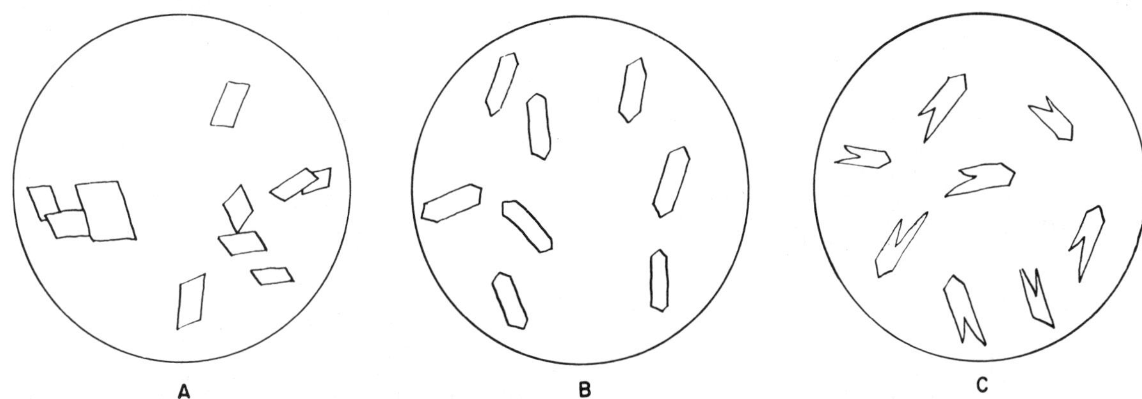

FIG. 28:07—Crystalline forms of free sterols. A: Cholesterol. B: Phytosterol. C: Mixed cholesterol-phytosterol

28.091 ***Apparatus***

(**a**) *Gas chromatograph.*—Barber-Colman Co. Model 5000 (replaced by Searle Analytic Series 4740), or equiv., with H flame ionization detector and 1 mv strip chart recorder. Temps (°): column, 220–260; flash heater and detector, 240–270; flow rates: N (ultra high purity grade), 20–25 psi (138–172 kPa) to elute β-sitosterol acetate in 16–20 min; H, ca 40–45 mL/min; air, 300–340 mL/min.

Adjust electrometer sensitivity so that 2.5 μg β-sitosterol acetate gives ca 50% deflection (10^{-9}–10^{-10} amp full scale deflection with 1 mv recorder). Repeat injections until const peak hts are obtained on successive injections of identical vols of std mixt.

(**b**) *Preparation of column.*—(*Caution: See* **51.039** and **51.040**.) Pack glass column, 1.8 m (6′) × 4 mm id, with com. 1–3% stationary phase on 100–120 mesh Gas-Chrom Q or dissolve 0.4–1.2 g polysiloxane in 200 mL toluene or CH_2Cl_2-toluene (1+1). Heat to dissolve (polysiloxane dissolves slowly in solv. mixt.). (*Caution:* Siloxanes are toxic. Wear disposable gloves and use effective fume removal device when handling.) Add soln to 40 g Gas-Chrom Q and let stand 10 min with occasional gentle stirring. Dry in rotary evaporator held in 50° bath or heat on steam bath with occasional gentle stirring and remove residual solv. in vac. oven at 50°.

Carefully wash inside of column and small amt glass wool with *5% soln dichlorodimethylsilane* in toluene, rinse with MeOH until rinsings are neut. to indicator paper, and air dry. Plug column exit with small plug of silanized glass wool and thru-hole septum, and plug injection side arm with ½ hole septum. Add coated packing material thru injection port, using funnel and plastic tubing and tapping column very gently during addn. Add ¼ packing material at time, remove funnel, and apply ca 5–10 psi (34.5–69 kPa) N to injection port while tapping gently to settle packing. Pack to 2.5 cm below injection side arm and plug with silanized glass wool.

(**c**) *Conditioning of column.*—Heat ≥8 hr at 260° with ca 5–10 psi (34.5–69 kPa) N flowing thru column. Shut off pressure, raise temp. to 290°, and continue heating ≥8 hr. Reduce temp. to 260°, adjust N to 5–10 psi, and heat addnl 8–12 hr.

(**d**) *Performance.*—Chromatograph ca 2 μL β-sitosterol acetate std soln to det. retention times and resolution of column. Min. of 1600 theoretical plates is required for β-sitosterol acetate peak.

$$\text{Theoretical plates} = (L/B)^2 \times 16,$$

where L = mm β-sitosterol acetate peak from injection point and B = mm triangulated base width of β-sitosterol acetate peak.

28.092 ***Determination***

Pipet 1.0 mL cholestane internal std soln into 3 dram vial contg sterol acetates, rotate vial to wash down sides, and swirl to dissolve. Inject 2–3 μL sample soln and 2–3 μL std mixt., (**f**), at least in duplicate. Identify β-sitosterol acetate peak in sample from retention time in std mixt. If ht of sample peak is >60% full scale, add addnl 1.0 mL internal std soln to sample soln, and rechromatograph sample and std mixt. solns. Measure peak hts of cholestane and β-sitosterol acetate peaks in mm.

$$\text{mg }\beta\text{-Sitosterol acetate/100 g sample} = (H_i/H_x) \times (C_x/C_i) \times (S_x/S_i) \times (Q_i/Q) \times 100,$$

where H_i and H_x = ht (mm) cholestane and β-sitosterol acetate peaks, resp., in std mixt.; S_x and S_i = ht (mm) β-sitosterol acetate and cholestane peaks, resp., in sample; C_x and C_i = μg β-sitosterol acetate and cholestane/μL, resp., in std mixt.; Q_i = μg cholestane/μL in sample; and Q = mg sample/μL.

Beta-Sitosterol in Butter Oil (*24*)—Official First Action

(Applicable to samples contg ≥4 mg free β-sitosterol/100 mg butter oil)

28.093 ***Principle***

Free 3-β-OH sterols are removed from butter oil by complexing with digitonin, and sterols are then removed from digitonide-Celite column by elution with dimethyl sulfoxide (DMSO). (*Caution:* DMSO can be harmful. Avoid skin contact by wearing heavy rubber gloves. Use effective fume removal device.) Butter oil has apparent range of 0–1 mg β-sitosterol/100 g and ice cream has apparent value of ca 4 mg/100 g fat from emulsifiers.

28.094 ***Reagents***

(**a**) *Diatomaceous earth.*—Celite 545, or equiv.

(**b**) *β-Sitosterol std soln.*—2 μg β-sitosterol/μL $CHCl_3$. Prep. from Applied Science Laboratories, Inc., std (95% β-sitosterol, 5% campesterol).

(**c**) *n-Hexane.*—Distil pure grade over KOH. (*Caution: See* **51.011**, **51.037**, **51.039**, and **51.061**.)

28.095 ***Apparatus***

(**a**) *Gas chromatograph.*—Operating conditions: temps (°): column 225–245 and injection port and flame ionization detector 265–285. Adjust N carrier gas flow (ca 50–60 mL/min) to obtain following retention times (min): cholesterol 16–18, campesterol 22–24, and β-sitosterol 28–30. Use 1.8 m (6′) × 4 mm id column contg 3% JXR silicone on 100–120 mesh Gas-Chrom Q and condition column 24 hr at 250° with 15–20 psi (103.4–138 kPa) N.

(**b**) *Performance.*—Monitor performance of gas chromatograph by noting sepn of campesterol and sitosterol expressed as peak resolution = $2D/(C + B)$, where D = distance between the 2 peak maxima, C = campesterol peak base width, and B = β-sitosterol peak base width. Peak resolution should be ≥1.6.

(**c**) *Injection technic.*—With 10 μL Hamilton microsyringe, draw 1 μL air into barrel, insert needle into soln, and draw desired amt into barrel. Remove needle from soln and draw 1 μL air into barrel. Note vol. on scale and adjust to desired vol., if necessary.

(**d**) *Preparation of std curve.*—Prep. std soln of 2 μg β-sitosterol/μL $CHCl_3$. (Det. composition of std as in **28.090(e)**.) Obtain std curves daily covering range 1–10 μg β-sitosterol, using ≥3 points. Plot area of β-sitosterol peak against μg β-sitosterol.

28.096 ***Preparation of Column***

Dissolve, with heating, 300 mg *digitonin* in 5 mL H_2O, add to mortar and pestle contg 10 g Celite, and mix thoroly. (Packing material can be kept several months if stored at 5° in tightly closed container.) Transfer 3 g Celite-digitonin mixt. to 2 × 12 cm tube with ca 5 mm id outflow tube and small glass wool pad at bottom, and closed with short length of gum rubber tubing and pinchcock. Pack firmly, using tamping rod. (Flow rate of tightly packed column is 0.5–0.75 mL/ min.) Sat. column with 5 mL *n*-hexane and let flow thru packing until n-hexane reaches top of packing material. Use column immediately. Do not let dry.

28.097 ***Preparation of Sample***

Dissolve 900 mg butter oil in 3 mL *n*-hexane. Quant. transfer soln, using disposable pipet, to digitonin-Celite column and let pass thru column until soln has entered packing material. Wash sample beaker twice with 2 mL *n*-hexane and add each wash to column, rinsing sides of tube. Wash column with five 2 mL portions *n*-hexane. After all hexane has entered column, wash with five 2 mL portions benzene. When last portion benzene reaches ca 1 cm above top of packing material, remove rubber tubing and wash inner and outer surface of column tip thoroly with benzene to remove traces of fat. (Failure to wash column sides and column tip with solv. will result in poor chromatograms due to interference from triglycerides.) Discard hexane and benzene. Begin elution with 10 mL DMSO before benzene falls below top of packing material. Collect DMSO eluate in 15 mL screw-cap centrf. tube.

Add 3 mL *n*-hexane to eluate, shake, and centrf. Transfer upper layer contg sterols to second screw-cap centrf. tube. Repeat extn of DMSO layer in first tube with two 4 mL portions *n*-hexane-benzene (1+1), carefully transferring upper layer to second tube each time. Vigorously shake pooled upper layers with 3 mL H_2O and centrf. until clear. Remove upper layer and evap. under N or filtered air in 30 mL beaker on steam bath. Transfer residue to 0.5 dram screw-cap vial with two 0.8 mL portions $CHCl_3$. After evapg solv. with N or filtered air over steam bath, redissolve sterols in 0.1 mL $CHCl_3$ for GLC analysis.

28.098 ***Determination***

Inject 2–8 μL extd sample and calc. β-sitosterol by converting peak area to wt, using daily std curve.

$$\text{mg } \beta\text{-Sitosterol/100 g butter oil} = (\mu\text{g from curve/1000}) \times (100/\mu\text{L injected}) \times (100/\text{g sample}).$$

Identify peaks from butter oil samples by comparing their retention times to retention times of known compds. Relative retention times are: cholesterol 1.0, campesterol 1.4, β-sitosterol 1.7.

Animal Fats in Vegetable Fats and Oils (Determination of Cholesterol) *(25)* Official Final Action

(Sterol fraction of some vegetable oils conts small amts of cholesterol. Sterol fraction of palm oil may contain considerable amt of cholesterol.)

28.099 ***Preparation of Sample***

Saponify and ext unsaponifiable matter from 2.5± 0.01 g fat as in par. 1 and 2, **28.081**. Discard aq. solns. Transfer ether ext to 250 mL beaker and evap. to dryness on steam bath under N. Dissolve unsaponifiable matter in 4–5 mL $CHCl_3$, transfer to 4 dram vial, and evap. to dryness. Rinse beaker with three 3 mL portions $CHCl_3$, taking special care to dissolve any material on sides of beaker. Transfer rinsings to vial and evap. to dryness under N. Store samples in freezer.

Isolation of Sterols by Thin Layer Chromatography

28.100 ***Reagents and Apparatus***

(**a**) *TLC plates.*—Prep. from silica gel PF 254 + 366 or HF 254 + 366 (Brinkmann Instruments, Inc., or equiv.) as in **28.101**, or use precoated plates available as "Uniplate" (precoated with silica gel HF 254 + 366, 500 μm thick; No. 2112) from Analtech, Inc., 75 Blue Hen Dr, Newark, DE 19711), or "Quanta Gram" (precoated with silica gel PQ1F with fluorescent indicator, 500 μm thick; No. 4811-830) from Whatman, Inc., 9 Bridewell Place, Clifton, NJ 07014.

(**b**) *Chloroform.*—Distd in glass (Burdick and Jackson Laboratories, Inc., or equiv.)

(**c**) *Ethyl ether.*—Anhyd., $\leqslant$0.01% alcohol (Fisher Scientific Co. E-138, or equiv.).

(**d**) *Petroleum ether.*—Distd in glass, bp 30–60° (Burdick and Jackson Laboratories, Inc., or equiv.).

(**e**) *β-Sitosterol std soln.*—3 μg/μL. Weigh 30.0 mg β-sitosterol std (Aldrich Chemical Co., Inc.) into 10 mL vol. flask and dil. to vol. with EtOAc. Com. material is mixt. of campesterol (earlier eluting component) and β-sitosterol.

(**f**) *Thin layer chromatographic apparatus.*—*See* **26.001(k)**.

(**g**) *Thin layer plate scraper.*—Optional; adapt from sealing tube with fritted disk (Corning Glassworks 39580, 30M). *See* Fig. **26:02**.

28.101 ***Preparation of Plates***

Align 5 matching 20 × 20 cm glass plates on mounting board, and just before coating, wipe plates with tissue dampened with alcohol to remove any dust or fingerprints. Adjust applicator to deliver 0.5 mm thick layer. Weigh 45 g silica gel into 500 mL erlenmeyer, add 130 mL H_2O, shake vigorously 25–30 sec, and pour into applicator. Immediately coat plates with silica gel suspension and let plates rest undisturbed until gelled (0.5–1 hr). Dry coated plates $\geqslant$2 hr at 110° and store in desiccating cabinet until just before use.

28.102 ***Thin Layer Chromatography***

(*Caution: See* **51.016**, **51.040**, and **51.056**.)

Line developing chamber with blotting paper and add 100 mL ether-pet ether (1+1) to chamber. Cover chamber and equilibrate 2 hr.

Draw line across plate 17 cm from bottom and ca 1 cm from each side. Spot 10 μL β-sitosterol std soln, (**e**), at point 2 cm from bottom edge and 3 cm from 1 side of plate. Dissolve unsaponifiable matter, **28.099**, in 200 μL $CHCl_3$ and spot entire sample in 10 μL portions on imaginary line 2 cm from bottom edge of plate so that spot centers are 0.75 cm apart. Rinse vial with ca 100 μL $CHCl_3$ and spot rinse soln in equal portions on top of sample spots.

Immediately insert plate into equilibrated chamber (position plate to expose coated surface to max. chamber vol.); cover chamber and seal with tape. Withdraw plate from chamber when solv. front reaches 17 cm stop line. Evap. solv. and view plate under longwave UV light in darkened room. Mark off sterol band (same R_f, 0.2–0.3, as β-sitosterol std) with needle, and remove sterol band as follows (do not remove β-sitosterol std): Scrape off sterol band with sq end of stainless steel spatula (Fisher No. 14-375-10, or equiv.) into 100 mL beaker and transfer with 20 mL $CHCl_3$ to 70 mm top diam. funnel contg folded 12.5 cm diam. filter paper (S&S 588, or equiv.). Ext sterols with five 10 mL portions $CHCl_3$ and evap. combined filtrate to near dryness on steam bath under N. Transfer residue to 3 dram vial (screw-cap with Al liner) with $CHCl_3$ and evap. to dryness under N. (Alternatively, remove sterol band with TLC plate scraper, elute sterols from silica gel with 70 mL $CHCl_3$ (fourteen 5 mL portions), and evap. solv. to near dryness on steam bath under N.)

Gas Chromatography of Sterols

28.103 ***Reagents***

Use reagents **28.090(a)**, **(b)**, **(c)**, and **(d)** and following:

(**a**) *Cholesterol std soln.*—1.2 μg/μL. Weigh 60.0 mg cholesterol std (Applied Science Laboratories, Inc.) into 50 mL vol. flask and dil. to vol. with EtOAc.

(**b**) *Cholestane-cholesterol std mixture.*—0.2 μg cholestane and 0.6 μg cholesterol/μL. Mix equal vols cholestane, **28.090(c)**, and cholesterol std solns.

(**c**) *Cholesterol-β-sitosterol std mixture.*—0.6 μg cholesterol and 1.5 μg β-sitosterol/μL. Mix equal vols cholesterol and β-sitosterol, **28.100(e)**, std solns.

(d) *Cholesteryl acetate std soln.*—0.6 μg/μL. Weigh 30.0 mg cholesteryl acetate std (ICN Pharmaceuticals, Inc., Life Sciences Group) into 50 mL vol. flask and dil. to vol. with EtOAc.

28.104 ***Apparatus***

(a) *Gas chromatograph.*—Barber-Colman Co. Model 5000 (replaced by Searle Analytic Series 4740), or equiv., with H flame ionization detector and 1 mv strip chart recorder. Temps (°): column, 220–250; detector and flash heater, 240–270; flow rates: N (ultra high purity grade), 20–25 psi (138–172 kPa) to elute cholesterol in 8–12 min; H, ca 40–45 mL/min; air, 300–340 mL/min. Electrometer sensitivity 1×10^{-9} amp full scale deflection with 1 mv recorder.

Adjust electrometer sensitivity so that 1.5 μg cholesterol gives ca 50% deflection. Repeat injections until const peak hts are obtained on successive injections of identical vols. of std mixt.

(b) *Preparation of column.*—*See* **28.091(b)**.

(c) *Conditioning of column.*—Heat 12–24 hr under conditions specified in **28.091(c)**.

(d) *Performance.*—Chromatograph ca 2 μL cholesterol-β-sitosterol std mixt. to det. retention times and resolution of column. Min. of 1600 theoretical plates is required for cholesterol peak; theoretical plates = $(L/B)^2 \times 16$, where L = cm cholesterol peak from injection point, and B = cm triangulated base width of cholesterol peak. In addn, sepn of cholesterol and campesterol peaks, expressed as peak resolution, should be $\geqslant$2.2. Peak resolution = $2D/(B + P)$, where D = distance in cm between cholesterol and campesterol peak max.; B = triangulated base width of cholesterol peak; and P = triangulated base width of campesterol peak. Det. peak resolution on sample having ca equal amts cholesterol and campesterol (ca equal peak areas); sample injected should give peak hts 25–50% of chart width.

28.105 ***Determination***

Pipet 1.0 mL cholestane internal std soln into 3 dram vial contg extd sterols, rotate vial to wash down sides with internal std soln, and swirl to dissolve sterols. Inject 2 μL sample at least in duplicate. Repeat with 2 μL cholestane-cholesterol std mixt. Identify cholesterol peak in sample from its retention time in std mixt. If cholesterol peak ht in sample is >60% full scale deflection, add addnl 1.0 mL cholestane internal std soln to sample and chromatograph sample and std mixt. as above. Measure cholestane and cholesterol peak hts in mm.

Calc. mg cholesterol/100 g sample, correcting for internal std, as follows:

$$\text{mg Cholesterol/100 g} = (H_i/H_x) \times (C_x/C_i) \times (S_x/S_i) \times (Q_i/Q) \times 100,$$

where H_i and H_x = ht (mm) cholestane and cholesterol peaks, resp., in std mixt.; S_x and S_i = ht (mm) cholesterol and cholestane peaks, resp., in sample; C_x and C_i = μg cholesterol and cholestane/μL, resp., in std mixt.; Q_i = μg cholestane/μL in sample; and Q = mg sample/μL.

28.106 ***Confirmatory Test***

Presence of cholesterol may be confirmed by GLC of sterol acetates. After detg cholesterol by GLC, evap. sample to dryness on steam bath under N. Cool and add 3 mL pyridine and 1 mL Ac_2O. Cap vial, swirl on steam bath until sterols dissolve, and continue heating on steam bath 1 hr. Evap., using N stream, until no odor of pyridine is detected. Chromatograph sterol acetates and cholesteryl acetate std solns and compare retention times of sample and cholesteryl acetate peaks.

Rosin Oil

28.107 ***Qualitative Test—Procedure***

Polarize pure oil, or definite diln with pet ether, in 200 mm tube. Rosin oil has polarization in 200 mm tube of +30 to +40°S, while most oils read between +1° and −1° (Lewkowitsch, "Chemical Technology and Analysis of Oils, Fats and Waxes," 6th Ed., **1**, 350(1921)).

Cottonseed Oil

28.108 ***Halphen Test (26)—Official Final Action***

(*Caution: See* **51.039**, **51.040**, and **51.048**.)

Mix CS_2 contg 1% S in soln with equal vol. amyl alcohol. Mix equal vols of this reagent and sample under examination, and heat in bath of boiling satd NaCl soln 1–2 hr. Presence of as little as 1% cottonseed oil produces pronounced characteristic red or orange-red soln. Depth of color is proportional, to certain extent, to amt of cottonseed oil present, and comparative tests with known mixts of cottonseed oil give approx. amt.

Different oils react with different intensities. Oils that have been heated to 200–210° (Allen, "Commercial Organic Analysis," 5th Ed., **2**, 177(1924)) and hydrogenated oils (Jamieson, "Vegetable Fats and Oils," 2nd Ed. (1943)) react with greatly diminished intensity. Heating 10 min at 250° renders cottonseed oil incapable of giving reaction (Abs. J. Soc. Chem. Ind. **18**, 711(1899)). Fat of animals fed on cottonseed meal or other cottonseed products may give pos. reaction by this test.

rv

Cyclopropene Fatty Acids (27)—Official First Action

28.109 ***Principle***

Oil is dissolved in mixt. of BuOH and 1% S in CS_2, and heated in presence of light in closed tube. "Halphen" pigments which are formed are measured spectrophtric.

28.110 ***Apparatus***

(a) *Tubes.*—Culture tubes, 20 × 150 mm with screw caps and Teflon liners, Pyrex No. 9825, or equiv., matched to within 0.01 A units when filled with H_2O.

(b) *Constant temperature oil bath.*—Maintained at 110°.

(c) *Spectrophotometer.*—Covering range 340–600 nm, with voltage regulation system. Bausch and Lomb Spectronic 20 is satisfactory if 0.75" tube adapter is enlarged slightly with sandpaper wrapped around conical figure.

28.111 ***Reagents***

(a) *n-Butanol.*—Redistil if color forms in solv. blank.

(b) *Dilute sulfur soln.*—1% pptd S in CS_2. Prep. daily.

(c) *Cyclopropene std.*—Cottonseed oil methyl esters contg known amt cyclopropene fatty acids (available from Supelco, Inc.).

28.112 ***Determination***

Accurately weigh ca 200 mg oil sample into screw cap tube. Pipet 20 mL BuOH and 5 mL 1% S in CS_2 into tube, cap tightly, and mix. Place in beaker contg propylene glycol maintained at 110° in oil bath in hood. Keep hood light on. Hold propylene glycol level above top of tube contents. After 2.5 hr, cool tube to room temp. in beaker contg flowing tap H_2O. Wipe tube dry and clean with soft paper towel. Measure A within 4 hr at max. ca 547 nm against blank prepd with corn oil or other cyclopropene fatty acid-free oil. If sample A is <0.04, increase sample size and oil blank up to 1 g and repeat detn. Det. amt of cyclopropene fatty acids from std curve prepd from cyclopropene std.

Peanut Oil

28.113 *Modified Renard Test (28)—Official Final Action*

(*Caution: See* **51.011**, **51.039**, and **51.054**.)

Weigh 20 g oil into erlenmeyer. Saponify with alc. KOH soln, **28.025**; neutze exactly with HOAc (1+3), using phthln; and wash into 800–1000 mL flask contg boiling mixt. of 100 mL H_2O and 120 mL *20% $Pb(OAc)_2$ soln.* Boil 1 min and then cool pptd soap by immersing flask in H_2O, swirling occasionally to cause soap to stick to sides. After cooling, decant H_2O and excess $Pb(OAc)_2$ soln, and wash Pb soap with cold H_2O and alcohol, 90% by vol. Add 200 mL ether, cork, and let stand until soap disintegrates; heat on H_2O bath, using reflux condenser, and boil ca 5 min. With oils, most of soap will be dissolved; with lards, which contain much stearin, part of soap will be left undissolved. Cool ether soln of soap to 15–17° and let stand until all insol. soaps sep. (ca 12 hr).

Filter on buchner and thoroly wash insol. Pb soaps with ether. Wash ether-insol. Pb soaps into separator with jet of ether, alternating with HCl (1+3) at end of operation if little of soap sticks to paper. Add enough HCl (1+3) so that total vol. of acid is ca 200 mL and enough ether to make its total vol. 150–200 mL, and shake vigorously several min. Let layers sep., drain off acid layer, and wash ether once with 100 mL HCl (1+3) and then with several portions of H_2O until H_2O washings are no longer acid to Me orange. If few undecomposed lumps of Pb soap remain (indicated by solid particles remaining after third washing with H_2O), break up by running off almost all H_2O layer, adding little HCl, and shaking; then continue washing with H_2O as before.

Distil ether from soln of insol. fatty acids and dry latter in flask by adding little absolute alcohol and evapg on steam bath. Dissolve dry fatty acids by warming with 100 mL 90% alcohol by vol. Cool slowly to 15°, shaking to aid crystn. Let stand 30 min at 15°.

In presence of peanut oil, crystals of arachidic acid sep. from soln. Filter, wash ppt twice with 10 mL alcohol, 90% by vol., and then with alcohol, 70% by vol., taking care to keep arachidic acid and wash solns at definite temp. in order to apply solubility corrections given below. Dissolve arachidic acid on filter with boiling absolute alcohol, evap. to dryness in weighed dish, dry, and weigh. To this wt add 0.0025 g/10 mL of 90% alcohol used in crystn and washing, if conducted at 15°; if conducted at 20°, add 0.0045 g/10 mL.

Mp of arachidic acid thus obtained is 71–72°. Wt arachidic acid × 20 = approx. wt peanut oil present. Arachidic acid has characteristic appearance and may be identified under microscope. As little as 5–10% peanut oil can be detected by this method.

Modified Bellier Test (29)—Official Final Action

(Applicable only in presence of olive, cottonseed, corn, and soybean oils)

28.114 ***Reagents***

(**a**) *Alcoholic potassium hydroxide soln.*—1.5*N*. Dissolve 10 g KOH in purified alcohol, **28.025**, and dil. to 100 mL with purified alcohol.

(**b**) *Hydrochloric acid.*—Sp gr 1.16. Dil. 83 mL concd acid (sp gr 1.19) to 100 mL with H_2O. Check with sp gr spindle.

(**c**) *Alcohol.*—70%. Dil. 700 mL alcohol to 950 mL with H_2O. Check by sp gr or refractive index and adjust if necessary.

28.115 ***Test***

Weigh 0.92 g or measure 1 mL sample into 125 mL erlenmeyer with ₸ outer joint. If oil is measured, use short Mohr pipet with fairly large opening at tip, drain to lower mark, hold until meniscus stops rising in pipet, and drain to mark again. Add 5 mL alc. KOH soln, and heat 5 min on steam bath, using air condenser to avoid loss of alcohol. Swirl once or twice during saponification. Add 50 mL 70% alcohol and 0.8 mL of the HCl. Warm to dissolve any ppt that may form.

Insert thermometer and cool with continuous agitation so that temp. falls ca 1°/min. Observe turbidity temp. or clouding point, which is temp. at which definite ppt first appears. (If temp. of soln is above room temp., cooling may be accomplished in air or by occasionally immersing soln in H_2O bath of temp. ≤5° below that of soln. Do not immerse flask below level of contents, and agitate continuously to prevent premature formation of turbidity by local cooling. Soln may be agitated by stirring with thermometer or by swirling flask. Observe turbidity temp. by looking thru soln toward good light, or toward dark background with good light coming from one side.)

If turbidity appears before temp. reaches 9° (olive oil) or 13° (cottonseed, corn, or soybean oils) presence of peanut oil is indicated. Confirm by **28.113**.

28.116 Cold Test (*30*)—Procedure

(Applicable to refined winterized salad oils)

Fill 4 oz oil sample bottle with oil at 25°, cork tightly, and seal with paraffin. Completely submerge bottle in bucket contg finely cracked ice and add H_2O until it rises to top of bottle. Keep bucket filled solidly with ice by removing any excess H_2O and adding ice when necessary. After 5.5 hr remove bottle and examine oil. If it is properly wintered, sample will be brilliant, clear, and limpid.

28.117 Tea Seed Oil in Olive Oil (*31*)—Official Final Action

For preliminary qual. test use following room temp. method: Measure exactly 0.8 mL Ac_2O, 1.5 mL $CHCl_3$, and 0.2 mL H_2SO_4 into test tube (18 × 150 mm is convenient). Mix, and cool to room temp. Add 7 drops of oil to be tested directly to reagents, mix, and cool again. (To measure test oil, use glass tubing, 4 mm od, and ca 2 mm id; 7 drops should weigh ca 0.22 g.) If soln of oil in reagents is cloudly after mixing and cooling, add Ac_2O dropwise, shaking after each addn until soln suddenly clears. Appreciable deviations from these amts, particularly in H_2SO_4, cause distinct variations in color intensities. Since mixed reagent deteriorates slowly, do not mix in advance of testing.

After 5 min, add 10 mL absolute ether from graduate and mix immediately by inverting once. Tea seed oil forms brown soln changing to intense red within min or so. This red reaches max. and then fades slowly within few min. Olive oil forms initial green soln on addn of ether. This color fades slowly to brown-gray, occasionally passing thru faint pink stage. Both olive oil and tea seed oil eventually fade to permanent light brown. Mixts of tea seed oil and olive oil show characteristic tea seed oil colors proportional in intensity to amt of tea seed oil present.

For approx. quant. estns, drop oil into reagents as described above and let remain at room temp. 5 min. In meantime, cool 10 mL portion absolute ether in ice-H_2O. After 5 min, place test tube contg oil and reagents in ice-H_2O 1 min, add cold ether (taking care that no H_2O falls into test tube), and mix. Return tube to ice-H_2O bath and let colors develop while it is immersed in ice-H_2O. Colors develop slowly and reach max. within ca 5 min.

Use deepest red colors produced as basis for comparison, and because of short period of stable max. intensity do not test >3 oils at one time. Stds contg known amts of tea seed oil in olive oil that give little or no pink with this test should be run simultaneously with sample. Preliminary room temp. test gives indication of stds to be used in ice-H_2O method.

Sesame Oil

28.118 ***Modified Villavecchia Test (32)—Official Final Action***

Add 2 mL furfural to 100 mL alcohol. Thoroly mix 0.1 mL of this soln with 10 mL HCl and 10 mL sample by shaking in test tube 15 sec. Let mixt. stand 10 min, observe color, add 10 mL H_2O, shake, and again observe color. If crimson color disappears, sesame oil is absent. (As furfural gives violet tint with HCl, it is necessary to use the very dil. soln specified.)

Foreign Fats Containing Tristearin in Lard (*33*) Official First Action

28.119 ***Principle***

Presence of beef fat, tallows, and similar fats, as well as hydrogenated and interesterified pork fat in pork fats and lard, is detected by detg difference between mp of crystd triglycerides and mp of fatty acids derived from these triglycerides. This value is large for pure pork fats and small for beef fats.

28.120 ***Determination***

Weigh 5 g melted and filtered lard into g-s graduate and add 20 mL warm acetone. Mix well, taking care that soln is clear and has temp. >30°. Let stand 16–18 hr at const temp. of 30°. Fine mass of crystals occupying ≤3 mL should then be found at bottom of graduate. Should vol. of crystals materially exceed 3 mL, take smaller amt of lard (3–4 g) for new test. If crystals obtained from 5 g lard are insufficient, increase wt lard and vol. acetone proportionately.

Decant supernate acetone soln from crystd glycerides. Add three 5 mL portions warm (30–35°) acetone from small wash bottle, taking care not to break up deposit in washing, and decant first 2 portions. Actively agitate third portion in graduate and by quick movement transfer crystals to small filter paper. Using wash bottle, wash crystals with 5 successive small portions of the warm acetone, and remove excess acetone by suction. Spread out paper and contents, breaking up any large lumps, and air dry at room temp.

Thoroly comminute mass and det. mp of crystals in closed 1 mm tube, using app. similar to that of Fig. **28:08**. Heat H_2O in beaker rapidly to ca 55° and maintain this temp. until thermometer carrying mp tube registers 50°; then heat again and raise temp. of outer bath rather quickly to 67°. Remove burner. Mp is reached when fused substance becomes perfectly clear and transparent.

When mp of glycerides obtained by this method is <63.6°, presence of beef fat or other fat should be suspected, and mp of ≤63.2° is evidence that sample is not pure lard. Conduct detn with control sample of pure lard.

Confirm presence of foreign fat by taking mp of fatty acids prepd from glycerides. After detg mp, transfer crystd glycerides to 50 mL beaker, add 25 mL ca 0.5*N* alc. KOH, and heat on steam bath until saponification is complete. Pour soln into separator contg 200 mL H_2O, acidify, add 75 mL ether, shake, and let stand. Drain aq. acid layer and wash ether soln ≥3 times with H_2O. Transfer ether soln to clean, dry 50 mL beaker, evap. ether on steam bath, and finally dry acids at 100°. Let acids remain at room temp. ca 2 hr and det. mp. If mp of glycerides,

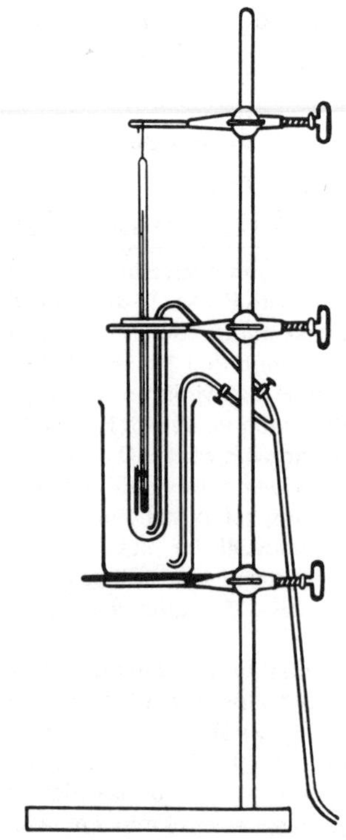

FIG. 28:08—Apparatus for determining melting point

plus twice difference between mp of glycerides and mp of fatty acids, is <73°, the lard is regarded as adulterated.

Conclusions may be confirmed further by precise detns of mean MW of sepd fatty acids. Dissolve acids in colorless, redistd alcohol, carefully neutzd immediately before use, and titr. with 0.5–0.2*N* KOH, using phthln. Mean MW = wt fatty acids × 1000/(mL × normality KOH used). If sample is pure lard, mean MW of fatty acids should correspond closely to that of fatty acids of β-palmitodistearin, 275.14. If sample is impure, mean MW should approach that of fatty acids from tristearin, 284.49.

28.121 Fish Oil and Marine Animal Oils in Presence of Vegetable Oils and in Absence of Metallic Salts (*34*)—Procedure

(*Caution: See* **51.047**.)

Dissolve 30 drops oil in 8 mL $CHCl_3$ in 50 mL beaker and add 10 mL Wijs soln, **28.020**. Add from buret, with const stirring, Br-HOAc (1+3–4) to end point where soln appears to bleach out, and then add slight excess. Mix, immediately pour into flat-bottom test tube, and let stand 1–3 hr until clear supernate is obtained. Measure ht of ppt with mm rule and compare with stds prepd with known amts of fish oil, including 0. Amt of insol. bromides is proportional to amt of fish oil up to ca 15% and as little as 1% fish oil can be detected by slight ppt on standing overnight.

Mineral Oil in Fats (*35*)

28.122 ***Qualitative Test—Procedure***

Place 1 mL oil or melted fat in erlenmeyer; add 1 mL KOH soln (3+2) and 25 mL alcohol. Boil under reflux air condenser, shaking occasionally, until saponification is complete (ca 5 min). Add 25 mL H_2O and mix. In presence of >0.5% mineral oil, distinct turbidity appears.

28.123 ***Quantitative Method—Official Final Action***

(*Caution: See* **51.011**, **51.039**, and **51.073**.)

Treat unsaponifiable residue, **28.081**, with H_2SO_4 as below. When very small amts of mineral oil are present, enough unsaponifiable residue for test may be obtained as follows:

Saponify 100 g fat by refluxing under air condenser 2 hr with 55 mL KOH soln (3+2) and 240 mL alcohol, with occasional shaking. Cool, add 300 mL pet ether (bp 35–60°), and transfer to separator. Rinse flask with 240 mL alcohol and add rinsings to separator. Add 480 mL H_2O and shake vigorously. Let layers sep., drain lower layer, and transfer upper layer to another separator. Repeat extn of saponified fat with 300 mL pet ether, and combine exts. Wash ext twice with 60 mL portions H_2O, using gentle agitation. Repeat washing with 60 mL 0.5*N* KOH, followed by vigorous agitation with successive 60 mL portions H_2O until washings are alkali-free. Evap. ext to small vol. and dry with anhyd. Na_2SO_4.

Filter pet ether soln thru small cotton plug into Babcock milk-test bottle, **16.060(a)**, add few small pieces broken porcelain, and remove solv. by heating on steam bath while passing current of air thru bottle. Cool, add 5 mL H_2SO_4, mix, and keep bottle in boiling H_2O bath 30 min, shaking occasionally. Remove bottle from bath, cool, and fill with H_2SO_4 until surface rises well into graduated neck. Centrf. 5 min at 1200 rpm and read vol. of unreacted residue. If enough mineral oil is available, obtain density as in **28.004**, using small Sprengel tube. Wt mineral oil can be closely approximated by multiplying vol. by 0.88. Refractive index of colorless residue should be <1.500 at 20°.

Hydrocarbons (*36*)—Official Final Action

AOCS–AOAC Method

(Applicable to satd hydrocarbons in glycerides)

28.124 ***Apparatus and Reagents***

(**a**) *Chromatographic tube.*—With Teflon stopcock, 25–35 mm diam. and 400 mm long.

(**b**) *Aluminum oxide.*—Activated alumina, Alcoa, grade F-20, 80–200 mesh (Aluminum Co. of America, or equiv.). Dry alumina ≥4 hr at 200° before using. Store in sealed bottles in desiccator. Alumina must have moisture content of 0–3% to retain glycerides.

28.125 ***Determination***

(*Caution: See* **51.011**, **51.039**, and **51.073**.)

Weigh 10±0.01 g melted, well mixed sample into 125 mL erlenmeyer, and dissolve in 50–100 mL pet ether, warming gently, if necessary.

Prep. column by tamping plug of glass wool into bottom of tube so that some of glass wool is in constricted portion above stopcock. Fill tube ca ⅔ full with pet ether (Fisher Scientific Co. No. E-139, or equiv.) and add 200 g alumina thru powder funnel. Tap side of tube to aid in packing. Cover with ca 1 cm anhyd. Na_2SO_4. Elute at rate of 80–90 drops (3.0–3.5 mL)/min, using stopcock for control.

When solv. head drops to ca 1 cm, add sample soln. Let solv. layer drop to ca 1 cm above alumina, collecting eluate in 500 mL erlenmeyer. Rinse sample flask with 50 mL pet ether and add to column. Repeat 3 times, adding each rinse to column when solv. head drops to ca 1 cm, and wash down sides of column on transferring. Continue adding pet ether to column until total of 400 mL has passed thru. (Inverted vol. flask can serve as convenient reservoir for final addn of solv.)

Evap. eluate on steam bath to 50–75 mL. Stirring rod placed in flask will help prevent superheating and consequent boiling over. Gentle air stream will aid solv. removal. Transfer to weighed 250 mL Soxhlet flask, rinsing with three 20 mL portions pet ether. Remove remaining solv. by evapn on warm surface with gentle air stream, keeping soln below bp. Cool to room temp. in desiccator and weigh.

Repeat with addnl heating periods of 20 min, cooling, and weighing until change in wt is <0.5 mg.

Conduct blank detn without sample.

$$\% \text{ Hydrocarbons} = (S - B) \times 100/C,$$

where S = g sample residue, B = g blank residue, and C = g sample.

28.126 ***Precision***

Following 95% confidence limits may be expected:

	% Hydrocarbon Content at Level of			
	0.0	0.05	0.5	5.0
Two single detns in 1 laboratory should differ ≤	0.06	0.09	0.14	0.33
Single detns in different laboratories should differ ≤	0.06	0.10	0.14	0.40

Confirm presence of hydrocarbons or mineral oil by comparison of IR spectrum of residue with that of pure hydrocarbons or mineral oil, USP.

Chick Edema Factor (Dioxins)

28.127 ★ ***Bioassay Method (37)—Official Final Action*** ★

Chick feeding test. See **28.113–28.117**, 12th ed.

Gas Chromatographic Method (38)—Official First Action

(*Caution: See* **51.011**, **51.015**, **51.030**, **51.039**, **51.040**, and **51.073**.)

28.128 ***Principle***

Fat, oil, fatty acid, or lipid is treated with H_2SO_4 and extd with pet ether. Ext is purified on Al_2O_3 column, further treated with H_2SO_4, and examined by electron capture GLC. Peaks with retention times relative to aldrin (R_a) between 8 and 45 indicate presence of chick edema factors (hexa-, hepta-, and octachlorodibenzo-*p*-dioxins).

28.129 ***Reagents and Apparatus***

(Rinse all glassware with appropriate solvs before use. Do not store solvs in polyethylene containers. Solvs available from Burdick and Jackson Laboratories, or equiv.)

(**a**) *Petroleum ether.*—Distd in glass, bp 30–60°.

(**b**) *Ethyl ether for alumina chromatography.*—Ether (≤2% alcohol) or absolute ether (≤0.01% alcohol).

(**c**) Carbon tetrachloride.—Distd in glass.

(**d**) *Isooctane.*—Distd in glass.

(**e**) *Aldrin std soln.*—0.05 μg/mL isooctane.

(**f**) *Chick edema factor low positive reference sample.*—1.5% Prep. from concd ref. toxic fat (available from Residue Analytical Chemistry Branch, Division of Chemistry and Physics, Bureau of Foods, Food and Drug Administration, Washington, DC 20204) in USP cottonseed or other vegetable oil. (*Caution:* Do not contact toxic fat.)

(**g**) *Activated alumina.*—Fisher Scientific Co. No. A-540; do not substitute. Activate 100 g portions by heating 4 hr at 260°. Transfer without cooling to dry container and close tightly. Check activity of Al_2O_3 by analysis of low pos. ref. sample, (**f**),

★ Surplus method—*see* inside front cover.

examining Al_2O_3 fractions 2 and 3. With sufficiently activated Al_2O_3, chick edema factor elutes predominantly or entirely in fraction 3 as indicated by gas chromatograms. (Chromatograms should show series of peaks with R_a between ca 8 and 45.)

(**h**) *Alumina chromatographic column.*—To dry tube, 17 (od) × 250 mm, fitted at bottom with coarse porosity fritted glass disk and Teflon stopcock (tube without disk but with glass wool plug at bottom may also be used), add redistd pet ether, dried before use with anhyd. Na_2SO_4, until tube is ⅔ full. Transfer 15 g Al_2O_3 to tube in small portions, tapping to settle. After last portion has settled and air bubbles stop rising to surface of solv., add 5 g anhyd. Na_2SO_4. Drain excess pet ether until it is just above surface of Na_2SO_4.

(**i**) *Gas chromatographic column.*—Glass, 2.1–2.7 m (7–9′) × ¼″, packed with 2.5% SE 52 silicone gum rubber on 60–80 mesh Gas-Chrom Q (Applied Science Laboratories, Inc.). Coat support with substrate as follows: Dissolve 2.5 g silicone gum rubber in 300 mL CH_2Cl_2-toluene (1+1) with heat. Add 97.5 g Gas-Chrom Q and let stand 10 min with occasional gentle stirring. Dry in rotary evaporator held in 50° bath. Apply vac. to chromatgc tube and add small amts of coated support while tapping tube at packing level after each addn. Fill to within 2.5 cm on exit side and 7.5 cm on entrance side and fill remaining space with silanized glass wool. Condition column at operating pressure 2–5 days at 250°.

(**j**) *Gas chromatograph.*—With tritium source concentric-type electron capture detector. Operate instrument in accordance with instructions of manufacturer. Obtain stable baseline before use. Choose operating voltage that will cause between 0.6 and full scale deflection for 0.1 ng aldrin (2 μL std aldrin soln) at sensitivity setting of 1×10^{-9} amp full scale. Keep column temp. at 200±1° and adjust N flow so that aldrin elutes in 1–1.5 min (0.25–0.33″ (6–8 mm)/min chart speed). Inject 2 μL aldrin std soln before each ref. or test sample.

28.130 ***Determination***

(**a**) *Analysis of reference toxic fat.*—Dissolve 2.5 g ref. 1.5% toxic fat in 10 mL CCl_4 in 500 mL g-s erlenmeyer and proceed as in (**b**), (**c**), and (**d**). Dissolve residue in 250 μL isooctane and inject 5 μL (equiv. to 50 mg original sample) into gas chromatograph. Resulting chromatogram should exhibit series of peaks with R_a ca 8–45. Peaks at 8–13 are due to hexachlorodibenzo-*p*-dioxin isomers; 2 peaks at 17–22, to the 2 hepta-isomers; and peak at 35–45, to octa-isomer.

(**b**) *Preliminary sulfuric acid cleanup.*—Dissolve 2.5 g sample in 10 mL CCl_4 in 500 mL g-s erlenmeyer. Add 10 mL H_2SO_4, stopper, and shake 30 sec. Add 125 mL pet ether, stopper, and shake vigorously ca 1 min. Let sep. and decant upper layer into 500 mL erlenmeyer, avoiding transfer of lower layer. Repeat extn with addnl 125 mL portion pet ether. Evap. combined pet ether exts to 5 mL.

(**c**) *Alumina chromatography.*—Before use, dry all solvs by shaking with anhyd. Na_2SO_4. Transfer evapd pet ether ext to alumina column, (**h**), using total of 10 mL pet ether. Let drain to just above level of Na_2SO_4. Keeping liq. level above Na_2SO_4 at all times, elute with 100 mL pet ether (fraction 1), 50 mL 5% Et ether in pet ether (fraction 2), and 100 mL 25% Et ether in pet ether (fraction 3). (Flow rates of 8–9 mL/min are satisfactory.) Discard fractions 1 and 2 and collect fraction 3 in 125 mL erlenmeyer. Add several boiling chips and evap. to ca 2 mL on steam bath. Transfer residue with small portions pet ether to 10 mL g-s graduate and further evap. to 3 mL under N.

(**d**) *Additional sulfuric acid cleanup.*—Add 2 mL H_2SO_4 to pet ether soln, stopper, and shake vigorously 30 sec. Let sep. and decant upper layer into 10 mL beaker, avoiding transfer of any H_2SO_4. Add 2 mL pet ether to graduate, swirl vigorously, let sep., and decant upper layer into beaker. Add 0.5 g solid $NaHCO_3$ to beaker and stir ca 0.5 min. Let stand 5 min and decant pet ether layer into 2 or 4 dram vial. Wash $NaHCO_3$ with 2 mL pet ether and decant washings into vial. Evap. solv. just to dryness at room temp. in vial under N.

(**e**) *Gas chromatography.*—Dissolve residue in 250 μL isooctane, stopper vial, and rotate to wet sides with solv. Inject 1 μL soln (equiv. to 10 mg sample) into gas chromatograph, (**j**). Peaks with R_a of 8–45 indicate presence of chick edema factor. Compare R_a values with those from ref. toxic fat, (**a**). If peaks indicative of chick edema factor are not observed, inject 5 μL soln (equiv. to 50 mg sample). (Types of samples found by experience to be free of components characteristic of toxic fats may be examined by initial injection of 5 μL.)

Perform reagent blank detn with each set of samples. Smooth baseline should be obtained in region R_a 8–45.

Synthetic Colors (*39*)—Official Final Action

28.131 ***Reagents***

(**a**) *Acid soln X.*—Mix 1 L HOAc with 200 mL HCl and 100 mL H_2O.

(**b**) *Acid soln Y.*—Cautiously add 400 mL H_2SO_4 to 100 mL H_2O. When cool, add 900 mL HOAc and mix.

(**c**) *Sodium hydroxide soln.*—Approx. 25%. Dissolve 250 g NaOH in H_2O and dil. to 1 L.

28.132 ***Separation and Identification***

(*Caution: See* **51.011**, **51.039**, and **51.073**.)

Place 125 mL oil and 250 mL pet ether in each of 6 separators. Shake contents of first with 50 mL Soln *X* and, as soon as layers sep., transfer lower layer to flask contg 250 mL H_2O. Mix, and immediately ext this dild acid soln by passing successively thru two 500 mL separators, each contg 75 mL pet ether. Shake vigorously, let layers sep., and discard lower aq. layer. Repeat this procedure with each of other 5 separators, using same pet ether to re-ext colors from the dild acid solns. Combine the 2 pet ether exts, wash with three 25 mL portions H_2O, and filter.

Ext combined pet ether soln with two 25 mL portions Soln *X*. Treat each acid ext sep. by mixing with 150 mL H_2O and re-extg quickly by passing thru two 250 mL separators, each contg 50 mL pet ether. Combine these pet ether solns, wash acid-free with 15 mL portions H_2O, and evap. to dryness on steam bath. Do not heat dish after removal of solv. Residue may contain Ext. D&C Yellow No. 9 or No. 10 (formerly FD&C Yellow No. 3 or No. 4, resp.) and possibly trace of Ext. D&C Orange No. 4 (formerly FD&C Orange No. 2) if latter dye was originally present in large amts. Identify color spectrophtric as in Chap. **34**.

Shake first separator contg dild oil with 25 mL Soln *Y*, let sep. 20 min, and transfer lower layer to flask contg 200 mL 25% NaOH. Mix, and add 200 mL H_2O. Cool, and remove color from this alk. soln by passing successive 100 mL portions thru two 250 mL separators, each contg 75 mL pet ether. Discard extd alk. soln. Continue this Soln *Y* treatment of oil in other 5 separators, and finally combine the 2 pet ether exts. Wash with three 50 mL portions H_2O and ext with two 20 mL portions Soln *Y*, letting layers sep. 5 min. Drain lower layers into flask contg 300 mL 25% NaOH, mix, and add 300 mL H_2O. Cool, and remove color from this alk. soln by passing successive 100 mL portions thru 2 separators, each contg 75 mL pet ether. Combine pet ether solns, wash free from alkali with H_2O, transfer to evapg dish, and remove solv. on steam bath. Residue may contain Ext. D&C Orange No. 4 and D&C Green No. 6. Remove former by dissolving in 3–5 mL portions 60% alcohol and filtering each portion thru small paper. Identify color spectrophtric as in Chapter **34**.

Dissolve residue on paper in 2–5 mL portions pet ether, collecting filtrate in original evapg dish. Remove solv. on steam bath. Blue residue indicates D&C Green No. 6. Dissolve residue in 15 mL alcohol and 10 mL H_2O, and add 0.5 mL HOAc. Identify color spectrophtric as in Chapter **34**.

Pink color in the various acid exts usually indicates synthetic dye. However, corn oil sometimes produces faint pink color in these exts. This is readily differentiated from synthetic colors spectrophtric. Chlorophyll may appear as green scum at interface in acid exts and as green residue on papers after filtration of pet ether solns.

MONO- AND DIGLYCERIDES

Glycerides in Monoglyceride Concentrates (*40*) Official Final Action

28.133 ***Apparatus***

(**a**) *Chromatographic tube.*—Reservoir, 250 mL, with Teflon stopcock attached thru ₸ 19/22 drip tip inner joint to column, 19 (id) × 290 mm, with outer ₸ 19/22 joint at top and with coarse fritted glass disk and inner ₸ 19/22 joint at bottom. Bottom joint connects to adapter consisting of outer ₸ 19/22 joint connected to Teflon stopcock. (Available from SGA Scientific Inc., from Print No. 580241-12.)

(**b**) *Mixer.*—Patterson-Kelley Twin Shell Blender, or equiv., for mixing adsorbent. (Available from Patterson-Kelley Co., Inc., 100 Burson St, East Stroudsburg, PA 18301.)

28.134 ***Preparation of Silica Gel***

Place ca 10 g silica gel (Fisher Scientific Co. No. S-679, grade 923, 100–200 mesh) in tared weighing bottle and cap immediately. Weigh to nearest mg and subtract tare wt. Remove cap and dry 2 hr at 200°. Remove from oven, cap immediately, and let cool 30 min at room temp. Raise cap momentarily to equalize internal pressure with atm. Weigh, reheat 5 min at 200°, cool, and reweigh. Repeat 5 min drying cycle until 2 consecutive wts agree within 10 mg. Calc. H_2O content as follows:

% H_2O in original silica gel = x = (loss in wt) × 100/sample wt. Adjust H_2O content of original silica gel to 5% as follows:

H_2O to be added = g original silica gel × $(5 - x)/95$.

Weigh silica gel to be adjusted in blender and add calcd amt H_2O to give final H_2O content of 5±0.1%. Blend 1 hr to ensure complete H_2O distribution and store in sealed container. Det. H_2O content of adjusted silica gel as above, and readjust if necessary.

28.135 ***Preparation of Sample***

(To avoid rearrangement of partial glycerides, use extreme caution in applying heat to samples. Do not heat >50°.)

(**a**) *Samples melting below 50°.*—Melt by warming at <50° for short periods (30 min max.).

(**b**) *Samples melting above 50°.*—Grind ca 10 g in mortar and pestle. If necessary, chill samples in solid CO_2.

Weigh 0.9–1.1 g prepd sample to 1 mg in 100 mL beaker. Add 15 mL $CHCl_3$ and warm if necessary for complete soln. Use only min. heat and do not heat >40°.

28.136 ***Preparation of Column***

Assemble chromatgc tube but without reservoir. Do not grease joints. Weigh 30 g prepd silica gel into 150 mL beaker and add 50–60 mL pet ether. Stir slowly with glass rod until all air bubbles are expelled. Place powder funnel in tube and transfer slurry. Open stopcock and let liq. level drop to ca 2 cm above silica gel. To transfer any silica gel slurry remaining in beaker, invert beaker over powder funnel at 45° and wash into tube with wash bottle, using min. amt pet ether. Rinse funnel and sides of tube; when solv. level drops to 2 cm above silica gel, close bottom stopcock. Remove powder funnel and carefully add sample. Open stopcock and adjust flow to 2 mL/min. Rinse beaker with 5 mL $CHCl_3$ and add rinse to column when level drops to 2 cm above silica gel.

(Keep temp. of work area below bp of most volatile solv. used, Et ether (34.6°). Higher temp. will cause sepn of column packing and permit solv. to channel.

Never let column become dry on top, and maintain 2 mL/min flow rate thruout elution. If necessary to interrupt elution, do so when very little glyceride is passing thru bottom stopcock. Avoid such interruptions, since solv. above bottom stopcock may cause pressure buildup and result in leakage thru stopcock or cracks in silica gel packing.)

28.137 ***Separation of Glycerides***

(*Caution: See* **51.011, 51.039, 51.040, 51.045**, and **51.054**.)

Attach reservoir to column, add 200 mL benzene, and collect eluate in tared 250 mL flask (triglyceride fraction). When all benzene has been added from separator and level in column drops to 2 cm above silica gel, add 200 mL 10% (v/v) ether in benzene and collect eluate in second tared 250 mL flask (diglyceride + free fatty acid (FFA) fraction). When all benzene-ether solv. has been added from separator and level in column drops to 2 cm above silica gel, add 200 mL ether, change to third tared 250 mL flask, and collect monoglyceride fraction.

(Addn of Et ether to column often creates internal pressure, resulting in increased flow rate and cracks in silica gel packing before fraction is completely eluted. Avoid by slightly sepg reservoir from column for ca 30 sec and letting solv. flow into column at same rate as eluate is collected.)

To ensure quant. sepn of fractions, rinse tip of column into receiver with same solv. used in elution just before changing flasks for next eluate.

Evap. collected tri-, di- plus FFA, and monoglyceride fractions on steam bath under stream of N or dry air. Let flasks cool at room temp. ≥15 min and weigh. Reheat samples on steam bath 5 min under N or dry air, let cool 15 min, and reweigh. Repeat 5 min evapn, cooling, and reweighing until 2 consecutive wts agree within 2 mg.

Any free fatty acid present is eluted with diglyceride fraction. To det. free fatty acid content of weighed diglyceride, add 25 mL warm neut. alcohol and 1 drop phthln indicator, and titr. with 0.05*N* NaOH.

28.138 ***Calculations***

% FFA (as oleic) = mL NaOH × Normality × 28.2/g sample
% Triglyceride = g triglyceride × 100/g sample
% Diglyceride = (g diglyceride × 100/g sample) − % FFA
% Monoglyceride = g monoglyceride × 100/g sample.

1-Monoglycerides (*41*)—Official First Action

American Oil Chemists' Society Method

28.139 ***Principle***

1-Monoglycerides are detd from HIO_4 consumed in the oxidn of adjacent hydroxyl groups. 2-Monoglycerides are not oxidized by HIO_4. Method is applicable to monoglyceride concs contg ≥15% 1-monoglyceride; not applicable to samples contg $CHCl_3$-sol. substances with ≥2 adjacent hydroxyl groups.

28.140 ***Reagents***

(**a**) *Periodic acid soln.*—Reagent grade (available from G. Frederick Smith Chemical Co.). Test as follows: To 0.5–0.6 g glycerol in 50 mL H_2O, add 50 mL HIO_4 soln from pipet. Prep. blank contg 50 mL H_2O. Let stand 30 min and titr. as in **28.142**. Titer of soln contg glycerol/titer of blank = 0.75–0.76 if reagent is satisfactory.

Dissolve 5.4 g HIO_4 in 100 mL H_2O, add 1900 mL HOAc, and mix thoroly. Store in g-s bottle in dark.

(**b**) *Starch indicator soln.*—Make homogeneous paste of 1.0 g sol. starch with H_2O. Add to 100 mL boiling H_2O, stir rapidly, and cool. Salicylic acid, 0.125 g/100 mL, may be added as preservative. Soln keeps longer if stored in refrigerator. Color of 2 mL starch soln dild with 100 mL H_2O contg 0.05 mL 0.1*N* I must be discharged by 0.05 mL 0.1*N* $Na_2S_2O_3$. Discard if end point from blue to colorless is no longer sharp.

(**c**) *Chloroform.*—Reagent or USP. Blanks on HIO_4 soln with and without $CHCl_3$ must check within 0.5 mL.

28.141 ***Preparation of Samples***

(Do not subject samples to excessive temps or monoglyceride content may be reduced.)

(**a**) *Solids in flake form.*—Mix without melting.

(**b**) *Solids not in flake form.*—Melt at $\leqslant$10° above mp, mix thoroly, and take sample. Do not test samples contg so much free glycerol that it seps on solidification.

(**c**) *Semisolids and liquids.*—Proceed as in (**b**).

28.142 ***Determination***

Accurately weigh 0.3–2 g sample calcd from equation: g = 30/% monoglyceride in sample, dissolve in $CHCl_3$, and transfer to 100 mL g-s vol. flask. Dil. to vol. with $CHCl_3$ and mix. Transfer entire soln to 500 mL g-s erlenmeyer (do not rinse) and add 100 mL H_2O. Stopper, and shake vigorously 1 min. Let stand until layers sep. and $CHCl_3$ layer is clear or only slightly cloudy (1–3 hr). If emulsions form, causing poor sepn, repeat detn, using 100 mL HOAc (5+95) instead of H_2O.

Pipet 50 mL HIO_4 soln into series of 400 mL beakers. Add 50 mL $CHCl_3$ to 2 and 50 mL H_2O to third as blanks (**28.140(c)**). Pipet 50 mL $CHCl_3$ sample soln into fourth, avoiding any aq. phase, and shake gently. (Solns must be cooled to <95°F (32°), if necessary.) Cover with watch glass and let stand 30 min.

Add 20 mL 15% KI soln, mix by gentle shaking, and let stand $\geqslant$1 min but $\leqslant$5 min, away from strong sunlight. Add 100 mL H_2O, and titr. with stdzd 0.1*N* $Na_2S_2O_3$, stirring continuously with mech. stirrer. After I color disappears from aq. layer, add 2 mL starch soln and continue titrn to disappearance of blue from aq. layer. Vigorous stirring is necessary to remove I from $CHCl_3$ layer.

If titer of sample is <0.8 titer of blanks, repeat detn, using smaller aliquot of $CHCl_3$ soln or smaller sample wt, to assure adequate excess of HIO_4.

$$\% \text{ Monoglyceride as monostearin} = (B - S) \times N \times 17.927/W,$$

where B = titer of $CHCl_3$ blank, S = titer of sample, N = normality of $Na_2S_2O_3$, W = g sample in $CHCl_3$ aliquot, and 17.927 = MW monostearin/20.

If content is to be calcd to monoglyceride other than monostearin, substitute for 17.927 MW of other monoglyceride/20. Alternatively, det. MW as follows: Sep. fatty acids as in first 2 par. of **28.014**. Accurately weigh ca 2 g fatty acids into 250 mL erlenmeyer and add 20–30 mL hot alcohol neutzd to faint pink of phthln. (SDA formula 30 or 3A is satisfactory.) Add 0.5 mL phthln and titr. immediately while shaking with 0.5*N* NaOH to pink that persists 30 sec. Calc. acid number (mg *KOH* required to neutze fatty acids in 1 g sample) = mL NaOH × normality × 56.1/g sample. Av. MW of fatty acids = 56104/acid number = *M*. MW monoglyceride = (M + 92.09) − 18.02.

Duplicate detns made on same day by 1 analyst should not differ (95% confidence limits) by more than ca 0.5, and 1.2% 1-monoglyceride at 40 and 90% levels; single detns and av. of duplicate detns made in 2 different laboratories should not differ by more than ca 1.2 and 3.2%, and 1.1 and 3.1%, resp., at same levels.

Revised Miner Method (42)

28.143 ***Principle***

Periodic acid oxidizes vicinal hydroxyl groups. Compds with =O, —OH, —NHR, and —NH_2 attached to adjacent C atoms will be oxidized by H_5IO_6; phospholipids can interfere. Such substances are absent from usual fat samples.

Samples are dissolved in $CHCl_3$ contg 5% dimethylformamide (to assure soln of glycerol) and aliquots are oxidized with excess H_5IO_6. H_5IO_6-H_2O soln exts and oxidizes free glycerol and H_5IO_6-MeOH soln oxidizes monoglyceride plus glycerol. Unused H_5IO_6 is detd iodometrically by reacting with KI and titrg with 0.05*N* std arsenite soln.

Calcn of monoglyceride is based on amt of H_5IO_6 consumed in oxidn of monoglyceride plus glycerol corrected for amt consumed in oxidn of free glycerol alone.

Method is applicable to fats, oils, shortenings, monoglycerides, and blends contg <15% 1-monoglycerides.

28.144 ***Reagents and Apparatus***

(**a**) *Periodic acid stock soln.*—Dissolve 12.0 g H_5IO_6 (G. Frederick Smith Chemical Co., reagent grade) in 100 mL H_2O. Store at room temp. in brown g-s bottle.

(**b**) *Periodic acid in 95% methanol.*—Mix 25 mL stock soln with 475 mL MeOH. Store at room temp. in brown g-s bottle and prep. fresh every 3–5 days.

(**c**) *Periodic acid in water.*—Mix 50 mL stock soln, (**a**), with 950 mL H_2O.

(**d**) *Potassium iodide soln.*—Dissolve 75 g KI and 50 g $NaHCO_3$ in H_2O.

(**e**) *Sodium arsenite.*—0.05*N*. *See* **50.005–50.006**.

(**f**) *Starch indicator.*—Make homogeneous paste of 0.50 g potato starch with 5 mL H_2O. Add to 200 mL boiling H_2O and boil 15 min, stirring constantly. Cool and store in g-s bottle. Prep. fresh daily.

(**g**) *Chloroform.*—I absorption should be <0.1 mL 0.1*N* $Na_2S_2O_3$/30 mL solv.

(**h**) *N,N-Dimethylformamide (DMF).*—25% soln in $CHCl_3$ (**g**). (*Caution:* This material is toxic. Avoid contact with skin or inhalation of vapors.)

(**i**) *Hot plate.*—Thermolyne, Model HP-A1915B, or equiv. (Thermolyne, 2555 Kerper Blvd, Dubuque, IA 52001).

28.145 ***Preparation of Samples***

See **28.141**.

28.146 ***Determination***

(*Caution: See* **51.018**, **51.040**, **51.053**, and **51.056**.)

Weigh sample into 100 mL beaker, calcg g required as:

$$S = K/(M' + 8G) = 50/(M' + 8G) = 4W_1 = 2W_2;$$

where M' = % monoglyceride expected; G = % free glycerol expected; K = const which dets % excess reagent [100 $T_1/(B_1 - T_1)$]; W_1 = aliquot wt for monoglyceride; W_2 = aliquot wt for free glycerol; B_1 = blank titrn for monoglyceride plus glycerol; B_2 = blank titrn for free glycerol; T_1 = sample titrn for monoglyceride plus glycerol; and T_2 = sample titrn for free glycerol.

For 20% excess, K = 70; 50% excess, K = 50 (preferred); and 100% excess, K = 42. Max. S should be 40 g/100 mL or, if preferred, 10 g can be weighed directly into reaction vessel.

(**a**) *Monoglyceride plus glycerol.*—Dissolve weighed sample in 20 mL 25% DMF. Use $CHCl_3$ to transfer quant. to 100 mL vol. flask and dil. to vol. Aliquots can be used for analysis of both monoglyceride plus glycerol and free glycerol.

Pipet 25 mL aliquot into 500 mL erlenmeyer and record sample wt in aliquot as W_1. Prep. 2 blanks in similar flasks by adding 5 mL 25% DMF and 20 mL $CHCl_3$ to each.

Pipet exactly 25 mL H_5IO_6-MeOH into the 25 mL aliquot and into each blank. (For samples low in monoglyceride, such as triglyceride fat or oil, vol. H_5IO_6-MeOH may be reduced from 25 mL to 10, 5, or even 3 mL; use same amt of reagent for blanks.) Add 2–3 glass beads to each sample and heat just to bp on hot plate, swirling several times during heating. (Do not heat blanks.) Let stand 30 min to cool, protected from sunlight or other strong illumination. Add 200 mL H_2O to each blank and sample, and swirl several times. Let sample stand 5 min ($\leq$45 min is permissible). Blanks may be analyzed immediately. Add 40 mL KI soln from graduate and swirl to mix. Let stand 1 min; then titr. with Na arsenite. After I color fades to pale yellow, add 2–3 mL starch indicator and continue titrn until starch-I color disappears. Record av. titrn of 2 blanks as B_1 and of sample as T_1. When >1 sample is run on same day with same reagents, av. titrn of 2 blanks which check within 0.1 mL can be used in all calcns. If 2 blanks do not check within 0.1 mL, third blank must be run. Excess H_5IO_6 must be 20–100%. If 100 $T_1/(B_1 - T_1)$ is <20%, repeat with smaller sample; if excess is much >100%, repeat with larger sample or use less H_5IO_6-MeOH. To complete H_5IO_6 oxidn, min. of 20% excess is required. If excess H_5IO_6-MeOH is much >100%, high apparent monoglyceride may result.

(**b**) *Free glycerol.*—Free glycerol must be extd completely from DMF layer into aq. layer. If glycerol is not in aq. layer when H_5IO_6-H_2O is added, or during standing time, results may be low.

Pipet 50 mL aliquot of weighed sample from (**a**) into 500 mL erlenmeyer. Record sample wt in aliquot as W_2. Prep. 2 blanks in similar flasks by adding 10 mL 25% DMF and 40 mL $CHCl_3$.

Add ca 100 mL H_2O to sample and blanks. Swirl ca 1 min, reversing direction several times. Pipet exactly 25 mL H_5IO_6-H_2O into each flask. Let stand at room temp. 30 min, swirling vigorously $\geq$30 sec at beginning and every 5 min during this period. Add 40 mL KI soln from graduate, swirl, and let stand 1 min. Titr. with 0.05N Na arsenite to starch-I end point as in (**a**), including blank titrns. Record sample titrn as T_2 and av. of blank titrn as B_2. Any excess >20% is permissible for H_5IO_6-H_2O.

28.147 ***Calculation***

$$\% \text{ Monoglyceride} = \{[(B_1 - T_1) - (W_1/W_2)(B_2 - T_2)] \times N \times MW \times 100\}/(W_1 \times 2 \times 1000),$$

where N is normality of Na arsenite soln, and MW is molecular wt of monoglyceride.

Monoglyceride content can be calcd as monostearin. Using exactly 0.05N Na arsenite, 358 as MW of monostearin, and sample wt of free glycerol equal to twice amt used for monoglyceride plus glycerol, following formula can be applied:

$$\% \text{ Monoglyceride (as monostearin)} = \{[(B_1 - T_1) - 0.5(B_2 - T_2)] \times 0.895\}/W_1.$$

Glycerides in Shortening (*43*)—Official Final Action

(Not generally applicable when emulsifiers other than mono- and diglycerides are present. *Caution: See* **51.011, 51.039, 51.040, 51.045**, and **51.054**.)

28.148 ***Apparatus***

See **28.133**.

28.149 ***Preparation of Silica Gel***

See **28.134**. Check each new lot of adsorbent for satisfactory sepn of glycerides. Collect last 15 mL of each eluate in weighed flask. If residue after evapn is >2 mg, increase amt of eluate until last 15 mL collected contains <2 mg. Once amts of eluates needed for complete sepn of glyceride fractions are established, only occasional checking of each lot of silica gel is required.

28.150 ***Preparation of Sample***

Melt entire sample in hot H_2O at 50° to avoid overheating, and mix well. Weigh 4.9–5.1 g prepd sample to 1 mg in 100 mL beaker. Add 10 mL benzene and warm if necessary for complete soln. Use only min. heat and do not heat >50°.

28.151 ***Preparation of Column***

Prep. column as in **28.136** and adjust flow to 2 mL/min. Begin collecting eluate in weighed 400 mL beaker. Rinse beaker with 10 mL benzene and add to column when level drops to 2 cm above silica gel. Repeat rinsing with 10 mL portions benzene, using total of 40 mL.

Observe precautions of last 2 par. of **28.136**.

28.152 ***Separation of Glycerides***

Attach reservoir separator to column, add 300 mL benzene, and collect eluate in weighed 400 mL beaker (triglyceride fraction). When all benzene has been added and level in column drops to 2 cm above silica gel, add 250 mL 10% (v/v) ether in benzene and collect eluate in second weighed 400 mL beaker (diglyceride fraction). When all benzene-ether solv. has been added and level in column drops to ca 2 cm above silica gel, add 200 mL ether and collect eluate in third weighed 400 mL beaker (monoglyceride fraction). Observe precaution of second par., **28.137**.

To ensure quant. sepn of fractions, rinse tip of column into receiver before changing beakers for next eluate. (Weighed 300 mL Soxhlet flasks can be used for collecting fractions, but 2 will be required for triglyceride eluate.)

Evap. tri-, di-, and monoglyceride fractions on steam bath under stream of clean N or dry air. Let beakers cool at room temp. $\geq$15 min and weigh. Replace beakers on steam bath 5 min, remove, cool 15 min, and reweigh. Repeat 5 min evapn, cooling, and reweighing until 2 consecutive wts agree within 2 mg.

28.153 ***Calculations***

% Triglyceride = g triglyceride × 100/g sample
% Diglyceride = g diglyceride × 100/g sample
% Monoglyceride = g monoglyceride × 100/g sample

High free fatty acid contents will give high results, since approx. 20% of free fatty acid is eluted with each of the tri- and monoglyceride fractions and 60% with diglyceride fraction. With most shortenings, effect is insignificant, since level of free fatty acids is <0.2%.

Nonhydroxy-derived glycerides, which may be formed by thermal exposure, may interfere. This material is found primarily in diglyceride fraction. Significant amts are not present in fresh shortenings. With used fats, diglyceride content of that fraction can be obtained from hydroxyl value.

FLAXSEED

28.154 ★ Oil by Refraction (*44*)—Official Final Action ★

(*Note:* Halogenated naphthalene may be harmful. *Caution: See* **51.084.**)

See **26.111–26.115**, 10th ed.

SELECTED REFERENCES

(*1*) Ind. Eng. Chem. **18**, 1347(1926); JAOAC **14**, 247(1931); **15**, 560(1932).

(*2*) Lewkowitsch, "Chemical Technology and Analysis of Oils, Fats and Waxes," 6th ed., **1**, 312(1921); J. Soc. Chem. Ind. **26**, 512(1907).

(*3*) USDA Bur. Chem. Bull, **13** (IV), p. 448; Lewkowitsch, "Chemical Technology and Analysis of Oils, Fats and Waxes," 6th ed., **1**, 325(1921); Wiley, "Principles and Practice of Agricultural Analysis," 2nd ed., **3**, 309(1906–14).

(*4*) JAOAC **25**, 726(1942).

(*5*) Compt. rend. **172**, 984(1921); Bull. soc. chim. (4), **29**, 745(1921); J. Am. Chem. Soc. **44**, 392(1922); JAOAC **10**, 323(1927).

(*6*) Ber. **34**, 3354(1901); J. Biol. Chem. **104**, 627(1934); Ind. Eng. Chem., Anal. Ed. **17**, 394(1945); AOCS Method Cd 13–60 (corrected 1961); JAOAC **48**, 131(1965).

(*7*) JAOAC **48**, 127(1965).

(*8*) J. Am. Oil Chem. Soc. **26**, 345(1949); AOCS Method Cd 8–53.

(*9*) JAOAC **55**, 846(1972).

(*10*) JAOAC **13**, 255(1930); **38**, 319(1955); **39**, 355(1956); **40**, 509(1957).

(*11*) JAOAC **39**, 212(1956); **40**, 531(1957).

(*12*) Cotton Oil Press **6**, No. 1, 41(1922); JAOAC **11**, 301(1928); **12**, 203(1929); **51**, 20(1968).

(*13*) JAOAC **40**, 487(1957); **42**, 42, 354(1959); AOCS Method Cd 7–58.

(*14*) IUPAC II.D.19, 5th ed. 4th suppl.; J. Am. Oil Chem. Soc. **45**, 103(1968); JAOAC **62**, 709(1979).

(*15*) JAOAC **62**, 709(1979); IUPAC II.D.25, 5th ed. 4th suppl.

(*16*) JAOAC **57**, 1161(1974).

(*17*) JAOAC **58**, 898(1975).

(*18*) JAOAC **61**, 1419(1978).

(*19*) JAOAC **48**, 437(1965); AOCS Method Cd 14–61.

(*20*) Analyst **58**, 203(1933); JAOAC **28**, 282(1945); **29**, 248(1946).

(*21*) JAOAC **26**, 499(1943); **28**, 282(1945); **29**, 247(1946).

(*22*) Netherlands Milk and Dairy J. **9**, 261(1955); JAOAC **38**, 338(1955); **41**, 268(1958).

(*23*) JAOAC **53**, 623(1970); **54**, 643(1971).

(*24*) J. Dairy Sci. **50**, 1764(1967); JAOAC **52**, 600(1969); **53**, 535(1970).

(*25*) JAOAC **52**, 774, 778(1969); **54**, 643(1971).

(*26*) J. Pharm. chim. 6th ser., **6**, 390(1897); Abs. Analyst **22**, 326(1897); Allen, "Commercial Organic Analysis," 5th ed., **2**, 177(1924); Conn. Agr. Expt. Sta. Rpt., **1900** (II), p. 143; Nature **178**, 372(1956); Chem. Rev. **64**, 497(1964).

(*27*) JAOAC **55**, 1288(1972); **56**, 82(1973).

(*28*) Compt. rend. **73**, 1330(1871); Lewkowitsch, "Chemical Technology and Analysis of Oils, Fats and Waxes," 6th ed., **2**, 316(1922).

(*29*) Analyst **62**, 96(1937); JAOAC **28**, 293(1945); **32**, 363(1949).

(*30*) JAOAC **12**, 203(1929).

(*31*) JAOAC **19**, 493(1936); **20**, 418(1937).

(*32*) J. Soc. Chem. Ind. **12**, 67(1893); **13**, 69(1894); JAOAC **6**, 441(1923).

(*33*) USDA Bur. Animal Ind. Circ. **132**; JAOAC **3**, 432(1920); **4**, 195(1920); **19**, 417(1936); Analyst **65**, 623(1940).

(*34*) J. Am. Oil Chem. Soc. **47**, 234(1970); JAOAC **57**, 1005(1974).

(*35*) JAOAC **28**, 285(1945).

(*36*) JAOAC **49**, 71, 232(1966).

(*37*) JAOAC **44**, 449, 456(1961); **45**, 231, 739(1962); **46**, 406(1963).

(*38*) JAOAC **46**, 384(1963); **48**, 433(1965); **50**, 874, 1338(1967); **51**, 940(1968); **53**, 628(1970); Nature **220**, 702(1968).

(*39*) JAOAC **25**, 726(1942); **34**, 235(1951).

(*40*) J. Am. Oil Chem. Soc. **35**, 325(1958); JAOAC **48**, **444**(1965).

(*41*) J. Am. Oil Chem. Soc. **34**, 301(1957); AOCS Method Cd 11–57 (revised 1971); JAOAC **49**, 816(1966).

(*42*) J. Am. Oil Chem. Soc. **31**, 466(1954); JAOAC **49**, 816(1966); **52**, 409, 602(1969).

(*43*) JAOAC **49**, 232, 812(1966).

(*44*) USDA Bull. **1471**(1927); JAOAC **20**, 421(1937).

SPECIAL REFERENCES

AMERICAN OIL CHEMISTS' SOCIETY, "Official and Tentative Methods," Champaign, IL (1973 and revisions).

"BAILEY'S Industrial Oil and Fat Products," 3rd ed., edited by Swern, Interscience Publishers, Inc., New York (1964); "Cottonseed and Cottonseed Products," Interscience Publishers, Inc., New York (1948).

BOEKENOOGEN, "Analysis and Characterization of Oils, Fats, and Fat Products," Vol. 1 (1964), Vol. 2 (1968), John Wiley and Sons, Inc., New York.

BRITISH STANDARDS INSTITUTION, "Methods of Analysis of Oils and Fats," British Standard **684**, London (1950).

CHAPMAN, "The Structure of Lipids," John Wiley and Sons, Inc., New York (1965).

COCKS AND VAN REDE, "Laboratory Handbook for Oil and Fat Analysis," Academic Press, New York (1966).

DEUEL, "The Lipids," Vol. 1, Interscience Publishers, Inc., New York (1951).

DEUTSCHE GESELLSCHAFT FÜR FETTWISSENSCHAFT E. V., "Deutsche Einheitsmethoden zur Untersuchung von Fetten, Fettprodukten und verwandten Stoffen," Wissenschaftliche Verlagsgesellschaft, Stuttgart (1950–).

ECKEY, "Vegetable Fats and Oils," Reinhold Publishing Co., New York (1954).

GUNSTONE, "An Introduction to the Chemistry and Biochemistry of Fatty Acids and Their Glycerides," 2nd ed., Chapman and Hall Ltd., London (1967).

HILDITCH AND WILLIAMS, "The Chemical Constitution of Natural Fats," 4th ed., John Wiley and Sons, Inc., New York (1964).

HOLMAN, "Progress in the Chemistry of Fats and Other Lipids," Vols. 1– (1952–) Pergamon Press, New York.

INTERNATIONAL UNION OF PURE AND APPLIED CHEMISTRY, "Standard Methods for the Analysis of Oils, Fats and Soaps," Butterworths, London (1966) and supplements.

KAUFMANN, "Analyse der Fette und Fettprodukte," 2 Vol., Springer-Verlag, Berlin (1958).

LUNDBERG, "Autoxidation and Antioxidants," Vol. 1 (1961); Vol. 2 (1962), Interscience Publishers, Inc., New York.

MARKLEY, "Fatty Acids, Their Chemistry, Properties, Production, and Uses," 2nd ed., Part 1 (1960); Part 2 (1961); Part 3 (1964); Part 4 (1967); Part 5 (1968); Interscience Publishers, Inc., New York.

MEHLENBACHER, "The Analysis of Fats and Oils," The Garrard Press, Champaign, Ill. (1960).

★ Surplus method—*see* inside front cover.

PARDUN, "Analyse der Nahrungsfette" Vol 16 of series "Grundlagen und Fortschritte der Lebensmitteluntersuchung und Lebensmitteltechnologie." Verlag Paul Parey in Berlin/Hamburg (1976).

PATTISON, "Fatty Acids and Their Industrial Applications," Marcel Dekker, Inc., New York (1968).

SCHULTZ, "Lipids and Their Oxidation," Avi Publishing Co., Inc., Westport, CT (1962).

WEISS, "Food Oils and Their Uses," Avi Publishing Co., Inc., Westport, CT (1970).

WILLIAMS, "Oils, Fats and Fatty Foods," 4th ed., American Elsevier Publishing Co., New York (1966).

29. Pesticide Residues

MULTIRESIDUE METHODS

GENERAL METHOD FOR ORGANOCHLORINE AND ORGANOPHOSPHORUS PESTICIDES (*1*)

29.001 ***Principle***

Thoroly mixed sample is extd with CH_3CN (high-H_2O foods) or aq. CH_3CN (low-H_2O or high sugar foods). Fat is extd from fatty foods and partitioned between pet ether and CH_3CN. Aliquot (nonfatty samples) or entire soln (fatty samples) of CH_3CN is dild with H_2O and residues are extd into pet ether. Residues are purified by chromatgy on Florisil column, eluting with mixt. of pet and Et ethers. Residues in concd eluates are measured by GLC and identified by combinations of gas, thin layer, or paper chromatgy.

Analyst competence in applying method for trace residues should be assured before analysis. Recoveries of added compds thru method should be ⩾80%.

Absence of interferences arising from laboratory and reagent contamination should also be assured by regular performance of reagent blanks. Solvs in particular, because of their concn during methods, can contribute significant interference if not sufficiently purified. Solvs of adequate purity are com. available from several manufacturers, but each batch must be tested under conditions of method in which it will be used.

Other reagents and app. (rubber, plastics, glass wool, etc.) are also potential source of interferences. *See* ref. (**1**) for recoveries obtained during collaborative and validation studies and Table **29:01** for commodities approved. *See* **29.008**, introductory par., and **29.008(c)** for GLC performance requirements:

Table 29:01 Compounds and Crops to Which General Method Applies

Compound	Official Final Action
Dieldrin Heptachlor epoxide	Group I nonfatty foods, dairy products, fish, vegetable oils, whole eggs
BHC p,p′-DDE p,p′-DDT p,p′-TDE(DDD)	Group I nonfatty foods, dairy products, fish, whole eggs
Lindane Methoxychlor Perthane	Group I nonfatty foods, dairy products, whole eggs
Aldrin Endrin Heptachlor Mirex	Group I nonfatty foods, whole eggs
o,p′-DDT	Group I nonfatty foods, dairy products
Diazinon Ethion Malathion Me parathion Parathion Ronnel	Group II nonfatty foods
	Official First Action
Polychlorinated biphenyls (PCB)	Poultry fat, fish, and dairy products

Group I nonfatty foods: apples*, apricots, barley*, beets, bell peppers, broccoli*, cabbage*, cantaloupes, cauliflower*, celery, collard greens, corn meal and silage, cucumbers*, eggplant, endive, grapes*, green beans, hay, kale*, mustard greens*, oats*, peaches, pears, peas, plums, popcorn, potatoes*, radishes, radish tops, spinach, squash*, strawberries, sugar beets, sweet potatoes, tomatoes*, turnips*, turnip greens*, wheat*

Group II nonfatty foods: Group I nonfatty foods marked with asterisk (*) plus carrots, green peppers, and lettuce

sensitivity, sepn capability, and linearity. Behavior of >200 pesticides and industrial chems in method is given in JAOAC **61**, 640(1978).

29.002 ***General Reagents***

Solvs must be purified and final distn conducted in all-glass app. (*Caution: See* **51.011, 51.039, 51.040, 51.043, 51.054, 51.061,** and **51.073.**) *See* **29.001**.

Solvent purity test.—Electron capture GLC requires absence of substances causing detector response as indicated by following test: Place 300 mL solv. in Kuderna-Danish concentrator fitted with 3-ball Snyder column and calibrated collection vessel, and evap. to 5 mL. Inject 5 μL conc. from 10 μL syringe into gas chromatograph, using conditions described in **29.008 (c)**. Conc. must not cause recorder deflection >1 mm from baseline for 2–60 min after injection.

(**a**) *Acetonitrile.—See solv. purity test.* Purify tech. CH_3CN as follows: To 4 L CH_3CN add 1 mL H_3PO_4, 30 g P_2O_5, and boiling chips, and distil in all-glass app. at 81–82°. Do not exceed 82°.

Some lots of reagent grade CH_3CN are impure and require distn. Generally vapors from such lots will turn moistened red litmus paper blue when held over mouth of storage container. Pronounced amine odor is detectable.

(**b**) *Acetonitrile saturated with petroleum ether.*— Sat. CH_3CN, (**a**), with redistd pet ether, (**m**).

(**c**) *Alcohol.*—USP, reagent grade, or MeOH, ACS.

(**d**) *Alcoholic alkali soln.*—2%. Dissolve 2 g NaOH or KOH in alcohol, and dil. to 100 mL.

(**e**) *Eluting solvent, 6%.*—Dil. 60 mL Et ether, (**h**), to 1 L with redistd pet ether, (**m**).

(**f**) *Eluting solvent, 15%.*—Prep. as in (**e**), using 150 mL Et ether.

(**g**) *Eluting solvent, 50%.*—Prep. as in (**e**), using 500 mL Et ether.

(**h**) *Ethyl ether.—See solv. purity test.* Redistd at 34–35°, and stored under N. Add 2% alcohol. Must be peroxide-free by test in *Definitions of Terms and Explanatory Notes,* item (3).

(**i**) *Florisil.*—60/100 PR grade, activated at 675°C (1250°F), available from Floridin Co. When 675°C activated Florisil is obtained in bulk, transfer immediately after opening to ca 500 mL (1 pt) glass jars, or bottles, with g-s or foil-lined, screw-top lids, and store in dark. Heat ⩾5 hr at 130° before use. Store at 130° in g-s bottles or in air-tight desiccator at room temp. and reheat at 130° after 2 days.

Prep. mixed pesticide std soln in hexane contg 1, 4, 1, 2, 1, 2, and 4 μg/mL, resp., of ronnel, ethion, heptachlor epoxide, parathion, dieldrin, endrin, and malathion.

Test each batch of activated Florisil by placing 1 mL mixed pesticide std on prepd column and eluting as in *Cleanup,* **29.015**. Conc. eluates from Florisil column to 10 mL. Inject aliquot (*see* **29.008**) of each eluate into gas chromatograph and det. quant. recovery of each compd as in **29.018**. Florisil that quant. elutes heptachlor epoxide, ronnel, and ethion in 6% eluate; dieldrin, endrin, and parathion in 15% eluate; and malathion in 50% eluate, is satisfactory.

Adsorptivity of lots of Florisil may be tested with lauric acid and size of column adjusted to compensate for variation in adsorptivity (JAOAC **51**, 29(1968)). Test adjusted column before use by performing elution test above.

(**j**) *Hexane.—See solv. purity test.* Reagent grade, redistd in all-glass app.

(**k**) *Magnesium oxide.*—Adsorptive magnesia (Fisher Scientific Co. No. S-120). Treat as follows: Slurry ca 500 g with H_2O, heat on steam bath ca 30 min, and filter with suction. Dry overnight at 105–130° and pulverize to pass No. 60 sieve. Store in closed jar.

(**l**) *Magnesia-Celite mixture.*—Mix treated MgO, (**k**), with Celite 545, 1+1 by wt. Pet ether ext of Celite should be free of electron-capturing substances.

(**m**) *Petroleum ether.—See solv. purity test.* Reagent grade, redistd in all-glass app. at 30–60°.

(**n**) *Sodium sulfate.*—Anhyd., granular.

29.003 ***Reagents for Thin Layer Chromatography***

(**a**) *Aluminum oxide.*—Neutral Al_2O_3 G (Type E, MC/B Manufacturing Chemists, Inc., No. 1090), or equiv., for TLC.

(**b**) *Developing solvents for organochlorine pesticides.—(1) n*-Heptane, com. grade. (*2*) *n*-Heptane contg 2% reagent grade acetone.

(**c**) *Chromogenic agent for organochlorine pesticides.*— Dissolve 0.100 g $AgNO_3$ in 1 mL H_2O, add 20 mL 2-phenoxyethanol (Practical, Eastman Kodak Co.), dil. to 200 mL with acetone, add very small drop 30% H_2O_2, and mix. Store in dark overnight and decant into spray bottle. Discard after 4 days.

(**d**) *Developing solvents for organophosphorus pesticides.— (1) Immobile.*—15 or 20% *N,N*-dimethylformamide (DMF) in ether. Dil. 75 or 100 mL DMF to 500 mL with ether and mix. (*2*) *Mobile.*—Methylcyclohexane.

(**e**) *Chromogenic agents for organophosphorus pesticides.— (1) Stock dye soln.*—Dissolve 1 g tetrabromophenolphthalein Et ester (Eastman No. 6810) in 100 mL acetone. (*2*) *Dye soln.*—Dil. 10 mL stock dye soln (*1*) to 50 mL with acetone. (*3*) *Silver nitrate soln.*—Dissolve 0.5 g $AgNO_3$ in 25 mL H_2O and dil. to 100 mL with acetone. (*4*) *Citric acid soln.*—Dissolve 5 g granular citric acid in 50 mL H_2O and dil. to 100 mL with acetone.

29.004 ★ ***Reagents for Paper Chromatography*** ★

(**a**) *Aqueous system.—(1) Immobile solvents.*— Mineral oil, USP heavy (corn, cottonseed, tung, or soya oil may also be used). Dissolve 25 mL in Et ether and dil. to 500 mL. (*2*) *Mobile solvents.*—Acetone, 2-methoxyethanol (Me Cellosolve), or MeOH, dil. 75 mL to 100 mL with H_2O; pyridine, dil. 40 mL to 100 mL with H_2O.

(**b**) *Nonaqueous system.—(1) Immobile solvents.*— Dil. 175 mL *N,N'*-dimethylformamide to 500 mL with Et ether; or dil. 50 mL 2-phenoxyethanol to 500 mL with ether. (*2*) *Mobile solvents.*—2,2,4-Trimethylpentane; mixed octanes.

(**c**) *Chromogenic agent.*—Place 1.7 g $AgNO_3$ in 200 mL vol. flask, dissolve in 5 mL H_2O, add 10 mL 2-phenoxyethanol, and dil. to vol. with reagent grade acetone (add 1 small drop 30% H_2O_2 soln to flask just before dilg to mark).

(**d**) *Pesticide std solns.*—1 mg/mL in EtOAc or hexane. (1μL = 1 μg.)

29.005 ***General Apparatus***

(**a**) *High-speed blender.*—Waring Blendor, or equiv.

(**b**) *Chromatographic tubes.*—With Teflon stopcocks and coarse fritted plate or glass wool plug; 22 mm id × 300 mm.

(**c**) *Chromatographic tubes without stopcocks.*—22 mm id × 300 or 400 mm.

(**d**) *Filter tubes.*—Approx. 22 mm id × 200 mm with short delivery tube and coarse fritted plate or glass wool plug.

(**e**) *Kuderna-Danish concentrators.*—500 and 1000 mL with Snyder distilling column and 5 or 10 mL plain, vol., and graduated receiving flasks (Kontes Glass Co. No. K-570000, K-621400, and K-570050, or equiv.).

(**f**) *Separators.*—1000 and 125 mL with Teflon stopcocks.

(**g**) *Micro-Snyder column.*—2-ball (Kontes Glass Co. No. K-569001, or equiv.).

(**h**) *Micro-Vigreux column.*—Kontes Glass Co. No. K-569251, or equiv.

29.006 ***Apparatus for Thin Layer Chromatography***

(**a**) *Desaga/Brinkmann standard model applicator, or equiv.*

(**b**) *Desaga/Brinkmann standard mounting board, or equiv.*

(**c**) *Desaga/Brinkmann drying rack, or equiv.*—Accommodates ten 8 × 8" plates.

(**d**) *Desaga/Brinkmann model 51 stainless steel desiccating cabinet, or equiv.*

(**e**) *Window glass.*—8 × 8", double strength window glass plates of uniform width and thickness; smooth off corners and edges with file or other tool.

(**f**) *Chromatographic tank and accessories.*—Available from Arthur H. Thomas Co. No. 2749-F05, or equiv., with metal instead of glass troughs.

(**g**) *Dipping tank and accessories.*—Stainless steel, 8½ × 8½ × ¼–3/16" inside width with metal supports and close-fitting U-shaped cover ca 9 × ½". Capacity ca 300 mL (Arthur H. Thomas Co. No. 2749–H50, or equiv.).

(**h**) *Spotting pipets.*—1 μL (Kontes Glass Co. No. K-422520).

(**i**) *Spray bottle.*—8 oz (Arthur H. Thomas Co. No. 2753–J10 or SGA Scientific, Inc., No. JC 2850, 250 mL).

(**j**) *Chromatography spray flask.*—250 mL (Microchemical Specialties Co., 1825 Eastshore Hwy, Berkeley, CA 94710, No. S-4530-D).

(**k**) *Tank liner.*—Cut 2 pieces, 12¼ × 8¾", from desk blotter, white or colored, and bend into L-shape to fit tank.

29.007 ★ ***Apparatus for Paper Chromatography*** ★

(**a**) *Chromatographic chamber.*—For ascending chromatgy with 8 × 8" sheets. Construct tanks, 9" long × 9" high × 3½" wide, from light stainless steel. From ¼" strips of the metal, form 2 supports and suspend flush with top from notches on sides at corners of tank. (Arthur H. Thomas Co. No. 2749-F10 has been found suitable.)

(**b**) *Pipets.*—Graduated 0.1 mL Mohr, and 1 μL spotting pipet long enough to reach bottom of conical centrf. tubes (Kontes Glass Co. No. K-422520).

(**c**) *Strong ultraviolet light source.*—Such as germicidal lamps (General Electric Co., Nela Park, Cleveland, OH 44112), either (*1*) two 30 watt, 36" tubes, No. G30T8, mounted in std 30 watt reflector fixture ca 20 cm above papers; or (*2*) two 15 watt, 18" tubes, No. G15T8, mounted in std 15 watt desk lamp fixture placed ca 10 cm above papers. Shield to protect eyes and skin at all times.

(**d**) *Chromatographic paper.*—Whatman No. 1, 8 × 8" sheets. With hard pencil, rule origin line 2.5 cm from bottom edge and make dot at 8–10 evenly spaced positions, with end dots 2.5 cm from sides of paper. With pencil, mark test number or other identification below each dot. Wash papers for aq. systems several times with *distd* H_2O and dry before use. (Papers for nonaq. systems need not be washed.) Any of following technics has been found satisfactory for washing papers:

(*1*) Hang paper clipped to glass rod in chromatgy tanks with lower edge in trough filled with distd H_2O; when H_2O rises to

★ Surplus method—*see* inside front cover.

top of paper, hang paper in hood and let dry. Repeat. Two papers may be clipped to each side of rod (4 papers per rod, 8 per tank).

(*2*) Wash by adaptation of continuous ascending paper chromatgy, using slit cover for box with 1 sheet per slit (JAOAC **40**, 1013(1957)). Let washing continue overnight; air dry papers without removing from cover.

(*3*) Place 10–12 papers in shallow pan, cover with distd H_2O, and let soak ca 15 min; then carefully pour off H_2O. Repeat 8–10 times. Dry papers, and weight pile with glass plate during storage.

(*4*) Place 10–25 papers in inclined shallow pan and let distd H_2O run slowly in one end and out other 2–3 hr; dry papers.

(*5*) Place papers in 8¼" sq stainless steel funnel with 8" sq perforated removable plate at bottom, let soak in distd H_2O 15–30 min, and drain off H_2O into suction flask; repeat several times, press papers between two 23 × 23 cm (9 × 9") glass or stainless steel plates, and dry overnight in forced-draft oven at 100–110°.

Paper, especially washed paper, must be dry. (All air-dried papers should be further dried 30 min at 100–110° before use.) If appreciable amt of moisture is in paper, it cannot absorb enough immobile solv. soln, and high R_f values result, as well as faint, indistinct chromatograms. Apparent air dryness is not enough; drying in forced-draft oven is necessary. Once dried, paper may be kept in ordinary dry storage without adverse result. This moisture effect is most critical with nonaq. systems.

29.008 *Apparatus for Gas Chromatography*

(*See also* JAOAC **47**, 326–342(1964); **49**, 8–21(1966).)

Gas chromatgc system when operated with column, (**b**), and approx. conditions described in *Gas Chromatography*, **29.018**, should be capable of producing ca ½ scale deflection for 1 ng heptachlor epoxide by electron capture detection and for 2 ng parathion by KCl-thermionic detection, and should resolve mixt. of heptachlor, aldrin, heptachlor epoxide, ethion, and carbophenothion into sep. peaks. Retention time for aldrin should be ca 4.5 min. Compds of interest must not be degraded by any part of GLC system.

(**a**) *Gas chromatograph*.—Instrument consisting of on-column injection system, all-glass column in oven controlled to ±0.1°, electron capture and thermionic detectors, each with independent power supply, electrometer, and appropriate mv recorder.

(**b**) *Column*.—Glass, 1.85 m (6') × 4 mm id packed with 10% DC-200 (w/w) on solid support: (*1*) 80–100 mesh Chromosorb W HP (Johns-Manville Products Corp., manufacturer, but available thru many GLC distributors); (*2*) 80–100 mesh Gas-Chrom Q (Applied Science Laboratories, Inc.); (*3*) 80–90 mesh Anakrom ABS (Analabs, Inc.). DC-200 may be replaced by OV-101 (available from many GLC distributors).

Weigh 2 g Dow Corning 200 silicone fluid (12,500 centistokes) or OV-101 into beaker. Dissolve in $CHCl_3$ and transfer to 300 mL Morton-type flask, using total of ca 100 mL $CHCl_3$. Add 18 g solid support, (*1*), (*2*) or (*3*), to flask. Swirl, and let stand ca 10 min. Place flask on rotary evaporator and remove solv. slowly with intermittent rotation, using 50° H_2O bath and slight vac. (Foaming may occur initially.) When solids appear damp, increase vac. Remove last traces of $CHCl_3$ without rotation or by air drying. Use only free-flowing material to fill column. Use care at all stages of column prepn to prevent fracturing solid support. Condition column at 250–260° with N flow of ca 100 mL/min ≥48 hr or until endrin exhibits single peak.

(**c**) *Electron capture detector (ECD)*.—Concentric design, for use with dc voltage supply and ^3H source (ca 150 mCi ^3H, U.S. Nuclear Regulatory Commission license is required.)

Det. detector operating characteristics as follows: Apply dc voltage to detector. After system becomes stable (overnight), det. current-voltage relationship at various voltages between 200 and 0 v. (Current measurements at voltages of 200, 150, 100, 75, 50, 40, 30, 25, 20, 15, 10, 8, 6, 4, 2, and 1 provide points for smooth curve.) Slightly lower, stable, standing current may be obtained after detector has been at operating temp. several hr. This is probably due to loss of some easily removed radioactive material. Det. and plot response-voltage relationship at 1×10^{-9} amp full scale sensitivity for 1 ng injections of heptachlor epoxide at same voltages used in obtaining current-voltage curve. Select as operating voltage that voltage at which heptachlor epoxide causes ca 40–50% full scale recorder deflection. Check linearity of system from 0.2 to 2.0 ng heptachlor epoxide.

Other electron capture detectors may be substituted for dc voltage concentric design ^3H detector, which is no longer marketed. Const current, variable frequency ^{63}Ni electron capture detectors are acceptable substitutes when operated at conditions to produce stable, reproducible, linear responses. Optimum conditions may produce more sensitive response than from ^3H detector. To maintain same method limit of quantitation of ^3H detector, inject proportionately smaller equiv. sample wt into ^{63}Ni detector system. The ^{63}Ni electron capture detector may provide different relative responses for pesticides than those obtained with ^3H electron capture detector. Use of Ar-CH_4 carrier gas, as recommended for most ^{63}Ni detectors, precludes use of KClTD dual detection system, (**d**), (**h**)–(**j**).

(**d**) *Potassium chloride thermionic detector (KClTD)*.—Flame ionization detector modified to incorporate coil with KCl coating prepd as in (*1*) or (*2*). Detector voltage is 300 v dc. Use in dual arrangement with electron capture detector.

All dual detector systems described are capable of comparable performance. In-series, (**h**), arrangement is preferred because of simplicity and ease of operation.

(*1*) *Coil with potassium chloride for in-series dual detector*.—*See* Fig. **29:01** (may be used with all detector arrangements). Wind Pt-Ir wire (B&S gage 26) on 7 mm diam. rod into 2 turn helix so that turns are touching. Approx. 5 mm below helix, continue to wind wire on 3 mm rod, or rod with same outside diam. as flame jet, making 3-turn spiral. Cut wire so that 7 mm helix is supported 4 mm above flame jet when 3 mm spiral is slipped over jet. Fill 30 mL tall-form Pt crucible ca ¼ full with KCl (ACS). Heat with Meker burner until all salt melts. Continue heating until bottom of crucible glows red, imparting pink glow to melt. Remove heat and begin dipping the 2-turn helix of coil into melt at 5 sec intervals as melt cools. (Make sure only 2-turn helix touches melt and do not raise coil above top of crucible.) When melt is at proper temp., salt clings to coil. Remove coil

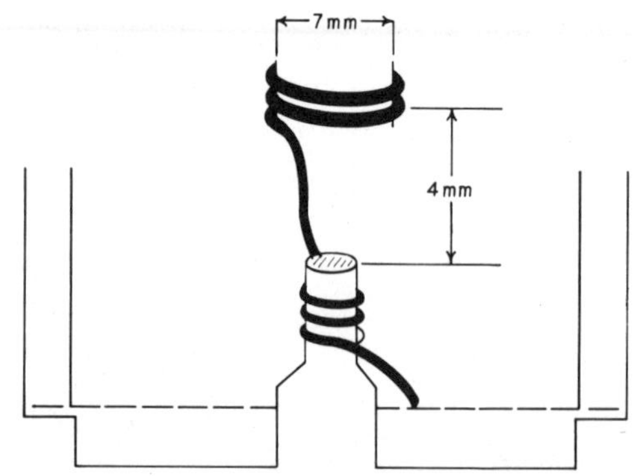

FIG. 29:01—KCl thermionic detector coil for in-series dual detection system

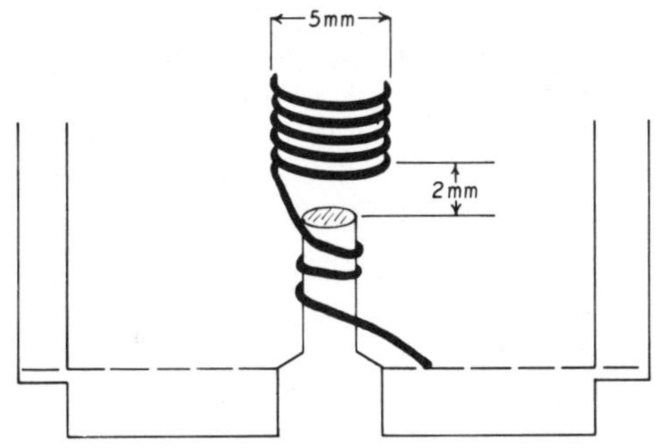

FIG. 29:02—KCl thermionic detector coil for parallel and in-series split dual detection systems

from melt. Place probe in center of coil while salt is molten. This causes crystn around probe tip. Remove center of coil. Remove any rough edges on coil coating by holding coil in burner flame 1 sec; id of properly coated coil is 5 mm. Position coil over flame jet.

(*2*) *Coil with potassium chloride for parallel and in-series split dual detectors.—See* Fig. **29:02**. Wind Pt-Ir wire (B&S gage 26) on 5 mm diam. rod into 5-turn helix so that turns are close together or touching. Continue to wind wire on 3 mm rod, or rod having same outside diam. as flame jet, making 3-turn spiral. Cut wire so that 5 mm helix is supported 2 mm above flame jet when 3 mm spiral is slipped over jet. Grasp formed wire by end opposite 5 mm helix with forceps. Dip 5 mm helix into satd KCl (recrystd twice from H_2O) soln, or apply KCl soln with dropper. Fuse in flame. (*Caution:* Use safety glasses; spattering occurs.) Repeat application of KCl soln 3–4 times until helix is coated with fused KCl. Coating should appear almost crystal clear. Position coil over flame jet.

(**e**) *Hydrogen.*—From generator or cylinder of compressed H gas (cylinder preferred). Equip cylinder with pressure drop of stainless steel capillary tubing (0.020" id) to restrict H flow to ca 30 mL/min at 20 lb delivery pressure. Place H source close to detector and use gas lines with min. dead vol. to reduce outgassing time in lines. (For fine precise control of H flow, insert Nupro Very Fine Metering Valve, "S" series (Nupro Co., 4800 E 345th Street, Willoughby, OH 44094; Part Number B-1S) between exit end of capillary tubing pressure drop and inlet of detector H line. *Caution:* Do not use Nupro valve as shut-off valve. Repeated tightening damages needle.) Use Swagelok fittings for all connections.

(**f**) *Air.*—Min. air requirement for thermionic detector is 300 mL/min. Cylinder of compressed air or aquarium air pump is recommended.

(**g**) *Capillary T-tube.*—(*See* Figs. **29:03** and **29:04**.) Prep. 1:1 stream splitter (*B*) for parallel and in-series split dual detection systems. Fit two 4.5 cm lengths of stainless steel capillary tubing, 0.010" id, 1/16" od, into 1 cm length of std wall, ⅛" stainless steel tubing. Fit 1" length of No. 16 hypodermic tubing at right angles in hole drilled into the piece of ⅛" tubing. Silver braze all connections. Prep. capillary T-tube (*E*) for introducing purge gas to parallel system. Fit two 2.5 cm lengths of No. 16 hypodermic tubing into 1 cm length of std wall, ⅛" stainless steel tubing. Fit 1 cm length of No. 16 hypodermic tubing at right angles in hole drilled into piece of ⅛" tubing. Silver braze as above.

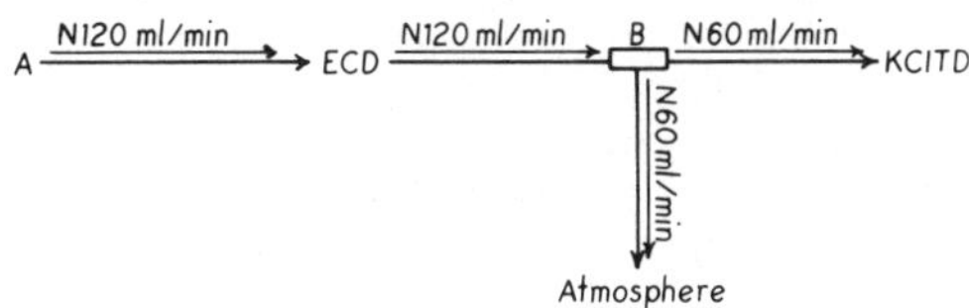

FIG. 29:03—In-series split dual detection system

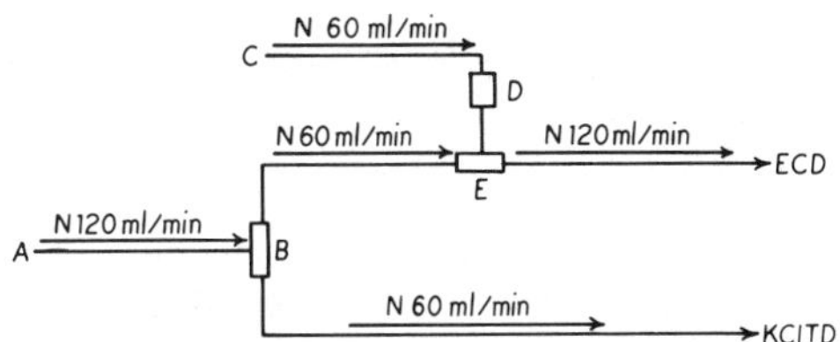

FIG. 29:04—Parallel dual detection system

(**h**) *Assembly of in-series dual detection system.*— Assemble as in Fig. **29:05**. Introduce column effluent (*A*) of 120 mL/min directly to ECD inlet. Connect ECD outlet directly to KCITD inlet, using No. 16 std wall Teflon tubing.

Note: For in-series, (**h**), and in-series split, (**i**), operation, thoroly check ECD for gas leaks, particularly at Teflon insulator.

(**i**) *Assembly of in-series split dual detection system.*—Assemble as in Fig. **29:03**. Introduce column effluent (*A*) of 120 mL/min directly to ECD inlet. Connect 1:1 stream splitter (*B*) between ECD outlet and KCITD inlet so that only 60 mL N/min enters KCITD and remaining 60 mL N/min exits to atm. Use No. 16 std wall Teflon tubing for all connections. *See Note* in (**h**).

(**j**) *Assembly of parallel dual detection system.*— Assemble as in Fig. **29:04**. Split column effluent (*A*) of 120 mL/min by passing thru 1:1 stream splitter (*B*) so that each detector receives 60 mL effluent/min. Increase flow to ECD by introducing 60 mL N/min from second N source (*C*) thru capillary T-tube (*E*). Preheat N from *C* by passing thru stainless steel capillary tube (*D*) (0.040" id) which extends 120 cm into column bath and returns to detector bath where addnl 35 cm of tubing is coiled into small helix. Connect capillary tubes and splitters to detectors with No. 16 std wall Teflon tubing. Measure flow at each end of splitter (*B*) to ensure exact 1:1 split.

(**k**) *Potassium chloride thermionic detector operation.*—Zero recorder with zero control before detector flame is ignited (no signal). Turn on H (ca 30 mL/min) and ignite flame. Adjust H with flame burning to give baseline current (BLC) of 0.2–0.8 × 10^{-8} amp. (Sensitivity to P compds is directly related to KCl temp., which depends on H concn in flame.) Select operational electrometer setting and adjust H concn to obtain 40–50% full scale recorder deflection for 2 ng parathion entering detector. When baseline has stabilized, measure BLC precisely, at electrometer setting of 1 × 10^{-8} amp full scale. Return to operational electrometer setting and zero recorder pen, using current balance control to "buck out" current generated by detector. Check linearity of system from 0.4 to 4.0 ng parathion. Monitor BLC frequently during operation. If drift occurs, readjust H concn to maintain same BLC. *For accurate quantitation, BLC must be identical during chromatgy of sample and std.*

Concentration Technics

29.009 ***Purified Extracts***

(Never evap. purified exts to dryness.)

(**a**) *To approximately 5 mL or more.*—Evap. on steam bath in Kuderna-Danish concentrator fitted with 3-ball Snyder column and vol. flask or graduated collection tube; 20-mesh boiling chip is necessary.

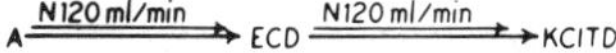

FIG. 29:05—In-series dual detection system

(b) *To less than 5 mL.*—Evap. to ca 5 mL as in (**a**). Remove collection tube from concentrator and fit tube with 2-ball micro-Snyder or micro-Vigreux column. Evap. to slightly less than desired vol., permit condensate to drain into tube, and remove column. Min. attainable vol. is 0.2–0.4 mL.

29.010 ***Extracts Containing Fats, Oils, or Plant Extractives***

(a) *Kuderna-Danish concentrator.*—Fitted with 3-ball Snyder column and vol. flask or graduated collection tube. Use on steam bath.

(b) *Flash evaporator.*—Keep flask in H_2O bath at room temp.

(c) *Beaker.*—Evap. in beaker in H_2O bath at 35–40° under stream of clean, dry air. Remove from heat and air stream as soon as last of solv. evaps. Let residual H_2O evap. spontaneously. Solvs may be evapd from fats on steam bath for short periods.

Preparation of Sample and Extraction

29.011 ***Nonfatty Foods***

(*Caution: See* **51.004, 51.011, 51.039, 51.040, 51.043**, and **51.073**.)

Pit *soft fruits*, if necessary. Chop or blend representative sample of *leafy or cole-type vegetables, pitted soft fruits, firm fruits, and roots*. Mix thoroly to obtain homogeneous sample before taking portions for analysis. Grind *dry or low moisture products*, e.g., hays, to pass No. 20 sieve and mix thoroly. Proceed as in (**a**), (**b**), (**c**), or (**d**).

(a) *High moisture (more than 75% H_2O) products containing less than 5% sugar.*—*(1) Products other than eggs.*—Weigh 100 g chopped or blended sample into high-speed blender jar, add 200 mL CH_3CN and ca 10 g Celite, and blend 2 min at high speed. Filter with suction thru 12 cm buchner fitted with sharkskin paper into 500 mL suction flask. Transfer filtrate to 250 mL graduate and record vol. (*F*). Transfer measured filtrate to 1 L separator, and proceed as in (**e**). *(2) Whole eggs.*—Discard shells and blend combined yolks and whites at *low* speed ≥5 min or until sample is homogeneous. Low-speed blending will minimize foaming or "whipping" of sample. Weigh ≤25 g thoroly mixed yolks and whites into high-speed blender jar, and proceed with addn of CH_3CN as in *(1)*.

(b) *High moisture (more than 75% H_2O) products containing 5–15% sugar.*—Add 200 mL CH_3CN and 50 mL H_2O to 100 g sample in blender and proceed as in (**a**). Transfer ≤250 mL filtered ext (record vol. (*F*)) to 1 L separator, and proceed as in (**e**).

(c) *High moisture (more than 75% H_2O) products containing 15–30% sugar, e.g., grapes.*—Heat mixt. of 200 mL CH_3CN and 50 mL H_2O to 75°, add to 100 g sample in blender, and immediately proceed as in (**a**). Before filtered ext cools, transfer ≤250 mL (record vol. (*F*)) to 1 L separator. Let cool to room temp. and proceed as in (**e**).

(d) *Dry or low-moisture products, e.g., hays.*—Add 350 mL 35% H_2O-CH_3CN (350 mL H_2O dild to 1 L with CH_3CN) to 20–50 g ground sample in blender (if larger sample is required, add enough addnl extn mixt. to wet sample and permit thoro blending). (*Caution: See* **51.004** and **51.043**.) Blend 5 min at high speed, and proceed as in (**a**), beginning "Filter with suction . . ." Transfer ≤250 mL filtered ext (record vol. (*F*)) to 1 L separator, and proceed as in (**e**).

(e) *Transfer of residues to petroleum ether.*—Carefully measure 100 mL pet ether and pour into separator contg filtrate. Shake vigorously 1–2 min and add 10 mL satd NaCl soln and 600 mL H_2O. Hold separator in horizontal position and mix vigorously 30–45 sec. Let sep., discard aq. layer, and gently wash solv. layer with two 100 mL portions H_2O. Discard washings, transfer solv. layer to 100 mL g-s cylinder, and record vol. (*P*). Add ca 15 g anhyd. Na_2SO_4 and shake vigorously. Do not let ext remain with Na_2SO_4 >1 hr or losses of organochlorine pesticides by adsorption may result. Transfer soln directly to Florisil column, **29.015**, or conc. to 5–10 mL in Kuderna-Danish concentrator for transfer.

(f) *Calculation for fruits and vegetables.*—Calc. g sample as $S \times (F/T) \times (P/100)$; where S = g sample taken; F = vol. filtrate; T = total vol. (mL H_2O in sample + mL CH_3CN added − correction in mL for vol. contraction); P = mL pet ether ext; and 100 = mL pet ether into which residues were partitioned. When 50 mL H_2O is added to CH_3CN for extn of high sugar products, total vol., T, is increased by 45, *i.e.*, T = 325 instead of 280 for samples contg 85% H_2O.

Example: 100 g sample contains 85 g H_2O; 200 mL CH_3CN is added; vol. contraction is 5 mL. Total vol., T, is 280 mL. If vol. filtrate is 235 mL, vol. pet ether ext is 85 mL, and residue is transferred to 100 mL pet ether, then $100 \times (235/280) \times (85/100) = 71$ g sample.

Consult refs on food composition for av. H_2O content. Water content of most fresh fruits and vegetables may be assumed to be 85%.

For 25 g whole eggs and 200 mL CH_3CN, use 215 as T.

(g) *Calculation for dry or low moisture products, e.g., hays.*—Calc. g sample as in fruits and vegetables, (**f**), except T = total vol. (mL H_2O in sample + mL 35% H_2O-CH_3CN added − correction in mL for vol. contraction). If H_2O content of sample is ≤10%, disregard and use vol. of extg mixt. as T.

29.012 ***Fat-Containing Foods***

(After isolation of fat, proceed with CH_3CN partitioning, **29.014**.)

(a) *Animal and vegetable fats and oils.*—If solid, warm until liq. and filter thru dry filter.

(b) *Butter.*—Warm at ca 50° until fat seps and decant fat thru dry filter.

(c) *Milk.*—(*Caution: See* **51.011, 51.039, 51.054**, and **51.073**.) To 100 mL fluid milk (dil. evapd milk 1+1 with H_2O) in 500 mL centrf. bottle, add 100 mL alcohol or MeOH and ca 1 g Na or K oxalate, and mix. Add 50 mL ether and shake vigorously 1 min; then add 50 mL pet ether and shake vigorously 1 min. Centrf. ca 5 min at ca 1500 rpm. Blow off solv. layer with wash bottle device, **16.220**, *Notes*, into 1 L separator contg 500–600 mL H_2O and 30 mL satd NaCl soln. Re-ext aq. residue twice, shaking vigorously with 50 mL portions ether-pet ether (1+1); centrf. and blow off solv. layer into separator after each extn. Mix combined exts and H_2O cautiously. Drain and discard H_2O. Rewash solv. layer twice with 100 mL portions H_2O, discarding H_2O each time. (If emulsions form, add ca 5 mL satd NaCl soln to solv. layer or include with H_2O wash.) Pass ether soln thru column of anhyd. Na_2SO_4, 50 × 25 mm od, and collect eluate in 400 mL beaker. Wash column with small portions pet ether and evap. solv. from combined exts at steam bath temp. under air current to obtain fat.

(d) *Cheese.*—Place 25–100 g (to provide 3 g fat) diced sample, ca 2 g Na or K oxalate, and 100 mL alcohol or MeOH in high-speed blender and blend 2–3 min. (If experience with product indicates emulsions will not be broken by centrfg, add 1 mL H_2O/2 g sample before blending.) Pour into 500 mL centrf. bottle, add 50 mL ether, and shake vigorously 1 min; then add 50 mL pet ether and shake vigorously 1 min (or divide between two 250 mL bottles and ext each by shaking vigorously 1 min with 25 mL each ether). Proceed as in (**c**), beginning "Centrf. ca 5 min at ca 1500 rpm."

(e) *Fish.*—(*Caution: See* **51.004**, **51.011**, **51.039**, and **51.073**.)

Weigh 25–50 g thoroly ground and mixed sample into high-speed blender. (If fat content is known or can be estd, adjust sample size so that max. of ca 3 g fat will be extd.) Add 100 g anhyd. Na_2SO_4 to combine with H_2O present and disintegrate sample. Alternately blend and mix with spatula until sample and Na_2SO_4 are well mixed. Scrape down sides of blender jar and break up caked material with spatula. Add 150 mL pet ether and blend at high speed 2 min. Decant supernate pet ether thru 12 cm buchner, fitted with 2 sharkskin papers, into 500 mL suction flask. Scrape down sides of blender jar and break up caked material with spatula. Re-ext residue in blender jar with two 100 mL portions pet ether and blend 2 min each time. (After blending 1 min, stop blender, scrape down sides of blender jar, and break up caked material with spatula; continue blending 1 min.) Scrape down sides of blender jar and break up caked material between extns. Decant supernate pet ether from repeat blendings thru buchner and combine with first ext. After last blending, transfer residue from blender jar to buchner, and rinse blender jar and material in buchner with three 25–50 mL portions pet ether. Immediately after last rinse, press residue in buchner with bottom of beaker to force out remaining pet ether. Pour combined exts thru 40 × 25 mm od column of anhyd. Na_2SO_4 and collect eluate in 500 or 1000 mL Kuderna-Danish concentrator with plain tube. Wash flask and column with small portions pet ether and evap. most of pet ether from combined exts and rinses in Kuderna-Danish concentrator. Transfer fat soln to tared beaker, using small amts pet ether. Evap. pet ether at steam bath temp. under current of dry air to obtain fat. When pet ether is completely removed, weigh and record wt of fat extd.

Record wt of fat taken for cleanup. ((Wt fat for cleanup/wt fat extd) × wt original sample = wt sample analyzed.) If it is known that ≤3 g fat will be extd from particular sample, do not isolate and weigh fat before CH_3CN partitioning. Detn is then on basis of wt of original sample.

Proceed as in general method, **29.001–29.028**, beginning with **29.014**.

29.013 ***Soil (2)***

(Official Final Action for aldrin, *p,p'*-DDE, *o,p'*-DDT, *p,p'*-DDT, dieldrin, endrin, heptachlor, heptachlor epoxide, lindane, and *p,p'*-TDE (DDD))

Weigh 10.0 g undried soil, sieved thru 2 mm sieve and mixed thoroly, into 250 mL erlenmeyer. Add 7 mL *0.2M NH_4Cl soln* (10.7 g/L) and let stand 15 min. Add 100 mL hexane-acetone (1+1), stopper tightly, and shake overnight (≥12 hr) on reciprocal or wrist-action shaker at 180 rpm.

Carefully pour supernate, avoiding aq.-clay phase, thru 2–3 cm column (22 mm id) of Florisil, **29.002(i)**, and collect eluate in 1 L separator. Rinse flask and soil with two 25 mL portions hexane-acetone and decant thru column. Rinse column with 10 mL hexane-acetone.

Add 200 mL H_2O to separator and shake gently ca 30 sec. Drain aq. phase into second separator and ext with 50 mL hexane. Combine hexane layers in first separator and wash with 100 mL H_2O. Drain and discard H_2O. Pour hexane thru 2 cm column (22 mm id) Na_2SO_4, conc. to 100 mL, and make preliminary injection of 5–10 μL into gas chromatograph. If peaks are present at retention times of DDE or dieldrin, conc. to 10 mL in Kuderna-Danish concentrator, **29.010(a)**, and sep. DDE or dieldrin as in **29.015**. (This cleanup may also be necessary with exts from high org. matter soils.) Proceed as in **29.018**, using ECD, (**b**). To calc. to dry basis, dry sep. sample of 10 g ca 16 hr at 105° to obtain % solids.

Cleanup Technics

29.014 ***Acetonitrile Partitioning***

(*Caution: See* **51.011**, **51.039**, and **51.073**. Different fats and oils may show varying tendencies to emulsion formation.)

Weigh ≤3 g fat into 125 mL separator, and add pet ether so that total vol. of fat and pet ether is 15 mL. Add 30 mL CH_3CN satd with pet ether, **29.002(b)**, shake vigorously 1 min, let layers sep., and drain CH_3CN into 1 L separator contg 650 mL H_2O, 40 mL satd NaCl soln, and 100 mL pet ether. Ext pet ether soln in 125 mL separator with 3 addnl 30 mL portions CH_3CN satd with pet ether, shaking vigorously 1 min each time. Combine all exts in the 1 L separator.

(If experience with particular sample (e.g., fish) indicates that cleanup may not be sufficient, perform partitioning as follows: Drain CH_3CN phase from first partitioning into second 125 mL separator contg 15 mL pet ether, shake vigorously 1 min, let layers sep., and drain CH_3CN into 1 L separator contg 650 mL H_2O, 40 mL satd NaCl soln, and 100 mL pet ether. Pass CH_3CN phase from each of 3 addnl partitionings thru same 15 mL pet ether in 125 mL separator. Shake vigorously each time and combine CH_3CN exts in the 1 L separator.)

Hold separator in horizontal position and mix thoroly 30–45 sec. Let layers sep. and drain aq. layer into second 1 L separator. Add 100 mL pet ether to second separator, shake vigorously 15 sec, and let layers sep. Discard aq. layer, combine pet ether with that in original separator, and wash with two 100 mL portions H_2O. Discard washings and draw off pet ether layer thru 50 × 25 mm od column of anhyd. Na_2SO_4 into 500 mL Kuderna-Danish concentrator. Rinse separator and then column with three ca 10 mL portions pet ether. Evap. combined ext and rinses to ca 10 mL in Kuderna-Danish concentrator for transfer to Florisil column.

29.015 ***Florisil Cleanup***

(*Caution: See* **51.011**, **51.039**, **51.040**, **51.054**, and **51.073**.)

Prep. 22 mm id Florisil column, **29.005(b)**, contg 10 cm, after settling (or amt detd by lauric acid test, **29.002(i)**), of activated Florisil topped with ca 1 cm anhyd. Na_2SO_4. Prewet column with 40–50 mL pet ether. Place Kuderna-Danish concentrator with vol. flask or graduated collection flask under column to receive eluate. Transfer pet ether ext or conc. to column, letting it pass thru at ≤5 mL/min. Rinse containers and Na_2SO_4, if present, with two ca 5 mL portions pet ether, pour rinsings onto column, rinse walls of tube with addnl small portions pet ether, and elute at ca 5 mL/min with 200 mL 6% eluting solv., **29.002(e)**. Change receivers and elute with 200 mL 15% eluting solv., **29.002(f)**, at ca 5 mL/min. Change receivers and elute with 200 mL 50% eluting solv., **29.002(g)**, at ca 5 mL/min.

Conc. each eluate to suitable definite vol. in Kuderna-Danish concentrator. When vol. <5 mL is needed, use 2-ball micro-Snyder or micro-Vigreux column.

First eluate (6%) contains *organochlorine pesticides* (aldrin, BHC, DDE, DDD (TDE), *o,p'*- and *p,p'*-DDT, heptachlor, heptachlor epoxide, lindane, methoxychlor, mirex, and Perthane), *industrial chems* (polychlorinated biphenyls (PCB)), and *organophosphorus pesticides* (ethion and ronnel) and is usually suitable for GLC directly. If further cleanup is necessary, repeat Florisil cleanup, using new column. Second eluate (15%) contains *organochlorine pesticides* (dieldrin and endrin) and *organophosphorus pesticides* (Diazinon, Me parathion, and parathion). If further cleanup is necessary, det. organophosphorus pesticides by GLC and TLC; then proceed with *Magnesia Cleanup*, **29.016**, and/or *Saponification*, **29.017**, which are applicable only to organochlorine pesticides in 15% eluate (organophosphorus pesticides are degraded). Third eluate (50%) contains *organophosphorus pesticide* malathion.

29.016 ***Magnesia Cleanup***

(Applicable only to organochlorine pesticides in 15% eluate when addnl cleanup is necessary)

Transfer ca 10 g MgO-Celite mixt., **29.002(l)**, to chromatgc tube without stopcock, **29.005(c)**, using vac. to pack. Prewash with ca 40 mL pet ether, discard prewash, and place Kuderna-Danish concentrator under column. Transfer 15% Florisil eluate, concd to ca 5 mL, to column, rinsing with small portions pet ether. Force pet ether into column with slight vac. or pressure. Then elute with 100 mL pet ether. Conc. eluate to suitable vol. Proceed with detn, or saponification, if required.

29.017 ***Saponification***

(Applicable only to organochlorine pesticides in 15% eluate if MgO-Celite eluate is not substantially free from oily materials.)

Transfer concd eluate to 125 mL g-s flask, rinsing with pet ether, and evap. just to dryness. Add 20 mL 2% alc. NaOH or KOH, **29.002(d)**, and reflux 30 min under air condenser. Transfer to 125 mL separator and rinse flask with three 10 mL portions pet ether, transferring each to separator. Add 20 mL H_2O and shake vigorously. Drain aq. layer into second separator contg 20 mL pet ether, shake vigorously, let sep., discard aq. layer, and add pet ether to first separator. Wash combined pet ether exts with three 20 mL portions aq. alcohol (1+1). (If initial aq. alcohol wash causes heavy emulsions, use H_2O only for addnl washes.) Discard aq. alcohol and dry pet ether layer thru 50 × 25 mm od column of anhyd. Na_2SO_4, rinsing with pet ether. Conc. solv., and rechromatograph on MgO-Celite column.

Detection Methods

29.018 ***Gas Chromatography—Tentative Identification and Quantitative Measurement***

(Applicable to organochlorine pesticides, organophosphorus pesticides, and polychlorinated biphenyls (PCB). Method is applicable to PCB residues when present alone in sample. If pesticidal or other compds are detected in chromatogram of the PCB residue, other chemical or physical operations must be applied to eliminate or minimize their interference before PCB quantitation.)

Inject suitable aliquot (3–8 μL) of concd eluate from Florisil or MgO-Celite column contg amt of compd within linear range into gas chromatograph, **29.008**, using 10 μL syringe. Tentatively identify residue peaks on basis of retention times. Measure area or ht of residue peak(s) and det. residue amt by comparison to peak area or ht obtained from known amt of appropriate ref. material(s). To ensure valid measurement of residue amt, size of peaks from residue and ref. std should be within ±25%. Chromatograph ref. material(s) immediately after sample.

Measure PCB residues by comparing total area or ht of residue peaks to total area or ht of peaks from appropriate Aroclor(s) (Analabs, Inc.) ref. materials. Measure total area or ht response from common baseline under all peaks. Use only those peaks from sample that can be attributed to chlorobiphenyls. These peaks must also be present in chromatogram of ref. material. Mixt. of Aroclors may be required to provide best match of GLC patterns of sample and ref.

Alternatively, det. PCB residues by individual peak area comparisons using Aroclor ref. material wt factors in Table **29:02**. Calc. each PCB peak against appropriate individual ref. peak with exactly same absolute retention. Sum individual peak values to obtain total ppm PCB. (This method is recommended for PCB residues with chromatgc patterns which are altered extensively from that of any Aroclor ref.)

(a) *Recommended operating conditions for 10% DC-200 or OV-101 column.*—Glass column, 1.8 m (6′) × 4 mm id. Temps (°): injector, 225; column 200; ^{3}H electron capture detector, 210 max.; carrier gas flow, 120 mL N/min.

(b) *Electron capture detection (ECD).*—(Use for detn of organochlorine pesticides in fruits, vegetables, and food contg fats and for detn of PCB in foods and paperboard.) Select for ^{3}H electron capture detector operating voltage that voltage (ca 50 v dc) at which 1 ng heptachlor epoxide produces 40–50% full scale recorder deflection at 1 or 3 × 10^{-9} amp full scale sensitivity.

Operate ^{63}Ni electron capture detector to produce stable, reproducible, linear response, and adjust amt of injected sample to accommodate differences in instrument sensitivity.

(c) *Potassium chloride thermionic and electron capture dual detection.*—(Use one of the 3 dual detection systems specified in **29.008(h)**, **(i)**, **(j)**, for detn of organophosphorus and organochlorine pesticides and PCB. In-series system, **(h)**, is preferred because of simplicity and ease of operation.) *(1) In-series dual detection.*—Operate ECD as in **(b)**. For KCITD, adjust H flow producing 0.2–0.8 × 10^{-8} amp baseline current and select electrometer setting at which 2 ng parathion produces 40– 50% full scale recorder deflection. *(2) In-series split dual detection.*—Same as *(3)*, *Parallel*, except ECD receives entire injection and KCITD receives ½ amt injected into column. *(3) Parallel dual detection.*— Same as *(1)*, *In-series dual*, except column effluent is split; therefore, inject twice as much sample to obtain desired limit of quantitation.

Table 29:02 Weight % factors for individual gas chromatographic peaks in Aroclor reference materials. Peaks are identified by their retention time relative to *p,p′*-DDE=100 at conditions consistent with 29.018(a) and (b).

	AROCHLOR				
R_{DDE}(100×)	1016 (77-029)[a]	1242 (71-696)[a]	1248 (71-697)[a]	1254 (71-698)[a]	1260 (71-699)[a]
11	0.2				
16	3.8	3.4	0.3		
21	8.1	10.3	1.1		
24	1.2	1.1	0.2		
28	16.8	15.8	6.0		
32	7.6	7.3	2.6		
37	18.5	17.0	8.7		
40	14.6	13.0	7.4		
47	11.6	9.9	15.7	7.1	
54	7.7	7.1	9.3	2.7	
58	6.4	4.4	8.3	1.2	
70	3.4	8.7	18.2	14.7	2.4
78		1.9	6.4		
84			4.6	18.6	3.6
98			3.4	8.3 }	2.8
104			3.3	14.1 }	
112			1.0		
117					4.4
125			2.3	15.6	11.0
146			1.2	9.0	13.3
160					5.5
174				7.4	10.0
203				1.3	10.9
232-244					11.2
280					12.5
332					4.2
360-372					5.4
448					0.8
528					2.0

[a] Food and Drug Administration Lot Nos. (Wt factors are valid only for these FDA Lot Nos.) Aroclor ref. materials are available from Food and Drug Administration, Division of Chemical Technology, HFF-420, 200 C St SW, Washington, DC 20204.

Thin Layer Chromatography—Confirmation of Identity

Method I

(Applicable to organochlorine and organophosphorus pesticides except where indicated)

29.019 ***Preparation of Adsorbent Layer***

Before coating, wash plates in hot soapy water and thoroly rinse with distilled H_2O. Press plates snugly into position on mounting board that has retaining ledge on one side and one end. Plastic board is mounted so that long side with raised ledge faces operator while short side with ledge is to right of operator. Before coating, wipe plates with few mL alcohol. Position applicator, trough open, with left edge 6 mm in from edge of first plate to be coated.

To coat 5 plates, weigh 30 g Al_2O_3 G, **29.003(a)**, into 250 mL ₮ erlenmeyer. Add 50 mL H_2O, stopper, and shake moderately 45 sec. Violent shaking produces bubbles, resulting in "pock-marked" layer.

Suspensions that contain adsorbents with binders set rapidly, and entire operation from prepn of slurry to final coating must be completed within 2 min.

After shaking, immediately pour slurry into applicator chamber. Rotate chamber by turning large lever handle thru 180°. After few sec, slurry begins to flow out of exit slit. Grasp applicator with both hands and pull it manually with steady motion across series of plates. Approx. 5 sec is required for actual coating operation. Immediately after application, tap edge of mounting board or shake entire board gently to smooth out slight ripples or imperfections in wet coating.

Let coated plates dry in position on mounting board 15 min. Then dry plates in forced-draft oven 30 min at 80°. Remove plates and cool.

Examine plates carefully in transmitted and reflected light for imperfections or irregularities in coating. Discard any plates showing extensive rippling or mottling of layer.

Prep. 5 more plates while first set is drying. Be sure applicator is thoroly cleaned and dried before reusing. The 10 coated and dried plates may be prewashed immediately.

29.020 ***Prewashing of Adsorbent Layer***

Scrape 1 cm of adsorbent off edge of plate with razor blade. Pour 15 mL 50% aq. acetone into metal trough inside chromatgc tank. Cut out 2 × 20 cm strip of Whatman No. 1 filter paper, wet with solv., and place over scraped off portion with 6 mm overlapping adsorbent layer. Place plate in chromatgc tank, seal tank with masking tape, and develop with 50% aq. acetone to within 4 cm from top of plate (75–90 min). Remove plate from tank, remove filter paper wick, invert plate, and dry in hood 5 min. Dry plate 45 min at 80°. Remove plate from oven, cool, and store in desiccator. Use prepd plates within 1 week after prepn.

29.021 ***Sample Spotting***

Make pencil mark 4 cm from bottom of plate at both sides. Imaginary line between the two points indicates sample spotting or origin "line." Draw line (which removes coating) completely across plate 14 cm from bottom edge; this line represents solv. front after development. On lower edge of adsorbent starting 2 cm in from left edge of plate, make 18 marks with pencil at 1 cm intervals. (Fewer marks with longer intervals may be used, if desired. Marks serve as horizontal guides to sample application. Identity of samples and stds may be etched directly into adsorbent layer above these marks above solv. front line.)

Imaginary spotting "line" is actually shadow line cast by strong light source from wooden ruler supported 2 cm above plate. Align ruler shadow on the two 4 cm marks on either edge of plate. Shadow line and 18 marks, resp., serve as vertical and horizontal guides for sample application.

For optimum semiquant. detn, spot aliquot of sample as follows:

(**a**) *Organochlorine pesticides*.—Adjust aliquot to give residue spot within range 0.005–0.1 μg. Spot stds and std mixts at 0.002, 0.005, 0.01, 0.02, 0.05, 0.1, and 0.2 μg. Sample spots >0.2 μg are difficult to det. quant. and <0.005 μg may be difficult to distinguish. Spot all 6% Florisil eluates on one plate and 15% Florisil eluates on another plate.

(**b**) *Organophosphorus pesticides*.—Adjust aliquots of sample and stds to give spot within range 0.1–0.5 μg. Spot 6, 15, and 50% Florisil eluates on same plate. Ronnel and ethion are not resolved; spot each std sep. Spot Diazinon, Me parathion, and malathion sep. or as mixt.

Vol. of sample ext spotted should be ≤10 μL, if possible, and spotting should be done repeatedly with 1, 2, or 3 μL Kontes spotting pipet. Spot std and sample solns with same pipet. For best results, keep size of spotted samples as small as possible.

29.022 ***Development***

(**a**) *Organochlorine pesticides*.—Place liners and metal trough in tank, **29.006(f)**. Presat. liner by pouring 75 mL developing solv., **29.003(b)**, into bottom of tank ≥30 min before developing plate. Presatn decreases development time and improves uniformity of R_f values.

For plates spotted with 6% Florisil eluates, pour 50 mL *n*-heptane into trough. Place lower edge of plate in metal trough with top of plate leaning against side of tank. Place glass cover plate on tank and seal with masking tape.

For plates spotted with 15% Florisil eluates, use acetone-*n*-heptane (2+98) as developing solv.

(**b**) *Organophosphorus pesticides*.—Prep. chromatgc tank, **29.006(f)**, after samples and stds have been spotted on plate. Place liners and metal trough in tank. Pour 50 mL methylcyclohexane, **29.003(d)**(*2*), into trough, and 75 mL into bottom of tank. Quickly fill dipping tank, **29.006(g)**, to within 4–5 cm from top with immobile solv., **29.003(d)**(*1*). Invert plate and dip with uncoated side touching back wall of tank to prevent front wall from scraping the adsorbent layer during dipping operation. Dip plate *just* to spotting line, remove, and immediately place in metal trough, with top portion of plate leaning against side of tank. Place glass cover plate on tank and seal with masking tape.

When solv. front in (**a**) or (**b**) *just* reaches pencil line 10 cm above spotting "line," remove plate and dry in hood 5 min.

29.023 ***Spraying***

(*Caution: See* **51.017**.)

(**a**) *Organochlorine pesticides*.—Support plate on one side and spray fairly heavily with chromogenic agent, **29.003(c)**, using lateral motions of spray bottle perpendicular to direction of solv. flow. Spray until plate appears translucent or soaked with reagent. Underspraying will result in poor sensitivity. After spraying, dry plate in hood 15 min; then immediately place under UV light source and proceed as in **29.024**.

(**b**) *Organophosphorus pesticides*.—Immediately spray plate moderately heavily and uniformly with dye soln, **29.003(e)**(*2*), using lateral motions of spray flask, **29.006(j)**, perpendicular to direction of solv. flow. Plate should be vivid blue after spraying. Using spray bottle, **29.006(i)**, overspray plate lightly and uniformly with $AgNO_3$ soln, **29.003(e)**(*3*) (at this point plate should be bluish purple and spots should be discernible).

After 2 min, overspray plate moderately and uniformly with citric acid soln, **29.003(e)**(*4*), using spray bottle, **29.006(i)**. After spraying, thiophosphate pesticides should immediately appear as vivid blue or purple spots against yellow background. Color of spots reaches max. intensity ca 5–10 min after citric acid spraying. After ca 10 min, background begins to change from yellow to greenish blue, masking spots. At this point, respraying plate with citric acid soln changes background back to yellow and makes spots stand out as well as or better than originally. Evaluate chromatogram ≤10 min after respraying. Blue spots fade completely and irreversibly after 30–40 min from time of original citric acid spraying.

29.024 ***Exposure***

(*Caution: See* **51.016.**)

Expose plate to UV light until spot for std of lowest concn appears; 5 ng of most organochlorine pesticides should be visible after 15–20 min exposure with equipment described under **29.007(c)**. Exposure times >30 min will not harm plates. For best results, place plates 8 cm from bottom edge of lamps.

Method II

(Applicable only to organochlorine pesticides)

29.025 ***Preparation of Adsorbent Layer***

Weigh 40 g Al_2O_3 G, **29.003(a)**, into 500 mL centrf. bottle. Add 80 mL 0.2% HNO_3, shake well, and centrf. at ca 1200 rpm 1–2 min. Decant supernate into 100 mL graduate, and record vol. (35–40 mL should be recovered). Add 80 mL H_2O, breaking up material on bottom of centrf. bottle with glass rod, if necessary. Shake well and centrf. as before. Decant and record vol. supernate recovered (60–70 mL). Add 2 addnl 80 mL portions H_2O, shake well, centrf., and decant.

Weigh the Al_2O_3 and H_2O that has been retained. (Wt should be ca 100 g.) Add 10 mL 1% $AgNO_3$ soln and enough H_2O to make total wt 120–130 g. Shake well, place in applicator, and prep. plates as in **29.019**. Let plates air dry in position on mounting board 15 min. Place in metal drying rack, in vertical position, 30 min at 100°.

29.026 ***Sample Spotting***

Spot as in **29.021**. Draw line across plate 4 cm from top (which removes coating). Next, scrape 6 mm of coating from each side of plate. (Irregularities in thickness of coating on these outer edges cause uneven flow of mobile solv.) Make pencil mark at each side of layer 2.5 cm from bottom of plate; imaginary line between these 2 points indicates sample spotting line. Spot samples and stds at 1 cm intervals.

29.027 ***Development and Exposure of Plates***

(*Caution: See* **51.016.**)

Develop plates as in **29.022**, except use only 25–30 mL mobile solv. in trough, since spotting line has been lowered to 2.5 cm. Use *n*-heptane to develop 6% Florisil eluates, and acetone-*n*-heptane (2+98) for 15% Florisil eluates.

Plates may be exposed to UV light after short drying period (ca 5 min) after removal from tank. Spots of aldrin, DDE, and isomers of DDT will appear within 5–10 min after exposure; lindane, endrin, dieldrin, and all others will require more time. Plates may be exposed 1.5–2 hr without appreciable darkening of background.

★ *Paper Chromatography* ★

29.028 ***Technic (3)***

(Once paper chromatgy is started, spot, develop, spray with chromogenic agent, and expose to UV light without delay; do not interrupt overnight. *Caution: See* **51.016.**)

Transfer 10 mL aliquot from column cleanup to 15 mL conical centrf. tube. (With most pesticides upper limit for good spots is ca 10 μg and optimum is ca 2 μg.) Evap. under gentle air stream at room temp. just to dryness (*Caution*). Wash down sides of tube with 0.5 mL ether, evap., and again wash down with 0.1–0.2 mL ether. Evap., take up residue (usually not visible) with 0.03–0.04 mL ether, and transfer to one of dots on origin line of chromatogram, **29.007(d)**, using 1 μL pipet repeatedly, until all residue is placed on 1 spot. Let spot dry after each application to restrict its size. Wash tube again with 0.03–0.04 mL ether and transfer to same spot.

Transfer std solns of known pesticides to other dots on same paper, adjacent to sample spots. (1 full μL pipet contains 1 μg compd. Use addnl pipetfuls to increase amt of pesticide on 1 spot.) For identification place several compds on sep. dots on same paper as unknown. For semiquant. estn place different amts of same compd, varying by 1–2 μg intervals, on sep. dots. (Experience and preceding analyses are guide to pesticide residues to be expected and thus to choice of pesticides to be used as stds for identification. If R_f values differ enough, several different pesticides may be placed on same dot; use 2–5 μg per pesticide.)

After samples and stds are spotted on paper, put 50 mL mobile solv. in trough; then fill dipping tank, **29.006 (g)**, with immobile solv. Hold paper by bottom, using spring clip, immerse it top down into soln of immobile solv. just to origin line, and immediately remove it. For aq. system, hang paper to dry 2–3 min; while paper is drying, clip glass rod, which supports paper in tank, to top of paper (opposite origin line). In nonaq. system, when paper is dipped in immobile solv., place in mobile solv. in chromatgc tanks as quickly as possible, allowing no time for drying. (As ether evaps, it may condense moisture on paper, which interferes with ability of pesticides to dissolve in immobile solv. *Excessive humidity and temp. tend to result in high R_f values and faint, indistinct chromatograms.*) Hang paper in tank so that origin end dips ca 1 cm into trough filled with mobile solv. Place glass plate on top of tank and seal with masking tape.

When mobile solv. has risen thru paper to within 2.5 cm of top (1.5–4 hr, depending on solv. system used), unseal tank, mark solv. front, and hang paper up until it appears dry. Uniformly spray dry paper with chromogenic agent (do not spray so heavily that it runs down paper). Dry paper until most of solv. is removed, and expose both sides to UV light until reduced Ag spots are developed. (Darkening of chromatogram background during storage may be largely prevented by washing finished chromatogram, after exposure to UV light, as follows: Suspend paper from glass rod with 3 or 4 clips, and thoroly play gentle stream of distd H_2O on both sides of sheet. Let suspended papers hang until dry (papers are very fragile when wet).)

It is advisable to evaluate chromatograms before washing them. Compare location, size, and intensity of spots from unknown with those from stds for identification and semiquant. estn of pesticides. Always chromatograph knowns and unknowns on same paper.

★ Surplus method—*see* inside front cover.

Endosulfan, Endosulfan Sulfate, Tetradifon, and Tetrasul (*4*)—Official Final Action

(Applicable to apples and cucumbers)

29.029 ***Principle***

Pesticides are extd with CH_3CN, partitioned with pet ether, eluted thru Florisil column with mixts of CH_2Cl_2, hexane, and CH_3CN, and detd by gas chromatgy. Method is variation of **29.001–29.018**, as it applies to nonfatty foods. Pesticides are eluted from Florisil column with different eluants to improve cleanup for these compds.

29.030 ***Apparatus***

See **29.005(a)–(h)** and **29.008(a)–(c)**.

29.031 ***Reagents***

(**a**) *Florisil.—See* **29.002(i)**.

(**b**) *Solvents.*—Hexane, CH_2Cl_2, and CH_3CN, all distd in glass and free from electron capturing substances (*see* **29.002**).

(**c**) *Eluant mixtures.—*(*1*) *Eluant I.*—20% CH_2Cl_2-hexane. Dil. 200 mL CH_2Cl_2 with hexane. Let mixt. reach room temp. and adjust vol. to 1 L with hexane. (*2*) *Eluant II.*—50% CH_2Cl_2-0.35% CH_3CN-49.65% hexane. Pipet 3.5 mL CH_3CN into 500 mL CH_2Cl_2, and dil. with hexane. Let mixt. reach room temp. and adjust to 1 L with hexane.

29.032 ***Preparation of Sample and Extraction***

See **29.011(a)**, **(b)**, **(e)–(g)**.

29.033 ***Column Chromatography***

(*Caution: See* **51.011**, **51.043**, and **51.061**.)

Add wt activated Florisil detd from lauric acid absorption value, **29.002(i)**, to 22 mm id chromatgc tube, **29.005(b)**. Gently tap chromatgc column to settle Florisil. Top column with ca 12 mm anhyd. granular Na_2SO_4. Wet column with 40–50 mL hexane. Use Kuderna-Danish concentrator with volumetric or graduated tube to collect eluate. Transfer pet ether or hexane soln of sample ext to column, and let it elute at ca 5 mL/min. Rinse container (and Na_2SO_4, if present) with 2 ca 5 mL portions hexane, transfer rinsings to column, and rinse walls of chromatgc tube with addnl small portions of hexane. Elute tetrasul at ca 5 mL/min with 200 mL eluant I. Change receivers and elute endosulfan I and II, endosulfan sulfate, and tetradifon at ca 5 mL/min with 200 mL eluant II. Conc. each eluate to suitable definite vol. in Kuderna-Danish concentrator. For evapn to <5 mL, use 2-ball micro Snyder or micro Vigreux column.

29.034 ***Determination***

See **29.008(a)–(c)**.

Using the 10% DC-200 column, retention times relative to aldrin are ca 1.6 for endosulfan I, 2.2 for endosulfan II, 2.5 for tetrasul, 2.7 for endosulfan sulfate, and 5.4 for tetradifon.

PCB in Paper and Paperboard (*5*)—Official First Action

29.035 ***Apparatus***

(**a**) *Gas chromatograph.*—Equipped with electron capture detector and 1.85 m (6′) × 4 mm id glass column contg either (*1*) 10% DC-200 or (*2*) 1+1 mixt. of 15% QF-1 + 10% DC-200 on 80–100 mesh Chromosorb W(HP). Operating conditions: temps (°)—column and detector 200, injector 225; flow rate, 120 mL N/min; concentric design electron capture detector operated at dc voltage to cause ½ full scale recorder deflection for 1 ng heptachlor epoxide when full scale deflection is 1×10^{-9} amp (*see* **29.008(c)**).

(**b**) *Chromatographic tubes.—See* **29.005(b)**.

(**c**) *Filter tube.—See* **29.005(d)**.

(**d**) *Kuderna-Danish concentrator.—See* **29.005(e)**, and **(g)**.

(**e**) *West condenser.*—400 mm jacket length with ₹ inner drip joint to fit 250 and 500 mL erlenmeyers.

29.036 ***Reagents***

(**a**) *Florisil.—See* **29.002(i)**.

(**b**) *Alcoholic potassium hydroxide soln.*—2% KOH in alcohol or redistd MeOH.

(**c**) *Petroleum ether.—See* **29.002(m)**.

(**d**) *Polychlorinated biphenyls.*—Com. mixts (Aroclors) for ref. in GLC detn (Analabs, Inc.).

29.037 ***Extraction***

(*Caution: See* **51.039**, and **51.073**.)

Cut paper sample representative of lot into pieces ca 6 × 6 mm and mix thoroly.

Weigh 10 g sample into 250 mL erlenmeyer. Do not pack tightly. (*See* note below if vol. of 10 g sample is >50 mL.) Add 60 mL 2% alc. KOH, and fit flask with West condenser cooled with circulating cold tap H_2O. Reflux gently on steam bath 30 min. Rinse inside of condenser with small amt of alcohol. Transfer soln thru glass wool plug in small funnel, to 250 mL separator, avoiding transfer of any paper material. Rinse paper and flask with three 40 mL portions pet ether, combining rinses in separator. Add 60 mL H_2O to separator and shake vigorously 30 sec. Drain lower aq. layer into second 250 mL separator. Add 60 mL pet ether to second separator and shake vigorously 30 sec. Discard aq. layer and combine pet ether layers in first separator. Rinse second separator with several small portions pet ether, collecting rinses in first separator. Wash pet ether with three 40 mL portions H_2O, discarding each wash. Dry pet ether thru 50 mm column, (**c**), of anhyd. Na_2SO_4, collecting eluate in Kuderna-Danish concentrator. Rinse separator and then column with 3 ca 20 mL portions pet ether, collecting rinses. Conc. combined pet ether ext and rinses on steam bath to ca 5 mL. Ext is ready for cleanup on Florisil column, **29.038**. If experience with particular sample types indicates that Florisil column cleanup is not required, proceed to GLC detn, **29.018**.

Note: Adequate extn of low density paper such as newspaper or tissue paper will require adjustment of either amt of sample to <10 g or vol. of reflux soln to >60 mL. Preferably, reduce sample to wt that is completely covered and wetted by 60 mL KOH soln. Increase in vol. of reflux soln >60 mL must be accompanied by proportional increases in vols of pet ether rinses of sample, H_2O diluent added to alc. reagent in separator, and size of erlenmeyers and separators.

29.038 ***Florisil Cleanup***

Proceed as in **29.015**, pars 1 and 2, except prep. 10 g column, pre-wet column with 20 mL pet ether, and elute at ca 5 mL/min with 150 mL pet ether. Concd eluate is suitable for analysis by GLC with electron capture detection, **29.018**.

Note: Waxes, if present in ext, can be removed before Florisil chromatgy by partitioning between pet ether and CH_3CN, **29.014**.

MULTIPLE RESIDUE METHODS FOR ORGANOPHOSPHORUS PESTICIDES

Carbon Column Cleanup Method (*6*)—Official Final Action

(CH_3CN extn and charcoal cleanup column using KCl thermionic or flame photometric detector for residues of parathion, paraoxon (diethyl *p*-nitrophenyl phosphate), carbophenothion and its O analog, and EPN (*O*-ethyl *O*-(*p*-nitrophenyl) phenylphosphonothioate) on apples and green beans)

29.039 ***Reagents***

(**a**) *Solvents.*—Redistd from glass (*see* **29.001**): EtOAc, CH_2Cl_2, benzene, hexane, CH_3CN, and isopropanol.

(**b**) *Acid-treated charcoal.*—Slurry 200 g Norit SG Extra (American Norit Co., Inc., 6301 Glidden Way, Jacksonville, FL 32208) or 100 g Nuchar C-190N (no longer marketed) with 500 mL HCl, cover with watch glass, and stir mag. while boiling 1 hr. Add 500 mL H_2O, stir, and boil addnl 30 min. Collect charcoal in buchner and wash with H_2O until washings are neut. to universal indicator paper. Dry at 130° in forced-draft oven.

(**c**) *Magnesium oxide.*—*See* **29.002**(**k**).

(**d**) *Adsorbent mixture.*—Mix 1 part acid-treated charcoal, 2 parts hydrated MgO, and 4 parts Celite 545, acid washed. Keep sealed.

(**e**) *Pesticide std solns.*—Prep. solns contg 1 μg/mL EtOAc of each of following: parathion, paraoxon, carbophenothion, carbophenothion O analog, and EPN.

(**f**) *Eluting soln.*—CH_3CN-benzene (1+1).

Purity test.—Reagents must be free of substances causing KCl thermionic detector response, as indicated by following test: Carry reagents thru entire method, and inject 5 μL from final conc. into gas chromatograph, using conditions described in **29.049**. Conc. must not cause recorder deflection >1 mm from baseline for 2–60 min after injection.

29.040 ***Apparatus***

See also **29.005** and **29.045**(**a**).

(**a**) *Vacuum adapter.*—Kontes Glass Co., No. K-954002, or equiv.

(**b**) *Gas chromatograph with potassium chloride thermionic detector.*—*See* **29.045**(**i**) and (**k**).

(**c**) *Column.*—*See* **29.045**(**j**).

(**d**) *Potassium chloride thermionic detector* (KCITD).—*See* **29.008**(**d**)(*1*) or (*2*), (**e**), (**f**), and (**k**). Also check linearity of GLC system to paraoxon and carbophenothion O analog.

(**e**) *Flame photometric detector* (*FPD*).—With P selective optical filter for 526 nm wavelength (Tracor, Inc., 6500 Tracor Ln, Austin, TX 78721). Equiv. to KCITD for detn of organophosphorus pesticides in fruits and vegetables. (*Note:* Older commercial models of FPD may give rise to adsorption and/or degradation of O analogs of organophosphorus pesticides within detector's gas mixing chamber. Design changes of detectors manufactured after mid-1973 have generally corrected this problem. Flameout in FPD, on injection of sample, can be avoided by letting H enter detector (lower part) so that H and GLC column effluent mix before burner area. Air-O enters detector thru upper part. This arrangement reverses that recommended by manufacturer. Specifications for physical modification of FPD to correct above problems are available from Division of Chemistry and Physics, Food and Drug Administration, Washington, DC 20204.) Use highly stabilized 0–750 v dc variable power supply capable of 10 ma output (Model 240 A; Keithley Instruments, Inc., 28775 Aurora Rd, Cleveland, OH 44139, or equiv.), 6.3 v ac ignitor power supply, electrometer with bucking capability of 1 × 10^{-6} amp (Tracor, Inc., or equiv.), and variable transformer capable of delivering 150 watts to control temp. of flame housing. Strip chart recorder should be compatible with electrometer.

(**f**) *Hydrogen.*—From cylinder of compressed H gas. Equip cylinder with regulator, delivery line, and variable flow controller capable of 200 mL/min delivery. Metering shut-off valve is required sep. from controller.

(**g**) *Air.*—Cylinder of compressed air equipped as in (**f**) to deliver up to 100 mL/min. Sep. shut-off valve is not needed.

(**h**) *Oxygen.*—Cylinder of compressed O gas equipped as in (**f**) to deliver up to 50 mL/min. Combine with air using std Swagelok tee before detector inlet.

(**i**) *Flame photometric detector operation.*—Adjust temp. of burner housing to ca 170–180° before igniting flame. Temp. will rise 20–30° after ignition. Do not allow detector to exceed 220°. Adjust gas flows at controllers to ca 150–300 mL/min H, 50–100 mL/min air, and 5–20 mL/min O. Adjust column effluent flow, **29.018**(**a**), to 120 mL N/min. Turn off H flow with metering shut-off valve (**f**). (*Caution:* Before attempting ignition, make certain H has been purged from detector with other gases. One min interval between ignition attempts is adequate.) Apply ca 750 v to photomultiplier tube from power supply. Zero recorder with electrometer set at appropriate sensitivity (ca 1 × 10^{-8} to 1 × 10^{-9} amp full scale). Push ignitor button and then slowly open H metering shut-off valve. Recorder pen will not return to zero baseline if flame ignites. If ignition is not effected, shut off H valve, increase O flow, and repeat ignition procedure. Establish proper baseline with buckout control after flame is lit. Operate at sensitivity that produces ½ full scale recorder deflection for 2 ng parathion. Reduce photomultiplier voltage to reduce sensitivity. Alternatively, use electrometer sensitivity and attenuator controls to achieve proper response. Check linearity of GLC system to paraoxon and carbophenothion O analog.

29.041 ***Preparation of Sample***

Blend and filter sample as in **29.011**(**a**), or (**b**). Transfer aliquot of CH_3CN ext (30–35 mL) equiv. to ca 10 g sample from suction flask to 125 mL separator, add equal vol. CH_2Cl_2, shake vigorously 30 sec, and set aside 10–15 min to sep. Calc. g sample in aliquot as g sample × [ml aliquot/(mL H_2O in sample + mL extg solv. added − correction in mL for vol. contraction)].

29.042 ***Charcoal Cleanup***

Fit 1-hole No. 5 rubber stopper onto tip of chromatgc tube, **29.005**(**b**), add side-arm vac. adapter and ₮ 24/40 receiving flask, open stopcock, and connect app. to open vac. line. Place 1 g Celite 545 in tube, tamp, add 6 g absorbent mixt., and tamp again. Add 2 cm glass wool plug on top of adsorbent. Prewash column with 100 mL eluting soln. Close stopcock when eluting soln is ca 2 cm above glass wool and maintain this head to ensure clean column. Disconnect vac., replace flask with 500 mL Kuderna-Danish flask equipped with 10 mL tube, **29.005**(**e**) (check calibration at 1 mL), and reconnect to open vac. line.

Drain lower CH_2Cl_2 layer in separator onto column, retaining H_2O layer (upper phase) in separator. Open column stopcock to vac. and adjust flow to ca 5 mL/min. Re-ext H_2O layer cautiously (do not shake vigorously) with two 10 mL portions CH_2Cl_2 and add exts to column. Discard H_2O phase. Elute column with 120 mL eluting soln (column may be taken to dryness). Disconnect app. and rinse column tip and vac. adapter with several mL EtOAc. Collect all rinses in same Kuderna-Danish concentrator with tube attached. Add 1 or 2 small boiling chips, attach Snyder column, and conc. cautiously over steam bath to ca 1 mL. (*Caution:* Begin heating very gently due to differences in densities and bps of individual solvs.) When cool, disconnect evaporative app. from Mills tube. Substitute column, **29.005**(**h**),

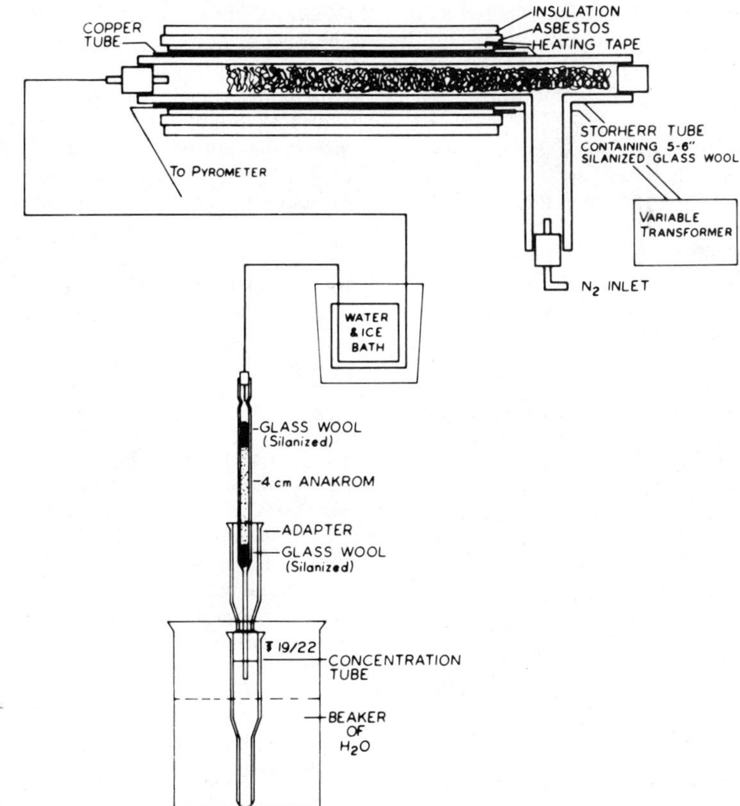

FIG. 29:06—Sweep co-distillation apparatus

on Mills tube, add boiling chips again, and conc. solv. to <1 mL. While app. is still immersed in steam bath, add 3–4 mL isopropanol (to remove CH_3CN azeotropically) and distil under gentle reflux. Repeat isopropanol addn and conc. to ca 0.5 mL. Remove from heat, cool, remove column, and adjust vol. to 1.0 mL with EtOAc.

29.043 ***Gas-Liquid Chromatography***

Proceed as in **29.049**, using recommended operating conditions *I* specified for column, **29.045(j)**(*1*). (*See* **29.040(e)–(i)** if using flame photometric detector.

Sweep Codistillation Method (*7*)—Official Final Action

(Sweep codistillation cleanup for parent organophosphorus residues of carbophenothion, *O,O*-diethyl-*O*-(2-isopropyl-6-methyl-4-pyrimidinyl) phosphorothioate (Diazinon®), ethion, malathion, Me parathion, and parathion in kale, endive, carrots, lettuce, apples, potatoes, and strawberries (fresh or non-sugared frozen); this cleanup is not adequate for electron capture gas chromatgc detector. Use only with KCl thermionic detector.)

29.044 ***Reagents***

(**a**) *Ethyl acetate*.—Redistd from glass. Check suitability of reagent by concg 100 mL to 2 mL. Inject 5 μL into GLC (KCl thermionic detector) with operating conditions specified in **29.045(i)**. Chromatogram should show no peaks to 20 min with chart speed of 1"/2 min.

(**b**) *Pesticide std soln*.—Prep. EtOAc soln contg 1 μg/mL of each of following: carbophenothion, Diazinon, ethion, malathion, Me parathion, and parathion.

29.045 ***Materials and Apparatus***

(**a**) *Glass wool*.—Silane-treated (available from Applied Science Laboratories, Inc.).

(**b**) *Anakrom ABS*.—80–90 mesh. Remove fines by stirring with EtOAc, decanting several times, and drying.

(**c**) *Teflon tubing*.—AWG No. 16, std, natural.

(**d**) *Disposable glass capillary pipets*.—145 mm long, 6 mm id, with capillary stem (Arthur H. Thomas Co. No. 7760-B10, or equiv.).

(**e**) *Syringes*.—1 mL Tuberculin Luer-Lok and 2 mL Luer-Lok with Luer-Lok 2" No. 25G needles.

(**f**) *High-speed blender*.—400 mL capacity. Omnimixer (available from DuPont Instruments/Sorvall, Peck's Ln, Newtown, CT 06470), or equiv.

(**g**) *Sweep co-distillation apparatus*.—*See* Fig. **29:06**. Following tubes are required: (*1*) *Storherr tube*. —24.5 cm long, 6 mm id (Kontes Glass Co., No. K-898600, or equiv.). (*2*) *Concentrating tube*.—10 mL calibrated to 0.5 mL. (*3*) *Adapter for extension of concentration tube*.—7 cm long, $ 19/22 (Kontes No. K-570100 (K-500750 part 355), or equiv.). Complete app. available from Kontes Glass Co. as No. K-500500.

(**h**) *Kuderna-Danish concentrators*.—500 mL with Snyder distilling column and 5 mL vol. and 10 mL graduated (Mills tube) receiving flasks, $ 19/22 (Kontes Glass Co., No. K-570000, K-621400, and K-570050, or equiv.).

(**i**) *Gas chromatograph with potassium chloride thermionic detector*.—*See* **29.008(a)**. Only thermionic detector, **29.008(d)**, is required.

Following conditions are important in operation of GLC and KCl thermionic detector:

(*1*) Every day before starting work change silane-treated glass wool plug insert in injection port of GLC column. Remove and replace only that portion affected by syringe.

(*2*) Every week before starting work reheat KCl spiral over gas burner and reinsert into detector. Detector must then equilibrate ca 2 hr before use.

(**j**) *Column*.—10% DC 200 or OV-101 on 80–100 mesh Chromosorb W HP in glass column 1.85 m (6′) × 4 mm id; *see* **29.008(b)**. Adjust column temp to give retention time for parathion of ca 5 min.

(*1*) *Recommended operating conditions: I*.—Temps (°): injection 225, column 200, detector 210; N flow 120 mL/min. Split column effluent with 1:1 stream splitter so that only 60 mL N/min enters KCITD. (*2*) *Recommended operating conditions II*.—Temps (°): column 220, injector and detector 240; N flow 60 mL/min.

(**k**) *Potassium chloride thermionic detector (KCITD)*.—*See* **29.008(d)**(*1*) or (*2*), (**e**), (**f**), and (**k**).

29.046 ***Preparation of Apparatus***

App. is constructed in 3 parts: removable Storherr tube, permanent heating coil, and distillate collector (*see* Fig. **29:06**). Com. model is available from Kontes Glass Co.

(**a**) *Preparation of removable Storherr tube*.—Pack Storherr tube with silane-treated glass wool. Use silane-treated glass wool as received. Do not pack glass wool too tightly; otherwise removal for cleaning is difficult. Only 13–15 cm portion from injection end requires packing. Insert injection septum and two 1-hole septums. Tube is now ready for use. Use clean tube for each sample. Clean tubes thoroly with soap and H_2O after use, rinse with acetone, and dry. Soak tubes difficult to clean in chromic acid cleaning soln before cleaning with soap and H_2O.

(**b**) *Preparation of permanent heating coil*.—Attach bimetallic wires of calibrated pyrometer directly to outside middle area of Cu tube (length 20 cm (8″) × 11 mm (7/16″) id). (Thermometer with stem covered with Al foil may also be used for temp. measurement.) Wrap heating tape (60 × 1.3 cm) uniformly around outside of Cu tubing and over bimetallic wires or thermometer, and secure ends. Cover heating tape with asbestos tape and secure with glass tape or glass thread. Cover asbestos with several layers of Al foil and secure with tape.

Place heating assembly on ring stand, using asbestos-covered 3-prong clamp. Orient and use heating coil in near horizontal position. Attach heating tape leads to variable transformer. Adjust transformer so pyrometer reads 180–185°. Use this setting or temp. for all crop cleanup.

Add N flow, 600 mL/min, to sidearm of Storherr tube. (For N pressure gage to give meaningful readings, add stainless steel capillary tube to reduce gas flow. Connect capillary tube directly to 1-hole septum in sidearm of tube with short length Teflon tubing.) Measure N flow with gas flow gage, and calibrate pressure regulator gage by this means.

(**c**) *Sample distillate collector*.—Construct in 3 parts: cooling coil, scrubber tube, and concn tube with extended adapter.

(*1*) *Cooling coil*.—Cut 120 cm length of Teflon tubing. Form this tubing into three 7 cm diam. loops having 2 arms of ca 20 cm lengths. Attach Teflon cooling coil and 1-hole septum directly to Storherr tube. Place coils in 250 mL beaker contg ice and H_2O. Place 250 mL beaker inside 400 mL beaker for insulation.

(*2*) *Scrubber tube*.—Insert silane-treated glass wool plug in constricted end of disposable pipet. On outside of pipet place marks 4 and 6 cm above top of glass wool plug. Add Anakrom ABS to 6 cm mark and pack Anakrom to 4 cm mark by compressing with 3 mm rod. Place silane-treated glass wool plug on top of packed Anakrom and 1-hole septum in pipet top. Connect exit arm of Teflon cooling coil directly into 1-hole septum in scrubber tube and extending ca 2 cm below septum. Secure scrubber tube on sep. ring stand with 3-prong clamp. Scrubber tube must be lower than cooling bath, especially in rinsing step.

(*3*) *Concentration tubes*.—Use 10 mL calibrated tubes, **29.045(h)**. Adapter, (**g**)(*3*), is needed for insertion into concn tube to prevent splash during sweep and rinsing steps. Place tip of scrubber thru adapter and into concn tube. If possible, place scrubber tip against wall of concn tube. Hold tube in place with clamp.

Adjust heat to 180–185° and N flow to 600 mL/min (measure before entering Storherr tube). Flush several 0.5 mL EtOAc injections thru entire system, using 2 mL syringe (used for all rinsings). Replace concn tube with clean tube and insert adapter; assembly is ready for use.

29.047 ***Extraction***

Ext all crops with EtOAc in *exact* order as follows: To high-speed blender, add 25 g chopped sample, 125 mL EtOAc from pipet, and 25 g anhyd. granular Na_2SO_4. Blend 5 min at slow speed; then 5 min at high speed with mixer cup immersed in ice-H_2O bath. Decant liq. thru 2.5 cm silane-treated glass wool plug contained in short glass chromatgc tube. (Do not add solids to glass wool plug.) Collect EtOAc ext (ca 100 mL) in 125 mL flask or bottle. Remove 50 mL aliquot (equiv. to 10 g original sample) and place in Kuderna-Danish concentrator with Snyder column, calibrated Mills tube, or 5 mL vol. receiving flask, and conc. to ca 5 mL. Adjust vol. to exactly 5.0 mL, using air jet or adding EtOAc. Use 1 mL aliquots (2 g sample) for sweep co-distn cleanup.

Store all stds and crop solns at ≤0° when not in use. Warm to room temp. ca 1 hr before use.

29.048 ***Sweep Co-Distillation Cleanup***

Assemble app. as in Fig. **29:06**, except position Storherr tube and heating unit so exit end of Storherr tube is ca 10° below horizontal to avoid backup of sample into N inlet arm. If sample backs up, *discard detn*. Check temp. (180–185°), N flow (600 mL/min), and receiver tube. Inject 1 mL (2 g) sample, using 1 mL Luer-Lok tuberculin syringe. Immediately follow sample with injection of 0.5 mL EtOAc sweeping solv. and repeat 0.5 mL EtOAc injection every 3 min for 21 min. After last injection wait 1 min until solv. has cleared cooling coil and scrubber tube; then disconnect cooling coil arm with septum from Storherr tube. Disconnect septum with attached cooling coil arm from scrubber tube and rinse 2 cm Teflon projection, collecting rinse in scrubber tube (still in position in concn tube). With septums in place on disconnected cooling coil arms, *reverse* coil arms and place that end formerly in Storherr tube into scrubber tube. Make certain that Teflon tubing in this arm extends 2 cm into scrubber tube below inserted septum (similar to position when cleaning up sample). Slowly inject 1 mL EtOAc rinse from 2 mL syringe directly into open end of cooling coil arm formerly in scrubber tube. Gently force rinse, using N flow from disconnected Storherr tube, thru cooling coil into scrubber tube and into concn tube. Repeat 1 mL EtOAc rinse 1–2 addnl times. Rinse scrubber tip end and inside of adapter, remove scrubber, disconnect adapter, and rinse ₸ joint. Collect all rinses in concn tube. Rinse down sides of concn tube and conc. to 1 mL, using N or air jet. Prevent H_2O condensation inside tubes by placing tube in room temp. H_2O bath during this step. If cleaned up soln is too concd for GLC detn (>2 μg/mL), dil. soln to 5 or 10 mL with EtOAc. If calibrations of Mills tube are incorrect (most usually are except for 1 mL mark), quant. transfer the concd soln to 5 or 10 mL vol. flask, using disposable pipet with attached rubber bulb. Rinse inside of tube with EtOAc and transfer rinse in same pipet. Repeat this rinse of tube and pipet several times; then rinse inside of pipet into flask, using EtOAc. Dil. to vol. Further diln with EtOAc or concn may be necessary to bring concn within measurement range.

Anakrom scrubber tube is used repeatedly without change. Final EtOAc rinses after each run keep it clean. However, if Anakrom becomes discolored, prep. new tube.

29.049 ***Determination by Gas-Liquid Chromatography***

Operate chromatograph under conditions specified for column, **29.045(j)**. Inject 3–8 μL aliquot concd, cleaned-up soln contg amt of pesticide within linear range of gas chromatgc system, (**i**), using 10 μL syringe. Tentatively identify residue peaks on basis of retention times. Det. amt of pesticide by comparing area under peak with that from known amt of appropriate std pesticide. For accurate detn, baseline current of sample and std must be identical during chromatgy.

Injections <3 μL are difficult to reproduce; injections >8 μL may cause flame blow-out. Sample wt is not critical—use injections equiv. to <1 mg or several hundred mg. Inject appropriate std immediately after every sample. Peak ht also may be used for detn, but only if ht of ref. std is ca same ht as sample unknown (width of base should then be same).

Single Sweep Oscillographic Polarographic Confirmatory Method (*8*)—Official Final Action

(Applicable to Diazinon, malathion, Me parathion, and parathion)

29.050 ***Apparatus***

(Wash all glassware with hot HNO_3 (1+1) and rinse with H_2O.)

(**a**) *Polarograph*.—Any voltammetric or polarographic instrument capable of linear sweep voltammetry at 10 ng pesticide/mL cell soln (equiv. to 0.01 ppm based on 1 g sample in 1 mL cell soln).

(**b**) *Silver wire electrode*.—Deposit very thin coating of AgCl on No. 20 or 22 gage Ag wire as follows: Dip wire in 10% HNO_3, rinse in H_2O, and then let stand 10 min in 1*N* HCl.

29.051 ***Reagents***

(*See* statement regarding solvs, **29.001**.)

(**a**) *Acetonitrile*.—Distd in glass at 82±1°.

(**b**) *Acetone*.—Distil at 56.5° with 0.25 g $KMnO_4$/L. Distn must be performed as directed.

(**c**) *Ethyl acetate*.—Distd in glass at 77±1°.

(**d**) *Petroleum ether*.—Distd in glass at 30–60°.

(**e**) *Nitrogen*.—Prepurified, H_2O-pumped.

(**f**) *Tetramethyl ammonium bromide*.—Eastman No. 670, or equiv.

(**g**) *Electrolyte solns*.—(*1*) *For Diazinon*.—Dissolve 7.7 g Me_4NBr in 300 mL H_2O. Add 115 mL HOAc and dil. to 500 mL with H_2O. (*2*) *For malathion*.—Dissolve 15.4 g Me_4NBr in 300 mL H_2O. Add 0.2 g LiCl and 4.1 mL HCl, and dil. to 500 mL with H_2O. (*3*) *For methyl parathion and parathion*.—Dissolve 2.2 g NaOAc $.3H_2O$ and 1.17 g NaCl in 100 mL H_2O and adjust to pH 4.8 with HOAc, using pH meter.

(**h**) *Pesticide std solns*.—(*1*) *Stock solns*.—Prep. individual solns contg 1.00 mg pesticide/mL EtOAc. Store at 0°. (*2*) *Intermediate solns*.—0.2 mg/mL. Transfer 5 mL stock soln to 25 mL vol. flask and dil. to vol. with pet ether for Diazinon, MeOH for malathion, and acetone for Me parathion and parathion.

29.052 ***Preparation of Standard Curves***

(**a**) *Diazinon*.—Transfer 0.0, 1.0, 2.0, 3.0, 4.0, and 5.0 mL intermediate std soln of Diazinon to individual 100 mL vol. flasks and dil. to vol. with pet ether. Transfer 1.0 mL of each soln to sep. 50 mL erlenmeyers and evap. to incipient dryness under gentle jet of dry air. Evap. remaining solv. with warmth of hand. Dissolve residue in 5.0 mL electrolyte soln, (**g**)(*1*). Transfer soln to polarographic cell, adjust to 25±1°, and bubble N thru soln 5 min. Polarograph between −0.70 and −1.2 v against either Hg pool or Ag wire ref. electrode.

Peak potential for Diazinon at 25° is −0.90±0.05 v against either electrode. Plot μg diazinon/mL cell soln against peak ht in units × instrument sensitivity setting.

(**b**) *Malathion*.—Transfer 0.0, 1.0, 2.0, 3.0, 4.0, and 5.0 mL intermediate std soln of malathion to individual 25 mL vol. flasks and dil. to vol. with MeOH. Transfer 2.0 mL of each soln to sep. 50 mL erlenmeyers and add 1.0 mL 0.1*N* KOH. After 3 min, add 2.0 mL electrolyte soln, (**g**)(*2*), mix well, and let stand 5 min. Transfer to polarographic cell, adjust to 25±1°, and bubble N thru soln 5 min. Polarograph between −0.5 and −1.0 v against either Hg pool or Ag wire electrode.

Peak potential for malathion at 25° is −0.82±0.05 v against Ag wire and −0.85±0.05 v against Hg pool ref. electrodes. Plot μg malathion/mL cell soln against peak ht in units × instrument sensitivity setting. (*Note:* Compd actually polarographed is fumaric acid resulting from basic hydrolysis of malathion.)

(**c**) *Parathion and methyl parathion*.—Transfer 0.0, 1.0, 2.0, 3.0, 4.0, and 5.0 mL intermediate parathion (or Me parathion) std soln to individual 100 mL vol. flasks and dil. to vol. with acetone. Transfer 5.0 mL aliquots of each soln to sep. 50 mL erlenmeyers, add 5.0 mL electrolyte soln, (**g**)(*3*), mix well, and transfer ca 5 mL to polarographic cell. Adjust to 25±1°, bubble N thru soln 5 min, and polarograph between −0.4 and −0.9 v against either Hg pool or Ag wire ref. electrode.

Peak potential for parathion and Me parathion at 25° is −0.68±0.05 v against Hg pool and −0.70±0.05 v against Ag wire ref. electrodes. Plot μg pesticide/mL cell soln (10 mL) against peak ht in units × instrument sensitivity setting. Cell soln vol. = 5 mL sample soln + 5 mL electrolyte soln.

29.053 ***Preparation of Sample Solution***

Prep., ext, and clean up samples as in **29.011–29.015**. Conc. 15% and 50% eluates from Florisil column to suitable definite vol. in Kuderna-Danish concentrator. All eluting solvs must be peroxide-free by test in *Definitions and Explanatory Terms,* item (3).

29.054 ***Determination***

(**a**) *Parathion and/or methyl parathion*.—Transfer aliquot of concd 15% Florisil eluate, equiv. to 5 g crop, to 50 mL erlenmeyer. Carefully evap. to dryness under gentle jet of air at room temp. Dissolve residue in 3.0 mL acetone. (*Note:* Since good polarograms can be obtained by using as little as 0.5 mL soln in cell, min. of 0.25 mL acetone can be used to dissolve residue.) Add 3.0 mL electrolyte soln, (**g**)(*3*), mix well, transfer to polarographic cell, and adjust to 25±1°. Bubble N thru soln 5 min and polarograph as in **29.052(c)**. Measure ht of wave whose peak potential corresponds to that of parathion, and det. concn from freshly prepd std curve or by comparing wave hts of sample soln with those of std soln polarographed immediately before or after sample. (Latter method is recommended for greater accuracy.)

Calc. μg/mL as follows:

$$C_{sample} = [(WH_{sample}) \times (IS_{sample}) \times (C_{std})]/[(WH_{std}) \times (IS_{std})]$$

where C = μg pesticide/mL cell soln; WH = wave ht; IS = instrument sensitivity setting.

ppm = (C_{sample} × mL sample soln)/g sample.

Limit of quant. detn is 0.01 ppm based on 1 g crop in 1 mL cell soln.

Me parathion, parathion, and paraoxon polarograph at ca same peak potential. If any one of these pesticides is present as indicated by multiple residue methods, it should be polarographed against that std. If these pesticides are present together, use mixed std contg ratio of pesticides as estd from analysis by multiple residue method. (Paraoxon will not be recovered by cleanup specified.)

Other pesticides known to give polarographic peak potentials similar to parathion are pentachloronitrobenzene (PCNB), 1,2,-4,5-tetrachloro-3-nitrobenzene (TCNB, tecnazene), and *O*-ethyl *O*-*p*-nitrophenyl phenylphosphonothioate (EPN). PCNB and TCNB are recovered in 6% Florisil eluate and will not interfere. Verify presence or absence of EPN by GLC or TLC.

(b) *Diazinon.*—Transfer aliquot of concd 15% Florisil eluate, equiv. to 5 g crop, to 50 mL erlenmeyer. Carefully evap. just to dryness, using gentle jet of dry air at room temp. Dissolve residue in 5.0 mL electrolyte soln, **(g)**(*1*). Transfer soln to polarographic cell and adjust to 25±1°. Bubble N thru soln 5 min and polarograph as in **29.052(a)**. Calc. amt of Diazinon present as in **(a)**.

Limit of quant. detn is 0.2 ppm based on 1 g crop sample in 1 mL cell soln.

(c) *Malathion.*—Transfer aliquot of concd eluate from 50% Florisil eluate, equiv. to 5 g crop, to 50 mL erlenmeyer. Carefully evap. just to dryness under gentle jet of dry air at room temp. Dissolve residue in 2.0 mL MeOH, add 1.0 mL 0.1*N* KOH, and let stand 3 min. Add 2.0 mL electrolyte soln, **(g)**(*2*), mix well, and let stand 5 min. Transfer to polarographic cell, adjust to 25±1°, bubble N thru soln 5 min, and polarograph as in **29.052(b)**. Calc. amt of malathion present as in **(a)**.

Limit of quant. detn is 0.3 ppm based on 1 g crop in 1.0 mL cell soln.

Note 1: If polarogram cannot be obtained because of high residual currents, check concd eluate for peroxides. If peroxides are present, transfer 5 mL concd eluate to small separator contg 25 mL 3% $FeSO_4$ soln; shake well and discard aq. layer. Transfer 1.0 mL ether layer to 50 mL erlenmeyer and proceed as in **(a)**, **(b)**, or **(c)**.

Note 2: All glassware used for polarographic detns should be thoroly washed with hot HNO_3 (1+1) and rinsed with distd H_2O.

29.055 ★ Cholinesterase Inhibition Method (*9*) ★ Official First Action

Nonspecific measure of H_2O-sol., cholinesterase inhibiting substances; applicable to alpha isomer of 2-carbomethoxy-1-methylvinyl dimethyl phosphate (Phosdrin®) in fruits and vegetables. *See* **29.049–29.055**, 12th ed.

MULTIPLE RESIDUE METHODS FOR FUMIGANTS

Volatile Fumigants in Grain (*10*)—Official First Action

(Applicable to $CHCl_3$, CCl_4, Cl_2CCClH, and BrH_2CCH_2Br in wheat and corn grain)

29.056 ***Apparatus and Reagents***

(a) *Column.*—4 m × 2.2 (id) mm stainless steel packed with 15% polypropylene glycol (LB 550X, Ucon fluid) on 60–80 mesh Chromosorb W.

(b) *Gas chromatograph.*—Isothermal with source-heated electron capture detector and glass-lined heated injection block. (100–200 mCi ^3H with Ar as β-ionization detector is more useful for multiresidue detns than ^{63}Ni and N.) Use 1 mv recorder with max. response time of 1 sec and chart speed of 0.5 cm/min. Operate electron capture detector with N at 25 psi (173 kPa) at 95° with polypropylene glycol column for CCl_4 (retention time, ca 6 min). Use 120° for $CHCl_3$ (3 min), Cl_2CCClH (4 min), and BrH_2CCH_2Br (8 min).

(c) *Acetone.*—Check for interfering peaks by gas chromatgy before use.

★ Surplus method—*see* inside front cover.

29.057 ***Determination***

(*Caution: see* **51.046.**)

Store sample at ≤5°. Quickly weigh 50 g and immerse in 150 mL acetone-H_2O (5+1) in 250 mL g-s flask, and stopper. Let stand 48 hr in dark at 20–25°, swirling at 24 hr. Decant 10 mL supernate into 25 mL g-s graduate, add 2 g NaCl, stopper, and shake vigorously 2 min. Let stand until layers sep. Pour 5 mL clear upper layer into 10 mL g-s graduate, add 1 g anhyd. $CaCl_2$, stopper, and shake 2 min. Let stand 30 min with occasional shaking.

Withdraw 0.5 μL aliquots from upper layer into 1 μL syringe. Inject into gas chromatograph. Dil. 10× or 100× with dry acetone, if necessary to avoid overloading detector. Inject all solns in triplicate and average results.

Construct calibration curve daily of peak hts against ng fumigant/125 mL acetone for suitable range.

MULTIPLE RESIDUE METHOD FOR ARYL *N*-METHYLCARBAMATE INSECTICIDES

Carbanolate (6-Chloro-3,4-xylyl methylcarbamate), Carbaryl (1-Naphthyl methylcarbamate), Carbofuran (2,3-Dihydro-2,2-dimethyl-7-benzofuranyl methylcarbamate), and Propoxur (*o*-Isopropoxyphenyl methylcarbamate)

Gas Chromatographic Method (11)—Official Final Action

(Applicable to apples, cabbage, collards, corn kernels, green beans, kale, and turnip tops. Rinse all glassware with acetone and then distd H_2O before use.)

29.058 ***Principle***

Residue is extd from crop with CH_3CN, and ext is purified by partitioning with pet ether and coagulating with H_3PO_4-NH_4Cl soln. Phenolic impurities are largely eliminated by partitioning CH_2Cl_2 ext with KOH soln. Carbamate residues are treated with 1-fluoro-2,4-dinitrobenzene to form ether derivative. Residues may be detd at levels ≥0.05 ppm. Recoveries range from 90 to 110%.

29.059 ***Reagents***

(a) *Borax.*—5% aq. soln.

(b) *Diatomaceous earth.*—Wash thoroly with acetone and dry 2 hr at 110°.

(c) *Coagulating soln.*—(*1*) *Stock soln.*—Dissolve 20 g NH_4Cl and 40 mL H_3PO_4 in 360 mL H_2O. (*2*) *Working soln.*—Dil. 100 mL stock soln to 1 L for coagulation.

(d) *1-Fluoro-2,4-dinitrobenzene soln.*—(Eastman Kodak Co.) Redistil at 128° and 1 mm pressure. Dissolve 1.5 mL in 25 mL acetone.

(e) *Pesticides.*—Best quality obtainable from manufacturer; anal. grades when available.

(f) *Potassium hydroxide soln.*—0.5*N* aq. soln.

(g) *Sodium chloride soln.*—30% aq. soln.

(h) *Solvents.*—Acetone, CH_2Cl_2, isooctane, CH_3CN, and pet ether (distd in glass; *see* statement regarding solvs, **29.001**); acetophenone and MeOH (anal. grade).

29.060 ***Gas Chromatographic Apparatus***

Gas chromatograph equipped with ^3H electron capture detector and 46 × 0.64 (od) cm (18 × ¼″) glass column contg 10% DC-200 (12,500 cst) on 60–70 mesh Anakrom ABS (Analabs, Inc.). Porous Teflon end plugs for ¼″ od glass tubing (Chemical Research Services, Inc., 852 Westgate Dr, Addison, IL 60101) are preferable, but glass wool can be used at outlet and omitted at inlet if necessary. (Glass wool at inlet tends to adsorb derivatives gradually and to release them later, giving rise to "ghost images" of compds.)

Equilibrate column 2 days at 250° and 2 weeks at 212°. Operating conditions: temps (°)—column 212, detector 218, standby temps 190 and 200, resp.; N carrier gas 60 mL/min; sensitivity 1×10^{-9} amp fuil scale; and detector potential either 25 or 50 V, depending on response level needed (⅓ to ⅔ full scale peak ht with injections of 4 ng carbamate).

Alternatively, use instrument with ^{63}Ni detector and 1.8 m (6′) × 4 mm id glass column contg 10% DC-200 on 60–70 mesh Anakrom ABS. Do not use glass wool at beginning of column. Operating conditions: temps (°)— column 232, detector 250, N carrier gas 80 mL/min, sensitivity 1×10^{-9} amp full scale, and detector potential 50 or 75 V.

29.061 ***Extraction of Pesticides***

(*Caution: See* **51.004**, **51.043**, and **51.073**)

Place 100 g sample and 200 mL CH_3CN (add 50 mL H_2O with fruit or other samples contg 5–15% sugar) in sq screw-top jar, and macerate in blender operated 2 min at moderate speed. Filter with suction into 500 mL r-b flask thru rapid paper in 11 cm buchner. Transfer aliquot equiv. to 40 g crop (mL aliquot = (mL H_2O in sample + mL CH_3CN added + mL H_2O added − 5 mL vol. contraction) × 40/100) to 250 mL separator. Shake 10 sec with 25 mL NaCl soln. Drain and discard aq. phase. Repeat with fresh NaCl soln. Add 100 mL pet ether, and shake 30 sec. Drain CH_3CN into 1 L separator. Strip pet ether by shaking 20 sec with 50 and 10 mL portions CH_3CN, draining each into the 1 L separator. Add 300 mL H_2O, 25 mL NaCl soln, and 50 mL MeOH. Ext mixt. with 100 mL and two 25 mL portions CH_2Cl_2, shaking each 20 sec, and drain lower layer into 500 mL r-b flask. Add 2 drops acetophenone, and evap. in rotary evaporator connected to aspirator pump. During evapn, keep H_2O bath within 40–50° range and remove flask from H_2O bath when ext vol. has been reduced to few mL, so that final evapn to dryness takes place at low temp.

Add 5 mL acetone, and swirl flask to dissolve residue. Add 50 mL coagulating soln, swirl to mix, add 1–2 g diat. earth, and swirl again to mix. Pour soln into 150 mL suction filter of medium porosity packed with 6 mm (¼″) diat. earth, and collect filtrate in 500 mL r-b flask. Break vac. immediately after liq. is drawn into diat. earth layer. Rinse sides of flask with 5 mL acetone, swirl, and repeat coagulation. Rinse flask with 20 mL coagulating soln, and add rinse to filter just after liq. of second coagulation is drawn into diat. earth layer. After filtration is complete (ca 5 min), transfer filtrate to 250 mL separator. Ext carbamates by shaking 20 sec with three 25 mL portions CH_2Cl_2, rinsing filter flask with each portion before adding to separator. Drain CH_2Cl_2 (lower) ext into another 250 mL separator. Soln may be held overnight at this point. Add 40 mL H_2O and 10 mL 0.5*N* KOH, mix briefly by gentle swirling, and shake 20 sec. Drain CH_2Cl_2 thru granular anhyd. Na_2SO_4 supported by glass wool in filter funnel, and collect filtrate in 250 mL erlenmeyer. Add 10 mL CH_2Cl_2 to separator, swirl gently, and drain org. phase. Repeat once. Rinse filter with two 10 mL portions CH_2Cl_2. Add 2 drops acetophenone, and evap. with same technic used in first evapn.

29.062 ***Determination***

Add 100 mL H_2O, 2 mL 0.5*N* KOH, and 1 mL 1-fluoro-2,4-dinitrobenzene soln. Stopper, and mix 20 min at high speed on mech. agitator. Add 10 mL 5% borax, swirl to mix, and heat on steam bath 20 min. Cool to room temp. by placing flasks in shallow H_2O bath 10 min. Add 5 mL isooctane, stopper, shake 3 min at high speed, and pour into 250 mL separator. Drain aq. phase, and rinse twice with H_2O. Drain isooctane soln thru funnel contg 6 mm glass wool plug into g-s test tube. Soln may be held overnight at this point. Inject 10 μL sample into gas chromatograph. If necessary to dil. sample, transfer 1 mL of isooctane ext to another test tube, dil. to exact vol. with isooctane, and shake to mix. Chromatograph std and sample solns at approx. same level of response.

Methylcarbamates, ppm = concn std × (peak ht sample/peak ht std) × (μL std/μL sample) × (diln vol./aliquot vol.) × 5/40.

29.063 ***Preparation of Standard Curves***

Dissolve 50 mg each carbamate in 100 mL benzene and store in brown bottles. Dil. 5 mL aliquots from these solns to 50 mL with benzene, and store in brown bottles. Transfer 50 μL to 250 mL erlenmeyer, and derivatize as in **29.062**. After extn of derivatives, solns will contain equiv. of 0.5 ng each carbamate/μL. Chromatograph 4, 6, 8, and 10 μL and plot mm response against ng carbamate. If response is nonlinear, adjust GLC parameters and/or prep. more dil. ref. soln, *e.g.*, equiv. of 0.25 μg carbamate/mL, and establish suitable linear working range.

METHODS FOR INDIVIDUAL RESIDUES

Benzene Hexachloride (Hexachlorocyclohexane, BHC)—Official Final Action

29.064 ***Multiple Residue Method***

See **29.001–29.028**.

29.065 ★ ***Colorimetric Method (12)*** ★

BHC is removed from sample by extg with CCl_4. After removal of solv., BHC is dechlorinated to benzene by action of Zn and HOAc in presence of malonic acid, which slowly liberates CO_2, sweeping benzene formed into nitrating mixt. Benzene is converted in const but not quant. (ca 85%) proportion to *m*-dinitrobenzene. After extn, *m*-dinitrobenzene is treated with butanone-2 and alkali, and *A* of magenta colored compd formed is measured at 565 nm.

See **24.101–24.105**, 10th ed. (*Caution: See* **51.011**, **51.039**, and **51.054**.)

29.066 ★ **Distinction Between Lindane and Technical BHC (*13*)—Official First Action** ★

BHC is extd with *n*-hexane. Ext is refluxed over fuming H_2SO_4 and BHC is extd with CH_3CN. Purified ext is chromatgd on paper to sep. and identify isomers. (*Caution: See* **51.004**, **51.011**, **51.016**, **51.030**, **51.031**, **51.039**, and **51.061**.)

See **24.107–24.110**, 10th ed.

Biphenyl (*14*)—Official Final Action

(Applicable to citrus fruit)

29.067 ***Principle***

Biphenyl is extd from blended peel or pulp by steam-liq.-liq. extn. Ext is subjected to TLC and biphenyl zone is completely

★ Surplus method—*see* inside front cover.

scraped from developed plate. Biphenyl is eluted from adsorbent with alcohol for spectrophtric detn.

29.068 ***Reagents***

(**a**) *Silica gel*.—GF-254 (Brinkmann Instruments, Inc. No. 7730).

(**b**) *Biphenyl std solns*.—(*1*) *Stock soln*.—Approx. 0.5 mg/mL. Dissolve ca 50 mg accurately weighed biphenyl in *n*-heptane and dil. to 100 mL with *n*-heptane. (*2*) *Limit soln*.—Approx. 0.01 mg/mL. Dil. 5 mL stock std to 250 mL with *n*-heptane.

Use stock std soln for spectrophtric quantitation after TLC step. Limit std soln aids in locating biphenyl zone and in estg small amts.

29.069 ***Apparatus***

(**a**) *Thin layer apparatus*.—See **19.041**; use 8 × 8″ glass plates.

(**b**) *Spotting pipet*.—100 μL (Kontes Glass Co. No. K-763800, or equiv.).

(**c**) *Tank liner*.—Whatman 3MM paper cut to fit tank.

(**d**) *Moisture test apparatus*.—Similar to lighter-than-H_2O volatile oil trap, **30.020(a)**, Fig. **30:01**, with cold finger condenser (SGA Scientific, Inc. No. JM-8590, or equiv.).

29.070 ***Preparation of TLC Plates***

Mix 40 g silica gel with 80 mL H_2O, shaking vigorously few sec, and finally swirling ca 30 sec to eliminate air bubbles. Spread slurry 0.3 mm thick over 5 plates. Let plates air dry in place ca 1 hr. Put plates in drying rack and place in 100° oven 2 min. Remove plates and store in desiccator over silica gel or $CaCl_2$ until used. Plates may be stored up to 30 days.

29.071 ***Preparation of Sample***

Sort out and discard rotten units. Completely peel ≥6 whole fruits (include all white material under peel in peel portion). Weigh peelings and peeled fruit, and calc. wt ratio of peelings to peeled fruit.

(**a**) *Peel*.—Grind combined peel in food grinder. Blend 200 g ground peel with 400 g H_2O at high speed 5 min (or in five 1 min increments if blender becomes very warm), using high-speed blender. (Larger batches may be blended with large blender as long as peel-H_2O ratio is same.)

(**b**) *Peeled fruit*.—Cut peeled fruit into small pieces and blend at high speed 5 min (or in five 1 min increments if blender becomes very warm).

29.072 ***Extraction***

Accurately weigh ca 300 g recently blended peel slurry or ca 100 g recently blended peeled fruit, and transfer to 1 L r-b ₸ 29/42 flask with enough H_2O to yield total vol. of ca 500 mL; add few boiling chips (6 mesh granular SiC is convenient). Connect extn unit of moisture test app. to flask and fill side arm with H_2O to overflowing. Place ca 3 mL *n*-heptane on top of H_2O layer and insert cold finger cooled with very rapid flow of cold H_2O. Gradually heat flask with mantle (controlled by variable transformer) until even boiling is obtained, then intensely enough to maintain vigorous boiling. Continue extn 3 hr from time mixt. starts boiling. (Wrap exposed portion of flask and connector arm between flask and extn unit with Al foil.) Initial carry-over of froth does not interfere. After 3 hr, discontinue heat and drain entire contents of extractor into 125 mL separator. Discard lower layer and drain heptane ext thru 2.5 cm column of granular anhyd. Na_2SO_4 (8–10 mm id column) into 10 mL vol. flask. Rinse separator with 1 mL *n*-heptane and add rinse to column. Rinse cold finger and extn unit with five 2 mL portions alcohol, collecting successive rinses in separator. Add 5 mL *n*-heptane to separator and shake vigorously few sec; add 50–75 mL H_2O and shake moderately few sec. Let layers sep. (lower layer may remain slightly cloudy) and discard lower layer. Pass heptane layer thru same Na_2SO_4 column into vol. flask. Rinse separator and column with enough *n*-heptane to dil. to vol.

29.073 ***Thin Layer Chromatography***

Pre-sat. tank contg liner with *n*-heptane ≥1 hr before use. Establish imaginary spotting line 3 cm from bottom edge of plate. For each intended spot, use tip of 100 μL pipet to scratch mark in adsorbent layer just size of pipet tip. (Space spots evenly with max. of 7 spots including blank.) Spot 100 μL each stock and limit std solns on extreme spots (one on far right and one on far left of plate). Spot 100 μL *n*-heptane as blank and 100 μL sample between std spots. Use same pipet for all spots, rinsing thoroly with *n*-heptane between applications. Keep size of spots uniform at 1.5–2 cm diam. by using following technic: Fill 100 μL pipet past mark with soln to be spotted. Carefully drain excess into absorbent towel until soln is at exact vol. mark. Press pipet tip against exposed glass in center of spotting mark on plate (hold pipet in vertical position at all times). Regulate size of spot by holding finger over top of pipet and pressing tip tightly against plate. Blow across spot (orally) only when necessary to regulate size of spot and never lift pipet from place once spotting is begun.

Pour 10–15 mL *n*-heptane in tank trough, insert plate, and seal tank. Develop until solv. is within 2.5 cm from top of plate (ca 30 min). Remove plate, air dry few min, and view under UV light. Biphenyl appears as bright blue spot on yellow background.

If no biphenyl appears in sample, end analysis at this point. If biphenyl is found, remove spots from plate without delay. Score upper and lower extremes of biphenyl zone horizontally across plate. Score vertical lines in adsorbent between biphenyl spots to include approx. equal area in each rectangle, scribing same area for ref. spot. Use razor blade to scrape off, and discard all adsorbent below biphenyl zone and outside extreme vertical lines. Use absorbent tissue and alcohol to clean exposed glass thoroly. Carefully scrape adsorbent from one extreme rectangular zone onto glazed paper and transfer to funnel inserted in 10 mL vol. flask; do not use solv. to rinse paper. Rinse off razor blade into funnel with small portion of alcohol. Tip plate at angle to facilitate rinsing of scraped area into funnel and rinse with several small portions alcohol. Rinse funnel and finally dil. to vol. with alcohol. Shake mixt. vigorously and let stand 5 min, shaking occasionally. Remove each biphenyl spot same way, working inward from each side of plate and cleaning and drying each previously removed zone. Filter each mixt. thru Whatman No. 44 paper, or equiv., and store filtrate in stoppered vessel for spectrophtric detn.

29.074 ***Spectrophotometry***

Det. A of each soln at 248 and 300 nm in 1 cm cell with alcohol as ref.

ppm Biphenyl = (ΔA_{248} sample/ΔA_{248} std) × (μg std spotted/g sample spotted), where $\Delta A_{248} = A_{248} - [A_{300} \times (A_{248}\text{ blank}/A_{300}\text{ blank})]$.

29.075 ★ ***2-(p-tert*-Butylphenoxy)-1-Methylethyl 2-Chloroethyl Sulfite (Aramite®) (*15*) Official Final Action** ★

Aramite is stripped from sample with benzene, soln is concd, and Aramite is hydrolyzed with KOH-isopropanol to form ethylene oxide. Evolved ethylene oxide is converted to HCHO with KIO_4, and HCHO is reacted with acetylacetone to form colored compd. which is detd. colorimetrically. *See* **29.067–29.071**, 12th ed.

Captan (N-(Trichloromethylthio)-4-Cyclohexene-1,2-Dicarboximide) (*16*)—Official Final Action

(Applicable to firm fruits such as apples, pears, peaches, and plums and to green vegetables)

29.076 ***Principle***

Captan is extd from crop with benzene; H_2O, color, and appreciable amts of waxes are removed, and red color is developed by fusion of captan with resorcinol at 135°; color changes to yellow on addn of HOAc.

29.077 ***Reagents***

(**a**) *Resorcinol.*—Must be free of discoloration and pass following tests: Fuse 0.5 g and dissolve in 25 mL HOAc. *A* at 425 nm is ≤0.015, against HOAc. 1.00 g should not lose >2 mg in 4 hr over H_2SO_4; if more is lost, dry over H_2SO_4 until test is satisfactory.

(**b**) *Cleanup mix.*—10 parts Nuchar, 5 parts Hyflo Super-Cel, and 5 parts anhyd. Na_2SO_4.

(**c**) *Captan std solns.*—(*1*) *Stock soln.*—3 mg/mL. Transfer 150 mg pure captan (available from Chevron Chemical Co., 940 Hensley St, Richmond, CA 94804) to 50 mL vol. flask and dil. to vol. with benzene. (*2*) *Intermediate soln.*—300 μg/mL. Pipet 10 mL stock soln into 100 mL vol. flask and dil. to vol. with benzene. (*3*) *Working soln.*—30 μg/mL. Pipet 10 mL intermediate std soln into 100 mL vol. flask and dil. to vol. with benzene.

29.078 ***Preparation of Sample***

(*Caution: See* **51.039**, **51.040**, and **51.045**.)

(**a**) *Fruits.*—Accurately weigh ca 500 g sample into clean, dry jar with screw cap faced with sheet cork gasket covered with wet filter paper, or other solv.-tight lid, and add 500 mL benzene. Multiples of sample-to-benzene ratio can be used. Agitate 15 min, drain benzene into container, and transfer to separator. (Transfer to separator may be omitted where there is no separable aq. layer.)

Transfer ca 100 mL sepd benzene layer to 250 mL g-s flask, and decolorize and dehydrate with 3–4 g cleanup mix, (**b**), by shaking vigorously ca 5 min. Filter thru folded paper, rejecting first 10–15 mL.

(**b**) *Green vegetables.*—Chop sample in food chopper such as Hobart Food Cutter, mix, and transfer 100 g to explosion-proof blender. Add 200 mL benzene and blend 2 min; add 20 g anhyd. Na_2SO_4 and blend 2 min more. Pour mixt. into 500 mL centrf. bottle, stopper with *cork*, and centrf. at ca 1400 rpm 5–10 min. Decant benzene layer into 250 mL g-s erlenmeyer, add ca 6 g cleanup mix, (**b**)/100 mL benzene, and shake vigorously ca 5 min. Filter thru folded paper, discarding first 10 mL. If water-white soln does not result, repeat cleanup treatment. Pipet 50 mL into 100 mL vol. flask and dil. to vol. with benzene.

★ Surplus method—*see* inside front cover.

29.079 ***Determination***

(*Caution: See* **51.018**, **51.040**, **51.041**, and **51.045**.)

Pipet 5 mL filtrate, **29.078**(**a**), or aliquot, (**b**), into 25 × 200 mm test tube and add 0.5±0.1 g resorcinol. Heat 20 min in oil bath at 135±5°, cautiously at first to evap. benzene; then immerse reaction tubes to depth of ca 5 cm but do not let them touch bottom of bath. Remove, and immediately add 10–15 mL HOAc, followed by rapid immersion in H_2O at room temp. Transfer quant. to 25 mL vol. flask, using HOAc, dil. to vol. with HOAc, and mix.

Det. *A* at 425 nm in 1 cm cell against HOAc within 1 hr. Calc. ppm from std curve.

29.080 ***Preparation of Standard Curve***

Prep. std curve simultaneously with samples. Pipet 0, 2, 4, and 5 mL aliquots of working std soln into 25 × 200 mm test tubes and add benzene to make total vol. of 5 mL in each tube. Add 0.5±0.1 g resorcinol and continue as in detn, beginning "Heat 20 min in oil bath . . ."

Note: One drop H_2O in reaction tube will cause apparent loss of ca 20% captan. Do not leave benzene aliquots in unstoppered reaction tubes where condensation of moisture will take place.

Carbaryl (1-Naphthyl N-Methylcarbamate) (Sevin®) Official Final Action

29.081 ***Multiple Residue Method***

See **29.058–29.063**.

Colorimetric Method (17)

29.082 ***Reagents***

(**a**) *Acetone.*—Redistd.

(**b**) *Coagulating soln.*—Dissolve 0.5 g NH_4Cl in 400 mL H_2O contg 1 mL H_3PO_4.

(**c**) *Color reagent.*—Dissolve 25 mg *p*-nitrobenzene-diazonium fluoborate in 5 mL MeOH and add 20 mL HOAc. Prep. just before use.

(**d**) *Methylene chloride.*—Redistd CH_2Cl_2.

(**e**) *Alcoholic potassium hydroxide soln.*—0.1*N* in MeOH.

(**f**) *Polyethylene glycol soln.*—Dil. 1 mL polyethylene glycol to 100 mL with CH_2Cl_2.

(**g**) *Carbaryl std solns.*—Ref. std material is available from Union Carbide Corp., PO Box 1906, Salinas, CA 93901. (*1*) *Stock soln.*—0.5 mg/mL. Place 50.0 mg in 100 mL vol. flask and dil. to vol. with CH_2Cl_2. (*2*) *Intermediate soln.*—50 μg/mL. Transfer 10 mL stock soln to 100 mL vol. flask and dil. to vol. with CH_2Cl_2. (*3*) *Working soln.*—5.0 μg/mL. Transfer 10 mL intermediate soln to 100 mL vol. flask and dil. to vol. with CH_2Cl_2.

29.083 ***Apparatus***

Evaporative concentrator.—See Fig. **29:07**. Vac. manifold connected thru stopcock to antisurge column, 250 × 19 mm od, contg glass marble, or Snyder column, attached to ₮ 24/40 erlenmeyer. Use surgical tubing wherever contact with sample is likely.

29.084 ***Preparation of Sample Solution***

Transfer 50 g sample to high-speed blender and add 150 mL CH_2Cl_2 and 100 g powd anhyd. Na_2SO_4. Blend at high speed 2 min and let settle 1 min. Decant solv. into 9 cm buchner fitted with Whatman No. 1, or equiv., paper covered with thin coat of Hyflo Super-Cel, or equiv., filter aid. Cautiously apply vac. until all solv. has filtered. Repeat extn with two 100 mL portions CH_2Cl_2. Treat combined filtrates as in (**a**) or (**b**):

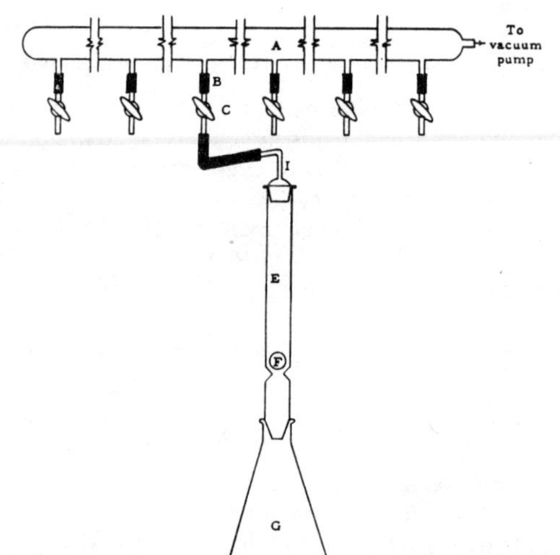

FIG. 29:07—Evaporative concentrator. A, glass manifold. B, pressure tubing. C, stopcock. D, adapter, ₮ 24/40. E, antisurge column, 25 cm × 19 mm od. F, glass marble. G, erlenmeyer, ₮ 24/40, 250 mL.

(**a**) Transfer combined filtrates to 500 mL ₮ erlenmeyer and add 1 mL polyethylene glycol soln. Connect to evaporative concentrator, place flask in H_2O bath at 25–30°, and carefully reduce pressure to ca 20 mm (2.7 kPa). After solv. evaps, immediately disconnect antisurge column from manifold. Rinse down walls of column and flask with 5 mL acetone from pipet, swirl flask, and warm gently under hot H_2O tap 30 sec. Add 50 mL coagulating soln thru column, and swirl. Remove column, let mixt. stand 30 min, and filter with vac. thru 3 mm layer of Super-Cel in No. 1 buchner. Wash flask and pad with two 15 mL portions coagulating soln.

Transfer filtrate to 125 mL separator, add 25 mL CH_2Cl_2, shake well, and let sep. completely. Drain lower layer into ₮ 250 mL erlenmeyer. Repeat extn of aq. layer with 25 mL CH_2Cl_2, adding ext to same 250 mL erlenmeyer. If combined exts are cloudy, add 5–10 g granular anhyd. Na_2SO_4, and shake. Decant solv. into clean 250 mL ₮ erlenmeyer, rinsing with small portion CH_2Cl_2. (If residue is expected to be >2 ppm, dil. exts to vol. in 100 mL vol. flask, and use appropriate aliquot.)

(**b**) Add 1 mL polyethylene glycol. Stopper, carefully reduce pressure to ca 150 mm, and warm on steam bath. When vol. is ca 5 mL, remove from steam bath and swirl until dry. Release vac., remove stopper, and let cool. Continue as in (**a**), beginning "Rinse down walls . . ." except column is not present.

29.085 ***Determination***

To soln in erlenmeyer add 1 mL polyethylene glycol soln and connect to column and evaporator. Evap. solv. as before, immediately disconnect, and remove column. Rinse down walls of flask with 2 mL 0.1*N* KOH in MeOH from pipet, rotating to ensure complete contact. Let stand 5 min, add exactly 17 mL HOAc, and with swirling add 1 mL color reagent. Let stand exactly 1 min and det. *A* in 1 cm cell at 475 nm against reagent blank processed along with sample as ref. Det. μg from std curve.

ppm Carbaryl = (μg/g sample) × (diln factor if aliquot was used).

29.086 ***Preparation of Standard Curve***

(*Caution: See* **51.018** and **51.041**.)

Pipet 0, 1, 3, 5, and 10 mL aliquots working std soln to 500 mL ₮ erlenmeyers, add 300 mL CH_2Cl_2 to each, and proceed as in **29.084**, beginning "Treat combined filtrates as in (**a**) or (**b**):" Plot *A* against μg carbaryl to obtain std curve.

Qualitative and Semiquantitative Method (18)
Official Final Action

(Applicable to apples and spinach)

29.087 ***Reagents***

(**a**) *Adsorbent*.—Al_2O_3 G (contains 10% $CaSO_4$). *See* **29.003**(**a**).
(**b**) *Coagulating soln.*—*See* **29.082**(**b**).
(**c**) *Chromogenic spray soln.*—Sat. diethylene glycol-alcohol soln (1+9) with *p*-nitrobenzene-diazonium fluoborate (practical grade, ca 25 mg/100 mL) by stirring ca 2 min. Filter, keep cold during use, and store in refrigerator. Do not use after 3 days.
(**d**) *Diethylene glycol soln.*—Dil. 10 mL diethylene glycol to 100 mL with redistd CH_2Cl_2.
(**e**) *Carbaryl std.*—Mp 141–142°. *See* **29.082**(**g**). Recrystallize from alcohol and H_2O, if necessary.

29.088 ***Apparatus***

(**a**) *TLC apparatus.*—App. suitable for 8 × 8" plates. *See* **29.006**.
(**b**) *Evaporative concentrator.*—Two chamber, ₮ 24/25, micro-Snyder column (Kontes Glass Co. K-569001); with 10 mL Mills tube, graduated (Kontes K-570050).

29.089 ***Extraction and Cleanup of Sample***

Transfer 25 g sample to blender. Add 150 mL CH_2Cl_2 and 100 g powd (150 g granular) anhyd. Na_2SO_4. Blend 2 min at low speed and let settle. Attach 9 cm buchner contg rapid paper to 500 mL filter flask. Cover paper with thin coat of Hyflo Super-Cel prepd as slurry in CH_2Cl_2. Decant ext into buchner and cautiously apply vac. Rinse blender with 50 mL CH_2Cl_2 and filter. Return residue to blender. (Complete sepn of residue from Super-Cel is unimportant.) Add 150 mL CH_2Cl_2, re-ext, filter, and rinse again with 50 mL CH_2Cl_2. Add 1 mL diethylene glycol soln to filter flask. Place flask with buchner contg original filter pad attached on steam bath and apply vac. When vol. in flask is ca 5 mL, remove flask from steam bath and swirl until dry. Release vac., remove buchner, and let flask cool.

Rinse down side of flask with 3 mL acetone from pipet and swirl to dissolve residue. While gently swirling flask, add 15 mL coagulating soln and let stand >10 min with occasional swirling. Filter, using vac., thru small fritted glass funnel, medium porosity, contg ca 6 mm layer of Hyflo Super-Cel and receive filtrate in 30 mL test tube. Wash ppt with three 2 mL portions acetone-H_2O soln (1+9), letting each washing remain in contact with ppt ca 15 sec before applying vac. Transfer filtrate and washings to 25 mL vol. flask, dil. to vol. with acetone-H_2O soln (1+9), and mix.

29.090 ***Determination***

(*Caution: See* **51.017**.)

Transfer 10 mL sample soln to 125 mL separator. Ext soln with two 5 mL portions CH_2Cl_2, shaking 5–10 sec each time. Combine exts in Mills tube, add small SiC chip (<0.01 mL vol.), fit with micro-Snyder column, and evap. to 0.1 mL on steam bath. (*Caution:* Samples may be lost by vigorous ebullition.)

Prepare 8 × 8" TLC plates coated with 250 μm layer Al_2O_3 adsorbent. Dry plates in forced-draft oven 30 min at 80°. Store in desiccator cabinet. Using 1 μL pipet, spot aliquots equiv. to 2 g sample and carbaryl stds (in CH_2Cl_2) to cover expected range.

Place trough in chromatgc tank lined with blotting paper. Add ca 50 mL acetone-benzene soln (1+4) to bottom of tank to sat. atm., and then add 50 mL same soln to trough. Place plate in trough and seal tank with masking tape. Develop plate until solv. front just reaches line drawn 10 cm from origin. Dry plate ca 15 min in hood. Spray moderately with 1.0*N* alc. KOH soln. Then spray moist plate with chromogenic soln. Blue spot with R_f value same as std carbaryl spot indicates carbaryl (R_f range, 0.52–0.60). Compare size and intensity of sample and std spots for semiquant. estn of amt of pesticide. It is possible to distinguish, for example, between 0.2 and 0.4 μg, but not between 0.3 and 0.4 μg. Optimum range for quant. estn is ca 0.1–0.4 μg. For amts >0.4 μg, spot smaller aliquot of remaining 80 μL soln. Then spot same vol. of std soln for valid comparison.

29.091 ★ *p*-Chlorophenyl Phenyl Sulfone (p-ClDPS; ★ Sulphenone®) (*19*)—Official Final Action

Hexane strip solns are extd with CH_3CN, which seps Sulphenone components from bulk of waxes, coloring matter, and to some extent from other pesticides. The CH_3CN residue is chromatographed on Magnesol column with hexane-anhyd. ether. Residue of fraction contg *p*-ClDPS is dissolved in isooctane for detn of UV *A*.

See **29.075–29.081**, 11th ed.

Diethyl Diphenyl Dichloroethane (Perthane) (*20*)—Official Final Action

(For low levels (less than ca 50 ng/GLC injection) and for confirmatory quantitation of higher levels of Perthane previously detd by **29.001–29.018**)

29.092 ***Principle***

Method is extension of general method for multiple residues, **29.001–29.018**. After electron capture GLC detn of Perthane and other organochlorine and organophosphorus pesticides, Perthane in 6% mixed ether eluate, **29.015**, is dehydrochlorinated to its olefin. Perthane olefin is extd from reaction mixt. into hexane and portion of hexane is injected into gas chromatograph with electron capture detector. Perthane olefin produces 10-fold increase in electron capture detector response over that of parent compd.

29.093 ***Reagents***

(a) *Hexane.—See* **29.002(j)**.
(b) *Carborundum chips.*—SiC, ca 20 mesh.
(c) *Alcoholic potassium hydroxide soln.*—Dissolve 2 g KOH in 100 mL alcohol.
(d) *Perthane std soln.*—50 μg/mL hexane. Perthane available from Rohm & Haas Co.
(e) *Perthane olefin std soln.*—5 μg/mL hexane.

29.094 ***Apparatus***

(a) *Reaction tube.*—12 or 15 mL graduated centrf. tube with No. 13 glass stopper (Corning Glass Works, No. 8084, or equiv.).
(b) *Heat source.*—Oil bath (100 mL beaker contg 80 mL paraffin oil) and mag. stirrer hot plate calibrated to maintain oil temp. at 100±5°.

29.095 ***Determination***

After electron capture GLC of Perthane and other organochlorine and organophosphorus pesticides, **29.001–29.018**, pipet entire 6% eluate, **29.015**, or aliquot contg ≤30 μg Perthane into reaction tube. Carefully evap. to dryness under gentle air current. Add 2 mL alc. KOH soln and 2–5 SiC chips. Place reaction tube in 100° oil bath to depth of ca 1.0 mL graduation and let soln reflux 15 min. (Conduct reaction in hood. Air flow thru hood will cool upper part of tube, which serves as condenser. Hood also removes odors escaping from hot oil.) Remove tube from oil bath, cool to room temp., and add 3 mL H_2O. Pipet vol. hexane (but ≥1 mL) into tube to give concn ca 5 μg Perthane olefin/mL. Shake vigorously ca 30 sec and let layers sep. Det. Perthane olefin in hexane layer as in **29.018**.

$$\text{ppm Perthane} = [(R \times W')/(R' \times W)] \times (307.25/270.78),$$

where R and R' = responses to Perthane olefin in sample and std, resp.; W' = ng std injected; W = mg equiv. sample injected; and 307.25 and 270.78 = MW Perthane and Perthane olefin, resp.

Dichloro Diphenyl Trichloroethane (DDT) (1,1,1-Trichloro-2,2-bis(chlorophenyl)ethane) Official Final Action

29.096 ***Multiple Residue Method***

See **29.001–29.028.**

★ Colorimetric Method (21) ★

29.097 ***Principle***

Com. DDT consists essentially of 2 isomers, *p,p'*- and *o,p'*-DDT, in proportion of ca 3:1. Dry isomers of DDT can be nitrated to tetranitro DDT, which can be extd by ether, dried, and taken up in measured vol. benzene. Treating this soln with stdzd anhyd. NaOMe soln produces reasonably stable colors—blue for *p,p'* and reddish purple for *o,p'* isomer. This reaction (Schechter-Haller) is fairly specific for DDT. Exceptions are nitrated or dehalogenated decomposition products of DDT and certain close analogs that can produce yellow to red and sometimes blue colors with NaOMe. If distinctly "off" colors are produced on samples of unknown spray history and cannot be removed from solv. by careful washing with alkali, analogs may be present, and special methods for their detection must be applied.

Principal known interfering insecticides are TDE (1,1-dichloro-2,2-bis(*p*-chlorophenyl)ethane), methoxychlor (1,1,1-trichloro-2,2-bis(*p*-methoxyphenyl) ethane), DNB and DNP (2-nitro-1,1-bis(*p*-chlorophenyl)butane and propane analogs of DDT). Other insecticidal compds, as well as limited amt of benzene-sol. plant extractives, are oxidized or degraded in nitration and are then removed from ether or pet ether soln by washing with alkali, or they do not react under conditions of method. Other org. material does not seriously interfere, but if >100 mg of extraneous org. matter is present, as in fats, special sepns must be made.

29.098 ***Preparation of Sample***

(*Caution: See* **51.004, 51.011, 51.039, 51.040, 51.043, 51.045**, and **51.073**.)

(a) *For all fresh or frozen fruits and vegetables, meat, and canned food except milk, and for all soft or wet materials generally: Beans (green), broccoli, brussels sprouts, cauliflower, cabbage, cherries, cranberries, grapes, lettuce, pea pods, spinach, squash, tomatoes, silage, etc.*—Finely chop 1 kg sample or entire contents of small unit package in suitable food chopper (powered mech. food chopper such as Hobart is satisfactory) and transfer well mixed 100 g portion to high-speed blender. Add 100 mL isopropanol and blend 2 min. Add 200 mL hexane or benzene and blend again 2 min. (To avoid splashing and

★ Surplus method—*see* inside front cover.

possible loss of sample, regulate blending speed with rheostat or variable transformer when necessary.)

Pour mixt. as completely as possible into 600–800 mL beaker and let solids settle. Pour solv. layer equally into two 250 mL centrf. bottles. With aid of stirring rod and funnel, distribute solid material equally between the 2 bottles. Stopper and centrf. 5 min at ca 1500 rpm. If solids pack firmly, decant supernate directly into 500 mL vol. flask. If solids pack loosely, transfer liq. thru siphon tube, **16.220**, *Notes.* Wash blender cup, cap, and beaker with two 100 mL portions isopropanol-hexane or -benzene (1+2). Distribute washings equally between the 2 bottles. Break up solid material with stirring rod, stopper bottles, and shake vigorously 2 min. Centrf. as before and add solv. layer to vol. flask. Dil. to vol. with isopropanol-hexane or -benzene (1+2). (Final soln should be clear.)

(**b**) *For hay, cured* (*dry*).—Chop 1 kg sample and mix well. Grind portion in Wiley or other mill to ca 20 mesh.

Measure 500 mL extg solv. (350 mL H_2O dild to 1 L with CH_3CN, **29.002(a)**, and mixed in graduate). Pour ca 350 mL into high-speed blender, add 50 g sample, and blend 2 min. Add remainder of extg solv. (total 500 mL) and blend addnl 3 min at highest speed attainable without splashing. Filter with vac. thru powder funnel contg wad of glass wool and press out free liq. with back of large spoon or other means. Measure and record vol. filtrate, and transfer to 2 L separator. Add 200 mL pet ether (boiling range 30–60°), and shake vigorously 1–2 min. Add ca 20 mL satd NaCl soln and ca 1200 mL H_2O, and mix gently but thoroly. Re-ext aq. layer with two 100 mL portions pet ether. Discard aq. layer, swirl combined pet ether, drain off any aq. phase closely, and transfer exts to beaker. Evap. just to dryness on steam bath with aid of gentle air current.

Wt sample represented in analysis = wt sample taken × vol. filtrate/vol. extg solv. added.

(**c**) *For flour, cereals, feeding stuffs, or other comparatively fine dry materials.*—Ext 25 g sample with ether or benzene in Soxhlet app. or shake larger samples with suitable amts of solv. in centrf. bottle, centrf., and decant solv. Repeat extn once or twice, according to size sample. If necessary, sep. fat and DDT as in (**d**), and det. DDT in ext by colorimetric method.

(**d**) *For milk, cream, cheese, butter, oils or fats, etc.*—As DDT is dissolved in fat phase of dairy products, first sep. fats as in **29.012**, then isolate DDT as in **29.014**, and det. by colorimetric method (3 g fat is upper limit). Proceed as in **29.102(b)**.

29.099 ***Reagents***

(*Caution: See* **51.011** and **51.039**.)

(**a**) *Ether.*—Peroxide- and aldehyde-free.

(**b**) *Redistilled ether-petroleum ether.*—(1+4).

(**c**) *Benzene.*—(*Caution: See* **51.045**.) Redistd. Distil until no more H_2O comes over, and discard distillate; replace condenser with dry one, and collect balance of distillate.

(**d**) *Nitrating mixture.*—(*Caution: See* **51.026**, **51.030**, and **51.031**.) Mix fuming HNO_3 (sp gr 1.49–1.50) with equal vol. H_2SO_4. Chill before using.

(**e**) *Sodium methylate soln.*—1.74*N*. 40 g Na/L MeOH. (*Caution: See* **51.034** and **51.038**.) Prep. anhyd. MeOH as follows: Place 75 mL "absolute" MeOH in flask provided with reflux condenser and add 5 g clean Mg turnings. Add 0.5 g I_2 and warm gently, if necessary, until vigorous evolution of H sets in; then reflux until most of Mg has been converted to $Mg(OMe)_2$. Add mixt. to ca 900 mL untreated MeOH, reflux 30 min, and distil with exclusion of atm. H_2O. Preserve in tightly stoppered bottles. (Or dehydrate by refluxing 2–4 hr with 25 g CaH_2/L and then distg.)

Place 20.0 g freshly cut Na in flask provided with reflux condenser and add enough purified MeOH portionwise thru condenser to dissolve all the Na, warming and refluxing if necessary. Rinse into 500 mL vol. flask with addnl purified MeOH, cool, dil. to vol., and mix thoroly. Chill, centrf. down any carbonate turbidity, and decant clear supernate into dispensing system that excludes atm. H_2O and CO_2. Adjust batches of NaOMe soln to std concn after titrn with std acid, and prep. new std curve for each batch as made.

Store in dispensing system with all outlets trapped against CO_2 and H_2O and with inner delivery tube to buret packed with dry, alkali-treated asbestos to filter soln immediately before use.

(**f**) *Pure p,p′ (mp 108–109°) and o,p′ (mp 74–74.5°) DDT.*—*p,p′* Isomer may be prepd from 200 g tech. DDT by recrystg 2 or 3 times from alcohol, and *o,p′*-DDT from mother liquors by concn, fractional crystn from *n*-pentane, and recrystn from MeOH. *o,p′*-DDT may be synthesized as in J. Am. Chem. Soc. **67**, 1591(1945).

(**g**) *DDT std solns.*—(*1*) *Pure soln.*—0.2 mg total DDT (0.15 mg *p,p′* and 0.05 mg *o,p′*)/mL. Weigh 50 mg of the 2 pure isomers into 2 sep. 50 mL vol. flasks and dil. to vol. with benzene. Pipet 15 mL *p,p′* soln and 5 mL *o,p′* soln into 100 mL vol. flask and dil. to vol. with benzene. (*2*) *Technical soln.*—0.2 mg tech. DDT/mL benzene.

29.100 ***Preparation of Standard Curves***

(**a**) *For 0—1.0 mg range.*—Measure 0, 1.00, 2.00, 3.00, 4.00, and 5.00 mL of either std DDT soln into 50 mL erlenmeyers and evap. solv. on steam bath. Remove residual vapors with gentle air current, weight flasks (small Pb rings are convenient), and immerse in pan of ice-H_2O. (Use pan shelved so that vessels do not rest directly on bottom; porcelain desiccator platform in pan of proper size makes convenient bath.) Thoroly chill flasks and to each slowly add 5 mL chilled nitrating mixt. Rotate flasks to wet all portions of residue; then place pan on hot plate or steam bath and heat so that solns reach ca 85° in 20–30 min. Remove flasks from pan, place directly upon active steam bath, and nitrate 30 min. Remove flasks and cool under tap or leave overnight.

Slowly pour chilled acid mixt. from each flask into separator contg ca 25 mL ice-cold H_2O, rinse flask with several portions of ice-H_2O, and pour rinsings into separator. Rinse again with 25 mL ether-pet ether (1+4), and finally with second 15 mL portion ether-pet ether (1+4), pouring last rinse into second separator. Ext by shaking first separator vigorously 1 min; then drain aq. layer into second separator and repeat extn. Discard aq. layer and drain second separator into first, rinsing with small portions of ether mixt. Bleed off any residual aq. layer as completely as possible, add 10 mL 10% KOH soln, and shake vigorously 30 sec. Drain off closely and wash with two 15 mL portions satd NaCl soln. Drain well and filter ext thru 1.2 cm layer of washed and dried glass wool previously wetted with ether mixt., held in filter tube, into 125 mL erlenmeyer contg glass bead. Rinse separator and filter with few small portions of ether mixt., evap. off ether on steam bath (gentle air current speeds evapn and controls bumping), and heat 1 hr at 100°.

Cool flask, making sure interior is thoroly dry, and take up residue with exactly 25 mL redistd benzene. Stopper flask and swirl 1 min to ensure complete soln of residue. (Procedure may be interrupted overnight at this stage.)

Transfer 5.00 mL aliquot to small flask and develop characteristic DDT color by adding exactly 10.0 mL NaOMe soln. Mix well, let stand 15 min, and then det. *A* at 600 nm in cell of appropriate length against benzene-NaOMe soln (1+2). (Readings in blue at 450 nm and in green at 510 nm should also be made to check presence of extraneous yellow and red colors when actual samples are read later.) If instrument used records in terms of T, convert to A (− log T).

Measure all colors of series in same (or similar) cells and plot A against μg DDT on linear coordinate paper to obtain std curve. Stopper cells with glass covers or stoppers. If test tubes are used, close with clean cork stoppers. Either cells with optically fused ends or cells constructed with alkali-resistant cement may be used, but if cemented cells are used, do not leave alk. solns in cells longer than necessary to make measurements, and clean cells immediately after use.

(**b**) *For 0—50 μg range.*—Add 0, 10, 20, 30, 40, and 50 μg DDT, in benzene soln, to series of 50 mL erlenmeyers, each contg 10 mg oleic acid in benzene soln, and evap. to dryness. (Small Pb rings are convenient for weighting flasks. Oleic acid serves as inert "keeper" material to prevent loss of micro amts of DDT.) Nitrate as in (**a**) and ext with redistd pet ether. Wash ext 3 times with 10% KOH soln, shaking vigorously 2 min each time. Heat final washed residues 1 hr at 100°, take up in 3.00 mL redistd benzene, and develop color with 6.00 mL of the NaOMe soln. Plot A against μg DDT as in (**a**).

29.101 ***Removal of Coloring Matter***

(*Caution: See* **51.011**, **51.030**, **51.031**, **51.039**, **51.040**, **51.045**, **51.049**, and **51.054**.)

(**a**) *Applicable to extracts of fruits, vegetables, and most other low-fat products.*—Evap. 200 mL aliquot prepd soln, **29.098**(**a**), or suitable aliquot of **29.098**(**c**), just to dryness in 400 mL beaker on steam bath with aid of small air current. Dissolve residue in 10 mL CCl_4 and transfer to column prepd as follows:

Grind 10 g Celite 545 thoroly with 3 mL 15–20% fuming H_2SO_4 in mortar, add 3 mL H_2SO_4, and grind well. Transfer at once to fritted glass funnel or tube (funnel: 40 mm id, 60 mL capacity, coarse porosity; tube: 30 mm disk, 130 mL capacity, coarse porosity (sulfur absorption tube, Arthur H. Thomas Co. No. 8815-K10 is satisfactory)). Pack adsorbent to firm level surface with flat-end glass rod. Add CCl_4 to column to wet adsorbent and let solv. drain until ca 2 mm layer remains on top of column.

Transfer 10 mL CCl_4 sample soln to column. Rinse sample beaker with three 10 mL portions CCl_4 and add rinsings to column. Collect eluate in 125 mL g-s flask. Let solv. drain until level just reaches surface of adsorbent and rinse walls of tube with 10 mL CCl_4. Repeat with second 10 mL portion CCl_4. After solv. drains to surface level, add 25 mL CCl_4 and let drain completely. At no time permit solv. to sink entirely into column (go dry) until this point is reached. Tamp surface of column with flat-end glass rod to remove all free liq.

(**b**) *Applicable to extracts of hay.*—Proceed as in (**a**), except use 20 g Celite 545 with 6 mL 15–20% fuming H_2SO_4 and 6 mL H_2SO_4 for column, and 170 mL CCl_4 for elution.

(**c**) *Applicable to extracts of fatty materials containing maximum of 3 g fat.*—Proceed as in (**a**), except use 30 g Celite 545 with 9 mL 15–20% fuming H_2SO_4 and 9 mL H_2SO_4, and 250 mL CCl_4 for elution.

29.102 ***Determination***

(*Caution: See* **51.011**, **51.039**, **51.040**, and **51.054**.)

(**a**) *Applicable to extracts of fruits, vegetables, and other low-fat products.*—Evap. solv. to dryness on steam bath with aid of small air current. Carefully nitrate residue as in **29.100**(**a**). To ensure thoro removal of interfering oxidn byproducts, wash ether mixt. with six 10 mL portions 10% KOH soln.

If amt of DDT is unknown, develop exploratory color with 5 mL aliquot and 10 mL NaOMe soln. If A is <0.20, check by taking 10–15 mL aliquot, evapg to dryness, redissolving in 5 mL benzene, and developing color; if A is >0.80, check by taking smaller aliquot, dilg to 5 mL with benzene, and developing color. In all cases, even if exploratory A reading falls in range 0.20–0.80, develop color on another aliquot of nitrated sample as check.

Det. A of final soln at 600 nm and also take readings at 510 and 450 nm to det. if gross amts of interfering red or yellow are present. Obtain total DDT in aliquot from std curve and calc. total DDT in sample in ppm.

(**b**) *Applicable to extracts of fatty materials containing maximum of 3 g fat.*—Proceed as in (**a**), except use all of nitrated sample to develop color, and use 0–50 μg std curve method, **29.100**(**b**).

Dichlone (2,3-Dichloro-1,4-naphthoquinone) (Phygon®) (22)—Official Final Action

(Applicable to fresh fruits and vegetables)

29.103 ***Reagents***

(**a**) *Dichlone std soln.*—0.2 mg/mL. Dissolve and dil. 40 mg dichlone (Eastman Kodak Co. No. 3836, or equiv.) to 200 mL with benzene.

(**b**) *Dimethylamine.*—25% aq. soln (Eastman Kodak Co. P601 or equiv.).

(**c**) *Florisil.*—60/100 mesh, PR Grade, activated at 1250°F (Floridin Co.). Heat ≥4 hr at 130° and store in stoppered flasks in desiccator prior to use.

29.104 ***Preparation of Standard Curve***

Place 0, 1.00, 2.00, 3.00, 4.00, and 5.00 mL dichlone std soln in 25 mL g-s graduates and dil. each to 10 mL with benzene. To each graduate add isopropanol to 20 mL mark and mix. Add 1 mL 25% Me_2NH soln, dil. to 25 mL with isopropanol, and mix.

Read A of stds against blank in covered 1 cm cells at 495 nm, and plot A against mg dichlone (0–1.0 mg range). Color is stable >1 hr.

29.105 ***Preparation of Column***

Fill 15 × 300 mm chromatgc tube, fitted with fritted glass disk or glass wool plug, with Florisil to ca ⅓ its length. (No stopcock is required.) Prewet Florisil with 30 mL benzene.

29.106 ***Determination***

(*Caution: See* **51.011**, **51.039**, **51.040**, and **51.045**.)

Strip weighed sample (ca 1 kg) with 500 mL benzene by gently turning or tumbling 10 min in suitable container (ca 4 L; 1 gal.). (Avoid breaking plant tissue.) Drain benzene into 1 L flask thru folded paper (ca 32 cm) contg ca 50 g anhyd. Na_2SO_4.

Add 200 mL dried benzene strip soln to prepd chromatgc column. Discard benzene eluate. Elute dichlone from column with 100 mL acetone-benzene eluting mixt. (1+99). Collect eluate in beaker and evap. to ca 15 mL. (Do not let sample overheat or go to dryness.) Rinse sample into graduate and dil. to 20 mL with benzene. Develop color in 10 mL of this soln as in **29.104**.

mg Dichlone from std curve × 5 = ppm dichlone (for 1 kg sample).

If visible color is present in benzene eluate, simultaneously develop color in remaining 10 mL aliquot, omitting Me_2NH and adding 1 mL H_2O. Subtract this blank A from that of developed sample to correct for sample blank.

★ *O,O*-Dimethyl *S*-(4-Oxo-1,2,3-benzotriazin-3-(4H)-yl Methyl) Phosphorodithioate (Guthion®) (*23*)—Official First Action ★

(Applicable to cole-type crops and to apples, plums, peaches, grapes, apricots, and cherries.)

29.107

Guthion is extd from crop with acetone and reextd with $CHCl_3$ from acetone after diln with H_2O. Solv. is removed by evapn; residue is dissolved in isopropanol and cleaned up on chromatgc column. Guthion is hydrolyzed in alk. soln to anthranilic acid, which is diazotized and coupled with *N*-(1-naphthyl) ethylenediamine.2HCl to form colored compd. Omission of alk. hydrolysis reveals presence of interfering materials except Et homolog of Guthion. *See* **29.102–29.107**, 12th ed.

Dodine (Cyprex®) (Dodecylguanidine Acetate) (DDGA) (*24*)—Official Final Action

(Applicable to apples, peaches, pears, pecans, and strawberries)

29.108 ***Reagents***

(**a**) *Bromocresol purple soln.*—Recrystallize indicator-grade bromocresol purple from boiling toluene (ca 2 g/100 mL). Dissolve 0.4 g recrystd material in 75 mL 0.01*N* NaOH; if necessary, add addnl 0.01*N* NaOH to bring pH to 6.0–6.1. Filter, if necessary, and dil. to 500 mL with CO_2-free H_2O. Store in brown bottle.

(**b**) *Buffer soln.*—pH 5.5. Dissolve 15.2 g $Na_2HPO_4.7H_2O$ and 74.0 g $NaH_2PO_4.H_2O$ in CO_2-free H_2O and dil. to 1 L.

(**c**) *Dodecylguanidine acetate (DDGA) std solns.*—(*1*) *Stock soln.*—130 μg/mL. Dissolve 32.5 mg Ref. Std (available from American Cyanamid Co.) in MeOH and dil. to 250 mL with MeOH. (*2*) *Working soln.*—13 μg/mL. Dil. 25 mL aliquot stock soln to 250 mL with MeOH.

29.109 ***Preparation of Sample***

Grind sample in high-speed blender with MeOH-$CHCl_3$ (2+1) in ratio of 400 mL solv./100 g sample. Filter with suction thru 2 Whatman No. 1, or equiv., papers in buchner, and wash pulp with MeOH-$CHCl_3$ (2+1), using 100 mL/100 g sample. Det. vol. of ext and transfer portion equiv. to 50 g sample to 400 mL beaker.

29.110 ***Determination***

Add several glass beads and 1 mL HCl to beaker, and evap. to 50 mL on steam bath. Add 30 mL 30% NaCl soln and 100 mL MeOH. Cool, transfer to 500 mL separator, and ext *gently* with 50 mL CCl_4 by inverting separator 6–8 times. Let phases sep. and discard CCl_4 layer. Repeat with 50 mL CCl_4, inverting separator ca twice as many times. Discard CCl_4; then ext with 50 mL CCl_4, shaking gently 30 sec. Finally, ext with 50 mL CCl_4, shaking vigorously 1 min, and again discard CCl_4.

Adjust pH of soln to ca 5.5 with 4*N* NaOH (pH meter), and add 20 mL pH 5.5 buffer and 20 mL bromocresol purple soln. Readjust pH to 5.5 and ext complex with two 50 mL portions $CHCl_3$, shaking 2 min each time. Shake combined ext 30 sec with 25 mL pH 5.5 buffer, and transfer $CHCl_3$ layer to another separator. Shake 1 min with 25 mL pH 5.5 buffer, let stand 10 min, and transfer $CHCl_3$ to another separator. Shake with 20 mL 0.05*N* NaOH to remove all combined indicator and any org. acids which may persist. Recomplex dodecylguanidine (in $CHCl_3$ as free base) by shaking 3 min with 5 mL bromocresol purple soln and 20 mL pH 5.5 buffer. Wash $CHCl_3$ with three 15 mL portions pH 5.5 buffer, shaking 1 min each time. Transfer $CHCl_3$ to dry 250 mL separator and shake 2 min with 20 mL 0.05*N* NaOH, measured by pipet. Read *A* of indicator in aq. soln at 590 nm, using Beckman spectrophtr, or equiv. Obtain μg DDGA from std curve.

29.111 ***Preparation of Standard Curve***

Add 0.5, 1.0, 2.0, 3.0, 4.0, and 5.0 mL std soln to series of separators contg 100 mL MeOH, 50 mL H_2O, 30 mL 30% NaCl soln, 20 mL bromocresol purple soln, and 20 mL pH 5.5 buffer. Adjust pH of each soln to 5.5 and continue as in **29.110**, par. 2, beginning "... and ext complex with two 50 mL portions $CHCl_3$, shaking 2 min each time." Read *A* of each aq. soln at 590 nm and plot against μg DDGA. No blank correction is necessary for stds.

ppm DDGA = μg DDGA in aliquot/g sample in aliquot.

Ethylenethiourea (ETU)

Gas Chromatographic Method (25) *Official First Action*

(Applicable to potatoes, spinach, applesauce, and milk. *Caution: See* **51.056** and **51.066**.)

29.112 ***Apparatus***

(**a**) *Chromatographic tube.*—Glass, 300 × 22 (id) mm, with coarse fritted disk and Teflon stopcock.

(**b**) *Filter paper.*—Sharkskin (Arthur H. Thomas Co., or equiv.).

(**c**) *Gas chromatograph.*—With flame photometric detector (Meloy Laboratories, Inc., 6715 Electronic Dr, Springfield VA 22151, or equiv.) contg S filter and 1.8 m × 4 (id) mm coiled glass column packed with 5% Carbowax 20M plus 2.5% KOH (prepd in MeOH) on 80–100 mesh Chromosorb W(HP). Condition new column 2 days at 210°. Typical operating conditions—temps (°): column 180, injection port 185, detector 185; flow rates (mL/min): N carrier gas 60, O 15, air 125, H 200; electrometer sensitivity 1×10^{-9} amp full scale deflection with 1 mv recorder. Approx. retention time of S-butylated ETU under these conditions is 4 min; 12 ng gives ca 50% full scale deflection. Change glass wool plug in injection port daily before use, and clean out inside of column at injection port weekly.

(**d**) *High-speed blender.*—Waring Blendor, or equiv. (*Caution: See* **51.004**.)

(**e**) *Pipets.*—Disposable glass capillary pipets, 145 × 6 (id) mm (Arthur H. Thomas Co., or equiv.).

(**f**) *Rotary evaporator.*—Use with 150 mm ₮ 24/40 Vigreux column and place vac. release valve in line. (*Caution: See* **51.004**.)

(**g**) *Silanized glass wool.*—Applied Science Laboratories, Inc., or equiv.

29.113 ***Reagents***

(**a**) *Aluminum oxide.*—Fisher No. A-540, or equiv., 80–200 mesh, for chromatgc adsorption. (Available from Fisher Scientific Co. as "Alumina, Adsorption, Fisher.") Use as received.

(**b**) *1-Bromobutane.*—Fisher Scientific Co., or equiv. Redistil between 101 and 101.5°.

(**c**) *Diatomaceous earth.*—Celite 545. Do not acid-wash.

(**d**) *Eluant.*—4% alcohol in $CHCl_3$. Dil. 40 mL alcohol to 1 L with $CHCl_3$, and mix well.

(**e**) *Solvents.*—$CHCl_3$, MeOH, and toluene, distd in glass (*see* statement regarding solvs, **29.001**).

(**f**) *Ethylenethiourea std solns.*—(*1*) *Stock soln.*—10 μg ETU/mL. Transfer 100 mg ETU ref. std (available from Pesticide Reference Standards Section, Registration Division, Environ-

★ Surplus method—*see* inside front cover.

mental Protection Agency, 401 M St, SW, Washington, DC 20460) to 100 mL vol. flask, and dil. to vol. with H_2O. Pipet 1 mL this soln into another 100 mL vol. flask, and dil. to vol. with H_2O. Prep. fresh monthly. (*2*) *Working soln.*—2 μg ETU/mL. Pipet 10 mL stock soln into 50 mL vol. flask, and dil. to vol. with H_2O. Prep. fresh weekly.

29.114 ***Extraction***

(Samples must be started and completed on same day.)

(**a**) *For crops, canned goods, and milk.*—Blend 100 g chopped crop (vegetables and fruits) or 100 g milk, 150 mL H_2O, 15 g NaCl, 10 g diat. earth, (**c**), and 200 mL MeOH in high-speed blender 2 min. Filter with vac. thru 1.3 cm bed of diat. earth spread dry and evenly on 9 cm double sharkskin filter paper in 91 mm (id) buchner. Transfer 87 mL (20 g) aliquot to previously weighed 500 mL ₮ 24/40 r-b flask. Add 50–70 mL MeOH, insert Vigreux column into flask, and conc. on rotary vac. evaporator immersed in 60–65° H_2O bath. If substantial initial frothing occurs, add 4–5 drops octanol. If much frothing occurs during last stages of concn, add addnl 4–5 drops octanol, 25 mL alcohol, or both. Conc. to ca 10 g. Disconnect flask, weigh, and add enough H_2O to bring wt to 13 g. Proceed immediately as in **29.115**.

(**b**) *Optional extraction for crops.*—(Applicable when presence of parent ethylenebisdithiocarbamate (EBDC) fungicide is suspected in sample. Provides measure of potential ETU residues which may be converted from EBDCs in home cooking.) Place 100 g chopped crop, 150 mL H_2O, and 1 mL NH_4OH in 1 L beaker, and record total wt. Cover with large watch glass, place on 600–720 watt hot plate turned to high, and heat 15 min, reducing heat to low after initial boiling. Cool, remove watch glass, and reweigh. Add H_2O to beaker to restore to original wt. Transfer quant. to high-speed blender, using 200 mL MeOH. Add 10 g diat. earth, (**c**), and blend 20 sec. Proceed as in (**a**), beginning "Filter with vac. thru 1.3 cm bed . . .", except conc. sample to ca 8 g and add H_2O to bring wt to 10 g. Proceed immediately as in **29.115**.

(**c**) *Optional extraction for milk.*—(Applicable when presence of parent EBDC fungicide is suspected in sample.) Place 100 g milk, 25 mL H_2O, 5 g NaCl, and 1 mL NH_4OH in 1 L beaker, and record total wt. Proceed as in (**b**), beginning "Cover with large watch glass, . . ." except use 275 mL MeOH, stir thoroly 1 min, and, after filtering, transfer 80 mL (20 g) aliquot to r-b flask. Proceed immediately as in **29.115**.

29.115 ***Cleanup***

Add 10 g Gas-Chrom S to sample ext, stopper, and shake vigorously until lump-free (30–60 sec), tapping on cork ring, if necessary. Add 50 mL eluant, (**d**), stopper, and shake 1–2 min. Pour mixt., including as much of Gas-Chrom S as possible, into chromatgc tube, **29.112**(**a**), contg 4–5 g Al_2O_3, (**a**), held in place with 1.3 cm glass wool plug. Rinse flask with 3 addnl 50 mL portions eluant, adding each rinse to tube. Collect eluate in 500 mL ₮ 24/40 r-b flask contg 10 mL H_2O and 20 mL alcohol. Conc. eluate to ca 20 mL using rotary vac. evaporator with Vigreux column. Add 5 mL H_2O and 20 mL alcohol, and conc. to 10 mL to eliminate $CHCl_3$. Rinse column and flask with 5 mL H_2O followed by 20 mL alcohol. Proceed immediately as in **29.116**.

29.116 ***Derivatization***

(**a**) *Sample.*—To sample flask add 1.5 g KOH, 2 mL l-bromobutane, (**b**), and 5–6 boiling chips. Reflux on pre-heated hot plate 10 min, using cold H_2O condenser and clamp to support flask. Cool, and transfer quant. to 250 mL separator with 10 mL H_2O followed by 50–60 mL $CHCl_3$. Shake 1–2 min, and let layers sep. completely (ca 5 min). Collect lower $CHCl_3$ layer in clean 250 mL ₮ 24/40 r-b flask. Add 2 drops HCl and evap. to near dryness on rotary vac. evaporator, using Vigreux column and 60–65° H_2O bath. Rinse neck of flask with 2–3 mL MeOH, and evap. again on rotary evaporator. Remove flask and evap. to dryness, using air jet for 2–3 min. *All MeOH must be removed by this final evapn or it will interfere with GLC detn.* Remove flask from air jet, pipet in 1 mL toluene and add 1.0–1.5 mL 10% KOH, stopper, and shake 1–2 min. Remove 0.5–0.7 mL of toluene layer with disposable pipet, (**e**), without collecting any of lower aq. layer. Place toluene sample ext in clean, dry calibrated test tube, and record vol. At this point, 1 mL ext is equiv. to 20 g sample. However, if final ext is dild for GLC, vol. recorded with respect to original 1 mL toluene must be used for sample wt. calcns:

Wt sample in final diln =

[(vol. obtained from 1 mL)/(1 mL toluene)] × 20 g

Do not conc. sample ext at this point due to volatility of butyl derivative of ETU.

(**b**) *Standard.*—Pipet 1 mL ETU working std soln into 500 mL ₮ 24/40 r-b flask. Add 15 mL H_2O, 20 mL alcohol, 1.5 g KOH, 2 mL l-bromobutane, and 5-6 boiling chips, and proceed as in (**a**), beginning "Reflux on preheated hot plate . . ."

29.117 ***Determination***

Initially, inject 4–6 μL std ext, **29.116**(**b**), into gas chromatograph, and then inject 5 μL sample ext, **29.116**(**a**). Adjust injection vol. of sample ext until peak hts of std and sample are approx. equal, and continue with alternate injections of sample and std. (S detector is non-linear; therefore, do not prep. std curve.)

$$\text{ETU, ppm} = (PH/PH') \times (W'/W),$$

where PH = peak ht of sample, PH' = peak ht of std, W' = ng ETU in std aliquot, and W = mg sample represented by sample aliquot.

29.118 ***Regeneration of Gas-Chrom S***

Shake all used Gas-Chrom S from cleanup column, **29.115**, into large beaker or flask. Discard Al_2O_3 and glass wool plug. Wash thoroly with H_2O, and decant after each wash. Wash thoroly with MeOH, decant, and vac. dry in large buchner. Air dry in hood and transfer to 80° oven overnight. Gas-Chrom S may now be re-used.

2-Heptadecyl Glyoxalidine Acetate (Glyodin) (*26*)—Official Final Action

(Applicable to apples and pears. Not applicable to fruits with extensive softening or decomposition. All glassware must be free of soap or detergent.)

29.119 ***Reagents***

(**a**) *Bromophenol blue soln.*—Prep. just before use. Transfer 50 mg bromophenol blue powder into 500 mL vol. flask with small amt of H_2O. Add 2 mL HOAc and swirl until dye is completely dissolved. Dil. to vol. with H_2O, and mix.

(**b**) *Glyodin std solns.*—Prep. from 2-heptadecyl glyoxalidine, purified grade (available from ICN-K&K Laboratories). (*1*) *Stock soln.*—1 mg/mL. Dissolve 100.0 mg 2-heptadecyl glyoxalidine in $CHCl_3$ in 100 mL vol. flask, dil. to vol. with $CHCl_3$, and mix. (*2*) *Working soln.*—0.05 mg free base/mL. Transfer 5.0 mL stock soln to 100 mL vol. flask, dil. to vol. with $CHCl_3$, and mix.

29.120 ***Preparation of Standard Curve***

Add 0, 2, 4, 6, 8, and 10 mL working std soln to six 50 mL vol. flasks. Add exactly 1 mL HOAc to each flask and dil. to vol. with

$CHCl_3$. Place 25 mL of each std, measured in graduate or fast-flow pipet, in 125 mL separator. Add 25 mL bromophenol blue soln, (**a**), from graduate or fast-flow pipet to each separator, and shake vigorously 1 min. Let sep. ≥20 min. Filter $CHCl_3$ layer thru pledget of glass wool in stem of separator into small g-s erlenmeyer. Det. *A* at 415 nm in spectrophtr, using 1 cm cells and 0 std as ref. Plot *A* against mg 2-heptadecyl glyoxalidine.

29.121 ***Preparation of Sample***

Fill tared wide-mouth gal. (3.8 L) glass jar with whole fruit so that little or no slack is present (to prevent battering of fruit). Weigh, and add 250 mL isopropanol. Screw cap on tightly with double thickness of cellophane placed over mouth of jar before cap is screwed on to help prevent leakage. Tumble or shake 10 min. Filter into 500 mL vol. flask thru small layer of glass wool in funnel. Drain off as much liq. as possible. Repeat stripping with second 250 mL portion of isopropanol, and filter into vol. flask. Wash glass wool and funnel with small portions of isopropanol and dil. to vol.

29.122 ***Determination***

Transfer 25 mL aliquot of strip soln to 50 mL beaker and evap. to dryness on steam bath under air jet. To residue add exactly 1 mL HOAc, allowing acid to drip slowly down sides of beaker so that all residue is wetted. Cover beaker with watch glass and heat gently on steam bath with swirling, until residue at bottom loosens and disintegrates. Thoroly rinse down sides with few mL $CHCl_3$ and transfer to 50 mL vol. flask. Rinse beaker with 4 addnl small portions $CHCl_3$, and transfer to vol. flask. Dil. to vol. with $CHCl_3$ (disregard turbidity and slight color in soln).

Transfer 25 mL $CHCl_3$ soln, measured in graduate or fast-flow pipet, to 125 mL separator. Proceed as in **29.120**, beginning, "Add 25 mL bromophenol blue soln, (**a**), . . ."

Perform detns along with prepn of std curve, using 0 std as ref. when detg sample *A*. Det. amt of 2-heptadecyl glyoxalidine in aliquot from std curve.

Glyodin (2-heptadecyl glyoxalidine acetate) = 2-heptadecyl glyoxalidine × 1.195.

Hexachlorobenzene (HCB) and Mirex in Fatty Products (*27*)—Official Final Action

29.123 ***Reagents***

(**a**) *Solvents.*—Hexane, methylene chloride, acetonitrile, and pet ether. *See* **29.002**.

(**b**) *Florisil.*—60–100 mesh PR grade. (*1*) *Unactivated, for partition chromatography.*—Use as received from manufacturer. (*2*) *Activated.*—*See* **29.002(i)**.

(**c**) *Eluant mixture.*—For Florisil column cleanup. Dil. 200 mL CH_2Cl_2 with hexane. Let reach room temp. and adjust to 1 L with hexane.

29.124 ***Apparatus***

(**a**) *Gas chromatograph.*—With electron capture detector. *See* **29.008(a)** and (**c**).

(**b**) *Column.*—1.85 m × 4 (id) mm glass column with 80–100 mesh Chromosorb W (HP) support, N flow 120 mL/min, and injection temp. 220°. For HCB analysis, use 15% OV-210 substrate; for Mirex, 3% OV-101. For HCB, use column temp. 180°, detector, 200°; for Mirex, use column temp. 210°, detector 220°. Operate ^3H electron capture detector at dc voltage which produces half scale deflection for 0.5 ng HCB or Mirex when electrometer sensitivity is 1×10^{-9} amp. Or, operate ^{63}Ni detector to produce stable, reproducible, linear response and adjust amt of injected sample, **29.018**, to accomodate difference in instrument sensitivity.

(**c**) *Chromatographic tubes.*—(*1*) *Plain.*—250 × 22 (id) mm. (*2*) *With stopcocks.*—*See* **29.005(b)**.

(**d**) *Kuderna-Danish concentrators.*—*See* **29.005(e)**.

(**e**) *Micro-Vigreux Column.*—See **29.005(h)**. Use for concn to vols < 5 mL.

29.125 ***Extraction of Fat***

Ext ≥3 g fat as in **29.012**. For products reported on fat basis, use 3 g fat. For products reported on as-is basis, record wt, *W*, of fat extd. Corresponding wt sample analyzed = (wt fat taken for cleanup/W) × wt original sample.

29.126 ***Cleanup***

(*Caution: See* **51.043** and **51.073**.)

Weigh 3 g fat into 250 mL beaker, add 20 g unactivated Florisil, and stir with spatula or glass rod until free-flowing powder is obtained. Place glass wool plug in bottom of plain chromatgc tube and add 3 g unactivated Florisil. Completely transfer fat-Florisil mixt. to tube. Settle column by repeatedly tapping tube. Place glass wool plug on top of Florisil. Place 1 L separator under column as receiver. Elute with 150 mL CH_3CN by gravity.

When elution is complete, add exactly 100 mL pet ether to separator, and shake vigorously 1–2 min. Add 10 mL satd NaCl soln and 500–600 mL H_2O, and shake vigorously 1 min. Let sep. and discard aq. (lower) layer. Wash pet ether with two 100 mL portions H_2O. Discard washings, transfer pet ether to 100 mL g-s graduate, and record vol., *P*. Calc.

Wt sample in eluate = (wt sample taken for cleanup × *P*/100, where 100 = mL pet ether added.

Complete cleanup on column of activated Florisil, **29.015**, using amt Florisil detd from lauric acid test, **29.002(i)**. Sample ext must be dry and free from polar solvs when placed on column. Elute at ca 5 mL/min with 200 mL eluant mixt., (**c**), and conc. Det HCB and Mirex as in **29.018**, using column, **29.124(b)**.

★ Malathion ★
(S-[1,2-bis(Ethoxycarbonyl)ethyl] O,O-Dimethyl Phosphorodithioate)

29.127 ***Multiple Residue Methods***

See **29.001–29.028**, **29.044–29.049**, and **29.050–29.054**.

29.128 ★ ***Colorimetric Method (28)—Official First Action*** ★

(Applicable to residues on surface of fruits and vegetables)

Malathion is extd with either CCl_4 or mixt. of CCl_4 and isopropanol and decomposed by alkali in CCl_4-alcohol soln into Na *O,O*-dimethyl phosphorodithioate, Na fumarate, and alcohol. Na *O,O*-dimethyl phosphorodithioate is converted to cupric salt which is sol. in CCl_4 with formation of intense yellow color. Color intensity is proportional to concn of *O,O*-dimethyl phosphorodithioic acid and is measured photometrically at 418 nm. *See* **29.116–29.120**, 12th ed.

Maleic Hydrazide (*29*)—Official Final Action

(Applicable to whole, dehydrated mashed, and frozen french fried potatoes, and potato chips; whole cranberries, onions, and peaches; and tobacco dust)

29.129 ***Principle***

Sample is boiled in alk. soln to drive off volatile basic interferences. Distn with Zn with N sweep expels hydrazine

★ Surplus method—*see* inside front cover.

liberated from maleic hydrazide. Hydrazine is reacted in acid soln with *p*-dimethylaminobenzaldehyde to form yellow compd.

29.130 ***Apparatus***

(**a**) *Distillation apparatus.—See* Fig. **29:08**. Flask is 300 mL capacity, flat-bottom, double thickness, with thermometer well. Thermometer is 90–220° (Tinius Olsen No. 718636 "Yellow Bak," or equiv. in temp. range and length; available on special order from Accuracy Scientific Instrument Co., 335 E Chew Ave, Philadelphia, PA 19120). Use 5" wire gauze with 4" diam. asbestos center. Centrf. tube receiver (50 mL) is graduated in 1 mL divisions.

(**b**) *Spectrophotometer.*—Beckman Model DU, or equiv.

29.131 ***Reagents***

(**a**) *p-Dimethylaminobenzaldehyde soln.*—Dissolve 2 g in 100 mL 1*N* H_2SO_4. Soln is stable.

(**b**) *Zn granules.*—"10 mesh."

(**c**) *Maleic hydrazide std soln.*—10 μg/mL. Dissolve 0.0100 g maleic hydrazide in 100 mL 0.1*N* NaOH and dil. to 1 L. Soln is stable.

29.132 ***Preparation of Sample***

Grind sample to soup-like consistency in high-speed blender, adding measured wt of H_2O if necessary. Prepd samples may be frozen for storage.

29.133 ***Determination***

Transfer 2 g ground sample to 300 mL distn flask. Dry socket neck joint, and add 50 g NaOH pellets, 1 mL *refined vegetable oil*, as anti-foaming agent, and 40 mL H_2O. Add 1 mL high bp oil to thermometer well and insert thermometer. Heat flask on high-temp. hot plate and swirl ca every 20 sec until pellets dissolve and gentle boiling begins. When temp. reads 160°, remove flask and let cool 5 min. Wipe socket joint clean and dry; add 0.5 g *ferrous chloride* and 5 mL (equiv. to ca 5 g) Zn.

Quickly grease socket joint with light film of high-vac. silicone grease and attach flask to app. (Fig. **29:08**). Center flask firmly on asbestos pad. Place 4 mL *p*-dimethylaminobenzaldehyde soln in 50 mL centrf. tube (ice-cooled) and immerse condenser tip. Adjust N flow (*dry N*) to 3 bubbles/sec in receiver. With rapid flow of condenser H_2O, heat flask with Bunsen burner, centering tip of outer cone of flame on asbestos pad. When boiling begins, adjust distance of burner so foaming contents fill ca ⅔ of flask. Distil until temp. reads 173°, *slowly* add H_2O from reservoir until temp. drops to 168°, turn off H_2O, and distil to 173°. Continue H_2O addn and distn at these temps until receiver contains ca 40 mL. Remove receiver. (If during distn receiver soln becomes turbid or ppt appears, add 2 drops H_2SO_4 and shake.)

Record vol. of distillate and det. *A* at 430, 460, and 490 nm, using 1 cm cells and 4 mL *p*-dimethylaminobenzaldehyde soln dild to 40 mL as ref.

After distn, remove hot distg flask from app. with heat-resistant gloves, remove thermometer, and seal well with small cork. Rinse N-H_2O inlet tube free of caustic with HCl from plastic squeeze bottle followed by H_2O. Then (with gloves and safety glasses) pour molten contents of distg flask into Fe can in sink to trap Zn granules. Rinse flask 3 times with H_2O and 2 times with HCl to remove encrusted caustic and Zn granules. Fill flask with HCl (1+9) to remain until next use. Rinse 3 times with H_2O before reuse. (Careful removal of *all* Zn granules with HCl is essential because residual Zn would cause premature destruction of maleic hydrazide in precook of next sample. Because of corrosion by the caustic soln, flasks may last for only ca 30 detns.)

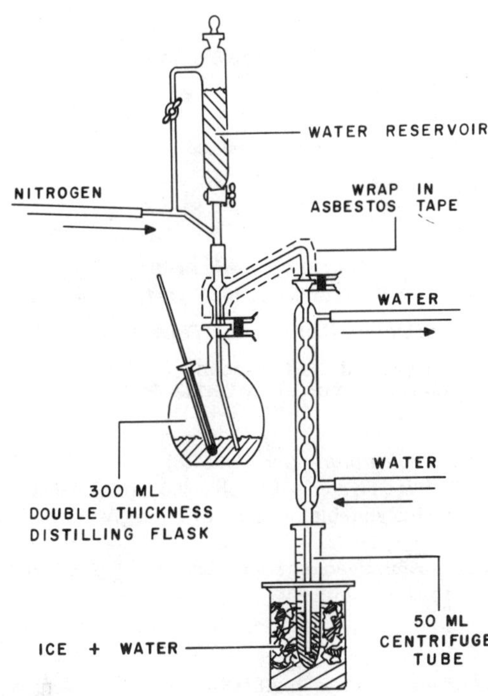

FIG. 29:08—Distillation apparatus for maleic hydrazide determination

29.134 ***Preparation of Standard Curve***

To clean 300 mL distn flasks, add 50 g NaOH pellets, 40 mL H_2O, and std soln equiv. to 0, 5, 10, 20, 30, 50, 100, 150, and 200 μg maleic hydrazide. Precook, distil, and measure *A* as in **29.133**. Det. ΔA for each std as follows:

$$\Delta A = [A_{460} - ((A_{430} + A_{490})/2)] \times \text{mL color soln}/40.$$

Plot ΔA of each std against μg maleic hydrazide to obtain std curve. If desired, derive simple factor from curve slope, *K*, converting ΔA to μg maleic hydrazide; thus, μg maleic hydrazide $= \Delta A \times K$.

29.135 ***Calculations***

Multiply ΔA of sample by *K* to derive μg maleic hydrazide; ppm = μg/sample wt (g).

Methoxychlor (2,2-Bis(*p*-Methoxyphenyl)-1,1,1-Trichloroethane)

29.136 ***Multiple Residue Methods***

See **29.001–29.028.**

29.137 ★ ***Colorimetric Method (30)*** ★ ***Official Final Action***

(Applicable to fruits and vegetables)

Pet ether soln of ext of sample is extd with CH_3CN to sep. methoxychlor from fats and plant waxes. Methoxychlor in concd ext is dehalogenated and converted by alk. hydrolysis to dehydrochloride, which is sepd by pet ether extn and reacted with 85% H_2SO_4 to produce red soln. *See* **24.149–24.152**, 10th ed. (*Caution: See* **51.011**, **51.039**, and **51.073**.)

★ Surplus method—*see* inside front cover.

Mirex

29.138 ***Multiple Residue Methods***

See **29.001–29.018**.

29.139 ***HCB and Mirex***

See **29.123–29.126**.

Monofluoroacetic Acid (Sodium Salt, "1080") (*31*)

Qualitative Test—Official Final Action

(Monochloroacetic acid also responds to this test. Confirm presence of org. F by **29.142–29.148**.)

29.140 ***Reagents***

(**a**) *Decolorizing carbon*.—*See* **16.027**(**b**).

(**b**) *Thiosalicylic acid soln*.—Dissolve 300 mg thiosalicylic acid (Eastman P2805 is suitable) in mixt. of 2 mL 1*N* NaOH and 18 mL H_2O.

(**c**) *Potassium ferricyanide soln*.—Dissolve 1 g $K_3Fe(CN)_6$ in H_2O and dil. to 50 mL with H_2O.

29.141 ***Test***

Prep. sample and ext as in **29.145–29.146**. If convenient, ext large enough sample to obtain 2–10 mg 1080. With very low levels of 1080, *e.g.*, 1–5 ppm, ext large enough sample to obtain ≥0.5 mg 1080.

Sep. ether ext from any aq. sludge which may have been carried over in extn, add ca 5 g anhyd. Na_2SO_4 and 0.5 g decolorizing C/100 mL ether, and shake vigorously. Let stand ca 15 min at room temp. with occasional shaking, and decant thru fluted paper into separator. Add ca 25 mL H_2O and enough NaOH soln (ca 1*N*) to make aq. layer alk. after vigorous shaking (outside test paper). Drain aq. layer into 125 mL erlenmeyer and aerate to remove dissolved ether. Using pH test paper and ca 1*N* solns of H_2SO_4 and NaOH, adjust to pH 4–6. Add 0.5 g C and place on steam bath for 15 min.

Cool under tap and filter thru fluted paper into ca 25 × 150 mm test tube. Add 1 mL thiosalicylic acid soln and 2 drops NaOH (1+1), and mix. Conc. soln to small vol. by placing on steam bath under gentle air current. Completely dry residue in oven at 130° or, if time is not factor, in 100° oven. (When convenient, overnight drying is satisfactory, with or without prior concn of soln.)

Dissolve *thoroly* dry residue in 2–3 mL H_2O, add 1 mL $K_3Fe(CN)_6$ soln, and mix. Red ppt, which forms at once when ≥1 mg 1080 is present, or upon standing when only fraction of mg is present, is pos. test for 1080.

Employ chromatgc instead of C purification in following cases:

(*1*) With pineapple juice when <2 mg 1080 can be extd.

(*2*) With grape juice even when ≥2 mg of 1080 can be conveniently extd.

(*3*) With any food or material when 1080 is strongly suspected and neg. test is obtained using C purification technic.

For chromatgc purification, follow **29.147** for sepg 1080 from other acids. Discard forerun, which may contain HOAc and other extraneous materials. Collect fraction large enough to contain all the 1080 as detd by preliminary detn. Ext fluoroacetic acid from eluate with 25 mL H_2O and enough alkali to cause aq. layer to retain alky after vigorous shaking (outside test paper). Drain org. layer and discard. Drain aq. layer into 125 mL erlenmeyer and aerate to remove $CHCl_3$. Pour soln into test tube and continue as above, beginning "Add 1 mL thiosalicylic acid soln . . ."

Quantitative Method—Official Final Action

29.142 ***Principle***

After suitable sample prepn, acid is extd with ether and sepd from inorg. fluorides (partially ether-sol.) by partition chromatgy on silicic acid, using 0.5*N* H_2SO_4 as immobile solv. and $CHCl_3$ contg 10% *tert*-amyl alcohol or *n*-BuOH as mobile solv. Monofluoroacetic acid in eluate is converted to its Na salt, and quantity is detd by micro F detn, **25.053**(**a**), **25.054**, and **25.055**.

29.143 ***Apparatus***

(**a**) *Chromatographic tubes*.—18 mm od × 250 mm long, prepd from Pyrex tubing.

(**b**) *Pressure source*.—Compressed air or cylinder of N or CO_2, and means of keeping pressure const, such as Hg column or diaphragm-type pressure regulator.

(**c**) *Mixer*.—High-speed blender.

29.144 ***Reagents***

(**a**) *Silicic acid*.—Mallinckrodt analytical reagent grade pptd powder, or equiv.

(**b**) *Mobile solvent*.—Add 100 mL *tert*-amyl alcohol or *n*-BuOH to 900 mL $CHCl_3$, and mix.

(**c**) *Phosphotungstic acid soln*.—Dissolve 20 g in H_2O and dil. to 100 mL.

29.145 ***Preparation of Sample***

This will vary with type of material. Dissolve sugars in H_2O, acidify with H_2SO_4, and ext directly. Following methods for different type materials will be suggestive. Simple H_2O wash may be adequate to prove contamination of certain foods.

(**a**) *Sugar*.—Dissolve 100 g sample in enough H_2O to give ca 350 mL.

(**b**) *Flour*.—Place 100 g sample in mixer, add 400 mL H_2O and 5 g *pancreatin*, and comminute ca 2 min. Adjust to pH 7–8, using *satd* $Na_3PO_4.12H_2O$ *soln* and suitable indicator paper. Transfer comminuted material to tared 1 L erlenmeyer, washing mixer with three 25 mL portions H_2O. Incubate mixt. ≥3 hr at 35–40°. Add 5 mL H_2SO_4 (1+1) and swirl. Add 20 mL phosphotungstic acid soln and swirl again. Dil. to 750 g with H_2O, stopper, and shake vigorously ca 2 min. Filter thru fluted paper or with suction thru buchner (16 cm size is convenient). Or, more quickly, centrf. and decant supernate. Use ≥375 g aliquot of filtrate. (Since sp gr of filtrate is very close to 1, measuring out aliquot in graduate is satisfactory.)

(**c**) *Wheat*.—Finely grind sample in suitable mill, such as Wiley mill. Proceed as in (**b**).

(**d**) *Corn meal*.—Proceed as in (**b**), except omit pancreatic digestion.

(**e**) *Corn*.—Grind sample and proceed as in (**d**).

(**f**) *Peanuts*.—Grind sample finely (like peanut butter) and proceed as in (**d**), except use 100 mL phosphotungstic acid soln. If necessary, refilter thru folded paper to remove oil.

(**g**) *Cheese*.—Proceed as in (**d**), except use 40 mL phosphotungstic acid soln.

(**h**) *Other foods such as chili peppers, cacao beans, etc.*—Treat in manner similar to one of preceding foods.

(**i**) *Biological tissue*.—If material is tough or fibrous, grind it twice thru food chopper. (Soft tissues, *e.g.*, brain and liver, need not be ground.) Place 100 g ground tissue in 800 mL beaker, add ca 300 mL H_2O, cover with watch glass, and boil gently ca 30 min. Transfer material to mixer, rinsing beaker with two 25 mL portions H_2O, and comminute thoroly (ca 2 min). Transfer comminuted material to tared 1 L erlenmeyer, rinsing mixer with two 25 mL portions H_2O. Add 5 mL H_2SO_4 (1+1) and mix.

Add enough phosphotungstic acid soln (50–75 mL) to ppt all proteins, then H_2O to make 600 g. Shake vigorously ca 2 min, and filter thru fluted paper or with suction thru buchner. If material does not filter rapidly, return mixt. to flask, add ca 10 mL addnl phosphotungstic acid soln, shake vigorously, and refilter.

Alternative method.—Place 100 g ground tissue in mixer, add 300 mL H_2O and 15 g pancreatin, and comminute thoroly (ca 2 min). Adjust to ca pH 8 with *satd* $Na_3PO_4.12H_2O$ *soln*, using suitable indicator paper. Transfer comminuted material from mixer to tared erlenmeyer, washing mixer with two 25 mL portions H_2O and incubate ca 3 hr at 35–40°. Ppt proteins and make to wt as directed previously.

29.146 ***Extraction***

Transfer soln (of sugar) or wt-aliquot of protein-free filtrate (of protein-contg materials) to 200 mL continuous extractor, Fig. **16:02.** (Tube is 115–120 cm long and 33–34 mm od, side arm, attached ca 63 cm from bottom, is 15–16 mm od; and inner tube is 12–13 mm od flared at top to ca 25 mm diam.; 1.5 L extractors of this type have been used successfully. Extra coarse fritted filter tip on bottom end of inner tube aids in getting smaller droplets of extg solv.) For each 50 g soln, add 1 mL H_2SO_4 (1+1). Ext with ether until all fluoroacetic acid has been extd (detd by preliminary experiment; usually 3–4 hr with 400 mL extractor). Transfer ether ext to separator of appropriate size.

To extn flask add ca 20 mL H_2O, 2 drops phthln, and enough 1.0*N* NaOH from buret to give strong alk. color of indicator after swirling. Pour rinse soln into separator and add addnl alkali until alk. color of indicator persists in aq. phase after vigorous shaking. Record vol. alkali required. Drain aq. layer into 100 mL beaker and wash ether with two 10 mL portions H_2O, rinsing extn flask each time with the H_2O before pouring it into separator. Add washings to beaker. Carefully adjust alky of ext just to alk. color of phthln with 0.1*N* H_2SO_4 and NaOH solns. Evap. neutzd ext to dryness on steam bath (current of air hastens evapn). If during evapn alk. color of indicator should disappear, add just enough 0.1*N* NaOH to give alk. color again. Do not continue heating after residue is apparently dry. Slightly moist residue is permissible.

29.147 ***Chromatography***

To 5 g silicic acid, (**a**), in mortar, add max. amt of 0.5*N* H_2SO_4 that it will hold without becoming sticky (50–80% of its wt). Mix well with pestle; then add ca 35 mL of the mobile solv. and work up into smooth slurry. (If SiO_2 agglomerates in solv., too much H_2SO_4 was used.) Place small cotton plug in bottom of chromatgc tube and pour in slurry, tilting tube slightly to avoid air bubbles. Let silicic acid pack down under 2–10 lb (14–69 kPa) pressure applied thru gas pressure regulator. When excess solv. has drained thru (column firm and viscous enough to resist pouring when tipped), column is ready for use. In prepg column take care to avoid cracking or drying out of the gel caused by leaving pressure on after column packs down and all solv. sinks into gel.

To dry or slightly moist residue in 100 mL beaker add enough H_2SO_4 (1+1) (ca 18*N*), usually 0.5–1.0 mL, to give excess of ca 0.25 mL over vol. necessary to convert all salts to free acid, as calcd from amt of 1*N* NaOH required to neutze acid extd by the ether. Wet salts *thoroly* with the acid, using small, narrow blade spatula (steel or Monel metal) to loosen salts from glass, and using flat-end glass rod to break up solid particles and mix resulting slurry. Add 5–10 g anhyd. granular Na_2SO_4 to take up excess liq. Stir well with tamping rod, breaking up any lumps. Add 10 mL mobile solv., (**b**), stir thoroly, and decant solv. carefully onto column.

Catch eluate in graduate. Apply pressure until all solv. sinks into gel; then release pressure. Add 5 mL mobile solv. to beaker and again stir thoroly. Carefully decant solv. onto column and, with aid of narrow-blade spatula, transfer bulk of material in beaker, mostly Na_2SO_4, to column. Renew pressure. When solv. passes ca halfway thru Na_2SO_4, release pressure. Rinse out beaker with addnl 5 mL solv. and transfer to column. After this washing sinks ca halfway into Na_2SO_4, fill tube with mobile solv. and complete collection, under pressure, of enough eluate to obtain all monofluoroacetic acid, as detd by test run on silicic acid used (ca 50 mL). Collect dropwise; 3–4 mL/min is convenient rate.

Transfer eluate to 125 mL separator; add ca 20 mL H_2O and enough 1.0*N* NaOH to give alk. color of phthln (phthln is present in eluate and no further addn is required) in aq. phase, after vigorous shaking. Drain aq. layer into 125 mL erlenmeyer and return solv. layer to separator. Wash solv. with two 10 mL portions H_2O and add washings to erlenmeyer. Aerate soln with current of air to remove traces of $CHCl_3$. (If excess $CHCl_3$ is not removed, excessive Cl may complicate F distn in next step.)

29.148 ***Determination***

Transfer aq. ext to Pt dish with little H_2O and mix with ca 20 mL lime suspension, **25.049**(**a**), evap. to *dryness*, and ash 15–20 min at 600°. (Little C in ash will not interfere in detn.) Proceed as in **25.053**(**a**), beginning "When clean ash is obtained, . . ." and **25.054–25.055** (100 mL Nessler tubes are preferable). Convert F results to fluoroacetic acid (× 4.11) or to Na monofluoroacetate (1080) (× 5.26) as desired, and correct for aliquot taken, if any, in extn. Ignore vol. occupied by insol. solids.

Naphthaleneacetic Acid (NAA) (*32*)
Official Final Action

(Applicable to apples and potatoes)

29.149 ***Apparatus***

(**a**) *Spectrophotometer.*—Cary 15 (current Model Cary 219, Varian Instruments), or equiv., with 5 cm cells.

(**b**) *Chromatographic tube.*—Glass, 22 mm id × 200 mm.

(**c**) *Food chopper.*—Hobart No. 84141 (Hobart Manufacturing Co., 711 Pennsylvania Ave, Troy, OH 45373), or equiv.

(**d**) *Blender cups.*—Stainless steel, 1 L capacity, with air-tight screw cover (Scientific Products, Inc. No. S8390) for high-speed blender.

29.150 ***Reagents***

(**a**) *Sodium phosphate soln.*—0.5*M*. 134 g $Na_2HPO_4.7H_2O$ or 70.5 g anhyd. salt/L.

(**b**) *Permanganate soln.*—0.02*M*. 31.6 g $KMnO_4$/L.

(**c**) *Florisil.*—60–100 mesh PR grade activated at 675° (1250°F) (Floridin Co.); use as received.

(**d**) *Naphthyleneacetic acid* (*NAA*) *soln.*—0.1 mg α-NAA/mL $CHCl_3$.

29.151 ***Extraction***

Chop sample in food chopper and transfer 200 g to blender cup. Add 20 mL 1*N* H_2SO_4 and 400 mL $CHCl_3$, screw top on blender, and blend 2 min at low speed. Pour mixt. into 500 mL centrf. bottle and centrf. 10 min at 1600 rpm. Take 200 mL aliquot from $CHCl_3$ layer.

29.152 ***Cleanup***

(**a**) *Apples*.—Place glass wool plug into chromatgc tube, add 10 cm Florisil, and top Florisil with glass wool plug. Transfer 200 mL $CHCl_3$ ext to column with min. amt $CHCl_3$. Rinse inside of tube twice with ca 5 mL $CHCl_3$. Elute column, in order, with 100 mL portions of CH_3CN, ether, NH_3-satd $CHCl_3$, and $CHCl_3$ and discard eluates. Using 500 mL separator as receiver, elute NAA with 100 mL 1% HOAc in $CHCl_3$ followed by 100 mL $CHCl_3$. Discard column, add 50 mL 1*N* H_2SO_4 to separator, and shake vigorously.Transfer $CHCl_3$ layer to 250 mL separator contg 50 mL H_2O and shake vigorously. Transfer $CHCl_3$ layer to 250 mL separator contg exactly 50 mL 0.5*M* Na_2HPO_4, shake vigorously, and discard $CHCl_3$ layer.

(**b**) *Potatoes*.—Proceed as in (**a**). Add 2 mL 85% H_3PO_4 and 2 mL 0.02*M* $KMnO_4$ to separator contg Na_2HPO_4 phase, mix, and let stand exactly 5 min. Ext NAA with two 25 mL portions $CHCl_3$, transfer $CHCl_3$ exts to 125 mL separator contg exactly 50 mL 0.5*M* Na_2HPO_4, shake vigorously, and discard $CHCl_3$ layer.

29.153 ***Determination***

(**a**) *Apples*.—Transfer 1 mL NAA std soln to 125 mL separator, add exactly 50 mL 0.5*M* Na_2HPO_4 and 50 mL $CHCl_3$, and shake vigorously. Let layers sep. and discard $CHCl_3$ layer. Obtain UV spectra (230–330 nm) of cleaned up apple ext and NAA std ext, using 5 cm cells, against 0.5*M* Na_2HPO_4. Use peak at 283 nm to compare apple ext and NAA std ext, correcting for baseline *A*, and calc. ppm NAA present.

(**b**) *Potatoes*.—Transfer 1 mL NAA std soln to 125 mL separator, add 50 mL 0.5*M* Na_2HPO_4 and 50 mL $CHCl_3$, and shake vigorously. Let layers sep. and discard $CHCl_3$ layer. Add 2 mL 85% H_3PO_4 and 2 mL 0.02*M* $KMnO_4$ to separator, mix, and let stand exactly 5 min. Ext NAA with two 25 mL portions $CHCl_3$, transfer $CHCl_3$ exts to 125 mL separator contg exactly 50 mL 0.5*M* Na_2HPO_4, shake vigorously, let layers sep., and discard $CHCl_3$ layer. Obtain UV spectrum and calc. ppm NAA as in (**a**). (If there is excessive interference in sample spectra, repeat 5 min oxidn for both sample and std, beginning with "Add 2 mL 85% H_3PO_4 . . .")

Nicotine (*33*)—Official Final Action

(Applicable to apples, cabbage, and spinach)

29.154 ***Reagents***

(**a**) *Dilute hydrochloric acid*.—Approx. 0.05*N*. Dil. 4.1 mL HCl to 1 L.

(**b**) *Nicotine std solns*.—(*1*) *Stock soln*.—1 mg/mL. Dil. 100 mg nicotine (Eastman Kodak Co. No. 1242, or equiv.) to 100 mL in vol. flask with ca 0.05*N* HCl. (*Caution:* nicotine is very toxic.) (*2*) *Working soln*.—0.01 mg/mL. Pipet 1 mL stock soln into 100 mL vol. flask and dil. to vol. with ca 0.05*N* HCl.

(**c**) *Stripping soln*.—Dil. 20 mL NH_4OH to 2 L in vol. flask. Prep. at time of use.

Leafy Crops

29.155 ***Preparation of Sample***

(*Caution: See* **51.040**, **51.045**, and **51.056**.)

Weigh 500 g chopped sample (spinach, cabbage) into clean, dry jar (3–5 gal.; 11–20 L). Add 800 mL benzene, 200 mL $CHCl_3$, and 10 mL NH_4OH. Close, tumble or roll ca 10 min, and drain soln as completely as possible into 1 L beaker. Filter thru folded 38.5 cm paper into flask and proceed immediately with detn.

29.156 ***Determination***

Place 400 mL filtered soln in 500 mL separator. Add 25 mL ca 0.05*N* HCl and 2 mL HCl, and shake vigorously. Let phases sep. (ca 5 min) and drain lower layer into 250 mL separator. Swirl large separator, let stand ca 2 min, and drain any addnl ext into 250 mL separator. Repeat several times. Then ext soln with 25, 25, 15, and 10 mL portions ca 0.05*N* HCl, repeating swirling as above. Drain all acid exts into 250 mL separator. Make exts just alk. to litmus with 10% NaOH soln. Ext with two 50 mL and four 25 mL portions $CHCl_3$, combining exts in 250 mL separator.

Add 2 mL HCl to exts and make sure soln is acid to litmus. Ext with 25, 25, 20, 10, and 5 mL portions ca 0.05*N* HCl, combining all exts in short-stem 125 mL separator. Wash exts with 15 mL pet ether. Drain aq. layer into second 125 mL separator and wash pet ether with 5 mL ca 0.05*N* HCl, adding wash to combined acid soln. Ext soln with another 15 mL pet ether, drain aq. layer into 100 mL vol. flask, and wash pet ether with 5 mL ca 0.05*N* HCl. Drain acid into vol. flask and dil. to vol. with ca 0.05*N* HCl. Mix, pour portion into 50 mL beaker, and let stand 10–15 min. Det *A* at 236, 259, and 282 nm with ca 0.05*N* HCl as ref. Confirm presence of nicotine by reading at 2 nm intervals and plot absorption curve, or use recording spectrophtr. Det. *A* of std nicotine soln against ca 0.05*N* HCl as ref.

Waxy Crops

29.157 ***Preparation of Sample***

Weigh 2–2.5 kg apples into clean, dry, jar (3–5 gal.; 11–20 L). Add 1 L stripping soln, tumble or roll ca 10 min, and drain carefully into 1 L beaker. Filter thru folded 38.5 cm paper into flask and proceed immediately with detn.

29.158 ***Determination***

Place 400 mL filtered soln in 500 mL separator. Add 50 mL $CHCl_3$, invert separator back and forth gently ca 2 min, and let phases sep. Drain clear portion of ext into 250 mL separator. (With fruits, emulsions may form which are very hard to break. Break emulsions by drawing $CHCl_3$ layer into *dry* 125 mL separator and shaking vigorously. Separator must be dry.) Let phases sep. and drain clear portion into the 250 mL separator. Add 35 mL $CHCl_3$ to the 125 mL separator, shake gently, and drain into the 500 mL separator. Ext as above and combine clear ext in the 250 mL separator. Ext with 35, 35, and 10 mL $CHCl_3$, combining exts in the 250 mL separator. Add $\geq$1 mL HCl to exts until definitely acid to litmus. Then ext with three 15 mL portions ca 0.05*N* HCl, combining acid exts in a 125 mL separator. Wash the 250 mL separator with 10 mL ca 0.05*N* HCl after each extn and add to 125 mL separator used to break emulsions. Shake, but do not attempt to break any emulsions in this separator. Combine all acid exts in 125 mL separator and shake with 15 mL pet ether. Let stand ca 5 min and drain aq. layer into another 125 mL separator. Wash pet ether with 5 mL ca 0.05*N* HCl (do not shake vigorously) and add washings to separator. Repeat washing with 15 mL pet ether and drain aq. ext into 100 mL vol. flask. Wash pet ether as before, add washings to flask, and let stand 10–15 min. Dil. to vol. with ca 0.05*N* HCl and det. *A* at 236, 259, and 282 nm, against ca 0.05*N* HCl as ref. Confirm presence of nicotine as in **29.156**.

Take *A* of std soln as:

$$A_{std} = A'_{259} - 0.5(A'_{236} + A'_{282})$$

and *A* of sample soln as:

$$A_{samp.} = A_{259} - 0.5(A_{236} + A_{282}).$$

Then:

$$\text{mg Nicotine} = (A_{samp.}/A_{std}) \times 2.5.$$

Parathion

29.159 ***Multiple Residue Methods***

See **29.001–29.024**, **29.039–29.043**, **29.044–29.049**, and **29.050–29.054**.

29.160 ★ ***Colorimetric Method (34)*** ★
Official Final Action

Parathion is extd with benzene or isopropanol-benzene and the strip soln is clarified. Parathion is brought into aq. soln and simultaneously reduced to its amine with Zn-HCl. The amine is diazotized and coupled with N-(1-naphthyl)ethylenediamine to form colored compd. *See* **29.139–29.144**, 11th ed.

Piperonyl Butoxide (*35*)
Official Final Action

(Applicable to Alaska peas, barley, hulled rice, oats, pinto beans, and wheat)

29.161 ***Principle***

Strong H_2SO_4 liberates HCHO, which is detd colorimetrically with chromotropic acid.

29.162 ***Reagents***

(**a**) *Chromotropic acid reagent*.—Dissolve 100 mg Na 1,8-dihydroxynaphthalene-3,6-disulfonate/mL of H_2O, filter, and keep in dark. Prep. daily. (1 mL required for each detn.)

(**b**) *Dilute sulfuric acid*.—Carefully mix 5 vols H_2SO_4 with 3 vols H_2O. Cool to room temp. and store in tight g-s container.

(**c**) *Methanolic potassium hydroxide*.—Dissolve 1.4 g KOH in 5 mL H_2O and add 95 mL MeOH (HCHO-free).

(**d**) *Methanol*.—If necessary, purify as follows: Reflux 1 L MeOH 1 hr with ca 10 g powd Al and ca 10 g NaOH and distil ca 800–900 mL.

(**e**) *Hexane*.—Redistd.

(**f**) *Chloroform*.—Reagent or redistd (for wheat extn).

(**g**) *Piperonyl butoxide std solns*.—(*1*) *Stock soln*.—1 mg/mL. Dissolve 0.1000 g in 100 mL benzene. (*2*) *Intermediate soln*.—100 μg/mL. Dil. 10 mL stock soln to 100 mL with benzene. (*3*) *Working soln*.—20 μg/mL. Dil. 20 mL intermediate soln to 100 mL with benzene.

29.163 ***Preparation of Standard Curve***

Add 0, 20, 40, 60, 80, and 100 μg piperonyl butoxide, resp., to each of 6 g-s test tubes (15 × 150 mm) (25–50 mL g-s centrf. tubes are also satisfactory) and evap. on steam bath with small air jet. Evap. last 1–2 mL benzene without heat.

Into each tube pipet both 1 mL chromotropic acid reagent and 5 mL dil. H_2SO_4, (**b**). Stopper loosely and place tubes in beaker of boiling H_2O 45 min, remove, and cool in beaker of cold H_2O. When cool, pipet 5 mL H_2O into each test tube, mix well, and read *A* in spectrophtr at 575 nm against reagent blank prepd similarly. Plot μg piperonyl butoxide against *A*.

29.164 ***Determination***

Ext sample as in **29.098(c)**, using $CHCl_3$. With current of air, evap. 25 mL (or suitable size aliquot) ext in small beaker just to dryness. Add 5 mL methanolic KOH. Warm gently just enough to melt wax (do not boil). Let stand 30 min, swirling vigorously at ca 10 min intervals. Transfer to small separator, rinse beaker with two 5 mL portions H_2O, and add to separator. Add 15 mL hexane to separator, shake vigorously 1 min, and let sep. Drain aq. layer and discard. Quant. transfer hexane layer to g-s test tube or centrf. tube and evap. to dryness with air jet. Small amt of heat may be used, but evap. last 1–2 mL with air alone. (Warmth of hand at this point is enough.)

Into dried residue pipet both 1 mL chromotropic acid reagent and 5 mL of the dil. H_2SO_4. Swirl vigorously to ensure that reagent contacts all of sample and place test tube in boiling H_2O bath. Stopper tube, lightly at first and then tighten. After 45 min in H_2O bath, remove, and cool to room temp. in beaker of cold H_2O. Pipet in 5 mL H_2O, mix well, and measure *A* in spectrophtr at 575 nm against reagent blank prepd similarly. From std curve, calc. piperonyl butoxide in aliquot.

Thiram (Tetramethylthiuram Disulfide) (*36*)
Official Final Action

(Applicable to corn, apples, tomatoes, strawberries, celery, and similar fruits and vegetables)

29.165 ***Principle***

Thiram is extd from sample with $CHCl_3$. Treatment with solid CuI results in formation of brown, $CHCl_3$-sol. Cu dimethyldithiocarbamate, and its *A* is measured at 440 nm. Other commonly used pesticides do not interfere, with exception of metal dithiocarbamates sol. in $CHCl_3$, such as ferbam or ziram. Moderate amts of color, waxes, and other extd plant matter do not interfere.

29.166 ***Reagents***

(**a**) *Chloroform*.—Either reagent or tech. grade may be used.

(**b**) *Thiram std solns*.—(*1*) *Stock soln*.—500 μg/mL. Dissolve 50.0 mg thiram (available from E. I. du Pont de Nemours & Co., Biochemicals Dept., 1007 Market St, Wilmington, DE 19898) in $CHCl_3$ and dil. to 100 mL with $CHCl_3$. (*2*) *Working soln*.—25 μg/mL. Dil. 5 mL stock soln to 100 mL with $CHCl_3$.

(**c**) *Cuprous iodide*.—If not available, prep. as follows: To soln of 10 g $CuSO_4.5H_2O$ in ca 100 mL H_2O, slowly add excess of KI soln. Remove liberated I_2 by adding $Na_2S_2O_3$ soln in slight excess. Filter, and wash ppt thoroly with H_2O and with alcohol. Dry at room temp. and crush to fine powder.

(**d**) *Attapulgus clay*.—Available from MC/B Manufacturing Chemists, No. AX1799.

29.167 ***Apparatus***

(**a**) *Spectrophotometer*.—Suitable for measuring *A* in UV and at 440 nm.

(**b**) *Glassware*.—Avoid contamination by rinsing with $CHCl_3$ and drying before use. Rinse app. that may have contained CuI from previous detns with dil. acid, H_2O, alcohol, and $CHCl_3$.

29.168 ***Preparation of Standard Curve***

(To minimize errors due to evapn of solv., keep flasks closed as much as possible, and cover funnels with watch glasses during filtrations.)

Using buret, add 2.0, 5.0, 10.0, and 15.0 mL working std soln to 25 mL vol. flasks. Dil. to vol. with $CHCl_3$, and mix. Solns contain 2, 5, 10, and 15 μg thiram/mL, resp.

Transfer ca 10 mL portions of std solns to 125 mL g-s erlenmeyers, add 10 mg CuI to each, stopper, and let stand 1 hr with occasional mixing. Filter, using 9 cm quant. paper, and read *A* at 440 nm against $CHCl_3$ as ref. Plot *A* against thiram concn in μg/mL.

29.169 ***Isolation***

(Avoid contact of solv. with rubber.)

(**a**) *Corn*.—Ext 200 g by shaking with 100 mL $CHCl_3$ 5 min in 500 mL g-s erlenmeyer. Decant ext thru small funnel (to retain corn kernels) into flask.

★ Surplus method—*see* inside front cover.

(**b**) *Apples, pears, and similar firm fruits.*—Weigh 2–3 kg into clean, dry jar (ca 3 gal.; 11 L). Add 500 mL $CHCl_3$ and stopper with tight-fitting cork, wooden bung, or plastic screw cap faced with gasket of sheet cork or other suitable solv.-resisting material. Ext 5 min by tumbling or other agitation. Decant ext into flask.

(**c**) *Tomatoes, berries, and similar soft fruits and vegetables.*—Weigh 1–3 kg into suitable container. Add 500 mL $CHCl_3$ and stopper with solv.-resisting closure. Ext 5 min by gentle shaking and decant into g-s erlenmeyer thru loose plug of glass wool.

(**d**) *Celery.*—Cut 2–3 kg into 3–8 cm pieces. Mix thoroly and ext 500 g sample with 500 mL $CHCl_3$ as above.

Add anhyd. Na_2SO_4, ca 5 g/100 mL, to decanted ext. Stopper flask, shake 5 min, and filter thru folded Whatman No. 12, or equiv., paper.

29.170 ***Determination***

(Thiram in $CHCl_3$ soln, particularly in presence of plant extractives, may decompose. Make detns as soon as possible.)

Transfer ca 10 mL filtered ext to g-s erlenmeyer and develop color as in **29.168**, beginning "... add 10 mg CuI ..." As ref., use another portion of filtered ext., untreated with CuI. From std curve, obtain thiram concn in $\mu g/mL$. If developed color is too intense, dil. with $CHCl_3$, making similar diln of ref. ext, and multiply thiram value found by appropriate diln factor.

ppm Thiram = (μg thiram/mL) × mL $CHCl_3$ used for extn/g sample.

29.171 ***Qualitative Test***

Adjust concn of ext, **29.169**, if necessary, to 10–15 μg thiram/mL by evapn on steam bath or by diln with $CHCl_3$. Add 0.25–1.0 g Attapulgus clay, depending on color of ext, to 50 mL of adjusted ext in beaker. Mix well and filter thru Whatman No. 12 folded paper, or equiv. Transfer 25 mL filtrate to g-s erlenmeyer, add 0.2 mL ca 0.1*N* $AgNO_3$ to ppt thiram and other $CHCl_3$-sol. dithiocarbamates, stopper, and shake vigorously 30 sec. Add ca 1 g anhyd. Na_2SO_4 and shake 30 sec. Let settle, decant carefully into 1 cm quartz cell, and *use as ref. soln*, adjusting to 0 *A* at 350 nm. Det. UV absorption curve over range 250–350 nm on clarified and filtered ext untreated with $AgNO_3$. Thiram gives curve with plateau at 270–283 nm, dropping sharply after peaking at ca 283. Ferbam and ziram give characteristic curves distinguishable from thiram.

SELECTED REFERENCES

(*1*) JAOAC **42**, 734(1959); **44**, 171(1961); **46**, 186(1963); **48**, 668(1965); **49**, 460, 463, 468(1966); **50**, 430, 623, 1205(1967); **51**, 311, 666, 892(1968); **52**, 1280(1969); **53**, 152, 355, 1300(1970); **54**, 325, 525(1971); **55**, 284(1972); **56**, 721, 1015(1973); **59**, 169(1976); **61**, 282(1978).
(*2*) JAOAC **56**, 728(1973); **57**, 604(1974).
(*3*) JAOAC **40**, 999(1957).
(*4*) JAOAC **59**, 209(1976).
(*5*) JAOAC **56**, 957(1973); **57**, 518(1974).
(*6*) JAOAC **54**, 513(1971); **57**, 930(1974).
(*7*) JAOAC **51**, 662(1968).
(*8*) JAOAC **52**, 811(1969).
(*9*) JAOAC **47**, 272(1964).
(*10*) Analyst **99**, 570(1974).
(*11*) JAOAC **56**, 713(1973); **58**, 562(1975).
(*12*) Anal. Chem. **24**, 544(1952); JAOAC **39**, 700 (1956).
(*13*) JAOAC **41**, 560(1958).
(*14*) JAOAC **50**, 934(1967).
(*15*) JAOAC **42**, 534(1959).
(*16*) JAOAC **40**, 219(1957); **46**, 143, 241(1963).
(*17*) JAOAC **47**, 283(1964); **48**, 676(1965).
(*18*) JAOAC **51**, 679(1968).
(*19*) JAOAC **41**, 572(1958).
(*20*) JAOAC **55**, 1042(1972); **56**, 721(1973).
(*21*) Ind. Eng. Chem., Anal. Ed. **15**, 383(1943); **17**, 704(1945); **19**, 51, 54(1947); JAOAC **29**, 112, 188 (1946); **30**, 337(1947); **31**, 355(1948); **33**, 585(1950); **51**, 892(1968).
(*22*) JAOAC **48**, 759(1965).
(*23*) JAOAC **46**, 229(1963).
(*24*) JAOAC **47**, 300(1964).
(*25*) JAOAC **60**, 1105, 1111(1977).
(*26*) JAOAC **46**, 238(1963).
(*27*) JAOAC **58**, 557(1975); **60**, 229(1977).
(*28*) JAOAC **40**, 230(1957); J. Sci. Food Agric. **20**, 4(1969).
(*29*) JAOAC **46**, 261(1963); **48**, 744(1965); **49**, 87(1966).
(*30*) JAOAC **40**, 235(1957).
(*31*) JAOAC **32**, 788(1949); **33**, 608(1950); **34**, 827(1951); **37**, 581(1954).
(*32*) JAOAC **53**, 149(1970).
(*33*) JAOAC **47**, 303(1964).
(*34*) Anal. Chem. **20**, 753(1948); JAOAC **38**, 673(1955).
(*35*) JAOAC **43**, 707(1960); **46**, 244(1963).
(*36*) JAOAC **42**, 545(1959); **45**, 410(1962).

SPECIAL REFERENCES

U.S. DEPT. OF HEW, FOOD AND DRUG ADMIN., "Pesticide Analytical Manual," Vols I and II. Available from FDA, Public Records and Documents Center HFI-35, 5600 Fishers Lane, Rockville, MD 20857.

BURKE, "Development of the Food and Drug Administration's Method of Analysis for Multiple Residues of Organochlorine Pesticides in Foods and Feeds." Residue Reviews **34**, 59–90(1971).

30. Spices and Other Condiments

SPICES

30.001 Preparation of Sample—Procedure

Grind sample to pass sieve with circular openings 1 mm diam. and mix thoroly. Since most spices lack uniformity and tend to stratify, use extreme care in weighing out portion for analysis. Stir material thoroly and weigh out the 2 g samples, using spoon with ca 2 g capacity. Dip spoonful from center of material, being careful to take ca required wt so as to avoid adding to or taking from portion on scale pan. In detn of starch in spices by diastase method, further reduce subsample as nearly as possible to impalpable powder.

Extractable Color (*1*)—Official First Action

(Applicable to capsicums and oleoresin paprika)

30.002 ***Apparatus and Reagents***

(**a**) *Spectrophotometer.*—Capable of accurately measuring *A* at 460 nm; with 1 cm stoppered cells.

(**b**) *Std color soln.*—Dry $CoSO_4(NH_4)_2SO_4.6H_2O$ 1 week in desiccator over Drierite. Dissolve 0.3005 g $K_2Cr_2O_7$ and 34.960 g dried $CoSO_4(NH_4)_2SO_4$ in 1.8*M* H_2SO_4 and dil. to 1 L with 1.8*M* H_2SO_4. *A* in 1 cm cell at 460 nm = 0.600.

(**c**) *Glass reference std.*—NBS SRM 2030, glass filter with *A* specified by NBS in range 0.4–0.6 at 465 nm.

30.003 ***Determination***

(**a**) *Capsicums.*—Grind capsicums to pass No. 40 (No. 18 if NBS std is used) sieve. Place accurately weighed sample contg 70–100 mg ground capsicums in 100 ml vol. flask, dil. to vol. with acetone, and stopper tightly. Shake flask and let stand 4 hr (16 hr if NBS std is used) at room temp. in dark. Shake flask again and let particles settle 2 min. Transfer portion of ext to spectrophtr cell with 10 mL pipet.

Det. *A* of sample at 460 nm, using acetone as blank. Det. *A* of std color soln at 460 nm, using 1.8*M* H_2SO_4 as blank, or of NBS std at 465 nm.

(**b**) *Oleoresin, using std color soln.*—Weigh, to nearest 0.1 mg, 50–80 mg sample on 5 cm sq glassine paper. Place paper with sample in 100 mL vol. flask and dil. to vol. with acetone. Ext $\geq$15 min with occasional shaking. Using 10 mL pipet, transfer 10 mL ext into another 100 mL vol. flask and dil. to vol. with acetone. Filter dild ext thru Whatman No. 40 paper, or equiv.; discard first 10–15 mL filtrate. Decant portion of filtrate into cell and measure *A* at 460 nm against acetone.

(**c**) *Oleoresin, using NBS std.*—Weigh, to nearest 0.1 mg, 70–100 mg sample and transfer to 100 ml vol. flask. Dil. to vol. with acetone, shake, and let stand 2 min. Pipet 10 ml ext into another 100 ml vol. flask, dil. to vol. with acetone, and shake. Transfer portion to cell and measure *A* at 460 nm against acetone.

30.004 ***Calculations***

To correct for instrument and cell variations, calc. correction factor, I_f = 0.600/*A* of std color soln at 460 nm, or I_f = declared *A* of NBS std at 465 nm/actual *A* of NBS std at 465 nm. Redet. I_f each time spectrophtr is turned on.

Range of *A* should be 0.30 to 0.70. Dil. exts with *A* >0.70 with acetone to ½ original concn. Discard exts with *A* <0.30 and ext larger sample.

ASTA color value for capsicum
$$= [(A_{ext} \text{ at } 460 \text{ nm}) \times (16.4\, I_f)]/\text{g sample}$$

ASTA color value for oleoresin
$$= [(A_{ext} \text{ at } 460 \text{ nm}) \times (164\, I_f)]/\text{g sample}$$

where 16.4 and 164 are conversion factors to American Spice Trade Association (ASTA) color values.

EOA (Essential Oils Association) color value for oleoresin = $[(A_{ext}$ at 460 nm) $\times$ 61,000 $I_f]$/g sample;

100 EOA color units = 2.69 ASTA color units.

30.005 Moisture (*2*)—Official Final Action

Clean distg tube receiver and condenser, **7.004**, with chromic acid soln, rinse thoroly with H_2O and then with ca 0.5*N* alc. KOH, and drain 10 min. Before cleaning, remove connecting stopper from condenser, to keep it dry. Place 40 g spice in distg flask and proceed as in **7.005**.

30.006 Ash (*2*)—Official Final Action

(**a**) *Most spices.*—Accurately weigh ca 2 g sample in flat-bottom dish, preferably Pt. Place dish in entrance of open furnace so that sample fumes off without catching fire. Then ash in furnace 30 min at 550°, break up ash with several drops H_2O, evap. carefully to dryness, and heat in furnace 30 min. If previous wetting showed ash to be C-free, remove dish to desiccator contg fresh, efficient desiccant (H_2SO_4 or anhyd. $Mg(ClO_4)_2$ is satisfactory), let cool to room temp., and weigh soon. If first wetting showed C, repeat wetting and heating until no specks of C are visible; then heat 30 min after disappearance of C. If C persists, leach ash with hot H_2O, filter thru quant. paper, wash paper thoroly, transfer paper and contents to ashing dish, dry, and ignite at 550° until ash is white. Cool dish, add filtrate, evap. to dryness on steam bath, and heat in furnace 30 min. Cool, and weigh as previously.

(**b**) *Nutmeg, mace, ginger, and cloves.*—Proceed as in (**a**), but heat at 600°.

(**c**) *Ground mustard or mustard flour.*—Ignite as in (**a**) and heat 30 min at 550°. Leach ash with hot H_2O, filter, and wash thoroly. Transfer paper and contents to ashing dish, dry, and heat in furnace 30 min. Remove dish, let cool, add 5–10 drops HNO_3, evap. to dryness, and heat in furnace 30 min. Repeat HNO_3 and heating treatment until residue is white. Add filtrate, evap. to dryness, and heat in furnace 30 min. Cool, and weigh as in (**a**).

30.007 Soluble and Insoluble Ash—Official Final Action

Proceed as in **31.015**, using ash obtained in **30.006**.

30.008 Ash Insoluble in Acid—Official Final Action

Boil H_2O-insol. residue, **30.007**, or total ash, **30.006**, with 25 mL HCl (2+5) 5 min, covering dish with watch glass to prevent spattering; collect insol. matter on gooch or ashless filter, wash with hot H_2O until washings are acid-free, ignite until C-free, cool, and weigh.

30.009 Calcium in Ash—Official Final Action

Ignite 2–4 g sample as in **30.006**, digest with hot HCl (2 + 5), evap. to dryness, moisten dry residue with dil. HCl, and again evap. to dryness to make SiO_2 insol. Treat residue with 5–10 mL HCl, add ca 50 mL H_2O, let stand on H_2O bath few min, filter, and wash insol. residue with hot H_2O. Det. CaO in combined filtrate and washings as in **3.015**.

30.010 Nitrogen—Official Final Action

Proceed as in **2.057**. Use 1 g sample for black or white pepper.

30.011 Nitrogen in Nonvolatile Ether Extract Official Final Action

(For black and white peppers)

(*Caution: See* **51.009**, **51.011**, **51.039**, and **51.054**.)

Ext 10 g pepper 20 hr in continuous extn app. with absolute ether, collecting ext in weighed 250 mL flask. Evap. ether, and dry first at 100° and finally to min. wt at 110°. Det. N in weighed ext as in **2.057**, digesting in same flask used for extn.

Crude piperine = N × 20.36.

30.012 Volatile and Nonvolatile Ether Extract (*3*) Official Final Action

(Not suitable for detn of volatile ether ext in spices high in volatile oils, such as cloves)

(*Caution: See* **51.009**, **51.011**, **51.039**, and **51.054**.)

Ext 2 g ground material 20 hr in continuous extn app. with anhyd. ether. Transfer ext to weighed capsule and let evap. at room temp. Store 18 hr over H_2SO_4 and weigh total ether ext. Heat ext gradually and then to min. wt at 110°. Loss is volatile ether ext; residue is nonvolatile ether ext.

30.013 Alcohol Extract (*4*)—Official Final Action

Place 2 g sample in 100 mL vol. flask and dil. to vol. with alcohol. Stopper, shake at 30 min intervals during 8 hr, and let stand 16 hr longer without shaking. Filter ext thru dry paper, evap. 50 mL aliquot filtrate to dryness in flat-bottom dish on steam bath, and heat to min. wt at 110°.

30.014 Copper-Reducing Substances by Direct Acid Hydrolysis—Official Final Action

Ext 4 g sample with five 10 mL portions ether on filter that will completely retain smallest starch granules. Let ether evap. from residue and wash with 150 mL alcohol, 10% by vol.

To avoid clogging of filter by glutinous mass that may result from washing with H_2O or dil. alcohol, omit all preliminary washings with cassia buds and cinnamon.

Carefully wash residue from paper into 500 mL flask with 200 mL H_2O, using small wash bottle and gently rubbing paper with tip of finger. Hydrolyze and det. Cu-reducing material as in **8.019**. Express results in terms of starch.

Starch—Official Final Action

30.015 *Method I*

Ext 4 g finely pulverized sample with ether and 500 mL 10% alcohol as in **30.014**, and det. starch by diastase method, **31.101**.

30.016 *Method II*

(Applicable to dry mustard)

Treat 2–3 g dry mustard flour as in **30.041**.

30.017 Crude Fiber—Official Final Action

Proceed as in **7.065**, and, before drying the crude fiber, remove all ether extractives by successive washings with ether.

Tannin (*5*)—Official Final Action

(For cloves and allspice)

30.018 *Reagents*

(**a**) *Oxalic acid soln.*—0.1*N*. 1 mL = 0.006235 g quercitannic acid or 0.0008 g O absorbed.

(**b**) *Potassium permanganate std soln.*—Dissolve 1.333 g $KMnO_4$ in 1 L H_2O and stdze against (**a**).

(**c**) *Indigo soln.*—Dissolve 6 g Na indigotin disulfonate in 500 mL H_2O by heating; cool, add 50 mL H_2SO_4, dil. to 1 L, and filter.

30.019 *Determination*

(*Caution: See* **51.009**, **51.011**, **51.039**, and **51.054**.)

Ext 2 g sample 20 hr with anhyd. ether. Boil residue 2 hr with 300 mL H_2O, cool, dil. to 500 mL, and filter. Measure 25 mL of this infusion into 2 L porcelain dish; add 20 mL indigo soln and 750 mL H_2O. Add std $KMnO_4$ soln, 1 mL at time, until blue soln changes to green; then add few drops at time until soln becomes golden yellow. Similarly titr. mixt. of 20 mL indigo soln and 750 mL H_2O. Multiply difference between 2 titrns by desired factor, **30.018(a)**, to obtain quercitannic acid or O absorbed.

Volatile Oil (*6*)—Official Final Action

30.020 *Apparatus*

(**a**) *Volatile oil traps.*—Clevenger-type with ₸ joints: (*1*) For oils with densities near or less than that of H_2O; and (*2*) for oils with densities greater than that of H_2O. (*See* Fig. **30:01**.)

(**b**) *Flask with magnetic stirrer.*—1 L r-b, shortneck with ₸ 29/42 joint; heavy duty mag. stirrer with egg-shaped stirring bar.

30.021 *Determination*

Prep. sample as in **30.001**, except use No. 20 sieve. Take precautions to prevent loss of volatile oil from heating during grinding.

Transfer enough weighed sample to 1 L flask to yield 2–4 mL volatile oil. Add H_2O to fill flask ca half full. Insert stirring bar and place flask in heating mantle set over mag. stirrer. Add antifoam agent, such as Dow Corning Antifoam Emulsion, ca size of pea. Clean trap and condenser with chromic acid soln just before use and fill trap with H_2O. Set app. so that condensate will not drop directly on surface of liq. in trap but will run down

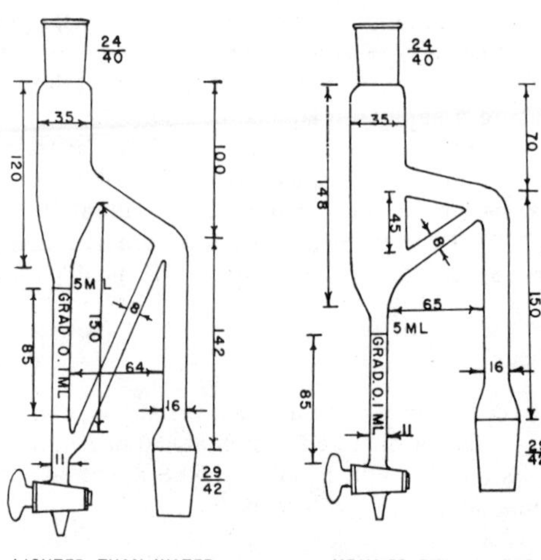

FIG. 30:01—Apparatus for volatile oil in spices (dimensions in mm)

side. Start stirrer and heat mantle thru variable transformer set at 90 volts (≤3 amp).

If oil seps in graduated portion of trap or clings to walls, add several drops satd aq. detergent soln thru top of condenser. Repeat, if necessary (usually once is enough). Distil 10 min after adding detergent to wash it out of trap. When density of oil is nearly 1, as in cassia, or if oil seps into 2 fractions in trap, as in nutmeg and allspice, add 1 mL xylene, accurately measured, to lighter-than-H_2O trap.

Distil until 2 consecutive readings taken at 1 hr intervals show no change in oil content (≥6 hr). Cool, and read vol. collected oil. If xylene was added, subtract its vol., and report oil as mL/100 g spice.

If required for further examination, drain oil into g-s tube or graduate, sepg from aq. layer. Let oil stand until clear, or dry with min. amt of anhyd. Na_2SO_4, and let settle before detg chem. and physical characteristics. Store in refrigerator.

30.022 Specific Gravity of Volatile Oil
Official Final Action

Det. sp gr at 25/25° as in **28.003** and **28.004**, using 1 mL Sprengel tube.

30.023 Refractive Index of Volatile Oil
Official Final Action

See **28.007** and **28.008**.

30.024 Eugenol in Volatile Oil—Official Final Action

Measure 2 mL volatile oil (transfer pipet) into Babcock milk bottle, **16.060(a)**. Add 20 mL 3% KOH soln, shake mixt. 5 min, heat 10 min in boiling H_2O bath, remove, and cool to room temp. When liqs sep. completely, add enough KOH soln to bring residual oil within graduated portion of neck and note vol. Calc. % by vol. from difference between vol. sample used and residual oil.

30.025 Volatile Oil and Resin in Ginger (*7*)
Official Final Action

(*Caution: See* **51.011**, **51.039**, and **51.054**.)

Place 50 g ground ginger in Soxhlet extractor and ext completely with ether (ca 4 hr). Transfer ext to 300 mL flask and evap. ether on steam bath until solv. is no longer detected. Add 50 mL H_2O to residue and det. yield of volatile oil (using trap for oils lighter than H_2O), sp gr, and refractive index, as in **30.021–30.023**.

Transfer residue in flask to separator and ext resin with ether. Transfer to tared beaker, evap. ether on steam bath, and dry to const wt in vac. desiccator.

Volatile Oil in Mustard Seed (*8*)—Official Final Action

30.026 ***Apparatus and Reagents***

(**a**) *Gas chromatograph.*—With flame ionization detector. Approx. operating conditions: Temps (°)— column 145, detector 200, injector 160; N flow rate 100 mL/min. Optimum conditions are obtained when ≥10 cm peak is obtained for 8 μL std soln injection.

(**b**) *Column and packing.*—3.7 m (12′) × 4 mm id, 5% Carbowax 4000 on Fluoropak 80, 20–40 mesh.

(**c**) *Allyl isothiocyanate std soln.*—30.5 mg/100 mL. Measure 30 μL allyl isothiocyanate in 50 μL syringe with 0.5% accuracy. Add to 50 mL 10% alcohol in 100 mL vol. flask and shake intermittently until dissolved. Dil. to vol. with H_2O.

30.027 ***Determination***

Grind ≥15 g seed to pass thru No. 20 sieve. Immediately weigh 6.0 g into 300 mL erlenmeyer, add 150 mL 5% alcohol, stopper tightly, and stir mag. 90±5 min in 37° H_2O bath.

(**a**) *Gas chromatographic method.*—Distil ca 70 mL into 100 mL vol. flask contg 20 mL 5% alcohol, taking care that end of condenser dips below surface of soln. Dil. to vol. with H_2O. Inject 4–10 μL into gas chromatograph. Compare peak ht of sample with that from same vol. std soln.

(**b**) *Titration method.*—Distil ca 60 mL into 100 mL vol. flask contg 10 mL NH_4OH (1+2), taking care that end of condenser dips below surface of soln. Add 20 mL 0.1*N* $AgNO_3$ to distillate and let stand overnight (*Caution: See* **51.044**); heat to bp on H_2O bath (boil behind safety barrier) to agglomerate Ag_2S, cool, dil. to 100 mL with H_2O, and filter. Acidify 50 mL filtrate with ca 5 mL HNO_3 and titr. with 0.1*N* NH_4SCN, using 5 mL 10% $FeNH_4(SO_4)_2.12H_2O$ soln as indicator. 1 mL 0.1*N* $AgNO_3$ = 0.004958 g allyl isothiocyanate.

Note: Before discarding Ag_2S and filter paper, treat with 25 mL 1*N* $Na_2S_2O_5$ in 1*N* NaOH.

Microscopic Examination—Procedure

30.028 ***General (9)***

Adulterants of vegetable origin in spices are best detected microscopically. General knowledge of vegetable histology and microscopic appearance of spices and spice adulterants is essential. Some std works on these subjects (***9***) are listed in Selected References.

30.029 ***Reagents***

(**a**) *Acidified chloral hydrate-glycerol soln.*—Dissolve 45 g chloral hydrate crystals in 25 mL HCl (1+8) and 10 mL glycerol.

(**b**) *Chloral hydrate soln.*—Dissolve 8 parts by wt chloral hydrate crystals in 5 parts H_2O.

(**c**) *Ferric acetate or chloride soln.*—Freshly prepd 1% aq. soln.

(**d**) *Iodine-potassium iodide soln* (*iodine soln*).— Dissolve 0.5 g I and 1.5 g KI in very small amt of H_2O and dil. to 25 mL.

(**e**) *Iodine-potassium iodide in zinc chloride soln.*— Dissolve 100 g $ZnCl_2$ in 60 mL H_2O in g-s bottle and add 20 g KI and 0.5 g I. Leave few I crystals in bottle to ensure satn and let soln stand few hr before use. Soln keeps for months. If color developed in tissue is too deep blue, dil. reagent slightly.

(**f**) *Millon reagent.—See* **7.125(g)**.

(**g**) *Potassium chlorate macerating soln.*—Mix 0.5 g $KClO_3$ with 50 mL HNO_3 (1+1) as needed.

(**h**) *Potassium hydroxide soln.*—Dissolve 5 g KOH in H_2O and dil. to 100 mL.

(**i**) *Sudan IV, saturated alcoholic soln.*—Approx. 0.09%.

30.030 ***Apparatus***

(**a**) *Wide-field stereoscopic microscope.*—Instrument with ca 10 to 60× magnification is useful for preliminary sepn.

(**b**) *Compound microscope.*—Instrument with ca 100 to 400× magnification. Eyepiece micrometer, mech. stage, and polarizing microscope are desirable for special types of work.

(**c**) *Sieves.*—Series of std mesh sieves from No. 10 to 100, and sieve with circular openings 1 mm diam.

(**d**) *Slides, cover glasses, needles, forceps, etc.*

30.031 ***Preparation of Sample***

Reduce 1 portion to fine powder in mortar. Sep. another portion into several grades of fineness by sieves of different mesh or by jarring on sheet of paper. In coarser grades, fragments of suspicious nature may often be seen with naked eye or under simple microscope; these should be picked out for subsequent examination under compd microscope.

30.032 ***Examination***

Mount small amt ground sample in H_2O and examine under compd microscope with both ordinary and polarized light. This gives general information as to nature of material and serves for detection and identification of starch granules and various tissues. Place small drop of I-KI soln at edge of cover glass, draw it into prepn with piece of filter paper placed at opposite edge of cover glass, and examine again. Starch granules are colored blue or blue-black; cellulose, yellow; and proteins, either brown or yellow.

Similarly, draw little KOH soln under cover glass and again examine. This treatment gelatinizes starch granules, dissolves proteins, saponifies fats, and in other ways clears prepn. It also imparts reddish color to tannins. If this treatment does not clear tissues satisfactorily, treat fresh portion for short time with acidified chloral hydrate-glycerol soln, heating gently, if necessary, or for some hours with the chloral hydrate soln.

Also examine crude fiber obtained in chem. analysis, as stone cells and other tissues are shown distinctly in this material.

To isolate stone cells, bast fibers, and other thick-wall cells, macerate portion of sample in $KClO_3$ macerating soln, varying proportions of $KClO_3$ and HNO_3 and heating long enough to secure desired results.

To distinguish cellulose from infiltrated substances (lignin, suberin, etc.), add freshly prepd I-KI in $ZnCl_2$ soln to H_2O mount. Cellulose is colored blue, and infiltrated substances are yellow.

To distinguish fats, oils, essential oils, resins, latex, and wax from other cell contents, place small amt of tissue on slide, add 2 drops Sudan IV soln and 2 drops glycerol or acidified chloral hydrate-glycerol soln, and heat gently; these substances are stained red. Treat sep. portion of tissue with ether, pet ether, or alcohol. Ether and pet ether dissolve fats, oils, essential oils, resins, latex, and wax. Alcohol dissolves essential oils and resins but usually affects fats, oils, latex, and wax slowly or not at all.

Test for proteins by warming cautiously on slide with drop of Millon reagent. Proteins are partially decomposed, gradually acquiring brick red color. To study form of aleurone (protein) granules, which in some plants are quite as characteristic as starch granules, prep. mount in pure glycerol or oil.

Test for tannins and tissues impregnated with them by adding $Fe(OAc)_3$ or $FeCl_3$ soln. Both reagents give green or blue color with tannins, but $Fe(OAc)_3$ acts more slowly and is preferred.

Crystals of Ca oxalate (J. Amer. Pharm. Assoc. **12,** 301(1923)) are recognized by their characteristic forms and by behavior to polarized light. To distinguish Ca oxalate from $CaCO_3$, treat with HOAc, which does not affect oxalate but dissolves carbonate with effervescence. Both are sol. in HCl.

Powd charcoal and charred shells resist bleaching action of KOH, chloral hydrate, and $KClO_3$ macerating soln.

PREPARED MUSTARD

30.033 Preparation of Sample—Procedure

Transfer entire contents of container to dish large enough to permit thoro stirring and make whole mass homogeneous. Preserve in g-s bottle. Stir well each time before removing portion for analysis.

30.034 Solids—Official Final Action

Weigh 5 g sample into flat-bottom Pt dish; distribute evenly over bottom of dish with little H_2O, place on steam bath until mixt. appears dry, and heat in oven at 100° to min. wt.

30.035 Total Chlorides (*10*)—Official Final Action

Weigh 3–4 g sample from weighing bottle, place in 300 mL erlenmeyer, and add excess std 0.1*N* $AgNO_3$ (usually 30 mL is enough). Mix thoroly, add 15 mL HNO_3, and bring to boil on hot plate. To boiling mixt. add 15 mL 5% $KMnO_4$ soln, 5 mL at time, rotating flask after each addn to mix contents. Add ca 50 mL H_2O and filter into 200 mL vol. flask. Wash filter free of $AgNO_3$ and dil. to vol. with H_2O. Mix thoroly and titr. 100 mL aliquot with 0.1*N* KSCN, using 2 mL satd Fe alum soln as indicator. Calc. chlorides as NaCl.

30.036 Ether Extract—Official Final Action

(*Caution: See* **51.009, 51.011, 51.039,** and **51.054.**)

Weigh 10 g sample into SiO_2, Al, or porcelain drying dish and mix with ca 30 g sand. Heat on H_2O bath until mixt. appears dry; then finish drying in oven at 100°. Grind until all lumps are broken up, and det. ether ext by extg 16 hr with anhyd. ether in Soxhlet extractor with Whatman single thickness or other close-texture thimble. Dry ext 30 min at 100°, cool, and weigh.

30.037 Total Nitrogen—Official Final Action

Det. N as in **2.057**, using 5 g sample.

30.038 Acidity—Official Final Action

Weigh 10 g sample into 200 mL vol. flask, dil. to vol. with H_2O, shake, filter thru dry paper, and det. acidity in 100 mL by titrn with 0.1*N* alkali, using phthln. Express result as HOAc. 1 mL 0.1*N* alkali = 0.0060 g HOAc.

30.039 ★ Sucrose—Official First Action ★

See **28.036–28.037**, 10th ed.

Starch—Official Final Action

30.040 ***Reagents***

(**a**) *Calcium chloride soln.*—30 g/100 mL soln adjusted to 0.01*N* alky.

(**b**) *Alcoholic sodium hydroxide soln.*—Mix 70 mL alcohol with 30 mL 0.1*N* NaOH.

(**c**) *Iodine-potassium iodide soln.*—Dissolve 2 g I and 6 g KI in 100 mL H_2O.

30.041 ***Determination***

Place 5 g prepd mustard in 500 mL erlenmeyer and pipet in 100 mL $CaCl_2$ soln, swirling flask gently until all lumps are broken. Add calcd vol. 1*N* NaOH to neutze acid in wt prepd mustard taken for analysis. Add glass beads. Connect to reflux condenser, first wetting inside of condenser and stopper with H_2O and draining 1 min. Heat gently (on asbestos board with center hole) to avoid initial foaming, and boil 15 min.

Leaving condenser connected, cool flask to room temp. in pan of cold H_2O. Remove flask, stopper, and shake vigorously. Pour contents into centrf. bottle and centrf. 5 min at 1500 rpm. Withdraw as much as possible of partially clarified middle layer (ca 75 mL) and filter thru 11 cm circle of absorbent cotton ca 5 cm thick placed in 60° funnel. Pipet 50 mL filtrate into second centrf. bottle contg 150 mL alcohol, stopper, and shake vigorously several min. Centrf. at 1500 rpm until clear (ca 5 min).

★ Surplus method—*see* inside front cover.

Decant liq. thru asbestos pad in Caldwell crucible, using suction, without transferring starch to crucible. Transfer pad to same centrf. bottle, and rinse all particles adhering to crucible into bottle with H_2O. Add several glass beads and H_2O to ca 100 mL. Stopper and shake vigorously until ppt is as finely dispersed as possible. Add slight excess I-KI soln (2–3 mL) and 30 mL satd $(NH_4)_2SO_4$ soln. Stopper and shake bottle. Rinse particles adhering to stopper into bottle, and centrf. until clear.

Decant supernate, with suction, thru asbestos pad in Caldwell crucible. Add 50 mL alc. NaOH soln to ppt in centrf. bottle. Stopper and shake vigorously. Wash stopper with 70% alcohol. Centrf. and decant supernate thru same pad as before. Repeat treatment with the NaOH soln until practically all blue disappears (usually 2–3 treatments). Without centrfg, transfer contents of bottle to Caldwell crucible, using 70% alcohol. Aspirate until pad is dry; then transfer pad to 500 mL Kjeldahl flask. Rinse bottle and crucible with 10 mL HCl (sp gr 1.1029) followed by five 10 mL portions H_2O, carefully removing all adhering particles. Attach Kjeldahl flask to reflux condenser, first adding glass beads to lessen bumping. Place on asbestos board with center hole and boil 1 hr. Cool, neutze with NaOH (1+1) (Me orange), and filter into 200 mL vol. flask; rinse flask and filter thoroly, and dil. to vol. with H_2O. Mix well, and det. glucose in 50 mL aliquot by **31.038**. (Blank on Fehling soln should be $\leq$0.3 mg.)

$$\% \text{ Starch} = [\text{g glucose} \times 0.9(100 + V + W) \times 8]/\text{wt sample},$$

where V = mL 1N NaOH used to neutze acidity, **30.038**, and W = g H_2O in sample taken (calcd from solids, **30.034**).

30.042 Crude Fiber (*11*)—Official Final Action

Weigh 10 g sample and transfer to 8 oz nursing bottle with 50 mL alcohol, stopper, and shake vigorously. Add 40 mL ether, shake, and let stand ca 5 min, shaking occasionally. Centrf. and decant alcohol-ether mixt. Treat twice more with 40 mL portions ether, shaking, centrfg, and decanting as before. Rest bottle on its side for short time, without heat, to let most of ether evap. Transfer material to 500 mL erlenmeyer, using 200 mL boiling H_2SO_4, **7.062(a)**, and proceed as in **7.065**, but in addn wash fiber with successive portions of ether before drying and weighing.

If preferred, treat sample with alcohol and ether in small beaker, transfer to hardened 11 cm filter paper, wash several times with ether, and transfer to 500 mL erlenmeyer with 200 mL boiling H_2SO_4.

30.043 Preservatives

See Chap. **20**.

DRESSINGS FOR FOODS (*12*)

30.044 Preparation of Sample—Procedure

(**a**) *Semisolid and emulsified dressings.*—Before removing any portion of sample for analysis, transfer to suitable container, such as glass fruit jar, of larger capacity than vol. of sample, and mix with spatula until homogeneous (2–3 min should be enough). Repeat mixing before each subsequent portion is removed for analysis if sample has stood for any appreciable time. For various detns, take approx. quantity directed and weigh. (Light 100 mL flask fitted with straight glass tube and oversized rubber bulb makes suitable weighing bottle.)

(**b**) *Separable dressings, small containers.*—Weigh bottle contg sample. Shake bottle 1 min, empty contents into high-speed blender, and let bottle drain 1 min. Weigh empty bottle to det. wt sample. Add 0.20 g egg albumen powder/100 g sample, cover blender, and blend 5 min; then transfer to suitable container of capacity larger than sample vol. Shake sample ca 20 times and stir with spatula or spoon ca 20 times before each portion is removed for analysis. Make all weighings immediately after sample prepn. Correct results for added emulsifier.

(**c**) *Separable dressings, large containers.*—Stir contents thoroly, adding 0.20 g egg albumen powder/100 g sample. Mech. stirrer of double-beater type is satisfactory. Continue stirring until powder is well dispersed thruout sample. Add sample in portions to high-speed blender and blend each portion ca 5 min. Transfer emulsified portions to jar of ca same size as original container and stir entire contents of sample to ensure uniform mixt. Transfer portion of prepd sample to suitable jar (ca 500 ml; 1 pt). Proceed as in (**b**), beginning "Shake sample ca 20 times . . ."

30.045 Total Solids—Official Final Action

Use 2 g sample and proceed as in **17.007(a)**.

30.046 Reducing Sugars Before Inversion Official Final Action

Weigh 20 g sample into wide-mouth 4 oz (120 mL) bottle and ext oil by adding ca 80 mL pet ether, shaking, and centrfg. Draw off as much as possible of pet ether soln (conveniently done by using suction and short-stem pipet), and repeat treatment with pet ether until all oil is removed (indicated by absence of color in solv.; usually 4 extns are required). Reserve ether soln for identification of oil. Remove pet ether from residue with air current and transfer residue with H_2O to 100 mL vol. flask. Add 5–10 mL *fresh soln of* HPO_3 (remove any white coating on HPO_3 by rinsing with H_2O, dissolve 5 g transparent lumps or sticks in cold H_2O, and dil. to 100 mL), mix thoroly, dil. to vol., and filter. Transfer 80 mL filtrate, or as large aliquot as possible, to 100 mL vol. flask; neutze with NaOH soln (1+1), using phthln; cool, dil. to vol., and det. reducing sugars on aliquot as in **31.038**. Calc. to invert sugar.

With dressings, particularly those contg starch, that cannot be clarified by above method, remove oil as in **16.059**, using 1 mL NH_4OH and 5 mL alcohol/g sample; transfer residue to 250 mL vol. flask with 50% alcohol, and proceed as in **7.079** and **31.038**.

30.047 Reducing Sugars After Inversion Official Final Action

Invert aliquot of soln, **30.046**, as in **31.026(b)** or (**c**), nearly neutze with NaOH soln (1+1), and det. reducing sugars in inverted soln as in **31.038**. Calc. to invert sugar from **52.019**.

30.048 Sucrose—Official Final Action

Subtract % invert sugar obtained before inversion, **30.046**, from that obtained after inversion, **30.047**, and multiply difference by 0.95.

30.049 Total Acidity—Official Final Action

Weigh ca 15 g sample into 500 mL erlenmeyer, dil. to ca 200 mL, and shake until all lumps are thoroly broken up. Titr. with 0.1N NaOH, using phthln, and calc. as HOAc. To recognize end point, have duplicate sample at hand so that, by comparison, first change of color may be noted.

30.050 Total Nitrogen—Official Final Action

Accurately weigh ca 15 g sample into 500 mL Kjeldahl flask and place on steam bath until egg is thoroly cooked and oil seps readily. Cool, and add ca 50 mL pet ether; mix, and decant pet ether thru small filter. Repeat pet ether treatment twice, rinsing out as much oil as possible. Wash filter with pet ether and add filter paper to sample in flask. Det. N, using 50 mL H_2SO_4 (more, if necessary) for digestion, as in **2.057**.

30.051 Total Phosphorus—Official Final Action

Use 10 g sample and proceed as in **17.023(a)** and **17.024**, except use Pt dish in place of beaker and burn off oil before ashing in furnace.

30.052 Total Fat—Official Final Action

(*Caution: See* **51.011**, **51.039**, **51.054**, and **51.073**.)

Thoroly mix sample, and accurately weigh ca 1 g, by difference, into Mojonnier tube. Add 10 mL HCl, shake, set tube in H_2O bath heated to 70°, and bring to bp. Boil 30 min, shaking tube thoroly every 5 min. Remove from H_2O bath, add H_2O to fill lower bulb of tube (but not neck), and cool to room temp.

To mixt. in Mojonnier tube add 25 mL ether and shake vigorously ≥1 min. Add 25 mL pet ether and again shake vigorously ≥1 min. To break emulsion centrf. 5–10 min at ca 300 rpm. Decant ether-fat soln into flask, contg porcelain chips or glass beads, that has been dried at 100°, allowed to cool in air to constant wt, and weighed against similar flask similarly treated as counterpoise. Rinse off mouth of tube with small vol. ether after each decantation, letting ether run into flask. Repeat ether extns twice, using only 15 mL of each ether for second and third extns. Again shake vigorously after addn of each ether and centrf. If necessary in order to decant all ether-fat soln after first extn, add more H_2O prior to second decantation.

Slowly evap. combined ether solns in flask, dry ca 90 min at 100° (placing counterpoise in oven at same time), cool in air to const wt, and weigh.

30.053 Identification of Oil—Official Final Action

Proceed as in Chapter **28**, using oil obtained by evapg pet ether exts from detn of reducing sugars, **30.046**. (*Caution: See* **51.011** and **51.073**.)

30.054 Gums in Mayonnaise and French Dressing (*13*) Official Final Action

(Not applicable in presence of starch)

(*Caution: See* **51.082**.)

Transfer 100 g sample to 250 mL beaker, add 35–40 mL hot H_2O, and mix thoroly. Heat to 65–70° in H_2O bath, add 10 mL *50% trichloroacetic acid soln,* and maintain at 65–70° until emulsion shows signs of breaking (never >10 min). Transfer mixt. to 250 mL (8 oz) nursing bottle and insert pipet guard (JAOAC **20**, 529(1937)) (wide-bore glass tube long enough to reach almost to bottom of centrf. bottle, with lower end loosely stoppered; tube is held in place by slotted rubber stopper). Centrf. 15–20 min at ca 1200 rpm. (This should sep. mixt. into lower aq. layer and upper oily layer, with layer of curd between. If sepn does not occur, add 30–40 mL toluene, mix, and repeat centrfg.) Using pipet inserted thru pipet guard, remove as much aq. layer as possible, and filter it into 600 mL beaker. Add 5 vols alcohol to filtrate and let stand overnight to ppt gums.

Decant or pipet off enough alcohol to leave ≤225 mL, transfer contents of beaker to 250 mL (8 oz) nursing bottle, centrf. until gum settles to bottom, and decant supernate alcohol as completely as possible. Dissolve residue in ≤50 mL hot H_2O, add 1 or 2 mL HOAc, and ppt by adding alcohol to 250 mL mark on nursing bottle. Let stand overnight, or until ppt flocculates, centrf. at 1200 rpm, and decant alcohol. (Heavy flocculent ppt at this point indicates presence of significant amt of gum. Slight ppt should not be considered positive test for gums, as spices present in most mayonnaises and french dressings usually give such ppt.) Confirm presence of gums as follows:

Add 35 mL hot H_2O to ppt in bottle, transfer to small beaker, add 5 mL HCl, and boil gently 2 min to hydrolyze gums to sugars. This soln may now be used for various qual. tests for monosaccharide sugars, as follows:

(a) *Copper reduction test.*—Transfer 1 mL hydrolyzed gum soln to test tube, neutze to litmus paper with ca 2*N* NaOH, and remove paper. Add 5 mL Benedict qual. soln, **16.269(a)**, and boil vigorously 1–2 min. Let cool spontaneously. Voluminous ppt, which may be green, yellow, or red, indicates reducing sugars.

(b) *Molisch test.*—Transfer 5 mL hydrolyzed gum soln to test tube, and add 2 drops *15% alc. α-naphthol soln.* Incline tube and slowly pour 3–5 mL H_2SO_4 down inner side so that 2 layers do not mix. Reddish-violet zone at point of contact indicates carbohydrates. (5% alc. thymol soln may be substituted for α-naphthol.)

Gums in Salad Dressing (*14*)—Official Final Action

(Applicable in presence of starch)

30.055 ***Reagents***

(a) *Calcium chloride soln.*—Sp gr 1.2 at 20°. If cloudy, let soln stand so insol. matter may ppt, and then filter.

(b) *Iodine soln.*—*See* **30.040(c)**.

30.056 ***Separation of Gums from Starch***

Defat 50 g salad dressing by heating on steam bath in 250 mL beaker until fat seps, cool, and ext with pet ether until last ether ext is colorless. Make alk. with $MgCO_3$ (2–2.5 g), testing with pH test paper. Heat mixt. in H_2O bath at 80° until residual ether and CO_2 are expelled. Add 100 mL $CaCl_2$ soln and heat in boiling H_2O bath 30 min, stirring occasionally. Pour into 250 mL Pyrex centrf. bottle, centrf., and decant as much of supernate as possible into 250 mL separator. Add 10 mL $CaCl_2$ soln to residue in bottle and shake well. Centrf. and decant supernate as before into separator. Swirl funnel gently and let oil sep. Drain all material below oil into another 250 mL Pyrex centrf. bottle. Centrf. and filter supernate thru 11 cm buchner fitted with Whatman No. 1, or equiv., paper precoated with layer of Celite filter-aid, or equiv. Collect filtrate in beaker within bell jar or in large test tube in suction flask. Add 10 mL $CaCl_2$ soln to residue in centrf. bottle, shake well, centrf., and decant supernate onto filter in buchner. Wash filter with enough $CaCl_2$ soln to make total vol. filtrate ca 110 mL.

Add slowly, with stirring, 20 mL I soln to clear ext to ppt starch-iodide. I should be present in considerable excess over amt required to react quant. with the starch. Considerable amts of reducing substances are present, which must be satisfied before starch can be quant. sepd. Add small amt of Celite filter-aid and let starch-iodide, which seps in finely divided condition, stand ca 1 hr. Filter by suction thru 11 cm Whatman No. 1, or equiv., paper, precoated with adequate layer of Celite. Use wire screen under paper to aid filtration. Do not wash pad. Test for excess I in filtrate with starch-iodide paper or starch soln. This test must be pos. to ensure removal of all starch. Add 4 vols alcohol to brown filtrate, and let stand overnight.

Centrf. off pptd crude gum. Wash twice with 70% alcohol. If possible, gum should be transferred to centrf. bottle, but in some cases gum adheres so firmly to wall of beaker that it can only be rinsed until washings are clear.

Heat on steam bath or in oven at 100° until alcohol is removed. Dissolve residue in 20 mL H_2O by heating in H_2O bath until no more material dissolves. Use rubber policeman to assist soln. (Be sure gum is dissolved or it will be lost here.) Centrf. to remove any insol. material. Decant supernate into another 250 mL centrf. bottle; add 1 drop HOAc and 1 drop $CaCl_2$ soln; and reppt with 4 vols alcohol. Let stand ≥1 hr or overnight. Centrf. and wash ppt twice with 70% alcohol by shaking well and centrfg.

Again evap. alcohol with aid of gentle air stream by heating in hot H_2O bath and dissolve ppt in 10 mL hot H_2O, using rubber policeman. (Heed warning in preceding par.) Centrf. to remove any insol. material and decant into 50 mL heavy duty Pyrex centrf. tube. (Short cone type is less likely to break.) Adjust vol. to 10 mL, add 1 drop HOAc and 1 drop $CaCl_2$ soln, and reppt with 40 mL alcohol. Let stand 1 hr, centrf., and wash with 70% alcohol as before. Heavy flocculent ppt at this point indicates presence of gums. Disregard very small amt of ppt adhering to walls of centrf. tube or appearing as mere turbidity, as spice gums present in most salad dressing usually give such ppt.

30.057 ***Detection of Gum***

To confirm presence of gums, remove residual alcohol by gentle heating in hot H_2O bath, dissolve residue in 10 mL hot H_2O, and centrf. to remove any insol. material. Decant supernate into 10 mL graduate, dil. to 10 mL with H_2O, and mix. To 1 mL of this soln add 1 or 2 drops basic $Pb(OAc)_2$ reagent, **31.021(a)**, 1 drop at time. Immediate flocculent, curdy, or gelatinous ppt is confirmation of presence of gums. Ppt may form on standing but this is to be disregarded.

Alginates (*15*)—Official First Action

(Applicable to mayonnaise, salad dressing, and french dressing)

30.058 ***Preparation of Sample***

Weigh, directly into 250 mL centrf. bottle, 2 g or enough sample to give 10–20 mg alginate (ca 2 g at 0.5% level). Disperse in 50 mL H_2O and fill bottle with acetone-alcohol (1+2). Shake vigorously and let stand until ppt begins to settle; then centrf. ca 10 min at 1600–1700 rpm. Decant, discard liq., disperse ppt in 50 mL H_2O, and reppt 2 more times. To ppt add 50 mL *dioxane*, shake well, and filter thru asbestos-matted gooch with suction. Transfer ppt to gooch, rinse bottle and ppt with several portions dioxane, and suck dry. Return ppt and asbestos mat to centrf. bottle, add 50 mL H_2O, disperse ppt, and adjust to pH 8–9 with 3% NaOH. (With french dressing add 0.25 g Celite 545, shake, and let stand 10 min, shaking several times. Centrf. 10 min at 1600–1700 rpm. Decant supernate, filtering if necessary to remove suspended particles.) To 10 mL aliquot in 50 mL centrf. tube, add 40 mL acetone-alcohol (1+2), stir vigorously, and let stand until ppt forms. If necessary, add 1 drop satd NaCl soln to start pptn. Centrf., discard liq., and dry ppt on steam bath.

30.059 ***Detection***

(Start detection at beginning of day so color changes can be observed.)

Moisten ppt with 3 drops 0.1*N* NaOH, rubbing thoroly with glass rod. Add 2 mL Fe-H_2SO_4 reagent, **13.058**, and let stand. Formation of purple-red color indicates presence of alginate. If brown color forms, repeat detection, using smaller aliquot for final pptn. Alginates are absent if no color develops on standing overnight.

Starch—Official Final Action

30.060 ***Reagents***

See **30.040.**

30.061 ***Determination***

Det. total acidity of prepd sample as in **30.049.** Place 4–5 g prepd sample in 500 mL erlenmeyer and add calcd vol. 0.1*N* NaOH, *V*, to neutze acid in wt sample taken. Pipet in 100 mL $CaCl_2$ soln, stopper flask, and swirl gently until all large lumps of dressing are broken up. Continue as in **30.041**, par. 1, beginning "Add glass beads." Calc. % starch from formula:

% Starch = [g glucose × 0.925(100 + V + W) × 8]/wt sample,

where W = g H_2O in sample taken (calcd from solids, **30.045.**)

VINEGARS (*16*)

(Unless otherwise directed, express results as g/100 mL.)

30.062 Organoleptic Examination—Procedure

Note appearance, color, odor, and taste. Neutze portion of sample with NaOH soln and note odor and taste. Ext neutzd vinegar with ether, evap. ether ext, and note odor and taste of residue. (Spices and pungent materials are indicated by characteristic odors and tastes.) Evap. portion of sample on H_2O bath. Odor of material as last of volatile matter evaps and appearance and taste of residue give information as to source and character of vinegar.

30.063 Preparation of Sample—Procedure

Mix thoroly and filter thru rapid paper.

30.064 Solids—Official Final Action

Measure 10 mL sample into weighed 50 mm diam., flat-bottom Pt dish, evap. on boiling H_2O bath 30 min, and dry exactly 2.5 hr in oven at temp. of boiling H_2O. Cool in desiccator and weigh. (To obtain concordant results it is necessary to use dish of size and shape stated and to dry exactly time specified.)

30.065 Ash—Official Final Action

Measure 25 mL sample into weighed Pt dish, evap. to dryness on H_2O or steam bath, and heat in furnace 30 min at 500–550°. Break up charred mass in Pt dish, add hot H_2O, filter thru ashless paper, and wash *thoroly* with H_2O. Return paper and contents to dish, dry, and heat 30 min at ca 525°, or until all C is burned off. Add filtrate, evap. to dryness, and heat 15 min at ca 525°. Cool in desiccator and weigh (wt *x*). Reheat 5 min at ca 525°, and cool ≤1 hr in desiccator contg efficient desiccant. Put 1 or 2 dishes (preferably only 1) in desiccator at a time. Place wt *x* on balance pan before removing dish from desiccator, and weigh rapidly to nearest mg. Calc. total ash from last wt.

30.066 Soluble and Insoluble Ash—Official Final Action

Treat ash, **30.065**, as in **31.015.**

30.067 Alkalinity of Soluble Ash—Official Final Action

Proceed as in **31.016**, using sol. ash obtained in **30.066.** Express result as number mL 1*N* acid required to neutze sol. ash from 100 mL vinegar. If relationship of ash to alky of sol. ash is abnormal, study composition of ash, especially content of chlorides, sulfates, phosphates, and alkalies (J. Amer. Chem. Soc. **22**, 218(1900)).

30.068 Soluble Phosphorus (*17*)—Official Final Action

Proceed as in **7.119**, or **8.033**, or **22.041★**, using soln obtained in **30.067**. If either volumetric or colorimetric method is used, stdze with sample of known phosphate content. Express results as mg P_2O_5/100 mL vinegar.

30.069 Insoluble Phosphorus (*17*)—Official Final Action

Dissolve H_2O-insol. ash, **30.066**, in ca 50 mL boiling HNO_3 (1+8) (use 25 mL H_2SO_4 (1+9) for colorimetric method) and proceed as in **7.119**, or **8.033**, or **22.041★**. If either volumetric or colorimetric method is used, stdze with sample of known phosphate content. Express result as mg P_2O_5/100 mL vinegar.

30.070 Total Phosphorus (*17*)—Official Final Action

Dissolve ash, **30.065**, or both sol. and insol. ash, **30.066**, in ca 50 mL boiling HNO_3 (1+8) (use 25 mL H_2SO_4 (1+9) for colorimetric method) and proceed as in **7.119**, or **8.033**, or **22.041★**. If either volumetric or colorimetric method is used, stdze with sample of known phosphate content. Express result as mg P_2O_5/100 mL vinegar. If desired, digest vinegar as in **22.041★**, instead of using ash from **30.065**.

30.071 Total Acids—Official Final Action

Dil. 10 mL sample with recently boiled and cooled H_2O until it appears only slightly colored and titr. with 0.5*N* alkali, using phthln. 1 mL 0.5*N* alkali = 0.0300 g HOAc.

30.072 Nonvolatile Acids—Official Final Action

Measure 10 mL vinegar into 200 mL porcelain casserole, evap. just to dryness, add 5–10 mL H_2O, and again evap.; repeat until ≥5 evapns have been made. Add ca 200 mL recently boiled and cooled H_2O, and titr. with 0.1*N* alkali, using phthln. 1 mL 0.1*N* alkali = 0.00600 g HOAc.

30.073 Volatile Acids—Official Final Action

Subtract nonvolatile acids, **30.072**, from total acids, **30.071**.

30.074 Total Reducing Substances Before Inversion Official Final Action

Measure 25 mL sample into 50 mL vol. flask and add enough NaOH soln (1+1) to nearly neutze acid. Cool, dil. to vol. with H_2O, and det. reducing substances in 20 mL soln as in **31.038**. If amt of reducing substances is very small, use 40 mL. Calc. result as invert sugar (for malt vinegar as glucose).

30.075 Total Reducing Substances After Inversion Official Final Action

Invert 25 mL sample in 50 mL vol. flask with 5 mL HCl, as in **31.026(b)** or (**c**). Nearly neutze with NaOH soln (1+1) and det. reducing substances as in **31.038**.

30.076 Nonvolatile Reducing Substances (Sugar) Official Final Action

(Useful in calcg nonsugar solids)

Evap. 50 mL sample on steam or H_2O bath to sirupy consistency, add 10 mL H_2O, and evap. again. Repeat with 10 mL H_2O. Transfer residue to 100 mL vol. flask with ca 50 mL warm H_2O. Cool, invert with 10 mL HCl as in **31.026(b)** or (**c**), and nearly neutze with NaOH soln (1+1). Cool, dil. to vol. with H_2O, and det. reducing substances in 20 mL or 40 mL, depending on amt present, as in **31.038**. Calc. result as invert sugar (for malt vinegar as glucose). If results for total reducing substances before and after inversion show absence of sucrose, inversion may be omitted here.

30.077 Volatile Reducing Substances (*18*)—Procedure

When sucrose is absent, subtract amt of nonvolatile reducing substances, **30.076**, from mean of total reducing substances before inversion, **30.074**, and after inversion, **30.075**. When sucrose is present, subtract amt of nonvolatile reducing substances, **30.076**, from amt of total reducing substances after inversion, **30.075**.

30.078 Alcohol—Official Final Action

Measure 100 mL sample into r-b distn flask. Make faintly alk. with NaOH soln (1+1), distil almost 50 mL, dil. to 50 mL at temp. of sample, and det. sp gr at 20/20° with pycnometer, **9.011**. Obtain % by vol. from **52.003**. Undue foaming may be avoided by adding small piece of paraffin, free from volatile constituents.

30.079 ★ Glycerol (*19*)—Official Final Action ★

All oxidizable org. material except glycerol is removed by evapn, pptn with $Ca(OH)_2$ and alcohol, absolute alcohol and ether, Ag_2CO_3, and basic $Pb(OAc)_2$. Residual glycerol is oxidized with dichromate in acid soln, and the excess is titrd with Fe^{+2}. *See* **30.079–30.080**, 12th ed.

30.080 Color—Official Final Action

Det. depth of color in Lovibond tintometer by good reflected daylight, using ½ or 1" cell and brewer's scale. Report result in terms of ½" cell and so state.

30.081 Polarization (*20*)—Official Final Action

Whenever possible, polarize in 200 mm tube without decolorizing. Report result on basis of 200 mm tube in °S, **31.020(a)**. When necessary, decolorize as follows:

(**a**) To 50 mL sample add measured vol. of satd neut. $Pb(OAc)_2$ soln, avoiding excess of Pb; filter, remove Pb with powd anhyd. K oxalate, and filter. Polarize and correct for diln with $Pb(OAc)_2$ soln.

(**b**) To 50 mL sample add decolorizing C, avoiding excess or too long treatment. Filter thru double paper and polarize.

30.082 Sulfates—Official Final Action

To 100 mL sample add 2 mL ca 1*N* HCl, heat to bp, and add 10 mL hot $BaCl_2.2H_2O$ soln (1 g/100 mL), dropwise. Continue boiling 5 min, keeping vol. ca const by adding hot H_2O as required. Let mixt. stand until supernate is clear (overnight is convenient, but this time should not be exceeded). Filter on ashless paper or weighed Munroe crucible (Z. Anal. Chem. **2**, 241(1888); J. Amer. Chem. Soc. **31**, 456, 928(1909)). Wash Cl-free with hot H_2O, dry, ignite at red heat (700–800°), cool, and weigh. Express result as mg SO_3/100 mL vinegar.

30.083 Dextrin (Qualitative Test)—Procedure

Evap. 100 mL sample to ca 15 mL. Slowly add 200 mL alcohol, with const stirring, and let stand overnight. Sep. ppt, preferably by centrfg, and wash with 80% alcohol. Dissolve in min. vol. H_2O and det. optical rotation. Distinct optical rotation indicates dextrin. Treat soln with several drops I soln of ca same color intensity. Formation of reddish brown color indicates dextrin.

30.084 Preservatives

See Chap. **20**.

Permanganate Oxidation Number (*21*) Official Final Action

(For differentiating between vinegar and com. HOAc)

★ Surplus method—*see* inside front cover.

30.085 ***Reagents***

(**a**) *Potassium permanganate soln.*—31 g/L. Prep. according to **50.025**; stdzn is unnecessary.

(**b**) *Sodium thiosulfate soln.*—0.5*N*. Accurately stdze against $K_2Cr_2O_7$ as in **50.038**, except use ca 0.5 g $K_2Cr_2O_7$, 10 g KI, 10 mL HCl, and 90 mL H_2O.

(**c**) *Potassium iodide soln.*—Dissolve 50 g KI in 100 mL H_2O and filter. Do not use unless colorless.

30.086 ***Determination***

Adjust sample to 4 g/100 mL acidity as HOAc. Steam distil 50 mL adjusted sample and collect 50 mL distillate. Regulate distn so that ca 45 mL remains in distg flask when 50 mL distillate has been collected. All-glass app. is preferable; if not available, cover cork or rubber stoppers with Sn or Al foil. App. illustrated in Fig. **18:02**, **18.050(a)**, is convenient. Keep distillate and reagents at 25°.

Transfer 50 mL distillate to 500 mL g-s erlenmeyer. Add 10 mL H_2SO_4 (1+1) and 25 mL $KMnO_4$ soln. Accurately measure $KMnO_4$ soln, draining pipet definite time. Hold at 25°, preferably in H_2O bath, exactly 1 hr. Then immediately add 20 mL KI soln and mix well. Titr. liberated I with 0.5*N* $Na_2S_2O_3$.

Conduct blank detn at same time, using 50 mL H_2O, 10 mL H_2SO_4 (1+1), and 25 mL $KMnO_4$ soln.

(mL 0.5*N* $Na_2S_2O_3$ required by blank − mL used in detn)/2 = permanganate oxidn number of vinegar. Report on basis of adjusted vinegar (4% acid).

If permanganate oxidn number is >15, repeat detn, using 25 mL adjusted vinegar + 25 mL H_2O. Repeat this reduction by ½ until mL $KMnO_4$ soln used is <15. Calc. permanganate oxidn number to basis of 50 mL adjusted vinegar.

SELECTED REFERENCES

(*1*) JAOAC **54**, 37(1971); **60**, 1(1977).
(*2*) JAOAC **24**, 667(1941).
(*3*) USDA Bur. Chem. Bull. **13**, (II), p. 165; JAOAC **23**, 581(1940).
(*4*) Conn. Agr. Expt. Sta. Rpt., 1898 (II), p. 187.
(*5*) USDA Bur. Chem. Bull. **13**, (II), p. 167; Anal. Chem. **27**, 1159(1955).
(*6*) JAOAC **17**, 70, 371(1934); **18**, 611(1935); **21**, 435(1938); **22**, 598(1939); **25**, 700(1942); **33**, 575(1950); **36**, 752(1953); **37**, 390(1954); **38**, 548(1955); **42**, 312(1959); **45**, 212(1962).
(*7*) JAOAC **19**, 98, 411(1936).
(*8*) JAOAC **4**, 525(1921); **53**, 1(1970).
(*9*) Winton, "Microscopy of Vegetable Foods," 2nd ed., 1916; Winton, "Structure and Composition of Foods," vol. IV, 1939; Youngken, "Textbook of Pharmacognosy," 6th ed., 1948; Food, Apr. 1956–Mar. 1957, inclusive, "Food Microscopy," parts 4–15; Claus, "Pharmacognosy," 4th ed., 1961; Parry, "Spices," 1962.
(*10*) JAOAC **24**, 703(1941); **25**, 97(1942).
(*11*) JAOAC **7**, 70(1923).
(*12*) JAOAC **5**, 248(1921); **7**, 138(1923); **16**, 77, 548(1933); **24**, 83, 695(1941); **34**, 267(1951); **35**, 231(1952); **36**, 758(1953); **37**, 393(1954).
(*13*) JAOAC **20**, 527(1937); **21**, 110(1938); **22**, 605(1939).
(*14*) Ind. Eng. Chem., Anal. Ed. **7**, 311(1935); JAOAC **27**, 260(1944); **28**, 249(1945); **29**, 250(1946); **35**, 358(1952).
(*15*) JAOAC **46**, 623(1963); **47**, 389(1964).
(*16*) JAOAC **8**, 150(1924); **9**, 440(1926); **10**, 490(1927); **11**, 499(1928); **14**, 507(1931); **15**, 535(1932); **16**, 536(1933); **17**, 360(1934); **21**, 430(1938); **23**, 586 (1940); **25**, 702(1942); **26**, 233(1943); **29**, 304 (1946); **32**, 336(1949); **45**, 562(1962).
(*17*) JAOAC **24**, 684(1941).
(*18*) J. Amer. Chem. Soc. **39**, 309(1917); J. Ind. Eng. Chem. **5**, 845(1913).
(*19*) USDA Bur. Chem. Bull. **137**, p. 61; JAOAC **3**, 411(1920); **15**, 535(1932); **18**, 82(1935).
(*20*) JAOAC **5**, 245(1921); **8**, 151(1924); **14**, 507(1931).
(*21*) JAOAC **27**, 263(1944); **32**, 336(1949); **34**, 262(1951); **35**, 229(1952).

31. Sugars and Sugar Products

SUGARS AND SIRUPS

31.001 Preparation of Sample—Official Final Action

(**a**) *Solids* (*sugars, etc.*).—Grind, if necessary, and mix to uniformity. Thoroly mix raw sugars with spatula in min. time. Break up any lumps either on glass plate with glass or iron rolling pin, or in large, clean, dry mortar, with pestle.

(**b**) *Semisolids* (*massecuites, etc.*).—Weigh 50 g sample, dissolve crystals of sugar in min. vol. of H_2O, wash into 250 mL vol. flask, dil. to vol., and mix thoroly; or weigh 50 g sample and dil. with H_2O to 100 g. If insol. material remains, mix uniformly by shaking before taking aliquots or weighed portions for detns.

(**c**) *Liquids* (*molasses, sirups, etc.*).—Mix materials thoroly. If crystals of sugar are present, dissolve them by heating gently (avoiding loss of H_2O by evapn), or by weighing whole mass, then adding H_2O, heating until completely dissolved, and after cooling, reweighing. Calc. all results to wt original substance.

Color of Raw Cane Sugars (*1*)—Official First Action

31.002 ***Reagent***

Filter-aid.—Celite, or equiv., analytical filter-aid.

31.003 ***Apparatus***

Fractionator.—Construct fractionator of 35 mm id, heavy-wall Pyrex tubing, 145 mm long from top to bottom shoulder where it is sealed to ₮ stopcock with 3 mm bore and 9 mm od tubing. Leave 55 mm stem below stopcock. Seal tube, 9 mm od, 45 mm long, to body of fractionator 45 mm below top. Connect to buchner and source of vac. thru "T" tube as shown in Fig. **31:01**. (Dimensions are not critical.)

31.004 ***Determination***

Place 60 g sample in flask, add 40 g boiling H_2O, and rotate flask until all sugar dissolves. Add 3 g Celite and shake mixt. vigorously 1 min. Assemble special filtration app., and connect to const vac. of 610 mm (81.3 kPa; 24"). With stopcock open, place paper, S&S 589 blue ribbon, 7 cm diam., in buchner, wet with H_2O, and suck excess H_2O thru filtering tube into flask. Close stopcock and pour well-shaken mixt. of sugar soln and Celite evenly over paper. Collect ca 10 mL of first filtrate, which is somewhat turbid, in filtering tube and run into flask by opening stopcock. Close stopcock, collect another 10 mL filtrate in filtering tube, and run into flask as before to wash inner walls of tube free from any small particles of turbidity. Keep bed of Celite well covered with sugar soln during entire filtration. *Do not let it run dry.* Collect final clear filtrate in filtering tube, transfer to small bottle or to small, g-s erlenmeyer, and mix thoroly. Det. refractometer Brix on portion of soln and calc. concn, c (g dry substance/mL soln), by multiplying Brix by corresponding true density and dividing by 100.

Det. % T at 560 nm on spectrophtr with wavelength and T scales that have been checked, preferably with std glass filter supplied by NBS. Use distd H_2O as the 100% T std. Cell thickness, b (in cm), used should be such that readings are within range 25–75% T.

Calc. attenuation index, $a_c^* = -(\log T)/bc$.

Moisture

31.005 *Vacuum Drying—Official Final Action*

(Applicable to cane and beet, raw and refined sugars)

Dry 2–5 g prepd sample, **31.001**(**a**), in flat dish (Ni, Pt, or Al with tight-fit cover), 2 hr at ≤70° (preferably 60°), under pressure ≤50 mm Hg (6.7 kPa). Bleed oven with current of air (dried by passing thru anhyd. $CaSO_4$, P_2O_5, or other efficient desiccant) during drying to remove H_2O vapor. Remove dish from oven, cover, cool in desiccator, and weigh. Redry 1 hr and repeat process until change in wt between successive dryings at 1 hr intervals is ≤2 mg.

31.006 *Drying at Atmospheric Pressure—Procedure*

(Applicable to cane and beet, raw and refined sugars)

Dry ca 5 g prepd sample, **31.001**(**a**), in flat dish (Ni, Pt, or Al with tight-fit cover), 3 hr at 100°. Remove dish, cover, cool in desiccator, and weigh. Redry 1 hr and repeat process until change in wt between successive dryings at 1 hr intervals is ≤2

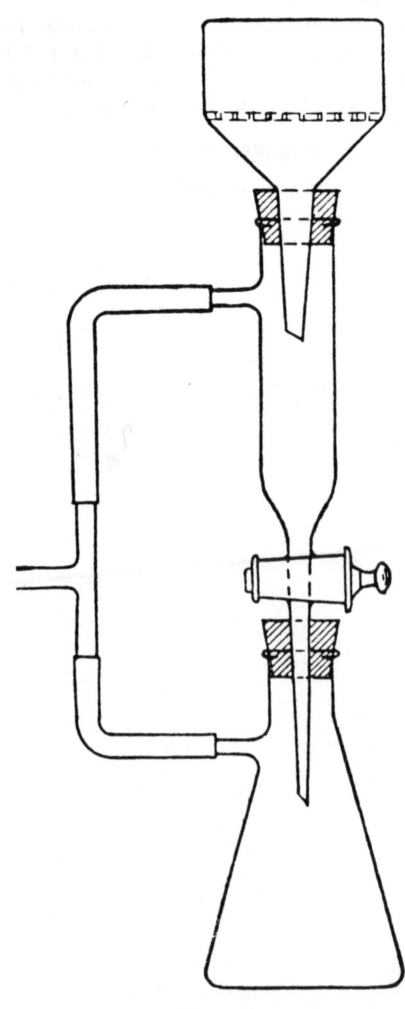

FIG. 31:01—Fractionator

mg. For large-grain sugars, increase temp. to 105–110° in final heating periods to expel last traces of occluded H_2O. Report loss in wt as H_2O.

31.007 ***Drying upon Pumice Stone—Official Final Action***

(Applicable to massecuites, molasses, and other liq. and semiliq. products)

Prep. pumice stone of 2 grades of fineness, one to pass thru 1 mm sieve, other thru 6 mm but not 1 mm sieve. Digest each 8 hr with H_2SO_4 (1+4) on steam bath. Wash acid-free and heat to 525°. Make detn in flat metal dish 60 mm diam. Place 3 mm layer of the fine pumice stone on bottom of dish, then 6–10 mm layer of coarse pumice stone; dry and weigh. Dil. sample with weighed portion of H_2O so that dild material contains 20–30% solid matter. Weigh, into prepd dish, amt of dild sample to yield ca 1 g dry matter. If this weighing cannot be made rapidly, use weighing bottle provided with cork thru which pipet passes. Dry at 70° under pressure ≤50 mm Hg (6.7 kPa), bleeding with dry air as in **31.005**. Make trial weighings at 2 hr intervals toward end of drying period until change in wt is ≤2 mg. Report loss in wt as H_2O. Substances contg little or no fructose or other readily decomposable substance may be dried in oven at 100°.

31.008 ***Drying upon Quartz Sand (2)—Official Final Action***

(Applicable to massecuites, molasses, and other liq. and semiliq. products)

Digest pure quartz sand that passes No. 40 but not No. 60 sieve with HCl, wash acid-free, dry, and ignite. Preserve in stoppered bottle. Place 25–30 g prepd sand and short stirring rod in dish ca 55 mm diam. and 40 mm deep, fitted with cover. Dry thoroly, cover dish, cool in desiccator, and weigh immediately. Add enough dild sample of known wt to yield ca 1 g dry matter and mix thoroly with sand. Heat on steam bath 15–20 min, stirring at 2–3 min intervals, or until mass becomes too stiff to manipulate readily. Dry at <70° (preferably 60°) under pressure ≤50 mm Hg (6.7 kPa), bleeding with dry air as in **31.005**. Make trial weighings at 2 hr intervals toward end of drying period (ca 18 hr) until change in wt is ≤2 mg.

For materials contg no fructose or other readily decomposable substance, dry 8–10 hr at atm. pressure in oven at 100°, cool in desiccator, and weigh, repeating heating and weighing until loss in 1 hr heating is ≤2 mg. Report loss in wt as H_2O.

As dry sand, as well as dried sample, absorbs appreciable moisture on standing over most desiccating agents, make all weighings as quickly as possible after cooling in desiccator.

Solids

31.009 ***By Means of Spindle—Official Final Action***

(Accurate only when applied to pure sucrose solns, but extensively used for approx. results with liq. sugar products contg invert sugar and other nonsucrose solids)

(a) *Direct.*—Density of juices, sirups, etc., is conveniently detd with Brix or Baumé hydrometer, preferably former as scale graduations agree closely with % total solids. Table for comparison of degrees Brix (% by wt of pure sucrose in pure solns), degrees Baumé (modulus 145), sp gr at 20/4°, and sp gr at 20/20° is given in **52.008**.

Use Brix spindle graduated in tenths and of appropriate range, and cylinder of sufficient diam. (≥12 mm larger than spindle bulb) to permit spindle to come to rest without touching sides. Soln should be at room temp. If this varies >1° from temp. at which spindle was graduated (20°), apply correction according to **52.010**. Before taking reading, let soln stand in cylinder until all air bubbles escape and all fatty or waxy materials come to top and are skimmed off. (Air bubbles may be conveniently removed by applying vac. to cylinder by means of tube passing thru stopper inserted in top of cylinder.) Lower spindle slowly into sirup; do not let sirup on spindle reach above sirup level.

(b) *Double dilution.*—If sample is too dense to det. density directly, dil. weighed portion with weighed amt of H_2O, or dissolve weighed portion and dil. to known vol. with H_2O. In first instance, % total solids is calcd by following formula:

$$\% \text{ Solids in undild material} = WS/w,$$

where S = % solids in dild material; W = wt dild material; and w = wt sample taken for diln.

When diln is made to definite vol., use following formula:

$$\% \text{ Solids in undild material} = VDS/w,$$

where V = vol. dild soln at given temp.; D = sp gr of dild soln at same temp.; S = % solids in dild soln at same temp.; and w = wt sample taken for diln.

Calcn is simplified by mixing equal wts sugar product and H_2O, and multiplying Brix of soln by 2.

31.010 ***By Means of Pycnometer (3)—Official Final Action***

(a) *Specific gravity (in vacuo or in air).*—Det. sp gr of soln at 20/4°, 20/20° *in vacuo,* or 20/20° in air as in **9.011**, using either pycnometers described in **9.009(b)** or other suitable type. Det. % by wt of solids as sucrose from appropriate table, **52.008** or **52.020**. When density of substance is too high for direct detn, dil. and then calc. sucrose content of original material as in **31.009(b)**.

(b) *Specific gravity of molasses.*—Use special calibrated 100 mL vol. flask with neck ca 8 mm id. Weigh empty flask and then fill with molasses, using long-stem funnel reaching below graduation mark, until level of molasses is up to lower end of neck of flask. (Flow of molasses may be stopped by inserting glass rod of suitable size into funnel so as to close stem opening.) Carefully remove funnel to prevent molasses from coming in contact with neck, and weigh flask and molasses. Add H_2O almost to graduation mark, running it down side of neck to prevent mixing with molasses. Let stand several hr or overnight for bubbles to escape. Place flask in const temp. H_2O bath, preferably at 20°, and leave until it reaches bath temp. Dil. to vol. at that temp. with H_2O. Weigh. Reduce wt molasses to *in vacuo* and calc. density. Obtain corresponding Brix or Baumé reading from **52.008**.

Example:	*grams*
X, wt H_2O content of flask at 20° *in vacuo*	= 99.823
Y, wt molasses at 20° *in vacuo*	= 132.834
Z, wt molasses and H_2O at 20° in vacuo	= 137.968
$X - (Z - Y)$ = wt H_2O occupying space of molasses *in vacuo*	= 94.689

$$\frac{132.834}{94.689} = 1.403 \text{ sp gr} \left(\frac{20°}{20°}\right) \text{ molasses.}$$

31.011 ***By Means of Refractometer (4) Official Final Action***

(Applicable only to liq. samples contg no undissolved solids)

Sol. solids by refractometric method is that concn by wt of sucrose in soln that has same n as soln analyzed. Use instrument with scale graduated at least in 0.001 units or 0.5% sucrose, permitting estn to $0.0002n$ or 0.25%, resp. Adjust instrument to read n of 1.3330 or 0% sucrose with H_2O at 20°.

Det. refractometer reading of soln at 20° and obtain corresponding % dry substance from either direct reading, if sugar refractometer is used, or from **52.012**, if instrument gives readings in terms of refractive index. Circulate H_2O at const temp., preferably 20°, thru jackets of refractometer or thru trough of immersion instrument, long enough to let temp. of prisms and of sample reach equilibrium, continuing circulation during observations and taking care that temp. is held const.

If detn is made at temp. other than 20°, or if humidity causes condensation of moisture on exposed faces of prisms, make measurements at room temp. and correct readings to std temp. of 20° from **52.016**. If soln is too dark to be read in instrument, dil. with concd sugar soln; never use H_2O for this purpose. Mix weighed amts of soln under examination and soln of pure sugar of about same strength, and calc. % dry substance in former = $[(W + B)C - BD]/W$, where W = wt (g) sample mixed with B; B = wt (g) sugar soln used in diln; C = % dry substance in mixt. $W + B$ obtained from refractive index; and D = % dry substance in pure sugar soln obtained from its refractive index.

For liq. products contg invert sugar, correct % solids obtained from **52.012** by adding 0.022 for each % invert sugar in sample.

Ash—Official Final Action

31.012 ***Method I***

Heat sample of appropriate wt for product being examined (usually 5–10 g) in 50–100 mL Pt dish at 100° until H_2O is expelled; add few drops pure olive oil and heat slowly over flame or under IR lamp until swelling stops. Place dish in furnace at ca 525° and leave until white ash is obtained. Moisten ash with H_2O, dry on steam bath and then on hot plate, and re-ash at 525° to const wt.

31.013 ***Method II***

Carbonize sample of appropriate wt for product being examined (usually 5–10 g) in 50–100 mL Pt dish at ca 525° and treat charred mass with hot H_2O to dissolve sol. salts. (In case of low-purity products, addn of few drops pure olive oil, as in **31.012**, may be desirable.) Filter thru ashless paper, ignite paper and residue to white ash, add filtrate of sol. salts, evap. to dryness, and ignite at ca 525° to const wt.

31.014 Sulfated Ash—Official Final Action

Weigh 5 g sample into 50–100 mL Pt dish, add 5 mL 10% (by wt) H_2SO_4, heat on hot plate until sample is well carbonized, and then ash in furnace at ca 550°. Cool, add 2–3 mL 10% H_2SO_4, evap. on steam bath, dry on hot plate, and again ignite at 550° to const wt. Express result as % sulfated ash.

31.015 Soluble and Insoluble Ash—Official Final Action

Ash sample as in **31.012** or **31.013**. Add 10 mL H_2O to ash in the Pt dish, heat nearly to boiling, filter thru ashless paper, and wash with hot H_2O until combined filtrate and washings measure ca 60 mL. Return paper and contents to Pt dish, ignite carefully, cool, and weigh. Calc. % H_2O-sol. and H_2O-insol. ash.

31.016 Alkalinity of Soluble Ash—Official Final Action

Cool filtrate from **31.015** and titr. with 0.1*N* HCl, **50.011–50.012**, using Me orange, **6.005(g)**. Express alky in terms of mL 1*N* acid/100 g sample.

31.017 Alkalinity of Insoluble Ash—Official Final Action

Add excess 0.1*N* HCl (usually 10–15 mL) to ignited insol. ash in Pt dish, **31.015**, heat to incipient boiling on hot plate, and cool. Transfer quant. to erlenmeyer and titr. excess HCl with 0.1*N* NaOH, using Me orange. Express alky in terms of mL 1*N* acid/100 g sample.

31.018 Mineral Adulterants in Ash (*5*)
Official First Action

In large porcelain evapg dish, mix 100 g sample with ca 35 g H_2SO_4 and evap. to sirupy consistency. Pass elec. current thru it while stirring by placing one Pt electrode in bottom of dish near one side and attaching other to lower end of glass rod with which contents are stirred. Begin with current of ca 1 amp and gradually increase to 4. In 10–15 min mass is reduced to fine, dry char that may be readily burned to white ash in original dish over free flame or in furnace.

Note: This method is preferred to ordinary method of heating with H_2SO_4, especially in case of molasses, because, if properly manipulated, material comes quickly into form of very finely divided char or powder that is especially adapted for subsequent quick ignition.

If elec. current is not available, treat 100 g sample in large porcelain dish, evap. to sirupy consistency with enough H_2SO_4 to carbonize mass thoroly, and ignite in usual manner.

Following adulterants may be present: salts of Sn, used in molasses to bleach; mineral pigments, such as $PbCrO_4$ in yellow confectionery; oxides of Fe, sometimes used to simulate color of chocolate; and Cu. These elements may be detected by usual qual. tests.

31.019 Nitrogen—Official Final Action

Det. N in 5 g sample as in **2.057**, using larger vol. of the H_2SO_4 if necessary for complete digestion.

Sucrose—Polarimetric Methods

31.020 ***General Procedure—Official Final Action***

(Rules of International Commission for Uniform Methods of Sugar Analysis (ICUMSA) (***6***))

(a) *Standardization of Saccharimeter Scale.*—Saccharimeter scale must be graduated in conformity with International Sugar Scale adopted by ICUMSA. Rotations on this scale are designated as degrees sugar (°S).

Basis of calibration of 100° point on International Sugar Scale is polarization of normal soln of pure sucrose (26.000 g/100 mL) at 20° in 200 mm tube, using white light and dichromate filter defined by Commission, **(b)**. This soln, polarized at 20°, must give saccharimeter reading of exactly 100°S. Temp. of sugar soln during polarization must be kept constant at 20°.

Following rotations hold for normal quartz plate of International Sugar Scale: Normal Quartz Plate = 100°S = 40.690° ±0.002° (λ = 5461 Å) at 20°

$$1° (\lambda = 5461 \text{ Å}) = 2.4576°S$$

Normal Quartz Plate = 100°S = 34.620°±0.002° (λ = 5892.5 Å) at 20°

$$1° (\lambda = 5892.5 \text{ Å}) = 2.8885°S$$

For existing saccharimeters graduated on Herzfeld-Schönrock scale, either change saccharimeter scale or use wt *w* of 26.026 g in 100 mL.

(b) *Directions for Raw Sugars.*—In general, make all polarizations at 20°. For countries where mean temp. is >20°, saccharimeters may be adjusted at 30° or any other suitable temp., under conditions specified above, provided sugar soln is dild to final vol. and polarized at this same temp.

In detg polarization of substances contg sugar, use only half-shade instruments, either single- or double-wedge, and either 200 or 400 mm instruments. During observation, keep app. in fixed position and so far removed from source of light that polarizing nicol is not warmed. As sources of light, use lamps that give strong white illumination or Na lamp. Whenever there is any irregularity in source of light, place thin ground-glass plate between source of light and polariscope so as to render illumination uniform.

Before and after each set of observations, det. correct adjustment of saccharimeter, using stdzd quartz plates; use calibrated wts, polarization flasks, and observation tubes and cover glasses. (Scratched or strained cover glasses must not be used.) Make several readings and take mean thereof but do not reject any reading.

Quartz plates are stdzd to second decimal place. Instrument and plate must be at same temp. (preferably 20°). Different points of scale, preferably 20°, 50°, 80°, and 100°S, should be tested against the plates.

In detg polarization, use whole normal wt (26±0.002 g) for 100 mL or multiple for any corresponding vol. Bring soln exactly to mark at proper temp. and after wiping out neck of flask with filter paper, add min. amt of *dry basic* $Pb(OAc)_2$, **31.021(c)**, shake to dissolve, and pour all clarified sugar soln on rapid, air-dry filter. Cover funnel at start of filtration. Reject first 25 mL filtrate and use remainder (must be perfectly clear) for polarization. In no case return whole soln or any part to filter. If filtrate is cloudy after 25 mL has been rejected, begin new detn. Polarize in 200 mm tube. If, after all means have been used to effect proper decolorization, soln is too dark to read, use 100 mm tube and multiply reading by 2.

Other permissible clarifying and decolorizing agents are alumina cream, **31.021(b)**, or concd alum soln. Do not use boneblack or decolorizing powders.

Whenever white light is used, it must be filtered thru soln of $K_2Cr_2O_7$ of such concn that % $K_2Cr_2O_7$ × length of column of soln in cm = 9. Double this concn in polarizing carbohydrate materials of high rotation dispersion, such as com. glucose, etc.

(c) *Normal Weights and Conversion Factors of Different Saccharimeter Scales.*—*(1) Herzfeld-Schönrock Scale.*—Normal wt = 26.026 g/100 mL soln. 1° = 0.34657° Angular Rotation D.*

(2) International Sugar Scale.—Normal wt = 26.000 g/100 mL soln. 1° = 0.34620° Angular Rotation D.*

(3) French Sugar Scale.—Normal wt = 16.269 g/100 mL soln. 1° = 0.21667° Angular Rotation D.*

31.021 *Preparation and Use of Clarifying Reagents (7) Official Final Action*

(*Caution: See* **51.084.**)

(a) *Basic lead acetate soln.*—Activate litharge by heating 2.5–3 hr at 650–670° in furnace (cooled product should be lemon color). Boil 430 g neut. $Pb(OAc)_2.3H_2O$, 130 g freshly activated litharge, and 1 L H_2O 30 min. Let mixt. cool and settle; then dil. supernate to sp gr of 1.25 with recently boiled H_2O. (Solid basic $Pb(OAc)_2$ may be substituted for the normal salt and litharge in prepn of soln. Because of error caused by vol. of ppt, this reagent is not recommended for clarifying products of low purity.)

(b) *Alumina cream.*—Prep. cold satd soln of alum in H_2O. Add NH_4OH with constant stirring until soln is alk. to litmus, let ppt settle, and wash by decantation with H_2O until wash H_2O gives only slight test for sulfates with $BaCl_2$ soln. Pour off excess H_2O and store residual cream in g-s bottle. (Alumina cream is suitable for clarifying light-colored sugar products or as adjunct to other agents when sugars are detd by polariscopic or reducing sugar methods.)

(c) *Dry basic lead acetate ACS.*—$3Pb(OAc)_2.2PbO$. Of this salt, ca 0.3 g = 1 mL basic $Pb(OAc)_2$ soln, **(a)**. In making clarification, add small amt of dry salt to sugar soln after dilg to vol., and shake; then add more salt and shake again, repeating addn until pptn is complete, but avoiding any excess. When molasses or any other substance producing heavy ppt is being clarified, add some dry, coarse sand to break up pellets of basic $Pb(OAc)_2$ and ppt. (Unless in excess, dry basic $Pb(OAc)_2$ does not cause vol. error.)

(d) *Neutral lead acetate soln.*—Prep. satd soln of neut. $Pb(OAc)_2$ and add to sugar soln before dilg to vol. (This reagent may be used for clarifying light-colored sugar products when sugars are detd by polariscopic methods, and its use is imperative when reducing sugars are detd in soln used for polarization.)

To remove excess Pb used in clarification, add anhyd. K or Na oxalate to clarified filtrate in small amts until test for Pb in filtrate is neg.; then refilter.

31.022 *Temperature Corrections for Polarization of Sugars (8)—Official First Action*

(a) *Refined sugars.*—Polarizations of sugars testing ≥99, when made at temp. other than 20°, may be calcd to polarizations at 20° by following formula:

$$P_{20} = p_t[1 + 0.0003\ (t - 20)],$$

where p_t = polarization at temp. read, t. (May be applied to beet sugar and raw cane sugars polarizing ≥96°S without appreciable error.)

(b) *Raw sugars.*—Polarization of raw cane sugars <96°S when made at temps other than 20°, may be calcd to polarizations at 20° by following formula:

$$P_{20} = p_t + 0.0015\ (p_t - 80)\ (t - 20),$$

where p_t and t are same as in **(a)**.

When % fructose in the sugar is known (in case of honeys and sugar cane products = ca ½ reducing sugars), use following formula:

$$P_{20} = p_t + 0.0003S\ (t - 20) - 0.00812F\ (t - 20),$$

where p_t *and* t are same as in **(a)**; S = % sucrose; and F = % fructose.

These formulas give results agreeing closely with polarizations obtained at 20° if sugar is of av. normal composition.

31.023 *Mutarotation—Procedure*

Products, such as honey and com. glucose, that contain glucose or other reducing sugars in cryst. form or in soln at high density may show mutarotation under conditions prevailing during analysis. Only const rotation should be used in polarimetric methods. To obtain this, let soln prepd for polarization stand overnight before making reading. If it is desired to make reading immediately, heat neut. soln (pH ca 7.0) to bp or add few drops NH_4OH, before dilg to vol.; or, if soln has been made to vol., add dry Na_2CO_3 until just distinctly alk. to litmus paper. (Do not let slightly alk. solns stand at such high temps or for such lengths of time as to cause destruction of fructose.) Det. completion of mutarotation by making readings at 15–30 min intervals until const.

Sucrose in Absence of Raffinose

By Polarization Before and After Inversion with Invertase (9)—Official Final Action

31.024 ★ *Reagent*

Invertase soln.—Com. invertase prepns are available (Invertase Scales (without melibiase), Wallerstein Co.). If it is desired to prep. soln in laboratory, method described in *(1)* may be

* Designation D refers to Na light of 589.2 nm.

used. In either case, prepn may be further purified and concd by ultrafiltration method described in (*3*). Com. prepns may also be purified by dialysis and then reconcd by evapg *in vacuo* at temp. ≤40°.

(*1*) *Crude invertase soln.*—Mix yeast with H_2O in proportion of 10 lb compressed bakers yeast to 5 L H_2O. Add 2 L toluene and stir thoroly at frequent intervals during first 24 hr. Let stand 7 days with occasional stirring, and filter by gravity thru large fluted papers. Mix residue with 2 L H_2O, filter, and combine filtrates. Purify (J. Ind. Chem. **16**, 562(1924)) by adding 15 g neut. $Pb(OAc)_2.3H_2O$ to each L of ext and filtering on paper after all $Pb(OAc)_2$ dissolves. Complete purification immediately by dialysis or by washing on ultrafilter as in (*3*).

(*2*) *Collodion ultrafilter* (***10***).—Dissolve 6 g sol. (in alcohol and ether mixt.) pyroxylin or nitrocellulose in mixt. of 50 mL absolute alcohol and 50 mL absolute ether by adding the alcohol to the cotton, letting mixt. stand in stoppered flask 10 min, adding the ether, and shaking. Let soln stand overnight. Pour ca 100 mL into 2 L graduate, and coat entire inside surface of graduate with the collodion. Drain, and dry 10 min. Fill graduate with H_2O, let stand 10–15 min, pour out H_2O, and remove collodion sack. Test for leaks by filling with H_2O. Slit open longitudinally and cut out circular piece 17–20 cm (7–8") diam. Cut bottom from 2 L bottle or erlenmeyer and grind edge smooth. Place it upon still moist collodion disk, fold edge of disk up around bottle, and cement it thereto with collodion that contains increased proportion of ether. Place 3 or 4 thicknesses of wet filter paper in 20 cm buchner. Place bottle with collodion membrane upon filter paper. Pour melted white petrolatum to depth of 2 cm between bottle and inside of funnel. Provide bottle with small mech. stirrer.

(*3*) *Washing and concentrating of invertase soln by ultrafiltration.*—Filter 4 L partially purified soln thru the ultrafilter, stirring continuously, until ca 1 L remains. Wash with distd H_2O added from const level device until filtrate is colorless (3 or 4 L of wash H_2O is required). Discard filtrate and transfer invertase soln to stoppered bottle. During entire process and in storage, preserve invertase soln with toluene.

(*4*) *Activity of invertase soln.*—Following test for activity of invertase soln is usually adequate: Dil. 1 mL invertase prepn to 200 mL. Transfer 10 g sucrose (granulated sugar) to sugar flask graduated at 100 and 110 mL, dissolve in ca 76 mL H_2O, add 2 drops HOAc, and dil. to 100 mL mark. To the 100 mL sugar soln add 10 mL dil. invertase soln and mix thoroly and rapidly, noting exact time at which solns are mixed. After exactly 60 min, make portions of soln just distinctly alk. to litmus paper with anhyd. Na_2CO_3 and polarize in 200 mm tube at 20°. If invertase soln is sufficiently active, alk. soln will polarize ca 31°S without correcting for diln to 110 mL and optical activity of invertase soln.

If more exact information concerning activity of invertase prepn is desired, det. its velocity const as follows: Dil. 1 mL invertase soln to 200 mL at 20°; place in const temp. bath at 20°; and when soln reaches this temp., pipet 20 mL into flask contg 200 mL sucrose soln (10 g/100 mL concn) previously made distinctly acid to Me red (corresponding to pH ca 4.6) by addn of HOAc and also brought to temp. of 20° in same bath. Mix thoroly and promptly, and note time at which invertase soln was added. Keep sucrose-invertase mixt. in const temp. bath; remove portions after 15, 30, and 45 min; immediately after removing, make each portion just distinctly alk. to litmus paper with anhyd. Na_2CO_3, and polarize at 20°. Correct all polarizations for polarization of invertase soln. Calc. velocity const, *k*, for each of polarizations (at time *t*) subsequent to initial polarization by following formula:

$$k = [\log_{10} 1.32\,R_0 - \log_{10}(R_t + 0.32\,R_0)]/t,$$

where k = unimolecular reaction velocity constant; t = number of min elapsing from time invertase and sucrose solns were mixed until inversion was stopped by addn of Na_2CO_3; R_0 = initial polarization (calcd by multiplying polarization of sucrose soln by 10/11 and correcting for polarization of invertase soln); and R_t = polarization at time t.

Invertase soln of sufficient activity (JAOAC **11**, 168 (1928); **16**, 79(1933); **17**, 74(1934)) should yield av. value for k (for various time periods) of ≥0.1, after multiplying k value directly obtained by 200 in order to correct for initial diln of invertase soln. Diln of invertase soln mentioned above is made solely for purpose of detg its activity; original, undild invertase soln is used as inverting reagent in detn of sucrose, **31.025**, unless activity of original invertase soln greatly exceeds k value of 0.1, and it is desirable to conserve invertase. In this case, dil. to k value of 0.1, which is done in same manner as dilg other solns to std strength. Activity of invertase prepn required for rapid inversion, **31.025(c)**, is same as that needed for overnight inversion, **31.025(b)**, but proportion of invertase prepn used in former case is twice that used in latter.

31.025 ***Determination***

(**a**) *Direct reading.*—Dissolve double normal wt of sample (52 g), or fraction thereof, in H_2O in 200 mL vol. flask; add necessary clarifying agent, **31.021(a)**, (**b**), or (**d**), avoiding excess; shake, dil. to vol. with H_2O, mix well, and filter, keeping funnel covered with watch glass. Reject first 25 mL filtrate.

If Pb clarifying agent was used, remove excess Pb from soln when enough filtrate collects by adding anhyd. Na_2CO_3, little at time, avoiding excess; mix well and refilter, rejecting first 25 mL filtrate. (Instead of weighing 52 g into 200 mL flask, two 26 g portions may be dild to 100 mL each, and treated exactly as described. Depending on color of product, multiples or fractions of normal wt may be used, and results calcd to basis of 26 g/100 mL.)

Pipet one 50 mL portion Pb-free filtrate into 100 mL vol. flask, dil. to vol. with H_2O, mix well, and polarize in 200 mm tube. Result, multiplied by 2, is direct reading (P of formula given below) or polarization before inversion. (If 400 mm tube is used, reading equals P.) If there is possibility of mutarotation, proceed as in **31.023**.

(**b**) *Invert reading.*—First det. vol. of HOAc necessary to make 50 mL of the Pb-free filtrate distinctly acid to Me red; then to another 50 mL Pb-free soln in 100 mL vol. flask add requisite vol. of acid and 5 mL invertase soln, fill flask with H_2O nearly to 100 mL, and let stand overnight (preferably at ≥20°).

Cool, and dil. to 100 mL at 20°. Mix well and polarize at 20° in 200 mm tube. If in doubt as to completion of hydrolysis, let portion of soln remain several hr and again polarize. If there is no change from previous reading, inversion is complete. Carefully note reading and temp. of soln. If it is necessary to work at temp. other than 20°, which is permissible within narrow limits, complete vols and make both direct and invert readings at same temp. Correct polarization for optical activity of invertase soln and multiply by 2. Calc. % sucrose, S, by following formula:

$$S = \frac{100(P - I)}{132.1 - 0.0833(13 - m) - 0.53(t - 20)},$$

where P = direct reading, normal soln; I = invert reading, normal soln; t = temp. at which readings are made; and m = g total solids from original sample in 100 mL inverted soln. To obtain m for liqs, det. total solids in original sample as % by wt, as in **31.011**, and multiply this figure by wt original sample in 100 mL invert soln.

(**c**) *Rapid inversion at 55–60°* (*11*).—If more rapid inversion is desired, proceed as follows: Prep. sample as in (**a**) and to 50 mL Pb-free filtrate in 100 mL vol. flask add enough HOAc to render soln distinctly acid to Me red, **31.024**(*4*). Det. vol. of HOAc required before pipetting 50 mL portion as in (**b**). Add 10 mL invertase soln, mix thoroly, place flask in H_2O bath at 55–60°, and let stand at that temp. 15 min, shaking occasionally.

Cool, add Na_2CO_3 until distinctly alk. to litmus paper, dil. to 100 mL at 20°, mix well, and det. polarization at 20° in 200 mm tube. Let soln remain in tube 10 min and again det. polarization. If there is no change from previous reading, mutarotation is complete. Carefully note reading and temp. of soln. Correct polarization for optical activity of invertase soln and multiply by 2. Calc. % sucrose by formula given in (**b**).

If soln has been made so alk. as to cause destruction of sugar, polarization, if neg., will in general decrease, since decomposition of fructose ordinarily is more rapid than that of other sugars present. If soln has not been made alk. enough to complete mutarotation quickly, polarization, if neg., will in general increase. As analyst gains experience he may omit polarization after 10 min if he has satisfied himself that he is adding enough Na_2CO_3 to complete mutarotation at once without causing any destruction of sugar during period intervening before polarization.

31.026 *By Polarization Before and After Inversion with Hydrochloric Acid (12)—Official Final Action*

(**a**) *Direct reading.*—Prep soln as in **31.025**(**a**). Pipet 50 mL Pb-free filtrate into 100 mL vol. flask; add 2.315 g NaCl and 25 mL H_2O. Dil. to vol. with H_2O at 20° and polarize in 200 mm tube at 20°. Multiply reading by 2 to obtain direct reading.

(**b**) *Invert reading.*—Pipet 50 mL portion Pb-free filtrate into 100 mL vol. flask and add 20 mL H_2O. Add, little by little, while rotating flask, 10 mL HCl (sp gr 1.1029 at 20/4° or 24.85° Brix at 20°). Heat H_2O bath and adjust heater to keep bath at 60°. Place flask in H_2O bath, agitate continuously ca 3 min, and leave flask in bath exactly 7 min longer. Place flask at once in H_2O at 20°.

When contents cool to ca 35°, dil. almost to mark. Leave flask in bath at 20° at least 30 min longer and finally dil. to mark. Mix well and polarize soln in 200 mm tube provided with lateral branch and H_2O jacket, keeping temp. at 20°. This reading must be multiplied by 2 to obtain invert reading. If it is necessary to work at temp. other than 20°, which is permissible within narrow limits, vols must be completed and both direct and invert polarizations must be made at exactly same temp.

Calc. % sucrose, S, by following formula:

$$S = \frac{100\,(P - I)}{132.56 - 0.0794(13 - m) - 0.53(t - 20)},$$

where P = direct reading, normal soln; I = invert reading, normal soln; t = temp. at which readings are made; and m = g total solids from original sample in 100 mL inverted soln. To obtain m for liqs, det. total solids in original sample as % by wt as in **31.011**, and multiply this figure by wt original sample in 100 mL invert soln.

(**c**) *Inversion at room temperature.*—Inversion may also be accomplished as follows: (*1*) Pipet 50 mL Pb-free filtrate into 100 mL vol. flask, add 20 mL H_2O and 10 mL HCl (sp gr 1.1029 at 20/4° or 24.85° Brix at 20°), and set aside 24 hr at ≥22°; or (*2*) set aside 10 hr if >28°. Dil. to 100 mL at 20° and polarize as in (**b**). Under these conditions formula must be changed to following:

$$S = \frac{100(P - I)}{132.66 - 0.0794(13 - m) - 0.53(t - 20)}.$$

Sucrose and Raffinose (*13*)

By Polarization Before and After Treatment with Two Enzyme Preparations—Official Final Action

31.027 *Reagents*

(**a**) *Invertase soln* (*top yeast extract*).—*See* **31.024**. This soln should be free from enzyme melibiase. Its invertase activity should be at least as great as that used for detn of sucrose in absence of raffinose, **31.024**(*4*). Com. available.

(**b**) *Invertase-melibiase soln* (*bottom yeast extract*). —Prep. as in **31.024**, using bottom fermenting brewers yeast instead of bakers yeast. Invertase activity should be at least as great as in (**a**). Obtainable only from brewers as a liq. Compress by filtering on buchner.

Test melibiase activity of soln as follows: Add 2 mL soln to be tested to 20 mL weakly acid melibiose soln polarizing +20.0°S and let stand 30 min at ca 20°. Add enough Na_2CO_3 to make soln slightly alk. to litmus paper. Prepn suitable for overnight hydrolysis of solns contg ≤0.2 g raffinose in 100 mL should have hydrolyzed 35% of melibiose present under conditions mentioned; prepn suitable for overnight hydrolysis of solns contg ≤0.65 g raffinose in 100 mL should have produced 50% hydrolysis of melibiose; and prepn suitable for overnight hydrolysis of solns contg 0.65–1.3 g raffinose in 100 mL should have hydrolyzed at least 70% of melibiose present under above conditions. Prepns of melibiose soln that polarize +20°S before hydrolysis will polarize +16.4°, +14.9°, and +12.9°S after 35, 50, and 70% hydrolysis, resp.

31.028 *Determination*

With sugar beet products, weigh material specified in Table **31:01**, transfer to 300 mL vol. flask, add vol. basic $Pb(OAc)_2$ soln, **31.021**(**a**), indicated in table, and dil. to vol. at 20°. Mix thoroly and filter thru fluted paper in closely covered funnel, rejecting first 25 mL filtrate. When enough filtrate collects, remove Pb from soln by adding $NH_4H_2PO_4$ in as small excess as possible, Table **31:01**. This condition is readily detd after little practice by appearance of $Pb_3(PO_4)_2$ ppt, which usually flocculates and settles rapidly in presence of slight excess of the salt. Mix well and filter, again rejecting at least first 25 mL filtrate.

Make direct polarization in 200 mm tube at 20° unless soln contains appreciable amt of invert sugar, in which case pipet 50 mL portion Pb-free filtrate into 100 mL flask, dil. with H_2O to vol., mix well, and polarize at 20°, preferably in 400 mm tube. This reading, calcd to normal wt of 26 g in 100 mL and 200 mm tube length, is direct reading (P) of formula given below for polarization before inversion.

Transfer two 50 mL portions of the Pb-free filtrate to 100 mL vol. flasks. To one add 5 mL invertase soln (top yeast ext) and to other 5 mL invertase-melibiase soln (bottom yeast ext); let stand overnight at room temp. (preferably ≥20°), dil. to vol., mix well, and polarize at 20°, preferably in 400 mm jacketed tube.

If rapid hydrolysis is desired, add 10 mL of each of the enzyme solns to 50 mL portions Pb-free filtrate in 100 mL vol. flasks and place in H_2O bath 40 min at 50–55°. Then add Na_2CO_3 until soln is slightly alk. to litmus paper, dil. to vol. at 20°, mix well, and polarize at 20°, preferably in 400 mm tube. Correct invert readings for optical activity of enzyme soln and calc. polarization to that of normal wt soln of 26 g/100 mL; also calc. reading to 200 mm tube length, if necessary.

Calc. % of anhyd. raffinose, R, and sucrose, S, from following formulas:

$$R = 1.354(X - Y);$$

$$S = \frac{(P - 2.202X + 1.202Y)100}{132.12 - 0.00718[132.12 - (P - 2.202X + 1.202Y)]},$$

where P = direct polarization, normal soln; X = corrected polarization after top yeast hydrolysis, normal soln; and Y = corrected polarization after bottom yeast hydrolysis, normal soln.

Quantities X and Y are treated algebraically.

31.029 *By Polarization Before and After Inversion with Hydrochloric Acid—Official Final Action*

(Of value chiefly in analysis of beet products)

If direct reading is >1° higher than % sucrose as calcd by formula given in **31.026(b)**, raffinose is probably present. Calc. sucrose and raffinose by following formulas (J. Ind. Eng. Chem. **13**, 793(1921)).

When polarizations are made at 20°:

$$S = (0.514P - I)/0.844, \text{ and } R = (0.33P + I)/1.563,$$

where P = direct reading, normal soln; I = invert reading, normal soln; S = % sucrose; and R = % anhyd. raffinose.

For all temps other than 20°:

$$S = \frac{P(0.478 + 0.0018t_2) - I(1.006 - 0.0003t_1)}{(0.908 - 0.0032t_2)(1.006 - 0.0003t_1)},$$

and

$$R = \frac{P(0.43 - 0.005t_2) + I(1.006 - 0.0003t_1)}{(1.681 - 0.0059t_2)(1.006 - 0.0003t_1)},$$

where t_1 = temp. of direct polarization; and t_2 = temp. of invert polarization.

31.030 Sucrose by Double Dilution Method (*14*) Official Final Action

(Applicable to substances in which vol. of combined insol. matter and ppt from clarifying agents is >1 mL from 26 g)

Weigh 13 g sample and dil. to 100 mL, using appropriate clarifier (basic $Pb(OAc)_2$ for dark-colored confectionery or molasses, and alumina cream for light-colored confectionery). Also weigh 26 g sample and dil. this second soln with clarifier to 100 mL. Filter both solns, and obtain direct polariscopic readings. Invert each soln as in **31.025(b)** or **(c)** or **31.026(b)** or **(c)** and obtain resp. invert readings.

True direct polarization of sample = 4 times direct polarization of dild soln minus direct polarization of undild soln. True invert polarization = 4 times invert polarization of dild soln minus invert polarization of undild soln. Calc. sucrose from true polarizations thus obtained, using formula in **31.025(b)** or **31.026(b)** or **(c)** corresponding to method of inversion used.

Sucrose—Chemical Methods

31.031 *From Reducing Sugars Before and After Inversion—Official Final Action*

Det. reducing sugars as in **31.038** (clarification having been effected with neutral $Pb(OAc)_2$ as in **31.021(d)**) and calc. to invert sugar from **52.019**. Invert soln as in **31.025(b)** or **(c)**, or **31.026(b)** or **(c)**; exactly neutze acid; and again det. reducing sugars, but calc. them to invert sugar from table, **52.019**, using invert sugar alone column. Deduct % invert sugar obtained before inversion from that obtained after inversion and multiply difference by 0.95 to obtain % sucrose. Dil. solns in both detns so that ≤230 mg invert sugar is present in amt taken for reduction. It is important that all Pb be removed from soln with anhyd. powd K oxalate before reduction.

Commercial Glucose (Approximate) Polarimetric Methods—Procedure

31.032 *Substances Containing Little or No Invert Sugar*

Com. glucose cannot be detd accurately, since amts of dextrin, maltose, and dextrose present vary. However, in sirups in which amt of invert sugar is too small to appreciably affect result, com. glucose may be estd approx. by following formula:

$$G = (a - S)100/211,$$

where G = % com. glucose solids; a = direct polarization, normal soln; and S = % cane sugar.

Express results in terms of com. glucose solids polarizing +211°S. (Result may be recalcd in terms of com. glucose of any polarization desired.)

Table 31:01 Amounts of Sample and Reagents Required for Clarification and Deleading of Beet Sugar-House Products

Material	Amount per 100 mL	Basic Lead Acetate (55° Brix)	Ammonium Dihydrogen Phosphate
	gram	*mL*	*gram*
Cossettes[a]	13	3	0.2
Pulp	100 mL[b]	2–4	0.2
Lime cake or sewer[c]	26.5	1.5	. . .[d]
Thin juice	52	2	0.2–0.3
Thick juice	26	4	0.3–0.4
White massecuite	13 or 26	3 or 6	0.3–0.7
High wash sirup	13 or 26	3 or 6	0.3–0.7
High green sirup	13 or 26	5 or 10	0.3–0.7
Raw or remelt massecuite	13	6	0.3–0.4
Raw or remelt sugar	26	3–4	0.3–0.4
Sugar melter	26	2–3	0.3–0.4
Low wash sirup	13	8–10	0.4–0.5
Low green sirup or molasses	13	10	0.4–0.5
Saccharate cakes and milk (carbonated)	26	4–6	0.3–04
Steffen waste and wash waters[c]	78 or 50 mL	2–3	0.2

[a] Usual method of extn, 26 g in 201.2 mL.
[b] Dil. to 110 mL.
[c] Neutze with HAOc before adding basic $Pb(OAc)_2$.
[d] As Ca in soln will be partly pptd by the phosphate, it is necessary to add enough phosphate to complete pptn of both Pb and Ca salts, and no definite quantity can be specified.

31.033 *Substances Containing Invert Sugar*

Prep. inverted half-normal soln of substance as in **31.026(b)**, except cool soln after inversion, make neut. to phthln with NaOH soln, slightly acidify with HCl (1+5), and treat with 5–10 mL alumina cream, **31.021 (b)**, before dilg to vol. Filter, and polarize at 87° in 200 mm jacketed metal tube. Multiply reading by 200 and divide by factor 196 to obtain amt of com. glucose solids polarizing +211°S. (Result may be recalcd in terms of com. glucose of any polarization desired.)

Invert Sugar—Chemical Methods

I. Lane-Eynon General Volumetric Method (15) Official Final Action

31.034 ***Reagents***

Soxhlet modification of Fehling soln.—Prep. by mixing equal vols of (**a**) and (**b**) immediately before use.

(**a**) *Copper sulfate soln.*—Dissolve 34.639 g $CuSO_4.5H_2O$ in H_2O, dil. to 500 mL, and filter thru glass wool or paper. Det. Cu content of soln (preferably by electrolysis, **31.044**) and so adjust that it contains 440.9 mg Cu/25 mL.

(**b**) *Alkaline tartrate soln.*—Dissolve 173 g KNa tartrate.$4H_2O$ (Rochelle salt) and 50 g NaOH in H_2O, dil. to 500 mL, let stand 2 days, and filter thru prepd asbestos, **31.037**.

(**c**) *Invert sugar std soln.*—1%. To soln of 9.5 g pure sucrose, add 5 mL HCl and dil. with H_2O to ca 100 mL. Store several days at room temp. (ca 7 days at 12–15° or 3 days at 20–25°); then dil. to 1 L. (Acidified 1% invert sugar soln is stable for several months.) Neutze aliquot with ca 1 *N* NaOH and dil. to desired concn immediately before use.

31.035 ***Standardization***

Accurately pipet 10 or 25 mL mixed Soxhlet reagent, or 5 or 12.5 mL each of Soxhlet solns **31.034(a)** and (**b**), into 300–400 mL erlenmeyer. (Amt of Cu taken differs slightly between 2 methods of pipetting, and method used must be consistent in stdzn and detn.) Prep. std soln of pure sugar of such concn that >15 mL and <50 mL is required to reduce all the Cu. Dispense from buret with offset tip to keep tube out of steam. To det. mg sugar required to completely reduce Cu at different concns, consult **52.017** and **52.018**. Add sugar soln within 0.5–1.0 mL of total required, heat cold mixt. to bp on wire gauze over burner, and maintain moderate boiling 2 min (coarse grains of C or other suitable inert material may be used to prevent bumping). Without removing flame add 1 mL *0.2% aq. methylene blue soln* (or 3–4 drops 1% soln) and complete titrn within total boiling time of ca 3 min by small addns (2–3 drops) of sugar soln to decoloration of indicator. (Maintain continuous evolution of steam to prevent reoxidn of Cu or indicator.) After complete reduction of Cu, methylene blue is reduced to colorless compd and soln resumes orange Cu_2O color which it had before addn of indicator.

Multiply titer by mg/mL std soln to obtain total sugar required to reduce the Cu. Compare with tabulated value in **52.017** or **52.018** to det. correction, if any, to be applied to table. Small deviations from tabulated values may arise from variations in technic or composition of reagents. If only approx. results (within 1%) are required, stdzn may be omitted, provided specifications of analysis are rigidly observed.

31.036 ***Determination***

(**a**) *Incremental method.*—If approx. concn of sugar in sample is unknown, proceed by incremental method of titrn. To 10 or 25 mL mixed Soxhlet soln, add 15 mL sugar soln and heat to bp over wire gauze. Boil ca 15 sec and rapidly add further amts of sugar soln until only faintest perceptible blue remains. Then add 1 mL 0.2% aq. methylene blue soln (or 3–4 drops 1% soln) and complete titrn by adding sugar soln dropwise. (Error resulting from this titrn will generally be ≤1%.)

(**b**) *Standard method.*—For higher precision repeat titrn, adding almost entire sugar soln required to reduce all Cu and proceed as in **31.035**. From **52.017** or **52.018** find total reducing sugar corresponding to titer and apply correction previously detd. Calc. as follows: total reducing sugar required × 100/titer = mg sugar in 100 mL.

II. Munson-Walker General Method (16) *Official Final Action*

31.037 ***Reagents***

Asbestos.—Digest asbestos, amphibole variety (*Caution: See* **51.086**), with HCl (1+3) 2–3 days. Wash acid-free, digest similar period with 10% NaOH soln, and then treat few hr with hot alk. tartrate soln, **31.034(b)** (alk. tartrate solns that have stood for some time may be used for this purpose). Wash asbestos alkali-free; digest several hr with HNO_3 (1+3); and after washing acid-free, shake with H_2O into fine pulp. In prepg gooch, make film of asbestos 6 mm thick and wash thoroly with H_2O to remove fine particles. If pptd Cu_2O is to be weighed as such, wash crucible with 10 mL alcohol and then with 10 mL ether; dry 30 min at 100°, cool in desiccator, and weigh.

Other reagents and solns used are described in **31.034**. Solns may be clarified by neut. $Pb(OAc)_2$ soln, **31.021(d)** (never basic $Pb(OAc)_2$). Remove excess Pb with dry Na oxalate.

31.038 ***Precipitation of Cuprous Oxide***

Transfer 25 mL each of $CuSO_4$ and alk. tartrate solns to 400 mL beaker of alkali-resistant glass and add 50 mL reducing sugar soln; or if smaller vol. of sugar soln is used, add H_2O to make flnal vol. 100 mL. Heat beaker on asbestos gauze over Bunsen burner, regulate flame so that boiling begins in 4 min, and continue boiling exactly 2 min. (It is important that these directions be strictly observed. To regulate burner for this purpose it is advisable to make preliminary tests, using 50 mL reagent and 50 mL H_2O, before proceeding with actual detn. Elec. heater may be used instead of burner.) Keep beaker covered with watch glass during heating.

Filter hot soln at once thru asbestos mat in porcelain gooch, using suction. Wash ppt of Cu_2O thoroly with H_2O at ca 60° and either weigh directly as Cu_2O, **31.039**, or det. amt of reduced Cu by one of methods described in **31.040–31.044**. Conduct blank detn, using 50 mL reagent and 50 mL H_2O, and if wt Cu_2O obtained is >0.5 mg, correct result of reducing sugar detn accordingly. Alk. tartrate soln deteriorates on standing, and wt Cu_2O obtained in blank increases.

Determination of Reduced Copper

31.039 *By Direct Weighing of Cuprous Oxide*

(Use only for detns in solns of reducing sugars of comparatively high purity. In products contg large amts of mineral or org. impurities, including sucrose, det. Cu in the Cu_2O by one of methods described in **31.040–31.044**, since the Cu_2O is likely to be contaminated with foreign matter.)

Prep. gooch as in **31.037**. Collect pptd Cu_2O on mat as in **31.038**; wash thoroly with hot H_2O, then with 10 mL alcohol, and finally with 10 mL ether. Dry ppt 30 min in oven at 100°, cool, and weigh. Obtain wt invert sugar equiv. to wt Cu_2O from **52.019**.

Number of mg Cu_2O reduced by given amt of reducing sugar varies, depending upon whether or not sucrose is present. In table, absence of sucrose is assumed except in entries under invert sugar and lactose, where, in addn to columns for these alone, columns are given for their mixts with sucrose in specified ratios in the case of lactose and in specified amts of total sugar in 50 mL soln in the case of invert sugar.

(Later Hammond table has replaced original Munson-Walker table, where applicable.)

By Titration with Sodium Thiosulfate (17)

31.040 ***Reagent***

Thiosulfate std soln.—Prep. soln contg 39 g $Na_2S_2O_3.5H_2O$/L. Accurately weigh 0.2–0.4 g pure electrolytic Cu and transfer to 250 mL erlenmeyer roughly marked at 20 mL intervals. Dissolve Cu in 5 mL HNO_3 (1+1), dil. to 20 or 30 mL, boil to expel red fumes, add slight excess satd Br-H_2O, and boil until Br is completely removed. Cool, and add 10 mL NaOAc soln (574 g trihydrate/L). Prep. 42 g/100 mL KI soln made very slightly alk. to avoid formation and oxidn of HI. Add 10 mL of the KI soln and titr. with $Na_2S_2O_3$ soln to light yellow. Add enough starch indicator, **6.005(f)**, to produce marked blue. As end point nears, add 2 g KSCN and stir until completely dissolved. Continue titrn until ppt is perfectly white. 1 mL $Na_2S_2O_3$ soln = ca 10 mg Cu.

It is essential for $Na_2S_2O_3$ titrn that concn of KI in soln be carefully regulated. If soln contains <320 mg Cu, at completion of titrn 4.2–5 g KI should have been added for each 100 mL total soln. If greater amts of Cu are present, add KI soln slowly from buret with const agitation in amts proportionately greater.

31.041 ***Determination***

Wash pptd Cu_2O, cover gooch with watch glass, and dissolve the Cu_2O with 5 mL HNO_3 (1+1) directed under watch glass with pipet. Collect filtrate in 250 mL erlenmeyer roughly marked at 20 mL intervals, and wash watch glass and gooch Cu-free. Proceed as in **31.040**, beginning, ". . . boil to expel red fumes, . . ." Obtain wt reducing sugar equiv. to wt Cu from **52.019**.

By Titration with Potassium Permanganate (18)

31.042 ***Reagents***

(**a**) *Potassium permanganate std soln.*—Approx. 0.1573*N*, and contg 4.98 g/L. Prep. and stdze as in **50.025–50.026**, using 0.35 g Na oxalate.

(**b**) *Ferric sulfate soln.*—Dissolve 135 g $FeNH_4(SO_4)_2.12H_2O$ or 55 g anhyd. $Fe_2(SO_4)_3$ in H_2O, and dil. to 1 L. Det. $Fe_2(SO_4)_3$ in stock supply by strong ignition to Fe_2O_3. Titr. 50 mL $Fe_2(SO_4)_3$ soln, acidified with 20 mL 4*N* H_2SO_4, with $KMnO_4$ soln, and use this titer as 0-point correction.

(**c**) *Ferrous phenanthroline indicator.*—Dissolve 0.7425 g *o*-phenanthroline.H_2O in 25 mL 0.025*M* $FeSO_4$ soln (6.95 g $FeSO_4.7H_2O$/L).

31.043 ***Determination***

Filter the Cu_2O thru gooch, and wash beaker and ppt thoroly. Transfer asbestos pad to beaker with glass rod. Add 50 mL $Fe_2(SO_4)_3$ soln and stir vigorously until Cu_2O is completely dissolved. Examine for complete soln, holding beaker above eye level. Cu_2O must be quant. transferred; if necessary, immerse crucible in soln and make sure adhering Cu_2O is dissolved. Remove crucible with glass rod and wash with H_2O. Add 20 mL 4*N* H_2SO_4 and titr. with std $KMnO_4$ soln. As end point approaches, add 1 drop ferrous phenanthroline indicator. At end point, brownish soln changes to green. Obtain wt reducing sugar equiv. to wt Cu from **52.019**.

31.044 ***By Electrolytic Deposition from Nitric Acid Solution (19)***

Decant hot soln, **31.038**, thru asbestos mat in gooch, and wash beaker and ppt thoroly with hot H_2O. Transfer asbestos mat from crucible to beaker with glass rod and rinse crucible with 14 mL HNO_3 (1+1), letting rinsings flow into beaker. After Cu_2O dissolves, dil. to 100 mL, heat to bp, and continue boiling ca 5 min to remove oxides of N. Cool, filter, transfer to 250 mL beaker, and dil. to 200 mL. Add 1 drop 0.1*N* HCl and mix thoroly.

For electrolysis use cylindrical electrodes of Pt gauze, ca 4 and 5 cm diam., resp., and ca 4.5 cm high, thoroly cleaned, ignited, cooled in desiccator, and weighed. Insert electrodes in Cu soln so that surface of cathode clears anode by ≥5 mm and both electrodes almost touch bottom of beaker. Cover with split watch glass to avoid loss by spattering. Electrolyze with current of 0.2–0.4 amp until deposition is complete, usually overnight. (Wash down sides of beaker and watch glass with H_2O, thus raising level of soln and exposing new surface of cathode; if new surface shows deposit of Cu, electrolysis is not complete.)

Without interrupting current, slowly lower beaker and at same time wash electrodes with stream of H_2O. Immediately immerse electrodes in another beaker of H_2O and break current. (Siphon can be used for washing, adding H_2O as soln is removed. Displacement of HNO_3 soln is complete when current ceases to flow.) Rinse cathode with alcohol and dry few min in oven at 100°. Cool in desiccator and weigh.

Electrolyte may be stirred by rotating anode or mech. stirrer. In this case, current may be increased to 1–2 amp, thus shortening time required for complete deposition of Cu to ca 1 hr.

If extreme care is taken to avoid spattering, Cu_2O can be dissolved by letting HNO_3 flow down walls of crucible. Keep crucible covered as much as possible with small watch glass. Collect filtrate in beaker, and wash watch glass and tip of pipet with jet of H_2O. Continue as above, beginning ". . . dil. to 100 mL, . . ." Obtain wt reducing sugars equiv. to wt Cu from **52.019**.

31.045 ★ ***III. Ofner Volumetric Method (20)*** ★
Official Final Action

(For materials contg small amts of invert sugar in presence of sucrose)

See **29.046–29.047**, 10th ed.

31.046 ★ ***IV. Meissl-Hiller Gravimetric Method*** ★
Official Final Action

(For materials contg >1.5% invert sugar and <98.5% sucrose)

See **29.048**, 10th ed.

31.047 ★ ***V. Quisumbing-Thomas Method (21)*** ★
Official First Action

See **31.048–31.049**, 11th ed.

VI. Berlin Institute Method (22)—Official First Action

(Applicable to dark-colored solns without defecation)

31.048 ***Reagent***

Müller's soln.—Dissolve 35 g $CuSO_4.5H_2O$ in 400 mL boiling H_2O. Sep. dissolve 173 g KNa tartrate.$4H_2O$ (Rochelle salt) and 68 g Na_2CO_3 in 500 mL boiling H_2O. Cool, mix the 2 solns, and dil. to 1 L. Shake with small amt of C and filter. If ppt forms on storage, refilter.

★ Surplus method—*see* inside front cover.

31.049 ***Determination***

Select amt of sample (10 g or less) contg ≤30 mg invert sugar. Pipet 10 mL Müller's soln and 100 mL sugar soln into 300 mL flask and cover. Mix thoroly and heat exactly 10 min in H_2O bath boiling so vigorously that immersion of flask does not interrupt boiling. Place flask so that H_2O level is ≥2 cm above surface of liq. in flask. After heating period, cool flask rapidly without agitation. Add 5 mL 5*N* HOAc to cooled soln, mix, and immediately add excess 0.0333*N* I soln (20–40 mL) from buret. After all Cu_2O ppt dissolves, titr. excess I with 0.0333*N* $Na_2S_2O_3$.

Apply following corrections to mL I soln consumed: (1) mL I required in blank with H_2O instead of sugar soln; (2) mL I required by sugar soln in detn conducted without heating; (3) 2.0 mL I for reducing action of 10 g sucrose or proportionate correction for smaller amt of sucrose. After these corrections 1 mL 0.0333*N* I = 1 mg invert sugar.

Glucose—Chemical Methods

31.050 ***Lane-Eynon General Volumetric Method***
Official Final Action

Proceed as in **31.036**, referring titer to **52.017** or **52.018**.

31.051 ***Munson-Walker General Method***
Official Final Action

Proceed as in **31.038** and obtain wt glucose from **52.019**.

Shaffer-Somogyi Micro Method—Official Final Action

31.052 ***Reagents***

(**a**) *Shaffer-Somogyi carbonate 50 reagent, 5 g KI.*—Dissolve 25 g each of anhyd. Na_2CO_3 and KNa tartrate.$4H_2O$ (Rochelle salt) in ca 500 mL H_2O in 2 L beaker. Add thru funnel with tip under surface, with stirring, 75 mL of soln of 100 g $CuSO_4.5H_2O$/L. Add 20 g $NaHCO_3$, dissolve, and add 5 g KI. Transfer soln to 1 L vol. flask, add 250 mL 0.100*N* KIO_3 (3.567 g dissolved and dild to 1 L), dil. to vol., and filter thru fritted glass. Age overnight before use.

(**b**) *Iodide-oxalate soln.*—Dissolve 2.5 g KI and 2.5 g $K_2C_2O_4$ in H_2O and dil. to 100 mL. Prep. fresh weekly.

(**c**) *Thiosulfate std soln.*—0.005*N*. Prep. daily from stdzd stock 0.1*N* soln, **50.037–50.038**.

(**d**) *Starch indicator.*—Rub 2.5 g sol. starch and ca 10 mg HgI_2 in little H_2O. Dissolve in ca 500 mL boiling H_2O.

31.053 ***Determination***

Pipet 5 mL soln contg 0.5–2.5 mg glucose into 25 × 200 mm test tube. Add 5 mL reagent, (**a**), and mix well by swirling. Prep. blank, using 5 mL H_2O and 5 mL reagent. Place tubes, capped with bulb or funnel, in boiling H_2O bath 15 min. Carefully remove tubes without agitation to running H_2O cooling bath 4 min. Remove caps and add down side of each tube 2 mL KI-$K_2C_2O_4$ soln and then 3 mL 2*N* H_2SO_4 (56 mL/L). (Do not agitate solns while alk.) Mix thoroly to ensure that all Cu_2O is dissolved, and let stand in cold H_2O bath 5 min, mixing twice during that time. Titr. with 0.005*N* $Na_2S_2O_3$, using starch indicator, (**d**). Subtract titrn of test soln from that of blank and det. amt glucose in 5 mL soln from Table **31:02**.

Make control detns with known amts of glucose and apply corrections for any deviations from tabulated equivs.

31.054 ★ ***Folin and Wu Micro Method (23)*** ★
Official First Action

See **31.054–31.055**, 12th ed.

Fructose—Chemical Methods—Official Final Action

31.055 ***Lane-Eynon General Volumetric Method***

Proceed as in **31.036**, referring titer to **52.017** or **52.018**.

31.056 ***Munson-Walker General Method***

Proceed as in **31.038** and **31.044**, and obtain wt fructose equiv. to wt Cu from **52.019**.

★ Surplus method—*see* inside front cover.

Table 31:02 Shaffer-Somogyi Dextrose-Thiosulfate Equivalents

mg glucose = (0.1099) (mL 0.005*N* $Na_2S_2O_3$) + 0.048

mL 0.005*N* $Na_2S_2O_3$	Tenths mL 0.005*N* Thiosulfate									
	0	0.1	0.2	0.3	0.4	0.5	0.6	0.7	0.8	0.9
	mg Dextrose in 5 mL of Soln									
3	0.378	0.389	0.400	0.411	0.422	0.432	0.444	0.455	0.466	0.477
4	0.488	0.499	0.510	0.521	0.532	0.543	0.554	0.565	0.576	0.587
5	0.598	0.608	0.619	0.630	0.641	0.652	0.663	0.674	0.685	0.696
6	0.707	0.718	0.729	0.740	0.751	0.762	0.773	0.784	0.795	0.806
7	0.817	0.828	0.839	0.850	0.861	0.872	0.883	0.894	0.905	0.916
8	0.927	0.938	0.949	0.960	0.971	0.982	0.993	1.004	1.015	1.026
9	1.037	1.048	1.059	1.070	1.081	1.092	1.103	1.114	1.125	1.136
10	1.147	1.158	1.169	1.180	1.191	1.202	1.213	1.224	1.235	1.246
11	1.257	1.268	1.279	1.290	1.301	1.312	1.323	1.334	1.345	1.356
12	1.367	1.378	1.389	1.400	1.411	1.422	1.433	1.444	1.455	1.466
13	1.477	1.488	1.499	1.510	1.521	1.532	1.543	1.554	1.565	1.576
14	1.587	1.598	1.609	1.620	1.631	1.642	1.653	1.664	1.675	1.686
15	1.697	1.707	1.718	1.729	1.740	1.751	1.762	1.773	1.784	1.795
16	1.806	1.817	1.828	1.839	1.850	1.861	1.872	1.883	1.894	1.905
17	1.916	1.927	1.938	1.949	1.960	1.971	1.982	1.993	2.004	2.015
18	2.026	2.037	2.048	2.059	2.070	2.081	2.092	2.103	2.114	2.125
19	2.136	2.147	2.158	2.169	2.180	2.191	2.202	2.213	2.224	2.235
20	2.246	2.257	2.268	2.279	2.290	2.301	2.312	2.323	2.334	2.345
21	2.356	2.367	2.378	2.389	2.400	2.411	2.422	2.433	2.444	2.455
22	2.466	2.477	2.488	2.499	2.510	2.521	2.532	2.543	2.554	2.565

J. Biol. Chem. **100**, 695(1933); **160**, 61(1945); JAOAC **42**, 341(1959); **43**, 645(1960).

Jackson-Mathews Modification of Nyns Selective Method (24)

31.057 ***Reagent***

Ost soln.—Dissolve 250 g anhyd. K_2CO_3 in ca 700 mL hot H_2O, add 100 g pulverized $KHCO_3$, and agitate mixt. until completely dissolved. Cool, and add, with very vigorous agitation, soln of 25.3 g $CuSO_4.5H_2O$ in 100–150 mL H_2O. Dil. to 1 L and filter.

31.058 ***Determination***

Transfer 50 mL Ost soln to 125 mL erlenmeyer and pipet in vol. sample soln contg ≤92 mg fructose or its equiv. of fructose-glucose mixt. (glucose has ca $^1/_{12}$ reducing power of fructose). Add H_2O to 70 mL. Immerse in H_2O bath regulated at 55°, preferably within 0.1°. Digest exactly 75 min, swirling at 10 or 15 min intervals.

Filter pptd Cu_2O on closely packed asbestos-mat gooch, and wash flask and ppt thoroly without attempting to transfer ppt quant. Det. Cu by one of methods described in **31.040–31.044**. As it is usually difficult to transfer Cu ppt quant. from erlenmeyer, select method of Cu analysis in which total Cu is dissolved in HNO_3 and detd by electrolysis or $Na_2S_2O_3$ titrn, or in $Fe_2(SO_4)_3$ soln followed by $KMnO_4$ titrn as in **31.043**.

See Table **31:03** for fructose equiv. If sample contained glucose in addn to fructose, anal. result is not true but "apparent" fructose, as glucose has appreciable reducing action under conditions of analysis. To det. correction for glucose, analyze sample also for total reducing sugars and compute true glucose and fructose by series of approximations. Calc. % reducing sugars in original sample and similarly % "apparent" fructose. Difference between these 2 percentages is "apparent" glucose. Divide apparent glucose by factor 12.4 and deduct result from apparent fructose to obtain new approximation to true fructose. Deduct new fructose % from total reducing sugar % to obtain more nearly correct value for true glucose and again divide by 12.4. Deduct quotient from original value of "apparent" fructose and continue approximation in same manner until % fructose remains essentially unaltered by 2 successive approximations.

If original sample contained sucrose, det. by means of Clerget method, **31.026**. Correct Cu for reducing action of sucrose before referring to Table **31:03**. 1, 2, 3, 4, and 5 g sucrose under conditions of analysis ppt 3.3, 5.7, 7.4, 8.5, and 9.0 mg Cu, resp.

Table 31:03 Copper-Fructose Equivalents According to Jackson and Mathews Modification of Nyns Selective Method for Fructose; Values Expressed in mg

(Linear interpolation yields accurate results)

Cu	Fructose	Cu	Fructose
5	2.5	130	39.3
10	4.5	140	42.0
15	6.2	150	44.7
20	7.9	160	47.4
25	9.5	170	50.0
30	11.0	180	52.6
35	12.5	190	55.2
40	13.9	200	57.9
45	15.4	210	60.6
50	16.8	220	63.4
55	18.3	230	66.4
60	19.7	240	69.4
65	21.2	250	72.5
70	22.5	260	75.7
80	25.4	270	79.0
90	28.1	280	82.4
100	30.9	290	85.9
110	33.7	300	89.5
120	36.5	310	93.2

Maltose—Chemical Methods—Official Final Action

31.059 ***Lane-Eynon General Volumetric Method***

Proceed as in **31.036**, referring titer to **52.017** or **52.018**.

31.060 ***Munson-Walker General Method***

Proceed as in **31.038** and **31.039**, and obtain wt maltose equiv. to wt Cu_2O from **52.019**.

Lactose—Chemical Methods—Official Final Action

31.061 ***Lane-Eynon General Volumetric Method***

Proceed as in **31.036**, referring titer to **52.017** or **52.018**.

31.062 ***Munson-Walker General Method***

Proceed as in **31.038** and **31.039**, and obtain wt lactose equiv. to wt of Cu_2O from **52.019**.

31.063 Arabinose, Galactose, and Xylose and Other Sugars—Official First Action

Proceed as in **31.053**, using appropriate heating time and equation for calcn from Table **31:04**. Make control detns with known amts of sugar and apply corrections for any deviations from equations.

Table 31:04 Shaffer-Somogyi Sugar-Thiosulfate Equivalents

y = mg sugar in 5 mL; x = mL 0.005*N* $Na_2S_2O_3$.

Sugar	Heating Time, min	Equation
L-Arabinose	30	$y = 0.1234x + 0.060$
Fructose	15	$y = 0.1113x + 0.079$
D-Galactose	30	$y = 0.1332x + 0.033$
Glucose	15	$y = 0.1099x + 0.048$
Lactose	35	$y = 0.2031x + 0.030$
Maltose	30	$y = 0.2199x + 0.0725$
D-Mannose	35	$y = 0.1148x + 0.084$
D-Ribose	25	$y = 0.1381x + 0.098$
L-Sorbose	15	$y = 0.1244x + 0.116$
D-Xylose	30	$y + 0.1103x + 0.044$

MOLASSES AND MOLASSES PRODUCTS (25)

31.064 ***Sampling—Procedure***

(a) *Liquid molasses.*—*(1) Molasses in barrels.*— Det. number of barrels to be sampled as follows: From lots of 1–10 barrels, sample all barrels; from lots of ≥11 barrels, sample 10 barrels. Take uniform amt from each barrel. Prep. composite from individual samples by mixing in container. Reduce composite to amt required and fill two ≥500 mL (1 pt) glass, stainless metal, or plastic jars. Close jars air-tight. Place one sample in cold storage (do not freeze) and put at disposal of second party as soon as possible. Send second sample to testing laboratory immediately after sampling.

(2) Molasses in small retail containers.—Content of intact and unopened container constitutes sample.

(3) Molasses in tank cars, tank trucks, or storage tanks.—(1) *Continuous drip sampling.*—Draw drip sample from pipeline as molasses is being pumped from vessel. From lot <5000 gal., collect ≥1 L (1 qt); from lot >5000 gal., draw 500 mL (1 pt) from each 5000 gal., but ≥1 L (1 qt).

(2) *Bacon bomb or thief sampling.*—Draw 2 similar complete samples of ca 1 L (1 qt) each consisting of continuous portion of core extending from top to bottom of tank. When for any reason such core cannot be obtained, draw three 1 L (1 qt) samples as follows: 1 portion from top just below surface of liq., 1 from center, and 1 from bottom of tank. Make composite for tank by combining samples from different levels as shown below.

Sample	Vessels of uniform cross section	Horizontal cylindrical tank (full)
Upper	1 part	1 part
Middle	3 parts	8 parts
Lower	1 part	1 part

Reduce composite to amt required and fill two ≥500 mL (1 pt) glass, stainless metal, or plastic jars. Close jars air-tight. Store and send for testing as in (**a**)(*1*).

(**b**) *Dried molasses.*—Proceed as in **7.001**. Divide composite into 2 equal portions and place each portion into sep. air-tight jar. Store and send for testing as in (**a**).

31.065 ***Transport of Samples***

Transport samples to laboratory as quickly as possible after sampling. Do not expose to direct sunlight or high temp. during transit.

31.066 ***Preparation of Sample***

Let samples come to ca room temp. before opening containers.

(**a**) *Dried products.*—Do not grind. Pass samples contg lumps thru No. 8 sieve and crush retains on glass plate with glass or metal rolling pin, or in clean, dry mortar, using pestle. Mix entire sample thoroly and place in air-tight container.

(**b**) *Liquids.*—See **31.001**(**c**).

31.067 ***Moisture—Official Final Action***

(**a**) *Dried products.*—*See* **31.005**.

(**b**) *Liquids.*—*See* **31.007** or **31.008**.

Moisture in Liquid Molasses (*26*)—Official Final Action

(Not applicable to molasses which fails to dissolve in MeOH within time specified for stability of end point of titrn assembly)

31.068 ***Apparatus***

Buret with automatic zero; reservoir for reagent; mag. stirrer; titrn vessel (300 mL Berzelius beaker with stopcock attached to side at bottom for withdrawing excess soln is recommended), electrodes, and circuitry for deadstop end point detection. All openings must be tightly closed or protected with drying tubes to prevent contamination from atm. H_2O. Various titrn assemblies may be obtained com. or one may be assembled.

Assemble titrn app. and follow manufacturer's instructions, setting for direct titrn. Set timer to give 30 sec end point. Add enough dry MeOH to cover electrodes on electrode probes and turn on stirrer. Adjust speed to obtain good stirring without splashing. Do not let stirrer bar contact electrodes. Titr. until satisfactory end point is reached. App. newly assembled or not recently used may require repetition of this step to dry out system. Test stability of end point obtained by continuing titrn beyond first 30 sec end point for same time required for titrn of test sample. Generally end point should persist for 5 min to be assured of protection from atm. H_2O contamination and instability of reagents.

31.069 ***Reagents***

(*Caution: See* **51.066**, **51.072**, and **51.081**.)

(**a**) *Karl Fischer reagent.*—Available com. or prep. as follows: Dissolve 133 g I in 425 mL dry pyridine in dry g-s bottle. Add 425 mL dry MeOH or ethylene glycol monomethyl ether. (Less trouble with stopcock leakage is obtained with ethylene glycol monomethyl ether.) Cool to <4° in ice bath and bubble in 102–105 g SO_2. Mix well and let stand 12 hr. Reagent is reasonably stable, but restdze for each series of detns.

(**b**) *Anhydrous methanol.*—Reagent grade MeOH contg <0.1% H_2O. Prep. by distg over Mg.

31.070 ***Determination***

Add ca 120 mg H_2O from weighing pipet or other suitable device and titr. with Karl Fischer reagent.

Calc. C = mg H_2O/mL reagent.

For titrn of molasses, C = ca 5 mg/mL. Weigh molasses estd to give 20–40 mL titer into titrn app. and titr.

% H_2O = (C × mL reagent)/(g sample × 10).

Drain excess liq. and repeat with succeeding samples. If time lapse occurs between titrn of samples, adjust liq. in titrn vessel to end point by titrn with reagent before adding next sample.

31.071 Specific Gravity—Official Final Action

See **31.010**(**b**).

31.072 Ash—Official Final Action

See **31.012**, **31.013**, or **31.014**.

31.073 Soluble and Insoluble Ash—Official Final Action

See **31.015**.

31.074 Mineral Adulterants in Ash—Official Final Action

See **31.018**.

31.075 Nitrogen—Official Final Action

See **31.019**.

31.076 Sucrose—Official Final Action

Polarimetric methods (when required by law). *See* **31.020–31.030**.

Total Sugars Expressed as Invert Sugar Official Final Action

Lane-Eynon Constant Volume Volumetric Method

31.077 ***Apparatus***

(**a**) *Electric heater.*—With white top and continuous temp. control over range 110–600°; attaining max. temp. within 5 min.

(**b**) *Buret.*—50 mL, graduated in 0.1 mL, with stopcock or pinchcock and offset delivery tube.

31.078 ***Reagents***

(**a**) *Soxhlet modification of Fehling soln.*—Prep. as in **31.034**(**a**) and (**b**).

(**b**) *Invert sugar std solns.*—(*1*) *Stock soln.*—10 mg/mL. Prep. as in **31.034**(**c**), using 5 mL HCl (sp gr 1.18 at 20/4°) and letting stand 3 days at room temp. (20–25°). (*2*) *Working soln.*—5 mg/mL. Pipet 100 mL stock soln into 200 mL vol. flask, add few drops phthln, and neutze with 20% NaOH. Dil. to vol. and mix well. Prep. fresh daily.

31.079 ***Preparation of Sample Solution***

(**a**) *Dried products containing not less than 30% total sugars.*—Weigh 8.00 g sample and transfer with 250 mL H_2O, preheated to 60±5°, into 500 mL vol. flask. Mech. shake flask 30 min. Let stand addnl 30 min and cool to 20°. Dil. to vol. with H_2O. Mix well and filter, using filter aid (Hyflo Super-Cel, or equiv.) and loose texture paper (Whatman No. 1, or equiv.). Discard first 25 mL filtrate. Cover funnel during filtration with watch glass to prevent evapn.

(**b**) *Liquids.*—Weigh 8.00 g sample and transfer with H_2O to 500 mL vol. flask. Dissolve, and dil. to vol. with H_2O. Proceed as in (**a**), beginning "Mix well . . ."

31.080 ***Standardization of Soxhlet Reagent***

Fill 50 mL buret with working std soln contg 5 mg invert sugar/mL.

Accurately pipet 10 mL each Soxhlet soln, (**a**) and (**b**), into 300 mL erlenmeyer, mix, and add 30 mL H_2O. Add from buret almost all std working soln (ca 19 mL) necessary to reduce the Cu. Add few boiling chips. Place cold mixt. on heater, regulate heat so that boiling will begin in ca 3 min, and maintain at moderate boil exactly 2 min, reducing heat, if necessary, to prevent bumping. Without removing flask from heater, add ca 4 drops *1% aq. methylene blue soln* and complete titrn within total boiling time of ca 3 min by dropwise addn of working std soln at intervals of ca 10 sec until boiling mixt. resumes bright orange appearance which it had before indicator was added. Maintain continuous evolution of steam to prevent reoxidn by air. Repeat stdzn several times. Factor *F* is av. number mL std sugar soln required to completely reduce 20 mL Soxhlet soln. Use av. of ≥3 titrns.

31.081 ***Inversion with Acid at Room Temperature***

Pipet 100 mL filtrate, **31.079**, into 200 mL vol. flask, and add 5 mL HCl (sp gr 1.18 at 20/4°). Let stand 24 hr at 20–25° or 10 hr at >25°. Add few drops phthln and neutze with 20% NaOH soln. Add few drops 0.5*N* HCl until red disappears. Dil. to vol. with H_2O and mix well.

31.082 ***Approximate Titration of Sample***

Det. approx. sugar content of sample as follows: Accurately pipet 10 mL each Soxhlet soln, (**a**) and (**b**), into 300 mL erlenmeyer, mix, and add 10 mL aliquot inverted sample soln. Add 40 mL H_2O so that vol. H_2O plus vol. sample soln is 50 mL, as in **31.080**. Mix without heating by swirling. Add few boiling chips. Place flask on heater, regulating heat so that boiling begins in ca 3 min. After liq. boils 10–15 sec, observe change in color of soln. If blue color persists, add working std sugar soln 0.5–1.0 mL at time, with few sec actual boiling after each addn until unsafe to add more without risk of passing end point. Add 3–4 drops methylene blue soln and continue adding sugar soln, ca 1 mL at time, at intervals of ca 10 sec, until indicator is completely decolorized. Calc. approx. % invert sugar in sample.

31.083 ***Titration of Sample***

Pipet 10 mL each of Soxhlet soln, (**a**) and (**b**), into 300 mL erlenmeyer, mix, and add aliquot inverted sample soln as indicated in Table **31:05**. Add mL H_2O specified in table so that vol. H_2O plus vol. sample soln is 50 mL, as in **31.080**, and mix without heating by swirling. Add few boiling chips. Place flask on heater, regulate heat so that boiling begins in ca 3 min, and during boiling, rapidly add working std invert sugar soln from buret, so that 0.5–1.0 mL is required to complete titrn. Continue as in **31.080**, beginning "Without removing flask . . ." Maintain moderate boiling.

$$\% \text{ Sugar as invert} = (F - M) \times I \times 100/W,$$

where *F* is Cu factor (mL std sugar soln required to reduce 20 mL mixed Soxhlet reagent); *M* is mL std sugar soln used in back-titrn of sample; *I* is g invert sugar in 1 mL working std sugar soln; and *W* is g sample in aliquot used. Report total sugars, expressed as invert.

Table 31:05 Aliquots for Cane Sirups and Molasses

mL H_2O	mL Aliquot	g Sample in Aliquot	Total Sugar as Invert, % Max.	Total Sugar as Invert, % Min.
40	10	0.08		73.00
35	15	0.12	82.00	58.00
30	20	0.16	61.00	41.00
25	25	0.20	49.00	35.00
20	30	0.24	41.00	29.00

Invert Sugar—Official Final Action

31.084 ***Preparation of Sample Solution***

Proceed as in **31.079**. Then pipet 100 mL filtrate into 200 mL vol. flask, dil. to vol. with H_2O, and mix well.

31.085 ***Titration of Sample***

Proceed as in **31.082–31.083**, except use aliquot of prepd sample soln without inversion as indicated in Table **31:06**.

Table 31:06 Aliquots for Cane Sirups and Molasses (Without Inversion)

mL H_2O	mL Aliquot	g Sample in Aliquot	Total Sugar as Invert, % Max.	Total Sugar as Invert, % Min.
40	10	0.16	61.00	40.00
35	15	0.24	40.00	30.00
30	20	0.32	30.00	24.00
25	25	0.40	24.00	20.00
20	30	0.48	20.00	15.00
10	40	0.64	15.00	12.00
–	50	0.80	12.00	8.00

Unfermentable Reducing Substances (27)
Official Final Action

(Applicable to molasses)

31.086 ***Reagents***

(**a**) *Bakers yeast, free from starch.*—Fleischmann, sold in 1 lb units by Standard Brands, Inc., is suitable. May be stored for few days in refrigerator.

(**b**) *Neutral lead acetate soln.*—Dissolve 20 g $Pb(OAc)_2.3H_2O$ in H_2O and dil. to 100 mL.

(**c**) *Soxhlet soln.*—*See* **31.034**(**a**) and (**b**). Mix equal vols (**a**) and (**b**) immediately before use.

(**d**) *Potassium iodide soln.*—Dissolve 20 g KI in H_2O and dil. to 100 mL.

(**e**) *Thiosulfate std soln.*—0.1*N*. *See* **50.037–50.038**.

31.087 ***Fermentation***

Transfer 12 g blackstrap molasses (or 8 g high-test molasses) to 500 mL vol. flask, using 75 mL H_2O. Add 25 g fresh yeast, coarsely chopped, and mix thoroly with molasses soln. Close flask with stopper provided with delivery tube, other end of which dips ca 1 cm below surface of H_2O in beaker; or use any other type of fermentation trap. Place flask in H_2O bath kept at 30° and let ferment ≥4 hr, shaking occasionally. (Incubator may be used and flask left overnight.)

When fermentation is complete, dil. mixt. with H_2O, clarify with 15 mL neut. $Pb(OAc)_2$ soln, dil. to vol. at 20°, add teaspoonful of Filter-Cel, or equiv., shake well, and filter, discarding first few mL. Delead entire filtrate with ca 0.5 g anhyd. K oxalate and filter again with aid of Filter-Cel. Test filtrate for Pb. If necessary, add addnl K oxalate and refilter.

31.088 ***Determination***

Transfer 25 mL final filtrate to 250 mL erlenmeyer, mix with 20 mL combined Soxhlet soln, and wash down wall of flask with 5 mL H_2O, making 50 mL total. Add few pieces of ignited pumice stone and place flask on wire gauze covered with asbestos plate that has center hole slightly smaller than bottom of flask. Heat with Bunsen burner, or, preferably, elec. heater with temp. control. Heat to boiling in 3 min and boil gently exactly 2 min longer. Immediately close flask with stopper provided with Bunsen valve and cool quickly under H_2O tap to prevent reoxidn. Add 15 mL KI soln and then 10 mL H_2SO_4 (1+3). Titr. liberated I at once with 0.1*N* $Na_2S_2O_3$, adding starch indicator toward end of titrn.

Det. blank with 75 mL H_2O instead of molasses soln, adding yeast, etc., as above. Deduct titer of sample from titer of blank, and find mg invert sugar corresponding to difference from Table **31:07**. Result, divided by 6 (in case of high-test molasses, by 4) gives directly % unfermentable reducing substances in the molasses, in terms of invert sugar.

Table 31:07 Milligrams Invert Sugar Corresponding to 0.1*N* Thiosulfate

0.1*N* Thiosulfate	Invert Sugar	0.1*N* Thiosulfate	Invert-Sugar
mL	*mg*	*mL*	*mg*
1	3.2	14	47.3
2	6.4	15	50.8
3	9.7	16	54.3
4	13.0	17	58.0
5	16.4	18	61.8
6	19.8	19	65.5
7	23.2	20	69.4
8	26.5	21	73.3
9	29.9	22	77.2
10	33.4	23	81.2
11	36.8	24	85.2
12	40.3	25	89.2
13	43.8	–	–

CONFECTIONERY

31.089 Preparation of Sample—Official Final Action

If composition of entire sample is desired, grind and mix thoroly. If sample is composed of layers or of distinctly different portions and it is desired to examine these individually, sep. with knife or other mech. means as completely as possible, and grind and mix each portion thoroly.

31.090 Moisture—Official Final Action

See **31.005**, **31.006**, **31.007**, or **31.008**.

31.091 Ash—Official Final Action

See **31.012** or **31.013**.

31.092 Soluble and Insoluble Ash—Official Final Action

See **31.015**.

31.093 Alkalinity of Soluble Ash—Official Final Action

See **31.016**.

31.094 Alkalinity of Insoluble Ash—Official Final Action

See **31.017**.

31.095 Mineral Adulterants in Ash—Official First Action

See **31.018**.

31.096 Nitrogen—Official Final Action

Det. N in 2–5 g sample as in **2.057**, using larger amt of H_2SO_4 if necessary for complete digestion.

Sucrose—Polarimetric Methods

31.097 ***In Absence of Raffinose—Official Final Action***

See **31.025**, **31.026**, or **31.030**.

Sucrose—Chemical Methods

31.098 ***By Reducing Sugars Before and After Inversion Official Final Action***

See **31.031**.

31.099 Commercial Glucose—Procedure

See **31.032** or **31.033**.

Starch—Official First Action

31.100 ***Reagent***

Malt extract.—Use clean, new barley malt of known efficacy and grind only as needed. Grind well, but not so fine that filtration is greatly retarded. Prep. infusion of freshly ground malt just before use. For every 80 mL malt ext required, digest 5 g ground malt with 100 mL H_2O at room temp. 2 hr, or 20 min if mixt. can be stirred by elec mixer. Filter to obtain clear ext, refiltering first portions of filtrate if necessary. Mix infusion well.

31.101 ***Determination***

Measure 25 mL of soln of uniform mixt. (representing 5 g sample) into 300 mL beaker, or add to beaker 5 g finely ground sample (previously extd with ether if sample contains much fat); add enough H_2O to make 100 mL; heat to ca 60° (avoiding, if possible, gelatinizing starch); and let stand ca 1 hr, stirring frequently to secure complete soln of sugars. Transfer to wide-mouth bottle, rinse beaker with little warm H_2O, and cool. Add equal vol. alcohol, mix, and let stand ≥1 hr.

Centrf. until ppt is closely packed on bottom of bottle and decant supernate thru hardened filter. Wash ppt with successive 50 mL portions of alcohol, 50% by vol., by centrfg and decanting thru filter until washings are sugar-free by following test: Add to test tube few drops of washings, 3 or 4 drops *20% alc. α-naphthol soln,* and 2 mL H_2O. Shake well, tip tube, let 2–5 mL H_2SO_4 flow down side of tube, and then hold tube upright. If sugar is present, interface of 2 liqs is colored faint to deep violet; on shaking, whole soln becomes blue-violet. Transfer residue from bottle and hardened filter to beaker with 50 mL H_2O.

Immerse beaker in boiling H_2O, and stir constantly 15 min, or until all starch is gelatinized; cool to 55°, add 20 mL malt ext, and hold at this temp. 1 hr. Heat again to boiling few min, cool to 55°, add 20 mL malt ext, and hold at this temp. 1 hr, or until residue treated with I soln shows no blue tinge upon microscopic examination. Cool, dil. to 250 mL, and filter.

Place 200 mL filtrate in flask, add 20 mL HCl (sp gr 1.125), connect with reflux condenser, and heat in boiling H_2O bath 2.5 hr. Cool, nearly neutze with 10% NaOH soln, finish neutzn with Na_2CO_3 soln, and dil. to 500 mL. Mix soln thoroly, pour thru dry filter, and det. glucose in aliquot as in **31.038**. Conduct blank detn on same vol. of malt ext as used with sample and correct wt glucose accordingly. Wt glucose obtained × 0.925 = wt starch.

Ether Extract—Official First Action

(*Caution: See* **51.011**, **51.039**, **51.054**, **51.073**, and **51.086**.)

31.102 ***Continuous Extraction Method***

Measure 25 mL 20% mixt. or soln into very thin, readily breakable glass evapg shell, or thin Pb or Sn foil contg 5–7 g freshly ignited asbestos fiber (*Caution:See* **52.086**); or, if possible to obtain uniform sample, weigh 5 g mixed, finely divided sample into dish and wash with H_2O onto asbestos in evapg shell, using small portion of asbestos fiber on stirring rod to transfer last traces of sample from dish to shell.

Dry to const wt at 100°, cool, wrap glass dish loosely in smooth paper, crush into rather small fragments between fingers, and carefully transfer crushed mass, including paper, to extn tube or fat extn cartridge. If metal dish is used, cut into small pieces and place in extn tube. Ext with anhyd. ether or pet ether (bp 45–60° and without weighable residue) in continuous extn app. ⩾25 hr. In most cases it is advisable to remove substance from extractor after first 12 hr, grind with sand to fine powder, and re-ext remaining 13 hr. Transfer ext to weighed flask, evap. solv., and dry to const wt at 100°.

31.103 ***Roese-Gottlieb Method***

Introduce 4 g sample, or amt of uniform soln equiv. to this wt dry substance, into Mojonnier fat extn tube or similar app.; dil. to 10 mL with H_2O, add 1.25 mL NH_4OH, and mix thoroly. Add 10 mL alcohol and mix; then add 25 mL ether and shake vigorously ca 30 sec; and finally add 25 mL pet ether (bp <60°) and shake again ca 30 sec. Let stand 20 min or until sepn of liqs is complete.

Draw off as much as possible of ether-fat soln (usually 0.5–0.8 mL is left) into weighed flask thru small, rapid filter. (Weigh flask with similar one as counterpoise.) Again ext liq. remaining in tube, this time with 15 mL each of ether and pet ether; shake vigorously ca 30 sec with each solv. and let settle. Proceed as above, washing mouth of tube and filter with few mL of mixt. of equal parts of the 2 solvs (previously mixed and freed from deposited H_2O).

For greater degree of accuracy, repeat extn. If previous solv.-fat solns have been drawn off closely, third extn usually yields ⩽1 mg fat, or ca 0.02% with 4 g sample. Slowly evap. solv. on steam bath and then dry fat in 100° oven to const wt. Test purity of fat by dissolving in little pet ether. If residue remains, wash fat out completely with pet ether, dry residue, weigh, and deduct wt.

31.104 Paraffin—Official First Action

To solv. ext in flask, **31.102** or **31.103**, add 10 mL alcohol and 2 mL NaOH soln (1+1); connect flask with reflux condenser; and heat 1 hr on H_2O bath, or until saponification is complete. Remove condenser and keep flask on bath until alcohol evaps and residue is dry. Dissolve residue as completely as possible in ca 40 mL H_2O and heat on bath, shaking frequently. Wash into separator, cool, and ext with 4 successive portions of pet ether, collecting exts in weighed flask or capsule. Evap. pet ether and dry to const wt at 100°. Any phytosterol or cholesterol present in fat would be extd with the paraffin but amt is so insignificant that it may generally be disregarded.

31.105 Shellac (*28*)—Official Final Action

(*Caution: See* **51.011**, **51.040**, and **51.045**.)

Place 50 g sample in 400 mL beaker. Add 50 mL mixt. of benzene and absolute alcohol (1+1), and cover with watch glass. Heat to bp on steam bath, and simmer few min, stirring occasionally. Decant liq. into tared, round 100 mL glass dish with flat bottom ca 7 cm diam. Ext once more with benzene-alcohol mixt., and finally rinse with two 25 mL portions absolute alcohol, simmering and stirring each time. With moist sugar candy, avoid overheating to prevent pieces from sticking together.

Add each ext to glass dish previously placed on steam bath. Evap. until alcohol is just removed, rotating dish as it goes to dryness in order to spread ext uniformly over bottom surface. Avoid baking shellac on dish. If fat appears to be present, wash with three 15 mL portions pet ether, stirring and warming. Decant thru rapid filter.

Add mixt. of 25 mL *isoamyl alcohol* (bp 129–132°) and 25 mL benzene to filter, and filter back into dish. Heat on steam bath with stirring, cool somewhat, and transfer soln with suspended matter to 125 mL separator. Rinse dish with 25 mL hot (ca 60°) H_2O, and add to separator; shake well and filter wash H_2O if necessary. Repeat washing with H_2O *twice* (or until washings are colorless), rinsing dish well around sides with first portions of liq. Finally, filter soln of shellac into tared dish, rinsing separator and filters with little absolute alcohol. Evap. to dryness on steam bath, rotating dish to give uniform film.

If much fat was extd in original benzene extn, wash final shellac residue with 25 mL pet ether, warming and stirring. Decant, dry on steam bath and in 100° oven, and weigh. After weighing, check for complete removal of sugars by thoroly rinsing dish and surface of shellac with hot H_2O, warming on steam bath, decanting, rinsing down with alcohol, and evapg with care to give uniform film on dish. Dry and reweigh.

31.106 Alcohol in Sirups Used in Confectionery ("Brandy Drops")—Official Final Action

Collect in beaker sirup from enough pieces of sample to yield 30–50 g, strain into weighed beaker, and weigh. Place sirup in 250–300 mL distg flask, dil. with half its vol. of H_2O, attach flask to vertical condenser, and distil almost 50 mL, or as much of liq. as possible without causing charring. Foaming may be prevented by adding little *tannin*, or piece of *paraffin* ca size of pea. Cool distillate, dil. to vol. with H_2O, and mix well. Det. sp gr as in **9.009–9.011**. Calc. % alcohol by wt or vol. in candy filling, using tables **52.003** and **52.005**.

HONEY

31.107 Preparation of Sample—Official Final Action

(**a**) *Liquid or strained honey.*—If sample is free from granulation, mix thoroly by stirring or shaking before weighing portions for detns; if granulated, place closed container in H_2O bath without submerging, and heat 30 min at 60°; then, if necessary, heat at 65° until liquefied. Occasional shaking is essential. Mix thoroly, cool rapidly as soon as sample liquefies, and weigh portions for detns. Do not heat honey intended for diastatic detn. If foreign matter, such as wax, sticks, bees, particles of comb, etc., is present, heat sample to 40° in H_2O bath and strain thru cheesecloth in hot H_2O funnel before weighing portions for analysis.

(**b**) *Comb honey.*—Cut across top of comb, if sealed, and sep. completely from comb by straining thru No. 40 sieve. When portions of comb or wax pass thru sieve, heat sample as in (**a**) and strain thru cheesecloth. If honey is granulated in comb, heat until wax is liquefied; stir, cool, and remove wax.

Color Classification (*29*)—Official First Action

31.108 ***Apparatus***

(**a**) *Containers.*—French sq bottles, screw finish, clear glass, 1.5 × 1.5", 2⁷/₃₂ oz. (Available from VirTis Co., Phoenix Precision Instrument Div., Rt 208, Gardiner, NY 12525.)

(**b**) *Comparator.*—All-metal boxes, ca 8 × 2 × 3" (20 × 5 × 7.5 cm), divided by thin partitions into 5 sq compartments, each of which has 2 windows, front and back, ca 1.2" (3 cm) sq. The 3 lighter glass stds (water white, extra white, and white) are mounted in 1 of comparator boxes on shelf against front windows in compartments 1, 3, and 5. The 3 darker stds (extra light amber, light amber, and amber) are mounted similarly in second comparator box. Place containers, (**a**), filled with H_2O (blanks) behind glass stds. With turbid honeys, substitute containers filled with suspensions of diat. earth (Hyflo Super-Cel, or equiv.) designated as "Cloudy 1," "Cloudy 2," and "Cloudy 3," contg 100, 200, and 400 mg/L H_2O, resp.

(**c**) *Glass stds.*—Use selected colored glasses tested and stdzd by USDA to correspond with color stds for honey.

Complete grading set is available from VirTis Co.

31.109 ***Determination***

Place clear blanks or cloudy suspensions in back of glass stds in compartments 1, 3, and 5 of 1 or both comparators. Pour sample (must be free from granulation) into clean, dry container, **31.108**(**a**). Place sample container in compartment 2 or 4 of either comparator. Hold comparator at convenient distance from eye and view by diffused light (e.g., north or overcast sky, diffused light from W lamp, or white or daylight fluorescent lamp). Move sample from compartment to compartment, interchanging blanks with cloudy suspensions if necessary. Det. classification as follows: If sample is equal to water white std in hue, or not as red (i.e., yellower), classify as water white; if perceptibly redder than water white std in hue but not redder than extra white std, classify as extra white, etc. If redder in hue than amber std, classify as dark amber. Hue (amber quality or redness) is attribute of color in classification.

Moisture—Official Final Action

31.110 ***Direct Drying***

Proceed as in **31.007** or **31.008**, using weighed sample sufficient to yield ca 1 g solids. Add, if necessary, few mL H_2O to incorporate sample thoroly with the sand. Dry at $<70°$ (preferably 60°) under pressure $\leqslant 50$ mm Hg (6.7 kPa).

31.111 ***By Means of Refractometer (30)***

Det. refractometer reading of honey at 20° and obtain corresponding % moisture from Table **31:08**. If detn is made at temp. other than 20°, correct reading to std temp. of 20° according to footnote.

31.112 Ash (*31*)—Official Final Action

Weigh 5–10 g honey into ignited and weighed Pt dish. Place under 375 watt IR lamp with variable voltage input and slowly increase applied voltage until sample is black and dry and there is no danger of loss by foaming. Ash in furnace at 600° to const wt (overnight). Cool and weigh.

31.113 Soluble Ash—Official Final Action

See **31.015**.

31.114 Alkalinity of Soluble Ash—Official Final Action

See **31.016**.

31.115 Nitrogen (*31*)—Official First Action

Det. N as in **47.021–47.023**, using 300 mg sample, 3.0±0.1 mL H_2SO_4, and 1 hr digestion after acid comes to true boil. Titr. with 0.01*N* HCl and calc. % N.

Proline (*32*)—Official First Action

31.116 ***Principle***

Proline, predominant free amino acid of honey, reacts with acid ninhydrin soln to form colored compd. Interference from other amino acids is negligible, $\leqslant 5\%$.

31.117 ***Reagents and Apparatus***

(**a**) *Ninhydrin soln.*—3%. Dissolve 3.0 g ninhydrin in 100 mL peroxide-free ethylene glycol monomethyl ether. Store solv., not reagent, over Zn metal in amber bottle.

(**b**) *L-(−)-Proline.*—Eastman No. 2488; dry in vac. oven and store in desiccator. Prep std solns as follows: (*1*) *Stock soln.*—0.5 mg/mL H_2O. Dil. 25 mg proline to 50 mL with H_2O. Refrigerate. (*2*) *Working soln.*—50 μg/mL. Dil. 10 mL stock soln to 100 mL with H_2O. Prep. fresh daily.

(**c**) *Reaction tubes.*—18×130 mm borosilicate screw-cap tubes with Teflon liners.

31.118 ***Determination***

Weigh 2.500 g honey, transfer to 50 mL vol. flask, and dil. to vol. with H_2O. Pipet 0.5 mL into each of 3 reaction tubes, add 0.25 mL HCOOH and 1.00 mL ninhydrin soln. Cap tightly, shake well, and place in boiling H_2O bath 15 min. Cool 5 min in 22° H_2O bath, remove cap, and pipet 5 mL aq. isopropanol (1+1) into each. Mix well and det. *A* at 520 nm against blank of H_2O carried thru method. Read all tubes within 35 min of cooling.

Correct for color of honey by detg *A* of soln contg 0.5 mL prepd honey soln, 1.25 mL H_2O, and 5.00 mL isopropanol (1+1). Subtract value from that of reacted sample before calcg.

Prep. calibration curve as in detn, using proline std soln instead of honey. *A* of 0.5 mL of soln of 50 μg proline/mL is ca 0.35 in 10 mm cell.

Calc. mg proline/100 g honey.

31.119 Direct Polarization—Official First Action

(**a**) *Immediate direct polarization.*—Transfer 26 g honey to 100 mL vol. flask with H_2O, add 5 mL alumina cream, **31.021**(**b**), dil. to vol. with H_2O at 20°, filter, and polarize immediately in 200 mm tube.

(**b**) *Constant direct polarization.*—Complete mutarotation as in **31.023**. If necessary to conserve sample, soln from tube used in immediate direct polarization, (**a**), may be returned to flask. Make final reading at 20° in 200 mm tube.

(**c**) *Mutarotation.*—Difference between (**a**) and (**b**) is measure of mutarotation.

Table 31:08 Relationship Between Refractive Index and Water Contents of Honeys[a]

Water Content, %	Refractive Index			Water Content, %	Refractive Index		
	20°C[b]	60°F[c]	40°C		20°C[b]	60°F[c]	40°C
13.0	1.5044	1.5053	1.4998	19.0	1.4890	1.4900	1.4845
13.2	1.5038	1.5048	1.4993	19.2	1.4885	1.4895	1.4840
13.4	1.5033	1.5043	1.4988	19.4	1.4880	1.4890	1.4835
13.6	1.5028	1.5038	1.4983	19.6	1.4875	1.4885	1.4829
13.8	1.5023	1.5033	1.4978	19.8	1.4870	1.4880	1.4824
14.0	1.5018	1.5027	1.4973	20.0	1.4865	1.4875	1.4819
14.2	1.5012	1.5022	1.4968	20.2	1.4860	1.4870	1.4814
14.4	1.5007	1.5017	1.4962	20.4	1.4855	1.4865	1.4809
14.6	1.5002	1.5012	1.4957	20.6	1.4850	1.4860	1.4804
14.8	1.4997	1.5007	1.4952	20.8	1.4845	1.4855	1.4799
15.0	1.4992	1.5002	1.4947	21.0	1.4840	1.4850	1.4794
15.2	1.4987	1.4997	1.4942	21.2	1.4835	1.4845	1.4788
15.4	1.4982	1.4992	1.4937	21.4	1.4830	1.4840	1.4783
15.6	1.4976	1.4986	1.4932	21.6	1.4825	1.4835	1.4778
15.8	1.4971	1.4981	1.4927	21.8	1.4820	1.4830	1.4773
16.0	1.4966	1.4976	1.4922	22.0	1.4815	1.4825	1.4768
16.2	1.4961	1.4971	1.4916	22.2	1.4810		
16.4	1.4956	1.4966	1.4911	22.4	1.4805		
16.6	1.4951	1.4961	1.4906	22.6	1.4800		
16.8	1.4946	1.4956	1.4901	22.8	1.4795		
17.0	1.4940	1.4951	1.4896	23.0	1.4790		
17.2	1.4935	1.4946	1.4891	23.2	1.4785		
17.4	1.4930	1.4940	1.4886	23.4	1.4780		
17.6	1.4925	1.4935	1.4881	23.6	1.4775		
17.8	1.4920	1.4930	1.4876	23.8	1.4770		
18.0	1.4915	1.4925	1.4870	24.0	1.4765		
18.2	1.4910	1.4920	1.4865	24.2	1.4760		
18.4	1.4905	1.4915	1.4860	24.4	1.4755		
18.6	1.4900	1.4910	1.4855	24.6	1.4750		
18.8	1.4895	1.4905	1.4850	24.8	1.4745		
				25.0	1.4740		

[a] Values for 20°C and 60°F are Wedmore's calculations (Bee World **36**, 197(1955)); 40°C values are calcd from Auerbach and Borries equation (Z. Nahr. Genussm. **22**, 353–358(1924)). Values >22.0% were extended by FAO/WHO Codex Committee on Methods of Analysis and Sampling (1968).
[b] If refractive index is measured at temp. above (below) 20°C, add (subtract) 0.00023/°C above (below) 20°C before using table.
[c] If refractive index is measured at temp. above (below) 60°F, add (subtract) 0.00013/°F above (below) 60°F before using table.

(**d**) *Direct polarization at 87°.*—Polarize soln obtained in (**b**) at 87° in jacketed 200 mm metal tube.

31.120 Reducing Sugars—Official Final Action

(**a**) *Munson-Walker method.*—Dil. 10 mL soln, **31.119(a)**, to 250 mL and det. reducing sugars in 25 mL of this soln by **31.038**. Calc. result to % invert sugar.

(**b**) *Lane-Eynon method.*—Dil. 10 mL soln, **31.119(a)**, to 500 mL and det. reducing sugars by const vol. method:

Stdze Fehling solns, **31.034**, so that 5.00 mL soln (**a**) and 5 mL soln (**b**) will react completely with 50 mg invert sugar std soln, **31.034(c)**, added as 25 mL of diln to 2 g/L.

Pipet 5 mL of each Fehling soln into 250 mL erlenmeyer. Add 7 mL H_2O, few boiling chips, and 15 mL dild honey soln from buret with offset tip. Heat to bp over wire gauze, and maintain moderate boil 2 min. Add 1 mL 0.2% methylene blue soln, or 3–4 drops 1% soln, while still boiling and complete titrn within total boiling time of 3 min by repeated small addns of dild honey soln until indicator is decolorized. (Observe color of supernate.) Note vol. honey soln used (x mL).

Repeat titrn, using 5 mL of each Fehling soln, $(25 - x)$ mL H_2O, and all but 1.5 mL dild honey soln (from buret) detd in preliminary titrn. Add honey soln to end point within 3 min and note vol. dild honey soln used (y mL). Duplicate titrns should agree within 0.1 mL.

% Invert sugar = 2000/(g honey sample × y).

31.121 Sucrose—Official Final Action

Proceed as in **31.031**. To det. reducing sugars after inversion, invert 50 mL soln, **31.119(a)**, as in **31.025(b)** or (**c**) or **31.026(b)** or (**c**), dil. 10 mL this soln with small amt of H_2O, neutze with Na_2CO_3, and dil. to 250 mL with H_2O. Use 50 mL of this soln, making detn as in **31.120(a)**.

31.122 Dextrin (Approximate)—Procedure

Using ≤4 mL H_2O, transfer 8 g sample (4 g for dark-colored honeydew honey) to 100 mL vol. flask by letting sample drain from weighing dish into flask and then dissolving residue in 2 mL H_2O. Add this soln to flask, and rinse weighing dish with two 1 mL portions H_2O, adding few mL absolute alcohol each time before decanting. Fill flask to vol. with absolute alcohol, shaking constantly. Set flask aside until dextrin collects on sides and bottom and liq. is clear.

Decant clear liq. thru filter paper and wash residue in flask with 10 mL alcohol, pouring washings thru same filter. Dissolve dextrin in flask with boiling H_2O and filter thru paper already used, receiving filtrate in weighed dish prepd as in **31.008**. Rinse flask and wash filter number of times with small portions of hot H_2O, evap. on H_2O bath, and dry to const wt at 70° under pressure ≤50 mm Hg (6.7 kPa).

Dissolve weighed alcohol ppt in H_2O and dil. to definite vol., using 50 mL H_2O for each 0.5 g ppt or part thereof.

Det. reducing sugars in soln both before and after inversion as in **31.031**, expressing results as invert sugar. Calc. sucrose from results thus obtained and subtract sum of reducing sugars before inversion and sucrose from wt total alcohol ppt to obtain wt dextrin.

Chromatographic Separation of Sugars
Method I (33)—Official Final Action

31.123 ***Principle***

By adsorption of honey sample on charcoal column, followed by elution into monosaccharide, disaccharide, and higher sugar fractions, interference of disaccharides in glucose and fructose detns is eliminated. Elution is by progressively higher alcohol concns, followed by detn of individual monosaccharides, sucrose, and reducing disaccharides collectively as maltose, and trisaccharides and higher sugars collectively after hydrolysis.

31.124 ***Preparation and Standardization of Absorption Column***

Column is 22 mm od × 370 mm long, with 1 L spherical section and ₸ 35/20 spherical joint at top. Adsorbent is 1 + 1 mixt. of Darco G-60 charcoal and rapid filter-aid (Celite 545 or Dicalite 4200). Insert glass wool plug, wet from below, and add enough dry adsorbent to dry tube (23–26 cm) to compress to 17 cm when vac. is applied with *gentle* tapping of column. Remove excess charcoal from walls of tube, and add filter-aid layer at top with *gentle* packing (1–1.5 cm). Wash column with 500 mL H_2O and 250 mL 50% alcohol, and let stand overnight with 50% alcohol on it. Flow rate should be 5.5–8.0 mL/min with H_2O at 9 lb/sq in. (62 kPa) pressure. Slower flow rates delay analyses excessively.

Alcohol content of eluting solns must be adjusted to retentive power of charcoal used. Wash column alcohol-free with 250 mL H_2O, quant. add 10 mL soln of 1.000 g anhyd. glucose to top, and draw it into column with suction (do not let dry). Add 300 mL H_2O to top, break suction, apply pressure (≤10 lb/sq in.; 69 kPa), and collect eluate in five 50 mL portions in tared beakers. Include 10 mL from sample introduction in first 50 mL fraction. Evap. fractions on steam bath, dry in vac. oven at 80–100°, and weigh.

Decant remaining H_2O from top of column, pass 50 mL 50% alcohol and then 250 mL H_2O thru column, and repeat chromatgy, using 1.000 g anhyd. glucose in 10 mL 1% alcohol, washing with 250 mL 1% alcohol as above. Select as *solv. 1* that which removes glucose in 150 mL. Repeat chromatgy with 2% alcohol, if necessary.

Wash column with 250 mL H_2O and then 20 mL 5% alcohol. To top, add 10 mL 5% alcohol soln contg 100 mg maltose and 100 mg sucrose. Elute as above with 250 mL 5% alcohol, weighing evapd 50 mL portions of filtrate. Repeat, if necessary, with 7, 8, and 9% alcohol to find *solv. 2* that will elute ≥98% disaccharides in 200 mL. *Solv. 1* previously selected must not elute disaccharides. Combinations found satisfactory with various charcoals are 1%, 7%; 2%, 8%; 2%, 9%. At conclusion, pass 100 mL 50% alcohol thru column, and store under layer of this solv.

31.125 ***Preparation of Fractions***

Wash column with 250 mL H_2O and decant any supernate. Pass 20 mL *solv. 1* thru column, and discard. Dissolve 1 g sample in 10 mL *solv. 1* in 50 mL beaker. Transfer sample (using long-stem funnel) onto column, and force into column. Use 15 mL *solv. 1* to rinse beaker and funnel, and add to column. Collect all eluate, beginning with sample introduction, in 250 mL vol. flask. Add 250 mL *solv. 1*, and collect exactly 250 mL total (fraction *1*, monosaccharides). Decant excess solv. from top, add 265–270 mL *solv. 2*, and collect 250 mL in vol. flask (fraction *2*, disaccharides). Decant excess, add 110 mL 50% alcohol (*solv. 3*), and collect 100 mL in vol. flask (fraction *3*, higher sugars). Mix each fraction thoroly. Column may be stored indefinitely, outlet closed, under 50% alcohol. Discard after 8 uses.

Fructose

31.126 ***Reagents***

Use reagents in **31.052** and following:

(**a**) *Iodine soln.*—0.05*N*. Dissolve 13.5 g pure I in soln of 24 g KI in 200 mL H_2O, and dil. to 2 L. Do not stdze.

(**b**) *Sodium sulfite soln.*—1%. Dissolve 1 g Na_2SO_3 in 100 mL H_2O. Make fresh daily.

(**c**) *Bromocresol green soln.*—Dissolve 150 mg bromocresol green in 100 mL H_2O.

31.127 ***Determination***

Pipet 20 mL fraction *1* into 200 mL vol. flask. Add 40 mL 0.05*N* I soln by pipet; then with vigorous mixing, add 25 mL 0.1*N* NaOH over 30 sec period, and immediately place flask in 18±0.1° H_2O bath. Exactly 10 min after alkali addn, add 5 mL 1*N* H_2SO_4 and remove from bath. Exactly neutze I with Na_2SO_3 soln, using 2 drops starch soln, **31.052(d)**, near end point. Back-titr. with dil. I if necessary. Add 5 drops bromocresol green and exactly neutze soln with 1*N* NaOH; then make just acid to indicator. Dil. to vol. and det. reducing value of 5 mL aliquots by Shaffer-Somogyi method, **31.053**.

Make duplicate blanks and detns. Deduct titrn from that of blank and calc. fructose:

% Fructose = 500[(titer × 0.1150) + 0.0915] × 100/mg sample

Fructose correction for glucose detn = f.c. = [(titer × 0.1150) + 0.0915] × 40. Bracketed quantity is mg fructose in 5 mL aliquot, valid between 0.5 and 1.75 mg fructose.

Glucose

31.128 ***Reagents***

Sodium thiosulfate soln.—0.05*N*. Prep. from stdzd stock 0.1000*N* soln, **50.037–50.038**.

31.129 ***Determination***

Pipet 20 mL fraction *1* into duplicate 250 mL erlenmeyers. Evap. to dryness on steam bath in air current. Add 20 mL H_2O, pipet in 20 mL 0.05*N* I, and slowly add 25 mL 0.1*N* NaOH, as in fructose detn. Immediately place in 18±0.1° H_2O bath. Exactly 10 min after alkali addn, add 5 mL 2*N* H_2SO_4, remove from bath, and titr. with 0.05*N* $Na_2S_2O_3$, using starch soln, **31.052(d)**.

Make duplicate blanks, using H_2O, subtract titrn value from that of blank, and calc. glucose:

% Glucose = 56.275[titer − (0.01215 × f.c.)] × 100/mg sample,

where f.c. = fructose correction from fructose detn. Equation is valid over range 10–15 mg glucose in 20 mL. In presence of glucose, 1 mg fructose requires 0.01215 mL 0.05*N* $Na_2S_2O_3$, in range 15–60 mg fructose.

Reducing Disaccharides as Maltose

31.130 ***Determination***

Pipet 5 mL aliquots of fraction *2* into 25 × 200 mm test tubes, and det. reducing value as in **31.053**, except boil tubes 30 min. Value for 15 min H_2O blank may be used here. Calc. % reducing disaccharides as maltose:

% "Maltose" = 50[(titer × 0.2264) + 0.075] × 100/mg sample.

Maltose correction for sucrose detn = m.c. = maltose titer × 0.92. Bracketed quantity is mg maltose in 5 mL aliquot, valid between 0.15 and 3.80 mg maltose. Reducing value of maltose at 15 min is 92% of final value.

Sucrose

31.131 ***Determination***

Pipet 25 mL fraction *2* into 50 mL vol. flask. Add 5 mL 6*N* HCl and 5 mL H_2O. Mix, let stand 17 min in 60° H_2O bath, cool, and neutze to bromocresol green with 5*N* NaOH (103 g/500 mL). (Polyethylene squeeze bottle is excellent for holding and delivering alkali.) Adjust to acid color of indicator, using 2*N* H_2SO_4 to correct over-run. Dil. to vol. and det. reducing value of 5 mL aliquots by Shaffer-Somogyi detn, **31.053**. Subtract titrn from blank, and calc. sucrose by ref. to curve constructed from following table:

Sucrose in 5 mL Aliquot Oxidized, mg	*0.005N $Na_2S_2O_3$ Required, mL*
0.255	1.75
0.502	3.95
1.004	8.72
1.260	11.28

From curve obtain S_1 = sucrose equiv. to maltose correction, **31.130**, and S_2 = sucrose equiv. of sucrose titer.

$$\% \text{ Sucrose} = 50(2S_2 - S_1) \times 100/\text{mg sample}.$$

Higher Sugars or "Dextrin"

31.132 ***Determination***

Pipet 25 mL aliquots of fraction *3* into 50 mL vol. flasks. Add 5 mL 6*N* HCl and 5 mL H_2O, and heat 45 min in boiling H_2O bath. Cool, neutze as for sucrose, dil. to vol., and det. reducing value by Shaffer-Somogyi detn, **31.053**. Subtract titrn value from blank and obtain glucose equiv. from curve constructed from following table:

Glucose, mg	*Titer, mL*
0.05	0.20
0.10	0.60
0.25	1.85
0.50	4.00
1.00	8.50
2.00	17.60

$$\% \text{ Higher sugars} = 40(\text{glucose equiv.}) \times 100/\text{mg sample}.$$

Notes: For most accurate work, Shaffer-Somogyi values must check within 0.04 mL. Calibration of all operations, including column, using known synthetic mixts of glucose, fructose, sucrose, maltose, and raffinose (corrected for moisture) is recommended for critical work. Sugar:mL $Na_2S_2O_3$ relations [(titer × 0.1150) + 0.0915] in equation for % fructose, and [(titer × 0.2264) + 0.075] in equation for % maltose, are obtained by analyzing known mixts of glucose and fructose for fructose, and known amts of maltose, resp., by method.

Efficiency of column sepn may be checked by paper chromatgy of fractions *1, 2,* and *3* as in **31.145**.

Alternative Method II (34)—Official First Action

31.133 ***Principle***

For use when sucrose is sugar of primary interest. Sugars are sepd by charcoal column, **31.124–31.125**. Glucose is detd in disaccharide fraction 2 by glucose oxidase before and after invertase hydrolysis and calcd to sucrose. Other sugars are detd by weighing residues of sepd fractions.

31.134 ***Reagents***

(**a**) *Column.*—Prep. as in **31.124**. Alternatively, use slurry prepn: Place glass wool plug at bottom of column and add ca 1 cm dry filter aid (Dicalite 4200, or equiv.). Wet filter aid layer from below. With outlet open, add slurry of 20 g adsorbent mixt. in 200 mL H_2O from top. Let drain 5 min and apply 27.6 kPa (4 psi) pressure until surface is stabilized. Then apply 69 kPa (10 psi) pressure, release, and remove excess adsorbent beyond 17 cm depth by suction from above. Add ca 1 cm filter aid. Wash column as in **31.124**.

(**b**) *Acetate buffer soln.*—0.1*M*, pH 4.5. Add 5.72 mL HOAc to 500 mL H_2O, adjust to pH 4.5 with 1*M* NaOH, and dil. to 1 L.

(**c**) *Tris buffer soln.*—pH 7.6. To 48.44 g tris(hydroxymethyl)aminomethane (available as Trizma base, No. T 1503, Sigma Chemical Co.) in 500 mL H_2O, add 384 mL 0.8*M* HCl, adjust to pH 7.6 if necessary, and dil. to 1 L.

(**d**) *Glucose oxidase-peroxidase reagent* (*GOP*).—Dissolve 120 mg glucose oxidase (Type II:purified, 15,000–20,000 units/g; Sigma Chemical Co. G 6125, or equiv.) and 32 mg peroxidase (Type I: from horseradish, salt-free powder; Sigma Chemical Co. P 8125, or equiv.) in 400 mL tris buffer, (**c**). Add soln of 270 mg *o*-tolidine.2HCl (available from Fisher Scientific Co. as Fisher certified T-320) in 520 mL H_2O. Refrigerate in brown bottle. Filter before use, if necessary. Stable ≥6 weeks.

(**e**) *Invertase reagent.*—Dissolve 12.5 mg invertase (Grade VI, from baker's yeast, essentially melibiase-free, activity ca 200 units/mg; Sigma Chemical Co. I 5875, or equiv.) in 50 mL pH 4.5 acetate buffer soln, (**b**).

(**f**) *Glucose std soln.*—0.1 mg/mL. Dissolve 25.0 mg glucose (SRM 41, NBS) in 25 mL H_2O in 250 mL vol. flask. Boil 2 min and dil. to vol. or dil. to vol. and hold final soln 2 hr before use.

31.135 ***Preparation of Fractions***

Proceed as in **31.125**.

31.136 ***Determination of Sugars***

(**a**) *Glucose.*—Dil. 5.00 mL fraction *1* to 100 mL and pipet 2 mL portions into each of two 18 × 150 mm test tubes. Place tube with 2 mL H_2O in rack, follow with 1 tube contg 2 mL std glucose soln (100 μg/mL), the 2 sample tubes, then 1 std. Repeat sequence if addnl detns are to be made. At intervals appropriate to measuring technic to be used (i.e., 30 or 60 sec with flow-thru cells; longer as needed for manual cells), add 5.00 mL glucose oxidase reagent at room temp. to each tube, beginning with H_2O tube, which will be reagent blank. After 60 min from addn of reagent, add 0.15 mL 4*N* HCl to first tube and mix thoroly with vortex mixer.

Continue same timing with other solns. Zero instrument with blank tube and det. *A* at 530 nm of each successive tube 1 min after addn of acid. Average *A* for each pair of sample tubes and calc. glucose concn, using av. *A′* of stds before and after corresponding sample tubes.

$$\mu\text{g Glucose in tube} = (A/A') \times \mu\text{g glucose in std tube}$$

$$\% \text{ Glucose in honey} = \mu\text{g glucose in tube} \times 2.5/\text{mg sample},$$

where factor 2.5 = 20 (diln factor) × 250 (vol. fraction)/(1000 μg/mg) × 2 (vol. in tube).

(**b**) *Sucrose.*—Pipet 2 mL fraction *2* into each of four 18×150 mm test tubes. Prep. 2 series, one control, other inverted. For each series, arrange in rack tube with 2 mL H_2O, 2 sample tubes, tube with 2 mL glucose std, 2 sample tubes, etc., finishing with 2 mL glucose std. To all tubes in control series add 0.50 mL H_2O; to all tubes in inverted series add 0.50 mL invertase reagent (or 0.50 mL pH 4.5 acetate buffer may be added to std tubes). Hold all tubes 30 min at room temp. Continue as in (**a**), beginning "At intervals appropriate . . .", beginning with inverted series followed by control series.

$$\mu\text{g Glucose} = (\mu\text{g glucose in std tube}) \times (A/A'),$$

$$\% \text{ Sucrose in honey} = 0.02375\ (\mu\text{g glucose in inverted tube} - \mu\text{g glucose in control tube})/\text{g sample},$$

where 0.02375 = μg glucose × 1.9 × 10^{-6} × (½) × 250 × 100; μg glucose × 1.9 = μg sucrose; 10^{-6} = μg/g; ½ = 2 mL analyzed; 250 = mL diln of sample; 100 = to convert to %.

31.137 ***Distribution of Sugars***

Filter fractions if filter aid is visible. Evap. to dryness, on steam bath with current of air or N, 50.0 mL fraction *1*, 100 mL fraction *2*, and entire fraction *3*, finally transfering each fraction to sep. weighed 50 mL beakers. Dry to const wt in vac. oven at ≤95°.

% Monosaccharides = g fraction *1* × 500/g sample,
% Disaccharides = g fraction *2* × 250/g sample,
% Higher sugars = g fraction *3* × 100/g sample.

High Pressure Liquid Chromatographic Method (35) *Official First Action*

31.138 ***Apparatus***

(a) *Chromatograph.*—Waters Associates Model ALC/GPC, or equiv., with Model 6000A solv. delivery system and model U6K injector.

(b) *Detector.*—Waters Associates R-401 refractive index detector, or equiv.

(c) *Recorder.*—Varian Aerograph Model A-25 dual pen recorder, or equiv.

(d) *Column.*—300 × 4 (id) mm μ-Bondapak/Carbohydrate (Waters Associates, No. 84038).

(e) *Sample clarification kit.*—Available in kit form from Waters Associates (No. 26865), or equiv.; 0.45 μm filters stable in org. solvs are suitable.

(f) *Syringes.*—10 μL No. 701-N point style No. 1, 2×0.020″ od, 25 gage needle (Hamilton Co.).

31.139 ***Reagents***

(a) *Mobile phase.*—Nonspectro acetronitrile (Burdick & Jackson Laboratories, Inc.) dild with H_2O (83+17). Degas mobile phase daily by mag. stirring 15 min under vac.

(b) *Sugar std soln.*—Place 3.804 g fructose (Mallinckrodt Chemical Works), 3.010 g glucose (Mallinckrodt Chemical Works), and 0.602 g sucrose into 100 mL vol. flask, dissolve in 50 mL H_2O, and add CH_3CN to vol. Composition of std approximates 5 g honey dissolved in 50 mL aq. CH_3CN (1+1).

31.140 ***Operating Conditions***

Fructose, glucose, and sucrose are baseline sepd and quantitated in 20 min under following conditions: flow rate, 1.0 mL/min (ca 500 psig; 3.45 MPa); temp., ambient (ca 23°); detector (R-401), 8× (fructose and glucose) and 2× (sucrose); attentuation, 10 mv on recorder, detector set so that 380 μg fructose gives full-scale deflection of pen; and chart speed, 0.1″/min. Mono-, di-, and trisaccharides are eluted from column in order of MW.

31.141 ***Preparation of Sample***

Weigh 5.000 g sample in small beaker and transfer to 50 mL vol. flask with 25 mL H_2O. Immediately dil. to vol. with CH_3CN and filter thru 0.45 μm filter, using sample clarification kit.

31.142 ***Chromatography***

Inject 10 μL std soln into chromatograph. Establish retention times, measure peak hts, and check reproducibility. Repeat for sample soln. Calc. glucose, fructose, and sucrose from integrator values or from peak hts as follows:

$$\text{Wt \% sugar} = 100 \times (PH/PH') \times (V/V') \times (W'/W)$$

where PH and PH' = peak hts (or integrator values) of sample and std, resp.; V and V' = mL sample and std (50 and 100) solns, resp,; and W and W' = g sample (5.000) and std, resp.

Commercial Glucose

Qualitative Test (36)—Official Final Action

31.143 ***Reagent***

Aniline-diphenylamine chromogenic reagent.—Dissolve 500 mg diphenylamine.HCl and 0.55 mL redistd aniline in 50 mL acetone. Add 5 mL 85% H_3PO_4. Prep. fresh daily.

31.144 ***Preparation of Sample***

Dil. sample with equal vol. H_2O. To 0.5 mL in small centrf. tube (11 × 100 mm test tube) add 4 mL absolute alcohol, shake, and centrf. Decant clear or slightly cloudy supernate, dissolve ppt in 0.5 mL H_2O, reppt with 4 mL absolute alcohol, and centrf. Decant, and dissolve ppt in 0.1 mL H_2O. Apply 2 μL to origin of chromatogram, as well as control spots of authentic honey and/or honeydew and corn sirup treated as above.

TLC method, **31.149(b)**, or paper chromatgc method, **31.145**, may be used.

31.145 ***Chromatography***

For details of performing paper chromatgy *see* **29.028** and JAOAC **40**, 999(1957).

Ascending or descending is satisfactory. Suitable solv. for latter is *n-PrOH-EtOAc-H₂O* (7+1+2). Equilibrate 45 min and irrigate ≥40 hr, letting solv. drip from serrated lower edge of paper. For shorter ascending use (ca 6 hr), roll paper into cylinder, staple edges, and set in cylindrical jar, using *isoamyl alcohol-pyridine-H₂O* (7+7+6). To obtain increased resolution, dry paper and repeat irrigation ≥1 time.

Irrigate with suitable solv., remove, and dry paper chromatogram. Dip in chromogenic reagent, let acetone evap., and heat ca 5–8 min at 85–95° until control spots of corn sirup treated as above become blue. Honey or honeydew sample contg 5% of com. glucose shows series of blue maltodextrin spots of low R_F, converging to origin. Honey and honeydew dextrin spots are distinctly brown or gray, not blue. If paper is heated excessively, both honey dextrin spots and maltodextrin spots will approach same shade of gray.

Commercial Invert Sugar (37)

Resorcinol Test (38)—Procedure

31.146 ***Reagent***

Resorcinol soln.—Dissolve 1 g resublimed resorcinol in 100 mL HCl (sp gr 1.18–1.19).

31.147 ***Test***

Dissolve 2 g honey in 10 mL H_2O and ext rapidly with washed ether 30 min in continuous extractor, Fig. **12:01B**. Conc. ether to ca 5 mL and transfer to test tube. Add 2 mL freshly prepd resorcinol soln, shake, and note color. Cherry red color appearing within 1 min indicates presence of com. invert sugar. Yellow to salmon shades have no significance.

Note: Resorcinol test, when neg., may not be regarded as conclusive evidence of absence of com. invert sugar sirup in honey.

High Fructose Corn Sirup

Thin Layer Chromatographic Method (39) *Official First Action*

31.148 ***Apparatus and Reagents***

(a) *Charcoal column.*—Use column and adsorbent as in **31.124**. Pack plug of fine glass wool in base of column; close outlet tube and partly fill column with H_2O. Open outlet and let H_2O flow thru column to remove any air bubbles. Close outlet when H_2O is ca 10 mL above glass wool; then add slurry of filter aid sufficient for ca 1 cm depth and let settle by gravity. Pour in slurry of 12 g adsorbent mixt. in 150 mL H_2O. Drain 5 min, apply 4 psi (27.6 kPa) pressure until surface stabilizes and then 10 psi (69 kPa). Clean excess adsorbent from surfaces by vac. Add slurry of filter aid sufficient for 1–2 cm depth, and wash column with 500 mL H_2O and 200 mL 50% alcohol, under which it may be stored. Before use, wash column with 250 mL H_2O. (Vac. operation may be used, but pressure is preferred.) Flow rate of 8.5 mL/min at 10 psi is commonly achieved.

(**b**) *Plates.*—Coated with 250 μ thickness of silica gel G. Store in desiccator.

(**c**) *Solvent—n*-Butanol-HOAc-H_2O (2+1+1).

(**d**) *Color reagent.*—Dissolve 1 mL redistd aniline and 1 g diphenylamine.HCl in 50 mL acetone and add 5 mL H_3PO_4. As alternative to redistg aniline, proceed as follows: Dissolve 1 g aniline in 50 mL acetone and decolorize with decolorizing carbon (not Darco G-60). Filter, dil. to 50 mL and add diphenylamine and H_3PO_4. Make fresh daily or store at 0°

31.149 ***Detection***

(**a**) *Preparation of sample.*—Weigh to nearest mg 1 g sample in 30 or 50 mL beaker. Add 10 mL H_2O to dissolve and place on top of column. Force into column with suction but do not let run dry. Rinse beaker with two 5 mL portions H_2O and force into column. Wash with 300 mL 7% alcohol, which is discarded, and then with 100 mL 50% alcohol. Evap. eluate in tared 50 mL beaker on steam bath in current of air or N, dry in vac. oven 0.5 hr at 65°, and weigh residue.

Transfer residue to 13 × 100 mm test tube with total of 1 mL H_2O. Evap to dryness in bath at ca 60° in current of air or N. Dissolve residue in 0.1 mL H_2O for each 10 mg material.

(**b**) *Chromatography.*—Place solv. in tank 15 min before inserting plate. Apply 2 and 6 (2 × 3 or 3 × 2) μL of test soln to plate. Apply control spots of pure and adulterated honey, prepd as above. Control solns may be preserved by freezing or drying. Place spotted plate in developing tank until solv. front approaches top of plate. Remove plate, dry, and spray thoroly with color reagent. (*Caution:* Avoid contact with spray.) Let acetone evap., and place in oven at 90–95° until spots are well developed (ca 7–10 min).

(**c**) *Interpretation.*—Pure honey will show 1 or 2 large blue-gray or blue-brown spots at R_f ca >0.35. When wt of isolated carbohydrate fraction is ≤15 mg (1.5%), any blue streaks or series of spots extending from origin provide conclusive evidence of presence of corn sirup, high fructose corn sirup (HFCS), including high fructose sirup derived from plant source other than corn. If wt is >15 mg, addnl test must be conducted to confirm adulteration. Repeat charcoal column pretreatment as follows: Prep. sample as in (**a**), except wash column with 100 mL 25% alcohol, discard this fraction, and wash with the 50% alcohol. Any blue streaks or series of spots extending from origin on TLC plate following this treatment provide conclusive evidence of adulteration.

Corn Sirup Products

Carbon Ratio Mass Spectrometric Method (40) *Official Final Action*

31.150 ***Principle***

Sample is burned completely to CO_2 and H_2O; CO_2 is purified, and ^{13}C to ^{52}C ratio is measured in isotope ratio mass spectrometer. Difference in $^{13}C/^{12}C$ values for honey (av. $\delta^{13}C = -25.4‰$ (parts per thousand)) and corn sirup (av. $\delta^{13}C = -9.7‰$) provides measure of corn sirup (including high fructose corn sirup (HFCS)) in honey.

31.151 ***Apparatus***

(**a**) *Combustion system.*—Vac.-tight glass manifold including quartz combustion tube ½ filled with CuO in tubular furnace, liq. N trap, automatic Toepler pump, and high-vac. source.

(**b**) *Purification system.*—Glass manifold interconnected with combustion system including trap, sample collection tube, and manometer (*see* Fig. **31:02** and Geochimica et Cosmochimica Acta **3**, 54–55(1953)).

(**c**) *Mass spectrometer.*—Micromass 602 (new model 602D) (Kearns Group, 58 Buckingham Dr, Stamford, CT 06902), Nuclide 6-60-RMS (Nuclide, 642 E College Ave, State College, PA 16801), Varian MAT G D150 (superceded by MAT 250) (Varian MAT Mass Spectrometry, 25 Hanover Rd., Florham Park, NJ 07932), or equiv. instrument designed or modified for isotope ratio measurement and capable of accuracy of 0.01% of abundance at mass 45.

31.152 ***Preparation of Sample***

Place 300–400 mg sample, weighed to nearest 0.1 mg, in ceramic boat, position boat in tube, and evacuate system. Admit to 600 mm Hg, tank O purified over CuO at 700°, followed by liq. N trap. Heat sample to ≥850° in manifold in tubular furnace, condensing CO_2 in liq. N trap. Recirculate gases over CuO 10–30 min at 850°. Isolate collection trap and purification system from combustion system and Toepler pump by valves, and pump off O. Cool purification trap with solid CO_2-acetone; cool sample tube with liq. N. Let collection trap warm, condensing impurities in solid CO_2 trap and CO_2 in sample tube.

31.153 ***Determination***

Operate mass spectrometer according to manufacturer's instructions. Calibrate with ≥2 stds such as NBS SRM 20 Solenhofen limestone ($\delta^{13}C = -1.06‰$ against Pee Dee belemnite (PDB)), NBS SRM 21 graphite ($\delta^{13}C = -27.8‰$), or NBS SRM 22 crude oil ($\delta^{13}C = -29.5‰$). Correct values obtained for zero enrichment in inlet system, mixing between sampling and std valves, tailing of major onto minor peak signal, and contribution of ^{17}O to mass 45 signal. Calc.:

$$\delta^{13}C\,(‰) = \left[\frac{^{13}C/^{12}C \text{ sample}}{^{13}C/^{12}C \text{ std}} - 1\right] \times 1000.$$

Convert laboratory analyses, relative to whatever std was used, to PDB base by following relationship:

$$\delta_{(X-PDB)} = \delta_{(X-B)} + \delta_{(B-PDB)} + 10^{-3}\,\delta_{(X-B)}\,\delta_{(B-PDB)},$$

where $(X - B)$ and $(X - PDB)$ refer to analyses of sample (X) relative to std (B) and relative to PDB, and $(B - PDB)$ is analysis of std (B) relative to PDB, all δ's in parts per thousand.

Sample with $\delta^{13}C$ value less negative than $-21.5‰$ relative to PDB is considered adulterated.

Diastatic Activity of Honey (*41*)—Official Final Action

(Do not heat sample for this detn.)

31.154 ***Principle***

Buffered sol. starch-honey soln is incubated and time required to reach specified end point is detd photometrically. Results are expressed as mL 1% starch hydrolyzed by enzyme in 1 g honey in 1 hr.

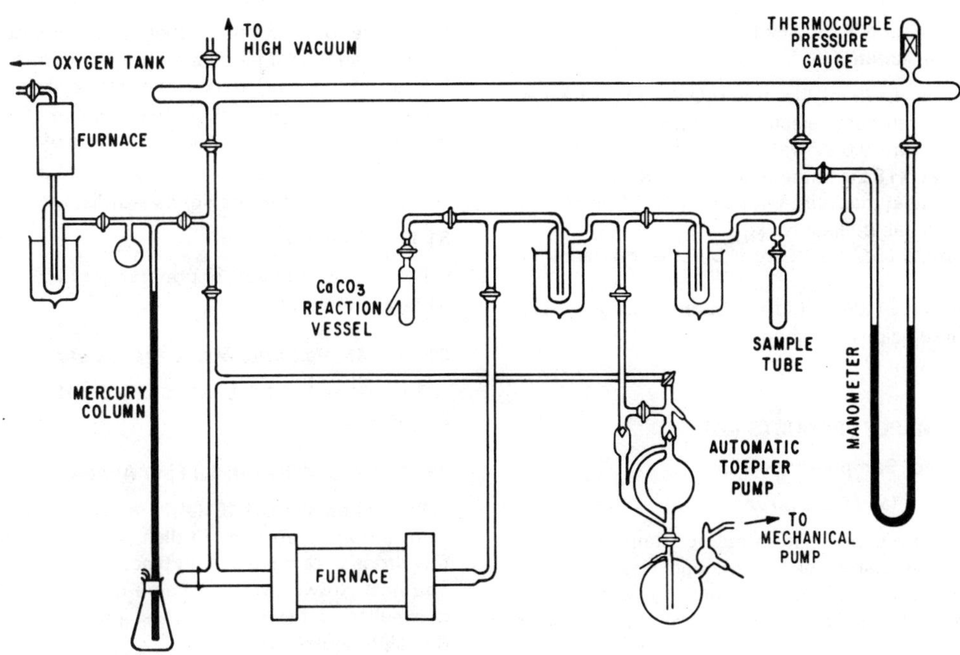

FIG. 31:02—Carbon combustion and purification system

Reprinted with permission from *Geochimica et Cosmochimica Acta,* **3**, 54 (1953).

31.155 ***Apparatus***

(**a**) *Reaction vessel.*—Attach sealed side arm, 18 × 60 mm, to 18 × 175 mm test tube. Lower side of side arm is attached 100 mm from bottom of tube, making 45° angle with lower portion of tube.

(**b**) *Photoelectric photometer.*—With 660 nm red filter or 600 nm interference filter and 1 cm cells.

31.156 ***Reagents***

(**a**) *Iodine stock soln.*—Dissolve 8.80 g resublimed I in 30–40 mL H_2O contg 22.0 g KI, and dil. to 1 L with H_2O.

(**b**) *Iodine soln.*—0.0007*N*. Dissolve 20 g KI and 5.00 mL I soln, (**a**), in H_2O and dil. to 500 mL. Prep. fresh every second day.

(**c**) *Acetate buffer soln.*—pH 5.3 (1.59*M*). Dissolve 87 g $NaOAc.3H_2O$ in 400 mL H_2O, add ca 10.5 mL HOAc in H_2O, and dil. to 500 mL. Adjust pH to 5.30 with NaOAc or HOAc, if necessary.

(**d**) *Sodium chloride soln.*—0.5*M*. Dissolve 14.5 g NaCl in H_2O and dil. to 500 mL.

(**e**) *Starch soln.*—Weigh 2.000 g sol. starch (special for diastatic power detn, available from ASBC) and mix with 90 mL H_2O in 250 mL erlenmeyer. Rapidly bring to bp, swirling soln as much as possible. Reduce heat and boil gently 3 min, cover, and let cool to room temp. Transfer to 100 mL vol. flask and dil. to vol. Observe details closely to limit variation in *A* values of starch-I blank.

31.157 ***Standardization***

Pipet 5 mL starch soln into 10 mL H_2O and mix well. Pipet 1 mL of this soln into several 50 mL graduates contg 10 mL dil. I soln. Mix well, and det. H_2O diln necessary to produce *A* value of 0.760±0.02. This is std diln for starch prepn used. Repeat when changing starch source.

31.158 ***Determination***

Weigh 5 g sample into 20 mL beaker, dissolve in 10–15 mL H_2O and 2.5 mL buffer soln, and transfer to 25 mL vol. flask contg 1.5 mL NaCl soln. Dil. to vol. (Soln must be buffered before addn to NaCl soln.)

Pipet 5 mL starch soln into side arm of reaction tube and 10 mL sample soln into bottom of tube, with care not to mix. Place tube in H_2O bath 15 min at 40±0.2°; then mix contents by tilting tube back and forth several times. Start stopwatch. At 5 min, remove 1 mL aliquot with 1 mL serological pipet and add rapidly to 10.00 mL dil. I soln in 50 mL graduate. Mix, dil. to previously detd vol., and det. *A* in photometer. Note time from mixing of starch and honey to addn of aliquot to I as reaction time. (Place 1 mL pipet in reaction tube for reuse when later aliquots are taken.) Continue taking 1 mL aliquots at intervals until *A* value of <0.235 is obtained.

The 5 min value gives approximation of end point as follows:

Absorbance	*End Point, min*
0.7	>25
0.65	20–25
0.6	15–18
0.55	11–13
0.5	9–10
0.45	7–8

31.159 ***Calculation***

Plot *A* against time (min) on rectilinear paper; draw straight line thru starting *A* and as many points as possible. From graph, det. time dild reaction-I mixt. reaches *A* of 0.235. Divide 300 by this time to obtain diastase no. (DN).

Notes: A 5-min reading is sufficient for approximating end point of sample of high DN (>35) if another value is taken soon enough to obtain *A* of ca 0.20. For accurate results, repeat detn, taking samples each min from start. With samples of low DN, another reading at 10 min will permit prediction of end point by plotting the data. No addnl readings need be taken until within few min of end point. Only 2 such readings are needed. The 5 min value will not accurately predict low DN.

31.160 Free, Lactone, and Total Acidity (*42*)
Official Final Action

Dissolve 10 g sample in 75 mL CO_2-free H_2O in 250 mL beaker. Stir with mag. stirrer, immerse electrodes of pH meter in soln, and record pH. Titr. with 0.05*N* NaOH at rate of 5.0 mL/min. Stop addn of NaOH at pH 8.50. Immediately pipet in 10 mL 0.05*N* NaOH, and without delay back-titr. with 0.05*N* HCl from 10 mL buret to pH 8.30. Calc. as milliequiv./kg:

Free acidity = (mL 0.05*N* NaOH from buret − mL blank) × 50/g sample;

Lactone = (10.00 − mL 0.05*N* HCl from buret) × 50/g sample;

Total acidity = free acidity + lactone.

MAPLE PRODUCTS (*43*)

31.161 Preparation of Sample—Procedure

(**a**) *Maple Sirup*

(*1*) *For solids determination.*—If sample contains no sugar crystals or suspended matter, decant enough clear sirup for detn. If sugar crystals are present, redissolve by heating at ca 50°. If suspended matter is present, filter sample thru cotton wool.

(*2*) *For other determinations.*—If sugar crystals are present, redissolve by heating. If other sediment is present, distribute it evenly thru sirup by shaking. Transfer ca 100 mL sirup, with its suspended sediment, to casserole or beaker, add ¼ vol. H_2O, and evap. over flame. When temp. of boiling sirup approaches 104°, draw small amt into thin-wall, ca 1 mL pipet, and cool to room temp. in running H_2O. Wipe outside of pipet, let possibly dild sirup in point escape, transfer some of remaining sirup to refractometer, and det. solids content of cooled sirup. Repeat operation from time to time until reading is obtained corresponding to 64.5% solids (n_{20} = 1.4521), or to such other value as in experience of analyst will give filtered sirup of 65.0% solids. Filter sirup thru filter that will let the 100 mL pass within 5 min and adjust filtrate to 65.0±0.5% solids (refractometric) by thoro mixing with appropriate amt of H_2O.

(**b**) *Maple Sugar and Other Solid or Semisolid Products*

(*1*) *For moisture and solids determination.*—Grind in mortar, if necessary, and mix thoroly.

(*2*) *For other determinations.*—To prep. sirup, dissolve ca 100 g sample in 150 mL hot H_2O, boil until temp. approaches 104°, and complete prepn of resulting sirup as in (**a**)(*2*), beginning ". . . draw small amt into thin-wall, ca 1 mL pipet, . . ."

Color Classification (*44*)—Official Final Action

31.162 ***Apparatus***

(**a**) *Containers.*—*See* **31.108(a)**. Internal thickness 1.24 × 1.24" (31.5 mm).

(**b**) *Comparator.*—*See* **31.108(b)**. Only 1 box is required with 3 glass color stds (light amber, medium amber, and dark amber). Place containers, (**a**), filled with H_2O behind each glass std.

(**c**) *Glass stds.*—Use selected colored glasses tested and stdzd by USDA to correspond with color stds for maple sirup.

Complete grading set is available from VirTis Co., Phoenix Precision Instrument Div., Rt 208, Gardiner, NY 12525.

31.163 ***Determination***

Proceed as in **31.109**. Det. classification as follows: If sample is equal to light amber std in hue, or not as red (*i.e.,* yellower), classify as light amber; if perceptibly redder than light amber std in hue, but not redder than medium amber std, classify as medium amber; if perceptibly redder than medium amber std, but not redder than dark amber std, classify as dark amber; if redder in hue than dark amber std, classify as "unclassified." Hue (redness or yellowness) is attribute of color in classification.

Moisture or Solids—Official Final Action

31.164 ***Maple Sugar***

Proceed as in **31.006**, or preferably **31.005**, using sample prepd as in **31.161(b)**(*1*).

31.165 ***Maple Sirup, Maple Cream, etc.***

Proceed as in **31.005**, **31.007**, or **31.011**, using prepd sample, **31.161(a)**(*1*).

31.166 Ash (*45*)—Official First Action

Prep. sirup as in **31.161(a)**(*2*) or (**b**)(*2*). Transfer 5–10 g sample from dropper into tared Pt dish (weigh to nearest 0.1 mg). Add few drops pure olive oil and place in oven 1 hr at 110°. Remove, and heat slowly over low flame or under IR lamp until all H_2O is expelled and swelling ceases. Ignite in furnace ≥3 hr at 600°. Reweigh and report % ash.

31.167 Soluble and Insoluble Ash—Official Final Action

See **31.015**.

31.168 Alkalinity of Soluble Ash—Official Final Action

See **31.016**.

31.169 Alkalinity of Insoluble Ash—Official Final Action

See **31.017**.

31.170 Alkalinity of Total Ash—Official Final Action

Add alkys of sol. and insol. portions from **31.168** and **31.169**.

Polarization—Official Final Action

31.171 ***Direct Polarization***

See **31.025(a)**.

31.172 ***Invert Polarization***

(**a**) *At 20°.*—Proceed as in **31.025(b)** or (**c**) or **31.026** (**b**) or (**c**).
(**b**) *At 87°.*—Proceed as in **31.033**.

31.173 Sucrose—Polarimetric Methods—Official Final Action

Proceed as in **31.025** or **31.026**, or calc. from results of **31.171** and **31.172(a)**, using appropriate formula from **31.025** or **31.026**.

Sucrose—Chemical Methods—Official Final Action

31.174 ***By Reducing Sugars Before and After Inversion***

See **31.031**.

31.175 Reducing Sugars as Invert Sugar
Official Final Action

(**a**) *Before inversion.*—Proceed as in **31.036** or **31.038**, using aliquot of soln used for direct polarization, **31.171**. If soln is clarified, only neut. $Pb(OAc)_2$ soln may be used, and excess of Pb must be removed with dry Na oxalate.

(**b**) *After inversion.*—Proceed as in **31.036** or **31.038**, using aliquot of soln used for invert polarization, **31.172(a)**. If soln is clarified, only neut. $Pb(OAc)_2$ soln may be used, and excess of Pb must be removed with dry Na oxalate.

31.176 Commercial Glucose—Procedure

See **31.032** or **31.033**.

Lead Number

31.177 ★ *Canadian Lead Number (Fowler Modification)(46)—Official Final Action* ★

See **29.147–29.148,** 10th ed.

Winton Lead Number (47)—Official Final Action

31.178 ***Reagent***

(**a**) *Basic lead acetate std soln.*—(*Caution: See* **51.084.**) Activate litharge by heating 2.5–3 hr to 650–670° in furnace (cooled product should be lemon color). In 500 mL erlenmeyer provided with reflux condenser, boil 80 g neut. $Pb(OAc)_2.3H_2O$ and 40 g freshly activated litharge with 250 g H_2O 45 min. Cool, filter off any residue, and dil. with recently boiled H_2O to density of 1.25 at 20°.

(**b**) *Dilute basic lead acetate std soln.*—To measured vol. reagent, (**a**), add 4 vols H_2O, and filter. Conduct blank with each set of detns.

31.179 ***Determination of Lead in Blank***

Transfer 25 mL dil. std basic $Pb(OAc)_2$ soln to 100 mL vol. flask, add few drops HOAc, and dil. to vol. with H_2O. Shake, and det. $PbSO_4$ in 10 mL soln as in **31.180**. Use of HOAc is imperative to retain all Pb in soln when reagent is dild with H_2O.

31.180 ***Determination***

Transfer 25 g sample with H_2O to 100 mL vol. flask. Add 25 mL dil. basic $Pb(OAc)_2$ std soln and shake. Fill to mark, shake, and let stand $\geq$3 hr before filtering. Pipet 10 mL clear filtrate into 250 mL beaker, add 40 mL H_2O and 1 mL H_2SO_4, shake, and add 100 mL alcohol. Let stand overnight, filter on weighed gooch, wash with alcohol, dry in 100° oven, and ignite in furnace at 550°, or over Bunsen burner, placing crucible in larger crucible, applying heat gradually at first, and heating until outside of crucible is barely visible red. Cool and weigh. Subtract wt $PbSO_4$ so found from wt $PbSO_4$ found in blank, **31.179,** and multiply by factor 27.33. Use of this factor gives Pb number directly (without various calcns otherwise required).

Conductivity Value (*48*)—Official Final Action

31.181 ***Apparatus***

(**a**) *Conductivity bridge.*—Use any com. available conductivity bridges, which are usually self-contained instruments with 2 external connections, one for connection to power source, usually 110 volt AC, and other to conductivity cell. In addn, some models have means for making adjustment for temp. and cell const. Leeds and Northrup Bridge No. 4961 (replaced by 4866-60) and cell No. 4924 (replaced by 4905-01-44-088) are commonly used and conductivity is read directly, corrected to 20° when in "SC" position. Instruments such as Beckman Instruments, Inc., 89 Commerce Rd, Cedar Grove, NJ 07009, without temp. compensator circuit must have sirup soln at exact temp. specified to be comparative.

Calibrate scale (slide wire) of conductivity bridge by use of external fixed resistor with external leads. This should have resistance of 1000 ohms which will approx. that of conductivity cell. Attach resistor to bridge connections for conductivity cell and set slide wire to same value as that of resistor. Meter should give 0 reading or response.

(**b**) *Conductivity cell.*—Made of resistance glass with platinized electrodes firmly fixed and adequately protected from displacement. Cell may be of dipping type, for immersing cell into test soln, or of vessel type, into which soln may be run and subsequently drained.

(**c**) *Constant temperature bath.*—To maintain or supply H_2O at 25±0.1° for controlling temp. of test soln and cell.

31.182 ***Determination of Cell Constant***

Dry 2–3 g KCl at 110° to const wt. Weigh 2 portions dried KCl, one 0.3728±0.0002 g and other 0.7456±0.0002 g, transfer to two 500 mL flasks, and dil. to vol. with H_2O at 20°. These solns will be 0.01 and 0.02*M* KCl, resp. Transfer portion of 0.01*M* KCl soln to beaker and adjust temp. to 25±0.1°.

If conductivity bridge has temp. compensating device, set it at 25°, the temp. of KCl solns. With leads of conductivity cell attached to conductivity bridge, place dipping conductivity cell in 0.01*M* KCl, taking care to completely immerse electrodes. Adjust slide wire of bridge to give null-point reading. Repeat until 3 successive and concordant slide wire values (ohms resistance) are obtained. Replace KCl soln with fresh portion before making next measurement, taking care to shake adhering drops of liq. from electrodes before immersing them.

Repeat, using 0.02*M* KCl.

Calc. cell const by multiplying observed resistances (scale readings in ohms) by 141.2 (specific conductivity of 0.01*M* KCl), and by 276.1 (specific conductivity of 0.02*M* KCl), resp. Average the 2 results.

31.183 ***Determination***

Add 70 mL H_2O to 100 mL g-s graduate and fill to vol. with maple sirup to be tested. Stopper, mix thoroly, adjust temp. to 25±0.1°, and measure resistance of dil. sirup with conductivity cell in same manner as used to calibrate cell. Repeat until 3 concordant observed scale readings (ohms) are obtained. Conductivity value = cell const/ohms.

Malic Acid (*49*)—Official Final Action

31.184 ***Apparatus***

(**a**) *Ion exchange tubes.*—Std wall Pyrex glass tubing, 10 (id) × 300 mm long, with 5 cm capillary tip.

(**b**) *Spectrophotometer.*—Suitable for measuring *A* at 390 nm, with matched 1 cm cells or matched test tubes.

31.185 ***Reagents***

(**a**) *Ion exchange resins.*—(*1*) *Cation exchange resin.*—Dowex-50 (60–80 mesh) (currently Dowex 50W-X8 (50–100 mesh)). (*2*) *Anion exchange resin.*—AG1-X8 (50–100 mesh) (Bio-Rad Labs, 32nd & Griffin Ave, Richmond, CA 94804 or Amberlite CG-400 AR, Type SB (100–200 mesh) (Mallinckrodt).

(**b**) *Ammonium carbonate soln.*—0.25*N*. Dissolve 14.26 g $(NH_4)_2CO_3.H_2O$ in H_2O and dil. to 1 L.

(**c**) *Ammonium carbonate soln.*—1.0*N*. Dissolve 57.05 g $(NH_4)_2CO_3.H_2O$ in H_2O and dil. to 1 L.

(**d**) *Sodium carbonate soln.*—1.0*N*. Dissolve 5.3 g Na_2CO_3 in H_2O and dil. to 100 mL.

(**e**) *Hydrochloric acid soln.*—5%. Dil. 12 mL HCl with 88 mL H_2O.

(**f**) *2,7-Naphthalenediol soln.*—Dissolve 1 g in 100 mL H_2SO_4.

★ Surplus method—*see* inside front cover.

(g) *Malic acid std soln.*—Dry Eastman L-malic acid 18 hr at 40°. Dissolve 0.2000 g in 500 mL H_2O. Dil. known vol. of this soln (ca 10 mL) to 100 mL so that final soln gives *A*, after reaction with color reagent as in detn, of 0.2–0.8.

31.186 ***Preparation of Ion Exchange Columns***

For each column add enough H_2O to 10 mL dry resin to make thin slurry and pour slurry into tube contg small plug of glass wool. Let H_2O drain to level of settled resin and wash with 2 mL portions H_2O to condition resins. To cation exchange resin (Dowex-50) add three or four 10 mL portions 5% HCl, letting acid drain to top of resin between each addn. Wash resin acid-free with 10 mL portions H_2O until effluent gives neg. test for chlorides. (Approx. 4 bed vols of H_2O are required.)

Treat anion exchange resin with three or four 10 mL portions 5% NaOH soln, draining liq. to top of resin between addns. Remove excess alkali with H_2O by washing with 10 mL portions until effluent gives neg. alkali test with indicator paper. Transform resin into carbonate form by addn of three or four 10 mL portions 1.0*N* Na_2CO_3 soln. Wash resin carbonate-free with 10 mL portions H_2O until effluent is neut. to indicator paper. Mount conditioned columns vertically with cation resin column directly above anion resin column, connecting tubes with 1-hole rubber stopper mounted in top of anion column. No stopcocks are required; close packing of fine resins prevents liq. from draining below surface of resins. Any portion of resin that becomes dry will be inactivated.

31.187 ***Separation of Malic Acid***

Transfer ca 10 mL sirup sample to tared 100 mL vol. flask and weigh to ±0.2 mg. Dil. to vol. with H_2O and transfer aliquot contg 6–20 mg malic acid (ca 15 mL) to cation exchange resin and let eluate pass onto anion exchange resin. Wash cation resin (upper column) with three 10 mL portions H_2O, again letting eluate pass directly onto anion resin. Remove upper column and wash anion resin column with three 10 mL portions H_2O to remove sugars and any loosely held acids present that might interfere with test. Elute column with five 10 mL portions 0.25*N* $(NH_4)_2CO_3$ to quant. remove all glycolic, glyceric, or lactic acids possibly present in original test soln. Elute malic acid from anion resin with five 10 mL portions 1*N* $(NH_4)_2CO_3$; collect 45–48 mL eluate in 250 mL vol. flask, and dil. to vol. with H_2O.

31.188 ***Determination***

Transfer 1 mL malic acid-$(NH_4)_2CO_3$ eluate to 18 × 150 mm culture tube and slowly add 6 mL 96% H_2SO_4 from buret, adding first 2 mL down walls of tube to avoid excessive evolution of CO_2. Add 0.1 mL 2,7-naphthalenediol soln and mix thoroly. Cap tubes with metal culture tube closures and heat in boiling H_2O bath (deep fat fryer is satisfactory) 25 min to develop color. Cool tubes, and measure *A* of colored solns within 30 min in 1 cm cell at 390 nm against blank of 1 mL H_2O, 6 mL H_2SO_4, and 0.1 mL reagent also heated 25 min in boiling H_2O bath.

Color developed follows Beer's law in which $a = A/Cb$, where *a* is absorptivity, *C* is concn in mg/mL, and *b* is cell thickness. Absorptivity may vary from day to day because of differences in blank; therefore, *a* must be established daily with duplicate portions of fresh std malic acid soln. Calc. *a* from *A* at 390 nm of colored soln resulting from reaction of soln of std malic acid and color reagent. Calc. amt of malic acid in sample from: $C = (A/ab) \times$ diln factor. Express value for malic acid in maple sirup in terms of std density (65.5° Brix) sirup.

Formaldehyde (*50*)—Official Final Action

31.189 ***Apparatus***

(a) *Distillation apparatus.*—30 mL micro Kjeldahl flask, with Ŧ 19/38 joint and 10 cm H_2O-cooled West condenser with Ŧ 19/38 inner joint bent at 90° angle. Prep. permanent insulation of bent portion of condenser by wrapping with ⅛" diam. asbestos cord from Ŧ joint to H_2O jacket. Install adjustable flask heater equipped with conical porcelain coil element and hand-controllable rheostat placed on underside (Cenco Instrument Corp. No. 16530-1, or equiv.).

(b) *Spectrophotometer.*—Suitable for measuring *A* at 415 nm; with matched 1 cm cells or matched test tubes.

31.190 ***Reagents***

(a) *Nash's Reagent "B".*—Dissolve 150 g NH_4OAc, 3 mL HOAc, and 2 mL acetylacetone in 200–300 mL H_2O in 1 L flask and dil. to vol.

(b) *Formaldehyde.*—Approx. 37% by wt. Assay by **6.349**.

31.191 ***Preparation of Standard Solutions***

(a) *Stock soln.*—1000 ppm. Weigh 5.35 g 37.4% CH_2O soln (for other concns, g CH_2O soln required = 200/% CH_2O) into 2 L vol. flask contg H_2O and dil. to vol. with H_2O.

(b) *Soln B.*—50 ppm. Pipet 10 mL *stock soln* into 200 mL vol. flask and dil. to vol. with H_2O.

(c) *Soln C.*—100 ppm. Pipet 10 mL *stock soln* into 100 mL vol. flask and dil. to vol. with H_2O.

(d) *Soln D.*—200 ppm. Pipet 10 mL *stock soln* into 50 mL vol. flask and dil. to vol. with H_2O.

(e) *Formaldehyde std solns.*—Prep. 1, 2, and 4 ppm std solns by pipetting 10 mL *Solns B, C, and D*, resp., into 500 g sirup and stirring mech. 15 min.

31.192 ***Determination***

Weigh 20±0.20 g sample into tared 30 mL micro Kjeldahl flask and insulate flask neck with asbestos cord as in **31.189(a)** from base of Ŧ joint down to body of flask. (This insulation is temporary; repeat after each washing and weighing.) Add 2 drops antifoam agent, and connect West condenser. Mount app., adjusting slope of condenser at 45° angle, with flask bottom centered in conical cavity and at such ht that sirup level in flask is even with top plate of heater, without touching hot element at any point; *see* Fig. **31:03**. Heat flask with heater, previously

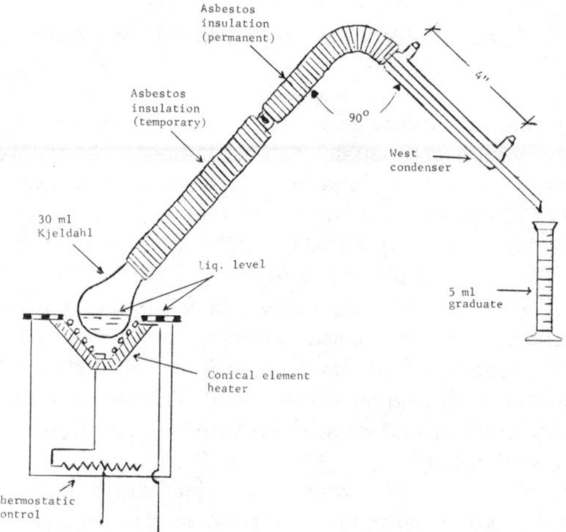

FIG. 31:03—Distillation apparatus for determining formaldehyde in maple sirup

adjusted with control knob in such position that exactly 3 mL H_2O is distd from sirup in 12–14 min. Collect 3 mL distillate in 5 mL graduate with funnel top. Using transfer pipets, place 1 mL distillate in 13 mm id test tube, and add 1 mL H_2O and 2 mL Nash's reagent. Heat 30 min in H_2O bath at 37±1° to develop color. Transfer colored soln to 1 cm cell and measure A at 415 nm against H_2O.

31.193 ***Blanks***

To det. A due to reagents, substitute 1 mL H_2O (from same source as used in detn) for 1 mL sample distillate. Subtract A of blank from that for sample to obtain A due to CH_2O. Or, as simpler operation, measure A of sample with instrument adjusted to 0 A for blank.

Obtain concn of CH_2O in sirup from A, using std curve.

31.194 ***Preparation of Standard Curve***

Construct std curve by plotting A obtained for sirups contg 1, 2, and 4 ppm CH_2O against concn of added CH_2O in ppm.

Straight line relationship is obtained for std curve. Project this line to Y axis (A); Y intercept indicates blank for sirup. Since sirup used to construct curve from A values may be atypical, draw and use parallel curve with 0 intercept. Correct ppm values obtained from this curve for av. sirup blank (ca 0.9 ppm).

Yeast Count (*51*)—Official Final Action

31.195 ***Apparatus***

(**a**) *Water bath.*—Const temp., capable of holding H_2O temp. at 27±1°.

(**b**) *Electric stirrer.*—Non-aerating (Kraft Apparatus, Inc., 402 Sagamore Ave, Mineola, NY 11501, Model S-25-25A, or equiv.).

(**c**) *Beakers.*—Tall-form, 300 and 500 mL. Cover with Al foil before sterilizing.

(**d**) *Hypodermic syringe.*—5 mL (Luer-Lok), or equiv., with hypodermic needle, 14 gage (Luer-Lok), 2" long.

(**e**) *Dilution bottles.*—160 mL, 45 × 140 mm.

(**f**) *Serological pipets.*—To deliver 1.0 mL with 0.1 mL graduations.

(**g**) *Petri dishes.*—100 × 15 mm.

Sterilize apparatus (**c**), (**d**), (**f**), and (**g**) 1 hr in hot air oven at 160°. Items (**f**) and (**g**) do not have to be sterilized when obtained as "single use" sterile plastic.

31.196 ***Culture Medium***

Wort agar culture medium.—Boil 15.00 g malt ext, 0.78 g peptone, 2.75 g dextrin, 2.35 g glycerol, 1.00 g K_2HPO_4, 1.00 g NH_4Cl, 12.75 g maltose, and 20.00 g agar in 1 L H_2O until dissolved. Autoclave 15 min at 121°.

31.197 ***Reagents***

(**a**) *Phosphate buffer stock soln.*—pH 7.2, 0.25*M*. *See* **4.023(e)**.

(**b**) *Phosphate buffer dilution water.*—*See* **4.023(f)**.

(**c**) *Hypochlorite germicide soln.*—200 ppm available Cl. Add 5 mL 5.25% NaClO soln to 1 gal. (3.8 L) H_2O.

31.198 ***Preparation of Sample Culture***

Sterilize stirrer head by submerging in 400 mL germicide soln in 500 mL tall-form beaker ≥10 min. Rinse by immersing in three 450 mL portions sterile H_2O in 500 mL tall-form beakers.

Warm bottle contg sirup to 80°F (26.7°) in H_2O bath set at 80±1.0°F. Transfer sirup to 300 mL sterile tallform beaker, place in 80°F constant temp. H_2O bath, and insert sterilized stirrer. Position stirrer near bottom of beaker and off center to prevent forming vortex. Cover with Al foil while stirring. Stir sirup 10 min at ca 500 rpm. If gas bubbles form, let sirup stand in H_2O bath until gas bubbles rise to surface.

Assemble sterile 14 gage needle and 5 mL syringe. Remove cover from sirup sample and with needle held ≥2.5 cm below surface of sirup, slowly draw 5.5–6.0 mL sirup into syringe. Invert syringe, holding needle vertically. Wipe excess sirup from needle with gauze pad wetted with alcohol. Holding pad around tip of needle, bring syringe plunger exactly to 5.0 mL graduation, expelling excess sirup and any air bubbles into sterile pad.

Make 10^{-1} diln of sirup by expelling 5 mL sirup completely from syringe into 45 mL sterile phosphate buffer diln blank, (**b**). Shake inoculated diln blank vigorously 10 sec, transfer 1 mL to petri dish with 1 mL pipet for 10^{-1} diln plate, and transfer 0.1 mL 10^{-1} diln with 1 mL pipet to petri dish for 10^{-2} diln plate. Transfer 1 mL of 10^{-1} diln to 99 mL sterile diln blank, (**b**), for 10^{-3} diln. Prep. 10^{-3} and 10^{-4} diln plates by using 1 and 0.1 mL vol. 10^{-3} sirup diln, resp. Transfer 1 mL 10^{-3} diln to 99 mL sterile diln blank, (**b**), to make 10^{-5} sirup diln. Prep. 10^{-5} and 10^{-6} diln plates by using 1 and 0.1 mL 10^{-5} diln, resp.

Pour 10–12 mL liquefied wort agar at 42–44° into each plate and mix with dild culture. After agar has solidified, invert plates and incubate 5 days at 21–25°. Count plates on 5th day, using Quebec Colony Counter, or equiv.

Bacterial Population of Maple Sap (*52*)
Official Final Action

31.199 ***Principle***

Resazurin is reduced to resorufin in direct proportion to bacterial action, with color change from purple to pink. Method permits rapid estimation of bacterial populations >1 × 10^6 cells/mL in maple sap.

31.200 ***Apparatus***

(**a**) *Serological pipets.*—To deliver 1 and 10 mL, with 1.0 mL graduations; sterilized.

(**b**) *Test tubes.*—150 × 16 mm, screw-top with molded plastic caps; sterilized.

(**c**) *Incubator or water bath with opaque cover.*— Constant temp., capable of maintaining 37.5±0.5°.

(**d**) *Bottles.*—200 mL amber, g-s.

31.201 ***Reagents***

(**a**) *Nonfat milk soln.*—Dissolve 100 g instant nonfat dry milk in 500 mL H_2O. Autoclave 15 min at 121 °.

(**b**) *Resazurin dye.*—Autoclave 200 mL H_2O in amber glass bottle 15 min at 121°. Using sterile forceps, add 1 std (certified by Biological Stain Commission) resazurin dye tablet (Allied Chemical Corp.) and shake to completely dissolve dye before H_2O cools. Store in cool, dark place. Prep. weekly.

(**c**) *Sterile maple sap control.*—Place 10 mL raw sap in test tube and autoclave 15 min at 121°.

31.202 ***Technic***

To sterile test tube, transfer 1 mL nonfat milk soln and 10 mL sample. Prep. control tube using 1 mL nonfat milk soln and 10 mL sterile maple sap control. Mix by capping and inverting tubes. Incubate 30 min at 37.5°, using incubator, **31.200(c)**. Remove tubes and, with sterile pipet, add 1 mL resazurin dye soln to each. Cap tubes, invert to mix thoroly, and incubate at 37.5°. Do not agitate tube before reading. Examine tube for color change to Munsell std bluish purple (new designation 4-P Matte) 2.5 P6/8 (Munsell Color Co., Inc., 2441 North Calvert St., Baltimore, MD 21218) end point at 0.5, 1, 2, 3, 4, and 5 hr. Color control should match Munsell std 7.5 PB6/10 and should remain stable for duration of test. Calc. bacterial cell population from: log $Y = 7.84 - 0.587\ X$, where Y = bacterial count, cells/mL, and X = time for color development in hr.

SUGAR BEETS

Sucrose

31.203 *Hot Water Digestion Method I (53)* *Official First Action*

(*Caution: See* **51.015**.)

Pass sample (usually in form of cossettes) thru meat grinder fitted with plate having 6 mm (¼") perforations and mix thoroly. Weigh 26 g prepd sample and rinse into 201.0 mL Kohlrausch flask, using ca 100 mL H_2O. Place flask under good vac. 5–10 min to remove air, carefully avoiding mech. loss when vac. is first applied. Add H_2O to ca 175 mL, and digest in H_2O bath at 80°, supporting flask so that body is entirely immersed but is not in contact with heating element. Remove flask 2 or 3 times during digestion, swirl contents, and after each agitation wash down pulp adhering to walls of flask with little H_2O at 80°.

After exactly 30 min digestion, fill flask to within 2–5 mL of mark with H_2O at 80° and continue digestion exactly 10 min longer. Cool to room temp. in H_2O bath. Add 6 mL basic $Pb(OAc)_2$ soln, **31.021(a)**, and H_2O to fill to mark. (Previous addns of H_2O and reagents should be so adjusted that ≤4 mL H_2O is required to dil. to vol.) Mix well by shaking, let stand 5 min, shake again, and filter. Let stand near saccharimeter at least 5 min, and polarize in 400 mm glass tube. If vol. adjustment and polariscopic observation are made at 20°, reading gives % sucrose directly; if at other temps, apply formula in **31.022(a)**.

Notes: The 1 mL >200 mL vol. is the detd vol. of marc for beets grown in Colorado and neighboring states. It should be detd for other localities. Beets of abnormally low purity may require 8–10 mL basic $Pb(OAc)_2$ soln for clarification. If foaming causes trouble, flask may be put under vac. second time after cooling, or few drops ether or 1 drop *amyl alcohol* may be added before soln is dild to vol.

31.204 *Hot Water Digestion Method II (54)* *Official First Action*

Use Ni-plated sheet Fe vessels, 11 cm high, 6 cm body diam., and 4 cm mouth diam.; use stoppers covered with Sn foil to fit.

Weigh 26 g prepd beet pulp, **31.203**, on watch glass (small enough to go into neck of beaker) and transfer to metal beaker; add 177 mL dil. basic $Pb(OAc)_2$ soln (5 parts basic $Pb(OAc)_2$ soln, **31.021(a)**, to 100 parts H_2O); shake, and stopper lightly. Submerge beaker in H_2O bath 30 min at 75–80°, shaking intermittently. When all air is expelled (generally after 5 min), tighten stopper. After 30 min, shake, cool to std temp., filter, add drop HOAc to filtrate, and polarize in 400 mm tube. Reading is % sugar in beet pulp.

STARCH CONVERSION PRODUCTS

31.205 Preparation of Sample—Official First Action

See **31.001**.

Moisture—Official First Action

31.206 ***Method I***

(Applicable to refined corn sugars)

See **31.005**.

31.207 ★ ***Method II (55)*** ★

(Applicable to corn sirups and crude corn sugars)

Vac. oven drying of sample absorbed on filter paper. *See* **31.193–31.194**, 12th ed.

Method III (56)

(Applicable to corn sirups and crude corn sugars)

31.208 ***Material and Apparatus***

(**a**) *Diatomaceous earth.*—Filter-Cel, or equiv. Preferably anal. grade. If com. grade is used, wash with HCl, then with H_2O to remove acid, and dry in oven at ca 105°. (Material should give neg. test for acid when moistened.)

(**b**) *Moisture dish.*—Al dish 25 mm high × 75 mm diam., with cover.

(**c**) *Pestle.*—Flat-end glass stirring rod ca 60 mm long.

31.209 ***Determination***

Place 10 g Filter-Cel in moisture dish contg pestle and dry to const wt. Weigh ca 5 g corn sirup or sugar in nickel scoop, dil. with ca 5 mL H_2O, and add to Filter-Cel. Wash scoop with three 2 mL portions H_2O and add washings to Filter-Cel. Thoroly incorporate soln with Filter-Cel by means of pestle, yielding *damp* workable mass. Dry to const wt in vac. oven at 100° for corn sirup or 70° for crude corn sugars.

Method IV (Corn Industries Research Foundation Method) (57)—Official Final Action

(Applicable to corn (glucose) sirups)

31.210 ***Material and Apparatus***

(**a**) *Diatomaceous earth.*—Hyflo Super-Cel *only.* Wash large portion on buchner with HCl (1+1000) until effluent is acid to litmus. Then wash with H_2O until pH of effluent is ≥4. Dry washed diat. earth in oven overnight at 105° and keep in closed container.

(**b**) *Moisture dish.*—Modify small A1 desiccator (Desicooler, Fisher Scientific Co., or equiv.) 76 mm high × 90 mm diam., with cover, to serve as container. Remove plastic handle from cover and close opening with rivet; also remove inner tray.

(**c**) *Stirrers.*—Pyrex test tubes, 100 × 13 mm. Make extensions for test tubes from stainless steel rods, 180 × 8 mm. Fit rods near one end with two rubber rings so spaced on rod that when it is inserted into test tube, snug fit is obtained near top and bottom of test tube.

(**d**) *Vacuum oven and vacuum pump.*—Capable of maintaining oven pressure of ≤3.3 kPa (25 mm Hg). Dry oven air by passing first thru gas scrubber contg H_2SO_4 and then thru anhyd. $CaSO_4$ (Drierite, or equiv.) in drying tower.

31.211 ***Determination***

Add 30 g previously dried diat. earth, (**a**), to moisture dish. Prep. tare dish with slightly less diat. earth than sample dishes. Place stirrers, (**c**), without extension rods in dishes. Dry sample dishes and covers, with covers off dishes, in vac. oven 5 hr at 100°, bleeding air thru drying train. Slowly release vac., remove dishes and covers from oven, quickly cover dishes, place in desiccator, and cool to room temp. Release covers of sample dishes and tare momentarily before weighing. Place tare on right hand pan of two-pan anal. balance and sample dish on left

★ Surplus method—*see* inside front cover.

hand pan. Add wts to tare until balance is obtained and record wt to nearest mg. If using single pan anal. balance, also weigh tare with sample dishes. Use any change in wt of tare which occurs between initial and final weighing of tare to correct final wt of sample dishes.

Accurately weigh 7–10 g sample (4–7 g dry substance) in 45 mL (40 × 50 mm) weighing bottle with ₮ cap style stopper. Add 10 mL warm H_2O and stir thoroly with small glass rod. Pour dild sample onto diat. earth in sample dish and complete quant. transfer of sample with three 5 mL portions of warm H_2O. Insert steel rod extension into stirring tube in sample dish and stir until sample is homogeneously dispersed thruout diat. earth. Remove rod, leaving stirring tube in dish, and place tare and sample dishes (with covers off) in vac. oven at 70° for corn sirups of >58 Dextrose Equivalent (D.E., reducing sugars as dextrose, dry basis), and at 100° for corn sirups of ≤58 D.E. Dry all fructose-contg sirups at 70°. Dry sample dishes in vac. oven 5 hr. Remove sample dishes from oven, insert stirring rod extension into stirring tube, and rework diat. earth until fine powder free of lumps is obtained. Return sample dishes to oven and heat 16 addnl hr under vac. Shut off vac. and slowly fill oven with air drawn thru drying train. Open oven, quickly cover tare and sample dishes, and place covered dishes in desiccator. Cool sample dishes and tare to room temp. and weigh as before.

Dry Substance—Official First Action

Method I—By Hydrometer (58)

31.212 ***Apparatus***

(**a**) *Water bath.*—Insulated H_2O bath with stirrer and thermostatic control, held at 60°.

(**b**) *Cylinders.*—Pyrex, 15 × 2¼", without lip.

(**c**) *Stopper seal.*—Consisting of 2 rubber stoppers that fit snugly into cylinder, sepd on metal rod by ca 8 cm. Rod is fixed in lower stopper but does not extend thru it. Top stopper is free to move on rod, altho tight enough to maintain predetd position, preventing evapn during heating.

(**d**) *Baumé hydrometers.*—Streamlined type, modulus 145, stdzd at 15.56° with range 35–45° Bé in 0.1° Bé; length over-all 12–13"; body diam. 0.77–0.79"; scale length 147–155 mm.

31.213 ***Determination***

Fill cylinder with sirup to within 10 cm of top, taking care that sides are free from sirup. Seal cylinder with stopper seal, placing bottom stopper within 1 cm of sirup surface and closing cylinder with top stopper. Immerse cylinder in H_2O bath at 60° (140°F) so that level of sirup is ca 5 cm below level of H_2O. Immerse hydrometer in H_2O bath. When sirup in cylinder is free of air and has reached temp. of bath (ca 90 min), raise cylinder until surface of sirup is at eye level. Remove stopper seal and insert previously dried hydrometer. After ca 10 min, read hydrometer. To obtain com. Baumé, add 1° Bé. to observed reading of hydrometer:

Com. Baumé = Bé. (140°F/60°F) + 1° Bé.

Det. corresponding dry substance from Table **31:09**.

31.214 ***Method II—By Refractometer (59)***

(Applicable only to liq. samples contg no undissolved solids)

Det. refractometer reading at 45°. Circulate H_2O thru jackets of refractometer long enough to let temp. of prisms and of sample reach equilibrium, continuing circulation during observation, and taking care that temp. is held const. From Table **31:10** obtain com. Baumé corresponding to observed refractive index. From Table **31:09** obtain corresponding dry substance.

Table 31:09 Commercial Table for Dry Substance in Corn Sirup and Corn Sugar Sirup

(Commercial Baumé = Bé. 140°F/60°F + 1° Bé.)

Commercial Baumé	Dextrose Equivalent and Ash							
	30.00 0.28	42.00 0.28	55.00 0.30	82.00 0.41	87.00 0.61	89.00 0.61	91.2 0.61	90.7 1.22
	Dry Substance (per cent)							
40.00	73.66	74.39	75.16	76.82	77.12	77.24	77.37	77.10
41.00	75.58	76.34	77.14	78.86	79.18	79.30	79.44	79.17
42.00	77.51	78.30	79.13	80.92	81.25	81.38	81.52	81.25
43.00	79.45	80.27	81.14	83.00	83.35	83.48	83.63	83.33
44.00	81.39	82.25	83.17	85.10	85.46	85.60	85.75	85.44
45.00	83.36	84.25	85.20	87.21	87.58	87.72	87.88	87.56
46.00	85.34	86.26	87.26	89.33	89.71	89.86	90.03	89.69
47.00	87.33	88.29	89.34	91.47	91.87	92.03	92.21	91.84

Table 31:10 Commercial Table of Refractive Indices of Corn Sirups and Corn Sugar Sirups at 45°C

(Commercial Baumé = Bé. 140 °F/60°F + 1° Bé.)

Commercial Baumé	Dextrose Equivalent and Ash									
	30.00 0.28	35.00 0.28	42.00 0.28	45.00 0.28	50.00 0.30	55.00 0.30	60.00 0.30	65.00 0.30	82.00 0.41	89.00 0.61
	Refractive Index at 45°									
40.00	1.4774	1.4773	1.4771	1.4770	1.4769	1.4768	1.4767	1.4766	1.4762	1.4760
41.00	1.4825	1.4824	1.4822	1.4821	1.4820	1.4820	1.4818	1.4817	1.4813	1.4811
42.00	1.4878	1.4877	1.4875	1.4874	1.4873	1.4873	1.4871	1.4869	1.4865	1.4863
43.00	1.4933	1.4931	1.4929	1.4928	1.4927	1.4926	1.4924	1.4923	1.4919	1.4916
44.00	1.4986	1.4985	1.4983	1.4982	1.4981	1.4980	1.4978	1.4977	1.4973	1.4971
45.00	1.5041	1.5040	1.5038	1.5037	1.5036	1.5036	1.5034	1.5033	1.5029	1.5027
46.00	1.5098	1.5097	1.5095	1.5094	1.5093	1.5092	1.5090	1.5089	1.5085	1.5083
47.00	1.5155	1.5154	1.5152	1.5151	1.5150	1.5149	1.5148	1.5147	1.5143	1.5142

31.215 Ash—Official First Action

(For most corn sugars and sirups it is unnecessary to re-ash.)

See **31.012**.

31.216 Sulfated Ash—Official First Action

See **31.014**. For most corn sirups and corn sugars, only a single sulfation is necessary

31.217 Acidity—Official First Action

Weigh 50 g sample, dissolve in 200 mL H_2O, and titr. with 0.1*N* NaOH, using phthln, to faint pink end point (pH 8.3). Calc. acidity as HCl.

31.218 Hydrogen-Ion Activity—Official First Action

Prep. soln of sample contg 40% total solids and det. pH potentiometrically. (Buffer capacity of product is normally such that no special provision need be made with regard to H_2O used for diln. If glass electrode is used, stdze against ref. buffer within 1.0 of detd pH.)

31.219 Nitrogen—Official First Action

See **2.057**.

31.220 Total Reducing Sugars—Official First Action

(**a**) *Lane-Eynon General Volumetric Method.—See* **31.036**. Use glucose as std.

(**b**) *Munson-Walker General Method.—See* **31.038**. Prep diln contg ca 1% reducing sugar.

Glucose by Steinhoff Methods—Official First Action

31.221 ★ *Zerban-Sattler Modification (60)* ★

Iodimetric titrn of pptd Cu_2O. *See* **31.206–31.207**, 12th ed.

31.222 ★ *Sichert-Bleyer Modification (61)* ★

Pptd Cu_2O dissolved in $FeNH_4(SO_4)_2$ and excess titrd with $KMnO_4$. *See* **31.208–31.209**, 12th ed.

Glucose by Glucose Oxidase Method (*62*)
Official Final Action

31.223 ***Principle***

Glucose is enzymatically oxidized with glucose oxidase to form H_2O_2, which reacts with a dye in presence of peroxidase to give stable colored product proportional to glucose concn.

31.224 ***Reagents***

(**a**) *Glucose test soln.*—Consists of (*1*) *Glucose oxidase.*—1000 glucose oxidase units/mL; purified (Miles Laboratories, Inc., or equiv.). (*2*) *Horseradish peroxidase.*—Available from Worthington Biochemical Co., Freehold, NJ 07728. (*3*) *Chromogen.*—*o*-Dianisidine.2HCl. (*4*) *Acetate buffer soln.*—pH 5.5, 0.1*M*. Dissolve 13.608 g $NaOAc.3H_2O$ and dil. to 1 L with H_2O. Add 2.7 mL HOAc and adjust pH with NaOAc or HOAc, if necessary.

Dissolve 40 mg chromogen, 40 mg horseradish peroxidase, and 0.4 mL glucose oxidase in 0.1*M* acetate buffer and dil. to 100 mL with buffer soln.

(**b**) *Glucose std soln.*—1 mg/mL. Dissolve 1.000 g NBS D-glucose, SRM 917 (previously dried 4 hr at 70° under vac.) in H_2O and dil. to 1 L in vol. flask. Mix and let stand 2 hr to permit mutarotation to occur. Prep. fresh on day of use.

★ Surplus method—*see* inside front cover.

31.225 ***Apparatus***

(**a**) *Spectrophotometer.*—Suitable for measuring *A* at 540 nm, with matching 1 cm cells.

(**b**) *Water bath.*—Capable of maintaining temp. at 30±1°.

31.226 ***Preparation of Standard Curve***

Pipet 1, 2, 3, and 4 mL aliquots std glucose soln into sep. 50 mL vol. flasks and dil. to vol. with H_2O. Mix and pipet 2 mL of each dild std into 18 × 150 mm test tubes (0.04, 0.08, 0.12, 0.16 mg glucose). Use 2 mL H_2O as blank. Place all tubes in 30° H_2O bath 5 min. At 0 time, start reaction by adding 1.0 mL glucose test soln to first tube. Allow 30–60 sec interval between enzyme addn to each subsequent tube. Mix tubes and let react exactly 30 min at 30°. Immediately stop reaction (30–60 sec intervals) by pipetting 10 mL H_2SO_4 (1+3) into each tube. Mix, cool to room temp., and measure *A* against reagent blank at 540 nm, using 1 cm cells. Plot *A* at 540 nm against mg glucose on linear coordinate paper.

31.227 ***Determination***

Weigh 1–5 g sirup sample to nearest 0.1 mg, using weighing bottle to prevent moisture loss during weighing. Dil. successively with H_2O to concn of 2.5–7.5 mg glucose/100 mL. Pipet 2 mL dild sample into 18 × 150 mm test tube. Proceed as in **31.226**, beginning "Place all tubes in 30° H_2O bath 5 min." Det. mg glucose from std curve and calc. % glucose in sample.

For results on dry substance basis, det. sample dry substance as in **31.212–31.213** or **31.214**.

Saccharides by Liquid Chromatography (*63*)

Corn Industries Research Foundation Method
Official First Action

(Applicable to corn (glucose) sirup)

31.228 ***Principle***

Corn sirup soln is passed thru cation exchange column. Sugars are sepd by mol. exclusion and selective adsorption, and detected wih differential refractometer. Peaks are quantitated against appropriate std with digital computing integrator. Psicose, fructose, dextrose, maltulose, other disaccharides (DP_2), DP_3, DP_4, etc. are detd in corn sirup with 50W-X4 resin. Alternative Q15-S column is suitable for detn of psicose, fructose, dextrose, total DP_2, DP_3, and DP_4+.

31.229 ***Apparatus***

(**a**) *Liquid chromatograph.*—Waters Associates Model 201 equipped with Model 6000 pump and Model R-401 refractive index detector (Waters Associates, Inc.), or equiv.

(**b**) *Recorder.*—Hewlett-Packard Model 7100B recorder with Model 17505A input module, or equiv.

(**c**) *Digital integrator.*—Spectra-Physics Autolab System I Computing Integrator with calcn capability, used according to manufacturer's "Method 1" (Spectra-Physics, 2905 Stender Way, Santa Clara, CA 95051), or equiv.

(**d**) *Circulating bath.*—45±0.005°. Haake Model FK (Haake, Inc., 244 Saddle River Rd, Saddle Brook, NJ 07662), or equiv.

(**e**) *Circulating bath.*—78±0.05°. Haake Model FS, or equiv. Dow Corning 200, 5cS viscosity silicone oil may be used as bath medium.

(f) *Syringe.*—100 μL Precision Sampling, Series B, Model 01-9264, PRESSURE-LOK (Precision Sampling Corp., 8275 West El Cajon, Baton Rouge, LA 70895), or equiv.

(g) *HPLC column.*—610 × 7 (id) mm (24 × ⅜"(od)) stainless steel column packed with Aminex 50W-X4, 20–30 μ, Ca resin (or, alternatively, Aminex Q15-S, 19–25 μ, Ca resin), and fitted with Waters Associates Model 98764 column temp. control block and ⅜", 10 μ frit, end fittings.

31.230 ***Reagents***

(a) *Mobile phase.*—Degassed H_2O, filtered thru 0.22 μ Millipore filter before use. Keep at ca 65° and stir slowly on hot plate-stirrer to remove dissolved gas.

(b) *Column packing.*—Aminex 50W-X4, 20–30 μ, or Q15-S, 19–25 μ, Ca form resin. Slurry required amt of Aminex 50W-X4, H form, or Q15-S, Na form cation exchange resin (Bio-Rad Laboratories) with H_2O, transfer to 350 mL medium porosity fritted glass funnel, and remove H_2O with vac. Wash each 10 g resin with 300 mL filtered (Whatman No. 4 paper, or equiv.) 0.3*M* $Ca(OAc)_2$ soln adjusted to pH 6.2 with HOAc. Wash each 10 g resin with 200 mL H_2O. Remove H_2O from treated resin with vac. and store in nonactinic bottle at room temp.

(c) *Mixed ion exchange resin.*—Exhaust (2 L 1.5*N* NaOH) and regenerate (2 L 1.5*N* HCl) ca 600 mL bed vol. Duolite C-3 (Diamond Shamrock Chemical Co, PO Box 829, Redwood City, CA 94064) cation resin. Repeat twice. Exhaust (2 L 1.5*N* HCl) and regenerate (once each with 2 L 1.5*N* NaOH, and 2 L 2*N* Na_2CO_3) ca 600 mL bed vol. Duolite ES-561 weak base anion exchange resin. Repeat twice. Wash final regenerated resins with H_2O to pH ranges of 4–5 (C-3) and 6–7 (ES-461). Air dry resins, combine equal wts of each, and mix. Avoid strong base resins which may promote alk. isomerization of sample.

(d) *Carbohydrate standards.*—Glucose (NBS); fructose (Pfanstiehl Laboratories, Inc., 1219 Glen Rock Ave., Waukegan, IL 60085); maltose.H_2O, Grade HHH (Hayashibara Biochemical Laboratories, Inc., 2–3, 1-CHOME, Shimoishii, Okayama, Japan); maltotriose (United States Biochemical Corp., 21000 Miles Pkwy, Cleveland, OH 44128); acid converted 42 Dextrose Equivalent (DE) corn sirup (available from member companies of Corn Refiners Association, Inc., (CRA), 1001 Connecticut Ave NW, Washington, DC 20036); psicose (Carb. Res. **16**, 383(1971)); maltulose (Cereal Science Today **17**, 180(1972)).

Est. corn sirup composition by detg level of each saccharide shown for given DE in CRA, Inc. Critical Data Tables, pp. 8–13. Det. DE as in **31.036** and **31.209**. Purity of given sugar may be detd by normalized LC analysis.

(e) *Mixed sugar standard.*—Prep. std sugar soln to contain ca 3 g dry carbohydrate substance/25 mL. Make dry basis % of each std sugar equiv. to level in typical sample of given type. Use 42 DE corn sirup to represent DP_{4+} fraction, adding dry wts of mono-, di-, and trisaccharide from 42 DE sirup to dry wts of pure glucose, maltose, and maltotriose used for std prepn. Add appropriate dry wt of each std sugar to tared 50 mL beaker. Record wt to fifth place. Add 20 mL H_2O, cover, and place on steam bath to dissolve. Transfer quant. to 25 mL vol. flask, dil. to vol., and mix. Add several drops toluene as preservative. Store at room temp. Avoid toluene layer when drawing up soln for std injection. Compute dry basis concn of each sugar:

$$\% \text{ sugar, dry basis} = \text{wt sugar} \times 100/(\text{wt glucose} + a + b) + (\text{wt fructose} + c) + [(\text{wt maltose} \times 0.94) + d + e] + [(\text{wt maltotriose} \times 0.94) + f + g + h] + \text{wt } DP_{4+},$$

where maltose and maltotriose wts are multiplied by 0.94 to account for H_2O of hydration and trace impurities; *a* and *b* = wt glucose from 42 DE sirup and maltulose; *c* = wt fructose from maltulose; *d* and *e* = wts of DP_2 from 42 DE sirup and maltulose; and *f*, *g* and *h* = DP_3 wts from 42 DE sirup, maltulose, and maltose.

31.231 ***Preparation of Column***

Place empty column vertically, and attach 380 × 7.7 (id) mm (15 × ⅜" (od)) stainless steel precolumn, using ⅜" union. Attach end fitting to bottom of column and vac. line to end fitting. Attach open-ended vessel (ca 500 mL) to precolumn with Tygon tubing and secure vessel in same plane as column. Slowly fill column, precolumn, and ca ⅓ of vessel with H_2O. Slurry ca 50 mL bed vol. of resin and add to vessel, using vac. Bring column to 78°. Pull vac. on column until resin level in vessel is const. Discontinue vac., disconnect vessel from precolumn, and pump solv. through precolumn and column at 0.5 mL/min (0.7 mL/min for Q15-S resin) overnight. Disconnect end fitting from precolumn and precolumn from column. Fill end fitting with ca 5 mm resin and attach to column. Cap end with fittings when storing column.

31.232 ***Operating Conditions***

Flow rate 0.4 mL/min (0.6 mL/min for Q15-S resin); column temp. 78°; detector temp. 45°; detector attenuation 8×; detector output 10 mv; recorder attenuation 1×, recorder range 10 mv; chart speed 2 in./hr. Program integrator to obtain trapezoidal baseline correction for each peak and to prevent erroneous baseline at valley point between fused peaks or on plateau created by fused peak cluster.

31.233 ***Standardization***

Inject 30 μL (ca 3.5 mg solids) of std soln. Integrate std sugar peaks in normalized mode. Sum DP_{4+} fractions obtained from normalized printout to obtain DP_{4+} normalized response. Divide known dry basis concn by normalized response for each component to obtain ratios. Divide each component ratio by glucose ratio to obtain System I KF values (calibration factors). Program component KF values in System I, **31.229(c)**, using Method 1 and glucose as ref. ($KF_{glucose}$ = 1). Enter DP_3 KF at both DP_3 retention time and at time 100 sec less than DP_3 time, to provide KF for panose, isomaltotriose, and linear DP_4 when 50W-X4 resin is used. List DP_{4+} KF as default KF for DP_{5+} calcn when 50W-X4 resin is used.

31.234 ***Preparation of Sample***

Det. approx dry substance as in **31.214**. Dil. sample by wt to ca 12% dry substance with H_2O. Add ca 0.3 g mixed exchange resin to ca 6 g dild sample and shake 10 min to remove possible interfering ionic material which elutes in DP_{4+} region.

31.235 ***Determination***

Rinse syringe with dild sample 4 times before injection. Inject 30 μL dild sample, **31.234**. Best accuracy is obtained when dry substance solids injected for sample and std are equiv. Integrate eluted peaks, using System I and Method I. After injection, wash syringe 4 times with warm tap H_2O, allowing air bubbles to scrub syringe walls. Wash syringe twice with H_2O.

31.236 ***Calculations***

Results are computed automatically when using **31.229(c)**. List fructose, glucose, maltulose, and other DP_2 results. Combine maltotriose, panose-isomaltotriose, and linear DP_4 results, and list sum as DP_{3-4}. Sum remaining results and list as DP_{5+}. Report results on ash-free, carbohydrate dry substance basis. In absence of computing integrator, list areas for fructose (*f*), glucose (*g*), maltulose, other DP_2, sum of maltotriose, panose-isomaltotriose and linear DP_4, and sum of DP_{5+}, and compute result by equation:

$$\% \text{ Component} = [(\text{Area component})(\text{KF component})] \times 100/\{[(\text{Area}_f)(\text{KF}_f)] + [(\text{Area}_g)(\text{KF}_g)] + \ldots + [(\text{Area}_{5+})(\text{KF}_{5+})]\}.$$

SELECTED REFERENCES

(*1*) JAOAC **37**, 292(1954).
(*2*) JAOAC **8**, 255(1925).
(*3*) JAOAC **15**, 195(1932); **18**, 83(1935).
(*4*) JAOAC **15**, 79(1932); **16**, 81(1933); **17**, 74(1934); **41**, 621(1958).
(*5*) Leach, 32nd Ann. Rept. Mass. Board Health, 1900, p. 563; Leach-Winton, "Food Inspection and Analysis," 4th ed., 1920, p. 654.
(*6*) Z. Ver. deut. Zucker-Ind. **50**, (N.F. 37), 357 (1900); **63**, (N.F. 50), 25(1913); J. Ind. Eng. Chem. **5**, 167(1913); JAOAC **18**, 162(1935); NBS Circular C **440**, 1942, pp. 768, 774; Int. Sugar J. **35**, 19(1933); **39**, 32S(1937).
(*7*) JAOAC **16**, 78(1933); **17**, 74(1934).
(*8*) Browne and Zerban, "Sugar Analysis," 1941, p. 395.
(*9*) JAOAC **8**, 256(1925).
(*10*) J. Ind. Eng. Chem. **16**, 170(1924).
(*11*) JAOAC **8**, 258(1925).
(*12*) JAOAC **8**, 400(1925).
(*13*) JAOAC **9**, 33(1926).
(*14*) Analyst **21**, 182(1896).
(*15*) J. Soc. Chem. Ind. **42**, 32T(1923); JAOAC **9**, 35(1926); **12**, 38(1929).
(*16*) J. Am. Chem. Soc. **28**, 663(1906); **26**, 541(1907); J. Research Natl. Bur. Standards **24**, 589(1940).
(*17*) JAOAC **12**, 38(1929); **18**, 83(1935); J. Am. Chem. Soc. **57**, 845(1935); Anal. Chem. **21**, 975(1949).
(*18*) J. Research Natl. Bur. Standards **15**, 493(1935); **19**, 691(1937); RP1057.
(*19*) JAOAC **23**, 558(1940); J. Research Natl. Bur. Standards, **22**, 697(1939); RP1213.
(*20*) Z. Zuckerind Czechoslovak Rep. **59**, 52, 63(1934); JAOAC **26**, 462(1943); **30**, 124(1947).
(*21*) J. Am. Chem. Soc. **43**, 1503(1921).
(*22*) JAOAC **38**, 594(1955).
(*23*) J. Biol. Chem. **41**, 367(1920); JAOAC **35**, 635(1952).
(*24*) JAOAC **15**, 79, 198(1932).
(*25*) JAOAC **51**, 755(1968); **52**, 564(1969); **53**, 347(1970).
(*26*) JAOAC **49**, 551(1966).
(*27*) "Methoden van Onderzoek bij de Java-Suikerindustrie," 6th Ed., 1931, p. 365; JAOAC **31**, 109(1948); **32** 102(1949).
(*28*) JAOAC **32**, 102(1949).
(*29*) USDA, Eastern Regional Research Lab., AIC-307, May 1951; JAOAC **39**, 919(1956).
(*30*) JAOAC **52**, 729(1969).
(*31*) JAOAC **45**, 548(1962).
(*32*) JAOAC **62**, 515(1979); J. Food Sci. **34**, 228(1969); J. Apicul. Res. **17**, 89(1978).
(*33*) JAOAC **37**, 466(1954); **39**, 1016(1956); **42**, 341(1959); **43**, 774(1960).
(*34*) JAOAC **62**, 515(1979).
(*35*) JAOAC **60**, 838(1977); **62**, 515(1979).
(*36*) JAOAC **42**, 346(1959); **43**, 638(1960).
(*37*) USDA Bur. Chem. Bull. **110** and **154**.
(*38*) USDA Bur. Chem. Bull. **154**, p. 15; JAOAC **15**, 78(1932), **45**, 213(1962).
(*39*) JAOAC **62**, 921(1979).
(*40*) JAOAC **61**, 746(1978); Geochim et Cosmochim Acta **12**, 133(1957).
(*41*) Food Research **23**, 446(1958); JAOAC **42**, 344(1959); **47**, 486(1964).
(*42*) JAOAC **45**, 548(1962); **46**, 148(1963).
(*43*) J. Am. Chem. Soc. **26**, 1523(1904); JAOAC **15**, 79(1932); **16**, 79(1933); **17**, 73(1934); **18**, 83(1935); Trans. Roy. Soc. Can. 1919, sec. 111, 221.
(*44*) JAOAC **44**, 330(1961).
(*45*) JAOAC **52**, 554(1969).
(*46*) JAOAC **4**, 437(1921); **16**, 80(1933); **17**, 74(1934).
(*47*) J. Am. Chem. Soc. **28**, 1204(1906); JAOAC **16**, 80, 158(1933); **17**, 74, 161(1934).
(*48*) JAOAC **49**, 508(1966).
(*49*) JAOAC **42**, 349(1959).
(*50*) JAOAC **47**, 548(1964); **56**, 132(1973).
(*51*) JAOAC **50**, 747(1967); **51**, 586(1968); **52**, 414(1969).
(*52*) JAOAC **52**, 714(1969); **55**, 119(1972); **57**, 544(1974).
(*53*) JAOAC **25**, 98(1942).
(*54*) USDA Bur. Chem. Bull. **146**, p. 19.
(*55*) Ind. Eng. Chem., Anal. Ed. **13**, 855(1941).
(*56*) Ind. Eng. Chem., Anal. Ed. **13**, 858(1941).
(*57*) JAOAC **60**,165(1977).
(*58*) Ind. Eng. Chem., Anal. Ed. **15**, 193(1943).
(*59*) Ind. Eng. Chem., Anal. Ed. **16**, 161(1944).
(*60*) Ind. Eng. Chem., Anal. Ed. **10**, 669(1938); Z. Spiritusind. **56**, 64(1933).
(*61*) Z. Anal. Chem. **107**, 328(1936); Z. Spiritusind. **56**, 64(1933).
(*62*) JAOAC **52**, 556(1969).
(*63*) JAOAC **62**, 527(1979).

32. Vegetable Products, Processed

CANNED PRODUCTS

Drained Weight—Procedure

32.001 ***Sieves***

See Definition of Terms and Explanatory Notes, item (16). Use 8" (20 cm) diam. for containers ≤3 lb (1.36 kg) or 12" (30 cm) diam. for containers >3 lb.

32.002 ***Determination***

Weigh full can, open, and pour entire contents on No. 8 sieve (use 7/16" sieve for canned tomatoes). Without shifting product, incline sieve at ca 17–20° angle to facilitate drainage. Drain 2 min, directly weigh either drained solids or free liq., and weigh dry empty can. From wts obtained, det. % liq. and % drained solid contents.

32.003 Preparation of Sample—Procedure

(**a**) *Products composed of solid and liquid portions.—See* **22.008(d)**. If only solid portion is required for analysis or examination, thoroly grind drained vegetables in mortar or food chopper. If composite of solid and liq. portion is required, thoroly grind entire contents of can in mortar or food chopper. In all cases, thoroly mix portion used and store balance in g-s container. Unless analysis is to be completed in reasonably short time, det. H_2O in portion of sample prepd as above. To prevent decomposition, dry remainder, grind, mix thoroly, and store in g-s container. (Second H_2O detn is required in this method.)

(**b**) *Comminuted products* (*tomato juice, tomato catsup, strained vegetables*).—Thoroly shake unopened container to incorporate any sediment. Transfer entire contents to large glass or porcelain dish, and mix thoroly, continuing stirring ≥1 min. Transfer well mixed sample to g-s container and shake or stir thoroly each time before removing portions for analysis.

Water Activity (*1*)—Official First Action

32.004 ***Principle***

Water activity, a_w, is ratio of vapor pressure of H_2O in product to vapor pressure of pure H_2O at same temp. It is numerically equal to 1/100 of relative humidity (RH) generated by product in closed system. RH can be calcd from direct measurement of partial vapor pressure or dew point or measured indirectly by sensors whose physical or elec. characteristics are altered by RH to which they are exposed. Instruments are checked or calibrated on basis of RH generated by std salt slushes.

32.005 ***Instruments and Systems***

(Select 1 of following instruments or systems to perform test. Each has different application limitations because of interferences from other volatile components of products being measured. Check with instrument manufacturer for more specific limitations.)

(**a**) *Change in electrical conductivity of immobilized salt soln.*—Instrument available from American Instrument Co.; Beckman Instruments, Inc., 89 Commerce Rd, Cedar Grove, NJ 07009; Nova Sina AG, Andreastrasse 7-11, CH 8050, Zurich, Switzerland; or Rotronic AG, CH 8047, Zurich, Switzerland. Immobilized salt sensors are affected by polyols such as glycerol and glycol and by volatile amines.

(**b**) *Change in electrical capacitance of polymer thin films.*—Instrument available from WeatherMeasure, 3213 Orange Grove, N Highlands, CA 95660 or General Eastern Corp., 36 Maple St, Watertown, MA 02172. *Note:* Polymer thin film sensors are affected by HOAc.

(**c**) *Dew point by chilled mirror technic.*—Instrument available from EG&G, Inc., Environmental Equipment Div., 151 Bear Hill Rd, Waltham, MA 02154 or General Eastern Corp. Dew point measurements can be affected by condensables with lower critical temp. than H_2O.

(**d**) *Longitudinal change in dimensions of water-sorbing fiber.*—Instrument available from Abbeon Cal, Inc., 123 Gray Ave, Santa Barbara, CA 93101 or G Lufft Metallbarometerfabrik, D-7, Postfach 692, Neue Weinsteige 22, Stuttgart, West Germany.

(**e**) *Partial water vapor pressure by manometric system.*—Partial H_2O vapor pressure measurements can be made useless by living products that respire, such as grains or nuts; by active fermentation; or by products that expand excessively when subjected to high vac.

(**f**) *Relative weight of moisture sorbed by anhydrous hydrophilic solid, e.g., microcrystalline cellulose.—See* J. Agr. Food Chem. **22**, 326(1974).

32.006 ***Apparatus and Reagents***

(As needed for instrument or system selected)

(**a**) *Dew point instrument.*—Equipped to measure temp. to ±0.1°. *See* **32.005(c)**.

(**b**) *Forced-draft cabinet.*—Const temp., set to maintain 25±1°; capacity ≥0.06 m^3 (2 cu ft); with access port to accomodate instrument sensor leads. Use in conjunction with (**c**).

(**c**) *Insulated box with cover.*—Large enough to hold test container, (**e**), and small enough to fit in forced-draft cabinet, (**b**); with access port to accomodate instrument sensor leads. Protect test container from short-term temp. fluctuations.

(**d**) *Manometric system.*—Sensitive to pressure differential of ±0.01 mm Hg (1.33 Pa). *See* **32.005(e)**.

(**e**) *Test containers.*—120 or 240 mL (4 or 8 oz) wide-mouth or Mason glass jars with Al- or Teflon-lined screw caps and gaskets. Check integrity of cap seals and sensor leads by any means available, e.g., ability of system to hold vac., using Tesla coil.

(**f**) *Water bath.*—Capable of maintaining temp. const within 0.1° at 25±1°; capacity sufficient to hold measuring chamber of selected app.

(**g**) *Hydrophilic solid.*—Microcryst. cellulose, Type PH-101 (FMC Corp., 2000 Market St, Philadelphia, PA 19103, or equiv.).

(**h**) *Reference salts.*—ACS reagent grade, fine crystal. *See* Table **32.01**.

Table 32:01 Water Activity of Reference Salt Slushes at 25°

Salt	a_w	Salt	a_w
$MgCl_2$	0.328	KBr	0.809
K_2CO_3	0.432	$(NH_4)_2SO_4$	0.810
$Mg(NO_3)_2$	0.529	KCl	0.843
NaBr	0.576	$Sr(NO_3)_2$	0.851
$CoCl_2$	0.649	$BaCl_2$	0.902
$SrCl_2$	0.709	KNO_3	0.936
$NaNO_3$	0.743	K_2SO_4	0.973
NaCl	0.753		

32.007 ***Preparation of Reference Salt Slushes***

Place selected ref. salt in test container to depth of ca 4 cm for more sol. salts (lower a_w), to depth of ca 1.5 cm for less sol. salts (higher a_w), and to intermediate depth for intermediate salts. Add H_2O in ca 2 mL increments, stirring well with spatula after each addn, until salt can absorb no more H_2O as evidenced by free liq. Keep free liq. to min. needed to establish satn of salt with H_2O. Slushes are ready for use upon completion of mixing, and are usable indefinitely (except for some high a_w salts susceptible to bacterial attack), if contained in manner to prevent substantial evapn losses. Some slushes, e.g., NaBr, may solidify gradually by crystal coalescence, with no effect on a_w.

32.008 ***Calibration***

Select ≥5 salts to cover a_w range of interest or range of sensor being used. Measure humidity generated by each salt slush in terms of instrument readout, as in **32.009**. Plot readout against a_w values given in Table **32:01** for selected salts, using cross-section paper scaled for reading to 0.001 a_w unit. Draw best av. smooth line thru plotted points. Use this calibration line to translate sensor instrument readout of samples to a_w or to check vapor pressure or dew point instruments for proper functioning.

32.009 ***Determination***

Place calibration slush or sample in forced-draft cabinet, (**b**), or H_2O bath, (**f**), until temp. is stabilized at 25±1°. Transfer salt slush or sample to test container, (**e**), seal container with sensing device attached, and place in temp. control device. Use vol. of sample or slush >1/20 total vol. sample container plus any associated void vol. of sensing system, but not so much as to interfere with operation of system. Record instrument response at 15, 30, 60, and 120 min after test container is placed in temp. control device, or record response on strip chart. Two consecutive readings, at indicated intervals, which vary by <0.01 a_w unit are evidence of adequately close approach to equilibrium. Continue readings at 60-min intervals, if necessary. Convert last reading to a_w by calcn from physical measurements or by ref. to calibration line. Make all measurements within range of calibration points; do not extrapolate calibration line. Make all measurements in same direction of change, and, if required by properties of sensor, expose sensor to controlled RH below ambient before starting each measurement.

32.010 Total Solids (*2*)—Official Final Action

To flat-bottom metal dish with tight-fitting cover, add ca 15 mg diat. earth filter-aid/sq cm, dry ca 30 min at 110°, cool in desiccator, weigh, and to each dish add sample of such size that dry residue will be ≥9 but ≤30 mg/sq cm. Weigh as rapidly as possible to avoid moisture loss. Mix with filter-aid and distribute uniformly over bottom of dish, dilg with H_2O if necessary to facilitate distribution. Bring sample to apparent dryness (remaining moisture not more than ca 50% dry solids) by one of following methods:

(1) Place sample on boiling H_2O bath and remove when samples reach apparent dryness.

(2) Place sample in forced-draft oven at 70°. Oven must have rapid air circulation and enough interchange of outside air to remove moisture rapidly. Examine dishes at intervals of ≤30 min, and remove as soon as they reach apparent dryness.

(3) Place sample in vac. oven at 70° with release cock left partly open to allow rapid flow of air thru oven at ≥310 mm Hg (41.3 kPa) pressure. Examine dishes at 30 min intervals and remove any that reach apparent dryness.

Place partially dried samples in vac. oven with bottoms of dishes in direct contact with shelf. Measure temp. of oven by thermometer in direct contact with shelf. Oven must be so constructed that temp. variations from one part of shelf to another does not exceed ca 2°. Admit dry air to oven at rate of 2–4 bubbles/sec by bubbling through H_2SO_4. Dry samples 2 hr at 69–71° (oven may be as low as 65° at start of drying, but must reach 69–71° before end of first hr) at pressure ≤50 mm Hg (6.6 kPa). As dried sample will absorb appreciable amt of moisture on standing over most desiccating agents, cover quickly, and weigh as soon as possible after sample reaches room temp.

32.011 Insoluble Solids (3)—Official Final Action

Wash 20 g sample repeatedly with hot H_2O, centrfg after each addn of H_2O and pouring clear supernate thru weighed filter paper on buchner. (Filter used is 1 of 2 such papers dried 2 hr at 100° and weighed in covered dish. Use second paper, if necessary, when first becomes clogged.) After 4 or 5 washings, transfer remaining insol. matter to filter, dry in uncovered dish 2 hr at 100°, cover, cool in desiccator, and weigh.

32.012 Alcohol-Insoluble Solids in Canned Peas (*4*)
Official Final Action

Pour sample on No. 8 screen, using 8" (20 cm) size for container of <3 lb net wt and 12" (30 cm) for larger amts. Spread peas evenly and let drain. Transfer peas to white pan and remove any foreign material. Add vol. H_2O equal to double vol. original sample.

Pour peas back on screen, spreading evenly, tilt screen as much as possible without shifting peas, and drain 2 min. With cloth, wipe surplus moisture from lower surface of screen. Grind drained peas in high-speed blender or food chopper until cotyledons are reduced to smooth paste, stir, and weigh 20 g ground material into 600 mL beaker. Add 300 mL 80% alcohol, stir, cover beaker, and bring to bp. Simmer slowly 30 min.

Fit buchner with filter paper of appropriate size (previously prepd by drying in flat-bottom dish 2 hr at 100°, covering with tight-fit cover, cooling in desiccator, and weighing at once). Apply suction and transfer contents of beaker to buchner so as to avoid running over edge of paper. Suck dry and wash material on filter with 80% alcohol until washings are clear and colorless.

Transfer paper and alcohol-insol. solids to dish used in prepn of paper, dry uncovered 2 hr at 100°, place cover on dish, cool in desiccator, and weigh at once. From this wt deduct wt dish, cover, and paper. Calc. % by wt of alcohol-insol. solids.

32.013 Soluble Solids—Official Final Action

% Total solids, **32.010** − % insol. solids, **32.011** = % sol. solids.

Soluble Solids in Tomato Products (*5*)
Official Final Action

32.014 ***Apparatus and Reagents***

(**a**) *Filters*.—Cut stems off 75 mm id glass or plastic funnels ca 1 cm from apex at 90° angle and firepolish ends. Set funnels in 150 mL jars, ca 55 mm id. If 150 mL beakers are used, close pouring spout with tape to prevent evapn. Insert folded paper, Whatman No. 2V, 12.5 cm, or equiv., in funnel.

(**b**) *Refractometer*.—Sensitive to 0.0001 n.

(**c**) *Ultracentrifuge*.—Centrf. should produce force of ca 150,000 × g (lesser force may be satisfactory for some samples). International No. B-60 or B-20A (Damon/IEC Div., 300 Second Ave, Needham Hts, MA 02194) are satisfactory.

(**d**) *Pectic enzyme.*—(*1*) *Dry preparation.*—In diat. earth base, e.g., Pectinol R-10 (Rohm and Haas Co.), Klerzyme® analytical (G.B. Fermentation Industries), or Spark-L® (Miles Laboratories, Inc). (*2*) *Soln.*—Prep. 0.4–1% aq. soln of (*1*); mix thoroly and let settle. Use clear supernate. Liq. prepns are also available commercially; dil., if necessary, before use.

32.015 ***Preparation of Sample***

(**a**) *Filtration without dilution.*—Weigh 100 g sample at room temp. and add weighed amt (0.2–1.0 g) dry enzyme prepn. Immediately mix with spoon or spatula to avoid evapn and transfer to filter. Tamp so sample is in close contact with paper and cover with petri dish (top or bottom portion) to form loose seal with top of funnel. Discard samples that do not filter in reasonable length of time (<1 hr). Mix 0.2–1.0 g dry enzyme prepn with 100 g fresh sample, seal in closed container, and incubate 30–60 min at ca 40°. Cool nearly to room temp. before opening container, remix sample, and transfer to filter. For samples that still do not filter within 1 hr, proceed as in (**b**).

(**b**) *Filtration with dilution.*—(Applicable to samples contg ≥35% solids that will not filter when treated as in (**a**).) Add 100 g enzyme soln to 100 g sample and immediately mix with spoon or spatula to avoid evapn. (Mech. mixer (e.g., Osterizer) with sealed blending container may be used.) Alternately blend and shake to dislodge and break up lumps sticking to container. Examine mixt. carefully for lumps and continue mixing until homogeneous. Transfer to filter and cover with petri dish.

(**c**) *Centrifugation.*—(Applicable to all samples.) Centrf. sample in ultracentrf. until reasonably clear serum is obtained (serum of some samples may be slightly turbid and/or red from presence of finely divided particles of pigment). Add dry enzyme as in (**a**) to decrease centrfg time. Protect sample from evapn during centrfg and before reading in refractometer.

32.016 ***Determination***

(**a**) *With filtration.*—Adjust refractometer for refractive index (*n*) of 1.3330 with H_2O at 20°. Let sample filter into jar or beaker until filtrate is clear (some color and turbidity may be tolerated). Quickly remove funnel and transfer large drop of filtrate directly from funnel to refractometer prism. (Tip of funnel may touch refractometer prism but should not scratch prism.) Replace funnel in jar. Read refractometer, preferably at 20°, but if humidity causes condensation of moisture on prism, make measurements at room temp. and correct readings to std temp. as in **52.016**. Read *n* or % sucrose on refractometer. If *n* is read, convert to % sucrose from **52.012**.

Let sample filter several min more. Repeat reading by removing funnel and transferring drop of filtrate to refractometer prism. The 2 readings should agree within 0.0002*n* or 0.1% sucrose. If not, repeat readings on successive portions of filtrate until agreement is obtained. Erratic readings indicate evapn of sample or faulty mixing and/or filtration technic.

Read clear supernate of 1% soln of dry enzyme on refractometer and convert to % sucrose. Subtract $1.15 \times B \times C$ from direct reading on sample (as % sucrose); where 1.15 = correction for insol. solids in weighed sample, assuming 12.5% total solids to be insol. solids; B = % enzyme prepn added to sample; and C = reading as sucrose obtained on 1% soln.

If dild sample is used, subtract $0.55 \times D \times C$ from reading on sample (as % sucrose); 0.55 = correction for insol. solids, as above, and D = % enzyme prepn added to diln H_2O. Multiply corrected reading for dild sample by 2 and add addnl correction according to following table:

Natural Tomato Sol. Solids as % Sucrose Corrected for Enzyme × 2	Correction
25.0	0.3
30.0	0.4
35.0	0.5
40.0	0.7
45.0	0.8
50.0	0.9

(**b**) *With centrifugation.*—Remove serum from rotor or centrf. tube with pipet or medicine dropper, and transfer to refractometer prism; avoid including solid particles as much as possible. If sharp line is not obtained on refractometer because of suspended solids, increase centrfg time or speed, or add enzyme to sample before centrfg. Calc. sol. solids as above.

(**c**) *Correction for added salt.*—(Use only when sample contains added salt and $R>S$.) Correct refractometer reading expressed as % sucrose at 20° for added salt by following formula: $S = (R - N) \times 1.016$ = total sol. solids as sucrose exclusive of added salt; where S = refractometer reading as sucrose corrected for added NaCl, R = total sol. solids as sucrose, and N = % total chlorides expressed as NaCl (detd by **32.023**).

32.017 Specific Gravity (*6*)—Official Final Action

(Applicable to comminuted tomato products)

Det. sp gr at 20/20°, using Gay-Lussac or similar small-neck bottle without cap. Clean and calibrate bottle at 20° as in **9.010**, strike off excess H_2O with straight edge, wipe bottle dry, and weigh immediately. Cool sample to 16–18°, fill bottle with the pulp, and centrf. 1 min at ca 1000 rpm. Add enough pulp to fill bottle to top and centrf. again. Remove bottle and take temp. of pulp, inserting thermometer so that no air is introduced. When temp. is just 20°, remove thermometer, add enough pulp at same temp. to have bottle slightly over full, and strike off even with straight edge. Clean outside of bottle and weigh at once to nearest 0.01 g.

Sp gr = wt pulp in bottle/wt H_2O at 20° that bottle holds.

32.018 Ash—Official Final Action

See **31.012** or **31.013**.

32.019 Alkalinity of Ash—Official Final Action

Proceed as in **22.027**. Express result as mL 1*N* acid required to neutze ash from 100 g sample.

Calcium (*7*)—Official Final Action

(Applicable to canned lima beans, potatoes, and tomatoes)

32.020 ***Reagents and Apparatus***

See **36.050** and **36.051**.

32.021 ***Preparation of Sample***

Thoroly comminute entire contents of can (representative portion if larger than No. 303 size can) in high-speed blender. Weigh 50 g sample (100 g in absence of declaration of added Ca) into Pt or porcelain dish. Evap. to dryness, using forced-draft oven, IR radiation, or other convenient means. Ash and treat as in **36.052**.

32.022 ***Determination***

Transfer 100 mL aliquot prepd sample soln to 250 mL beaker and adjust to pH 3.5 with 10% KOH soln added dropwise, using pH meter and mag. stirrer. Pass sample soln thru resin column

(column is in chloride form), collecting effluent in 400 mL beaker at flow rate of 2–3 mL/min. Wash column with two 50 mL portions H_2O, passing first portion thru at same rate as sample soln and second at 6–7 mL/min. Finally pass enough H_2O freely thru column to make 250–300 mL final vol. Adjust to pH 12.5–13.0, using pH meter and mag. stirrer, with KOH–KCN soln, **1.022(b)**. Add 0.100 g ascorbic acid and 200–300 mg hydroxynaphthol blue indicator. Titr. immediately with 0.01*M* EDTA soln thru pink to deep blue end point, using mag. stirrer.

% Ca = mL EDTA × (molarity EDTA soln/0.01) × 0.4008 × 2 × 100/mg sample.

Sodium Chloride—Official Final Action

32.023 ***Method I***

Proceed as in **3.072** or **3.074**, using HNO_3 soln of ash, **3.071**. Calc. and report results as % NaCl.

32.024 ***Method II (Rapid Method) (8)***

Weigh ca 5 g material, transfer with 80% alcohol to 100 mL vol. flask, and add enough 80% alcohol to give vol. of ca 50 mL. Shake well to suspend all insol. material. Add 1 mL HNO_3 and with pipet add excess of 0.1*N* $AgNO_3$ soln. Dil. to 100 mL with alcohol. Transfer mixt. to centrf. bottle and centrf. 5 min at ca 1800 rpm. Pipet 50 mL supernate into 300 mL erlenmeyer, add 2 mL satd $FeNH_4(SO_4)_2$ soln and 2 mL HNO_3, and titr. to permanent light brown with 0.1*N* NH_4SCN.

% NaCl = [(mL 0.1*N* $AgNO_3$/2) − mL 0.1*N* NH_4SCN] × 0.5844 × 100/50 × *W*,

where *W* = g sample.

Method III (Potentiometric Method) (9)

32.025 ***Principle***

Product is dispersed with H_2O and acidified; sol. chlorides are titrd potentiometrically with $AgNO_3$. Applicable to levels ≥0.03% NaCl. For convenience in calcns, wts or vols and normality are specified so that 1 mL $AgNO_3$ = 0.1% NaCl. If balance permitting rapid weighing of specified wt is not available, convenient wt sample and normality $AgNO_3$ soln may be used.

32.026 ***Apparatus***

(**a**) *Balance*.—Capacity, ≥200 g, taring range, ≥100 g, readability, ≤0.01 g. Mettler No. P1200 (superseded by P1210) (Mettler Instrument Corp., PO Box 100, Princeton, NJ 08540), or equiv., is convenient.

(**b**) *Electrodes*.—Ag billet combination electrode (Beckman No. 39261, or equiv.), or sep. indicating Ag (Beckman 39604, Orion 94-17, Fisher 13-639-122, or equiv.), and glass ref. (Beckman 40455, Orion 90-02, Fisher 9-313-216, or equiv.) electrodes. Before initial use and before each day's use, if necessary, clean Ag billet electrode tip with scouring powder or other suitable material and rinse thoroly with H_2O. (Hot H_2O may be required with some kinds of samples.) Clean other electrodes as recommended by manufacturer. Reclean as frequently as necessary to prevent drifting of end point reading. With some samples, periodically rinse electrodes with H_2O and wipe with tissue to prevent accumulation of film. It is unnecessary to coat Ag billet electrodes with AgCl.

(**c**) *Magnetic stirrer*.—Operating thru variable transformer to permit range of speed which, once set, is const.

(**d**) *pH meter*.—Preferably direct reading, with scale divisions 10 mv or less; range at least ±700 mv, e.g., digital type.

32.027 ***Reagents***

(**a**) *Nitric acid, dilute*.—(1+49). Dil. 20 mL HNO_3 to 1 L with H_2O.

(**b**) *Silver nitrate std soln*.—0.0856*N*. Dissolve 14.541 g $AgNO_3$ in H_2O and dil. to 1 L in vol. flask. Stdze as in **32.028**, and adjust to exact normality specified so that with indicated sample wt, 1 mL = 0.1% NaCl. Store in Pyrex container out of direct sunlight. Soln is stable in room light.

(**c**) *Sodium chloride std soln*.—0.0856*N*. Dissolve in H_2O 5.000 g NaCl (if assay is <100.0% NaCl, divide 5.000 g by % NaCl/100 to obtain corrected wt), previously dried 2 hr at 110°, and dil. to 1 L in vol. flask.

(**d**) *Water*.—Distd or deionized, halogen-free by following test: Add 1 mL ca 0.1*N* $AgNO_3$ and 5 mL HNO_3 (1+4) to 100 mL of the H_2O. No more than slight turbidity should be produced.

32.028 ***Standardization***

Pipet 25 mL NaCl std soln into 250 mL beaker, dil. to ca 50 mL with H_2O, and add 50 mL HNO_3 (1+49). Insert electrodes, start mag. stirrer, and stir throughout titrn at const rate producing vigorous agitation without splashing. Titr. with $AgNO_3$ std soln, adjusting increments with rate of voltage change so that accurate plot of mv against mL $AgNO_3$ soln can be prepd. Add total of 50 mL $AgNO_3$ soln to obtain complete curve.

Det. inflection point by drawing 2 straight lines with 45° slope with respect to axes and tangent to titrn curve at the 2 points of greatest curvature. Inflection point is at intersection of titrn curve with line drawn parallel to, and midway between, other 2 lines. From vol. $AgNO_3$ soln used, calc. normality and adjust to 0.0856*N*. Restdze occasionally. Use inflection point as end point in titrg samples. Recheck end point potential occasionally, and redet. when either individual electrode, combination electrode, or pH meter is replaced by prepg new titrn curve.

For greatest accuracy, when series of detns on same food is performed, det. and use end point from titrn curve of that food rather than using end point obtained with NaCl std soln.

32.029 ***Preparation of Sample***

(**a**) *Clear liquids with low viscosity*.—(Fruit juices, clear soups, wines, etc.) Use directly.

(**b**) *Comminuted products*.—(Tomato juice, tomato catsup, strained vegetables, etc.) Thoroly shake unopened container to incorporate any sediment. Transfer entire contents to large glass or porcelain dish and mix thoroly, continuing stirring ≥1 min. Transfer to g-s container, and shake or stir thoroly each time before removing portions for analysis.

(**c**) *General method for heterogeneous (fish, meat, etc.), low moisture (cereal products, etc.), and hard-to-disperse, homogeneous (cheese, peanut butter, etc.) foods*.—Weigh 50.0 g sample into 1 L (qt) container of high-speed blender and add 450 g H_2O. Cover, start blender at low speed by use of variable transformer for initial dispersion, and blend thoroly at high speed (1–2 min is usually adequate). Equiv. of 5 g sample is conveniently dispensed thru 50 mL pipet with tip cut off. Thoroly mix sample suspension immediately before pipetting aliquot for analysis so that solid material is uniformly suspended.

(**d**) *Other types of foods*.—Prep. sample by method (**a**), (**b**), (**c**), or other suitable method.

To preserve samples or sample suspensions for future analysis, add 0.5 mL ca 37% HCHO soln/100 g sample or sample suspension, mix well, and store at room temp. Correct for diln by HCHO soln by multiplying % NaCl by 1.005.

32.030 ***Determination***

(**a**) *For products containing less than 5 per cent salt.*—Place 5.00 g (or 5.00 mL if concn is to be expressed on w/v basis) prepd sample from (**a**) or (**b**) or 50.0 g from (**c**) into tared 250 mL beaker; add H_2O to ca 50 mL if (**a**) or (**b**) is used. (Use boiling H_2O with samples such as butter to melt fat.) Add 50 mL HNO_3 (1+49). Titr. as in **32.028**, using 10 mL buret if salt content is ≤1%.

$$\% \text{ NaCl} = \text{mL } 0.0856N \text{ AgNO}_3/10.$$

(**b**) *For products containing 5 or more per cent salt.*—Place 5.00 g (or 5.00 mL if concn is to be expressed on w/v basis) prepd sample from (**a**) or (**b**) into 100 mL vol. flask and dil. to vol. with H_2O. Mix, and transfer aliquot contg 50–250 mg NaCl to 250 mL beaker. If sample is prepd by (**c**), transfer weighed aliquot contg 50–250 mg NaCl to tared 250 mL beaker. Proceed as in **32.028**, beginning ". . . dil. to ca 50 mL with H_2O, . . ."

$$\% \text{ NaCl} = F \times \text{mL } 0.0856N \text{ AgNO}_3/10,$$

where F = diln factor = 100/mL aliquot titrd if sample is prepd by (**a**) or (**b**) or 50/g aliquot titrd if prepd by (**c**).

(**c**) *General case.*—Accurately weigh approx. sample wt stated. (If % NaCl ≥5%, weigh <5 g sample rather than dilg to 100 mL, if more convenient.) Use ca 0.1*N* $AgNO_3$ soln, accurately stdzd as in **32.028**, without adjusting to specific normality, and titr. as in **32.028**.

$$\% \text{ NaCl} = \text{mL AgNO}_3 \times N \text{ AgNO}_3 \times 0.05844 \times 100/\text{g sample}.$$

If sample is overtitrd, add NaCl std soln, and complete titrn. Correct for vol. of std soln added.

32.031 Reducing Sugars Before Inversion
Official Final Action

Weigh 20 g sample into 200 mL vol. flask, dil. with ca 100 mL H_2O, clarify with slight excess of neut. $Pb(OAc)_2$ soln, **31.021(d)**, dil. to vol., and filter. Remove excess Pb with anhyd. Na_2SO_4 or with dry Na or K oxalate. Filter, and det. reducing sugars as in **31.038**. Express result as % invert sugar.

32.032 Reducing Sugars After Inversion
Official Final Action

Transfer 50 mL filtrate, **32.031**, to 100 mL vol. flask, add 5 mL HCl, and let stand overnight, as in **31.026(c)**. Nearly neutze with NaOH soln, cool, dil. to vol., and det. reducing sugars in aliquot as in **31.038**. Express result as % invert sugar.

32.033 Sucrose—Official Final Action

See **31.031**.

32.034 Total Acids—Official Final Action

Proceed as in **22.060** or **22.061**, using 5 g sample. Express result as mL 1*N* alkali required to neutze 100 g sample.

Oxalic Acid (*10*)—Official Final Action

32.035 ***Reagents***

(**a**) *Indicator paper.*—Short-range Alkacid (No. 2, pH 3.5–5.5, Fisher Scientific Co., or equiv.).

(**b**) *Potassium permanganate solns.*—(*1*) *Approx. 0.1N.*—Prep. and stdze as in **50.025–50.026**. (*2*) *Approx. 0.01N.*—Dil. 100 mL 0.1*N* to 1 L. Prep. fresh before use.

(**c**) *Acetate buffer soln.*—pH 4.5. Dissolve 2.5 g anhyd. $CaCl_2$ in 50 mL HOAc (1+1) and add to soln of 33 g $NaOAc.3H_2O$ dild to 50 mL.

(**d**) *Wash liquid.*—Dil. 12.5 mL HOAc to 250 mL with H_2O. Add powd Ca oxalate, shake, and let stand. Repeat addn and shaking to satn. Cool to 4° and store in refrigerator. Just before use, filter amt needed. Keep cold during filtration and use.

(**e**) *Tungstophosphoric acid reagent.*—Dissolve 2.5 g $Na_2WO_4.2H_2O$ in mixt. of 4 mL H_3PO_4 and 50 mL H_2O, and dil. to 100 mL with H_2O.

(**f**) *Lanthanum soln.*—5%. Wet 5.9 g La_2O_3 with H_2O, very slowly add 25 mL HCl to dissolve, and dil. to 100 mL with H_2O.

(**g**) *Calcium std solns.*—(*1*) *1 mg/mL.* Slurry 2.497 g $CaCO_3$ (primary std grade) in 1 L vol. flask with 300 mL H_2O. Carefully add 10 mL HCl. After CO_2 is completely released, dil. to vol. with H_2O. (*2*) *0.05 mg/mL.*—Dil. 5.0 mL soln (*1*) to 100 mL with H_2O.

32.036 ***Apparatus***

Atomic absorption spectrophotometer.—Perkin-Elmer Model 303, or equiv. double beam instrument. Typical operating parameters for this app. are given in Table **32:02**. Operator must be familiar with optimum settings for app. and use table only as guide. (*Caution: See* **51.006**.)

32.037 ***Preparation of Sample***

Det. net wt of contents of can. Transfer quant. to high-speed blender, rinsing can with 100 mL H_2O added from buret or pipet. Homogenize 15 min and cool to room temp.

Accurately weigh ca 35 g slurry into 800 mL beaker. Add H_2O to bring total wt to ca 300 g; then add 55 mL 6*N* HCl. Add 2 drops *caprylic alcohol*, and boil 15 min. Cool, transfer quant. to 500 mL vol. flask, dil. to vol. with H_2O, mix, and let stand overnight. Mix, and filter thru fast quant. paper, discarding first 100 mL filtrate.

32.038 ***Precipitation of Oxalic Acid***

Pipet 25 mL filtrate into 50 mL erlenmeyer, add 5.0 mL tungstophosphoric acid reagent, mix, and let stand ≥5 hr. Filter thru Whatman No. 30 quant. paper, or equiv. Pipet 20 mL filtrate into 50 mL conical centrf. tube and add NH_4OH dropwise to pH 4–4.5, using indicator paper, (**a**). Add 5 mL buffer soln, (**c**), and stir with glass rod. Rinse rod into centrf. tube with small stream of H_2O and let stand overnight.

Centrf. ≥15 min at 1700 rpm to compact ppt. Decant supernate with one smooth continuous inversion of centrf. tube. Hold tube upside down and let remaining supernate drip completely onto clean filter paper. Do not disturb Ca oxalate ppt. Wash ppt by completely breaking it into fine suspension with fine jet stream of 20 mL filtered cold wash liq., (**d**). Repeat centrfg and decanting steps, taking care that ppt is drained completely. Discard paper. Add 5 mL H_2SO_4 (1+9) to ppt. Proceed with permanganate titrn or AA detn.

32.039 ***Determination by Permanganate Titration***

Heat sample and blank (5 mL H_2SO_4 (1+9) in 50 mL centrf. tube) prepd solns in boiling H_2O bath. Titr. *hot* soln with 0.01*N* $KMnO_4$ until first pink persists ≥30 sec.

$$\text{mg Oxalic acid/100 g product} = \text{mL } 0.01N \text{ KMnO}_4 \times 1350 \times (\text{net wt} + 100\text{ g})/(\text{wt slurry taken} \times \text{net wt})$$

where 1350 = 0.45 (mg anhyd. oxalic acid equiv. to 1 mL 0.01*N* $KMnO_4$) × [(30/20) × (500/25) (diln factors)] × 100 (to convert to 100 g product).

32.040 ***Determination by Atomic Absorption***

Quant. transfer entire contents of centrf. tube to 10 mL vol. flask with H_2SO_4 (1+9) and dil. to vol. with same soln (*soln I*). Pipet 2 mL *soln I* into 50 mL vol. flask contg 10.0 mL La soln, (**f**). Dil. to vol. with H_2O (*soln II*). Transfer 15.0 mL *soln II* to 25 mL vol. flask contg 2 mL La soln. Dil. to vol. with H_2O.

Pipet 0, 2.0, 4.0, 6.0, 8.0, 10.0, and 12.0 mL $CaCO_3$ soln, (**g**)(*2*), into sep. 50 mL vol. flasks. Pipet 10 mL La soln into each and dil. to vol. with H_2O.

Set instrument to previously established optimum conditions or according to manufacturer's instructions. Det. *A* of sample and std solns, taking ≥2 std readings before and after sample readings. Flush burner with H_2O and check 0 point between readings. Correct for reagent blank reading, if significant, and det. Ca concn from std curve obtained by plotting *A* against μg Ca/mL.

mg Oxalic acid/100 g product = (μg Ca/mL) × 2807.5 × (net wt + 100 g)/(wt slurry taken × net wt),

where 2807.5 = 2.246/1000 (to convert μg Ca to mg oxalic acid) × [25 × (50/15)× (10/2) × (30/20) × (500/25) (diln factors)] × 100 (to convert to 100 g product).

Table 32:02 Operating Parameters for Oxalic Acid Determination

Wavelength, nm	422.7
Slit width, mm	1-setting 4
Hollow Zn-Ca cathode lamp, ma	15–20
Air, aspirating	9.0 (scale divisions)
Acetylene fuel	9.5 (scale divisions)
Flame	reducing
Ht, burner to light path, in.	ca 0.5
Sample uptake, mL/min	5
Optimum concn range, μg/mL	0–10

Lactic Acid—Official Final Action

32.041 ***Preparation of Solution***

Weigh 50 g ground and mixed sample into tared centrf. bottle and add 100 mL H_2O. Make acid to Congo red paper with 1*N* H_2SO_4. Adjust wt of contents of bottle to 200 g by addn of H_2O, shake vigorously, and centrf. Decant supernate and weigh 100 g into 100–110 mL vol. flask. Dil. to 110 mL mark with H_2O, shake, and pipet 50 mL into continuous extractor (Fig. **16:01**). Add 0.5 mL H_2SO_4 (1+1) and 2 mL 20% $Na_2WO_4.2H_2O$ soln, and proceed as in **16.030**.

If sample contains HOAc added in course of manufacture (*e.g.*, catsup), transfer extd material, after evapn of ether, to beaker, add ca 50 mL H_2O, and evap. to 20 mL. Again add 50 mL H_2O and evap. to 20 mL. Neutze with satd $Ba(OH)_2$ soln and proceed as in **16.031**.

32.042 ★ Field Corn in Canned Mixtures ★ of Field and Sweet Corn (*11*) Official Final Action

See **30.016**, 10th ed.

DRIED VEGETABLES

Water (*12*)—Official Final Action

(Dry all glassware in oven.)

32.043 ***Preparation of Sample***

Grind sample to pass No. 30 sieve and store in tightly sealed container.

★ Surplus method—*see* inside front cover.

Near-Infrared Spectrophotometric Method

(*Caution: See* **51.053**.)

32.044 ***Apparatus***

Spectrophotometer.—Beckman Instruments DK2A, or equiv., near-IR recording instrument.

32.045 ***Preparation of Standard Curve***

Accurately weigh 200, 300, 400, 500, and 600 mg H_2O into sep. 125 mL g-s erlenmeyers. Pipet 100 mL *N,N-dimethylformamide* (DMF) into each flask. Record *A* of solns in matched quartz or silica cells from 1.8 to 2.1 μm, using for ref. same lot DMF as used for prepn of std solns. Draw baseline between minima at ca 1.82 μm and 2.0 μm. *A* of std soln at max., ca 1.92 μm = total *A* at max. − baseline *A* at max. Plot corrected baseline *A* against mg H_2O/100 mL DMF.

32.046 ***Determination***

Accurately weigh sample contg ca 70–100 mg H_2O into 50 mL g-s erlenmeyer. Pipet in 20 mL DMF. Tape stopper securely to flask and heat 60±1 min at 90±1° in oven. Mech. shake flask 10 min. Cool to room temp. Decant soln into g-s centrf. tube and centrf. at 1500 rpm until soln is clear (ca 5 min). Record *A* of soln and calc. *A* at max. as in **32.045**.

% H_2O = (mg H_2O from std curve× 100)/(5 × mg sample)

Karl Fischer Method

32.047 ***Apparatus***

Titrimeter.—Fisher Scientific Co. Model 36, Manual K-F Titrimeter, or equiv., with 2 Pt electrodes. See **31.068**.

32.048 ***Reagents***

(**a**) *Karl Fischer reagent*.—Stabilized, with H_2O equiv. of ca 5 mg H_2O/mL reagent. Available com. or prep. as in **31.069(a)**, using ethylene glycol monomethyl ether. Place 50 mL formamide, practical grade, into 200 mL Berzelius beaker contg mag. stirrer. Place in titrimeter and titr. (Titr. slowly near end point until 0.1 mL addn causes meter to deflect to right of 0 and remain 60 sec.) Quickly add accurately weighed amt (0.250–0.350 g) disodium tartrate.$2H_2O$. Titr. immediately to same end point. Repeat detn and calc. av.

mg H_2O/mL reagent = (mg $Na_2C_4H_4O_6.2H_2O$ × 0.1566)/mL reagent.

(**b**) *Sodium tartrate dihydrate*.—"60 mesh."

32.049 ***Determination***

Accurately weigh 2.0–2.5 g sample into 50 mL g-s erlenmeyer. Pipet in 20 mL *N,N-dimethylformamide* (DMF). Ext and centrf. as in **32.046**.

Place 50 mL formamide into 200 mL Berzelius beaker and titr. to end point as in stdzg Karl Fischer reagent. Quickly pipet 10 mL sample soln into beaker and titr. to same end point. Det. blank by titrg 10 mL DMF in same manner as sample, Repeat blank detn and calc. av.

% H_2O in sample = [200 (mL reagent for sample − blank titer) (mg H_2O/mL reagent)]/mg sample.

FROZEN VEGETABLES

Net Contents of Frozen Food Containers (*13*)—Procedure

32.050 ***Apparatus***

(**a**) *For packages up to 5 pounds.*—Use scale of adequate capacity with sensitivity of 0.01 oz.

(**b**) *For packages over 5 pounds.*—Use scale of adequate capacity with sensitivity of 0.025 oz.

32.051 ***Procedure***

Set scale on firm support and level. Adjust 0 load indicator or rest point and check sensitivity.

(**a**) *Unglazed frozen foods.*—Remove package from low temp. storage, remove frost and ice from outside of package, and weigh immediately (W). Open package; remove contents, including any product particles and frost crystals. Air-dry empty package at room temp. and weigh (E). Wt contents = $W - E$.

(**b**) *Glazed frozen foods.—See* **18.001**(**a**).

32.052 Thawing Frozen Vegetables (*14*)—Procedure

(*FAO/WHO Method*)

See **22.006**. Use (**a**), (**b**), or following, as appropriate to product; e.g., for corn, use air thawing or indirect contact to avoid leaching solids. Do not use direct contact if there is indication of off flavors or odors.

Direct contact thawing.—(Applicable to vegetables having few cut surfaces such as brussels sprouts, asparagus, or green beans.) Remove product from package and immerse in H_2O at $\leq 30°$. As soon as individual units can be sepd, drain on screen to remove excess H_2O, and place on tray for air thawing and examination.

Total Solids in Frozen Spinach (*15*)
Official Final Action

32.053 ***Apparatus***

(**a**) *Drying dish.*—Al, with tight-fitting cover, 33 × 70 mm id.

(**b**) *Drying oven.*—Mech. air circulation or gravity convection, 105°.

32.054 ***Preparation of Sample***

Transfer frozen contents of package, including any product particles and frost crystals, to 2 L beaker. Cover with plastic wrap to prevent evapn and thaw by placing beaker in ca 30° H_2O bath. Transfer contents to high-speed blender and reduce to smooth, uniform puree while stirring constantly with rubber spatula to maintain proper action of blender. Return blended sample to original beaker and stir to pick up residual H_2O. Transfer ca 200 g sample to small, sealed container for analysis.

32.055 ***Determination***

Add ca 15 mg diat. earth filter-aid/sq cm to drying dish. Dry ca 1 hr at 105°, cool in desiccator, and weigh. Add amt sample so dry residue will be >12 but <30 mg/sq cm. Weigh as rapidly as possible to avoid moisture loss. Mix with filter-aid and distribute slurry uniformly over bottom of dish; dil. with H_2O if necessary to aid distribution. Wash solids on stirring rod into dish. Dry sample by one of following methods:

(**a**) Place sample in 105° oven with mech. air circulation and provision for interchange with outside air to remove moisture. Dry 4 hr and weigh. Repeat drying and weighing until wt loss in 1 hr drying is ≤ 1 mg.

(**b**) Place sample in 105° gravity convection oven. Monitor temp. at point near air outlet where temp. will gradually rise at rate proportional to load in oven. When temp. reaches 100° (4–6 hr), continue heating 1 hr and weigh. Repeat drying and weighing as in (**a**).

When dry, quickly remove dish from oven, cover, and place in desiccator to cool. Weigh as soon as possible after sample reaches room temp.

$$\% \text{ Solids} = [(W_3 - W_1) \times 100]/(W_2 - W_1),$$

where W_1 = tare wt of dish and diat. earth, W_2 = wt of dish and wet sample, and W_3 = wt of dish and dried sample.

Alcohol-Insoluble Solids in Frozen Peas (*16*)
Official Final Action

32.056 ***Reagents and Apparatus***

(**a**) *Alcohol solns.*—(*1*) *Extracting soln.*—SDA 3-A (5% MeOH) or reagent (3-A–isopropanol (95+5)). (*2*) *Washing soln.*—80%. Dil. 8 L 3-A or reagent alcohol to 9.5 L with H_2O.

(**b**) *Drying dish.*—Flat-bottom, with tight-fitting cover.

(**c**) *Drying oven.*—Well ventilated, thermostatically controlled at 100±2°.

32.057 ***Preparation of Sample***

Transfer frozen contents of package to plastic bag; tie bag securely and immerse in H_2O bath with continuous flow at room temp. Avoid agitation of bag during thawing by using clamps or wts. When sample completely thaws, remove bag, blot off adhering H_2O, and transfer peas to No. 8 sieve, using 8" (20 cm) for container <3 lb (1.36 kg) net wt and 12" (30 cm) for larger amts. If sauce is present, remove with gentle H_2O spray at room temp. Without shifting peas, incline sieve to aid drainage; drain 2 min. With cloth, wipe surplus H_2O from lower screen surface. Weigh 250 g peas into high-speed blender, add 250 g H_2O, and blend to smooth paste. For <250 g sample, use entire sample with equal wt H_2O.

32.058 ***Determination***

Weigh 20 g ±10 mg paste into 250 mL distn flask, add 120 mL extg soln, and reflux 30 min on steam or H_2O bath or hot plate. Fit buchner with paper of appropriate size (previously prepd by drying in flat-bottom dish 2 hr at 100°, covering with tight-fit cover, cooling in desiccator, and weighing). Apply vac. and transfer flask contents to buchner so as to avoid running over edge of paper. Suck dry and wash material on filter with 80% alcohol until washings are clear and colorless.

Transfer paper and alcohol-insol. solids to dish used to prep. paper, dry uncovered 2 hr at 100°, cover tightly, cool in desiccator, and weigh at once. From this wt deduct wt dish, cover, and paper. Calc. % by wt of alcohol-insol. solids.

Fibrous Material in Frozen Green Beans (*17*)
Official Final Action

32.059 ***Apparatus***

(**a**) *Mixer.*—Overhead rotor, drink mixer type with 2 scalloped buttons 2.5 cm diam., spaced ca 2.5 cm apart on mixer spindle. No-load rating $\geq$12,000 rpm. Equipped with metal mixer cup.

(**b**) *Macerating plunger rod.*—No. 7 rubber stopper attached with flat head screw, in inverted position, to end of 0.5" (12.7 mm) wood dowel, 25–30 cm long.

(**c**) *Fiber sieve assembly.*—Fit 85 mm diam. stainless steel or Monel screen, 30 mesh (595 μm) 32 gage, to wide mouth Mason jar closure ring. Attach to glass funnel prepd by cutting off bottom half of wide mouth Mason jar, leaving ca 12 cm side on closure side.

(**d**) *Fiber washing assembly*.—Glass tube nozzle 75 mm (3″) long × 3 mm (⅛″) id inserted into rubber hose ≤6 mm (¼″) id which is connected to H_2O source at controlled pressure such that assembly will deliver H_2O from nozzle at 1650±50 mL/min.

32.060 ***Preparation of Sample***

Place ≥250 g (9 oz) sample on ≥8″ No. 8 sieve and place under gentle stream of H_2O (30–40°) to thaw bean units and wash away any sauce. Remove any extraneous material, including stem end of any unsnipped bean unit.

Place thawed sample in utensil with enough boiling H_2O to cover. Cover utensil and boil 15 min after H_2O returns to boil. Drain on No. 8 sieve, cool to room temp. under cold H_2O, and drain.

32.061 ***Determination***

Place ca 250 g cooked sample on tray, break open pods, and remove and discard seeds. Collect on sieve, to permit drainage, enough pods to provide 200 g sample. Cover accumulated pods to prevent drying.

Prep. several clean fiber sieves before starting detn. Remove each used screen from ring, brush with stiff bristle brush to loosen fibrous residue, and rinse under stream of H_2O. Reset in ring, dry 1 hr at 100°, cool in desiccator, and weigh to 0.2 mg (T g).

Transfer 200±0.5 g deseeded beans to mixer cup and mash with plunger rod. Remove rod and wash adhering material into cup with 275 mL hot H_2O. Heat almost to bp, carefully add 40 mL 50% (w/w) NaOH soln, with stirring, and bring to boil, adding ≤1 mL *capryl alcohol* if necessary to control foaming. Boil 5 min, in fume hood, stirring occasionally.

Transfer cup to mixer and stir 5 min at speed ≥9000 rpm that does not cause spillage. (Control speed with variable transformer set at 80–90 v, measured with voltmeter.) Add capryl alcohol dropwise as necessary to control foaming. Sample spillage may be prevented by use of large polyethylene funnel with stem removed to pass mixer spindle and with notch at upper cup bracket so that funnel rests on rim of mixer cup.

Attach weighed screen and ring assembly to glass funnel to provide tight joint. Place on ring clamp, and pour mixt. from cup slowly thru screen, washing simultaneously with moving stream of H_2O from washing assembly until mat is free from pulp. Transfer funnel assembly to warm H_2O bath to leach remaining NaOH. Return funnel assembly to ring and place few drops phthln on mat. If red color develops, continue washing until alk.-free.

Detach funnel and rest ring and sieve against side wall of a tray to let H_2O drain. Place ring and sieve assembly in 100° oven, providing free circulation of air thru screen. Dry 3 hr at 100°; cool 15 min in desiccator contg fresh 8–20 mesh $CaCl_2$, $CaSO_4$, or silica gel. Weigh rapidly to 0.5 mg (W g).

$$\% \text{ Fibrous material} = (W - T) \times 100/\text{g sample}.$$

Report results to 0.001%.

Aldehydes as Acetaldehyde (*18*)—Official First Action

32.062 ***Apparatus***

Steam distilling apparatus.—Consists of 500 mL Kjeldahl flask, spray trap, and condenser, preferably all-glass with ₸ joints (Cat. No. JD 1710, SGA Scientific, Inc., is satisfactory). App. with rubber stoppers and connections is suitable if satisfactory blanks are obtained. (Some rubber yields neg. blanks.)

32.063 ***Reagents***

(**a**) *Sodium thiosulfate std soln*.—0.05N. Prep. daily by dilg 0.1N soln, **50.037–50.038**. 1 mL 0.05N $Na_2S_2O_3$ = 1.1 mg AcH.

(**b**) *Iodine std soln*.—0.05–0.0515N. Prep. as in **50.018**, stdze against $Na_2S_2O_3$ soln, (**a**), and adjust concn, if necessary.

(**c**) *Sodium bisulfite std soln.*—0.05N in ca 10% alcohol. Dissolve 2.60 g $NaHSO_3$ in 500 mL H_2O in 1 L vol. flask. Add 100 mL alcohol, mix, and dil. to vol. with H_2O. Stdze against I soln, (**b**), and adjust concn, if necessary, so as to be slightly weaker than that of the I soln, but not <0.0485N. Prep. fresh daily.

(**d**) *Aldehyde-free alcohol*.—Use alcohol contg <2 ppm AcH; if greater, purify as in **19.071(a)**. Det. aldehydes as in **32.064**, using 300 mL freshly boiled and cooled H_2O and 35 mL of the alcohol, beginning "Pipet in 25 mL $NaHSO_3$ soln . . ." Det. blank similarly but without alcohol. Difference in titrns × 31 = ppm aldehydes as AcH.

32.064 ***Determination***

Sharply strike package of frozen vegetable on surface or edge of table to break up block. Mix well and grind ca 150 g thru food chopper.

Transfer 50 g sample to Kjeldahl flask with ca 150 mL H_2O. Add 1–2 drops *Dow-Corning Antifoam*, or equiv., and steam distil into 500 mL erlenmeyer, immersed in ice bath and contg 100 mL chilled, freshly boiled H_2O to cover end of delivery tube. Collect ca 300 mL within 12–15 min. To distillate add 35 mL aldehyde-free alcohol. Pipet in 25 mL $NaHSO_3$ soln and let stand 30 min, shaking occasionally. Pipet in 25 mL I soln, and titr. with $Na_2S_2O_3$ soln, using 5 mL starch indicator, **32.065(g)**. Det. blank on 300 mL freshly boiled and cooled H_2O. Difference in mL × 1.1 = mg AcH; mg AcH × 1000/wt sample = ppm.

Catalase (*19*)—Official First Action

32.065 ***Reagents***

Relatively Stable Reagents

(**a**) *Phosphate buffer soln*.—0.1M, pH 6.95±0.15. Dissolve 15.22 g $K_2HPO_4.3H_2O$ and 4.54 g KH_2PO_4 in H_2O and dil. to 1 L.

(**b**) *Sulfuric acid containing molybdate.—2N*. Add 55 mL H_2SO_4 to ca 800 mL H_2O, cool, add 0.1 g finely ground $(NH_4)_6Mo_7O_{24}.4H_2O$, agitate until completely dissolved, and dil. to 1 L with H_2O.

(**c**) *Sodium thiosulfate (ca 0.01N) in 10% potassium iodide soln*.—Dissolve 100 g KI, 2.50 g $Na_2S_2O_3.5H_2O$, and ca 1 g Na_2CO_3 in 500 mL H_2O and dil. to 1 L. (Need not be stdzd.)

(**d**) *Iodine std soln.—0.01N*. Prep. as in **50.018**. Stdze against std $Na_2S_2O_3$ *soln*, **50.037–50.038**. (Avoid exposure to excessive light even while in buret.)

Relatively Unstable Reagents

(**e**) *Hydrogen peroxide*.—0.1N. Dil. 0.58 mL 30% H_2O_2 to 100 mL with cold H_2O. Keep in refrigerator or ice bath when not in use. *Prep. daily.*

(**f**) *20% soln of glucose in buffer soln*.—Dissolve 20 g glucose in 100 mL phosphate buffer soln, (**a**). Keep refrigerated and prep. weekly.

(**g**) *Starch indicator*.—Add 1.0 g sol. starch to 100 mL cold H_2O, stir thoroly, and heat to boiling. Prep. biweekly.

32.066 ***Preparation of Extract***

To avoid contamination with oxides of heavy metals, handle samples only with nonmetallic or stainless steel spatulas.

(**a**) *Undried or frozen vegetables*.—Comminute 50 g portions in high-speed blender 3 min with ca 1 g $CaCO_3$ and enough H_2O

to make total vol. 200 mL. Remove larger particles by filtering thru 15 cm (6") gauze-backed cotton milk filter. Assay filtrate within 30 min.

(**b**) *Dried vegetables*.—Rehydrate 5 g sample and ext as in (**a**).

32.067 ***Determination***

(**a**) *To demonstrate presence or absence of catalase*.—To 10 mL ext (or less, depending on activity) add H_2O to total vol. of 43 mL and 5 mL glucose soln, (**f**). Mix, and add 2 mL 0.1*N* H_2O_2. *Immediately* after addn of H_2O_2, mix thoroly, quickly remove "0-time" aliquot of completed reaction mixt. with rapid-flow pipet, and blow it into 125 mL erlenmeyer contg 10 mL H_2SO_4-molybdate soln. Count "0-time" from time delivery of aliquot from pipet is started. Remove 10 mL aliquots at 5 and 10 min. (Temp. of reaction mixt. must remain at <20°.) At any time within 1 hr add 5 mL $Na_2S_2O_3$-KI soln to each flask and mix. Let stand 3–5 min; then titr. excess $Na_2S_2O_3$ with 0.01*N* I, using ca 10 drops starch indicator.

Perform blank in exactly same manner, except add H_2O instead of H_2O_2, and do not remove 5 and 10 min aliquots. Differences between titer value of blank and of values obtained in presence of H_2O_2 are I soln equivs of H_2O_2 present at respective times. "Zero-time" titer value should be 0.5–2 mL I soln; differences between blank-titer value and "0-time" titer value should be 3.0–4.5 mL 0.01*N* I. Difference of <3.0 mL (*i.e.*, I titer values >2 mL) indicates that the H_2O_2 was too weak or that catalase activity was so high that large amt of H_2O_2 was decomposed before "0-time" aliquot was removed. In latter case, differences corresponding to 5 and 10 min may be nearly 0, even when large amts of catalase are present. In such case, catalase content of ext can be detd by method (**b**), if desired. If 10 mL aliquots of ext are used, blank-titer value is 4–6 mL, and "0-time" titer value is <2 mL, catalase is indicated to be absent (within experimental error) when titer values for 5 and 10 min do not differ from "0-time" titer value by >0.20 mL and 0.40 mL, resp.

(**b**) *To accurately determine catalase activity of sample in terms of K_f*.—"Katalase Fähigkeit," K_f, is k, first order reaction const (log base 10) detd at 0°, divided by g sample/50 mL reaction mixt. That is, $K_f = k/g$, and is therefore expression of catalase activity of prepn. Pure catalase has K_f of 40,000–60,000, depending on source. If K_f is to be detd, make assay exactly as in (**a**), except maintain reaction mixt. at 0°. It is generally desirable to obtain 15 min titer value in addn to those described in (**a**). If sample is enzyme prepn of high activity rather than a vegetable, dissolve suitable amt in dil. buffer, pH 6.5–7.5, preferably contg 2% glucose.

32.068 ***Calculation of K_f***

Value for K_f for 0–5 min and 5–10 min periods should check at 0°, but at higher temps K_f (5–10 min) may be <K_f (0–5 min), because catalase is inactivated by H_2O_2 at significant rate at higher temps. K_f is given by following formula:

$$K_f = \frac{\left(\dfrac{1}{t_b - t_a}\right)\log\left(\dfrac{\text{blank titer} - \text{titer at } t_a}{\text{blank titer} - \text{titer at } t_b}\right)}{\text{g sample/50 mL reaction mixt.}}$$

where t_a and t_b are initial and final times for 2 titer values under consideration. For exts of undried vegetables prepd as in **32.066**, the g sample in reaction mixt. is obtained with enough accuracy by multiplying mL ext used by 0.25. For most nearly accurate results, enzyme concn should be adjusted so that difference between blank titrn and t_0 titrn is 3–4 mL, and difference between blank titrn and t_{10} titrn is 0.5–1 mL I soln.

Peroxidase (*20*)—Official Final Action

32.069 ***Reagents***

Relatively Stable Reagents

(**a**) *Phosphate-oxalate buffer soln*.—0.1*M*, pH 6.0. Dissolve 14.2 g Na_2HPO_4 (or 26.81 g $Na_2HPO_4.7H_2O$) and 12.6 g $H_2C_2O_4.2H_2O$ in H_2O with heat, cool, adjust pH to 6.0 with 1*N* NaOH, and dil. to 1 L.

(**b**) *Oxalic acid soln*.—1*M*. Dissolve 126 g $H_2C_2O_4.2H_2O$ in H_2O and dil. to 1 L.

(**c**) *Sodium chloride soln*.—2.0%. Dissolve 20 g NaCl in H_2O and dil. to 1 L. Cool to 0° and store at 0°.

Relatively Unstable Reagents

(**d**) *Hydrogen peroxide soln*.—0.1*N*. Dil. 0.58 mL 30% H_2O_2 to 100 mL with cold H_2O. Stdze iodometrically as follows: To 25 mL 0.1*N* H_2O_2 add 10 mL 4*N* H_2SO_4, 6 mL 1*N* KI, and 3 drops 1*N* $(NH_4)_2Mo_7O_{24}$. Titr. soln with 0.1*N* $Na_2S_2O_3$ to starch end point. Store in refrigerator when not in use. Prep. weekly.

(**e**) *Indophenol soln*.—0.001*N*. Dissolve 200 mg 2,6-dichloroindophenol (LaMotte Chemical Products Co., Chestertown, MD 21620) or 175 mg Na salt (Eastman Kodak Co.), or equivs, in H_2O and dil. to 1 L. Stdze against 0.01*N* $Na_2S_2O_3$ by titrg I liberated by 50 mL dye after addn of 10 mL 1*N* KI and 10 mL 4*N* H_2SO_4. Store in refrigerator. Prep. weekly.

(**f**) *Ascorbic acid soln*.—0.05*M*. Dissolve 880 mg L-ascorbic acid in 0.1*M* buffer, (**a**), and dil. to 100 mL. Prep. daily.

32.070 ***Preparation of Extract***

Comminute 50 g portions fresh or frozen vegetable tissue in high-speed blender with 200 mL cold 2% NaCl soln. Remove larger particles by filtering thru 15 cm (6") gauze-backed cotton milk filter. Assay filtrate within 30 min.

32.071 ***Determination***

Into 400 mL beaker place 75 mL buffer, (**a**), 50 mL dye, 5 mL ascorbic acid, and enough H_2O to make total vol. of 250 mL after addn of tissue ext and H_2O_2. Adjust to 25±0.5° by warming or cooling as necessary. Place beaker on mag. stirrer and stir mixt. 30 sec at speed just below that which would cause excessive aeration. From pipet add 1–3 mL ext (equiv. to 0.2–0.4 g tissue) and rapidly add 5 mL H_2O_2 from blowout pipet. Start stopwatch immediately on addn of H_2O_2. Continue mixing during addn of H_2O_2 and until first aliquot is removed.

Within 15–30 sec after adding H_2O_2, remove 25 mL aliquot of reaction mixt. with 25 mL rapid-flow pipet adjusted to empty by blowing out in 5 sec, and discharge into 5 mL oxalic acid soln in 125 mL erlenmeyer. Take 4–5 subsequent samples at 1 min intervals and blow out into other 125 mL flasks each contg 5 mL oxalic acid soln. Record time as time pipet is emptied. Titr. residual ascorbic acid with dye soln and calc. first order reaction rate const. Adjust enzyme activity so that const is of order of magnitude of 15–20 × 10^{-2} and express peroxidase activity, K_f, as K_1/g tissue used. Perform all titrns beyond fading end point to clearly visible pink, permanent 1 min. Adjust all titrns to same end point by comparison with first flask of each series. Add dye rapidly at first and more slowly later.

32.072 ***Calculation of K_1 and K_f***

Under optimal conditions, initial titrn value is 35–40 mL dye and subsequent titrn values decrease to 20–25 mL in 5 min. Calc. first order reaction rate const as for catalase, **32.068**, or take from slope of plot of log mL dye against time. Divide av. K_1 value for several intervals of time (0–1, 1–2, 2–3 min) by wt of vegetable tissue corresponding to vol. of ext in reaction mixt.

SELECTED REFERENCES

(*1*) JAOAC **61,** 1166(1978).
(*2*) JAOAC **47,** 492(1964).
(*3*) USDA Bur. Chem. Bull. **152,** 118(1911).
(*4*) JAOAC **21,** 244(1938); **22,** 370(1939).
(*5*) JAOAC **52,** 1050(1969); **55,** 809(1972).
(*6*) N.C.A. Bull. **27–L,** Revised 1966, p. 26; JAOAC **19,** 254(1936).
(*7*) JAOAC **49,** 287(1966); **50,** 787(1967); **51,** 796(1968); **53,** 720(1970).
(*8*) JAOAC **22,** 765(1939); **23,** 353(1940); **24,** 424(1941); **25,** 466(1942).
(*9*) JAOAC **54,** 471(1971); **57,** 1209(1974).
(*10*) JAOAC **56,** 164, 1030(1973).
(*11*) JAOAC **11,** 136(1928); **12,** 39(1929); **15,** 167(1932).
(*12*) JAOAC **50,** 701(1967); **52,** 416(1969).
(*13*) JAOAC **46,** 30(1963).
(*14*) FAO/WHO Food Standards Program CAC/RM 32-1970.
(*15*) JAOAC **54,** 52(1971).
(*16*) JAOAC **54,** 54(1971).
(*17*) JAOAC **57,** 701(1974).
(18) JAOAC **39,** 282(1956).
(*19*) JAOAC **30,** 76, 413(1947).
(*20*) JAOAC **46,** 712(1963).

33. Waters; and Salt

WATER

33.001 Specific Gravity—Official Final Action

Det. sp gr at 20/20°, using pycnometer, as in **9.011**.

Specific Conductance (*1, 2*)

33.002 ***Principle***

Conductivity of sample is compared with that of std KCl soln. Method is applicable to drinking, surface, and saline waters, and domestic and industrial wastes.

Synthetic H_2O samples contg increments of inorg. salts analyzed by 41 analysts in 17 laboratories showed following results:

Increment as sp conductance, μmhos/cm	Std deviation		Bias	
	%	μmhos/cm	%	μmhos/cm
100	7.6	7.55	−2.0	− 2.0
106	7.7	8.14	−0.8	− 0.8
808	7.5	66.1	−3.6	−29.3
848	9.4	79.6	−4.5	−38.5
1640	6.5	106	−5.4	−87.9
1710	7.0	119	−5.1	−86.9

33.003 ***Apparatus and Reagent***

(**a**) *Conductivity meter.*—Self-contained, Wheatstone bridge-type, capable of being read to ±1%.

(**b**) *Specific conductance cell.*—Choose cell according to expected sp conductance so that measured cell resistance is 500–10,000 ohms. Cell const should be ca 0.1 for solns of low conductivity (<100 μmhos), 1 for moderate, and 10 for highly conducting, such as brines. Check complete assembly with KCl solns of known conductance shown in Table **33:01**. Clean new cells with chromic acid cleaning soln and platinize new electrodes before use. Reclean and platinize electrodes whenever readings become erratic or if inspection shows any Pt black has flaked off. To platinize, connect both electrodes together to neg. terminal of 1.5 v dry cell and immerse in soln of 1 g chloroplatinic acid and 12 mg $Pb(OAc)_2$ in 100 mL H_2O. Connect pos. terminal to piece of Pt wire and dip into soln. Control current so that only small amt gas is evolved. Discontinue electrolysis when both electrodes are coated. Soln may be saved for subsequent use. Rinse electrodes thoroly and keep immersed in H_2O when not in use.

(**c**) *Potassium chloride std soln.*—0.01*M*. Dissolve 745.6 mg KCl in freshly boiled double-distd H_2O and dil. to 1 L at 25°. Soln has sp conductance of 1413 μmhos at 25°. It is satisfactory for most waters when using cell with const of 1–2. With other cells, use soln in Table **33:01** and corresponding sp conductance in calcn. Store in g-s Pyrex bottle.

33.004 ***Determination***

Temp. must be const thruout detn since sp conductance varies ca 2%/degree. Use 25° if possible; otherwise use near room temp. but between 20–30°.

Place 4 tubes std KCl soln and 2 tubes of each sample in H_2O bath and let stand 30 min. Rinse cell in 3 tubes of KCl soln and measure resistance of soln 4, R_{KCl}. Rinse cell thoroly with tube 1 of sample and measure resistance of tube 2, R_s. Do not repeat measurement of KCl soln unless temp. drift of more than few tenths degree occurs. If samples differ in conductivity by factor of ≥5, minimize carry-over by rinsing in 2 tubes of sample and measuring third.

33.005 ***Calculation***

Calc. cell const, *C*, in mhos/cm = R_{KCl} × 0.001413 at 25°. Specific conductance of sample at 25° = C/R_s in mhos/cm. Multiply by 10^6 to obtain μmhos/cm.

If temp. is not exactly 25°, measure R_{KCl} and R_s at same temp. and calc. sp conductance = 1413 × R_{KCl}/R_s in μmhos/cm.

pH (*1, 2*)

33.006 ***Principle***

pH, which is accepted measure of acidity or alky, is detd by change in potential of glass-satd calomel electrodes, as measured by com. app. stdzd against std buffer solns whose pH values are assigned by NBS. pH of most natural H_2O falls within 4–9. Majority of waters are slightly basic from presence of CO_3-HCO_3 system.

Table 33:01 Conductances of KCl Solns at 25°

Concn, *M*	Conductance, μmhos/cm	
	Equiv.	Specific
0	149.85	
0.0001	149.43	14.94
0.0005	147.81	73.90
0.001	146.95	147.0
0.005	143.55	717.8
0.01	141.27	1,413
0.02	138.34	2,767
0.05	133.37	6,668
0.1	128.96	12,900
0.2	124.08	24,820
0.5	117.27	58,640
1.0	111.87	111,900

Method is applicable to drinking, surface, and saline waters, and domestic and industrial wastes. Oils and greases, by coating electrodes, may cause sluggish response.

Buffered synthetic H_2O samples analyzed by 44 analysts in 20 laboratories showed following results:

pH	Std deviation, pH units	Bias, pH units
3.5	0.10	−0.01
3.5	0.11	0.00
7.1	0.20	+0.07
7.2	0.18	−0.002
8.0	0.13	−0.01
8.0	0.12	+0.01

33.007 ***Apparatus and Reagent***

(**a**) *pH meter.*—Com. instrument with flow-type electrodes (preferred for relatively unbuffered samples such as condensates) or immersion electrodes. Operate in accordance with manufacturer's instructions.

(**b**) *Std buffer solns.*—*See* **50.007** and Table **50:02**.

33.008 ***Determination***

Thoroly wet electrodes and prep. in accordance with manufacturer's instructions. Stdze instrument with std buffer with pH near that of sample and then with 2 others to check linearity of electrode response.

Analyze sample as soon as possible, preferably within few hr. Do not open sample bottle before analysis. With immersion electrodes, wash 6–8 times with portions of sample, particularly when unbuffered soln follows buffered soln. Equilibrium, as shown by absence of drift, must be established before readings are accepted.

Acidity (*1, 2*)

33.009 ***Principle***

Sample is titrd to pH 8.3, using phthln as indicator, and results are reported as mg $CaCO_3$/L. Method is applicable to drinking and surface waters, domestic and industrial wastes, and saline waters. Synthetic H_2O contg increments of HCO_3 analyzed by 40 analysts in 17 laboratories showed following results:

Added,	Std deviation		Bias	
mg $CaCO_3$/L	%	mg $CaCO_3$/L	%	mg $CaCO_3$/L
20	9.0	1.79	+2.8	+0.55
21	8.2	1.73	+0.5	+0.11

33.010 ***Apparatus***

(**a**) *Illumination.*—Daytime fluorescent lamps provide uniform lighting conditions.

(**b**) *Potentiometric equipment.*—Automatic titrators and pH meters, suitably calibrated, may be substituted for visual titrn and end point.

33.011 ***Reagents***

(**a**) *Carbon dioxide-free water.*—If pH is <6.0, prep. as in **50.033(a)**. Deionized H_2O may be substituted if conductance is <2 μmhos/cm and pH >6.0.

(**b**) *Sodium hydroxide std soln.*—0.02*N*. Dil. 20.0 mL 1*N* NaOH with CO_2-free H_2O to 1 L. Store in tightly stoppered Pyrex bottle protected by soda-lime tube. Prep. weekly. Stdze against 0.0200*N* KH phthalate soln (4.085 g/L) or against stdzd 0.02*N* HCl or H_2SO_4. Use vol. soln to give acidity approx. that of samples titrd, dild to vol. of sample, with same vol. indicator, and same time intervals as in detn. 1 mL 0.0200*N* NaOH = 1.00 mg $CaCO_3$/1.00 mL.

33.012 ***Preparation of Samples***

Collect and store samples in Pyrex or polyethylene bottles. Refrigerate at 4° and perform detn as soon as possible, preferably within 24 hr.

33.013 ***Determination***

Use sample vol. requiring <25 mL titrant. If indicator is used, remove free Cl with 1 drop 0.1*N* $Na_2S_2O_3$, **50.037**.

To 50 or 100 mL sample in white porcelain casserole or in erlenmeyer over white surface, add 0.15 mL phthln. Titr. with stdzd 0.02*N* NaOH to faint pink (pH 8.3).

mg $CaCO_3$/L = mL NaOH × normality NaOH × 50,000/mL sample.

Alkalinity (*1, 2*)

33.014 ***Principle***

Unaltered (undild, unconcd, unfiltered) sample is titrd potentiometrically to pH 4.5. Applicable to drinking and surface waters, domestic and industrial wastes, and saline waters. Suitable for all concn ranges.

Synthetic H_2O contg increments of HCO_3 analyzed by 40 analysts in 17 laboratories showed following results:

Added,	Std deviation		Bias	
mg $CaCO_3$/L	%	mg $CaCO_3$/L	%	mg $CaCO_3$/L
8	16	1.3	+10.6	+0.85
9	12	1.1	+22.3	+2.0
113	4.7	5.3	− 8.2	−9.3
119	4.5	5.4	− 7.4	−8.8

33.015 ***Apparatus***

See **33.010(b)**.

33.016 ***Reagents***

(**a**) *Carbon dioxide-free water.*—*See* **33.011(a)**.

(**b**) *Acid std soln.*—0.02*N*. Prep. ca 0.1*N* stock soln by dilg 8.3 mL HCl or 2.8 mL H_2SO_4 to 1 L. Dil. 200 mL stock soln to 1 L with CO_2-free H_2O. Stdze against 0.02*N* Na_2CO_3 (1.060 g Na_2CO_3/L, **50.016(c)**) or stdzd 0.02*N* NaOH, **33.011(b)**. Use vol. soln to give alky approx. that of samples titrd, dild to vol. of sample, with same vol. indicator and same time intervals as in detn. 1 mL 0.02*N* acid = 1.00 mg $CaCO_3$/L.

33.017 ***Preparation of Samples***

See **33.012**.

33.018 ***Determination***

Use sample vol. requiring <25 mL titrant. Titr. potentiometrically to pH 4.5.

mg $CaCO_3$/L = ml acid × normality acid × 50,000/ mL sample.

Biochemical Oxygen Demand (BOD) (*1, 3*)

33.019 ***Principle***

Sample is incubated 5 days at 20° in presence of acclimated biological system. Comparison of O content of sample at beginning and end of incubation is measure of BOD.

Method is applicable to raw or treated domestic wastes, industrial water, and industrial waste water. Following classes of materials exert O demand: (*1*) org. material usable as food by aerobic organisms (source of BOD of many waste waters); (*2*) oxidizable N from nitrites, NH_3, and org. N compds which serve as food for specific bacteria (e.g., *Nitrosomonas* and *Nitrobacter*) (a source of some of O demand of biologically treated effluents); (*3*) chemically oxidizable materials (e.g., Fe^{+2}, S^{-2}, SO_3^{-2}) (when present, test must be based upon calcd initial dissolved O content).

Many synthetic org. components of industrial wastes are not degraded by common organisms. Without special seeding material, effect is manifested as retardation of aerobic metabolism because of toxic effect or deficiency or absence of appropriate microorganism. Toxic compds in distd H_2O, frequently Cu, may result in low BOD.

Distd H_2O contg known increments of oxidizable org. material analyzed by 74 analysts in 50 laboratories showed following results:

Increment org. material,	Std deviation		Bias	
mg/L	%	mg/L	%	mg/L
2.2	33	0.7	− 4	− 0.08
194	15	26	−10	−19

33.020 ***Apparatus***

(**a**) *Incubation bottles.*—250 or 300 mL with glass stoppers.

(**b**) *Incubator.*—Air or H_2O bath maintained at 20±1° and which excludes light. (*Caution:* Check H_2O bath to assure that it is electrically grounded.)

33.021 ***Reagents***

(**a**) *Water.*—Contg ≤0.01 mg Cu/L, obtained by double demineralization of distd H_2O or distn from all-glass or Sn-lined system.

(**b**) *Calcium chloride soln.*—27.5 g anhyd. $CaCl_2$/L.

(**c**) *Ferric chloride soln.*—0.25 g $FeCl_3.6H_2O$/L.

(**d**) *Magnesium sulfate soln.*—22.5 g $MgSO_4.7H_2O$/L.

(**e**) *Phosphate buffer soln.*—pH 7.2. Dissolve 8.50 g KH_2PO_4, 21.75 g K_2HPO_4, 33.40 g $Na_2HPO_4.7H_2O$, and 1.70 g NH_4Cl in ca 500 mL H_2O and dil. to 1 L.

(**f**) *Seeding material.*—Satisfactory seed may sometimes be obtained or developed from supernate of domestic sewage stored 24–36 hr at 20°, from receiving H_2O downstream from point of discharge, or, in case of industrial wastes contg org. compds not amenable to oxidn by domestic sewage seed, from acclimated seed developed in laboratory.

(**g**) *Sodium hydroxide soln.*—50 g NaOH/L.

(**h**) *Sodium sulfite soln.*—1.575 g Na_2SO_3/L. Prep. fresh as needed.

33.022 ***Preparation of Dilution Water***

Store H_2O, **33.021(a)**, in cotton-plugged bottles long enough to sat. with atm. O at 20°, or aerate with air filtered to remove any oil from compressor (≤1 hr may be required for 19 L (5 gal.)). Add desired vol. of O-satd H_2O to suitable bottle and add 1 mL each of phosphate buffer, $MgSO_4$, $CaCl_2$, and $FeCl_3$ solns/L. Seed this diln H_2O with seeding material and with vol. found by experience to be most satisfactory for particular waste being examined. Use seeded diln H_2O within 24 hr of prepn.

Periodically check quality of diln H_2O, effectiveness of seed, and technic with particular org. compd if known to be present in waste or, for general work, with mixt. of glucose and glutamic acid (150 mg each/ L) which should show BOD ca 220±30 mg/L in 95% of detns. Appreciable divergence requires examination of quality of H_2O, viability of seeding material, or technic.

33.023 ***Preparation of Samples***

Keep time between collection of sample and start of analysis to absolute min. Protect samples from atm. O. If necessary, pretreat samples as follows:

(**a**) *Acidity or caustic alkalinity.*—Neutze to ca pH 7 with dil. H_2SO_4 or 5% NaOH, using pH meter or bromothymol blue as external indicator. pH of seeded diln H_2O should not be changed by diln of sample.

(**b**) *Residual chlorine.*—Let stand 1–2 hr to dissipate Cl. If not effective, use Na_2SO_3 treatment. Det. vol. to be used by adding 10 mL HOAc (1+1) or H_2SO_4 (1+49) and 10 mL 10% KI to 1 L sample. Titr. to starch-I end point with Na_2SO_3 soln. Add indicated vol. to sample, and test small portion with starch-I soln to check that treatment is complete.

(**c**) *Toxic substances.*—Remove or neutze. Test for toxicity as follows: Add same amt seed to duplicate set of BOD bottles. Add diln H_2O to each bottle, leaving room for amt of sample to give final concns of 0.06, 0.12, 0.25, 0.50, 1.0, 2.5, 5, 10, 20, and 40%. Neutze sample, add required vol. sample to duplicate bottles, and fill with diln H_2O. Det. dissolved O in 1 series ca 15 min after prepn of diln. Det. dissolved O in second series after 3 days. Plot consumption of dissolved O against concn. Magnitude of O concn change will depend on amt of food available and toxicity of sample. If toxicity is factor, O consumption will decrease at higher concns.

(**d**) *Supersaturation with oxygen.*—Samples contg >9.2 mg O/L at 20° may be encountered during winter or where algae are actively growing. To prevent loss of O during incubation, reduce O content to satn by transferring sample at ca 20° to partially fill bottle and shake vigorously.

33.024 ***Determination***

Sample must be dild with seeded diln H_2O so that at least 1 diln will achieve dissolved O depletion of 1 mg/ L (ppm) during 5 day test period but will not reduce residual dissolved O to <1 mg/L. (Preliminary chemical O demand (COD) detn, **33.034–33.040**, may serve as guide to est. range of BOD.)

Carefully siphon seeded diln H_2O into 1 or 2 L graduate, filling it ½ full. Add vol. of carefully mixed sample to desired diln and fill to mark with diln H_2O. Mix well with plunger-type mixing rod, avoiding entrainment of air. If possible BOD range is large, prep. geometric series of dilns to cover possible range. Siphon, with continued mixing, dild sample to completely fill 3 BOD bottles—1 for incubation, 1 for detn of dissolved O content, and 1 for detn of immediate dissolved O demand (IDOD). Insert stoppers without entrainment of any bubbles. Det. dissolved O by method indicated in **33.027**.

Alternatively, prep. dild samples directly by pipetting sample with wide-tip pipet into BOD bottles of known capacity and filling bottles with seeded diln H_2O. If diln >1:100 is required, prep. in graduate before adding to BOD bottles.

Prep. blank of seeded diln H_2O contg vol. used for diln of samples for detn of initial dissolved O content. Prep. control of 2 BOD bottles with unseeded diln H_2O. Stopper and H_2O-seal 1 bottle for incubation. (If special H_2O-sealed bottles are not used, H_2O-seal by immersion in tray of H_2O.) Det. dissolved O in other bottle before incubation. Quality of unseeded diln H_2O is satisfactory if depletion obtained is ≤0.2 mg/L, preferably ≤0.1. Do not use this value as blank correction.

If diln H_2O is seeded, det. O depletion of seed used in such diln that will result in 40–70% depletion in 5 days. Use this depletion, not seeded blank, to calc. correction due to small amt of seed in diln H_2O.

Incubate prepd mixts, H_2O-sealed, 5 days at 20±1° and det. final dissolved O content.

33.025 ***Calculation***

Calc. in mg/L (ppm) as follows:

Immediate dissolved O demand ($IDOD$) = $(D_C - D_1)/P$.

When seeding is not required, $BOD = (D_1 - D_2)/P$.

When using seeded diln H_2O, $BOD = [(D_1 - D_2) - (B_1 - B_2)f]/P$.

Including $IDOD$, if small or not detd, $BOD = (D_C - D_2)/P$.

Where

D_0 = dissolved O (DO) of original diln H_2O,

D_1 = DO in dild sample 15 min after prepn,

D_2 = DO of dild sample after incubation,

S = DO of original undild sample,

D_C = DO available in diln at zero time = $(D_0p) + SP$,

p = decimal fraction of diln H_2O used,

P = decimal fraction of sample used,

B_1 = DO of the diln of seed control before incubation,

B_2 = DO of the diln of seed control after incubation,

f = ratio of seed in sample to seed in control = (% seed in D_1)/(% seed in B_1).

33.026 ***Interpretation***

Arbitrary std 5 day incubation period is satisfactory measurement of the O load on receiving water for raw or treated domestic sewage. It may be misleading for wastes contg org. compds not easily amenable to biological oxidn. Studies with 3 incubation periods on series of dilns of the waste will provide information on lag periods, suitability of inocula, rate of biochem. oxidn, ultimate O demand, and amenability to biochem. self-purification. Particularly important is ratio of 5 day BOD to ultimate O demand.

Dissolved Oxygen (*1*)

(*Caution: See* **51.018**.)

33.027 ***Applications***

Azide (Alsterberg) method is ordinarly used; it is not affected by most common interference, nitrite, but most other oxidizing or reducing agents should be absent. Effect of Fe^{+3} is eliminated with F^-. Permanganate (Rideal-Stewart) method is used in presence of Fe^{+2} but not org. matter. Pomeroy-Kirshman-Alsterberg method is used for waters supersatd with O or contg high org. matter content.

Method I, Azide Method

33.028 ***Reagents***

(**a**) *Alkaline iodide-sodium azide soln.*—Dissolve 500 g NaOH (or 700 g KOH) and 135 g NaI (or 150 g KI) in H_2O, dil. to 950 mL, and cool. Slowly, with stirring, add soln of 10 g NaN_3 in 40 mL H_2O. Dild and acidified soln must not give color with starch indicator. Store in dark bottle with rubber stopper.

(**b**) *Manganese sulfate soln.*—Dissolve 364 g $MnSO_4.H_2O$ in H_2O, filter, and dil. to 1 L. No more than trace of I should be liberated when soln is added to acidified KI soln.

(**c**) *Potassium biiodate std soln.*—0.025*N*. Dissolve 0.8125 g $KH(IO_3)_2$ in H_2O in 1 L vol. flask and dil. to vol.

(**d**) *Potassium fluoride soln.*—40 g $KF.2H_2O$/100 mL. (*Caution:* KF is toxic and corrosive. *See* **51.084**.)

(**e**) *Sodium thiosulfate std solns.*—(*1*) *0.1N*.—Dissolve 25 g $Na_2S_2O_3.5H_2O$ in H_2O, add 1 g NaOH or 5 mL $CHCl_3$, and dil. to 1 L. Stdze against $KH(IO_3)_2$ or $K_2Cr_2O_7$, **50.038**. (*2*) *0.025N*.—Dil. 250 mL 0.1*N* to 1 L. 1 mL = 0.2 mg O.

(**f**) *Starch indicator soln.*—Disperse 5–6 g potato or arrowroot starch in mortar with few mL H_2O. Pour into 1 L boiling H_2O, boil few min, and let settle overnight. Decant clear soln and preserve with 1.3 g salicylic acid or few drops toluene.

33.029 ***Determination***

(Add all reagents, except H_2SO_4, well below surface of sample from 10 mL pipets graduated in 0.1 mL, with tips elongated ca 50 mm.)

Add 2.0 mL $MnSO_4$ soln and 2.0 mL alk. I-NaN_3 soln to sample in 250 or 300 mL BOD bottle, replace stopper, excluding air bubbles, and invert several times to mix. Let floc settle and repeat mixing. (Water with high chloride concn requires 10 min contact with ppt.) After floc has settled, leaving ≥100 mL clear supernate, remove stopper and add 2.0 mL H_2SO_4 down neck of bottle. (If >100 ppm Fe^{+3} is present, add 1.0 mL KF soln before acidifying.) Restopper and mix by inversion until I_2 is uniformly distributed. Immediately titr. 203 mL (3 mL is allowance for added reagents) with 0.025*N* $Na_2S_2O_3$ to pale straw yellow. Add 1–2 mL starch indicator and titr. to disappearance of blue. Disregard reappearance of blue.

ppm dissolved O = (mL 0.025*N* $Na_2S_2O_3$ × 0.2/200) × 1000.

Method II, Permanganate Method

33.030 ***Reagents***

(**a**) *Alkaline iodide soln.*—Prep. as in **33.028(a)**, except omit NaN_3.

(**b**) *Potassium oxalate soln.*—2%. Dissolve 2 g $K_2C_2O_4.H_2O$ in 100 mL H_2O. 1 mL equiv. to 1.1 mL $KMnO_4$ soln, (**c**).

(**c**) *Potassium permanganate soln.*—6.3 g/L.

33.031 ***Determination***

Add to sample 0.70 mL H_2SO_4 and then 1.0 mL $KMnO_4$ soln. If sample is high in Fe, also add 1.0 mL KF soln, **33.028(d)**. If necessary, add addnl $KMnO_4$ soln to maintain violet tinge 5 min. (If >5 mL is required, prep. stronger $KMnO_4$ soln to avoid diln of sample.) After 5 min, decolorize with just enough oxalate soln (usually 0.5–1.0 mL) within 2–10 min. Add 2.0 mL $MnSO_4$ soln, **33.028(b)**, and 3.0 mL alk. I_2 soln, **33.030(a)**. Stopper bottle and mix. Let ppt settle, remix 20 sec, and let settle until ≥100 mL clear supernate is present. Acidify with 2.0 mL H_2SO_4. Titr., using vol. of 205 mL, and calc. as in **33.029**.

Method III, Pomeroy-Kirshman-Alsterberg Method

33.032 ***Reagent***

Alkaline iodide-sodium azide soln.—Dissolve 400 g NaOH in 500 mL freshly boiled and cooled H_2O. Cool slightly and then add 900 g NaI; mix. Dissolve 10 g NaN_3 in 40 mL H_2O. Add slowly, with stirring, to alk. I_2 soln, bringing total vol. to ≥1 L.

33.033 ***Determination***

To sample add 2.0 mL $MnSO_4$ soln, **33.028(b)**, and 2.0 mL alk. I_2-NaN_3 soln, **33.032**. Stopper and mix by inversion. After ppt has settled, add 2.0 mL H_2SO_4 and mix. Titr., using vol. of 203 mL, and calc. as in **33.029**.

Chemical Oxygen Demand (COD) (*1, 3*)

33.034 ***Principle***

Org. substances are oxidized by $K_2Cr_2O_7$ in H_2SO_4 (1+1) at reflux temp. with Ag_2SO_4 as catalyst and $HgSO_4$ to remove Cl interference. Excess dichromate is titrd with Fe^{+2}, using ortho-phenanthroline as indicator. Method is independent detn of org. matter in sample and has no definable relationship to biological oxygen demand (BOD).

Method is applicable to surface and saline waters and industrial wastes. Apply *Method I*, using 0.25*N* reagents, to samples contg >50 mg COD/L; apply low level modification, *Method II*, using 0.025*N* reagents, to samples in range 5–50 mg/L; apply special modification, *Method III*, to saline waters contg >1000 mg Cl/L and >250 mg COD/L.

Org. matter from glassware, atm., and distd H_2O must be excluded. Condition glassware by using it for blank detn to eliminate org. matter.

Distd H_2O contg known increments of oxidizable org. material analyzed by 89 analysts in 58 laboratories showed following results:

Increment org. material, mg/L	Std deviation		Bias	
	%	mg/L	%	mg/L
12.3	34	4	0	0
270	7	18	−2	−5

33.035 ***Preparation of Sample***

Collect samples in glass bottles if possible; plastic may be used if it contributes no org. material to sample. Test biologically active samples as soon as possible. Mix or homogenize samples contg settleable materials. Samples may be preserved with H_2SO_4, 2 mL/L.

33.036 ***Apparatus and Reagents***

(**a**) *Reflux apparatus.*—500 mL erlenmeyer or 300 mL r-b flask with ₸ joint connected to 30 cm (12") Allihn condenser.

(**b**) *Distilled water.*—Low in org. matter. Ordinary distd H_2O is satisfactory; do not use deionized H_2O.

(**c**) *Potassium dichromate std solns.*—(*1*) *0.25N.*—Dissolve 12.259 g $K_2Cr_2O_7$, primary std grade, previously dried 2 hr at 103°, in distd H_2O and dil. to 1 L. (*2*) *0.025N.*—Dil. 100 mL 0.25*N* to 1 L with H_2O.

(**d**) *Sulfuric acid reagent.*—Dissolve 23.5 g Ag_2SO_4 in 9 lb (4.1 kg) bottle H_2SO_4. (1–2 days may be required for dissoln.)

(**e**) *Ferrous ammonium sulfate std soln.*—(*1*) *0.25N.*—Dissolve 98 g $Fe(NH_4)_2(SO_4)_2.6H_2O$ in H_2O, add 20 mL H_2SO_4, cool, and dil. to 1 L. Stdze daily against 0.25*N* $K_2Cr_2O_7$, (**c**)(*1*). (*2*) *0.025N.*—Dil. 100 mL 0.25*N* to 1 L with H_2O. Stdze daily against 0.025*N* $K_2Cr_2O_7$, (**c**)(*2*).

(**f**) *Phenanthroline ferrous sulfate (ferroin) indicator soln.*—Dissolve 1.48 g 1,10-(ortho)-phenanthroline.H_2O and 0.70 g $FeSO_4.7H_2O$ in 100 mL H_2O.

33.037 ***Standardization of Ferrous Solutions***

(**a**) *Concentrated soln.*—Dil. 25.0 mL 0.25*N* $K_2Cr_2O_7$, (**c**)(*1*), to ca 250 mL with H_2O. Add 75 mL H_2SO_4 and cool. Titr. with 0.25*N* $Fe(NH_4)_2(SO_4)_2$, using 10 drops ferroin indicator. Normality = (mL $K_2Cr_2O_7$ × normality)/mL $Fe(NH_4)_2(SO_4)_2$.

(**b**) *Dilute soln.*—To 15 mL H_2O add 10.0 mL 0.025*N* $K_2Cr_2O_7$, (**c**)(*2*). Add 20 mL H_2SO_4 and cool. Titr. with 0.025*N* $Fe(NH_4)_2(SO_4)_2$, using 1 drop ferroin indicator. Blue-green to reddish brown color change is sharp. Calc. normality as in (**a**).

33.038 ***Method I—High Level***

(*Caution: See* **51.065** and **51.079**.)

Place several boiling chips and 1 g $HgSO_4$ in reflux flask. Add 5.0 mL H_2SO_4 and swirl until $HgSO_4$ dissolves. Place in ice bath and slowly add, with swirling, 25.0 mL 0.25*N* $K_2Cr_2O_7$. Slowly, and with swirling, add 70.0 mL H_2SO_4-Ag_2SO_4 reagent. While still in bath, pipet in 50 mL sample (or aliquot dild to 50 mL) with continuous mixing. Attach condenser and reflux 2 hr. (Shorter period may be used on waste H_2O of const or known composition where time of max. oxidn has been detd previously.)

Cool, and wash down condenser with ca 25 mL H_2O. If r-b flask has been used, quant. transfer soln to 500 mL erlenmeyer. Dil. to ca 300 mL with H_2O, and let cool to ca room temp. Add 8–10 drops ferroin indicator, and titr. excess $K_2Cr_2O_7$ with 0.25*N* $Fe(NH_4)_2(SO_4)_2$ to sharp, reddish end point (*S* mL). Perform blank detn with all reagents, including refluxing, on distd H_2O in place of sample and det. mL 0.25*N* $Fe(NH_4)_2(SO_4)_2$ required (*B* mL).

$$\text{mg COD/L} = (B - S) \times N \times 8000/V,$$

where *N* = normality $Fe(NH_4)_2(SO_4)_2$ soln and *V* = vol. sample used.

33.039 ***Method II—Low Level***

Proceed as in high level detn, **33.038**, except use 0.025*N* $K_2Cr_2O_7$ and $Fe(NH_4)_2(SO_4)_2$.

33.040 ***Method III—Saline Waters***

Pipet 50 mL sample of 250–800 mg COD/L and Cl^- >1000 mg/L (or aliquot dild to 50 mL with *distd* H_2O having Cl^- concn equal to that of sample) into 500 mL erlenmeyer and add 25.0 mL 0.25*N* $K_2Cr_2O_7$ and 5.0 mL H_2SO_4. Add 10 mg $HgSO_4$/mg Cl in sample and swirl until dissolved. Carefully add 70.0 mL H_2SO_4-Ag_2SO_4 reagent with swirling. Add several boiling chips, attach condenser, and reflux 2 hr. (If volatile org. compds are present in sample, attach condenser prior to addn of H_2SO_4-Ag_2SO_4 reagent and add reagent thru condenser while cooling flask in ice bath.)

Cool, and proceed as in low level detn, **33.039**, including blank. Disregard reappearance of blue-green after end point is reached.

For saline waters, prep. std curve of COD against mg Cl^-/L, using NaCl solns with intervals of ≤4000 up to 20,000 mg Cl^-/L, carried thru entire detn.

$$\text{COD, mg/L} = [(B - S) \times N \times 8000 - 50D] \times 1.20/V,$$

where *D* = Cl^- correction from std curve, and 1.20 is compensation factor to account for extent of Cl^- oxidn which is dissimilar in org. and inorg. systems. Other symbols are defined in **33.038**.

33.041 Total Solids—Official Final Action

Thoroly shake sample, and pipet 100 mL unfiltered sample into weighed Pt dish. If sample contains much suspended matter, shake, pour rapidly into 100 mL graduate, and immediately transfer to weighed Pt dish. Evap. to dryness and heat to const wt at 100°.

33.042 Solids in Solution—Official Final Action

Let sample stand until all sediment settles and filter if necessary to secure perfectly clear liq. (Occasionally, clear filtrate can be obtained only by use of alumina cream, **31.021(b)**; avoid if possible.) Evap. 100–250 mL to dryness in weighed Pt dish. Heat to const wt at 100°.

33.043 Ignited Residue—Official Final Action

Ignite residue from **33.041** at 525–550° in furnace or over burner until dish shows dull red glow and ash is white or nearly so. Note any odor or change in color produced during ignition. Det. wt ignited residue and calc. loss on ignition.

Organic Carbon (*1, 3*)

33.044 ***Principle***

Carbonaceous material of water sample is oxidized to CO_2 in stream of O or air in catalytic combustion tube at 950°. Calibrated IR analyzer measures CO_2.

Method is applicable to 1–150 mg org. C in surface and saline waters and domestic and industrial wastes. Preliminary treatment of sample defines type of C measured: (*1*) sol., nonvolatile org. C (e.g., natural sugars); (*2*) sol., volatile org. C (e.g., mercaptans); (*3*) insol., partially volatile C (e.g., oils); (*4*) insol., particulate carbonaceous materials (e.g., cellulose fibers); (*5*) sol. or insol. carbonaceous materials adsorbed or entrapped on insol. inorg. suspended matter (e.g., oily matter adsorbed on silt particles).

Since usefulness of method is in assessing potential O-demanding load of org. material, CO_3 and HCO_3 carbon must be removed before analysis or subtracted from final result.

Distd H_2O analyzed by 28 analysts in 21 laboratories showed following results on exact increments of oxidizable org. compds:

Added total org. C, mg/L	Std deviation		Bias	
	%	mg/L	%	mg/L
4.9	80	3.9	+15	0.75
107	8	8.3	+ 1	1.1

33.045 ***Preparation of Sample***

Glass bottles are preferable storage containers but polyethylene and Cubitainers (Hedwin Corp., 1209 E Lincoln Way, La

Port, IN 46390) may be used if tests show no contribution of C to samples. Keep interval between collection and analysis at min., store at 4°, and protect from light and O. If samples cannot be analyzed within 2 hr, acidify to pH <2 with HCl or H_2SO_4.

33.046 ***Apparatus***

(**a**) *Organic carbon analyzer.*—Dow-Beckman Carbonaceous Analyzer (single channel) or Model No. 915 (dual channel) (Beckman Instruments), or equiv., with air pump, purification train, flow controls, nondispersive-type IR stream analyzer specific for CO_2, and recorder.

(**b**) *Syringes.*—(*1*) 0–50 μL, needle opening ca 150 μm, Hamilton No. 705N, or equiv.; (*2*) 0–500 μL, needle opening ca 400 μm, for samples with large particulates, Hamilton No. 750N, or equiv.; or (*3*) push button syringes which ensure uniformity of injection rate, 20 or 200 μL size, Hamilton No. CR700-20 or CR700-200, or equiv.

33.047 ***Reagents***

(*Caution: See* **51.086**.)

(**a**) *Water.*—For diln of samples and prepn of stds, blanks, and reagents. Use CO_2-free, double distd H_2O; do not use H_2O purified by ion exchange.

(**b**) *Organic carbon std solns.*—(*1*) *Stock phthalate soln.*—1000 mg C/L. Dissolve 0.2128 g KH phthalate, **50.033(c)**, in H_2O, and dil. to 100 mL. (*2*) *Working solns.*—Prep. solns contg 10, 20, 30, 40, 50, 60, 80, and 100 mg C/L by dilg 1.0, 2.0, 3.0, 4.0, 5.0, 6.0, 8.0, and 10.0 mL stock soln to 100 mL with H_2O.

(**c**) *Carbonate carbon std solns.*—(*1*) *Stock soln.*— 1000 mg C/L. Dissolve 0.3500 g $NaHCO_3$ and 0.4418 g Na_2CO_3 in H_2O and dil. to 100 mL. (*2*) *Working solns.*—Prep. identical series with concns as in (**b**)(*2*).

(**d**) *Packing for total carbon tube.*—Dissolve 20 g $Co(NO_3)_2.6H_2O$ in 50 mL H_2O and add to 15 g long fiber asbestos in porcelain evapg dish. Mix, and evap. to dryness on steam bath. Place in cold furnace, heat to 950°, and hold at this temp. 1–2 hr. Cool, break up any lumps, and mix adequately but not excessively. With combustion tube held vertically, taper joint up, add ca 1 cm untreated asbestos and then ca 1 g catalyst transferred in small amts with forceps. As it is added, tap or push material with 6 mm glass rod, using only wt of rod to compress material. Do not force packing. When completed, length of packing should be ca 5–6 cm. Test packed tube by measuring flow rate of gas thru it at room temp. and at 950°. Rate should drop <20%.

(**e**) *Packing for carbonate tube* (*dual channel instrument*).—Place small wad of quartz wool or asbestos near exit of carbonate evolution tube. From entrance end add 6–12 mesh quartz chips to length of 10 cm. Add H_3PO_4 while holding tube vertically and let excess drain.

33.048 ***Adjustment of Instrument***

Turn on IR analyzer, recorder, and furnaces, setting total C furnace at 950° and carbonate furnace at 175°. Let warm up >2 hr; leave on continuously for daily operation. Adjust O flow to 80–100 mL/min thru total C tube. With recorder set at appropriate mv range, adjust amplifier gain so that 20 μL sample of 100 mg C/L std gives peak ht ca half scale. Noise level should be <0.5% full scale; if higher, analyzer or recorder may need servicing.

If single channel unit is equipped with large diam. combustion tube and dual channel unit with Hastalloy tube for total C channel, use 100 μL sample in range 1–30 mg C/L.

33.049 ***Calibration***

(**a**) *Dual channel instrument.*—Rinse syringe several times with std soln, fill, and adjust to 20 μL. Wipe off excess with soft paper tissue, taking care that no lint adheres to needle. Remove plug from syringe holder, insert syringe, and inject soln into tube with single, rapid movement of index finger. Leave syringe in holder until flow rate returns to normal; then replace it with plug. Run duplicate detns on each std soln and on blank. Read ht of each peak. Let recorder return to baseline between injections. Subtract blank from each peak and prep. std curve of corrected peak ht against mg C/L.

Turn 4-way valve to direct flow thru low temp. tube and analyzer. Adjust flow to 80–100 mL/min and let baseline stabilize. Inject in duplicate 20 μL each of 20, 40, 60, 80, and 100 mg inorg. C/L std solns and blank. Prep. std curve of corrected peak ht against mg inorg. C/L.

(**b**) *Single channel instrument.*—Prep. std curve as in (**a**), par. 1.

33.050 ***Determination***

(**a**) *Dual channel instrument.*—Mix sample thoroly and dil. to bring C content within range of std curve. Inject 20 μL sample in duplicate as in **33.049(a)** and det. peak hts corresponding to total and inorg. C. Convert to concn and subtract inorg. C from total C to obtain total org. C. Results may be verified by operating unit as single channel system, injecting acidified, N-purged sample into high temp. furnace, and comparing results.

Filter 100 mL aliquot sample thru prerinsed 0.45 μm fritted glass filter and repeat detn to obtain dissolved C values. Subtract dissolved or inorg. C to obtain dissolved org. C. Results may be verified by operating unit as single channel system, injecting acidified, N-purged, filtered sample into high temp. furnace, and comparing results.

(**b**) *Single channel instrument.*—Transfer 10–15 mL sample to 30 mL beaker. If sample is not acid-preserved, add 2 drops HCl to reduce pH to ≤2 and purge with CO_2-free N ca 5–10 min. (Do not use plastic tubing.) Place beaker on mag. stirrer and withdraw 20 μL aliquot while stirring. Inject as in **33.049(a)**. Prep. and inject filtered samples. Calc. total, inorg., and dissolved C as in (**a**).

Total Nitrogen—Kjeldahl Method (*1, 4*)

33.051 ***Principle***

Sample is digested with H_2SO_4 to convert org. N to NH_3, which is distd after alkalinization and detd by nesslerization or titrimetry. Preserve samples by addn of 40 mg $HgCl_2$/L and store at 4°. Analyze as soon as possible, as conversion of org. N to NH_3 may occur even with preservation.

Method is applicable to surface and saline waters and domestic and industrial wastes. Some industrial wastes contg materials such as amines, nitro compds, hydrazones, oximes, semicarbazones, and some refractory tertiary amines may not be converted to NH_3.

Natural H_2O analyzed by 31 analysts in 20 laboratories showed the following results on exact increments of org. N:

Method	Added, mg N/L	Std deviation		Bias	
		%	mg N/L	%	mg N/L
Colorm.	0.20	100	0.20	+15.5	0.03
Colorm.	0.31	81	0.25	+ 5.5	0.02
Titr.	4.10	26	1.06	+ 1.0	0.04
Titr.	4.61	26	1.19	− 1.7	−0.08

33.052 ***Apparatus***

(**a**) *Digestion apparatus.—See* **2.056**(**a**).

(**b**) *Distillation apparatus.—See* **2.056**(**b**); or use all-glass app. with 800 or 1000 mL distg flask and 500 mL g-s erlenmeyers, marked at 350 and 500 mL, as receivers. Prep. for use by distg mix.. ‿. NaOH-$Na_2S_2O_3$ soln and H_2O (1+1) until distillate is NH_3-free by Nessler reagent, (**j**). Repeat each time app. is out of service ≥4 hr.

(**c**) *Nessler tubes.*—Matched, ca 300 mm long, 17 mm id, and marked at 225±1.5 mm inside measurement from bottom.

(**d**) *Spectrophotometer or filter photometer.*—For use at 425 nm.

33.053 ***Reagents***

(*Caution: See* **51.065**, **51.079**, and **51.084**.)

(**a**) *Water.*—Distd, NH_3-free. Pass thru ion exchange column of mixed strongly acidic cation and strongly basic anion exchange resins. Regenerate resins according to manufacturer's instructions.

(**b**) *Mercuric sulfate soln.*—Dissolve 8 g red HgO in 50 mL H_2SO_4 (1+5) and dil. to 100 mL with H_2O.

(**c**) *Digestion soln.*—Dissolve 267 g K_2SO_4 in 1300 mL H_2O and add 400 mL H_2SO_4. Add 50 mL $HgSO_4$ soln, (**b**), and dil. to 2 L.

(**d**) *Sodium hydroxide-sodium thiosulfate soln.*—Dissolve 500 g NaOH and 25 g $Na_2S_2O_3.5H_2O$ in H_2O and dil. to 1 L.

(**e**) *Phenolphthalein indicator soln.*—Dissolve 5 g phthln in 500 mL alcohol or isopropanol and add 500 mL H_2O. Add 0.02*N* NaOH until faint pink.

(**f**) *Sulfuric acid std soln.*—0.02*N*. Prep. and stdze as in **50.039–50.041**. 1.00 mL = 0.28 mg N.

(**g**) *Ammonia std solns.*—(*1*) *Stock soln.*—1.00 mg N/mL. Dissolve 3.819 g NH_4Cl in H_2O and dil. to 1 L. (*2*) *Working soln.*—0.01 mg N/ml. Dil. 10 mL stock soln to 1 L.

(**h**) *Boric acid soln.*—Dissolve 20 g H_3BO_3 in H_2O and dil. to 1 L.

(**i**) *Mixed indicator.*—Mix 2 vols 0.2% alc. Me red with 1 vol. 0.2% alc. methylene blue. Prep. fresh every 30 days. SDA 3-A or 30 denatured alcohol may be used.

(**j**) *Nessler reagent.*—Dissolve 100 g HgI_2 and 70 g KI in small amt H_2O. Add slowly, with stirring, to cooled soln of 160 g NaOH in 500 mL H_2O, and dil. to 1 L. Reagent is stable 1 year if stored in Pyrex container out of direct sunlight. Reagent should give characteristic color, but no ppt, with 0.04 mg NH_3-N in 50 mL H_2O within 10 min.

33.054 ***Digestion and Distillation***

Det. sample size as follows:

mg N/L	*mL sample*
0– 5	500
5– 10	250
10– 20	100
20– 50	50.0
50–100	25.0

Place sample, or residue from NH_3 detn (for org. Kjeldahl N only), into 800 mL Kjeldahl flask. Dil., if necessary, to 500 mL and add 100 mL digestion soln, (**c**). Boil until SO_3 fumes are evolved and soln becomes colorless or pale yellow. Cool, and dil. with 300 mL H_2O. Add NaOH-$Na_2S_2O_3$ soln slowly down neck of tilted flask to underlay acid soln in amt sufficient to make final soln strongly alk. as shown by phthln (60 mL NaOH-$Na_2S_2O_3$ soln will neutze 20 mL H_2SO_4). Connect flask to condenser, with tip of condenser dipping into 50 mL 2% H_3BO_3 soln in 500 mL g-s erlenmeyer. If soln is to be titrd, 100 or 200 mL H_3BO_3 may be used. Mix solns and distil 300 mL at 6–10 mL/min. If NH_3 concn is ≥1 mg/L, det. titrimetrically, **33.055**; if less, det. colorimetrically, **33.056**.

33.055 ***Titrimetric Determination***

Add 3 drops mixed indicator, (**i**), to distillate and titr. with 0.02*N* H_2SO_4, (**f**), matching end point against blank contg same vol. NH_3-free H_2O, H_3BO_3 soln, and indicator.

mg Total N/L = [(mL std H_2SO_4 for sample − mL std H_2SO_4 for reagent blank) × normality std H_2SO_4 × 14.01 × 1000]/mL sample digested.

33.056 ***Colorimetric Determination***

Prep. series of stds contg 0.0, 0.2, 0.5, 1.0, 1.5, 2.0, 3.0, and 4.0 mL NH_3 working std soln, (**g**)(*2*), dild to 50 mL with NH_3-free H_2O (contains 0.0, 0.04, 0.10, 0.20, 0.30, 0.40, 0.60, and 0.80 mg NH_3 N/L). Add 1 mL Nessler reagent, (**j**), and mix. After 20 min, read *A* at 425 nm against 0.0 (blank) std, and plot *A* against concn to obtain std curve. Distil 1 or more high and low std solns daily to ensure adequate recoveries.

As estd by preliminary detn, det. NH_3 in 50 mL aliquot, or aliquot dild to 50 mL, as above, and read NH_3 concn from std curve.

mg Total N/L = [(mg NH_3-N from curve × 1000)/ mL sample taken for distn] × (mL final distillate, including H_3BO_3 soln/mL distillate taken for nesslerization).

Ammonia Nitrogen (*1, 4*)

33.057 ***Principle***

Sample buffered at pH 9.5 is distd into H_3BO_3 soln. Depending upon concn, NH_3 is detd colorimetrically (0.05–1.0 mg N/L) by nesslerization or titrimetry (1.0–25 mg N/L). Hg, if present as preservative, and residual Cl must be removed by addn of $Na_2S_2O_3$ before distn.

Method is applicable to surface and saline waters and domestic and industrial wastes. A number of volatile amines will cause turbidity with Nessler reagent. Some volatile compds, such as certain ketones, aldehydes, and alcohols, may cause off color on nesslerization. Some of these, such as HCHO, may be eliminated by boiling at pH 2–3 before distn. Volatile compds, such as hydrazine, influence titrimetric results.

Natural and distd H_2O analyzed by 24 analysts in 16 laboratories showed the following results on exact increments of ammonium salt:

		Added,	Std deviation		Bias	
Method	Type	mg N/L	%	mg N/L	%	mg N/L
Colorm.	Distd.	0.21	58	0.122	− 5.54	−0.01
Colorm.	Nat.	0.26	27	0.070	−18.12	−0.05
Titr.	Distd.	1.71	14	0.244	+ 0.46	+0.01
Titr.	Nat.	1.92	15	0.279	− 2.01	−0.04

33.058 ***Apparatus***

See **33.052**(**b**), (**c**), and (**d**).

33.059 ***Reagents***

See **33.053**(**a**), (**f**)–(**j**), and following:

(**a**) *Borate buffer.*—pH 9.5. Add 88 mL 0.1*N* NaOH to 500 mL 0.025*M* $Na_2B_4O_7$ (5.0 g anhyd. salt/L), and dil. to 1 L.

(**b**) *Sodium hydroxide soln.*—1*N*. Dissolve 40 g NaOH in NH_3-free H_2O and dil. to 1 L.

(**c**) *Dechlorinating reagent.*—Dissolve 3.5 g $Na_2S_2O_3$ in NH_3-free H_2O and dil. to 1 L. 1 mL will remove 0.5 mg residual Cl in 500 mL sample.

33.060 ***Distillation***

Add 500 mL NH_3-free H_2O and few boiling chips previously treated with NaOH soln to Kjeldahl distg flask.

Adjust 400 mL sample to pH 9.5 with 1*N* NaOH, using pH meter or short range test paper. If sample contains residual Cl, remove by adding equiv. amt dechlorinating reagent, (**c**). Transfer to distg flask and add 25 mL buffer, (**a**). Distil 300 mL at 6–10 mL/min into 50 mL H_3BO_3 soln, **33.053(h)**. Dil. distillate to 500 mL in receiving flask. Det. NH_3 in 50 mL aliquot as in colorimetric detn. If NH_3 concn is $\geq$1 mg/L, det. titrimetrically, **33.061**; if less, det. colorimetrically, **33.062**.

33.061 ***Titrimetric Determination***

Proceed as in **33.055**, using remaining 450 mL distillate.

mg NH_3-N/L = (mL 0.02*N* H_2SO_4 × 1000)/equiv. mL sample in aliquot titrd.

33.062 ***Colorimetric Determination***

Proceed as in **33.056**.

mg NH_3-N/L = (NH_3 concn from std curve × 1000)/(0.8 × mL distillate taken for detn).

Nitrate Nitrogen (*1, 4*)

Brucine Colorimetric Method

33.063 ***Principle***

Nitrate ion reacts with brucine in H_2SO_4 at 100° to form colored compd whose *A* is measured at 410 nm. Temp. control of reaction is critical. Applicable to 0.1–2 mg NO_3-N/L in surface and saline waters and domestic and industrial wastes.

Org. matter developing color with H_2SO_4 and natural color are compensated for by blank; effect of salinity is compensated for by addn of NaCl. Strong oxidizing and reducing agents interfere. Det. presence of free Cl with *o*-tolidine reagent. Eliminate residual Cl by addn of $NaAsO_3$ soln. Effect of Fe^{+2}, Fe^{+3}, and Mn^{+4} is negligible at <1 mg/L.

Natural H_2O analyzed by 27 analysts in 15 laboratories showed the following results on exact increments of inorg. nitrate:

Added, mg N/L	Std deviation		Bias	
	%	mg N/L	%	mg N/L
0.16	58	0.092	−6.8	−0.01
0.19	44	0.083	+8.3	+0.02
1.08	23	0.245	+4.1	+0.04
1.24	17	0.214	+2.8	+0.04

33.064 ***Apparatus***

(**a**) *Spectrophotometer or filter photometer.*—Capable of accommodating 25 mm diam. tubes and measuring *A* at 410 nm.

(**b**) *Tubes.*—Matched tubes for conducting reaction and measuring *A*.

(**c**) *Racks.*—Neoprene, wire coated, evenly spaced, to permit uniform flow of bath H_2O between tubes.

(**d**) *Water baths.*—(*1*) *100°.*—Boiling H_2O bath of sufficient size so that when tubes are inserted, temp. drop is $\leq$1–2°. Should have tight-fit cover, preferably of gable construction, with circulator or stirrer to maintain uniform temp. *Uniform temp. control of this bath is critical.* (*Caution:* Check H_2O bath to assure it is electrically grounded.) (*2*) *10–15°.*—For cooling tubes.

33.065 ***Reagents***

(**a**) *Water.*—Use distd or deionized H_2O for prepn of all reagents and stds.

(**b**) *Salt soln.*—Dissolve 300 g NaCl in H_2O and dil. to 1 L.

(**c**) *Sulfuric acid.*—13*N*. Carefully add 500 mL H_2SO_4 to 125 mL H_2O. Cool, and keep tightly stoppered.

(**d**) *Brucine-sulfanilic acid reagent.*—Dissolve 1 g brucine sulfate.$7H_2O$ and 0.1 g sulfanilic acid.H_2O in 70 mL H_2O. Stored in dark bottle at 5°, soln is stable several months. Slowly developing pink does not affect usefulness.

(**e**) *Nitrate std solns.*—(*1*) *Stock soln.*—100 mg N/L. Dissolve 0.7218 g KNO_3 in H_2O and dil. to 1 L. (*2*) *Working soln.*—1 mg/L. Dil. 10 mL stock soln to 1 L. Prep. fresh weekly.

33.066 ***Determination***

(*Caution: See* **51.018** and **51.030.**)

Preserve samples with 40 mg $HgCl_2$/L and store at 4°. Adjust pH to ca 7 with HOAc (1+3) and, if necessary, filter thru 0.45 μm filter.

Prep. set of matched tubes for blanks, stds, and samples. If necessary to correct for color or for org. matter which will cause color on heating, add extra set of tubes to which all reagents except brucine will be added.

Pipet 10 mL sample, or aliquot dild to 10 mL, into sample tubes. For saline sample, add 2.0 mL 30% NaCl soln to samples, stds, and blank tubes. Swirl tubes and place in 0–10° bath. Pipet 10 mL 13*N* H_2SO_4 into each tube and swirl. Let all tubes come to thermal equilibrium. Pipet 0.5 mL brucine reagent to all tubes except color control tubes and swirl. Then place entire rack contg all tubes in boiling H_2O bath for exactly 25 min. Remove rack and transfer to cold H_2O bath and let cool to 20–25°. Dry tubes and read *A* against reagent blank at 410 nm.

Prep. set of stds contg 0.1–2 mg N/L and conduct stds along with samples. Color may not follow Beer's law. If necessary, subtract *A* of color controls from *A* of samples.

Chloride (*1, 2*)

Mercuric Nitrate Method

33.067 ***Principle***

Chloride titrd with mercuric ions forms sol., slightly dissociated $HgCl_2$. In pH range 2.3–2.8, diphenylcarbazone indicates end point by forming purple complex with excess Hg^{+2}. Xylene cyanol FF serves as pH indicator and background color to facilitate end point detection. $NaHCO_3$ added to both blank and sample followed by const amt of HNO_3 added with indicators provides pH of 2.5±0.1. Increasing strength of titrant and modifying indicator mixt. permits detn of high Cl concns common in waste water.

Br and I titr. as chloride. Chromate, Fe^{+3}, and SO_3^{-2} interfere when present at >10 mg/L. Sulfites may be removed with 0.5–1 mL H_2O_2/50 mL sample. Methods are applicable to drinking, surface, and saline waters, and domestic and industrial wastes at all Cl concns. However, to avoid large titrn vols, use sample contg <20 mg Cl/50 mL.

Synthetic H_2O samples analyzed by 42 analysts in 18 laboratories showed the following results on exact increments of Cl:

Added, mg Cl/L	Std deviation		Bias	
	%	mg Cl/L	%	mg Cl/L
17	9.1	1.54	+2.2	+0.4
18	7.3	1.32	+3.5	+0.6
91	3.2	2.92	+0.1	+0.1
97	3.3	3.16	−0.5	−0.5
382	3.1	11.7	−0.6	−2.3
398	3.0	11.8	−1.2	−4.7

33.068 ***Reagents***

(**a**) *Sodium chloride std soln.*—0.0141*N*. Dissolve 824.1 mg NaCl, dried at 140°, in Cl-free H_2O, and dil. to 1 L. 1 mL = 0.500 mg Cl.

(**b**) *Chlorine-free water.*—Redistd or deionized.

For Low Chloride Concentration

(**c**) *Indicator-acidifier reagent.*—(Neutzes 150 mg $CaCO_3$/L in 100 mL sample.) Dissolve, in order given, 250 mg *s*-diphenylcarbazone, 4.0 mL HNO_3, and 30 mg xylene cyanol FF in 100 mL alcohol or isopropanol. Store in dark bottle in refrigerator. For routine analysis of samples with very high or low alky, HNO_3 concn may be adjusted so that final pH when added to samples is 2.5±0.1.

(**d**) *Mercuric nitrate std soln.*—0.0141*N*. Dissolve 2.3 g $Hg(NO_3)_2$ or 2.5 g $Hg(NO_3)_2.H_2O$ in 100 mL H_2O contg 0.25 mL HNO_3. Dil. to just under 1 L. Stdze as in **33.069**(**a**), using 5.00 mL aliquot NaCl std soln, (**a**), and 10 mg $NaHCO_3$, dild to 100 mL. Adjust soln to exactly 0.0141*N* and perform final stdzn. Store in dark bottle away from light. 1 mL = 0.500 mg Cl.

For High Chloride Concentration

(**e**) *Mixed indicator.*—Dissolve 5 g *s*-diphenylcarbazone and 0.5 g bromophenol blue in 750 mL alcohol or isopropanol and dil. to 1 L with same solv.

(**f**) *Mercuric nitrate std soln.*—0.141*N*. Dissolve 25 g $Hg(NO_3)_2.H_2O$ in 900 mL H_2O contg 5.0 mL HNO_3. Dil. to just under 1 L. Stdze as in **33.069**(**b**), using 25.00 mL aliquots NaCl std soln, (**a**), and 25 mL H_2O. Adjust soln to exactly 0.141*N* and perform final stdzn. Store in dark bottle away from light. 1 mL = 5.00 mg Cl.

33.069 ***Determination***

(**a**) *For low chloride (drinking water).*—To ≤100 mL sample contg ≤10 mg Cl, add 1.0 mL indicator-acidifier, (**c**). Color should be green-blue. If not, adjust pH of sample to 8 before addn of reagent. Titr. with 0.0141*N* $Hg(NO_3)_2$ to definite purple end point. (Soln becomes blue few drops before end point.) Det. blank by titrn of equal vol. H_2O contg 10 mg $NaHCO_3$.

(**b**) *For high chloride.*—To 50.0 mL sample (5.00 mL if ≥5 mL titrant needed) in 150 mL beaker, add 0.5 mL mixed indicator, (**e**), and mix well. Color should be purple. Add 0.1*N* HNO_3 dropwise until just yellow. Titr. with 0.141*N* $Hg(NO_3)_2$ to first permanent dark purple. Det. blank by titrn of equal vol. H_2O.

(**c**) *Calculation.*—mg Cl/L = [(mL sample titrn − mL blank titrn) × normality $Hg(NO_3)_2$ × 35,340]/mL sample.

mg NaCl/L = (mg Cl/L) × 1.65.

Fluoride (*5*)—Official Final Action

33.070 ***Reagents***

(**a**) *Fluoride std soln.*—0.01 mg F/mL. Dissolve 2.21 g NaF (min. purity 98%) in 1 L H_2O. Dil. 10 mL of this soln to 1 L.

(**b**) *Thorium nitrate soln.*—Dissolve 0.25 g $Th(NO_3)_4.12H_2O$ or 0.2 g $Th(NO_3)_4.4H_2O$ in 1 L H_2O.

(**c**) *Alizarin red indicator.*—0.01% aq. soln Na alizarin sulfonate (alizarin red S).

(**d**) *Hydrochloric acid.*—Exactly 0.05*N*.

(**e**) *Sodium hydroxide soln.*—Exactly 0.05*N*.

(**f**) *Hydroxylamine hydrochloride soln.*—1.0 g/100 mL.

33.071 ***Apparatus***

(**a**) *Claisen flask.*—250 mL.

(**b**) *Nessler tubes.*—6 long-form 50 mL tubes with double optically plane disks fused to tubes. Match tubes for length and test for optical similarity as follows: Add ca 40 mL H_2O, 1 mL indicator, 2 mL 0.05*N* HCl, and H_2O to mark on tube. To 1 tube add amt of $Th(NO_3)_4$ soln such that, after dilg to mark and mixing, color is barely changed to faint pink. Note amt of $Th(NO_3)_4$ soln used. Add same amt of $Th(NO_3)_4$ soln to each of remaining 5 tubes. Reject tubes showing detectable differences in shade or intensity.

See also **25.051**.

33.072 ***Preparation of Sample***

If sample has odor of H_2S, oxidize with 0.1 mL 30% H_2O_2 soln before evapn.

Place 100 mL sample in porcelain or Pt dish, make alk. to phthln with 10% NaOH soln (avoid excess), and evap. to 20 mL over burner at temp. just below bp. During evapn keep sample alk. by adding small amts of 0.05*N* NaOH from time to time. Transfer the 20 mL evapd sample to Claisen flask contg glass beads or boiling tube previously rinsed with boiling 10% NaOH soln to eliminate all traces of gelatinous SiO_2 accumulating in flask.

Place flask contg sample on insulating board (15 × 15 × 0.6 cm with 2.5 cm center hole) over burner adjusted for medium flame. Close straight neck of flask with 2-hole rubber stopper thru which pass thermometer and stem of small separator with outlet constricted to 2 mm diam. (Adjust thermometer and outlet tube of separator to extend almost to bottom of flask.) Close other neck of flask with solid rubber stopper. (Alternatively, all-glass distn assembly may be used.)

Connect flask with H_2O condenser; add 20 mL 60% $HClO_4$ (*Caution: See* **51.028**(**a**) and (**d**)) to flask, rinsing evapg dish and separator; then add amt of *satd $AgClO_4$ soln* that will ppt chlorides (detd previously by titrn with std $AgNO_3$ soln), and distil at 132±3°, adding H_2O dropwise thru separator to maintain temp. during distn. Collect nearly 200 mL distillate. Dil. to vol. (200 mL) and mix well. To det. acidity, use 40 mL distillate, add 1 mL indicator, mix thoroly, and note mL 0.05*N* NaOH required for neutzn.

Repeat prepn and distn, using 100 mL H_2O in place of sample, to det. blank.

33.073 ***Determination***

Prep. 1 std, 1 color comparison tube, and 1 or more sample tubes as follows:

(**a**) *Color comparison tube.*—To 40 mL H_2O add 2 mL 0.05*N* HCl, 1 mL alizarin red indicator, 1 mL $NH_2OH.HCl$ soln, and enough $Th(NO_3)_4$ soln to give faint but definite pink end point. Compare all end point colors with this color.

(**b**) *Sample tube.*—To sample tube contg 40 mL distillate add 1 mL indicator, 1 mL $H_2NOH.HCl$ soln, and vol. 0.05*N* HCl such that total vol. acid in tube (acidity previously detd plus vol. 0.05*N* HCl added) equals 2 mL 0.05*N* HCl. Dil. to vol. and mix. If in preliminary acidity detn it is found that the 40 mL distillate requires >2 mL 0.05*N* NaOH soln for neutzn, do not add the HCl soln to sample tube, but add to std tube same amt of acid as was found present in sample tube. If 40 mL distillate requires >5 mL 0.05*N* NaOH, repeat distn under conditions favorable to low acidity. From 10 mL buret, graduated to 0.05 mL, add $Th(NO_3)_4$ soln with frequent mixing until faint pink appears, comparable to comparison tube, (**a**). Note vol. $Th(NO_3)_4$ soln used.

(**c**) *Std tube.*—To std tube contg 40 mL H_2O add 1 mL indicator, 1 mL $H_2NOH.HCl$ soln, and ≥2 mL 0.05*N* HCl, as was required in sample tube in (**b**). If aliquot chosen for detn already contains 2–5 mL 0.05*N* acid, add exactly same amt to std tube. Add exactly same amt of $Th(NO_3)_4$ soln as was added to sample tube. To std tube (now more highly colored than sample tube), add std F soln from 10 mL buret with mixing until color matches that of sample tube. Dil. contents of both std and sample tubes to same vol. Mix soln in each tube and let all air bubbles escape before making color comparisons. Check end point by adding 1–2 drops std F soln to std tube. Distinct color change should develop.

33.074 ***Calculation***

Subtract mL F soln required by blank from mL F soln required by sample.

$$\frac{\text{mL F soln} \times \text{mL total distillate} \times 10}{\text{mL aliquot titrd} \times \text{wt sample taken}} = \text{F (ppm)}.$$

Example: 100 mL sample, evapd and distd to 200 mL, of which 40 mL aliquot corresponds to 5 mL F soln, gives:

$$(5 \times 200 \times 10)/(40 \times 100) = 2.5 \text{ F (ppm)}.$$

★ Hydrogen Sulfide (*6*)—Official Final Action ★

33.075 ***Iodometric Method***

See **31.016–31.017**, 10th ed.

33.076 Carbonate and Bicarbonate—Official Final Action

To 100 mL sample add few drops phthln, and if pink is produced, titr. with 0.05*N* HCl or H_2SO_4, adding drop every 2–3 sec until color disappears. Multiply buret reading by factor 3 to obtain mg CO_3 ion in 100 mL. To colorless soln from this titrn, or to original soln if no color is produced with phthln, add 1–2 drops Me orange, continue titrn without refilling buret, and note total reading. If CO_3 is absent, multiply total buret reading by factor 3.05 to obtain value of HCO_3 ion in mg/100 mL. If CO_3 is present, multiply reading with phthln by 2 and subtract from total reading of buret. Multiply difference by 3.05 to obtain HCO_3 ion in mg/100 mL. Express results as mg/L.

33.077 Silica—Official Final Action

Make preliminary examination, using 100–250 mL sample, to det. approx. amt of Ca and Mg present, in order to det. amt of sample to be evapd for final analysis.

Evap. amt of sample equiv. to 0.1–0.6 g CaO or 0.1–1 g $Mg_2P_2O_7$ (usually 1–5 L). Acidify sample with HCl and evap. on steam bath to dryness in Pt dish. Continue drying ca 1 hr. Thoroly moisten residue with 5–10 mL HCl. Let stand 10–15 min and add enough H_2O to bring sol. salts into soln. Heat on steam bath until salts dissolve. Filter to remove most of SiO_2 and wash thoroly with hot H_2O. Evap. filtrate to dryness and treat residue with 5 mL HCl and enough H_2O to dissolve sol. salts, as before. Heat, filter, and wash thoroly with hot H_2O. Designate filtrate as *Soln X*.

Transfer the two residues to Pt crucible, ignite, heat over blast lamp, and weigh. Moisten contents of crucible with few drops H_2O, add few drops H_2SO_4 and few mL HF, and evap. on steam bath under hood. Repeat treatment if all SiO_2 is not volatilized. Dry carefully on hot plate, ignite, heat over blast lamp, and weigh. Difference between the two wts is wt SiO_2. Add wt residue (Fe_2O_3 + Al_2O_3) to that of Al_2O_3 and Fe_2O_3 obtained in **33.078**. (If residue weighs >0.5 mg, $BaSO_4$ may be present in sample. If so, make necessary correction and add to wt Fe_2O_3 and Al_2O_3 in **33.078**.)

★ Surplus method—*see* inside front cover.

33.078 Iron and Aluminum—Official Final Action

Conc. *Soln X*, **33.077**, to 200 mL; while still hot, slowly add NH_4OH, stirring constantly, until alk. to Me orange. Boil, filter, and wash 3 times with hot H_2O. Dissolve ppt in hot HCl (1+1). Dil. to ca 25 mL, boil, and again ppt with NH_4OH. Filter, wash thoroly with hot H_2O, dry, ignite, and weigh as Al_2O_3 and Fe_2O_3. (In presence of H_3PO_4, wt of this residue must be corrected for P_2O_5 equiv. to H_3PO_4 found in **33.115**, allowing for difference in vols of the water used for these detns.) Designate filtrate as *Soln Y*.

Iron—Official Final Action

33.079 ***Colorimetric Method***

(Iron <1 mg; not applicable in presence of phosphates)

Fuse, in Pt crucible, ignited ppt of Fe_2O_3 and Al_2O_3, **33.078**, with fused $KHSO_4$, dissolve in H_2O, and ppt Fe and Al with NH_4OH. Filter, dissolve ppt on filter paper in HCl and HNO_3, dil. soln, add 3 mL 5% NH_4SCN soln, dil. to suitable vol., and compare color developed with that of calibrated color disks or stds contg known amts of Fe treated similarly.

33.080 ***Volumetric Method***

(*Caution: See* **51.059**.)

Fuse residue of Fe_2O_3 and Al_2O_3, **33.078**, in Pt crucible with ca 1 g fused $KHSO_4$. (Fusion takes only few min, and must not be continued beyond time actually needed.) When fusion is complete, set crucible aside to cool. Add H_2SO_4 (1+4) and heat crucible until fused mass dissolves. Evap. on steam bath as far as possible; then heat gradually until copious fumes of SO_3 evolve. Dissolve in H_2O and let stand on steam bath. Cool, transfer to erlenmeyer, and dil. to such vol. that soln contains ≤2.5% free H_2SO_4.

Pass H_2S thru soln to reduce Fe and ppt any Pt contaminating residue from fusion. (Zn may be used instead of H_2S for reducing Fe.) Filter, wash, and again pass H_2S thru soln to reduce all Fe. Expel H_2S by boiling, at same time passing current of CO_2 thru soln. Test escaping gas with $Pb(OAc)_2$ paper to confirm complete removal of H_2S. Discontinue boiling and let flask cool without discontinuing current of CO_2. Titr. reduced Fe with std $KMnO_4$ soln (1 mL = 1 mg Fe) and calc. as Fe.

Hardness (*1, 2*)

33.081 ***Calculation Method***

Calc. hardness as sum of $CaCO_3$ equivs (mg/L) obtained by multiplying concn (mg/L) found of following cations by factor shown:

Cation	*Factor*	*Cation*	*Factor*
Ca	2.497	Al	5.564
Mg	4.116	Zn	1.531
Sr	1.142	Mn	1.822
Fe	1.792		

EDTA Titrimetric Method

33.082 ***Principle***

Ca and Mg at pH 10 in presence of dye eriochrome black T are wine red. When completely complexed with EDTA, soln becomes blue. Mg must be present for satisfactory end point and is added as MgEDTA. End point sharpness increases with pH, but high pH may cause pptn of $Ca(OH)_2$ or $Mg(OH)_2$ and cause color changes of dye. pH of 10.0±0.1 is satisfactory compromise. Limit of 5 min for titrn minimizes pptn. Heavy metal interference is minimized by complexing with cyanide.

Method is applicable to drinking and surface waters and domestic and industrial wastes. To avoid large titrn vols, use aliquot contg <25 mg $CaCO_3$.

Synthetic H_2O samples contg exact increments of Ca and Mg salts analyzed by 43 analysts in 19 laboratories showed the following results:

Increment, total hardness as mg $CaCO_3$/L	Std deviation		Bias	
	%	mg $CaCO_3$/L	%	mg $CaCO_3$/L
31	9.4	2.9	−0.87	− 0.003
33	7.6	2.5	−0.73	− 0.24
182	2.7	4.9	−0.19	− 0.4
194	1.5	3.0	−1.04	− 2.0
417	2.3	9.7	−3.35	−13.0
444	2.0	8.7	−3.23	−14.3

33.083 ***Reagents***

(**a**) *Buffer soln.*—Dissolve 16.9 g NH_4Cl in 143 mL NH_4OH, add 1.25 g MgEDTA, and dil. to 250 mL with H_2O. (1.179 g Na_2 EDTA.$2H_2O$ and 0.780 g $MgSO_4.7H_2O$ or 0.644 g $MgCl_2.6H_2O$ dissolved in 50 mL H_2O may be substituted for 1.25 g MgEDTA.) Store in tightly stoppered Pyrex or plastic bottle. Dispense from bulb-operated pipet. Discard after 1 month or when 1–2 mL added to sample fails to produce pH 10.0±0.1 at end point of titrn.

(**b**) *Indicator.*—Mix 0.5 g eriochrome black T and 100 g NaCl to prep. dry powd mixt. If end point change is not clear and sharp, prep. new mixt.

(**c**) *EDTA std soln.*—0.01*M*. Weigh 3.723 g $Na_2EDTA.2H_2O$ and dil. to 1 L with H_2O. Stdze against Ca std soln as in **33.084**. Store in polyethylene bottle and restdze periodically.

(**d**) *Calcium std soln.*—1.000 mg $CaCO_3$/mL. Weigh 1.000 g $CaCO_3$ (primary std or special reagent low in heavy metals, alkalis, and Mg) into 500 mL erlenmeyer. Place funnel in neck and add, little at a time, HCl (1+1) until all $CaCO_3$ has dissolved. Add 200 mL H_2O and boil few min to expel CO_2. Cool, add few drops Me red indicator, and adjust to intermediate orange with 3*N* NH_4OH or HCl (1+1), as required. Transfer quant. to 1 L vol. flask and dil. to vol.

33.084 ***Determination***

Dil. 25 mL sample (or such vol. as to require <15 mL titrant) to ca 50 mL with H_2O in porcelain casserole, add 1–2 mL buffer soln, 250 mg NaCN (pH of soln should be 10±0.1), and ca 200 mg indicator powder, and titr. with EDTA std soln slowly, with continuous stirring, until last reddish tinge disappears, adding last few drops at 3–5 sec intervals. Color at end point is blue in daylight and under daylight fluorescent lamp. Complete titrn within 5 min from time of buffer addn.

For waters of low hardness (<5 mg/L), use 100–1000 mL sample, proportionately larger amts of reagents, microburet, and blank of distd H_2O equal to sample vol.

Hardness (EDTA) as mg $CaCO_3$/L = $T \times B \times 1000$/mL sample, where T = mL EDTA std soln and B = mg $CaCO_3$ equiv. to 1.00 mL EDTA std soln.

33.085 Aluminum—Official Final Action

To obtain wt Al_2O_3, in absence of phosphates, subtract from wt Fe_2O_3 and Al_2O_3, **33.078**, the Fe, **33.079** or **33.080**, calcd as Fe_2O_3. Calc. as Al.

33.086 Calcium—Official Final Action

Conc. *Soln Y*, **33.078**, to 150–200 mL, and to this soln, contg equiv. of ≤0.6 g CaO or 1 g $Mg_2P_2O_7$, add 1–2 g $H_2C_2O_4.2H_2O$ and enough HCl (1+1) to clear soln. Heat to bp and neutze with NH_4OH, stirring constantly. Add NH_4OH in slight excess and let stand 3 hr in warm place. Filter supernate and wash ppt once or twice by decantation with 1% $(NH_4)_2C_2O_4$ soln. Dissolve ppt in HCl (1+1), dil. to 100–200 mL, add little more $H_2C_2O_4$, and ppt as above. After letting ppt stand 3 hr, filter, wash with 1% $(NH_4)_2C_2O_4$ soln, dry, ignite, heat over blast lamp at ≥950°, and weigh as CaO and SrO. From this wt subtract wt SrO equiv. to the Sr, **33.087**. Difference is wt CaO. Calc. as Ca. Designate combined filtrates and washings as *Soln Z*.

As check on CaO, evap. to dryness filtrate from the $Sr(NO_3)_2$ in **33.087**, beginning "Filter, and wash with ether-alcohol mixt. . . ." Dissolve the $Ca(NO_3)_2$ in H_2O, ppt as oxalate, filter, wash, ignite at 950°, and weigh as CaO. CaO × 0.7147 = Ca.

33.087 Strontium (*7*)—Official Final Action

Dissolve oxides, **33.086**, in HNO_3 (1+1) and test with spectroscope for Sr. If Sr is present, transfer HNO_3 soln to small erlenmeyer. Evap. nearly to dryness over low flame, and heat 1–2 hr at 150–160° after H_2O is evapd. Break up dried material with stirring rod and add 10–15 mL mixt. of absolute alcohol and ether (1+1) to dissolve the $Ca(NO_3)_2$. Cork flask and let stand with frequent shaking ≥2 hr. Decant soln thru 5.5 cm filter, reserving filtrate. Wash residue several times by decantation with small portions of the ether-alcohol mixt. Dry residue and paper, and repeatedly wash paper with small portions of hot H_2O, collecting filtrate in flask contg main portion of $Sr(NO_3)_2$ residue. Add 1 or 2 drops HNO_3 (1+1), evap., dry, pulverize, and treat with 10–15 mL ether-alcohol mixt. Cork flask and let stand ca 12 hr, shaking occasionally.

Filter, and wash with ether-alcohol mixt. until few drops filtrate evapd on watch glass leave practically no residue. Dry paper and ppt. Dissolve $Sr(NO_3)_2$ in few mL hot H_2O. Add few drops H_2SO_4 and then add vol. alcohol equal to vol. soln and let stand 12 hr. Filter, ignite, weigh as $SrSO_4$, and calc. to Sr. Test spectroscopically for Ca and Ba. If these elements are present, det. amt and make necessary correction.

33.088 Magnesium—Official Final Action

Conc. *Soln Z*, **33.086**, to 200 mL, acidify with HCl (1+1), and add 2–3 g $(NH_4)_2HPO_4$ and enough HCl (1+1) to produce clear soln when all $(NH_4)_2HPO_4$ is dissolved. When cold, make slightly alk. with NH_4OH, stirring constantly. Add 2 mL excess of NH_4OH and let stand ca 12 hr. Filter supernate and wash 4 times by decantation with NH_4OH (1+10). Dissolve ppt in HCl (1+1), dil. to ca 150 mL, add little $(NH_4)_2HPO_4$, and ppt with NH_4OH as before. Let stand 12 hr, filter, wash Cl-free with NH_4OH (1+10), place in porcelain crucible, ignite, heat over blast lamp, and weigh as $Mg_2P_2O_7$. Calc. to Mg. $Mg_2P_2O_7$ × 0.21842 = Mg.

Cadmium, Chromium, Copper, Iron, Lead, Magnesium, Manganese, Silver, Zinc

Atomic Absorption Method (8)
Official First Action

33.089 ***Principle***

Metals in soln are detd directly by AA spectrophotometry; suspended metals are sepd by membrane filtration, or suspension is dissolved and analyzed; Pb and Cd in low concn are chelated, concd, and then extd with org. solv. prior to AA detn. Applicable to surface and saline waters, and domestic and industrial wastes. Three synthetic water samples contg between 0.05 and 1.0 mg each metal/L analyzed by 8–23 laboratories showed results given in Table **33:02**.

33.090 ***Apparatus***

(Use Pyrex glassware exclusively; clean thoroly with detergent and H_2O; rinse with chromic acid cleaning soln, H_2O, dil. HNO_3, and H_2O, in that order. Use deionized distd H_2O wherever H_2O is specified in method.)

Atomic absorption spectrophotometer.—Spectrophtr capable of operating at conditions given in Table **33:03**. Operator must become familiar with settings and operations of his app., using table only as guide. Use Boling burner for aq. solns, and premix burner with solv. (*Caution: See* **51.006**).

33.091 ***Reagents***

(**a**) *Deionized distilled water.*—*See* **33.053**(**a**).

(**b**) *Nitric acid.*—Dil. 500 mL redistd HNO_3 to 1 L with H_2O. (*Caution:* Perform distn in hood with protective sash in place.)

(**c**) *Hydrochloric acid.*—Dil. 500 mL HCl to 1 L with H_2O and distil in all-Pyrex app.

(**d**) *Metal std solns.*—(*1*) *Stock solns.*—Accurately weigh amt of metal specified in Table **33:04** into beaker and add dissolving medium. When metal is completely dissolved, transfer quant. to 1 L vol. flask and dil. to vol. with H_2O. (*2*) *Working solns.*—Prep. daily. Dil. aliquots of stock solns with H_2O to make ≥4 std solns of each element within range of detn, Table **33:03**. Add 1.5 mL HNO_3/L to all working std solns before dilg to vol. Add 1 mL $LaCl_3$/10 mL Mg working std soln.

(**e**) *Lanthanum stock soln.*—50 g La/L ca 5% HCl. Slowly add 250 mL HCl to 58.65 g La_2O_3 (99.99%, Ventron Corp., Alfa Products, 8 Congress St, Beverly, MA 01915, or equiv.), dissolve, and dil. to 1 L.

(**f**) *Ammonium pyrrolidine dithiocarbamate* (*APDC*) *soln.*—Dissolve 1 g APDC in 100 mL H_2O. Prep. fresh daily.

Table 33:02 Bias and Standard Deviations of Determination of Metals by Atomic Absorption

Metal	Added, mg/L	Std deviation %	Std deviation mg/L	Bias %	Bias mg/L
Cd	0.01	53	0.007	+27.5	+0.003
	0.01 (extn)	61	0.006	0.0	0.0
	0.05	8	0.004	+ 2.0	+0.001
	0.05 (extn)	10	0.005	+ 1.2	+0.001
	0.10	8	0.008	+ 3.4	+0.003
	0.10 (extn)	52	0.045	−15.0	−0.015
Cr	0.05	26	0.013	− 2.3	−0.001
	0.10	22	0.021	− 2.9	−0.003
	0.20	12	0.024	− 3.0	−0.006
Cu	0.05	42	0.023	+ 8.3	+0.004
	0.25	8	0.020	+ 2.2	+0.006
	1.00	6	0.060	+ 0.6	+0.006
Fe	0.10	34	0.032	− 5.3	−0.005
	0.30	18	0.050	− 5.0	−0.015
	0.50	6	0.031	+ 1.1	+0.006
Pb	0.05	76	0.036	− 5.0	−0.002
	0.05 (extn)	53	0.028	+ 3.0	+0.002
	0.10	67	0.057	−16.0	−0.016
	0.10 (extn)	55	0.053	− 5.0	−0.005
	0.20	30	0.052	−14.0	−0.028
	0.20 (extn)	48	0.088	− 8.0	−0.017
Mg	0.05	10	0.006	+ 8.5	+0.004
	0.10	10	0.011	+ 8.2	+0.008
	0.20	7	0.014	+ 5.0	+0.010
Mn	0.05	14	0.007	+ 6.0	+0.003
	0.25	12	0.030	+ 4.4	+0.011
	0.50	8	0.043	+ 1.3	+0.007
Ag	0.05	17	0.010	+10.6	+0.005
	0.10	11	0.010	− 7.1	−0.007
	0.20	8	0.016	+ 7.3	+0.015
Zn	0.05	46	0.021	− 9.3	−0.005
	0.50	3	0.016	+ 1.4	+0.007
	1.00	5	0.051	− 0.1	−0.001

Table 33:03 Operating Parameters

Metal	Wavelength, nm	Flame	Optimum range, mg/L
Cd	328.1	Oxidizing air–C_2H_2	0.1 – 2
Cr	357.9	Sl. reducing air–C_2H_2	1 –200
Cu	324.7	Oxidizing air–C_2H_2	0.1 – 10
Fe	248.3	Oxidizing air–C_2H_2	0.1 – 20
Pb	217.0	Sl. oxidizing air–C_2H_2	1 – 10
Mg[a]	285.2	Reducing air–C_2H_2	0.01– 2
Mn	279.5	Oxidizing air–C_2H_2	0.1 – 20
Ag	328.1	Oxidizing air–C_2H_2	0.1 – 20
Zn	213.9	Oxidizing air–C_2H_2	0.1 – 2

[a] With 1% La soln.

33.092 ***Preparation of Sample***

(**a**) *Dissolved metals.*—As soon as practicable after collection, filter known vol. sample thru 0.45 μm membrane. Use first 50–100 mL to rinse flask and discard. Collect filtrate and preserve soln by adding 3 mL HNO_3 (1+1)/L.

(**b**) *Suspended metals.*—Transfer residue and membrane from (**a**) to 250 mL beaker and add 3 mL HNO_3. Cover with watch glass and heat gently to dissolve membrane. Increase heat and evap. to dryness. Cool, and add 3 mL HNO_3, and heat until digestion is complete, generally indicated by light colored residue. Add 2 mL HCl (1+1), and heat gently to dissolve residue. Wash watch glass and beaker with H_2O and filter. Wash filter and discard. Dil. filtrate with H_2O to concn within range of instrument.

(**c**) *Total metal.*—Transfer aliquot of well mixed sample to beaker and add 3 mL HNO_3. Heat, and evap. to dryness. (Do not boil.) Continue as in (**b**), beginning "Cool, and add 3 mL HNO_3, . . ."

33.093 ***Determination***

(P interference in Mg detn is eliminated by adding La stock soln to sample and working std solns so that final dilns contain 1% La.)

(**a**) *General method.*—Set up instrument as in Table **33:03**, or previously established optimum settings. Secondary or less sensitive lines (*Spectrochim Acta* **17**, 710(1961)) may be used to reduce necessary diln, if desired. Read 4 std solns within range before and after each group of 6–12 samples, and re-establish 0 *A* each time. Prep. calibration curve from av. of each std before and after sample group. Read sample concn from plot of *A* against mg/L.

(**b**) *Special extraction method.*—When Pb or Cd concn is too low for direct detn, transfer sample aliquot to 250 mL beaker and dil. to 100 mL with H_2O. Prep. blank and stds in same manner. Adjust pH of sample and std solns to 2.5 with HCl, using pH meter. Transfer quant. to 200 mL vol. flask, add 2.5 mL APDC soln, and mix. Add 10 mL methyl isobutyl ketone and shake vigorously 1 min. Let layers sep.; then add H_2O until ketone layer is in neck of flask. (Centrfg may be necessary.) Aspirate ketone layer and record readings of stds and samples

Table 33:04 Preparation of Metal Standard Solutions

Metal[a]	Wt, g	Compd	Dissolving medium (1 L total)
Cd	1.142	CdO	5 mL redistd HNO_3
Cr	1.923	CrO_3	H_2O + 10 mL redistd HNO_3
Cu	1.000	Cu, electrolytic	5 mL redistd HNO_3
Fe	1.000	Fe wire	5 mL redistd HNO_3
Pb	1.599	$Pb(NO_3)_2$	H_2O + 10 mL redistd HNO_3
Mg	0.829	MgO	10 mL redistd HNO_3[b]
Mn	1.583	MnO_2	10 mL HCl
Ag	1.575	$AgNO_3$	H_2O + 10 mL redistd HNO_3
Zn	1.000	Zn	10 mL HNO_3

[a] Final concn = 1000 mg/L except for Mg (500 mg/L).
[b] Add 1 mL La stock soln to 10 mL working std soln.

against blank. (Fuel-to-air ratio should be adjusted to as blue a flame as possible, since org. solv. adds to fuel supply.) Prep. calibration curve from av. of each std and read sample concn from plot (mg/L).

33.094 ***Calculations***

(**a**) *General method.*—mg Metal/L = (mg metal in aliquot/L) × *F* where *F* = final diln/mL aliquot.

(**b**) *Special extraction method.*—mg Metal/L = mg metal in aliquot/L.

Mercury

Flameless Atomic Absorption Method (9)
Official Final Action

33.095 ***Principle***

Org. Hg is oxidized to inorg. Hg by $KMnO_4$, $K_2S_2O_8$, and heat. The Hg is reduced to elemental state with stannous ion, and Hg is aerated from soln thru measuring cell in closed system. *A* is measured in AA spectrophtr.

Method is applicable to detn of 0.2–10 μg Hg/L of drinking, surface, and saline waters and domestic and industrial wastes. Interference from Cl or ≤20 mg S/L is eliminated by oxidn with $KMnO_4$; 10 mg Cu/L does not interfere. Analysis without reagents will det. if absorbing interfering volatile org. compds are present.

Natural waters analyzed by 76–82 laboratories showed the following results on exact increments of org. and inorg. Hg compds:

Added, μg Hg/L	Std deviation		Bias	
	%	μg Hg/L	%	μg Hg/L
0.21	79	0.28	+66	+0.14
0.27	67	0.28	+53	+0.14
0.51	79	0.54	+32	+0.16
0.60	55	0.39	+18	+0.11
3.4	44	1.5	+ 0.34	0.0
4.1	29	1.1	− 7.1	−0.3
8.8	42	3.7	− 0.4	0.0
9.6	39	3.6	− 5.2	−0.5

33.096 ***Apparatus***

(Rinse all glassware with chromic acid cleaning soln or HNO_3 (1+1) and Hg-free H_2O before use.)

(**a**) *Atomic absorption spectrophotometer.*—Equipped with Hg hollow cathode lamp and gas flow-thru cell (Fig. **33:01**), 115 × 25 (id) mm with quartz windows cemented in place. Use at 253.7 nm with operating conditions specified by manufacturer.

(**b**) *Air pump.*—Peristaltic pump capable of delivering ca 1 L air/min. Use Tygon tubing for all connections.

(**c**) *Flowmeter.*—Capable of measuring air flow of 1 L/min.

(**d**) *Lamp.*—Small reading lamp contg 60 watt bulb to prevent condensation of moisture inside cell. Position lamp to warm cell (*See* Fig. **33:01**.). Alternatively, use $Mg(ClO_4)_2$-filled drying tube, **33.097**(**a**).

(**e**) *Digestion flask.*—250 mL flat-bottom boiling flask fitted with 2-hole rubber stopper. Use straight glass frit of coarse porosity for gas inlet.

33.097 ***Reagents***

(**a**) *Magnesium perchlorate.*—Place 20 g $Mg(ClO_4)_2$ in 150 × 18 (id) mm drying tube (Fig. **33:01**); replace as needed. (*Caution: See* **51.064**.)

(**b**) *Mercury absorbing media.*—Add one of following to 250 mL gas-washing bottle fitted with 2-hole rubber stopper and attach to aeration app. as by-pass (*See* Fig. **33:01**): (*1*) *Potassium permanganate-sulfuric acid soln.*—Equal vols 0.1*N* $KMnO_4$ and H_2SO_4 (1+9). (*2*) *Iodine-potassium iodide soln.*—0.25% I_2-3% KI soln. Alternatively, vent Hg vapor into exhaust hood.

(**c**) *Sodium chloride-hydroxylamine sulfate soln.*—Dissolve 120 g NaCl and 120 g $(NH_2OH)_2.H_2SO_4$ in H_2O and dil. to 1 L.

(**d**) *Stannous sulfate soln.*—Disperse 100 g $SnSO_4$ in H_2O contg 14 mL H_2SO_4 and dil. to 1 L. Stir suspension with mag. stirrer continuously during use.

(**e**) *Mercury std solns.*—(*1*) *Stock soln.*—1000 μg/mL. Dissolve 0.1354 g $HgCl_2$ in 75 mL H_2O, add 10 mL HNO_3, and dil. to 100 mL with H_2O. (*2*) *Intermediate soln.*—10 μg/mL. Pipet 10 mL stock soln into 500 mL H_2O, add 2 mL HNO_3, and dil. to 1 L with H_2O. Prep. fresh daily. (*3*) *Working soln.*—0.1 μg/mL. Pipet 10 mL intermediate soln into 500 mL H_2O, add 2 mL HNO_3, and dil. to 1 L with H_2O. Prep. fresh daily.

33.098 ***Preparation of Sample***

(**a**) *Dissolved mercury.*—Proceed as in **33.092**(**a**).

(**b**) *Suspended mercury.*—Transfer residue and membrane from (**a**) to digestion flask and proceed as in **33.099**.

(**c**) *Total mercury.*—Preserve soln by adding 2 mL HNO_3/L and proceed as in **33.099**.

33.099 ***Determination***

Transfer 100 mL sample or aliquot dild to 100 mL, contg ≤1.0 μg Hg, to digestion flask. Slowly add 5 mL H_2SO_4 and 2.5 mL HNO_3, with mixing. Add 15 mL *5%* $KMnO_4$ *soln,* shake, and add addnl $KMnO_4$ until purple color lasts ≥15 min. Add 8 mL *5%* $K_2S_2O_8$ *soln*, heat 2 hr in 95° H_2O bath, and cool to room temp.

Adjust output of pump to ca 1 L/min and connect app. as in Fig. **33:01**, except for gas inlet. With pump working and spectrophtr zeroed, add 6 mL NaCl-$(NH_2OH)_2.H_2SO_4$ soln to reduce excess $KMnO_4$ (purple color disappears); let stand 30 sec, and add 5 mL $SnSO_4$ soln. Immediately connect digestion flask gas inlet to aeration app. and aerate without manual agitation. *A* will reach max. within 30 sec. Record *A*. When pen levels off (ca 1 min), open by-pass valve and continue aeration until *A* returns to min. value. Close bypass valve, remove stopper and frit from digestion flask, and continue aeration to flush system.

Check for interfering volatile org. compds by placing same vol. sample or dild sample into digestion flask. Connect flask to aeration app. and aerate without manual agitation and measure *A* after 30 sec. Subtract *A* from reading obtained on sample with reagents added.

Prep. std curve by dilg 0, 0.5, 1.0, 2.0, 5.0, and 10.0 mL aliquots Hg working std soln to 100 mL, and adding to series of digestion flasks. Proceed as in par. 1, beginning "Slowly add 5 mL H_2SO_4 . . ."

Plot *A* against μg Hg. Det. μg Hg in sample from curve.

$$\mu g\ Hg/L = W \times (1000/V),$$

where *W* = μg Hg in sample and *V* = mL sample.

Barium—Official Final Action

(It is not necessary to look for Ba if sulfate is present in appreciable amt unless sample contains large amt of bicarbonate or chloride, which may hold in soln small amts of both sulfate and Ba.)

Gravimetric Method (10)

33.100 ***Reagents***

(**a**) *Ammonium dichromate soln.*—Dissolve 100 g of the SO_4-free salt in H_2O and dil. to 1 L.

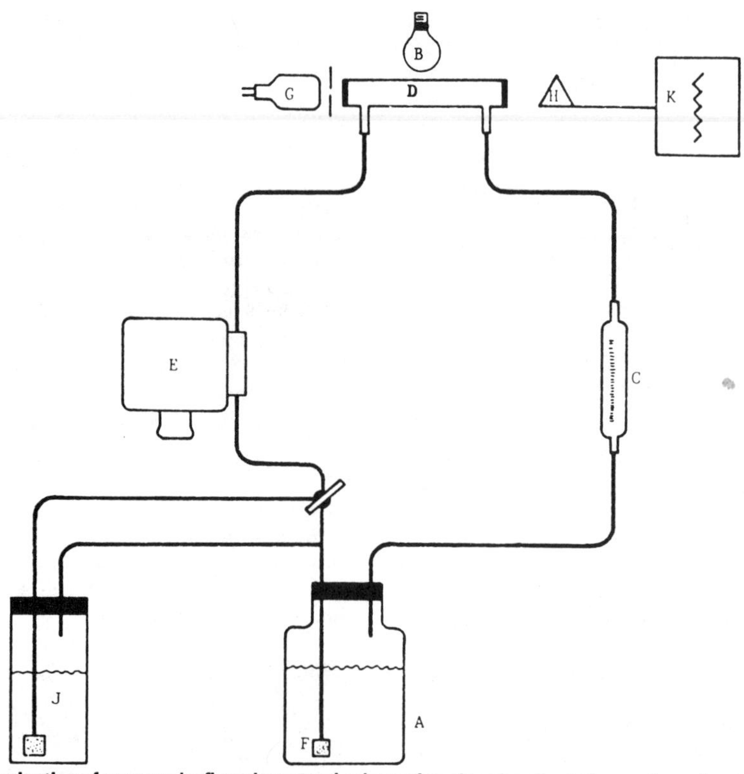

FIG. 33:01—Apparatus for determination of mercury by flameless atomic absorption closed recirculating system: A, reaction flask; B, 60 watt light bulb; C, rotameter, 1 L air/min; D, absorption cell with quartz windows; E, air pump, 1 L air/min; F, glass tube with fritted end; G, hollow cathode Hg lamp; H, atomic absorption detector; J, gas washing bottle contg 0.25% I_2 in 3% KI soln; K, recorder, any compatible model.

(**b**) *Ammonium acetate soln.*—Dissolve 300 g of the salt in H_2O, neutze with NH_4OH, and dil. to 1 L.

(**c**) *Dilute ammonium acetate wash soln.*—Dil. 20 mL (**b**) to 1 L.

(Reaction of acetate solns should be alk. rather than acid.)

33.101 ***Determination***

Acidify 1–5 L portion of sample with HCl and conc. to ca 200 mL. (If ppt forms, filter off and test for Ba.) Add ca 0.5 g NH_4Cl, and ppt Fe and Al with NH_4OH. Boil, filter, and wash. To filtrate, add excess (10 mL) NH_4OAc soln, (**b**), keeping total vol. ca 200 mL. Heat to bp, and add, with stirring, ca 5 mL $(NH_4)_2Cr_2O_7$ soln. Let settle and cool. Decant clear liq. thru filter and wash ppt by decantation with dil. NH_4OAc soln until filtrate is no longer perceptibly colored (ca 100 mL wash soln).

Place beaker under funnel, dissolve ppt on paper with warm HNO_3 (1+1), using as little as possible, and wash paper. Add little more acid to dissolve ppt in beaker, and then NH_4OH until ppt that forms no longer redissolves. Heat to bp; add, with stirring, 10 mL NH_4OAc soln, (**b**), and 2 mL $(NH_4)_2Cr_2O_7$ soln; let cool slowly, and wash ppt free of chromate with dil. NH_4OAc soln by decantation and filtration. Dry ppt, ignite moderately to const wt, and weigh as $BaCrO_4$. Calc. as Ba, using factor 0.5421.

33.102 ***Volumetric Method***

Proceed as in **33.101** thru "... wash ppt free of chromate with dil. NH_4OAc soln ..." (after second pptn). Dissolve ppt in ca 10 mL HCl (1+1) and hot H_2O. Wash filter, dil. soln to ca 400 mL, and add ca 50 mL freshly prepd 10% KI soln. Mix carefully and titr. liberated I_2 after 3 or 4 min with 0.1*N* $Na_2S_2O_3$. 1 mL 0.1*N* $Na_2S_2O_3$ = 4.578 mg Ba.

Potassium (*1, 2*)

Atomic Absorption Method

33.103 ***Principle***

Method is applicable to detn of 0.01–2 mg K/L of surface and saline waters and domestic and industrial wastes. Na may interfere if present at much higher levels than K but effect may be avoided by approx. matching Na concn of stds with that of sample.

Synthetic H_2O analyzed by 19 analysts in 10 laboratories showed the following results on exact increments of K salt:

Added, mg K/L	Std deviation		Bias	
	%	mg K/L	%	mg K/L
1.5	11	0.17	+4.8	0.07
1.4	16	0.22	+6.6	0.09
8.0	8	0.64	+7.6	0.60
7.5	9	0.66	+8.7	0.64
20.0	6	1.11	+7.4	1.5
19.0	8	1.58	+7.4	1.4

33.104 ***Apparatus***

Atomic absorption spectrophotometer.—Equipped with Boling-type burner, set at 766.5 nm.

33.105 ***Reagents***

(**a**) *Deionized distilled water.—See* **33.053**(**a**). Use for prepn of reagents and stds, and as diln H_2O.

(**b**) *Potassium std solns.*—(*1*) *Stock soln.*—100 mg K/L. Dissolve 0.1907 g KCl, dried at 110°, in H_2O, and dil. to 1 L. (*2*) *Working solns.*—Prep. dil. std solns in range of interest at time of analysis. If HNO_3 is used to preserve samples, add corresponding amt to working std solns.

33.106 ***Determination***

(*Caution: See* **51.006**.)

Follow manufacturer's instructions for app. operation. Optimize conditions for max. absorption and stability. Beginning with blank and working toward highest std, aspirate solns and record readings. Repeat std solns and samples enough times to secure reliable av. reading for each soln. If necessary, dil. sample with H_2O to bring into range for direct reading.

For instruments which read directly in concn, set curve corrector to read out proper concn. Otherwise, plot calibration curve, using concn range producing absorption of 0–80%. Before plotting, convert % absorption to absorbance: A = log (100/% T) = 2 − log % T, where % T = 100 − % absorption. Curves are frequently nonlinear. Increase number of stds in that portion of curve.

Read mg K/L from calibration curve or directly from readout system.

mg K/L in sample = (mg K/L) in aliquot × D; D = (mL aliquot + mL H_2O added)/mL aliquot.

Sodium (*1, 2*)

Atomic Absorption Method

33.107 ***Principle***

Method is applicable to detn of 1–200 mg Na/L in surface and saline waters and domestic and industrial wastes.

Synthetic H_2O analyzed by 22 analysts in 12 laboratories showed the following results on exact increments of Na salts:

Added,	Std deviation		Bias	
mg Na/L	%	mg Na/L	%	mg Na/L
4.1	3.4	0.14	+1.9	0.07
3.8	5.0	0.19	+2.9	0.11
55.0	3.6	1.99	+0.9	0.5
52.0	3.7	1.93	+0.8	0.4
155	2.4	3.75	+0.0	0.0
149	2.7	3.97	−0.1	0.0

33.108 ***Apparatus***

Atomic absorption spectrophotometer.—See **33.104**. Use Na hollow cathode lamp, 330.2 nm, Bolling burner, and oxidizing air-C_2H_2 flame. For greater sensitivity (0.005–0.2 mg/L), use 589.0 nm line.

33.109 ***Reagents***

(**a**) *Deionized distilled water.—See* **33.053**(**a**).

(**b**) *Sodium std solns.*—(*1*) *Stock soln.*—1000 mg Na/L. Dissolve 2.542 g NaCl, dried at 140°, in H_2O, and dil. to 1 L. (*2*) *Working solns.*—Prep. dil. std solns in range of interest at time of analysis. If HNO_3 is used to preserve samples, add corresponding amt to working std solns.

33.110 ***Determination***

Proceed as in **33.106**, using Na parameters and std solns.

Phosphorus (*1, 4*)

33.111 ***Definitions***

(**a**) *Phosphorus.*—(*P*). All P present in sample, regardless of form, measured by persulfate digestion method. (*1*) *Orthophosphate.*—(*P, ortho*). Inorg. P, (PO_4^{-3}), in sample as measured by direct colorimetric analysis. (*2*) *Hydrolyzable phosphorus.*—(*P, hydro*). P as measured by H_2SO_4 hydrolysis method minus orthophosphate; includes polyphosphates, $(P_2O_7)^{-4}$, $(P_3O_{10})^{-5}$, and some org. P. (*3*) *Organic phosphorus.*— (*P, org*) = *P* − [(*P, ortho*) + (*P, hydro*)].

(**b**) *Dissolved phosphorus.*—(*P-D*). P present in filtrate of sample filtered thru 0.45 μm pore filter, measured by persulfate digestion method. (*1*) *Dissolved orthophosphate.*—(*P-D, ortho*). Inorg. P as measured by direct colorimetric method. (*2*) *Dissolved hydrolyzable phosphorus.*—(*P-D, hydro*). P as measured by H_2SO_4 hydrolysis − (*P-D, ortho*). (*3*) *Dissolved organic phosphorus.*—(*P-D, org*) = (*P-D*) − [(*P-D, ortho*) + (*P-D, hydro*)].

(**c**) *Insoluble phosphorus.*—(*P-I*). When sufficient amt is present, calc. following: (*1*) *P-I* = (*P*) − (*P-D*). (*2*) *Insoluble orthophosphate.*—(*P-I, ortho*) = [(*P, ortho*) − (*P-D, ortho*)]. (*3*) *Insoluble hydrolyzable phosphorus.*—(*P-I, hydro*) = [(*P, hydro*) − (*P-D, hydro*)]. (*4*) *Insoluble organic phosphorus.*—(*P-I, org*) = [(*P, org*) − (*P-D, org*)].

33.112 ***Principle***

Ammonium molybdate and K antimonyl tartrate react in acid soln with dil. solns of PO_4^{-3} to form Sb phosphomolybdate complex which is reduced to intensely blue complexes by ascorbic acid. Method is specific for orthophosphate and for compds that can be convered to orthophosphate. Various forms of P are detd, depending on pretreatment, in range 0.01–0.5 mg P/L.

Method is applicable to surface and saline waters and domestic and industrial wastes. Most commonly measured forms are total P, dissolved P, orthophosphate, and dissolved orthophosphate. Hydrolyzable P is normally found only in sewage-type samples. Concns of Cu, Fe, silicate, and arsenate many times greater than those in sea water do not interfere. Interference of $HgCl_2$, used as preservative, is overcome by adding min. of 50 mg NaCl/L to samples.

Natural H_2O analyzed by 33 analysts in 19 laboratories showed following results on exact increments of org. phosphate:

Added,	Std deviation		Bias	
mg P/L	%	mg P/L	%	mg P/L
0.110	30	0.033	+ 3.1	+0.003
0.132	39	0.051	+12.0	+0.016
0.772	17	0.130	+ 3.0	+0.023
0.882	15	0.128	− 0.9	−0.008

Natural H_2O analyzed by 26 analysts in 16 laboratories showed following results on exact increments of orthophosphate:

Added,	Std deviation		Bias	
mg P/L	%	mg P/L	%	mg P/L
0.029	34	0.010	−5.0	−0.001
0.038	21	0.008	−6.0	−0.002
0.335	5.4	0.018	−2.8	−0.009
0.383	6.0	0.023	−1.8	−0.007

33.113 ***Apparatus***

(**a**) *Glassware.*—Wash all glassware with hot HCl (1+1) and rinse with H_2O. Remove last traces of P by filling with H_2O contg all color-developing reagents. Use treated glassware only for P detns and after use, rinse with H_2O and keep covered until used again. Under such conditions, hot HCl and reagent treatment need be applied only occasionally. *Never use com. detergents on glassware.*

(**b**) *Photometer.*—Spectrophtr or filter photometer measuring at 880 nm, using ⩾2.5 cm light path.

33.114 ***Reagents***

(**a**) *Dilute sulfuric acid.*—5*N*. Dil. 70 mL H_2SO_4 to 500 mL.

(**b**) *Potassium antimonyl tartrate soln.*—Weigh 1.3715 g $K(SbO)C_4H_4O_6.0.5H_2O$, dissolve in ca 400 mL H_2O, and dil. to 500 mL. Store in dark g-s bottle at 4°.

(**c**) *Ammonium molybdate soln.*—Dissolve 20 g $(NH_4)_6Mo_7O_{24}.4H_2O$ in 500 mL H_2O. Store in plastic bottle at 4°.

(**d**) *Ascorbic acid soln.*—0.1*M*. Dissolve 1.76 g in 100 mL H_2O. Stable 1 week at 4°.

(**e**) *Combined reagent.*—Warm reagents (**b**)–(**d**) to room temp., and add with mixing in following order: 50 mL 5*N* H_2SO_4, 5 mL K antimonyl tartrate soln, 15 mL NH_4 molybdate soln, and 30 mL ascorbic acid soln. If turbidity forms, shake, and let stand few min before proceeding. Stable 1 week at 4°.

(**f**) *Hydrolyzing acid soln.*—Slowly add 310 mL H_2SO_4 to 600 mL H_2O, cool, and dil. to 1 L.

(**g**) *Phosphorus std solns.*—(*1*) *Stock soln.*—50 mg P/L. Dissolve and dil. 0.2197 g KH_2PO_4, dried at 105°, to 1 L. (*2*) *Intermediate soln.*—0.5 mg/L. Dil. 10.0 mL stock soln to 1 L. (*3*) *Working solns.*—Dil. 0.0, 1.0, 3.0, 5.0, 10.0, 20.0, 30.0, 40.0, and 50.0 mL intermediate soln to 50 mL to prep. std solns contg 0.0, 0.01, 0.03, 0.05, 0.10, 0.20, 0.30, 0.40, and 0.50 mg P/L.

33.115 ***Determination***

Store samples in plastic or Pyrex containers. If analysis cannot be performed on day of collection, preserve with 40 mg $HgCl_2$/L and refrigerate at 4°. In such case, add 50 mg NaCl/L before analysis.

(**a**) *Phosphorus.*—Add 1 mL hydrolyzing acid soln to 50 mL sample in 125 mL erlenmeyer. Add 0.4 g NH_4 persulfate, and boil gently on preheated hot plate 30–40 min or until vol is 10 mL. Do not let sample evap. to dryness. Alternatively, autoclave 30 min at 121°. Cool, add few drops phthln, adjust to pink with 1*N* NaOH, and then to colorless with 1 drop hydrolyzing acid soln. Cool, and dil. to 50.0 mL. If turbid, filter. Proceed as in (**c**), beginning "Add 8.0 mL combined reagent, . . ."

(**b**) *Hydrolyzable phosphorus.*—Proceed as in (**a**), except omit addn of NH_4 persulfate.

(**c**) *Orthophosphate.*—Add 1 drop phthln to 50.0 mL sample; if red develops, add hydrolyzing acid soln dropwise until color is discharged. Add 8.0 mL combined reagent, and mix thoroly. After specific time within 10–30 min, measure *A* at 880 nm against reagent blank as ref.

(**d**) *Std curve and calculation.*—Process stds and blank as in (**c**) and plot *A* against mg P/L. Include blank and ≥2 std solns with each series of samples. If stds do not agree with std curve within ±2%, prep. new std curve. Obtain mg P/L sample directly from std curve.

Automated Method (1)

33.116 ***Principle***

See **33.111–33.115**. Developed color is measured automatically.

Natural H_2O analyzed by 6 laboratories showed following results on exact increments of orthophosphate:

Added, mg P/L	Std deviation %	Std deviation mg P/L	Bias %	Bias mg P/L
0.04	47	0.019	+16.7	+0.007
0.04	35	0.014	− 8.3	−0.003
0.29	30	0.087	−15.5	−0.05
0.30	22	0.066	−12.8	−0.04

33.117 ***Apparatus***

(**a**) *Glassware.*—*See* **33.113(a)**.

(**b**) *Automatic analyzer.*—AutoAnalyzer with following modules (Technicon Instruments Corp.): Sampler I, manifold, proportioning pump, 50° bath, colorimeter with 50 mm tubular flowcell and 650 nm filter, and recorder. *See* Fig. **33:02**.

33.118 ***Reagents***

Prep. reagents **33.114(a)**, (**d**), and (**f**), and following:

(**a**) *Potassium antimonyl tartrate soln.*—Weigh 0.3 g $K(SbO)C_4H_4O_6.0.5H_2O$, dissolve in ca 50 mL H_2O, and dil. to 100 mL. Store in dark g-s bottle at 4°.

(**b**) *Ammonium molybdate soln.*—Dissolve 4 g $(NH_4)_6Mo_7O_{24}.4H_2O$ in 100 mL H_2O. Store in plastic bottle at 4°.

(**c**) *Combined reagent.*—Prep. as in **33.114(e)**. 100 mL is enough for 4 hr operation. Prep. fresh for each series.

(**d**) *Wash water.*—Add 40 mL hydrolyzing acid soln, **33.114(f)**, to ca 1 L H_2O and dil. to 2 L (not used when only orthophosphate is detd).

(**e**) *Phosphorus std solns.*—(*1*) *Stock soln.*—0.1 mg P/L. Dissolve and dil. 0.4393 g KH_2PO_4, dried at 105°, to 1 L. (*2*) *Intermediate soln 1.*—0.01 mg P/L. Dil. 100 mL stock soln to 1 L. (*3*) *Intermediate soln 2.*— 0.001 mg P/L. Dil. 100 mL intermediate soln *1* to 1 L. (*4*) *Working solns.*—Dil. 0.0, 2.0, 5.0, and 10.0 mL intermediate soln *2* and 2.0, 5.0, 8.0, and 10.0 mL intermediate soln *1* to 100 mL to prep. std solns contg 0.00, 0.02, 0.05, 0.10, 0.20, 0.50, 0.80, and 1.00 mg P/L, resp.

33.119 ***Determination***

Store and prep. samples as in **33.115**.

(**a**) *Phosphorus.*—Proceed as in **33.115(a)**, but det. orthophosphate as in (**c**), below.

(**b**) *Hydrolyzable phosphorus.*—Proceed as in **33.115(a)**, omitting addn of NH_4 persulfate, and det. orthophosphate as in (**c**), below.

(**c**) *Orthophosphate.*—Set up manifold as in Fig. **33:02**. Let colorimeter and recorder warm up 30 min. Run baseline with all reagents but with H_2O thru sample line. Adjust dark current and operative opening on colorimeter to obtain stable baseline. Place wash H_2O, (**d**), in sampler in pairs, for other than ortho-P, and H_2O for ortho-P, leaving every third position vacant. Set sample timing at 1 min. Place std solns in sampler in vacant positions in order of decreasing concn and complete filling of sampler tray with unknown samples. Change sample line from H_2O to sampler and begin analysis.

(**d**) *Std curve and calculation.*—Prep. std curve by plotting peak hts against mg P/L. Obtain sample concn from peak ht. Reanalyze any sample whose computed value is <5% of its immediate predecessor.

Sulfate

Turbidimetric Method (1, 2)

33.120 ***Principle***

Sulfate is pptd in dil. HCl with $BaCl_2$ under controlled conditions to form $BaSO_4$ crystals of uniform size. *A* of suspension is measured and sulfate concn is obtained from std curve.

Method is applicable to drinking and surface waters and domestic and industrial wastes. Dil. samples to concn of ≤40 mg SO_4/L. Color and suspended matter interfere. Some suspended matter is removed by filtration. Remaining interference is corrected by blank which omits $BaCl_2$.

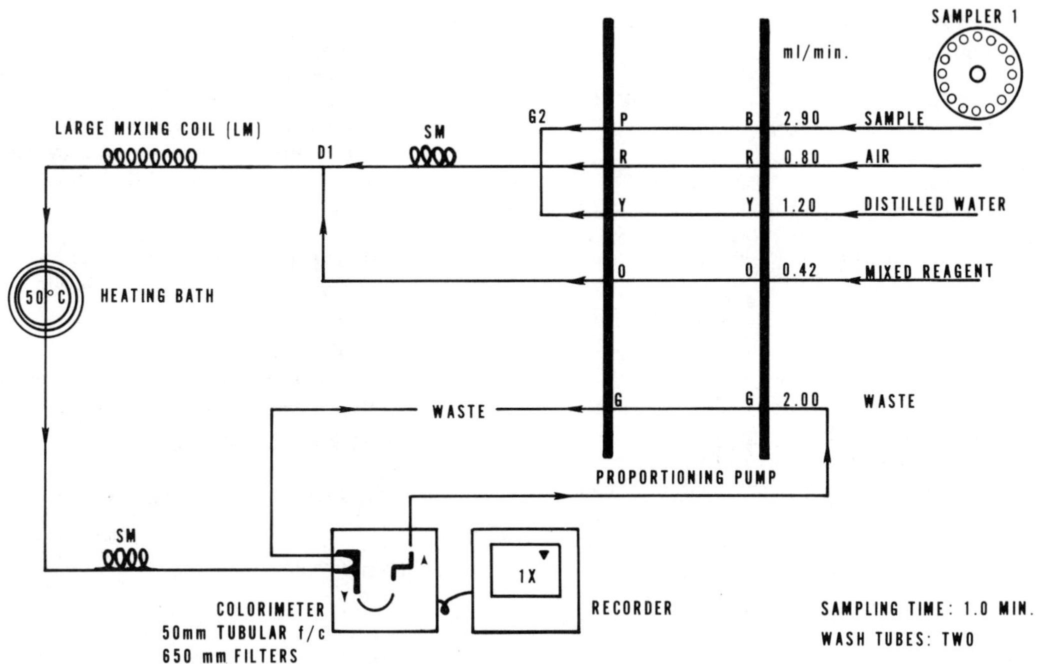

FIG. 33:02—Phosphorus manifold

Synthetic H_2O samples contg exact increments of inorg. SO_4 analyzed by 34 analysts in 16 laboratories showed following results:

Increment as mg SO_4/L	Std deviation		Bias	
	%	mg SO_4/L	%	mg SO_4/L
8.6	27	2.3	−3.7	−0.3
9.2	20	1.8	−8.3	−0.8
110	7.1	7.9	−3.0	−3.3
122	6.1	7.5	−3.4	−4.1
188	5.1	9.6	0.0	+0.1
199	5.9	11.8	−1.7	−3.4

33.121 *Apparatus*

(**a**) *Magnetic stirrer.*—Adjustable, but once set must operate at const speed. Stirring bars must be of identical shape and size. Exact speed is not critical, but it should be const for each series of samples and stds and should be at max. at which no splashing occurs. Timing device to permit operation for exactly 1 min is desirable.

(**b**) *Photometer.*—Nephelometer, spectrophtr set at 420 nm with 4–5 cm cell, or filter photometer with filter having max. *T* near 420 nm with 4–5 cm cell.

33.122 *Reagents*

(**a**) *Conditioning reagent.*—Mix 50 mL glycerol with soln of 30 mL HCl, 300 mL H_2O, 100 mL alcohol or isopropanol, and 75 g NaCl.

(**b**) *Barium chloride.*—Crystals, 20–30 mesh. Dispense from 0.2–0.3 mL measuring spoon.

(**c**) *Sulfate std soln.*—100 μg SO_4/mL. Dil. 10.41 mL 0.0200*N* H_2SO_4 to 100 mL, or dissolve 147.9 mg anhyd. Na_2SO_4 in H_2O and dil. to 1 L.

33.123 *Determination*

Pipet 5 mL conditioning reagent into 100 mL sample or aliquot dild to 100 mL in 250 mL erlenmeyer, and mix on mag. stirrer. While stirring, add spoonful of $BaCl_2$ crystals and begin timing. Stir exactly 1 min at const speed. Immediately transfer some soln into cell and measure turbidity at 30 sec intervals for 4 min. Record max. reading. Conduct blank detn without $BaCl_2$ and subtract reading.

Prep. std curve by carrying 0–40 mg SO_4/L, in 5 mg increments, thru entire detn. Introduce std soln with every 3–4 samples.

mg SO_4/L = mg SO_4 from curve × 1000/mL sample.

33.124 *Gravimetric Method*

Make preliminary examination, using 100–250 mL sample, to det. approx. amt of sulfates. (Alkali salts present can be approximated by calcg amt of Na necessary to combine with excess of acids—HCl, H_2SO_4, and H_2CO_3—over Ca and Mg.)

Take enough sample (usually 1–5 L) to yield ≤1 g $BaSO_4$ and ≤0.5 g mixed chlorides. Acidify with HCl (1+1), evap. to dryness in Pt dish, and remove SiO_2 by 2 evapns as in **33.077**, using ≤2 mL HCl for final soln. Combine filtrate and washings from SiO_2 detns and conc. to 150–200 mL. Heat to bp and ppt with slight excess of 10% $BaCl_2.2H_2O$ soln, added very slowly and with const stirring. Cover, and let stand on steam bath ca 12 hr. Filter, thoroly wash $BaSO_4$ ppt with hot H_2O until Cl-free, dry, ignite over Bunsen burner and weigh.

If sulfate content of sample is unusually large, proceed as far as concn of SiO_2 filtrates, as above. Add 50 mL HCl, heat to bp, and ppt with $BaCl_2$ soln as before. Evap. to dryness, take up in H_2O and few drops HCl, digest until ppt settles, wash by decantation, filter, ignite, and weigh. Calc. to SO_4 ion.

33.125 Preparation of Sample—Manganese, Iodine, Bromine, Arsenic, and Boric Acid—Official Final Action

Evap. 0.5–2 L sample to dryness after addn of small amts of solid Na_2CO_3. Boil residue thus obtained with H_2O, transfer to filter, and wash thoroly with hot H_2O. Use residue remaining on filter for detn of Mn. Dil. alk. filtrate to definite vol. and use for detn of I, Br, As, and H_3BO_3.

Manganese—Official Final Action

Persulfate Method

33.126 ***Reagents***

(**a**) *Silver nitrate soln*.—Dissolve 2 g $AgNO_3$ in H_2O and dil. to 1 L.

(**b**) *Manganese std soln*.—0.1 mg/mL. Dissolve 0.2877 g $KMnO_4$ in ca 100 mL H_2O, acidify soln with H_2SO_4 (1+1), and slowly heat to bp. Slowly add enough 10% $H_2C_2O_4.2H_2O$ soln to discharge color. Cool, and dil. to 1 L.

33.127 ***Determination***

Dissolve insol. residue, **33.125**, in excess HNO_3 (1+1), evap. to dryness, treat with H_2O, and add ca 1 mL HNO_3 and little of the $AgNO_3$ soln. If ppt of AgCl appears, add addnl $AgNO_3$ soln until all Cl is pptd. Add excess of ca 10 mL $AgNO_3$ soln for each mg Mn present in sample. Filter, add 1 g $(NH_4)_2S_2O_8$ to filtrate, and place beaker or flask contg soln on steam bath until pink color develops (ca 20 min). Compare color developed with stds similarly prepd by treating solns contg known amts of std Mn soln with dil. HNO_3, $AgNO_3$ soln, and $(NH_4)_2S_2O_8$.

33.128 ★ Bismuthate Method (11) ★

See **31.037–31.038**, 10th ed.

Iodide and Bromide—Official First Action

(This method is qual. and approx. quant. For accurate quant. methods for iodides, *see* **33.149**.)

33.129 ***Determination***

(*Caution: See* **51.039**, **51.040**, **51.047**, and **51.048**.)

Evap. aliquot of alk. filtrate, **33.125**, to dryness; add 2–3 mL H_2O to dissolve residue and enough alcohol to make ca 90% alcohol. (This ppts chlorides.) Heat to bp, filter, and repeat soln and pptn once or twice. Add 2 or 3 drops 10% NaOH soln to combined alc. filtrates and evap. to dryness. Dissolve last residue in 2–3 mL H_2O and repeat pptn with alcohol, heating, and filtering. Add drop of 10% NaOH soln to this alc. filtrate and evap. to dryness.

Dissolve residue in little H_2O, acidify with H_2SO_4 (1+5), using 3 or 4 drops excess, and transfer to small flask. Add 4 drops *0.2% $NaNO_2$ soln* and ca 5 mL CS_2. Shake until all I is extd and filter off acid soln from CS_2. Wash flask, filter, and contents with cold H_2O and transfer CS_2 contg the I in soln to Nessler tube, using ca 5 mL CS_2. In washing filter, make contents of tube to definite vol., usually 12–15 mL, and compare color with that of other tubes contg known amts of I dissolved in CS_2. Prep. these std tubes by treating measured amts of soln of known KI content as above, beginning ". . . acidify with H_2SO_4 (1+5), . . ."

Sep. transfer acid soln of sample and stds from which I has been removed to small flasks. To stds add definite measured amts of bromide soln of known concn, and to each flask contg sample and stds add 5 mL CS_2. Add *satd and freshly prepd Cl-H_2O*, 1 mL at time, shaking after each addn until all Br is set free. Avoid large excess of Cl, as a bromo-chloride may form and change color reaction.

Filter off aq. soln from CS_2 thru moistened filter, wash contents of filter 2 or 3 times with H_2O, and then transfer to Nessler tube with ca 1 mL CS_2. Repeat extn of filtrate twice, using 3 mL CS_2 each time. Combined CS_2 exts usually total 11.5–12 mL. Add enough CS_2 to tubes to make definite vol., usually 12–15 mL, and compare sample with stds. If, when using this method near its upper limit, amts of CS_2 recommended do not ext all Br, make 1 or 2 addnl extns with CS_2, transfer exts to another tube, and compare color with some of lower stds. Add readings thus obtained to others.

Results closely approximating true values for I and Br can be obtained in shorter time on most samples by omitting extns with alcohol and comparing color of CS_2 solns directly in extn flasks.

33.130 ★ Bromide in Presence of Chloride but not Iodide (*12*)—Official First Action ★

See **31.040–31.043**, 10th ed.

33.131 ★ Bromide in Presence of Chloride and Iodide (*13*)—Official Final Action ★

See **31.044–31.046**, 10th ed.

Arsenic—Official Final Action

33.132 ***Reagents and Apparatus***

See **25.006** and **25.007**.

33.133 ***Determination***

Take portion of alk. filtrate, **33.125**, contg $\leq$0.03 mg As_2O_3. If amt taken is >10 mL, evap. soln to ca that vol. on steam bath. Transfer soln into generator of app., **25.007**, with aid of ca 10 mL H_2O, add 20 mL H_2SO_4 (1+2), and proceed as in **25.010** or **25.012**, beginning with addn of KI reagent.

★ Boric Acid ★

33.134 ***Qualitative Test—Procedure***

See **31.049**, 10th ed.

33.135 ***Quantitative Method (14)—Official First Action***

Titrn with NaOH in presence of mannitol. *See* **31.050–31.051**, 10th ed.

33.136 Lead

See **25.095–25.100**.

33.137 Method of Reporting Results (*15*)—Procedure

Report radicals and anhyd. salts in mg/L or, in case of highly concd waters, in g/L. For benefit of physicians, in case of medicinal waters, also report salts in terms of grains/qt, using factor 0.014600 to convert mg/L to grains/qt. In reporting salts in terms of grains/qt, convert salts that have H_2O of crystn to hydrated form as expressed in USP and in NF, and convert $Mg(HCO_3)_2$ to $MgCO_3$ and $Ca(HCO_3)_2$ to $CaCO_3$. Use following factors in these calcns:

$$Na_2SO_4 \times 2.2683 = Na_2SO_4.10H_2O$$
$$MgSO_4 \times 2.0477 = MgSO_4.7H_2O$$
$$CaSO_4 \times 1.2647 = CaSO_4.2H_2O$$
$$Mg(HCO_3)_2 \times 0.5762 = MgCO_3$$
$$Ca(HCO_3)_2 \times 0.6174 = CaCO_3.$$

When complete analysis is made, report error of analysis and state how it is distributed. Report only significant figures.

Report Fe and Al together when present in unimportant amts and in calcns consider them as Fe. When Fe and Al are present in larger amts, make sepn and report each sep.

In calcg hypothetical combinations of anions and cations, join NO_2, NO_3, BO_3, and AsO_4 to Na; I and Br to K; and PO_4 to Ca. Assign residual cations in following order: NH_4, Li, K, Na, Mg,

★ Surplus method—*see* inside front cover.

Ca, Sr, Mn, Fe, and Al; to residual anions in following order: Cl, SO_4, CO_3, and HCO_3. When not enough HCO_3 is present to join with all Ca, residual Ca is joined to SiO_2 to form $CaSiO_3$, and Mn, Fe, and Al are calcd to oxides Mn_3O_4, Fe_2O_3, and Al_2O_3, resp.

Use equiv. combining wts or their reciprocals in uniting radicals and, when necessary for purpose of comparison, in reducing salts to radicals and reuniting radicals in order specified above. *See* Table **33:05**.

Equiv. combining wt of radical is obtained by dividing its wt by its valence. Equiv. combining wt of salt is obtained by dividing its MW by product of valence of basic element and number of atoms of basic element in the salt.

Procedure in calcg hypothetical combinations by use of equiv. combining wts and their reciprocals is as follows:

Multiply wts obtained, expressed in mg/L, or, for highly concd waters, in g/L, for each radical to be combined, by corresponding reciprocal of equiv. combining wts. If Na and K are to be detd by calcn, as is frequently the case, subtract sum of values obtained (reacting values) for basic radicals from sum of reacting values for acid radicals. Difference represents reacting value of undetd Na and K.

When all constituents in water have been detd, sums of reacting values of acid and basic radicals should be very nearly equal. In this case, if difference is reasonable and well within limit of accuracy of methods used, it may be distributed equally among all radicals detd, or among those believed to be less accurately detd than others. If difference is unreasonably great, repeat analysis in whole or in part. Sums of reacting values of acid and basic radicals must be equal before calcn is made. Obtain reacting values of the salts by subtracting in succession reacting values of radicals in specified order. To convert these values to mg/L of respective salts, multiply each of them by the equiv. combining wt of respective salt.

SALT (*16*)

33.138 Preparation of Sample—Procedure

If sample is coarser than "20 mesh," grind so that all will pass No. 20 sieve, but avoid undue grinding so that as much as possible will be retained on No. 80 sieve. Mix sample by quartering and weigh all needed portions as nearly at same time as possible.

33.139 Moisture—Official First Action

Place ca 10 g sample in dry, weighed 200 mL erlenmeyer. Weigh flask and sample. Spread sample evenly over bottom of

Table 33:05 Equivalent Combining Weights and Their Reciprocals Based on International Atomic Weights, 1973

Neg. Radicals	Equiv. Combining Wts	Reciprocals of Equiv. Combining Wts	Pos. Radicals	Equiv. Combining Wts	Reciprocals of Equiv. Combining Wts
NO_3	62.0049	0.01613	NH_4	18.0383	0.05544
BO_2	42.81	0.02336	Li	6.941	0.14407
AsO_4	46.3064	0.02160	K	39.0983	0.02558
I	126.9045	0.00788	Na	22.98977	0.04350
Br	79.904	0.01252	Mg	12.153	0.08228
PO_4	31.6571	0.03159	Ca	20.04	0.04990
HS	33.07	0.03024	Sr	43.81	0.02283
S	16.03	0.06238	Ba	68.67	0.01456
SiO_3	38.042	0.02629	Mn	27.4690	0.03640
O	7.9997	0.12500	Fe^{++}	27.924	0.03581
Cl	35.453	0.02821	Fe^{+++}	18.616	0.05372
SO_4	48.03	0.02082	Al	8.9938	0.11119
CO_3	30.005	0.03333	Cu	31.773	0.03147
HCO_3	61.017	0.01639			

Salts	Equiv. Combining Wts	Reciprocals of Equiv. Combining Wts	Salts	Equiv. Combining Wts	Reciprocals of Equiv. Combining Wts
NH_4Cl	53.491	0.01869	$MgCl_2$	47.606	0.02101
LiCl	42.394	0.02359	$MgSO_4$	60.18	0.01662
Li_2SO_4	54.97	0.01819	$MgCO_3$	42.157	0.02372
Li_2CO_3	36.946	0.02707	$Mg(HCO_3)_2$	73.170	0.01367
$LiHCO_3$	67.958	0.01471	$Mg(NO_3)_2$	74.157	0.01348
KCl	74.551	0.01341	$CaCl_2$	55.49	0.01802
K_2SO_4	87.13	0.01148	$CaSO_4$	68.07	0.01469
K_2CO_3	69.103	0.01447	$CaCO_3$	50.04	0.01998
$KHCO_3$	100.115	0.00999	$Ca(HCO_3)_2$	81.06	0.01234
KI	166.003	0.00602	$CaSiO_3$	58.08	0.01722
KBr	119.002	0.00840	$Ca_3(PO_4)_2$	51.70	0.01934
NaCl	58.443	0.01711	$SrSO_4$	91.84	0.01089
NaBr	102.894	0.00972	$SrCO_3$	73.81	0.01355
NaI	149.8942	0.00667	$Sr(HCO_3)_2$	104.83	0.00954
Na_2SO_4	71.02	0.01408	$BaSO_4$	116.70	0.00857
Na_2CO_3	52.994	0.01887	$Ba(HCO_3)_2$	129.69	0.00771
$NaHCO_3$	84.007	0.01190	$MnSO_4$	75.50	0.01325
$NaNO_2$	68.9952	0.01449	$MnCO_3$	57.474	0.01740
$NaNO_3$	84.9946	0.01177	$Mn(HCO_3)_2$	88.486	0.01130
$NaBO_2$	65.80	0.01520	$FeSO_4$	75.95	0.01317
Na_3AsO_4	69.2961	0.01443	$Fe_2(SO_4)_3$	66.64	0.01501
NaF	41.9881	0.02382	$FeCO_3$	57.928	0.01726
NaHS	56.06	0.01784	$Fe(HCO_3)_2$	88.941	0.01124
Na_3PO_4	54.6488	0.01830	Fe_2O_3	26.615	0.03757
Na_2S	39.02	0.02563	$Al_2(SO_4)_3$	57.02	0.01754
Na_2SiO_3	61.032	0.01638	Al_2O_3	16.9935	0.05885

flask by shaking gently and insert small funnel in neck. Heat flask and sample for periods of 1 hr each at ca 250° until 2 consecutive weighings agree within 5 mg. Occasionally shake flask so that sample will dry evenly. Report loss of wt as H_2O.

33.140 Matters Insoluble in Water—Official First Action

Place 10 g sample in 250 mL beaker, add 200 mL H_2O at room temp., and let stand 30 min, stirring frequently. Filter thru weighed gooch with asbestos mat dried at 110°. Transfer residue to gooch with aid of policeman, using total of ≤50 mL H_2O. Wash residue with ca ten 10 mL portions H_2O, until 10 mL filtrate shows only faint opalescence upon addn of few drops $AgNO_3$ soln. Dry crucible and contents to const wt at 110°. Report increase in wt gooch as "matters insol. in H_2O" and report results in % on H_2O-free basis. If matters insol. in H_2O are >0.1%, det. their nature.

33.141 Matters Insoluble in Acid (*17*) Official First Action

Treat 10 g sample with 200 mL HCl (1+19), boil 2–3 min, and let stand 30 min, stirring frequently. Filter thru gooch with mat dried at 110°. Wash, dry at 110°, cool, and weigh. Express results in %.

33.142 Preparation of Solution for Sulfate, Calcium, and Magnesium—Procedure

Weigh ca 20 g sample, transfer to 400 mL beaker, and dissolve in 200 mL HCl (1+3). Cover beaker, heat to bp, and continue boiling gently 10 min. Filter thru paper and wash residue with small amts of hot H_2O until filtrate is Cl-free. Unite filtrate and washings, cool, and dil. to 500 mL (*Soln X*).

33.143 Sulfate—Official First Action

Place 250 mL *Soln X*, **33.142**, in 400 mL beaker, heat to bp, and add slight excess hot *10% $BaCl_2$ soln* dropwise while stirring. Conc. by heating gently and finally evap. to dryness on steam bath. Facilitate removal of free acid by stirring partly dried residue. Wash ppt by decantation with small amts of hot H_2O, finally transferring ppt to close-grain filter paper with aid of policeman and stream of hot H_2O. Test filtrate for presence of Ba. Wash ppt on paper until filtrate is Cl-free. Dry and ignite paper contg ppt over Bunsen flame. Report % SO_4 in sample on H_2O-free basis.

33.144 Calcium—Official First Action

Place remainder of *Soln X* in 400 mL beaker. Add excess of *10% $H_2C_2O_4.2H_2O$ soln* (10 mL usually is enough). Add few drops Me orange; neutze while hot by adding NH_4OH dropwise, stirring constantly. Add ca 1 mL excess NH_4OH, stir, and let stand in warm place 3 hr. Decant supernate thru filter, reserving filtrate for detn of Mg. Test filtrate for Ca with $(NH_4)_2C_2O_4$ soln. Wash ppt in beaker once with 10 mL *1% $(NH_4)_2C_2O_4$ soln*, decanting thru filter paper. Combine filtrate and washings. Dissolve ppt on paper with hot HCl (1+1), using same beaker; dil. to 100 mL, add little more $H_2C_2O_4$ soln, and ppt as before. Let stand 3 hr, filter, and wash with 1% $(NH_4)_2C_2O_4$ soln as before, reserving filtrate and washings. Transfer ppt to crucible, dry, ignite, and heat over blast lamp to const wt (CaO). Report as % Ca on H_2O-free basis.

33.145 Magnesium—Official First Action

Combine filtrates and washings from Ca detn, conc. if necessary by boiling gently to ca 150 mL, and proceed as in **33.088**. Report as % Mg on H_2O-free basis.

33.146 Lead

See **25.095–25.100**.

Iodine in Iodized Salt (*18*)—Official Final Action

33.147 ***Reagents***

(**a**) *Bromine water*.—(*Caution: See* **51.047**.) For alternative method, **33.149(b)**, det. approx. concn (mg Br/mL) by adding measured vol. from buret to flask contg 50 mL H_2O, 5 mL 10% KI soln, and 5 mL H_2SO_4 (1+9), and titrg liberated I with 0.1*N* $Na_2S_2O_3$.

(**b**) *Sodium thiosulfate*.—0.005*N*. Prep. daily by dilg 0.1*N* soln, **50.037–50.038**.

(**c**) *Starch soln*.—1% (freshly prepd). *See* **2.144(b)**.

(**d**) *Potassium iodide control soln*.—0.3270 g KI/250 mL. Dil. 50 mL to 250 mL, and use 5 mL (= 1.0 mg I and 1.308 mg KI) for control.

33.148 ***Preparation of Sample***

Dissolve 50 g sample in H_2O and dil. to 250 mL in vol. flask. Take 25, for **33.149(a)**, or 50 mL, for **33.149(b)**, aliquot for analysis.

33.149 ***Determination***

(**a**) *Application when $Na_2S_2O_3$ content is ≤0.5%*.— Place sample aliquot in 600 mL beaker and dil. to ca 300 mL. Neutze to Me orange with H_3PO_4 and add 1 mL excess. Proceed as in **7.115**, third par.

(**b**) *Alternative method. Not applicable in presence of $Na_2S_2O_3$*.—Pipet 50 mL sample soln into 200 mL erlenmeyer. Neutze to Me orange with 2*N* H_2SO_4. Add Br-H_2O dropwise from buret in amt equiv. to 20 mg Br. After few min destroy greater portion of remaining free Br by adding 1% Na_2SO_3 soln *dropwise while mixing*. Wash down neck and sides of flask with H_2O and complete removal of Br by adding 1 or 2 drops 5% phenol soln. Add 1 mL 2*N* H_2SO_4 and 5 mL 10% KI soln, and titr. liberated I with $Na_2S_2O_3$ soln, adding 1 mL starch indicator near end of titrn. Correct detn for blank on reagents and make 1 or more control detns, using 50 mL 20% reagent grade NaCl soln to which has been added appropriate amts of dil. control KI soln. 1 mL 0.005*N* $Na_2S_2O_3$ = 0.1058 mg I and 0.1384 mg KI.

33.150 Method of Reporting Results—Procedure

(In absence of added drying agents such as $MgCO_3$, Ca phosphate, etc.)

Convert sulfate to $CaSO_4$ and unused Ca to $CaCl_2$, unless sulfate in sample exceeds amt necessary to combine with Ca, in which case convert Ca to $CaSO_4$ and unused sulfate first to $MgSO_4$ and remaining sulfate, if any, to Na_2SO_4. Convert unused Mg to $MgCl_2$. Add percentages of $CaCl_2$ and $MgCl_2$. Report on H_2O-free basis % of matter insol. in H_2O, of SO_4, of Ca, of Mg, of $CaSO_4$, of $CaCl_2$, and of $MgCl_2$. Also report results of qual. examination of matters insol. in H_2O, if amt is >0.1% on H_2O-free basis.

SELECTED REFERENCES

(*1*) Methods for Chemical Analysis of Water and Wastes, 1971.
(*2*) FWPCA Method Study 1; Mineral and Physical Analyses, June 1969.
(*3*) Method Research Study 3; Demand Analyses, 1971.
(*4*) Method Study No. 2; Nutrient Analyses, Manual Methods, 1970.
(*5*) JAOAC **22**, 482(1939).

(*6*) JAOAC **9,** 29(1926).
(*7*) Chem. Ztg. **35,** 337(1911); JAOAC **1,** 97, 458(1915); **2,** 113(1916).
(*8*) Water Metals No. 4, Study No. 30 (1968), Analytical Reference Service, Public Health Service.
(*9*) ASTM STP 573, 1975, pp. 566–580.
(*10*) Morse, "Exercises in Quantitative Chemistry," p. 417; JAOAC **4,** 86(1920).
(*11*) J. Am. Chem. Soc. **34,** 1379(1912); JAOAC **4,** 85(1920).
(*12*) J. Ind. Eng. Chem. **11,** 954(1919).
(*13*) J. Ind. Eng. Chem. **12,** 358(1920); JAOAC **5,** 29(1921).
(*14*) Ind. Eng. Chem., Anal. Ed. **4,** 38(1932); Methods of Analysis used in Rubidoux Laboratory, USDA Bur. Plant Ind., 5th Ed., 22(1947).
(*15*) JAOAC **5,** 385(1922).
(*16*) JAOAC **5,** 384(1922).
(*17*) JAOAC **5,** 385(1922); **6,** 129(1923).
(*18*) Biochem. Z. **138,** 383(1923); **174,** 364(1926); JAOAC **26,** 440(1943).

Note: Ref. (*1*) is available from Superintendent of Documents, Washington, DC 20402, Stock No. 055-001-00067-7, $5; Refs. (*2*), (*3*), (*4*), and (*8*) are available from National Environmental Research Center, Environmental Protection Agency, Cincinnati, OH 45268.

34. Color Additives

(Number in brackets following name of a color represents number of that color as listed in Society of Dyers and Colourists' "Colour Index," third edition, 1971.

In conformity with common usage, thruout this chapter the reagent designated as "amyl alcohol" is actually "isoamyl alcohol.")

SEPARATION AND IDENTIFICATION OF COLOR ADDITIVES IN FOODS, DRUGS, AND COSMETICS

34.001 ★ PIGMENTS AND LAKES PROCEDURE ★

See **34.001**, 11th ed.

SOLUBLE COLOR ADDITIVES AND THEIR LAKES: SEPARATION BY IMMISCIBLE SOLVENTS (*1*)

34.002 ★ Synthetic Organic Color Additives in General—Official Final Action ★

See **34.002**, 11th ed.

34.003 ★ Oil-Soluble Dyes (*2*) ★ Official First Action

Immiscible solv. method. *See* **34.003**, 11th ed.

34.004 ★ Water-Soluble Dyes (*1*) ★ Official Final Action

Immiscible solv. method. *See* **34.004–34.006**, 11th ed.

SYNTHETIC ORGANIC COLOR ADDITIVES IN FOODS (*3*)

(Amaranth*, ponceau 3R*, ponceau SX*, erythrosine, orange I*, light green SF yellowish*, fast green FCF, guinea green B*, brilliant blue FCF, indigotine, naphthol yellow S*, sunset yellow FCF, tartrazine, yellow AB*, yellow OB*, orange SS*, and oil red XO*.)

34.005 ★ *Immiscible Solvent Method* ★ *Official First Action*

See **34.007–34.008**, 11th ed.

Chromatographic Method

34.006 Identification—Procedure

(a) *Oil-soluble dyes.*—Prep. soln of the isolated dye of suitable concn in $CHCl_3$. Det. spectrophtric curve of this soln and compare curve with those of known dyes in $CHCl_3$ solns detd on same instrument under same conditions. If spectrophtric data cannot be correlated with that of known color, unknown color may be mixt. In such cases, proceed as in **34.009–34.013**.

(b) *Water-soluble dyes.*—Prep. ca neut. soln of the dye in concn suitable for spectrophtric analysis with cells and instruments available. Divide soln into 3 portions and to 1 portion add few crystals of NH_4OAc. To second portion add HCl to make ca 0.1*N*. To third portion add NaOH soln to make ca 0.1*N*. Det. spectrophtric curves of the 3 solns and compare with corresponding curves of known dyes detd under same conditions on same instrument.

If spectrophtric data of unknown color cannot be correlated with that of a known color, unknown color may be mixt. In such cases subject unknown color soln to chromatgy. For oil-sol. colors, paper chromatgc procedure of JAOAC **35**, 423(1952); **36**, 802(1953), or following column chromatgc method may be used.

34.007 ***Preparation of Column***

Lightly tamp glass wool plug into constricted end of chromatgc tube ca 100 cm long × 2.54 cm diam. Prep. thin aq. slurry of ca 40 g *powd cellulose,* such as SolkaFloc BW 40 (Brown Co., Berlin, NH 03570), and pour into column. Let liq. drain as cellulose settles and add more slurry as needed until all is added. When liq. level drops almost to top of adsorbent bed, add wash of 20% NaCl soln. Just before last of this soln enters adsorbent, close constricted end of column. Column may be used immediately or may be stored for several weeks before use. (Column described is adequate for 0.5–2.0 mg total dye. Column size may be varied if more or less dye is present.)

34.008 ***Chromatographic Separation***

To neut. aq. soln of the color add enough NaCl to make 20% soln. Pour soln into column so that adsorbent bed is not disturbed; then open constricted end of tube. When last of soln is ready to pass into adsorbent bed, add few mL 20% NaCl soln. If any color moves down column at moderate rate, continue washing with 20% NaCl soln. If all color remains at or near top of column, change to 10% NaCl soln. If this soln fails to move any color down column, change to 5% NaCl soln. Continue lowering NaCl concn by half until concn is found which moves color down column at moderate rate.

Continue adding appropriate concn of NaCl soln until color is eluted and collected. If color seps into 2 or more bands as it progresses down column, collect each band sep. In some cases it may be necessary to change to still more dil. NaCl soln to elute upper bands of color. If $\geqslant 2$ bands of color are found, examine each spectrophtric as in **34.006(b)**. If this procedure gives no indication that >1 color is present, it may be assumed that color is not mixt.

Chromatographic Separation of Oil-Soluble Color Additives (*4*)—Official First Action

34.009 ***Principle***

Eleven oil-sol. color additives are sepd chromatgc. Colors in fractions are identified spectrophtric. Steps are given in Table **34:01**.

34.010 ***Apparatus***

Chromatographic tubes.—20 (id) × 300 mm, with stopcock and fritted glass plate (or glass fiber disk over glass wool plug). With device to deliver air pressure at top.

34.011 ***Reagents***

(a) *Florisil.*—60–100 mesh. Activated at 650° (1200°F) by manufacturer (Floridin Co). Store at 130° in g-s bottle. For use, add 1.5 mL H_2O to 100 g Florisil in g-s bottle, shake to break up lumps, and mix thoroly. Let stand overnight before use.

(b) *Alumina.*—80–200 mesh. Adsorption, for chromatgc analysis. Heat 100–200 g 1 hr at 400°. Store in tightly stoppered bottle in desiccator.

(c) *Adsorptive magnesia.*—Fisher Scientific Co. No. S-120.

(d) *Celite 545.*—Johns-Manville Products Corp.

(e) *Silicic acid.*—100 mesh. For chromatgy (Mallinckrodt Chemical Co. No. 2847, or equiv.).

(f) *Solvents.*—Reagent grade. Pet ether, ether, alcohol, $CHCl_3$, *n*-hexane, benzene, and CH_3CN. Redistil CH_3CN from H_3PO_4 and P_2O_5, if necessary.

* No longer permitted in United States.
★ Surplus method—*see* inside front cover.

34.012 ***Preparation of Columns***

(Place plug of glass wool or piece of Teflon-coated nylon on top of each column.)

(**a**) *Florisil column.*—Fill tube to ht of 10 cm, tapping to pack and remove air. Wash with pet ether and drain to top level of column.

(**b**) *Alumina column.*—Add 50 mL pet ether to closed tube, add 18 g alumina, and work plunger to break lumps and remove air. Drain to top level.

(**c**) *Magnesia column.*—Mix equal wts of MgO and Celite 545. Prep. as for (**b**), using 9 g of mixt. Compress column with slight air pressure.

(**d**) *Silicic acid column.*—Add ca 10 cm of mixt. of equal wts silicic acid and Celite 545 to column, using suction. Tamp and smooth upper surface, and wash with *n*-hexane, using pressure.

34.013 ***Determination***

(*Caution: See* **51.011**, **51.039**, **51.040**, **51.043**, **51.045**, **51.054**, **51.056**, and **51.061**.)

Dil. 10 mL oil-based sample with 10 mL pet ether and place on Florisil column. Elute with pet ether. Discard colorless portion and begin collection when color appears. Continue elution until eluate (No. 1) is colorless. Set eluate aside, change receivers, and elute with ether until eluate (No. 2) is colorless. Set eluate No. 2 aside, start elution with alcohol-ether (1+3), and watch eluting colors. Change receivers when eluate color changes. (Identify receivers by position in scheme. Usually first eluate is yellow from natural color of base oil and has no distinctive spectrophtric curve. Discard this eluate.) Next eluate is D&C Violet No. 2 (if present); then D&C Yellow No. 11.

When alcohol-ether eluate is colorless, begin elution with CH_3CN. (This will elute last trace of D&C Yellow No. 11; also Toluidine Red.)

Evap. individual alcohol-ether and CH_3CN eluates to dryness, dissolve residues in $CHCl_3$, and dil. to vols suitable for spectrophtr. Scan between 350–700 nm, and compare against curves of known colors. (Sepn of D&C Violet No. 2 and D&C Yellow No. 11 may not be complete but colors can be identified because adsorption peaks are widely sepd. These colors may be sepd by extg D&C Yellow No. 11 with 70% alcohol from soln of their mixt. in pet ether.) Evap. original ether eluate (No. 2) to remove all ether, add pet ether eluate (No. 1), and evap. to ca 15 mL.

Transfer carefully to alumina column. When all soln enters column, wash with 50 mL pet ether and discard eluate. Add two 10 mL portions $CHCl_3$. If $CHCl_3$ eluate is green or blue, add it to following alcohol-$CHCl_3$ eluate; if $CHCl_3$ eluate is colorless, discard it. Continue elution with alcohol-$CHCl_3$ (1+3) until eluate is colorless. Evap. solv. completely and dissolve residue in pet ether.

Carefully add soln to MgO column, dropwise at side of tube, with pipet. Apply slight pressure until soln just passes into adsorbent; then wash column with 25 mL pet ether, and discard pet ether wash. Elute with $CHCl_3$ and watch for colors, collecting sep. fractions. (First fraction may contain D&C Green No. 6 and Hexyl Blue. Second may contain Orange SS and Oil Red XO. Continue to colorless eluate and change receivers; then elute with alcohol-$CHCl_3$ (1+3), changing receivers as different colors appear (Oil Red OS, Yellows AB and OB, and D&C Red No. 17). Evap. individual solns, dissolve each in $CHCl_3$, and scan from 350 to 700 nm. Compare curves with those from known colors. If curve for blue-green portion does not conform to known color, use following sepn:

Evap. $CHCl_3$ and dissolve residue in *n*-hexane. Put on silicic acid column, and elute with *n*-hexane-benzene (1+1). Collect eluate until colorless and continue elution with benzene until eluate is colorless.

(If curve for D&C Red No. 17 has min. at 385 nm, Yellows AB and OB may be present. Sep. yellows from Red No. 17 as follows: Evap. $CHCl_3$. Dissolve residue in min. vol. pet ether. Put on MgO column, and elute with alcohol-$CHCl_3$ (1+3). Collect sep. fractions as color changes.)

Det. color present by evapg solv. in fraction, dilg to vol. with $CHCl_3$, and scanning from 350 to 700 nm. Compare curves with known color on same chart.

★ NATURAL COLORING MATTERS ★

34.014 Identification by Color Reactions
Official First Action

See **34.017–34.020** and Table **34:2**, 11th ed.

★ Surplus method—*see* inside front cover.

Table 34:01 Scheme for Separation and Identification of Oil-Soluble Color Additives

Column	Eluent	Eluate
A Florisil column	Pet ether	Colorless (Discard)
	Ether	Colored } To column **B**
		Colored } To column **B**
	Alcohol-ether	Yellow (Natural color, discard)
		D&C Violet No. 2 [60725]
		D&C Yellow No. 11 [47000]
	CH_3CN	Traces of D&C Yellow No. 11
		Toluidine Red [12120]*
B Alumina column	Pet Ether	Discard
	$CHCl_3$	Colorless (Discard)
	Alcohol-$CHCl_3$	Colored } To column **C**
		Colored } To column **C**
C Magnesia column	Pet ether	Discard
	$CHCl_3$	D&C Green No. 6 [61565] } To Column **D**
		Hexyl Blue [61555]* } To Column **D**
		Orange SS [15510]*
	Alcohol-$CHCl_3$	Oil Red XO [12140]*
		Oil Red OS [26125]*
		Yellow AB [11380]* and Yellow OB [11390]*
		D&C Red No. 17 [26100]
D Silicic acid column	*n*-Hexane-benzene	D&C Green No. 6
	Benzene	Hexyl Blue No. 5

* No longer permitted in the United States.

ANALYSIS OF COMMERCIAL SYNTHETIC ORGANIC COLOR ADDITIVES

34.015 Specifications for Certifiable Synthetic Organic Color Additives

Color Additive Amendment of 1960 to Federal Food, Drug, and Cosmetic Act provides for listing of color additives that are safe for use in foods, drugs, or cosmetics, and for certification of batches of those colors. "Code of Federal Regulations," Title 21, Part 74 provides listings of such color additives; provisionally listed colors are found in Part 81. Colors must be free from impurities to extent avoidable by good manufacturing practice. Color certification examines each batch for color content, subsidiary colors, intermediates, heavy metals, volatile matter, and inorg. salts.

Methods no longer used and colors and their specifications applicable to colors previously certifiable will be found in 9th, 10th, 11th, and 12th eds of *Official Methods of Analysis.* (*See* also Tables (**e**), (**f**), (**g**), and (**h**) below.)

(a) *Determinations To Be Made on All Straight Colors*

Det. Pb as in **34.081–34.083, 34.084–34.086,** or **34.087.**

(b) *Straight Colors—FD&C*

	Method
FD&C Blue No. 1 (Brilliant Blue FCF)	
Volatile matter (135°)	**34.028**
NaCl, Na_2SO_4	**(1)**
H_2O-insol. matter	**34.029**
Leuco base	**(2)**
o, m, and *p*-sulfobenzaldehydes	**34.046**
N-Ethyl, *N*-(m-sulfobenzyl)sulfanilic acid	**34.046**
Subsidiary colors	**(3)**
Chromium	**(4)**
Total color	**34.019(c) & 34.027**
FD&C Blue No. 2 (Indigotine)	
Volatile matter (135°)	**34.028**
H_2O-insol. matter	**34.029**
NaCl, Na_2SO_4	**(1)**
Subsidiary colors	**(5)**
Total color	**34.019(c) & 34.027**
FD&C Green No. 3 (Fast Green FCF)	
Volatile matter (135°)	**34.028**
H_2O-insol. matter	**34.029**
NaCl, Na_2SO_4	**(1)**
Leuco base	**(2)**
Chromium	**(4)**
Total color	**34.019(c) & 34.027**
FD&C Red No. 3 (Erythrosine)	
Volatile matter (135°)	**34.028**
NaCl, Na_2SO_4	**(1)**
H_2O-insol. matter	**34.029**
NaI	—
Unhalogenated intermediates	—
Triiodoresorcinol	—
2-(2′,4′-Dihydroxy-3′,5′-diiodobenzoyl) benzoic acid	—
Monoiodofluoresceins	—
Other lower iodinated fluoresceins	—
Total color	**34.020(a) & 34.027**
FD&C Red No. 4 (Ponceau SX)	
Volatile matter (135°)	**34.028**
H_2O-insol. matter	**34.029**
NaCl, Na_2SO_4	**(1)**
Total color	**34.019(c) & 34.027**

	Method
Citrus Red No. 2	
Volatile matter (100°)	**34.028**
H_2O-sol. matter	**34.100**
Matter insol. in CCl_4	**34.030**
Uncombined intermediates	—
Subsidiary colors	—
Total color	**34.019(e) & 34.027**
FD&C Red No. 40	
Volatile matter (135°)	**34.028**
H_2O-insol. matter	**34.029**
NaCl, Na_2SO_4	**(1)**
Uncombined intermediates	**34.063**
Subsidiary colors	—
Total color	**34.019(c) & 34.027**
FD&C Yellow No. 5 (Tartrazine)	
Volatile matter (135°)	**34.028**
NaCl, Na_2SO_4	**(1)**
H_2O-insol. matter	**34.029**
Phenylhydrazine-*p*-sulfonic acid	—
Other uncombined intermediates	—
Subsidiary colors	—
Total color	**34.019(c) & 34.027**
FD&C Yellow No. 6 (Sunset Yellow FCF)	
Volatile matter (135°)	**34.028**
H_2O-insol. matter	**34.029**
NaCl, Na_2SO_4	**(1)**
Intermediates	**34.053**
Subsidiary dye	—
Total color	**34.019(a) & 34.027**
Orange B	
Volatile matter (135°)	**34.028**
H_2O-insol. matter	**34.029**
NaCl, Na_2SO_4	**(1)**
1-(4-Sulfophenyl)-3-ethylcarboxy-5-hydroxypyrazolone and 1-(4-Sulfophenyl)-3-carboxy-5-hydroxypyrazolone	—
Naphthionic acid	—
Phenylhydrazine-*p*-sulfonic acid	—
Trisodium salt of 1-(4-Sulfophenyl)-3-carboxy-4-(4-sulfonaphthylazo)-5-hydroxypyrazole	—
Other subsidiary dyes	—
Total color	**34.019(c) & 34.027**
Lakes	
Volatile matter (135°)	**34.028**
H_2O-insol. matter	**34.029**
Total color	*See individual colors*

(c) *Straight Colors—D&C*

D&C Blue No. 4 (Alphazurine FG)	Method
Volatile matter (135°)	**34.028**
H_2O-insol. matter	**34.029**
NH_4Cl, $(NH_4)_2SO_4$	**(1)**
Chromium	**(4)**
Leuco base	**(2)**
Subsidiary colors	**(3)**
Intermediates	**34.046**
Total color	**34.019(c) & 34.027**

D&C Blue No. 6 (Indigo)	Method
Volatile matter (135°)	**34.028**
Intermediates	—
Total color	**34.019(g)**

D&C Blue No. 9 (Carbanthrene Blue)	Method
Volatile matter (135°)	**34.028**
Intermediates	—
Matter extractable by alc. HCl	—
Organically combined Cl in pure dye	—
Total color	—

D&C Brown No. 1 (Resorcin Brown)	Method
Volatile matter (135°)	**34.028**
H_2O-insol. matter	**34.029**
NaCl, Na_2SO_4	**(1)**
Intermediates	—
Subsidiary colors	—
Total color	**34.019(c) & 34.027**

D&C Green No. 5 (Alizarin Cyanine Green F)	Method
Volatile matter (135°)	**34.028**
H_2O-insol. matter	**34.029**
NaCl, Na_2SO_4	**(1)**
Subsidiary colors	**(6)**
Intermediates	—
Total color	**34.019(b) & 34.027**

D&C Green No. 6 (Quinizarin Green SS)	Method
Volatile matter (135°)	**34.028**
H_2O-sol. matter	**34.100**
Matter insol. in CCl_4	**34.030**
Subsidiary colors	—
Intermediates	—
Total color ($CHCl_3$)	**34.027**

D&C Green No. 8 (Pyranine Concentrated)	Method
Volatile matter (135°)	**34.028**
H_2O-insol. matter	**34.029**
$CHCl_3$-sol. matter	**34.101**
Pyrene	**34.071**
NaCl, Na_2SO_4	**(1)**
Intermediates	—
Total color	**34.027**

D&C Orange No. 4 (Orange II)	Method
Volatile matter (135°)	**34.028**
H_2O-insol. matter	**34.029**
NaCl, Na_2SO_4	**(1)**
Subsidiary colors	—
Intermediates	—
Total color	**34.019(c)**

D&C Orange No. 5 (Dibromofluorescein)	Method
Volatile matter (135°)	**34.028**
Insol. matter (alk. soln)	**34.037**
Subsidiary colors	—
Intermediates	—
Total color	**34.020(b)**

D&C Orange No. 10 (Diiodofluorescein)	Method
Volatile matter (135°)	**34.028**
Insol. matter (alk. soln)	**34.037**
Subsidiary colors	—
Intermediates	—
Total color	**34.020(b)**

D&C Orange No. 11 (Erythrosine Yellowish NA)	Method
Volatile matter (135°)	**34.028**
H_2O-insol. matter	**34.029**
NaCl, Na_2SO_4	**(1)**
Subsidiary colors	—
Intermediates	—
Total color	**34.020(a)**

D&C Orange No. 17 (Permatone Orange, Permanent Orange)	Method
Volatile matter (135°)	**34.028**
Insol. matter (in toluene)	**34.031**
Subsidiary colors	—
Intermediates	—
Total color ($CHCl_3$)	**34.027**

D&C Red No. 6 (Lithol Rubin B)	Method
Volatile matter (135°)	**34.028**
Subsidiary colors	—
Intermediates	—
Total color	**34.019(c) & 34.027**

D&C Red No. 7 (Lithol Rubin BCA)	Method
Volatile matter (135°)	**34.028**
Subsidiary colors	—
Intermediates	—
Total color	**34.019(f) & 34.027**

(1) JAOAC **57,** 353; 356(1974).
(2) JAOAC **57,** 963(1974)
(3) JAOAC **56,** 947(1973)
(4) JAOAC **53,** 916(1970)
(5) JAOAC **53,** 250(1970)
(6) JAOAC **56,** 1188(1973)
(7) JAOAC **50,** 1199(1967)
(8) JAOAC **50,** 1198(1967)
(9) JAOAC **54,** 215(1971)
(10) JAOAC **36,** 930(1953)
(11) JAOAC **50,** 1297(1967)
(12) JAOAC **44,** 733(1961)

(Continued)

(c) *Straight Colors—D&C—(Continued)*

	Method
D&C Red No. 8 (Lake Red C)	
Volatile matter (135°)	**34.028**
Subsidiary colors	**(7)**
Intermediates	—
Total color	**34.019(f) & 34.027**
D&C Red No. 9 (Lake Red CBA)	
Volatile matter (135°)	**34.028**
Sol. Ba	—
Subsidiary colors	**(7)**
Intermediates	—
Total color	**34.019(f) & 34.027**
D&C Red No. 17 (Toney Red)	
Volatile matter (135°)	**34.028**
Insol. matter (in toluene)	**34.031**
Subsidiary colors	**(8)**
Intermediates	—
Total color ($CHCl_3$)	**34.019(e) & 34.027**
D&C Red No. 19 (Rhodamine B)	
Volatile matter (135°)	**34.028**
H_2O-insol. matter	**34.029**
Subsidiary colors	—
Intermediates	—
Total color (H_2O)	**34.027**
D&C Red No. 21 (Tetrabromofluorescein)	
Volatile matter (135°)	**34.028**
Insol. matter (alk. soln)	**34.037**
Subsidiary colors	—
Intermediates	—
Total color	**34.020(b) & 34.027**
D&C Red No. 22 (Eosin YS)	
Volatile matter (135°)	**34.028**
H_2O-insol. matter	**34.029**
NaCl, Na_2SO_4	**(1)**
Subsidiary colors	—
Intermediates	—
Total color	**34.020(a) & 34.027**
D&C Red No. 27 (Tetrachlorotetrabromofluorescein)	
Volatile matter (135°)	**34.028**
Insol. matter (alk. soln)	**34.037**
Subsidiary colors	—
Intermediates	—
Total color	**34.020(b) & 34.027**
D&C Red No. 28 (Phloxine B)	
Volatile matter (135°)	**34.028**
H_2O-insol. matter	**34.029**
NaCl, Na_2SO_4	**(1)**
Subsidiary colors	—
Intermediates	—
Total color	**34.020(a) & 34.027**
D&C Red No. 30 (Helindone Pink CN)	
Volatile matter (135°)	**34.028**
Insol. matter (in xylene)	**34.036**
Total color	**34.019(g), 34.027, & (9)**

	Method
D&C Red No. 31 (Brilliant Lake Red R)	
Volatile matter (135°)	**34.028**
Intermediates	—
Total color	**34.019(f) & 34.027**
D&C Red No. 33 (Acid Fuchsin D, Naphthalene Red B)	
Volatile matter (135°)	**34.028**
H_2O-insol. matter	**34.029**
NaCl, Na_2SO_4	**(1)**
Subsidiary colors	**(10)**
Intermediates	—
Total color	**34.019(c) & 34.027**
D&C Red No. 34 (Deep Maroon, Fanchon Maroon)	
Volatile matter (135°)	**34.028**
Intermediates	—
Total color	**34.019(f) & 34.027**
D&C Red No. 36 (Flaming Red)	
Volatile matter (135°)	**34.028**
Insol. matter (in toluene)	**34.031**
Total color ($CHCl_3$)	**34.027**
D&C Red No. 37 (Rhodamine B Stearate)	
Volatile matter (80°)	**34.028**
Insol. matter (in benzene)	**34.032**
Subsidiary colors	—
Intermediates	—
Total color (H_2O)	**34.027**
D&C Red No. 39 (Alba Red)	
Volatile matter (135°)	**34.028**
Insol. matter (in acetone)	**34.033**
Subsidiary colors	—
Intermediates	—
Total color	—
D&C Violet No. 2 (D&C Blue No. 3, Alizurol Purple SS)	
Volatile matter (135°)	**34.028**
Insol. matter	—
Subsidiary colors	—
Intermediates	**(11)**
Total color ($CHCl_3$)	**34.027**
D&C Yellow No. 7 (Fluorescein)	
Volatile matter (135°)	**34.028**
Insol. matter (alk. soln)	**34.037**
Subsidiary colors	—
Intermediates	—
Pure dye (alk. aq. soln)	**34.019(e) & 34.027**
D&C Yellow No. 8 (Uranine)	
Volatile matter (135°)	**34.028**
H_2O-insol. matter	**34.029**
NaCl, Na_2SO_4	**(1)**
Subsidiary colors	—
Intermediates	—
Total Color (H_2O)	**34.019(e) & 34.027**

(Continued)

(c) *Straight Colors—D&C—(Continued)*

D&C Yellow No. 10 (Quinoline Yellow WS)	Method
Volatile matter (135°)	**34.028**
H_2O-insol. matter	**34.029**
NaCl, Na_2SO_4	**(1)**
Subsidiary colors	**(12)**
Intermediates	—
Total color	**34.021(a) or 34.023**

D&C Yellow No. 11 (Quinoline Yellow SS)	Method
Volatile matter (135°)	**34.028**
Insol. matter (in alcohol)	**34.034**
Subsidiary colors	—
Intermediates	—
Total color ($CHCl_3$)	**34.027**

Phthalocyaninato (2-) Copper	Method
Volatile matter (135°)	**34.028**
Salt content (as NaCl)	**(1)**
Alcohol-sol. matter	—
Org. chlorine	**34.092**
Aromatic amines	—
Total color	—

Lakes	
Volatile matter (135°)	**34.028**
Subsidiary colors	*See individual colors*
Intermediates	*See individual colors*
Total color	*See individual colors*

(d) *Straight Colors—Ext D&C*

Ext. D&C Violet No. 2 (Alizurol Purple)	Method
Volatile matter (135°)	**34.028**
Water-insol.matter	**34.029**
NaCl, Na_2SO_4	**(1)**
Subsidiary colors	—
Intermediates	—
Total color	**34.019(b) & 34.027**

Ext. D&C Yellow No. 7 (Naphthol Yellow S)	Method
Volatile matter (135°)	**34.028**
H_2O-insol. matter	**34.029**
NaCl, Na_2SO_4	**(1)**
Subsidiary colors	—
Intermediates	—
Martius Yellow	**34.075**
Total color	**34.019(c) & 34.027**

Lakes	
Volatile matter (135°)	**34.028**
Subsidiary colors	*See individual colors*
Intermediates	*See individual colors*
Total color	*See individual colors*

See page 571 for references.

(e) *Specifications and Applicable Methods for Following Previously Listed Colors Appear in Ninth Edition:*

FD&C Designation	C.I. No.	Common Name
FD&C Red No. 1	16155	Ponceau 3R
D&C Blue No. 5	61530	Alizarin Astrol B
D&C Blue No. 8	42052	Patent Blue CA
D&C Green No. 4	42095	Light Green CF Yellowish
D&C Green No. 7	42100	Fast Acid Green B
D&C Orange No. 3	16230	Orange G
D&C Orange No. 6	45370	Dibromofluorescein NA
D&C Orange No. 7	45370	Dibromofluorescein K
D&C Orange No. 8	45365	Dichlorofluorescein
D&C Orange No. 9	45365	Dichlorofluorescein NA
D&C Orange No. 12	45425	Erythrosine Yellowish K
D&C Orange No. 13	45455	Erythrosine Yellowish NH
D&C Orange No. 14	45456	Orange TR
D&C Orange No. 15	58000	Alizarin
D&C Orange No. 16	45371	Diiododibromofluorescein
D&C Red No. 14	15500	Lake Red D
D&C Red No. 15	15500	Lake Red DBA
D&C Red No. 16	15500	Lake Red DCA
D&C Red No. 18	26125	Oil Red OS
D&C Red No. 20	45170	Rhodamine B Acetate
D&C Red No. 23	45380	Eosin YSK
D&C Red No. 24	45366	Tetrachlorofluorescein
D&C Red No. 25	45366	Tetrachlorofluorescein NA
D&C Red No. 26	45366	Tetrachlorofluorescein K
D&C Red No. 29	45457	Bluish Orange TR
D&C Red No. 35	12120	Toluidine Red
D&C Red No. 38	12350	Toluidine Maroon
D&C Yellow No. 9	45350	Uranine K
Ext. D&C Black No. 1	26370	Coomassie Fast Black B
Ext. D&C Blue No. 1	52015	Methylene Blue
Ext. D&C Blue No. 2	52015	Methylene Blue-Zinc Dichloride
Ext. D&C Blue No. 3	42080	Erioglaucine X
Ext. D&C Blue No. 4	63010	Alizarin Saphirol
Ext. D&C Blue No. 5	61555	Hexyl Blue
Ext. D&C Orange No. 1	11725	Hansa Orange
Ext. D&C Orange No. 2	45395	Indelible Orange
Ext. D&C Orange No. 4	12100	Orange SS
Ext. D&C Red No. 1	18055	Amidonaphthol Red 6B
Ext. D&C Red No. 2	16105	Pigment Scarlet NA
Ext. D&C Red No. 3	45190	Violamine R
Ext. D&C Red No. 4	45435	Dichlorotetraiodofluorescein
Ext. D&C Red No. 5	45435	Rose Bengale TD
Ext. D&C Red No. 6	45435	Rose Bengale TDK
Ext. D&C Red No. 7	58005	Alizarin Carmine
Ext. D&C Red No. 9	14830	Bordeaux Red
Ext. D&C Red No. 10	14720	Azo Rubin Extra
Ext. D&C Red No. 11	18050	Fast Crimson GR
Ext. D&C Red No. 12	15570	Royal Scarlet
Ext. D&C Red No. 13	27290	Croceine Scarlet MOO
Ext. D&C Red No. 14	12140	Oil Red XO
Ext. D&C Violet No. 1	61710	Alizarin Violet 12
Ext. D&C Yellow No. 2	13065	Metanil Yellow CA
Ext. D&C Yellow No. 4	18950	Polar Yellow 5G
Ext. D&C Yellow No. 5	11680	Hansa Yellow
Ext. D&C Yellow No. 6	14010	Dupont Yellow
Ext. D&C Yellow No. 8	10316	Naphthol Yellow S Potassium Salt
Ext. D&C Yellow No. 9	11380	Yellow AB
Ext. D&C Yellow No. 10	11390	Yellow OB

(f) *Specifications and Applicable Methods for Following Previously Listed Colors Appear in Tenth Edition:*

FD&C Designation	C.I. No.	Common Name
FD&C Green No. 1	42085	Guinea Green B
FD&C Green No. 2	42095	Light Green SF Yellowish
D&C Black No. 1	20470	Naphthol Blue Black
D&C Blue No. 7	42052	Patent Blue NA
D&C Red No. 5	16150	Ponceau 2R
Ext. D&C Orange No. 3	14600	Orange 1
Ext. D&C Red No. 8	15620	Fast Red A
Ext. D&C Red No. 15	16155	Ponceau 3R
Ext. D&C Red No. 24	14700	Ponceau SX
Ext. D&C Yellow No. 3	18820	Fast Light Yellow

(g) *Specifications and Applicable Methods for Following Previously Listed Colors Appear in Eleventh Edition:*

FD&C Designation	C.I. No.	Common Name
FD&C Violet No. 1	42640	Wool Violet 5BN

(h) *Specifications and Applicable Methods for Following Previously Listed Colors Appear in Twelfth Edition:*

FD&C Designation	C.I. No.	Common Name
FD&C Red No. 2	16185	Amaranth
D&C Red No. 10	15630	Lithol Red
D&C Red No. 11	15630	Lithol Red CA
D&C Red No. 12	15630	Lithol Red BA
D&C Red No. 13	15630	Lithol Red SR
Ext. D&C Green No. 1	10020	Naphthol Green B
Ext. D&C Yellow No. 1	13065	Metanil Yellow

34.016 Preparation of Sample—Official Final Action

Thoroly mix and promptly weigh portion required. If weighing cannot be made directly into dish in which detn is to be made, use weighing bottles, placing in each bottle amt approximating wt required, and weighing immediately.

Pure Dye

By Titration with Standard Titanous Chloride Solution—Official Final Action

34.017 ***Apparatus***

See Fig. **34:01.**

34.018 ***Reagents***

(**a**) *Titanous chloride std soln.*—0.1*N*. *See* **50.042–50.043**. *See* Tables **34:02** and **34:03** for factors.

(**b**) *Potassium dichromate std soln.*—*See* **50.024.**

(**c**) *Indicator.*—For many dyes $TiCl_3$ titrn end point is indicated by sharp decoloration. For some dyes change is so gradual that excess of $TiCl_3$ ($\leq$0.3 mL ca 0.1*N* soln) is required, and suitable std soln of some other dye must be used for back-titrn (methylene blue serves well). In other cases it is better to use indicator that is reduced after original dye has reacted with the $TiCl_3$. Known amt of FD&C Green No. 2 serves well for this purpose.

34.019 ***Determination***

(**a**) Prep. 1.0% soln of sample in H_2O and place vol. soln equiv. to ca 20 mL 0.1*N* $TiCl_3$ in 500 mL wide-mouth erlenmeyer. Add 15 g Na citrate and H_2O to bring vol. to 150–200 mL. Heat to bp and titr. with std $TiCl_3$ soln.

(**b**) Prep. 0.5% soln of sample in alcohol. Proceed as in (**a**), substituting 50% alcohol for H_2O.

(**c**) Proceed as in (**a**), substituting 15 g Na acid tartrate for Na citrate.

(**d**) Proceed as in (**c**), using as indicator vol. FD&C Green No. 2 soln (freshly prepd) contg ca 10 mg dye. Det. $TiCl_3$ soln equiv. to vol. indicator soln used and deduct this vol. from total required for titrn.

(**e**) Prep. 0.5% soln of sample in alcohol. Proceed as in (**d**), substituting 50% alcohol for H_2O.

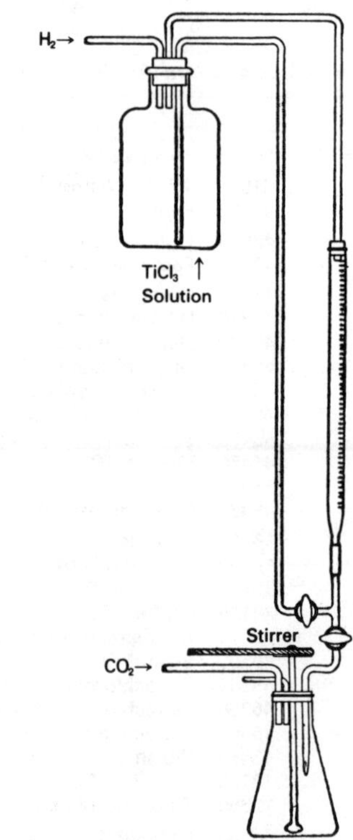

FIG. 34:01—Titanous chloride titration apparatus

(f) (JAOAC **24,** 904(1941); **32,** 644(1949)). In wide-mouth erlenmeyer dissolve 0.2 g sample in 5 mL H_2SO_4, using stirring rod to break up any lumps, and mix well. Dil. with 100 mL alcohol and heat, with stirring, until all dye is in soln. Dissolve 20 g Na acid tartrate in 100 mL boiling H_2O and add 20 mL 30% NaOH soln. Stirring rapidly, add this soln to alc. dye soln. Titr. resulting soln with std $TiCl_3$ soln.

(g) Place sample equiv. to ca 20 mL 0.1*N* $TiCl_3$ in 50 mL beaker, and pour 2 mL *fuming* H_2SO_4 (20% free SO_3) down side of beaker. Stir well with glass rod and place on steam bath. After 30 min pour sulfonated product into 500 mL wide-mouth erlenmeyer contg 100 g ice. Add few g cracked ice to material remaining in beaker and wash all color into flask. Add 50 mL alcohol and 20 g Na acid tartrate, heat, and titr. in usual manner.

(h) Proceed as in (g), but sulfonate at room temp.

Table 34:02 $TiCl_3$ Titration Factors

Color	MW	g Color/mL 0.1*N* $TiCl_3$	mL 0.1*N* $TiCl_3$/g Color
FD&C Blue No. 1	792.8	0.03965	25.2
FD&C Blue No. 2	466.4	0.02332	42.9
FD&C Green No. 3	808.9	0.04045	24.7
FD&C Red No. 4	480.4	0.01201	83.3
Citrus Red No. 2	308.3	0.00771	129.7
FD&C Red No. 40	496.4	0.01241	80.58
FD&C Yellow No. 5	534.4	0.01336	74.9
FD&C Yellow No. 6	452.4	0.01131	88.4
Orange B	590.4	0.01476	67.75
D&C Blue No. 4	783.0	0.03915	25.5
D&C Blue No. 6	262.3	0.01312	76.3
D&C Brown No. 1	448.4	0.00561	178.4
D&C Green No. 5	622.6	0.03113	32.1
D&C Green No. 6	418.5	0.02093	47.8
D&C Orange No. 4	350.3	0.00876	114.2
D&C Red No. 6	430.3	0.01076	92.9
D&C Red No. 7	424.5	0.01061	94.2
D&C Red No. 8	398.8	0.00997	100.3
D&C Red No. 9	444.5	0.01111	90.0
D&C Red No. 17	352.4	0.00441	227.0
D&C Red No. 19	479.0	0.02395	41.8
D&C Red No. 30	393.3	0.01967	50.8
D&C Red No. 31	311.3	0.00778	128.5
D&C Red No. 33	467.4	0.01169	85.6
D&C Red No. 34	460.5	0.01151	86.9
D&C Red No. 36	327.7	0.00328	305.1
D&C Red No. 37	727.0	0.03635	27.5
D&C Red No. 39	329.4	0.00824	121.4
D&C Yellow No. 7	332.3	0.01662	60.2
D&C Yellow No. 8	376.3	0.01882	53.2
Ext. D&C Violet No. 2	431.4	0.02157	46.4
Ext. D&C Yellow No. 7	358.2	0.00299	335.0

Table 34:03 Conversion Factors—Precipitated Color Acids to Specified Salts

Color	Factor
FD&C Red No. 3	1.074[a]
D&C Red No. 22	1.068
D&C Red No. 28	1.056
D&C Orange No. 11	1.075

[a] Includes 1 molecule H_2O of crystn.

34.020 ***Gravimetrically—Official Final Action***

(a) Prep. 1.0% soln of sample in H_2O. Transfer 50 mL aliquot to 500 mL beaker, heat to bp, add 25 mL HCl (1+49), and again bring to bp. Wash down sides of beaker with little H_2O, cover with watch glass, and keep on steam bath several hr or overnight. Cool to room temp., transfer ppt to weighed gooch with HCl (1+199), and wash with two 10–15 mL portions H_2O. Dry crucible and ppt 3 hr at 135°, cool in desiccator, and weigh.

% Pure dye = wt ppt × conversion factor (Table **34:03**) × 100/wt sample

(b) Prep. 1.0% soln of sample in ca 0.1*N* NaOH and proceed as in (a). No factor is required since colors for which this method is specified are not salts.

★ ***From Nitrogen Content—Official Final Action*** ★

34.021 Micro-Kjeldahl Method

See **34.027–34.029**, 11th ed.

★ ***From Sulfur Content*** ★

34.022 ***Fusion Method—Official Final Action***

See **34.030**, 11th ed.

34.023 ***Perchloric Acid Digestion Method (5) Official First Action***

See **34.031–34.032**, 11th ed.

By Spectrophotometric Measurement (6) Official Final Action

34.024 ***Apparatus***

(a) *Spectrophotometer.*—Capable of accurate measurement of solns in region 400–750 nm; preferably with effective slit width of ≤10 nm.

(b) *Two or more matched absorption cells.*

34.025 ***Reagents***

(a) *Std sample of dye to be determined.*—Std samples should be carefully prepd and of highest attainable purity. Pure dye content of std samples must be accurately known for quant. results.

(b) *Solvents.*—Free from suspended matter.

34.026 ***Standardization***

Prep. series of solns of known concns of std sample and det. $A(=\log(1/T))$ of solns, corrected for A due to solv. and cell, at suitable wavelength. (Wavelength at which A is max. is usually selected.) Adjust concns of solns to give A values of 0.4–1.0 with instrument and cells used. Plot or tabulate data obtained.

34.027 ***Determination***

Prep. sample soln in solv. used in stdzn. (Soln must be of such concn that A obtained will be in range covered by stds examined.) Det. A of this soln under same conditions used in stdzn.

Calc. "pure dye" content of sample from A of sample soln and A′ of std soln:

Pure dye = (A/concn sample)(concn std/A′) × purity of std.

If straight line does not result when A' and concn data obtained from examination of std soln are plotted, *i.e.,* if Beer's law does not hold, det. concn of "unknown" soln by comparison with data obtained from known soln of very nearly same concn.

34.028 Volatile Matter—Official Final Action

Accurately weigh ca 2 g sample into tared weighing bottle ca 4 cm diam., and dry in air oven at temp. prescribed, **34.015**, 6 hr or overnight. Cool over efficient desiccant and reweigh. Report loss in wt as volatile matter.

★ Surplus method—*see* inside front cover.

INSOLUBLE MATTER

34.029 Water-Insoluble Matter—Official Final Action

Dissolve 2 g sample in 200 mL hot H_2O and let soln cool to room temp. Filter thru gooch, fitted with glass fiber disk, dried at 135°, and weighed. Wash with cold H_2O until washings are colorless, dry 3 hr at 135°, cool in desiccator, and weigh. Report increase in wt as H_2O-insol. matter.

34.030 Carbon Tetrachloride-Insoluble Matter Official Final Action

(*Caution: See* **51.040** and **51.049**.)

Mix 0.2–0.5 g sample with 100 mL CCl_4 in 250 mL beaker, stir, and heat to bp. Filter hot soln thru weighed gooch, transfer residue in beaker to filter, and wash with 10 mL portions CCl_4 until washings are colorless. Dry 3 hr at 100–105° and weigh. Report increase in wt as CCl_4-insol. matter.

34.031 Toluene-Insoluble Matter—Official Final Action

Proceed as in **34.030**, but substitute toluene for CCl_4.

34.032 Benzene-Insoluble Matter—Official Final Action

(*Caution: See* **51.039**, **51.040**, and **51.045**.)

Proceed as in **34.030**, but substitute benzene for CCl_4.

34.033 Acetone-Insoluble Matter—Official First Action

Proceed as in **34.030**, but substitute acetone for CCl_4.

34.034 Alcohol-Insoluble Matter—Official First Action

Proceed as in **34.030**, but substitute alcohol for CCl_4.

34.035 ★ Carbon Tetrachloride—Insoluble Matter ★ Official First Action

See **34.046**, 11th ed.

34.036 Xylene-Insoluble Matter—Official First Action

Proceed as in **34.030**, but substitute xylene for CCl_4.

34.037 Insoluble Matter (Alkaline Solution) Official First Action

Proceed as in **34.029**, but use 1% NaOH soln or NH_4OH (1+14) instead of H_2O.

EXTRACTS

34.038 ★ Isopropyl Ether Extract (*7*) ★ Official Final Action

See **34.049**, 11th ed.

34.039 ★ Matter Extractable by Alcoholic Hydrochloric ★ Acid—Official First Action

See **34.050**, 11th ed.

★ Ether Extracts—Official Final Action ★

34.040 *By Extraction in Separator*

See **34.051–34.052**, 11th ed.

34.041 *By Extraction in Continuous Extractor*

See **34.053**, 11th ed.

★ Surplus method—*see* inside front cover.

34.042 ★ Ether Extracts from Alkaline Solution ★ Official Final Action

See **34.054**, 11th ed.

34.043 Petroleum Ether Extract (*7*)—Official Final Action

See **34.055**, 11th ed.

INTERMEDIATES

34.044 ★ Volatile Amines (*8*)—Official Final Action ★

See **34.056–34.057**, 11th ed.

34.045 ★ Nonvolatile Unsulfonated Amines (*9*) ★ Official Final Action

See **34.058**, 11th ed.

Intermediates in FD&C Blue No. 1 (*10*) Official Final Action

34.046 ***Principle***

FD&C Blue No. 1 (C.I. No. 42090) is more strongly adsorbed on cellulose from concd $(NH_4)_2SO_4$ soln than are dye intermediates. Benzaldehyde sulfonic acids (SB), i.e., composite of *ortho* (OSB), *meta* (MSB), and *para* (PSB) isomers, and *N*-ethyl-*N*-(3-sulfobenzyl) sulfanilic acid (ESBSA) can be estd from UV absorption spectra of eluate fractions between 350 and 230 nm.

34.047 ***Apparatus***

(**a**) *Chromatographic tube.*—400 mm long × 24 mm id with sealed-in coarse fritted disk. Attach short length of clean, rubber tube with pinchcock.

(**b**) *Spectrophotometer.*—Suitable for use in quartz UV region. (Recording spectrophtr is preferred.)

34.048 ***Reagents***

(**a**) *Eluant.*—Dissolve 400 g $(NH_4)_2SO_4$ in H_2O and dil. to 1 L. Eluant should be free of Fe and other UV absorbing impurities. Test for purity as follows: Slurry eluant with 1/5 its wt of cellulose powder and filter. *A* should be ≤0.08 in the 350–230 nm region when measured in 1 cm cell against H_2O.

(**b**) *Cellulose powder.*—Whatman "Ashless Powder Chemically Prepared, Standard Grade," or equiv.

(**c**) *Ammonium sulfate.*—Grind to fine powder.

34.049 ***Preparation of Chromatographic Column***

Slurry 24 g cellulose powder in 140 mL eluant. Close pinchcock and pour slurry into tube. Open pinchcock and let eluate drain at ≤5 mL/min until liq. is only 1–2 mm above level of packed cellulose. Close cock.

34.050 ***Separation of Intermediates***

Place 0.200 g sample in 50 mL beaker. Add 10 mL H_2O and stir to dissolve. Add 2 g cellulose powder and mix. Add 7 g $(NH_4)_2SO_4$ powder and mix well. Transfer mixt. to top of prepd column. Rinse beaker with 5 mL eluant and add washings to column. Let column drain until flow nearly ceases. Add eluant to column and adjust flow rate to ≤5 mL/min. Immediately collect 10.0±0.05 mL fractions. Collect as many 10.0 mL fractions as necessary to remove compds from column; 30 fractions should be enough, but exact number can be detd by inspection of fractions. Record spectra from 350 to 230 nm against eluant in 1.00 cm fused silica absorption cells, dilg fractions with eluant if necessary.

34.051 ***Calculations***

Examine spectra to det. compds present. Calc. to nearest 0.01%, with min. report of "<0.05%."

OSB, MSB, and PSB elute together and generally appear between fractions 7 and 15 with absorption max. near 252, 246, and 251 nm, resp. Calc. as SB at 252 nm, i.e., isoabsorptive point of OSB and MSB.

If *o*-chlorobenzoic acid and/or *o*-sulfobenzoic acid are present in sample, they will be eluted just ahead of SB; sepn may not be complete. Benzoic acids are identified by small max. or shoulders near 270 nm, but are not estd by this method. To calc. fraction as SB, ratio A_{252}/A_{274} must be $\geqslant$2.0.

ESBSA generally appears between fractions 15 and 30 and has absorption max. near 274 nm.

Any fraction whose absorption cannot be attributed to above compds should be noted and A at peak reported.

% SB = 0.0969 $\times$ ΣA_{252}, where ΣA_{252} = sum of A (corrected for diln if dild) of all fractions contg SB; and 0.0969 = 100/(51.6 $\times$ 20.0 $\times$ 1), where 100 = factor for conversion to %, 51.6 = A at 252 nm of mixt. of 92% (OSB + MSB) + 8% PSB, 20.0 = effective sample concn in g/L, and 1 = path length in cm.

% ESBSA = 0.0806 $\times$ ΣA_{274}, where ΣA_{274} = sum of A of all fractions contg ESBSA; and 0.0806 = 100/(62.0 $\times$ 20.0 $\times$ 1), where 100 = factor for conversion to %, 62.0 = ESBSA A at 274 nm, 20.0 = effective sample concn in g/L, and 1 = path length in cm.

% Other absorbers = 0.10 $\times$ ΣA_x, where ΣA_x = sum of A at wavelength max. of detected absorber; and 0.10 = 100/(50 $\times$ 20.0 $\times$ 1), where 100 = factor for conversion to %, 50 = assumed a, 20.0 = effective sample concn in g/L, and 1 = path length in cm.

34.052 ★ Lake Red C Amine in D&C Red Nos. 8 and 9 (*11*)—Official Final Action ★

See **34.065–34.066**, 11th ed.

Intermediates in FD&C Yellow No. 6 (*12*)
Official First Action

34.053 ***Principle***

FD&C Yellow No. 6 (C.I. No. 15985) is more strongly adsorbed on cellulose from concd $(NH_4)_2SO_4$ soln than are dye intermediates. Sulfanilic acid and Schaeffer's salt elute sep. with 40% $(NH_4)_2SO_4$; 6,6′-oxybis(2-naphthalenesulfonic acid) (DONS) elutes with 20% $(NH_4)_2SO_4$. Each intermediate is detd by UV spectrophotometry.

34.054 ***Apparatus***

(**a**) *Chromatographic tube.*—Approx. 20 (id) $\times$ 400 mm with sealed-in coarse fritted disk (Corning No. 38450, or equiv.). Attach short length of clean rubber tube with pinchcock.

(**b**) *Spectrophotometer.—See* **34.047(b)**; with 5 cm cells.

34.055 ***Reagents***

(All reagents must be free of UV-absorbing impurities. Test for purity as follows: Conduct blank as in detn. A of each fraction should be $\leqslant$0.4 in 210–370 nm region in 5 cm cell against H_2O.)

(**a**) *Ammonium sulfate solns.—(1) 40%.*—Dissolve 400 g in H_2O and dil. to 1 L in vol. flask. *(2) 20%.*— Dissolve 400 g in H_2O and dil. to 2 L in vol. flask.

(**b**) *Cellulose powder.*—Whatman CF 11, or equiv.

★ Surplus method—*see* inside front cover.

34.056 ***Preparation of Chromatographic Column***

Slurry 30 g cellulose powder in 200 mL 40% $(NH_4)_2SO_4$ soln. With pinchcock open, pour slurry into tube and let eluant drain to surface of cellulose. Wash column with 200 mL same eluant, let drain until liq. is 1–2 mm above level of packed cellulose, and close pinchcock.

34.057 ***Separation of Intermediates***

Place 0.500 g sample in 100 mL vol. flask. Dissolve in H_2O, dil. to vol. with H_2O, and mix. Pipet 5 mL into 50 mL beaker. Add 2 g cellulose powder and mix. Add 7 g $(NH_4)_2SO_4$ powder and mix. Transfer quant. to tube, using ca 5 mL 40% $(NH_4)_2SO_4$ soln, and let drain just to surface of cellulose. Open pinchcock, add 250 mL 40% $(NH_4)_2SO_4$, and immediately begin collecting 50$\pm$1 mL fractions. After eluant has just passed into column, elute with 20% $(NH_4)_2SO_4$ and collect 50 mL fractions until color elutes (ca 1 L).

Record spectra in 5 cm cells from 370 to 210 nm against 40% $(NH_4)_2SO_4$ soln for fractions 1–8 and 20% $(NH_4)_2SO_4$ soln for remaining fractions, dilg with respective eluant, if necessary.

34.058 ***Calculations***

Examine spectra to det. compds present. Calc. to nearest 0.01%, with min. report of "<0.02%."

Sulfanilic acid normally elutes in fractions 3–6; Schaeffer's salt in fractions 8–10; and DONS in fractions 16–23.

% Sulfanilic acid (as Na salt, MW 195.2)
$$= 0.496 \times \Sigma[(A_1 - A_2)_{250} - (A_3 - A_4)_{360}]$$

% Schaeffer's salt (as Na salt, MW 246.2)
$$= 0.131 \times \Sigma[(A_1 - A_2)_{232} - (A_3 - A_4)_{360}]$$

% DONS (as di-Na salt, MW 474.4)
$$= 0.234 \times \Sigma[(A_1 - A_2)_{240} - (A_4)_{360}],$$

where $\Sigma[(A_1 - A_2) - (A_3 - A_4)]$ = sums of A of eluates (A_1, A_3) at indicated wavelengths, corrected for solv. blanks (A_2, A_4), if necessary, of all fractions contg the appropriate compd; 0.496 = 100/(80.7 $\times$ 5 $\times$ 0.5), 0.131 = 100/(305 $\times$ 5 $\times$ 0.5), and 0.234 = 100/(171 $\times$ 5 $\times$ 0.5), where 100 = factor for conversion to %, 0.5 = effective sample concn in g/L, 5 = path length in cm, and 80.7, 305, and 171 = a (L/g-cm) of sulfanilic acid, Schaeffer's salt, and DONS, resp.

4,4′-(Diazoamino)dibenzenesulfonic Acid (DAADBSA) in FD&C Yellow No. 6

High Pressure Liquid Chromatographic Method (13)
Official First Action

34.059 ***Apparatus and Reagents***

(**a**) *Liquid chromatograph.*—DuPont Model 830 with gradient elution accessory and Model 835 multiwavelength detector with 365 nm filter (No. 835052907), or equiv. system. Operating conditions: chart speed, 0.5″/min; eluant flow rate, 1.00 mL/min; detector sensitivity, 0.02 A unit full scale (AUFS); temp., ambient; gradient, 0–100% secondary eluant run in nonlinear, slow start mode (function 4, clockwise) at 1%/min; injection vol., 5 μL. Since peak size varies with eluant flow rate, check flow before injecting each sample, and adjust as necessary.

(**b**) *Liquid chromatographic column.*—No. 316 stainless steel, 1000 $\times$ 2.1 (id) mm, packed with DuPont No. 820960005 SAX (strong anion exchange) resin. Ready-to-use column is available as DuPont No. 830950405.

(**c**) *Eluants.—(1) Primary eluant.*—0.01*M* aq. $Na_2B_4O_7$ (2 g/L). *(2) Secondary eluant.*—0.01*M* aq. $Na_2B_4O_7$ (2 g/L) in 0.50*M* aq. $NaClO_4.H_2O$ (70.2 g/L).

34.060 ***Sample Preparation and Resolution***

Accurately weigh ca 1.000 g sample into 10 mL vol. flask, and dissolve and dil. to vol. with primary eluant.

Before injecting first sample, run blank (0–100%) gradient; then pump primary eluant thru column 14 min. Immediately inject 5.0 μL sample soln into chromatograph, using μL syringe. Start 0–100% gradient at once and maintain final composition until chromatogram is complete (ca 50 min). Pump primary eluant thru column 14 min; then inject next sample. (*Blank* 0–100% gradient can be run at 10%/min; however, sample gradients must be run at 1%/min.)

34.061 ***Calibration***

Accurately weigh ca 0.2000 g (100% basis) DAADBSA into 5 mL vol. flask, and dissolve and dil. to vol. with primary eluant. Prep. soln of ca 1.000 g DAADBSA-free FD&C Yellow No. 6 in 10 mL primary eluant, as in **34.060**. Transfer 5 μL DAADBSA soln to DAADBSA-free FD&C Yellow No. 6 soln with μL syringe, mix, and inject. Add 2 more 5 μL portions DAADBSA soln, mix, and inject into chromatograph after each addn. This provides min. of 3 stds (0.02, 0.04, and 0.06% DAADBSA). Addnl stds contg 0.005, 0.03, and 0.05% DAADBSA are desirable.

34.062 ***Calculations***

Det. area (peak ht $\times$ width at half ht, in sq mm) of DAADBSA peak in each spiked sample. Correct area for any area due to DAADBSA in FD&C Yellow No. 6, plot area against % DAADBSA added, and use this plot to det. % DAADBSA in samples. Report results to nearest 0.001% as DAADBSA disodium salt, MW 401.32.

Intermediates in FD&C Red No. 40 (*14*)
Official First Action

34.063 ***Principle***

FD&C Red No. 40 (C.I. No. 16035) is more strongly adsorbed on cellulose from concd $(NH_4)_2SO_4$ soln than are dye intermediates. 5-Amino-4-methoxy-2-toluenesulfonic acid (CSA) and Schaeffer's salt elute sep. with 40% $(NH_4)_2SO_4$; 6,6′-oxybis(2-naphthalensulfonic acid) (DONS) elutes with 20% $(NH_4)_2SO_4$. Each intermediate is detd by UV spectrophotometry.

34.064 ***Apparatus***

See **34.054**.

34.065 ***Reagents***

See **34.055**.

34.066 ***Preparation of Chromatographic Column***

See **34.056**. Prep. and elute similar column as blank. Blank need be repeated only when new reagents are introduced.

34.067 ***Separation of Intermediates***

Weigh 0.100 g sample into 50 mL beaker. Add 5 mL H_2O and stir to dissolve. Proceed as in **34.057**, beginning "Add 2 g cellulose powder . . .", except elute with ca 1.5 L 20% $(NH_4)_2SO_4$.

34.068 ***Calculations***

See **34.058**. CSA normally elutes in fractions 4–6, Schaeffer's salt in fractions 8–10, and DONS in fractions 16–30.

% CSA (as free acid, MW 217.2)

$$= 0.186 \times \Sigma[(A_1 - A_2)_{252} - (A_3 - A_4)_{360}]$$

% Schaeffer's salt (as Na salt, MW = 246.2)

$$= 0.395 \times \Sigma[(A_1 - A_2)_{282} - (A_3 - A_4)_{360}]$$

% DONS (as di-Na salt, MW 474.4)

$$= 0.0585 \times \Sigma[(A_1 - A_2)_{240} - (A_3 - A_4)_{360}]$$

Effective sample concn is 2 g/L; 53.8, 25.3, and 171 = *a* (L/g-cm) of CSA, Schaeffer's salt, and DONS, resp; *see* **34.058** for calcn of constants.

★ β-Naphthol—Official Final Action ★

34.069 ***Method I***

Extn, coupling with diazotized sulfanilic acid, and titrn with $TiCl_3$. *See* **34.067– 34.068**, 11th ed.

34.070 ***Method II***

Extn, coupling with benzenediazonium chloride, and spectrophthric detn at 490 nm. *See* **34.066–34.068**, 12th ed.

34.071 Pyrene in D&C Green No. 8—Official First Action

(*Caution: See* **51.011**, **51.039**, and **51.054**.)

H_2O-insol. matter, **34.029**, contains all of pyrene as well as other H_2O-insol. material. Ext this residue with 50 mL ether, filter into weighed dish, wash filter with ether, and add washings to filtrate. Evap. ether at 40– 50°, dry over H_2SO_4 in desiccator 3 hr, and weigh. Increase in wt is pyrene.

★ Phthalic Acid Derivatives (*15*) ★
Official Final Action

(Applicable to FD&C Red No. 3; D&C Orange Nos. 5, 10, 11, and 17; D&C Red Nos. 21 and 22; D&C Yellow Nos. 7 and 8.)

34.072 ***Spectrophotometric Method***

See **34.076–34.078**, 11th ed.

34.073 ***Applicable to D&C Yellow No. 10***

See **34.079**, 11th ed.

34.074 ***Applicable to D&C Red No. 19 and D&C Yellow No. 11***

See **34.080**, 11th ed.

SUBSIDIARY AND LOWER SULFONATED DYES

34.075 Martius Yellow—Official First Action

Dissolve 5 g sample in 150 mL H_2O, add 5 mL HCl, and shake vigorously in separator 1 min with 50 mL pet ether (sp gr 0.65). Sep. solns and again ext aq. liq. with 25–30 mL solv. Combine pet ether exts, decant into clean separator, and wash with 25 mL portions 0.25*N* HCl until washings are colorless. Remove Martius Yellow by shaking with few portions 5% NaOH soln. Neutze alk. dye soln with *tartaric acid,* add 5 g Na tartrate, and titr. with std $TiCl_3$ soln, **50.042–50.043**, using as indicator ca 10 mg FD&C Green No. 2 from freshly prepd soln. Det. blank on tartrate, FD&C Green No. 2, and H_2O.

1 mL 0.1*N* $TiCl_3$ = 0.002134 g Martius Yellow.

★ Subsidiary Dyes in FD&C Yellow No. 5 (*16*) ★
Official Final Action

34.076 ***Lower Sulfonated Dyes***

Spectrophtric detn. *See* **34.085–34.086**, 11th ed.

★ Surplus method—*see* inside front cover.

★ **Subsidiary Dyes in FD&C Yellow No. 6** ★

34.077 ***Lower Sulfonated Dyes (17)***
Official First Action

Spectrophtric detn. *See* **34.087–34.088**, 11th ed.

34.078 ***Higher Sulfonated Dyes (18)***
Official Final Action

Isolation by extn from acid soln by amyl alcohol, and spectrophthric detn at appropriate wavelength. *See* **34.078–34.079**, 12th ed.

34.079 ★ **Subsidiary Dyes in D&C Red Nos. 6 and 7** ★
Official First Action

Distillation and $KBrO_3$ titrn. *See* **34.091–34.092**, 11th ed.

34.080 ★ **4-Toluene-azo-2-naphthol- 3-carboxylic Acid in D&C Red Nos. 6 and 7 (*19*)—Official First Action** ★

Solubilized by refluxing with HCl in ethylene glycol monomethyl ether, extn with isopropanol, and spectrophthric detn at 507 nm. *See* **34.081**, 12th ed.

METALS

Lead—Official Final Action

Method I (20)

(Applicable to colors not contg Ca, Ba, or Sr)

34.081 ***Reagents***

(**a**) *Lead std solns.—See* **25.095(a)**.

(**b**) *Dilute nitric acid.*—1%. *See* **25.095(b)**.

(**c**) *Citric acid soln.*—50%. Special grade—low in Pb. *See* **25.095(d)**.

(**d**) *Diphenylthiocarbazone (dithizone) soln.*—Stock soln of purified dithizone in $CHCl_3$ contg 1.00 mg/mL. Also working soln contg 20 mg/L. *See* **25.095(e)**.

(**e**) *Potassium cyanide soln.*—10%. Dissolve 50 g phosphate-free KCN in H_2O and dil. to 500 mL. (*Caution: See* **51.050**.)

(**f**) *Hydroxylamine hydrochloride soln.*—10%. Dissolve 10 g $H_2NOH.HCl$ in 20 mL H_2O and make slightly alk. with NH_4OH. Ext Pb with dithizone. Remove excess dithizone with $CHCl_3$ and boil off any $CHCl_3$ remaining in aq. phase. Acidify with HCl and dil. to 100 mL.

(**g**) *Thymol blue indicator.*—0.1%. Dissolve 0.1 g thymol blue in H_2O, add enough 0.1*N* NaOH to change color to blue, and dil.to 100 mL.

34.082 ***Preparation of Sample***

(*Caution: See* **51.019**, **51.026**, **51.028**, and **51.030**.)

Transfer 5.00 g sample to 500 mL Kjeldahl flask, add 10 mL H_2SO_4 and 10 mL HNO_3, and heat. When SO_3 fumes begin to evolve, add 5 mL HNO_3 and heat until SO_3 again evolves. Repeat addn of HNO_3 each time SO_3 fumes appear until dye is completely in soln and digest is yellow. Then add 10 mL of mixt. of HNO_3 and 60–70% $HClO_4$ (1+1), and continue heating until digest is colorless or pale yellow and bulk of H_2SO_4 is evapd.

Cool flask under running H_2O and neutze soln by addns of small portions of NH_4OH. Add 20 mL citric acid soln and adjust to pH 8.5–9 with NH_4OH, using 4 drops thymol blue indicator. Add 5 mL 10% KCN soln.

★ Surplus method—*see* inside front cover.

Transfer alk. soln to 250 mL Pyrex separator. Ext Pb with 20 mL portion dithizone soln contg 20 mg/L. (*Note:* If enough Fe is present to cause excessive oxidn of dithizone as indicated by yellow color in $CHCl_3$ layer, add 10 mL 10% $H_2NOH.HCl$ soln to reduce the Fe.) Let $CHCl_3$ layer settle and drain into another separator. Wash down floating globules of $CHCl_3$ with two 5 mL portions of less concd dithizone soln (4 mg/L) and add to receiving separator. Repeat extns with the more concd dithizone soln until no more red Pb dithizonate is observed. Make 2 more extns with 10 mL portions less concd dithizone soln.

Add 25 mL 1% HNO_3 to separator contg combined dithizone exts. Shake, let settle, and drain green dithizone layer into another separator contg addnl 25 mL 1% HNO_3. Shake, let layers sep., and discard $CHCl_3$ fraction. Combine 1% HNO_3 exts.

34.083 ***Determination***

Det. Pb in combined 1% HNO_3 exts as in **25.100**.

Method II (21)

(Applicable to Al lakes)

34.084 ***Apparatus***

See Fig. **34:02**. Pptn tube *B* is fitted with inlets for addn of sample and of H_2S and for release of H_2S and transfer of pptd PbS to filter in *C* (fine porosity fritted glass covered with Celite

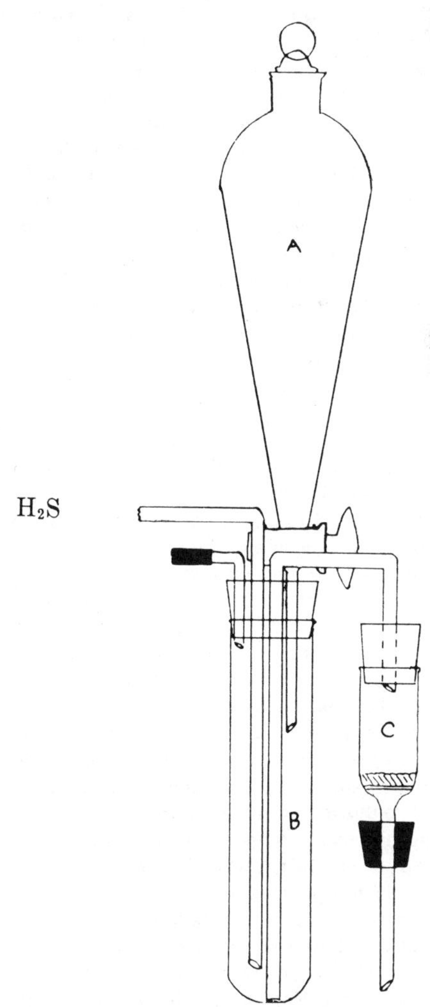

FIG. 34:02—Sulfiding apparatus (full scale)

or other similar filter-aid). For 20–300 μg Pb, ca 0.5 g filter-aid is enough to allow rapid filtration with complete retention of ppt. Filter must be thoroly washed with HNO_3 followed by H_2O before use.

Wash all glassware successively with scouring powder, H_2O, HNO_3, and again with H_2O. Wash pptn app. with HNO_3 and H_2O between detns.

34.085 ***Reagents***

All reagents should be Pb-free. *See* **25.095**. Any source of H_2S may be used. Scrub gas first with H_2SO_4 (1+1), and then with H_2O before passing into soln.

34.086 ***Determination***

(*Caution: See* **51.019**, **51.026**, **51.028**, **51.030**, and **51.059**.)

Weigh 2 g sample into 500 mL Kjeldahl flask, add 10 mL H_2SO_4 and 10 mL HNO_3, and digest over low flame until SO_3 fumes appear. Add 5 mL portions HNO_3 (waiting until SO_3 fumes appear before adding each succeeding portion) until all org. matter is in soln. Slowly add 5–10 mL mixt. of HNO_3 and 60–70% $HClO_4$ (1+1), and continue digestion until white ppt formed shows first signs of spattering. Let flask cool, and cautiously add 5 mL H_2O and then few drops NH_4OH. Vigorously swirl flask and cool under running H_2O. Add 20 mL citric acid soln, **34.081(c)**, and adjust to pH 3.0–3.4 (bromophenol blue) with NH_4OH. Add 1 mL *$CuSO_4$ soln* (1 mg Cu/mL) and transfer soln to pptn tube, *B*, of sulfiding app., Fig. **34:02**. Bubble H_2S thru soln 3–5 min at ca 2 bubbles/sec and filter resulting suspension thru *C* at rate of ca 1 drop/sec. When filtration is complete, remove receiver contg filtrate and attach suction test tube.

Add 3 mL hot HNO_3 thru separator *A* and draw thru filter; follow with 2 mL hot H_2O. Detach filter and pass addnl 3 mL hot HNO_3 thru filter, wetting all sides. Again follow with 2 mL hot H_2O. If filter is still colored with PbS, wash again with hot HNO_3 and H_2O. Wash dissolved sulfides into pptn tube *B*, wetting all sides to take up any residual PbS and then into 50–100 mL g-s erlenmeyer. Stopper, and shake few sec; remove stopper and boil until soln clears, to remove last traces of H_2S and to coagulate any free S present.

Transfer soln to 250 mL separator. Wash flask with two 5 mL portions H_2O and add washings to main soln. Add 10 mL citric acid soln, 5 mL 10% KCN soln, and few drops of $H_2NOH.HCl$ soln, **34.081(f)**, to prevent oxidn of dithizone; adjust pH to 8.5–9.5 (thymol blue) with NH_4OH.

Immediately ext with 20 portions dithizone, **34.081(d)**, using the more dil. soln unless exceptionally large amts of Pb are present. Shake 20–30 sec, let layers sep., and note color of $CHCl_3$ phase. (Pb dithizone complex is red, but color may be masked by excess green dithizone, giving intermediate hues of purple and crimson. Color of $CHCl_3$ ext gives first indication of amt of Pb present, and progress of extn can be followed by noting color of successive exts.)

Drain $CHCl_3$ layer into 125 mL short-stem separator contg 25–30 mL H_2O made ammoniacal with *one drop* NH_4OH (sp gr 0.90). Continue extn until 2 successive exts with small portions of more dil. dithizone solns show the neg. color (green, not bluish or purple), combining exts in smaller separator. Shake, let layers sep., drain $CHCl_3$ fraction into another small separator, and repeat washing process as before. Drain $CHCl_3$ fraction as cleanly as possible into 100 or 150 mL beaker, and pass small portion of dil. dithizone soln thru separators in succession so as to wash out small portions of ext persisting in aq. fraction. Add to beaker and evap. $CHCl_3$ with gentle heat on steam bath. Take up dry residue with 3–4 mL HNO_3, and heat by swirling over low flame. Dil. to ca 25 mL and continue heating 1–2 min to expel oxides of N. Add small piece of litmus paper, neutze with NH_4OH, and dil. to 50 mL. Add 0.5 mL HNO_3 and proceed as in **25.100**.

34.087 ***Method III* (*21*)**

(Applicable to Ca, Ba, and Sr lakes)

Place 2 g sample, 4 g Na_2CO_3, 6 g K_2CO_3, and 0.5 g $NaNO_3$ in Pt crucible and mix thoroly. Heat carefully until sample is carbonized; then heat to ca 850° and hold at that temp. 15 min. (If temp.-controlled furnace is available, it is only necessary to place fusion mixt. in cold furnace and raise temp. gradually to 850° over 2 hr period. Usually 15 min heating at 850° will complete fusion.)

Let crucible and contents cool to $<100°$; then add 2 or 3 mL H_2O and heat over low flame, using care to prevent spattering, until contents can be sepd from crucible. Transfer fused mixt. to 150 mL beaker with aid of ca 25 mL hot H_2O. Boil until caked material is completely disintegrated, and filter thru retentive paper. Wash residue on filter with two 15 mL portions hot 5% Na_2CO_3 soln. Pb will be in both filtrate and residue. Transfer filtrate to separator and ext Pb from filtrate as in **34.086**.

Dissolve residue on filter in 10–20 mL HCl (2+5), wash filter with H_2O, and add washings to filtrate. Boil soln to expel CO_2; then transfer to separator and ext Pb as above. Combine with $CHCl_3$ exts from sol. portion of fusion products and det. total Pb as in **34.086**.

34.088 ★ Sulfated Ash—Official Final Action ★

See **34.104**, 11th ed.

34.089 ★ Mixed Oxides (Fe, Al, Ca, and Mg) ★ Official Final Action

See **34.105**, 11th ed.

★ HALOGENS IN PURE COLORS ★

34.090 Iodine (*22*)—Official Final Action

See **34.106–34.107**, 11th ed.

34.091 Bromine (*23*)—Official Final Action

See **34.108–34.109**, 11th ed.

34.092 Chlorine (*24*)—Official Final Action

See **34.110**, 11th ed.

34.093 Chlorine in Presence of Bromine (*22*) Official Final Action

See **34.111–34.113**, 11th ed.

FREE HALOGENS—OFFICIAL FIRST ACTION

34.094 ★ Free Chlorine or Bromine ★

See **34.114–34.115**, 11th ed.

★ INORGANIC SALTS—OFFICIAL FINAL ACTION ★

34.095 Sodium Chloride in Acid Dyes (*25*)

See **34.116–34.118**, 11th ed.

34.096 Sodium Chloride in Basic Dyes (*25*)

See **34.119–34.120**, 11th ed.

★ Surplus method—*see* inside front cover.

34.097 Sodium Sulfate (*25*)

See **34.121–34.122**, 11th ed.

34.098 Sodium Halides in Halogenated Fluorescein Colors

See **34.123**, 11th ed.

34.099 Sodium Acetate

See **34.124–34.126**, 11th ed.

SOLUBLE MATTER—OFFICIAL FIRST ACTION

34.100 Water-Soluble Matter

Place 5 g well powd sample in 500 mL erlenmeyer or wide-mouth bottle, add 200 mL H_2O, stopper, and shake vigorously. Repeat mixing several times during 2 hr period. Filter, and evap. 100 mL filtrate in weighed Pt dish on steam bath. Dry in oven at 100–105°, cool in desiccator, and weigh. Report increase in wt as H_2O-sol. matter. Test small portions of remainder of filtrate for chlorides, sulfates, and nitrates. If more than traces are present, make proper analyses on aliquot portions of filtrate.

34.101 Chloroform-Soluble Matter

Weigh 5 g sample into cellulose thimble and ext in Soxhlet app. with $CHCl_3$ 16 hr. Transfer ext to separator and wash with 30 mL portions H_2O until washings are practically colorless. Ext combined washings with ca 30 mL $CHCl_3$ and add washings to main ext. Drain $CHCl_3$ ext into weighed dish. Wash separator with few mL $CHCl_3$ and add washings to dish. Evap. at room temp., dry in desiccator to const wt (±0.5 mg), and weigh. Report as $CHCl_3$ ext.

34.102 ★ Matter Soluble in One Per Cent ★ Aqueous Hydrochloric Acid

See **34.129**, 11th ed.

MISCELLANEOUS

34.103 ★ Melting Point—Official Final Action ★

See **34.130–34.131**, 11th ed.

34.104 ★ Free Acid—Official First Action ★

See **34.132**, 11th ed.

SELECTED REFERENCES

(*1*) USDA Bur. Chem. Bull. **448;** USDA Bur. Chem. Circs. **25** and **63;** Allen, "Commercial Organic Analysis," 4th ed., 1911, Vol. 5; Leach-Winton, "Food Inspection and Analysis," 4th ed., 1920; Girard, "Analyse des Matières Alimentaires et Recherche de leurs Falsifications," 2nd ed., 1904; USDA Bur. Animal Ind. Circ. **180;** J. Ind. Eng. Chem. **8,** 1123(1916); **9,** 955(1917).

(*2*) USDA Bur. Chem. Bull. **65,** p. 152; Ann. fals. **3,** 293(1910); USDA Bur. Chem. Circs. **25** and **63;** Abs. Chem. Centr. **69,** (*2*) 943(1898); J. Ind. Eng. Chem. **8,** 614(1916); **10,** 436(1918).

(*3*) USDA Bull. **1390,** Supplement 1 (1930).

(*4*) JAOAC **49,** 674(1966).

(*5*) JAOAC **26,** 182(1943).

(*6*) JAOAC **27,** 576(1944); **30,** 522(1947); **31,** 598, 674(1948); **32,** 130, 635(1949).

(*7*) JAOAC **25,** 936(1942).

(*8*) JAOAC **31,** 592(1948); **32,** 613(1949).

(*9*) JAOAC **31,** 594(1948); **32,** 624(1949).

(*10*) JAOAC **50,** 526(1967).

(*11*) JAOAC **35,** 419(1952).

(*12*) JAOAC **55,** 723(1972).

(*13*) JAOAC **60,** 168(1977).

(*14*) JAOAC **56,** 700(1973).

(*15*) JAOAC **33,** 398(1950); **34,** 407(1951).

(*16*) JAOAC **33,** 937(1950).

(*17*) JAOAC **32,** 672(1949).

(*18*) JAOAC **37,** 805(1954).

(*19*) JAOAC **46,** 344(1963).

(*20*) JAOAC **30,** 552(1947); **32,** 622(1949).

(*21*) JAOAC **31,** 677(1948); **32,** 621(1949).

(*22*) JAOAC **25,** 755(1942); **32,** 680(1949).

(*23*) JAOAC **26,** 433(1943); **28,** 757(1945).

(*24*) JAOAC **26,** 433(1943); **32,** 609(1949).

(*25*) JAOAC **25,** 958(1942).

★ Surplus method—*see* inside front cover.

35. Cosmetics

GENERAL METHODS

Water and Ethyl Alcohol (*1*)—Official First Action

35.001 ***Principle***

Sample is dissolved or dispersed in ethylene glycol monomethyl ether, which also serves as internal std, and H_2O and alcohol are detd by GLC, using relatively inert column, perfluorocarbon substrate coated with high MW polyethylene glycol, to minimize tailing.

35.002 ***Apparatus***

Gas chromatograph.—With thermal conductivity detector operated at following temps (°): Detector ca 250, injection port ca 260, oven, ca 100; He flow rate, 50 mL/min; bridge current, as directed by manufacturer.

35.003 ***Standard Solutions***

Prep. 3 std solns in 125 mL g-s flasks contg H_2O and absolute alcohol, weighed to 0.1 mg, in ethylene glycol monomethyl ether weighed to 10 mg, as follows:

H_2O, mg	Alcohol, mg	Ethylene Glycol Monomethyl Ether, g
125	375	24.50
250	250	24.50
375	125	24.50

H_2O content of ethylene glycol monomethyl ether should be <0.05%. Use same batch for stds and samples. Com. product is usually satisfactory, but because of hygroscopicity, *expose solns to air as little as possible.*

35.004 ***Preparation of Column***

Weigh 10 g polyethylene glycol 20000 (Carbowax 20M) into 800 mL beaker, dissolve completely in ca 400 mL warm CH_2Cl_2, and cool to ca 0°. Slurry cold soln with 190 g precooled (ca 0°) Fluoropak 80, 40–60 mesh (Applied Science Laboratories). Transfer to 15 cm crystg dish, place in hood, and evap. to dryness at room temp. with occasional stirring. Recool to ca 0° and screen thru No. 40 on No. 60 precooled screen. Pack fraction remaining on No. 60 in 4.6 m (15′) × ¼″ precooled Cu column, using vibrator. (Use of cooled column packer (Press-Pak, available from Alltek Associates, 202 Campus Dr, Arlington Hts, IL 60004) at 35 lb/sq in. (240 kPa) N pressure allows packing of cooled, precoiled column.)

35.005 ***Standardization***

Inject 3 µL of one of std solns with 10 µL syringe and det. elution time of ethylene glycol monomethyl ether. (Order is alcohol, H_2O, and glycol ether.) Adjust oven temp., if necessary, so latter elutes in 15–20 min. With satisfactory column, pen will return to within 1% of recorder 0 between alcohol and H_2O peaks. Det. sample size for each std soln such that response for smallest peak is ≥¼ full scale on ×1 attenuation. Det. all attenuations necessary to keep all peaks on chart scale. (Too large samples will overload column and skew glycol ether peak.)

With some gas chromatographs, alcohol peak response will vary with time interval between emergence of glycol ether of previous injection and injection of sample. Thus, inject all samples (std curves and actual detns) at same time interval after emergence of glycol ether. This requires use of preliminary sample. If time sequence is broken, inject another preliminary sample to re-establish sequence.

Obtain chromatograms, in duplicate, and on same day, for each std soln, using sample sizes and attenuations detd above. Duplicate sample sizes to 0.1 µL and use same technic for injecting and withdrawing syringe needle. Det. peak ht of each component, correcting for attenuation.

Calc. ratios: peak ht H_2O/peak ht ethylene glycol monomethyl ether (R_{PW}), and wt H_2O/wt ethylene glycol monomethyl ether (R_{WW}). Average the 2 R_{PW} values for each std soln and plot av. R_{PW} values against corresponding R_{WW} values. Draw best straight line thru 3 points. Make same calcns for alcohol stds, and plot corresponding R_{PA} and R_{WA} values. (Curves should be straight lines intersecting x or y axis near origin.)

35.006 ***Determination***

Accurately weigh sample contg ca 100–400 mg H_2O and/or alcohol into 125 mL g-s flask, add 24.50±0.1 g ethylene glycol monomethyl ether, and mix thoroly. (Complete soln is unnecessary but glycol ether phase should contain all the H_2O and alcohol.) Det. proper sample size as in **35.005**, recording necessary attenuations. From good chromatogram, calc. R_{PW} and R_{PA} values. Read R_{WW} and R_{WA} values from std curves. From latter values prep. *final std soln* of 24.50 g ethylene glycol monomethyl ether plus H_2O and/or alcohol which approximates (within 10%) curve of sample. Det., in sequence, (*a*) curve of proper size sample, (*b*) curve of adjusted *final std soln,* and repeat (*a*) and (*b*), in that order. Det. av. R_{PW} and R_{PA} values of unknown and final std solns, then R_{WW} and R_{WA} of std soln.

For H_2O: R_{WW} (sample) = R_{PW} (sample) × R_{WW} (std)/R_{PW} (std); wt H_2O (sample) = wt ethylene glycol monomethyl ether (sample) × R_{WW} (sample); and % H_2O (sample) = (wt H_2O/wt sample) × 100.

For alcohol: R_{WA} (sample) = R_{PA} (sample) × R_{WA} (std)/R_{PA} (std); wt alcohol (sample) = wt ethylene glycol monomethyl ether (sample) × R_{WA} (sample); and % alcohol (sample) = (wt alcohol/wt sample) × 100.

Propylene Glycol (*2*)—Official Final Action

(Applicable to all types of cosmetics)

35.007 ***Apparatus***

(a) *Distillation apparatus.*—All-glass, with ₸ 20/40 joints: 250 mL r-b flask, elec. heating mantle, 20 mL Barrett H_2O trap with ₸ stopper, and driptip condenser.

(b) *Gas chromatograph.*—With H flame detector and capable of operating at ca 200°.

(c) *GLC column.*—1.8 m (6′) × ¼″ od Cu or Al column packed with 80–100 mesh Chromosorb 101. Pack resin in column, using vibrator and column packer, **35.004**, operated at 25–35 lb (170–240 kPa) pressure. Heat column overnight at 240° with He flow rate ca 100 mL/min. Condition column with propylene glycol as in **35.010**. Inject enough aq. soln of propylene glycol-trimethylene glycol (1+1) to give ≥½ full-scale response. If column is satisfactory, 2 symmetrical peaks will be obtained. Reject batches of Chromosorb 101 which give unsymmetrical peaks.

35.008 ***Reagents***

(a) *Propylene glycol.*—Eastman Kodak Co. No. 1321, or equiv.; assay by periodate oxidn as in **19.009 (a)**.

(**b**) *Trimethylene glycol.*—Propylene glycol-free.

(**c**) *Isooctane (2,2,4-trimethylpentane).*—Bp 99–100°.

(**d**) *Propylene glycol and trimethylene glycol std solns.*—10 mg/mL. Prep. sep. std solns. Accurately weigh ca 1.0 g std, dissolve in H_2O, transfer to 100 mL vol. flask, and dil. to vol.

35.009 ***Separation of Propylene Glycol by Co-distillation***

(*Caution: See* **51.011**, **51.039**, and **51.062**.)

Accurately weigh sample contg ca 2–40 mg propylene glycol into 250 mL r-b flask. Add 8–10 mL H_2O and few boiling chips. Connect flask to distn app. and add, thru condenser, enough isooctane to fill H_2O trap and provide 25–40 mL isooctane in distn flask. Adjust voltage on heating mantle so that isooctane distils at 5–10 mL/min. Continue distn 30 min after all H_2O appears to be collected in trap. Drain as much H_2O as possible (leave ca 0.25 mL in H_2O trap) into small g-s container. (Stoppered 25 mL graduate is convenient.) Remove heat from distn flask and, when boiling stops, disconnect flask from app. and add 5 mL H_2O. Reconnect to app. and distil as before. Drain distillate into container contg first H_2O distillate. Repeat with second 5 mL portion H_2O. Mix combined distillates.

35.010 ***Preparation of Instrument***

With Chromosorb 101 column in gas chromatograph, set column temp. at ca 180°, injection port and detector temps at ca 300°, and He flow rate near 70 mL/min. If necessary, adjust column temp. to elute propylene glycol in ca 6 min. Condition column by initial 0.5 μL injection of propylene glycol. Column must be conditioned in this manner once a day before use for detg propylene glycol. Use 5 μL aq. test soln contg ca 1 mg propylene glycol/mL and adjust H and air flow to flame detector until max. response is obtained. (*See* manufacturer's directions.) Note range and attenuation settings needed to keep peak on scale.

Establish rough calibration curve of peak ht response against wt propylene glycol by injecting known amts propylene glycol and observing response.

35.011 ***Determination***

Det. approx. propylene glycol content of aq. soln, obtained by codistn of sample with isooctane, by injecting known amt distillate into chromatograph. To sample soln add known aliquot of std trimethylene glycol soln (preferably sample soln should contain approx. equal wts propylene glycol and trimethylene glycol). Prep., from accurately measured aliquots of stds, soln contg approx. same wt propylene glycol and trimethylene glycol as prepd sample and dil. to approx. same vol. as sample soln.

Det., by trial injections, resp. vols of sample and std solns required to give nearly equal responses of ca ¾ full-scale for propylene glycol. Alternately inject these vols sample and known solns, making ≥2 injections of each soln. Det. sample and its corresponding std at same range and attenuation settings.

35.012 ***Calculations***

From chromatograms, calc. following peak ht ratios for sample, R, and std, R', resp.:

R = peak ht propylene glycol/peak ht trimethylene glycol

R' = peak ht propylene glycol/peak ht trimethylene glycol,

Using av. values of R and R', calc. amt propylene glycol in sample.

mg Propylene glycol = (R/R') × mg propylene glycol (std) × [mg trimethylene glycol (sample)]/[mg trimethylene glycol (std)]

(If same aliquot of trimethylene glycol is used for prepd sample and std, last factor = 1.)

DEODORANTS AND ANTIPERSPIRANTS

Aluminum and Zinc (*3*)—Official Final Action

35.013 ***Reagents***

(**a**) *8-Hydroxyquinoline soln.*—Dissolve 5.0 g 8-hydroxyquinoline in 12 mL HOAc, dil. to 100 mL with H_2O, and filter if not clear. Prep. fresh soln ≤2 weeks.

(**b**) *Ammonium acetate soln.*—Approx. 2*N*. Dissolve 150–160 g NH_4OAc in 1 L H_2O and filter if not clear.

(**c**) *Hydrochloric acid.*—Approx. 2*N* (1+5).

(**d**) *Ammonium hydroxide.*—Approx. 2*N*. Vol. of NH_4OH required to neutze 20 mL 2*N* HCl, (**c**), should be known to within ±2 mL.

35.014 ***Preparation of Sample***

(**a**) *Liquids.*—Dil. 5 mL sample to 250 mL with H_2O in vol. flask. If perfume oils sep., filter before taking aliquot for analysis.

(**b**) *Creams and pastes.*—Accurately weigh 2–3 g sample into 250 mL beaker. Add 5 mL HCl (HNO_3 if chlorides are to be detd) and ca 50 mL H_2O, and heat until oils liquefy and sep.; cool until oils solidify, and decant aq. layer thru fluted paper into 250 mL vol. flask. Return filter to original beaker and macerate thoroly. Repeat above extn twice, decant as before, and finally thoroly wash residue and paper with H_2O. (It is unnecessary to return filter paper to beaker after these extns.) Cool combined exts to room temp., dil. to vol. with H_2O, and mix.

(**c**) *Solids.*—Accurately weigh 2–3 g sample into 250 mL beaker, add 5 mL HCl (HNO_3 if chlorides are to be detd) and ca 50 mL H_2O, and heat to bp. Cool, and filter thru fluted paper into 250 mL vol. flask. If filtrate is cloudy, refilter thru fine quant. paper. Thoroly wash beaker and paper with H_2O. Cool flask and contents to room temp., dil. to vol. with H_2O, and mix.

35.015 ***Determination***

(**a**) *Interfering metals absent.*—Take aliquot of sample soln contg 12–25 mg Al or 20–60 mg Zn. Add 1–2 drops phthln, and then add 2*N* NH_4OH until neut. or until faint permanent turbidity results. Add 5 mL HOAc (1+9), dil. to ca 100 mL, and heat to 70–90°. Add 10 mL 8-hydroxyquinoline soln and then slowly add NH_4OAc soln until 20 mL (*see Note*) in excess of vol. required to produce permanent ppt has been added. If permanent ppt forms on addn of 8-hydroxyquinoline, add only 20 mL NH_4OAc soln. Heat below bp 2–5 min and set aside 30–60 min. (Moderate excess of 8-hydroxyquinoline is required for complete pptn. If enough reagent has been added, soln will be yellow at this point; if it is not, repeat detn, using larger vol. of 8-hydroxyquinoline soln.) Filter thru tared gooch, wash thoroly with H_2O, dry 1–2 hr at 130–140°, cool, and weigh. Dry again 30 min, cool, and weigh. Repeat to const wt (±0.3 mg). (Alternatively, ppt may be dried overnight.)

Wt ppt × 0.05871 = Al;
Wt ppt × 0.1848 = Zn

Note: Final pH of soln from which metals are pptd should be 4.9–5.1. Vol. of NH_4OAc soln required to produce this pH should be detd experimentally each time new set of reagents is prepd. If NH_4OAc is of usual purity, ca 20 mL soln will be required.

(**b**) *In presence of magnesium.*—Ppt as in (**a**) and set aside ca 30 min. Decant most of liq. thru quant. paper (part or all of ppt may be transferred to paper if necessary) and discard filtrate. Place beaker used for pptn under funnel and dissolve ppt on paper in hot 2*N* HCl (20 mL is usually enough if added in several small portions). Wash paper and funnel with 20–30 mL H_2O. Add 2 mL 8-hydroxyquinoline soln, 5 mL HOAc (1+9), and vol.

of 2*N* NH_4OH equiv. to 2*N* HCl used to dissolve ppt (do not use excess). Dil. to ca 100 mL, heat to 70–90°, and proceed as in (**a**), beginning ". . . slowly add NH_4OAc soln . . ."

Zinc (*4*)—Official Final Action

35.016 ***Reagent***

8-Hydroxyquinaldine soln.—Dissolve 5.0 g 8-hydroxyquinaldine in 12 mL HOAc, dil. to 100 mL with H_2O, and filter if soln is not clear. (Soln is stable ca 1 week. If only tech. grade base is available, purify by recrystn from alcohol (2+1), using 6 mL solv. for each g base, before prepg soln.)

35.017 ***Determination***

Pipet aliquot of sample soln, **35.014**, contg 20–50 mg Zn, into 400 mL beaker. Adjust soln to slight acidity, add 1 g NH_4 tartrate if Al is present, and then add 2 mL 8-hydroxyquinaldine soln for each 10 mg Zn present; dil. to 200 mL and heat to 60–80°. Neutze excess acid by adding NH_4OH (1+4) until Zn complex salt that forms on addn of each drop just redissolves on stirring. Slowly add, with stirring, 45 mL NH_4OAc soln, **35.013(b)**, and let mixt. come to room temp.

Det. pH of soln; if pH is not 5.7–5.9, adjust with the NH_4OH soln, and let mixt. stand 10–20 min to achieve equilibrium. Decant thru tared gooch and wash ppt in beaker twice with hot H_2O, decanting each wash into crucible. Finally transfer ppt to crucible and again wash with hot H_2O. (Total vol. washings should be >200 mL.) Dry crucible and ppt 2 hr at 130–140°, cool, and weigh. Reheat 30 min at 130–140°; cool, reweigh, and repeat heating, cooling, and weighing to const wt. Wt ppt × 0.1712 = wt Zn.

35.018 Aluminum—Official Final Action

Multiply wt Zn found, **35.017**, by 5.411 to obtain equiv. wt 8-hydroxyquinoline salt, multiply by appropriate factor for aliquot taken, and subtract from wt combined Al and Zn salts, **35.015**. Difference × 0.05871 = wt Al.

Soluble Zirconium in Antiperspirant Aerosols

Colorimetric Method (5)—Official First Action

35.019 ***Reagents***

(**a**) *Alizarin red S (sodium alizarin sulfonate) soln.*—Dissolve 1.5 g alizarin red S indicator (Allied Chemical Corp., or equiv.) in 300 mL hot H_2O. Cool and filter thru double layer of rapid, medium porosity paper (Whatman No. 12, 24 cm folded, or equiv.). Dil. filtrate to 1 L with H_2O, and refilter. Soln is stable ≥1 month.

(**b**) *Zirconyl chloride octahydrate.*—Fisher No. Z-80, or equiv. Assay as in **35.020**.

35.020 ***Assay of Standard***

Accurately weigh 500–600 mg $ZrOCl_2.8H_2O$ into 400 mL beaker and dissolve in 50 mL H_2O. Add 4 g NH_4NO_3 and warm on steam bath to ca 50°. Slowly add, with stirring, 100 mL NH_4OH and continue heating 20 min. Filter while hot thru 15 cm Whatman No. 42, or equiv., paper. Complete transfer of ppt with 2–3 portions 2% NH_4NO_3 in NH_4OH (2+98). Carefully fold paper and place in ca 50 mL Pt crucible. Dry in oven at 105°. Partially cover crucible and gently heat with Meker burner until paper is well charred. Continue heating at max. burner temp. to const wt.

$$\% \text{ Zr} = \text{ZrO residue} \times 74.03/\text{wt } ZrOCl_2.8H_2O$$

35.021 ***Preparation of Standard Curve***

Dissolve $ZrOCl_2.8H_2O$ contg 200 mg Zr in 70 mL H_2O in 200 mL vol. flask. Add 110 mL HCl, cool, and dil. to vol. with H_2O. Prep. this 1 mg/mL stock soln fresh weekly. Pipet 2, 5, 10, and 15 mL stock soln into 100 mL vol. flasks. Dil. each to vol. with HCl (55+45), and mix. Pipet 5 mL each dil. std and, as blank, 5 mL HCl (55+45) into sep. 100 mL vol. flasks for color development (0, 100, 250, 500, and 750 μg Zr/100 mL). Add to each flask 10.0 mL alizarin red S soln, (**a**), and 8 mL H_2O. Swirl and place in 75±3° H_2O bath. Monitor temp. of solns with thermometer in 100 mL vol. flask contg 23 mL H_2O added at room temp. and placed simultaneously in bath. Swirl flasks occasionally while heating. After solns reach 70°, keep flasks in bath addnl 6.5±1 min. Remove and let cool 20 min at room temp. Dil. each to vol. with H_2O and mix. Measure *A* in 2 cm cells against blank at 525 nm, scanning on recording spectrophtr from 700–460 nm. Plot *A* against μg Zr/100 mL.

(If 750 μg Zr/100 mL cannot be read on *A* scale, use higher range of spectrophtr or 14.0 mL aliquot (700 μg Zr/100 mL).)

35.022 ***Preparation of Sample***

Remove cap and any paper wrapping from aerosol can. Record wt of can to nearest 0.01 g. Replace cap and freeze contents by placing inverted can in beaker contg mixt. of solid CO_2 and acetone and cooling ≥1 hr. Transfer can to smaller beaker in exhaust hood and cautiously open bottom end with can opener, keeping end partially attached to can. Let volatile gases escape at room temp. Remove dip tube after initial thawing when gas evolution has subsided, but keep tube with can in beaker. Place beaker on steam bath, and heat gently to evolve higher boiling gases. Increase heat slowly and maintain until bubbling subsides. Place beaker contg can and dip tube in 70° forced-draft oven 45 min. Raise temp. to 115° and maintain 2.5 hr, stirring occasionally with stainless steel spatula. Remove from oven and let cool to room temp. Thoroly mix contents, including any portion clinging to sides, to form homogeneous conc. Weigh can plus contents, spatula, and dip tube. Stir contents ca 1 min and weigh again. Repeat stirring and weighing until wt is const to within 0.01 g. Record wt and immediately transfer contents to g-s weighing bottle (quant. transfer unnecessary). Stopper bottle and protect from further wt loss by opening only when necessary.

Remove cap from can and thoroly remove remaining contents from can, spatula, and dip tube with H_2O and alcohol. Dry cap, can, spatula, and dip tube to const wt at 110°. Obtain wt of conc. by subtracting latter wt from wt previously recorded after drying contents. Obtain wt of intact can contents by subtracting wt of clean, dry can (without cap) and dip tube from gross wt initially recorded.

35.023 ***Determination***

Record gross wt of prepd sample in weighing bottle. Mix sample briefly and remove ca 1 g with spatula. Calc. wt removed as difference in gross wt.

Transfer sample as completely as possible from spatula to lower half of 600 mL beaker. Thoroly wipe spatula with small piece of filter paper and add paper to beaker. Add 5 mL alcohol and break up sample with glass rod. Slowly add 200 mL HCl while stirring vigorously. Heat to bp on steam bath. Boil 2–3 min and immediately transfer thru funnel to 1 L vol. flask. Complete transfer with 200 mL and 150 mL portions hot HCl. Warm flask on steam bath and shake vigorously 3–4 min. Rinse beaker with 450 mL H_2O, add to flask, and mix thoroly. Cool to room temp., dil. to vol. with HCl, and mix thoroly. Let undissolved material settle and coagulate. Filter portion thru double layer of

24 cm Whatman No. 12, or equiv., folded paper, discarding first 50 mL. Make appropriate dilns with HCl (55+45) to obtain Zr concn of 40–100 μg/mL. Pipet 5 mL into 100 mL vol. flask, and proceed as in **35.021**, beginning "Add to each flask 10.0 mL alizarin red . . ."

$$\% \text{ Zr in intact can contents} = (C/W_s) \times (W_c/W_i) \times (F/10^4),$$

where C = μg Zr/100 mL read from std curve; W_s, W_c, and W_i = g sample, prepd conc., and intact can contents, resp.; and F = appropriate diln factor.

Boric Acid (*6*)—Official Final Action

35.024 ***Preparation of Ion Exchange Column***

Provide glass tube 58 cm long × 2 cm diam. (23 × 0.75") with stopcock and outlet tube. Tamp 3 cm glass wool plug into bottom of tube, fill tube with H_2O, and add Amberlite IR-120(H) ion exchange resin slowly to form 20 cm column. Wash with HCl (1+9) and then with 50 mL portions H_2O until effluent gives neg. Cl test.

Regenerate after use by transferring accumulated resin from number of detns to large glass tube and washing with HCl (1+9) until effluent gives neg. test for adsorbed cations, *e.g.,* Zn, Al. Then remove HCl from resin by washing with H_2O until effluent gives neg. Cl test.

35.025 ***Determination***

Place sample contg 50–200 mg H_3BO_3 in 250 mL casserole, add 2 drops phthln, and make alk. with 10% NaOH soln. Evap. to dryness on steam bath under gentle air current, dry residue 1 hr at 140° in oven, and ash 1 hr at 550°. Cool to room temp., add ca 50 mL hot H_2O, acidify cautiously with HCl, and filter hot soln thru quant. paper into 250 mL beaker. Wash paper with little hot H_2O and reserve filtrate (may be slightly cloudy).

Transfer paper to same casserole and make alk. by wetting with ca 10 mL H_2O and few drops 10% NaOH soln. Evap. to dryness on steam bath, dry 1 hr at 140°, and ash 2 hr at 550°. Cool, add ca 50 mL hot H_2O, acidify with HCl, and filter into reserved filtrate. Wash casserole and paper thoroly with hot H_2O, and discard paper. (Total vol. soln should be ca 200 mL.)

Cool soln; add NH_4OH until barely alk. to litmus paper or until flocculent ppt appears. Reacidify with HCl until slightly acid to litmus paper or until ppt just redissolves. Pass soln thru ion exchange column into 1 L flask at rate requiring 10–15 min for passage. Follow sample soln with several 50 mL portions H_2O until effluent is only slightly acid to pH test paper. Add 5 drops Me red, **2.091(b)**, make alk. with freshly prepd 10% NaOH soln, and then barely acid with HCl.

Connect flask to H_2O-cooled reflux condenser and boil 5 min. Wash down condenser with little H_2O and cool soln to room temp. under running H_2O. Neutze to Me red with 0.1*N* NaOH, **50.034**; add 4–5 g mannitol and ca 0.5 mL phthln. Titr. with 0.1*N* NaOH to pink color, add more mannitol, and if pink disappears, continue titrn until it reappears. Repeat addn of mannitol until there is no further change in color.

Det. blank as follows: To ca 350 mL H_2O add vol. of freshly prepd 10% NaOH soln equal to that required to neutze sample after passing thru column. Barely acidify with HCl and proceed as above, beginning "Connect flask to H_2O-cooled reflux condenser . . ." Subtract blank titrn from sample titrn and calc. H_3BO_3 content of sample. 1 mL 0.1*N* NaOH = 0.00618 g H_3BO_3.

35.026 Chlorides (*7*)—Official Final Action

Pipet aliquot of sample soln, **35.014**, contg ca 100 mg Cl into 250 mL beaker. Dil. to 150 mL with H_2O, neutze to litmus with NH_4OH (1+1), and acidify with 1 mL HNO_3 (1+1). If any undissolved ppt remains, add more HNO_3 (1+1) until clear soln is obtained. Add dropwise, stirring constantly, slight excess of 0.1*N* $AgNO_3$. (Excess should be ≤5 mL.) Pptn and succeeding operations must be carried out in subdued light. Heat mixt. to 90–95° and stir until ppt coagulates. Let ppt settle; add 1–2 drops 0.1*N* $AgNO_3$ to supernate to ensure presence of excess Ag. Let mixt. stand 1–2 hr in dark.

Decant thru tared gooch, wash ppt 2–3 times with 0.01*N* HNO_3 by decantation, and finally transfer ppt to gooch with 0.01*N* HNO_3. Continue washing ppt with 0.01*N* HNO_3 until washing gives neg. test for Ag when 1 drop 0.1*N* HCl is added. Complete washing by removing most of the HNO_3 with two 10 mL portions H_2O. Dry crucible 2 hr at 120–130° and weigh. Repeat drying to const wt (0.2 mg). Wt AgCl × 0.2474 = wt Cl.

35.027 Sulfates (*7*)—Official Final Action

Pipet aliquot of sample soln, **35.014**, contg ca 100 mg sulfate into 600 mL beaker. Dil. to 350 mL with H_2O, neutze to litmus with NH_4OH (1+1), and acidify with 2 mL HCl. If any undissolved ppt remains, add more HCl until soln is clear.

Heat 50 mL *1% $BaCl_2$ soln* almost to bp and add rapidly with stirring to sulfate soln which has also been heated to near bp. Let ppt settle, and add little $BaCl_2$ soln to ensure excess of Ba. Let mixt. stand 1–2 hr on steam bath. Decant thru tared gooch, wash ppt 4–5 times with small portions of warm H_2O by decantation, and finally transfer ppt to gooch with warm H_2O. Continue washing ppt with warm H_2O until washing gives neg. test for Cl. Dry crucible 2 hr at 110–120° and weigh. Repeat drying to const wt (0.2 mg). Wt $BaSO_4$ × 0.4116 = wt sulfate.

Hexachlorophene (*8*)—Official Final Action

35.028 ***Apparatus***

(**a**) *Chromatographic equipment.*—Insert 2 cm plug of glass wool in bottom of tube 55 cm long × 2.5 cm od with constricted tip 2.5 cm long and 8 mm od. Provide with brass tamper of diam. slightly smaller than id of tube, and fittings, including pressure gage, for applying pressure to top of column.

(**b**) *Spectrophotometer.*—Capable of isolating band ≤5 nm in region 220–360 nm.

35.029 ***Reagents***

(**a**) *Silanized Celite.*—Weigh ca 700 g Celite 545 into 4 L beaker, add 3 L HCl (1+4), and stir thoroly. Heat on steam bath several hr, stirring occasionally. Filter slurry thru buchner under vac. and wash with H_2O until washings are Fe- and Cl-free. Suck dry, transfer to beaker, and dry ca 15 hr at 135°. Transfer ca 150 g dried Celite to crystg dish, and let stand in air 30 min. In well ventilated hood, pour 25 mL GE SC-77 Dri-Film (General Electric Co., 1 River Rd, Schenectady, NY 12305) into bottom of large glass desiccator. Place dish contg Celite on porcelain support in desiccator, and let stand in closed desiccator 4 hr. Remove dish, and let stand in hood until residual HCl dissipates.

(**b**) *Immobile solvent.*—Mix equal vols CCl_4 and *n*-heptane.

(**c**) *Eluting solns.*—In sep. 250 mL vol. flasks, add 1 mL HCl to 25, 87.5, and 150 mL alcohol and dil. each to vol. with H_2O (10, 35, and 60% alcohol, resp.).

(**d**) *Hexachlorophene std solns.*—(*1*) *Stock soln.*— 0.6 mg/mL. Accurately weigh ca 60 mg hexachlorophene USP and dil. to vol. in 100 mL vol. flask with acidified 60% alcohol, (**c**). (*2*) *Working std solns.*—Dil. 5, 10, and 20 mL aliquots stock soln to 100 mL with acidified 60% alcohol, (**c**) (0.03, 0.06, and 0.12 mg/mL).

35.030 ***Preparation of Sample***

(**a**) *For products containing sulfated surface-active agents.*—Accurately weigh, in weighing bottle, ca 1 g sample and transfer quant. to ₮ 250 mL r-b flask with 75 mL 20% alcohol. Add 10 mL HCl and few boiling chips, attach H_2O-cooled condenser, and reflux 15 min. Cool to room temp. and transfer to 250 mL separator with ca 25 mL H_2O. Rinse flask with 30 mL $CHCl_3$ and transfer to separator. Shake well and drain $CHCl_3$ into another 250 mL separator. Rinse beaker with two addnl 30 mL portions $CHCl_3$, ext aq. soln with each, and combine $CHCl_3$ exts in 250 mL separator. Wash combined exts with 10 mL H_2O acidified with HCl, and filter thru $CHCl_3$-wetted plug of cotton in powder funnel into 250 mL beaker. Wash cotton with 20 mL $CHCl_3$, and evap. $CHCl_3$ to ca 10 mL on steam bath under air current. Complete evapn to dryness at room temp. under air current.

(**b**) *For products not containing sulfated surface-active agents.*—Accurately weigh, in weighing bottle, ca 1 g sample and transfer quant. to 250 mL separator with 40 mL warm H_2O. Acidify with HCl, and ext with three 30 mL portions $CHCl_3$. Wash combined $CHCl_3$ exts with 10 mL H_2O acidified with HCl, and continue as in (**a**), beginning, ". . . and filter thru $CHCl_3$-wetted plug . . ."

35.031 ***Isolation of Hexachlorophene***

Weigh two 12 g portions silane-treated Celite. To 1 portion in 250 mL beaker, add 7 mL CCl_4-*n*-heptane (1+1), mix well, and pack mixt. gently but firmly with tamper into chromatgc tube in ca 4 g portions.

To residue from **35.030**(**a**) or (**b**), add 7 mL CCl_4-*n*-heptane (1+1), and stir well to dissolve or disperse residue. Add the second 12 g portion silane-treated Celite, stir thoroly, and pack mixt. into tube as before. Wipe beaker, stirring rod, and tamper with small piece of glass wool and lightly tamp it on top of completed column.

Elute column with 100 mL acidified 10% alcohol, then with 200 mL acidified 35% alcohol, and finally with 250 mL acidified 60% alcohol. Maintain flow at ca 2 mL/min with aid of air pressure and do not permit level of eluting liqs to fall below glass wool plug. Collect two 100 mL portions and then 50 mL portions in vol. flasks. Hexachlorophene should elute with acidified 60% alcohol.

35.032 ***Determination***

Add 1 drop HCl to each eluate in vol. flasks and obtain spectra over 220–360 nm in 1 cm cell against corresponding eluting soln. If necessary, dil. with corresponding eluting soln. Obtain spectra of working std solns similarly.

From curves, identify eluates contg hexachlorophene. Calc. hexachlorophene in each eluate by comparing A at 297 nm of sample with that of std, using straight line background correction. Add amts in eluates to obtain amt in sample.

Methenamine (*9*)—Official Final Action

35.033 ***Reagent***

Borax-carbonate soln.—Dissolve 5.0 g Na_2CO_3 and 4.0 g $Na_2B_4O_7.10H_2O$ in 100 mL H_2O.

35.034 ***Determination***

Pipet aliquot of sample soln, **35.014**, contg 150–200 mg methenamine into 500 mL r-b flask and dil. to 30 mL with H_2O. Neutze to litmus with either NaOH soln or dil. H_2SO_4; then acidify with 1 mL H_2SO_4. Connect flask to H_2O-cooled condenser and reflux 30 min to hydrolyze methenamine. Dil. to 175 mL by adding H_2O thru top of condenser, and disconnect condenser. Connect flask thru Kjeldahl trap to efficient straight-wall condenser and distil into 200 mL vol. flask contg 10 mL freshly prepd *10% $NaHSO_3$ soln.* Continue distn until residual vol. is ca 5 mL, taking care to avoid charring.

Wash down condenser with little H_2O and cool distillate to room temp. Dil. distillate to vol. with H_2O, mix well, and let stand 30 min. Pipet 20 mL aliquot into wide-mouth 250 mL erlenmeyer, add 3–4 mL starch indicator, **6.005**(**f**), and destroy excess bisulfite with ca 1*N* I soln. Carefully adjust to starch-I end point with 0.5% $NaHSO_3$ soln and 0.05*N* I. Dil. to 50 mL with H_2O, add 10 mL borax-carbonate soln, and titr. with 0.05*N* I to permanent blue. 1 mL 0.05*N* I consumed in alk. titrn = 0.5841 mg methenamine.

Phenolsulfonates—Official Final Action

35.035 ★ ***Bromination Method (9)*** ★

See **35.025–35.026**, 11th ed.

Spectrophotometric Method (10)

35.036 ***Apparatus and Reagents***

(**a**) *Spectrophotometer.*—*See* **35.028**(**b**).

(**b**) *Zinc phenolsulfonate std soln.*—10 mg/L in ca 0.1*N* NaOH. Dissolve 100 mg Zn phenolsulfonate, NF XI (equiv. to 62.67 mg phenolsulfonic acid), in 100 mL H_2O. Dil. 10 mL aliquot to 100 mL with H_2O. Pipet 10 mL aliquot into 100 mL vol. flask, add 4 mL freshly prepd 10% NaOH soln, and dil. to vol. with H_2O.

35.037 ***Determination***

(**a**) *In presence of sulfated surface-active agents.*—Accurately weigh sample contg 5–10 mg phenolsulfonic acid into 250 mL erlenmeyer. Add 10 mL H_2O and 2 mL HCl, connect to H_2O-cooled condenser, and reflux 0.5 hr. Cool to room temp., transfer quant. to 100 mL separator with 20 mL H_2O, and proceed as in (**b**), beginning ". . . ext with three 30 mL portions $CHCl_3$."

(**b**) *In absence of sulfated surface-active agents.*—Accurately weigh, in weighing bottle, sample contg 5–10 mg phenolsulfonic acid. Transfer quant. to 100 mL separator with aid of 30 mL H_2O. Acidify with HCl and ext with three 30 mL portions $CHCl_3$. Discard $CHCl_3$ exts. Filter aq. soln thru moistened quant. paper into 100 mL vol. flask and dil. to vol. with H_2O. Pipet 10 mL aliquot into 100 mL vol. flask, neutze to litmus paper with freshly prepd 10% NaOH soln, add 4 mL excess, and dil. to vol. with H_2O. Det. A of sample soln and A' of std soln at 253 nm in 1 cm cells, using 0.1*N* NaOH as blank.

$$\% \text{ phenolsulfonic acid} = C \times A/[10\,A' \times (\text{g sample})],$$

where C = concn phenolsulfonic acid (mg/L) in std soln.

35.038 Urea (*7*)—Official Final Action

Pipet aliquot of sample soln, **35.014**, contg 50–100 mg urea into ₮ 100 mL r-b flask. Acidify with HCl, adding 0.5 mL excess. Immerse flask in steam bath and evap. to dryness. Add 10 g cryst. $MgCl_2.6H_2O$ and 1 mL HCl, and connect flask to reflux condenser. Carefully heat mixt. with small flame until $MgCl_2$ dissolves in its H_2O of crystn, and reflux slowly 2 hr so that rate of return of liq. from condenser is 9–14 drops/ min.

Let soln cool, add H_2O thru top of condenser, disconnect flask, and if necessary, heat to dissolve solids. Transfer soln to 1 L flat-bottom flask, dil. to ca 400 mL with H_2O, make alk. with 10% NaOH soln, and distil ca 275–300 mL into suitable portion of 0.1*N* H_2SO_4 contg several drops of Me red, **50.014**(**a**). Titr. excess acid with ca 0.1*N* NaOH, using more indicator if necessary.

★ Surplus method—*see* inside front cover.

Stdze the 0.1*N* NaOH against the std 0.1*N* H_2SO_4, using Me red as indicator.

Correct for blank by refluxing 10 g cryst. $MgCl_2 .6H_2O$ and 1 mL HCl and proceeding as above. 1 mL 0.1*N* H_2SO_4 = 3.003 mg urea.

DEPILATORIES

35.039 Sulfides in Powders (*11*)—Official Final Action

(*Caution: See* **51.018** and **51.078.**)

Pipet 50 mL 0.1*N* As_2O_3 soln, **50.006**, into 250 mL g-s vol. flask. Weigh sample contg <0.12 g sulfide calcd as H_2S and transfer to flask, washing down any material on sides of flask with H_2O. Add 20 mL HCl (1+1), stopper immediately, and shake vigorously until sample decomposes. (If sample contains $CaCO_3$, slowly add the 20 mL acid thru dropping funnel fitted with rubber stopper to fit flask. Shake gently, letting liberated CO_2 bubble up thru acid. When reaction subsides, drain remainder of acid into flask, remove funnel, stopper flask, and shake vigorously.)

Cool to room temp. and dil. to vol. with H_2O. Filter thru dry paper into dry flask. Pipet 100 mL filtrate into 300 mL erlenmeyer; add 5 mL starch soln, **2.144(b)**, and enough I soln to form blue soln. Make alk. with $NaHCO_3$, adding 1–2 g excess. Titr. to permanent blue with 0.1*N* I, **50.018**. Subtract mL 0.1*N* I consumed in alk. titrn from mL 0.1*N* As_2O_3 present in aliquot. 1 mL 0.1*N* As_2O_3 = 0.005411 g CaS or 0.01271 g BaS.

★ FACE POWDERS (*12*) ★

35.040 ★ Fats and Fatty Acids as Stearic Acid ★ Official Final Action

Pet. ether extn. *See* **35.032**, 11th ed.

35.041 ★ Boric Acid—Official Final Action ★

Aq. extn and titrn in presence of mannitol. *See* **35.033**, 11th ed.

35.042 ★ Total Zinc—Official Final Action ★

Sepn as carbonate, pptn as phosphate, and ignition to $Zn_2P_2O_7$. *See* **35.034–35.035**, 11th ed.

35.043 ★ Acid-Soluble Calcium ★ Official Final Action

Isolation of Ca, pptn as oxalate, and titrn with $KMnO_4$. *See* **35.036**, 11th ed.

35.044 ★ Acid-Soluble Magnesium ★ Official Final Action

Det. Mg in filtrate from acid-sol. Ca as in **33.088**. $Mg_2P_2O_7 \times 0.3622 = MgO$.

35.045 ★ Barium Sulfate—Official Final Action ★

Fusion, and sepn and detn as $BaSO_4$. *See* **35.038–35.039**, 11th ed.

35.046 ★ Total Titanium and Iron ★ Official Final Action

Reduction with amalgamated Zn and $KMnO_4$ titrn. *See* **35.040–35.041**, 11th ed.

★ Surplus method—*see* inside front cover.

35.047 ★ Total Iron—Official Final Action ★

Titrn of Fe with $TiCl_3$. *See* **35.042–35.043**, 11th ed.

35.048 ★ Total Titanium—Official Final Action ★

% total (TiO_2 + Fe_2O_3) − % total Fe_2O_3 = % total TiO_2.

35.049 ★ Total Oxides of Iron, Titanium, ★ and Aluminum—Official Final Action

Pptn with NH_4OH and ignition. *See* **35.045**, 11th ed.

35.050 ★ Total Aluminum—Official Final Action ★

% Total (Al_2O_3 + Fe_2O_3 + TiO_2) − % total (Fe_2O_3 + TiO_2) = % total Al_2O_3.

35.051 ★ Acid-Insoluble Calcium ★ Official Final Action

Det. Ca in filtrate from NH_4OH ppt, **35.049**, as in **6.055**, beginning ". . . heat to boiling . . ."

35.052 ★ Acid-Insoluble Magnesium ★ Official Final Action

Det. Mg in filtrate from acid-insol. Ca as in **33.088**. $Mg_2P_2O_7 \times 0.3622 = MgO$.

35.053 ★ Silica—Official Final Action ★

Fusion, $HClO_4$ pptn, ignition, and HF treatment. *See* **35.049**, 11th ed.

35.054 ★ Starch—Official Final Action ★

Weigh ca 5 g sample into 500 mL Florence flask (preferably ₮). Moisten with 10 mL alcohol. Acid-wash as in **8.020**, hydrolyze starch as in **8.019** (but filter hydrolyzed mixt. before and not after dilg to vol.), and det. glucose as in **31.038** and **31.039**.

HAIR PREPARATIONS

2,5-Diaminotoluene in Hair Dyes and Rinses (*13*) Official Final Action

35.055 ★ *Acetylation Method* ★

See **35.051**, 11th ed.

35.056 ★ *Dichlorimide Method* ★

See **35.052–35.053**, 11th ed.

Paraphenylenediamine in Hair Dyes and Rinses Official Final Action

35.057 ★ *Acetylation Method* (*14*) ★

See **35.054–35.055**, 11th ed.

35.058 ★ *Dichlorimide Method* ★ (*Benzoquinone Method*) (*15*)

See **35.056**, 11th ed.

Potassium Bromate and Sodium Perborate in Cold Wave Neutralizers—Official Final Action

35.059 *Qualitative Tests* (*16*)

(**a**) *General tests.*—$KBrO_3$ and $NaBO_3$ are white cryst. salts sol. in H_2O. Aq. soln of $KBrO_3$ is slightly acid; of $NaBO_3$, slightly alk. In flame test, using Pt wire in slightly darkened room, $KBrO_3$

gives reddish violet flame when viewed thru Co glass; $NaBO_3$, typical yellow Na flame. Both compds give following test: Dissolve 0.1 g sample in 10 mL H_2O, acidify with HCl, and add 0.5 g KI. Liberation of I indicates presence of oxidizing agent.

(**b**) *Confirmatory test for bromate.*—To 1 mL 5% soln of sample in test tube, slowly add 2 mL H_2SO_4 with vigorous shaking. Note odor and color of liberated gas. (*Caution.*) Cool test tube, *carefully* add 2 mL CS_2, and shake. CS_2 layer becomes yellow or red if Br is present.

(**c**) *Confirmatory test for boron.*—Moisten 0.2 g sample in porcelain crucible with 1–2 drops H_2SO_4, add 2 mL MeOH, stir well, and ignite. Green flame indicates presence of B.

★ Pyrogallol in Hair Dyes (*17*) ★ Official Final Action

35.060 ***Qualitative Test***

Reaction with $NaHSO_3$, isolation, and detn of mp. *See* **35.058**, 11th ed.

35.061 ***Colorimetric Method***

See **35.059–35.061**, 11th ed.

35.062 ★ Resorcinol in Hair Lotions (*18*) ★ Official Final Action

Bromate titrn. *See* **35.062–35.063**, 11th ed.

35.063 ★ Salicylic Acid in Hair Lotions (*19*) ★ Official Final Action

Bromate titrn. *See* **35.064**, 11th ed.

Thioglycolate Solutions in Cold Permanent Waves (*16*) Official Final Action

35.064 ***Qualitative Test***

(*Caution: See* **51.018**. $Cd(OAc)_2$ is toxic.)

Dil. 2 mL sample to 10 mL with H_2O, acidify with 10% HOAc, add 5 mL excess, and shake well. Add 2 mL *10% $Cd(OAc)_2.2H_2O$ soln,* and shake. White gelatinous ppt forms if thioglycolic acid is present. Add excess of NH_4OH (2+3) and shake. Ppt of Cd thioglycolate will dissolve.

35.065 ***Quantitative Method***

(Applicable in absence of reducing substances other than thioglycolates)

Pipet sample aliquot contg 250–300 mg thioglycolic acid into wide-mouth 250 mL erlenmeyer. Dil. to 50 mL with H_2O, add 2–3 drops Me red, **2.115(c)**, and make slightly acid with HCl. Add 3–4 mL starch indicator, **6.005(f)**, and titr. with 0.1*N* I to purple end point. 1 mL 0.1*N* I = 0.009212 g thioglycolic acid.

Dithiodiglycolic Acid (*20*)—Official Final Action

35.066 ***Principle***

Soln contg mixt. of thioglycolic (TGA) and dithiodiglycolic (DTDGA) acids is titrd with std 0.1*N* I soln, which selectively titrs TGA. DTDGA is reduced to TGA in Jones reductor. Resulting total TGA is titrd; increased TGA represents DTDGA.

35.067 ***Reagents***

(**a**) *Zinc metal.*—20–30 mesh. Mallinckrodt Chemicals Analytical Reagent grade has been found suitable.

(**b**) *Mercuric salt soln.*—2% aq. soln of $Hg(NO_3)_2$ or $HgCl_2$. (*Caution: See* **51.079**.)

35.068 ***Apparatus***

(**a**) *Jones reductor.*—Glass tube, 50–65 cm long, 2 cm id, with stopcock, preferably Teflon, and delivery tip extending ca 8 cm below stopcock.

(**b**) *Magnetic stirrer.*—With glass- or Teflon-covered stirring bar.

35.069 ***Preparation of Jones Reductor***

Place 300 g Zn in 800 mL beaker; add 300 mL Hg soln and 2 mL HNO_3. Stir 10 min with glass rod. Decant supernate and repeat amalgamation with fresh portion Hg soln and 2 mL HNO_3. Wash amalgamated Zn 3 times, by decantation, with H_2O. (Zn should have silvery luster.) Maintain H_2O layer over Zn thruout.

Fill tube with H_2O; then slowly add prepd Zn, draining excess H_2O. Pass 500 mL H_2O thru column, maintaining H_2O layer over Zn.

Det. suitability of reductor as follows: Pass 20 mL H_2O thru column, followed by 200 mL H_2SO_4 (1+9), then 100 mL H_2O. Titr. combined washings as in **35.070(c)**. If titrn is >0.2 mL, wash column with addnl H_2O.

Det. reductor efficiency by treating ca 350 mg DTDGA, accurately weighed, in 5 mL H_2O as in **35.070(b)**. Recovery must be ⩾97%. Lower recovery indicates unsuitable reductor.

Prepd reductor may be stored 3 months before use, provided amalgamated Zn is always kept covered with H_2O. Prewash column with 200 mL H_2SO_4 (1+9) before use after overnight storage.

35.070 ***Determination***

(**a**) *Titration 1.*—Pipet sample aliquot contg 350–400 mg TGA and DTDGA into 500 mL Phillips flask contg mag. stirring bar; dil. to 100 mL with H_2O, add 2 drops Me red indicator, **2.115(c)**, and just acidify with H_2SO_4 (1+1). Add starch indicator soln, **6.005(f)**, and titr. soln with 0.1*N* I std soln, **50.018**.

1 mL 0.1*N* I = 9.212 mg TGA.

(**b**) *Reduction.*—Arrange reductor column to deliver into 1 L suction flask contg mag. stirring bar. Connect flask to vac. outlet which can be regulated to desired flow rate.

Dil. sample aliquot equal to that used in *Titration 1* with 200 mL H_2SO_4 (1+9).

Add 50 mL H_2SO_4 (1+19) to column, apply gentle suction, and elute at ca 10 mL/min. When liq. reaches top of amalgam, immediately add dild sample soln, increase vac., and elute at ca 17–20 mL/min. When liq. reaches top of amalgam, rinse sample container with 100 mL H_2SO_4 (1+19) in several portions and add to column. Follow with three 100 mL portions H_2O at ca 50 mL/min. Release vac., rinsing column tip into flask with H_2O.

(**c**) *Titration 2.*—Place suction flask contg reduced sample soln on mag. stirrer; add 5 drops Me red indicator, **2.115(c)**, and set stirrer at medium speed. Add NH_4OH to yellow indicator color (ca 70 mL); then add H_2SO_4 (1+1) dropwise just to indicator red color. Stopper flask and place in ice bath. Cool sample soln with min. swirling to ⩽25°. Add 5 mL starch indicator, **6.005(f)**, place on mag. stirrer, and titr. with 0.1*N* I to purple end point.

Perform sep. blank detns for *Titrations 1* and *2* and make appropriate corrections.

mg DTDGA in sample aliquot = 9.111 ($N - M$),

where M = mL 0.1*N* I from *Titration 1* corrected for blank and N = mL 0.1*N* I from *Titration 2* corrected for blank.

★ Surplus method—*see* inside front cover.

SUNTAN PREPARATIONS

Amyl *p*-Dimethylaminobenzoate (*21*)
Official Final Action

35.071 ***Apparatus***

(**a**) *Spectrophotometer.*—Cary Model 11 (replaced by Models 14 and 17) recording spectrophtr, or equiv., with 1 cm quartz cells.

(**b**) *Chromatographic equipment.*—(*1*) Glass chromatgc tube, 55 cm × 22 mm id with glass wool plug in constricted tip. (*2*) Brass tamper to fit chromatgc tube. (*3*) Source of variable air pressure to regulate column elution rate at ca 2 mL/min.

35.072 ***Reagents***

(**a**) *Solvent.*—(*1*) *Immobile solvent.*—*n*-Heptane-CCl_4 (1+1). (*2*) *Mobile solvents.*—Acidified 50% and 60% alcohol, contg 2 mL HCl/500 mL.

(**b**) *Silanized Celite.*—*See* **35.029**(**a**).

(**c**) *Amyl p-dimethylaminobenzoate.*—0.01 mg/mL. Dil. 10 mg std (available as Escalol 506 from Van Dyk and Co., Inc., Belleville, NJ 07109) to 1 L with NH_4OH-60% alcohol (1+99).

35.073 ***Preparation of Samples***

(*Caution: See* **51.011**, **51.040**, and **51.056**.)

In weighing bottle, weigh sample contg 10–20 mg amyl *p*-dimethylaminobenzoate. Transfer quant. to 250 mL separator with 50 mL H_2O, slightly acidify with HCl, using test paper, and ext with four 35 mL portions $CHCl_3$. Combine exts, wash with 10 mL H_2O, and filter thru $CHCl_3$-washed cotton plug in powder funnel, into 250 mL beaker. Wash cotton with 10 mL $CHCl_3$. Evap. to ca 1 mL on steam bath under air jet. Remove beaker from steam bath and continue evapn under air jet until all $CHCl_3$ has evapd. Reserve prepd residue for chromatgy.

35.074 ***Chromatography***

(**a**) *Column preparation.*—Prep. column in 2 layers as in **35.031**, par. 1 and 2. (Proper prepn of columns may be checked by eluting known amt of std from column, noting recovery.)

(**b**) *Elution.*—Elute column first with 100 mL acidified 50% alcohol at 2 mL/min, then with 350 mL acidified 60% alcohol at same flow rate. Collect eluates in consecutively numbered 50 mL vol. flasks. Add few drops NH_4OH to each flask, mix well, test for alky, and dil. to vol.

35.075 ***Determination***

Obtain spectra at 220–360 nm for each eluate. For blanks, use corresponding alcohol solns consisting of either NH_4OH-50% alcohol (1+99) or NH_4OH-60% alcohol (1+99). Dil. as necessary with NH_4OH-alcohol solns of proper concn. For quant. detn, obtain spectra of this compd in basic soln, not acid soln. Calc. amt material in each eluate by comparing *A* at 314 nm of sample with std amyl *p*-dimethylaminobenzoate soln in NH_4OH-60% alcohol (1+99), (**c**), using straight line background correction.

VANISHING CREAM (*22*)

35.076 Test for Type of Emulsion—Official Final Action

Dust small amts of finely ground oil-sol. and H_2O-sol. dyes on sep. portions of sample. If color of oil-sol. dye spreads rapidly, H_2O-in-oil emulsion is indicated; if color of H_2O-sol. dye spreads, oil-in-H_2O emulsion is indicated.

35.077 Water—Official Final Action

Transfer 5–20 g sample to erlenmeyer; add 50 mL toluene, few glass beads, and ca 2 g *lump rosin.* Connect flask to Dean and Stark distg tube receiver, and distil until no more H_2O collects in receiver. Cool, read vol. H_2O under the toluene at room temp., and from this vol., calc. % H_2O.

35.078 Ash—Official Final Action

Place 2–10 g sample in flat-bottom Pt dish, and remove H_2O and volatile material by placing dish on steam bath or in 100° oven. Ignite sample at low temp. and finally at 600° to const wt.

35.079 Chloroform-Soluble Material
Official Final Action

(*Caution: See* **51.011**, **51.040**, and **51.056**.)

Place 2–10 g sample in separator, add 25–50 mL H_2O, acidify slightly with H_2SO_4 (1+9), and ext with successive portions $CHCl_3$, collecting all exts in second separator. (Usually 4–5 portions $CHCl_3$, each ca 35 mL, are enough to remove all $CHCl_3$-sol. material.) Wash combined $CHCl_3$ exts with 10 mL H_2O, filter thru cotton plug placed in separator stem, and collect filtrate in weighed dish. Shake aq. washing with small vol. of $CHCl_3$, and filter this $CHCl_3$ into dish. Evap. $CHCl_3$ on steam bath and dry residue for 15 min intervals at 100° to const wt.

Glycerol—Official Final Action

35.080 ***Reagents***

(**a**) *Potassium periodate soln.*—0.02*M*. Dissolve 4.6 g KIO_4 in ca 500 mL hot H_2O. Dil. to ca 900 mL with H_2O, cool to room temp., and dil. to 1 L.

(**b**) *Sodium hydroxide std soln.*—0.02*N*. *See* **50.034–50.036.**

(**c**) *Bromocresol purple indicator.*—Dissolve 0.1 g bromocresol purple in 100 mL alcohol.

(**d**) *Propylene glycol.*—Bp 85–86°/10 mm.

(**e**) *Arsenious oxide soln.*—0.02*N*. Dil. 100 mL 0.1*N* As_2O_3, **50.006**, to 500 mL with H_2O.

35.081 ***Isolation and Oxidation of Glycerol***

(**a**) *Isolation of glycerol.*—Place 2–10 g sample in separator, add 25–50 mL H_2O, acidify slightly with H_2SO_4 (10 g/100 mL), and ext with successive portions $CHCl_3$. (Usually 4–5 portions, each ca 35 mL, remove all $CHCl_3$-sol. material.) Wash combined $CHCl_3$ exts with 10 mL H_2O. Filter aq. soln and wash H_2O thru cotton plug to remove droplets of $CHCl_3$, and collect filtrate in 250 mL vol. flask. Add 3 drops bromocresol purple indicator to filtrate and neutze with CO_2-free alkali (0.1*N* NaOH is satisfactory), making final adjustment with 0.02*N* NaOH. Dil. almost to vol. with H_2O, and if necessary, add more alkali to keep soln light but definite purple; then complete diln to vol. and mix.

(**b**) *Periodate oxidation.*—Transfer aliquot neut. soln, preferably contg 30–40 mg glycerol, to 100 mL vol. flask, and add 50 mL KIO_4 soln. Dil. to vol. with H_2O and let stand ca 1 hr. Test for excess periodate, which must be present in oxidn mixt., by adding $NaHCO_3$ and KI to test portion. If excess is present, I is liberated.

35.082 ***Determination***

(**a**) *By titration of formic acid.*—(Applicable in absence of substances yielding acid on periodate oxidn.) Transfer 50 mL aliquot of oxidized mixt. to titrn flask, add 10 drops propylene glycol (ca 0.5 mL), mix well, wash down sides of flask with H_2O, and let stand 10 min. Add 3 drops bromocresol purple indicator and titr. with NaOH soln to light purple end point. 1 mL 0.02*N* NaOH = 1.842 mg glycerol.

(**b**) *From periodate consumed.*—Transfer 20 mL aliquot of oxidized mixt., **35.081(b)**, to titrn flask and dil. with ca 50 mL H_2O. Add ca 1.0 g $NaHCO_3$, 0.5 g KI, and 5 mL starch indicator, **2.144(b)**. Titr. immediately with As_2O_3 soln to disappearance of blue. Stdze 10 mL KIO_4 similarly. Difference between the 2 titrns represents amt of periodate reduced in 20 mL aliquot taken. To obtain amt of periodate reduced in original aliquot obtained from 250 mL flask, multiply above difference by 5.

1 mL 0.02*N* As_2O_3 = 0.4605 mg glycerol.

BIOASSAY

35.083 Eye Irritation Test (*23*)—Official First Action

Use 6 albino rabbits of either sex, weighing 2.0–2.5 kg, randomly selected, for each substance. Facilities must be designed and maintained so as to exclude extraneous materials that might produce eye irritation. Examine both eyes of each animal before testing. Use only animals without defects or eye irritation.

Hold animal firmly but gently until quiet. Instill 0.1 mL test material onto cornea so that it flows into conjunctival sac of 1 eye of each animal by gently pulling lower lid away from eyeball to form cup into which test substance is dropped. Hold lids gently together 1 sec and release animal. Other eye, untreated, serves as control.

Examine eyes grossly or microscopically and record grade of ocular reaction of cornea, iris, and conjunctiva at 24, 48, and 72 hr, and 7 days. After 24 hr observation, further examine eyes after applying fluorescein-impregnated paper strips (Barnes-Hind, Ayerst, etc.). Eyes may be washed with sterile isotonic NaCl soln after 24 hr reading.

Independently grade each portion of eye (cornea, iris, and conjunctiva) without reference to total score, using definitions and color photographs in "Illustrated Guide for Grading Eye Irritation by Hazardous Substances," Superintendent of Documents, Government Printing Office, Washington, DC 20402. (*Note:* Color photographs in JAOAC **56**, 912–3(1973) do not have correct color. Use photographs in reprints supplied by AOAC, Box 540, Benjamin Franklin Station, Washington, DC 20044.)

Consider animal as exhibiting pos. reaction if test substance produces, at any of the readings, ulceration of cornea (other than fine stippling), or opacity of cornea (other than slight dulling of normal luster), or inflammation of iris (other than slight deepening of folds (or rugae) or slight circumcorneal injection of blood vessels), or if substance produces in conjunctivae (excluding cornea and iris) obvious swelling with partial eversion of lids or diffuse crimson-red with individual vessels not easily discernible. Basis for irritation is grade ≥1 for cornea and iris and ≥2 for redness and chemosis.

Sample is eye irritant if ≥4 of 6 rabbits have irritation. Sample is not eye irritant if 0 or 1 of 6 rabbits has irritation. For combined parameters, eye is considered irritated if ≥1 parameter has a grade considered to be eye irritant. If 2 or 3 animals exhibit pos. reaction, repeat test with 6 different animals. Second test is considered pos. if ≥3 animals exhibit pos. reaction. If only 1 or 2 animals in second test exhibit pos. reaction, repeat test with 6 different animals. In third test, substance is considered irritant if any animal exhibits pos. reaction.

SPECIAL REFERENCE

"Newburger's Manual of Cosmetic Analysis," 2nd ed., AOAC, Box 540 Benjamin Franklin Station, Washington, DC 20044(1977).

SELECTED REFERENCES

(*1*) JAOAC **49**, 718(1966).
(*2*) JAOAC **53**, 82(1970).
(*3*) Ind. Eng. Chem., Anal. Ed. **10**, 212(1938); JAOAC **28**, 734(1945).
(*4*) Ind. Eng. Chem., Anal Ed. **16**, 387(1944); JAOAC **33**, 371(1950).
(*5*) JAOAC **59**, 830, 1421(1976); **60**, 663(1977).
(*6*) Anal. Chem. **24**, 182(1952); JAOAC **36**, 791(1953).
(*7*) JAOAC **34**, 298, 299(1951).
(*8*) JAOAC **57**, 563(1974).
(*9*) JAOAC **35**, 279(1952).
(*10*) JAOAC **37**, 798(1954).
(*11*) JAOAC **23**, 437(1940); **25**, 113(1942); **27**, 112(1944).
(*12*) JAOAC **25**, 909(1942); **32**, 50, 601(1949); **33**, 359(1950).
(*13*) JAOAC **22**, 158(1939); **26**, 116(1943); **28**, 739(1945); **33**, 374(1950).
(*14*) JAOAC **23**, 717(1940); **33**, 374(1950).
(*15*) JAOAC **22**, 158(1939); **25**, 113(1942); **27**, 112(1944).
(*16*) JAOAC **35**, 285(1952).
(*17*) Analyst **48**, 2(1923); **50**, 49(1925); JAOAC **28**, 744(1945); **30**, 512(1947); **31**, 577(1948); **32**, 592(1949).
(*18*) JAOAC **25**, 897(1942); **30**, 517(1947).
(*19*) JAOAC **25**, 112(1942); **26**, 354(1943); **27**, 112(1944).
(*20*) JAOAC **53**, 78(1970).
(*21*) JAOAC **53**, 84(1970).
(*22*) JAOAC **25**, 903(1942); **26**, 249(1943); **27**, 462(1944); **30**, 507, 651(1947); **31**, 580(1948); **33**, 362, 367(1950).
(*23*) JAOAC **56**, 905(1973).

36. Drugs: General

GENERAL DIRECTIONS

36.001 Extraction with Lighter-Than-Water Solvents

Perform preliminary steps directed in method prior to extn. Ext. aq. soln in separator with specified vols of solv. (ether, pet ether, etc.) by shaking ⩾1 min. Let sep. completely, swirl to remove H_2O droplets, transfer lower aq. layer to second separator, and decant solv. layer thru pledget of solv.-washed cotton or glass wool in short-stem funnel inserted in neck of third separator. Wash mouth of separator with fine stream of solv. Repeatedly shake aq. soln with addnl portions of solvs until substance sought is extd, using second and first separators alternately for shaking, collecting solvs by filtering into third. If aq. soln is to be further examined, dry cotton pledget in funnel by drawing air thru stem, and wash with 5 mL H_2O into main aq. ext.

36.002 Purified Diatomaceous (Siliceous) Earth for Partition Chromatography

Celite 545, acid-washed (Johns-Manville Products Corp.), or equiv., is usually suitable for column chromatgy. When interfering materials are present, purify as follows: Place pad of glass wool in base of chromatgc tube ⩾100 mm diam. and add siliceous earth to ht ca 5 times diam. Add vol. HCl equal to ca ⅓ vol. of earth, and let percolate. Wash with MeOH, using small vols at first to rinse walls of tube, and then until washings are neut. to moistened indicator paper. Extrude into shallow dishes, heat on steam bath to remove MeOH, and dry at 105° until material is powdery and MeOH-free. Store in tightly closed containers.

Sampling (*1*)—Official Final Action

Methods for drugs involve analysis of sample portions stated: individual dosage form or fraction of composite, depending on information needed. Implication of results depends upon sampling procedure used.

36.003 I. Tablets and Pills

Methods described below are typical random sampling schemes designed for obtaining analysis representative of particular lot of tablets or pills.

(**a**) *Bulk lots.*—Mix lot thoroly without mutilating contents. Count, weigh, and thoroly powder ⩾100 units. Calc. av. wt/unit.

(**b**) *Containers of 1000 or more units.*—Open and cautiously mix contents without mutilation. Count, weigh, and powder ⩾30 units selected at random.

(**c**) *Containers of 100—500 units.*—Remove from one container ⩾20 units selected at random, weigh, and powder.

36.004 II. Soft Capsules

Count and weigh ⩾20 capsules and det. gross wt/capsule. Open capsules and transfer as much of contents as possible to weighing bottle. Clean capsules (cutting in 2 if necessary) and wash by agitating with alternate portions of alcohol and ether. (Few drops of HOAc mixed with alcohol aids cleaning.) Remove ether before fan or air blast. Deduct wt cleaned, empty capsules from gross wt, and calc. av. net contents.

36.005 III. Ampuls

Before opening ampuls, dislodge any liq. in neck. With file, or other suitable instrument, mark level of liq. on neck. Open each near tip, transfer bulk of contents to small flask, and mix. To det. vol. contents, wash and dry empty ampuls, and fill to mark with H_2O from buret or graduated pipet.

SOLVENTS

Acetone and Isopropyl and Ethyl Alcohols

36.006 ★ Qualitative Tests (*2*)—Official Final Action ★

Acetone, in absence of other ketones, is identified as 2,4-dinitrophenylhydrazone, mp 128°. Alcohols, if present at >5%, are concd by distn, dried with Na_2SO_4, and identified as 3,5-dinitrobenzoates: isopropyl, mp 122°; Et, 92°. For lower concns, acetone is removed by refluxing with alk. paraformaldehyde. Distd alcohols are oxidized to acetone, pptd by dinitrophenylhydrazone to confirm isopropanol, and to HOAc, forming colored complex with La to confirm EtOH. If acetone and isopropanol are absent, EtOH is detected by iodoform reaction. *See* **36.006–36.010**, 12th ed.

Gas Chromatographic Method (3)—Official Final Action

(Applicable to liq. prepns contg ethanol with isopropanol or acetone or individual compds)

36.007 ***Reagents and Apparatus***

(**a**) *Ethanol std stock soln.*—(*1*) *2% (v/v).*—Dil. 5.0 mL absolute alcohol to 250 mL with H_2O. (*2*) *0.2% (v/v).*—Dil. 10.0 mL soln (*1*) to 100 mL with H_2O.

(**b**) *Isopropanol std stock soln.*—2% (v/v). Dil. 5.0 mL isopropanol to 250 mL with H_2O.

(**c**) *Acetone std stock soln.*—2% (v/v). Dil. 5.0 mL acetone to 250 mL with H_2O.

(**d**) *Acetonitrile internal std stock soln.*—2% (v/v). Dil. 5.0 mL CH_3CN to 250 mL with H_2O.

(**e**) *Gas chromatograph.*—With 1.8 m (6′) × 4 mm id glass column, packed with 80–100 mesh Porapak Q (Waters Associates, Inc.) and H flame ionization detector. Approx. operating conditions: temps (°)— column 135, detector 155, injection port 165; N carrier gas flow rate 120 mL/min. CH_3CN peak should elute in 5 min. Adjust H and air flow rates and electrometer sensitivity so that 5 μL 0.2% EtOH std soln gives 50–70% scale deflection.

36.008 ***Preparation of GC Column***

Carefully plug column exit with small pad of glass wool. Apply vac. to exit and slowly add packing material thru inlet, tapping very gently to pack firmly. Pack to within 1 cm of area heated by injection port. Plug with glass wool and condition overnight at 235° with slow N stream.

36.009 ***Preparation of Sample***

(**a**) *Ethanol.*—Prep. soln contg ca 2% (v/v) EtOH by stepwise diln with H_2O. Proceed as in **36.010**.

(**b**) *Isopropanol.*—Prep. soln contg ca 2% (v/v) isopropanol by stepwise diln with H_2O. Proceed as in **36.010**.

★ Surplus method—*see* inside front cover.

(c) *Acetone.*—Prep. soln contg ca 2% (v/v) acetone by stepwise diln with H_2O. Proceed as in **36.010**.

If acetone concn is unknown, prep. 50% diln of product with H_2O, prep. acetone std soln, and inject sample and std as in **36.010**. To det. amt acetone, adjust product and std dilns to give comparable peak hts; % internal std added to the 2 solns should be equal to % acetone present in std soln.

36.010 ***Determination***

Pipet 10 mL sample soln into 100 mL vol. flask. Pipet 10 mL each std stock soln needed into sep. 100 mL vol. flask. Pipet 10 mL internal std stock soln into each flask and dil. to vol. with H_2O.

Inject 5 μL sample and std solns, each in duplicate, using 10 μL syringe. Approx. retention times of peaks relative to CH_3CN internal std peak are as follows: EtOH, 0.76; acetone, 1.32; isopropanol, 1.40.

Calc. % EtOH, acetone, or isopropanol in sample as

$$\% C = C' \times (H/H') \times (I'/I) \times f,$$

where C and C' = % component in sample and std, resp., H = av. sample peak ht or area in sample chromatogram, H' = av. std peak ht or area in std chromatogram, I and I' = resp. values for internal std, and f = sample diln factor.

36.011 ★ Ether (*4*)—Official Final Action ★

(Not applicable in presence of essential oils)

Dichromate oxidn of aspirated sample. *See* **32.370–32.374**, 10th ed.

36.012 ★ Propylene Glycol (*5*)—Official Final Action ★

Periodate oxidn of propylene glycol isolated by codistn with cyclohexane. *See* **36.016–36.017**, 12th ed.

HALOGENATED COMPOUNDS

Chlorinated Hydrocarbons (*6*)—Official First Action

36.013 ***Apparatus***

(a) *Infrared spectrophotometer.*—Double beam, with wavelength range 2–16 μm with 1 mm sealed cells.

(b) *Device for filling pipet or buret by pressure.*— Fit 2-hole rubber stopper (No. 1 fits 8 oz medicine bottle) with 1 glass tube extending just thru stopper and with other end attached to tubing for application of pressure. Thru other hole fit straight glass tube extending to bottom of container and attach to other end short piece of rubber tubing to connect to delivery tip of buret or pipet. When not transferring, prevent evapn with pinch clamps.

36.014 ***Reagents***

(*Caution: See* **51.011** and **51.040**.)

(a) *Chloroform std soln.*—Wash $CHCl_3$ 3 times with H_2O, and dry with Na_2SO_4. Pipet 10 mL dried $CHCl_3$ into 200 mL vol. flask contg 185 mL alcohol, dil. to vol. with alcohol, and mix. Using air pressure, transfer 20 mL of this soln to 200 mL vol. flask contg 170 mL alcohol (keep tip below surface), dil. to vol. with alcohol, and mix.

(b) *Carbon tetrachloride std soln.*—Prep. as in (a), using dilns of 5 to 200 and 10 to 200 mL.

(c) *Trichloroethylene std soln.*—Redistil $HClC{:}CCl_2$, collecting fraction boiling at 86–88°. Prep. as in (a), using dilns of 10 to 200 and 10 to 200 mL.

★ Surplus method—*see* inside front cover.

(d) *Tetrachloroethylene std soln.*—Redistil $Cl_2C{:}CCl_2$, collecting fraction boiling at 119–121°. Prep. as in (a), using dilns of 10 to 200 and 10 to 200 mL.

(e) *Reference soln.*—Mix 10 mL alcohol with 75 mL 10% sucrose soln and ext with 10, 10, and 5 mL CS_2. Combine exts in 25 mL vol. flask and dil. to vol. with CS_2. (CS_2 exts are dry enough to be placed in NaCl cells.) Use in ref. cell for reading both stds and samples.

36.015 ***Preparation of Standard Curves***

(Use air pressure to fill pipet or covered buret.)

Transfer 10–30 mL of each std soln to separators contg 5 vols 10% sucrose soln and 10 mL CS_2, keeping delivery tip just below surface of liq. Quickly stopper separator and ext 1–2 min by very gently inverting 50–60 times/min. (Do not release pressure thru stopcock.) Let layers sep. and drain CS_2 layer into 25 mL vol. flask or stoppered graduate. Repeat extn with 10 and 5 mL CS_2, combine all exts, and dil. to vol. with CS_2. (Exts may be held at room temp. overnight if tightly stoppered, but samples and stds must be read on same day.)

Obtain spectrum of each std soln from 2 to 16 μm against ref. soln, (e). (Thruout entire series, gain and position of comb adjustments must not be altered.) If desired, obtain %T (or A) at wavelengths of interest (*see* Table **36:01**), making shortened runs of remaining solns, and combining some of them on 1 chart. Det. %T (or A) of both peak and baseline; convert each to A; and plot ΔA against mL std in aliquot taken for extn on linear paper. If %T is preferred, plot original values of %T on semilog paper.

Table 36:01 Infrared Wavelengths of Chlorinated Hydrocarbons

Compound	Wavelength, μm	
	Peak	Baseline
Chloroform	8.25	7.70– 8.70
Carbon tetrachloride	12.80	12.10–13.90
Trichloroethylene	10.77	10.30–11.00
Tetrachloroethylene	11.10	10.50–11.50

36.016 ***Preparation of Sample***

(a) *Encapsulated liquids.*—Det. gross wt of representative number of capsules. Open capsules and transfer contents to g-s flask. Weigh dried empty capsules and det. av. net contents. Transfer 1 mL aliquot, using air pressure, to 200 mL vol. flask contg ca 195 mL alcohol (keep tip below surface), dil. to vol. with alcohol, and mix. For $CHCl_3$, use soln direct; for CCl_4, dil. 25 mL to 100 mL with alcohol; for tri- and tetrachloroethylene, dil. 50 mL to 100 mL with alcohol.

(b) *Preparations such as cough sirups.*—Shake well and let bubbles clear before opening container. Take aliquot contg chlorinated hydrocarbon vol. approx. that of std, using alcohol for diln if necessary.

36.017 ***Determination***

Transfer aliquot of sample or sample diln to separator contg 5 vols 10% sucrose soln and 10 mL CS_2 (keep tip beneath surface). Proceed as in **36.015**. Det. identity of chlorinated hydrocarbons present by comparison with std spectra and det. amt from std curves.

Chlorobutanol (1,1,1-Trichloro-2-methyl-2-propanol)

36.018 ★ *Gravimetric Method (7)* ★
Official Final Action

Isolation of chlorobutanol by steam distn, if necessary, liberation of ionic Cl by saponification under pressure, and gravimetric detn of Cl as AgCl. *See* **36.023–36.024**, 12th ed.

Gas Chromatographic and Infrared Method (8)
Official Final Action

(*Caution: See* **51.039**, **51.040**, **51.048**,and **51.049**.)

36.019 ***Reagents***

(**a**) *Diatomaceous earth.—See* **36.002**.

(**b**) *Chlorobutanol.*—USP. Store over soln satd with both sugar and salt; product contains ½ mole H_2O of hydration.

(**c**) *Glass wool.*—Fine; washed with CS_2 and dried.

(**d**) *Dichlorodimethylsilane.*—Dissolve 5 mL in 100 mL toluene. (*Caution:* Dichlorodimethylsilane is toxic. Avoid contact with skin or eyes. Use effective fume removal device.)

36.020 ***Apparatus***

(**a**) *Chromatographic tube.*—23 × 400 mm with drip tip small enough to fit into 10 mL vol. flask, and with close-fitting tamping rod.

(**b**) *Infrared spectrophotometer.*—With matched 1 mm path length, liq.-filled NaCl cells.

(**c**) *Gas chromatograph.*—With 1.8 m (6′) × 4 mm glass column, packed with Carbowax 6000 on 100–110 mesh Anakrom ABS, H flame ionization detector, and strip chart recorder.

36.021 ***Preparation of GLC Column***

Carefully wash inside of column and small amt of glass wool with dichlorodimethylsilane soln, rinse with MeOH, and dry. Slowly sprinkle ca 25 g Anakrom ABS into 400 mL beaker almost filled with CCl_4. Remove fine particles remaining at surface with vac. line and trap. Decant solv., oven-dry support, and transfer 20.0 g to 500 mL filter flask fitted with trap and stopper. Dissolve 5.0 g polyethylene glycol (Carbowax 6000) in 100 mL toluene, warming if necessary. Add Carbowax soln to flask and apply vac. 5 min, swirling occasionally. Return to atm. pressure and let stand 5 min. Transfer slurry with rapid swirling to buchner fitted with coarse paper. Maintain reduced pressure on funnel 5 min; then dry coated support by spreading on smooth surface. Air dry 1 hr. Oven-dry addnl hr at 90°.

Carefully plug column exit with small pad fine glass wool and thru-hole septum. Apply vac. to exit port and slowly add coated support thru injection port, tapping very gently to pack firmly. Pack to within 1 cm of area heated by flash heater. Plug with fine glass wool and condition ca 3 days at 200° with slow N stream.

36.022 ***Preparation of Standard Solutions***

Dissolve ca 0.5 g chlorobutanol.½H_2O, accurately weighed, in 1 mL alcohol and transfer to 100 mL vol. flask with 8 mL alcohol. Dil. to vol. with H_2O. Using 5 mL aliquots, prep. duplicate diat. earth columns with trap layers as in **36.023**. Prep. and elute columns individually. Calc. mg anhyd. chlorobutanol/mL CS_2 = C_{hyd} × 0.9517. (Chlorobutanol is appreciably volatile at room temp.; expose to atm. as little as possible.)

36.023 ***GLC Determination***

Weigh 3 g diat. earth, add 2 mL 1*N* HCl, and mix until uniform. Transfer to chromatgc tube plugged with small pad glass wool and tamp moderately tight.

Calc. vol. sample contg ca 25 mg chlorobutanol. Weigh diat. earth equal to 1 g/mL sample. Pipet sample into diat. earth, and mix (ca 1 min) until uniform. Transfer quant. to same column, dry washing with small amt of dry diat. earth, and tamp firmly. Pack as few portions as possible, each portion ≤5 g diat. earth. Rinse beaker with small portions CS_2 and transfer to column until sample portion is wet with CS_2. Let each portion sink into column before adding next. Add 20 mL CS_2 to column and collect eluate in 10 mL vol. flask. Rinse column tip with few drops CS_2 (pipet) when 8–9 mL collects. Continue to collect eluate to vol., stopper flask, and mix. This should yield proper concn for either GLC or IR detns. (Tightly stoppered solns of chlorobutanol in CS_2 may be stored overnight.)

Inject, as below, 6 μL sample soln and est. concn from std curve.

36.024 ***GLC Standard Curve***

Operating conditions: temps (°)—column 135, detector 215, flash heater 230; N flow rate, ca 35 mL/min to elute chlorobutanol in ca 6 min; and H flow rate, 30 mL/min.

Adjust electrometer sensitivity so that 12 μg chlorobutanol gives ca 50% deflection. Inject 4, 5, 6, 7, 8, and 9 μL of each std eluate from 10 μL syringe. Read vol. in syringe before and after injection; take difference as vol. injected. Plot net (Δ) % deflection against μg anhyd. chlorobutanol injected.

36.025 ***Preparation of Infrared Standard***

Record spectrum of each std eluate from 9 to 15 μm, using quant. instrument settings and CS_2 in ref. beam. Det. av. *A* of max. at 12.5–12.6 μm, using baseline technics with min. ca 9.5 and ca 14.2 μm as base. (Δ*A* is linear from 0.5 to 4.5 mg chlorobutanol/mL CS_2.)

36.026 ***Infrared Determination***

Det. *A* of sample soln at 12.5–12.6 μm, as above.

mg Chlorobutanol in sample aliquot = (Δ*A* sample eluate/Δ*A* std eluate) × mg chlorobutanol in 10 mL CS_2 std.

36.027 ★ Chloroform or Carbon Tetrachloride (*9*) ★
Official Final Action

(*See* **36.013–36.017**.)

Decomposition under pressure to inorg. Cl and detn by Volhard titrn. *See* **36.355–36.357**, 11th ed.

36.028 ★ Tetrachloroethylene in Mixtures (*10*) ★
Official Final Action

(*See* **36.013–36.017**.)

Na reduction and detn of total Cl. *See* **36.434–36.435**, 11th ed.

36.029 ★ Trichloroethylene (*11*)—Official Final Action ★

(*See* **36.013–36.017**.)

Reduction under pressure and detn of total Cl. *See* **36.437–36.439**, 11th ed.

Iodoform (*12*)—Official Final Action

36.030 ***Reagents***

(**a**) *Ammonium thiocyanate std soln.*—0.05*N*. Stdze against 0.1*N* $AgNO_3$, using equal vol. alcohol and 3 mL $FeNH_4(SO_4)_2$ soln as indicator.

★ Surplus method—*see* inside front cover.

(b) *Ferric ammonium sulfate indicator.*—Dissolve 8 g $FeNH_4(SO_4)_2.12H_2O$ in 100 mL H_2O.

36.031 ***Determination***

Accurately weigh ca 0.25 g CHI_3 and transfer quant. to 200 mL erlenmeyer. Add 40 mL alcohol, swirl gently until CHI_3 dissolves, filter if necessary, and immediately add 40 mL 0.1*N* $AgNO_3$ and 10 mL HNO_3. Swirl gently ca 5 min, let stand at room temp. 2–3 hr, and then swirl occasionally as aid in flocculating the AgI. Titr. excess $AgNO_3$ with 0.05*N* NH_4SCN, using 3 mL of the $FeNH_4(SO_4)_2$ indicator. 1 mL 0.1*N* $AgNO_3$ = 0.01312 g CHI_3. Or: Proceed as in **36.032**, last par. beginning "Collect AgI on weighed gooch, . . ."

36.032 Iodoform in Ointments (*13*)
Official Final Action

Transfer ca 2.5 g sample to tared 50 mL beaker and weigh. Add 5 mL $CHCl_3$, stir gently with glass rod, and transfer bulk of undissolved ointment and $CHCl_3$ soln to 250 mL g-s flask. Add 5 mL $CHCl_3$ to ointment remaining in beaker and stir until dissolved. Add soln to flask and finally wash beaker 3 times, using ≤5 mL $CHCl_3$ each time, and add washings to flask. Or: weigh sample in small, tared glass capsule, drop capsule with contents into 250 mL g-s flask, and add ≤20 mL $CHCl_3$. (Use glass capsule only in volumetric detn.) Swirl gently until all ointment dissolves. Add 40 mL 0.1*N* *alc. $AgNO_3$* and swirl to wash down any CHI_3 that adheres to sides of flask. Slowly add 10 mL HNO_3 and let stand at room temp. ca 18 hr. Titr. excess of 0.1*N* alc. $AgNO_3$ with 0.05*N* NH_4SCN, **36.030(a)**, using 3 mL $FeNH_4(SO_4)_2$ indicator, **36.030(b)**, vigorously shaking mixt. near end of titrn. 1 mL 0.1*N* $AgNO_3$ = 0.01312 g CHI_3.

For gravimetric detn use ordinary erlenmeyer instead of g-s flask. Weigh ointment base into 100 mL beaker and add $CHCl_3$. After ointment base dissolves, filter thru gooch, using suction. Wash beaker and crucible once with alcohol. Wash crucible several times with $CHCl_3$ without suction. Collect filtrate in erlenmeyer and add 40 mL 0.1*N* $AgNO_3$ and 10 mL HNO_3 in small portions. Let mixt. stand 18 hr. Collect AgI on weighed gooch, using suction. Wash with H_2O and then with alcohol. Finally, wash repeatedly with $CHCl_3$ without suction. Dry gooch and contents at ca 125° to const wt. 1 g AgI = 0.5590 g CHI_3.

36.033 Iodoform on Gauze (*14*)—Official Final Action

Weigh, in tared g-s weighing bottle, sample of CHI_3 gauze contg ca 1 g CHI_3. (CHI_3 gauze is usually moist and loses wt rapidly when exposed to air.) Transfer to 150 mL beaker, add ca 75 mL alcohol, and stir until CHI_3 dissolves. Filter into 200 mL vol. flask, draining alc. soln by pressing on gauze. Wash with four or five 25 mL portions alcohol, filter washings, and finally dil. to vol. with alcohol. Pipet 40 mL aliquot into 200 mL erlenmeyer and immediately add 40 mL 0.1*N* $AgNO_3$ and 10 mL HNO_3. Proceed as in **36.032**, beginning ". . . let stand at room temp. ca 18 hr."

INORGANIC DRUGS

★ Arsenic in Iron-Arsenic Tablets (*15*) ★
Official Final Action

36.034 ***Reagent***

Std soln of potassium bromate (*or of iodine*).— Stdze against pure As_2O_3. (Concn of this soln is matter of choice. 0.5625 g $KBrO_3$ dissolved in H_2O and dild to 1 L gives soln that is 0.02021*N*; 1 mL = 1 mg As_2O_3.)

36.035 ***Apparatus***

Use either Ramberg-Sjöström As flask, Fig. **36:01A**, consisting of 300 mL Kjeldahl flask provided with special outlet tube connected with flask by means of ₸ joint, or 300 mL Kjeldahl flask provided with 13 mm id outlet tube, with constricted tip ca 5 mm, connected with flask by means of rubber stopper, Fig. **36:01B**.

36.036 ***Determination***

(*Caution: See* **51.019**, **51.026**, **51.030**, and **51.078**.)

Weigh and place in flask tablets or pills equiv. to 25 mg As_2O_3, add 10–15 mL H_2O, and let soak 30 min. Add, in small portions at time, 20 mL fuming HNO_3, cooling if necessary to prevent loss by frothing. When reaction ceases, carefully add, in small portions at time, 25–28 mL H_2SO_4. Place flask in inclined position on asbestos mat and heat over small flame. When most of HNO_3 is driven off, and while still heating, drop in 8 mL fuming HNO_3 thru suitably placed separator and heat over larger flame until SO_3 evolves. If after cooling, pptd sulfates are not colorless or pale yellow and are not free from gray or black particles, heat contents of flask further with addnl 10 mL fuming HNO_3. (All org. matter must be destroyed.)

To cooled mixt. add 30 mL *satd $(NH_4)_2C_2O_4$ soln;* heat until fumes of SO_3 evolve, and to ensure complete destruction of oxalic acid, for 10 min longer over low flame; cool, and add 20 mL H_2O while gently swirling flask. Dry neck of flask over small flame and add 30 g NaCl, 5 g $FeSO_4.7H_2O$ (or 1 g $N_2H_4.H_2SO_4$), 1 g NaBr, and 25 mL HCl. Mix, and connect delivery tube. If

★ Surplus method—*see* inside front cover.

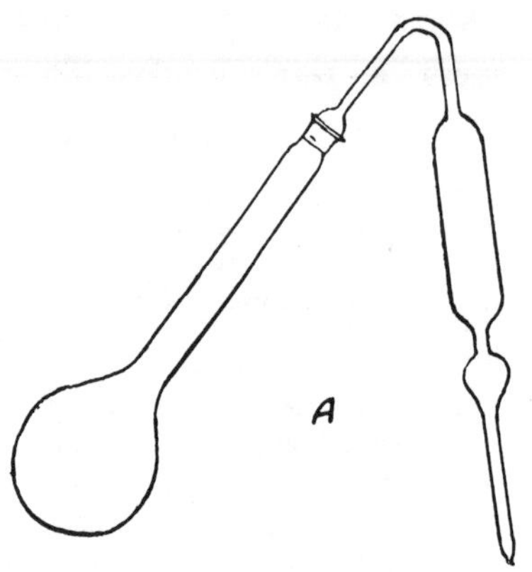

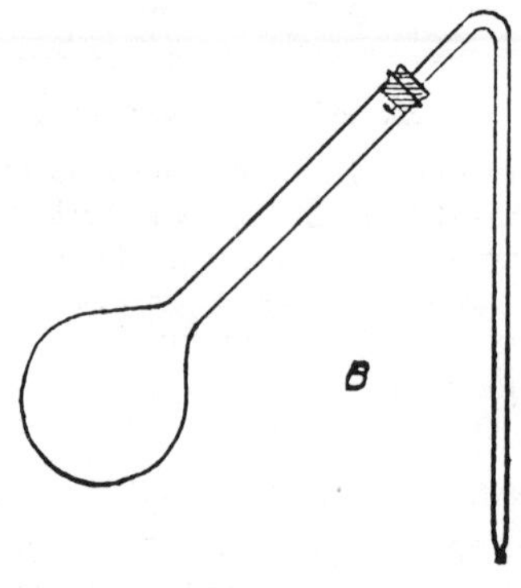

FIG. 36:01—Apparatus for determining arsenic in iron-arsenic tablets

Ramberg-Sjöström app. is used, moisten ground-glass joint with 1 drop H_2SO_4. Fix flask in inclined position with tip of outlet tube ca 1 cm under surface of 150 mL H_2O in erlenmeyer surrounded by ice or by cold H_2O.

Distil at such rate that bend at top of tube becomes warm in 4 min and lower end in ca 8 min from time heat is applied. Discontinue distn after 10 min, but before removing flame, lift distn flask until tip of outlet tube is above H_2O in receiving flask. Let outlet tube drain, remove receiver, and either titr. with std $KBrO_3$ soln, using 2 drops Me orange (red of indicator at end point may fade slowly, but color should persist $\geq$1 min upon addn of another drop of indicator); or nearly neutze with NaOH, add 4–5 g $NaHCO_3$, and titr. with std I soln, **6.005(b)**, using starch indicator, **6.005(f)**.

36.037 ★ Arsenic in Iron Methylarsenate (*16*) ★ Official Final Action

(*Caution: See* **51.078.**)

Transfer suitable amt of sample (0.2 g, if practicable) to Kjeldahl flask. Add 10 g K_2SO_4, 0.3 g starch, and 20 mL H_2SO_4. Digest over low heat until frothing ceases and continue digestion over slightly higher flame until mixt. is colorless. Cool, and add 20 mL H_2O. Dry neck of flask over small flame, cool contents, and add 30 g NaCl, 5 g $FeSO_4.7H_2O$, 1 g NaBr, and 25 mL HCl. Distil as in **36.036**. Conduct blank, using same amts of reagents.

Arsenic in Cacodylate Injections

Differential Pulse Polarographic Method (17) *Official Final Action*

36.038 ***Apparatus***

(**a**) *Polarograph.*—Capable of effectively scanning −0.15 to −0.9 v in differential pulse mode. Typical instrument settings: scan rate, 2 mv/sec; scan direction, "−"; range, 1.5 v; initial potential, −0.15 v; modulation amplitude, 50 mv; operation mode, differential pulse; current range, 0.05 ma, or as needed; output offset, as required; display direction, "+"; drop time, 1 sec; low pass filter, off; selector, off; pushbutton, initial; recorder: X-axis, 0.1 v/in., Y-axis, 1 v/in.

(**b**) *Cells.*—Std cell bottom with satd calomel ref. electrode (SCE), C rod counter electrode, and dropping Hg indicating electrode.

(**c**) *Pipet.*—100 μL Eppendorf pipet, or equiv.

36.039 ***Reagents***

(**a**) *Supporting electrolyte.*—1*M* HCl. Add 82 mL HCl to ca 500 mL H_2O in 1 L vol. flask, dil. to vol. with H_2O, and mix.

(**b**) *Arsenic std soln.*—2.000 mg As/mL. Dissolve 0.2640 g As_2O_3, dried 1 hr at 105°, in ca 25 mL 1*N* NaOH in 100 mL vol. flask, acidify to litmus with 1*M* HCl, and dil. to vol. with H_2O.

36.040 ***Digestion***

Transfer to 100 mL borosilicate beaker accurately measured vol. of injection, dild if necessary, and contg ca 29 mg Na cacodylate (ca 10 mg As), and add 1.0 g $Mg(NO_3)_2.6H_2O$ and 1 mL HNO_3. Heat on hot plate at low heat until H_2O is evapd; then at high heat to dry residue. Complete digestion by placing beaker in furnace at 450° until no brown fumes are evolved (30 min). Remove from furnace and let cool to room temp. Perform blank similarly.

36.041 ***Reduction of Arsenic***

Add to residue 20 mL 5*M* HCl (2+3) and swirl to dissolve, warming on steam bath, if necessary; then add 5 mL 40% HBr and 0.3 g $H_2NNH_2.H_2SO_4$. Cover beaker with watch glass and place on steam bath 30 min. Cool to room temp., transfer with H_2O to 100 mL vol. flask, dil. to vol. with H_2O, and mix.

36.042 ***Determination***

Add to polarographic cell 20 mL supporting electrolyte and bubble N thru soln 5 min; then direct gas to sweep over soln. Switch selector to "Cell", and allow sufficient time for recorder pen to come to rest. Depress "Scan" pushbutton and record polarogram from −0.15 to −0.9 v. Pipet 2 mL of sample soln into cell, bubble N thru soln 1 min, direct gas to sweep over soln, and record polarogram as before, using same instrumental settings. Repeat operations on 2 addnl 100 μL aliquots of std soln. Polarograph blank similarly. Plot std addn curve as follows: mg std added, 0, 0.2, and 0.4, on X-axis and first As peak ht which appears at ca −0.37 v against SCE on Y-axis. Extrapolate linear plot to X-axis to obtain mg As in aliquot. Correct for blank, if necessary. Stds need not be polarographed beyond ca −0.60 v, since anal. peak is at ca −0.37 v against SCE.

36.043 ★ Arsenic in Sodium Cacodylate (*18*) ★ Official Final Action

Digestion with H_2SO_4, distn, and titrn with I. *See* **36.044**, 12th ed.

Bismuth Compounds

36.044 *Gravimetric Method (19)*—Official Final Action

(Applicable in absence of Pb. *Caution: See* **51.011**, **51.026**, and **51.059.**)

Thoroly mix sample and weigh 0.5 g into 500 mL Kjeldahl flask. Ignite gently over small flame, using wire gauze under flask, and increase heat towards end. Let cool, add 15–20 mL HNO_3, evap. to dryness, and ignite as before until yellow or orange Bi_2O_3 is formed. Cool residue and dissolve in 10–15 mL warm HNO_3, using few mL 3% H_2O_2 if residue does not dissolve readily. Boil off excess H_2O_2 and wash into 400 mL beaker with H_2O, rinsing flask well. Dil. to ca 200 mL, make just neut. to litmus with NH_4OH, and add 5 mL HCl. Ppt with *H_2S* completely.

Transfer ppt to filter paper and wash once with HCl (5+200) and then several times with H_2O. Dissolve ppt of Bi_2S_3 on filter with hot HNO_3 (1+2). Small residue of S (and HgS if Hg salts are present) usually remains. Neutze filtrate with NH_4OH (2+3) and ppt with 25 mL 20% $(NH_4)_2CO_3$ soln. Conc. to ca 150 mL (by boiling, if desired) and let stand on steam bath 1–2 hr. Collect ppt in previously ignited, weighed gooch, wash with small amt of H_2O, dry, ignite in furnace at ca 550°, and weigh as Bi_2O_3.

Polarographic Method (*20*)—Official Final Action

36.045 ***Apparatus***

(**a**) *Polarograph.*—*See* **20.001**. Capable of scanning 0 to −1.0 v and measuring 0.040 μa/mm.

(**b**) *Cells.*—Microcell with satd calomel or Hg pool ref. electrode.

36.046 ***Reagents***

(**a**) *Supporting electrolyte.*—1*M* HCl. Add 171 mL HCl to ca 1 L H_2O in 2 L vol. flask and mix. Cool to room temp., dil. to vol. with H_2O, and mix.

(**b**) *Gelatin maximum suppressor.*—1 mg/mL. Accurately weigh 100 mg gelatin (Difco Laboratories, No. 0143-01; or Knox Gelatine Inc., Johnstown, NY 12095, unflavored gelatine No. 1)

★ Surplus method—*see* inside front cover.

into small beaker and dissolve in small amt of H_2O on steam bath. Transfer quant. to 100 mL vol. flask and dil. to vol. with H_2O. Prep. fresh daily.

(**c**) *Bismuth std solns.*—(*1*) *Stock soln.*—1 mg/mL. Transfer 122.2 mg Bi subcarbonate, equiv. to 100 mg Bi (mg Bi subcarbonate × 0.8182 (factor derived from primary std) = mg Bi), to 100 mL vol. flask with supporting electrolyte, (**a**). Dil. to vol. with same soln. (*2*) *Working soln.*—0.2 mg/mL. Pipet 20.0 mL stock soln into 100 mL vol. flask, add 1.0 mL gelatin max. suppressor, (**b**), and dil. to vol. with supporting electrolyte, (**a**). Mix thoroly.

36.047 ***Preparation of Sample***

(**a**) *Tablets.*—Det. av. wt/tablet. Grind to pass No. 60 sieve. Quant. transfer amt tablet material contg 10 mg Bi, accurately weighed, to 50 mL vol. flask with aid of 1*M* HCl, (**a**). Add 0.5 mL gelatin max. suppressor, (**b**), and dil. to vol. with 1*M* HCl. Shake thoroly or use sonic vibrator. Filter thru rapid paper just before polarographic detn.

(**b**) *Magma, emulsions, and injectables.*—Mix *thoroly* to disperse suspension. Immediately transfer aliquot contg ca 100 mg Bi to 100 mL vol. flask. Rinse inside of pipet with 1*M* HCl, (**a**), and dil. to vol. with same soln. Pipet 10 mL into 50 mL vol. flask, add 0.5 mL gelatin max. suppressor, (**b**), and dil. to vol. with 1*M* HCl. Mix thoroly.

(**c**) *Powder.*—Transfer entire contents of vial, or amt material equiv. to 200 mg Bi for bulk powders or capsules, to 200 mL vol. flask. Wash vial into flask and dil. sample to vol. with 1*M* HCl, (**a**). Proceed as for magma, beginning "Pipet 10 mL . . ."

36.048 ***Determination***

Transfer soln to cell and bubble N thru soln 10 min. Record polarogram from 0 to −1.0 v against satd calomel ref. electrode. Measure ht of diffusion current (I_d) at half-wave potential ($E_{1/2}$), and det. Bi concn by comparing wave hts of sample soln with those of std soln polarographed immediately before and after samples. Do all detns at same current sensitivity and consecutively.

$E_{1/2}$ value is qual. identification of Bi.

Calc. concn of Bi as follows:

(**a**) *Tablets.*—mg Bi/tablet = $50 \times (I/I') \times C \times (W/W')$;

(**b**) *Magma, emulsions, and injectables.*—mg Bi/mL = $500 \times (I/I') \times (C/V)$;

(**c**) *Powder.*—mg Bi/mg sample = $1000 \times (I/I') \times (C/W')$;

where I and I' = diffusion currents of sample and std, resp.; C = mg Bi/mL working soln, (**c**)(*2*); W and W' = av. tablet wt and wt sample taken (mg), resp.; and V = mL liq. prepn taken.

36.049 ***Measurement of Diffusion Current***

Measure diffusion current (I_d at $E_{1/2}$). Draw lines tangent to tops of residual and limiting currents. Draw third line tangent to vertical slope. Measure its length, mark off half-way point at $I_d/2$; then drop perpendicular thru this point and thru abscissa (applied voltage). Diffusion current is perpendicular portion of this line cutting thru limiting current and residual current tangent lines.

Calcium and Magnesium (*21*)—Official Final Action

(Applicable to pharmaceuticals and vitamin-mineral prepns)

36.050 ***Reagents***

Use H_2O redistd from glass (preferable) or deionized H_2O, reagents **1.022(a)**, (**b**), (**c**), and in addn:

(**a**) *Calcium carbonate.*—Primary std grade, dried 2 hr at 285°.

(**b**) *Hydroxy naphthol blue.*—Ca indicator (Mallinckrodt Chemical Works No. 5630 in dispenser bottle ready for use, or equiv.). Store in dark and replace after 1 year.

(**c**) *Calmagite.*—Ca + Mg indicator (Mallinckrodt No. 4283 in dispenser bottle ready for use, or equiv.). Store in dark and replace after 1 year.

(**d**) *Disodium dihydrogen ethylenediamine tetraacetate* (*EDTA*) *std soln.*—0.01*M*. Dissolve 3.72 g $Na_2H_2EDTA.2H_2O$ (99+ % purity) in H_2O in 1 L vol. flask, dil. to vol., and mix. Accurately weigh enough $CaCO_3$ (ca 40 mg) to give ca 40 mL titrn with 0.01*M* EDTA and transfer to 400 mL beaker. Add 50 mL H_2O and enough HCl (1+3) to dissolve the $CaCO_3$. Dil. to ca 150 mL with H_2O and add 15 mL 1*N* NaOH, disregarding any ppt or turbidity. Add ca 200 mg hydroxy naphthol blue indicator and titr. from pink to deep blue end point, using mag. stirrer. Add last few mL EDTA soln dropwise. Molarity EDTA soln = mg $CaCO_3$/(mL EDTA × 100.09).

36.051 ***Apparatus***

(**a**) *Titration stand.*—Fluorescent illuminated.

(**b**) *Ion exchange column.*—Approx. 20 × 600 mm, fitted with coarse porosity fritted glass disk and Teflon stopcock. Place 30–40 g moist Amberlite IR-4B resin (anion exchange resin with high phosphate capacity) from fresh bottle in 600 mL beaker and exhaust with three 250 mL portions 5% Na_2CO_3 or NaOH. Wash with H_2O until excess base is removed. Treat resin with three 250 mL portions 5% HCl (3+22), mixing thoroly after each treatment. Rinse with H_2O until color is removed, and transfer with H_2O to column. Column is ready for use after draining H_2O to top of resin column. (Exchange capacity for phosphate is ca 1500 mg; therefore, number of aliquots can be passed thru column before regeneration is necessary. Rinse column with ca 250 mL H_2O before each use until eluate is colorless.)

36.052 ***Preparation of Sample***

Transfer 2 g well mixed sample to 100 mL Pt or porcelain dish. Ash at ≤525° until apparently C-free (gray to brown). Cool, add 20 mL H_2O, stir with stirring rod, and add 10 mL HCl cautiously under watch glass. Rinse off watch glass into dish and evap. to dryness on steam bath. Add 50 mL HCl (1+9), heat on steam bath 15 min, and filter thru quant. paper into 200 mL vol. flask. Wash paper and dish thoroly with hot H_2O. Cool filtrate, dil. to vol., and mix.

36.053 ***Determination***

Transfer 50 mL aliquot prepd sample to 250 mL beaker and adjust to pH 3.5 with 10% KOH soln added dropwise, using pH meter and mag. stirrer. Pass sample thru resin column (column is in Cl form), collecting effluent in 250 mL vol. flask and adjusting flow rate to 2–3 mL/min. Wash column with two 50 mL portions H_2O, passing first portion thru at same rate as sample soln and second at 6–7 mL/min. Finally, pass enough H_2O freely thru column to dil. to vol. Mix thoroly. Pipet two 100 mL aliquots into 400 mL beakers.

Titration 1 (*calcium + magnesium*).—Adjust first aliquot to pH 10 (using pH meter and mag. stirrer) with pH 10 buffer soln, **1.022(a)** (ca 5 mL). Add 2 mL 2% KCN soln, **1.022(c)**, and 200 mg Calmagite indicator, and titr. immediately with 0.01*M* EDTA soln thru red to deep blue end point, using mag. stirrer.

Titration 2 (*calcium*).—Adjust second aliquot to pH 12.5–13.0 (using pH meter and mag. stirrer) with KOH-KCN soln, **1.022(b)** (ca 10 mL). Add 0.100 g ascorbic acid and 200–300 mg hydroxy naphthol blue indicator. Titr. immediately with 0.01*M* EDTA soln thru pink to deep blue end point, using mag. stirrer.

$$\% Ca = Y \times F \times 0.4008 \times 10 \times 100/\text{mg sample};$$
$$\% Mg = (X - Y) \times F \times 0.2431 \times 10 \times 100/\text{mg sample};$$

where X and Y = mL EDTA soln from titrns *1* and *2*, and F = molarity EDTA soln/0.01.

36.054 Calcium Gluconate (22)—Official Final Action

(Applicable to prepns whose aq. solns are neut. and which do not contain salts of other optically active hydroxy acids. *Caution: See* **51.083** and **51.084**.)

Weigh two 0.5 g portions Ca gluconate or two 1 g portions powd tablets contg ≤50% of the salt. If chocolate or fatty base is present, wash samples several times on hardened filter with absolute ether and warm residue until ether is driven off.

Transfer each portion to sep. 25 mL vol. flasks, add 15 mL H_2O, and warm until Ca salt dissolves. (Samples contg cocoa will have undissolved residue.) Cool mixt. to room temp.

To one flask (No. 1) add 3.5 g *finely pulverized uranyl acetate*, stopper, and shake mech. 1 hr. (If agitation is not vigorous enough, >1 hr of shaking may be required.) Let other flask (No. 2) stand. If sample contains chocolate, add little alumina cream, **31.021(b)**, to each flask. Cool to room temp., dil. flask No. 1 to vol. with *uranyl acetate soln* (10 g shaken with 95 mL H_2O until satd and then filtered), and flask No. 2 with H_2O. Filter, and polarize each soln in 200 mm tube, using 50 mm tube contg *1.8% $K_2Cr_2O_7$ soln* as light filter. If soln is too dark to read in 200 mm tube, make reading in 100 mm tube and multiply result by 2. If X = rotation in °S of Soln No. 2 and Y = rotation of Soln No. 1, with 1 g sample: % $Ca(C_6H_{11}O_7)_2 = 4.34 \times (Y - X)$; and with 0.5 g sample: % $Ca(C_6H_{11}O_7)_2 = 8.52 \times (Y - X)$.

Calcium, Potassium, and Sodium in Electrolyte Replenishers

Atomic Absorption–Flame Photometric Method (23) Official Final Action

(Applicable to Ringer's and Lactated Ringer's Injections)

36.055 ***Reagents***

(Use H_2O of ≥0.5 megohms resistivity for all rinsing and diln. Use borosilicate volumetric glassware, including pipets, meeting NBS tolerances. Use ≥4 mL single transfer pipets for all dilns, except that Class A 5 mL Mohr pipets may be used to complete intermediate and final dilns. Clean all glassware with HNO_3 (1+3) until washings show no Na at 589 nm when compared with H_2O used in Na detn.)

(**a**) *Buffer soln.*—0.25*M* EDTA + 25 mg La_2O_3/mL. (Required in AA detn of Ca and K only.) Transfer 73.1 g EDTA into 1 L erlenmeyer. Add ca 100 mL H_2O, and shake cautiously with just enough NH_4OH to dissolve. Transfer 25.0 g low-Ca La_2O_3 to 500 mL erlenmeyer, add 25 mL H_2O, and very cautiously dissolve with 70% $HClO_4$. Cool both solns. Pour $HClO_4$ soln into EDTA soln, and wash mixt. into 1 L vol. flask. Dissolve completely and adjust to pH slightly alk. to *Me orange,* using NH_4OH or 70% $HClO_4$, as needed. Dil. to vol. with H_2O, mix, and store in clean, dry polyethylene or Teflon bottle.

(**b**) *Calcium std soln.*—10 mg/mL. Dry $CaCO_3$ (low in alkalis) ≥2 hr at 285° (*Caution:* Higher temp. may convert $CaCO_3$, in part, to CaO.), cool in desiccator, and transfer 24.975 g to 1 L vol. flask. Add ca 150 mL H_2O and acidify cautiously with 45 mL HCl from freshly opened bottle. Cool to room temp., dil. to vol. with H_2O, and mix. Store in clean, dry polyethylene or Teflon bottle.

(**c**) *Potassium std soln.*—1 mg/mL. Dry KCl ≥2 hr at 500–600°, cool in desiccator, and transfer 1.9070 g to 1 L vol. flask. Dissolve and dil. to vol. with H_2O, mix, and store in clean, dry polyethylene or Teflon bottle.

(**d**) *Sodium std soln.*—10 mg/mL. Dry NaCl ≥2 hr at 500–600°, cool in desiccator, and transfer 25.420 g to 1 L vol. flask. Dissolve and dil. to vol. with H_2O, mix, and store in clean, dry polyethylene or Teflon bottle.

(**e**) *Mixed cation std soln.*—(5 μg Ca + 10 μg K + 200 μg Na)/mL. Pipet 10 mL Ca std soln, (**b**), into 200 mL vol. flask, dil. to vol. with H_2O, and mix. Pipet 10 mL this dild soln into 1 L vol. flask, pipet in 10 mL K std soln, (**c**), and 20 mL Na std soln, (**d**), dil. to vol. with H_2O, and mix. Store in clean, dry polyethylene or Teflon bottle. Stable ≥1 month. (Proportionate vols may be prepd.)

36.056 ***Instrumental Requirements***

(*Caution: See* **51.006** and **51.007**.)

Use spectrophtr in AA or flame emission mode. Keep *A* readings between 0.100 and 0.820 units, or emission readings between 20 and 95% *T* by adjusting sample dilns, if necessary.

Prep. sufficient std solns to bracket sample detns. Readings of all stds must be on linear portion of std curve. Linearity is detd by running intermediate test std which must agree to within 1% of reading indicated by straight line relationship between the bracketing std points.

Spectrophtr must pass following precision test: Read, sequentially, low std, sample, and high std. Repeat twice and average readings of each soln. Results are acceptable if each individual reading differs from av. value for particular soln by ≤1.4%.

36.057 ***Determination***

(**a**) *Calcium.*—(*1*) *For absorption.*—Pipet 5 mL sample and 4 mL buffer soln into 100 mL vol. flask, dil. to vol. with H_2O, and mix. Prep. "median range std" by dilg mixed cation std soln, including 4.00 mL buffer soln in each 100 mL std soln. Analyze sample and std solns at 422.7 nm, and est. no. and concn of stds needed for final detn as required in **36.056**, par. 2. (*2*) *For emission.*—Proceed as in (*1*), omitting buffer soln.

(**b**) *Potassium.*—(*1*) *For absorption.*—Pipet 5 mL sample to 100 mL vol. flask, dil. to vol. with H_2O, and mix. Pipet 10 mL this soln into 50 mL vol. flask, pipet in 2 mL buffer soln, dil. to vol. with H_2O, and mix. Prep. "median range std" by dilg mixed cation std soln, including 2.00 mL buffer soln in each 50 mL final soln. Analyze sample and std solns at 766.5 nm, and est. no. and concn of stds needed for final assay as required in **36.056**, par. 2. (*2*) *For emission.*—Proceed as in (*1*), omitting buffer soln.

(**c**) *Sodium.*—Pipet 5 mL sample into 100 mL vol. flask, dil. to vol. with H_2O, and mix. Pipet 4 mL this soln into 500 mL vol. flask, dil. to vol. with H_2O, and mix. Prep. "median range std" by dilg mixed cation std soln. Analyze sample and std solns at 589.0 nm, and est. no. and concn of stds needed for final assay as required in **36.056**, par. 2.

(**d**) *Calculations.*—Det. concn of each cation from std curve. Calc. concn of each cation as mg Cl salt/100 mL sample.

★ Calcium, Phosphorus, and Iron in Vitamin Preparations (24)—Official Final Action ★

36.058 ***Reagents***

(**a**) *Molybdate soln.*—(*1*) Thoroly mix 50 g MoO_3 (99.5–100%) and 140 mL H_2O and dissolve by addn of 72 mL NH_4OH with stirring; (*2*) dissolve 50 g powd tartaric acid in 140 mL H_2O; (*3*) mix 295 mL colorless HNO_3 with 400 mL H_2O. When solns are cool, pour soln (*1*) into soln (*2*) with stirring, and then pour combined solns into soln (*3*). Keep in warm place (ca 40°)

★ Surplus method—*see* inside front cover.

overnight, filter thru asbestos, and store in bottle with loosely stoppered, plastic screw cap. When free from phosphates, soln is practically colorless.

(b) *Ammonium nitrate soln.*—Dissolve 500 g NH_4NO_3 in H_2O and dil. to 1 L.

(c) *Carbon dioxide-free water.*—Recently boiled and cooled H_2O.

(d) *Sodium hydroxide and hydrochloric acid std solns.*—0.1*N*. Prep. as in **50.032–50.036**, and **50.011–50.013**.

36.059 ***Determination***

Transfer representative portion of well mixed sample contg ≥10 mg P, 50 mg Ca, and 1 mg Fe to 100 mL Pt or porcelain dish. Ash at ≤525° until apparently C-free (gray to brown). Cool, moisten with 20 mL H_2O, break up ash with stirring rod, and cautiously add 10 mL HCl under watch glass. Rinse off watch glass into dish and evap. to dryness on steam bath. Add 50 mL HCl (1+9), heat on steam bath 15 min, and filter thru quant. paper into 200 mL vol. flask. Thoroly wash filter and dish with hot H_2O, cool filtrate, dil. to vol., and mix.

(a) *Phosphorus.*—Transfer aliquot contg 2–5 mg P to 300 mL erlenmeyer, and dil. to ca 50–60 mL. Add 20 mL NH_4NO_3 soln and heat in H_2O bath to 45–50°. Add 20 mL freshly filtered molybdate soln (this vol. will ppt up to 20 mg P_2O_5) and let flasks remain in bath 30 min at 45–50°, swirling contents at ca 5 min intervals. To prevent tipping, weight flask with Pb rings or by other means.

For filtration, use filter tube (so-called carbon filter), ca 28 mm id, fitted with removable, perforated porcelain disk from Caldwell crucible. (Caldwell crucible or gooch may also be used.) Prep. quick filtering pad 3–4 mm thick, using short-fiber asbestos. (*Caution: See* **51.086**.) For convenience in washing and in transferring filter tubes, provide suction flask with rubber stopper having hole somewhat larger than stem of filter tube.

With full suction, filter ppt and wash flask and then filter tube with ca 6 portions cold H_2O, using 150–200 mL total. Test for complete washing by passing 25 mL CO_2-free H_2O thru flask and filter tube into clean suction flask. Immediately disconnect suction and add 1 drop each of 0.1*N* NaOH and phthln, which should yield strong pink color.

Loosen pad and porcelain disk with wire or narrow rod inserted in stem end, and transfer to flask. Place filter tube in neck of flask, dissolve any ppt on walls with measured vol. std alkali, and rinse down filter tube with ca 25 mL CO_2-free H_2O. (Enough std alkali must have been added to dissolve ppt.) Stopper flask, swirl, and let stand, mixing occasionally, until yellow ppt completely dissolves. Dil. to ca 75 mL with CO_2-free H_2O, add 10 drops phthln, and titr. with std acid to complete disappearance of pink, matching end point with another flask contg H_2O and asbestos only. If alkali adheres to fragments of asbestos, making end point uncertain, add slight excess of std acid and complete titrn with std alkali. 1 mL 0.1*N* NaOH = 0.3086 mg P_2O_5. Subtract alkali consumed in blank detn.

(b) *Calcium.*—Transfer aliquot contg 20–40 mg Ca to beaker, dil. to 100 mL, and proceed as in **3.015**. Correct for $KMnO_4$ consumed in blank detn.

(c) *Iron.*—Transfer aliquot contg 0.2–0.5 mg Fe to 100 mL vol. flask, add enough HCl (1+9) to yield 2 mL concd acid, and dil. to vol. Proceed as in **14.013(a)**, beginning "Pipet 10 mL aliquot into 25 mL vol. flask . . ." Det. Fe in sample by comparison with stds prepd as in **14.012**.

36.060 ★ Effervescent Potassium Bromide with Caffeine (*25*)—Official Final Action ★

KBr is detd by Volhard titrn; caffeine is detd by extn from alk. soln with $CHCl_3$ and weighing. *See* **36.057–36.058**, 12th ed.

Elixir of Five Bromides (*26*)—Official Final Action

36.061 ***Preparation of Dilution***

Transfer 50 mL sample to 1 L vol. flask, dil. to vol., and mix. Measure aliquots of this diln at original temp. of sample.

36.062 ***Determinations***

(a) *Ammonium bromide.*—Place 200 mL aliquot of diln in Kjeldahl flask; add small piece of *paraffin* and excess 10% NaOH soln (ca 5 mL). Distil NH_3 into excess std acid (40 mL 0.1*N* usually is enough). Titr. excess acid with 0.1*N* NaOH, using Me red. 1 mL 0.1*N* acid = 0.00979 g NH_4Br.

(b) *Calcium bromide.*—Pipet 100 mL aliquot of diln into casserole or Pt dish and evap. to dryness. Ignite at dull red (ca 525°) until org. matter is thoroly charred. Cool, add 5 mL HCl (1+3) to dissolve Ca salts, filter, and wash well with hot H_2O. Return filter and unoxidized C to casserole or dish and ignite at 600° until residue is white. Treat residue with 5 mL HCl (1+3), filter, and wash with hot H_2O, combining filtrates.

Det. Ca as in **3.015**, and reserve filtrate for detn of Na, K, and Li. If 0.1*N* $KMnO_4$ is used, 1 mL = 0.0100 g $CaBr_2$.

(c) *Lithium bromide.*—Dil. filtrate and washings from Ca detn to 200 mL and mix. Evap. 100 mL aliquot to dryness and drive off all NH_4 salts by heating to faint red (ca 525°) in Pt dish. Treat residue with little H_2O, filter into Pt dish, add few mL HCl, and evap. to dryness.

Complete conversion of alkali bromides to chlorides by treating residue with Cl-H_2O and evapg to dryness. Repeat addn and evapn of Cl-H_2O twice more, or until there is no apparent darkening of soln due to liberation of Br.

Dissolve mixed chlorides in min. amt of cold H_2O (ca 1.5 mL is more than enough for 0.5 g salts), in tall 200 mL beaker. Add 1 drop HCl, and then gradually add 20 mL absolute alcohol, dropping alcohol into center of beaker (not on sides) while rotating soln. (NaCl and KCl should be pptd in perfectly uniform granular condition.) In similar manner add 60 mL ether (sp gr 0.716–0.717 at 25°) and let mixt. stand ca 5 min or until ppt is well agglomerated and supernate is almost clear, rotating mixt. occasionally. Filter with suction thru weighed gooch into erlenmeyer, using bell jar arrangement, washing beaker thoroly with mixt. of alcohol and ether (1+5), and collecting all ppt on gooch with aid of policeman. Thoroly wash ppt on gooch, set crucible aside, and rinse funnel with alcohol-ether mixt. to wash any adhering Li soln into flask contg filtrate. Evap. filtrate to dryness on steam bath, using air current.

Treat residue with 10 mL absolute alcohol, warming if necessary, so that practically all residue dissolves. If slight film remains on bottom and sides of flask, remove with policeman. Then, while rotating soln in flask, add 50 mL ether (sp gr 0.716–0.717 at 25°), followed by 1 drop HCl. Let stand 30 min, rotating soln frequently. When fine ppt has agglomerated (only very small amt is usually pptd), filter into tall beaker with suction thru gooch contg first ppt. Wash combined ppts with the ether-alcohol mixt., taking same precautions as in first pptn. Air dry gooch and contents; then dry in oven, ignite gently, cool, and weigh to obtain combined wt NaCl and KCl. Reserve crucible and contents for K detn.

Evap., on steam bath, ether-alcohol filtrate and washings contg the Li. Dissolve residue in little H_2O, add slight excess of H_2SO_4 (1+1), and transfer to weighed porcelain or Pt dish. Evap. as far as possible on steam bath and then gently ignite residue over flame. (By placing dish on triangle over asbestos gauze and using low flame, soln can be evapd without spattering.) Finally ignite carefully over full flame, cool, and weigh. If charring

★ Surplus method—*see* inside front cover.

has occurred, repeat ignition with H_2SO_4. Calc. to LiBr, using factor 1.5800.

(**d**) *Sodium bromide.*—Remove combined KCl and NaCl from gooch by washing with hot H_2O, dil. to 50 mL, and use 5 mL aliquot for detn of Na. Proceed as in **3.028**, beginning ". . . add 100 mL Mg uranyl acetate soln . . ." Calc. to NaBr, using factor 0.0688.

(**e**) *Potassium bromide.*—To 25 mL aliquot of soln of KCl and NaCl, add enough Pt soln (0.105 g H_2PtCl_6/mL) to convert KCl and NaCl to K_2PtCl_6 and Na_2PtCl_6, and evap. to dryness. Treat residue with 80% alcohol by vol., filter, and wash until excess of H_2PtCl_6 and Na_2PtCl_6 is removed. Dry filter and ppt, dissolve residue in hot H_2O, and transfer to weighed Pt dish. Evap. on steam bath, dry 30 min in oven at 100°, cool, and weigh as K_2PtCl_6. Calc. to KBr, using factor 0.4898.

(**f**) *Total bromine.*—Transfer 20 mL of diln to 500 mL flask. Add 100 mL H_2O, 2 mL HNO_3, and excess of 0.1*N* $AgNO_3$ (usually 30 mL). Titr. excess $AgNO_3$ with 0.1*N* NH_4SCN, using Fe alum indicator. 1 mL 0.1*N* $AgNO_3$ = 0.00799 g Br.

36.063 ★ Elixir of Three Bromides (*26*) ★ Official Final Action

NH_3 is detd by distn into excess std acid and back titrating; K is detd gravimetrically as K_2PtCl_6; Na is detd gravimetrically as Na-Mg uranyl acetate; and total Br is detd by Volhard titrn. *See* **36.061–36.062**, 12th ed.

★ Hypophosphites in Sirups (*27*) ★ Official Final Action

(Applicable in absence of phosphates; if phosphates are present, make suitable correction.)

36.064 *Method I*

Hypophosphites are oxidized to phosphate with HNO_3; phosphate is pptd with molybdate soln; phosphomolybdate is dissolved in NH_4OH, and phosphate is repptd as $MgNH_4PO_4$ which is detd gravimetrically as $Mg_2P_2O_7$. Ca is pptd as oxalate and ignited to $CaSO_4$ in presence of H_2SO_4. *See* **36.063**, 12th ed.

36.065 *Method II*

(Not applicable in presence of other reducing agents or of phenolic compds)

Oxdn of hypophosphites with excess std bromate; residual bromate liberates I which is titrd with $Na_2S_2O_3$. *See* **36.064–36.065**, 12th ed.

36.066 Iodine (*28*)—Official Final Action

Transfer sample contg ≤0.1 g iodide (0.05 g is ample) to crucible, preferably Ni. If sample contains only slight amt of org. material, add 1 g starch. Add 2–3 g solid KOH. If sample is solid, add 10–15 mL alcohol before adding KOH. Alkali must be thoroly mixed with sample to prevent loss of I in furnace (either stir, leaving stirring rod in crucible, or heat and swirl on steam bath until KOH is in soln). Dry and char thoroly. (Use as low temp. as possible to prevent loss of I; ≤525°.) Ext charred mass with hot H_2O, filter into erlenmeyer, and wash well with hot H_2O.

Neutze filtrate with H_2SO_4 (1+1), make alk. again with 4% NaOH soln, and add 1 mL excess. Heat to bp and slowly add satd $KMnO_4$ soln until $KMnO_4$ color remains after several min of boiling. Then add ca 0.5 mL excess, continue boiling ca 5 min, and let cool. Add enough $KMnO_4$ to completely oxidize all iodide to iodate so that $KMnO_4$ color, not brown MnO_2 color, is present at end of boiling period. Add few mL alcohol and place on steam bath. ($KMnO_4$ color should be bleached; if it is not, add little more alcohol.) When ppt has settled, filter, and wash with hot *1% NH_4Cl soln.* If filtrate is not clear, digest on steam bath until the MnO_2 can be retained on filter. After cooling, add 1–2 g KI, acidify with HCl, and titr. with 0.1*N* $Na_2S_2O_3$. 1 mL 0.1*N* $Na_2S_2O_3$ = 0.00277 g KI, 0.00250 g NaI, or 0.00212 g I.

36.067 Iodine Ointment (*29*)—Official Final Action

(**a**) *Free iodine.*—Weigh (to 1 mg) ca 2 g ointment, and transfer to 250 mL I flask. Melt on H_2O bath (≤70°), add 30 mL $CHCl_3$, mix well, and then add 30 mL H_2O. (All of base should be dissolved in $CHCl_3$ before H_2O is added.) Titr. with 0.1*N* $Na_2S_2O_3$, using starch indicator, **6.005(f)**. Approach end point dropwise, shaking flask vigorously to ensure that all I has been extd from $CHCl_3$ layer. 1 mL 0.1*N* $Na_2S_2O_3$ = 0.01269 g I.

(**b**) *Potassium iodide.*—Pour liqs from free I detn, (**a**), into 500 mL I flask, rinsing flask with 200 mL H_2O, added in several portions. (It is desirable to maintain this vol. within rather narrow limits.) Add 0.5 mL *0.2% alc. p-ethoxychrysoidin indicator* and 1–4 drops 0.1*N* NaOH (to neutze). (Aq. layer should now be clear yellow.) Titr. with 0.1*N* $AgNO_3$, approaching end point dropwise and swirling frequently. ($AgNO_3$ soln causes turbidity due to formation of colloidal AgI and development of reddish-brown color similar to that observed in over-titrd Volhard detn. End point, which is produced by 1 drop $AgNO_3$ soln, is characterized by flocculation of colloidal AgI and complete disappearance of reddish brown tinge, leaving almost clear, pale yellow supernate.) mL 0.1*N* $AgNO_3$ − mL 0.1*N* $Na_2S_2O_3$, (**a**) = mL consumed by iodide originally present. 1 mL 0.1*N* $AgNO_3$ = 0.0166 g KI.

Iron

Spectrophotometric Method (30)—Official Final Action

(Applicable to drugs listed in Table **36:02**. Rinse all glassware with deionized H_2O before use to avoid Fe contamination from tap H_2O.)

Table 36:02 Conditions for Analysis of Various Iron Preparations

Preparation	Initial Solv.	Diln Solv.	Color Develop. Temp.
Ferrous ammonium sulfate, powder	(1)	H_2O	Room
Ferrous sulfate, powder, tablets	(1)	H_2O	Room
Ferrous gluconate, powder, tablets	(1)	H_2O	Room
Ferrous fumarate, powder, tablets	(1)	H_2O	Heat
Ferric ammonium citrate, powder	(1)	H_2O	Heat
Ferric glycerophosphate, powder	(1)	H_2O	Room
Iron cacodylate, powder, injection[a]	(1)	H_2O	Heat
Iron peptonate, powder	H_2O	(2)	Heat
Soluble ferric pyrophosphate, powder	H_2O	(2)	Room
Ferrous sulfate, elixir	H_2O	(2)	Room
Iron sorbitex, injection (1.00 mL sample)	H_2O	(2)	Heat
Iron dextran, injection (1.00 mL sample)	H_2O	(2)	Heat

Solv. (1) = 100 mL H_2O contg 4 mL HCl, dil. to vol. with H_2O
Solv. (2) = 2 mL HCl, dil. to vol. with H_2O
[a] For iron cacodylate injection, use sample contg 5–6 mg Fe and use initial diln directly for detn.

★ Surplus method—*see* inside front cover.

36.068 ***Principle***

Sample is dissolved in dil. HCl or H_2O and dild to concn of 3 mg/100 mL. Fe^{+2} is detd by complexing with α,α'-dipyridyl at pH 4.5 and measuring A at 523 nm. Total Fe is detd by reducing Fe^{+3} to Fe^{+2} with ascorbic acid and complexing with dipyridyl. Fe^{+3} is detd by difference.

36.069 ***Reagents***

(**a**) *Dipyridyl soln.*—Dissolve 0.1 g α,α'-dipyridyl in H_2O and dil. to 100 mL. Soln is stable up to 4 months if stored in cool, dark place.

(**b**) *Iron std solns.*—(*1*) *Stock soln.*—0.3 mg Fe/mL. Accurately weigh ca 0.3 g std Fe powder (99.999%, A. D. Mackay, Inc., 198 Broadway, New York, NY 10038, or equiv.), dissolve in 100 mL H_2O and 20 mL HCl by heating on steam bath, if necessary, dil. to 1 L with H_2O, and mix. (Complete soln may require as long as 5 hr heating.) (*2*) *Working soln.*—0.03 mg/mL. Dil. 50.0 mL stock soln to 500 mL with H_2O.

(**c**) *Acetate buffer soln.*—pH 4.5. Dissolve 273 g NaOAc.3H_2O in H_2O, add 240 mL HOAc, and dil. to 2 L with H_2O.

36.070 ***Preparation of Sample***

(Complete immediately to avoid oxidn of Fe^{+2} to Fe^{+3}.)

(**a**) *Powders.*—Accurately weigh sample contg ca 60 mg Fe, transfer to 200 mL vol. flask, and dissolve and dil. to vol. with initial solv. specified in Table **36:02**. Dil. 10.0 mL aliquot to 100.0 mL with specified diln solv.

(**b**) *Tablets.*—Accurately weigh portion powd tablets or individual tablets contg ca 60 mg Fe into 200 mL vol. flask, add 100 mL H_2O and 4 mL HCl, heat on steam bath 30 min (Fe gluconate and $FeSO_4$ do not require heat; place 5–10 min in ultrasonic bath), cool to room temp., and dil. to vol. with H_2O. Filter thru Whatman No. 1 paper, or equiv. Dil. 10.00 mL filtrate to 100.0 mL with H_2O.

(**c**) *Elixirs, sirups, and injections.*—Pipet sample (use "to contain" pipet and rinse, if sample is viscous) contg ca 60 mg Fe into 200 mL vol. flask, dil. to vol. with H_2O, and mix. Pipet 10 mL into 100 mL vol. flask, add 2 mL HCl, and dil. to vol. with H_2O.

36.071 ***Determination***

(**a**) *Ferrous iron.*—Pipet duplicate 10 mL aliquots sample soln (1 as sample blank) and 10 mL working std soln, contg ca 300 μg Fe, into sep. 100 mL vol. flasks. Transfer 10 mL reagent blank soln, prepd by dilg 4 mL HCl to 2 L with H_2O, into fourth 100 mL vol. flask. To all solns, add 15 mL buffer soln and ca 20 mL H_2O, and mix. To 1 sample soln, std, and reagent blank, add 5 mL dipyridyl soln. To std soln, add 20–25 mg *USP ascorbic acid powder.* Dil. all solns to vol. with H_2O, and mix. Let stand 3 hr.

Record A of working std soln, sample soln, and sample blank soln (no addn of dipyridyl soln) from 700 to 500 nm against reagent blank soln, setting spectrophtr at 0 A at 523 nm against reagent blank soln. Use A at max., ca 523 nm.

$$\% \text{ Fe in powder} = [(A - A_0)/A'] \times C \times (200/W),$$

where A, A_0, and A' refer to sample, sample blank, and std, resp.; C = concn working std soln in μg/mL; and W = mg sample.

$$\text{mg Fe/tablet} = [(A - A_0)/A'] \times C \times (2/W) \times T,$$

where T = av. mg/tablet.

mg Fe in original aliquot elixir, sirup, or injection taken for assay $= [(A - A_0)/A'] \times C \times 2$,

$$\text{mg Fe compd} = (\text{mg Fe} \times \text{MW})/55.85,$$

where MW = molecular wt of Fe compd.

(**b**) *Total iron.*—Proceed as in (**a**), adding ascorbic acid to sample, sample blank, and std solns. Develop color 3 hr at room temp. or 1 hr, without delay, on steam bath as specified in Table **36:02**, heating before dilg solns to vol. Det. A as in (**a**), and calc. % total Fe or mg/dose or aliquot.

(**c**) *Ferric iron.*—Fe^{+3} = total Fe − Fe^{+2}, all expressed in same units.

Ferrous Sulfate

Semiautomated Method (31)—Official First Action

36.072 ***Principle***

$FeSO_4$ in tablets, capsules, or liqs is dissolved in 2% H_2SO_4, mixed with 1,10-phenanthroline in acetate buffer to form stable Fe^{+2} complex, and A is measured in flowcell at 502 nm.

36.073 ***Apparatus***

(**a**) *Automatic analyzer.*—AutoAnalyzer with following modules (Technicon Instruments Corp.: Sampler II with 30/hr (3:1) cam; 2 proportioning pumps (I or II); manifold; colorimeter I, with 15 mm tubular flowcell and matched 502 nm filters, or spectrophtr; compatible recorder (*see* Fig. **36:02**).

(**b**) *Shaker.*—Wrist action (Burrell Corp., model BT, or equiv.).

(**c**) *Ultrasonic generator.*—Model 11, 150 watt (Heat Systems-Ultrasonic, Inc., 38 E Mall, Plainview, NY 11803), or equiv.

36.074 ***Reagents***

(Use deaerated, deionized H_2O thruout.)

(**a**) *1,10-Phenanthroline reagent.*—35 mg/100 mL. Dissolve 350 mg 1,10-phenanthroline.H_2O in 500 mL H_2O, dil. to 1 L with H_2O, and add 10 drops wetting soln, (**c**).

(**b**) *Sulfuric acid.*—2% (w/v). Dil. 11.4 mL H_2SO_4 to 1 L with H_2O.

(**c**) *Acetate buffer.*—pH 4.6–4.7. Dissolve 136.08 g NaOAc in mixt. of 57 mL HOAc and 500 mL H_2O. Dil. to 2 L with H_2O, add 20 drops of wetting soln, (**d**), and mix well.

(**d**) *Wetting soln.*—30% soln (w/v) polyoxyethylene lauryl ether in H_2O (Brij-35, Technicon No. T21-0110).

(**e**) *Iron std soln.*—60 mg Fe/100 mL. Accurately weigh ca 60 mg Fe wire and transfer to 100 mL vol. flask. Add 10 mL H_2O and 1.3 mL H_2SO_4, heat on steam bath until dissolved, and dil. to vol. with H_2O.

36.075 ***Preparation of Sample***

Place individual tablet or capsule, liq. aliquot, or weighed composite in accurately measured vol. 2% H_2SO_4 to give Fe concn of 0.6 mg/mL. Use ultrasonic generator to disintegrate solid dosage formulations. After complete disintegration, agitate 15 min on mech. shaker. Let settle 2 hr.

36.076 ***Analytical System***

Sample is withdrawn and dild with air-segmented stream of H_2O in double mixer, resampled, and mixed with acetate buffer. 1,10-Phenanthroline reagent is added and, after mixing in double mixer, soln is debubbled and passed thru 15 mm flowcell, where A is measured at 502 nm.

36.077 ***Start-Up and Shut-Down Operations***

Place all lines in resp. solns and pump until steady baseline is obtained (ca 15 min). To shut down system, place all lines in H_2O and pump 10 min. Remove lines from H_2O reservoir and pump system dry. If irregular bubble pattern occurs during sample run, pump soln contg 10 drops wetting soln/L H_2O thru system ca 5 min before finally flushing with H_2O for shut-down.

36.078 ***Determination***

Fill sample cups in following order: 3 cups std soln, 5 cups sample soln, 1 cup std soln, 5 cups sample soln, etc., ending with 3 cups std soln. (First 2 cups of std soln are used to equilibrate system, but are not included in calcns.) Start Sampler II. After last cup has been sampled, let system operate until steady baseline is obtained. Draw tangent to initial and final

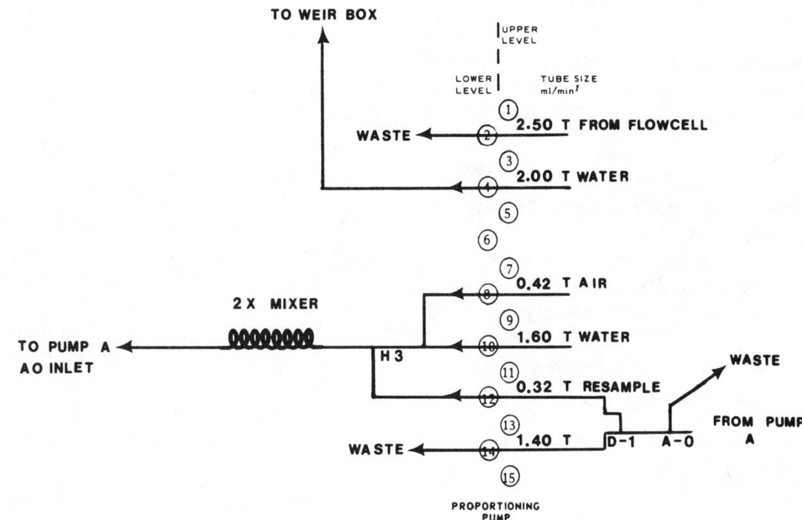

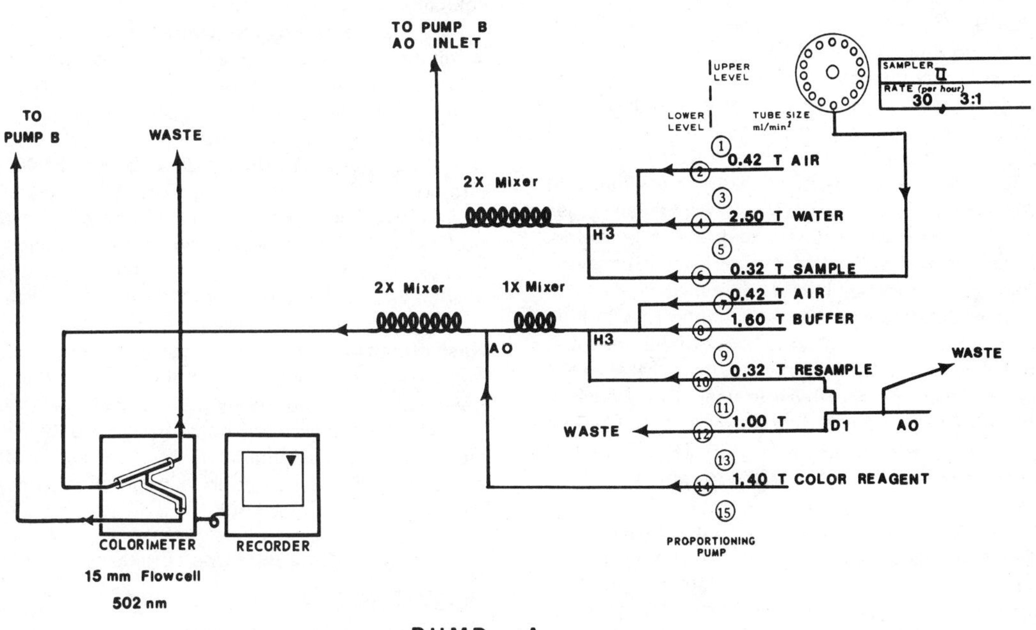

FIG. 36:02—Flow diagrams for semiautomated analysis for ferrous sulfate

baselines. Subtract baseline to det. net A and A' for each sample and std peak, resp. Discard values for first 2 and last std peaks and calc. av. std A'.

$$\text{mg Fe in portion taken} = (A/A') \times C \times D,$$

where C = concn of std in mg/mL and D = diln factor.

Mercury (*32*)—Official Final Action

(Applicable to Hg in phenylmercuric chloride, HgI_2, nitromersol, HgO ointment, and calomel tablets. *Caution: See* **51.079**.)

36.079 ***Reagents***

(**a**) *Strychnine sulfate soln.*—Approx. 0.01*M*; 4.3 g/500 mL.

(**b**) *Valser's reagent.*—Dissolve 10 g KI in H_2O and dil. to 100 mL. Sat. with HgI_2 (ca 14 g) and filter.

36.080 ***Apparatus***

(**a**) *Digestion flask.*—Acetylation or r-b, 100 mL, fitted to H_2O-cooled straight-tube condenser with ₮ joint.

(**b**) *Gooch crucibles.*—Fitted with 21 mm filter paper disks, covered with thin layer of asbestos (*Caution: See* **51.086**), and dried at 105°. Use to filter and weigh ppt of strychnine.HI.HgI_2.

36.081 ***Preparation of Samples***

(*Caution: See* **51.047**.)

Accurately weigh (avoid use of metal containers) or measure sample contg 20–100 mg Hg (optimal ca 50 mg) and treat as follows:

(**a**) *Solns of organic mercurials.*—Transfer sample to beaker and evap. just to dryness with low heat (60–70°) and air current. Dissolve residue in ca 5 mL 10% NaOH soln and transfer to digestion flask. Rinse beaker with four 3–4 mL portions H_2O and add rinsings to digestion flask. Add excess liq. Br to soln and connect flask to condenser. Boil 4–5 min and add 3 mL HCl thru top of condenser. Continue to heat soln until Br collects in condenser tube. Remove heat and cool until Br returns to soln in digestion flask.

Alternately heat and cool until Br has almost completely dissipated. (After 3 intervals of heating, flow of H_2O thru condenser may be discontinued to aid in removing Br.) Let flask cool, and rinse inside of condenser with ca 5 mL H_2O. Disconnect flask and rinse tip of condenser with small stream of H_2O from wash bottle. Filter thru 9 cm paper into 150 mL beaker, and rinse flask and filter with four 5 mL portions H_2O.

(**b**) *Ointments.*—Transfer sample to digestion flask and add 5 mL HCl (1+3) followed by 5 mL satd Br-H_2O. Add small pieces of porcelain, SiC, or few glass beads to prevent bumping. Connect flask to condenser and fit flask over hole cut in asbestos board so that bottom extends just below undersurface of board. Heat over low flame, maintaining slow and continuous boiling ca 10 min, and then cool to room temp. Disconnect flask and decant aq. portion thru 9 cm paper into 150 mL beaker. Take precautions to retain all ointment base in flask. Rinse neck of flask into filter with few drops of H_2O from wash bottle. Add 1 mL HCl (1+3), 1 mL satd Br-H_2O, and 8 mL H_2O to flask and reflux. Again cool contents of flask and decant aq. phase thru filter.

Repeat refluxing and decanting with two 10 mL portions H_2O and finally rinse condenser tube into flask with ca 5 mL H_2O. Disconnect flask, rinse condenser tip, and decant rinsings thru filter. Rinse filter with 2 small portions H_2O from wash bottle.

Test for complete removal of Hg by adding 5 mL H_2O and 2 drops HCl (1+3) to digestion flask and refluxing as before. Pass this soln thru original filter into 50 mL beaker. To filtrate add 1 drop 10% KI soln and 1 drop strychnine sulfate soln. No turbidity should be produced. If extn is incomplete, repeat refluxings with H_2O until all Hg is removed. Reserve all test solns showing presence of Hg to add to major portion after pptn of Hg.

(**c**) *Calomel tablets.*—Det. av. wt/tablet. Grind to fine powder and transfer accurately weighed portion to digestion flask. Add 10 mL satd Br-H_2O and 5 mL HCl (1+3). Connect flask to reflux condenser and gently boil contents until most of Br vapors collect in condenser. Discontinue heating until Br returns to soln in flask. Repeat alternate heating and cooling until Br vapors are dissipated. Cool flask and contents to room temp. and rinse condenser tube with ca 10 mL H_2O. Disconnect flask and rinse condenser tip into flask. Filter soln thru gooch into 150 mL beaker. Rinse flask with three 5 mL portions H_2O and pass rinsings thru crucible, and finally rinse crucible with fine stream of H_2O.

(**d**) *Tablets containing purgative drugs.*—If tablets contain purgative drugs, add 10 mL alcohol to weighed sample in flask. Heat on steam bath with gentle agitation until alcohol begins to boil. Remove flask, cool under tap, and filter supernate thru gooch fitted with asbestos mat. Retain as much of insol. residue in flask as possible. Rinse flask and contents with three 10 mL portions alcohol and two 5 mL portions H_2O, and decant thru crucible as above. Remove asbestos mat with fine wire or needle and transfer to flask. Rinse crucible with 10 mL satd Br-H_2O and 5 mL HCl (1+3), and add rinsings to flask. Connect flask to condenser, and treat as in (**c**).

36.082 ***Determination***

Add 10 mL 10% KI soln to filtrate, and if necessary, evap. on steam bath under air current to ca 50 mL. If soln has not previously been acidified, add 3 mL HCl (1+3). Add 1% $NaHSO_3$ soln until I color is discharged, and keep soln free from I color by addn of $NaHSO_3$ soln until final filtration is made. Add strychnine sulfate soln slowly from buret or pipet until ppt coagulates and settles rapidly. (Strychnine sulfate soln may be added as rapidly as it will flow from buret if theoretical amt is used, based on 1 mL soln for each 4 mg Hg expected to be present.) Avoid undue excess of strychnine because of slight solubility of its hydriodide.

Let ppt settle and test for complete pptn by adding 2–3 drops strychnine sulfate soln to clear supernate. If pptn is incomplete, indicated by cloudiness around the drops, add strychnine sulfate soln in 1 mL increments until pptn is complete. Let ppt remain in beaker with occasional stirring 0.5–1 hr.

Decant supernate thru weighed gooch, **36.080(b)**. Wash ppt into crucible with fine stream of H_2O. Completely transfer ppt to crucible, and wash residue and crucible with three 5 mL portions H_2O. Scrub beaker thoroly with policeman. Transfer crucible and holder to another small suction flask and wash residue with 2–3 mL H_2O. Test filtrate for complete removal of strychnine by addn of Valser's reagent. If necessary, continue washing ppt with small portions H_2O until last washings give no more than faint opalescence upon addn of Valser's reagent. Always test main filtrate by addn of ca 1 mL strychnine sulfate soln to assure complete pptn of Hg. If pptn was incomplete, repeat detn. Dry crucible 1 hr at 105°, cool in desiccator, and weigh. Calc. % Hg compd in sample on basis of MW of 916.74 for ppt of strychnine.HI.HgI_2.

Merbromin (Mercurochrome®) (*33*)

36.083 ***Tests for Purity—Procedure***

(**a**) Acidify portion of merbromin soln with 10% H_2SO_4 and filter off ppt. Filtrate is only slightly yellow.

(**b**) Pass H_2S (*Caution: See* **51.059**) into portion of filtrate. No ppt or coloring occurs.

(c) Add few mL 10% HNO_3 to another portion of filtrate and add $AgNO_3$ soln. No ppt forms.

36.084 *Total Solids in Solution—Official Final Action*

Pipet 10 mL merbromin soln into tared, extra-wide-form weighing bottle and evap. to dryness on steam bath. Let dry overnight in open bottle in desiccator contg H_2SO_4. Weigh.

36.085 *Determination of Mercury—Official Final Action*

(*Caution: See* **51.019**, **51.030**, **51.039**, **51.040**, **51.048**, **51.049**, **51.059**, **51.080**, and **51.086**.)

Pipet 10 mL ca 2% merbromin soln into 500 mL tall beaker and evap. to dryness on steam bath (or accurately weigh ca 0.2 g powder). Dissolve residue in 4 mL H_2O and slowly add, with const mixing, 10 mL H_2SO_4. Incline beaker and cautiously add small portions finely powd $KMnO_4$, mixing after each addn, until deep purple color shows that considerable excess has been added. Let stand 30 min, mixing occasionally. Mixt. should still be purple.

Add 100 mL H_2O and mix thoroly. Add small portions finely powd oxalic acid, mixing after each addn, until soln is clear. Filter thru small filter into 400 mL beaker, wash original beaker and filter until filtrate measures ca 200 mL, and pass H_2S thru soln 20 min. Warm on steam bath until ppt of HgS settles quickly after stirring, and again pass H_2S thru warm soln 5 min. Immediately filter soln into weighed gooch; thoroly wash ppt on filter with H_2O, 3 times with alcohol, and then with 4 or 5 portions CCl_4 or CS_2, letting liq. run thru crucible without suction; finally wash with ether. Dry ppt to const wt at 100° and weigh as HgS. HgS $\times$ 0.8622 = Hg.

Qual. test dried ppt for Hg and other heavy metals. If slow filtration occurs during washing with H_2O, let ppt drain, and wash once with alcohol; then continue as directed.

36.086 Mercurous Chloride (Calomel) in Ointments (*34*) Official Final Action

Accurately weigh ca 1 g ointment, transfer to 250 mL g-s erlenmeyer, and treat with ca 50 mL $CHCl_3$. When base is dissolved, decant thru dry, closely packed asbestos mat in Caldwell crucible (*Caution: See* **51.086**), using light suction. Wash flask and contents several times with 20–30 mL portions $CHCl_3$, decanting thru crucible. Let any residual $CHCl_3$ in flask evap., and transfer asbestos mat and contents to flask, wiping sides of crucible and mouth of flask with damp piece of filter paper and adding it to flask. Add 2.5 g KI and 30 mL std 0.1*N* I, **50.018** (stdzd against $Na_2S_2O_3$), stopper, and mix well. Let stand ca 1.5 hr or until soln of calomel is complete, agitating frequently and fairly vigorously. Titr. with 0.1*N* $Na_2S_2O_3$, **50.038**, adding 1 or 2 mL excess and using starch indicator, **6.005(f)**. When all traces of I disappear, back-titr. with std I soln to blue color. 1 mL 0.1*N* I = 0.02360 g Hg_2Cl_2.

36.087 Mercurous Chloride (Calomel) in Tablets (*35*) Official Final Action

Count and weigh representative number of tablets. Powder tablets and accurately weigh well mixed sample contg 0.19–0.26 g (3–4 grains) Hg_2Cl_2. Transfer to 200 mL g-s erlenmeyer, add ca 50 mL H_2O, acidify with HOAc, and after sol. fillers dissolve, decant with aid of suction thru tightly packed asbestos mat placed on plate of Caldwell crucible (*Caution: see* **51.086**). Wash once with H_2O by decantation and then successively with alcohol and ether. Transfer removable plate holding mat and insol. material to original flask, washing into flask any insol. material adhering to sides of crucible. Add 2.5 g KI, 10 mL H_2O, and then 30 mL std 0.1*N* I soln, **50.018**. Complete detn as in **36.086**.

36.088 Mercurous Iodide in Tablets (*36*) Official Final Action

Accurately weigh well mixed powd sample contg 0.19–0.26 g (3–4 grains) Hg_2I_2. Transfer sample to 200 mL g-s flask, and proceed as in **36.087**, omitting addn of H_2O after the KI. 1 mL 0.1*N* I = 0.03275 g Hg_2I_2.

Note: Some com. tablets are difficult to filter thru asbestos mat without loss of Hg_2I_2. Placing few drops of alumina cream, **31.021(b)**, on mat before filtration is started (wash free from NH_3), satisfactorily prevents loss, tho it retards filtration.

36.089 Mercury in Mercurial Ointment (*37*) Official Final Action

(*Caution: See* **51.011** and **51.026**.)

After mixing ointment thoroly with glass rod, avoiding contact with metals, weigh 1 g sample into erlenmeyer. Add 20 mL H_2O and 20 mL HNO_3, and heat gently over small flame until red fumes cease to evolve. Cool, and decant aq. soln from ointment base into separator. Wash ointment base with 50 mL boiling H_2O, cool, and decant into separator. Repeat washing until all Hg is removed.

Shake combined solns in separator with 50 mL ether. Transfer aq. soln to erlenmeyer. Wash ether soln with three 10 mL portions H_2O until Hg is removed, adding washings to flask. Add 3 mL $FeNH_4(SO_4)_2$ soln, **36.036(b)**, and titr. with 0.1*N* NH_4SCN. 1 mL 0.1*N* NH_4SCN = 0.01003 g Hg.

36.090 ★ Mercury in Ointment of Mercuric Nitrate (*38*) ★ Official Final Action

(*Caution: See* **51.011** and **51.026**.)

Transfer, to 200–300 mL erlenmeyer, 3–5 g sample, accurately weighed, using glass or bone spatula. Add 40 mL HNO_3 (1+1) and few glass beads, and insert short-stem funnel into neck of flask. Boil gently 1–1.5 hr on hot plate or over low flame. (With latter, use piece of asbestos with circular hole under asbestos wire gauze.) Add 30 mL H_2O, using part to wash funnel. Cool enough (ca 20° or below) to cause solidification of unconsumed fat. Filter thru 11 cm paper into 200 mL vol. flask. Wash fat, flask, and filter, using ca 100 mL 1% HNO_3. Dil. to vol. and mix well. Reserve fat to test for complete extn as below.

Test for complete extn of Hg from fat and its removal from filter, etc., by repeating HNO_3 digestion ca 30 min on residual fat in flask or on filter, completing this as sep. detn, including $KMnO_4$ digestion. Add any titrn in excess of 1–2 drops (0.05–0.08 mL 0.1*N* NH_4SCN) resulting from this test portion to that obtained by titrg main ext.

Transfer 100 mL aliquot to 500 mL erlenmeyer. Add 7 mL HNO_3, 5 mL H_2SO_4, and 2 g powd $KMnO_4$, and rotate to dissolve. Heat just to bp over low flame or on hot plate. Boil gently 45 min, maintaining excess of $KMnO_4$, indicated by dark purple color. (Excess is essential.) When adding $KMnO_4$ to boiling liq., use smaller portions (ca 0.5 g or less) to avoid loss due to frothing.

Caution: Use of greater excess of $KMnO_4$ than necessary is not objectionable, but proportionately more H_2O_2 is required to remove it and MnO_2 at end of digestion. Usually ca 10 g is required. Rate of consumption and total $KMnO_4$ consumed appear to vary with temp., org. matter present, and period of heating. Large amt of MnO_2 formed may lead to wrong conclusion concerning color indicative of excess of $KMnO_4$. Frequent examination of soln is necessary. Observation of this color is aided by looking thru supernate toward white background while inclining container.

★ Surplus method—*see* inside front cover.

Remove excess $KMnO_4$ and dissolve MnO_2 by adding H_2O_2 (5–10%, prepd from 30%) dropwise to hot soln. When colorless, add 2% $KMnO_4$ soln slowly until faint pink or brown persists ca 1 min. If large amt of MnO_2 forms at this point, again use H_2O_2 sparingly; then use $KMnO_4$ to discharge the H_2O_2. Discharge color from last addn of $KMnO_4$, including weak brown from MnO_2, by adding dropwise just enough *8% $FeSO_4.7H_2O$ soln.* Cool to ca 20°, add 3 mL ca 0.5*N* $FeNH_4(SO_4)_2.12H_2O$, and titr. with std 0.1*N* NH_4SCN. 1 mL 0.1*N* NH_4SCN = 0.01003 g Hg.

Nitrites in Tablets—Official Final Action

36.091 ★ ***Hydrazine Method (39)*** ★

(Applicable in presence or absence of nitrates or chlorides)

Nitrites react with excess std hydrazine sulfate and excess is titrd with std I soln. *See* **36.080–36.081**, 12th ed.

Silver Proteinates (*40*)—Official Final Action

36.092 ***Total Silver***

(*Caution: See* **51.011** and **51.026.**)

Place 1 g sample, accurately weighed, in 500 mL Kjeldahl flask; add 15 mL H_2SO_4 and then 10 mL HNO_3. Place on steam bath few min, with occasional rotation, to ensure homogeneous mixt., and boil to white fumes. Add more HNO_3, boil again to clear colorless soln, and cool. Add 100 mL H_2O and boil until free of N oxides. Cool, dil. to 300 mL, add 5 mL HNO_3 and 5 mL $FeNH_4(SO_4)_2$ soln, **36.030(b)**, and titr. with 0.1*N* NH_4SCN. 1 mL 0.1*N* NH_4SCN = 0.01079 g Ag.

36.093 ***Ionizable Silver Compounds***

Weigh strip of com. dialyzing tubing 55 mm wide and ca 30 cm long, wet with H_2O until uniformly pliable, shake free of adhering H_2O, and partially dry by rolling in clean paper towel. Reweigh while still moist and place in 250 mL beaker. (Sheets of dialyzing parchment paper may be used in place of tubing. Over one end of glass tube 10 cm long and ca 2.5 cm od, fold and secure with rubber band sq piece of parchment paper in form of sack large enough to hold sample soln. Dialyzing material should be kept in humid container to prevent breaking when handled.)

Weigh 1 g sample, dissolve in 15 mL H_2O, and transfer to dialyzing tube. Calc., and add enough H_2O to beaker to make 100 mL (this ensures 20 mL in dialyzing tube and 80 mL in beaker). Adjust tubing to form "U" in beaker, cover with watch glass, and keep cool and in dark 24 hr.

(**a**) *Qualitative test.*—Test few mL clear, colorless soln from beaker for Ag ions by addn of few drops HCl (1+3) and trace of HNO_3.

(**b**) *Determination.*—If Ag ions are present, remove 50 mL clear, colorless soln (representing 0.5 g sample) from beaker, dil. to 100 mL, and add 2 mL $FeNH_4(SO_4)_2$ soln, **36.030(b)**, and 2 mL colorless HNO_3. Titr. with 0.01*N* NH_4SCN and calc. to % by wt ionizable Ag. 1 mL 0.01*N* NH_4SCN = 0.001079 g Ag.

MYDRIATICS AND MYOTICS

36.094 ★ ***Cat-Eye Bioassay Method (41)*** ★ ***Official Final Action***

Contraction of pupil of cat eye treated with sample is compared to that of eye treated with control std prepn, with untreated eye as control, all exposed to 100 watt elec. lamp at 1′ distance. *See* **36.084–36.088**, 12th ed.

★ Surplus method—*see* inside front cover.

MICROSCOPIC TESTS

Microchemical Tests

For Alkaloids and Related Amines—Official Final Action

36.095 ***Reagents***

(**a**) *Ammoniacal silver nitrate soln.*—Mix 2.5 mL 4% $AgNO_3$ soln with 2.5 mL NH_4OH (1+5). Prep. fresh.

(**b**) *Ammonium hydroxide soln.*—10% NH_3 (2+3).

(**c**) *Ammonium thiocyanate soln.*—Dissolve 5 g NH_4SCN in 100 mL H_2O.

(**d**) *Bismuth iodide soln.*—(*1*) Prep. stock concd $Bi(NO_3)_3$ soln by dissolving 50 g Bi subnitrate in 70 mL HNO_3 (1+1) and dilg to 100 mL with H_2O. (*2*) Dissolve 1.25 g KI in 4.5 mL H_2O and add 0.5 mL stock concd $Bi(NO_3)_3$ soln. Prep. fresh when soln darkens appreciably.

(**e**) *Bismuth iodide in diluted sulfuric acid soln.*— Dissolve 1.25 g KI in 2.0 mL H_2O, and add 2.5 mL H_2SO_4 (1+3) and 0.5 mL stock concd $Bi(NO_3)_3$ soln, (**d**)(*1*). Prep. fresh daily.

(**f**) *Disodium phosphate soln.*—Dissolve 5 g $Na_2HPO_4.12H_2O$ in 100 mL H_2O.

(**g**) *Gold bromide in hydrochloric acid soln.*—Dissolve 1 g $HAuCl_4.3H_2O$ and 1.5 mL 40% HBr in 18 mL HCl. (Satd aq. NaBr soln may be substituted for the HBr.)

(**h**) *Gold chloride soln.*—Dissolve 1 g $HAuCl_4.3H_2O$ in 20 mL H_2O.

(**i**) *Hydrochloric acid.*—5% (1+6).

(**j**) *Iodine-potassium iodide soln.*—Dissolve 1.27 g I and 2 g KI in 5 mL H_2O, and dil. to 100 mL.

(**k**) *Lead iodide soln.*—To aq. KOAc soln (1+3) add 1 drop Me red and HOAc until yellow changes to orange; then, while gently warming, sat. with PbI_2, cool, and filter.

(**l**) *Mercuric chloride soln.*—Dissolve 5 g $HgCl_2$ in 100 mL H_2O.

(**m**) *Mercuric chloride-sodium chloride soln.*—Dissolve 5 g $HgCl_2$ and 0.75 g NaCl in 100 mL H_2O.

(**n**) *Platinic chloride soln.*—Dissolve 5 g $H_2PtCl_6.6H_2O$ in 100 mL H_2O.

(**o**) *Potassium cadmium iodide soln.*—Dissolve 3 g CdI_2 in 18 mL H_2O contg 6 g KI.

(**p**) *Potassium ferrocyanide soln.*—Dissolve 5 g $K_4Fe(CN)_6.3H_2O$ in 100 mL H_2O.

(**q**) *Potassium hydroxide soln.*—Dissolve 5 g KOH in 100 mL H_2O.

(**r**) *Potassium iodide soln.*—Dissolve 5 g KI in 100 mL H_2O.

(**s**) *Potassium permanganate soln.*—Dissolve 1 g $KMnO_4$ in 100 mL H_2O.

(**t**) *Reinecke salt soln.*—Dissolve 0.1 g $NH_4[Cr(NH_3)_2(SCN)_4].H_2O$ and 0.03 g $H_2NOH.HCl$ in 10 mL alcohol. Filter, and store in refrigerator. (Reagent is stable ≥6 months.)

(**u**) *Sodium benzoate soln.*—Dissolve 5 g Na benzoate in 100 mL H_2O.

(**v**) *Sodium carbonate soln.*—Dissolve 5 g $Na_2CO_3.H_2O$ in 100 mL H_2O.

(**w**) *Sodium iodide soln.*—Dissolve 5 g Naji in 100 mL H_2O.

(**x**) *Sodium nitroprusside.*—$Na_2Fe(CN)_5NO.2H_2O$ crystals.

(**y**) *Zinc chloride soln.*—Dissolve 5 g $ZnCl_2$ in 100 mL H_2O.

(**z**) *Zinc potassium iodide soln.*—Dissolve 5 g $Zn(OAc)_2.3H_2O$ and 20 g KI in 100 mL H_2O.

36.096 ***Preparation of Samples***

(**a**) *Usual controls.*—Dissolve 0.4 or 0.2 mg pure alkaloid salt in 0.04 mL H_2O to make ca 1:100 or 1:200 soln.

(**b**) *Alkaloids in compounds.*—Sep. alkaloid in pure form by extg it from ammoniacal soln with suitable immiscible solv., and evap. solv. Dissolve little of residue in min. of 0.1*N* HCl and dil. with H_2O, if necessary, to ca alkaloid concn specified in (**a**) or in test.

(**c**) *Hypodermic tablets.*—Dissolve portion of tablet in drop of H_2O to ca same alkaloid concn specified in (**a**) or in test.

36.097 ***Identification***

Place drop (ca 0.04 mL) of alkaloid soln on glass slide, add drop of reagent, and without stirring or covering, examine under microscope, using magnification of ca 100–500×. Note kind of crystals formed. Compare their characteristics with descriptions given, Table **36:03**, and with a control. Use polarizing microscope if available, and note characteristics such as birefringence and dichroism.

For Barbiturates (62)—Official Final Action

36.098 ***Reagent***

Iodine-potassium iodide soln.—Dissolve 5 g I and 80 g KI in enough H_2O (ca 78 mL) to make 100 mL. Dil. with 2 parts by vol. of H_3PO_4. Prep. dild reagent every 2–3 weeks.

36.099 ***Identification***

Dissolve little barbiturate in drop H_2O on slide. If present as Na salt, it dissolves readily; if present as acid, add little droplet 1% NaOH on stirring rod and mix. Add 1 full drop reagent and let stand until crystn occurs (immediate with some compds, 0.5–1 hr with secobarbital). Free acid may ppt or crystallize.

Table 36:03 Characteristics of Microchemical Tests for Alkaloids and Related Amines

Alkaloid	Reagent	Description of Crystals
Aconitine (*42*)	Sodium carbonate	In 1:3000 soln heated to 50° in test tube. Small, transparent, hexagonal plates; also rods in contact.
Amylocaine (*43*)	1 drop HCl and 1 drop gold chloride	1:50. Dendritic crystals.
Apomorphine (*44*)	Potassium iodide	1:50. Small crystals that have sharp, clear-cut angles like those of diamond.
	Gold chloride	Red-brown, fine needles, in dense masses in all solns to 1:10,000.
	Hydrochloric acid	1:50. Small rods singly and in clusters.
Arecoline (*42*)	Bismuth iodide	Red, rhombic crystals.
Atropine (*45*)	Iodine potassium iodide	Small, dark rods and triangular plates form in great numbers, singly and in groups.
Benzylmorphine (*46*) (Peronine)	Potassium iodide	1:200. Dense rosettes of needles. Crystals are formed readily in dil. solns (1:1000) in form of sheaves of needles.
	Ammonium thiocyanate	1:200. Rosettes and sheaves of needles in acid or neut. soln.
	Hydrochloric acid	1:100. Rods, usually notched at ends and often in rosettes, are formed on stirring.
Berberine (*47*)	Hydrochloric acid	Satd soln; fine yellow needles. (Avoid excess reagent.)
Brucine (*48*)	Potassium iodide	Long masses of transparent, rectangular plates; also rosettes of thin plates.
	Mercuric chloride	Small, dense rosettes.
Choline (*49*)	Reinecke salt	Add 1 drop acetone to 1 drop H_2O soln of base. Stir, add 1 drop reagent, and stir again. 1:100. Thin, hexgonal plates and star-shaped forms. 1:1000–1:10,000. Six-sided, more coffin-shaped plates; sometimes rosette aggregates of plates on edge, resembling needles.
	Platinic chloride and sodium iodide	1:100 in H_2O. Add 1 drop H_2PtCl_6 soln, stir, and add small drop NaI soln without stirring. Small black rectangular prisms and slender black rods.
Cinchonidine (*50*)	Sodium benzoate	Rosettes and sheaves of needles spreading to large size.
	Platinic chloride	Rosettes of transparent plates.
	Sodium carbonate	Spherical crystals, but not needles as in cinchonine.
Cinchonine (*50*)	Sodium carbonate	Dark rosettes, composed of radiating needles, form immediately.
	Disodium phosphate	Similar to crystals formed by Na_2CO_3, but more burr-shaped.
Cocaine (*51*)	Platinic chloride	Delicate, feathery crystals, later becoming heavier in structure.
Codeine (*51*)	Potassium cadmium iodide	Silvery, circular masses, crystg into dark rosettes of irregular outline.
	Iodine potassium iodide	Heavy, red-brown ppt; crystallizes very slowly in yellow blades extending in branches (never red).
Cotarnine (*47*)	Platinic chloride	1:200. Hair-like crystals, yellow and curving.
	Mercuric chloride	Colorless, long, branching needles.
	Potassium ferrocyanide	Acidify with 1 drop 5% HCl; globules that develop into dense, burr-shaped crystals; also amber-brown plates.
Dihydromorphinone (*52*)	Sodium nitroprusside	To minute amt (<1 mg) in 2 drops H_2O add minute fragment of reagent. Elongated 6-sided prisms; also in aggregates.
Ephedrine (*53*)	Bismuth iodide in dild sulfuric acid	1:200. Long, brownish orange, radiating and interlacing needles and branching rods.
Ethylhydrocupreine (*54*)	Ammonium thiocyanate	1:100 in 0.1*N* HCl. Long, straight needles.
Ethylmorphine (*46*)	Iodine potassium iodide	1:200. Groups of yellow needles, branching later.
	Mercuric chloride	Transparent plates, often with notched ends; singly and in groups. Stir to start crystn.
Heroin (*55*) (Diacetyl-morphine)	Platinic chloride	Spherical clusters of golden yellow needles form slowly around nucleus; cluster disintegrates on standing.
Homatropine (*56*)	Gold chloride	1:200. Green-gold blades, often with pointed ends and united in pairs; surfaces appear etched on long standing.
Hydrastine (*44*)	1 drop 5% HCl and 1 drop potassium ferrocyanide	1:100. Spheres of radiating crystals. Shake slide to start crystn. Avoid excess reagent.

(*Continued*)

Table 36:03 Characteristics of Microchemical Tests for Alkaloids and Related Amines—*Continued*

Alkaloid	Reagent	Description of Crystals
Hydrastinine (*46*)	Potassium permanganate	1:500. Immediate red plates, often with serrated edges. In concd soln, great number of large red or brown plates with deeply cut edges.
	Mercuric chloride	1:500. Transparent needles forming branches rapidly in neut. and acidified solns.
	1 drop 5% HCl and 1 drop potassium ferrocyanide	1:200. Yellow rhombic plates and tree-like crystals.
Hyoscyamine (*56*)	Gold chloride	Thin, transparent, nearly colorless irregular plates, often curved. Crystals form slowly in 1:100 to 1:200 soln. Shaking slide aids crystn.
Morphine (*51*)	Potassium cadmium iodide	Silvery, gelatinous ppt, crystg in dense masses of fine needles.
	Iodine potassium iodide	Small drop of reagent produces heavy, red-brown ppt, slowly crystg in shining, red, overlapping plates extending in branches.
Narceine (*47*)	Iodine potassium iodide or zinc potassium iodide	1:400. Blue, radiating needles, sometimes with yellow dichroism.
	Platinic chloride	Beautiful feathery rosettes develop in all solns.
Nicotine (*57*)	Mercuric chloride	Radiating, transparent blades form in presence of slight excess of H_2SO_4; feather-like blades form in presence of HCl.
	Mercuric chloride-sodium chloride	Radiating, transparent blades.
Noscapine (*47*) (l-Narcotine)	Potassium hydroxide or ammonium hydroxide	1:200. White, amorphous ppt that crystallizes slowly; dense rosettes of needles.
Papaverine (*58*)	Zinc chloride	Thin, rectangular plates in excess HCl.
Physostigmine (*59*)	Lead iodide	1:100. Radiating, serrated plates.
	Gold bromide in HCl	1 mg in 1 drop H_2O. Brown, dendritic aggregates.
Pilocarpine (*45*)	Platinic chloride	Crystals form slowly; layers of thin, yellow, triangular plates of delicate structure.
Procaine (*58*)	Platinic chloride	Spherical crystals of radiating branches.
	Gold chloride and HCl	Irregular, radiating branches.
Quinidine (*50*)	Potassium iodide	Small, triangular crystals in great numbers; best in 1:1000 diln; sol. in excess reagent.
Quinine (*50*)	Disodium phosphate	Silvery, sheaf-like crystals.
Racephedrine (*60*) (*dl*-Ephedrine)	Bismuth iodide in dild sulfuric acid	1:200. Large orange plates and red prisms and grains.
Scopolamine (*56*) (Hyoscine)	Gold chloride	Clusters of pale yellow, transparent blades, with coarse, saw-toothed edges form immediately on shaking slide. Crystals grow to large size in 1:200 soln.
Sparteine (*57*)	Gold chloride	Large numbers of blade-like crystals varying in size according to concn.
Strychnine (*61*)	Platinic chloride	Crystals form immediately in clusters and singly in small, wedge-shaped needles that move about field.
	Potassium cadmium iodide	Silvery masses, slowly forming rosettes.
Yohimbine (*42*)	Sodium carbonate	In 1:1000 soln heated to 50°. Fine needles in sheaf-like bundles and rosettes.

However, I reaction crystals are easily distinguished by their color, often coupled with strong dichroism. Det. birefringence with polarizing microscope. Cover glass is usually not needed but may be used for observation at high magnification and when slide stands >1 hr; on standing, KI may crystallize as sq, colorless, isotropic crystals.

Note crystals formed and compare characteristics with descriptions, Tables **36:04** and **36:06**.

For Sympathomimetics (60)—Official Final Action

36.100 ***Reagents***

(**a**) *Bismuth iodide in diluted sulfuric acid soln.*— See **36.095(e)**.

(**b**) *Gold chloride in diluted phosphoric acid soln.*— Dissolve 1 g $HAuCl_4.3H_2O$ in 20 mL H_3PO_4 (1+2).

(**c**) *Platinic chloride in diluted phosphoric acid soln.*—Dissolve 1 g $H_2PtCl_6.6H_2O$ in 20 mL H_3PO_4 (1+3).

(**d**) *Sodium tetraphenylboron soln.*—Aq. soln (1+20).

36.101 ***Identification***

(**a**) *Direct test.*—Add drop of reagent to little of powd solid or crushed tablet and spread out on slide with little stirring. Do not stir to homogeneity as local concns and dilns will assist crystn. Let stand to evap. to higher acid concn if necessary for crystal formation.

(**b**) *Volatility test.*—Place small amt of substance or crushed tablet in depression of cavity slide, add drop 5% NaOH soln, and stir briefly. Place very small drop of reagent on thin slide, invert over cavity slide, and let stand. As crystals appear, examine with inverted slide in place. After observing crystals or after ≥1 hr exposure, if only few or no crystals form, reinvert thin slide with hanging drop, and let stand for gradual evapn of H_2O from reagent drop. Examine for crystals. Compare with descriptions, Table **36:05**.

For Synthetics—Official Final Action

(*See* Table **36.06**.)

Table 36:04 Characteristics of Microchemical Tests for Barbiturates

Barbiturate	Crystal Form	Dichroism or Pleochroism	Remarks
Allylbarbital (5-Allyl-5-isobutylbarbituric acid) "Itobarbital"	Immediate crystn in rods, splinters, and leaflike crystals with pointed ends.	Red to black dichroism.	Free acid may crystallize out.
5-Allyl-5-(2-cyclopenten-1-yl) barbituric acid	Gradual crystn in dichroic straight-edged blades, brown-yellow to brown-orange.	—	Very bright birefringence; free acid as colorless rods, splinters, needles.
Amobarbital (5-Ethyl-5-isoamylbarbituric acid)	Dil. soln: fairly large brown blades. Concd soln: multitudes of little pale-colored flakes.	—	Examine at 200×; sensitive test.
Aprobarbital (5-Allyl-5-isopropylbarbituric acid)	Light orange-brown rod-blades, birefringent.	Yellow to brown-orange dichroism.	—
Barbital (5,5-Diethylbarbituric acid)	Form very soon; fairly large, rectangular or splinter blades.	Extreme pleochroism by transmitted polarized light.	Beetle-green iridescence by reflected light.
* Bemegride (4-Ethyl-4-methyl-2,6-piperidinedione)	Small light-colored dichroic rods or blades and flakes or plates, orangish brown to colorless or yellowish.	—	Birefringence is bright and plates that are sq or nearly so extinguish diagonally.
Butabarbital Sodium (Sodium 5-sec-butyl-5-ethylbarbiturate)	Dil. soln: red-brown irregular plates. Concd soln: brown blades in clusters.	Slightly dichroic; dichroism yellow to red-brown.	Free acid: colorless blades.
Butethal (5-Butyl-5-ethylbarbituric acid)	Small plate crystals basically rhomboids. "Propeller-type" of elongate pointed blades.	Strong dichroism, light yellow to black.	—
Cyclobarbital (5-(1-Cyclohexenyl)-5-ethylbarbituric acid)	Dil. soln: rosettes of little pointed crystals; larger are red-brown plates.	Red-brown plates of variable dichroism frequently four-bladed.	Sensitive test.
Diallyl barbituric acid (5,5-Diallylbarbituric acid)	Crystallizes quickly in branching twigs, splinters, and blades.	Extreme black to "white" dichroism by polarized light.	Golden-beetle iridescence by reflected light.
Heptabarbital (5-(1-Cyclohepten-1-yl)-5-ethylbarbituric acid)	Little red-brown plates in great numbers, often 4-parted; good birefringence.	—	Sensitive.
Hexobarbital Sodium (Sodium 5-(1-cyclohexen-1-yl)-1,5-dimethylbarbiturate	Dichroic blades and broad splinters in groups, varying to curving threads and needles in rosettes.	Very strong dichroism; black to light brownish yellow.	Sensitive for I reaction crystals as well as for free acid.
Metharbital (5,5-Diethyl-1-methylbarbituric acid)	Dark needles, small to large, and splintery narrow blades.	Dichroism black to brown.	Good birefringence with crossed nicols.
5-Methyl-5-phenylbarbituric acid	Red-brown irregular platy forms appear after free acid is pptd.	Gradually strongly dichroic rods or blades.	Test fairly sensitive for dil. soln.
Phenobarbital (5-Ethyl-5-phenylbarbituric acid)	Soon crystallizes in little dark grains; also a few larger red blades and dark splinter-rods in clusters.	—	Free acid may also crystallize out.
Probarbital (5-Ethyl-5-isopropylbarbituric acid)	Scattered iodine-reaction crystals form in various jagged shapes, color dark brown to black dichroism, or red-black with but little dichroism.		Free acid thrown out, forming long rods with pointed ends.
Secobarbital (5-Allyl-5-(1-methylbutyl)barbituric acid)	Crystallizes in plates or elongate and rectangular but mostly distorted into any shape after 1 hr.	Light yellow to orange or red dichroism by polarized light.	Distinctly birefringent.
Sodium Pentobarbital (Sodium 5-ethyl-5-(1-methylbutyl) barbiturate)	Crystallizes quickly in great numbers of small red-brown plates.	Minute light-colored flakes exhibit dichroism; dark brown or black to yellow.	—
Talbutal (5-Allyl-5-sec-butylbarbituric acid)	Amorphous ppt crystallizes in large needles and dichroic blades, lighter to deeper brown, in dendrites; then gray-black curled sheaves of threads.	—	Excellent test. Both types of crystals have good birefringence
Vinbarbital (5-Ethyl-5-(1-methyl-1-butenyl) barbituric acid)	Multitudes of small dark crystals, tiny grains and rods with dichroism brown to black. In quite dil. soln possible to get good small crystals, little dark rods with dichroism red to black, and small plates tending to be sq, generally appearing red but with same red to black dichroism, and with sq extinction (not diagonal).		Very sensitive.

* This drug has barbiturate-type formula (although there is only one N) but is central nervous stimulant instead of depressant.

36.102 ***Reagents***

(**a**) *Acetic acid.*—Dil. 6 mL HOAc to 100 mL with H_2O.

(**b**) *Ammoniacal nickel acetate soln.*—Mix 1 vol. 5% $Ni(OAc)_2.4H_2O$ soln with 1 vol. NH_4OH (2+3). Use clear supernate.

(**c**) *Ammoniacal silver nitrate soln.—See* **36.095(a)**.

(**d**) *Ammonium thiocyanate soln.—See* **36.095(c)**.

(**e**) *Barium hydroxide soln.*—Satd aq. soln.

(**f**) *Benzaldehyde.*—USP quality.

(**g**) *Bismuth iodide soln.—See* **36.095(d)**.

(**h**) *Bromide-bromate soln.*—Dissolve 0.3 g $KBrO_3$ and 1.2 g KBr in H_2O, and dil. to 100 mL.

(**i**) *Glycerol-alcohol mixture.*—(1+1).

(**j**) *Gold bromide in hydrochloric acid soln.—See* **36.095(g)**.

(**k**) *Gold chloride soln.—See* **36.095(h)**.

(**l**) *Iodine-potassium iodide soln.—See* **36.095(j)**.

(**m**) *Lead acetate soln.*—Dissolve 5 g $Pb(OAc)_2.3H_2O$ in H_2O and dil. to 100 mL.

(**n**) *Lead triethanolamine soln.*—Add 1 mL triethanolamine (tech. 90% is satisfactory) to soln of 1 g $Pb(OAc)_2.3H_2O$ in 20 mL H_2O. Slight turbidity does not interfere.

(**o**) *Magnesia mixture.*—Dissolve 5.5 g $MgCl_2.6H_2O$ and 14.0 g NH_4Cl in H_2O. Add 13.05 mL NH_4OH and dil. to 100 mL with H_2O.

(**p**) *Mercuric chloride soln.—See* **36.095(l)**.

(**q**) *Mercurous nitrate soln.*—Dissolve 15 g $HgNO_3.H_2O$ in mixt. of 90 mL H_2O and 10 mL HNO_3 (1+9). Store in dark, amber bottle contg small globule of Hg.

(**r**) *Nitric acid.*—(1+1).

Table 36:05 Characteristics of Microchemical Tests for Sympathomimetics

Sympathomimetic	Reagent	Test	Description of Crystals
		Volatile Substances	
dl-Amphetamine	Gold chloride in dild phosphoric acid	direct or volatility	Very irregular plates, with irregular blade-arms especially after evapn; sq if perfect.
	Platinic chloride in dild phosphoric acid	volatility	Irregular blades and needles, very low birefringence; after evapn, characteristic plates with narrow irregular arms of blades.
d-Amphetamine	Gold chloride in dild phosphoric acid	direct or volatility	Long yellow rods and blades; with evapn, some crystals as with *dl* may form.
	Platinic chloride in dild phosphoric acid	volatility	Long needles, often bent, very little birefringence; after some evapn, long rectangular blades. (*l*-Ephedrine in direct test gives similar crystals which are more sol.; it is less volatile and does not normally form crystals in hanging drop.)
Epinephrine	Sodium tetraphenylboron	volatility	$MeNH_2$ liberated; birefringent X's or 4-arm crystals; also thick blades with central rib, pointed ends, pos. elongation.
Isoproterenol	Sodium tetraphenylboron	volatility	Isopropylamine liberated; plates tending to nonregular hexagons; no birefringence where plates lie flat but there are rods which are birefringent.
Methamphetamine and *dl*-Methamphetamine (*d*- and *dl*-Desoxyephedrine)	Gold chloride in dild phosphoric acid	direct or volatility	Long blades and jointed crystals, fairly high birefringence.
	Platinic chloride in dild phosphoric acid	volatility	Grains with sharp edges which aggregate in chains and short prisms. Birefringent.
dl-Methamphetamine (*dl*-Desoxyephedrine)	Bismuth iodide in dild sulfuric acid	volatility	Drops, crystg in orange-red prisms with conspicuously slanting ends; inclined extinction ca 20°; also "mossy" formation of grains and some large deep red grains.
	Freshly prepd gold chloride in dild phosphoric acid	volatility	Right-angled crossed blades with serrated and/or lobed edges.
	Aged (≥4 months) gold chloride in dild phosphoric acid	volatility	X blade formation with highly birefringent ribs visible in thin crystals or thickened X blades. Right-angled crossed blades are not present.
Methamphetamine (*d*-Desoxyephedrine)	Bismuth iodide in dild sulfuric acid	volatility	Drops, long orange splinters, blades, needles; also deep red angular grains (red prisms only after evapn).
	Freshly prepd gold chloride in dild phosphoric acid	volatility	Numerous multiple "V"-shaped blades, few single "V"-shaped blades.
	Aged (≥4 months) gold chloride in dild phosphoric acid	volatility	Numerous single "V"-shaped blades.
		Slightly Volatile Substances	
dl-Ephedrine (racephedrine)	Gold chloride in dild phosphoric acid	direct or volatility	Irregular plates based on the sq, growing along diagonals in 4 arms; some birefringent, some not.
	Bismuth iodide in dild sulfuric acid	volatility	Orange rods or sticks, short and stubby, some plates; more irregular plates on evapn.
l-Ephedrine	Gold chloride in dild phosphoric acid	direct or volatility	Long needles or splinters and long jointed forms; strong birefringence.
	Bismuth iodide in dild sulfuric acid	volatility	Long brownish orange needles, often branching or in sheaves; also, especially with evapn, orange irregular blades.
Pseudoephedrine	Gold chloride in dild phosphoric acid	direct or volatility (2 hr)	Thin branching sticks, many like combs; some broaden to blades or spear-head plates; very high birefringence.

(Continued)

Table 36:05 Characteristics of Microchemical Tests for Sympathomimetics—*Continued*

Sympathomimetic	Reagent	Test	Description of Crystals
Phenylpropanolamine	Gold chloride in dild phosphoric acid	direct	Plates and blades of extremely high birefringence, elongate hexagonal or diamonds, very bright colors. Branch into 4 or 6 irregular arms.
		volatility (2 hr)	After definite drying, pyramidal grains to blades and plates with irregular arms, very birefringent.
Phenmetrazine	Gold chloride in dild phosphoric acid	direct or volatility	Rectangular plates joined in jagged arms of strongly birefringent crystals, often in X forms, very characteristic.
	Bismuth iodide in dild sulfuric acid	volatility	Orange-red blades, usually pointed ends, often in rosettes; also with needles in branching aggregates; also red prisms.

(**s**) *Phosphotungstic acid soln.*—Dissolve 5 g $P_2O_5.24WO_3.xH_2O$ in 100 mL H_2O.

(**t**) *Picric acid.*—Crystals.

(**u**) *Picrolonic acid soln.*—Dissolve 250 mg 1-(*p*-nitrophenyl)-3-methyl-4-nitropyrazolone in 25 mL alcohol.

(**v**) *Platinic chloride soln.—See* **36.095(n)**.

(**w**) *Potassium cadmium iodide soln.—See* **36.095(o)**.

(**x**) *Potassium ferrocyanide soln.—See* **36.095(p)**.

(**y**) *Silicotungstic acid soln.*—Dissolve 5 g $4H_2O.SiO_2.12WO_3.22H_2O$ in 100 mL ca 6*N* H_2SO_4.

(**z**) *Silver nitrate soln.*—Dissolve 1 g $AgNO_3$ in 20 mL H_2O.

(**aa**) *Sodium nitrite soln.*—Dissolve 10 g $NaNO_2$ in H_2O and dil. to 100 mL.

(**bb**) *Zinc pyridine soln.*—Add 1 mL pyridine to soln of 1 g $Zn(OAc)_2.2H_2O$ in 20 mL H_2O.

Table 36:06 Characteristics of Microchemical Tests for Synthetics

Synthetic	Solvent	Concentration of Synthetic	Reagent	Description of Tests and Crystals
Acetanilid (*63*)	HCl (1+3)	1:100	Phosphotungstic acid	Rosettes of prisms.
	HCl (1+3)	1:100	Bromide-bromate soln	Small prisms.
Aminopyrine (*65*)	H_2O	1:100	Mercuric chloride	Long, slender, radiating crystals, often curved.
			Potassium cadmium iodide	Groups of spiny branches.
Amobarbital (*54*)	NH_4OH (1+9)	1:50	Acetic acid	Long, branching needles; some hexagonal plates in groups.
	NH_4OH (1+9)	1:25	Acetic acid	Groups of rectangular plates.
Antipyrine (*66*)	H_2O	1:100	Potassium ferrocyanide	Add 1 drop HCl (1+39). Acicular and prismatic crystals form.
Aspirin (Acetylsalicylic acid) (*64*)	2% triethanolamine	1:50	Silver nitrate	Fine, curling, hair-like crystals form first near edge of drop.
Barbital (*54*)	—	Approx. 1 mg powder	Ammoniacal silver nitrate	Stir to aid soln and crystn. Very small, twined crystals and larger tufts.
	NH_4OH (1+9)	1:50	Acetic acid	Dark burrs (stirring hastens crystn).
Benzocaine (Ethyl aminobenzoate) (*67*)	0.1*N* HCl	1:100	Potassium ferrocyanide	Colorless, irregular plates and rods.
Benzoic acid (*64*)	—	Dry powder	Lead triethanolamine	Stir small amt of synthetic into 1 drop reagent. Stir thoroly to induce crystn. 4-sided plates, singly and in groups.
	—	Dry powder	Zinc pyridine	Stir small amt of synthetic into 1 drop reagent. Stir thoroly to induce crystn. Hexagonal crystals.
	2% triethanolamine	1:100 to 1:200	Silver nitrate	Rods or curving blades with irregular ends.
Cinchophen (*67*)	0.1*N* NaOH. Add H_2O and make slightly acid with HCl	1:1000	Gold chloride	Dark clusters of needles. Few short, rhombic crystals.
Diallybarbituric acid (*68*)	—	Dry powder	Lead triethanolamine	Stir small amt of synthetic into 1 drop reagent. Rods singly and in clusters.
	—	Dry powder	Barium hydroxide	Stir small amt of synthetic into 1 drop reagent. Rods singly and in groups.
Dinitrophenol (*65*)	Small amt of 0.1*N* NaOH	1:100	HCl	Plates with 4 branches. In more dil. soln, single rectangular plates.
Diphenhydramine hydrochloride (*69*)	Glycerol-alcohol (1+1) or H_2O	Approx. 0.2 mg powder or tablet material or 1:100	Platinic chloride	Aggregates of platy crystals form readily in glycerol-alcohol, gradually in H_2O. Plates with jagged edges, tendency to twin, forming X-shaped aggregates, hour-glass forms, and dendritic structures. First order gray polarization colors; symmetrical or parallel extinction. Plates show pos. elongation.
Hydrochlorothiazide (71)	5% NaOH	—	Iodine-potassium iodide, **36.098**	Burrs, with iodine-colored centers and highly birefringent peripheral blades or dichroic rods, iodine-colored to colorless[a]

(Continued)

Table 36:06 Characteristics of Microchemical Tests for Synthetics—*Continued*

Synthetic	Solvent	Concentration of Synthetic	Reagent	Description of Tests and Crystals
8-Hydroxyquinoline sulfate (*67*)	Dissolve salt in H_2O. Dissolve free base in HCl (1+3), avoiding excess	1:500	Magnesia mixt.	Small, elliptical grains. Few burr-shaped crystals on standing.
Mandelic acid (*68*)	H_2O	1:100	Lead acetate	Rosettes of thin, curving plates.
	H_2O	1:100	Mercurous nitrate	Burr-shaped groups of needles.
Methenamine (*66*)	H_2O	1:500	Silicotungstic acid	Thin, transparent, rectangular crystals.
Neocinchophen (*63*)	HCl (1+3)	Satd soln	Ammonium thiocyanate	Rosettes of needles. (Gentle agitation by tipping slide back and forth hastens crystn.)
	HCl (1+3)	Satd soln	Platinic chloride	Needles in clusters.
Pentylenetetrazol (*70*)	H_2O	—	Mercuric chloride (1:10)	Rods, many almost needle-like; frequency in groups; also in radiating aggregates.
	H_2O	1:100	Silicotungstic acid	Amorphous, changes to elongated prisms; also long needles.
Phenacetin (Acetophenetidin (*63*)	—	Approx. 1 mg powd material	HNO_3	Add 1 drop HNO_3, let stand few sec, then add 1 drop H_2O. Bright yellow, curving, branched crystals.
	HCl (1+3)	Satd soln	Iodine-potassium iodide	Large, irregular plates.
Phenazopyridine.HCl (*67*)	Dissolve salt in H_2O. Dissolve free base in HCl (1+3), avoiding excess	1:1000	Ammonium thiocyanate	Small, red-brown, dense sheaves.
Phenobarbital (*54*)	—	Approx. 1 mg powder	Ammoniacal nickel acetate	Stir to aid soln and crystn. Single rectangular crystals.
Pyrilamine maleate (*69*)	Glycerol-alcohol (1+1) or H_2O	1:1000 or ca 0.1 mg powder	Platinic chloride	Needles in rosette aggregates, sheaves, and singly. Needles show second order blue and green, and first order red and yellow polarization colors; parallel extinction and neg. elongation.
Salicylic acid (*64*)	HCl (1+3)	Dry powder	Bromide-bromate soln	Stir few crystals into 1 drop of the HCl. Add 1 drop reagent. Fine needles appear to grow from the crystals of salicylic acid.
	—	Dry powder	Lead triethanolamine	Stir few crystals into 1 drop reagent. Rods or needles grow from the crystals of salicylic acid.
	2% triethanolamine	1:100 to 1:200	Silver nitrate	Small, irregular plates; few short rods.
Sulfadiazine (*49*)	H_2O	—	Gold bromide in HCl	Red, circular masses composed of fine needles.
Sulfanilamide (*68*)	—	Dry powder	Benzaldehyde	Thoroly stir small amt into 1 drop reagent. 4-sided plates.
	0.1*N* HCl	Satd soln	Sodium nitrite	Yellow needles.
Sulfapyridine (*52*)	Acetone + H_2O	—	Gold chloride	Yellow rods or blades; also X-shaped aggregates.
Sodium sulfapyridine monohydrate (*52*)	H_2O	1:100	Gold chloride	Yellow rods in X-shaped aggregates.
Sulfathiazole (*70*)	50% alcohol	—	Picric acid	Long, fine, yellow needles, many curved, occur in dense rosettes; also short, stout rods in groups or singly.
	50% alcohol (or no solv.)	—	Picrolonic acid	Distinct rosettes of very fine needles; also single needles.
Triethanolamine (*66*)	H_2O	1:100	Bismuth iodide	Oily globules changing to large, red, hexagonal plates and prismatic crystals.
Tripelennamine hydrochloride (*69*)	Glycerol-alcohol (1+1) or H_2O	1:1000 or ca 0.1 mg powder or tablet material	Platinic chloride	Small needles and bladed crystals in dense rosette aggregates and singly. Needles show first order white and yellow polarization colors, parallel extinction, and pos. elongation.

[a] Official First Action.

For Xanthine Group Alkaloids (60)
Official First Action

36.103 ***Reagents***

(**a**) *Bismuth iodide soln.*—*See* **36.095(d)**(*2*).

(**b**) *Gold bromide in dilute hydrochloric acid.*—Dissolve 1 g $HAuCl_4.3H_2O$ in 1.5 mL 40% HBr and add HCl (1+3) to make 45 mL.

(**c**) *Iodine-potassium iodide soln* (*5–14*).—Dissolve 5 g I and 14 g KI in H_2O and dil. to 100 mL with H_2O.

36.104 ***General Test***

(Murexide reaction)

To small amt of substance in small porcelain crucible add very small crystal $KClO_3$ and 1 drop HCl (1+1). Set on hot plate at ca 100°, or hot enough to boil off H_2O in short time. Soon after drying, residue becomes orange to red. Add 1 drop NH_4OH. Purple color is produced in presence of caffeine, theobromine, theophylline, and related xanthine derivatives.

36.105 ***Identification***

(**a**) *Bismuth iodide soln.*—Add 1 drop reagent to little dry material on slide and cover.

(**b**) *Gold bromide in dilute hydrochloric acid.*—Place 1 drop reagent beside very small amt of dry substance on slide and apply cover glass so that reagent flows over substance.

(**c**) *Iodine-potassium iodide soln* (*5–14*).—In depression of cavity slide dissolve little of substance in small drop 1% NaOH soln and stir in excess $NaHCO_3$ (some undissolved). Add large drop reagent and stir slightly. Add several crystals KCl. Examine center and edge as soln evaps.

See Table **36:07**.

Optical-Crystallographic Examination of Crystalline Substances (*72*)—Official Final Action

(General knowledge of microscopy and crystallography is necessary for application of this technic. Some of std works on this subject are listed in Selected References (*72*). Optical-crystallographic properties of antihistamines, alkaloids, antibiotics, barbiturates, hallucinogens, steroids, sulfonamides, sympathomimetic amines and tranquilizers are given in Tables **52.024** and **52.025**.)

36.106 ***Apparatus***

(**a**) *Polarizing microscope.*—Fitted with polarizing prisms below and above rotating, graduated circular stage and with accessories (Bertrand lens or pinhole eyepiece, first order red or quartz wedge compensators) for observation of interference figures, optic sign, and sign of elongation.

(**b**) *Refractometer.*—For measuring refractive indices of liqs at 20° or 25° from 1.300 to 1.840 with precision of ±0.0005.

36.107 ***Reagents***

Immersion media.—Ideally immersion media for refractive index detn should have same color and intensity of color as substance being examined and be chemically stable. Refractive indices should not vary perceptibly with ordinary changes of temp. with exception of special liqs used in index-variation methods. Permanent set of liqs covering range 1.430–1.790 in 0.005 intervals made with following mixts is useful for both inorg. and org. substances:

Mixture	n_D *(20°)*
Kerosene and mineral oil	1.435–1.480
Mineral oil and α-monochloronaphthalene	1.485–1.640
α-Monochloronaphthalene and methylene iodide	1.645–1.740
Methylene iodide and sulfur	1.740–1.790

Substances sol. in these liqs require prepg special set of liqs.

36.108 ***Determinations***

Refractive indices.—Det. refractive indices by mounting cryst. material in suitable immersion liqs and observing Becke line. Successively suspend crystals or crystal fragments of substance in immersion liqs of known refractive indices. Greater the difference between refractive indices of crystal and liq., the more prominently one stands out in bold relief from other. By repeatedly mounting such crystals in oils of successively lower or higher index, ultimately zone of contact of crystal and liq. becomes practically invisible, demonstrating that refractive indices of liq. and solid have been matched.

In case of substances crystg in isometric (cubic) system, there is only 1 refractive index, designated by n. Such substances are not doubly refractive when examined with crossed nicols. Substances crystg in other systems, hexagonal, tetragonal, monoclinic, triclinic, and orthorhombic, in ideal cases, have >1 measurable refractive index. With uniaxial substances such as those crystg in hexagonal and tetragonal systems, 2 significant indices can be detd, designated as n_ϵ and n_ω. Substances crystg in monoclinic, triclinic, and orthorhombic systems, in ideal cases, have 3 refractive indices, designated as n_α, n_β, and n_γ.

Table 36:07 Characteristics of Microchemical Tests for Xanthine Alkaloids

Alkaloid	Reagent	Description of Crystals
Caffeine	Gold bromide in dil. HCl	Outer part: brownish needles with bright white birefringence. Inner part: small rods to sticks, little grains and plates with weak yellow birefringence.
	Bismuth iodide	Small brownish orange rods or blades growing from sample or nearby in rosettes; also some orange grains.
	Iodine-potassium iodide (5–14)	Grains, dark red to black, sometimes yellow or orange-brown; generally sq or cubical; birefringent with fairly strong light; some irregular dichroic blades.
Dyphylline	Gold bromide in dil. HCl	Needles, scattered and in rosettes; fairly bright birefringence.
	Bismuth iodide	Very small grains, flakes, blades in multitudes, birefringent.
	Iodine-potassium iodide (5–14)	Fuzzy brown dense rosettes thruout drop, birefringent around rims; excess reagent must be used; 5 min required to form crystals.
Theobromine	Gold bromide in dil. HCl	Grains or plates in dense groups; bright birefringence at edge of cluster.
	Bismuth iodide	Brown needles in rosettes.
	Iodine-potassium iodide (5–14)	Orange-brown chips; also rectangular plates with opposite sides incised; smaller crystals: grains, often lens shaped or diamonds; birefringent, somewhat dichroic.
Theophylline	Gold bromide in dil. HCl	Long needles in sheaves; fairly bright birefringence.
	Bismuth iodide	Grains and short prisms, often rectangular; brightly birefringent.
	Iodine-potassium iodide (5–14)	Black needles in rosettes around edge; birefringent; when larger, blades or rods, dichroic black vertically to yellow horizontally.

Extinction and extinction angle of anisotropic substances.—Anisotropic crystals, when rotated through 360° on stage, become dark 4 times. Positions of darkness are known as extinction positions and correspond to positions in which vibrations of birefringent rays produced by crystal are mutually parallel to vibration directions of polarizer and analyzer indicated by cross hairs in eyepiece. If crystal extinguishes when crystal edge or face is parallel to one of cross hairs, extinction is *parallel*. If bisector of silhouette angle is parallel to one of cross hairs, extinction is *symmetrical*. Crystals showing extinction differing from these 2 have *inclined* extinction. Measure extinction angles on those crystals showing inclined extinction by rotating crystal so that crystal edge or face is parallel to 1 of cross hairs. Rotate stage until crystal extinguishes. Read on stage vernier extinction angle between face or edge at extinction and nearest cross hair. Express extinction angles with relationship to principal vibration directions of light and crystallographic axes.

Elongation.—Many crystals are frequently elongated in 1 direction. Relationship between direction of elongation and vibration directions of slow and fast rays of anisotropic crystal is sometimes of determinative value. If substance is length slow, *i.e.,* slow ray or higher refractive index is parallel to direction of elongation, sign of elongation is pos.; if substance is length fast, sign is neg.

Sign of elongation (+ or −) is detd with gypsum plate and crossed nicols. A long and narrow crystal, showing very little color with crossed nicols, is so oriented that its long dimension is parallel to direction "z" of plate (slow ray) which is inserted in slit of microscope tube. (Direction "z" is indicated by arrow on plate.) If crystal appears blue or other color of higher order than red-violet due to plate, elongation is +; if crystal appears yellow, white, or gray, *i.e.,* of lower order color than red-violet field, elongation is −.

Optic character and optic sign.—Det. optic character (uniaxial or biaxial) and optic sign (+ or −), using first order red or quartz wedge compensators in conjunction with interference figures. Obtain interference figures from conoscopic images of crystals suitably oriented. In absence of interference figures, det. these properties from relationship of principal refractive indices. When $(n_\beta - n_\alpha)$ is $<(n_\gamma - n_\beta)$, optic sign is +. When $(n_\beta - n_\alpha)$ is $>(n_\gamma - n_\beta)$, optic sign is −.

Optic axial angle (2V).—Calc. axial angle (2V) from values of 3 refractive indices (here designated α, β, and γ) according to formulas:

$$\text{Cos}^2\, V_\alpha = \frac{\gamma^2(\beta^2 - \alpha^2)}{\beta^2(\gamma^2 - \alpha^2)} \text{ (for − optic sign), or}$$

$$\text{Cos}^2\, V_\gamma = \frac{\alpha^2(\gamma^2 - \beta^2)}{\beta^2(\gamma^2 - \alpha^2)} \text{ (for + optic sign),}$$

where $2V_\alpha$ is axial angle about α, and $2V_\gamma$ is axial angle about γ. Alternatively, est. approx. value of 2V from curvature of isogyre referring to diagrams of substances with known angles. Angle ranges from small (0–25°, sharply curved) to medium (26–60°, moderately curved) to large (61–90°, nearly straight isogyre).

SELECTED REFERENCES

(*1*) JAOAC **10,** 99(1927).
(*2*) JAOAC **25,** 839(1942).
(*3*) JAOAC **56,** 684(1973).
(*4*) JAOAC **11,** 360(1928); **12,** 288(1929); **13,** 326(1930); **16,** 348(1933); **17,** 440(1934); **18,** 532(1935).
(*5*) JAOAC **36,** 734(1953).
(*6*) JAOAC **45,** 616(1962); **46,** 652(1963).
(*7*) JAOAC **19,** 535(1936); **21,** 557(1938); **22,** 730(1939).
(*8*) JAOAC **50,** 669(1967).
(*9*) JAOAC **12,** 264(1929); **14,** 360(1931); **22,** 761(1939).
(*10*) JAOAC **17,** 451(1934); **18,** 519(1935).
(*11*) JAOAC **32,** 549(1949).
(*12*) JAOAC **14,** 370(1931).
(*13*) JAOAC **15,** 434(1932).
(*14*) JAOAC **15,** 441(1932).
(*15*) JAOAC **10,** 343(1927).
(*16*) JAOAC **11,** 326(1928).
(*17*) JAOAC **60,** 1015(1977).
(*18*) JAOAC **9,** 286(1926).
(*19*) JAOAC **15,** 422(1932).
(*20*) JAOAC **55,** 155(1972).
(*21*) JAOAC **49,** 287(1966); **50,** 663, 787(1967); **51,** 275(1968).
(*22*) JAOAC **15,** 456, 461(1932); **16,** 379(1933); **17,** 425(1934).
(*23*) JAOAC **60,** 929(1977).
(*24*) JAOAC **25,** 441(1942); **27,** 88(1944); **32,** 114, 558(1949).
(*25*) JAOAC **21,** 571(1938).
(*26*) JAOAC **24,** 842(1941); **25,** 847(1942).
(*27*) JAOAC **18,** 525(1938); **19,** 516(1936); **20,** 555(1937); **21,** 529(1938); **22,** 712(1939).
(*28*) JAOAC **15,** 419(1932); **32,** 555(1949).
(*29*) JAOAC **24,** 833(1941).
(*30*) JAOAC **59,** 1156(1976).
(*31*) JAOAC **61,** 968(1978).
(*32*) JAOAC **40,** 819(1957).
(*33*) JAOAC **17,** 75, 432(1934).
(*34*) JAOAC **14,** 312(1931).
(*35*) JAOAC **10,** 367(1927); **11,** 343(1928); **12,** 280(1929).
(*36*) JAOAC **12,** 280(1929).
(*37*) JAOAC **18,** 520(1935).
(*38*) JAOAC **22,** 743(1939).
(*39*) JAOAC **38,** 651(1955).
(*40*) JAOAC **8,** 551(1925); **9,** 312(1926); **10,** 374(1927).
(*41*) JAOAC **10,** 383(1927); **11,** 362(1928).
(*42*) JAOAC **15,** 413(1932).
(*43*) JAOAC **23,** 746(1940).
(*44*) JAOAC **20,** 551(1937); **21,** 91(1938).
(*45*) JAOAC **11,** 353(1928); **14,** 316(1931); **18,** 521(1935).
(*46*) JAOAC **21,** 525(1938).
(*47*) JAOAC **22,** 706(1939).
(*48*) JAOAC **13,** 315(1930).
(*49*) JAOAC **26,** 96(1943).
(*50*) JAOAC **12,** 282(1929).
(*51*) JAOAC **10,** 370(1927); **11,** 353(1928).
(*52*) JAOAC **24,** 830(1941).
(*53*) JAOAC **14,** 316(1931).
(*54*) JAOAC **20,** 553(1937).
(*55*) JAOAC **5,** 154(1921); **10,** 370(1927).
(*56*) JAOAC **18,** 521(1935).
(*57*) JAOAC **16,** 345(1933).
(*58*) JAOAC **17,** 433(1934).
(*59*) JAOAC **23,** 746(1940); **24,** 830(1941).
(*60*) JAOAC **43,** 262(1960); **61,** 1435(1978).
(*61*) JAOAC **11,** 353(1928).
(*62*) JAOAC **45,** 600(1962).
(*63*) JAOAC **19,** 514(1936).
(*64*) JAOAC **21,** 528(1938).
(*65*) JAOAC **18,** 523(1935).
(*66*) JAOAC **17,** 435(1934).
(*67*) JAOAC **16,** 391(1933).
(*68*) JAOAC **22,** 709(1939).
(*69*) JAOAC **35,** 576(1952).
(*70*) JAOAC **25,** 830(1942).
(*71*) JAOAC **61,** 1435(1978).
(*72*) Stewart and Stolman, editors, "Toxicology, Mechanisms and Analytical Methods," Vol. 1, pp. 660–713(1960); Hart-

shorne and Stuart, "Crystals and the Polarizing Microscope," 3rd ed., 1960; Chamot and Mason, "Handbook of Chemical Microscopy," Vol. **1**, 1958; NF XIII, First Supplement; Bloss, "Introduction to the Methods of Optical Crystallography," 1961; Wahlstrom, "Optical Crystallography," 1969.

GENERAL REFERENCES

BANES, "Principles of Regulatory Drug Analysis," AOAC, Box 540 Benjamin Franklin Station, Washington, DC 20044 (1966).

BANES, "A Chemist's Guide to Regulatory Drug Analysis," AOAC, Box 540, Benjamin Franklin Station, Washington, DC 20044 (1974).

37. Drugs: Acidic

ACIDS

Benzoic and Salicylic Acids—Official Final Action

37.001 ★ ***Titrimetric Method (1)*** ★

(Applicable to ointments. *Caution: See* **51.011**, **51.039**, **51.040**, **51.054**, and **51.056**.)

Extn of both acids from acid soln and titrn with std alkali. Bromination of salicylic acid with std $KBrO_3$ and calcn of benzoic acid by difference. *See* **37.001**, 12th ed.

Chromatographic Method (2)

37.002 ***Apparatus***

(**a**) *Chromatographic tubes.*—Fuse 6 cm length of 5–6 mm tubing to piece of 25 mm tubing ca 25 cm long (25 × 200 mm test tube may be used). Constrict stem slightly ca 2 cm below seal. Com. tubes with dimensions ±10% are satisfactory. Pack wad of Pyrex glass wool in base as support.

(**b**) *Tamping rod.*—Flatten end of glass rod to circular head with clearance of ca 1 mm in tube (**a**). Or use disk of stainless steel, Al, etc., of diam. ca 1 mm less than id of column, (**a**), attached to 30–45 cm (12–18") rod.

37.003 ***Reagents***

(**a**) *Ferric chloride-urea soln.*—Dissolve, without heating, 18 g reagent grade urea in 2.5 mL 60% $FeCl_3.6H_2O$ (available from MC/B Manufacturing Chemists) and 12.5 mL 0.05*N* HCl. Prep. fresh daily.

(**b**) *Phosphoric acid.*—30%. Dil. 30 mL 85% H_3PO_4 to 85 mL with H_2O.

(**c**) *Sodium bicarbonate.*—1*N*. Dissolve 2.5 g $NaHCO_3$ in 30 mL H_2O. Use only freshly prepd soln.

(**d**) *Diatomaceous earth.*—*See* **36.002**.

(**e**) *Benzoic acid std soln.*—Accurately weigh 40–100 mg benzoic acid (depending on concn benzoic acid in sample), dissolve in $CHCl_3$, and dil. to 100 mL with $CHCl_3$. Shortly before use, transfer 5 mL to 50 mL vol. flask; add 4 drops HCl, 1 mL HOAc, 5 mL ether, and 7 mL MeOH; and dil. to vol. with $CHCl_3$.

(**f**) *Salicylic acid std soln.*—Dissolve 50 mg salicylic acid in $CHCl_3$ and dil. to 100 mL. Transfer 5 mL to 100 mL vol. flask; add 2 drops HCl, 2 mL HOAc, 10 mL MeOH, and 20 mL ether; and dil. to vol. with $CHCl_3$.

37.004 ***Preparation of Sample***

(**a**) *Ointments.*—Dissolve ca 1 g sample, accurately weighed, in $CHCl_3$ and dil. to 100 mL. If necessary, dil. aliquot to prep. final soln contg 0.15–0.25 mg salicylic acid/mL $CHCl_3$.

(**b**) *Liquids.*—Dil. aliquot of liq. contg 150–250 mg salicylic acid to 100 mL with MeOH. Dil. 10 mL methanolic soln to 100 mL with $CHCl_3$.

37.005 ***Preparation of Columns***

Column I.—Lower stage: mix 1 g diat. earth with 0.5 mL 30% H_3PO_4 to uniform fluffy mixt. Transfer to tube and tamp to uniform mass with gentle pressure. *Upper stage:* Similarly mix 5 g diat. earth with 3 mL $FeCl_3$ urea reagent. (Mix thoroly, as nonuniform column may cause difficulty in elution of salicylic acid.) Transfer to tube directly above H_3PO_4 layer. Cover with glass wool.

Column II.—Mix 2 g diat. earth with 1 mL freshly prepd 1*N* $NaHCO_3$ soln.

37.006 ***Determination***

(Use H_2O-satd solvs.)

Mount *Column I* directly above *Column II*. Pipet 10 mL dild sample into small beaker. Pour onto upper column, washing beaker with 10 mL $CHCl_3$ in small portions. Let sample sink into column and wash column with 75 mL $CHCl_3$. If purple salicylic acid band reaches H_3PO_4 layer, repeat with smaller sample. Sep. columns and wash *Column II* with 50 mL ether. Discard wash. Elute *Column I* into 100 mL vol. flask (contg 10 mL MeOH and 2 drops HCl) with 2 mL HOAc in 20 mL ether followed by enough 1% HOAc in $CHCl_3$ to bring to vol. Measure *A* of eluate and salicylic acid std at max., ca 306 nm, and calc. concn salicylic acid.

Elute *Column II* into 50 mL vol. flask (contg 7 mL MeOH and 4 drops HCl) with 0.5 mL HOAc in 5 mL $CHCl_3$ followed by enough 1% HOAc in $CHCl_3$ to bring to vol. Measure *A* of eluate and benzoic acid std at max., ca 275 nm, and calc. concn benzoic acid.

37.007 ★ **Salicylic Acid in Presence of Other Phenols (*3*)—Official Final Action** ★

See **32.184–32.185**, 10th ed. (*Caution: See* **51.011**, **51.040**, and **51.056**.)

Mandelic Acid (*4*)—Official Final Action

37.008 ***Qualitative Tests***

(Applicable to free acid)

See Microchemical Tests, Table **36:06**.

37.009 ***Determination***

(*Caution: See* **51.011**, **51.039**, **51.040**, **51.054**, and **51.056**.)

(**a**) *Tablets.*—Weigh amt of powd sample contg 0.4–0.5 g mandelic acid and transfer to separator contg 10 mL H_2O. Acidify with HCl (1+3) and add 2 mL excess. Ext with six 20 mL portions $CHCl_3$-ether (2+1); wash each portion in second separator with 2 mL H_2O, and pass soln thru cotton plug, previously satd with solv., into 250 mL beaker. Wash outer surface of separator stem with few mL solv. and add to main portion. Test for complete extn with 15 mL addnl solv. and evap. in sep. beaker. Wash any residue thus obtained into beaker contg main ext with few mL solv. Evap. to dryness at $\leqslant 40°$ with aid of air current. Dissolve residue in 25 mL CO_2-free H_2O, **50.033(a)**, and titr. with 0.1*N* NaOH, using phthln. 1 mL 0.1*N* NaOH = 0.01522 g mandelic acid ($C_6H_5CHOHCOOH$); 0.01692 g NH_4 mandelate, 0.01741 g Na mandelate, 0.01712 g Ca mandelate, and 0.01633 g Mg mandelate.

After titrn, mandelic acid may be re-extd and ext used for mp detns or qual. tests.

(**b**) *Liquid preparations.*—Measure 1 mL sample, or aliquot of diln contg 0.4–0.5 g mandelic acid, into separator and acidify with HCl (1+3). Proceed as in (**a**).

★ Surplus method—*see* inside front cover.

ANTIPYRETIC DRUGS

Acetaminophen (5)—Official Final Action

37.010 ***Reagents***

(**a**) *Bicarbonate-carbonate buffer.*—pH 10.1. Weigh 1.0 g $NaHCO_3$ and 4.5 g Na_2CO_3 into 100 mL vol. flask and dil. to vol. with H_2O.

(**b**) *Acidic methanol.*—1.0 mL 0.1*N* HCl/100 mL MeOH. Prep. enough to ensure same MeOH is used thruout for std and sample.

(**c**) *Diatomaceous earth.*—*See* **36.002.**

(**d**) *Acetaminophen std soln.*—0.008 mg/mL. Accurately weigh 40 mg acetaminophen std into 100 mL vol. flask. Dil. to vol. with acidic MeOH and mix well. Transfer 2.0 mL to 100 mL vol. flask and dil. to vol. with acidic MeOH.

37.011 ***Preparation of Sample***

(**a**) *Sirup.*—Transfer 15.0 mL 0.1*N* NaOH to 25 mL vol. flask. Dil. to vol. with acetaminophen sirup, avoiding wetting flask neck above graduation mark while adding sirup, and mix. Transfer 10.0 mL of this diln to 100 mL vol. flask, dil. to vol. with H_2O, and mix.

(**b**) *Tablets.*—Det. av. wt/tablet and pulverize. Accurately weigh portion of powder contg ca 240 mg acetaminophen and transfer to 250 mL vol. flask. Add 2 mL 1.0*N* NaOH and ca 100 mL H_2O. Shake, dil. to vol. with H_2O, and mix.

37.012 ***Preparation of Chromatographic Column***

Pack fine glass wool plug in base of chromatgc tube (25 × 250 mm) with aid of tamping rod ca 45 cm long and having disk with diam. ca 1 mm less than tube. To 3.0 g diat. earth, add 2.0 mL buffer soln and mix until fluffy. Transfer mixt. to column and tamp gently to compress to uniform mass. Transfer 2.0 mL sample soln to 100 mL beaker, add 1 drop HCl, and mix. Add 3.0 g diat. earth, mix thoroly, and transfer to column. Scrub beaker with 1 g diat. earth and 2 drops H_2O. Transfer to column, tamp, and top with fine glass wool pad.

37.013 ***Determination***

(*Caution: See* **51.011**, **51.039**, and **51.054**.)

(Use H_2O-washed solvs thruout.)

Pass 100 mL $CHCl_3$ thru column and discard eluate. Elute acetaminophen with 150 mL ether, collecting eluate in 400 mL beaker. Evap. soln to dryness on steam bath under air stream. Dissolve residue in acidic MeOH, transfer quant. to 50 mL vol. flask, and dil. to vol. with same solv. Transfer 10.0 mL of this soln to 50 mL vol. flask, dil. to vol. with acidic MeOH, and mix. Scan spectra of sample and std solns from 350 to 240 nm in 1 cm cells, using acidic MeOH as blank.

mg Acetaminophen in portion of sirup or tablet taken

$$= 31.25 \times C \times (A/A'),$$

where C = mg/mL std soln, and A and A' refer to sample and std, resp., at max., ca 249 nm.

Acetaminophen and Salicylamide (6)—Official Final Action

(Applicable in presence of antihistamines, barbiturates, caffeine, ascorbic acid, prednisone, and belladonna alkaloids. Aspirin interferes in salicylamide detn.)

37.014 ***Apparatus***

(**a**) *Chromatographic tube.*—Plain, 250 × 25 mm i.d.

(**b**) *Tamping rod.*—*See* **37.002(b)**; use for packing columns.

(**c**) *UV spectrophotometer.*—Preferably recording, with matched 1.0 cm cells.

(**d**) *Infrared spectrophotometer.*—With equipment suitable for prepg KBr disks.

37.015 ***Reagents***

(**a**) *Tripotassium phosphate.*—20%. Dissolve 10.0 g K_3PO_4 in H_2O and dil. to 50 mL.

(**b**) *Water-washed chloroform.*—Shake equal vols $CHCl_3$ and H_2O in separator 1 min. Use within 1 day.

(**c**) *Water-washed ethyl acetate.*—Shake equal vols EtOAc and H_2O in separator 1 min. Discard lower phase.

(**d**) *Acetic acid in chloroform.*—(*1*) 10%.—Dil. 10.0 mL HOAc to 100 mL with $CHCl_3$. (*2*) 1%.—Dil. 10.0 mL 10% soln to 100 mL with $CHCl_3$. Prep. ca 375 mL for each sample and 225 mL for std solns.

(**e**) *Diatomaceous earth.*—*See* **36.002.**

(**f**) *Acetaminophen std soln.*—0.6 mg/100 mL. Accurately weigh ca 60 mg USP Ref. Std Acetaminophen; dissolve and dil. with alcohol in 100 mL vol. flask. Dil. 10.0 mL of this soln to 100 mL with alcohol. Dil. 10.0 mL of second diln to 100 mL with alcohol.

(**g**) *Salicylamide std soln.*—2 mg/100 mL. Accurately weigh ca 50 mg USP Ref. Std Salicylamide; dissolve and dil. with 1% HOAc-$CHCl_3$ in 100 mL vol. flask. Dil. 4.0 mL of this soln to 100 mL with 1% HOAc-$CHCl_3$.

37.016 ***Preparation of Sample***

Det. av. wt of tablets or capsules, reduce to powder passing No. 60 sieve.

37.017 ***Preparation of Columns***

Column I.—Place small piece of glass wool in chromatgc tube. Mix 1.0 g diat. earth, (**e**), and 0.5 mL HCl (1+1) in beaker until fluffy, and pack in tube. Accurately weigh portion powd sample contg ca 50 mg acetaminophen into 100 mL beaker and thoroly wet with 2.0 mL HCl (1+1). Add 3.0 g diat. earth, mix until fluffy, transfer quant. to column, and pack. Scrub sample beaker with 1.0 g diat. earth and 0.5 mL HCl (1+1), and pack on column. Wipe all utensils and sample beaker with glass wool and pack on column.

Column II.—Place small piece of glass wool in chromatgc tube. Mix 3.0 mL 20% K_3PO_4 and 5.0 g diat. earth until fluffy, and pack on column. Cover diat. earth with small piece of glass wool.

37.018 ***Determination***

Mount columns so that *I* elutes into *II*. Place waste beaker under column *II*. Add 100 mL H_2O-washed $CHCl_3$ to column *I*. After all $CHCl_3$ has passed thru both columns, sep. columns, rinsing stem of top column with 5 mL H_2O-washed $CHCl_3$ into bottom column. Elute column *II* with addnl 25 mL H_2O-washed $CHCl_3$. Rinse stem of column *II* with $CHCl_3$ after all $CHCl_3$ has passed thru. Discard wash $CHCl_3$.

Place 250 mL vol. flasks under each column. Elute acetaminophen from column *I* with 100 mL H_2O-washed EtOAc. Do not let column run dry until entire 100 mL has passed into column. Rinse column stem with EtOAc (not H_2O-washed) into flask. Add 5 mL alcohol, mix, and dil. to vol. with EtOAc (not H_2O-washed). Pipet 15 mL into 50 mL vol. flask and dil. to vol. with EtOAc (not H_2O-washed). Pipet 10 mL of this soln into 100 mL beaker and evap. to dryness with gentle air current. Do not use heat. Dissolve residue in alcohol and transfer quant. to 100 mL vol. flask with several portions alcohol; dil. to vol. with alcohol. Det. *A* of sample and std, (**f**), solns at 248 nm in 1.0 cm cell against alcohol as ref. If recording spectrophtr is available, scan soln from 320 to ca 210 nm in 1.0 cm cells against alcohol.

mg Acetaminophen in portion sample taken

$$= 83.33(A/A') \times C,$$

where A and A' refer to sample and std solns, resp., at 248 nm; and C = exact concn of ref. std soln in mg/100 mL final soln.

Elute salicylamide from column *II* by passing 10.0 mL 10% HOAc-$CHCl_3$ thru column, followed by 100 mL 1% HOAc-$CHCl_3$. After complete elution, rinse stem of column into flask with 1% HOAc-$CHCl_3$ and dil. to vol. with same solv. Pipet aliquot contg ca 2 mg salicylamide into 100 mL vol. flask and dil. to vol. with 1% HOAc-$CHCl_3$. Det. A of sample and std, (**g**), solns at 308 nm in 1.0 cm cells against 1% HOAc-$CHCl_3$ as ref. If recording spectrophtr is used, scan solns from 370 to ca 260 nm in 1.0 cm cells against 1% HOAc-$CHCl_3$.

mg Salicylamide in portion sample taken

$$= (250/B) \times (A/A') \times C,$$

where B = vol. (mL) aliquot taken to contain 2 mg salicylamide; A and A' refer to sample and ref. std solns, resp., at 308 nm; and C = exact concn of ref. std soln in mg/100 mL final soln.

37.019 ***Identification***

Prep. KBr disks of each ingredient from eluates by evapg, with gentle air current only, aliquot contg ca 1 mg each ingredient. Be sure no detectable odor of HOAc is present from salicylamide aliquot before prepg KBr disk.

Compare IR spectrum of each with its respective std from 2.0 μm (5000 cm^{-1}) to 15 μm (660 cm^{-1}).

★ Acetanilid and Acetophenetidin (Phenacetin) (*7*) ★

37.020 ***Qualitative Test for Acetophenetidin—Procedure***

See **32.129**, 10th ed.

37.021 ***Quantitative Methods—Official Final Action***

(**a**) *Acetophenetidin.*—(*1*) *Volumetric. See* **32.131(a)**(1), 10th ed. (*2*) *Gravimetric. See* **32.131(a)**(2), 10th ed.

(**b**) *Acetanilid.—See* **32.131(b)**, 10th ed. (*Caution: See* **51.011**, **51.040**, and **51.056**.)

37.022 ★ Acetanilid and Caffeine (*8*) ★ Official Final Action

See **32.132–32.134**, 10th ed. (*Caution: See* **51.011**, **51.040**, and **51.056**.)

37.023 ★ Acetanilid, Caffeine, and Codeine (*9*) ★ Official Final Action

See **32.135–32.136**, 10th ed. (*Caution: See* **51.011**, **51.040**, and **51.056**.)

37.024 ★ Acetanilid, Caffeine, and Quinine (*9*) ★ Official Final Action

See **32.137–32.139**, 10th ed. (*Caution: See* **51.011**, **51.040**, and **51.056**.)

37.025 ★ Acetanilid, Caffeine, Quinine, and Morphine (*10*) ★ Official Final Action

See **32.140–32.141**, 10th ed. (*Caution: See* **51.011**, **51.040**, and **51.056**.)

★ Surplus method—*see* inside front cover.

37.026 ★ Acetanilid and Sodium Salicylate (*11*) ★ Official Final Action

See **32.142–32.143**, 10th ed. (*Caution: See* **51.011**, **51.040**, and **51.056**.)

Acetophenetidin, Acetylsalicylic Acid, and Caffeine (APC)—Official Final Action

(For antihistamines in combination with APC—*See* **38.136**.)

37.027 ★ *Method I (For Acetylsalicylic Acid Only)* (*12*) ★

$CHCl_3$ extn, hydrolysis to salicylic acid, and pptn as tetraiodophenylenequinone. *See* **36.190**, 11th ed.

37.028 ★ *Method II* (*13*) ★

Removal of acetylsalicylic acid with $NaHCO_3$ soln. Gravimetric detn of most of acetophenetidin from dil. H_2SO_4, hydrolysis of remaining acetophenetidin to phenetidin sulfate, extn of caffeine, and regeneration of residual acetophenetidin. *See* **36.191–36.192**, 11th ed.

Chromatographic Method (*14*)

37.029 ***Reagents***

(**a**) *Sodium bicarbonate soln.*—1*M*. Dissolve 4.2 g $NaHCO_3$ in 48 mL H_2O.

(**b**) *Washed ether.*—Wash USP ether with equal vol. H_2O in separator. Filter thru paper, rejecting first 15 mL. Use within 3 days. Approx. 70 mL required for each sample.

(**c**) *Chloroform.*—USP. A against H_2O at 276 nm $\leq$0.050. Use same lot thruout.

(**d**) *Washed chloroform.*—Wash and filter $CHCl_3$ as in (**b**). Use within 3 days. Use same lot thruout. Approx. 700 mL is required for stds and 170 mL for each sample.

(**e**) *Isooctane.*—A against H_2O at 286 nm $\leq$0.050. Use same lot thruout.

(**f**) *Acetophenetidin std soln.*—7 mg/100 mL. Dissolve 70.0 mg pure acetophenetidin in $CHCl_3$ and dil. to 100 mL with $CHCl_3$. Dil. 10 mL aliquot to 100 mL with isooctane.

(**g**) *Caffeine std soln.*—1.4 mg/100 mL. Dissolve 140.0 mg caffeine in washed $CHCl_3$ and dil. to 100 mL. Dil. 10 mL aliquot to 100 mL; dil. 10 mL aliquot of this soln to 100 mL with washed $CHCl_3$.

(**h**) *Acetylsalicylic acid std soln.*—5 mg/100 mL. Dissolve 100.0 mg acetylsalicylic acid in washed $CHCl_3$ and dil. to 100 mL. To 5 mL aliquot add 1.0 mL HOAc and dil. to 100 mL with washed $CHCl_3$. Prep. fresh daily.

(**i**) *Salicylic acid std soln.*—2.5 mg/100 mL. Dissolve 100.0 mg salicylic acid in washed $CHCl_3$ and dil. to 100 mL. Dil. 25 mL aliquot to 100 mL; to 10 mL aliquot of this soln, add 1.0 mL HOAc and dil. to 100 mL with washed $CHCl_3$.

37.030 ***Apparatus***

See **37.002**.

37.031 ***Preparation of Sample***

Weigh powd sample contg ca 100 mg acetylsalicylic acid and transfer to 100 mL vol. flask. Add 60 mL $CHCl_3$ and shake well. Add 0.2 mL HOAc and dil. to vol. with $CHCl_3$.

37.032 ***Preparation of Chromatographic Column***

Loosely pack small amt of fine glass wool in base of chromatgc tube so as to support diat. earth, but not cause irregularity in thickness of diat. earth layer.

To 2.0 g diat. earth, **36.002**, in 100 mL beaker, or glass mortar, add 2.0 mL H_2SO_4 (1+9). Mix well with metal spatula. Transfer to chromatgc tube, and with packing rod, compress lightly to uniform mass. Mix 2.0 g diat. earth with 2.0 mL 1*M* $NaHCO_3$ and place in column above acid layer. Wash column with 15–20 mL washed ether and discard washings.

37.033 ***Separation***

(Use washed ether and washed $CHCl_3$ thruout, except for dissolving acetophenetidin residue.)

(**a**) *Acetophenetidin.*—Dil. 5 mL aliquot prepd sample soln with 20 mL ether and pass thru column, receiving eluate in 100 or 150 mL beaker. After soln has passed into adsorbent, wash with five 5 mL portions ether, letting each portion pass into adsorbent before adding next. Wash tip of outlet with $CHCl_3$ and evap. total eluate to dryness by gentle heating on steam bath with air current. Dissolve acetophenetidin residue in 5 mL USP $CHCl_3$ and dil. with isooctane to 50 mL.

(**b**) *Caffeine.*—Immediately after passage of last portion of ether thru column, replace beaker with 50 mL vol. flask. Pass 48 mL $CHCl_3$ thru column, wash tip with $CHCl_3$ and dil. eluate to vol.

(**c**) *Acetylsalicylic acid and salicylic acid.*—Immediately replace receiver with 100 mL vol. flask. Pass soln of 0.5 mL HOAc in 5 mL $CHCl_3$ thru column, followed by 90–92 mL 1% soln of HOAc in $CHCl_3$. Wash tip with $CHCl_3$ and dil. eluate to vol.

37.034 ***Determination***

Immediately det. *A* of acid fraction and of acetylsalicylic and salicylic acid std solns at 280 and 310 nm against 1% HOAc in $CHCl_3$. Det *A* of acetophenetidin fraction and std at 286 nm against isooctane-USP $CHCl_3$ (9+1) and that of caffeine fraction and std at 276 nm against washed $CHCl_3$ blank.

Calc. amt of each ingredient in sample. Acetylsalicylic and salicylic acids may be calcd by successive approximations as follows: Attributing entire *A* at 310 nm to salicylic acid, use ratio of salicylic acid std readings at the 2 wavelengths to calc. *A* due to salicylic acid at 280 nm, and deduct from total *A* at 280 nm. Attributing remainder to acetylsalicylic acid, use ratio of acetylsalicylic acid std readings to calc. *A* due to acetylsalicylic acid at 310 nm. Deduct this *A* from total at 310 nm. Use remainder to calc. amt of salicylic acid in sample and also to recalc. *A* due to salicylic acid at 280 nm. Deduct latter from total *A* at 280 nm and use remainder to calc. amt of acetylsalicylic acid in sample. Alternatively, calc. these two ingredients by simultaneous equations. Amt of acetylsalicylic acid hydrolyzed may be calcd by multiplying amt of salicylic acid by 1.3044.

37.035 Codeine in APC Tablets

See **38.012–38.013**.

37.036 ★ Acetophenetidin, Acetylsalicylic Acid, ★ and Salol (Phenyl Salicylate) (*15*) Official Final Action

See **32.153**, 10th ed. (*Caution: See* **51.011**, **51.040**, and **51.056**.)

37.037 ★ Acetophenetidin, Aminopyrine, and ★ Caffeine (*16*)—Official Final Action

See **32.154**, 10th ed. (*Caution: See* **51.011**, **51.040**, and **51.056**.)

37.038 ★ Acetophenetidin, Aminopyrine, Caffeine, ★ and Phenobarbital (*17*)—Official Final Action

See **32.155**, 10th ed.

37.039 ★ Acetophenetidin (Phenacetin) and ★ Caffeine (*18*)—Official Final Action

(*Caution: See* **51.011**, **51.040**, and **51.056**.)

See **36.202–36.203**, 11th ed.

★ Acetophenetidin (Phenacetin) and Salol (Phenyl ★ Salicylate) (*19*)—Official Final Action

37.040 ***Acid Hydrolysis Method***

See **32.158**, 10th ed.

37.041 ***Alkaline Hydrolysis Method***

See **32.159**, 10th ed.

Acetylsalicylic Acid (*20*)—Official Final Action

37.042 ★ *Melting Point* ★

See **36.206**, 11th ed.

37.043 ★ *Free Salicylic Acid* ★

Colorimetric method. *See* **36.207**, 11th ed.

37.044 ★ *Total Salicylate* ★

(**a**) Gravimetric method as tetraiodophenylenequinone. *See* **36.209(a)**, 11th ed.

(**b**) Volumetric bromination method. *See* **36.209(b)**, 11th ed.

37.045 ★ *Combined Acetic Acid (21)* ★

See **36.210**, 11th ed.

★ *Double Titration Method (22)* ★

37.046 ***Preparation of Solution***

(**a**) *Dry extraction method (applicable in all cases).*—Treat weighed sample contg ≥0.3 g acetylsalicylic acid with small portions $CHCl_3$, filter into beaker, and wash residue with $CHCl_3$ until completely extd. Evap. bulk of $CHCl_3$ on steam bath, finishing with aid of elec. fan without heat.

(**b**) *Wet extraction method (applicable in absence of acids and alkalies, or alkaline earth carbonates).*—Transfer accurately weighed sample contg ≥0.3 g acetylsalicylic acid to small separator contg ca 20 mL H_2O. Ext repeatedly with $CHCl_3$, using 30, 25, 20, 15, 10, and 5 mL portions, and test for completeness of extn by evapg portion of final ext on watch glass. Filter combined $CHCl_3$ portions thru cotton, and wash funnel and cotton with $CHCl_3$. Evap. bulk of $CHCl_3$ on steam bath, finishing with aid of elec. fan without heat.

(**c**) *Acetylsalicylic acid and uncoated tablets containing no excipient.*—Dissolve sample directly in 10 mL neut. alcohol.

37.047 ***Determination***

Dissolve the dry $CHCl_3$ ext in 10 mL neut. alcohol, and immediately and rapidly titr. with 0.1*N* alkali, using phthln. Use first persistent pink as end point, since any slight excess of alkali tends to hydrolyze ester quickly. Add vol. of the 0.1*N* alkali equal to that used in first titrn and then add 5 mL more. Heat on steam bath 15 min. Back-titr. with 0.1*N* acid. If product is pure, total vol. of alkali consumed will be twice that of first titrn. 1 mL 0.1*N* alkali consumed in 2 titrns = 0.0090 g acetylsalicylic acid.

★ Surplus method—*see* inside front cover.

Acetylsalicylic Acid and Phenobarbital (*23*)
Official Final Action

37.048 ***Apparatus***

(**a**) *Spectrophotometer.*—Capable of isolating spectrum of ≤2 nm in region 230–300 nm.

(**b**) *Chromatographic tube and tamping rod.*—*See* **37.002**.

37.049 ***Reagents***

(**a**) *Dibasic potassium phosphate soln.*—Approx. 2*M*. Dissolve 35 g K_2HPO_4 in H_2O, cool to room temp., and dil. to 100 mL.

(**b**) *Diatomaceous earth.*—*See* **36.002**.

(**c**) *Washed chloroform.*—Wash USP $CHCl_3$ with ½ vol. H_2O in separator.

(**d**) *Acetylsalicylic acid std soln.*—5 mg/100 mL. Dissolve 100 mg acetylsalicylic acid in $CHCl_3$ and dil. to 100 mL with $CHCl_3$. Dil. 5 mL aliquot to 100 mL with $CHCl_3$.

(**e**) *Phenobarbital std soln.*—1 mg/100 mL. Dissolve 100 mg phenobarbital in NH_4OH (1+27) and dil. to 500 mL with NH_4OH (1+27). Dil. 5 mL aliquot to 100 mL with NH_4OH (1+27).

37.050 ***Preparation of Sample Solution***

Transfer accurately weighed portion of finely ground tablets contg 60–120 mg phenobarbital to 100 mL vol. flask. Dissolve in $CHCl_3$ by shaking vigorously and dil. to vol. with $CHCl_3$.

37.051 ***Preparation of Chromatographic Column***

Pack small pledget of glass wool in constricted portion of stem of tube and place pad of glass wool ca 5 mm thick in bottom of large portion of tube. Fasten piece of rubber tubing with attached screw clamp to outlet to limit flow during packing. Clamp tube in vertical position.

To 10 g diat. earth in mortar add 50 mL $CHCl_3$, and mix with pestle to form slurry. Distribute 10 mL 2*M* K_2HPO_4 soln, (**a**), over surface of slurry and mix thoroly until homogeneous, adding more $CHCl_3$ if necessary. Add this slurry to tube, ca ⅕ at time, alternately packing and forming flocculent suspension by working packing rod up and down. Diat. earth must be covered with $CHCl_3$ at all times.

After column is packed, remove rubber tube from stem and rinse stem with $CHCl_3$. Check flow rate of column with $CHCl_3$ level ca 5 cm above surface of column. Adjust rate of flow to 2–5 mL/min by tightening or loosening glass wool pledget in constricted portion of stem. When level of solv. just reaches surface of column, place 100 mL vol. flask under stem.

37.052 ***Determination of Phenobarbital***

Add 5 mL prepd sample soln, **37.050**, from pipet to side of tube near diat. earth surface. When level of sample soln reaches surface of column, add 5 mL washed $CHCl_3$, let sink into column, and repeat with another 5 mL washed $CHCl_3$. After last rinse enters column, add washed $CHCl_3$ to tube and keep level of 4–8 cm $CHCl_3$ above column during elution.

Collect 95 mL eluate in the 100 mL vol. flask. Dil. to vol. with $CHCl_3$, mix, and transfer 20 mL aliquot to 100 mL beaker. Evap. to dryness on steam bath under air current. Dissolve residue in NH_4OH (1+27) and transfer to 100 mL vol. flask. Rinse, and dil. to vol. with NH_4OH (1+27). Det. *A* at max., ca 240.5 nm, against blank prepd by passing 5 mL $CHCl_3$ thru column as with sample soln.

$$\text{g Phenobarbital in sample} = 10A/a,$$

where *a* is absorptivity of phenobarbital at 240.5 nm obtained by dividing *A* of std phenobarbital soln in 1 cm cell at 240.5 nm by its concn (0.01 g/L).

37.053 ***Determination of Acetylsalicylic Acid***

Dil. 5 mL original sample soln, **37.050**, to 100 mL with $CHCl_3$ in vol. flask. Dil. 10 mL aliquot of this soln to 100 mL with $CHCl_3$. Det. *A* of final diln on spectrophtr at 278 nm against $CHCl_3$ blank.

$$\text{g Acetylsalicylic acid in sample} = 20A_{278}/a_{278},$$

where a_{278} is absorptivity of acetylsalicylic acid at 278 nm obtained by dividing *A* of std acetylsalicylic acid soln in 1 cm cell at 278 nm by its concn (0.05 g/L).

37.054 ★ Acetylsalicylic Acid and Phenolphthalein ★ in Tablets (*24*)—Official Final Action

(*Caution: See* **51.011**, **51.039**, **51.040**, **51.054**, and **51.056**.)

Accurately weigh powd sample, prepd as in **36.003**, contg 0.05–0.1 g phthln. Ext repeatedly with 20 mL portions ether, and filter into separator. Test for complete extn (5–8 extns required).

(**a**) *Acetylsalicylic acid.*—Shake ether soln, ≥1 min each time, with two 20 mL portions 4% $NaHCO_3$ soln (temp. ≤20°). Transfer soln to second separator. Wash ether with two 10 mL portions H_2O and add to $NaHCO_3$ soln. Ext $NaHCO_3$ soln with 20 mL ether. Drain lower aq. layer into 100 mL vol. flask. Wash ether with small portions H_2O, rinse into flask, and dil. to vol. Add wash ether to bulk of solv. in original separator. Reserve ether soln for detn of phthln.

Transfer aliquot $NaHCO_3$ soln contg ≥0.3 g acetylsalicylic acid to separator. (Acid must be sepd from $NaHCO_3$ soln as rapidly as possible to prevent hydrolysis.) Acidify with HCl (1+3) and ext liberated acetylsalicylic acid with 30, 20, 20, 10, and 10 mL portions $CHCl_3$-ether (3+2). Wash each ext with 2 mL H_2O in second separator and filter thru cotton pledget, moistened with $CHCl_3$-ether mixt., into counterpoised weighed beaker. Test for complete extn. Evap. filtrate to 10–15 mL on H_2O bath, and complete evapn without heat. Dry residue to const wt at room temp. Wt may be checked by double titrn method, **37.047**.

(**b**) *Phenolphthalein.*—Ext original ether soln with 20 mL portions 3% NaOH soln until all phthln is removed (indicated by color). Transfer these alk. exts to second separator, acidify with HCl (1+3), and ext with $CHCl_3$-ether (3+2). Wash each ext in third separator with 2 mL H_2O to which has been added 1 or 2 drops HCl (1+3). Filter exts into counterpoised weighed beaker, using cotton pledget moistened with the $CHCl_3$-ether mixt. in stem of funnel. Evap. on H_2O bath and dry to const wt at 120°. Wt may be checked by tetraiodo method, **37.136**.

Aminopyrine—Official Final Action

37.055 ***Qualitative Tests (25)***

(**a**) Dissolve 0.01 g sample in 2 mL H_2O and add few drops of yellow HNO_3 (contg HNO_2). Purplish blue soln is produced.

(**b**) Dissolve 0.01 g sample in 2 mL H_2O and add 1 mL 10% $FeCl_3$ soln. Purple to violet color develops, which becomes red on addn of H_2SO_4 (1+9).

(**c**) Dissolve 0.1 g sample in 2 mL H_2O and add few drops of 5% $AgNO_3$ soln. After few sec, purple to violet color is produced, and on standing, deposit of metallic Ag results (useful for detecting aminopyrine in antipyrine).

(**d**) Dissolve 0.1–0.2 g sample in 2 mL H_2O, add 1 or 2 drops 0.2% $NaNO_2$ soln and few drops of H_2SO_4 (1+9), and shake few sec. Purplish blue color develops and then gradually fades, leaving colorless soln. Excess $NaNO_2$ destroys aminopyrine color. On addn of few more drops of $NaNO_2$ soln and dil. H_2SO_4,

★ Surplus method—*see* inside front cover.

yellowish green color remains after purple disappears if antipyrine is present. (Useful for detecting antipyrine in presence of aminopyrine.)

37.056 ***Quantitative Method (26)***

(*Caution: See* **51.011**, **51.040**, and **51.056**.)

Place 1 g powd sample in 100 mL vol. flask, add 60 mL 1*N* H_2SO_4, and shake several min to ensure complete soln of aminopyrine. Dil. to vol. with 1*N* H_2SO_4. Filter, if not clear, thru dry filter, rejecting first part of filtrate. Pipet 20 mL aliquot of soln or filtrate into separator; make distinctly alk. with either NH_4OH or 5% NaOH; and ext with 20, 15, 10, 10, and 5 mL portions $CHCl_3$. Combine $CHCl_3$ exts in second separator and wash with 2 mL H_2O. Filter $CHCl_3$ soln into weighed beaker thru cotton pledget satd with $CHCl_3$. Ext wash H_2O with 5 mL $CHCl_3$ and add this to combined $CHCl_3$ exts. Evap. combined $CHCl_3$ exts just to dryness on H_2O bath with aid of air current and dry residue 10 min at 100°. Cool in desiccator, and weigh as aminopyrine. Identify aminopyrine by its mp, 106.5–109°, and qual. tests, **37.055**, or microchem. tests, Table **36:06**.

HYPNOTIC DRUGS

Acetylcarbromal and Bromisovalum (*27*) Official Final Action

37.057 ***Principle***

Acetylcarbromal is eluted with heptane-CCl_4 and bromisovalum with H_2O-satd $CHCl_3$ from diat. earth column. Eluates are dried; acetylcarbromal residue is dissolved in CCl_4 and bromisovalum residue in $CHCl_3$. Concns are detd by IR spectrometry at 5.8 μm. Identification is made from residues in KBr disks.

37.058 ***Apparatus***

(**a**) *Infrared spectrophotometer*.—Beckman IR-5, (current model Acculab 5), or equiv., with 1 mm liq. cells.

(**b**) *Chromatographic tube*.—*See* **37.002**.

37.059 ***Reagents***

(**a**) *Diatomaceous earth*.—*See* **36.002**.

(**b**) *Reference std solns*.—1.00 mg/mL. Completely dissolve 50.0 mg acetylcarbromal (mp 109°) in CCl_4 in 50 mL vol. flask and dil. to vol. with CCl_4. Completely dissolve 50.0 mg bromisovalum (mp 148–149°) in $CHCl_3$ in 50 mL vol. flask and dil. to vol. with $CHCl_3$.

37.060 ***Column Chromatography***

(*Caution: See* **51.011**, **51.040**, **51.049**, and **51.056**.)

Pack small wad of fine glass wool into bottom of tube. Thoroly mix 4 g diat. earth with 5 mL HCl (2+1), transfer to tube, and tamp to uniform mass with tamping rod.

Det. av. wt/tablet and pulverize. Accurately weigh portion of powder contg 10–30 mg acetylcarbromal, and mix in beaker with 1 g diat. earth and 1 mL H_2O. Transfer to tube, dry-rinse beaker with small portion diat. earth, and tamp to uniform mass. Wash beaker with few portions H_2O-satd CCl_4-heptane (1+1) and pour thru column. Elute acetylcarbromal with CCl_4-heptane mixt., collecting 50 mL eluate in beaker. Immediately, without letting column go dry, elute bromisovalum with 100 mL H_2O-satd $CHCl_3$, collecting eluate in beaker. Evap. both eluates to complete dryness on steam bath with air current.

Dissolve acetylcarbromal residue with several portions of CCl_4 (dried with anhyd. Na_2SO_4) and dil. to concn of 1 mg/mL. Dissolve bromisovalum residue in several portions of $CHCl_3$ (dried with anhyd. Na_2SO_4) and dil. to concn of 1 mg/mL. Using their resp. solvs as ref. solns, det. IR spectrum at 5–7 μm. For calcn, use *A* of max. at ca 5.8 μm, using baseline technic:

$$\% \text{ Compd} = (100 \times A \times C \times V)/(A' \times W),$$

where *A* and *A'* refer to sample and std solns, resp., *C* = concn of std soln (mg/mL), *V* = final vol. sample soln, and *W* = mg sample.

37.061 ***Identification***

Evap. 1 mL each of std and sample soln, and prep. KBr disk from each of residues, using ca 200 mg KBr. Scan IR spectra for identification.

Carbromal (*28*)—Official Final Action

37.062 ***Apparatus***

See Fig. **37:01**. Consists of 100 mL r-b flask with 24/40 § inner joint; condenser with jacket ca 130 mm long; and absorption flask with 2 bulbs. Condenser is equipped with 12/30 and 24/40 § inner joints. Small dropping funnel is fused to tube above jacket. Absorption flask has outer 12/30 § joint. Small springs (not shown) are attached to hooks on joints to keep app. tightly connected during use.

FIG. 37:01—Bromine apparatus

37.063 ***Determination***

Place sample calcd to contain 40–60 mg Br in oxidn flask and dissolve in 2 mL 10% NaOH soln and 8 mL H_2O. Lubricate joints of app. with H_3PO_4 and connect flask to condenser. Place ca 15 mL 1% *$N_2H_4.H_2SO_4$ soln* and 5 mL 10% NaOH soln in absorption flask and connect to app. (Use <20 mL absorbing soln if app. has smaller absorption bulbs than indicated.)

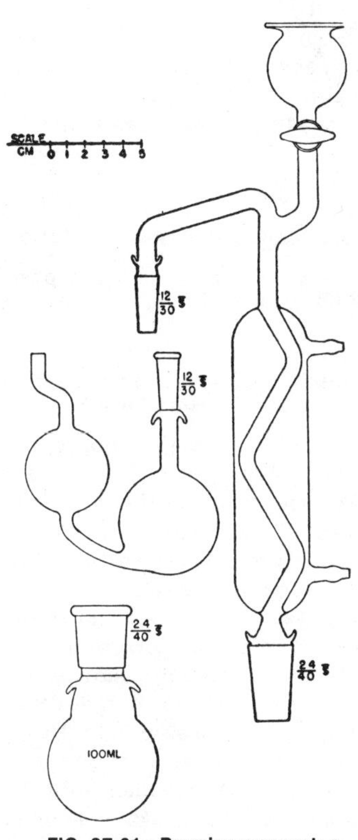

FIG. 37:01—Bromine apparatus

Add 5 mL *CrO_3 soln (1+1)* thru addn tube, wash down with 2–3 mL H_2O, and then slowly add 10 mL H_2SO_4. If vigorous reaction begins, let it subside before heating flask; if reaction does not begin as acid is added, heat gently with small flame, but remove flame before reaction becomes too vigorous, otherwise reaction mixt. may foam up into condenser. When reaction subsides, heat mixt. to boiling. When foaming subsides, add 5 mL H_2SO_4 thru dropping funnel, boil 10 min, add another 5 mL H_2SO_4, and boil again 10 min. Drain H_2O from condenser and boil reaction mixt. until 2–3 drops H_2O distil into absorber.

Disconnect absorption flask, wash contents into 500 mL I flask, and dil. to ca 100 mL with H_2O. Add ca 12 mL H_3PO_4, 5 mL *3% KCN soln,* and 15 mL *3% $KMnO_4$ soln,* wetting sides of flask with each reagent as it is added. Stopper flasks and mix by gentle swirling, wetting entire inside surface. Let stand ≥7 min; then add ca 2 g solid $FeSO_4.(NH_4)_2SO_4.6H_2O$. Wash down sides of flask and mix. (Clear, nearly colorless soln should result.) If any $KMnO_4$ or MnO_2 remains, add more $Fe(NH_4)_2(SO_4)_2.6H_2O$ (2 g excess does no harm).

Add ca 2 g KI and immediately titr. liberated I with 0.05*N* $Na_2S_2O_3$, using starch indicator. (End point is disappearance of starch-I color; avoid over-titrn as color of soln remains light blue.) 1 mL 0.05*N* $Na_2S_2O_3$ = 0.001998 g Br or 0.00593 g carbromal.

37.064 Carbromal and Pentobarbital (*28*)
Official Final Action

(*Caution: See* **51.011**, **51.040**, and **51.056**.)

Transfer 0.5–0.7 g sample to separator, and add 15 mL H_2O and 0.5 mL 1*N* NaOH from pipet. Ext carbromal with at least five 25 mL portions $CHCl_3$, washing each portion in second separator contg 10 mL H_2O and 2 drops 0.1*N* NaOH. Filter $CHCl_3$ thru cotton and transfer to tared flask or beaker. Test for complete extn. Evap. $CHCl_3$ soln of carbromal nearly but not quite to dryness on steam bath in air current. Remove container and let stand in air to const wt.

Combine aq. solns and proceed as in **37.065**, beginning "Acidify to litmus paper . . ." Wt pentobarbital × 1.097 = wt Na pentobarbital in portion taken for assay. Det. mp of dried exts. Carbromal melts at 116–119° and pentobarbital at 126–130°.

Barbiturates—Official Final Action

(*See also* **38.111–38.117** for barbital and phenobarbital and **39.113–39.116** for mannitol hexanitrate and phenobarbital.)

37.065 *Method I (29)*

(Applicable in absence of stearic acid. *Caution: See* **51.011**, **51.040**, and **51.056**.)

Accurately weigh 0.3–0.5 g sample into separator, add 10 mL H_2O, and shake well. Add 5 mL 0.5*N* NaOH and shake again. Acidify to litmus paper with HCl (1+3), added dropwise, and add ca 1 mL excess. Ext with successive 40, 30, 20, 20, and 10 mL portions $CHCl_3$. Test for complete extn by shaking with addnl 10 mL solv. and evapg in sep. beaker.

Combine solv. in second separator and wash with 2 mL H_2O acidified with 1 drop HCl. Filter solv. thru cotton pledget into small weighed beaker. Evap. on steam bath with aid of air current, heat 10 min at 80–90°, cool in desiccator, and weigh. Add 2 or 3 mL anhyd. ether and evap. solv. (Usually 2 treatments with 2 mL each of anhyd. ether are enough to remove last traces of $CHCl_3$ and to produce cryst. residue.) Dry at 80–90°, cool, and weigh. Repeat treatment with anhyd. ether and evapn to const wt. Det. mp to check purity of residue.

37.066 *Method II (30)—Official Final Action*

(Applicable in presence of stearic acid)

Dissolve residue obtained in **37.065** in 10 mL alcohol, add 20 mL *satd $Ba(OH)_2$ soln,* and stir well. Filter into separator, and wash residue and filter with two or three 10 mL portions of the $Ba(OH)_2$ soln. Acidify filtrate with HCl (1+3) and proceed as in **37.065**, beginning "Ext with successive . . ."

37.067 *Microscopic Tests—Official Final Action*

See **36.098–36.099**, Tables **36:04** and **36:06**, and **36.106–36.108**.

★ Amobarbital Sodium and Secobarbital Sodium (*31*)—Official Final Action ★

37.068 ***Reagents***

(**a**) *Sodium secobarbital std.*—Assay by **37.065**.

(**b**) *Phosphate buffer soln.*—pH 6.85–6.90. Dissolve 6.80 g KH_2PO_4 in ca 500 mL H_2O in 1 L vol. flask. Add 23.6 mL 1.00*N* NaOH soln and dil. to vol. with H_2O.

37.069 ***Preparation of Standard Curve***

Accurately weigh ca 100 mg Na secobarbital, transfer to 25 mL vol. flask, dil. to vol. with H_2O, and mix well. Calc. equiv. barbituric acid/mL std soln as follows:

mg Barbituric acid/mL = (mg Na secobarbital/25)
× (% Na secobarbital (from assay)/100) × (128.09/260.27).

Pipet 0.5, 1.0, and 2.0 mL aliquots into 50 mL vol. flasks, dil. to vol. with buffer soln, and mix. Det. *A* of each soln at 237 nm against buffer soln. Plot *A* against mg barbituric acid.

Include 1 or 2 stds with each set of detns.

37.070 ***Determination of Total Barbiturates***

Accurately weigh sample contg ca 400 mg total Na amobarbital and Na secobarbital, transfer to 100 mL vol. flask, and dil. to vol. with H_2O. Mix, and let stand 10 min with occasional shaking. Filter thru quant. paper retentive enough to produce clear soln, discarding first 10–15 mL filtrate. Pipet 2 mL filtrate into 50 mL vol. flask, dil. to vol. with buffer soln, and mix well. Det. *A* at 237 nm against buffer soln. Det. total barbituric acid in aliquot by ref. to std curve and calc. to mg total barbituric acid in sample.

37.071 ***Determination of Sodium Secobarbital***

Pipet 50 mL filtrate into I flask and add 10.0 mL 0.1*N* KBr-$KBrO_3$, **50.020**. Add 5 mL HCl, stopper at once, and let stand 5 min, shaking occasionally. Add 10 mL 10% KI soln, stopper, and shake. Rinse stopper and neck of flask with H_2O, add starch indicator, and titr. liberated I with 0.1*N* $Na_2S_2O_3$, **50.037**, using 10 mL buret. 1 mL 0.1*N* KBr-$KBrO_3$ consumed = 13.01 mg Na secobarbital. Calc. to mg Na secobarbital in sample.

37.072 ***Determination of Sodium Amobarbital (by Difference)***

mg Na amobarbital in sample = [mg total barbituric acid
− (mg Na secobarbital × 0.492)] × 1.94.

Phenobarbital and Aminophylline (*32*) Official Final Action

37.073 ***Reagents***

(**a**) *Dilute ammonium hydroxide soln.*—0.1% NH_3. Dil. 4 mL NH_4OH to 1 L with H_2O.

★ Surplus method—*see* inside front cover.

(**b**) *Phenobarbital std soln.*—10 μg/mL. Dissolve 100.0 mg phenobarbital in the dil. NH_4OH soln in 500 mL vol. flask, dil. to vol. with the dil. NH_4OH, and mix. Transfer 5 mL aliquot to 100 mL vol. flask, dil. to vol. with the dil. NH_4OH, and mix.

(**c**) *Theophylline std soln.*—10 μg/mL. Dissolve 100.0 mg theophylline in HCl (1+18) in 500 mL vol. flask. Dil. to vol. with HCl (1+18) and mix. Transfer 5 mL aliquot to 100 mL vol. flask, dil. to vol. with H_2O, and mix.

37.074 ***Separation of Aminophylline and Phenobarbital***

Transfer weighed portion of powd sample contg ca 15 mg phenobarbital to separator contg 25 mL HCl (1+1). Add 60 mL ether, shake, and let stand to clear. Pass aq. soln successively thru 2 other separators, each contg 50 mL ether, shake, and let stand to clear. Transfer ether-washed aq. soln to 500 mL vol. flask. Wash the 3 ether solns successively with three 10 mL portions HCl (1+1) and one 10 mL portion H_2O, and add these washes to the vol. flask. Reserve for detn of theophylline.

37.075 ***Determination of Phenobarbital***

(*Caution: See* **51.011**, **51.039**, and **51.054**.)

Combine ether solns and evap. to dryness. Dissolve residue in ca 100 mL of the dil. NH_4OH and transfer to 200 mL vol. flask. Dil. to vol. with the dil. NH_4OH and mix. Filter, if necessary, transfer 10 mL aliquot to 100 mL vol. flask, dil. to vol. with the dil. NH_4OH, and mix. Det. A_P at max., ca 240.5 nm, against dil. NH_4OH. Read this soln same day it is prepd.

Det. A'_P of std phenobarbital soln, (**b**), at same wavelength, using the dil. NH_4OH as blank. Calc. $a_p = A'_P/cb$, where c = 0.01 g/L, and b = cell length in cm. Phenobarbital (g/L sample soln) = A_P/a_P.

If stearates are present, proceed as above, dissolving residue in ca 100 mL of the dil. NH_4OH and dilg to ca 190 mL with the dil. NH_4OH. Acidify with HCl, testing with litmus paper. Dil. to vol. with H_2O, mix, and filter. Transfer 10 mL aliquot to 100 mL vol. flask, add 1 drop NH_4OH (1+1), dil. to vol. with the dil. NH_4OH, and det. A_P at 240.5 nm.

37.076 ***Determination of Theophylline***

Dil. aq. soln in vol. flask to vol. with H_2O and mix. Transfer aliquot contg 0.5–1.0 mg theophylline to 100 mL vol. flask, dil. to vol. with H_2O, and mix. Det. A_T at 271 nm against blank soln contg same vol. HCl. Det. A'_T of std theophylline soln, (**c**), and calc. a_T as in **37.075**. Theophylline (g/L sample soln) = A_T/a_T. Aminophylline, $C_{16}H_{24}N_{10}O_4.2H_2O$ = 1.267 × theophylline.

Phenobarbital and Diphenylhydantoin (*33*)
Official Final Action

37.077 ***Reagents***

(**a**) *Water-saturated soln of 15% n-amyl alcohol in $CHCl_3$.*—Sat. 500 mL 15% n-amyl alcohol in $CHCl_3$ with 25 mL H_2O and let stand 30 min. Det. suitability of reagent by passing 80 mL thru prepd column followed by 25 mL H_2O-satd $CHCl_3$, evapg to dryness on steam bath with air current, dilg to 25.0 mL with alcohol, and reading A in 1 cm cell on recording spectrophtr from 320 to 250 nm. If $(A_{258} - A_{263}) \leq 0.190$, make blank correction. Higher ΔA indicates better grade reagent must be used.

(**b**) *Acetic acid-chloroform soln.*—1% HOAc in H_2O-satd $CHCl_3$.

37.078 ***Preparation of Standards***

(**a**) *Phenobarbital std soln.*—Weigh and transfer 20 mg phenobarbital, USP, to 50 mL vol. flask; dissolve and dil. to vol. with alcohol. Pipet 10 mL into 125 mL g-s erlenmeyer and evap. to dryness on steam bath with air current (4 mg/100 mL 0.1*N* NaOH has A of ca 1.30 at max., ca 253 nm, in 1 cm cell).

(**b**) *5,5-Diphenylhydantoin std soln.*—Weigh and transfer 90 mg diphenylhydantoin (Eastman), to 50 mL vol. flask; dissolve and dil. to vol. with alcohol. Pipet 10 mL into 125 mL g-s erlenmeyer and evap. to dryness on steam bath with air current (18 mg/25 mL alcohol has A of ca 1.90 at max., ca 258 nm, in 1 cm cell).

37.079 ***Preparation of Sample***

Accurately weigh powd sample contg ca 90 mg diphenylhydantoin and transfer to 50 mL vol. flask. Add 1.5 mL alcohol, 0.1 mL HOAc, and ca 25 mL reagent, **37.077(a)**. Heat on steam bath with swirling until $CHCl_3$ boils. Remove from heat and swirl 5 min. Heat to boiling as before, remove, and let stand 15 min with frequent agitation. Let cool and dil. to vol. with reagent (**a**). (Diphenylhydantoin dissolves with difficulty. Turbidity of soln may persist because of insol. excipients.)

37.080 ***Preparation of Column***

Use glass tube 25 mm diam. × 15–30 cm long, with stem plugged with glass wool, and glass tamping rod weighing ca 32 g and having 20–22 mm ram head.

(**a**) *Column packing.*—(*1*) *Bottom layer.*—Mix 2 g diat. earth, **36.002**, and 1 mL *12% $BaCl_2$ soln.* (*2*) *Top layer.*—Mix 4 g diat. earth, **36.002**, and 3 mL *satd Na_3PO_4 soln.*

(**b**) *Packing technic.*—*Column must be packed exactly as follows:* Transfer sep. bottom and top packing layers to tube in 1–2 g portions and tamp 10–15 times with tamping rod after addn of each portion by dropping rod from 2.5 cm above packing surface.

Place glass wool pad over diat.earth mixt. and pass 25 mL reagent (**a**) thru column at 5–10 mL/min, discarding eluate.

37.081 ***Determination***

(*Caution: See* **51.011**, **51.022**, **51.040**, and **51.056**.)

Place 125 mL g-s erlenmeyer under column and pipet 10 mL sample soln directly over glass wool pad. Let drain into column, and wash column with three 10 mL portions reagent (**a**), letting each drain into column. Add addnl 40 mL reagent (**a**). Pass 25 mL H_2O-satd $CHCl_3$ thru column, wash stem with $CHCl_3$, and evap. eluate to dryness on steam bath with air current. (Odor of *n*-amyl alcohol must be absent.) Residue is diphenylhydantoin.

Place 125 mL g-s erlenmeyer under column and add to column 5 mL HOAc in $CHCl_3$ (1+4). Let drain into column. Add 20 mL reagent, **37.077(b)**, let drain into column, and add 70 mL more. Wash stem with $CHCl_3$ and evap. eluate to dryness on steam bath with air current. Residue is phenobarbital.

Add 25 mL alcohol by pipet to both sample and std diphenylhydantoin residues. Stopper and warm with swirling. Let stand, swirling occasionally, until solid matter is completely dissolved. Det A of sample and std solns against reagent, **37.077(a)**, on recording spectrophtr from 320 to 250 nm in 1 cm cell.

mg Diphenylhydantoin/capsule

$$= C \times (K/W) \times (A_{258} - A_{263})/(A'_{258} - A'_{263}),$$

where A_{258} and A_{263} = max. and min. A of sample soln at ca 258 and 263 nm, resp.; A'_{258} and A'_{263} = max. and min. A of std soln at 258 and 263 nm, resp.; C = mg std diphenylhydantoin; K = av. capsule content wt (mg); and W = mg sample. Diphenylhydantoin × 1.087 = Na diphenylhydantoin.

Add 100 mL 0.1*N* NaOH by pipet to both sample and std phenobarbital residues. Stopper and shake vigorously 2 min.

Immediately read A of solns on recording spectrophtr from 350 to 230 nm in 1 cm cell.

$$\text{mg Phenobarbital/capsule} = C \times (K/W) \times (A_{253}/A'_{253}),$$

where A_{253} and A'_{253} = A of sample and std solns, resp., at max., ca 253 nm; C = mg std phenobarbital; K = av. capsule content wt (mg); W = mg sample.

Phenobarbital and Theobromine (*34*)—Official Final Action

37.082 ***Reagents***

(**a**) *Theobromine std soln.*—1.00 mg/100 mL. Dissolve 100 mg theobromine in H_2SO_4 (1+4), and dil. to 100 mL with this acid. Transfer 5.0 mL aliquot to 500 mL vol. flask, add 200 mL 5% NaOH soln, and cool to room temp. Dil. to vol. with H_2O and mix thoroly.

(**b**) *Phenobarbital std soln.*—1.50 mg/100 mL. Dissolve 75.0 mg phenobarbital in $CHCl_3$ and dil. to 100 mL with $CHCl_3$. Dil. 10 mL aliquot to 50 mL with $CHCl_3$. Transfer 10 mL aliquot of latter soln to 100 mL vol. flask, dil. to vol. with $CHCl_3$, and mix.

37.083 ***Separation of Theobromine and Phenobarbital***

(*Caution: See* **51.011**, **51.039**, and **51.054**.)

Transfer portion of well mixed sample contg ≥15 mg phenobarbital to 125 mL separator, add 15 mL 5% NaOH soln, and ext with three 30 mL portions $CHCl_3$. Wash each $CHCl_3$ ext with 10 mL 5% NaOH soln in second separator. Discard $CHCl_3$.

Add 30 mL H_2SO_4 (1+4) to alk. mixt. in first separator, cool thoroly, and shake with 50 mL ether. Transfer aq. layer contg dissolved theobromine to second separator, cool, and shake with 40 mL ether. Remove lower phase to third separator and wash with another 40 mL portion ether. Repeat extn thru the 3 separators, using two 40 mL portions H_2SO_4 (1+4) and two 20 mL portions H_2O. Collect aq. exts in 250 mL vol. flask, dil. to vol. with H_2O, and mix. Reserve for theobromine detn.

Filter ether solns thru cotton pledget into beaker, washing the 3 separators and filter successively with three 5 mL portions ether. Evap. carefully to dryness, and dissolve residue in $CHCl_3$.

37.084 ***Spectrophotometric Determinations***

(**a**) *Theobromine.*—Pipet aliquot contg 4–8 mg theobromine into 500 mL vol. flask, add 200 mL 5% NaOH soln, and cool to room temp. Dil. to vol. with H_2O and mix. Det. A at 274 nm of this soln and of std theobromine soln, (**a**), A', relative to soln prepd by dilg 10 mL 5% NaOH soln to 25 mL. Calc. theobromine content of sample.

$$\text{mg Theobromine in aliquot} = 5.0\,A/A'.$$

(**b**) *Phenobarbital.*—Transfer $CHCl_3$ soln to vol. flask and dil. with $CHCl_3$ to obtain soln contg 20–40 mg phenobarbital/100 mL. Place 5.0 mL in 100 mL vol. flask, dil. to vol. with $CHCl_3$, and mix. Transfer 20 mL aliquot of latter soln to separator contg 25 mL NH_4OH (1+24). Similarly treat 20 mL aliquot std phenobarbital soln, (**b**), and 20 mL portion $CHCl_3$ as blank. Shake vigorously ≥1 min, sep., and discard $CHCl_3$. Let aq. ext stand 30 min. Det. A at 241 nm of clear aq. solns of sample, and of std, A', relative to blank, using same cell for std and sample. Calc. phenobarbital content of sample.

$$\text{mg Phenobarbital in final aliquot} = 0.30A/A'.$$

In presence of salicylates, proceed as in (**c**):

(**c**) *Phenobarbital in presence of salicylates.*—Prep. chromatgc column as in **37.051**, and adjust flow to 2–4 mL/min.

When $CHCl_3$ just stops flowing from tube, pipet 5 mL original $CHCl_3$ soln, (**b**), (equiv. to 1–2 mg phenobarbital) into tube, and collect eluate in 100 mL vol. flask. As level of $CHCl_3$ soln reaches top of column, add ca 5 mL $CHCl_3$, and repeat with second $CHCl_3$ wash. Add enough $CHCl_3$ to keep column of solv. 2–5 cm high, and collect ca 95 mL eluate. Wash outside surface of stem with stream of $CHCl_3$ and collect washings in vol. flask. Dil. to vol. with $CHCl_3$ and mix thoroly. Det. phenobarbital in eluates as in (**b**), beginning "Transfer 20 mL aliquot of latter soln . . ."

Sodium Butabarbital (*35*)—Official Final Action

37.085 ***Reagents***

(**a**) *Sodium carbonate soln.*—1*M*. Dissolve 10.6 g Na_2CO_3 and dil. to 100 mL with H_2O.

(**b**) *Mixed solvent.*—Isooctane-ether (4+1). Wash mixed solv. with equal vol. H_2O.

(**c**) *Ether.*—H_2O-satd. Use thruout.

(**d**) *Dilute ammonium hydroxide.*—Dil. 30 mL NH_4OH to 1 L with H_2O.

(**e**) *Diatomaceous earth.*—*See* **36.002.**

(**f**) *Dimethylsulfoxide* (*DMSO*).—Spectral grade (Fisher Scientific Co. D-136; M/CB Manufacturing Chemists MX 1457).

(**g**) *Butabarbital std solns.*—(*1*) *Stock soln.*—0.1 mg/mL. Dissolve 20 mg USP Ref. Std in ≤1 mL MeOH and dil. to 200 mL with dil. NH_4OH. (*2*) *Working soln.*—0.01 mg/mL. Dil. 10 mL stock soln to 100 mL with dil. NH_4OH.

37.086 ***Preparation of Sample***

Det. av. wt/tablet and pulverize. Transfer accurately weighed portion contg ca 20 mg butabarbital to 100 mL beaker. Add 1 mL *DMSO* and 2 drops HCl, and swirl to dissolve active ingredient. Add 1 mL H_2O and 3 g diat. earth, and mix thoroly until uniform.

37.087 ***Preparation of Column***

Place small glass wool plug at base of 250 × 25 mm chromatgc tube. Transfer uniform mixt. of 4 g diat. earth and 3 mL Na_2CO_3 soln to tube and tamp to uniform mass. Transfer sample prepn to column, drywash beaker with 1 g diat. earth, transfer wash to column, and tamp.

37.088 ***Determination***

Pass 75 mL mixed solv. thru column and discard. Elute butabarbital with 100 mL ether, collecting eluate in 250 mL separator. Rinse tip of column with ether. Ext eluate with three 50 mL portions dil. NH_4OH, collect extns in 200 mL vol. flask, and adjust to vol. with dil. NH_4OH. Dil. 10.0 mL of this soln to 100.0 mL with dil. NH_4OH. Read A of sample and std solns at max. ca 239 nm against dil. NH_4OH as ref. and calc. Na butabarbital.

Sodium Diphenylhydantoin in Capsules (*36*)
Official Final Action

37.089 ***Reagents***

(**a**) *Sodium carbonate.*—0.5*M*. Dissolve 5.3 g Na_2CO_3 and dil. to 100 mL.

(**b**) *Mixed solvent.*—Isooctane-$CHCl_3$ (7+3). Wash mixed solv. with equal vol. H_2O.

(**c**) *Chloroform.*—H_2O-satd. (*Caution: See* **51.056**.)

(**d**) *Acid-alcohol.*—Dil. 1 mL HCl (1+99) with 50 mL alcohol.

(**e**) *Diatomaceous earth.*—*See* **36.002.**

(**f**) *Diphenylhydantoin std soln.*—0.25 mg/mL. Dissolve 25 mg USP Ref. Std in 100 mL acid-alcohol.

37.090 ***Preparation of Sample***

Remove, as completely as possible, contents of capsules and weigh. Det. av. net contents. Mix, and transfer accurately weighed portion contg ca 100 mg Na diphenylhydantoin to 25 mL vol. flask. Add 2 mL *DMSO,* **37.085(f)**, and swirl mixt. ca 3 min. Add 4 drops HCl, swirl to mix, and immediately but cautiously add 0.5*M* Na_2CO_3 to vol. Mix, and filter thru rapid paper.

37.091 ***Preparation of Column***

Place small glass wool plug at base of 250 × 25 mm chromatgc tube. Mix 3 g diat. earth and 2 mL 0.5*M* Na_2CO_3, and transfer to tube; tamp. Mix 3 g diat. earth and 2.0 mL prepd sample soln, and transfer to column. Dry-wash beaker with ca 1 g diat. earth, and transfer wash to column. Place pad of glass wool on top of column.

37.092 ***Determination***

Pass 75 mL mixed solv. thru column, and discard. Elute diphenylhydantoin with 75 mL $CHCl_3$, collecting eluate in 125 mL g-s erlenmeyer. Rinse tip of column with $CHCl_3$. Evap. solv. to dryness on steam bath under air current. Dissolve residue in 25.0 mL acid-alcohol. Det. *A* of sample and std solns at max., ca 258 nm, against acid-alcohol as ref. Calc. Na diphenylhydantoin content. Diphenylhydantoin × 1.087 = Na diphenylhydantoin.

Chloral Hydrate (*37*)—Official Final Action

37.093 ***Principle***

Quinaldine ethyl iodide reacts with chloral hydrate to produce stable blue cyanine dye with *A* max. at ca 605 nm. Other polychlorinated compds do not interfere.

37.094 ***Reagents***

(**a**) *Quinaldine ethyl iodide soln.*—1.5%. Dissolve 1.5 g quinaldine ethyl iodide in H_2O and dil. to 100 mL. Filter if necessary.

(**b**) *2-Aminoethanol soln.*—0.1*N*. Dissolve 6.1 g 2-aminoethanol in H_2O and dil. to 1 L.

(**c**) *Chloral hydrate std soln.*—100 μg/mL. Dissolve 0.2500 g chloral hydrate USP in H_2O and dil. to 250 mL. Dil. 10 mL aliquot to 100 mL with H_2O.

37.095 ***Apparatus***

Recording spectrophotometer.—400–800 nm range with matched 1 cm cells.

37.096 ***Preparation of Sample***

(**a**) *Capsules.*—Place counted number of capsules contg ca 2.5 g chloral hydrate in g-s 250 mL flask, add 25 mL H_2O, stopper, and heat on steam bath with frequent swirling until dissolved. Cool, and transfer quant. to 250 mL vol. flask with H_2O. Dil. to vol., mix, and dil. stepwise to ca 100 μg/mL with H_2O.

(**b**) *Solns.*—Prep. soln contg ca 100 μg chloral hydrate/mL by stepwise diln with H_2O.

37.097 ***Determination***

Pipet 10 mL sample soln contg ca 1 mg chloral hydrate into 100 mL vol. flask and pipet 10 mL std chloral hydrate soln into second 100 mL vol. flask. Pipet 10 mL H_2O into third 100 mL vol. flask as blank. To each flask add 10 mL quinaldine ethyl iodide soln and 60 mL isopropanol, and mix. Add 5 mL 0.1*N* 2-aminoethanol and dil. to vol. with H_2O. Place in H_2O bath 1 hr at 60°. Cool, and record spectra of sample and std from 400 to 800 nm against blank. Do not exceed 120 nm/min near max. Det *A* max. at ca 605 nm, using baseline technic with ca 430 and ca 770 nm as base.

mg Chloral hydrate in sample aliquot
= (net *A* of sample soln/net *A* of std soln)
× mg chloral hydrate in 10 mL std soln.

37.098 ★ **(2-Isopropyl-4-Pentenyl) Urea** ★ **(Sedormid®) (*38*)—Official Final Action**

Direct $CHCl_3$ extn. *See* **32.237**, 10th ed.

37.099 ★ **Sulfonmethane (Sulfonal®) or** ★ **Sulfonethylmethane (Trional®) (*39*) Official Final Action**

Direct ether extn. *See* **32.238**, 10th ed. (*Caution: See* **51.011**, **51.039**, and **51.054**.)

Ethchlorvynol (1-Chloro-3-ethyl-1-penten-4-yn-3-ol) (*40*) Official Final Action

37.100 ***Reagents***

(**a**) *Ethchlorvynol.*—(*Caution: See* **51.011** and **51.015**.) Purify by vac. distn (62° at ca 10 mm) or assay by titrn as follows: Transfer ca 110 mg ethchlorvynol, accurately weighed, to 250 mL erlenmeyer contg 50 mL 2.5% $AgNO_3$ soln in 70% alcohol. Immediately titr. with 0.05*N* NaOH, using 8–10 drops Me red-methylene blue, (**e**). Perform blank detn and make any necessary correction. 1 mL 0.05*N* NaOH = 7.230 mg ethchlorvynol. (*Caution:* Protect pure ethchlorvynol from excessive exposure to light and air.) Store at <10° in glass containers with polyethylene or Teflon stopper liners.

(**b**) *Ethchlorvynol stock soln.*—10 mg/mL. Accurately weigh ca 0.5 g ethchlorvynol and dissolve in 5 mL alcohol. Transfer quant. to 50 mL vol. flask with 10 mL alcohol. Dil. to vol. with H_2O.

(**c**) *Internal std soln.*—2.0%. Dissolve 2.0 g 1,3-dichloro-2-propanol in 10 mL alcohol and dil. to 100 mL with H_2O.

(**d**) *Dichlorodimethylsilane soln.*—Dissolve 5 mL dichlorodimethylsilane in 100 mL toluene. (*Caution:* Dichlorodimethylsilane causes severe burns. Vapor is harmful. Avoid contact with skin, eyes, or clothing. Use effective fume removal device. *See also* **51.040**.)

(**e**) *Methyl red-methylene blue mixed indicator.*—Dissolve 0.3 g Me red in 60 mL alcohol and dil. to 100 mL with H_2O. Dissolve 0.2 g methylene blue in 100 mL 50% alcohol and add to Me red soln.

37.101 ***Apparatus***

Gas chromatograph.—With 1.2 m (4') × 4 mm glass column, packed with Carbowax 20M on 100–120 mesh Gas-Chrom Q, and H flame ionization detector. *Operating conditions:* temps (°)—column 115, detector 190, injection port 200; flow rates (mL/min)—N 50, H 92, air ca 500. Adjust column temp. to elute ethchlorvynol in 12–15 min (relative retention time of internal std is ca 0.8). Adjust H and air flow rates to give stable flame and good sensitivity. Adjust electrometer sensitivity so that 12 μg ethchlorvynol gives 50–70% deflection.

37.102 ***Preparation of GLC Column***

Carefully wash inside of column and small amt of fine glass wool with dichlorodimethylsilane soln, rinse with alcohol, and dry thoroly. Dissolve 5.0 g Carbowax 20M in 100 mL $CHCl_3$. Add Carbowax soln to 10.0 g 100–120 mesh Gas-Chrom Q in 250 mL

★ Surplus method—*see* inside front cover.

filter flask fitted with trap and stopper. Slowly apply vac. and maintain 5 min. Swirl slurry rapidly and transfer in small portions to buchner fitted with 9 cm Whatman No. 4 paper. Maintain vac. 5 min after last portion is added; then air dry coated support 1 hr by spreading on smooth surface. Oven dry addnl hr at 100°.

Carefully plug column exit with small pad of glass wool. Apply vac. to exit end and slowly add coated support thru inlet, tapping very gently to pack firmly. Pack to within 1 cm of area heated by injection port. Plug with glass wool and condition overnight at 220° with slow N stream.

37.103 ***Preparation of Sample***

(**a**) *Capsules (200—500 mg).*—Place counted number of capsules contg ca 2.5 g ethchlorvynol in 250 mL vol. flask; add 75 mL H_2O and 30 mL alcohol, stopper, and heat on steam bath with frequent swirling until dissolved. Cool and dil. to vol. with H_2O.

(**b**) *Capsules (100 mg).*—Place 10 capsules in 100 mL vol. flask, add 50 mL H_2O and 15 mL alcohol, stopper, and heat on steam bath with frequent swirling until dissolved. Cool and dil. to vol. with H_2O.

(**c**) *Solutions.*—Prep. soln contg ca 10 mg ethchlorvynol/mL by stepwise diln with 20% alcohol.

37.104 ***Determination***

Pipet 10 mL sample soln contg ca 100 mg ethchlorvynol into 50 mL vol. flask; pipet 10 mL ethchlorvynol stock soln into second 50 mL vol. flask. Pipet 10 mL internal std soln into each flask and dil. to vol. with H_2O.

Rinse 10 μL syringe with 50% alcohol and draw up 1 μL 50% alcohol. Draw in 1 μL air followed by 6 μL sample. Draw in 1 μL air and note sample vol. Insert needle thru septum of gas chromatograph, quickly depress plunger, and retract syringe needle. Inject 6 μL of each soln. Run std before and after sample. Calc. amt of ethchlorvynol in 10 mL sample aliquot as follows:

$$C = C' \times (X/X') \times (I'/I),$$

where C and C' = mg ethchlorvynol in 10 mL sample aliquot and std stock soln, resp.; X = area ethchlorvynol peak in sample chromatogram; X' = av. area ethchlorvynol peak in std chromatograms; I = area internal std peak in sample chromatogram; and I' = av. area internal std peak in std chromatograms.

Paraldehyde (*41*)—Official Final Action

37.105 ***Reagents***

(**a**) *Paraldehyde std.*—USP. Redistil twice and collect only fraction distg 120.5–123°. Store in amber g-s bottle. (*Caution:* Paraldehyde is toxic. Use effective fume removal device.)

(**b**) *Paraldehyde std solns.*—(*1*) *Stock soln.*—0.05 mL/mL. Pipet 5 mL std paraldehyde into 100 mL vol. flask, add 8.0 mL internal std, and dil. to vol. with acetone. (*2*) *Working std soln.*—0.005 mL/mL. Pipet 5 mL stock soln into 50 mL vol. flask and dil. to vol. with acetone.

(**c**) *Isoamyl alcohol.*—(M/CB Manufacturing Chemists). Check purity by injecting 5 μL into gas chromatograph. If any interfering peaks are present, redistil. (*Caution: See* **51.011**.)

(**d**) *Internal std.*—Dil. isoamyl alcohol, (**c**), with equal vol. acetone.

37.106 ***Apparatus***

(**a**) *Gas chromatographic column.*—2% cyclohexane dimethanol succinate (HIEFF-8BP) plus 20% Carbowax 20M on 80–100 mesh Diatoport S (Hewlett-Packard Co., Avondale, PA 19311) or Chromosorb W (HP). Prep. as follows: Weigh 500 mg HIEFF-8BP plus 5.0 g Carbowax 20M into 500 mL Morton flask. Add 200 mL $CHCl_3$ and, if necessary, heat on steam bath with swirling to dissolve liq. phase. Add 20 g 80–100 mesh Diatoport S (or Chromosorb W (HP)) and evap. $CHCl_3$ under reduced pressure on rotating evaporator. Remove last traces $CHCl_3$ in 100° oven. Pack 1.8 m (6′) × 4 mm id glass column and condition column 16 hr at 190° with N flow of 60 mL/min before use.

(**b**) *Gas chromatograph.*—Packard Model 7800 (replaced by 5700) with flame ionization detector and Hewlett-Packard Model 3370A (replaced by 3380) electronic integrator, or equivs. GLC conditions: temps (°)—column 110, injection port 125, detector 125; flow rates (mL/min)—N carrier gas 60, air 600, H 60; sensitivity 1 × 10^{-8} amp; and chart speed 26″/hr.

37.107 ***Preparation of Sample***

Pipet amt elixir contg 2.5 mL paraldehyde into 50 mL vol. flask. Add 4.0 mL internal std and dil. to vol. with acetone. Pipet 5 mL this soln into 50 mL vol. flask and dil. to vol. with acetone.

37.108 ***Determination***

Inject ca 4 μL std and sample solns into gas chromatograph operated as in **37.106(b)**. Make ⩾3 injections of sample and std solns and take av.

Calc. amt paraldehyde in sample as follows:

$$\% \text{ Paraldehyde} = (R_x/R_s) \times C \times DF,$$

where R_x = ratio of sample to internal std peak area in sample soln, R_s = ratio of std to internal std peak area in std soln, C = concn of std (%, v/v), and DF = sample diln factor.

Since GLC peaks for paraldehyde are narrow, symmetrical, and well defined, peak hts may be used in place of peak area.

Phenaglycodol (*42*)—Official Final Action

37.109 ***Apparatus***

Recording infrared spectrophotometer.—With two 1.0 mm liq. cells with NaCl windows (preferably matched) and KBr disk holder.

37.110 ***Reagents***

(**a**) *Phenaglycodol std.*—Available from Eli Lilly & Co., or equiv.

(**b**) *Carbon disulfide.*—Spectral grade.

(**c**) *Cotton.*—Wash thoroly with $CHCl_3$ and dry.

37.111 ***Determination***

(*Caution: See* **51.011**, **51.040**, and **51.056**.)

Det. av. wt/tablet or capsule, pulverize, and sieve to obtain uniform sample. Accurately weigh sample contg ca 200 mg phenaglycodol and transfer to 125 mL separator with 50 mL $CHCl_3$. Add 15 mL 0.5*N* NaOH, shake 1 min, and filter sepd $CHCl_3$ layer thru cotton into 150 mL beaker. Ext alk. soln with two addnl 25 mL portions $CHCl_3$, filtering each sepd $CHCl_3$ layer into beaker. Evap. combined exts just to dryness, using gentle current of air, at temp. <50°. Dissolve residue in CS_2, transfer quant. to 50 mL vol. flask, and dil. to vol. with CS_2.

Accurately weigh ca 200 mg std phenaglycodol, transfer to 125 mL separator with 50 mL $CHCl_3$, and ext as above.

Det. baseline *A* of sample and std solns against CS_2 at ca 9.85 μm. Draw baseline between minima at ca 9.75 μm and ca 10.0 μm. Calc. phenaglycodol content of sample.

Prep. KBr disk by grinding 2 mg residue and 200 mg spectroscopic grade KBr in Mullite mortar and press in die with hydraulic press. Record spectrum at 2–15 μm and compare with spectrum of extd std residue to det. identity of sample.

PHENOLIC DRUGS

p-Aminosalicylic Acid (PAS) and Isonicotinylhydrazine (INH) (*43*)—Official Final Action

37.112 ***Reagents***

(**a**) *Benzaldehyde.*—USP or reagent grade.

(**b**) *Concentrated phosphate buffer.*—pH 7. Dissolve 34 g anhyd. KH_2PO_4 in 136 mL 1*N* NaOH and dil. to 1 L with H_2O.

37.113 ***Extraction of Tablets***

(**a**) Accurately weigh sample of powd tablets contg 35–40 mg INH and transfer to 150 mL beaker. Stir with 20 mL H_2O, add 1.5 g $NaHCO_3$, and continue stirring until effervescence stops. Filter with vac. thru medium porosity fritted glass filter (3.5 cm diam. is convenient) precoated with ca 3 mm layer of diat. earth, **36.002**. Rinse beaker thoroly with 5 mL H_2O, break vac., transfer rinsings to funnel, washing down inside wall, and reapply vac. Repeat washing of beaker and funnel with 3 addnl 5 mL portions H_2O. Quant. transfer filtrate to 50 mL vol. flask with aid of small portions H_2O, dil. to vol., and mix. Proceed immediately with detn of PAS. Det. INH as soon as practicable, preferably $\leq$4 hr after prepn of $NaHCO_3$ soln.

(**b**) (*Applicable when filtration with vacuum is not feasible.*)—Weigh sample as in (**a**), and transfer quant. to 40–50 mL r-b centrf. tube. Cautiously add, in small portions, freshly prepd soln of 1.5 g $NaHCO_3$ in 20 mL H_2O. Agitate well after each addn, avoiding loss from foaming by occasionally adding few drops of ether. After all $NaHCO_3$ soln is added, continue agitation until effervescence stops. Centrf. 5–10 min at ca 2000 rpm and decant supernate into 50 mL vol. flask. Add 10 mL H_2O to tube, using rubber policeman to wash down wall, to disintegrate residual cake, and to secure uniform suspension. Centrf. as before, and combine supernate wash with original ext. Repeat washing with three 5 mL portions H_2O, dil. combined aq. phases to vol., mix, and filter thru fluted paper. Proceed as in (**a**).

37.114 ***p-Aminosalicylic Acid (PAS)***

From aq. $NaHCO_3$ ext, transfer aliquot contg ca 150 mg PAS to 500 mL vol. flask and dil. to vol. with H_2O. Transfer 10 mL aliquot to 250 mL vol. flask, add 12.5 mL concd pH 7 buffer, and dil. to vol. with H_2O. Measure *A* of this diln in 1 cm cell at 299 (max.), 244 (min.), and 325 nm against 1 + 19 diln of the buffer. (With instruments suitable for *A* readings in range 1.0–1.5, use 2 cm cell thruout method or modify diln so that concn of substance is twice that specified.) Calc. baseline A_B:

$$A_B = A_{299} - (0.3210\,A_{244} + 0.6790\,A_{325}).$$

Accurately weigh ca 50 mg finely powd pure PAS, dissolve in 2 mL alcohol, add 5 mL 0.1*N* NaOH, and dil. with H_2O to exactly 500 mL. Transfer 25 mL aliquot to 200 mL vol. flask, add 10 mL concd pH 7 buffer, and dil. to vol. with H_2O. Det. *A* at 244, 299, and 325 nm as above. Det. A_B, and from this value and that obtained from sample soln, calc. amt PAS in sample.

37.115 ***Isonicotinylhydrazine (INH)***

(*Caution: See* **51.011**, **51.040**, and **51.056**.)

Transfer 20 mL aliquot of the $NaHCO_3$ ext to 125 mL separator, add 0.5 mL benzaldehyde, shake 15 min, and let stand 10 min. Ext with six 20 mL portions $CHCl_3$, filter exts thru compact pledget of absorbent cotton into 150 mL beaker, and evap. filtrate on steam bath in air current until residue has only faint odor of benzaldehyde. Rinse down wall of beaker with little $CHCl_3$ to conc. residue at bottom, and evap. to dryness. Add 1–2 mL $CHCl_3$, evap. again to dryness on steam bath in air current, and heat residue few min. Repeat $CHCl_3$ and heating treatment until hot residue of benzylidine isonicotinylhydrazine (BINH) is odorless, or has at most very faint odor of benzoic acid (there must be no sweet odor or odor of benzaldehyde; take care to avoid loss from spattering).

Dissolve residue in $CHCl_3$ and transfer quant. to separator with addnl solv. Add $CHCl_3$ to vol. of 20–30 mL, shake with 10 mL freshly prepd 5% $NaHCO_3$, and filter $CHCl_3$ layer thru compact pledget of absorbent cotton. Wash aq. soln with three 10 mL portions $CHCl_3$, passing each wash thru filter, and evap. combined $CHCl_3$ exts to dryness on steam bath in air current.

Dissolve residue of BINH in alcohol without heat, and dil. to exactly 100 mL with alcohol. Dil. 5 mL aliquot of this soln to exactly 200 mL with alcohol, and det. *A* of diln (1 cm cell; alcohol blank) at 302 (max.) and 375 nm. Subtract reading at 375 (background *A* from impurities) from that at 302 nm. Difference represents *A* from BINH at 302 nm.

Dissolve ca 20 mg, accurately weighed, of pure BINH in alcohol and dil. to exactly 100 mL. Dil. 10 mL aliquot of this soln to exactly 250 mL with alcohol and det. *A* at 302 nm. Using this value and that due to BINH obtained from sample, calc. equiv. amt of BINH in sample. BINH $\times$ 0.6088 = INH.

37.116 ★ Dinitrophenol (or Its Sodium Compound) (*44*)—Official Final Action ★

Bromination method. *See* **32.331–32.332**, 10th ed.

Glyceryl Guaiacolate (*45*)—Official Final Action

Polarographic Method

(Not applicable in presence of salicylate)

37.117 ***Apparatus***

(**a**) *Polarograph.*—*See* **20.001**.

(**b**) *Micro or std cell, H-shaped.*—Satd calomel electrode, with 3% KCl-agar plug.

(**c**) *Water bath.*—Maintain at 65±1° in freely circulating H_2O bath.

37.118 ***Reagents***

(**a**) *Potassium nitrate soln.*—1*M*. Weigh 50.5 g KNO_3 into 500 mL vol. flask, dil. to vol. with H_2O, and mix.

(**b**) *Dilute sulfuric acid soln.*—10% (v/v). Dil. 20 mL H_2SO_4 (1+1) to 100 mL with H_2O and mix.

(**c**) *Gelatin maximum suppressor.*—1 mg/mL. Accurately weigh 100 mg gelatin (Difco Laboratories No. 0143-01; or Knox Gelatine Inc., Johnstown, NY 12095, unflavored gelatin No. 1) into 100 mL vol. flask, and dissolve in small amt H_2O on steam bath. Cool, dil. to vol. with H_2O, and mix. Prep. fresh daily, as needed.

(**d**) *Supporting electrolyte.*—pH 10.4. Weigh 53.5 g NH_4Cl into 1 L vol. flask, add 400 mL NH_4OH, mix to dissolve, and dil. to vol. with H_2O.

(**e**) *Glyceryl guaiacolate std soln.*—1 mg/mL. Accurately weigh 25 mg glyceryl guaiacolate std into 25 mL vol. flask. Dil. to vol. with H_2O and mix.

37.119 ***Preparation of Sample***

(**a**) *Sirups.*—Quant. transfer accurately measured portion of sample contg ca 100 mg glyceryl guaiacolate to 125 mL separator, add 10 mL dil. H_2SO_4, and ext with four 20 mL portions $CHCl_3$, and then with 15 mL $CHCl_3$. Collect $CHCl_3$ exts in second separator and wash with 10 mL H_2O. Filter $CHCl_3$ layer thru pledget of $CHCl_3$-washed cotton into 100 mL vol. flask. Rinse

★ Surplus method—*see* inside front cover.

separator with 2–3 mL $CHCl_3$ and add wash to vol. flask. Dil. to vol. with $CHCl_3$ and mix.

(b) *Tablets.*—Det. av. wt/tablet. Grind without loss to pass No. 60 sieve. Accurately weigh powder contg ca 50 mg glyceryl guaiacolate and transfer to 125 mL separator. Add 10 mL H_2O and shake 2 min. Proceed as in **(a)**, beginning ". . . add 10 mL dil. H_2SO_4, . . ."

37.120 ***Derivative Formation***

Pipet duplicate 10 mL aliquots for sirups or 20 mL aliquots for tablets of prepd soln into sep. 100 mL vol. flasks and carefully evap. to dryness with aid of air only. Add 10 mL H_2O to each and shake to dissolve glyceryl guaiacolate. Label flasks as sample and blank. Pipet 10 mL glyceryl guaiacolate std soln into third 100 mL vol. flask and label as std.

Pipet 3 mL H_2SO_4 (1+1) into each flask. Pipet 3 mL 1*M* KNO_3 into std and sample flasks and 3.0 mL H_2O into blank flask. Place flasks in 65° const temp. bath. When solns reach 65°, heat addnl 60 min. Remove from bath and cool to room temp. Into each flask pipet 25 mL electrolyte soln and 5 mL gelatin soln, cool to room temp., dil. to vol. with H_2O, and mix thoroly.

37.121 ***Polarography***

Transfer soln to polarographic cell and bubble N thru for 5 min with micro H cell or 10 min with std H cell at moderate rate. Polarograph from −0.2 to −0.9 v against satd calomel ref. electrode. Measure ht of diffusion current (I_d) at half-wave potential as follows: Draw line tangent to top of residual current extending to half-wave potential point. Draw line along top of limiting current extending to half-wave potential point. Measure vertical drop at half-wave potential between the 2 lines in convenient units.

Det. glyceryl guaiacolate concn by comparing wave ht of sample soln with those of std and blank solns.

Subtract diffusion current (I_d^b) of blank, if any, from sample only. Perform all detns at same current sensitivity and within same time span.

37.122 ***Calculations***

(a) *Sirup.*—mg Glyceryl guaiacolate/mL

$$= 100 \times (I_d - I_d^b) \times C/(I_d' \times V),$$

(b) *Tablets.*—mg Glyceryl guaiacolate/tablet

$$= 50 \times (I_d - I_d^b) \times C \times W_t/(I_d' \times W_s),$$

where I_d, I_d^b, and I_d' = diffusion current of sample, blank, and std solns, resp.; C = mg glyceryl guaiacolate/mL std soln; W_t and W_s = av. tablet wt and wt sample taken, resp.; and V = mL liq. prepn taken.

Guaiacol *(46)*—Official Final Action

37.123 ***Reagent***

Hydriodic acid.—Sp gr 1.7. Boil HI 30 min under reflux with excess of hypophosphorous acid. When cool, transfer to dark, g-s bottle. Do not leave bottle unstoppered more than few min.

37.124 ***Apparatus***

Methoxyl apparatus.—*See* Fig. **47:07**.

37.125 ***Determination***

Place aliquot of alk. guaiacol soln (guaiacol dissolved in 1% NaOH) contg 0.03–0.06 g guaiacol in boiling flask and evap. soln just to dryness on steam bath in air current. For solid guaiacol compds, weigh 0.06–0.10 g and transfer directly to flask. Complete detn by method for methoxyl group, **47.050**, beginning "Add 2.5 mL melted *phenol* from wide-tip pipet . . ." Boil 30 min and titr. with 0.1*N* $Na_2S_2O_3$. 1 mL 0.1*N* I = 0.00207 g guaiacol; 0.00229 g guaiacol carbonate; 0.00404 g K guaiacol sulfonate.

Hexylresorcinol *(47)*—Official Final Action

37.126 ***Reagents***

(a) *Sodium thiosulfate std soln.*—0.1*N*. Prep. as in **50.037**.

(b) *Purified methanol.*—Purify if necessary as follows: Add enough Br to com. MeOH to give bright yellow soln, heat to bp on H_2O bath, and boil 5 min. Cool, and carefully decolorize by adding 10% $NaHSO_3$ soln dropwise until just colorless.

37.127 ***Standardization of Thiosulfate***

Add 30 mL 0.1*N* KBr-$KBrO_3$, **4.002(g)**, and 10 mL purified MeOH to 150 mL g-s flask. Wet stopper. Add 5 mL HCl, stopper flask, immediately place under running tap H_2O, and swirl until flask cools to room temp.; continue to shake 5 min after adding HCl. Cautiously loosen stopper and add 5 mL 20% KI soln. Swirl gently to liberate I, wash stopper, and titr. with $Na_2S_2O_3$ soln. Add starch paste when soln is pale yellow.

37.128 ***Determination***

Transfer 0.07–0.09 g sample to 150 mL g-s flask. Add 10 mL MeOH, **(b)**, and swirl gently to dissolve sample. Add 30 mL 0.1*N* KBr-$KBrO_3$. Moisten stopper, add 5 mL HCl, stopper flask, and immediately hold under running H_2O while swirling vigorously. When cooled to room temp. (ca 1 min), remove from tap and shake vigorously 5 min after adding HCl. Cautiously loosen stopper and add 5 mL 20% KI soln. Swirl gently, wash stopper with little H_2O, add 1 mL $CHCl_3$, and titr. with $Na_2S_2O_3$ soln while swirling flask gently. Near end point, stopper flask and shake vigorously to remove halogen from $CHCl_3$. When soln becomes pale yellow, add starch paste and continue titrn. End point is reached when starch-I color does not return during 30 sec of vigorous shaking. 1 mL 0.1*N* KBr-$KBrO_3$ soln = 0.00486 g hexylresorcinol.

8-Hydroxyquinoline Sulfate (Oxyquinoline) *(48)* Official Final Action

Method I

(For amts of hydroxyquinoline sulfate between 25 and 250 mg. Use this method whenever nature of sample permits.)

37.129 ***Extraction***

(a) *Interfering substances absent.*—Dissolve sample in ca 75 mL H_2O and add 5 mL HCl.

(b) *Nonoily preparations.*—Ext preferably from soln alk. with $NaHCO_3$ or borax. If extn from such medium is impracticable, or if compds of NH_3 or heavy or alk. earth metals are present, add Me red, **50.014(a)**, and adjust with NaOH and/or HCl to slight acidity. Add $NaOAc.3H_2O$ in proportion of 1 g/100 mL soln. If heavy or alk. earth metals are present, also add 2 mL HOAc/100 mL soln.

Ext adjusted soln with enough 20 mL portions $CHCl_3$. For alk. or slightly acid soln, usually 6 extns suffice; when extra HOAc has been added, 10–12 extns are needed. Test for complete extn by adding little HCl (1+9) to last portion, evapg $CHCl_3$ on steam bath, adjusting to 70°, and adding drop of 0.01*N* KBr-$KBrO_3$ and then drop of Me red; Me red should be bleached immediately.

Ext combined $CHCl_3$ exts with five 10 mL portions HCl (1+9). If salicylic acid, volatile oils, etc., are present, wash each acid portion with same 10 mL ether. If sample contains phenol or other volatile interfering substances not completely removed by preceding process, boil acid soln to remove them, keeping vol. ca const by adding more H_2O.

(c) *Ointments, etc.*—Transfer sample to separator with 50 mL ether, and ext with five 10 mL portions HCl (1+9). If salicylic acid, etc., is present, wash each acid portion with same 10 mL ether. Add Me red; make just alk. with 10% NaOH soln, then just acid with dil. HCl, and proceed as in (**b**), beginning "Add $NaOAc.3H_2O$ . . ."

37.130 ***Determination***

Adjust acid soln (**a**), (**b**), or (**c**), to 50° and keep at this temp. during titrn by reheating occasionally. Add drop (or more) Me red **50.014(a)**, *from buret* and titr. with 0.1*N* KBr-$KBrO_3$, **4.002(g)**. (Color of liq. gradually changes from brown-orange to yellow; add more indicator whenever soln becomes yellow. At slightly beyond halfway point, dibromohydroxyquinoline may crystallize and adsorb dye. Disregard color of ppt and judge by that of soln. By dilg to ≤0.1 g hydroxyquinoline sulfate/100 mL, formation of ppt can be avoided.) End point is reached when, after waiting 10 sec for absorption of last drop of KBr-$KBrO_3$ soln and adding drop of indicator, it is bleached almost immediately. Timing for addn of drop of indicator at end point is important, as proper conditions prevail only brief period.

Read vols of 2 solns consumed. Measure 10 mL Me red into erlenmeyer, add 2 mL HCl, and titr. with 0.1*N* KBr-$KBrO_3$. Correct main titrn for vol. of Br consumed by measured vol. indicator used in titrn. 1 mL 0.1*N* KBr-$KBrO_3$ = 0.00508 g $(C_9H_7NO)_2.H_2SO_4.H_2O$.

37.131 ***Method II***

(For amts between 2 and 10 mg)

Ext as in **37.129**. Start titrn as in **37.130**, using 0.01*N* KBr-$KBrO_3$, and dild Me red (1 vol. Me red, **50.014(a)**, 4 vols H_2O, and enough NaOH to dissolve dye) instead of stronger reagents. Use as little indicator as possible. When near end point, shown by more rapid consumption of indicator, heat to 70°, and complete titrn at this temp.

Methyl Salicylate (*49*)—Official Final Action

37.132 ***Reagents***

(**a**) *Salicylic acid std soln.*—20 μg/mL. Dissolve 0.2500 g reagent grade salicylic acid in 95 mL $CHCl_3$ in 250 mL vol. flask and dil. to vol. with alcohol. Dil. 2.00 mL to 100 mL with alcohol.

(**b**) *Sodium bicarbonate soln.*—Dissolve 5 g $NaHCO_3$ in 100 mL of H_2O to which 1 drop HCl has been added.

37.133 ***Determination***

Prep. sample diln, if necessary, to contain ca 5% Me salicylate. Pipet 5 mL sample or diln into 50 mL ether-pet ether mixt. (1+1) in separator and wash with two 5 mL portions cold, freshly prepd $NaHCO_3$ soln. Discard unemulsified aq. phases. Ext org. layer with two 5 mL portions 5% NaOH soln followed by two 5 mL portions H_2O. Let phases sep. 5 min and drain unemulsified aq. layers into another separator. Wash combined exts with 10 mL pet ether and drain aq. phase into another separator. Acidify cautiously with HCl (litmus paper) and ext with four 20 mL and one 15 mL portions $CHCl_3$. Filter each ext thru $CHCl_3$-moistened plug of cotton into 250 mL vol. flask. Dil. to vol. with alcohol and transfer 2.00 mL aliquot to 100 mL vol. flask.

Dil. to vol. with alcohol and det. *A* at max. (ca 305 nm). Calc. as salicylic acid by comparison with *A* of std soln. Salicylic acid × 1.1016 = Me salicylate.

Phenolphthalein in Chocolate Preparations (*50*)
Official Final Action

37.134 ***Reagents***

(**a**) *Potassium hydroxide soln.*—5±0.1*N*.

(**b**) *Iodine soln.*—0.5*N*. Dissolve 12.7 g KI in 10 mL H_2O, add 6.35 g I, and when dissolved add 12 mL KOH soln, (**a**). Dil. to 100 mL with H_2O.

(**c**) *Sodium sulfite soln.*—Dissolve 12.6 g anhyd. Na_2SO_3 in H_2O and dil. to 100 mL with H_2O.

37.135 ***Preparation of Alcoholic Extract***

Chill sample until hard; then reduce to granules by grating, shaving, or grinding. Mix thoroly. Accurately weigh amt of prepd sample contg ca 0.1 g phthln into gooch with thin asbestos mat or fritted glass disk. Ext fat with 5, 4, and 3 mL CCl_4, using slight suction towards end. Place crucible on bell jar app. Ext phthln from sample with several portions hot alcohol, collecting filtrate in 300 mL tall beaker. Wash underside of crucible free from phthln with hot alcohol (ca 50 mL is enough for extn and washings). Evap. combined alc. exts to dryness on steam bath.

37.136 ***Determination***

Dissolve residue at room temp. in 1–1.5 mL KOH soln. (Alk. phthln soln is unstable in air, and phthln should be converted to tetraiodo compd within 1 hr.) Add piece of ice (ca 40 g) and 7–8 mL I soln. Add HCl dropwise from buret, using stirring rod, to complete pptn. If ppt and supernate are not brown, add addnl I soln to ensure excess. Again dissolve ppt by adding KOH from buret dropwise, with stirring. Wash down any unreacted phthln adhering to sides of beaker with little H_2O. (Soln should now be blue to blue-purple.)

Repeat pptn with acid and resoln with alkali 3 more times, adding small piece of ice if necessary. Then add 1–1.5 mL Na_2SO_3 soln to blue alk. soln and filter into 250 mL beaker thru gooch with *thin* asbestos mat or *coarse* fritted glass disk. Wash crucible several times with H_2O. Acidify filtrate with HCl, using few mL excess, and heat on steam bath 20–30 min, stirring occasionally. Decant hot supernate thru weighed gooch (with asbestos mat or medium fritted glass disk). Wash white to cream-colored ppt in beaker by decantation with hot H_2O few times. Completely transfer ppt to the gooch and wash with hot H_2O until filtrate is clear and gives neg. test for Cl. When app. has cooled and ppt has been sucked fairly dry, wash ppt several times with pet ether, using suction toward end. Dry tetraiodophenolphthalein to const wt at 110–130°. Wt ppt × 0.3873 = wt phthln.

37.137 **Phenolphthalein in Emulsions (*51*)**
Official Final Action

Shake sample well, preferably in mech. shaker, 10 min. Accurately weigh amt of sample contg ca 0.1 g phthln from weighing buret directly into centrf. bottle. Add 100 mL alcohol-ether (1+3), stopper bottle, shake vigorously, and then centrf. until clear. Decant into separator. Wash residue in bottle twice with 10 mL portions solv. mixt., adding these washings to separator. Dissolve residue in bottle in few mL H_2O and reppt gums with 50 mL solv. mixt. Shake and centrf. as before, decanting into separator. Wash residue and bottle with three 10 mL portions solv. mixt. and add these to separator. Dissolve residue in few mL H_2O and test for complete extn with NaOH.

Shake exts in separator repeatedly with 25 mL portions ca 0.1*N* NaOH until phthln is completely removed, as shown by absence of color. Combine alk. exts in another separator and acidify soln with dil. H_2SO_4 (1+15).

Ext phthln by shaking acid mixt. repeatedly with 10 mL portions ether. Test for complete extn with NaOH soln. Combine ether exts in 150 mL beaker, evap. to dryness, and det. phthln as in **37.136**, omitting filtration of alk. soln.

Phenolphthalein in Tablets

37.138 ★ ***Ether Extraction Method (52)*** ★
Official Final Action

See **37.138**, 12th ed.

37.139 ★ **Phenolsulfonates (*53*)—Official Final Action** ★

Bromination method. *See* **32.342**, 10th ed.

Thymol (*54*)—Official Final Action

37.140 ***Preparation of Solution***

Weigh 2 g pulverized thymol, transfer to 500 mL vol. flask, and add 25 mL 25% NaOH soln. Agitate until thymol is dissolved and dil. to vol. at 20° with H_2O.

37.141 ***Method I*** ***Determination***

Transfer 25 mL aliquot thymol soln to 250 mL g-s erlenmeyer, add 20 mL hot HCl (1+1), and immediately add 1–3 mL less than theoretical vol. 0.1*N* KBr-$KBrO_3$, **4.002(g)**. Warm to 70–80°, add 2 drops 0.1% aq. Me orange, and titr. slowly with KBr-$KBrO_3$ soln, swirling vigorously after each addn. When red of Me orange has been bleached, add 2 drops titrg soln, stopper, shake vigorously 10 sec, add 1 drop Me orange, and again shake vigorously 10 sec. Continue addn of KBr-$KBrO_3$ soln, 2 drops at time, shaking each time until red disappears. Add 1 drop Me orange, shake vigorously, and if red does not disappear, repeat alternate addn of 2 drops KBr-$KBrO_3$ soln and 1 drop Me orange, shaking after each addn as before until red disappears. Calc. mL KBr-$KBrO_3$ soln used to % thymol. 1 mL 0.1*N* KBr-$KBrO_3$ = 0.003756 g thymol. Reserve mixt. in titrg flask for **37.142**.

37.142 ***Method II***

To cooled mixt. from titrn, **37.141**, add 3–5 mL addnl KBr-$KBrO_3$ soln. (If sample has not been previously analyzed by **37.141**, det. approx. vol. of KBr-$KBrO_3$ soln to use by adding 20 mL HCl (1+1) to 25 mL soln, **37.140**, heating to ca 80°, and titrg slowly with KBr-$KBrO_3$ soln, while vigorously swirling flask, to yellow color maintained 1 min.) Stopper, shake, add 1 g solid KI, wash sides of flask and stopper with H_2O, and titr. I liberated by excess KBr-$KBrO_3$ soln with 0.1*N* $Na_2S_2O_3$, using starch soln, **6.005(f)**, as indicator. Calc. vol. $Na_2S_2O_3$ soln used in terms of KBr-$KBrO_3$ soln, deduct from total vol. KBr-$KBrO_3$ soln added, and calc. to % thymol.

37.143 **Thymol in Antiseptics (*55*)—Official Final Action**

(*Caution: See* **51.011**, **51.039**, and **51.054**.)

If alc. content is not known, make preliminary alcohol detn.

Transfer 50 mL sample (or aliquot contg 0.05–0.10 g thymol) to Pt or porcelain evapg dish. Add 6–7 mL 50% NaOH soln, mix well, and carefully dealcoholize by placing dish on steam bath before elec. fan. Evap. vol. slightly more than amt of alcohol present. (If >30% alcohol is present, dil. with H_2O to alc. content of 25%. In no case should evapn be carried >70% of original vol.) Transfer soln to 125 mL separator, washing out evapg dish with enough H_2O to bring vol. to ca 75 mL.

★ Surplus method—*see* inside front cover.

Ext alk. soln with two 20 mL portions pet ether. Wash combined exts once with 5–10 mL 5% NaOH soln and add washings to aq. layer. Ext aq. soln contg thymol, together with Na salts of boric, benzoic, and salicylic acids, with ether as in **36.001**, using 20, 15, 15, 10, and 10 mL. Use 8–10 extns if prepn contains glycerol. Combine ether exts, transfer to 250 mL g-s erlenmeyer, and add 5 mL recently prepd alc. KOH soln, **28.025**. Evap. most of ether, using steam bath and elec. fan but do not evap. entirely to dryness. Leave 6–8 mL residue and add to it 75 mL hot H_2O (80–90°) and 10 mL HCl.

Immediately add 1–3 mL less than theoretical vol. 0.1*N* KBr-$KBrO_3$, **4.002(g)**, swirling constantly. Add 2 drops aq. 0.1% Me orange and titr. slowly with KBr-$KBrO_3$ soln as in **37.141**.

Test for complete extn by shaking aq. layer with two 15–20 mL portions ether and titrg the thymol, if any, in ether exts. Add this titrn to that obtained for main ether ext.

If theoretical amt of thymol present is not known, add 2 drops Me orange and titr. slowly, swirling constantly during addn of KBr-$KBrO_3$ soln until red color is bleached. Continue as in **37.141**, beginning ". . . add 2 drops titrg soln, stopper, shake vigorously . . ."

Caution: To avoid loss of thymol by volatilization, both evapn of alcohol and later evapn of ether must be done carefully.

Acenocoumarol, Dicumarol (Bishydroxycoumarin), Phenprocoumon, Potassium Warfarin, and Sodium Warfarin (*56*)—Official Final Action

37.144 ***Principle***

Basic soln of drug is acidified and extd with $CHCl_3$ or $CHCl_3$-pyrimidine-propylene glycol (for dicumarol), and *A* of extd material is read in flowcell at 308 nm.

37.145 ***Apparatus***

(**a**) *Automatic analyzer.*—AutoAnalyzer with following modules (Technicon Instruments Corp.): Sampler II with 20/hr (2:1) cam; proportioning pump I; manifold (Fig. **37:02**).

(**b**) *Filter.*—Fill 50 × 5 mm id glass tubing completely, but loosely, with glass wool.

(**c**) *Spectrophotometer.*—Double-beam spectrophtr which records *A* at fixed wavelength, with 10 mm flowcell (Arthur H. Thomas Co., No. 8495-L10) (2 mm flowcell (Beckman Instruments, No. 565411) for dicumarol).

(**d**) *Ultrasonic generator.*—Model 11, 150 watt (Heat Systems-Ultrasonic, Inc., 38 E Mall, Plainview, NY 11803).

37.146 ***Reagents***

(**a**) *Chloroform.*—H_2O-washed and filtered thru paper. Prep. fresh daily. (Use in all except dicoumarol detn.)

(**b**) *Chloroform-pyridine-propylene glycol soln.*—Mix 50 mL pyridine with 50 mL propylene glycol and dil. to 1 L with $CHCl_3$. Use in dicumarol assay.

(**c**) *Acenocoumarol std soln.*—0.08 mg/mL. Accurately weigh ca 20 mg acenocoumarol std in 250 mL vol. flask. Dissolve in ca 100 mL 0.01*N* NaOH with aid of ultrasonic generator and dil. to vol. with 0.01*N* NaOH.

(**d**) *Dicumarol (bishydroxycoumarin) std soln.*—0.25 mg/mL. Accurately weigh ca 25 mg USP Ref. Std Bishydroxycoumarin in 100 mL vol. flask. Dissolve in ca 50 mL 0.01*N* NaOH with aid of ultrasonic generator and dil. to vol. with same solv. Prep. fresh daily.

(**e**) *Phenprocoumon std soln.*—0.12 mg/mL. Accurately weigh ca 30 mg USP Ref. Std Phenprocoumon in 250 mL vol. flask. Dissolve in ca 100 mL 0.01*N* NaOH with aid of ultrasonic generator and dil. to vol. with 0.01*N* NaOH.

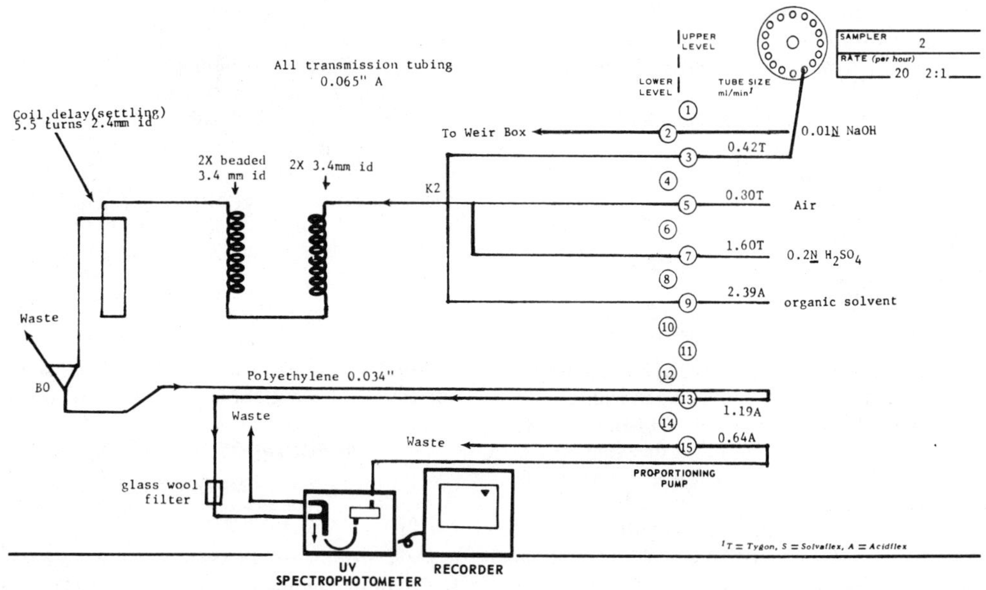

FIG. 37:02—Flow diagram for automated analysis for acenocoumarol, dicumarol, phenprocoumon, potassium warfarin, and sodium warfarin

(**f**) *Warfarin std soln.*—0.1 mg/mL. Accurately weigh ca 25 mg USP Ref. Std Warfarin into 250 mL vol. flask, and dissolve and dil. to vol. with 0.01*N* NaOH.

37.147 ***Preparation of Sample***

Disintegrate individual tablet or capsule or disperse weighed composite in accurately measured vol. 0.01*N* NaOH to give drug concn (mg/mL) as follows: acenocoumarol 0.08, dicoumarol 0.25, phenprocoumon 0.12, Na or K warfarin 0.10. Use ultrasonic generator ca 10 min to assure tablet disintegration. Let suspension stand 1.5 hr with occasional mixing.

37.148 ***Analytical System***

Sample is withdrawn, segmented with air, and acidified with 0.2*N* H_2SO_4. Solv., (**a**) or (**b**), is added, mixed in beaded coil, and phases are sepd in BO fitting. Org. phase contg extd drug is debubbled, and *A* of soln at 308 nm is measured in 10 mm flowcell (2 mm flowcell for dicumarol).

37.149 ***Start-Up***

Pump alcohol thru solv. line 10 min; then pump solv. thru line 5 min. Place remaining tubes in their resp. solns and let system equilibrate 20–30 min. Calibrate spectrophtr at 2 or 3 absorbances. Adjust mask in ref. compartment of spectrophtr to set desired baseline.

37.150 ***Shut-Down***

Place acid, base, and sampling lines in H_2O, leave solv. line in its reservoir, and pump 5 min. Remove acid, base, and sampling lines from H_2O and continue pumping 5 min to purge system of H_2O. Place solv. line in alcohol and pump 5 min. Remove line and pump system dry.

37.151 ***Determination***

Fill sample cups in following order: 4 cups std soln, 5 cups sample soln, 1 cup std soln, 5 cups sample soln, etc. Place 2 cups std soln at end of each run. (Extra cups of std solns at start and end of sampling pattern are used to overcome carryover effect in transitions from wash soln to std soln and vice versa. Three extra cups at beginning and 1 extra cup at end should suffice, but det. exact number needed for equilibrium by experiment. System should give uniform response for at least final pair of extra std cups before sample pattern is started.) Start Sampler II. After last cup has been sampled, let system operate until steady baseline is obtained. Draw tangent to initial and final baselines. Subtract baseline to det. net *A* and *A'* for each sample and std peak, resp. Discard values for first 3 and last std peaks and calc. av. std *A'*.

mg Na (or K) warfarin in portion taken = 1.071 (or 1.124) × $(A/A') \times C \times D$, where 1.071 and 1.124 = ratios of MW of Na and K warfarin to warfarin, resp.; C = concn of std in mg/mL, and D = diln factor.

mg Acenocoumarin, dicumarol, or phenprocoumon in portion taken = $(A/A') \times C \times D$.

SULFONAMIDE DRUGS

Mixtures of Sulfonamides

★ Paper Chromatographic Method (57) ★
Official First Action

37.152 ***Apparatus***

(**a**) *Chromatographic chamber.*—*See* **29.006(f)**; with trays approx. 3.8 × 31.6 cm (1.5 × 8.5"), glass lid, and fasteners for ascending chromatgy.

(**b**) *Chromatographic paper.*—8 × 8" (20 × 20 cm) sheets, Whatman No. 1, or equiv.

(**c**) *Viewing apparatus.*—Use light source having 160 microwatts/sq cm at 253.7 nm at distance of 46 cm suspended ≥23 cm above paper. Fluorescence Analysis Cabinet C-3F with model C-81 lamps is convenient (Spectronics Corporation, 956 Brush Hollow Rd, Westbury, NY 11590).

37.153 ***Reagents***

(Use reagent grade materials except as noted.)

(**a**) *Mobile solvent.*—50 mL CH_2Cl_2.

(**b**) *Immobile solvent.*—Dissolve 30 mL redistd formamide in 70 mL acetone. Prep. fresh daily.

★ Surplus method—*see* inside front cover.

(c) *Sodium nitrite soln.*—0.1%. Prep. fresh daily.

(d) *Ammonium sulfamate soln.*—0.5%.

(e) *N-(1-naphthyl) ethylenediamine dihydrochloride (NED) soln.*—See **42.017(d)**.

(f) *Dilute hydrochloric acid.*—Approx. 0.12*N*. Dil. 10 mL HCl to 1 L.

(g) *Chromatographic rinse soln.*—Dil. 9 vols. MeOH with 1 vol. NH_4OH (2+5).

(h) *Sulfacetamide, sulfadiazine, sulfamerazine, and sulfamethazine.*—USP Ref. Stds.

(i) *Sulfathiazole std.*—NF XI grade, or equiv.

37.154 ***Preparation of Standards***

(a) Prep. sep. std solns for each component of sample under test. Accurately weigh ca 10 mg Ref. Std, transfer quant. with MeOH rinses to 10 mL vol. flask contg 0.3 mL NH_4OH, dissolve, and dil. to vol. with MeOH. Transfer 1.0 mL of this soln to 100 mL vol. flask and dil. to vol. with 0.12*N* HCl. MeOH solns of stds are stable ≥1 week; acid solns, ≥1 month.

(b) Prep. mixed chromatgc std soln by transferring 1 mL of each MeOH soln of required stds to small g-s flask and mixing. This std is used to identify components of test sample on chromatogram.

37.155 ***Preparation of Sample***

Det. av. wt/tablet and pulverize. Accurately weigh amt powder contg ca 50 mg of each sulfonamide and transfer with MeOH rinses to 50 mL vol. flask contg 3 mL NH_4OH. Shake occasionally during 15 min and dil. to vol. with MeOH. Mix thoroly.

37.156 ***Determination***

Draw pencil line parallel to and 2.5 cm from bottom of paper. Mark line at points 2.5 and 5 cm from each edge of paper. Impregnate paper by dipping it in immobile solv. 30 sec. (For convenience, roll paper and dip rolled sheet into 100 mL graduate contg immobile solv.) Remove paper, drain 10 sec, and blot between filter papers. Place impregnated paper on dry filter paper and air dry 3–5 min. With 100 μL pipet and by repeated applications, streak sample soln along starting line, limiting delivery to ca 20 μL/streak. Evap. solv. with gentle air current between applications. Keep within marks 5 cm from either edge, and make streak as narrow as possible by uniform motion of pipet along starting line. Rinse outside tip of pipet with drop (ca 10 μL) of chromatgc rinse soln, and streak rinse along starting line between 5 and 2.5 cm points at right edge. Repeat rinsing twice and finally blow out pipet. (Restricting application of rinse to sep. area prevents diffusion of major streak.) Apply 10 μL spot of mixed chromatgc std soln at mark 2.5 cm from left edge. Dry paper 5 min before developing it.

Place mobile solv. in tray in chromatgc tank, cover tank, and let equilibrate ca 15 min. Remove cover, and without delay, place 7–10 mL H_2O in second tray and suspend paper so that it dips into mobile solv. Seal edges of lid to tank with masking tape and develop chromatogram 1 hr. Remove paper from tank and air dry 5 min.

Place chromatogram on dry sheet of filter paper and view it under shortwave UV light. Sulfacetamide (lowest R_f) is light-sensitive and must be protected from excessive exposure. Circle sulfacetamide band and cover circled area with dry sheet of filter paper. Outline remaining bands and confirm identity of sample components by matching R_f values with those of spots from chromatgc stds.

Cut marked zones from paper. Cut each zone into 5 or 6 pieces and place in 50 mL g-s conical flask. Add 20.0 mL 0.12*N* HCl to each flask. Let stand 15–30 min; swirl each flask ≥5 times. Filter solns thru dry glass wool into test tube, discarding first 4–5 mL filtrate. Pipet 5 mL aliquot of each sample soln into sep. 10 mL vol. flasks. Pipet 3 mL aliquot of each required std soln into sep. 10 mL vol. flasks. To each flask, and to blank flask contg 5 mL 0.12*N* HCl, add 1 mL $NaNO_2$ soln and 0.10 mL HCl. Let stand 5 min with frequent swirling. Then add 1 mL NH_4 sulfamate soln, swirl frequently, and let stand 5 min. Finally add 1 mL NED soln, swirl, adjust to vol. with H_2O, mix, and let stand ≥15 but ≤60 min. Record spectra of sample and std solns between 440 and 700 nm against blank. Draw baseline, and det. corrected *A* at max., ca 545 nm.

mg Individual sulfonamides/g sample taken

$$= 2000 \times (A/A') \times (C/W),$$

where *A* and *A'* refer to sample and std solns, resp. (baseline-corrected), *C* = mg std in aliquot taken, and *W* = g sample.

Trisulfapyrimidines (*58*)—Official Final Action

Total Trisulfapyrimidines

37.157 ***Principle***

Total trisulfapyrimidines in sample are detd by coupling with *N*-1-naphthyl ethylenediamine.2HCl (NED), recording spectra of samples and stds between 660 and 480 nm. Individual sulfonamides are sepd by TLC and their ratios detd spectrophtric after coupling with NED.

37.158 ***Reagents***

(a) *Ammonia-methanol soln.*—Dil. 5 mL NH_4OH to 100 mL with MeOH.

(b) *Sulfamerazine std soln.*—Approx. 6 μg/mL acid soln. Accurately weigh calcd amt USP Ref. Std Sulfamerazine, previously dried, and dissolve in NH_4OH-MeOH soln; dil. quant. and stepwise with MeOH to obtain soln contg ca 120 μg/mL. Transfer 5.0 mL to 100 mL vol. flask and dil. to vol. with 0.12*N* HCl, **37.153 (f)**. Acidic soln is stable ≥1 month.

(c) *Dilute ammonia soln.*—Dil. 400 mL NH_4OH to 1 L with H_2O.

(d) *N-1-naphthyl ethylenediamine dihydrochloride (NED) soln.*—0.1%. Prep. fresh before use.

37.159 ***Preparation of Sample***

(a) *Tablets.*—Accurately weigh finely powd portion contg ca 180 mg total sulfonamides and transfer to 50 mL vol. flask, using 10 mL dil. NH_4OH, (c). Let stand ca 15 min, mixing occasionally, dil. to vol. with MeOH, and centrf. portion to clarify (Soln I). Dil. 5.0 mL clarified soln to 250 mL with H_2O; dil. 4.0 mL of this soln to 50 mL with H_2O (Soln II).

(b) *Suspensions.*—Shake in original container to ensure homogeneity, let stand long enough for entrapped air to rise, and invert carefully just before removing portion for weighing. Det. sp gr by weighing 100 mL in tared 100 mL vol. flask. Thoroly mix and weigh portion contg 180 mg total sulfonamides and proceed as in (a).

37.160 ***Determination***

Pipet 5.0 mL aliquots sulfamerazine std soln and prepd Soln II into sep. 10 mL vol. flasks. Add 1.0 mL HCl (1+1) to each flask, mix, and cool. (Solns must be at room temp. for quant. results.) Add 1.0 mL *0.1% $NaNO_2$*, mix well, and let stand 2 min. Add 1.0 mL 0.5% *NH_4 sulfamate,* and mix. After 2 min, add 1.0 mL NED soln, (f). Mix and adjust to vol. with H_2O. Record spectra of samples and stds against H_2O between 660 and 480 nm (peak ca 545 nm) within 15–60 min. Correct *A* by subtracting *A* at 660 nm from peak *A* at ca 545 nm.

mg Total sulfapyrimidines in sample = $(A/A') \times 31.25C$, where A and A' = corrected A of dild assay soln and sulfamerazine std soln, resp., and C = μg sulfamerazine/mL std soln.

Ratio of Sulfadiazine:Sulfamerazine:Sulfamethazine

37.161 ***Reagents and Apparatus***

(**a**) *Chromatographic identification standards.*—Prep. sep. solns of USP Ref. Std Sulfadiazine, Sulfamerazine, and Sulfamethazine in NH_4OH-MeOH soln, **37.158(a)**, to contain ca 1 mg/mL each.

(**b**) *Developing solvent.*—$CHCl_3$-MeOH-NH_4OH (30+12+1).

(**c**) *Thin layer plate.*—20 × 20 cm, coated 0.25 mm thick with silica gel GF (Brinkmann Instruments, Inc.). Divide into 2 approx. equal parts by scraping thin vertical line thru coating.

37.162 ***Thin Layer Chromatography***

Line suitable chromatgc tank with blotting paper. Wet bottom of tank and paper with developing solv., seal tank, and let equilibrate 30 min. Apply ca 50 μL centrfd Soln I to starting line of thin layer plate in streak ca 8 cm long (not to extend within 1 cm of plate edge or center line), using N stream. (It is not necessary to spot accurately measured vol.) On other half of plate, spot sep. 10 μL chromatgc identification stds, evenly spaced, under N stream. Develop plate in tank equilibrated 0.5 hr, letting solv. migrate 10–15 cm above starting line. Air dry plate, locate bands under shortwave UV light, and circle with stylus. Remove silica gel from each band by scraping onto glazed weighing paper, and transfer to sep. 50 mL g-s centrf. tubes. Add 10.0 mL 0.1*N* NaOH to each tube, shake 3 min, and centrf. Transfer 5.0 mL aliquots of each supernate to 10 mL vol. flasks. Add 1.0 mL HCl (1+1) to each flask, mix, and cool. (Soln must be at room temp. for quant. results.) Develop color and record spectra as in **37.160**.

37.163 ***Calculations***

Calc. fraction of each sulfapyrimidine in total sulfapyrimidines as follows:

Sulfadiazine fraction = $0.947A_d/T$

Sulfamerazine fraction = A_r/T

Sulfamethazine fraction = $1.053A_m/T$,

where A_d, A_r, and A_m = corrected A of the sulfadiazine, sulfamerazine, and sulfamethazine bands, resp., and $T = 0.947A_d + A_r + 1.053A_m$.

Sulfadiazine and Sulfamerazine (*59*)—Official Final Action

37.164 ***Reagents***

(**a**) *Citrate buffer soln.*—Dissolve 37 g $Na_3C_6H_5O_7 .2H_2O$ in H_2O, add 32 mL HCl, and dil. to 250 mL with H_2O.

(**b**) *2-Thiobarbituric acid* (*TBA*) *soln.*—Recrystallize acid twice from H_2O. Dissolve 5 g recrystd acid in 20 mL 1*N* NaOH dild with 500 mL H_2O. Add 250 mL citrate buffer soln and adjust to pH 2.0. Reagent is stable when stored in g-s bottle in refrigerator.

37.165 ***Determination***

(**a**) *Sulfadiazine.*—To powd sample contg ca 0.1 g mixed sulfonamides, add 50 mL 1*N* HCl. Shake intermittently 10 min, filter if necessary, and dil. filtrate and washings to 100 mL with H_2O. To 5 mL aliquot, add 7.5 mL 1*N* HCl and dil. to 100 mL. Designate this soln (contg ca 5 mg mixed sulfonamides/100 mL 0.1*N* HCl) as *Soln X*. To 1.0 mL aliquot *Soln X* in g-s test tube, add 10.0 mL TBA soln, stopper, and heat 1 hr at 100°. Weigh tube before and after heating, and compensate for any loss by addn of H_2O. Similarly treat 1.0 mL std contg 25 μg sulfadiazine in 0.1*N* HCl and blank contg 0.1*N* HCl. Det. A of sample and of std, A', at 532 nm against blank.

mg Sulfadiazine in sample taken = $50\,A/A'$.

(**b**) *Sulfamerazine.*—Det. A_T of *Soln X*, and A'_D and A'_M of solns contg 5.0 mg pure sulfadiazine and sulfamerazine, resp., in 100 mL 0.1*N* HCl, at 305 nm against 0.1*N* HCl blank. Then A of *Soln X* due to sulfadiazine (A_D) = A'_D × (mg sulfadiazine in *Soln X*/5.0), and A due to sulfamerazine (A_M) = $A_T - A_D$.

mg Sulfamerazine in sample taken = $100\,A_M/A'_M$.

37.166 Sulfadiazine in Presence of Other Sulfonamides (*57*)—Official Final Action

Det. sulfadiazine as in **37.165(a)** from soln prepd to contain ca 25 μg sulfadiazine/mL 0.1*N* HCl.

37.167 ★ Sulfanilamide (*60*)—Official Final Action ★

Hydrolysis and distn and titrn of NH_3 produced. *See* **36.483**, 11th ed.

OTHER IMIDE DRUGS

Bendroflumethiazide (*61*)—Official First Action

37.168 ***Principle***

Bendroflumethiazide is eluted from 0.1*M* Na_2CO_3-diat. earth column with HOAc-$CHCl_3$ and measured directly by UV spectrophotometry.

37.169 ***Apparatus***

(**a**) *Chromatographic tube and tamping rod.*—*See* **37.002**.

(**b**) *Diatomaceous earth.*—*See* **36.002**.

37.170 ***Reagents***

(**a**) *Sodium carbonate soln.*—0.1*M*. Dissolve 10.6 g Na_2CO_3 in H_2O, dil. to 1 L with H_2O, and mix.

(**b**) *Bendroflumethiazide std solns.*—(*1*) *Stock soln.*—0.4 mg/mL. Accurately weigh ca 20 mg USP Bendroflumethiazide Ref. Std into small beaker, add 5 mL DMSO, and mix with glass rod until dissolved. Transfer quant. to 50 mL vol. flask with MeOH and dil. to vol. with MeOH. (*2*) *Working soln.*—0.012 mg/mL. Transfer 3.0 mL stock soln to 100 mL vol. flask contg 2 mL MeOH and 2 drops HCl. Dil. to vol. with $CHCl_3$.

37.171 ***Preparation of Sample***

Finely powder tablets to pass No. 60 sieve. Transfer portion contg 15–20 mg bendroflumethiazide to 50 mL vol. flask. Add 5 mL DMSO, wetting entire sample. (*Caution:* DMSO can be harmful. Avoid skin contact by wearing heavy rubber gloves. Use effective fume removal device.) Let stand 10 min with frequent mixing. Dil. to vol. with 0.1*M* Na_2CO_3. Filter portion thru paper, discarding first few mL.

37.172 ***Preparation of Columns***

(**a**) *Lower layer.*—Mix 2 g diat. earth with 1 mL 0.1*M* Na_2CO_3 in 150 mL beaker, transfer to tube, and tamp to uniform mass.

(**b**) *Upper layer.*—Mix 4 g diat. earth with 3.0 mL sample soln, transfer to tube, and tamp. Dry-wash flask contg sample mixt. with 1 g diat. earth and 2–3 drops H_2O; transfer to column and tamp. Top with glass wool pad.

★ Surplus method—*see* inside front cover.

37.173 ***Determination***

(Use H_2O-washed solvs thruout. Caution: See **51.039** and **51.062**.)

Let 75 mL isooctane elute thru column and discard eluate. Use 100 mL vol. flask contg 2 drops HCl in 5 mL MeOH as receiver, and elute column with 90 mL *$CHCl_3$-HOAc (98+2)*. Dil. to vol. with $CHCl_3$.

Det. *A* of sample and working std solns at max., ca 271 nm (a = 48.8), in 1 cm cells with spectrophtr against $CHCl_3$-HOAc (98+2) as ref.

37.174 ***Identification***

Macerate portion finely powd tablets contg 4–5 mg bendroflumethiazide with H_2O. Transfer to 125 mL separator, using small portions H_2O, and dil. to ca 15 mL. Ext with three 20 mL portions $CHCl_3$, collecting $CHCl_3$ in 100 mL beaker. Evap. to dryness on steam bath with aid of air current. Dissolve residue in small vol. MeOH and evap. to dryness. Compare IR spectrum in KBr matrix of residue with that of ref. std previously recrystd from alcohol.

Methimazole (1-Methyl-2-Mercaptoimidazole) (*62*)
Official Final Action

(*Caution: See* **51.011**, **51.040**, and **51.056**.)

37.175 ***Apparatus***

(**a**) *Chromatographic tube.*—200 × 22 mm.

(**b**) *Spectrophotometer.*—Recording double-beam IR spectrophtr, with 2 mm cells and NaCl windows.

37.176 ***Reagents***

(**a**) *Diatomaceous earth.—See* **36.002**.

(**b**) *Methimazole std.*—Store in desiccator over P_2O_5 when not in use.

37.177 ***Column Chromatography***

Transfer amt of freshly ground tablet mixt. contg 10 mg methimazole to 100 mL beaker, add 3 mL H_2O, and mix thoroly to wet sample. Add 4 g diat. earth and mix thoroly. Transfer in 2 equal portions to chromatgc tube contg pledget of glass wool and pack tightly. Rinse beaker with 0.5 g diat. earth and add to column; top with glass wool pad. Rinse beaker with 150 mL H_2O-washed isooctane (redistd) and add rinses to column. Let last drops of isooctane drain from column before proceeding. Discard isooctane eluate.

Rinse beaker with three 5 mL portions H_2O-washed $CHCl_3$ and add rinses to column. Collect eluate. Elute methimazole with 200 mL H_2O-washed $CHCl_3$, maintaining solv. head ≤75 mm (3″) during elution. Combine $CHCl_3$ eluates, and evap. at ca 40–60° with air stream to ca 10 mL, washing down sides of beaker with small portions $CHCl_3$ during evapn. Do not heat excessively, since methimazole may oxidize. Quant. transfer conc. to 30 mL beaker with several small portions $CHCl_3$. Evap. solv. at ca 30–40° under air stream. (Make certain all traces of isooctane are removed.) Dry residue in vac. over anhyd. P_2O_5 30 min. (If necessary, store residue over desiccant in dark; methimazole oxidizes on standing.)

37.178 ***Determination***

Add 5 mL CS_2 to residue in beaker, cover with watch glass, and warm to dissolve. Cool and quant. transfer soln to 10 mL vol. flask with CS_2. Repeat with two 2 mL portions CS_2, cool, transfer to flask, and dil. to vol.

Prep. std soln methimazole in CS_2, with warming, to contain exactly 1.00 mg/mL. Record quant. IR spectra of sample and std solns between 7.6 and 8.4 μm in 2 mm NaCl cells. Measure baseline *A* values of 7.83 μm max., using minima at 7.7 and 8.3 μm.

mg Methimazole/tablet = $A \times (C'/A') \times 10 \times (T/W)$,

where *A* and *A′* = baseline values for sample and std, resp.; *C′* = mg/mL std soln; *T* and *W* = av. wt/tablet and sample wt, resp., in mg.

Identify samples by comparing IR spectra of quant. solns with spectrum of std over 2–15 μm, using CS_2 as blank.

Methyldopa and Chlorothiazide in Combination (*63*)
Official Final Action

37.179 ***Reagents and Apparatus***

(**a**) *Ion exchange resin.*—AG 50W-X4, 100–200 mesh, H^+ form (BioRad Laboratories, 32nd and Griffin Aves, Richmond, CA 94804). Strongly acidic nuclear sulfonic groups on polystyrene lattice.

(**b**) *Acidic methanol.*—Add 1 drop HCl to 500 mL anhyd. MeOH. (Dissoln of thiazides is retarded by >2 drops.)

(**c**) *Methanolic hydrochloric acid.*—1*N*. Dil. 42 mL HCl to 500 mL with anhyd. MeOH.

(**d**) *Ion exchange tube.*—150 × 12 mm id, with replaceable coarse fritted glass disk, Teflon stopcock, and Buna-N "O" ring seal (Kontes Glass Co., No. K-422280, or equiv.).

(**e**) *Methyldopa std soln.*—30 μg/mL. Accurately weigh ca 3 mg std, previously dried at 105° overnight, and dissolve in 100.0 mL 1*N* methanolic HCl.

(**f**) *Chlorothiazide std soln.*—10 μg/mL. Accurately weigh ca 1 mg std, previously dried 1 hr at 105°, and dissolve, with heat if necessary, in 100.0 mL acidic MeOH.

37.180 ***Preparation of Column***

Prep. slurry of 2 g resin with 20–25 mL anhyd. MeOH and transfer to tube with stopcock closed and contg plug of glass wool under fritted disk. Let resin settle by gravity; then top with small pledget of glass wool. Column need not be tamped. Drain solv., wash column with several portions anhyd. MeOH, and discard all washings. Prevent column from drying before use by maintaining head of 2–3 mL MeOH or H_2O.

When resin is being used for first time and on completion of sepns, wash thoroly with 15–20 mL HCl-MeOH (1+1) to recondition resin. With stopcock closed and glass wool removed, stir resin to obtain slurry, let settle, and drain. Repeat twice. Finally, wash resin first with H_2O until excess acid is removed and then with several portions anhyd. MeOH. Store under H_2O.

37.181 ***Preparation of Sample***

Det. av. wt/tablet and pulverize to pass No. 80 sieve. Accurately weigh amt contg ca 25 mg chlorothiazide into 50 mL beaker. Add 15 mL acidic MeOH and heat carefully on steam bath ca 30 min to dissolve active ingredients. Cool, transfer to 50 mL vol. flask, and dil. to vol. with acidic MeOH.

37.182 ***Determination***

(**a**) *Chlorothiazide.*—Collect eluate in 100 mL vol. flask at rate of 2–3 drops/sec. Transfer 10.0 mL sample soln to prepd column. After sample soln has entered column, rinse down sides with three 2 mL portions anhyd. MeOH, letting each portion sink into resin completely before next addn. Do not agitate column mech. or by addn of solv. Complete elution with 50 mL anhyd. MeOH. Rinse column tip with acidic MeOH. Add 1 drop HCl to eluate and dil. to vol. with anhyd. MeOH. Further dil. 5.0 mL to 25.0 mL with acidic MeOH. Scan sample and std solns between 235 and

360 nm against acidic MeOH. Calc. chlorothiazide from *A* at max., ca 277 nm. Proceed immediately to methyldopa detn before column dries.

(**b**) *Methyldopa.*—Place another 100 mL vol. flask under column after elution in (**a**). Elute with 50 mL 1*N* methanolic HCl at 2–3 drops/sec. Rinse column tip with 1*N* methanolic HCl. Dil. to vol. with 1*N* methanolic HCl and further dil. to concn of ca 30 μg methyldopa/mL. Scan sample and std solns between 230 and 360 nm against 1*N* methanolic HCl. Calc. methyldopa from *A* at max., ca 280 nm.

Nikethamide

Gas Chromatographic Method (64)—Official First Action

37.183 ***Principle***

Nikethamide prepn is dild with acetone contg anthracene as internal std and detd by GLC with flame ionization detector. Method is applicable to levels of nikethamide normally encountered in injectable prepns (25% w/v). Store all solns contg anthracene in low-actinic glassware and complete detn within 1 day.

37.184 ***Apparatus and Reagents***

(*Caution: See* **51.046**.)

(**a**) *Gas chromatograph.*—Packard Model 838, or equiv., with flame ionization detector and 1.8 m (6′) × 4 mm id glass tube packed with 4% XE-60 on 80–100 mesh Gas-Chrom Q (Applied Science Laboratories, Inc., precoated, or equiv., or prep. as in **37.185**). Operating conditions: temps (°)—column 180, injection port 210, detector 210; gas flows (mL/min)—N carrier gas 56, air 200, H 25; sensitivity 10^{-9} amp full scale, attenuation 1×. Before use, condition column 24 hr at 240–250° with 100±20 mL N/min. If necessary, vary column temp. or gas flow to attain retention times of ca 6 and 4–5 min for anthracene and nikethamide, resp. Also vary detector sensitivity or injection vol. (4–7 μL) to attain peak hts of 50–90% full scale.

(**b**) *Internal std soln.*—0.8 mg/mL. Accurately weigh ca 0.8 g anthracene, heat ca 15 min on steam bath with acetone to dissolve, and dil. to 100 mL with acetone.

(**c**) *Nikethamide std solns.*—(*1*) *Stock soln.*—Approx. 1.0 mg nikethamide (ICN-K&K Laboratories)/mL acetone, accurately prepd. (*2*) *Working soln.*— Approx. 0.5 mg nikethamide/mL acetone. Accurately measure equal vols (≥5.0 mL each) of (**b**) and (**c**)(*1*) and mix thoroly.

37.185 ***Preparation of Column***

Wash tube and small amt fine glass wool with 5% (v/v) dichlorodimethylsilane in toluene; rinse with acetone and dry thoroly at room temp. (*Caution:* Dichlorodimethylsilane is toxic. Avoid contact with skin and eyes. Use effective fume removal device.) Dissolve 3.0 g XE-60 in 100 mL $CHCl_3$. Transfer soln to 250 mL beaker and slowly add 20.0 g 80–100 mesh Gas-Chrom Q with const but gentle stirring. Continue stirring ca 30 sec after adding all support. Place beaker under bell jar and apply vac. Carefully increase vac. and hold at max. ca 1 min to degas.

Swirl slurry rapidly and transfer in small portions to buchner fitted with 9 cm Whatman No. 4 paper. Maintain vac. 5 min after last portion is added. Air dry coated support 1 hr by spreading on smooth surface, and oven-dry addnl hr at 105°.

Plug column exit with small wad of silanized fine glass wool and thru-hole septum. Apply vac. to exit and slowly add coated support thru injection end, tapping very gently to aid compaction. Pack to within *1 cm* of area heated by flash heater. Plug inlet with ≤3 mm wad of silanized fine glass wool and condition as in **37.184**(**a**).

37.186 ***Determination***

Pipet 5 mL sample (25% w/v com. prepn) into 250 mL vol. flask, dil. to vol. with acetone, and mix. Dil. 20.0 mL to 100 mL with acetone (dil. sample soln). Prep. assay soln by mixing equal vols of dil. sample soln and internal std soln. Inject 5 μL working std soln into gas chromatograph and record chromatogram; then inject 5 μL assay soln and record.

$$\% \text{ Nikethamide (w/v)} = (P \times I' \times C' \times 100)/(P' \times I \times C),$$

where P and P' = peak hts (or areas) of nikethamide in assay soln and working std soln, resp.; I and I' = peak hts (or areas) of anthracene (internal std) in assay soln and working std soln, resp.; C' = g nikethamide/mL working std soln; and C = mL sample/mL assay soln.

37.187 Propylthiouracil (*65*)—Official Final Action

Start and complete detn on same day.

Transfer accurately weighed sample contg ca 150 mg propylthiouracil to 200 mL vol. flask, and transfer 150.0 mg pure propylthiouracil to another 200 mL vol. flask as std. To each flask add 150 mL NH_4OH (1+13), washing down necks. Shake flasks moderately and continuously 1 min to dissolve propylthiouracil. Dil. to vols with NH_4OH (1+13) and mix.

Filter sample soln, discarding first 25 mL filtrate. Dil. 20 mL aliquot clear filtrate to 200 mL with H_2O in vol. flask (or 25 mL aliquot to 250 mL) and mix. Dil. 20 mL aliquot of this soln to 200 mL in vol. flask (or 25 mL aliquot to 250 mL) and mix. Prep. same double diln of std soln to obtain final concn of 0.0075 mg/mL.

Det. *A* of final solns of std and sample against H_2O blank in silica cells in spectrophtr at 234 nm. Apply cell corrections unless same cell is used for both std and sample. Calc. propylthiouracil content of sample.

37.188 ★ Thiouracil (2-Mercapto-4-hydroxypyrimidine) ★ (*66*)—Official First Action

Bromination method. *See* **32.394**, 10th ed.

Thiazides (*67*)—Official Final Action

37.189 ***Principle***

Benzthiazide, hydrochlorothiazide, or hydroflumethiazide is eluted from 0.2*N* NaOH-diat. earth column with HOAc-ethyl ether, extd into 0.2*N* NaOH, and detd by UV spectrophotometry. Chlorothiazide is eluted from 0.2*M* K_2HPO_4-diat. earth column with HOAc-ethyl ether, extd into 0.2*N* HCl, and detd by UV spectrophotometry. Methyclothiazide is eluted from 0.1*M* $NaHCO_3$-diat. earth column with $CHCl_3$ and measured directly by UV spectrophotometry.

37.190 ***Apparatus and Reagents***

(**a**) *Chromatographic tube and tamping rod.*—*See* **37.002**.

(**b**) *Diatomaceous earth.*—*See* **36.002**.

(**c**) *Dipotassium phosphate solns.*—0.2 and 0.1*M*, 34.85 and 17.43 g K_2HPO_4/L, resp.

(**d**) *Benzthiazide, hydrochlorothiazide, and hydroflumethiazide std solns.*—Prep. with ether-satd 0.2*N* NaOH. (*1*) *Benzthiazide.*—3.0 mg USP Ref. Std/200 mL. (*2*) *Hydrochlorothiazide.*—2.0 mg USP Ref. Std/ 200 mL. (*3*) *Hydroflumethiazide.*—2.0 mg USP Ref. Std/200 mL.

(**e**) *Chlorothiazide std solns.*—(*1*) *Stock soln.*—1.4 mg/mL. Accurately weigh ca 70 mg USP Chlorothiazide Ref. Std into small beaker, add 2 mL dimethylsulfoxide (DMSO), and mix with

★ Surplus method—*see* inside front cover.

glass rod until dissolved. Transfer quant. to 50 mL vol. flask, using 0.2*M* K_2HPO_4, and dil. to vol. with same solv. (*2*) *Working soln.*—0.014 mg/mL. Dil. 2.0 mL stock soln to 200 mL with 0.2*N* HCl.

(**f**) *Methyclothiazide std solns.*—(*1*) *Stock soln.*—0.2 mg/mL. Accurately weigh 20 mg USP Methyclothiazide Ref. Std into 100 mL vol. flask and dil. to vol. with MeOH. (*2*) *Working soln.*—0.01 mg/mL. Dil. 10 mL stock soln to 200 mL with $CHCl_3$.

37.191 ***Preparation of Sample***

Finely powder to pass No. 60 sieve.

(**a**) *Benzthiazide, hydrochlorothiazide, or hydroflumethiazide.*—Transfer portion contg 75 mg benzthiazide or 50 mg hydrochlorothiazide or hydroflumethiazide to 50 mL vol. flask, using 0.2*N* NaOH. Shake to dissolve completely and dil. to vol.

(**b**) *Chlorothiazide.*—Transfer portion contg ca 70 mg to small beaker and add 2.0 mL DMSO. Mix thoroly 2–3 min with glass rod to dissolve completely. Transfer to 50 mL vol. flask, using 0.2*M* K_2HPO_4, and dil. to vol. with same solv. Mix thoroly.

(**c**) *Methyclothiazide.*—Transfer portion contg ca 2 mg to 150 mL beaker. Add 2 mL MeOH and mix thoroly. Add 2 mL 0.1*M* $NaHCO_3$ and mix.

37.192 ***Preparation of Columns***

(**a**) *Benzthiazide, chlorothiazide, hydrochlorothiazide, or hydroflumethiazide.*—(*1*) *Lower layer.*—Mix 2 g diat. earth with 1 mL 0.2*N* NaOH (1 mL 0.1*M* K_2HPO_4 for chlorothiazide) in 150 mL beaker, transfer to tube, and tamp to uniform mass.

(*2*) *Upper layer.*—Mix 3 g diat. earth with 2 mL sample soln, transfer to tube, and tamp. Dry-wash flask contg sample mixt. with 1 g diat. earth and 2–3 drops H_2O; transfer to column and tamp. Top with glass wool pad.

(**b**) *Methyclothiazide.*—(*1*) *Lower layer.*—Mix 3 g diat. earth with 2 mL 0.1*M* $NaHCO_3$ in 150 mL beaker, transfer to tube, and tamp to uniform mass.

(*2*) *Upper layer.*—Proceed as in (**a**)(*2*), except use 4 g diat. earth.

37.193 ***Determination***

(Use H_2O-satd solvs thruout.)

(**a**) *Benthiazide, hydrochlorothiazide, and hydroflumethiazide.*—Pass 50 mL $CHCl_3$, followed by 50 mL ether, thru column; discard eluate. Using 250 mL separator as receiver, elute column with 0.1 mL HOAc in 100 mL ether. Wash tip of column with ether. Add 65 mL isooctane to eluate and ext org. phase with three 50 mL portions 0.2*N* NaOH; combine NaOH soln in 200 mL vol. flask and dil. to vol.

Det. *A* of sample and std solns in 1 cm cells with spectrophtr against 0.2*N* NaOH as ref.

(**b**) *Chlorothiazide.*—Proceed as in (**a**), except use 0.25 mL HOAc in 100 mL ether, 50 mL isooctane, and 0.2*N* HCl instead of NaOH. Use 0.2*N* HCl as ref. solv.

(**c**) *Methyclothiazide.*—Pass 75 mL isooctane-ether (9+1) thru column; discard eluate. Use 200 vol. flask as receiver and elute column with 100 mL $CHCl_3$. Wash tip of column with ether. Add 10 mL MeOH and dil. to vol. with $CHCl_3$. Use $CHCl_3$ as ref. solv.

Wavelength of max. *A*, and *a* of individual compds are as follows:

Compd	λ Max., nm	Absorptivity
Benzthiazide	295	29.6
Chlorothiazide	278	32.4
Methyclothiazide	268	51.8
Hydrochlorothiazide	273	49.1
Hydroflumethiazide	273	45.4

37.194 ***Identification***

(**a**) *Benzthiazide, hydrochlorothiazide, and hydroflumethiazide.*—Acidify portion sample soln with 1*N* HCl and ext with 50 mL ether. Evap. ether to dryness, add 5 mL alcohol, and evap. again. Compare IR spectrum in KBr matrix of residue with that of ref. std previously recrystd from alcohol.

(**b**) *Chlorothiazide.*—Transfer 5 mL prepd soln, **37.191(b)**, to 125 mL separator, add 10 mL H_2O, acidify with 1*N* HCl, and ext with 75 mL ether. Evap. ether to dryness. Add 5 mL alcohol to residue and evap. to dryness. Compare IR spectrum in KBr matrix of residue from 400 to 600 cm^{-1} with that of ref. std previously recrystd from alcohol.

(**c**) *Methyclothiazide.*—Transfer portion sample contg ca 4 mg active ingredient to 125 mL separator, add 20 mL 0.1*M* $NaHCO_3$, and ext with ca 75 mL ether. Proceed as in (**b**).

Polythiazide (*68*)—Official Final Action

(Applicable to formulations contg vanillin)

37.195 ***Principle***

Vanillin, which interferes in method, is condensed thru aldehyde group with primary amine group of sulfanilic acid to form strongly polar and H_2O-sol. Schiff's base, which is retained in aq. immobile phase of column. Less polar polythiazide is eluted with mobile phase, ether-isooctane, and detd by UV spectrophotometry.

37.196 ***Apparatus and Reagents***

(Use H_2O-washed solvs thruout.)

(**a**) *Chromatographic tube and tamping rod.*—*See* **37.002**.

(**b**) *Diatomaceous earth.*—*See* **36.002**.

(**c**) *Dilute ammonium hydroxide.*—1*N*. Dil. 17 mL NH_4OH to 250 mL with H_2O.

(**d**) *Ammonium sulfanilate soln.*—6%. Dissolve 6.0 g sulfanilic acid in 1*N* NH_4OH and dil. to 100 mL with 1*N* NH_4OH.

(**e**) *Polythiazide std soln.*—10 μg/mL. Accurately weigh ca 100 mg polythiazide, transfer to 100 mL vol. flask, and dil. to vol. with MeOH. Further dil. 10 mL of this soln to 100 mL with MeOH and 10 mL dild soln to 100 mL with MeOH.

37.197 ***Preparation of Sample***

Accurately weigh sample contg ca 1 mg polythiazide and transfer to 150 mL beaker. Add 0.25 mL dimethylsulfoxide (DMSO) and mix thoroly to wet entire sample. Let stand 3–4 min.

37.198 ***Preparation of Column***

(**a**) *Lower layer.*—Mix 6 g diat. earth, (**b**), and 5 mL NH_4 sulfanilate soln in 150 mL beaker, transfer to tube, and tamp to uniform mass.

(**b**) *Upper layer.*—Add 4 mL NH_4 sulfanilate soln to sample soln, and mix. Add 4 g diat. earth, mix, transfer to tube, and tamp to uniform mass. Dry-wash beaker with 1 g diat. earth and few drops H_2O, transfer to tube, and tamp. Top with glass wool pad.

37.199 ***Determination***

Pass 100 mL isooctane thru column; discard eluate. Elute polythiazide with 100 mL isooctane-ether (1+1), receiving eluate in 250 mL beaker. Immediately evap. eluate to dryness. Dissolve residue in small amt MeOH and transfer quant. to 100 mL vol. flask. Dil. to vol. with MeOH. Filter thru glass wool, discarding first 20 mL. Det. *A* of sample and std solns against MeOH in 1 cm cell at max., ca 268 nm.

SELECTED REFERENCES

(*1*) JAOAC **28**, 723(1945); **31**, 558(1948).
(*2*) JAOAC **50**, 666(1967).
(*3*) JAOAC **13**, 344(1930).
(*4*) JAOAC **22**, 757(1939).
(*5*) JAOAC **53**, 591(1970).
(*6*) JAOAC **54**, 895(1971).
(*7*) JAOAC **2**, 66(1916).
(*8*) JAOAC **2**, 59(1916).
(*9*) JAOAC **2**, 72(1916).
(*10*) JAOAC **2**, 73(1916).
(*11*) JAOAC **2**, 70(1916).
(*12*) JAOAC **8**, 506(1925).
(*13*) JAOAC **22**, 723(1939).
(*14*) JAOAC **43**, 241(1960).
(*15*) JAOAC **23**, 752(1940).
(*16*) JAOAC **24**, 809(1941).
(*17*) JAOAC **25**, 809(1942).
(*18*) JAOAC **2**, 63(1916).
(*19*) JAOAC **2**, 68(1916).
(*20*) JAOAC **5**, 581(1922).
(*21*) JAOAC **8**, 499(1925); **9**, 278(1926).
(*22*) JAOAC **5**, 583(1922).
(*23*) JAOAC **38**, 635(1955).
(*24*) JAOAC **21**, 560(1938); **22**, 732(1939).
(*25*) JAOAC **7**, 29(1923); **8**, 40(1924); **8**, 544(1925).
(*26*) JAOAC **11**, 51, 350(1928); **23**, 60, 742(1940).
(*27*) JAOAC **51**, 621(1968).
(*28*) JAOAC **26**, 433(1943); **28**, 757(1945); **34**, 570(1951).
(*29*) JAOAC **8**, 47, 510(1925); **25**, 799(1942); **26**, 101(1943).
(*30*) JAOAC **19**, 508(1936).
(*31*) JAOAC **38**, 630(1955).
(*32*) JAOAC **38**, 624(1955).
(*33*) JAOAC **48**, 582(1965).
(*34*) JAOAC **32**, 533(1949); **34**, 566(1951).
(*35*) JAOAC **55**, 152(1972).
(*36*) JAOAC **55**, 170(1972).
(*37*) JAOAC **51**, 626(1968).
(*38*) JAOAC **27**, 357(1944); **28**, 708(1945).
(*39*) JAOAC **15**, 426(1932); **16**, 366(1933).
(*40*) JAOAC **53**, 834(1970).
(*41*) JAOAC **55**, 166(1972).
(*42*) JAOAC **51**, 631(1968).
(*43*) JAOAC **41**, 496(1958).
(*44*) JAOAC **18**, 464(1935); **20**, 592(1937).
(*45*) JAOAC **57**, 756(1974).
(*46*) JAOAC **21**, 543(1938); **22**, 721(1939).
(*47*) JAOAC **16**, 384(1933); **20**, 564(1937).
(*48*) JAOAC **28**, 699(1945); **29**, 280(1946).
(*49*) JAOAC **43**, 239(1960); **44**, 152(1961).
(*50*) JAOAC **31**, 547(1948); **33**, 203(1950).
(*51*) JAOAC **25**, 843(1942); **26**, 311(1943).
(*52*) JAOAC **7**, 14(1923).
(*53*) JAOAC **13**, 364(1930); **14**, 351(1931); **16**, 364(1933).
(*54*) JAOAC **12**, 296(1929); **14**, 330(1931).
(*55*) JAOAC **13**, 332(1930); **14**, 330(1931); **15**, 418(1932).
(*56*) JAOAC **56**, 692(1973); **58**, 80(1975).
(*57*) JAOAC **47**, 194, 474(1964).
(*58*) JAOAC **56**, 689(1973).
(*59*) JAOAC **37**, 697(1954).
(*60*) JAOAC **22**, 748(1939).
(*61*) JAOAC **59**, 90(1976).
(*62*) JAOAC **50**, 674(1967).
(*63*) JAOAC **54**, 603(1971).
(*64*) JAOAC **59**, 93(1976).
(*65*) JAOAC **35**, 572(1952).
(*66*) JAOAC **31**, 544(1948).
(*67*) JAOAC **55**, 161(1972).
(*68*) JAOAC **57**, 716(1974).

38. Drugs: Alkaloid and Related Bases

ALKALOIDS, OPIUM

38.001 Microchemical Tests—Official Final Action

See **36.095–36.097** and Table **36:03**, and **36.106–36.108**.

38.002 General Titration Method (*1*)—Official Final Action

(*Caution: See* **51.011**, **51.040**, and **51.056**.)

Det. av. wt/tablet or other unit and grind to fine powder. Accurately weigh sample equiv. to 100–200 mg alkaloid and transfer to separator with ca 20 mL H_2O. Add 1 mL H_2SO_4 (1+9) and ext with three 25 mL portions $CHCl_3$. (Extn from acid soln is not necessary in absence of $CHCl_3$-sol. acidic or neut. components.) Add ca 1 mL NH_4OH (use excess solid $NaHCO_3$ for apomorphine or physostigmine) and ext with four 25 mL portions $CHCl_3$ (use CH_2Cl_2 for ephedrine and $CHCl_3$-isopropanol (4+1) for morphine). Use correspondingly larger vols of solv. if larger vols aq. soln are required, as in case of sirups or with excessive amts of excipients. Check alky of soln after first extn by touching indicator paper to stopper. If not distinctly alk., add addnl NH_4OH. Check for complete extn by evapg 1 mL final ext to dryness; if more than trace of residue remains, ext with addnl portions solv. Filter ext thru plug of cotton or fine glass wool, previously wet with $CHCl_3$, into 200 mL erlenmeyer. Complete detn by either of following methods ((**a**) must be used for arecoline and cocaine):

(**a**) Evap. combined exts on steam bath with air current to ca 10 mL. Add measured excess 0.02*N* H_2SO_4 and continue evapn to remove solv. Cool, add Me red, and titr. excess acid with 0.02*N* NaOH.

(**b**) Evap. combined exts on steam bath with air current to dryness. Dissolve residue in ca 2 mL MeOH, heating if necessary. Add Me red, and titr. with 0.02*N* H_2SO_4 to faint pink. If alkaloid is not completely dissolved, heat gently to complete soln. Add ca 40 mL freshly boiled, cooled H_2O, and complete titrn.

See Table **38:01** for titrn factors.

38.003 Apomorphine in Tablets—Official Final Action

See **38.002**.

38.004 Codeine in Tablets—Official Final Action

See **38.002**.

Codeine in Presence of Antihistamines (*2*) Official Final Action

(Applicable to sirups contg codeine with pyrilamine, methapyrilene, prophenpyridamine, and similar antihistamines)

38.005 ***Apparatus***

See **37.002**.

38.006 ***Reagents***

(**a**) *Triethylamine.*—If blank *A*, **38.008**, is >0.010, purify as follows: Reflux 100 mL Et_3N with 20 mL H_2O and 2 g Na hydrosulfite ≥8 hr. Wash with four or five 20 mL portions H_2O, dry by either distg into Dean-Stark trap or by salting-out with anhyd. K_2CO_3, and then distil, collecting first 75 mL. Store over anhyd. Na_2CO_3 or K_2CO_3. (*Caution: See* **51.011**, **51.040**, and **51.052**.)

(**b**) *Codeine std soln.*—Accurately weigh ca 100 mg codeine sulfate.$5H_2O$ (or other salt), dissolve in MeOH, transfer to 100

Table 38:01 Titration Factors for Alkaloids

Alkaloid	Formula	mg/mL 0.02*N* H_2SO_4
Apomorphine hydrochloride	$C_{17}H_{17}O_2N.HCl.\frac{1}{2}H_2O$	6.25
Arecoline hydrobromide	$C_8H_{13}O_2N.HBr$	4.72
Atropine	$C_{17}H_{23}NO_3$	5.79
Atropine sulfate	$(C_{17}H_{23}NO_3)_2.H_2SO_4.H_2O$	6.95
Cocaine hydrochloride	$C_{17}H_{21}O_4N.HCl$	6.80
Codeine sulfate	$(C_{18}H_{21}O_3N)_2.H_2SO_4.5H_2O$	7.87
Codeine phosphate	$C_{18}H_{21}O_3N.H_3PO_4.1\frac{1}{2}H_2O$	8.49
Emetine hydrochloride	$C_{29}H_{40}O_4N_2.2HCl$	5.54
Ephedrine	$C_{10}H_{15}ON$	3.30
Ephedrine hydrochloride	$C_{10}H_{15}ON.HCl$	4.03
Ephedrine sulfate	$(C_{10}H_{15}ON)_2.H_2SO_4$	4.29
Ethylmorphine hydrochloride	$C_{19}H_{23}O_3N.HCl.2H_2O$	7.72
Homatropine hydrobromide	$C_{16}H_{21}O_3N.HBr$	7.13
Homatropine hydrochloride	$C_{16}H_{21}O_3N.HCl$	6.24
Hydrocodone hydrochloride	$C_{18}H_{21}O_3N.HCl.H_2O$	7.08
Hydrocodone bitartrate	$C_{18}H_{21}O_3N.C_4H_6O_6.2\frac{1}{2}H_2O$	9.89
Morphine hydrochloride	$C_{17}H_{19}O_3N.HCl.3H_2O$	7.52
Morphine sulfate	$(C_{17}H_{19}O_3N)_2.H_2SO_4.5H_2O$	7.59
Physostigmine salicylate	$C_{15}H_{21}O_2N_3.C_7H_6O_3$	8.27
Physostigmine sulfate	$(C_{15}H_{21}O_2N_3)_2.H_2SO_4$	6.49
Pilocarpine hydrochloride	$C_{11}H_{16}O_2N_2.HCl$	4.89
Pilocarpine nitrate	$C_{11}H_{16}O_2N_2.HNO_3$	5.43
Procaine hydrochloride	$C_{13}H_{20}O_2N_2.HCl$	5.46
Strychnine	$C_{21}H_{22}O_2N_2$	6.69
Strychnine sulfate	$(C_{21}H_{22}O_2N_2)_2.H_2SO_4.5H_2O$	8.57
Strychnine nitrate	$C_{21}H_{22}O_2N_2.HNO_3$	7.95

mL vol. flask, and dil. to vol. with MeOH. 1 mL = 0.8067 mg codeine.H_2O.

(**c**) *Chloroform.*—Use $CHCl_3$ satd with H_2O thruout.

(**d**) *Diatomaceous earth.*—*See* **36.002**.

38.007 ***Preparation of Sample***

Prep. following 3 columns (columns II and III need not be quant.):

(**a**) *Column I.*—Pipet 2.0 mL sample, draining thoroly, into small beaker. Add 0.5 mL 1*N* NaOH and 3 g diat. earth. Mix thoroly and transfer quant. to tube, **37.002**(**a**). Dry-wash beaker with small portion diat. earth and few drops H_2O, and add to tube. Tamp column firmly with tamping rod, and press pad of glass wool on top.

(**b**) *Column II.*—Mix 3 g diat. earth and 2 mL 1*N* HNO_3, and prep. column as in (**a**).

(**c**) *Column III.*—Mix 3 g diat. earth and 2 mL 1*N* H_2SO_4, and prep. column as in (**a**).

38.008 ***Determination***

Arrange columns so that effluent from *I* flows into *II* and then into *III*. Pass 100 mL $CHCl_3$ over columns. Discard Column *I* which retains excipients.

Pass 50 mL $CHCl_3$ thru Column *II* (which retains antihistamine) onto *III*; then pass 25 mL $CHCl_3$ over *III*. Remove Column *II*.

To recover codeine, place 50 mL vol. flask contg 10 mL MeOH and 1 mL HCl under Column *III*. Pass 5 mL $CHCl_3$ contg 1 mL Et_3N over column followed by 32 mL 1% Et_3N in $CHCl_3$. Dil. to vol. with $CHCl_3$ and det. *A* at 287 nm against $CHCl_3$. (Film of Et_3N.HCl may adhere to walls of cells. Rinse cells carefully with H_2O and alcohol; then wipe clean before use.) Correct for blank *A* of mixt. of 10 mL MeOH, 1 mL Et_3N, and 1 mL HCl dild to 50 mL with $CHCl_3$. Also det. *A'* of std prepd by dilg 5 mL std soln contg 1 mg codeine salt/mL MeOH, to 50 mL with $CHCl_3$ and 5 drops HCl.

$$\text{mg Codeine salt in sample} = 5AC/A',$$

where *A* and *A'* refer to corrected *A* of sample and std, resp., and *C* = mg codeine salt/mL std soln.

Codeine and Terpin Hydrate in Elixirs (*3*) Official Final Action

38.009 ***Reagents***

(**a**) *Color reagent.*—Either Folin-Denis reagent, **9.098**(**a**), or phosphotungstic-phosphomolybdic acid reagent prepd as follows: To 100 g pure Na tungstate and 20 g phosphomolybdic acid (free from nitrates and NH_4 salts), add 100 g H_3PO_4 and 700 mL H_2O. Boil over free flame 1.5–2 hr, cool, filter if necessary, and dil. to 1 L with H_2O. Equiv. amt of pure molybdic acid may be substituted for phosphomolybdic acid.

(**b**) *Terpin hydrate std soln.*—Accurately weigh ca 80 mg terpin hydrate, add 2 mL HOAc, and stir until terpin hydrate is almost dissolved. Add 10 mL alcohol, stir, and transfer to 100 mL vol. flask. Rinse dish with three 10 mL portions alcohol. Finally rinse few times with H_2O and dil. to vol. with H_2O. Soln keeps indefinitely.

(**c**) *Codeine std soln.*—*See* **38.006**(**b**).

(**d**) *Water-saturated ether.*—Add 100 mL H_2O to 200 mL ether in separator, shake, let stand 30 min, and discard H_2O.

(**e**) *Acidified water-saturated chloroform.*—Sat. 300 mL $CHCl_3$ with H_2O. After 30 min standing, transfer $CHCl_3$ to flask contg 3 mL HOAc.

(**f**) *Diatomaceous earth.*—*See* **36.002**.

38.010 ***Determination of Terpin Hydrate***

Pipet 5 mL sample into distg flask and add 100 mL satd NaCl soln, 35 mL alcohol, 2 mL HOAc, and 10 mL H_2O. Distil, collecting 100 mL distillate.

Pipet 5 mL color reagent into 50 mL vol. flask. Cool under running H_2O while slowly adding 5 mL H_2SO_4. Let mixt. come to room temp. and then add exactly 2 mL sample distillate. Place flask in boiling H_2O 20 min. Cool under H_2O to room temp. and dil. to vol. with dil. alcohol (1+3). Shake every few min until soln is clear (10–15 min). (If soln fails to clear, phosphomolybdic acid used to prep. color reagent is unsatisfactory.)

Let stand 0.5 hr and det. *A* at 725 nm against reagent blank prepd without sample. Det. *A'* of std soln prepd simultaneously with sample, beginning "Pipet 5 mL color reagent . . ."

Terpin hydrate (g/100 mL elixir) = $A \times C \times 20/A'$; where *C* = g terpin hydrate/100 mL std soln.

38.011 ***Determination of Codeine***

Pipet 5 mL sample into 100 mL beaker, add 0.5 g *p-toluenesulfonic acid,* and stir with glass rod. Add 6 g diat. earth, mix to fluffy mass, and transfer to tube, **37.002**(**a**), contg plug of glass wool at base. Tamp firmly, and cover with glass wool. Pass H_2O-satd ether over column and discard ether (Column *I*).

Mix 2 g diat. earth and 1 mL 1*N* $NaHCO_3$ (8.4 g/100 mL). Add to second tube (*II*), tamp, and cover with glass wool. Mount Column *I* over Column *II* and place 100 mL vol. flask contg 10 mL MeOH and 4 drops HCl under *II*. Add in 4 equal portions enough acidified H_2O-satd $CHCl_3$ to Column *I* to fill vol. flask to mark. Completely drain each portion before adding next.

Prep. std codeine soln contg 10 mL std soln, (**c**), and 2 drops HCl dild to 50 mL with H_2O-satd $CHCl_3$.

Det. *A* and *A'* at 287 nm of sample and std solns, resp., against mixt. of 10 mL MeOH and 2 drops HCl dild to 50 mL with H_2O-satd $CHCl_3$.

Codeine.H_2O, mg/100 mL elixir = $A \times C \times 20/A'$, where *C* = mg codeine.H_2O in 100 mL std soln.

Codeine in APC Tablets (*4*)—Official Final Action

(Wash all ether with H_2O and wash 0.1*N* H_2SO_4 with ether before use in prepn of reagents and in detn.)

38.012 ***Reagents***

(**a**) *Phosphate-citrate buffer.*—pH 5.1. *See* **38.197** (**d**).

(**b**) *Di-(2-ethylhexyl)phosphoric acid (DEHP) soln.*—Prep. daily 1% soln in ether. (Compd available from ICN-K&K Laboratories, Inc. *Caution:* Avoid contact with skin.)

(**c**) *Codeine std soln.*—120 μg codeine salt/mL 0.1*N* H_2SO_4. Prep. fresh daily from phosphate or sulfate salt. Dissolve 60 mg codeine salt in 0.1*N* H_2SO_4 and dil. to 50 mL. Dil. 10 mL aliquot of this soln to 100 mL with 0.1*N* H_2SO_4.

38.013 ***Determination***

Grind sample to pass No. 60 sieve.

Pack small glass wool plug in base of 200 × 22 mm id chromatgc tube. Mix 2 g diat. earth, **36.002**, and 1 mL pH 5.1 buffer, transfer to tube, and tamp. Accurately weigh ground sample contg 12 mg codeine for 0.5 and 1 grain tablets, 6 mg for 0.25 and 0.125 grain tablets, and 2.5 mg for 1 mg tablets into 100 mL beaker. Add 2.0 mL pH 5.1 buffer and mix to smooth suspension. Add 3 g diat. earth and mix well. Quant. transfer mixt. to tube, above pH 5.1 layer, with aid of scoop-type spatula. Wipe beaker and spatula with glass wool, add to tube, and tamp.

Add 50 mL ether to sample beaker, swirl, and transfer to column. Elute with 4 addnl 50 mL portions ether, letting each portion pass into column before adding next. Rinse tip of column with 2–3 mL $CHCl_3$. Discard rinse and eluate which contain aspirin, acetophenetidin, and caffeine (APC).

Wash column with 50 mL ether and discard eluate. Rinse tip of column with 2–3 mL $CHCl_3$ and dry tip with tissue paper. Place 125 mL separator under column and elute codeine with 50 mL 1% DEHP soln. After soln passes into column, elute with 50 mL ether. Rinse column tip with 5–10 mL ether into separator. Ext with three 10 mL portions 0.1*N* H_2SO_4, collecting exts in vol. flask (100 mL flask for 1 and 0.5 grain codeine, 50 mL flask for 0.25 and 0.125 grain codeine), and dil. to vol. with 0.1*N* H_2SO_4. (For tablets contg 1 mg codeine, use 10, 10, and 4 mL 0.1*N* H_2SO_4 and dil. to 25 mL.) Det. *A* of sample and std solns at max., ca 284 nm, against 0.1*N* H_2SO_4. Calc. codeine salt content of tablets.

38.014 ★ Codeine, Acetanilid, and Caffeine ★
Official Final Action

See **37.023**.

38.015 Ethylmorphine (Dionine) in Sirups
Official Final Action

See **38.002**.

Hydrocodone (Dihydrocodeinone)—Official Final Action

38.016 *General Method*

See **38.002**.

In Presence of Antihistamines (5)

(*Caution: See* **51.011**, **51.040**, and **51.056**.)

38.017 ***Apparatus and Reagents***

(**a**) *Chromatographic tubes and tamping rod.—See* **37.002**.
(**b**) *Column I.*—Thoroly mix 4 g acid-washed diat. earth, **36.002**, and 3 mL ca 2*N* HCl. Transfer to tube and tamp to uniform mass, using gentle pressure.
(**c**) *Column II.*—Mix and tamp layers as in (**b**). (*1*) *Lower layer.*—2 g diat. earth and 1 mL 1*N* $NaHCO_3$. (*2*) *Upper layer.*—4 g diat. earth and 3 mL 6% succinic acid.
(**d**) *Equilibrated sulfuric acid.*—Thoroly shake 1*N* H_2SO_4 with small vol. H_2O-satd $CHCl_3$.
(**e**) *Hydrocodone std soln.*—175 μg hydrocodone bitartrate/mL. Dissolve 17.5 mg hydrocodone bitartrate in equilibrated H_2SO_4 in 100 mL vol. flask and dil. to vol. with equilibrated H_2SO_4. Shake ca 20 mL std soln with ca 75 mL H_2O-satd $CHCl_3$. Det *A'* of aq. phase from 360 to 250 nm.

38.018 ***Determination***

Mount Column *I* directly over Column *II*. Transfer 10.0 mL sample (or vol. contg ca 3–4 mg hydrocodone bitartrate) to separator. Add 5 mL H_2O and 1 mL ca 1*N* NaOH, and ext with four 30 mL portions of $CHCl_3$. Pass each ext thru columns; let individual exts drain completely into both columns. Wash with 50 mL H_2O-satd $CHCl_3$. Discard Column *I*. Wash Column *II* with addnl 100 mL H_2O-satd $CHCl_3$. Discard eluate.

Add mixt. of 3.5 g diat. earth and 3 mL NH_4OH to Column *II*, directly onto packing. Tamp. Pass 150 mL H_2O-satd $CHCl_3$ thru column. Evap. eluate to ca 75 mL or until NH_3 is completely removed (test vapors with moistened indicator paper). Quant. transfer to separator contg 20.0 mL equilibrated H_2SO_4 and shake thoroly. Det. *A* of aq. phase from 360 to 250 nm, using max., ca 282 nm, for calcn.

$$\text{mg Hydrocodone bitartrate in mL sample taken} = (A/A') \times C \times V,$$

where *A* and *A'* refer to sample and std, resp., *C* = mg hydrocodone bitartrate/mL in std, and *V* = vol. H_2SO_4 (20 mL).

38.019 Morphine in Sirups and Tablets
Official Final Action

See **38.002**.

Morphine in Opium and Paregoric (*6*)—Official Final Action

(*Caution: See* **51.011, 51.039, 51.040, 51.052, 51.054**, and **51.056**.)

38.020 ***Apparatus***

(**a**) *Chromatographic tubes.—See* **37.002**.
(**b**) *Diatomaceous earth.—See* **36.002**.

38.021 ***Reagents***

(**a**) *Triethylamine.*—Purified as in **38.006(a)**.
(**b**) *Morphine std soln.*—0.08 mg anhyd. morphine/mL. Accurately weigh morphine base or salt equiv. to 4 mg anhyd. morphine into 50 mL vol. flask. Add 10 mL MeOH, 1 mL HCl, and 1 mL Et_3N, and dil. to vol. with $CHCl_3$. Alternatively, prep. stock soln by dissolving accurately weighed std equiv. to ca 40 mg anhyd. morphine in 0.5 mL Et_3N in 100 mL vol. flask, and dil. to vol. with MeOH. Pipet 10 mL of this stock soln into 50 mL vol. flask, add 1 mL Et_3N and 1 mL HCl, and dil. to vol. with H_2O-satd $CHCl_3$.
(**c**) *Citrate buffer.*—0.1*M*, pH 4.4. Mix equal vols 0.1*M* Na citrate (2.94 g $Na_3C_6H_5O_7.H_2O$/100 mL) with 0.1*M* citric acid (2.10 g $H_3C_6H_5O_7.H_2O$/100 mL).

38.022 ***Preparation of Sample***

(**a**) *Opium.*—Accurately weigh ca 2 g opium into 100 mL vol. flask. Add 20 mL dimethyl sulfoxide (DMSO) and heat in beaker of boiling H_2O or in steam bath ca 15 min. Swirl gently to dissolve, keeping opium particles in contact with DMSO and not letting particles remain on walls. Inspect soln carefully. If undissolved material remains, continue heating. Small amt insol. material, such as fine leaf fragments, sandlike particles, and gelatinous particles, may remain undissolved; add more DMSO, if necessary. Cool, add H_2O to ca 90 mL, and mix. Let soln reach room temp., dil. to vol. with H_2O, and mix. (If foaming occurs on mixing, use 1 drop ether or alcohol to dispel foam.)

If sample is in pieces too large to fit in neck of vol. flask, accurately weigh into 250 mL beaker, add 20 mL DMSO, and heat in boiling H_2O or steam bath. Use stirring rod to disperse sample while heating. Decant into 100 mL vol. flask. If undissolved opium remains in beaker, heat with addnl 3 mL portions DMSO as needed until soln is complete as possible (DMSO concn in final soln can vary over wide range without adverse effect.) Dil. to vol. with H_2O as above.

Filter prepd soln thru paper, rejecting first 20 mL filtrate. Use 2 mL aliquot for prepn of Column *I*.

(**b**) *Paregoric.*—Evap. 10.0 mL paregoric, contg ca 4 mg morphine, to ca 2 mL on steam bath under stream of air. If evapn continues beyond 2 mL, dil. to 2 mL with H_2O. Cool soln to room temp. and then use for prepn of Column *I*.

38.023 ***Preparation of Columns***

(**a**) *Column I.*—(*1*) *Lower layer.*—Mix 3 g diat. earth and 2 mL citrate buffer; transfer to tube and tamp as in **38.007**. (*2*) *Upper layer.*—Add 0.5 mL citrate buffer to 2.0 mL aliquot of sample ext, **38.022(a)** or (**b**). Add 3 g diat. earth, mix, and transfer to

★ Surplus method—*see* inside front cover.

tube. Dry-wash beaker with 1 g diat. earth and add to column; tamp and add glass wool pad.

(b) *Column II.*—Mix 3 g diat. earth and 2 mL 1.0*M* K_2HPO_4 (17.42 g/100 mL); transfer to tube, tamp, and add glass wool pad.

(c) *Column III.*—Mix 3 g diat. earth and 2 mL 0.5*M* NaOH; transfer to tube, tamp, and add glass wool pad.

38.024 ***Determination***

(Use H_2O-satd solvs thruout. Rinse each column tip with $CHCl_3$ before discarding columns or changing receivers.)

Pass 100 mL ether, followed by 100 mL $CHCl_3$, thru Column *I*. Discard eluates. Mount Columns *II* and *III* in series below Column *I*. Pass thru columns 5 mL 20% (v/v) Et_3N in $CHCl_3$, followed by four 10 mL portions 1% Et_3N in $CHCl_3$. Let each portion pass thru completely before next addn. Continue elution without delay. Discard Column *I*, and pass three 5 mL portions 1% Et_3N in $CHCl_3$ thru remaining columns. Discard Column *II*. Wash Column *III* successively with 10 mL 1% Et_3N in $CHCl_3$, 50 mL $CHCl_3$, 2 mL 10% HOAc in $CHCl_3$, and 50 mL 1% HOAc in $CHCl_3$. Discard all eluates.

Place as receiver under Column *III* 50 mL vol. flask contg 10 mL MeOH and 1 mL HCl. (Remove metal leashes from vol. flasks to prevent contamination during transfer to cells.) Elute column with 5 mL 20% Et_3N in $CHCl_3$, followed by 33 mL 1% Et_3N in $CHCl_3$. Dil. eluate to vol. with $CHCl_3$.

Scan spectrum of eluate and morphine std from 360 to 255 nm, using $CHCl_3$ as ref. (Film of $Et_3N.HCl$ may adhere to walls of cells. Rinse cells carefully with H_2O and alcohol; then wipe clear before scanning.) Correct *A* at max., ca 285 nm, by extrapolating baseline from 340 to 310 nm to this wavelength.

mg Anhyd. morphine in aliquot taken = $(W' \times A/A') \times f$,

where W' = mg morphine in std soln, A and A' = corrected A of sample and std, resp., and f = factor to convert wt std to its equiv. in anhyd. morphine (if hydrated morphine or morphine salt is used as std).

38.025 ★ Morphine, Acetanilid, Caffeine, and Quinine ★ Official Final Action

See **37.025**.

ALKALOIDS, OTHER THAN OPIUM

38.026 ★ Aconitine in Aconite Root ★ Qualitative Test (*7*)—Procedure

See **32.028**, 10th ed.

38.027 Arecoline Hydrobromide—Official Final Action

See **38.002**.

Atropine in Tablets—Official Final Action

38.028 *Extraction and Titration Method*

See **38.002**.

Infrared Method (8)

38.029 ***Apparatus***

IR spectrophtr for operation in 2–15 μm region, with 2 NaCl cells 1.0 mm thick, suitable for CS_2 solns. *A* of cells when filled with CS_2 should match to within 0.05; use cell having higher *A* for sample soln.

★ Surplus method—*see* inside front cover.

38.030 ***Determination***

Transfer enough tablets to yield 5–10 mg atropine to small separator. Dissolve in 5 mL H_2O, add 1 mL NH_4OH and 20 mL $CHCl_3$, and shake 1 min. Let sep. and filter $CHCl_3$ layer thru cotton pledget moistened with $CHCl_3$ into 50 mL g-s flask. Repeat extn with three 10 mL portions $CHCl_3$. Evap. combined $CHCl_3$ exts to dryness on steam bath with aid of air current.

Transfer ca 25 mg atropine, USP, accurately weighed, to 50 mL g-s flask. By pipet, add to sample and std flasks measured vols of CS_2 to produce concns of ca 3 mg/mL. Stopper flasks, mix well, and immediately det. *A* of sample and std solns relative to CS_2 at max. of 9.68 μm, using baseline between minima at 9.14 and 9.87 μm. Calc. atropine sulfate content of sample; atropine $\times$ 1.20 = atropine sulfate.

Record spectra of sample and std solns from 2 to 15 μm and compare for identity of sample.

Belladonna and Stramonium Alkaloids in Ointments (*9*) Official Final Action

38.031 ★ *Method I* ★

(*Caution: See* **51.011**, **51.040**, and **51.056**.)

Solv. extn method. *See* **32.037**, 10th ed.

38.032 ★ *Method II* ★

Acid extn method. *See* **32.038**, 10th ed.

38.033 Caffeine

(a) *Microchemical tests.—See* Table **36:07**.
(b) *With acetanilid.—See* **37.022★**.
(c) *With acetanilid and codeine.—See* **37.023★**.
(d) *With acetanilid and quinine.—See* **37.024★**.
(e) *With acetanilid, morphine, and quinine.—See* **37.025★**.
(f) *With acetophenetidin.—See* **37.039★**.
(g) *With acetophenetidin and aminopyrine.—See* **37.037★**.
(h) *With acetophenetidin, aminopyrine, and phenobarbital.—See* **37.038★**.
(i) *With acetophenetidin and aspirin.—See* **37.027★**, **37.028★**, and **37.029–37.034**.
(j) *With acetophenetidin, aspirin, and codeine.—See* **38.012–38.013**.
(k) *With effervescent potassium bromide.—See* **36.060★**.

38.034 Cocaine—Official Final Action

See **38.002**.

38.035 Emetine Hydrochloride in Tablets Official Final Action

See **38.002**.

38.036 ★ Ephedra, Alkaloids in (*10*) ★ Official Final Action

(*Caution: See* **51.011**, **51.039**, and **51.054**.)

See **32.047**, 10th ed.

Ephedrine in Inhalants—Official Final Action

38.037 ★ *Method I* (*11*) ★

(*Caution: See* **51.011**, **51.039**, and **51.054**.)

Extn into acid, making alk. and extn into ether, and titrn. *See* **36.067**, 11th ed.

38.038 ***Method II (12)***

(*Caution: See* **51.011**, **51.040**, and **51.056**.)

(**a**) *Oily inhalants containing oxazolidines (products of reaction of ephedrine with carbonyl compounds).*—Accurately weigh or otherwise measure sample contg ca 100 mg ephedrine. (With most inhalants, sample size will be ca 10 mL. Altho sample contg as little as 20 mg of the drug may be used if necessary, larger sample should be employed when practicable.) Quant. rinse sample into 125 mL erlenmeyer (lipped flask will facilitate later transfer to separator) with small portions benzene totaling ca 5 mL, add 10 mL H_2SO_4 (1+35), and boil gently 10 min with frequent agitation and swirling. (Boiling is best done on hot plate, taking care to avoid superheating, bumping, and loss of sample.)

Cool, transfer contents to 125 mL separator, and rinse flask with portions benzene totaling ca 1.5 times vol. sample to remove all oily matter from flask. Shake separator contg the acid and benzene rinsings, drain acid layer into second separator, and vigorously swirl first separator to force down addnl acid and ensure more nearly complete phase sepn. Drain into second separator any acid layer that further seps, and ext benzene-oil phase with the three 5 mL portions H_2O previously used to rinse flask. Swirl first separator each time after main portion of H_2O has been drained into second separator. (In transfer of ephedrine from org. solv. to aq. phase, and *vice versa,* shake $\geq$1 min and as vigorously as possible without causing emulsions.)

Wash acid soln of ephedrine sulfate with 3 mL $CHCl_3$ and discard $CHCl_3$ washings. Make soln alk. to litmus with 20% NaOH soln (ca 2.5 mL); then add 0.5 mL excess and ext ephedrine by shaking *vigorously* with six 15 mL portions $CHCl_3$. If >50 mg ephedrine is present, filter exts thru cotton pledget into tared 100 mL beaker previously dried at 110° and cooled in desiccator. After fourth extn, rinse filter funnel and its tip with $CHCl_3$ (letting rinsings drain into beaker), float 5 drops (0.2 mL) HCl onto surface of combined exts, and evap. on steam bath in air current until beaker can easily accommodate remaining exts. To test for complete extn, shake alk. phase with seventh and eighth 15 mL portions $CHCl_3$, filter these thru cotton into small beaker, float 2 drops HCl on surface, and evap. to dryness on steam bath in air current. If *cryst.* residue results, combine it with main exts, using small amt MeOH for transfer, and repeat test if considered necessary.

Continue evapn of main exts to 1 or 2 mL. Then cautiously heat on bath, but without air current, until no HCl odor remains and residue of ephedrine.HCl is apparently dry. Heat beaker 30 min at 110°, cool in desiccator, and weigh. Wt residue × 0.8192 = wt ephedrine base.

If <50 mg ephedrine is present in sample, carry out extn to completion as described above, and evap. filtered exts in untared beaker until $CHCl_3$ (but not excess HCl) has been removed. Direct fine stream redistd MeOH around inside of beaker to dissolve ephedrine salt, and immediately repeat process with stream of $CHCl_3$. Transfer MeOH-$CHCl_3$ soln to tared 20 mL beaker, previously dried at 110° and cooled in desiccator, and repeat MeOH and $CHCl_3$ rinsings until ephedrine.HCl has been quant. transferred. Evap. soln on steam bath, in air current, until the salt begins to crystallize. Continue solv. removal by cautious heating alone, to avoid loss from decrepitation, until residue is apparently dry and there is no odor of HCl. Dry and weigh as above.

(**b**) *Oily inhalants or petroleum jelly preparations containing free ephedrine only.*—If product is oil, quant. transfer suitable sample, (**a**), to 125 mL separator with portions benzene totaling ca 1.5 times vol. sample, and ext mixt. with 5 mL H_2SO_4 (1+16) and then with four 5 mL portions H_2O, swirling separator each time as in (**a**), and continue assay as in (**a**), par. 3, beginning "Wash acid soln of ephedrine sulfate . . ." If product is petroleum jelly prepn, dissolve sample in enough benzene to obtain soln of suitable fluidity (30 mL should be enough for 10 g sample) and proceed as for oily inhalants.

38.039 ★ Ephedrine in Water-Soluble Jellies, ★ Sirups, and Solutions of Ephedrine Salts Official Final Action

Extn with ether from alk. soln, extn by acid, re-extn by $CHCl_3$ from alk. soln, and gravimetric detn by **38.038**. *See* **38.039**, 12th ed.

Ephedrine in Tablets and Capsules—Official Final Action

38.040 ***Method I***

See **38.002**.

38.041 ★ ***Method II (12)*** **★**

Extn with ether from Na_2CO_3 soln. *See* **38.041**, 12th ed.

Ergotamine (*13*)—Official Final Action

(Applicable in presence of caffeine, acetophenetidin, phenobarbital, and belladonna alkaloids)

38.042 ***Reagents***

(**a**) *Tartaric acid soln.*—1%. Dissolve 10 g tartaric acid in H_2O and dil. to 1 L.

(**b**) *Alcoholic tartaric acid soln.*—Mix equal vols tartaric acid soln, (**a**), with alcohol. Prep. fresh daily.

(**c**) *Sodium bicarbonate soln.*—10%. Dissolve 100 g $NaHCO_3$ in H_2O and dil. to 1 L.

(**d**) *Citric acid soln.*—(1+1). Mix equal wts of citric acid and H_2O.

(**e**) *Alum soln.*—0.25*M*. Dissolve 12 g $KAl(SO_4)_2 \cdot 12H_2O$ in H_2O and dil. to 1 L. pH should be 3.5±0.2.

(**f**) *Color reagent.*—Dissolve 1.25 g *p*-dimethylaminobenzaldehyde in cooled mixt. of 650 mL H_2SO_4 and 350 mL H_2O. Add 0.5 mL 9% $FeCl_3$ soln.

(**g**) *Diatomaceous earth.*—*See* **36.002**.

(**h**) *Ergotamine tartrate std soln.*—50 μg/mL. Dissolve 25 mg ergotamine tartrate, USP, in enough tartaric acid soln, (**a**), to make 500 mL.

38.043 ***Preparation of Chromatographic Column***

Chromatographic tube.—Prep. chromatgc tube as in **37.002(a)**. Fit with packing rod, **37.002(b)**. Place small wad of glass wool in bottom of tube.

Ergotamine-retaining layer.—Add ca 4 g diat. earth to 3 mL citric acid soln in beaker. Mix thoroly with scoop-shaped spatula until mixt. appears fluffy and uniform, and transfer to chromatgc tube. Tap side of tube gently to settle mixt. Press down firmly with packing rod.

Ergonovine-retaining layer.—Add ca 2 g diat. earth to 2 mL alum soln, mix, and transfer to tube on top of citric acid layer. Press down firmly and evenly.

Water layer.—Add ca 2 g diat. earth to 2 mL H_2O, mix, and transfer to tube on top of alum layer. Press down firmly and evenly and top with pad of glass wool.

38.044 ***Preparation of Sample***

(**a**) *Tablets.*—Det. av. wt and reduce to fine powder. Accurately weigh portion contg ca 2.5 mg ergotamine tartrate into beaker.

★ Surplus method—*see* inside front cover.

Mix thoroly with 5 mL 1% tartaric acid soln and let stand 30 min. Add 5 mL $CHCl_3$ and 1 mL 10% $NaHCO_3$ soln, and mix. (Aq. phase must be alk.) Add ca 7 g diat. earth and stir thoroly until mass appears uniform and does not stick to beaker. (It may be necessary to wash down sides of beaker with small amts of $CHCl_3$.) Add and mix more diat. earth as may be necessary to make mixt. workable. Quant. transfer mixt. to another chromatgc tube fitted with glass wool plug, in several portions, pressing down firmly with packing rod. Wash packing rod, spatula, and sides of beaker with small amt (ca 5 mL) of $CHCl_3$. Add enough diat. earth to make mixt. workable. Scrub sides of beaker and add mixt. to tube. Again rinse rod, spatula, and beaker with $CHCl_3$ and pour wash onto column.

(**b**) *Suppositories.*—Place suppositories contg 3–5 mg ergotamine tartrate in 125 mL separator. Add 10 mL 0.2*N* H_2SO_4 and 75 mL ether. Shake until sample dissolves and then 1 min more. Drain acid layer into second separator. Complete extn with three 10 mL portions acid. Discard ether layer. Combine exts and make alk. with NH_4OH. Promptly ext alkaloids with four 10 mL portions $CHCl_3$. Pass each $CHCl_3$ ext directly onto prepd column, **38.043**. Let column drain completely between addn of successive exts. Proceed as in **38.045**, second par.

38.045 ***Separation of Ergotamine***

Place tube contg sample so that effluent will flow directly onto water layer of second column. Add 50 mL H_2O-satd ether to top column and receive eluate from bottom column in 250 mL erlenmeyer. Follow with 50 mL H_2O-satd $CHCl_3$. (Since effluent may flow faster thru sample column than thru second column, do not add too much $CHCl_3$ at a time.) Rinse tip of sample column with $CHCl_3$ from wash bottle and discard sample column.

Let column drain completely and then rinse down sides with small amt of $CHCl_3$. Pass thru addnl 25 mL H_2O-satd $CHCl_3$ into same flask and rinse tip of column with alcohol. Discard effluent if ergotamine was properly retained. (*See Note.*)

Inspect column for proper retention of ergotamine and for presence of H_2O-sol. alkaloids by holding column under UV light *very briefly.* (*Caution: See* **51.016**.) Blue fluorescent band must not be at bottom of column. (*See Note.*) Extrude column into 400 mL beaker. Rinse tube with H_2O. Add 8 g $NaHCO_3$ and ca 25 mL H_2O to form aq. liq. layer. Break up column with spatula and mix. Wash mixt. with H_2O from wash bottle into 250 mL separator. Add 10 mL $CHCl_3$ and shake. Check aq. layer to assure that it is alk. Be sure that layers are well sepd. It may be necessary to break $CHCl_3$ bubbles with wire. Drain $CHCl_3$ layer thru glass wool filter into 100 mL vol. flask. Ext aq. layer with four 10 mL portions $CHCl_3$ and filter solv. layers into the 100 mL vol. flask. Dil. to vol. with $CHCl_3$, and mix.

38.046 ***Determination***

Evap. 10 mL aliquot $CHCl_3$ soln in 50 mL erlenmeyer to dryness with air current. Do not heat. (Ergotamine is easily decomposed. If assay cannot be completed in 1 day, dried residue after evapn of $CHCl_3$ may be stored in refrigerator overnight.) Dissolve residue, equiv. to 0.25 mg ergotamine tartrate, in 5.0 mL alc. tartrate soln. Pipet 5.0 mL std soln into 50 mL erlenmeyer. Add, to each, 10 mL color reagent dropwise while swirling continuously in ice-H_2O bath. After 30, but <60 min, det. *A* of sample and of std, *A'*, at 550 nm against blank prepd by mixing 5 mL H_2O and 10 mL reagent.

mg Ergotamine tartrate in sample weighed = $(A/A') \times 2.5$.

Note: Ergot alkaloids fluoresce bright blue when exposed to UV light at ca 360 nm. If fluorescent band has reached bottom of trap layer, sample must be discarded. If desired, sample can be salvaged by combining column and effluent, shaking with $CHCl_3$, and passing thru another acid trap. Use of eluant which is not H_2O-satd will cause loss of ergotamine from column. Blue fluorescent ring at top of alum layer indicates presence of H_2O-sol. ergot alkaloids. If detn of H_2O-sol. alkaloid content is desired, repeat detn on new portion of sample, changing citric acid trap to one prepd by mixing 3 g diat. earth with 3 mL alum soln. Cover alum layer with mixt. of 2 g diat. earth and 2 mL H_2O.

Paper Chromatographic Identification (14)
Official Final Action

38.047 ***Reagents***

(**a**) *Mobile solvent.*—Dissolve 7.1 g Na citrate in H_2O and dil. to 100 mL. Adjust pH to ca 4.7 with 2*N* HCl and transfer to separator. Add 70 mL formamide and 9 mL dimethylphthalate. Shake vigorously, let sep., and drain and discard lower layer. Adjust to pH 5.2 with 2*N* HCl or NaOH.

(**b**) *Immobile solvent.*—Dimethylphthalate-$CHCl_3$ (1+9). Prep. immediately before use.

(**c**) *Ergotamine std solns.*—Accurately weigh 10 mg ergotamine tartrate, USP, into small separator contg 5 mL 1% tartaric acid soln and mix gently. Make alk. with few drops 10% $NaHCO_3$ soln, add 2.0 mL $CHCl_3$, and shake vigorously. Draw off $CHCl_3$ layer (*std soln 1*). Dil. 1.0 mL *std soln 1* to 25 mL with $CHCl_3$ (*std soln 2*).

38.048 ***Identification***

For details of app. and technic *see* **29.007** and **29.028**. Blotter paper liners must be used in tank and tank must be sealed.

Equilibrate mobile solv. in sealed tank ≥3 hr with liners dipping into solv. Just before use, quickly dip marked 8 × 8" paper once in freshly prepd immobile solv. and let dry 15 min.

Prep. soln of ergotamine in $CHCl_3$, as in **38.045**, contg 2.5 mg/0.5 mL (remainder of $CHCl_3$ soln from assay may be evapd to this concn). Spot 10 μL each of sample and std solns on paper and let solv. evap. Place paper in tank, seal tank, and let chromatogram develop until solv. front is ca 2.5 cm from top (ca 3 hr). Let paper dry overnight in hood and examine under UV light. There should be one yellow primary spot (and there may be a "tail," probably as result of ergotamine changing to ergotaminine during developing) corresponding to 50 μg ergotamine spot (*std 1*) in position and intensity. If any other spot is more intense than that of *std 2*, >2 μg other ergot alkaloids, expressed as ergotamine tartrate, are present.

Note: Ergot alkaloids produce blue fluorescence which on overnight contact with formamide and air changes to yellow fluorescence. Paper must be completely dry and *std 2* spot clearly visible. In humid weather it may be necessary to dry developed paper 2–3 days in well ventilated hood.

38.049 Homatropine in Tablets—Official Final Action

See **38.002**.

Ipecac Alkaloids (*15*)—Official Final Action

(Applicable to sirup, fluidextract, and powd prepns)

(*Caution: See* **51.011**, **51.052**, **51.054**, **51.056**, and **51.062**.)

38.050 ***Principle***

Principal ipecac alkaloids, phenolic cephaeline and its Me ether emetine, constitute over 90% of total alkaloids of ipecac. They occur in ratios varying from 3:1 to 1:3 in the several species and constitute total of ca 2–3% of wt of root. Minor alkaloids, mainly psychotrine, *o*-methyl psychotrine, and emetamine, are closely related structurally to emetine, differing principally by presence of addnl double bonds, which affect their UV spectra.

Four-column system isolates emetine and cephaeline from ipecac sirup, fluidext, and powd root. Prepn of sample itself, made alk. with $NaHCO_3$, constitutes immobile phase in first column. Ether eluate of this column, contg total alkaloids together with other ether extractives from sample, is passed thru phosphate buffer column 1*N* with respect to chloride ion. Alkaloids are retained in column while nonalkaloidal extractives are partly washed thru column. Major purification is achieved in next step in which mixt. of $CHCl_3$ and ether selectively removes emetine and cephaeline (with perhaps trace amts of other alkaloids) from phosphate column, and carries them onto pH 4.0 column, on which they are retained. Purification achieved in this step is 2-fold: (*1*) Phosphate buffer column retains alkaloids (presumably emetamine and psychotrine) which absorb in UV region between 380 and 300 nm, in which region emetine and cephaeline do not absorb. (Retained alkaloids can be recovered in part by elution with $CHCl_3$, and remainder with ether soln of di(ethylhexyl)phosphoric acid, which is very effective counter-ion for extn of alkaloids.) (*2*) Eluate from phosphate column carries thru pH 4.0 column material which absorbs in UV. This material, if not removed, would accompany emetine and thus give spuriously high assay values. This is especially significant in the case of ipecac sirup, which contains large amt of substance, provisionally identified as 5-hydroxymethyl-2-furaldehyde, spectrum of which closely resembles that of emetine.

Emetine and cephaeline are sepd in final partition step. Combined alkaloids are eluted from pH 4.0 column after raising pH to >8 *in situ* with soln of Et_3N in mixt. of ether and isooctane. This eluate continues thru 0.5*N* NaOH column which retains phenolic alkaloid cephaeline. Finally, cephaeline is eluted directly with $CHCl_3$ from NaOH column, with no adjustment of pH.

Respective eluates are extd with 0.5*N* H_2SO_4 and *A* of acid solns are measured at 283 nm. Since only emetine std is available, and inasmuch as cephaeline and its Me ether emetine have essentially same molar *A*, this std is used for both emetine and cephaeline.

38.051 *Reagents*

(a) *Triethylamine.*—Must pass following test: Transfer 3.0 mL to 50 mL graduate or vol. flask contg 15 mL 4*N* H_2SO_4, dil. to vol. with 0.5*N* H_2SO_4, and mix. Scan spectrum from 350 to 240 nm against 0.5*N* H_2SO_4 as blank. If *A* at ca 250 nm is >0.040, purify as in **38.006(a)**.

(b) *Dimethyl sulfoxide (DMSO).*—Spectral grade (Fisher Scientific Co., or equiv.).

(c) *Ethyl ether.*—Peroxide-free. *See* Definitions of Terms and Explanatory Notes, item 3.

(d) *Phosphate buffer.*—Mix 3 vols 0.5*M* KH_2PO_4 with 1 vol. 0.5*M* K_2HPO_4, and adjust to pH 6.0±0.05. Dissolve 7.46 g KCl/100 mL mixt.

(e) *Citrate buffer.*—Mix equal vols 0.5*M* citric acid and 0.5*M* Na citrate, and adjust to pH 4.0±0.05.

(f) *Emetine std soln.*—Accurately weigh ca 3 mg emetine.2HCl.3H_2O and dissolve in 50 mL 0.5*N* H_2SO_4 (1 mg emetine.2HCl.3H_2O is equiv. to 0.79 mg emetine base). If alkaloid content of std is not known, det. as in **38.002**.

38.052 *Preparation of Sample*

(a) *Sirup.*—Pipet 10 mL H_2O into 25 mL vol. flask. Using 20 mL pipet, add sirup to vol., avoiding wetting neck of flask above graduation mark, and mix. Use 4.0 mL for prepn of Column *I*.

(b) *Fluidextract.*—Pipet 5 mL fluidext into 50 mL vol. flask, dil. to vol. with H_2O, and mix. Pipet 2 mL into 150 mL beaker. Evap. almost to dryness on steam bath, using gentle stream of air to remove alcohol. Add 3 mL H_2O and ca 1 g $NaHCO_3$, and mix. Proceed as in **38.053(a)**, beginning ". . . add 6 g diat. earth, and mix."

(c) *Powdered ipecac.*—Accurately weigh ca 200 mg powd ipecac (60 mesh) in 150 mL beaker, add 2 mL DMSO, and mix thoroly with flattened stirring rod to assure complete wetting of powder. Let stand ca 30 min. Add 2 mL H_2O and ca 1 g $NaHCO_3$, and mix. Proceed as in **38.053(a)**, beginning ". . . add 6 g diat. earth, and mix."

38.053 *Preparation of Columns*

Transfer specified soln to 150 mL beaker, add specified wt acid-washed diat. earth, and mix until uniform fluffy mixt. is obtained.

(a) *Column I.*—To 4.0 mL sample soln, add 1 g $NaHCO_3$, mix, add 6 g diat. earth, and mix. Dry-wash beaker with 1 g diat. earth and add to column. (Since emetine is unstable in alk. soln and in $CHCl_3$, proceed with detn without delay.)

(b) *Column II.*—Add 3 g diat. earth to 2 mL phosphate buffer and mix.

(c) *Column III.*—Add 3 g diat. earth to 2 mL citrate buffer and mix.

(d) *Column IV.*—Add 3 g diat. earth to 2 mL 0.5*N* NaOH and mix.

Quant. transfer mixts to sep. chromatgc tubes, **37.002**. Tamp each to uniform mass and top with glass wool pad.

38.054 *Determination*

(Use H_2O-satd solvs thruout. Rinse tips of columns with ether before discarding columns and when changing solvs. Remove metal leashes from separators and vol. flasks.)

Mount Column *II* under Column *I*. Pass three 50 mL portions ether thru columns. Discard eluate and Column *I*. Mount Column *III* below Column *II*. Pass three 50 mL portions $CHCl_3$-ether (3+1) thru columns. Let each portion pass thru completely before next addn. Continue elution without delay. Discard eluate and Column *II*. Pass 25 mL $CHCl_3$-ether (3+1) thru Column *III*. Discard eluate. Pass 25 mL ether-*isooctane* (1+1) thru Column *III*. Discard eluate. Prewash Column *IV* with 20 mL 2% Et_3N in ether-isooctane (1+1) and discard eluate. Mount Column *IV* below Column *III*. Collect emetine eluate in 125 mL separator contg 15 mL 4*N* H_2SO_4 by passing 10 mL 20% Et_3N in ether-isooctane (1+1), followed by three 10 mL portions 2% Et_3N in ether-isooctane (1+1) thru Columns *III* and *IV*. Discard Column *III*. Pass two 10 mL portions of 2% Et_3N in ether-isooctane (1+1) thru Column *IV*, collecting eluate in same 125 mL separator. Shake separator, and transfer acid layer to 50 mL vol. flask. Ext solv. with two 10 mL portions 0.5*N* H_2SO_4 and combine in vol. flask. Dil. to vol. with 0.5*N* H_2SO_4.

Elute cephaeline from Column *IV* with 75 mL $CHCl_3$. Collect eluate in 250 mL separator contg 20 mL 0.5*N* H_2SO_4 and 150 mL ether. Shake and transfer acid layer to 50 mL vol. flask. Ext solv. with 2 addnl 10 mL portions 0.5*N* H_2SO_4 and combine in vol. flask. Dil. to vol. with 0.5*N* H_2SO_4.

Scan spectra of emetine std and sample fractions from 350 to 240 nm against 0.5*N* H_2SO_4. Correct *A* at 283 nm by subtracting *A* at 350 nm for samples (ΔA) and for stds ($\Delta A'$).

38.055 *Calculations*

(a) *Sirup.*—Calc. mg drug/100 mL = $0.1 \times (\Delta A/\Delta A') \times C \times D \times F$, where C = concn std in μg/mL, D = diln factor = $(25/15) \times (50/4) = 20.8$, and F for emetine = 0.79 if emetine.2HCl.3H_2O is used as std; if H_2O content differs from 3H_2O, recalc. factor from MW of anhyd. salt = 554. F for cephaeline = 0.79 × 0.971 = 0.767, where 0.971 is ratio of MW of emetine and cephaeline.

(**b**) *Fluidextract.*—Calc. mg drug/100 mL as in (**a**), using D = (50/2) × (50/5) = 250.

(**c**) *Powdered ipecac.*—Calc. % drug = $(\Delta A/\Delta A') \times (F \times 5C/W)$, where C and F are defined in (**a**), and W = mg sample.

Norepinephrine (Arterenol) in Preparations of Epinephrine (Adrenalin) (*16*)—Official Final Action

38.056 ***Apparatus***

(**a**) *Chromatographic tube and tamping rod.*—See **37.002**.

(**b**) *Hypodermic syringe.*—1 mL without needle, graduated in 0.01 mL.

38.057 ***Reagents***

(**a**) *Diatomaceous earth.*—See **36.002**.

(**b**) *Glass wool.*—Pyrex No. 3950.

(**c**) *Benzene.*—Distil reagent grade benzene in all-glass app. Shake distillate with H_2O 2–3 min and filter benzene layer thru paper. Use this H_2O-satd solv. unless dry benzene is specified. (*Caution: See* **51.011**, **51.039**, **51.040**, and **51.045**.)

(**d**) *Concentrated phosphate buffer.*—pH 6. Dil. 50.0 mL 0.2M KH_2PO_4 soln, **50.009**(**b**), and 5.64 mL 0.2M NaOH, **50.009**(**d**), to 100 mL with H_2O.

(**e**) *Iodine-potassium iodide soln.*—Dissolve 2 g I and 6 g KI in H_2O, and dil. to 100 mL.

(**f**) *Norepinephrine std soln.*—0.100 mg norepinephrine base/mL. Dissolve 19.9 mg *l*-norepinephrine (levarterenol) bitartrate.H_2O in exactly 100 mL H_2O. Discard after 8 hr.

38.058 ***Preparation of Sample***

(**a**) *Aqueous solns of epinephrine.HCl containing bisulfite and chlorobutanol.*—If soln is 0.1% with respect to "total epinephrine" (epinephrine + norepinephrine), pipet 30 mL sample into 125 mL separator provided with tightly fitting stopper and stopcock. If soln is more concd, use sample contg 30 mg "total epinephrine," and dil. to 30 mL with H_2O.

(**b**) *Suspensions of epinephrine in oil.*—Mix suspension by gentle swirling and agitation; add to separator accurately measured vol. contg ca 30 mg epinephrine and 25 mL pet ether, and swirl until oily base dissolves. Add 10 mL 0.05N H_2SO_4 and ext epinephrine by shaking 1 min. Drain aq. layer into 125 mL separator, and wash pet ether layer with two 10 mL portions H_2O. Add washes to acid ext, wash combined aq. layers with two 10 mL portions CCl_4, and discard CCl_4. Rinse stopper and mouth of separator with few drops H_2O and let rinsings drain into separator. Proceed as in **38.059**, beginning "Add 2.10 g $NaHCO_3$ . . ."

(**c**) *Ointments of epinephrine bitartrate (petrolatum base).*—Transfer to separator accurately weighed sample contg ca 60 mg epinephrine bitartrate. Add 25 mL benzene and swirl until ointment base dissolves. Proceed as in (**b**), beginning "Add 10 mL 0.05N H_2SO_4 . . ." except if bisulfite is present, it must be removed with I, as below, before proceeding with acetylation.

38.059 ***Acetylation***

(*Caution: See* **51.011**, **51.040**, and **51.056**.)

Add 25 mL CCl_4 and shake vigorously to ext chlorobutanol. After layers sep. completely, drain and discard solv., and repeat extn with two 25 mL portions CCl_4. After each extn, drain as much solv. as possible. Rinse stopper and mouth of separator with few drops of H_2O, and let rinsings drain into separator. Add 4 drops starch indicator, **38.153**(**b**); then, while swirling, destroy $NaHSO_3$ by adding I-KI soln, (**e**), *dropwise* until soln remains blue. Immediately discharge blue color by adding 0.1N $Na_2S_2O_3$ dropwise. Add 2.10 g $NaHCO_3$ (prevent it from contacting wet mouth of separator) and swirl few sec to dissolve most of $NaHCO_3$. Immediately, using hypodermic syringe, rapidly inject into separator exactly 1 mL Ac_2O (prevent reagent from contacting mouth of funnel). Stopper separator at once and shake vigorously until evolution of CO_2 stops (ca 7–8 min). Release pressure as necessary by momentarily inverting separator and cautiously opening stopcock.

Let mixt. stand 5 min; then ext with six 30 mL portions $CHCl_3$. Filter each ext thru $CHCl_3$-washed compact pledget of absorbent cotton into beaker, and evap. combined exts to small vol. or to dryness on steam bath under air current. Quant. transfer residue with small portions $CHCl_3$ to tared 50 mL beaker and continue evapn until solv. is removed. Dry 30 min at 105°, let cool in desiccator, and weigh. Wt mixed amorphous triacetyl derivatives of epinephrine and norepinephrine × 0.5923 = E = "total epinephrine."

38.060 ***Chromatographic Separation of Acetylation Product***

(*Caution: See* **51.011**, **51.039**, **51.040**, **51.045**, and **51.056**.)

Place wad of glass wool in chromatgc tube and compress it tightly at juncture of tube and stem, using packing rod.

Place 10 g diat. earth and ca 175 mL benzene in 250 mL beaker. While stirring vigorously and continuously, add 7.0 mL H_2O, dropwise, to produce uniform solid phase. Transfer to chromatgc tube ca 1/10 of the solid, under benzene, and compress it firmly and evenly with packing rod. While keeping column of benzene above solid in tube, add remainder of solid in beaker in ca 5 equal portions and compress each portion firmly and evenly before adding next. Properly prepd column is ca 65 mm high and permits flow of ca 2–4 mL benzene/ min under head of 8 cm solv. With wad of absorbent cotton affixed to stiff wire, remove any solid adhering to tube above column. Keep layer of benzene above column until used.

To beaker contg mixt. of triacetyl derivatives, add exactly 6 mL *dry* benzene. Warm gently and dissolve residue completely by stirring and swirling. Cover beaker with watch glass to retard evapn, and cool to room temp.

Remove supernate benzene from tube by careful aspiration, pipet onto top of column accurately measured aliquot of soln of derivative equiv. to 20–25 mg total epinephrine, and immediately place graduate under tube. As soon as last of benzene soln is absorbed by column, rinse down wall of tube with three 2 mL portions benzene, delivered conveniently from pipet. Let each rinse be completely absorbed before adding next portion. Then carefully add benzene into tube to ht of ca 8 cm above top of column, and maintain level of the benzene with suitable constant level device. After 160 mL effluent (contg triacetylepinephrine) collects, thoroly rinse tip of tube with $CHCl_3$ and discard effluent and rinsings, or reserve for qual. tests.

Remove layer of benzene above column by aspiration, place clean receiver under tube, and let $CHCl_3$ pass thru column until 100 mL effluent (contg triacetylnorepinephrine) collects. Evap. effluent to dryness and transfer to 50 mL beaker, confining residue near bottom of beaker.

38.061 ***Determination of Norepinephrine***

Add exactly 10 mL 0.50N HCl to residue of triacetylnorepinephrine, warm gently, and dissolve by stirring and rubbing with rubber policeman. Pour soln into g-s test tube (15 × 150 mm is convenient), place tube in boiling H_2O bath, and stopper loosely. After 5 min, stopper tightly and maintain 30 addnl min at 100°. Remove tube and cool to room temp., lifting stopper slightly from time to time to keep vac. from forming.

Thoroly mix contents and transfer 1 mL aliquot to another g-s test tube. Neutze acid by adding exactly 42 mg $NaHCO_3$. (Ensure that *all* $NaHCO_3$ is delivered to bottom of tube, and that none adheres to wall above acid layer.) After effervescence stops, add 1.5 mL H_2O and 2.5 mL buffer, (**d**). Mix by swirling, and add 4 drops 0.1*N* I. Swirl, and after exactly 3 min (timed by stopwatch) from addn of I, add 6 drops 0.1*N* $Na_2S_2O_3$, stopper, and mix thoroly. Measure *A* at 520 nm, 3±0.5 min after addn of $Na_2S_2O_3$ soln, in 1 cm cells against the pH 6 buffer blank in Beckman Model DU spectrophtr, or equiv.

Transfer 1.5 mL aliquot std soln to g-s test tube. Add 1 mL H_2O and 2.5 mL pH 6 buffer, (**d**), and swirl. Develop color and measure *A'* at 520 nm as above.

Calc. amt norepinephrine in sample originally taken for analysis, and from this value and *E*, **38.059**, calc. % norepinephrine in "total epinephrine."

38.062 ★ Physostigmine (Eserine) in Ointments (*17*) ★ Official Final Action

See **32.089**, 10th ed.

38.063 Physostigmine Salicylate in Tablets Official Final Action

See **38.002**.

38.064 Pilocarpine Hydrochloride in Tablets Official Final Action

See **38.002**.

38.065 Quinine—Official Final Action

(**a**) *Microchemical tests.—See* Table **36:03**.
(**b**) *Optical crystallographic properties.—See* **52.024** and **52.025**.
(**c**) *With acetanilid and caffeine.—See* **37.024★**.
(**d**) *With acetanilid, caffeine, and morphine.—See* **37.025★**.
(**e**) *With diacetylmorphine.—See* **40.007★**.

38.066 ★ *Spectrophotometric Method (18)* ★ *Official Final Action*

Spectrophtric detn in UV. *See* **38.066–38.067**, 12th ed.

38.067 ★ Quinine Ethylcarbonate (*19*) ★ Official Final Action

Saponification, extn from alk. soln, and gravimetric and titrimetric detn. *See* **38.068**, 12th ed.

Elixirs of Iron, Quinine, and Strychnine

36.068 ★ *Method I (20)—Official Final Action* ★

Chromatgc sepn. *See* **38.069–38.074**, 12th ed.

Method II (21)—Official Final Action

38.069 ***Apparatus***

See **37.002**.

★ Surplus method—*see* inside front cover.

38.070 ***Reagents***

(**a**) *Strychnine sulfate std solns.—(1) Stock soln.*—250 μg/mL. Dissolve 25.0 mg strychnine sulfate in MeOH and dil. to 100 mL with MeOH. (*2*) *Working soln.*—50 μg/mL. To 10 mL stock soln add 5 drops HCl and dil. to 50 mL with $CHCl_3$.
(**b**) *Triethylamine.—See* **38.006**(**a**).

38.071 ***Preparation of Sample and Columns***

Sample.—Pipet 10 mL sample into 100 mL beaker, add 0.2 g *p*-toluenesulfonic acid, and heat on steam bath under gentle air current to remove alcohol.

Column I.—Add 2 mL 2*N* NaOH to 3 g diat. earth, **36.002**. Mix thoroly by kneading with flexible spatula, transfer to column, and tamp, using gentle pressure, to uniform mass. Add 8 g diat. earth to alcohol-free sample. (If sample is too sirupy from excess evapn of H_2O, add small amt of H_2O.) Mix thoroly, transfer to column above NaOH layer, and tamp. Dry-wash with ca 1 g diat. earth for quant. transfer.

Column II.—Mix 3 g diat. earth and 2 mL 2*N* NaOH, and tamp as above. Mix 8 g diat. earth and 7 mL 1*N* HCl, transfer to column above NaOH layer, and tamp.

Column III.—Mix 3 g diat. earth and 2 mL 1*N* tartaric acid, and tamp as above.

Place small pad of glass wool above each column.

38.072 ***Determination***

(Use H_2O-satd solvs thruout.)

Pass 100 mL ether thru Column *I*, discarding eluate contg aromatic flavoring components and bulk of transformation product of quinine which forms in aged prepns.

Mount columns so that eluate from *I* passes thru *II* onto *III*. Pass 100 mL $CHCl_3$ thru columns and discard Column *I*. Pass 50 mL $CHCl_3$ thru Column *II* onto *III* and finally pass 50 mL $CHCl_3$ thru Column *III*. Discard eluate. Column *II* may be used for quinine detn as in **38.074★**, 12th ed.

Place 50 mL vol. flask contg 10 mL MeOH and 1 mL HCl under Column *III* which contains strychnine. Pass thru column 5 mL $CHCl_3$ contg 1 mL triethylamine, followed by 32 mL 1% triethylamine in $CHCl_3$. Dil. to vol. with $CHCl_3$. Det. *A* at 350, 320, and 288 nm against $CHCl_3$ or, preferably, record spectrum over this region. (Film of $Et_3N.HCl$ may adhere to walls of cells. Rinse cells carefully with H_2O and alcohol; then wipe clean before use.) Background *A* at 310–360 nm should be <0.02. Deduct av. reading at 320 and 350 nm from reading at inflection at 288 nm. (Max. *A* of strychnine is at ca 255 nm but nature of solvs makes it undesirable to use this wavelength.)

Deduct *A* of blank of 10 mL MeOH, 1 mL triethylamine, and 1 mL HCl dild to 50 mL with $CHCl_3$. Compare net *A* with that of dild strychnine sulfate std soln, *A'*, and calc. strychnine content.

Reserpine

Method I (22)—Official Final Action

38.073 ***Reagents***

(**a**) *Sulfamic acid soln.*—2.5%. Prep. fresh every 2–3 days.
(**b**) *Alcoholic sodium nitrite soln.*—Dissolve 10 g $NaNO_2$ in 100 mL H_2O. Store in refrigerator. Mix 1 mL of this aq. soln with 50 mL alcohol.
(**c**) *Reserpine std soln.*—50 μg/mL. Dissolve 25 mg USP Reserpine Ref. Std, previously dried 3 hr at 60°, in ca 40 mL boiling alcohol, cool, and dil. to 100 mL with alcohol. Dil. 10 mL of this stock soln to 50 mL with alcohol. When stored in tightly stoppered brown bottle in dark, solns are stable for weeks.

38.074 ***Determination***

(**a**) *Crystalline reserpine.*—Accurately weigh ca 25 mg reserpine, dissolve in ca 40 mL boiling alcohol, cool, and dil. to 100 mL with alcohol. Transfer 10.0 mL to separator contg 50 mL *1% $NaHCO_3$ soln.* Ext with 20, 10, and 10 mL $CHCl_3$, washing each $CHCl_3$ ext in second separator with 50 mL *2% citric acid soln.* Filter $CHCl_3$ exts thru cotton into 50 mL vol. flask contg 5 mL alcohol, dil. to 50 mL with $CHCl_3$, and mix.

Transfer duplicate 5.0 mL aliquots to 25 mL vol. flasks contg 15 mL alcohol. Transfer duplicate 5.0 mL aliquots dil. reserpine std soln to 25 mL vol. flasks contg 10 mL alcohol and 4.5 mL $CHCl_3$. Add 1.0 mL alc. $NaNO_2$ soln to 1 std and 1 sample soln. Add 10 drops HCl to all flasks, swirl, and let stand 30 min. Add 1.0 mL sulfamic acid soln, dil. with alcohol to 25 mL, and mix. Let stand 15 min and det. A in matched 1 cm cells at 390 nm against alcohol.

mg Reserpine in sample weighed $= 25 \times (A - A_0)/(A' - A_0')$, where A and A_0 refer to nitrite-treated and untreated sample, resp., and A' and A_0' refer to corresponding std aliquots.

(**b**) *Tablets.*—Transfer accurately weighed portion powd tablets contg ca 5 mg reserpine to 100 mL beaker. Add 20 mL alcohol, cover with watch glass, and heat to simmering. Boil gently 20 min, stirring occasionally, adding small portions alcohol to maintain vol. Cool to <50°, add 10 mL $CHCl_3$, and mix. Filter thru pledget of cotton, and collect filtrate in 50 mL vol. flask. Wash filter and solids with several portions $CHCl_3$. Cool, dil. to 50 mL, and mix. Transfer 25 mL aliquot to separator contg 50 mL 1% $NaHCO_3$. Add 5 mL $CHCl_3$ and shake vigorously. Transfer $CHCl_3$ layer to separator contg 50 mL *2% citric acid soln,* and shake. Repeat extns with two 10 mL portions $CHCl_3$. Filter exts thru cotton and collect in 50 mL vol. flask contg 5 mL alcohol. Proceed as in (**a**), second par., after dilg to vol. with $CHCl_3$.

mg Reserpine in portion powd tablets weighed

$$= 5 \times (A - A_0)/(A' - A_0').$$

Method II (23)—Official Final Action

38.075 ***Reagents***

(Prep. std, sample, and blank solns from same lots of $CHCl_3$ and MeOH.)

(**a**) *Treated fiberglass.*—Soak Pyrex fiberglass, Corning Glass Works No. 3950, in $CHCl_3$, rinse several times with $CHCl_3$, and air dry on filter paper or dry in forced-draft oven.

(**b**) *Dimethylsulfoxide (DMSO).*—*See* **37.085(f)**.

(**c**) *Sodium nitrite in dilute methanol soln.*—0.3% in MeOH (1+1). Stable ≥1 month when stored in refrigerator. Bring to room temp. before use.

(**d**) *Methanolic hydrochloric acid soln.*—Dil. 6.0 mL HCl to 100 mL with MeOH.

(**e**) *Reserpine std soln.*—20 μg/mL. Dissolve 25.0 mg accurately weighed USP Reserpine Ref. Std, previously dried 3 hr at 60°, in 0.25 mL $CHCl_3$. Mix with ca 30 mL MeOH, previously warmed to 50°; transfer mixt. to 250 mL vol. flask with warm MeOH. Cool soln to room temp., dil. to vol. with MeOH, and mix. Protect soln from light. Just prior to use, pipet 10 mL into 50 mL vol. flask, add 36 mL $CHCl_3$, and dil. to vol. with MeOH.

(**f**) *Diatomaceous earth.*—*See* **36.002**.

38.076 ***Preparation of Column***

Place small pledget of treated fiberglass in base of 200 × 22 mm id tube. *Lower layer:* Mix 1 g diat. earth, **36.002**, with 0.5 mL freshly prepd 2% $NaHCO_3$, transfer to column, and tamp to uniform mass. *Acid layer:* Mix 1 g diat. earth with 0.5 mL freshly prepd 0.5% citric acid soln, transfer to column, and tamp. *Water layer:* Mix 1 g diat. earth with 0.5 mL H_2O; transfer to column, and tamp.

Proceed with entire assay *quickly,* without interruption, avoiding exposure of sample to direct light. Read UV spectrum immediately after column elution is completed.

38.077 ***Chromatography***

Powder tablets and pass thru No. 60 sieve. Transfer accurately weighed amt, contg ca 1 mg reserpine, but ≤1 g of the powder, to 150 mL beaker. Dry-mix powder with ca 500 mg diat. earth. Add 1 mL DMSO and wet sample thoroly by mixing with spatula. Let mixt. stand, with spatula remaining in beaker, 5 min. Add addnl 500 mg diat. earth and mix thoroly. Add addnl diat. earth to total wt of 2 g and mix thoroly. Quant. transfer to column thru wide-mouth funnel. Dry-wash beaker with ca 1 g diat. earth and transfer to column. Wipe beaker, spatula, and funnel with small pledget of treated glass wool. Tamp sample, drywash, and glass wool firmly. Pass ca 45 mL $CHCl_3$ thru sample column. Collect eluate in 50 mL vol. flask contg 14 mL MeOH, rinsing tip of column with $CHCl_3$, and dil. sample to vol. with $CHCl_3$.

Prep. and elute blank column exactly as above, replacing sample layer with 1 mL DMSO + 2 g diat. earth.

38.078 ***UV Assay***

Scan UV absorption spectrum of sample eluate from 250 to 350 nm, against column blank eluate. Likewise, scan spectrum of std soln in same range against ref. blank of 3.6 parts $CHCl_3$ and 1.4 parts MeOH.

mg Reserpine in sample portion $= (A/A') \times (C \times 50)$,

where A and A' refer to sample and std, resp., at 268 nm, and C = mg reserpine/mL in std soln (0.02).

38.079 ***Colorimetric Assay***

Pipet duplicate 5.0 mL aliquots of sample eluate and std soln into sep. 10 mL vol. flasks. Add 2.0 mL methanolic HCl soln to each flask and swirl. To one std and one sample flask, add 1.0 mL MeOH (1+1) (blanks). To remaining std and sample flasks, add 1.0 mL 0.3% $NaNO_2$ soln and mix. Let stand exactly 30 min. Add 0.5 mL freshly prepd 5% *NH_4 sulfamate* soln to each flask, dil. with MeOH, and let stand ≥10 min. Read A from 450 to 350 nm for each soln against blank of 3.6 parts $CHCl_3$, 5.4 parts MeOH, and 1 part H_2O.

mg Reserpine in sample portion

$$= [(A - A_0) \times C \times 50)]/(A' - A_0'),$$

where A, A_0, A', and A_0' refer to sample, sample blank, std, and std blank, resp., at 390 nm and C = mg reserpine/mL in std soln (0.02).

Single Tablet Assay (24)—Official Final Action

38.080 ***Reagents***

(**a**) *Vanadium pentoxide-phosphoric acid (VP-PA) solns.*—(*1*) *Stock soln.*—Sat. 85% H_3PO_4 with V_2O_5 by shaking mech. 2 hr. Filter thru medium porosity fritted glass funnel. (Satd soln contains ca 0.8 mg V_2O_5/mL.) Soln is stable ca 1 month. (*2*) *Working soln.*—Dil. 10 mL stock soln to 100 mL with H_2O. Prep. fresh daily.

(**b**) *Reserpine std solns.*—(*1*) *Stock soln.*—0.1 mg/ mL. Accurately weigh ca 10 mg USP Reserpine Ref. Std, previously dried 3 hr at 60°, into 100 mL vol. flask. Dissolve in 0.1 mL $CHCl_3$; then add 30 mL alcohol previously warmed to 50°. Cool to room temp. and dil. to vol. with alcohol. (*2*) *Working soln I.*—0.002 mg/mL. Transfer 2.0 mL stock soln to 100 mL vol. flask contg ca 50 mL alcohol. Add following vols $CHCl_3$: for 1 mg tablets, 1.0 mL; 0.5 mg, 2 mL; 0.25 mg, 2.4 mL. Dil. to vol. with alcohol. (*3*) *Working soln II.*—0.001 mg/mL. Transfer 1.0 mL stock soln to 100 mL vol. flask contg ca 50 mL alcohol, add 2.0 mL $CHCl_3$, and dil. to vol. with alcohol. Protect all std solns from light as in **38.073(c)**.

38.081 ***Apparatus***

Spectrophotofluorometer.—Adjusted so that reserpine working std solns *II* and *I* give ca 40 and 80% *F*, resp. Wavelengths of max. excitation and fluorescence of reserpine treated with VP-PA are 400 and 500 nm, resp. (*Caution: See* **51.008**.)

38.082 ***Preparation of Sample***

Drop single tablet into 100 mL vol. flask. Add 2 mL H_2O, crush tablet with fire-polished glass rod, and, leaving rod in flask, heat on steam bath ca 15 min or until tablet is dispersed. Frequently crush particles with rod to aid soln. Cool. Rinse rod into flask with following vols $CHCl_3$: 2 mL for 0.1 mg tablets; 3 mL for 0.25; and 5 mL for 0.5 and 1. Remove rod. Protect $CHCl_3$ solns of reserpine from light. Vigorously shake flask ca 2 min. Dil. to vol. with alcohol, shake vigorously, and filter thru rapid paper, discarding first 25 mL filtrate. Collect remaining filtrate in g-s erlenmeyer. Further dil. filtrate as follows: For 0.1 mg tablets, use directly; 0.25 mg, dil. 20 mL to 25 mL; 0.5, 20 to 50; and 1, 10 to 50.

38.083 ***Determination***

Transfer 5.0 mL std soln *II* (for 0.1 mg tablets) or std soln *I* (for all others) and 5.0 mL final sample diln to sep. 50 mL g-s erlenmeyers. Add 5.0 mL VP-PA working soln to each flask, shake vigorously, and let stand 15–60 min. Det. fluorescence of sample and std solns. (Blank is unnecessary, since its reading is negligible compared to sample and std solns.)

Relative fluorescence = %F × meter multiplier reading.

mg Reserpine/tablet = $(R/R') \times C \times f$,

where R and R' = relative fluorescence of sample and std solns, resp., C = concn reserpine *stock* soln, and factor f = 1, 2.5, 5, and 10 for 0.1, 0.25, 0.5, and 1 mg tablets, resp.

Semiautomated Fluorometric Method (25)
Official Final Action

38.084 ***Principle***

Reserpine is dissolved in 0.25*M* H_3PO_4 soln contg 20% MeOH and mixed with V_2O_5, and fluorescence of oxidized reserpine is detd.

38.085 ***Apparatus***

(Other equiv. instruments may be used.)

(**a**) *Automatic analyzer.*—AutoAnalyzer with following modules (Technicon Instruments Corp.): Sampler II with 30/hr (2:1) cam; proportioning pump I; manifold (*see* Fig. **38:01**).

(**b**) *Ratio fluorometer.*—Equipped with flowcell and Corning No. 5113 filter for 395 nm excitation and Wratten No. 8 filter for 495 nm emission.

(**c**) *Recorder.*—Texas Instruments Servo/Riter II (Texas Instruments, Inc., PO Box 1444, Houston, TX 77001), or equiv.

38.086 ***Reagents***

(**a**) *Phosphoric acid-methanol soln.*—Add 20 mL H_3PO_4 to 200 mL MeOH and dil. to 1 L with H_2O.

(**b**) *Vanadium pentoxide-phosphoric acid (VP-PA) solns.*—(*1*) *Stock soln.*—Sat. 85% H_3PO_4 with V_2O_5 by stirring mag. 3 hr. Let settle overnight. (Satd soln contains ca 0.8 mg V_2O_5/mL.) Soln is stable ca 1 month. (*2*) *Working soln.*—Dil. 200 mL stock soln to 1 L with H_2O. Prep. fresh daily.

(**c**) *Reserpine std solns.*—(*1*) *Stock soln.*—0.125 mg/mL. Accurately weigh ca 25 mg USP Reserpine Ref. Std, previously dried 3 hr at 60°, into 200 mL vol. flask, dissolve in H_3PO_4-MeOH soln, and dil. to vol. (*2*) *Working soln I.*—0.0025 mg/mL. Dil. 5.0 mL stock soln to 250 mL with H_3PO_4-MeOH soln. (*3*) *Working soln II.*—0.002 mg/mL. Dil. 4.0 mL stock soln to 250 mL with H_3PO_4-MeOH soln.

38.087 ***Preparation of Sample***

Place tablet in suitable vol. flask to give reserpine concn of 0.002–0.0025 mg/mL. Add H_3PO_4-MeOH soln to ca ½ vol. of flask and place in ultrasonic generator to disintegrate tablet. After complete disintegration, agitate 15 min on mech. shaker. Dil. to vol. and mix. Let soln settle 2 hr.

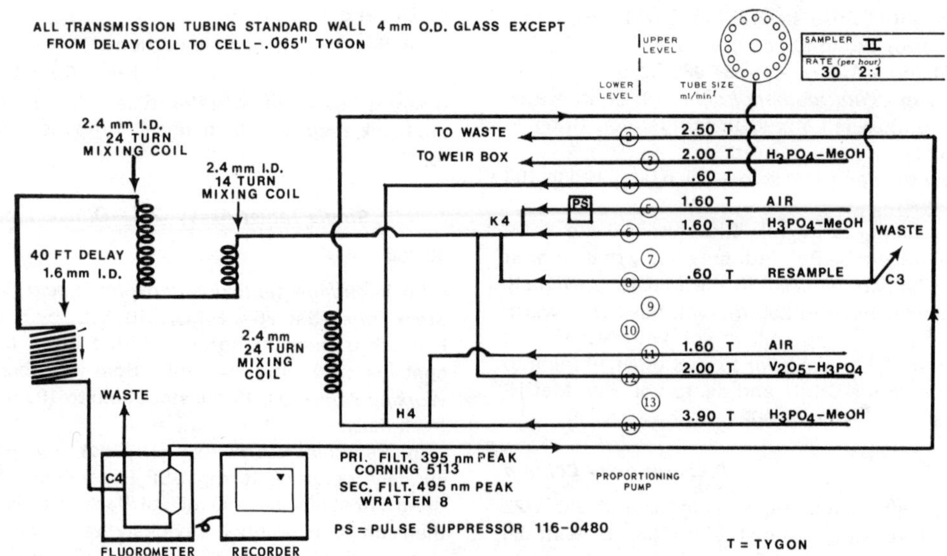

FIG. 38:01—Flow diagram for semiautomated fluorometric analysis for reserpine

38.088 ***Analytical System***

Sample is withdrawn, segmented with air, and dild with H_3PO_4-MeOH soln. Soln is resampled into stream of solv. that has been segmented with air and then mixed with VA-PA working soln. After flowing thru full delay coil (ca 10 min delay), soln is debubbled and passed thru flowcell, and fluorescence is measured at excitation and emission wavelengths of 395 and 495 nm, resp.

38.089 ***Start-Up and Shut-Down Operations***

Place all tubes in resp. solns and pump until steady baseline is obtained. To shut down system, place all lines in H_2O and pump 15 min. Remove lines from H_2O reservoir and pump system dry.

38.090 ***Determination***

Fill 3 mL sample cups in following order: 5 cups std soln, 5 cups sample solns, 1 cup std soln, 5 cups sample solns, etc., ending with 2 cups std soln. Start Sampler II. After last cup has been sampled, let system operate until steady baseline is obtained. Draw tangent to initial and final baselines. Subtract baseline to det. net fluorescence for each sample, F, and std, F', peak, resp. Using av. of 2 stds which bracket sample peak, calc. reserpine as follows:

$$\text{mg Reserpine in sample taken} = (F/F') \times C \times D,$$

where C = concn of std in mg/mL and D = diln factor.

Reserpine-Rescinnamine Group Alkaloids in *Rauwolfia serpentina*

Spectrophotofluorometric Method (26)
Official Final Action

38.091 ***Principle***

Reserpine-rescinnamine is extd with DMSO-MeOH. After addn of H_2SO_4, drug is extd into $CHCl_3$, then sepd from interfering materials by chromatgy on 0.1*N* NaOH-diat. earth and silica gel columns. Reserpine-rescinnamine is eluted from latter column with $CHCl_3$-MeOH and detd by spectrophotofluorometry against std treated similarly.

38.092 ***Apparatus***

(**a**) *Chromatographic tube and tamping rod.*—200 × 22 (id) mm. *See* **37.002**.

(**b**) *Shaker.*—Wrist action (Model BT, Burrell Corp., or equiv.).

(**c**) *Spectrophotofluorometer.*—Excitation and emission wavelengths 400 and 502 nm (uncorrected), resp. Use excitation and emission slit widths consistent with good quantitation according to manufacturer's recommendations. Sensitivity setting depends upon slit widths. (*Caution: See* **51.008**.)

38.093 ***Reagents***

(**a**) *Acidic alcohol soln.*—Add 10 mL 85% H_3PO_4 to 40 mL H_2O and 50 mL alcohol. Mix well and cool before use.

(**b**) *Chloroform-methanol mixture.*—(1+1). Mix equal vols $CHCl_3$ and MeOH; 105 mL/detn is required.

(**c**) *Diatomaceous earth.*—*See* **36.002**.

(**d**) *Dimethyl sulfoxide-methanol mixture.*—(1+1). Mix equal vols DMSO and MeOH. 10 mL/detn is required. (*Caution:* DMSO can be harmful. Avoid skin contact by wearing heavy rubber gloves. Use effective fume removal device.)

(**e**) *Silica gel for column chromatography.*—0.063–0.2 mm. *See* **26.027**(**a**).

(**f**) *Sulfuric acid.*—0.5*N*. Add 7 mL H_2SO_4 to 500 mL H_2O, and mix well.

(**g**) *Vanadium pentoxide-phosphoric acid* (*VP-PA*) *solns.*—(*1*) *Stock soln.*—0.8 mg V_2O_5/mL. Sat. 85% H_3PO_4 with V_2O_5 by shaking mech. 2 hr. Filter thru medium porosity fritted glass funnel. Soln is stable ca 1 month. (*2*) *Working soln.*—0.08 mg V_2O_5/mL. Dil. 10 mL stock soln and 40 mL H_2O to 100 mL with alcohol. Prep. fresh daily.

(**h**) *Reserpine std solns.*—(*1*) *Stock soln.*—40 μg/mL. Accurately weigh 20 mg USP Reserpine Ref. Std, previously dried 3 hr at 60°, into 500 mL vol. flask. Dissolve with 50 mL hot alcohol, cool, and dil. to vol. with alcohol. Protect soln from direct sunlight. Soln, when stored in g-s brown glass bottle, is stable for weeks. (*2*) *Working soln.*—2 μg/mL. Pipet 5 mL stock soln into 100 mL vol. flask, and dil. to vol. with alcohol. Prep. fresh daily.

38.094 ***Preparation of Sample***

Grind tablets to pass No. 60 sieve. Mix well. Use powd root samples as received.

38.095 ***Preparation of Columns***

(**a**) *Column I.*—Mix 2 mL 0.1*N* NaOH with 3 g diat. earth. Transfer to chromatgc tube plugged with glass wool, and tamp. Cover with pad of glass wool.

(**b**) *Column II.*—Pour silica gel into chromatgc tube (plugged with glass wool) to ht of ca 4 cm. Tap side of tube lightly with tamping rod. Cover silica gel with pad of glass wool. Arrange columns so that eluate from Column I flows directly into Column II. Wet columns with 25 mL freshly prepd H_2O-satd $CHCl_3$.

38.096 ***Cleanup***

(Perform in subdued light.)

Accurately weigh prepd sample contg ca 200 mg *Rauwolfia serpentina* and transfer to 50 mL g-s centrf. tube. Add 10.0 mL DMSO-MeOH (1+1), stopper, and shake vigorously by hand until entire sample is thoroly wetted. Shake mech. 30 min at most vigorous setting. (Wrap tube with Al foil if shaker is not in dark place.) Centrf. 5 min at 1200 rpm. Pipet 5 mL aliquot of supernate into 125 mL separator contg 50 mL 0.5*N* H_2SO_4. (*Caution:* DMSO can be harmful. Do not use mouth suction to fill pipet.) (Do not pipet any undissolved residue.) Ext with four 25 mL portions $CHCl_3$.

In second separator contg 25 mL 0.5*N* H_2SO_4, shake each 25 mL $CHCl_3$ ext individually, and drain into Column I. Let each ext sink entirely into both columns before adding next 25 mL ext. After draining fourth ext into second separator, rinse tip of first separator into second with 1–2 mL $CHCl_3$. Then rinse tip of second separator into Column I, and tip of Column I into Column II. Discard all $CHCl_3$ eluted from Column II. Sep. columns and discard Column I.

Place 100 mL vol. flask under Column II, and elute with ca 90 mL $CHCl_3$-MeOH (1+1). Rinse tip of Column II into vol. flask with ca 5 mL $CHCl_3$-MeOH (1+1), and dil. eluate to vol. with $CHCl_3$-MeOH (1+1).

38.097 ***Determination***

Transfer duplicate 5.0 mL aliquots $CHCl_3$-MeOH eluate to sep. 25 mL vol. flasks. Transfer duplicate 5.0 mL aliquots working std soln to sep. 25 mL vol. flasks, each contg 5 mL $CHCl_3$-MeOH (1+1). Add 5.0 mL VP-PA working soln, (**g**)(*2*), to 1 flask of each set, and mix well. Add 5.0 mL acidic alcohol soln, (**a**), to other (blank) flasks, dil. to vol. with alcohol, and mix well. Det. fluorescence intensity of each soln within 15–60 min.

38.098 ***Calculations***

(**a**) *Tablets.*—Calc. % reserpine-rescinnamine group alkaloids in labeled amt *Rauwolfia serpentina*/tablet:

$$[(F - F_0)/(F' - F_0')] \times (C/W) \times (T/L) \times 100 \times D,$$

where F and F' = fluorescence of sample and std, resp.; F_0 and F_0' = fluorescence of sample and std blanks, resp.; C = mg reserpine/mL in working std soln (0.002); W = g sample; T = av. tablet wt in g; L = labeled mg *Rauwolfia serpentina*/tablet; and D = sample diln factor (200 mL).

(**b**) *Powdered root.*—Calc. % reserpine-rescinnamine group alkaloids in *Rauwolfia serpentina* powd root:

$$[(F = F_0)/(F' - F_0')] \times (C/W) \times 100 \times D,$$

where symbols are defined in (**a**).

Spectrophotometric Method (27)—Official Final Action

38.099 ***Reagents***

(**a**) *1,1,1-Trichloroethane.*—(*Caution:* Trichloroethane is toxic. *See* **51.040**.) Redistil in all-glass app., collecting fraction boiling at 73–76°.

(**b**) *Reserpine std soln.*—20 μg/mL. Dissolve 20.0 mg USP Reserpine Ref. Std, previously dried 3 hr at 60°, in 25 mL hot alcohol, cool, and dil. to 50 mL with alcohol. Dil. 5 mL of this soln to 100 mL with alcohol.

(**c**) *Dilute sulfuric acid.*—0.5*N*. Dissolve ca 30 mL H_2SO_4 in 2 L H_2O.

(**d**) *Sulfamic acid soln.*—5% aq. soln. Prep. fresh every 2–3 days.

38.100 ***Apparatus***

Soxhlet extraction apparatus.—Medium size extractor with 250 mL flask and 35 × 80 mm thimble is most convenient, although smaller app. may be used.

38.101 ***Determination***

Ext 2–3 g finely powd *Rauwolfia serpentina* root, or equiv. in powd tablets, in Soxhlet extn app. 4 hr, using ca 100 mL vigorously boiling alcohol. Protect flask and thimble, and all solns of rauwolfia alkaloids, from strong or direct light.

Wash ext into 100 mL vol. flask with alcohol, cool, dil. to vol., and mix. Transfer 20 mL aliquot to separator contg 200 mL 0.5*N* H_2SO_4, mix, and ext with three 25 mL portions trichloroethane. Drain lower solv. phase as completely as possible. Wash each trichloroethane ext in second separator contg 50 mL 0.5*N* H_2SO_4, and discard.

Ext main aq. soln with 25, 15, 15, 10, 10, and 10 mL $CHCl_3$. Wash each $CHCl_3$ ext with the acid in second separator, and then with two 10 mL portions 2% $NaHCO_3$ soln in third and fourth separators. Filter $CHCl_3$ exts thru cotton into 100 mL vol. flask contg 10 mL alcohol. Dil. to 100 mL with $CHCl_3$ and mix.

Transfer duplicate 10.0 mL aliquots to 18 × 150 mm test tubes and mix each with 4 mL alcohol. Add two or three "20-mesh" SiC boiling chips, and heat to boiling in H_2O bath at ca 70°. Gradually raise bath temp. to 100°, or until boiling in tube *just* stops (avoid prolonged heating in absence of solv.). Wipe outsides of warm tubes, place in vac. desiccator, and evap. to dryness under vac. Dissolve residues by agitating with 5.0 mL alcohol.

Take duplicate 5 mL aliquots reserpine std soln, and add 2.0 mL 0.5*N* H_2SO_4 to one sample tube and to one std tube (blanks). To other tubes add 1.0 mL 0.5*N* H_2SO_4 and 1.0 mL 0.3% $NaNO_2$ soln. Mix contents of each tube, and warm in H_2O bath 20 min at 50–60°. Cool, add 0.5 mL sulfamic acid soln to each tube, and mix. Let stand 15 min and det. A in matched 1 cm cells at 390 nm against alcohol-H_2O (2+1).

mg Reserpine-rescinnamine alkaloids in sample weighed

$$= 5 \times (A - A_0)/(A' - A_0'),$$

where A and A_0 refer to nitrite-treated and untreated samples, resp., and A' and A_0' refer to std soln aliquots.

Rescinnamine (*28*)—Official Final Action

38.102 ***Reagents***

(**a**) *Ammonium sulfamate soln.*—2.5%. Prep. fresh every 2–3 days.

(**b**) *Alcoholic sodium nitrite soln.*—*See* **38.073**(**b**).

(**c**) *Rescinnamine std soln.*—40 μg/mL. Dissolve 20.0 mg USP Rescinnamine Ref. Std in 0.5 mL $CHCl_3$, transfer to 50 mL vol. flask, and dil. to vol. with alcohol. Protect all rescinnamine solns from direct or strong light. Alc. soln is stable several weeks in dark. Dil. 5.0 mL std soln to 50 mL with $CHCl_3$.

38.103 ***Determination***

(**a**) *Crystalline rescinnamine.*—Accurately weigh ca 20 mg sample, dissolve in 0.5 mL $CHCl_3$, transfer to 50 mL vol. flask, and dil. to vol. with alcohol. Pipet 5 mL aliquot into separator contg 50 mL 0.5*N* H_2SO_4, add 22 mL $CHCl_3$ and 3 mL alcohol, and shake vigorously 2 min. Transfer $CHCl_3$ layer to second separator contg 50 mL 1% $NaHCO_3$ soln, and shake again. Filter $CHCl_3$ layer thru cotton previously washed with $CHCl_3$ into 50 mL vol. flask contg 5.0 mL alcohol. Ext acid and alk. solns with 2 addnl 10 mL portions $CHCl_3$, filter into vol. flask, and dil. to vol. with $CHCl_3$.

Transfer duplicate 10 mL aliquots prepd sample soln and std soln, (**c**), to 25 mL vol. flasks, each contg 10 mL alcohol. Add 1 mL alc. $NaNO_2$ soln, **38.073**(**b**), to 1 flask of each set; to remaining flasks add 1 mL alcohol. Add 10 drops HCl to all flasks, swirl, and let stand 30 min. Add 1 mL 2.5% NH_4 sulfamate soln, dil. to vol. with alcohol, mix, and let stand 10 min.

Det A in matched 1 cm cells at 390 nm against mixt. of $CHCl_3$, alcohol, and H_2O (9+15+1) as ref.

mg Rescinnamine in sample weighed

$$= 20 \times (A - A_0)/(A' - A_0'),$$

where A and A_0 refer to nitrite-treated and untreated sample, resp., and A' and A_0' refer to corresponding std aliquots.

(**b**) *Tablets.*—Transfer accurately weighed portion powd tablets contg ca 2.5 mg rescinnamine to 50 mL beaker. Insert small glass rod and cover with watch glass. Add 10 mL alcohol, mark vol., and boil gently 20 min with occasional stirring, maintaining original vol. by adding alcohol when necessary. Cool to <50°, add 5 mL $CHCl_3$, and filter thru pledget of cotton previously washed with $CHCl_3$ into 25 mL vol. flask. Wash filter and solids with $CHCl_3$, cool, and dil. to vol. Mix, and let settle ca 10 min. (If soln is not clear, transfer to g-s graduate and let settle 10 min more.)

Pipet 20 mL aliquot into separator contg 50 mL 0.5*N* H_2SO_4, add 10 mL $CHCl_3$, and shake vigorously 2 min. Transfer $CHCl_3$ to second separator contg 50 mL 1% $NaHCO_3$ soln, and shake again. Filter $CHCl_3$ layer thru cotton previously washed with $CHCl_3$ into 50 mL vol. flask contg 5.0 mL alcohol. Ext acid and alk. solns with two 10 mL portions $CHCl_3$, filter into vol. flask, and dil. to vol. with $CHCl_3$.

Proceed as in (**a**), second par.

mg Rescinnamine in sample weighed

$$= 2.5 \times (A - A_0)/(A' - A_0').$$

38.104 ***Determination of Total Alkaloids***

Transfer 10 mL aliquot prepd sample soln and 10 mL std soln, (**c**), to sep. 25 mL vol. flasks, and dil. to vol. with alcohol. Det. spectrum of each soln in region 250–360 nm against blank of 9 mL $CHCl_3$ dild to 25 mL with alcohol.

mg Total alkaloids in sample weighed = $2.5 \times T/S$,

where T and S are A of sample and std solns at max. near 304 nm, resp.

Presence of other alkaloids is indicated by difference between the 2 spectra; presence of reserpine in particular is indicated by difference between colorimetric and UV detns.

38.105 Strychnine in Liquid Preparations (*29*)
Official Final Action

(Other alkaloids absent. *See* **38.068★**.)

Into evapg dish measure 50 mL sample, or enough to yield ≥0.065 g strychnine, and remove alcohol by evapn. Transfer to separator, add 1 mL NH_4OH, or enough to render soln alk., and proceed as in **38.002**, beginning "... ext with four 25 mL portions $CHCl_3$ (use ..."

38.106 Strychnine in Tablets—Official Final Action

(Other alkaloids absent)

See **38.002**.

Theobromine in Theobromine-Calcium Salicylate (*30*)
Official Final Action

38.107 ***Method I***

Dry ca 0.5 g sample at 110° to const wt. Weigh 0.2 g dried substance into g-s 100 mL vol. flask, add 2 mL HOAc, and warm on steam bath. Add 10 mL boiling H_2O and shake until dissolved, adding more boiling H_2O if necessary. Cool soln to room temp. (Soln should be clear or nearly so.) Add 50 mL 0.1*N* I, 20 mL satd NaCl soln, and 2 mL HCl. Shake well and dil. to vol. with H_2O. Shake again and let stand overnight. Filter, discarding first 10 mL filtrate. Titr. 50 mL filtrate with 0.1*N* $Na_2S_2O_3$, using starch soln, **6.005(f)**, as indicator. 1 mL 0.1*N* I = 0.00450 g theobromine, $C_7H_8O_2N_4$.

Method II (31)

38.108 ***Indicator***

Phenol red indicator.—Triturate 0.1 g phenol red in agate mortar with 15 mL 0.02*N* NaOH until dissolved and dil. soln to 200 mL with recently boiled H_2O.

38.109 ***Determination***

Weigh 0.5 g powd tablets, 0.4 g powder, or 0.2 g theobromine alkaloid into 300 mL beaker and add 100 mL H_2O. Warm moderately over flame and add 15 mL ca 0.1*N* H_2SO_4. Heat to boiling to ensure complete soln and to remove CO_2. Cool to room temp. Add 1.5 mL phenol red indicator and make slightly alk. with ca 0.1*N* NaOH (violet-red); then titr. carefully to acid reaction with 0.1*N* H_2SO_4 (yellow). To this soln add 25 mL (an excess) neut. 0.1*N* $AgNO_3$, **50.027**, and immediately titr. liberated HNO_3 with 0.1*N* NaOH to distinct violet-red. Cautiously titr. dropwise with const stirring near end point. 1 mL 0.1*N* NaOH = 0.01802 g $C_7H_8O_2N_4$.

38.110 ★ Theophylline (*32*)—Official Final Action ★

(Applicable to solns and tablets. *Caution: See* **51.011**, **51.040**, and **51.056**.)

Extn from acid soln and gravimetric detn. *See* **38.101**, 12th ed.

OTHER BASES

Selected Drug Combinations by
Ion Exchange Chromatography (*33*)
Official Final Action

(Applicable to 14 antihistamines, antitussive agents, expectorants, and sedatives, alone or combined. *See* Tables **38:02** for alphabetical listing of compds and **38:03** for analyzable combinations.)

38.111 ***Principle***

Nitrogenous bases are sepd from excipients by retention on sulfonated polystyrene resin column. Bases are eluted with HCl and detd by UV absorption. Org. acids are retained on quaternary NH_4 anion resin, eluted with HCl, and detd by UV absorption.

38.112 ***Apparatus***

(**a**) *Chromatographic tubes.*—250 and 150 × 12 mm id Chromaflex (Kontes Glass Co., K-422281, sizes 25-12 and 15-12) with 125 mL glass reservoir (K-422450), 2 replaceable coarse fritted glass disks (K-952050, 12 mm size), 2 Teflon stopcock adapters with ₸ inner drip joint (K-422400, 12 mm size), 2 Teflon stopcock adapters with non-₸ drip tip (K-422400, 12 mm size), Buna-N "O" rings (K-758200, 12 mm size) to seal adapter to column, and 2 clamps (K-675000, 12 mm size); or equiv.

(**b**) *Recording spectrophotometer.*—Suitable for measurement in 250–350 nm range, with 1 and 5 cm cells.

38.113 ***Reagents***

(**a**) *Hydrochloric acid.*—1.2*N*. Dil. 10.0 mL HCl to 100 mL in vol. flask and stdze as in **50.012**. Use normality to calc. vol. concd HCl needed to prep. eluting solns, (**b**)(*2*).

(**b**) *Alcoholic hydrochloric acid solns.*—(*1*) *Washing soln.*—6*N*. Dil. 50 mL HCl to 100 mL with alcohol (normality not critical). (*2*) *Eluting solns.*—0.055, 0.27, 0.30, 0.60, 1.00, and 2.50*N*. Add 500 mL alcohol to sep. 1 L vol. flasks and add enough HCl to each to give exact normality when dild to vol. Cool to room temp., dil. to vol. with H_2O, and mix.

(**c**) *Buffers.*—(*1*) *Concentrated alkaline borate buffer soln.*—pH 9; **42.025(a)**, pHydrion buffers (Micro Essential Laboratory, Inc., 4224 Ave H, Brooklyn, NY 11210), USP alk. borate buffer, or equiv., may be used. (*2*) *Diluted soln.*—Dil. 5 mL concd soln with 95 mL isopropanol (1+1). (*3*) *pH 6 buffer.*—pHydrion buffer (Micro Essential Laboratory, Inc.), phosphate buffer, **50.010**, or equiv.

(**d**) *Cation exchange resin.*—Bio-Rad AG 50W-X4, 100–200 mesh, H-form (Bio-Rad Laboratories, 32nd and Griffin Aves, Richmond, CA 94804), or equiv. (This is washed and sized Dowex 50W-X4 resin with max. impurities (ppm): Fe 1.00, Cu 0.8, Ni 0.05, Pb 0.2, and Al 15.)

(**e**) *Anion exchange resin.*—Bio-Rad AGI-X2, 200– 400 mesh, Cl-form, or equiv. (This is washed and sized Dowex 1-X2 resin with max. impurities (ppm): Fe 0.5, Cu 0.2, Ni 0.05, Pb 0.005, and Al 5.)

(**f**) *Isopropanol.*—Undild and dild (1+1).

★ Surplus method—*see* inside front cover.

38.114 ***Preparation of Columns***

(**a**) *Column I.*—Place fritted glass disk over small glass wool pad in ₮ adapter. Seal adapter to 250 mm column with Buna-N "O" ring. Hold in place with metal clamp and tighten thumb screw on clamp. Mix 3.0 g cation exchange resin with 15 mL H_2O in beaker. Add slurry to 250 mm tube contg some H_2O. Rinse beaker with H_2O and add wash to column.

Pretreat column by adding five 10 mL portions 6*N* alc. HCl. Stir gently few sec after each addn and let soln pass to level of resin before further addn. Follow with H_2O, stirring gently few sec until pH of eluate is 4–7. Condition resin by washing with 200 mL, followed by 10 mL 2.5*N* alc. HCl. Collect each eluate sep. and mix each. Scan 200 mL eluate against 10 mL eluate, using 1 cm cells, over 360–220 nm to det. whether any adsorbing material is being eluted from resin bed. If A is >0.05 at 258 and 310 nm, repeat conditioning. Pass H_2O thru column until neutzd to pH 4–7. Drain to level of resin. Column is ready for use.

(**b**) *Column II.*—Place fritted glass disk over small glass wool pad in non-₮ adapter. Seal adapter to 150 mm length tube with Buna-N "O" ring. Hold in place with metal clamp and tighten thumb screw on clamp. Mix 1.5 g anion exchange resin with 15 mL H_2O in beaker. Add slurry to 150 mm tube contg some H_2O. Rinse beaker with H_2O and add to column.

Pretreat column as in (**a**) and wash until pH of eluate is 4–7. Condition resin by washing with 50 mL isopropanol (1+1). Drain to level of resin. Column is ready for use.

(**c**) *Regeneration (both columns).*—(Repeat after each analysis.) Add five 10 mL portions 6*N* alc. HCl. Stir gently few sec after each addn. Let soln drain to level of resin before further addn to column. Follow with H_2O and stir gently until pH of eluate is 4–7. Store with H_2O on each column. Drain H_2O to level of resin before use.

38.115 ***Preparation of Standard Solutions***

Prep. stds fresh daily as in Table **38:02**, using USP ref. stds, where available.

38.116 ***Preparation of Samples***

(**a**) *Powders and tablets.*—From Table **38:02** and final vol. in **38.117**, calc. amt of finely pulverized sample to weigh accurately. Transfer to 50 mL Florence or vol. flask with three 5 mL portions alcohol followed by three 5 mL portions isopropanol (1+1). Warm 5 min on steam bath and mix on mech. wrist-action shaker until sample is thoroly dispersed. Filter onto indicated ion exchange column, **38.117**, thru Whatman No. 541 dry paper, rinse flask and funnel with 4 portions warm isopropanol (1+1), and add rinses to column.

(**b**) *Individual tablet assay.*—Crush tablet and completely transfer to 50 mL Florence or vol. flask and continue as in (**a**).

(**c**) *Capsules.*—From Table **38:02**, final vol. in **38.117**, and amt of sample available, calc. amt of active ingredients and final vol. (V). Quant. transfer capsule contents to erlenmeyer. Place emptied capsules in beaker, add ($V/4$) mL cold H_2O to cover, and let stand 10 min with frequent agitation. Transfer soln in beaker to erlenmeyer, rinse beaker with four 5 mL portions cold H_2O, and add rinses to flask. Add equal vol. undild isopropanol to flask and mix. Warm erlenmeyer on steam bath 5 min and mix contents until thoroly dispersed. Filter soln into vol. flask thru Whatman No. 541 dry paper and wash paper with four 5 mL portions warm isopropanol (1+1). Cool, dil. to vol. with isopropanol (1+1), and mix.

(**d**) *Sirups or viscous liquids.*—Using 25 mL "to contain" pipet, draw sirup or viscous liq. just to meniscus and transfer to 50 mL vol. flask. Dil. to vol. with appropriate solv. and mix. (Solv. may be H_2O, alcohol, undild isopropanol, or dild isopropanol (1+1). Test small portion sirup for solubility in each solv. If alcohol ppts Me cellulose (excipient), filter and take portion clear filtrate for analysis.) From Table **38:02** and final vol. in **38.117**, calc. vol. aliquot to pipet from vol. flask onto ion exchange column.

(**e**) *Aqueous liquids.*—From Table **38:02** and final vol. in **38.117**, calc. vol. sample to pipet onto ion exchange column.

38.117 ***Determination***

Complete sample prepn and detn within same day. No flow rate adjustment for columns is necessary except for amphetamine sulfate. Elute columns with stopcocks fully opened.

(**a**) Arrange columns so eluate from Column *I* flows thru Column *II* into 200 mL vol. flask. Let sample soln pass thru columns until it sinks into resin. Pass ca 150 mL isopropanol (1+1) thru columns. (To prevent resin disturbance, establish ca 5 mL solv. head on Column *II* before each elution as follows: Break seal between columns. Close Column *II* stopcock and let eluate from Column *I* drain onto *II* until 5 mL is added. Close Column *I* stopcock. Re-establish seal between columns and open both stopcocks. Each eluate should pass completely thru resin in both columns before next eluate is added.) Remove Column *II*.

Add 10.0 mL concd pH 9.0 buffer to the vol. flask, dil. to vol. with isopropanol (1+1), and mix. This flask contains barbital Na or phenobarbital. Dil. sample solns with dild pH 9.0 buffer to

Table 38:02 Preparation of Standards (Use 100 mL Volumetric Flasks)[a]

Std	Abbrev.	Solv. (and Column Eluant)	Concn. mg/mL	Detd by Method 38.108
Amphetamine sulfate (USP)	AS	0.60*N* alc. HCl	0.15	a
Barbital sodium (ICN-K&K Laboratories, Inc.)	BS	[b]	0.01	a, c
Codeine phosphate	CP	0.30*N* alc. HCl	0.10	d
Dextromethorphan.HBr (USP)	DM	1.00*N* alc. HCl	0.10	f, g
Ephedrine sulfate (USP)	ES	0.60*N* alc. HCl	0.15	a
Glyceryl guaiacolate	GG	isopropanol (1+1)	0.04	g
Methapyrilene.HCl (USP)	MP	2.50*N* alc. HCl	0.02	a, b
Phenobarbital (USP)	PB	[b]	0.01	a, c
Phenylephrine.HCl (USP)	PE	0.30*N* alc. HCl	0.05	e, f, g
Phenylpropanolamine.HCl (USP)	PP	0.60*N* alc. HCl	0.15	e, f, g
Potassium guaiacolsulfonate	PG	0.055*N* alc. HCl	0.04	d, e, f
Promethazine.HCl (USP)	PZ	2.50*N* alc. HCl	0.04	d, e
Pyrilamine maleate (USP)	PM	2.50*N* alc. HCl	0.02	a, b, f, g
Tripelennamine citrate (USP)	TC	2.50*N* alc. HCl	0.025	a, b

[a] Use 1 cm cell for detn, except for AS, ES, and PP where 5 cm is used.
[b] Weigh std into 100 mL vol. flask, dissolve in 5.0 mL concd pH 9 buffer soln, and dil. to vol. with isopropanol (1+1).

give final concn ca 1 mg/100 mL. Scan sample and std solns from 350 to 220 nm against dild pH 9.0 buffer. Det. A at max., ca 240 nm, and calc. sample soln concn.

Wash Column *I* with 50 mL 0.055*N* alc. HCl. Follow with 10.0 mL 0.27*N* alc. HCl to elute excipients and any remaining color. Discard wash. Place 100 mL vol. flask beneath column and elute amphetamine sulfate or ephedrine sulfate with 100 mL 0.60*N* alc. HCl. (Use max. gravity flow for ephedrine but adjust flow to 2–3 mL/min for amphetamine sulfate.) Scan sample and std solns from 350 to 220 nm in 5 cm cells against 0.60*N* alc. HCl. Calc. sample soln concn by drawing baseline between min. at ca 265 and 255 nm. Measure A between max. and baseline at ca 258 nm.

For methapyrilene.HCl, pyrilamine maleate, or tripelennamine citrate, place 250 mL vol. flask beneath Column *I*, elute antihistamine with 250 mL 2.50*N* alc. HCl, and mix. Dil. sample with 2.50*N* alc. HCl to give concn ca 2.5 mg/100 mL. Scan sample and std solns from 360 to 220 nm against 2.50*N* alc. HCl. Det. A at max., ca 310 nm, and calc. sample soln concn.

In absence of barbiturate, omit Column *II*, and proceed as in par. 3.

In absence of antihistamine, omit par. 4.

(b) Proceed as in **(a)**, omitting Column *II* and 0.60*N* alc. HCl eluant.

(c) Proceed as in **(a)**, omitting pars 3 and 4.

(d) Arrange columns so eluate from Column *II* flows thru Column *I* and into beaker. Proceed as in **(a)**, until columns are sepd.

Promethazine.HCl and codeine phosphate are retained on Column *I*; K guaiacolsulfonate is retained on Column *II*.

For K guaiacolsulfonate, place 250 mL vol. flask beneath Column *II* and elute guaiacolsulfonate anion with 250.0 mL 0.055*N* alc. HCl. Dil. to vol. with 0.055*N* alc. HCl and mix. Further dil. with 0.055*N* alc. HCl to give concn ca 0.04 mg/mL. Scan sample and std solns from 350 to 240 nm in 1 cm cells against 0.055*N* alc. HCl as ref. Calc. sample soln concn by drawing baseline tangent from 350 to 290 nm and extended to 240 nm. Measure A between max. and baseline at ca 278 nm.

For codeine phosphate, place 250 mL vol. flask beneath Column *I* and elute with 250.0 mL 0.30*N* alc. HCl. Dil. to vol. with 0.30*N* alc. HCl and mix. Further dil. with 0.30*N* alc. HCl to give concn ca 0.10 mg/mL. Scan sample and std solns between 350 and 220 nm in 1 cm cells against 0.30*N* alc. HCl as ref. Calc. sample soln concn by drawing baseline tangent from ca 300 to

Table 38:03 Determinative Table of Methods Applicable to Drugs, Combinations, and Dosage Forms[a]

Compd(s)	AS	BS	CP	DM[b]	ES	GG	MP	PB	PE	PG	PM	PP[b]	PZ	TC
AS+	s(a)	s(a)					s(a)	s(a)			s(a)			s(a)
AS+BS+							s(a)				s(a)			s(a)
AS+PB+							s(a)				s(a)			s(a)
BS+		s(c)			s(a)		s(a)				s(a)			s(a)
BS+ES+							s(a)				s(a)			s(a)
CP+			(d)							(d)				
CP+PG+													(d)	
DM[b]+				s(f)		s(g)			s(f)	s(f)	s(f)	f(f)		
DM+GG+									(g)			(g)		
DM+GG+PE+											s(g)			
DM+GG+PM+									s(g)			f(g)		
DM+PE+										s(f)	s(f)			
DM+PE+PG+											s(f)			
DM+PG+									s(f)			(f)		
DM+PG+PM+									s(f)			(f)		
DM+PM+									s(f)			(f)		
ES+					(a)		s(a)	s(a)			s(a)			s(a)
ES+MP+								s(a)						
ES+PB+							s(a)	s(a)			s(a)			s(a)
GG+									(g)		(g)	f(g)		
GG+PE+											(g)			
GG+PM+									(g)			f(g)		
MP+							s(b)							
PB+								s(c)						
PE+									(e)	(e)			(e)	
PE+PG+											(f)		(e)	
PG+												f(e)		
PG+PM+												f(f)		
PG+PZ+												f(e)		
PM+											(b)			
PP[b]+												f(e)		
PZ+													(d)	
TC+														s(b)

[a] *Explanation:* Single compds will be found at intersection of identical column and row heads. For combinations of ⩾2 compds (n), arrange compds alphabetically in order of their abbreviations. Locate the first group of 1 less than total number present ($n - 1$) in first column; entire combination is given at intersection of row list of ($n - 1$) compds with column headed by last compd. *Abbreviations*—dosage forms: s = solid prepn (tablet, capsule, or powder); f = fluid prepn (elixir, sirup, or aq. soln). *Method:* appropriate sec. in **38.117** given in parentheses, **(a)**–**(g)**. When only the method sec. appears as entry, both solid and fluid prepns, except in footnote *b* below, can be analyzed.

[b] DM can be detd in s form only; PP can be detd in f form only.

260 nm. Measure *A* between max. and baseline at ca 285 nm.

For promethazine.HCl, place 250 mL vol. flask beneath Column *I* and elute with 250.0 mL 2.50*N* alc. HCl. Dil. to vol. with 2.50*N* alc. HCl and mix. Further dil. with 2.50*N* alc. HCl to give concn ca 0.04 mg/mL. Scan sample and std solns between 360 and 240 nm in 1 cm cells against 2.50*N* alc. HCl as ref. Det. *A* at max., ca 300 nm, and calc. sample soln concn.

In absence of K guaiacolsulfonate, omit Column *II*.

In absence of codeine phosphate, omit 0.30*N* alc. HCl eluate.

In absence of promethazine.HCl, omit 2.50*N* alc. HCl eluant.

(**e**) Arrange columns so eluate from Column *I* flows thru Column *II* and into beaker. Proceed as in (**d**) until K guaiacolsulfonate has been detd. Phenylephrine.HCl or phenylpropanolamine.HCl and promethazine.HCl are retained on Column *I*.

Wash Column *I* with 50 mL 0.055*N* alc. HCl to elute excipients and any remaining color, and discard wash. Place 100 mL vol. flask beneath column and elute phenylephrine.HCl or phenylpropanolamine.HCl with 100.0 mL 0.30*N* alc. HCl. Dil. to vol. with 0.30*N* alc. HCl and mix. Further dil. with 0.30*N* alc. HCl to give concns ca 0.05 and 0.10 mg/mL, resp. For phenylephrine.HCl, scan sample and std solns between 350 and 220 nm in 1 cm cells against 0.30*N* alc. HCl as ref. Calc. sample soln concn by using baseline drawn tangent from 295 to 240 nm. Measure *A* between max. and baseline at ca 272 nm.

For phenylpropanolamine.HCl, scan sample and std solns between 350 and 220 nm in 5 cm cells against 0.30*N* alc. HCl as ref. Calc. sample soln concn by using baseline drawn tangent from ca 265 to 255 nm. Measure *A* between max. and baseline at ca 258 nm.

For promethazine.HCl, proceed as in (**d**).

(**f**) Proceed as in (**e**) until phenylephrine.HCl or phenylpropanolamine.HCl has been detd.

For dextromethorphan.HBr, place 200 mL vol. flask beneath Column *I* and elute with 120.0 mL 1.00*N* alc. HCl. Dil. to vol. with 1.00*N* alc. HCl and mix. Further dil. with 1.00*N* alc. HCl to give concn ca 0.10 mg/ mL. Scan sample and std solns between 350 and 235 nm in 1 cm cells against 1.00*N* alc. HCl as ref. Calc. sample soln concn by using baseline drawn tangent from 350 to 300 nm and extended to 235 nm. Measure *A* between max. and baseline at ca 280 nm.

For pyrilamine maleate, place 250 mL vol. flask beneath Column *I* and elute with 250.0 mL 2.50*N* alc. HCl. Dil. to vol. with 2.50*N* alc. HCl and mix. Further dil. with 2.50*N* alc. HCl to give concn ca 0.020 mg/mL. Scan sample and std solns from 360 to 220 nm against 2.50*N* alc. HCl as ref. Det. *A* at max., ca 310 nm, and calc. sample soln concn.

In absence of dextromethorphan.HBr, omit 1.00*N* alc. HCl eluant.

In absence of phenylephrine.HCl or phenolpropanolamine.HCl, discard 0.30*N* alc. HCl eluant.

In absence of pyrilamine maleate, omit 2.50*N* alc. HCl eluant.

(**g**) Proceed as for phenylephrine.HCl or phenylpropanolamine.HCl, etc. in (**e**) except arrange columns so eluate from Column *II* flows thru Column *I* and into 250 mL vol. flask. Let sample soln flow thru column until it sinks into resin. Pass ca 150 mL isopropanol (1+1) thru columns. (To prevent resin disturbance, establish ca 5 mL solv. head on Column *I* before each elution as in (**a**).) Remove Column *II* and wash Column *I* with 50.0 mL 0.055*N* alc. HCl; collect eluate in same vol. flask. Dil. glyceryl guaiacolate to vol. with isopropanol (1+1) and mix. Further dil. sample with isopropanol (1+1) to give concn ca 0.04 mg/mL. Scan sample and std solns from 350 to 220 nm against isopropanol (1+1) as ref. Det. *A* at max., ca 274 nm, and calc. sample soln concn.

In absence of dextromethorphan.HBr, omit 1.00*N* alc. HCl eluant.

In absence of pyrilamine maleate, omit 2.50*N* alc. HCl eluant.

In absence of phenylephrine.HCl or phenylpropanolamine.HCl, discard 0.30*N* alc. HCl eluant.

38.118–38.119 Reserved

Amphetamine (*34*)—Official Final Action

38.120 ★ *Titrimetric Method* ★

Extn from alk. soln and titrn. *See* **38.116**, 12th ed.

38.121 ★ *Confirmatory Gravimetric Determination* ★

Acetylation and gravimetric detn of acetylamphetamine. *See* **38.117**, 12th ed.

Spectrophotometric Method (*35*)—Official First Action

(Applicable in presence of thyroid, phenobarbital, atropine, and aloin)

38.122 ***Apparatus***

(**a**) *Spectrophotometer.*—Capable of isolating bands ≤1 nm in 225–300 nm region; with 1 cm cells.

(**b**) *Distillation apparatus.*—Use following or equiv.: 500 mL Kjeldahl flask (Kontes Glass Co., No. K-742000) to which is fitted bulb-type distg head (K-517000). Attach connector (K-169500) from distg head to H_2O-cooled West condenser (K-452000). Attach adapter to bottom of condenser to dip below surface of liq. in 300 mL erlenmeyer. All joints are ₮ 24/40. Lightly coat flask joint with Dow Corning high vac. grease to prevent freezing.

38.123 ***Preparation of Standard Solution***

Accurately weigh 80–90 mg amphetamine sulfate of known purity, transfer to 100 mL vol. flask, and dissolve in 1*N* H_2SO_4. Dil. to vol. with 1*N* H_2SO_4 and mix well.

38.124 ***Preparation of Sample***

Det. av. wt of tablets or capsule contents. Grind tablets or capsule contents to pass No. 60 sieve without appreciable loss.

38.125 ***Determination***

Accurately weigh portion prepd sample contg ca 20–22 mg amphetamine sulfate (or equiv. of other salt). Transfer to Kjeldahl flask, add 25 mL 1*N* H_2SO_4, ca 0.5 g granulated Zn, and 100 mL H_2O, and heat on steam bath ca 5 min. Swirl occasionally to completely disperse sample. Cool and wash down sides of flask with 75 mL H_2O contg small amt of antifoam agent such as Dow Corning Antifoam A spray. Place 300 mL erlenmeyer contg 50 mL 0.5*N* H_2SO_4 under condenser so that adapter extends nearly to bottom of flask.

Place Kjeldahl flask on wire gauze sq from which 4 cm circle of asbestos has been removed. Add 25 mL 10% NaOH soln to flask and quickly connect distn app. Make sure all joints are tight. Begin heating with Bunsen burner and bring to rolling boil (shield receiver from excessive heat). Collect 150–175 mL distillate or enough so total vol. in receiver is 200–225 mL. Distil 60±15 min.

When distn is complete, remove connector first, then burner. Rinse condenser and adapter into receiver with few mL H_2O. Transfer distillate to 500 mL separator, washing flask with few mL H_2O, and add washing to separator. Make soln alk. with 25 mL 10% NaOH soln, immediately add 50 mL $CHCl_3$, and shake

★ Surplus method—*see* inside front cover.

cautiously but thoroly 2 min. Let layers sep. completely. Carefully drain $CHCl_3$ ext into clean, dry 250 mL separator and re-ext alk. soln with 50, 25, 25, and 25 mL $CHCl_3$. Add 25 mL 1*N* H_2SO_4 by pipet to separator contg combined $CHCl_3$ exts and shake vigorously 2–3 min. Let layers sep. completely and discard $CHCl_3$. Obtain UV spectrum of aq. phase in 1 cm cell between 225 and 300 nm against ref. soln of $CHCl_3$-satd 1*N* H_2SO_4.

Shake 250 mL H_2O and 175 mL $CHCl_3$ in 500 mL separator 1–2 min. Withdraw clear $CHCl_3$ layer into separator contg 25 mL std soln. Shake vigorously 2–3 min. Obtain UV spectrum of aq. phase in 1 cm cell as above.

38.126 ***Calculations***

mg Amphetamine sulfate/g sample taken

$$= (A/A') \times (\text{mg std per mL/g sample}) \times 25,$$

where $A = A_{max.}$ of sample at ca 257 nm − ($A_{min.}$ at ca 254 nm + $A_{min.}$ at ca 262 nm)/2 and A' is corresponding value for std.

★ Stereochemical Composition of Amphetamines (*36*) ★

38.127 ***Polarimetric Method***

Accurately weigh 90 mg acetyl derivative, **38.121★**, transfer quant. to 5 mL vol. flask, and dil. to vol. with $CHCl_3$. Det. optical rotation of soln in semimicro 2 dm (200 mm) tube (bore, ca 4.5 mm; vol., 3–4 mL) at same temp. at which soln was dild to vol. Acetyl-*d*-amphetamine is levorotatory in $CHCl_3$.

In measuring rotation with polariscope, take 10 readings on soln and calc. av. to 0.001°. Det. av. reading with same tube filled with $CHCl_3$ similarly, and use av. zero-point reading thus obtained to correct av. reading of soln. If saccharimeter is used instead of polariscope, est. all readings to 0.05 division, calc. av. to 0.01 division, correct for zero-point, and multiply value so obtained by appropriate factor, **31.020(c)**, or by 0.3462 (°S) to obtain rotation, α, in angular degrees.

Calc. sp rotation, $[\alpha]$ (to 0.1°) $= 100\alpha/c \times l$,

in which c = acetylamphetamine concn in g/100 mL and l = tube length in decimeters.

% Dextroamphetamine $= 50 + (50[\alpha]/44)$,

in which $[\alpha]$ = sp rotation of acetyl derivative from sample, and 44 = sp rotation of pure acetyl-*d*-amphetamine; sign of rotation is ignored.

38.128 ***Confirmatory Thermal Analysis***

In mp tube, 2–3 mm id at bottom and ca 70 mm long, place enough finely powd acetyl-*dl*-amphetamine (ca 8 mg) to form column 5–6 mm high after tube and contents have been tapped firmly several times on hard surface.

Select thermometer with 90–130° range, with graduations permitting readings to 0.5° with aid of low-power hand lens. Thermometer need not be calibrated, but if not, same thermometer must be used in detg std mp curve and mp of derivative from sample.

Securely fix mp tube to thermometer by 2 small rubber bands, one near top of tube and other as far down as possible without letting liq. in bath touch band. (Bands may be cut from rubber tubing of proper size.) Adjust tube so that middle of column of specimen coincides approx. with middle of thermometer bulb.

Support assembly in mech.-stirred mp bath. Rapidly raise temp. of bath until it is ca 5° below anticipated mp (temp. at which specimen becomes entirely clear liq.); then regulate heating carefully so that rise in temp. is ≤0.5°/min. After specimen begins to melt, stir continuously with chromel wire (0.4 mm diam.; flatten ca 3 mm of lower end and bend flattened portion at right angle ca 1 mm from tip so as to form hoe-like stirrer) while carefully inspecting it with ca 10× hand lens. (Observation is facilitated by passing beam of light thru specimen from rear.) Note temp. at which last crystal disappears, and record this as mp. Remove tube and thermometer from bath, induce melt to solidify by stirring (seeding if necessary), and repeat detn. Replicate detns will not differ by >1° if carefully performed. Following same procedure, det. mp of pure acetyl-*d*-amphetamine.

Prep. series of std mixts of acetyl-*d*- and acetyl-*l*-amphetamine with following compositions, expressed in mg: 80*d* + 20*dl*, 60*d* + 40*dl*, 40*d* + 60*dl*, and 20*d* + 80*dl*. These mixts contain, resp., 90, 80, 70, and 60% *d*-isomer. In each case, accurately weigh each component into small (18 × 55 mm) test tube, hold tube in bath heated to 130–135° until contents melt completely, stir molten contents with small stainless steel spatula until well mixed, and then withdraw tube from bath and continue to stir until melt solidifies completely. Transfer solidified material as completely as possible to small mortar, powder finely, and mix thoroly. Det. mp of each mixt. as above. In each mixt., beginning of fusion (softening, appearance of liq. phase) will be noted at ca same temp. (ca 93°), but temp. at which system becomes entirely liq. (mp) will depend on composition of mixt. Unlike mp detns of pure *dl*- and *d*-derivatives, it is not important to stir mixts continuously after first evidence of fusion. After considerable liq. phase forms, stir sample occasionally as solid phase diminishes. Stir continuously during ca last 2 min of detn, *i.e.,* during inspection in anticipation of disappearance of last portion of cryst. matter. Push down any solids adhering to walls of tube above melt into melt with wire stirrer.

Using coordinate paper, plot av. mp (ordinate) of each specimen against composition (abscissa) expressed as % acetyl-*d*-amphetamine, and draw best smooth curve thru the 6 plotted points.

Det. mp of derivative obtained from sample and est. % *d*-isomer present from std curve.

Gas-Liquid Chromatographic Method (37)
Official Final Action

38.129 ***Apparatus***

(a) *Gas chromatograph.*—Equipped with flame ionization detector. Operate at sensitivity such that proline derivative from 10 μg *d*-amphetamine sulfate gives peak 70–90% full scale. Adjust injection zone and detector temps to 230°.

(b) *Column.*—Glass, 2 m × 4 mm id, packed with 1% Carbowax 20M on 80–100 or 100–120 mesh Gas-Chrom Q (Applied Science Laboratories, Inc.). Condition column 24 hr at 210° before use. Operate at 185° and adjust N carrier gas flow rate so that proline derivative of *d*-amphetamine is eluted in ca 15 min (ca 60 mL/min).

(c) *Chromatographic tube.*—22 × 300 mm, without stopcock.

38.130 ***Reagents***

(a) *Diatomaceous earth.—See* **36.002**.

(b) *Proline reagent.*—(Prep. reagent at <30°.) To 1.0 g *l*-proline (Sigma Chemical Co.) in 125 mL g-s conical flask, add 5 g trifluoroacetic anhydride (Eastman Kodak Co.) and swirl until proline is dissolved. Evap. excess trifluoroacetic anhydride under stream of dry N. Add 5 mL thionyl chloride, let stand 15 min, and evap. excess under stream of dry N. Dissolve residue in 100 mL CH_2Cl_2 and refrigerate when not in use. Properly prepd reagent will give *l*-amphetamine ratio, **38.132**, ≤0.02 with *d*-amphetamine sulfate. (*Caution:* Trifluoroacetic anhydride and

★ Surplus method—*see* inside front cover.

thionyl chloride are toxic. Wear rubber gloves and eye protection and use effective fume removal device for evapn.)

(**c**) *Std soln I.*—0.5 mg USP Ref. Std Dextroamphetamine Sulfate/mL H_2O.

(**d**) *Std soln II.*—0.5 mg *dl*-amphetamine sulfate (ICN–K&K Laboratories, Inc.)/mL H_2O. Recrystallize *dl*-amphetamine sulfate from alcohol and dry under vac. at 100° before use.

38.131 ***Preparation of Wash Column***

Mix 3.0 mL 1*N* NaOH with 5.0 g diat. earth and transfer to chromatgc tube contg small glass wool plug. Place glass wool pad on top of diat. earth and tamp firmly.

38.132 ***Preparation of Standard Curve***

Prep. series of *l*-amphetamine sulfate stds contg total of ca 10 mg amphetamine sulfate in 20 mL H_2O in 125 mL separators as follows: 0% *l*-amphetamine sulfate from 20 mL std soln *I* and 0 mL std soln *II*; 12.5%, 15 mL *I* and 5 mL *II*; 25%, 10 mL *I* and 10 mL *II*; 37.5%, 5 mL *I* and 15 mL *II*; and 50%, 0 mL *I* and 20 mL *II*. Treat each soln as follows: Add 5 mL 1*N* NaOH and ext with two 25 mL portions $CHCl_3$. Filter $CHCl_3$ exts thru absorbent cotton into dry 150 mL beaker. Add 3 mL proline reagent, (**b**), and let stand 30 min; then transfer to wash column. Collect eluate in 150 mL beaker. Pass addnl 25 mL $CHCl_3$ thru column. Evap. on steam bath with aid of N stream, dissolve residue in 5 mL $CHCl_3$, and transfer to g-s flask. Inject 5 μL and calc.

$$l\text{-amphetamine ratio} = H_l \times R_l/[(H_d \times R_d) + (H_l \times R_l)],$$

where *H* and *R* = peak ht and retention time, resp., of *d*- and *l*-amphetamine derivatives. Plot *l*-amphetamine ratio against % *l*-amphetamine.

38.133 ***Determination***

Transfer finely powd sample contg ca 10 mg amphetamine sulfate to 100 mL beaker, add 2 g diat. earth, and mix. Add 3.0 mL 1*N* NaOH and mix to uniform slurry. Add 3.0 g diat. earth, mix well, and pack into chromatgc tube contg small glass wool plug. Place 150 mL beaker under column and elute with 100 mL $CHCl_3$. Proceed as in **38.132**, beginning "Add 3 mL proline reagent, (**b**), . . ." Calc. *l*-amphetamine ratio and det. *l*-amphetamine from std curve.

38.134 Amphetamine in Presence of Antihistamines and Barbiturates and Other Drugs Official Final Action

See **38.111–38.117.**

Antihistamines in Presence of Acetophenetidin, Acetylsalicylic Acid, and Caffeine (APC) (*38*) Official Final Action

(Applicable to thonzylamine.HCl, pheniramine maleate, and chlorpheniramine maleate in combination with APC)

38.135 ***Preparation of Standard Solutions***

Prep. sep. std solns of thonzylamine.HCl, pheniramine maleate, and chlorpheniramine maleate by dissolving 250 mg antihistamine salt, accurately weighed, in 50.0 mL H_2O. Pipet 5 mL of each soln into sep. 100 mL vol. flasks and dil. to vol. with ca 0.1*N* H_2SO_4. Transfer 10 mL of each acid soln to sep. 100 mL vol. flasks and dil. to vol. with ca 0.1*N* H_2SO_4. (Concn = 2.5 mg/100 mL.) Det. *A'* of thonzylamine.HCl at 314 nm, pheniramine maleate at 265 nm, and chlorpheniramine maleate at 264 nm.

38.136 ***Determination***

Place accurately weighed powd sample contg ca 10 mg antihistamine in 125 mL separator. Add 15 mL H_2O and ca 0.5 mL H_2SO_4 (1+1). Ext with $CHCl_3$, using 30, 20, 20, and 20 mL portions. Re-ext by passing $CHCl_3$ exts successively thru 2 separators, each contg 10 mL ca 0.1*N* H_2SO_4, shaking vigorously each time. Discard $CHCl_3$ and combine aq. solns.

Make combined solns alk. with 10% NaOH and ext with 30, 20, 20, and 20 mL portions $CHCl_3$. Again pass $CHCl_3$ exts successively thru 2 separators, each contg 20 mL ca 0.1*N* H_2SO_4, shaking vigorously each time. Discard $CHCl_3$, combine acid aq. solns, and dil. to vol. with ca 0.1*N* H_2SO_4 in 100 mL vol. flask. Transfer 25 mL aliquot to 100 mL vol. flask and dil. to vol. with ca 0.1*N* H_2SO_4. Det. *A* at wavelength of max. absorption against ca 0.1*N* acid as ref.

% Thonzylamine.HCl = $(A \times 2.5 \times 4 \times 100)/(A' \times \text{mg sample})$.

% Pheniramine or chlorpheniramine maleate

$$= 1.018 \times (A \times 2.5 \times 4 \times 100)/(A' \times \text{mg sample}),$$

where 1.018 corrects for absorbance of maleate moiety of std.

38.137 Antipyrine and Benzocaine—Official Final Action

See **38.144–38.148.**

Benzocaine (Ethyl *p*-Aminobenzoate)—Official Final Action

Colorimetric Method (*39*)

38.138 ***Principle***

Benzocaine is diazotized with $NaNO_2$, excess nitrite is removed with NH_4 sulfamate, and product is coupled with N-1-naphthylethylenediamine.2HCl. Colored soln has max. at 540 nm. Method is not applicable in presence of sulfonamides. Benzocaine must be sepd from inorg. I to avoid interference. Antipyrine in 10-fold excess does not interfere.

38.139 ***Reagents***

Benzocaine std solns.—(*1*) *Stock soln.*—0.25 mg/mL. Dissolve 25.0 mg benzocaine USP in 25–50 mL H_2O in 100 mL vol. flask. Add 3 mL HCl, shake gently, and dil. to vol. with H_2O. (*2*) *Working soln.*—5 μg/mL. Pipet 10 mL stock soln into 100 mL vol. flask and dil. to vol. with H_2O. Pipet 20 mL of this soln into 100 mL vol. flask and dil. to vol. with H_2O.

38.140 ***Preparation of Standard Curve***

Pipet 0.0, 2.0, 6.0, and 10.0 mL working std soln into sep. 25 mL vol. flasks. To each flask add 1 mL HCl (1+1). Dil. to 15 mL with H_2O, add 1 mL 0.1% $NaNO_2$ soln, **37.153(c)**, mix, and let stand 5 min, swirling several times during standing. Add 1 mL 0.5% NH_4 sulfamate soln, **37.153(d)**, and let stand 5 min, swirling several times during standing. Add 1 mL colorless 0.1% N-1-naphthylethylenediamine.2HCl soln, **42.017(d)**, let stand 15 min, swirling several times during standing, and dil. to 25.0 mL with H_2O.

Det. *A* of each soln in matched 1 cm cells in spectrophtr at 540 nm against H_2O as ref. (Avoid collection of N bubbles on cell walls.) To obtain ΔA, subtract reading of soln contg *no* std from each of other std readings. Plot ΔA against benzocaine concn.

38.141 ***Preparation of Samples***

(**a**) *Liquid preparation in water-soluble bases.*—Weigh sample contg 100 mg benzocaine, transfer to 250 mL vol. flask, and add 75 mL alcohol. Add 3 mL HCl, dil. to vol. with H_2O, and mix well. Pipet 10 mL into 100 mL vol. flask, dil. to vol. with H_2O, and mix well. Pipet 10 mL of diln into 100 mL vol. flask, dil. to vol. with H_2O, and mix well.

(**b**) *Tablets or troches.*—Weigh powd sample contg 7.5–10 mg benzocaine. Transfer to 100 mL beaker, wet with 2–3 mL alcohol, stir with glass rod to slurry, add 5 mL H_2O and 2 mL HCl, stir, and let stand at room temp. 5 min. Dil. with 25 mL H_2O, transfer quant. to 100 mL vol. flask, and dil. to vol. If soln is cloudy, filter thru dry paper, discarding first 10 mL filtrate. Pipet 10 mL clear filtrate into 100 mL vol. flask, dil. to vol. with H_2O, and mix well.

(**c**) *Suppositories in water-soluble bases.*—Weigh sample contg 50–100 mg benzocaine into 100 mL beaker, add 15 mL H_2O and 3 mL HCl, and let stand at room temp. 15 min, stirring occasionally with rod. Transfer quant. to 250 mL vol. flask, dil. to vol., and mix well. Pipet 10 mL into 100 mL vol. flask, dil. to vol., and mix well. Pipet 10 mL of diln into 100 mL vol. flask, dil. to vol., and mix well.

38.142 ***Determination***

Pipet 2 aliquots of final diln specified in **38.141** contg 20–30 μg benzocaine into sep 25 mL vol. flasks. Label one flask "sample" and the other "sample blank." Proceed as in **38.140**, beginning "To each flask add 1 mL HCl (1+1)." except do not add $NaNO_2$ to "sample blank."

Det. A at 540 nm for each soln against H_2O as ref. Subtract A of "sample blank" from "sample" reading. Det. μg benzocaine in aliquot from std curve.

$$\% \text{ Benzocaine} = (B \times F)/(W \times 10),$$

where B = μg benzocaine from std curve, F = diln factor, and W = mg sample.

38.143 ★ ***Bromination Method (40)*** ★

See **38.139**, 12th ed.

Benzocaine and Antipyrine (*41*)—Official Final Action

(Applicable in presence of glycerol and propylene glycol bases)

38.144 ***Principle***

Benzocaine and antipyrine are extd by column partition chromatgy. Antipyrine is retained on $FeCl_3$ column and benzocaine on HCl column. Max. A are detd in $CHCl_3$ eluates at 272 nm for antipyrine and 283 nm for benzocaine. To identify compds, IR spectra of KBr dispersions are compared to stds.

38.145 ***Apparatus and Reagents***

(**a**) *Chromatographic column and tamping rod.—See* **37.002**.

(**b**) *Syringe.*—10 mL syringe with 14 gage 4" laboratory cannula.

(**c**) *Ferric chloride.*—9%. Dissolve 9 g anhyd. $FeCl_3$ in H_2O and dil. to 100 mL.

(**d**) *Diatomaceous earth.—See* **36.002.**

(**e**) *Chloroform, washed.*—Shake 4 vols $CHCl_3$ with 1 vol. H_2O.

(**f**) *Mixed solvent.*—H_2O-satd $CHCl_3$-ether-isooctane (10+25+65).

(**g**) *Antipyrine std soln.*—1 mg/100 mL. Accurately weigh antipyrine std, previously dried 2 hr at 60°, and dil. with $CHCl_3$ to give concn of 0.1 mg/mL. Pipet 10 mL into 100 mL vol. flask contg 10 mL MeOH and 1.0 mL mixed solv., and dil. to vol. with washed $CHCl_3$.

(**h**) *Benzocaine std soln.*—0.4 mg/100 mL. Accurately weigh USP Benzocaine Ref. Std, previously dried 3 hr over P_2O_5, and dil. with $CHCl_3$ to concn of 0.04 mg/mL. Pipet 10 mL into 100 mL vol. flask contg 10 mL MeOH and 1.0 mL mixed solv., and dil. to vol. with washed $CHCl_3$.

(**i**) *Photometric blank.*—Pipet 10 mL MeOH and 1 mL mixed solv. into 100 mL vol. flask, dil. to vol. with washed $CHCl_3$, and mix.

(**j**) *Potassium bromide.*—Anhyd. spectrophtric grade.

38.146 ***Sample Density***

(Altho sample is weighed because of viscosity of prepns, report results on wt/vol. basis.)

Slowly withdraw 10 mL sample with syringe, keeping air bubbles to min., and transfer to previously weighed 10 mL vol. flask without touching sides of flask above mark. Let any air bubbles present rise before filling to final vol. Weigh flask and contents, and calc. sample density.

38.147 ***Preparation of Chromatographic Columns***

Loosely pack small amt glass wool uniformly in base of 3 chromatgc tubes to support diat. earth.

Bottom column.—Mix 3 g diat. earth with 2 mL 2N HCl to form uniform fluffy mixt. Transfer mixt. to column and tamp firmly to uniform mass.

Middle column.—Mix 5 g diat. earth with 3 mL $FeCl_3$ soln and transfer to column as above.

Top column.—Accurately weigh sample contg 20 mg antipyrine into 100 mL beaker. Add 2 mL H_2O and then 3 g diat. earth. Mix thoroly, transfer to column, and tamp firmly to uniform mass. Dry-wash beaker with 1 g diat. earth and tamp as above.

Top each column with small loose pad of glass wool.

38.148 ***Determination***

(*Caution: See* **51.011**, **51.040**, and **51.056**.)

(**a**) *Separation of antipyrine and benzocaine.*—Arrange 3 columns in series. Rinse beaker that contained sample with 50 mL mixed solv. and transfer to top column. Elute columns with 3 addnl 25 mL portions mixed solv. Discard eluate. (Middle column contains antipyrine and bottom column contains benzocaine.) Sep. columns, and elute middle and bottom columns sep. with four 25 mL portions washed $CHCl_3$, collecting eluates in 100 mL vol. flasks. Dil. to vol. with washed $CHCl_3$.

(**b**) *Determination of antipyrine.*—Pipet 5 mL from antipyrine flask into 100 mL vol. flask contg 10 mL MeOH and dil. to vol. with washed $CHCl_3$. Det. A of final diln against photometric blank, (**i**), at 272 nm, using 1 cm cells. Similarly, det. A' of std antipyrine soln and calc. amt of antipyrine in sample.

(**c**) *Determination of benzocaine.*—Pipet aliquot of eluate contg 0.4 mg benzocaine into 100 mL vol. flask contg 10.0 mL MeOH and dil. to vol. with washed $CHCl_3$. Det. A of final diln against photometric blank, (**i**), at 283 nm. Similarly, det. A' of std benzocaine soln and calc. amt of benzocaine in sample.

(**d**) *Identification of antipyrine and benzocaine.*—Transfer remaining $CHCl_3$ eluates from antipyrine and benzocaine sepn to sep. 150 mL beakers. Place beakers in 30–40° H_2O bath and evap. to dryness with gentle air current. (*Caution:* Benzocaine is volatile.)

Prep. KBr disk of each residue, using 0.8 mg residue and 200 mg KBr. Record IR spectrum of each between 2 and 16 μm and qual. compare these spectra with IR spectra of antipyrine and benzocaine stds.

Benztropine Mesylate (*42*)—Official Final Action

(Not applicable in presence of compds reacting with bromophenol blue, e.g., quaternary ammonium compds)

★ Surplus method—*see* inside front cover.

38.149 ***Principle***

Benztropine is extd from acid soln by bromophenol blue-$CHCl_3$ soln, forming dye complex with max. *A* at ca 410 nm.

38.150 ***Reagents and Apparatus***

(**a**) *Dye soln.*—Weigh 100 mg reagent bromophenol blue into 1 L vol. flask, add ca 750 mL $CHCl_3$, stir mech. 10 min to dissolve, and dil. to vol. with $CHCl_3$. Filter thru small pad of glass wool. Dil. 50 mL to 500 mL with $CHCl_3$. Prep. fresh daily.

(**b**) *Benztropine mesylate std soln.*—1 mg/100 mL. Weigh 100 mg USP Ref. Std into 100 mL vol. flask and dissolve and dil. to 100 mL with 0.2*N* H_2SO_4. Dil. 10 mL aliquot to 100 mL with 0.2*N* H_2SO_4 and further dil. 10 mL dild soln to 100 mL with 0.2*N* H_2SO_4. Prep. fresh daily.

(**c**) *Spectrophotometer.*—Recording, with 5 cm matched cells.

38.151 ***Preparation of Sample***

(**a**) *Tablets.*—Transfer accurately weighed ground portion contg ca 1 mg benztropine mesylate to 100 mL vol. flask, using ca 70 mL 0.2*N* H_2SO_4. Shake mech. 15 min and filter thru Whatman No. 541 paper wetted with 0.2*N* H_2SO_4 into 100 mL vol. flask. Rinse flask and filter with three 5 mL portions 0.2*N* H_2SO_4, rinse filter with several small portions 0.2*N* H_2SO_4, adding rinses to soln, and dil. to vol. with 0.2*N* H_2SO_4.

(**b**) *Injections.*—Transfer aliquot contg ca 1 mg benztropine mesylate to 100 mL vol. flask and dil. to vol. with 0.2*N* H_2SO_4.

38.152 ***Determination***

Perform detn on same day sample and std solns are prepd. Place 25 mL each sample soln and std soln and 0.2*N* H_2SO_4 for blank into sep. 250 mL separators and treat similarly. Add 50 mL dye soln and shake vigorously 1 min. Let sep. and drain lower layer into 125 mL separator contg 25 mL 0.2*N* H_2SO_4. Wash by inverting 5 times and let stand ca 20 min. Filter lower $CHCl_3$ layer thru glass wool wetted with $CHCl_3$ into 100 mL vol. flask, covering funnel with watch glass. Re-ext aq. soln in 250 mL separator with 50 mL dye soln, shake vigorously 1 min, drain into same 125 mL separator, and wash and filter as before, rewetting glass wool with $CHCl_3$ if necessary. Dil. to vol. with $CHCl_3$, mix, and place in dark 40 min.

Record spectra of std and sample solns against blank in matched 5 cm cells, and det. *A* at max., ca 410 nm.

$$\text{mg Benztropine mesylate/100 mL} = (A/A') \times C,$$

where *A* and *A'* refer to sample and std solns, resp; and *C* = concn std soln in mg/100 mL.

Butacaine Sulfate (*43*)—Official Final Action

38.153 ***Reagents***

(**a**) *Potassium iodide soln.*—20%. Prep. fresh.

(**b**) *Starch indicator.*—Make 1.5 g sol. starch into paste with few mL H_2O, and add slowly, with stirring, to 300 mL boiling H_2O.

(**c**) *Picrolonic acid soln.*—2.5% in alcohol.

38.154 ***Determination***

(*Caution: See* **51.011**, **51.040**, and **51.056**.)

(**a**) *Ointments containing butacaine sulfate in petrolatum or other greasy base.*—Into 125 mL separator accurately weigh sample contg ca 50 mg butacaine sulfate. Add 25 mL benzene and swirl until ointment base dissolves; then add 10 mL HCl (1+7) and shake separator gently ca 1 min. Let layers sep., drain aq. phase into second separator, and repeat extn 4 times with 10 mL portions H_2O. Wash combined aq. exts with 5 mL CCl_4 and discard washing. Neutze soln with NH_4OH, add 2 mL excess, and ext butacaine base by shaking with five 15 mL portions $CHCl_3$. Filter each ext thru cotton pledget into 100 mL beaker, and evap. combined exts on steam bath under air current until no $CHCl_3$ odor remains.

Rinse down beaker wall with 2 mL alcohol delivered from pipet, warm until oily base dissolves completely, and add 1 drop HCl. Tilt and rotate beaker to wet with acidic soln any liq. on wall of beaker, and add 1 drop Me red. If soln does not react strongly acid, add addnl HCl dropwise. Dil. with few mL H_2O, and wash quant. into 500 mL I flask with more H_2O.

To soln add, from pipet, 10 mL KBr-$KBrO_3$ soln, **4.002(g)**, dil. to 200 mL with H_2O, and add 10 mL HCl. Immediately stopper flask and swirl 5 min or until ppt coagulates. After 5 min, add 5 mL KI soln to flask, stopper, and shake vigorously. Rinse stopper and neck of flask with little H_2O, and titr. soln with 0.1*N* $Na_2S_2O_3$, **50.037**, until color is discharged. Add 15 mL starch indicator and 20 mL $CHCl_3$, stopper flask, and shake vigorously. Continue titrn, vigorously shaking stoppered flask after each addn of $Na_2S_2O_3$ soln. Add $Na_2S_2O_3$ soln dropwise as end point approaches. (During titrn, mixt. passes thru series of color changes; at end point aq. phase is colorless and emulsified $CHCl_3$ layer is nearly so.) 1 mL 0.1*N* KBr-$KBrO_3$ = 0.00889 g $(C_{18}H_{30}N_2O_2)_2.H_2SO_4$.

To isolate bromination product for identification, transfer titrd mixt. to separator, make alk. with NH_4OH, and shake vigorously. Drain emulsified $CHCl_3$ layer, and to break emulsion, filter with suction thru 0.5 cm layer Hyflo Super-Cel (or similar filter-aid) supported on paper in buchner. Shake aq. phase remaining in separator with 25 mL $CHCl_3$, and pass $CHCl_3$ ext thru filter. Transfer combined filtrates to separator, filter $CHCl_3$ layer thru cotton pledget into beaker, and evap. on steam bath under air current.

To oily residue of dibromobutacaine add 2 mL picrolonic acid soln and stir. Filter ppt on Hirsch funnel, wash with 2–3 mL alcohol, dry at 105°, and det. capillary mp, alone and in admixt. with authentic dibromobutacaine picrolonate (mp 158–160° with decomposition). If ppt does not form on adding picrolonic acid soln to bromination product, seed with small crystal of dibromobutacaine picrolonate; if ppt still does not form, butacaine is absent.

(**b**) *Tablets.*—Det. av. wt/tablet. To 125 mL separator add accurately weighed, finely powd tablet mixt. contg ca 200 mg butacaine sulfate, add 25 mL H_2O, and swirl separator until sample dissolves. Add 2 mL NH_4OH and ext with six 15 mL portions $CHCl_3$. Shake each ext with 5 mL H_2O in second separator, and then filter thru cotton pledget into beaker. (If emulsion forms in aq. phase in first separator, more than 6 extns may be required. Test for complete extn by evapg seventh ext on steam bath; if appreciable residue is obtained, dissolve it in $CHCl_3$, combine with previous exts, and continue extns until complete. If aq. phase in first separator tends to emulsify, break emulsion by addn of Na_2SO_4 or by other means.) Evap. filtrate to small vol. on steam bath and complete detn by one of following methods:

(*1*) Quant. transfer concd soln of butacaine base to tared 50 mL beaker with $CHCl_3$, remove solv. on steam bath in air current, dry 30 min at 105°, cool in desiccator, and weigh. Wt residue × 1.160 = wt butacaine sulfate, $(C_{18}H_{30}N_2O_2)_2.H_2SO_4$.

Gravimetric detn may be checked acidimetrically as follows: Rinse down wall of beaker with 2 mL neut. alcohol delivered from pipet, warm beaker on steam bath until butacaine base dissolves completely, add 1 drop Me red, and rinse down beaker wall with another 2 mL alcohol. Titr. soln with 0.1 *N* H_2SO_4, **50.040** or **50.041**, almost to point of color change; rinse down wall of beaker with H_2O, dil. to ca 45 mL, and complete titrn. 1 mL 0.1*N* H_2SO_4 = 0.0355 g $(C_{18}H_{30}N_2O_2)_2.H_2SO_4$.

(*2*) Det. gravimetrically as in (*1*); then proceed as in (**a**), beginning "Rinse down beaker wall with 2 mL alcohol . . ." except use 50 mL instead of 10 mL KBr-$KBrO_3$ soln.

(*3*) Completely remove solv. on steam bath, and proceed as in (*1*), second par. Then wash titrd soln into 500 mL I flask, pipet in 50 mL KBr-$KBrO_3$ soln, **4.002(g)**, dil. to 200 mL with H_2O, add 10 mL HCl, and proceed as in (**a**), beginning "Immediately stopper flask . . ."

(**c**) *Crystals.*—Accurately weigh ca 200 mg sample into 125 mL separator, add 25 mL H_2O, and swirl separator until sample dissolves. Continue as in (**b**), beginning "Add 2 mL NH_4OH . . ."

(**d**) *Solns.*—Transfer to 125 mL separator aliquot contg ca 200 mg butacaine sulfate, and if necessary, dil. to 25 mL with H_2O. Proceed as in (**b**), completing detn by (**b**)(*1*), (*2*), or (*3*) if chlorobutanol is absent, and only by (**b**)(*3*) if chlorobutanol is present.

★ Cinchophen—Official Final Action ★

38.155 ***In Presence of Salicylates (44)***

Quant. iodination. *See* **38.151–38.152**, 12th ed.

38.156 ***In Presence of Sodium Bicarbonate (45)***

Extn from acid soln and titrn. *See* **38.153–38.154**, 12th ed.

Meperidine (Demerol®, Pethidine) *(46)*—Official Final Action

38.157 ★ Distillation Method ★

See **36.093–36.095**, 11th ed.

38.158 ***Extraction Method***

Accurately weigh portion of powd sample contg ca 0.1 g meperidine, and macerate 2 hr with 10 mL H_2O and 1 mL 1*N* H_2SO_4. Decant liq. thru small filter into separator. Macerate residue 20 min with 5 mL H_2O, filter thru same filter, and wash residue and filter with small portions of H_2O.

Sat. soln with NaCl; then add 5 mL 1*N* NaOH and ext with 25 mL and six 20 mL portions ether as in **36.001**. Wash combined ether exts with two 5 mL portions H_2O; ext this H_2O with 10 mL ether and add this ether to main ether ext. Ext ether soln first with 20.0 mL 0.02*N* H_2SO_4, and then successively with 10 and 5 mL H_2O. Combine H_2SO_4 and H_2O exts in beaker and warm on H_2O bath until no ether odor is detected. Cool soln, and titr. excess acid with 0.02*N* NaOH, using Me red. 1 mL 0.02*N* H_2SO_4 = 0.005676 g meperidine.HCl, $C_{15}H_{21}O_2N.HCl$.

Mephentermine Sulfate (*N*,α,α-Trimethylphenethylamine Sulfate) *(47)*—Official First Action

38.159 ***Principle***

Mephentermine sulfate is sepd on ion exchange column, eluted with alcoholic HCl, and measured by UV spectrophotometry.

38.160 ***Apparatus***

(**a**) *Chromatographic tube.*—Glass, 150 × 12 (id) mm, fitted with replaceable coarse fritted glass disk, Teflon stopcock, and Buna-N "O" ring seal (Kontes Glass Co., No. K-422280, or equiv.).

(**b**) *Ion exchange resin.*—*See* **38.113(d)**.

★ Surplus method—*see* inside front cover.

38.161 ***Reagents***

(**a**) *Alcoholic hydrochloric acid.*—(*1*) 1.5*N*.—Mix 1 part HCl with 7 parts alcohol-H_2O (1+1). (*2*) 6*N*.—Mix 1 part HCl with 1 part alcohol-H_2O (1+1).

(**b**) *Mephentermine sulfate std soln.*—0.5 mg/mL. Accurately weigh ca 25 mg mephentermine sulfate, previously dried 1 hr at 105°, into 50 mL vol. flask. Dissolve and dil. to vol. with 1.5*N* alcoholic HCl, (**a**)(*1*), and mix.

38.162 ***Preparation of Column***

Prep. slurry of 2 g resin, (**b**), with 20–25 mL alcohol-H_2O (1+1), and transfer to tube, (**a**), with stopcock closed and plug of glass wool under fritted disk. Let resin settle by gravity; then top with small pledget of glass wool. (Column need not be tamped.) Drain solv., wash column with three 10–20 mL portions alcohol-H_2O (1+1) followed by 20 mL H_2O, and discard all washings. Prevent column from drying out before use by maintaining head of 2–3 mL alcohol-H_2O (1+1) or H_2O.

When using column for first time and upon completion of sepns, wash thoroly with 15–20 mL 6*N* alcoholic HCl, (**a**)(*2*), to recondition resin. With stopcock closed, stir resin to obtain slurry, let settle, and drain. Repeat twice. Finally, wash resin with alcohol-H_2O (1+1) until excess acid is removed and then with three 10–20 mL portions H_2O. Store under H_2O when not in use.

Perform blank detn on new column, beginning in **38.163** with "Elute mephentermine with three 5 mL portions . . ." If UV spectrum has *A* >0.05 at 258 nm, recondition column again or prep. new column, using different bottle of resin.

38.163 ***Preparation of Sample***

(**a**) *Tablets.*—Grind tablets to pass No. 80 sieve. Accurately weigh amt powder contg ca 25 mg mephentermine sulfate into 50 mL beaker. Add 10 mL H_2O, heat on steam bath 2–3 min, cool, and filter thru 9 cm Whatman No. 541 paper into prepd column, **38.162**. Column flow rate should be ca 2–3 drops/sec. Thoroly wash filter paper with three 5–10 mL portions H_2O, letting each portion pass into column before addn of next. Wash column with 25 mL alcohol-H_2O (1+1). Discard all washings. Elute mephentermine with three 5 mL portions 1.5*N* alcoholic HCl, then with 30 mL 1.5*N* alcoholic HCl. Let each portion just enter column before adding next, introducing eluant down sides of column so as not to disturb resin. Collect eluate in 50 mL vol. flask, rinse liq. from tip of column into flask, and dil. to vol.

(**b**) *Elixir.*—Add sample vol. contg ca 25 mg mephentermine sulfate to prepd column, **38.162**, and proceed as in (**a**), beginning "Elute mephentermine with three 5 mL portions . . ." If sample contains parabens, wash column with 25 mL alcohol before eluting.

38.164 ***Determination***

Scan sample and std solns from 220–300 nm against 1.5*N* alcohol-HCl as ref. blank. Draw baseline connecting min. *A* at ca 254 and 262 nm, and use max. *A* at 258 nm to calc. potency of mephentermine sulfate:

$$\text{mg Mephentermine sulfate/tablet} = (A/A') \times (X/\text{g sample}) \times W,$$

where *A* and *A'* refer to sample and std, resp.; *X* = av. g/tablet; and *W* = mg std in 50.0 mL 1.5*N* alcoholic HCl; or

$$\text{mg Mephentermine sulfate/mL} = (A/A') \times (F/\text{mL sample}) \times W,$$

where *F* = diln factor.

Methapyrilene in Expectorants (*48*)—Official Final Action

(See also **38.111–38.117**.)

38.165 ***Reagent***

Methapyrilene hydrochloride std soln.—0.015 mg methapyrilene.HCl/mL. Transfer 60 mg methapyrilene.HCl, accurately weighed, to 200 mL vol. flask. Dissolve in ca 0.1*N* H_2SO_4 and dil. to vol. with ca 0.1*N* H_2SO_4. Transfer 5 mL aliquot to 100 mL vol. flask and dil. to vol. with ca 0.1*N* H_2SO_4.

38.166 ***Determination***

Pipet 10 mL sample into separator, make alk. with NH_4OH, and ext with four 20 mL portions $CHCl_3$. Combine $CHCl_3$ exts in 100 mL vol. flask and dil. to vol. with $CHCl_3$. Transfer aliquot contg 1–3 mg methapyrilene to small beaker and evap. just to dryness on steam bath with air current. Dissolve residue in ca 0.1*N* H_2SO_4, transfer to 100 mL vol. flask, and dil. to vol. with ca 0.1*N* H_2SO_4. Det. *A* of this soln and *A'* of std against ca 0.1*N* H_2SO_4 blank at 315 nm.

mg Methapyrilene.HCl/100 mL sample
$= (A \times 1.5 \times 100 \times 10)/(A' \times \text{vol. aliquot})$.

Neostigmine (Prostigmine®)

38.167 ★ ***Distillation Method (49)*** ★
Official Final Action

See **38.159**, 12th ed.

Chromatographic Method (50)—Official Final Action

38.168 ***Apparatus***

(**a**) *Spectrophotometer.*—Suitable for measurement in range 265–400 nm.

(**b**) *Chromatographic tube and tamping rod.*—*See* **37.002**.

38.169 ***Reagents***

(**a**) *Phosphate buffer.*—pH 5.8. Mix 1 vol. 1*M* K_2HPO_4 (17.4 g/100 mL) with 4 vols. 1*M* KH_2PO_4 (13.6 g/100 mL). Adjust pH, using pH meter, to 5.80±0.05 with either component.

(**b**) *Washed chloroform.*—Shake equal vols $CHCl_3$ and H_2O in separator. Let layers sep. 5 min and discard upper layer.

(**c**) *Washed ether.*—Shake equal vols ether and H_2O in separator. Let layers sep. 5 min and discard lower layer.

(**d**) *Bis(2-ethylhexyl) hydrogen phosphate (DEHP) soln.*—2.5% Mix. 2.5 mL DEHP with 97.5 mL H_2O-washed $CHCl_3$.

(**e**) *Diatomaceous earth.*—*See* **36.002**.

(**f**) *Neostigmine std soln.*—Dry neostigmine bromide 3 hr in 105° oven. Accurately weigh ca 5 mg dry std, using microbalance, and transfer to 150 mL beaker. Add 2.0 mL pH 5.8 phosphate buffer, mix by swirling gently, and proceed as in **38.171**.

38.170 ***Preparation of Sample***

(**a**) *Tablets.*—Accurately weigh portion powd tablets contg 5 mg neostigmine bromide into 150 mL beaker, add 2.0 mL pH 5.8 phosphate buffer, mix by swirling gently, and proceed as in **38.171**.

(**b**) *Individual tablets.*—Transfer tablet to 50 mL centrf. tube, powder if coated, and add 6.0 mL pH 5.8 phosphate buffer by pipet. Stopper, shake mech. 30 min, and centrf. 5 min at high speed. Pipet 2.0 mL clear supernate into 150 mL beaker and proceed as in **38.171**.

(**c**) *Ophthalmic soln.*—Dil. accurately measured vol. sample soln to 2.5 mg neostigmine bromide/mL with pH 5.8 phosphate buffer soln. Pipet 2.0 mL dild sample soln into 150 mL beaker and proceed as in **38.171**.

38.171 ***Determination***

(*Caution: See* **51.011**, **51.054**, **51.056**, and **51.062**. Use H_2O-washed solvs thruout.)

Treat std and sample solns similarly. Add 3.0 g diat. earth, mix with metal spatula until fluffy, and transfer quant. in 3 portions to chromatgc tube contg 1 g diat. earth mixed with 0.5 mL pH 5.8 phosphate buffer. Pack uniformly. Dry-wash beaker with 0.2 g diat earth, transfer wash to tube, and pack uniformly. Wipe beaker and all app. used in column prepn with glass wool and add to column. Proceed without delay.

Wash column with 75 mL ether and then with 75 mL $CHCl_3$. Discard washings. Elute neostigmine bromide with 75 mL 2.5% DEHP soln into 500 mL separator contg 20 mL 0.1*N* H_2SO_4. Complete elution with 25 mL $CHCl_3$. Add 175 mL isooctane to eluate and shake vigorously 2 min. Let stand ≥5 min to completely sep. layers. Transfer lower aq. layer to 250 mL beaker. Repeat extn with two 20 mL portions 0.1*N* H_2SO_4, and combine aq. layers in the 250 mL beaker.

Add 10 mL *10% NaOH soln* to beaker, mix by swirling gently, cover with watch glass, and heat 45 min on vigorous steam bath. Cool, transfer quant. to 100 mL vol. flask, dil. to vol. with H_2O, and mix. Centrf. portions of std and sample solns. Record spectra of clear sample and std solns between 400 and 255 nm against 1% NaOH soln in 1 cm cells. Det. ΔA of each soln by subtracting *A* at 340 nm from *A* at max., ca 293.5 nm.

mg Neostigmine bromide in final soln = $(\Delta A/\Delta A') \times C \times 100$, where C = mg neostigmine bromide std/mL, and ΔA and $\Delta A'$ refer to sample and std, resp.

Neostigmine Methylsulfate (*51*)—Official Final Action

(Applicable only to injections)

38.172 ***Apparatus and Reagents***

(**a**) *Recording spectrophotometer.*—Suitable for measurement in range 230–350 nm.

(**b**) *Neostigmine methylsulfate std soln.*—0.5 mg/mL. Accurately weigh 50 mg neostigmine methylsulfate of known purity, transfer to 100 mL vol. flask, add 1 mL 1*N* H_2SO_4, and dil. to vol. with H_2O.

38.173 ***Preparation of Sample***

(**a**) *Interfering UV-absorbing preservatives absent.*—Transfer aliquot contg 5.0 mg neostigmine methylsulfate to 150 mL beaker and hydrolyze as in **38.175**.

(**b**) *Injection solns containing phenol or parabens.*—Proceed as in **38.174**.

38.174 ***Extraction of Interferences***

Transfer sample aliquot (or sample diln if necessary) contg 5.0 mg neostigmine methylsulfate to 125 mL separator, add 1 mL 1*N* H_2SO_4, and add H_2O to total vol. of 21 mL. Add 35 mL $CHCl_3$ and shake vigorously 2 min. Transfer $CHCl_3$ layer into second 125 mL separator contg wash soln of 10 mL H_2O and 1 mL 1*N* H_2SO_4; shake, let layers sep. completely, and discard $CHCl_3$ phase. Repeat extn with 5 addnl 35 mL portions $CHCl_3$. Rinse stem of each separator with $CHCl_3$ after last extn and discard $CHCl_3$. Combine aq. layers in 150 mL beaker. Rinse each separator in succession with two 5 mL portions H_2O, rinse stem

★ Surplus method—*see* inside front cover.

of each separator with H_2O, transfer rinsings to beaker, and proceed as in **38.175**.

38.175 ***Hydrolysis***

Add 25 mL 10% NaOH soln and H_2O to ca 80 mL. Cover with watch glass and heat 30 min on vigorous steam bath. Cool, quant. transfer soln thru loose glass wool plug, prewashed with 1% NaOH soln, to 250 mL vol. flask, and dil. to vol. with H_2O. In sep. beaker, similarly treat 10 mL aliquot std neostigmine methylsulfate soln. Perform blank detn, omitting neostigmine methylsulfate. Proceed as in **38.176**.

38.176 ***Determination***

Record spectra of sample and std solns, relative to blank, in 1 cm cells, from 350 to 230 nm. Det. ΔA of each soln by subtracting A at 350 nm from A at max., ca 239 nm.

mg/mL Neostigmine methylsulfate in sample

$$= (\Delta A/\Delta A') \times 0.5 \times (10/\text{mL sample aliquot}),$$

where ΔA and $\Delta A'$ refer to sample and std, resp.

38.177 ★ Pamaquine (Plasmochin®) (*52*) ★ Official Final Action

Extn from alk. soln and titrn. *See* **38.169–38.170**, 12th ed.

Phenazopyridine Hydrochloride (Pyridium®, Mallophene®) (*53*)—Official Final Action

38.178 ***Reagents***

(**a**) *Titanium trichloride std soln.*—Prep. as in **50.042** and stdze as in **50.043**.

(**b**) *Light green SF yellowish soln.*—Dissolve 1 g FD&C Green No. 2 in H_2O and dil. to 1 L.

38.179 ***Preparation of Solution***

(*Caution: See* **51.011**, **51.040**, and **51.056**.)

(**a**) *Solns.*—To vol. contg ca 0.1 g phenazopyridine.HCl, add 10 mL 0.1*N* HCl and dil. to 100 mL.

(**b**) *Tablets and jelly.*—Accurately weigh sample (powd in case of tablets) contg ca 0.1 g phenazopyridine.HCl, add 10 mL 0.1*N* HCl, and dil. to 100 mL.

(**c**) *Ointments.*—Accurately weigh, in 100 mL beaker, sample contg ca 0.1 g phenazopyridine.HCl, stir with ether until ointment base dissolves, and wash into separator with ether and H_2O. Shake thoroly, and drain aq. layer into second separator contg 25 mL ether. Shake, and drain aq. layer into third separator contg 25 mL ether. Shake, and transfer aq. layer to 250 mL beaker. Wash ether layers with alternate 10 mL portions HCl (1+1) and H_2O until no more color is removed, successively passing each portion of the HCl or H_2O thru the 3 separators and finally into beaker. Nearly neutze combined acid exts with NH_4OH, cool, wash into separator, make ammoniacal, and ext with 25 mL portions $CHCl_3$ until no more color is removed, filtering $CHCl_3$ thru cotton pledget in stem of separator. Evap. combined $CHCl_3$ exts just to dryness, take up in 10 mL 0.1*N* HCl, and dil. to 100 mL.

38.180 ***Determination***

Heat soln to bp, add 15 g *Na acid tartrate,* and boil 2 min. Add 10 mL light green SF yellowish soln and titr. hot with std $TiCl_3$ soln in current of CO_2. End point is change from green to pale yellow. Perform blank titrn with 10 mL 0.1*N* HCl, 90 mL H_2O, 15 g Na acid tartrate, and 10 mL light green SF yellowish soln, and subtract from vol. $TiCl_3$ previously found. 1 mL 0.1*N* $TiCl_3$ = 0.00624 g phenazopyridine.HCl, $C_{11}H_{11}N_5$.HCl.

★ Surplus method—*see* inside front cover.

Phenethylamines (*54*)—Official Final Action

(Applicable to amphetamine, methamphetamine, mephentermine, phenylpropylmethylamine (Vonedrine®), and ephedrine)

38.181 ***Apparatus***

Spectrophotometer.—Suitable for measurement in region 250–270 nm; with 1 cm cells of quartz or fused Si (preferably matched pair); or recording spectrophtr.

38.182 ***Preparation of Standard Solution***

Accurately weigh 500–700 mg phenethylamine salt of known purity, transfer to 100 mL vol. flask, and dissolve in 0.1*N* H_2SO_4. Dil. to vol. with the H_2SO_4 and mix well.

38.183 ***Determination***

Accurately weigh powd sample contg 25–50 mg amine base and transfer to 40–50 mL g-s centrf. tube contg 3–3.5 g NaCl and 6–7 glass beads. Dissolve sample by adding 5 mL 1*N* H_2SO_4, and swirl gently to aid escape of any liberated CO_2. Test for acidity with litmus paper, adding more acid if necessary. Pipet in 25 mL $CHCl_3$ and 4 mL 2*N* NaOH, stopper securely, and shake 3–5 min. To second 40–50 mL centrf. tube contg 3–3.5 g NaCl and 6–7 glass beads, add 10 mL std soln, **38.182**. Swirl to dissolve salt, pipet in 25 mL $CHCl_3$ and 1 mL 2*N* NaOH, stopper securely, and shake 3–5 min.

Centrf. tubes 3–5 min at 1500–1800 rpm. Withdraw 10 mL clear $CHCl_3$ layer by closing upper end of 10 mL pipet with index finger while lowering tip thru aq. layer. Wipe off outer portion of pipet, and transfer 10 mL $CHCl_3$ layer to second 40–50 mL centrf. tube contg 25 mL 0.1*N* H_2SO_4 and 6–7 glass beads. Stopper securely, shake, and centrf. as above.

Prep. acid blank soln by shaking 25 mL 0.1*N* H_2SO_4 with 3–5 mL $CHCl_3$ and centrfg to obtain clear acid soln. Read A of portions of clear acid soln obtained from aliquots of std and of sample solns against acid blank prepd as above in ref. cell, using 1 cm cells in range 252–255 for first min., 256–258 for max., and 260–262 for second min.

38.184 ***Calculations***

Calc. A difference (ΔA) between A at maximum and A of 2 minima: $\Delta A = A_{max} - 0.5(A_{min\ 1} + A_{min\ 2})$.

Calc. absorptivity differential (Δa) produced by 1 g/L (1 mg/mL) of std amine base or salt:

$$\Delta a_{std} = \Delta A_{std} \times 100/\text{wt std},$$

where ΔA_{std} = A difference for std soln; 100 = mL std soln measured; and wt = mg std in aliquot measured.

mg Amine/unit of sample

$$=(\Delta A_{sample} \times 25 \times 25 \times \text{av. wt of unit in mg})/(\Delta a_{std} \times 10 \times \text{wt sample in mg}).$$

Phenothiazine (*55*)—Official First Action

38.185 ***Reagents and Apparatus***

(All $CHCl_3$ solns must be protected from light and assay must be completed within 8 hr.)

(**a**) *Phenothiazine std soln.*—Dissolve phenothiazine in 10 parts toluene with heat. Add 0.1 g activated charcoal for each 4 g phenothiazine. Boil 10 min under reflux and filter while hot thru heated filter. Cool soln, and collect phenothiazine crystals on buchner or fritted glass filter. Dry crystals at 100° and then in vac. desiccator contg paraffin chips. Repeat recrystn, if necessary, until mp is 184–185°. Dissolve 100.0 mg purified phenothiazine in $CHCl_3$ in 50 mL vol. flask and dil. to vol. with $CHCl_3$.

(**b**) *Internal std soln.*—Dissolve 125 mg promethazine.HCl in $CHCl_3$ in 25 mL vol. flask and dil. to vol. with $CHCl_3$.

(**c**) *Chromatographic column.*—Slurry 20 g Gas-Chrom Q, 100–120 mesh, with 100 mL $CHCl_3$ in 500 mL r-b flask. Add, with stirring, 1.0 g Apiezon L dissolved in 50 mL $CHCl_3$. Evap. to dryness in 70° H_2O bath, using rotary vac. evaporator. Apply vac. (ca 50 cm Hg) to one end of 1.2 m (4′) glass column (4 mm id) and, with gentle tapping only, fill tube with coated support. Condition column by heating 48 hr at 240° with N flow of ca 10 mL/min.

(**d**) *Gas chromatograph.*—Any gas chromatograph with H flame ionization detector capable of using specified column.

38.186 ***Determination***

Grind representative sample portion to pass No. 60 sieve. Accurately weigh sample contg ca 200 mg phenothiazine and transfer to 100 mL vol. flask. Add 80 mL $CHCl_3$ and shake vigorously until phenothiazine is completely dissolved (ca 20 min). Dil. to vol. with $CHCl_3$, mix thoroly, and let stand 15 min. Pipet 5 mL aliquots of clear supernate and phenothiazine std soln into sep. 25 mL g-s erlenmeyers. Pipet 4 mL aliquots of promethazine.HCl internal std soln into each flask.

About 1 hr before initial injection, adjust app. to following temps: column 215°, detector 230°, injector 230°. Set N carrier gas flow rate to give phenothiazine retention time of ca 8 min (ca 20 psig regulator outlet pressure). Retention time of internal std will be ca 17 min. Inject similar vol. of sample and std soln contg ca 10 μg phenothiazine, using sensitivity setting that gives 70–90% of full-scale deflection.

% Phenothiazine in original sample

$$= (M/W)(P_u/P_a) \times (P_b/P_p) \times 200,$$

where M = mg phenothiazine used to prep. std soln, W = mg sample, P_u = phenothiazine sample soln peak area, P_a = promethazine.HCl sample soln peak area, P_b = promethazine.HCl std soln peak area, and P_p = phenothiazine std soln peak area.

Phenylephrine Hydrochloride

38.187 ★ Acetylation Method (*56*)—Official First Action ★

Acetylation on diat. earth column and detn by UV spectrophotometry in eluate. *See* **36.108–36.111**, 11th ed.

Colorimetric Method (57)—Official Final Action

(Not applicable in presence of tetracycline, acetaminophen, salicylamide, phenolic compds, and Zn salts)

38.188 ***Reagents***

Prep. (**a**), (**b**), and (**d**)(*2*) fresh on day of use.

(**a**) *4-Aminoantipyrine hydrochloride soln.*—(Eastman) 3% in H_2O.

(**b**) *Potassium ferricyanide soln.*—4% $K_3Fe(CN)_6$ in H_2O.

(**c**) *Sodium borate soln.*—2% $Na_2B_4O_7.10H_2O$ in H_2O.

(**d**) *Phenylephrine hydrochloride std solns.*—(*1*) *Stock soln.*—Approx. 2.5 mg/mL. Weigh ca 125 mg phenylephrine.HCl to nearest 0.1 mg into 50 mL vol. flask and dil. to vol. with H_2O. Soln is stable several months under refrigeration. (*2*) *Working std soln.*—Approx. 0.25 mg/mL. Dil. 5 mL stock soln to 50 mL with H_2O.

★ Surplus method—*see* inside front cover.

38.189 ***Preparation of Samples***

(**a**) *Tablets and capsules.*—Det. av. wt/unit. Grind tablets to powder and mix, or mix contents of capsules. Weigh portion contg ca 12.5 mg phenylephrine.HCl into 50 mL vol. flask, add ca 30 mL H_2O, and shake vigorously. Dil. to vol., shake again, and filter if soln is not clear.

(**b**) *Powders for oral suspensions, oral suspensions, sirups, solns, etc.*—Reconstitute powders for oral suspension as directed on label or use solns, sirups, and oral suspensions as is. Transfer aliquot contg ca 12.5 mg phenylephrine.HCl into 50 mL vol. flask and proceed as in (**a**).

38.190 ***Determination***

(Reaction is time dependent; assay samples one at a time.)

Transfer 2 mL aliquot sample soln to 50 mL vol. flask (omit sample for reagent blank), add 1.0 mL 4% $K_3Fe(CN)_6$ soln, and swirl. Dil. to ca 48 mL with $Na_2B_2O_7$ soln and add 1.0 mL aminoantipyrine soln. Immediately dil. to vol. with $Na_2B_2O_7$ soln and shake vigorously. Immediately det. A of soln at 490 nm against reagent blank, in matched 1 cm cells.

Calc. sample concn, $S = CFA/A'$, where C = mg std/mL, F = diln factor, and A and A' refer to sample and std. resp.

Report mg phenylephrine.HCl/tablet, capsule, or vol. liq. dose.

Automated Method (*58*)—Official Final Action

38.191 ***Principle***

Oxidn products of phenylephrine with $K_3Fe(CN)_6$ form colored complex with 4-aminoantipyrine in borate soln. Method is automated version of **38.188–38.190** and is not applicable in presence of tetracycline, acetaminophen, salicylamide, phenolic compds, and Zn salts.

38.192 ***Apparatus***

Automatic analyzer.—AutoAnalyzer with following modules (available from Technicon Corp.): (*1*) *Sampler II.*—With 50/hr (2:1) cam. (*2*) *Proportioning pump.* (*3*) *Colorimeter.*—With 15 mm tubular flowcell and matched 490 nm filters. (*4*) *Recorder.* (*5*) *Manifold.*

Assemble app. as shown in Fig. **38:02**. Make sample and resample pump tubes as short as possible by cutting each end 6 mm from color-coded shoulders. Sample line is 20 cm. Reduce vol. at point of debubbling and flowcell by constricting lower arm of C-5 debubbler with Tygon tubing to give push fit with 0.015 × 2.5″ polyethylene tubing leading to flowcell as shown in Fig. **38:03**.

Prewash system with H_2O before placing reagent lines in their appropriate reagent container. When tubes are pumping satisfactorily and system is equilibrated (ca 15 min), adjust colorimeter and recorder to produce steady baseline.

38.193 ***Reagents***

See **38.188**(**a**), (**b**), (**c**), (**d**)(*1*) (2.5 mg/mL), and in addn:

(**a**) *Wetting agent.*—Add 0.5 mL polyoxyethylene lauryl ether (Brij 35) to 1 L H_2O.

38.194 ***Preparation of Sample***

Proceed as in **38.189**, except weigh portion contg ca 125 mg in (**a**) and transfer aliquot (dild if necessary) contg 125 mg in (**b**).

38.195 ***Stream Flow***

See Fig. **38:02**. Sample solns are withdrawn from sample cups, segmented with air, and dild in manifold. Stream is

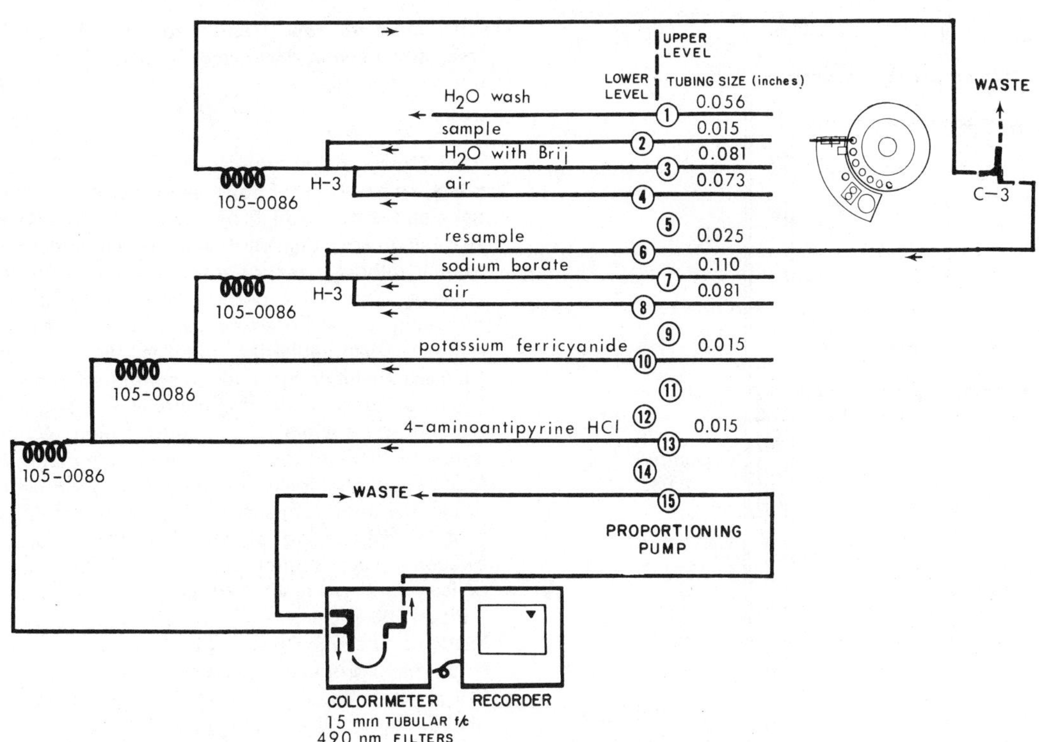

FIG. 38:02—Flow diagram for phenylephrine hydrochloride

debubbled and resampled. Resultant stream is buffered with air-segmented stream of borate soln. $K_3Fe(CN)_6$ is added and mixed, and color reagent is added and mixed. Stream is debubbled and *A* is measured at 490 nm.

38.196 ***Determination***

Fill 2 mL sample cups with prepd solns and aspirate at 2:1 sample-to-wash ratio, picking up sample with 0.016" stainless steel probe. Include 2 std solns (2.5 mg/mL) at beginning and end of each run of 5 samples in duplicate (10 detns). Draw line between baseline at beginning and end of run, if necessary. Subtract baseline *A* from max. *A* to obtain net *A* (ΔA) for each peak. Calc. mg phenylephrine.HCl/unit dose as in **38.190** from ΔA, using av. of duplicate detns.

Ion-Pair Column Partition Method (59)
Official Final Action

(Not applicable in presence of phenolic nitrogenous bases)

38.197 ***Apparatus and Reagents***

(**a**) *Recording spectrophotometer.*—With matched 1 cm cells.

(**b**) *Chromatographic tubes.—See* **37.002**.

(**c**) *Phosphate buffer.*—pH 5.80±0.05. Mix 1 vol. 1*M* K_2HPO_4 (174 g/L) and 4 vols 1*M* KH_2PO_4 (136 g/L) and adjust pH with either component.

(**d**) *Phosphate-citrate buffer.*—pH 5.10±0.05. Mix 2 vols 1*M* K_2HPO_4 and 1 vol. 1*M* citric acid (192 g $C_6H_8O_7$ or 210 g $C_6H_8O_7.H_2O$/L) and adjust pH with either component.

(**e**) *Diatomaceous earth.—See* **36.002**.

(**f**) *Bis-(2-ethylhexyl) hydrogen phosphate (DEHP) soln.*—Reagent grade. 2.4% v/v in H_2O-satd ether. Prep. fresh daily.

(**g**) *Sulfuric acid.*—0.1*N*, ether-satd. Prep. fresh daily.

(**h**) *Chloroform and ether.*—H_2O-satd. Prep. fresh daily and use thruout detn.

(**i**) *Phenylephrine hydrochloride std solns.*—(*1*) *Stock soln.*—1 mg/mL. Accurately weigh ca 100 mg USP Phenylephrine.HCl Ref. Std in 100 mL vol. flask and dil. to vol. with H_2O. (*2*) *Working soln.*—0.04 mg/mL. Dil. 2 mL stock soln to 50 mL with 0.1*N* NaOH and use to obtain spectrum between 400 and 200 nm (or as far as instrument permits) along with sample detn.

38.198 ***Preparation of Samples***

(**a**) *Samples containing about 1 mg phenylephrine.HCl/mL sirup.*—Pipet 4.0 mL pH 5.8 buffer into 10 mL vol. flask. Carefully add sirup to vol. Do not wet flask above mark.

(**b**) *Samples containing more than 1 mg phenylephrine .HCl/mL sirup.*—Dil. to 1 mg/mL and proceed as in (**a**).

(**c**) *Tablets.*—Weigh ground sample contg ca 2 mg phenylephrine into 50 mL beaker. If components of tablets are H_2O-sol., add 2 mL H_2O, warm slightly to dissolve, and add 1 mL pH 5.8 buffer. If some components are not H_2O-sol. (e.g., acetaminophen), add 1 mL dimethylsulfoxide, warm to dissolve, and then add 2 mL pH 5.8 buffer. For tablets contg antacids (e.g., $Mg(OH)_2$ and $Al(OH)_3$), heat powd sample contg ca 2 mg phenylephrine with 5 mL alcohol and 1 mL HCl to dissolve alk. material; add 10 mL *n*-BuOH and evap. to dryness. Dissolve residue in 1 mL dimethylsulfoxide and add 2 mL pH 5.8 buffer.

(**d**) *Capsules.*—Take portion of contents contg ca 2 mg phenylephrine and proceed as in (**c**). Grind sample if necessary.

38.199 ***Determination***

Pack small glass wool plug in base of chromatgc tube as support. Transfer mixt. of 1 g diat. earth with 0.8 mL pH 5.1 buffer to tube and tamp to uniform mass. Mix 4 g diat. earth with 3.0 mL aliquot prepd sample and carefully transfer directly above pH 5.1 layer, tamping gently. Dry-wash beaker with 1 g diat. earth, add to column, and tamp. Cover with small glass wool pad. Pass 75 mL $CHCl_3$ thru column followed by 125 mL ether, and discard eluates. Place 125 mL separator contg ca 20

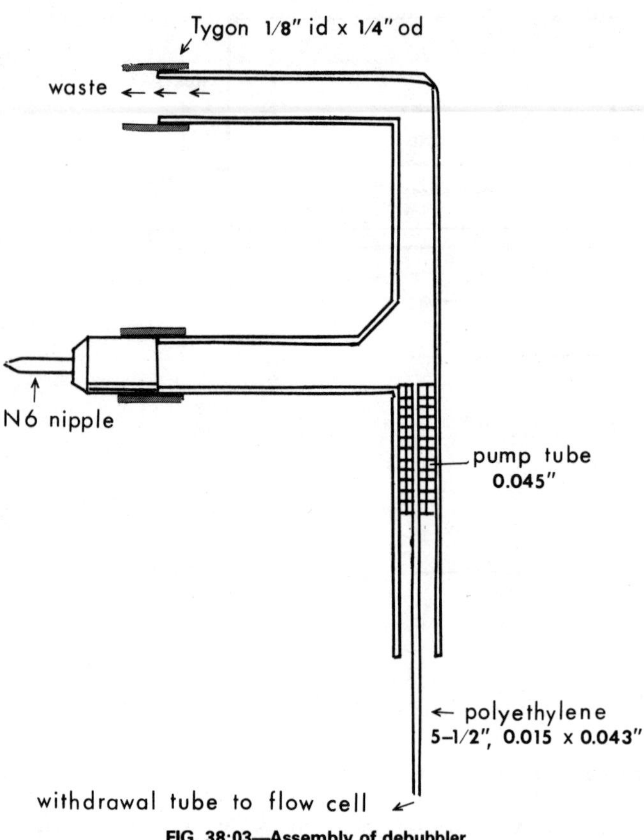

FIG. 38:03—Assembly of debubbler

mL 0.1*N* H_2SO_4 as receiver under column. Elute column with 50 mL DEHP-ether soln and then with 25 mL ether, collecting in same separator. Shake separator and transfer aq. phase to 50 mL vol. flask contg 6 mL 1*N* NaOH. Re-ext ether with 15 mL 0.1*N* H_2SO_4. Combine exts and dil. to vol. with H_2O. Obtain spectrum between 200 and 400 nm on same day as elution.

38.200 ***Calculations***

Det. corrected *A* (ΔA) of both std and sample as follows: Construct baseline representing background *A* extension obtained from 400 to ca 250 nm. (Constructed baseline *A* value at wavelength of max. *A*, ca 290 nm, is designated as A_B.) Subtract A_B from total A_{max} observed at wavelength peak.

For std, calc. $a = \Delta A'/bc$, where b = cell pathlength (1 cm), and c = concn in g/L.

For samples, calc. $c = (\Delta A \times F)/ab$, where F = diln factor.

Report mg phenylephrine.HCl/tablet, capsule, or vol. liq. dose.

Phenylpropanolamine Hydrochloride—Official Final Action

Chromatographic Method (60)

38.201 ***Apparatus***

See **37.002**.

38.202 ***Reagents***

(**a**) *Chloroform.*—*A* at 258.5 nm, measured against H_2O blank, <0.200.

(**b**) *Diatomaceous earth.*—*See* **36.002**.

38.203 ***Preparation of Column***

Fix pledget of glass wool in stem of chromatgc tube above constriction. Clamp tube vertically. In small beaker mix 3 g diat. earth and 2 mL H_2O. Transfer to tube with metal spatula and press down evenly with packing rod.

38.204 ***Determination***

(**a**) *Capsules and tablets.*—To 150 mL beaker transfer accurately weighed amt of powd sample contg ca 50 mg phenylpropanolamine.HCl. Add 5 mL NH_4OH (1+4) and mix by gentle swirling. Add 5 g diat. earth and mix with metal spatula. Transfer to tube without loss thru powder funnel, in 4 or more portions, pressing down each portion evenly with packing rod. When removing funnel from tube each time, tap it lightly in tube to remove loosely adhering particles; then hang it in beaker of such size that it does not touch bottom. After using packing rod, scrape off most of adhering material into tube with spatula, and tap rod and spatula over mouth of tube. When laying down implements, place them in position such that their ends do not touch anything. Finally use smooth, intact rubber policeman to sweep material from beaker and funnel into tube. Rub beaker, spatula, and packing rod with three ca 1 g portions diat. earth, sweeping each portion thru funnel into tube, using rubber policeman. Press down each portion with packing rod.

Place 100 mL vol. flask in receiving position. Wash down inside of tube with $CHCl_3$, adding enough (ca 20 mL) to moisten column and produce only few drops of eluate. Elute with 95 mL $CHCl_3$, wash tip of tube with little $CHCl_3$, and dil. to vol. with $CHCl_3$. Measure *A* at 258.5 nm, 2–5 min after pouring into silica cell, against portion of same $CHCl_3$ used for elution.

To 150 mL beaker transfer ca 50 mg pure phenylpropanolamine.HCl, accurately weighed. Proceed as with sample, beginning "Add 5 mL NH_4OH (1+4) . . ." Det. *A* of sample and std eluates at ca same time, on same setting of wavelength dial. Use same cell for both eluates, and same cell for both blanks. Calc. phenylpropanolamine.HCl content.

(**b**) *Aqueous solns.*—Prep. column as in **38.203**. Into 150 mL beaker pipet vol. sample contg ca 50 mg phenylpropanolamine.HCl, or pipet 10 mL, whichever is less. Add 1 mL NH_4OH and mix by gentle swirling. Add number of g diat. earth equal to total number mL of liq. and mix with metal spatula. Proceed as in (**a**), beginning "Transfer to tube without loss . . ."

Extraction Method (61)

38.205 ***Determination***

Proceed as in **38.183–38.184**.

Phenylalkanolamine Salts Including Phenylpropanolamine Hydrochloride and Ephedrine Sulfate in Elixirs and Sirups (62)—Official Final Action

(Applicable to individual phenylalkanolamines when only one is present, except for phenylephrine, which does not interfere and which is not detd by this method.)

38.206 ***Principle***

Phenylalkanolamine is eluted with CH_2Cl_2 from weakly basic diat. earth column, retained on weakly acidic column, and converted to benzaldehyde by on-column periodate reaction. Benzaldehyde is detd by UV spectrometry and is proportional to amt alkanolamine salt in sample.

38.207 ***Reagents and Apparatus***

(**a**) *Phosphate-chloride soln.*—Dissolve 5 g KH_2PO_4 and 7.5 g KCl in 100 mL H_2O.

(**b**) *Sodium metaperiodate soln*.—Dissolve 2 g $NaIO_4$ in 20 mL H_2O. Store in dark.

(**c**) *Water-saturated methylene chloride*.—Sat. ca 400 mL spectral grade CH_2Cl_2 by shaking 1 min with equal vol. H_2O. Use thruout.

(**d**) *Diatomaceous earth*.—*See* **36.002**.

(**e**) *Phenylalkanolamine salt std soln*.—0.4 mg/mL. Accurately weigh ca 100 mg phenylalkanolamine salt and dissolve and dil. to 250 mL with H_2O.

(**f**) *Recording spectrophotometer*.—With matched 1 cm cells.

(**g**) *Chromatographic tubes and tamping rod*.—*See* **37.002**.

38.208 ***Preparation of Sample and Chromatographic Columns***

Sample.—Accurately dil. sample with H_2O to final concn of ca 0.4 mg/mL.

Column I.—Add 2.0 mL dild sample to 300 mg K_2HPO_4 in 150 mL beaker. Swirl to dissolve. Add 3 g diat. earth, mix, transfer quant. to column, and tamp. Dry-wash beaker with 1 g diat. earth, add wash to column, and tamp. Cover with small glass wool plug. If acidic compds such as acetaminophen or theophylline are present, underlay sample-diat. earth mixt. with mixt. of 3 g diat. earth and 2 mL 10% NaOH.

Column II.—Mix 3 g diat. earth and 2 mL phosphate-chloride soln, and transfer to column. Tamp and cover with small glass wool pad.

Column III.—Mix 0.5 mL H_2O and 1 g diat. earth, transfer to column, and tamp. Mix 3 g diat. earth and 2 mL $NaIO_4$ soln, transfer to column, tamp, and cover with glass wool pad.

38.209 ***Preparation of Standard***

Prep. sep. column *III* as above. Mix 2.0 mL phenylalkanolamine salt std soln and 3 g diat. earth, transfer quant. to column, and tamp. Dry-wash beaker with 1 g diat. earth, transfer wash to column, tamp, and cover with glass wool pad. Place 100 mL vol. flask under column. Wet column with 10 mL CH_2Cl_2. With pipet, evenly distribute 1.0 mL NH_4OH onto surface of column packing. Elute column with four 25 mL portions CH_2Cl_2; let each portion sink entirely into surface. Rinse tip of column into flask and dil. eluate to vol. with CH_2Cl_2. Elute with addnl 25 mL CH_2Cl_2 and collect eluate for use as blank.

38.210 ***Determination***

Mount columns so that eluate from *I* flows onto *II*. Elute combined columns with four 25 mL portions CH_2Cl_2; let each portion sink entirely into surface of both columns. Rinse tip of Column *I* into *II* with CH_2Cl_2 and discard *I*. Elute Column *II* with addnl 25 mL CH_2Cl_2. Discard all eluates.

Mount Column *II* above *III* and place 100 mL vol. flask under *III*. With pipet, evenly distribute 1.0 mL NH_4OH onto surface of Column *II* packing. Elute combined columns with four 25 mL portions CH_2Cl_2; let each portion sink entirely into surface of each column. Rinse tip of Column *II* into *III* with ca 1 mL CH_2Cl_2. Discard Column *II* and continue to elute Column *III* until 100 mL eluate is collected.

Scan spectra of sample and std eluates from 350 to 230 nm, against column blank eluate. If liq. is cloudy, let soln clear (ca 1 min) before detg A. Calc. net A for sample and std solns, ΔA and $\Delta A'$, resp., at min. A, ca 267 nm, and max. A, ca 246 nm.

$$\text{mg Phenylalkanolamine salt/mL} = (\Delta A/\Delta A') \times C \times F,$$

where C = mg std/mL and F = diln factor.

Piperazine—Official Final Action

Chromatographic Method (*63*)

(Applicable to aq. solns)

38.211 ***Apparatus***

Chromatographic tube.—40 × 300 mm, with stopcock and fritted glass disk or plug of glass wool as support.

38.212 ***Determination***

(*Caution: See* **51.011**, **51.040**, and **51.056**.)

Prep. layered column with tamped layer of 5 g diat. earth, **36.002**, on bottom; add layer of 5 g diat. earth thoroly mixed with 5 mL H_2O, and tamp. Thoroly mix 25 g diat. earth and 5 g $NaHCO_3$ in 600 mL beaker, add 25 mL aliquot of piperazine soln contg ca 100 mg piperazine, and again mix thoroly. Add 2 mL Ac_2O and mix 5 min, transferring to another beaker to ensure thoro mixing. Add mixt. to column, using large funnel to prevent loss, and tamp. Dry-wash the 2 beakers with 5 g diat. earth, add to column, and tamp. Place pad of glass wool on top.

Pass 200 mL $CHCl_3$ thru column, adjusting flow to ca 7 mL/min, and collect eluate in 250 mL beaker, previously dried at 80°, cooled in desiccator, and weighed. Evap. $CHCl_3$ on steam bath with air current, and dry to const wt in convection oven at 80° (ca 3 hr). Piperazine = diacetylpiperazine × 0.5061.

Check for complete extn by passing another 100 mL portion $CHCl_3$ thru column, evapg to dryness, and noting if residue is present.

Det. mp of diacetylpiperazine, which should be ca 140°.

Near-Infrared Method (*64*)

38.213 ***Apparatus and Reagents***

(**a**) *Near-infrared spectrophotometer*.—With 5 cm Si cells.

(**b**) *Drying tube*.—Approx. 3.5 cm diam. × 9 cm long. Pack with glass wool and ca 6 cm granular anhyd. Na_2SO_4 prewetted with ca 30 mL reagent grade $CHCl_3$.

(**c**) *Piperazine dihydrochloride*.—Anal. std. (Available from Pfaltz & Bauer Inc, 375 Fairfield Ave, Stamford CT 06902.) Store above Si gel.

38.214 ***Preparation of Standard***

Accurately weigh std piperazine equiv. to ca 3.5–3.8 g anhyd. base, transfer to 100 mL vol. flask with H_2O, dil. to vol., and mix. Transfer 10.0 mL of this soln and exactly 5 mL H_2O to separator. Add 25 mL *NaOH soln* (1+1) and swirl. *Final concn of NaOH must be* >30%. Cool separator under tap, add 30 mL $CHCl_3$, and shake carefully ca 2 min. Drain $CHCl_3$ layer thru drying tube, (**b**), into 100 mL vol. flask. Ext with three 20 mL portions $CHCl_3$, draining thru drying tube into vol. flask. Rinse tube with $CHCl_3$ and dil. to vol. Prep. blank as above, using 15 mL H_2O.

38.215 ***Preparation of Sample***

(**a**) *Powders*.—Transfer sample contg ca 250–300 mg piperazine base thru small funnel to separator contg exactly 5 mL H_2O. Rinse funnel with exactly 10 mL H_2O from pipet. Mix, and proceed as in **38.214**, beginning, "Add 25 mL *NaOH soln* . . ." Dil. $CHCl_3$ exts to 100 mL.

(**b**) *Sirups*.—Transfer sample contg ca 500 mg piperazine base to separator. Add H_2O to total vol. of exactly 15 mL. Proceed as in **38.214**, beginning "Add 25 mL *NaOH soln* . . ." *except* use 200 mL vol. flask to collect $CHCl_3$ exts, and ext with three 50 mL portions $CHCl_3$, finally rinsing inside of separator with several 10–15 mL portions $CHCl_3$ before dilg to 200 mL.

38.216 ***Determination***

Using 5 cm cells, scan from 1600 to 1450 nm against blank. (Max. is ca 1520 nm.) Draw baseline between min. at ca 1460 and 1565 nm and det. net *A*.

$(A/A') \times$ (mg base in std/mL $CHCl_3$)
= (mg base in sample)/(mL final $CHCl_3$ soln)

where *A* and *A'* refer to sample and std, resp. Convert sample from base to known salt formula, if desired.

Procaine—Official Final Action

38.217 ***Qualitative Tests***

See Microchemical Tests, **36.095–36.097**.

Quantitative Methods

Method I—with or without Propoxycaine (65)

(Applicable in presence of parabens and phenolic vasoconstrictors)

38.218 ***Apparatus and Reagents***

(**a**) *Chromatographic tubes and tamping rod.—See* **37.002**.

(**b**) *Bromide-citrate buffer.*—Mix equal vols 0.5*M* Na citrate (147 g $2H_2O$/L) and 0.5*M* citric acid (105 g $1H_2O$/L). Adjust to pH 4.0±0.2, using pH meter, by addn of appropriate citrate soln. Add 10.3 g NaBr/100 mL soln (1.0*M* Br) and mix.

(**c**) *Chloroform-isooctane solvent.*—65% $CHCl_3$ in isooctane. Do not sat. with H_2O before use. Dil. 65 parts $CHCl_3$ in graduate to 100 parts with isooctane and mix.

(**d**) *Phosphate buffer.*—pH 7.0±0.2. Mix equal vols 0.5*M* KH_2PO_4 (68.0 g/L) and 0.5*M* K_2HPO_4 (87.1 g/L).

(**e**) *Procaine hydrochloride and propoxycaine hydrochloride std solns.*—Pep. sep. aq. solns contg 10 μg/mL.

38.219 ***Preparation of Sample and Column***

Pipet 1 mL sample soln contg 20 mg procaine.HCl or 4 mg propoxycaine.HCl into beaker, add 1.0 mL phosphate buffer, and mix. Add 3 g diat. earth, **36.002**, and mix.

Place small glass wool plug in base of chromatgc tube. Mix 4 g diat. earth and 3 mL bromide-citrate buffer in small beaker, transfer to column, and tamp with gentle pressure. Mix 2 g diat. earth and 1 mL 0.1*N* NaOH, add to column, and tamp. Quant. transfer sample mixt. to column and tamp. Scrub beaker with 1 g diat. earth and 2–3 drops phosphate buffer, add to column, and tamp. Cover with pad of glass wool.

38.220 ***Determination***

(Perform elution for propoxycaine even in its absence.)

(**a**) *Propoxycaine.*—Place 200 mL vol. flask under column and elute with 150 mL 65% $CHCl_3$ in isooctane. Dil. to vol. with $CHCl_3$ and mix. Pipet 10 mL aliquot into 100 mL beaker, add 4 drops HOAc, and evap. nearly to dryness on steam bath under gentle air current, then to dryness with reduced heat. Pipet 20 mL H_2O into beaker and dissolve residue.

(**b**) *Procaine.*—Place 200 mL vol. flask under column and elute with 125 mL $CHCl_3$. Dil. to vol. with $CHCl_3$ and mix. Pipet 10 mL aliquot into 100 mL beaker and evap. to dryness as in (**a**), but without addn of HOAc. Dissolve residue in H_2O and transfer quant. to 100 mL vol. flask, dil. to vol. with H_2O, and mix.

(**c**) *Spectrophotometry.*—Record spectra of sample and std solns from 350 to 250 nm and det. *A* of samples and *A'* of stds at max., ca 302 and 290 nm, for propoxycaine and procaine, resp.

$$C = C' \, (A/A') \, D,$$

where *C* and *C'* = concns (μg/mL) of sample and std, resp., and *D* = appropriate diln factor.

38.221 ★ ***Method II (66)*** ★

(Dets as procaine any *p*-aminobenzoic acid formed by decomposition)

Bromination method. *See* **38.211**, 12th ed.

38.222 ***Method III***

(Dets only undecomposed procaine)

See **38.002**.

38.223 ★ ***Method IV (67)*** ★

(Applicable in presence of chlorobutanol, cocaine, codeine, heroin, lactose, and morphine)

Distn into excess std acid and back-titrn. *See* **32.096**, 10th ed.

Procainamide Hydrochloride

Spectrophotometric Method (68)—Official First Action

38.224 ***Principle***

Procainamide is extd from acid soln with $CHCl_3$. After evapn of solv., residue is dissolved in alk. soln and max. *A* detd at ca 272 nm.

38.225 ***Reagent***

Procainamide hydrochloride std solns.—Stock soln.—1 mg/mL. Assay std as in USP XX. Accurately weigh ca 100 mg procainamide.HCl (ICN-K&K Laboratories, Inc., No. 17158) into 100 mL vol. flask, and dissolve and dil. to vol. with 0.01*N* NaOH. *Working soln.*—1 mg/100 mL. Pipet 1 mL stock soln into 100 mL vol. flask and dil. to vol. with 0.01*N* NaOH. Prep. fresh daily.

38.226 ***Preparation of Sample***

(**a**) *Capsules.*—Proceed as in **36.004**. Mix, and transfer accurately weighed portion contg ca 100 mL procainamide.HCl to 125 mL separator. Add 10 mL HCl (1+9) and shake to disperse. Add 15 mL H_2O.

(**b**) *Tablets.*—Det. av. wt. Reduce tablets to fine powder. (For tablets with coatings that do not reduce to powder, carefully peel off and discard coatings, and reduce tablets to fine powder.) Mix, and transfer accurately weighed portion contg ca 100 mg procainamide.HCl to 125 mL separator. Add 10 mL HCl (1+9) and shake to disperse. Add 15 mL H_2O.

(**c**) *Injections.*—Dil. soln, if necessary, with HCl (1+9) to give ca 100 mg procainamide.HCl/mL. Pipet 1 mL into 125 mL separator, add 10 mL HCl (1+9), and shake. Add 15 mL H_2O.

38.227 ***Determination***

(*Caution: See* **51.011** and **51.056**.)

Ext sample soln with three 25 mL portions $CHCl_3$ and discard $CHCl_3$. To aq. soln add 5 mL NH_4OH and ext with five 25 mL portions $CHCl_3$, collecting exts in 250 mL beaker and rinsing tip of separator into beaker after each extn. Evap. $CHCl_3$ to dryness on steam bath with air current. Quant. transfer residue to 100 mL vol. flask with 0.01*N* NaOH, and dil. to vol. with same solv.

★ Surplus method—*see* inside front cover.

Pipet 1 mL dild soln into another 100 mL vol. flask and dil. to vol. with 0.01*N* NaOH. Record spectra of std and sample solns against 0.01*N* NaOH and det. *A* at max., ca 272 nm.

mg Procainamide.HCl/capsule or tablet

$$= (A/A') \times C \times D \times (W/W'),$$

where *A* and *A'* refer to sample and std solns, resp.; *C* = concn of std soln in mg/mL; *D* = sample diln factor in mL; *W* = av. mg/capsule or tablet; and *W'* = mg sample.

For injections, mg procainamide.HCl/mL

$$= (A/A') \times C \times D/V,$$

where *V* = mL sample aliquot.

Pyrilamine in Cough Sirup (*48*)—Official Final Action

(*See also* **38.111–38.117.**)

38.228 ***Reagent***

Pyrilamine std soln.—0.015 mg pyrilamine maleate/mL. Transfer 150 mg pyrilamine maleate to 500 mL vol. flask, dissolve in ca 0.1*N* H_2SO_4, and dil. to vol. with ca 0.1*N* H_2SO_4. Transfer 5 mL aliquot to 100 mL vol. flask and dil. to vol. with ca 0.1*N* H_2SO_4.

38.229 ***Determination***

Proceed as for detn of methapyrilene, **38.166**, but measure *A* at 314 nm.

mg Pyrilamine maleate/100 mL sample

$$= (A \times 100 \times 1.5 \times 10)/(A' \times \text{mL aliquot}),$$

where *A* and *A'* refer to sample and std, resp.

Quinacrine Hydrochloride (Atabrine®)

38.230 ★ ***Volumetric Method (69)—Official Final Action*** ★

Oxidn with $K_2Cr_2O_7$ and titrn of excess. *See* **38.216–38.217**, 12th ed.

Fluorometric Method (70)—Official Final Action

(*Caution: See* **51.008.**)

38.231 ***Apparatus***

Spectrophotofluorometer.—Scanning, with 1 cm cell path, Xe lamp, excitation wavelength 420 nm, and sensitivity to produce 80% fluorescence intensity (*F*) for std soln.

38.232 ***Reagent***

Quinacrine hydrochloride std soln.—0.00050 mg/mL. Weigh 5.0 mg USP Quinacrine.HCl Ref. Std in 1 L vol. flask and dil. to vol. with H_2O. Mix well and dil. 10.0 mL to 100 mL with 0.1*N* HCl. Alternatively, weigh 50.0 mg quinacrine.HCl into 1 L vol. flask and dil. to vol. with H_2O. Mix well and dil. 10.0 mL to 1 L with 0.1*N* HCl. Prep. fresh daily.

38.233 ***Preparation of Sample***

(**a**) *Tablets and powders.*—Weigh amt of well mixed or well ground sample contg 100 mg quinacrine.HCl into 200 mL vol. flask. Dil. to vol. with 0.1*N* HCl, mix 2 min, and filter if necessary. Dil. 10.0 mL clear sample soln to 1 L with H_2O and mix. Finally dil. 10 mL to 100 mL with 0.1*N* HCl to obtain sample soln.

(**b**) *Liquids.*—Pipet accurate sample contg ca 100 mg quinacrine.HCl into 200 mL vol. flask. Proceed as in (**a**), beginning "Dil. to vol. with 0.1*N* HCl, . . ."

★ Surplus method—*see* inside front cover.

38.234 ***Determination***

Adjust spectrophotofluorometer to ca 80% fluorescence intensity (*F*) at 500 nm with std soln. Transfer ca 3 mL sample soln to 10 × 10 mm clean cell and read % *F*, using 0.1*N* HCl as blank.

Calc. as follows:

Liqs: mg quinacrine.HCl/mL = $200{,}000 \times C \times (F/F') \times (1/V)$

Solids: % by wt quinacrine.HCl = $200{,}000 \times C \times (F/F') \times (100/W)$

where *C* = mg/mL std soln; *F* and *F'*, resp., = fluorescence of sample and std solns at 500 nm, each corrected for blank; *W* = mg sample; and *V* = mL sample.

38.235 ***Identification***

Set emission wavelength monochromator at wavelength of max. fluorescence, i.e., 500 nm. Scan std and sample solns used for quantitation with excitation wavelength monochromator from 200 to 750 nm.

Use same instrument parameters as for quantitation except set sensitivity at ca 40. Sample and std spectra exhibit identical max. and min.

SELECTED REFERENCES

(*1*) JAOAC **44,** 293(1961).
(*2*) JAOAC **44,** 285(1961).
(*3*) JAOAC **42,** 459(1959); **48,** 607(1965).
(*4*) JAOAC **55,** 142(1972).
(*5*) JAOAC **50,** 655(1967); **51,** 494(1968).
(*6*) JAOAC **51,** 1315(1968); **53,** 603(1970).
(*7*) JAOAC **15,** 402(1932).
(*8*) JAOAC **41,** 504(1958).
(*9*) JAOAC **15,** 83, 442(1932).
(*10*) JAOAC **12,** 290(1929); **13,** 329(1930); **14,** 327(1931).
(*11*) JAOAC **14,** 327(1931).
(*12*) JAOAC **30,** 467(1947); **31,** 528(1948).
(*13*) JAOAC **43,** 224(1960); **46,** 634(1963).
(*14*) JAOAC **44,** 288(1961).
(*15*) JAOAC **54,** 609, 614(1971).
(*16*) JAOAC **39,** 639(1956).
(*17*) JAOAC **31,** 526(1948); **32,** 530(1949).
(*18*) JAOAC **25,** 524(1942); **26,** 238(1943).
(*19*) JAOAC **30,** 464(1947).
(*20*) JAOAC **42,** 455(1959).
(*21*) JAOAC **45,** 595(1962).
(*22*) JAOAC **41,** 488(1958).
(*23*) JAOAC **52,** 113(1969); **53,** 1106(1970).
(*24*) JAOAC **55,** 149(1972).
(*25*) JAOAC **59,** 289(1976).
(*26*) JAOAC **59,** 811(1976).
(*27*) J. Am. Pharm. Ass., Sci. Ed. **45,** 708(1956); JAOAC **40,** 64(1957).
(*28*) JAOAC **44,** 303(1961).
(*29*) JAOAC **3,** 379(1920); **4,** 572(1921).
(*30*) JAOAC **19,** 534(1936).
(*31*) JAOAC **21,** 555(1938); **22,** 729(1939).
(*32*) JAOAC **20,** 577, 631(1937).
(*33*) JAOAC **52,** 854(1969); **53,** 847(1970); **57,** 741(1974).
(*34*) JAOAC **37,** 685(1954).
(*35*) JAOAC **52,** 507(1969).
(*36*) JAOAC **37,** 685(1954).
(*37*) JAOAC **55,** 146(1972).
(*38*) JAOAC **41,** 495(1958).
(*39*) JAOAC **51,** 612(1968).
(*40*) JAOAC **28,** 706(1945).

(*41*) JAOAC **51,** 624(1968).
(*42*) JAOAC **56,** 681(1973).
(*43*) JAOAC **32,** 548(1949); **33,** 206(1950).
(*44*) JAOAC **21,** 554(1938).
(*45*) JAOAC **20,** 589(1937).
(*46*) JAOAC **28,** 711(1945); **31,** 540(1948).
(*47*) JAOAC **61,** 60(1978).
(*48*) JAOAC **42,** 466(1959).
(*49*) JAOAC **25,** 814(1942); **28,** 686(1945).
(*50*) JAOAC **57,** 725(1974).
(*51*) JAOAC **54,** 21(1971).
(*52*) JAOAC **30,** 476(1947).
(*53*) JAOAC **21,** 552(1938).
(*54*) JAOAC **40,** 824(1957); **49,** 237(1966).
(*55*) JAOAC **49,** 857(1966); **50,** 682(1967); **51,** 273(1968).
(*56*) JAOAC **48,** 579(1965).
(*57*) J. Pharm. Sci. **52,** 802(1963); JAOAC **52,** 500(1969).
(*58*) JAOAC **54,** 596, 600(1971).
(*59*) JAOAC **53,** 120(1970).
(*60*) JAOAC **41,** 499(1958).
(*61*) JAOAC **41,** 509(1958); **58,** 852(1975).
(*62*) JAOAC **56,** 100(1973); **58,** 852(1975).
(*63*) JAOAC **44,** 312(1961).
(*64*) JAOAC **48,** 590(1965).
(*65*) JAOAC **58,** 88, 93(1975).
(*66*) JAOAC **5,** 163, 589(1922).
(*67*) JAOAC **23,** 776(1940).
(*68*) JAOAC **59,** 807(1976).
(*69*) JAOAC **27,** 354(1944); **31,** 538(1948).
(*70*) JAOAC **53,** 117(1970).

39. Drugs: Neutral

STEROIDS AND RELATED HORMONES

Conjugated Estrogens (*1*)—Official Final Action

39.001 ***Reagents***

(**a**) *Iron-Kober reagent*.—Dissolve 1.054 g $FeSO_4.(NH_4)_2SO_4.6H_2O$ (Mohr salt) in ca 20 mL H_2O; add 1 mL H_2SO_4 and 1 mL 30% H_2O_2. Mix, heat until effervescence ceases, and dil. to exactly 50 mL. To 3 vols of the Fe soln in vol. flask, add H_2SO_4, with cooling, to make 100 vols.

Redistil phenol, discarding first 10% and last 5%. (*Caution:* Phenol may be harmful. Avoid contact with skin and eyes and breathing vapors.) Collect distillate with exclusion of moisture in dry, tared g-s flask of ca twice vol. of the phenol. Place stoppered flask in ice bath to solidify phenol, breaking top crust with glass rod to ensure complete crystn. Dry and weigh flask.

Add to phenol 1.13 times its wt of Fe-H_2SO_4 soln, stopper flask, and let stand without cooling but with occasional mixing until phenol is liquefied (≤30 min). Shake mixt. vigorously until homogeneous and let stand in dark 16–24 hr. Add to mixt. 23.5% its wt of H_2SO_4 (10+11). Shake vigorously to homogeneity. Transfer to dry g-s bottles. Stored in dark and protected from absorption of moisture, this reagent is stable for months.

(**b**) *Dicyclohexylamine acetate*.—Dissolve 50 g dicyclohexylamine in 150 mL acetone, cool in ice bath, and add, with stirring, 18 mL HOAc dissolved in 150 mL acetone. Filter ppt on buchner, wash with small amt acetone, and air dry.

(**c**) *Girard reagent T* (*trimethylacethydrazide ammonium chloride*).—Recrystallize com. samples twice from absolute alcohol and dry under vac. at room temp. Recrystd material should be white and practically odorless. Store in tightly stoppered bottle in desiccator.

(**d**) *Estrone std soln*.—50 μg/mL. Dissolve ca 5.0 mg USP Estrone Ref. Std, accurately weighed, in benzene, and dil. to 100 mL with benzene.

(**e**) *Equilin std soln*.—20 μg/mL. Dissolve ca 2.0 mg USP Equilin Ref. Std, accurately weighed, in benzene, and dil. to 100 mL with benzene.

39.002 ***Preparation of Sample***

(*Caution: See* **51.011**, **51.039**, **51.040**, **51.045**, and **51.056**.)

Reduce tablets to fine powder without loss. Weigh sample contg ca 7 mg Na estrone sulfate and transfer to 250 mL beaker. Add 6 g diat. earth, **36.002**, and mix thoroly. Add 4 mL H_2O and mix until uniform. Transfer quant., with aid of small amt of dry diat. earth, **36.002**, to 25 × 150 mm chromatgc tube. Tamp moderately tight and wash column with 100 mL H_2O-satd ether, discarding ether wash. Add 100 mg dicyclohexylamine acetate, (**b**), dissolved in 5 mL $CHCl_3$, to column, and collect eluate in 250 mL g-s flask. Wash column with several 5 mL portions $CHCl_3$ and finally with enough solv. to produce 150 mL total eluate. Evap. to dryness on steam bath with aid of air current.

Dissolve residue in 25 mL absolute MeOH, add 1 mL HCl and few boiling chips, stopper loosely, and boil 5 min. Cool, transfer to 125 mL separator with 70 mL H_2O, and ext with four 25 mL portions $CHCl_3$. Evap. combined $CHCl_3$ exts just to dryness on steam bath with aid of air current.

Dissolve residue in 5 mL $CHCl_3$ and transfer, using ≤5 mL $CHCl_3$, to 125 mL separator contg 50 mL isooctane. Add 10 mL 10% NaOH soln and shake 1 min. Transfer aq. layer to second 125 mL separator. Ext with two addnl 10 mL portions 10% NaOH soln, adding each to second separator. Discard $CHCl_3$-isooctane soln. Acidify alk. ext with dil. H_2SO_4, cool, add 25 mL benzene, and shake 1 min. Transfer aq. layer to second separator contg 25 mL benzene, shake 1 min, and drain and discard aq. layer. Wash each benzene layer successively with 10 mL 10% Na_2CO_3 soln and two 10 mL portions H_2O. Filter benzene layers thru cotton plug previously washed with benzene into 100 mL vol. flask. Wash separators and funnel with benzene, filter washings into vol. flask, dil. to vol., and mix (*Soln I*).

Evap. 50 mL aliquot *Soln I* to ca 5 mL and transfer to 25 mL g-s erlenmeyer with small vol. $CHCl_3$. Evap. to dryness on steam bath with air current. Reserve remainder of *Soln I* for detn of total estrogens. Add 100 mg Girard Reagent T and 0.5 mL HOAc to flask, stopper loosely, and heat on steam bath 5 min, swirling several times to ensure complete mixing. Cool, and transfer to 125 mL separator with ca 25 mL ice-H_2O. Add 5 mL 5% NaOAc soln and ext immediately with three 10 mL portions $CHCl_3$. Combine $CHCl_3$ exts in second separator, wash with 5 mL ice-H_2O, and discard $CHCl_3$. Add H_2O wash to aq. soln in first separator. Add 3 mL H_2SO_4 (1+2), mix well, and let stand 30 min. Ext aq. soln with three 25 mL portions $CHCl_3$, combine exts in second separator, wash with 5 mL H_2O, and filter thru cotton pad previously washed with $CHCl_3$ into 150 mL beaker. Wash separator and filter with little $CHCl_3$, and add to main ext. Evap. $CHCl_3$ soln to dryness on steam bath with air current. Dissolve residue in little benzene, transfer quant. to 50 mL vol. flask, and dil. to vol. with benzene (*Soln II*).

39.003 ***Determination of Total Estrogens as Sodium Estrone Sulfate***

Transfer duplicate 1 mL aliquots *Soln I* and estrone std soln, using same pipet, to 16 × 150 mm g-s test tubes. Add few boiling chips to each tube, evap. to dryness in steam bath, and cool in vac. desiccator. To each tube and to blank tube, add 1.0 mL Fe-Kober reagent, **39.001**(**a**), stopper, and place in boiling H_2O bath. Heat ca 1 min, shake tubes to mix, and release pressure by removing stopper momentarily. Heat 90 min, cool in H_2O bath, add 10.0 mL H_2SO_4 (1+2), and mix.

Det. *A* of std and sample solns against blank between 400 and 700 nm, and det. baseline *A* at 520 nm, drawing baseline between min. at ca 400 and 700 nm.

Total estrogens as Na estrone sulfate, mg/g

$$= (A_B/S_1) \times (C_1/w) \times 138 + d/2;$$

where A_B = baseline-corrected *A* of sample soln, S_1 = baseline-corrected *A* of std soln, C_1 = mg estrone in std aliquot, *w* = g sample, and *d* = Na equilin sulfate in mg/g from **39.004**. Conversion factors are Na estrone sulfate:estrone = 1.38 and Na equilin sulfate:equilin = 1.38.

39.004 ***Determination of Equilin as Sodium Equilin Sulfate***

Transfer duplicate 1 mL portions *Soln II* and equilin std soln (larger aliquots may be used for samples low in equilin; do not exceed 25–30 μg equilin), using same pipet, to 16 × 150 mm g-s test tubes. Add few boiling chips to each tube, evap. just to dryness in steam bath, and cool in vac. desiccator. To each tube and to blank tube add 0.10 mL alcohol and rotate tube to dissolve ketosteroids. Add 1.0 mL Fe-Kober reagent, **39.001**(**a**), to each tube, mix thoroly, stopper, and heat 25 min in boiling

H_2O bath. Cool, add 3.00 mL H_2SO_4 (1+2) to each tube, and mix thoroly. Det. *A* against blank at 620 nm.

Na equilin sulfate, mg/g = $(A_2/S_2) \times (C_2/w) \times 138$;

where A_2 = A of sample soln, S_2 = *A* of std soln, C_2 = mg equilin in std aliquot, and *w* = g sample.

39.005 ***Determination of Estrone as Sodium Estrone Sulfate***

Transfer duplicate 1 mL aliquots *Soln II*, estrone std soln, and equilin std soln to 16 × 150 mm g-s test tubes. Proceed as in **39.003**, beginning, "Add few boiling chips . . ." except heat 2 hr instead of 90 min. Det. *A* against blank at 520 nm. Correct *A* of sample soln for equilin *A* as follows:

$$A_3\ (\text{corr.}) = A_3 - (S_4 \times A_2)/S_2;$$

Na estrone sulfate, mg/g = $(A_3(\text{corr.})/S_3) \times (C_1/w) \times 138$;

where A_3 = *A* of sample soln, S_3 = *A* of estrone std soln, S_4 = *A* of equilin std soln, C_1 = mg estrone in std aliquot, and *w* = g sample.

39.006 ★ Ketosteroids (*2*)—Official First Action ★

Extn of oils from alk. soln followed by extn of ketosteroids from acid soln, and reaction with Girard reagent T. Product extd from neut. soln is used for β-estradiol detn. After acidification, ketosteroids are extd with $CHCl_3$, evapd to dryness, and residue dissolved in alcohol. Aliquot reacted with BQC to det. equilenin, with benzenesulfonyl chloride to det. equilin, and with Fe-Kober reagent to det. estrone. *See* **39.006–39.012**, 12th ed.

39.007 ★ Beta-Estradiol (*2*)—Official First Action ★

Colorimetric method. *See* **36.249–36.254**, 11th ed.

Estradiol Valerate (*3*)—Official Final Action

39.008 ***Principle***

Oils are eluted with heptane from CH_3NO_2-diat. earth column. Estradiol valerate is eluted with addnl heptane, and detd by fluorometry at max. intensity, ca 328 nm.

39.009 ***Apparatus***

(**a**) *Recording spectrophotofluorometer*.—With 1 cm cell path, excitation wavelength 285 nm, and sensitivity to produce 70% fluorescence for std soln at 328 nm.

(**b**) *Glass chromatographic tubes*.—250 × 25 mm id.

39.010 ***Reagents***

(**a**) *Heptane*.—Redistd.

(**b**) *Nitromethane*.—Spectral grade, or equiv.

(**c**) *Diatomaceous earth*.—*See* **36.002**.

(**d**) *Estradiol valerate std solns*.—(*1*) *Stock soln*.—0.4 mg/mL. Accurately weigh ca 40 mg USP Estradiol Valerate Ref. Std in 100 mL vol. flask and dil. to vol. with absolute alcohol. (*2*) *Working soln*.—16 μg/mL. Dil. 2 mL stock soln to 50 mL with absolute alcohol.

39.011 ***Preparation of Sample***

Using "to contain" pipet (or hypodermic syringe fitted with 1½", 18 gage needle), transfer accurately measured vol. sample contg ca 40 mg estradiol valerate to 100 mL vol. flask. Wash pipet with heptane and add wash to vol. flask. Dil. to vol. with heptane and mix.

★ Surplus method—*see* inside front cover.

39.012 ***Preparation of Column***

Place glass wool plug in base of chromatgc tube. To 10 g diat. earth in 250 mL beaker, add 11 mL CH_3NO_2. (*Caution:* CH_3NO_2 is toxic and flammable. Wear resistant rubber gloves when using it. Use effective fume removal device.) Mix until fluffy and add to tube in portions, packing moderately after each addn. Top column with glass wool pad and prewash column with 50 mL heptane.

39.013 ***Determination***

Transfer 2 mL sample soln to column. Wash with 5, 5, 10, 10, and 40 mL heptane (70 mL total), allowing each portion to pass thru column before adding next. Discard eluate. (*Caution: See* **51.011** and **51.039**.) Change receiver to 250 mL beaker and continue eluting with heptane, collecting ca 150 mL. Evap. eluate to dryness and quant. transfer residue to 50 mL vol. flask, using absolute alcohol. Dil. to vol. with absolute alcohol.

Adjust spectrophotofluorometer to ca 70% fluorescence intensity at 328 nm with working std soln. Scan sample and std solns from ca 280 to 450 nm, reading % fluorescence at max., ca 328 nm. Use absolute alcohol as blank.

mg Estradiol valerate/mL = $100 \times C \times (F/F') \times (1/V)$,

where *C* = concn of std soln (mg/mL); *F* and *F'* = fluorescence of sample and std solns, resp., at 328 nm, each corrected for blank; and *V* = vol. of sample taken.

Diethylstilbestrol (*4*)—Official Final Action

39.014 ***Reagent and Apparatus***

(**a**) *Diethylstilbestrol std soln*.—Accurately weigh suitable amt of USP Diethylstilbestrol Ref. Std, dissolve in alcohol, and prep. soln contg 20.0 μg/mL by accurate stepwise diln with alcohol. Prep. working std soln by mixing 25 mL of this soln with 25 mL 1.8% K_2HPO_4 soln.

(**b**) *Irradiation containers*.—Quartz cells ⩾4 mL capacity with clear sides, or 18 × 150 mm Vycor test tubes, held in rack that does not obstruct effective light beam of cylindrical 15 watt germicidal lamp, may be used conveniently.

39.015 ***Preparation of Assay Solution***

(**a**) *Oil solns containing 2 mg or less diethylstilbestrol/mL*.—Using accurately calibrated hypodermic syringe, transfer vol. sample contg 2 mg diethylstilbestrol to separator contg 50 mL isooctane. Shake mixt. with 10 mL 1*N* NaOH and transfer well defined aq. layer as completely as possible to second separator contg 50 mL isooctane. Shake vigorously and transfer clear aq. layer to third separator. Repeat extn of the 2 isooctane layers successively with two 10 mL portions 1*N* NaOH, collect aq. layers in third separator, and discard extd isooctane layers.

Acidify combined aq. exts with 3 mL H_2SO_4 (1+1), cool, and ext diethylstilbestrol with three 30 mL portions $CHCl_3$. Wash $CHCl_3$ exts successively in 2 separators, first contg 20 mL 1% $NaHCO_3$ soln and second, 20 mL H_2O.

Filter washed $CHCl_3$ exts thru cotton pledget moistened with $CHCl_3$ into 100 mL vol. flask, dil. to vol. with $CHCl_3$, and mix.

Transfer 10.0 mL $CHCl_3$ soln, contg 200 μg diethylstilbestrol, to small erlenmeyer and evap. just to dryness on steam bath with aid of air current. Cool in vac. desiccator 10 min. Add 10.0 mL alcohol, stopper, and dissolve residue by swirling. After 15 min, mix with 10.0 mL *1.8% K_2HPO_4* to prep. assay soln.

(**b**) *Oil solns containing more than 2 mg diethylstilbestrol/mL*.—Dil. convenient accurately measured vol. oil soln with $CHCl_3$ to obtain soln contg 0.5 mg diethylstilbestrol/mL. Transfer

4 mL aliquot to separator contg 50 mL isooctane and proceed as in (**a**), beginning "Shake mixt. with 10 mL 1*N* NaOH . . ."

(**c**) *Tablets.*—Transfer accurately weighed portion powd material contg 2 mg diethylstilbestrol to separator contg 30 mL $CHCl_3$. Add 10 mL H_2O and 1 mL H_2SO_4 (1+1) and shake vigorously. Drain $CHCl_3$ layer into second separator, wash with 5 mL H_2O, and filter thru cotton pledget moistened with $CHCl_3$ into 100 mL vol. flask. Repeat extn with three 20 mL portions $CHCl_3$, dil. combined exts to 100 mL, and mix.

Proceed as in (**a**), fourth par.

39.016 ***Irradiation***

(*Caution:* Protect eyes from direct rays of UV light.)

Test transparency of several irradiation containers as follows: Transfer convenient vols of working std soln to tubes, place them ca 7 cm from 15 watt germicidal lamp, and irradiate soln transversely ca 10 min. Measure *A* of yellow solns at 418 nm in suitable spectrophtr in matched 1 cm cells, against H_2O. Re-irradiate for 1–3 min intervals, and note irradiation time required for max. *A*. Repeat irradiation process, varying distance of tubes from lamp, and det. most convenient conditions for developing stable, repeatable colors of max. *A* (ca 0.7 at 418 nm).

Transfer portions of working std soln and assay soln to clean, dry irradiation containers, and irradiate under optimum conditions previously detd. Calc. wt diethylstilbestrol in sample.

39.017 ***Total Phenols***

Transfer 20 mL $CHCl_3$ ext, **39.015**, contg 400 μg diethylstilbestrol to beaker. Transfer alc. soln contg 400.0 μg USP Diethylstilbestrol Ref. Std to similar beaker, and treat both solns as follows: Evap. to dryness on steam bath with aid of air current. Dissolve residues in 2.0 mL HOAc with gentle warming. Cool to room temp., add 10 drops H_2SO_4 (1+1), and mix. Cool, add 5 drops *10% $NaNO_2$ soln*, and let stand 45 min with occasional mixing. Wash quant. into 25 mL vol. flask with ca 20 mL alc. NH_4OH soln, prepd by mixing equal vols alcohol and dil. NH_4OH (4+6). Cool in ice bath, and let stand at room temp. 1 hr. Dil. to vol. with the alc. NH_4OH soln, and mix. If ppt forms, filter thru dry paper, rejecting first few mL filtrate. Det. *A* of clear, yellow alk. solns at 420 nm in tightly stoppered 1 cm cells, in suitable spectrophtr, against alcohol (1+2). Calc. % total phenols, as diethylstilbestrol, in sample.

Dienestrol (*5*)—Official Final Action

(*Caution: See* **51.011, 51.018, 51.045, 51.054, 51.062**, and **51.066.**)

39.018 ***Reagents***

(**a**) *Dienestrol std soln.*—Approx. 15 μg/mL. Accurately weigh USP Dienestrol Ref. Std, dissolve in MeOH, and serially dil. to concn. Store in low-actinic vol. flask.

(**b**) *Methanolic sulfuric acid.*—Carefully add, with swirling, 50 mL H_2SO_4 to 50 mL cold MeOH, while continuously chilling mixt. in ice-H_2O. Use reagent at room temp. Reagent is stable 3–4 days in g-s flask.

(**c**) *Ethyl ether.*—Test as follows on day of use: Evap., with gentle heat and air stream, mixt. of 10.0 mL dienestrol std soln in ca 200 mL H_2O-washed ether. Dissolve residue in 10.0 mL MeOH. Proceed as in **39.021**, using this soln and 5.0 mL dienestrol std soln. Resulting solns should be clear and exhibit single max. at ca 303 nm, and corrected *A*, **39.022**, should differ $\leqslant$3%. If necessary, wash 750 mL ether with three 50 mL portions 10*N* KOH in 1 L separator. Percolate upper ether layer thru 300 × 22 mm glass chromatgc tube contg glass wool plug and 20 g diat. earth thoroly mixed with 15 mL 10*N* KOH and tamped moderately tight. Discard first 30 mL eluate and collect remainder for use. Column will only purify max. of 1 L ether.

(**d**) *Diatomaceous earth.*—*See* **36.002.**

39.019 ***Preparation of Columns***

Trap column.—Mix 4 g diat. earth and 3 mL *0.25M KOH* and transfer to 200 × 22 mm glass chromatgc tube contg glass wool plug. Tamp mixt. tightly and top with glass wool pad. Prewash column with 25 mL H_2O-washed ether, followed by 25 mL benzene.

Sample column.—Accurately weigh freshly ground sample contg ca 400 μg dienestrol into 150 mL beaker. Add 3 mL *0.3M K_3PO_4* and wet sample completely. Add 5 g diat. earth and mix thoroly with spatula. Transfer quant. in 2 equal portions to 200 × 22 mm glass chromatgc tube contg glass wool pad, tamping each portion moderately tight. Dry-rinse beaker with 1–2 g diat. earth and add rinse to column. Wipe tamper, spatula, and beaker with glass wool pad and add pad to top of column.

39.020 ***Chromatography***

Arrange columns so that eluate from sample column passes into trap column. Add 25 mL benzene to trap column; then add 175 mL benzene-isooctane (9+1) to sample column, using several portions to rinse sample beaker. Maintain layer of eluant over trap column. (To maintain this reservoir in trap column, connect the 2 columns with air-tight stopper, i.e., hollow No. 4 Nalgene stopper with hole drilled to accommodate stem of sample column.) Discard sample column when elution is complete. Wash trap column with addnl 25 mL benzene-isooctane (9+1) and discard eluates.

Elute dienestrol from trap column with 225 mL H_2O-washed ether into 250 mL g-s conical flask contg 10 mL absolute alcohol. Without delay, evap. to near dryness, using air stream and gentle heat. Rinse flask walls with small amt of absolute alcohol and evap. soln to dryness. Pipet 25 mL MeOH into flask, stopper tightly, and let stand several min with frequent vigorous swirling.

39.021 ***Isomerization***

Into sep. 25 mL g-s conical flasks, pipet 5 mL dienestrol std soln, 5 mL sample prepn, and 5 mL MeOH as reagent blank. Add 5.0 mL methanolic H_2SO_4 to each flask with swirling (solns will become warm). Stopper flasks tightly and shake vigorously; then let cool $\geqslant$25 min at room temp.

39.022 ***Determination***

Det. *A* of sample and std solns between 400 and 240 nm in 1 cm cells against reagent blank. Correct *A* at ca 303 nm by subtracting *A* at 360 nm.

$$\text{mg Dienestrol/tablet} = [(A/A') \times C \times V \times W]/Q,$$

where *A* and *A'* refer to sample and std solns, resp.; *C* = exact concn of std in mg/mL; *V* = mL sample diln (25 mL); *W* = av. tablet wt (g); and *Q* = sample wt (g).

Hexestrol (4,4'-(1,2-Diethylethylene Diphenol)) (*6*) Official Final Action

39.023 ***Determination***

Grind tablets to fine powder. Weigh amt powder contg ca 5 mg hexestrol into 125 mL separator contg 25 mL H_2O and 1 mL HCl (1+9). Ext with 25, 15, 10, and 10 mL $CHCl_3$. Drain each ext thru $CHCl_3$-satd cotton pledget into 100 mL beaker. Evap. combined exts to ca 25 mL on steam bath in air current. Check for completeness of extn by evapg addnl 10 mL ext to dryness.

Quant. transfer concd $CHCl_3$ exts to 125 mL separator contg 10 mL isooctane. Ext with 25, 15, 15, and 10 mL ca 0.1*N* NaOH, rolling or shaking separator gently 90 sec each time; emulsions may form. Drain lower org. layer into second 125 mL separator, each time including any small emulsion layer present. Continue alk. extn of org. phase, draining it alternately into two 125 mL separators and combining alk. exts by pouring each time into original separator. Discard org. phase.

Make combined alk. exts acid with HCl. Ext with 25, 15, 15, and 10 mL $CHCl_3$, collecting combined exts in 125 mL separator. Wash $CHCl_3$ exts with two 15 mL portions H_2O. Discard H_2O washes.

Pass combined $CHCl_3$ exts thru 1 cm column of granular anhyd. Na_2SO_4 in coarse fritted glass funnel, ca 3.5 cm id, into 100 mL vol. flask. Rinse column and stem tip with small portions $CHCl_3$. Dil. to vol. with $CHCl_3$. Place 50.0 mL aliquot in g-s flask and evap. just to dryness on steam bath, with aid of air current. Remove last traces of $CHCl_3$ with air current and without heat. Pipet 50 mL alcohol onto dry residue; shake 1 min to dissolve. This is sample soln.

Prep. std soln by dissolving pure hexestrol in enough alcohol to make concn ca 2.5 mg/50.0 mL. Use alcohol as ref. blank with sample and std solns.

Det. baseline *A* of sample and std solns at 280 nm with spectrophtr. If recording UV spectrophtr is used, record spectra between 320 and 240 nm. Adjust instrument to begin at 320 nm with zero *A*, and record spectra to 240 nm.

$$\text{mg Hexestrol in assay sample} = (A/A') \times (\text{mg/mL std soln}) \times \text{total mL sample soln},$$

where *A* refers to sample and *A'* refers to std soln at 280 nm.

39.024 ***Qualitative Identification***

(**a**) *Ultraviolet spectra*.—Dil. alc. soln of sample and std previously used for quant. assay to ca 20 μg/mL with alcohol. Compare UV spectrum from 215 to 320 nm with similar spectrum from authentic hexestrol.

(**b**) *Infrared spectra*.—Prep. KBr disk contg 0.3–0.6% hexestrol from residue obtained by evapg portion of remaining $CHCl_3$ sample soln from assay. Compare IR spectrum from 2 to 16 μm with similar spectrum from authentic hexestrol. (Extraneous peak at 5.85 μm appears in spectra of tablet prepns that does not appear in std.)

Ethinyl Estradiol (*7*)—Official Final Action

39.025 ***Reagents***

(**a**) *Methanol-sulfuric acid*.—In ice bath, cautiously add chilled H_2SO_4 in small increments, with mixing, to 60 mL chilled anhyd. MeOH in 200 mL vol. flask. Cool to room temp., dil. to vol. with H_2SO_4, and mix. Reagent is stable at room temp. ca 1 month. (*Caution:* Wear face shield and heavy rubber gloves to protect against splashes.)

(**b**) *Washed chloroform*.—Vigorously shake ca 500 mL $CHCl_3$ with 30 mL H_2SO_4 in 1 L separator ca 2 min. Discard H_2SO_4 (bottom) layer. Wash $CHCl_3$ with 400 mL H_2O by shaking vigorously 1 min; discard H_2O. Repeat H_2O washing 3 times as above. Filter clear $CHCl_3$ layer thru funnel contg pad of glass wool covered with ca 50 g granular anhyd. Na_2SO_4. Prep. fresh daily. Use same batch of washed $CHCl_3$ for all samples and stds thruout series.

(**c**) *Ethinyl estradiol std solns*.—(*1*) *Stock soln*.—0.8 mg/mL. Accurately weigh ca 40 mg USP Ref. Std Ethinyl Estradiol, dissolve in anhyd. MeOH in 50 mL vol. flask, dil. to vol. with MeOH, and mix. (*2*) *Intermediate soln*.—20 μg/mL. Pipet 5.0 mL stock soln into 200 mL vol. flask, dil. to vol. with isooctane, and mix. (*3*) *Working soln*.—4 μg/mL. Pipet 20 mL intermediate soln into 100 mL vol. flask, dil. to vol. with isooctane, and mix. (This soln is stable at room temp. ca 3 weeks.)

(**d**) *Diatomaceous earth*.—*See* **36.002**.

39.026 ***Preparation of Column***

Trap layer.—Transfer ca 5 g granular anhyd. Na_2SO_4 to 25 × 250 mm chromatgc tube contg pad of glass wool in base. Thoroly mix 3 mL *10% NaOH soln* with 3 g diat. earth in 100 mL beaker. Transfer mixt. to tube in 1 portion and tamp moderately.

Sample layer.—Accurately weigh portion of ground tablet composite contg ca 40 μg ethinyl estradiol into 100 mL beaker. Add 3 mL $CHCl_3$ and 2 mL H_2O, and stir frequently 2 min to dissolve max. amt of sample. Mix with 4 g diat. earth 1 min, transfer quant. to tube in 1 portion, and tamp moderately. Dry-wash beaker with ca 0.5 g diat. earth and transfer wash to column. Wipe tamper, spatula, and beaker with glass wool and place glass wool on column.

39.027 ***Chromatography***

Rinse tamper, spatula, and beaker with 25 mL isooctane and add rinse to column. Discard eluate. Using total of 55 mL $CHCl_3$-isooctane (1+9), repeat rinsing as above and discard eluate. Wash column with 15 mL isooctane and discard eluate. Finally, elute ethinyl estradiol with 50 mL washed $CHCl_3$, followed by 25 mL isooctane, collecting eluate in 250 mL separator.

39.028 ***Determination***

Pipet 10 mL each of std soln and isooctane (reagent blank) into sep. dry 250 mL separators. To each add 50 mL washed $CHCl_3$ and 15 mL isooctane, and mix gently. Pipet 10 mL MeOH-H_2SO_4 into sample, blank, and std separators, letting pipet drain completely. (*Caution: See* **51.018** and **51.030**.) Shake *vigorously* 4 min, and let layers sep. ca 15 min; protect from strong light. Within 30 min, scan spectra between 700 and 500 nm of pink (lower) phases of std and sample in 1 cm cells against reagent blank as ref., set at 0 at 700 nm.

$$\mu\text{g Ethinyl estradiol in final soln} = (A/A') \times C \times 10\ (\text{mL}),$$

where *A* and *A'* refer to sample and std solns, resp., at max., ca 537 nm; and $C = \mu$g/mL std soln.

Mestranol (*8*)—Official Final Action

(Applicable in presence of norethindrone and norethynodrel; not applicable in presence of ethynodiol diacetate or chlormadinone acetate)

39.029 ***Reagents***

(**a**) *Diatomaceous earth*.—*See* **36.002**.

(**b**) *Immobile solvent*.—Mix equal vols DMF and formamide (either redistd or stabilized formamide may be used).

(**c**) *n-Heptane*.—Redistd (may be prepd by fractionating thru all-glass column). *A* against alcohol in 1 cm cells should be <0.500 in range 250–360 nm (limit of aromatic content). Residue from evapn of 25 mL distillate, dissolved in 10 mL alcohol, should have $A \leq 0.01$ in range 230–360 nm (nonvolatile residue limit).

(**d**) *Spectrophotometric solvent*.—Transfer 10.0 mL $CHCl_3$ to 100 mL vol. flask, add ca 80 mL *n*-heptane, warm to room temp., and dil. to vol. with *n*-heptane.

(**e**) *Mestranol std soln*.—0.06 mg/mL. Dissolve accurately weighed amt USP Mestranol Ref. Std in $CHCl_3$ and dil. quant. to ca 0.6 mg mestranol/mL. Transfer 10.0 mL aliquot to 100 mL vol. flask, add ca 80 mL *n*-heptane, warm to room temp., and dil. to vol. with *n*-heptane.

39.030 ***Preparation of Assay Mixture***

Finely powder tablets. Transfer accurately weighed portion contg ca 0.6 mg mestranol to 100 mL beaker. Add 2.0 mL immobile solv., mix, and warm 5 min on steam bath with occasional stirring with spatula to ensure that powder is thoroly wetted. Cool, add 4 g diat. earth, and mix with spatula until fluffy.

39.031 ***Column Chromatography***

Pack pledget of fine glass wool in base of 25 × 250 mm chromatgc tube. Transfer 3.0 mL immobile solv. to 100 mL beaker, add 1 g anhyd. Na_2SO_4, and mix by swirling. Add 5 g diat. earth and mix until fluffy. Transfer to tube and tamp gently to compress to uniform mass. Quant. transfer prepd sample to column, scrub beaker with 0.5 g diat. earth, and tamp as before. Wipe beaker, spatula, and funnel with pad of glass wool. Place pad on top of column and tamp lightly.

Add *n*-heptane to column. Discard first 20 mL eluate and then collect ca 99 mL eluate in 100 mL vol. flask. Wash tip of column with heptane, dil. eluate to vol. with heptane, and mix. Transfer 50.0 mL aliquot to 125 mL g-s conical flask and evap. on steam bath with aid of air current to ca 1 mL. (*Caution:* Use effective fume removal device when evapg heptane.) Remove last traces of solv. without heat. Wash sides of flask with ca 2 mL alcohol and evap. solv. on steam bath as before, removing last traces of solv. without heat. Add 5.0 mL spectrophtric solv. to flask, stopper, let stand ca 5 min, and swirl to ensure soln of residue.

39.032 ***Determination***

Record *A* of sample and std solns in 1 cm cells against spectrophtric solv. Construct baseline by extending line passing between points on spectrum at 302 and 315 nm. Det. baseline-corrected *A* of sample (ΔA) and std ($\Delta A'$) at max., ca 287 nm.

mg Mestranol in portion of tablets taken = $10C \times (\Delta A/\Delta A')$, where C = exact concn, mg/mL, of mestranol std.

Mestranol in Combination with Ethynodiol Diacetate

Spectrophotometric Method (9)—Official Final Action

39.033 ***Principle***

Mestranol is sepd on partition column, eluted with *n*-heptane, and extd into $MeOH\text{-}H_2SO_4$ reagent to form colored steroid complex with max. *A* at ca 540 nm.

39.034 ***Apparatus and Reagents***

(*Caution:* Dimethyl sulfoxide (DMSO) and formamide can be harmful. Avoid skin contact by wearing heavy rubber gloves. Use effective fume removal device.)

(**a**) *Chromatographic tubes and tamping rod.*—Glass, 25 (od) × 300 mm. *See* **37.002**.

(**b**) *Formamide.*—Reagent grade contg no stabilizing agent or H_2O. Use recently opened bottle.

(**c**) *Washed n-heptane.*—Vigorously shake *n*-heptane (bp 98–99°) with ca 10% of its vol. of H_2SO_4 in separator ≥5 min. Discard H_2SO_4 (lower) layer and wash heptane with H_2O until washings are neut. to pH test paper. Filter thru firm plug of absorbent cotton covered with ca 50 g anhyd. Na_2SO_4, discarding first 5 mL. Use same batch of washed heptane for all samples and stds thruout series.

(**d**) *Methanol-sulfuric acid reagent.*—Cautiously add in small increments, with mixing, chilled H_2SO_4 (min. 95%) to 60 mL chilled anhyd. MeOH in 200 mL vol. flask in ice bath. Adjust to room temp., dil. to vol. with H_2SO_4, and mix. Reagent is stable at room temp. ca 1 month. (*Caution: See* **51.030** and **51.066**.)

(**e**) *Mestranol std solns.*—(*1*) *Stock soln.*—1 mg/mL. Dissolve ca 25 mg USP Ref. Std Mestranol, accurately weighed, with 3 mL $CHCl_3$ in 25 mL vol. flask, dil. to vol. with *n*-heptane, and mix well. (*2*) *Intermediate soln.*—30 μg/mL. Pipet 3 mL stock soln into 100 mL vol. flask, dil. to vol. with *n*-heptane, and mix. (*3*) *Working soln.*—0.75 μg/mL. Pipet 5 mL intermediate soln into 200 mL vol. flask, dil. to vol. with *n*-heptane, and mix. Prep. fresh daily.

39.035 ***Preparation of Column***

Thoroly mix 3 g diat. earth, **36.002**, and 1 mL H_2O in 100 mL beaker, transfer to chromatgc tube contg pledget of glass wool at base, and tamp moderately tight.

Thoroly mix 7 g diat. earth and 3.5 mL DMSO (spectral grade)-formamide (10+9) in 150 mL beaker, transfer to tube in 2 portions, and tamp each moderately tight.

Accurately weigh portion of ground tablets contg ca 150 μg mestranol into 100 mL beaker. Add 2 mL formamide and stir continuously 2 min to wet and disperse sample completely. Mix thoroly with 4 g diat. earth, transfer quant. to column in 1 portion, and tamp moderately tight. Scrub beaker with ca 0.5 g diat. earth and transfer to column. Wipe tamper, spatula, and beaker with glass wool, and place as pad above column contents.

39.036 ***Determination***

Rinse tamper, spatula, and beaker with 65 mL *n*-heptane, and pour rinse into column. Discard eluate contg ethynodiol diacetate. Elute mestranol with total of 135 mL *n*-heptane, collecting eluate in 200 mL vol. flask. Dil. to vol. with *n*-heptane and mix.

Pipet 50 mL each of mestranol working std soln and sample eluate in sep. dry 250 mL separators. Pipet 10 mL $MeOH\text{-}H_2SO_4$ (*Caution: See* **51.018**.) reagent into each, draining pipet completely. Shake vigorously 4 min and let stand 45 min, protected from light. Within ≤25 min, scan pink (lower) phase in each separator between 700 and 500 nm in 10 mm cells against $MeOH\text{-}H_2SO_4$ reagent as ref., setting instrument to 0 *A* at 700 nm for each scan.

μg Mestranol in sample taken = $200 \times C \times (A/A')$,

where 200 = mL sample diln, C = μg mestranol std/mL std soln, and A and A' refer to sample and std, resp., at max., ca 540 nm.

Progestational Steroids (*10*)—Official Final Action

39.037 ***Principle***

$CHCl_3$ ext of norethindrone, norethindrone acetate, dimethisterone, or medroxyprogesterone acetate is treated directly with isonicotinic acid hydrazide to produce stable color measured at 380 nm. Norethynodrel in $CHCl_3$ ext is isomerized with HCl prior to same reaction.

39.038 ***Reagents***

(**a**) *Isonicotinic acid hydrazide (INH) soln.*—Transfer 100 mg INH (mp 171–173°) to 200 mL vol. flask. Add ca 150 mL MeOH and 0.1 mL HCl. Shake to dissolve, and dil. to vol. with MeOH.

(**b**) *Washed cotton.*—Wash absorbent cotton with $CHCl_3$ and air dry.

(**c**) *Washed chloroform.*—Shake $CHCl_3$ with equal vol. H_2O in separator. After $CHCl_3$ layer clears, filter thru pledget of washed cotton covered with bed of ca 50 g anhyd. Na_2SO_4. Use thruout method.

(**d**) *Methanolic HCl soln.*—Dil. 3.0 mL HCl to 50 mL with MeOH.

(e) *Std soln.*—Dissolve accurately weighed amt std drug in $CHCl_3$ and dil., if necessary, with $CHCl_3$ to ca 10 mg/100 mL.

39.039 ***Preparation of Sample***

Finely powder tablets. Transfer accurately weighed portion of powder contg ca 10 mg steroid to 125 mL separator contg 10 mL H_2O. Add 25 mL $CHCl_3$, shake continuously 5 min, and filter ext thru pledget of cotton and ca 30 g anhyd. Na_2SO_4 into 100 mL vol. flask. Repeat extn with two 25 mL portions $CHCl_3$, combine exts, rinse filter with $CHCl_3$, and dil. filtrate to vol. with $CHCl_3$.

39.040 ***Determination***

(**a**) *Norethindrone, norethindrone acetate, dimethisterone, and medroxyprogesterone acetate.*—To sep. 50 mL g-s conical flasks, transfer 5.0 mL sample ext, 5.0 mL std soln, and 5.0 mL $CHCl_3$ as blank. To each flask add 25.0 mL INH soln, stopper, mix, and let stand 30 min. Record spectra from 500 to 350 nm against reagent blank.

$$\text{mg Steroid/tablet} = (A/A') \times W' \times (T/W),$$

where A and A' refer to sample and std, resp., at max., ca 380 nm; and W, W', and T = mg sample, mg std/100 mL, and av. tablet wt in mg, resp.

(**b**) *Norethynodrel.*—Add 1.0 mL methanolic HCl to sep. flasks contg 100 mL sample ext, 100 mL norethynodrel std, and 100 mL $CHCl_3$ as blank. Shake vigorously 3 min (mixts may be hazy) and let stand 70 min. Add 1.0 mL MeOH to each flask and mix thoroly (mixts become clear).

Transfer 5.0 mL each soln to sep. 50 mL g-s conical flasks and continue as in (**a**).

Single Tablet Assay (11)—Official Final Action

39.041 ***Principle***

Principle is same as in **39.037**, except that before colorimetric detn, sample is eluted from H_2O-diat. earth column with $CHCl_3$. Elution vols and vols of isonicotinic acid hydrazide used vary with individual tablet dosage levels ranging from 0.35 to 10 mg.

39.042 ***Apparatus and Reagents***

(**a**) *Glass chromatographic tube and tamping rod.* —250 × 25 (od) mm. *See* **37.002**.

(**b**) *Isonicotinic acid hydrazide (INH) soln.*—Prep. 500 mL as in **39.038**(**a**), using 500 mL vol. flask and 2.5-fold amts of all reagents.

(**c**) *Washed chloroform.—See* **39.038**(**c**).

(**d**) *Methanolic hydrochloric acid soln.*—10%. Dil. 5.0 mL HCl to 50 mL with MeOH.

(**e**) *Std solns.*—Dissolve in individual vol. flasks accurately weighed amt of each std material in $CHCl_3$, and dil. with $CHCl_3$ to ca 0.035 mg norethindrone/mL, 0.025 mg norgestrel/mL, and 0.25 mg norethynodrel/mL. Prep. fresh daily.

39.043 ***Preparation of Column***

Soak 1 accurately weighed tablet with 1 mL H_2O in 100 mL beaker. Thoroly mix 1 g diat. earth, **36.002**, with 0.5 mL H_2O in another 100 mL beaker with small metal spatula, transfer to chromatgc tube contg small pledget of glass wool at base, and tamp tight. Carefully triturate tablet with spatula, add 3 mL $CHCl_3$, and mix gently to dissolve as much as possible of tablet. Mix sample thoroly with 3 g diat. earth, transfer to tube in 1 portion, and tamp tight. Scrub beaker with ca 0.5 g diat. earth and transfer to tube. Wipe tamper, spatula, and beaker with small pledget of glass wool and add to column.

39.044 ***Elution***

(**a**) *Norethindrone (0.35 mg/tablet).*—Pipet 15 mL INH soln into 25 mL vol. flask and place to collect eluate from column. Rinse tamper, spatula, and beaker with 10 mL $CHCl_3$, and pour rinse into column. When elution stops, continue elution by adding 1 mL portions $CHCl_3$ until eluate fills flask to within ca 0.5 mL of mark. Gently swirl flask occasionally during elution without detaching it from column. Detach flask from column, add $CHCl_3$ to vol., mix, and let stand 45 min before colorimetric detn.

For >0.35 mg norethindrone, increase elution vol. and/or dil. eluate.

(**b**) *Norgestrel (0.5 mg/tablet).*—Pipet 30 mL INH soln into 50 mL vol. flask and place it to collect eluate from column. Rinse tamper, spatula, and beaker with 10 mL $CHCl_3$, and pour rinse into column. When elution stops, continue elution by adding 2 mL portions $CHCl_3$ until eluate fills flask to within ca 0.5 mL of mark. Continue as in (**a**).

(**c**) *Norethynodrel (2.5–5.0 mg/tablet).*—Place 100 mL vol. flask marked to indicate ca 75 mL vol. to collect eluate from column. Rinse tamper, spatula, and beaker with 10 mL $CHCl_3$, and pour rinse into column. When elution stops, continue elution by adding 5 mL portions $CHCl_3$ until eluate fills flask to 75 mL mark. Pipet 10 mL norethynodrel std soln into another 100 mL vol. flask and mix with 65 mL $CHCl_3$. Add 75 mL $CHCl_3$ into third 100 mL vol. flask as blank. Add ca 5 small boiling chips and 1.0 mL methanolic 10% HCl into each flask. Stopper, and shake vigorously 1–2 min. Remove stoppers and heat soln to bp on steam bath. Continue heating 15 min with occasional swirling. Remove flasks and cool to room temp. Dil. each to vol. with $CHCl_3$ and mix. ($CHCl_3$ solns should be completely clear.)

39.045 ***Determination***

(**a**) *Norethindrone.*—Into 25 mL vol. flask, pipet 10 mL norethindrone std soln and 15.0 mL INH soln. Stopper, and shake ca 1 min. Into another 25 mL vol. flask, pipet 10 mL $CHCl_3$ and 15 mL INH soln as blank for both norethindrone and norgestrel. Stopper flask and mix. Let all flasks stand 1 hr.

(**b**) *Norgestrel.*—Pipet 20 mL norgestrel std soln into 50 mL vol. flask and add 30.0 mL INH soln. Stopper, and shake ca 1 min. Let soln and blank, (**a**), stand 1 hr.

(**c**) *Norethynodrel.*—Into sep. 25 mL vol. flasks, pipet 10 mL each of isomerized sample, std, and blank. Add 15.0 mL INH soln to each. Stopper, shake ca 1 min, and let stand 1 hr.

Record spectra of samples and stds from 550 to 350 nm within next hr, against corresponding ref. blank, setting instrument to 0 A at 550 nm for each scan.

$$\mu\text{g Progestin/tablet} = (A/A') \times C \times (\overline{W}/W),$$

where A and A' refer to sample and std, resp., at ca 380 nm; C = μg of corresponding std in 10.0 mL norethindrone or norgestrel std soln, or 20.0 mL norethynodrel std soln; $\overline{W}$ = av. tablet wt; and W = individual tablet wt.

39.046 ★ Ethisterone (17α-Ethynyltestosterone) (*12*) ★ Official First Action

KBr Disk Method

Column chromatgc sepn and IR spectrophtric detn. *See* **39.043–39.046**, 12th ed.

★ Surplus method—*see* inside front cover.

Dexamethasone Phosphate (*13*)—Official First Action

39.047 ***Reagents***

(**a**) *Borate buffer.*—pH 8.2. Dissolve 6.2 g boric acid in H_2O, and dil. to ca 1 L. Adjust pH to 8.6 with 50% (w/w) NaOH soln. Add 10.2 g $MgCl_2.6H_2O$ and dissolve. (pH will decrease to 8.2.)

(**b**) *Alkaline phosphatase soln.*—Dissolve 100 mg intestinal alk. phosphatase enzyme (Worthington Biochemical Corp., Rte 9, Freehold, NJ 07728), ⩾1.4 units/mg, in 50 mL borate buffer.

(**c**) *Tetramethyl ammonium hydroxide soln.*—Dil. 10 mL 10% soln of $(Me)_4NOH$ to 100 mL with alcohol.

(**d**) *Blue tetrazolium soln.*—Dissolve 0.5 g blue tetrazolium in 100 mL alcohol and filter. Store protected from light.

(**e**) *Dexamethasone phosphate std soln.*—Accurately weigh ca 12 mg USP Dexamethasone Phosphate Ref. Std into 100 mL vol. flask. Add H_2O, shake to dissolve, and dil. to vol. with H_2O.

39.048 ***Extraction***

(**a**) *Creams and ointments.*—Weigh portion contg ca 2.5 mg dexamethasone phosphate into 125 mL separator. Add 15 mL *5% NaCl soln* and 25 mL CH_2Cl_2. Shake well to disperse sample. Continue shaking 2 min. Let phases sep., and transfer CH_2Cl_2 layer to second separator contg 6 mL 5% NaCl soln. Shake well 1 min, let phases sep., and discard CH_2Cl_2 layer. Repeat wash with addnl 25 mL CH_2Cl_2, washing each aq. phase in succession. Discard CH_2Cl_2. Transfer aq. phase in first separator to 25 mL vol. flask. Rinse first separator with contents of second and transfer rinse to vol. flask. Rinse both separators with same 2 mL 5% NaCl soln and add rinse to vol. flask. Dil. to vol. with 5% NaCl, if necessary.

(**b**) *Solutions.*—Accurately dil. soln to concn ca 0.1 mg dexamethasone phosphate/mL. Place 25 mL dild soln and 25 mL CH_2Cl_2 in 125 mL separator, shake, let layers sep., and discard CH_2Cl_2.

39.049 ***Enzymatic Reaction and Extraction***

Pipet 3 mL of each aq. sample and std soln into sep. 125 mL separators. Add 8 mL alk. phosphatase, mix, and let stand 2 hr at room temp. (⩾25°). Ext with two 25 mL portions CH_2Cl_2. Filter CH_2Cl_2 layers into 100 mL beaker thru small pledget of cotton. Evap. CH_2Cl_2 at room temp. in current of air in hood. (Do not use air current strong enough to cool CH_2Cl_2 and cause moisture to collect in beaker.) Dissolve residue in 10 mL alcohol. Transfer quant. to 25 mL vol. flask, rinsing beaker with three 5 mL portions alcohol. Prep. blank by evapg 50 mL CH_2Cl_2 and dissolving residue in 25 mL alcohol.

39.050 ***Determination***

Pipet 10 mL blank soln into 20 mL g-s test tube or flask. Add 1.0 mL $(Me)_4NOH$ soln and 1.0 mL blue tetrazolium soln. Stopper and set aside, protected from light, *exactly* 45 min. At 1–3 min intervals, repeat above operations with 10 mL each sample and std soln. (Series of samples can be analyzed using 1 blank and 1 std soln.) Det. A of each soln at 515 nm *exactly* 45 min after addn of blue tetrazolium, against alcohol as ref.

39.051 ***Calculations***

(**a**) *Creams and ointments.*—

mg Dexamethasone phosphate/g = $(A/A') \times C \times (25/W)$.

(**b**) *Solns.*—

mg Dexamethasone phosphate/mL = $(A/A') \times C \times D$,

where A and A' refer to sample and std solns, resp., corrected for blank; C = mg/mL std soln; W = g sample; and D = diln factor.

Prednisolone or Prednisone

Semiautomated Method (14)—Official Final Action

39.052 ***Principle***

Alcoholic soln of drug is extd with $CHCl_3$ and reacted with tetramethylammonium hydroxide and blue tetrazolium. A of resulting complex is read in flowcell at 525 nm.

39.053 ***Apparatus***

(**a**) *Automatic analyzer.*—AutoAnalyzer with following modules (Technicon Instruments Corp.): Sampler II with 30/hr (3:1) cam; proportioning pump I; colorimeter I, equipped with 15 mm tubular flowcell and matched 525 nm filters; recorder compatible with colorimeter I; manifold (*see* Fig. **39.01**).

(**b**) *Shaker.*—Model BT, wrist-action (Burrell Corp.).

(**c**) *Ultrasonic generator.*—150 watt.

39.054 ***Reagents***

(**a**) *Blue tetrazolium (BT) reagent.*—0.15%. Dissolve 1.5 g BT in 50 mL MeOH and dil to 1 L with alcohol. Store in light-resistant bottle.

(**b**) *Tetramethylammonium hydroxide (TMAH) reagent.*—0.15%. Dil. 15.0 mL 10% TMAH soln to 1 L with alcohol.

(**c**) *Prednisolone std soln.*—(*1*) *Stock soln.*—0.4 mg/mL. Accurately weigh ca 40 mg USP Prednisolone Ref. Std into 100 mL vol. flask, dissolve in 50% alcohol, and dil to vol. (*2*) *Working soln.*—0.10 mg/mL. Pipet 25 mL stock soln into 100 mL vol. flask and dil. to vol. with 50% alcohol.

(**d**) *Prednisone std soln.*—(*1*) *Stock soln.*—0.2 mg/mL. Accurately weigh ca 20 mg USP Prednisone Ref. Std into 100 mL vol. flask, dissolve in 50% alcohol, and dil. to vol. (*2*) *Working soln.*—0.05 mg/mL. Pipet 25 mL stock soln into 100 mL vol. flask and dil. to vol. with 50% alcohol.

39.055 ***Preparation of Sample***

Disintegrate individual tablet or disperse weighed composite in accurately measured vol. 50% alcohol to give prednisolone concn of 0.1 mg/mL or prednisone concn of 0.05 mg/mL. Use ultrasonic generator until tablet is disintegrated and shake mech. 15 min. Let soln settle ⩾2 hr.

39.056 ***Analytical System***

Sample is withdrawn and extd with air-segmented stream of $CHCl_3$ in double mixer, and org. phase is sepd in BO fitting. BT and TMAH reagents are added to org. phase and mixed. Soln is passed thru delay coil and A is detd at 525 nm in 15 mm flowcell.

39.057 ***Start-Up and Shut-Down Operations***

Pump alcohol thru $CHCl_3$ line 10 min; then pump $CHCl_3$ thru line 5 min. Place remaining tubes in their resp. solns and let system equilibrate 20–30 min or until steady baseline is obtained. To shut down system, place $CHCl_3$, BT, and TMAH lines in alcohol and remove all other lines from their solns. After 15 min, remove remaining lines from alcohol soln and pump system dry.

39.058 ***Determination***

Fill sample cups in following order: 3 cups std soln, 5 cups sample soln, 1 cup std soln, 5 cups sample soln, etc. Place 2 cups std soln at end of each series. (First 2 cups of std solns are used to equilibrate system, but are not included in calcns.) Start Sampler II. After last cup has been sampled, let system operate until steady baseline is obtained. Draw tangent to initial and final baselines. Subtract baseline to det. net A and A' for each sample and std peak, resp. Discard values for first 2 and last std peaks and calc. av. std A'.

mg Drug in portion taken = $(A/A') \times C \times D$,

where C = concn of std in mg/mL and D = diln factor.

NONALKALOIDAL VEGETABLE DRUGS AND THEIR DERIVATIVES

Digitoxin (*15*)—Official Final Action

39.059 ***Reagents***

(**a**) *Formamide.*—Shake 1 L $HCONH_2$ (99% grade) with ca 30 g anhyd. K_2CO_3 15 min and filter. Distil under vac. in all-glass app. Reject first portion of distillate contg H_2O, and collect fraction boiling at ca 101°/12 mm Hg (1.6 kPa) (115°/25 mm Hg; 3.3 kPa). Store over H_2SO_4 until odor of NH_3 is no longer detected.

(**b**) *Alkaline picrate reagent.*—Mix 20 mL 1% aq. picric acid soln with 10 mL 5% NaOH soln, dil. to 100 mL with H_2O, and mix. Reagent is stable 2–3 days.

(**c**) *Digitoxin std soln.*—0.04 mg/mL. Dissolve 20.0 mg USP Digitoxin Ref. Std in alcohol, and dil. to 50 mL with alcohol. Dil. 10.0 mL of this stock soln to 100 mL with alcohol.

(**d**) *Diatomaceous earth.—See* **36.002**.

39.060 ***Preparation of Chromatographic Column***

Chromatographic tube.—See **37.002**.

Wash layer.—Add ca 2 g diat. earth to 1 mL H_2O in 100 mL beaker. Mix thoroly with stirring rod or scoop until the mixt. appears fluffy and uniform, and transfer to chromatgc tube. Press down lightly with packing rod. (Wash layer should be 15–20 mm thick.)

Trap layer.—Add 3 g diat. earth to 3 mL formamide-H_2O soln (2+1) in 150 mL beaker, mix thoroly, and transfer to tube containing wash layer. Press trap layer down lightly and evenly.

39.061 ***Preparation of Sample***

(**a**) *Crystalline digitoxin.*—Dissolve 20 mg digitoxin, accurately weighed, in 20 mL $CHCl_3$. Transfer to 100 mL vol. flask with several portions of benzene, dil. to vol. with benzene, and mix. Transfer 10.0 mL to chromatgc column, **39.060**. When liq. has passed into column, proceed as in **39.062**.

(**b**) *Tablets.*—Thoroly mix accurately weighed powd sample contg 2 mg digitoxin with 2 mL H_2O in 250 mL beaker. Add 4 mL formamide, stir thoroly, and cover beaker with watch glass. Heat mixt. 20 min on steam bath, with frequent stirring. Cool; add 2 mL H_2O and ca 8 g diat. earth. Stir thoroly until mass appears uniform and does not stick to beaker. Quant. transfer mixt. to prepd chromatgc tube, **39.060**, thru powder funnel in several portions, pressing it down with stirring rod. Use rubber policeman to sweep adhering particles from beaker and funnel into tube. Scrub beaker and stirring rod with ca 1 g diat. earth, and add dry washings to tube thru funnel. Repeat washing with 2 addnl portions diat. earth. Place cotton pad in tube and press it down on column with packing rod, sweeping diat. earth on sides of tube before it. (Over-all ht of column should be 120–150 mm.)

39.062 ***Separation of Digitoxin***

Elute digitoxin with ca 240 mL benzene-$CHCl_3$ (3+1), collecting eluate in 250 mL vol. flask at rate ≤4 mL/min. Wash stem with stream of $CHCl_3$, dil. to 250 mL with $CHCl_3$, and mix.

Continue elution as in **39.064**.

39.063 ***Colorimetric Determination***

Transfer 25 mL aliquot eluate to small erlenmeyer and evap. to dryness on steam bath with aid of air current. Moisten residue with ca 0.5 mL alcohol, and again evap. to dryness. Add 5.0 mL alcohol to cooled flask, stopper, and let stand 15 min with occasional shaking.

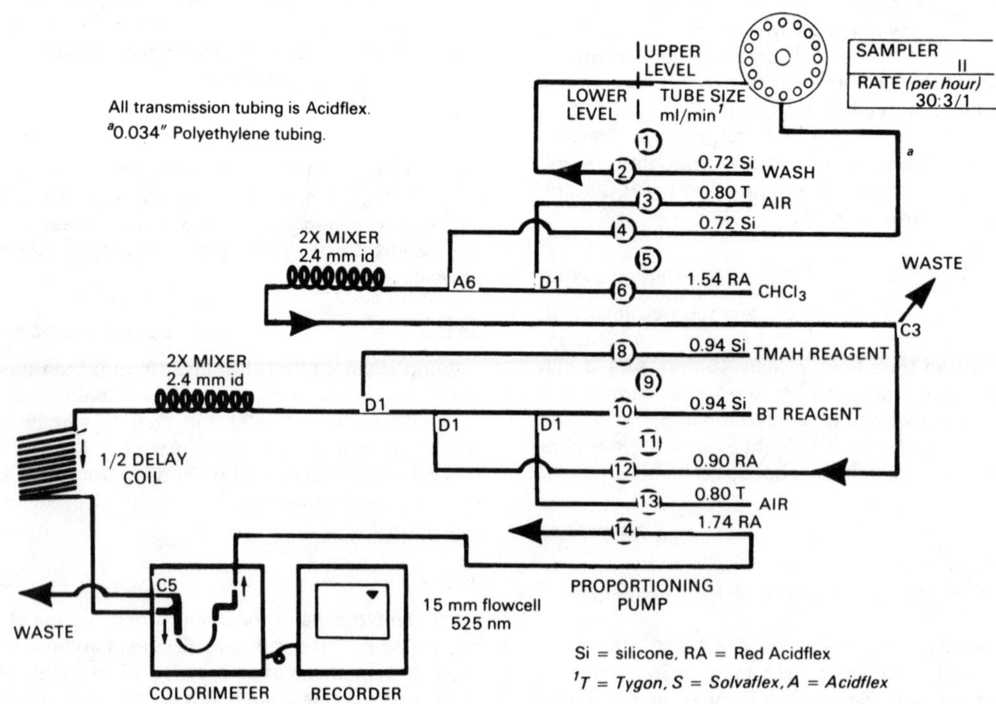

FIG. 39:01—Flow diagram for semiautomated analysis for prednisolone or prednisone

Transfer 5.0 mL aliquot dild std digitoxin soln to small flask and 5 mL alcohol to another flask as blank. Add 3.0 mL alk. picrate reagent to each flask, and mix by swirling. Protect soln from intense light. After 10 min, det. *A* of std and sample solns relative to blank at 495 nm, repeating measurements at 2 min intervals until max. values are attained. Calc. digitoxin content of sample.

39.064 ***Tests for Other Digitoxosides***

(*Caution: See* **51.011**, **51.040**, and **51.056**.)

After digitoxin seps, elute other digitoxosides with 200 mL $CHCl_3$, collecting eluate in separator. Shake with 100 mL H_2O. Transfer lower layer to beaker, ext H_2O with 30 mL $CHCl_3$, and add $CHCl_3$ washings to beaker. Evap. to dryness. Pipet 5 mL dild digitoxin std soln into second beaker and evap. to dryness. Add 4 mL Keller-Kiliani reagent, **39.073(b)**, to each of the cooled residues and mix thoroly. After 15 min, filter thru glass wool if necessary, and det. *A* of *clear* sample and std relative to reagent blank, at 590 nm; repeat measurements at 5 min intervals until max. values are attained. Calc. content of other digitoxosides in sample as digitoxin.

Digoxin

Automated Method (16)—Official Final Action

39.065 ***Principle***

KIO_4 oxidizes *cis*-2-deoxy sugars to malonyldialdehydes which are condensed with 2-thiobarbituric acid to yield stable, intensely colored methine dyes. Glycoside moiety of digoxin consists of 3 molecules of digitoxose, 2,6-dideoxy-D-ribohexose, which yields colored compd with max. *A* at 530 nm.

39.066 ***Apparatus***

(**a**) *Automatic analyzer.*—AutoAnalyzer with following modules (Technicon Instruments Corp.): Sampler II with 40/hr (2:1) cam; proportioning pump I; manifold; const temp. bath (75°) with two 40′ × 1.6 mm id coils; Model 1 colorimeter, with 50 mm tubular flowcell, matched 530 nm filters; Bristol recorder linear in *T*, and paper printed in *A* units. (*See* Fig. **39:02**.)

(**b**) *Shaker.*—Model BT, wrist-action (Burrell Corp.).

(**c**) *Ultrasonic generator.*—150 watt.

39.067 ***Reagents***

(**a**) *Arsenic trioxide soln.*—Add 20.0 g As_2O_3 and 7.0 g NaOH pellets to 100 mL H_2O, and heat to bp to dissolve. (*Caution: See* **51.078**.) Add 800 mL H_2O and 60 mL HCl, and dil. to 1 L.

(**b**) *Potassium metaperiodate soln.*—Add 3.6 g KIO_4 to 900 mL H_2O. Heat and stir to dissolve. Cool. Add 3.0 mL H_2SO_4 and dil. to 1 L.

(**c**) *Thiobarbituric acid (TBA) soln.*—Add 15.0 g TBA and 4.5 g NaOH pellets to 900 mL H_2O, and stir to dissolve. Add HCl slowly to pH 3.5–4.0. Filter and dil. to 1 L.

(**d**) *Digoxin std solns.*—(*1*) *Stock soln.*—0.05 mg/ mL. Accurately weigh ca 25 mg USP Digoxin Ref. Std into 500 mL vol. flask and dil. to vol. with 50% alcohol. (*2*) *Working soln.*—5 μg/mL. Pipet 10 mL stock soln into 100 mL vol. flask and dil. to vol. with 50% alcohol. Prep. fresh daily.

39.068 ***Preparation of Sample***

Disintegrate individual tablet or disperse weighed composite in accurately measured vol. 50% alcohol to give digoxin concn of 5 μg/mL. Use ultrasonic generator ≥5 min to assure tablet disintegration. Shake mech. 1 hr. Let soln settle ≥2 hr.

39.069 ***Analytical System***

Sample is withdrawn, segmented with air, and oxidized with KIO_4 in mixing coil. As_2O_3 is added to remove excess KIO_4; then TBA is added. Color is developed in 75° heating bath, and *A* of soln at 530 nm is measured in 50 mm flowcell.

39.070 ***Start-Up***

Place all lines in their resp. solns, and let system equilibrate 30 min.

39.071 ***Shut-Down***

Place KIO_4, As_2O_3, and TBA lines in H_2O. Remove all other lines from their solns. After 10 min, remove remaining lines from H_2O and pump system dry.

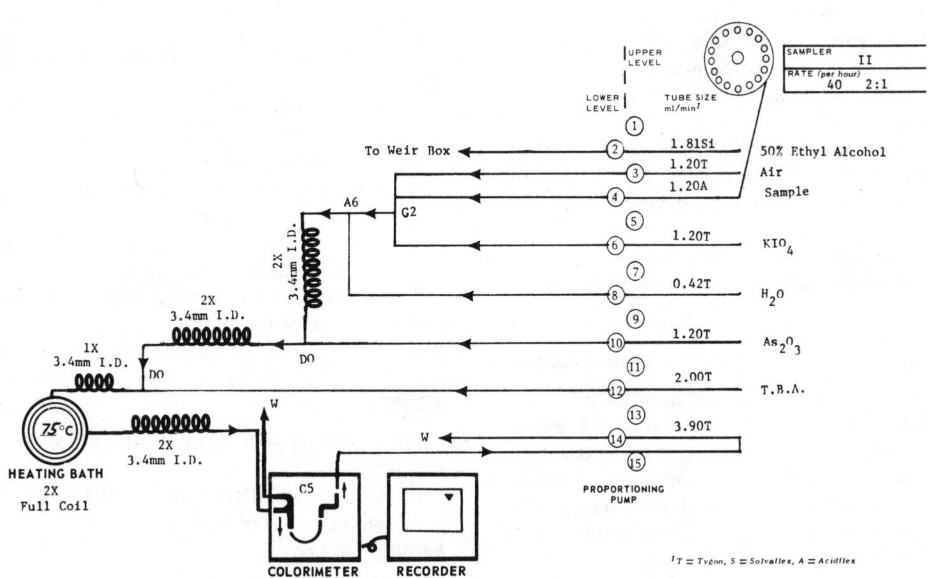

FIG. 39:02—Flow diagram for automated analysis for digoxin

39.072 ***Determination***

Fill sample cups in following order: 4 cups std soln, 5 cups sample soln, 1 cup std soln, 5 cups sample soln, etc. Place 2 cups std soln at end of each run. (Extra cups of std solns at start and end of sampling pattern will eliminate carryover effect in transitions from wash soln to std soln and vice versa. Three extra cups at start and 1 extra cup at end should suffice, but det. number needed for equilibrium by experiment. System should give uniform response for at least final pair of extra std cups before sample pattern is started.) Start Sampler II. After last cup has been sampled, let system operate until steady baseline is obtained. Draw tangent to initial and final baselines. Subtract baseline to det. ΔA and $\Delta A'$ for each sample and std peak, resp. Discard values for first 3 and last std peaks and calc. av. $\Delta A'$.

$$\text{mg Digoxin in portion taken} = (\Delta A/\Delta A') \times C \times D,$$

where C = concn of std in mg/mL and D = diln factor.

Digoxin and Total Digitoxosides (*17*)—Official Final Action

39.073 ***Reagents***

(**a**) *Alkaline dinitrobenzene soln.*—(*1*) Prep. 5% soln *m*-dinitrobenzene in benzene, and store in g-s brown glass bottle. (*2*) Mix 1 mL 10% tetramethyl ammonium hydroxide soln with 140 mL absolute alcohol, titr. with 0.01*N* HCl, using Me red, and adjust to 0.008*N* with absolute alcohol. Just before use, mix 60 mL (*1*) with 40 mL (*2*).

(**b**) *Keller-Kiliani reagent.*—Mix 60 mL HOAc with 1 mL 9% $FeCl_3.6H_2O$ soln and 5 mL H_2SO_4, and cool.

(**c**) *Digoxin std soln.*—25.0 μg/mL. Dissolve 25.0 mg USP Digoxin Ref. Std, $C_{41}H_{64}O_{14}$, in hot alcohol, cool, dil. to 100 mL, and mix. Dil. 10.0 mL of this soln to 100 mL with alcohol and mix.

39.074 ***Preparation of Sample***

(**a**) *Crystalline digoxin.*—Prep. alc. soln contg 125 μg digoxin/mL. Transfer 10.0 mL to separator, add 50 mL H_2O and 1 mL 2*N* H_2SO_4, and ext with three 30 mL portions $CHCl_3$. Wash each $CHCl_3$ ext in second separator by shaking with 10 mL H_2O and 1 g powd *anion-cation exchange resin* (Amberlite MB-1, anal. grade, indicator-free, has been found satisfactory; available as Mallinckrodt Cat. No. 3325), and filter thru pledget of cotton moistened with $CHCl_3$ into 100 mL vol. flask. Dil. to vol. with $CHCl_3$ and mix well. This soln is *Assay Soln*.

(**b**) *Elixirs and injections.*—Transfer aliquot contg 1.25 mg digoxin to separator, and proceed as in (**a**), beginning: "... add 50 mL H_2O and 1 mL 2*N* H_2SO_4, ..."

(**c**) *Tablets.*—Accurately weigh, into 100 mL beaker, portion of powd tablets contg 1.25 mg digoxin. Add 10 mL alcohol, cover with watch glass, and heat to bp on steam bath. Let simmer 20 min with frequent stirring. Cool, wash quant. into separator with 30 mL $CHCl_3$ and 50 mL H_2O, add 1 mL 2*N* H_2SO_4, and proceed as in (**a**), beginning: "... ext with three 30 mL portions $CHCl_3$."

39.075 ***Determination***

(**a**) *Digoxin.*—Pipet 5.0 mL digoxin std soln and 10.0 mL assay soln into similar erlenmeyers, and evap. to dryness on steam bath with aid of air current. Cool, and to each flask add 5.0 mL freshly prepd alk. dinitrobenzene reagent. Let stand 5 min at ≤30°, with frequent mixing. Det. A of developing blue colors relative to reagent blank at 620 nm at 1 min intervals, using matched 1 cm cells and spectrophtr. Record max. A of aliquot of assay soln and that of digoxin std soln, A'. Digoxin (mg in assay soln) = 1.25 A/A'.

(**b**) *Other digitoxosides.*—Pipet 20 mL assay soln and 10 mL digoxin std soln into sep. beakers and evap. to dryness on steam bath with aid of air current. Cool, add 4.0 mL Keller-Kiliani reagent at ≤30° to each beaker, and mix thoroly. After 15 min, det. A of sample and std at 590 nm relative to reagent blank at 5 min intervals. Record max. A of sample and that of std, A'. Total digitoxosides calcd as digoxin (mg in sample soln) = 1.25 A/A'. Difference between this value and that obtained in (**a**) is amt of other digitoxosides in sample soln.

39.076 ★ Camphor (*18*)—Official Final Action ★

(Not applicable to synthetic camphor)

Steam distn, benzene extn, and polarimetric detn. *See* **39.061**, 12th ed.

39.077 ★ Camphor in Spirits (*19*) ★ Official Final Action

Gravimetric detn as 2,4-dinitrophenylhydrazone. *See* **39.062–39.063**, 12th ed.

Camphor (*20*)—Official Final Action

39.078 ***Apparatus***

(**a**) *Gas chromatograph.*—With H flame ionization detector and strip chart recorder. Operate instrument in accordance with manufacturer's instructions. Operating conditions: temps (°)—column 180, detector 220, flash heater 250; N flow rate ca 60 mL/min adjusted to elute phenol in ca 9 min. Approx. retention time of camphor is 2.5 min. Adjust electrometer sensitivity so that 2.5 μg phenol gives ca 50% deflection.

(**b**) *GLC column.*—(Material available from Applied Science Laboratories, Inc. has been found satisfactory.) Dissolve 1.2 g Carbowax 20M in ca 50 mL CH_2Cl_2 on steam bath. (*Caution:* Use effective fume removal device when heating or evapg CH_2Cl_2.) Add 10 g 100–140 mesh Gas-Chrom P and stir as solv. evaps. Dry 1 hr at 105°. Pour dry, coated packing material into 1.8 m (6') × 4 mm glass tube, vibrating with hand vibrator. Place glass wool plugs at each end; then insert septums. Condition prepd column overnight at 200° with N flow.

39.079 ***Reagents***

(**a**) *Camphor std soln.*—0.5 mg/mL. Dissolve and dil. 100 mg camphor to 200 mL with $CHCl_3$.

(**b**) *Phenol internal std soln.*—1 mg/mL. Dissolve and dil. 100 mg phenol to 100 mL with $CHCl_3$.

(**c**) *Menthol internal std soln.*—0.5 mg/mL. Dissolve and dil. 100 mg menthol to 200 mL with $CHCl_3$.

(**d**) *Methyl salicylate internal std soln.*—1 mg/mL. Dissolve and dil. 100 mg Me salicylate to 100 mL with $CHCl_3$.

(**e**) *Working std soln.*—Pipet equal vols of appropriate internal std soln, (**b**), (**c**), or (**d**), and camphor std soln, (**a**), into g-s flask. Phenol is preferred internal std but sample must not contain substance selected as internal std.

39.080 ***Preparation of Sample***

(**a**) *Oily solns.*—Dil. aliquot of sample with $CHCl_3$ to ca 0.5 mg camphor/mL.

(**b**) *Ointments.*—Dissolve weighed sample in $CHCl_3$, warming very slightly if necessary. Dil. with $CHCl_3$ to ca 0.5 mg camphor/mL.

★ Surplus method—*see* inside front cover.

39.081 ***Determination***

Pipet equal vols sample soln and internal std into g-s flask. Inject 5 μL into gas chromatograph and record chromatogram. Inject 5 μL working std soln and record chromatogram. Measure ht of each peak above baseline.

Concn (mg/mL or mg/g) in sample

$$= (P \times I' \times C')/(P' \times I \times C),$$

where P' and P = hts std and sample peaks, resp.; I' and I = hts internal std peak in std and sample, resp.; C' = mg std/mL std soln used to prep. working std; and C = mL or g sample/mL sample soln.

39.082 ★ Camphor, Monobromated, in Tablets (*21*) ★ Official Final Action

Liberation of inorg. Br with Na amalgam and gravimetric detn as AgBr. *See* **39.068–39.069**, 12th ed.

39.083 ★ Menthol (*22*)—Official Final Action ★

Acetylation and quant. saponification of derivative. *See* **39.070**, 12th ed.

39.084 ★ Aloin (*23*)—Official Final Action ★

Extn with dil. H_2SO_4 and transfer of impurities into $CHCl_3$. Aloin is salted out into $CHCl_3$-alcohol and detd gravimetrically. *See* **39.071**, 12th ed.

39.085 ★ Podophyllum (*24*)—Official Final Action ★

Extn with alcohol, pptn with cold dil. HCl, and gravimetric detn. *See* **39.072**, 12th ed.

39.086 ★ Chenopodium Oil (*25*)—Official Final Action ★

Titrn with $TiCl_3$. *See* **39.073–39.074**, 12th ed.

Santonin in Mixtures—Official Final Action

39.087 ★ *Langer Method (Modified) (26)* ★

See **36.515**, 11th ed.

Dinitrophenylhydrazine Method (27)

39.088 ***Reagent***

Dinitrophenylhydrazine sulfate soln.—Dissolve 1 g 2,4-dinitrophenylhydrazine in mixt. of 90 mL H_2O and 10 mL H_2SO_4 by warming; cool, and filter.

39.089 ***Determination***

(*Caution: See* **51.011**, **51.039**, **51.040**, and **51.045**.)

Weigh 2.5 g ground sample into gooch and wash with ca 100 mL pet ether satd with santonin. Discard washings. Ext with ca 100 mL benzene, collecting filtrate in beaker. Evap. to dryness, warm residue with alcohol until dissolved, transfer to 100 mL vol. flask, cool, dil. to vol. at 20° with alcohol, and filter if necessary. To 25 mL of this soln add 50 mL dinitrophenylhydrazine sulfate soln and let stand 48 hr in dark. Collect ppt in gooch and wash with ca 150 mL alcohol (1+2). Dry residue 1 hr at 100°, cool, and weigh. Wt ppt × 0.5775 = wt santonin.

Ultraviolet Absorption Method (28)

(Applicable in presence of starch and calomel)

39.090 ***Reagent***

Santonin std soln.—10 μg/mL. Weigh 50 mg santonin NF XI, transfer to 50 mL vol. flask, dissolve in alcohol, and dil. to vol. with alcohol. Pipet 2 mL aliquot into 200 mL vol. flask and dil. to vol. with alcohol.

39.091 ***Determination***

Accurately weigh portion powd sample contg ca 35 mg santonin, transfer to 100 mL vol. flask, dil. to vol. with alcohol, and shake frequently during 15 min. Let settle ca 15 min, transfer 5 mL aliquot supernate to 200 mL vol. flask, dil. to vol. with alcohol, and mix. Det. A of this soln and of std soln, A', against alcohol at 240 nm.

Grains santonin/tablet = (wt std, mg) × A × 4000 × tablet wt (mg)/A' × mg sample × 64.8.

39.092 ***Identification***

Ext portion of powd tablets with alcohol or use alc. soln from detn and evap. to dryness. Santonin gives white tabular crystals, mp 170–173°.

Infrared Method (29)—Official Final Action

(Applicable to tablets in presence of calomel)

39.093 ***Apparatus***

Infrared spectrophotometer.—For operation in 2–15 μm region; equipped with 2 matched NaCl cells 1.0 mm thick, suitable for CS_2 solns. (Cells of shorter path length are not suitable because of low solubility of santonin.)

39.094 ***Determination***

(Caution: See **51.011**, **51.018**, **51.039**, **51.040**, **51.048**, and **51.056**.)

Transfer 25 mg Santonin NF XI, accurately weighed, to 125 mL separator contg ca 15 mL H_2O. Ext as for sample.

Transfer accurately weighed portion powd tablets, contg ca 25 mg santonin, to 125 mL separator contg ca 15 mL H_2O. Make just ammoniacal with NH_4OH (1+9) (ca 1 drop) and ext with four 25 mL portions $CHCl_3$. Filter each ext thru cotton plug, moistened with $CHCl_3$, in long-stem glass funnel into 250 mL beaker. Evap. combined $CHCl_3$ exts to ca 5 mL on steam bath with aid of air current. Transfer quant. to 25 mL g-s erlenmeyer with ca 10 mL $CHCl_3$ in 2 mL portions, and evap. to dryness. Wash down sides of flask with few mL anhyd. ether, repeating if necessary to form dry residue. Use caution to avoid loss of sample by spattering. Add 10 mL CS_2 from pipet, stopper flask, and mix by swirling. Filter any insol. material thru cotton, and immediately det. baseline A of sample and std (A') solns relative to CS_2 at max. of 9.75 μm, drawing baseline between minima of 9.6 and 9.95 μm.

% Santonin = A × mg std × 100/A' × mg sample.

Record spectra of sample and std solns from 2 to 15 μm and compare for sample identity.

39.095 ★ Santonin in Santonica (Levant Worm ★ Seed) (*30*)—Official Final Action

(*Caution: See* **51.011**, **51.039**, **51.040**, and **51.045**.)

Extn with benzene, cleanup with alcohol, $Ba(OH)_2$, acid, and $CHCl_3$ extn. Detn by dinitrophenylhydrazine method. *See* **39.083**, 12th ed.

★ Surplus method—*see* inside front cover.

Rutin (*31*)—Official Final Action

39.096 ***Reagents***

(**a**) *Acid-alcohol reagent.*—Mix 550 mL alcohol with 50 mL HOAc and dil. to 1 L with H_2O.

(**b**) *Rutin std soln.*—0.02 mg/mL. Accurately weigh 100 mg rutin (obtainable from ICN–K&K Laboratories, Inc.) and dissolve in 50 mL acid-alcohol. Transfer to 250 mL vol. flask with small portions acid-alcohol. Dil. to vol. with reagent and mix well. Pipet 5 mL aliquot into 100 mL vol. flask and dil. to vol. with H_2O.

(**c**) *Quercetin std soln.*—0.01 mg/mL. Prep. as in (**b**), using 50 mg quercetin. Pure quercetin may be prepd as in J. Am. Pharm. Assoc., Sci. Ed. **42**, 66(1953).

39.097 ***Apparatus***

(**a**) *Spectrophotometer.*—Capable of isolating 338.5, 352.5, and 366.5 nm, with isolated spectrum ≤5 nm.

(**b**) *Absorption cells.*—Matched 1 cm.

(**c**) *Glass stirring rods.*—Of small enough diam. to dislodge material from tips of 50 mL conical centrf. tubes.

39.098 ***Preparation of Sample Solution***

Weigh directly into 50 mL centrf. tube number of tablets required to give 0.05–0.50 g rutin (≥5 tablets). Record number and wt. (If tablets are coated, dissolve coating with distd H_2O after weighing, discard aq. washings, and transfer rutin-contg core to centrf. tube.) Add 20 mL acid-alcohol reagent and break up tablets with stirring rod. After tablets are thoroly disintegrated, heat mixt. 10 min in H_2O bath held at 70–80°, resuspending material occasionally by stirring. Remove stirring rod, rinse with acid-alcohol reagent, and centrf. 15 min. at ca 2000 rpm.

Decant supernate into 250 mL vol. flask, using funnel and decanting with one smooth motion, and let tube drain ca 10 sec. While still inverted, rinse mouth of tube with acid-alcohol reagent. Ext twice more, starting with "Add 20 mL acid-alcohol reagent . . ." After third extn, dil. combined supernates to 250 mL with acid-alcohol reagent. Any insol. material may be removed by filtration after diln if first 15–20 mL filtrate is discarded. Depending on original wt rutin taken, make diln with H_2O to give final concn of 0.01–0.03 g rutin/L. Ppts forming during aq. diln may be removed by filtration if first portion of filtrate is discarded to guard against concn changes due to adsorption.

39.099 ***Determination***

Det. A of sample soln against H_2O blank at 338.5, 352.5, and 366.5 nm. Also det. A of std rutin soln, A'_R, and std quercetin soln, A'_Q, against H_2O blank at 352.5 and 366.5 nm. (In absence of std quercetin, values $A'_{Q,352.5} = 0.553$ and $A'_{Q,365.5} = 0.631$ may be used. Any error introduced by use of these predetd values should be of second order.) Calc. as follows:

$$R_1 = A_{338.5}/A_{352.5};$$

and

$$R_2 = A_{366.5}/A_{352.5}.$$

If $R_1 = 0.914 \pm 0.009$ and $R_2 = 0.842 \pm 0.013$, extd material can be considered pure rutin and wt rutin/tablet can be calcd:

$$\text{mg Rutin/tablet} = A_{352.5} \times d \times W \times 0.02/A'_{R,352.5} \times w,$$

where d = sample diln factor; W = av. wt/tablet; and w = wt sample.

(Value of R_1 beyond its upper limit while R_2 remains within its range indicates interfering absorption which diminishes rapidly enough to be ineffective at 352.5 nm. Under this condition, A observed at 352.5 nm is accepted as correct, and rutin content is calcd as for pure rutin. Increase in R_2 while R_1 remains within or below its limits usually indicates presence of quercetin. Simultaneous increase or decrease of both ratios beyond their respective limits indicates invalidating condition.) Amts of rutin and quercetin may be calcd by solution of following simultaneous equations:

$$A_{352.5} = (A'_{R,352.5} \times r/0.02) + (A'_{Q,352.5} \times q/0.01)$$

$$A_{366.5} = (A'_{R,366.5} \times r/0.02) + (A'_{Q,366.5} \times q/0.01)$$

where r = mg rutin/mL in sample soln, and q = mg quercetin/mL in sample soln.

39.100 ★ **Gums, Identification (*32*)—Official Final Action** ★

(*See* also **16.290–16.296.**)

Spot tests. *See* **39.088–39.090**, 12th ed.

39.101 ★ **Ipomea (*33*)—Official Final Action** ★

Proceed as in **39.102**.

39.102 **Jalap (*33*)—Official Final Action**

Place 10 g sample, as "60-mesh" powder, in 250 mL erlenmeyer and add 50 mL alcohol. Fit flask with stopper thru which is inserted glass tube ca 1 m long to act as condenser, and heat gently on simmering steam bath 30 min, shaking occasionally. Transfer contents to small percolator and percolate slowly with warm alcohol until ca 95 mL collects.

To test for complete extn, collect 10 mL more percolate and pour few drops into cold H_2O; if more than faint cloudiness appears, continue percolation with warm alcohol until test for resin fails. Conc. the addnl percolate by evapn and add to flask before dilg to vol. Cool percolate to room temp. and dil. to 100 mL with alcohol. Mix well.

Evap. 25 mL of the prepd tincture (representing 2.5 g drug) on H_2O bath in beaker or flask and dry residue until alcohol-free. Add 15 mL H_2O, bring mixt. to bp, let cool ca 3 min, and stir well with flat-end rod 2 min to ensure thoro washing of resin. Cool mixt. by placing container in jar of ice-cold H_2O and decant wash H_2O onto 9 cm filter. Repeat washing of resin with another 15 mL portion H_2O, boiling and cooling mixt., kneading resin as before, and decanting washings into filter as before. Repeat washing and kneading process with hot H_2O third time.

Dissolve residue in container in 10 mL warm alcohol and pour soln onto filter, collecting filtrate in weighed beaker or flask. Use enough hot alcohol in small portions to completely transfer soln of resin to filter and ensure thoro washing of filter. Evap. combined filtrate and washings to apparent dryness, add 1 mL absolute alcohol, and evap. solv., taking care to rotate container in inclined position as last portions of solv. are dissipated. Dry residue at 80° to const wt.

39.103 ★ **Volatile Acidity of Tragacanth (*34*)** ★ **Official Final Action**

Steam distn and titrn of distillate. *See* **39.093**, 12th ed.

MISCELLANEOUS

★ Nitroglycerin (Glyceryl Trinitrate)—Official Final Action ★

Reduction Method (35)

39.104 ***Apparatus***

(**a**) *Connecting bulb.*—Hopkins style, ca 7.6 cm diam. This style has long inlet tube with opening on side of tube.

★ Surplus method—*see* inside front cover.

(**b**) *Condenser.*—Water-cooled, 56 cm long, and preferably of Pyrex glass.

(**c**) *Adapter tube.*—Approx. 2.25 cm diam. at top and with narrow outlet.

(**d**) *Scrubber-trap.*—Any efficient trap in which all vapor is washed thoroly with H_2O before it leaves distg flask (*see* Fig. **39:03.**).

39.105 ***Extraction***

(**a**) *Ether extraction.*—Place in 50 mL beaker weighed sample contg ca 0.0324 g (0.5 grain) nitroglycerin. If sample consists of tablets, count those taken; if of powd material, mix thoroly before weighing. Add 10 mL ether, and to facilitate extn, reduce tablets to fine powder, using flat-end stirring rod. Stir thoroly. Decant ether thru dry 7 cm quant. paper into 250 mL beaker contg 10 mL alcohol. Hold paper in place in funnel with the stirring rod and pour ether down rod. Make 4 addnl extns in same way. Dissolve ether-insol. residue in small amt of H_2O, transfer soln to separator, and ext with two 10 mL portions ether. Filter these exts, add to first exts, and evap. combined ether soln to ca 10 mL with fan. Transfer soln to 800 mL Kjeldahl flask, rinsing beaker first with 10 mL alcohol and then with little H_2O. Dil. to ca 300 mL with recently boiled and cooled NH_3-free H_2O.

(**b**) *Alcohol extraction.*—Weigh into g-s erlenmeyer sample contg ca 0.065 g (1 grain) nitroglycerin. If sample consists of tablets, count those taken; if of powd material, mix thoroly before weighing portion taken for analysis. Pipet in 50 mL alcohol. To facilitate extn, reduce tablets to fine powder with flat-end rod. Stopper flask and shake. Let mixt. settle, transfer 25 mL aliquot of clear soln to 800 mL Kjeldahl flask, and dil. to ca 300 mL with NH_3-free H_2O.

39.106 ***Determination***

Place flask on wire gauze with asbestos center. Add thru funnel 2 g *Devarda alloy,* ca 4 cm *heavy* (ca 16 gage) *Al wire,* and 10–15 mL alc. KOH soln (15 g KOH dild to 100 mL with alcohol). Immediately after adding alkali, place little H_2O in scrubber trap (A and B, Fig. **39:03**), and insert rubber stopper carrying scrubber trap and connecting bulb into neck of flask. Connect outlet tube of connecting bulb with upright condenser fitted with adapter tube dipping to bottom of 500 mL erlenmeyer contg measured vol. (ca 25 mL) 0.02*N* HCl or H_2SO_4 and 10–15 mL H_2O, and so inclined that tip of adapter is submerged as far as practicable under surface of liq. in flask.

Heat distn flask ca 1 hr, using small flame and regulating heat so that rapid evolution of H, but no appreciable distn, takes place. Gradually increase heat until distn begins; when active foaming ceases, continue distn with large flame until ca 40 mL liq. remains in distg flask. Lower flame toward end of distn to avoid cracking flask. Remove receiver contg distillate, add enough Me red to make soln red, and titr. excess acid with 0.02*N* NaOH soln. From difference between this excess and amt added, after making correction shown by blank with same amt of reagents distd in same manner, calc. % nitroglycerin in sample. 1 mL 0.02*N* acid = 0.001514 g nitroglycerin.

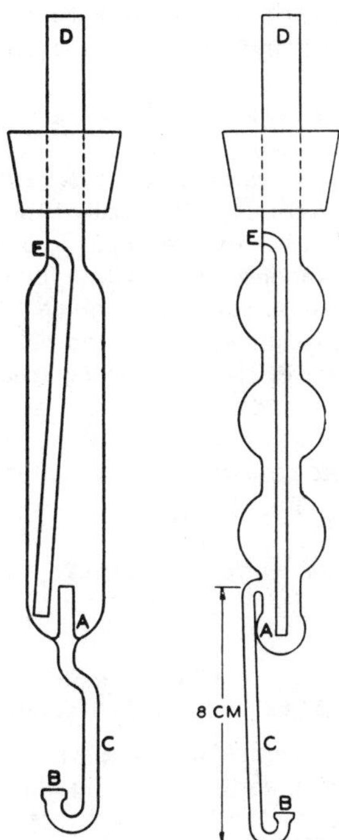

FIG. 39:03—Scrubber trap for ammonia distillation

Infrared Method (36)

39.107 ***Reagent***

Nitroglycerin std.—Absorbate on lactose contg ca 10% nitroglycerin. Stdze by **39.104–39.106**. This product is stable indefinitely in tightly stoppered bottle.

39.108 ***Determination***

(*Caution: See* **51.011**, **51.039**, **51.040**, and **51.048**.)

Transfer number of tablets contg ca 5 mg nitroglycerin to small separator. Dissolve or suspend in 5 mL H_2O, add 20 mL CS_2, shake 1 min, and let sep. Filter CS_2 layer thru pledget of cotton previously washed with CS_2 and collect in 100 mL beaker. Repeat extn with three 10 mL portions CS_2. Evap. combined exts to ca 3 mL, using gentle current of air, at temp. $\leq 50°$. Transfer quant. to 5 mL vol. flask and dil. to vol. with CS_2.

Accurately weigh amt std absorbate contg ca 5 mg nitroglycerin. Transfer to small separator and ext as above.

Det. baseline A_B of sample and std solns relative to CS_2 at 7.89 μm, drawing baseline between min. at 7.5 and 8.3 μm. Calc. nitroglycerin content of sample. Record spectra of sample and std solns from 2 to 15 μm and compare for identity of sample.

Nitrate Esters—Official Final Action

Infrared Method (37)

(Applicable to mannitol hexanitrate, erythritol tetranitrate, or pentaerythritol tetranitrate)

39.109 ***Apparatus***

(**a**) *Recording infrared spectrophotometer.*—With two 1.0 mm liq. absorption cells with NaCl windows, preferably matched or of known *A* difference, and KBr disk holder.

(**b**) *Chromatographic tube.*—25 × 200 mm with 5 × 40 mm stem.

(**c**) *Die and hydraulic press.*—Suitable for prepg KBr disks.

39.110 ***Preparation of Standard Solution***

Ext ester from com. absorbate (usually 10% on lactose or other inert diluent) with ether, filter, and evap. to dryness with aid of air current at temp. $\leq 50°$. Dry in vac. desiccator 1 hr. Prep. std soln contg 0.5 mg ester/mL $CHCl_3$.

Caution: Pure crystalline nitrate esters are very explosive, especially pentaerythritol tetranitrate. Do not use sample contg >5 mg pure compd.

39.111 ***Preparation of Sample***

Reduce tablets to fine powder. Weigh sample contg ca 25 mg nitrate ester and transfer to 125 mL separator with ca 5 mL H_2O. Make distinctly acid with H_2SO_4 (1+9). Proceed as in (**a**) in absence of phenobarbital, or (**b**) in presence of phenobarbital.

(**a**) Add 10 mL $CHCl_3$ to separator, shake vigorously several min, and let sep. Transfer $CHCl_3$ layer to 50 mL vol. flask. Ext aq. soln with three addnl 10 mL portions $CHCl_3$ and transfer each ext to vol. flask. Dil. to vol. with $CHCl_3$, mix, and filter.

(**b**) Add 15 mL $CHCl_3$ to separator, shake vigorously several min, and let sep. Transfer $CHCl_3$ layer to chromatgc column contg 4 mL 1*M* K_3PO_4 soln adsorbed on 5 g diat. earth, **36.002**, collecting eluate in 50 mL vol. flask. Ext. aq. soln with three addnl 10 mL portions $CHCl_3$, and pass each ext thru column, collecting eluate in vol. flask. Dil. to vol. with $CHCl_3$, mix, and filter.

39.112 ***Determination***

(Store $CHCl_3$ to be used in IR measurements in stoppered flask.)

Transfer 5 mL aliquot $CHCl_3$ soln to 25 mL g-s erlenmeyer, evap. to dryness with aid of air current at temp. $\leq 50°$, and complete drying in vac. desiccator. Add 5.00 mL $CHCl_3$ to residue, stopper flask tightly, and let stand 30 min with occasional shaking to ensure complete soln. Det *A* of std and sample solns against $CHCl_3$ at max. (ca 6.0 μm) and calc. amt of ester per tablet.

Evap. another portion $CHCl_3$ soln to dryness as above. Prep. KBr disk by grinding together in agate mortar 1 mg residue with 200 mg IR spectral grade KBr and pressing in die and hydraulic press. Record spectrum from 2 to 15 μm and compare with spectrum of std nitrate ester to det. identity of sample.

Mannitol Hexanitrate; Mannitol Hexanitrate and Phenobarbital (*38*)—Official Final Action

(Ascorbic acid interferes. *See also* **39.109–39.112**.)

39.113 ***Reagents***

(**a**) *Phenoldisulfonic acid.*—Heat 5 g colorless phenol, 30 mL H_2SO_4, and 15 mL fuming H_2SO_4 (ca 20% free SO_3) on steam bath 2 hr. (*Caution: See* **51.030** and **51.031**.)

(**b**) *Nitrate std soln.*—Dissolve 100 mg KNO_3 or $NaNO_3$ in ca 1 mL H_2O and dil. to 100 mL with HOAc.

(**c**) *Phenobarbital std soln.*—In 100 mL vol. flask dissolve 100 mg phenobarbital and dil. to vol. with HOAc. Pipet 5 mL of this soln and 15 mL HOAc into 100 mL vol. flask, dil. to vol. with H_2O, and filter, discarding first 5 mL filtrate.

39.114 ***Preparation of Sample***

Transfer accurately weighed sample contg ca 30 mg mannitol hexanitrate to 50 mL vol. flask, and dil. to vol. with HOAc. Shake well and filter, discarding first 5 mL filtrate.

39.115 ***Determination of Mannitol Hexanitrate***

Transfer 1.0 mL aliquots of sample, std, and HOAc (blank) to individual 100 mL vol. flasks, add 2.0 mL phenoldisulfonic acid to each, and let stand 15 min. Dil. with H_2O to ca 60 mL, add NH_4OH (ca 10 mL) until max. yellow color appears, cool to room temp., dil. to vol. with H_2O, and mix. Det. *A* of sample and std, *A'*, relative to blank at 408 nm.

% Mannitol hexanitrate = $(A \times R_2 \times k \times 50)/(A' \times R_1)$;

where R_1 is mg sample, R_2 is mg std/mL, and *k* is 88.66 for $NaNO_3$ and 74.56 for KNO_3 std.

39.116 ***Determination of Phenobarbital***

Pipet 10 mL aliquot sample soln into 50 mL vol. flask, dil. to vol. with H_2O, shake, and filter, discarding first 5 mL filtrate. Prep. blank by dilg 10.0 mL HOAc to 50 mL with H_2O and filtering. Dil. sep. 20 mL aliquots of std, sample, and blank solns to 100 mL with NH_4OH (1+9), adjusting to room temp. before dilg. to vol. (Final pH of soln, 9.0–9.6.) Det. *A* of sample and std relative to blank at 240 nm, and calc. phenobarbital content.

39.117 **Pentaerythritol Tetranitrate (*39*)**
Official Final Action

(Applicable in presence of meprobamate)

Accurately weigh powd sample contg ca 40 mg pentaerythritol tetranitrate into 50 mL g-s vol. flask. Add ca 30 mL HOAc, shake ca 1 min, and dil. to vol. with HOAc. Filter, discarding first 5 mL filtrate. Proceed as in **39.115**.

% Pentaerythritol tetranitrate = $(A \times R' \times k \times 50)/(A' \times R)$;

where *A* and *A'* refer to sample and std, resp.; *R* and *R'* are mg sample and mg std/mL, resp.; and *k* is 92.99 for $NaNO_3$ or 78.18 for KNO_3 std.

Pentaerythritol Tetranitrate (PETN) and Meprobamate (*40*)—Official Final Action

(*Caution:* PETN may explode when heated strongly, even when dissolved.)

39.118 ***Apparatus***

See **39.109**.

39.119 ***Reagents***

(*Caution: See* **51.011**, **51.040**, and **51.056**.)

(**a**) *Dilute phosphoric acid.*—3 + 1. Dil. 3 vols 85% H_3PO_4 with 1 vol. H_2O.

(**b**) *Water-washed benzene.*—Shake equal vols benzene and H_2O 1 min in separator. Discard lower phase. Use within 2 days of prepn.

(**c**) *Water-washed chloroform.*—Shake equal vols. $CHCl_3$ and H_2O 1 min in separator. Discard upper layer. Use within 2 days of prepn.

(**d**) *Anhydrous chloroform.*—Filter H_2O-washed $CHCl_3$ thru anhyd. Na_2SO_4.

(**e**) *Pentaerythritol tetranitrate (PETN) std soln.*—10 mg/50 mL. Ext PETN from com. PETN (usually 10% on lactose or other inert diluent) with $CHCl_3$ to give ca 20 mg pure PETN. Filter and evap. to dryness under air current with little or no heat. Dry in vac. desiccator 2 hr. Accurately weigh ca 10 mg, using microbalance, dissolve in anhyd. $CHCl_3$, and dil. to 50 mL with this solv. Destroy excess PETN by dissolving in acetone and burning in large vessel behind safety barrier, using effective fume removal device.

(**f**) *Meprobamate std soln.*—80 mg/100 mL. Dissolve 80 mg USP Meprobamate Ref. Std in anhyd. $CHCl_3$ and dil. to 100 mL with this solv.

(**g**) *Diatomaceous earth.*—*See* **36.002**.

39.120 ***Determination***

(Use H_2O-washed solvs unless designated anhyd. *Caution: See* **51.011**, **51.039**, **51.040**, **51.045**, and **51.056**.)

Loosely pack small amt of fine glass wool in base of chromatgc tube to support diat. earth. Weigh 3 g diat. earth into 100 mL beaker, add 2.0 mL 1*N* NaOH, mix with metal spatula until fluffy, and pack uniformly in tube. Weigh 5 g diat. earth into 250 mL beaker, add 7.0 mL dil. H_3PO_4, mix until fluffy, and pack uniformly on column. (Do not pack too tightly as column will elute too slowly.) Accurately weigh portion powd sample contg ca 10 mg PETN into 150 mL beaker. Add 4 mL benzene and heat gently with swirling ca 1 min. Cool, add 4 g diat. earth, mix until fluffy, transfer quant. to column, and pack uniformly. Dry-wash beaker with 1 g diat. earth and 0.5 mL benzene, transfer to column, and pack uniformly. Wipe sample beaker and all app. used in column prepn with glass wool, and pack on column.

Pass 75 mL benzene thru column and collect eluate in 150 mL beaker until elution ceases. Rinse column tip with small portions benzene into beaker and set aside. This fraction contains PETN.

Place 250 mL beaker under column. Add 4.0 mL H_2O to column and let it be absorbed. Pass 150 mL $CHCl_3$ thru column and collect eluate in 250 mL beaker. Rinse column tip with $CHCl_3$ into beaker. This fraction contains meprobamate.

Evap. each fraction on steam bath under gentle air current to ca 10 mL and take to dryness with little or no heat from steam bath. Place beakers in vac. oven 30 min at 30° and $\leq$380 mm (15") Hg. Remove from oven. Add ca 10 mL anhyd. $CHCl_3$ to PETN beaker and heat gently to dissolve residue. Quant. transfer with anhyd. $CHCl_3$ to 50 mL vol. flask and dil. to vol. with anhyd. $CHCl_3$.

Dissolve meprobamate residue with ca 20–25 mL anhyd. $CHCl_3$. If theoretical wt of meprobamate in sample wt taken is 100 mg, transfer quant. to 100 mL vol. flask with anhyd. $CHCl_3$ and dil. to vol. with this solv. If theoretical wt of meprobamate is ca 200 mg, use 250 mL vol. flask and proceed as above.

Scan sample and std solns in 1.0 mm cells from 5.0 to 6.5 μm (2000–1540 cm^{-1}) on IR spectrophtr against anhyd. $CHCl_3$ as ref.

Calc. PETN by subtracting A at 5.5 μm (1818 cm^{-1}) from A at ca 6.02 μm (1660 cm^{-1}) and compare with std A. (*Note:* PETN sample solns may contain very small peak at ca 5.8 μm (1722 cm^{-1}). This is contaminant of meprobamate and does not interfere with PETN detn. Also, a peak may appear at ca 6.25 μm (1600 cm^{-1}). This is H_2O peak. Disregard this peak in calcg PETN net A.)

Calc. meprobamate by subtracting A at 5.5 μm (1818 cm^{-1}) from A at ca 5.82 μm (1718 cm^{-1}) and compare with std A.

39.121 ***Identification***

(**a**) *PETN.*—Prep. both std and sample KBr disks from respective assay solns. Evap. 4–5 mL of each soln in small mortar, add 200 mg KBr, mix thoroly, and press. Scan spectrum from 2 to 15 μm (5000–667 cm^{-1}). Compare sample and std curves. (*Note:* Sample IR curve may deviate from std curve. This deviation is caused by meprobamate contaminant. However, all major peaks in std and sample should be evident.)

(**b**) *Meprobamate.*—Prepare KBr disks as above from 1 mL sample and std assay solns. Scan and compare as in (**a**).

Menadione Sodium Bisulfite (*41*)—Official Final Action

(Applicable to injections)

39.122 ***Principle***

Aq. menadione.$NaHSO_3$ soln is mixed with diat. earth and placed in chromatgc column over lower layer of HCl-diat. earth. Excipients are eluted with $CHCl_3$ and menadione with NH_3-$CHCl_3$. Excess NH_3 which could decompose menadione is neutzd by acidic lower layer. Menadione is detd by UV spectrophotometry.

39.123 ***Reagents***

(**a**) *Chloroform.*—Use H_2O-washed $CHCl_3$ thruout.

(**b**) *Ammoniacal chloroform.*—Mix 1 part NH_4OH with 25 parts $CHCl_3$ as needed.

(**c**) *Menadione std soln.*—50 μg/mL. Dissolve 50 mg USP Menadione Ref. Std in $CHCl_3$ and dil. to 100 mL with $CHCl_3$. Dil. 10 mL aliquot to 100 mL with $CHCl_3$.

39.124 ***Determination***

Mix 1 mL HCl (1+3) with 1.5 g diat. earth, **36.002**, and pack into chromatgc tube, **37.002**. Dil. aq. sample soln to contain ca 5 mg menadione.$NaHSO_3.3H_2O$/mL, mix 2.0 mL this soln with 3 g diat. earth in beaker, and pack into tube. Dry-wash beaker with 1 g diat. earth, add to tube, tamp until compressed, and overlay with piece of glass wool used to wipe beaker.

Wash column with 100 mL $CHCl_3$ and discard $CHCl_3$. Wash tip of column with few mL $CHCl_3$. With 100 mL vol. flask as receiver, add 5 mL NH_4OH-$CHCl_3$, let sink into diat. earth, and elute menadione with 90 mL $CHCl_3$. Rinse tip of column with $CHCl_3$ and dil. to vol. with $CHCl_3$. Scan soln and std soln from 280 to 400 nm against $CHCl_3$ and det. A at max., ca 334 nm.

$$\text{mg Menadione.NaHSO}_3.3\text{H}_2\text{O/mL dild assay soln} = 0.05 \times 1.918 \times C \times (A/A');$$

where 1.918 is factor to convert menadione to menadione .$NaHSO_3.3H_2O$; C = μg menadione/mL std soln; and A and A' refer to sample and std solns, resp.

Meprobamate (*42*)—Official Final Action

39.125 ***Apparatus***

(**a**) *Spectrophotometer.*—Recording IR spectrophtr, effective over 0.75–3.5 μm range, with 1 cm matching near-IR silica cells. Peak at ca 2.91 μm for meprobamate must be resolved.

(**b**) *Chromatographic tubes.*—Glass, 20 × 300 mm.

39.126 ***Reagents***

(**a**) *Alcohol-free chloroform.*—Thruout detn use only $CHCl_3$ prepd daily as follows: Ext alcohol by passing $CHCl_3$ successively thru three 500 mL separators, each contg 50–75 mL H_2O. Pack 2 chromatgc tubes half-full with alumina (80–200 mesh, Fisher No. A-540, or equiv.) activated by heating 2 hr at 300°. Mount one column above other and pass $CHCl_3$ thru both columns. Pass $\leq$500 mL $CHCl_3$ at one time. If more $CHCl_3$ is needed, repeat purification with fresh alumina.

(**b**) *Meprobamate std soln.*—0.5 mg/mL. Accurately weigh ca 25 mg USP Meprobamate Ref. Std and transfer to 50 mL vol. flask. Dissolve in and dil. to vol. with $CHCl_3$. Absorptivity should be ca 1.0 if 2.91 μm peak is properly resolved.

39.127 ***Preparation of Sample***

Finely pulverize tablets, accurately weigh portion contg ca 50 mg meprobamate, and transfer to dry 100 mL vol. flask. Add 50 mL $CHCl_3$, shake 15–20 min, and dil. to vol. with $CHCl_3$. Filter soln thru dry Whatman No. 1 paper, or equiv. Discard first 20–25 mL and collect remainder in dry g-s erlenmeyer.

39.128 ***Determination***

Zero instrument at 2.914 μm with $CHCl_3$ in both cells. Scan sample and std solns against $CHCl_3$ between 3.000 and 2.790 μm. Measure baseline A values at max., ca 2.91 μm, from straight line drawn between minima at ca 2.980 and 2.875.

$$\text{mg Meprobamate/tablet} = A_{sample} \times (C/A_{std}) \times 100 \times (T/W);$$

where A refers to baseline values; C = mg meprobamate/mL std soln; T and W = av. wt/tablet and sample wt, resp., in mg.

39.129 Meprobamate and Pentaerythritol Tetranitrate

See **39.118–39.121**.

Dichlorophene (*43*)—Official Final Action

39.130 ***Principle***

Dichlorophene is extd from acid soln with $CHCl_3$ and detd by measuring *A* in alc. NaOH soln at 305 nm.

39.131 ***Reagent***

Dichlorophene std solns.—(*1*) *Stock soln.*—600 μg/mL. Dissolve 60 mg dichlorophene (ICN–K&K Laboratories, Inc.) in alcohol and dil. to 100 mL. (*2*) *Working soln.*—15 μg/mL. Dil. 5.0 mL stock soln to 200 mL with 0.1*N* NaOH. Prep. fresh daily.

39.132 ***Preparation of Sample***

(**a**) *Soft gelatin capsules.*—Select representative number (5–20) of capsules. Treat each capsule, one at a time, as follows: Using sharp scalpel, cut capsule lengthwise and transfer to funnel placed in neck of 500 mL vol. flask. Thoroly rinse capsule contents, scalpel, and funnel with alcohol. Remove funnel and carefully transfer opened capsule to vol. flask. Dil. to vol. with alcohol and mix. Prep. soln contg ca 0.3 mg dichlorophene/mL by stepwise diln with alcohol.

(**b**) *Suspension.*—Mix thoroly. Using 10 mL "to contain" pipet with wide orifice (Duopette pipet, Scientific Products, Inc., No. P4615-1X, or equiv.), withdraw suspension to TC mark. Drain pipet into 250 mL vol. flask, using pressure applied from rubber bulb. Thoroly rinse pipet into flask with alcohol, dil. to vol., and mix. Prep. soln contg ca 0.3 mg dichlorophene/mL by stepwise diln with alcohol.

39.133 ***Determination***

Transfer 10 mL aliquot prepd sample soln to 125 mL separator contg 10 mL H_2O. Add 3 mL 1*N* NaOH, mix well, and ext with 10 mL *n*-hexane. Let sep. and transfer lower aq. layer to second separator. Ext with another 10 mL portion *n*-hexane. Transfer aq. layer to third separator. Combine *n*-hexane exts in first separator and ext with 10 mL 50% alcohol. Discard hexane. Add alc. wash to aq. layer in third separator. Add 7 mL 1*N* HCl and mix well. (Soln should be distinctly acid to litmus paper.) Ext acid soln with four 25 mL portions $CHCl_3$. Filter each ext thru $CHCl_3$-washed cotton into 250 mL beaker. Rinse funnel and cotton with ca 5 mL $CHCl_3$ and carefully evap. *just* to dryness on steam bath, using gentle air jet. Let beaker and contents cool. Dissolve residue of dichlorophene in 5.0 mL alcohol and transfer to 200 mL vol. flask, using 0.1*N* NaOH. Dil. to vol. with 0.1*N* NaOH and mix.

Record spectra of sample and std solns from 370 to 225 nm, using 1 cm cells and 5 mL alcohol dild to 200 mL with 0.1*N* NaOH as ref.

Det. *A* of std and sample solns at peak wavelength ca 305 nm and calc. dichlorophene content of sample.

39.134 ***Identification***

Dil. aliquots of sample assay soln, working std soln, and ref. soln with equal vols 0.1*N* NaOH. Obtain *A* between 370 and 225 nm.

Spectra should be similar and exhibit maxima at 245 and 305 nm. Ratio (A_{245}/A_{305}) of sample does not differ appreciably from that of std.

Methenamine (Hexamethylenetetramine) in Tablets (*44*)—Official Final Action

39.135 ***Reagent***

Modified Nessler reagent.—(*1*) Dissolve 10 g $HgCl_2$, 30 g KI, and 5 g acacia in 200 mL H_2O, and filter thru cotton; (*2*) dissolve 15 g NaOH in 100 mL H_2O. Mix 20 mL soln (*1*) with 10 mL soln (*2*).

39.136 ***Determination***

Weigh 0.5 g powder, prepd as in **36.003**, into r-b flask, and add 100 mL H_2O and 25 mL HCl (1+2.5). Connect with reflux condenser (preferably of worm type) and boil gently 15 min. Cool, wash condenser tube with little H_2O, transfer contents of flask to 250 mL vol. flask, and dil. to vol.

Chill 30 mL Nessler reagent and add 10 mL aliquot of hydrolyzed sample soln. Wash neck of container with jet of H_2O and let stand $\geq$1 min. Add 10 mL HOAc (1+1.5) so that inside of neck is completely washed by reagent, mix quickly and thoroly by rotating and tilting flask, and immediately add 20 mL 0.1*N* I from buret or pipet. Titr. excess I with 0.1*N* $Na_2S_2O_3$, adding 5–10 drops starch indicator, **6.005(f)**, toward end of titrn, until blue disappears. Final color of soln is pale straw-green. If preferred, end point may be detd by reappearance of faint blue when drop of the I soln is added. 1 mL 0.1*N* I = 0.00117 g methenamine.

Methenamine and Methenamine Mandelate Automated Method (*45*)—Official Final Action

39.137 ***Principle***

Methenamine is hydrolyzed to HCHO and NH_4^+ in acid soln. Free HCHO condenses with chromotropic acid in strong acid soln to form colorless hydroxydiphenylmethane derivative which is further oxidized to colored *p*-quinoidal compd with max. *A* at 570 nm. Method is applicable to methenamine, methenamine mandelate, and methenamine with NaH_2PO_4.

39.138 ***Reagents and Apparatus***

(Use deionized H_2O or equiv. thruout.)

(**a**) *Dilute ammonia.*—Dil. 5 mL NH_4OH to 1 L with H_2O.

(**b**) *Dilute sulfuric acid.*—72%. Slowly add H_2SO_4 to 600 mL H_2O to total vol. of 1.5 L (when cool).

(**c**) *Chromotropic acid* (*CTA*) *color reagent.*—Suspend 500 mg CTA, di-Na salt (ICN–K&K Laboratories, Inc., Eastman Kodak Co., or equiv.), in 20 mL H_2O and *slowly* add 30 mL H_2SO_4 in small portions (overheating produces deep violet color and inactivates reagent). Cool, and mix into 1.5 L 72% H_2SO_4.

(**d**) *Methenamine std soln.*—Dissolve enough methenamine, previously dried over P_2O_5 and stdzd (USP), in dil. NH_4OH to give concn of std appropriate for dosage level analyzed (Table **39:01**).

(**e**) *Automatic analyzer.*—AutoAnalyzer with following modules (Technicon Instruments Corp.): Sampler II with 20/hr (2:1) cam; proportioning pump I; heating bath set at 90° with two 40′ coils, 1.6 mm id; colorimeter with 15 mm tubular flowcell and matched 570 nm filters; recorder with semilog paper; manifold (Fig. **39:04**). Wire down all tube connections carrying H_2SO_4.

Table 39:01 Sample Pump Tube Sizes and Methenamine Std Concns for Various Tablet Dosage Levels

Product	Dosage, mg/ tablet	Pump Tube Size, mL/min	Std, mg/100 mL
Methenamine mandelate	250	1.00	2.50
Methenamine mandelate	500	0.60	5.00
Methenamine	300, 325	0.60	6.00, 6.50
Methenamine	500	0.23	5.00
Methenamine mandelate	1000	0.23	10.00

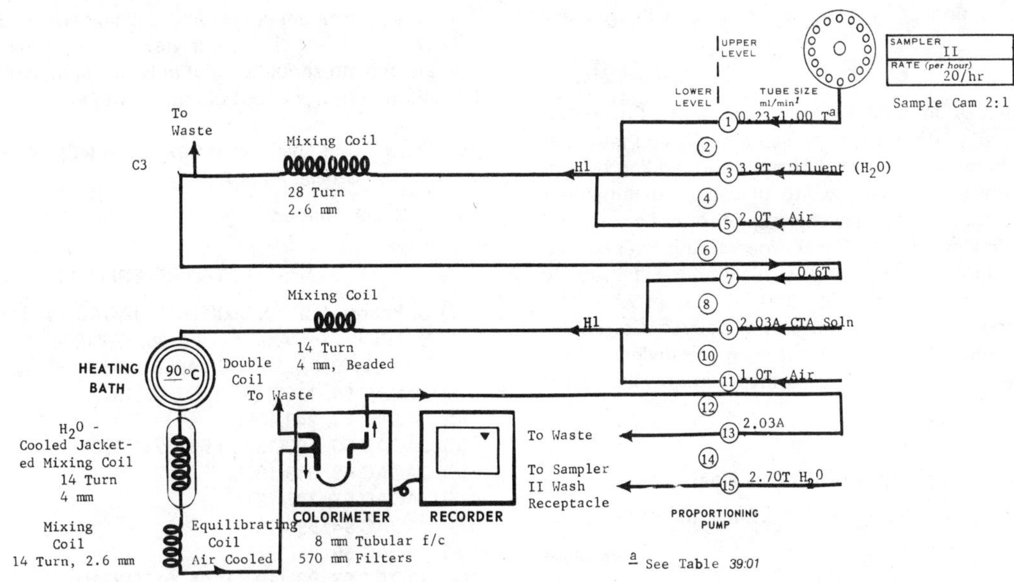

FIG. 39:04—Flow diagram for automated analysis of methenamine and methenamine mandelate

39.139 ***Preparation of Sample***

Disintegrate uncoated tablets contg equiv. of 250–500 mg methenamine by intermittent shaking in 100 mL dil. NH_4OH. Crush coated tablets and hard uncoated tablets before addn of solv. Ultrasonic bath may be used to hasten soln. Dil. 1.0 mL sample soln to 50 mL with dil. NH_4OH.

Samples of all dosage levels can be prepd in 125 mL (4 oz) glass, snap-cap vials provided with Parafilm seal if appropriate sampling pump tube is used (*see* Table **39:01**). A 1+50 diln may be accomplished with 1.00 mL Thomas-Seligson vac. diln pipet mounted beneath automatic 50.0 mL delivery pipet. Est. increase in vol. resulting from dissolving 1 tablet in 100 mL solv., using vol. flask and graduated pipet.

39.140 ***Analytical System***

See Fig. **39:04** and Table **39:01**. Sample solns are withdrawn from sample cups, segmented with air, and dild in manifold with H_2O. CTA soln is added and stream is passed thru beaded coil into 90° heating bath for color development. Stream is cooled in H_2O-jacketed coil and equilibrated at room temp. in mixing coil. Stream is debubbled and passed into colorimeter equipped with 570 nm filters and 15 mm tubular flowcell for *A* measurement. Inlet and outlet tubing of flowcell should be ca same id.

39.141 ***Start-Up and Shut-Down Operations***

Turn on heating bath (3 hr), cooling H_2O in jacketed coil (30 min), and colorimeter (30 min) in advance. Prewash system 5 min with H_2O and then pump all reagents thru their resp. lines. Let equilibrate 20–30 min and adjust colorimeter and recorder to produce steady baseline. To shut down system, flush 10–15 min with H_2O and pump all lines dry.

39.142 ***Determination***

Fill 8.5 mL sample cups with prepd solns and aspirate thru 0.034″ stainless steel probe at 20/hr with sample-to-wash ratio of 2:1. Include 1 std soln between each 5 sample solns, and insert 3 std solns at beginning and end of each 10–30 samples. Draw line between baseline at beginning and end of run. Subtract av. baseline *A* from max. *A* to obtain net *A* (ΔA) for each peak. Calc. av. $\Delta A'$ for std solns, disregarding first and last 2 std peaks.

$$\text{mg Methenamine/unit dose} = (\Delta A/\Delta A') \times C \times D,$$

where C = mg methenamine/mL std soln and D = diln factor.

Methylene Blue (Methylthionine Chloride) (*46*)
Official Final Action

39.143 ***Preparation of Solution***

(**a**) *Foreign material absent.*—Into 50 mL beaker weigh 0.1–0.14 g powd sample, **36.003**, and transfer to 200 mL vol. flask with 100–140 mL H_2O. Dissolve completely by heating 30 min on steam bath with frequent shaking.

(**b**) *Oils or water-insoluble material present.*—(*Caution: See* **51.040** and **51.049**.) To 50 mL beaker transfer weighed amt of prepd sample, **36.003**, contg 0.1–0.14 g methylene blue. Add 15 mL CCl_4, warm on steam bath few min, and stir with glass rod to dissolve oils. Transfer to 100 mL separator, using ca 50 mL hot H_2O and little CCl_4, if necessary. Cool, shake, and let sep. Transfer CCl_4 with undissolved material to second separator for further treatment. (Clear aq. soln of dye should now remain in first separator. If not clear, ext with another 15 mL portion CCl_4, transferring any remaining insol. material in similar manner to second separator.) Add ca 10 mL CCl_4 to second separator and remove methylene blue by shaking vigorously with 20–40 mL portions H_2O until practically no more dye is extd. (Few drops of HOAc hasten this extn.) To aq. exts in 400 mL beaker, add main soln from first separator, cover with inverted watch glass on glass rods, and evap. to ca 50 mL. Proceed as in (**c**). CCl_4 soln may be reserved for qual. tests for oils.

(**c**) *Water-soluble material present.*—Either use aq. soln from (**b**), or weigh portion of sample contg 0.1–0.14 g methylene blue into 150 mL beaker, add ca 50 mL H_2O, and heat 30 min on steam bath with occasional shaking. Transfer to 100 mL separator, keeping vol. as small as possible. Ext with *α-dichlorohydrin,* using 10, 5, 3, and 2 mL portions. Combine dichlorohydrin exts in 200–300 mL separator, add 3 or 4 times their vol. CCl_4, and ext dye with H_2O by repeated vigorous shaking with 30–50 mL portions. (Few drops of HOAc hasten removal.) From combined aq. exts, remove any traces of dichlorohydrin by shaking once with ca 15 mL CCl_4 and draining after settling 5–10 min. Evap. aq. exts to ca 50 mL over flame, covering beaker as in (**b**) with inverted watch glass. Transfer to 200 mL vol. flask. Dissolve completely by heating 30 min on steam bath with frequent shaking.

39.144 ***Determination***

Conduct blank as in detn, including filtration. Cool soln, **39.143(a)** or (**c**), add 50 mL HOAc, shake thoroly, and let stand ≥25 min. Add 30 mL 0.2*N* I, **50.018**, from buret, adding first 10 mL by fast drops with const rotating of flask and remaining 20 mL at full speed, and continue shaking. Stopper flask and let stand 50 min, shaking thoroly 5 or 6 times during interval. Dil. to vol. with H_2O, shake, and let stand 10 min longer. Filter rapidly thru dry, folded, 12 cm paper. Titr. 100 mL aliquot with 0.1*N* $Na_2S_2O_3$, with or without starch indicator as desired. Correct for blank titrn. 1 mL 0.2*N* I = 0.01496 g methylene blue, $C_{16}H_{18}N_3ClS.3H_2O$; or 0.01279 g anhyd. methylene blue, $C_{16}H_{18}N_3ClS$.

Sodium Fluorescein (*47*)—Official Final Action

(Applicable to solns. *Caution: See* **51.008** and **51.016**.)

39.145 ***Apparatus***

(**a**) *Fluorometric apparatus.*—Spectrophotofluorometer or fluorocolorimeter. With cell path ≥1 cm, excitation wavelength 460 nm, emission wavelength 515 nm, and sensitivity to yield ≥85% *T* for most concd std soln. Warm lamp ≥20 min before making measurements.

(**b**) *Thin layer sheets.*—Silica gel (100 μm) with fluorescent indicator (Eastman Kodak Co. Chromagram sheets for TLC, No. 6060, or equiv.).

39.146 ***Reagents***

(**a**) *Acriflavine hydrochloride soln.*—Dissolve 5 mg salt (J. T. Baker Chemical Co., or equiv.) in 0.5 mL H_2O and dil. to 5 mL with alcohol.

(**b**) *Fluorescein diacetate.*—Mp 206–208° (Eastman Kodak Co. No. 1688, or equiv.). If material is impure, indicated by low mp or other evidence, recrystallize from alcohol.

(**c**) *Sodium fluorescein std solns.*—(*1*) *Stock soln.*—903.6 μg Na fluorescein/mL. Accurately weigh 100 mg fluorescein diacetate (equiv. to 90.36 mg Na fluorescein), dried 1 hr at 100°, and transfer to 100 mL vol. flask with ca 10 mL alcohol. Add 2 mL 10% NaOH and heat on steam bath at ca boiling temp. 20 min. Swirl frequently. After hydrolysis, cool flask, dil. to vol. with H_2O, and mix. (*2*) *Intermediate soln.*—0.9036 μg Na fluorescein/mL. Dil. 1 mL clear stock soln to 1 L with H_2O and mix. (*3*) *Working solns.*—0.000, 0.009, 0.018, 0.027, 0.036, and 0.045 μg Na fluorescein/mL. Transfer 0.0, 1.0, 2.0, 3.0, 4.0, and 5.0 mL intermediate soln to sep. 100 mL vol. flasks, add 20 mL pH 9 buffer to each, and dil. to vol. with H_2O.

(**d**) *Boric acid buffer.*—pH 9. Prep. ca 200 mL soln 0.05*M* in boric acid and 0.05*M* in KCl. Adjust to pH 9 with 0.2*M* NaOH.

39.147 ***Preparation of Sample***

Quant. dil. sample with H_2O to obtain ca 1 μg Na fluorescein/mL and transfer 3.0 mL aliquot to 100 mL vol. flask contg 20 mL pH 9 buffer. Dil. to vol. with H_2O and mix.

39.148 ***Determination***

Measure fluorescent intensity (*I*) of all working std solns and plot std curve (μg Na fluorescein against *I*). Det. *I* of sample soln and calc. concn of sample.

39.149 ***Purity and Identification***

Dil. concd sample and hydrolyzed stock solns with alcohol to contain ca 1 mg Na fluorescein/mL.

Spot 10 μL each of above solns and acriflavine.HCl soln on fluorescent silica gel sheets and develop with *n*-BuOH-alcohol-H_2O (2+1+1). Dry sheet and view under longwave UV light. Sample and std should exhibit only one spot, which has similar but different R_f from spot obtained with acriflavine.HCl.

39.150 ★ **Cod Liver Oil in Emulsions (*48*)** ★
Official Final Action

See **32.299**, 10th ed.

SELECTED REFERENCES

(*1*) J. Pharm. Sci. **50**, 550(1961); JAOAC **44**, 317(1961).
(*2*) J. Am. Pharm. Ass., Sci. Ed. **35**, 176(1946); **39**, 37, 544(1950); **42**, 167(1953); JAOAC **34**, 581(1951); **37**, 702(1954).
(*3*) JAOAC **54**, 1192(1971); **56**, 86(1973).
(*4*) JAOAC **43**, 248(1960).
(*5*) JAOAC **55**, 190(1972); **56**, 674(1973).
(*6*) JAOAC **48**, 613(1965).
(*7*) JAOAC **57**, 747(1974).
(*8*) JAOAC **54**, 590(1971).
(*9*) JAOAC **58**, 75(1975).
(*10*) JAOAC **53**, 831(1970); **54**, 617(1971).
(*11*) JAOAC **60**, 922(1977).
(*12*) JAOAC **46**, 646(1963).
(*13*) JAOAC **57**, 731(1974).
(*14*) JAOAC **60**, 27(1977).
(*15*) J. Am. Pharm. Ass., Sci. Ed. **43**, 580(1954); JAOAC **41**, 487(1958).
(*16*) JAOAC **58**, 70(1975).
(*17*) JAOAC **42**, 453(1959).
(*18*) JAOAC **9**, 52, 288(1926).
(*19*) JAOAC **28**, 719(1945); **31**, 535(1948).
(*20*) JAOAC **55**, 610(1972).
(*21*) JAOAC **5**, 587(1922).
(*22*) JAOAC **12**, 300(1929); **14**, 337(1931).
(*23*) JAOAC **15**, 407(1932).
(*24*) JAOAC **16**, 375(1933); **18**, 555(1935).
(*25*) JAOAC **14**, 341(1931).
(*26*) JAOAC **14**, 321(1931).
(*27*) J. Pharm. Chim. 8th ser. **16**, 49(1932); JAOAC **18**, 526(1935).
(*28*) JAOAC **45**, 593(1962).
(*29*) JAOAC **48**, 592(1965).
(*30*) Quart. J. Pharmacol. **5**, 369(1932); JAOAC **18**, 526(1935); **19**, 517(1936).
(*31*) JAOAC **35**, 566(1952); **36**, 85, 699(1953).
(*32*) JAOAC **20**, 588(1937); **22**, 726(1939).
(*33*) JAOAC **15**, 448(1932); **16**, 375(1933).
(*34*) USDA Bur. Chem. Circ. **94**, p. 4; J. Ind. Eng. Chem. **4**, 374(1912); JAOAC **2**, 74(1916).
(*35*) JAOAC **9**, 316(1926); **10**, 376(1927); **15**, 140(1932); **20**, 569(1937); **21**, 541(1938).
(*36*) JAOAC **41**, 504(1958).
(*37*) JAOAC **43**, 259(1960).
(*38*) JAOAC **41**, 493(1958).
(*39*) JAOAC **47**, 469(1964).
(*40*) JAOAC **53**, 594(1970).
(*41*) JAOAC **54**, 593(1971).
(*42*) JAOAC **51**, 616(1968).
(*43*) JAOAC **55**, 163(1972).
(*44*) JAOAC **3**, 374(1920).
(*45*) JAOAC **56**, 647, 1295(1973).
(*46*) JAOAC **7**, 20(1923).
(*47*) JAOAC **52**, 110(1969).
(*48*) JAOAC **22**, 739(1939).

★ Surplus method—*see* inside front cover.

40. Drugs: Illicit

40.001 Microchemical Tests—Official Final Action

See **36.095–36.108** (Diacetylmorphine (heroin), diacetylmorphine.HCl, lysergic acid diethylamide tartrate, 4-methyl-2,5-dimethoxyamphetamine.HCl (STP.HCl, DOM), and psilocybin).

Cocaine Hydrochloride

Gas Chromatographic Method (1)—Official First Action

40.002 ***Principle***

Cocaine is extd from weakly basic, aq. soln with $CHCl_3$ contg internal std, and then sepd by GLC from other amines, org.-sol. neutrals, and internal std.

40.003 ***Apparatus and Reagents***

(**a**) *Gas chromatograph.*—With H flame detector and 1.8 m (6′) × 4 (id) mm glass column packed with 3% OV-1 on 100–120 mesh Chromosorb W(HP) (Applied Science Laboratories, Inc.). Typical operating conditions: temps (°): column 225, detector and injector 240; N carrier gas flow rate, 60 mL/min. Adjust column temp. to elute cocaine in 3±0.5 min. Adjust H and air flow rates and electrometer sensitivity so that 4 μL cocaine std soln gives 40–60% full scale deflection. Retention time of cocaine relative to internal std is ca 0.65.

(**b**) *Dibasic potassium phosphate.*—10%. Dissolve 5 g K_2HPO_4 in 50 mL H_2O, and mix well.

(**c**) *Dilute hydrochloric acid.*—0.1*N*. Dil. 7.0 mL HCl to 1 L with H_2O, and mix well.

(**d**) *Internal std soln.*—0.8 mg/mL. Dissolve 80 mg tetracosane in 100 mL $CHCl_3$, and mix well.

(**e**) *Cocaine hydrochloride std soln.*—1 mg/mL. Accurately weigh ca 10 mg cocaine.HCl into 10 mL vol. flask, and dil. to vol. with internal std soln. Prep. fresh every 3 months. Store in refrigerator.

40.004 ***Preparation of GLC Column***

Plug column exit with silanized glass wool. Apply vac. to exit end, and slowly add packing material thru column inlet while gently tapping column. Fill to within 1 cm of column inlet, and plug with silanized glass wool. Condition column overnight at 260° with slow stream of N. Sat. column with cocaine by making successive 4 μL injections of cocaine std soln until cocaine: internal std ratio differs by <3% from preceding std injection.

40.005 ***Determination***

Accurately weigh ca 250 mg finely ground sample and dil. quant. with 0.1*N* HCl to estd cocaine.HCl concn of 1 mg/mL. Mix well and let any insol. material settle. Pipet 2 mL sample prepn, 2 mL internal std soln, and 1 mL 10% K_2HPO_4 into test tube; stopper, and shake vigorously. Let layers sep. Pipet 2 mL cocaine std soln, 2 mL 0.1*N* HCl, and 1 mL 10% K_2HPO_4 soln into another test tube, stopper, and shake vigorously. Let layers sep. Inject 4 μL $CHCl_3$ (bottom) layer of sample and std solns, each in duplicate, using 10 μL syringe.

$$\% \text{ Cocaine.HCl} = (P/P') \times (B'/B) \times (C/W) \times D \times 100,$$

where P and P' = av. areas or peak hts of sample and std cocaine.HCl, resp.; B and B' = av. areas or peak hts of internal std in sample and std, resp.; C = mg cocaine.HCl/mL in std soln; W = mg sample; and D = diln factor for sample.

$$\text{mg Cocaine.HCl/tablet} = \% \text{ cocaine.HCl} \times \text{av. tablet wt in mg}/100$$

40.006 ★ Diacetylmorphine (Heroin) in Tablets (*2*) ★ Official Final Action

Extn and titrn. *See* **36.022**, 11th ed.

40.007 ★ Diacetylmorphine and Quinine (*3*) ★ Official Final Action

UV spectrophtric detn in NaOH-MeOH soln. *See* **40.003–40.005**, 12th ed.

★ Lysergic Acid Diethylamide (LSD) (*4*) ★ Official First Action

(*Caution:* LSD is strong psychotomimetic agent. Use rubber gloves and effective fume removal device to avoid skin contact and breathing dusts of materials suspected or known to contain LSD.)

40.008 ***Reagents and Apparatus***

(**a**) *Indicator paper.*—Sat. filter paper (Whatman No. 1, or equiv.) with 2% *p*-dimethylaminobenzaldehyde in alcohol, air dry, and cut into strips 4–5 cm wide. Store in tightly capped amber glass bottles.

(**b**) *Chromatographic paper saturated with immobile solvent.*—Sat. 8 × 8″ (20 × 20 cm) Whatman No. 1 chromatgc paper with MeOH soln of 25% formamide (stabilized reagent grade or recently distd) and 1% benzoic acid. Place wet paper between 2 Whatman No. 1 sheets and remove excess solv. by blotting lightly; then suspend paper from glass rod ca 15 min to let MeOH evap. (paper remains slightly moist with formamide).

(**c**) *Chromatographic mobile solvent.*—Sat. ether with formamide by shaking in separator. Let reagents sep. and discard lower formamide layer.

(**d**) *Reference stds.*—LSD tartrate (USP authentic substance *d*-lysergic acid diethylamide tartrate) and USP Ergonovine Maleate Ref. Std.

(**e**) *Spectrophotometer.*—Preferably capable of recording spectrum continuously from 400 to ca 200 nm.

40.009 ***Presumptive Test***

Ext LSD (ca 40 μg) from ground powder with enough MeOH to provide ca 5 drops liq. ext. Decant clear liq. into beaker. Transfer 1 or 2 drops liq. (contg ca 5–10 μg LSD) to prepd indicator paper with eye dropper and let MeOH evap. Add 1 drop HCl and let paper stand, supported so that HCl does not touch any surface. If LSD is present, violet-red or violet-blue spot develops and slowly diffuses to edge of ring to form colored ring. Compare test with MeOH blank and LSD ref. soln in MeOH.

Test can detect 1 μg LSD. Larger amt LSD gives faster reaction and more pronounced, more stable color ring.

★ Surplus method—*see* inside front cover.

40.010 ***Paper Chromatography***

(Spot solns from (**a**) and (**b**) and chromatograph simultaneously on same chromatgc paper.)

Arrange chromatgc chamber for ascending chromatgy. To mobile solv. trough in chamber, add enough mobile solv. to develop chromatogram and equilibrate chamber with solv. vapor. Cover chamber and let equilibrate ca 15 min.

(**a**) *Paper chromatography of LSD.*—Prep. sample soln by extg ca 60 μg LSD from ground sample with 5 mL MeOH and filtering. Evap. ca ½ filtrate to dryness in 10–15 mL centrf. tube by warming on steam bath under gentle air stream. Wash sides of tube with 10 μL MeOH. Sep. spot 3 μL (10 μg LSD) concd sample soln and equiv. (10 μg) LSD ref. std MeOH soln on prepd chromatgc paper. Apply soln in portions (ca 0.5 μL) and let dry before reapplication; spot size should be <10 mm diam. Altho method is applicable to as much as 100 μg LSD, vol. ext spotted must be minimal.

After spotting is complete and spot is dry, apply enough immobile solv. (ca 5–10 μL) to cover spot. Spotting removes immobile solv.; it must be replenished to prevent streaking. Check adequacy of sample spot by comparing intensity of fluorescence with that of std under UV light. If sample spot fluoresces weakly, indicating insufficient LSD, overspot more sample ext from centrf. tube as above.

Place spotted paper in equilibrated chromatgc chamber and seal with tape. Develop chromatogram until mobile solv. reaches within ca 5 cm of top of paper (ca 0.5 hr). Withdraw paper and let air dry. Observe under UV light (long and short wavelength).

(**b**) *Paper chromatography of products of partial racemization of LSD by base.*—In 25 mL erlenmeyer, add remaining filtered sample soln from (**a**) and adjust vol. to ca 5 mL. Treat equiv. LSD ref. std soln similarly. Add equal vol. 1*N* NaOH, cover, and heat on steam bath 5 min. Remove from steam bath, cool, transfer to separator, and dil. with ca 20 mL H_2O. Ext LSD with 15 mL $CHCl_3$, wash $CHCl_3$ with 15 mL H_2O, and discard H_2O wash. Evap. $CHCl_3$ to dryness and dissolve residue in 10 μL MeOH as in (**a**). Spot and develop MeOH soln and degraded LSD ref. std soln as in (**a**).

Racemization, which produces iso-LSD, causes 2 spots to appear on paper. Iso-LSD has lower R_f value than LSD.

40.011 ***Determination***

(Perform assay as rapidly as possible and away from direct sunlight. Use freshly prepd std soln.)

Place accurately weighed portion powd sample in 50.0 mL alcohol and shake. Filter to remove insol. material, discarding first few mL filtrate. Take aliquot of filtrate contg ca 0.2 mg LSD and evap. almost to dryness under air current on steam bath with min. heat. Dissolve residue in several mL 0.1*N* HCl and transfer to separator with several portions 0.1*N* HCl to make total vol. ca 25 mL. Make soln alk. with NH_4OH. Ext LSD with four 15 mL portions $CHCl_3$. Evap. combined $CHCl_3$ ext to dryness with min. heat in air current. Dissolve residue in 10 mL 1% HOAc in alcohol.

Prep. std soln by accurately weighing LSD tartrate std and dilg to 20 μg/mL with 1% alc. HOAc.

Scan sample and std solns from 400 to 200 nm and compare *A* at max., ca 312 nm, using 1% alc. HOAc as blank. Calc. as follows:

$$\text{LSD (free base, anhyd.)} (\mu g/g) = (A/A') \times (C/W) \times 10 \text{ (mL)} \times 0.811;$$

where *A* and *A'* refer to sample and std solns, resp.; *C* is concn of std in μg/mL; and *W* is g sample in aliquot filtrate taken.

Accurately weigh ≥5 mg (microbalance) USP Ergonovine Maleate Ref. Std, dissolve in 1% alc. HOAc, and dil. with 1% alc. HOAc to ca 20 μg/mL. Measure *A* between 400 and 200 nm. Calc. LSD concn, using *A* at max., ca 312 nm:

$$\text{LSD (free base, anhyd.)} (\mu g/g) = (A/A') \times (C/W) \times 10 \text{ (mL)} \times 0.733.$$

Marihuana (Cannabis)

Duquenois-Levine Qualitative Test (5)
Official Final Action

40.012 ***Reagent***

Duquenois reagent.—Dissolve 12 drops acetaldehyde (fresh) and 1 g vanillin in 50 mL alcohol.

40.013 ***Test***

Ext ca 100 mg sample with 25 mL pet ether, filter into white porcelain dish, and evap. to dryness on steam bath. Add 2 mL Duquenois reagent and stir to dissolve residue. Add 2 mL HCl, stir, and let stand 10 min. Note color, transfer soln to test tube, add 2 mL $CHCl_3$, and shake. Let sep. and note color in $CHCl_3$ layer; purple color is pos. test.

Methaqualone (2-Methyl-3-*o*-tolyl-4(3*H*)-quinazolinone) in Pharmaceutical and Clandestine Preparations

Gas Chromatographic Method (6)—Official First Action

40.014 ***Apparatus and Reagents***

(**a**) *Gas chromatograph.*—With flame ionization detector and 1.8 m × 4 (id) mm glass column packed with 3% OV-1 on 100–120 mesh Chromosorb W(HP). Typical operating conditions: temps (°): column 235, detector and injector 260; flow rates (mL/min): N carrier gas 60, H 30, air 300; set column temp. and flow rate to give methaqualone retention time of 2.5±0.5 min.

(**b**) *Sodium bicarbonate soln.*—1*M*. Dissolve 7 g $NaHCO_3$ in 100 mL H_2O.

(**c**) *Internal std soln.*—Dissolve tetraphenylethylene (Eastman Kodak Co.) in $CHCl_3$ to give concn of 4 mg/mL. Each analysis requires 25 mL.

(**d**) *Methaqualone hydrochloride std soln.*—4 mg/mL. Accurately weigh methaqualone.HCl and dil. with internal std soln to give concn of 4 mg/mL.

40.015 ***Determination***

Condition new column overnight at 270° with slow stream of N. Sat. column immediately before analysis by making three 3 μL injections of methaqualone.HCl std soln.

Accurately weigh sample contg ca 100 mg methaqualone.HCl and transfer quant. to 50 mL erlenmeyer. Pipet in 25 mL internal std soln and add ca 10 mL 1*M* $NaHCO_3$ soln. Heat on steam bath 5–8 min, cool to room temp., stopper, and shake. Let sep. and inject 1–2 μL of $CHCl_3$ (bottom) layer into gas chromatograph.

$$\% \text{ Methaqualone.HCl} = (P/P') \times (B'/B) \times (C/W) \times 2500,$$

where *P* and *P'* = areas or peak hts of sample and std methaqualone.HCl, resp.; *B* and *B'* = areas or peak hts of sample and std internal std, resp.; *C* = mg methaqualone.HCl/mL in std soln; and *W* = mg sample.

Phencyclidine (7)—Official First Action

(Applicable to powders only)

40.016 ***Principle***

Phencyclidine is extd from weakly basic, aq. soln with $CHCl_3$ contg internal std. Phencyclidine is sepd by GLC from other amines, org. sol. neutral compds, and internal std.

40.017 ***Reagents and Apparatus***

(**a**) *Internal std soln.*—Dissolve 80 mg eicosane ($C_{20}H_{42}$) in 100 mL $CHCl_3$.

(**b**) *Phencyclidine hydrochloride std soln.*—Weigh 10.0 mg phencyclidine.HCl (USP Authentic Substance) and dissolve in 10.0 mL internal std soln. Store in refrigerator and replace every 3 months.

(**c**) *Gas chromatograph.*—With 1.8 m (6') × 4 mm (id) glass column, packed with 3% OV-1 on 100–120 mesh Chromosorb W HP (Applied Science Laboratories, Inc.), and H flame detector. Typical operating conditions: temps (°): column 190, detector 240, injection port 240; N carrier gas flow rate 60 mL/min. Adjust column temp. to elute phencyclidine in 3±0.5 min. Adjust H and air flow rates and electrometer sensitivity so that 4 μL phencyclidine std soln gives 40–60% full scale deflection. Retention time of phencyclidine relative to internal std is ca 0.75.

(**d**) *Column.*—Plug column exit with plug of silanized glass wool. Apply vac. to exit end and slowly add packing thru inlet end while tapping gently. Fill to within 1 cm of inlet and plug with silanized glass wool. Condition column overnight at 260° with slow flow of N while disconnected from detector. Sat. column by making successive phencyclidine injections until phencyclidine/internal std ratio differs by <3% from that of preceding injection.

40.018 ***Determination***

Accurately weigh ca 250 mg finely ground sample, dissolve in 0.1*N* HCl, and quant. dil. to estimated phencyclidine.HCl concn of 1 mg/mL. Let any insol. material settle. Pipet 2 mL aliquots sample soln and 2 mL std soln into sep. test tubes. Add 2.0 mL internal std soln and 1.0 mL 10% K_2HPO_4 soln to sample tube, stopper, and shake vigorously. Add 2.0 mL 0.1*N* HCl and 1.0 mL 10% K_2HPO_4 to std tube, stopper, and shake vigorously. Let sep. Inject duplicate 4 μL aliquots of lower $CHCl_3$ layers into gas chromatograph from 10 μL syringe.

% Phencyclidine.HCl = $(H/H')\ (C'/W)\ (B'/B) \times DF \times 100$,

where H and H' = av. peak ht or area of sample and std, resp.; C' = mg std phencyclidine.HCl/mL in std soln; W = mg sample; B and B' = av. peak ht or area of internal std in sample and std, resp.; and DF = diln factor for sample.

mg Phencyclidine.HCl/tablet
= % Phencyclidine.HCl × av. tablet wt (mg)/100.

SELECTED REFERENCES

(*1*) JAOAC **61**, 473, 683(1978).
(*2*) JAOAC **5**, 154(1921); **5**, 573(1922); **7**, 6(1923).
(*3*) JAOAC **38**, 849(1955); **42**, 458(1959).
(*4*) JAOAC **51**, 1318(1968).
(*5*) JAOAC **45**, 597(1962).
(*6*) JAOAC **60**, 935(1977).
(*7*) JAOAC **62**, 560(1979).

41. Drugs and Feed Additives in Animal Tissues

ANOT (3-Amino-5-nitro-*o*-toluamide) (*1*)
Official Final Action

41.001 ***Principle***

ANOT, metabolite of zoalene, is liberated from ground tissue by enzymatic digestion with ficin. Digest is treated with $NaHCO_3$ and extd with acetone. $CHCl_3$ is added to sep. soln into 2 layers. Org. layer is concd and passed thru alumina column. Adsorbed ANOT is washed with $CHCl_3$ and eluted with 80% alcohol. Alcohol soln is passed thru cation exchange resin and ANOT is eluted with 4*N* HCl. Colored compd formed by diazotization and coupling with *N*-1-naphthylethylenediamine is measured at 540 nm.

41.002 ***Apparatus***

(**a**) *Chromatographic tube.*—600 × 16 mm id.

(**b**) *Ion exchange columns for Dowex resin.*—180 × 11 mm id.

(**c**) *Mixer.*—High speed, high shear mixer with explosion-proof motor, and ca 1 L container.

(**d**) *Spectrophotometer.*—Beckman Model DU (replaced by Models 24/25), or equiv.

41.003 ***Reagents***

(**a**) *Alumina.*—Activated, Alcoa grade F-20, 80–200 mesh.

(**b**) *3-Amino-5-nitro-o-toluamide.*—ANOT, anal. std. Available from Ag-Organics Dept., Dow Chemical Co.

(**c**) *Ammonium sulfamate soln.*—1.0%. Prep. fresh weekly.

(**d**) *Coupling reagent.*—0.25% aq. soln. of *N*-1-naphthylethylenediamine.2HCl. Prep. fresh weekly and store in dark bottle.

(**e**) *Dowex 50W-X8 cation exchange resin.*—Hydrogen form, 200–400 mesh. Bio-Rad Laboratories, 32nd and Griffin Ave, Richmond, CA 94804.

(**f**) *Ficin.*—ICN Pharmaceuticals, Inc., Life Sciences Group. (*Caution:* Ficin is potent proteolytic enzyme which attacks living tissues. Avoid contact with skin and eyes and breathing dust.)

(**g**) *Sodium nitrite soln.*—0.25%. Prep. fresh daily.

41.004 ***Preparation of Alumina Column***

Insert small plug of glass wool into chromatgc tube and compress in lower end of tube. Add 60 g alumina and pack by gently tapping tube on rubber stopper to ht of ca 30 cm. Add 100 mL $CHCl_3$ and drain to just above level of alumina. Do not drain $CHCl_3$ below level of alumina.

41.005 ***Preparation of Ion Exchange Column***

Heat 100 g Dowex 50W-X8 on steam bath with 400 mL 6*N* HCl 2–3 hr. Filter on buchner and wash with H_2O until washings are acid-free. Wash resin with 100 mL 80% alcohol. Then mix resin with 250 mL 80% alcohol. Pour enough resin slurry into ion exchange column to give bed ht of ca 5 cm after settling. Wash resin with 25 mL 80% alcohol. Slight air pressure can be used to increase flow of liq. thru resin. Do not let liq. level drain below top of resin bed.

41.006 ***Preparation of Standard Curve***

Accurately weigh 100 mg ANOT into 1 L vol. flask, dissolve in 50 mL acetone, and dil. to vol. with H_2O. Dil. 10 mL of this stock soln to 100 mL with H_2O to give working soln of 10 μg/mL. Pipet 0, 2, 4, 6, 8, and 10 mL aliquots of this soln into sep. 50 mL vol. flasks. Dil. each to ca 40 mL with 4*N* HCl. Proceed as in **41.007**, beginning "Add 1 mL 0.25% $NaNO_2$ . . ." Plot *A* at 540 nm against μg ANOT.

41.007 ***Determination***

(*Caution: See* **51.011**, **51.040**, and **51.056**.)

Collect tissue, freeze with solid CO_2, and keep frozen until analyzed. Grind tissue while at least partially frozen and weigh 50 g into 1 qt (1 L) Mason jar. Add 125 mL H_2O, 15 mL 1*N* HCl, and 5 g ficin, and mix with mixer ca 5 min. Cover jar loosely and keep 24 hr at 30°. Then keep 30 min in bath at 70–80°, remove, and cool.

Weigh ca 10 g $NaHCO_3$ and slowly add to jar with stirring, taking care that sample does not foam over top of jar. When foaming has subsided, add 500 mL acetone and mix 5 min with mixer.

Filter on buchner into 1 L filter flask, using 11 cm paper and ca 5 g Super-Cel as filter pad. Wash residue with 200 mL acetone, collecting washings in same flask. Transfer filtrate to 2 L separator and add 1 L $CHCl_3$. Shake ext in separator vigorously and let stand until layers sep. Drain $CHCl_3$ layer into 2 L beaker. Ext aq. layer with 200 mL $CHCl_3$ and combine $CHCl_3$ washing with original ext. Evap. $CHCl_3$ ext to ca 50 mL under heat lamp with air current. Add 100 mL $CHCl_3$ and again evap. to 50 mL. If soln is not clear, repeat addn and evapn of $CHCl_3$ to remove H_2O.

Add clear $CHCl_3$ soln to alumina column and drain to level of alumina. Wash with four 50 mL portions $CHCl_3$. Discard washings. Add 90 mL 80% alcohol to column to elute ANOT. Discard first 30 mL effluent and collect 60 mL in 100 mL beaker. Transfer this soln to ion exchange column. Slight air pressure may be used to increase flow of soln. After soln has drained to top of resin bed, wash with 50 mL 80% alcohol followed by 50 mL H_2O. Discard washings. Add 45 mL 4*N* HCl and collect effluent in 50 mL vol. flask.

Add 1 mL 0.25% $NaNO_2$, mix, and let stand 5 min. Add 1 mL 1% NH_4 sulfamate soln, mix, and let stand 5 min. Add 1 mL coupling reagent, mix, dil. to vol. with 4*N* HCl, and mix thoroly. Let stand 15 min and read *A* at 540 nm, using 1 cm cells, against H_2O as ref.

41.008 ***Calculations***

Obtain μg of ANOT corresponding to *A* from std curve.

ppm ANOT in sample = μg ANOT/g sample.

Total Arsenic (*2*)—Official Final Action

(Complete analysis in 1 day; otherwise stop after ashing step.)

41.009 ***Reagents and Apparatus***

(**a**) *Silver diethyldithiocarbamate* (*AgDDC*).—See **25.006(m)**. Reagent is stable several months at room temp.

(**b**) *Arsenic std solns.*—(*1*) *Stock soln.*—500 μg/mL. Accurately weigh 0.660 NBS As_2O_3 SRM, or equiv., dissolve in 25 mL 2*N* NaOH, and dil. to 1 L with H_2O. (*2*) *Working solns.*—0–2 ppm. Just before use, prep. by dilg stock soln with H_2O.

(**c**) *Zinc.*—Shot, contg ≤0.00001% As (Fisher Scientific Co., No. Z-12, or granules of equiv. purity).

(**d**) *Cellulose powder.*—Whatman CF-11 fibrous (H. Reeve Angel & Co., Inc.).

(**e**) *Distillation apparatus.*—(*1*) *Flask.*—250 mL erlenmeyer. (*2*) *Connecting tube.*—L-shaped 8 mm od glass tube with 11 and 7 cm sides. Plug shorter end with 2 pieces of glass wool satd with 10% $Pb(OAc)_2$ soln and dried (replace plugs when discolored). (*3*) *Delivery tube.*—L-shaped 6 mm od glass tube with 22 and 5 cm sides. Constrict end of longer side to 1 mm opening. (*4*) *Receiver.*—8 cm length of 15 mm glass tube sealed to open end of 100 × 10 mm od test tube.

Connect flask thru 1-hole rubber stopper with 11 cm side of connecting tube. Attach connecting tube to 5 cm side of delivery tube with rubber tube sleeve. Fit constricted end of delivery tube into bottom of receiver.

41.010 ***Dry Ashing***

Blend liver and kidney in high-speed blender. Pass fibrous tissues such as muscle and skin thru meat grinder, and divide and quarter. Weigh 10 g tissue into 100 mL Coors crucible. Add 3 g MgO and 20 mL cellulose powder (10 mL beaker is convenient measure) to liver, kidney, and skin samples and 10 mL cellulose powder to muscle samples. Mix thoroly and char cautiously over open flame until evolution of smoke ceases. (*Caution:* Rapid rise in temp. will cause crucibles to crack; avoid overheating samples to prevent loss of As.)

Cool, add 3 g $Mg(NO_3)_2.6H_2O$, and place in cold furnace preset at 555°. After furnace reaches operating temp., ash 2 hr. Cool, moisten ash with 10 mL H_2O, and transfer quant. to 250 mL erlenmeyer with 90 mL 6*N* HCl. Dil. to 175 mL with H_2O. (Presence of black carbonaceous particles does not interfere.)

41.011 ***Distillation***

Add 2 mL 15% KI soln, and swirl. Add 1 mL *$SnCl_2$ soln,* **25.006(g)**, and swirl. Cool in freezer or ice bath 45 min or until sample reaches 4°. Prep. blank contg 90 mL 6*N* HCl and 85 mL H_2O, and treat similarly.

Prep. trapping soln by pipetting 3 mL AgDDC reagent into receiving tube and place in ice bath. Attach delivery tube to connecting tube and insert delivery tube into AgDDC soln. Add 10 g Zn shot or granules to cooled erlenmeyer, immediately connect flask to connecting tube, and let distn proceed 1 hr at room temp. Det. *A* against reagent blank in 1 cm cell at 540 nm; det. As content from std curve.

Calc. As concn in sample by multiplying *A* at 540 nm by reciprocal slope of std curve, disregarding *y* intercept term.

41.012 ***Preparation of Standard Curve***

Add As working std solns (but <2 mL soln) to 10 g tissue to provide curve over desired range (usually 0–2 ppm As). Carry these samples thru ashing and distn. Det. best fitting straight line from ≥4 sets of detns for each tissue by method of least sqs, *Definitions of Terms and Explanatory Notes,* Item (24).

Clopidol (3,5-Dichloro-2,6-dimethyl-4-pyridinol) (*3*)
Official Final Action

Gas Chromatographic Method

(Diazomethane is toxic, can cause specific sensitivity, and is potentially explosive. Prep. diazomethane reagent, methylate, and evap. in hood. Avoid ground glass joints, etched or scratched glassware, and sharp edges. Store diazomethane solns in freezer; do not expose to direct sunlight or strong artificial light.)

41.013 ***Principle***

Tissues and eggs are extd with MeOH; ext is filtered and cleaned up on alumina and anion exchange columns. Eluate is methylated with diazomethane, producing Me ether of clopidol (3,5-dichloro-4-methoxy-2,6-lutidine), which is detd by electron capture GLC. Applicable to ≥0.1 ppm in chicken tissues and ≥0.05 ppm in eggs.

41.014 ***Apparatus***

(**a**) *Centrifuge.*—Clinical (Model CL, International Equipment Co., Needham Heights, MA 02194), or equiv., with head and cups to accommodate 13 × 100 mm tubes.

(**b**) *Flask.*—500 mL r-b ₮ 29/42 neck. Make 6 irregularly spaced 6 mm projections into flask by heating spot ca 2 cm diam. with torch and pushing spot in with blunt instrument.

(**c**) *Gas chromatograph.*—With electron capture detector. Operating conditions: temps (°)—column 155, injection port 220, detector 220; flow rates—N carrier gas 120 mL/min; sensitivity 3×10^{-10} amp; and chart speed 20″/hr.

(**d**) *Gas chromatographic column.*—25% DC-200 silicone oil (Dow Corning Corp.) on 80–100 mesh Chromosorb W (AW) (Applied Science Laboratories, Inc.). Prepd column available from Applied Science Laboratories, or prep. as follows: Weigh 12 g Chromosorb W (AW), from which fines have been removed on No. 100 sieve, into specially modified r-b flask, (**b**), contg 100 mL $CHCl_3$ and 3 g DC-200 fluid. Dry on rotary evaporator under vac. Use heat lamp or hot H_2O to aid evapn. Sieve and discard fines passing No. 100 sieve. Pack 1.9 m (74″) × 3 mm id U-shaped borosilicate glass column and condition ≥18 hr at 200° with N flow of 75–100 mL/min before use. Add packing to column, tapping on floor to settle. Insert glass wool plug at effluent end. Level of packing in injection arm should be few mm below depth of needle point at inlet.

(**e**) *Liquid chromatographic columns.*—(*1*) *Alumina column.*—Add 6 g (1 heaping 5 mL beaker) alumina, **41.015(a)**, to 300 × 18 mm id column, with coarse fritted disk and 30 × 5 mm id stem. (*2*) *Anion exchange column.*—Place 1 cm (after settling) AG1-X8 resin, **41.015(b)**, in 170 × 10 mm id column, with coarse fritted disk and 30 × 5 mm id stem, using MeOH to transfer resin. Rinse column with 2 mL MeOH, applying air pressure from squeeze bulb.

(**f**) *Homogenizer.*—*See* **41.002(c)**, or equiv., for use with Brockway 4 oz (125 mL) sq powder jar (No. 72 G1333, with 38 mm Polyseal caps, Brockway Glass Co., Inc., McCullough Ave, Brockway, PA 15824) and pt (500 mL) or qt (1 L) Mason jars.

(**g**) *Meat grinder.*—With stainless steel attachment.

(**h**) *Shaker.*—Wrist-action (Model BT, Burrell Corp., or equiv.).

(**i**) *Culture tubes.*—13 × 100 mm (Corning Glass Co., No. 9825), with 13 mm foil-lined plastic screw caps.

41.015 ***Reagents***

(**a**) *Alumina.*—Alcoa F-20, 80–200 mesh (Fisher Scientific Co.).

(**b**) *Anion exchange resin.*—Bio-Rad AG1-X8, 100–200 mesh, acetate form (Bio-Rad Laboratories, 32nd and Griffin Aves, Richmond, CA 94804).

(**c**) *Diazomethane reagent.*—Approx. 18 mg/mL in Et ether. Add 35 mL 2-(2-ethoxy-ethoxy) ethanol (Aldrich Chemical Co., Inc.) and 10 mL ether to soln of 6 g KOH in 10 mL H_2O in 125 mL long-neck distg flask. Place mag. stirring bar in flask and mount above H_2O bath on top of hot plate mag. stirrer. Attach dropping funnel and efficient condenser connected in series to 250 and 50 mL erlenmeyers. Place 25 mL ether in second flask and place inlet tubing below surface of ether. Cool both receiving flasks in ice. Place soln of 21.5 g *N*-methyl-*N*-nitroso-*p*-toluenesulfonamide (Diazald; Aldrich Chemical Co., Inc.) dissolved in 140 mL ether in dropping funnel. Heat H_2O bath to 55° and raise it to heat distn flask. Stir contents of flask while adding Diazald soln over 20 min. Interrupt distn when distillate is nearly colorless. Combine contents of the 2 receivers and store at 0° in culture tubes with foil-lined screw caps. Reagent is stable several weeks if kept in freezer in full, closed tubes. Alternatively, diazomethane reagent may be prepd as in Anal Chem. **32,** 1412–1414(1960).

(**d**) *Methanolic hydrochloric acid.*—5%. Add 25 mL HCl to 475 mL MeOH.

41.016 ***Standard Solutions***

(**a**) *Clopidol std solns.*—(*1*) *Stock soln.*—100 μg/mL. Accurately weigh ca 100 mg Clopidol Anal. Std (available from Sampling Coordinator, Ag-Organics Dept, Dow Chemical USA) in weighing bottle, transfer to 1 L vol. flask with MeOH, to total vol. of ca 950 mL. Stir mag. to dissolve clopidol (may take 2–3 hr). Dil. to vol. at room temp., and mix well. (*2*) *Intermediate soln.*—10 μg/mL. Pipet 10 mL stock soln into 100 mL vol. flask, dil. to vol. with MeOH, and mix. (*3*) *Working soln.*—1 μg/mL. Pipet 10 mL intermediate soln into 100 mL vol. flask, dil. to vol. with MeOH, and mix.

(**b**) *3,5-Dichloro-4-methoxy-2,6-lutidine (clopidol methyl ether) std solns.*—(*1*) *Stock soln.*—1 mg clopidol equiv./mL. Weigh 107.3 mg 3,5-dichloro-4-methoxy-2,6-lutidine anal. std (available from Sampling Coordinator, Ag-Organics Dept., Dow Chemical USA) in weighing bottle. Transfer to 100 mL vol. flask with benzene, dil. to vol. with benzene, and mix well. (*2*) *Intermediate soln I.*—10 μg clopidol equiv./mL. Pipet 1 mL stock soln into 100 mL vol. flask, dil. to vol. with benzene, and mix. (*3*) *Intermediate soln II.*—1.0 μg clopidol equiv./mL. Pipet 10 mL intermediate soln *I* into 100 mL vol. flask, dil. to vol. with benzene, and mix. (*4*) *Working solns.*—Prep. series of std solns contg 0.01 to 0.20 μg clopidol equiv./mL by dilg portions of intermediate soln *II* with benzene.

41.017 ***Chromatography of Standards***

Fill syringe needle with benzene, avoiding entrapped air, draw 3 μL sample aliquots of clopidol methyl ether working soln into syringe, and inject onto column. Measure peak hts (*PH*) in terms of % full-scale deflection, and plot *PH* against μg/mL. Prep. std curve daily and check by injecting std soln after every 1 or 2 samples.

41.018 ***Determination***

(**a**) *Muscle, liver, and kidney.*—Homogenize by grinding thru meat grinder. Accurately weigh ca 20 g tissue into 4 oz (125 mL) jar. Add 50 mL MeOH and 3 g HyFlo Super-Cel filter aid for muscle; use 12 g filter aid for liver and kidney. Attach jar to homogenizer and blend 3 min at max. speed. Filter thru 2 g pad of filter aid in 60 mL coarse fritted glass buchner mounted on filter assembly. Collect filtrate in 100 mL graduate, and wash jar and filter cake with MeOH to nearly 100 mL. If filter cake goes dry, break up with spatula during addn of more MeOH to prevent channeling. Dil. to 100 mL at room temp., stopper, and mix well.

Place anion exchange column under alumina column. Pipet 20 mL ext onto alumina column and let elute thru both columns into beaker. Wash columns with 10 mL MeOH added to alumina column, rinsing sides. Remove alumina column and beaker. Place 25 mL vol. flask under anion exchange column and elute clopidol with two 10 mL portions 5% HCl in MeOH. Dil. eluate to vol. with MeOH, and mix well. Pipet 1 mL aliquot into 13 × 100 mm tube and evap. to dryness (4–5 min) by mounting tube in 70° H_2O bath so H_2O level is at same ht as soln in tube. Direct very small jet of air down tube using rubber tubing and medicine dropper tip, or equiv. Remove tube, add 0.2 mL 80% MeOH, and heat briefly to redissolve residue. Add 1 mL diazomethane reagent, seal with screw cap, and heat gently 2 min by mounting tube as before in 70° H_2O bath. Remove tube, and let cool 5 min before removing cap. Add small SiC boiling chip and evap. reagents gently by mounting tube with only extreme rounded bottom portion touching H_2O of 70° bath. Continue heating 2–3 min until ether is evapd. Add 0.1 mL 1*N* NaOH, 5 mL H_2O, and 1.0 mL benzene, cap tube, and vigorously shake mixt. 1 min. Centrf. 3 min. Dil. further by adding more benzene, if necessary. Inject 3 μL of benzene layer as in **41.017**. Det. *PH* and interpolate μg/mL clopidol in benzene ext from std curve.

(**b**) *Eggs.*—Accurately weigh ca 20.0 g sample into 4 oz. (125 mL) jar, and add ca 12 g Hyflo Super-Cel. Shake mech. 15 min. Proceed as in (**a**), beginning "Filter thru 2 g pad . . ." Elute with 9.5 mL 5% HCl in MeOH and collect eluate in 10 mL vol. flask.

(**c**) *Recovery factor.*—Accurately weigh 20.0 g samples of homogenized clopidol-free tissue, and add equiv. of 0.0, 0.1, and 0.5 ppm clopidol working std soln (0.0, 2.0, and 10.0 mL, resp.). Proceed as in (**a**) and calc. av. recovery factor, *R* = (ppm found from std curve)/(ppm added). For eggs, use 20 g samples, add equiv. of 0.00, 0.05, and 0.2 ppm (0.0, 1.0, and 4.0 mL working std soln, resp.), proceed as in (**b**), and calc. av. recovery factor, *R.*

$$\text{ppm Clopidol in tissues} = 6.25\,(G - G')/R$$
$$\text{ppm Clopidol in eggs} = 2.5\,(G - G')/R$$

where G = μg/mL from std curve of sample, and G′ = μg/mL from std curve of blank.

Decoquinate (Ethyl 6-*n*-decyloxy-7-ethoxy-4-hydroxy-3-quinoline carboxylate) (*4*)—Official Final Action

(Applicable to chicken tissues at ≤2.5 ppm level)

41.019 ***Principle***

Tissue is homogenized in MeOH-$CHCl_3$. After addn of metaphosphoric acid, decoquinate is extd into $CHCl_3$ and sepd from interfering materials by chromatgy on Florisil. Decoquinate is eluted from column with $CaCl_2$-MeOH and detd by fluorometry against std treated similarly. Range 0.1–2.2 ppm; sensitivity 0.1 ppm.

41.020 ***Apparatus***

(**a**) *Fluorometer.*—Aminco-Bowman SPF, or equiv.

(**b**) *Chromatographic columns.*—Prep. as in **42.053(a)**, except use 0.4±0.02 g Florisil.

41.021 ***Reagents***

(**a**) *Methanol-chloroform soln.*—Mix 4 parts MeOH, redistd in all-glass app., and 1 part $CHCl_3$, spectral grade.

(**b**) *Decoquinate std solns.*—(*1*) *Stock soln.*—200 μg/mL. Weigh 20 mg Decoquinate Ref. Std (available from Hess & Clark Laboratories). Dissolve and dil. to 100 mL with $CHCl_3$. (*2*) *Working soln.*—10 μg/mL. Pipet 5 mL stock soln into 100 mL vol. flask and dil. to vol. with $CHCl_3$. (*3*) *Fluorescence reference soln.*—0.2 μg/mL. Pipet 2 mL working soln into 100 mL vol. flask and dil. to vol. with elution solv., (**c**). Solns are stable ≥1 month.

(**c**) *Elution solvent.*—Dissolve 10 g anhyd. $CaCl_2$ in 1 L redistd MeOH. Let stand 24 hr. Decant from any insol. residue.

(**d**) *Metaphosphoric acid soln.*—5%. Dissolve 50 g metaphosphoric acid pellets (J. T. Baker Chemical Co., No. 0252) in 1 L H_2O. Refrigerate at 5° and use cold.

(**e**) *Florisil.*—100–200 mesh (Fisher Scientific Co., No. F-101).

41.022 ***Preparation of Standard Curve***

Add 55 mL (50 g) MeOH-$CHCl_3$ (4+1) soln to each of four 250 mL separators. Add 0.0, 0.1, 0.3, and 0.5 mL working soln contg 0, 1, 3, and 5 μg decoquinate, resp. Proceed with *Determination,* beginning "Add 100 mL 5% metaphosphoric acid, . . .", adding entire $CHCl_3$ ext to column. Construct std curve by plotting fluorescence against μg decoquinate/mL.

41.023 ***Determination***

Weigh 20 g tissue into high-speed blender. Add 80±1 g MeOH-$CHCl_3$ (4+1) (weigh on top-loading balance). Blend 1 min. Transfer to centrf. bottle and centrf. 5 min at ca 2000 rpm. Decant and weigh 50 g supernate (equiv. to 10 g tissue) into 250 mL separator. Add 100 mL 5% metaphosphoric acid, invert 50 times, let phases sep. 10 min, and drain and retain $CHCl_3$ layer. Add 10 mL addnl $CHCl_3$ to separator, shake, and let sep. as before. Combine $CHCl_3$ exts, add 2 mL MeOH, and dil. to 25 mL with $CHCl_3$.

Depending on expected decoquinate content, add 5, 10, or 25 mL ext (2, 4, or 10 g tissue, resp.) to chromatgc column. Normally use 10 mL for liver, kidney, skin, and fat, and 25 mL for muscle samples. Wash column with 10 mL MeOH. Elute with 15 mL elution solv., (**c**), collecting in tube marked at 15 mL. Mix and transfer to fluorometer cell. Set activation wavelength at 270 nm and emission wavelength at 390 nm. With fluorescence ref. std in cell, adjust microphotometer controls to give reading of 80 on rel. intensity scale. Det. fluorescence of samples, and calc. μg decoquinate from std curve.

Ethoxyquin (1,2-Dihydro-6-ethoxy-2,2,4-trimethylquinoline) (*5*)—Official First Action

(Applicable to chicken tissues and eggs)

41.024 ***Apparatus***

(**a**) *Photofluorometer.—(Caution: See* **51.008**.) Instrument with primary filter passing only 365 nm Hg line and secondary filter passing light between 410 and 580 nm (but not below 410 nm). Photovolt Corp., 1115 Broadway, New York, NY 10010, Model 540 with BHgl primary filter and B470 secondary filter is suitable.

(**b**) *Separators.*—250 mL with Teflon stopcocks.

41.025 ***Reagents***

(**a**) *Isooctane.*—Fluorescence <2% that of soln contg 0.020 μg quinine sulfate/mL 0.1*N* H_2SO_4. If necessary, purify isooctane by passing thru 30 × 2 cm activated alumina column.

(**b**) *Sulfuric acid-sodium sulfate soln.*—0.3*N* H_2SO_4 contg 2% Na_2SO_4.

(**c**) *Ethoxyquin std solns.—(1) Stock soln.*—10 μg/mL. Place 10 mg com. grade ethoxyquin in 1 L vol. flask; dissolve and dil. to vol. with isooctane. Store in refrigerator. *(2) Working solns.*—0.010, 0.020, 0.030, and 0.050 μg/mL. Transfer 1, 2, 3, and 5 mL aliquots stock soln to 1 L vol. flasks and dil. to vol. with isooctane. Prep. fresh on day of use.

41.026 ***Preparation of Standard Curve***

Prep. std curve at time of analysis of final ethoxyquin exts. Read ethoxyquin stds with photofluorometer set at 0 with shutters closed and at 100 with most concd std. Plot instrument reading against μg ethoxyquin on linear graph paper.

41.027 ***Preparation of Sample and Extraction***

(All glassware must be free of stopcock grease.)

(**a**) *Egg yolk.*—Carefully break egg to avoid rupturing yolk and sep. as much of egg white from yolk as possible. Wash yolk in running H_2O to remove most of remaining egg white. Dry yolk on absorbent paper, break yolk sac, pour yolk into bottle, and stopper.

Weigh bottle contg yolk and pour ca 5 g yolk into mortar contg 25 g anhyd. granular Na_2SO_4 and 3 g anhyd. powd Na_2CO_3. Reweigh bottle and record wt yolk added. (Several samples may be prepd from same yolk.) Grind mixt. in mortar until uniform and dry 1 hr in desiccator contg Drierite.

Transfer dried mixt. to 4 oz (125 mL) screw-cap bottle and shake 30 min with 50 mL isooctane. Centrf. and filter supernate thru Whatman No. 1 paper into 250 mL separator. Repeat extn with second 50 mL isooctane and add ext to separator.

Gently shake isooctane ext 1 min each with two 50 mL portions 0.3*N* H_2SO_4-Na_2SO_4 soln. Combine acid exts and add 10 mL 6*N* NaOH. Ext alk. soln with two 50 mL portions isooctane. Combine isooctane exts and dry 15 min over anhyd. Na_2SO_4; decant, and dil. to 100 mL with isooctane.

(**b**) *Tissue (muscle and liver).*—Accurately weigh ca 5 g muscle or 1 g liver and add to 15 g anhyd. Na_2SO_4 and 2 g anhyd. Na_2CO_3 in mortar. Grind until uniform and place in desiccator 1 hr.

Shake dried mixt. 30 min in 4 oz (125 mL) screw-cap bottle with 100 mL isooctane. Centrf., and filter into 250 mL separator. Continue as in (**a**), 4th par., beginning "Gently shake isooctane ext . . ."

(**c**) *Fat.*—Accurately weigh ca 1 g frozen fat and add to 10 g granular, anhyd. Na_2SO_4 and 1 g anhyd. Na_2CO_3 in *glass* mortar. Grind mixt. thoroly. Add 20 mL isooctane and continue grinding several min. Decant isooctane into 4 oz (125 mL) screw-cap bottle. Repeat grinding with isooctane 3 times. Transfer isooctane ext to bottle, shake, and centrf.

Decant supernate isooctane layer into 250 mL separator and continue as in (**a**), 4th par., beginning "Gently shake isooctane ext . . ."

41.028 ***Determination***

Det. fluorescence of isooctane soln and calc. ethoxyquin content from std curve.

ppm Ethoxyquin = (μg/mL ethoxyquin) × (mL ext/g sample).

Melengestrol Acetate (MGA)

Gas Chromatographic Method (6)—Official Final Action

41.029 ***Principle***

MGA is extd from lean tissue with CH_3CN and ext is partitioned with hexane. MGA in fatty tissues is extd with hexane and then transferred into CH_3CN. Residue from either ext, after evapn of solv., is chromatgd on Florisil to remove interfering lipid materials with hexane and hexane-acetone (95+5). MGA is eluted with hexane-acetone (80+20). Residue is dissolved in hexane-acetone, and detd by GLC.

For those liver samples where MGA is poorly resolved on chromatogram, hexane-acetone is evapd, partitioned with aq. 70% MeOH-hexane, transferred into $CHCl_3$, and evapd. Dry residue is dissolved in hexane-acetone and reinjected onto GLC column.

41.030 ***Apparatus***

(**a**) *Adapters.*—₮ 24/40, Nos. 5225-10 and 5205 (Ace Glass, Inc., or equiv.).

(**b**) *High-speed blender.*—Waring Blendor Model 702-B with 1 L glass bowl having polyethylene gaskets (*see* (**i**)), or equiv.

(**c**) *Chromatographic tubes.*—Glass, 400 × 19 mm id, fitted with medium porosity fritted glass disks, Teflon stopcocks, and ₮ 24/40 tops.

(**d**) *Containers.*—Plastic, Romac No. AP06C with No. LA-16P lids (Romac Container, Inc., 33625 Pen Oak Pkwy, Avon Lake, OH 44012), or equiv. For storage of frozen tissues.

(**e**) *Flasks.*—R-b, 50, 500, and 1000 mL.

(**f**) *Funnels.*—Medium porosity fritted glass funnels, 350 mL.

(**g**) *Gas chromatograph.*—F&M Model 402, replaced by

HP 5700 series, (available from Hewlett-Packard Co., Rt 41, Avondale, PA 19311), or equiv., with all-glass on-column injection system, ^{63}Ni electron capture detector, and 1 mv strip chart recorder. Operating conditions: temps (°)—column 240–250, injection port 240–250, detector 270–275; flow rates—He carrier gas 60–80 mL/min (40 psi, 3.0–3.5 rotameter setting), Ar-CH_4 purge gas (95+5) 135–150 mL/min (40 psi); attenuation 16× or 32×; pulse interval 150; electrometer sensitivity 1×10^{-12} amp full scale deflection with 1 mv recorder. Approx. retention time of MGA under these conditions is 5–6 min.

(**h**) *Gas chromatographic column*.—Use borosilicate glass tubing, 0.2362±0.013" (6.00±0.33 mm) od and 0.118±0.01" (3.00±0.25 mm) id (Wilkens-Anderson Co., 4525 W Division St, Chicago, IL 60651, or equiv.). Bend 0.9 m (3') piece of tubing into proper design for instrument. Pack column with 1% OV-17 on 100–120 mesh Gas Chrom Q (max. operating temp., 350°, Applied Science Laboratories, Inc., or equiv.), and plug both ends with 0.5 cm loosely packed silanized glass wool. Pack far enough from ends so that no part of column packing or glass wool is inside injection port or detector inlet fittings. Connect column to injection port and cap detector inlet. Condition column 1 hr at 240° with He carrier gas at 40 mL/min, and then 16 hr at 275° with He carrier gas at 80 mL/min. Remove cap and connect column to detector.

(**i**) *Gaskets*.—Polyethylene, cut from 1 qt (1 L) freezer containers.

(**j**) *Nitrogen pressure manifold for columns*.—(Optional). Adapters No. 5205 (Ace Glass, Inc., or equiv.) connected thru manifold regulated at 3 psi (20.7 kPa), with individual control valve.

(**k**) *Pipets*.—Transfer pipets, 9" Dispo-pipettes (Scientific Products, Inc., or equiv.).

(**l**) *Reservoirs*.—250 mL ₮ 24/40 r-b flasks with ₮ 24/40 male joint in bottom, or equiv.

(**m**) *Rotary evaporator*.—4–6 small size Rinco evaporators (Rinco Instrument Co., 503 S Prairie St, Greenville, IL 62246), or equiv., controlled with 4 mm bore stopcocks connected to manifold that leads to 2 condensation traps connected in series to vac. pump with free air capacity of 140 L/min. Cool traps with solid CO_2-alcohol mixt. Connect each sample in r-b flask with 2 adapters in series to evaporator, and heat in thermostatically controlled H_2O bath at 45°.

(**n**) *Separators*.—With Teflon stopcocks, 500 and 1000 mL.

(**o**) *Silanized glass wool*.—Applied Science Laboratories, Inc., or equiv.

(**p**) *Syringe*.—10 μL, Hamilton No. 701N, or equiv.

41.031 *Reagents*

(All solvs must show no impurities when processed thru entire detn in absence of tissues.)

(**a**) *Argon-methane, 95+5*.—Purge gas (Matheson Gas Products, PO Box 85, 932 Paterson Plank Rd, Lyndhurst, NJ 07071, or equiv.).

(**b**) *Diatomaceous earth*.—Celite 545 (Johns-Manville Products Corp., or equiv.).

(**c**) *Florisil*.—60–100 mesh (available from Floridin Co.). Activated by manufacturer at 650° (1225–1250°F). Heat in oven at 130° ≥48 hr before use.

(**d**) *Glassware cleaner*.—Haemo Sol (Scientific Products, Inc., or equiv.).

(**e**) *Helium*.—99.5% min. purity (Matheson Gas Products, or equiv.).

(**f**) *Solid carbon dioxide*.

(**g**) *Solvents*.—Acetone, CH_3CN, benzene, $CHCl_3$, hexane, and MeOH. Distd-in-glass grade (Burdick & Jackson Laboratories, Inc., or equiv.).

(**h**) *Solvent mixtures*.—(v/v). (*1*) *Hexane-acetone*.—(8+2). (*2*) *Hexane-acetone*.—(95+5). (*3*) *70% Methanol*.

(**i**) *Anhydrous sodium sulfate*.—Mallinckrodt Chemical Works, or equiv. Wash with $CHCl_3$, dry in 110° oven, and store in g-s bottle until used.

41.032 *MGA Standard Solutions*

(**a**) *Stock solns*.—(*1*) *A*.—1 mg/mL; 1000 ppm. Dissolve 100.0 mg melengestrol acetate (99.5% purity, Upjohn Co.) in 100 mL acetone. Soln is stable 2–3 months. (*2*) *B*.—100 ppm. Dil. 10.0 mL soln *A* to 100 mL with MeOH. Prep. soln fresh daily. (*3*) *C*.—10 ppm. Dil. 10.0 mL soln *B* to 100 mL with MeOH. Prep. soln fresh daily.

(**b**) *Intermediate solns*.—(*1*) *D*.—0.5 ppm. Dil. 5.0 mL soln *C* to 100 mL with MeOH. (*2*) *E*.—1.0 ppm. Dil. 10.0 mL soln *C* to 100 mL with MeOH. (*3*) *F*.—1.5 ppm. Dil. 15.0 mL soln *C* to 100 mL with MeOH.

(**c**) *Working solns*.—0.25, 0.50, 0.75 ppm. Transfer 5.0 mL solns *D*, *E*, and *F* into sep. 50 mL r-b flasks and evap. on rotary evaporator. Dissolve residues in 10.0 mL portions hexane-acetone (8+2).

41.033 *Extraction*

(Wash all glassware in detergent and rinse in H_2O to remove traces of cleaning agent. Then rinse with MeOH, acetone, or $CHCl_3$. *Caution: See* **51.004**, **51.043**, **51.046**, and **51.061**. Store samples in freezer.)

(**a**) *From fat*.—Transfer 25.0 g sample to 250 mL beaker. Add 150 mL hexane and warm on steam bath without boiling. Stir with spatula until fat dissolves. Place 20 g diat. earth (2 heaping tablespoons) in fritted funnel and wash with 100 mL CH_3CN. Discard wash. Filter warmed fat soln thru cake on funnel with vac. into 1 L filter flask. Rinse beaker with <50 mL hexane to remove solids, and transfer to funnel. Remove top 3 mm diat. earth cake and transfer to blender bowl. (Some diat. earth is left in funnel for next filtration.)

Add 150 mL hexane and homogenize 3 min at low speed. Filter soln thru diat. earth cake into filter flask. Rinse blender bowl with enough hexane to remove solids, and transfer to funnel. Adjust combined filtrates to ca 400 mL with hexane in filter flask. Rinse beaker and blender bowl with two 50 mL portions CH_3CN, and transfer to funnel. (Rinse cake thoroly, since MGA may adsorb onto diat. earth from hexane.) Warm filter flask on steam bath in hood and transfer filtrate to 1 L separator. Rinse flask with 5–15 mL CH_3CN, and transfer to separator. Shake vigorously 1 min. Let layers sep. 30 min. Drain lower layer into 1 L r-b flask. Add 100 mL CH_3CN to separator. Repeat extn and sepn twice. Add 50 mL benzene to r-b flask and evap. on rotary evaporator.

(**b**) *From muscle, liver, and kidney*.—Transfer 25.0 g frozen tissue to blender bowl. Let thaw 5–10 min at room temp. Add 150 mL CH_3CN, 20 g diat. earth (2 heaping tablespoons), and 50 g anhyd. Na_2SO_4 (2 tablespoons). Homogenize at low speed 3 min. Place 20 g diat. earth into fritted funnel and wash with 100 mL CH_3CN. Discard wash. Filter soln thru cake with vac. into 1 L filter flask. Rinse blender bowl with <50 mL CH_3CN to remove remaining solids. Sep. tissue cake from filter pad and transfer to blender. (Do not disturb diat. earth below tissue cake. Household fork is good transfer tool.)

Add 10 g diat. earth, 25 g anhyd. Na_2SO_4, and 150 mL CH_3CN to blender bowl. Homogenize 3 min at low speed, filter, and rinse. Transfer combined filtrate to 1 L r-b flask and add 50 mL benzene. Evap. to dryness in rotary evaporator. (*Caution:* Bumping may occur.) To dry residue, add 200 mL hexane and 100 mL CH_3CN thru adapter. Remove adapter, and transfer solv. mixt.

to 1 L separator. Add another 200 mL portion hexane to r-b flask and transfer to separator. Shake vigorously 1 min. Let layers sep. 30 min. Drain lower layer into 1 L r-b flask. Add 100 mL CH_3CN to separator. Repeat extn and sepn twice. Add 50 mL benzene and evap. on rotary evaporator.

41.034 ***Column Chromatography***

Before analysis of samples, confirm, using MGA std soln, that hexane-acetone (8+2) elutes MGA completely, as follows: Pipet 1 mL 1 ppm MGA std soln into 50 mL r-b flask and evap. solv. on rotary evaporator. Chromatograph on Florisil column as indicated below. Det. recovery of MGA. If recovery is <95%, det. new elution vol. or obtain new batch of Florisil.

To 19 mm id glass tube, add cooled Florisil to ht of 10 cm with tapping. Push small wad of glass wool into tube until it touches Florisil. Place reservoir on top of column. Consecutively prewash column with 100 mL hexane, 100 mL acetone, and 100 mL hexane. (N pressure may be used to speed up this washing.) Remove reservoir.

Dissolve sample residue in 20 mL hexane and transfer to top of column. Replace reservoir and consecutively wash flask with 20 mL hexane, 200 mL hexane, and 300 mL hexane-acetone (95+5), and add each washing to column; if N pressure is used, add adapter. When last of solv. has reached top of column, place 500 mL r-b flask under column, wash r-b flask with 150–170 mL hexane-acetone (8+2), and transfer to column for MGA elution. Elute sample until column goes dry, using N pressure to blow out last of solv. Evap. to dryness on rotary evaporator. Quant. transfer dried residue with five 2 mL portions acetone to 50 mL r-b flask and evap. on rotary evaporator. Dil. sample to 1.0 mL with hexane-acetone (8+2).

MGA gives poorly resolved chromatogram with some liver samples. Following addnl cleanup is necessary to remove interferences: Evap. remainder of 1 mL hexane-acetone soln on rotary evaporator. To dried residue, add three 20 mL portions hexane and transfer to 500 mL separator. Add 50 mL 70% MeOH, shake vigorously 1 min, let sep. 15 min, and drain lower layer into second 500 mL separator. Add 50 mL 70% MeOH to first separator. Repeat extn and sepn twice. To MeOH layer in second separator, add 1.0 mL satd Na_2SO_4 soln, 100 mL deionized H_2O, and 50 mL $CHCl_3$. Shake vigorously 1 min. (*Caution:* Vent frequently.) Let layers sep. 15 min and drain lower layer into 500 mL r-b flask. Add 50 mL $CHCl_3$ to separator and repeat extn and sepn twice. Evap. $CHCl_3$ on rotary evaporator. Quant. transfer dried residue with five 2 mL portions acetone to 50 mL r-b flask and evap. on rotary evaporator. Add 1.0 mL hexane-acetone (8+2) and reinject on column.

41.035 ***Gas Chromatography***

Alternately inject 2–4 μL aliquots sample blank and 0.25 ppm MGA std soln until reproducible peak hts are obtained for std. Inject 1–4 μL 0.25 ppm MGA std soln. Adjust gas flow and attenuation until 20–25 mm peak ht is obtained. Use this std soln for measurement and calcn of samples at ca 10 ppb (ng/g) level, 0.5 ppm std soln for samples at ca 20 ppb, and 0.75 ppm std soln for samples at 30 ppb.

Inject same sample vol. as used for std soln to obtain 20–25 mm response. Measure peak ht of std, H', and sample, H, at retention time of MGA by baseline technic.

$$\text{ppb MGA} = (H/H') \times C \times (V/I)/\text{g sample},$$

where C = ng MGA std injected on column; V = total mL soln (sample + solv.) in r-b flask (1.0 mL); and I = mL sample soln injected onto column.

Nalidixic Acid (7)—Official Final Action

(Applicable to chicken liver and muscle contg ≥100 ppb nalidixic acid)

41.036 ***Principle***

Nalidixic acid is extd from aq. tissue homogenate with EtOAc. EtOAc is collected, concd, and passed thru alumina column which retains nalidixic acid. Nalidixic acid is removed from column with borate buffer, acidified, and re-extd with $CHCl_3$. After $CHCl_3$ removal, residual nalidixic acid is made to fluoresce with H_2SO_4 and resultant fluorescence is measured with spectrofluorometer.

41.037 ***Apparatus***

(**a**) *Spectrofluorometer.*—(*Caution: See* **51.008.**) Aminco-Bowman 4-8202, or equiv., with Xe lamp, IP 28 photomultiplier tube, and operated with manufacturer's slit arrangement No. 3. Precise wavelength settings for excitation and emission may vary slightly between instruments. Det. optimal wavelengths (ca 325 and 408 nm) after evapn of 2 mL working std soln (1 μg nalidixic acid) and soln of residue in 10 mL 21.5*N* H_2SO_4, **41.038(c)**(*1*).

(**b**) *Chromatographic tubes.*—160 × 11.5 (id) mm (Kontes Glass Co., No. K-420000, or equiv.).

(**c**) *Shaker.*—Reciprocating (Sargent-Welch Scientific Co., No. S-74060, or equiv.).

41.038 ***Reagents***

(**a**) *Phosphate buffer soln.*—pH 6.0. Weigh 28 g $NaH_2PO_4.H_2O$ into 1 L beaker, add ca 600 mL H_2O, and adjust pH potentiometrically with aq. NaOH. Dil. to 1 L.

(**b**) *Borate buffer soln.*—pH 10.0. Dissolve 30 g H_3BO_3 in ca 600 mL H_2O and adjust pH potentiometrically with aq. NaOH. Dil. to 1 L.

(**c**) *Dilute sulfuric acid.*—(*Caution: See* **51.030.**) (*1*) *21.5N.*—Measure 200 mL H_2O into 1 L flask and gradually add, with cooling, 300 mL H_2SO_4. Use soln at room temp. (*2*) *7N.*—Dil. 1 vol. (*1*) with 2 vols. H_2O.

(**d**) *Alumina.*—Neut. (Fisher Scientific Co., No. A-950, or equiv.).

(**e**) *Nalidixic acid std solns.*—(*1*) *Stock soln.*—500 μg/mL. Dissolve 50.0 mg nalidixic acid anal. std (available from Sterling Winthrop Research Institute, Rensselaer, NY 12144) in 100 mL MeOH. (*2*) *Intermediate soln.*—5.0 μg/mL. Dil. 2.0 mL stock soln to 200 mL with MeOH. (*3*) *Working soln.*—0.5 μg/mL. Dil. 10.0 mL intermediate soln to 100 mL with MeOH.

41.039 ***Determination***

(*Caution: See* **51.005, 51.039, 51.056,** and **51.057.**)

Transfer 10 g chicken liver or muscle to high-speed blender. Add 100 mL phosphate buffer and blend 2–3 min. Transfer homogenate to 500 mL g-s extn bottle and add 300 mL EtOAc.

Add 100 mL phosphate buffer to each of five 500 mL g-s extn bottles. Transfer 0, 1.0, 2.0, 3.0, and 4.0 mL working soln contg 0.0, 0.50, 1.0, 1.5, and 2.0 μg nalidixic acid, resp. Add 300 mL EtOAc to each. Mech. shake all bottles contg sample and std 10–15 min and centrf. ca 5 min at 2500 rpm. Withdraw 250 mL EtOAc supernate from each and transfer to sep. 600 mL beakers. Evap. each under air current on steam bath to ca 60 mL.

Prep. adsorption column for sample and each std as follows: Place glass wool plug at bottom of chromatgc tube and add alumina to depth of 3 cm (ca 3 g). Place another glass wool pad at top of column. Wash each column with 25 mL EtOAc. Transfer tissue and std exts from beakers to respective columns. Rinse each beaker with 25 mL EtOAc followed by two 25 mL portions ether and two 25 mL portions MeOH. Transfer each solv. rinse to corresponding column and discard all eluates.

Add two 25 mL portions borate buffer and collect eluate in 50 mL graduate. Transfer eluate from graduate to 125 mL separator with Teflon stopcock. Ext with 25 mL ether and discard ether. Acidify aq. soln with 10 mL 7*N* H_2SO_4. Thoroly ext with 25 mL and 10 mL $CHCl_3$. Withdraw each $CHCl_3$ ext and combine in 100 mL beaker. (Do not introduce any aq. phase.) Evap. solv. just to dryness on steam bath.

Add 10.0 mL 21.5*N* H_2SO_4 to each beaker. Mix thoroly ≥10 min. Det. relative fluorescence (product of linear scale meter reading and meter multiplier setting) of processed blank, stds, and tissue sample in 1 cm cell at excitation 325 nm and emission, 408 nm. Subtract relative fluorescence of reagent blank from relative fluorescence of all std and sample prepns.

Prep. std curve with reagent blank-corrected relative fluorescence values of processed stds as ordinate and corresponding μg nalidixic acid as abscissa. From std curve, det. amt nalidixic acid (x) which corresponds to reagent blank-corrected relative fluorescence of processed tissue sample.

ppb (ng/g) Nalidixic acid = $(x \times 1000)/10$ g (tissue wt).

Zoalene (3,5-Dinitro-*o*-toluamide) (*1*)
Official Final Action

41.040 ***Principle***

Ground tissue is extd with acetone, and benzene is added to sep. soln into 2 layers. Org. layer is concd, and passed thru alumina column. Absorbed zoalene is washed with $CHCl_3$ and eluted with 80% alcohol. Alc. soln is evapd just to dryness and residue dissolved in alc. DMF soln. Colored complex formed by addn of 1,3-diaminopropane is measured at 560 nm.

41.041 ***Apparatus***

See **41.002(a)**, **(b)**, and **(d)**.

41.042 ***Reagents***

(a) *Acetone-benzene soln.*—Mix 35 parts acetone with 65 parts benzene.

(b) *Alumina.*—*See* **41.003(a)**.

(c) *1,3-Diaminopropane.*—Aldrich Chemical Co.

(d) *Dimethylformamide-alcohol soln.*—Mix 4 parts DMF with 1 part absolute ethanol.

(e) *Zoalene.*—Anal. std. (Available from Agricultural Dept., Dow Chemical Co.)

41.043 ***Preparation of Alumina Column***

See **41.004**.

41.044 ***Preparation of Standard Curve***

Accurately weigh 100 mg zoalene into 1 L vol. flask, dissolve in 50 mL acetone, and dil. to vol. with H_2O. Dil. 10 mL of this stock soln to 100 mL with H_2O to give working soln of 10 μg/mL. Pipet 0, 2, 4, 6, 8, and 10 mL aliquots working soln into sep. 100 mL beakers and evap. just to dryness under heat lamp. Add 5 mL alc. DMF soln to each beaker and stir 1–2 min. Add 5 mL 1,3-diaminopropane. After 10 min, measure *A* of soln at 560 nm, using 1 cm cells against H_2O as ref. Prep. std curve by plotting *A* against μg zoalene.

41.045 ***Determination***

(*Caution: See* **51.004, 51.011, 51.039, 51.040, 51.045**, and **51.046**.)

Collect tissue, freeze with solid CO_2, and keep frozen until analyzed. Grind tissue while at least partially frozen and weigh 50 g into 1 qt (1 L) Mason jar. Add 250 mL acetone and mix with high-speed mixer ca 5 min. Filter on buchner into 1 L filter flask, using 11 cm paper and ca 5 g Super-Cel as filter pad. Wash residue with 100 mL acetone, collecting washings in same flask. Transfer filtrate to 1 L separator and add 500 mL benzene.

Vigorously shake ext in separator and let stand until layers sep. Swirl funnel and let stand again until layers sep. Drain aq. layer into 250 mL centrf. bottle. Transfer org. layer to 1 L beaker. Rinse separator with 100 mL acetone-benzene soln and add to centrf. bottle. Stopper, shake vigorously, and centrf. 20 min at ca 1700 rpm. Remove lower layer with suction tube and transfer org. layer to 1 L beaker.

Evap. to 10 mL under heat lamp with air current. Add 100 mL $CHCl_3$ and evap. to 50 mL. If soln is not clear, repeat addn and evapn of $CHCl_3$ to remove H_2O.

Add clear $CHCl_3$ soln to alumina column and drain to level of alumina. Wash with four 50 mL portions $CHCl_3$. Discard washings. Add 90 mL 80% alcohol to column to elute zoalene. Discard first 30 mL effluent and collect 60 mL in 100 mL beaker. Evap. soln under heat lamp with air current until residue no longer flows. Do not heat residue after beaker is dry.

Add 5 mL alc. DMF soln to beaker and warm with stirring to ca 45° to dissolve residue. When completely in soln, add 5 mL 1,3-diaminopropane to develop color. Filter thru small fluted paper. After 10 min, measure *A* of soln at 560 nm, using 1 cm cells against H_2O as ref.

41.046 ***Calculations***

Obtain μg zoalene corresponding to *A* from std curve.

ppm Zoalene in sample = μg zoalene/g sample.

SELECTED REFERENCES

(*1*) J. Agr. Food Chem. **9**, 201(1961); JAOAC **49**, 708(1966).
(*2*) JAOAC **56**, 793(1973).
(*3*) JAOAC **57**, 914(1974).
(*4*) JAOAC **56**, 71(1973).
(*5*) JAOAC **50**, 844(1967); **51**, 453, 537(1968).
(*6*) JAOAC **59**, 507(1976).
(*7*) JAOAC **53**, 464(1970).

42. Drugs in Feeds

(Medicated feeds may deteriorate under improper storage conditions. When possible, use reasonably fresh samples, store them in the cold, and grind just before analysis.)

Qualitative Tests for Furazolidone and Zoalene (*1*)
Official First Action

42.001 ***Apparatus***

See **7.124**.

42.002 ***Reagents***

(**a**) *Dimethylformamide* (*DMF*).—Reagent grade.

(**b**) *Alcoholic potassium hydroxide soln.*—4%. Dissolve 4 g KOH in 100 mL alcohol. If premixed with DMF (1+9), prep. fresh daily.

(**c**) *Ethylenediamine.*—Use in hood.

42.003 ***Preparation of Sample***

Gently grind pellet, cube, or crumble forms with mortar and pestle. Sieve thru nest of Nos. 10, 20, and 30 sieves with pan. Drugs usually are concd in portion in pan.

42.004 ***Identification***

(**a**) *DMF test.*—Place 9 drops DMF and 1 drop alc. KOH soln in each of 3 depressions of white spot plate. Sprinkle ca 0.01 g fine feed material into each soln from tip of spatula while observing reaction under microscope. Furazolidone produces intense blue color, easily detected at ≥0.0025%. Zoalene gives bright green, easily detected at ≥0.0025%. Color of minute particles of zoalene fades rapidly; color of larger particles persists 3–5 min.

(**b**) *Ethylenediamine test.*—Place dry filter paper at bottom of petri dish and sprinkle ca 0.5 g fine feed evenly over paper. Dispense 2–4 mL ethylenediamine under edge of paper so as to wet entire paper and sample. Examine under stereoscopic microscope at 10× for particles developing bright purple, indicating zoalene, or deep red, indicating furazolidone. (Blood meal, frequently used in livestock feed, also gives deep red color with reagent.)

Total Arsenic (*2*)—Official Final Action

42.005 ***Reagents***

(**a**) *Arsenic trioxide.*—NBS As_2O_3 SRM 83, or equiv.

(**b**) *Magnesium oxide-magnesium nitrate slurry.*—Suspend 75 g MgO and 105 g $Mg(NO_3)_2.6H_2O$ in enough H_2O to make 1 L. Agitate vigorously before addn to sample. (Freshly prepd slurry gives ash which is easily disturbed by air currents.)

(**c**) *Stannous chloride soln.*—**25.006**(**g**). Effective as long as it discharges yellow color in sample ext.

(**d**) *Absorbing soln.*—Transfer with graduate 25 mL 1.5% $HgCl_2$ soln, and with pipet 3.75 mL 6*N* H_2SO_4 and 3.75 mL 0.03*N* $KMnO_4$, into 250 mL graduate. Dil. to 250 mL with H_2O and mix. Prep. fresh daily.

(**e**) *Ammonium molybdate reagent.*—Dissolve 1 g $(NH_4)_2MoO_4$ in 100 mL 5.4*N* H_2SO_4. Soln keeps several weeks. (Prep. 5.4*N* H_2SO_4 by dilg 6*N* (9+1).)

(**f**) *Hydrazine sulfate reagent.*—0.15%. Dissolve 0.15 g $N_2H_4.H_2SO_4$ in 100 mL H_2O. Soln keeps several weeks.

42.006 ***Apparatus***

(Do not clean app. and glassware with detergents, as they interfere with color development. Haemo-Sol, available from Scientific Products, Inc., or equiv., is satisfactory.)

(**a**) *Evaporating dishes.*—70 mL; Coors No. 430, size 00A, or equiv.

(**b**) *Arsine evolution apparatus.*—Bend 6 mm id glass tubing at 120° angle ca 10 cm from one end and at 60° angle ca 15 cm from other end. Plug shorter end with glass wool impregnated with satd $Pb(OAc)_2$ soln and insert in rubber stopper, placed in top of 125 mL erlenmeyer, so that end of tube projects just below stopper. Plug other end with unimpregnated glass wool and connect thru rubber tubing to glass tube, constricted at lower end, that reaches to bottom of 50 mL large neck vol. flask, or if preferred, 50 mL centrf. tube, marked exactly at 50 mL and approx. at 20 mL.

42.007 ***Preparation of Sample Solution***

Weigh ground sample contg ≤50 μg As (unless aliquot is to be taken from digested soln) into 70 mL ashing dish. If >2.5 g sample is used, increase amt of slurry and size of ashing dish. Add ca 10 mL well mixed slurry, (**b**), and enough H_2O to permit thoro mixing with stirring rod. Rinse stirring rod, and dry sample at 100°. Ash 2–4 hr at 550–600°. (Slight C residue does not interfere. Use care to avoid loss of ash.)

Cool, and moisten residue with H_2O. Cover dish with watch glass and add ca 15 mL HCl (1+1). Let stand overnight, or heat on H_2O bath with agitation until ash dissolves. Filter thru Whatman No. 30 paper into 125 mL erlenmeyer. Rinse filter with enough hot H_2O, in several portions, to obtain ca 60 mL filtrate.

42.008 ***Preparation of Standard Curve***

Dissolve 0.660 g As_2O_3 in 25 mL 10% NaOH soln, dil. to 1 L with H_2O, and mix. Dil. 10 mL aliquot to 1 L with H_2O (1 mL = 5 μg As). Transfer 0, 2, 4, 6, 8, 10, 12, and 14 mL aliquots from buret into 125 mL erlenmeyers. Dil. each to ca 60 mL with H_2O and proceed as in **42.009**. Plot *A* against μg As.

42.009 ***Arsine Evolution***

Add ca 10 mL HCl, 2 mL KI soln, **25.006**(**f**), and 0.5 mL $SnCl_2$ soln, (**c**). Swirl, heat in H_2O bath 5 min, and cool. Have all parts of evolution app. ready for immediate assembly, with ca 20 mL absorbing soln, (**d**), in 50 mL vol. flask or centrf. tube marked at 50 mL. Add 5–6 g Zn, **25.006**(**j**), to digested soln; quickly insert stopper contg glass tubing into erlenmeyer and place delivery tube against bottom of vol. flask or centrf. tube so that bubbles will be small. Use few drops of H_2O to test for leaks between rubber stopper and erlenmeyer. Connecting glass tube must be large enough so bubbles will not carry over Pb compds from impregnated glass wool plug into absorption flask.

42.010 ***Color Development***

After 30 min, disconnect rubber tubing, leaving delivery tube in receiving vessel so that any Hg arsenide on tube will be exposed to color-developing reagents. Add 1.0 mL NH_4 molybdate reagent, (**e**), and mix by forcing air thru delivery tube. Add 1.0 mL hydrazine sulfate reagent, (**f**), and again mix. Heat in boiling H_2O bath 20 min. Rinse delivery tube with H_2O and remove. Cool to room temp., dil. to 50 mL, and mix. Filter thru tight glass wool plug in funnel or centrf. (Do not use filter paper, as color will be adsorbed.) Read A against H_2O at ≥750 nm. Max. A is at 840 nm. Det. As content from std curve.

As × 2.90 = arsanilic acid; As × 2.24 = arsenosobenzene; As × 3.51 = 3-nitro-4-hydroxyphenylarsonic acid; As × 3.3 = 4-nitrophenylarsonic acid; As × 3.47 = *p*-ureidobenzenearsonic acid.

★ 2-Acetylamino-5-nitrothiazole (Cyzine®) (*3*) ★
Official Final Action

42.011 *Principle*

2-Acetylamino-5-nitrothiazole is extd from finished feeds by hot dimethylformamide (DMF). Aliquot of filtered ext is passed thru alumina column. Impurities are removed by washing with DMF, and 2-acetylamino-5-nitrothiazole is eluted with acidified MeOH. A of yellow soln, developed by action of NaOH on compd, is detd spectrophtric at 410 nm.

42.012 *Apparatus*

(**a**) *Spectrophotometer.*—For use at 410 nm with 1 cm cells.
(**b**) *Chromatographic tubes.*—10 (id) × 300 mm; Corning Glass Works No. 38450.
(**c**) *Filter grip.*—New York Laboratory Supply Co. No. 35050.
(**d**) *Filter disks.*—Glass fiber, 5.5 cm; Reeve Angel No. 934AH.

42.013 *Reagents*

(**a**) *Acidified methanol.*—Add 2 mL 5*N* HCl to 100 mL MeOH.
(**b**) *Alcoholic sodium hydroxide soln.*—Add 2.5 mL 10*N* NaOH to 100 mL alcohol. Let stand 2 days for carbonates to settle.
(**c**) *Aluminum oxide.*—Alcoa F-20, for chromatgc adsorption. (Available from Fisher Scientific Co., as "Alumina, Adsorption, Fisher.") It is unsuitable for use as received and must be prepd as in **42.014**(**a**).

42.014 *Preparation of Chromatographic Column*

(**a**) *Preparation of alumina.*—To 250 g alumina in 2 L beaker add 1.5 L H_2O, stir, let settle 10 min, and decant as much H_2O as possible. Add 1.5 L 1*N* HCl, stir well, and let stand ≥1 hr, stirring at 10–15 min intervals. Decant, including fines, and add 1.5 L H_2O. Stir, let settle, and decant H_2O, including fines. Continue washing and decanting to include fines with 1.5 L portions of H_2O *until pH of wash H_2O is same as that of H_2O being used for wash.* (Universal indicator paper is satisfactory for pH detn. When taking pH, H_2O should be essentially free from suspended fines.) Transfer alumina to buchner and air dry ca 1 min, using gentle vac. Transfer alumina to wide, shallow dish and dry at 100–150° ≥16 hr, stirring several times during drying. Alumina should be free of lumps and should pour freely; if not, dry further. During drying, other materials must not be present in oven.

(**b**) *Preparation of column.*—Fit 0.6 cm section of 0.25" natural rubber tubing 1–2 cm from end of stem of 75 mm glass funnel with ca 3 mm stem bore thruout length. Fit funnel into top of 10 × 300 mm chromatgc tube, forming tight seal. Fit 5 cm piece of rubber tubing to end of tube and 8 cm piece of tapered glass tubing or 3 mm bore glass stopcock to tubing. Control flow of liq. to ca 1 drop/sec by stopcock or pinch clamp.

★ Surplus method—*see* inside front cover.

Remove funnel and fill tube with DMF to ca 0.6 cm above end of funnel stem after funnel is replaced. Make slurry of previously prepd alumina, using 3 vols DMF to 1 vol. alumina. Heat slurry on hot plate (do not boil) to expel adsorbed gases and cool to room temp. Prep. fresh before using; do not use slurry which has stood overnight. Swirl beaker to suspend alumina and add portions thru affixed funnel to tube until alumina is 275 mm high. After each addn, gently tap side of tube to disperse alumina evenly. Keep ca 1 cm DMF over alumina until ready for use.

42.015 *Determination*

(*Caution: See* **51.018**, **51.040**, and **51.053**.)

Weigh 20.0 g well mixed, freshly ground feed and transfer to 250 mL beaker. To second 250 mL beaker, add 60 mL DMF from graduate, and bring to bp on hot plate under hood. Add boiling DMF to sample, boil 2 min, stirring constantly, and cool to room temp. Filter, using gentle suction, into 200 mL Kohlrausch flask by decanting thru 5.5 cm buchner fitted with glass fiber filter disk. (Adapt buchner to flask by means of filter grip.)

Repeat extn with 60 mL boiling DMF as above, transferring entire cooled contents of beaker to buchner. Rinse beaker with two 30 mL portions cold DMF, adding each to buchner. Cool flask to room temp. and dil. to vol. with DMF. Stopper and mix well.

Pipet 10 mL aliquot DMF ext thru funnel onto column and let it elute at ca 1 drop/sec. Just before ext reaches top of column, add 10 mL DMF and let it run thru. Repeat wash with two 10 mL portions DMF and discard all DMF eluates.

Pass four 10 mL portions acidified MeOH thru column to elute 2-acetylamino-5-nitrothiazole. Make each addn, including first, just before preceding one reaches top of column. Do not let column go dry at any time. Collect eluate in 50 mL g-s vol. flask until ca 2 mL of last acidified MeOH portion remains on top of column. To ca 40 mL eluate in vol. flask, add exactly 0.5 mL 5*N* HCl and mix. Soln should become distinctly lighter. Add MeOH to vol. and mix thoroly.

Pipet 20 mL aliquots into each of two 25 mL g-s vol. flasks. Dil. first to vol. with MeOH, stopper, and mix well (blank). To second flask add 5 mL alc. NaOH soln (sample soln). Prep. reagent blank by adding 5 mL alc. NaOH to third 25 mL vol. flask and dilg to vol. with MeOH. Det. A of blank (A_0) and sample (A) soln at 410 nm in 1 cm cell against reagent blank. Altho developed color is stable ca 0.5 hr, do not prep. sample solns until just before reading.

42.016 *Calculations*

% 2-Acetylamino-5-nitrothiazole
$$= [(A - A_0) \times 25 \times 50 \times 200 \times 100]/(a \times 100 \times 20 \times 10 \times \text{g sample})$$
$$= 1.25 \times (A - A_0)/\text{g sample},$$
for a (1%, 1 cm) = 1000.

Det. a as follows: Accurately weigh ca 100 mg purified 2-acetylamino-5-nitrothiazole and transfer to 100 mL vol. flask with small portions DMF. Add total of ca 20 mL DMF and dissolve by warming on steam bath. After soln is complete, cool to room temp., dil. to vol. with DMF, stopper, and mix well. Dil. 5 mL aliquot to 200 mL with DMF, add 10 mL aliquot to prepd alumina column, **42.014**(**b**), and proceed as in detn to det. A'.

$$a = (A' \times 25 \times 50 \times 200 \times 1000)/(20 \times 10 \times 5 \times \text{mg sample})$$
$$= A' \times 250{,}000/\text{mg sample}.$$

Aklomide (2-Chloro-4-nitrobenzamide) (2,4-CNBA) (*4*)—Official Final Action

(Applicable in presence of sulfanitran or roxarsone)

42.017 ***Reagents***

(**a**) *Titanous chloride soln.*—4% aq. Prep. fresh on day of use from 20% soln or solid $TiCl_3$.

(**b**) *Sodium nitrite soln.*—0.1% aq. Prep. fresh on day of use.

(**c**) *Ammonium sulfamate soln.*—0.5%. Dissolve 500 mg $NH_4SO_3NH_2$ in H_2O and dil. to 100 mL. Prep. fresh weekly.

(**d**) *Coupling reagent.*—0.1% aq. *N*-naphthylethylenediamine.2HCl. Prep. fresh weekly and store in dark glass bottle in refrigerator.

(**e**) *Aklomide std solns.*—2-Chloro-4-nitrobenzamide, purified for std use, available from Salsbury Laboratories. (*1*) *Stock soln.*—1 mg/mL. Transfer 100 mg aklomide to 100 mL vol. flask, dissolve in ca 75 mL MeOH, dil. to vol. with MeOH, and mix well. (*2*) *Intermediate soln.*—10 μg/mL. Pipet 10 mL stock soln into 100 mL vol. flask, dil. to vol. with MeOH, and mix. Pipet 5 mL into 50 mL vol. flask. Evap. to dryness on H_2O bath with aid of gentle air stream and cool to room temp. Add ca 30 mL 0.15*N* HCl, shake 10 min intermittently, dil. to vol. with 0.15*N* HCl, and mix well. (*3*) *Working solns.*—0, 0.4, 0.8, 1.2, 1.6, and 2.0 μg/mL. Transfer 0, 1, 2, 3, 4, and 5 mL intermediate soln to sep. 25 mL vol. flasks and dil. to vol. with 0.15*N* HCl.

42.018 ***Preparation of Standard Curve***

Transfer 4 mL aliquot from each working std soln to sep. colorimetric tubes and proceed with reduction, color development, and measurement as in **42.019**. Tubes contain 0, 1.6, 3.2, 4.8, 6.4, and 8.0 μg aklomide/tube, equiv. to 0, 0.008, 0.016, 0.024, 0.032, and 0.040% aklomide in feed when 5 g sample is taken. Plot *A* against % aklomide.

42.019 ***Determination***

Weigh 5 g sample contg ca 0.025% aklomide into 100 mL vol. flask, add 75 mL MeOH, and heat 30 min in 60° H_2O bath, shaking occasionally. Remove flask, cool to room temp., and dil. to vol. with MeOH. Mix thoroly and let stand 40 min to settle feed particles.

Pipet 5 mL clear supernate into 50 mL vol. flask and dil. to vol. with 0.15*N* HCl. Mix well and filter thru Whatman No. 4 paper into 125 mL erlenmeyer. (If filtrate is cloudy, refilter.) Pipet 4 mL filtrate into each of 2 tubes, add 2 drops 4% $TiCl_3$ from dropper, mix, and let stand 2 min. Add 2 drops 10*N* NaOH from dropper, mix until white ppt persists, and acidify with 2.0 mL HCl. Mix and let stand until soln clears. Add 0.5 mL $NaNO_2$ to one tube and 0.5 mL H_2O to second tube as blank; mix. After 3 min, add 0.5 mL 0.5% NH_4 sulfamate to each tube and mix. After 2 min, add 0.5 mL coupling reagent to each, mix, and let color develop 15 min. Read *A* of soln at 545 nm in colorimeter or spectrophtr. Subtract reading of feed blank. Det. % aklomide in feed directly from std curve.

Thin Layer Chromatographic Qualitative Test

42.020 ***Reagents***

(**a**) *Spray reagent.*—Dissolve and dil. 0.1 g *p*-(dimethylamino)cinnamaldehyde (DMC) (available from J. T. Baker Chemical Co.) to 100 mL with 1.0*N* HCl. (Soln is stable ≥1 month.) Just before use, add 1 mL 20% $TiCl_3$ to 25 mL DMC soln and mix. Discard after 1 hr.

(**b**) *Aklomide reference std.*—1 mg/mL. *See* **42.017(e)**(*1*).

42.021 ***Test***

Ext 10 g sample with 25 mL MeOH, shaking occasionally during 15 min. Filter thru Whatman No. 4 paper into 50 mL beaker. Conc. filtrate to ca 2 mL on steam bath. Spot ca 10 μL on 250 μm silica gel G TLC plate along with ref. std and develop ca 30 min, in ether. Remove from tank and air dry ca 15 min. Spray plate with DMC-$TiCl_3$ reagent. (*Caution: See* **51.017**.) Aklomide forms reddish pink spot. Compare R_f value to that of ref. std.

p-Aminobenzoic Acid (*5*)—Official Final Action

42.022 ***Preparation of Standard Solution***

Transfer 0.100 g *p*-aminobenzoic acid (99+% purity, available from ICN Pharmaceuticals Inc., Life Sciences Group) to 100 mL vol. flask, dissolve in 5 mL 1*N* NaOH, and dil. to vol. with H_2O. Dil. 5 mL aliquot to 200 mL with H_2O (1 mL = 25 μg). Place 2, 4, and 6 mL aliquots dild soln (50, 100, 150 μg) in 100 mL vol. flasks, add 3 mL HCl to each, dil. to vol. with H_2O, and mix.

42.023 ***Determination***

Transfer 5 g freshly ground feed to 250 mL vol. flask, add 135 mL H_2O, making slurry of first 10 mL to wet sample completely, and then add 15 mL HCl. Mix, and place on steam bath 25 min, swirling occasionally until soln darkens. Cool, dil. to 250 mL with H_2O, and let feed particles settle. Pipet 50 mL into 100 mL vol. flask, dil. to vol. with H_2O, and mix thoroly. Pour soln into 250 mL beaker, add filter-aid, and filter thru 18.5 cm Whatman No. 2 paper, or equiv., discarding first 10–15 mL, if turbid.

Pipet two 10 mL aliquots into 50 mL beakers, add 5 mL H_2O and 2 mL *fresh 0.10% $NaNO_2$ soln,* mix, and let stand 3 min. Add 2 mL *0.50% NH_4 sulfamate soln,* mix, and let stand 2 min. Then add, to one beaker only, 1 mL coupling reagent, **42.017(d)**, and to other 1 mL H_2O. Mix solns and wait 10 min. Det. *A* against H_2O at 545 nm in spectrophtr. (Avoid false readings due to N bubbles on cell walls.) Subtract blank *A* from sample *A* and calc. μg found by ref. to std curve.

% *p*-aminobenzoic acid in feed = μg found/1000.

K *p*-aminobenzoate = *p*-aminobenzoic acid × 1.278.

Prep. stds by treating 10 mL aliquots of 3 final std solns, representing 5, 10, and 15 μg, as in detn, beginning ". . . add 5 mL H_2O . . ." Plot *A* at 5, 10, and 15 μg and draw straight line.

42.024 ***Qualitative Tests***

(To differentiate *p*-aminobenzoic acid, arsanilic acid, and sulfaquinoxaline)

Place 10 mL prepd sample filtrate in separator. Ext with 10 mL peroxide-free ether by vigorous shaking 30 sec. Let layers sep., and drain aq. layer into another separator. Re-ext with 10 mL ether and drain aq. layer into third separator for third extn with same vol. ether. After final extn, drain aq. layer into fourth separator, add 5 mL H_2O, mix, and couple soln as in **42.023**, second par. Wait 10 min, add 5 drops HCl and 10 mL isoamyl alcohol, and ext gently ca 30 sec. Let stand until layers sep. Red color in solv. is due to *p*-aminobenzoic acid; that in lower layer, to arsanilic acid. Drain as much aq. layer as possible and again ext with 10 mL solv. Arsanilic acid remains as distinct color in aq. layer, not as mere trace due to incomplete removal of *p*-aminobenzoic acid. Combine ether exts, wash with 5 mL H_2O, discard, and ext with 10 mL 1% Na_2CO_3 soln; acidify, and couple again to prove presence of sulfaquinoxaline.

★ 2-Amino-5-nitrothiazole (Enheptin®) (*6*) ★
Official Final Action

42.025 ***Reagents***

(**a**) *Borate buffer.*—pH 9.0. Dil. 50.0 mL H_3BO_3-KCl soln, **50.009(c)**, and 21.40 mL 0.2*M* NaOH, **50.009** (**d**), to 200 mL with H_2O.

(**b**) *Sodium hydrosulfite soln.*—Prep. 1% soln of Na hydrosulfite in borate buffer, (**a**), and use within 5 min of prepn.

42.026 ***Determination***

Transfer 2 g ground feed to 50 mL wide-mouth vol. flask, add 10 mL acetone, and let stand 2 min, swirling occasionally. Dil. to vol. with H_2O, mix, and filter immediately thru *coarse* paper. Transfer 25 mL aliquot to 50 mL vol. flask, add 15 mL 5% NH_4Cl soln, and mix. Dil. to vol. with H_2O, mix, and filter thru Whatman No. 42 paper, or equiv., discarding first 10 mL filtrate.

Place 4 mL aliquot in each of 2 small beakers. To first, add 0.5 mL freshly prepd Na hydrosulfite soln. Dil. contents of both beakers to 10 mL and immediately read both solns in spectrophtr against H_2O at 388.5 nm. Subtract *A* of reduced soln from that of unreduced soln. From std curve read μg Enheptin corresponding to this difference.

μg Enheptin × 0.00125 = % Enheptin in sample.

42.027 ***Preparation of Standard Curve***

Dissolve 100 mg 2-amino-5-nitrothiazole std in 100 mL acetone and dil. to 1 L with H_2O. Transfer aliquots of 4, 8, 12, 16, and 20 mL to 100 mL vol. flasks and dil. to vol. with H_2O. Treat 5 mL aliquots of each diln as above, and read *A* of unreduced soln against reduced soln as blank, obtaining readings corresponding to 20, 40, 60, 80, and 100 μg.

Amprolium (1-(4-Amino-2-*n*-propyl-5-pyrimidinylmethyl)-2-picolinium chloride hydrochloride) (*7*)—Official Final Action

42.028 ***Principle***

Amprolium is extd from feed with aq. MeOH. Ext is purified by chromatgy on alumina, and amprolium reacts with 2,7-naphthalenediol, $K_3Fe(CN)_6$, KCN, and NaOH in MeOH to form colored compd with absorption max. at 530 nm. There is no interference from usual components of com. feeds, vitamins, antibiotics, picolines, or pyrimidines. Nithiazide, Enheptin A, and nitrofurazone show some interference.

42.029 ***Reagents***

(*Caution: See* **51.050**.)

(**a**) *Alcoholic sodium hydroxide soln.*—Dil. 15.0 mL aq. NaOH soln, (**i**), with anhyd. MeOH to 200 mL. Stopper, and mix well.

(**b**) *Alumina.*—Reagent grade suitable for chromatgy. Should pass following test: Vigorously shake 10 g alumina with 100 mL H_2O in 250 mL g-s flask ≥2 min. Let settle, decant, and det. pH potentiometrically. pH should be 9.5–10.5.

(**c**) *Amprolium std soln.*—25 μg/mL. Weigh 25.0 mg Amprolium Ref. Std (available from Merck & Co.) into 50 mL vol. flask, dissolve in dil. MeOH, (**e**), dil. to vol., and mix. Dil. 5 mL to 100 mL in vol. flask with dil. MeOH. Soln is stable 1 week.

(**d**) *Color developing reagent.*—Add 5 mL $K_3Fe(CN)_6$ soln to 90 mL naphthalenediol soln, (**f**), in 250 mL g-s flask, and mix well. Add 5 mL KCN soln, (**g**), stopper, mix well, and let stand 30–35 min. Add 100 mL alc. NaOH soln, (**a**), and mix. Use within 75 min, filtering thru medium porosity fritted glass filter just before use.

(**e**) *Dilute methyl alcohol.*—Mix 2 vols anhyd. MeOH with 1 vol. H_2O. Cool to room temp. before use.

(**f**) *Naphthalenediol soln.*—Dissolve 25 mg 2,7-naphthalenediol (Eastman Kodak Co.) in 1 L anhyd. MeOH.

(**g**) *Potassium cyanide soln.*—Dissolve 1.0 g KCN in 100 mL H_2O. Kept tightly stoppered, soln is stable 2 weeks.

(**h**) *Potassium ferricyanide soln.*—Dissolve 200 mg $K_3Fe(CN)_6$ in 100 mL H_2O. Kept tightly stoppered, soln is stable 2 weeks.

(**i**) *Sodium hydroxide soln.*—Dissolve 2.25 g NaOH in 200 mL H_2O.

42.030 ***Extraction***

Accurately weigh amt ground feed (≤15 g) contg 1.5–2.5 mg amprolium and transfer to 250 mL g-s flask. Add 100.0 mL dil. MeOH, stopper, and stir mag. or shake mech. 60 min. Filter thru Whatman No. 42, or equiv., paper and collect 25–40 mL clear filtrate, rejecting first 10–15 mL. Filtrate should be clear. Refilter, if necessary, thru fresh paper or centrf. until clear.

42.031 ***Chromatography***

(**a**) *Preparation of alumina.*—To 200 g Al_2O_3, (**b**), add 1 L H_2O. Stir mixt. 30 min. Filter slurry thru fast paper on buchner funnel. Wash Al_2O_3 on filter with three 100 mL portions of anhyd. MeOH. Air-dry under vac. until Al_2O_3 reaches room temp. Prepd Al_2O_3 should be free-flowing. Store in g-s bottle.

(**b**) *Preparation of column.*—Constrict end of 40 cm length of 9–10 mm id glass tubing by rotating in hot flame until opening is 4–5 mm. Insert small plug of Pyrex glass wool in lower end of tube and compress with glass rod to thickness ca 2–3 mm. Transfer 5.0 g prepd alumina to dry tube and pack by gentle tapping of tube. Prep. sep. column for each sample.

(**c**) *Chromatography of feed extract.*—Pipet 25 mL clear ext onto column and let pass thru column by gravity. Reject first 3 mL eluate and collect next 5 mL for color development.

42.032 ***Determination***

Mark 3 sep. 15 mL centrf. tubes as *X, S,* and *B*. To *X* add 4.00 mL clear eluate from column; to *S* add 4.00 mL amprolium std soln, and to *B* add 4.00 mL dil. MeOH as blank. Add 10.0 mL color developing reagent to each tube, stopper, mix, and let stand 20 min. Centrf. 2–3 min, decant into 1 cm cells, and cover. (If solns are not clear and free from suspended particles, decant into cells thru small plug of Pyrex glass wool.) Det. *A* of solns *X* and *S* in spectrophtr or colorimeter at 530 nm against soln *B* as ref. within 20–25 min after adding color developing reagent.

% Amprolium in feed = $(2.5A \times C)/(A' \times W)$;

where *A* and *A'* refer to sample and std, resp., *C* = mg amprolium in final aliquot of std soln (0.100 mg), and *W* = g original sample.

Fluorometric Method (8)—Official Final Action

(Applicable in absence of antibiotics except procaine penicillin and chlortetracycline)

42.033 ***Reagents***

(**a**) *Amprolium std solns.*—(*1*) *Stock soln.*—0.20 mg/mL. Weigh 20.0 mg Amprolium Ref. Std (available from Merck & Co.) and dissolve in enough TCA soln, (**d**), to make 100.0 mL. (*2*) *Working soln.*—1 μg/mL. Dil. 5.00 mL stock soln to 100 mL with TCA soln and mix well. Further dil. 10 mL of this soln to 100 mL with H_2O, and mix well.

★ Surplus method—*see* inside front cover.

(b) *Potassium ferricyanide soln.*—Dissolve 2 g $K_3Fe(CN)_6$ in 100 mL H_2O.

(c) *Silver nitrate soln.*—Dissolve 5 g $AgNO_3$ in 100 mL H_2O.

(d) *Trichloroacetic acid (TCA) soln.*—Dissolve 5 g CCl_3COOH in 100 mL H_2O.

42.034 ***Extraction***

Grind feed sample to pass No. 20 sieve and mix thoroly. (High-speed blender grinds most feeds to desired fineness in ca 3 min.) Weigh sample contg ca 750 μg amprolium and transfer to 250 mL g-s flask. Add 100.0 mL TCA soln, stopper, and agitate 30 min on mag. stirrer or mech. shaker.

Filter by gravity thru Whatman No. 42 paper, rejecting first 5 mL. Collect $\geq$10 mL clear filtrate. Transfer 5.00 mL clear ext to 50 mL vol. flask, dil. to vol. with H_2O, and mix well. This is dild sample ext.

42.035 ***Development of Fluorophor***

Mark three 50 mL centrf. tubes *X, Y,* and *Z.* To tube *X* add 15.00 mL dild sample ext; to tube *Y* add 1.50 mL TCA soln and 13.50 mL H_2O as blank soln; and to tube *Z* add 15.00 mL amprolium working std soln. To all tubes add 5.00 mL *NaOH soln* (3+10), stopper with polyethylene stoppers, and mix well. Immediately add 0.50 mL $AgNO_3$ soln to all tubes, stopper, and mix well. Let all tubes stand 2 min. Then to all tubes add 3.0 mL $K_3Fe(CN)_6$ soln, stopper, mix, and let stand 3.0 min.

During this 3 min wait, add 15 mL *n*-BuOH to all tubes, as overlay, and stopper. After 3 min, vigorously shake all tubes 1.0 min, and centrf. 1 min. Transfer 10.0 mL aliquots of upper BuOH layer from all tubes to test tubes. Add 1.00 mL absolute alcohol to each tube and mix well.

42.036 ***Measurement of Fluorescence***

(*Caution: See* **51.008.**)

(a) *For instruments designed to accommodate 10 × 10 mm cells and using monochromatic light for excitation.*—Set activation wavelength at 400 nm (uncorrected) and emission wavelength at 455 nm (uncorrected). Transfer ca 2.0 mL fluorophor BuOH ext to cell and read.

(b) *For instruments designed to accommodate 10 × 40 mm cells and using filters to adjust wavelengths for excitation and emission.*—Use Corning Glass Works 5840 (CS-7-60) filter placed after light source to adjust excitation wavelength and Corning Glass Works 3385 (CS-3-71) filter placed behind cell to adjust emission wavelength. Transfer entire contents of test tube contg extd fluorophor to cell and read.

42.037 ***Calculations***

$$\% \text{ Amprolium in feed} = (X - Y) \times C/[150 \times (Z - Y) \times W],$$

where *X, Y,* and *Z* are fluorescence readings of sample, reagent blank, and std, resp.; $C = \mu$g in 15 mL std soln (15.0); and W = g sample.

Arsanilic Acid (*p*-Aminobenzenearsonic Acid) (*9*) Official Final Action

(Applicable in absence of sulfonamides)

42.038 ***Determination***

Transfer 4.0 g freshly ground sample to 200 mL vol. flask, and add ca 80 mL H_2O and 4 mL 0.5*N* NaOH. Place flask on steam bath ca 5 min, swirling occasionally. Carefully add 20 mL HCl, mix, and cool to room temp. Dil. to vol. with H_2O, mix, pour into 250 mL beaker, add some Filter-Cel, or equiv., and filter thru Whatman No. 42, or equiv., paper, discarding first 5 mL.

Pipet 5 mL aliquots of clear filtrate into each of two 20 × 175 mm test tubes. To each tube add 2 mL *0.1% $NaNO_2$ soln,* mix, and let stand 5 min. Add 2 mL *0.5% NH_4 sulfamate soln* and let stand 2 min. Then add, to 1 tube only, 1 mL coupling reagent, **42.017(d)**, mix, and let stand 10 min before dilg both solns to vol. of 15 mL. Mix well (if bubbles appear, filter thru glass wool), and det. *A* against H_2O at 538 nm in spectrophtr or with 540 nm filter in photometer. Subtract *A* of blank from sample *A*. Det. μg arsanilic acid in aliquot (equiv. to 100 mg sample) from std curve.

42.039 ***Preparation of Standard Curve***

Transfer 0.100 g pure *arsanilic acid* to 100 mL vol. flask, add ca 20 mL H_2O and 2 mL 0.5*N* NaOH, and dissolve. Dil. to vol. with H_2O and mix well. Transfer 10 mL to 100 mL vol. flask, dil. to vol. with H_2O, and mix well. Dil. 5 mL of this soln to 250 mL with H_2O in vol. flask, and mix well (1 mL = 2 μg arsanilic acid). Pipet aliquots of 0, 2, 3, 5, and 8 mL of this std soln into 20 × 175 mm test tubes, add 1 mL HCl (1+1) to each tube, and continue as in **42.038**, beginning "To each tube add 2 mL *0.1% $NaNO_2$ . . .*" Subtract blank *A* from *A* of stds and plot differences against 4, 6, 10, and 16 μg arsanilic acid in aliquots.

42.040 **Bifuran—Official Final Action**

See **42.075–42.076.**

42.041 ★ **Bithionol (2,2′-Thiobis(4,6-dichlorophenol))** ★ **(*10*)—Official Final Action**

Bithionol is extd from acid soln with hexane, re-extd into alk. soln, and reacted with 4-aminoantipyrine and $K_3Fe(CN)_6$. Colored product is extd into BuOH and detd spectrophtric at 500 nm. *See* **38.035–38.037**, 11th ed.

Buquinolate (Ethyl 4-hydroxy-6,7-diisobutoxy-3-quinolinecarboxylate) (*11*)—Official Final Action

42.042 ***Principle***

Buquinolate is extd from feed with $CHCl_3$, concd to small vol., and sepd from interfering substances by TLC utilizing 2 solv. systems. Buquinolate is eluted from substrate and detd fluorometrically.

42.043 ***Reagents***

(a) *Alcohol, 80%.*—Dil. 84.3 mL alcohol to 100 mL with H_2O.

(b) *Developing solvent.*—Mix $CHCl_3$ with alcohol (10+1). Prep. fresh daily.

(c) *Buquinolate std solns.*—(*1*) *Stock soln.*—0.5 mg/mL. Dissolve 50.0 mg Buquinolate Ref. Std (available from Norwich Pharmacal Co., Norwich, NY 13815) in $CHCl_3$ to make 100 mL. Warm mixt. on steam bath as necessary. Soln is stable 1 month if protected from evapn. (*2*) *Working soln.*—100 μg/mL. Pipet 5 mL stock soln into 25 mL vol. flask, dil. to vol. with $CHCl_3$, and mix well. Prep. fresh daily.

42.044 ***Apparatus***

(a) *Developing tanks.*—Line developing tanks (Brinkmann Instruments, Inc. No. 25-10-200-2, or equiv., for plates $\leq$20 × 20 cm) with Whatman 3 MM paper. Add 100 mL $CHCl_3$ to one tank; add 100 mL developing solv., (b), to second tank. Prep. each tank fresh daily.

★ Surplus method—*see* inside front cover.

(**b**) *Plates for TLC.*—Clean plates thoroly with alkyl benzene sulfonate-type detergent (Ajax, or equiv.) and brush; rinse plates with H_2O and then with acetone. Let plates air dry. Slurry 60 g silica gel G (Brinkmann No. 68-00-261-3) with 120 mL H_2O. Pour into suitable applicator and spread 0.500 mm layer on 20 × 20 cm plates. Air dry 15–30 min; then dry 2 hr at 110°. Cool and store plates in desiccator until used.

(**c**) *Fluorometer.*—Either spectrophotofluorometer or filter fluorometer may be used. (Suitable filters are: excitation, Baird Atomic, Inc. type UV-7E (UV Spectrum Filters, Nos. 59-07-9); emission, Corning Glass Works 0–52 + 7–60.) (*Caution: See* **51.008**.)

42.045 ***Determination***

(*Caution: See* **51.016**.)

Grind ca 100 g sample to pass No. 30 sieve and mix thoroly. Accurately weigh sample contg 1.25 mg buquinolate into 250 mL g-s erlenmeyer. Pipet 100 mL $CHCl_3$ into sample flask. Shake mech. 1 hr. Filter ext thru Whatman No. 54 paper on buchner with mild vac. (Take care to prevent solv. loss by evapn.) Transfer exactly 80 mL ext to 150 mL beaker and evap. almost to dryness on steam bath. Take up residue in small portion $CHCl_3$ and transfer to 10 mL vol. flask with small portions $CHCl_3$. Dil. to vol. with $CHCl_3$ and mix well.

Apply 250 μL sample ext and 250 μL working std soln to TLC plate. Place spots ca 25 mm from bottom of plate and 40 mm apart. (Do not touch pipet to plate.) Develop plate in $CHCl_3$ developing tank, (**a**), until solv. front nearly reaches top of plate (ca 1 hr). Observe plate under short wavelength UV light: Buquinolate remains at origin; feed background migrates. Transfer air-dried (5–10 min) plate to tank contg developing solv., (**b**). Let plate develop until solv. front advances 12 cm. Air dry 5–10 min. Examine plates under short wavelength UV light. Buquinolate migrates from origin (R_f, 0.4–0.6). With spatula, outline each buquinolate spot plus blank spot of equiv. area and R_f. Remove adsorbent from around buquinolate spots and discard. Quant. transfer each spot to sep. g-s 25 mL erlenmeyers. Pipet 10 mL 80% alcohol, (**a**), into each flask, shake mech. 20 min, and centrf.

Det. intensity of fluorescent radiation (I) of sample, std, and blank in 10 × 10 mm silica cells, at excitation and emission wavelengths of 265 and 375 nm, resp.

$$\% \text{ Buquinolate} = [(I_{sample} - I_{blank})/(I_{std} - I_{blank})] \times (0.125/\text{g sample}).$$

42.046 ★ Cadmium Anthranilate (*12*) ★
Official Final Action

Spectrophtric detn of dithizone complex. *See* **42.046–42.047**, 12th ed.

Carbadox (Methyl 3-(2-Quinoxalinylmethylene) Carbazate-N^1, N^4-dioxide, Mecadox) (*13*)—Official First Action

(Applicable to levels ≥0.0055%. Carbadox solns are light sensitive. Exts must be protected from direct sunlight or artificial light.)

42.047 ***Apparatus***

(**a**) *Filter aid.*—Celite 545 or Millipore prefilter pad (No. AP2504700, Millipore Corp., Ashby Rd, Bedford, MA 01730), or equiv.

(**b**) *Spectrophotometer.*—For use at 520 nm.

★ Surplus method—*see* inside front cover.

42.048 ***Reagents***

(**a**) *Carbadox std solns.*—(*1*) *Stock soln.*—1.10 mg/mL. Weigh 110.0 mg Carbadox Ref. Std (available from Pfizer, Inc., Quality Control, Agricultural Div., 1107 S Rt 291, Lee's Summit, MO 64063) into 100 mL vol. flask, dissolve in $CHCl_3$-MeOH (3+1), and dil. to vol. with same solv. Ultrasonic bath speeds dissoln. Prep. fresh daily. (*2*) *Working soln.*—0.110 mg/mL. Pipet 10 mL stock soln into 100 mL vol. flask, dil. to vol. with $CHCl_3$-MeOH (3+1), and mix well. Prep. fresh daily.

(**b**) *Methanolic hydrochloric acid soln.*—1*N*. Dil. 85 mL HCl to 1 L with MeOH.

(**c**) *Methanolic sodium hydroxide soln.*—0.05*N*. Dissolve 2.0 g NaOH in MeOH and dil. to 1 L with MeOH. Prep. fresh weekly or sooner if ppt forms.

(**d**) *Potassium phosphate soln.*—1*M*. Dissolve 136 g KH_2PO_4 in H_2O and dil. to 1 L.

(**e**) *Sodium hydroxide-sodium chloride soln.*—Dissolve 100 g NaCl in 0.1*N* NaOH and dil. to 1 L with 0.1*N* NaOH.

(**f**) *Stannous chloride soln.*—Prep. immediately before use. Add 8.0 g $SnCl_2.2H_2O$ to 100 mL methanolic 1*N* HCl. Place in 55–60° H_2O bath and swirl intermittently until soln is clear (ca 20 min). Stopper and cool to room temp. Use within 2 hr.

42.049 ***Preparation of Samples***

(*Caution: See* **51.056** and **51.066**)

Weigh duplicate portions ground feed into 250 mL erlenmeyers: 2.000 g for 0.0330–0.0606% carbadox; 5.000 g, 0.0110–0.0330%; and 20.00 g, 0.0055–0.0110%. Wet each portion with 10 mL H_2O, let stand 5 min, and add 140 mL $CHCl_3$-MeOH (3+1). Add 15.0 mL working std soln to 1 portion. Stopper both flasks loosely or with polyethylene stopper with pinhole, and boil gently 1 hr. Cool to room temp.

Using three 25 mL portions $CHCl_3$-MeOH (3+1), quant. transfer mixt. to buchner precoated with Celite or contg prefilter pad, collecting filtrate under vac. in 250 mL vol. flask. Dil. to vol. with $CHCl_3$-MeOH (3+1), and mix well. Pipet 100 mL aliquot into 250 mL separator contg 50 mL NaOH-NaCl soln. Shake 10 sec and discard lower $CHCl_3$ layer. Add 50 mL $CHCl_3$, shake 10 sec, and discard $CHCl_3$ layer. Add 10 mL KH_2PO_4 soln, and ext with three 50 mL portions $CHCl_3$, combining exts in r-b flask. Do not let any solids at interface drain into flask. Evap. to dryness, using rotary evaporator and 60° H_2O bath.

Conduct reagent blank of H_2O and $CHCl_3$-MeOH (3+1) thru boiling, filtration, extns, and evapn, omitting addn of feed and carbadox.

42.050 ***Determination***

Dissolve residue in flask from sample, sample plus std, and blank in 5.00 mL 0.05*N* methanolic NaOH. Add 20.0 mL $SnCl_2$ soln, swirl gently, and let stand 10 min for complete color development. If necessary, clarify soln by filtration thru small glass wool plug. Within 15 min after completion of color development, det. A of clear solns at 520 nm against MeOH as ref. solv. Subtract A of blank from A of sample and A' of sample plus std.

$$\% \text{ Carbadox} = (A/\text{g sample}) \times [1/(A' - A)] \times (\text{mg carbadox/mL working std soln}) \times (1\text{ g}/1000\text{ mg}) \times 15\text{ mL aliquot} \times 100.$$

Decoquinate (Ethyl 6-*n*-decyloxy-7-ethoxy-4-hydroxy-3-quinolinecarboxylate) (*14*)—Official Final Action

42.051 ***Principle***

Decoquinate is extd from feed with 1% $CaCl_2$-MeOH soln. After addn of H_2O and acid, drug is extd into $CHCl_3$, then sepd from interfering materials by chromatgy on Florisil. Decoquinate is eluted from column with 1% $CaCl_2$-MeOH and detd by fluorometry against std treated similarly.

42.052 ***Reagents***

(**a**) *Calcium chloride-methanol soln.*—1%. Dissolve 10 g anhyd. $CaCl_2$, reagent grade, in 1 L MeOH, spectral grade (MC/B Manufacturing Chemists) or equiv. redistd, reagent grade, anhyd. MeOH. Filter thru Whatman No. 2 paper.

(**b**) *Decoquinate std solns.*—*(1) Stock soln.*—300 μg/mL. Weigh 30 mg Decoquinate Ref. Std (available from Hess & Clark Laboratories). Dissolve and dil. to 100 mL with 1% $CaCl_2$-MeOH soln. Prep. fresh monthly. *(2) Working soln.*—6 μg/mL. Pipet 5 mL stock soln into 250 mL vol. flask and dil. to vol. with 1% $CaCl_2$-MeOH soln. Check *A* of this soln in 1 cm quartz cells at 265 nm against spectral grade MeOH (ca 0.660). Prep fresh std when *A* is outside range 0.620–0.700. Soln is stable ≥1 week. *(3) Fluorescence reference soln.*—1.5 μg/mL. Pipet 25 mL working std soln into 100 mL vol. flask and dil. to vol. with spectral grade MeOH. Check *A* at 265 nm as above. Prep. fresh std when *A* is outside range 0.150–0.190.

(**c**) *Florisil.*—100–200 mesh (Fisher No. F-101).

42.053 ***Apparatus***

(**a**) *Chromatographic columns.*—Draw 30 cm length of 9 mm tubing (7 mm id) to drip tip. Insert small glass wool plug to support adsorbent. Close drip end with short piece of tubing and pinch clamp. Add 5 mL $CHCl_3$ to column, then 0.5±0.01 g Florisil. Add 2 mL addnl $CHCl_3$ and stir with thin glass rod to settle adsorbent. Remove tubing and wash down sides of tube with $CHCl_3$. Prep. just before use.

(**b**) *Separators.*—125 or 250 mL with Teflon stopcocks.

(**c**) *Fluorometer.*—(*Caution: See* **51.008**.) Either spectrofluorometer or filter fluorometer may be used. Excitation filter: Baird Atomic, Inc. UV-2 (UV Spectrum Filters No. 14-16-8, 325 nm); emission filter: Baird Atomic S/UV (UV Spectrum Filters No. 14-01-4, 390 nm).

42.054 ***Determination***

Weigh 10 g sample into 125 mL erlenmeyer, add exactly 50 mL 1% $CaCl_2$-MeOH soln, stopper, and shake mech. 20 min. Decant soln into centrf. tube and centrf. 5 min at moderate speed. Pipet 10 mL clear supernate into 125 mL separator. Prep. std by pipetting 10 mL working std soln into another separator. Add exactly 10 mL $CHCl_3$ to each funnel by pipet and swirl to mix. Add 100 mL dil. HCl (1+19) to each funnel. Shake gently by inverting 25 times; then allow 15 min for phases to sep. Drain $CHCl_3$ layer into centrf. tube and centrf. 5 min. Remove by aspiration any droplets of floating H_2O phase that seps.

Pipet 5 mL $CHCl_3$ sample soln onto Florisil column. Pipet 5 mL $CHCl_3$ std soln onto another column. Pipet 5 mL $CHCl_3$ onto third column (reagent blank). Pass two 10 mL portions anhyd. MeOH thru each column. Let MeOH drain to surface of Florisil and discard column effluent. Elute with 15 mL 1% $CaCl_2$-MeOH soln, collecting in tube marked at 15 mL. Mix well, centrf. if not clear, and transfer to fluorometer cells. Set activation wavelength of fluorometer at 325 nm and emission wavelength at 390 nm. Set fluorometer sensitivity with fluorescence ref. std to give convenient scale reading (e.g., 100). Det. fluorescence of samples, std, and reagent blank. Subtract reagent blank correction, if any, from reading of std and samples.

% Decoquinate in feed = (0.003 × corrected fluorescence of sample)/corrected fluorescence of std.

Dibutyltin Dilaurate (DBTD, Butynorate®)

Atomic Absorption Spectrophotometric Method (15) *Official Final Action*

42.055 ***Principle***

DBTD is extd from feed with $CHCl_3$, ext is filtered to remove feed particles, and aliquot is concd in presence of MeOH until $CHCl_3$ is removed. MeOH soln is dild and filtered to remove feed interference, and Sn is detd by AA using air-C_2H_2 flame.

42.056 ***Apparatus and Reagents***

(**a**) *Atomic absorption spectrophotometer.*—Double beam, operated at 286.3 nm with air-C_2H_2 flame and direct readout using 10 mv recorder. Optimize instrument according to manufacturer's instructions.

(**b**) *Hot plate.*—Regulated to ±3°.

(**c**) *Mechanical shaker.*—Wrist-action type (Burrell Corp., or equiv.).

(**d**) *Tin std solns.*—*(1) Stock soln.*—500 μg/mL. Accurately weigh ca 0.217 g dibutyltin bis(2-ethylhexanoate) (NBS SRM No. 1057 or Eastman Kodak No. 10427, % Sn certified) into 100 mL vol. flask, and dissolve and dil. to vol. with MeOH. *(2) Working soln.*—10 μg/mL. Pipet 2 mL stock soln into 100 mL vol. flask, add 1.0 mL HCl, and dil. to vol. with MeOH.

42.057 ***Preparation of Sample and Extraction***

Grind sample in high-speed blender to pass No. 20 sieve (ca 3 min), and mix thoroly. Accurately weigh aliquot contg ca 10 μg Sn/mL in final soln (*see* Table **42:01**), and transfer to 125 mL erlenmeyer. Add 50 mL $CHCl_3$, mix, and place flask in 55–60° H_2O bath. Let sample reach bath temp.; then stopper tightly. Continue heating addnl 30 min, swirling occasionally. Remove from H_2O bath and shake mech. 20 min. Filter thru Whatman No. 4 paper, and collect ≥30 mL filtrate in 50 mL erlenmeyer.

Pipet 25 mL filtrate into 100 mL graduated beaker, add 2 boiling chips and 0.25 mL HCl, and conc. to ca 10 mL at gentle boil on hot plate. Add 20 mL MeOH and conc. sample to ca 10 mL again; then repeat with addnl 20 mL and 30 mL portions MeOH. (Raise temp. of hot plate to maintain gentle boiling as ratio of MeOH to $CHCl_3$ increases.) Remove from heat and let cool to room temp. Transfer MeOH soln to 25 mL vol. flask, washing beaker and funnel with 2–3 five mL portions MeOH, dil. to vol. with MeOH, and mix thoroly. Filter thru Whatman No. 42 paper and collect filtrate in another 25 mL vol. flask.

Prep. blank by dilg 1 mL HCl to 100 mL with MeOH.

42.058 ***Determination***

(*Caution: See* **51.006**.)

Let spectrophtr warm up thoroly and equilibrate by aspirating MeOH 15 min, using air-C_2H_2 flame and triple slot burner head. Zero spectrophtr by aspirating blank; then aspirate sample and std solns, using conditions given in (**a**). Repeat sequence for each sample.

$$\% \text{ DBTD} = A \times C \times 50 \times 5.32 \times 10^{-6} \times (100/A') \times W$$
$$= (A/A') \times (0.266/W),$$

Table 42:01 Sample Weights for DBDT-Containing Feeds

%DBDT	Feed Sample, g
0.020 (Polystat)	13.00
0.0375 (Tinostat)	7.00
0.0700 (Wormal)	3.75
0.1400 (Wormal)	2.00

where A and A' refer to sample and std, resp.; C = g std/mL; and W = g sample.

Diethylstilbestrol (DES) (*16*)—Official First Action

42.059 ***Reagent***

Diethylstilbestrol std soln.—55 μg/mL. Prep. stock soln contg 0.55 mg USP Ref. Std Diethylstilbestrol/mL $CHCl_3$. Dil. 10 mL of this stock soln to 100 mL with $CHCl_3$.

42.060 ***Apparatus***

(**a**) *Lamp.*—UV or germicidal lamp. Wattage of lamp and distance from cell should be such that peak absorption results with min. rise in temp. of soln, preferably ≤1°. (*Caution: See* **51.016**.)

(**b**) *Spectrophotometer.*—With W lamp and matched 1 cm absorption cells. Cells must be silica or quartz, if used for irradiation.

(**c**) *Cells.*—Matched 1 cm quartz absorption cells or transparent quartz tubes, 16 × 150 mm for irradiation.

42.061 ***Standardization***

Place quartz cells or tubes in suitable holder, rigidly fixed, so that cells or tubes are irradiated transversely and at fixed distance from lamp. (Do not irradiate from top.) Distance may be 15 cm or whatever gives irradiation max. between ca 5–12 min. Cells or tubes must be clean and dry for each detn. Det. optimum irradiation time by irradiation in quartz cells of ca 3 mL HOAc contg DES at time intervals of 1 min increments to find approx. irradiation max. Depending on source of irradiation, more exact irradiation time for max. A may result with shorter time intervals.

Pipet 1 mL std soln into 100 mL beaker, evap. in air current, add 10 mL HOAc, stir, and transfer ca 3 mL portions to each of 2 or 3 cells for irradiation. Cool, if necessary, and det. A at 415 nm as in **42.062**. Alternatively, use mixt. of alcohol and 0.1*M* K_2HPO_4 (1+1) as solv.

Irradiation is critical and conditions must be carefully observed. Check frequently against std soln, and use exact same conditions for samples. Time of exposure may be longer with feed ext than with pure DES soln.

42.062 ***Determination***

Accurately weigh 20 g "40-mesh" sample, add 2–3 g *Dicalite* or other diat. earth, mix well, transfer to extn thimble (33 × 94 mm), and place piece of absorbent cotton in top of thimble. To extn flask add 140 mL solv. mixt. contg 7% v/v EtOH in $CHCl_3$, and ext 16 hr or overnight at rate of ≥100 drops/min in Soxhlet extractor. After extn, leave part of $CHCl_3$ in upper part of app. and transfer it to another flask. If insol. material is present in main ext, filter into 100 mL vol. flask (glass wool in funnel is suitable), rinse with rest of $CHCl_3$ from other flask, cool, dil. to vol. with $CHCl_3$, and mix.

Pipet 25 mL into 125 mL separator (aliquot *1*). Transfer another 25 mL into second 125 mL separator (aliquot *2*). Into second separator pipet 1.0 mL DES std soln, contg 55 μg. Add 25 mL $CHCl_3$ and 25 mL 1*N* H_2SO_4 to each separator and wash by inverting funnel with rotary motion 6 times rather vigorously. Transfer lower $CHCl_3$ layer to another 125 mL separator, add 10 mL $CHCl_3$ to acid soln, and wash again as before. Combine $CHCl_3$ solns, discarding aq. soln.

Add 10 mL 1*N* NaOH and invert separator with rotary motion rather vigorously ca 12 times but not hard enough to cause serious emulsions. Drain $CHCl_3$ layer into another 125 mL separator. Again ext this $CHCl_3$ with 10 mL 1*N* NaOH in same way. Discard $CHCl_3$ layer and combine alk. exts in separator.

To combined alk. exts add 5 mL $CHCl_3$, shake few sec, discard lower $CHCl_3$ layer, and repeat 3 or 4 times in same way until $CHCl_3$ exts are colorless. Transfer washed alk. ext to 100 mL beaker. To this separator add 5 mL H_2O, shake, and add to combined alk. ext. Add 10 mL 2*N* H_3PO_4, cool to room temp., and adjust to pH 9.0±0.1 with 2*N* H_3PO_4. (*Caution:* Rinse separators that contained combined NaOH exts at least twice with H_2O to remove all alky.)

Return pH-adjusted soln to original separator (alk.-free) from which it was taken, rinsing beakers with two 2 mL portions H_2O. Rinse beakers with 15 mL $CHCl_3$, shake 30–60 sec carefully to avoid emulsions, transfer lower $CHCl_3$ layer to clean, dry separator, and ext pH-adjusted soln twice more in same way with 15 mL portions $CHCl_3$. Combine all $CHCl_3$ exts, add 25 mL H_2O, and shake briefly. Filter $CHCl_3$ ext thru 30 mL fritted glass funnel (ca 20 × 100 mm), medium porosity, contg 2 cm anhyd. Na_2SO_4, into 50 mL vol. flask. Wash the H_2O with small portions $CHCl_3$ and use to rinse Na_2SO_4 and funnel. Continue to rinse funnel with $CHCl_3$ to 50 mL vol. Mix, and pipet 25 mL aliquot into 150 mL beaker previously rinsed with $CHCl_3$. Evap. just to dryness on steam bath with aid of air current (manifold arrangement works well on series of samples). Evap. last of $CHCl_3$ with air current only.

Pipet 10 mL HOAc, or alcohol-0.1*M* K_2HPO_4 (1+1), into the beaker. Stir with glass rod to ensure soln of DES. Transfer ca 3 mL into each of 2 or 3 matched quartz cells (1 cm thickness). Read A at 415 nm before irradiation. Immediately place cells in front of lamp, as in **42.061**, and irradiate under same conditions. Read A. If quartz tubes are used, readings before irradiation can be made on remaining 4 mL of soln for blank correction.

Calc. by increment method for each solv., where A refers to sample after irradiation; A_0, before; B = A of sample plus added DES after irradiation; B_0, before.

mg DES/lb feed = $(A - A_0) \times 4.99/[(B - B_0) - (A - A_0)]$

Alternative calculations.—Prep. std curve from 27.5, 41.25, 55.0, 82.5, and 110 μg DES. After correcting for blank, det. μg DES from A reading.

mg DES/lb feed = μg × 0.1815

1,2-Dimethyl-5-nitroimidazole (Dimetridazole) (*17*)
Official First Action

42.063 ***Principle***

Dimetridazole is extd from feeds with MeOH, sepd from interfering substances by two alumina chromatgc steps, and detd spectrophtric at its UV wavelength max. Nihydrazone, furazolidone, zoalene, 2-chloro-4-nitrobenzamide, tylosin, and large amts procaine (from procaine penicillin) interfere.

42.064 ***Apparatus and Reagents***

(**a**) *Spectrophotometer.*—For use in UV.

(**b**) *Chromatographic tubes.*—13 × 150 mm and 15 × 250 mm, constricted at bottom to hold glass wool plug and 6 mm od delivery tube.

(**c**) *Aluminum oxide.*—Suitable for chromatgy, **42.029(b)**. To det. suitability of alumina, perform detn on feed that does not contain dimetridazole or other imidazole drugs. If feed appears to contain >0.004% dimetridazole, use another batch of alumina.

(**d**) *1,2-Dimethyl-5-nitroimidazole* (*dimetridazole*) *std solns.*—(*1*) *Stock soln.*—0.1 mg/mL. Weigh 100 mg dimetridazole std (available from Salsbury Laboratories) into 100 mL vol. flask. Dissolve in H_2O by shaking frequently ca 20 min. Dil. to vol. with H_2O and mix. Pipet 20 mL into 200 mL vol. flask, dil. to vol. with H_2O, and mix. (*2*) *Working solns.*—Pipet 5, 10, 20, 30, and 40 mL stock soln into sep. 100 mL vol. flasks. Add 5.0 mL 3*N* HCl to each, immediately dil. to vol. with H_2O, and mix. Pipet 5 mL each soln and 5 mL 0.10*N* NaOH into sep. 50 mL erlenmeyers. Stopper and mix. These solns contain 2.5, 5, 10, 15, and 20 μg dimetridazole/mL.

42.065 ***Preparation of Standard Curve***

Proceed as in **42.068**, using working std solns and blank prepd by mixing 5 mL 0.15*N* HCl with 5 mL 0.10*N* NaOH.

Read *A* against blank for recording or manual spectrophtrs. Construct std curve by plotting *A* against μg dimetridazole/mL.

42.066 ***Preparation of Sample***

Weigh portion finely ground feed contg 0.5–2.0 mg dimetridazole (usually 5 g) into 100 mL vol. flask. Add 70–75 mL MeOH and place in 60° const temp. bath 30 min. Make certain that H_2O level covers flask to ca 3 mm below MeOH level. Swirl flask 2 or 3 times during first 5 min to heat evenly. Cool to room temp., dil. to vol. with MeOH, and mix. Let stand 5–10 min to let coarse feed particles settle.

42.067 ***Chromatography***

Place small glass wool plug in bottom of 250 × 15 mm chromatgc tube and add 8 cm layer alumina; pack column tightly to prevent streaking. (If streaks enter effluent, pos. bias is introduced.) Decant methanolic ext onto column so that settled feed particles are not disturbed. Collect ca 30 mL eluate in 50 mL vol. flask. Stopper until ready for use.

(*Note:* Dimetridazole sublimes at temps >70°; manner of solv. removal is critical.) For feed contg 0.015% dimetridazole, pipet 15 mL effluent (4 mL if feed contains 0.06%; 3 mL if feed contains 0.10%) into 125 mL suction or r-b flask and evap. under reduced pressure from H_2O aspirator. If 15 mL is taken, use hot plate (low heat) or H_2O-bath to reduce to 3–4 mL. Shake to prevent bumping. When vol. approaches 3–4 mL remove flask from heat and remove last 3–4 mL only with heat from palm of hand. Continue shaking to prevent bumping. Do not attempt to attain complete dryness because part of the 2–3 drops of oily residue is dimetridazole.

Wash down walls of flask, beginning at base of neck, with 5.0 mL 0.10*N* NaOH. Swirl to wash walls. Let stand 5 min and add 5.0 mL 0.15*N* HCl. Swirl to mix and wash flask walls. Stopper until ready for chromatgy.

42.068 ***Determination***

Prep. second alumina column by inserting small glass wool plug into bottom of 150 × 13 mm chromatgc tube, add 4 cm layer alumina, and tap gently to pack column lightly. Pour entire 10 mL soln onto column and let pass thru by gravity. Collect effluent in 50 mL erlenmeyer. Force out liq. adhering to column by applying air pressure with rubber bulb. Swirl flask to mix. Stopper until ready to read. Pass blank soln of 5 mL 0.15*N* HCl and 5 mL 0.10*N* NaOH thru sep. 4 cm alumina column as above.

(**a**) *Using recording spectrophotometer.*—Fill matched pair silica cells with reagent blank and with sample soln (always use same cell for blank) and scan from 330 to 310 nm. Read *A* at peak and obtain concn of soln in μg/mL from std curve.

$$\% \text{ Dimetridazole} = [(\mu g/mL \text{ from std curve}) \times \text{diln factor} \times 100]/(g \text{ sample} \times 10^6),$$

where diln factor = 1.335×10^{-3} for feeds contg 0.015%; 5×10^{-3}, 0.06%; and 6.66×10^{-3}, 0.1%.

(**b**) *Using manual spectrophotometer.*—Locate peak *A* of sample soln (ca 318 nm), using matched pair silica cells, and set wavelength at peak. Read *A* of sample and blank solns and correct sample for blank. Obtain concn of soln in μg/mL from std curve, and calc. % in feed as above.

Ethopabate (Methyl 4-acetamido-2-ethoxy-benzoate) (*18*)
Official Final Action

42.069 ***Principle***

Ethopabate is extd from feed by 50% MeOH at room temp. Clear filtrate is acidified with dil. HCl and extd with $CHCl_3$. Most interfering substances (amines, *p*-aminobenzoic acid, procaine) are sepd. $CHCl_3$ ext is washed with Na_2CO_3 soln to remove sulfaquinoxaline, acetyl-(*p*-nitrophenyl) sulfanilamide, and chlortetracycline. Ethopabate is converted to free amine by controlled acid hydrolysis. Free amine is diazotized and coupled; colored complex is extd with *n*-BuOH and read at 550 nm.

42.070 ***Reagents***

(**a**) *Dilute hydrochloric acid.*—0.3*N*. Dil. 25 mL HCl with H_2O to 1 L.

(**b**) *Sodium carbonate soln.*—Dissolve 40 g anhyd. Na_2CO_3 in H_2O and dil. to 1 L.

(**c**) *Coupling reagent (NED).*—Dissolve 50 mg *N*-(1-naphthyl)ethylenediamine.2HCl in 25 mL H_2O. Prep. fresh as needed.

(**d**) *Ethopabate std solns.*—(*1*) *Stock soln.*—0.400 mg/mL. Weigh 40.0 mg Ethopabate Ref. Std (available from Merck & Co.) into 100 mL vol. flask, dissolve in MeOH, and dil. to vol. (*2*) *Intermediate soln.*—40 μg/mL. Pipet 10 mL stock soln into 100 mL vol. flask, dil. to vol. with aq. MeOH (1+1), and mix well. Stored in tightly stoppered flasks, solns are stable ≥1 month. (*3*) *Working soln.*—16.0 μg/20.0 mL. Pipet 5 mL intermediate soln into 250 mL vol. flask, dil. to vol. with aq. MeOH (1+1), and mix well.

42.071 ***Extraction***

Grind feed sample to pass No. 20 sieve and mix thoroly. (High-speed blender grinds most feeds to desired fineness in ca 3 min.) Accurately weigh sample contg ca 80 μg ethopabate (do not exceed 20 g). Transfer to 250 mL g-s flask. Add 100.0 mL aq. MeOH (1+1) and mag. stirrer bar, stopper tightly, and stir 1 hr. (Mech. shaker that provides vigorous agitation may be used.) Centrf., or filter portion of ext thru fast paper. Collect only enough filtrate to supply aliquot for test. If necessary, store exts overnight at room temp. in tightly stoppered flasks.

42.072 ***Removal of Interferences***

Pipet 20 mL clear ext into 50 mL centrf. tube. Add 5.0 mL dil. HCl (1+9) and 10 mL $CHCl_3$, stopper with polyethylene stopper, and shake vigorously 3 min on mech. shaker. Centrf., and carefully transfer bottom $CHCl_3$ layer into clean 50 mL centrf. tube, using syringe with long needle. Repeat extn with two more 10 mL portions $CHCl_3$. Add 10 mL Na_2CO_3 soln to combined $CHCl_3$ exts, stopper, and shake 3 min. Centrf., and without disturbing interface, draw off most of top aq. layer, using syringe, and discard. Repeat washing with another 10 mL Na_2CO_3 soln, discarding washing. Add 10 mL H_2O to $CHCl_3$ ext, stopper, shake vigorously ca 1 min, and centrf. Draw off aq. layer and discard. Repeat with another 10 mL H_2O. (To avoid loss of drug and low results, do not disturb interface on $CHCl_3$, and complete extn and washings in shortest time possible. Prolonged contact with HCl and Na_2CO_3 may cause partial hydrolysis of ethopabate.)

Pipet 20 mL aq. MeOH (1+1) into 50 mL centrf. tube, add 5.0 mL dil. HCl (1+9), and proceed as for sample (reagent blank).

Pipet 20 mL ethopabate working std soln (16.0 μg) into 50 mL centrf. tube, add 5.0 mL dil. HCl (1+9), and proceed as for sample (std).

42.073 ***Conversion of Ethopabate to Free Amine***

Quant. transfer washed $CHCl_3$ exts to sep. 100 mL beakers. Rinse each centrf. tube with two 3 mL portions aq. MeOH (1+1), adding rinsings to beaker. Place beaker on steam bath and evap. $CHCl_3$ to vol. of ca 2 mL. Add 5.0 mL aq. MeOH (1+1) and swirl beaker to dissolve completely.

Quant. transfer soln to r-b centrf. tube. Rinse beaker with 10, 10, and 5 mL portions 0.3*N* HCl. Immerse tube in boiling H_2O bath so that level of liq. in tube is just below level of H_2O bath. Heat 45 min. Remove tube from hot H_2O bath and cool to 10–15° in cold H_2O bath.

42.074 ***Development and Measurement of Color***

Remove tubes from cold H_2O bath. Add 1.0 mL *freshly prepd 0.2% $NaNO_2$ soln* to each tube, mix, and let stand 2 min. Add 1.0 mL 1.0% NH_4 sulfamate soln, mix, and let stand 2 min. Add 1.0 mL NED soln, mix, and let stand 10 min. Add 5.0 g NaCl and 5.00 mL *n*-BuOH, stopper, and shake vigorously until NaCl dissolves. Centrf., carefully transfer portion of clear, colored alc. layer to 1 cm cell, and read *A* at 555 nm against *n*-BuOH. Correct for reagent blank.

% Ethopabate in feed = $0.008 \times (A - A_B)/[(A' - A_B) \times W]$, where A, A_B, and A' refer to sample, reagent blank, and std, resp., and W = g original sample.

Furazolidone (*N*-[5-Nitro-2-furfurylidene]-3-amino-2-oxazolidone), Bifuran (Mixture of Furazolidone and Nitrofurazone), or Nitrofurazone (5-Nitro-2-furaldehyde semicarbazone) (*19*)—Official Final Action

42.075 ***Reagents***

(**a**) *Phenylhydrazine hydrochloride soln.*—Dissolve 0.5 g phenylhydrazine.HCl in 50 mL H_2O. Prep. fresh daily. Mix equal vol. of this soln with HCl.

(**b**) *Furazolidone std solns.*—(*1*) *Stock soln.*—0.55 mg/mL. Weigh 55 mg furazolidone std (available from Hess & Clark) into 100 mL vol. flask, dil. to vol. with dimethylformamide (DMF), and mix. Soln is stable several months when protected from light. (*2*) *Working soln.*—Prep. working std corresponding to label declaration. For feeds contg 0.011% furazolidone, pipet 2 mL stock soln into 100 mL vol. flask, add 48 mL DMF, and dil. to vol. with H_2O. For feeds contg 0.00275% furazolidone, pipet 0.5 mL stock soln into 100 mL vol. flask, add 49.5 mL DMF, and dil. to vol. with H_2O.

(**c**) *Nitrofurazone std solns.*—(*1*) *Stock soln.*—0.56 mg/mL. Weigh 56 mg nitrofurazone std (available from Hess & Clark) into 100 mL vol. flask, dil. to vol. with DMF, and mix. Soln is stable several months when protected from light. (*2*) *Working soln.*—Prep. working std corresponding to label declaration. For feeds contg 0.0056% nitrofurazone, pipet 1 mL stock soln into 100 mL vol. flask, add 49 mL DMF, and dil. to vol. with H_2O. For feeds contg 0.0112% nitrofurazone, pipet 2 mL stock soln into 100 mL vol. flask, add 48 mL DMF, and dil. to vol. with H_2O.

(**d**) *Bifuran std solns.*—(*1*) *Stock soln.*—0.1285 mg/mL. Pipet 20 mL nitrofurazone stock soln and 3 mL furazolidone stock soln into 100 mL vol. flask and dil. to vol. with DMF. (*2*) *Working soln.*—For feeds contg 0.0064% total nitrofurans, prep. working std by pipetting 5 mL bifuran stock soln into 100 mL vol. flask, adding 45 mL DMF, and dilg to vol. with H_2O.

(**e**) *Adsorbent.*—To 100 parts alumina, **42.029(b)**, in screw cap bottle, add 4 parts $Mg(OH)_2$, shake until thoroly mixed, then add 5 parts H_2O, and mix until all lumps disappear. Store in tightly sealed container.

42.076 ***Determination***

(*Caution: See* **51.018**, **51.040**, and **51.053**.)

Grind coarse or pelleted feeds to "20 mesh" thru cutting-type mill such as Wiley Intermediate. Finer feeds need not be ground. Weigh 10 g sample into 125 mL erlenmeyer, add exactly 50 mL DMF, stopper loosely, and place in boiling H_2O bath 5 min. Mech. shake 10 min and filter thru rapid paper. To 25 mL filtrate add 25 mL H_2O and mix.

Prep. ca 20 mm diam. adsorption column, contg adsorbent, to ht of 5 cm. Pass the 50% DMF sample soln thru column, discarding first 3 mL eluate. (If column flow stops, break up gummy film at top of adsorbent, using long thin glass rod.) Pipet 5 mL aliquots of eluate into each of 2 numbered test tubes. Protect one tube from light. To other tube, add 3 drops *freshly prepd 2% soln of Na hydrosulfite* and let stand 20 min, shaking at ca 5 min intervals. Treat 5 mL aliquots of working std soln in exactly same manner.

Pipet 5 mL phenylhydrazine.HCl soln into each of the numbered test tubes contg samples and stds. Mix and place tubes in 70° H_2O bath 25 min; cool in 15° H_2O bath 5 min. Add exactly 10 mL toluene to each tube, stopper, and shake vigorously 40 times. Centrf. or filter toluene soln directly into absorption cell thru cotton wad inserted in stem of small funnel. Read *A* of solns at 440 nm.

$$\% \text{ Furazolidone} = [(A_{\text{samp.}} - A_{\text{red. samp.}}) \times 0.011 \text{ (or } 0.00275)]/(A_{\text{std}} - A_{\text{red. std}})$$

$$\% \text{ Total nitrofurans (bifuran)} = [(A_{\text{samp.}} - A_{\text{red. samp.}}) \times 0.0064]/(A_{\text{std}} - A_{\text{red. std}})$$

$$\% \text{ Nitrofurazone} = [(A_{\text{samp.}} - A_{\text{red. samp.}}) \times 0.0056 \text{ (or } 0.011)]/(A_{\text{std}} - A_{\text{red. std}})$$

42.077 ★ **Glycarbylamide (4,5-Imidazoledicarboxamide) (*20*)—Official Final Action** ★

Glycarbylamide is extd from feed with dimethylformamide. Ext is purified by chromatgy on alumina and anion exchange resin, and traces of residual impurities are oxidized with Br. *A* of glycarbylamide is measured at 283 nm in alk. soln against portion of same soln from which glycarbylamide has been removed by adsorption on HgO. *See* **38.066–38.071**, 11th ed.

Ipronidazole (1-Methyl-2-isopropyl-5-nitroimidazole) (*21*) Official First Action

42.078 ***Principle***

Ipronidazole is extd from feed with warm 0.2*N* HCl, transferred to benzene after alkalinization, and measured by GLC with electron capture detector.

42.079 ***Apparatus***

(**a**) *Gas chromatograph.*—With electron capture detector. Conditions: temps (°)—column 180±2 (isothermal), injection 240±2, detector 210±2; N flow 60 mL/min (install 3′ (0.9 m) × ¼″ molecular sieve 5A trap in N line).

(**b**) *Recorder.*—Texas Instruments (PO Box 1444, Houston, TX 77001) 0–1 mv input and 1.0 sec full scale deflection, chart speed 0.75″/min, or equiv.

(**c**) *Gas chromatographic column.*—0.9 m (3′) × ⅛″ od stainless steel tubing packed with 5% Carbowax 20M-terephthalic acid (TPA) on 100–120 mesh Chromosorb G, acid-washed and

★ Surplus method—*see* inside front cover.

dichlorodimethylsilane-treated (Applied Science Laboratories, Inc.).

(**d**) *Column preparation.*—Dissolve 1.0 g Carbowax 20M-TPA in 30 mL $CHCl_3$ and let stand over 19.0 g Chromosorb G 3 days with occasional swirling. After standing, evap. $CHCl_3$ under N and dry 1 hr in 70° oven. After packing, condition column 2 days at 200° in slow stream of N before use.

42.080 ***Reagents***

(**a**) *Benzene.*—Redistil from all-glass app., discarding first and last 10%. (*Caution: See* **51.011**, **51.039**, **51.040**, and **51.045**.)

(**b**) *Ipronidazole.*—Available from Hoffmann-La Roche, Inc.; prep. std soln contg 0.3 μg ipronidazole/mL benzene.

42.081 ***Chromatography of Standard***

Inject 5 μL std ipronidazole soln into gas chromatograph and adjust conditions to obtain ca 5 min retention time. Det. area under ipronidazole peak as product of peak ht (cm) and width (cm) at half ht, using slope baseline technic. After satisfactory performance of column is established, inject at least duplicate 5 μL aliquots of std soln (1.5 ng/5 μL) at beginning of work day and periodically thereafter (e.g., after each 5–6 sample injections). Measure ipronidazole peak area in each case.

42.082 ***Preparation of Sample***

(*Caution: See* **51.018** and **51.045**.)

Ext mash-type feeds without prior grinding. Grind pelleted feeds to pass No. 30 sieve before extn. (Method for feeds is described for 0.0060% level of ipronidazole with modifications indicated for 0.0030 and 0.0090% levels.)

Transfer 10 g sample into 500 mL vol. flask (for 0.0030% level, use 20 g sample) and add exactly 200 mL 0.2*N* HCl previously warmed to 40±3°. Stopper flask and shake mech. 20 min. Let settle few min. Centrf. portion of supernate and pipet 10 mL (for 0.0090% level, transfer 5.0 mL and add 5 mL 0.2*N* HCl) to g-s centrf. tube. Place tube in cold H_2O bath and add 0.5 mL 5*N* NaOH to make alk. (pH = 10–12.5; check with Accutint pH paper; do not hold eluate at high pH for prolonged time). Pipet 20 mL benzene into tube, stopper, shake mech. 5 min, and centrf. 10 min at 2500 rpm. Pipet 5 mL clear benzene ext into 25 mL vol. flask, dil. to vol. with benzene, and mix. This is sample soln.

42.083 ***Determination***

Inject 5 μL sample soln into chromatograph. Measure area of ipronidazole peak obtained from chromatogram.

$$\% \text{ Ipronidazole} = (B \times C \times D)/(B' \times 10{,}000),$$

where B and B' = areas under ipronidazole peak for sample and std solns, resp.; C = μg ipronidazole/mL in std soln (0.3); and D = diln factor (0.0030% level, D = 100; 0.0060%, 200; and 0.0090%, 400).

★ Nequinate (Methyl 7-benzyloxy-6-butyl-1,4-dihydro-4-oxo-3-quinolinecarboxylate) (*22*) ★ Official Final Action

42.084 ***Principle***

Coccidiostat nequinate is used in feed at 20 μg/g. Drug is extd from feed with 1% HCOOH in $CHCl_3$ and filtered; ext is dild with $CHCl_3$. Methanesulfonic acid (MSA) is added and fluorescence is measured against std treated in same manner.

★ Surplus method—*see* inside front cover.

42.085 ***Apparatus***

(**a**) *Spectrophotofluorometer.*—With sufficient energy at 270 nm.

(**b**) *Automatic dilutor.*—0.1 mL dild to 20 mL with $CHCl_3$; reproducibility ±0.1% (Labindustries, 620 Hearst Ave, Berkeley, CA 94710, No. 82001).

42.086 ***Reagents***

(**a**) *Chloroform.*—Check each bottle before use to det. that it has fluorescence background ≤10% fluorescence of ref. std soln after addn of MSA.

(**b**) *Methanesulfonic acid (MSA) soln.*—Contg 50 mg MSA (Eastman Kodak Co. No. 6320)/mL $CHCl_3$; prep. fresh daily.

(**c**) *Formic acid.*—97–100% (MC/B Manufacturing Chemists, FX 440, or equiv.).

(**d**) *Diethylamine (DEA) soln.*—Contg 50 mg DEA (bp 55–56°)/mL $CHCl_3$; prep. fresh daily.

(**e**) *Nequinate std solns.*—(*1*) *Stock soln.*—1 mg/mL. Weigh 100 mg nequinate into 100 mL vol. flask. Dissolve and dil. to vol. with 1% HCOOH in $CHCl_3$. (*2*) *Working soln.*—4.0 μg/mL. Dil. 10 mL stock soln to 100 mL with 1% HCOOH in $CHCl_3$. Further dil. 4.0 mL of this soln to 100 mL with same solv.

42.087 ***Determination***

Grind pelleted or coarse feed to pass No. 30 sieve. Weigh 5 g sample into 40 mL centrf. tube with Teflon-lined screw cap. Add exactly 25 mL 1% HCOOH in $CHCl_3$ (25 mL automatic pipet is convenient). Stopper tube and shake mech. 15 min. Filter small portion ext thru medium porosity fritted glass filter with aid of pressure. (Since <1.0 mL filtrate is required for next step, it is not necessary for all of ext to pass thru filter. Feed ext theoretically contains 4 μg/mL.)

Dil. 2 fractions filtered ext to calcd concn of 0.02 μg/mL $CHCl_3$. Use either automatic dilutor (0.1 mL to 20 mL) or perform diln by transferring 0.5 mL filtered feed ext to 100 mL vol. flask, using Hamilton or tuberculin syringe, and dilg to vol. with $CHCl_3$. To one fraction, S^+, add 0.02 mL MSA soln/10 mL. To second fraction, S^-, add 0.02 mL DEA soln/10 mL. Dil. 2 fractions working std soln (4.0 μg/mL) to 0.02 μg/mL in same manner. To one fraction, R^+, add 0.02 mL MSA soln/10 mL. To second fraction, R^-, add 0.02 mL DEA soln/10 mL. (MSA and DEA solns can be added most easily by use of micrometer buret.)

Using ref. std, R^+, adjust monochromators for max. fluorescence, excitation wavelength near 270 nm, and emission wavelength near 372 nm. Adjust gain to read ca 70% full scale and det. fluorescence of ref. stds (R^+ *and* R^-) and samples (S^+ and S^-).

$$\mu\text{g Nequinate/g sample} = [(F_{S+} - F_{S-})/(F_{R+} - F_{R-})] \times (100/W_S),$$

where $F_S{}^+$, $F_S{}^-$, $F_R{}^+$, and $F_R{}^-$ = fluorescence of S^+ (sample with MSA), S^- (sample with DEA), R^+ (ref. std with MSA), and R^- (ref. std with DEA), resp.; and W_S = g sample.

Nicarbazin (4,4′-Dinitrocarbanilide.2-hydroxy-4,6-dimethylpyrimidine) (*23*)—Official Final Action

(Presence of furazolidone, nitrofurazone, or nihydrazone may cause high results. Confirm presence of nicarbazin by Identification Test, **42.093**.)

42.088 ***Reagents***

(**a**) *Dimethylformamide (DMF).*—Reagent grade.

(**b**) *Alumina.*—*See* **42.029**(**b**).

(**c**) *Alcohol.*—Formulas SDA Nos. 2B, 3A, or 30 may be used.

(**d**) *Alcoholic sodium hydroxide soln.*—Dil. 2.0 mL clear 50%

NaOH soln, **50.033(b)**, to 100 mL with alcohol. Centrf. in stoppered tube. Prep. fresh daily.

(**e**) *Nicarbazin std solns.*—(*1*) *Stock soln.*—Weigh 25.0 mg Nicarbazin Ref. Std (available from Merck & Co.) into 500 mL vol. flask, and dissolve in ca 150 mL DMF with aid of gentle heat. Cool, dil. to vol. with DMF, and mix well. Store protected from light. (*2*) *Working soln.*—12.5 μg/mL. Transfer 25.0 mL stock soln to 100 mL vol. flask and dil. to vol. with DMF. Mix well.

42.089 ***Preparation of Column***

Use glass tube 22 mm id, ca 50 cm long, constricted at lower end. Place plug of glass wool in constricted end and add 30 g alumina in 3 portions. Tamp each portion with glass rod while applying gentle suction. Wash column with 25 mL DMF, draining to point 1–2 cm above bed level before adding sample to column. Prep. column for each sample and std.

Never let column run dry; keep head of liq. at all times.

42.090 ***Preparation of Sample***

(*Caution: See* **51.011**, **51.040**, and **51.053**.)

Weigh 10.0 g sample into 250 mL erlenmeyer and add 100.0 mL DMF. Heat *just to bp* on hot plate in hood with intermittent stirring. Cool to room temp. by immersing in H_2O bath. Decant supernate into centrf. tubes and centrf. 3 min.

42.091 ***Determination***

(*Caution: See* **51.018**, **51.040**, and **51.053**.)

Pipet 25.0 mL clear ext onto column and let pass thru column with aid of gentle suction. Wash column with three 10 mL portions DMF and reject washings. Elute with nine 5 mL portions alcohol, discarding first 15 mL eluate and collecting next 25 mL eluate in 25 × 200 mm tube. Quant. transfer eluate into 50 mL vol. flask and dil. to vol. with alcohol. Mix well.

Pipet 25.0 mL working std soln onto another column and proceed as for sample.

Pipet two 15.0 mL portions sample soln into sep. 25 mL vol. flasks. To one add 5.0 mL alc. NaOH soln and adjust vol. of both solns to 25 mL with alcohol. Read *A* of yellow soln formed in first flask within 5 min in spectrophtr or colorimeter at 430 nm against second soln as blank. Calc. wt nicarbazin from std curve.

42.092 ***Preparation of Standard Curve***

Pipet 10, 15, and 20 mL aliquots of chromatgd working std soln into sep. 25 mL vol. flasks, add 5 mL alc. NaOH, and dil. to vol. with alcohol. Mix well. Measure *A* within 5 min at 430 nm against alcohol.

Prep. std curve by plotting *A* against μg nicarbazin.

42.093 ***Identification Test***

Place alcohol in 1 cm quartz cell and clear chromatgd sample soln in matched cell. Det. *A* at 2 nm intervals from 340 to 349 nm with Beckman Model DU spectrophtr, or equiv., at min. slit width. Absorption max. at 344±4 nm confirms presence of nicarbazin.

Nicotine (*24*)—Official Final Action

(Applicable in the presence of phenothiazine, dibutyltin dilaurate, and 2,2′-dihydroxy-5,5′-dichlorodiphenylmethane)

42.094 ***Principle***

Nicotine is extd with alkali, steam distd, extd with $CHCl_3$, and detd spectrophtric in acidic soln.

42.095 ***Reagents***

(**a**) *Dilute hydrochloric acid.*—0.05*N*. Dil. 4.1 mL HCl to 1 L with H_2O.

(**b**) *Nicotine std soln.*—0.012 mg/mL. Accurately weigh ca 100 mg nicotine and dil. to 100 mL in vol. flask with 0.05*N* HCl. Transfer 3.0 mL aliquot to 250 mL vol. flask and dil. to vol. with 0.05*N* HCl. (*Caution:* Nicotine is very toxic.)

(**c**) *Antifoam.*—Antifoam A (Dow Corning Corp.), or equiv.

42.096 ***Apparatus***

(**a**) *Distillation flask.*—250 mL r-b flask and Claisen distg head or 250 mL Claisen flask.

(**b**) *Condenser.*—Graham coil type with 300 mm jacket (Corning No. 2500, or equiv.). Must be used in vertical position.

(**c**) *Ultraviolet recording spectrophotometer.*—Double beam, capable of scanning UV spectrum from 220 to 300 nm, with 1 cm cells.

42.097 ***Determination***

(Detn can be interrupted at any step where soln is acidic.)

Accurately weigh representative portion of feed, ground thru No. 20 sieve, contg ca 3 mg nicotine and transfer to 250 mL centrf. bottle. Add 100 mL 0.5% NaOH soln, stopper (Neoprene or rubber), and shake vigorously 1 min. Centrf. ca 5 min at 1500 rpm. Decant free flowing and viscous liq. into 400–600 mL beaker. Rinse lip and centrf. bottle into beaker with few mL H_2O, being careful not to dislodge solid material. Repeat extn, centrfg, and rinsing twice, combining supernates in beaker. Adjust soln to pH 2–3 with HCl and evap. on hot plate to ca 100 mL. Cool, adjust to pH 10–14 with NaOH (1+1), and transfer quant. to distn flask, using min. of H_2O. Vol. must be ≤125 mL. Add 10 drops antifoam to flask. Place tip of condenser below surface of 7 mL H_2SO_4 (1+5) in 500 mL flask or beaker (container must be tilted at first to obtain sufficient depth). Steam distil at rate of ≥8 mL/min. (It will be necessary to heat Claisen flask as distn proceeds to avoid condensation of steam in flask.) Collect ca 300 mL distillate. When distn is complete, rinse condenser into receiver with ca 5 mL H_2O.

Transfer distillate to 500 mL separator, rinse with H_2O, make distinctly alk. (pH 10–14) with NaOH (1+1), and ext with five 20 mL portions $CHCl_3$. Combine $CHCl_3$ exts in 250 mL separator. Ext nicotine from $CHCl_3$ with 20, 20, 15, 15, and 15 mL portions 0.05*N* HCl. Combine HCl exts in 125 mL separator and shake gently few sec with 15 mL pet ether to remove any remaining $CHCl_3$. Drain clear HCl layer into 250 mL vol. flask and wash pet ether with addnl 10 mL 0.05*N* HCl. Drain acid layer into vol. flask, dil. to vol. with 0.05*N* HCl, and record UV spectrum from 220 to 300 nm in 1 cm cell against 0.05*N* HCl in recording spectrophtr. Draw line tangent to 2 min. obtained (ca 226 and 280 nm), drop perpendicular from point of max. *A* (ca 259 nm) to tangent line, and det. net *A*. Similarly det. net *A*′ of std soln.

% Nicotine in feed = (Net *A* × mg nicotine in final std soln × 100)/(Net *A*′ × g sample × 1000).

Nifursol (3,5-Dinitrosalicylic acid (5-nitrofurfurylidene) hydrazide) (*25*)—Official First Action

42.098 ***Principle***

Nifursol is extd from feed with dimethylformamide (DMF). Feed interferences are removed from DMF soln by column chromatgy on alumina. Drug is reacted with phenylhydrazine to form 5-nitrofurfural phenylhydrazone, which is extd into toluene and detd spectrophtric at 555 nm immediately after addn of methylbenzethonium hydroxide.

42.099 ***Apparatus***

(**a**) *Chromatographic tubes.*—400 × 20 mm id, with glass wool plug.

(**b**) *Spectrophotometer.*—For use at 555 nm.

42.100 ***Reagents***

(**a**) *N,N-Dimethylformamide (DMF) solns.*—*(1) 95% DMF.*—Dil. 95 parts DMF (MC/B Manufacturing Chemists, DX1730, or equiv.) with 5 parts H_2O. *(2) 50% DMF.*—Dil. 50 parts DMF with 50 parts H_2O.

(**b**) *Alumina.*—To 100 parts 80–200 mesh alumina (Alcoa F-40, Fisher Scientific Co., A-540), add 6 parts powd $Mg(OH)_2$. Shake mixt. in screw-cap bottle until thoroly mixed. Add 8 parts H_2O and immediately mix until all lumps disappear.

(**c**) *Phenylhydrazine soln.*—Prep. immediately before use by dissolving 0.25 g phenylhydrazine.HCl crystals in 25 mL H_2O. Add 25 mL HCl.

(**d**) *Hyamine® hydroxide 10-X (methylbenzethonium hydroxide).*—1*M* soln in MeOH (Packard Instrument Co., Inc., 2200 Warrenville Rd, Downers Grove, IL 60515, No. 6003005).

(**e**) *Nifursol std solns.*—*(1) Stock soln.*—0.25 mg/mL. Weigh 25 mg nifursol (mp 224–226°, Salsbury Laboratories) into 100 mL vol. flask. Add 5 mL DMF, mix until all material is dissolved, and dil. to vol. with MeOH. *(2) Working soln.*—6.25 μg/mL. Pipet 5.0 mL stock soln into 200 mL vol. flask, add 100 mL 95% DMF, and dil. to vol. with H_2O. (Nifursol solns are not stable for long periods of time; prep. fresh as needed.)

42.101 ***Extraction***

Weigh 5.00 g finely ground feed into 250 mL erlenmeyer. Add exactly 50 mL 95% DMF, stopper, and shake gently 5 min on mech. shaker. Place sample 30 min in 60° H_2O bath, remove, and shake vigorously 30 min on mech. shaker. Filter thru rapid paper in buchner, using vac. Transfer 40.0 mL aliquot of filtrate to beaker, add 40.0 mL H_2O, stir, and let stand 30 min in dark.

42.102 ***Chromatography***

Add 7 cm specially prepd alumina to chromatgc tube contg glass wool plug. Tap column walls to settle alumina; then add 1.5 cm *Ottawa sand* (available from Sargent-Welch Scientific Co.). Prewash column with 50 mL 50% DMF *just* before use. Add DMF sample soln to column, discard first 60 mL eluate, and collect next 12 mL. (Decrease in flow rate may occur with some feed exts due to accumulation of fine ppt that settles on surface of alumina. Increase flow rate by stirring top of alumina and sand to break up ppt layer or by applying gentle air pressure to top of column.)

42.103 ***Determination***

Pipet 5 mL aliquot into 20 mL test tube. Add 5 mL freshly prepd phenylhydrazine soln to tube, mix, and place 20 min in 40° H_2O bath. Cool tube under cold tap H_2O (<20°) 5 min, add exactly 5 mL toluene, stopper tube, and shake vigorously. (*Caution:* Do not use black rubber stoppers.) Centrf. 5 min to clear toluene layer and transfer 3.0 mL toluene to 1 cm cell. Add 0.1 mL methylbenzethonium hydroxide to cell and mix immediately. Read sample within 1 min at 555 nm on spectrophtr. Det. concn of nifursol from std curve.

42.104 ***Preparation of Standard Curve***

Pipet 0, 2, 3, 4, and 5 mL aliquots working soln (equiv. to 0.000, 0.0050, 0.0075, 0.0100, and 0.0125% in feed) into sep. 20 mL test tubes. Dil. to 5 mL with 50% DMF. Develop color as in **42.103** and plot *A* against % drug in feed.

Nihydrazone (5-Nitro-2-furfuraldehyde acetylhydrazone) *(26)*—Official Final Action

42.105 ***Reagents***

(**a**) *95% Dimethylformamide (DMF).*—Dil. 95 parts DMF (Eastman Kodak Co. No. 5870, or equiv.) with 5 parts H_2O. (*Caution: See* **51.053**.)

(**b**) *Nihydrazone std solns.*—*(1) Stock soln.*—Weigh 110 mg cryst. nihydrazone (available from Norwich Pharmacal Co., Norwich, NY 13815) into 100 mL vol. flask, dissolve in DMF, and dil. to vol. with DMF. Protected from light, soln is stable several months. *(2) Working soln.*—For feeds contg 0.011% nihydrazone, pipet 1 mL aliquot stock soln into 100 mL vol. flask, add 50 mL DMF, and dil. to vol. with H_2O.

42.106 ***Determination***

Weigh 10 g sample into 125 mL erlenmeyer, add exactly 50 mL 95% DMF, stopper loosely, and place in boiling H_2O bath 5 min (or until temp. of solv. reaches 90°). Shake mech. 10 min and filter thru rapid paper. To 25 mL filtrate add 25 mL H_2O and mix. Let stand, protected from light, ≥30 min. (Some solids may sep.; standing for longer time is permissible.)

Prep. ca 20 mm diam. adsorption column contg adsorbent, **42.075(e)**, to ht of 5 cm. (With highly colored feeds, use somewhat longer column.) Use plug of cotton or glass wool to support column, and similar plug or layer of washed sea sand on top. Pass sample soln thru column, collecting ca 15 mL eluate. Pipet 5 mL aliquots into each of 2 tubes. Protect 1 tube from light; to other add 3 drops *freshly prepd 2% Na hydrosulfite soln,* mix, and let stand 5 min. Treat 5 mL aliquots dild std soln similarly.

Pipet 5 mL phenylhydrazine soln, **42.075(a)**, into all test tubes, mix, and heat 20 min in 40° H_2O bath. Cool by placing tubes in 15° H_2O bath 5 min. Add exactly 10 mL toluene to each tube, stopper, and shake vigorously 40 times. Sep. and centrf. toluene layer, and read *A* at 440 nm.

$$\% \text{ Nihydrazone} = [(A_{\text{samp.}} - A_{\text{red. samp.}}) \times 0.011]/(A_{\text{std}} - A_{\text{red. std}}).$$

Nithiazide (1-Ethyl-3-(5-nitro-2-thiazolyl) urea) *(27)* Official Final Action

42.107 ***Reagents***

(**a**) *Dimethylformamide (DMF).*—Reagent grade. If *A* of reagent blank as detd in **42.110** is >0.050, purify as follows: Add 1 g activated charcoal, NF XI/100 mL DMF. Shake ca 2 min, and filter. Refilter if not clear. (*Caution: See* **51.018**, **51.040**, and **51.053**.)

(**b**) *Alumina.*—*See* **42.029(b)**.

(**c**) *Procaine soln.*—Dissolve 100 mg procaine.HCl, USP, in 70 mL H_2O, add 20.0 mL HCl, mix well, cool to room temp., dil. to 100 mL with H_2O, and mix well.

(**d**) *Coupling reagent.*—*See* **42.017(d)**. Prep. fresh daily.

(**e**) *Nithiazide std solns.*—*(1) Stock soln.*—0.400 mg/mL. Weigh 40.0 mg nithiazide into 100 mL vol. flask, and dissolve in and dil. to vol. with DMF. Protected from light, soln is stable ca 6 weeks. *(2) Working soln.*—10 μg/mL. Pipet 5 mL stock soln into 200 mL vol. flask, dil. to vol. with DMF, and mix well.

42.108 ***Extraction***

Accurately weigh amt of ground sample (≤4 g) contg ca 0.5 mg nithiazide and transfer to 100 mL vol. flask. Add 50.0 mL DMF, stopper loosely, and heat 10 min at 60–75° (not >75°) in H_2O bath or on steam bath, swirling frequently. Remove flask and mech. shake 15 min. Cool to room temp., transfer mixt. to 50 mL centrf. tube, and centrf.

42.109 ***Chromatography***

(**a**) *Preparation of alumina.*—Transfer 200 g alumina to 1 L beaker. Add 500 mL H_2O and agitate 5 min with mech. stirrer. Let settle 5 min and decant supernate. Repeat washing with 2 addnl 500 mL portions H_2O and decant supernate as completely as possible. Add 300 mL MeOH to alumina and agitate ca 3 min. Filter thru buchner, continue to apply suction ca 5 min, and dry 4 hr at 110°. Store in tightly stoppered bottle.

(**b**) *Preparation of column.*—Prep. chromatgc tube as in **42.031(b)**. Transfer 3.0 g prepd alumina to tube in 2 equal portions. Lightly tamp each portion with glass rod while applying gentle suction. Wash column with 10.0 mL DMF and drain liq. to ca 5 mm above bed level prior to adding sample soln. Do not permit column to run dry; keep 5 mm head of liq. at all times. Prep. sep. column for each sample, std, and reagent blank.

(**c**) *Chromatography of feed extract.*—Pipet 20 mL clear feed ext onto column and let it pass thru column by gravity. Do not let column run dry; keep 5 mm head of liq. Wash inner walls of tube and alumina with three 4.0 mL portions DMF added from pipet. Let final DMF wash drain thru column until no further liq. appears at tip of column. Dry tip of column with filter paper.

Elute column by gravity with 4 mL portions H_2O. Collect first 1.0 mL eluate in graduate and reject; then collect eluate in 25 mL vol. flask until liq. level is just below mark. Adjust with H_2O to mark, stopper, and mix well. (Required time for elution should be $\leq$60 min; appreciably longer time indicates improper column prepn.)

42.110 ***Determination***

Pipet 10 mL clear eluate into 25 mL vol. flask. Add 5.0 mL 1*N* NaOH, mix well, and let stand 10 min at 20–25°. Add 5.0 mL procaine soln, mix well, and let stand 2 min at 20–25°; then add enough coupling reagent to mark, stopper, mix, and let stand 15 min. (If colored soln is not clear, filter thru clean fritted glass funnel of medium or fine porosity.) Det. *A* of purple-red soln, in 1 cm cell in spectrophtr or colorimeter at 540 nm, against H_2O as ref.

Prep. reagent blank by transferring 20.0 mL DMF onto freshly prepd column and proceeding in exactly same manner as for sample.

Prep. std by transferring 20.0 mL nithiazide working std onto freshly prepd column and proceeding in exactly same manner as for sample.

% Nithiazide in feed = $5C(A - A_0)/8W(A' - A_0)$,

where A refers to sample, A' to std, A_0 to reagent blank, C = mg nithiazide in final aliquot of std (0.080 mg), and W = g original sample.

Nitrodan (3-Methyl-5-(*p*-nitrophenylazo) rhodanine) (*28*) Official Final Action

(Not applicable in presence of interfering nitro compds)

42.111 ***Reagents***

(**a**) *N,N-Dimethylformamide (DMF)-alcohol solvent.*—(1+1). Mix equal vols DMF and alcohol (anhyd. or SDF 3A). Store in tightly closed container.

(**b**) *Nitrodan std solns.*—(*1*) *Stock soln.*—200 μg/mL. Weigh exactly 50 mg nitrodan (available from Pet Products, Div. of Cooper Laboratories, Inc., Brentwood, NY 11717). Rinse into 250 mL vol. flask with DMF-alcohol solv., and dil. to ca 150 mL. Break up nitrodan particles with flattened stirring rod and shake to facilitate soln or dissolve, using mag. stirrer. (Be sure all particles are dissolved.) Dil. to vol. and mix. (*2*) *Working soln.*—10 μg/mL. Pipet 5 mL stock soln into 100 mL vol. flask, dil. to vol. with DMF-alcohol solv., and mix.

Prep. all std solns same day as std curve.

42.112 ***Preparation of Standard Curve***

Pipet 5, 10, 15, and 20 mL (50, 100, 150, and 200 μg nitrodan) working soln into four 50 mL vol. flasks. Dil. almost to vol. with DMF-alcohol solv. and mix. Just before reading, add 1 drop 2*N* NaOH to each flask, dil. to vol. with DMF-alcohol, and mix. Read *A* in 1 cm cells at 575 nm against solv. Plot *A* against concn (μg/mL).

42.113 ***Preparation of Sample***

(**a**) *Meals and pellets.*—Grind sample to pass sieve with 1 mm circular openings and mix thoroly.

(**b**) *Expanded dog food.*—Grind ca 3 oz (85 g) representative sample in high-speed blender until chunks are broken (30–60 sec). Transfer to mixing jar and brush in fines that adhere to blender. Mix thoroly.

42.114 ***Determination***

Weigh 2.0 g sample (or larger if necessary) and transfer to small glass mortar. Add ca 15 mL DMF-alcohol and grind with pestle to ensure complete contact of drug and solv. Quant. transfer mixt. to medium porosity fritted glass funnel connected to 250 mL suction flask. Filter and wash with small portions of solv. until washings and residue are no longer violet. (Avoid unnecessary delay.) Transfer filtrate to vol. flask of vol. to yield final concn of 1–4 μg nitrodan/mL. Add 1 drop 2*N* NaOH just before reading, dil. to vol. with solv., and mix. Measure *A* within 10 min in 1 cm cell at 575 nm against solv.

% Nitrodan in sample = [(μg nitrodan/mL final soln) (from std curve) × 100]/(g sample/mL final soln) × 10^6.

42.115 Nitrofurazone—Official Final Action

See **42.075–42.076**.

Nitromide (3,5-Dinitrobenzamide) (3,5-DNBA) (*29*) Official Final Action

42.116 ***Reagents***

(**a**) *Diethylamine reagent (DEA), aged.*—(1 year or older.) Fresh DEA may be artifically aged as follows: Place 1 L DEA in dry 2 L flask with 40 g Na or K fluosilicate. Connect flask to 60 cm (24") bulb reflux condenser and reflux on sand bath 2–3 days in hood. When reagent is sufficiently "aged," 2 mL clear DEA added to 8 mL dimethylsulfoxide contg 50 μg 3,5-DNBA should develop max. color in ca 40 min. *A* as read on Beckman DU spectrophtr at 560 nm should be ca 0.375; on Klett-Summerson photoelec. colorimeter with No. 56 filter, ca 200. Reagent must be free from turbidity. Prep. new std curve for each batch of DEA.

(**b**) *3,5-Dinitrobenzamide (DNBA) std solns.*—(*1*) *Stock soln.*—1 mg/mL. Weigh 100 mg 3,5-DNBA into 100 mL flask and dil. to vol. with MeOH. (*2*) *Working soln.*—20 μg/mL. Transfer 2.0 mL stock soln to 100 mL vol. flask and dil. to vol. with MeOH.

42.117 ***Preparation of Standard Curve***

Place 1.0, 2.0, 3.0, and 5.0 mL working soln contg 20, 40, 60, and 100 μg, resp., of 3,5-DNBA in 4 colorimeter tubes. Evap. to dryness at 50° in air current. Dissolve residue in 8 mL dimethylsulfoxide at 70°, cool, and add 2 mL DEA reagent. Place in dark at 20–25° and read after 1 hr. Plot std curve, using *A* as ordinate and concn as abscissa.

42.118 ***Preparation of Sample***

Weigh 5.0 g feed, contg 0.025% 3,5-DNBA, into 100 mL vol. flask and dil. to vol. with MeOH. Shake frequently 20 min and let stand 40 min to permit feed particles to settle.

If feed contains 0.075% 3,5-DNBA, use 2 g finely ground feed; if 0.15%, use 1 g in 100 mL or 5 g in 500 mL MeOH. Prep. premixes by weighing appropriate sample and serially dilg MeOH ext.

42.119 ***Determination***

Pipet 4 mL aliquot of ext into g-s test tube. Place tube in 50° H_2O bath and evap. to dryness with air current directed onto surface of MeOH. Add 8 mL dimethylsulfoxide and heat to 70° to hasten soln; cool, and add 2 mL DEA reagent. Place in dark 1 hr at 20– 25°. Det *A* at 560 nm in Beckman DU spectrophtr, Klett-Summerson photoelec. colorimeter with No. 56 filter, or similar instrument, against dimethylsulfoxide as ref.

Det. amt of 3,5-DNBA in tube from std curve.

% 3,5-DNBA in feed

= μg 3,5-DNBA in tube × 25 × 100/5,000,000;

or μg 3,5-DNBA in tube × 5 = μg 3,5-DNBA/g feed or ppm.

★ Nitrophenide (m,m′-Dinitrodiphenyldisulfide) (*30*) ★
Official Final Action

(Applicable in presence of arsanilic acid)

42.120 ***Reagent***

Buffer soln.—pH 6.6. Dissolve 41.29 g anhyd. Na_2HPO_4 in H_2O and dil. to 1 L. Dissolve 11.47 g citric acid.H_2O in H_2O and dil. to 1 L. Mix in equal proportions.

42.121 ***Determination***

Transfer 2 g ground sample to 300 mL erlenmeyer, add 0.5 g $Na_2S_2O_4$ and 50 mL buffer soln, and place in boiling H_2O bath 20 min. Remove flask, slowly add 10 mL HCl, and replace flask in boiling H_2O bath 5 min. (This heating destroys arsanilic acid and ppts colloidal S.) Remove flask, connect to compressed air or vac. manifold, and aerate vigorously 15 min. Transfer to 100 mL vol. flask, cool, dil. to vol. with H_2O, and mix. Filter thru Whatman No. 42 paper, or equiv., discarding first 15 mL filtrate if turbid.

Pipet 5 mL portions of clear filtrate into each of two 50 mL beakers; to each add 2 mL *freshly prepd 0.1% $NaNO_2$ soln.* After 5 min, add 2 mL *0.50% aq. NH_4 sulfamate soln,* and let stand 2 min. Add 1 mL coupling reagent, **42.017(d)**, to first beaker and 1 mL H_2O to second. Thoroly mix solns after adding each reagent. After 10 min, add 15 mL H_2O to each beaker and mix. Read *A* of both solns against H_2O blank in spectrophtr at 545 nm. Subtract *A* of feed blank from sample *A* and det. amt of nitrophenide from std curve. Divide by 1000 to obtain % nitrophenide.

42.122 ***Preparation of Standard Curve***

Transfer 0.10 g pure nitrophenide to 100 mL vol. flask, dissolve in 50 mL acetone, and dil. to vol. with acetone. Pipet 10 mL aliquot into another 100 mL vol. flask and dil. to vol. with acetone. Pipet 2, 3, 4, 5, and 6 mL portions of this dild soln into sep. 100 mL vol. flasks and carefully evap. in gentle air stream. To each flask add 0.5 g $Na_2S_2O_4$ and 50 mL buffer soln, and proceed as in **42.121**, aerating 20 min. Plot std curve representing 10, 15, 20, 25, and 30 μg nitrophenide against *A*.

Note: Detn may be performed in 100 mL vol. flasks, if care is taken to add HCl *slowly* and in *small portions* with const swirling, after reduction, in order to avoid excessive foaming and loss of soln.

★ Surplus method—*see* inside front cover.

4-Nitrophenylarsonic Acid (Nitarsone) (*31*)
Official Final Action

42.123 ***Principle***

Nitarsone is extd from feed with 50% dimethylsulfoxide (DMSO) and sepd from interferences by alumina chromatgy. Nitro group is reduced with $TiCl_3$ and resulting amine assayed colorimetrically at 530 nm with Bratton-Marshall reaction. Arsanilic acid and carbarsone interfere.

42.124 ***Reagents***

(a) *Nitarsone std solns.*—(*1*) *Stock soln.*—1 mg/mL. Weigh 100 mg nitarsone std (available from Salsbury Laboratories) into 100 mL vol. flask and dil. to vol. with 4% NaOH. (*2*) *Working soln.*—50 μg/mL. Dil. 10 mL stock soln to 200 mL with 4% NaOH.

(b) *Activated alumina.*—Alcoa grade F-20, 80–200 mesh (available from Fisher Scientific Co. as Alumina, adsorption, Fisher No. A-540). To det. suitability of alumina, perform entire detn on 100 μg nitarsone. Recovery should be >95%.

(c) *Dimethylsulfoxide* (*DMSO*) *soln.*—50%. Dil. with equal vol. H_2O. (*Caution:* DMSO can be harmful. Avoid skin contact by wearing heavy rubber gloves. Use effective fume removal device.)

(d) *Titanous chloride soln.*—4% aq. Prep. fresh daily from 20% soln open ≤3 months and kept refrigerated, or from solid $TiCl_3$. If >1 min is required for color disappearance in detn, use fresh source of $TiCl_3$. (*Caution:* $TiCl_3$ is corrosive. Wear disposable plastic or rubber gloves. Avoid contact with eyes.)

(e) *Sodium nitrite soln.*—0.1% aq. Prep. weekly.

42.125 ***Preparation of Standard Curve***

Pipet 0, 2, 5, 10, 15, 20, and 25 mL working soln into sep. 100 mL vol. flasks and dil. to vol. with 4% NaOH. Pipet 10 mL from each flask into sep. 50 mL vol. flasks, add 15 mL 4% NaOH, and dil. to vol. with H_2O. Pipet 4 mL from each flask into sep. test tubes and develop color as in **42.127**, beginning ". . . add 2 drops 4% $TiCl_3$ . . ." Std concns correspond to 0, 0.004, 0.010, 0.020, 0.030, 0.040, and 0.050% nitarsone in feeds. Plot std curve of *A* against % drug in feed.

42.126 ***Preparation of Sample***

Accurately weigh 5 g finely ground feed into 100 mL vol. flask. Add 75 mL 50% DMSO, place sample on wrist action mech. shaker, and shake at room temp. 30 min. Dil. to vol. with 50% DMSO and mix. Transfer 30–40 mL to 50 mL centrf. tube and centrf. 10 min at 2000 rpm.

42.127 ***Determination***

(*Caution: See* **51.018.**)

Add alumina to 20 × 400 mm chromatgc tube with fritted glass disk to depth of 7 cm. Tap tube wall to settle alumina; then add 1 cm layer of sand. Prewash column with 50 mL 50% DMSO before use.

Pipet 10 mL supernate from prepn of sample onto prewashed column. For feeds contg >0.04% nitarsone, use smaller aliquot.

Let sample enter column and then wash into column with several 5 mL portions H_2O. Wash column with 75 mL H_2O and discard eluate.

Elute nitarsone with 65 mL 4% NaOH, discarding first 15 mL. Collect remaining eluate in 100 mL vol. flask, letting column run dry. Nitarsone is eluted with ca 25–30 mL eluant. Dil. eluate to vol. with H_2O and mix.

Pipet 4 mL dild eluate into 2 test tubes, add 2 drops 4% $TiCl_3$ to each with mixing, and shake or mix on Vortex mixer until black color disappears. Add 2 mL HCl to each and mix thoroly. Add 0.5 mL 0.1% $NaNO_2$, **(e)**, and mix. After 5 min, add 0.5 mL 0.5% NH_4 sulfamate, **42.017(c)**, and mix. After 2 min, add 0.5 mL 0.1% coupling reagent, **42.017(d)**, to one tube and 0.5 mL H_2O to second tube for blank. Let color develop 15 min; then read *A* of sample and blank at 530 nm on spectrophtr. Correct sample *A* for blank *A* and det. amt nitarsone in sample from std curve.

Phenothiazine (*32*)—Official Final Action

42.128 ***Reagent***

Phenothiazine std soln.—Dissolve 10 mg recrystd (from 10% soln in toluene) phenothiazine in 50 mL alcohol and dil. to 100 mL with alcohol. For working stds, dil. with equal vol. of alcohol. (1 mL dild soln = 50 μg phenothiazine.) Use freshly prepd soln; alc. solns gradually develop rose tint within few hr.

42.129 ***Determination***

Place 1 g ground sample in 100 mL vol. flask, add 50 mL alcohol, and heat on steam bath 15 min. Cool, dil. to vol. with alcohol, mix, and let settle (ca 15 min) until supernate is clear.

Place 2 mL aliquot in 25 mL vol. flask and add 10 mL alcohol. To flask add, in order given, 1 mL *1% alc. p-aminobenzoic acid soln,* 1 mL *aq. 2% $NaNO_2$ soln*, and 1 mL HCl (1+3). Dil. to vol. with alcohol. Read *A* of green soln at 600 nm in spectrophtr against reagent blank. Det. amt of phenothiazine from std curve.

% Phenothiazine = μg/200.

Prep. std curve, using 1, 2, and 3 mL dil. std soln, as above.

Piperazine (*33*)—Official Final Action

42.130 ***Principle***

Piperazine or piperazine salt is quant. extd from feed into slightly acidic aq. soln. Dild filtrate is reacted with equal vol. benzoquinone soln at 80°. Colored complex formed is detd spectrophtric at 490 nm.

Applicable to detn of 0.05–0.5% piperazine, usually present as one of its salts, in animal feeds. Amines give similar color reaction. Alkalies produce increased color; pH adjustment in method overcomes interference of this kind.

42.131 ***Apparatus***

(a) *Water bath.*—Approx. 25 cm (10") diam. with 15–20 cm (6–8") depth H_2O. Thermostatically controlled at 80±0.1°. (Viscosity bath is satisfactory.)

(b) *Test tubes.*—Pyrex, 15 × 125 mm, with rubber stoppers, and rack capable of supporting tubes when immersed in H_2O bath.

42.132 ***Reagents***

(a) *Quinone soln.*—Dissolve 0.5 g *p*-benzoquinone in 2.5 mL HOAc and little alcohol in dry 100 mL vol. flask and dil. to vol. with alcohol. Keep soln in ice bath or refrigerator. Prep. fresh daily. (*Note: p*-Benzoquinone is lachrymator; avoid breathing vapor and contact with skin and clothing.) If blanks are high or variable, purify *p*-benzoquinone by steam distn in hood.

(b) *Piperazine std solns.*—(*1*) *Stock soln.*—Dissolve exactly 185 mg pure piperazine.2HCl (equiv. to 100 mg piperazine) in H_2O and dil. to 250 mL. (*2*) *Working soln.*—20 μg/mL. Dil. 25.0 mL stock soln to vol. in 500 mL vol. flask.

42.133 ***Preparation of Standard Curve***

Using working soln, add, by microburet or pipets, 20, 40, 60, 80, and 100 μg piperazine equiv. and intermediate values, if required, into test tubes. Dil. to 5 mL in each test tube with H_2O. Include H_2O blank with each detn.

Add 5 mL quinone reagent to each std and blank. Stopper tubes and mix by inverting. Remove stoppers and immerse in H_2O bath at 80±0.1° exactly 10 min. (Bath temp. can be varied; use same temp. for samples and stds.) Immediately immerse tubes in ice bath 3 min. Let stand at room temp. ≥20 min, but ≤40 min. Read *A* at 490 nm in 1.0 cm cells, using reagent blank to zero instrument. Plot *A* of each std against μg piperazine.

42.134 ***Determination***

Weigh 10.00 g well mixed feed (grind pellets in mortar) into 500 mL (16 oz) wide-mouth, screw-cap bottle. Add exactly 200 mL H_2O from graduate and adjust to pH 4–5 (0.15 mL H_2SO_4 (1+2) is usually enough for 10 g feed). Cap or stopper bottle and place in wrist-action shaker 30 min. Add ca 5 g Celite (*Note:* some grades may retain piperazine) as slurry to buchner contg 9.0 cm Whatman No. 3 paper and pull down under full vac. Wash pad with small portion feed ext and discard washing. Rapidly filter remaining feed ext and reserve filtrate for color development. (Do not delay; turbidity may form.)

Pipet 25.0 mL filtrate into 250 mL vol. flask and dil. to vol. with H_2O. Pipet 5 mL aliquot into test tube and immediately proceed with color development as in **42.133**. Include H_2O blank with each detn.

Prep. sample color blank for each feed as follows: Pipet 5 mL aliquot dild ext into test tube and 5 mL H_2O into another test tube as ref. To each, add 5 mL soln contg 2.5 mL HOAc dild to 100 mL with alcohol. Mix by inverting and omit heating. Read *A* at same wavelength and subtract from sample reading. Include 1 or 2 stds with each detn to detect shift in std curve; adjust accordingly. Obtain μg piperazine from std curve.

% Piperazine = (μg piperazine × 10^{-4})/g sample in aliquot.

Pyrantel Tartrate (E-1,4,5,6-Tetrahydro-1-methyl-2-[(*trans*-2-(2-thienyl)vinyl]pyrimidine tartrate, Banminth®)

Spectrophotometric Method (*34*)—Official First Action

(Applicable to range 0.0106–0.8811%. Pyrantel tartrate solns are light sensitive. Exts must be protected from direct sunlight or artificial light.)

42.135 ***Apparatus***

(a) *High-speed blender.*—Waring Blendor, or equiv.

(b) *Centrifuge.*—International Model EXD-2 (Damon/IEC Div., 300 Second Ave, Needham Hts, MA 02194), or equiv., equipped to hold 50 mL g-s centrf. tubes.

(c) *Filter aid.*—Celite 545, acid-washed, or Millipore prefilter pad (No. AP2507500, Millipore Corp., Ashby Rd. Bedford, MA 01730), or equivs.

(d) *Filtrator.*—Fisher No. 9-788, low form (Fisher Scientific Co.), or equiv.

(e) *Mixer.*—Vortex Genie mixer (Scientific Products), or equiv.

(f) *Spectrophotometer.*—For use at 311 nm, with 1 cm cells.

42.136 ***Reagents***

(**a**) *Hydrochloric acid.*—0.1*N*. Dil. 8.33 mL HCl to 1 L with H_2O.

(**b**) *Leaching soln.*—Dissolve 100 g NaCl in 1 L H_2O, add 1 L MeOH, and mix vigorously. Prep. fresh daily.

(**c**) *Perchloric acid.*—0.24*M*. Dil. 20 mL $HClO_4$ to 1 L with H_2O.

(**d**) *Sodium hydroxide.*—0.1*N*. Dissolve 4 g NaOH in H_2O and dil. to 1 L with H_2O.

(**e**) *Pyrantel tartrate std solns.*—(*1*) *Stock soln.*—0.80 mg/mL. Weigh 80.0 mg Pyrantel Tartrate Ref. Std (available from Pfizer, Inc., Quality Control, Agricultural Div., 1107 S MO Rt 291, Lee's Summit, MO 64063) into 100 mL vol. flask, dissolve in leaching soln, (**b**), and dil. to vol. with same solv. Use ultrasonic bath to speed soln. If std does not dissolve readily, remake. Prep. fresh daily. (*2*) *Working soln.*—0.16 mg/mL. Pipet 20 mL stock soln into 100 mL vol. flask, dil. to vol. with leaching soln, and mix well. Prep. fresh daily.

42.137 ***Preparation of Samples***

Weigh duplicate portions feed ground in high-speed blender, (**a**), into 125 mL erlenmeyers: 15.000±0.010 g for 0.0106% pyrantel tartrate; 1.800±0.010 g, 0.0881%; and 1.000±0.010 g, 0.881%. Add 60 mL leaching soln to 1 portion; add 50 mL leaching soln and, by pipet, 10 mL working std soln, (**e**)(*2*), to other portion of 0.0106% or 0.0881% pairs or 10 mL stock std soln, (**e**)(*1*), to other of 0.881% pair. Cap with polypropylene stopper and shake mech. 1 hr.

Quant. transfer mixt. to buchner precoated with Celite or contg prefilter pad, (**c**), rinsing flask with small portions leaching soln, (**b**), and collecting filtrate under vac. with Filtrator, (**d**), contg 250 mL erlenmeyer, until vol. filtrate is 150 mL. Transfer filtrate to 200 mL vol. flask, and dil. to vol. with leaching soln. For 0.881% level, pipet 50 mL dild filtrate into 250 mL vol. flask, and dil. to vol. with leaching soln.

42.138 ***Determination***

Pipet 25 mL prepd sample soln into 250 mL separator contg 5 g finely ground KI, and shake to dissolve. Pipet in 100 mL $CHCl_3$ and shake 45 sec. Transfer lower $CHCl_3$ layer to another 250 mL separator contg 25 mL 0.24*M* $HClO_4$, and shake 10 sec. Transfer ca 35 mL lower $CHCl_3$ layer to 50 mL g-s centrf. tube contg 10.0 mL 0.1*N* NaOH. Stopper tube, and mix on vortex mixer, (**e**), 15 sec while shaking back and forth. Centrf. 10 min at 990 × *g* (1800 rpm). Pipet 25 mL lower $CHCl_3$ layer from tube into another 50 mL g-s centrf. tube contg 10.0 mL 0.1*N* HCl. Stopper tube, mix, and centrf. as before. Rapidly record *A* of upper aq. layer at 311 nm against $CHCl_3$-satd 0.1*N* HCl as ref. solv.

% Pyrantel tartrate = $(A/W) \times [W'/(A' - A)] \times F \times 100$, where *A* and *A'* refer to absorbance of sample and spiked sample, resp.; *W* = g feed, supplement, or conc.; *W'* = g pyrantel tartrate ref. std used to prep. std soln; $F = [(1/100 \text{ mL}) \times (20 \text{ mL}/100 \text{ mL}) \times 10 \text{ mL}]$ for 0.0106% and 0.0881% levels; and $F = [(1/100) \times 10]$ for 0.881% level.

★ Racephenicol (*dl*-Threo-2,2-dichloro-N-[β-hydroxy-α-(hydroxymethyl)-*p*-(methylsulfonyl) phenethyl] acetamide) ★ Official Final Action

42.139 ***Method I (35)***

(Applicable to levels ⩾0.002%)

Racephenicol is extd from feed with acetone, and the dichloroacetamido group is converted to amine compd by alk. hydrolysis. After cleanup, amine is oxidized with periodate to *p*-methylsulfonylbenzaldehyde, which is detd by UV spectrophotometry. With blank correction, method will measure levels as low as 0.002%. *See* **42.128–42.131**, 12th ed.

42.140 ***Method II (36)***

(Applicable to levels ⩾0.0005%; *Caution: See* **51.011**, **51.018**, **51.039**, **51.040**, and **51.043**.)

Samples are extd with hot CH_3CN. Fats are selectively removed with hexane and CH_3CN is volatilized. Nonvolatile material remaining is hydrolyzed to remove dichloracetamido group of racephenicol. Soln is cleaned up with $CHCl_3$ and oxidized with periodate, converting residual amine compd to *p*-methylsulfonylbenzaldehyde, which is measured by UV spectrophotometry, using curvature inversion technic. *See* **42.133–42.136**, 12th ed.

Reserpine (*37*)—Official Final Action

(Applicable at 0.2–2.0 ppm level)

42.141 ***Reagents***

(**a**) *Citric acid soln.*—Dissolve 2.0 g citric acid.H_2O in H_2O and dil. to 100 mL.

(**b**) *Sodium nitrite soln.*—Dissolve 0.1 g $NaNO_2$ in 50 mL H_2O and dil. to 100 mL with MeOH. Prep. fresh daily.

(**c**) *Sodium bicarbonate soln.*—Dissolve 1.0 g $NaHCO_3$ in H_2O and dil. to 100 mL.

(**d**) *Dilute sulfuric acid.*—Add 3.0 mL H_2SO_4 to ca 1 L H_2O and let cool to room temp.

(**e**) *Quinine sulfate soln.*—0.5 μg/mL. Dissolve 50 mg quinine sulfate in dil. H_2SO_4 and dil. to 100 mL with dil. H_2SO_4 (*Soln 1*). Dil 2 mL *Soln 1* to 100 mL with dil. H_2SO_4 (*Soln 2*). Dil 5 mL *Soln 2* to 100 mL with dil. H_2SO_4 (*Soln 3*).

(**f**) *Reserpine std soln.*—2 μg/mL. Dissolve 50 mg reserpine in $CHCl_3$ and dil. to 50 mL (*Soln 1*). Dil. 4 mL *Soln 1* to 100 mL with $CHCl_3$ (*Soln 2*). Dil. 5 mL *Soln 2* to 100 mL with $CHCl_3$ (*Soln 3*). Prep. all solns fresh daily.

(**g**) *Desicote.*—Beckman Instruments No. 18772.

42.142 ***Apparatus***

(**a**) *Photofluorometer.*—With primary filter PC-6 (Corning Glass Works No. 7–51) and secondary filter PC-9A (Corning No. 3–71). Wavelengths of max. excitation and fluorescence of reserpine treated with HNO_2 are 390 and 510 nm, resp. (*Caution: See* **51.008**.)

(**b**) *Separators.*—500, 125, and 60 mL Squibb-type with Teflon stopcocks. Coat 500 mL separators with Desicote as precaution to prevent adsorption of reserpine by glass during *n*-hexane-citric acid extn. Adsorption is particularly significant in 8 μg std. Add 10–20 mL Desicote fluid to one 500 mL separator and shake until entire inner surface is wetted. Drain Desicote into other 500 mL separator and repeat. Dry separators by passing air current thru them. Remove any visible film by rinsing with CCl_4. Discard CCl_4 and air dry separators as before. (*Caution:* Desicote may be harmful. Avoid contact with skin and eyes. Use effective fume removal device.)

(**c**) *Funnel.*—Buchner with fritted disk, coarse porosity, 60 mL.

(**d**) *Filter bell.*—New York Laboratory Supply Co. No. 35070, or equiv.

42.143 ***Extraction***

(All glassware must be scrupulously clean. Wash with $CHCl_3$ and/or MeOH and dry. Complete all assays in 1 day. Keep exposure of reserpine in $CHCl_3$ to light at min.)

★ Surplus method—*see* inside front cover.

Accurately weigh 2 ca 40 g samples. (Grind pelletized feed in high-speed blender ca 5 min.) Treat each sep. as follows: Press sample down firmly in funnel, (**c**). Add 15–20 mL $CHCl_3$ (do not stir) to each funnel and collect filtrate in 100 mL vol. flask in filter bell with mild vac. Continue extns with 10–15 mL portions $CHCl_3$ until ca 100 mL collects; dil. to 100 mL with $CHCl_3$ and mix well.

(**a**) *For 2.0 ppm (0.0002%).*—Pipet 10 mL $CHCl_3$ ext of each sample and 30 mL $CHCl_3$ into sep. 500 mL separators.

(**b**) *For 1.0 ppm (0.0001%).*—Pipet 20 mL $CHCl_3$ ext of each sample and 20 mL $CHCl_3$ into sep. 500 mL separators.

(**c**) *For 0.2 ppm (0.00002%).*—Transfer 100 mL $CHCl_3$ ext to 500 mL r-b flask, rinsing with several small portions $CHCl_3$, and evap. to ca 20 mL under vac. at $\leq 60°$ in rotating vac. evaporator. Transfer each concd ext to sep. 500 mL separators. Rinse flasks with two 10 mL portions $CHCl_3$ and add rinsings to separators.

Add 400 mL *n*-hexane to each separator and mix well. To each of 2 addnl 500 mL separators, add exactly 4 mL std reserpine *Soln 3,* 36 mL $CHCl_3$, and 400 mL *n*-hexane. Treat both samples and stds similarly and simultaneously. Ext with three 20 mL portions citric acid soln by shaking each ext *gently* for total of 5 min. (To avoid emulsions, shake 1 min and let sep.; repeat shaking twice for 2 min, and let sep. after each shaking.) Combine citric acid exts in 125 mL separator and ext with three 10 mL portions $CHCl_3$ by shaking *gently* ca 1 min for each extn. Combine $CHCl_3$ exts in 60 mL separator, add 5 mL $NaHCO_3$ soln, and shake gently 1 min. Let sep., and withdraw lower $CHCl_3$ layer into 50 mL vol. flask. Dil. to vol. with MeOH, and mix well.

42.144 ***Determination***

Pipet two 15 mL portions of each feed ext and two 15 mL portions of each extd std into sep. 25 mL vol. flasks (total of 8 flasks). To each add 0.5 mL HCl and swirl gently. To 1 flask from each feed extn and to 1 from each std, add 1.0 mL $NaNO_2$ soln from pipet and swirl gently (total of 4 flasks). To other flasks (blanks), add 1 mL dil. MeOH (1+1). Let stand 30 min, swirling occasionally, and dil. to vol. with MeOH.

Adjust photofluorometer to give galvanometer readings of 100 with quinine sulfate *Soln 3* and to 0 with dil. H_2SO_4. (With other suitable instruments, set 4.0 mL unextd std reserpine *Soln 3*, dild and developed as above for extd stds, to 60–80.) Det. fluorescence of std prepns, S; feed prepns, F; and resp. blanks, S_0 and F_0.

(**a**) For 2.0 ppm:
% Reserpine = $(F - F_0)/[(S - S_0) \times 125 \times W]$.

(**b**) For 1.0 ppm:
% Reserpine = $(F - F_0)/[(S - S_0) \times 250 \times W]$.

(**c**) For 0.2 ppm:
% Reserpine = $(F - F_0)/[(S - S_0) \times 1{,}250 \times W]$,
where W = g feed sample.

Ronnel (*O,O*-Dimethyl-*O*-(2,4,5-trichlorophenyl) phosphorothioate)

Gas Chromatographic Method (38)—Official Final Action

42.145 ***Apparatus***

Gas chromatograph.—With electron capture detector. Operating parameters: Column 1.2–1.8 m (4–6′) glass, 3–4 mm id packed with 5% (w/w) SF-96 silicone fluid on 60–80 mesh Chromosorb W; temps (°): column 195, inlet 220; carrier gas Ar-CH_4 (95+5), 60 mL/min; and attenuation to give ca 50% scale deflection with 1 ng ronnel. (Retention time for ronnel should be 5–10 min. Adjust column temp. if necessary.) Significant variations in replicate injections indicate instability of instrument or faulty injection, and these should be rechecked.

42.146 ***Reagents***

(**a**) *Hexane.*—Spectral grade.

(**b**) *Ronnel std solns.*—(*1*) *Stock soln.*—1 mg/mL. Dissolve 0.1000 g ronnel std sample (available from Dow Chemical USA, Ag-Organics Dept.) in hexane and dil. to 100 mL. (*2*) *Intermediate soln.*—20 μg/mL. Dil. 2.0 mL stock soln to 100 mL with hexane. (*3*) *Working soln.*—1 ng/5 μL. Dil. 1.0 mL intermediate soln to 100 mL with hexane.

42.147 ***Determination***

Weigh 10.0 g sample into 8 oz (250 mL) screw-cap extn bottle, or equiv. Add 200.0 mL acetone and shake 4 hr. Remove from shaker and centrf. portion 10 min. Pipet 1.0 mL into 100 mL vol. flask and dil. to vol. with hexane.

Inject 5 μL portions in following sequence: ronnel working std soln, dild sample ext, duplicate of dild sample ext, and ronnel working std soln. Record chromatogram of each.

Measure ronnel peak hts and calc. % ronnel, using av. peak hts from std replicates (PH′) and ext replicates (PH) for each detn:

$$\% \text{ Ronnel} = (PH/PH') \times 0.04.$$

Sample wt and aliquot specified are for feeds contg 0.04% ronnel. With feeds contg other levels of ronnel, use 10.0 g sample but select aliquot or aliquots to give expected ronnel concn of 1 ng/5 μL final diln.

% Ronnel = (PH/PH′) × g ronnel in std injected × F × 100, where F = 1/[(g sample/mL in final diln) × (μL sample injected × 10^{-3})].

Ultraviolet Method (39)—Official Final Action

(For mineral feed mixts contg 1–40% ronnel)

42.148 ***Principle***

Ronnel is extd from feed with MeOH, cleaned up with ion exchange resin, and detd by UV measurement.

42.149 ***Reagents***

(**a**) *Methanol.*—Absolute. Coefficient C as detd in calibration with MeOH should be 0.0322–0.0330. If outside this range, adjust to this value by adding 5–15 drops HCl/L MeOH. Det. C on same day samples are analyzed.

(**b**) *Ronnel std solns.*—*See* **42.146**(**b**).

(**c**) *Ion exchange resin.*—Dowex 2-X8, 50–100 mesh. Obtainable in chloride form. Convert to acetate form as follows: Plug 10 × 300 mm chromatgc tube, equipped with Teflon stopcock, with glass wool. Fill with aq. slurry of resin to ht of ca 120 mm. Wash resin with ca 500 mL 10% aq. NaOAc soln until effluent gives only faint test for Cl with $AgNO_3$ after acidification with HNO_3. (Use ca 4 lb/sq in. (276 kPa) N pressure to speed washing.) Keep resin covered with liq. during prepn, storage, and analysis. Extrude or wash resin into 100 mL beaker; wash 3 times with H_2O by decantation, then 3 times with MeOH. Pour MeOH slurry back into tube and wash with 50 mL HOAc-MeOH (1+4), followed by 50 mL MeOH. Keep resin column (now ready for use) covered with MeOH.

Resin can be used repeatedly unless samples contain considerable salt. Check activity periodically by passing 10 mL of soln of 50 mg trichlorophenol in 100 mL MeOH thru column, washing with three 10 mL portions MeOH, and dilg eluate to 100 mL with MeOH. If soln has noticeable peaks at 292 and 298 nm, discard resin. To prep. larger amts of resin, use larger column. Store resin in closed container under MeOH. It is stable ≥1 month.

42.150 ***Calibration***

Weigh 0.1000 g ronnel std into 100 mL vol. flask, dissolve in MeOH, dil. to vol., and mix. Dil. 10.0 mL to 100 mL with MeOH. Det A against MeOH in 1 cm Si cell at 302, 282, and 262 nm.

Calc. coefficient C (g ronnel/100 mL final soln/A unit) = $0.01/\Delta A$, where ΔA is $A_{282} - [(A_{302} + A_{262})/2]$. Coefficient C should be ca 0.0326.

42.151 ***Determination***

(*Caution: See* **51.018** and **51.040**.)

Weigh 10.0 g sample into 8 oz (250 mL) extn bottle, or equiv., add 100.0 mL MeOH, stopper, and shake vigorously 15 min on mech. shaker. Decant thru folded 18.5 cm Whatman No. 2V paper, or equiv., into 500 mL vol. flask. Repeat extn twice, shaking 3 min each time with 100 mL MeOH. Wash residue from bottle onto paper and wash thoroly with three 50 mL portions MeOH. Dil. to vol. with MeOH and mix. Pipet 20 mL aliquot onto ion exchange column, (**c**), and collect eluate in 250 mL vol. flask. Wash column with three 10 mL portions MeOH (do not let MeOH level drop below resin surface). Dil. to 250 mL with MeOH and mix. (If sample is reasonably fresh or if presence of 2,4,5-trichlorophenol is not suspected, ion exchange resin cleanup step may be omitted.) Det. ΔA against MeOH as in **42.150**.

% Ronnel = $(\Delta A \times C \times 100)$/g sample in 100 mL final soln

Sample wt and aliquot specified are for mineral mixts contg 5% ronnel. With mineral mixts contg other levels of ronnel use 10.0 g sample but select aliquot to give expected ronnel concn of 0.01 g ronnel/100 mL of final diln. Calc. % ronnel from above formula.

42.152 ***Gas Chromatography***

If GLC measurement of ronnel is desired, dil. 1.0 mL undild MeOH sample ext to 100 mL with hexane. (Dil. aliquot of MeOH ext with hexane same day to avoid hydrolysis of ronnel in MeOH.) Dil. 1.0 mL of this dild ext to 50 mL with hexane. Measure response from 5 μL injections of ronnel working std soln and final diln of ext as in **42.147**.

% Ronnel = (PH/PH′) × 5,

where PH and PH′ are peak hts of sample and std resp.

Sample wt and aliquots specified are for mineral mixts contg 5% ronnel. With mineral mixts contg other levels of ronnel use 10.0 g sample but select aliquot to give expected ronnel concn of 1 ng/5 μL final diln. Calc. % ronnel by general formula given in **42.147**.

Roxarsone
(4-Hydroxy-3-nitrobenzenearsonic acid)
(*40*)—Official Final Action

(Not applicable to pelleted feeds contg hemicellulose ext)

42.153 ***Principle***

Roxarsone is extd from feed with 2% K_2HPO_4. Proteins are pptd at isoelec. point and removed by centrfg. Ext is treated with activated C at pH 12 to remove interferences and roxarsone is detd spectrophtric at 410 nm.

42.154 ***Apparatus***

(**a**) *Centrifuge.*—International Model V, or equiv.

(**b**) *Mechanical shaker.*—Burrell wrist-action (Burrell Corp.), or equiv.

42.155 ***Reagents***

(**a**) *Potassium phosphate, dibasic, soln.*—2%. Dissolve 2 g K_2HPO_4 in 100 mL H_2O.

(**b**) *Dilute hydrochloric acid.*—Dil. 45 mL HCl to 200 mL with H_2O.

(**c**) *Sodium hydroxide soln.*—Dissolve 24 g NaOH in 100 mL H_2O.

(**d**) *Charcoal adsorbent.*—Activated (Darco G-60, or equiv.).

(**e**) *Roxarsone std soln.*—300 μg/mL. Accurately weigh 300 mg Roxarsone Ref. Std (Salsbury Laboratories) into 1 L vol. flask. Dissolve and dil. to vol. with 2% K_2HPO_4 soln.

42.156 ***Preparation of Sample***

Grind sample in high-speed blender to pass No. 20 sieve (ca 3 min) and mix thoroly. Weigh 15.0 g ground sample into 125 mL erlenmeyer, add 50.0 mL 2% K_2HPO_4 soln, place on mech. shaker, and shake vigorously 5 min at room temp. Immediately transfer to 100 mL centrf. tube and centrf. 10 min at 3000 rpm. Perform extn and centrfg with min. delay.

Decant 30 mL aliquot supernate into 50 mL graduated centrf. tube, pipet in 1 mL dil. HCl, stopper, and mix thoroly. Let sample stand until protein flocculates (ca 15 min) and centrf. 10 min at 3000 rpm.

42.157 ***Purification***

Pipet 25 mL clear supernate into 125 mL erlenmeyer. Pipet in 1 mL NaOH soln, and mix thoroly. Add 2.0 g activated C and swirl sample several times during 30 min standing. Filter thru Whatman No. 42 fluted paper into 50 mL erlenmeyer. Repeat C treatment with second 2.0 g portion.

42.158 ***Determination***

Place 3 mL filtrate in cell and det. A at 410 nm against H_2O blank. Add 2 drops concd HCl from dropper (or 5 mL serological pipet), mix, and reread A. Difference in A of acidic and basic samples represents roxarsone present. Det. amt from std curve.

42.159 ***Preparation of Standard Curve***

Pipet 0, 1, 3, 5, 7, and 10 mL aliquots std roxarsone soln into 100 mL vol. flasks and dil. to vol. with 2% K_2HPO_4 soln. Pipet 30 mL aliquot from each flask into sep. erlenmeyers, pipet 1 mL dil. HCl into each flask, and mix. Pipet 25 mL aliquot this soln into sep. 50 mL erlenmeyers, pipet in 1 mL NaOH soln, and mix thoroly. Transfer 3 mL soln from erlenmeyers into sep. cells and det. A at 410 nm against H_2O blank. Add 2 drops concd HCl from dropper (or 5 mL serological pipet), mix, and reread A. Plot difference in A of std solns against concn of solns expressed as 0, 0.001, 0.003, 0.005, 0.007, and 0.010% roxarsone in feed when 15 g sample is used.

42.160 ***Determination in Premix***

Weigh appropriate size sample of premix, place in 200 mL vol. flask, and add 50 mL 2% K_2HPO_4 soln and 4.0 mL NaOH soln. Let stand 20 min, shaking occasionally; then dil. to vol. with 2% K_2HPO_4 soln and let feed particles settle 30 min. Proceed as in **42.156**, par. 2, using appropriate aliquots and dilns to give final concns in range of std curve.

(*Example:* 5% Premix.—Place 5 g thoroly mixed premix in 200 mL vol. flask and ext as above. Transfer 10 mL aliquot ext to 100 mL vol. flask, dil. to vol. with H_2O, and mix thoroly. Transfer 10 mL aliquot this soln to another 100 mL vol. flask and dil. to vol. with H_2O. Diln factor for this premix is 1200.)

After diln, transfer 30 mL aliquot to 125 mL erlenmeyer. Pipet in 1 mL dil. HCl and mix. Transfer 25 mL this soln to 125 mL erlenmeyer, pipet in 1 mL NaOH soln, mix thoroly, add 2.0 g activated C, shake several times during 30 min, and filter. Repeat C treatment. Read A of filtrate and det. concn of roxarsone as in **42.158**, multiplying by diln factor.

Sulfonamide Drugs (*41*)—Official First Action

(Applicable to premixes and concs)

42.161 ***Determination of Absorptivities***

Prep. sep. std solns of sulfathiazole (SZ), sulfamerazine (SM), and sulfamethazine (SH) by accurately weighing ca 50 mg each compd and transferring to sep. 50 mL vol. flasks; add 5 mL alcohol and 2 mL NH_4OH, and swirl to dissolve. For sulfaquinoxaline (SQ), weigh 45 mg, warm on steam bath to dissolve, and cool. Dil. each flask to vol. with alcohol, and mix. Evap. 2 mL aliquots to dryness in sep. small beakers, transfer to sep. 200 mL vol. flasks (100 mL for SQ) with several small portions 0.1*N* NaOH, and dil. to vol. with 0.1*N* NaOH. Also dil. 25 mL aliquot SQ soln to 50 mL with 0.1*N* NaOH. Obtain spectrum of each soln in 1 cm cell against 0.1*N* NaOH from 400 to 220 nm.

Calc. a_{255} (1.00 mg/100 mL) $= A \times 50/W$,

where A is reading at max., ca 255 nm, corrected for A at 400 nm, if any, and W is mg compd weighed. (For SQ, use A of dild soln.)

For SQ, also calc. a_{358} (2.00 mg/100 mL) $= A \times 50/W$, where A is reading at max., ca 358 nm, corrected for A at 400 nm, if any, of more concd soln.

42.162 ***Preparation of Sample***

(**a**) *Solids.*—Transfer accurately weighed sample contg ca 50 mg sulfonamide with lowest concn to 50 mL vol. flask, add 5 mL alcohol and 2 mL NH_4OH, and warm 10 min on steam bath. Cool to room temp., dil. to vol. with alcohol, and mix.

(**b**) *Liquid concentrates.*—Pipet aliquot contg ca 200 mg sulfonamide with lowest concn into 200 mL vol. flask, dil. to vol. with alcohol, and mix.

For each sulfonamide declared, calc. an R value to 2 decimal places by dividing its labeled amt by that of sulfonamide with lowest labeled amt, whose R = 1.00. Calc. to 2 decimal places. Designate each ratio as R_{SQ}, R_{SZ}, R_{SM}, and R_{SH}, and their sum as R_T. (If 4 sulfonamides are present in equal amts, all R = 1.00 and R_T = 4.00.)

42.163 ***Determination of Sulfaquinoxaline***

Pipet 5 mL sample soln into g-s flask and add accurately measured vol. alcohol so that total mL of final soln $= 10 \times R_T$ (*Soln I*). Mix, pipet 10 mL into small beaker, and evap. to dryness on steam bath. Transfer residue to 100 mL vol. flask with several small portions 0.1*N* NaOH, dil. to vol. with 0.1*N* NaOH, and mix (*Soln II*). Obtain spectrum from 400 to 300 nm, and det. A at max., ca 358 nm.

$$\% \text{ SQ} = [A_{358} \times 2 \times R_T \times (V/5) \times 100]/(a_{358} \times S),$$

where V = mL original sample soln (50 or 200), and S = mg original sample (for solids) or mL × 1000 (for liqs).

If Na salt declared, NaSQ = SQ/0.9318.

42.164 ***Determination of Total Sulfonamides***

Dil. 20.0 mL *Soln II* to 100 mL with 0.1*N* NaOH. Obtain spectrum from 400 to 230 nm and det. A_T at max., ca 255 nm.

$$\% \text{ Total sulfonamides} = [A_T \times V \times R_T^2 \times 100]/[(R \times a)_{SQ} + (R \times a)_{SZ} + (R \times a)_{SM} + (R \times a)_{SH}] \times S.$$

If Na salts are present, multiply each a by appropriate factor: NaSQ, 0.9318; NaSZ, 0.9207; NaSM, 0.9232; and NaSH, 0.9268.

Separation by Thin Layer Chromatography

42.165 ***Preparation of Plates***

(**a**) *Plates A.*—Weigh 30 g silica gel H or HF 254 (Brinkmann Instruments, Inc.) into 250 mL g-s flask. (Add 100 mg fluorescent indicator H 254 if silica gel H is used.) Add 70 mL H_2O and shake well 1 min. Coat five 20 × 20 cm plates with 0.25 mm layer and air dry. Do not dry in oven and do not store in presence of drying agent.

(**b**) *Plates B.*—Proceed as in (**a**) but use 0.1*N* NaOH instead of H_2O to slurry silica gel.

42.166 ***Preparation of Blanks***

Develop a plate A in $CHCl_3$-MeOH (97+3) to ht of ca 15 cm. Scrape 2 spots, each ca 2 sq cm, from developed section of plate, into centrf. tubes and ext with 10 mL 0.1*N* NaOH. Scrape 2 addnl spots, each ca 4 sq cm, from developed portion and ext with 50 mL 0.1*N* NaOH. Centrf. the 4 exts 5 min at high speed and decant most of soln into sep. small beakers, being careful not to disturb sediment.

Develop a plate B in $CHCl_3$-MeOH (90+10) and proceed as above.

Det. A at max., ca 255 nm, of all 8 exts. A should be ≤ 0.04. If readings are low and reproducible, average each set of 4 values for 2 and 4 sq cm exts, resp. If readings are high or not reproducible, recentrf. exts at higher speed, and be very careful to exclude sediment during decanting. Av. blank A may be used for all detns which use same batch of silica gel and same speed of centrfg.

42.167 ***Thin Layer Chromatography***

Spot 100 μL sample soln on plate A and plate B by repeated application of adjacent drops on line 4 cm long, drying each drop with gentle air current before applying another drop at same place. Develop plate A in $CHCl_3$-MeOH (93+7) and plate B in (90+10) until solv. front reaches top of plate.

View plates under shortwave UV light and delineate each spot with dissecting needle, including small margins whenever possible. Plate A should have 2 completely sepd spots, designated as c (lower: SZ) and d (upper: SM+SH+SQ); plate B should have 3 completely sepd spots designated as f (lower: SQ+SZ), h (middle: SM), and p (top: SH). If less than indicated no. of spots are sepd, spot another aliquot over slightly longer line and develop as before.

Use collection tube consisting of 7–8 cm of 8 mm od glass tubing with short constriction at one end and medium fritted glass disk fused near center. Clean tube with strong air current and attach wide tube to vac. Draw as much of spot as possible into tube, using narrow tube to loosen adsorbent layer. Without disconnecting vac., transfer tube to 10 mL vol. flask for spot c and 50 mL for spot d. Release vac., and transfer material to flask with repeated gentle tapping. Repeat until entire spot has been transferred; then blow out tube into flask with gentle air current to remove last of particles.

Fill each flask ca ½ full with 0.1*N* NaOH, swirl well 1 min, dil. to vol. with 0.1*N* NaOH, and mix. Centrf. all or ≥ 10 mL each soln at same speed used for blanks and carefully decant ca 8 mL into small beakers. Obtain spectrum of each soln from 400 to 230 nm and record A_c of spot c ext and A_d of spot d ext at max., ca 255 nm. Correct A_c for av. blank of 2 sq cm exts and A_d for av. blank of 4 sq cm exts.

Calc. recovery factor, $F = [(5 \times A_d) + A_c]/(R_T \times A_T)$.

$$\% \text{ SZ} = (A_c \times V \times 100)/(a_{SZ,255} \times F \times S)$$

$$\% \text{NaSZ} = \% \text{SZ}/0.9207$$

From plate B, transfer spot f to 50 mL vol. flask and spot h and p to 10 mL vol. flasks. Obtain blank corrected A_f, A_h, and A_p as for exts of plate A.

Calc. recovery factor $F' = [(5 \times A_f) + A_h + A_p]/(R_T \times A_T)$

$$\%SM = (A_h \times V \times 100)/(a_{SM} \times F' \times S)$$
$$\%SH = (A_p \times V \times 100)/(a_{SH} \times F' \times S)$$
$$\%\ NaSM = \%\ SM/0.9232$$
$$\%\ NaSH = \%\ SH/0.9268$$

Sulfadimethoxine (N^1-(2,6-Dimethoxy-4-pyrimidinyl)sulfanilamide (*42*)—Official First Action

42.168 ***Reagents and Apparatus***

See **42.017(b)**, (**c**), and (**d**), and in addn:

(**a**) *Ficin soln.*—0.2%. Disperse 500 mg ficin (Calbiochem, fig latex) in H_2O (preheated to 40°) and dil. to 250 mL. Use 10 mL of this warm soln in detn. (*Caution:* Ficin is very potent proteolytic enzyme which attacks living tissues. Avoid contact with skin and eyes and breathing dust.)

(**b**) *Petroleum ether.*—Bp 35–60°, purified on silica gel column.

(**c**) *Trichloroacetic acid soln.*—3%. Dissolve 30 g CCl_3COOH in H_2O and dil. to 1 L. (*Caution: See* **51.082**.)

(**d**) *Sulfadimethoxine std soln.*—Accurately weigh 125 mg sulfadimethoxine USP Ref. Std and transfer quant. to 100 mL vol. flask. Add ca 70 mL acetone and shake until completely dissolved. Dil. to vol. with acetone and mix. Pipet 20 mL soln into 200 mL vol. flask, dil. to vol. with acetone, and mix. Pipet 10 mL (or 5 mL if working at 0.00625% level) of last diln into 200 mL vol. flask contg 10 mL 0.2% ficin soln. Add ca 120 mL acetone and 2 mL 40% NaOH soln, and mix. Dil. to vol. with acetone and mix. Pipet 25 mL final diln into 50 mL g-s centrf. tube, evap. almost to dryness under N stream in 50° H_2O bath, and proceed as in **42.169**, beginning "Pipet 15 mL pet ether into centrf. tube . . ." Resulting clear filtrate is std soln.

(**e**) *Reagent blank.*—Into 200 mL vol. flask pipet 10 mL 0.2% ficin soln and 2 mL 40% NaOH soln. Dil. to vol. with acetone and mix. Pipet 25 mL of this soln into 50 mL g-s centrf. tube, evap. almost to dryness under N stream in 50° H_2O bath, and proceed as in **42.169**, beginning "Pipet 15 mL pet ether into centrf. tube . . ." Resulting clear filtrate is blank soln.

(**f**) *Spectrophotometer.*—With 5 cm cells, or photoelec. colorimeter with 540 nm filter, or equiv.

42.169 ***Preparation of Sample***

(*Caution: See* **51.004**, **51.018**, **51.039**, and **51.046**.)

Pipet 10 mL 0.2% ficin soln into high-speed blender. Accurately weigh 10 g sample into blender, spreading carefully on surface of liq. Let sample soak 10 min.

Add ca 120 mL acetone. Blend 2 min, adjusting speed with variable transformer, so that acetone does not wet screw cap. (*Caution:* To release pressure, stop blending after 3–4 sec and unscrew cap momentarily.) Blend 2 min and remove screw cap. Push down into acetone all solid particles adhering to container wall, using rubber policeman. Replace screw cap and continue blending 1 min. Remove screw cap, pipet 2 mL 40% NaOH soln into container, and continue blending 2 min. Push down into acetone all solid particles adhering to wall of container, using rubber policeman.

Quant. transfer blender contents to 250 mL g-s graduate, using small portions acetone to total vol. of 200 mL. Stopper, mix well, and let liq. and solids sep. Wrap tip of 50 mL pipet with glass wool and transfer ca 40 mL ext to 50 mL g-s centrf. tube. Centrf. 5 min at 2000 rpm. Pipet 25 mL clear acetone ext into another centrf. tube and evap. almost to dryness (only few drops of oily, sirupy liq. left) under N stream in 50° H_2O bath. Pipet 15 mL pet ether into centrf. tube and dissolve or disperse residue in it.

Pipet 25 mL 0.2*N* NaOH into centrf. tube, stopper, and shake mech. 5 min. Centrf. 10 min at 2000 rpm. By pipet, transfer lower NaOH layer (ca 24 mL) into another centrf. tube and centrf. 10 min at 2000 rpm. Pipet 20 mL clear soln into 100 mL vol. flask. Dil. to vol. with 3% CCl_3COOH soln. Mix and let stand 10 min. Filter entire soln thru Whatman No. 42 paper, discarding first 10 mL filtrate. If turbid, filter thru second paper. Clear filtrate is sample soln.

42.170 ***Determination***

(**a**) *Reading on spectrophotometer with 5 cm cells.*—Pipet following vols (mL) of indicated solns into 6 sep. labeled 25 mL vol. flasks:

Soln	*Sample 1*	*Sample 2*	*Sample Blank*	*Std 1*	*Std 2*	*Reagent Blank*
Sample	15	15	15	—	—	—
Std	—	—	—	15	15	—
Blank	—	—	—	—	—	15

Pipet 1 mL 0.1% $NaNO_2$ soln, **42.017(b)**, into each, mix, and let stand 3 min. Pipet 1 mL 0.5% NH_4 sulfamate soln, **42.017(c)**, into each, mix, and let stand 2 min. Pipet 1 mL 0.1% coupling reagent, **42.017(d)**, into all except sample blank, and 1 mL H_2O into sample blank. Mix and let stand 10 min in dark. Dil. each flask to vol. with H_2O and mix. Measure A of each soln at 540 nm in 5 cm cell against reagent blank in ref. cell.

(**b**) *Reading on photoelectric colorimeter.*—Proceed as in (**a**) except do not dil. after standing, but read at existing vol.; 50 mL g-s centrf. tubes may be used in place of vol. flasks. Transfer solns from flasks or tubes to matched colorimeter tubes. Set instrument with 540 nm filter to 100% T (0 A) with tube contg reagent blank. Det. A (= 2 − log (%T)) of each of other tubes contg samples, sample blank, and stds.

(**c**) *Calculation.*—Higher levels of sulfadimethoxine:

$$\%\ Sulfadimethoxine = [(A - A_0) \times S]/(1000 \times A' \times W).$$

Lower levels of sulfadimethoxine:

$$\%\ Sulfadimethoxine = [(A - A_0) \times S]/(2000 \times A' \times W),$$

where A, A_0, and A' refer to sample, reagent blank, and std, resp.; W = g original sample; and S = mg std weighed.

42.171 Sulfaguanidine (*43*)—Official First Action

Weigh 1 g ground sample into 250 mL vol. flask, and add 100 mL H_2O and 2.5 mL 0.50*N* NaOH. Heat in H_2O bath 15 min with occasional swirling, cool, dil. to vol., and mix well. Let material settle, pipet 25 mL into 100 mL vol. flask, add 10 mL *1.00% $ZnSO_4.7H_2O$ soln,* dil. to vol., mix well, and let stand 1 min. Filter thru 18.5 cm Whatman No. 2 paper, discarding first 10 mL filtrate. (Filtrate must be free of turbidity.)

Pipet 2 mL clear filtrate into 25 mL vol. flask; add 2.5 mL 0.50*N* HCl and 2 mL 0.1% $NaNO_2$ soln, **42.017(b)**. Let stand 3 min. Add 2 mL 0.50% NH_4 sulfamate soln, **42.017(c)**, and wait addnl 2 min. Add 2 mL coupling reagent, **42.017(d)**, and dil. to vol. Swirl flask after addn of each reagent. Prep. blank, using H_2O and same vols reagents dild to 25 mL. Shake vigorously. Measure A of colored soln in spectrophtr at 545 nm against reagent blank, and det. amt of sulfaguanidine present by ref. to std curve.

$$\%\ Sulfaguanidine = \mu g\ sulfaguanidine \times 0.05.$$

Prep. std curve as follows: Dissolve 0.010 g pure sulfaguanidine in 2.5 mL 0.50*N* NaOH and 100 mL H_2O in 250 mL vol. flask by heating 15 min in boiling H_2O bath. Cool, and dil. to vol. with H_2O. Pipet 25 mL of this soln into 100 mL vol. flask, add 10 mL $ZnSO_4$ soln, dil. to vol., and filter (1 mL = 10 μg sulfaguanidine). Pipet 1, 2, 3, and 4 mL portions of this dild soln (equiv. to 10, 20, 30, and 40 μg sulfaguanidine, resp.) into sep. 25 mL vol. flasks, dil. to 10 mL with H_2O, and proceed as in second par. beginning "... add 2.5 mL 0.50*N* HCl ..." Plot *A* against μg sulfaguanidine.

Sulfamethazine (*N*-(4,6-Dimethyl-2-pyrimidinyl) sulfanilamide) (*44*)—Official First Action

(Applicable to feeds contg procaine penicillin)

42.172 ***Reagents***

See **42.017(b)**, **(c)**, and **(d)** and in addn:

(a) *50% Methanol soln.*—50% (v/v) aq. soln of MeOH.

(b) *Sulfamethazine std solns.*—*(1) Stock soln.*—Accurately weigh 0.100 g pure sulfamethazine (available from American Cyanamid Co.) into 100 mL vol. flask. Add 50 mL 50% MeOH soln and shake until dissolved. Dil. to vol. with 50% MeOH soln. Soln is stable at least several weeks. *(2) Intermediate soln.*—Pipet 5 mL stock soln into 200 mL vol. flask, dil. to vol. with 50% MeOH, and mix well. Soln is also stable several weeks. *(3) Working soln.*—2.5 μg/mL. Pipet 10 mL intermediate soln into 100 mL vol. flask, add 1 mL HCl and 50 mL 50% MeOH, dil. to vol. with H_2O, and mix well. Soln is stable ca 2 weeks.

42.173 ***Preparation of Sample***

Weigh 5.00 g sample into 250 mL g-s erlenmeyer. Add 100.0 mL 50% MeOH soln, shake well on mech. shaker 1 hr, and centrf. Pipet aliquot supernate contg ca 250 μg sulfamethazine into 100 mL vol. flask, add 50% MeOH, if necessary, to vol. of ca 60 mL, followed by 1.0 mL HCl, and 10 mL *1% $ZnSO_4$ soln.* Let stand 10 min, dil. to vol. with H_2O, and mix.

42.174 ***Determination***

Filter portion of prepd soln thru Whatman No. 42 paper, or equiv., into 250 mL flask. Filtrate should be clear. Pipet two 10 mL aliquots filtrate and 10 mL working std soln into sep. 50 mL centrf. tubes. To each tube add 1.0 mL 0.1% $NaNO_2$ soln, mix and let stand 3 min. Add 1.0 mL 0.5% NH_4 sulfamate soln; mix and let stand 2 min. Add 1.0 mL 0.1% *N*-(1-naphthyl)ethylenediamine.2HCl soln to one of sample solns and to std soln. To second sample soln add 1.0 mL H_2O (sample blank). Mix all solns well and let stand 10 min.

To sample, sample blank, and std soln add ca 10 mL $CHCl_3$, stopper, and shake *vigorously* 30 sec (30 sec is required to ensure complete removal of procaine dye). Add 0.8 mL 10*N* NaOH to sample, sample blank, and std soln. Stopper and shake vigorously ≥1 min to ensure complete removal of procaine dye. Centrf. solns at 2000 rpm 5 min or until aq. layer is completely clear. Remove 10.0 mL aq. phase with pipet and transfer to 50 mL erlenmeyer or 50 mL beaker. Add 1.0 mL HCl and remove fumes formed in flask with aspirator or air stream.

Read *A* of sample, sample blank, and std (*A'*) at 540 nm in spectrophtr, against H_2O blank. Correct *A* of sample by subtracting that of sample blank.

% Sulfamethazine = (A/A') × (2.5 μg/mL) × (100 mL/mL ext aliquot taken) × (100 mL/5 g) × (1 g/10^6 μg) × 100.

Sulfanitran (Acetyl-(*p*-nitrophenyl)sulfanilamide; APNPS) (*45*)—Official Final Action

42.175 ***Reagents***

See **42.017(b)**, **(c)**, and **(d)** and in addn:

Sulfanitran std solns.—*(1) Stock soln.*—100 μg/mL. Accurately weigh 100 mg pure APNPS (available from Salsbury Laboratories) into 1 L vol. flask, add enough 1*N* NaOH for complete soln, and dil. to vol. with H_2O. *(2) Working soln.*—10 μg/mL. Dil. 10 mL stock soln to 100 mL with H_2O.

42.176 ***Preparation of Standard Curve***

Pipet 0, 4, 6, 8, and 10 mL aliquots working std soln into sep. 50 mL vol. flasks. Add 0.5 mL HCl and adjust vol. with H_2O to ca 15 mL. Place flasks in boiling H_2O bath 1 hr to deacetylate. Cool, and dil. to vol. Transfer 5 mL aliquot from each flask to sep. colorimeter tubes. Develop color by adding 0.5 mL 0.1% $NaNO_2$ soln (not >5 days old, stored in refrigerator), 0.5 mL 0.5% NH_4 sulfamate soln, and 0.5 mL coupling reagent. Det. *A* at 540 nm against reagent blank (0 mL aliquot).

(To establish most reliable std curve, make detns on 3 sep. days and use av. values.)

42.177 ***Extraction and Deacetylation***

(For premixes, use proper dilns to give 5–10 μg APNPS in final aliquot, taking dilns into consideration in final calcn.)

Weigh 5.0 g sample into 100 mL vol. flask and add 80 mL MeOH. Place flask in 60° H_2O bath until MeOH is hot. Repeatedly remove and immerse flask during 20 min, shaking frequently. Cool to room temp., and dil. to vol. with MeOH. Shake thoroly, and let stand 40 min to permit particles to settle.

Pipet 25 mL aliquot MeOH ext into 50 mL vol. flask. Add 10 mL H_2O, 5 mL *1.0% $ZnSO_4$ soln,* and ca 3 drops 1*N* NaOH to improve flocculation. (Keep near neutrality.) Place flask in boiling H_2O bath 2 min to aid pptn; then cool to room temp., dil. to vol., mix thoroly, and filter thru Whatman No. 42 paper, or equiv. Discard first 5 mL filtrate.

Pipet 10 mL aliquot filtrate into 50 mL vol. flask contg 8.0 mL H_2O and 0.5 mL HCl. Place flask in boiling H_2O bath 1 hr to evap. MeOH and deacetylate APNPS, shaking frequently during first 15 min. Cool to room temp. and dil. to vol. with H_2O. Centrf. if turbidity appears.

42.178 ***Determination***

Place 5.0 mL aliquot in each of 2 colorimeter tubes. To 1 tube (blank) add 1.0 mL H_2O and 0.5 mL coupling reagent. To other tube add 0.5 mL 0.1% $NaNO_2$ soln; after 3 min, add 0.5 mL 0.5% NH_4 sulfamate soln, wait 2 min, and add 0.5 mL coupling reagent. Close tube with thumb and invert immediately after adding each reagent. Let stand 10 min for color development and det. *A* of sample and blank at 540 nm in spectrophtr or colorimeter against H_2O. Det. amt APNPS from std curve after subtracting *A* of blank.

% APNPS in sample = μg APNPS in tube × 200 × 100/(5,000,000 × μg sample) = μg APNPS × 0.004.

Sulfaquinoxaline (*46*)

Method I—Official First Action

(Applicable only to nonpelleted feeds contg arsanilic acid. In absence of arsanilic acid, use **42.184**.)

42.179 ***Principle***

Sulfaquinoxaline is extd from feed with DMF and sepd from interfering substances by column chromatgy on alumina. Isolated sulfaquinoxaline is acidified, diazotized, and coupled in presence of Zr, and colored complex is extd with BuOH and measured at 550 nm. Arsanilic acid remains in final aq. soln and can be measured at 540 nm and compared with std treated similarly.

42.180 ***Reagents***

See **42.017(b)**, **(c)**, and **(d)** and in addn:

(a) *Alkaline salt soln.*—Dissolve 2.0 g NaOH and 100.0 g NaCl in 500 mL H_2O.

(b) *Zirconium soln.*—Dissolve 5.0 g zirconyl chloride, $ZrOCl_2.8H_2O$ (Fisher Scientific Co.), in 100 mL H_2O.

(c) *Sulfaquinoxaline std solns.*—*(1) Stock soln.*—Weigh 40.0 mg Sulfaquinoxaline Ref. Std (available from Merck & Co., Inc.) and dissolve in 50.0 mL DMF. Soln is stable at least 1 month if kept tightly stoppered and protected from light. *(2) Intermediate soln.*—80 μg/mL. Dil. 5 mL stock soln to 50 mL with DMF. *(3) Working soln.*—8 μg/mL. Dil. 5 mL intermediate soln to 50 mL with DMF. Prep. from freshly prepd intermediate soln just before use.

(d) *Butanol mixture.*—Mix 100 mL *n*-hexane with 400 mL *n*-BuOH.

42.181 ***Preparation of Sample***

Weigh 4.00 g ground feed sample into 100 mL vol. flask. Add 50.0 mL DMF, stopper, and agitate by mag. stirrer or mech. shaker 60 min. Transfer mixt. to 50 mL centrf. tube and centrf. 5 min at 2500 rpm.

42.182 ***Chromatography***

(a) *Preparation of column.*—Constrict end of 50–60 cm length of 9–11 mm id glass tubing by rotating in hot flame until opening is 4–5 mm. Insert small plug of Pyrex glass wool in lower end and compress with glass rod to thickness of 2–3 mm. Transfer 5.0 g alumina, **42.029(b)**, to dry tube and pack by gentle tapping while applying vac.

(b) *Separation.*—Pipet 10 mL clear ext onto column and let pass thru by gravity. Do not let column run dry; keep 5 mm head of liq. Wash inner walls with two 5.0 mL portions $CHCl_3$. Let final washing drain until no further liq. appears at tip. Discard effluent and washings. Attach column tip to vac. and draw air thru until alumina is dry, indicated by tube returning to room temp. Elute column by gravity with 25 mL alk. salt soln, collecting eluate in 25 mL vol. flask. Add 1.0 mL HCl to eluate, dil. to vol. with H_2O, and mix well.

Prep. reagent blank by transferring 10 mL DMF onto fresh column and proceeding as for sample. Prep. std by transferring 10.0 mL sulfaquinoxaline working std soln onto fresh column and proceeding as for sample.

42.183 ***Determination***

Transfer 10 mL aliquots of each eluate to sep. centrf. tubes. Add 2.0 mL Zr soln and mix. Add 1.0 mL *0.1% $NaNO_2$ soln,* mix, and let stand 2 min. Add 1.0 mL *0.5% NH_4 sulfamate soln,* mix, and let stand 2 min. Add 1.0 mL coupling reagent, **42.017(d)**, mix, and let stand 10 min. Add 2.0 g NaCl and 10.0 mL BuOH mixt., stopper, and shake vigorously until NaCl dissolves. Centrf., carefully transfer portion of clear, colored top solv. layer to 1 cm cell, and read *A* at 550 nm against BuOH mixt. Correct for reagent blank.

$$\% \text{ Sulfaquinoxaline} = 0.04 \times (A/A')/W,$$

where *A* and *A'* refer to sample and std (blank corrected), resp., and *W* = g sample.

42.184 ***Method II—Official Final Action***

(Applicable in absence of arsanilic acid)

Weigh 5 g ground sample into 250 mL vol. flask, add 150 mL H_2O and 5 mL 0.5*N* NaOH, and place in boiling H_2O bath 15 min. Remove, cool, dil. to vol. with H_2O, mix, and let settle. Transfer 50 mL supernatant to 100 mL vol. flask, add 3 mL HCl, and dil. to vol. Mix, and filter thru 18.5 cm Whatman No. 2 paper (or equiv.), discarding first 15 mL filtrate if turbid.

To 10 mL filtrate in each of two 50 mL beakers add 2 mL *freshly prepd 0.1% $NaNO_2$ soln* and let stand 3 min. Add 2 mL *0.5% NH_4 sulfamate soln* and let stand 2 min. Add 1 mL coupling reagent, **42.017(d)**, to first beaker and 1 mL H_2O to second beaker. Mix thoroly after adding each reagent. After 10 min, read *A* in spectrophtr at 545 nm. Subtract *A* of feed blank from sample *A* and det. amt of sulfaquinoxaline from std curve. Divide by 1000 to obtain % sulfaquinoxaline.

Prep. std curve as follows: Dissolve 0.250 g pure sulfaquinoxaline in 5 mL 0.5*N* NaOH and 50 mL H_2O in 500 mL vol. flask, and dil. to vol. with H_2O. Pipet 5 mL aliquot of this soln into 100 mL vol. flask and dil. to vol. with H_2O. Pipet 2, 4, 6, 8, and 10 mL portions of this dild soln (equiv. to 50, 100, 150, 200, and 250 μg sulfaquinoxaline, resp.) into sep. 100 mL vol. flasks, add 3 mL HCl to each flask, and dil. to vol. with H_2O. Treat 10 mL aliquots of these final dilns as in second par. Det. *A* at 545 nm against H_2O blank, and plot *A* against μg sulfaquinoxaline.

Thiabendazole (2-(4-Thiazolyl)-benzimidazole) (47)
Official Final Action

Method I

(Applicable to all feeds)

42.185 ***Principle***

Thiabendazole is extd from feed with 0.1*N* HCl. Interferences are removed by adjusting ext to pH 5–6 with Na citrate and extg with $CHCl_3$. Thiabendazole is re-extd with 0.1*N* HCl and reduced with Zn slurry in 30% glycerol in presence of *p*-phenylenediamine. Oxidn with ferric iron yields blue complex which is extd with BuOH and measured at 605 nm.

42.186 ***Reagents***

(a) *Zinc dust.*—Reagent grade. Crush fine lumps with spatula immediately before use.

(b) *Zinc slurry.*—Weigh 50 mg *p*-phenylenediamine.2HCl (*Caution: p*-phenylenediamine may be harmful; *see* **51.084**) and 2 g Zn dust into dry 100 mL g-s graduate. Add 100 mL 30% (v/v) glycerol soln, stopper, and shake ca 30 sec to suspend Zn dust uniformly. (There must be no agglomeration of Zn.) Prep. just before use and use immediately.

(c) *Ferric soln.*—Dissolve 15.0 g $FeNH_4(SO_4)_2.12H_2O$ in 75 mL H_2O, add 10.0 mL 1*N* H_2SO_4, dil. to 100 mL, and mix.

(d) *Thiabendazole std solns.*—*(1) Stock soln.*—0.5 mg/mL. Dissolve 50.0 mg Thiabendazole Ref. Std (available from Merck & Co.) in 0.1*N* HCl and dil. to 100 mL. Soln is stable ≥1 month. *(2) Intermediate soln.*—50 μg/mL. Dil. 10 mL stock soln to 100 mL with 0.1*N* HCl. Soln is stable ≥1 month. *(3) Working soln.*—5 μg/mL. Dil. 20.0 mL intermediate soln to 200 mL with 0.1*N* HCl. (Use same 0.1*N* HCl as in extn of feed.)

42.187 ***Determination***

Grind ca 100 g well mixed sample to pass No. 30 sieve and mix. (3 min in high-speed blender should be enough.)

Weigh 2.000 g ground sample into 250 mL ₸ 24/40 flat-bottom extn flask. (For feeds contg <0.025% thiabendazole, weigh 5.000 g.)

Add 100.0 mL 0.1*N* HCl to sample and add mag. stirring bar. Connect flask to reflux condenser (Allihn, drip tip) and reflux gently on mag. hot plate, while stirring, 30 min. Cool, transfer mixt. to centrf. tube, and centrf. ca 5 min. Dil. measured aliquot of supernate to concn of 5 μg thiabendazole/mL (serial dilns may be necessary). Such dilns det. "dilution factor," *DF*:

Declaration, %	Sample wt, g	Dilution(s)	DF
0.01	5	none	1
0.025	2	none	1
0.1	2	25–100	4
1.0	2	10–100; 25–100	40
6.0	2	10–100; 10–250	250

Mark series of 50 mL centrf. tubes 1, 2, 3, 4, etc. Place 20.0 mL 0.1*N* HCl in tube 1 and 20.0 mL (100 μg) working std soln in tubes 2 and 3. Place 20.0 mL aliquots of sample solns in tubes 4, 5, etc. Add 3 g Na citrate, 3 g NaCl, and 20.0 mL $CHCl_3$ to each tube, stopper tightly with polyethylene stopper, and shake mech. 5 min. Centrf. ca 5 min and discard top layers. With pipet, transfer 10 mL $CHCl_3$ ext to dry, marked, centrf. tubes, add 25.0 mL 0.1*N* HCl to each, stopper, and shake 5 min. Centrf., and transfer, with pipet, 15 mL of top acid layer to another marked tube. (Because of timing, handle ≤10 tubes at one time.)

With rapid delivery pipet, add 5 mL freshly prepd Zn slurry, (**b**), to each tube. (5 mL pipet with tip cut off to give delivery in ca 5 sec is suitable. Hold pipet directly over center of soln.) Do not shake tube but *immediately stopper* tightly and let stand 4 min. Start timing after delivery of slurry to first tube.

After 4 min, add 5.0 mL ferric soln, (**c**), to each tube with rapid pipet, stopper, and mix by inverting tube. Let stand 5 min; then shake vigorously and centrf. ca 3 min. With pipet, transfer 15 mL clear, colored soln to marked, dry, centrf. tubes. Let stand 45 min from addn of ferric soln. Then add 5.00 mL *n*-BuOH and 3 g anhyd. Na_2SO_4 to each tube. Stopper, and immediately shake each tube ca 5 sec to avoid caking of Na_2SO_4; then shake all tubes ca 3 min or until Na_2SO_4 is completely dissolved, and centrf.

Transfer clear BuOH soln (top layer) to dry 1 cm cell and read *A* at 605 nm against *n*-BuOH as ref.

% Thiabendazole in feed = $(A - A_0)(C)(DF)/360(A' - A_0)W$,

where A refers to sample, A_0 to reagent blank (tube 1), A' to std, C = μg thiabendazole std in final 15.0 mL colored soln (18 μg), DF = diln factor, and W = g original sample.

Method II

(Applicable to cattle supplements and premixes contg >1% thiabendazole. Principle is same as **42.185**, except that single extn at room temp. with 0.1*N* HCl is used. Not applicable to feeds, premixes, or cattle supplements contg high levels of protein.)

42.188 ***Reagents***

See **42.186** except:

(**a**) *Thiabendazole working soln.*—2 μg/mL. Dil. 10.0 mL thiabendazole intermediate soln, **42.186(d)**(*2*), to 250 mL with 0.1*N* HCl.

42.189 ***Determination***

Prep. sample as in **42.187**, except use ca 50 g representative sample.

Weigh 2.000 g ground sample into 1 L vol. flask and add 750 mL 0.1*N* HCl. Add mag. stirring bar, stopper, and mix vigorously on mag. stirrer 1 hr at room temp. (Mech. shaker providing vigorous agitation may be used.) Remove and rinse bar, and dil. to vol. with 0.1*N* HCl. Mix, centrf., and dil. aliquots of clear ext with 0.1*N* HCl to concn of 2 μg thiabendazole/mL. Diln factors, *DF*, are as follows (*see* **42.187**):

Declaration, %	Dilution	DF
1.0	10–100	10
2.5	4.0–100	25
6.0	4.0–250	62.5

Develop color in exts as soon as possible after extn. (Acid exts of some feeds deteriorate upon standing.)

Mark series of 50 mL centrf. tubes (≤10) as in **42.187**. Add 15.0 mL 0.1*N* HCl to tube 1, and 15.0 mL working soln, (**a**), to tubes 2 and 3. Add 15.0 mL sample exts to other tubes. Then with rapid delivery pipet, add 5.0 mL freshly prepd Zn slurry as in **42.187**. Proceed as in **42.187** with addn of ferric soln, observing same technics and time precautions. Read final clear BuOH ext, as above, in 1 cm cell at 605 nm.

% Thiabendazole in feed = $(A - A_0)(C)(DF)/90(A' - A_0)W$,

where symbols are as defined in **42.187**.

Zoalene (3,5-Dinitro-*o*-toluamide) (*48*)
Official Final Action

(Not applicable in presence of furazolidone, nitrofurazone, and nihydrazone)

42.190 ***Principle***

Zoalene is extd from feeds, premixes, and concs contg 0.004–25% with 85% CH_3CN. For mixes contg <1%, alumina is added. After filtration and diln, zoalene is detd colorimetrically after reaction with ethylenediamine.

42.191 ***Reagents***

(**a**) *Acetone.*—95%. Add 5 mL H_2O to 95 mL acetone.

(**b**) *Acetonitrile.*—85%. Add 850 mL practical grade CH_3CN to 150 mL H_2O (deionized or distd).

(**c**) *Activated alumina.*—Alcoa grade F 20, 80–200 mesh. (Available from Fisher Scientific Co. "Alumina, Adsorption, Fisher.")

(**d**) *Dimethylformamide* (*DMF*).—95%. Add 5 mL H_2O to 95 mL tech. DMF. Prep. fresh daily, since old solns may cause cloudiness.

(**e**) *Ethylenediamine.*—98–100%. (MC/B Manufacturing Chemists). Reagent must be practically colorless.

(**f**) *Zoalene std soln.*—40 μg/mL. Weigh 40.0 mg Zoalene Ref. Std (available from Dow Chemical USA, Ag-Organics Dept.) into 1 L vol. flask, dil. to vol. with 85% CH_3CN, and mix.

42.192 ***Determination***

Weigh 10.0 g sample into 250 mL erlenmeyer and add 65 mL 85% CH_3CN. Warm on steam bath to 50±5°, swirling occasionally. Let cool to room temp. (ca 30 min). Add 20 g alumina and swirl occasionally ca 3 min. (Addn of alumina is unnecessary for concs contg ≥1% zoalene.) Filter with suction on medium or fine porosity 40 mm diam. fritted glass funnel, transferring as much solids as possible. Transfer remaining solids with min. vol. 85% CH_3CN, and suck dry. Suspend cake in funnel with min. vol. 85% CH_3CN and slight stirring but without suction. Then filter with suction and repeat suspension and filtering, keeping total vol. <100 mL. Transfer combined filtrates to 100 mL vol. flask (or vol. flask may be used to collect filtrates directly), dil. to vol. with 85% CH_3CN, and mix.

Based on zoalene concn, make addnl dilns with 95% acetone and use aliquots indicated in Table **42:02**.

Pipet indicated aliquots into three 50 mL beakers, X, Y, and Z, for concns <0.25%; omit X for samples >0.25%. Pipet 1 mL std soln into beaker Z and evap. all solns to dryness with air current. (Heat may be used but temp. must not exceed 60°.) Pipet 10 mL 95% DMF into X and 2 mL each into Y and Z. Swirl intermittently during 5 min to dissolve zoalene. Pipet 8 mL ethylenediamine into Y and Z and mix. If turbidity persists after 2 min, filter thru small Reeve Angel No. 804, or equiv., paper. Read *A* of solns at 560 nm in stoppered 1 cm cells against 95%

Table 42:02 Dilution of Sample for Determination

% Zoalene in Sample	Addnl Diln	Aliquot Size, mL	Multiplication Factor *M*
0.004– 0.012	None	4	1
0.012– 0.025	None	2	2
0.025– 0.050	10 to 100	10	4
0.050– 0.10	10 to 100	5	8
0.10 – 0.25	10 to 100	2	20
0.25 – 0.5	1 to 100	10	40
0.5 – 1.0	1 to 100	5	80
1.0 – 2.5	1 to 100	2	200
2.5 – 5.0	1 to 1000	10	400
5.0 –10.0	1 to 1000	5	800
10.0 –25.0	1 to 1000	2	2000

DMF 5 min after addn of ethylenediamine. Keep cell compartment of spectrophtr at <30° to avoid rapid fading of color. If A is >1, reanalyze, using greater diln or smaller aliquot.

$$\% \text{ Zoalene} = (A_Y - A_X) \times M/100\ (A_Z - A_Y).$$

Caution: CH_3CN and ethylenediamine are toxic. Handle in hood and avoid contact with skin.

ANTIBIOTICS

Microscopic Test for Chlortetracycline (*49*)
Official Final Action

42.193 ***Apparatus***

Microscopes.—See **7.124(a)** and **(b)**.

42.194 ***Reagent***

Modified Sakaguchi reagent.—Dissolve 5 g H_3BO_3 in 150 mL H_2O and add 350 mL H_2SO_4. Store in g-s bottle in refrigerator. Use cold.

42.195 ***Determination***

Grind sample as in **7.002**. Pipet ca 10 mL Sakaguchi reagent into 9 cm petri dish. Place No. 60 sieve over petri dish. With top of spatula, sprinkle ca 0.5 g sample on sieve, and gently tap it to obtain good distribution of particles over liq. surface. Place under stereoscopic microscope and examine with transmitted light at ca 15×. If substage illumination is not available, place petri dish on white surface and illuminate with blue light.

As particles of antibiotic slowly dissolve, diffusing chlortetracycline turns intense purple. Color fades in 5–10 min.

MICROBIOLOGICAL METHODS (*50*)

42.196 ***Culture Media***

(Deionized H_2O may be used for prepn of media.)

(a) *Agar medium A.*—(Antibiotic Medium 1.) Dissolve 6.0 g pancreatic digest of gelatin, 4.0 g pancreatic digest of casein, 3.0 g yeast ext, 1.5 g beef ext, 1.0 g anhyd. glucose, and 15 g agar in H_2O, and dil. to 1 L. Adjust with 1*N* NaOH or HCl (1+9) so that after sterilization pH is 6.5–6.6. (Difco Penassay Seed Agar and BBL Seed Agar have been found satisfactory.)

(b) *Agar medium B.*—(Antibiotic Medium 4.) Dissolve 6.0 g pancreatic digest of gelatin, 3.0 g yeast ext, 1.5 g beef ext, 1.0 g anhyd. glucose, and 15 g agar in H_2O, and dil. to 1 L. Adjust with 1*N* NaOH or HCl (1+9) so that after sterilization pH is 6.5–6.6. (Difco and BBL Yeast Beef Agar have been found satisfactory.)

(c) *Agar medium C.*—(Antibiotic Medium 2.) Dissolve 6.0 g pancreatic digest of gelatin, 3.0 g yeast ext, 1.5 g beef ext, and 15 g agar in H_2O, and dil. to 1 L. Adjust with 1*N* NaOH or HCl (1+9) so that after sterilization pH is 6.5–6.6. (Difco Penassay Base Agar and BBL Base Agar have been found satisfactory.)

(d) *Agar medium D.*—(Antibiotic Medium 8.) Use agar medium C adjusted with 1*N* NaOH or HCl (1+9) so that final pH is 5.7–5.9. (Difco Antibiotic Medium 8 and BBL Base Agar with low pH have been found satisfactory.)

(e) *Agar medium E.*—(Antibiotic Medium 5.) Use agar medium C adjusted with 1*N* NaOH so that final pH is 7.8–8.0. (Difco Streptomycin Assay Agar and BBL Streptomycin Assay Agar with Yeast Extract have been found satisfactory.)

(f) *Agar medium F.*—Adjust agar medium A with 3.5*N* NaOH (2.8–3.8 mL/L) so that after sterilization pH is 8.9–9.1.

(g) *Agar medium G.*—(Antibiotic Medium 32.) Use agar medium A to which is added 300 mg $MnSO_4.H_2O$ or 0.4 mL 1% $MnCl_2$ soln/L.

(h) *Agar medium H.*—Dil. 1 L agar medium A to 1.2 L and adjust to pH 8.1.

(i) *Agar medium I.*—Dissolve 9.4 g pancreatic digest of gelatin, 4.7 g yeast ext, 2.4 g beef ext, 10.0 g NaCl, 10.0 g anhyd. glucose, 13.0 g anhyd. KH_2PO_4, 1 g $Na_2HPO_4.7H_2O$, and 23.5 g agar in H_2O, and dil. to 1 L. After sterilization pH is 5.3–5.5. (BBL Nystatin Assay Agar supplemented with 13.0 g anhyd. KH_2PO_4 and 1 g $Na_2HPO_4.7H_2O$ has been found satisfactory.)

(j) *Agar medium J.*—(Antibiotic Medium 11.) Use agar medium A adjusted with 1*N* NaOH so that final pH is 7.9–8.0. (Difco and BBL Neomycin Assay Agar have been found satisfactory.)

(k) *Agar medium K.*—To each L agar medium J add 12.5 mL 2*M* $CaCl_2$ after autoclaving and just before pouring plates.

(l) *Agar medium L.*—Dissolve 0.69 g K_2HPO_4, 0.45 g KH_2PO_4, 2.5 g yeast ext, 10.0 g anhyd. glucose, and 15.0 g Purified Agar No. L 28 (Oxoid Canada Ltd, 145 Bentley Ave, Ottawa, Ontario K2E 6T7, Canada) in H_2O and dil. to 1 L. Adjust to pH 6.0 with HCl before use.

(m) *Agar medium M.*—Dissolve 2.5 g yeast ext, 10.0 g glucose, 0.69 g K_2HPO_4, 0.45 g KH_2PO_4, and 20.0 g agar in H_2O and dil. to 1 L. Before adding inoculum, adjust liquified medium to pH 6.0 with 1*N* HCl (ca 2 mL/L).

(n) *Broth medium A.*—(Antibiotic Medium 3.) Dissolve 5.0 g pancreatic digest of gelatin, 1.5 g yeast ext, 1.5 g beef ext, 3.5 g NaCl, 1.0 g anhyd. glucose, 3.68 g anhyd. K_2HPO_4, and 1.32 g anhyd. KH_2PO_4 in H_2O, and dil. to 1 L. Adjust with 1*N* NaOH or HCl (1+9) so that after sterilization pH is 6.95–7.05. (Difco Penassay Broth and BBL Antibiotic Assay Broth have been found satisfactory.)

(o) *Broth medium B.*—Dissolve 5.0 g pancreatic digest of casein, 5.0 g pancreatic digest of animal tissues, and 20 g anhyd. glucose in H_2O, and dil. to 1 L. Adjust with 1*N* NaOH or with HCl (1+11) so that after sterilization pH is 5.6–5.7. (Difco Fluid Sabouraud Medium and BBL Sabouraud Liquid Broth Modified have been found satisfactory.)

42.197 ***Reagents***

(a) *Phosphate-bicarbonate buffer.*—pH 8. Dissolve 16.73 g anhyd. K_2HPO_4, 0.523 g anhyd. KH_2PO_4, and 20 g $NaHCO_3$ in H_2O and dil. to 1 L.

(b) *Phosphate buffer.*—pH 8; 0.1*M*. Dissolve 16.73 g anhyd. K_2HPO_4 and 0.523 g anhyd. KH_2PO_4 in H_2O and dil. to 1 L.

(c) *Phosphate buffer.*—pH 7.0; 0.1*M*. Dissolve 13.6 g anhyd. K_2HPO_4 and 4.0 g anhyd. KH_2PO_4 in H_2O and dil. to 1 L.

(d) *5% Phosphate buffer.*—pH 6.5. Dissolve 22.15 g anhyd. K_2HPO_4 and 27.85 g anhyd. KH_2PO_4 in H_2O and dil. to 1 L.

(e) *10% Phosphate buffer.*—pH 6. Dissolve 80 g anhyd. KH_2PO_4 and 20 g anhyd. K_2HPO_4 in H_2O and dil. to 1 L.

(f) *1% Phosphate buffer.*—pH 6. Dissolve 8.0 g anhyd. KH_2PO_4 and 2.0 g anhyd. K_2HPO_4 in H_2O and dil. to 1 L.

(**g**) *Phosphate buffer.*—pH 4.5; 0.1*M*. Dissolve 13.6 g anhyd. KH_2PO_4 in H_2O and dil. to 1 L.

(**h**) *Pyridine-buffer soln.*—Mix 9 vols pyridine and 31 vols pH 6.0 buffer, (**f**).

(**i**) *40% Pyridine-buffer soln.*—Mix 4 vols pyridine (2° boiling range), 3 vols 5% phosphate buffer, (**d**), and 3 vols H_2O.

(**j**) *Acid-acetone.*—Mix 1 vol. 4*N* HCl, 13 vols acetone, and 6 vols H_2O.

(**k**) *Acid-methanol.*—Mix 1 vol. HCl and 50 vols MeOH.

(**l**) *Ethyl acetate.*—99% undenatured grade.

(**m**) *Buffer-acetone extractant.*—Mix equal vols pH 6 buffer, (**f**), and acetone.

(**n**) *Tris buffer.*—pH 8.0, 0.05*M*. Dissolve 6.05 g tris(hydroxymethyl)aminomethane (THAM, primary std, available from Fisher Scientific Co.) in 900 mL H_2O, adjust pH to 8.0 with HCl, and dil. to 1 L.

(**o**) *Calcium chloride soln.*—2*M*. Dissolve 294.04 g $CaCl_2.2H_2O$ in H_2O and dil. to 1 L.

(**q**) *Sodium hypochlorite soln.*—5.25%. Use freshly opened bottle com. soln. (Clorox has been found satisfactory.) Store in dark at 2–10°.

(**r**) *Sterile isotonic saline soln.*—Dissolve 9.0 g NaCl in H_2O and dil. to 1 L. Autoclave 20 min at 121°.

(**s**) *Lead acetate soln.*—Dissolve 303 mg $Pb(OAc)_2.3H_2O$ in H_2O and dil. to 1 L with H_2O.

42.198 *Apparatus*

(High-speed blender jars, after disassembling, must be cleaned with great care to eliminate all traces of antibiotics. All app. which contacts sample and solns must be thoroly cleaned and be detergent-free.)

(**a**) *Cylinders.*—Polished open stainless steel cylinders, 8±0.1 mm od, 6±0.1 mm id, and 10±0.1 mm high (obtainable from S & L Metal Products Corp., 58–29 57th Drive, Maspeth, NY 11378).

(**b**) *Petri dishes* (*plates*).—Glass or plastic; 100 mm wide × 20 mm deep. Porcelain covers glazed on outside or cover lids with filter pad inserts are satisfactory for absorbing H_2O of syneresis. Glass or plastic covers may be used if they are raised slightly to allow escape of H_2O.

(**c**) *Cylinder dispenser.*—Cylinders, (**a**), may be placed on plates with Shaw Dispenser, available from E. C. Condit, PO Box 75, Middle Haddam, CT 06456 or Arthur E. Farmer, PO Box 1785, Trenton, NJ 08618.

(**d**) *Heating mat.*—Masonite, 20 × 24 × 5/16" (available from Electrozot Corp., PO Box 1059, Monroe, NC 28110), or equiv.

(**e**) *Aluminum air sparger.*—Construct from 2.8 m (110") length of 0.25" Al tubing. Make 3 semicircular bends 64, 132, and 200 cm (25, 52, and 79") from short end and 70° bend 17 cm (6.5") from beginning of long end. Support sparger on 2 lengths of wood 44 × 2.5 × 1.3 cm (17.5 × 1 × 0.5"); drill 16 holes with 0.2 cm (1/16") drill between supports 10 cm (3.75") apart and 8 other holes outside of supports so all holes will be centered over dishes they aerate. Connect both ends of sparger to glass Y-tube with Tygon tubing. Connect to air line supplying 276–345 kPa (40–50 lb/sq in.) and equipped with H_2O trap.

42.199 *Stock Cultures and Preparation of Test Organism Suspensions*

For appropriate test organism designated below, prep. slant culture on ≥1 tube of agar medium A. Incubate overnight at indicated temp. held constant to ±0.5°, and then store in dark at 2–10°. Do not use if >2 weeks old.

Prep. suspensions of test organisms as follows:

(**a**) *Micrococcus flavus.*—ATCC No. 10240. Incubate stock culture at 32–35°. Wash growth from stock culture with ca 3 mL broth medium A and transfer liq. to surface of 300 mL agar medium A in Roux bottle. Spread suspension evenly over entire surface, using sterile glass beads, and incubate overnight at 32–35°. Wash growth from agar surface with ca 25 mL sterile isotonic saline soln. Store bulk suspension at 2–10°. Use for bacitracin assay.

(**b**) *Sarcina subflava.*—ATCC No. 7468. Incubate stock culture at 32–35°. Prep. suspension as in (**a**) and use as alternative organism for bacitracin assay.

(**c**) *Bacillus cereus.*—ATCC No. 11778. Incubate stock culture at 30°. Wash growth from stock culture with ca 3 mL sterile H_2O, transfer to surface of 300 mL agar medium A, and incubate 7 days at 30°. Wash growth from agar surface with ca 25 mL sterile H_2O and heat suspension 30 min at 65°. Centrf. and decant. Wash residual spores 3 times with sterile H_2O, centrfg and decanting each time. Discard wash H_2O. Heat residual spores 30 min at 65° and resuspend in sterile H_2O. Store this stock suspension at 2–10°. Use for chlortetracycline and oxytetracycline assays.

(**d**) *Bacillus subtilis.*—ATCC No. 6633. Incubate stock culture at 37°. Wash growth from stock culture with ca 3 mL sterile isotonic saline soln, transfer to surface of 300 mL agar medium G in Roux bottle, and incubate 7 days at 37°. Wash growth from agar surface with ca 50 mL sterile isotonic saline soln into centrf. bottle. Heat suspension 30 min in 65° H_2O bath to destroy vegetative cells. Centrf., decant, and resuspend cells in ca 50 mL sterile isotonic saline soln. Repeat heating, centrfg, and suspending twice, or until supernate is clear. Final suspension is stock spore suspension. Store at 2–10°. Use for hygromycin B, monensin, and streptomycin assays.

(**e**) *Sarcina lutea.*—ATCC No. 9341. Incubate stock culture at 26–30°. Prep. organism suspension by one of following methods:

(*1*) *Roux bottle culture.*—Wash growth from 24 hr slant culture with ca 3 mL broth medium A, and transfer liq. to surface of 300 mL agar medium A in Roux bottle. Spread suspension evenly over entire surface, using sterile glass beads, and incubate 24 hr at 26–32°. Wash growth from agar surface with ca 15 mL sterile isotonic saline soln. Store bulk suspension ≤2 weeks at 2–10°.

(*2*) *Broth culture.*—Wash growth from stock culture with ca 3 mL broth medium A, and transfer liq. to 100 mL broth medium A. Incubate 48 hr at 26–32° with continuous mech. agitation. This 48 hr culture is inoculum. Store ≤2 weeks at 2–10°.

Use for erythromycin, lincomycin, novobiocin feed supplement, oleandomycin, penicillin, and tylosin assays.

(**f**) *Staphylococcus epidermidis.*—ATCC 12228. Incubate stock culture at 32°. Inoculate 30 mL broth medium A in 300 mL flask with 1 loop from stock culture, and incubate overnight at 26–32°. Prep. daily. Use for neomycin and for novobiocin final feed assays.

(**g**) *Saccharomyces cerevisiae.*—ATCC No. 9763. Incubate stock culture on agar medium I at 37°. Prep. inoculum by one of following methods:

(*1*) *Broth culture.*—Inoculate 100 mL broth medium B with 1 loop from stock culture and incubate overnight at 37°. This culture is inoculum. Store ≤2 weeks at 2–10°.

(*2*) *Roux bottle culture.*—Wash growth from stock culture with ca 3 mL sterile isotonic saline soln, and transfer liq. to surface of 300 mL agar medium I in Roux bottle. Spread suspension evenly over entire surface, using sterile glass beads, and incubate 24 hr at 37°. Wash growth from agar surface with ca 15 mL sterile isotonic saline soln. Store ≤2 weeks at 2–10°.

Use for nystatin assay.

(**h**) *Escherichia coli.*—UC 527 (available from The Upjohn Co.).

Incubate at 36°. Inoculate 30 mL broth medium A in 250 mL flask from stock culture of *E. coli* and grow 18–24 hr at 36°. Prep. daily. Use for spectinomycin assay.

42.200 ***Preparation of Standard Response Line***

Prep. concns of Ref. Std (described for each antibiotic) simultaneously with assay soln. Use indicated concn as ref. concn.

Prep. plates with appropriate base agar layer and/or appropriate seed agar layer (described for each antibiotic). Distribute agar evenly by tilting plates from side to side with circular motion, and let harden. *Use plates same day prepd.*

Place 6 cylinders on each plate at ca 60° intervals on 2.8 cm radius. Fill 3 alternate cylinders with ref. concn and other 3 cylinders with one of other concns of std. Use 3 plates for each concn required for std response line, except ref. concn. Incubate plates overnight at appropriate temp., and measure diams of zones of inhibition as accurately as possible. (In most cases, it is possible to est. zone diams to nearest 0.1 mm.) Values given in each method for zones of inhibition to be obtained with ref. concns of antibiotics are for guidance only, but it is important that lowest concn on std response line give measurable zone and that slope of response line be adequate. In each set of 3 plates average the 9 readings of ref. concn and the 9 readings of concn being tested. Av. of all 36 readings of ref. concn from 12 plates is correction point for response line. Correct av. value obtained for each concn to appropriate figure if ref. concn reading on that set of 3 plates was same as correction point.

For example, if in correcting second concn of std response line, av. of 36 readings of ref. concn is 20.0 mm, and av. of 9 readings of ref. concn of this set of 3 plates is 19.8 mm, correction is +0.2 mm. If av. reading of second concn on same 3 plates is 17.0 mm, corrected value is 17.2 mm. Plot corrected values, including correction point, on semilog graph paper, using logarithmic scale for concn and arithmetic scale for av. zone diams. Draw line of best fit by inspection or calc. as follows:

$$L = (3a + 2b + c - e)/5$$

$$H = (3e + 2d + c - a)/5$$

where L and H = calcd zone diams for low and high concns, resp., of std response line; a, b, c, d, and e = corrected av. zone diams for each concn on std response line.

For methods specifying 3 doses of std, calc. as follows:

$$L = (5a + 2b - c)/6$$

$$H = (5c + 2b - a)/6.$$

For methods specifying 4 doses of std, calc. as follows:

$$L = (7a + 4b + c - 2d)/10$$

$$H = (7d + 4c + b - 2a)/10.$$

Formulae for calcg L and H are applicable only when std doses are spaced at equal intervals on log scale; i.e., interval between successive log doses is same.

Plot values for L and H and connect with straight line. Ref. point is zone size intercept on arithmetic scale for ref. concn with plotted response line. Alternatively, det. slope B of std response line = $(H - L)/(\log h - \log l)$, where h and l are high and low std concns, resp., and B is the increase in zone size for each 10× increase in drug concn.

42.201 ***Determination of Potency***

Use 3 plates for each assay soln. On each plate fill 3 alternate cylinders with ref. concn and fill other 3 cylinders with assay soln. Incubate plates overnight at appropriate temp. and measure diam. of zones of inhibition. Average the 9 readings of ref. concn and the 9 readings of assay soln. If assay soln gives larger av. than ref. concn, add difference between them to ref. point on std response line. If assay soln gives smaller value than ref. concn, subtract difference between them from ref. point on std response line. Using corrected value of assay soln, det. amt of antibiotic from std response line.

Alternatively, det. log relative potency $M' = (\bar{y}_u - \bar{y}_s)/B$, where $\bar{y}_u$ and $\bar{y}_s$ are av. of 9 readings of assay soln and ref. concn, resp., and B is slope of std response line. Antilog M' = potency of assay soln relative to std; and (antilog M') × 100 = potency of assay soln as % of std ref. concn.

For calcns, 1 ton = 908,000 g; ppm × 0.908 = g/ton.

Bacitracin—Official Final Action

For Feed Supplements (50)

(Applicable to supplements contg ≥6 g/lb)

42.202 ***Standard Solutions***

(a) *Bacitracin stock soln.*—Dry ca 40 mg USP Zinc Bacitracin Ref. Std 3 hr at 60° in vac. oven at ≤5 mm (0.66 kPa) pressure. Det. accurate dry wt and dissolve in enough 0.01*N* HCl to give concn of exactly 100 units/mL. Prep. fresh daily. (1 g bacitracin = 42,000 units.)

(b) *Std response line.*—Dil. appropriate aliquots of stock soln, **(a)**, with enough pH 6 buffer, **42.197(f)**, to obtain concns of 0.05, 0.10, 0.20, 0.40, and 0.80 unit/mL. Ref. concn is 0.20 unit/mL.

42.203 ***Plates***

(a) *Base layer.*—Add 10 mL melted agar medium C to sterile petri dishes, distribute evenly, and let harden on *perfectly level surface.*

(b) *Seed layer.*—Before assay, det. by prepn of trial plates optimum concn (usually 0.1–0.5%) of suspension of *M. flavus*, **42.199(a)**, or *S. subflava*, **42.199(b)**, to be added to agar medium A to obtain zones of inhibition of adequate size (20 mm±10% with 0.2 unit/mL) and sharpness. For actual assay add appropriate amt of suspension to agar medium A previously melted and cooled to 48°. Mix thoroly and add 4.0 mL to each plate contg base layer.

42.204 ***Assay Solution***

Obtain and prep. sample as in **7.001** and **7.002**. Place 2 g feed supplement conc. in 150 mL beaker, add 5 mL HCl (2+5), and stir 1 min. Check pH; if pH is >2, add more acid until pH 2 is reached. Add 45 mL pyridine buffer soln, **42.197(h)**, and transfer mixt. to centrf. tube. Shake well 5 min and centrf. ca 15 min at 2000 rpm. Dil. aliquot of clear soln with enough pH 6 buffer, **42.197(f)**, to obtain estd concn of 0.20 unit/mL. Designate soln obtained as assay soln.

42.205 ***Assay***

Using bacitracin std response line, assay soln, and plates, proceed as in **42.200–42.201**, incubating at 32–35°.

For Mixed Feeds (51)—Official First Action

(Applicable to feeds contg ≥20 g bacitracin/ton)

42.206 ***Standard Solutions***

(a) *Working soln.*—Dil. stock soln, **42.202(a)**, with enough pH 6.5 buffer, **42.197(d)**, to obtain concn of 10 units/mL. Prep. daily.

(b) *Std response line.*—Dil. appropriate aliquots of working soln, **(a)**, with enough pH 6.5 buffer, **42.197 (d)**, to obtain concns of 0.025, 0.05, 0.10, and 0.20 unit/mL. Ref. concn is 0.1 unit/mL.

42.207 ***Plates***

Use single inoculated agar layer prepd as in **42.203** (**b**), except add 10.0 mL to each plate and refrigerate ≥1 hr before use. Zone of 17.5 mm±10% should be obtained with 0.1 unit/mL.

42.208 ***Assay Solution***

Transfer 10.0 g mixed feed contg ≥20 g bacitracin/ton to 150 mL beaker. Add 20 mL acetone, stir, and let stand few min. Decant most of liq. into 50 mL r-b centrf. tube (guide stream with stirring rod). Add 20 mL acetone to residue in beaker, stir, let stand few min, and decant again into centrf. tube. Centrf. 2–3 min at 1800 rpm, decant carefully, and discard supernate acetone. Place centrf. tube in 37° incubator and dry sediment. Tilt beaker contg acetone-soaked solids and spread solids with stirring rod to hasten solv. evapn. Dry beaker and rod in 37° incubator (ca 1 hr).

Add 25 mL HCl (1+32) to dried residue in centrf. tube. Stir, and transfer acid to dry feed in beaker. Add 25 mL 40% pyridine buffer soln, **42.197(i)**, and stir. Pour contents of beaker back and forth from beaker to tube to combine and mix entire sample. Centrf. mixt. 5 min at 1800 rpm. Pipet 15 mL supernate into 50 mL g-s graduate and add MeOH to vol. of 30.0 mL. Stopper, shake, and let proteins settle few min. Transfer mixt. to 50 mL centrf. tube and centrf. 2–3 min at 1800 rpm. Carefully pipet 10 mL supernate and transfer to petri dish with pour lip.

Center each dish on heating mat, **42.198(d)**, under corresponding hole in Al air sparger, **42.198(e)**. Slowly open air stopcock until open area ca 5–8 cm diam. is formed in liq. Aerate until dry. Add 3 mL 5% buffer, **42.197(d)**, and loosen and stir residue with neoprene policeman. Transfer to 25 mL g-s graduate, guiding soln with diagonal edge of policeman. Wash dish and policeman with four 1 mL portions 5% buffer, **42.197(d)**, pouring each wash into graduate. Add 1.0 mL 1*N* NaOH, stopper, and mix. Adjust to pH 6.50±0.05, returning portions used for checking pH to graduate. Dil. to 10.0 mL (dil. 40 g/ton samples to 20.0 mL) with 5% buffer, **42.197(d)**. Transfer liq. to 15 mL centrf. tube and centrf. 5 min at 1800 rpm. Use clear supernate as assay soln.

42.209 ***Assay***

Using bacitracin std response line, **42.206(b)**, assay soln, **42.208**, and plates, **42.207**, proceed as in **42.200–42.201**, except use 4 plates for each concn required for std response line (total of 12 plates) and for each assay soln. Incubate at 37°.

42.210 ***Calculation***

g/ton = (unit/mL assay soln) × (a/10) × (30/15) × (50/g sample) × (908,000/42,000),

where a = 10 for 20 g/ton and 20 for 40 g/ton samples; 10 = mL aliquot dried; 30 = vol. after addn of MeOH; 15 = vol. supernate; 50 = vol. HCl and 40% pyridine buffer; 908,000 = number of g in ton; and 42,000 = number of units/g of bacitracin.

Chlortetracycline (CTC) Hydrochloride (*52*)
Official Final Action

(Applicable to feeds contg ≥10 ppm)

42.211 ***Standard Solutions***

(**a**) *Chlortetracycline stock soln.*—Accurately weigh ca 40 mg CTC.HCl USP Ref. Std and dissolve in enough 0.01*N* HCl to give concn of exactly 1000 μg/mL. Store in dark ≤5 days at 2–10°.

(**b**) *Std solns and response line for samples containing more than 50 ppm chlortetracycline.HCl.*—Dil. appropriate aliquots of stock soln, (**a**), with enough pH 4.5 buffer, **42.197(g)**, to obtain concns of 0.01, 0.02, 0.04, 0.08, and 0.16 μg/mL. Ref. concn is 0.04 μg/mL.

(**c**) *Std solns and response line for samples containing 10–50 ppm chlortetracycline.HCl.*—Prep. as in (**b**), but dil. with inactivated diluent, (**d**), instead of buffer soln and include concns of 0, 0.005, and 0.32 μg CTC.HCl/mL. Draw best line of fit by inspection.

(**d**) *Inactivated diluent.*—To 10 mL acid-acetone feed ext (prepd from feed under test as in **42.213(b)**) in 600 mL beaker, add 90 mL pH 4.5 phosphate buffer, **42.197(g)**, and adjust to pH 4.5–4.7 with 1*N* NaOH. Add 1.0 mL fresh 5.25% NaOCl soln, **42.197(q)**, and stir 1–2 min, rinsing sides of beaker. *Heat, stirring thoroly at 10 min intervals, in uncovered beaker in boiling H_2O bath 30 min.* Cool to room temp. under tap H_2O stream and transfer quant. to 100 mL vol. flask. Rinse beaker with 6 mL acetone, add rinsings to vol. flask, and dil. to vol. with pH 4.5 buffer. Transfer quant. to another flask and dil. with enough pH 4.5 buffer so that final concn of feed ext is same as that in assay soln.

42.212 ***Plates***

(**a**) *Base layer.*—Add 6.0 mL melted agar medium D to sterile petri dishes, distribute evenly, and let harden on *perfectly level surface.*

(**b**) *Seed layer.*—Before assay, det. by prepn of trial plates optimum concn (usually 0.03–0.10%) of organism suspension of *B. cereus*, **42.199(c)**, to be added to agar medium D to obtain zones of inhibition with as little as 0.01 μg CTC.HCl/mL for assaying samples contg >50 ppm and 0.005 μg/mL for samples contg ≤50 ppm CTC.HCl. Zone of 20 mm±10% should be obtained with 0.04 μg/mL. For actual assay add appropriate amt of suspension to agar medium D previously melted and cooled to 48°. Mix thoroly and add 4.0 mL to each of plates contg base layer.

42.213 ***Assay Solution***

(Solv. losses may occur from evapn of volatile solvs in open containers. Carefully measure and record vols of solvs, and make appropriate mathematical corrections for any losses in vol.)

(**a**) *Samples containing more than 50 ppm chlortetracycline .HCl.*—Obtain and prep. sample as in **7.001** and **7.002**. Place 2, 10, or 20 g sample, resp., contg CTC.HCl ≥10 g/lb (>2%), >400 ppm to 2%, or 50–400 ppm in 150 mL beaker and pipet in 40 mL acid-acetone soln, **42.197(j)**. Stir ca 2 min with glass rod, let stand 2 min, and stir. Adjust pH to 1.0–1.2 with HCl, if necessary, and note vol. HCl added. Transfer to 1 qt (1 L) high-speed blender jar, using addnl 20 mL (minus vol. equiv. to HCl added in adjusting pH) acid-acetone to rinse beaker and pH meter electrodes. Cover jar and blend 3 min at high speed. Transfer mixt. to 100 mL centrf. tubes. Wash blender jar with 40 mL acid-acetone and combine washings with ext in centrf. tubes. Shake well 5 min. Centrf. ca 15 min at 2000 rpm. Combine and mix clarified exts. Adjust 10 mL aliquot to pH 4.5 with 1*N* NaOH. Dil. adjusted soln with enough pH 4.5 buffer, **42.197(g)**, to obtain estd concn of 0.04 μg/mL. Designate soln as assay soln.

(**b**) *Samples containing 10–50 ppm chlortetracycline.HCl.*—Obtain and prep. sample as in **7.001** and **7.002**. Place 50 g sample in 250 mL beaker and pipet in 100 mL acid-acetone soln, **42.197(j)**. Stir, adjust pH, and blend as in (**a**), using 50 mL (less vol. equiv. to HCl added in adjusting pH) acid-acetone to transfer to blender jar. After blending, transfer quant. to 250 mL centrf. bottle, rinsing jar with 50 mL acid-acetone soln. Shake thoroly and centrf. ca 15 min at 2000 rpm. Pipet 5 mL clear supernate into 50 mL beaker, add ca 40 mL pH 4.5 buffer, **42.197(g)**, mix, and adjust pH to 4.5–4.7 with 1*N* NaOH. Transfer quant. to flask, rinse beaker and pH meter electrodes with pH 4.5 buffer, and add rinsings to flask. Add enough pH 4.5 buffer to obtain estd concn of 0.04 μg/mL. Designate as assay soln.

42.214 ***Assay***

Using CTC.HCl std response line, assay soln, and plates, proceed as in **42.200–42.201**, incubating at 30°.

Turbidimetric Method (53)—Official First Action

(Applicable to feed supplements contg ≥20 g/lb)

42.215 ***Apparatus and Reagents***

(**a**) *Assay broth.*—Prep. as in **42.196(n)**, but in 1.7× quantity.

(**b**) *Homogenizer.*—Omni-Mixer (Du Pont Co. Sorvall Operations, Newtown, CT 06470), or equiv.

(**c**) *For manual assay.*—(*1*) *Spectrophotometer.*—Turner Model 330 (Turner Associates, 2524 Pulgas Ave, Palo Alto, CA 94303), or equiv. Response time must be rapid, <4 sec. (*2*) *Flowcell.*—10 mm light path and 0.25 mL vol. (No. 8495-L10, Arthur H. Thomas Co., or equiv.) and adapter (No. 8475-F50, Arthur H. Thomas Co., or equiv.) to hold cell assembly in spectrophtr. Polyethylene tubing, 0.055″ (1.4 mm) id, is used as inlet and outlet. Fit inlet tube with short length of stainless steel tube and connect outlet to vac. thru solenoid valve (EQ-0724, Elanco Products Co., PO Box 1750, Indianapolis, IN 46206, or equiv.). Adjust vac. to obtain flow rate of 1.0 mL/sec. Flowcell must be rigidly held in its holder and holder rigidly fixed in adapter. (*3*) *Water bath and heater.*—Part of AUTOTURB System, (**d**), or equiv. (*4*) *Constant voltage transformer.*—Sola transformer, wave form corrected, for stabilizing current voltage (Elanco Products Co., or equiv.); connected to spectrophtr. (*5*) *Filling unit.*—Filamatic single nozzle filler (National Instrument Co., Inc., 4119 Fordleigh Rd, Baltimore, MD 21215), or equiv. Use with Teflon tubing, 0.063″ (1.6 mm) id, to fill assay tubes. (*6*) *Digital voltmeter.*—3½ or 4½ digit. Newport Model 400AS3 (Newport Laboratories, Inc., 630 E Young St, Santa Ana, CA 92705), or equiv. Connect to spectrophtr output to measure % *T*.

(**d**) *For automated assay.*—AUTOTURB System (Elanco Products Co.).

42.216 ***Standard Solutions***

(**a**) *For manual assay.*—Dil. aliquots of stock soln, **42.211(a)**, in enough pH 4.5 buffer, **42.197(g)**, to give concns of 0.02, 0.04, 0.06, 0.08, and 0.10 μg CTC.HCl/mL.

(**b**) *For automated system.*—Prep. concns of 0.2, 0.4, 0.6, and 0.8 μg CTC.HCl/mL as in (**a**).

42.217 ***Preparation of Inoculum***

Inoculate 200 mL broth medium A, **42.196(n)**, with 1 loop from 24 hr stock culture of *Staphylococcus aureus,* ATCC 9144, and incubate overnight at 37° on rotary shaker. Store ≤2 weeks at 2–10°.

42.218 ***Preparation of Samples***

Weigh 2 g sample into 250 mL glass or plastic centrf. bottle. Add 50 mL acid-acetone, **42.197(j)**. Stopper or cap immediately, agitate intermittently 5 min, and adjust to pH 1.0–1.2 with HCl, if necessary, using pH meter. Note vol. HCl used. Add 50 mL (minus vol. HCl used) of acid-acetone. Insert blades of homogenizer into centrf. bottle and blend 3 min at high speed while keeping bottle covered. Rinse blades into bottle with 100 mL acid-acetone. Tightly cap bottle and centrf. ca 15 min at 2000 rpm. Filter thru Whatman No. 2V paper, or equiv. Make further dilns with pH 4.5 buffer, **42.197(g)**, to ca 0.09 and 0.06 μg CTC.HCl/mL for manual assay, and 0.6 for automated assay.

42.219 ***Assay***

(**a**) *Manual method.*—Inoculate assay broth, **42.196(n)**, with 0.5–1.0 mL inoculum, **42.217**/100 mL. Incubate at 37° (20–30 min) until *A* is ca 0.05 at 600 nm in 10 mm flowcell, using uninoculated broth as blank.

Completely fill test tube carrier with 18 × 150 mm test tubes contg medium even tho assay may require only portion of these tubes. These tubes are included only to maintain uniform H_2O flow in bath.

Pipet 1 mL pH 4.5 buffer, **42.197(g)**, into each of 4 blank tubes and into each of 4 zero level std tubes. Pipet into each of 4 tubes 1 mL of each std and each sample soln. Add 9.0 mL inoculated assay broth to all tubes. Refrigerate blank tubes. Incubate all other tubes at 37° until % *T* of zero level tubes is ca 30 at 600 nm (3–4 hr). Do not remove tubes from bath during incubation to observe growth. Use extra tubes for this purpose and after inspection, replace in bath but do not measure. Stop growth in all tubes by heating 1–2 min at 80°; then cool rapidly in cold H_2O. Shake each tube by placing thumb over tube and inverting once. Do not shake mech. Measure turbidity at 600 nm in static suspension. Let culture flow ca 4 sec, stop flow ca 2 sec to dislodge air bubbles, and let flow again ca 3 sec. Stop flow and read % *T*. Average the 4 readings for each std and sample.

(**b**) *Automated method.*—System pipets two 0.10 and two 0.15 mL portions of sample soln and std solns into assay tubes, dils with inoculated broth, and reads % *T* at 600 nm. Average the 2 readings.

42.220 ***Calculations***

(**a**) *Manual assay.*—Convert av. % *T* to *A* and plot log *A* against μg CTC.HCl/mL on semi-log paper. Draw std response line. Read μg CTC.HCl/mL in sample from line.

(**b**) *Automated assay.*—Read μg CTC.HCl/mL from graph made as in (**a**) for 0.10 mL vols and for 0.15 mL vols. Average results.

g/lb = μg CTC.HCl (from curve) $\times D \times 454 \times 10^{-6}$/g sample, where D = diln factor, 454×10^{-6} = conversion of μg/g to g/lb.

Erythromycin (*54*)—Official First Action

(Applicable to feeds contg 9.25 and 92.5 g/ton without pelleting adjuvants and ≥ 92.5 g/ton with bentonite or Masonex)

42.221 ***Reagent***

Dimethoxymethane (*methylal*).—Tech., $CH_2(OCH_3)_2$ (MC/B Manufacturing Chemists, No. MX-650; or Eastman Kodak No. 525).

42.222 ***Standard Solution***

(**a**) *Erythromycin stock soln.*—Accurately weigh amt USP Erythromycin Ref. Std and dissolve in enough methylal-MeOH (4+1) to give concn of 1000 μg erythromycin base/mL. (1 μg base is equiv. to 1.08 μg of the thiocyanate.) Dil. further with pH 8 buffer, **42.197(b)**, to final concn of 100 μg/mL. Store in refrigerator ≤1 week.

(**b**) *Std response line.*—Dil. appropriate aliquots of stock soln, (**a**), with enough pH 8 buffer, **42.197(b)**, to obtain concns of 0.05, 0.1, 0.2, 0.4, and 0.8 μg erythromycin base/mL. Ref. concn is 0.2 μg/mL.

42.223 ***Plates***

Before assay, det. by prepn of trial plates optimum concn (usually 0.05–0.2%) of organism suspension of *Sarcina lutea,* **42.199(e)**(*1*), to be added to agar medium J, **42.196(j)**, to obtain zones of inhibition of adequate size (17.5 mm±10% with ref. concn) and sharpness. For actual assay add appropriate amt suspension to agar medium J previously melted and cooled to 48°. Place 10 mL inoculated medium in each of required number of plates, let harden, and refrigerate in inverted position until just before use.

42.224 ***Assay Solution***

Accurately weigh ca 10 g sample contg equiv. of ≥92.5 g erythromycin base/ton or 40 g contg equiv. of 9.25 g erythromycin base/ton and transfer to 250 mL g-s erlenmeyer.

For feeds contg no pelleting adjuvants add 20.0 mL H_2O and 80.0 mL methylal-MeOH (4+1) soln. For feeds contg bentonite or Masonex, add 20.0 mL 5% phosphate buffer, **42.196(b)**, and 15.0 mL MeOH. Mix and let feed slurry stand 10 min before adding 65.0 mL methylal. Stopper and mix 1 hr on mag. stirrer or mech. shaker (add glass beads for adequate mixing on shaker).

Let feed settle and dil. to 0.203 μg erythromycin base/mL as in (**a**) or (**b**) below:

(**a**) *Feeds containing equivalent of, or more than 92.5 g erythromycin base/ton.*—Dil. 2.0 mL ext to 100 mL with pH 8 buffer, **42.197(b)**.

(**b**) *Feeds containing equivalent of 9.25 g erythromycin base/ton.*—Dil. 5 mL ext to 100 mL with pH 8 buffer.

42.225 ***Assay***

Using erythromycin std response line, **42.222(b)**, assay soln, **42.224**, and plates, **42.223**, proceed as in **42.200–42.201**, except use 4 plates for each concn required for std response line (total of 16 plates) and for each assay soln. Incubate at 30°.

Hygromycin B (*55*)—Official Final Action

(Applicable to feeds contg ≥6000 units/lb)

42.226 ***Standard Solutions***

(**a**) *Hygromycin B stock soln.*—Accurately weigh amt of Hygromycin B Ref. Std (available from Elanco Analytical Laboratory, Dept. MC 757, Elanco Products Co. Division of Eli Lilly & Co., Indianapolis, IN 46206) contg 50,000 units, transfer to 50 mL vol. flask, and dil. to vol. with pH 7 phosphate buffer, **42.197(c)**. Store in refrigerator ≤2 weeks.

(**b**) *Std response line.*—Dil. appropriate aliquots of stock soln daily with enough pH 7 buffer, **42.197(c)**, to obtain concns of 15, 25, 50, and 75 units/mL. Ref. concn is 25 units/mL.

42.227 ***Plates***

(**a**) *Base layer.*—Add 10 mL melted agar medium E to sterile petri dishes, distribute evenly, and let harden *on perfectly level surface.*

(**b**) *Seed layer.*—Before assay, det. by prepn of trial plates optimum concn (usually 0.2% of 1:10 diln) of spore suspension of *B. subtilis,* **42.199(d)**, to be added to agar medium E. Zone of 16 mm±10% should be obtained with 25 units/mL. For actual assay add appropriate amt of spore suspension to agar medium E which has been melted and cooled to 48°. Mix thoroly and add 4.0 mL to each plate contg base layer. Store plates at 2–10° until just before use.

42.228 ***Assay Solution***

(**a**) *Preparation of ion exchange resin column.*—Slurry ca 1 lb (450 g) Amberlite IRC-50 ion exchange resin with 2 L 1*N* H_2SO_4 3 hr. Wash until neut. with H_2O and gradually add solid LiOH with stirring until pH remains at 7–8. Let stand overnight and wash with H_2O ≥5 times. Neutze to pH 7.0 with 1*N* H_3PO_4. Store under H_2O in glass container.

Place glass wool plug at bottom of 6 mm id × 140 mm long tube fitted with valve to control flow and 50 mL reservoir at top. Fill tube with H_2O and add wet resin to within 20 mm of top of tube. Drain H_2O to within 5 mm of resin surface. Wash with 25 mL sterile H_2O immediately before use.

(**b**) *Preparation of assay soln.*—Obtain and prep. sample as in **7.001** and **7.002**. Weigh 50 g sample contg 6000–12,000 units/lb (30 g for 18,000–24,000 units/lb, 20 g for >24,000) into jar of high-speed blender. Add 300 mL (500 for the higher potency feeds) pH 7 phosphate buffer, **42.197(c)**, and blend 5 min, operating blender from variable transformer set at 70. Centrf. 10 min at 2600 rpm. Adjust 125 mL supernate to pH 5.0 with HCl (ca 0.5 mL). Add 50 mL $CHCl_3$ previously washed with pH 7.0 buffer, stopper, and shake thoroly. Centrf. mixt. 10 min at 2600 rpm. Remove aq. phase, adjust to pH 7.0 with 40% NaOH soln (ca 0.7 mL), and centrf.

Transfer 100 mL neutzd soln (75 mL if feed contains ≥42,000 units/lb) to ion exchange column and adjust flow rate to 40 drops/min. Wash column with four 20 mL portions sterile H_2O. Elute hygromycin B with 50 mL NH_4OH (1+9) into 100 mL Pyrex beaker. Evap. to 3–5 mL and adjust to pH 7.0 with 1*N* HCl. Transfer to 10 mL vol. flask, dil. to vol. with pH 7.0 phosphate buffer, and designate as assay soln. (Final concn should be ca 25 units/mL.)

42.229 ***Assay***

Using hygromycin std response line, assay soln, and plates, proceed as in **42.200–42.201**, except use 6 plates for each concn required for std response line (total of 18 plates) and for each assay soln. Equations for *L* and *H* cannot be used. Incubate at 37°.

42.230 ***Calculation***

Units/lb = [1.1 × (units/mL assay soln) × 454 × mL pH 7 buffer (300 or 500) × 10 × (125 + mL HCl + mL 40% NaOH)]/[125 mL × g sample × mL neutzd soln put on column].

Lasalocid

Microbiological Method (56)—Official First Action

42.231 ***Reagents and Apparatus***

See **42.198(a)–(c)**, **42.306(a)**, and following:

(**a**) *Ethyl acetate.*—Purify by passage over silica gel and distil.

(**b**) *Methanol.*—75% and 19.4% by vol. in H_2O.

(**c**) *Automatic pipetting machine.*—Brewer (available from BBL, Div of Bioquest), or equiv.

42.232 ***Standard Solutions***

(**a**) *Lasalocid sodium stock soln.*—100 μg/mL. Accurately weigh suitable amt Lasalocid Na Ref. Std (available from Hoffmann-La Roche Inc.) and dil. to appropriate vol. with anhyd. MeOH.

(**b**) *Std response line.*—Dil. aliquots stock soln, (**a**), using anhyd. MeOH and H_2O, to obtain concns of 0.25, 0.5, 1.0, 2.0, and 4.0 μg/mL in 25% MeOH (v/v). Ref. concn is 1 μg/mL. Solns are stable ≤1 month at room temp.

42.233 ***Stock Culture and Preparation of Inoculum***

Prep. slant culture of *Bacillus subtilis,* ATCC 6633, on ≥1 tube of agar medium A, **42.196(a)**. Incubate 16–24 hr at 37°. Wash growth from stock culture with ca 3 mL sterile distd H_2O, transfer liq. to surface of 300 mL agar medium G, **42.196(g)**, in Roux bottle, and incubate 7 days at 37°. Wash growth from agar surface with ca 25 mL sterile distd H_2O into centrf. bottle. Heat suspension 30 min in 65° H_2O bath. Centrf., decant, and resuspend cells in ca 25 mL sterile distd H_2O. Repeat centrfg and suspending 3 times, discarding H_2O washings. Heat residual spores 30 min in 65° H_2O bath. Resuspend spores in ca 35 mL sterile distd H_2O. Suspension may be kept 1 yr at ca 5°. Before use, dil. suspension with sterile distd H_2O (usually 1+50) to read 20% *T* on spectrophtr at 530 nm; store ≤1 week at 5°.

42.234 ***Plates***

Seed layer.—Use single inoculated agar layer. Before assay, det. by prepn of trial plates optimum concn (usually 5 mL for each 100 mL seed agar) of dild suspension of *B. subtilis,* **42.233**, to be added to agar medium M to obtain zones of inhibition of adequate size (17.5±2.5 mm with 1.0 μg/mL) and sharpness. For actual assay, add appropriate amt of suspension to agar medium M previously melted, adjusted to pH 6.0, and cooled to 60°. Mix thoroly and add 6.0 mL to each plate. Distribute evenly and let harden *on perfectly level surface.* Prep plates 2.5–3 hr before use.

42.235 ***Assay Solution***

(**a**) *Premixes, 15%.*—Accurately weigh 1.0 g premix, transfer to 200 mL vol. flask, add 100 mL MeOH, shake vigorously 3 min, and dil. to vol. with MeOH. Dil. 4.0 mL of this diln to 100 mL with MeOH. Further dil. 3.0 mL of last diln with 22 mL MeOH and H_2O to 100 mL (1 mL = ca 1 μg lasalocid Na/mL 25% MeOH).

(**b**) *Final feed, 0.0075%.*—Weigh 20 g mash feed or pellets ground to pass No. 20 sieve and transfer to 500 mL vol. flask. Add 12 mL pH 4.7 buffer and wet feed thoroly. Immerse flask 5 min in 70° H_2O bath. Cool to room temp. Add 200 mL EtOAc, stopper, and shake mech. 10 min. Centrf. ca 100 mL EtOAc ext 10 min at 2000 rpm. Pipet 60 mL clear EtOAc ext into 200 mL vol. flask, add 8 mL 1.5*N* HCl, and shake 10 min. Let layers sep., transfer EtOAc layer to 100 mL g-s centrf. tube, and centrf. 10 min at 2000 rpm. Pipet 40 mL clear EtOAc ext into another 100 mL g-s centrf. tube and add 2 mL 40% NaOH soln. Stopper and shake briefly by hand, add 8 g anhyd. Na_2SO_4, and shake again. Centrf. 10 min at 2000 rpm and decant 25 mL clear supernate into 50 mL g-s graduate. Evap. all EtOAc under stream of N with graduate immersed in 60° H_2O bath. Dissolve residue in 5 mL hexane, add exactly 25 mL 75% MeOH (v/v), stopper, and shake vigorously 1 min. Transfer to 125 mL separator and let stand ca 1 hr. Withdraw lower (MeOH) layer into 25 mL beaker, pipet 5 mL into 50 mL vol. flask, and dil. to vol. with 19.4% (v/v) MeOH.

42.236 ***Assay***

Using lasalocid Na std response line, assay soln, and plates, proceed as in **42.200–42.201**, incubating at 35±1°. Calc. L and H and fit straight line by simplified least square method, **42.200**.

Lincomycin (*57*)—Official First Action

Method I

(Applicable to feeds contg ≥3.63 g/ton)

42.237 ***Standard Solutions***

(**a**) *Lincomycin stock soln.*—Accurately weigh ca 40 mg USP Lincomycin.HCl Ref. Std and dissolve in enough pH 8 buffer, **42.197(b)**, to give concn of exactly 100 μg lincomycin base/mL. Store ≤30 days at 2–10°.

(**b**) *Std response line.*—Dil. aliquots stock soln, (**a**), with enough pH 8 phosphate buffer, **42.197(b)**, to obtain concns of 0.2, 0.4, 0.8, 1.6, and 3.2 μg lincomycin base/mL. Ref. concn is 0.8 μg/mL.

42.238 ***Plates***

(**a**) *Base layer.*—Add 10 mL melted agar medium E to sterile petri dishes, distribute evenly, and let harden *on perfectly level surface.*

(**b**) *Seed layer.*—Before assay, det. by prepn of trial plates optimum concn of organism suspension of *S. lutea* (usually 0.02–0.05% of suspension prepd as in **42.199(e)**(*1*) or 0.2–1% as in **42.199(e)**(*2*)) to be added to agar medium J to obtain zones of inhibition of adequate size (16 mm±10% with 0.8 μg/mL) and sharpness. For assay, add appropriate amt of organism suspension to agar medium J previously melted and cooled to 48°. Mix thoroly and add 4.0 mL to each plate contg base layer.

42.239 ***Assay Solution***

Obtain and prep. sample as in **7.001** and **7.002**. Accurately weigh ca 10 g ground sample and transfer to 250 mL g-s, r-b flask, add 20 mL H_2O, and shake 10 min on wrist-action shaker. Add 50 mL *0.1N HCl-MeOH* (*1+4*) and shake 10 min. Filter thru Whatman No. 4 paper, using 42 mm buchner and 500 mL flask. Repeat extn twice, using 50 mL HCl-MeOH each time. (Do not add more H_2O.) Alternatively, conduct extns in 250 mL centrf. bottle and centrf. to clarify.

Transfer combined filtrates to 500 mL r-b flask and evap. to 15–20 mL, using rotary evaporator. (Do not heat >60°.) Transfer aq. ext to 125 mL separator. Rinse flask successively with 10 mL Skellysolve B, **3.029(o)**, 7–8 mL phosphate buffer, **42.197(b)**, and 10 mL Skellysolve B. Add all rinsings to separator, shake, and let sep. Drain aq. phase, ext Skellysolve B twice with 7–8 mL buffer, and adjust combined exts to pH 8.0 with dil. NaOH soln. Adjust vol. with pH 8 buffer to 0.6–1.0 μg lincomycin base/mL.

42.240 ***Assay***

Using lincomycin std response line and assay soln, proceed as in **42.200–42.201**, incubating at 32°.

Method II

(Applicable to feeds, feed supplements, and vitamin-mineral premixes contg 20-2600 g/ton)

42.241 ***Standard Solutions***

Std response line (*for monolayer plates*).—Dil. aliquots stock soln, **42.237(a)**, with enough pH 8 phosphate buffer, **42.197(b)**, to obtain concns of 0.15, 0.3, 0.6, 1.2, and 2.4 μg lincomycin base/mL. Ref. concn is 0.6 μg/mL.

42.242 ***Plates***

Monolayer.—Proceed as in **42.238(b)**, except zones of inhibition should be 18.5 mm±10% with 0.6 μg/mL; add 7.5 mL final mixt. to each plate, distribute evenly, and let harden *on perfectly level surface.*

42.243 ***Assay Solution***

Obtain and prep. sample as in **7.001** and **7.002**.

(**a**) *For 20–80 g/ton.*—Accurately weigh ca 10–20 g ground sample (*see* Table **42:03**), and transfer quant. to 250 mL centrf.

Table 42:03 Examples of Sample Size and Dilution of Extract

Assay soln. **42.243**	Feed level of lincomycin, g/ton	μg/g	Sample size, g	Total extn vol., mL	Aliquot vol., mL	Final vol., mL	Final concn, μg/mL
(a)	20	22	20.0	75	5.0	50	0.59
(a)	40	44	10.0	75	5.0	50	0.59
(a)	80	88	10.0	75	2.5	50	0.59
(b)	80	88	6.0	100	1.0	10	0.53
(b)	140	154	6.0	100	1.0	15	0.62
(b)	200	220	6.0	100	1.0	25	0.53
(b)	400	440	6.0	100	1.0	50	0.53
(b)	1000	1100	4.0	100	1.0	100	0.44
(b)	2600	2860	4.0	100	1.0	200	0.57

bottle. Add 75.0 mL 0.1N HCl-MeOH (1+4), and shake 20 min on mech. shaker. Centrf. 5 min at ca 2500 rpm to clarify. Decant supernate into 250 mL separator, add 75 mL hexane, and shake moderately 1 min. Let layers sep. ≥15 min. Drain lower aq. layer into 100 mL beaker, and pipet 2.5–5 mL aliquot into 50 mL mixing cylinder. Adjust vol. to ca 40 mL with pH 8 phosphate buffer, **42.197(b)**, and add 1 drop 4*N* NaOH. Stopper and shake vigorously. If necessary, adjust to pH 8 and dil. to 50 mL with pH 8 buffer. Final concn should be 0.5–0.8 μg lincomycin base/mL.

(**b**) *For 80–2600 g/ton.*—Accurately weigh 4–6 g ground sample (*see* Table **42:03**), and transfer quant. to 250 mL centrf. bottle. Add 50.0 mL 0.1*N* HCl-MeOH (1+4), shake 20 min on mech. shaker, and add 50 mL pH 8 buffer. Shake mech. 5 min and centrf. 5 min at ca 2500 rpm to clarify. Dil. 1.0 mL aliquot with pH 8 buffer to 0.4–0.8 μg lincomycin base/mL.

42.244 ***Assay***

Using lincomycin std response line and assay soln, proceed as in **42.200–42.201**, incubating at 32°, except use 2 plates instead of 3 and 6 readings instead of 9. Av. of all 24 readings of ref. concn from 8 plates is correction point for response line.

Monensin—Official First Action

Method I (58)

(Applicable to feeds contg ≥90 g/ton)

42.245 ***Standard Solutions***

(**a**) *Monensin std solns.*—(*1*) *Stock soln.*—1 mg/mL. Accurately weigh enough Monensin Na Salt Ref. Std (Elanco Analytical Laboratory, Dept. MC757, Elanco Products Co. Division of Eli Lilly & Co., Indianapolis, IN 46206) into 100 mL vol. flask to give concn of 1 mg free acid/mL. Dil. to vol. with anhyd. MeOH. Store at 5°; discard after 2 weeks. (*2*) *Working soln.*—100 μg/ mL. Dil. 1 mL stock soln to 10 mL with aq. MeOH (1+1). Prep. fresh daily.

(**b**) *Std response line.*—Dil. aliquots of working soln, (**a**)(*2*), with enough aq. MeOH (1+1) to obtain concns of 0.25, 0.5, 1.0, and 2.0 μg monensin/mL. Ref. concn is 0.5 μg/mL.

42.246 ***Plates***

Seed layer.—Use single inoculated agar layer. Before assay, det. by prepn of trial plates optimum concn (usually 0.5 mL for each 100 mL seed agar) of suspension of *B. subtilis,* **42.199(d)**, to be added to agar medium L to obtain zones of inhibition of adequate size (17.5±2.5 mm with 0.5 μg/mL) and sharpness. Before use, dil. suspension with sterile H_2O to read 20% *T* on spectrophtr at 530 nm; prep. dild suspension daily. For actual assay, add appropriate amt of suspension to agar medium L previously melted and cooled to 48–50°. Mix thoroly and add 6.0 mL to each plate. Cover and refrigerate ≥1 hr before use.

42.247 ***Assay Solution***

Place glass wool plug at bottom of 19 mm id × 500 mm chromatgc tube and add ca 75 mm alumina, **41.003(a)**, with gentle tapping. Accurately weigh sample (20 g finished feed, 5 g premix) and add to column. Elute column with MeOH-H_2O (9+1), using 200 mL vol. flask as receiver. Do not restrict flow. Collect 200 mL eluate, mix, and dil. with aq. MeOH (1+1) to 0.5 μg monensin/mL. Designate soln obtained as assay soln.

42.248 ***Assay***

Use 10 seeded agar plates for std curve. Place 4 stainless steel cylinders, **42.198(a)**, on each plate at 90° intervals. Fill 1 cylinder on each plate with different concn of std soln, (**b**), and incubate all plates 16–18 hr at 35–37°. Measure diams of zones of inhibition. Calc. av. zone diam. at each std concn and fit straight line by simplified least squares method, **42.200**.

42.249 ***Determination***

Use 5 plates for each assay soln and align cylinders at 90° intervals. On each plate fill alternate cylinders with ref. concn and fill other cylinders with assay soln. Incubate plates 16–18 hr at 35–37° and measure diams of zones of inhibition to nearest 0.1 mm. Average 10 readings of ref. concn and 10 readings of assay soln. Proceed as in **42.201**.

Turbidimetric Method (59)

42.250 ***Apparatus and Reagents***

(**a**) *Assay broth.*—In 500 mL erlenmeyer, dissolve 9.0 g low K ion medium (N-Z Case, Humko-Sheffield Chemical, PO Box 398, Memphis TN 38101), 3.0 g yeast ext, and 8.0 g glucose in 100 mL H_2O while heating to bp. Cool immediately, and add to bottle contg 1500 mL sterile H_2O, 4.5 mL 10% soln of polysorbate 80, and 12.5 mL citrate buffer soln, (**c**). pH should be 5.2±0.1; adjust if necessary.

(**b**) *Automated turbidimetric system.*—Autoturb® (Elanco Products Co., Division of Eli Lilly and Co., 740 S Alabama St, Indianapolis, IN 46206), or equiv. System pipets samples into assay tubes, dils with inoculated broth, incubates, and measures turbidity.

(**c**) *Citrate buffer soln.*—pH 4.0. Dissolve 105 g citric acid.H_2O, 142 g Na citrate.$2H_2O$, and 1.9 g KCl in H_2O and dil. to 1 L with H_2O.

(**d**) *Monensin std solns.*—(*1*) *Stock soln.*—1 mg free acid/mL. Accurately weigh enough Monensin Na Salt Ref. Std (Elanco Analytical Laboratory, Department MC757, Elanco Products Co.) into 100 mL vol. flask to give concn of 1 mg free acid/mL. Add MeOH to dissolve salt, dil. to vol. with MeOH, and stopper tightly. (Soln is stable at room or refrigerator temp. 1 month, except for gain in potency from loss of MeOH. Warm refrigerated soln to room temp. before pipetting.) (*2*) *Intermediate soln.*—10 μg/mL. Dil. 1.0 mL stock soln to 100 mL with MeOH. (*3*) *Autoturb working solns.*—Using pipets and vol. flasks, prep. solns contg 0.25, 0.50, 0.75, and 1.0 μg/mL MeOH. (*4*) *Manual working solns.*—Dil. stock soln to 10.0 μg/mL with MeOH. Prep. std solns of 0.0, 0.05, 0.10, 0.15, and 0.20 μg/mL by adding appropriate vols of 10.0 μg/mL soln to vol. flasks, adding enough MeOH so that final MeOH concn is 20% in each flask, and adjusting to vol. with H_2O.

42.251 ***Preparation of Inoculum***

Use *Streptococcus faecalis* (ATCC 8043) as assay organism in either frozen suspension or freshly grown inoculum. Prep. latter by inoculating flask of broth medium A, **42.196(n)** (Difco No. 3 Broth), in afternoon and leaving flask overnight at room temp. Use 10–20 mL inoculum/L assay medium. Let assay medium inoculated with frozen suspension stand at room temp. 45 min before using. (This treatment prevents drift within test.)

42.252 ***Preparation of Samples***

Grind ≥100 g feed sample, and mix. Accurately weigh 10.0 g representative well ground sample, and transfer to 4 oz (125 mL) jar fitted with Al foil-lined cap. Add 100.0 mL MeOH and tightly cap jar. Shake well and let stand overnight or ≥8 hr. Approx. 30 min before dilg, shake once more and let solids settle.

(**a**) *Autoturb system measurement.*—Dil. 1.0 mL ext to 20.0 mL with MeOH to prep. soln to be dild by system.

(**b**) *Manual measurement.*—Dil. ext 100-fold (1+99) and 66-fold (3+197) to obtain approx. assay concns of 0.10 and 0.15 μg/mL by adding aliquots of sample to sep. vol. flasks, adding MeOH to 20% final concn, and dilg to vol. with H_2O. These solns are stable ≥1 week at room temp.

42.253 ***Assay***

(**a**) *Autoturb system measurement.*—Place assay tube carrier in diluter unit. Place total of 20 sample tubes in sample turntable (including 5 tubes contg the 4 std levels and 1 tube with MeOH) in middle of test series. Fill remaining places in turntable with samples dild to estd concn of 0.6 μg/mL. When diluter unit has processed tubes, place carrier in 37.5° H_2O bath 3–4 hr or until turbidity of 0 tube measures 40% *T* or slightly less. Stop growth by heating carrier with tubes in 80° H_2O bath 1–2 min. Cool and read at 650 nm.

(**b**) *Manual measurement.*—(*1*) *Std curve.*—Prep. series of culture tubes, in triplicate, by adding 0.5 mL of each working std soln to sep. tubes. Add 9.5 mL inoculated assay broth to each tube. (*2*) *Samples.*—Prep. 2 dilns for each sample to contain ca 0.1 and 0.15 μg monensin activity/mL soln. Add 0.5 mL of each diln to 3 sep. tubes, and add 9.5 mL inoculated assay broth to each tube. Sample levels are ca 0.05 and 0.075 μg/tube.

Incubate std and sample tubes 4–5 hr at 37.5° or until turbidity of control std tubes (0.0 monensin) measures ca 30% *T* at 650 nm. Terminate growth by heating tubes ≥2 min at 80°. Cool tubes, and measure turbidity of each tube at 650 nm.

42.254 ***Preparation of Standard Curve***

(**a**) *Autoturb system measurement.*—Prep. 2 dose-response curves, 1 for 0.1 mL loop and other for 0.15 mL loop. Prep. graph of log % *T* against concn. Use av. turbidity of each pair of tubes in prepg std curves. Assay each sample in duplicate at 2 concns, 0.10 mL and 0.15 mL sample. Average readings from 0.10 mL loop for sample and obtain monensin equiv. by interpolation from 0.10 mL std curve. Repeat for 0.15 mL loop and use 0.15 mL std curve.

(**b**) *Manual measurement.*—Prep. only single std curve. Prep. graph of log % *T* against concn. Average 3 readings obtained for each diln of sample. Obtain monensin equiv. for each sample diln by interpolation from std curve.

42.255 ***Calculations***

(**a**) *Autoturb system measurement.*—Average 2 readings of 0.10 mL vols for feed sample and obtain monensin equiv. by interpolation from 0.10 mL std curve (P_1). Repeat for 0.15 mL sample vols to obtain P_2.

μg Monensin activity/mL = $(P_1 + P_2)/2 = P_A$
μg Monensin/g feed = $P_A \times 200$
g Monensin activity (free acid/ton feed) = $P_A \times 200 \times 0.908$

(**b**) *Manual measurement.*—Multiply av. monensin equiv. for each of the 2 sample dilns (M_1 = 0.10 mL diln, M_2 = 0.15 mL diln) by its respective diln factor (e.g., 100 and 66). Average the 2 values to obtain potency of original material (P_A).

μg Monensin activity/mL = $(M_1 + M_2)/2 = P_A$
μg Monensin/g feed = $P_A \times 200$
g Monensin activity (free acid/ton feed) = $P_A \times 200 \times 0.908$

Neomycin (*60*)—Official First Action

(Applicable to feeds contg ≥28 g neomycin base/ton; soybean content >40% reduces accuracy of method.)

42.256 ***Standard Solutions***

(**a**) *Stock soln.*—Dry USP Neomycin Sulfate Ref. Std 3 hr in vac. oven at ≤5 mm (0.66 kPa). Accurately weigh enough dried std (10–50 mg) and dissolve in Tris buffer, **42.197(n)**, to give concn of 100 μg neomycin base/mL. (Neomycin sulfate equiv. to neomycin base is given on container.) Store ≤4 weeks at 2–10°.

(**b**) *Std response line.*—Dil. aliquots of stock soln (**a**) with enough inactivated feed ext, **42.258(b)**, to obtain 0.50, 0.75, 1.13, 1.69, and 2.53 μg neomycin base/mL. Prep. std response line for each feed sample.

42.257 ***Plates***

(**a**) *Base layer.*—Add 10 mL melted agar medium K to petri dishes, distribute evenly, and let harden *on perfectly level surface*.

(**b**) *Seed layer.*—Add appropriate amt (usually 0.5–2%) broth culture of *S. epidermidis*, **42.199(f)**, to agar medium K previously melted and cooled to 48°. Mix thoroly and add 4.0 mL to each plate contg base layer. Distribute agar evenly by tilting plates from side to side with circular motion and let harden. *Use plates same day prepd.* Zone of inhibition of 18 mm±15% should be obtained with 1.13 μg/mL.

42.258 ***Assay Solution***

(**a**) *Preparation of sample.*—Obtain and prep. sample as in **7.001** and **7.002**. Weigh 20 g sample into 500 mL r-b flask. Add 100.0 mL NaCl-$CaCl_2$ soln, **42.197(p)**, and shake 15 min on wrist-action shaker. Transfer to 250 mL centrf. bottle (*do not rinse*), centrf. 15 min at 1800–2000 rpm, and decant supernate into beaker. Transfer 20 mL aliquot to 100 mL beaker and set aside to prep. std response line diluent. Using pH meter, adjust remaining portion with HCl to pH 2.0. Wait ≥5 min; then readjust to pH 8.0 with 10*N* NaOH. (High concns of acid and base are used to avoid significant changes in vol.) Centrf. 30–35 mL 15 min at 1800–2000 rpm. Dil. ext soln with Tris buffer according to neomycin content in feed as in Table **42:04** (diln I).

(**b**) *Preparation of std response line diluent.*—Inactivate the 20 mL aliquot from (**a**) by adjusting to pH 4.5–4.7 with 2*N* HCl.

Add 1.5 mL fresh 5.25% NaOCl soln, **42.197(q)**, and heat 45 min in boiling H_2O bath, stirring thoroly at least every 10 min during heating period. Cool to room temp., adjust to pH 8.0 with 3.5*N* NaOH, and dil. to 20 mL with H_2O. Dil. inactivated ext with Tris buffer, **42.197(n)**, according to neomycin content in feed as in diln II column of Table **42:04**.

Use dild soln to prep. std response line solns.

42.259 ***Assay***

Using neomycin std response line, assay soln, and plates, proceed as in **42.200–42.201**, incubating at 32–35°. Result may be calcd as neomycin sulfate by multiplying neomycin base by 1.428 (1.0 mg neomycin sulfate is equiv. to 0.7 mg neomycin base).

Table 42:04 Dilution of Extract

Neomycin Base, g/ton	Sample Extract, Diln I	Neomycin Base, Final Concn, μg/mL	Inactivated Extract, Diln II
140	1 to 20	1.54	10 to 200
70	1 to 10	1.54	20 to 200
35	1 to 10	0.77	20 to 200

Novobiocin (*61*)—Official Final Action

(Applicable to feeds contg ⩾350 ppm)

42.260 ***Standard Solutions***

(**a**) *Novobiocin stock soln.*—Dry USP Novobiocin Ref. Std 3 hr at 60° in vac. oven at ⩽5 mm (0.66 kPa). Accurately weigh ca 30 mg dried std, dissolve in 10 mL absolute alcohol, and dil. with enough pH 8 phosphate buffer, **42.197(b)**, to give concn of 1 mg/mL. Store ⩽3 weeks at 2–10°.

(**b**) *Std response line for feed supplements.*—Dil. aliquots of stock soln, (**a**), with enough pH 6 buffer, **42.197(f)**, to obtain concns of 1.9, 2.4, 3.0, 3.8, and 4.7 μg/mL. Ref. concn is 3.0 μg/mL.

(**c**) *Std response line for finished feeds.*—Dil. aliquots of stock soln, (**a**), with enough pH 6 buffer, **42.197(f)**, to obtain concns of 0.128, 0.16, 0.20, 0.25, and 0.312 μg/mL. Ref. concn is 0.20 μg/mL.

42.261 ***Plates***

(**a**) *For feed supplements.*—(*1*) *Base layer.*—Add 21 mL melted agar medium C to sterile petri dishes, distribute evenly, and let harden *on perfectly level surface*.

(*2*) *Seed layer.*—Before assay, det. by prepn of trial plates optimum concn of organism suspension of *S. lutea* (usually 0.2–0.5% of suspension prepd as in **42.199(e)**(*1*) or 2–5% as in **42.199(e)**(*2*)) to be added to agar medium C to obtain zones of inhibition of adequate size (14 mm±10% with 3.0 μg/mL) and sharpness. For actual assay, add appropriate amt of organism suspension to agar medium C, previously melted and cooled to 48°. Mix thoroly and add 5.0 mL to each plate contg base layer.

(**b**) *For final feed.*—(*1*) *Base layer.*—Prep. as in (**a**) (*1*), using 15 mL melted agar medium C.

(*2*) *Seed layer.*—Add appropriate amt (usually 0.5– 2%) broth culture of *S. epidermidis*, **42.199(f)**, to agar medium C previously melted and cooled to 48°. Mix thoroly and add 5 mL to each plate contg base layer. Zone of 14 mm±10% should be obtained with 0.20 μg/mL.

42.262 ***Assay Solution***

(**a**) *For feed supplements containing 50 mg/g.*— Obtain and prep. sample as in **7.001** and **7.002**. Accurately weigh suitable size sample and add enough absolute alcohol to give estd concn of 2 mg/mL. Let stand 30 min, shaking occasionally. Add equal vol. pH 8 phosphate buffer, **42.197(b)**, and mix. Dil. to estd concn of 3 μg/mL with pH 6 buffer, **42.197(f)**, and use as assay soln.

(**b**) *For final feed containing not less than 350 μg/g.*—Obtain and prep. sample as in **7.001** and **7.002**. Weigh 1 g sample into 50 mL g-s graduate; ext twice with 20 mL EtOAc, shaking vigorously 2 min. Decant supernate into second 50 mL g-s graduate. Dil. to 50 mL with EtOAc. Transfer 2.0–4.0 mL aliquot to 100 mL vol. flask, add 5.0 mL pH 8 phosphate buffer, **42.197(b)**, and mix thoroly. Dil. to vol. with pH 6 buffer, **42.197(f)**, and shake vigorously to dissolve all EtOAc. Final concn of novobiocin should be 0.15–0.30 μg/mL.

42.263 ***Assay***

Using proper novobiocin std response line, assay soln, and plates, proceed as in **42.200–42.201**, incubating at 32–35°.

Nystatin (*62*)—Official First Action

(For feeds contg ⩾50 g/ton)

42.264 ***Standard Solutions***

(**a**) *Nystatin stock soln.*—Dry ca 25 mg USP Nystatin Ref. Std 2 hr at 40° in vac. oven at ⩽5 mm (0.66 kPa). Accurately det. dry wt and add enough MeOH to give concn of exactly 500 units/mL. Dissolve by shaking on mech. shaker 0.5 hr (soln may be slightly hazy). Prep. fresh daily. (1 g nystatin = 2,800,000 units.)

(**b**) *Std response line.*—Dil. aliquots stock soln, (**a**), with enough inactivated feed ext, **42.266(b)**, to obtain concns of 10, 20, and 40 units/mL. Prep. std response line for each feed sample. Ref. concn is 20 units/mL.

42.265 ***Plates***

Seed agar.—Use single inoculated agar layer. Before assay, det. by prepn of trial plates optimum concn of organism suspension of *Sacch. cerevisiae* (usually 2.5% of suspension prepd as in **42.199(g)**(*1*)), to be added to agar medium I, **42.196(i)**, to obtain zones of inhibition of adequate size (18 mm±10% for 20 units/mL) and sharpness. For actual assay, add appropriate amt of organism suspension to agar medium I, previously melted and cooled to 48°. Mix thoroly and add 10 mL to each sterile petri dish.

42.266 ***Assay Solution***

(**a**) *Preparation of sample.*—Obtain and prep. sample as in **7.001** and **7.002**. Weigh amt sample contg ca 50 g nystatin/ton (ca 7700 units total), into 500 mL erlenmeyer. Add 150 mL anhyd. MeOH, mix thoroly by hand, and then shake 1 hr on rotary shaker. Centrf. briefly. Dil. 4 parts ext with 6 parts 10% phosphate buffer, **42.197(e)**. Set aside 10 mL as sample test soln and use remainder to prep. response line diluent.

(**b**) *Preparation of std response line diluent.*—Measure vol. of remaining dild ext soln from (**a**). Place soln in cotton-plugged erlenmeyer having twice capacity of vol. to be contained, and autoclave 15 min at 121° (slow exhaust). Cool to room temp. and restore to original vol. by adding anhyd. MeOH. Mix thoroly and use dild soln to prep. std response line solns.

42.267 ***Assay***

Use 10 plates for each sample. On each plate, fill alternate cylinders, each with 1 of std response line solns, and fill other

3 cylinders with sample test soln. Incubate plates overnight at 30–37°; then measure diams of zones of inhibition to nearest 0.1 mm. Calc. av. zone diam. at each std concn; plot values on semilog graph paper and draw line as in **42.200**. Calc. av. zone diam. of sample test soln. Using this value, det. potency of antibiotic from std response line.

Oleandomycin (*63*)—Official Final Action

(For feeds contg ≥2 g/ton)

42.268 ***Standard Solutions***

(**a**) *Oleandomycin stock soln.*—250 μg/mL. Accurately weigh Oleandomycin Chloroform Adduct Ref. Std (available from Quality Control, Pfizer, Inc., 630 Flushing Ave, Brooklyn, NY 11206) or USP Ref. Std. Dissolve in ca 5 mL MeOH and dil. with enough pH 8.0 phosphate-bicarbonate buffer, **42.197(a)**, to give concn of 250 μg/mL. Prep. fresh daily.

(**b**) *Intermediate std soln.*—5 μg/mL. Dil. 5.0 mL stock soln to 250 mL in vol. flask with pH 8.0 phosphate-bicarbonate buffer, **42.197(a)**.

(**c**) *Std response line.*—Dil. intermediate std soln with pH 8.0 buffer, **42.197(a)**, to obtain concns of 0.025, 0.05, 0.10, 0.20, and 0.40 μg/mL. Ref. concn is 0.10 μg/mL.

42.269 ***Assay Solution***

Obtain and prep. sample as in **7.001** and **7.002**. Accurately weigh 20 g sample contg ≥2 g oleandomycin/ ton into 500 mL boiling flask, add 200 mL pH 8.0 phosphate-bicarbonate buffer, **42.197(a)**, and shake mech. 45 min. Let settle, decant into 50 mL centrf. tube, and centrf. 5 min at 2000 rpm. Dil. supernate with addnl pH 8.0 buffer to approx. ref. concn of 0.1 μg/mL. Use sample ext same day prepd.

42.270 ***Plates***

Use single inoculated agar layer. Before assay, det. by prepn of trial plates optimum concn of organism suspension of *S. lutea* (usually 0.05–0.1% of suspension prepd as in **42.199(e)**(*1*)) to be added to agar medium J to obtain zones of inhibition of adequate size (16 mm±10% with 0.1 μg/mL) and sharpness. For actual assay, add appropriate amt of organism suspension to agar medium J previously melted and cooled to 48°. Mix thoroly and add 10.0 mL to each petri dish.

42.271 ***Assay***

Using oleandomycin std response line, assay soln, and plates, proceed as in **42.200–42.201**, incubating plates at 37°.

Oxytetracycline (*64*)—Official Final Action

(Applicable to feeds contg ≥10 g/ton)

42.272 ***Standard Solutions***

(**a**) *Oxytetracycline stock soln.*—Accurately weigh ca 40 mg Oxytetracycline USP Ref. Std and dissolve in enough 0.1*N* HCl to give exact concn of 100 μg oxytetracycline/mL. (1 μg base is equiv. to 1.08 μg of the hydrochloride.) Store in dark ≤5 days at 2–10°.

(**b**) *Std response line.*—Dil. appropriate aliquots stock soln, (**a**), with enough pH 4.5 buffer, **42.197(g)**, to obtain concns of 0.05, 0.10, 0.20, 0.40, and 0.80 μg oxytetracycline/mL. Ref. concn is 0.20 μg/mL.

Method I

(Applicable to >220 mg/lb)

42.273 ***Assay Solution***

(Solv. losses may occur from evapn of volatile solvs in open containers. Carefully measure and record vols. of solvs, and make appropriate mathematical corrections for any losses in vol.)

Obtain and prep. sample as in **7.001** and **7.002**. Using mortar and pestle or high-speed blender, grind 2 g sample with 50 mL acid-MeOH, **42.197(k)**, and transfer mixt. to 100 mL centrf. tube. Wash mortar and pestle or blender jar with 50 mL acid-MeOH and combine washings with ext in centrf. tube. Shake well 5 min. Centrf. ca 15 min at 2000 rpm. Remove 10 mL clear soln and adjust to pH 4.5 with 1*N* NaOH. Dil. adjusted soln with enough pH 4.5 buffer, **42.197(g)**, to obtain estd concn of 0.20 μg/mL. Designate as assay soln.

42.274 ***Assay***

Using oxytetracycline std response line and assay soln, and chlortetracycline plates, **42.212(b)**, proceed as in **42.200–42.201**, incubating at 30°.

Method II

(Applicable to ≤220 mg/lb)

42.275 ***Plates***

Use single inoculated agar layer. Before assay, det. by prepn of trial plates optimum concn (usually 0.03–0.10%) of stock suspension of *B. cereus,* **42.199(c)**, to be added to agar medium D, **42.196(d)**, to obtain zones of inhibition with as little as 0.05 μg oxytetracycline/mL. Zone of 18 mm±10% should be obtained with 0.20 μg/mL. For actual assay add appropriate amt of inoculum to agar medium D previously melted and cooled to 48°. Mix thoroly, and add 9.0 mL to each plate.

42.276 ***Assay Solution***

(Solv. losses may occur from evapn of volatile solvs in open containers. Carefully measure and record vols of solvs, and make appropriate mathematical corrections for any losses in vol.)

Accurately weigh 20 g ground finished feed into 250 mL extn flask, add 100 mL acid-MeOH, **42.197(k)**, stopper, and shake mech. 5 min. Centrf. ca 5 min at 2000 rpm. Remove 20 mL supernate and adjust to pH 4.5 with 1*N* NaOH. Dil. adjusted soln with enough pH 4.5 buffer, **42.197(g)**, to obtain estd concn of 0.20 μg/mL and filter thru Whatman No. 2V paper, or equiv. Designate as assay soln.

42.277 ***Assay***

Using oxytetracycline std response line, assay soln, **42.276**, and plates, proceed as in **42.200–42.201**, incubating at 28–30°. Calc. result as oxytetracycline.HCl by multiplying oxytetracycline base by 1.08.

Procaine Penicillin (*65*)—Official Final Action

(Applicable to feeds contg ≥1.5 g/ton)

42.278 ***Standard Solutions***

(**a**) *Penicillin stock soln.*—Accurately weigh, in atm. of ≤50% relative humidity, ca 30 mg USP Potassium or Sodium Penicillin G Ref. Std. Dissolve in enough pH 6 buffer, **42.197(f)**, to give known concn of 100–1000 units/mL. Store in dark ≤2 days at 2–10°.

(**b**) *Std response line.*—Dil. appropriate aliquots of stock soln, (**a**), with enough pH 6 buffer, **42.197(f)**, to obtain concns of 0.0125, 0.025, 0.05, 0.10, and 0.20 unit/mL. Ref. concn is 0.05 unit/mL.

42.279 ***Plates***

(**a**) *Base layer.*—Add 10 mL melted agar medium A to sterile petri dishes, distribute evenly, and let harden on *perfectly level surface.*

(**b**) *Seed layer.*—Before assay, det. by prepn of trial plates optimum concn of organism suspension of *S. lutea* (usually 0.2–0.5% of suspension prepd as in **42.199(e)**(*1*) or 2–5% as in **42.199(e)**(*2*)) to be added to agar medium B to obtain zones of inhibition of adequate size (19 mm±10% with 0.05 unit/mL) and sharpness.

For actual assay, add appropriate amt of organism suspension to agar medium B previously melted and cooled to 48°. Mix thoroly and add 4.0 mL to each plate contg base layer.

42.280 ***Assay Solution***

(Solv. losses may occur from evapn of volatile solvs in open containers. Carefully measure and record vols of solvs, and make appropriate mathematical corrections for any losses in vol.)

Obtain and prep. sample as in **7.001** and **7.002**. Vary amts of sample and extractant according to penicillin content of feed as follows:

Penicillin Content	*Sample Size, g*	*Vol. Extractant, mL*
≥100 g/lb	1	100
1–100 g/lb	3	100
0.1–1 g/lb	10	100
<0.1 g/lb (200 g/ton)	50	200

Ext appropriate amt of sample with pH 6 buffer-acetone extractant, **42.197(m)**, in suitable container, using either wrist-action or reciprocating mech. shaker 30 min or high-speed blender 2 min; let settle and decant supernate. Centrf. if more than slightly turbid. Dil. aliquot of supernate with enough pH 6 buffer, **42.197(f)**, to obtain estd concn of 0.05 unit/mL.

42.281 ***Assay***

Using penicillin std response line, assay soln, and plates, proceed as in **42.200–42.201**, incubating at 26–32°. Calc. result in terms of units or wt (1 unit is antibiotic activity of 0.6 μg Na penicillin G; 1 mg Na salt = 1667 units; 1 mg K salt = 1595 units).

42.282 ***Identity***

To aliquot of supernate assay soln, **42.280**, add enough *penicillinase soln* to inactivate penicillin by incubating mixt. 1 hr at 37°. Further dil. with enough pH 6 buffer, **42.197(f)**, to give same diln factor as in **42.280**. Assay as in **42.281**. Absence of zone of inhibition indicates that activity in sample is due to penicillin. (*See* **16.141**.)

Spectinomycin (*66*)—Official First Action

(Applicable in presence of lincomycin to feeds contg ≥18 g/ton)

42.283 ***Standard Solutions***

(**a**) *Spectinomycin stock soln.*—1 mg spectinomycin base/mL. Accurately weigh amt of Spectinomycin.HCl.5H_2O Ref. Std (available from Agricultural Division, The Upjohn Co., Kalamazoo, MI 49001) and dissolve in enough H_2O to give concn of exactly 1.0 mg spectinomycin base/mL. Store in dark ≤30 days at 2–10°.

(**b**) *Std response line.*—Dil. stock soln with Tris buffer, **42.197(n)**, to obtain concn of 100 μg/mL. Dil. this soln with Tris buffer to obtain 2.8, 4.4, 7.0, 11.0, and 17.4 μg spectinomycin base/mL. Prep. daily. Ref. concn is 7.0 μg/mL.

42.284 ***Plates***

Before assay, det. by prepn of trial plates optimum concn of culture of *E. coli,* **42.199(h)** (usually ca 0.04%) to be added to agar medium F to obtain zones of inhibition of adequate size and sharpness. Zones of 13±1 and 23±1 mm should be obtained for 2.8 and 17.4 μg/mL, resp.

For actual assay, add appropriate amt of culture to agar medium F, previously melted and cooled to 48°. Mix thoroly and add 7.0 mL to each plate.

42.285 ***Assay Solution***

Weigh 20 g feed into 250 mL centrf. tube and add 100 mL acid-MeOH (20 mL 1*N* HCl dild to 1 L with MeOH). Shake 15 min on wrist-action shaker, or equiv., centrf. 5 min at 2000 rpm, and decant into 500 mL r-b flask. Repeat extn twice, combining exts in r-b flask. Evap. ext under vac. until all MeOH and most of H_2O have been removed. Do not exceed 60° and do not evap. to complete dryness. Add 30 mL $Pb(OAc)_2$ soln, **42.197(s)**, to flask, shake vigorously 2 min, and transfer quant. to 100 mL beaker. Rinse flask with 10–15 mL Tris buffer and add rinse to beaker. Adjust to pH 8.0 with 3.5*N* NaOH. Transfer quant. to 100 mL graduate, rinsing beaker with buffer, and dil. to 100 mL with buffer. Mix thoroly, and let sample stand 30 min. Centrf. 30–50 mL 10 min at 2000 rpm. Decant supernate into test vials for storage (≤2 days) until assay. Designate soln obtained as assay soln.

42.286 ***Assay***

Using spectinomycin std response line, assay soln, and plates, proceed as in **42.200–42.201**, incubating at 26°.

g Spectinomycin/ton
= (μg spectinomycin base/mL assay soln) × 4.54.

If zone size is plotted against g/ton instead of μg base/mL working stds as follows, calcns are not necessary.

μg Base/mL	g/ton
2.8	12.7
4.4	20.0
7.0	31.8
11.0	50.0
17.4	79.0

Streptomycin (*67*)—Official Final Action

Method I

(Applicable to feeds contg ≥30 g/ton)

42.287 ***Standard Solutions***

(**a**) *Streptomycin stock soln.*—Dry ca 40 mg USP Streptomycin Sulfate Ref. Std 3 hr at 60° in vac. oven at ≤5 mm (0.66 kPa). Det. accurate dry wt and dissolve in enough H_2O to give concn of exactly 100 μg streptomycin base/mL. Store ≤30 days at 2–10°.

(**b**) *Std response line.*—Dil. aliquots of stock soln, (**a**), with enough pH 8 buffer, **42.197(b)**, to obtain concns of 0.64, 0.80, 1.0, 1.25, and 1.56 μg streptomycin base/mL. Ref. concn is 1.0 μg/mL.

42.288 ***Plates***

(**a**) *Base layer.*—Add 12 mL melted agar medium E to sterile petri dishes. Distribute agar evenly and let harden on *perfectly level surface.*

(**b**) *Seed layer.*—Before assay, det. by prepn of trial plates optimum concn (usually 0.05–0.2%) of spore suspension of *B. subtilis,* **42.199(d)**, to be added to agar medium E. For actual assay, sharp zones of inhibition (14 mm±10%) should be obtained with 0.64 μg streptomycin base/mL. Add appropriate amt of spore suspension to agar medium E which has been melted and cooled to 48°. Mix thoroly and add 4.0 mL to each plate contg base layer.

42.289 ***Assay Solution***

Obtain and prep. sample as in **7.001** and **7.002**. Using 10.0 g sample and 200 mL 0.5*N* HCl, shake mech. 30 min or blend 2 min in high-speed blender. Centrf. ca 15 min at 2000 rpm. Transfer aliquot of supernate to beaker, add ca 25 mL pH 8 buffer, **42.197(b)**, and adjust to pH 8±0.1 with 5*N* and 1*N* NaOH. Transfer quant. to suitable vol. flask, dil. to vol. with pH 8 buffer, **42.197(b)**, and mix. Dil. aliquot with enough pH 8 phosphate buffer to obtain estd concn of 1.0 μg streptomycin base/mL. Filter dild soln without suction thru Whatman No. 2V paper, or equiv. Designate as assay soln.

42.290 ***Assay***

Using streptomycin std response line, assay soln, and plates, proceed as in **42.200–42.201**, incubating at 37°.

Method II

(Applicable to feeds contg 5–30 g/ton)

42.291 ***Standard Solutions***

Std response line.—Dil. aliquots of stock soln, **42.287(a)**, with enough pH 8 buffer, **42.197(b)**, to obtain concns of 0.19, 0.24, 0.30, 0.38, and 0.47 μg streptomycin base/mL. Ref. concn is 0.30 μg/mL.

42.292 ***Plates***

(**a**) *Base layer.*—Prep. as in **42.288(a)**, except use 10 mL agar medium E.

(**b**) *Seed layer.*—Prep. as in **42.288(b)**, except that sharp zones of inhibition (11 mm±10%) should be obtained with 0.19 μg/mL std.

42.293 ***Assay Solution***

Proceed as in **42.289**, using 40 g sample and dilg to estd final concn of 0.3 μg streptomycin base/mL. Let soln stand 1 hr before filtering.

Note: Feeds may produce considerable gas during acid extn. When using mech. shaker, let each sample stand in acid extractant ca 1 hr with occasional swirling before placing on shaker. When using high-speed blender, use jar with lid cover rather than sealed jar, and hold lid down by hand at start of blending.

42.294 ***Assay***

Using streptomycin std response line, assay soln, and plates, proceed as in **42.200–42.201**, incubating at 22–25°.

Tylosin (*68*)—Official Final Action

(Applicable to feeds containing ≥11 g/ton)

42.295 ***Standard Solutions***

(**a**) *Tylosin stock soln.*—Dry Tylosin base Ref. Std (available from Elanco Analytical Laboratory, Dept. MC757, Elanco Products Co. Division of Eli Lilly and Company, Indianapolis, IN 46206) 4 hr at 70° and store in desiccator over fresh P_2O_5. Accurately weigh suitable amt (10–15 mg) of dried std and dissolve in 5 mL MeOH. Adjust vol. with pH 7 phosphate buffer, **42.197(c)**, to give concn of 1000 μg/mL. Store in refrigerator ≤2 weeks.

(**b**) *Std response line.*—Dil. appropriate aliquots of stock soln with mixt. of MeOH and pH 8 phosphate buffer, **42.197(b)**, (4+6), to obtain concns of 0.125, 0.25, 0.50, 1.0, and 2.0 μg/mL. Ref. concn is 0.50 μg/mL.

42.296 ***Plates***

(**a**) *Base layer.*—Add 10 mL melted agar medium H to petri dishes, distribute evenly, and let harden on *perfectly level surface*.

(**b**) *Seed layer.*—Before assay, det. by prepn of trial plates optimum concn of organism suspension of *S. lutea* (usually 0.05–0.2% of suspension prepd as in **42.199(e)**(*1*) or 0.5–2% as in **42.199(e)**(*2*)) to be added to agar medium H to obtain zones of inhibition of adequate size (15 mm±10% with 0.50 μg/mL) and sharpness. For actual assay, add appropriate amt of organism suspension to agar medium H melted and cooled to 48°. Mix thoroly and add 5.0 mL to each plate contg base layer. Refrigerate plates until just before application of assay solns.

42.297 ***Assay Solution***

Obtain and prep. sample as in **7.001** and **7.002**. Accurately weigh 10 g feed premix or 20 g final feed into 250 mL homogenizer cup or blender jar. Add 90 mL hot (70–80°) pH 8 phosphate buffer, **42.197(b)**, and place on steam bath 10 min. Blend 5 min, add 60 mL MeOH, and blend addnl 5 min. Centrf. or filter thru Whatman No. 1 paper and dil., if necessary, with mixt. of MeOH and pH 8 phosphate buffer, **42.197(b)**, (4+6), to concn of 0.5 μg tylosin/mL.

42.298 ***Assay***

Prep. 10 plates for std response line and 5 for each sample. Place 5 cylinders on each std response line plate at 72° intervals on 2.8 cm radius. Place 4 cylinders on each sample plate at 90° interval . Fill cylinders on each of 10 std plates with each concn of std response line. On each sample plate fill 2 diagonally opposite cylinders with ref. concn and remaining 2 cylinders with assay soln. Incubate plates overnight at 30°. Measure zones of inhibition to nearest 0.1 mm. Record av. zone diam. for each concn of std on std plates and proceed as in **42.200**.

Average the 10 readings of ref. concn on sample plates and the 10 readings of assay soln. Proceed as in **42.201**.

CHEMICAL METHODS

Griseofulvin (*69*)—Official Final Action

(Applicable to concns ≥10 mg/oz.
Caution: See **51.011**, **51.040**, and **51.056**.)

42.299 ***Reagents***

(**a**) *Activated alumina.*—Alcoa grade F-20.

(**b**) *Solvent mixture.*—Pet ether-$CHCl_3$ (65+35).

(**c**) *Griseofulvin std soln.*—10 μg/mL. Accurately weigh ca 25 mg USP Griseofulvin Ref. Std into 250 mL vol. flask; dissolve and dil. to vol. with solv. mixt. Dil. 10 mL of this soln to 100 mL in vol. flask.

42.300 ***Apparatus***

(**a**) *Chromatographic tube.*—20 × 400 mm, with fritted disk and stopcock.

(**b**) *High-speed blender.*—Waring-type, or equiv., 1 L capacity.

(**c**) *Spectrophotometer.*—Capable of accurate readings at 290 and 320 nm.

42.301 ***Preparation of Sample***

Grind 250 g feed pellets or mash in high-speed blender 5 min. Accurately weigh ca 14 g finely powd feed into fat-free thimble and ext in Soxhlet app. 2 hr with 100 mL $CHCl_3$. Evap. ext to 10 mL on steam bath, dil. with 100 mL pet ether, and chromatograph.

42.302 ***Preparation of Chromatographic Column***

Place 50 mL solv. mixt., (**b**), in tube and add 45 mL activated alumina portionwise, with tapping to ensure uniform packing. Place small glass wool pad on top of alumina and drain solv. to just below top of pad.

42.303 ***Determination***

Add pet ether-$CHCl_3$ sample ext to column. As last of ext passes thru glass wool pad, rinse sample flask with solv. mixt., add to column, and begin elution with solv. mixt. Adjust liq. head to give flow rate of 15–20 mL/min. Start collecting 25 mL fractions when green eluate first appears (discard yellow and almost colorless eluates which precede). When *A* of fractions at 290 nm exceeds *A* at 320 nm, stop fractionating, and collect next 700 mL eluate. Dil. eluate to vol. in 1 L vol. flask with solv. mixt. Det. *A* of this soln and of griseofulvin std soln at 290 and 320 nm against solv. mixt. blank.

$$\text{mg Griseofulvin/oz} = (A_{290} - A_{320})(W')(10)(28.35)/(A'_{290} - A'_{320})(25)(\text{g sample}),$$

where *A* refers to sample eluate, *A'* to std soln, and *W'* = mg ref. std griseofulvin used to prep. std soln.

Lasalocid

Spectrofluorometric Method (*70*)

Official Final Action

42.304 ***Principle***

Compd is extd from pH 4.7 soln with EtOAc, fluorescent impurities are removed by acid and alkali treatments, and compd is detd fluorometrically, correcting for nonspecific fluorescence by complexing with H_3BO_3. Monensin and ethoxyquin do not interfere.

42.305 ***Apparatus***

Spectrofluorometer.—With 10 mm fused quartz cells. Excitation and emmission wavelengths, ca 310 and 419 nm, resp. Accurately det. peak excitation and emission wavelengths using std soln I, following manufacturer's directions. Do not change wavelength settings between readings.

For routine setting and checking of instrument, use std soln I.

Adjust settings to compensate for decreased intensity with age from dulled reflecting surfaces and lamp.

42.306 ***Reagents***

(**a**) *Acetate buffer soln.*—pH 4.7. Dissolve 5.0 g NaOAc in ca 50 mL H_2O, adjust to pH 4.7 with HOAc, and dil. to 100 mL with H_2O.

(**b**) *Ethyl acetate.*—Must have ca 0 fluorescence. If necessary, purify as follows: Elute 1 gal. EtOAc thru 9–10 cm (od) column packed with ca 100 cm silica gel (activated desiccant, 100–200 mesh, Grade H, W. R. Grace & Co., Davison Chemical Div., PO Box 2117, Baltimore, MD 21203) topped with 5 cm layer of $NaHCO_3$. Redistil eluate from all-glass app. with 60 cm jacketed distg column, discarding first and last 10%. (*Caution: See* **51.011** and **51.057**.) To redistd EtOAc add 40% aq. NaOH and mix briefly. Follow with anhyd. Na_2SO_4 and shake again. (Ratio of EtOAc:40% NaOH:Na_2SO_4 is 1000:50:200 or multiple thereof.)

(**c**) *Methanolic boric acid soln.*—Dissolve 20.0 g H_3BO_3 in MeOH and dil. to 500 mL with MeOH. Prep. fresh daily.

(**d**) *Lasalocid std solns.*—(*1*) *Std soln I.*—Dissolve 30.0 mg Lasalocid Ref. Std (available from Hoffmann-La Roche Inc.) in EtOAc and dil. to 100 mL with EtOAc. Pipet 4 mL into 100 mL vol. flask, dil. to vol. with EtOAc, and mix. Pipet 25 mL final diln into 50 mL g-s centrf. tube contg 2.4 mL pH 4.7 buffer. Shake mech. 25–30 min and centrf. 10 min at 2000 rpm. Pipet 2 mL clear EtOAc ext into 100 mL vol. flask, dil. to vol. with EtOAc, and mix. (*2*) *Std soln II.*—Pipet addnl 2 mL clear EtOAc ext into another 100 mL vol. flask contg 10 mL methanolic H_3BO_3 soln, dil. to vol. with EtOAc, and mix.

42.307 ***Preparation of Sample***

(**a**) *Feeds.*—Grind 200 g sample (mash, pellets, or crumbles) to pass No. 30 sieve, and mix thoroly. Accurately weigh ca 4 g sample into 50 mL g-s centrf. tube contg 2.4 mL pH 4.7 buffer. Turn and shake tube by hand to wet uniformly. Immerse tube 4–5 min in 70° H_2O bath. Cool to room temp. and add 25 mL EtOAc by pipet. Stopper tube and shake briefly but vigorously by hand to disperse sample. If necessary, break up lumps with narrow-tip spatula or glass rod. Stopper tube and shake mech. 25–30 min. Centrf. 10 min at 2000 rpm. Pipet 15 mL clear EtOAc ext into 50 mL centrf. tube. Add 2 mL 1.5*N* HCl and shake 10 min. Centrf. 10 min at 2000 rpm. Pipet 10 mL clear EtOAc ext into another 50 mL g-s centrf. tube and add 0.5 mL 40% NaOH soln. Shake briefly by hand, add 2 g anhyd. Na_2SO_4, and shake again. Centrf. 10 min at 2000 rpm. If EtOAc soln is not clear or fine particles are present at surface, swirl tube gently by hand and recentrf. Pipet 2 mL EtOAc layer into 100 mL vol. flask without disturbing aq. alk. soln, dil. to vol. with EtOAc, and mix. Designate as *Sample soln I*. Pipet another 2 mL aliquot EtOAc layer into second 100 mL vol. flask contg 10 mL methanolic H_3BO_3 soln, dil. to vol. with EtOAc, and mix. Designate as *Sample soln II*.

Pipet 25 mL EtOAc into 50 mL g-s centrf. tube contg 2.4 mL pH 4.7 buffer and proceed as above, beginning "Stopper tube and shake briefly . . ." Designate final solns as *Reagent blank soln I* and *Reagent blank soln II*.

(**b**) *Premixes.*—Accurately weigh 2.00 g 15% premix and transfer into 500 mL vol. flask. Add exactly 250 mL EtOAc and shake 25 min on mech. shaker. Centrf. aliquot, and dil. with EtOAc as in (**a**) to obtain *Sample soln I* and *Sample soln II* (complex) contg ca 0.24 μg lasalocid/ml EtOAc. Proceed with fluorescence measurements as in **42.308**. (*Note:* Omit treatment with pH 4.7 buffer for both premix and std.)

42.308 ***Determination***

Set excitation and emission wavelengths of app. at max. Adjust instrument with std. soln I, (**d**)(*I*), in cell to microammeter reading of 0.400. Check this ref. point before and after each reading, using same cell for all ref. readings. Because of decomposition in UV, discard and replace std soln I after every second reading. Measure fluorescence at 419 nm in order: *Sample soln I* (U_1), *Std soln I* (S_1), *Reagent blank soln I* (R_1), *Sample soln II* (U_2), *Std soln II* (S_2), and *Reagent blank soln II* (R_2). If reading of std soln I drifts, adjust gain to initial setting. If drift is beyond 0.393–0.407, recheck readings of all solns.

Altho fluorescence response of std is linear from 0.12 to 0.48 μg/mL, concn of lasalocid in sample soln should be ±25% of that of std soln.

42.309 ***Calculations***

(**a**) % Lasalocid Na in feed $= [(U_1 - R_1) - (U_2 - R_2)] \times D \times S/[(S_1 - R_1) - (S_2 - R_2)] \times W \times 96 \times 100$,

where U, S_1, S_2, and R are defined in **42.308**; D = diln factor ($25 \times 100/2 = 1250$); S = concn of lasalocid in *Std soln I* (= 0.24 μg/mL); W = g sample; and 96 = % recovery. When S = 0.24 μg/mL, W = 4.00 g, and R_1 and R_2 = *0*,

% Lasalocid Na in feed $= (U_1 - U_2) \times 0.00781/(S_1 - S_2)$

(**b**) % Lasalocid Na in premix $= [(U_1 - R_1) - (U_2 - R_2)] \times D \times S/[(S_1 - R_1) - (S_2 - R_2)] \times W \times 10{,}000$,

where U, S_1, S_2, and R are defined in **42.308**; D = diln factor ($250 \times 50 \times 50 \times 100/5 \times 5 \times 2 = 1{,}250{,}000$); S = concn of lasalocid in *Std soln I* (= 0.24 μg/mL); W = g sample. When S = 0.24 μg/mL, W = 2.00 g and R_1 and R_2 = 0,

% Lasalocid Na in 15% premix $= (U_1 - U_2) \times 15/(S_1 - S_2)$

SELECTED REFERENCES

(*1*) JAOAC **56,** 762(1973).
(*2*) Ind. Eng. Chem., Anal. Ed. **15,** 408(1943); **24,** 1821(1952); Sandell, "Colorimetric Determination of Traces of Metals," 3rd ed., 1959; JAOAC **40,** 455(1957).
(*3*) JAOAC **44,** 26(1961); **46,** 463(1963).
(*4*) JAOAC **52,** 438(1969).
(*5*) JAOAC **47,** 214(1964).
(*6*) JAOAC **36,** 219(1953); **37,** 257(1954).
(*7*) JAOAC **44,** 5(1961).
(*8*) JAOAC **48,** 285(1965).
(*9*) JAOAC **37,** 257(1954); **40,** 452(1957).
(*10*) JAOAC **43,** 301(1960).
(*11*) JAOAC **50,** 264(1967).
(*12*) JAOAC **46,** 467(1963).
(*13*) JAOAC **60,** 1059(1977).
(*14*) JAOAC **51,** 1279(1968).
(*15*) JAOAC **60,** 1054(1977).
(*16*) JAOAC **39,** 327(1956); **40,** 459(1957); **41,** 316(1958); **42,** 250(1959).
(*17*) JAOAC **48,** 301(1965); **53,** 646(1970).
(*18*) JAOAC **47,** 221(1964); **48,** 280(1965).
(*19*) JAOAC **40,** 463(1957); **41,** 333(1958); **43,** 310(1960); **44,** 30 (1961); **52,** 233, 421(1969).
(*20*) JAOAC **43,** 284(1960).
(*21*) JAOAC **54,** 72(1971).
(*22*) JAOAC **54,** 69(1971).
(*23*) JAOAC **39,** 321(1956); **40,** 469(1957); **41,** 326(1958).
(*24*) JAOAC **47,** 226(1964).
(*25*) JAOAC **54,** 66(1971).
(*26*) JAOAC **44,** 2(1961).
(*27*) JAOAC **43,** 295(1960).
(*28*) JAOAC **50,** 261(1967).
(*29*) JAOAC **42,** 239(1959).
(*30*) JAOAC **35,** 552(1952); **36,** 219(1953); **39,** 307(1956).
(*31*) JAOAC **53,** 641(1970).
(*32*) JAOAC **41,** 338(1958); **42,** 254(1959).
(*33*) JAOAC **50,** 268(1967).
(*34*) JAOAC **61,** 296(1971).
(*35*) JAOAC **49,** 329(1966).
(*36*) JAOAC **51,** 752(1968).
(*37*) JAOAC **43,** 291(1960); **44,** 13(1961); **45,** 589(1962); **46,** 448 (1963).
(*38*) JAOAC **52,** 435(1969); **53,** 634(1970).
(*39*) JAOAC **49,** 241, 318(1966); **53,** 634(1970).
(*40*) JAOAC **54,** 80(1971).
(*41*) JAOAC **57,** 345(1974).
(*42*) JAOAC **53,** 638(1970).
(*43*) JAOAC **34,** 559(1951).
(*44*) JAOAC **51,** 1282(1968); **52,** 423(1969).
(*45*) JAOAC **46,** 452(1963).
(*46*) JAOAC **33,** 156(1950); **38,** 229(1955); **39,** 307(1956); **56,** 758 (1973).
(*47*) JAOAC **49,** 312(1966).
(*48*) JAOAC **44,** 18(1961); **45,** 294(1962).
(*49*) JAOAC **51,** 750(1968).
(*50*) JAOAC **40,** 857(1957).
(*51*) JAOAC **48,** 256(1965).
(*52*) JAOAC **40,** 857(1957); **50,** 446(1967).
(*53*) JAOAC **60,** 1119(1977).
(*54*) JAOAC **54,** 940, 944(1971); **60,** 176(1977).
(*55*) JAOAC **43,** 213(1960).
(*56*) JAOAC **57,** 978(1974); **58,** 941(1975).
(*57*) JAOAC **50,** 442(1967); **61,** 1107(1978).
(*58*) JAOAC **55,** 718(1972).
(*59*) JAOAC **55,**114(1972); **60,** 179(1977).
(*60*) JAOAC **53,** 60(1970).
(*61*) JAOAC **45,** 310(1962).
(*62*) JAOAC **57,** 536(1974).
(*63*) JAOAC **56,** 1149(1973); **57,** 823(1974).
(*64*) JAOAC **51,** 548(1968).
(*65*) JAOAC **50,** 450(1967).
(*66*) JAOAC **56,** 834(1973).
(*67*) JAOAC **54,** 116(1971); **55,** 714(1972).
(*68*) JAOAC **45,** 317(1962).
(*69*) JAOAC **49,** 494(1966).
(*70*) JAOAC **58,** 507(1975).

43. Vitamins and Other Nutrients

CHEMICAL METHODS

Vitamin A in Margarine (*1*)—Official First Action

43.001 ***Principle***

Unsaponifiable portion of margarine is chromatgd on adsorption column consisting of 2 segments of activated and stdzd alumina sepd by middle segment of alk. alumina. (If eluate fraction contg vitamin A is colored, it must be further chromatgd on column of MgO.) Top segment of alumina column prevents caking and initiates sepn of vitamin A from carotene and other interfering substances. Middle section of alk. alumina seps persistent interference that cannot be sepd by other adsorbents. Final portion of column is nonfluorescent and provides suitable background for observing vitamin A fluorescence on column, thus facilitating control of the chromatgy.

Carotene elutes from column first, second fraction of eluate is discarded, and third fraction contains vitamin A. Better control of chromatgy than is possible by observing colored and fluorescent bands on column is achieved by observing fluorescence in 1 mL portions from final parts of fluorescent and colored eluates. This technic achieves sepn of vitamin A from impurities that cause erroneously high values. Adequacy of sepn is detd from ratio of *A* of chromatgd vitamin A soln at 310 and 325 nm.

A of sample soln at 325 nm multiplied by factor 18.3 gives concn of vitamin A in units/mL.

43.002 ***Apparatus***

(**a**) *Spectrophotometer and cells.*—UV spectrophtr with suitable source of UV light is required. (Incandescent lamp is not suitable source.) Spectrophtr (such as Beckman DU, or equiv.) with continuous spectrum source and reading to 200 nm is recommended. Matched quartz cells with 1.0 cm internal light path are preferable. If cells are not matched, suitable corrections must be made. Periodically check wavelength and *A* scales of spectrophtr. (*See* Definitions of Terms and Explanatory Notes, item (23).)

(**b**) *Chromatographic tubes.*—(*1*) 12 mm od × 90 mm with sealed-in disk of medium porosity and with funnel on upper end and stem on lower end, 8 mm od × 40 mm. (Available from SGA Scientific, Inc.) (*2*) 8 mm od × 250 mm long with lower 50 mm pulled out to form tapered constricted exit 2 mm id. Plug ca 10 mm of upper part of constricted section with glass wool. Fuse flared tube, 18 mm od × 140 mm to top of 6 mm section.

(**c**) *Vacuum gage with bleeder valve or pinchcock regulator.*—Use vac. micro bell jar large enough to hold 100 mL beaker or flask for applying vac. and collecting eluates. Control vac. from line or H_2O aspirator by gage and stopcock or screw-clamp bleeder on T-tube.

(**d**) *Long wavelength ultraviolet lamp.*—Use lamp source of *weak* UV for observing fluorescent bands on chromatgc columns. Lamp should provide radiation in long (300 nm) wavelength region. (Suitable lamp is available from Ultra-Violet Products, Inc., No. UVSL-55: LW 240.) With com. lamps, narrow aperture or screen may be necessary to reduce amt of destructive radiation. (Vitamin A is readily destroyed by too intense UV light.)

43.003 ***Reagents***

(**a**) *Potassium hydroxide soln.*—50% w/w (780 g/L).

(**b**) *Alcohol.*—Absolute and 95%. Shall not show *A* >0.05 when measured at 300 nm in suitable spectrophtr in 1.0 cm quartz cell against H_2O. Isopropanol USP reagent of same spectral purity may be substituted for absolute alcohol in *A* measurements.

(**c**) *Ethyl ether.*—Peroxide-free. Use USP, freshly distilled, discarding first and last 10% of distillate; or use USP anesthesia grade in 0.5 lb cans. Must meet same *A* requirement as for alcohol, (**b**).

(**d**) *Petroleum ether.*—Bp 30–60°, free from fluorescence and with *T* at 300 nm >85% when measured against air in quartz spectrophtr fitted with 1 cm cell. This solv., available in 5 lb cans, should be suitable for chromatgc purposes. Also, in adsorbent activity test, eluant effect of 10 mL pet ether by itself must cause movement of visible color ≤1 cm below surface of column. To meet these requirements, purification by adsorption and/or distn may be necessary.

(**e**) *Eluting solns.*—(*1*) 16% redistd ether in pet ether; (*2*) 25% redistd ether in pet ether; (*3*) 10% absolute alcohol in pet ether. Dry (*1*) and (*2*) with anhyd. Na_2SO_4 and store over bright Cu strip or turnings to inhibit peroxide formation.

(**f**) *Sodium sulfate.*—Anhyd., granular; 10% soln must not be acid (red) to Me red. Must not adsorb vitamin A.

(**g**) *Alumina.*—Alcoa grade F-20 or Fisher "Alumina, Adsorption," Cat. No. A-540. Before working with alumina it is essential to det. that following specifications for particle size have been met: Not >50% of alumina should pass No. 160 sieve; ca 50% should pass No. 100 sieve, but not No. 160 sieve. Remainder (≤20%) which does not pass thru No. 100 sieve should pass No. 60 sieve. Blend thoroly before use.

(**h**) *Standardized alumina.*—Heat portion of alumina 3 hr in furnace at 600°, and after partial cooling, place in tightly closed screw-cap glass jar. Cool to room temp., pass thru No. 80 sieve, weigh, and place in weighed screw-cap glass jar of such size that only ⅔ of vol. is used. Add H_2O dropwise, with frequent shaking of capped bottle, until alumina contains 3% by wt of added H_2O. (Proportion of H_2O required may vary from 2 to 4%; 3% is usually sufficient for new alumina and 2% for rejuvenated material.) Continue shaking ≥15 min until no lumps remain and material is uniform. Transfer batch to several small, tightly capped jars.

Det. adsorption index as in **43.004**, after alumina has remained in tightly capped jar overnight. (Since change in moisture content will affect adsorptivity of reagent, container must be kept tightly closed, except while removing portion of contents for use.) Adsorption index of stored material decreases with time and should be checked periodically. Alumina suitable for chromatgy has adsorption index of 30–40; extremely retentive alumina with index >50 will not permit clean-cut sepns. When index is <10, adsorbent has lost most of its retentiveness. Decreased retentiveness may be due to excess H_2O content or to changed physical state caused by overheating.

(**i**) *Standardized alkaline alumina.*—Mix portion of alumina, (**g**), with equal wt of 10% (w/w) aq. KOH soln in evapg dish. Decant excess liq., and dry moist alumina overnight at 100°. Pass dry material thru No. 60 sieve and place in capped bottle filled ≤⅔ full. Add H_2O dropwise with frequent shaking until alumina contains 3% by wt of added H_2O. Det. adsorption index as in **43.004**. To be suitable for use, alk. alumina should have index of 7–12. If desired adsorption index is not attained with

3% H_2O, add addnl H_2O in 2% increments to index of 7–12. Store in tightly capped jars.

(**j**) *Standardized adsorptive magnesia.*—(Westvaco Sea Sorb 43, Fisher Scientific Co., No. S-120.) Heat portion of magnesia 4 hr at 600°. After cooling, mix with equal portion of Hyflo Super-Cel (Celite), in ½ full, tightly closed jar. Det. adsorption index as in **43.005**. To be suitable for use, the magnesia-Celite mixt. should have index of 20–35.

(**k**) *Ext. D&C Yellow No. 10 soln.*—Dissolve 20 mg dye (Yellow OB; formerly FD&C Yellow No. 4; Colour Index No. 11390) in 1 L pet ether.

43.004 *Determination of Adsorption Index of Alumina*

Place adsorbent to be tested in chromatgc tube 8 mm od × 220 mm contg glass wool plug at bottom. Tap material into settled position, making column 10 cm high, and attach to vac. controlled bell jar. Add 1.0 mL dye soln, (**k**), to top of column. From accurately filled 50 mL graduate, add small portions of eluting soln, 16% ether in pet ether. Apply slight vac. (5″ (16.9 kPa); or 635 mm Hg pressure). Accurately det. vol. of eluant required to elute dye completely from column. This vol. in mL is adsorption index. For easier recognition of end point, collect eluate until all apparent color on column has been removed, and then collect 2 mL fractions in small beakers until colorless fraction is obtained.

43.005 *Determination of Adsorption Index of Magnesia*

Place magnesia-Celite mixt. to be tested in chromatgc tube 12 mm od × 90 mm, and fitted with sealed-in fritted glass disk. Apply 25″ (635 mm; 84.7 kPa) vac. (125 mm, 16.7 kPa pressure) and, with aid of tamper of suitable diam., tightly pack column to ht of 1.5 cm. Release vac., and add 1.0 mL dye soln, (**k**). From accurately filled 50 mL graduate add small (ca 2 mL) portions eluting soln, 10% absolute alcohol in pet ether. Apply 20″ (510 mm; 68.0 kPa) of vac. (250 mm, 33.3 kPa pressure) and continue to add portions of eluant until most of color is eluted. Collect final eluates in 1.0 mL portions under 5″ (130 mm; 17.3 kPa) of vac. (630 mm, 84.0 kPa pressure). Vol. in mL of eluant required to produce first colorless 1 mL fraction is adsorption index of MgO-Celite mixt. (Removal of individual fractions is easily accomplished at 5″ (130 mm; 17.3 kPa) of vac. by slipping edge of micro bell jar over edge of its base plate.)

43.006 *Sampling*

Store sample in refrigerator. Remove outer layers from 1 lb prints and take sample from interior. Remove end slices from ¼ lb prints and take sample from remainder.

43.007 *Determination*

(*Caution: See* **51.011, 51.016, 51.039, 51.054**, and **51.073**.)

(**a**) *General precautions.*—Protect vitamin A from strong illumination by working in subdued light or by using nonactinic glassware. Avoid undue exposure of vitamin A solns to air. Perform chromatgc steps in completely darkened room to make possible adequate monitoring of chromatgc columns with UV light. Complete all steps as promptly as possible.

(**b**) *Saponification.*—Weigh 10±0.1 g sample into wide-mouth 500 mL erlenmeyer equipped with cold finger condenser, and add 75 mL 95% alcohol and 25 mL 50% KOH soln. Heat on elec. hot plate and stir to break up lumps and completely disperse sample. Maintain soln at vigorous boil 5 min. Remove heat and let stand at room temp. 20 min with occasional stirring. Avoid rapid cooling.

(**c**) *Extraction.*—Transfer soln to 500 mL separator. Rinse saponification flask with 100 mL H_2O in several portions and add rinsings to separator. Add 100 mL ether, shake vigorously, and let stand ca 2 min. Transfer aq. portion to another 500 mL separator and ext with four 50 mL portions ether. (In case of slow sepn, add 2–5 mL 95% alcohol and swirl gently.) Combine ether exts, pour two 100 mL portions H_2O into combined ether exts, swirl gently, and sep. Ext these 2 combined rinses with 2 consecutive 50 mL portions ether, adding ether to original ether exts. Pour two 100 mL portions H_2O thru combined ether exts and discard each washing without shaking. Add ca 10 mL 0.02*N* KOH, shake vigorously, and discard after sepn. Rinse with successive 50 mL portions H_2O, with gentle agitation, until rinse H_2O is alkali-free to phthln. Let ether soln stand 5 min, discard sepd H_2O, transfer with rinsing to 400–500 mL tall beaker, add 3–5 g anhyd. Na_2SO_4, and stir gently to remove traces of H_2O. Decant ether ext into another clean 400–500 mL beaker, and rinse Na_2SO_4 thoroly (ca 6 times) with small portions ether. Combine rinses with ext.

(**d**) *Preparation of soln for chromatography.*—Evap. ext on steam bath to vol. of ca 25 mL. Transfer to 50 mL beaker and continue evapn on steam bath until viscous oily residue forms which, when stirred with small rod, shows no indication of volatilizing liq. Heat ca 20 sec, but ≤2 min, until droplets of oil form. Remove from steam bath and immediately apply stream of *nitrogen* 1 min. Add 5 mL pet ether, transfer to 10 mL vol. flask, and dil. to vol. with pet ether. This is sample soln.

(**e**) *Alumina chromatography.*—Pack each adsorbent in chromatgc tube 12 mm od × 90 mm by gravity and slight tapping. Add stdzd alumina to ht of 1 cm, then segment of alk. alumina 2 cm high, and another segment of stdzd alumina 4 cm high. Apply 5″ (130 mm; 17.3 kPa) of vac. (630 mm, 84.0 kPa pressure), and add 5 mL pet ether, followed by 5 mL sample soln, then another 5 mL pet ether. As last of soln disappears into column, add 5 mL portions 16% ether eluant until all carotene elutes from column. Det. completeness of elution by collecting final part of eluate in 1 mL beakers and observing color against white background. Elution is complete when carotene color cannot be seen in last 1 mL fraction observed. Combine all carotene fractions and reserve for concn, below.

Continue elution with 5 mL portions 16% ether. Examine column regularly with UV lamp and observe progress of fluorescent vitamin A band. (Total time required to elute vitamin A should be ≤20 min. If it is desirable to accelerate movement of vitamin A down column, use 25% ether eluting solv. in 3 mL portions.) Discard eluate that collects after carotene fraction has been collected and before vitamin A band begins to elute. Collect all of vitamin A eluate in sep. beaker. Elution of vitamin A is complete when 1 mL portion of eluate collected in 1 mL beaker shows no vitamin A fluorescence when examined with UV lamp. Detn of cut-off point for collection of vitamin A fraction is very important. If it goes too far, extraneous material absorbing at 325 nm will be present, giving erroneously high results; if chosen too early, vitamin A values will be low. Combine all vitamin A-contg fractions. (*Note:* Some food dyes may not be sepd from vitamin A by alumina chromatgy. Whenever the fluorescent vitamin A eluate is colored, rechromatograph on magnesia column as in (**f**).)

Treat carotene eluate and vitamin A eluate sep., maintaining identity of each soln.

Reduce vol. of carotene eluate and of vitamin A eluate to ca 2 mL by evapn on steam bath. Completely remove remaining solv. by evapn at temp. ≤40° under vac. or with stream of N. Dissolve carotene in 5 mL pet ether, transfer to 10 mL vol. flask, and dil. to vol. with pet ether. This is carotene soln for spectrophtric measurement.

If vitamin A eluate shows no indication of color, dissolve residue in 5 mL absolute alcohol, transfer to 10 mL vol. flask, and dil. to vol. with absolute alcohol. If vitamin A eluate is colored, dissolve residue in ca 2 mL pet ether and proceed with chromatgy on magnesia-Celite.

(f) *Magnesium oxide chromatography.*—Pack magnesia-Celite mixt. in chromatgc tube 12 mm od × 65 mm, using full vac. and light tapping. Column should be 4 cm high. Add 5 mL pet ether and apply 15″ (380 mm; 50.8 kPa) of vac. (380 mm, 50.8 kPa pressure). When pet ether disappears into column, add pet ether sample soln. Rinse container with three 2 mL portions pet ether and add each rinse to column. Elute vitamin A from column with 0.5% absolute alcohol in pet ether. Use technic of adding eluant, observing movement of vitamin A fluorescence, and collecting vitamin A eluate similar to that described for alumina chromatgy. This sepn should take ≤10 min. Loss of vitamin A may result if this chromatgc step is too slow. Evap. solv. as before, dissolve residue in 5 mL absolute alcohol, transfer to 10 mL vol. flask, and dil. to vol. with absolute alcohol.

(g) *Spectrophotometric measurements and calculations.*—(*1*) *Carotene.*—Det. A of pet ether soln of carotene at 450 nm in 1 cm cell.

$$\mu g\ \text{Carotene/lb} = A \times 4.17 \times 454/W;$$

$$\text{carotene as units vitamin A/lb} = A \times 6.95 \times 454/W;$$

where W = g sample/mL soln.

(*2*) *Vitamin A.*—Det. A of absolute alcohol soln of vitamin A at 310 nm and at 325 nm in 1 cm cell.

$$\mu g\ \text{Vitamin A/lb} = A_{325} \times 5.5 \times 454/W;$$

$$\text{units vitamin A/lb} = A_{325} \times 18.3 \times 454/W;$$

where A_{325} = A at 325 nm and W = g sample/mL soln.

Det. ratio of A at 310 and 325 nm; this ratio is usually ≤1.

Vitamin A in Mixed Feeds, Premixes, and Foods (*2*)
Official First Action

(Not applicable to products contg provitamin A (carotene) as predominant source of vitamin A activity nor to high potency vitamin A concs used for feed, premix, and food manufacture)

43.008 ***Apparatus***

(a) *Photoelectric colorimeter.*—Evelyn or similar low-light transmitting colorimeter or spectrophtr with direct-reading deflecting-type galvanometer and optical mechanism or filter for 620 nm wavelength (vitamin A) and 440 nm (carotene). Use matched absorption tubes. Instrument providing linearity between A and concn is preferable.

(b) *Carr-Price reagent dispenser.*—9 or 10 mL all-glass app. with 3–4 mm diam. opening for rapid reagent delivery. Hypodermic syringe, pipet, automatic pipet, or glass cylinder may be used. Keep app. clean and moisture-free.

(c) *Chromatographic tubes.*—18 × 200 mm (ca 12 mm id), sealed to tube 5 × 100 mm.

(d) *Eluate receiver.*—Fraction collector, or 100 mL lipless graduate fitted with 2-hole stopper, with stem of chromatgc tube inserted thru one hole and bent glass tube connected to vac. source thru other. Use H_2O aspirator for vac.

(e) *Alkaline digestion (hydrolysis) apparatus.*—H_2O-cooled refluxing app. connected to *long-neck* ₮ boiling flask, 250 or 500 mL. Calibrate at convenient vol. in neck (e.g., 250 mL flask at 260 mL). Heat on boiling H_2O or steam bath, or hot plate with mag. stirrer.

(f) *Extraction apparatus.*—50–60 mL heavy duty centrf. tube, g-s or screw-cap *with Teflon liner* (check for leakage). For extg larger vol. needed for low potency samples, use 125 or 250 mL separator (no rubber stoppers).

(g) *Ultraviolet light.*—Longwave, 360 nm (Model UVL-22, Ultra-Violet Products, Inc., or equiv.). Use *only* low-intensity lamp.

(h) *Evaporation assemblies.*—Modify 2 arms of Y-tube to U-shape, and attach stoppers wrapped with tinfoil or Teflon ribbon (pipe seal). Connect top arm to H_2O aspirator. Use back-flow safety bottle, and manometer or gage for measuring vac., and 2-way stopcock in system to open and close vac. Heat colorimeter tubes contg ≤10 mL vitamin A soln, attached 2 at a time to app., in H_2O bath at 60–65°, shaking gently to prevent bumping and speed evapn. Optionally use partial vac. and N. To conc. larger vol. ext, use simple 50–200 mL vac. app. consisting of 3-way stopcock, single arm to flask, second to vac. thru trap, and third sealed to small vertical reservoir made from test tube for adding solv. when vac. is broken, or use rotary evap. app.

43.009 ***Reagents***

(a) *Adsorbent.*—Woelm alumina, neutral, activity grade 1 (ICN Pharmaceuticals Inc., Life Sciences Group). Place 5 g H_2O in small g-s bottle, add 95 g alumina, and mix by shaking until no lumps are observed. Let stand and cool ≥2 hr before use. Adjust activity if necessary as in **43.010**. Store in small, well filled, tightly closed bottles. Moisture content must be controlled; do not expose original or prepd alumina to air.

(b) *Chloroform.*—Reagent grade. If not clear, purify by distn, discarding first and last 10%. Discard distd $CHCl_3$ after 1 week. (*Caution: See* **51.011**, **51.040**, and **51.056**.)

(c) *Hexane.*—Reagent, or high quality, com. grade, redistd from all-glass app., saving 64–68° fraction. Must be free of alcohols, esters, and ketones. (*Caution: See* **51.011**, **51.039**, and **51.061**.)

(d) *Alcohol.*—95%. SDA No. 3-A, or No. 30; aldehyde-free by Schiff's test.

(e) *Acetone in hexane soln.*—4 and 15%. Dil. reagent grade acetone with hexane, (**c**).

(f) *Soln for removing antimony trichloride from colorimeter tubes.*—Wash tubes with HCl, or soak in 10% Rochelle salt soln to which small amt detergent is added. Wash thoroly in hot detergent soln.

(g) *Potassium hydroxide soln.*—Dissolve 70 g reagent grade KOH in 70 mL H_2O, mix, and cool. Prep. fresh each time.

(h) *Antimony trichloride (Carr-Price) reagent.*—20%. (*Caution:* $SbCl_3$ is toxic and corrosive; avoid contact.) Use reagent grade $SbCl_3$ crystals from unopened, tightly sealed bottle. Do not use if bottle contains fluids or colored products, or if crystals are moist and sticky. Add 100 g $SbCl_3$ crystals to $CHCl_3$ and dil. to 500 mL. Warm and shake to dissolve. Cool, and add 15 mL Ac_2O. (*Caution: See* **51.022**.) If soln is not clear, filter, centrf., or let settle and decant. Work rapidly with min. exposure of crystals or prepd reagent to atm. Reagent is stable ≥2 months when stored in tight g-s brown bottle.

(i) *Vitamin A reference soln.*—Use USP Ref. Std Soln which contains cryst. all-*trans* retinyl acetate in cottonseed oil, equiv. to 30 mg retinol (vitamin A alcohol)/g oil (or as stated when purchased).

(j) *Carotene reference crystals.*—Pure α- and β-carotene are available from Sigma Chemical Co. Crystals should dissolve in hexane without residue and have characteristic spectrophtric curve. Det. concn as in **43.017**, using spectrophtr.

43.010 ***Adsorption Column***

Place *small* glass wool or cotton plug at bottom of chromatgc tube. Pack with adsorbent added in small portions, tamping lightly, to ht 5–6 cm. (Vac. helps in packing.) Top with 0.5 cm powd, anhyd. Na_2SO_4, level, and pack lightly. Use immediately; do not expose to air flow.

Test column for recovery of vitamin A as follows: Hydrolyze and ext 100–200 mg USP Vitamin A Ref. Std as in **43.013(a)**(*2*) and (**b**). Prep. soln to contain 30–40 μg extd vitamin A and 50–100 μg carotene, dild to 15 mL with hexane. Wash prepd column with 20 mL hexane and adjust vac. (only slight vac. required) for elution rate of ca 2 drops/sec. Add vitamin A-carotene mixt. before top of column runs dry. Elute carotene with 4% acetone in hexane (20–30 mL normally required). Locate vitamin A band by brief inspection with UV light. Band should be ≤2 cm below top of alumina. (*Caution:* Avoid looking at radiations. Use only low-intensity UV lamp.)

Elute vitamin A with 15% acetone in hexane (30–35 mL normally required). Inspect last few mL eluate for vitamin A fluorescence. If necessary, elute with more solv. until fluorescence no longer is observed in eluate. If vitamin A elutes too slowly, prep. adsorbent using 1–2% more H_2O, **43.009(a)**, and test again; if vitamin A elutes too rapidly, use less H_2O. Evap. suitable aliquot of eluate to dryness under vac. or N, add 1 mL $CHCl_3$ to dissolve residue, and det. vitamin A as in **43.013(d)**. Compare result with that for hydrolyzed vitamin A not chromatgd. Recovery should be ≥90%.

43.011 ***Standardization***

Det. blank on all reagents, including cottonseed oil. *A* of blank should be almost 0.

(**a**) *Preparation of std vitamin A curve.*—Cut tip from capsule contg USP Ref. Std Soln of vitamin A and express oil into small tared beaker or watch glass. Weigh accurately. Transfer oil to vol. flask and dil. to vol. with $CHCl_3$. Use soln as soon as possible; discard after 8 hr. Work in subdued light or use low-actinic glassware. Make ≥5 dilns of vitamin A soln with $CHCl_3$ so that 1 mL aliquots treated as in **43.013(d)** give *T* in 20–85% range (*A,* 0.7–0.07) at 620 nm. Plot *T* or *A* against μg vitamin A. If plot of *A* is straight line, factor may be calcd for detg vitamin A in samples.

(**b**) *Preparation of std carotene curve.*—Prep. series of dilns of carotene in hexane. Plot *A* at 440 nm against μg carotene. Use curve or factor to det. carotene concn of samples.

(**c**) *Determination of correction factor for yellow pigment in vitamin A eluate.*—Monohydroxy carotenoids (e.g., cryptoxanthol) elute with hydrolyzed vitamin A (vitamin A alcohol). Correct for pigment when present in more than traces, as follows: Hydrolyze 30–40 g ground yellow corn as in **43.013(a)**(*1*). Ext 50 mL soln with two 50 mL portions hexane in separator. Wash ext with H_2O, dry with anhyd. Na_2SO_4, and conc. to 15–20 mL. Chromatograph as in **43.013(c)**, and save fraction eluting with 15% acetone in hexane. Make ≥5 dilns so that *A* values at 440 nm are in 0.1–0.6 range (conc. soln if necessary). Evap. 10 mL of each soln in colorimeter tubes as in **43.008(h)**, dissolve residue in 1 mL $CHCl_3$, and develop and read blue color at 620 nm as in **43.013(d)**. Plot *A* at 440 nm against *A* at 620 nm. Use this curve to calc. *A* of carotenoid pigment-$SbCl_3$ product in vitamin A detn at 620 nm, based on *A* of carotenoid at 440 nm. If plot is linear, calc. factor to correct for vitamin A equiv. to pigment in vitamin A detn.

43.012 ***Storage and Preparation of Sample***

(**a**) *Dry mixed feed and premixes.*—Collect 600–800 g bulk sample. Refrigerate in dark in tightly closed glass or plastic containers. Immediately before analysis, warm to room temp., grind entire sample so that ≥95% passes No. 20 sieve, mix by rolling on paper, or by equiv. method, regrind, and remix. (Grinding helps fracture and disperse high-potency beadlet-type vitamin A products in sample.) Sample, avoiding loss of fine particles. Some high-potency products (e.g., ≥30 μg vitamin A/g) contg stabilized vitamin A are sampled better if dild with freshly ground cereal grain before initial grinding and sampling. Do not store ground sample >1 week.

(**b**) *Foods.*—Proceed as in (**a**), except bulk sample of 400 g is enough for products not contg stabilized vitamin A. Sticky pastries, prepd drink mixes, canned pet foods, etc., may require special sampling, e.g., use of sections of crushed pastry, individual pack of food, or as directed for official tests.

(**c**) *Liquid feed supplements and premixes.*—Store in cool place, but at ≥8°, in tightly closed glass or plastic containers. Warm to 35–40° immediately before analysis. Mix thoroly by repeated pouring or stirring before sampling.

43.013 ***Determination***

(Work in subdued light; avoid high laboratory temp. Complete all steps of method as rapidly as consistent with careful following of directions.)

(*1*) *For products containing less than 5000 USP units vitamin A/lb* (ca 1500 μg/lb or 3000 μg/kg), weigh ≥40 g sample prepd as in **43.012**, into 500 mL long-neck boiling flask. (*2*) *For products containing 5000–20,000 unit/lb,* use 20–40 g sample and 250–500 mL flask. (*3*) *For products containing 20,000–80,000 unit/lb,* use 10–20 g sample and 250 mL flask.

To low-fat products, add 1 g *fresh* cottonseed or peanut oil to boiling flask before alk. digestion. Proceed as in (**a**)(*1*) or (*2*).

(**a**) *Alkaline digestion (hydrolysis).*—(*1*) *Mixed dry samples, premixes, and semimoist foods.*—Add vol. (mL) alcohol equal to 4 times wt (g) sample, but ≥40 mL. Mix thoroly. Slowly add, with mixing, vol. KOH soln equal to g sample, but ≥10 mL. Place stirring bar in flask. Reflux 30 min at ca 2 drops/sec. Agitate flasks ≥3 times during refluxing to disperse any aggregates formed, or use hot plate with mag. stirring. (Hand agitation with stirring bar gives better dispersion on some samples than does mag. stirring.) Cool rapidly to room temp. Add alcohol-H_2O soln (3+1) up to 20–30 mL below calibration mark. Shake to mix thoroly. Add alcohol-H_2O soln to calibration mark, and mix again. (Use size flask to have vitamin A concn convenient for further steps of method; do not over-dil.) Let suspended matter settle. After standing, if soln in flask is single, homogeneous phase, proceed to (**b**); if not, *see* (**b**)(*2*). (Sticky film on walls of flask when sample has high sugar content apparently causes no difficulty if contents are well mixed.)

(*2*) *Liquid samples (supplements containing molasses, liquid breakfast drinks, etc.).*—If sample is viscous, mix thoroly with equal vol. warm H_2O. Add slowly, with mixing, vol. (mL) KOH soln equal to wt (g) sample. Add slowly, with mixing, vol. (mL) alcohol equal to 4 times wt (g) sample. Digest sample as in (*1*), beginning with "Place stirring bar in flask."

(**b**) *Extraction.*—(*1*) *For products containing more than 1500 μg vitamin A/lb.*—Transfer 5.0–15.0 mL soln, depending on vitamin A concn, free of suspended matter, to the 50–60 mL centrf. tube. Add 2 mL H_2O for each 5 mL soln, and add 20.0 mL hexane. Ext vitamin A by shaking vigorously ≥1 min. Let phases sep. and centrf. briefly. If amt of vitamin A in ext is <1 mg and if hexane layer is clear, with only traces of yellow color, draw lower layer from bottom of centrf. tube with pipet and filler bulb, and discard; if hexane layer is yellow, proceed to (**c**). Wash ext in tube once with 20 mL H_2O, let layers sep., and centrf. briefly. Transfer 1.0–10.0 mL hexane ext, as required for satisfactory color development, to colorimeter tube and proceed to vitamin A detn, (**d**). Avoid loss of hexane by evapn. If vitamin A recovery is low, again ext soln contg vitamin A, and combine exts before washing.

(*2*) *For solns of* (**a**)(*1*) *separating into two liquid phases.*—Shake vigorously and remove portion for extn before sepn occurs, and proceed as in (*1*), or transfer total contents, without diln with alcohol-H_2O, to separator. Add vol. (mL) H_2O equal to 2 times wt (g) sample; ext once with vol. (mL) hexane equal to 3 times wt (g) sample and again with 2 vols hexane. Combine exts and wash with two 100 mL portions H_2O, or until free of alkali. Dil. to smallest suitable vol. Centrf. portion, or dry with anhyd. Na_2SO_4 and dil. to previous vol. Proceed to (**c**) or transfer 1.0–10.0 mL to colorimeter tube and proceed to (**d**) if no pigments are present.

(*3*) *For products containing less than 1500 µg vitamin A/lb that require extraction of more than 15 mL hydrolyzed soln, or those with measurable carotenoid pigments.*—Use separator, increasing H_2O and hexane vols proportionally. Ext twice, combine exts, dil. to vol., wash, and centrf. or dry as in (*2*). Proceed to (**c**), or transfer 1.0–10.0 mL to colorimeter tube and proceed to (**d**) if no pigments are present.

(**c**) *Chromatography.*—If yellow pigments are present, chromatograph sample. If possible, use aliquot contg 25–60 µg vitamin A in 10–15 mL hexane ext. Conc. portion hexane ext under vac., **43.008(h)**, if necessary to obtain suitable vitamin A concn. Wash packed column with 20 mL hexane, and add ext contg vitamin A just before top of column runs dry. Elute at ca 2 drops/sec. Elute carotene with 4% acetone in hexane, and vitamin A with 15% acetone in hexane as in **43.010**. Cryptoxanthin and related pigments elute with vitamin A.

(**d**) *Colorimetry.*—If carotene was sepd during chromatgy, det. concn as in **43.017**.

If vitamin A eluate in 15% acetone-hexane soln contains yellow pigment, read *T* (or *A*) as carotene with 440 nm filter. Calc. correction, **43.011(c)**, to apply to *A* of blue-color reaction with vitamin A, using necessary diln factor if 1:10 vol. at 620 and 440 nm was not used.

Evap. soln as in **43.008(h)** under vac. in H_2O bath at 60–65°. Dissolve residue in 1 mL $CHCl_3$. Adjust colorimeter to 100% *T* (or 0% *A*) at 620 nm, using 1 mL $CHCl_3$ and measured vol. (9 or 10 mL) $SbCl_3$ reagent. (This point must remain const for series of detns; readjust as required.) Place tube contg 1 mL $CHCl_3$ soln of vitamin A in instrument. Add measured vol. $SbCl_3$ reagent in 1–2 sec. Read *T* (or *A*) as first transitory pause point (*T* should be in 20–85% range). Read quickly; color begins to fade and *T* increases slowly after 3–5 sec. Instrument *cannot* be adjusted to make reading after $SbCl_3$ is added. Examine tube contents within short time; soln should be blue, without turbidity, and blue should fade.

Det. recovery factor, *R*, for vitamin A detn by adding known amt vitamin A to samples (or blank feeds or foods when available) of general types analyzed, carrying analysis thru entire method.

(**e**) *Calculation of vitamin A content.*—

$$\mu g \text{ Vitamin A/g} = (C_u - C_c) \times [V/(W \times R)];$$

or

$$\mu g \text{ Vitamin A/lb} = (C_u - C_c) \times V \times [454/(W \times R)];$$

where C_u = uncorrected concn vitamin A from curve or factor; C_c = correction for yellow pigment in vitamin A eluate; V = final vol. sample ext; W = g sample; and R = recovery factor for vitamin A.

(*Note:* If solids are present in flask after hydrolysis, results may be increased slightly. Ignore vol. of solids unless sample is large and vol. soln in flask is relatively small, in which case difference could be ≤5%. Correction for vol. of solids is difficult because some samples leave considerable unhydrolyzed residue and others, none. Max. correction is based on 10 g feed reducing vol. in hydrolysis flask by 3 mL. Apply estd correction, if necessary.)

Carotenes in Fresh Plant Materials and Silages (*3*)
Official Final Action

(*Caution: See* **51.004, 51.011, 51.039, 51.046,** and **51.061**.)

43.014 ***Reagents***

(**a**) *Acetone.*—Dry, alcohol-free. To dry, treat with anhyd. Na_2SO_4 and distil over granular ca "10 mesh" Zn.

(**b**) *Commercial hexane.*—Bp 60–70°; distilled over KOH.

(**c**) *Adsorbent.*—Activated magnesia (Sea Sorb 43; Fisher Scientific Co., No. S-120).

(**d**) *Diatomaceous earth.*—Hyflo Super-Cel.

43.015 ***Extraction***

Finely cut material with scissors or knife, or grind in food chopper to assure representative sample. If analysis cannot be performed immediately, blanch in boiling H_2O 5–10 min and store in frozen condition. Place 2–5 g weighed sample in high-speed blender; add 40 mL acetone, 60 mL hexane, and 0.1 g $MgCO_3$, and blend 5 min. Filter with suction or let residue settle and decant into separator. Wash residue with two 25 mL portions acetone, then with 25 mL hexane, and combine exts. Wash acetone from ext with five 100 mL portions H_2O, transfer upper layer to 100 mL vol. flask contg 9 mL acetone, and dil. to vol. with hexane. If desired, alcohol may be used instead of acetone for extn. Use 80 mL alcohol and 60 mL hexane in blender; other vols same as for acetone.

43.016 ***Separation of Pigments***

Pack activated magnesia-diat. earth mixt. (1+1) in chromatgc tube 22 mm od × 175 mm sealed to 10 mm od tube at bottom. To prep. column, place small glass wool or cotton plug inside tube, add loose adsorbent to 15 cm depth, attach tube to suction flask, and apply full vac. of H_2O pump. Use flat instrument (such as inverted cork mounted on rod or tamping rod) to gently press adsorbent and flatten surface (packed column should be ca 10 cm deep). Place 1 cm layer anhyd. Na_2SO_4 above adsorbent.

With vac. continuously applied to flask, pour ext into column. Use 50 mL acetone-hexane (1+9), or slightly more, if necessary, to develop chromatogram and wash visible carotenes thru adsorbent. Keep top of column covered with layer of solv. during entire operation (conveniently done by clamping inverted vol. flask full of solv. above column with neck 1–2 cm above surface of adsorbent).

Collect entire eluate. (Carotenes pass rapidly thru column; bands of xanthophylls, carotene oxidn products, and chlorophylls should be present in column when operation is complete.) Transfer eluate, which has been reduced in vol. by loss of vapor thru H_2O pump, to 100 mL vol. flask, dil. to vol. with acetone-hexane (1+9), and det. carotene content photometrically.

43.017 ***Determination***

Det. *A* of soln as soon as possible with spectrophtr at 436 nm or with instrument having suitable filter system, such as Klett photometer with No. 44 filter, or Evelyn photoelec. colorimeter with 440 nm filter. Calibrate these instruments first with solns of high purity β-carotene as shown by characteristic absorption curve (J. Biol. Chem. **144,** 21(1942)). Prep. calibration chart and convert *A* of soln to be detd to carotene concn from chart.

When detns are made with properly calibrated spectrophtr at 436 nm,

$$C = (A \times 454)/(196 \times L \times W),$$

where C = concn carotene (mg/lb) in original sample, L = cell length in cm, and W = g sample/mL final diln. Report results as mg β-carotene/lb. Multiply by 2.2 to give ppm or by 1667 to give International Units/lb.

Carotenes and Xanthophylls in Dried Plant Materials and Mixed Feeds (*4*)—Official Final Action

(*Caution: See* **51.011**, **51.018**, **51.037**, **51.039**, and **51.046**.)

43.018 ***Apparatus***

(**a**) *Chromatographic tube.*—12.5 mm id × 30 cm, Pyrex, with bottom capillary tube 2 mm id × ca 10 cm to extend into neck of 25 mL vol. flask.

(**b**) *Vacuum filtration device.*—For collection of eluate in vol. flask (Fisher Scientific Co. "Filtrator," or equiv.). Attach rubber stopper to column to fit device.

43.019 ***Reagents***

(**a**) *Acetone.*—Dry, alcohol-free. Distil over Zn (granular, ca 10 mesh).

(**b**) *Hexane.*—Com.; Phillips Petroleum Co. "high purity," or equiv.

(**c**) *Extractant.*—Hexane-acetone-absolute alcohol-toluene (10 +7+6+7).

(**d**) *Adsorbent I.*—Mix in mech. blender 1–2 hr 1+1 (w/w) silica gel G (according to Stahl; Brinkmann Instruments, Inc.) and diat. earth (Hyflo Super-Cel).

(**e**) *Adsorbent II.*—Mix in mech. blender 1–2 hr 1+1 (w/w) activated magnesia (Sea Sorb 43; Fisher Scientific Co.) and diat. earth (Hyflo Super-Cel).

(**f**) *Methanolic potassium hydroxide.*—40%. Dissolve 40 g KOH in MeOH, cool, and dil. to 100 mL with MeOH.

(**g**) *Sodium sulfate soln.*—10%. Dissolve 10 g anhyd. Na_2SO_4 in 100 mL H_2O.

(**h**) *Eluants.*—(*1*) *Carotenes.*—Hexane-acetone (96+4). (*2*) *Monohydroxy pigments* (*MHP*).—Hexane-acetone (90+10). (*3*) *Dihydroxy pigments* (*DHP*).—Hexane-acetone (80+20). (*4*) *Total xanthophylls* (*TX*).—Hexane-acetone-MeOH (80+10+10).

(**i**) *1-(Phenylazo)-2-naphthol (C.I. Solvent Yellow 14; Sudan I) std solns.*—(*1*) *Stock soln.*—1.0 millimolar (*mM*). Recrystallize std (Aldrich Chemical Co., or MC/B Manufacturing Chemists) from hot absolute alcohol. Dry crystals to const wt in 70° vac. oven. Dissolve 0.1241 g in 500 mL acetone-isopropanol (1+1). (*2*) *Working soln.*—0.04*mM*. Dil. 20 mL stock soln to 500 mL with acetone-isopropanol (1+1). Store in dark.

43.020 ***Preparation of Sample***

Grind sample to pass No. 40 sieve. Accurately weigh sample (2 g corn gluten or alfalfa meal; 50 mg marigold meal; 4 g mixed feed) into 100 mL vol. flask. Pipet 30 mL extractant into flask, stopper, and swirl 1 min. For low-moisture samples, e.g., marigold meal, dehydrated alfalfa, or corn gluten (not air-dried samples), also pipet 1 mL H_2O/2 g sample into flask, stopper, and swirl 1 min. For high-moisture (air-dried) samples, omit addn of H_2O.

(**a**) *Hot saponification.*—(For rapid extn and for samples contg xanthophyll esters.) Pipet 2 mL (4 mL for 4 g sample of mixed feed) 40% methanolic KOH into flask, swirl 1 min, and place flask in 56° H_2O bath 20 min. Attach air condenser or cool neck of flask to prevent loss of solv. Cool sample, and let stand in dark 1 hr. Pipet 30 mL hexane into flask, swirl 1 min, dil. to vol. with 10% Na_2SO_4 soln, and shake vigorously 1 min. Let stand in dark 1 hr before chromatgy. Upper phase is 50 mL.

(**b**) *Cold (overnight) saponification.*—(For samples not contg xanthophyll esters.) Let mixt. stand in dark ca 16 hr. Pipet 2 mL 40% methanolic KOH into flask and swirl 1 min; let stand in dark 1 hr; then proceed with hexane addn as in (**a**).

43.021 ***Chromatography***

With column on Filtrator, place absorbent cotton or glass wool plug in bottom and add ca 12 cm layer Adsorbent I. Apply full vac. and add more adsorbent to give 7 cm layer. Use flat instrument such as inverted cork on glass rod to press and flatten surface of adsorbent. Place 2 cm layer anhyd. Na_2SO_4 above adsorbent and press firmly.

(**a**) *Total carotenes.*—With 25 mL vol. flask as receiver, pipet 5 mL (or 10 mL if low pigment) of upper phase onto column and adjust vac. for flow of 2 or 3 drops/sec. Needle valve in vac. line helps control flow rate. Add carotene eluant as last of soln enters adsorbent and continue until carotene band is collected in flask. Keep adsorbent covered with solv. at all times. Release vac., place carotene soln in dark until it reaches room temp., and dil. to vol. with carotene eluant. Invert flask several times to mix; then det. *A* immediately, as in **43.022**.

Xanthophylls remain on column. For sepn of monohydroxy from dihydroxy pigments (both free from epoxy and polyoxy pigments), or for total xanthophylls, proceed as in (**b**) or (**c**).

(**b**) *Separation of xanthophylls.*—(*1*) With 25 mL vol. flask in Filtrator and vac. applied to column, let eluant level approach adsorbent surface; then immediately add MHP eluant. Band of monohydroxy pigments (zeinoxanthin, cryptoxanthin) and any persistent mono- or di-esters should move down column ahead of other bands. When elution of MHP band is complete, place flask in dark to attain room temp. before dilg to vol. with MHP eluant and detg *A*. (*2*) Proceed as in (*1*), using DHP eluant to collect pigments of next band (lutein, zeaxanthin, and their isomers) in 25 (or 50) mL vol. flask. Violaxanthin, neoxanthin, and other polyoxy pigments (POP) remain on column.

(**c**) *Total xanthophylls.*—If value for total xanthophylls is desired, pipet fresh aliquot from upper phase of original ext onto 7 cm column of Adsorbent II, and elute carotenes with hexane-acetone (90+10) and total xanthophylls with hexane-acetone-MeOH (80+10+10).

43.022 ***Determination***

Measure *A* promptly to minimize isomerization and autoxidn losses. First, check calibration of spectrophtr by reading working std soln at 1 nm intervals between 469 and 479 nm. If max. value is not at 474 nm, recalibrate instrument. When instrument shows max. *A* at 474 nm and slit width is 0.03, working soln readings should be 0.561 (474) and 0.460 (436). Correct calcns from equations below, for instrument deviation factor. If instrument lacks controllable slit, est. concn by assuming that working std soln of dye, (**i**)(*2*), has same *A* as 2.35 mg carotenes/L at 436 nm and 2.38 mg xanthophylls/L at 474 nm.

Det. *A* of carotene fraction at 436 nm and MHP and DHP fractions at 474 nm. For highest accuracy, control soln vols to give *A* between 0.25 and 0.75.

43.023 ***Calculations***

Following equations are applicable to *A* data obtained from calibrated spectrophtrs that operate with narrow slit width. Values 196 and 236 are *a* for *trans*-β-carotene and *trans*-lutein at prescribed wavelengths; b = cell length in cm; d = diln factor = (g sample × mL ext on column)/(50 mL upper phase × mL final diln); and f = instrument deviation factor = 0.460/observed A_{436} or 0.561/observed A_{474}.

Carotene fraction concn (mg/lb)

$$= (A_{436} \times 454 \times f)/(196 \times b \times d).$$

MHP fraction concn (mg/lb), or DHP fraction concn (mg/lb), or total xanthophylls (mg/lb)

$$=(A_{474} \times 454 \times f)/(236 \times b \times d).$$

Thiamine (Vitamin B_1)

(Methods not applicable in presence of materials that adsorb thiamine or which contain extraneous materials which affect thiochrome fluorescence)

Fluorometric Method (5)—Official Final Action

43.024 ***Reagents and Apparatus***

(**a**) *Double-normal sodium acetate.*—Dissolve 272 g NaOAc $.3H_2O$ in enough H_2O to make 1 L.

(**b**) *Bromocresol green pH indicator.*—Dissolve 0.1 g indicator by triturating in agate mortar with 2.8 mL 0.05*N* NaOH, and dil. to 200 mL with H_2O. Transition range: 4.0 (green)–5.8 (blue).

(**c**) *Bromophenol blue indicator.*—Dissolve 0.1 g indicator by triturating in agate mortar with 3.0 mL 0.05*N* NaOH, and dil. to 250 mL with H_2O. Transition range: 3.0 (yellow)–4.6 (blue).

(**d**) *Enzyme soln.*—Prep., on day on which it is to be used, 10% aq. soln of enzyme prepn potent in diastatic and phosphorolytic activity. (Among enzymes available for this purpose are Mylase P (Wallerstein Co.), and Clarase (Miles Laboratories, Inc.)).

(**e**) *Base-exchange silicate.*—Purify artificially prepd silicate of base-exchange type, in form of granular powder of "50–80 mesh" size, as follows: Place convenient amt (100–500 g) of base-exchange silicate in suitable beaker, add enough hot 3% HOAc to cover, and boil 10–15 min, stirring continuously. Let settle and decant supernate. Repeat washing 3 times, then wash similarly 3 times with hot neut. KCl soln, (**g**), and finally wash with boiling H_2O until last washing gives no reaction for Cl. Dry material at ca 100° and store in well closed container. (Purified base-exchange silicate may be purchased as "Thiochrome Decalso," Fisher Scientific Co., No. T-97.)

(**f**) *Chromatographic columns.*—Use glass chromatgc tubes (ca 275 mm overall length, with reservoir capacity ca 60 mL) consisting of 3 parts fused together with following approx. dimensions (od × length, mm): (*1*) reservoir at top, 35 × 95, (*2*) adsorption tube in middle, 8 × 145, drawn into (*3*) capillary at bottom 35 mm long and of such diam. that when tube is filled, rate of flow will be ≤1 mL/min. Prep. tubes for use as follows: Over upper end of capillary, with aid of glass rod, place pledget of fine glass wool. To adsorption tube, add H_2O suspension of 1.0–2.0 g purified base-exchange silicate, taking care to wash down all silicate from walls of reservoir. To keep air out of adsorption column, keep layer of liq. above surface of silicate during adsorption process. (Prevent tube from draining by placing rubber cap, filled with H_2O to avoid inclusion of air, over lower end of capillary.)

(**g**) *Neutral potassium chloride soln.*—Dissolve 250 g KCl in H_2O to make 1 L.

(**h**) *Acid potassium chloride soln.*—Add 8.5 mL HCl to 1 L of the neut. KCl soln.

(**i**) *Sodium hydroxide soln.*—15%. Dissolve 15 g NaOH in H_2O to make 100 mL.

(**j**) *Potassium ferricyanide soln.*—1%. Dissolve 1 g $K_3Fe(CN)_6$ in H_2O to make 100 mL. Prep. soln on day it is used.

(**k**) *Oxidizing reagent.*—Mix 4.0 mL of the 1% $K_3Fe(CN)_6$ soln with the 15% NaOH soln to make 100 mL. Use soln within 4 hr.

(**l**) *Isobutyl alcohol.*—Redistd in all-glass app. Use redistd product as anhyd. or H_2O-satd.

(**m**) *Quinine sulfate stock soln.*—Use quinine sulfate soln to govern reproducibility of fluorometer. Prep. stock soln by dissolving 10 mg quinine sulfate in 0.1*N* H_2SO_4 to make 1 L. Store in light-resistant containers.

(**n**) *Quinine sulfate std soln.*—Dil. 1 vol. quinine sulfate stock soln with 39 vols 0.1*N* H_2SO_4. (Soln fluoresces to ca same degree as does isobutanol ext of thiochrome obtained from 1 μg thiamine.HCl.) Store soln in light-resistant containers.

(**o**) *Thiamine hydrochloride std solns.*—(*1*) *Stock soln.*—100 μg/mL. Accurately weigh 50–60 mg USP Thiamine Hydrochloride Ref. Std that has been dried to const wt over P_2O_5 in desiccator. (Ref. std is hygroscopic; avoid absorption of moisture.) Dissolve in 20% alcohol adjusted to pH 3.5–4.3 with HCl, and dil. to 500 mL with the acidified alcohol. Add enough addnl acidified alcohol to make concn exactly 100 μg thiamine.HCl/mL. Store at ca 10° in g-s, light-resistant bottle.

(*2*) *Intermediate soln.*—10 μg/mL. Dil. 100 mL stock soln to 1 L with 20% alcohol adjusted to pH 3.5–4.3 with HCl. Store at ca 10° in g-s, light-resistant bottle.

(*3*) *Working soln.*—1 μg/mL. To 10 mL intermediate soln, add ca 50 mL ca 0.1*N* HCl, digest or autoclave as in **43.025(a)**(*1*), cool, and dil. to 100 mL with the 0.1*N* HCl. Prep. fresh soln for each assay.

For materials contg free thiamine, dil. 20 mL working soln to 100 mL with 0.1*N* HCl. Designate as assay std soln and proceed directly to oxidn, **43.028**.

For materials contg thiamine pyrophosphate, take 20 mL working soln and proceed as in **43.026**, beginning ". . . dil to ca 65 mL . . ." Designate final 25 mL eluate (equiv. to 5 μg USP Thiamine.HCl Ref. Std) from **43.027** as assay std soln and proceed as in **43.028**.

43.025 ***Extraction***

(**a**) *For materials containing free thiamine (not applicable in presence of thiamine pyrophosphate).*—Place measured amt of sample in flask of suitable size, prep. sample by (*1*), (*2*), or (*3*), and proceed directly to oxidn, **43.028**.

(*1*) *For dry or semidry materials containing no appreciable quantity of basic substances.*—Add vol. 0.1*N* HCl equal in mL to ≥10 times dry wt sample in g. Comminute and evenly disperse material in liq. if it is not readily sol. If lumping occurs, agitate vigorously so that all particles come in contact with liq.; then wash down sides of flask with 0.1*N* HCl. Digest 30 min at 95–100° in steam bath, or in boiling H_2O, with frequent mixing; or autoclave mixt. 30 min at 121–123°. Cool, and if lumping occurs, agitate mixt. until particles are evenly dispersed. Dil. with 0.1*N* HCl to measured vol. contg ca 0.2 μg thiamine/mL. Designate as Assay Sample Soln.

(*2*) *For dry or semidry materials containing appreciable amounts of basic substances.*—Add dil. HCl to adjust mixt. to ca pH 4.0. Add amt of H_2O such that total vol. liq. is equal in mL to ≥10 times dry wt sample in g. Add equiv. of 1 mL 10*N* HCl/100 mL liq. and proceed as in (*1*), beginning with second sentence.

(*3*) *For liquid materials.*—Adjust material to ca pH 4.0 with dil. HCl, or, with vigorous agitation, NaOH soln, and proceed as in (*2*), beginning with second sentence.

(**b**) *For materials containing thiamine pyrophosphate.*—Proceed as in (**a**)(*1*), but dil. with 0.1*N* HCl to measured vol. contg 0.2–5.0 μg thiamine/mL, followed by enzyme hydrolysis and purification, **43.026–43.027**.

43.026 ***Enzyme Hydrolysis***

Take aliquot contg ca 10–25 μg thiamine, dil. to ca 65 mL with 0.1*N* HCl, and adjust pH to 4.0–4.5 with ca 5 mL 2*N* NaOAc, using pH meter or bromocresol green indicator and spot plate.

End point should be definitely on blue side of color change. Add 5 mL enzyme soln, mix, and incubate 3 hr at 45–50°. Cool, adjust to ca pH 3.5, using bromophenol blue indicator or pH meter, dil. to 100 mL with H_2O, and filter thru paper known not to adsorb thiamine (ash-free papers have been found satisfactory).

43.027 ***Purification***

Pass aliquot of filtered soln contg ca 5 μg thiamine thru prepd chromatgc column, and wash column with three 5 mL portions of almost boiling H_2O. Do not permit surface of liq. to fall below surface of base-exchange silicate.

Elute thiamine from base-exchange silicate by passing five 4.0–4.5 mL portions almost boiling acid-KCl soln thru column. Do not permit surface of liq. to fall below surface of silicate until final portion of acid-KCl soln has been added. Collect eluate in 25 mL vol. flask, cool, and dil. to vol. with acid-KCl soln. Designate this as Assay Sample Soln.

43.028 ***Oxidation of Thiamine to Thiochrome***

To each of ≥4 ca 40 mL tubes (or reaction vessels) add ca 1.5 g NaCl or KCl and 5 mL assay std soln. (*Precision and accuracy of results depend upon uniform technic in conducting following oxidn.* Protect soln from light which destroys thiochrome. Use pipet that delivers 3 mL in 1–2 sec for addn of oxidizing reagent.) Place tip of pipet contg oxidizing reagent in neck of tube and hold it so that stream of soln does not hit side of tube. Gently swirl tube to produce rotary motion in liq. and immediately add 3 mL oxidizing reagent. Remove pipet and swirl tube again to ensure adequate mixing. *Immediately* add 13 mL isobutanol, stopper, and shake tube vigorously ≥15 sec. Similarly treat ≥1 tube and treat each of ≥2 remaining tubes (std blanks) similarly except replace oxidizing reagent with 15% NaOH soln.

To each of ≥4 similar tubes add 5 mL Assay Sample Soln. Treat these tubes in same manner as directed for tubes contg working std soln.

After isobutanol has been added to all tubes, shake again ca 2 min. (Tubes may be placed in shaker box for this addnl shaking.) Centrf. tubes at low speed until clear supernate can be obtained from each. Pipet or decant ca 10 mL isobutanol ext (upper layer) from each tube into cell for thiochrome fluorescence measurement.

43.029 ***Thiochrome Fluorescence Measurement***

(Thiamine content of oxidized Assay Soln is detd by comparing intensity of fluorescence of ext of this soln with that from oxidized std soln. Intensity of fluorescence is proportional to amt of thiamine present and may be measured with suitable fluorometer. Input filter of narrow T range with max. ca 365 nm and output filter of narrow T range with max. ca 435 nm have been found satisfactory. Use quinine sulfate std soln to govern reproducibility of fluorometer. *Caution: See* **51.008**.)

Measure fluorescence (I) of isobutanol ext from oxidized Assay Sample Soln. Next measure fluorescence (b) of ext from Assay Sample Soln which has been treated with 3 mL 15% NaOH soln. Then measure fluorescence (S) of ext from oxidized assay std soln. Finally, measure fluorescence (d) of ext from assay std soln which has been treated with 3 mL 15% NaOH soln (std blank).

43.030 ***Calculation***

Calc. as follows:

μg Thiamine.HCl in 5 mL Assay Soln = $(I - b)/(S - d)$.

Rapid Fluorometric Method (6)—Official Final Action

(Applicable to detn thiamine in enriched flour, farina, corn meal, macaroni, and noodle products, or where bound thiamine or thiamine pyrophosphate is not significant)

43.031 ***Reagents***

See **43.024(c)**, **(i)**, **(j)**, **(k)**, **(l)**, **(m)**, **(n)**, and **(o)**.

43.032 ***Preparation of Standard Solution***

Dil. 5 mL thiamine.HCl intermediate soln, **43.024(o)**(*2*), to 250 mL with ca 0.1*N* HCl (1 mL = 0.2 μg thiamine.HCl). Designate this as working std soln. If NaCl is to be added to sample for extn, add NaCl to working std soln, before final diln, to give final concn of ca 5% (w/v). Proceed as in **43.034**.

43.033 ***Extraction***

Weigh enough sample to give final Assay Soln with thiamine concn of ca 0.2 μg/mL (e.g., 4.54 g enriched flour for 100 mL or 9.07 g for 200 mL final vol.) and proceed by one of following methods:

(a) *95–100° Digestion.*—Place measured amt of sample in bottle or flask of suitable size. (Addn of NaCl to give final concn of ca 5% (w/v) aids in subsequent sepn of sample soln. Thoroly mix flour and salt with stirring rod before adding 0.1*N* HCl.) Add in 2 portions, with vigorous stirring, vol. ca 0.1*N* HCl in proportion ca 15 mL acid to 1 g sample, using part of acid to wash down sides of vessel. Place vessel in H_2O bath previously heated to 95–100°. Stir at frequent intervals to keep solids in suspension during thickening stage (5–8 min) and occasionally during balance of total heating time of 30 min.

After hydrolysis has proceeded ca 10 min, place drop of soln on spot plate and test with thymol blue. Soln should be distinctly red (pH 1.0–1.2). If not enough (indicating presence of basic substances in sample), add ca 1*N* HCl in 1.0 mL portions until desired acidity is reached. Note vol. of 1*N* acid required to supplement the 0.1*N* acid and *repeat digestion* with new sample wt and necessary mixt. of 1*N* and 0.1*N* acids. Cool, and dil. with 0.1*N* HCl to measured vol. contg ca 0.2 μg thiamine/mL.

Centrf. mixt. until supernate is clear or practically so and/or filter thru paper known not to adsorb thiamine (ash-free papers have been found satisfactory), or filter thru fritted glass funnel, using suitable anal. filter-aid (ash-free filter pulp and Celite Analytical Filter-Aid have been found satisfactory). Discard first $^1/_{10}$ part of filtrate. Designate remainder of filtrate as Assay Sample Soln.

(b) *Autoclaved digestion.*—Proceed as in **(a)** without addn of NaCl, except to autoclave 20 min at 5 lb (34.5 kPa) pressure (108–109°) with total heating time ≤35 min including 5–10 min to attain desired pressure and ca 5 min to reduce pressure. (It may be necessary to preheat autoclave to ca 100° before inserting samples.)

43.034 ***Oxidation***

Proceed as in **43.028**, except add ca 2.5 g NaCl or KCl to each tube (or reaction vessel) before addn of 5 mL working std soln, **43.032**, or 5 mL Assay Sample Soln, **43.033**. After addn of working std soln or Assay Sample Soln, gently swirl each tube until most of salt is dissolved. Measure fluorescence of isobutanol exts as in **43.029**, and calc. thiamine.HCl content as in **43.030**.

Alternative blank reading.—Use following technic on samples giving extremely high blank readings with 15% NaOH soln: After reading fluorescence of all tubes, add 1 drop (0.05 mL) HCl (1+1) to each tube of isobutanol ext from oxidized Assay and

Std Solns, swirl, and take addnl reading. This quenches thiochrome fluorescence and provides blank reading for each tube. Use av. values obtained for Std and Assay Solns in place of *b* and *d* in **43.030**.

Thiamine in Bread (*7*)—Official Final Action

43.035 ***Reagents and Apparatus***

Use reagents and app. as in **43.024** and following:

(**a**) *Thiamine hydrochloride working soln.*—1 μg/mL. Pipet 20 mL thiamine.HCl intermediate soln, **43.024(o)**(*2*), into 200 mL vol. flask and dil. to vol. with ca 0.1*N* HCl. Prep. fresh daily.

(**b**) *Procedural std soln.*—Pipet 40 mL working soln, (**a**), into one of the acid digestion containers, dil. to ca 150 mL with ca 0.1*N* HCl, and continue as under sample treatment (1 mL = 0.2 μg thiamine.HCl in final vol.). (To be used for recovery experiments to test efficiency of method.)

(**c**) *Direct std soln.*—0.2 μg/mL. Pipet 40 mL working soln, (**a**), into 200 mL vol. flask, add ca 16 mL H_2O, and dil. to vol. with eluting acid KCl soln, **43.024(h)**.

43.036 ***Acid and Enzyme Digestions***

Weigh (±0.05 g) amt of air-dried bread, **14.107**, contg ca 40 μg thiamine and transfer to 250 mL digestion flask or centrf. bottle. Add 150 mL ca 0.1*N* HCl, stirring with glass rod to provide homogeneous mixt. with ca ½ of acid and using remainder to wash down side of container. Digest 30 min in boiling H_2O bath. Stir enough to prevent lumping or clotting, especially during first 5–10 min. Cool to room temp. and adjust pH to 4.5 by adding 2*N* NaOAc, **43.024(a)**, using pH meter or bromocresol green indicator, **43.024(b)**, and spot plate; end point should be definitely on blue side of green blue change. Alternatively, use const amt of hydrolyzing acid and previously detd amt of NaOAc soln required to adjust to pH 4.5.

Add 5 mL enzyme soln, **43.024(d)**, mix, warm to 45°, and digest in H_2O bath 1 hr at 45–50°. Stir at 10–15 min intervals. Cool, transfer to 200 mL vol. flask, and dil. to vol. with 0.1*N* HCl. Mix, and filter thru paper known not to adsorb thiamine. (Paper can be tested by comparing filtered and nonfiltered procedural std soln, **43.035(b)**. Ash-free papers have been found satisfactory.) Check pH of filtrate, using bromophenol blue indicator, **43.024(c)**, and spot plate, or pH meter (should be ca 3.5 for subsequent base-exchange sepn), and purify as in **43.027**.

43.037 ***Oxidation of Thiamine to Thiochrome***

Pipet duplicate 5 mL aliquots of direct std soln, **43.035(c)**, and duplicate 5 mL aliquots of Assay Sample Soln into ca 40 mL tubes or reaction vessels, and proceed as in **43.028**.

43.038 ***Thiochrome Fluorescence Measurement***

Thiamine content of oxidized Assay Soln is detd by comparing intensity of fluorescence of ext of this soln with that from oxidized direct std soln, **43.035(c)**, correcting for blank fluorescence of each of these solns. Intensity of fluorescence is linear in range 0–2 μg thiamine and may be measured with fluorometer as in **43.029**.

Correct for blank of Assay Solns giving extremely high blank fluorescence readings with 15% NaOH soln by alternative technic, **43.034**.

$$\text{mg Thiamine.HCl/lb (fresh basis)} = (I/B) \times (40 \times 454 \times F/W \times 1000),$$

if specified aliquots have been used, where I = corrected reading of assay soln; B = corrected reading of std soln; W = g air-dried bread sample; and F = air-dry wt:fresh wt ratio.

Riboflavin (Vitamin B_2) (*8*)

Fluorometric Method—Official Final Action

43.039 ***Apparatus***

Photofluorometer.—Use fluorometer suitable for accurately measuring fluorescence of solns contg riboflavin in concns of 0.05–0.2 μg/mL. Input filter of narrow *T* range with max. ca 440 nm and output filter of narrow *T* range with max. ca 565 nm have been found satisfactory.

43.040 ***Reagents***

(Do not shake std solns stored under toluene.)

(**a**) *Riboflavin std solns.*—(*1*) *Stock soln.*—100 μg/mL. Dissolve 50 mg USP Riboflavin Ref. Std, previously dried and stored in dark in desiccator over P_2O_5, in 0.02*N* HOAc to make 500 mL. (To facilitate soln, warm with ca 300 mL 0.02*N* HOAc on steam bath with constant stirring until dissolved, cool, and add 0.02*N* HOAc to make 500 mL.) Store under toluene at ca 10°.

(*2*) *Intermediate soln.*—10 μg/mL. Dil. 100 mL stock soln to 1 L with 0.02*N* HOAc. Store under toluene at ca 10°.

(*3*) *Working soln I.*—1 μg/mL. Dil. 10 mL intermediate soln to 100 mL with H_2O. Prep. fresh for each assay. Use as std soln in **43.042**.

(*4*) *Working soln II.*—0.1 μg/mL. Dil. 10 mL intermediate soln to 1 L with H_2O. Prep. fresh for each assay. Use as std soln in **43.043**.

(**b**) *Sodium hydrosulfite.*—High purity and stored to avoid undue exposure to light and air. Check suitability as follows: To each of ≥2 tubes add 10 mL H_2O and 1 mL std riboflavin soln contg 20 μg/mL, and proceed as in **43.042** with respect to addn of HOAc, $KMnO_4$ soln, and H_2O_2 soln. Then when 8 mg $Na_2S_2O_4$ is added with mixing, riboflavin should be completely reduced in ≤5 sec.

(**c**) *Extraction soln.*—Mix 300 mL MeOH, 100 mL pyridine, 100 mL H_2O, and 10 mL HOAc. (Proportionate amts may be prepd.)

43.041 ***Preparation of Sample Solution***

(Thruout all stages, protect solns from undue exposure to light and keep at pH <7.0. Where directed to filter thru paper, use paper known not to adsorb riboflavin (ash-free papers have been found satisfactory).)

Place measured amt of sample in suitable size flask and proceed by one of following methods:

(**a**) *For dry or semidry materials containing no appreciable amount of basic substances.*—Add vol. 0.1*N* HCl equal in mL to ≥10 times dry wt sample in g; resulting soln must contain ≤0.1 mg riboflavin/mL. If material is not readily sol., comminute so that it may be evenly dispersed in liq. Then agitate vigorously and wash down sides of flask with 0.1*N* HCl.

Heat mixt. in autoclave 30 min at 121–123° and cool. If lumping occurs, agitate until particles are evenly dispersed. Adjust, with vigorous agitation, to pH 6.0–6.5 with NaOH soln; then immediately add dil. HCl until no further pptn occurs (usually ca pH 4.5, isoelec. point of many proteins).

Dil. mixt. to measured vol. contg >0.1 μg riboflavin/mL and filter thru paper. (In case of mixt. difficult to filter, centrfg and/or filtering thru fritted glass, using suitable anal. filter-aid, may often be substituted for, or may precede, filtering thru paper. Ash-free filter paper pulp and Celite Analytical Filter-Aid have been found satisfactory.) Take aliquot of clear filtrate and check for dissolved protein by adding dropwise, first dil. HCl, and if no ppt forms, then, with vigorous agitation, NaOH soln, and proceed as follows:

(*1*) If no further pptn occurs, add, with vigorous agitation,

NaOH soln to pH 6.8, dil. soln to final measured vol. contg ca 0.1 μg riboflavin/mL, and if cloudiness occurs, filter again.

(*2*) If further pptn occurs, adjust soln again to point of max. pptn, dil. to measured vol. contg >0.1 μg riboflavin/mL, and then filter. Take aliquot of clear filtrate and proceed as in (*1*).

If riboflavin content of sample is so low that these requirements cannot be met, conc. clear filtrate obtained at ca pH 4.5 to suitable vol. with heat under reduced pressure. Filter if necessary and proceed as in (*1*).

(b) *For dry or semidry materials containing appreciable amounts of basic substances.*—Adjust mixt. to pH 5.0–6.0 with dil. HCl. Add amt of H_2O such that total vol. liq. is equal in mL to ≥10 times dry wt sample in g. (Resulting soln must contain ≤0.1 mg riboflavin/mL.) Then add equiv. of 1.0 mL 10*N* HCl/100 mL liq. and proceed as in **(a)**, beginning with second sentence.

(c) *For liquid materials.*—Adjust pH to 5.0–6.0 with dil. HCl or, with vigorous agitation, NaOH soln, and proceed as in **(b)**, beginning with second sentence.

(d) *For concentrates, premixes, and multivitamin supplements.*—Place measured amt of sample in flask and add vol. extn soln equal in mL to ≥10 times dry wt sample in g; resulting soln must contain ≤0.1 mg riboflavin/mL. If sample is not readily sol., comminute so that it may be dispersed evenly in liq. Then agitate vigorously and wash down sides of flask with extn soln.

Reflux mixt. 1 hr and cool. If lumping occurs, agitate mixt. until particles are dispersed evenly. Dil. mixt. to measured vol. with extn soln and let any undissolved particles settle, or filter or centrf., if necessary. Take aliquot of clear soln and dil. with H_2O to measured vol. contg ca 0.1 μg riboflavin/mL and filter if soln is not clear. Proceed with detn, **43.043**.

43.042 ***Determination***

To each of ≥4 tubes (or reaction vessels) add 10 mL sample soln. (If fluorometer is type that requires tubular cuvets, all reactions may be carried out in matched set of these cuvets.) To each of ≥2 tubes add 1 mL std riboflavin working soln I, **(a)**(*3*), and mix, and to each of ≥2 remaining tubes, add 1 mL H_2O and mix. To each tube add 1 mL HOAc and mix; add, with mixing, 0.5 mL 4.0% $KMnO_4$ soln (vol. may be increased for sample solns that contain excess of oxidizable material, but ≤0.5 mL in excess of that required to complete oxidn of foreign material should be added). Let stand 2 min; then to each tube add, with mixing, 0.5 mL 3.0% H_2O_2 soln; permanganate color must be destroyed within 10 sec. Shake vigorously until excess O is expelled. If gas bubbles remain on sides of tubes after foaming stops, remove by tipping tubes so that soln flows slowly from end to end.

In fluorometer, measure fluorescence (X) of sample soln contg 1 mL added std riboflavin working soln I. Next, measure fluorescence (B) of sample soln contg 1 mL added H_2O. Add, with mixing, 20 mg *powd* $Na_2S_2O_4$ to ≥2 tubes, measure min. fluorescence (C) within 5 sec. Calc. on basis of aliquots taken as follows:

mg Riboflavin/mL final sample soln

$$= [(B - C)/(X - B)] \times 0.10 \times 0.001.$$

(Value of $(B - C)/(X - B)$ must be ≥0.66 and ≤1.5.)

Note: Quantity of $Na_2S_2O_4$ appreciably >20 mg may reduce foreign pigments and/or foreign fluorescing substances, thereby causing erroneous results.

43.043 ***Alternative Determination—Official Final Action***

(Applicable to high potency samples)

Add 10 mL sample soln to ≥2 cuvets. Add 10 mL working std soln II, **(a)**(*4*), to each of another set of ≥2 cuvets. Add 1 mL HOAc to each tube and mix. Measure fluorescence of sample and std solns in fluorometer. Add, with mixing, 20 mg *powd* $Na_2S_2O_4$ to 1 tube each of std and sample and measure min. fluorescence within 5 sec. Calc. on basis of aliquots taken as follows:

mg Riboflavin/mL final sample soln

$$= [(I - Q)/(I' - Q')] \times (0.1 \times 0.001),$$

where I and I' = fluorescence intensities of sample and std, resp., and Q and Q' = fluorescences of sample and std, resp., after $Na_2S_2O_4$ addn.

Niacin (Nicotinic Acid) and Niacinamide (Nicotinamide)
Official Final Action

Colorimetric Method (9)

43.044 ***Reagents***

(a) *Niacin std solns.*—(*1*) *Stock soln.*—100 μg/mL. Dissolve 50 mg USP Niacin Ref. Std, previously dried and stored in dark in desiccator over P_2O_5, in 25% alcohol to make 500 mL. Store at ca 10°.

(*2*) *Working soln I.*—10 μg/mL. Remove small portion stock soln and let come to room temp. Dil. 10 mL to 100 mL with H_2O. Use as std soln in **43.045(c)**.

(*3*) *Working soln II.*—4 μg/mL. Dil. 2 mL stock soln, allowed to come to room temp. as in (*2*), to 50 mL with H_2O. Use as std soln in **43.045(b)** and **43.046(a)**.

(b) *Dilute ammonium hydroxide.*—Dil. 5 mL NH_4OH to 250 mL with H_2O.

(c) *Dilute hydrochloric acid.*—1 + 5.

(d) *Phosphate buffer soln.*—pH 8. Dissolve 60 g $Na_2HPO_4.7H_2O$ and 10 g KH_2PO_4 in warm H_2O and dil. to 200 mL.

(e) *Cyanogen bromide soln.*—10%. Prep. under hood. Warm 370 mL H_2O to 40° in large flask and add 40 g CNBr. Shake until dissolved, cool, and dil. to 400 mL. Do not let CNBr or soln come in contact with skin. Store in refrigerator.

(f) *10% Sulfanilic acid soln.*—Add NH_4OH in 1 mL portions to mixt. of 20 g sulfanilic acid and 170 mL H_2O until acid dissolves. Adjust to pH 4.5 with HCl (1+1), using bromocresol green indicator, **43.024(b)**, and spot plate. Dil. to 200 mL. Soln should be almost colorless. Use in **43.046(a)**.

(g) *55% Sulfanilic acid soln.*—Add 27 mL H_2O and 27 mL NH_4OH to 55 g sulfanilic acid and shake until dissolved, warming if necessary. Adjust to pH 7 with few drops NH_4OH or 5*N* HCl and dil. to 100 mL. Store in dark. Use in **43.046(b)**.

43.045 ***Preparation of Sample and Standards***

(a) *Pharmaceutical preparations.*—Disperse ≥5 tablets or capsules in small vol. H_2O with heat. Tablets may be ground first. Cool, transfer to vol. flask, and dil. to vol. Soln should contain 50–200 μg niacin/mL. Pipet 10 mL aliquot into 250 mL erlenmeyer and add 10 mL HCl. Evap. on hot plate to ca 2 mL, cool, add ca 25–50 mL H_2O, and adjust to pH 2.5–4.5 with 40% NaOH or KOH soln. Transfer to vol. flask of such size that soln contains ca 4 μg niacin/mL. Filter, if necessary, discarding first 10 mL filtrate. Proceed as in **43.046(a)**.

(b) *Noncereal foods and feeds.*—Weigh 1 oz (28.35 g) sample into 1 L erlenmeyer, add 200 mL 1*N* H_2SO_4, mix, and heat 30 min in autoclave at 15 lb (104 kPa) pressure. Cool, adjust to pH 4.5 with 10*N* NaOH, using bromocresol green as outside indicator, dil. to 250 mL with H_2O, and filter. Weigh 17g $(NH_4)_2SO_4$ into 50 mL vol. flask, pipet in 40 mL sample soln, dil. to vol. with H_2O, and shake vigorously. Filter, mix well, and use 1 mL for color development. In case of samples contg 16 mg niacin/lb, final soln contains 3.2 μg/mL.

Pipet 40 mL working soln II, (**a**)(*3*), into 17 g $(NH_4)_2SO_4$ in 50 mL vol. flask, and dil. to vol. with H_2O. This std contains 3.2 μg/mL. Proceed as in **43.046(a)**.

(**c**) *Cereal products.*—Run 1 reagent blank and 5 levels of working soln I, (**a**)(*2*), with samples thruout detn.

Place 1.5 g $Ca(OH)_2$ into each of six 250 mL erlenmeyers. From pipet add 0, 5, 10, 15, 20, and 25 mL working soln I, resp. Accurately weigh ca 2.5 g sample contg ca 100 μg niacin into another flask contg ca 1.5 g $Ca(OH)_2$. To all flasks add H_2O to ca 90 mL, shake to mix, and autoclave 2 hr at 15 lb (104 kPa) pressure. Mix thoroly while still hot. Cool to ca 40°, transfer to 100 mL vol. flasks, and dil. to vol. (When necessary, sample may be stored in refrigerator few days.)

Transfer ca 50 mL supernate from each vol. flask to sep. centrf. tubes and place in ice bath 15 min or in refrigerator ≥2 hr. Centrf. 15 min and pipet 20 mL supernate from each tube into sep. centrf. tubes contg 8 g $(NH_4)_2SO_4$ and 2 mL phosphate buffer soln. Shake to dissolve and warm to 55–60°. Centrf. 5 min and filter thru Whatman No. 12 paper, or equiv., refiltering if necessary to obtain clear soln. Proceed as in **43.046(b)**.

43.046 *Determination*

(**a**) *For pharmaceutical preparations and noncereal foods and feeds.*—Add 10% sulfanilic acid soln, (**f**), and CNBr soln under hood from burets or pipets filled by mech. suction. (*Caution: CNBr is toxic.*) Use working soln II, (**a**)(*3*). Prep. tubes as follows:

Standard Blank	*Sample Blank*
1.0 mL std soln	1.0 mL sample soln
5.0 mL H_2O	5.0 mL H_2O
0.5 mL dil. NH_4OH	0.5 mL dil. NH_4OH
2.0 mL 10% sulfanilic acid	2.0 mL 10% sulfanilic acid
0.5 mL dil. HCl	0.5 mL dil. HCl

Standard Soln	*Sample Soln*
1.0 mL std soln	1.0 mL sample soln
0.5 mL dil. NH_4OH	0.5 mL dil. NH_4OH
5.0 mL CNBr	5.0 mL CNBr
2.0 mL 10% sulfanilic acid	2.0 mL 10% sulfanilic acid
0.5 mL H_2O	0.5 mL H_2O

Prep. sep. sample blank for each sample.

Pipet std soln and sample soln into respective tubes; add 5 mL H_2O for std blank and sample blank. Add all subsequent solns to single tube and read color before proceeding with next tube. Starting with std blank, swirl tube to impart rotary motion in liq., immediately add dil. NH_4OH, swirl again, add sulfanilic acid, and swirl. Immediately add 0.5 mL dil. HCl, mix again, place in photoelec. colorimeter, and adjust instrument to 0 *A* at any specific wavelength between 430 and 450 nm within ca 30 sec after addn of sulfanilic acid soln. Treat std soln in same way as std blank with respect to addn of dil. NH_4OH. Immediately swirl tube, add CNBr soln, and swirl again. At 30 sec after addn of CNBr soln, swirl tube, add sulfanilic acid soln, and swirl again. Immediately add 0.5 mL H_2O, mix again, and stopper. With instrument set at 0 *A* for std blank, as above, read *A* of std soln at max. (Color reaches max. in ca 1.5 min after addn of sulfanilic acid soln, remains at peak ca 2 min, and then fades slowly.)

With sample blank set at 0 *A*, det. *A* of sample soln similarly. Niacin content is proportional to *A* if std and sample solns are ca same concn.

(**b**) *For cereal products.*—In each of 2 tubes place 5 mL std and in each of 2 addnl tubes place 5 mL sample soln. In addnl tube to be used as reagent blank, place 5 mL H_2O. To one std tube and one sample tube to be used as their respective blanks, add 10 mL H_2O. Let all tubes stand 30 min in bath of finely crushed ice, preferably in refrigerator. To remaining sample and std tubes and to reagent blank, consecutively add 10 mL cold CNBr, followed in 30 sec by 1.0 mL 55% sulfanilic acid soln, (**g**). Mix immediately after addn of each reagent (most conveniently done by swirling), and stopper tubes contg CNBr. Replace all tubes in ice bath. To std and sample blank add 1.0 mL 55% sulfanilic acid soln.

Set colorimeter to 0 *A* at 470 nm with std blank, and read *A* of other tubes 12–15 min after addn of sulfanilic acid. Tubes must be cooled uniformly and each tube must be wiped dry just before placing in colorimeter. If tubes fog, dip momentarily in hot H_2O and wipe before reading.

Plot std curve of *A* of std minus that of reagent blank against niacin concn in μg/mL, drawing straight line of best fit. From this line read concn, *C*, corresponding to *A* of sample corrected for sample blank and reagent blank.

$$\text{mg Niacin/100 g sample} = C/(10 \times \text{g sample}).$$

Automated Method (10)—Official Final Action

43.047 *Principle*

Niacin and niacinamide are extd from cereal products with $Ca(OH)_2$. Pyridine groups are cleaved by CNBr and reacted with sulfanilic acid to form yellow complex whose *A* is read at 470 nm.

43.048 *Apparatus and Reagents*

(**a**) *Automatic analyzer.*—AutoAnalyzer AAII with following modules (Technicon Instruments Corp.): Sampler IV, proportioning pump, colorimeter with 470 nm filters, recorder, and manifold No. 116-D137. *See* Fig. **43:01**.

(**b**) *Cyanogen bromide soln.*—10%. See **43.044(e)**.

(**c**) *Phosphate buffer soln I.*—pH 8. *See* **43.044(d)**.

(**d**) *Phosphate buffer soln II.*—pH 8. Dissolve 60 g $Na_2HPO_4.7H_2O$ and 10 g KH_2PO_4 in warm H_2O and dil. to 2 L. Add 1 mL Brij-35 (Technicon Instruments Corp. No. T21-0110) and mix.

(**e**) *Sulfanilic acid soln.*—10%. Add 100 g sulfanilic acid to beaker contg 500 mL H_2O. Mix on mag. stirrer and slowly add NH_4OH until acid dissolves (ca 40 mL). Adjust to pH 7 with HCl (1+3) and dil. to 1 L.

(**f**) *Niacin std solns.*—(*1*) *Stock soln.*—100 μg/mL. *See* **43.044(a)**(*1*). (*2*) *Working soln.*—25 μg/mL. Remove small portion stock soln and let come to room temp. Dil. 25 mL to 100 mL with H_2O. (*3*) *Calibration soln.*—2.5 μg/mL. Dil. 10 mL working std soln to 100 mL with H_2O.

43.049 *Preparation of Samples and Standards*

Run 4 levels of working std soln with samples thruout detn.

Place 1.5 g $Ca(OH)_2$ into each of four 250 mL erlenmeyers. From pipet add 5, 10, 15, and 20 mL working std soln, resp. Accurately weigh ca 5 g sample contg ca 150–400 μg niacin into another flask contg 1.5 g $Ca(OH)_2$. To all flasks add H_2O to ca 90 mL, shake to mix, and autoclave 2 hr at 15 lb (104 kPa) pressure. Mix thoroly while still hot. Cool to ca 40°, transfer to 100 mL vol. flasks, add 1 drop Brij-35, and dil. to vol. (When necessary, soln may be stored in refrigerator few days.)

Transfer ca 35 mL supernate from each vol. flask to sep. centrf. tubes and place in ice bath 15 min or in refrigerator 2 hr. Centrf. 15 min, pipet 20 mL supernate from each tube into sep. centrf. tubes, add 2 mL phosphate buffer soln I, mix thoroly, and filter thru Whatman No. 2 paper, or equiv.

43.050 ***Determination***

(System should be operated under hood. If this is not possible, take following precautions to minimize CNBr fumes: Remove only portion of CNBr soln from refrigerator (usually 100 mL in 100 mL vol. flask is sufficient). Place tubing (polyethylene preferred) into flask and wrap opening with Al foil. Suspend waste lines from flowcell into 1 L erlenmeyer contg ca 100 mL 25% NaOH soln. Cover opening of flask with wet paper towel.)

Establish steady baseline with all reagents pumping thru system. Adjust 2.5 μg/mL std soln (250 μg/100 mL) to 50 scale units on recorder by using "Std Cal" control on colorimeter. Fill sample cups in following order: stds, samples, and 2.5 μg/mL std soln after every 10 samples. Dialyzer in system results in low blanks for most samples. Det. blank as follows: Place CNBr line into H_2O and flush system free of CNBr (ca 30 min). Keep all other tubing in resp. reagents and "Std Cal" setting locked in position as in analysis. Establish steady baseline and repeat detn on samples and stds in same order as in analysis.

43.051 ***Calculations***

Plot std curve of A (chart units) of std minus blank against niacin concn in μg/mL, drawing line of best fit. Read concn, C, corresponding to A of sample corrected for blank and any shift in baseline during run.

For diln to 100 mL for both samples and stds,

mg Niacin/100 g = $C/(10 \times \text{g sample})$,

where $C = (\mu g/mL) \times 100$.

Niacinamide in Multivitamin Preparations (*11*)
Official Final Action

43.052 ***Principle***

Niacinamide is extd in KH_2PO_4 soln at pH ca 4.5 and allowed to react with CNBr and barbituric acid. Reaction product is measured spectrophtric. Niacin does not interfere unless present at 3 times concn of amide.

43.053 ***Reagents***

(**a**) *Cyanogen bromide soln.*—10%. *See* **43.044**(**e**). Let come to room temp. before use.

(**b**) *Potassium dihydrogen phosphate solns.*—(*1*) 3%. Dissolve and dil. 30 g KH_2PO_4 to 1 L with H_2O. (*2*) *0.3%.*—Dil. soln (*1*) with H_2O (1+9).

(**c**) *Barbituric acid buffered soln.*—Prep. vol. required for each batch of assays by adding 2 g reagent grade barbituric acid to each 100 mL 3% KH_2PO_4 soln. Stir mech. 1 hr and filter before use.

(**d**) *Niacinamide std solns.*—(*1*) *Stock soln.*—250 μg/mL. Dissolve and dil. 50 mg USP Niacinamide Ref. Std to 200 mL with 60% alcohol. Store at ca 10°. (*2*) *Working soln.*—5 μg/mL. Let small portion stock soln warm to room temp. Dil. 2 mL to 100 mL with 0.3% KH_2PO_4 soln.

43.054 ***Preparation of Samples***

Take 5 tablets or capsules or appropriate vol. of liq. for each assay. Grind tablets to fine powder. Place accurately weighed sample in erlenmeyer (for sealed gelatin capsules, add ca 2 mL ethylene chloride to aid dispersion). Add vol. 0.3% KH_2PO_4 soln equal in mL to at least twice mg niacinamide expected. If sample is not readily sol., shake to disperse and heat 15 min in boiling H_2O bath or in autoclave at 15 lb (104 kPa) pressure. Dil. to ca 5 μg/mL with 0.3% KH_2PO_4 soln. Filter if necessary.

43.055 ***Determination***

Prep. sep. sample blank for each sample by replacing CNBr with H_2O.

To 1 mL working std soln or assay soln in spectrophtr tube, add 0.5 mL CNBr soln, mix, stopper, and let stand 25–30 min. (To avoid standing >30 min when analyzing several samples, allow regular interval of 1–2 min between addns of CNBr.) Add 10 mL barbituric acid soln and swirl. (If barbituric acid soln cannot be added after 30 min, transfer tubes to crushed ice bath to stabilize CNBr reaction.)

Set spectrophtr to 0 A at 550 nm with appropriate blank in which CNBr is replaced by H_2O. Read A of reaction product at max. color development (ca 2–4 min after addn of barbituric acid soln; color remains stable ca 1 min, then fades slowly).

mg Niacinamide in original wt sample taken

$= (A \times 5 \times \text{diln factor})/(A' \times 1000)$,

where A and A' refer to sample and std soln, resp., and 5 = μg

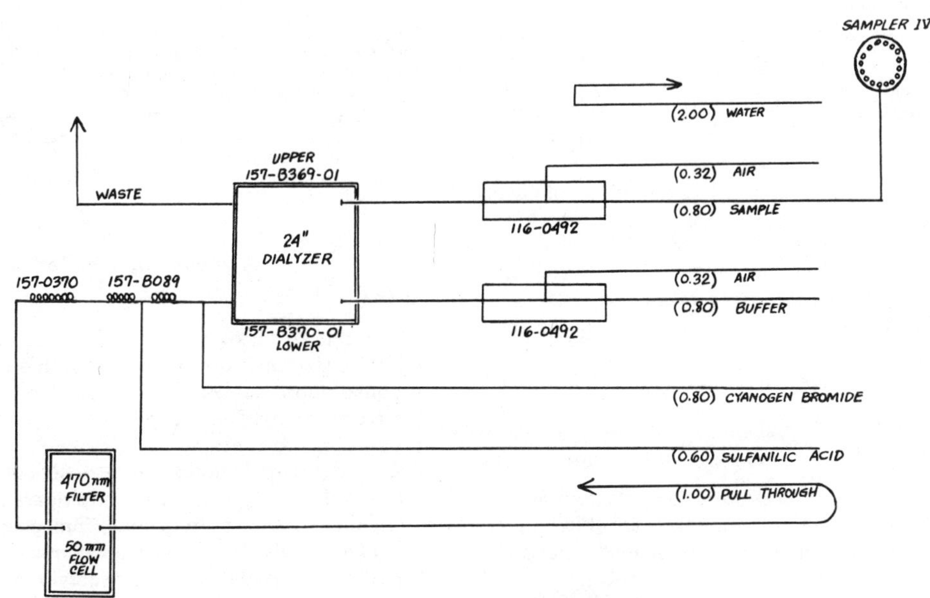

FIG. 43:01—Flow diagram for automated analysis for niacin and niacinamide

niacinamide/mL working std soln. Report mg niacinamide/tablet, capsule, or g or mL of liq.

Vitamin C (Ascorbic Acid)—Official Final Action

2,6-Dichloroindophenol Method (12)

(Applicable to detn of reduced ascorbic acid. Not applicable in presence of ferrous Fe, stannous Sn, cuprous Cu, SO_2, sulfite, or thiosulfate. *See Note.*)

43.056 ***Principle***

Ascorbic acid reduces oxidn-reduction indicator dye, 2,6-dichloroindophenol, to colorless soln. At end point, excess unreduced dye is rose pink in acid soln. Vitamin is extd and titrn performed in presence of HPO_3-HOAc or HPO_3-HOAc-H_2SO_4 soln to maintain proper acidity for reaction and to avoid autoxidn of ascorbic acid at high pH.

43.057 ***Reagents***

(**a**) *Extracting solns.*—(*1*) *Metaphosphoric acid-acetic acid soln.*—Dissolve, with shaking, 15 g HPO_3 pellets or freshly pulverized stick HPO_3 in 40 mL HOAc and 200 mL H_2O; dil. to ca 500 mL, and filter rapidly thru fluted paper into g-s bottle. (HPO_3 slowly changes to H_3PO_4, but if stored in refrigerator, soln remains satisfactory 7–10 days.) (*2*) *Metaphosphoric acid-acetic acid-sulfuric acid soln.*—Proceed as in (*1*), except use 0.3*N* H_2SO_4 in place of H_2O.

(**b**) *Ascorbic acid std soln.*—1 mg/mL. Accurately weigh 50 mg USP Ascorbic Acid Ref. Std that has been stored in desiccator away from direct sunlight. Transfer to 50 mL vol. flask. Dil. to vol. *immediately before use* with HPO_3-HOAc soln, (**a**)(*1*).

(**c**) *Indophenol std soln.*—Dissolve 50 mg 2,6-dichloroindophenol Na salt (Eastman Kodak Co. No. 3463), that has been stored in desiccator over soda lime, in 50 mL H_2O to which has been added 42 mg $NaHCO_3$; shake vigorously, and when dye dissolves, dil. to 200 mL with H_2O. Filter thru fluted paper into amber g-s bottle. Keep stoppered, out of direct sunlight, and store in refrigerator. (Decomposition products that make end point indistinct occur in some batches of dry indophenol and also develop with time in stock soln. Add 5.0 mL extg soln contg excess ascorbic acid to 15 mL dye reagent. If reduced soln is not practically colorless, discard, and prep. new stock soln. If dry dye is at fault, obtain new supply.)

Transfer three 2.0 mL aliquots ascorbic acid std soln to each of three 50 mL erlenmeyers contg 5.0 mL HPO_3-HOAc soln, (**a**)(*1*). Titr. rapidly with indophenol soln from 50 mL buret until light but distinct rose pink persists $\geq$5 sec. (Each titrn should require ca 15 mL indophenol soln, and titrns should check within 0.1 mL.) Similarly titr. 3 blanks composed of 7.0 mL HPO_3-HOAc soln, (**a**)(*1*), plus vol. H_2O ca equal to vol. indophenol soln used in direct titrns. After subtracting av. blanks (usually ca 0.1 mL) from stdzn titrns, calc. and express concn of indophenol soln as mg ascorbic acid equiv. to 1.0 mL reagent. Stdze indophenol soln daily with freshly prepd ascorbic acid std soln.

(**d**) *Thymol blue pH indicator.*—0.04%. Dissolve 0.1 g indicator by triturating in agate mortar with 10.75 mL 0.02*N* NaOH and dil. to 250 mL with H_2O. Transition range: 1.2 (red)–2.8 (yellow).

43.058 ***Preliminary Test for Appreciable Amount of Basic Substances***

Grind representative sample or express contents from capsule and add ca 25 mL HPO_3-HOAc soln, (**a**)(*1*). Test pH by placing drop thymol blue pH indicator on pestle or by using spot plate. (pH >1.2 indicates appreciable amts of basic substances.) For liq. prepns, dil. representative sample ca two-fold with HPO_3-HOAc soln, (**a**)(*1*), before testing with indicator.

43.059 ***Preparation of Sample Assay Solution***

(**a**) *For dry materials containing no appreciable amount of basic substances.*—Pulverize sample by gentle grinding, add HPO_3-HOAc soln, (**a**)(*1*), and triturate until sample is in suspension. Dil. with HPO_3-HOAc soln, (**a**)(*1*), to measured vol. Designate this vol. as *V* mL.

(Use ca 10 mL extg soln/g dry sample. Final soln should contain 10–100 mg ascorbic acid/100 mL.)

(**b**) *For dry materials containing appreciable amounts of basic substances.*—Pulverize sample by gentle grinding, add HPO_3-HOAc-H_2SO_4 soln, (**a**)(*2*), to adjust pH to ca 1.2, and triturate until sample is in suspension. Dil. with HPO_3-HOAc soln, (**a**)(*1*), to measured vol. Designate this vol. as *V* mL.

(Use ca 10 mL extg soln/g dry sample. Final soln should contain 10–100 mg ascorbic acid/100 mL.)

(**c**) *For liquid materials.*—Take amt of sample contg ca 100 mg ascorbic acid. If appreciable amts of basic substances are present, adjust pH to ca 1.2 with HPO_3-HOAc-H_2SO_4 soln, (**a**)(*2*). Dil. with HPO_3-HOAc soln, (**a**)(*1*), to measured vol. contg 10–100 mg ascorbic acid/100 mL. Designate this vol. as *V* mL.

(**d**) *For fruit and vegetable juices.*—Prep. juice as in **22.008**(**a**). Add aliquots of $\geq$100 mL prepd juice to equal vols of HPO_3-HOAc soln, (**a**)(*1*). Designate total vol. as *V* mL. Mix, and filter thru rapid folded paper (Eaton-Dikeman No. 195, 18.5 cm, or equiv.).

43.060 ***Determination***

Titr. 3 sample aliquots each contg ca 2 mg ascorbic acid and make blank detns for correction of titrns as in **43.057**(**c**), using proper vols of HPO_3-HOAc soln, (**a**)(*1*), and H_2O. If ca 2 mg ascorbic acid is contained in sample aliquot <7 mL, add HPO_3-HOAc soln to give 7 mL for titrn.

mg Ascorbic acid/g, tablet, mL, etc. = $(X - B) \times (F/E) \times (V/Y)$,

where X = av. mL for sample titrn, B = av. mL for sample blank titrn, F = mg ascorbic acid equiv. to 1.0 mL indophenol std soln, E = number of g, tablets, mL, etc. assayed, V = vol. initial assay soln, and Y = vol. sample aliquot titrated.

Note: Products contg ferrous Fe, stannous Sn, and cuprous Cu give values in excess of their actual ascorbic acid content by this method. Following are simple tests to det. whether these reducing ions are present in such amts as to invalidate test: Add 2 drops *0.05% aq. soln of methylene blue* to 10 mL freshly prepd mixt. (1+1) of sample soln and HPO_3-HOAc reagent and mix. Disappearance of methylene blue color in 5–10 sec indicates presence of interfering substances. Stannous Sn does not give this test and may be tested for as follows: To another 10 mL sample soln to which 10 mL HCl (1+3) has been added, add 5 drops *0.05% aq. soln of indigo carmine* and mix. Disappearance of color in 5–10 sec indicates presence of stannous Sn or other interfering substance.

Microfluorometric Method (13)

43.061 ***Principle***

Ascorbic acid is oxidized to dehydroascorbic acid in presence of Norit. Oxidized form is reacted with *o*-phenylenediamine to produce fluorophor having activation max. at ca 350 nm and fluorescence max. at ca 430 nm. Fluorescence intensity is proportional to concn.

Development of fluorescent derivative of vitamin is prevented by forming H_3BO_3-dehydroascorbic acid complex prior to addn of diamine soln. Any remaining fluorescence is due to extraneous materials. This serves as "blank."

Ascorbic plus dehydroascorbic acid is calcd by comparing corrected fluorescence reading for sample with that of std similarly oxidized and treated.

43.062 ***Reagents***

(**a**) *Extracting solns.*—Prep.: (*1*) HPO_3-HOAc and (*2*) HPO_3-HOAc-H_2SO_4 solns as in **43.057(a)**.

(**b**) *Ascorbic acid std soln.*—100 μg/mL. Dil. 10 mL ascorbic acid std soln, **43.057(b)**, to 100 mL with HPO_3-HOAc soln, (**a**)(*1*).

(**c**) *o-Phenylenediamine soln.*—For each 100 mL soln required, weigh 20 mg *o*-phenylenediamine.2HCl (Eastman Kodak Co. No. 678). Dil. to vol. with H_2O immediately before use.

(**d**) *Thymol blue pH indicator.*—Prep. as in **43.057(d)**.

(**e**) *Sodium acetate soln.*—Dissolve 500 g $NaOAc.3H_2O$ in H_2O and dil. to 1 L.

(**f**) *Boric acid-sodium acetate soln.*—Dissolve 3 g H_3BO_3 in 100 mL NaOAc soln. Prep. fresh for each assay.

(**g**) *Acid-washed Norit.*—Add 1 L HCl (1+9) to 200 g Norit Neutral (Fisher Scientific Co., Carbon, decolorizing, C-170), heat to bp, and filter with vac. Remove cake to large beaker. Add 1 L H_2O, stir, and filter. Repeat washing with H_2O and filtering. Dry overnight at 110–120°.

43.063 ***Apparatus***

(**a**) *Automatic pipetting machine.*—Brewer, BBL Div. of Bioquest, or equiv. Calibrate to deliver 5 mL aliquots.

(**b**) *Vortex mixer.*—Scientific Industries, Inc., 70 Orville Dr, Bohemia, NY 11716, or equiv.

(**c**) *Fluorometer.*—Aminco Fluoro-Microphotometer (American Instrument Co.) with lamp F4T4/BL and cuvet adapter B12-63019 to accept 18 × 150 mm test tubes, or equiv. Use as primary filter Corning Glass Works Nos. 7380 (C.S. No. 0-52) and 5860 (C.S. No. 7-37) and as secondary filter Corning Nos. 5113 (C.S. No. 5-58) and 3389 (C.S. No. 3-73). (*Caution: See* **51.008**.)

(**d**) *Fluorescence reading tubes.*—Stdzd 18 × 150 mm test tubes.

43.064 ***Preliminary Test for Appreciable Amount of Basic Substances***

Proceed as in **43.058**.

43.065 ***Preparation of Sample Assay Solution***

(**a**) *For dry materials containing no appreciable amount of basic substances.*—Proceed as in **43.059(a)**. Dil. with HPO_3-HOAc soln, **43.057(a)**(*1*), to ca 100 μg ascorbic acid/mL. Designate this vol. as *V* mL. Filter solns contg large amts of suspended solids thru Whatman No. 12 paper, or equiv. Designate as sample assay soln.

(**b**) *For dry materials containing appreciable amounts of basic substances.*—Proceed as in **43.059(b)**. Then proceed as in (**a**), beginning "Dil. with . . ."

(**c**) *For liquid materials.*—Proceed as in **43.059(c)**. Then proceed as in (**a**), beginning "Dil. with . . ."

(**d**) *For gelatin-encapsulated pharmaceutical products.*—Place sample in small beaker and heat gently with enough proper extg soln, **43.057(a)**(*1*) or (*2*), to cover. If capsules do not disintegrate readily, crush with glass rod. Cool rapidly to room temp. If appreciable amts of basic substances are present, adjust pH to ca 1.2 with HPO_3-HOAc-H_2SO_4 soln, **43.057(a)**(*2*). Proceed as in (**a**), beginning "Dil. with . . ."

Note: For samples difficult to filter, proceed as in applicable section, (**a**), (**b**), (**c**), or (**d**), except dil. sample assay soln with HPO_3-HOAc soln to ca 50 μg ascorbic acid/mL. Compare with std soln prepd by dilg 5 mL ascorbic acid std soln, **43.057(b)**, to 100 mL with HPO_3-HOAc soln. (1 mL = 50 μg ascorbic acid.)

43.066 ***Determination***

Following steps must be performed consecutively without delay.

Transfer 100 mL std and sample assay solns to 300 mL erlenmeyers. Add 2 g acid-washed Norit, shake vigorously, and filter thru Whatman No. 12 paper, or equiv., discarding first few mL. Transfer 5 mL each filtrate to sep. 100 mL vol. flasks, contg 5 mL H_3BO_3-NaOAc soln. Let stand 15 min, swirling occasionally. Designate as std or sample blank solns, resp.

During 15 min period, transfer 5 mL of each filtrate to sep. 100 mL vol. flasks contg 5 mL NaOAc soln and ca 75 mL H_2O. Dil. to vol. with H_2O. Transfer 2 mL of each soln to each of 3 fluorescence reading tubes. Designate as std or sample tubes, resp.

At appropriate time, dil. blank solns to vol. with H_2O. Transfer 2 mL of these solns to each of 3 fluorescence reading tubes. Designate as std or sample blank tubes, resp.

Using automatic pipetting machine, add 5 mL *o*-phenylenediamine soln to all tubes. Use Vortex mixer to swirl tubes. Protect from light and let stand 35 min at room temp.

43.067 ***Fluorometry***

Measure fluorescence of std tube (*C*), std blank tube (*B*), sample tube (*X*), and sample blank tube (*D*).

mg Ascorbic acid/g, tablet, mL, etc.

$$= [(\text{av. } X - \text{av. } D)/(\text{av. } C - \text{av. } B)] \times (20 \times S \times V/E),$$

where V = initial assay soln vol., E = number of g, tablets, mL, etc., and S = concn of std in mg/mL added to reading tube.

Vitamin D (*14*)—Official Final Action

(Avoid exposure of solns to actinic light thruout entire detn)

43.068 ***Principle***

Specific steps required depend upon whether prepn contains oils or not, if other fat-sol. vitamins are present, and concn of vitamin D, as shown in Table **43:01**.

(**a**) *Vitamin D concentrates without other vitamins.*—Prepn is saponified and extd, and unsaponifiable material is treated with maleic anhydride to remove *trans*-isomers; however, certain other antirachitic-inactive isomers such as isotachysterol, if present, are not removed and are included in result. (Resin is treated directly with maleic anhydride without previous saponification and extn.) After maleic anhydride treatment, soln is reacted with $SbCl_3$ and *A* is detd at 500 nm. By confirmation

Table 43:01 Scheme for Analysis of Preparations of Vitamin D With and Without Other Fat-Soluble Vitamins[a]

Prepns	IU/g	Steps for prepns without other vitamins	Steps for prepns contg vitamin A and tocopherols
Oily solns	500–100,000 ≥100,000	A + E + I A + I	A + E + F + H
Powders, capsules, tablets, and aq. dispersions	200–25,000 ≥25,000	B + E + I B + I	B + E + F + H
Vitamin D resin	≥20,000,000	C + G + I	

[a] All assays except vitamin D resin include diln (step D) and, prior to colorimetric detn (steps H or I), maleic anhydride addn (step G).

test, **43.078**, values ≤5% are considered neg. for isotachysterol. (Any appropriate technic for identification of isotachysterol may be used.) Vitamin D concs include vitamin D resins contg ≥20,000,000 IU/g, vitamin D in oily solns contg ≥100,000 IU/g, and vitamin D in powders and aq. dispersions contg ≥25,000 IU/g.

(**b**) *Vitamin D in multivitamin preparations*.—Prepn is saponified and extd, and unsaponifiable material is chromatgd successively on phosphate-treated alumina to remove tocopherols, carotene, and BHT, if present; and on polyethylene glycol 600-Chromosorb W and Florex to sep. vitamin A, if present. Purified sample is treated with maleic anhydride to remove biologically inactive *trans*-isomers. Vitamin D is detd colorimetrically by $SbCl_3$ reaction, modified to correct for interfering decomposition products of vitamin A still present in final soln.

43.069 ***Reagents***

(**a**) *Solvents*.—≥95% Ac_2O, alcohol, toluene-free benzene, peroxide- and acid-free ether, acid-free isooctane, peroxide- and acid-free polyethylene glycol 600, and acid-free toluene.

(**b**) *Petroleum ether*.—Reflux over KOH pellets and collect fraction distg between 40 and 60°. (*Caution: See* **51.011**(**a**).)

(**c**) *Ethyl ether-petroleum ether eluants*.—8 and 30% ether in pet ether.

(**d**) *Ethylene dichloride*.—Nanograde, or purify reagent grade as follows: Reflux 1 L CH_2ClCH_2Cl with 50 g KOH pellets and ca 50 sq cm Al foil 2 hr. Remove KOH and Al. Shake CH_2ClCH_2Cl with 5 g powd P_2O_5 and distil (bp 82°), discarding first 50 mL.

(**e**) *Acetyl chloride*.—Available in ampuls. Soln must be colorless and freshly redistd.

(**f**) *Column chromatography materials*.—(*1*) *Alumina*.—Type 1076 (E. Merck, Darmstadt, Germany). (*2*) *Disodium hydrogen phosphate*.—$Na_2HPO_4.2H_2O$. (*3*) *Diatomaceous earth*.—Acid-washed Chromosorb W, 80–100 mesh (150–180 μm). (*4*) *Granular fuller's earth*.—Florex-XXS (Floridin Co.). Sieve and retain 150–250 μm fraction.

(**g**) *Color-inhibiting soln*.—Isooctane-toluene-Ac_2O (1+1+1).

(**h**) *Sodium ascorbate soln*.—20%. Dissolve 3.5 g ascorbic acid in 20 mL 1*N* NaOH. Prep. fresh daily.

(**i**) *Potassium hydroxide solns*.—3, 6 (w/v), and 50 (w/w)% in H_2O.

(**j**) *Pyrogallol soln*.—20%. Dissolve 20 g in alcohol and dil. to 100 mL with alcohol.

(**k**) *Sodium sulfide soln*.—10%. Dissolve 12 g $Na_2S.9H_2O$ in 20 mL H_2O and dil. to 100 mL with 87% glycerol.

(**l**) *β-Carotene soln*.—0.01% in isooctane.

(**m**) *Maleic anhydride solns*.—(*1*) *Stock soln*.—10%. Dissolve 10 g maleic anhydride (distd, bp 196°) in 100 mL toluene (clear soln, stable ca 1 month). (*2*) *Working soln*.—*1*%. Just before use, dil. aliquot with toluene to obtain 1% soln.

(**n**) *Color reagent*.—(*Caution:* $SbCl_3$ is toxic and corrosive. Avoid contact with skin and eyes and breathing vapor.) Prep. 2 stock solns as follows: (*1*) *Soln A*.—Dissolve ca 110 g $SbCl_3$ (dry, crystalline, and, if necessary, distd) in 400 mL CH_2ClCH_2Cl. Add ca 2 g anhyd. alumina, mix, and filter thru paper into 500 mL vol. flask. Dil. to vol. with CH_2ClCH_2Cl and mix. *A* of soln, detd in 2 cm cell at 500 nm with spectrophtr against CH_2ClCH_2Cl, should be ≤0.070. (*2*) *Soln B*.—Mix under hood 100 mL colorless, distd AcCl and 400 mL CH_2ClCH_2Cl and store in cool place.

Mix 90 mL *Soln A* and 10 mL *Soln B*. Store in brown, g-s bottle, and use in ≤7 days; discard if any color develops.

(**o**) *Vitamin standards*.—USP Ref. Std Ergocalciferol (if sample is labeled as contg vitamin D_2) or cholecalciferol (if sample is labeled as contg vitamin D or D_3). Dissolve ca 25 mg calciferol ref. std, accurately weighed, in 100 mL 20% toluene in isooctane soln contg 0.5 mg butylated hydroxytoluene (BHT)/mL. Soln is stable ≤1 month, if kept in dark at room temp. On day of assay, pipet 2 mL concd std soln into 100 mL vol. flask and dil. to vol. with 20% toluene in isooctane.

(**p**) *Butylated hydroxytoluene* (*BHT*) *Soln*.—0.1% in toluene.

(**q**) *Ethoxyquin soln*.—0.05 mg/mL in pet ether.

43.070 ***Column I***

(**a**) *Chromatographic tube*.—Seal coarse fritted glass disk in lower end of 20 (id) × 150 mm tube and 250 mL bulb at upper end. Fit constricted portion at lower end with Teflon stopcock.

(**b**) *Preparation and deactivation of phosphate-treated alumina*.—Sieve alumina and collect 50–150 μm fraction. Heat 250 g sieved alumina with 1.6 L H_2O and 20 g $Na_2HPO_4.2H_2O$ in 2 L erlenmeyer 30 min on steam bath, swirling occasionally. Cool, swirl gently, and decant upper layer, which sometimes contains suspension of finest particles. Filter residue by suction on paper in buchner. Transfer alumina to 22 cm diam. porcelain disk. Dry in 150° oven 3 hr, mixing occasionally to prevent lumping. Cool disk on asbestos plate in vac. desiccator. Store activated alumina in air-tight (rubber-stoppered) container. Weigh 30 g dried alumina into each of three 100 mL erlenmeyers. Pipet in 0.6, 1.2, and 1.8 mL H_2O into the 3 flasks, resp., and stopper. Heat 5 min on steam bath. Vigorously shake warm flasks until powder is free flowing. Cool, and let stand 15 min.

Prep. 3 columns from the 3 deactivated phosphate-treated alumina portions, as in (**c**). Pipet 5 mL sample soln contg ca 4000 IU vitamin A alcohol in pet ether onto each column, and elute each column in 10 mL portions with 200 mL 8% (v/v) ether-pet ether. Discard eluates. Examine columns under 360 nm UV light with portable lamp. Column thru which green fluorescent vitamin A alcohol band has passed ca ⅓ way contains desired H_2O content in alumina. Elute this column with 150 mL 30% (v/v) ether-pet ether, and examine under 360 nm UV light. Column should not show any fluorescence. Prep. deactivated phosphate-treated alumina with desired H_2O content, and prep. column as in (**c**). Check activity of deactivated phosphate-treated alumina with chosen H_2O content by column performance test, **43.073**. If performance is <97%, repeat deactivation, using different vol. of H_2O. If performance remains <97%, distil pet ether as in **43.069**(**b**).

(**c**) *Preparation of column*.—Add 40 mL pet ether to deactivated alumina, swirl, and transfer to tube, using pet ether. Let packing settle, maintain head of ≥0.5 cm liq. on column thruout assay, and use N to regulate flow rate at 4–5 mL/min. (Phosphate-treated alumina column can be used for only 1 assay.)

43.071 ***Column II***

(**a**) *Chromatographic tube,*—Constrict lower end (ca 5 cm) of 20 (id) × 300 mm tube to 8 mm diam. and insert coarse fritted glass disk at point of constriction. Fit constricted portion with Teflon stopcock.

(**b**) *Preparation of polyethylene glycol 600-Chromosorb W mixture*.—Weigh 10 g polyethylene glycol 600 in 1 L g-s erlenmeyer, and dissolve in 100 mL benzene. Add 20 g acid-washed Chromosorb W and swirl. Add 300 mL pet ether in small portions, and mix by swirling vigorously. Let settle, and decant upper layer. Wash slurry with two 100 mL portions pet ether, decanting upper layer each time.

(**c**) *Preparation of column*.—Connect lower end of tube to aspirator, and fill tube nearly to top with pet ether. Pour small portion of slurry, (**b**), into tube, and let settle by gravity. Pack column by intermittent suction, closing stopcock when 3–4 mL liq. is left on column. Fill tube again with pet ether, and repeat packing, beginning "Pour small portion . . ." Pack column at upper end with disk plunger while effluent keeps running off. Close stopcock when 3–4 mL liq. is left on column. Gently tap tube to make upper layer of column horizontal. Wash column with 100 mL isooctane to elute pet ether. Space under fritted glass disk must be empty. Check packing of column with 1 mL β-carotene soln, which should pass thru column as horizontal band. Otherwise, repeat packing. Check recovery by column performance test, **43.073**, together with Florex column, **43.075(b)** (Florex should have been checked previously as in **43.072(b)**). Use 1000 IU vitamin A alcohol as detector.

When polyethylene glycol 600-Chromosorb W column is dirty and gives poor performance test, wash Chromosorb W with three 200 mL portions alcohol, and decant upper layer. Wash again with two 200 mL portions ether. Evap. to dryness in r-b flask under vac. by swirling. Use cleaned-up Chromosorb W to prep. new polyethylene glycol 600-Chromosorb W mixt., (**b**), and column.

43.072 ***Column III***

(**a**) *Chromatographic tube.*—Use same tube as column I.

(**b**) *Preparation and deactivation of Florex.*—Eliminate small particles as follows: Suspend 200 g Florex in 500 mL alcohol and boil few min in 1 L r-b flask. Decant upper layer contg colloidal suspension. Shake with 250 mL alcohol and decant upper layer. Repeat washing with two 250 mL portions of ether. (*Caution:* Perform ether washing and evapn under effective fume removal device.) Dry suspension on steam bath at 100°, using aspirator, and store in air-tight container. Weigh 10 g dried Florex into 50 mL erlenmeyer. Add 1.6 mL H_2O by pipet, stopper flask, and heat 5 min on steam bath. Gently swirl warm flask to obtain free-flowing powder. Cool, and let stand 15 min. Check activity of deactivated Florex (16% H_2O) by column performance test, **43.073**. If performance is <97%, repeat deactivation, using different vol. H_2O.

(**c**) *Preparation of column.*—Add 20 mL pet ether to flask, swirl, and transfer Florex with pet ether to tube; let packing settle. Regulate flow rate at 2 mL/min with stopcock. Elute with 50 mL isooctane and discard eluate. Maintain head of 1 cm liq. on column thruout assay.

43.073 ***Column Performance Test***

Pipet 10 mL soln contg 5 μg cryst. cholecalciferol (or ergocalciferol)/mL pet ether onto column, and elute as in **43.075(a)** or (**b**), collecting eluate in 250 mL r-b flask. Evap. to dryness under vac. in ca 40° H_2O bath. Evap. 10.0 mL untreated calciferol soln in same way. Cool and restore atm. pressure with N. Without delay, sep. dissolve each residue in 10.0 mL 20% toluene in isooctane and measure as follows: Pipet 2 mL into 2 cm cell, add 5 mL color reagent from rapid delivery pipet, and mix. Measure A at 500 nm against blank consisting of 2 mL 20% toluene in isooctane and 5 mL color reagent.

% Performance = 100 (A/A_r), where A and A_r refer to A of soln with and without chromatgy, resp.

This column performance test can also be used to check the 3 columns together. Result of performance tests should be between 97 and 103%; if not, repeat deactivation of column materials with different vols of H_2O and recheck by performance test.

43.074 ***Preparation of Sample***

(*Caution: See* **51.018**, **51.045**, and **51.073**.)

(**a**) *Step A. Isolation of unsaponifiable matter from oils.*—Factor m is nearest integral number, indicating number of 1 g samples taken. Factor r is nearest integral number, indicating multiple of 100 μg (4000 IU) vitamin D in sample taken.

For concs contg >2.5 mg (100,000 IU) vitamin D/g, accurately weigh ca 1 g sample into saponification flask. Define $m(= 1)$ and r.

For low potency prepns contg 12.5–2500 μg (500–100,000 IU) vitamin D/g, accurately weigh amt of sample ≥1 g equiv. to ca $r \times$ *100 μg* ($r \times$ 4000 IU) vitamin D and contg ≤75 mg α-tocopheryl acetate into saponification flask. Define m and r. Add $m \times$ 10 mL 20% pyrogallol soln, $m \times$ 1 mL 20% Na ascorbate soln, $m \times$ 25 mL alcohol, and $m \times$ 4 mL 50% aq. KOH soln, and reflux 30 min on steam bath, using air condenser. Add $m \times$ 5 mL 20% pyrogallol soln to hot soln and then cool. Add, without delay, $m \times$ 100.0 mL benzene, mix, and transfer to separator *without rinsing*. Add $m \times$ 40 mL 6% aq. KOH soln, shake vigorously 10 sec, let layers sep. (2–3 min), and discard still turbid aq. layer. Wash benzene layer with 1 portion of $m \times$ 40 mL 3% aq. KOH soln and $m \times$ 40 mL portions of H_2O until discarded H_2O is neut. to phthln (usually 4–5 washings). Drain last few drops of H_2O, add $m \times$ 2 sheets of 9 cm filter paper (in strips) to funnel, and shake until benzene layer is clear. Store this soln in stoppered flask and continue as in (**d**).

(*Note:* During washing, turbid aq. layer contains droplets of benzene. As droplets have same vitamin D concn as benzene layer, detn of concn of vitamin D in benzene layer, **43.077(a)** or (**b**), is not influenced by loss of these droplets.)

(**b**) *Step B. Isolation of unsaponifiable matter from powders, capsules, tablets, and aqueous dispersions.*—Factor n is nearest integral number, indicating number of 5 g samples of powder, 5 g samples of capsules or tablets, or 2 g samples of aq. dispersions taken. Factor r is nearest integral number, indicating multiple of 100 μg (4000 IU) vitamin D in sample taken.

For concs contg ≥625 μg (25,000 IU) vitamin D/g, accurately weigh ≥0.1 g sample into saponification flask. Define $n(= 1)$ and r.

For low potency prepns contg 5–625 μg (200–25,000 IU) vitamin D/g, accurately weigh amt of sample or take known number (W) of capsules or tablets, contg ca 100 μg (4000 IU) vitamin D and contg ≤75 mg α-tocopheryl acetate into saponification flask. Define $r(= 1)$ and n.

For capsules or tablets, warm sample with $n \times$ 10 mL 20% Na ascorbate soln ca 10 min on steam bath, swirling occasionally. Crush remaining solid with blunt glass rod, warm 5 min longer, and add $n \times$ 3 drops of Na_2S soln. Add dropwise, with gentle swirling, $n \times$ 20 mL 20% pyrogallol soln and then, all at once, $n \times$ 10 mL 50% aq. KOH soln, followed by dropwise addn, with gentle swirling, of $n \times$ 25 mL alcohol; reflux 30 min on steam bath. Add $n \times$ 5 mL 20% pyrogallol soln and $n \times$ 80 mL alcohol to hot soln, with swirling; then cool. Add, without delay, $n \times$ 100.0 mL benzene, mix, and transfer to separator *without rinsing*. Add $n \times$ 200 mL 6% aq. KOH soln, shake vigorously 10 sec, let layers sep. (2–3 min), and discard still turbid aq. layer. Wash benzene layer once with $n \times$ 40 mL portion of 3% aq. KOH soln and then with $n \times$ 40 mL portions of H_2O until discarded H_2O is neut. to phthln (usually 4–5 washings). Drain last few drops of H_2O, add $n \times$ 2 sheets of 9 cm filter paper (in strips) to funnel, and shake until benzene layer is clear. Store this soln in g-s flask and continue as in (**d**).

For dry prepns and aq. dispersions, warm 3–4 min at 35° with $n \times$ 10 mL 20% Na ascorbate soln, swirl, and add $n \times$ 3 drops Na_2S soln to sample. Proceed as above, par. 4, beginning with "Add dropwise, . . ."

(**c**) *Step C. Preparation of vitamin D resin in tins.*—Factor r is as defined in (**a**) and (**b**).

For resins contg ca 25,000,000 IU vitamin D/g, scatter sample by sharp blows on outside of container. Into 50 mL flask, accurately weigh ca 0.8 g (contg ca 20,000,000 IU vitamin D) of largest lumps from lower part of container. (Caution: Resin sample must *never* be powdered.) Dissolve sample in toluene and dil. to mark. Dil. aliquot to exactly *r* times its vol. with pet ether. Pipet 25 mL, contg 50 μg (2000 IU) vitamin D, into r-b flask. Evap. aliquot to dryness under vac. by swirling in H_2O bath at <40°. Cool, restore atm. pressure with N, and continue without delay as in **43.076**.

(**d**) *Step D. Preparation of aliquot of unsaponifiable matter.*— Factors *m, n,* and *r* are as defined in (**a**) and (**b**).

For concs without other vitamins, dil. aliquot of benzene soln from (**a**) or (**b**) to exactly *r* times its vol. with benzene or pet ether and pipet 50 mL, contg 50 μg (2000 IU) vitamin D, into r-b flask. Evap. as in (**c**), and continue without delay as in **43.076**.

For concs of multivitamin prepns, dil. aliquot of benzene soln from (**a**) or (**b**) to exactly *r* times its vol. with benzene or pet ether and pipet 75 mL contg 75 μg (3000 IU) vitamin D into r-b flask. Add 1 mL ethoxyquin soln. Evap. as in (**c**), and continue without delay as in **43.075**.

For low potency multivitamin prepns, pipet aliquot of benzene soln from (**a**) or (**b**), $m \times 75.0$ mL or $n \times 75.0$ mL, resp., contg 75 μg (3000 IU) vitamin D into r-b flask. Add 1 mL ethoxyquin soln. Evap. as in (**c**), and continue without delay as in **43.075**.

For low potency prepns without other vitamins, pipet $m \times 50.0$ mL or $n \times 50.0$ mL, contg 50 μg (2000 IU) vitamin D, into r-b flask. Evap. aliquot to dryness under vac. by swirling in H_2O bath at <40°. Cool, restore atm. pressure with N, and continue without delay as in **43.075**.

43.075 ***Column Chromatography***

(**a**) *Step E. Alumina.*—Dissolve residue from **43.074**(**d**) in 5 mL pet ether. Transfer to column I with aid of 10 mL pet ether, let liq. drain, and wash with 10 mL pet ether. Elute column, in 10 mL portions, with 200 mL 8% ether-pet ether and discard eluate. Elute column with 150 mL 30% ether-pet ether, collecting eluate in r-b flask. Add 1 mL ethoxyquin soln. Evap. eluate to dryness under vac. at 40°. Cool, restore atm. pressure with N, and continue without delay as in (**b**). (For prepns without other vitamins, continue as in **43.076**.)

(**b**) *Step F. Polyethylene glycol 600-Chromosorb W and Florex.*—Dissolve residue from (**a**) in 3.00 mL isooctane. Let solv. drain from column II. Just as meniscus of solv. reaches surface of column, pipet 2 mL sample soln onto column. When meniscus of soln reaches surface of column, add 1 mL isooctane and elute thru column; repeat this elution twice. When last of isooctane enters column, continue adding isooctane from dropping funnel or in 10 mL portions, keeping flow rate to ca 2 mL/min. Let eluate drain into column III, keeping $\geq$1 cm soln on column III by means of stopcock. Examine column II $\leq$1 sec under UV light (360 nm) with portable UV lamp at intervals during chromatgy, and stop when front of fluorescent vitamin A band is located 3 cm from bottom of column II. Remove column II. Vitamin D is on column III. Discard eluate of column III. Elute all vitamin A from column II with isooctane. Column II is now ready for another vitamin D detn.

Elute column III with 150 mL benzene, collecting eluate in r-b flask, and add 1 mL ethoxyquin soln. Evap. to dryness under vac. at 40°, cool, restore atm. pressure with N, and continue without delay.

43.076 ***Inactivation of Tachysterol***

Step G. Maleic anhydride addition.—Dissolve residue from **43.074**(**c**) or (**d**) or **43.075**(**a**) or (**b**), contg preferably ca 2000 IU vitamin D, in 2.00 mL 1% maleic anhydride soln in r-b flask; stopper flask and swirl. Let stand 30 min in dark at room temp. Add 8.00 mL isooctane by buret or pipet to soln (sample prepn).

43.077 ***Colorimetric Determination***

(**a**) *Step H. Multivitamin sample preparations.*— Designate 3 suitable, matched colorimetric tubes ca 20 mm id as *1, 2,* and *3,* resp. Pipet 2 mL sample prepn from **43.076** into tube *1,* 2 mL std soln into tube *2,* and 1 mL sample prepn and 1 mL color-inhibiting soln into tube *3*. To each tube add quickly, and preferably from automatic pipet, 5.0 mL color reagent, and mix. After 45 sec, accurately timed from addn of color reagent, det. *A* of the 3 solns at 500 nm, with spectrophtr, using blank of 2 mL 20% toluene in isooctane and 5 mL color reagent. Make second reading at 550 nm 45 sec after first reading for each soln. (*Note:* Some batches of color reagent develop max. color after 45 sec. Check this first with std prepn. Other batches give max. after 45–120 sec. Use exact time of max. and measure 45 sec later at 550 nm.) Designate *A* as $A_{1(500)}$, $A_{2(500)}$, $A_{3(500)}$, $A_{1(550)}$, $A_{2(550)}$, and $A_{3(550)}$, resp., in which subscripts indicate number of tube and wavelength (in parentheses).

Calc. μg or IU vitamin D/g sample, capsule, or tablet as follows:

$$\text{Potency} = C \times (V_S/W) \times (A_D/A_{2(500)}),$$

where C = μg or IU cholecalciferol or ergocalciferol/mL in std soln (1 μg = 40 IU), W = g sample or number of capsules or tablets, V_S = final vol. of sample ($r \times 20$ mL), and r = diln factor for sample, **43.074**(**a**), (**b**), (**c**), and (**d**); and

$$A_D = [q/(q-p)] \times A_{1(500)} - [1/(q-p)] \times A_{1(550)},$$

where $p = A_{2(550)}/A_{2(500)}$ and $q = A_{3(550)}/A_{3(500)}$.

In spectrophtr with $\leq$10 nm band pass, *A* of std soln at 550 nm will be negligible. Then *p* is <0.01 and, for this spectrophtr, $A_D = A_{1(500)} - (A_{1(550)}/q)$. If *q* is <1, it should be taken as 1, to avoid systematic errors.

(**b**) *Step I. Sample preparations without other vitamins.*— Designate 2 suitable, matched colorimetric tubes ca 20 mm id as *1* and *2*, resp. Pipet 2 mL sample prepn from **43.076** into tube *1* and 2 mL std soln into tube *2*. To each tube add quickly, and preferably from automatic pipet, 5.0 mL color reagent, and mix. Then 60 sec, accurately timed (see *Note* in (**a**)), after addn of color reagent, det. *A* of the 2 solns at 500 nm, with spectrophtr, using blank of 2 mL 20% toluene in isooctane and 5 mL color reagent. Designate *A* as $A_{1(500)}$ and $A_{2(500)}$, resp., in which subscripts indicate number of tube and wavelength (in parentheses).

Calc. μg or IU vitamin D/g sample as follows:

$$\text{Potency} = C \times (V_s/W) \times (A_{1(500)}/A_{2(500)}),$$

where C, V_S, and W are as defined in (**a**).

43.078 ***Confirmation of Identity in Concentrates***

Prep. sample residue, as in **43.074**, contg ca 2.5 mg vitamin D (100,000 IU) and dissolve in 10.00 mL 0.1% BHT soln, (**p**). Pipet 4 mL of this soln into each of two 10 mL vol. flasks. To one flask add 2 mL 10% maleic anhydride soln, (**m**)(*1*). Place plastic tube over neck of flask. Fill flask with N and close tube with pinch cock. Heat 3 hr in dark in 100° H_2O bath, and cool. Dil. solns (treated with maleic anhydride and untreated) to vol. with 0.1% BHT soln. Quant. transfer untreated soln to 200 mL vol. flask and dil. to vol. with 0.1% BHT soln. Det. *A* of treated and dild untreated solns colorimetrically with color reagent as in **43.077**(**b**).

$$\text{Residual color value (\%)} = 5 \times (A/A_u),$$

where A and A_u refer to *A* of treated and dild untreated solns, resp. Residual color values $\leq$5% are considered neg. for isotachysterol.

High Performance (Pressure) Liquid Chromatographic Method (*15*)—Official First Action

(Applicable to oils contg ≥100,000 IU cholecalciferol or vitamin D_3/g, and powders and aq. dispersions (≥25,000 IU cholecalciferol/g))

43.079 ***Principle***

Dry concs and aq. dispersions are saponified and extd. Vitamin D resins and oil solns are dissolved in solv. Vitamin D and previtamin D are sepd from impurities by HPLC. Previtamin D concn is calcd as vitamin D using calibration factor. Vitamin D is sum of vitamin D and previtamin D.

43.080 ***Apparatus***

(**a**) *Liquid chromatograph.*—Hewlett Packard 1010 A, or equiv. with 254 nm UV detector. Typical operating conditions: chart speed, 1 cm/min; eluant flow rate, 2 mL/min (ca 100 atm.); detector sensitivity, 0.128 AUFS; temp., ambient; and valve injection vol., 20 μL.

(**b**) *Chromatographic column.*—Stainless steel, 150 × 4.6 (id) mm, packed with 5 μm particle size LiChrosorb Si 60, passing system suitability test. Before entering this column, mobile phase must be pumped thru 100 cm × 4 mm stainless steel column contg 50–250 μ silica, dried 4 hr at 250°. Different column lengths and brands of packing may be substituted, and injection vol. may be varied between 10–30 μL, provided system suitability test is met.

43.081 ***Reagents***

(**a**) *n-Hexane.*—Spectroquality. Dry by passing thru column 60 × 8 cm diam. contg 500 g 50–250 μ silica dried 4 hr at 150°.

(**b**) *n-Amyl alcohol.*—Reagent grade.

(**c**) *Mobile phase.*—*n*-Hexane and *n*-amyl alcohol (997 + 3). Adjust ratio of components, if necessary, to meet suitability test.

(**d**) *Toluene.*—Reagent or Nanograde.

(**e**) *Vitamin D std soln.*—Accurately weigh ca 80 mg USP Cholecalciferol Ref. Std into 50 mL amber vol. flask. Dissolve without heat in toluene, and dil. to vol. with toluene. Prep. fresh daily.

(**f**) *Suitability std soln.*—Prep. soln contg 2 mg vitamin D_3 and 0.2 mg trans-vitamin D_3/g vegetable oil. Dissolve 0.25 g this soln in 10 mL toluene-mobile phase (1+1). Peaks of trans-vitamin D_3 and previtamin D_3 should have ca same peak ht. If necessary, previtamin D_3 content can be increased by warming oil soln at 90° ca 45 min. Store oil at 5°.

(**g**) *Sodium ascorbate soln.*—Dissolve 3.5 g ascorbic acid in 20 mL 1*N* NaOH. Prep. fresh daily.

(**h**) *Sodium sulfide soln.*—Dissolve 12 g $Na_2S.9H_2O$ in 20 mL H_2O and dil. to 100 mL with 87% glycerol.

(**i**) *Potassium hydroxide solns.*—(*1*) *50% (w/w).*—Dissolve 50 g KOH in 50 mL H_2O and cool. Prep. fresh. (*2*) *3% in alcohol.*—Dissolve 3 g KOH in H_2O, add 10 mL alcohol, and dil. to 100 mL with H_2O. Prep. fresh.

(**j**) *Ether.*—Acid- and peroxide-free.

43.082 ***System Suitability Test***

Chromatograph 20 μL portions suitability std soln 6 times. Det. constancy of peak ht by calcg std deviation and then relative std deviation = std deviation × 100/mean peak ht. Relative std deviation should be ≤1%.

Det. peak resolution (*R*) between previtamin D_3 and trans-vitamin D_3:

$$R = 2D/(B + C),$$

where D = distance between peak max. of previtamin D_3 and trans-vitamin D_3; B = peak width of previtamin D_3; and C = peak width of trans-vitamin D_3. Peak resolution should be ≥1.0 for previtamin D_3/trans-vitamin D_3.

43.083 ***Determination of Calibration Factor***

Pipet 4 mL vitamin D std soln, (**e**), into 25 mL vol. flask. Add 1 mL toluene and dil. to vol. with mobile phase. Store in ice bath. Inject 20 μL onto column thru sampling valve and adjust operating conditions of detector to obtain max. on scale peak hts. Repeat injection and average peak hts (=*K*).

Pipet 5 mL vitamin D std soln, (**e**), into 25 mL vol. flask, add few crystals *butylated hydroxytoluene*, displace air with N, and attach reflux condenser. Heat in 90° H_2O bath in dark under N, and cool. Dil. to vol. with mobile phase. Inject 20 μL onto column under same conditions as above. Det. peak ht of heated vitamin D (*L*) and of previtamin D formed (*M*). Calc.:

$$CF = [(5K/4) - L]/M.$$

43.084 ***Preparation of Sample***

(**a**) *Resins.*—Shatter sample by sharp blows on outside of container. Into 100 mL flask, accurately weigh ca 0.8 g (contg ca 20,000,000 IU vitamin D) of largest lumps from lower part of container. (*Caution:* Resin sample must never be powdered.) Dissolve in toluene and dil. to vol. with toluene. Pipet 5 mL into 100 mL vol. flask, add 15 mL toluene, and dil. to vol. with mobile phase. (Concn = 10,000 IU or 0.25 mg vitamin D/mL.)

(**b**) *Vitamin D in oil.*—Accurately weigh amt of oil contg ca 500,000 IU into 50 mL vol. flask. Dissolve in 10.0 mL toluene, and dil. to vol. with mobile phase.

(**c**) *Dry preparations and aqueous dispersions.*—Accurately weigh into saponification flask amt sample contg ca 100,000 IU cholecalciferol. Add in small portions, with gentle swirling, 25 mL alcohol, 2 mL Na ascorbate soln, (**g**), and 5 mL KOH soln, (**i**)(*1*). Reflux on H_2O bath 30 min and cool rapidly under running H_2O. Transfer soln to separator with aid of two 15 mL portions H_2O, and two 50 mL portions ether.

Shake vigorously 30 sec and let stand until clear. Transfer aq. (lower) phase to second separator and shake with 10 mL alcohol and 50 mL *n*-pentane. Let sep., and transfer lower aq. layer to third separator and upper pentane phase to first separator, washing second separator with two 10 mL portions pentane, adding washings to first separator. Shake aq. phase in third separator with 50 mL pentane, discard aq. phase, and add pentane to first separator. Wash combined pentane exts with three 50 mL portions 3% KOH soln, (**i**)(*2*), shaking vigorously, and then wash with successive 50 mL portions H_2O until last washing is neut. to phthln. Drain last few drops of H_2O, add 2 sheets of 9 cm filter paper in strips to funnel, and shake. Transfer washed pentane ext to r-b flask, rinsing separator and paper with pentane.

Evap. soln to dryness under vac. by swirling in H_2O bath at ≤40°. Cool under running H_2O and restore atm. pressure with N. Dissolve residue immediately in 2.0 mL toluene, transfer to 10 mL amber vol. flask, rinsing with 1 mL portions mobile phase, and dil. to vol. with mobile phase.

43.085 ***Determination***

Inject 20 μL vitamin D std soln and prepd sample soln onto column thru sampling valve with detector adjusted as in **43.083**. Measure peak hts of vitamin D and previtamin D. Repeat injections and re-inject std soln after every 4 sample injections to verify that response remains const.

43.086 ***Calculations***

Average peak hts obtained for std replicates and sample duplicates.

IU vitamin D/g = $([P_D + (P_P \times CF)]/P_R)(W'/W)(V/V') \times 40{,}000$, where P_D, P_P, and P_R = peak ht of vitamin D in sample, previtamin D in sample, and vitamin D in std, resp.; CF = calibration factor previtamin D/vitamin D; W' = wt std in mg; W = wt sample in g; V = total mL sample soln; V' = total mL std soln (= 25 × 50/4); and 40,000 = IU vitamin D/mg USP ref. std.

43.087 **Nomenclature for Vitamin E (*16*)**
Official First Action

(**a**) Term *vitamin E* should be used as generic descriptor for all tocol and tocotrienol derivatives qual. exhibiting biological activity of α-tocopherol. Thus phrases such as "vitamin E activity," "vitamin E deficiency," and "vitamin E in form of . . ." represent preferred usage

(**b**) Term *tocopherols* should be used as generic descriptor for all Me tocols. Thus term "tocopherol" is not synonymous with term "vitamin E."

(**c**) Compd 5,7,8-trimethyltocol should be designated α-tocopherol. The trivial name α-tocopherol without stereochem. designation should never be used to refer to specific material. Important diastereoisomers and mixts of diastereoisomers of α-tocopherol are further named below.

(**d**) Compd identical to that isolated from natural sources, 2*R*,4'*R*,8'*R*-α-tocopherol with structure in Fig. **43:02**, formerly known as *d*-α-tocopherol, should be designated *RRR*-α-tocopherol.

(**e**) Totally synthetic α-tocopherol obtained from totally synthetic phytol or isophytol as starting material is mixt. of 8 diastereoisomers as 4 racemates or pairs of enantiomers in unspecified proportions. It was formerly known as *dl*-α-tocopherol and should be designated *all-rac*-α-tocopherol.

(**f**) Mixt. of *RRR*-α-tocopherol and 2-*epi*-α-tocopherol obtained by synthesis using natural phytol (and as acetate ester formerly known as "synthetic racemic α-tocopheryl acetate" and formerly the International Std for vitamin E) should be designated as 2-*ambo*-α-tocopherol. Such an asymetric reaction would only by chance result in formation of equimolar amts of the 2 possible epimers. However, 2-*ambo*-α-tocopherol obtained as described above closely approaches equimolar proportions of its epimers.

(**g**) Compd 2*S*,4'*R*,8'*R*-α-tocopherol, also known as the epimer of *d*-α-tocopherol, or 2*l*-α-tocopherol, or *l*-α-tocopherol, should be designated 2-*epi*-α-tocopherol.

(**h**) Esters of tocopherols and tocotrienols should be designated tocopheryl esters and tocotrienyl esters, resp.

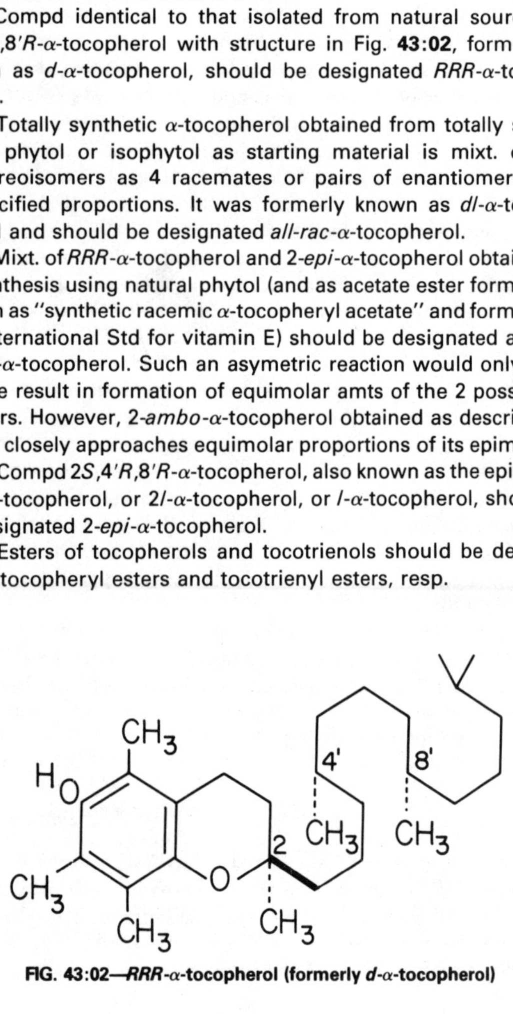

FIG. 43:02—*RRR*-α-tocopherol (formerly *d*-α-tocopherol)

alpha-Tocopherol and alpha-Tocopheryl Acetate (*17*)
Official Final Action

(Applicable to foods and feeds)

43.088 ***Principle***

Following methods are designed to det. vitamin E in foods and feeds in the several forms in which it may occur. Unsupplemented food or feed will contain *natural* α-tocopherol associated with many other reducing substances. This type of sample is extd, lipid residue saponified, and α-tocopherol isolated by TLC and detd colorimetrically. Foods or feeds may be supplemented with α-tocopheryl acetate added either as oil or in various dry forms. Assay for *total* α-tocopherol (natural plus supplemental) follows same operations described above. To specifically det. α-tocopheryl acetate, sample is extd, reducing substances, including natural α-tocopherol, are removed by oxidative chromatgy, α-tocopheryl acetate is saponified, and resulting α-tocopherol is detd colorimetrically.

Calcn of assay results for supplemented foods and feeds in terms of International Units (IU) is complicated by fact that natural and synthetic α-tocopheryl acetates have different wt-activity factors. α-Tocopherol occurring naturally is in *RRR*-form. With samples supplemented with *RRR*-α-tocopheryl acetate (natural), resulting total α-tocopherol is all in *RRR*-form and IU potency of sample can readily be detd by using appropriate factor. With samples supplemented with *all-rac*-α-tocopheryl acetate (synthetic), resulting total α-tocopherol is mixt. of *RRR*- and *all-rac*-forms. To convert to IU, level of supplementation with *all-rac*-α-tocopheryl acetate must be detd specifically and natural α-tocopherol is detd by difference. Appropriate factors are then sep. applied to detd levels of *RRR*- and *all-rac*-forms and results are added to det. IU potency of sample. If isomeric nature of supplement is not known, it must be detd sep., **43.097–43.105**, before IU potency of supplemented samples can be detd.

Precautions.—Evap. tocopherol solns with N stream or under vac. Do not use air stream. Do not let soln of tocopherol evap. to dryness for >2–3 sec because tocopherol in thin film is subject to oxidn. Perform TLC, including detection step (except for UV light), in darkness or very subdued light. Complete all steps as promptly as possible. If analysis cannot be completed in 1 day, store solns at −20°.

43.089 ***Apparatus***

(**a**) *Spectrophotometric colorimeter.*—Bausch & Lomb Spectronic 20 colorimeter with matched 13 mm test tubes, or equiv.

(**b**) *Spectrophotometer.*—Beckman Model DU with incandescent light source and matched cells (1 cm light path; 4.5 or 1.6 mL capacity), or equiv. (If cell holder does not elevate larger cells so liq. is in light path, use small plugs (usually 1 cm) in bottom of holder.)

(**c**) *Extractor.*—Hot alcohol extn app. (*Anal. Chem.* **20**, 1221(1948)), Goldfisch extractor (Labconco Corp.), or equiv.

(**d**) *Chromagram®* sheet.—Type X6062. Alumina absorbent without fluorescent indicator, for AOAC vitamin E assay (Eastman Kodak Co.). If activation is necessary, heat 30 min at 105° in air oven.

(**e**) *Pipets.*—Ultra-micro, measuring pipets, 50 μL capacity (VWR Scientific, No. 53477-089, or equiv.).

(**f**) *Developing chamber.*—Corning Glass Works Pyrex 6944, or equiv.

(**g**) *Sprayer.*—Aerosol propellant (VWR Scientific No. 21434 -086, or equiv.).

(**h**) *Vials.*—Glass 1.8 mL (½ dram) with screw caps (Demuth Glass, Inc., Parkersburg, WV 26101) and 25 mL (7 dram) with polyethylene stoppers (Kimble Products No. 60975-L, or equiv.).

(**i**) *Ultraviolet lamps.*—366 nm wavelength (longwave) (Blak-Ray UVL-21, Ultra-Violet Products, Inc.) or 254 nm wavelength (shortwave) (Spectronics Corp, 956 Brush Hollow Rd, Westbury, NY 11590, Model R-51, or equiv.). (*Caution: See* **51.016**.)

(**j**) *Chromatographic tubes.*—18 (id) × 270 mm.

43.090 ***Reagents***

(**a**) *Petroleum ether.*—(*1*) *Purified.*—Boiling range 35–60° (Skellysolve F, Getty Refining and Marketing Co, or equiv.). Redistil from KOH pellets and Zn granules or dust, discarding first and last 5%. (*Caution: See* **51.011(a)**, **51.039**, and **51.073**.) (*2*) *High boiling.*—Boiling range 60–71° (Skellysolve B, or equiv.).

(**b**) *Alcohol.*—Absolute or SDA 3-A (absolute). If significant reducing substances are present, redistil from Al and KOH. (*Caution: See* **51.011**, **51.039**, and **51.055**.)

(**c**) *Petroleum ether-absolute alcohol mixture.*—Dil. 600 mL pet ether, (**a**)(*2*), to 1 L with absolute alcohol.

(**d**) *RRR-alpha-Tocopherol.*—Eastman grade or equiv. purity. Prep. 1 mg/mL std soln in absolute alcohol and store at 5°.

(**e**) *2′,7′-Dichlorofluorescein soln.*—Dissolve 4 mg dye (Eastman 373) in 100 mL absolute alcohol.

(**f**) *Anhydrous ether.*—Redistil from KOH pellets and Al granules or dust, discarding first and last 5%. (*Caution: See* **51.011(a)**, **51.039**, and **51.054**.)

(**g**) *Bathophenanthroline soln.*—0.003*M*. Dissolve 100 mg 4,7-diphenyl-1,10-phenanthroline (bathophenanthroline, G. Frederick Smith Chemical Co.) in 100 mL absolute alcohol. Store in amber or opaque glassware at 5°. Prep. fresh soln every 3 weeks.

(**h**) *Ferric chloride soln.*—0.002*M*. Dissolve 55 mg $FeCl_3.6H_2O$ in 100 mL absolute alcohol. Store in amber or opaque glassware at 5°.

(**i**) *Orthophosphoric acid.*—0.172*M*. Dil. 1.1 mL 86% H_3PO_4 to 100 mL with absolute alcohol.

(**j**) *Anhydrous sodium sulfate.*—Granular and powd.

(**k**) *Concentrated potassium hydroxide soln.*—Dissolve 80 g KOH pellets in 50 mL H_2O.

(**l**) *Phenolphthalein soln.*—Dissolve 1 g phthln in 100 mL absolute alcohol.

(**m**) *Isopropyl ether.*—Eastman 1193, or equiv.

(**n**) *Water-saturated n-butanol.*—Mix 800 mL *n*-BuOH with 160 mL H_2O.

(**o**) *Ascorbic acid.*—Eastman 4640, or equiv.

(**p**) *Cyclohexane.*—Eastman 702, or equiv.

(**q**) *Fuller's earth.*—Florex AA-RVM grade, 60–100 mesh (Floridin Co.).

(**r**) *Ceric sulfate-treated fuller's earth.*—To 4.8 g $Ce(HSO_4)_4$ (G. Frederick Smith Chemical Co.) add mixt. of 0.5 mL H_2SO_4 and ca 5 mL H_2O, and stir. Dil. to 100 mL with H_2O. Warm in hot H_2O bath and shake until almost all $Ce(HSO_4)_4$ is dissolved. Cool to ca 35–40° and use promptly ($Ce(HSO_4)_4$ ppts on standing at room temp.). Spread 200 g fuller's earth in large glazed porcelain dish. Distribute 100 mL $Ce(HSO_4)_4$ soln on fuller's earth, stir gently but thoroly, and dry 48 hr in 60° oven. Store in tightly capped bottle.

(**s**) *Diatomaceous earth.*—Celite 501, or equiv. inert filter-aid.

(**t**) *Benzene.*—Eastman grade, or product of equiv. purity without addnl purification.

(**u**) *Olive oil.*—USP, contg 1.5 mg total reducing substances/g, or equiv. oil.

43.091 ***Preparation of Sample and Extraction***

(*Caution: See* **51.009**, **51.011**, **51.015**, **51.039**, **51.054**, **51.055**, and **51.073**.)

(Use for detn of natural α-tocopherol, total α-tocopherol (natural α-tocopherol + supplemental α-tocopheryl acetate), or supplemental α-tocopheryl acetate.)

Sample size of 10 g is convenient for most foods and feeds. Use 40 g with dry feeds and foods supplemented with high potency prepns at low levels (1 IU/100 g). Min. wt is 1 g, contg 0.1 IU of total α-tocopherol or supplemental α-tocopheryl acetate; if assay for both is performed on same initial sample, min. amt is 0.2 IU for each component.

(**a**) *Fat or oil.*—Gently warm solid fat to liquefy, mix thoroly, and weigh. To det. total α-tocopherol, place sample in ₮ 125 mL r-b flask for saponification as in **43.092**. To det. supplemental α-tocopheryl acetate, proceed directly as in **43.107**.

(**b**) *Milk and milk products.*—Measure exactly 60 mL milk or reconstituted powd or concd milk product, add equal vol. absolute alcohol, and shake to mix. Add 150 mL ether, shake 30 sec, add 150 mL pet ether, (**a**)(*1*), and shake 30 sec. Let layers sep. and remove ether layer. Repeat extn ≥2 times, using 25 mL absolute alcohol, 100 mL ether, and 100 mL pet ether each time. Combine ether layers and evap. to 50 mL. Take 10 mL aliquot, evap. solv., and weigh lipid. Transfer remaining 40 mL or aliquot contg ca 1 g lipid and ≥0.1 IU vitamin E to ₮ 125 mL r-b flask. Evap. solv. under N on steam bath. To det. total α-tocopherol, proceed immediately to saponification as in **43.092**. To det. supplemental α-tocopheryl acetate, proceed as in **43.107**.

(**c**) *Wet products.*—Place accurately weighed sample in large mortar and grind thoroly with 2–3 times its wt of anhyd. powd Na_2SO_4 until dry mixt. is obtained. Quant. transfer mixt. to ≥1 Soxhlet thimbles, using absolute alcohol as rinsing liq., and proceed as in (**d**).

(**d**) *Dry products.*—(Applicable to products such as premixes, feed concs, and feeds which may or may not be supplemented with α-tocopheryl acetate, either in dry carrier or added directly to product, but not in gelatin, vegetable gum, or dextrin matrix.) If coarse particles are present, grind sample. Place accurately weighed sample into Soxhlet thimble. Place 100 mL absolute alcohol and boiling chip in flask and either mark liq. level or weigh flask and contents. Assemble hot ethanol extn app., attach condenser, and ext over steam bath 16 hr (overnight). (Use 4 hr extn with Goldfisch extractor.) Stopper flask, cool ext to room temp., and add absolute alcohol, if necessary, to restore to ca original vol.

Transfer ext to separator, rinse flask with 100 mL H_2O followed by 50 mL pet ether, (**a**)(*2*), and ca 0.5 g granular anhyd. Na_2SO_4, and add rinses to separator. Shake separator 10 min, let layers sep., and drain and discard aq. layer. Dil. pet ether ext to 50 mL; take 10 mL aliquot, evap. solv., and weigh lipid. Continue as in (**b**), beginning "Transfer remaining 40 mL or . . ."

(**e**) *Dry products supplemented with alpha-tocopheryl acetate in gelatin, vegetable gum, or dextrin matrix.*—Proceed as in (**d**), thru ". . . discard aq. layer." Retain pet ether ext. Quant. transfer contents of Soxhlet extn thimble to ₮ r-b flask, with total of 50 mL 2.5*N* H_2SO_4. Attach reflux condenser and reflux 30 min on hot plate. Cool to room temp. and transfer to separator, rinsing flask with 50 mL absolute alcohol. Ext with two 75 mL and one 50 mL portions pet ether, (**a**)(*2*). Combine pet ether exts and pet ether ext obtained from hot alcohol extn. Evap. under N to <50 mL and dil. to 50 mL. Take 10 mL aliquot, evap. solv., and weigh lipid. Continue as in (**b**), beginning "Transfer remaining 40 mL or . . ." except that **43.107** is not applicable to det. supplemental α-tocopheryl acetate.

(**f**) *Expanded dog foods and baked dog biscuits supplemented* *before expansion, processing, or baking.*—Grind sample. Place accurately weighed portion in ₮ 250 mL r-b flask connected to H_2O condenser. Add 25 mL H_2O-satd *n*-BuOH. Insert condenser, heat soln to bp over steam bath, and reflux 1 hr, swirling every 10 min. Cool, and evap. to absolute dryness under vac. at 60°. Quant. transfer dried sample to ≥1 Soxhlet extn thimbles, using absolute alcohol as rinsing liq., and proceed as in (**d**).

43.092 *Saponification and Re-extraction*

(*Caution: See* **51.011**, **51.039**, and **51.054**.)

Prep. sample as in **43.091** or **43.108**. For each g (or fraction of g) of lipid residue in ₮ 125 mL r-b flask, add 4 mL absolute alcohol and 0.3 g ascorbic acid. Attach reflux condenser and heat to bp in boiling H_2O bath. Raise condenser and add 1 mL concd KOH soln for each g (or fraction of g) of lipid residue, replace condenser, and reflux 15 min. (*Note:* Exclusion of air is essential, since tocopherols in alk. solns are easily oxidized.)

Stopper and cool rapidly under cold running H_2O. Transfer soln to separator, using 20 mL H_2O/g (or fraction of g) of lipid residue. Ext unsaponifiable matter by rinsing saponification flask and shaking with each of three 25 mL portions ether for each g (or fraction of g) of lipid residue. (*Caution:* Emulsions may form; add salt to break.) Combine ether exts and wash with equal vols H_2O until soln is neut. to phthln. Filter washed ether ext thru anhyd. granular Na_2SO_4 into erlenmeyer, rinsing with ether. Conc. ether soln to ca 5 mL under N with gentle warming. Transfer soln to 10 mL vol. flask, rinse, and dil. to vol. with ether. Use one aliquot of this ether soln for TLC, **43.093**, and another aliquot for detn of total reducing substances, **43.094**.

(*Note:* If samples contain ethoxyquin or BHA, wash ether unsaponifiable ext (before H_2O wash) twice with equal vol. H_2SO_4 (1+1). Then proceed with H_2O wash of ether. *Caution:* If ether is visible in the H_2SO_4 (1+1), wash the H_2SO_4 (1+1) once with ether and combine this ether with original ether.)

43.093 *Thin Layer Chromatography of Unsaponifiable Matter and Elution of alpha-Tocopherol*

(*Caution: See* **51.016** and **51.017**.)

Perform TLC of α-tocopherol in darkness or subdued light.

(**a**) *Establishment of recovery factor.*—(TLC method is sensitive to ambient humidity.) Based on ambient relative humidity, treat alumina sheet and select solv. systems as given in Table **43:02** to obtain R_f for α-tocopherol of 0.5–0.7.

Using micropipet, quant. transfer 10 μL std soln (10 μg α-tocopherol) slowly to form small spot ca 2 cm from lower and left-hand edges of alumina sheet. Use small amt of ether to rinse micropipet and add to spot. Dry spot with N jet during spotting.

Immediately place sheet in chamber and develop in first dimension, using predetd first dimension solv. system (Table **43:02**). Develop chromatogram until solv. front has moved ca 15–16 cm from bottom of sheet, remove sheet from chamber, and dry with N. Turn sheet 90° counterclockwise, immediately place in second chamber, and develop with predetd second dimension solv. system until solv. front is ca 15–16 cm from bottom of sheet.

Table 43:02 Humidity Conditions for TLC of alpha-Tocopherol

		Solvent Systems	
Relative Humidity, %	Activation of Sheet	1st Dimension Benzene-Ether	2nd Dimension Pet Ether, (**a**)(1)–IsoPr Ether
<20	No	60 + 40 + 1% H_2O	50 + 50 + 1% H_2O
20	No	60 + 40	50 + 50
40	No	90 + 10	80 + 20
60	No	100 + 0	90 + 10
>60	Yes	cyclohexane-benzene, 20 + 80	100 + 0

Remove sheet from chamber and dry with N. Spray sheet lightly with alc. dichlorofluorescein soln. When sheet is completely dry (ca 5 min), locate tocopherol spots under UV light. (*Warning:* Excessive use of UV light can destroy tocopherol.)

Circle tocopherol spot (allowing safety margin of ca 5 mm around spot) and also circle spot of comparable size from unused but sprayed portion of sheet for blank. Cut out both spots and place in sep. 25 mL vials contg 1.4 mL bathophenanthroline soln, (**g**), replace cap, swirl, and let stand 15 min for elution. Proceed as in **43.094**(**a**) for colorimetry.

Recovery factor(s) = μg α-tocopherol recovered from sheet/μg-tocopherol taken as sample. (Recovery factors should be const within a laboratory but may range from ca 75 to 85%.)

(**b**) *TLC of sample.*—Pipet aliquot of ether soln of unsaponifiable matter, contg ca 10–20 μg α-tocopherol, into 1.8 mL screw-cap vial. Evap. ether with N until 0.1–0.2 mL remains. Using micropipet, transfer entire contents of vial slowly to form small spot ca 2 cm from lower and left-hand edges of alumina sheet. Use few drops ether to rinse vial and transfer this soln to same spot. Dry spot with jet of N during spotting.

Immediately place sheet in chamber and develop as in (**a**). (If ethoxyquin has not been completely removed in **43.092**, it will be very bright blue fluorescent spot located ca 1 cm above α-tocopherol spot (dark purple with no fluorescence).)

Elute α-tocopherol spot as in (**a**). (Most desirable way to identify α-tocopherol spot correctly is to chromatograph α-tocopherol std with ext aliquot. In first dimension, spot std ca 2 cm from lower and righthand edges of sheet. In second dimension, spot std ca 2 cm from lower and left-hand edges of sheet *after* sheet has been turned 90° counterclockwise.)

43.094 *Colorimetry of alpha-Tocopherol*

(Method (**a**) is applicable only to Beckman spectrophtr and samples low in fat; (**b**) is applicable to any spectrophtr using working vol. of ≤6 mL in colorimeter tube and sample may contain considerable fat.)

(**a**) *Colorimetry after TLC.*—Take 1.0 mL from 1.4 mL bathophenanthroline soln from each vial. Place in 15 mL centrf. tube, add 0.3 mL $FeCl_3$ soln, (**h**), dropwise, and swirl. Exactly 15 sec after addn of last drop, add 0.3 mL H_3PO_4 soln, (**i**), and swirl. After 3 min, color formed is stable 90 min.

If necessary, centrf. to settle adsorbent particles. Add supernate to sep. cells and measure *A* in Beckman spectrophtr at 534 nm against *A* of blank spot.

Det. amts of α-tocopherol in circled spot, using response factor or calibration curve prepd by colorimetry above and recovery factor detd in **43.093**(**a**).

(**b**) *Colorimetry of alpha-tocopherol or total reducing material.*—Select colorimeter tubes matched with 6 mL pet ether, (**a**)(*2*)-absolute alcohol (3+2). Maintain const subdued lighting conditions thruout colorimetry.

(*1*) *Calibration curve.*—Place exactly 4 mL pet ether, (**a**)(*2*)-absolute alcohol (3+2) contg 5 μg pure α-tocopherol in 25 mL vial. Add exactly 1.0 mL bathophenanthroline soln, swirl, add exactly 0.5 mL $FeCl_3$ soln dropwise, and swirl. Exactly 15 sec after addn of last drop of $FeCl_3$ soln, add exactly 0.5 mL H_3PO_4 soln and swirl. After 3 min, color formed is stable 90 min.

Transfer soln to matched colorimeter tube and measure *A* in spectrophtr at 534 nm against reagent blank prepd in same manner but without addn of α-tocopherol.

Repeat steps 5 times, using 5–50 μg α-tocopherol; plot A against μg α-tocopherol/6 mL on linear graph paper. Draw best fitting smooth curve thru 6 points and origin. Check calibration curve daily and prep. new curve when new reagent solns are prepd.

(*2*) *Colorimetric determination.*—Accurately transfer sample or aliquot contg ca 20 μg α-tocopherol or equiv. amt of reducing substances to 25 mL vial. Evap. to dryness under N, immediately add exactly 4 mL pet ether, **(a)**(*2*)-absolute alcohol (3+2), and swirl until sample is dissolved. Proceed as in (*1*), beginning "Add exactly 1.0 mL bathophenanthroline soln, . . ."

If sample contains appreciable amts (>100 mg) of lipid or unsaponifiable matter, transfer soln to colorimeter or centrf. tube and centrf. ca 10 min at ca 2500 rpm before colorimetric detn. If color formed is too great for accurate A detn, dil. soln with reagent blank soln and read A again.

Det. α-tocopherol or α-tocopherol equiv. of reducing substances from previously established std curve in μg α-tocopherol/6 mL.

43.095 ***Calculations***

(a) *For TLC.*—mg α-Tocopherol/sample = μg α-tocopherol measured × (1.4/1.0) × (x/y) × (v/w) × (1/1000), where 1.4 and 1.0 = mL bathophenanthroline used for elution and taken from eluate, resp.; x = total mL ext before saponification; y = mL of x used for saponification; v = total mL unsaponifiable ext; w = mL of v used for spotting on TLC, 1/1000 = factor to convert μg to mg.

(b) *For total reducing material.*—mg α-Tocopherol equiv./sample = μg α-tocopherol measured × (x/y) × (d/e) × (1/1000), where symbols are defined in **(a)**, d = total mL unsaponifiable ext, and e = mL of d used for colorimeter reading.

43.096 ***Calculation of IU Potency***

(a) *For products not containing added alpha-tocopheryl acetate.*—IU/g sample = (mg α-tocopherol in sample/wt sample in g) × 1.49.

(b) *For products supplemented with RRR-alpha-tocopheryl acetate* (*natural*).—Calc. as in **(a)**.

(c) *For products supplemented with all-rac-alpha-tocopheryl acetate* (*synthetic*).—mg *all-rac-α*-Tocopherol/g sample = (mg *all-rac-α*-tocopherol in sample (**43.110(c)**)/wt sample in g).

mg *RRR-α*-Tocopherol/g sample = (mg α-tocopherol in sample (**43.095**)/wt sample in g) − (mg *all-rac-α*-tocopherol/wt sample in g).

IU/g sample = (mg *RRR-α*-tocopherol/wt sample in g) × 1.49 + (mg *all-rac-α*-tocopherol/wt sample in g) × 1.10.

Identification of *RRR*- or *all-rac-alpha*-Tocopherol (*18*) Official First Action

43.097 ***Principle***

To calc. vitamin E in International Units (IU), it is necessary to know or to identify α-tocopherol or α-tocopherol ester as *RRR* or *all-rac* form. Sample is extd and saponified, and extraneous color is removed by chromatgy. Optical rotation of ferricyanide oxidn product of resulting α-tocopherol is negligible for *all-rac* forms and pos. for *RRR* form.

Applicable to pharmaceutical prepns and food or feed supplements contg α-tocopherol esters if the α-tocopherol is present at or can be concd to ≥200 mg α-tocopherol/g before oxidn step.

Precautions.—*See* **43.088**.

43.098 ***Apparatus***

See **43.089(a)** and **(j)**, and following:

High precision polarimeter.—Reading to ≤0.002° (Rudolph Model 85, Rudolph Instruments, PO Box 161, Little Falls, NJ 07424, or equiv.); with 2.8 mL semimicro glass tube, 4.0 mm bore, 20 cm long, and central tubulation.

43.099 ***Reagents***

See **43.090** and following:

(a) *Magnesium silicate.*—Florisil grade 60–100 mesh (Floridin Co.).

(b) *Petroleum ether-ether mixture.*—Dil. 200 mL anhyd. ether, **43.090(f)**, to 1 L with pet ether, **43.090(a)**(*1*).

(c) *Isooctane.*—ACS UV grade.

(d) *Potassium ferricyanide soln.*—Dissolve 5.0 g $K_3Fe(CN)_6$ in 50 mL 0.2*N* NaOH. (*Caution:* Avoid residual acetone on glassware. If soln is brown, discard.)

43.100 ***Preparation of Sample and Extraction***

(*Caution: See* **51.011, 51.015, 51.039, 51.045, 51.054, 51.055**, and **51.073**.)

See **43.091** and following:

(a) *Oily forms.*—Weigh sample contg 100–120 IU vitamin E and place in ₮ 125 mL r-b flask. Saponify as in **43.101**.

(b) *Dry forms and hard-shell multivitamin capsules.*—(If necessary, grind in mortar to fine powder.) Place accurately weighed sample of dry product or capsule contents contg 100–120 IU vitamin E in ₮ flask and add 50 mL 2.5*N* H_2SO_4. Attach reflux condenser and reflux 30 min on hot plate. Cool to room temp. and transfer to separator, rinsing flask with 50 mL absolute alcohol. Ext with two 75 mL and one 50 mL portions high boiling pet ether, **43.090(a)**(*2*). Combine pet ether exts, and evap. under N to <50 mL. Transfer to ₮ 125 mL r-b flask and evap. solv. under N on steam bath. Saponify as in **43.101**.

(c) *Soft-shelled multivitamin capsules.*—(*1*) *Preparation of column.*—Place in order, on top of small glass wool plug in chromatgc tube: 3 g fuller's earth, 3 g $Ce(HSO_4)_4$-treated fuller's earth, 3 mm layer fuller's earth, 3 g $Ce(HSO_4)_4$-treated fuller's earth, 4 g fuller's earth, and 5 mm layer diat. earth on top. Tap gently after addn of each portion of adsorbent to ensure even packing. Wash column under suction with ca 200 mL pet ether, **43.090(a)**(*1*). Keep layer of solv. above top of adsorbent at all times. Use new column for each assay.

(*2*) *Elution of vitamin E.*—Weigh sample of capsule contents contg 100–120 IU vitamin E, dissolve in 4 mL pet ether, **43.090(a)**(*1*), and quant. transfer to top of chromatgc column, using elongated dropper. If aliquot contains <500 mg lipid, add olive oil as necessary to give this min. amt lipid. Use five ca 1.0 mL portions pet ether, **43.090(a)**(*1*), as rinses for quant. transfer. To prevent column from running dry, do not use vac. during sample transfer. Elute column with 100 mL benzene. Evap. benzene eluate to ca 4 mL on steam bath under N stream and then to dryness under N with reduced heat. Saponify as in **43.101**.

43.101 ***Saponification and Re-extraction***

Proceed as in **43.092**. Use 0.2 mL of this ether soln to det. α-tocopherol as in **43.102(a)** or **(b)**, and purify remainder as in **43.103**.

43.102 ***Determination of alpha-Tocopherol***

(a) *By colorimetry.*—Proceed as in **43.094(b)**. Calc. as follows:

mg α-Tocopherol equiv./sample

= μg α-tocopherol measured × (d/e) × (1/1000),

where d = total mL unsaponifiable ext, e = mL of d used for colorimetric reading, and (1/1000) = factor to convert μg to mg.

(**b**) *By gas-liquid chromatography.*—Proceed as in **43.111–43.118**. Det. mg α-tocopherol equiv./sample.

43.103 ***Chromatographic Purification***

(*Caution: See* **51.011**, **51.054**, and **51.073**.)

(If sample is one of pure forms of vitamin E (USP), omit this step. Evap. ether, add exactly 4.8 mL isooctane, and proceed as in **43.104**. *Caution:* Avoid residual acetone on glassware.)

(**a**) *Preparation of column.*—Place in order, on top of small glass wool plug in chromatgc tube: 10 g Mg silicate and 5 mm layer diat. earth on top. Tap gently after addn of each portion to ensure even packing. Wash column under suction with ca 200 mL pet ether, **43.090(a)**(*1*). Keep layer of solv. above top of adsorbent at all times. Use new column for each assay.

(**b**) *Elution of purified tocopherols.*—Quant. transfer 9.8 mL ether soln of tocopherols, **43.101**, to 15 mL centrf. tube. Evap. to dryness under N and dissolve residue in 5 mL pet ether, **43.090(a)**(*1*). Quant. transfer pet ether soln to top of chromatgc column, using elongated dropper, and five ca 1.0 mL portions pet ether as rinses. To prevent column from running dry, do not use vac. during sample transfer. Develop column with ca 100 mL pet ether and discard pet ether. Elute column with ca 100 mL of pet ether-ether mixture, (**b**). Evap. pet ether-ether mixt. eluate to ca 2 mL on steam bath under N stream. Quant. transfer to 5 mL centrf. tube and evap. to dryness under N with reduced heat. Add exactly 5 mL isooctane. This is *Soln I*. Quant. remove 0.2 mL of *Soln I* and det. mg tocopherols/mL as in **43.102**. Using remaining 4.8 mL of *Soln I*, proceed as in **43.104**.

43.104 ***Oxidation and Polarimetry***

(**a**) *Direct measurement.*—Measure optical rotation of *Soln I*. Calc. specific rotation before oxidn as in **43.105**.

(**b**) *Oxidation.*—Quant. transfer exactly 4 mL *Soln I* to 250 mL separator, using 50 mL pet ether, **43.090(a)**(*1*). Add 10 mL $K_3Fe(CN)_6$ soln, stopper, and shake 3 min. Discard aq. layer; wash solv. layer by gentle shaking with two 50 mL portions H_2O. Dry washed soln with anhyd. granular Na_2SO_4. Transfer quant. to flask and evap. under N with gentle warming to ca 2 mL. Transfer quant. to 5 mL centrf. tube and evap. to dryness under N with reduced heat. Add exactly 3 mL isooctane and measure optical rotation. Calc. specific rotation after oxidn as in **43.105**.

43.105 ***Calculations***

(**a**) *Specific rotation.*—Calc. in terms of α-tocopherol:

$$[a]_D^{25} = (r \times V)/(C \times l),$$

where $[a]_D^{25}$ = specific rotation at 25° with Na light; r = observed rotation; V = mL soln resulting from diln; C = g tocopherols in soln; and l = length of tube in dm (= 2).

(*1*) *Before oxidation.*—V = 4.8;

$$C = [(4.8/1000) \times (\text{mg tocopherols/mL})];$$

(*2*) *After oxidation.*—V = 3.0;

$$C = [(4.0/1000) \times (\text{mg tocopherols/mL})];$$

where 4.8 = mL of *Soln I* remaining after removal of aliquot for α-tocopherol detn; mg tocopherol/mL refers to *Soln I*; 1000 = factor to convert mg to g; 3.0 = vol. oxidized soln resulting from diln; and 4.0 = vol. of *Soln I* used for oxidn.

(**b**) *Specific rotation ratio.*—Calc. ratio

$$= ([a]_D^{25} \text{ after oxidn} - [a]_D^{25} \text{ before oxidn})/25.5,$$

where 25.5 is specific rotation of oxidn product of pure *RRR*-α-tocopherol. If ratio = 1.0±0.30, sample is identified as *RRR*-α-tocopherol; if ratio = 0.00±0.10, sample is identified as *all-rac*-α-tocopherol.

(**c**) *International Units.*—(*1*) If *RRR*-α-tocopherol is present:

IU vitamin E/g sample = (mg α-tocopherol equiv. in sample/g sample) × 1.10.

(*2*) If *all-rac*-α-tocopherol is present:

IU vitamin E/g sample = (mg α-tocopherol equiv. in sample/g sample) × 1.10.

Supplemental alpha-Tocopheryl Acetate in Foods and Feeds (*17*)—Official Final Action

43.106 ***Modified Extraction for Supplemental alpha-Tocopheryl Acetate Only***

(*Caution: See* **51.011**, **51.015**, **51.039**, and **51.073**.)

(Methods for sample prepn and extn described in **43.091** are usually sufficient. Following modified extn technics may be used for special cases.)

(**a**) *Wet products.*—Place accurately weighed sample in large mortar and grind thoroly with 2–3 times its wt anhyd. powd Na_2SO_4 until dry mixt. is obtained. Quant. transfer mixt. to g-s flask, add 50 mL purified ether, shake thoroly 15 min, and let solids settle. Take 10 mL aliquot of clear ext, evap. solv., and weigh lipid. Transfer ≤30 mL aliquot contg ca 1 g lipid and ca 0.1 IU supplemental vitamin E to ₮ 125 mL r-b flask, evap. solv. under N on steam bath, and proceed as in **43.107**.

(**b**) *Expanded dog foods and baked dog biscuits supplemented before expansion, processing, or baking.*—Proceed as in **43.091(f)**, except after refluxing, cool soln and let solids settle. Assume that vol. liq. present equals vol. H_2O-satd *n*-BuOH added plus H_2O content of sample extd. Take aliquot of H_2O-satd *n*-BuOH ext contg ca 0.1 IU supplemental vitamin E and evap. to dryness under vac. in 60° H_2O bath. Quant. transfer dried aliquot to Soxhlet extn thimble, using purified pet ether, (**a**)(*1*), as rinsing liq. Re-ext residue in Soxhlet 45 min with 50 mL purified pet ether, (**a**)(*1*). Evap. under N to <50 mL and dil. to 50 mL. Take 10 mL aliquot, evap. solv., and weigh lipid. Transfer remaining 40 mL or aliquot contg ca 1 g lipid and 0.1 IU supplemental vitamin E to ₮ 125 mL r-b flask, evap. solv. under N on steam bath, and proceed as in **43.107**.

43.107 ***Oxidative Chromatography***

(**a**) *Preparation of column.—See* **43.100(c)(1)**.

(**b**) *Elution of α-tocopheryl acetate.*—Quant. transfer test sample or aliquot contg ca 0.1 IU supplemental α-tocopheryl acetate from **43.091** or **43.106** in 4 mL pet ether, (**a**)(*1*) (aliquot may be evapd just to dryness under N and residue then dissolved in pet ether, (**a**)(*1*)) to top of chromatgc column, using elongated dropper. If aliquot contains <500 mg lipid, add olive oil as necessary to give this min. amt of lipid. Use ca five 1.0 mL portions pet ether, (**a**)(*1*), as rinses for quant. transfer. To prevent column from running dry, do not use vac. during sample transfer. Elute column with 100 mL benzene. Evap. benzene eluate to ca 4 mL on steam bath under N stream and then to dryness under N with reduced heat. Dissolve residue and dil. to 10 mL with pet ether, (**a**)(*2*)-absolute alcohol (3+2). Use ≤5 mL to det. reducing substances before saponification as in **43.109(a)**. Use ≤4 mL for saponification in **43.108**.

43.108 ***Saponification***

Accurately transfer ≤4 mL aliquot of pet ether, (**a**)(*2*)-absolute alcohol (3+2) contg ca 20 μg α-tocopherol to ₮ 125 mL r-b flask. Evap. to dryness under N and saponify as in **43.092**, except that entire dry ether ext should be concd to small vol. in 25 mL vial. Proceed as in **43.109(b)**.

43.109 ***Colorimetry***

(**a**) *Before saponification.*—Using ≤5 mL pet ether, (**a**)(*2*)-absolute alcohol soln from **43.107**, det. α-tocopherol equiv. of extraneous reducing substances not removed in oxidative chromatgy by colorimetry as in **43.094**(**b**).

(*Note:* If α-tocopherol equiv. of reducing substances before saponification (μg/g sample) exceeds 15% of α-tocopherol after saponification (μg/g sample), repeat assay, using ≥2 oxidative chromatgc columns, or equiv. With unusually high levels of antioxidants, solv. partition or other purification steps may be necessary.)

(**b**) *After saponification.*—Assay concd ether exts in 25 mL vial from **43.108** for α-tocopherol as in **43.094**(**b**).

(*Note:* If excessive amts of non-α-tocopheryl acetate (>15%) are present in feed supplement or supplemented feed, det. α-tocopherol as follows: After oxidative chromatgy as in **43.107** and saponification as in **43.092**, use aliquot of ether ext for TLC, **43.093**. Apply ratio of α-tocopherol in **43.094**(**a**) to total tocopherols as detd in **43.109**(**b**) as correction factor to mg α-tocopherol/g sample in **43.110**(**c**).)

43.110 ***Calculations***

(**a**) mg Reducing substances before saponification/sample = μg substances measured × (x/y) × $(10/w)$ × (1/1000), where x = total mL ext from **43.091**; y = mL ext used for chromatgy, **43.107**; 10 = mL soln after chromatgy; w = mL taken for colorimetry; and 1/1000 = factor to convert μg to mg.

(**b**) mg α-Tocopherol after saponification/sample = μg α-tocopherol measured × (x/y) × $(10/v)$ × (1/1000), where symbols are defined in (**a**), 10 = mL soln after chromatgy, and v = mL taken for saponification.

(**c**) mg α-Tocopherol/sample = (mg α-tocopherol/sample, after saponification) − (mg reducing substances/sample, before saponification).

(**d**) mg α-Tocopheryl acetate/g sample = (mg α-tocopherol in sample/wt sample in g) × 1.098.

(**e**) Det. IU added vitamin E/g sample as follows:

If *RRR*-α-tocopheryl acetate is present: IU vitamin E/g sample = (mg α-tocopheryl acetate/wt sample in g) × 1.36.

If *all-rac*-α-tocopheryl acetate is present: IU vitamin E/g sample = (mg α-tocopheryl acetate/wt sample in g) × 1.00.

Vitamin E (*19*)—Official Final Action

(Applicable to pharmaceutical prepns)

43.111 ***Apparatus***

(**a**) *Gas chromatograph.*—Equipped with either H flame or β-Ar ionization detector; capable of accepting glass column and glass-lined sample introduction system or on-column injection. Typical operating conditions: temps (°)—column 270–285, injection system 295, detector 295; N or Ar carrier gas flow adjusted so α-tocopheryl acetate peak appears 23–27 min after sample introduction; satisfactory recorder chart speed 0.33″/min; and β-Ar detector 900 v dc.

(**b**) *Filter assembly.*—Consisting of Millipore filter holder, No. XX 1004700, and microfiber glass prefilter disk, No. AP 2004200 (Millipore Corp., Ashby Rd, Bedford, MA 01730); and Filtrator, Fisher Scientific Co. No. 9-788.

43.112 ***Reagents***

(**a**) *n-Hexane.*—Pure grade, Phillips Petroleum Co.

(**b**) *RRR- or all-rac-alpha-Tocopherol.*—Eastman Kodak Co. No. 6340; or Hoffmann-La Roche, Inc. No. 60524.

(**c**) *RRR- or all-rac-alpha-Tocopheryl acetate.*—Eastman No. 6679; or Hoffmann-La Roche No. 60526.

(**d**) *RRR- or all-rac-alpha-Tocopheryl hydrogen succinate.*—Eastman No. 6347; or Hoffmann-La Roche No. 60540.

(**e**) *Internal std soln.*—Dissolve 500 mg hexadecyl palmitate (cetyl palmitate, primary internal std, Analabs No. LMS-067, or equiv.) or, alternatively 500 mg dotriacontane (Eastman Kodak Co., No. 3555) in *n*-hexane in 500 mL vol. flask and dil. to vol. with *n*-hexane.

(**f**) *Vitamin E std solns.*—Prep. desired vitamin E analog(s) Ref. Std(s) by transferring 100 mg analog into 100 mL vol. flask and dissolve and dil. to vol. with internal std soln or with *n*-hexane (for external std method). Refrigerate all std solns in *amber* Pyrex vol. flasks under N.

43.113 ***Preparation of Column***

Fill 2.4 m (8′) × 4 mm id (uniform bore) Pyrex tube with 5% SE-30 on 100–120 mesh Gas-Chrom Q to within 10 cm of injection point and 2.5 cm of column exit. Vibrate column while filling. Insert glass wool plugs, one extending to top of carrier gas inlet arm at column injection end and another filling space between packing and septum at exit.

Condition column 24 hr at 285° and 80 mL/min carrier gas flow. Let column cool with gas flowing. Connect column outlet to detector; bring chromatograph to operating temp. and carrier gas flow rate. Record baseline to check instrument stability. Baseline drift should be ≤1% in 30 min.

(Pretested column available from Applied Science Laboratories.)

(Occasionally column is rendered unusable for 1–4 hr following direct injection. If this situation arises, either increase column temp. for short time to drive off sample contaminants or wait until baseline stabilizes at column operating temp.)

43.114 ***Preparation of Sample***

(*Caution: See* **51.011** and **51.061**.)

(**a**) *Tablets.*—Grind in mortar and ext with four 25 mL portions *n*-hexane. Filter thru filter assembly into receiver. (*1*) *Internal std method.*—Evap. hexane under N stream and dil. with internal std soln to such vol. that final concn is 1 mg vitamin E/mL. (*2*) *External std method.*—Dil. with hexane to such vol. that final concn is 1 mg vitamin E/mL based on label claim.

(**b**) *Capsules.*—Dissolve in *n*-hexane under N, heating slightly if needed. If capsules do not disintegrate, cut open and remove contents with *n*-hexane. Open slip-capsules and place contents and capsule parts in *n*-hexane. Continue as in (**a**).

(**c**) *Injectables and liquids.*—Dil. with internal std soln (for internal std method) or with *n*-hexane (for external std method) so that final concn is 1 mg vitamin E/mL. If product is not miscible with *n*-hexane, inject μL aliquots of product directly onto GLC column and use external std method for detn.

(**d**) *Other preparations.*—If sample is not directly extractable with *n*-hexane, disperse with H_2O and dissolve in suitable solv. Evap. solv. under N and proceed as in (**a**).

43.115 ***Injection Technic***

(**a**) *Internal std method.*—Injection technic is not critical.

(**b**) *External std method.*—Use following injection technic with 10 μL Hamilton microsyringe: Draw 1 μL air into barrel, insert needle into sample, and draw desired amt into barrel; remove needle from soln, and draw 1 μL air into barrel. Check sample vol. between same μL range on calibration scale each time sample is obtained to ensure uniformity in vol.

43.116 ***Performance Check***

Monitor instrument and column performance by observing sepn of α-tocopherol and α-tocopheryl acetate peaks expressed as peak resolution.

Peak resolution = $2D/(B + C)$, where D = distance between analog peak maxima, B = α-tocopheryl acetate peak base width, and C = α-tocopherol peak base width.

Det. these values with mixt. of equal wts α-tocopherol and α-tocopheryl acetate, using sample size so that ht of peaks is ca 50% full scale. If peak resolution is ≥1.0, column and instrument are satisfactory. All columns will show gradual loss in peak resolution; when value is <1.0, install new column.

(**a**) *Internal std method.*—Calibrate instrument by injecting amt (usually 2–5 μL) std soln(s) to produce peaks for vitamin E analogs and internal std that give ca 50% full scale deflection. Measure area of analog(s) and internal std peaks with integrator, or by peak ht times width at half peak ht, recording sensitivity and retention times. Calc. relative response factor, *RF*, for std soln = (Q_s/Q_d), where Q_s and Q_d are peak areas of specific vitamin E analog and internal std, resp. Repeat calibration until *RF* is const (within 2%) for 3 consecutive injections and other parameters are stabilized. Repeat calibration for each vitamin E analog of interest.

(**b**) *External std method.*—Prep. std curve of 2–5 μg of each analog of interest daily. Plot response in area against μg injected, using ≥3 points in duplicate for each analog to be measured.

43.117 ***Peak Identification***

Compare retention times of samples and stds. Distinguish α-tocopherol from α-tocopheryl hydrogen succinate in sample exts (these vitamin E analogs have similar retention times) as follows: Obtain GLC analysis of ext. Add 1 mL Ac_2O-pyridine (2+1) to ext, and shake 10 min. Evap. soln under N stream, dil. to original vol. with *n*-hexane, and obtain GLC analysis. If peak shifts to α-tocopheryl acetate position, sample contains alcohol; if it does not shift, sample contains α-tocopheryl hydrogen succinate. Relative retention times are: α-tocopheryl acetate, 1.0; α-tocopherol, 0.9; α-tocopheryl hydrogen succinate, 0.9.

Relative to hexadecyl palmitate and dotriacontane, resp., in internal std method, retention times are: α-tocopherol, 0.53 and 0.75; α-tocopheryl hydrogen succinate, 0.54 and 0.76; α-tocopheryl acetate, 0.62 and 0.86.

43.118 ***Determination***

(**a**) *Internal std method.*—Inject vol. sample soln, **43.114**, prepd on basis of label claim, to give expected response comparable to that of std soln(s) as in **43.116(a)**. Measure area of peak(s) of vitamin E analog(s) and internal std.

mg Vitamin E analog(s)/tablet, capsule, or mL
= (Q_x/Q_d) × (declared potency/*RF*),
where Q_x and Q_d are peak areas of vitamin E analog from sample and internal std, resp., and *RF* is detd as in **43.116(a)**.

If label claims are stated as International Units (IU), convert to wt, using following conversion factors:

1 mg *all-rac*-α-tocopheryl acetate = 1 IU; 1 mg *all-rac*-α-tocopherol = 1.1 IU; 1 mg *RRR*-α-tocopheryl acetate = 1.36 IU; 1 mg *RRR*-α-tocopherol = 1.49 IU; 1 mg *RRR*-α-tocopheryl hydrogen succinate = 1.21 IU.

(**b**) *External std method.*—Inject 2 μL sample ext. Det. area of each peak with electromech. or electronic integrator, or by triangulation, i.e., peak ht × peak width at half ht. Convert peak area to amt vitamin E analog, using sp calibration plot.

mg Vitamin E analog(s)/tablet, capsule, or mL = $(X/N)(V/U)$, where X = μg read from calibration curve, N = μL injected (normally 2), V = vol. total ext (mL), and U = number tablets, capsules, or mL initially used. If necessary, convert to IU as in (**a**).

43.119 ★ **Calcium Pantothenate (*20*)** ★
Official First Action

Pantothenate molecule is cleaved with acid and resulting β-alanine is treated with chlorinating soln and then with KI. Free I is measured spectrophtric. *See* **43.086–43.090**, 12th ed.

Menadione Sodium Bisulfite
(Water-Soluble Vitamin K_3) (*21*)
Official Final Action

43.120 ***Principle***

Menadione is extd as menadione.$NaHSO_3.3H_2O$ with MeOH and converted to menadione by on-column pyrolytic GLC.

43.121 ***Apparatus***

(**a**) *Gas chromatograph.*—With flame ionization detector. Operating conditions: temps (°)—column 135, injection port 250, detector block 235; flow rates (mL/min)—N 25, H 25, air 300. Adjust conditions to give ≥0.5 full scale deflection for 0.5 mg menadione/mL.

(**b**) *Column.*—Pyrex or stainless steel 120 × 0.64 cm (4′ × ¼″) or 180 × 0.32 cm (6′ × ⅛″), with glass-lined sample introduction system or on-column injection, packed with (*1*) 2% OV-17 on 80–100 mesh acid-washed Chromosorb W (Supelco, Inc.) silylated with BSA (*N,O*-bis-(trimethylsilyl) acetamide)-TMCS (trimethyl chlorosilane), 5 + 1; or (*2*) 3% Dexsil 300 on 100–120 mesh Gas Chrom Q. Condition 2% OV-17 column (*1*) 12 hr at 250° with N. (*Caution:* Silanes are toxic. Wear disposable gloves and use effective fume removal device when handling.)

43.122 ***Standard Solutions***

(**a**) *Menadione std soln.*—(*1*) *Stock soln.*—4 mg/mL. Dissolve 200 mg USP Menadione Ref. Std in MeOH and dil. to 50 mL with MeOH. Store in dark; prep. fresh daily. (*2*) *Working solns.*—Prep std solns, each contg 1.0 mg diethyl phthalate (DEP)/mL, as follows:

	mg Menadione/mL				
Soln	0.8	0.6	0.5	0.4	0.2
MeOH	3	7	15	4	9
Stock soln	2	3	5	1	1
DEP soln	5	10	20	5	10
Final vol., mL	10	20	40	10	20

(**b**) *Menadione sodium bisulfite std soln.*—(*1*) *Stock soln.*—2 mg/mL. Dissolve 200 mg menadione .$NaHSO_3.3H_2O$ (94+%, ICN Pharmaceuticals, Inc., Life Sciences Group) in MeOH and dil. to 100 mL with MeOH. Prep. weekly. (*2*) *Check soln.*—Mix equal parts soln (**b**)(*1*) and (**c**); final concn is 1.0 mg menadione .$NaHSO_3.3H_2O$ and 1.0 mg DEP/mL.

(**c**) *Diethyl phthalate (DEP) internal std soln.*—2 mg/mL. Dissolve 1.0 g DEP (Aldrich Chemical Co., Inc.) in MeOH and dil. to 500 mL with MeOH.

43.123 ***Preparation of Sample***

Accurately weigh 5.0 g feed premix contg ca 5.0 g menadione/lb (16 g menadione.$NaHSO_3.3H_2O$/lb) and transfer

★ Surplus method—*see* inside front cover.

to 200 mL g-s erlenmeyer. Add 50 mL internal std soln, (**c**), mix gently 10 min, and let stand 5 min. Dil. 5 mL aliquot with 5 mL MeOH, mix, and centrf. For premixes with different menadione levels, adjust extn technic to obtain final concn so that equiv. menadione content is ca 0.5 mg/mL and soln contains 1.0 mg DEP/mL.

43.124 ***Calibration***

Inject 2 μL 0.5 mg menadione-DEP working std soln into gas chromatograph. Adjust to give ≥0.5 full scale deflection. Det. menadione/DEP peak response ratio (R_1), using integrator or peak areas as follows:

$$R_1 = PA_1/PA_2$$

where PA_1 and PA_2 = peak areas of menadione (0.5 mg/mL) and DEP (1.0 mg/mL), resp.

Inject 2 μL aliquot of each menadione std soln and det. menadione/DEP peak response ratios. Prep. std curve by plotting mg menadione/mL against menadione/DEP peak response ratio for each std soln. Adjust instrument to obtain linear std curve.

Prior to sample analysis, check injection port temp. for on-column pyrolysis of menadione.$NaHSO_3.3H_2O$ compd to menadione by injecting 2 μL aliquot menadione.$NaHSO_3.3H_2O$ check std soln. Det. menadione (pyrolytic product)/DEP peak response ratio (R_2) and calc. % menadione in menadione.$NaHSO_3.3H_2O$ check std soln

$$=(MD_1/MSB_2) \times (R_2/R_1) \times 100$$

where MD_1 = mg menadione/mL in std soln, and MSB_2 = mg menadione.$NaHSO_3.3H_2O$/mL in check std soln.

43.125 ***Determination***

Check chromatgc conditions daily by injecting 2 μL 0.5 mg/mL std soln ≥3 times and det. av. peak response ratio, R_1, which should be within ±10% of std curve. If not, readjust temps and flow rates.

Inject 2 μL sample soln ≥2 times and det. av. menadione/DEP peak response ratio, R_x.

g Menadione/g sample = $(MD_1/PM_x) \times (R_x/R_1)$,

where PM_x = mg sample/mL sample soln.

g Menadione/lb sample

= (g menadione/g premix) × (453.7 g/lb).

MICROBIOLOGICAL METHODS

Vitamins—Official Final Action

(Thruout all stages, except where otherwise directed, protect solns from undue exposure to light.)

43.126 ***Stock Solutions for Basal Media***

(Store all solns in dark at ca 10°. Store all solns except those contg alcohol under toluene. Proportionate amts may be prepd.)

(**a**) *Acid-hydrolyzed casein soln.*—(*Caution: See* **51.011** and **51.015**.) Mix 400 g vitamin-free casein with 2 L const-boiling HCl (ca 5*N*) and either reflux 8–12 hr, or autoclave 8–12 hr at 121–123°. Remove HCl from mixt. by distn under reduced pressure until thick paste remains. Redissolve paste in H_2O, adjust soln to pH 3.5±0.1 with ca 10% NaOH soln, and dil. with H_2O to 4 L. Add 80 g activated charcoal, stir 1 hr, and filter. Repeat treatment with activated charcoal. Filter soln if ppt forms upon storage. (Some com. sources of vitamin-free acid-hydrolyzed casein have been found satisfactory.)

(**b**) *Adenine-guanine-uracil soln.*—Dissolve 1.0 g each of adenine sulfate, guanine.HCl, and uracil in 50 mL warm HCl (1+1), cool, and dil. with H_2O to 1 L.

(**c**) *Asparagine soln.*—Dissolve 10 g L-asparagine.H_2O in H_2O and dil. to 1 L.

(**d**) *Cystine soln.*—Suspend 2 g L-cystine in ca 750 mL H_2O, heat to 70–80°, and add HCl (1+1), dropwise, with stirring, until solid dissolves. Cool, and dil. with H_2O to 1 L.

(**e**) *Cystine-tryptophan soln.*—Suspend 8 g L-cystine and 2 g L-tryptophan (or 4 g D,L-tryptophan) in ca 1.5 L H_2O, heat to 70–80°, and add HCl (1+1), dropwise, with stirring, until solids dissolve. Cool, and dil. with H_2O to 2 L.

(**f**) *Manganese sulfate soln.*—Dissolve 2 g $MnSO_4.H_2O$ in H_2O and dil. to 200 mL.

(**g**) *Photolyzed peptone soln.*—Dissolve 100 g peptone in 625 mL H_2O, add soln of 50 g NaOH in 625 mL H_2O, and mix in vessel (such as crystg dish) of such size that depth of soln is 1–2 cm. Place 100–500 watt bulb, fitted with reflector, ca 30–50 cm from soln, and expose soln, with occasional stirring, to light from bulb until riboflavin is destroyed (4–10 hr may be enough). Maintain soln at ≤25° during this treatment. Adjust soln to pH 6.0–6.5 with HOAc, add 18 g anhyd. NaOAc, stir until solid dissolves, dil. with H_2O to 2 L, and filter if soln is not clear.

(**h**) *Polysorbate 80 soln.*—Dissolve 25 g polysorbate 80 (polyoxyethylene sorbitan monooleate) in alcohol to make 250 mL.

(**i**) *Salt soln A.*—Dissolve 50 g anhyd. KH_2PO_4 and 50 g anhyd. K_2HPO_4 in H_2O, dil. to 1 L, and add 10 drops HCl.

(**j**) *Salt soln B.*—Dissolve 20 g $MgSO_4.7H_2O$, 1 g NaCl, 1 g $FeSO_4.7H_2O$, and 1 g $MnSO_4.H_2O$ in H_2O, dil. to 1 L, and add 10 drops HCl.

(**k**) *Tryptophan soln.*—Suspend 2.0 g L-tryptophan (or 4.0 g D,L-tryptophan) in 700–800 mL H_2O, heat to 70–80°, and add HCl (1+1), dropwise, with stirring, until solid dissolves. Cool, and dil. with H_2O to 1 L.

(**l**) *Vitamin soln I.*—Dissolve 25 mg riboflavin, 25 mg thiamine.HCl, 0.25 mg biotin, and 50 mg niacin in 0.02*N* HOAc to make 1 L.

(**m**) *Vitamin soln II.*—Dissolve 50 mg *p*-aminobenzoic acid, 25 mg Ca pantothenate, 100 mg pyridoxine.HCl, 100 mg pyridoxal.HCl, 20 mg pyridoxamine.2HCl, and 5 mg folic acid in 25% alcohol to make 1 L.

(**n**) *Vitamin soln III.*—Dissolve 10 mg *p*-aminobenzoic acid, 40 mg pyridoxine.HCl, 4 mg thiamine.HCl, 8 mg Ca pantothenate, 8 mg niacin, and 0.2 mg biotin in ca 300 mL H_2O. Add 10 mg riboflavin dissolved in ca 200 mL 0.02*N* HOAc. Then add soln contg 1.9 g anhyd. NaOAc and 1.6 mL HOAc in ca 40 mL H_2O, and dil. with H_2O to 2 L.

(**o**) *Vitamin soln IV.*—Dissolve 20 mg riboflavin, 10 mg thiamine.HCl, and 0.04 mg biotin in 0.02*N* HOAc to make 1 L.

(**p**) *Vitamin soln V.*—Dissolve 10 mg *p*-aminobenzoic acid, 20 mg Ca pantothenate, and 40 mg pyridoxine.HCl in 25% alcohol to make 1 L.

(**q**) *Vitamin soln VI.*—Dissolve 10 mg *p*-aminobenzoic acid, 50 mg niacin, and 40 mg pyridoxine.HCl in 25% alcohol to make 1 L.

(**r**) *Xanthine soln.*—Suspend 1.0 g xanthine in 150–200 mL H_2O, heat to ca 70°, add 30 mL NH_4OH (2+3), and stir until solid dissolves. Cool, and dil. with H_2O to 1 L.

(**s**) *Yeast supplement soln.*—Dissolve 20 g H_2O-sol. yeast ext in 100 mL H_2O, add soln of 30 g Pb subacetate in 100 mL H_2O (soln is turbid), and mix. Filter, and adjust filtrate to pH 10 with NH_4OH (1+2). Filter, and adjust filtrate to pH 6.5 with HOAc. Ppt excess Pb with H_2S, filter, and dil. filtrate with H_2O to 200 mL.

43.127 ***Culture and Suspension Media***

(**a**) *Liquid culture medium.*—Dissolve 15 g peptonized milk, 5 g H_2O-sol. yeast ext, 10 g anhyd. glucose, and 2 g anhyd. KH_2PO_4 in ca 600 mL H_2O. Add 100 mL filtered tomato juice, and adjust to pH 6.5–6.8 with NaOH soln. Add, with mixing, 10 mL polysorbate 80 soln, (**h**), and dil. with H_2O to 1 L. Add 10 mL portions soln to test tubes, cover to prevent contamination, sterilize 15 min in autoclave at 121–123°, and cool tubes as rapidly as practicable to keep color formation at min. Store in dark at ca 10°. (Difco Lactobacilli Broth AOAC, Difco Laboratories, has been found satisfactory.)

(b) *Agar culture medium.*—To 500 mL liq. culture medium, **(a)**, add 5.0–7.5 g agar, and heat with stirring on steam bath until agar dissolves. Add ca 10 mL portions hot soln to test tubes, cover to prevent contamination, sterilize 15 min in autoclave at 121–123°, and cool tubes in upright position as rapidly as practicable to keep color formation at min. Store in dark at ca 10°. (Difco agar culture medium for AOAC microbiological assays (Lactobacilli Agar AOAC) has been found satisfactory.)

(c) *Suspension medium.*—Dil. measured vol. appropriate basal medium stock soln, Table **43:03**, with equal vol. H_2O. Add 10 mL portions dild medium to test tubes, cover to prevent contamination, sterilize 15 min in autoclave at 121–123°, and cool tubes as rapidly as practicable to keep color formation at min. Store in dark at ca 10°.

43.128 *Stock Cultures of Test Organisms*

For appropriate test organism, designated below, prep. stab culture in ≥1 tubes of *agar culture medium,* **43.127(b)**. Incubate 6–24 hr at any selected temp. between 30 and 40° held const to within ±0.5°, and finally store in dark at ca 10°. Before using new culture in assay, make several successive transfers of culture in 1–2 week period.

Prep. fresh stab culture ≥1 time weekly and do not use for prepg inoculum if >1 week old.

Activity of slow-growing culture may be increased by daily or twice-daily transfer of stab culture, and is considered satisfactory when definite turbidity in liq. inoculum can be observed 2–4 hr after inoculation. Slow-growing culture seldom gives suitable response curve and may cause erratic results.

(a) *Lactobacillus leichmannii.*—ATCC No. 7830. For use in assay of cobalamin.

(b) *Streptococcus faecalis (faecium).*—ATCC No. 8043. For use in assay of folic acid.

(c) *Lactobacillus plantarum.*—ATCC No. 8014. For use in assay of niacin and pantothenic acid.

(d) *Lactobacillus casei* subsp. *rhamnosus.*—ATCC No. 7469. For use in assay of riboflavin.

43.129 *Assay Tubes*

Meticulously cleanse by suitable means (Na lauryl sulfate USP has been found satisfactory as detergent), hard-glass test tubes, ca 20 × 150 mm, and other necessary glassware. (Test organisms are highly sensitive to minute amts of growth factors and to many cleansing agents. Therefore, it may be preferred to follow cleansing by heating 1–2 hr at ca 250°. This is of particular importance in cobalamin assay.)

Prep. tubes contg appropriate std soln as follows: To test tubes add, in duplicate (or replicate), 0.0 (for uninoculated blanks), 0.0 (for inoculated blanks), 1.0, 2.0, 3.0, 4.0, and 5.0 mL, resp., of std soln.

Prep. tubes contg appropriate assay soln as follows: To similar test tubes add, in duplicate (or replicate), 1.0, 2.0, 3.0, and 4.0 mL, resp., of assay soln.

To each tube of std soln and assay soln add H_2O to make 5.0 mL. Then add 5.0 mL appropriate basal medium stock soln, Table **43:03**, and mix. Cover tubes suitably to prevent bacterial contamination, and sterilize (10 min for titrimetric method, **43.130**; or 5 min for turbidimetric method, **43.132**) in autoclave at 121–123°, reaching this temp. in ≤10 min. Cool as rapidly as

Table 43:03 Basal Media Stock Solutions for 250 mL (Proportionate Amounts May be Prepared)[a]

Ingredients (Stock Solutions, **43.126**)	**(a)** Cobalamin (Vitamin B_{12} Activity)	**(b)** Folic Acid (Pteroylglutamic Acid)	**(c)** Niacin and Niacinamide	**(d)** Pantothenic Acid	**(e)** Riboflavin (Vitamin B_2)
	mL	mL	mL	mL	mL
(a) Acid-hydrolyzed casein soln	25	25	25	25	
(b) Adenine-guanine-uracil soln	5	2.5	5	5	
(c) Asparagine soln	5	15			
(d) Cystine soln					25
(e) Cystine-tryptophan soln			25	25	
(f) Manganese sulfate soln		5			
(g) Photolyzed peptone soln					50
(h) Polysorbate 80 soln	5	0.25		0.25	
(i) Salt soln A	5		5	5	5
(j) Salt soln B	5	5	5	5	5
(k) Tryptophan soln		25			
(l) Vitamin soln I	10				
(m) Vitamin soln II	10				
(n) Vitamin soln III		50			
(o) Vitamin soln IV			5	5	
(p) Vitamin soln V			5		
(q) Vitamin soln VI				5	
(r) Xanthine soln	5	5			
(s) Yeast supplement soln					5
Solids	grams	grams	grams	grams	grams
Ascorbic acid	1				
L-Cysteine.HCl.H_2O		0.19			
L-Cystine	0.1				
Glucose, anhyd.	10	10	10	10	15
Glutathione		0.0013			
K_2HPO_4, anhyd.		1.6			
NaOAc.3H_2O	8.3		8.3	8.3	
Na citrate.2H_2O		13			
D,L-Tryptophan	0.1				

[a] Some com. sources of basal media have been found satisfactory.

practicable to keep color formation at min. Take precautions to keep sterilizing and cooling conditions uniform thruout assay. Too close packing of tubes in autoclave, or overloading of it, may cause variation in heating rate.

Aseptically inoculate each tube, except 1 set of duplicate (or replicate) tubes contg 0.0 mL std soln (uninoculated blanks), with 1 drop appropriate inoculum. Incubate for time period designated in titrimetric method, **43.130**, or turbidimetric method, **43.132**, at any selected temp. between 30 and 40° held const to within ±0.5°. Contamination of assay tubes with any foreign organism invalidates assay.

Titrimetric Method

43.130 ***Determination***

Incubate tubes 72 hr, and then titr. contents of each tube with 0.1*N* NaOH, using bromothymol blue indicator, or to pH 6.8 measured potentiometrically.

Disregard results of assay if response at inoculated blank level is equiv. to titrn of >1.5 mL greater than that at uninoculated blank level. Response at 5.0 mL level of std soln should be equiv. to titrn of ca 8–12 mL.

Prep. std concn-response curve by plotting titrn values, expressed in mL 0.1*N* NaOH for each level of std soln used, against amt of ref. std contained in respective tubes.

Det. amt of vitamin for each level of assay soln by interpolation from std curve. Discard any observed titrn values equiv. to <0.5 mL or >4.5 mL, resp., of std soln. Proceed as in **43.133**.

Turbidimetric Method

(Not applicable in presence of extraneous turbidity or color in amt that interferes with turbidimetric measurements)

43.131 ***Calibration of Photometer***

Using inoculum and std stock soln as prescribed for appropriate vitamin in following table, and using suspension medium **43.127(c)**, proceed as directed below.

Vitamin	Inoculum	Std Stock Soln
Cobalamin	**43.136**[a]	**43.135(a)**
Folic acid	**43.144**	**43.143(b)**
Niacin	**43.156**	**43.151(a)**
Pantothenic acid	**43.165**	**43.160(a)**
Riboflavin	**43.174**	**43.169(a)**

[a] Proceed as in **43.136**, except replace fifth sentence with the following: "Dil 0.2–1.0 mL aliquot of this suspension with 10 mL sterile suspension medium."

Aseptically add 1 mL inoculum to ca 300 mL sterile suspension medium contg 1.0 mL std stock soln, and incubate mixt. for same period and at same temp. to be employed in detn, **43.132**. After incubating, centrf. and wash cells 3 times with ca 50 mL portions 0.9% NaCl soln; then resuspend cells in the NaCl soln to make 25 mL.

Evap. 10 mL aliquot of cell suspension on steam bath, and dry to const wt at 110° in vac. oven. Correcting for wt of NaCl, calc. dry wt of cells in mg/mL of suspension.

Dil. second measured aliquot of cell suspension with 0.9% NaCl soln so that each mL is equiv. to 0.5 mg dry cells. To test tubes add, in triplicate, 0.0 (for blanks), 0.5, 1.0, 1.5, 2.0, 2.5, 3.0, 4.0, and 5.0 mL, resp., of this dild cell suspension. To each tube add 0.9% NaCl soln to make 5.0 mL. Then add 5.0 mL appropriate basal medium stock soln, Table **43:03**, mix (1 drop of suitable *antifoam agent* may be added; 1–2% soln of Dow Corning Antifoam AF Emulsion or Antifoam B has been found satisfactory), and transfer to optical cell. With blanks set at 100% *T*, measure % *T* of each tube under same conditions to be used in respective assay. Prep. curve by plotting % *T* readings for each level of dild cell suspension used against cell content (mg dry wt) of respective tubes.

Repeat appropriate calibration step at least twice more for photometer to be used in respective assay. Draw composite curve, best representing 3 or more individual curves, relating % *T* to mg dried cell wt for photometer under conditions of respective assay. Once appropriate curve for particular instrument is established, all subsequent relationships between % *T* and cell wt are detd directly from this curve. Respective assay limits expressed as mg dried cell wt/tube are so detd.

43.132 ***Determination***

Incubate tubes 16–24 hr until max. turbidity is obtained, as demonstrated by lack of significant change during 2 hr addnl incubation period in tubes contg highest level of std soln.

Det. *T* of tubes as follows: Thoroly mix contents of each tube (1 drop of suitable antifoam agent soln may be added; 1–2% soln of Dow Corning Antifoam AF Emulsion or Antifoam B has been found satisfactory), and transfer to optical cell. Agitate contents, place cell in photometer set at any specific wavelength between 540 and 660 nm, and read % *T* when steady state is reached.

Steady state is observed few sec after agitation when galvanometer reading remains const ⩾30 sec. Allow ca same time interval for reading on each tube.

With *T* set at 100% for uninoculated blank level, read % *T* of inoculated blank level. If this reading corresponds to dried cell wt >0.6 mg/tube, disregard results of assay. Then with *T* reset at 100% for inoculated blank level, read % *T* for each of remaining tubes. Disregard results of assay if % *T* observed at 5.0 mL level of std soln (against inoculated blank) is equiv. to that for dried cell wt of <1.25 mg/tube.

Prep. std concn-response curve by plotting % *T* readings for each level of std soln used against amt of ref. std contained in respective tubes.

Det. amt of vitamin for each level of assay soln by interpolation from std curve. Discard any observed *T* values equiv. to <0.5 mL or >4.5 mL, resp., of std soln. Proceed as in **43.133**.

43.133 ***Calculation for Both Titrimetric and Turbidimetric Methods***

For each level of assay soln used, calc. vitamin content/mL of assay soln. Calc. av. of values obtained from tubes that do not vary by >±10% from this av. If number of acceptable values remaining is <⅔ of original number of tubes used in the 4 levels of assay soln, data are insufficient for calcg potency of sample. If number of acceptable values remaining is ⩾⅔ of original number of tubes, calc. potency of sample from av. of them.

Cobalamin (Vitamin B_{12} Activity) *(22)*

(Applicable to materials contg ca ⩾0.1 μg of vitamin B_{12} activity/g or mL)

43.134 ***Basal Medium Stock Solution***

Using ingredients in amts prescribed for cobalamin, Table **43:03(a)**, proceed as directed below.

Dissolve L-cystine and D,L-tryptophan in 10 mL 1*N* HCl. Using solns prepd as in **43.126**, add, with mixing, and in following order: adenine-guanine-uracil soln, **(b)**; xanthine soln, **(r)**; vitamin soln I, **(l)**; vitamin soln II, **(m)**; salt soln A, **(i)**; salt soln B, **(j)**; asparagine soln, **(c)**; and acid-hydrolyzed casein soln, **(a)**. Add ca 100 mL H_2O and add, with mixing, anhyd. glucose, $NaOAc.3H_2O$, and ascorbic acid. When soln is complete, adjust to pH 6.0 with NaOH soln, add, with mixing, polysorbate 80 soln, (**h**), and dil. with H_2O to 250 mL.

Titrimetric Method

43.135 ***Cyanocobalamin Standard Solutions***

(**a**) *Stock soln.*—100 ng/mL. Accurately weigh, in closed system, USP Cyanocobalamin Ref. Std equiv. to 50–60 μg cyanocobalamin, that has been dried to const wt and stored in dark over P_2O_5 in desiccator. Dissolve in 25% alcohol, and dil. with addnl 25% alcohol to make cyanocobalamin concn exactly 100 ng/mL. Store in dark at ca 10°.

(**b**) *Intermediate soln.*—1 ng/mL. Dil. 10 mL stock soln, (**a**), with 25% alcohol to 1 L. Store in dark at ca 10°.

(**c**) *Working soln.*—Dil. suitable vol. intermediate soln, (**b**), with H_2O to measured vol. such that after incubation as in **43.129** and **43.130**, response at 5.0 mL level of this soln is equiv. to titrn (as described in **43.130**) of ca 8–12 mL. Designate this as std soln. (This concn is usually 0.01–0.04 ng cyanocobalamin/mL std soln.) Prep. fresh std soln for each assay.

43.136 ***Inoculum***

Make transfer of cells from stock culture of *Lactobacillus leichmannii,* **43.128(a)**, to sterile tube contg 10 mL liq. culture medium, **43.127(a)**. Incubate 6–24 hr at any selected temp. between 30 and 40° held const to within ±0.5°. Under aseptic conditions, centrf. culture and decant supernate. Wash cells with 3 ca 10 mL portions sterile 0.9% NaCl soln or sterile suspension medium, **43.127(c)**. Resuspend cells in 10 mL sterile 0.9% NaCl soln or sterile suspension medium. Dil. aliquot with sterile 0.9% NaCl soln or sterile suspension medium to give *T* equiv. to that for dried cell wt (as described in **43.131**) of 0.50–0.75 mg/tube when read against suspension medium set at 100% *T*. Cell suspension so obtained is inoculum.

43.137 ***Assay Solution***

Prep. aq. extg soln just before use contg, in each 100 mL, 1.3 g anhyd. Na_2HPO_4, 1.2 g citric acid.H_2O, and 1.0 g *anhyd. Na metabisulfite,* $Na_2S_2O_5$. Place measured amt of sample in flask contg ≥25 mL extg soln for each g or mL sample taken. If sample is not readily sol., comminute to disperse it evenly in liq.; then agitate vigorously and wash down sides of flask with H_2O.

Autoclave mixt. 10 min at 121–123° and cool. If lumping occurs, agitate mixt. until particles are evenly dispersed. Dil. mixt. to measured vol. with H_2O, and let any undissolved particles settle, or filter or centrf. if necessary. Take aliquot of clear soln, add H_2O, adjust to pH 6.0, and dil. with addnl H_2O to measured vol. contg, per mL, cobalamin activity ca equiv. to that of std soln, **43.135(c)**. Designate this as assay soln. Excess of bisulfite may affect test organism. Therefore, assay soln must contain ≤0.03 mg $Na_2S_2O_5$/mL.

43.138 ***Assay***

Using std soln, **43.135(c)**, assay soln, **43.137**, basal medium stock soln, **43.134**, and inoculum, **43.136**, proceed as in **43.129**, **43.130**, and **43.133**.

Turbidimetric Method

43.139 ***Cyanocobalamin Standard Solution***

Dil. suitable vol. cyanocobalamin intermediate std soln, **43.135(b)**, with H_2O to measured vol. such that after incubation as in **43.129** and **43.132**, with inoculated blank set at 100% *T*, % *T* at 5.0 mL level of this soln is equiv. to that for dried cell wt (as described in **43.131**) of ≥1.25 mg. Designate this as std soln. (This concn is usually 0.01–0.04 ng cyanocobalamin/mL std soln.) Prep. fresh std soln for each assay.

43.140 ***Assay Solution***

Proceed as in **43.137**, except that where ref. is made to concn of cyanocobalamin activity ca equiv. to that of std soln, **43.135(c)**, replace by concn of cyanocobalamin activity ca equiv. to that of std soln, **43.139**. Designate soln so obtained as assay soln.

43.141 ***Assay***

Using std soln, **43.139**, assay soln, **43.140**, basal medium stock soln, **43.134**, and inoculum, **43.136**, proceed as in **43.129**, **43.132**, and **43.133**.

Folic Acid (Pteroylglutamic Acid) (*23*)

(Applicable only to materials contg free forms of folic acid)

43.142 ***Basal Medium Stock Solution***

Using ingredients in amts prescribed for folic acid, Table **43:03(b)**, proceed as directed below.

Using solns prepd as in **43.126** add, with mixing, and in following order: acid-hydrolyzed casein soln, (**a**); tryptophan soln, (**k**); adenine-guanine-uracil soln, (**b**); xanthine soln, (**r**); asparagine soln, (**c**); vitamin soln III, (**n**); and salt soln B, (**j**). Add ca 50 mL H_2O, and add, with mixing, cysteine, anhyd. glucose, Na citrate dihydrate, anhyd. K_2HPO_4, and glutathione. When soln is complete, adjust to pH 6.8 with NaOH soln, add, with mixing, polysorbate 80 soln, (**h**), and $MnSO_4$ soln, (**f**), and dil. with H_2O to 250 mL.

Titrimetric Method

43.143 ***Folic Acid Standard Solutions***

(Do not shake std solns stored under toluene.)

(**a**) *Stock soln.*—100 μg/mL. Accurately weigh, in closed system, USP Folic Acid Ref. Std, equiv. to 50–60 mg folic acid, that has been dried to const wt and stored in dark over P_2O_5 in desiccator. Dissolve in ca 30 mL 0.01*N* NaOH, add ca 300 mL H_2O, adjust to pH 7–8 with HCl soln, and dil. with addnl H_2O to make folic acid concn exactly 100 μg/mL. Store under toluene in dark at ca 10°.

(**b**) *Intermediate soln I.*—1 μg/mL. To 10 mL stock soln, (**a**), add ca 500 mL H_2O, adjust to pH 7–8, and dil. with addnl H_2O to 1 L. Store under toluene in dark at ca 10°.

(**c**) *Intermediate soln II.*—100 ng/mL. To 100 mL intermediate soln I, (**b**), add ca 500 mL H_2O, adjust to pH 7–8, and dil. with addnl H_2O to 1 L. Store under toluene in dark at ca 10°.

(**d**) *Working soln.*—Dil. suitable vol. intermediate soln II (**c**), with H_2O to measured vol. such that after incubation as in **43.129** and **43.130**, response at 5.0 mL level of this soln is equiv. to titrn (as described in **43.130**) of ca 8–12 mL. Designate this as std soln. (This concn is usually 1.0–4.0 ng folic acid/ml std soln.) Prep. fresh std soln for each assay.

43.144 ***Inoculum***

Make transfer of cells from stock culture of *Streptococcus faecalis,* **43.128(b)**, to sterile tube contg 10 mL liq. culture medium, **43.127(a)**. Incubate 6–24 hr at any selected temp. between 30 and 40° held const to within ±0.5°. Under aseptic conditions, centrf. culture and decant supernate. Wash cells with 3 ca 10 mL portions sterile 0.9% NaCl soln or sterile suspension medium, **43.127(c)**. Resuspend cells in 10 mL sterile 0.9% NaCl soln or sterile suspension medium. Cell suspension so obtained is inoculum.

43.145 ***Assay Solution***

Place measured amt of sample in flask and add vol. H_2O equal in mL to ≥10 times dry wt sample in g; resulting soln must contain ≤1.0 mg folic acid/mL. Add equiv. of 2 mL NH_4OH (2+3)/100 mL liq. If sample is not readily sol., comminute to disperse it evenly in liq.; then agitate vigorously and wash down sides of flask with 0.1*N* NH_4OH.

Autoclave mixt. 15 min at 121–123° and cool. If lumping occurs, agitate mixt. until particles are evenly dispersed. Dil. mixt. to measured vol. with H_2O, and let any undissolved particles settle, or filter or centrf. if necessary. Take aliquot of clear soln, add H_2O, adjust to pH 6.8, and dil. with addnl H_2O to measured vol. contg, per mL, folic acid ca equiv. to that of std soln, **43.143(d)**. Designate this as assay soln.

43.146 ***Assay***

Using std soln, **43.143(d)**, assay soln, **43.145**, basal medium stock soln, **43.142**, and inoculum, **43.144**, proceed as in **43.129**, **43.130**, and **43.133**.

Turbidimetric Method

43.147 ***Folic Acid Standard Solution***

Dil. suitable vol. folic acid intermediate soln II, **43.143(c)**, with H_2O to measured vol. such that after incubation as in **43.129** and **43.132**, with inoculated blank set at 100% *T*, % *T* at 5.0 mL level of this soln is equiv. to that for dried cell wt (as described in **43.131**) of ≥1.25 mg. Designate this as std soln. (This concn is usually 0.5–2.0 ng folic acid/mL std soln.) Prep. fresh std soln for each assay.

43.148 ***Assay Solution***

Proceed as in **43.145**, except that where ref. is made to folic acid concn ca equiv. to that of std soln, **43.143(d)**, replace by folic acid concn ca equiv. to that of std soln, **43.147**. Designate soln so obtained as assay soln.

43.149 ***Assay***

Using std soln, **43.147**, assay soln, **43.148**, basal medium stock soln, **43.142**, and inoculum, **43.144**, proceed as in **43.129, 43.132**, and **43.133**.

Niacin and Niacinamide (Nicotinic Acid and Nicotinamide) (*24*)

43.150 ***Basal Medium Stock Solution***

Using ingredients in amts prescribed for niacin, Table **43:03(c)**, proceed as below.

Using solns prepd as in **43.126**, add, with mixing, and in following order: acid-hydrolyzed casein soln, (**a**); cystine-tryptophan soln, (**e**); adenine-guanine-uracil soln, (**b**); vitamin soln IV, (**o**); vitamin soln V, (**p**); salt soln A, (**i**); and salt soln B, (**j**). Add ca 100 mL H_2O, and add, with mixing, anhyd. glucose and $NaOAc.3H_2O$. When soln is complete, adjust to pH 6.8 with NaOH soln, and dil. with H_2O to 250 mL.

Titrimetric Method

43.151 ***Niacin Standard Solutions***

(**a**) *Stock soln.*—100 μg/mL. Accurately weigh, in closed system, 50–60 mg USP Niacin Ref. Std that has been dried to const wt and stored in dark over P_2O_5 in desiccator. Dissolve in 25% alcohol, and dil. with addnl 25% alcohol to make niacin concn exactly 100 μg/mL. Store in dark at ca 10°.

(**b**) *Intermediate soln I.*—10 μg/mL. Dil. 100 mL stock soln, (**a**), with 25% alcohol to 1 L. Store in dark at ca 10°.

(**c**) *Working soln.*—Dil. suitable vol. intermediate soln, (**b**), with H_2O to measured vol. such that after incubation as in **43.129** and **43.130**, response at 5.0 mL level of this soln is equiv. to titrn (as described in **43.130**) of ca 8–12 mL. Designate this as std soln. (This concn is usually 0.1–0.4 μg niacin/mL std soln.) Prep. fresh std soln for each assay.

43.152 ***Inoculum***

(**a**) *Liquid culture medium.*—Dil. measured vol. basal medium stock soln, **43.150**, with equal vol. aq. soln contg 0.2 μg niacin/mL. Add 10 mL portions dild medium to test tubes, cover to prevent contamination, sterilize 15 min in autoclave at 121–123°, and cool tubes as rapidly as practicable to avoid color formation from overheating. Store in dark at ca 10°.

(**b**) *Inoculum.*—Make transfer of cells from stock culture of *Lactobacillus plantarum*, **43.128(c)**, to sterile tube contg 10 mL liq. culture medium, (**a**). Incubate 6–24 hr at any selected temp. between 30 and 40° held const to within ±0.5°. Under aseptic conditions, centrf. culture and decant supernate. Wash cells with 3 ca 10 mL portions sterile 0.9% NaCl soln or sterile suspension medium, **43.127(c)**. Resuspend cells in 10 mL sterile 0.9% NaCl soln or sterile suspension medium. Cell suspension so obtained is inoculum.

43.153 ***Assay Solution***

Place measured amt of sample in flask and proceed as below. Designate final measured vol. so obtained as assay soln.

(**a**) *For dry or semidry materials containing no appreciable amount of basic substances.*—Add vol. 1*N* H_2SO_4 equal in mL to ≥10 times dry wt sample in g; resulting soln must contain ≤5.0 mg niacin/mL. If sample is not readily sol., comminute to disperse it evenly in liq. Then agitate vigorously and wash down sides of flask with 1*N* H_2SO_4.

Autoclave mixt. 30 min at 121–123° and cool. If lumping occurs, agitate mixt. until particles are evenly dispersed. If dissolved protein is not present, adjust mixt. to pH 6.8 with NaOH soln, dil. with H_2O to final measured vol. contg, per mL, niacin ca equiv. to that of std soln, **43.151(c)**, and filter if soln is not clear.

If dissolved protein is present, adjust mixt., with vigorous agitation, to pH 6.0–6.5 with NaOH soln; then immediately add dil. HCl until no further pptn occurs (usually ca pH 4.5, isoelec. point of many proteins). Dil. mixt. to measured vol. with H_2O, and filter. (In case of mixt. difficult to filter, centrfg and/or filtering thru fritted glass, using suitable anal. filter-aid, may often be substituted for, or may precede, filtering thru paper. Ash-free filter paper pulp and Celite Analytical Filter-Aid have been found satisfactory.) Take aliquot of clear filtrate and check for dissolved protein by adding dropwise, first dil. HCl, and if no ppt forms, then, with vigorous agitation, NaOH soln, and proceed as follows with this aliquot:

(*1*) If no further pptn occurs, add, with vigorous agitation, NaOH soln to pH 6.8, and dil. with H_2O to final measured vol. contg, per mL, niacin ca equiv. to that of std soln, **43.151(c)**. If cloudiness occurs, refilter.

(*2*) If further pptn occurs, adjust mixt. again to point of max. pptn, dil. with H_2O to measured vol., and then filter. Take aliquot of clear filtrate and proceed as in (*1*).

(**b**) *For dry or semidry materials containing appreciable amounts of basic substances.*—Adjust mixt. to pH 5.0–6.0 with dil. H_2SO_4. Add vol. H_2O equal in mL to ≥10 times dry wt sample in g; resulting soln must contain ≤5.0 mg niacin/mL. Then add equiv. of 10 mL 10*N* H_2SO_4/100 mL liq. and proceed as in (**a**), beginning with second sentence, "If sample is not readily sol., . . ."

(**c**) *For liquid materials.*—Adjust mixt. to pH 5.0–6.0 with H_2SO_4 soln or NaOH soln and proceed as in (**b**), beginning with second sentence, "Add vol. H_2O . . ."

43.154 ***Assay***

Using std soln, **43.151(c)**, assay soln, **43.153**, basal medium stock soln, **43.150**, and inoculum, **43.152(b)**, proceed as in **43.129**, **43.130**, and **43.133**. Value so obtained is potency of sample expressed as niacin. Multiply this value by 0.992 if potency is to be expressed as niacinamide.

Turbidimetric Method

43.155 ***Niacin Standard Solutions***

(**a**) *Intermediate soln II.*—1.0 μg/mL. Dil. 10 mL niacin std stock soln, **43.151(a)**, with 25% alcohol to 1 L. Store in dark at ca 10°.

(**b**) *Working soln.*—Dil. suitable vol. intermediate soln II, (**a**), with H_2O to measured vol. such that after incubation as in **43.129** and **43.132**, with inoculated blank set at 100% *T*, % *T* at 5.0 mL level of this soln is equiv. to that for dried cell wt (as described in **43.131**) of $\geqslant$1.25 mg. Designate this as std soln. (This concn is usually 0.01–0.04 μg niacin/mL std soln.) Prep. fresh std soln for each assay.

43.156 ***Inoculum***

Proceed as in **43.152(b)**.

43.157 ***Assay Solution***

Proceed as in **43.153**, except that where ref. is made to niacin concn ca equiv. to that of std soln, **43.151(c)**, replace by niacin concn ca equiv. to that of std soln, **43.155(b)**. Designate soln so obtained as assay soln.

43.158 ***Assay***

Using std soln, **43.155(b)**, assay soln, **43.157**, basal medium stock soln, **43.150**, and inoculum, **43.156**, proceed as in **43.129**, **43.132**, and **43.133**. Value so obtained is potency of sample expressed as niacin. Multiply this value by 0.992 if potency is to be expressed as niacinamide.

Pantothenic Acid (*25*)

(Applicable only to materials contg Ca pantothenate or other free forms of pantothenic acid)

43.159 ***Basal Medium Stock Solution***

Using ingredients in amts prescribed for pantothenic acid, Table **43:03(d)**, proceed as below.

Using solns prepd as in **43.126**, add, with mixing, and in following order: acid-hydrolyzed casein soln, (**a**); cystine-tryptophan soln, (**e**); adenine-guanine-uracil soln, (**b**); vitamin soln IV, (**o**); vitamin soln VI, (**q**); salt soln A, (**i**); and salt soln B, (**j**). Add ca 100 mL H_2O and add, with mixing, anhyd. glucose and $NaOAc.3H_2O$. When soln is complete, adjust to pH 6.8 with NaOH soln, add, with mixing, polysorbate 80 soln, (**h**), and dil. with H_2O to 250 mL.

Titrimetric Method

43.160 ***Pantothenic Acid Standard Solutions***

(Do not shake std solns stored under toluene.)

(**a**) *Stock soln.*—40 μg/mL. Accurately weigh, in closed system, 45–55 mg USP Calcium Pantothenate Ref. Std that has been dried to const wt and stored in dark over P_2O_5 in desiccator. Dissolve in ca 500 mL H_2O, add 10 mL 0.2*N* HOAc and 100 mL 0.2*N* NaOAc, and dil. with addnl H_2O to make Ca pantothenate concn exactly 43.47 μg/mL (40 μg pantothenic acid/mL). Store under toluene in dark at ca 10°.

(**b**) *Intermediate soln.*—1.0 μg/mL. To 25 mL stock soln, (**a**), add ca 500 mL H_2O, 10 mL 0.2*N* HOAc, and 100 mL 0.2*N* NaOAc, and dil. with addnl H_2O to 1 L. Store under toluene in dark at ca 10°.

(**c**) *Working soln.*—Dil. suitable vol. of intermediate soln, (**b**), with H_2O to measured vol. such that after incubation as in **43.129** and **43.130**, response at 5.0 mL level of this soln is equiv. to titrn (as described in **43.130**) of ca 8–12 mL. Designate this as std soln. (This concn is usually 0.005–0.020 μg pantothenic acid/mL std soln.) Prep. fresh std soln for each assay.

43.161 ***Inoculum***

(**a**) *Liquid culture medium.*—Dil. measured vol. basal medium stock soln, **43.159**, with equal vol. aq. soln contg 0.04 μg pantothenic acid/mL. Add 10 mL portions dild medium to test tubes, cover to prevent contamination, sterilize 15 min in autoclave at 121– 123°, and cool tubes as rapidly as practicable to avoid color formation from overheating. Store in dark at ca 10°.

(**b**) Make transfer of cells from stock culture of *Lactobacillus plantarum*, **43.128(c)**, to sterile tube contg 10 mL liq. culture medium, (**a**). Incubate 6–24 hr at any selected temp. between 30 and 40° held const to within ±0.5°. Under aseptic conditions, centrf. culture and decant supernate. Wash cells with 3 ca 10 mL portions sterile 0.9% NaCl soln or sterile suspension medium, **43.127(c)**. Resuspend cells in 10 mL sterile 0.9% NaCl soln or sterile suspension medium. Cell suspension so obtained is inoculum.

43.162 ***Assay Solution***

(Thruout all stages, keep soln below pH 7.0 to prevent loss of pantothenic acid.)

Place measured amt of sample in flask and proceed as below. (Where directed to filter thru paper, use paper known not to adsorb pantothenic acid. Ash-free papers have been found satisfactory.) Designate final measured vol. so obtained as assay soln.

(**a**) *For dry or semidry materials containing no appreciable amount of basic substances.*—Add vol. H_2O equal in mL to $\geqslant$10 times dry wt sample in g; resulting soln must contain $\leqslant$5 mg pantothenic acid/mL. Adjust mixt. to pH 5.65±0.05 with HOAc soln or NaOAc soln. If sample is not readily sol., comminute so that it may be evenly dispersed in liq. Then agitate vigorously and wash down sides of flask with aq. soln contg in each liter 10 mL 0.2*N* HOAc and 100 mL 0.2*N* NaOAc.

Autoclave mixt. 5–7 min at 121–123° and cool. Then proceed as in **43.153(a)**, beginning with second sentence in second par., "If lumping occurs, . . ." except where ref. is made to niacin concn ca equiv. to that of std soln, **43.151(c)**, replace by pantothenic acid concn ca equiv. to that of std soln, **43.160(c)**.

(**b**) *For dry or semidry materials containing appreciable amounts of basic substances.*—Adjust mixt. to pH 5.0–6.0 with HOAc soln. Add vol. H_2O equal in mL to $\geqslant$10 times dry wt sample in g; resulting soln must contain $\leqslant$5 mg pantothenic acid/mL. Then proceed as in (**a**), beginning with second sentence: "Adjust mixt. to pH 5.65±0.05 . . ."

(**c**) *For liquid materials.*—Adjust mixt. to pH 5.0–6.0 with HOAc soln or NaOAc soln and proceed as in (**b**), beginning with second sentence: "Add vol. H_2O . . ."

43.163 ***Assay***

Using std soln, **43.160(c)**, assay soln, **43.162**, basal medium stock soln, **43.159**, and inoculum, **43.161(b)**, proceed as in **43.129**, **43.130**, and **43.133**. Value so obtained is potency of sample expressed as D-pantothenic acid. Multiply this value by 1.087 if potency is to be expressed as Ca D-pantothenate. Multiply this value by 1.100 if potency is to be expressed as Na pantothenate.

Turbidimetric Method

43.164 ***Pantothenic Acid Standard Solution***

Dil. suitable amt of pantothenic acid intermediate soln, **43.160(b)**, with H_2O to measured vol. such that after incubation as in **43.129** and **43.132**, with inoculated blank set at 100% *T*, % *T* at 5.0 mL level of this soln is equiv. to that for dried cell wt (as described in **43.131**) of ≥1.25 mg. Designate this as std soln. (This concn is usually 0.003–0.012 μg pantothenic acid/mL std soln.) Prep. fresh std soln for each assay.

43.165 ***Inoculum***

Proceed as in **43.161(b)**.

43.166 ***Assay Solution***

Proceed as in **43.162**, except that where ref. is made to pantothenic acid concn ca equiv. to that of std soln, **43.160(c)**, replace by pantothenic acid concn ca equiv. to that of std soln, **43.164**. Designate soln so obtained as assay soln.

43.167 ***Assay***

Using std soln, **43.164**, assay soln, **43.166**, basal medium stock soln, **43.159**, and inoculum, **43.165**, proceed as in **43.129**, **43.132**, and **43.133**. Value so obtained is potency of sample expressed as D-pantothenic acid. Multiply this value by 1.087 if potency is to be expressed as Ca D-pantothenate.

Riboflavin (Vitamin B_2) *(26)*

(Not applicable in presence of materials which adsorb riboflavin)

43.168 ***Basal Medium Stock Solution***

Using ingredients in amts prescribed for riboflavin, Table **43:03(e)**, proceed as below.

Using solns prepd as in **43.126**, add, with mixing, and in following order: photolyzed peptone soln, (**g**); cystine soln, (**d**); yeast supplement soln, (**s**); salt soln A, (**i**); and salt soln B, (**j**). Add ca 100 mL H_2O, and add anhyd. glucose with mixing. When soln is complete, adjust to pH 6.8 with NaOH soln, and dil. with H_2O to 250 mL.

Titrimetric Method

43.169 ***Riboflavin Standard Solutions***

(Do not shake std solns stored under toluene.)

(**a**) *Stock soln.*—100 μg/mL. Accurately weigh, in closed system, 50–60 mg USP Riboflavin Ref. Std that has been dried to const wt and stored in dark over P_2O_5 in desiccator. Suspend in ca 300 mL 0.02*N* HOAc and warm on steam bath, with stirring, until solid dissolves. Cool, and dil. with 0.02*N* HOAc to make riboflavin concn exactly 100 μg/mL. Store under toluene in dark at ca 10°.

(**b**) *Intermediate soln I.*—10 μg/mL. Dil. 100 mL stock soln, (**a**), with 0.02*N* HOAc to 1 L. Store under toluene in dark at ca 10°.

(**c**) *Working soln.*—Dil. suitable vol. intermediate soln, (**b**), with H_2O to measured vol. such that after incubation as in **43.129** and **43.130**, response at 5.0 mL level of this soln is equiv. to titrn (as described in **43.130**) of ca 8–12 mL. Designate this as std soln. (This concn is usually 0.05–0.20 μg riboflavin/mL std soln.) Prep. fresh std soln for each assay.

43.170 ***Inoculum***

(**a**) *Liquid culture medium.*—Dil. measured vol. basal medium stock soln, **43.168**, with equal vol. aq. soln contg 0.1 μg riboflavin/mL. Add 10 mL portions dild medium to test tubes, cover to prevent contamination, sterilize 15 min in autoclave at 121–123°, and cool tubes as rapidly as practicable to avoid color formation from overheating. Store in dark at ca 10°.

(**b**) Make transfer of cells from stock culture of *Lactobacillus casei*, **43.128(d)**, to sterile tube contg 10 mL liq. culture medium, (**a**). Incubate 6–24 hr at any selected temp. between 30 and 40° held const to within ±0.5°. Under aseptic conditions, centrf. culture and decant supernate. Wash cells with 3 ca 10 mL portions sterile 0.9% NaCl soln or sterile suspension medium, **43.127(c)**. Resuspend cells in 10 mL sterile 0.9% NaCl soln or sterile suspension medium. Cell suspension so obtained is inoculum.

43.171 ***Assay Solution***

(Thruout all stages, keep solution below pH 7.0 to prevent loss of riboflavin.)

Place measured amt of sample in flask and proceed as below. (Where directed to filter thru paper, use paper known not to adsorb riboflavin. Ash-free papers have been found satisfactory.) Designate final measured vol. so obtained as assay soln.

(**a**) *For dry or semidry materials containing no appreciable amount of basic substances.*—Add vol. 0.1*N* HCl equal in mL to ≥10 times dry wt sample in g; resulting soln must contain ≤0.1 mg riboflavin/mL. If sample is not readily sol., comminute so that it may be evenly dispersed in liq. Then agitate vigorously and wash down sides of flask with 0.1*N* HCl.

Then proceed as in **43.153(a)**, beginning with second par., "Autoclave mixt. 30 min . . ." except that where ref. is made to niacin concn ca equiv. to that of std soln, **43.151(c)**, replace by riboflavin concn ca equiv. to that of std soln, **43.169(c)**.

If riboflavin content of sample is so low that these requirements cannot be met, conc. clear filtrate obtained at ca pH 4.5 to suitable vol. with heat under reduced pressure. Filter if necessary, and proceed as in **43.153(a)**(*1*).

(**b**) *For dry or semidry materials containing appreciable amounts of basic substances.*—Adjust mixt. to pH 5.0–6.0 with dil. HCl. Add vol. H_2O equal in mL to ≥10 times dry wt sample in g; resulting soln must contain ≤0.1 mg riboflavin/mL. Then add equiv. of 1.0 mL 10*N* HCl/100 mL liq. and proceed as in (**a**), beginning with second sentence, "If sample is not readily sol., . . ."

(**c**) *For liquid materials.*—Adjust mixt. to pH 5.0– 6.0 with dil. HCl, or with vigorous agitation, NaOH soln, and proceed as in (**b**), beginning with second sentence, "Add vol. H_2O . . ."

43.172 ***Assay***

Using std soln, **43.169(c)**, assay soln, **43.171**, basal medium stock soln, **43.168**, and inoculum, **43.170(b)**, proceed as in **43.129**, **43.130**, and **43.133**.

Turbidimetric Method

43.173 ***Riboflavin Standard Solutions***

(Do not shake std solns stored under toluene.)

(**a**) *Intermediate soln II.*—1.0 μg/mL. Dil. 10 mL riboflavin stock soln, **43.169(a)**, with 0.02*N* HOAc to 1 L. Store under toluene in dark at ca 10°.

(**b**) *Std soln.*—Dil. suitable vol. intermediate soln II, (**a**), with H_2O to measured vol. such that after incubation as in **43.129** and **43.132**, with inoculated blank set at 100% *T*, % *T* at 5.0 mL level of this soln is equiv. to that for dried cell wt (as described in **43.131**) of ≥1.25 mg. Designate this as std soln. (This concn is usually 0.01–0.04 μg riboflavin/mL std soln.) Prep. fresh std soln for each assay.

43.174 ***Inoculum***

Proceed as in **43.170(b)**.

43.175 ***Assay Solution***

Proceed as in **43.171**, except that where ref. is made to riboflavin concn ca equiv. to that of std soln, **43.169(c)**, replace by riboflavin concn ca equiv. to that of std soln, **43.173(b)**. Designate soln so obtained as assay soln.

43.176 ***Assay***

Using std soln, **43.173(b)**, assay soln, **43.175**, basal medium stock soln, **43.168**, and inoculum, **43.174**, proceed as in **43.129**, **43.132**, and **43.133**.

Amino Acids (27)—Official First Action

(Applicable only to materials contg free forms of amino acids in absence of appreciable amt of protein)

43.177 ***Stock Solutions for Basal Media***

(Store all solns under toluene; in addn, store vitamin and amino acid solns in dark at ca 10°.)

(**a**) *Amino acid soln.*—Prep. stock soln of each amino acid as in Table **43:04**. Use amino acids of highest purity available. (DL form may be preferred since it is less likely to be contaminated with other amino acids.) If DL form is used, double wt given in table. Dissolve amino acid with heat, if necessary, and dil. to indicated vol. with H_2O. Where special solvs are indicated, dissolve amino acid in vol. initial solv. specified, and dil. to final vol. with H_2O.

(**b**) *Adenine-guanine-uracil soln.—See* **43.126(b)**.

(**c**) *Salt soln A.*—Dissolve 50 g anhyd. K_2HPO_4 and 50 g anhyd. KH_2PO_4 in H_2O, dil. to 500 mL, and add 5 drops HCl.

(**d**) *Salt soln B.*—Dissolve 20 g $MgSO_4.7H_2O$, 1 g NaCl, 1 g $FeSO_4.7H_2O$, and 1 g $MnSO_4.H_2O$ in H_2O, dil. to 500 mL, and add 5 drops HCl.

(**e**) *Vitamin soln I.*—Dissolve 25 mg riboflavin, 25 mg thiamine.HCl, 50 mg niacin, and 0.15 mg biotin in 0.02*N* HOAc to make 1 L.

(**f**) *Vitamin soln II.*—Dissolve 50 mg pyridoxal, 50 mg pyridoxamine.HCl, 25 mg Ca pantothenate, 5 mg *p*-aminobenzoic acid, and 0.25 mg folic acid in 25% alcohol to make 1 L.

43.178 ***Basal Medium***

Complete assay medium is given in Table **43:05**. In prepg medium for given assay, omit particular amino acid to be assayed from medium. Concn of all ingredients in basal medium is twice what it will be in assay tube after addn of sample or std soln and H_2O. Table lists amts of ingredients required for 50, 100, 150, and 200 tubes. Prep. fresh for each assay.

To combined solns add glucose and NaOAc with mixing. When soln is complete, adjust to pH 6.8 and dil. to vol. (*Note:* Amts of glucose and NaOAc depend upon organism used in assay.)

43.179 ***Culture and Suspension Media***

(**a**) *Agar culture medium.—See* **43.127(b)**. (Available from Difco Laboratories as Lactobacilli Agar AOAC.)

(**b**) *Liquid culture medium.*—Dil. measured vol. of complete amino acid basal medium, **43.178**, with equal vol. H_2O. Add 10 mL portions to test tubes, cover to prevent contamination (or screw-cap tubes may be used), sterilize 15 min in autoclave at 121–123°, and cool tubes as rapidly as practicable to keep color formation at min. Store in dark at ca 10°.

(**c**) *Liquid suspension medium.*—Dil. measured vol. appropriate basal medium (without amino acid being assayed), **43.178**, with equal vol. H_2O. Add 10 mL portions to test tubes, cover to prevent contamination, sterilize 15 min at 121–123°, and cool as rapidly as practicable to keep color formation at min. Store in dark at ca 10°.

Table 43:04 Amino Acid Stock Solns

	Amino Acid	Weight	Initial Solvent	Final Volume	Final Concn
		g	mL	mL	mg/mL
(a)	L-Alanine	5.000	900 H_2O	1000	5
(b)	L-Arginine.HCl	12.095	400 H_2O	500	20
(c)	L-Asparagine	5.000	400 H_2O	500	10
(d)	L-Aspartic acid	10.000	100 1*N* NaOH	1000	10
(e)	L-Cysteine.HCl	5.000	100 2*N* HCl	1000	5
(f)	L-Cystine	5.000	100 2*N* HCl	1000	5
(g)	L-Glutamic acid	10.000	100 1*N* NaOH	1000	10
(h)	Glycine	10.000	400 H_2O	500	20
(i)	L-Histidine.HCl	12.351	400 H_2O	500	20
(j)	L-Hydroxyproline	5.000	150 H_2O	250	20
(k)	L-Isoleucine	5.000	900 H_2O	1000	5
(l)	L-Leucine	10.000	900 H_2O	1000	10
(m)	L-Lysine.HCl	6.248	400 H_2O	500	10
(n)	L-Methionine	5.000	900 H_2O	1000	5
(o)	L-Norleucine	5.000	100 2*N* HCl	1000	5
(p)	L-Phenylalanine	5.000	900 H_2O	1000	5
(q)	L-Proline	5.000	150 H_2O	250	20
(r)	L-Serine	5.000	900 H_2O	1000	5
(s)	L-Threonine	5.000	900 H_2O	1000	5
(t)	L-Tryptophan	5.000	50 1*N* NaOH	500	10
(u)	L-Tyrosine	5.000	50 1*N* NaOH	500	10
(v)	L-Valine	5.000	900 H_2O	1000	5

Table 43:05 Composition of Basal Medium

	Ingredients (Stock solns, **43.177**)	250 mL	500 mL	750 mL	1 L
		mL	mL	mL	mL
(a)	Amino Acid Solns:				
	L-Alanine	10	20	30	40
	L-Arginine.HCl	5	10	15	20
	L-Asparagine	5	10	15	20
	L-Aspartic acid	5	10	15	20
	L-Cysteine.HCl	5	10	15	20
	L-Cystine	5	10	15	20
	L-Glutamic acid[a]	25	50	75	100
	Glycine	5	10	15	20
	L-Histidine.HCl	5	10	15	20
	L-Hydroxyproline	2.5	5	7.5	10
	L-Isoleucine	10	20	30	40
	L-Leucine	5	10	15	20
	L-Lysine.HCl	5	10	15	20
	L-Methionine	10	20	30	40
	L-Norleucine	10	20	30	40
	L-Phenylalanine	10	20	30	40
	L-Proline	2.5	5	7.5	10
	L-Serine	10	20	30	40
	L-Threonine	10	20	30	40
	L-Tryptophan	5	10	15	20
	L-Tyrosine	10	20	30	40
	L-Valine	10	20	30	40
(b)	Adenine-guanine-uracil	5	10	15	20
(c)	Salt Soln A	2.5	5.0	7.5	10
(d)	Salt Soln B	2.5	5.0	7.5	10
(e)	Vitamin Soln I	10	20	30	40
(f)	Vitamin Soln II	10	20	30	40
	Glucose, anhyd.				
	with *S. faecalis*	5 g	10 g	15 g	20 g
	with *L. plantarum* or *P. cerevisiae*	10 g	20 g	30 g	40 g
	NaOAc, anhyd.				
	with *S. faecalis*	3 g	6 g	9 g	12 g
	with *L. plantarum* or *P. cerevisiae*	6 g	12 g	18 g	24 g

[a] For methionine assay use DL-glutamic acid, since L-glutamic acid often contains methionine.

43.180 ***Stock Cultures of Test Organisms***

Prep. and test cultures as in **43.128**. Use following organisms:

(**a**) *Streptococcus faecalis* (*faecium*).—ATCC No. 9790. For use in assay of isoleucine, leucine, threonine, tryptophan, valine, arginine, and histidine.

(**b**) *Lactobacillus plantarum.*—ATCC No. 8014. For use in assay of isoleucine, leucine, methionine, phenylalanine, tryptophan, and valine.

(**c**) *Pediococcus cerevisiae* (*acidilactici*).—ATCC No. 8042. For use in assay of lysine, methionine, phenylalanine, tyrosine, cystine, and histidine.

43.181 ***Inoculum***

Make transfer of cells from fresh stock culture of appropriate organism to sterile tube contg 10 mL liq. culture medium, **43.179(b)**. Incubate 16–24 hr at 34± 0.5°. Under aseptic conditions, centrf. and decant supernate. Suspend cells in 10 mL appropriate sterile suspension medium, **43.179(c)**.

43.182 ***Reference Standard Solutions of Amino Acids***

Dry stdzd amino acids (available from ICN Pharmaceuticals, Inc., Life Sciences Group) to const wt over P_2O_5 and store in desiccator over P_2O_5. Prep. stock soln of each amino acid by accurately weighing amt designated in Table **43:06** in closed system and dilg to final vol. with H_2O. Prep. std working soln by dilg aliquot std stock soln to designated vol. with H_2O. Store std stock solns under toluene in dark at ca 10°. Prep. std working solns fresh for each assay. (Do not shake std solns stored under toluene.)

43.183 ***Calibration of Photometer***

Using inoculum, **43.181**, and std stock solns, Table **43:06**, proceed as in **43.131**, incubating 16–24 hr at 34±0.5°. In measurement, use basal medium, **43.178**, for dilg.

43.184 ***Preparation of Sample***

(**a**) *Liquids containing free amino acids.*—Dil. with H_2O to concn required to obtain assay soln.

(**b**) *Dry or semidry materials.*—Add H_2O equal in mL to ≥10 times dry wt in g of sample. Heat 10 min in autoclave at 121–123°. Cool, dil. to vol., and filter if necessary to obtain assay soln.

43.185 ***Assay***

Proceed as in **43.129** (disregard ref. to titrimetric method), using working std solns, Table **43:06**, assay soln, **43.184**, and basal medium, Table **43:05** (omitting amino acid being assayed). Incubate 16–24 hr at 34± 0.5°.

43.186 ***Determination***

Proceed as in **43.132**.

43.187 ***Calculation***

Proceed as in **43.133**.

Table 43:06 Preparation of Reference Stock and Standard Amino Acid Solutions

Amino Acid	mg	Std Stock Soln final vol. mL	concn μg/mL	aliquot mL	Std Working Soln final vol. mL	concn μg/mL
L-Arginine.HCl	121	500	200	5	200	5
L-Cystine (dissolve in 100 ml 1N HCl)	100	1000	100	15	500	3
L-Histidine.HCl.H_2O	135	1000	100	15	500	3
L-Isoleucine	100	1000	100	5	100	5
L-Leucine	100	1000	100			
(with *L. plantarum*)				5	100	5
(with *S. faecalis*)				10	100	10
L-Lysine.HCl	251	1000	200	15	200	15
L-Methionine	50	1000	50	10	250	2
L-Phenylalanine	100	1000	100	5	100	5
L-Threonine	100	1000	100	5	100	5
L-Tryptophan (dissolve in 100 ml 0.1N NaOH)	40	1000	40	5	250	0.8
L-Tyrosine (dissolve in 100 ml 0.1N NaOH)	100	1000	100			
(with *L. plantarum*)				5	250	2
(with *P. cerevisiae*)				10	250	4
L-Valine	100	1000	100			
(with *L. plantarum*)				10	200	5
(with *S. faecalis*)				10	100	10

Vitamin B_6 (Pyridoxine, Pyridoxal, Pyridoxamine) in Food Extracts (*28*)
Official Final Action

43.188 ***Reagents***

(Work in subdued light with all solns contg vitamin B_6.)

(a) *Potassium acetate buffers.*—(*1*) *0.01M, pH 4.5.*—Dissolve 0.981 g KOAc in H_2O and dil. to 1 L. Adjust pH with HOAc. (*2*) *0.02M, pH 5.5.*—Dissolve 1.96 g KOAc in H_2O and dil. to 1 L. Adjust pH with HOAc. (*3*) *0.04M, pH 6.0.*—Dissolve 3.92 g KOAc in H_2O and dil. to 1 L. Adjust pH with HOAc. (*4*) *0.1M, pH 7.0.*—Dissolve 9.815 g KOAc in H_2O and dil. to 1 L. Adjust pH with HOAc or KOH soln.

(b) *Potassium chloride-phosphate buffer.*—pH 8.0. Dissolve 74.6 g KCl and 17.4 g K_2HPO_4 in 800 mL H_2O and adjust pH with HOAc. Dil. to 1 L.

(c) *Ion exchange resin.*—Dowex AG 50W-X8, 100–200 mesh.

(d) *Acid-hydrolyzed casein soln.*—100 mg/mL. (*Caution: See* **51.011** and **51.015**.) Mix 100 g vitamin-free casein with 500 mL const-boiling HCl (ca 5N HCl, 208 mL HCl dild to 500 mL with H_2O) and reflux 8 hr. Remove HCl from mixt. by distn under vac. until very thick sirup remains, keeping H_2O bath temp. <80°. Dissolve sirup in H_2O and conc. again in same manner. Redissolve sirup in H_2O.

Adjust to pH 4 with 40% NaOH, add H_2O to ca 600 mL, add 40 g activated C, stir 4 hr, and filter with vac. thru buchner with thin pad of HCl-washed Filter-Cel. Continue following activated C treatments only if soln is not clear and colorless: Add 20 g activated C to filtrate, stir 1 hr, and refilter. Repeat with fresh 10 g portion activated C and filter. When soln is clear and colorless, dil. to 1 L with H_2O. (Before soln is dild to vol., 2–3 mL 6N HCl may be added to extend time before microbial growth occurs.) Store in refrigerator.

(e) *Vitamin soln I.*—Dissolve 10 mg thiamine and 1 g inositol in ca 200 mL H_2O and dil. to 1 L. Store in refrigerator. (1 mL = 10 μg thiamine and 1 mg inositol.)

(f) *Vitamin soln II.*—Dissolve 10 mg biotin in 100 mL 50% alcohol. Store in refrigerator. (1 mL = 100 μg biotin.) Dissolve 200 mg Ca pantothenate and 200 mg niacin in ca 200 mL H_2O; add 8 mL biotin soln and dil. to 1 L with H_2O. Store in refrigerator. (1 mL = 200 μg each Ca pantothenate and niacin and 0.8 μg biotin.)

(g) *Salt soln I.*—Dissolve 17 g KCl, 10.3 g $MgSO_4.7H_2O$, 100 mg $FeCl_3.6H_2O$, and 100 mg $MnSO_4.H_2O$ in ca 800 mL H_2O. Add 2 mL HCl. Dissolve 5 g $CaCl_2.2H_2O$ in ca 100 mL H_2O, add to first soln, and dil. to 1 L with H_2O. Store in refrigerator. (1 mL = 17 mg KCl, 10.3 mg $MgSO_4.7H_2O$, 100 μg $FeCl_3.6H_2O$, 100 μg $MnSO_4.H_2O$, and 5 mg $CaCl_2.2H_2O$.)

(h) *Salt soln II.*—Dissolve 22 g KH_2PO_4 and 40 g $(NH_4)_2HPO_4$ in H_2O and dil. to 1 L. Store in refrigerator. (1 mL = 22 mg KH_2PO_4 and 40 mg $(NH_4)_2HPO_4$.)

(i) *Polysorbate 80 soln.*—Weigh 2.5 g polysorbate 80 (Tween 80) in small beaker. Transfer with warm (45°) H_2O and dil. to 500 mL. Store in refrigerator. (1 mL = 5 mg polysorbate 80.)

(j) *Citric acid soln.*—(1+1). Dissolve 50 g citric acid in 50 mL H_2O. Store at room temp. in bottle with plastic stopper.

(k) *Ammonium phosphate soln.*—(1+2). Dissolve 25 g $(NH_4)_2HPO_4$ in 50 mL H_2O. Store at room temp. in bottle with plastic stopper.

(l) *Pyridoxine, pyridoxal, and pyridoxamine std solns.*—Prep. sep. solns for each as follows: (*1*) *Stock soln.*—10.0 μg/mL. Dissolve 12.16 mg pyridoxine.HCl, 12.18 mg pyridoxal.HCl, and 14.34 mg pyridoxamine.HCl, resp., in 1N HCl and dil. to 1 L with 1N HCl. Store in g-s bottles in refrigerator.

(*2*) *Intermediate soln.*—1.0 μg/mL. Dil. 10 mL stock soln to 100 mL with H_2O.

(*3*) *Working soln.*—1.0 ng/mL. Dil. 5 mL intermediate soln to 500 mL with H_2O and mix. Dil. 10 mL to 100 mL with H_2O. Prep. fresh for each assay.

(m) *Mixed pyridoxine, pyridoxal, pyridoxamine solns* (*for liquid broth culture.*).—Pipet 2 mL of each intermediate soln (1.0 μg/mL) into 1 L vol. flask and dil. to vol. with H_2O.

(n) *Citrate buffer soln.*—Dissolve 100 g K citrate and 20 g citric acid in H_2O and dil. to 1 L. Store in refrigerator. (1 mL = 100 mg K citrate and 20 mg citric acid.)

(o) *Basal medium stock soln* (*for 200 tubes*).—To make 1 L medium, add to ca 400 mL H_2O: 100 mL citrate buffer, 100 mL hydrolyzed casein soln, 50 mL vitamin soln I, 25 mL vitamin soln II, 50 mL salt soln I, and 50 mL salt soln II. Dissolve 100 g glucose in this soln. Dissolve 22 mg DL-tryptophan, 27 mg L-histidine.HCl, 100 mg DL-methionine, 216 mg DL-isoleucine, and 256 mg DL-valine in 10 mL HCl (1+9) in small beaker and add to above. Add 20 mL polysorbate 80 soln. Adjust to pH 4.5 with citric acid (1+1) or $(NH_4)_2HPO_4$ (1+2) solns. Dil. to 1 L with H_2O. Store in Pyrex bottle plugged with cotton in refrigerator. Prep. ≤24 hr before use. When ready, steam 10 min and cool.

(p) *Test organism.*—*Saccharomyces uvarum* (ATCC No. 9080). Maintain by weekly transfers on wort agar slants (**q**). Incubate these freshly seeded agar slants 24 hr at 30° and refrigerate.

(**q**) *Agar culture medium.*—Suspend 25 g Bactowort agar in ca 400 mL H_2O in marked 500 mL wide-mouth erlenmeyer. Cover to prevent contamination, steam ca 10 min to dissolve agar, and adjust vol. to 500 mL. Pipet hot agar in ca 10 mL portions into 20 × 150 mm test tubes, plug with absorbent cotton, and autoclave 15 min at 121°. Since this medium has acid reaction, avoid overheating, which results in softer medium. Tilt hot agar tubes to form slants and cool in this position.

(**r**) *Liquid culture medium.*—Pipet 5 mL mixed soln, (**m**), into 16 × 150 mm test tubes contg two 4 mm glass beads, cover to prevent contamination, and autoclave 10 min at 121°. Add 5 mL steamed vitamin B_6-free basal medium, (**o**), under aseptic conditions. Store tubes in refrigerator.

(**s**) *Inoculum rinse.*—Pipet 5 mL H_2O into test tubes, cover to prevent contamination, and autoclave 10 min at 121°. Add 5 mL steamed vitamin B_6-free basal medium, (**o**), under aseptic conditions. Store tubes in refrigerator.

43.189 ***Assay Inoculum***

(*Caution: See* **51.005**.)

Incubate cells for inoculum on agar 24 hr at 30° before use. Transfer these cells under aseptic conditions to liq. broth culture tubes. Plug with absorbent cotton held on with masking tape (or other cover to prevent contamination) and place tubes on shaker 20 hr in 30° room. Replace cotton plugs aseptically with sterile rubber stoppers; centrf. 1.5 min at 2500 rpm. Decant liq. and resuspend in 10 mL inoculum rinse. Sep. by centrfg 1.5 min at 2500 rpm. Decant liq., resuspend in second 10 mL sterile inoculum rinse, centrf. 1.5 min, and decant. Cells suspended in third 10 mL inoculum rinse are assay inoculum.

43.190 ***Preparation of Exchange Resin and Column***

To 250 g Dowex AG 50W-X8 (100–200 mesh) in H form, add excess 6*N* KOH until supernate is blue to litmus. Let settle, decant, and rinse resin with H_2O until supernate is clear. Add ca 600 mL 3*N* HCl, stir, and heat 0.5 hr in boiling H_2O bath. Decant and repeat treatment with 3*N* HCl twice. Rinse resin until rinse H_2O is neut. Add 6*N* KOH until pH is strongly basic and stir 1 hr. Rinse with H_2O until rinse H_2O is neut. Suspend in 2*M* KOAc and store in refrigerator until needed. Just before use, wash resin with H_2O until H_2O is green to bromothymol blue. Resin can be regenerated, beginning with 3*N* HCl treatment.

Prep. tubes by sealing capillary stopcock, 1.5 mm bore and 50 mm side arms, to 22 mm od × ≥400 mm tube. Pour 5–10 mL H_2O into tube. Place glass wool plug in bottom of tube and remove bubbles from capillary and glass wool. Rinse measured 30 mL prepd resin, settled out of H_2O suspension, into tube with H_2O. After resin settles in tube, place glass wool plug on top of resin. Rinse column with 50 mL hot H_2O followed by two 50 mL portions hot 0.01*M* KOAc (pH 4.5). pH of last buffer rinse from column should be 4.5; otherwise, more rinsing with buffer is required. Do not permit liq. level on column to fall below top glass wool plug at any time.

43.191 ***Preparation of Sample***

Weigh 1–2 g dry product into 500 mL erlenmeyer. For plant products, add 200 mL 0.44*N* HCl and for animal products, add 200 mL 0.055*N* HCl. Autoclave plant soln 2 hr at 121°, and animal soln 5 hr at 121°. Cool to room temp., adjust to pH 4.5 with 6*N* or satd KOH, and dil. to 250 mL with H_2O in vol. flask. Filter thru Whatman No. 40 paper. Take 40–200 mL filtered aliquot for chromatgy.

43.192 ***Chromatography***

Place desired amt of filtered ext on ion exchange column in ca 50 mL portions and let pass completely thru with no flow regulation. Wash beaker and column 3 times with ca 5 mL portions hot 0.02*M* KOAc (pH 5.5), followed by similar washing to column sides. Wash column with same soln until total of 100 mL 0.02*M* KOAc (pH 5.5) soln is used. Elute pyridoxal with two 50 mL portions boiling 0.04*M* KOAc (pH 6.0), using 100 mL vol. flask as receiver. Elute pyridoxine with two 50 mL portions boiling 0.1*M* KOAc (pH 7.0), using 100 mL vol. flask as receiver. Elute pyridoxamine with two 50 mL portions boiling KCl-K_2HPO_4 (pH 8.0) soln, using 250 mL beaker as receiver. Adjust pH to 4.5. Dil. pyridoxine and pyridoxal eluates to 100 mL and pyridoxamine eluate to 200 mL with H_2O unless otherwise desired.

For std pyridoxine, pyridoxal, and pyridoxamine, mix 10 mL each intermediate soln, neutze with KOH, and adjust to pH 4.5 with HOAc. Put this soln on column, wash, and elute fractions as above. Dil. eluted pyridoxine and pyridoxal stds to 100 mL and dil. eluted pyridoxamine, after pH is adjusted to 4.5, to 200 mL with H_2O. Dil. eluted stds to 1.0 ng/mL with H_2O.

43.193 ***Assay***

Heat clean tubes and glass beads 2 hr at 260°. Place two 4 mm glass beads in each 16 × 150 mm screw-cap glass culture tube. For std curve, pipet into triplicate tubes appropriate freshly prepd std working solns to give 0.0, 0.0, 1.0, 2.0, 3.0, 4.0, and 5.0 ng pyridoxine, pyridoxal, or pyridoxamine/tube. Similarly prep. set of tubes for eluted stds, omitting blanks. Dil. sample eluates from chromatgc column to contain ca 1 ng vitamin B_6 component/mL. Pipet 1, 2, 3, 4, and 5 mL dild eluates into triplicate tubes. Pipet H_2O into all tubes to bring vol. to 5 mL/tube. Cap tubes with plastic caps with 3 mm (1/8") hole thru top. Autoclave entire set 10 min at 121°. Cool tubes to room temp. Using automatic pipet with sterilized delivery attachments, pipet 5 mL steamed medium, (**o**), thru hole in cap. Cover tubes with sterile cheesecloth and place in refrigerator. Remove from refrigerator 1 hr before inoculation. Aseptically inoculate thru cap of each tube, except first set of 0.0 level for std curves, with 1 drop assay inoculum of *S. uvarum* suspended cells. Take care to maintain uniform cell suspension, since cells may settle out during inoculation step. Incubate tubes on const rotary shaker 22 hr in temp.-regulated room (30°). Steam tubes in autoclave 5 min, cool, and remove caps. Read % *T* at 550 nm on spectrophtr. Set 100% *T* with H_2O to read uninoculated blank. Set 100% *T* with uninoculated blank to read inoculated blank. Mix 9 inoculated blank tubes, and with this mixt. set at 100% *T* on instrument, read all other tubes.

Average readings of triplicate tubes and plot % *T* against ng eluted std pyridoxine, pyridoxal, or pyridoxamine/tube on semilog paper. Det. amt of pyridoxine, pyridoxal, or pyridoxamine/sample tube by interpolation. Report μg pyridoxine, pyridoxal, and pyridoxamine/g sample.

BIOASSAY METHODS

Thiamine Hydrochloride (Vitamin B_1) (*29*)

43.194 ★ ***Growth Method—Official Final Action*** ★

See **39.108–39.115**, 10th ed.

★ Surplus method—*see* inside front cover.

Vitamin D (*30*)—Official Final Action

(Not applicable to products offered for poultry feeding)

43.195 ***Definitions***

Assay group means group of rats to which assay sample (vitamin D sample) is administered during assay period. *Assay sample* means sample under examination for vitamin D potency. *Assay soln* means soln of sample in oil prepd for feeding after saponification. *Assay period* means interval in life of rat between last day of depletion period and eighth or eleventh day thereafter. *Assemble* means procedure by which rats are selected and assigned to groups for purposes of feeding, care, and observation. *Daily* means each of first 6 or 8 days of assay period. *Depletion period* means interval in life of rat between last day of preliminary period and first day of assay period. *Dose* means amt of ref. oil or of assay milk or other supplement to be fed daily to rat during assay period. *Feed* means make readily available to rat or administer to rat by mouth. *Group* means 7 or more rats maintained on same required dietary regime during assay period. *Preliminary period* means interval in life of rat between seventh day after birth and first day of depletion period.

43.196 ***Reagents***

(**a**) *Ground gluten.*—Clean, sound product made from wheat flour by almost complete removal of starch, contg ≤10% H_2O and, calcd on H_2O-free basis, ≥14.2% N, ≤15% N-free ext (using protein factor 5.7), and ≤5.5% starch (detd by diastase method, **7.081**).

(**b**) *Reference oil.*—USP Ergocalciferol or Cholecalciferol Ref. Std.

(**c**) *Cottonseed oil.*—USP grade meeting following addnl requirements: Saponify 10 g oil as in **43.200**, and dissolve unsaponifiable residue in 10 mL pet ether. In sep. container place 0.4 mL $FeCl_3$ soln (1+1000) and 12 mL soln of α,α-dipyridyl in absolute alcohol (1+6000), mix, and 5 min later read *A* in 1.0 cm cell at 520 nm, using suitable spectrophtr, against absolute alcohol. Then add 0.2 mL soln of unsaponifiable residue in pet ether to entire colored soln, and after 5 min read *A*. Difference between first and second *A* values is ≥0.125.

(**d**) *Rachitogenic diet.*—Mix 76% whole yellow corn, ground to pass No. 30 sieve; 20% gluten, ground to pass No. 30 sieve; 3% $CaCO_3$; and 1% NaCl.

43.197 ***Preservation of Sample***

Store samples so as to minimize exposure to heat, light, and air. Deliver milk samples in original container immediately after collection or store under refrigeration in iced container until delivered. After delivery to assayer, preserve in homogeneous state by refrigeration at ≤10° for ≤10 days, or for ≤30 days by addn of 2 drops 10% HCHO soln to 1 qt milk in addn to refrigeration at ≤10°. Preserve evapd and reconstituted milk in same manner as fluid milk. Soured or curdled sample is unsuitable for assay. Preserve sample of dried milk, after being opened by assayer, by refrigeration at ≤10°.

43.198 ***Sample***

Sample shall consist of ≥10 g food, 10 capsules or tablets, or sufficient vol. of liqs to satisfy needs of entire assay.

If amt of vitamin D in sample is such that aliquot to be fed contains <5 mg P, sample may be fed directly. If aliquot contains >5 mg P, sample must be saponified.

All manipulations and dilns of vitamin sample must be made with materials known to be free of vitamin D.

43.199 ***Preparation of Sample for Direct Feeding***

(**a**) *Feed concentrates and tablets.*—Thoroly grind weighed sample. Promptly weigh aliquot of ground powder and grind it again with equal wt of edible vegetable oil. To this add amt of powd sucrose such that assay dose will be contained in 1–2 g. Mix thoroly by grinding again and proceed as in assay period, **43.205**.

(**b**) *Capsules.*—Open weighed capsules and transfer contents as completely as possible into container. Thoroly mix combined contents and promptly weigh aliquot. Proceed as in (**a**). Obtain sample wt by subtracting wt empty ether-washed capsules from total wt capsules.

(**c**) *Oils.*—Add amt of edible vegetable oil that will produce diln contg assay dose in vol. equal to vol. ref. diln.

(**d**) *Water-miscible liquids.*—Dil. as for oils, using H_2O, glycerol, or propylene glycol to facilitate feeding.

43.200 ***Preparation of Sample by Saponification***

(*Caution: See* **51.011**, **51.039**, and **51.054**.)

Weigh sample and transfer to saponification flask. (For milk, see **43.201**.)

In case of capsules or tablets, place ≥10 in small reflux flask, add 10 mL H_2O, and heat on steam bath ca 10 min. Crush each capsule or tablet with blunt glass rod and warm 5 min more. Add 2 mL cottonseed oil and vol. of KOH (50% w/w) soln representing 2.5 mL for each g total wt of sample plus cottonseed oil, but ≥15 mL. Add 50 mL alcohol and reflux vigorously 30 min in 100° bath. Cool soln and transfer to Squibb-type separator, using 50 mL H_2O. Ext with four 30 mL portions peroxide-free ether (USP anesthesia ether is suitable), using more H_2O or small portions alcohol to break any emulsions that may form. Wash combined ether exts 4 times with H_2O as follows: (*1*) 100 mL with very gentle swirling; (*2*) 100 mL with gentle swirling; (*3*) 50 mL with gentle shaking; (*4*) 50 mL with vigorous shaking. Dry ether ext with two 75 mL portions satd NaCl soln, shaking vigorously both times. Transfer ether ext to beaker and evap. on steam bath to convenient vol. If H_2O is present, dry with 3–5 g anhyd. Na_2SO_4. Decant into weighed container, rinse beaker and Na_2SO_4 with 3–5 addnl portions ether, and combine all washings in weighed container. Evap. ether on steam bath until no ether odor is detectable, and weigh fat. Multiply by 1.10 to det. vol., and add amt of edible vegetable oil that will produce convenient final diln for feeding. Mix thoroly (mag. stirrer is desirable).

43.201 ***Preparation of Milk Samples***

Proceed as in **43.200** with following modifications: Use 50–100 mL alcohol and 10 g KOH pellets per 100 mL sample. Swirl until all KOH dissolves. Reflux 40–60 min. (To minimize bumping and scorching of sample, place several short pieces of glass stirring rod in saponification flask and use oil or H_2O bath at 100°.) Use 50–100 mL ether for first extn. Only small part of butterfat is saponified, but fat may be fed without affecting results. Where unusually large amt (>0.5 g) of fat would have to be fed in every dose, ext from which ether has been evapd may be resaponified as in **43.200**.

43.202 ***Preliminary Period***

Thruout preliminary period each rat must be raised under immediate supervision of, or according to directions specified by, assayer. Thruout preliminary period, keep rats on dietary regimen that provides for normal development in all respects, except to limit supply of vitamin D to such degree that rats weighing 40–60 g at age of 21–30 days and subsisting 18–25 days on suitable rachitogenic diet show evidence of severe rickets.

43.203 *Depletion Period*

Rat is suitable for depletion period when its age is ≤30 days, and its body wt is >44 g but ≤60 g, provided it shows no evidence of injury, disease, or anatomical abnormality that might hinder growth and development. Thruout depletion period provide each rat with rachitogenic diet and H_2O or USP H_2O *ad libitum,* and permit no other dietary supplement to be available.

43.204 *Assembling Rats into Groups for Assay Period*

Assemble rats that are suitable for assay period into groups. For each sample provide ≥1 assay group. In assay of one sample at least one ref. group must be provided, but this ref. group may be used for concurrent assay of ≥1 assay sample. (Where 2 ref. groups are desired, dose levels must be selected so that ratio of higher to lower dose is not <1.5 or >2.5. Dosage levels for samples based upon single assumed potency for each sample may be equiv. to ref. levels or at midlevel equal to sq root of product of the 2 dosage levels of the ref.) On any one day during interval of assembling rats into groups, total number of rats assigned to make up any one group must not exceed by >2 the number of rats that have been assigned to make up any other group. When assembling of all groups is completed, total number of rats in each group must be same. Assign not >3 rats from 1 litter to assay group unless equal number of rats from same litter is assigned to ref. group. There must be enough animals in each group to meet requirements specified in **43.208**.

43.205 *Assay Period*

Rat is suitable for assay period provided depletion period is >18 days but ≤25 days, and provided rat shows evidence of rickets characterized by distinctive wobbly rachitic gait and enlarged joints. Presence of rickets may also be established by examination of leg bone of one member of litter by "line test," **43.206**, or by X-ray examination of animals selected for assay. Keep each rat in individual cage, provided with rachitogenic diet and H_2O *ad libitum.* On any calendar day of assay period, assay and ref. groups must receive rachitogenic diet compounded from same lots of ingredients.

Following optional methods of feeding ref. oil soln and sample soln are permissible, but both ref. oil soln and sample soln must be fed according to same method in any 1 assay. Supplements may be fed on first day of assay period, or in equal portions on first, third, and fifth days, or on first and third days, or on first and fourth days of 7 day or 10 day assay period, or on first 6 days of 7 day assay period, or on first 8 days of 10 day assay period; supplements may be fed admixed with amt of basal ration that will be consumed within first 5 days of 7 day assay period or within first 8 days of 10 day assay period. In each case make unsupplemented ration available during remainder of assay period.

Feed amt of ref. oil found by experience to cause extent and degree of calcification of rachitic metaphysis equiv. to 4 on line test chart. Feed that vol. of sample soln which is calcd to contain, on basis of claimed or assumed potency, same number of units of vitamin D as contained in amt of ref. oil fed.

After assay period, kill each rat and examine ≥1 leg bone for healing of rachitic metaphysis according to "line test," **43.206**.

Ref. oil may be dild with edible vegetable oil free from vitamins A and D before being fed. Dild oil must be stored in dark at temp. ≤10° for ≤30 days. Do not feed >0.2 mL of dild oil as daily dose. During assay period, keep all conditions of environment (particularly physiologically active radiations) as uniform as possible with respect to assay and ref. groups.

43.206 *Line Test*

Make line test on proximal end of tibia or distal end of radius or ulna. Remove end of desired bone from animal and clean off adhering tissue. Make longitudinal median section thru end of bone with clean, sharp blade to expose plane surface thru junction of epiphysis and diaphysis. In any one assay use same bone of all animals and section thru same plane. Rinse both sections of bone in H_2O and immerse in 2% $AgNO_3$ soln 1 min. Then rinse sections in H_2O and expose sectioned surfaces in H_2O to daylight or other source of actinic light until calcified areas have developed clearly defined stains without marked discoloration of uncalcified areas. Immediately record extent and degree of calcification of rachitic metaphysis of every section.

Staining procedure may be modified to differentiate more clearly between calcified and uncalcified areas. Suitable alternative procedure is to take freshly sectioned bone and proceed as follows: (*1*) Soak in ether-acetone mixt. (3+1) ≥5 min (at this stage, after bone sections are dry, they may be mounted for convenience and ease of handling on std microscope slides with aid of rubber cement and remainder of procedure performed in Coplin staining jars); (*2*) soak in alcohol 10 min; (*3*) soak in acetone 10 min; (*4*) soak 40 min in H_2O which is completely changed after 1, 10, 20, and 30 min; (*5*) stain with 2% $AgNO_3$ soln 60 sec; and (*6*) wash 40 min with H_2O in dark with complete changes after 1, 10, 20, and 30 min. Expose stained sections in H_2O to daylight or other source of actinic light until stains have developed.

Score degree of calcification of rachitic metaphysis in each rat according to scale shown in Fig. **43:03**. Because lines pictured in chart differ somewhat from line of healing being scored, it is necessary to visualize calcification as if it were compact and continuous in comparing it with appropriate figure in chart. Use of chart is illustrated by accompanying photographs of actual sections of radii, Fig. **43:04**.

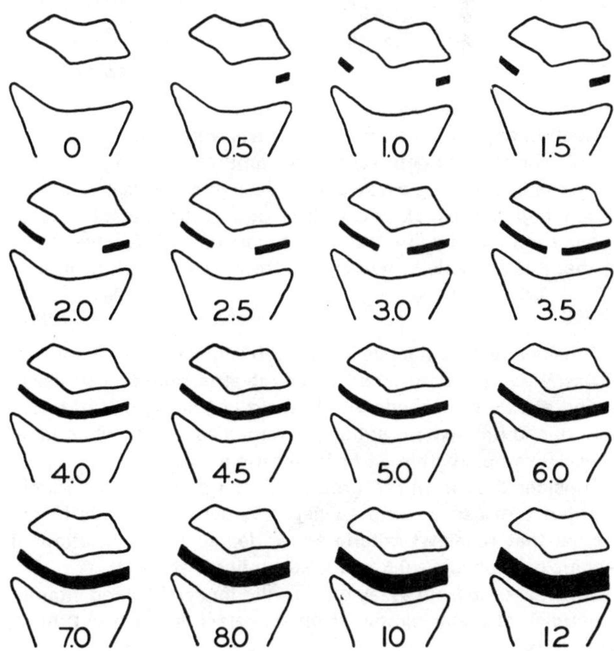

FIG. 43:03—Line test chart

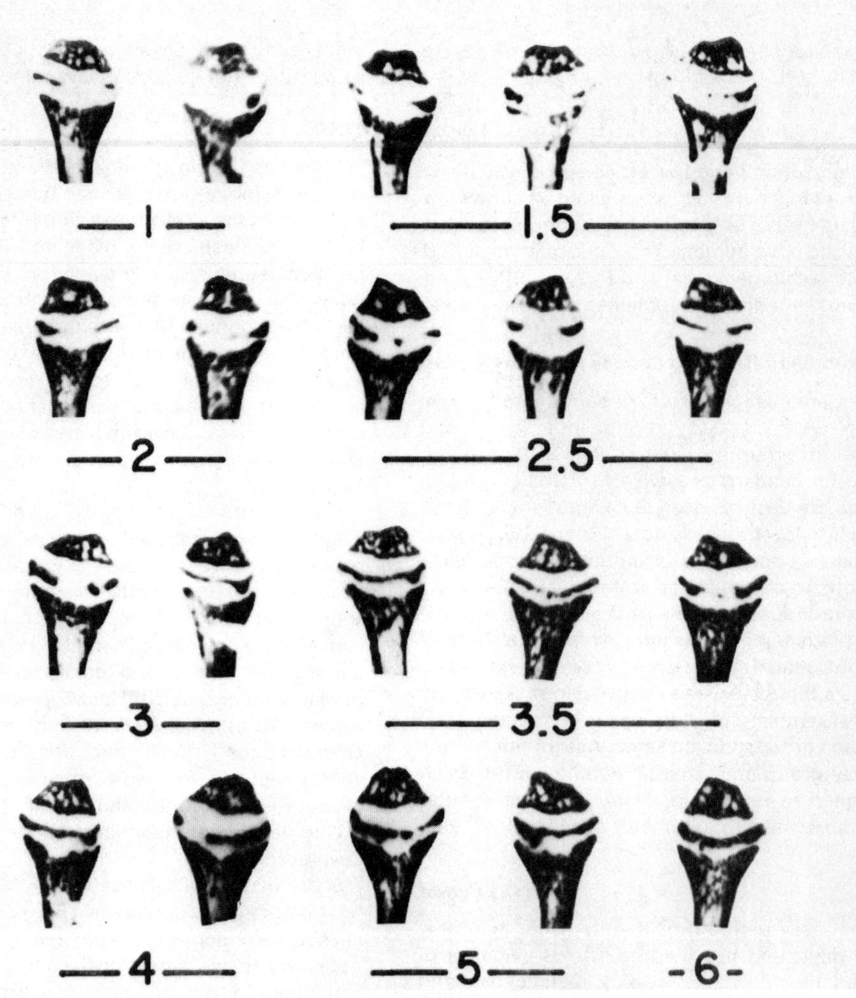

FIG. 43:04—Photographs of radii sections scored according to line test chart. For illustrative purposes only; should not be used as scoring scale

43.207 ***Recording of Data***

On day beginning assay period and on seventh or tenth day thereafter, depending on duration of assay period, record body wt of each rat. Keep record of amt of rachitogenic diet consumed/rat during assay period. Assign numerical values to extent and degree of calcification of rachitic metaphyses of bones examined by line test by comparison with line test chart so that it is possible to average performance of each group.

43.208 ***Potency of Assay Sample***

Consider data from rat valid for establishing vitamin D potency of assay sample only when wt of rat at termination of assay period equals or exceeds wt of rat on beginning day of assay period, and only when rat has consumed each prescribed dose of assay sample within 24 hr from time it was fed.

Consider data from ref. group valid for establishing vitamin D potency of assay sample when $\geqslant 2/3$ but not <7 rats in ref. groups that meet wt criteria show degree of calcification of rachitic metaphysis $\geqslant 0.5$ and $\leqslant 8.0$ on line test chart.

Consider data from assay group valid for establishing vitamin D potency of assay sample when $\geqslant 7$ rats in assay group meet wt criteria.

When av. response of assay group equals or exceeds av. response of ref. group, consider that vitamin D content of sample fed during assay period equals or exceeds vitamin D content of ref. oil fed during assay period. When av. response of assay group is less than av. response of ref. group, and $<1/2$ of rats in assay group show degree of calcification of rachitic metaphysis $\geqslant 0.5$ on line test chart, consider vitamin D content of sample fed during assay period to be less than vitamin D content of ref. oil fed during assay period. When av. response of assay group (A) is less than av. response of ref. group (R) and if $\geqslant 1/2$ rats in assay group show degree of calcification of rachitic metaphysis $\geqslant 0.5$ on line test chart, and:

(1) *Rats in assay and reference groups are unpaired by litter mates, then:*

$$t^2 = C_u(\overline{Y}_R - \overline{Y}_A)^2/S_u^2$$

where:

$$C_u = n_A n_R/(n_A + n_R)$$

$$S_u^2 = (\Sigma Y^2 - n_R\overline{Y}_R^2 - n_A\overline{Y}_A^2)/(n_A + n - 2)$$

$\overline{Y}_R$ = av. score for ref. group, $\overline{Y}_A$ = av. score for assay group, ΣY^2 = sum of squares of all individual scores, n_A = number of rats in assay group, and n_R = number of rats in ref. group. Find t^2 in table, where d.f. = degrees of freedom = $n_A + n_R - 2$. Or:

(2) *Rats in assay and reference groups are paired by litter mates,* subtract each response in assay group from associated litter mate response in ref. group. Maintain sign of difference.

Then:

$$t^2 = n_P\bar{D}^2/S_{\bar{D}}^2$$

where: n_P = number of pairs, $\bar{D}^2$ = square of av. difference, $\bar{D}$ = av. of differences, $S_{\bar{D}}^2$ = variance of differences = $(\Sigma D^2 - n_P\bar{D}^2)/(n_P - 1)$, and ΣD^2 = sum of squares of differences. Find t^2 in Table **43:07**, where d.f. = $n_P - 1$.

If calcd t^2 exceeds t^2 in table, consider vitamin D content of sample fed during assay period to be less than vitamin D content of ref. oil fed during assay period; otherwise consider that vitamin D content of sample equals or exceeds vitamin D content of ref. oil, provided S_u^2 is <1.5, or $S_{\bar{D}}^2$ is <2.5. If S_u^2 or $S_{\bar{D}}^2$ is >1.5 or 2.5, resp., data of this assay are inadequate to establish potency of assay sample. (Assay must then be extended or repeated.)

Calcn of t^2 and S^2 is illustrated as follows:

(1) *For unpaired data:*

Healing Scores

	Reference	Assay
	3.62	4.00
	3.12	4.37
	6.00	2.37
	5.50	2.00
	4.25	3.75
	5.50	2.50
	4.75	4.00
Average = $\bar{Y}$ =	4.68	3.28

$\Sigma Y^2 = 240.9901$

$C_u = (n_A \times n_R)/(n_A + n_R)$

$= (7 \times 7)/(7 + 7) = 3.5$

$S_u^2 = (\Sigma Y^2 - n_R\bar{Y}_R^2 - n_A\bar{Y}_A^2)/(n_A + n_R - 2)$

$= [240.9901 - 7(4.68)^2 - 7(3.28)^2]/12$

$= 1.0304$

$t^2 = (C_u/S_u^2)(\bar{Y}_R - \bar{Y}_A)^2$

$= (3.5/1.0304)(4.68 - 3.28)^2 = 6.658$

d.f. $= n_R + n_A - 2 = 12$

Tabular t^2 for d.f. = 12 is 3.176

Calcd t^2 (6.658) exceeds value in table for d.f. = 12 (3.176); therefore, vitamin D content of assay sample is less than vitamin D content of ref. oil. Since S_u^2 (1.0304) is <1.50, assay is valid.

(2) *For paired data:*

Litter	Healing Scores Reference	Assay	Difference
1	4.02	4.40	− 0.38
2	3.52	4.77	− 1.25
3	6.40	2.77	+ 3.63
4	5.90	2.40	+ 3.50
5	4.65	4.15	+ 0.50
6	5.90	2.90	+ 3.00
7	5.15	4.40	+ 0.75
Average = $\bar{D}$		=	1.39
ΣD^2		=	36.9463

$S_{\bar{D}}^2 = (\Sigma D^2 - n_P\bar{D}^2)/(n_P - 1)$

$= [36.9463 - 7(1.39)^2]/6 = 3.9036$

$t^2 = (n_P\bar{D}^2)/(S_{\bar{D}}^2)$

$= 7(1.39)^2/3.9036 = 3.4647$

d.f. $= n_P - 1 = 6$

Tabular t^2 for d.f. = 6 is 3.775

Altho calcd value of t^2, 3.4647, is less than tabular value for d.f. = 6 of 3.775, indicating that vitamin D content of assay sample equals or exceeds vitamin D content of ref. oil, *assay must be repeated* since value for $S_{\bar{D}}^2$ of 3.9036 is >2.5. Available data are inadequate to establish potency of sample.

Table 43:07 t^2 **Values**

d.f.	t^2	d.f.	t^2	d.f.	t^2
6	3.775	14	3.101	22	2.948
7	3.591	15	3.073	23	2.938
8	3.460	16	3.049	24	2.928
9	3.360	17	3.028	25	2.917
10	3.283	18	3.007	26	2.910
11	3.226	19	2.989	27	2.900
12	3.176	20	2.976	28	2.893
13	3.136	21	2.962	29	2.887
				30	2.880

(If desired, potency of vitamin D_2 may be calcd from multiple level assays by statistical procedure of USP XIX, p. 605, or corresponding procedure of USP XX.)

Vitamin D_3 in Poultry Feed Supplements (*31*)
Official Final Action

(Applicable to fish and fish liver oils and their exts, and to materials used for supplementing vitamin D content of feeds. Not applicable to irradiated ergosterol products or to irradiated yeast unless recommended for poultry. This assay is comparison, under conditions specified, of efficacy of product under assay with that of USP Cholecalciferol Ref. Std in controlling ash content of bones of growing chicks.)

43.209 ***Basal Rachitic Ration***

The basal ration is uniform mixt. in proportions designated of following ingredients, which have been finely ground:

	per cent
Yellow corn, ground	58
Wheat flour middlings or wheat gray shorts	25
Casein, crude, domestic, acid pptd	12
Calcium phosphate, tribasic	2
Salt, iodized (0.02% KI)	1
Yeast, non-irradiated (7% min. N)	2

To each kg of above mixt. add 0.22 g $MnSO_4.5H_2O$.

43.210 ***Determination***

Provide cages with screen bottoms and keep chicks away from sunshine or other source of actinic light that may influence calcification. Keep cages in rooms in which wide variations in temp. are prevented (const temp. preferred). Unless temp. of room is adequately controlled, provide each cage with suitable elec. heating device. Start all birds to be used in one assay on same day and keep all conditions of environment uniform for all groups in assay.

Make assay on groups of 1- or 2-day-old White Leghorn chicks as specified below. Provide for ≥1 neg. control group that receives no vitamin D, ≥3 pos. control groups that receive graduated levels of vitamin D from USP Vitamin D Ref. Std, and ≥1 assay group for each product to be assayed. Have pos. control and assay groups consist of ≥20 birds each, and neg. control consist of ≥10 birds.

Prep. rations for all groups in assay from one batch of basal ration. Add Ref. Std to basal ration in such amts as to produce measurable increase in % bone ash above that obtained in neg. control group (it is not possible to make comparisons if max. bone ash is obtained). Add assay product to basal ration in such amts as to permit direct comparison in response of assay and pos. control groups.

To basal ration of neg. control group add corn oil equal in amt to max. amt of oil fed to any group in assay, and add corn oil to rations of other groups until total amt of corn oil and oil contg vitamin D is equal to amt of corn oil added to ration of neg. control group.

Feed chicks in respective groups prescribed ration and H_2O (natural or distd) *ad libitum* 21 days. Discard all chicks that show abnormality or disease not related to vitamin D deficiency. At least 15 chicks must remain in each ref. or assay group used in calcg vitamin D potency of assay product.

Thruout any one assay, consistently use the specific method, (**a**) or (**b**), adopted for extg, drying, and ashing of bones.

(**a**) Kill chicks; remove left tibia of each bird and clean off adhering tissue. (To facilitate removal of adhering tissue, bones may be placed in boiling H_2O ≤2 min. Bones may be preserved in alcohol for extn.) Completely ext bones with suitable fat solv. or solvs (20 hr with hot alcohol followed by 20 hr with ether is suitable, and bones should be crushed to facilitate extn). Dry extd bones to const wt at 95–100° under pressure <100 mm Hg (13.3 kPa) (ca 5 hr), cool in desiccator, and weigh. Ash H_2O- and fat-free bones from each group of birds in furnace to const wt at any given temp. between 450 and 550°, or if preferred, 1 hr at ca 850°. (Ash detn may be made on individual bones if desired.)

(**b**) Alternatively, use toe ash measurement of response to vitamin D: Excise middle toe from each foot by cutting thru joint between second and third tarsal bones from distal end. Use entire toe for sample. Remove any dirt, but not tissue, and do not ext with solv. Composite samples of group, dry 8 hr at 100° in air oven, and ash 4 hr at 600° in furnace.

43.211 ***Interpretation of Results***

One international chick unit of vitamin D is equal in biological activity to one unit vitamin D in USP Vitamin D Ref. Std in this method of assay. Product under assay meets its declared vitamin potency in international chick units of vitamin D if % ash in H_2O- and fat-free bone produced in assay groups by given number of units of vitamin D is equal to or is greater than % ash produced by same number of units of vitamin D from USP Ref. Std.

Biological Evaluation of Protein Quality (Protein Efficiency Ratio)(*32*)—Official Final Action

(Applicable to materials contg >1.80% N)

43.212 ***Reagents***

(**a**) *ANRC reference casein.*—Available from Humko Sheffield Chemical, PO Box 398, Memphis TN 38101.

(**b**) *Salt mixture USP.*—Either USP salt mixt. or salt mixt. having essentially same proportions of the elements. Prep. USP XIX (p. 612) salt mixt. (or corresponding USP XX item) as follows: Grind in mortar portion of 139.3 g NaCl with 0.79 g KI. Similarly grind together remainder of the NaCl with 389.0 g KH_2PO_4, 57.3 g $MgSO_4$ anhyd., 381.4 g $CaCO_3$, 27.0 g $FeSO_4.7H_2O$, 4.01 g $MnSO_4.H_2O$, 0.548 g $ZnSO_4.7H_2O$, 0.477 g $CuSO_4.5H_2O$, and 0.023 g $CoCl_2.6H_2O$, finally adding the NaCl-KI mixt. Reduce entire mixt. to fine powder.

(**c**) *Vitamin mixture.*—

	mg/100 g ration
Vitamin A (dry, stabilized)	2000 (IU)
Vitamin D (dry, stabilized)	200 (IU)
Vitamin E (dry, stabilized)	10 (IU)
Menadione	0.5
Choline	200
p-Aminobenzoic acid	10
Inositol	10
Niacin	4
Ca D-pantothenate	4
Riboflavin	0.8
Thiamine.HCl	0.5
Pyridoxine.HCl	0.5
Folic acid	0.2
Biotin	0.04
Vitamin B_{12}	0.003
Glucose, to make	1000

(**d**) *Cottonseed oil.*

(**e**) *Cellulose.*—Cellu Flour, Solka Floc, or equiv.

(**f**) *Protein evaluation basal diet.*—

Sample	X*
Cottonseed oil	$8 - \frac{X \times \text{\% ether extract}}{100}$
Salt mixture USP	$5 - \frac{X \times \text{\% ash}}{100}$
Vitamin mixture	1
Cellulose	$1 - \frac{X \times \text{\% crude fiber}}{100}$
Water	$5 - \frac{X \times \text{\% moisture}}{100}$
Sucrose or corn starch, to make 100	

$$^*X = \frac{1.60 \times 100}{\text{\% N of sample}}$$

All % figures refer to sample. Proximate analysis is needed to adjust diet so that all comparisons between samples and ref. material shall be made with diets having same content of N, fat, ash, moisture, and crude fiber. These suggested levels of fat, ash, moisture, and crude fiber are desirable whenever proximate analysis of sample permits.

43.213 ***Experimental Animals***

Laboratory rats, males, shall be from same colony, and maintained during period before weaning upon diet and under environmental conditions that will provide for normal development in all respects; weaned; ≥21 days of age but ≤28 days of age; range of individual rat wts among animals used shall be ≤10 g. When animals are transported from breeding colony to test laboratory, acclimation period of ≥3 days but <7 should precede test.

43.214 ***Assay Groups***

Assemble groups of ≥10 rats. In assay of each material provide 1 group that will receive ANRC ref. casein. One ref. casein group may be used for concurrent assay of >1 assay material. When assembling of all groups is complete, total number of rats in each group must be the same, and av. wt of rats in any 1 group on day beginning assay period must not exceed by >5 g av. wt of rats in any other group.

43.215 ***Assay Period***

Throughout assay period keep each rat in individual cage and provide with appropriate assay diet and H_2O *ad libitum.* During assay period maintain all conditions of environment as uniform as possible with respect to each of groups being compared to ANRC ref. casein. Record body wt of each rat on beginning day of assay period and body wt and food intake of each rat at regular intervals, not >7 days, and on 28th day after beginning of assay period.

43.216 ***Calculation and Tabulation of Results***

Calc. av. 28 day wt gain and protein (N × 6.25) intake per rat for each group. Calc. Protein Efficiency Ratio (PER) (wt gain/protein intake) for each group. Det. ratio × 100 of PER for each assay group to PER for ANRC casein ref. group. Tabulate 28 day wt gains, protein intake, PER, and ratio × 100 of sample PER to ANRC Ref. Casein PER for each assay group. Report protein quality of sample as ratio × 100 of sample PER to ANRC Ref. Casein PER.

Hemoglobin Repletion Test for Iron (*33*)
Official First Action

43.217 ***Apparatus and Reagents***

(**a**) *Colorimeter.*—Bausch & Lomb Spectronic 20, or equiv.
(**b**) *Basal diet.*—(Antibiotic may be added if desired.)

Ingredient	%
Glucose.H_2O	49.38
Vitamin-free casein	20.00
Degermed yellow corn meal	15.00
Gelatin	5.00
Corn oil	5.00
Monosodium phosphate	2.00
Calcium carbonate	2.00
KCl	0.50
Iodized salt	0.50
Trace mineral premix, (**c**)	0.27
Choline chloride	0.15
Vitamin premix, (**d**)	0.10
dl-Methionine	0.10

(**c**) *Trace mineral premix.*—

Mineral	*g/2 kg Trace Mineral Premix*	*g/100 g Trace Mineral Premix*	*g/kg Diet*
$MgSO_4$, anhyd.	1476.32	73.816	1.9819
$ZnSO_4.7H_2O$	393.14	19.657	0.5278
$MnSO_4.H_2O$	114.66	5.733	0.1539
$CuSO_4.5H_2O$	14.63	0.7315	0.0196
KIO_3	1.25	0.0625	0.0017

(**d**) *Vitamin premix.*—

Component	*g/2 kg Vitamin Premix*	*g/100 g Vitamin Premix*	*g/kg Diet*
Vitamin A, stabilized, 500,000 IU/g	20.00	1.00	0.0100
Vitamin D_3, stabilized, 200,000 ICU/g	15.00	0.75	0.0075
α-Tocopheryl acetate	100.00	5.00	0.0500
Menadione	0.80	0.04	0.0004
Thiamine.HCl	6.00	0.30	0.0030
Riboflavin	6.00	0.30	0.0030
Pyridoxine.HCl	20.00	1.00	0.0100
Calcium pantothenate	20.00	1.00	0.0100
Niacin	60.00	3.00	0.0300
Folic acid	2.00	0.10	0.0010
Vitamin B_{12}, 0.1% in gelatin	40.00	2.00	0.0200
Sucrose	1710.20	85.51	0.8551

(**e**) *Drabkin's soln.*—Dissolve 1 g $NaHCO_3$, 52 mg KCN, and 198 mg $K_3Fe(CN)_6$ in H_2O, and dil. to 1 L. Store in brown bottle in dark. Soln is stable indefinitely in dark. Discard when cloudiness occurs or ppt forms.

43.218 ***Hemoglobin Determination***

Pipet 5 mL Drabkin's soln into colorimeter tubes and to each add 0.02 mL whole blood drawn from tail vein of rat. Rinse pipet several times with soln in tube. Mix by inverting. Reserve 1 tube for blank to zero instrument. Let stand 10 min. Set wavelength at 540 nm, place blank tube in instrument, and set at 100% *T*. Replace blank with sample soln and read % *T*. Use Table **43:08** to obtain concn of sample in g hemoglobin/100 mL blood.

43.219 ***Assay***

Place male weanling rats, ≤21 days old, from fast growing strain on diet, (**b**). Keep diet and suitable H_2O (naturally low in Fe or distd) before experimental animals at all times.

After rats have been on basal diet 4 weeks, check hemoglobin of blood of representative rats to det. that animals are anemic. (Rats are satisfactorily depleted when hemoglobin is <6 g/100 mL.) If animals are not depleted, continue basal diet and retest at intervals.

After animals are satisfactorily depleted, divide them into groups of ≥8 comparable animals each, house them in individual stainless steel cages or cages otherwise protected against readily available Fe, and place them on test diets. Use $FeSO_4.7H_2O$ as ref. std. Place groups of test animals on 0, 6, 12, and 24 mg Fe/kg diet, supplied by ref. std $FeSO_4.7H_2O$. Place other groups on diets that contain levels of samples expected to give comparable responses.

Place 3 groups of depleted animals on each sample. Analyze test samples by **14.011–14.013** to det. Fe content so that known amts Fe can be added to test diets.

After 2 weeks on test diets, take individual blood samples and det. hemoglobin, **43.218**.

Interpret results as parallel lines-type assay (Bliss and White, Chap. 2 in "The Vitamins," 2nd ed., Vol. 6, edited by P. Gyorgy and W. N. Pearson, Academic Press, New York, 1967, pp. 50–57). Report bioavailability of samples against $FeSO_4.7H_2O$ = 100.

Table 43:08 Conversion of % *T* to g Hemoglobin/100 mL Blood[a]

T	0	1	2	3	4	5	6	7	8	9
0										
10										
20	22.3	21.6	21.0	20.3	19.7	19.2	18.6	18.0	17.6	17.1
30	16.6	16.1	15.7	15.3	14.9	14.5	14.1	13.7	13.4	13.0
40	12.6	12.3	12.0	11.6	11.4	11.0	10.7	10.4	10.1	9.8
50	9.5	9.3	9.0	8.7	8.5	8.2	8.0	7.7	7.5	7.2
60	7.0	6.8	6.5	6.4	6.1	5.9	5.7	5.5	5.3	5.1
70	4.9	4.7	4.5	4.3	4.1	3.9	3.8	3.6	3.4	3.2
80	3.0	2.9	2.7	2.5	2.4	2.2	2.0	1.9	1.7	1.6
90	1.4	1.3	1.1	1.0	0.8	0.7	0.5			

[a] Example: Transmission reading on scale = 47. Concentration found opposite 40, under 7 = 10.4.

NUTRITIONALLY RELATED COMPONENTS

Sodium in Foods for Special Dietary Use

Ion Selective Electrode Method (34)
Official Final Action

(Applicable to foods contg ≤100 mg Na/100 g)

43.220 ***Apparatus***

(**a**) *Electrode.*—Sodium combination ion selective electrode (Model 96-11, Orion Research, Inc., or equiv.).

(**b**) *Graph paper.*—Gran's plot paper, 10% vol. corrected (No. 90-00-90, Orion Research, Inc., or equiv.).

(**c**) *Magnetic stirrer.*—*See* **7.110(b)**.

(**d**) *pH meter.*—With expanded mv scale (Model 701/701A, Orion Research, Inc., or equiv.).

43.221 ***Reagents***

(**a**) *Buffer soln.*—pH 10.2. Total ionic strength adjustment buffer (TISAB), 0.5*M* triethanolamine. Dissolve 74.6 g triethanolamine in ca 900 mL H_2O, adjust pH to 10.2 with HCl, and dil. to 1 L with H_2O.

(**b**) *Sodium std solns.*—(*1*) *Stock soln.*—10 mg/mL. Accurately weigh 2.5421 g NaCl, previously dried overnight at 100°, into 100 mL vol. flask. Dissolve and dil. to vol. with H_2O, and mix. (*2*) *Working solns.*— 0.1, 1.0, and 2.0 mg/mL. Pipet 1, 10, and 20 mL stock soln into sep. 100 mL vol. flasks, dil. each to vol. with buffer soln, and mix.

43.222 ***Preparation of Sample***

Blend entire contents of can, including H_2O. Weigh 10.0 g sample and dil. to 100 mL with buffer soln. Mix and transfer to 150 mL beaker.

43.223 ***Determination***

(**a**) *For foods with 0–5 mg declared Na/100 g.*—Immerse electrode in sample beaker and stir mag. 2–5 min to equilibrate. Record mv potential on expanded mv scale. From 10 mL buret, add five 1.0 mL portions 0.1 mg Na/mL working std soln to beaker, stirring mag. 30 sec after each addn. Plot mv reading for 0, 1, 2, 3, 4, and 5 mL on graph paper, (**b**). Follow plotting instructions, **5.007(b)**, except plot most pos. mv reading at top of vertical axis. Draw best straight line thru points, extrapolate line to horizontal axis, and read mg Na in sample.

Perform blank detn on 100 mL buffer soln, adding five 1.0 mL portions 0.1 mg Na/mL working std soln, as above. Plot mv readings on graph paper, omitting 0 mL reading, such that 5 mL reading falls near top of paper. Draw best straight line thru points, extrapolate line to horizontal axis, and read mg Na in blank.

$$\text{mg Na/100 g food} = [(S - B) \times 100]/W,$$

where S = mg Na in sample, B = mg Na in blank, and W = g sample.

(**b**) *For foods with 5–50 mg declared Na/100 g.*—Proceed as in (**a**), except use 1.0 mg Na/mL working std soln.

(**c**) *For foods with 50–100 mg declared Na/100 g.*— Proceed as in (**a**), except use 2.0 mg Na/mL working std soln.

Available Lysine (*35*)—Official Final Action

43.224 ***Principle***

1-Fluoro-2,4-dinitrobenzene (DNFB) reacts with free ε-amino groups in proteins, forming DNFB-ε-amino lysine which is stable to acid hydrolysis. Sample is acid hydrolyzed and unavailable lysine is detd with amino acid analyzer; total lysine is detd on untreated sample. Available lysine, which was bound by DNFB, is detd by difference.

43.225 ***Reagents***

(Use deionized H_2O thruout.)

(**a**) *Sodium citrate buffer.*—pH 2.20±0.03. Dissolve 19.6 g Na citrate.$2H_2O$ in H_2O, add 16.5 mL HCl, 5.0 mL thiodiglycol (TG), 1.0 g Brij-35 dissolved in H_2O by heating, and 0.1 mL *n*-caprylic acid, and dil. to 1 L. Filter before using.

(**b**) *Sodium citrate buffer.*—pH 5.28±0.02. Dissolve 137.26 g Na citrate.$2H_2O$ in H_2O, add 26.0 mL HCl, 4.0 g Brij-35 dissolved in H_2O by heating, and 0.4 mL *n*-caprylic acid, and dil. to 4 L. Filter before using.

(**c**) *Sodium citrate buffer with 2% n-propanol.*—pH 5.28±0.02. Prep. as in (**b**), but add 80 mL *n*-propanol before diln to 4 L.

(**d**) *Sodium acetate buffer.*—4*N*, pH 5.51±0.03. Add 1088 g NaOAc.$3H_2O$ to 800 mL H_2O. Stir while heating on steam or H_2O bath until soln is complete and cool to room temp. Add 200 mL HOAc and stir. Add H_2O to final vol. of 2 L, adjust pH, if necessary (1 g NaOH/2 L causes change of 0.02 pH), and filter before using.

(**e**) *Regeneration reagent.*—Prep. 0.2*N* NaOH contg 1 g Brij-35/L.

(**f**) *Ninhydrin reagent.*—Prep. and introduce into reservoir in absence of O. Bubble slow stream of N thru soln while mixing and stirring to displace any air. Use mag. stirrer with seamless Teflon bar, 0.5 × 3″. Add 3 L filtered peroxide-free Methyl Cellosolve (colorless soln must be produced when 3 mL is mixed with 3 mL 4% KI soln) to 1 L filtered 4*N* NaOAc buffer soln, and stir mag. 15 min while bubbling N thru soln at ca 1 cu ft/hr. Add 80 g ninhydrin (*Caution:* Weigh in hood) and stir mag. with N bubbling until ninhydrin is completely dissolved (usually 6–10 min). Weigh exactly 1.600 g $SnCl_2.2H_2O$ and add to soln, rinsing with Methyl Cellosolve to final vol. Reagent turns deep ruby red as $SnCl_2$ dissolves but color fades after ca 2 hr to yellow-green when fresh and yellow-brown later. Continue stirring with N bubbling until $SnCl_2$ dissolves completely (ca 3–8 min).

43.226 ***Preparation of Protein Hydrolysate***

Grind sample in Wiley mill with No. 20 screen and mix well. Weigh 0.1–1.0 g sample into No. 5/0 crucible (1.3 mL). (Calc. sample wt to give final concn of 0.72–0.88 mg protein/mL after diln with 100 mL Na citrate buffer, pH 2.2.

$$\text{mg Sample to use} = (\text{final concn desired (mg/mL)} \times 100\ (\text{mL}))/(\%\ \text{protein in sample}/100),$$

but do not use >1 g.)

Place sample or sample and crucible in 500 mL boiling flask and add 4–5 glass beads. Add 10 mL freshly prepd 10% $NaHCO_3$ soln, 10 mL alcohol, and 0.4 mL dinitrofluorobenzene (DNFB). Stopper flask and shake mech. >3 hr. Carefully acidify with 6*N* HCl (ca 2 mL). Evap. to oily dryness at 40° in vac. rotary evaporator. Release vac. very slowly to avoid disturbing residue. Add 50–75 mL anhyd. ether, decant, and re-evap. in rotary evaporator at 40° without vac. Repeat washing with ether and evapn 3 addnl times. (*Caution: See* **51.011** and **51.054**.)

Add ca 125 mL 6*N* HCl. Heat carefully until all CO_2 is released, and then boil under reflux 18 hr, maintaining const stream of H_2O-pumped or prepurified N thru Tygon capillary tube which comes to ca 2.5 cm of surface of soln. Cool 1 hr and wash down residue in condenser. Evap. to sticky paste in vac. rotary evaporator at 40°. Repeat addn of 100 mL H_2O and evapn 4 addnl times, evapg to dryness during last evapn.

43.227 ***Preparation of Protein Hydrolysate Without DNFB***

Weigh sample to give final concn of 0.18–0.22 mg protein/mL after diln with 100 mL Na citrate buffer, pH 2.2, into 5/0 crucible.

Place sample or sample and crucible into 500 mL boiling flask and add 4–5 glass beads. Add 200 mL 6*N* HCl and distl off 100 mL. Hydrolyze under reflux 24 hr, maintaining const stream of N as in **43.226**. Evap. to sticky paste in vac. rotary evaporator at 40°. Repeat addn of 100 mL H_2O and evapn 5 addnl times, evapg to dryness during last evapn.

Proceed as in **43.228**, except use protein concn of 0.18–0.22 mg/mL and 6 cm prepd column.

43.228 ***Determination***

Pipet in 100 mL Na citrate buffer, pH 2.2. Stopper flask, shake 5 min, and filter thru Whatman No. 43 paper into storage bottle. Use 1.0 mL filtrate contg 0.72–0.88 mg protein/mL on 12 cm column of Beckman Custom Research Resin Type PA-35, regenerated after NH_3 peak of each sample with regeneration reagent and equilibrated with Na citrate buffer with 2% *n*-PrOH.

Operate automatic amino acid analyzer (Beckman Model 120C, or equiv.) in accordance with instructions of manufacturer. Identify lysine peak by comparison with calibration run with lysine or std calibration mixt. under same operating conditions as used in analysis.

Det. area under curve for lysine or use integrator, and compare areas of samples with those from calibration stds contg known concn of lysine (e.g., 2.500±0.004 μm/mL 0.1*N* HCl).

To calc. % available lysine, subtract % lysine of DNFB-treated sample from % lysine of non-DNFB-treated sample.

Cholesterol in Multicomponent Foods

Gas Chromatographic Method (36)—Official Final Action

43.229 ***Principle***

Lipid is extd from sample by mixed solv. and saponified. Unsaponifiable fraction contg cholesterol and other sterols is extd with benzene. Sterols are derivatized to form trimethylsilyl (TMS) ethers which are detd quant. by GLC, using 5α-cholestane as internal std.

43.230 ***Apparatus***

(**a**) *Centrifuge tubes*.—Pyrex No. 13, 15 mL. Silanize tubes as follows: Rinse clean tubes with anhyd. MeOH and dry 30 min at 110°. Transfer tubes to desiccator. Fill tubes with 10% soln of dimethyldichlorosilane (DMCS) in toluene, stopper tubes, and let stand 1 hr. Drain tubes and rinse thoroly with anhyd. MeOH. Dry in 110° oven before use. After use, clean tubes with MeOH, H_2O, and MeOH, in that order. Dry tubes in 100° oven before use. Tubes can be re-used without silylation as long as strong alkali wash is avoided.

(**b**) *Gas chromatograph*.—With H flame ionization detector, on-column injection system, and 2.4 m (8′) × 3 mm id U-shaped glass column packed with 0.5% Apiezon L (No. 08304, Applied Science Laboratories, Inc.) on 80–100 mesh Gas-Chrom Q (No. 02002, Applied Science Laboratories, Inc.). Alternative column: 1.8 m (6′) × 4 mm id U-shaped glass column packed with 1% SE-30 on 100–120 mesh Gas-Chrom Q (No. 12409, Applied Science Laboratories, Inc.). Operating conditions: temps (°)—flash heater 275, detector 275, column 230; flow rates (mL/min)—N (ultra high purity grade) ca 50, to elute cholesterol in 9–11 min, H ca 35, air 350; electrometer sensitivity 1×10^{-9} amp full-scale deflection with 1 mv recorder.

(**c**) *Homogenizer*.—Sorvall Omnimixer (IVA Sorvall, Inc., Norwalk, CT 06852), or equiv., for use with 12 oz (350 mL) wide-mouth screw-cap jars.

(**d**) *Magnetic stirrer-hot plate*.—With variable speed and heat controls.

(**e**) *Rotary evaporator*.—With glass condenser flask between concn flask and metal shaft.

(**f**) *Test tube mixer*.—Vortex-Genie mixer (No. 12-812, Fisher Scientific Co.), or equiv.

43.231 ***Reagents***

(*Caution:* Silanes are toxic. Avoid contact with skin and eyes. Use effective fume removal device.)

(**a**) *Cholesterol std solns*.—Std cholesterol available as No. 21502, Applied Science Laboratories, Inc. (*1*) *Stock soln*.—1.0 mg/mL DMF. (*2*) *Working solns*.—Dil. stock soln with DMF to obtain concn range from 0.05 to 0.5 mg/mL.

(**b**) *5α-Cholestane internal std solns*.—Std 5α-cholestane available as No. 19505, Applied Science Laboratories, Inc. (*1*) *Stock soln*.—1.0 mg/mL *n*-heptane. (*2*) *Working soln*.—0.2 mg/mL. Dil. stock soln with *n*-heptane to obtain concn of 0.2 mg/mL.

(**c**) *Dimethyldichlorosilane*.—No. 18008, Applied Science Laboratories, Inc., or equiv.

(**d**) *Dimethylformamide*.—Distd in glass (Burdick & Jackson Laboratories, Inc.; Anspec Co., Inc., PO Box 7044, Ann Arbor, MI 48107; or equiv.).

(**e**) *Glass wool*.—Silane-treated (No. 14502, Applied Science Laboratories, Inc., or equiv.).

(**f**) *n-Heptane*.—Distd in glass (Burdick & Jackson Laboratories, Inc., Eastman Kodak Co., No. 2215, or equiv.).

(**g**) *Hexamethyldisilazane* (*HMDS*).—No. 18006, Applied Science Laboratories, Inc., Pierce Chemical Co., or equiv.

(**h**) *Concentrated potassium hydroxide soln*.—Dissolve 60 g KOH in 40 mL H_2O.

(**i**) *Reagent alcohols*.—EtOH-MeOH-isopropanol (90+5+5). Following reagent alcohols are satisfactory: No. 3945–1GL, Harleco, Division of American Hospital Supply Corp., 480 Democrat Rd, Gibbstown, NJ 08027; Wilkens-Anderson Co., 4525 W Division St, Chicago IL 60651; No. 7019 or No. 7006, Mallinckrodt Chemical Works.

(**j**) *Toluene*.—Nanograde, distd in glass (Mallinckrodt Chemical Works, or equiv.).

(**k**) *Trimethylchlorosilane* (*TMCS*).—No. 18010, Applied Science Laboratories, Inc., or equiv.

(**l**) *Trimethylsilyl* (*TMS*) *reagent*.—HMDS-TMCS-pyridine (9+6+10).

43.232 ***Preparation and Packing of Gas Chromatographic Column***

(*Caution: See* **51.025** and **51.062**.)

Attach empty column to aspirator and draw thru 5% HF soln. Stop vac. with pinch clamp, quickly cap both ends of column with rubber stoppers, and let column stand filled with 5% HF soln 10 min.

Attach column to aspirator again, draw off 5% HF soln, and rinse with ca 150 mL H_2O followed by 150 mL anhyd. MeOH. Finally, rinse column with 150 mL isooctane. Draw air thru column until dry. Fill column with TMS reagent, (l), by pulling it thru slowly with aspirator. Plug both ends of column and let stand 30 min. Draw TMS reagent thru and rinse immediately with 100 mL anhyd. MeOH, followed by 200 mL isooctane. Let column dry under vac.

Use com. prepd column packing of 0.5% Apiezon L on 80–100 mesh Gas-Chrom Q (Applied Science Laboratories, Inc.), or prep. as follows: Weigh 0.5 g Apiezon L into 100 mL beaker, add 80 mL toluene, stir mag. until it dissolves completely, and transfer to 500 mL erlenmeyer, rinsing beaker with four 5 mL portions toluene. Weigh 10 g 80–100 mesh Gas-Chrom Q and add to

Apiezon L soln. Stopper flask and shake to make slurry. Immediately pour slurry thru buchner-type fritted glass Pyrex filter (medium porosity) under vac., stirring continuously until all liq. is drawn off. Measure filtrate in graduate and det. amt Apiezon L adsorbed. Let stand under vac., stirring occasionally until almost dry. Transfer packing to porcelain evapn dish and dry completely in 110–120° oven. Store in glass bottle until ready to use.

Heat packing 15 min in 100° oven. Plug detector end of silanized column with 6 mm silanized glass wool and attach to aspirator. Add warm packing thru funnel attached to column and gently tap column. Finally, plug injection port end with silanized glass wool. Condition column 24 hr at 235° with N flow.

43.233 ***Moisture Determination***

Accurately weigh ca 5.0 g sample into tared Al dish, place in circulating-type 100° air oven, and dry overnight or 3 hr at 110°. Cover, and let cool in desiccator. Weigh accurately and det. moisture content to adjust for H_2O to be added in **43.234**.

43.234 ***Extraction of Lipid***

(*Caution: See* **51.011, 51.054, 51.056, 51.066**, and **51.074**.)

(**a**) *For foods other than dried whole egg solids, mayonnaise, and nonfat dry milk.*—Accurately weigh known amt sample contg ca 0.5–1 g fat and transfer quant. to homogenizer cup with 100.0 mL anhyd. MeOH. On basis of moisture detn, add enough H_2O to bring total H_2O content in extn to 40 mL. Add 50 mL $CHCl_3$ and blend 3 min at high speed. (Ratio of $CHCl_3$-MeOH-H_2O must be 50–100–40 in this single-phase extn.) Add addnl 50 mL $CHCl_3$ and blend 0.5 min at medium speed. Then add 50 mL H_2O and again blend 0.5 min at medium speed. Filter homogenate under vac. into 1 L suction flask thru buchner fitted with Whatman No. 1 paper contg 2 g diat. earth, **36.002**. Pour filtrate into 500 mL graduate. Re-ext filter cake and paper with ca 90 mL $CHCl_3$ and filter ext without diat. earth. Rinse cup and filter cake with two 15 mL portions $CHCl_3$. Add these rinses to original filtrate and let layers sep. (If emulsion develops, centrf. filtrate 5 min at 2500 rpm.) Record vol. of $CHCl_3$ (lower) layer and aspirate aq. alcohol layer. (Total vol. of $CHCl_3$ layer should be ca 200 mL.) Proceed as in **43.235**.

(**b**) *For dried whole egg solids.*—Use acid hydrolysis, **17.012(b)**, and proceed as in **43.235**, par. 2.

(**c**) *For mayonnaise.*—Accurately weigh ca 1.2–1.5 g sample and transfer quant. to homogenizer cup with 100.0 mL anhyd. MeOH. Add 40 mL H_2O and 50 mL $CHCl_3$ and blend 3 min at medium speed. Add addnl 50 mL $CHCl_3$ and blend 0.5 min at medium speed. Then add 50 mL H_2O and again blend 0.5 min at medium speed. Transfer homogenate to 500 mL separator. Rinse cup with three 20 mL portions $CHCl_3$ and add these rinses to separator. Mix by gently rotating separator end to end. Let layers sep. Drain $CHCl_3$ (lower) layer into graduate. Rinse aq. MeOH layer with 40 mL $CHCl_3$, add rinse to graduate, and mix. Record vol. of $CHCl_3$ layer. Proceed as in **43.235**, using 150 mL aliquot $CHCl_3$-lipid ext and 250 mL beaker.

(**d**) *For nonfat dry milk.*—Accurately weigh ca 25 g sample and transfer quant. to 300 mL erlenmeyer contg 100 mL H_2O. Stir to mix thoroly, and refrigerate overnight. Pour reconstituted milk into 1 L separator, add 100 mL reagent alcohol, (**i**), and shake 1 min. Add 100 mL ether and shake 1 min. Add 100 mL pentane and shake 1 min. Let layers sep. Drain aq. (lower) layer into second separator. Repeat extn with 100 mL ether and 100 mL pentane, shaking 1 min after each addn. If layers do not sep., add 40 mL reagent alcohol, gently rotate end over end 10 times, and let stand 5 min. Discard aq. layer. Filter combined ether exts thru column of anhyd. Na_2SO_4 into 600 mL beaker. Evap. to ca 10 mL under gentle N stream on 70° H_2O bath. Transfer ext to 300 mL g-s erlenmeyer, rinsing beaker with pentane. Evap. to dryness under gentle N stream on steam bath, and proceed as in **43.235**, par. 2.

43.235 ***Saponification and Extraction of Unsaponifiable Fraction***

(*Caution: See* **51.011, 51.018, 51.045**, and **51.073**.)

Filter 100 mL aliquot $CHCl_3$-lipid ext thru glass funnel contg small pledget of glass wool and ca 25 g anhyd. Na_2SO_4 into 150 mL beaker. Rinse Na_2SO_4 with 15 mL $CHCl_3$ and evap. ext to dryness under gentle N stream on 90° H_2O bath or steam bath. Dissolve residue in ca 70 mL pet ether and filter thru Whatman No. 1 paper contg ca 20 g anhyd. Na_2SO_4 into 300 mL g-s erlenmeyer. Rinse beaker and Na_2SO_4 with several 10 mL portions pet ether. Evap. to dryness under gentle N stream on steam bath.

Introduce mag. stirring bar into erlenmeyer and place on mag. stirrer-hot plate. With gentle stirring, slowly add 8 mL concd KOH soln, (**h**), and 40 mL reagent alcohol, (**i**). Attach condenser, turn on mag. stirrer-hot plate, and reflux soln 1 hr. Turn off heat and add 60 mL reagent alcohol thru condenser into saponified soln while stirring and cooling. When sample ceases to reflux, remove condenser, and pipet 100 mL benzene into sample while slowly stirring. Remove stirring bar, stopper flask, and shake vigorously 30 sec.

Pour into 500 mL separator without rinsing. Add 200 mL 1*N* KOH and shake vigorously 10 sec. Let layers sep. and discard aq. (lower) layer (will be turbid). Wash benzene layer with 40 mL 0.5*N* KOH, rotate gently end to end 10 sec, and discard aq. (lower) layer. Pour benzene layer into 250 mL separator. Back-wash benzene layer with 40 mL H_2O by gently rotating separator end to end 10 times. Repeat H_2O wash 3 more times. pH of last H_2O wash should be ca 7. Pour benzene ext from top of separator, filtering thru Whatman No. 4 paper contg ca 15 g anhyd. Na_2SO_4 into 125 mL g-s erlenmeyer. Add ca 20 g anhyd. Na_2SO_4; stopper and shake flask vigorously. Let stand 15 min.

Pipet 50 mL aliquot into 100 mL r-b g-s flask and evap. to dryness on rotary evaporator at 40°. Add 3 mL acetone and again evap. to dryness. Dissolve residue in 3 mL DMF.

43.236 ***Derivatization of Cholesterol Standards and Gas Chromatographic Calibration***

Transfer 1.0 mL of each cholesterol working std soln, **43.231(a)**(*2*), to 15 mL silanized centrf. tube. (Keep DMCS-silanized centrf. tubes clean and dry.) Add 0.2 mL HMDS and 0.1 mL TMCS. Stopper tube and shake vigorously on test tube mixer, (**f**), or by hand for 30 sec. Let soln stand undisturbed 15 min. Add 1.0 mL 5α-cholestane internal std working soln, **43.231(b)**(*2*), and 10 mL H_2O to tube. Shake vigorously 1 min and centrf. 2 min.

Inject duplicate 3 μL or other appropriate vols (use same vol. thruout for all stds and samples) heptane layer into gas chromatograph. Adjust GLC parameters to give retention times of ca 5 min for 5α-cholestane and 10 min for cholesterol. Det. area of each peak by using ht-width measurement or digital integrator. Divide cholesterol peak area by internal std peak area to obtain std response ratio. Average results for duplicate detns. Plot av. response ratio (y-axis) against cholesterol concn (mg/mL) (x-axis). Std response ratio plot should bracket sample response ratio.

43.237 ***Derivatization and Analysis of Samples***

Transfer 1.0 mL sample soln, **43.235**, to 15 mL silanized centrf. tube and proceed as in **43.236**, beginning "Add 0.2 mL HMDS . . ." If GLC response is beyond scope of std calibration, dil. sample soln and derivatize again.

mg Cholesterol/100 g sample =
(mg/mL cholesterol in sample from std curve × 100)/
(g/mL sample used for derivatization)

SELECTED REFERENCES

(*1*) JAOAC **43**, 6(1960); **45**, 442(1962).

(*2*) JAOAC **33**, 615(1950); **34**, 370(1951); **35**, 706(1952); **36**, 812(1953); **37**, 742(1954); **38**, 692, 695(1955); **39**, 126(1956); **40**, 865(1957); **41**, 593(1958); **42**, 422, 520(1959); **43**, 30(1960); **49**, 250(1966); **57**, 897(1974); Analyst **89**, 7(1964).

(*3*) Ind. Eng. Chem., Anal. Ed. **13**, 600(1941); **15**, 18(1943); **16**, 513(1944); **19**, 170(1947); J. Biol. Chem. **164**, 2(1946); JAOAC **25**, 573, 886(1942); **26**, 77(1943); **27**, 542(1944); **28**, 563(1945); **29**, 18(1946); **30**, 412(1947); **31**, 459, 621, 623, 633, 776(1948); **32**, 480, 766, 775, 804(1949); **33**, 647(1950); **34**, 387, 460(1951); **35**, 736, 826(1952); **36**, 857(1953); **37**, 753, 756, 880, 887, 894(1954); **38**, 694(1955); **39**, 139(1956); **40**, 865(1957); **41**, 600(1958); **42**, 528(1959); **45**, 219(1962); **53**, 181, 186(1970).

(*4*) JAOAC **53**, 181, 186(1970); **56**, 748(1973); **57**, 511(1974).

(*5*) JAOAC **25**, 456(1942); **27**, 534(1944); **28**, 554(1945); **31**, 455(1948); **43**, 45, 55(1960).

(*6*) JAOAC **36**, 837(1953); **37**, 122, 757(1954); **38**, 722(1955).

(*7*) JAOAC **40**, 843(1957); **41**, 603(1958); **43**, 47(1960).

(*8*) JAOAC **23**, 346(1940); **24**, 413(1941); **25**, 459(1942); **26**, 81(1943); **27**, 540(1944); **30**, 392(1947); **31**, 701(1948); **32**, 108, 461(1949); **33**, 88, 632(1950); **37**, 770(1954); **43**, 42(1960); **53**, 542(1970).

(*9*) Anal. Chem. **23**, 983(1951); JAOAC **34**, 380(1951); **36**, 1018(1953); **42**, 625(1959); **44**, 431(1961); **45**, 449(1962); **51**, 506, 828(1968).

(*10*) JAOAC **58**, 799(1975).

(*11*) J. Pharm. Sci. **50**, 926(1961); JAOAC **51**, 828(1968).

(*12*) J. Biol. Chem. **103**, 687(1933); **112**, 625(1936); **116**, 409, 563(1936); **126**, 771(1938); Biochem. J. **27**, 580(1933); **30**, 2273(1936); **36**, 115(1942); Physiol. Rev. **16**, 238(1936); J. Am. Med. Ass. **111**, 1290(1938); Biochem. Z. **301**, 229(1939); JAOAC **27**, 537(1944); **28**, 559(1945); **29**, 69(1946); **30**, 673(1947); **32**, 479(1949); **34**, 380(1951); **36**, 1127(1953); **38**, 514(1955); **50**, 798(1967).

(*13*) JAOAC **48**, 1248(1965); **50**, 798(1967).

(*14*) JAOAC **54**, 1168(1971); **57**, 1349(1974); **58**, 330(1975); **60**, 151(1977).

(*15*) JAOAC **62**, 129(1979).

(*16*) Eur. J. Biochem. **46**, 217(1974); Nutr. Abstrs. and Rev. **48**, 831(1978); J. Nutr. **109**, 8(1979).

(*17*) Anal. Chem. **20**, 1221(1948); **28**, 376(1956); **33**, 849(1961); Analyst **84**, 356(1959); J. Chromatogr. **30**, 502(1967); JAOAC **45**, 425(1962); **49**, 1060(1966); **54**, 1(1971).

(*18*) JAOAC **58**, 585(1975).

(*19*) JAOAC **50**, 809(1967); **52**, 442(1969); **55**, 1211(1972).

(*20*) JAOAC **48**, 1217(1965); **52**, 448(1969).

(*21*) JAOAC **56**, 1277(1973).

(*22*) JAOAC **35**, 161, 169, 726(1952); **36**, 846(1953); **37**, 781(1954); **38**, 711(1955); **39**, 167, 172(1956); **40**, 856(1957); **41**, 61, 587(1958); **42**, 529(1959).

(*23*) Science **100**, 295(1944); J. Biol. Chem. **157**, 303(1945); **163**, 447, 449(1946); Ann. N.Y. Acad. Sci. **48**, 261(1946); Analyst **72**, 84(1947); JAOAC **31**, 466(1948); **32**, 464(1949); **33**, 633(1950); **39**, 172(1956); **40**, 855, 856(1957); **41**, 61, 587, 591(1958); **42**, 529(1959).

(*24*) JAOAC **27**, 105(1944); **30**, 82(1947); **32**, 110, 479(1949); **39**, 172(1956); **40**, 856(1957); **41**, 61, 587(1958); **42**, 529(1959).

(*25*) JAOAC **28**, 567(1945); **35**, 103, 722(1952); **37**, 779(1954); **38**, 710(1955); **39**, 172(1956); **40**, 853, 856(1957); **41**, 61, 587, 739(1958); **42**, 525, 529(1959); J. Biol. Chem. **192**, 181(1951).

(*26*) JAOAC **23**, 346(1940); **24**, 413(1941); **25**, 459(1942); **26**, 81(1943); **27**, 540(1944); **28**, 560(1945); **29**, 25(1946); **30**, 79, 391(1947); **31**, 701(1948); **32**, 105, 461(1949); **33**, 88, 631(1950); **37**, 770(1954); **39**, 172(1956); **40**, 856(1957); **41**, 61, 587(1958); **42**, 529(1959).

(*27*) JAOAC **41**, 420, 679(1958); **43**, 34(1960).

(*28*) JAOAC **44**, 426(1961); **47**, 750(1964); **53**, 546(1970).

(*29*) JAOAC **21**, 305, 622(1938); **22**, 662(1939); **23**, 653(1940); **24**, 147, 403(1941); **25**, 456(1942); **27**, 534(1944).

(*30*) JAOAC **19**, 248(1936); **20**, 213(1937); **21**, 243(1938); **22**, 468(1939); **23**, 341(1940); **32**, 480, 801(1949); **38**, 165(1955); **39**, 141(1956); **41**, 588(1958); **43**, 59(1960); **46**, 160(1963); Anal. Chem. **24**, 1841(1952).

(*31*) JAOAC **15**, 222, 660(1932); **16**, 184(1933); **17**, 180(1934); **18**, 341, 357, 471(1935); **19**, 628, 637, 647(1936); **20**, 438, 450(1937); **21**, 607(1938); **22**, 445, 656(1939); **23**, 648, 665(1940); **24**, 190, 432, 858, 961(1941); **25**, 213, 459, 518(1942); **26**, 263, 516(1943); **27**, 283, 289(1944); **29**, 396(1946); **30**, 190(1947); **32**, 801(1949); **33**, 645(1950); **35**, 27, 715(1952); **51**, 591(1968).

(*32*) JAOAC **43**, 38(1960); **48**, 847(1965).

(*33*) JAOAC **57**, 513(1974).

(*34*) JAOAC **59**, 1131(1976).

(*35*) JAOAC **58**, 599(1975).

(*36*) JAOAC **58**, 804(1975); **59**, 46(1976).

44. Extraneous Materials: Isolation

GENERAL

44.001 ***Definition of Terms***

(**a**) *Extraneous materials.*—Any foreign matter in product associated with objectionable conditions or practices in production, storage, or distribution; included are filth (*see* (**b**)–(**f**)), decomposed material (decayed tissues due to parasitic or non-parasitic causes), and miscellaneous matter such as sand and soil, glass, rust, or other foreign substances. Excluded are bacterial counts.

(**b**) *Filth.*—Any objectionable matter contributed by animal contamination of product such as rodent, insect, or bird matter; or any other objectionable matter contributed by insanitary conditions.

(**c**) *Suggested format for reporting identified filth.*—

Method(s): AOAC (1980) method(s) used for analysis of product.

Code(s): Manufacturer's or distributor's identification marks.

Subdivision numbers: Use inspector's subdivision number when given

Amount of subdivision examined: Amt of sample portion analyzed.

Findings: Use *only* those captions that apply to findings.

(*1*) Whole insects or equiv. (total no.). Give identity of insects if known, and state whether alive or dead. Give size.

(a) Adults including flies
(b) Pupae
(c) Maggots
(d) Larvae, other than maggots
(e) Adult heads
(f) Larval heads
(g) Pupal cast skins
(h) Larval cast skins
(i) Larval head capsules

(*2*) No. insect fragments, identified. Give size range and identity.

(*3*) No. insect fragments, unidentified. Give size range.

(*4*) No. insect eggs (give kind).

(*5*) No. aphids, thrips, psocids, spiders, scale insects, mites, etc.

Fragments of above.

(*6*) No. setae (if fly, state).

(*7*) No. insect excreta pellets (identify as to insect order if known).

(*8*) No. rat or mouse excreta pellets (state which or give length; give wt if from condimental seeds and spices).

(*9*) No. rat or mouse excreta pellet fragments.

(*10*) No. rat or mouse hairs and hair fragments (give sizes or range).

(*11*) No. other hairs (give size and kind, if known).

(*12*) No. feather fragments (give size).

(*13*) Other extraneous materials (describe).

(*14*) Rodent urine on bagging or food beneath (give dimensions of stain).

(*15*) Bird excreta on bagging or food beneath.

Except where total is called for, there should be no duplication in various elements. For example, setae are insect fragments but report only under setae. Similarly where fragments can be identified as from mites, aphids, thrips, and scale insects, report under that heading, not under insect fragments. It is important to report whether or not infestation is due to live insects and whether or not sample was fumigated before shipment or upon receipt at laboratory.

(**d**) *Heavy filth.*—Heavier filth material sepd from product by sedimentation based on different densities of filth, food particles, and immersion liqs such as $CHCl_3$, CCl_4, etc. Examples of such filth are insect and rodent excreta pellets and pellet fragments, sand, and soil.

(**e**) *Light filth.*—Lighter filth particles that are oleophilic and are sepd from product by floating them in an oil-aq. liq. mixt. Examples are insect fragments, rodent hairs, and feather barbules.

(**f**) *Sieved filth.*—Filth particles of specific size ranges sepd quant. from product by use of selected sieve mesh sizes.

44.002 ***Apparatus***

(Avoid use of polyethylene beakers, funnels, containers, etc., as insect fragments and rodent hairs adhere to app. made from this material.)

(**a**) *Aerator, water.*—For attachment to faucet to provide smooth-flowing, aerated H_2O stream. Remove lower screen. (Available from Fisher Scientific Co., No. 91-404, or Arthur H. Thomas Co., No. 4551-F10.)

(**b**) *Autoclave.*—(*1*) *Slow exhaust type.*—Set "slow exh" to lower pressure from 15 to 0 in 15–20 min. (*2*) *Non-slow exhaust.*—Let cool to 0 psi before opening or venting.

(**c**) *Blenders.*—(*1*) *High-speed.*—*See* "Definitions of Terms and Explanatory Notes," item (18). Use 1 L, 4-lobe jar fitted with 4-blade assembly, 2 blades tilted upward ca 30° with diam. 60 mm and 2 blades tilted downward ca 25° with diam. 55 mm. Operate at 3000–3500 rpm thru variable transformer. To measure speed, attach 1-hole No. 8 rubber stopper to sq rotor shaft and insert tachometer. (Later attachment of jar does not appreciably alter speed.) (*2*) *High-speed overhead*—Alternative to high-speed blender: Mixer with 6 canted, sharp-edge stainless steel blades rotating on shaft of suspended motor and speed control. Blades rotate at bottom of stainless steel cup having 4 indentations, forming lobes. Sorvall Omni-Mixer (Ivan Sorvall, Inc., Newtown, CT 06470), or equiv., meets these requirements.

(**d**) *Blood counting cell.*—Depth 0.1 mm, preferably ruled in the Thoma or old Neubauer system. Cell with "improved" Neubauer system, equipped with optically worked cover glass, may also be used.

(**e**) *Bolting cloth.*—Silk cloth woven to std size opening and thickness which is used in flour mills. Number of silk specifies number of mesh/linear in. "X," "XX," or "XXX" after number refers to thickness of thread from which cloth is woven; this also affects size of opening in cloth. Therefore, follow designation exactly as to both number and "X" of bolting cloth. (Available from Tetko, Inc., 420 Saw Mill Rd, Elmsford, NY 10523.)

Prep. disks by boiling large squares of silk before cutting them into circles. Circles cut from unboiled silk shrink and become misshapen. Make rulings ca 5–7 mm apart with India ink or other permanent marking material, using fine pen, on boiled and pressed cloth marked off in circles ca 85 mm diam.

When needed, dye ruled cloth by placing in hot (80–85°) soln of 50 mg FD&C Blue No. 1 in 1 L H_2O contg 2.5 mL HOAc, and holding at this temp. ca 15 min with frequent stirring. Rinse well and store in dark.

(**f**) *Butter stirrer.*—*See* Fig. **44:01**.

(**g**) *Compound microscope.*—*See* (**q**)(*1*).

(**h**) *Cyclone.*—Laboratory cyclone or pulper consists of cylindrical perforated metal screen in which revolves paddle which forces soft material from food product out thru openings in screen. Tough materials such as seeds, skins, and stems are moved along and out opening in end of cylinder. Use as power source ¼ horsepower, 110 v, 1725 rpm elec. motor. Screen is 22 gage material, 400 holes/sq in., each 0.027″ diam. Screen is 2.5″ id and length of effective screen is 3″. Paddle has 2 fins, each 25/32″ wide, set alternately and extending 13/16″ from center of shaft. Pulper is fed thru hopper which leads into basin 3.5″ long and 2.5″ id. Portion of paddle with fins inserted at 30° angle forces material from basin into screening compartment. Cyclone is so constructed that waste opening may be closed, as needed. Sieved material is caught in shield and delivered thru spout to container. Machine may be readily disassembled for washing. (Blueprints available from Div. Microbiology, Food and Drug Administration, Washington, DC 20204.)

(**i**) *Extraction vessels.*—(*1*) *Kilborn funnel.*—1 L, 3.5″ od by 9.5″ high, 8 mm opening at tip. Rubber tubing ⅜″ id and pinch clamp provides convenient cut-off.

(*2*) *Percolator.*—2 L, Corning Glass Works No. 7040, or equiv., conforming to following general size and shape: 115 mm id × 400 mm long, ca 90 mm id at 200 mm down from top, with 8–9 mm bore tip, with cut-off as in (*1*). Use stirring rod 370 × 10 mm diam, when specified, to prevent compacting of sample in drain opening.

(*3*) *Trap flask.* (*a*) *Wildman.*—Consists of 1 or 2 L erlenmeyer into which is inserted close-fitting rubber stopper supported on stiff metal rod 5 mm (3/16″) diam. and ca 10 cm longer than ht of flask. (Rod of greater diam. is not desirable because of its greater displacement of liq.) Rod is threaded (#10–32) at lower end and furnished with nuts and washers to hold it in place on stopper. Countersink lower nut and washer in the rubber to prevent striking flask. *See* **44.004**(**a**) and Fig. **44:02**. Or: (*b*) *Wafer stopper.*—(Entomological Supplies, Inc., 5655 Oregon Ave, Baltimore, MD 21227).

(**j**) *Filter paper.*—Use smooth, high wet-strength, rapid-acting filter paper ruled with oil-, alcohol-, and water-proof lines 5 mm apart. S&S No. 8 is satisfactory.

(**k**) *Filter paper defatting cup.*—Center S&S 588 folded filter paper, or equiv., over bottom of smaller beaker specified in method. Partially shape paper over bottom of beaker and gently insert beaker and paper into larger specified beaker. Remove smaller beaker and transfer weighed sample into formed paper cup.

(**l**) *Funnels for filtration with suction.*—Use funnels with filter papers or bolting cloth cupped up on sides to eliminate loss of solids. Use rapid filter paper for filtration thru Hirsch funnel.

Use of wire screen or bolting cloth between perforated funnel plate and filter paper accelerates filtration and gives more uniform distribution of solids.

(**m**) *Greenough-type* (*widefield stereoscopic*) *microscope for filth examination.*—*See* (**q**)(*2*).

(**n**) *Illuminators for widefield stereoscopic microscopes.*—(*1*) *Filth examination.*—Illuminator for this purpose should have: compactness and flexibility; transformer or resistor to vary light intensity; focusing adjustment to give uniformly lighted field of view; blue-white color from cool low-voltage source. (*2*) *Rot fragment counting.*—Use small substage illuminator fitted with daylight or blue ground-glass filter and 15 watt bulb.

(**o**) *Howard mold-counting apparatus.*—(*1*) *Howard mold-counting slide.*—Glass slide of one-piece construction with flat plane circle ca 19 mm diam. or rectangle 20 × 15 mm surrounded by moat and flanked on each side by shoulders 0.1 mm higher than plane surface. Cover glass is supported on shoulders and leaves depth of 0.1 mm between underside of cover glass and plane surface. Central plane, shoulders, and cover glass have optically worked surfaces. To facilitate calibration of microscope, newer slides are engraved with circle 1.382 mm diam. or with 2 fine parallel lines 1.382 mm apart.

(*2*) *Accessory disk for mold counting.*—Glass disk that fits into microscope eyepiece, ruled into squares each side of which

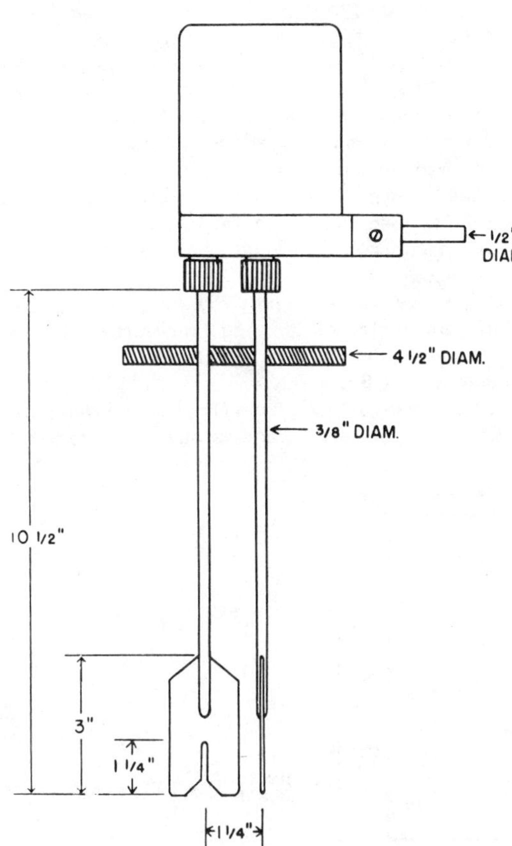

FIG. 44:01—Mechanical butter stirrer

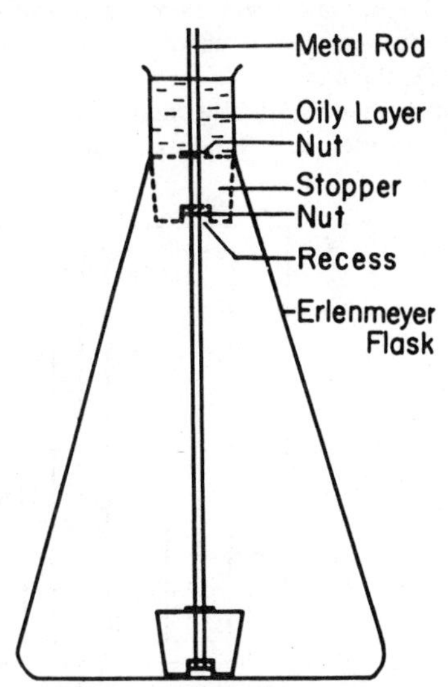

FIG. 44:02—Wildman trap flask

is equal to 1/6 of diam. of field. Since limiting diaphragm is eyepiece field stop, rulings equal 1/6 of this diaphragm opening. Field viewed on slide with mold-counting microscope has diam. of 1.382 mm at magnification of 90–125×.

(3) *Method of illumination of compound microscope for mold counting.*—Unless microscope has built-in light source, fasten lamp and microscope securely to baseboard so that they are used and maintained as unit. Adjust mirror pivot so that it is not easily moved, and hold microscope in place by screws or cleats.

(p) *Magnetic stirring bar and stirrer-hot plate.*—Teflon-covered bars ca 47 mm long × 9 mm od; use with hot plate having independent, continuously variable heat and speed controls. *See* also **44.004(b)**.

(q) *Microscopes.*—(*1*) *Compound microscope.*—For mold counting and other filth and decomposition work, microscope should have following min. specifications: binocular body with inclined oculars; 4 parfocal achromatic objectives of ca 5, 10, 20, and 40×; revolving 4-place nosepiece; achromatic condenser with N.A. of 1.40 in centerable mount; 10× Huygenian eyepieces; fine adjustment; mech. stage preferably with adjusting buttons at sides of stage (if photomicrographs are to be made, revolving stage is more satisfactory); stdzd field of view of 1.382 mm diam. at 90–125×; equipped with drop-in ocular disk ruled in squares, each of which is 1/6 of field diam.

(2) *Widefield stereoscopic microscope for filth and rot fragment examination.*—Microscope should have following min. specifications: binocular body with inclined oculars; sliding or revolving nosepiece to accommodate 3 objectives; 3 parfocal objectives 1×, 3×, and 6 or 7.5×; paired 10× and paired 15× widefield oculars; mounted on base and capable of illumination by transmitted or reflected light. 30× is ordinarily used for routine examination of filter papers. Verification at higher magnification may be required.

(r) *Petri dishes.*—Use to hold filter papers, bolting cloths, etc., for microscopic examination; low-edge (10 mm high) type.

(s) *Pipet for tissue transfer.*—Use 1 mL measuring pipet with bore 3.0±0.5 mm and tip cut off at 1.0 mL mark. In pipetting, draw material slightly above 0.5 mL mark and let it drop slowly to mark.

(t) *Rot fragment counting plate and cover preparation.*—Glass plate; 55 × 100 mm, 1.5–4.0 mm thick with cover 50 × 85 mm, ca 1.5 mm thick. Carefully paint on coat of resist over the entire surface, avoiding pinholes. Asphaltum varnish makes excellent resist; paraffin wax may also be used. Carefully scribe crosswise parallel lines, 4.5 mm apart with 15 mm space at each end, thru resist. If asphaltum varnish is used, lines may be scribed with new steel-wheel glass cutter.

Place coated scribed slides face down over HF in polyethylene container. Det. proper acid fume exposure by trial and error. Following etching, remove resist by placing slide in H_2O contg detergent. If resist is not easily scrubbed off, use toluene for cleanup.

Alternatively, use clear plastic plate; 55 × 100 mm, 4–6 mm thick with glass cover 50 × 85 mm, ca 2 mm thick. With sharp needle, carefully scribe crosswise parallel lines, 4.5 mm apart with 15 mm spaces at each end. Several slides can be made at one time by using strip of plastic 100 mm wide and any multiple of 55 mm long, allowing extra length to compensate for each cut of 2–3 mm thickness.

Fasten ½ of square cover slip, ca 22 mm on side and ca 0.25 mm thick, at each end of counting plate to raise cover plate above ruled plate. *See* Fig. **44:03**. Glass slides are available on special order from Ace Glass, Inc.

(u) *Sieves.*—*See* "Definitions of Terms and Explanatory Notes," item (16). Sieves of No. 100 or finer should be "plain (not twill) weave" of stainless steel. Plain weave is woven with one wire alternately over and under next.

44.003 ***Reagents***

(a) *Acetic acid.*—Practical glacial HOAc is satisfactory.

(b) *Acetone.*—Practical acetone is suitable unless otherwise specified.

(c) *Acid-alcohol soln.*—HCl and 60% alcohol (1+9) or HCl and 40% isopropanol (1+9).

(d) *Alcohol.*—95% com. ethanol (not denatured) unless otherwise specified. Make all dilns by vol.

(e) *60% Alcohol-calcium chloride soln.*—To each 3 L 60% alcohol (amt for 1 analysis), add 200 g anhyd. $CaCl_2$. Stir until salt dissolves. Cloudiness from traces of $CaCO_3$ will clear up during analysis when soln is acidified.

(f) *Algin soln for rot fragment determination.*—Proceed as for stabilizer solns, **(gg)**; then adjust final mixt. to pH 7.0–7.5 with NaOH soln.

(g) *Antifoam soln.*—1 g Dow Corning Antifoam A compd dild with 20 mL EtOAc. Use supernate and keep tightly closed.

(h) *Borax.*—Household borax is satisfactory. This is usually $Na_2B_4O_7.10H_2O$, which is not very sol. in cold H_2O. If >5% borax soln is desired, it must be kept hot.

(i) *Calgon.*—Na hexametaphosphate (obtainable from Calgon Corp., PO Box 1346, Pittsburgh, PA 15230).

(j) *Carbon tetrachloride.*—Tech. grade is suitable unless otherwise specified.

(k) *Carob bean soln.*—Blend 0.75% carob bean gum in H_2O. Boil 2 min and cool to 20–25°. Add 2 mL HCHO/100 mL and stir gently. Let settle and use clear supernate.

(l) *Castor oil.*—USP.

(m) *Chloral hydrate.*—Aq. soln (1+1) or *see* Hertwig's soln.

(n) *Chloroform.*—Tech. grade is suitable unless otherwise

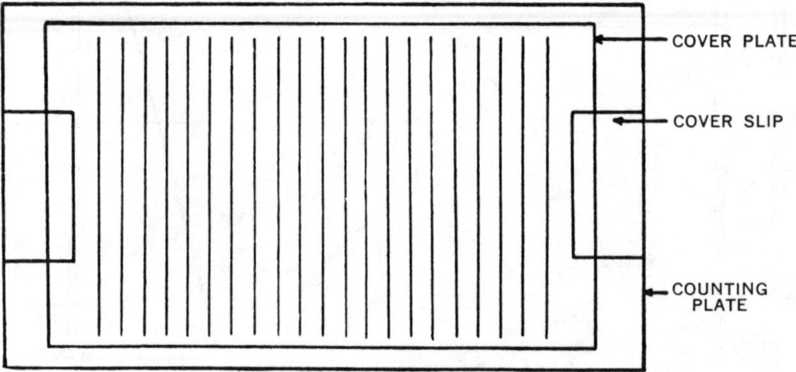

FIG. 44:03—Rot fragment counting slide

specified. Mixt. of pet ether and tetrachloroethylene (CCl_2CCl_2), adjusted to sp gr of $CHCl_3$, 1.5, may be used instead of $CHCl_3$ in sedimentation, but not in defatting, steps.

(**o**) *Chloroplatinic acid soln.*—Dissolve 5 g H_2PtCl_6 in 100 mL H_2O.

(**p**) *Crystal violet soln.*—Dissolve 10 g dye (Colour Index 42555) in 100 mL alcohol and filter.

(**q**) *Detergent soln.*—Prep. aq. Na lauryl sulfate soln as required.

(**r**) *Emulsifiers.*—Nonionic, H_2O-sol. surfactants. (*1*) *Nonylphenoxypoly(ethyleneoxy)ethanol.*—Igepal CO-730 (GAF Corp.). (*2*) *Dialkylphenoxypoly(ethyleneoxy)ethanol.*—Igepal DM-710 (GAF Corp.). (*3*) *Nonylphenoxypoly(ethyleneoxy)ethanol.*—Igepal CO-630 (GAF Corp.).

(**s**) *Flotation liquid.*—Mineral oil, (**y**), and heptane, (**u**), (85+15).

(**t**) *Formaldehyde soln.*—Use USP reagent soln. Strength is expressed as % by vol. of USP soln.

(**u**) *Heptane.*—Com. *n*-heptane contg <8% toluene.

(**v**) *Hertwig's soln.*—Useful for clearing plant and insect materials; action continues on standing. Use only for temporary mounts, not for permanent slides. Dissolve 45 g chloral hydrate crystals in 25 mL HCl (1+8) and 10 mL glycerol.

(**w**) *Isopropanol saturated with heptane.*—To 600 mL isopropanol add 45 mL heptane and 430 mL H_2O, mix, and let stand overnight. Siphon from below interface.

(**x**) *Kerosene, deodorized.*—Refinol No. 9 (Standard Oil of Indiana), Dispersol (Shell Oil Co.), or equiv. insecticide grade.

(**y**) *Mineral oil.*—Paraffin oil, white, light, 125/135 Saybolt Universal Viscosity (38°), sp gr 0.840–0.860 (24°). Fisher Scientific Co. No. O-119, or equiv.

(**z**) *Pancreatin soln.*—Use USP or sol. pancreatin kept refrigerated at 10°. Use fresh soln. Mix at rate of 5 g/100 mL H_2O at ≤40°. Use special soln for cheese, 10 g/100 mL. Stir with malted milk unit or blender 10 min, or let stand 30 min with frequent shaking. Centrf. at 1500 rpm and filter supernate thru S&S No. 8 paper, or equiv. Alternatively, filter thru cotton pads 10–13 cm thick and then thru rapid No. 8 paper in Hirsch funnel with suction.

(**aa**) *Phosphoric acid.*—Tech. grade.

(**bb**) *Sodium carbonate.*—Tech. grade. If hydrated salt is used, calc. to anhyd. basis.

(**cc**) *Sodium chloride.*—Tech. grade.

(**dd**) *Sodium oleate.*—Tech. grade.

(**ee**) *Sodium phosphate soln.*—Tech. grade Na_3PO_4. Prep. 5% soln.

(**ff**) *Sodium sulfite.*—Tech. grade. If hydrated salt is used, calc. to anhyd. basis.

(**gg**) *Stabilizer solns.*—0.5% Na carboxymethylcellulose preferred (Cellulose Gum CMC-7H3SF, Hercules Inc., Cellulose and Protein Products Dept., Wilmington, DE 19899). Place 500 mL boiling H_2O in high-speed blender. With blender running, add 2.5 g Cellulose Gum and 10 mL HCHO, and blend ca 1 min. Alternatives: 3–5% pectin or 1% algin. Add required amt of stabilizer directly to H_2O while agitating in high-speed blender. Treat soln with vac. or heat to remove air bubbles. Add 2 mL HCHO/100 mL soln as preservative. (If blender is not available, mix dry stabilizer with alcohol to facilitate incorporation with H_2O.) Adjust to pH 7.0–7.5. Filter soln thru 8 μm membrane filter (Millipore No. SCWP-047-00, or equiv.) using suitable vac. filtration app. (Millipore No. XX15-047-00, or equiv.).

(**hh**) *Tween 80—60% alcohol soln.*—To 40 mL polysorbate 80 (ICI United States, Inc.), add 210 mL 60% alcohol, mix, and filter. (Proportionate vols may be prepd.)

(**ii**) *Tetrasodium EDTA soln.*—Dissolve 5 g Na_4EDTA in 100 mL H_2O, add 150 mL alcohol, mix, and filter. (Proportionate vols may be prepd.)

(**jj**) *Wetting agents.*—(*1*) *Tergitol Anionic 7.*—Na heptadecyl sulfate (Union Carbide Corp.). (*2*) *Triton X-114.*—Alkylaryl polyether alcohol (Rohm & Haas Co.).

44.004 ***Special Technics***

(**a**) *Operation of Wildman trap flask.*—Unless otherwise directed in specific method, cool mixt. in flask to room temp. Bring vol. of liq. to ca 900 mL in 2 L flask and to ca 600 mL in 1 L flask. Add vol. of flotation liq. as stated in method by pouring down stirring rod. Tilt flask ca 45° from vertical and mix 1 min at rate of 200–250 strokes/min with brisk rotary motion so that liq. is brought to a roll. Avoid splashing thru surface of liq. with rubber stopper. Add enough liq. to bring flotation liq. well into neck of flask.

Unless otherwise stated, let mixt. stand 30 min, intermittently stirring bottom layer every 3–6 min during first 20 min of standing. Spin stopper to remove sediment and trap off by raising stopper as far as possible into neck of flask, being sure that oil layer and ≥1 cm of liq. below interface are above stopper. Hold stopper in place and pour off liq. into beaker. Rinse out material on rod and in neck of flask with liq. extn medium in which floating was performed and add to beaker.

Do not wash out neck of flask with 95% alcohol or other liq. which may interfere with surface relationships of the 2 phases; this will cause loss in recovery in subsequent trappings.

Filter trapped material and rinsings with suction thru rapid paper in Hirsch funnel. Add flotation liq. as specified to trap flask and stir vigorously. Add enough liq. extn medium to bring flotation liq. into neck of flask. Trap off again, rinse, and filter as above.

(**b**) *Operation of magnetic stirrer.*—To disperse flotation liq. thru sample, dil. liq. extn medium to vol. specified in method and bring to proper temp. Add mag. stirring bar, **44.002(p)**, and proper vol. of flotation liq. Slowly bring unit to max. speed that does not produce visible or audible splashing (central portion of stirring bar is usually just visible at bottom of vortex) and stir for time stated in method. Time stirring interval after achieving proper speed and vortex.

(**c**) *Tween 80-Na_4EDTA extraction.*—Add 300 mL 60% alcohol to sample in 2 L trap flask. Successively, without interruption, add 250 mL Tween 80–60% alcohol soln, **44.003(hh)**; mix and quickly add 250 mL EDTA-60% alcohol soln, **44.003(ii)**, followed by 70 mL heptane, **44.003(u)**. Mix 1 min as in (**a**), and rapidly fill flask with 60% alcohol.

During first 20 min of standing, gently stir settled material occasionally. After 20 min, rotate rod to remove debris from stopper surface and clamp unrinsed rod so that stopper is above level of settled material. Let stand undisturbed 1 addnl hr. Trap off as in (**a**), without disturbing interface while manipulating rod. Rinse with 60% alcohol. Add 40 mL heptane, let stand 1.5 hr, and perform second trapping.

(**d**) *Filtration technic.*—(Treatment of trapped-off material.) If material trapped off in beaker contains appreciable starchy debris, add enough HCl to make soln 1–2% of HCl (1+99–49), bring to boil, and filter while hot. If fats or colloidal material retard filtration, hasten by playing stream of hot H_2O over paper during filtration.

(**e**) *Clearing of plant materials.*—With sedimentation or flotation procedures, some food material may be trapped off with filth particles. By proper clearing, filth may be made to stand out in contrast with white background of filter paper by one of following technics:

(*1*) For heavy filth, moisten paper with H_2O or 50% alcohol. (This method does not clear material completely, but it leaves rodent pellets and other filth soft and pliable.)

(*2*) For light filth examination, wet paper with glycerol-alcohol (1+1) immediately after filtering. Place enough liq. on paper to fill fibers but not enough to cause flowing of extd materials. This clearing agent does not harden filth material on paper, as do many oils which might be used as clearing agents.

(*3*) Clove oil can be used for clearing plant materials. This oil has high refractive index and clears more completely than does alcohol-glycerol soln.

(f) *Illumination for the widefield stereoscopic microscope.*—(*1*) *By direct light.*—Focus and adjust light to strike paper at ca 70° angle from horizontal. Light may come from right or left.

(*2*) *By transmitted light.*—In cases where transmitted light is necessary, use mirror on microscope stand. Mirror with white surface instead of conventional silvered mirror is particularly useful.

In counting rot fragments, remove mirror and metal contrast plate and replace with box-type substage lamp. Place lamp, **44.002(n)**(*2*), so that center of glass filter is directly below objective and within 2 cm of glass microscope plate.

(g) *Microscopic examination of filter papers.*—Make examination at 30× (unless otherwise specified), using widefield stereoscopic microscope, on properly cleared paper. Continually tease and probe particles while observing thru microscope. Turn over all large pieces of material, such as bran, which might obscure filth elements. Examine all doubtful pieces of material at 60–75×. At least twice magnification used in original examination is necessary to show new details not observable at lower power. If doubt still remains, mount piece, clear thoroly, and examine under compd microscope. *Thoro knowledge of appearance of authentic materials is assumed.*

BEVERAGES AND BEVERAGE MATERIALS

Carbonated and Noncarbonated Soft Drinks

44.005 *Geotrichum* Mold (*1*)—Official First Action

Det. net vol., *v*, of container and transfer contents to 3″ No. 230 sieve, **44.002(u)**. Transfer residue from sieve to 50 mL graduated centrf. tube, and proceed as in **44.079(a)** and **(d)**.

Express results as mycelial fragments/350 mL (12 fl oz) = 7000 S/v, where S = total no. mycelial fragments on the 2 slides.

Cocoa, Chocolate, and Press Cake

Light Filth (*2*)—Official First Action

44.006 *Apparatus and Reagent*

(a) *Hirsch porcelain funnel with plug.*—Size 0, fitted with fixed perforated filtering plate. Diam. at top, 94 mm; diam. of plate, 56 mm. Fit stem end of funnel with rubber tubing ca 10 cm (4″) long which can be plugged with plastic or cork stopper.

(b) *Sodium hypochlorite soln.*—Approx. 0.25%. Dil. 5 mL com. NaOCl soln, 5.25% by wt, with 95 mL H_2O. Prep. fresh daily.

44.007 *Determination*

(a) *Cocoa.*—Mix 50 g cocoa into 500 mL hot (55–70°) 2% detergent soln, **44.003(q)**, or 500 mL hot 2% Igepal CO-630, **44.003(r)**(*3*). Pour portionwise onto No. 230 sieve, **44.002(u)**, and wash with forcible stream of 55–70° tap H_2O, using aerator, **44.002(a)**. Remove fat by tilting sieve ca 20° and play H_2O thru liq. which collects at side. When fat and fine material have washed thru and foam is gone, transfer residue to 2 L trap flask, **44.002(i)**(*3*), with H_2O. Add ca 500 mL H_2O and boil 10 min. Cool to room temp. and add H_2O to total vol. of 1 L. Pour 50 mL heptane, **44.003(u)**, down stirring rod. Lower mag. stirring bar, **44.002(p)**, into flask on stirring rod stopper. Raise rod above liq. and secure with clamp. Stir mag., **44.004(b)**, 5 min. After stirring, fill flask with H_2O. Let stand 30 min, gently stirring bottom layer every 4–5 min with stirring bar for first 20 min. Trap off heptane. Add 35 mL more heptane, stir by hand gently 1 min, let stand 15 min, and again trap off. Filter combined trappings, using Hirsch funnel. Remove paper and examine microscopically. If debris on filter paper is excessive, proceed as in **(d)** after examining paper for hairs only.

(b) *Chocolate.*—Use 100 g finely shaven chocolate and proceed as in **(a)**.

(c) *Press cake.*—(*1*) *Method I.*—Heat sample (usually very hard lumps) 2–3 hr at 60–70° and break into ≤0.5″ (1 cm) pieces. Mix 50 g into 500 mL hot 2% detergent soln, **44.003(q)**, or 500 mL hot 2% Igepal CO-630, **44.003(r)**(*3*), in 800 mL beaker. Stir with butter stirrer, **44.002(f)**, or mag. stirrer, at low speed 2–3 hr until completely dispersed, or let soak overnight. Stir thoroly, pour portionwise onto No. 230 sieve, **44.002(u)**, and proceed as in **(a)**.

(*2*) *Method II* (*3*).—Break sample into ≤1 cm (0.5″) pieces, using hammer or similar implement. Weigh 50 g into 1 L beaker and add 100 mL peanut oil. Add mag. stirring bar, and heat with gentle stirring to 150°. Transfer to cool mag. stirring unit and stir 10 min at speed where no splashing occurs. Add 500 mL aq. 5% Triton X-114 soln, **44.003(jj)**(*2*), and stir 5 min. Proceed as in **(a)**, beginning "Pour portionwise onto No. 230 sieve, . . ." If oil drops are visible after completion of sieving, wash material on sieve with 2% aq. Triton X-114 soln by spraying from wash bottle. Continue sieving until surfactant is removed and proceed as in **(a)**.

(d) *Bleaching technic* (*4*).—Return paper to Hirsch funnel in suction flask. Wash thoroly with H_2O. (If paper contains alcohol and glycerol from examination for hairs, wash first with alcohol and then with H_2O.) Apply vac. until paper appears dry, turn off vac., and plug rubber tubing with stopper. Cover paper with ca 3 mm (5–7 mL) NaOCl soln and let stand until bleaching of cocoa tissue is complete, but <30 min. Maintain level of soln entire period and do not let soln flow over rim of paper. Turn on vac., which will remove stopper. Wash paper with H_2O. Examine microscopically for insect fragments and other extraneous materials other than hairs.

Ground Coffee and Coffee Substitutes

(*Caution: See* **51.011**, **51.040**, and **51.056**.)

44.008 Filth—Official First Action

(a) *Heavy filth, sand, and soil.*—Weigh 100 g sample in 600 mL beaker, add 350 mL $CHCl_3$, and boil 15 min, stirring occasionally. Wash down sides of beaker with $CHCl_3$. Let mixt. cool and settle 15 min with occasional stirring of top layer. Carefully decant $CHCl_3$ and floating tissue onto smooth ca 15 cm filter paper in buchner without disturbing heavy residue on bottom of beaker. Repeat decanting with small amts of $CHCl_3$ until practically no plant tissue remains with residue on bottom of beaker. (Sp gr of $CHCl_3$ may be increased by addn of CCl_4, if necessary to float plant tissue. Do not add CCl_4 beyond 1 part CCl_4 to 1 part $CHCl_3$.) Transfer residue from beaker to ashless filter paper and examine for filth. If residue is appreciable, ignite filter and det. wt sand, soil, etc.

(b) *Light filth* (*ground coffee*) (*4*)—(*Caution: See* **51.056**.) Make filter paper cup from 24 cm paper and 150 and 250 mL beakers, **44.002(k)**. Weigh 25 g sample into this cup. Add 100 mL $CHCl_3$ by pouring most of liq. outside paper cup into the 250 mL beaker. Press cup down into $CHCl_3$ and place on steam bath.

Boil gently 5 min, avoiding excessive loss of $CHCl_3$. Lift paper, clamp with clothespin, and let drain to slow drip. Discard solv. and repeat extn with two 100 mL portions $CHCl_3$. Position paper on Hirsch funnel and aspirate to apparent dryness. Complete by drying (*1*) overnight in hood, (*2*) 1 hr in 80° convection oven, or (*3*) 30 min in 80° vac. oven at >5" (13 cm, 16.9 kPa) vac.

Wash sample into 2 L trap flask with total of 400 mL H_2O. Boil gently 15 min, remove from hot plate, and set aside. Dil. to 600 mL with H_2O, add 400 mL undild isopropanol while stirring mag., heat to bp, and boil 2–3 min. Add 40 mL mineral oil, **44.003(y)**, and heat to vigorous boil. Transfer to cool stirrer and stir mag., **44.004(b)**, 5 min. Slowly fill flask with 40% isopropanol by letting liq. flow down rod while top of stopper is held just above contents. Stir with rotary swirl to resuspend solids, and trap off after 2 min. Filter onto ruled paper. Add 30 mL mineral oil, stir by hand 30 sec, and trap off after 5 min. Filter onto another ruled paper and examine papers microscopically.

If filter paper debris is excessive, examine for rodent hairs and then bleach as in **44.007(d)**.

(c) *Light filth (other substitutes except chicory)*.— Air dry decanted material on paper overnight or for 1 hr in oven at ca 80°, transfer dried material to 2 L trap flask, and add 400 mL hot H_2O. Boil 15 min and, if necessary, add small amts cold H_2O intermittently to prevent foaming. Cool mixt. to <20°. Trap off twice, using 35 and 25 mL portions heptane, **44.003(u)**, resp. In first trapping, after stirring heptane, let stand 5 min before filling flask. Filter and examine microscopically.

(d) *Light filth (ground chicory)* (*5*).—Add 50 g sample to 1 L beaker contg soln of 5 g Na lauryl sulfate and 10 g $NaHCO_3$ in 500 mL H_2O. Stir and place *in* steam bath. Heat 20 min, stirring twice at 5 min intervals, and wash down sides with few mL H_2O after each stirring. Transfer to No. 230 sieve and wash until foam is gone. Rinse sieve retainings with ca 100 mL 40% isopropanol. Transfer (use of teaspoon suggested) to 2 L trap flask with 40% isopropanol. Dil. to 800–900 mL with 40% isopropanol. Boil 4 min with gentle stirring. Add 50 mL mineral oil and heat until boiling starts again. Move to cool mag. stirrer and stir 5 min. Fill trap flask with 40% isopropanol added down rod with stopper held just above liq. Stir immediately to resuspend settlings. Stir 2 more times at 3 min intervals. Raise rod; wash with few mL 40% isopropanol and clamp with stopper ca 75 mm below interface. Let stand 4 min. Trap off, rinse neck, and filter onto ruled paper. Add 25–30 mL mineral oil, stir by hand 45 sec at moderate speed, and add 15–20 mL H_2O. Let stand 20 min, trap off, rinse flask neck with undild isopropanol, and filter onto sep. ruled papers. Examine papers at 20–30×.

Aphids in Hops

Light Filth (*6*)—Official First Action (AOAC-ASBC Method)

44.009 ***Reagents and Apparatus***

(a) *Flotation soln*.—Satd $Na_2B_4O_7$ soln, 100 g borax/L H_2O.

(b) *Iodine stain*.—Dissolve 0.5 g I and 1.5 g KI in 25 mL H_2O.

(c) *Blender*.—"Intensifier" Twin Shell Blender, Patterson-Kelley Co., Inc., 100 Burson St, East Stroudsburg, PA 18301, or equiv.

44.010 ***Preparation of Sample***

Place sample in blender, using 4 qt (3.8 L) size shell for small samples or 8 qt (7.6 L) size shell for large samples. Activate blender and "intensifier" for 1 min intervals until blending and breakage of sprigs are complete. Draw off 10 g samples from bottom plate.

44.011 ***Determination***

Mix 10 g representative sample in 100 mL satd borax soln in 2 L Wildman trap flask. Bring to *slow* boil. Keep mixt. from boiling onto sides of flask by keeping boiling to min. and by washing down sides with H_2O. Boil 1.5 hr, and cool to room temp. Fill flask to 1600 mL with H_2O and 35 mL heptane, **44.003(u)**, and stir vigorously 10 sec. Fill flask with H_2O, let stand 30 min, and trap off. Perform second trapping, using 25 mL heptane, stirring 10 sec, and letting flask stand 15 min. Wash neck of flask with isopropanol. Pour trappings onto ruled paper(s), add 10–12 drops I stain, and examine microscopically. If excess plant tissue is present in trappings, pour trappings thru 5" No. 10 sieve held over paper. Wash plant tissue on sieve with alcohol onto filter paper to remove any adhering insects.

Count as aphid any whole aphid or part contg head. Count individually aphid cast skins and other insects.

Tea—Official First Action

44.012 Gross Contamination

See **44.119**.

44.013 Heavy and Light Filth

See **44.120**.

DAIRY PRODUCTS

Sediment Test on Milk (*7*)—Official Final Action

44.014 ***Apparatus and Materials***

(a) *Tester*.—Simply constructed, easily cleaned, and adjustable between samplings to permit sanitary removal of used disk and replacement with clean disk. Before using, check tester for reproducibility as in **44.015**. Milk or sediment must not bypass disk. Select type according to method of sampling:

(*1*) *For mixed sample method*.—Pressure, gravity, or vac. type: (a) For 1 gal. sample use any suitable device that will filter sample thru disk with exposed area 1⅛" diam. (b) For 1 pt sample, equip single-unit, off-bottom tester with No. 125 BNC 0.40" safety head (available from Sediment Testing Supply Co., 1512 Jarvis Ave, Chicago, IL 60626) having filtering area 0.40" diam., or use any suitable device having filtering area 0.40" diam.

(*2*) *For off-bottom method*.—Single-unit type for intake of 1 pt on upstroke of plunger and discharge thru disk on down stroke, or 2-unit type, contg 1 unit for removal of 1 pt milk from bottom of can and another for filtering sample. Use sampling device long enough to permit reaching bottom of milk can, with filtering area 1⅛" diam.

(b) *Cotton sediment disks*.—Std lintine cotton disks or pads, 1¼" diam., for use over flat wire screen in tester to expose filtration area 1⅛" diam. Disk must not contain phenolic resins or other chem that may contaminate milk.

Test sediment disks as follows: Filter 12 mg std sediment mixt. (60 mL aliquot (**d**)) thru pad, using clean flask to catch filtrate. Transfer filtrate to beaker, rinse flask 3 times with H_2O, and add rinsings to beaker. Filter fitrate thru 7 or 9 cm S&S White Ribbon paper (or equiv.) that has been washed with ca 200 mL H_2O, dried to constant wt at 100°, and cooled in covered dish in desiccator before weighing. Thoroly rinse beaker and paper with H_2O and dry to const wt as above. Test ≥3 disks; av. wt sediment passing thru each disk should be ≤2.8 mg. In addn, std disk prepd from fine mixt. should not appear to have sediment buried beneath surface.

(c) *Sediment filtering apparatus*.—(*1*) *For 1⅛" diameter stds*.—App. must hold 1¼" sediment disk and have effective filtering area 1⅛" diam. This 1⅛" area must be unobstructed except for wire screen or wire screen and perforated plate support for filter disk. App. should be supported in filter flask so vac. can be used for rapid filtration or flask air outlet can be closed to stop filtration. App. should have ca 80° funnel with capacity of ≥80 mL but ≤450 mL. Test app. by filtering H_2O suspension of C thru std disk. Disk should have clean, sharply defined border. When sediment suspension is filtered, sediment should be evenly distributed over disk with no pattern formation. Figs **44:04** and **44:05** show suitable app.

(*2*) *For 0.40" diameter stds.*—Vac. type that holds 1¼" sediment disk and uses only 0.40" diam. filtering area. Test app. as in (*1*).

(**d**) *Preparation of coarse std sediment disks.*—Prep. uniform mixt. of oven-dried (100°) materials which meet following screening specifications. Grind all materials by hand with mortar and pestle.

	Per cent
Cow manure, thru No. 40	53
Cow manure, thru No. 20, retained on No. 40	2
Garden soil, thru No. 40	27
Charcoal, thru No. 40	14
Charcoal, thru No. 20, retained on No. 40	4

Place 2.00 g above mixt. in 100 mL vol. flask, thoroly wet with 4–6 mL *0.1% Aerosol OT soln* (prep. 1–2% soln in acetone and dil. with H_2O) or other suitable wetting agent, add 46 mL 0.75% carob bean gum soln prepd as in **44.003(k)**, and bring level of liq. just into neck of flask by adding *50% (by wt) sucrose soln.* Let stand ≥30 min, add few drops alcohol, and dil. to vol. with the sucrose soln. Mix thoroly, pour into 250 mL beaker or other suitable container, and stir with mech. or mag. stirrer at speed (ca 200–300 rpm) such that mixt. is thoroly agitated but very little air is whipped into suspension. Observe with bright reflected light to see that suspension is uniformly stirred.

Transfer, while stirring, 10 mL portion (200 mg std sediment) with large-tip, graduated pipet to 1 L vol. flask, and dil. to vol. with the 50% sucrose soln. When thoroly mixed, each mL contains 0.2 mg sediment. Mix, pour into 1.5 L beaker, and stir as above. If particles accumulate on side of beaker, wash down with portions of sediment suspension or push under with tip of pipet. While stirring, pipet definite vols of sediment mixt. and add to ¾ pt filtered sweet skim milk. Mix thoroly and pass mixt. thru std sediment disk in filtering app., (**c**)(*1*). Gently pour milk down side of filtering app. and filter with very little or no suction. Wash container promptly with ¼ pt filtered skim milk. Let last portion of milk flow thru pad with no suction applied. If sediment does not appear to be evenly distributed over pad, add 15 or 20 mL skim milk and let it filter thru without suction. Repeat addn until sediment appears evenly distributed. Suck air thru disk ca 1 min to remove excess skim milk.

For permanent record, mount and spray disks with 40% HCHO soln or with alc. soln contg 2.5 g each of menthol and thymol in 100 mL. Alternatively, if most of milk is removed by thoro aspiration, no preservative is needed. Dried pads may be coated with colorless plastic cement dild with 1–3 vols acetone so that mixt. is thin enough to pour easily. If acetone dissolves pigment from paper and stains pads, place pads on flat glass plate for

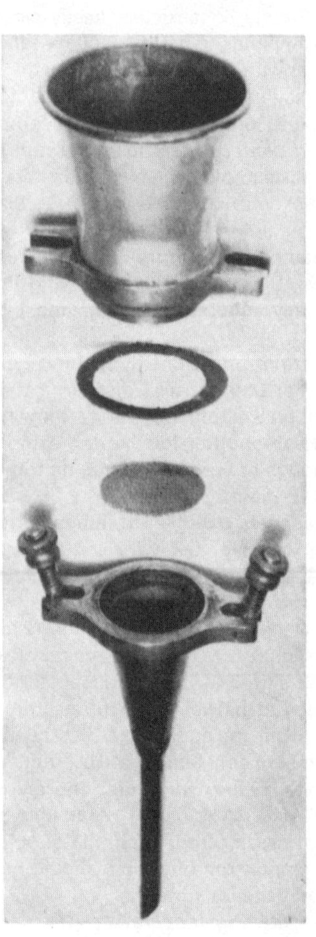

FIG. 44:04—Sediment filtering apparatus, unassembled

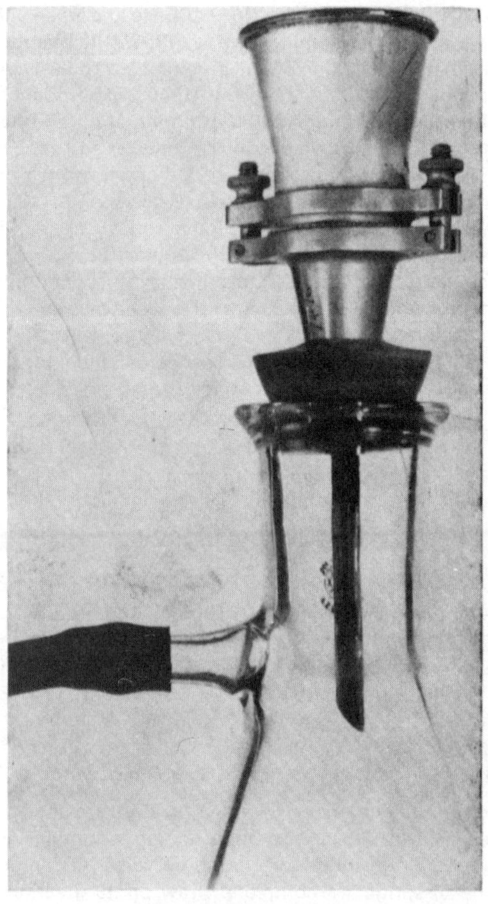

FIG. 44:05—Sediment filtering apparatus, assembled

treating with dild cement. Move pads while drying to prevent sticking to glass. When pads are almost dry, place light wt (*e.g.,* petri dish) directly on them to prevent curling. Pads may be mounted with plastic cement. (Std disks made from manure contg large amt of chlorophyll cannot be coated with plastic cement, as solv. exts chlorophyll and stains pad green. Use this method of preserving pads only if there is no leaching of pigment from sediment on addn of dild plastic cement.)

Following above method, prep. series of disks contg sediment remaining from 0.0, 0.2, 0.5, 1.0, 2.0, 3.0, 4.0, 5.0, 6.0, 7.0, 8.0, 9.0, 10.0, 12.0, and 14.0 mg std mixt. Mark disks to show mg of sediment used to prep. each pad. Do not use as std any pad on which sediment is not evenly distributed.

For comparison with tests on samples, entire series of disks may be used, but usually it is more convenient to select few disks denoting variations in grade that are applicable to particular investigations being made. If grading charts are prepd and reports made, indicate on chart and report whether mixed or off-bottom sample was used. If stds are to be handled or used for appreciable length of time, place them under glass, transparent plastic sheets, or other suitable materials. In using stds, use either of following methods: (*1*) Grade sediment disk to nearest std disk regardless of whether actual amt of sediment is above or below std; or (*2*) grade sediment disk of sample as "more than __ mg" or "less than __ mg." Choose stds to fit method of grading. When grading disks, disregard gross pieces of material (whole flies, hairs, large chunks of dirt or manure, etc.) but if such matter is present, list each sep. on report.

(**e**) *Preparation of fine std sediment disks.*—(*1*) *1⅛" diameter stds.*—Grind oven-dried (100°) cow manure, garden soil, and wood charcoal (not powd) in impact mill, Wiley mill, or other suitable type, using fine screen in mill. Pass cow manure thru Wiley mill or similar type 2 or 3 times. Sift materials sep. in max. batches of 50 g as follows: Dry 25–50 g at 100° for 3–4 hr. While still warm, place in 8" No. 140 sieve nested over No. 230. Add cover and receiver. Shake nested sieves by hand 5 min at ca 120 strokes/min. Sep. sieves and brush off material adhering to underside of No. 230 and discard before emptying sieve. Dry material retained on No. 230 ca 2 hr (max. batch 20 g) and resift 5 min as above. Sep. sieves and brush off material adhering to underside of No. 230 before emptying. Use "on 230" fractions from second siftings and mix uniformly in following proportions: cow manure 66%, garden soil 28%, and charcoal 6%.

Combine above 2 "on 140" fractions of each of the 3 materials and resift as above, except use No. 120 sieve nested over No. 140. Resift new "on 140" fraction, retaining "on 140" fraction from second sifting. (Dry before each sifting and brush material from underside of No. 140 sieve before emptying.) Mix manure, soil, and charcoal in above proportions.

Place 1.80 g mixt. from "on 230" fractions and 0.20 g mixt. from "on 140" fractions in 100 mL vol. flask. Proceed as in (**d**), beginning ". . . thoroly wet with 4–6 mL *0.1% Aerosol OT soln* . . ." except use H_2O instead of 50% sucrose soln for dilg 10 mL aliquot to 1 L.

Where (**d**) states "While stirring, pipet definite vols . . ." proceed as follows: Det. approx. funnel capacity of filtering app., (**c**)(*1*), by pouring H_2O into assembled app. with filter flask air outlet closed. Include H_2O that filters thru as part of funnel capacity. While stirring, pipet aliquots of sediment suspension into beakers. Add H_2O to make total vol. 20–50 mL less than funnel capacity, using total vol. of ≥60 mL but ≤400 mL.

With filter flask air outlet closed to prevent filtration, mix dild aliquot and pour into app., (**c**)(*1*), fitted with wet std disk, (**b**). (Use alcohol or wetting agent if necessary to wet disk.) Add 20–50 mL H_2O to beaker and rinse by swirling. Pour into funnel, keeping lip of beaker touching surface of H_2O if possible. (Rinse H_2O should nearly fill funnel if capacity is ≤450 mL.) Open flask air outlet. After H_2O has filtered thru pad, apply vac. and aspirate disk for ca 1 min. Remove pad and let dry in covered dish. If sediment is not evenly distributed, discard pad. After some practice, ca 75% of pads prepd should be acceptable. No preservative is required. Pads may be coated with dild plastic cement and used as in (**d**).

(*2*) *0.40" diameter stds.*—While stirring, pipet 100 mL above dild fine suspension into suitable container and dil. to 800 mL with H_2O. Each mL contains 0.025 mg sediment and when filtered thru 0.40" diam. area is equiv. to 0.2 mg filtered thru 1⅛" diam. area. Prep. series of stds by filtering suitable aliquots thru disks in app., (**c**)(*2*). Dil. each aliquot to 50–60 mL and filter with min. suction. Rinse beaker with small vol. H_2O and add to funnel. Carefully rinse side of funnel with small vol. H_2O. Use min. suction necessary to remove excess H_2O from disk. Designate 0.40" diam. stds as "__ mg equiv." and use in grading 1 pt mixed sample test disks in same manner as 1⅛" diam. stds are used.

(**f**) *Photographic stds.*—Photographic stds (obtainable from Photography Div., Office of Information, US Dept. of Agriculture, Washington, DC 20250) may be used as guide in grading sediment pads, but it is preferable to use actual disks prepd as in (**d**) or (**e**). Stds that more nearly resemble disk being graded should be used in each case. Do not use photographs that have become faded, stained, soiled, or otherwise damaged.

44.015 ***Checking Sediment Testers***

To check sediment testing devices, proceed as follows: Measure actual vol. of milk delivered to assure that 1 pt is withdrawn and passes thru disk. Transfer 10 mL 2% sediment suspension in sucrose soln, **44.014(d)**, using large-tip, graduated pipet, to 10 gal. clean filtered H_2O in clean milk can. After thoroly agitating mixt., remove 1 pt with clean pt measure and filter thru 1⅛" diam. area of sediment disk, **44.014(b)**, mounted on suitable funnel of correct size, *e.g.,* **44.014(c)**(*1*). After thoro agitation of contents of milk can, again remove pt sample with the sediment testing device and pass thru sediment disk in exactly same manner as for testing milk. Repeat this operation with the tester several times to det. whether all disks so obtained give same sediment as disk obtained by filtering thru funnel, **44.014(c)**(*1*).

44.016 ***Collection of Sample***

(**a**) *Mixed sample method.*—For retail containers, 5 to 10 gal. cans, and storage tanks, use 1 pt or 1 gal. samples. Before mixing milk, transfer with small strainer any floating extraneous matter, such as flies, hairs, large chunks of debris, etc., to mounted disk, **44.017(a)**, or mount on sep. disk, properly identified. Thoroly mix milk in container before removing test portion. Avoid contamination of sample with foreign matter on stirrers or by any other means. For retail containers take 1 pt from mixed container or composite sufficient number to make 1 gal. Proceed as in **44.017(a)**.

(**b**) *Off-bottom method.*—For 5 to 10 gal. cans take pt sample with either type of off-bottom tester from unstirred can of milk. Before withdrawing sample, remove with small strainer any floating extraneous matter as in (**a**). Take sample ≤¼" off bottom of unstirred can of milk by inserting sampler and, during upstroke of plunger, drawing head of instrument once across diam. of can bottom or around circumference if can has high center. Expel milk with gun in can and then with short stroke remove excess fluid from pad. Proceed as in **44.017(b)**.

44.017 ***Determination***

(**a**) *Mixed samples.*—Pass sample thru properly adjusted disk, **44.014(b)**, held in correct position in tester. Warm 1 pt sample to 90–100°F and filter thru restricted area 0.40" diam., **44.014(a)**(*1*). If single-unit off-bottom tester with special head is used, warm sample larger than 1 pt to 90–100°F and withdraw 1 pt with tester while stirring, or draw 1 pt into tester and warm milk by holding tester under running hot H_2O before discharging milk thru disk.

Warm 1 gal. sample to 80–90°F or filter cold thru 1⅛" diam. area of disk, **44.014(b)**. If milk is filtered at temp. <90°F, rinse disk by filtering ca ½ pt sediment-free warm (90–100°F) H_2O thru disk before removing from tester. If milk is to be salvaged, do not dil. with H_2O. (Milk varies in its rate of flow thru disks; pasteurized milk may be more difficult to filter than raw milk. Other factors influencing rate of flow are temp., fat content, degree of clumping of fat globules, stage of lactation, presence of mastitic milk, and amt of sediment in sample.)

Remove disk from tester and mount on special sized paper or store in individual transparent waxed envelope. (If disk is placed on paper or in envelope while still moist, drying milk acts as adhesive.) Grade by comparison with std disks, **44.014(d)** or **(e)**, and indicate on report whether pad was graded wet or dry. (Character of sediment may be detd by microscopic examination.)

To prevent decomposition on storage, disk may be sprayed with HCHO soln or alc. menthol-thymol soln as in **44.014(d)**. Do not use glue to affix disk to paper; if disk becomes detached, moisten with few drops H_2O and remount. Protect from contamination.

(b) *Off-bottom samples.*—Remove disk from tester, **44.016(b)**, and proceed as in **(a)**, third par., beginning ". . . mount on special sized paper . . ."

Filth in Butter, Cheese, Cheese Products, Dried Milk Products, and Dairy Products in General—Official First Action

Use following methods independently or in various combinations. Weigh 225 g, except in **44.022**, into suitable container and use S&S ruled No. 8 paper for filtration. Cut hard cheese into small pieces.

44.018 ***Butter***

Place container in H_2O bath or oven at ca 80°. When fat seps, filter directly thru paper with suction, retaining most of curd and H_2O in container. After fat passes thru, filter remaining material. To facilitate filtration of curd, wash paper with near boiling H_2O during filtration. (For butter not filterable by this process, use **44.020**.) Examine paper microscopically.

44.019 ***Evaporated Milk, Condensed Milk, Sweet Cream, Spray-Dried Whole or Skim Milk***

Reconstitute dried or concd products. Dil. reconstituted product with equal vol. hot H_2O, hot 3% $Na_2C_2O_4$ soln, or hot 2% Na_2CO_3 soln, and filter with suction. During filtration, continually wash paper with stream of near boiling H_2O to prevent accumulation of layer of particles which clogs paper. Examine paper microscopically.

44.020 ***Soft and Semi-Soft Cheese and Sour Cream; Some Dried Whole and Skim Milks; and Butter That Cannot Be Filtered by 44.018***

Cut 225 g cheese into 6 mm cubes and add to 800–1000 mL boiling H_3PO_4 (1+40) in 1.5–2 L beaker, stirring continuously with slow speed mech. stirrer, **44.002(f)**, or on mag. stirrer-hot plate, **44.002(p)**, with stirring bar ca 75 × 12 mm, until sample is dispersed (usually >20 min). Filter, without letting mixt. accumulate on paper, and continually wash filter with stream of near boiling H_2O to prevent clogging. When filtration is impeded, add H_2O, dil. (1–5%) alkali, H_3PO_4 (1+40), or hot alcohol, until paper clears; then resume addn of sample suspension and H_2O. Examine paper microscopically.

44.021 ***Hard Cheeses, Hard Skim, Part Skim Milk Cheeses (Romano, Ricotta, Feta, Pecorino, Sardo, Goats' Milk Cheeses, Sbrinz, Goya, Whey Cheeses, etc.) (8)***

(Not applicable to cheese contg herbs, spices, or molds thruout)

Prep. cheese for sampling by trimming and discarding thin layers to remove all "old" cut surfaces and to keep paraffin coating and mold out of sample. Cut and break up 225 g trimmed cheese into 4 L beaker. Add ca 700 mL ca 55° filtered H_2O. Set beaker under mech. stirrer, **44.002(f)**, and stir 15 min, maintaining mixt. at 55°. Add 100 mL 20% aq. Na_4EDTA soln, stir, and adjust mixt. to pH 8 with NH_4OH or dil. HCl (1+2). Rinse sides of beaker free of adhering cheese particles with ca 60° H_2O. Maintain pH 8 by addn of NH_4OH and keep adding ca 60° H_2O to dil. cheese mixt. to ca 3 L. If foaming occurs, place wet vegetable parchment Patapar paper, 27 lb wt (available from Paterson Parchment Paper Co., Bristol, PA 19007), or Parafilm M (Cat. No. 13-374, Fisher Scientific Co.), split to accommodate stirrer blades, over top of beaker to break foam. Continue stirring until cheese becomes finely dispersed.

Cool dispersion to 40° and adjust to pH 8 with NH_4OH or HCl (1+2). Add 300 mL pancreatin soln, **44.003(z)**, (except use 600 mL pancreatin soln for ricotta). Let mixt. digest at ≤40° with continued stirring ca 1.5 hr. Maintain pH 8 by addn of NH_4OH.

After digestion, place beaker on hot plate and heat to 65–68°, continuing mech. stirring. Adjust to pH 6.0±0.2 with HCl (1+2). Carefully adjust stirrer blades close to bottom of beaker to pick up any cheese particles which settle. Continue stirring 15 min or until cheese appears completely solubilized. Rinse inside of beaker, stirrer blades, etc., with ca 65° H_2O and filter thru ruled paper, using ca 65° H_2O and then alcohol to rinse beaker. If filtration becomes slow (e.g., cream cheese), let paper clear, wash with alcohol, and use addnl paper. Mixt. will filter more easily if No. 60 screen (ca 5 cm diam.) is placed under paper and small amt of mixt. is allowed to suck dry before filtering is continued. Examine paper microscopically.

44.022 ***Casein (9)***

Weigh 50 g sample into 1 L beaker. Slowly stir in 170 mL 20% Na_4EDTA soln until well mixed with sample. With constant stirring, bring vol. to 1 L with hot tap H_2O (55–70°). Wet sieve on No. 230 sieve, **44.002(u)**, with forcible spray of hot tap H_2O until foam subsides. Wash sieve retainings into beaker and pour onto ruled filter paper. Examine papers microscopically.

44.023 ***Cheese Containing Mold, Plant Tissues, and Spices***

Disperse cheese by **44.020** or first par. of **44.021**. Pour thru No. 140 sieve, **44.002(u)**, washing thoroly with forcible stream of H_2O. Transfer material retained on sieve to beaker. Add 200 mL H_3PO_4 (1+49), boil until lumpy residue dissolves, and pour again thru No. 140 sieve, washing thoroly with forcible stream of hot H_2O. Transfer material on sieve with ca 200 mL 60% alcohol to trap flask and cool. Trap off, using heptane, **44.003(u)**, and H_2O, filter, and examine microscopically.

44.024 Sediment in Cream, Butter, Cheese, Cheese Products, Dried Milk Products, and Dairy Products in General Official First Action

(a) *Rapid method for sweet cream and cream in which curd* *is easy to disperse and in absence of mold.*—Place 1 pt (500 mL) sample in beaker or pan of convenient size, ca 2 L, and add ca 500 mL hot H_2O (70–90°). More or less H_2O may be added so that mixt. when ready for filtration is at 45–60°. Remove whole flies or other large filth particles which float to surface and which would be broken up by stirrer. Place these on sediment pad when completed. Place pan under malted milk stirrer, and add, while stirring, 25 mL 40% Calgon soln, **44.003(i)**; if necessary, add more Calgon soln to make mixt. alk. to litmus. Stir 30–60 sec or until curd is broken up. Filter with vac. thru std sediment disk, **44.014(b)**. If pad clogs, filter remaining portion thru fresh disk. Rinse pan and funnel with hot H_2O onto sediment disk.

(b) *Other dairy products.*—Proceed as in **44.020** or **44.021**, and filter thru std sediment disk, **44.014(b)**. Violent mech. agitation, such as is provided by malted milk stirrer, may be used to facilitate dispersion of product.

Compare with std sediment disks, **44.014(d)**, **(e)**(*1*), or **(f)**.

44.025 ★ Mold in Butter (*10*)—Official Final Action ★

See **40.024**, 11th ed.

NUTS AND NUT PRODUCTS

Shelled Nuts (Except Pecans)

44.026 Light Filth (*11*)—Official First Action

(*Caution: See* **51.039**, **51.040**, **51.055**, and **51.056**.)

Nutmeats, all sizes, except pecans.—Weigh 100 g sample into 1.5 L beaker. Add 600 mL $CHCl_3$; boil 15 min. Prep. ≥24 cm paper for 100 mm plate diam. buchner by moistening with H_2O and forming around base of 1 L beaker. Place 7 cm disk of bolting cloth, **44.002(e)**, (mesh size not critical) in buchner, insert paper, apply vac., and press moistened paper until good seal is obtained. Rinse paper with isopropanol. Quant. transfer nutmeats and $CHCl_3$ onto previously prepd paper. Maintain suction on nutmeats in buchner 5 min after visible dripping ceases. Release vac., add isopropanol until nutmeats are covered, let stand few min, and reapply vac. until dripping ceases. Repeat isopropanol wash step and aspirate 5 min after visible dripping ceases. Quant. transfer nutmeats on paper to 2 L trap flask, **44.002(i)**(*3*) Scrape all fines from paper with spatula and finally rinse paper clean with 60% alcohol-$CaCl_2$ soln, **44.003(e)**. Bring vol. to 1 L with 60% alcohol-$CaCl_2$ soln and add 50 mL HCl. Add mag. stirring bar, **44.002(p)**, to flask, place flask on mag. stirring hot plate, and heat to *full boil* with gentle stirring. Immediately transfer flask to cool stirring unit and add 40 mL mineral oil, **44.003(y)**, by pouring down stirring rod. Stir mag., **44.004(b)**, 2 min.

Fill with 60% alcohol-$CaCl_2$ soln and gently stir 5–10 sec with stirring rod. Let stand 2 min and trap off. Add 25 mL mineral oil, hand stir gently 30 sec, and let stand 10 min. Repeat trapping. Wash flask neck thoroly with isopropanol, and transfer washings to beaker with trappings. Filter onto ruled paper and examine microscopically.

Pecans, All Sizes—Official First Action

44.027 Light Filth (*11*)

(*Caution: See* **51.040** and **51.056**.)

Form cup, using 32 cm paper with 1–1.5 L beaker, **44.002(k)**. Weigh 100 g sample into filter paper cup and place in 1.5 L beaker. Add 400 mL $CHCl_3$ and boil 5 min. After cooling few min, lift paper and drain. Repeat 5 min boil and drain with two addnl 400 mL portions $CHCl_3$. Proceed as in **44.026**, beginning "Place 7 cm disk of bolting cloth, . . ."

44.028 Heavy Filth

(*Caution: See* **51.011**, **51.039**, and **51.073**.)

Weigh 100 g sample into 600 mL beaker. Add ca 350 mL pet ether and boil gently 30 min, adding pet ether to maintain original vol. Decant solv., taking care not to lose any coarse nut tissue, and discard. Add ca 300 mL $CHCl_3$ to beaker and let settle 10–15 min. Pour off floating nutmeats and ca ⅔ of the $CHCl_3$, and discard. Repeat sepn with smaller vols of mixt. of $CHCl_3$ and CCl_4 (1+1) until residue in beaker is relatively free of nutmeat particles. Transfer residue in beaker to ashless paper and examine for heavy filth. If appreciable amt of sand and soil is present, ignite paper in weighed crucible at ca 500° and weigh.

44.029 Curculio Larvae in Pecan Pieces (*12*)

Weigh 115 g (ca ¼ lb) sample into 1.5 L beaker and add mag. stirring bar, **44.002(p)**. Add 300 mL undild isopropanol and stir on mag. stirrer 5–10 sec. Add H_2O (200 mL for midget pieces and 300 mL for small, small medium, medium, and mixed pieces) and stir 5–10 sec on stirrer. After few sec, gently agitate settled nutmeats with stirring rod to release any entrapped curculio. Remove all floating material and examine for curculio larvae. Reclaim flotation soln by pouring thru No. 12 sieve and use for one addnl sample.

Shredded Coconut

44.030 Filth—Official First Action

(a) *Heavy filth.*—Proceed as in **44.043**, using 100 g sample in 800 mL beaker.

(b) *Light filth.*—Weigh 100 g sample into 1.5 or 2.0 L beaker. Add 1 L detergent soln, **44.033**. Heat in steam bath 10 min, stirring immediately and after ca 5 min.

Pour entire sample onto 8" No. 230 sieve, rinse beaker with hot H_2O, and add rinse to sieve. Wash sieve with forcible stream of hot H_2O until all foam is gone; then rinse well with 40% isopropanol and let drain. Place wide stem funnel in 2 L trap flask, and transfer bulk of sample to flask with spoon. Rinse remaining material to edge of sieve with aerator spray, and transfer quant. to trap flask with 40% isopropanol. Dil. to 1 L with 40% isopropanol, add mag. stirring bar, **44.002(p)**, and place on mag. stirrer-hot plate, **44.002(p)**. Add 40 mL mineral oil, **44.003(y)**, and stir vigorously 1 min. Turn stirrer to slow rate, add 50 mL HCl, and heat to vigorous boil (*Caution:* Soln may froth violently upon reaching bp with high heat input.

Place sample flask on cool stirrer and stir mag., **44.004(b)**, 3 min. Let stand 2 min; then slowly fill flask with 40% isopropanol added down stirring rod to bring oil interface 1 cm above fully raised stopper or wafer. Lower stopper to midpoint of flask, clamp, and let stand undisturbed 2 min. Trap off into beaker, rinsing neck of trap flask with 40% isopropanol. Add 25 mL flotation liq. **44.003(s)**, and stir vigorously by hand 1 min. Adjust oil level as above, and let stand undisturbed 10 min. Trap off into second beaker, rinsing neck of flask well with isopropanol.

Filter each trapped off layer onto sep. identified papers, rinsing beakers with isopropanol, and examine papers microscopically at 30×.

Peanut Butter

44.031 ★ Preparation of Sample ★ Official First Action

See **40.031**, 11th ed.

★ Surplus method—*see* inside front cover.

44.032 ★ Water-Insoluble Inorganic Residue ("WIIR") ★ and Excreta—Official First Action

Defatting, floating off nut tissues, dissolving sol. minerals and NaCl in dil. HCl, and igniting residue. *See* **40.032**, 11th ed.

Light Filth (*13*)—Official First Action

44.033 ***Reagent***

Detergent soln—Dissolve sep. 20 g USP Na lauryl sulfate and 10 g tech. $Na_2B_4O_7.10H_2O$ in H_2O, combine, and dil. to 1 L.

44.034 ***Determination***

Weigh 100 g sample into 1.5 L beaker and heat on steam bath until softened. Add 1 L filtered hot detergent soln, and stir well. Heat 10 min *in* steam bath. Stir well, pour portionwise onto No. 230 sieve, **44.002(u)**, and wash with forcible stream of 55–70° tap H_2O, using aerator, **44.002(a)**. When foam is gone, transfer material on sieve to 2 L trap flask, **44.002(i)**(*3*), with 55% alcohol (or 40% isopropanol) and bring vol. to 1 L. Add 50 mL HCl. Lower mag. stirring bar into flask on stirring rod stopper. Heat to bp and boil 10 min while slowly stirring on mag. stirring hot plate **44.002(p)**.

Transfer flask to unheated stirring unit and immediately add 40 mL mineral oil, **44.003(y)**, by pouring down stirring rod. Stir mag. 2 min. Fill with deaerated 55% alcohol (or 40% isopropanol) and gently stir 5–10 sec with stoppered rod. Let stand 5 min. Trap off. Add 25 mL mineral oil, stir by hand gently 30 sec, and let stand 5 min. Repeat trapping. Wash flask neck thoroly with isopropanol. Filter onto ruled paper and examine microscopically.

44.035 ★ Rocks and Decomposed Peanuts in ★ Coarse Peanut Butter—Official First Action

Floating off nut tissue and examining residue. *See* **44.035**, 11th ed.

44.036 ★ Glass—Procedure ★

Dispersing sample with detergent soln, decanting, floating off nut tissue, and examining residue. *See* **40.036**, 11th ed.

GRAINS AND THEIR PRODUCTS

Grains and Seeds

44.037 Internal Insect Infestation—Official First Action

Mix grain by passing 6 times thru Jones sampler, recombining sepns before each pass. Sep. slightly >100 g and weigh 100 g. Transfer weighed sample, small amt at time, to 5" or 8" No. 12 sieve, and with stiff bristle brush, work insects thru sieve as completely as possible.

Grind screened sample in cutting-type mill set at 0.061". (Dry damp or tempered grain in forced-draft oven 1 hr at 70–80° or 2 hr in oven without draft.) Transfer cracked grain, including any residue in mill, to 2 L trap flask, **44.002(i)**(*3*), trap as in **44.004(a)**, using 60% isopropanol satd with heptane, **44.003(w)**, and heptane, **44.003(u)**, as solvs, and filter on 10XX bolting cloth, **44.002(e)**. If considerable starchy material is in ext, hydrolyze with HCl as in **44.004(d)**. Examine as in **44.004(g)** except use 15× as lower limit of magnification. Count only whole insects, insect heads, cast skins, and head capsules.

Unpopped Popcorn, Cereal Grains, Peas, Beans, Etc.

44.038 External Light Filth—Procedure

Transfer 225 g sample to 2 L trap flask, **44.002(i)**(*3*). Add 600 mL 40% alcohol and boil gently, with frequent stirring, 5 min. Cool, trap off, using heptane, **44.003(u)**, and 40% alcohol, filter, and examine microscopically.

Popped Popcorn

44.039 Filth—Procedure

Weigh 50 g sample into 2 L trap flask. Add 500 mL hot H_2O, boil 15 min, and cool to room temp. Add 35 mL heptane, **44.003(u)**, mix, and let stand 5 min. Fill with H_2O, trap off, filter, and examine microscopically.

Brewer's Grits

44.040 Rodent Excreta—Procedure

See **44.043.**

44.041 Light Filth—Official First Action

See **44.044.**

White and Yellow Corn Meal, Cracked Wheat, and Rye, Pumpernickel, and Buckwheat Flours

44.042 Light Filth (*14*)—Official Final Action

(*Caution: See* **51.011**, **51.040**, and **51.056**.)

Weigh 25 g sample into 94 × 33 mm Soxhlet thimble and cover with pad of glass wool. Add ca 300 mL $CHCl_3$ and 3–4 glass beads to 500 mL Soxhlet extn flask. Ext in Soxhlet extractor at medium rate ca 90 min (counting time from first overflow and siphoning ca every 5 min). Place extn thimble in 250 mL beaker and dry with air on steam bath until no $CHCl_3$ odor remains.

Quant. transfer contents of thimble and any material adhering to glass wool, with spatula and acid-alcohol rinses, **44.003(c)**, to 1 L trap flask for trap flask method, **(a)**, or to 1–1.5 L beaker for percolator method, **(b)**.

Place trap flask or beaker on mag. stirrer, add stirring bar, and slowly add acid-alcohol soln, stirring constantly to form smooth slurry. Dil. to ca 600 mL with acid-alcohol soln and add ca 40 mL mineral oil, **44.003(y)**. Mag. stir mixt. 10 min, **44.004(b)**. Continue as in **(a)** or **(b)**.

(a) *Trap flask method.*—At end of stirring period, fill flask with acid-alcohol soln and let stand 30 min; stir gently every 3–4 min for first 25 min. Trap off, rinsing neck of flask with acid-alcohol soln. Add ca 30 mL mineral oil and stir mag. ca 5 min. Let stand 30 min, stirring and trapping as above. Combine trappings in beaker and transfer quant. to Kilborn funnel, **44.002(i)**(*1*) or percolator (*2*), contg ca 125 mL H_2O. Retain beaker. Add tap H_2O to ca 1 cm from top of funnel. Let oil layer sep. 5–10 min and drain until interface is ca 5 cm above constriction, discarding lower aq. layer. Repeat H_2O washes until lower phase is clear. Drain interface-oil layer into retained beaker, washing sides of funnel with ca 50–100 mL H_2O. If product residue is present in retained beaker contents, add ca 10 mL HCl. Boil ca 5 min on hot plate and filter thru ruled paper. After mineral oil layer has passed thru paper, rinse all glassware used (except trap flask) with alcohol followed by H_2O, then 5% detergent soln, **44.003(q)**, and finally with H_2O. Filter rinses thru original filter paper. Examine microscopically.

(b) *Corning percolator method.*—Place stirring rod in drain opening inside percolator, **44.002(i)**(*2*). Add ca 250 mL H_2O to percolator. Quant. transfer beaker contents to percolator. Add acid-alcohol soln to ca 6 cm from top. Let stand ca 30 min;

★ Surplus method—*see* inside front cover.

gently stir contents with stirring rod every 3–4 min during first 25 min in such manner as to prevent product dropping into drain opening. After 30 min, raise stirring rod and drain, discarding lower layer but leaving ca 250 mL in percolator. Rinse stirring rod with acid-alcohol soln and add rinsings to percolator contents. Retain stirring rod for further rinsings.

Add acid-alcohol soln to percolator to ca 6 cm from top and let stand ca 30 min, stirring as before. Drain and discard lower layer as before to 250 mL. Add H_2O to ca 6 cm from top and proceed as in (**a**), beginning "Let oil layer sep. 5–10 min . . ."

Whole and Degerminated Corn Meal (for Rodent Excreta Only), Corn Grits, Rye Meal, Wheat Meal, Whole Wheat Flour, Farina, and Semolina

44.043 Rodent Excreta (*15*)—Official First Action

(*Caution: See* **51.040**, **51.049**, and **51.056**.)

Weigh 50 g sample in 250 mL hooked-lip beaker. Add $CHCl_3$ to within ca 1 cm of top, mix thoroly, and let settle ≥30 min, stirring surface layer occasionally. Carefully decant $CHCl_3$ and float tissue onto buchner, without disturbing heavy residue in bottom of beaker. Before decanting, take care that floating layer has not become so compact as to render this operation difficult. Add amt of CCl_4 equal to amt of $CHCl_3$ and tissue left in beaker, let settle again, and decant as before. Repeat this process with mixt. of equal parts $CHCl_3$ and CCl_4 until very little tissue remains in beaker. Do not decant any rodent excreta fragments that may be present. Wash residue in beaker onto 7 cm ruled paper with stream of $CHCl_3$ or CCl_4 and examine microscopically.

44.044 Light Filth—Official First Action

(Not applicable to whole and degerminated corn meal)

Draw air thru material in buchner, **44.043**, until liq. evaps. Air dry overnight, or dry in oven at ca 80°. (*Caution:* In oven drying, phosgene is liberated and adequate ventilation must be provided.) Transfer residue to 1 L trap flask, **44.002(i)**(*3*). Add 100 mL 60% isopropanol satd with heptane, **44.003(w)**, and mix thoroly. Wash down sides of flask with isopropanol-heptane soln until ca 400 mL is added, and soak 30 min. Trap off twice with 20–30 mL heptane, **44.003(u)**, for each trapping and 60% isopropanol satd with heptane as liq. extn medium. In first trapping, let stand 5 min after stirring in heptane before filling flask. Filter, and examine both trappings microscopically.

White Flour

Light Filth (*16*)—Official First Action

44.045 *Acid Digestion Method*

Digest 50 g flour in 2–2.5 L beaker with ca 600 mL HCl (3+97) by autoclaving 5 min at 121°. Immediately transfer digest to 1 L beaker, using HCl (3+97) at room temp. to assist in transfer. Add 50 mL mineral oil, **44.003(y)**, and stir mag., **44.004(b)**, 5 min. Quant. transfer to Kilborn funnel, **44.002(i)**(*1*), or percolator, (*2*), retaining beaker. Let stand 30 min, stirring gently with long glass rod several times during first 10 min. Drain lower layer to ca 3 cm of interface, wash sides with cold tap H_2O, and let layers sep. ca 2–3 min. Repeat drain and H_2O wash until lower phase is clear. After final wash, drain oil layer into retained beaker, rinsing sides of funnel with H_2O and alcohol. Add HCl to ca 3% (v/v) and boil 3–4 min on hot plate. Filter hot soln thru ruled paper, and thoroly rinse beaker and funnel with H_2O, alcohol, and 5% detergent soln, **44.003(q)**. Filter each rinse sep. thru same paper. Examine microscopically.

Corn Flour

Light and Heavy Filth—Official First Action

44.046 *Pancreatin Digestion Method*

(**a**) *Light filth.*—Weigh 50 g flour into 600 mL beaker; stir into smooth slurry with 50 mL pancreatin soln, **44.003(z)**, dild with 100 mL H_2O. Dil. with H_2O to total vol. of ca 400 mL, and adjust to pH 8 with Na_3PO_4 soln, **44.003(ee)**. Readjust pH after ca 15 min and again in ca 45 min. Add, with stirring, 3 drops HCHO soln and digest 16–18 hr at room temp. or ≤40°. Transfer to 2 L trap flask and ext as in **44.004(a)**, using 30 and 20 mL deodorized kerosene, **44.003(x)**, and H_2O as solvs. Combine trappings and rinsings in beaker, transfer to 2 L trap flask, and trap off as above. If considerable starchy material is in ext, hydrolyze with HCl as in **44.004(d)**. Examine papers microscopically.

(**b**) *Rodent excreta.*—Proceed as in **44.043**.

44.047 *Acid Hydrolysis Method (17)*

Light filth.—Disperse 50 g flour in 1 L beaker with ca 400 mL HCl (5+95) and 20 mL mineral oil, **44.003(y)**. Place on hot plate, bring to rolling boil with stirring, and boil 10 min. Remove from heat and transfer quant. to extn vessel, **44.002(i)**(*1*) or (*2*). Rinse beaker and rod with ≤50 mL hot H_2O, transfer rinsings to extn vessel, and retain beaker and rod. Fill extn vessel with cold H_2O to ca 3 cm from top. Let settle 30 min, and drain carefully without forming vortex, until upper layer is ca 5 cm from bottom. Add 25 mL kerosene, **44.003(x)**, to extn vessel and drain oil layer into retained beaker. If excessive starchy material has sepd with oil layer, hydrolyze with 100–200 mL HCl (5+95) before continuing. Wash sides of extn vessel with 5% detergent soln, **44.003(q)**, in wash bottle, and collect washings in retained beaker. Filter entire contents of beaker thru ruled paper, **44.002(j)**, in Hirsch funnel. Rinse beaker with 5% detergent soln, and filter. Examine microscopically at 30×.

Soy Flour

44.048 Light Filth (*18*)—Official First Action

Weigh 50 g sample into 500 mL beaker and add ca 50 mL isopropanol, with stirring. Add mag. stirring bar and, with stirring, slowly add 300 mL satd NaCl soln at room temp. Stir to thin slurry and transfer in small increments to No. 230 sieve, **44.002(u)**. Wash residue with forceful stream of cold H_2O, using aerator, **44.002(a)**, until effluent is clear and foaming has subsided. Let residue drain in sieve. Wash residue with isopropanol and let drain. Transfer residue to 1.5 L beaker with 40% isopropanol and dil. to 800 mL with 40% isopropanol. Heat to bp with mag. stirring, and add 50 mL mineral oil, **44.003(y)**. Stir mag., **44.004(b)**, 3 min while continuing to boil.

Transfer quant. to 2 L percolator, **44.002(i)**(*2*). Retain 1.5 L beaker as vessel to fill percolator with H_2O during refill cycles. Fill percolator with 40% isopropanol to within 3 cm of top. Let stand 5 min and drain contents to within 3 cm of bottom of oil layer. Repeat drain and refill steps at 3 min intervals with hot tap H_2O (55–70°) until aq. phase is clear. Drain most of aq. phase and discard. Drain oil layer into 400 mL beaker. Wash percolator with alternate washes of H_2O and isopropanol, and collect washings in 400 mL beaker. Filter onto ruled paper and examine microscopically.

44.049 Insect Eggs (*19*)—Official First Action

Transfer 50 g flour to No. 100 sieve (if >ca 0.1 g residue is obtained, No. 60 or No. 80 sieve should be used to prevent slow filtration after digestion) and sift gently until no more flour passes thru. Transfer residue on sieve to 250 mL beaker and wet with 2–3 mL alcohol. Add 30 mL H_2SO_4 (1+19), cover beaker, and heat on steam bath 10 min. Filter thru paper on suction funnel, using min. suction necessary to filter. Keep beaker partially inverted over funnel and rinse with H_2O. Turn off suction. Add 15–20 mL ca 0.1*N* I to paper in funnel. Allow 10–15 sec for I to stain contents. Apply gentle suction. After I passes thru filter, wash paper with 25–30 mL 1% H_2SO_4, followed by several small H_2O washes. Transfer paper to petri dish and examine at once under 20× magnification.

44.050 Insect Excreta (*20*)—Official First Action

(**a**) *Optional for 1–4 samples.*—Weigh 0.20 g flour on weighed flat glass disk 7–7.5 cm diam. Add clove oil and spread mixt. into thin uniform layer. (Enough oil should be present to clear flour and present smooth surface of oil, but not so much that mixt. flows off disk.) Place wire grid over disk and examine microscopically with dark background and intense reflected light. Depending upon size of plate, larger amts of flour and ruled glass plate can be used and oil-flour mount covered with glass, *e.g.,* use 0.5 g flour on tomato rot count plate, **44.002(t)**. Weigh flour in counterbalanced scoop or directly on plate. Thoroly sat. flour on counting plate, cover with glass, and count insect excreta. To move or turn suspected particles, gently apply pressure or move cover slightly while observing thru microscope.

(**b**) *Optional in multiple-sample schedule.*—Tare 2–8 small numbered vials on each balance pan and weigh by shifting weights from one side to other. (If desired, larger portion may be weighed in beaker and some of flour floated off in $CHCl_3$-ether or $CHCl_3$-toluene mixt., sp gr 1.40, before transferring to filter paper.) Rinse contents of each vial onto smooth-surface, ruled paper in Hirsch funnel with $CHCl_3$ or CCl_4. Transfer paper to petri dish, flood with clove oil, and examine with dark background and intense reflected light.

Wheat Germ, Raw or Processed

Light Filth (*21*)—Official Final Action

(*Caution: See* **51.040** and **51.056.**)

44.051 ***Determination***

Form paper cup, using 32 cm paper and 250 and 400 mL beakers, **44.002(k)**. Tare 400 mL beaker and paper, weigh 50 g sample into filter paper in beaker, and add ca 150 mL $CHCl_3$. Boil on steam bath 5 min, occasionally rinsing down sides of filter paper with $CHCl_3$ to maintain original level. Remove from heat. Carefully lift paper contg sample from beaker so as to prevent any loss of sample. Let most of $CHCl_3$ drain into beaker; then discard drainings. Repeat operation 2 addnl times beginning ". . . add ca 150 mL $CHCl_3$." After last $CHCl_3$ defatting, place paper contg sample in buchner. Apply vac. until draining slows to drip. Rinse sides of paper and sample with undild isopropanol and apply vac. until draining has ceased. Turn off vac. Add ca 50–60 mL undild isopropanol to sample. Let stand 2 min; then apply vac. until dripping ceases and sample appears dry.

Transfer sample from paper to 1 L beaker with hot tap H_2O (55–70°). Fold filter paper in half and rub together; then wash with hot tap H_2O into beaker. Repeat several times until paper appears clean. Discard paper and bring vol. of hot H_2O to 600 mL. Add 30 mL HCl and 1 mL antifoam, **44.003(g)**. Boil on stirrer-hot plate, **44.002(p)**, 10 min with const stirring; then remove from heat. Pour contents of beaker onto No. 230 sieve, **44.002(u)**, and wash with forcible hot H_2O spray (55–70°), **44.002(a)**, until all starchy material has passed thru and only bran remains (color of sample will change from light tan to dark brown). Transfer material from sieve to 2 L trap flask with 55% alcohol or 40% isopropanol, dil. to ca 1 L, and add 50 mL HCl. Heat to 60–70° on hot plate (do not boil), remove flask from heat, and add 50 mL mineral oil, **44.003(y)**. Stir mag., **44.004(b)**, 3 min. Fill flask with same dil. alcohol used previously, stir gently by hand 1 min, let flask stand 10 min, and trap off, rinsing neck of flask with same dil. alcohol used previously. Perform second extn, using 25 mL mineral oil. Stir gently by hand 1 min, let stand 15 min, and trap off. Rinse neck of flask with undild isopropanol or alcohol. Filter trappings thru ruled paper and examine microscopically.

Wheat Gluten

44.052 Light Filth (*22*)—Official First Action

Add 900 mL 40% isopropanol, 100 mL HCl, and mag. stirring bar to 2 L trap flask, **44.002(i)**(*3*). Using mag. stirrer, without heat, stir at max. speed where no splashing occurs, and slowly add 50 g sample thru long-stem funnel with wide diam. bore to avoid getting sample on stoppered rod or sides of trap flask. Stir 3 min, and then boil 15 min with gentle stirring on mag. stirrer-hot plate. Immediately transfer flask to cool stirring unit and add 40 mL light mineral oil, **44.003(y)**. Stir mag., **44.004(b)**, 3 min. Slowly fill flask with 40% isopropanol by letting liq. flow down stoppered rod while top of stopper is maintained just above flask contents. After filling flask, gently stir settled material 5–10 sec with stoppered rod. Let stand undisturbed 5 min and immediately trap off. Add 25 mL light mineral oil, stir gently by hand 30 sec, and let stand 10 min. Repeat trapping. Wash flask neck thoroly with isopropanol and transfer washings to beaker contg trappings. Filter onto ruled paper and examine microscopically.

Starch

44.053 Light Filth (*23*)—Official First Action

Weigh 225 g sample into 2 L beaker, add 1.2 L cold H_2O, and stir well to disperse lumps. Pour onto No. 230 sieve, **44.002(u)**, and wash with forcible stream of cold tap H_2O, using aerator, **44.002(a)**. (If excessive residue remains on sieve, wash into beaker with H_2O, add HCl to make to (1+9), bring to bp, and repeat sieving.) Quant. transfer sieve retainings to beaker, filter onto ruled paper, and examine microscopically.

BAKED GOODS

High Bran Content Breads (24)

44.054 Light Filth—Official First Action

Post-milling contamination.—Add 225 g sample to 2 L beaker contg ca 1 L H_2O and 50 mL HCl. Stir well. Add 1 mL antifoam soln, **44.003(g)**. Autoclave ca 20 min as in **44.002(b)**(*1*) or ca 15 min as in (*2*). Transfer digest in small portions onto No. 140 sieve, **44.002(u)**, with hot tap H_2O (55–70°) until amt of residue remains const. Place sieve in pan, cover residue to depth of ca 2 cm with alcohol or isopropanol, let stand 5 min, and drain. Repeat this step 3 times with $CHCl_3$, then twice more with alcohol or isopropanol, and drain completely. Promptly transfer sieve retainings quant. to 1 L beaker with acid-alcohol, **44.003(c)**, dilg contents to ca 600 mL with acid-alcohol. Add 50 mL mineral oil, **44.003(y)**, and stir mag., **44.004(b)**, 5 min.

Completely transfer beaker contents to percolator, **44.002(i)**(*2*), or Kilborn funnel, (*1*), retaining beaker. Let stand 30 min, stirring gently ca every 5 min with long glass stirring rod for first 20 min; drain contents to ca 250 mL. Add acid-alcohol to ca 3 cm of top and let stand 30 min, stirring as before. Again drain to ca 250 mL. Fill funnel with cold tap H_2O, let settle ca 1.5 min, and drain to ca 250 mL. Continue drain and refill cycles until lower aq. phase is clear and free of suspended material.

After last wash, drain oil-H_2O interface into retained beaker. Promptly wash sides of percolator with 50–100 mL portions hot tap H_2O, isopropanol or alcohol, and 5% detergent soln, **44.003(q)**, if necessary. Filter thru ruled paper, washing sides of beaker as above, using rubber policeman, if necessary. Examine microscopically.

Baked Goods with Fruit and Nut Tissues

Light Filth—Official First Action

44.055 ***Pancreatin Digestion Method***

Post-milling contamination.—Weigh 225 g sample into 2 L beaker, add enough hot H_2O to soften and sat. material, and proceed as in (**a**). If lumps persist or if H_2O is not immediately absorbed uniformly thru entire mass, proceed as in (**b**).

(**a**) Adjust mixt. to pH 7–8 with ca 5% Na_3PO_4 soln. Stir and break up material as much as possible. Cool to 40° and add 100 mL pancreatin soln, **44.003(z)**. Stir thoroly and readjust to pH 7–8. Let stand 30 min, stir, and readjust pH.

(**b**) Est. vol. of mixt. and add HCl to ca 1 + 49 concn. Boil until solids become finely divided and so digested that mixt. will not froth over when covered during boiling. Neutze to ca pH 6 with NaOH soln; then add Na_3PO_4 soln to pH 8 and continue as in (**a**).

For white flour products, add 0.2 mL or 4 drops HCHO and digest overnight. For products made from whole wheat and rye flours and from similar materials of high bran content, digest only 2–3 hr.

Pour digested material thru 5″ or 8″ No. 140 sieve, **44.002(u)**. While pouring, play forcible stream of hot H_2O from tap on this material. Wash well with large stream of hot H_2O. After complete washing (no starchy material visible unattached to bran), wash twice alternately with alcohol and $CHCl_3$ in that order, and then rinse thoroly with alcohol and finally with H_2O.

Transfer material to filter paper if little residue remains or to 1 or 2 L trap flask, **44.002(i)**(*3*), if large amt remains. Transfer bulk of material with spoon. Rinse residue from screen with 60% alcohol from wash bottle. Wash screen with forcible stream of hot H_2O, collecting final residue at one edge of screen and transferring to trap flask with stream of 60% alcohol as above. Add 400 or 900 mL 60% alcohol, depending on size of trap flask.

Boil 20 min. Cool to <20° and add 20 or 40 mL heptane, **44.003(u)**; fill flask with 60% alcohol, and trap off twice. Use care in stirring and adding alcohol to prevent emulsions or inclusion of air. If residue in flask tends to rise, stir material down 2 or 3 times. Filter trapped-off material and examine microscopically.

44.056 ***Acid Hydrolysis Method (25)***

(Rapid method; also applicable to flours)

Post-milling contamination.—Add 225 g sample to 2 L beaker contg ca 1 L H_2O and 30 mL HCl. Wet product completely and, for flour, stir until slurry is practically lump-free. Add antifoam soln, **44.003(g)**, cover with watch glass, and heat 15–20 min in autoclave at 121°. Let pressure fall to 0 before opening vent valve. Transfer digest in small portions to 5″ or 8″ No. 140 sieve, **44.002(u)**, washing thoroly between addns with needle spray from aerator. After all sample has been transferred, continue washing until there is no further reduction in amt of residue. Proceed as in **44.055**, par. 5, beginning "After complete washing . . ."

44.057 ★ **Pre- and Post-Milling Contamination** ★

Direct trapping. *See* **44.056**, 12th ed.

White Breads and High-Fat Products

44.058 Light Filth (*26*)—Official First Action

Add 1 L hot (55–70°) tap H_2O to 2 L beaker. Add 20 mL emulsifier, **44.003(r)**(*2*), and 5 mL (**r**)(*1*), and mix well. Add 225 g sample, breaking any crust to <1 sq in. Stir well. Proceed with either autoclave, (**a**), or steam bath, (**b**), digestion.

(**a**) *Autoclave.*—Add 30 mL HCl with stirring. Add 1 mL antifoam soln, **44.003(g)**. Autoclave as in **44.002** (**b**)(*1*) or (**b**)(*2*) for 30 min at 121°.

(**b**) *Steam bath.*—Add 90 mL HCl with stirring. Heat in steam bath 10 min. Add 1 mL antifoam soln. Boil 15 min on mag. stirrer-hot plate, **44.002(p)**, keeping beaker covered with watch glass.

Wet sieve on No. 230 plain weave sieve, **44.002(u)**, with hot H_2O (55–70°). Sieve until effluent is clear and foam is gone. Transfer sieve retainings to original beaker. (*Caution:* Do not allow sample in beaker or sieve to cool.) Add 30 mL HCl and dil. to 1 L with H_2O. Stir on stirrer-hot plate, and bring to bp. Boil 6 min, add 50 mL mineral oil, **44.003(y)**, and continue heating until boiling resumes. Transfer beaker to cool mag. stirrer and stir mag., **44.004(b)**, 3 min.

Promptly transfer beaker contents to percolator, **44.002(i)**(*2*), contg ca 250 mL H_2O. Rinse beaker into percolator and bring vol. to 1700 mL mark with H_2O. After 1 min, stir percolator contents with glass rod. Place rod in beaker and set aside to receive final oil drain. Let stand 2 min. Drain oil to 250 mL mark and discard drainings. Refill percolator with H_2O. Continue drain and refill cycles until lower aq. phase is almost clear. Drain oil to 250 mL mark. Drain oil into original beaker. Wash percolator sides with min. of 50 mL H_2O and alcohol or isopropanol. If sides do not appear clean, follow with H_2O and 5% detergent wash, **44.003(q)**. Filter onto ruled paper and examine microscopically.

Breading of Frozen Food Products (*27*)
Official First Action

44.059 ***Light Filth***

Remove breading from product as in **18.002**. Weigh 50 g sepd breading in 1 L beaker. Add ca 300 mL hot tap H_2O (55–70°), 5 mL emulsifier CO-730, **44.003(r)**(*1*), 20 mL emulsifier DM-710, **44.003(r)**(*2*), and 60 mL HCl. Fill beaker to 600 mL with hot tap H_2O, stir well, and heat beaker in steam bath 20 min, stirring at 5 min intervals. Add 1 mL antifoam soln, **44.003(g)**. Boil 15 min on preheated hot plate, keeping beaker covered with watch glass. Wet-sieve on No. 230 plain weave sieve, **44.002(u)**, with hot H_2O, until effluent is clear and foam has dispersed. Transfer sieve retainings to original beaker with HCl-60% alcohol soln (1+9), and bring vol. to ca 600 mL. Add 50 mL mineral oil, **44.003(y)**, and stir mag., **44.004(b)**, 10 min. Place stirring rod in drain opening of percolator, **44.002(i)**(*2*), and add ca 250 mL acid-alcohol soln. Quant. transfer beaker contents to percolator. Add acid-alcohol soln to ca 6 cm from top, let stand 5 min, resuspend solids with stirring rod, and let stand addnl 5 min. Drain to ca 250 mL mark, refill percolator to original vol. with acid-alcohol soln, and repeat previous steps until lower aq. phase is almost clear. Drain oil to 250 mL mark and transfer to original beaker. Wash percolator sides with 50 mL H_2O, and alcohol or isopropanol. If sides do not appear clean, follow with

★ Surplus method—*see* inside front cover.

H_2O and 5% detergent wash, **44.003(q)**. Filter onto ruled paper and examine microscopically.

Alimentary Pastes

44.060 Light Filth (*28*)—Official First Action

Weigh 225 g sample into 1.5–2.0 L beaker. Add 1 L HCl (30+970) and 0.3 mL antifoam soln, **44.003(g)**. (For spaghetti, break into lengths that will not lie flat on bottom of beaker.) Autoclave 30 min at 121° as in either **44.002(b)**(*1*) or (*2*).

Wet sieve on No. 230 sieve, **44.002(u)**, with hot tap H_2O (50–70°) to remove all original liq. and major portion of fine material.

Return sieve retainings to original beaker with hot H_2O (60–100°), dilg to ca 1 L. Add 30 mL HCl, mag. stirring bar, and 50 mL mineral oil, **44.003(y)**.

Stir mag., **44.004(b)**, 6 min. Promptly transfer to percolator, **44.002(i)**(*2*), contg ca 250 mL H_2O. Rinse beaker into percolator with hot tap H_2O to bring to 1700 mL. After 3 min, drain oil interface to 250 mL. Discard drainings and refill by pouring hot tap H_2O down percolator sides to loosen adhering material and refill to 1700 mL mark. After 2–3 min, drain and refill for 2 more cycles. (Lower layer should be almost free of suspended material after last refill; if not, continue thru ≥1 recycles.) Finally, drain oil-H_2O interface to 250 mL mark, change to original beaker, and drain. Promptly wash down sides successively with ≥50 mL portions hot tap H_2O, isopropanol or alcohol, and hot tap H_2O. Use 5% detergent soln, **44.003(q)**, if necessary.

Transfer beaker contents to ruled filter paper with min. of 50 mL washes of hot H_2O, alcohol or isopropanol, and H_2O or detergent, using rubber policeman if necessary to clean sides of beaker.

BREAKFAST CEREALS

Corn and Rice, Ready-to-Eat and Corn Chip Products

44.061 Light Filth (*29*)—Official First Action

(*Caution: See* **51.039**.)

(**a**) *Cereals and food products containing no fats or oils.*—(Check ingredient label.) To 1–1.5 L beaker (depending on bulk of product), add 50 g sample, 500 mL hot (55–70°) tap H_2O, and 40 mL HCl. Bring mixt. to full boil on mag. stirrer-hot plate, **44.002(p)**, using slow stirring speed. Boil 20 min and wet sieve immediately on No. 230 sieve, **44.002(u)**, with forceful hot (55–70°) H_2O spray until residue no longer passes thru sieve and H_2O is clear. Wash sieve retainings either into 2 L Wildman trap flask, **44.002(i)**(*3*), or back into original beaker if Kilborn, (**i**)(*1*), or percolator, (**i**)(*2*), is to be used, using 40% isopropanol.

(*1*) *Trap flask.*—Bring vol. to 800 mL with 40% isopropanol and add 30 mL HCl. Raise stirring rod plunger and secure above liq. with clamp. Add mag. stirring bar, **44.002(p)**, and stir at slow speed while bringing mixt. to bp. Boil 5 min. Add 50 mL mineral oil, **44.003(y)**, and stir mag., **44.004(b)**, 3 min.

Remove from heat and fill with 40% isopropanol. Let stand 10 min and trap off, rinsing neck of flask and rod with isopropanol or alcohol. Filter trappings thru ruled paper.

(*2*) *Kilborn or percolator.*—Bring vol. in original beaker to 600 mL with 40% isopropanol and add 25 mL HCl. Bring to bp with slow stirring, boil 5 min, add 50 mL mineral oil, and stir mag. 3 min, **44,004(b)**.

Transfer from beaker to separator, rinsing beaker into separator with 40% isopropanol. If residue in separator is heavy, resuspend with glass rod. Rinse rod into separator.

Let stand 3 min and drain contents to within 3 cm of bottom of oil layer. Refill with hot (55–70°) tap H_2O. Repeat drain and refill steps with 3 min intervals, until H_2O phase is free of plant material. Discard drainings. Drain oil layer into original beaker, rinsing sides of separator alternately with isopropanol or hot H_2O and alcohol, using rubber policeman to clean sides. Filter contents of beaker thru ruled paper.

(**b**) *Cereals and food products containing natural and synthetic fats or vegetable oils.*—Proceed as in (**a**), beginning "... 500 mL hot (55–70°) tap H_2O, . . ." but also add to this mixt. 20 mL emulsifier, **44.003(r)**(*2*); then proceed as in (**a**) with no further changes.

Whole Wheat

44.062 Light Filth (*30*)—Official First Action

Weigh 50 g sample into 1 L beaker. Add 500 mL H_2O and 40 mL HCl. Boil 20 min with mag. stirring to keep solids from scorching. Immediately after boiling, wet-sieve on No. 230 sieve, **44.002(u)**, with hot (55–70°) tap H_2O until effluent is clear. Transfer sieve retainings with isopropanol to preshaped filter paper cup, using ≥24 cm paper and 150 and 250 mL beakers, **44.002(k)**. Transfer paper and retainings to Hirsch funnel. Apply vac. to apparent dryness. Turn vac. off, add 150 mL isopropanol, and vac. dry. Repeat isopropanol washing and vac. drying 2 more times.

Transfer filter paper retainings with 40% isopropanol to 2 L trap flask contg 25 mL oleate soln (10 g Na oleate, **44.003(dd)**, dild to 100 mL with 40% isopropanol and stirred in at room temp.). Bring vol. of flask to 800 mL with 40% isopropanol. Boil 5 min with mag. stirring. Cool contents of flask to 23±2° with either air or H_2O cooling. Add 50 mL flotation liq., **44.003(s)**, and stir mag. 3 min, **44.004(b)**. Fill flask with 40% isopropanol by slowly running isopropanol down rod onto top of stopper, held ca 3 mm above liq. Let stand 3 min and trap off. Add 50 mL flotation liq. and stir ca 15 sec. Add 40% isopropanol as needed to fill flask. Let stand 20 min and perform second trapping. Combine trappings. Filter thru ruled filter paper and examine microscopically.

EGGS AND EGG PRODUCTS (*31*)
OFFICIAL FIRST ACTION

(Eggs may be contaminated with chicken excrement, dirt, sand, metal fragments, hairs, and feathers, depending upon condition of the eggs, method of manufacture, and storage conditions. Method of isolation of contaminants depends upon nature of product (whole, whites, or yolks) and physical state (fresh, frozen, or dried).)

44.063 ***Reagents***

(**a**) *Anionic surfactant.*—Na *N*-methyl-*N*-tall oil acid taurate, Igepon TK-32 (GAF Corp.), or equiv.

(**b**) *Phenolphthalein soln.*—Prep. 5% soln in alcohol, dil. with equal vol. H_2O, and filter.

(**c**) *Disodium phosphate soln.*—Filtered satd soln (ca 100 g anhyd. salt/L), and filtered 6% (anhyd. basis) aq. soln.

(**d**) *Trisodium phosphate soln.*—Filtered satd soln.

(**e**) *Tetrasodium EDTA soln.*—10% filtered aq. soln of Na_4-EDTA.

44.064 Light and Heavy Filth and Other Extraneous Materials

(**a**) *Whole eggs or yolks.*—Thaw frozen sample at room temp. or in cold running H_2O. Weigh 100 g thawed sample into 250 mL centrf. bottle. Add 30 mL 6% Na_2HPO_4 and stir. Shake vigorously 1.5–2.0 min, add addnl 30 mL 6% Na_2HPO_4, and shake ca 2 min. Dil. with 6% reagent to fill bottle and centrf. whole eggs 5 min at 1500 rpm and yolks 5 min at 800 rpm. Decant ca ⅔ liq. into

1.5 or 2.0 L beaker and isolate light filth as in (**b**). Add ca equal vol. 6% Na_2HPO_4 soln to residue in bottle, shake well, and recentrf. Decant closely. To sediment in bottle add ca ½ vol. H_3PO_4 and warm on steam bath. Transfer to 250 mL beaker, boil 3–5 min, and filter while boiling. Examine at 30× for metal and glass fragments, and chicken excrement. Check amorphous white material for uric acid as in **44.177**.

(**b**) *Egg whites.*—Use decanted whole egg or yolk material from (**a**) or weigh 100 g thawed whites into 1.5 or 2.0 L beaker and add ca 300 mL 6% Na_2HPO_4 soln in small portions with thoro stirring. Add 16 mL Na_4EDTA soln, (**e**), then 12 mL phthln, (**b**). Let stand 10 min; then adjust to pH 7.6–8.0, using H_3PO_4 (1+9) or Na_3PO_4 soln as needed. Add 2 mL surfactant, (**a**), and readjust to pH 7.6–8.0, using short range pH paper. Add 200 mL pancreatin soln, **44.003(z)**, and readjust to 7.6–8.0.

Place in 37–38° H_2O bath to ca depth of digestion mixt.; stir, and adjust to pH 7.6–8.0 at ca 15 min intervals for ca 2 hr. Add 2 mL surfactant and dil. to 1.0–1.2 L with H_2O. Adjust to pH 8.0 and place in incubator at 37° overnight. Readjust to pH 8.0 and let stand 15–20 min without stirring. Decant in small portions onto ruled paper, using full suction, while washing paper with hot tap H_2O. Examine paper microscopically.

(**c**) *Dried egg yolks.*—Defat egg yolks as follows: Weigh 25 g sample into 150 mL tall-form beaker, add 50 mL pet ether, and stir thoroly (until smooth). While stirring, add solv. to almost fill beaker. Stir top again after 1 min, let stand 1 min, and decant solv. into larger beaker. Repeat defatting step twice more with pet ether. Filter combined washes thru smooth textured paper, air dry paper thoroly, and hold for pancreatin digestion. Discard solv. (*Caution: See* **51.011**.) Place 150 mL beaker on steam bath and remove solv. completely from residue with continuous stirring to prevent bumping. Transfer dried residue in beaker and dried residue on paper, using spatula, to 600 mL beaker and proceed as in (**d**).

(**d**) *Dried whole eggs.*—Weigh 25 g sample into 600 mL beaker, or continue with dried yolk residue from (**c**). Add mixt. of 90 mL satd soln of Na_2HPO_4 and 10 mL alcohol in small portions with stirring. (Suspension must be smooth and finely divided at this point.) With stirring, add 12 mL Na_4EDTA soln, (**e**), then 5 mL phthln, (**b**). If intense red develops, discharge with H_3PO_4 (1+9). Adjust to pH 7.6–8.0 with satd Na_3PO_4 soln, using short range indicator paper. Add 200 mL pancreatin soln, **44.003(z)**, to suspension. Continue as in (**b**), beginning "Place in 37–38° H_2O bath . . ."

(**e**) *Dried whites.*—Weigh 25 g sample into 250 or 400 mL beaker. Dil. 4.5 mL surfactant, (**a**), to 35 mL with H_2O and add to beaker in portions of 5 mL, rotating and shaking beaker until sample absorbs each portion. Let soak 10–15 min; then add 20 mL H_2O in 4–5 portions with thoro stirring after each addn. Stir to smooth slurry. (Material must be finely dispersed before proceeding.) Add 7 mL Na_4EDTA soln, (**e**), then 3 mL phthln, (**b**). Transfer to 1.5 or 2 L beaker and dil. with H_2O to 700–800 mL. Adjust to pH 7.2–7.6 and add 200 mL pancreatin soln, **44.003(z)**. Continue as in (**b**), beginning "Place in 37–38° H_2O bath . . ."

44.065 Sedimentation Method for Chicken Excrement and Heavy Filth

(**a**) *Frozen whole eggs or yolks.*—Examine by **44.064(a)**.

(**b**) *Dried egg yolk.*—Add 25 g sample in small portions with continuous stirring to mixt. of 75 mL H_3PO_4 (1+9) and 5 mL surfactant, **44.063(a)**, in 150 mL tall-form beaker. Stir to smooth paste and add H_3PO_4, few mL at time, to fill beaker while stirring. Stir top layer 1 min and let stand 5 min. Decant ca ⅔ vol. into 250 mL beaker and add H_3PO_4 (1+9) to both beakers equal to vol. present. Stir contents of both beakers 1 min and let stand 5 min. Again stir top layers 1 min and slowly add H_3PO_4 with stirring to fill both beakers. Let stand 5 min and repeat stirring and standing. Decant both beakers closely into 1 L beaker.

Dil. material in 1 L beaker with H_2O, stirring continuously, until full. Stir top layer 1 min and let stand 5 min, and repeat stirring and standing. Decant closely, discarding supernates. Composite all residues in 250 mL beaker by transferring with H_3PO_4 (1+9) from wash bottle. Decant acid and floating egg material and transfer residue to ruled paper with H_2O, using min. suction Wash residue with two 30 mL portions H_2O, using min. suction. Examine microscopically, keeping paper moist. Check amorphous white material for uric acid as in **44.177**.

POULTRY, MEAT, AND FISH AND OTHER MARINE PRODUCTS

44.066 ★ Filth and Sand in Chicken Giblet Paste ★ Procedure

See **40.063**, 11th ed.

44.067 ★ Glass in Meat Scraps—Procedure ★

Floating off tissues and examining residue. *See* **40.065**, 11th ed.

Shellfish

44.068 Shell in Canned Crabmeat (*32*)—Official First Action

Weigh 57 g (2 oz) representative sample into 400 mL beaker. Add 150 mL 1.5% NaOH soln and stir to break up lumps. Add 10 drops *1% aq. Alizarin Red S* indicator. Heat until meat has been digested (10 min at ca 80°), stirring 3 or 4 times. Pour on No. 12 sieve nested in No. 60 sieve, **44.002(u)**, and wash with H_2O. Wash shell from both sieves onto weighed paper, dry at 100°, and cool to room temp. Weigh and count shell. Report shell as number of pieces and wt/lb.

44.069 Light Filth in Canned Crabmeat (*33*) Official First Action

Transfer entire contents of ≤7 oz (200 g) can (or 7 oz portion of larger sample) to 2 L trap flask, **44.002(i)**(*3*). Thoroly wash can (and parchment, if present) with tap H_2O and add washings to flask. Add ca 800 mL hot (55–70°) tap H_2O. With mag. stirring, **44.004(b)**, heat to bp. Add 50 mL mineral oil, **44.003(y)**, and stir mag. 3 min while continuing to boil. Remove flask from heat, fill with hot tap H_2O, and let stand 30 min, stirring gently by hand at 10 and 20 min. Trap off into 400 mL beaker. Add 30 mL mineral oil to trap flask. With stirring bar spinning at max. speed, disperse oil thruout aq. (lower) phase, stirring by hand. Stir mag. 5 min at max. speed. Fill flask with hot tap H_2O and let stand 20 min, stirring gently by hand at 10 min. Trap off into same beaker. Wash mouth of trap flask with isopropanol and decant washings into beaker.

Transfer to 2 L percolator, **44.002(i)**(*2*), contg ca 250 mL H_2O. Rinse beaker into percolator and bring vol. to ca 1700 mL with H_2O at room temp., ca 20°. Let stand 3 min. Drain oil to 250 mL mark and discard drainings. Repeat fill and drain cycle ≥2 more times. Drain remaining oil and H_2O into original 400 mL beaker. Wash percolator sides with 1% detergent soln, **44.003(q)**, and isopropanol, and collect washings in beaker. Filter onto ruled paper and examine microscopically. If filtering action slows, use new filter paper.

★ Surplus method—*see* inside front cover.

44.070 Shell in Canned Clams and Oysters (*32*)
Official First Action

Weigh 57 g (2 oz) representative sample into 600 mL beaker. Continue as in **44.068**, except digest by boiling ca 15 min.

Canned Fish and Fish Products

44.071 Light Filth (*34*)—Official First Action

For ≤8 oz (225 g) samples, transfer entire contents of can (or 8 oz portion of larger sample) to 1.5 L beaker and break up lumps with spatula. Wash can thoroly with small amt of isopropanol and add washings to beaker. Add 50 mL HCl and H_2O to make 800 mL. With mag. stirring, heat to bp and boil 20 min. (If product foams, add H_2O occasionally.) Add 50 mL mineral oil, **44.003(y)**, and stir mag., **44.004(b)**, 5 min while continuing to boil.

Transfer to 2 L percolator, **44.002(i)**(*2*), contg ca 250 mL H_2O. Retain the 1.5 L beaker to fill percolator with H_2O during refill cycles. Fill percolator with hot tap H_2O (55–70°) to within 3 cm of top. Let stand 3 min and drain contents to ca 3 cm of bottom of oil layer. (If large amt of suspended solids is present, let stand longer to permit sepn of oil.) Repeat drain and refill steps at 3 min intervals until aq. phase appears clear. Finally, slowly drain percolator to min. vol. of aq. phase without loss of oil phase. Drain oil layer into 600 mL beaker. Wash percolator with warm H_2O, 5% detergent soln, **44.003(q)**, H_2O, and isopropanol in sequence, using ca 50 mL per wash, and collect washings in 600 mL beaker. Filter onto ruled paper and examine microscopically.

Canned Shrimp

44.072 Light Filth (*35*)—Official First Action

For shrimp <2.5 cm long, place entire contents of can into 2 L beaker contg mag. stirring bar. For larger shrimp, skewer on probe, and wash each shrimp with hot (55–70°) H_2O from plastic squeeze bottle over 2 L beaker contg stirring bar. Discard shrimp. Wash can thoroly, pouring washings into beaker. Bring H_2O level in beaker to ca 925 mL with hot tap H_2O. Add 25 mL HCl and 50 mL light mineral oil, **44.003(y)**. Boil and stir mag., **44.004(b)**, 3 min. Transfer promptly to percolator, **44.002(i)**(*2*), which has its rubber hose fitting clamped shut as close to tubulation opening as possible and contg ca 200 mL hot tap H_2O. Reserve beaker. Add ca 800 mL addnl hot tap H_2O. Let stand 10 min. Drain oil layer to ca 7.5 cm from bottom, using rod to force shrimp tissue thru tubulator, if necessary. Remove rod, and wash with hot H_2O into reserved beaker. Reserve rod for further washings. Drain percolator to 300 mL mark, let stand 1 min and slowly drain and discard remaining aq. phase until min. vol. remains. Do not let vortex form, as it may cause loss of oil. Drain oil layer into reserved beaker. Filter thru ruled paper. Wash paper with 55–70° hot tap H_2O. Alternately wash percolator and rod with 5% detergent soln, **44.003(q)**, and hot tap H_2O. Filter onto the ruled filter paper and examine microscopically.

Uncooked Pork Sausage and Ground Beef or Hamburger

44.073 Enzyme Digestion Method (*36*)
Official First Action

Grind sausage, using meat grinder with end plate having 3/16" holes. Weigh 225 g sample into 1.5–2 L beaker. Add 980 mL warm H_2O and 20 mL emulsifier, **44.003(r)**(*1*), and stir 5 min. Add 20 mL HCl and stir 1 min. Proceed with overnight digestion, (**a**), or rapid digestion, (**b**).

With ground beef, use only overnight digestion with 5.0 g 1:10,000 or 10 g NF pepsin. In flotation, (**c**), omit addn of 50 mL HCl and subsequent boiling. After addn of light mineral oil, let stand 20 min, instead of 10 min.

(**a**) *Overnight digestion.*—Add 0.5 g 1:10,000 pepsin (Difco Laboratories, or equiv.) or 2.0 g NF pepsin and stir 1 min. Digest in 50° H_2O bath or incubator 18 hr. Add 5 mL Triton X-114, **44.003(jj)**(*2*), and stir 1 min. Keep all samples at digestion temp. in bath until ready to sieve. Sieve portionwise on No. 230 sieve with hot H_2O spray. Transfer to ruled filter paper if small amt residue remains on sieve or proceed with flotation, (**c**).

(**b**) *Rapid digestion.*—Add 2.0 g 1:10,000 pepsin or 10 g NF pepsin and stir 1 min. Digest in 62° H_2O bath 2 hr. Add 5 mL Triton X-114, **44.003(jj)**(*2*), and stir 1 min. Keep all samples at digestion temp. until ready to sieve. Sieve portionwise on No. 230 sieve. Proceed with flotation, (**c**).

(**c**) *Flotation.*—Wet residue on sieve with 40% isopropanol and immediately transfer quant. to 2 L trap flask, using 40% isopropanol. Bring vol. to 1 L with 40% isopropanol and add 50 mL HCl. Add mag. stirring bar, **44.002(p)**, and, with gentle stirring, boil 10 min on mag. stirrer-hot plate. Cool to room temp. in cold H_2O bath and add 40 mL flotation liq., **44.003(s)**. Stir mag. 3 min, **44.004(b)**. Let oil phase sep. 1 min, and slowly fill flask with 40% isopropanol by letting liq. flow down stoppered rod while top of stopper is maintained just above flask contents. After filling flask, gently stir settled plant material with stoppered rod 5–10 sec. Let stand undisturbed 5 min and immediately trap off. Add 25 mL light mineral oil, **44.003(y)**, stir gently by hand 30 sec, and let stand 10 min. Repeat trapping. Wash flask neck thoroly with isopropanol and transfer washings to beaker contg trappings. Filter onto ruled paper and examine microscopically.

44.074 Alternative Method for Sausages (*37*)
Official First Action

(*Caution: See* **51.056**.)

(**a**) *Bulk or link sausages that are easily teased apart.*—Weigh 225 g sample into 1.5–2 L beaker. Add 1 L 10% Tergitol soln, **44.003(jj)**(*1*), and 75 × 12 mm stirring bar; stir mag., 5 min, or until thoroly dispersed. Sieve portionwise on No. 230 sieve, **44.002(u)**. Form filter paper around 1 L beaker, **44.002(k)**, moistening with H_2O to make paper pliable. Insert paper into buchner, 91 mm id plate, wash with isopropanol, and aspirate to near dryness.

Wet residue on sieve with isopropanol and quant. transfer to filter paper cup with isopropanol. Add enough isopropanol to cover residue and, after 1 min, apply vac. until dripping ceases. Transfer paper cup to 1 L beaker and add 300 mL $CHCl_3$. Boil on steam bath 5 min. Let soln cool few min, lift paper, drain, and transfer to 300 mL fresh $CHCl_3$. Repeat 5 min boil and drain. Return paper cup to buchner and apply vac. until dripping ceases. Cover residue with isopropanol for 1 min, reapply vac., and continue to aspirate 5 min. Quant. transfer residue to 2 L trap flask, using 40% isopropanol, and proceed as in **44.073(c)**, second sentence.

(**b**) *Link sausages compressed into casings so that product is not easily teased apart.*—Remove casing and weigh 225 g sample into 2 L beaker. Add 1 L 10% Tergitol soln, **44.003(jj)**(*1*), and stir with mech. stirrer, **44.002(f)**, at max. speed at which no splashing occurs, 15 min or until thoroly dispersed. Proceed as in (**a**), beginning, "Sieve portionwise on No. 230 sieve, . . ."

FRUITS AND FRUIT PRODUCTS

Apple Butter

44.075 Rot—Official Final Action

Make mold count as in **44.096**, after first dilg 50 mL well-mixed sample with 50 mL stabilizer soln, **44.003(gg)**.

44.076 Light Filth—Official First Action

Weigh 100 g well mixed sample into 400 mL beaker, add enough cold H_2O to obtain uniform dispersion, and transfer to 2 L trap flask, **44.002(i)**(*3*). Add 35 mL heptane, **44.003(u)**, and stir. Add cold H_2O to bring heptane into neck of flask. Let stand 30 min with occasional stirring, and trap off. Transfer trapping to second flask contg ca 1 L H_2O, stir, fill flask with H_2O, and let stand 15 min with occasional stirring. Trap off, filter onto ruled paper, and examine paper microscopically.

★ *Dried Apple Chops—Official First Action* ★

44.077 Heavy Filth

See **40.069**, 11th ed.

44.078 Insects and Light Filth

See **40.070**, 11th ed.

Canned Fruits and Juices

44.079 *Geotrichum* Mold (*1*)—Official First Action

(Applicable to products where mold is not masked by large amts of tissues)

Det. net wt (g) of can contents. Drain contents 3 min on 8″ No. 8 sieve, **44.002(u)**, in pan. Remove fruit from sieve with spoon and discard. Wash can and sieve with ca 300 mL H_2O from wash bottle, saving liq. and washings. Quant. transfer combined liq. and washings onto 5″ No. 16 sieve resting in 2 L beaker. Wash residue on sieve with ca 50 mL H_2O, and discard residue. Quant. transfer combined liq. and washings onto 5″ No. 230 sieve, tilted at ca 30° angle, and discard liq. and washings. Wash tissue to lower edge of sieve with H_2O.

With wash bottle and spatula, transfer residue from sieve to 50 mL graduated thick-walled centrf. tube with min. vol. H_2O. For vols $\leq$10 mL, use (**a**); $>$10 mL but $\leq$30 mL, use (**b**); and $>$30 mL, use (**c**).

(**a**) Dil. to 10 mL. Add 1 drop crystal violet staining soln, **44.003(p)**, and mix thoroly. Add 10 mL stabilizer soln, **44.003(gg)**, to bring total vol. to 20 mL. Proceed as in (**d**).

(**b**) Dil. to 40 mL. Add 3 drops crystal violet soln. Mix well. Centrf. ca 6 min at ca 2200 rpm, **44.082**. Decant and discard supernate. Bring vol. of sediment in centrf. tube to nearest 5 mL graduation by adding H_2O. Note combined vol. of sediment and H_2O, add equal vol. stabilizer soln, and mix thoroly but gently. Record mL total vol. of mixt. in centrf. tube, (V). Proceed as in (**d**).

(**c**) Transfer to 100 mL g-s graduate. Dil. to 100 mL and mix well. Quickly pour off two 25 mL aliquots into sep. centrf. tubes and proceed as in (**b**). Keep final vols equal; V = sum of vol. in both tubes.

(**d**) Pipet 2 sep. 0.5 mL portions, using pipet, **44.002(s)**, and apply as streak ca 4 cm long to each of 2 rot fragment counting slides, **44.002(t)** (4 in case of (**c**)). With transmitted diffused light, examine each slide at 30–45×, using stereoscopic microscope. Count recognizable *Geotrichum* mycelial fragments (usually $\geq$3 characteristic hyphal branches) on each of 2 slides. Record total on 2 slides.

(**e**) *Calculations.*—Calc. mycelial fragments/500 g product: $N = [S \times V \times 500]/W$, where S = total mycelial fragments on 2 slides; V = mL total vol. of mixt. in centrf. tube; and W = net wt product sample in g.

Blackberries, Blueberries, Loganberries, Raspberries, and Cherries; Fresh, Canned, and Frozen

44.080 Rot in Blackberries, Raspberries, and Other Drupelet Berries—Official Final Action

(**a**) *Frozen with or without sugar.*—Pulp berries thru cyclone, **44.002(h)**, and mix thoroly. Mix 25 g pulp with 50 mL stabilizer soln, **44.003(gg)**. Make mold count as in **44.096**.

(**b**) *Frozen in sirup, canned in sirup or water.*— Drain berries 2 min on No. 20 sieve. Pulp, dil., and make mold count as in (**a**).

44.081 Maggots in Blueberries and Cherries—Procedure

Weigh 567 g (20 oz) fresh fruit or use No. 2 can of processed fruit. Add 100 mL H_2O to fresh or frozen fruit and boil 5 min, with frequent stirring. (Omit this step with canned fruit.) Transfer 1 cm layer of fruit to No. 6 sieve immersed in pan of H_2O. Shake loose maggots and debris thru sieve. Carefully mash fruit under H_2O to rub any remaining maggots thru sieve. Rinse and discard any pulp and seeds. Repeat process with another portion of fruit.

After all fruit is screened, transfer mixt. to black-bottom pan. (With cherries, transfer first to No. 6 sieve resting in ca 3 cm H_2O, shake sieve until maggots drop thru, and discard pulp on sieve.) Slowly decant H_2O and pulp from pan. Add more H_2O and repeat decantation. Pick out and count maggots by examination of contents of pan. Transfer contents of this pan to white-bottom pan and count maggots in pan.

Citrus and Pineapple Juices, Canned, Single Strength

44.082 Mold Count—Official Final Action

Pour contents of can into beaker and mix thoroly by pouring back and forth between beaker and can $\geq$12 times. After mixing, transfer 50 mL juice to graduated 50 mL conical-bottom centrf. tube. Centrf. 10 min at 2200 rpm, using International type SB, size 1 centrf., (Damon/IEC Div., 300 Second Ave, Needham Hts, MA 02194) with 8-place No. 240 head (distance from center of centrf. head to center of cups (at rest) is 5¼″), or other centrf. giving equiv. centrifugal force as computed by following formula: $N_1^2r_1 = N_2^2r_2$, where N = rpm, and r = radius of centrf. arm. Check speed with tachometer, since rheostat does not necessarily indicate speed in rpm.

Spontaneously let centrf. come to complete stop before removing tubes and read vol. sediment in centrf. tube. Remove tube and decant supernate without disturbing sediment. With pineapple juice, add 0.5 mL HCl (to dissolve oxalate crystals). Add H_2O to tube to bring level to 10 mL mark and then add 5 mL stabilizer soln, **44.003(gg)**. Thoroly mix sediment, H_2O, and stabilizer soln and pour into small beaker. Mix by pouring back and forth between beaker and tube $\geq$6 times. Stir mixt. thoroly in beaker and proceed as in **44.096**. In addn to checking microscopic fields, indicate those fields positive due to *Geotrichum candidum*.

44.083 Fly Eggs and Maggots—Official First Action

Filter 250 mL thoroly mixed sample thru buchner fitted with 10XX bolting cloth, **44.002(e)** (wire mesh screen under bolting

★ Surplus method—*see* inside front cover.

cloth facilitates filtration). Pour juice slowly to avoid accumulation of excess pulp on cloth (2 or 3 cloths may be necessary). Examine filters microscopically.

44.084 Light Filth—Official First Action

To 250 mL juice in 2 L trap flask add 15 mL castor oil, **44.003(l)**, and fill with enough hot H_2O (ca 70°), stirring vigorously, to bring oil layer into neck of flask. Let stand 30 min. Trap off, filter, and examine.

Cranberry Sauce

44.085 Mold—Official Final Action

(**a**) *Strained sauce.*—Immerse unopened can of sauce in boiling H_2O bath 30–45 min to facilitate breaking gel. Remove can from bath and open carefully to avoid loss of sauce thru sudden release of pressure. Transfer contents into beaker (1 L for No. 2 can). Stir sauce to break gel. (Slow-speed mech. mixer (350–450 rpm) may be used.) Thoroly mix 50 g stirred sauce with 50 g stabilizer soln, **44.003(gg)**. Make mold count of mixt. as in **44.096**.

(**b**) *Whole sauce (seeds and skins included).*—Pulp contents of container (if considerably >1 lb (500 g), such as No. 10 can, remove well-mixed aliquot of 1 lb) thru cyclone to remove skins and seeds, and prep. homogeneous pulp. Mix 50 g of this pulp with 50 g stabilizer soln, **44.003(gg)**. Make mold count as in **44.096**.

Fig and Fruit Paste

44.086 Light and Heavy Filth (*38*)—Official First Action

(**a**) *Light filth.*—Weigh 100 g paste into 1 L beaker. Add 400 mL boiling H_2O and mag. stirring bar. Boil on mag. stirrer-hot plate, **44.002(p)**, until all lumps are disintegrated. Wet sieve mixt. on 8″ No. 140 sieve, **44.002(u)**, with hot tap H_2O to remove fine and sol. material. Transfer residue from sieve to 2 L trap flask, **44.002(i)**(*3*), with H_2O. Add H_2O to bring vol. to ca 900 mL, and ext twice with 35 and 25 mL kerosene, **44.003(x)**, as in **44.004(a)**. Examine papers microscopically as in **44.004(f)**(*1*) and (**g**).

(**b**) *Heavy filth.*—Empty remaining trap flask contents and rinsings onto 8″ No. 140 sieve. Wet sieve with hot tap H_2O to remove kerosene as completely as possible. Transfer material from sieve to 1 L beaker and add hot H_2O to ca 400 mL. Boil vigorously 15 min, frequently adding 10% Na_4EDTA soln to keep pH ca 8. (Check with pH paper.) Transfer hot mixt. to 8″ No. 140 sieve. Wet sieve until seeds are completely sepd from fig tissue. Return residue on sieve to the 1 L beaker. Add H_2O to ca 300 mL, swirl, and quickly decant suspended fig tissue and filth elements onto ruled paper in Hirsch funnel, retaining seeds in beaker. Add H_2O and repeat decanting, changing paper as necessary. Examine papers for heavy filth elements at ca 30×.

44.087 Alternative Method for Light Filth (*39*) Official First Action

Weigh 100 g paste into 1 L beaker. Break paste into small lumps. Add 400 mL boiling H_2O and mag. stirring bar. Boil and stir on mag. stirrer-hot plate, **44.002(p)**, until all lumps are disintegrated. Wet-sieve mixt. on 8″ No. 140 sieve, **44.002(u)**, with hot tap H_2O to remove fine and sol. material. Transfer residue from sieve to 2 L trap flask, **44.002(i)**(*3*), with H_2O. Add H_2O to bring vol. to ca 900 mL, add 35 mL kerosene, **44.003(x)**, and ext as in **44.004(a)**. Make second extn with 25 mL kerosene.

If trapped material is relatively free of plant tissue, filter on ruled paper. Examine microscopically for whole and equiv. insects only, as in **44.001(c)**(*1*). Det. insect head count for fig paste from number of whole or equiv. forms of lepidoptera and coleoptera.

If trapped material contains excessive plant tissue, transfer with ca 150 mL H_2O to percolator, **44.002(i)**(*2*), contg ca 250 mL H_2O. Fill percolator to within 5 cm of top, let kerosene layer sep., and drain slowly to 250 mL mark. Repeat refill and drain cycle if necessary. Drain remaining liq. into original beaker, rinsing percolator alternately with H_2O and acetone; filter and examine as above.

Jam and Jelly

44.088 Light Filth—Official First Action

(**a**) *Jam.*—Empty contents of jar into dish and mix thoroly. Weigh 100 g into beaker, add 200 mL H_2O (ca 50°), transfer to 1 L trap flask, **44.002(i)**(*3*), add 10 mL HCl, and boil ca 5 min. Cool to room temp., add 25 mL heptane, **44.003(u)**, and stir thoroly. Trap off, filter, and examine microscopically.

(**b**) *Jelly.*—Empty contents of jar into dish and mix thoroly. Weigh 100 g into beaker and add 300–400 mL hot H_2O; warm beaker, with stirring, until jelly dissolves, filter, and examine microscopically.

When so-called "jellies" contg small amts of fruit tissue will not filter thru paper, proceed as in (**a**).

Raisins

44.089 Light Filth (*40*)—Official First Action

(*Caution: See* **51.040** and **51.056**.)

Add 500 mL $CHCl_3$ to 225 g sample in 1 L beaker and boil on steam bath 10 min, keeping $CHCl_3$ vol. at ca 500 mL. Decant $CHCl_3$, holding back raisins with glass rod, onto 7.5 cm ruled filter paper in Hirsch funnel. Retain paper. Repeat 10 min $CHCl_3$ boil and decant. Using H_2O, wash filter retainings from paper back into beaker contg raisin tissue. Bring vol. in beaker to 700 mL with hot H_2O (55–70°) and rehydrate *in steam bath* 30 min. Sieve portionwise onto 8″ No. 8 sieve nested in 8″ No. 140 sieve, **44.002(u)**. Thoroly wash each portion with stream of hot H_2O while gently rubbing raisins over sieve with fingers. Microscopically examine any decomposed raisins for fly eggs and maggots.

Wet retainings on No. 140 sieve with 25% isopropanol, transfer to 2 L trap flask, **44.002(i)**(*3*), with 25% isopropanol, and bring vol. to 1 L. Add 70 mL HCl and mag. stirring bar to flask, heat to boiling, and continue for 10 min, slowly stirring on mag. stirrer-hot plate, **44.002(p)**. Cool to <25° in cold H_2O bath. Add 40 mL flotation oil (mix kerosene, **44.003(x)**, and mineral oil, **44.003(y)**, (1+2)) and stir mag., **44.004(b)**, 5 min. Let stand 1 min after gentle 10–15 sec stir with stoppered rod (*see* **44.004(a)**). Fill with deaerated 25% isopropanol by slowly running alcohol down rod onto top of stopper maintained ca 3 mm above liq. Let stand 15 min, gently stirring mixt. 2–3 times during first 10 min. Trap; filter first and second extns sep. Add 25 mL flotation oil and gently hand stir 1 min. Let stand 1 min; gently disturb oil-alcohol interface with several up-and-down strokes of stoppered rod to cause fine plant material to settle. Let stand 10 min. Perform second trapping. Thoroly wash flask neck with isopropanol. Pour trappings onto ruled filter paper and examine at 30×. If second extn is difficult to filter, pour onto No. 230 sieve, **44.002(u)**, and wash twice alternately with undild isopropanol and hot H_2O. Wash sieve retainings into 400 mL beaker with hot H_2O and add 7 mL HCl/100 mL H_2O. Boil 10 min and pour onto ruled filter paper.

Strawberries (Frozen)

44.090 Mold—Official Final Action

Pulp thawed berries thru cyclone and mix thoroly. (Pour juice thru cyclone last.) If necessary, remove air bubbles with suction or by mixing ca 100 g pulp with 3–5 drops *capryl alcohol.* Again mix thoroly and make mold count as in **44.096**.

Acid-Insoluble Residue (Soil) (*41*) Official Final Action

(Applicable to frozen fruits and vegetables)

44.091 ***Determination***

Remove frozen sample from container. Place in weighed plastic bag, reweigh, and seal tightly with rubber band. Thaw sample by immersing bag in hot H_2O and transfer contents to high-speed blender, washing inside of bag. Blend until sample is disintegrated and transfer to 2 L beaker. Nearly fill beaker with H_2O and mix contents thoroly by swirling. Let stand 10 min and decant supernate into second 2 L beaker. Refill first beaker with H_2O and repeat mixing. Fill second beaker with H_2O and mix by swirling. After 10 min, decant second beaker into third and first into second. Continue operation, decanting from third beaker into sink until vegetable material is washed from sample. If many seeds settle, float them off with hot 15% NaCl soln, increasing NaCl concn if necessary to complete flotation. Remove NaCl residue with hot H_2O. Collect mineral residue from the 3 beakers on ashless filter paper, and discard filtrate. Ignite paper in weighed porcelain crucible over medium Bunsen flame and place in furnace 1 hr at ca 600°. Cool, add 5 mL HCl, and heat to bp. Cool, add 10 mL H_2O, and reheat to bp. Filter and wash free from acid. Ignite, ash as before, and weigh to det. acid-insol. residue. Calc. % insol. residue = wt acid-insol. residue (g) × 100/net wt sample (g).

SUGARS AND SUGAR PRODUCTS

Candy

44.092 Filth—Official First Action

(**a**) *In hard candy, gum drops, gum, starch, or pectin-base candies.*—Dissolve in boiling HCl (1+70), filter thru rapid paper on Hirsch funnel, and examine microscopically.

(**b**) *In hard candy difficult to filter by* (**a**) *(e.g., licorice candy).*—Proceed as in (**c**).

(**c**) *All water-insoluble candy except those containing confectioners corn flakes, wheat bran, or other cereal fillers, and those whose major constituent, excluding chocolate coating, consists primarily of finely ground nutmeats (e.g., peanut butter, almond paste, etc.).* (**42**)—Weigh 225 g sample into 1.5–2 L beaker. Add 1 L 5% soln of Tergitol, **44.003(jj)**(*1*), and heat *in* steam bath 10 min. Stir 5–10 min on mag. stirrer-hot plate. Sieve portionwise on No. 230 sieve, **44.002(u)**. If residue on sieve is small, transfer directly to ruled filter paper; otherwise, transfer quant. to 2 L trap flask, using 40% isopropanol. Bring vol. to 1 L with 40% isopropanol and add 50 mL HCl. Gently stir on mag. stirrer-hot plate while heating *to full boil*. Immediately transfer flask to cool stirring unit and add 40 mL light mineral oil, **44.003(y)**. Stir mag., **44.004(b)**, 2 min. Let stand 1 min; then slowly fill flask with 40% isopropanol by running liq. down stoppered rod while top of stopper is maintained just above liq. After filling flask, gently stir settled plant material 5–10 sec with stoppered rod. Let stand undisturbed 2 min and immediately trap off. Add 25 mL light mineral oil, stir by hand gently 30 sec, and let stand 10 min. Repeat trapping. Wash flask neck thoroly with isopropanol and transfer washings to beaker contg trappings. Filter onto ruled paper and examine microscopically.

(**d**) *Water-insoluble candies containing confectioners corn flakes, wheat bran, or other cereal fillers, and those whose major constituent, excluding the chocolate coating, consists primarily of finely ground nutmeats (e.g., peanut butter, almond paste, etc.).* (**42**)—(*Caution: See* **51.011**, **51.040**, and **51.056**.) Proceed as in (**c**) thru sieving on No. 230 sieve. Wash residue on sieve with isopropanol. Form filter paper around 600 mL beaker, **44.002(k)**, moistening with H_2O to make paper pliable. Insert paper into 91 mm buchner, wash with isopropanol, and aspirate to near dryness. Quant. transfer residue on sieve to filter paper cup with isopropanol and add enough isopropanol to cover residue. After 1 min, apply vac. until dripping ceases. Place paper cup contg sieved residue in 1 L beaker, add 200 mL $CHCl_3$, and boil 5 min on steam bath. After few min of cooling, lift paper, drain, and transfer to 200 mL fresh $CHCl_3$. Repeat 5 min boil and drain. Return paper cup to buchner and apply vac. until dripping ceases. Cover residue with isopropanol 1 min, reapply vac., and continue to aspirate 5 min after visible dripping ceases. Proceed as in (**c**), beginning with "... transfer quant. to 2 L trap flask, using 40% isopropanol." Continue as in (**c**), except after bringing contents of flask to full boil, cool to room temp. in cold H_2O bath, and use flotation liq., **44.003(s)**, in place of mineral oil.

(**e**) *In chocolate candy coating.*—Heat 400 mL CH_2Cl_2 in 800 mL beaker to 30–35° and keep at this temp. Place portion of candy in wire basket (ca 8 cm diam. × 3 cm high) made from No. 8 screen and with wire handles. Move basket up and down thru CH_2Cl_2 until chocolate coating dissolves. Rinse each candy center with fine stream of CH_2Cl_2 from wash bottle and save center. Repeat with balance of sample. Stir CH_2Cl_2-chocolate suspension and pour thru No. 140 sieve. Transfer residue from sieve to filter paper and examine microscopically. Examine candy centers by appropriate method, (**a**), (**b**), (**c**), or (**d**).

Chewing Gum

44.093 ★ Filth—Procedure ★

See **44.082**, 11th ed.

Sirups, Molasses, and Honey

44.094 Filth—Official First Action

(**a**) Mix sample thoroly and dissolve 200 g in 200 mL hot H_2O acidified with 5 mL HNO_3. Filter at once thru rapid paper in Hirsch funnel. Wash with min. amt of hot H_2O and examine microscopically.

(**b**) *Alternative method.*—Dissolve 200 g in 500 mL hot H_2O. Filter at once thru 10XX bolting cloth in Hirsch funnel. Wash with min. amt of hot H_2O and examine microscopically.

Sugars

44.095 Filth—Official First Action

Dissolve 100 g sample in ca 200 mL hot H_2O. Boil, and filter at once thru rapid paper in Hirsch funnel. Examine microscopically.

VEGETABLES AND VEGETABLE PRODUCTS

Tomato Products (Not Dehydrated)

44.096 Molds (*43*)—Official Final Action

In making mold counts of tomato products, use juice as it comes from container. For catsup, place 50 mL stabilizer soln,

★ Surplus method—*see* inside front cover.

44.003(gg), in 100 mL graduate, add 50 mL well mixed catsup sample by displacement, and mix thoroly. In case of puree and paste, add H_2O to make mixt. with tomato sol. solids content that gives refractive index of 1.3448–1.3454 at 20° (1.3442–1.3448 at 25°). Add 2–6 drops capryl alcohol to each 100 mL mold count prepn to reduce or eliminate air bubbles on Howard mold counting slide.

Clean Howard cell, **44.002(o)**(*1*), so that Newton's rings are produced between slide and cover glass. Remove cover and with knife blade or scalpel, place portion of well mixed sample upon central disk; with same instrument, spread evenly over disk, and cover with glass so as to give uniform distribution. Use only enough sample to bring material to edge of disk. (It is of utmost importance that portion be taken from thoroly mixed sample and spread evenly over slide disk. Otherwise, when cover slip is put in place, insol. material, and consequently molds, may be more abundant at center of mount.) Discard any mount showing uneven distribution or absence of Newton's rings, or liq. that has been drawn across moat and between cover glass and shoulder.

Place slide under microscope and examine with such adjustment that each field of view covers 1.5 sq mm. (This area, which is essential, may frequently be obtained by so adjusting drawtube that diam. of field becomes 1.382 mm. When such adjustment is not possible, make accessory drop-in ocular diaphragm with aperture accurately cut to necessary size. Diam. of area of field of view can be detd by use of stage micrometer. When instrument is properly adjusted, vol. of liq. examined per field is 0.15 cu mm.) Use magnification of 90–125×. In those instances where identifying characteristics of mold filaments are not clearly discernible in std field, use magnification of ca 200× (8 mm objective) to confirm identity of mold filaments previously observed in std field. *See* Figs. **44:06–44:08.**

From each of ≥2 mounts examine ≥25 fields taken in such manner as to be representative of all sections of mount. Observe each field, noting presence or absence of mold filaments and recording results as pos. when aggregate length of ≤3 filaments present exceeds ⅙ of diam. of field. Calc. proportion of pos. fields from results of examination of all observed fields and report as % fields contg mold filaments.

44.097 ★ Yeasts and Spores—Official Final Action ★

See **40.086**, 11th ed.

44.098 Rot in Canned Tomatoes—Official Final Action

Drain contents of can 2 min on No. 2 sieve. For containers of <3 lb net wt, use 8" diam. sieve; for containers of ≥3 lb net wt, use 12" sieve. Examine drained tomatoes and record number and size of any rotten portions present. Pass drained tomatoes thru laboratory cyclone, **44.002(h)**. Make mold counts on both drained juice and pulped tomatoes as in **44.096**.

★ Surplus method—*see* inside front cover.

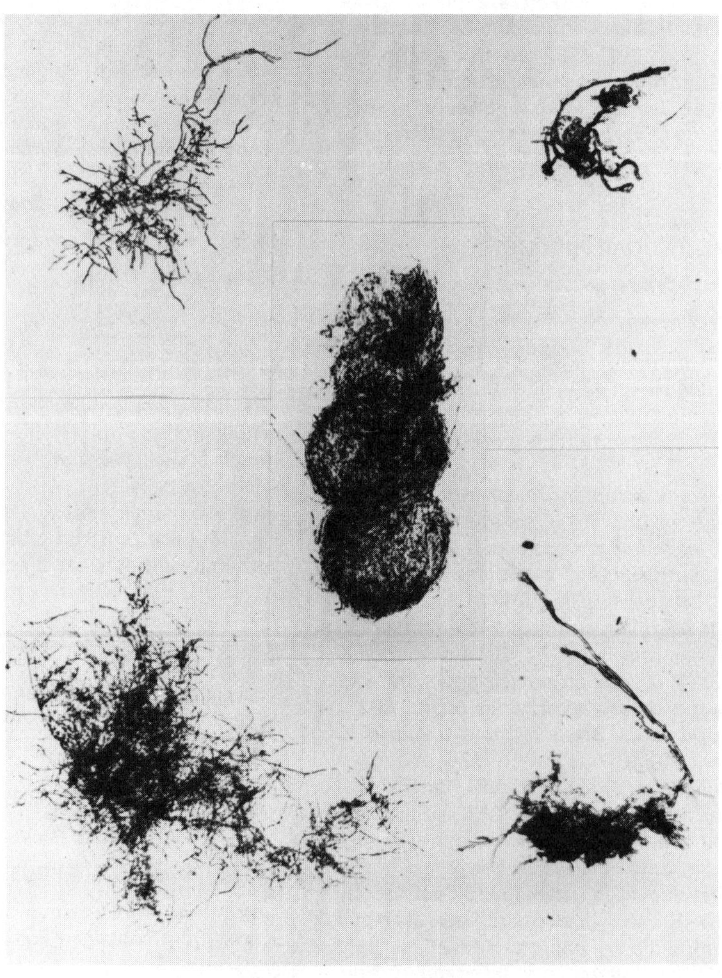

FIG. 44:06—Rot fragments from tomato puree. 40×

44.099 Rot Fragments in Comminuted Tomato Products (*44*)—Official Final Action

Weigh 10 g juice or 5 g catsup or sauce, and transfer with 100 mL H_2O to 400 mL beaker. In case of puree or paste add H_2O to make mixt. of tomato sol. solids content that gives refractive index of 1.3448–1.3454 at 20° (1.3442–1.3448 at 25°). Use 5 g mixt. for sample.

Add 10 drops crystal violet soln, **44.003(p)**, stir, and let stain 3 min. Add 200 mL H_2O and spread evenly over surface of 3" No. 60 sieve. Rinse beaker with 200 mL H_2O, and pour H_2O evenly over tomato tissue on sieve. Tilt sieve to ca 30° angle and wash tissue to lower edge with H_2O. Let tissue drain, and transfer with spatula to bottom of graduated tube ca 12 × 3 cm. Transfer remaining tissue by washing down with H_2O from dropper and immediately taking up tissue in wash H_2O before it has run thru sieve. Bring vol. of H_2O and tissue to 10 mL with H_2O. Add stabilizer soln, **44.003(gg)**, to bring vol. to 20 mL and mix well. Pipet 2 sep. 0.5 mL portions and spread evenly over 2 counting slides, **44.002(t)**, using pipet, **44.002(s)**. Let material flow slowly onto slide, spreading uniformly in center of slide to cover area ca 6 × 2 cm. Touch lower end of pipet to slide several times to ensure complete removal of material. Blow out last drop if necessary. Examine each slide at 30–45×, using transmitted light. Count number of rot fragments on each of the 2 slides, add results, and multiply by 2 (for 10 g sample) or 4 (for 5 g sample) to obtain number of rot fragments per g juice, catsup, sauce, or dild puree or paste. Rot fragment is defined as particle of tomato cellular material with one or more mold filaments attached. Some may appear as almost solid masses of mold. *See* Figs. **44:06–44:08**.

44.100 Fly Eggs and Maggots—Official First Action

(**a**) *Comminuted products.*—Thoroly mix sample and transfer 100 g to 2 L separator. Add 20–30 mL heptane and shake thoroly, releasing pressure as necessary. Fill separator with H_2O in such manner as to produce max. agitation. Place separator in ring stand and let settle; at 15 min intervals during 1 hr, drain 15–20 mL from separator, and gently shake separator with rotary motion to facilitate settling out of fly eggs and maggots. If drained liq. contains seeds, pass it thru No. 10 sieve, and thoroly rinse seeds and sieve, recovering both liq. portion and rinse H_2O in beaker. Filter thru 10XX bolting cloth, pretreated and dyed as in **44.002(e)**, in Hirsch funnel. Examine for eggs and maggots at ca 10×. If fly eggs or maggots are found in this examination, continue sepg and draining, as above, addnl hr.

(**b**) *Canned tomatoes.*—Pulp entire contents of can in such way that min. number of eggs and maggots are crushed or broken. (This may be done by passing material thru No. 6 or No. 8 sieve and adding seeds and residue remaining on sieve to pulp.)

Place 500 g of the well mixed pulped tomatoes in 6 L separator. Add 125–150 mL heptane, **44.003(u)**, and ca 1 L H_2O and shake

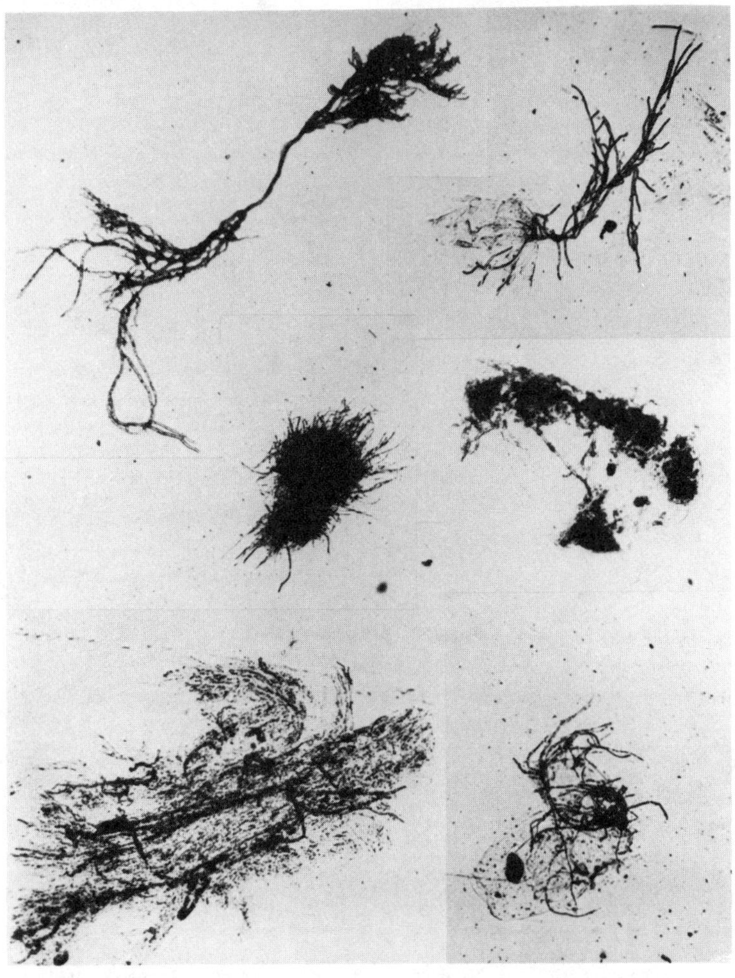

FIG. 44:07—Rot fragments from tomato puree. 40×

vigorously, releasing pressure as necessary. Fill separator with H_2O. Place separator in ring stand and let layers sep. At 15 min intervals during 1 hr, drain 25–30 mL from bottom of separator, and gently shake separator with rotary motion to facilitate settling of fly eggs and maggots. Each portion may be examined at once or combined with subsequent portions. Pass drained portions thru No. 10 sieve and thoroly rinse seeds and sieve, recovering both liq. portion and rinse H_2O in beaker. Filter thru 10XX bolting cloth in Hirsch funnel. Examine cloth for eggs and maggots at ca 10×. If fly eggs or maggots are found in this examination, continue sepg and draining, as above, addnl hr.

44.101 Light Filth

(**a**) *Comminuted products* (*Official First Action*).— Place 200 g of any tomato product except paste (where 100 g is used) in trap flask, **44.002(i)**(*3*), with 20 mL castor oil and mix well. Add enough hot tap H_2O (ca 70°) to fill flask. (At first, bubbles of air tend to bring up tomato tissues, but after several stirrings these begin to settle out, leaving H_2O layer near oil fairly clear.) Let stand with occasional gentle stirring 30 min; then trap off into beaker. Wash out neck of flask with heptane to remove adhering castor oil. Add little more hot H_2O to flask, stir, let stand 10 min, and then trap off again. (Occasionally it may be necessary to transfer trapped-off material to another trap flask and rewash to eliminate tomato tissue.) Filter trapped-off portion; thoroly wash beaker, sides of funnel, and paper with heptane to dissolve oil and speed filtration. Examine paper at 20–30×.

(**b**) *Canned tomatoes* (*Procedure*).—Drain entire can on No. 6 sieve, saving drained juice. (For cans contg <3 lb use 8" sieve; use larger sieve for larger cans or drain and rinse portionwise.) Rinse portion on sieve with hot H_2O (ca 70°) from wash bottle and transfer drained juice, fragments, and washings to 1 or more 2 L Wildman trap flasks (max. 900 mL/flask; No. 10 cans require ≥2). Bring vol. in flasks to ca 900 mL with H_2O (70°) and add 20–25 mL castor oil. Tilt flask to ca 45° and mix 1 min with brisk rotary motion (200–250 strokes/min). Avoid splashing thru surface with stopper. Add hot H_2O to bring oil layer into neck and let stand 30 min with occasional stirring. Trap off into beaker oil-H_2O layer and any debris that rises. Wash out oil in neck with heptane. Add ca 10 mL hot H_2O to flask, stir, let stand 10 min, and trap into same beaker. Add 25–30 mL heptane to

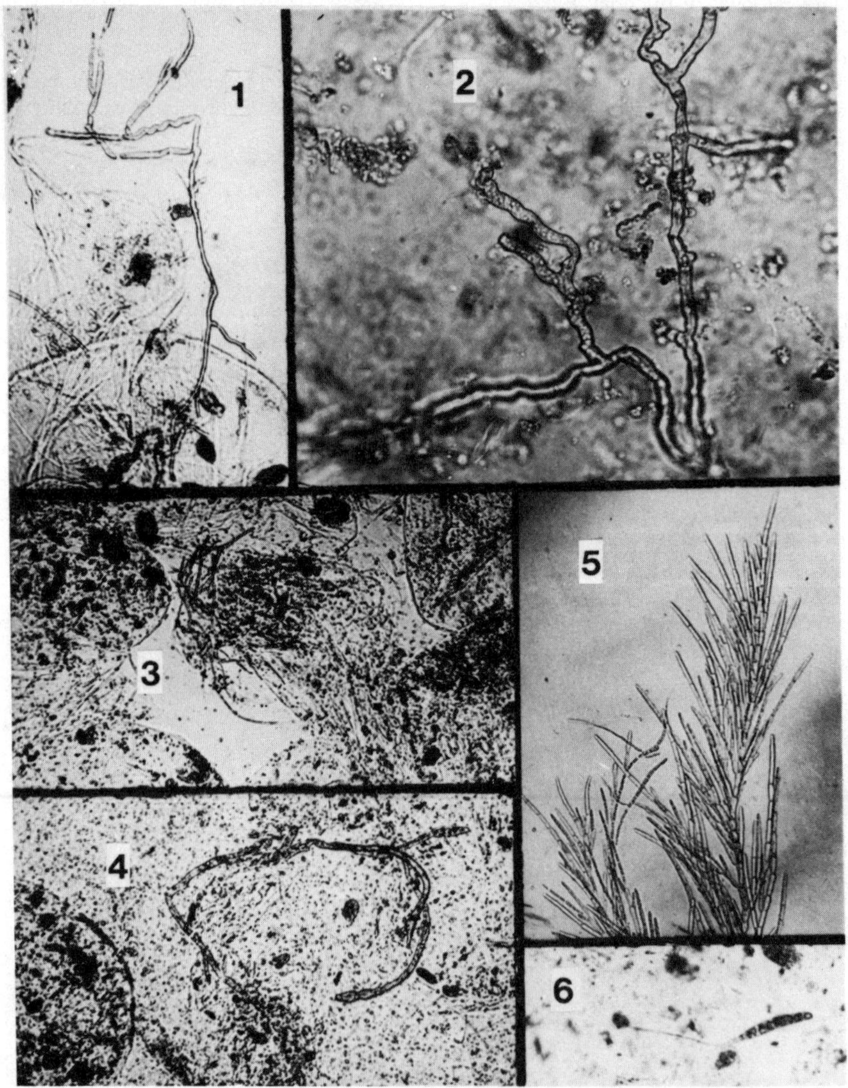

FIG. 44:08—Mold filaments in tomato products (100×). 1, branching mold and tomato cells. 2, coarse mold showing nonparallel and parallel walls, branching, granulation, and blunt tips. 3, very fine mold. 4, mold showing beginning of sporulation at end of hypha. 5, *Geotrichum* mold showing cross walls and feathery appearance characteristic of slimy machinery. 6, *Alternaria* spore with attached hypha.

beaker and stir to dissolve oil. Filter thru paper (use hot H_2O or heptane if necessary) and examine paper microscopically.

Tomato Soup, Canned Spaghetti, Pork and Beans, and Other Similar Products Containing Tomato Sauce

44.102 Mold—Official Final Action

(**a**) *Tomato soup.*—Place unopened can in hot H_2O and heat until contents are thoroly warmed; then open. Transfer 10 mL thoroly mixed soup to 50 mL centrf. tube and add 3 mL NaOH soln (1+1). If starch is absent, omit the NaOH. Stir until starch dissolves and tissues clear. Add enough H_2O to fill tube, and centrf. (Time required to centrf. sample varies greatly. With centrf. arm length of 5¼" and speed of ca 1600 rpm, ca 20 min is required for av. sample. In heavy soups, gelatinizing of much starch sometimes interferes with proper settling out of solids during centrfg. If liq. remains cloudy, it may be necessary to discard sample and start again by adding 3 mL NaOH soln to only 5 mL soup.) When supernate is clear, pour off; if not entirely clear, check supernate for mold before discarding. Add enough H_2O to residue in tube to bring to original vol. of soup, mix, and count mold as in **44.096**.

(**b**) *Tomato sauce in pork and beans, spaghetti, ravioli, chili con carne, tamales, etc.*—Place unopened can in hot H_2O and heat until contents are thoroly warmed. Open can and transfer contents onto No. 6 sieve. Drain until major portion of liq. passes thru. (With some products, sauce runs thru at once, but in case of some beans and spaghetti, ≥10 min may be required.) Mix sauce thoroly, place 10 mL in centrf. tube, and proceed as in (**a**). Use care in counting products contg meat so as not to confuse mold filaments and muscle fibers that superficially resemble each other; muscle fibers are usually much thicker and striations are often visible.

(**c**) *Tomato sauce packing medium on fish.*—Place unopened can in hot H_2O (ca 90–95°) until contents are thoroly warmed. Open can and drain contents on No. 6 sieve until major portion of sauce and oil passes thru. Mix liq., place up to 50 mL in 50 mL centrf. tube, and centrf. as in (**a**). Record vol. of lower oil-free sauce layer, and discard oil and part of mold-free aq. layer. Add H_2O to bring to recorded vol., mix, and count mold as in **44.096**, removing bits of fish tissue from slide, if necessary, before counting.

(**d**) *Tomato powder, dehydrated (Official First Action)* (**45**).—Weigh 17.0 g thoroly mixed sample into high-speed blender, **44.002(c)**, contg 150 mL H_2O to produce mixt. equiv. to tomato puree. Blend 30 sec and, with rubber policeman, rub down any material adhering to walls. Rinse walls with 50.0 mL H_2O to bring total vol. to 200 mL, and blend 1 min. Add 2 drops capryl alcohol to break foam and count mold as in **44.096**.

Pureed Infant Food

44.103 Molds—Official Final Action

Proceed as in **44.096**. Add ca 0.2 g NaOH to ca 6 g product before counting, and stir thoroly until NaOH is dissolved.

44.104 Light Filth—Official First Action

Transfer contents of 2 cans or jars (ca 250 g) of food to 1 L trap flask, **40.002(i)**(*3*), previously rinsed with H_2O. Thoroly mix in ca 20 mL of the oil. Fill with deaerated H_2O either at room temp. or at 50–70°. Let mixt. stand 30 min, stirring 4–6 times during this period to release filth from layer of food. Trap off and examine microscopically.

Use type of oil and temp. indicated in following table:

Food	*Oil*	*Temp.*
All fruits Asparagus Beets Carrots Green beans Peas	Light mineral oil	Room
Spinach	Light mineral oil	50–70°
Squash	Castor oil	50–70°

44.105 Fly Eggs and Maggots—Official First Action

Transfer residue in trap flask, **44.104**, to 2 L separator. Add ca 100 mL heptane, **44.003(u)**, and shake vigorously. Let material settle ca 2 hr, occasionally stirring surface layer to permit any eggs and maggots to settle out. Withdraw ca 200 mL from bottom of separator and filter this material thru 10XX bolting cloth, **44.002(e)**, using several cloths if there is large accumulation of sediment. Examine microscopically at 15–20×.

44.106 *Geotrichum* Mold in Canned Vegetables and Vegetable Juices—(*1*)—Official First Action

See **44.079**.

Peas and Beans

44.107 Weevils—Official First Action

Microscopic examination.—If peas or beans are canned and of normal texture, pour on No. 8 sieve in pan filled with enough H_2O to stand 2–3 cm above mesh of sieve. Mash peas thru sieve with fingers. After as much as possible of material has been worked thru, remove sieve from pan and shake excess H_2O back into pan. Transfer material retained on sieve to 2 L beaker. Pour material that passed thru No. 8 sieve onto No. 40 sieve, discarding that which passes thru. Let material on sieve drain few min, and shake lightly to remove free H_2O from solid material. (If peas are unusually hard, or have tough skins, pass contents of can thru meat or food chopper directly onto No. 40 sieve.) Discard any excess H_2O passing thru this sieve. Cook dried or frozen peas before maceration.

Add material retained on the No. 40 sieve to the beaker. Add ca 130 mL heptane, **44.003(u)**, to this material and mix thoroly with large spoon. Rinse any material remaining on sieve into beaker with H_2O. Stir material in beaker and pick out any insects that may rise to top of H_2O layer. Repeat stirring and searching several times until no more larvae are recovered.

Add enough H_2O to bring contents of beaker to within 1–2 cm of top. Pick out any larvae visible at surface. Stir again, and let mixt. stand ca 5 min; then skim off heptane and upper part of H_2O layer with spoon and place in trap flask, **44.002(i)**(*3*), previously filled ca ¼ full of H_2O. Add 90–100 mL heptane to material remaining in beaker, and stir vigorously. Let stand ca 5 addnl min, skim off heptane and upper part of H_2O layer as before, and add to material already in trap flask.

Fill flask with H_2O. Trap off as much heptane as possible and filter into Hirsch funnel. Lower stopper into flask, and, to rinse sides of trap flask, apply vac. ca 5 min by fitting large rubber stopper and glass tube over mouth of flask. (As ordinary erlenmeyer collapses under vac. of 20" of Hg (50 cm; 67.7 kPa), use either less vac. or heavy-wall flask.) Release vac., add H_2O, and trap off. Add trapped-off portion to that already on filter. Examine microscopically.

Potato Chips

44.108 Filth—Official First Action

Weigh 100 g sample into 1.5 L beaker. Crush chips into small pieces and cover with pet ether. Let stand ca 5 min and decant thru filter. Add pet ether and decant again thru filter. Let pet ether evap. from chips. Transfer to 2 L trap flask, add 500 mL 60% alcohol, and boil ca 30 min, replacing alcohol lost by evapn. Cool, add 35 mL heptane, **44.003(u)**, mix, let stand ca 5 min, and fill with 60% alcohol. Let stand, trap off twice, and filter as usual. Examine papers microscopically.

Dehydrated Potato Products

44.109 Light Filth (*46*)—Official First Action

Weigh 50 g sample into 1.5–2 L beaker. Add 1 L hot HCl (1+9) and mag. stirring bar. Boil 10 min with gentle stirring on mag. stirrer-hot plate, **44.002(p)**. Sieve portionwise on No. 230 sieve, **44.002(u)**. Wet residue on sieve with 40% isopropanol and transfer quant. to 2 L trap flask, **44.002(i)**(*3*), using 40% isopropanol. Bring vol. to 1 L with 40% isopropanol and add 50 mL HCl. Add mag. stirring bar, heat, and boil 10 min with gentle mag. stirring. Immediately transfer flask to cool stirring unit and add 40 mL mineral oil, **44.003(y)**. Stir mag., **44.004(b)**, 3 min. Slowly fill flask with 40% isopropanol by letting liq. flow down stoppered rod while top of stopper is held just above liq. After filling flask, gently stir settled plant material by hand 5–10 sec with stoppered rod. Let stand undisturbed 5 min and immediately trap off. Add 25 mL mineral oil, gently stir by hand 30 sec, and let stand 10 min. Repeat trapping. Wash flask neck thoroly with undild isopropanol and transfer washings to beaker contg trappings. Filter onto ruled paper and examine microscopically.

Frozen Green Leafy Vegetables

44.110 Light Filth (*47*)—Official Final Action

Thaw and accurately weigh 100 g sample. Chop into ca 2.5 cm (1″) pieces and mix thoroly. Transfer to 2 L trap flask, **44.002(i)**(*3*) for collard and mustard greens or beaker for other products. Add *1% anhyd. Na_2SO_4 soln* to cover product to depth of 2.5 cm, cover, and boil 30–40 min. Add H_2O as required to maintain original vol. Remove from heat, add 1% Na_2SO_4 soln to ca 1.2–1.4 L, and add 35 mL light mineral oil, **44.003(y)**. Stir mag. 10 min, **44.004(b)**. Proceed as in **(a)** or **(b)**.

(a) *Percolator method.*—Quant. transfer contents to percolator, **44.002(i)**(*2*), and reserve beaker. Stir gently with long glass stirring rod at 5 and 10 min. Let stand *undisturbed* 5 min; then drain to ca 250 mL. Add ca 1 L 1% Na_2SO_4 soln, and repeat drain and refill cycles until lower aq. phase is clear and free of suspended material.

After last cycle, drain oil-H_2O interface into reserved beaker. Immediately wash sides of percolator with 100–200 mL portions hot tap H_2O, isopropanol or alcohol, and 5% detergent soln, **44.003(q)**, if necessary. Filter thru ruled paper, washing sides of beaker as above and using rubber policeman if needed. Examine paper microscopically.

(b) *Trap flask method.*—After mixing, add trap flask rod and fill flask slowly with 1% Na_2SO_4 soln, letting soln run down rod. Let stand 10 min, stirring gently with rod several times during first 5 min. Secure rod above settled debris during last 5 min. Trap as in **44.004(a)**, and rinse neck of flask with H_2O. Add 25 mL light mineral oil and clamp rod above settled debris. Stir mag. 30 sec and repeat trapping. Make final trap after 10 min, rinsing flask neck with alcohol or isopropanol. Filter thru ruled paper and examine microscopically.

44.111 Acid-Insoluble Residue (Soil) in Frozen Spinach (*41*)—Official Final Action

See **44.091**.

44.112 Light Filth in Canned Leafy Greens (*48*) Official First Action

(Applicable to whole or chopped kale, turnip, mustard, and collard greens.)

Drain can contents on No. 8 sieve 2 min and reserve brine. Immediately take 100 g from sieve. If pieces are ≤1 cm in length, place in 2 L trap flask. Cut larger pieces on small cutting board to this size to avoid interference with mag. stirring. Wash residue from cutting into trap flask with 40% isopropanol. Add 40% isopropanol to fill trap flask to 1 L mark. Add mag. stirring bar (13 × 76 mm). Add 50 mL light mineral oil, **44.003(y)**. Place flask on mag. stirrer, **44.004(b)**. Slowly bring stirrer to max. speed at which stirring bar is just visible at bottom of vortex, avoiding visible or audible splashing. Proper stirring will produce vertical rolling of contents. Stir 5 min, remove flask from stirrer, and let stand 1 min. Add 40% isopropanol down rod to fill flask. Manually stir material in bottom of flask with rotary motion ca 15 sec. Repeat stirring at two 5 min intervals. Raise stirring rod from bottom of flask and clamp. Let stand addnl 10 min and trap off into beaker. Repeat trapping with 35 mL oil, stirring manually 1 min. Filter onto ruled papers.

Filter reserved brine on sep. papers. Examine papers for aphids and other extraneous materials at 10–30X. Det. number of aphids, etc. in 100 g of drained greens and add to this number in proportionate amt of drained liq. calcd as follows:

$$\frac{\text{100 g sample}}{\text{total g drained wt}} \times \text{total number aphids, etc. in liq.}$$

44.113 *Canned Broccoli—Official First Action*

(a) *Insects.*—Transfer contents of can to pan of suitable size and chop up leaves into pieces 2–5 cm long. Weigh 100 g well mixed sample into 1 L beaker. Add 500–600 mL H_2O and boil 5 min. Pour H_2O and sample into 2 L trap flask, **44.002(i)**(*3*). Add 35 mL heptane, **44.003(u)**, and stir thoroly to ensure contact between heptane and all portions of leaves. Fill flask with deaerated H_2O, let stand 30 min, trap off heptane layer, filter, and examine microscopically. Add 40 mL heptane to flask and repeat extn.

If plant tissue rises to interface, place No. 8 sieve, 6–8″ diam., in suitable size evapg dish contg enough H_2O to cover screen ca 1 cm. Pour entrapped heptane from trap flask onto sieve as it is held under the H_2O. Move sieve gently up and down to let insects pass thru into the H_2O. Remove screen and filter contents of dish. Repeat washing to free any insects left on greens on screen, and filter washings. Examine papers microscopically.

(b) *Aphids and Thrips.*—Det. drained wt of contents of canned greens as in **44.098**, reserving drained liquor. Chop drained leaves into pieces 2–5 cm long and weigh 100 g well mixed sample into 1 L beaker. Add H_2O to cover adequately, followed by 25 g neut. $Pb(OAc)_2.3H_2O$ crystals (or equiv. soln of $Pb(OAc)_2$) and 10 mL HOAc. Boil on hot plate 5–10 min, cool, and transfer to 2 L trap flask, **44.002(i)**(*3*). Add 35 mL heptane, **44.003(u)**, and mix thoroly to ensure contact between heptane and all portions of leaves. Fill flask with deaerated H_2O. Let settle few min for most of vegetable matter to sink to bottom. To force any tissue that rises (probably held by entrapped globules of heptane) to sink, pivot lower end of trap-rod on bottom of flask, and rotate upper part of rod around neck of flask to knock globules from vegetable tissue without at same time breaking interface and thus rewetting tissue with heptane. Again let flask stand, trap off heptane layer, and filter.

Re-ext with 20 mL heptane, trap off, and filter (usually possible on same paper). Det. total number of aphids or other light filth in entire liquor drained from can by subjecting it to heptane flotation as usual. (Normally liquor does not present any difficulty and use of $Pb(OAc)_2$ is unnecessary.) Count total number of aphids and thrips including parts contg heads. Count cast skins and other insects sep. Calc. on basis of 100 g of drained material.

44.114 Heavy Filth—Official First Action

Recover heavy filth such as soil, maggots (especially those of spinach leaf miner), and rodent excreta, that sink to bottom of trap flask, as follows: Transfer contents of trap flask, **44.113(a)** or (**b**), by rinsing with H_2O into 4–6 L pail. Add H_2O to pail until ca full. Stir, let stand short time, and decant ca half pail contents. Refill pail with H_2O and repeat operation until most of floating greens are removed. Wash heavy filth left in pail into black shallow pan and examine visually for larvae, stones, and other debris, picking material out with forceps.

Sauerkraut

44.115 Filth—Official First Action

Use entire contents of container of <2 lb (900 g). Use 24 oz (700 g) well mixed sample from larger containers. Wash small portion at time on nested 8" Nos. 8, 20, and 140 sieves, **44.002(u)**. Wash material remaining on No. 20 sieve with washings passing thru No. 140 sieve. Transfer material on No. 20 sieve to paper and examine at ca 10× for whole insects or large body parts. Transfer material remaining on No. 140 sieve to paper and examine microscopically.

Mushrooms

Canned, Fresh, Frozen, Freeze-Dried, and Dehydrated (*49*)
Official First Action

(For maggots, mites, etc.)

44.116 ***Insects***

(**a**) *Canned mushrooms*.—Pour contents of can evenly over weighed No. 8 sieve. Use 8" sieve, for containers of net wt <3 lb (1.4 kg) and 12" sieve for larger containers. Drain 2 min, and reweigh sieve and mushrooms to det. drained wt mushrooms.

Rinse container, and use rinsings and several addnl portions H_2O to rinse mushrooms on sieve (ca 500 mL total). Combine drained liq. with rinsings and filter thru ruled paper. Examine residue on paper microscopically and det. total number of maggots in liq.

Place 100 g drained mushrooms in high-speed blender, **44.002(c)**. Add 300 mL H_2O and blend 30–45 sec at ca 3000 rpm. Attain proper speed quickly by using setting of 1.5–2× final setting on variable transformer for few sec at start. Fragments of mushrooms after blending should be ≤3–5 mm long. Pour mixt. into nested set of 8" Nos. 20, 40, and 140 sieves, **44.002(u)**. Rinse tissue 2–3 min with spray of tap H_2O from aerator, **44.002(a)**. Discard material on No. 20 sieve. Transfer residue from No. 40 sieve to 600 mL beaker with H_2O and bring total vol. to ca 100 mL. Add 5 mL *sat. aq. crystal violet soln* and heat to bp. Pour stained mixt. into No. 40 sieve. Wash mushroom tissue, and maggots, if any, to edge of sieve and remove excess stain with tap H_2O from aerator. Using wash bottle contg com. 5.25% NaOCl soln, and gentle spray of tap H_2O from aerator, alternately spray tissue with H_2O and NaOCl soln until stain has been removed from mushroom tissue. Wash tissue into 600 mL beaker and transfer to ruled paper, using vac. Avoid obscuring maggots with mushroom tissues. (Not more than 2–3 papers should be necessary.)

Transfer residue from No. 140 sieve to 600 mL beaker with H_2O and repeat staining, bleaching, and filtering as above.

Examine papers for maggots and other extraneous materials at 10–30×. Maggots are stained dark violet. Det. number of maggots in 100 g drained mushrooms and add to this value the number in proportionate amt of drained liq. calcd as follows: (100/total g drained mushrooms) × total number of maggots in liq.

(**b**) *Fresh, frozen, freeze-dried, and dehydrated mushrooms*.—For fresh and frozen mushrooms weigh 170 g sample, and for dried mushrooms weigh 15 g sample, into suitable container, and add enough H_2O to immerse mushrooms. Soften mushroom tissue by soaking several hours or, alternatively, by heating on steam bath or simmering 1½–2 hr as necessary, followed by cooling 30–60 min to fully rehydrate. Quant. transfer contents to high-speed blender and proceed as in (**a**), beginning "... blend 30–45 sec at ca 3000 rpm."

Dried (Not Powdered)

44.117 ***Light and Heavy Filth—Procedure***

Thoroly mix sample and weigh 100 g portion. Transfer mushrooms to trap flask, **44.002(i)**(*3*), add H_2O, and let soak several hr, preferably overnight on steam bath, or boil 30 min. Cool to room temp., add 30 mL heptane, **44.003(u)**, and churn contents by hard, rapid pounding of mushrooms against bottom of flask, using vertical movement of rubber plunger. Trap off twice, filter, and examine microscopically.

Canned Whole and Cream-Style Corn (50)
Official First Action

44.118 Macroscopic and Microscopic Examination

Place 200 g well mixed sample in 1.5 L beaker and add 1 L 40% isopropanol. Bring to bp, stirring mag., **44.004(b)**, add 50 mL mineral oil, **44.003(y)**, and boil and stir 3 min more. Transfer immediately to percolator contg ca 100 mL 40% isopropanol and glass or metal rod for forcing corn thru spout. Retain stirring bar in beaker. Rinse bar with undild isopropanol. Add ca 900 mL 40% isopropanol to beaker, stir, and add to percolator, **44.002(i)**(*2*). Reserve beaker. After ca 5 min standing, drain percolator to within 8 cm of bottom onto 8" No. 20 sieve nested in large white enamel tray of ca 2 L capacity. Use rod to force corn thru percolator drain spout. Withdraw rod after removing corn from percolator and wash with small amt of undild isopropanol into reserved beaker. Discard isopropanol collected in tray. Leave sieve in place with retained corn material. Using reserved beaker, add ca 1.5 L hot tap H_2O (50–70°) to percolator. Let phases sep. ca 3 min and make final drain. Discard all but last 5 cm oil-aq. phase. Drain into 600 mL beaker. Wash sides of percolator with alternate isopropanol and H_2O rinses, and collect in same beaker. Add rest of corn from can to corn retained on sieve, sieve portionwise if necessary, and wash with tap H_2O to remove starch and fine particles. Reverse sieve into white enamel tray. Wash corn into tray with forceful spray of H_2O (ca 22°) to 3 cm depth in tray. Let corn settle and examine under H_2O for worm-eaten or rotten kernels and whole worms, heads, or large fragments. Add these to trappings previously obtained from percolator. Tip tray and slowly decant H_2O while carefully observing flowing H_2O for insect fragments. Refill tray with 3 cm H_2O (ca 22°) and repeat decantation, examining closely for objectionable material. Discard pan contents. Filter beaker contents thru ruled filter paper and examine microscopically. If filtration is impeded by excessive starch material, proceed as in **44.004(d)**.

SPICES AND OTHER CONDIMENTS

Ground Allspice, Anise, Curry Powder, Dill Seed, Fennel, Fenugreek, Poppy Seed, Savory, and Condiments; Heavy Filth Only: Caraway Seed, Cardamon, Celery Seed, Cloves, Coriander, Cumin, Ginger, Mace, Marjoram, Mustard, Oregano, Rosemary, Sage, and Thyme

44.119 Gross Contamination—Official First Action

Sift 200–400 g ground spice thru No. 20 sieve. Transfer any insects or other filth retained on sieve to suitable dish and examine with Greenough microscope.

44.120 Heavy and Light Filth for Products Lacking Specific Method—Official First Action

(*Caution: See* **51.011**, **51.039**, **51.040**, **51.056**, and **51.073**.)

(**a**) *Heavy filth and sand.*—Weigh 10 g sample into 250 mL beaker. Add 150 mL pet ether and boil gently 15 min on steam bath in hood. Occasionally add pet ether to keep vol. const. Decant pet ether onto smooth 7 cm paper in buchner. Add 150 mL $CHCl_3$ to beaker and let stand 30 min with occasional stirring. Decant spice and $CHCl_3$ onto funnel, leaving heavy residue of sand and soil, if any, in beaker. If appreciable spice tissue remains on bottom of beaker, add successive portions of $CHCl_3$ mixed with CCl_4 to give increasingly higher sp gr until practically all spice tissue is floated off. Transfer residue from beaker to ashless paper and examine microscopically. If there is appreciable amt of residue, place paper in weighed crucible, ignite, and weigh sand and soil.

(**b**) *Light filth.*—Thoroly dry material in buchner and transfer, including fine material that must be scraped from paper, to 1 L trap flask, **44.002(i)**(*3*). Add ca 150 mL H_2O, heat to bp, and simmer 15 min, with stirring; wash down inside of flask with H_2O; and cool to $<20°$. Add 25 mL heptane, **44.003(u)**, mix thoroly, and let stand 5 min; then fill flask with H_2O and let stand 30 min. Stir every 5 min, trap off, and filter. Add ca 15 mL heptane and mix thoroly; trap off and filter second time after 15 min. If second extn yields appreciable amt of filth, decant most of liq. from flask, add 15 mL heptane, and make third extn. Examine papers microscopically.

Light Filth (*57*)—Official First Action

(*See* Table **44:01** for applicability and parameters for specific spices.)

44.121 *Reagents*

(**a**) *Tween 80–40% isopropanol.*—To 40 mL polysorbate 80 (ICI United States, Inc.) add 210 mL 40% isopropanol, mix, and filter. (Proportionate vols may be prepd.)

(**b**) *Tetrasodium EDTA soln.*—Dissolve 5 g Na_4EDTA in 100 mL H_2O, add 150 mL isopropanol, mix, and filter. (Proportionate vols may be prepd.)

44.122 *Pretreatment*

(*Caution: See* **51.056**.)

Form filter paper cup, 400 mL–1 L, **44.002(k)**, and weigh sample into cup.

(**a**) *Isopropanol extraction.*—Add 400 mL isopropanol to sample beaker contg cup, and boil gently on hot plate 10 min. Transfer cup to buchner and aspirate to slow drip. Repeat twice with 400 mL isopropanol. Proceed with isolation step specified in Table **44:01**.

(**b**) *Chloroform-isopropanol extraction.*—Add 400 mL $CHCl_3$ to cup in sample beaker, and boil gently on hot plate in fume hood 10 min. Transfer cup to buchner and aspirate to slow drip. Repeat twice with 400 mL $CHCl_3$. Turn off vac., cover sample with isopropanol, and let stand 1 min. Aspirate to slow drip. Repeat isopropanol extn. Proceed with isolation step specified in Table **44:01**.

(**c**) *For crushed red peppers.*—Weigh 25 g sample into filter paper cup formed in 250 mL beaker. Place in 80–85° H_2O bath or on top of steam bath. Add 100 mL isopropanol and heat 5 min. Lift paper cup and let drain. Discard drainings, avoiding contact with liq.

Add 100 mL isopropanol and repeat extn and draining. Place cup in Hirsch funnel and wash with ca 100 mL isopropanol. Aspirate to near dryness.

(**d**) *For ground mace and ground caraway seed.*—Add 400 mL $CHCl_3$ to cup in sample beaker, and boil gently on hot plate in fume hood 10 min. Transfer cup to buchner and aspirate to slow drip. Return cup to empty beaker, add 400 mL isopropanol, and boil gently 5 min. Transfer cup to buchner and aspirate to slow drip.

44.123 *Isolation*

(**a**) *Mineral oil-n-heptane* (*85+15*).—Quant. transfer sample to 2 L trap flask, **44.002(i)**(*3*), with 40% isopropanol. Dil. to 400 mL with 40% isopropanol and boil gently 10 min with mag. stirring. Cool in H_2O bath to 20–25°. Add mixt. 50 mL Tween 80, **44.121(a)**, and 50 mL Na_4EDTA, **44.122(b)**, slowly down stirring rod. (Omit for parsley, rosemary, and bay leaves.) Hand stir 1 min, using gentle rotary motion, and let stand 5 min. Dil. to 800 mL with 40% isopropanol, add 50 mL flotation liq., **44.003(s)**, and stir mag., **44.004(b)**, 5 min. Fill flask with 40% isopropanol, and let stand 30 min with intermittent stirring.

Trap off, rinsing neck of flask with 40% isopropanol. Add 35 mL flotation liq. Hand stir solids on bottom with vigorous rotary motion. Fill flask with 40% isopropanol. Let stand 20 min. Trap off, rinse neck with isopropanol, and filter onto ruled paper. Examine microscopically at 30×.

(**b**) *Mineral oil.*—Place filter cup with sample in No. 230 sieve, **44.002(u)**, and wash sample into sieve with gentle stream of hot tap H_2O. Sieve with forceful spray of hot (55–70°) tap H_2O until rinse is clear. Wet residue on sieve with 40% isopropanol and transfer quant. to 2 L trap flask, **44.002(i)**(*3*), using 40% isopropanol. Dil. to 400 mL with 40% isopropanol and boil gently 10 min with mag. stirring. Remove from heat and immediately add mixt. 50 mL Tween 80, **44.121(a)**, plus 50 mL Na_4EDTA, **44.121(b)**, slowly down stirring rod. Hand stir 1 min with gentle rotary motion. Let stand undisturbed 5–10 min. Dil. to 800 mL with 40% isopropanol, add 50 mL mineral oil, **44.003(y)**, and stir mag., **44.004(b)**, 3 min. Fill flask with 40% isopropanol, and let stand 30 min with intermittent stirring. Trap off, and repeat as in (**a**), using 35 mL mineral oil for second trapping.

(**c**) *For crushed red peppers.*—Transfer bulk of sample directly to 2 L trap flask, **44.002(i)**(*3*), by scraping from paper with spatula. Complete transfer by rinsing paper with 40% isopropanol, and finally dil. to ca 800 mL. Stir and heat to vigorous boil for ca 5 min (*Caution:* Watch for excessive foaming! Control with cold H_2O from wash bottle.). Transfer to cooling bath until temp. drops to 20–25°.

Add 40 mL flotation liq., **44.003(s)**, and stir mag., **44.004(b)**, 5 min. Let stand 5 min while mixing 50 mL Tween 80, **44.121(a)**, and 50 mL Na_4EDTA, **44.121(b)**, with 200 mL of 40% isopropanol.

Slowly add mixt. down rod with top of stopper held just *below* top of liq. Gently swirl upper portion of liq. using particular care not to disturb settlings at this time.

Let stand 5 min. Raise rod and spin stopper with gentle rotary motion to free suspended material. With top of stopper just *above* oil phase, slowly fill flask with 40% isopropanol. Swirl top portion of liq. gently, avoiding any disturbance of settled material.

Clamp rod and stopper about midpoint of flask. Let stand 5 min, spin stopper to dislodge material on it, and let stand 20–30 min undisturbed. Trap off and rinse neck with 40% isopropanol.

Add 35 mL flotation liq. and swirl rapidly to suspend plant material without incorporating air. Let stand ca 20 min. Trap off and filter onto ruled paper. Examine microscopically at 30×.

(**d**) *For ground mace and ground caraway seed.*—Proceed as in (**b**), except after adding 50 mL mineral oil, stir mag. 5 min.

Ground Cinnamon

44.124 Heavy and Light Filth—Official First Action

(**a**) *Heavy filth and sand.*—Weigh 2 g sample into 50 mL centrf. tube and add ca 45 mL CCl_4. Centrf. 5 min at 800 rpm in International size I, type SB, centrf., using No. 240 head with arm length of 5.25", or equiv. Stir layer at top of liq. and repeat centrfg. Decant ca ⅔ of liq. and floating layer, and add fresh CCl_4 up to 45 mL. Mix thoroly and again centrf. Decant as much of liq. and floating layer as possible without disturbing residue in centrf. tube. Wash residue onto 11 cm ashless paper with

Table 44:01 Methods for Spices; for Those not Listed, use 44.120(a) and (b) for Ground Form of Product

	Form	Sample, g	Pretreatment **44.122**	Isolation **44.123**	Method Heavy	Light Filth
Allspice	Ground	10			**44.120(a)**	**44.120(b)**
Anise	"	10			**44.120(a)**	**44.120(b)**
Annato	"	25				**44.153**
Basil	Whole (**1**)	25	**b**	**a**		
Bay leaves	" (**1**)	25	**b**	**a**		
Capsiciums[a]	Ground	25			**44.132**	**44.133**
Caraway seed	" (**4**)	10	**d**	**d**		
Cardamon	"	10			**44.120(a)**	**44.126**
Celery leaves	Whole (**1**)	25	**b**	**a**		
seed	Ground	10			**44.120(a)**	**44.127**
Chervil	Whole (**1**)	10	**a**	**a**		
Chives	" (**1**)	5	**a**	**a**		
Cinnamon	Ground	—			**44.124(a)**	**44.124(b)**
	Unground	100				**44.143**
Cloves	Ground (**1**)	10	**a**	**b**		
Condimental seeds	Whole	200			**44.152** (Excreta)	
Coriander	Ground	10			**44.120(a)**	**44.127**
Cumin	" (**1**)	10	**a**	**b**		
Curry powder	Powder	10			**44.120(a)**	**44.120(b)**
Fennel	Ground	10			**44.120(a)**	**44.120(b)**
Fenugreek	"	10			**44.120(a)**	**44.120(b)**
Dill seed	"	10			**44.120(a)**	**44.120(b)**
Weed	Whole (**1**)	25	**b**	**a**		
Garlic	Powder	50			**44.130(a)**	**44.130(b)**
Ginger	Ground	10				**44.127**
Mace	Ground (**4**)	10	**d**	**d**		
Marjoram	" (**1**)	10	**b**	**b**		
Mint	Flakes (**1**)	25	**a**	**a**		
Mustard seed	Ground (**1**)	10	**a**	**b**		
Nutmeg	"	10				**44.128**
	Reconditioned	see method				**44.144**
Onion	Powder	50			**44.130(a)**	**44.130(b)**
Oregano	Ground (**1**)	10	**b**	**b**		
	Unground	10				**44.145**
Paprika	Ground	25			**44.139**	
Parsley	Whole (**1**)	10	**a**	**a**		
Pepper						
Black	Ground	see method			**44.125**	**44.126**
White	"	see method			**44.125**	**44.127**
Red	Crushed (**2**)	25	**c**	**c**		
Poppy seed	Ground	10			**44.120(a)**	**44.120(b)**
Rosemary	" (**1**)	10	**a**	**b**		
	Whole (**1**)	25	**b**	**a**		
Sage	Ground (**1**)	10	**b**	**b**		
	Rubbed	25			**44.150**	
Savory	Ground	10			**44.120(a)**	**44.120(b)**
Tarragon	Whole (**1**)	10	**a**	**a**		
Thyme	Ground (**1**)	10	**a**	**b**		
	Whole (**1**)	25	**a**	**a**		
Turmeric	Ground (**3**)	10	**a**	**b**		
Vegetables	Flakes (**1**)	25	a	a		

[a] Excluding paprika.
Ref. JAOAC; (**1**): **58**, 447(1975); (**2**): **58**, 445(1975); (**3**): **58**, 451(1975); (**4**): **59**, 827(1976).

CCl_4. Examine under low-power microscope for filth. If there is appreciable residue, place paper in weighed crucible, ignite, and weigh sand and soil.

(b) *Light filth* (**52**).—(Where alcohol and 60% alcohol are specified, isopropanol and 40% isopropanol, resp., may be substituted. Use same alcohol thruout method.) Weigh 50 g sample into 800 mL beaker. Add 500 mL hot (55–70°) tap H_2O and 50 mL HCl. Stir several min with stirring bar at high speed on mag. stirrer-hot plate, **44.004(b)**, holding temp. without boiling until gel is dispersed (suspension will become less viscous and vortex will become more pronounced). Sieve portionwise onto No. 230 sieve, **44.002(u)**, with forceful stream of hot tap H_2O, using aerator, **44.002(a)**. After fine material has passed thru sieve, wash residue alternately with alcohol and hot tap H_2O until most foam and color have passed thru.

Transfer residue to 1.5 L beaker with 60% alcohol, using spoon to transfer bulk of material. Dil. to 1 L with 60% alcohol. Add 50 mL HCl and heat (do not boil) while stirring with mag. stirrer to prevent charring. When mixt. is hot (ca 55°), add 50 mL mineral oil, **44.003(y)**, and stir mag., **44.004(b)**, 4 min. Transfer beaker contents to 2 L percolator, **44.002(i)**(*2*), rinse beaker well with 60% alcohol, and add rinsings to percolator. Bring vol. in percolator to ca 1.7 L with 60% alcohol. Resuspend material in percolator by vigorously stirring with glass rod, and rinse rod into percolator with 60% alcohol. Let settle 3 min, and immediately drain material in percolator to within several cm of bottom of mineral oil layer. Refill percolator with hot tap H_2O, adding H_2O rapidly to thoroly resuspend material in percolator. Let settle 3 min, and drain again. Repeat hot H_2O rinses until aq. medium is practically free of suspended matter with max. of 7 rinses. Discard hot H_2O rinses. Drain mineral oil layer into 800 mL beaker and rinse sides of percolator with alternate rinses of 95% alcohol and hot (55–70°) tap H_2O (use rubber policeman if necessary). Pour mineral oil and final rinses onto ruled paper and examine microscopically.

Ground Black and White Pepper

44.125 Heavy Filth and Sand—Official First Action

(*Caution: See* **51.040** and **51.049**.)

Weigh 50 g sample into 600 mL beaker. Add 400 mL CCl_4 and let beaker stand ≥1 hr with occasional stirring. Decant pepper and solv. onto 15 cm paper in buchner, leaving heavy residue of sand and soil in beaker. Repeat decantation with CCl_4 if necessary to secure practically complete sepn of spice materials from any heavy residue. Transfer residue from beaker to ashless paper and examine for filth. If there is appreciable residue, place paper in weighed crucible, ignite, and weigh sand and soil.

44.126 Light Filth (Ground Black Pepper Only) (*53*) Official First Action

Weigh 50 g sample (or use floated material from **44.125** before ignition) into 400 mL beaker and add enough hot H_2O (55–70°) to make thin slurry. Pour slurry onto No. 230 sieve, **44.002(u)**, and wash residue with forceful stream of hot H_2O, using aerator, **44.002(a)**, until effluent is clear. Wash sieve residue with ca 100 mL isopropanol and let drain. Transfer residue from sieve with 40% isopropanol into 2 L trap flask. Dil. to 800 mL with 40% isopropanol. Bring to rolling boil with mag. stirring. Cool to room temp. in H_2O bath. Add 40 mL flotation liq., **44.003(s)**, and stir mag. 3 min, **44.004(b)**. Let oil phase sep. 5 min and then fill flask with 40% isopropanol by letting liq. flow down stirring rod. Let stand 20 min, with gentle stirring at 5 min intervals, and trap off. Repeat trapping with 20 mL flotation liq.; stir gently after addn to avoid disturbing bottom layer. Let stand 10 min and trap off. Filter onto ruled paper and examine microscopically.

Ground Cardamon, Celery Seed, Coriander, Ginger, and White Pepper

44.127 Light Filth (*54*)—Official First Action

Weigh 10 g sample (25 g for white pepper) into 800 mL beaker contg 400 mL isopropanol. Add mag. stirring bar, place on stirrer, **44.002(p)**, and stir mag. 6 min, keeping all solids in motion. Pour mixt. onto No. 230 sieve, **44.002(u)**, and wash residue with H_2O until washings are clear. Transfer residue from sieve with 40% isopropanol into 2 L trap flask, **44.002(i)**(*3*). Add 760 mL 40% isopropanol and 40 mL HCl. Bring to vigorous boil on hot plate with mag. stirring. Cool to 20–25° in cold H_2O bath. Add 40 mL flotation liq., **44.003(s)**, and stir mag., **44.004(b)**, 5 min. Let stand 5 min and then slowly fill flask with 40% isopropanol by letting liq. flow down stirring rod with top of stopper just below oil layer. Resuspend material at bottom of flask without disturbing oil (upper) layer. Let stand 20 min, stirring bottom occasionally, and trap off. Add 30 mL flotation liq., and stir mag., **44.004(b)**, 30 sec while pushing oil into aq. (lower) layer; continue stirring 4.5 min. Let stand 15 min, trap off, filter onto ruled paper, and examine microscopically at 30×. If filtering action slows, use new filter paper.

Filth in Ground Nutmeg (*55*)—Official First Action

44.128 *Pretreatment*

Form 32 cm filter paper defatting cup, 400–800 mL, **44.002(k)**. Weigh 10 g sample into cup, add 400 mL $CHCl_3$, and simmer 10 min. Drain or aspirate and discard $CHCl_3$. Return cup to beaker, add 400 mL isopropanol, and heat to vigorous boil.

44.129 *Isolation*

Immediately wet-sieve on No. 230 sieve, **44.002(u)**, until washings are clear. Rinse material on sieve with 40% isopropanol and let drain. Quant. transfer to 2 L trap flask, **44.002(i)**(*3*), with 40% isopropanol and dil. to 800 mL. Add stirring bar, **44.002(p)**, and heat to vigorous boil while stirring. Add 40 mL mineral oil, **44.003(y)**, and continue heating to vigorous boil.

Transfer flask to cool stirrer, and mag. stir, **44.004(b)**, 5 min. Set aside and fill with 40% isopropanol down stirring rod to bring oil just into neck of flask. Stir to suspend settlings. Stir after 5 min and clamp wafer at ca midpoint of flask. After 5 min adjust oil level to 1 cm above fully raised stopper, and swirl interface. Let stand 5 min and trap off into beaker. Rinse neck with 40% isopropanol and add rinse to trappings.

Add 30 mL mineral oil and hand stir 1 min. Let stand 10 min and trap off. Rinse neck of flask with isopropanol and add rinse to beaker. Filter onto ruled paper(s). Examine papers at 30X.

Ground Onion and Garlic Powders

44.130 Heavy and Light Filth—Official First Action

(*Caution: See* **51.040** and **51.049**.)

(a) *Heavy filth and sand.*—Weigh 50 g sample into 250 mL hook-lip beaker. Add 200 mL CCl_4, stir thoroly, and let stand 30 min with occasional stirring. Decant plant tissue onto 15 cm paper in buchner, add 100 mL CCl_4, and repeat decantation until practically no plant tissue remains with sand and soil on bottom of beaker. Transfer residue in beaker to ashless paper with stream of CCl_4 from wash bottle and examine for filth. If there is appreciable residue, place paper in weighed crucible, ignite, and weigh sand and soil.

(**b**) *Light filth.*—Dry residue of plant tissue from buchner, (**a**), overnight or in oven 1 hr at 80°, and transfer to 2 L trap flask, **44.002(i)**(*3*). Add 250 mL Tween 80–60% alcohol soln, **44.003(hh)**, mix well, and let stand 15–30 min. Add 60% alcohol to 800 mL and trap off twice in 60% alcohol with 75 and 35 mL heptane, **44.003(u)**, resp., as in **44.004(a)**. Let stand 1–1.5 hr for each extn and avoid stirring except for few circular upward strokes immediately after filling flask with 60% alcohol. Filter, and examine microscopically.

Garlic Powder

44.131 Rot (Based on Mold Count) (*56*) Official First Action

Proceed as in **44.136**.

Ground Capsicums (Red and Cayenne Pepper, Chili Powder, etc.)

44.132 Heavy Filth—Official First Action

(*Caution: See* **51.040** and **51.049**.)

(**a**) *Heavy filth and sand.*—Isolate gross filth such as large larvae, adult insects, clumps of webbing, and insect and rodent excreta pellets by sifting pepper thru No. 10 sieve.

Weigh 50 g sifted sample into 600 mL beaker and add 400 mL pet ether. Boil gently 30 min, occasionally adding pet ether to keep vol. constant. Decant pet ether onto smooth 15 cm paper in buchner. Add 400 mL CCl_4 and let stand 30 min with occasional stirring. Decant pepper and solv. onto same 15 cm paper in buchner, leaving heavy residue of sand and soil in beaker. Repeat decantation with CCl_4 if necessary to secure practically complete sepn of spice tissues from heavy residue. Transfer residue from beaker to ashless paper and examine for filth. If there is appreciable residue, place paper in weighed crucible, ignite, and det. sand and soil.

Light Filth in Ground Capsicums Excluding Paprika (*57*) Official First Action

(Complete analysis without overnight interruptions.)

44.133 *Reagent*

Premixed Tween 80-alcohol-tetrasodium EDTA soln.—Measure 840 mL 60% alcohol in 1 L graduate. Add 160 mL Tween 80 (polysorbate 80, ICI United States, Inc.) to 250 mL g-s graduate. Invert 250 mL graduate over 3 L beaker and drain briefly. Rinse 250 mL graduate with several portions of the 840 mL 60% alcohol, pouring each into beaker. Add rest of 60% alcohol to beaker and start mag. stirring. Add 20 g Na_4EDTA to beaker while stirring rapidly. Add 1 L 60% alcohol and stir until uniform. Store in nonmetal containers. Mixed reagent is stable several weeks.

44.134 *Pretreatment*

Proceed as in **44.122(a)**, using 25 g sample.

44.135 *Isolation*

Wet-sieve on No. 230 sieve with warm tap H_2O until drainings are clear. Transfer sample with spoon thru wide-stem funnel into 2 L trap flask, **44.002(i)**(*3*). Rinse remaining material to edge of sieve and transfer quant. to trap flask with 60% alcohol. Dil. to 600 mL with 60% alcohol.

Simmer 10 min on hot plate. Alternatively, place on preheated hot plate, bring to boil, and then transfer to 3–4 cm deep boiling H_2O bath for 10 min and simmer. This technic avoids severe frothing encountered in hot plate boiling. Cool to ≥20° but <25°. Remove from bath and add 40 mL flotation liq., **44.003(s)**. Dil. to 800 mL with 60% alcohol and stir mag. 5 min, **44.004(b)**. Set aside, add 100 mL premixed Tween 80-alcohol-Na_4EDTA soln, and mix thru liq. by gently swirling stopper (wafer) 1 min. Let stand 3 min. Slowly add 60% alcohol down trap rod, maintaining stopper above oil layer, until oil just reaches neck of flask. Swirl stopper thru lower portion of trap flask to suspend settlings (dark material may rise halfway up in trap flask). Add 60% alcohol down rod to bring bottom of oil layer to level 1 cm above fully raised stopper.

Clamp rod with stopper at ca midpoint of flask. Let stand 15 min; then gently swirl stopper thru upper half of liq. to hasten rising of oil droplets. Let stand 15 min undisturbed and trap off into beaker, rinsing neck of flask with 60% alcohol. Filter onto labeled ruled paper.

Add 30 ml flotation liq. and stir manually 1 min. Clamp rod at midpoint and let stand 10 min. Swirl gently thru upper half of liq. and adjust oil level. Let stand 15 min and trap off. Rinse neck of flask with 95% alcohol or isopropanol. Filter onto second ruled paper and examine papers at 30×.

44.136 Rot (Based on Mold Count)—Official Final Action

Weigh 10 g thoroly mixed sample of ground capsicums and transfer to high-speed blender. Add 200 mL 1% NaOH soln in 3 or 4 successive portions, stirring after each addn, washing down with final portion any material that may stick to walls of blender. Agitate mixt. in blender 1 min at ca 13,000 rpm. With rubber policeman, rub down into mixt. any material sticking to walls and repeat blending 2 min longer. Add 2 or 3 drops *capryl alcohol* to break foam. Mix 100 g of this mixt. with 50 g stabilizer soln, **44.003(gg)**, and count with Howard mold-counting slide, **44.002(o)**(*1*), as in **44.096**.

Occasionally blended mixt. contains particles of seed tissue that make it difficult to obtain Newton's rings in prepg slide for mold counting. Clamp devised for holding cover slip in place to obviate this difficulty consists of metal plate with circular opening, 2.5 cm diam., in center of plate; 2 clips attached to edge of plate hold cover slip in position when slide is placed on plate.

Paprika—Official First Action

44.137 Gross Contamination

See **44.119**.

Light Filth in Ground Paprika (*58*)

44.138 *Reagents*

See **44.121(a)**, (**b**), and in addn:

Premixed Tween 80–40% isopropanol-tetrasodium EDTA soln.—Mix 250 mL Tween 80–40% isopropanol, **44.121(a)**, and 250 mL Na_4EDTA soln, **44.121(b)**. Mixed reagent is stable several weeks. Store in nonmetal containers.

44.139 *Pretreatment*

Form 32 cm filter paper (rapid flow) cup around 400 mL beaker, as in **44.002(k)**. Remove paper, place in 1 L beaker, and add 25 g sample.

Pour 400 mL isopropanol into the 1 L beaker, distributing liq. equally inside and outside cup. Place on preheated hot plate and boil gently exactly 10 min. (Alternatively, bring to boil on hotter hot plate; then set aside *in* steam bath opening for 10 min boil.) Remove cup from beaker without delay, and let drain or place on buchner and aspirate to slow drip. Discard liq.

Replace cup in 1 L beaker and repeat twice with 400 mL isopropanol.

44.140 ***Isolation***

Wash sample from cup into No. 230 sieve, **44.002(u)**, with gentle H_2O stream, avoiding splashing and loss of sample. Wet sieve with forceful stream of warm H_2O from aerator until washings are clear. (Ignore foam or froth produced by action of strong spray on paprika.)

Add 400 mL 40% isopropanol to wash bottle. Place wide-stem powder funnel in trap flask. Transfer bulk of sieved sample to trap flask, using portion of 40% isopropanol. Wash remaining material on sieve to edge with warm H_2O and complete quant. transfer to trap flask with 40% isopropanol. Wash walls of flask with 40% isopropanol. Pour remainder of 400 mL 40% isopropanol into trap flask.

Place on hot plate and boil gently 10 min; swirl to rinse material from walls of flask. (Do not allow material to accumulate and dry on flask walls.) Remove from hot plate and immediately add 100 mL premixed Tween 80–40% isopropanol-Na_4EDTA soln, **44.138**. Stir gently ca 1 min. Let stand 10 min. Dil. to 800 mL with 40% isopropanol added slowly down stirring rod, positioned with stopper just above liq. level. Add 50 mL mineral oil, **44.003(y)**, and stir mag., **44.004(b)**, 3 min, with stopper located above liq. level.

Add 40% isopropanol slowly down stirring rod to bring oil into neck of flask. Let stand ca 10 min. Raise stopper to middle of flask and swirl gently to cause movement of upper liq. and hasten rising of oil droplets. Rinse rod with 40% isopropanol and clamp so that stopper is at midpoint of flask. Add 40% isopropanol down rod to bring bottom of oil layer to level 1 cm above fully raised stopper. Let stand 10 min and swirl gently again. Let stand 10 min undisturbed and trap off into beaker.

Add ca 35 mL mineral oil and hand stir 1 min at speed sufficient to keep oil moving thru trap flask. Add ca 20 mL 40% isopropanol, stir gently at ca 5 min intervals for 20–25 min, then let stand undisturbed 5–10 min. Trap off into second beaker and rinse neck of trap flask with alcohol or undild isopropanol.

Filter solns from both beakers onto sep. ruled filter papers in Hirsch funnel, rinsing each beaker carefully with isopropanol. Examine microscopically at 30×.

★ *Whole Spices* ★

44.141 Filth by Flotation—Official First Action

See **40.115**, 11th ed.

Whole, Cracked, or Pieces of Allspice, Anise, Caraway, Celery Seed, Cloves, Coriander, Cumin, Dill Seed, Fennel Seed, Fenugreek, Ginger, Mace, Marjoram, Mixed Pickling Spice, Mustard, Nutmeg, Black Pepper, White Pepper, Poppy Seed, Savory, and Turmeric

44.142 Filth—Official First Action

Weigh 25 g sample into 400 mL beaker and proceed as in **44.120(a)** and **(b)**, except use more reagent, and where necessary, 2 L trap flask, and add 400 mL hot H_2O and 20 mL HCl; also use 35 mL heptane, instead of 25 mL.

Unground Cinnamon, Crude and Reconditioned

44.143 Light Filth (*59*)—Official First Action

If sample is reconditioned or if pieces are not rolled and are 8 cm (3") long, weigh 100 g sample directly into 1.5 L beaker. If sample consists of quills, break open quills into lengths of ≤8 cm and transfer broken pieces, including dust and small particles, to 1.5 L beaker. Add 1 L hot tap H_2O and 50 mL HCl. Heat on hot plate to ca 60°. Pour portionwise onto No. 6 over No. 230 sieve, **44.002(u)**, and rinse well with forcible stream of hot tap H_2O, using aerator, **44.002(a)**, while turning larger pieces with glass rod. Discard material on No. 6 sieve and transfer residue on No. 230 sieve to 2 L trap flask, **44.002(i)**(*3*), with hot tap H_2O, using spoon if necessary. Fill trap flask to 1 L with H_2O and add 50 mL HCl. Heat with stirring to ca 60–70°. Add 50 mL mineral oil, **44.003(y)**, and stir mag., **44.004(b)**, 2 min. Fill with H_2O, let stand 5 min, and trap. Add 25 mL mineral oil, gently stir with stopper 1 min, let stand 5 min, and again trap. Rinse neck of flask with alcohol or isopropanol. Filter trappings onto ruled filter paper and examine for insects and other arthropods, hairs, excreta, etc.

★ Surplus method—*see* inside front cover.

Nutmegs, Reconditioned (60)—Official First Action

44.144 Light Filth

(*Caution: See* **51.011**, **51.040**, and **51.056**.)

Weigh 100 g sample into 1.5 L beaker (50 g if finely ground product is used). Add 400 mL $CHCl_3$ and boil 5 min. Prep. 32 cm folded S&S 588 filter paper, by moistening with H_2O and forming around base of 1 L beaker. Place 7 cm disk of bolting cloth (mesh size not critical) in 10 cm plate diam. buchner, insert paper, apply vac., and press moistened paper until good seal is obtained. Rinse paper with isopropanol, and aspirate until nearly dry. Quant. transfer nutmeg to paper, and aspirate off $CHCl_3$. Transfer paper contg spice tissue back to original beaker, add 400 mL fresh $CHCl_3$, and boil 5 min. After cooling few min, lift paper, and drain and discard $CHCl_3$. Replace paper in beaker, add 400 mL $CHCl_3$, and repeat 5 min boiling third time.

Replace paper in buchner and aspirate off $CHCl_3$, maintaining suction ca 5 min after visible dripping ceases. Release vac.; add isopropanol until spice is covered, let stand few min, and reapply vac. until visible dripping ceases. Repeat isopropanol wash step and aspirate ca 5 min after visible dripping ceases.

Quant. transfer retained spice to 8" diam. No. 230 sieve, **44.002(u)**, with copious rinses of hot tap H_2O. Wash material on sieve with forceful stream of hot H_2O from aerator, **44.002(a)**, until no more spice tissue passes sieve. Transfer most of sieve contents with spoon and quant. transfer remaining material to 2 L trap flask with 60% alcohol-$CaCl_2$ soln, **44.003(e)**, from wash bottle. Add mag. stirring bar, bring vol. to 1 L with 60% alcohol-$CaCl_2$ soln, add 50 mL HCl, and place flask on mag. stirrer-hot plate, **44.002(p)**. Heat to *full boil* with gentle stirring. Immediately transfer flask to cool stirring unit and add 40 mL light mineral oil, **44.003(y)**, by pouring down stirring rod. Stir 2 min with mag. stirrer, **44.004(b)**. Fill with 60% alcohol-$CaCl_2$ soln and gently stir 5–10 sec with stirring rod. Let stand 2 min and trap off. Add 35 mL light mineral oil, stir by hand gently 30 sec, and let stand 10 min. Repeat trappings. Wash flask neck thoroly with isopropanol and transfer washings to beaker with trappings. Filter onto ruled paper and examine microscopically.

Unground Oregano

Light Filth (*61*)—Official First Action

44.145 ***Reagents***

(**a**) *Polysorbate 80-tetrasodium EDTA mixture* (*1+1*).—Prep. from Tween 80–60% alcohol soln, **44.003(hh)**, and Na_4EDTA–60% alcohol soln, **44.003(ii)**.

(**b**) *15% Alcohol.*—Prep. ca 1700 mL/sample prior to analysis.

44.146 ***Determination***

Weigh 10 g sample into 2 L trap flask, **44.002(i)**(*3*), add 400 mL 60% alcohol, and boil gently 10 min, occasionally swirling flask gently and/or using plunger to prevent material from accumulating on wall of flask above surface of liq. Immediately add 100 mL Tween 80-Na_4EDTA mixt., and swirl few sec, again using plunger to clear material from wall of flask. Let stand 10 min in cold H_2O bath. Dil. to 800 mL with 15% alcohol. Add 50 mL mineral oil, **44.003(y)**, and stir mag., **44.004(b)**, 2 min. Fill with 15% alcohol and hand stir every 2–3 min for 20 min. Clamp stirring rod in place so that plunger is held above sediment at bottom of flask. Leave flask undisturbed 10 min. Trap, filter onto ruled paper, and examine microscopically.

★ ***Unground Fermented Crushed Peppers*** ★

44.147 Light and Heavy Filth—Official First Action

See **40.121**, 11th ed.

★ ***Pepper Sauce*** ★

44.148 Light and Heavy Filth—Official First Action

See **40.122**, 11th ed.

Prepared Mustard

44.149 Light Filth (*62*)—Official First Action

Weigh 100 g well mixed sample into 1 L beaker, and slowly add 400 mL HCl (3+97) and 20 mL mineral oil, **44.003(y)**, with constant stirring until smooth slurry forms. Place on hot plate and bring to *rolling boil;* hold at *rolling boil* ca 10 min. Transfer quant. to Kilborn funnel, **44.002(i)**(*1*); retain beaker and stirring rod for rinsing. Fill separator to ca 1 cm from top with cold H_2O.

After 1.5–2 min, gently stir contents of separator; let oil layer sep. again ca 1.5–2 min, and slowly drain and discard lower layer until interface is ca 5 cm above constriction. Fill separator with cold H_2O to ca 1 cm from top; let oil sep. 1.5–2 min, and slowly drain and discard lower aq. layer until interface is ca 5 cm above constriction. Repeat H_2O wash until lower layer is clear.

Filter mineral oil and H_2O retained in separator thru ruled paper, **44.002(j)**, using Hirsch funnel. After mineral oil layer has passed thru paper, rinse all glassware thoroly with alcohol, followed by H_2O, then 5% detergent soln, **44.003(q)**, and cold H_2O. Filter each rinse sep. thru same paper. Rinse final papers with enough alcohol to remove yellow color. Examine papers at 30×.

Light Filth in Rubbed Sage (*63*)—Official First Action

44.150 ***Pretreatment***

Form 32 cm filter paper cup over 400 mL beaker and insert into 1 L beaker, **44.002(k)**. Place 25 g sample into cup. Add 400 mL $CHCl_3$, ca equally between cup and beaker. Boil gently 10 min in hood. (Alternatively, bring to bp on hot plate and continue heating 10 min total on steam bath.) Transfer cup to buchner and aspirate to slow drip. Return cup to beaker and repeat extn with two 400 mL portions $CHCl_3$. After third $CHCl_3$ aspiration, turn off vac., cover sample with isopropanol, let stand 1 min, and aspirate to slow drip. Repeat isopropanol extn once.

44.151 ***Isolation***

Transfer sample from paper cup to No. 230 sieve, **44.002(u)**, with gentle stream of hot tap H_2O. Sieve with forceful spray of *hot* (55–70°) tap H_2O until rinse is clear. Wash residue to edge of sieve and let drain momentarily. Rinse sieve with ca 100 mL of alcohol delivered from wash bottle. Let stand 1 min. Again wash sieve residue with hot tap H_2O until drainings are colorless; then wet well with 40% isopropanol.

Add mag. stirring bar, **44.002(p)**, to 2 L trap flask, **44.002(i)**(*3*). Place wide stem funnel in flask opening and transfer bulk of sample with spoon. Rinse remaining material to edge of sieve with aerator spray and quant. transfer to flask with total of 400 mL 40% isopropanol. Stir gently while boiling 10 min on hot plate. (Alternatively, bring to boil on hot plate and continue heating 10 min in ca 40 mm boiling water bath.) Remove from heat and immediately add 100 mL premixed Tween 80-Na_4EDTA, **44.133**, slowly down rod and mix by gentle swirling 1 min.

Cool in H_2O bath at 20–25°. Add 50 mL mineral oil, **44.003(y)**. Dil. to 800 mL with 40% isopropanol added slowly down stirring rod to avoid mixing or agitation of flask contents.

Stir mag., **44.004(b)**, 5 min, and let stand 3 min. Add 100 mL premixed Tween 80-Na_4EDTA and very gently swirl thru top of liq. 1 min.

Fill flask with 40% isopropanol, added slowly down stirring rod to minimize agitation of liq. Let stand 20 min *undisturbed.* Trap off, rinsing neck of flask with 40% isopropanol, and add to trappings in beaker.

Add 35 mL mineral oil and hand stir 1 min. Let stand ca 1 min. Slowly fill flask with 40% isopropanol. Let stand 7 min, spin stopper to free of settlings, adjust oil level to ca 1 cm above fully raised stopper and let stand 8 min. Trap off into beaker, rinsing neck of flask well with isopropanol. Transfer trappings to ruled filter paper, rinsing beaker well with isopropanol. Examine papers at 30X.

Condimental Seeds

44.152 Rodent and Insect Excreta—Official First Action

Prep. liq. with sp gr of 1.16–1.19 by mixing $CHCl_3$ or CCl_4 with alcohol or pet ether. Mix 200 g sample with 500–700 mL of the liq. in 1 qt (1 L) drug percolator. Let stand 30 min, stirring at ca 5 min intervals. Trap sediment in lower end of percolator with cork plug and remove lower cork so as to deliver all sediment into beaker. Lift upper cork slightly and rinse tube and cork by letting small amt of liq. pass. After stirring top layer, make 2 more sepns at 5 min intervals. Transfer contents of beaker to filter paper, drain liq., and examine. Sep. rodent excreta and insect excreta, air dry, and weigh each sep. to nearest mg.

Ground Annatto

44.153 Light Filth—Official First Action

See **44.133–44.135.**

44.154 ★ **Whole Tamarind Pulp** ★

See **40.125**, 11th ed.

Whole Pickles

44.155 Filth—Official First Action

Pour entire contents of jar onto No. 8 sieve nested in No. 140 sieve, **44.002(u)**. Wash jar thoroly to remove any filth adhering to sides, and pour washings thru sieves. Wash pickles thoroly with stream of hot H_2O, turning from time to time. Transfer material on No. 140 sieve directly to ruled paper and examine microscopically.

★ Surplus method—*see* inside front cover.

Chopped Pickles and Relish

44.156 Filth—Official First Action

Add 200 mL H_2O to 100 g sample in trap flask or beaker, boil 15 min, and cool. If boiling is done in beaker, transfer to trap flask, **44.002(i)**(*3*). Trap off twice, using 25 and 15 mL heptane, **44.003(u)**. Filter, and examine microscopically.

Dressings for Food

(Salad dressing, french dressing, and related products)

44.157 Filth—Official First Action

Weigh 200 g sample into 800 mL beaker, stir in 50 mL H_3PO_4, and mix thoroly. Thin with ca 600 mL H_2O, and again mix thoroly. If possible, filter thru S&S No. 8 ruled paper with suction; otherwise thru No. 140 sieve, **44.002(u)**, and transfer to ruled paper. Examine papers microscopically.

Prepared Horseradish (*64*)—Official First Action

44.158 ***Determination***

Weigh 100 g sample into 600 mL beaker. Add 200 mL H_2O and transfer to 2 L trap flask with H_2O. Dil. to 1 L, add 50 mL HCl, and stir few sec. Add mag. stirring bar, **44.002(p)**, and 50 mL flotation liq., **44.003(s)**, and stir mag., **44.004(b)**, 3 min. Slowly fill flask with distd H_2O by running liq. down stoppered rod while stopper is maintained just above liq. After filling flask, gently stir settled material 5–10 sec with stoppered rod. Let stand undisturbed 5 min; then trap off. Add 35 mL flotation liq., stir gently by hand 30 sec, and let stand 10 min. Repeat trapping. Wash flask neck thoroly with isopropanol and transfer washings to beaker contg trappings. Filter onto ruled paper and examine microscopically.

ANIMAL EXCRETIONS

Urine Stains on Foods and Containers (65)
Official First Action

44.159 Preliminary Examination with Ultraviolet Light

(*Caution: See* **51.016**.)

Examine suspected stains in dark room under long wave UV light (366 nm). (Dried urine on textiles usually fluoresces blue-white, but color varies somewhat, depending upon natural color of textile and type of lamp and filter used.) Run check patches with known types of urine. For microchem. analysis, outline stained area with pencil under the UV light. When odor of urine is detected, report this finding.

44.160 Urease Test for Urea

Cut out portion of stained area and transfer 1 or 2 threads to 5 mL crucible or beaker. Save balance of cloth to confirm urine by **44.162–44.164**. Leach 10 min in just enough warm H_2O to cover material. Remove threads and squeeze out as much liq. as possible with clean, flat-tip forceps.

Transfer 2 or 3 drops to microculture slide with deep cylindrical depression. Add small drop *urease mixt.* (suspension of ¼ of 25 mg urease tablet in 0.5–0.7 mL H_2O). Place small drop *10% H_2PtCl_6 soln* on cover slip and invert over the depression, with hanging drop at center of depression opening. (Cover slip may be sealed on with petrolatum if only minute amts of urea are suspected.)

With evolution of NH_3, brilliant, highly refractive, octahedral crystals of $(NH_4)_2PtCl_6$ are formed in hanging drop. Time required for crystals to form varies from few sec to 30 min, or even longer in some instances, according to conditions. Crystals may be visible to naked eye and are readily detected under microscope at 100×. Certain org. compds that are volatile and H_2O-sol. may yield crystals in the hanging drop, and if reagent soln is too concd, H_2PtCl_6 may crystallize. However, crystal habits of these substances are different from those of $(NH_4)_2PtCl_6$. (Stained patches of the food material can be tested by method similar to above.)

44.161 Xanthydrol Test for Urea (*66*)
Official First Action

(Not applicable in presence of dried skim milk)

Place portion of stained cloth, ca 3 mm sq (stain located by fluorescence) on microscope slide. Add drop of HOAc (2+1) and stir. (Or instead of cutting out a patch of cloth, rinse stained material with H_2O or other suitable solv. such as HOAc, acetone, or hot alcohol, evap. soln to dryness, dissolve residue in little HOAc (2+1), and place drop on slide.)

Transfer droplet with stirring rod to another place on slide and dil. with drop of HOAc (2+1). To both drops add very small amt of *xanthydrol* and stir into soln. If urea is present, crystals of dixanthylurea form very shortly. Examine with magnification of ca 100–120× (higher power may be used for closer examination if crystals formed are quite small). Use of polarizing microscope is desirable but not essential.

Crystals may be either or both of 2 kinds, depending on concn of urea present: (*a*) most prevalent are clusters of narrow feather-blades of low birefringence which form thruout soln at ca 1:200 to 1:25,000 concn (under low power they may appear to be needles or threads); (*b*) straight needles, often in sheaves or clusters, of much greater birefringence, forming chiefly at or near edge as drop evaps, at concns from 1:50 to 1:1,000. Both kinds have neg. elongation (observed with polarizing microscope, using red plate). Crystals should be noted before drop dries, but remain when it dries. Response is given by fresh urine solids content of ≥4 μg in drop. Test material from portion of sample other than fluorescent spot as blank.

TLC Method (*67*)—Official First Action

44.162 ***Apparatus***

(**a**) *Thin layer apparatus.—See* **29.006** and **29.007(c)**.

(**b**) *Blender.*—High-speed, with stainless steel semi-micro jar (Arthur H. Thomas Co., No. 3392-G15, or equiv.).

44.163 ***Reagents***

(**a**) *Urea std soln.*—20 mg/mL H_2O.

(**b**) *Allantoin std soln.*—2 mg/mL H_2O.

(**c**) *Indoxyl sulfate* (*indican*) *std soln.*—Approx. 0.1 mg/mL H_2O (Sigma Chemical Co.). Store in dark.

(**d**) *Tryptophan soln.*—1 mg/mL 50% aq. acetone (used as longwave fluorescent marker with R_f approx. that of urea in developing solv.).

(**e**) *p-Dimethylaminobenzaldehyde* (*pDAB*) *spray.*—Mix 75 mL MeOH and 25 mL HCl, and cool to 70°. Add 2 g reagent grade pDAB to cooled mixt. and dissolve with stirring. (*Caution:* Spray reagent is toxic and corrosive. *See* **51.017**.)

(**f**) *Sodium acetate spray.*—Satd aq. soln.

(**g**) *Developing solvent.*—*n*-BuOH-HOAc-H_2O (10+5+5); prep. fresh daily.

(**h**) *Cellulose powder.*—TLC grade, MN300 (Brinkmann Instruments, Inc., No. 66 00 100-8).

44.164 ***Determination***

On previous day prep. plates for overnight drying. Equilibrate tanks ca 1 hr before extg samples.

(**a**) *Preliminary examination.*—Check samples as in **44.159** for fluorescent areas. Mark fluorescent spots as well as nearby equiv. nonfluorescent areas as controls. Transfer selected spots to test tubes.

(**b**) *Extraction.*—Add 10 mL acetone to test tube, place in hot H_2O bath, and simmer 5 min, avoiding excess loss of solv. Decant acetone into 13 or 15 mL conical centrf. tube preheated in beaker of hot H_2O on steam bath. Repeat extn and transfer 3 addnl times, keeping centrf. tubes hot to avoid bumping. Conc. final soln to 0.1–0.15 mL. Chromatograph without appreciable delay, holding ext in dark until ready to spot.

(**c**) *Preparation of TLC tank.*—Add ca 150 mL satd $NaHSO_4$ soln to lined tank; then add ca 15 g addnl solid $NaHSO_4$ to bottom of tank. Place empty solv. trough in bottom of tank and cover tank.

(**d**) *Preparation of thin layer plates.*—(*1*) *Brinkmann-DeSaga.*—Add 15 g cellulose to 100 mL H_2O in blender operating at ca 90 v setting of variable transformer. Use small spatula to work powder into H_2O. Turn variable transformer to 120 v (line voltage) and blend ≥1.5 min. Apply slurry as 0.375 mm layer to 5 plates and air dry plates overnight.

(*2*) *Quickfit plate leveler and spreader.*—Add 12 g cellulose to 75 mL H_2O in blender operating at 90 v setting of variable transformer. Use small spatula to work powder into H_2O. Turn transformer to 120 v (line voltage), add 15 mL H_2O, and blend ≥1.5 min. Using 0.50 mm slot, spread slurry on 5 plates and air dry plates overnight.

(*3*) *Prepared plates.*—Plates prepd from MN300 cellulose (Analtech, Inc., 75 Blue Hen Dr, Newark, DE 19711) have been found satisfactory.

(**e**) *Spotting of plates.*—Spot on TLC plate placed directly on heated surface (70°). (Det. surface temp. as follows: Add 125 mL glycerol to 250 mL conical flask. Thru hole in cork stopper insert 76 mm (3") immersion thermometer until tip contacts bottom.) Spot sample conc. ca 25 mm from edge of plate at ca 15 mm intervals. Keep sample spots to min. size. Add 50 μL acetone to tube, shake well, and transfer to sample spot.

(**f**) *Cleanup.*—If there is appreciable color and/or other visible material, clean up with benzene. Line TLC chamber with heavy blotting paper, or equiv. Add 40–60 mL benzene to bottom of tank and cover. (For frequent use, coat ground glass surfaces of tank with high viscosity silicone grease.) Add 20–25 mL benzene to trough in tank. Place spotted plate in trough and let rise ca 25 mm above spotting line. Remove, fan dry, and repeat rise and drying. Place plate in tank third time and let rise ca 13 cm to carry most of interfering material above 10 cm line. Remove from tank and scratch wide line in layer at 10 cm above spotting line.

(**g**) *Development of plates.*—Dry washed plate 5 min in 80° forced-draft oven. Promptly place warm plate in empty solv. trough of TLC tank. Let stand 20 min. Slide cover aside just enough to place tip of long-stem funnel in solv. trough. Slowly add 20 mL developing solv., (**g**), to trough, close lid, and develop in dark to 10 cm line (65–70 min). Dry plate 5 min in 80° forced-draft oven.

(**h**) *Color development.*—Spray plate with pDAB reagent until distinctly moist but not shiny wet and again heat 5 min in 80° forced-draft oven. Strong yellow-to-orange area at R_f 0.75–0.80 is urea. Pale yellow smaller spot at R_f 0.45–0.50 is allantoin. Mark each area as color develops, since colors fade from one step to next. Place under longwave black light, **29.007**(**c**), in darkened room and check for pale yellow fluorescent area between urea and allantoin. Spray satd NaOAc soln (ca 1–2 mL/plate) in space between urea and allantoin until yellow of *both* has faded. Let plate air dry ca 10 min in hood (do not heat), and check plate under longwave black light. Weak fluorescent pink-to-orange color against very pale blue fluorescent background confirms presence of urinary indican.

Urine in Grain (68)—Official First Action

44.165 ***Principles***

Grain is sprayed with Mg uranyl acetate soln. If rodent urine is present, its Na content reacts to cause greenish fluorescence on kernel when sample is viewed under short-wave UV light.

44.166 ***Reagents***

(**a**) *Magnesium uranyl acetate soln.*—Prep. reagents **3.027**(**a**) and (**b**) in 1/10 amts, mix, add 22 mL glycerol, mix, and filter thru washed, dried paper.

(**b**) *Urease soln.*—Wet 0.2 g urease powder with small amt of H_2O, stir into paste, and dil. to 10 mL with H_2O.

(**c**) *Bromothymol blue soln.*—Rub 0.15 g indicator powder in mortar with 2.4 mL 0.1*N* NaOH soln. After indicator dissolves, wash mortar and pestle with H_2O, and dil. to 50 mL with H_2O. Soln should be green; pH ca 7.0.

(**d**) *Urease-bromothymol blue test paper.*—Mix 10 mL indicator soln, (**c**), with 10 mL urease soln, (**b**). Pour mixt. into watch glass. Using clean tweezers, dip pieces of heavy filter paper (Whatman No. 5, S&S No. 598, or 589 green ribbon have been found satisfactory) in soln. (To avoid uneven distribution of indicator and enzyme, wet entire paper at once by laying it on surface of soln.) Hang paper to dry in place free from NH_3 fumes, strong air currents, or heat. Paper should be orange when dry. Store dry paper in well-stoppered, dark glass bottle in cool place.

(**e**) *Xanthydrol.*—Eastman Kodak Co. No. 1559, crystals.

44.167 ***Apparatus***

(**a**) *Ultraviolet lamp.*—Short wave, 253.7 nm, with filters to eliminate most visible light.

(**b**) *Chromatographic sprayer.*—250 mL, to deliver fine spray from air supply (Kontes Glass Co., K-422500, or equiv.). Hand-operated atomizer is satisfactory if it delivers fine spray.

44.168 ***Ultraviolet Test***

Spread 50 g grain in shallow tray, or on sheet of waxed paper on tray. Place in hood or well ventilated area, and spray evenly with Mg uranyl acetate reagent, making several sweeps horizontally and vertically across sample. Let stand 1–3 min, and examine under short-wave UV light. With clean tweezers, transfer kernels showing greenish fluorescent areas to spot plate. (Avoid prolonged exposure to UV light and do not touch grains with bare fingers (use gloves). Perspiration may cause false fluorescence.)

Use as blanks 1 or 2 kernels showing no green fluorescence under UV light.

44.169 ***Urease-Bromothymol Blue Test***

Add 1–4 drops H_2O to each suspect kernel on spot plate. Let stand 3–5 min. Place strip of test paper, (**d**), on glass microscope slide, transfer drop of ext to paper with stirring rod, and cover with second slide. Blue spots, slowly developing over 2–4 min, indicate urea. (As reagent is slightly acid, color may not appear for several min, depending on how heavily grain was sprayed.)

44.170 ***Confirmatory Test***

Transfer 1–2 drops aq. ext of suspect kernels to microscope slide and evap. to dryness. Add drop of HOAc (2+1) and very small amt of xanthydrol crystals. If urea is present, characteristic crystals of dixanthylurea form quickly, and are visible at 60× or lower with wide-field stereoscopic microscope.

Bromothymol Blue-Agar Test (69)—Official First Action

44.171 ***Apparatus***

(**a**) *Disposable trays.*—Microtiter® plates, flexible vinyl, flat-bottom (Dynatech Laboratories inc., 900 Slaters Ln, Alexandria, VA 22314), or equiv.

(**b**) *Culture tubes.*—6 (od) × 50 mm.

44.172 ***Reagents***

(**a**) *Bromothymol blue (BTB) indicator soln.*—Sol. form (Fisher Scientific Co., B-100, or equiv.). Transfer 50 mg BTB to 20 mL g-s test tube and add 10 mL H_2O. Add 1 drop H_3PO_4 (1+9) and dissolve completely by stirring. Add ca 0.1*N* NaOH dropwise to dark green (pH 5.8–6.0). (This prepn is enough for 1 batch of test agar.)

(**b**) *Urease suspension.*—Grind 0.30 g urease in small mortar, add few mL H_2O, and continue grinding. Slowly dil. to 15 mL with stirring.

(**c**) *Test agar.*—Add 0.75 g bacteriological grade agar and 0.30 g Na benzoate to 300 mL cold H_2O with vigorous stirring, and place on mag. stirrer-hot plate, **44.002**(**p**); heat with stirring and boil gently 1 min. Cool to 45–48°, add BTB soln, (**a**), and adjust to pH 5.5 (yellow-green), using 0.9–1.1*N* NaOH or H_2SO_4. Add urease suspension to pH-adjusted, 45–48° agar and readjust pH, if necessary. Divide agar into 2 equal portions in beakers. To one portion add 0.5 mL 0.1*N* $AgNO_3$. To other portion add 0.1*N* H_2SO_4 (ca 0.2 mL) to adjust to match color shade or pH of first portion. Mix each portion thoroly and let stand ca 5 min.

Agar sensitivity test.—Prep. known urea-contaminated seeds by spotting each seed with 0.5 μL 0.25% aq. soln of urea and let dry. Test these known samples as in **44.173**. If no color response is obtained with known grains, either obtain new lot of urease or increase urease content after checking activity as in **7.033**(**b**) and **7.034** so that suspension contains enough urease to convert 0.80 g urea, and repeat sensitivity test.

44.173 ***Test***

Initially check sample for free alkali, using test agar contg $AgNO_3$ soln (45–48°), by (**a**) or (**b**) below:

(**a**) *For immediate use.*—Add grain, or unknown sample, to wells of disposable tray, **44.171**(**a**), and, using dropping pipet, add agar until object is covered.

(**b**) *For storage and/or intermittent use.*—Add agar to culture tubes, **44.171**(**b**), to ½ ht. Transfer tubes to heat-sealable plastic bags, seal, and store at 4±1°. Agar can be stored ≤120 days. To use, let stand 1 hr at room temp. Use small glass rod to force test object below surface of agar. Remove rod and shake down agar. Observe frequently for color change near surface of object.

If test for free alkali is neg. (no color change of indicator), proceed with $AgNO_3$-free test agar, analyzing sample in similar manner. (Grains must be totally immersed during test.) Color change of indicator is yellow → green → blue, depending on concn of NH_3 produced. Reaction usually requires 1–3 min to give detectable color. Time varies inversely with urea concn. Spots from higher levels of urea continue to develop and enlarge for 10–12 min and then fade gradually.

TLC Method (*70*)—Official Final Action

44.174 ***Apparatus***

See **44.162** and following:

(**a**) *Soxhlet extractor.*—250 mL extn flask; extn chamber 39 (id) × 115 mm with top joint ₮ 45/50 and bottom joint ₮ 24/40; 35 × 90 mm thimbles; condenser joint ₮ 45/50 (Arthur H. Thomas Co., No. 4406-E34, or equiv.).

(**b**) *Kuderna-Danish concentrator.*—*See* **29.005**(**e**).

44.175 ***Reagents***

See **44.163**.

44.176 ***Determination***

(*Caution, See* **51.011**, **51.039**, and **51.046**.)

On previous day prep. plates for overnight drying. Equilibrate tanks ca 1 hr before extg samples.

(**a**) *Soxhlet extraction.*—Ext 18 g sample with 60 mL acetone 1 hr at 3–4 min/siphon. Transfer ext to 100 mL g-s graduate, dil. to vol., and take aliquot equiv. to 9 g sample. Conc. as in (**c**).

(**b**) *Alternative extraction.*—Place 18 g sample in 50 mL beaker or erlenmeyer. Add 1 mL acetone/g sample and boil gently 5 min, avoiding excessive loss of acetone. Decant thru glass wool pad into 100 mL g-s graduate. Repeat acetone boil and decanting 3 addnl times, and dil. to 100 mL. Conc. aliquot equiv. to 9 g as in (**c**).

(**c**) *Concentration.*—Conc. aliquot to ca 0.2 mL in Kuderna-Danish concentrator as in **29.009**(**b**); or, alternatively, place empty 13 mL graduated conical centrf. tube in beaker of boiling H_2O. When tube is hot, slowly transfer portions ext, using syringe fitted with long needle, to evapn tube. Let each portion evap. before next is added. Evap. to ca 0.20 mL. Chromatograph without appreciable delay.

(**d**) *Preparation of tank and plates.*—*See* **44.164**(**c**) and (**d**).

(**e**) *Spotting of plates.*—Spot sample conc. as band ca 25 mm long on line 15 mm up and 15 mm in from edge of plate. Wash sides of evapn tube with ca 50 μL acetone and transfer wash to sample band area. Repeat 50 μL washings and transfers until last transfer is colorless (ca 4 transfers). Spot 1 μL each of std solns (**a**)–(**d**) ca 10 mm apart along line 15 mm to left of center of plate and 15 mm from edge of plate.

(**f**) *Development of plates.*—Place plate in trough contg ether in lined tank presatd with ether. Let ether travel to top of plate. Remove plate and let air dry. Immediately draw intersecting lines to divide plate into 4 equal sqs. Dry plate 5 min in 80° forced-draft oven. Remove plate from oven and promptly place in dry solv. trough in TLC tank with spotted band down. Close tank and let stand 20 min. Slide top aside just enough to introduce long-stem funnel into solv. trough. Slowly add 20 mL developing solv., (**g**), to trough. Close lid and develop in dark to line of first direction. Dry plate 5 min in 80° forced-draft oven.

Rotate warm plate to place chromatographed stds in upper left quarter of plate and promptly place in dry trough in tank. Let stand 20 min without touching any liq. in closed tank. Then slide cover aside just enough to introduce long-stem funnel into solv. trough and slowly add 20 mL developing solv. Let front move to line in this second dimension. Dry plate 5 min in 80° forced-draft oven.

(**g**) *Color development.*—Proceed as in **44.164**(**h**).

Bird Excrement in Food and Containers (71)
Official Final Action

44.177 ***Test for Uric Acid***

(Not suitable for minute residues from suspect areas of food containers)

Transfer white, amorphous, grainy particles to depression of spot plate preheated to ca 100° on hot plate or in oven. Add small drop of HNO_3 (1+1) to sides of depression so that it will run down to wet particles; then evap. to dryness in 0.5–1.0 min.

Heat 1–3 min. If particles turn orange-red to deep red with heat, uric acid and/or its salts may be present.

To confirm: Cool plate until there is no perceptible heat to back of hand; then streak across colored area with small glass rod wetted with 50% NaOH soln. Intense purple will develop almost immediately.

Modification for particles less than 1 mg.—Position microscope or strong magnifying glass to observe 18 mm No. 2 cover glass placed on metal surface heated to ca 110–120°. Place suspect particle on glass, add 5–10 μL HNO_3, evap. to dryness, and heat in oven 5–7 min at 135–140°. Remove to cool white surface under magnifier and observe baked reaction residue. Pos. reaction shows yellow-orange to orange-red ring.

To confirm: With 1 mm glass rod place small drop 50% NaOH soln on edge of cover glass. Wipe rod and transfer small portion of drop to edge of baked residue. *Do not flood.* Purple-violet color develops promptly with uric acid or its salts.

Insect Excrement

Uric Acid in Flour (*72*)—Official Final Action

(Applicable to levels ≥4 mg/100 g)

44.178 ***Apparatus***

(**a**) *Spectrophotometer.*—Beckman Model DU, or equiv.

(**b**) *Centrifuge.*—Desk centrf. with multiple head to hold 15 mL polyethylene test tubes.

(**c**) *Incubator or water bath.*—Capable of maintaining temp. of 37±1°.

44.179 ***Reagents***

(**a**) *Uric acid std soln.*—100 μg/mL. Dissolve 100 mg uric acid in 1 L 5% NaOAc soln. (If necessary, warm in H_2O bath at 60–70°.) Filter and store in brown bottle; discard after 1 week. (Do not use com. uric acid std solns, as they may contain uricase inhibitors.)

(**b**) *Sodium borate buffer.*—0.01*M*, pH 9.2. Dissolve 3.8 g $Na_2B_4O_7.10H_2O$ in H_2O and dil. to 1 L.

(**c**) *Sodium acetate soln.*—5%. Dissolve 100 g anhyd. NaOAc in H_2O and dil. to 2 L. If necessary, adjust pH to 8.8–9.2 with HOAc or NaOH.

(**d**) *Glutathione soln.*—10 mg/mL in H_2O. Use within 30 min.

(**e**) *Uricase soln.*—Prep. suspension of 10 mg dried uricase in 50 mL 0.01*M* Na borate buffer. Use within 1 hr. (Clean all glassware that comes in contact with uricase enzyme with chromic acid soln; adsorbed uricase on glass surface produces low results.)

44.180 ***Preliminary Tests***

(**a**) *Test for purity of reagents.*—Dil. 5.0 mL uric acid std soln to 25 mL with 5% NaOAc soln. Place 5 mL in each of 3 test tubes. To 1 tube add 5 mL Na borate buffer, invert several times, and measure *A* at 292 nm. *A* should be ≥0.72, which corresponds to 0.072 *A* unit/μg uric acid/mL final soln. Test std uric acid soln daily.

(**b**) *Test for efficiency of uricase soln.*—Label remaining 2 tubes in (**a**) as No. 1 and No. 2; label a third test tube No. 3. Add 5 mL uricase soln to tubes No. 1 and No. 3. Close mouth of tube No. 1 with piece of cellophane sheet under thumb and invert. Stopper all 3 tubes with clean rubber stoppers and incubate 2 hr at 37°. After incubation, mix contents of tubes No. 2 and No. 3 by repeatedly pouring (6 times) from one tube to other, and immediately (within 60 sec) read *A* of combined solns at 292 nm, using soln in tube No. 1 as blank. *A* should be ≥0.648 for ≥90% of theoretical efficiency of uricase. If efficiency is <90%, incubate 4 hr. If increased incubation does not increase efficiency to 90%, discard uricase sample.

44.181 ***Preparation of Standard Curve***

Pipet 0.0, 2.5, 5.0, 10.0, and 15.0 mL uric acid std soln into 5 beakers (corresponds to 0.0, 1.0, 2.0, 4.0, and 6.0 μg uric acid/mL in final soln, resp.), and perform all steps as in **44.182**, except omit flour.

44.182 ***Determination***

Add 25 mL 1*N* HCl and 5 mL glutathione soln to 4 g flour in 250 mL beaker. Mix well with glass rod and let stand overnight (≥16 hr). Add 25 mL 1*N* NaOH with stirring and adjust pH to 9.0–9.3 with 1*N* NaOH or 1*N* HCl. Transfer to 100 mL g-s graduate, carefully scraping all material sticking to sides of beaker with glass rod. Rinse beaker with 6 small portions 5% NaOAc and dil. to 100 mL with 5% NaOAc. Shake *gently* by inverting graduate several times every 10 min for 1 hr. (Vigorous shaking tends to produce turbid soln.) Transfer aliquot to 15 mL polyethylene test tube and centrf. 30 min at 3000 rpm. Decant supernate into small erlenmeyer, mix well, and pipet 4 mL into each of 2 test tubes, No. 1 and No. 2. To each tube, add 1 mL Na borate buffer and mix by rotating between palms of hands. (Mix soln with Na borate buffer within 15 min to avoid turbid soln.) Label third tube as No. 3. Add 5 mL uricase soln to tubes No. 1 and No. 3. Mix contents of tube No. 1 as in **44.180(b)**. Stopper all 3 tubes with rubber stoppers and incubate 2 hr at 37°. Combine solns in tubes No. 2 and No. 3, as in **44.180(b)**, and read *A* immediately (within 60 sec) at 292 nm against soln No. 1 (blank). (If flour ext appears very turbid after centrfg, dil. centrfd ext 1 + 4 with Na borate buffer and pipet 5.0 mL into each of 2 test tubes, No. 1 and No. 2. Add 5 mL uricase to each tube (No. 1 and No. 3) and proceed with detn as above.)

Reading, *A*, corresponds to amt of uric acid present in 4 mL portions of centrfd soln; amt of uric acid obtained from std curve × diln factor = amt of uric acid in sample.

Uric Acid from Bird and Insect Excreta

Thin Layer Chromatographic Method (73)
Official First Action

(Applicable to suspect material not suitable for detn by **44.177** and/or to confirmation of **44.177** when adequate material is available.)

44.183 ***Apparatus and Reagents***

(**a**) *Thin layer cellulose plates.*—*See* **44.164(d)**(*1*)–(*3*).

(**b**) *Cellulose powder.*—*See* **44.163(h)**.

(**c**) *Detection sprays.*—(*1*) *Spray reagent A.*—Prep. satd aq. soln of Na_3PO_4, and filter. (*2*) *Spray reagent B.*—Weigh 50 g Na_2WO_4 into 500 mL ₮ 24/40 boiling flask, add 10 g anhyd. Na_2HPO_4 and 100 mL H_2O, and heat until solids are dissolved. Add 50 mL cool (room temp.) H_2SO_4 (1+3) very slowly with swirling to the tungstate soln. Reflux 1 hr, cool to room temp., and dil. to 250 mL.

(**d**) *Developing solvent.*—*n*-BuOH-MeOH-H_2O (4+4+3). Measure vols sep. and mix well to form stable single phase. To 30 mL this soln add fresh daily 1 mL HOAc, and mix well.

(**e**) *Dye mixture.*—Dissolve 8 mg each of FD&C Red No. 2 and FD&C Yellow No. 6 in 250 mL H_2O, and mix well.

(**f**) *Lithium carbonate soln.*—1 mg/mL H_2O.

(**g**) *Phenolphthalein soln*—1% in alcohol-H_2O (1+1).

(**h**) *Uric acid std soln.*—(*1*) *Stock soln.*—1 mg/mL. Dry 105 mg uric acid in 100° oven overnight, and cool to room temp. in desiccator. Accurately weigh 60 mg Li_2CO_3 and transfer to 100 mL vol. flask. Accurately weigh 100 mg cool uric acid and transfer quant. to the 100 mL vol. flask with ca 50 mL H_2O. Place in 60° H_2O bath and agitate until soln clears. Cool immediately under tap H_2O to room temp. and dil. to vol. with H_2O. For short term use (<3 days), store in refrigerator; for extended use, place portions in small containers and store hard frozen. (*2*) *Working soln.*—100 μg/mL. Pipet 10 mL stock soln into 100 mL vol. flask and dil. to vol. with H_2O. Prep. fresh daily.

44.184 ***Preparation of Sample***

(**a**) *Insect excreta.*—Transfer material to small test tube, crush with glass rod, and add 0.05–0.1 mL Li_2CO_3 soln, (**c**). Let soak ca 10 min, and centrf. Obtain clear supernate, and proceed as in **44.185**.

(**b**) *Paper bags or cartons.*—Cut ca 5–6 mm diam. portion from suspect area, and place in small test tube. Add ca 0.1 mL Li_2CO_3 soln, (**c**), and agitate with small stirring rod. Let soak ca 10 min, and proceed as in **44.185**.

(**c**) *Other suspect material.*—Transfer small portion to test tube, add ca 0.1 mL Li_2CO_3 soln, (**c**), and stir with glass rod. Let soak ca 10 min, and centrf. Obtain clear supernate, and proceed as in **44.185**.

44.185 ***Determination***

(**a**) *Spotting of plates.*—Place coated plate on heated metal slab (*see* **44.164(e)**). Place infrared lamp or forced hot air source (hair dryer, etc.) above the plate to speed drying of spots. Spot 1 μl uric acid working std soln, (**h**)(*2*), at each edge and at center of plate ca 15–20 mm up from bottom. Overspot each of 3 working std spots with 1 μL dye mixt., (**e**). Spot samples along same line at ca 10 mm intervals. Keep spots to min. size by drying well between successive small addns.

(**b**) *Development of plates.*—Develop in conventional tank without pre-equilibration or, alternatively, form sandwich chamber with uncoated plate and develop. Dry plate on heated metal slab or in forced draft oven ca 5 min at 75–80°. Along line parallel to origin, place two 1 μL spots phthln soln, (**g**), between each upper and lower set of dye spots.

(**c**) *Color development.*—Observe plate under shortwave (254 nm) black light in darkened room, marking quenching (dark) spots with circle. High levels of uric acid should appear as 4–5 mm areas at R_f = 0.40±0.05, depending upon conditions of development. Spray plate in hood with spray reagent A, (**c**) (*1*), until strong phthln spots appear and background darkens slightly. (*Caution: See* **51.017**.) Spray with spray reagent B, (**c**) (*2*), until plate is damp or just shiny wet. Place immediately in horizontal position, and dry as in (**b**). If all spots have not responded, respray again with spray reagent A until strong phthln spots appear. Pale blue color at R_f of std, which darkens slightly upon heating, confirms presence of uric acid. Prolonged heating fades color.

MISCELLANEOUS

Plant Gums, Crude

44.186 Light Filth (*74*)—Official First Action

(If av. particle is ≤5 mm, proceed with method. If particle size is >5 mm, break into pieces by hand or by dropping small amts at a time into high-speed blender until desired size is reached. Where 95% and 40% alcohol are specified, isopropanol and 30% isopropanol, resp., can be substituted.)

Weigh 50 g sample into 2 L beaker, add 1.2 L H_2O and 15 mL HCl, and stir well. Autoclave 1 hr at 121°. Slow vent. (Arabic and guar gums will completely dissolve in 15–30 min in 1.2 L H_2O + 25 mL HCl when placed on mag. stirrer-hot plate or in steam bath.) Sieve portionwise on No. 230 sieve, **44.002(u)**, using forcible stream of hot (55–70°) tap H_2O from aerator, **44.002(a)**, until all gum has passed thru. Transfer directly to ruled filter paper if negligible amts of plant tissue remain on sieve. If large amts of plant debris remain on sieve, transfer to 1 L trap flask with 40% alcohol. Bring vol. to 500 mL with 40% alcohol and add 25 mL HCl. Heat to ca 60° on mag. stirrer-hot plate with stirring. Add 25 mL mineral oil, **44.003(y)**, and stir mag. 2 min, **44.004(b)**. Fill flask with 40% alcohol and gently swirl contents with stopper. Let stand 10 min and perform first trapping. Add 25 mL mineral oil, and gently stir with stopper 1 min. Let stand 5 min and perform second trapping. Rinse neck of flask with 95% alcohol and pour trappings onto ruled filter paper. Examine at 30×.

Leafy Crude Drugs—Official First Action

44.187 Gross Contamination

See **44.119**.

44.188 Heavy and Light Filth

See **44.120**.

Papain, Crude and Refined

44.189 Light Filth (*75*)—Official First Action

Weigh 50 g sample into 1.5 L beaker. (*Caution:* Weigh under effective fume removal device to avoid breathing dust. Avoid skin contact.) Add 1 L hot H_2O and small amt of Antifoam A spray. Boil 20 min with stirring. Wet sieve forcefully on No. 230 sieve until all whitish material passes thru sieve and only plant debris and extraneous materials remain. If small amt of material remains on sieve, transfer directly to ruled filter paper. If large amt of plant tissue remains, transfer to 1 L trap flask with 40% isopropanol or 55% alcohol (use same alcohol thruout method). Bring vol. to 500 mL with alcohol and add 25 mL HCl. Boil 5 min, add 25 mL mineral oil, **44.003(y)**, stir mag. 2 min, **44.004(b)**, fill with alcohol, and trap off after 10 min. Perform second trapping, using 15 mL mineral oil, stir by hand 1 min, and trap off after 10 min. Filter trappings thru ruled paper and examine microscopically.

44.190 *Direction of Insect Penetration thru Packaging Materials (76)—Official First Action*

(**a**) **Entrance Characteristics**

(*1*) *Kraft paper, paper box.*

(*a*) *Surface fraying.*—Consists of paper fibers cut and lifted from surface of packaging material by mandibular activity. Represents first activity of hole formation. May occur at random on "entrance" surface of packaging materials. *See* Fig. **44:09(B)**.

(*b*) *Terraced depression.*—Consists of "step effect" formed when *secondary depression* is superimposed on *initial depression; see* Fig. **44:09(D)**. This terracing may be present around entire perimeter of final hole or at one or more points around it.

(*c*) *Tapered hole.*—Diam. of hole is greater on entrance side than exit side. This feature is most obvious on thicker packaging materials. *See* Fig. **44:09(E)**.

(*2*) *Foil, Cellophane, polyethylene plastic, waxed paper.*

(*a*) *Mandibular scratches.*—Found on Al foil, Cellophane, and polyethylene plastic. Consists of small, short surface scratches or grooves formed by pincerlike action of mandibles. Frequently observed around perimeter of hole or in localized groups at random on entrance surface. *See* Fig. **44:09(F)**.

(*b*) *Upturned edges.*—Present around perimeter of holes in

Al foil and polyethylene plastic materials. Appear as continuous irregularly upturned edge in foil (Fig. **44:09(G)**) and generally as upturned fraying of plastic (Fig. **44:09(H)**) in polyethylene materials. Not observed on waxed paper and Cellophane materials.

(*c*) *Roughened surface.*—Observed around perimeter of holes or randomly on surface of polyethylene plastic and waxed paper. Consists of surface fraying or pulled up tufts resulting from mandibular action on material. Distinct mandibular scratches may be observed around or in roughened areas.

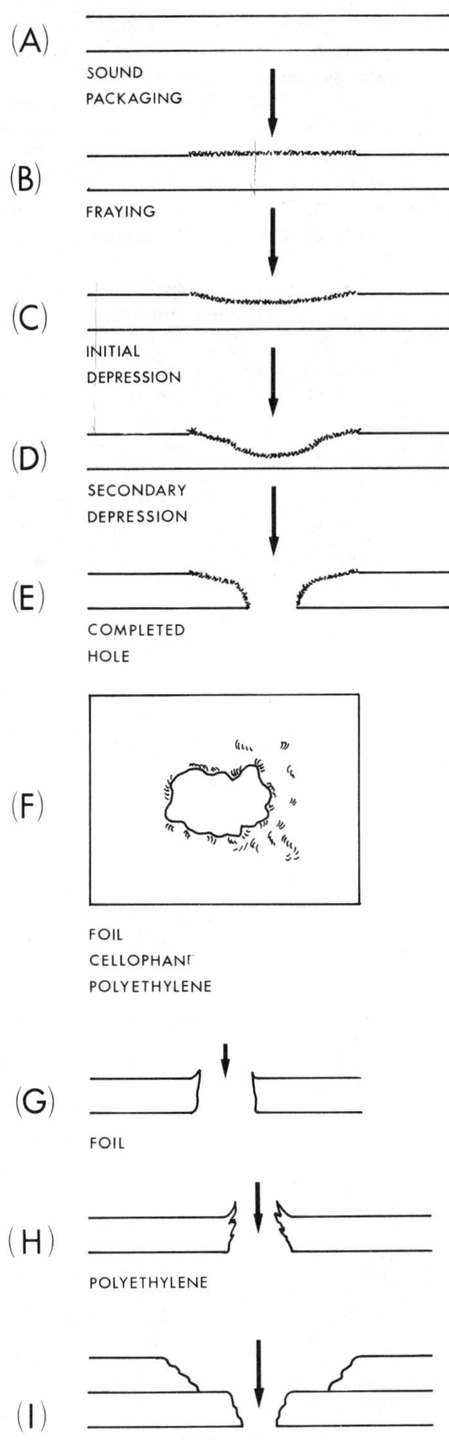

FIG. 44:09—Insect penetration of packaging.

(*3*) *Foil/paper, foil/plastic, or other laminates.*

(*a*) *Entrance characteristics.—See* specific materials.

(*b*) *Terracing of laminates.*—Quite common on entrance side of these materials. Observed as larger hole bored in laminate material on entrance surface and smaller hole in exit side of material. *See* Fig. **44:09(I)**.

(b) Exit Characteristics

All types of packaging materials.

(*1*) Clean-cut hole perimeter.

(*2*) Diam. of hole smaller than on entrance side.

(*3*) No surface fraying, scratches, or depressions (*see* Fig. **44:09(E)**).

SELECTED REFERENCES

(*1*) JAOAC **57**, 957(1974).
(*2*) JAOAC **48**, 543(1965); **50**, 496(1967).
(*3*) JAOAC **54**, 567(1971).
(*4*) JAOAC **55**, 57(1972); **58**, 1302(1975).
(*5*) JAOAC **54**, 571(1971).
(*6*) JAOAC **50**, 499, 520(1967).
(*7*) JAOAC **35**, 340(1952); **36**, 310(1953); **37**, 117(1954); **48**, 559(1965); Am. J. Pub. Health **37**, 728(1947).
(*8*) JAOAC **50**, 501(1967).
(*9*) JAOAC **53**, 552(1970).
(*10*) JAOAC **20**, 93(1937); **2**, 495(1939); **23**, 468, 693(1940); **24**, 183, 550(1941); **25**, 609(1942); Food Ind. **7**, 441(1935).
(*11*) JAOAC **53**, 553(1970).
(*12*) JAOAC **53**, 550(1970).
(*13*) JAOAC **51**, 531(1968).
(*14*) JAOAC **53**, 723(1970); **54**, 903(1971).
(*15*) Cereal Chem. **18**, 655(1941).
(*16*) JAOAC **55**, 514(1972).
(*17*) JAOAC **48**, 554(1965).
(*18*) JAOAC **55**, 60(1972).
(*19*) Food Ind. **12**, 36(1940).
(*20*) JAOAC **26**, 257(1943).
(*21*) JAOAC **53**, 560(1970).
(*22*) JAOAC **55**, 64(1972).
(*23*) JAOAC **55**, 62(1972).
(*24*) JAOAC **55**, 516(1972).
(*25*) JAOAC **45**, 660(1962).
(*26*) JAOAC **53**, 562(1970).
(*27*) JAOAC **58**, 441(1975).
(*28*) JAOAC **52**, 463(1969).
(*29*) JAOAC **53**, 558(1970).
(*30*) JAOAC **54**, 573(1971).
(*31*) JAOAC **43**, 565(1960).
(*32*) JAOAC **51**, 504(1968).
(*33*) JAOAC **59**, 825(1976).
(*34*) JAOAC **55**, 69(1972).
(*35*) JAOAC **57**, 691(1974).
(*36*) JAOAC **56**, 631(1973); **59**, 51(1976).
(*37*) JAOAC **55**, 66(1972).
(*38*) JAOAC **47**, 897(1964).
(*39*) JAOAC **58**, 443(1975).
(*40*) JAOAC **52**, 19(1969).
(*41*) JAOAC **54**, 581(1971).
(*42*) JAOAC **54**, 568(1971).
(*43*) Bur. Chem. Circ. **68** (1911); Food and Drug Adm. Leaflet, July 1942; Amer. Can Co. Bull. (1954); Natl. Canners Ass. Tomato Products Tables, 2nd rev. (Feb. 1966); JAOAC **49**, 572(1966); **53**, 366(1970).
(*44*) JAOAC **35**, 337(1952); **53**, 366(1970); Natl. Canners Ass. Tomato Products Tables, 2nd rev. (Feb. 1966).
(*45*) JAOAC **55**, 73(1972).

(*46*) JAOAC **55,** 71(1972).
(*47*) JAOAC **57,** 693(1974).
(*48*) JAOAC **62,** 600(1979).
(*49*) JAOAC **49,** 576(1966); **50,** 514(1967); **59,** 353(1976).
(*50*) JAOAC **56,** 634(1973).
(*51*) JAOAC **58,** 445, 447, 451(1975); **59,** 827(1976).
(*52*) JAOAC **51,** 518(1968).
(*53*) JAOAC **55,** 83(1972).
(*54*) JAOAC **60,** 117(1977).
(*55*) JAOAC **62,** 595(1979).
(*56*) JAOAC **55,** 78(1972).
(*57*) JAOAC **61,** 900(1978).
(*58*) JAOAC **60,** 114(1977).
(*59*) JAOAC **52,** 469(1969).
(*60*) JAOAC **54,** 575(1971).
(*61*) JAOAC **52,** 21(1969).
(*62*) JAOAC **51,** 522(1968).
(*63*) JAOAC **62,** 598(1979).
(*64*) JAOAC **56,** 629(1973).
(*65*) JAOAC **25,** 772(1942).
(*66*) JAOAC **42,** 473(1959).
(*67*) JAOAC **57,** 689(1974).
(*68*) JAOAC **46,** 685(1963).
(*69*) JAOAC **55,** 76(1972).
(*70*) JAOAC **56,** 637(1973).
(*71*) JAOAC **45,** 659(1962); **47,** 516(1964).
(*72*) JAOAC **49,** 899(1966); **50,** 776(1967); **52,** 833(1969).
(*73*) JAOAC **61,** 903(1978).
(*74*) JAOAC **52,** 17(1969).
(*75*) JAOAC **54,** 565(1971).
(*76*) JAOAC **56,** 640(1973).

GENERAL REFERENCES

(*1*) Microscopic-Analytical Methods in Food and Drug Control. Food and Drug Tech. Bull. No. 1. (Out of print; under revision.)
(*2*) Annotated Bibliography of Methods for Examination of Foods. JAOAC **29,** 420(1946); JAOAC **38,** 1016(1955).
(*3*) Insect Contaminants of Foods. JAOAC **33,** 898(1950).
(*4*) Insect Setae. JAOAC **37,** 960(1954).
(*5*) Radiographic Applications. JAOAC **37,** 148(1954).
(*6*) "Identification of Stored Products by the Micromorphology of the Exoskeleton." A series published in JAOAC (reprints are no longer available): Elytral patterns **38,** 776(1955); Adult antennas **39,** 879(1956); Larval fragments **39,** 990(1956); Adult legs **40,** 973(1957); Adult and larval beetle mandibles **41,** 460(1958); Adult labral characteristics **41,** 472(1958); Head, thorax, abdomen **41,** 828(1958); Adult moths **43,** 444(1960); Larvae of moths **41,** 704(1958); Cockroach fragments **41,** 886(1958); Miscellaneous insects **41,** 206(1958).
(*7*) "Micro-Analytical Entomology for Food Sanitation Control." AOAC, Box 540, Benjamin Franklin Station, Washington, DC 20044 (1962).
(*8*) Winton, A. L. and Winton, K. B., "The Structure and Composition of Foods." John Wiley & Sons (4 Vols: 1932–1939).
(*9*) "Food Microscopy." A series published in Food **25**(1956)–**28**(1959).
(*10*) "Training Manual for Analytical Entomology in the Food Industry." AOAC, Box 540 Benjamin Franklin Station, Washington, DC 20044 (1977).

45. Forensic Sciences

Latent Fingerprints

Powder Brushing Method (1)—Official Final Action

(Applicable to development of latent images deposited on nonporous surfaces within 120 hr and not subjected to extreme temp. or humidity changes)

45.001 ***Determination***

Pour small amt fingerprint powder (Hi-Fi Volcano, Sirchie Fingerprint Laboratories, Inc., Gravelly Hollow Rd, Medford, NJ 08055, or equiv.) into shallow dish or onto piece of paper. Pick up small amt with end of camel hair brush. Hold brush over surface to be dusted, and tap handle lightly to permit powder to drift onto surface. Brush surface lightly until image begins to appear. Continue with light strokes, following ridge direction in pattern as it forms. Apply addnl powder, if necessary, to obtain good contrast, but retain ridge detail. When sufficient detail and contrast are obtained, remove excess powder with ostrich feather duster. Preserve image by photographing and then taping over, leaving tape in place if practical. If not, pull off tape slowly and evenly, and place on 3 × 5" card of contrasting color.

Chemical Development Method (2)—Official First Action

(Applicable to forced development of latent images deposited on bond and newsprint papers)

45.002 ***Apparatus and Reagent***

(**a**) *Steam iron.*—With heat indicator.

(**b**) *Ninhydrin soln.*—0.5%. Dissolve 0.5 g 1,2,3-indantrione $.H_2O$ in 100 mL acetone, mix, and let stand 15 min.

45.003 ***Pretreatment***

(If evidence contains handwriting, printing, or typewriting to be examined by document examiner, protect area by brushing pretreatment, allowing for migration of ninhydrin soln. In general, spray large objects.)

Perform one of following pretreatments on papers:

(**a**) *Dipping.*—Pour small vol. ninhydrin soln into flat dish, pick up paper with tweezers, submerge paper in soln until satd, hold paper above dish, letting excess liq. drip into dish, and place paper on clean blotter to air dry.

(**b**) *Brushing.*—With paint brush or cotton swab on wooden stick, pick up small vol. ninhydrin soln from flat dish, paint paper until surface is coated, transfer to clean blotter, and let air dry.

(**c**) *Spraying.*—Pour ca 30 mL ninhydrin soln into spraying cannister. Use com. compressed air or inert gas, or compressed air from laboratory line as propellant. Place papers in exhaust hood or similar cabinet. Hold spraying cannister upright ca 8–10" (20–25 cm) from paper and spray until paper is coated. Transfer paper to blotter and let air dry.

Discard ninhydrin soln in flat dish. Return ninhydrin spraying soln to supply bottle for future use.

45.004 ***Development***

Fill steam iron with H_2O and turn heat indicator to "Steam". Place papers on clean blotter. When steam is being ejected from sole plate holes, hold iron ca 1" (2.5 cm) above papers and move iron around to distribute heat and steam evenly. Vary ht above paper with rate steam is being projected beneath iron. Steam should just reach papers before rising to sole plate. Wipe sole plate frequently to prevent condensate from dripping on paper. Images will begin to develop in ca 45 sec and continue to intensify until plum or purple color is obtained. Move paper to clean blotter and let air dry; as alternative, after steam development of prints, shut off steam, wipe bottom of iron free of moisture, and then lightly pass iron over developed prints to enhance images. (Use caution not to burn or scorch papers.) Continue with each paper until all have been treated. When papers are dry, place each in appropriately labeled envelope or plastic protector, handling with tweezers.

Characterization and Matching of Glass Fragments by Dispersion Microscopy

Double Variation Method (3)—Official Final Action

45.005 ***Principle***

Refractive indices (n) of glass and stdzd liqs are matched at different wavelengths by varying temp. of mixt. The n of glass remains relatively const with temp. change; those of liqs decrease with increasing temp. Plot of wavelength, where n of glass and liq. match, against temp. for specific stdzd liq., is characteristic of particular glass.

45.006 ***Apparatus***

(**a**) *Microscope.*—Compd, transmitted light type, with illumination system capable of restricted substage aperture or, preferably, phase contrast optics which permits easier matching, with provision for long working distance.

(**b**) *Hot stage.*—Capable of attaining, holding, and indicating temp. accurately (±0.1°) and permitting use of required illumination (Mettler FP-5, Mettler Instrument Corp., 20 Nassau St, Princeton, NJ 08540, or equiv.).

(**c**) *Monochromatic light source.*—Accurately calibrated (±1 nm at 486) with sufficient intensity in small beam of low angular aperture over range at least 460–680 nm (continuous interference filter, 400–700 nm, band width ca 15 nm, No. 50 09 00, Carl Zeiss, Inc., 444 Fifth Ave, New York, NY 10018, is satisfactory).

(**d**) *Graph paper.*—Hartmann net (linear temp., nonlinear wavelength resulting in straight line) preferable; available from Walter C. McCrone Associates, Inc., 2820 S Michigan Ave, Chicago, IL 60616. If unavailable, use ordinary graph paper.

45.007 ***Reagents***

(**a**) *Refractive index liquids.*—Calibrated immersion liqs, range 1.50–1.65 (R. P. Cargille Laboratories, 55 Commerce Rd, Cedar Grove, NJ 07009), or NBS SRM 1823 silicone liqs. Use high dispersion set with most glasses.

(**b**) *Collodion soln.*—Dil. 1 mL 3% collodion, flexible (Fisher Scientific Co., No. C-409), to 100 mL with amyl acetate.

45.008 ***Preparation of Samples***

(All particles examined must be ≤100 μm in major dimension.)

(**a**) *Single small flake.*—Arrange 3 small (2–3 mm) cover slip flakes at corners of ca 1 cm triangle near end of ⅝ × 3" microscope slide and cement in place by placing drop of dild collodion soln outside of triangle and drawing soln to each fragment in turn with fine tungsten needle. With very small drop of dild collodion soln, cement test fragment on slide within triangle, near 1 of fragments as locator. Avoid touching collodion cementing cover slip fragments. Second fragment can be cemented close by for simultaneous and direct comparison. Excessive collodion interferes with index readings; if necessary, thin collodion around test fragment with amyl acetate. Place cover slip on the 3 supports, and place small drop of liq. of known n at edge to be drawn around fragments by capillary attraction. After n measurement, clean slide, if necessary to change liq., by removing cover slip and rinsing tilted slide held over waste containers with drops of benzene added from dropper.

(**b**) *Many small flakes.*—Obtain many small flakes by crushing in anvil-striker type hammer mill. Place few flakes on slide without cementing, cover with cover slip, and add small drop of liq. at edge of cover slip. New prepn may be used for each liq. or slide may be cleaned by removing cover, pushing particles to side with razor cut edge of filter paper, adding drop of new liq., pushing again to side, and adding drop of fresh liq.

45.009 *Determination*

Choose immersion liq. which matches n of glass at far red end of spectrum at temp. slightly above room temp., ca 30°. With such match, all subsequent temp.-wavelength matches will be <60°, requiring small temp. corrections. Use narrow beam of light parallel to optic axis passing thru closed down substage aperture, but open enough to see Becke lines. (There will be best iris setting for each wavelength.) Place mounted sample on hot stage set at lowest even degree temp. at which wavelength match is observed (ca 660 nm). Darkened room and intense illumination are advantageous. Record av. of several matching wavelengths for that temp. Set temp. at successively higher even degree intervals, let equilibrate 30 sec, and read wavelength. Repeat match several times and det. av. Continue increasing temp. until no match can be obtained (ca 450 nm). Let hot stage cool, and recheck 1–2 of lower temp. matches. Difference indicates change in liq. at high temp. and requires repeat of second half of data at higher temp. with fresh liq. Rate should be 1 data point/min. Plot data on Hartmann net or ordinary graph paper.

Table 45:01 Refractive Indices and Temperature Coefficients of Cargille Liquids

n^{25}_F	n^{25}_D	n^{25}_C	dn/dt (25–35°)
	A Series		
1.46594	1.460	1.45762	0.00037
1.47666	1.470	1.46735	0.00037
1.48739	1.480	1.47709	0.00037
1.49812	1.490	1.48682	0.00038
1.50884	1.500	1.49656	0.00038
1.51957	1.510	1.50629	0.00038
1.53030	1.520	1.51603	0.00038
1.54103	1.530	1.52576	0.00038
1.55175	1.540	1.53550	0.00039
1.56248	1.550	1.54523	0.00039
1.57321	1.560	1.55497	0.00039
1.58393	1.570	1.56470	0.00039
1.59466	1.580	1.57444	0.00040
1.60539	1.590	1.58417	0.00040
1.61611	1.600	1.59391	0.00040
	High Dispersion Series		
1.5134	1.500	1.4943	0.00045
1.5247	1.510	1.5039	0.00046
1.5360	1.520	1.5134	0.00046
1.5451	1.530	1.5242	0.00047
1.5557	1.540	1.5339	0.00047
1.5664	1.550	1.5437	0.00047
1.5770	1.560	1.5534	0.00047
1.5877	1.570	1.5632	0.00047
1.5983	1.580	1.5729	0.00047
1.6090	1.590	1.5827	0.00047
1.6196	1.600	1.5924	0.00047
1.6303	1.610	1.6021	0.00047
1.6410	1.620	1.6119	0.00047
1.6516	1.630	1.6216	0.00047
1.6623	1.640	1.6314	0.00047

Reprinted with permission of Ann Arbor Science Publishers Inc., Ann Arbor, MI.

45.010 *Calculations*

From graph, read temp. corresponding to 486.1 (F), 589.3 (D), and 656.3 (C) nm. From Table **45:01**, obtain n of liq. used at these wavelengths and temp. coefficient to be used in correcting table values at 25° to actual matching temp. Report matching temp. and corrected refractive index (n^t) for each of the 3 wavelengths specified.

Example: Using Cargille liq. 1.520:

Wavelength	*Matching temp. from graph*	*n at this wavelength (Table **45:01**) at 25°*	*Calcd n at matching temp.*
486	42.8	1.53030	1.52354
589	33.6	1.52000	1.51673
656	29.6	1.51603	1.51428

Calcd n is obtained by using dn/dt = 0.00038/° in equation: $n^t = n_{25} - (\text{matching temp.} - 25)(dn/dt)$

$$n_{486} = 1.53030 - (42.8 - 25)(0.00038)$$
$$= 1.53030 - 0.00676 = 1.52354.$$

Repeat for 589 and 656 nm.

Mineral Wool Insulation (*4*)
Interim Official First Action

45.011 *Apparatus and Reagents*

(**a**) *Microscopes.*—(*1*) Phase contrast, with provision for long working distances; (*2*) Low power inspection type.

(**b**) *Illuminators.*—White and UV (253.7 nm) incident light sources.

(**c**) *Monochromator.*—*See* **45.006(c)**, or High Intensity Monochromator (Bausch & Lomb, Inc.), or equiv, for transmitted light illumination.

(**d**) *Hot Stage.*—*See* **45.006(b)**.

(**e**) *Graph paper.*—*See* **45.006(d)**

(**f**) *Annealing oven.*—650°. Controlled temp. muffle furnace.

(**g**) *Refractive index liquids.*—*See* **45.007(a)**.

45.012 *Microscopic Examination*

Compare known and unknown source materials under low power microscope in incident light to det. color of resin, if any, and disposition of resin on fibers (e.g. evenly coated, in globs, etc). Compare diams of fibers, and relative abundance of slugs and shot.

45.013 *Annealing*

Place known source and unknown source fibers and slugs in porcelain crucibles with covers and heat to 650° (1200°F) in controlled temp. muffle furnace. Hold at 650° ≥10 min; then lower temp. at rate of ca 28° (50°F)/30 min to ca 365° (690°F) when rate of cooling becomes immaterial.

45.014 ***Comparison of Properties***

(**a**) *Fluorescence*.—If enough material is available, compare fluorescence of annealed fibers under UV light, (**b**). Note color and brightness of fluorescence.

(**b**) *Solubility in acid*.—Place annealed fibers on glass slide under low power microscope, add drop HCl (1+3), and note solubility. Repeat, if indicated, with concd HCl.

(**c**) *Optical properties*.—Place representative fibers and slugs from annealed known and unknown source materials on microscope slides under cover slips. Introduce refractive index liq., (**g**), under cover slip. Insert on hot stage and adjust temp. until fibers essentially disappear when viewed thru phase microscope and monochromator set near red end of visible spectrum (near 656 nm). Note temp. and monochromator setting. Increase temp. in 5° (9°F) increments to find ≥3 match points of glass and oil within 656–486 nm range. Plot results on graph paper, (**e**), on which oil dispersion curves have been plotted and calibrated. If variations along fibers or among fibers and slugs have been observed, curve for material is best expressed by band covering all match points observed.

Because of wide variation of *n* among mineral wool insulations, it may be necessary to make several trials before appropriate oil is found. If fibers are clearly visible in all wavelengths of light at temps between 35 and 90°, choose different oil. Repeat trial-and-error procedure until oil is found in which fibers match oil at 3 different wavelengths beween 656 and 486 nm.

Compare properties of known and unknown source materials.

Voice Print Identification (*5*)—Official Final Action

45.015 ***Principle***

Voice print method of speaker identification consists of aural and visual comparison of one or more known voices to unknown or questioned voice. Aural examination dets if acoustic properties of known and unknown voices exhibit preponderance of similarities or differences. Visual analysis with speech spectrograms compares spectrographic features of similar sounds in both known and unknown voices.

45.016 ***Apparatus***

(**a**) *Sound spectrograph*.—Model 4691 or 700 from Voice Identification, Inc., PO Box 714, Somerville, NJ 08876, or Voice Scan Spectrograph Model LGK 100 from Audio Intelligence Devices, PO Box 23130, Ft Lauderdale, FL 33307, or equiv.

(**b**) *Tape recorders*.—(*1*) Model 110 Sony cassette (ac capability, 115–120 v, 60 Hz; frequency response, 50–10,000 Hz), or equiv. (*2*) Multitrack, for aural evaluation (optional).

(**c**) *Patch cord*.

(**d**) *Spectrograph paper*.

45.017 ***Determination***

Record unknown and known voices onto spectrograph. Use patch cord to record speech samples from cassette recorder to spectrograph. Adjust signal peaks to zero volume units (VU) for proper record level, and monitor recording.

Listen to known and questioned voices until familiar with context of each call and each speaker's voice. Set spectrograph modes for normal (bar), wide-band, expanded linear frequency scale with high shaping. Adjust scan playback level to zero VU for production of each spectrogram. Label unknown spectrogram by call number. Label known spectrogram by name given for each speaker. Properly label all speech sounds produced on each spectrogram.

Aurally compare questioned and known voices, using multitrack recorder, or 2 recorders. Visually examine similar sounds between unknown and known voices as displayed in speech spectrograms. Conduct aural and visual examinations simultaneously in arriving at conclusion, without limitations on time or restrictions on number of speech samples necessary.

Make 1 of 5 alternative judgments: (1) positive identification; (2) positive elimination; (3) probable identification; (4) probable elimination; (5) unable to arrive at conclusion. Base all positive judgments on ≥10 pairs of like sounds in known and unknown voices.

SELECTED REFERENCES

(*1*) JAOAC **57,** 662(1974); **58,** 126(1975).
(*2*) JAOAC **59,** 1003(1976)
(*3*) JAOAC **56,** 1223(1973); **57,** 668(1974).
(*4*) JAOAC **60,** 772(1977); **62,** 792(1979).
(*5*) JAOAC **58,** 453(1975); **59,** 927(1976).

SPECIAL REFERENCE

(*1*) McCrone, W. C. and Delly, J. G., "The Particle Atlas," 2nd ed., Vol. 4, Ann Arbor Science Publishers, PO Box 1425, Ann Arbor, MI 48106 (1973), Table: Optical Constants for Cargille Refractive Index Liquids.

46. Microbiological Methods

(When preparing culture media, use distd or deionized H_2O such as Purified Water USP XX, found to be free from traces of dissolved metals, and bactericidal or inhibitory compds. Use anhyd. salts unless otherwise specified.)

Cross Reference Tables

46.001 ***Methods for Examination of Foods***

- Beef, ground
  - Virus — **46.120**
- Candy and candy coatings
  - Salmonella — **46.071**
- Coconut
  - Salmonella — **46.071**
- Eggs and egg products
  - Coliform organisms — **46.009**
  - Direct microscopic count — **46.012**
  - Fungi — **46.011**
  - Plate counts
    - Std — **46.008**
    - Spiral — **46.110–46.116**
  - Salmonella
    - Cultural — **46.056**
    - Fluorescent antibody (FA) — **46.071**
  - Staphylococci, hemolytic — **46.010**
  - Streptococci — **46.010**
- Fish meal
  - Salmonella — **46.071**
- Foods, canned, low-acid
  - Commercial sterility — **46.018–46.025**
- Foods, chilled, frozen, precooked, or prepd, and food ingredients
  - Aerobic plate count
    - Std — **46.015**
    - Spiral — **46.110–46.116**
  - Coliform organisms — **46.016**
  - *Escherichia coli* — **46.016**
  - Salmonella, fluorescent antibody — **46.071**
  - *Staphylococcus aureus,* coagulase pos.
    - Tube cultural — **46.017**
    - Surface plating — **46.075–46.076**
- Foods, outbreak
  - *Clostridium botulinum* and toxins — **46.037–46.045**
  - *Clostridium perfringens* — **46.031–46.036**
    - Alpha-toxin — **46.046–46.053**
  - *Staphylococcus aureus* — **46.017, 46.075–46.076**
    - Staphyloccal enterotoxin — **46.077–46.085**
- Frog legs
  - Salmonella — **46.071**
- Garlic powder
  - Salmonella — **46.056**
- Meat and meat products
  - Salmonella — **46.071**
- Milk, fluid
  - Somatic cell count — **46.086–46.109**
- Milk products, dried
  - Salmonella
    - Cultural — **46.056**
    - Fluorescent antibody (FA) — **46.071**
- Nut meats, tree
  - Aerobic plate count
    - Std — **46.015**
    - Spiral plate — **46.110–46.116**
  - Coliform organisms — **46.016**
  - *Escherichia coli* — **46.016**
- Onion powder
  - Salmonella — **46.056**
- Sugars
  - Thermophilic bacterial spores — **46.026–46.030**
- Yeast
  - Dried active
    - Salmonella — **46.056**
  - Dried inactive
    - Salmonella — **46.071**

46.002 ***Methods for Examination for Organisms***

- *Clostridium botulinum*
  - Foods, prepared and canned — **46.037–46.045**
- *Clostridium perfringens*
  - Foods, chilled, frozen, precooked, or prepd — **46.031–46.036**
- Coliform organisms
  - Eggs and egg products — **46.009**
  - Foods, chilled, frozen, precooked, or prepd — **46.016**
  - Nut meats, tree — **46.016**
  - Shellfish, growing waters — **46.117–46.119**
- *Escherichia coli*
  - Foods, chilled, frozen, precooked, or prepd — **46.016**
  - Nut meats, tree — **46.016**
  - Shellfish, growing waters — **46.117–46.119**
- Fungi
  - Eggs and egg products — **46.011**
- Salmonella
  - Candy and candy coatings — **46.071**
  - Coconut — **46.071**
  - Eggs and egg products — **46.056, 46.071**
  - Fish meal — **46.071**
  - Foods, chilled, frozen, precooked or prepd, and food ingredients — **46.071**
  - Frog legs — **46.071**
  - Garlic powder — **46.056**
  - Meat and meat products — **46.071**
  - Milk products, dried — **46.056, 46.071**
  - Onion powder — **46.056**
  - Yeast, dried
    - Active — **46.056**
    - Inactive — **46.071**
- Somatic cells
  - Milk, fluid — **46.086**
- Staphylococci, hemolytic
  - Eggs and egg products — **46.010**
- *Staphylococcus aureus*
  - Coagulase pos. — **46.075**
  - Foods, chilled, frozen, precooked, or prepd — **46.017, 46.076**
  - Nut meats, tree — **46.017, 46.076**
- Streptococci
  - Eggs and egg products — **46.010**
- Thermophilic bacterial spores
  - Sugars — **46.026–46.030**
- Virus
  - Ground beef — **46.120–46.122**

EXAMINATION OF EGGS AND EGG PRODUCTS (1)

("Compendium of Methods for the Microbiological Examination of Foods." Prepd by the APHA Intersociety/Agency Committee on Microbiological Methods for Foods. 1976. Marvin L. Speck, Ed., should be used as guide for further study of microorganisms obtained in culturing technics described.)

Sampling—Official Final Action

46.003 ***Equipment***

(**a**) *Liquid eggs.*—Sampling tube or dipper, sterile sample containers with tight closures (pt (500 mL) Mason jars or friction top cans are most practical), alcohol, alcohol lamp or other burner, absorbent cotton, clean cloth or towel, and H_2O pail.

(**b**) *Frozen eggs.*—Elec. (high-speed) or hand drill with 1 × 16" auger, hammer and steel strip (12×2×0.25"), or other tool for opening cans; tablespoon, hatchet or chisel, precooled sterile containers, etc., as in (**a**).

(**c**) *Dried eggs.*—Grain trier long enough to reach to bottom of containers to be sampled. Clean sample containers with tight closures (pt (500 mL) Mason jars or paperboard cartons), clean cloth or towel, and tablespoon.

46.004 ***Methods***

Take samples from representative number of containers in lot, **17.001**. Sterilize sampling tube or dipper, auger, spoon, and hatchet by wiping with alcohol-soaked cotton and flaming over alcohol lamp or other burner. Between samplings, thoroly wash instruments, dry, and resterilize. Open and sample all containers under as nearly aseptic conditions as possible.

(**a**) *Liquid eggs.*—Thoroly mix contents of container with sterile sample tube or dipper, and transfer ca 400 mL (0.75 pt) to sterile sample container. Keep samples at <5° but avoid freezing. Observe and record odor of each container sampled as normal, abnormal, reject, or musty.

(**b**) *Frozen eggs.*—Remove top layer of egg with sterilized hatchet or chisel. Drill 3 cores from top to bottom of container: first core in center, second core midway between center and periphery, and third core near edge of container. Transfer drillings from container to sample container with sterile spoon. Examine product organoleptically by smelling at opening of fourth drill-hole made after removal of bacteriological sample. (Heat produced by elec. drill intensifies odor of egg material, thus facilitating organoleptic examination.) Record odors as normal, abnormal, reject, or musty. Refrigerate samples with solid CO_2 or other suitable refrigerant if analysis is to be delayed or sampling point is at some distance from laboratory.

(**c**) *Dried eggs.*—For small packages, take entire parcel or parcels for sample. For boxes and barrels, remove top layer with sterile spoon or other sterile instrument, and with sterile trier remove ≥3 cores as in (**b**). (Samples should consist of ca 400 mL (0.75 pt).) Aseptically transfer core to sample container with sterile spoon or other suitable instrument. Store samples under refrigeration or in cool place.

Culture Media—Official Final Action

46.005 ***Standard Methods Media***

(**a**) *Dilution water.*—To prep. stock soln, dissolve 34 g KH_2PO_4 in 500 mL H_2O, adjust to pH 7.2 with 1*N* NaOH (ca 175 mL), and dil. to 1 L with H_2O. To prep. buffered H_2O for dilns, dil. 1.25 mL stock soln to 1 L with boiled and cooled H_2O. Autoclave 15 min at 121°.

(**b**) *Buffered glucose broth (MR-VP medium).*—For Me red-Voges Proskauer (MR-VP) tests. Dissolve 7.0 g proteose peptone, 5.0 g glucose, and 5.0 g K_2HPO_4 in ca 800 mL H_2O with gentle heat and occasional stirring. Filter, cool to 20°, and dil. to 1 L. Dispense 10 mL portions into test tubes and autoclave 12–15 min at 121°. Max exposure to heat should be ≤30 min. Final pH, 6.9±0.2.

(**c**) *Endo medium.*—Suspend 3.5 g K_2HPO_4, 10.0 g peptone, 20.0 g agar, and 10 g lactose in 1 L H_2O. Boil to dissolve, add H_2O to original vol., and clarify if necessary. Dispense in 100 mL portions and autoclave 15 min at 121°. Final pH, 7.4±0.1. Before use, melt and add 0.25 g Na_2SO_3 and 1.0 mL filtered 5% alc. soln basic fuchsin.

(**d**) *Eosin methylene blue agar (Levine).*—Dissolve 10.0 g peptone, 2.0 g K_2HPO_4, and 15.0 g agar in 1 L H_2O. Boil to dissolve and add H_2O to original vol. Dispense in 100 or 200 mL portions and autoclave 15 min at 121°. Final pH, 7.1±0.1. Before use, melt and to each 100 mL add 5 mL sterile 20% lactose soln, 2.0 mL 2% aq. Eosin Y soln, and 1.3 mL 0.5% aq. methylene blue soln.

(**e**) *Koser's citrate broth.*—Dissolve 1.5 g $NaNH_4HPO_4.4H_2O$, 1.0 g K_2HPO_4, 0.2 g $MgSO_4.7H_2O$, and 3.0 g Na citrate.$2H_2O$ in 1 L H_2O. Dispense in 10 mL portions into test tubes and autoclave 15 min at 121°. Final pH, 6.7±0.1.

(**f**) *Lactose broth.*—Dissolve on H_2O bath, with stirring, 3.0 g beef ext and 5.0 g polypeptone or peptone in 1 L H_2O. Add 5.0 g lactose. Dispense into fermentation tubes and autoclave 15 min at 121°. Max. exposure to heat should be ≤30 min. Final pH, 6.9±0.2.

(**g**) *Plate count agar (tryptone glucose yeast agar).*—Suspend 5.0 g peptone-tryptone (pancreatic digest of casein), 2.5 g yeast ext, 1.0 g glucose, and 15.0 g agar in 1 L H_2O. Heat and boil until all ingredients are dissolved. Autoclave 15 min at 121°. Final pH, 7.0±0.1.

(**h**) *Tryptophane broth.*—Dissolve by heating, with stirring, 10.0 g tryptone or trypticase in 1 L H_2O. Dispense in 5 mL portions into test tubes and autoclave 15 min at 121°. Final pH, 6.9±0.2.

46.006 ***Other Media***

(**a**) *Malt agar.*—Dissolve by boiling 30 g malt ext (Difco) and 15.0 g agar in 1 L H_2O. Autoclave 15 min at 121°. Just before use, melt malt agar and acidify with 85% lactic acid to pH 3.5. Do not reheat medium after addn of acid.

(**b**) *Milk protein hydrolysate glucose agar.*—BBL dehydrated, or prep. from 9.0 g milk protein hydrolysate, 1 g glucose, 15 g agar, and 1 L H_2O; adjust to pH 7.0. Autoclave 15 min at 121°, cool to room temp., and readjust pH to 7.0, if necessary.

(**c**) *Physiological salt soln.*—Dissolve 8.5 g NaCl in 1 L H_2O. Autoclave 15 min at 121° and cool to room temp.

(**d**) *Veal infusion agar.*—Mix 500 g ground lean veal and 1 L H_2O. Infuse overnight in refrigerator and strain thru cheesecloth without pressure. Dil. to original vol. with H_2O and skim off any fat. Steam in Arnold sterilizer 30 min and filter thru paper. Add 10.0 g peptone (Difco), 5.0 g NaCl, and 15.0 g agar.

Steam in Arnold sterilizer to dissolve ingredients. Adjust to pH 7.6 and steam in Arnold sterilizer 15 min. Filter thru buchner with paper pulp mat, with suction. (Use egg albumen for clarification when necessary. Add fresh white of 1 egg previously beaten with 50 mL medium or its equiv. in desiccated egg white (1.5 g) to each L of medium before adjusting pH and after cooling to 50°. Shake thoroly to ensure soln of egg white. Let stand 20 min. Heat in Arnold sterilizer 15 min to coagulate egg white. Shake vigorously and reheat. Filter, adjust to pH 7.6, steam in Arnold sterilizer 15 min, and filter.)

Place 10 mL portions in test tubes or 80 mL portions into bottles. Autoclave 20 min at 121°; final pH, 7.4.

For hemolytic tests, cool melted agar to 45° and add 5% defibrinated horse, sheep, or rabbit blood prior to pouring plates (0.5 mL blood/10 mL medium).

Operating Technic (2)

46.007 ***Preparation of Sample—Official Final Action***

(**a**) *Liquid eggs.*—Thoroly mix sample with sterile spoon or sterile mech. stirrer and prep. 1:10 diln by aseptically weighing 11 g egg material into sterile wide-mouth g-s or screw-cap bottle; add 99 g sterile diln H_2O, **46.005(a)**, or sterile physiological salt soln, **46.006(c)**, and 1 tablespoonful sterile glass shot. Thoroly agitate 1:10 diln to ensure complete soln or distribution of egg material in diluent by shaking each container rapidly 25 times, each shake being up-and-down movement of ca 30 cm, time interval not exceeding 7 sec. Let bubbles escape. Transfer representative portion from 1:10 diln for higher serial dilns as needed. Proceed as in **46.008–46.012(a)**. Pour all plates and inoculate other media within 15 min after prepn of first diln to avoid growth or death of microorganisms.

(**b**) *Frozen eggs.*—Thaw frozen egg material as rapidly as possible to avoid increase in number of microorganisms present and at temp. low enough to prevent destruction of the microorganisms (≤45° for ≤15 min). (Frequent rotary shaking of sample container aids in thawing frozen material. Thawing temp. may be maintained by use of H_2O bath or bacteriological incubator.) Proceed as in (**a**).

(**c**) *Dried eggs.*—Thoroly mix sample with sterile spoon or spatula. Prep. 1:10 diln as in (**a**). If material is relatively insol. (stored samples), use 0.1*N* LiOH as diluent. Prep. serial dilns as in (**a**) and proceed as in **46.008–46.012(b)**.

46.008 ***Plate Counts—Official Final Action***

Inoculate one set of petri plates with 1 mL portion of each suitable diln. Pour plates with tryptone glucose yeast agar or milk protein hydrolysate glucose agar previously cooled to 42–45°. Incubate inoculated plates 3 days at 32°. Count plates with aid of Quebec colony counter, if available. Express final results as number of viable microorganisms/g egg material.

46.009 ***Incidence of Coliform Group—Official Final Action***

(**a**) Inoculate 1.0 mL portions from suitable dilns of egg material into fermentation tubes of lactose broth. Incubate 24–48 hr at 35°. Streak eosin methylene blue or Endo medium plates from all lactose broth cultures showing gas production. Incubate plates 24–48 hr at 35°. Examine plates of differential media for colonies of microorganisms of coliform group. Record number of coliform bacteria/g egg material as reciprocal of highest diln showing pos. confirmation on differential media.

(**b**) *Biochemical reaction (optional).*—Inoculate from colonies of coliform types of bacteria appearing on differential agar plates to agar slants, **46.005(g)** or **46.006(b)**. Incubate 24 hr at 35°. Purify cultures for further study. Obtain IMViC biochem. reactions of purified cultures by following tests:

Kovac test (indole production), **46.016(a)**;

Acid production in Me red indicator, **46.016(b)**;

Acetylmethylcarbinol production, **46.016(b)**;

Koser sodium citrate test (utilization of Na citrate as sole source of C), **46.016(c)**.

Note: Follow methods for biochem. reactions recommended in "Standard Methods for Examination of Water and Waste Water," 14th ed., 1976, American Public Health Association, 1015 18th St NW, Washington, DC 20036.

46.010 ***Incidence of Hemolytic Staphylococci and Streptococci—Procedure***

Inoculate petri plates with 1 mL portions of suitable dilns of sample. Pour plates with veal infusion agar contg 5% defibrinated horse, sheep, or rabbit blood (0.5 mL blood/10 mL medium). Cool agar to 45° and add blood just before pouring plates. Incubate plates 24 hr at 35°. Confirm presence of coccus types of microorganisms by microscopic examination of smears taken from representative colonies and stained by Gram method. Express final results as number/g.

46.011 ***Tests for Fungi—Procedure***

Inoculate petri plates with 1 mL portions of suitable dilns of sample. Pour inoculated plates with malt agar, **46.006(a)**, previously cooled to 42–45°. Incubate plates 5 days at 20° or at room temp., if 20° incubator is not available. Express final results as number of fungi/g egg material. Confirm yeast colonies by microscopic examination of smears stained by Gram method.

46.012 ***Direct Microscopic Counts—Official Final Action***

North aniline oil-methylene blue stain.—Mix 3.0 mL aniline oil with 10.0 mL alcohol, and slowly add 1.5 mL HCl with const agitation. Add 30.0 mL satd alc. methylene blue soln, dil. to 100.0 mL with H_2O, and filter.

(**a**) *Liquid and frozen eggs.*—Place 0.01 mL undild egg material on clean, dry microscopic slide and spread over area of 2 sq cm (circular area with diam. of 1.6 cm suggested). Let film prepn dry on level surface at 35–40°. Immerse in xylene ≤1 min; then immerse in alcohol ≤1 min. Stain ≥45 sec in North aniline oil-methylene blue stain (10–20 min preferred; exposure up to 2 hr does not overstain). Wash slide by repeated immersions in H_2O and dry thoroly before examination. Observe subsequent operations and precaution as in "Standard Methods for Examination of Dairy Products," 14th ed., 1978, American Public Health Association. Express final result as number of bacteria/g egg material (double microscopic factor, since 2 sq cm area is used).

(**b**) *Dried eggs.*—Place 0.01 mL of 1:10 or 1:100 diln of dried egg material on clean, dry microscopic slide and spread over 2 sq cm.

Note: 0.1*N* LiOH may be used as diluent and is preferred for samples that are relatively insol. Circular area with diam. of 1.6 cm is preferable. Addn of drop of H_2O to each film facilitates uniform spreading.

Proceed as in (**a**). Double microscopic factor, since area of 2 sq cm is used, and multiply count by 10 or 100, depending on whether film was prepd from 1:10 or 1:100 diln.

EXAMINATION OF FROZEN, CHILLED, PRECOOKED, OR PREPARED FOODS (3)—OFFICIAL FIRST ACTION

(For the detn of aerobic plate count, most probable number of coliform bacteria and *Escherichia coli,* and staphylococcus in products such as frozen cooked meat, poultry, and vegetable products; cooked and/or breaded seafood; bakery products; salads; tree nut meats; and ingredients of food samples collected during sanitation inspections of food producing establishments, unless specific directions are given for that product.

46.013 ***Media and Reagents***

Ingredients and reagents used to prep. following media may be product of any manufacturer if comparative tests show that satisfactory results are obtained. Use pure carbohydrates suitable for biological use; ACS reagent grade inorg. chemicals; and dyes certified by "Biological Stain Commission" for use in media.

For convenience, dehydrated media of any brand equiv. to formulation may be used. Test each lot of medium for sterility and growth-promoting qualities of suitable organisms (e.g., inoculate media contg lactose with coliform bacteria, staphylococcus media with staphylococcus, etc.).

Det. pH before autoclaving with pH meter stdzd against std

buffers, **50.007**. Adjust pH, when necessary, by adding 1*N* NaOH or 1*N* HCl so that stated final pH results after autoclaving.

Use sterile glass or plastic, 100 × 15 mm, petri dishes.

(**a**) *Plate count agar.—See* **46.005(g)**.

(**b**) *Lauryl sulfate tryptose broth.*—Dissolve 20.0 g trypticase or tryptose (pancreatic digest of casein), 5.0 g NaCl, 5.0 g lactose, 2.75 g K_2HPO_4, 2.75 g KH_2PO_4, and 0.1 g Na lauryl sulfate in 1 L H_2O with gentle heat, if necessary. Dispense 10 mL portions into 20 × 150 mm test tubes contg inverted fermentation tubes 10 × 75 mm. Autoclave 15 min at 121°. Final pH, 6.8±0.1.

(**c**) *Brilliant green lactose bile (BGLB) broth.*—Dissolve 10.0 g peptone and 10.0 g lactose in ca 500 mL H_2O. Add soln (pH 7.0–7.5) of 20 g dehydrated oxgall or oxbile in 200 mL H_2O. Dil. to 975 mL and adjust pH to 7.4. Add 13.3 mL 0.1% soln of brilliant green, and dil. to 1 L with H_2O. Filter thru cotton and dispense 10 mL portions into 20 × 150 mm test tubes contg inverted 10 × 75 mm fermentation tubes. Autoclave 15 min at 121°. Final pH, 7.2±0.1.

(**d**) *Eosin methylene blue agar (Levine).—See* **46.005(d)**.

(**e**) *Baird-Parker medium (egg tellurite glycine pyruvate agar, ETGPA).*—(*1*) *Basal medium.*—Suspend 10.0 tryptone, 5.0 g beef ext, 1.0 g yeast ext, 10 g Na pyruvate, 12.0 g glycine, 5.0 g $LiCl.6H_2O$, and 20.0 g agar in 950 mL H_2O. Heat to bp with frequent agitation to dissolve ingredients completely. Dispense 95 mL portions into screw-capped bottles. Autoclave 15 min at 121°. Final pH, 7.0±0.2 at 25°. Store ≤1 month at 4±1°.

(*2*) *Enrichment.*—Bacto EY tellurite enrichment (Difco Laboratories) or prep. as follows: Soak fresh eggs ca 1 min in diln of satd $HgCl_2$ soln (1+1000). Aseptically crack eggs and sep. yolks from whites. Blend yolk and physiological saline soln, **46.006(c)**, (3+7, v/v) in high-speed blender ca 5 sec. To 50 mL egg yolk emulsion add 10 mL filter sterilized 1% K tellurite soln. Mix and store at 4±1°.

(*3*) *Complete medium.*—Add 5 mL warmed enrichment to 95 mL molten basal medium cooled to 45–50°. Mix well, avoiding bubbles, and pour 15–18 mL into sterile 100 × 15 mm petri dishes. Store plates at room temp. (≤25°) for ≤5 days before use. Medium should be densely opaque; do not use nonopaque plates. Dry plates before use by 1 of following methods: (*a*) in convection oven or incubator 30 min at 50° with lids removed and agar surface downward; (*b*) in forced-draft oven or incubator 2 hr at 50° with lids on and agar surface upward; (*c*) in incubator 4 hr at 35° with lids on and agar surface upward; or (*d*) on laboratory bench 16–18 hr at room temp. with lids on and agar surface upward.

(*4*) *Interpretation.*—Colonies of *S. aureus* are typically circular, smooth, convex, moist, 2–3 mm in diam. on uncrowded plates, gray-black to jet-black, frequently with light-colored (off-white) margin, surrounded by opaque zone (ppt) and frequently with outer clear zone; colonies have buttery to gummy consistency when touched with inoculating needle. Occasional non-lipolytic strains may be encountered which have same appearance, except that surrounding opaque and clear zones are absent. Colonies isolated from frozen or desiccated foods which have been stored for extended periods are frequently less black than typical colonies and may have rough appearance and dry texture.

(**f**) *Trypticase (tryptic) soy broth with 10% sodium chloride.*—Add 95 g NaCl to 1 L of soln of 17.0 g trypticase or tryptose (pancreatic digest of casein), 3.0 g phytone (papaic digest of soya meal), 5.0 g NaCl, 2.5 g K_2HPO_4, and 2.5 g glucose. Heat gently if necessary. Dispense into 16–20 mm diam. tubes to depth of 5–8 cm. Autoclave 15 min at 121°. Final pH, 7.3±0.2.

(**g**) *EC broth.*—Dissolve 20.0 g trypticase or tryptose (pancreatic digest of casein), 1.5 g Bacto bile salt No. 3 or bile salt mixt., 5.0 g lactose, 4.0 g K_2HPO_4, 1.5 g KH_2PO_4, and 5.0 g NaCl in 1 L H_2O. Dispense 8 mL into 16 × 150 mm test tubes contg inverted 10 × 75 mm fermentation tube. Autoclave 15 min at 121°. Final pH, 6.9±0.1.

(**h**) *Brain-heart infusion.—See* **46.054(r)**. Dispense into bottles or tubes for storage and autoclave 15 min at 121°.

(**i**) *Desiccated coagulase plasma (rabbit) with EDTA.*—Reconstitute according to manufacturer's directions. If not available, reconstitute *desiccated coagulase plasma (rabbit)* and add Na_2H_2EDTA to final concn of 0.1% in reconstituted plasma.

(**j**) *Tryptophane broth.—See* **46.005(h)** but dispense in 10 mL portions.

(**k**) *Buffered glucose broth.—See* **46.005(b)**. BBL, Division of Bioquest, or Difco dehydrated medium may be used.

(**l**) *Koser's citrate broth.—See* **46.005(e)**.

(**m**) *Butterfield's buffered phosphate diluent.*—(*1*) *Stock soln.*—Dissolve 34.0 g KH_2PO_4 in 500 mL H_2O, adjust to pH 7.2 with ca 175 mL 1*N* NaOH, and dil. to 1 L. Store in refrigerator. (*2*) *Diluent.*—Dil. 1.25 mL stock soln to 1 L with H_2O. Prep. diln blanks with this soln, dispensing enough to allow for losses during autoclaving. Autoclave 15 min at 121°.

46.014 *Preparation of Sample*

(Prep. all decimal dilns with 90 mL sterile diluent plus 10 mL previous diln unless otherwise specified. Shake all dilns 25 times in 30 cm arc. Pipets must accurately deliver required vol. Do not use to deliver <10% of their total vol. For example, to deliver 1 mL, do not use pipet >10 mL; to deliver 0.1 mL, do not use pipet >1 mL.)

(**a**) *Frozen and/or prepared foods.*—Use balance with capacity of ≥2 kg and sensitivity of 0.1 g to aseptically weigh 50 g unthawed (if frozen) sample into sterile high-speed blender jar. Add 450 mL diluent, (**m**)(*2*), and blend 2 min. (If necessary to temper frozen sample to remove 50 g portion, hold ≤18 hr at 2–5°.) Not >15 min should elapse from time sample is blended until all dilns are in appropriate media.

If entire sample consists of <50 g, weigh portion equiv. to ½ sample and add vol. of sterile diluent required to make 1:10 diln. Total vol. in blender jar must completely cover blades.

(**b**) *Tree nut meat halves and larger pieces.*—Aseptically weigh 50 g sample into sterile jar. Add 50 mL diluent, (**m**)(*2*), and shake vigorously (50 times thru 30 cm arc) to obtain 10^0 diln. Let stand 3–5 min and shake just before making serial dilns and inoculations.

(**c**) *Nut meal.*—Aseptically weigh 10 g sample into sterile jar. Add 90 mL diluent, (**m**)(*2*), to obtain 10^{-1} diln.

46.015 *Aerobic Plate Count*

Seed duplicate petri dishes in dilns of 1:10, 1:100, 1:1000, etc., using plate count agar, (**a**). Ordinarily 1:100 thru 1:10,000 are satisfactory. Place 1 mL appropriate diln in each plate, and add molten agar (cooled to 42–45°) within 15 min from time of original diln. Incubate 48±2 hr at 35° and count duplicate plates in suitable range (30–300 colonies). If plates do not contain 30–300 colonies, record diln counted and note number of colonies found. Average counts obtained and report as aerobic plate count/g.

46.016 *Coliform Group and E. coli* *Official Final Action for Tree Nut Meats*

Seed 3-tube most probable number (MPN) series into lauryl sulfate tryptose broth, (**b**), using 1 mL inocula of 1:10, 1:100, and 1:1000 dilns, with triplicate tubes at each diln. (For nut meats (halves and larger pieces), begin MPN detn with 10^0 diln;

for nut meal, begin with 10^{-1} diln.) Incubate 48±2 hr at 35° for gas formation as evidenced by displacement of liq. in insert tube or by vigorous effervescence when tubes are shaken *gently.* Examine tubes for gas formation at 24 and 48 hr intervals. Transfer, using 3 mm loop, from gassing tubes to BGLB, (**c**) (omit this transfer for tree nuts), and EC broth, (**g**), at time gas formation is noted.

Incubate BGLB broth 48±2 hr at 35°. Using MPN Table **46:01**, compute MPN on basis of number of tubes of BGLB broth producing gas by end of incubation period. Report as MPN of coliform bacteria/g.

Incubate EC broth 48±2 hr at 45.5±0.05° in covered H_2O bath. Submerge broth tubes in bath so that H_2O level is above highest level of medium. Examine tubes for gas formation at 24 or 48 hr intervals. Streak gas-pos. tubes on Levine's eosine methylene blue agar plates, (**d**), and incubate plates 24±2 hr at 35°.

Pick 2 or more well isolated typical colonies from Levine's eosine methylene blue agar plates and transfer to agar slants prepd from agar medium, (**a**). Incubate 18–24 hr at 35°. If typical colonies are not present, pick 2 or more colonies most likely to be *E. coli.* Pick ≥2 from every plate.

Transfer growth from plate count agar slants into following broths for identification by biochem. tests:

(**a**) *Tryptophane broth, (j).*—Incubate 24±2 hr at 35° and test for indole by adding 0.2–0.3 mL Kovacs reagent, **46.055(a)**, to 24 hr culture. Test is pos. if upper layer turns red.

(**b**) *MR-VP medium, (k).*—Incubate 48±2 hr at 35°. Aseptically transfer 1 mL culture to 13 × 100 mm test tube to test for acetylmethylcarbinol. Add 0.6 mL 5% alc. α-naphthol soln, 0.2 mL KOH soln (4+10), and few crystals of creatine. Shake and let stand 2 hr. Test is pos. if eosin pink develops. Alternatively, *see* **46.062(c)**(*1*).

Incubate remainder of MR-VP medium for addnl 48 hr and test for Me red reaction by adding 5 drops Me red soln to culture. Test is pos. if culture turns red; neg., if yellow. (Prep. Me red soln by dissolving 0.1 g Me red in 300 mL 90% alcohol and dilg to 500 mL with H_2O.)

(**c**) *Koser citrate broth, (l).*—Incubate 96 hr at 35° and record growth as + or −.

(**d**) *Lauryl sulfate tryptose broth, (b).*—Incubate 48±2 hr at 35°. Examine tubes for gas formation.

(**e**) *Gram stain.*—Perform Gram stain on 18 hr agar slant (Standard Methods for the Examination of Water and Waste Water, 14th ed., 1976). Coliform organisms will stain red (neg.); Gram-pos. organisms will stain blue-black.

(**f**) *Classification.*—Classify biochem. types as follows:

Indole	*MR*	*VP*	*Citrate*	*Type*
+	+	−	−	Typical *E. coli*
−	+	−	−	Atypical *E. coli*
+	+	−	+	Typical Intermediate
−	+	−	+	Atypical Intermediate
−	−	+	+	Typical *Enterobacter aerogenes*
+	−	+	+	Atypical *Enterobacter aerogenes*

Other groupings may appear; in such cases cultures are usually mixed. Restreak to det. their purity.

Compute MPN of *E. coli*/g, considering Gram neg., nonspore-forming rods producing gas in lactose and producing ++−− or −+−− IMViC patterns as *E. coli.*

46.017 ***Staphylococcus aureus—Official Final Action***

(Applicable to detection and enumeration of small numbers of *S. aureus* in raw food ingredients and non-processed foods expected to contain large population of competing species.)

Inoculate 3 tubes of trypticase soy broth with 10% NaCl, (**f**), at each test diln with 1 mL aliquots of decimal dilns of sample. Max. diln of sample must be high enough to yield neg. end point. Incubate 48 hr at 35–37°.

Using 3 mm loop, transfer 1 loopful from each growth-pos. tube to dried Baird-Parker medium plates, (**e**)(*3*). Streak so as to obtain isolated colonies. Incubate 45–48 hr at 35–37°.

From each plate showing growth, pick ≥1 colony suspected to be *S. aureus,* (**e**)(*4*). Transfer colonies to tubes contg 0.2 mL brain heart infusion (BHI) broth, **46.054(r)**, and emulsify thoroly. Withdraw 1 loopful of resulting culture suspension and transfer to agar slant contg any suitable maintenance medium, e.g., **4.037(b)**. Incubate BHI culture suspensions and slants 18–24 hr at 35–37°. Retain slant cultures at room temp. for ancillary or repeat tests, in case coagulase test results are questionable.

To BHI cultures add 0.5 mL reconstituted coagulase plasma with EDTA, (**i**), and mix thoroly. Incubate at 35–37° and examine periodically over 6 hr interval for clot formation. Any degree of clot formation is considered pos. reaction. Small or poorly organized clots may be observed by gently tipping tube so that liq. portion of reaction mixt. approaches lip of tube; clots will protrude above liq. surface. Coagulase-pos. cultures are considered to be *S. aureus.* Test pos. and neg. controls simultaneously with cultures of unknown coagulase reactivity. Recheck doubtful

Table 46:01 Most Probable Numbers (MPN) per 1 g of Sample, Using 3 Tubes with Each of 0.1, 0.01, and 0.001 g Portions

Positive Tubes				Positive Tubes				Positive Tubes				Positive Tubes			
0.1	0.01	0.001	MPN	0.1	0.01	0.001	MPN	0.1	0.01	0.001	MPN	0.1	0.01	0.001	MPN
0	0	0	<3.	1	0	0	3.6	2	0	0	9.1	3	0	0	23.
0	0	1	3.	1	0	1	7.2	2	0	1	14.	3	0	1	39.
0	0	2	6.	1	0	2	11.	2	0	2	20.	3	0	2	64.
0	0	3	9.	1	0	3	15.	2	0	3	26.	3	0	3	95.
0	1	0	3.	1	1	0	7.3	2	1	0	15.	3	1	0	43.
0	1	1	6.1	1	1	1	11.	2	1	1	20.	3	1	1	75.
0	1	2	9.2	1	1	2	15.	2	1	2	27.	3	1	2	120.
0	1	3	12.	1	1	3	19.	2	1	3	34.	3	1	3	160.
0	2	0	6.2	1	2	0	11.	2	2	0	21.	3	2	0	93.
0	2	1	9.3	1	2	1	15.	2	2	1	28.	3	2	1	150.
0	2	2	12.	1	2	2	20.	2	2	2	35.	3	2	2	210.
0	2	3	16.	1	2	3	24.	2	2	3	42.	3	2	3	290.
0	3	0	9.4	1	3	0	16.	2	3	0	29.	3	3	0	240.
0	3	1	13.	1	3	1	20.	2	3	1	36.	3	3	1	460.
0	3	2	16.	1	3	2	24.	2	3	2	44.	3	3	2	1100.
0	3	3	19.	1	3	3	29.	2	3	3	53.	3	3	3	>1100.

coagulase test results on BHI cultures which have been incubated at 35–37° for >18 but ≤48 hr.

Report most probable number (MPN) of *S. aureus*/g from tables of MPN values, Table **46:01**.

COMMERCIAL STERILITY OF LOW ACID CANNED FOODS (4) OFFICIAL FINAL ACTION

(Personnel with beards, mustaches, or sideburns below ear lobe should not perform sterility examination unless these are completely covered with sterile caps and masks. Wear clean laboratory coat for examination.)

46.018 ***Principle***

"Low acid foods" means any food with finished equilibrium pH value >4.6. Method applies only to containers which show no distention of either end. Incubate containers ≥10 days at 21–35° before examination.

Com. sterility is defined as that condition achieved by application of heat which renders food free of viable forms of microorganisms having public health significance, as well as microorganisms not of health significance capable of reproducing in the food under normal non-refrigerated conditions of storage and distribution.

46.019 ***Media and Reagents***

See also **46.013**.

(**a**) *Tryptone broth.*—(Aerobic medium.) Dissolve 10.0 g tryptone or trypticase, 5.0 g glucose, 1.25 g K_2HPO_4, 1.0 g yeast ext, and 2.0 mL 2% alc. soln of bromocresol purple in 1 L H_2O with gentle heat, if necessary. Dispense 10 mL portions into 20 × 150 mm screw-cap test tubes and autoclave 20 min at 121°. Do not exhaust before using.

(**b**) *Modified PE-2 medium.*—(Anaerobic medium.) Dissolve 20.0 g peptone, 3.0 g yeast ext, and 2.0 mL 2% alc. soln of bromocresol purple in 1 L H_2O with gentle heat, if necessary. Dispense 19 mL portions into 20 × 150 mm screw-cap test tubes contg 8–10 *untreated* Alaska seed peas (Rogers Brothers Co., Seed Div., PO Box 2188, Idaho Falls, ID 83401, No. 423; Northrup King Seed Co., 1500 NE Jackson St, Minneapolis, MN 55413; or hardware store). Autoclave 30 min at 121°. If not freshly prepd, heat to 100° and cool to 55° before using.

(**c**) *Glucose starch agar.*—(Aerobic medium; Difco dehydrated, or equiv.) Dissolve 15.0 g proteose peptone No. 3, 2.0 g glucose, 10.0 g sol. starch, 5.0 g NaCl, 3.0 g Na_2HPO_4, 20.0 g gelatin, and 10.0 g agar in 1 L H_2O, heat to bp, and autoclave 15 min at 121° in erlenmeyer. Aseptically pour into sterile petri dishes and allow to solidify.

(**d**) *Nutrient agar.*—(Aerobic medium for spore production; Difco dehydrated, or equiv.) Dissolve 3.0 g beef ext, 5.0 g peptone, and 15.0 g agar in 1 L H_2O, heat to bp, and autoclave 30 min at 121°.

(**e**) *Detergent sanitizer soln.*—pHisoHex (3% hexachlorophene), or equiv.

46.020 ***Apparatus***

(**a**) *Can opener.*—Bacti-Disc Cutter (Wilkens-Anderson Co., 4525 W Division St, Chicago, IL 60651, No. 10810-01), bacteriological can opener (Marmora Machine Co., 1956 N Latrobe Ave, Chicago, IL 60639), or equiv.

(**b**) *Caps.*—Disposable, operating room-type (American Hospital Supply Corp., 1450 Waukegan Rd, McGaw Park, IL 60085, No. 47315-110, or equiv.).

(**c**) *Pipets.*—Straight wall, 200–250 mm long × 7 mm id, 9 mm od (Scientific Products, Inc., No. G6100–9, cut and fire polished, or equiv.).

46.021 ***Sampling***

Conduct test in clean room. (If necessary, open room may be used but outside windows must be closed and direct drafts across work area must be eliminated.) If available, use laminar flow cabinet. Strip labels from cans, examine cans for external defects, and record descriptions. Wash cans with soap (or detergent sanitizer soln) and H_2O, and dry with clean paper towels. Wipe counter top with 100 ppm Cl soln (e.g., Clorox or dild NaOCl soln) immediately before placing washed and dried can on it. Place code end of can in down position and number cans in ink or with $CuSO_4$ marking soln to right of side seam.

Wash hands and face with soap, and rewash hands and face with detergent sanitizer soln. Completely cover hair with clean disposable operating room cap.

Hold noncoded end of can over large Meker burner, just above blue portion of flame. Heat this end of can until all condensation is evapd; then return can to table in former position. Clean handle and blade of special can opener, (**a**), with paper towel moistened with 70% alcohol, flame metal portion enough to destroy all microorganisms, and use it to make 4 cm (1.5") diam. hole in noncoded, heated end of can. Immediately and without moving can, use straight-wall sterile glass pipet, (**c**), to transfer ca 2 g food to sep. tubes, 2 each of aerobic and 2 of anaerobic media (4 total). (No other transferring tool may be substituted.) Preloosen screw cap and hold it between little and ring fingers while transfer is being made. Flame lips of media tubes both before and after addn of food. When transferring food to anaerobic tubes, food must be inoculated into lower portion of medium. Tighten screw caps after inoculation, incubate tubes 72 hr at 35°, and observe daily. Record results for each tube sep.

Remove addnl ≥10 g food sample from each container with sterile pipet and place in sterile 25 × 200 mm screw-cap test tube. Use pipet like spatula, if necessary, for this operation (thermophilic contamination unlikely). Number tube to correspond to can and refrigerate for later testing, if necessary.

46.022 ***Contamination Control***

Use sterile loop or glass rod to streak plate of glucose starch agar, (**c**). On table, open plate of glucose starch agar for time equal to longest duration that any medium tube or plate is exposed. Incubate plates 72 hr at 35°, and observe daily.

46.023 ***Microscopic Examination***

With pair of metal cutting shears, enlarge hole in can and record odor. Microscopically (oil immersion) examine heat-fixed thin smear of food, stained 10 sec with 1% gentian (or crystal) violet and washed in running tap H_2O, or, alternatively, examine wet mounts with phase contrast microscope. If food contains appreciable fat, xylol should be dripped across food smear while it is still hot from heat fixing. Compare stained smear with one made from normal product, if possible.

46.024 ***pH Determination***

Det. pH with pH meter, using ref. buffer near normal pH of food. Record both ref. buffer pH and sample pH. Compare to normal can of food, if available.

46.025 ***Confirmation of Results***

If there is any abnormal odor, abnormal appearance, abnormal pH, numbers of bacteria on microscopic examination, and/or growth in media from any can of food, subculture corresponding refrigerated tube as follows: Flame lip of tube and, with straight-wall sterile glass pipet, (**c**), transfer ca 2 g food to 2 tubes each of aerobic and anaerobic media (4 total). Flame lips of media tubes both before and after addn of food. Tighten caps after inoculation, incubate tubes 72 hr at 55°, and observe daily. Record results for each tube sep.

Any organisms isolated from normal cans having obvious vac. which produce gas in anaerobic medium at 35° should immediately be suspected as being from laboratory contamination. Aseptically inoculate growing organism into another normal can, close hole with solder, and incubate 14 days at 35°. Any swelling of container indicates that organism was not in original sample. Record as laboratory contamination and review results of addnl cans to verify finding of contamination.

Growth in aerobic medium at 35° from normal cans indicates either non-com. sterility or laboratory contamination. Unless there is abnormal odor, abnormal appearance, abnormal pH, and/or numbers of bacteria on microscopic examination from product in original can, record results as laboratory contamination and review results of addnl cans to verify finding of contamination. Otherwise, observe subculture results at 55°. Growth at 35° and absence of growth at 55° confirm nonsterility of original container. Check growth under aerobic conditions on nutrient agar plates, (**d**), at 55° and confirm for spores after 72 hr. Confirmation indicates nonsterility due to flat sour spoilage. Record growth at 55° under anaerobic conditions with gas production as com. sterile. Growth is caused by dormant spores incapable of growth at normal temps of storage and distribution.

If only one of duplicate tubes is pos. after incubation and streaked glucose starch agar is also neg., record as laboratory contamination. Growth on air control plate of glucose starch agar also indicates potential laboratory contamination.

THERMOPHILIC BACTERIAL SPORES IN SUGARS (*5*)
OFFICIAL FIRST ACTION

(Sugar, both beet and cane, may carry spores of all 3 groups of thermophilic bacteria that are important as spoilage agents in low-acid canned foods, i.e., flat sour bacteria (*Bacillus stearothermophilus*), thermophilic anaerobes not producing H_2S (*Clostridium thermosaccharolyticum*), and sulfide spoilage bacteria or thermophilic anaerobes producing H_2S (*C. nigrificans*). These bacteria are not of health significance, but excessive numbers may survive com. heat processes.)

46.026 *Sampling*

Take 225 g (0.5 lb) samples from 5 sep. bags or barrels of shipment or lot, place in clean containers, and seal.

Sample liq. sugar by drawing 5 sep. 200–250 mL (6–8 oz) portions during pumping transfer from tank trucks to storage tanks or at refinery during filling of tank trucks.

Number of samples will vary in relation to size of shipment or lot. If there is significant variability in lot, this fact will become evident, in majority of cases, thru individual tests on the 5 samples.

46.027 *Preparation of Sample*

(**a**) *Dry sugar.*—Place 20 g sample in sterile 150–250 mL erlenmeyer marked to indicate 100 mL. Add sterile H_2O to 100 mL mark. Bring rapidly to bp, and boil 5 min. Replace liq. evapd with sterile H_2O.

(**b**) *Liquid sugar.*—Add sample contg 20 g dry sugar, detd on basis of °Brix (e.g., 29.41 g 68° Brix (%) liq. sugar is equiv. to 20 g dry sugar), to sterile 250 mL flask and proceed as in (**a**).

46.028 *Culture Media*

(**a**) *Glucose tryptone agar.*—For detection of flat sour bacteria. Use com. stdzd dehydrated medium (Bacto-Dextrose Tryptone Agar) preferably, or prep. as follows: Suspend 10.0 g tryptone, 5.0 g glucose, 15.0 g agar, and 0.04 g bromocresol purple in 1 L H_2O, and mix thoroly. Final pH, 6.7±0.1. Autoclave 30 min at 121° and cool to 55°.

(**b**) *Liver broth.*—For detection of thermophilic anaerobes not producing H_2S (*C. thermosaccharolyticum*). Mix 500 g chopped beef liver with 1 L H_2O. Slowly boil mixt. 1 hr, adjust to ca pH 7.0, and boil addnl 10 min. Press boiled material thru cheesecloth and dil. liq. to 1 L. To broth, add 10.0 g peptone and 1.0 g K_2HPO_4, and adjust to pH 7.0. To test tube, add 1–2 cm previously boiled ground beef liver and 10–12 mL broth. Sterilize 20 min at 121°. Before using medium, unless freshly prepd, exhaust by subjecting to flowing steam ≥20 min, and, after inoculation, stratify with 5–6 cm layer of plain nutrient agar (common formula) that has been cooled to 50°.

(**c**) *Sulfite agar, modified.*—For detection of sulfide spoilage bacteria. Suspend 10.0 g tryptone, 1.0 g Na_2SO_3, and 20.0 g agar in 1 L H_2O, and mix thoroly. At time agar is added to tube, place clean iron strip or nail in each tube. No adjustment of reaction is necessary. Prep. medium and Na_2SO_3 soln, if used in place of solid Na_2SO_3, fresh weekly. Autoclave medium 20 min at 121° and cool to 55°.

46.029 *Culture Technic*

(**a**) *Flat sour spores.*—Into 5 sep. petri dishes, pipet 2 mL boiled sugar soln. Cover, and mix inoculum with glucose tryptone agar. Incubate plates 35–48 hr at 55° and, to prevent drying of agar, humidify incubator. Combined count from 5 plates represents number of spores in 2 g original sugar. Multiply this count by 5 to express results in terms of number of spores/10 g sugar.

Characteristic colonies are round, 1–5 mm in diam., with typical opaque central "spot," and, usually, surrounded by yellow halo in field of purple. This halo may be insignificant or missing with certain low acid-producing types or if plate is so thickly seeded that entire plate has yellow tinge. Typical subsurface colonies are compact and may approach "pin point" conditions.

If identity of subsurface colonies is doubtful, observe nature of surface colonies. If they show reasonable purity of formed flora, assume that subsurface colonies have been formed by similar bacterial groups. If plate is heavily seeded, counts may not be accurate and colony structure and size may be atypical. If plates are so heavily seeded that counting is impractical, dil. original soln and repeat procedure.

To det. if typical subsurface colonies are flat sour organisms, apply streak from colonies to agar plates to det. surface characteristics.

(**b**) *Thermophilic anaerobes not producing hydrogen sulfide.*—Divide 20 mL boiled sugar soln equally among 6 liver broth tubes and stratify liq. medium with plain nutrient agar. After agar has solidified, preheat to 55° and incubate 72 hr at that temp.

Thermophilic anaerobes not producing H_2S are identified by splitting of agar, presence of acid, and, occasionally, cheesy odor. Method is suitable as qual. test but provides only rough estn; results cannot be expressed as number of spores/unit wt sugar.

(**c**) *Sulfide spoilage bacteria.*—Divide 20 mL boiled sugar soln equally among 6 freshly exhausted tubes contg modified sulfite agar. Incubate 48 hr at 55°.

In sulfite agar, sulfide spoilage bacteria form characteristic blackened spherical areas. Due to solubility of H_2S and its fixation by Fe, no gas is noted. Some thermophilic anaerobes not producing H_2S generate relatively large amts of H, which splits agar and reduces sulfite, thereby causing general blackening of medium. This condition, however, is readily distinguishable from restricted blackened area mentioned above. Count blackened areas to obtain quant. results.

46.030 ***Reporting Results***

Report flat sour and sulfide spoilage results as number of spores/10 g sugar. Report thermophilic anaerobes not producing H_2S as number of tubes pos. or neg. (+ or −).

CLOSTRIDIUM PERFRINGENS (*6*)
OFFICIAL FINAL ACTION

(Applicable to examination of outbreak foods in which relatively large numbers of vegetative cells are expected to be present)

46.031 ***Apparatus***

(**a**) *Pipets.*—1.0 mL serological with 0.1 mL graduations and 10.0 mL with 1.0 mL graduations.

(**b**) *Colony counter.*—Quebec, or equiv., dark field model.

(**c**) *High-speed blender.*—Waring Blendor, or equiv., multispeed model, with low-speed operation at 13,000 rpm, and 1 L glass or metal blender jars with covers. One jar is required for each sample.

(**d**) *Anaerobic jars.*—BBL Gas-Pak jars equipped with Gas-Pak H + CO_2 generator envelopes are recommended. Anaero-jar (Pfizer Diagnostics, 1407 N Dayton St, Chicago, IL 60622) with replacement of air by purified N or N-CO_2 (9+1) is satisfactory.

(**e**) *Freezer, ultra-low temperature.*—REVCO Model ULT-107 (REVCO, Inc., 1100 Memorial Dr, W Columbia, SC 29169), or equiv., capable of maintaining temp. of −68°.

(**f**) *Shipping container.*—Heavy duty styrofoam, including hermetically sealable metal canister (friction-fit paint can is satisfactory).

46.032 ***Reagents***

(**a**) *Peptone dilution water.*—Dissolve 2.0 g peptone (Difco B118) in 2 L H_2O for each sample, and adjust to pH 7.0±0.1. Dispense enough vol. in 175 mL (6 oz) bottles to give 90±1 mL and in 750 mL erlenmeyers to give 450±5 mL after autoclaving 15 min at 121°.

(**b**) *Nitrite test reagents.*—(*1*) *Reagent A.*—Dissolve 8 g sulfanilic acid in 1 L 5*N* HOAc (2+5). (*2*) *Reagent B.*—Dissolve 5 g α-naphthol in 1 L 5*N* HOAc.

(**c**) *Buffered glycerol-salt soln.*—Dissolve 4.2 g NaCl in 900 mL H_2O. Add 12.4 g anhyd. K_2HPO_4, 4.0 g anhyd. KH_2PO_4, and 100 mL glycerol. Mix well to dissolve, and adjust pH to 7.2. Autoclave 15 min at 121°. For double-strength glycerol soln (20%), use 200 mL glycerol and 800 mL. H_2O.

46.033 ***Culture Media***

(Sizes of culture media containers (test tubes, flasks, and petri dishes) are specified for each medium. All media except tryptose-sulfite-cycloserine (TSC) agar are incubated in air at 35°. Media not used ≤4 hr after prepn must be heated 10 min in boiling H_2O or flowing steam to expel O and cooled rapidly in tap H_2O without agitation just before use.)

(**a**) *Tryptose-sulfite-cycloserine agar.*—15.0 g tryptose, 20.0 g agar, 5.0 g soytone, 5.0 g yeast ext, 1.0 g Na metabisulfite, and 1.0 g ferric ammonium citrate (NF Brown Pearls) dild to 1 L with H_2O (SFP agar base, Difco 0811-01, is satisfactory). Adjust to pH 7.6±0.1, dispense 250 mL portions into 500 mL flasks, and sterilize 15 min at 121°. Before plating, add 20.0 mL 0.5% filter-sterilized soln of D-cycloserine to each 250 mL sterile melted medium at 50°. To make egg yolk-contg plates, add 20 mL 50% egg yolk emulsion, (**c**), to 250 mL sterile medium contg D-cycloserine. Dispense 15 mL portions into 100 × 15 mm sterile petri dishes. Cover plates with towel and let dry overnight at room temp. before use.

(**b**) *D-Cycloserine soln.*—Dissolve 1 g D-cycloserine (Sigma Chemical Co. or Serva Feinbiochemicia, Heidelberg, West Germany) without heating in 200 mL 0.05*M* phosphate buffer (pH 8.0±0.1) and sterilize by filtering thru 0.45 μm membrane filter.

(**c**) *Egg yolk emulsion.*—Wash fresh eggs with stiff brush and drain. Soak 1 hr in 70% alcohol. Aseptically remove yolk and mix with equal vol. sterile 0.85% NaCl soln. Store at 4°.

(**d**) *Buffered motility-nitrate medium.*—3.0 g beef ext, 5.0 g peptone, 5.0 g KNO_3, 2.5 g Na_2HPO_4, 3.0 g agar, 5.0 g galactose, and 5.0 g glycerol dild to 1 L with H_2O. Adjust to pH 7.3±0.1, dispense 11 mL portions into 150 × 16 mm tubes, and sterilize 15 min at 121°.

(**e**) *Lactose-gelatin medium.*—15.0 g tryptose, 10.0 g yeast ext, 10.0 g lactose, 5.0 g Na_2HPO_4, 0.05 g phenol red, and 120.0 g gelatin dild to 1 L with H_2O. Adjust to pH 7.5±0.1 before adding lactose and phenol red. Dispense 10 mL portions into 150 × 16 mm screw-cap tubes and sterilize 15 min at 121°.

(**f**) *Sporulation broth.*—15.0 g polypeptone, 3.0 g yeast ext, 3.0 g sol. starch, 0.1 g $MgSO_4$, 1.0 g Na thioglycolate, and 11.0 g Na_2HPO_4 dild to 1 L with H_2O. Adjust to pH 7.8±0.1, dispense 15 mL portions into 150 × 20 mm screw-cap tubes, and sterilize 15 min at 121°.

(**g**) *Polypeptone-yeast extract* (*PY*) *medium.*—20.0 g polypeptone, 5.0 g yeast ext, and 5.0 g NaCl dild to 1 L with H_2O. Adjust to pH 6.9±0.1, dispense 9 mL portions into 125 × 16 mm screw-cap tubes, and sterilize 15 min at 121°.

(**h**) *Fluid thioglycolate medium.*—(BBL-01-140, Difco 0256, Oxoid CM173). Dispense 10 mL portions into 150 × 16 mm screw-cap tubes. Sterilize 15 min at 121°, and cool quickly. Final pH is 7.1±0.1.

46.034 ***Preparation of Sample***

(**a**) *For storage and shipping.*—Using aseptic technic, transfer 50 g sample to sterile container such as Whirl-Pak plastic bag and add 50 g sterile buffered glycerol-salt soln. Mix well by kneading bag or stirring with sterile pipet. Let soln penetrate solid foods 10 min before freezing. Treat liq. samples such as beef juice or gravy with double-strength (20% glycerol) soln to obtain final concn of 10% glycerol. Freeze samples as quickly as possible in ultra-low temp. freezer at −68° or, alternatively, by placing in sealable metal canister and storing with solid CO_2 in insulated shipping container. To ship samples, place in sealable metal canister and pack in well insulated styrofoam shipping carton with sufficient solid CO_2 to keep samples frozen during transit. Ship by most rapid means possible. Upon receipt, transfer samples to ultra-low temp. freezer at −68° or replenish solid CO_2 in shipping carton to maintain temp. at ca −56° until samples can be examined. Thaw samples and proceed as in (**b**) without delay.

(**b**) *For analysis.*—Using aspetic technic, weigh 50 g food sample into sterile blender jar. Add 450 mL peptone diln H_2O and homogenize 2 min at low speed (13,000 rpm). Use this 1:10 diln to prep. serial dilns from 10^{-2} to 10^{-6} by transferring 10 mL of 1:10 diln to 90 mL diln blank, mixing well with gentle shaking, and continuing until 10^{-6} diln is reached.

46.035 ***Plate Count Technic***

Pour ca 5 mL TSC agar without egg yolk into each of ten 100 × 15 mm petri dishes and spread evenly by rapidly rotating dish. When agar has solidified, label plates and aseptically pipet 1 mL of each diln of homogenate in duplicate onto agar surface in center of dish. Pour addnl 15 mL TSC agar without egg yolk into dish and mix well with inoculum by gently rotating dish.

Alternatively, with sterile glass rod spreader, spread 0.1 mL diln over previously poured plates of TSC agar contg egg yolk emulsion. Let plates absorb inoculum 5–10 min; then overlay with 10 mL TSC agar without egg yolk. (TSC agar contg egg yolk is preferred for foods which may also contain other sulfite-reducing *Clostridium* sp.)

When agar has solidified, place plates in upright position in anaerobic jar. Produce anaerobic conditions, and incubate jar 20 hr at 35° for TSC agar without egg yolk and 24 hr at 35° for TSC agar with egg yolk. After incubation, remove plates from jar and observe macroscopically for growth and black colony production. Select plates showing estd 20–200 black colonies. Using Quebec colony counter with piece of white tissue paper over counting area, count black colonies and calc. number of *Clostridium* sp./g food. *C. perfringens* colonies in medium contg egg yolk are black and usually surrounded by 2–4 mm zone of white ppt due to lecithinase activity. However, since a few strains are weak or neg. for lecithinase, count any black colonies suspected to be *C. perfringens* and confirm identity as in **46.036**.

46.036 ***Confirmation Technic***

Select 10 characteristic colonies from countable plates (20–200 colonies), inoculate each into tube of fluid thioglycolate medium, and incubate 18–24 hr at 35°. Make Gram-stained smear of fluid thioglycolate cultures and check for purity and presence of short, thick, Gram-pos. bacillus characteristic of *C. perfringens.* Streak contaminated cultures on TSC agar contg egg yolk and incubate plates anaerobically 24 hr at 35° to obtain pure cultures. Stab-inoculate buffered motility-nitrate and lactose gelatin media with 2 mm loopfuls of pure fluid thioglycolate culture or portion of isolated colony from TSC agar plate. Inoculate sporulation broth with 1 mL fluid thioglycolate culture and incubate 24 hr at 35°. Examine tubes of buffered motility-nitrate medium by transmitted light for type of growth along stab. Nonmotile organisms produce growth only in and along line of stab. Motile organisms produce diffuse growth out into medium away from stab.

Test buffered motility-nitrate medium for presence of nitrite by adding 0.5 mL Reagent A and 0.2 mL Reagent B. Orange which develops within 15 min indicates presence of nitrites. If no color develops, add few grains of powd Zn metal, and let stand 10 min. No color change after addn of Zn indicates that nitrates are completely reduced; change to orange indicates that organism is incapable of reducing nitrates.

Examine lactose-gelatin medium for gas and color change from red to yellow, indicating that lactose is fermented with production of acid. Chill tubes 1 hr at 5° and check for gelatin liquefaction. If medium solidifies, reincubate addnl 24 hr at 35° and repeat test for gelatin liquefaction. Make Gram-stained smear from sporulation broth and examine microscopically for spores. Report whether or not spores are produced. Store sporulated cultures at 4° if further testing of isolates is desired.

Nonmotile, Gram-pos. bacilli which produce black colonies in TSC agar, reduce nitrates to nitrites, produce acid and gas from lactose, and liquefy gelatin within 48 hr are provisionally identified as *C. perfringens*.

Organisms suspected to be *C. perfringens* that do not meet criteria stated above must be confirmed by further testing. Subculture into fluid thioglycolate medium isolates that do not liquefy gelatin or which are atypical in other respects. Incubate 24 hr at 35°, make Gram-stained smear, and check for purity. Inoculate 1 tube of PY medium, (**g**), contg *1% salicin* and 1 tube contg *1% raffinose* with 0.1 mL fluid thioglycolate culture. Incubate media 24 hr at 35° and check PY-salicin for acid and gas. Transfer 1.0 mL culture to test tube and add 1–2 drops *0.04% phenol red.* Yellow indicates acid is produced from salicin. (Salicin usually is not fermented by *C. perfringens* but is rapidly fermented with production of acid and gas by closely related species.) Reincubate media addnl 48 hr and test both media for production of acid. Acid is usually produced from raffinose by *C. perfringens* but not by closely related species. Acid is produced from salicin in PY medium by a few strains of *C. perfringens.*

Calc. number of *C. perfringens* in sample on basis of % colonies tested that are confirmed as *C. perfringens.* (*Example:* If av. plate count of 10^{-4} diln was 85, and 8 of 10 colonies tested were confirmed as *C. perfringens,* number of *C. perfringens*/g food is 85 × (8/10) × 10,000 = 680,000.) (*Note:* Diln factor with plates contg egg yolk is 10-fold higher than diln plated.)

Clostridium botulinum and its Toxins (7)
Official Final Action

(*Caution: See* **51.018**)

46.037 ***Principle***

Mice injected intraperitoneally (IP) with food ext contg ≥1 min. lethal dose (MLD) of botulinum toxin die within 72 hr after exhibiting sequence of symptoms characteristic of botulinum intoxication. Homologous antitoxin will protect mice from symptoms while other antitoxins will not, thus detg serological type. Viable spores in food will grow in suitable culture medium and produce toxin, which is detected and typed.

46.038 ***Apparatus***

(**a**) *Can opener.—See* **46.020**(**a**).

(**b**) *Anaerobic jars.*—Gas-Pak (BBL) or Case-nitrogen replacement.

(**c**) *Petri dishes.*—100 mm diam. Dry prepd plates ca 24 hr at 35° before streaking.

(**d**) *Centrifuge.*—High-speed, refrigerated.

(**e**) *Syringes.*—1.0 or 3.0 mL with 25 gage ⅝" needles for inoculating mice.

46.039 ***Media and Reagents***

(**a**) *Cooked meat broth.*—Use either liver or heart medium. (*1*) *Chopped liver broth.*—Grind 500 g fresh beef liver into 800 mL H_2O. Heat to bp and simmer 1 hr. Cool, adjust to pH 7.0, and boil 10 min. Filter thru cheesecloth, pressing out excess liq. To broth add 10 g peptone, 1 g K_2HPO_4, and 1 g sol. starch. Adjust to pH 7.0 and dil. to 1 L with H_2O. Filter thru coarse paper. (If desired, broth and liver may be stored sep. in freezer for future use.) To 18 or 20 × 150 mm test tubes, add liver to ht of 1–2 cm and 10–12 mL liq. Autoclave 20 min at 121°. (*2*) *Cooked meat medium.*—Use com. medium of following formula: beef heart 454 g, proteose peptone 20 g, dextrose 2 g, and NaCl 5 g. Suspend 12.5 g medium in 100 mL cold H_2O. Mix thoroly and let stand until particles are thoroly wetted (ca 15 min). (Alternatively, add 1.25 g solid medium into test tubes, add 10 mL cold H_2O, and mix thoroly to wet all particles.) Autoclave 15 min at 121°. Final pH, 7.2±0.1.

(**b**) *Trypticase-peptone-glucose-yeast extract broth with trypsin* (*TPGYT*).—Dissolve 50 g trypticase, 5 g Bacto-peptone, 20 g yeast ext, 4 g dextrose, and 1 g Na thioglycolate in 1 L H_2O, and dispense 15 mL portions into 20× 150 mm culture tubes or 100 mL portions into 6 fl oz prescription bottles. Autoclave 10 min (tubes) or 15 min (bottles) at 121°. Final pH, 7.0±0.1. Refrigerate, and discard if not used within 2 weeks. Immediately before use, steam or boil 10–15 min to remove O, cool quickly, and aseptically add 1.0 mL trypsin soln/15 mL broth.

Prep. trypsin soln by dissolving 1.5 g trypsin (Difco 1:250) in 100 mL H_2O. Sterilize by filtering thru 0.45 μm Millipore or equiv. filter, and refrigerate.

(c) *Liver-veal-egg yolk agar or anaerobic egg yolk agar.*—(*1*) *Liver-veal-egg yolk agar* (*LVEY*).—Wash 2 or 3 eggs with stiff brush, and drain. Soak eggs in 0.1% $HgCl_2$ soln 1 hr. Drain $HgCl_2$ soln and replace with 70% alcohol, soaking 30 min. Remove eggs, crack aseptically, and discard whites. Remove yolk with syringe, place in sterile container, and add equal vol. sterile 0.85% NaCl soln. Mix thoroly. To each 500 mL prepd sterile com. dehydrated liver veal agar at 50°, add 40 mL egg yolk-NaCl suspension. Mix thoroly and pour plates. Dry plates 2 days at room temp. or 24 hr at 35°. Discard contaminated plates, and store sterile plates in refrigerator. (*2*) *Anaerobic egg agar.*—Dissolve 5 g yeast ext, 5 g tryptone, 20 g proteose peptone, 5 g NaCl, and 20 g agar in 1 L H_2O. Adjust to pH 7.0, dispense 500 mL into 1 L flask, and autoclave 20 min at 121°. To 500 mL melted agar at 45–50°, add 40 mL egg yolk-NaCl suspension, prepd as in (*1*). Mix, and pour plates immediately. Dry and store sterile plates as in (*1*).

(d) *Gel-phosphate buffer.*—pH 6.2. Dissolve 2 g gelatin and 4 g Na_2HPO_4 in 1 L H_2O with gentle heat. Dispense into 100 mL milk diln bottle. Autoclave 20 min at 121°.

(e) *Clostridium botulinum antitoxin preparations.*—Types A thru F or polyvalent A–F. Available from Scientific Resources Branch, Laboratory Division, Center for Disease Control, Atlanta, GA 30333.

46.040 *Preparation of Sample*

(a) *Preliminary examination.*—Keep samples refrigerated. Unopened canned foods, unless badly swollen and in danger of bursting, need not be refrigerated. Record code and condition of container. Clean and identify container.

(b) *Solid foods.*—Aseptically transfer portion, with little or no free liq., to sterile mortar. Add equal amt sterile gel-phosphate buffer, (d), and grind with sterile pestle. Alternatively, inoculate small pieces of sample with sterile forceps directly into enrichment broth.

(c) *Liquid foods.*—Inoculate with sterile pipets directly into enrichment broth.

(d) *Canned foods.*—Prep., disinfect with alc. I soln, and open cans as in **46.021**. If can has swelled, position can so vertical side seam is away from operator. If can has buckled ends, chill before opening, and flame cautiously to avoid bursting can.

(e) *Visual examination.*—Note appearance, odor, and any evidence of decomposition. DO NOT TASTE PRODUCT under any circumstances.

(f) *Reserve sample.*—After culturing, aseptically remove portion to sterile sample jars for further tests which may be needed later.

46.041 *Detection of Viable C. botulinum*

(a) *Enrichment.*—Remove dissolved O from media before inoculation by steaming 10–15 min and cooling quickly without agitation. Inoculate 2 tubes of cooked meat broth, (a), with 1–2 g solid or 1–2 mL liq. food or ext/15 mL broth, introducing inoculum slowly beneath surface of broth. Incubate at 35°. Similarly inoculate 2 tubes of TPGYT broth, **46.039(b)**, and incubate at 26°.

(b) *Examination.*—After 5 days, examine cultures for turbidity, gas production, digestion of meat particles, and odor. Also examine microscopically by wet mount under high power phase contrast or by bright field illumination of smear stained by Gram stain, crystal violet, or methylene blue. Observe morphology of organisms and note existence of typical clostridial cells, occurrence and relative extent of sporulation, and location of spores within cells.

(c) *Further treatment.*—Usually 5 day incubation produces active growth and highest concn of toxin, as well as peak sporulation. Retain culture in refrigerator for pure culture isolation. If there is no growth after 5 days, incubate addnl 10 days to detect possible delayed germination of *C. botulinum* spores before discarding culture as sterile.

46.042 *Isolation of Pure Cultures*

If good sporulation has occurred, *C. botulinum* is more readily isolated from mixed flora in enrichment culture or from original sample.

(a) *Pretreatment.*—Add equal vol. filter-sterilized absolute alcohol to 1–2 mL culture or sample in sterile screw-cap tube. Mix well and incubate at room temp. 1 hr. Alternatively, heat 1–2 mL enrichment culture 10–15 min at 80° to destroy vegetative cells. (Do not use heat treatment for nonproteolytic type *C. botulinum.*)

(b) *Plating.*—With inoculating loop, streak 1 or 2 loopfuls of alcohol or heat-treated cultures, dild if necessary, to either or both liver veal egg yolk agar or anaerobic egg yolk agar dried plates in manner to obtain isolated colonies. Incubate plates ca 48 hr at 35° under anaerobic conditions of Case anaerobic jar or Gas-Pak systems, or equivs.

(c) *Selection of colonies.*—Typical colonies are raised or flat, smooth or rough, and commonly show some spreading and have irregular edge. On egg yolk media, colonies usually exhibit surface iridescence when examined by oblique light. This luster zone is referred to as "pearly layer." Zone usually extends beyond and follows irregular contour of colony. Besides pearly zone, colonies of types C, D, and E are ordinarily surrounded by wide (2–4 mm) zone of yellow ppt. Colonies of types A and B generally show smaller zone of pptn. Not all typical colonies will produce toxin. Some members of genus *Clostridium* have typical morphological characteristics but do not produce toxins.

(d) *Cultures.*—With sterile transfer loop, inoculate each of 10 selected colonies into tube of sterile medium: (*1*) TPGYT broth for *C. botulinum* Type E, incubating 5 days at 26°; and (*2*) cooked meat broth for other toxin types, incubating 5 days at 35°. Use cultures for confirmation as in (e) and for detection and identification of toxin as in **46.043**.

(e) *Confirmation.*—Streak culture from (d) in duplicate on egg yolk agar plates, incubating 1 plate anaerobically and other plate aerobically at 35°. If colonies typical of *C. botulinum* are found on anaerobic plate and no growth is found on aerobic plate, culture may be pure. Failure to isolate *C. botulinum* from ≥1 of selected colonies may indicate that its population relative to mixed flora is low. Repeated serial transfers thru addnl enrichment steps, **46.041(a)**, may increase numbers sufficiently to permit isolation. Store pure culture, (d), either under refrigeration, on glass beads, or lyophilized.

46.043 *Detection of Toxin*

(a) *Preparation of sample.*—Ext solid foods with equal vol. gel-phosphate buffer, **46.039(d)**, macerating with sterile, prechilled mortar and pestle. Centrf. ext and liq. foods contg suspended solids under refrigeration. Rinse empty containers suspected of having held toxic foods with few mL gel-phosphate buffer. Use min. vol. to avoid diln of toxin.

(b) *Trypsin treatment.*—Toxins of nonproteolytic types, if present, may need trypsin activation to be detected. Do not use trypsin treatment with TPGYT culture which already contains trypsin. Further treatment may degrade any fully activated toxin present in culture.

Adjust portion of food supernate, (**a**), liq. food, or cooked meat culture, if necessary, to pH 6.2 with 1*N* NaOH or HCl. Prep. satd trypsin treated and untreated materials. Dil. portions of un- in clean culture tube. Mix 0.2 mL trypsin soln with 1.8 mL liq. to be tested. Incubate 1 hr at 37° with occasional gentle agitation.

(**c**) *Toxicity testing.*—Conduct each test in duplicate, *i.e.* on trypsin treated and untreated materials. Dil. portions of untreated and treated food supernate, liq. food, or culture 1:2, 1:10, and 1:100, resp., with gel-phosphate buffer. Inject sep. pairs of mice, ca 15–20 g, IP with original and dild fluids, treated and untreated, using syringe, (**e**). Heat 1.5 mL original untreated fluid 10 min at 100° for control. Cool, and inject pair of mice each with 0.5 mL heated fluid. These mice should not die because botulinum toxin, if present, is inactivated by this heat treatment.

Observe mice periodically for 72 hr, recording symptoms and time of deaths. Typical symptoms of botulism usually begin within 24 hr with ruffling of fur, followed in sequence by labored breathing, weakness of limbs, and finally total paralysis with gasping for breath, followed by death due to respiratory failure. Death without symptoms of botulism is not sufficient evidence that injected material contained botulinum toxin. Deaths may occur from chems present in fluid or from trauma.

If after 72 hr, all but mice receiving heated prepn have died, repeat toxicity test, using higher dilns of fluids. It is necessary to have dilns that kill as well as dilns that do not kill to establish an end point or MLD (min. lethal dose) as est. of amt of toxin present. MLD is contained in highest diln killing both (or all) mice inoculated. Calc. MLD/mL.

46.044 ***Typing of Toxin***

Dil. monovalent antitoxins to types A, B, E, and F in 0.85% NaCl soln to concn of 1 International Unit/0.5 mL. Prep. enough dild antitoxin to inject 0.5 mL into each of 2 mice for each diln of prepn to be tested.

Use toxic prepn which gave greatest number of MLD, either treated or untreated. If untreated, same prepn can be used as was used for toxicity testing; if trypsinized prepn was most lethal, prep. freshly trypsinized fluid since continued action of trypsin may destroy toxin. Prep. dilns to cover range of at least 10, 100, and 1000 MLD below previously detd end point of toxicity.

Inject several groups of mice IP, each mouse receiving 0.5 mL of 1 of dild antitoxins, 30–60 min before challenging them with IP injection of toxic prepns.

Inject pairs of mice protected by specific monovalent antitoxin injection IP with each diln of toxic prepn. Also inject pair of unprotected mice (no injection of antitoxin) with each toxic diln as control. (This protocol requires 30 mice: 3 pairs for each of the 4 monovalent antitoxins (A, B, E, and F), each pair to receive challenge of 1 of the 3 dilns of toxic prepn ($2 \times 3 \times 4 = 24$) plus 1 pair of unprotected mice for each diln of toxic material as control ($2 \times 3 = 6$).

Observe mice 72 hr for symptoms of botulism and record time of deaths. If results indicate that toxin was not neutzd, repeat test, using monovalent antitoxins to types C and D, plus polyvalent antitoxin pool of types A thru F.

46.045 ***Interpretation***

Toxin in food means that product, if consumed without thoro heating, could cause botulism. Presence of toxin in food is required for botulism to occur. Viable *C. botulinum* but no toxin in food is not proof that food in question caused botulism. Ingested organisms may be found in alimentary tract, but are considered to be unable to multiply and produce toxin *in vivo.*

Presence of botulinum toxin and/or organisms in low-acid (pH >4.6) canned foods means that items were underprocessed or were contaminated thru post-processing leakage. Swollen cans are more likely than flat cans to contain botulinum toxin since organism produces gas during growth. Presence of toxin in flat can may imply that seams were loose enough to let gas escape. Toxin in canned foods is usually of type A or of proteolytic type B strain, since spores of proteolytics can be among more heat resistant bacterial spores. Spores of nonproteolytics, types B, E, and F, generally are of low heat resistance and would not normally survive even mild heat treatment.

Protection of mice from botulism and death with 1 of monovalent botulinum antitoxins confirms presence of botulinum toxin and dets serological type of toxin in sample.

If mice are not protected by 1 of monovalent antitoxins, there may be too much toxin in sample, there may be more than 1 kind of toxin present, or deaths may be due to some other cause. In such cases, retesting at higher dilns of test fluids is required and mixts of antitoxins must be used in place of monovalent antiserum. If mice are still not protected, some other toxic material, which is not heat labile, could be responsible if both heated and unheated fluids cause death. It is also possible that heat stable toxic substance could mask botulinum toxin.

Estimation of *Clostridium perfringens,* alpha-Toxin Method (*8*)—Official Final Action

(Applicable to examination of outbreak foods in which relatively large numbers of vegetative cells are expected to be present)

46.046 ***Apparatus***

(**a**) *Centrifuge.*—High-speed, preferably refrigerated, with 250 mL bottles.

(**b**) *Seitz filter.*—100–250 mL with sterilizing filter pads.

(**c**) *High-speed blender.*—Waring Blendor or Omni-Mixer homogenizer (DuPont Co., Sorvall Operations, Newtown, CT 06470), with blending vessels.

(**d**) *Vacuum flask.*—Sidearm 1 L erlenmeyer fitted with 1-hole rubber stopper to receive 200 mm glass tubing with 125 cm of 6 mm od (3 mm id) rubber tubing attached.

(**e**) *Tubing.*—Stainless steel thin wall (No. 9 surgical), 3 (od) × 180 mm (Tubesales, 175 Tubeway St, Forrest Park, GA 30050).

(**f**) *Dialysis tubing.*—1.21" flat width (Fisher Scientific Co., No. 8667C).

46.047 ***Reagents***

(**a**) *N-2-Hydroxyethyl piperazine-N'-2-ethane sulfonic acid (HEPES) buffer soln.*—Dissolve 6.0 g HEPES (Calbiochem) and 11.7 g NaCl in 500 mL H_2O. Adjust to pH 8.0 with 3*N* NaOH and store at 4°.

(**b**) *Lecithovitellin soln.*—Mix 1 egg yolk with 250 mL saline soln, (**e**), and clarify by centrfg 20 min at 14,000×*g* at 4°. Filter-sterilize supernate with Seitz filter and store at 4°.

(**c**) *Saline agar base.*—Add 15.0 g purified agar (Difco Laboratories) and 8.5 g NaCl to 1 L H_2O. Adjust to pH 7.0, heat to dissolve agar, dispense in 100 mL portions, and autoclave 15 min at 121°.

(**d**) *Washed red blood cells.*—Wash packed human red blood cells 3 times by mixing with 4 vols saline soln, (**e**). Centrf. 10 min at low speed (2500 rpm) to sediment cells. Remove supernate with vac. flask. Resuspend cells in addnl saline soln and repeat these steps twice. After final wash, mix cells with equal vol. saline soln. Use sterile precautions.

(**e**) *Sterile saline soln.*—Dissolve 8.5 g NaCl in 1 L H_2O. Adjust to pH 7.0, dispense 250 mL portions into Pyrex containers, and autoclave 15 min at 121°.

(f) *Polyethylene glycol soln.*—30%. Dissolve 120 g polyethylene glycol (Carbowax Compound 20M, Union Carbide Corp., PO Box 8361, S Charleston, WV 25303) in 400 mL H_2O.

(g) *Antiserum.*—*Clostridium perfringens* Type A diagnostic serum (Wellcome Reagents, Burroughs-Wellcome Co., 3030 Cornwallis Rd, Research Triangle Park, NC 27709).

46.048 ***Preparation of Hemolysin Plates***

Melt 100 mL saline agar base, (**c**), cool to 50°, and add 11 mL washed red cells, (**d**). Mix thoroly and dispense 7 mL into 15 × 100 mm sterile plastic petri dishes. Dry plates overnight at room temp. and store at 4°. Just before use, cut test wells by applying vac. to sterile stainless steel tube, (**e**), and plunging tube into agar. Using template, space 9 test wells 3 cm apart and 2 cm from edge, and place 2 addnl wells 3 cm apart near center of plate.

46.049 ***Toxin Extraction***

Homogenize 25 g food (do not include fat) in 100 mL HEPES buffer soln, (**a**), 1 min in high-speed blender. Centrf. homogenate 20 min at 14,000–20,000×*g* at 5°. Filter supernate thru Whatman No. 31 paper, or equiv., to remove fat (chill ext centrfd without refrigeration 1 hr at 4° before filtering). Discard solids. Rinse Seitz filter pad with 15 mL saline soln. Discard saline soln and filter-sterilize ext, rinsing filter pad with 10 mL saline soln.

46.050 ***Concentration***

Soak 90 cm dialysis tubing 1 hr in H_2O. Tie one end and fill with saline soln. Check for leaks and rinse out twice with saline soln. Transfer sterile ext to dialysis sack and conc. to <10 mL by dialyzing 4–5 hr against 400 mL 30% polyethylene glycol, (**f**), at 4°. Rinse outside of sack with tap H_2O and collect concd ext in sterile tube.

46.051 ***Toxin Testing***

Adjust vol. of concd ext to 10±0.5 mL with saline soln. Set up 10 sterile 13 × 100 mm test tubes and add 0.5 mL saline soln to all tubes except first and last. Add 0.5 mL ext to first and second tubes. Mix ext and saline soln in second tube and transfer 0.5 mL to third tube, etc., to serially dil. ext from 0 to 1+255. Change pipet after 3 dilns to prevent excessive carry-over. Mix 0.25 mL ext, 0.25 mL saline soln, and 0.1 mL antiserum, (**g**), in last tube. Fill 1 peripheral well of duplicate hemolysin plates with each diln of ext, using fine-tipped Pasteur pipet. Fill 1 center well of each plate with ext-antiserum mixt. and the other with saline soln. Add 0.5 mL lecithovitellin soln, (**b**), to remainder of dild ext in each tube, including ext-antiserum mixt. Mix well, and incubate tubes and plates (in plastic bag) 24 hr at 35°.

46.052 ***alpha-Toxin Titer***

After incubation, refrigerate plates 2 hr at 4°. Measure hemolytic zone (width from edge of well in mm). Last 3 dilns before end point should exhibit ca 1 mm reduction in width for each 2-fold diln. If not, repeat α-toxin test. Hemolytic zone 1 mm in width is end point of titrn.

Examine ext-lecithovitellin mixt. in tubes for lecithinase activity and record results. Max. reaction (++++) is white pellicle 4–5 mm thick over clear liq. Activity decreases with diln to (+) reaction (opaque soln with no pellicle). This diln is end point of lecithovitellin test. Hemolytic and lecithinase activities neutzd by antiserum are due to α-toxin.

46.053 ***Population Estimate***

Compare titer of α-toxin present in ext with data in Table **46:02** to est. population of *C. perfringens.* Hemolysin (HI) plate titer is preferred for this because lecithovitellin (LV) test is less sensitive with some food exts.

Table 46:02 Correlation between Population Levels of *C. perfringens* and Amount alpha-Toxin Produced in Food[a]

α-Toxin titer[b]		Estd *C. perfringens* population/g × 10^6
HI plate	LV test	
Undild		1.2
1+1	Undild	2.5
1+3	1+1	6.5
1+7	1+3	9.5
1+15	1+7	25
1+31	1+15	55
1+63	1+31	80
1+127	1+127	150
1+255	1+255	210

[a] Based on viable counts obtained with 6 strains in chicken broth.
[b] Diln which produces 1 mm zone of hemolysis in HI plate or one + reaction in LV test.

SALMONELLA (*9*)—OFFICIAL FINAL ACTION

(Applicable to the detection and identification of *Salmonella* from dried active yeast, dried whole egg, dried egg yolk, and dried egg white, nonfat dry milk and dry whole milk, and onion and garlic powders. Method described is minimal. Depending upon history of sample, addnl types of examinations may be applied. Use *Identification of Enterobacteriaceae*, P. R. Edwards and W. H. Ewing, Burgess Publishing Co., Minneapolis, MN 55415, 3rd ed., 1972, as guide for further study of isolated microorganisms. For food sampling plans and initial sample handling, refer to Chapter 1, *FDA Bacteriological Analytical Manual*, 5th ed., 1978.)

46.054 ***Culture Media***

(Sizes of culture media containers (test tubes, flasks, and petri dishes) are specified in prepn of each medium. Different size containers may be used if they give identical results. All media containers must have covers, caps, or plugs which prevent contamination but maintain aerobic conditions unless otherwise directed.)

(**a**) *Lactose broth.*—*See* **46.005**(**f**). Dispense 225 mL portions into 500 mL screw-cap bottles or flasks.

(**b**)(*1*) *Selenite cystine broth.*—Suspend 5.0 g tryptone or polypeptone, 4.0 g lactose, 10.0 g Na_2HPO_4, 4.0 g $NaHSeO_3$, and 0.01 g L-cystine in 1 L H_2O and mix thoroly. Heat with frequent agitation. Dispense 10 mL portions into sterile 16 × 150 mm test tubes. Heat 10 min in flowing steam. *Do not autoclave*. Final pH, 7.0±0.2. Medium is not sterile. Use same day as prepd.

(*2*) *Selenite cystine broth* (*North and Bartram*).—Prep. as in (*1*), using 5.0 g polypeptone or 4.0 g tryptone, 4.0 g lactose, 4.0 g $NaHSeO_3$, 5.5 g Na_2HPO_4, 4.5 g KH_2PO_4, and 1 mL 1% L-cystine (10 mg) soln prepd by dissolving 1.0 g L-cystine in 15 mL 1*N* NaOH and dilg to 100 mL with sterile H_2O.

(**c**) *Tetrathionate broth* (*with iodine and brilliant green*).—Suspend 5.0 g polypeptone, 1.0 g bile salts, 10 g $CaCO_3$, and 30 g $Na_2S_2O_3.5H_2O$ in 1 L H_2O, mix thoroly, and heat to bp. (Ppt will not dissolve completely.) Cool to <45° and store at 5–8°. Prep. I-KI soln by dissolving 5 g KI in 5 mL sterile H_2O, adding 6 g resublimed I, dissolving, and dilg to 20 mL with sterile H_2O. Prep. brilliant green soln by dissolving 0.1 g dye in sterile H_2O and dilg to 100 mL. On day medium is used, add 20 mL I-KI soln and 10 mL brilliant green soln per 1 L basal broth. Resuspend ppt by gentle agitation and aseptically dispense 10 mL portions into 20 or 16 × 150 mm sterile test tubes. *Do not heat medium after addn of I-KI and dye solns.*

(d) *Brilliant green agar.*—Use com. dehydrated medium contg 3.0 g yeast ext, 10 g proteose peptone No. 3 or polypeptone, 5.0 g NaCl, 10 g lactose, 10 g sucrose, 0.08 g phenol red, 5 mL 0.25% brilliant green (12.5 mg) soln, and 20 g agar. Suspend medium in 1 L H_2O, mix thoroly, and heat with occasional agitation. Boil 1 min to dissolve. Autoclave 1 L portions 12 min at 121°. (Addnl heating decreases selectivity of medium; less heating increases selectivity.) Cool to 45–50° and pour 20 mL portions into 15 × 100 mm petri dishes. Let dry ca 2 hr with covers partially removed; then close plates. Final pH, 6.9±0.2.

(e) *Salmonella-Shigella agar.*—Suspend 5.0 g beef ext, 5.0 g polypeptone or proteose peptone, 10 g lactose, 8.5 g bile salts mixt., 8.5 g Na citrate.$2H_2O$, 8.5 g $Na_2S_2O_3.5H_2O$, 1.0 g ferric citrate, 13.5 g agar, 0.33 mL 0.1% brilliant green (0.33 mg) soln, and 2.5 mL 1% neutral red (25 mg) soln in 1 L H_2O, and mix thoroly until homogeneous. Heat with occasional agitation and boil 1–2 min until ingredients dissolve. Cool to 45–50° and pour 20 mL portions into 15 × 100 mm petri dishes. Let dry ca 2 hr with covers partially removed; then close plates. Final pH, 7.0±0.2. *Do not autoclave.*

(f) *Bismuth sulfite agar (Wilson and Blair).*—Suspend 10 g polypeptone or peptone, 5.0 g beef ext, 5.0 g glucose, 4.0 g Na_2HPO_4, 0.3 g $FeSO_4$, 8.0 g $Bi_2(SO_3)_3$ indicator, 0.025 g brilliant green, and 20 g agar in 1 L H_2O, mix thoroly, and heat with occasional agitation. Boil ca 1 min to obtain uniform suspension. (Ppt will not dissolve.) Cool to 45–50°. Suspend ppt by gentle agitation and pour 20 mL portions into 15 × 100 mm petri dishes. Let dry ca 2 hr with covers partially removed; then close plates. Final pH, 7.6±0.2. *Do not autoclave.* Prepare plates day before streaking and store in dark at room temp. Selectivity of plates decreases 48 hr after prepn.

(g) *Triple sugar iron agar (TSI agar).*—Suspend ingredients *(1)* or *(2)* in 1 L H_2O, mix thoroly, and heat with occasional agitation. Boil ca 1 min until ingredients dissolve. Fill 16 × 150 mm tubes ⅓ full and cap or plug so that aerobic conditions are maintained during use. Autoclave 12 min at 121°. Before medium solidifies, place tubes in slanted position so that deep butts (ca 3 cm) and adequate slants (ca 5 cm) are formed on solidification.

(1) 20 g polypeptone, 5.0 g NaCl, 10 g lactose, 10 g sucrose, 1 g glucose, 0.2 g $Fe(NH_4)_2(SO_4)_2.6H_2O$, 0.2 g $Na_2S_2O_3$, 0.025 g phenol red, and 13 g agar. Final pH, 7.3±0.2.

(2) 3.0 g beef ext, 3.0 g yeast ext, 15 g peptone, 5.0 g proteose-peptone, 1.0 g glucose, 10 g lactose, 10 g sucrose, 0.2 g $FeSO_4$, 5.0 g NaCl, 0.3 g $Na_2S_2O_3$, 0.024 g phenol red, and 12 g agar. Final pH, 7.4±0.2.

(h) *Tryptophane broth.—See* **46.005(h)**. Use 16 or 20 × 150 mm test tubes.

(i) *Buffered glucose broth (MR-VP medium).—See* **46.005(b)**. Use 16 or 20 × 150 mm test tubes.

(j) *Simmon's citrate agar.*—Dissolve 2.0 g Na citrate, 5.0 g NaCl, 1.0 g K_2HPO_4, 1.0 g $NH_4H_2PO_4$, 0.2 g $MgSO_4$, 0.08 g bromothymol blue, and 15 g agar in 1 L H_2O, and heat gently with occasional agitation. Boil 1–2 min until ingredients dissolve. Final pH, 6.9±0.2. Fill 13 or 16 × 150 mm test tubes ⅓ full and cap or plug so that aerobic conditions are maintained during use. Autoclave 15 min at 121°. Before medium solidifies, place tubes in slanted position so that deep butts (ca 2 or 3 cm, resp.) and adequate slants (ca 4 or 5 cm, resp.) are formed on solidification.

(k)*(1)* *Urea broth.*—Dissolve 20 g urea, 0.1 g yeast ext, 9.1 g KH_2PO_4, 9.5 g Na_2HPO_4, and 4.0 mL 0.25% phenol red (10 mg) soln in 1 L H_2O. *Do not heat.* Sterilize by filtration and aseptically dispense 1.5–3 mL portions into 13 × 100 mm sterile test tubes. Final pH, 6.8±0.2.

(2) *Rapid urea broth.*—Prep. as in *(1)*, using 0.091 and 0.095 g phosphate salts, resp.

(l) *Malonate broth.*—Dissolve 1.0 g yeast ext, 2.0 g $(NH_4)_2SO_4$, 0.6 g K_2HPO_4, 0.4 g KH_2PO_4, 2.0 g NaCl, 3.0 g Na malonate, 0.25 g glucose, and 0.025 g bromothymol blue in 1 L H_2O, heating if necessary until dissolved. Dispense 3 mL portions into 13 × 100 mm test tubes and autoclave 15 min at 121°. Final pH, 6.7±0.2.

(m)*(1)* *Lysine iron agar (Edwards and Fife).*—Dissolve 5.0 g gelysate or peptone, 3.0 g yeast ext, 1.0 g glucose, 10 g L-lysine, 0.5 g ferric ammonium citrate, 0.04 g anhyd. $Na_2S_2O_3$, 0.02 g bromocresol purple, and 15 g agar in 1 L H_2O, heating until dissolved. Dispense 4 mL portions into 13 × 100 mL test tubes and cap or plug so that aerobic conditions are maintained during use. Autoclave 12 min at 121°. Before medium solidifies, place tubes in slanted position so that 4 cm butts and 2.5 cm slants are formed on solidification. Final pH, 6.7±0.2.

(2) *Lysine decarboxylase broth (Falkow).*—Dissolve 5.0 g gelysate or peptone, 3.0 g yeast ext, 1.0 g glucose, 5.0 g L-lysine, and 0.02 g bromocresol purple in 1 L H_2O, heating until dissolved. Dispense 5 mL portions into 16 × 125 mm screw-cap test tubes. Autoclave, loosely capped, 15 min at 121°. Screw caps on tightly for storage and after inoculation. Final pH, 6.5–6.8.

(n) *Motility test medium (semisolid medium).*—Dissolve 3.0 g beef ext, 10 g peptone or gelysate, 5.0 g NaCl, and 4.0 g agar in 1 L H_2O and heat gently with occasional agitation. Boil 1–2 min to dissolve. If medium is to be stored, dispense 20 mL portions into screw-cap containers, replacing caps loosely. Autoclave 15 min at 121°. Cool to 45°. To store, screw caps on tightly and refrigerate at 5–8°. To use, remelt in boiling H_2O or flowing steam and cool to 45°. Aseptically dispense 20 mL portions into 15 × 100 mm petri dishes and let solidify with dish completely covered. Use plates same day as prepd. Final pH, 7.4±0.2.

(o) *Potassium cyanide (KCN) broth.*—Dissolve 3.0 g proteose peptone No. 3 or polypeptone, 5.0 g NaCl, 0.225 g KH_2PO_4, and 5.64 g Na_2HPO_4 in 1 L H_2O. Autoclave 15 min at 121°. Cool and refrigerate at 5–8°. Final pH, 7.6±0.2. Dissolve 0.5 g KCN in 100 mL cold (5–8°) sterile H_2O. Using sterile bulb pipet or sterile syringe (*do not pipet by mouth*), aseptically add 15 mL cold KCN soln per L cold, sterile basal broth. Mix thoroly with gentle agitation and aseptically dispense 1.0–1.5 mL portions into sterile 13 × 100 mm test tubes. Using aseptic technic, immediately stopper tubes with No. 2 corks impregnated with paraffin. Prep. corks by boiling in paraffin ca 5 min. Place corks in tubes so that paraffin does not flow into broth but forms good seal between rim of tube and cork. Medium stored at 5–8° is usually stable ca 2 weeks.

(p)*(1)* *Phenol red carbohydrate broth.*—Dissolve 10 g trypticase or proteose peptone No. 3, 5.0 g NaCl, 1.0 g beef ext (optional), and 7.2 mL 0.25% phenol red (18 mg) soln in 1 L H_2O and heat with gentle agitation until dissolved. Dissolve 5 g dulcitol, 10 g lactose, or 10 g sucrose (as specified in title of test) in this basal broth. Dispense 2.5 mL portions into 13 × 100 mm test tubes contg inverted 6 × 50 mm fermentation tubes. Autoclave 10 min at 118° (12 psi). Final pH, 7.3±0.2. Alternatively, dissolve ingredients, omitting carbohydrate, in 800 mL H_2O with heat and occasional agitation. Dispense 2.0 mL portions into 13 × 100 mm test tubes contg inverted fermentation tubes. Autoclave 15 min at 118° and let cool. Dissolve carbohydrate in 200 mL H_2O and sterilize by passing soln thru bacteria-retaining filter. Aseptically add 0.5 mL sterile filtrate to each tube of sterilized broth after cooling to $<45°$. Shake gently to mix. Final pH, 7.4±0.2.

(2) *Purple carbohydrate broth.*—Prep. as in *(1)*, using as basal

broth 10 g proteose peptone No. 3 or gelysate, 5.0 g NaCl, and 0.015 or 0.020 g bromocresol purple. Final pH, 6.8±0.2.

(q) *MacConkey agar*.—Suspend 3.0 g proteose peptone or polypeptone, 17 g peptone or gelysate, 10 g lactose, 1.5 g bile salts No. 3 or bile salts mixt., 5.0 g NaCl, 3.0 mL 1% neutral red (30 mg) soln, 1 mL 0.1% crystal violet (1.0 mg) soln, and 13.5 g agar in 1 L H_2O and mix thoroly until homogeneous. Heat, with occasional agitation, and boil 1–2 min until ingredients dissolve. Autoclave 15 min at 121°. Cool to 45–50° and pour 20 mL portions into 15 × 100 mm petri dishes. Let dry ≥2 hr with plates covered. Do not use wet plates. Final pH, 7.1±0.2.

(r) *Brain-heart infusion broth*.—Dissolve infusion from 200 g calf brain and from 250 g beef heart, 10.0 g proteose peptone or gelysate, 5.0 g NaCl, 2.5 g $Na_2HPO_4.12H_2O$, and 2.0 g glucose in 1 L H_2O, heating gently if necessary. Dispense 5 mL portions into 16 × 150 mm test tubes and autoclave 15 min at 121°. Final pH, 7.4±0.2.

(s) *Trypticase soy-tryptose broth*.—Combine 15 g com. dehydrated trypticase soy broth medium (contg 17.0 g trypticase, 3.0 g phytone, 5.0 g NaCl, 2.5 g K_2HPO_4, and 2.5 g glucose), 13.5 g com. dehydrated tryptose broth medium (contg 20 g tryptose, 5 g NaCl, and 1.0 g glucose), 3 g yeast ext, and 1 L H_2O. Heat, if necessary, until dissolved. Dispense 5 mL portions into 16 × 150 mm test tubes and autoclave 15 min at 121°. Final pH, 7.2±0.2.

(t) *Trypticase (tryptic) soy broth*.—Prep. as in **46.013(f)**, but omit NaCl.

(u) *Lauryl sulfate tryptose broth*.—Prep. as in **46.013(b)**.

46.055 ***Diagnostic Reagents***

(a) *Kovacs reagent for indole test*.—Dissolve 5 g *p*-dimethylaminobenzaldehyde in 75 mL amyl alcohol and slowly add 25 mL HCl.

(b) *Voges-Proskauer (VP) test reagents*.—*(1) Alpha-naphthol soln*.—5%. Dissolve 5.0 g α-naphthol in 100 mL absolute alcohol. *(2) Potassium hydroxide soln*.—40%. Dissolve 40 g KOH in H_2O and dil. to 100 mL.

(c) *Sodium hydroxide soln*.—1*N*. Dissolve 42.11 g 95% reagent NaOH in sterile H_2O and dil. to 1 L.

(d) *Hydrochloric acid soln*.—1*N*. Dil. 89 mL to 1 L with sterile H_2O.

(e) *Methyl red indicator*.—Dissolve 0.10 g Me red in 300 mL alcohol and dil. to 500 mL with H_2O.

(f) *Sterile physiological saline soln*.—*See* **46.006(c)**.

(g) *Formalinized physiological saline soln*.—Add 6 mL HCHO soln (36–38%) to 1 L sterile saline soln, **(f)**, mix, and store in tightly stoppered containers.

(h) *Salmonella polyvalent somatic (O) antiserum**.—("Serological Identification of the *Salmonella* Serotypes," No. 0168, Difco Laboratories, October 1977, p. 13, or equiv.) Contains agglutinins for at least somatic (O) antigens 1, 2, 3, 4, 5, 6, 7, 8, 9, 10, 11, 12, 13, 14, 15, 16, 19, 22, 23, 24, 25, 34, and Vi. They are agglutinins for somatic (O) groups: A, B, C_1, C_2, D, E_1, E_2, E_3, E_4, F, G_1, G_2, H, I, and Vi.

(i) *Salmonella individual somatic (O) antisera**.—(*See* ref. in **(h)**.) For at least each of the somatic (O) groups listed in **(h)**.

(j) *Salmonella polyvalent flagellar (H) antiserum Poly a-z**.—(*See* p. 12 of ref. in **(h)**.) Contains agglutinins for at least the following flagellar (H) antigens: a, b, c, d, e, f, g, h, i, k, l, m, n, p, q, r, s, t, u, v, w, x, y, z, z_4, z_6, z_{10}, z_{13}, z_{15}, z_{23}, z_{24}, z_{28}, z_{29}, z_{32}, 1, 2, 5, 6, 7.

* Conform to specifications issued by Diagnostic Products Evaluation Branch, Biological Products Div., Bureau of Laboratories, Center for Disease Control, Atlanta, GA 30333.

(k) *Salmonella "Spicer-Edwards" flagellar (H) antisera**.—(From pp. 11 and 12 of ref. in **(h)**.) Consists of 7 pooled or polyvalent antisera which react as in Table **46:03**.

(l) *pH Test paper*.—Min. range 6.0–7.6 with max. gradations of 0.4 pH unit per color change.

(m) *Sterile distilled water*.—Dispense 1 L H_2O into 2 L wide-mouth flask or wide-mouth jar; plug or cap loosely. Autoclave 20 min at 121°.

(n) *Brilliant green dye soln*.—1%. Dissolve 1 g in sterile H_2O and dil. to 100 mL. (Since some batches of dye are unusually toxic, test all batches of dye before use and use only those producing satisfactory results when tested with known pos. and neg. test organisms.)

(o) *Bromcresol purple soln*.—0.2%. Dissolve 0.2 g in 100 mL sterile H_2O.

Detection

46.056 ***Preparation of Sample***

(a) *Dried whole egg, dried egg yolk, and dried egg white*.—Aseptically open sample container and aseptically weigh 25 g sample into sterile, empty, wide-mouth, screw-cap pt (500 mL) jar. Add ca 15 mL sterile lactose broth, **46.054(a)**. Stir with sterile glass rod, sterile spoon, or sterile tongue depressor to smooth suspension. Add 3 addnl portions lactose broth, 10, 10, and 190 mL for total of 225 mL. Stir after each addn until sample is suspended without lumps. Cap jar securely and let stand at room temp. 60 min. Mix well by shaking, and det. pH with test paper, **46.055(l)**. Adjust pH, if necessary, to 6.8±0.2 with sterile 1*N* NaOH or HCl, **46.055(c)** or **(d)**, capping jar securely and mixing well before detg final pH. Loosen jar cap ca ¼ turn and incubate 24±2 hr at 35°.

(b) *Nonfat dry milk and dry whole milk*.—Aseptically weigh 25 g sample into sterile, wide-mouth screw-cap 500 mL (1 pt) jar. Add 225 mL sterile H_2O and mix well. Cap jar securely and let stand 1 hr at room temp. Mix well by swirling and det. pH with test paper, **46.055(l)**. Adjust pH, if necessary, to 6.8±0.2 with sterile 1*N* NaOH or HCl, **46.055(c)** or **(d)**. Add 0.45 mL of 1% aq. brilliant green dye soln, **46.055(n)**, and mix well. Loosen jar cap ca ¼ turn and incubate 24±2 hr at 35°.

Table 46:03 Salmonella H Antisera Spicer-Edwards and H Antigens with Which Each Reacts

	Salmonella H Antisera Spicer-Edwards			
H Antigens	1	2	3	4
a	+	+	+	−
b	+	+	−	+
c	+	+	−	−
d	+	−	+	+
eh	+	−	+	−
G Complex[a]	+	−	−	+
i	+	−	−	−
k	−	+	+	+
r	−	+	−	+
y	−	+	−	−
z	−	−	+	+
z_4 Complex[b]	−	−	+	−
z_{10}	−	−	−	+
z_{29}	−	+	+	−

H Antigens	Salmonella H Antisera
enx, enz_{15}	EN complex
lv, lw, lz_{13}, lz_{28}	L complex
1, 2; 1, 5; 1, 6; 1, 7	1 complex

[a] The G complex component of Salmonella H antisera Spicer-Edwards 1 and 4 reacts with antigens f, g, m, p, q, s, t, and u.
[b] The z_4 complex component reacts with z_4, z_{23}, z_{24}, and z_{32}.
(From Difco Laboratories)

(**c**) *Dried active yeast.*—Aseptically weigh 25 g sample into sterile, empty, wide-mouth, screw-cap pt (500 mL) jar. Add 225 mL sterile trypticase (tryptic) soy broth, **46.013(f)** (*omit 10% NaCl*), and let yeast form smooth suspension. Det. pH with test paper, **46.055(l)**. Adjust pH, if necessary to 6.8±0.2 with sterile 1*N* NaOH or HCl, **46.055(c)** or (**d**), capping jar securely and mixing well before detg final pH. (If pH is adjusted before yeast is evenly suspended, final pH will be less than desired.) Incubate 24±2 hr at 35°.

(**d**) *Onion powder and garlic powder.*—Aseptically weigh 25 g sample into sterile, wide-mouth, screw-cap 500 mL (1 pt) jar. Add 225 mL sterile trypticase (tryptic) soy broth, **46.013(f)** (omit 10% NaCl from media but add 0.5% K_2SO_3 prior to autoclaving), and mix thoroly using sterile glass rod or spoon. Let stand 60 min and det. pH with test paper, **46.055(l)**. Adjust pH, if necessary, to 6.8±0.2 with sterile 1*N* NaOH or 1*N* HCl, **46.055(c)** or (**d**). Incubate 24±2 hr at 35°.

46.057 ***Isolation***

(**a**) *Growth in selective broth.*—Gently shake incubated sample mixt., **46.056**, and transfer 1 mL to 10 mL selenite cystine broth, **46.054(b)**(*1*) or (*2*), and addnl 1 mL to 10 mL tetrathionate broth, **46.054(c)**. Incubate 24±2 hr at 35°. (For dried active yeast, substitute lauryl sulfate tryptose broth, **46.013(b)**, for selenite cystine broth, **46.054(b)**(*1*) or (*2*).)

Streak 3 mm loopful of incubated selenite cystine broth on selective media plates of brilliant green agar, **46.054(d)**, Salmonella-Shigella agar, **46.054(e)**, and $Bi_2(SO_3)_3$ agar, **46.054(f)**. Repeat with 3 mm loopful of incubated tetrathionate broth. Incubate plates 24±2 hr at 35°.

(**b**) *Appearance of typical Salmonella colonies.*—(*1*) *On brilliant green agar.*—Colorless, pink to fuchsia, translucent to opaque, with surrounding medium pink to red. Some *Salmonella* appear as transparent green colonies if surrounded by lactose- or sucrose-fermenting organisms which produce colonies that are yellow-green or green.

(*2*) *On Salmonella-Shigella agar.*—Uncolored to pale pink, opaque, transparent or translucent, but some strains produce black-centered colonies.

(*3*) *On bismuth sulfite agar.*—Brown, gray to black, sometimes with metallic sheen. Surrounding medium is usually brown at first, turning black with increasing incubation time. Some strains produce green colonies with little or no darkening of surrounding medium.

If plates do not have typical or suspicious colonies or do not contain growth, incubate addnl 24 hr.

46.058 ***Treatment of Typical or Suspicious Colonies***

(**a**) *Inoculation of triple sugar iron (TSI) agar and lysine iron agar (LIA).*—Pick with needle 2 or more typical or suspicious colonies, if present, from each brilliant green, Salmonella-Shigella, and $Bi_2(SO_3)_3$ agar plates having growth. Inoculate TSI agar slant, **46.054(g)**, with portion of each colony by streaking slant and stabbing butt. After inoculating TSI agar with needle, do not obtain more inoculum from colony and do not heat needle, but inoculate LIA, **46.054(m)**(*1*), as in **46.061(a)**. Store picked selective plates at 5–8° or at room temp. (ca 26°).

(**b**) *Presumptive positive reactions.*—Incubate TSI slants 24±2 hr at 35°. Presumptive pos. *Salmonella* cultures have alk. (red) slants and acid (yellow) butts, with or without H_2S (blackening of agar). (H_2S-neg. TSI cultures which otherwise appear to be salmonellae cannot be excluded from further examination.) TSI cultures which otherwise appear not to be salmonellae (including yellow slants) cannot be excluded from further examination and should be treated as presumptive pos. TSI agar cultures if corresponding LIA gives typical *Salmonella* reaction. Discard TSI cultures that appear to be non-*Salmonella* when corresponding LIA agar (acid in butt of tube) is not typical for *Salmonella*. LIA is useful in detection of lactose- or sucrose-fermenting *Salmonella* or lactose-fermenting *Salmonella arizonae* organisms which give neg. TSI reactions. Further test lysine decarboxylase-pos. cultures to det. if they are *Salmonella* sp., **46.062(e)**(*1*), or *Salmonella arizonae* organisms, **46.062(e)**(*2*).

If TSI fails to give typical *Salmonella* reaction, pick addnl suspicious colonies from selective medium plate not giving presumptive pos. culture and inoculate TSI and LIA slants as in (**a**).

(**c**) *Selection for identification.*—Apply biochem. and serological identification tests to 3 presumptive pos. TSI agar cultures picked from selective agar plates streaked from selenite cystine broth and to 3 presumptive pos. TSI agar cultures picked from selective agar plates streaked from tetrathionate broth.

If 3 presumptive pos. TSI agar cultures are not isolated from 1 set of selective agar plates, test other presumptive pos. TSI agar cultures, if isolated, by biochem. and serological tests. A min. of 6 TSI cultures are examined for each 25 g sample tested.

Identification

46.059 ***Cultures***

Pure cultures on TSI agar are required for inoculation of biochem. test media.

(**a**) *Pure cultures.*—Proceed to **46.060**.

(**b**) *Mixed cultures.*—Streak any culture that appears to be mixed on MacConkey agar, **46.054(q)**, or brilliant green agar, **46.054(d)**. Incubate 24±2 hr at 35°.

(**c**) *Appearance of Salmonella colonies.*—(*1*) *On MacConkey agar.*—Typical colonies appear transparent and colorless, sometimes with dark centers. *Salmonella* will clear areas of pptd bile caused by other organisms sometimes present in medium.

(*2*) *On brilliant green agar.—See* **46.057(b)**(*1*).

Pick with needle ≥2 typical or suspicious colonies and inoculate TSI slants by streaking the slant and stabbing the butt as in **46.058(a)**. Retest purified cultures as in **46.058(b)**, and proceed with identification.

As alternative to conventional tube system for *Salmonella*, any one of the 3 commercial biochem. systems (API, Enterotube, or Minitek) may be used for presumptive generic identification of foodborne *Salmonella*. *See* **46.072–46.074**.

46.060 ***Subcultures***

(**a**) *Urease test.*—Subculture small amt of growth from presumptive pos. TSI agar culture to urea broth, **46.054(k)**(*1*), and incubate 24±2 hr at 35° or inoculate rapid urea broth, **46.054(k)**(*2*) with two 3 mm loopfuls of growth from each presumptive-pos. TSI agar slant culture, and incubate 2 hr in H_2O bath at 37±0.5°. Discard all cultures that give pos. test (purple-red color). Salmonellae are urease neg. (no change in orange color of medium).

(**b**) *Serological flagellar (H) screening test.*—To reduce number of presumptive pos. TSI agar cultures carried thru identification tests, perform serological flagellar (H) screening test by transferring one 3 mm loopful of each urease-neg. TSI agar culture to either:

(*1*) Brain-heart infusion broth, **46.054(r)**, (for test on same day) and incubate at 35° until visible growth occurs (ca 4–6 hr); or

(*2*) Trypticase soy-tryptose broth, **46.054(s)**, (for test on following day) and incubate 24±2 hr at 35°.

To 5 mL of each of the 6 broth cultures add ca 2.5 mL formalinized physiological saline soln, **46.055(g)**. Select 2 formalinized broth cultures and test with *Salmonella* flagellar (H) antisera, **46.055(j)** or (**k**), as in **46.066** or **46.067**.

If selected formalinized broth cultures are pos., perform addnl tests on these cultures, beginning with **46.061**, except step **46.061(d)** may be omitted.

If both formalinized broth cultures are neg., perform serological test on the 4 additional broth cultures (**46.060(b)**(*1*) or (*2*)) to obtain, if possible, 2 pos. cultures for addnl testing, **46.061**.

If all urease-neg. TSI cultures from sample are *Salmonella* serological flagellar (H) test neg., then perform addnl tests, beginning with **46.061**, on these cultures.

46.061 *Testing Urease-Negative Cultures*

Using needle, transfer portion of presumptive pos. TSI agar culture to lysine iron agar medium and small amt of growth from the TSI agar culture to each of other media:

(**a**) *Lysine iron agar*, **46.054(m)**(*1*).—Streak slant and stab butt. Replace tube cap *loosely* and incubate 48±2 hr at 35°. Examine at least every 24 hr. Most salmonellae give purple color of alk. reaction thruout medium (final color is slightly darker than original purple color of medium). If H_2S is produced, butt of medium is blackened. Neg. test is purple or red slant and yellow butt. If LIA test, **46.058(a)**, was satisfactory, it need not be repeated. Use lysine decarboxylase broth for final detn of lysine decarboxylase if culture gives doubtful LIA reaction.

If liq. medium is preferred, inoculate tube of lysine decarboxylase broth, **46.054(m)**(*2*). Close tube cap *tightly* after inoculation and incubate 96±2 hr at 35°. Examine at least every 24 hr. Salmonellae give purple color of alk. reaction thruout broth (final color is slightly darker than original purple color of medium). Sometimes tubes which have yellow color after 8–12 hr of incubation change to purple later. Neg. test is permanent yellow color thruout broth. If medium appears to be discolored (neither purple nor yellow) add few drops of 0.2% bromcresol purple dye **46.055(o)**, and re-read tube reactions.

(LIA is incubated loosely capped so that aerobic conditions are maintained, while lysine decarboxylase broth is incubated tightly closed to exclude air.)

(**b**) *Phenol red dulcitol broth*, **46.054(p)**(*1*).—Incubate 48±2 hr at 35°. Examine at least every 24 hr. Most salmonellae give pos. test indicated by gas formation (displacement of liq. in inverted tube) and/or acid reaction (yellow). Neg. test is alk. reaction (red) and no gas formation.

(Purple broth base with dulcitol, **46.054(p)**(*2*), may be substituted. Pos. test is acid reaction (yellow) and gas. Neg. test is alk. reaction (purple).)

(**c**) *Tryptophane broth*, **46.054(h)**.—Incubate 24±2 hr at 35° and test as follows:

(*1*) Transfer 3 mm loopful, excluding all solid particles, to KCN broth, **46.054(o)**. Heat rim of tube to form good seal when restoppered. Incubate 48±2 hr at 35°. Salmonellae do not grow in this broth as shown by lack of turbidity (neg. test).

(*2*) Transfer 3 mm loopful to malonate broth, **46.054(l)**, and incubate 48±2 hr at 35°. Salmonellae give neg. test as shown by green color (unchanged). Pos. test (alk. reaction) is shown by blue color.

(*3*) Transfer 5 mL to empty test tube and add 0.2–0.3 mL Kovac's reagent, **46.055(a)**. Pos. test for indole is shown by deep red color in reagent on surface of broth. Most salmonellae are indole-neg.

(**d**) *Trypticase soy-tryptose broth*, **46.054(s)**.—Incubate 24±2 hr at 35°. To 5 mL broth culture add ca 2.5 mL formalized physiological saline soln, **46.055(g)**. Refrigerate formalized broth at 5–8° if test is to be performed on another day. Perform *Salmonella* serological flagellar (H) test, **46.066**, or "Spicer-Edwards" flagellar (H) test tube test, **46.067**, using formalized broth culture as flagellar (H) antigen to be tested.

(**e**) *Tests indicating absence of Salmonella*.—Discard, as not *Salmonella*, cultures that show either:

(*1*) Pos. indole test (red) and neg. *Salmonella* serological flagellar (H) test.

(*2*) Pos. KCN broth test (growth) and neg. lysine decarboxylase test (yellow).

(**f**) *Testing of TSI agar cultures*.—Use *Salmonella* serological somatic (O) test, **46.064**.

(**g**) *Classification*.—Classify as *Salmonella* sp. cultures that have all characteristics shown in Table **46:04**. If 1 TSI culture from 25 g sample is classified as *Salmonella* sp., further testing of other TSI cultures from same 25 g sample is unnecessary.

(**h**) *Special cases*.—Cultures that contain demonstrable *Salmonella* antigens as shown by pos. *Salmonella* serological somatic (O) test and pos. flagellar (H) test but do not have biochem. characteristics of salmonellae should be purified as in **46.059(b)** and retested, beginning with **46.060**.

46.062 *Additional Biochemical Tests*

Perform addnl tests on cultures that do not give identical test results as in Table **46:04** and do not classify as *Salmonella* sp. Transfer 1 loopful of culture from each unclassified TSI agar slant to each of following media:

(**a**) *Phenol red lactose broth*, **46.054(p)**(*1*).—Incubate 48±2 hr at 35°. Examine inoculated broth at least every 24 hr. Pos. test is shown by gas formation (displacement of liq. in inverted tube) and acid reaction (yellow). Most salmonellae give neg. test shown by alk. reaction (red) and no gas formation.

Discard, as not *Salmonella*, cultures that give pos. phenol red lactose broth test, except: (*1*) Cultures described in **46.058(b)**, and (*2*) cultures that also give pos. malonate broth test. Cultures that are phenol red lactose broth pos. or neg. and malonate broth pos. are tested further to det. if they are *Salmonella arizonae*, **46.062 (e)**(*2*).

(Purple lactose broth, **46.054(p)**(*2*), may be substituted. Pos. test is acid reaction (yellow) and gas. Neg. test is alk. reaction (purple) and no gas formation.)

(**b**) *Phenol red sucrose broth*, **46.054(p)**(*1*).—Incubate and read as in (**a**) above. Discard, as not *Salmonella*, cultures that give pos. test, except cultures described in **46.058(b)**. (Purple sucrose broth may be substituted and read as in (**a**) above.)

(**c**) *Buffered glucose broth* (*MR-VP medium*, **46.054(i)**).—Incubate 48±2 hr at 35°.

(*1*) Perform Voges-Proskauer (VP) test at room temp. by transferring 1 mL 48-hr culture to test tube and adding 0.6 mL α-naphthol soln, **46.055(b)**(*1*), and 0.2 mL 40% KOH soln, **46.055(b)**(*2*). Shake after each addn. To intensify and speed reaction, add few creatine crystals to test medium. Read results 4 hr after adding reagents. Pos. VP test is development of eosin pink color. Salmonellae give neg. test.

Table 46:04 Characteristics of Salmonella

Test or Substrate	Results[a]
Urease, **46.060(a)**	Negative (orange-red)
Lysine decarboxylase, **46.061(a)**	Positive (alk.; purple thruout medium)
Phenol red dulcitol broth, **46.061(b)**	Positive (yellow and gas)[b]
KCN broth, **46.061(c)**(*1*)	Negative (no growth)
Malonate broth, **46.061(c)**(*2*)	Negative (unchanged green)[c]
Indole test, **46.061(c)**(*3*)	Negative (no red color)
Polyvalent flagellar test, **46.060(b)**, **46.061(d)**	Positive (visible agglutination)
Polyvalent somatic test, **46.061(f)**	Positive (visible agglutination)

[a] +, ≥90% pos. in 1–2 days; −, ≥90% neg. in 1–2 days.
[b] Majority of *S. arizonae* cultures are neg.
[c] Majority of *S. arizonae* cultures are pos.

(*2*) Incubate remainder of MR-VP medium addnl 48±2 hr at 35°. Perform Me red test by transferring 5 mL culture to test tube and adding 5–6 drops Me red soln, **46.055(e)**, and read results immediately. Salmonellae give pos. test (red). Neg. test is indicated by yellow color.

(d) *Simmon's citrate agar*, **46.054(j)**.—Inoculate by streaking slant and stabbing butt. Incubate 96±2 hr at 35°. Salmonellae usually give pos. test shown by growth and color change from green to blue (alk.). Color change usually appears first on slant and then spreads thru medium. Neg. test is indicated by no or very little growth and no change in color of medium.

(e) *Classification*.—Classify cultures according to results listed in Table **46:05**. If 1 TSI culture from 25 g sample is classified as *Salmonella* sp., further testing of other TSI cultures from same 25 g sample is unnecessary.

(*1*) *Salmonella* sp.—Cultures that have reaction patterns of Table **46:05**.

(*2*) *Salmonella arizonae* sp.—Cultures that have reaction pattern of Table **46:05**, except footnote reactions [b] and [c].

(*3*) *Non-Salmonella* sp.—Discard, as not *Salmonella*, cultures that give results listed in any 1 subdivision of Table **46:06**.

(f) *Tests indicating absence of Salmonella.*—Discard, as not *Salmonella*, cultures that give following 3 results:

(*1*) Pos. KCN broth test (growth),

(*2*) Pos. Voges-Proskauer test (red), and

(*3*) Neg. Me red test (yellow).

46.063 *Summary of Classification of Non-Salmonella Cultures*

Classify, by performing addnl tests described in *Identification of Enterobacteriaceae,* any culture that is not clearly identified as *Salmonella* sp. or *Salmonella arizonae* by classification schemes in Tables **46:04** and **46:05** or not eliminated from these groups by test reactions listed in Table **46:06**.

If neither of 2 TSI cultures carried thru biochem. tests, **46.061–46.062** and Tables **46:04–46:06**, confirms as *Salmonella,* perform biochem. tests, beginning with **46.061**, on remaining urease-neg. TSI cultures from same 25 g sample.

Salmonella Serological Tests

(Follow manufacturer's instructions for reconstitution, mixing, diln, and operation of *Salmonella* antisera. Dil. and pretest all *Salmonella* serological antisera with known test cultures to ensure reliability of results with unknown cultures. *Caution:* Handle viable cultures carefully to prevent contaminating environment.)

46.064 *Polyvalent Somatic (O) Slide or Plate Test*

Using wax pencil, mark off 2 sections ca 1 × 2 cm on inside of glass or plastic petri dish. Place ½ of 3 mm loopful of culture from 24- or 48-hr TSI agar slant on dish in upper part of each marked section. Add 1 drop saline soln, **46.055(f)**, to lower part of one section only. Add 1 drop *Salmonella* polyvalent somatic (O) antiserum, **46.055(h)**, to other section only. With clean, sterile transfer loop or needle, emulsify culture in saline soln for one section and repeat for other section contg antiserum. Tilt mixt. in both sections back and forth 1 min and observe against dark background. Any degree of agglutination is pos. reaction.

Classify polyvalent somatic (O) test as:

(a) *Positive.*—Agglutination in culture-saline-serum mixt. and no agglutination in culture-saline mixt.

(b) *Negative.*—No agglutination in culture-saline-serum mixt. (Polyvalent somatic antisera do not contain agglutinins for antigens of some salmonellae isolated from foods. Neg. somatic reactions occur with salmonellae serotypes whose corresponding agglutinins are not contained in the antisera, i.e., *S. cerro,* group K(18); *S. minnesota,* group L(21); *S. alachua,* group O(35).)

(c) *Non-specific.*—Both mixts agglutinate. Requires addnl testing as in *Identification of Enterobacteriaceae.*

46.065 *Determination of Somatic Grouping (Optional)*

Perform serological somatic (O) test on culture as in **46.064**, using individual group somatic (O) antiserum (including Vi), **46.055(i)**, instead of *Salmonella* polyvalent somatic (O) antiserum. Repeat test, using each group somatic antiserum or until culture reacts with specific group antiserum.

Suspend cultures pos. with Vi antiserum by emulsifying growth from slant surface in 1 mL physiological saline soln, **46.055(f)**, to make heavy suspension. Heat in boiling H_2O 20–30 min and let cool. Retest heated suspension, using somatic group D, C_1, and Vi antisera. Vi-pos. cultures which react with somatic group D antiserum are probably *Salmonella typhi,* and Vi-pos. cultures which react with somatic group C_1 antiserum are probably *Salmonella paratyphi C.* For these cultures to be classified as *Salmonella* sp., they must have characteristics of salmonellae as in Table **46:04** or **46.05**. Heated Vi-pos. cultures which do not react with any individual somatic serum but continue to react with Vi antiserum probably belong to *Citrobacter* and are not *Salmonella.* Confirm conclusion by biochem. tests listed in Table **46:05**.

Table 46:05 Biochemical and Serological Reactions of *Salmonella*

Test or substrate	Positive	Negative	*Salmonella* reaction[a]
Glucose (TSI), **46.058(b)**	yellow butt	red butt	+
H_2S (TSI), **46.058(b)**	blackening	no blackening	+
Urease, **46.060(a)**	purple-red color	no color change	−
Lysine decarboxylase broth, **46.061(a)**	purple color	yellow color	+
Phenol red dulcitol broth, **46.061(b)**	gas; yellow color	no gas; no color change	+[b]
KCN broth, **46.061(c)**(*1*)	turbidity	no turbidity	−
Malonate broth, **46.061(c)**(*2*)	blue color	no color change	−[c]
Indole test, **46.061(c)**(*3*)	violet color at surface	yellow color at surface	−
Polyvalent flagellar test, **46.060(b)**, **46.061(d)**	agglutination	no agglutination	+
Polyvalent somatic test, **46.061(f)**	agglutination	no agglutination	+
Phenol red lactose broth, **46.062(a)**	gas; yellow color	no gas; no color change	−[c]
Phenyl red sucrose broth, **46.062(b)**	gas; yellow color	no gas; no color change	−
Voges-Proskauer test, **46.062(c)**(*1*)	pink to red color	no color change	−
Methyl red test, **46.062(c)**(*2*)	diffuse red color	diffuse yellow color	+
Simmon's citrate, **46.062(d)**	growth; blue color	no growth; no color change	v

[a] +, ⩾90% pos. in 1–2 days; −, ⩾90% neg. in 1–2 days; v, variable.
[b] Majority of *S. arizonae* cultures are neg.
[c] Majority of *S. arizonae* cultures are pos.

Table 46:06 Criteria for Discarding Non-Salmonella Cultures

Test(s) or Substrate(s)	Results
(a) Urease test, **46.060(a)**	Positive (purple-red)
(b) Indole test, **46.061(c)**(*3*)	Positive (red)
Polyvalent flagellar test, **46.060(b)**, **46.061(d)**, or Spicer-Edwards flagellar (H) test, **46.067**	Negative (no agglutination)
(c) Lysine decarboxylase test, **46.061(a)**	Negative (yellow)
KCN broth, **46.061(c)**(*1*)	Positive (growth)
(d) Phenol red lactose broth[a], **46.062(a)**	Positive (gas and/or acid)[b]
(e) Phenol red sucrose broth, **46.062(b)**	Positive (gas and/or acid)[b]
(f) KCN broth, **46.061(c)**(*1*)	Positive (growth)
Voges-Proskauer test, **46.062(c)**(*1*)	Positive (red)
Methyl red test, **46.062(c)**(*2*)	Negative (yellow)

[a] Malonate broth positive cultures are tested further to det. if they are *Salmonela arizonae*, **46.062(e)**(*2*)

[b] Do not discard pos. broth cultures if corresponding LIA cultures give typical Salmonella reactions; test further to det. if they are *Salmonella* sp. *See* **46.058(a)**

Cultures that give pos. somatic (O) test with any individual somatic (O) antiserum are recorded as pos. for that somatic (O) group; cultures that do not react with any individual somatic (O) antiserum are recorded as neg. for individual group somatic (O) test.

46.066 ***Polyvalent Flagellar (H) Test Tube Test***

Place 0.5 mL appropriately dild *Salmonella* polyvalent flagellar (H) antiserum, **46.055(j)**, in 10 × 75 or 13 × 100 mm serological test tube and add 0.5 mL antigen to be tested: formalinized brain-heart infusion broth, **46.060(b)**(*1*), or formalinized trypticase soy-tryptose broth, **46.060(b)**(*2*) or **46.061(d)**. If formalinized culture contains granular particles, pellicles, or sediment, also prep. saline control by mixing 0.5 mL formalinized saline soln, **46.055(g)**, with 0.5 mL formalinized trypticase soy-tryptose broth culture in same size serological test tube. Incubate mixts 1 hr in H_2O bath at 48–50°. Observe preliminary results at 15 min intervals and read final results at 1 hr.

Classify polyvalent flagellar (H) test as:

(**a**) *Positive.*—Agglutination in culture-formalinized saline-serum mixt. and no agglutination in culture-formalinized saline mixt.

(**b**) *Negative.*—No agglutination in culture-formalinized saline-serum mixt. (Polyvalent flagellar antiserum does not contain agglutinins for antigens of some salmonellae isolated from foods. Neg. flagellar reactions occur with *Salmonella* serotypes whose corresponding agglutinins are not contained in the antisera (i.e., *S. simsbury,* z_{27}; *S. chittagong,* z_{35})).

(**c**) *Non-specific.*—Both mixts agglutinate. Requires addnl testing as in *Identification of Enterobacteriaceae.*

Cultures that give typical biochem. results as salmonellae but do not agglutinate in *Salmonella* flagellar (H) antisera must be tested to det. if enough flagellar (H) antigens are present. Test motility of culture as follows:

Inoculate petri dish contg motility test medium, **46.054(n)**, with 3 mm loopful TSI culture by stabbing medium once, 10 mm from edge of plate to depth of 2–3 mm. (Do not stab to bottom of plate with inoculum.) Do not inoculate any other portion of plate. Incubate 24 hr at 35°. When organism has migrated 40 mm or more toward other side of plate, it is sufficiently motile to retest.

Transfer 3 mm loopful of growth which migrated farthest from inoculation point into tube of trypticase soy-tryptose broth, **46.061(d)**. Retest this culture by adding ½ vol. formalized physiological saline soln, **46.055(g)**, and repeat *Salmonella* serological flagellar (H) test, **46.066** or **46.067**.

Incubate cultures that are not motile after first 24 hr incubation for addnl 24 hr at 35°. If still neg., incubate 5 days at 25° before classifying as nonmotile (flagellar (H) antigen not detected).

Cultures that are non-motile or cultures that are *Salmonella* serological flagellar (H) test-neg., when retested, are classified according to results of other tests in *Identification of Enterobacteriaceae.*

46.067 ***"Spicer-Edwards" Flagellar (H) Test Tube Test***

(Alternative to polyvalent flagellar (H) test tube test, **46.066**, to det. presence or absence of flagellar (H) antigens)

Test each culture, using each of the 7 "Spicer-Edwards" flagellar (H) antisera, **46.055(k)**. Perform test as in **46.066**, using 1 of the 7 "Spicer-Edwards" (H) antisera for each test instead of *Salmonella* polyvalent flagellar (H) antiserum. Since there are 7 "Spicer-Edwards" antisera, each culture must be tested 7 times.

Pos. agglutination indicates presence of flagellar (H) antigen. Identify by comparing pattern of agglutination reactions obained with agglutinins known to be present in each of the 7 'Spicer-Edwards" (H) antisera. Results of these reactions are shown in Table **46:03**.

If culture produces pos. agglutination when tested with each of the 4 "Spicer-Edwards" antisera 1, 2, 3, and 4 (4 plus pattern), then results indicate presence of non-specific antigen other than *Salmonella* antigen or presence of more than single *Salmonella* H antigen which cannot be identified with this antisera until antigens are sepd.

Fluorescent Antibody (FA) Method (*10*)
Official Final Action

46.068 ***Precautions***

Method is screening test for presence of *Salmonella*; it is not confirmatory test, since conjugate will react with some other members of enterobacteriaceae.

Enrichment broths from samples pos. by FA method must be streaked on selective media as in **46.057** and typical or suspicious colonies identified as in **46.058–46.067**.

Method must be followed rigorously since errors in prepn of sample, smears, conjugate, and other reagents can lead to invalid results. Microscopic observation of stained smears must be performed with critically aligned and properly functioning equipment.

Visual estimation of degree of fluorescence of stained cells is somewhat subjective and should be conducted by analyst with prior training or experience in both FA methodology and in cultural technic for detection of *Salmonella.*

If sample prepn does not normally include pre-enrichment step (as with meat, poultry, and certain environmental samples), 4 hr post-enrichment incubation period may not be sufficient for development of number of *Salmonella* cells required for detection by FA method. Therefore, include pre-enrichment step or extend post-enrichment incubation time. In some cases when pre-enrichment step is not used, sample is not adequately dild and carryover of debris into post-enrichment broth may interfere with observation of FA stained cells.

46.069 ***Apparatus***

(**a**) *Multiwell coated slides.*—Clean thin (1.0–1.2 mm) slides thoroly with detergent and rinse with distd H_2O and alcohol. Apply double row of 4 sep. drops of glycerol (8 drops total) to each of series of slides and spray with fluorocarbon coating material (Fluorolube, Fisher Scientific Co.). After few min, rinse off each slide individually under tap and then with distd H_2O, and stand on end in rack to dry. (Prepd slides are available from Cell-Line Associates, Minotola, NJ 08341 and Clinical Sciences, Inc., 30 Troy Rd, Whippany, NJ 07981.)

(**b**) *Fluorescent microscope.*—With exciter filter with wavelength transmission of 330–500 nm and barrier filter with wavelength reception >400 nm.

46.070 ***Reagents***

(**a**) *Phosphate-buffered saline (PBS) soln.*—pH 7.5; 0.01*M*; 0.85% NaCl. Dissolve 12.0 g anhyd. Na_2HPO_4, 2.2 g $NaH_2PO_4.H_2O$, and 85.0 g NaCl in H_2O and dil. to 1 L. Dil. 100 mL this soln to 1 L with H_2O. Adjust pH to 7.5 with 0.1*N* HCl or 0.1*N* NaOH, if necessary.

(**b**) *Carbonate buffer.*—pH 9.0. Mix 4.4 mL 0.5*M* Na_2CO_3 (5.3 g in 100 mL H_2O) with 100 mL 0.5*M* $NaHCO_3$ (4.2 g in 100 mL H_2O). pH should be 9.0; if not, adjust by addn of 0.5*M* Na_2CO_3.

(**c**) *Glycerol saline soln.*—pH 9.0. Mix 9 mL glycerol with 1 mL carbonate buffer, (**b**). pH decreases on storage; prep. weekly.

(**d**) *Salmonella polyvalent fluorescent antibody conjugate.*—Fluorescein isothiocyanate-labelled Salmonella OH globulin, polyvalent, contg antibodies for all antigens within *Salmonella* O groups A–S, and meeting specifications of Center for Disease Control, Atlanta, GA 30333 (1975). (Available from Difco Laboratories; Clinical Sciences, Inc., 30 Troy Rd, Whippany, NJ 07981) Before use, titer each lot to det. appropriate routine test diln (RTD). Use pure cultures of *Salmonella* representative of several somatic groups. Prep. 5 dilns (1:2, 1:4, 1:8, 1:16, and 1:32) of conjugate in PBS soln, (**a**). Stain duplicate smears from cultures with each diln and det. intensity of fluorescence. RTD is that diln one less than highest diln giving 4+ fluorescence with representative *Salmonella* cultures. Store stock (undild) conjugate of known titer frozen, and dil. when needed. Dild conjugate can be stored at 4° for few weeks as long as control cultures remain pos.

46.071 ***Determination***

(**a**) *Pre-enrichment.*—Pre-enrich product in noninhibitory broth to initiate growth of salmonellae. Methods used vary with product as in (*1*)–(*8*). In all cases loosen jar caps ¼ turn and incubate 24±2 hr at 35°. Except where selenite cystine and tetrathionate broths, **46.054**(**b**)(*1*) or (*2*) and (**c**), resp., have already been used ((*2*)(b) and (*5*)), transfer 1 mL incubated mixts to selenite cystine broth and tetrathionate broth for selective enrichment as in **46.057**(**a**). Where these broths have already been used ((*2*)(b) and (*5*)), proceed directly to post-enrichment, (**b**).

(*1*) *Dried yeast (inactive).*—Weigh 25 g into sterile, wide-mouth, screw-cap, 500 mL (pt) jar, add 225 mL sterile trypticase (tryptic) soy broth, **46.054**(**t**), and mix well. If pH is <6.6, adjust to 6.8±0.2 with 1*N* NaOH.

(*2*) *Meats, animal substances, glandular products, and fish meal.*—(*a*) *Heated, processed, and dried products.*—Weigh 25 g into sterile blending jar, add 225 mL sterile lactose broth, **46.005**(**f**), and blend 2 min at 8000 rpm. If product is powd., ground, or comminuted, blending may be omitted. Transfer aseptically to sterile, wide-mouth, screw-cap, 500 mL (pt) jar and adjust pH to 6.8±0.2 with 1*N* NaOH. If product contains large amt of fat, add 2.2 mL of steamed (15 min) Tergitol Anionic 7, **44.003**(**jj**)(*1*).

(*b*) *Raw and highly contaminated products.*—Weigh duplicate 25 g samples into sep. sterile blending jars. Add 225 mL of selenite cystine broth to one jar and 225 mL of tetrathionate broth to other, and blend 2 min. Transfer aseptically to sterile, wide-mouth, screw cap, 500 mL (pt) jars.

(*c*) *Raw frog legs.*—Aseptically place 2 legs into single sterile, wide-mouth, screw cap, 500 mL (pt) jar contg 225 mL sterile lactose broth, **46.005**(**f**).

(*3*) *Dry nonfat and dry whole milk.*—Weigh 25 g into sterile, wide-mouth, screw cap, 500 mL (pt) jar, add 225 mL sterile distd H_2O, and mix well. Adjust pH to 6.8±0.2 with 1*N* NaOH, if necessary. Add 0.45 mL 1% aq. brilliant green soln and mix well.

(*4*) *Dried whole eggs, yolks, and whites; pasteurized liquid and frozen eggs; prepared powdered mixes (cake, cookie, donut, biscuit, and bread); and infant formula.*—If product is frozen, thaw rapidly at ≤45° for ≤15 min or overnight at 5–10°. Weigh 25 g into sterile, wide-mouth, screw cap jar. Add 225 mL lactose broth, little at time with mixing, cap jar, and let stand at room temp. 60 min. Mix well and adjust to pH 6.8±0.2 with 1*N* NaOH or HCl.

(*5*) *Nonpasteurized frozen egg products.*—Thaw as in (*4*). Weigh duplicate 25 g samples into sep. sterile, wide-mouth, screw cap, 500 mL (pt) jars. Add 225 mL selenite cystine broth to one jar and 225 mL tetrathionate broth to other, and mix well. Adjust pH to 6.8±0.2 with 1*N* NaOH.

(*6*) *Egg-containing foods (noodles, egg rolls, etc.)*—Proceed as in (*2*)(*a*).

(*7*) *Coconut.*—Proceed as in (*2*)(*a*), using Tergitol Anionic 7, but omitting blending.

(*8*) *Candy and candy coatings.*—Weigh 25 g into sterile blending jar. Add ca 225 mL from 1 L sterile reconstituted skim milk (100 g nonfat dry milk dispersed in 1 L H_2O), and blend 2 min. Adjust pH to 6.8±0.2 with 1*N* NaOH, if necessary. Add 0.45 mL 1% aq. brilliant green soln and mix well.

(**b**) *Postenrichment.*—Transfer 1 mL of incubated selenite cystine enrichment broth to 10 mL of sterile selenite cystine broth as post-enrichment. (Other vols may be used if 1:10 diln ratio is maintained.) Take aliquot from upper third of selective enrichment cultures to minimize product carryover. Similarly transfer 1 mL of incubated tetrathionate enrichment broth to 10 mL of sterile selenite cystine broth. Incubate 4 hr in 35° H_2O bath.

(**c**) *Staining.*—Transfer ca 0.0075 mL of each post-enrichment medium with sterile 2 mm loop into sep. wells of multiwell coated slide, and dry thoroly in air at room temp. Fix by immersion in bath of alcohol-$CHCl_3$-formalin (60+30+10) 3 min. Rinse 2 or 3 times in alcohol, and air dry at room temp. Change alcohol periodically to prevent cell carryover (250 mL alcohol will rinse 5–10 slides). Slides may also be fixed and rinsed by flooding. Apply solns to one end of slide and allow to flow into wells.

Cover dried smears with titered *Salmonella* polyvalent FA conjugate and let stain in moist chamber 15–30 min. *FA conjugate must not dry on smear.* (Covered plastic petri dish contg piece of filter paper moistened with H_2O is excellent staining chamber.) Drain excess conjugate by standing slide on edge few sec. (Avoid mixing conjugate from one well on slide to another.) Immediately rinse slides in PBS soln, **46.070**(**a**). Then soak slides 10 min in fresh PBS soln and rinse briefly with H_2O. Air-dry smears again at room temp. and then mount by placing drop of glycerol saline soln, (**b**), directly onto each smear and covering with No. 1 glass cover slip. Add enough glycerol saline soln to smear to ensure adequate, but not excessive, coverage of all wells after cover slips have been placed. Do not trap air bubbles under cover slip.

(**d**) *Examination.*—Examine smears with fluorescent microscope. Scan entire smear using 40–50× oil immersion objective to locate fluorescent cells. When found, change objective to

100× oil immersion lens for definitive detn of cell morphology and fluorescence. Objectives with iris diaphragm for adjusting numerical aperture are helpful for control of contrast between cells and background. Estimate degree of fluorescence of cells on scale of neg. to 4+ as follows:

4+ = Max. fluorescence; brilliant yellow-green; clearcut cell outline; sharply defined cell center.

3+ = Less brilliant yellow-green fluorescence; clearcut cell outline; sharply defined cell center.

2+ = Definite but dim fluorescence; cell outline less well defined.

1+ = Very subdued fluorescence; cell outline indistinguishable from cell center in most instances.

− = Negligible or complete lack of fluorescence.

Typical pos. smears for salmonellae exhibit ≥2 short to medium rod-shaped cells per field, using 100× objective. Cells should be distributed thruout entire smear. Intensity of fluorescence should be in range of 3+ to 4+. Occasionally cells are observed with proper morphology and cell distribution, but fluorescence is rated 2+. Sometimes 3+ to 4+ fluorescence is observed, but distribution is poor and not all fields contain cells, due to improper processing of slides. Score both cases pos. and subject to confirmatory tests.

Each time samples are tested, carry culture of known *Salmonella* strain thru all cultural, staining, and observation steps as control.

Report: (1) morphological characteristics of fluorescent cells; (2) number of typical cells per field under 100× oil immersion objective; and (3) degree of fluorescence of cells (1+ to 4+).

Presumptive Generic Identification Using Commercial Biochemical Kits (11)—Official First Action

(Use of com. biochem. kit as alternative to **46.060–46.063** is based upon demonstration in analyst's laboratory of adequate correlation between com. biochem. kit intended for use and **46.060–46.063**.)

46.072 ***Kits***

(**a**) *API.*—Available from Analytab Products Inc., 200 Express St, Plainview, NY 11803. Consists of series of 20 plastic microtubes contg biochem. test substrate affixed to plastic strip for conducting following 22 tests: urease; oxidase; tryptophan deaminase; *o*-nitrophenyl-*β-D*-galactosidase (ONPG); lysine and ornithine decarboxylase; arginine dihydrolase; gelatinase; citrate utilization; H_2S production; indole production; acetoin production (Voges-Proskauer or VP test); nitrate reduction; and fermentation of amygdalin, arabinose, glucose, inositol, mannitol, melibiose, rhamnose, sorbitol, and sucrose. Required reagents include Kovacs reagent, **46.055(a)**; 10% $FeCl_3$ soln (for phenylalanine deaminase test); VP test reagents (5% α-naphthol soln and 40% KOH soln), **46.055(b)**; nitrate reduction reagents (solns of sulfanilic acid and *N,N*-dimethyl-α-naphthylamine); sterile mineral oil; oxidase test reagents (1% *N,N,N',N'*-tetramethyl-*p*-phenylenediamine.2HCl soln and 0.2% ascorbic acid soln); sterile H_2O; and 1.5% H_2O_2.

(**b**) *Enterotube.*—Available from Roche Diagnostics, Div. of Hoffman-La Roche, Inc. Consists of self-contained sterile compartmental plastic tube contg 12 different conventional media and enclosed inoculating needle for conducting following 15 tests: lysine and ornithine decarboxylase; phenylalanine deaminase; urease; Voges-Proskauer (VP); citrate utilization; H_2S production; indole production; and utilization of dulcitol, lactose, adonitol, arabinose, sorbitol, and glucose (acid and gas). Kovacs reagent, **46.055(a)** (for indole test) and VP reagents, **46.055(b)**, are also required.

(**c**) *Minitek.*—Available from BBL, Div. of BioQuest. Consists of system for differentiation of microorganisms by observation of their effect upon chem. substrates impregnated into paper disks for conducting following 25 tests: urease; *o*-nitrophenyl-*β-D*-galactosidase (ONPG); phenylalanine deaminase; lysine and ornithine decarboxylase; arginine dihydrolase; nitrate reduction; citrate utilization; H_2S production; indole production; malonate utilization; Voges-Proskauer (VP) test; and fermentation of adonitol, arabinose, dulcitol, esculin, glucose, inositol, lactose, mannitol, raffinose, rhamnose, salicin, sorbitol, and sucrose. In addition to inoculum broth, required reagents include Kovacs reagent, **46.055(a)**, 10% $FeCl_3$ soln (for phenylalanine deaminase test); VP test reagents (5% α-naphthol soln and 40% KOH soln), **46.055(b)**; nitrate reduction reagents (solns of sulfanilic acid and *N,N*-dimethyl-α-naphthylamine); and sterile mineral oil. Required apparatus includes Minitek pipetter, disposable pipet tips, color comparator cards, disk dispenser, plastic multiwell plates, humidor with sponges for incubation of disks in plates after adding inoculum broth contg test culture, and paper disks impregnated with individual substrates for performing biochem. tests.

Systems (**a**)–(**c**) are also available from Scientific Products, Inc., and Fisher Scientific Co. Systems (**b**) and (**c**) are also available from VWR Scientific, Inc.

46.073 ***Isolation***

Prep. samples and isolate presumptive cultures by **46.056–46.058**.

46.074 ***Identification***

Assemble supplies and prep. reagents required for utilizing kit. Inoculate each unit according to directions supplied by manufacturer, incubating for time and temp. specified. Add reagents, observe, and record results. For presumptive identification, classify cultures according to flow charts and tables supplied by manufacturer as *Salmonella* or non-*Salmonella* sp.

For confirmation of cultures presumptively identified as *Salmonella* sp., perform *Salmonella* serological somatic (O) test, **46.064**, and *Salmonella* serological flagellar (H) test, **46.066**, or "Spicer-Edwards" flagellar (H) test, **46.067**, and classify cultures according to following guidelines:

(**a**) Cultures classified as presumptive *Salmonella* sp. with com. biochem. kits are confirmed as *Salmonella* sp. when culture demonstrates pos. *Salmonella* somatic (O) test and pos. *Salmonella* (H) test.

(**b**) Cultures classified as presumptive non-*Salmonella* sp. with com. biochem. kits are confirmed as non-*Salmonella* sp. when culture demonstrates neg. *Salmonella* somatic (O) test and neg. *Salmonella* (H) test.

(**c**) Cultures which do not conform to (**a**) or (**b**) should be classified according to addnl tests specified in *Identification of Enterobacteriaceae,* P. R. Edwards and W. H. Ewing, Burgess Publishing Co., Minneapolis, MN 55415, 3rd ed., 1972, or sent to ref. typing laboratory for definitive serotyping and identification.

Surface Plating Method for Isolation and Enumeration of *Staphylococcus aureus* in Food (*12*) Official First Action

(Applicable for general purpose use in testing foods expected to contain ≥10 cells of *S. aureus*/g. For small numbers, *see* **46.017**.

46.075 ***Apparatus***

Sterile, bent glass streaking rods.—Hockey stick or hoe-shape, with fire-polished ends, 3–4 mm diam., 15–20 cm long, with angled spreading surface 45–55 mm long.

46.076 ***Determination***

At each diln plated, aseptically transfer 1 mL of sample suspension, **46.014(a)**, to triplicate plates of Baird-Parker medium, **46.013(e)**(*3*), and equitably distribute the 1 mL inoculum over the triplicate plates (e.g., 0.4 mL–0.3 mL–0.3 mL). Spread inoculum over surface of agar using sterile, bent glass streaking rods. Avoid extreme edges of plate. Retain plates in upright position until inoculum is absorbed by medium (ca 10 min on properly dried plates). If inoculum is not readily absorbed, plates may be placed in incubator in upright position ca 1 hr before inverting. Invert plates and incubate 45–48 hr at 35–37°. Select plates contg 20–200 colonies, unless only plates at lower dilns (>200 colonies) have colonies with typical appearance of *S. aureus,* **46.013(e)**(*4*). If several types of colonies are observed which appear to be *S. aureus,* count number of colonies of each type and record counts sep. When plates at lowest diln plated contain <20 colonies, these may be used. If plates contg >200 colonies have colonies with typical appearance of *S. aureus* and typical colonies do not appear at higher dilns, use these plates for enumeration of *S. aureus,* but do not count non-typical colonies. Select ≥1 colony of each type counted and test for coagulase production, **46.017**. Add number of colonies on triplicate plates represented by colonies giving pos. coagulase test and multiply by sample diln factor. Report this number as number of *S. aureus*/g of food tested.

Staphylococcal Enterotoxin

Microslide Gel Double Diffusion Test (13)
Official Final Action

(Detects 0.1–0.01 μg enterotoxin/mL and is applicable to detection of enterotoxin in culture fluids and concd food exts)

46.077 ***Principle***

Pptn line occurs when serological type of enterotoxin diffuses thru gel and reacts with its specific antibody. Coalescence with ref. pptn line which results from serological reactivity of enterotoxin serotype and specific antibody confirms identity.

46.078 ***Apparatus***

(**a**) *Debubblers.*—Fine glass rods. Prep. by pulling glass tubing very fine, as in making capillary pipets. Break into ca 6 cm lengths and seal ends in flame.

(**b**) *Electrical tape.*—Insulating tape, 0.25 × 19.1 mm (Scotch Brand, 3M Co., Electro-Products Division, St Paul, MN 55110, or equiv.).

(**c**) *Microscope slides.*—Plain glass, pre-cleaned, 7.62 × 2.54 cm (3 × 1″), 0.96–1.06 mm thick.

(**d**) *Pasteur pipets.*—Prep. by drawing out ca 7 mm od glass tubing or use disposable 30 or 40 μL pipets (Kensington Scientific Corp., 1399 64th St, Emeryville, CA 94608, or equiv.).

(**e**) *Petri dishes.*—20 × 150 mm and 15 × 100 mm.

(**f**) *Plastic templates.*—*See* Fig. **46:01**. (Available from Division of Microbiology, Food and Drug Administration, 200 C St, SW, Washington, DC 20204.)

(**g**) *Silicone lubricant.*—High vac. grease (Dow Corning Corp., or equiv.).

(**h**) *Staining jars.*—Coplin or Wheaton jars.

(**i**) *Sterile bent glass spreaders.*—Bend glass rods like hockey sticks and fire polish.

(**j**) *Water-saturated synthetic sponge strips.*—Approx. 1.5 × 1.5 × 6.5 cm H_2O-satd absorbent cotton is also satisfactory.

46.079 ***Media and Reagents***

(**a**) *Agar soln for coating slides.*—0.2%. Add 2 g bacteriological grade agar to 1 L boiling H_2O and heat until agar dissolves. Pour 20–30 mL portions agar into 180 mL (6 oz) prescription bottles or equiv. containers and store at room temp. Remelt when needed for coating slides.

(**b**) *Brain-heart infusion (BHI) agar.*—0.7% (w/v). Adjust BHI broth to pH 5.3; add bacteriological grade agar to prep. 0.7% concn and dissolve by boiling gently. Distribute in 25 mL portions into 25 × 200 mm test tubes, and autoclave 10 min at 121°. Immediately before use, aseptically empty tubes of sterile medium into 15 × 100 mm petri dishes.

(**c**) *Enterotoxin antisera.*—Dil. lyophilized sera (Makor Chemical Ltd., P.O. Box 6570, Jerusalem, Israel, or Division of Microbiology, Food and Drug Administration, 200 C St, SW, Washington, DC 20204) with normal physiological saline according to specific instructions of supplier. Store liq. stocks (highly concd) and working dilns of antisera at 4°; for long term storage, freeze-drying or freezing is recommended.

(**d**) *Enterotoxin references.*—Rehydrate lyophilized enterotoxin prepns, (**c**), according to specific instructions of supplier.

(**e**) *Gel diffusion agar.*—Add 1.2% purified agar (Noble special agar, Difco Laboratories) to boiling fluid base (0.85% NaCl–0.80% Na barbital with final concn of 1:10,000 merthiolate (Eli Lilly and Co., or equiv.) adjusted to pH 7.4). Filter hot agar thru 2 layers of anal. grade paper and store in 15–25 mL portions in screw-cap bottles.

(**f**) *Staining soln.*—0.1% Thiazine Red R stain (MC/B Manufacturing Chemists, or equiv.) in 1% HOAc.

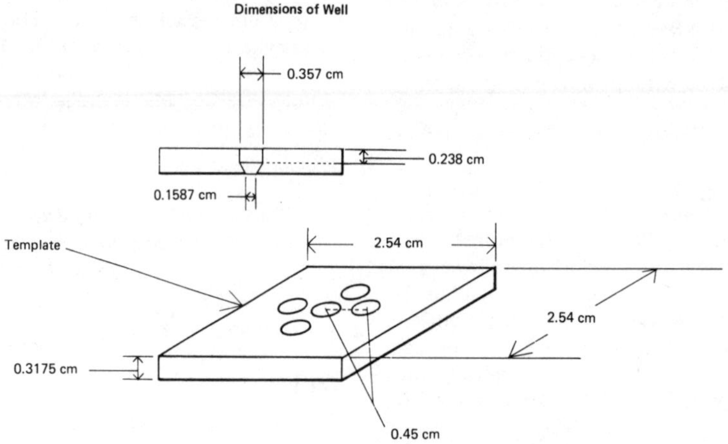

FIG. 46:01—Plastic template schematic for microslide assembly

(**g**) *Sterile distilled water.*—Dispense 5 mL distd H_2O into tubes and autoclave 15 min at 121°. Normal physiological saline may be substituted for H_2O.

(**h**) *Turbidity std.*—1% $BaCl_2$–1% H_2SO_4 (1+99) (No. 1 of McFarland nephelometer scale).

46.080 ***Preparation of Sample***

Select ≥4 isolated staphylococcal colonies from enumeration and recovery media, and streak nutrient media agar slants, or equiv. Incubate slants 18–24 hr at 35–37°. Add loopful of growth from agar slants to 5.0 mL sterile distd H_2O or saline and prep. aq. suspension of organisms from each slant which is equiv. to turbidity of No. 1 tube of McFarland nephelometer scale (ca 3 × 10^8 organisms/mL). Inoculate surface of semisolid BHI agar with 4 drops aq. suspension of organisms delivered from sterile 1.0 mL pipet. Spread drops of aq. culture suspension over entire surface of semisolid agar with sterile glass rod and incubate plates upright 48 hr at 35–37°. Transfer contents of petri dish to 50 mL centrf. tube with aid of wood applicator stick and centrf. 10 min at 32,800 *g* to remove agar and organisms. Examine culture fluid for presence of serologically identifiable enterotoxins.

46.081 ***Preparation of Slides***

Wrap double layer of elec. tape around pre-cleaned microscope slide, leaving 2.0 cm space in center, as follows: Start piece of tape ca 9.5–10 cm long ca 0.5 cm from edge of bottom surface of slide and wrap tightly around slide twice. Wipe area between tapes with cheesecloth soaked with alcohol, and dry with dry cheesecloth. Coat upper surface area between tapes with 0.2% bacteriological grade agar as follows: Melt 0.2% agar, and maintain at ≥55° in screw-cap bottle. Hold slide over beaker on hot plate adjusted to 65–85° and pour or brush 0.2% agar over slide between 2 pieces of tape. Let excess agar drain off, wipe bottom surface of slide, and collect agar in beaker for reuse. Place slide on tray and dry in dust-free atm. (e.g., incubator). If slides are not clean, agar will not coat slides uniformly.

46.082 ***Preparation of Slide Assemblies***

Prep. plastic templates according to specifications in Fig. **46:01**. Spread *thin* film of silicone grease on side of template that will be placed next to agar (i.e., side with smaller holes). Place ca 0.4 mL melted and cooled (55–60°) 1.2% gel diffusion agar between tapes. Immediately lay silicone-coated template on melted agar and edges of bordering tapes. Place 1 edge of template on 1 piece of tape, and bring opposite edge to rest gently on other piece. Sat. strips of synthetic sponge (ca 1.5 × 1.5 × 6.5 cm) with H_2O, and place 2 strips on periphery of each 20 × 150 mm petri dish. Place slide in prepd petri dish (2–4 slide assemblies/dish) soon after agar hardens, and label slide.

46.083 ***Slide Gel Diffusion Test***

To prep. record of assay, draw hole pattern of template on record sheet and indicate number (same as that used for slide) and contents of each well. Place suitable diln of antiserum or sera in central well, homologous ref. enterotoxin in peripheral well(s), and material under examination in well adjacent to that contg ref. enterotoxin. See Fig. **46:02**(*1*) for reagent arrangement for simultaneous detection of 2 enterotoxin types (bivalent detection system). Prep. control slide with only ref. toxin and antienterotoxin serum to det. proper reactivity of reagents. Fill wells to convexity with reagents, using Pasteur or disposable 30 or 40 µL pipet. Partially fill capillary pipet with soln and remove excess liq. by touching pipet to edge of sample tube. Slowly lower pipet into well until it touches agar surface, and fill to convexity. Remove trapped air bubbles from *all* wells by probing with debubbler, (**a**), against dark background. Let slides incubate 48–72 hr at room temp. in covered petri dishes contg moist sponge strips (24 hr slide incubation at 35° is generally sufficient for testing of culture fluids). Carefully remove template by sliding it to 1 side. If necessary, clean slide by dipping in H_2O and wiping bottom of slide. Enhance lines of pptn by immersing slide in staining soln, (**f**), 5–10 min. To preserve slide as permanent record, rinse any reactant liq. remaining on slide by dipping in H_2O and then immerse slide in each of following baths 10 min: staining soln, 1% HOAc, 1% HOAc, and 1% HOAc

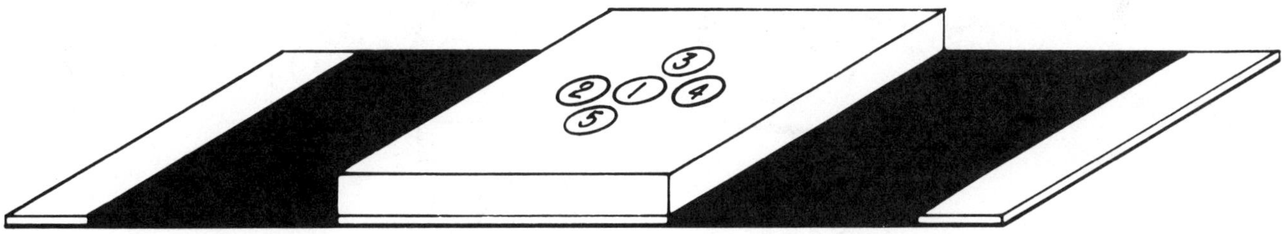

(1) Bivalent

1. Combination Antisera (e.g., Anti A and B)
2. Prepn under test
3. Ref. enterotoxin (e.g., Type A)
4. Prepn under test
5. Ref. enterotoxin (e.g., Type B)

(2) Monovalent

1. Antiserum (e.g., Anti A)
2. Dilns of prepn under test
3. Ref. enterotoxin (e.g., Type A)
4. Dilns of prepn under test
5. Dilns of prepn under test

FIG. 46:02—Arrangement of antisera and homologous reference enterotoxins (*1*) when assaying preparation(s) under test for presence of 2 staphylococcal enterotoxins simultaneously (bivalent detection system) or (*2*) when assaying dilutions of preparation under test with apparent enterotoxin excess (monovalent detection system)

contg 1% glycerol. Drain excess fluid from slide and dry in 35° incubator. After prolonged storage, lines of pptn may not be visible until slide is immersed in H_2O.

46.084 *Interpretation*

Examine slide for lines of pptn by holding at oblique angle to light source against dark background. Coalescence of test sample lines of pptn with ref. line(s) of pptn indicates pos. reaction. Fig. **46:03** shows microslide gel diffusion test as bivalent detection system: Antisera to enterotoxins A and B are in well 1; known ref. enterotoxins A and B are in wells 3 and 5, resp., to produce ref. lines of A and B; prepns under test are in wells 2 and 4. Interpret 4 reactions as follows: (1) No line development between test prepns—absence of enterotoxins A and B; (2) coalescence of test prepn line from well 4 with enterotoxin A ref. line (intersection of test prepn line with enterotoxin B ref. line)—absence of enterotoxins A and B in well 2, presence of enterotoxin A and absence of enterotoxin B in well 4; (3) presence of enterotoxin A and absence of enterotoxin B in both test prepns; and (4) absence of enterotoxins A and B in test prepn in well 2, presence of enterotoxins A and B in well 4. Operator can simplify assay by testing only 1 prepn for presence of 2 different enterotoxins on same set of slides.

If concn of enterotoxin in test material is excessive, formation of ref. line will be inhibited because of fast migration of toxin thru gel, thus localizing antibody in its well. Fig. **46:04**(*A*) shows this inhibition of ref. line formation when 10 and 5 μg enterotoxin/mL, resp., are used. Figs. **46:04**(*B*)–**46:04**(*F*) show ppt patterns when successively less enterotoxin is used. If test prepn inhibits formation of ref. line as in Fig. **46:04**(*A*), dil. test material, utilizing monovalent system shown in Fig. **46:05**. Reactant arrangement for assaying dilns of prepn under test is shown in Fig. **46:02**(*2*). Figure **46:05** shows microslide gel diffusion test as monovalent system in which antiserum is placed in well 1; ref. enterotoxin in well 3; and dilns of test prepn in wells 2, 4, and 5. Do not make starting diln of culture fluid (test material) so high as to dil. beyond reactive concn of enterotoxin.

Occasionally, atypical ppt patterns form which may be difficult for inexperienced analysts to interpret. One of most common atypical reactions is formation of lines not related to toxin, but caused by other antigens in test material. Examples of such patterns are given in Fig. **46:06**, which shows microslide gel diffusion test as bivalent detection system. (*See* reactant arrangement in Fig. **46:02**(*1*).) In ppt pattern **46:06**(*1*), test prepn in well 4 produced atypical reaction indicated by nonspecific line of pptn (lines of nonidentity with enterotoxin refs A and B), which intersects enterotoxin ref. lines. In ppt pattern **46:06**(*2*), both test prepns (wells 2 and 4) are neg. for enterotoxins A and B but produce nonspecific lines of pptn which intersect enterotoxin A and B ref. lines of pptn.

46.085 *Slide and Template Recovery*

To recover slides for reuse, clean without removing tape. Rinse slides with tap H_2O to remove agar gel, boil 3–5 min in tap H_2O contg mild detergent, rinse in tap H_2O and then in distd H_2O, immerse momentarily in alcohol, and wipe dry with cheesecloth. Wash templates with hot (not boiling) H_2O contg moderately strong detergent, using cheesecloth to remove silicone film. Rinse templates with tap H_2O, distd H_2O, and alcohol; dry with cheesecloth, and tap alcohol out of wells. In cleaning plastic templates, avoid exposure to excessive heat or plastic-dissolving solvs. Templates and especially wells must be dry before reuse.

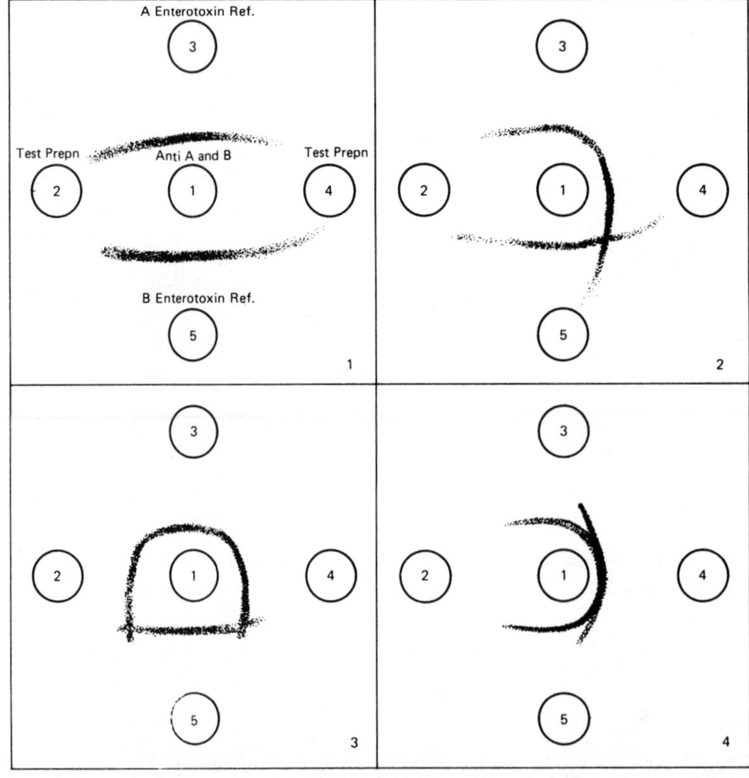

FIG. 46:03—Examples of 4 possible reactions in bivalent detection system. *See* 46.084 for explanation of reactions

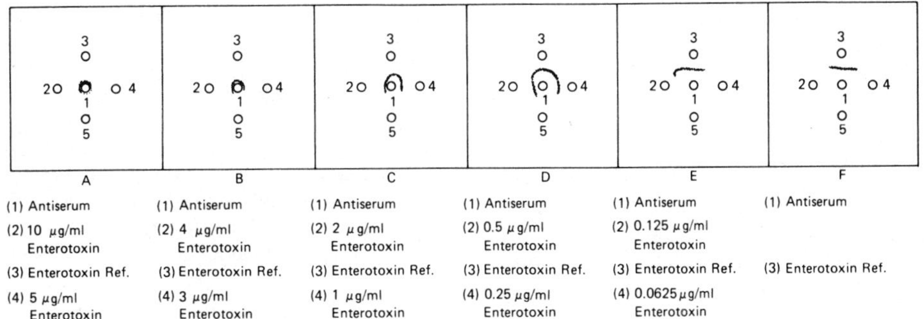

FIG. 46:04—Effect of amount of enterotoxin in test preparation on development of reference line of precipitation. ***See*** **46.084 for explanation of reactions**

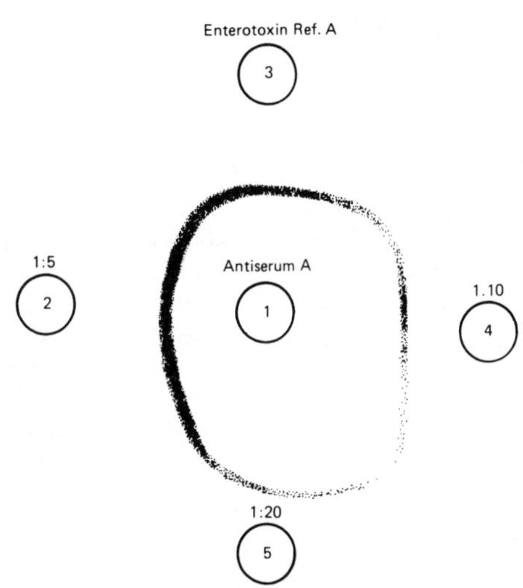

FIG. 46:05—Appearance of microslide gel diffusion test as monovalent system

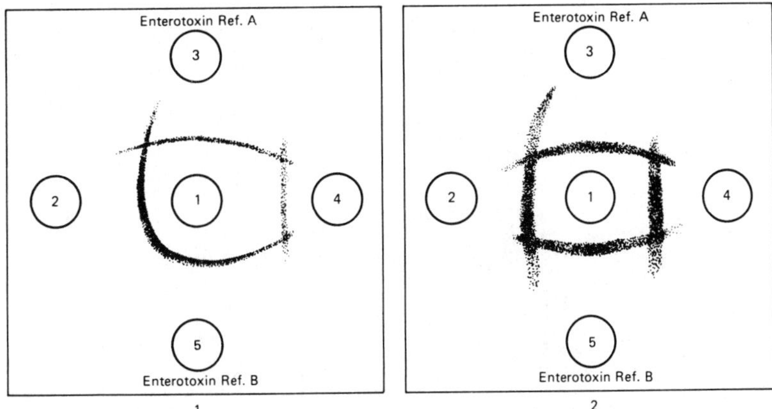

FIG. 46:06—Precipitate patterns in microslide gel diffusion test demonstrating nonspecific (atypical) lines of precipitation

OPTICAL SOMATIC CELL COUNTING (OSCC)

Method I (*14*)—Official Final Action

46.086 ***Principle***

Prefixed milk samples are automatically measured into, then sequentially and automatically reacted with, reagent matrix which dissolves fat, carbohydrates, etc., in milk, leaving somatic cells in suspension. Mixt. is then pumped into cell counter which counts cells as they pass thru stage of dark field microscope. Samples are compared with ref. suspension of turkey erythrocytes and results are recorded on strip chart.

46.087 ***Apparatus***

(**a**) *Automatic analyzer.*—AutoAnalyzer with following modules (Technicon Instruments Corp.): Sampler IV, proportioning pump II, const temp. bath with two 40′ glass coils (set at 60°), optical somatic cell counter, recorder with strip chart, sample cups, and 1 manifold (Fig. **46:07**).

(**b**) *Pipets.*—Disposable, 4 mL, for sampling, and 1 mL, graduated to 0.1 mL.

46.088 ***Reagents***

(*Caution: See* **51.037**, **51.040**, and **51.066**.)

(**a**) *Fixative.*—Mix 40 mL 37% HCHO soln with 60 mL H_2O.

(**b**) *Diluent.*—Dil. 5 g 50% glutaraldehyde soln to 1 L with H_2O, add 1 mL 50% methanolic Triton X-100, (**f**), and mix.

(**c**) *Wetting agent.*—30% aq. BRIJ-35® soln (polyoxyethylene surfactant, Technicon Instrument Corp.).

(**d**) *Methanolic potassium hydroxide.*—Dissolve 350 g KOH in absolute MeOH, and dil. to 1 L with absolute MeOH.

(**e**) *Methanolic hydroxylamine hydrochloride.*—Dissolve 120 g $H_2NOH.HCl$ in 900 mL absolute MeOH, and dil. to 1 L with absolute MeOH.

(**f**) *Methanolic Triton X-100.*—Mix 500 mL Triton X-100® (Rohm & Haas Co.) in 50 mL absolute MeOH.

(**g**) *EDTA, tetrasodium salt.*—Dissolve 200 g Na_4EDTA in H_2O, dil. to 1 L, and filter thru Whatman No. 1 paper.

(**h**) *Clarification reagent.*—Cool 600 mL methanolic KOH, (**d**), to 2°. Slowly add in 100 mL portions to 1.5 L methanolic $H_2NOH.HCl$, (**e**), cap, and shake vigorously after each addn. (*Caution:* Do not let pressure build up in container.) Cool to 10°, shaking every 15 min during cooling. Refrigerate overnight. Filter with vac. thru coarse porosity fritted glass funnel. Add 2 L filtrate to 1 L methanolic Triton X-100, add 1 L EDTA soln, cap, and mix. If ppt appears upon standing, refilter. Soln is stable 30 days at 10°. Rate of consumption is 520 mL/hr. (Prepd components, in proper vols and containers, are available from Technicon Instruments Corp.)

(**i**) *Wash water.*—0.1 mL wetting agent, (**c**)/L. Rate of consumption is 520 mL/hr.

(**j**) *Reference cells.*—Fixed turkey erythrocytes (Technicon Instruments Corp.). *Note:* Lots may vary; therefore, check each lot No. against known lot No. before use. Check comparative threshold curves and cell counts, and compare with 5 milk samples of various somatic cell counts, against direct microscopic somatic cell counts. Use each vial for $\leq$8 samplings and $\leq$2 days; do not freeze or refrigerate, as refrigeration causes cells to clump and freezing causes lysis.

46.089 ***Analytical System***

Use std Solvaflex pump tubing thruout system, unless otherwise specified (Fig. **46:07**). Pump sample at 0.3 mL/min. Pump diluent at 7.8 mL/min thru pulse suppressor and segment with air pumped thru pulse suppressor at 7.8 mL/min; add to sample in HO fitting. Pass dild sample thru double glass mixing coil to T fitting where clarification reagent is introduced thru Solvaflex tubing and pulse suppressor at 15 mL/min. Pump stream thru single mixing coil into 60° heating bath. Pass clarified dild sample thru debubbler tube, and then thru flowcell in optical somatic cell counter.

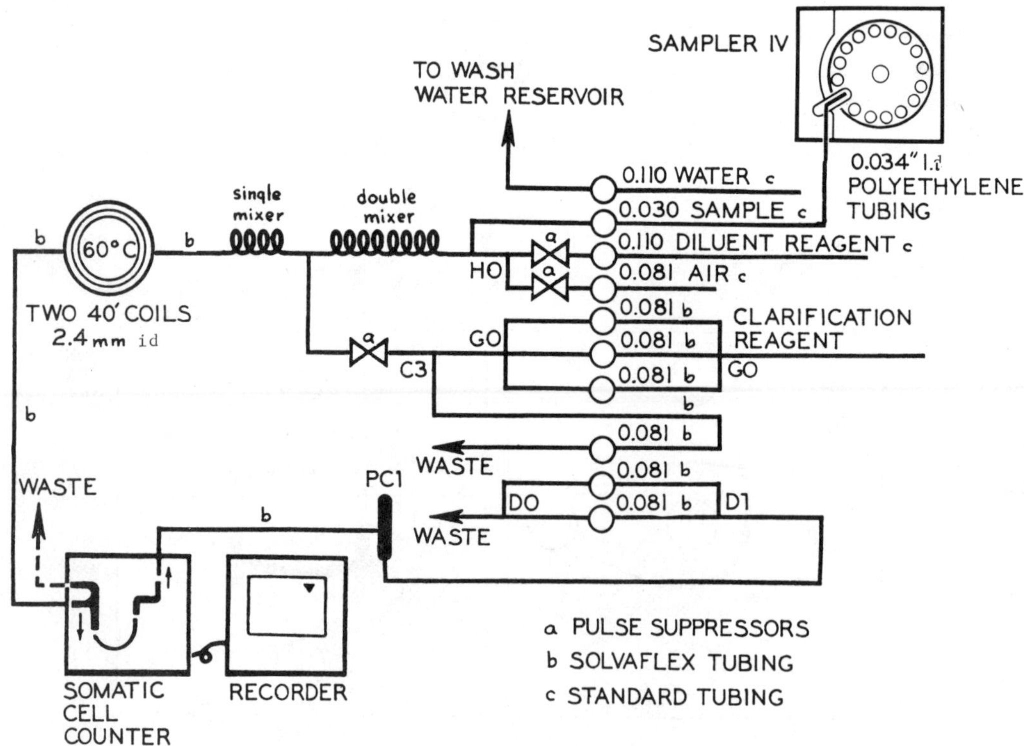

FIG. 46:07—Optical somatic cell counter flow diagram

46.090 ***Start-Up Procedure***

Place all reagent lines in appropriate solns and sampling line in wash H_2O. Check bath temp. (60°). Turn on power switch for each module. Latch platen into position and pump reagents thru system until oscilloscope on cell counter indicates particle-free flow stream (ca 15 min). Set threshold control to 21. Turn on recorder chart drive. Set reagent baseline to 0 and record baseline 5 min.

46.091 ***Shut-Down Procedure***

Turn off sampler manually, or with stop pin, after last sample has been aspirated. Turn off recorder chart drive when pen returns to baseline after last sample peak. Place clarification reagent line in 75% MeOH wash soln. Place diluent and sampling lines into wash H_2O. Pump cleaning solns thru system 20 min. Remove all lines from wash solns. Release platen, relax pump tubes, and turn module switches off. Heating bath may be left on to avoid warm-up time following day.

46.092 ***Checks and Calibration***

Proceed as in **46.090** and obtain reagent baseline. Thoroly mix one tube of ref. cells by inverting 30 times, letting siliconized glass beads fall completely thru liq. until cells are evenly distributed. Place sampling probe into ref. tube, keeping end of probe ≥5 mm from bottom of tube, and continually aspirate ref. into system. When cell pulses appear on oscilloscope, adjust recorder pen to 50% full scale, using cell counter sensitivity control. Record 2 min, turn off chart drive, set threshold control to 8, wait 2 min, turn on chart drive, record 30 sec, and turn off chart drive. Manually advance paper 0.5″. Set threshold control to 24, wait 2 min, turn on chart drive, record 30 sec, and turn off chart drive. Manually advance paper 0.5″. Set threshold to 21, wait 2 min, turn on chart drive, and record 2–5 min. Return probe to sampler arm, and turn off chart drive. Difference between readings at threshold settings of 8 and 24 should be ≤5% full scale deflection. Excessive threshold difference may be due to blockage in flowcell or tube system, optics out of focus, or inadequate mixing of ref. cells.

46.093 ***Preparation of Sample***

(Protect samples from freezing before analysis to avoid irreversible coagulation of protein, resulting in high counts. Take extreme care not to contaminate samples with extraneous particulate matter.)

Pipet 4 mL fresh milk <36 hr from time of collection into sampling tubes. Add 0.1 mL fixative reagent, stopper, and invert 10 times for mixing. Let tube stand 18 hr at 20±3°, or incubate 55 min in 55° H_2O bath, remove, and let cool to room temp.

46.094 ***Determination***

Place H_2O in first cup and ref. cells in next 3 cups. Place untreated milk sample, for reagent control (response should be similar to H_2O response), in fifth cup.

Continue with samples, inserting H_2O cup every 10–15 samples and ref. cell cup every 30 samples. Set sampling rate to either 30 or 60/hr, with 1:1 sample-to-wash ratio. Activate sampler. As first ref. peak appears on chart, adjust peak to correspond to assigned value of ref. tube, using sensitivity control. Each scale division on strip chart should be equiv. to 20,000 somatic cells, e.g., ref. assigned value of 1.4×10^6 = 70% full scale.

Calc. results for each sample by multiplying peak ht in scale divisions × 20,000. Report as optical somatic cell count (OSCC)/mL. If peak ht exceeds full scale, report as OSCC = >2,000,000/mL. If peak ht is not clear, e.g., from instrument lag time when sample with high cell count is followed by sample with low cell count at 60/hr sampling rate, reanalyze doubtful sample to obtain well defined peak ht.

Method II (15)—Official First Action

46.095 ***Principle***

See **46.086**.

46.096 ***Apparatus***

(**a**) *Automatic analyzer.*—AutoAnalyzer with following modules (Technicon Instruments Corp.): Sampler IV, proportioning pump III, const temp. bath cartridge with 3.5 min hold time at 65°, optical somatic cell counter, recorder with strip chart, and 1 manifold (Fig. **46:08**).

(**b**) *Pipets.—See* **46.087**(**b**).

(**c**) *Sample tubes.*—Disposable plastic or glass to fit sampler tray.

46.097 ***Reagents***

(*Caution: See* **51.037**, **51.040**, and **51.066**.)

(**a**) *Fixative.*—See **46.088**(**a**).

(**b**) *Methanolic Triton X-100.*—50%. Mix 500 mL Triton X-100® (Rohm & Haas Co.) in 500 mL absolute MeOH.

(**c**) *Diluent/wash soln.*—Add 2 mL methanolic Triton X-100, (**b**), to 1 L H_2O, and mix.

(**d**) *Clarification reagent.*—Dissolve 36.2 g KOH in 1 L H_2O. Add 192 mL NH_4OH and mix well. Dissolve 120 g Na_4EDTA in the soln. Mix 1.5 L MeOH with 300 mL Triton X-100. Combine the 2 solns and mix well. Dil. to 4 L with H_2O and mix well. Filter as in **46.088**(**h**), if necessary. Reagent must be free of particulate matter ≥2–3 μm.

(**e**) *Reference cells.—See* **46.088**(**j**). Use each vial for ≤8 samplings and within 2 days; do not freeze or refrigerate, as refrigeration causes cells to clump and freezing causes lysis.

46.098 ***Analytical System***

Use std Solvaflex pump tubing thruout system, unless otherwise specified (Fig. **46:08**). Pump sample at 0.32 mL/min; pump diluent at 1.20 mL/min, and segment with air pumped at 0.32 mL/min; add to sample in HO fitting. Pass dild sample thru double Kel-F mixing coil to resample fitting where clarification reagent is introduced thru Solvaflex tubing at 2.50 mL/min. Pump stream thru double Kel-F mixing coil into 65° heating bath. Pass clarified dild sample thru single Kel-F mixing coil, and then thru flowcell in optical somatic cell counter.

46.099 ***Start-Up Procedure***

Place all reagent lines in appropriate solns and sampling line in wash H_2O. Turn on power switch for each module. Latch platen into position and pump reagents thru system until oscilloscope in counter indicates particle-free flow stream (ca 10 min). Fill PC1 valve ½ full by inversion. Check that flowcell pull-thru line is free of bubbles. Adjust resample fitting so that small portion of every air bubble is pulled thru. Examine for leaks. Check bath temp. (65±1°). Set threshold control to 21. Turn on recorder chart drive. Set reagent baseline to 0 and record baseline 5 min. Clamp off sample waste.

46.100 ***Shut-Down Procedure***

Proceed as in **46.091**, except place clarification reagent line in 30% MeOH wash soln.

46.101 ***Checks and Calibration***

Proceed as in **46.092**, except follow start-up in **46.099**, not **46.090**. Perform threshold checks at beginning of each day's operation. If threshold is not within specifications or if sudden change in sensitivity occurs, examine system to locate malfunction.

46.102 ***Preparation of Sample***

(Protect samples from freezing before analysis to avoid irreversible coagulation of protein, resulting in high counts. Take extreme care not to contaminate samples with extraneous particulate matter.)

Shake each sample container 25 times thru arc of 30 cm in 7 sec to obtain uniform mixing. Let foam settle, and pipet 4 mL fresh milk ≤36 hr from time of collection into sampling tube. Add 0.1 mL fixative reagent, stopper, and invert 10 times for mixing. Incubate 55 min in 55° H_2O bath, remove, and let tube cool to room temp. Analyze within 48 hr after "fixing".

46.103 ***Determination***

Proceed as in **46.094**, except set sampling rate to either 80 or 120/hr. Est. count for samples with OSCC >2,000,000/mL by reducing sensitivity setting and recalibrating accordingly; report as estd OSCC/mL.

46.104 ***Damping***

When damping of signal is required, move damping control from rapid position to 80, 60, or 40 (depending on rate of analysis), as soon as pen reaches max. and is plotting at steady state. Amt of damping time varies from 20 sec at 80/hr to ca 30 sec at 40/hr. Do not use damping on wash in or wash out; damping should end ca 2–3 sec before wash out begins. Do not activate damping switch unless timer switch is in set position. When no damping is desired, place damping switch in rapid position and timer switch at "set". No damping is possible at sampling rates of 120 or 200/hr.

Method III (16)—Official Final Action

46.105 ***Principle***

Fresh or preserved milk samples are automatically sampled at 40°, mixed with buffer and dye, and stirred. Portion of mixt. is transferred to rotating disk which serves as object plane for microscope. Xe arc lamp excites somatic cell nuclei-dye complex to emit fluorescent light, and energy emitted by each nucleus is measured as elec. pulse.

46.106 ***Apparatus***

Optical somatic cell counter.—Fossomatic (manufactured by Foss Electric Co., Hillerod, Denmark, and available from Foss America, Inc., PO Box 504, Rt 82, Fishkill, NY 12524) consisting of heating coils, rotating table, stirrer, syringes for delivering buffer and dye, rotating disk, microscope equipped to detect fluorescence, and totalizing circuit and printer (*see* Fig. **46:09**).

46.107 ***Reagents***

(**a**) *Ethidium bromide dye soln.*—(*1*) *Stock soln.*—0.1%. Dissolve 1.00 g ethidium bromide (Aldrich Chemical Co., Inc., or equiv.) in 1 L H_2O by heating to 40–50° and mixing thoroly. Stock soln is stable 60 days in light-proof, air-tight bottle. (*2*)

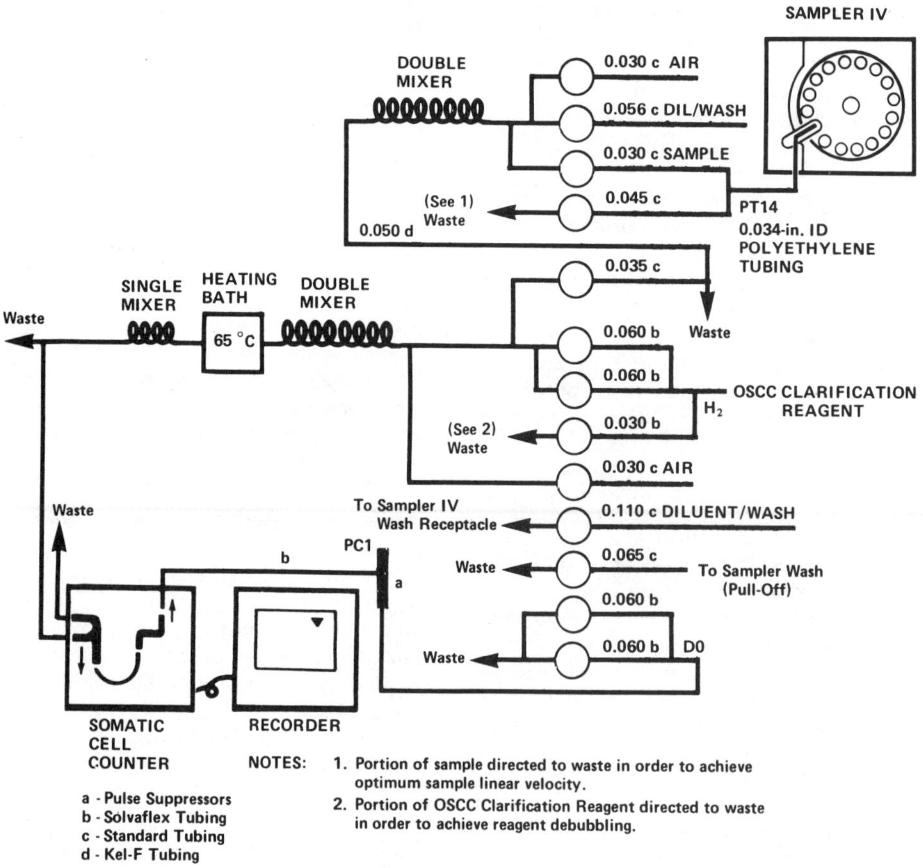

a - Pulse Suppressors
b - Solvaflex Tubing
c - Standard Tubing
d - Kel-F Tubing

NOTES: 1. Portion of sample directed to waste in order to achieve optimum sample linear velocity.
2. Portion of OSCC Clarification Reagent directed to waste in order to achieve reagent debubbling.

FIG. 46:08—Optical somatic cell counter flow diagram

Working soln.—0.002%. Dil. 20 mL dye stock soln to 1 L with KH phthalate buffer soln, (**c**), and mix thoroly.

(**b**) *Rinsing liquid.*—(*1*) *Stock soln.*—1% Triton X-100 (Rohm & Haas Co., or equiv.). Dissolve 10 mL Triton X-100 in 1 L H_2O. Stock soln is stable 25 days in air-tight container. (*2*) *Working soln.*—Add 10 mL stock soln to 25 mL NH_4OH (1+3), dil. to 10 L with H_2O, and mix thoroly.

(**c**) *Potassium hydrogen phthalate buffer soln.*—0.025*m*. Dissolve 51.0 g KH phthalate and 13.75 g KOH in 10 L H_2O by heating to 50° and mixing thoroly. Add 10 mL 1% Triton X-100, (**b**)(*1*), and again mix thoroly. Store ≤7 days in air-tight container.

46.108 ***Analytical System***

Two fl oz (60 mL) milk sample is heated to 40°, placed on self-feeding rack, and stirred to ensure even cell distribution just before 200 μL milk is withdrawn. Sample is combined with 1.800 mL 60° buffer soln and 2.000 mL 60° dye soln. Final mixt. is stirred continuously until 20 μL is spread 10 μm deep on edge of rotating disk, 0.5 mm wide along effective length of 3500 mm. Field is viewed with 15× microscope objective. Cell-dye complex is excited by filtered blue light (400–570 nm) from Xe lamp to emit red fluorescence, and filtered fluorescence (590–700 nm) over background (removed by discriminator) is sensed by photomultiplier. Each pulse is transformed and reading of total cells/20 μL is digitized on display as well as on printer. Rinsing liq. is used to flush system between milk samples to ensure no carryover effect of sample.

Somatic cells/mL milk = No. pulses × 1000

46.109 ***Standardization***

Perform direct somatic cell counts (DMSCC) on 3 std milk samples within range 300,000–2,000,000 cells/mL as in **46.086–46.094** or **46.095–46.104**. (Before analysis, obtain 3 subsamples of each std to avoid excessive reheating.) To arrive at optimum discriminator setting, compare stds over ≥5 discriminator settings having increments of 0.25–0.5 between settings. Choose initial setting near previous operating point and additional settings to provide ≥1 set of readings above and ≥1 below apparent optimum. Optimum is setting at which deviations of Fossomatic readings from those of stds are minimal, with 1 of opposite sign from rest. Check instrument every 700–800 samples or after each 4 hr of operation against std milk samples preserved with 0.05% $K_2Cr_2O_7$.

Spiral Plate Method for Bacterial Count (*17*)
Official First Action

(Applicable to foods and cosmetics)

46.110 ***Principle***

Bacterial suspension from prepd sample of food or cosmetic is deposited continuously on surface of rotating agar plate. Resultant track on surface is in form of Archimedes spiral. Vol. is decreased while dispensing stylus moves from center to edge so that exponential relationship exists between vol. deposited and radius of agar. On incubation, colonies develop along lines where liq. was deposited. Counting grid is calibrated for sample vol. associated with different areas of agar. No. colonies per known area is counted and calcd to bacterial concn.

46.111 ***Apparatus***

Spiral plating machine.—For use with 150 × 15 mm petri dishes and adjusted to deliver total vol. of 0.035 mL/plate. Platform carrying plate is rotated at ca 50 rpm and is connected mech. to lead screw driving hollow syringe dispenser. Backflow syringe, 2-way valve, and vac. trap control loading and dispensing of sample, disposal of residual sample, and rinsing of system. Liq. is dispensed from backflow syringe thru thin wall Teflon tubing thru stylus to surface of agar plate. (Available com. from Spiral Systems Marketing, 4853 Cordell Ave, Suite A10, Bethesda, MD 20014.)

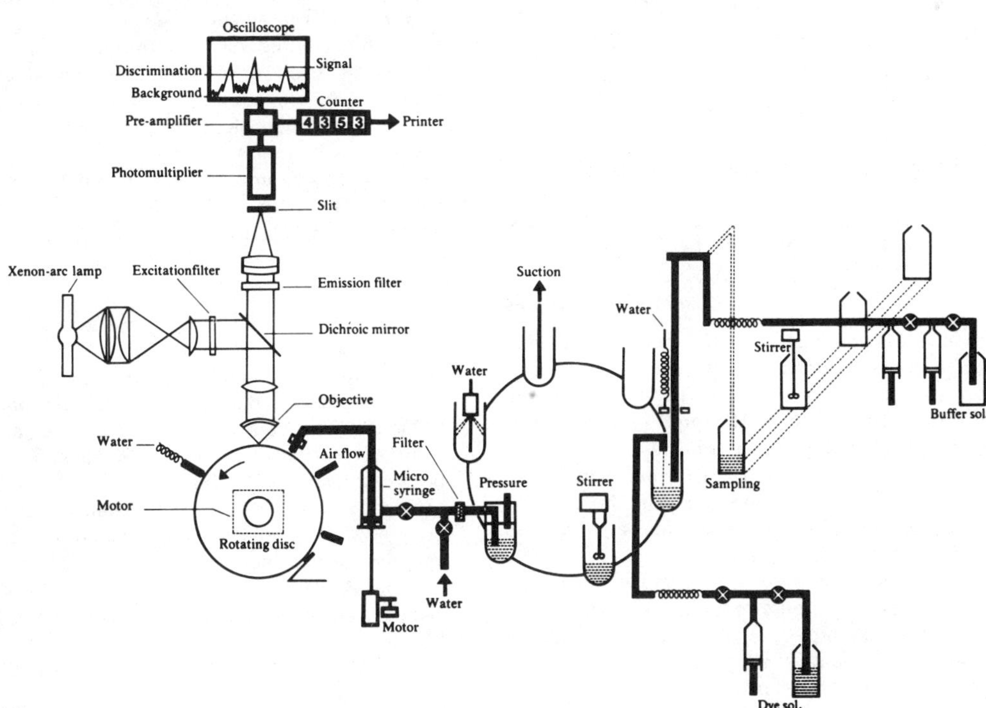

FIG. 46:09—Optical somatic cell counter flow diagram (Fossomatic)

46.112 ***Plates***

Pour 40–45 mL portions plate count agar, **46.005(g)**, into 150 × 15 mm petri dishes; let harden and dry to smooth, even surface.

46.113 ***Calibration of Spiral Counters***

To det. vol. associated with different parts of counting grid, prep. 11 bacterial suspensions by dilg 1:1 from 10^6 to 10^3 cells/mL (use nonspreaders). Plate all dilns in duplicate by both **46.015** and spiral plater, using same medium and incubator. Count spiral plates as in **46.116** and divide by av. count/mL by **46.015** to calc. vol. of counted grid area.

$$\text{mL in counted area} = \frac{\text{No. spiral colonies on area}}{\text{count/mL by } \mathbf{46.015}}$$

46.114 ***Preparation of Samples***

Weigh 50 g sample into sterile blender jar, add 450 mL diln H_2O, **46.005(a)**, and blend 2 min. If necessary, let settle few min before removing portion of supernate for spiral plating. (Presence of particles may clog tubing.)

Liqs may be used directly or after dilg 1+9 with diln H_2O.

46.115 ***Operation***

Check stylus tip angle by letting vac. hold microscope cover slip against face of stylus tip at 1 mm above platform. Cover slip should be parallel to rotating platform in all directions. Adjust angle if necesary. Check stylus at start position.

Clean stylus tip before use and between plating each sample by rinsing 1 sec with com. 5.25% NaOCl soln and then 1 sec with sterile H_2O. Identify 3 disposable polyethylene sample cups and fill with com. 5.25% NaOCl soln, sterile H_2O, and sample. Turn vac. filling valve to "on" and move sample holder into position under stylus tip. Lower stylus into NaOCl soln and lift out twice. Repeat with H_2O. Lower stylus into sample soln. Draw soln thru stylus until continuous column of liq. is present in tube above vac. filling valve. With tip of stylus still below surface of sample, close vac. valve. Raise stylus and move sample holder out of way.

Identify lid of agar plate and remove lid. Place dish on turntable, and lower stylus until tip rests freely on agar surface. Start app. and let rotate until stylus is lifted and app. stops automatically. Remove dish and replace cover. Incubate 48±3 hr at 35±1°.

After all samples have been plated, flush app. with NaOCl soln and H_2O. When not in use, leave filled with H_2O.

46.116 ***Counting Spiral Plates***

Transparent viewing grid consists of 13.2 cm circle divided into 5 areas by 4 concentric circles equidistant along diam. (marked 1 (furthest) and 4 (nearest) to center) and into eight 45° wedges or octants, marked A thru H. Thus, each octant is subdivided by 4 arcs linearly equidistant from each other. Outer ring of 2 opposite octants (e.g., A and E) is further subdivided in half by arc in middle (marked ½), and outer ring thus formed is divided in half by line toward center. Addnl lines are provided for use with 10 cm plates.

After incubation, center plate over grid. Choose any octant sector and count colonies from outer edge toward center until 20 colonies have been counted. Continue counting remaining colonies contained in segment in which 20th colony was observed. Record this count together with No. segment that included 20th colony (i.e., ½, 1, 2, 3, or 4). Count opposite similar segment and add together. If 20 colonies are not contained in an octant, count all colonies on plate and designate as T (total). If total No. colonies counted exceeds 75 in completing count in segment contg 20th colony, count will generally be low because of coincidence error associated with crowding of colony. In this case, count circumferentially adjacent annular segments starting with sector 1 until ≥50 colonies are counted, and complete count of remaining colonies in segment in which 50th colony was observed.

Divide No. colonies counted (or sum of 2 sector counts) by corresponding vol. sectors counted in mL to obtain bacterial count/mL. Use as vol. that calcd for that sector(s) from calibration, **46.113**, based on std plate count.

Fecal Coliforms (*18*)—Official Final Action

(Applicable to enumeration of fecal coliforms and also as presumptive test for *Escherichia coli* in shellfish growing waters)

46.117 ***Apparatus***

(**a**) *Pipets.*—1.0 mL serological with 0.1 mL graduations and 10.0 mL with 0.1 mL graduations. Pipets conforming to APHA stds as given in "Standard Methods for the Examination of Dairy Products," 14th ed., 1978, American Public Health Association, 1015 18th St, NW, Washington, DC 20036, may also be used.

(**b**) *Incubator.*—Air, 35±0.5°.

(**c**) *Water bath.*—Covered, circulating, 44.5±0.2°.

(**d**) *Dilution bottles or tubes.*—Borosilicate glass, with glass or rubber stoppers or polyethylene screw caps equipped with Teflon liners.

46.118 ***Media***

(**a**) *Butterfield's buffered phosphate diluent.—See* **46.013(m)**.

(**b**) *Medium A-1 broth.*—Dissolve 5 g lactose, 20 g tryptone, 5 g NaCl, and 0.5 g salicin in 1 L H_2O. Heat to dissolve ingredients, pipet in 1 mL Triton X-100 (Rohm & Haas Co.), and adjust pH to 6.9±0.1. For 10 mL sample aliquots, prep. and use double strength medium. To achieve approx. same level of medium and inoculum in all tubes, dispense 10 mL portions of single strength broth into 150 × 18 mm tubes contg inverted fermentation vials; use 175 × 22 mm tubes contg inverted fermentation vials for double strength broth. Autoclave 10 min at 121°. Formation of flocculent ppt, particularly in double strength medium, is common and does not impair performance. Store in dark at room temp. and use within 7 days. Store dehydrated ingredients and/or medium under conditions that will prevent absorption of moisture.

46.119 ***Determination***

Shake sample and each successive diln bottle vigorously using 25 complete up and down movements of ca 30 cm in 7 sec. Inoculate H_2O sample directly into tubes contg A-1 medium in suitable decimal dilns using 3 or 5 tubes/diln with Butterfield's buffered phosphate diluent. Place inoculated tubes into air incubator and incubate 3 hr at 35±0.5°. Transfer tubes to H_2O bath and incubate 21±2 hr at 44.5±0.2°. Maintain H_2O level in bath above level of liq. in inoculated tubes. Presence of gas in inverted vial or of dissolved gas which can be removed by slight agitation of tube constitutes pos. test. Use std Most Probable Number (MPN) tables, Table **46:01** or Table **46:07**, to det. MPN values. Report results as fecal coliform MPN/100 mL sample.

Virus in Ground Beef (*19*)—Official Final Action

46.120 ***Media and Reagents***

(**a**) *Diethylaminoethyl (DEAE) dextran sulfate soln.*—Add 1 g

Table 46:07 Most Probable Numbers per 100 mL of Sample, Planting 5 Portions in Each of 3 Dilutions in Geometric Series

Number of Positive Tubes			MPN	Number of Positive Tubes			MPN	Number of Positive Tubes			MPN	Number of Positive Tubes			MPN	Number of Positive Tubes			MPN	Number of Positive Tubes			MPN
10 mL	1 mL	0.1 mL		10 mL	1 mL	0.1 mL		10 mL	1 mL	0.1 mL		10 mL	1 mL	0.1 mL		10 mL	1 mL	0.1 mL		10 mL	1 mL	0.1 mL	
0	0	0		1	0	0	2.0	2	0	0	4.5	3	0	0	7.8	4	0	0	13	5	0	0	23
0	0	1	1.8	1	0	1	4.0	2	0	1	6.8	3	0	1	11	4	0	1	17	5	0	1	31
0	0	2	3.6	1	0	2	6.0	2	0	2	9.1	3	0	2	13	4	0	2	21	5	0	2	43
0	0	3	5.4	1	0	3	8.0	2	0	3	12	3	0	3	16	4	0	3	25	5	0	3	58
0	0	4	7.2	1	0	4	10	2	0	4	14	3	0	4	20	4	0	4	30	5	0	4	76
0	0	5	9.0	1	0	5	12	2	0	5	16	3	0	5	23	4	0	5	36	5	0	5	95
0	1	0	1.8	1	1	0	4.0	2	1	0	6.8	3	1	0	11	4	1	0	17	5	1	0	33
0	1	1	3.6	1	1	1	6.1	2	1	1	9.2	3	1	1	[illegible]	4	1	1	21	5	1	1	46
0	1	2	5.5	1	1	2	8.1	2	1	2	12	3	1	2	[illegible]	4	1	2	26	5	1	2	64
0	1	3	7.3	1	1	3	10	2	1	3	14	3	1	3	20	4	1	3	31	5	1	3	84
0	1	4	9.1	1	1	4	12	2	1	4	17	3	1	4	23	4	1	4	36	5	1	4	110
0	1	5	11	1	1	5	14	2	1	5	19	3	1	5	27	4	1	5	42	5	1	5	130
0	2	0	3.7	1	2	0	6.1	2	2	0	9.3	3	2	0	14	4	2	0	22	5	2	0	49
0	2	1	5.5	1	2	1	8.2	2	2	1	12	3	2	1	17	4	2	1	26	5	2	1	70
0	2	2	7.4	1	2	2	10	2	2	2	14	3	2	2	20	4	2	2	32	5	2	2	95
0	2	3	9.2	1	2	3	12	2	2	3	17	3	2	3	24	4	2	3	38	5	2	3	120
0	2	4	11	1	2	4	15	2	2	4	19	3	2	4	27	4	2	4	44	5	2	4	150
0	2	5	13	1	2	5	17	2	2	5	22	3	2	5	31	4	2	5	50	5	2	5	180
0	3	0	5.6	1	3	0	8.3	2	3	0	12	3	3	0	17	4	3	0	27	5	3	0	79
0	3	1	7.4	1	3	1	10	2	3	1	14	3	3	1	21	4	3	1	33	5	3	1	110
0	3	2	9.3	1	3	2	13	2	3	2	17	3	3	2	24	4	3	2	39	5	3	2	140
0	3	3	11	1	3	3	15	2	3	3	20	3	3	3	28	4	3	3	45	5	3	3	180
0	3	4	13	1	3	4	17	2	3	4	22	3	3	4	31	4	3	4	52	5	3	4	210
0	3	5	15	1	3	5	19	2	3	5	25	3	3	5	35	4	3	5	59	5	3	5	250
0	4	0	7.5	1	4	0	11	2	4	0	15	3	4	0	21	4	4	0	34	5	4	0	130
0	4	1	9.4	1	4	1	13	2	4	1	17	3	4	1	24	4	4	1	40	5	4	1	170
0	4	2	11	1	4	2	15	2	4	2	20	3	4	2	28	4	4	2	47	5	4	2	220
0	4	3	13	1	4	3	17	2	4	3	23	3	4	3	32	4	4	3	54	5	4	3	280
0	4	4	15	1	4	4	19	2	4	4	25	3	4	4	36	4	4	4	62	5	4	4	350
0	4	5	17	1	4	5	22	2	4	5	28	3	4	5	40	4	4	5	69	5	4	5	430
0	5	0	9.4	1	5	0	13	2	5	0	17	3	5	0	25	4	5	0	41	5	5	0	240
0	5	1	11	1	5	1	15	2	5	1	20	3	5	1	29	4	5	1	48	5	5	1	350
0	5	2	13	1	5	2	17	2	5	2	23	3	5	2	32	4	5	2	56	5	5	2	540
0	5	3	15	1	5	3	19	2	5	3	26	3	5	3	37	4	5	3	64	5	5	3	920
0	5	4	17	1	5	4	22	2	5	4	29	3	5	4	41	4	5	4	72	5	5	4	1,600
0	5	5	19	1	5	5	24	2	5	5	32	3	5	5	45	4	5	5	81				

DEAE dextran sulfate, 2 × 10^6 MW (Pharmacia Fine Chemicals, Inc., 800 Centennial Ave, Piscataway, NJ 08854), to H_2O, dil. to 100 mL, mix on mag. stirrer, and filter thru 0.22 μm filter.

(**b**) _Magnesium chloride soln._—Add 50.75 g $MgCl_2.6H_2O$ to H_2O, dil. to 100 mL, mix on mag. stirrer, and filter thru 0.22 μm filter.

(**c**) _Neutral red soln._—Add 1 g neutral red to 1 L H_2O, mix overnight on mag. stirrer, autoclave 15 min at 121°, and dispense into 100 mL bottles for storage at 10°.

(**d**) _Sodium bicarbonate soln._—pH 8.0. Add 75 g $NaHCO_3$ to H_2O, dil. to 1 L, and filter thru 0.22 μm filter.

(**e**) _Tissue culture._—Propagate Vero monkey kidney cell cultures (ATCC CCL 81) in 6 oz (45 sq cm) prescription bottles contg growth medium, (**f**). After cell sheets are confluent, ca 7 days, decant medium, add 10 mL 0.02% Na_4EDTA in phosphate buffered saline soln, **46.070**(**a**), and shake. When cells resuspend, ca 20 min, pour suspension into centrf. tube, centrf. 15 min at 700 rpm in International PR-2, rotor 259, and decant supernate. Add 146 mL growth medium to cell pellet, mix, and distribute into 8 prescription bottles. Repeat propagation until enough cultures are prepd to perform analysis.

(**f**) _Growth medium._—To Leibovitz medium (L-15) (Grand Island Biological Co., 3175 Staley Rd, Grand Island, NY 14072) add equal vol. Eagle's minimum essential medium (MEM) with Hank's salt (Grand Island Biological Co.). Add 10% fetal bovine serum (Flow Laboratories, 1710 Chapman Ave, Rockville, MD 20852). To final mixt. add 10 mL of 7.5% $NaHCO_3$ soln, (**d**). Medium will maintain cells 15 days without having to be changed.

(**g**) _Virus._—Poliovirus 1, Chat, attenuated (ATCC VR-192). Passage in Vero cell cultures. Prep. virus pool and titer. Dil. pool to provide 10–50 plaque forming units (pfu)/g.

(**h**) _High antibiotic minimum essential medium (HAMEM)._—Prep. MEM with nonessential amino acids in Hank's salt soln contg in each L: 20 mL fetal bovine serum, 5.0 mL $MgCl_2$ soln, (**b**), 10 mL DEAE dextran sulfate soln, (**a**), 4.643 g K penicillin G, 5.0 g streptomycin sulfate, 0.25 g tetracycline.HCl, and 5.0 mg amphotericin B. Adjust to pH 8.5 with 1_N_ NaOH for elution of virus and to prevent coagulation of sample slurry.

(**i**) _Agar medium._—Mix 400 mL "2×" MEM (filtered thru 0.22 μm filter), 20 mL fetal bovine serum, 30 mL $NaHCO_3$ soln, (**d**), 15 mL neutral red soln, (**c**), 10 mL DEAE dextran sulfate soln, (**a**), 10 mL $MgCl_2$ soln, (**b**), 2 mL amphotericin B soln (10 μg/mL), 2 mL tetracycline.HCl soln (50 μg/mL), 5 mL K penicillin G soln (1435 units/mL), and 6 mL streptomycin sulfate soln (1 mg/mL).

(**j**) _Agar overlay medium._—Add 9.5 g Oxoid Ion agar No. 2 (Flow Laboratories) or 12 g Difco purified agar to H_2O, dil. to 490 mL, mix on mag. stirrer, autoclave 15 min at 121°, and temper in 47° H_2O bath. Add tempered agar to 500 mL agar medium, (**i**), and temper in 43° H_2O bath. Add 10 mL canned sterile milk

(Real-fresh, Inc., PO Box 1551, Visalia, CA 93277) just before use.

46.121 ***Preparation of Sample***

Place 100 g sample in plastic Whirl-Pac bag (Fisher Scientific Co.) and add 200 mL HAMEM, (**h**). Shake vigorously by hand, adjust pH of slurry to 8.5, and let stand 1 hr at room temp, shaking vigorously 1 min every 20 min. Readjust pH to 8.5 and pour thru funnel contg 5 g Pyrex glass wool pretreated with HAMEM. Let filter 1 hr (ca 180 mL filtrate is obtained) and compress glass wool and slurry with wooden tongue depressor to express remaining liq.

46.122 ***Assay***

Inoculate 1 mL filtrate into each of 10 bottles of Vero cell monolayers, (**e**), rotating bottles to obtain even distribution of inoculum. Incubate 1 hr at 36°. Return bottles to room temp. Dispense 18 mL agar overlay medium, (**j**), into each bottle against inside surface away from cell sheet. Cap bottles and turn so overlay gently floods cell surface. Let solidify at room temp. 30 min with bottles covered to exclude light. Turn bottles so that overlay side is up, and incubate in dark at 36°. Remove bottles daily from incubator, and count and mark plaques until no new plaques appear in 48 hr. Discard after 14 days.

Plaque forming units (pfu)/100 g sample = (Av. plaque count/bottle) × (total vol. filtrate/mL filtrate inoculated per bottle).

SELECTED REFERENCES

(*1*) JAOAC **22,** 625(1939).
(*2*) JAOAC **36,** 91, 316(1953).
(*3*) JAOAC **49,** 270, 276(1966); **51,** 865, 867(1968); **58,** 1154(1975).
(*4*) JAOAC **55,** 613(1972).
(*5*) JAOAC **19,** 439(1936); **21,** 457(1938); **55,** 445(1972).
(*6*) JAOAC **59,** 606(1976).
(*7*) JAOAC **60,** 541(1977).
(*8*) JAOAC **57,** 91(1974).
(*9*) JAOAC **50,** 753(1967); **51,** 870(1968); **52,** 455(1969); **56,** 1027(1973).
(*10*) JAOAC **58,** 828(1975).
(*11*) JAOAC **61,** 1043(1978).
(*12*) JAOAC **58,** 1154(1975).
(*13*) JAOAC **59,** 594(1976).
(*14*) JAOAC **56,** 950(1973).
(*15*) JAOAC **61,** 1328(1978).
(*16*) JAOAC **61,** 779(1978).
(*17*) JAOAC **60,** 807(1977).
(*18*) JAOAC **61,** 1317(1978).
(*19*) JAOAC **58,** 576(1975).

SPECIAL REFERENCE

FDA Bacteriological Analytical Manual (BAM) 5th edition (1978) AOAC, Box 540, Benjamin Franklin Station, Washington DC 20044.

47. Microchemical Methods

Molecular Weight (MW) (*1*)—Official Final Action

Thermoelectric-Vapor Pressure Method

(Applicable to materials with MW <500)

47.001 ***Apparatus and Reagents***

(**a**) *Molecular weight apparatus.*—Vapor pressure osmometer, Hewlett-Packard; MW app., Hitachi Perkin-Elmer, available as Corona/Wescan Model 232 A from (Wescan Instruments, Inc., 3018 Scott Blvd, Santa Clara, CA 95050; isothermal distn app., Arthur H. Thomas Co.; or equiv. equipment using vapor pressure equilibrium technic. Instrument must use sensitive bridge system to measure temp. difference between solv. and test soln drops suspended on thermistors in const temp. cell whose atm. is satd with solv. vapor.

(**b**) *Standards.*—Benzil, MW 210.23, mp 94.5–95.5°, and C and H analyses within 0.2% of theoretical values (C, 79.99; H, 4.79). Recrystallize from EtOAc, acetone, or $CHCl_3$, if necessary.

If sample is ionizable salt sol. in H_2O, use reagent grade KCl as std. If sample is not a salt and sol. only in H_2O, use sucrose as std.

(**c**) *Solvents.*—Use reagent grade solv. from same lot and preferably from same bottle to sat. cell and to prep. sample and std solns. Solv. must completely dissolve sample, preferably without heating. (Proper choice of solv. and std is critical.) Preferred solvs are (number indicates order of choice):

Solvent	Nature of Sample: Unknown	Neutral	Acidic	Basic	Salt
Acetone	2	1	1	–	–
Ethyl acetate	1	2	2	1	–
Chloroform	3	3	–	2	–
Water	–	–	–	–	1

For samples not sol. in solvs listed, test solubility in H_2O (if thermistor wiring is completely encased in glass or plastic), *n*-heptane, and benzene. Other solvs that may be used are: alcohol, CCl_4, methylethyl ketone, dioxane, cyclohexane, CH_2Cl_2, dimethyl formamide, toluene, and CH_3CN. Use solvs such as esters, ketones, or alcohols for samples which tend to form dimers thru H bonding, e.g., org. acids.

47.002 ***Determination***

Follow manufacturer's instructions, including recommended concn range for solns, instrument operation, and reading of ΔR response.

Adjust cell temp. so vapor pressure of solv. is 150–350 mm, preferably 200–300 mm. If instrument is not equipped to cool cell, cell temp. must be enough above ambient (ca 5°) so thermostatic control maintains const cell temp.

Construct calibration curve with std and solv. to be used in analysis. Det. ΔR response at 4 std concns in recommended range and plot ΔR against mole fraction (MF). Prep. sample soln in recommended range and obtain 3 ΔR readings. Use median ΔR value to calc. MW. If calibration curve is straight line, calc. MW of sample by:

$$MW = (g\ solute)(MW\ solv.)(K - \Delta R)/(\Delta R)(g\ solv.),$$

where K = (ΔR std)/(MF std) and

$$MF\ std = [(g\ std)/(MW\ std)]/[(g\ std/MW\ std) + (g\ solv./MW\ solv.)]$$

If ΔR–MF plot yields curved line, interpolate MF of sample from calibration curve and calc. MW by:

$$MW = (g\ solute)(MW\ solv.)(1 - MF)/(MF)(g\ solv.)$$

Bromine, Chlorine, and Iodine

Carius Combustion Method (2)—Official Final Action

(Do not alter combustion conditions such as temp., size of sample, vol. of acid, etc. Variations from specified conditions present dangerous explosion hazard.)

47.003 ***Reagents***

(**a**) *Fuming nitric acid.*—Reagent grade, halogen-free, sp gr 1.50.

(**b**) *Silver nitrate.*—Reagent grade, powd.

47.004 ***Apparatus (3)***

(**a**) *Combustion tubes.*—Fig. **47:01**. Use clean, heavy- or std-wall Pyrex tubes, free from flaws, with round seal at bottom, and with following specifications. (Vol. HNO_3 and temp. depend on combustion tube used.)

Dimensions	Heavy-Wall	Std-Wall
Wall thickness, mm	2.3±0.3	1.2±0.2
Outside diam., mm	13±0.8	13±0.7
Length, mm	210±10	240±10
Length of sealed tube between bottom and start of taper at shoulder, mm	150–175	180–210
Vol. HNO_3 (sp gr 60°F, ca 1.5), mL	0.5	0.3
Temp., °C	250	300

(**b**) *Furnace.*—Elec., to hold ≥4 tubes at ca 45° angle. Must maintain temp. of 250±10° or 300±10° for ≥5 hr, with ≤5° difference between any 2 points on a tube or ≤5° difference between similar points on any 2 tubes. Must have variable resistor or other device to adjust furnace to desired temp. Open end of furnace wells must have safety device to retain glass in furnace in case tube explodes, and device must be provided for removing individual tubes from wells (*2*).

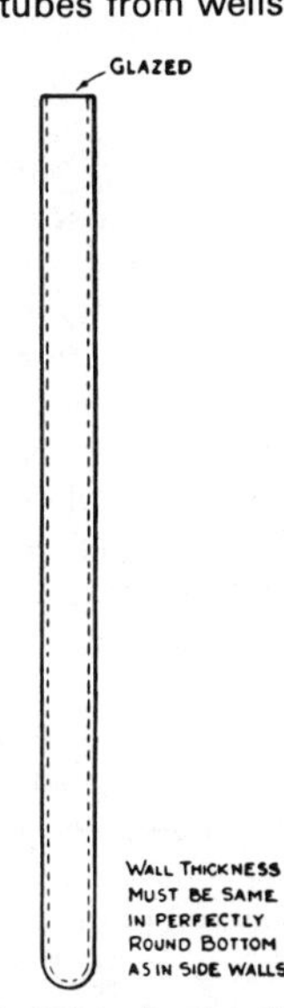
GLAZED
WALL THICKNESS
MUST BE SAME
IN PERFECTLY
ROUND BOTTOM
AS IN SIDE WALLS.

FIG. 47:01—Combustion tube

(c) *Filter tubes.*—Micro 3 mL filter tube with medium-coarse porosity fritted disk (av. pore diam. 15–25 μm) (**3**).

(d) *Siphon.*—Make from 3 mm od glass tubing, with parallel arms, one 50 and other 250 mm long, and with 110 mm connecting section rising with 13° slope to longer arm (**3**).

47.005 ***Sample***

Using microchem. balance, weigh 5–20 mg sample contg min. of 1.5 mg Cl, 2.5 mg Br, or 3.2 mg I; or using semimicrochem. balance, weigh 10–20 mg sample contg min. of 2.5 mg Cl, 4.5 mg Br, or 5.7 mg I.

(a) *Solid samples.*—Weigh by difference in weighing tube (**3**).

(b) *Viscous liquids or gummy solids.*—Weigh in porcelain boat.

(c) *Volatile liquids.*—Weigh in 5 cm sealed glass tube, 1–2 mm id with capillary tip. Break off tip of capillary before placing in combustion tube, sealed end down.

47.006 ***Determination***

Place weighed sample in combustion tube, add powd $AgNO_3$ 100% in excess of amt estd to be necessary, and add 0.5±0.05 or 0.3±0.03 mL fuming HNO_3, depending on type of combustion tube, **47.004 (a)**. Using blast lamp and holding at 30–40° angle, slowly rotate tube in flame until wall thickens, pull out, and seal off narrow neck of tube. Wall of seal should be ≥¾ of thickness of tube wall and sealed tube should have length shown in table. (If sample and HNO_3 react at room temp., immediately cool bottom of tube in ice-H_2O or solid CO_2-acetone bath, remove, and seal at once.) Immediately place tube in furnace and heat 5 hr at 250 or 300±10°, according to tube size.

Observe following precautions before and during opening of combustion tubes: (*a*) Place asbestos glove on hand used to hold small burner or hand torch; (*b*) protect face by transparent face mask or work behind safety shield; (*c*) be certain tube has cooled to room temp.; (*d*) force tip of tube 2–5 cm out of furnace well; (*e*) gently flame end to drive all acid from tip and upper walls; and (*f*) soften tip with small hot flame until pressure in tube is released by blowing out softened glass.

Remove vented tube from furnace and cut off constricted end by scratching tube with file ca 1 cm from shoulder of open end, moistening scratch, and touching with tip of very hot glass rod. Remove end of tube with care and fire polish to avoid contaminating ppt with glass splinters.

Rinse walls of tube with H_2O until tube is ca ¾ full, place in steam or boiling H_2O bath, protected from light, and digest until ppt coagulates (ca 30 min). Longer digestion is required for I than for Br or Cl since eutectic mixt. of $AgNO_3$ and AgI is formed, which melts below temp. of steam bath and persists as heavy yellow oil on bottom of tube. Stirring with glass rod speeds up soln of $AgNO_3$ and greatly reduces digestion time, which *must* be continued until ppt is in form of *fine powder.* If excessive amts of $AgNO_3$ have been used, greater dilns than specified are required for complete pptn. Therefore, after digestion appears complete, pipet few drops of clear supernate aq. soln into test tube contg several mL H_2O. If turbidity occurs, entire supernate must be dild with H_2O until pptn stops, and digestion to coagulate ppt must be repeated. If no turbidity occurs on diln, pipetted portion may be discarded.

Place previously washed, dried, and weighed filter tube in 1-hole stopper in suction flask, connect short arm of siphon tube to filter tube thru small rubber stopper, and adjust tube so that long arm of siphon almost touches ppt. Transfer ppt to filter tube by suction. Rinse tube and ppt alternately with 1% HNO_3 and alcohol, using 2 or 3 mL portions for each rinse.

Remove siphon, rinse tip and stopper with alcohol, and rinse filter tube and ppt first with the acid, then with alcohol. Wipe outside of filter tube with moist chamois (or cheesecloth) and dry 30 min at 125° in air oven or 30 min at 80° in vac. oven; cool to room temp. (ca 30 min) and weigh. Handle dry tube with chamois finger cots or tweezers. Make blank detn and subtract any correction from wt sample ppt.

$$\% \text{ Cl} = (\text{wt ppt} - \text{blank}) \times \frac{\text{Cl}}{\text{AgCl}} \times \frac{100}{\text{wt sample}}$$

$$\% \text{ Br} = (\text{wt ppt} - \text{blank}) \times \frac{\text{Br}}{\text{AgBr}} \times \frac{100}{\text{wt sample}}$$

$$\% \text{ I} = (\text{wt ppt} - \text{blank}) \times \frac{\text{I}}{\text{AgI}} \times \frac{100}{\text{wt sample}}$$

Oxygen Flask Combustion Method (*4*)
Official Final Action

47.007 ***Apparatus and Reagents***

(a) *s-Diphenylcarbazone indicator.*—1.5% alc. soln. Heat to dissolve, if necessary. Prep. fresh daily.

(b) *Bromophenol blue indicator.*—0.05%. Dil. 5 mL 1% alc. soln to 100 mL with alcohol.

(c) *Mercuric nitrate std soln.*—Dissolve 1.7 g $Hg(NO_3)_2.H_2O$ in 500 mL H_2O contg 2 mL HNO_3 and dil. to 1 L. Adjust to pH 1.7, using pH meter, by adding HNO_3 dropwise. Stdze as follows: Accurately weigh 4–6 mg KCl and transfer to 250 mL erlenmeyer. Add 20 mL H_2O and 80 mL alcohol, and stir mag. at moderate speed. Add 5 drops bromophenol blue indicator and 0.5*N* HNO_3 to yellow end point; then add 3 drops excess. Add 5 drops *s*-diphenylcarbazone indicator and titr. at ≤5 mL/min with $Hg(NO_3)_2$ std soln to orchid-pink. Subtract reagent blank. Repeat stdzn ≥3 times.

$$\text{Normality} = \text{mg KCl}/(74.551 \times \text{mL } Hg(NO_3)_2)$$

(d) *Hydrogen peroxide soln.*—30%.

(e) *Hydrazine sulfate soln.*—Satd aq. soln.

(f) *Buret.*—Graduated to 0.01 mL. Tip should be fine enough that 1 drop is ca 0.015 mL.

47.008 ***Determination***

Accurately weigh sample contg 1.5–3 mg Cl, 3–6 mg Br, or 6–9 mg I and fold in paper carrier. Insert carrier in Pt holder in stopper of 500 mL Schöniger flask, **47.041(b)**. Add 2.0 mL 0.5*N* KOH, 4 drops satd aq. hydrazine sulfate soln, and 10 mL H_2O to flask. Flush flask ≥3 min with rapid stream of O. Add 1 drop long-chain alcohol (e.g., dodecanol) to carrier in basket (not on tail) just before combustion. Ignite carrier and immediately insert into flask. (*Caution:* Use safety barrier and reinforced gloves. Remote control igniting device is available.) After combustion is complete, shake stoppered flask 10 min or until all visible cloudiness disappears. Let stoppered flask stand 5 min at room temp. Add ca 3 mL H_2O at funnel portion of stoppered flask as H_2O seal and stopper wash. Remove stopper, and rinse stopper, Pt holder, and flask walls with ca 15 mL H_2O. Add 8 drops 30% H_2O_2 to flask and boil until small bubbles no longer evolve (ca 10 min). (Do not let contents go to dryness. Add H_2O if necessary.) Cool to *room temp.* and proceed within 5 min.

Rinse walls of flask with enough H_2O to bring to ca 75 mL; then add 150 mL alcohol. Stir mag. at moderate speed. Add 15 drops bromophenol blue indicator, and proceed as in stdzn, **(c)**, beginning ". . . and 0.5*N* HNO_3 . . .", taking as end point change in color from faint yellow to orchid-pink. Subtract paper blank from vol. used. Typical blank is 0.15 mL $Hg(NO_3)_2$.

$$\% \text{ Halogen} = [\text{mL } Hg(NO_3)_2 \times \text{atomic wt of halogen} \times \text{normality} \times 100]/\text{mg sample.}$$

Carbon and Hydrogen (*5*)—Official Final Action

47.009 ***Reagents***

(**a**) *Copper oxide.*—Wire form, ca 1 mm diam. and 3–4 mm long; discard material finer than "20-mesh." Ignite 1 hr at 800–900° before placing in combustion tube.

(**b**) *Platinum gauze, 52 mesh.*—From three 3 × 5 cm sections, make 3 rolls, each 30 mm long × 7 mm od. Boil 15 min in HNO_3 (1+1) and ignite in nonluminous Bunsen flame.

(**c**) *Asbestos.*—Gooch asbestos; ignite 30 min at 800–900° and store in wide-mouth bottle. (*Caution: See* **51.086**.)

(**d**) *Silver.*—Fine wire or ribbon; if tarnished, reduce in stream of H at 350–450°. (*Note:* H ignites explosively in O. Flush reduction app. with CO_2 or N before and after H use. Vent exhaust gas into effective fume removal device. Perform reduction behind safety barrier.)

(**e**) *Lead dioxide.*—Pellets, 1–2 mm diam., special grade for microanalysis; or prep. by digesting com. grade powder 2 hr in HNO_3, let stand 1 hr, decant, wash with H_2O until acid-free, evap. to dryness, and cut into 2 mm cubes. Roll cubes in jar to round corners and sieve out powder.

(**f**) *Glass wool.*—Pyrex, pliable.

(**g**) *Dehydrite or Anhydrone.*—($Mg(ClO_4)_2$, anhyd.) Break pieces to <3 mm long; discard portion passing thru No. 40 sieve.

(**h**) *Ascarite.*—(NaOH on asbestos.) Use com. prepn of "8–20 mesh."

47.010 ***Apparatus (See Fig. 47:02)***

(**a**) *Oxygen.*—Cylinder with pressure regulator adjustable from 0 to 10 lb pressure (69 kPa) on low-pressure side and with needle-valve control.

(**b**) *Preheater.*—Specifications as recommended by Committee on Microchemical Apparatus, Div. Anal. Chem. (ACS) (*3*), except with 12/2 ball joint. Rubber connectors may be used.

(**c**) *Bubble counter and U-tube.*—According to recommended specifications (*3*), except with ball joints. Rubber connectors may be used.

(**d**) *Combustion tube.*—Fused quartz (or Vycor), dimensions according to recommended specifications (*3*) but with 12/2 ball joint on side arm and 5/12 or 7/15 inner joint on exit end. Rubber connectors may be used. Pyrex glass tubes may be used, but furnace temps should be ≤725°.

(**e**) *Absorption tubes.*—Pregl-type, according to recommended specifications (*3*) but with 5/12 joints; alternatively, Prater-type, semimicro size with 7/15 joints. Rubber connectors may be used.

(**f**) *Bubble counter or flowmeter.*—Any convenient arrangement to measure 10–30 mL/min gas flow from exit end of second absorption tube.

(**g**) *Preheater furnace.*—Elec., 12–14 mm id × 13 cm (5") long, maintained at 600±25°. Gas heaters may be used for all furnaces but specified temps should be maintained. Temps of furnaces are measured at center of furnace inside empty combustion tube with one end stoppered.

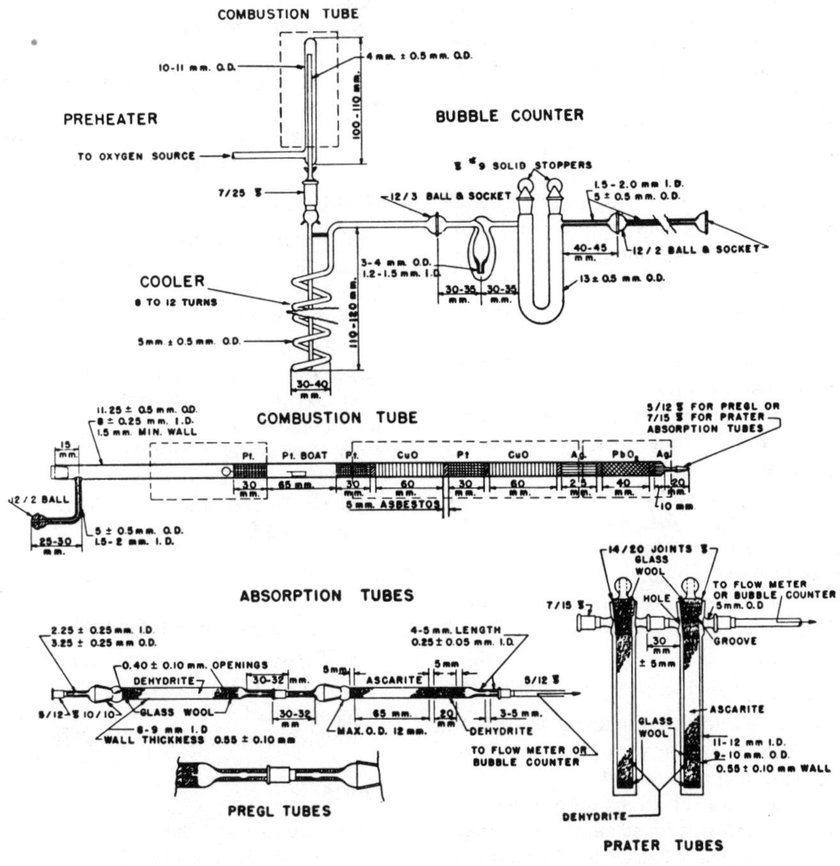

FIG. 47:02—Carbon and hydrogen apparatus

(**h**) *Burning furnace.*—Elec., 13–14 mm id × 10 cm (4″) long. Furnace should reach 600–700° in 5 min, ca 800° in 15 min, with max. of 850° in 30 min. *See* (**g**).

(**i**) *Long furnace.*—Elec., 13–14 mm id × 20 cm (8″) long; maintained at 775–800°. *See* (**g**).

(**j**) *Constant temperature mortar.*—Elec., 13–14 mm id × 8 cm (3″) long, thermostatically controlled at 177±2°. *See* (**g**).

47.011 ***Preparation of Apparatus***

(**a**) *Preheater.*—Place CuO in preheater tube, connect spiral cooling coil, immerse coil in beaker of H_2O, and support assembly by suitable clamps and stand. Place furnace over preheater tube and maintain at ca 600°. Connect side arm of combustion unit to needle valve of O pressure regulator by suitable tubing, rubber or Tygon.

(**b**) *Bubble counter-U-tube.*—Fill bubble counter and U-tube by placing glass wool plug at bottom of U, fill side next to bubble counter with Dehydrite to within 12 mm of side arm, and cap with another glass wool plug. Place Ascarite layer in other side to within 38 mm of side arm; then insert glass wool plug, ca 25 mm of Dehydrite, and finally second plug. Cement in stoppers with glass cement or paraffin; then with medicine dropper add H_2SO_4 to bubbler until level is 3–4 mm above bubbler tip. Connect to preheater with pressure clamp.

(**c**) *Combustion tube.*—Clean and dry combustion tube. Place 10 mm roll of Ag in exit end with 1 or 2 strands reaching to open end of ground joint. Insert loose asbestos plug (not choking plug), 40 mm PbO_2, asbestos plug, and second Ag roll 25 mm long, which should extend into long furnace ca 12 mm. Insert asbestos plug, 60 mm CuO, asbestos plug, 30 mm Pt gauze roll, asbestos plug, 60 mm CuO, asbestos plug, and finally 30 mm Pt gauze, which should extend about 10 mm beyond end of long furnace. Place prepd tube in furnaces with exit end protruding far enough beyond const temp. mortar to permit connecting absorption tubes. Connect side arm to bubble counter-U-tube.

(**d**) *Absorption tubes.*—Place glass wool plug in end of H_2O absorption tube, fill tube to within 12 mm of other end with Dehydrite or Anhydrone, and cap with second glass wool plug. If Pregl tubes are used, seal ground-glass joint with enough glass cement to give clear seal, and remove any excess on outer surface of tube with cotton dipped in benzene or other solv. If Prater tubes are used, lubricate lower ⅔ of inner joint with min. of light stopcock grease and insert in outer tube.

Prep. CO_2 absorption tube by placing glass wool plug in end and fill tube to within ca 38 mm of other end with Ascarite. Insert 6 mm glass wool plug, add 20 mm layer of Dehydrite, and cap filling with another glass wool plug. Complete assembly of absorption tube as for H_2O absorption tube. Connect absorption tubes to combustion tube with ground joints (use no lubricant) or with special impregnated rubber tubing.

Attach calibrated bubble counter or flowmeter to exit end of CO_2 absorption tube.

47.012 ***Determination***

(**a**) *Conditioning apparatus.*—Condition prepd and assembled app. by heating combustion tube 3–4 hr with long furnace at 775–800° and with O flowing thru app. at rate of 15–20 mL/min. Use 3–4 lb (21–28 kPa) O pressure on low pressure side of regulator. At the same time, make 2 simulated sample burnings, without sample, with burning furnace at 825–850°. (Temp. must be ca 100° lower if Pyrex combustion tubes are used.)

Burn unweighed 10–15 mg sample to condition combustion and absorption tubes. With absorption tubes connected, adjust needle valve on regulator so that O flow is 15–20 mL/min and place burning furnace ca 75 mm from long furnace. Place micro Pt boat contg sample in combustion tube ca 50 mm from long furnace. Insert third Pt roll 25 mm from boat, and stopper tube. Turn on burning furnace and let it reach ca 600° before starting sample combustion by moving furnace over sample at rate of 25 mm in 6–8 min. Move burning furnace across sample only once, taking 18–24 min for full travel of furnace. Turn off burning furnace 5 min after it reaches long furnace but continue to sweep O thru tube for addnl 15 min before disconnecting absorption tubes.

Remove absorption tubes and place by balance to equilibrate. Handle tubes only with clean chamois finger cots. If Prater tubes are used, turn joints ¼ turn to seal. If rubber connections are used, wipe only tips of tubes with moist, then dry, chamois before placing them by balance. Wait 10 min if ground joints were used or 15 min if rubber connections were made; then weigh CO_2 absorption tube first and H_2O absorption tube next, using glass tare with vol. and surface approx. equal to that of absorption tubes. Record wts of tubes and reconnect to combustion tube for subsequent analysis.

(**b**) *Proving the apparatus.*—Replace boat with one contg 10–15 mg sample of std compd such as NBS microchem. std, weighed to nearest 0.01 mg. Repeat combustion and weighing as in (**a**). Calc. % C and H in std sample from increase in wt of CO_2 and H_2O absorption tubes. Repeat analysis until results from 2 consecutive runs are within 0.30% of theoretical values and means of C and H results are within 0.20% of theoretical value for the std compd. (Humidity conditions of room may make it necessary to correct apparent wt of H_2O by subtracting a blank value.)

When app. meets this test, analyze samples as above.

$$\%C = \text{wt } CO_2 \times 0.2729 \times 100/\text{wt sample}$$
$$\%H = \text{wt } H_2O \times 0.1119 \times 100/\text{wt sample}$$

Carbon, Hydrogen, and Nitrogen Automated Method (*6*)—Official Final Action

47.013 ***Apparatus***

(**a**) *Automatic carbon-hydrogen-nitrogen (C-H-N) analyzer.*—Model 185 (FM) (current model 185B; Hewlett-Packard, Rte 41, Avondale, PA 19311), Perkin-Elmer 240 (PE) (current model 204B; Perkin-Elmer Corp.), or equiv.

(**b**) *Helium.*—Cylinder with pressure regulator and needle valve control. Preheater and purifier optional.

(**c**) *Oxygen.*—For PE only. Cylinder with pressure regulator and needle valve control.

(**d**) *Line voltage regulator.*—Optional; 50 amp, output 115 v±0.25%.

(**e**) *On-line computer or integrator.*—Mandatory for FM app. but optional for PE app.

47.014 ***Reagents***

(*See* instrument instruction manuals.)

(**a**) *Catalyst.*—Solid oxidn catalyst (oxides of Co, W, or Ag) required for FM; optional for PE if time and temp. meet conditions specified.

(**b**) *Std compounds.*—NBS acetanilide, or equiv.

47.015 ***Preparation of Apparatus***

Prep. and assemble app. as in manual. Adjust preliminary settings and regulate He flow (He and O for PE). Set and let temp. systems equilibrate until const. Use combustion temp. >1080° for FM and 980–1000° for PE. Use specified 500° and 650° reduction temps, resp., for FM and PE. Maintain detector column suboven within 5–15° of main oven. Adjust bridge current to value specified. After sweeping air "slug" from combustion chamber, use 20–50 sec range combustion period (gas flow diverted) for FM (40–50 sec for samples difficult to burn). Use extended "Hold 30 sec" combustion period for PE. Add Co_3O_4 + Ag_2WO_4, Ag_2O + Ag_2WO_4, or CoO + WO_3 to combustion tube filling of PE. However, if PE is in optimum condition, only 2 of 3 required conditions (temp., time, and catalyst) need be adhered to.

47.016 ***Determination***

Burn 2 unweighed samples ca 2 mg (PE) or 0.6 mg (FM) to condition app. Make $\geqslant$2 blank runs (simulated sample runs without sample) to check and adjust timing of each phase where necessary, to check pattern of final measurements, and to obtain blank factors if required in calcns. Then run std and sample compds, weighed to nearest 0.001 mg or better for PE and 0.0001 mg for FM. Calc. factors as suggested in manual. Rerun std to check factors. Different type std may be used for this rerun. Initially check factors until 2 of 3 detns are within 0.3% of theoretical value. Calc. % C, H, and N, using factors obtained from std compds.

47.017 ***Special Precautions for Volatile Samples***

Weigh volatile samples in capillaries, Al capsules, or Al weighing pans. During sweeping period, volatile samples must be in cooler portion of combustion tube, as near orifice as possible.

Fluorine (7)—Official Final Action

47.018 ***Reagents***

(**a**) *Sodium alizarin sulfonate indicator.*—(Alizarin red S) 0.035% aq. soln.

(**b**) *Sodium fluoride std soln.*—0.01*N*. Dissolve 0.4200 g NaF in H_2O and dil. to 1 L.

(**c**) *Thorium nitrate std soln.*—0.01*N*. Dissolve 1.38 g $Th(NO_3)_4.4H_2O$ in H_2O and dil. to 1 L. Stdze by titrg against 0.01*N* NaF, using 1, 2, 3, 4, 5, 6, 7, 8, 9, and 10 mL portions and plotting curve.

47.019 ***Apparatus***

(**a**) *Schöniger combustion flask.*—500 mL with filter paper carriers.

(**b**) *Distillation apparatus.*—*See* Fig. **47:03**. Attach to steam generator. Steam enters thru joint, J_1, passes thru 2 concentric tubes, IT_1 and ET_1, and enters distn flask, *D*, thru 2 openings. Vapors enter condenser, *C*, which consists of 3 concentric tubes. In IT_2 and ET_2, vapors are condensed; in ET_3, cooling H_2O is circulated. Distillate drains off on right thru descending tube. Ground joint, J_2, serves as opening for addn of soln and as seat for thermometer which records temp. of liq., *L*. Elec. heating jacket, *H*, surrounds section of distn flask contg liq. and is prepd from 600 cm Nichrome wire, *W*, of 2.120 ohms/foot, 420 cm of which is wound on 48 mm diam. glass cylinder covered with Al foil and asbestos, then covered with insulating cement, asbestos, and another layer of cement. Jacket is held in place with ring, *R*, and temp. is controlled with 7.5 amp variable transformer.

47.020 ***Determination***

(**a**) *In absence of arsenic, mercury, and phosphorus.*—Place sample contg 0.5–0.7 mg F on filter paper carrier. (Weigh liq. samples in gelatin or Me cellulose capsules and place closed capsule on paper carrier.) Add ca 15–20 mg Na_2O_2, wrap mixt. in filter paper, and place in Pt basket carrier in stopper of Schöniger flask. Place 20 mL H_2O in flask, introduce O several min, ignite sample, and immediately insert into flask. (*Note:* Use safety barrier and reinforced gloves. Remote control igniting device is available.) After combustion is complete, shake vigorously until cloudiness disappears, and let flask stand undisturbed ca 15 min to ensure complete absorption of oxidn products. (If enough I is present to give yellow soln, warm on steam bath to dispel color.) Wash soln into titrg vessel, adjust to pH 3.0±0.05 with 1*N* and 0.1*N* HCl and 0.1*N* NaOH, using pH meter, and add 2 mL Na alizarin sulfonate indicator. (pH adjustment is critical, since alizarin sulfonate is also acid-base indicator.) Titr. with std $Th(NO_3)_4$ soln to pink end point, preferably using photoelec. photometer with 520 nm filter. Use entire soln rather than aliquot. If visual titrn is used, compare color with controls in fluorescent light. Det. mg F from std curve.

$$\% \text{ F} = \text{mg F} \times 100/\text{mg sample.}$$

(**b**) *In presence of arsenic, mercury, and phosphorus.*—Burn sample as in (**a**) and transfer soln to distn app. thru joint J_2 with as little H_2O as possible. Add 20 mL 70–72% $HClO_4$, 1 mL *25% $AgClO_4$ soln,* and ca 12 glass beads. Heat mixt. by means of jacket, and as temp. rises, start steam generation. Maintain temp. of mixt. at 135±2° after raising temp. to this point as quickly as possible by adjusting transformer. Collect distillate in 250 mL vol. flask. (Practice is required for successful manipulation of distn. To avoid sucking back of soln, keep vol. in flask at min. and keep steam generation const. Addn of phthln and small amt of 0.1*N* NaOH to generator provides means of detg if suck-back has occurred.) (Clean distn app. between detns by replacing steam generator with bottle or flask connected to suction and immersing distillate delivery tube in F-free H_2O, which is sucked thru entire system.)

Transfer distillate to titrg vessel, adjust to pH 3.0± 0.05, add 2 mL Na alizarin sulfonate indicator, and titr. as in (**a**).

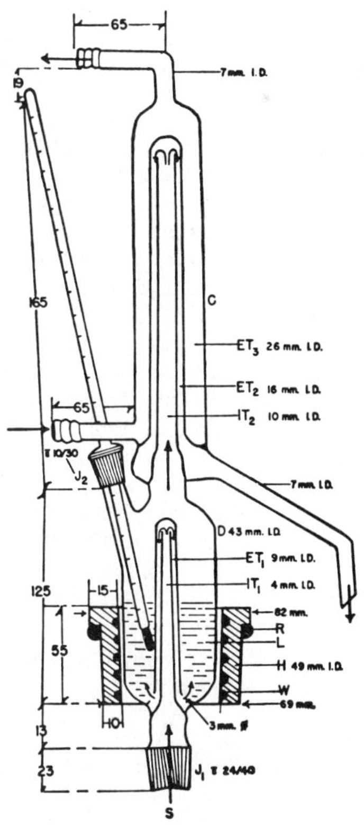

FIG. 47:03—Upper section of distilling apparatus. From Anal. Chem. 29, 141(1957)

Nitrogen (*8*)

Micro-Kjeldahl Method—Official Final Action

(Not applicable to material contg N–N or N–O linkages)

47.021 ***Reagents***

(**a**) *Sulfuric acid.*—Sp gr 1.84, N-free.

(**b**) *Mercuric oxide.*—N-free.

(**c**) *Potassium sulfate.*—N-free.

(**d**) *Sodium hydroxide-sodium thiosulfate soln.*—Dissolve 60 g NaOH and 5 g $Na_2S_2O_3.5H_2O$ in H_2O and dil. to 100 mL or add 25 mL 25% $Na_2S_2O_3.5H_2O$ to 100 mL 50% NaOH soln.

(**e**) *Boric acid soln.*—Satd soln.

(**f**) *Indicator soln.*—(*1*) *Methyl red-methylene blue.*—Mix 2 parts 0.2% alc. Me red soln with 1 part 0.2% alc. methylene blue soln; or (*2*) *Methyl red-bromocresol green soln.*—Mix 1 part 0.2% alc. Me red soln with 5 parts 0.2% alc. bromocresol green soln.

(**g**) *Hydrochloric acid.*—0.02*N*. Prep. as in **50.011** and stdze as in **50.015** or **50.017**.

47.022 ***Apparatus (9)***

(**a**) *Digestion rack.*—With either gas or elec. heaters which will supply enough heat to 30 mL flask to cause 15 mL H_2O at 25° to come to rolling boil in ≥2 but <3 min.

(**b**) *Distillation apparatus.*—One-piece or Parnas-Wagner distn app. recommended by Committee on Microchemical Apparatus, ACS (*9*).

(**c**) *Digestion flasks.*—Use 30 mL regular Kjeldahl or Soltys-type flasks (*9*). For small samples, 10 mL Kjeldahl flasks may be used.

47.023 ***Determination***

Weigh sample requiring 3–10 mL 0.01 or 0.02*N* HCl and transfer to 30 mL digestion flask. If sample wt is <10 mg, use microchem. balance (max. wt 100 mg dry org. matter). Use charging tube for dry solids, porcelain boat for sticky solids or nonvolatile liqs, and capillary or capsule for volatile liqs. Add 1.9±0.1 g K_2SO_4, 40±10 mg HgO, and 2.0±0.1 mL H_2SO_4. If sample wt is >15 mg, add addnl 0.1 mL H_2SO_4 for each 10 mg dry org. matter >15 mg. Make certain that acid has sp gr ≥1.84 if sample contains nitriles. (10 mL flasks and ½ quantities of reagents may be used for samples <7 mg.) Add boiling chips which pass No. 10 sieve. If boiling time for digestion rack heaters is 2–2.5 min, digest 1 hr after all H_2O is distilled and acid comes to true boil; if boiling time is 2.5–3 min, digest 1.5 hr. (Digest 0.5 hr if sample is known to contain no refractory ring N.)

Cool, add min. vol. of H_2O to dissolve solids, cool, and place thin film of Vaseline on rim of flask. Transfer digest and boiling chips to distn app. and rinse flask 5 or 6 times with 1–2 mL portions H_2O. Place 125 mL Phillips beaker or erlenmeyer contg 5 mL satd H_3BO_3 soln and 2–4 drops indicator under condenser with tip extending below surface of soln. Add 8–10 mL NaOH-$Na_2S_2O_3$ soln to still, collect ca 15 mL distillate, and dil. to ca 50 mL. (Use 2.5 mL H_3BO_3 and 1–2 drops indicator, and dil. to ca 25 mL if 0.01*N* HCl is to be used.) Titr to end point. Make blank detn and calc.

%N = [(mL HCl − mL blank) × normality × 14.007 × 100]/mg sample.

Oxygen (*10*)—Official Final Action

47.024 ***Principle***

Org. O compds are thermally decomposed in inert atm. to H_2O, CO, and CO_2. At 1120°, following reactions are complete: $C + CO_2 \rightarrow 2CO$; $H_2O + C \rightarrow H_2 + CO$. The CO is converted to CO_2 by reaction with CuO and CO_2 is detd gravimetrically.

47.025 ***Reagents***

(**a**) *Copper oxide.*—See **47.009**(**a**).

(**b**) *Ascarite.*—*See* **47.009**(**h**).

(**c**) *Dehydrite or Anhydrone.*—*See* **47.009**(**g**).

(**d**) *Nitrogen.*—Purify high purity N by passing thru series of scrubbing bottles contg different solid desiccants ($CaCl_2$, anhyd. $Mg(ClO_4)_2$, and P_2O_5), then thru tube contg closely packed reduced Cu turnings at 600°, thru Anhydrone, and finally thru bubble counter and U-tube.

(**e**) *Carbon.*—Fisher, C-198, lampblack, or equiv. Pelletize by swirling constantly while adding CCl_4 dropwise; dry in oven at 100–120°. Purify by digesting with HCl. Add large vol. H_2O, stir mech., let C settle, and decant H_2O. Repeat until H_2O wash is Cl-free. Dry C, place in quartz tube, and heat in slow stream of N, (**d**), several hr, increasing temp. gradually to 550°.

(**f**) *Quartz chips.*—Clean chips with HF, rinse with H_2O, and dry in oven.

47.026 ***Apparatus (See Figs. 47:04 and 47:05)***

(**a**) *Long stationary furnace, 675°.*—**47.010**(**i**), except maintained at 675±5°; (*A*).

(**b**) *Long stationary furnace, 1120°.*—*See* (**c**); (*B*).

(**c**) *Short movable furnace, 1120°.*—This furnace (*C*) and that in (**b**) may be available as unit.

(**d**) *Nitrogen purification train.*—Preheater furnace (*D*), **47.010**(**g**), with section of combustion tubing, quartz, Vycor, or Pyrex glass No. 1720, or equiv., packed with ca 10 cm reduced Cu turnings.

(**e**) *Bubble counter and U-tube.*—*See* **47.010**(**c**) and **47.011**(**b**).

(**f**) *Cap.*—$ 14/35 cap with 2 mm stopcock; (*F*).

(**g**) *Thermal decomposition tube.*—Clear fused quartz, solar radiation grade, 7.5–8 mm id, 10–11 mm od, and 60 cm long, exclusive of capillary tube; (*G*). At one end is $ 14/35 male joint. About 1 cm from joint is bent side arm, 6–7 mm od and 2–4 mm id. At other end is 15 cm capillary tube 6–7 mm od and 1–2 mm id. Wash tube with HF and H_2O, and dry.

Fill tube as shown in Fig. **47:05**, with repeated tapping to avoid channeling. The C must *at all times* be in section of furnace that is at 1120°.

(**h**) *By-pass stopcocks.*—3 way T-type with § ball joint on side arm; (*H*) and (*H'*).

(**i**) *Spiral by-pass tube.*—Glass tube (*I*), contg spiral, for flexibility, and § socket joints on each end. Length should be sufficient to connect to § ball joints on § stopcocks, (*H*) and (*H'*).

(**j**) *Quartz tube.*—Filled with reduced Cu; (*J*).

(**k**) *Short stationary furnace, 900°.*—**47.010**(**h**), except capable of maintaining 900°; (*K*).

(**l**) *Scrubber tube.*—Any type of drying tube fitted with crushed KOH pellets or Ascarite, (*L*), for removing halogens and S.

(**m**) *Drying tube.*—*See* **47.010**(**e**), or use U-tube. Fill with Anhydrone only, as in **47.011**(**d**); (*M*).

(**n**) *Carbon dioxide absorption tube.*—Fill with Ascarite and Anhydrone as in **47.011**(**d**); (*N*).

(**o**) *Oxidation tube.*—Tube, 30–40 cm, exclusive of tip, similar to that in (**d**) except packed with ca 25 cm CuO wire. Let 5 cm extend beyond furnace. Maintain at 675±5° to oxidize CO to CO_2; (*O*).

(**p**) *Guard tube.*—Glass tube 110–120 mm × 10–12 mm od, 1 mm wall, contg Anhydrone; (*P*).

(**q**) *Mariotte bottle.*—Glass 2 L bottle. Place 1-hole rubber stopper in top of bottle. Insert glass tube to 7–10 cm of bottom of bottle. Attach 3-way stopcock to top of tube. In bottom

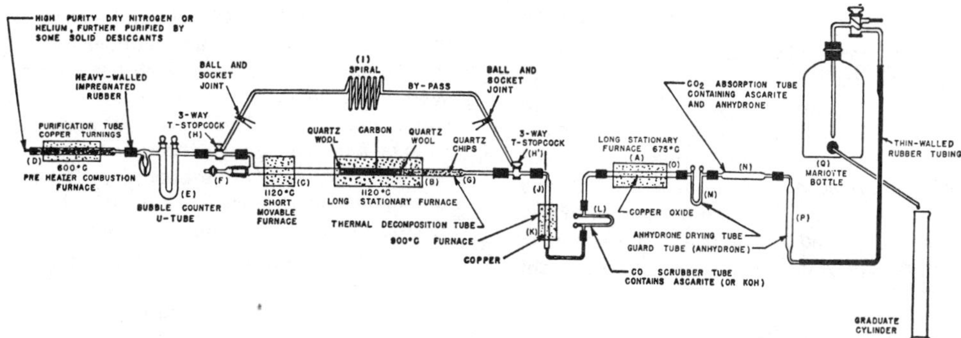

FIG. 47:04—Gravimetric setup for oxygen determination. (Note: (1) All rubber connections made of heavy-walled impregnated rubber except Mariotte bottle. (2) Tubes marked (M) and (L) may be replaced with regulation absorption tubes)

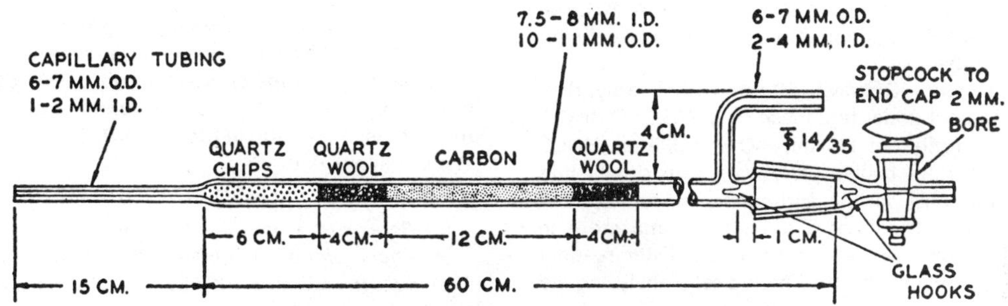

FIG. 47:05—Quartz reaction tube and filling for oxygen determination

opening insert 1-hole rubber stopper contg drain tube to 1 L graduate. Fill bottle with H_2O; (*Q*).

(**r**) *Safety trap.*—Gas washing bottle, 125 mL, Drechsel tall-form, Kimble Products No. 15060 or equiv. Connect T-tube to top of center tube. Fill bottle ca ⅓ with Hg and connect by T-tube between preheater and N supply. (Gas pressure valve, Friedrich, or other regulator may also be used.)

(**s**) *Nitrogen tank.*—Use tank of high purity N equipped with pressure reducing valve, and safety valve to blow off at set pressure.

47.027 *Assembling Apparatus*

Assemble as in Fig. **47:04**, starting with N tank (**s**), not shown, and connecting as follows, using ground glass joints and paraffin-impregnated heavy-wall tubing: Safety trap (**r**), not shown; purification train (*D*); bubble counter and U-tube (*E*); thermal decomposition tube (*G*); spiral by-pass tube (*I*); quartz tube (*J*); U-tube (*L*); oxidn tube (*O*); drying tube (*M*); CO_2 absorption tube (*N*); guard tube (*P*); and Mariotte bottle (*Q*).

47.028 *Conditioning Apparatus*

Assemble app. up to CO_2 absorption tube; set various furnaces in place. Pass slow stream of N (10 mL/ min) thru system 1–2 hr at *room temp.* Heat all units to specified temps and continue N stream 2 days. Attach remainder of app. with arm of Mariotte bottle slightly below horizontal, and adjust ht of Hg in safety trap (**r**) to obtain 10 mL N/min thru system with all parts at operating temp. Record rates of bubble flow thru bubble counter and Mariotte bottle.

C in thermal decomposition tube (**g**) must be at 1120°. Best results are obtained by keeping furnaces at specified temp. at all times, even when not in use.

47.029 *Determination*

Adjust N flow to 10 mL/min with all furnaces heated to specified temp. Cool short movable furnace (*C*) to room temp. Weigh enough sample to produce 1.0–1.3 mg O; if solid, weigh directly in Pt boat; if liq., weigh in capillary tube, preferably quartz, and insert in Coombs-Alber Pt sleeve or long Pt boat. Turn stopcocks (*H*) and (*H'*) and open stopcock on cap (*F*) to let N flow in reverse direction thru tube (*G*). Remove cap (*F*), and insert Pt boat contg sample to within ca 7 cm of long furnace (*B*) with aid of Pt hook on end of glass rod. Immediately replace cap (*F*) with its stopcock open and let reverse flow of N continue ca 20 min to expel all air.

Weigh CO_2 absorption tube (*N*) as in **47.012(a)** and attach in position. Close stopcock on cap (*F*) and turn stopcocks (*H*) and (*H'*) so N flows forward thru decomposition tube (*G*). Open stopcock on Mariotte bottle (*Q*) and let N flow thru entire system at 10 mL/min. Heat movable furnace (*C*) to ca 1120°, move to within ca 3 cm of sample, and turn on automatic drive to pyrolyze sample slowly. About 25–30 min is required for furnace (*C*) to reach furnace (*B*). Move furnace forward and heat parts of tube insulated by walls of furnaces 5–10 min to pyrolyze any material condensed in cooler portions of tube. Return furnaces to original positions. Let furnace (*C*) cool. Continue flow of N until ca 700 mL has passed thru from beginning of pyrolysis, using exactly same amt in detn and blank. Remove CO_2 absorption tube *N*, and reweigh as in **47.012(a)**.

Perform blank detn with empty Pt boat and subtract wt CO_2 of blank from that of detn. (Well-functioning app. gives zero blank.)

$$\% O = \text{Wt } CO_2 \times 0.3635 \times 100/\text{wt sample.}$$

47.030 ***Cleaning Reaction Tube***

When visibility becomes poor on thermal decomposition tube from deposited C, remove as follows: With entire app. assembled (with absorption tube and Mariotte bottle attached), close stopcock (*H*) to both (*G*) and (*I*). Turn stopcock (*H'*) to connect (*G*) to (*J*). Open cap stopcock (*F*), lower arm of Mariotte bottle, and suck air thru reaction tube. Heat movable furnace to 1120° and move it over against long furnace; C will be burned off in few min. Close stopcock of cap (*F*), and turn stopcock (*H*) to connect reaction tube (*G*) with N supply. Pass N thru system overnight to remove air.

Phosphorus (*11*)—Official Final Action

47.031 ***Reagents***

(**a**) *Nitric-sulfuric acid mixture.*—Slowly pour 420 mL HNO_3 into 580 mL H_2O; then slowly add 30 mL H_2SO_4.

(**b**) *Ammonium nitrate soln.*—2%. Prep. 2% soln of NH_4NO_3 in H_2O, add 2 drops HNO_3, and store in g-s bottle. Filter immediately before use.

(**c**) *Molybdate reagent.*—Dissolve 150 g powd NH_4 molybdate in 400 mL H_2O and cool under tap. Place 50 g $(NH_4)_2SO_4$ in 1 L vol. flask, dissolve in mixt. of 105 mL H_2O and 395 mL HNO_3, and cool under tap. Pour cooled molybdate soln slowly into $(NH_4)_2SO_4$ soln with const stirring and cooling under tap. Dil. soln to 1 L, store in refrigerator 3 days, filter, and store in paraffin-lined, g-s, brown bottle in refrigerator. Filter reagent immediately before use and check by periodically analyzing std sample.

47.032 ***Apparatus***

(**a**) *Kjeldahl digestion flasks (30 mL), rack, and manifold.*—*See* **47.022**(**a**) and (**c**).

(**b**) *Filter tubes and filtration assembly.*—*See* **47.004**(**c**) and (**d**).

(**c**) *Rubber stoppers.*—Two or three small, solid rubber stoppers to loosen ppt from walls of flask.

47.033 ***Determination***

Weigh 3–20 mg sample, depending on P content and whether microchem. or semimicrochem. balance is used (max. wt ppt = 50 mg). Weigh in charging tube, if possible, and transfer to Kjeldahl flask. Use porcelain boat for sticky solids and viscous liqs, and glass capillary for volatile liqs.

Add 0.5 mL H_2SO_4 followed by 4–5 drops HNO_3. Heat on digestion rack to white SO_3 fumes and cool under tap. Add 4–5 drops HNO_3, repeat digestion, and cool under tap. Add 4–5 drops HNO_3 and again digest to SO_3 fumes. Cool to room temp.; add 2 mL acid mixt., (**a**), and 12.5 mL H_2O, rinsing down neck of flask. (If porcelain boat was used to add sample, remove boat with Pt wire; if glass capillary was used, filter digestion mixt. to remove capillary. Rinse filter and boat or capillary with 12.5 mL H_2O used to dil. sample.)

Place flask on steam bath 15 min to convert P to H_3PO_4. Remove from steam bath and pipet 15 mL molybdate reagent, (**c**), into center of digest, not down walls of flask. Let stand 2–3 min; then gently swirl to mix contents, being careful to prevent reagents from splashing on neck of flask. Cover flask and set in dark place overnight.

Condition filter tube as described below and weigh empty tube. Connect tared filter tube to filtration assembly and transfer ppt to filter thru siphon tube. Wash flask alternately with 1–2 mL portions of the NH_4NO_3 soln and alcohol. Add 2–3 small rubber stoppers to digestion flask, shake to loosen any ppt, and transfer with the NH_4NO_3 soln and alcohol. Disconnect siphon tube; rinse ppt from tip and stopper into filter tube with the NH_4NO_3 soln and alcohol. Wash ppt with more NH_4NO_3 soln, alcohol, and finally with acetone, and suck dry. Wipe filter tube with chamois skin, place in vertical position in vac. desiccator contg no desiccant, and evacuate to 1 mm for 30 min with mech. vac. pump in continuous operation. Release vac. and weigh *immediately* to nearest 0.1 mg. (Rapid weighing is essential because of hygroscopic nature of ppt.)

$$\% \text{ P} = \text{mg ppt} \times 0.014524 \times 100/\text{mg sample}$$

Sulfur

Titrimetric Carius Combustion Method (12) *Official Final Action*

(Not applicable in presence of P)

47.034 ***Reagents***

(**a**) *Fuming nitric acid.*—Reagent grade, sp gr 1.50.

(**b**) *Sodium chloride.*—Reagent grade, fine crystals.

(**c**) *Barium chloride soln.*—Approx. 0.02*N*. Stdze by titrg 5–7 mg freshly dried K_2SO_4, ACS (weighed to nearest 0.01 mg), by method used for sample titrn, **47.037**. Correct titrn for indicator error by blank detn.

$$\text{Normality} = \text{mg } K_2SO_4/174.258 \text{ (mL } BaCl_2 \text{ soln} - \text{mL blank)}$$

(**d**) *Potassium sulfate.*—ACS, powd and dried.

(**e**) *Phenolphthalein soln.*—0.5% soln in 50% alcohol.

(**f**) *Sulfate indicator.*—"THQ" sulfate indicator (Betz Laboratories, Inc., 4636 Somerton Rd, Trevose, PA 19047) or mix 0.1 g K rhodizonate with 15 g sucrose by grinding in mortar.

47.035 ***Apparatus***

(**a**) *Combustion tubes and furnace.*—*See* **47.004**(**a**) and (**b**).

(**b**) *Titration assembly.*—5 mL buret graduated in 0.01 mL; rectangular titrn cell ca 2 × 4 × 5 cm with min. capacity of 50 mL; and std orange-red glass color filter (Corning Glass Works No. 3482, CS 3-67) selected to have 37% *T* at 550 nm. (Alternatively, use ref. titrn cell contg 30 mL of soln of 20 g $Na_2Cr_2O_7$/L H_2O.) Place cell and filter side by side on milk glass window illuminated from below, preferably by fluorescent light. Mask light source so that only cells and filter are illuminated. For best results use no overhead illumination. Place microscope slides (1–3) with ground glass surface (prepd by grinding with H_2O suspension of fine SiC) over glass filter to compensate for increased turbidity.

47.036 ***Sample***

Using microchem. balance, weigh 5–20 mg sample contg ⩾0.75 mg S, or using semimicrochem. balance, weigh 10–20 mg sample contg ⩾0.75 mg S (1.5 mg for gravimetric detn). Weigh samples as in **47.005**.

47.037 ***Determination***

Place weighed sample in combustion tube, add NaCl 100% in excess of amt equiv. to S in sample, and proceed as in **47.006**, beginning ". . . and add . . . fuming HNO_3, . . ." thru end of third par. ". . . with glass splinters."

Transfer contents of tube to 50 mL beaker, rinsing tube 4–6 times with 3–5 mL portions H_2O. Evap. to dryness on steam bath.

Dissolve residue in 10 mL H_2O, pour soln into titrn cell, add 1 drop phthln, and make just alk. with ca 0.1*N* NaOH, then acid with ca 0.02*N* HCl, adding 1 drop excess. Add ca 0.15 g of the sulfate indicator, stir to dissolve, and rinse beaker 2 or 3 times, using enough alcohol so that final soln contains ca 50%. Titr. with std $BaCl_2$ soln from 5 mL buret until stable color of soln immediately after stirring matches std glass color filter. Make certain end point taken is real and not pseudo end point which fades on standing 1–2 min. (Addn of 1–2 drops $BaCl_2$ soln develops definite red.) Det. blank on reagents and correct titrn.

% S = (mL $BaCl_2$ − mL blank) × normality × 16.032 × 100/mg sample.

Gravimetric Carius Combustion Method (13)
Official Final Action

(Applicable in presence of P)

47.038 ***Apparatus (3)***

Crucible and filter stick.—Porcelain crucible, ca 15 mL capacity, with black inside glaze, wt ca 10 g; with porcelain filter stick, with unglazed bottom, wt ca 2 g. (Altho filter stick is weighed with crucible, it is removed before addn of soln of residue.)

47.039 ***Determination***

Dissolve residue, **47.037**, in 3 mL H_2O, pour into previously ignited and weighed (with filter stick) porcelain crucible, and rinse beaker with four 2 mL portions H_2O. Place crucible on steam bath until soln is near bp. If vol. exceeds 10–11 mL, evap. to this vol. Add dropwise 0.5 mL *10% $BaCl_2$ soln* (1 mL for samples contg >5 mg S), digest ≥15 min, and cool 15 min.

Connect porcelain filter, previously ignited and weighed with crucible, to arm of siphon with rubber tubing. Connect other arm of siphon to suction flask thru rubber stopper. Lower filter into crucible, slowly draw off soln, and rinse ppt, walls of crucible, and filter with five or six 3 mL portions HCl (1+300), drawing off as much liq. as possible. Carefully detach filter, place in crucible, wipe outside of crucible and end of filter with moist chamois or cheesecloth, and handle thereafter with crucible tongs. Place crucible and filter in larger crucible and dry in oven 10 min at ca 110°. Ignite in furnace 10 min at 700–750° (ppt may also be ignited by heating larger crucible contg crucible and filter to dull red heat with Meker burner), cool on metal block 30 min or in desiccator 1 hr, and weigh. Det. blank on reagents.

% S = (wt $BaSO_4$ − blank) × 0.1374 × 100/wt sample

Oxygen Flask Combustion Method (14)
Official First Action

(Not applicable in presence of P)

47.040 ***Reagents***

(**a**) *Barium chloride soln.*—Approx. 0.02*N*. Stdze as follows: Accurately weigh 3.5–5.5 mg K_2SO_4 into titrn cell, dissolve in 15 mL H_2O, add 0.15 g sulfate indicator, (**f**), and dissolve; dil. soln to 30 mL with alcohol. Titr. to end point (same color as ref. glass) with $BaCl_2$ soln, making certain end point taken is real; *see* **47.042**. Titr. blank. Calc. normality as in **47.034(c)**.

(**b**) *Hydrogen peroxide soln.*—30% (Fisher Scientific Co. No. H-325, or equiv. purity). (*Caution: See* **51.070**.)

(**c**) *Oxygen cylinder.*—With regulator and connections for filling combustion flask.

(**d**) *Potassium sulfate.*—ACS, powd and dried.

(**e**) *Phenolphthalein soln.*—0.5% soln in 50% alcohol.

(**f**) *Sulfate indicator.*—Tetrahydroxyquinone (THQ) sulfate indicator (Betz Laboratories, Inc., 4636 Somerton Rd, Trevose, PA 19047) or mix 0.1 g K rhodizonate with 15 g sucrose by grinding in mortar. Vac.-dry overnight at room temp.

47.041 ***Apparatus***

(**a**) *Mechanical shaker.*—Optional.

(**b**) *Oxygen flask combustion apparatus.*—Thomas-Ogg infrared igniter (Arthur H. Thomas Co. No. 6516-G10) and 500 mL thick wall combustion flask (No. 6514-F10), black sample wrappers (No. 6514-F65), Pt sample carrier, stopper, and clamp to avoid loss of sample during pressure changes which occur during combustion. App. is completely shielded within hinged cabinet. Precautions used when employing other manually operated elec. units should include proper safety shielding and reinforced gloves. Flasks must be free of org. solvs to avoid explosion.

(**c**) *Titration assembly.*—*See* **47.035(b)**.

47.042 ***Determination***

Weigh sample contg ca 0.75 mg S and fold into paper carrier. Add 5 mL 0.1*N* NaOH and 3 drops H_2O_2 to 500 mL combustion flask. Flush flask with O ≥2 min. Place paper carrier contg sample in Pt basket, hang on hook of stopper, and insert stopper in flask. Ignite. Shake 30 min. (If gas phase has not cleared, let stand 10 min.) Open flask, and rinse stopper and Pt sample basket with H_2O. Transfer soln to 100 mL beaker, rinsing flask with min. vol. H_2O. Acidify with 2 mL 0.5*N* HNO_3 (≥1 mL in excess of base) and evap. to dryness on steam bath. Dissolve acid-free residue in ca 5 mL H_2O and transfer to titrn cell. Rinse beaker with ca 5 mL H_2O. Add 1 drop phthln and make just alk. with ca 0.1*N* NaOH; then acidify with ca 0.02*N* HNO_3. Add ca 0.15 g THQ indicator, stir to dissolve, and rinse beaker 2–3 times with enough alcohol so that final soln in cell contains ca 50% alcohol. Titr. with std $BaCl_2$ soln from 5 mL buret until stable color of soln immediately after stirring matches std glass color filter as in **47.037**.

% S = [(mL $BaCl_2$ − mL blank) × normality × 16.032 × 100]/mg sample

Alternative Oxygen Flask Combustion Method (15)
Official First Action

(Not applicable in presence of P. All reagents must be as pure as possible, since high concns of Cl, F, NO_3, PO_4, K, and Na interfere. Useful in absence of titrn assembly necessary for THQ titrn.)

47.043 ***Reagents***

(**a**) *Barium perchlorate std soln.*—Approx. 0.01*N*. Accurately weigh ca 6 g $Ba(ClO_4)_2.3H_2O$ and dissolve in 200 mL H_2O. Add 2 drops HCl and dil. to 1 L. Stdze as follows: Accurately weigh ca 3.8 mg *S*-benzylisothiourea.HCl, (**e**), and proceed as in **47.045**, beginning "... and fold into paper carrier." and continuing to "... and correct titrn values." Calc. factor *F*, mg S/mL $Ba(ClO_4)_2$.

F = (mg *S*-benzylisothiourea.HCl × 0.1582)/[mL $Ba(ClO_4)_2$ − mL blank],

where 0.1582 is fraction S in *S*-benzylisothiourea.HCl.

(**b**) *Hydrogen peroxide soln.*—6%. Dil. 20 mL 30% H_2O_2 (Fisher Scientific Co., No. H-325, or equiv. purity) to 100 mL with H_2O. (*Caution: See* **51.070**.)

(**c**) *Methylene blue indicator soln.*—Approx. 0.0125%. Dissolve 12.5 mg methylene blue (J. T. Baker Chemical Co., or equiv.) in 100 mL H_2O.

(**d**) *Oxygen cylinder.*—*See* **47.040(c)**.

(**e**) *S-Benzylisothiourea.HCl.*—Purity equiv. to NBS specifications.

(**f**) *Thorin indicator soln.*—Approx. 0.2%. Dissolve 200 mg thorin (J. T. Baker Chemical Co., or equiv.) in 100 mL H_2O.

47.044 ***Apparatus***

(**a**) *Mechanical shaker*.—Optional.

(**b**) *Oxygen flask combustion apparatus*.—*See* **47.041(b)**.

47.045 ***Determination***

Weigh sample contg ca 0.60 mg S and fold into paper carrier. Add 10 mL 6% H_2O_2 soln to 500 mL combustion flask. Flush flask with O ≥2 min. Place paper carrier contg sample in Pt basket, hang on hook of stopper, and insert stopper in flask. Ignite. Shake 30 min. (If gas phase has not cleared, let stand addnl 10 min.) Open flask, and rinse stopper and Pt sample basket with alcohol. Transfer soln to 200 mL beaker, rinsing flask with alcohol. Place mag. stirring bar in beaker. Add alcohol to 100 mL mark. Add 2 drops thorin indicator soln and 2 drops methylene blue indicator soln, and titr. with $Ba(ClO_4)_2$ soln to faint pink end point, stirring mag. Det. blank on reagents and correct titrn values. Calc. % S, using factor *F* from **47.043(a)**.

$$\% \; S = [(mL \; Ba(ClO_4)_2 - mL \; blank) \times F \times 100]/mg \; sample$$

47.046 ★ ***Titrimetric Catalytic Combustion Method (12)*** ★ ***Official Final Action***

See **38.031–38.034**, 10th ed.

47.047 ★ ***Gravimetric Catalytic Combustion Method (13)*** ★ ***Official Final Action***

See **38.035**, 10th ed.

Alkoxyl Groups (*16*)—Official Final Action

47.048 ***Reagents***

(**a**) *Acetic acid-potassium acetate-bromine soln*.— Dissolve 10 g KOAc in enough HOAc to make 100 mL, and add 3 mL Br. Prep. fresh.

(**b**) *Sodium acetate soln*.—Dissolve 25 g $NaOAc.3H_2O$ in enough H_2O to make 100 mL.

(**c**) *Starch indicator*.—Mix ca 2 g finely powd potato starch with cold H_2O to thin paste; add ca 200 mL boiling H_2O, stirring constantly. Add ca 1 mL Hg, shake, and let soln stand over the Hg.

(**d**) *Sodium thiosulfate std soln*.—0.02*N*. Prep. daily by dilg 0.1*N* soln, **50.037–50.038**.

(**e**) *Hydriodic acid*.—Place 250 mL constant boiling HI (57%, sp gr 1.7) in 500 mL r-b flask connected by ₮ joint to air condenser, and reflux 2 hr while stream of CO_2 or N bubbles thru from glass tube extending to bottom. Do not let acid vapors come in contact with org. material. As soon as refluxing stops, discontinue gas flow. Cool, and store in g-s bottle.

47.049 ***Apparatus***

Use modified Clark app., Figs. **47:06** and **47:07**.

47.050 ***Determination***

Fill scrubber halfway with NaOAc soln, and fill receiver ⅔ full with freshly prepd KOAc-Br soln. Weigh enough sample in Pt boat to require ca 8 mL $Na_2S_2O_3$ soln in detn, and place in bottom of boiling flask. Add 2.5 mL melted *phenol* from wide-tip pipet and 5 mL of the HI, and connect boiling flask. Pass CO_2 thru app. from side arm of flask at uniform rate of 15 mL/min. Let reaction mixt. remain at room temp. 30 min. With manteled microburner, boil liq. at such rate that vapors of boiling liq. rise into condenser, but not more than halfway; continue boiling 60 min (first 30 min with H_2O circulating thru condenser and last 30 min with H_2O drained from condenser). Disconnect flask, remove receiver, and rinse delivery tube and contents of receiver into 125 mL erlenmeyer contg 5 mL NaOAc soln. Adjust vol. to

★ Surplus method—*see* inside front cover.

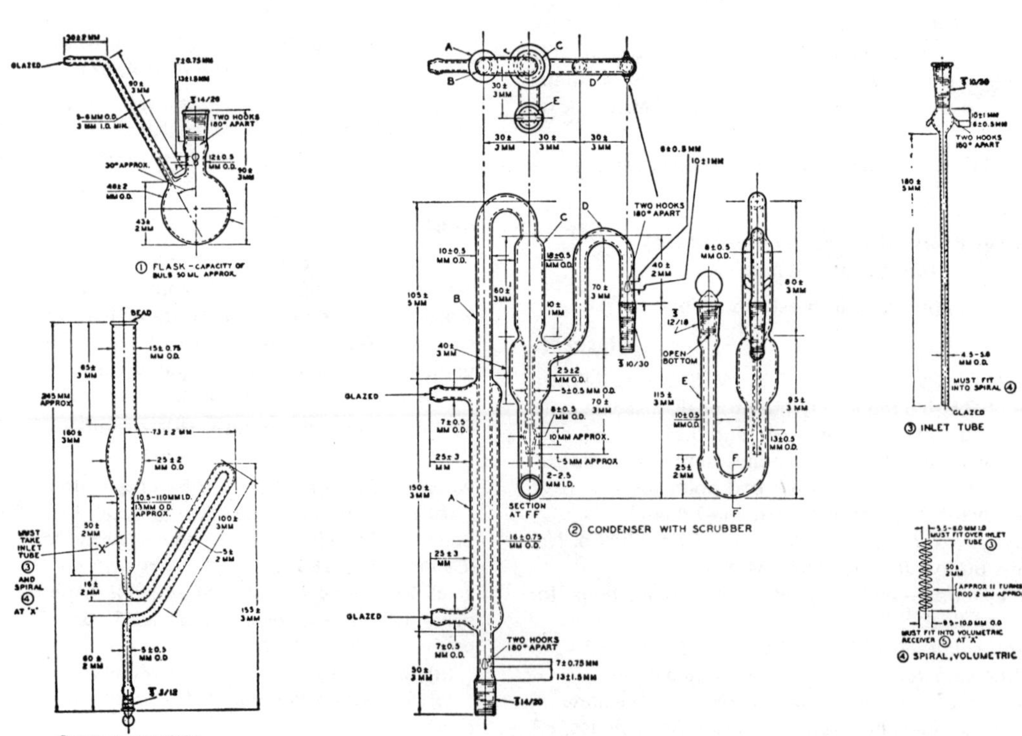

FIG. 47:06—Details of modified Clark apparatus

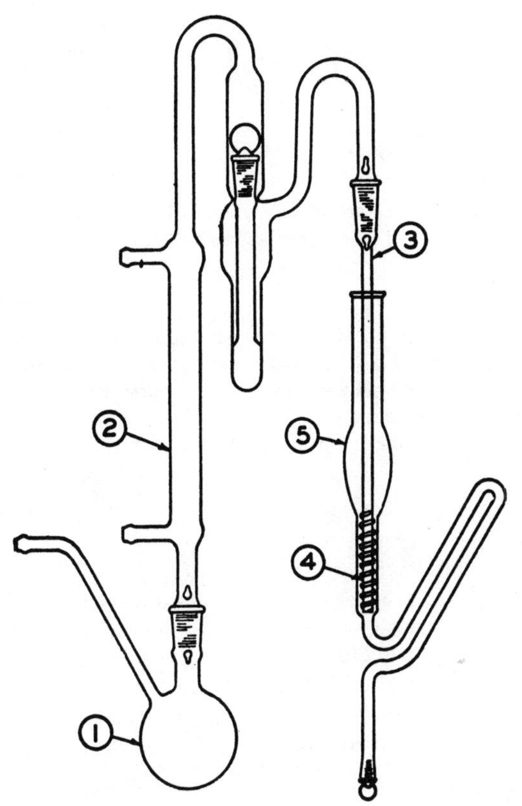

FIG. 47:07—Modified Clark apparatus

ca 50 mL and add *formic acid* dropwise until excess Br is destroyed.

Remove any Br vapors by blowing air over liq.; then add 0.5 g KI and 5 mL 10% H_2SO_4. Swirl soln to dissolve KI and mix contents; then titr. liberated I with the $Na_2S_2O_3$ soln, using starch indicator as in stdzn.

Det. blank on all reagents by making detn without sample.

% Alkoxyl group = (mL in detn − mL in blank) × normality × equiv. wt × 100/mg sample.

Equiv. wt: methoxyl = 5.173; ethoxyl = 7.510.

SELECTED REFERENCES

(*1*) JAOAC **51,** 992, 1231(1968); **52,** 430(1969).
(*2*) JAOAC **35,** 291(1952); **36,** 91, 319(1953); **40,** 381(1957); **41,** 297(1958); Anal. Chem. **23,** 1689(1951).
(*3*) Anal. Chem. **21,** 1555(1949).
(*4*) JAOAC **56,** 888(1973); **57,** 26(1974).
(*5*) JAOAC **32,** 561(1949); **34,** 94, 607(1951); Anal. Chem. **23,** 911(1951).
(*6*) JAOAC **54,** 808(1971); **55,** 676(1972).
(*7*) JAOAC **44,** 258(1961).
(*8*) JAOAC **32,** 561(1949); **33,** 179(1950); **43,** 689(1960).
(*9*) Anal. Chem. **23,** 523(1951).
(*10*) Steyermark, A., "Quantitative Organic Microanalysis," 2nd Ed., Academic Press, New York (1961); JAOAC **46,** 559(1963).
(*11*) JAOAC **40,** 386(1957).
(*12*) JAOAC **35,** 305(1952); **36,** 94, 335(1953).
(*13*) JAOAC **38,** 377(1955).
(*14*) JAOAC **58,** 146(1975).
(*15*) JAOAC **59,** 1135(1976).
(*16*) JAOAC **39,** 108, 401(1956).

48. Radioactivity

48.001 ★ **Qualitative Test—Official Final Action** ★

(Applicable to solids)

See **40.001**, 10th ed. (alpha ray electroscope).

Quantitative Methods

48.002 ★ ***Emanation or Radon Method*** ★ ***(1)—Official Final Action***

(Applicable only to Ra in amts $<10^{-9}$ g. Limit is arbitrary, depending on particular equipment used and accuracy required.)

See **40.002–40.005**, 10th ed. (*Caution: See* **51.011** and **51.025**.)

48.003 ★ ***Gamma Ray Method Using Electroscope*** ★ ***(2)—Official Final Action***

(Applicable only to Ra in amts $>10^{-5}$ g. Limit is arbitrary, depending on particular equipment used and accuracy required.)

See **40.006–40.010**, 10th ed.

48.004 ★ ***Gamma Ray Method Using Geiger-Muller*** ★ ***Counter (3)—Official Final Action***

(Applicable only to Ra in amts $>10^{-7}$ g. Limit is arbitrary, depending on particular equipment used and accuracy required.)

See **40.011–40.015**, 10th ed.

Tritium in Water (*4*)—Official Final Action

48.005 ***Principle***

Sample is distd to remove quenching materials and nonvolatile radioactive materials. Distn is to dryness to ensure complete transfer of ^3H to distillate. Aliquot of distillate is mixed with scintillation soln and counted in liq. scintillation spectrometer (coincidence-type). Std ^3H and background samples are prepd and counted alternately to nullify errors produced by aging of scintillation medium or instrument drift.

48.006 ***Apparatus***

(a) *Liquid scintillation spectrometer.*—Coincidence-type. Available from Searle Analytic, Inc, 2000 Nuclear Dr, Des Plaines, IL 60018; Packard Instrument Co., 2200 Warrenville Rd, Downers Grove, IL 60515; and others.

(b) *Liquid scintillation vial.*—20 mL; low-K glass, polyethylene, nylon, or equiv. bottles, available from manufacturers under **(a)**.

48.007 ***Reagents***

(a) *Scintillation soln.*—Thoroly mix 4 g PPO (2,5-diphenyloxazole), 0.05 g POPOP (1,4-di-2-(5-phenyloxazolyl) benzene), and 120 g solid naphthalene in 1 L spectral grade 1,4-dioxane. (Available from manufacturers under **48.006(a)**.) Store in dark bottles. Soln is stable 2 months.

(b) *Tritium std soln.*—Pipet 4 mL H_2O of known ^3H activity and 16 mL scintillation soln into scintillation vial, tightly cover vial with screw cap, and mix thoroly by shaking.

(c) *Background soln.*—Mix 4 mL distd H_2O (free of ^3H activity to be measured in samples) with 16 mL scintillation soln as in **(b)**.

★ Surplus method—*see* inside front cover.

48.008 ***Preparation of Sample***

Distil 20–30 mL sample to dryness. Mix 4 mL sample distillate with 16 mL scintillation soln as in **48.007(b)**.

48.009 ***Determination***

Prior to counting, dark-adapt and cool sample, background, and std solns ca 3 hr in instrument freezer at $>2°$ (to prevent solidification of soln with time), or at ambient temp. if ambient temp. liq. scintillation spectrometer is used. Count solns for total of 200,000 counts or 100 min, whichever is sooner.

48.010 ***Calculation***

Counting efficiency, $E = (S - B)/D$;

^3H, pCi (picocuries)/mL $= (C - B)/(E \times 4 \times 2.22)$,

where S = gross cpm (counts/min) of std, B = cpm background, D = dpm (disintegrations/min) of ^3H activity in std, and C = gross cpm for sample.

Strontium-90 in Water (*5*)—Official Final Action

48.011 ***Principle***

Applicable to H_2O, and to sewage and industrial waste if org. matter is destroyed and interfering ions are eliminated.

Added carrier Sr along with radionuclides are sepd from other radioactive elements and inactive sample solids by pptn as $Sr(NO_3)_2$ from fuming HNO_3. Sr is finally pptd as $SrCO_3$, which is dried, weighed, and set aside ca 2 weeks for ingrowth of ^{90}Y. Ppt is then dissolved and ^{90}Y is prepd for counting by (*a*) extn by tributyl phosphate and evapg on planchet, or (*b*) addn of Y carrier and pptg as oxalate.

Radioactive Ba and Ra which interfere are removed by addn of Ba carrier. Ca interferes with Sr pptn, but is removed by HNO_3 pptn and acetone treatment.

48.012 ***Apparatus***

(a) *Counting pans.*—Stainless steel, ca 50 mm diam. and 7 mm deep.

(b) *Filtration assembly.*—For mounting ppts for counting. Consists of (*1*) 2-piece filtering app. for 2.4 cm filter such as stainless steel filter holder (Interex Corp., 3 Strathmore Rd, Natick, MA 01760, No. 12-103; ICN Pharmaceuticals, Inc., Life Sciences Group, No. 83012), Teflon filter holder, or equiv. (*2*) Nylon (Zytel 101) disk with ring for mounting ppt (Control Molding Corp., PO Box F, Mariners Harbor Station, Staten Island, NY 10303, No. J-356).

(c) *Film, Mylar.*—To cover ppts during counting and storage, ca 1 mil (0.025″) thick. Available in rolls 1.5″ (3.8 cm) wide as manufacturer's No. 92A, E. I. du Pont de Nemours, Film Dept, Wilmington, DE 19898.

(d) *Glass fiber filter paper.*—No. 934-AH, 2.4 cm diam., available from H. Reeve Angel and Co.

(e) *Centrifuge tubes.*—40 mL, heavy duty with short cone bottom and pour-out lip.

(f) *Beta particle counter.*—Low background, shielded, anticoincidence counter. Det. counter efficiency for ^{90}Y as oxalate and ^{89}Sr as carbonate for specific counter and geometry.

48.013 ***Reagents***

(**a**) *Dilute acetic acid.*—6*N*. Add 345 mL HOAc to H_2O and dil. to 1 L.

(**b**) *Ammonium acetate buffer.*—pH 5.5. Dissolve 154 g NH_4OAc in 700 mL H_2O, add 57 mL HOAc, adjust pH to 5.5 with dropwise addn of either HOAc or 6*N* NH_4OH, as necessary, and dil. to 1 L.

(**c**) *Dilute ammonium hydroxide.*—6*N*. Dil. 400 mL NH_4OH to 1 L with H_2O.

(**d**) *Barium carrier soln.*—10 mg Ba/mL. Dissolve 19.0 g $Ba(NO_3)_2$ in H_2O and dil. to 1 L.

(**e**) *Dilute hydrochloric acid.*—6*N*. Add 500 mL HCl to H_2O and dil. to 1 L.

(**f**) *Fuming nitric acid.*—21*N*. Sp gr 1.48, 90% HNO_3.

(**g**) *Dilute nitric acid.*—(*1*) *14N.*—Add 875 mL HNO_3 to H_2O and dil. to 1 L. (*2*) *6N.*—Add 384 mL HNO_3 to H_2O and dil. to 1 L. (*3*) *0.1N.*—Add 6.25 mL HNO_3 to H_2O and dil. to 1 L.

(**h**) *Oxalic acid soln.*—Satd. Approx. 11 g $H_2C_2O_4.2H_2O$ in 100 mL H_2O.

(**i**) *Mixed rare earth carrier soln.*—Dissolve 12.8 g $Ce(NO_3)_3.6H_2O$, 14 g $ZrOCl_2.8H_2O$, and 25 g $FeCl_3.6H_2O$ in 600 mL H_2O contg 10 mL HCl, and dil. to 1 L. (*Caution:* $Ce(NO_3)_3$ is toxic. Wear resistant rubber or plastic gloves.)

(**j**) *Sodium carbonate soln.*—2*N*. Dissolve 142 g $Na_2CO_3.H_2O$ in H_2O and dil. to 1 L.

(**k**) *Sodium chromate soln.*—0.5*M*. Dissolve 117 g $Na_2CrO_4.4H_2O$ in H_2O and dil. to 1 L.

(**l**) *Sodium hydroxide soln.*—6*N*. Dissolve 240 g NaOH in H_2O and dil. to 1 L.

(**m**) *Strontium carrier soln.*—10 mg Sr/mL. Dissolve 24.16 g $Sr(NO_3)_2$ in H_2O and dil. to 1 L. Stdze by pipetting (in triplicate) 10 mL soln into 40 mL centrf. tubes and adding 15 mL 2*N* Na_2CO_3. Stir and heat in boiling H_2O bath 15 min. Filter thru weighed, fine porosity, fritted glass, 15 mL crucible. Wash with three 5 mL portions H_2O and three 5 mL portions absolute alcohol or acetone, wipe crucible with absorbent tissue, and dry to const wt at 110° (ca 20 min). Cool in desiccator and weigh.

$$\text{mg Sr/mL} = \text{mg } SrCO_3 \times 0.5935/10.$$

(**n**) *Tributyl phosphate* (*TBP*), *equilibrated.*— Shake TBP with equal vol. 14*N* HNO_3. Sep. and discard lower acid phase.

(**o**) *Yttrium carrier soln.*—10 mg Y/mL. Dissolve 12.7 g Y_2O_3 in 30 mL HNO_3 by stirring and heating. Add addnl 20 mL HNO_3 and dil. to 1 L with H_2O. 1 mL = 34 mg $Y_2(C_2O_4)_3.9H_2O$. Det. exact equivalence as in **48.014**(**f**) or (**g**).

48.014 ***Determination***

(*Caution: See* **51.026** and **51.031**.)

(**a**) *Precipitation as carbonate.*—To 1 L drinking H_2O (or less, but contg ≥25 pCi ^{90}Sr) or filtered raw H_2O sample in beaker, add 2.0 mL HNO_3 and mix. Add 2.0 mL each of Ba and Sr carrier solns and mix well. (Ppt of $BaSO_4$ will not cause difficulty.) Heat to bp, and add 20 mL 6*N* NaOH and 20 mL 2*N* Na_2CO_3. Stir, and let simmer ca 1 hr at 90–95°. Let cool until ppt has settled (1–3 hr). Decant and discard supernate. Transfer ppt to 40 mL centrf. tube, centrf., and discard supernate.

(**b**) *Purification as nitrate.*—Cautiously add 4 mL HNO_3 dropwise to ppt. Heat to bp, stir, and cool under running H_2O. Add 20 mL fuming HNO_3, cool 5–10 min in ice bath, stir, and centrf. Discard supernate. Add 4 mL H_2O to residue, stir, and heat to bp to dissolve $Sr(NO_3)_2$. Centrf. while hot and decant supernate into clean centrf. tube. Add 2 mL 6*N* HNO_3 to residue, heat to bp, centrf. while hot, and combine supernate with aq. supernate. Discard insol. residue of $BaSO_4$, SiO_2, etc.

Cool combined supernates, add 20 mL fuming HNO_3, cool 5–10 min in ice bath, stir, centrf., and discard supernate. Add 4 mL H_2O to ppt and dissolve by heating, cool, add 20 mL fuming HNO_3, cool 5–10 min in ice bath, stir, centrf., and discard supernate. If >200 mg Ca is present in sample, repeat H_2O soln and fuming HNO_3 pptn.

(**c**) *Removal of rare earths.*—After last HNO_3 pptn, invert tube in beaker ca 10 min to drain off most of excess HNO_3. Add 20 mL acetone to ppt. Stir thoroly, cool, centrf., and discard supernate. Dissolve ppt of Sr and Ba nitrates in 10 mL H_2O and boil 30 sec to remove any remaining acetone.

Add 0.25 mL mixed rare earth carrier soln and ppt rare earth hydroxides by making soln basic with 6*N* NH_4OH. Digest in boiling H_2O bath 10 min. Cool in ice bath, centrf., decant supernate to clean tube, and discard ppt. Repeat addn of rare earth carrier soln, pptn, and decantation. Note time as beginning of ^{90}Y ingrowth period.

(**d**) *Removal of barium.*—Add 2 drops Me red indicator and then 6*N* HOAc, dropwise with stirring, until soln is red. Add 5 mL acetate buffer soln, heat to bp, and add 2 mL Na_2CrO_4 soln dropwise with stirring. Digest in boiling H_2O bath 5 min. Cool in ice bath, centrf., decant supernate into clean tube, and discard residue.

(**e**) *Precipitation as strontium carbonate.*—Add 2 mL 6*N* NaOH to supernate; then add 5 mL 2*N* Na_2CO_3 and heat to bp. If pH is <9, add addnl NaOH soln. Cool in ice bath ca 5 min, centrf., and discard supernate. Add 15 mL H_2O to ppt, stir, centrf., and discard wash H_2O. Repeat washing and weigh $SrCO_3$ as in (*1*) or (*2*):

(*1*) Slurry ppt with small vol. H_2O, and transfer to weighed stainless steel pan. Dry under IR lamp, cool, and weigh. (*2*) Transfer ppt to weighed paper or glass filter mounted in 2 piece funnel. Let settle by gravity for uniform deposition; then apply suction. Wash ppt with three 5 mL portions H_2O, three 5 mL portions alcohol, and three 5 mL portions ether or acetone. Dry 15–30 min in 110–125° oven, cool, and weigh.

Store ppt ≥2 weeks to permit ingrowth of ^{90}Y. Sep. and count ^{90}Y by (**f**) or (**g**).

(**f**) *Separation by TBP extraction.*—If $SrCO_3$ is weighed in pan, place pan in small funnel in mouth of 60 mL separator and carefully add 1 mL 6*N* HNO_3 dropwise. Tilt pan to empty, and rinse with two 2 mL portions 6*N* HNO_3.

If $SrCO_3$ is weighed on filter, dislodge bulk of ppt into small funnel in mouth of 60 mL separator. Cautiously add 1 mL 6*N* HNO_3 dropwise to dissolve remaining ppt. Rinse filter and funnel with two 2 mL portions of 6*N* HNO_3.

Remove pan or filter and add 10 mL fuming HNO_3 to separator thru funnel. Remove funnel and add 1 mL Y carrier soln to separator. Add 5.0 mL TBP, shake thoroly 3–5 min, let sep., and transfer aq. layer to second 60 mL separator. Add 5.0 mL TBP to second separator, shake 5 min, let sep., and transfer aq. layer to third 60 mL separator. Combine TBP exts and wash with two 5 mL portions 14*N* HNO_3. Record time as beginning of ^{90}Y decay. (Combine acid washings with aq. phase in third separator if second ingrowth of ^{90}Y is desired.)

Back-ext ^{90}Y from combined org. phase with 10 mL 0.1*N* HNO_3 5 min. Either (*1*) repeat TBP extn as above, beginning "Add 5.0 mL TBP, . . ." and finally back-extg ^{90}Y into 10 mL 0.1*N* HNO_3 and continue as in (**g**), line 10 beginning "Gradually . . ."; or (*2*) transfer aq. phase to 50 mL beaker and evap. on hot plate to 5–10 mL. Transfer residual soln to weighed stainless steel counting pan and evap. Rinse with two 2 mL portions 0.1*N* HNO_3, add rinsings to counting pan, evap. to dryness, and weigh. Count in internal proportional or end window counter and calc. ^{90}Sr as in **48.015**.

(**g**) *Separation by yttrium oxalate precipitation.*— Dissolve $SrCO_3$ by cautiously adding 2 mL 6*N* HNO_3 dropwise, and transfer to 40 mL centrf. tube, rinsing with 0.1*N* HNO_3. Add 1 mL Y carrier soln, 2 drops Me red, and NH_4OH dropwise to Me red end point. Add addnl 5 mL NH_4OH and record time as end of ^{90}Y ingrowth and beginning of decay. Centrf. and decant supernate into beaker. (Save supernate and washings for second ingrowth, if desired.) Wash ppt with two 20 mL portions hot H_2O. Add 5–10 drops 6*N* HNO_3, stir to dissolve ppt, add 25 mL H_2O, and heat in H_2O bath at 90°. Gradually add 15–20 drops satd oxalic acid soln with stirring, and adjust pH to 1.5–2.0 (pH meter or indicator paper) with dropwise addn of NH_4OH. Digest ppt 5 min; then cool in ice bath with occasional stirring.

Transfer ppt to weighed glass fiber filter in 2-piece funnel. Let ppt settle by gravity for uniform deposition and then apply suction. Wash ppt with 10–15 mL H_2O, three 5 mL portions alcohol, and then three 5 mL portions ether. Air dry ppt 2 min with suction, weigh, mount on nylon disk and ring with Mylar cover, count, and calc. ^{90}Sr as in **48.015**.

48.015 ***Calculations***

(**a**) *Strontium-90 calculation.—*

$$^{90}Sr, pCi/L = net\ cpm/(abcdfg \times 2.22),$$

where a = counting efficiency for ^{90}Y; b = chem. yield (fraction) of extd or pptd ^{90}Y; c = mg final Y oxalate ppt/mg Y oxalate in 1 mL carrier; d = chem. yield (fraction) of Sr detd as in **48.014(e)** (20 mg Sr equiv. to 33.6 mg $SrCO_3$) or by flame photometry; f f = vol., L, original sample; g = ^{90}Y decay factor = $e^{-\lambda t}$; e = base of natural logarithms; $\lambda = 0.693/T_{1/2}$; $T_{1/2}$ = 64.2 hr for ^{90}Y; and t = time, hr, between sepn and counting.

(**b**) *Counting efficiency.*—Prep. curve from various wts Y oxalate ppt spiked with $^{90}Sr/^{90}Y$, pptd as in **48.014(g)**.

(**c**) *Correction for carrier recovery.*—If sample contains more than trace stable Sr, it will act as carrier and will result in >100% yield. In such case det. Sr by flame photometry.

Strontium-89 and Strontium-90 in Milk

Ion Exchange Method (6)—Official Final Action

48.016 ***Principle***

Fresh milk samples are preserved with HCHO and stored to obtain ^{90}Y ingrowth. After storage, Y, Sr, and Ba carriers and citrate soln are added. Citrate forms Y complex which is adsorbed on anion exchange resin. Y is desorbed and sepd from radionuclides by tributyl phosphate extn. Y is re-extd into dil. HNO_3 and pptd as oxalate, which is weighed and counted for ^{90}Y activity to calc. ^{90}Sr.

Radio-Sr is desorbed along with Ca and radio-Ba; Ca, radio-Ba, and rare earth radionuclides are sepd by repetitive pptns; Sr is pptd as $SrCO_3$ and counted. Total radio-Sr minus ^{90}Sr by ^{90}Y measurement yields value for ^{89}Sr.

Milk contg known increments of ^{89}Sr and ^{90}Sr detd in triplicate by 11 laboratories showed following results (av. of triplicates):

Amt Present, pCi/L		Std Dev.		Bias	
		%	pCi/L	%	pCi/L
^{89}Sr	29.0	10.0	2.9	+7.0	+2.0
	197.0	3.4	7.2	+1.5	+3.0
^{90}Sr	32.4	0.9	0.3	+0.3	+0.1
	151.2	2.8	4.2	−0.9	−1.3

48.017 ***Operating Notes***

Radio-Ba and La radionuclides will interfere without purification. Purification from Ca is important for recovery tests but need not be as thoro if Sr recovery is detd by ^{85}Sr tracer or flame photometry. Thoroly desorb columns before re-use and test periodically to assure complete desorption.

48.018 ***Apparatus***

See **48.012(b)–(f)**, plus following:

Ion exchange system.—Consists of 1 L graduated separator, 250 mL separator with fritted glass disk as cation exchange column, and 30 mL separator with fritted glass disk as anion exchange column (Kontes Glass Co., No. K-427530).

48.019 ***Reagents***

See **48.013(c)**, **(e)–(g)**, plus following:

(**a**) *Ammonium acetate buffer.*—pH 5.0. Dissolve 153 g NH_4OAc in 900 mL H_2O. Adjust pH to 5.0 with HOAc, using pH meter, and dil. to 1 L.

(**b**) *Anion exchange resin.*—Dowex 1-X8 (Cl form), anal. grade, 50–100 mesh size, available from Bio-Rad Laboratories, 32nd and Griffin Aves, Richmond, CA 94804.

(**c**) *Barium carrier soln.*—20 mg Ba/mL. Dissolve 38.1 g $Ba(NO_3)_2$ in H_2O, add 1 mL HNO_3, and dil. to 1 L.

(**d**) *Cation exchange resin.*—Dowex 50W-X8 (Na form), anal. grade, 50–100 mesh size, available from Bio-Rad Laboratories. Convert com. available H form into Na form by passing 1.5 L 4*N* NaCl thru 170 mL resin placed in column and rinsing with ca 500 mL H_2O until wash H_2O is Cl-free when tested with 1% $AgNO_3$.

(**e**) *Citrate soln.*—2*M*. Dissolve 384 g anhyd. citric acid (420 g monohydrate) in H_2O, adjust to pH 6.5 with dil. NaOH soln, and dil. to 1 L.

(**f**) *Oxalic acid soln.*—2*N*. Dissolve 126 g $H_2C_2O_4.H_2O$ in warm H_2O, cool, and dil. to 1 L.

(**g**) *Silver nitrate soln.*—1%. Dissolve 1 g $AgNO_3$ in H_2O and dil. to 100 mL. Store in brown bottle.

(**h**) *Sodium chloride soln.*—4*N*. Dissolve 236 g NaCl in H_2O and dil. to 1 L.

(**i**) *Sodium carbonate soln.*—3*N*. Dissolve 159 g Na_2CO_3 in H_2O and dil. to 1 L.

(**j**) *Sodium chromate soln.*—1*N*. Dissolve 81 g Na_2CrO_4 in H_2O and dil. to 1 L.

(**k**) *Strontium carrier soln.*—20 mg Sr/mL. Dissolve 48.3 g $Sr(NO_3)_2$ in H_2O, add 1 mL HNO_3, and dil. to 1 L. Stdze by pipetting 1 mL portions into six sep. 40 mL centrf. tubes contg 15 mL H_2O. Adjust pH (indicator paper or meter) to 8.5–9.0 with 6*N* NH_4OH. Add, with stirring, 3–5 mL 3*N* Na_2CO_3 and digest 5 min in near boiling H_2O bath. Cool to room temp. and process ppt as in **48.022(d)** or **(e)**.

(**l**) *Tributyl phosphate (TBP), pre-equilibrated.*— Add 150 mL H_2O and 30 mL 3*N* Na_2CO_3 to 300 mL TBP in 1 L separator. Shake 2–3 min and let sep. Discard lower aq. phase. Add 150 mL H_2O to separator, shake 2–3 min, and let sep. Discard lower aq. phase. Add 150 mL 14*N* HNO_3 and shake 5 min. Let sep. and discard lower aq. phase. Repeat 14*N* HNO_3 treatment twice.

(**m**) *Yttrium carrier soln.*—10 mg Y/mL. Dissolve 12.7 g Y_2O_3 in 50 mL HNO_3 by heating (avoid boiling). Dil. to 900 mL with H_2O, adjust pH to 2.0 with NH_4OH, and dil. to 1 L with H_2O. Stdze by pipetting 1 mL portions into each of six 40 mL centrf. tubes contg 15 mL H_2O. Add 5 mL 2*N* oxalic acid and adjust pH to 1.5 with 6*N* NH_4OH, using pH meter. Digest in hot H_2O bath 10 min, and cool to below room temp. Centrf. and discard supernate. Process ppt as in **48.022(d)** or **(e)**.

Use Y_2O_3 of 99.999% purity (Ventron Corp., Alfa Products, 8 Congress St, Beverly, MA 01915). Material of lower purity may require purification because of radioactive contaminants.

48.020 ***Preparation of Sample***

Preserve freshly drawn sample with ca 3 mL HCHO soln for each L milk and refrigerate for known period of time up to 2 weeks to allow ^{90}Y ingrowth. Thoroly mix preserved, stored sample. If homogeneous, transfer 1 L to separator, **48.018**. If nonhomogeneous, before transfer, filter thru loose bed of Pyrex glass wool to prevent clogging of resin columns.

48.021 ***Removal of Radioelements by Ion Exchange***

Combine 1.00 mL each of Y, Sr, and Ba carriers with 10 mL citrate soln, (**e**) in small beaker or vial. Transfer quant. to 1 L sample in separator, and mix well.

Add 170 mL Dowex 50W-X8, (**d**), to 250 mL separator filled with H_2O. Add 15 mL Dowex 1-X8, (**b**), to 30 mL separator filled with H_2O. Connect all separators together in order sample (top), anion column, cation column (bottom), and place beaker to collect effluent. Open stopcocks of sample, anion, and cation separators, in that order, and note time. Control effluent rate at 10 mL/min with anion column stopcock. Check and adjust effluent flow periodically.

Stop flow when milk level reaches top of each resin bed and note time. Record as mean time the av. period of effluent flow. This time is taken as beginning of ^{90}Y decay. Do not permit unnecessary delay during elution. Discard eluate.

Connect separator contg 300 mL warm H_2O, continue elution at 10 mL/min as above, and discard.

48.022 ***Yttrium-90 Separation, Purification, and Determination***

Connect separator contg 100 mL 2*N* HCl to top of anion separator. Open upper stopcock and then lower stopcock, and control effluent flow at 2 mL/min. Collect 15 mL eluate. Close both stopcocks and remove top separator. Stir resin thoroly with glass stirring rod, and rinse into resin column with small vol. 2*N* HCl. Reconnect separator, and continue 2*N* HCl elution, collecting total of 70 mL Y eluate. Retain eluate.

Adjust flow rate to 10 mL/min for remaining 30 mL acid to recharge separator. Discard this eluate. Wash resin with $\geq$100 mL H_2O until Cl-free by $AgNO_3$ test. Separator is ready for next detn.

Add 5 mL 2*N* oxalic acid to retained eluate and adjust pH to 1.5 with 6*N* NH_4OH, using pH meter. Stir, heat to near bp in H_2O bath, cool in ice bath, centrf., decant, and discard supernate. Proceed as in (**a**) or (**b**), depending on whether ^{140}Ba-^{140}La is absent or present from gamma analysis of sample.

(**a**) *If fresh fission products are absent.*—Dissolve ppt in 1 mL 6*N* HCl, add 15 mL H_2O, and filter thru Whatman No. 541 paper into 40 mL centrf. tube. Wash paper, collecting washings in tube, discard paper, and continue as in (**c**).

(**b**) *If fresh fission products are present.*—Dissolve ppt in 10 mL HNO_3; transfer soln to 60 mL separator, washing centrf. tube with addnl 10 mL HNO_3. Add 10 mL equilibrated TBP, (**I**), shake 2–3 min, let sep., and drain and discard lower acid phase. Add 15 mL 14*N* HNO_3 to separator, shake 2–3 min, let sep., and drain and discard lower acid phase. Repeat 14*N* HNO_3 treatment to remove light lanthanide elements, particularly ^{140}La. Add 15 mL H_2O to separator and shake 2–3 min. Let sep., and drain aq. phase contg most of Y into 40 mL centrf. tube. Repeat wash, using 15 mL 0.1*N* HNO_3, adding it to centrf. tube.

(**c**) *Preparation of yttrium oxalate.*—Add 5 mL 2*N* oxalic acid to purified Y soln from (**a**) or (**b**), and adjust to pH 1.5 with NH_4OH, using pH meter. Digest soln in hot H_2O bath 10 min with occasional mixing. Cool in ice bath, centrf., and discard supernate. Sep. and count ^{90}Y oxalate as in (**d**) or (**e**), stdze carrier by the same technic used for sample, and calc. ^{90}Sr activity from ^{90}Y count as in **48.024(a)**.

(**d**) *Filtration method.*—Place 2.8 cm glass fiber filter on stainless steel planchet and weigh together. Transfer tared filter to filter holder, **48.012(b)**(*1*), and assemble.

With H_2O spray, quant. transfer Y oxalate ppt to filter funnel, using min. of suction so that ppt is distributed uniformly over filter area. Increase suction as necessary after most of ppt is on filter. Wash ppt with three 10 mL portions warm H_2O, three 5 mL portions alcohol, and three 5 mL portions ether. Continue suction ca 2–3 min. Carefully remove filter, place on original planchet, and let stand at room temp. 10–15 min. Weigh and calc. yield Y oxalate (likely $Y_2(C_2O_4)_3.9H_2O$) by dividing this wt by wt obtained on stdzn of carrier, **48.019(m)**.

Remove filter from planchet, place on top of nylon disk, cover with piece of Mylar film, place nylon ring over Mylar film, and press ring onto nylon disk. Cut off excess film. Count ^{90}Y activity, without undue delay, in low background anticoincidence beta counter. Repeat counting after 3 days to confirm purity of ^{90}Y by its rate of decay. Record dates and time of counting.

(**e**) *Direct dispersion method.*—Wash ppt twice with 20 mL portions warm H_2O, cool to below room temp., centrf., and discard supernate. Quant. transfer ppt to tared stainless steel dish. Uniformly disperse ppt over dish bottom and dry under IR lamp to const wt. Count in β particle counter.

48.023 ***Strontium-89 Separation, Purification, and Determination***

(*Caution: See* **51.026** and **51.031**.)

Connect 1 L separator contg 1 L 4*N* NaCl to cation separator. Open upper stopcock and then lower stopcock, and control effluent flow at 10 mL/min. Collect ca 1 L eluate in 2 L beaker, but leave resin covered with 2–3 mL soln. Retain eluate.

Wash cation separator with 500 mL H_2O from top separator at rate of 10 mL/min. Discard wash H_2O. If resin becomes clogged with milk solids, back-wash separator or transfer resin to beaker, agitate with H_2O, and decant.

Dil. retained eluate to 1.5 L with H_2O, heat to 85–90° on hot plate, and add 100 mL 3*N* Na_2CO_3 with gentle stirring. Remove from heat and cool to room temp. Decant bulk of clear supernate. Quant. transfer ppt to 250 mL centrf. bottle with H_2O and centrf.; discard supernate. Add 50 mL H_2O and disperse ppt. Centrf., discard supernate, and repeat. Dry ppt 4 hr in oven at 110°.

Dissolve ppt with vigorous stirring by adding ca 4 mL 6*N* HNO_3 in small amts (mag. stirrer is helpful). Filter thru Whatman No. 541 paper into 40 mL graduated centrf. tube. Rinse bottle with 4 mL 6*N* HNO_3 and pour washing thru paper. Discard paper. Add 20 mL 21*N* HNO_3 to filtrate. Stir and cool in ice bath; centrf. and discard supernate. ($Sr(NO_3)_2$ pptn is critical in obtaining good recovery of Sr adequately sepd from Ca.) Recoveries from single pptn are as follows:

[HNO_3]	*Sr Rec., %*	*Ca Rec., %*
14*N*	81±4	2.6±0.9
16*N*	98±1.4	11 ±2
18*N*	100±1.7	51 ±3

Dissolve ppt in 5 mL H_2O and adjust to pH 5.0 with NH_4OH, using pH meter. Add 5 mL NH_4OAc buffer. Heat in H_2O bath, add 1 mL 1*N* Na_2CrO_4, and mix well. Digest in bath 5 min. Centrf. and decant supernate into small beaker. Evap. to ca 2 mL, add 2 mL 6*N* HNO_3, and transfer to 40 mL centrf. tube, using one 3 mL H_2O rinse. Add 20 mL 21*N* HNO_3, stir, cool in ice bath, centrf., and discard supernate. Add 3 mL H_2O and 5 mL 6*N* HNO_3 to dissolve ppt. Add 20 mL 21*N* HNO_3, stir, cool in ice bath, centrf., and discard supernate. Record time as beginning of ^{90}Y ingrowth.

Dissolve ppt in few mL H_2O and adjust pH to 8.5–9.0 with 6*N* NH_4OH. Add 3–5 mL 3*N* Na_2CO_3 to ppt $SrCO_3$. Centrf., and discard supernate. Disperse ppt in 10 mL H_2O, centrf., and discard supernate. Sep. and count $SrCO_3$ as in **(a)** or **(b)**:

(a) *Filtration method.*—Proceed as in **48.022(d)**, but wash ppt with three 5–10 mL portions H_2O, transfer to original planchet, and dry 30 min in oven at 110°. Cool in desiccator and weigh. Count as in **48.022(d)**, record time of counting, and calc. ^{89}Sr as in **48.024(b)**.

(b) *Direct dispersion method.*—Wash ppt twice with ca 10 mL portions H_2O, dispersing ppt, centrf., and decant and discard supernate. Quant. transfer ppt to tared stainless steel dish. Uniformly disperse ppt over dish bottom, dry 30 min in 110° oven. Cool in desiccator and weigh. Count in β particle counter. Record time of counting and calc. ^{89}Sr as in **48.024(b)**

48.024 ***Calculations***

(a) *For strontium-90 activity.*—

$$^{90}Sr \text{ activity, pCi/L} = (\text{cpm} \pm \sigma)/R_S R_Y E_Y D_Y I_Y V,$$

where cpm = net beta count rate of ^{90}Y

$$\sigma = \sqrt{\frac{N_s}{t_s} + \frac{N_b}{t_b}}$$

N_s = sample count rate
N_b = background count rate
t_s = sample counting time
t_b = background counting time
R_S = fraction Sr carrier recovered
R_Y = fraction Y carrier recovered
E_Y = counter efficiency for ^{90}Y as Y oxalate, cpm/pCi
D_Y = decay correction factor ($= e^{-\lambda t}$, defined in **48.015(a)**) for ^{90}Y, where t is time of sepg ^{90}Y from Sr to time of counting, **48.022(d)** or **(e)**
I_Y = ingrowth correction factor ($= 1 - e^{-\lambda t}$) for degree of equilibrium attained during ^{90}Y ingrowth period, where t is time from start of ingrowth period to time of sepg ^{90}Y from Sr
V = sample vol., L.

(b) *For strontium-89 activity.*—

$$^{89}Sr \text{ activity, pCi/L} = \frac{1}{E_S D_S}\left[\frac{N_s + \sigma}{R_S V} - C_S(a_S E'_S + E_Y I_Y)\right]$$

where E_S = counter efficiency for ^{89}Sr as $SrCO_3$, cpm/pCi
D_S = decay correction factor ($= e^{-\lambda t}$) for ^{89}Sr, where t is time from sample collection to time of counting

$$\sigma = \sqrt{\frac{N_S}{t_S} + \frac{N_b}{t_b}}$$

R_S = fraction Sr carrier recovered
N_S = net counts/min of observed radio-Sr
V = sample vol., L
C_S = ^{90}Sr activity, pCi/L
a_S = absorption factor for ^{90}Sr as $SrCO_3$ obtained from self-absorption calibration curve. (Self-absorption curves for ^{89}Sr and ^{90}Sr derived by pptg series of carrier $SrCO_3$ concns over expected recovery range in presence of const amt of ^{89}Sr and Y-free ^{90}Sr, resp. Ordinate is ratio of count rate for each thickness to count rate at 0 sample thickness and abcissa is sample wt for given type of sample mount.)
E'_S = counter efficiency for ^{90}Sr as $SrCO_3$, cpm/pCi
E_Y = counter efficiency for ^{90}Y as Y oxalate, cpm/pCi
I_Y = correction factor ($= 1 - e^{-\lambda t}$) for degree of equilibrium attained during ^{90}Y ingrowth period, where t is time ^{90}Y was sepd from $SrCO_3$ to time of counting, **48.023(a)** or **(b)**.

Cesium-137 in Milk by Gamma-Ray Spectroscopy, Using Simultaneous Equations (7)—Official Final Action

48.025 ***Principle***

Applicable to ^{137}Cs in fluid milk preserved with HCHO. Known vol. is placed in counting vessel positioned over and around right cylinder scintillation crystal detector, NaI(Tl), of multichannel gamma spectrometer. Gamma radiation is counted for given time. Accumulated pulses of ^{137}Cs from its selected photon energy range are sepd from other gamma-emitting radionuclides and background radiation by simultaneous equations. ^{131}I and ^{140}Ba may be present and ^{40}K is always present as natural contaminant. They may contribute counts in 1 or more of photopeak ranges.

In special cases, newly formed fission products may be present, e.g., ^{133}I and ^{135}I, which may interfere either thru direct overlapping of photopeaks or by contributing Compton-continuum counts. Such interference may be minimized by waiting for decay of short-lived radionuclides, by addnl counting following decay, or by chem. sepn.

Milk contg known increments of ^{137}Cs detd in triplicate by 25 laboratories showed following results (av. of triplicates):

Amt ^{137}Cs Present, pCi/L	*Std Deviation*		*Bias*	
	%	*pCi/L*	*%*	*pCi/L*
52	10.2	5.3	+1.9	+ 1
305	5.9	18.1	−3.3	−10

48.026 ***Apparatus***

(a) *Alignment sources.*—Gamma ray energies, at least 1 near ^{137}Cs spectrum, with well known energies and abundance of gamma rays in photopeaks, for alignment. Solid sources, ca 0.1 μCi, are preferred over liq. sources. ^{207}Bi is satisfactory single source with several photopeaks; ^{137}Cs and ^{60}Co are good pair.

(b) *Counter.*—Low level gamma spectrometer consisting of shielded Tl-activated NaI scintillation detector, 4 × 4″, coupled to multichannel pulse-ht analyzer and readout system.

(c) *Counting vessel (Marinelli beaker).*—Use 3.5 L beaker, Fig. **48:01**, for 4 × 4″ detector. Beaker and lid available from plastic laboratory-ware suppliers such as Bel-Art Products, Pequannock, NJ 07440, No. F26862 for beaker and No. 26872 for lid.

48.027 ***Reagents***

(*Caution: See* **51.075**.)

(a) *Carrier solns.*—10 mg/mL. Prep. solns of CsCl (1.267 g/100 mL), NaI (1.181 g/100 mL), and $BaCl_2.2H_2O$ (1.779 g/100 mL). Store in polyethylene or glass bottles.

(b) *Stock std solns.*—10,000 pCi/mL. Dil. calibrated solns of ^{137}Cs, ^{131}I, and ^{140}Ba to approx. indicated strength.

(c) *Potassium-40 stock std soln.*—1.89 dpm (disintegrations/min) ^{40}K/mg K. Dissolve 240 g KCl (equiv. to 126 g K) in 3 L H_2O in Marinelli beaker and dil. to 3.5 L.

(d) *Calibrating solns.*—For Cs and Ba, add 3–5 mL carrier soln, **(a)**, to 3 L H_2O in Marinelli beaker, mix, add convenient amt of stock std soln, **(b)**, sufficient to reduce counting error to ca 1% when counted within 10–100 min, mix, adjust pH to 3.5–4.5, and dil. to 3.5 L. Prep. I soln similarly, but adjust pH to 8.5.

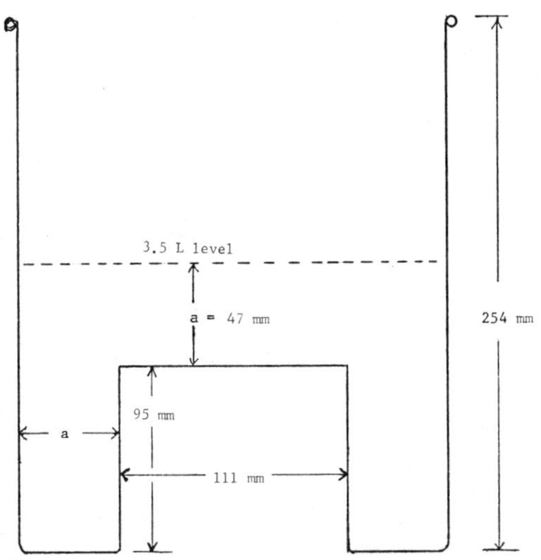

FIG. 48:01—Cross-section of Marinelli beaker.

48.028 ***Determination***

Using alignment sources centered on detector, adjust spectrometer to cover range at least between 0 and 2 MeV, in intervals (channels) of 10 or 20 keV. Adjust voltage or gain control so that the 2 gamma photopeaks of std fall in their appropriate channels. Check and adjust alignment daily.

Place Marinelli beaker contg 3.5 L calibrating soln, (**d**), over detector, and count std for time (10–100 min) sufficient to reduce counting error to ca 1%. Repeat with each calibrating soln and with H_2O. Recalibrate spectrometer yearly or more frequently if gamma ray resolution changes.

Transfer 3.5 L well mixed milk sample at room temp. into Marinelli beaker, place over detector, and count 100 min or time sufficient to give desired counting statistics.

48.029 ***Calculations***

(**a**) *Counter efficiency.*—Total individual counts observed in channels of photopeak range for each calibrating soln. Subtract total background count for same photopeak range. Divide net count by counting time in min and amt of radionuclide in pCi, and record cpm/ pCi for each.

(**b**) *Interference coefficients.*—When counting std soln of each interfering radionuclide, ^{131}I, ^{140}Ba, ^{40}K, ratio of net counting rate in ^{137}Cs energy range to net counting rate in its own photon energy range gives its fractional interfering coefficients for ^{137}Cs energy range.

Designate counting rate for ^{131}I, ^{140}Ba, ^{137}Cs, and ^{40}K with symbols I, B, C, and K, resp. Designate net counting rates (observed − background) in their resp. photon energy ranges as N_i, N_b, N_c, and N_k, resp. Then, f, fractional coefficients or contributions of nuclide in particular range, is designated by 2 lower case subscripts; first one indicates nuclide photon energy range (column) and second, nuclide (row). Then following 4 equations:

$$N_i = I + f_{bi} B + f_{ci} C + f_{ki} K \quad (1)$$
$$N_b = f_{ib} I + B + f_{cb} C + f_{kb} K \quad (2)$$
$$N_c = f_{ic} I + f_{bc} B + C + f_{kc} K \quad (3)$$
$$N_k = f_{ik} I + f_{bk} B + f_{ck} C + K \quad (4)$$

can be solved simultaneously by matrix algebra, using inversions to provide numerical consts W, X, Y, and Z in equations 5, 6, 7, and 8. These consts are used to solve for ^{137}Cs concn and ≤3 of other nuclides in sample. Net counting rate for each nuclide is:

$$^{131}I = I = W_1N_i + W_2N_b + W_3N_c + W_4N_k \quad (5)$$
$$^{140}Ba = B = X_1N_i + X_2N_b + X_3N_c + X_4N_k \quad (6)$$
$$^{137}Cs = C = Y_1N_i + Y_2N_b + Y_3N_c + Y_4N_k \quad (7)$$
$$^{40}K = K = Z_1N_i + Z_2N_b + Z_3N_c + Z_4N_k \quad (8)$$

Calibration to derive values for consts in equations 5, 6, 7, and 8 is applicable as long as instrument alignment and mode of operation remain const and gamma-emitting nuclides are limited to the 4 elements in matrix. Long-hand inversion of 4 × 4 matrix is tedious and subject to mistakes. Use of computer is recommended to provide numerical consts for equations 5–8. Thereafter, desk calcns can det. concns of ^{131}I, ^{140}Ba, ^{137}Cs, and ^{40}K in samples in absence of computer by summing counts in each photopeak, subtracting background, and applying equations 5–8.

(**c**) *Cesium-137 activity.*—From spectral gamma counts of sample, substitute net value in equation 7 and convert net counts/min for ^{137}Cs to pCi/L milk at time of counting:

$$^{137}Cs\ (pCi/L) = \text{net cpm}/(E \times V),$$

where E = counting efficiency/pCi from std solns, and V = sample vol., L.

Radioactive Contamination—Procedure

Emergency Level Procedure (*8*)

48.030 ***Apparatus***

(**a**) *Portable count-rate meter.*—Consists of: (*1*) *Self-quenching glass Geiger-Müller tube,* side wall ≤32 mg/cm², mounted in slide opening metal shield; threshold ca 800 v, operated at ca midpoint of voltage plateau, slope of which is ≤10%, connected with coaxial cable to (*2*) *Suitable power supply and electronic amplifier unit* with meter calibrated in milliroentgens (mr)/hr, connected thru sensitivity switch providing 3 ranges of scale reading, *e.g.,* 0–20, 0–2, and 0–0.2 mr/hr; linear response within each range.

(**b**) *Comparison std.*—Induces meter response identical to that from surface of H_2O contaminated with fission products decaying at rate of 2×10^5 dmp/mL (emergency tolerance level for H_2O to be consumed for ≤10 day period). Construct such std as follows: Uniformly suspend suitable amt of "60-mesh" $UO_2(OAc)_2.2H_2O$ (ca 3 g, adjusted by trial; *Caution: See* **51.083** and **51.084**) in 5 g liq. casting plastic, level, and solidify in shallow container, such as lid of ointment tin, ca 80 mm diam. and side wall 15 mm deeper than layer of plastic. Base of ointment tin, fitted with indented ring 15 mm below its edge, serves as container for liqs and finely divided solids to be tested, and to protect comparison std when not in use. Supplementary std of ½ this activity may be prepd similarly for monitoring supplies to be consumed over 30 day period.

48.031 ***Determination***

With selectivity switch set for highest range (*e.g.,* 0–20 mr/hr), and with shield open, place G-M tube diametrically across std in contact with edge of container at 2 points. Adjust meter pointer to convenient value ca midway of scale with calibration screw and record reading as av. of fluctuations over 1–2 min. Duplicate reading should check within ±5%. Avoid extraneous radiation, such as that from luminous dial watch.

Fill sample container with liq. or finely divided solid to level of indented ring and obtain duplicate readings. Sample readings within ±100% of std reading are of practical quant. significance for monitoring under emergency conditions.

SELECTED REFERENCES

(*1*) Rev. Sci. Instrum. **4,** 216(1933); **6,** 99(1935); Phys. Rev. **55,** 931(1939).
(*2*) JAOAC **19,** 101(1936).
(*3*) JAOAC **25,** 103, 618(1942).
(*4*) JAOAC **52,** 90(1969).
(*5*) JAOAC **56,** 208(1973).
(*6*) JAOAC **56,** 213(1973); **57,** 37(1974).
(*7*) JAOAC **56,** 204(1973).
(*8*) JAOAC **38,** 678(1955).

49. Spectroscopic Methods

EMISSION SPECTROGRAPHIC METHODS OFFICIAL FIRST ACTION

Aluminum, Barium, Boron, Calcium, Copper, Iron, Magnesium, Manganese, Molybdenum, Phosphorus, Potassium, Sodium, Strontium, and Zinc in Plants (*1*)

49.001 ***General Recommendations***

(**a**) *Instrumental technic.*—If, because of equipment limitations, described methods cannot be followed in detail, or if detn of other elements is desired, following protocol is recommended: Det. experimentally, with available facilities, potentials of various sample prepns and excitation conditions with relation to element detectability and general concn requirements. Select analysis lines on basis of desirable intensity and freedom from spectral interference by other elements, as detd by prepg spectrum of each component element at av. concn at which it occurs in samples to be analyzed. Line and phototube characteristics are usually detd by instrument manufacturer.

(**b**) *Precision.*—Stdze all conditions of technic and det. reproducibility of results by making ca 20 successive exposures on sample of representative composition. For each element, calc. std deviation of single exposure and divide by square root of number of individual exposures that will be averaged in practice to constitute 1 detn. From this est. of std deviation of single detn, calc. coefficient of variation for each element. Following upper limits for precision error of spectrographic detns in analysis of plant material are satisfactory in relation to other routine methods or to practical requirements: Coefficients of variation (%)— Ca, Mg, Mn, and Mo, 3–7; B, Ba, Cu, K, P, and Zn, 7–15; and Al, Fe, and Na, >15. Coefficients of variation vary from instrument to instrument for each element; above values were obtained from std plant tissue by 11 different instruments.

(**c**) *Accuracy.*—Precise technic is essential but not only factor involved in accuracy. Reliability and appropriateness of stds and judgment used in ref. method are of utmost importance. Failure in any of these respects can result in serious calibration error for otherwise satisfactory method.

Carefully prep. synthetic stds from highet grade H_2O-free analyzed chems, collectively blanked for minor and trace elements. Preferably confirm values assigned to natural stds by results of >1 laboratory.

Matrix similarity between stds and samples, or closely controlled correction system for matrix differences, is essential. Check correction scales frequently against stds which closely match particular types of plant materials being analyzed.

Precision error of technic applies to ref. exposures as well as to samples. For this reason, base fiducial adjustments on as many ref. exposures as may be feasibly included in each series of samples.

Direct Reading Method—Official First Action

49.002 ***Apparatus***

(**a**) *Spark excitation source.*

(**b**) *Spectrograph.*—1.5 m grating spectrograph with spark stand and disk attachment rotating at 30 rpm.

(**c**) *Electrode sharpener.*

(**d**) *Disk electrode.*—High purity graphite disk 0.492″ diam. and 0.200″ thick.

(**e**) *Upper (pin) electrode.*—Point appropriate lengths of std grade spectrographic C rods, 0.180″ diam., in pencil sharpener equipped with pin stop to produce 1/16″ diam. flat tip.

(**f**) *Porcelain boat.*—60 mm long, 10 mm wide, and 8 mm high (Coors No. 2, or equiv.).

49.003 ***Reagents***

(**a**) *Buffer.*—Dissolve 50 g Li_2CO_3 in 200 mL HNO_3, and dil. to 1 L with H_2O. (*Caution: See* **51.026**.)

(**b**) *Element stock std solns.*—On basis of expected sample concn range, prep. stock solns from individual pure nitrates, chlorides, or carbonate salts, or metal of resp. elements, as indicated in Table **49:01**.

(**c**) *Mixed element std solns.*—Prep. 5 std solns contg % or ppm element indicated in Table **49:02** as follows: Dissolve 50 g Li_2CO_3 in 200 mL HNO_3, pipet in indicated aliquots, and dil. to 1 L with H_2O. Prep. fresh every 6 months.

49.004 ***Preparation of Sample***

Dry plant material 24 hr at 80° and grind in Wiley mill with No. 20 stainless steel sieve. Store in air-tight containers or in coin envelopes in dry atm.

Weigh 1.0 g prepd sample into 30 mL high form crucible (porcelain is satisfactory). Ash ≥4 hr at 500° with crucible resting on asbestos plate rather than on floor of furnace. Cool, add 5.0 mL buffer soln, (**a**), stir, and let stand 30 min.

49.005 ***Determination***

(**a**) *Excitation.*—Align and space electrodes 4 mm apart in holders; position pin electrode over disk electrode. Set source parameters to give uniform breakdown voltage at tandem air gap with operating parameters at 4 breaks/cycle and 4 amp (parameters may vary with source for best operating efficiency).

Table 49:01 Preparation of Stock Standard Solutions

Element	Salt	Element, g/L	Salt, g/L	Solvent
K	KCl	125	238.36	H_2O
Ca	$CaCO_3$	40	99.89	1*N* HNO_3
Mg	MgO	20	33.16	1*N* HNO_3
P	H_3PO_4	10	31.64	H_2O
Na	NaCl	10	25.42	H_2O
Fe	Fe metal	1	1.00	1*N* HNO_3
Mn	MnO	1	1.29	1*N* HNO_3
Al	Al metal	1	1.00	1*N* HNO_3
Zn	Zn metal	1	1.00	1*N* HNO_3
Cu	Cu metal	1	1.00	1*N* HNO_3
Ba	$BaCl_2$	1	1.52	H_2O
Sr	$SrCO_3$	1	1.68	1*N* HNO_3
B	H_3BO_3	1	5.72	H_2O
Mo	$(NH_4)_6Mo_7O_{24}.H_2O$	0.1	1.29	H_2O

Table 49:02 Preparation of Mixed Element Standard Solutions

Element	Element, g/L	Standard Solution Number 1	2	3	4	5
				mL to give (%)[a]		
K	125	2(0.5)	4(1.0)	8(2.0)	12(3.0)	20(5.0)
Ca	40	100(2.0)	50(1.0)	30(0.6)	10(0.2)	15(0.3)
Mg	20	100(1.0)	70(0.7)	50(0.5)	20(0.2)	10(0.1)
P	10	2(0.1)	4(0.2)	6(0.3)	10(0.5)	14(0.7)
				mL to give (ppm)[a]		
Na	10	1(50)	2(100)	10(500)	20(1000)	40(2000)
Fe	10	10(500)	4(200)	2(100)	1(50)	6(300)
Mn	10	0.4(20)	1(50)	2(100)	4(200)	10(500)
Al	10	0.6(30)	1(50)	2(100)	4(200)	10(500)
Zn	1	2(10)	4(20)	6(30)	10(50)	20(100)
Cu	1	1(5)	2(10)	4(20)	10(50)	14(70)
Ba	1	20(100)	10(50)	4(20)	2(10)	1(5)
Sr	1	40(200)	20(100)	10(50)	6(30)	3(15)
B	1	1(5)	2(10)	4(20)	10(50)	14(70)
Mo	0.1	2(1)	4(2)	8(4)	12(6)	20(10)

[a] Concn based on 1 g sample taken up in 5 mL buffer.

Place aliquot of prepd soln in porcelain boat, set boat on arc stand, and raise to immerse 1/16" of disc in soln. Spark 10 sec to condition electrodes and photomultiplier tubes and then spark addnl 30 sec for integration.

(**b**) *Calibration.*—Calibration technic varies with instrument. Use mixed element std solns and known plant tissue stds to calibrate spectrograph by same technic as for samples. Prep. std curves to cover desired concn range, using ratio to internal std and background correction for best results.

★ Surplus method—*see* inside front cover.

49.006 ★ *Direct Current Arc Excitation Method* ★

See **44.003–44.006**, 11th ed.

49.007 ★ *Alternating Current Spark Excitation Method* ★

See **44.007–44.011**, 11th ed.

SELECTED REFERENCES

(*1*) JAOAC **36,** 411(1953); **37,** 721(1954); **58,** 764(1975).

50. Standard Solutions and Materials

50.001 General Directions (*1*)

Use accurately calibrated equipment, which meets NBS specifications. Because alk. and other corrosive solns dissolve glass, to avoid vol. errors do not store such solns in calibrated app. burets used continuously with such solns should be recalibrated periodically.

Working temp. of std soln should approximate that of its temp. during stdzn. If temp. corrections are necessary, sufficient accuracy may be obtained by use of Table **50:01**.

Ammonium and Potassium Thiocyanates (*2*)
Official Final Action

50.002 ***Reagents***

(**a**) *Purified silver nitrate.*—Dissolve 50 g $AgNO_3$ in 20 mL boiling H_2O contg ca 5 drops HNO_3. Heat to dissolve, filter while still hot thru fritted glass filter, using suction, and collect filtrate in clean Pyrex beaker. Wash beaker and filter with ca 5 mL hot H_2O, adding washings to filtrate. Cool in ice bath, stirring to induce crystn, and place in refrigerator at ca 10° until equilibrium is reached. Decant liq. thru fritted glass filter and transfer crystals to filter. Cover filter with watch glass and draw air thru filter to remove adhering liq. Transfer crystals to small, clean Pyrex beaker. Cover beaker with watch glass and place inside larger covered Pyrex beaker. Dry at 105° and fuse at 220–250° (mp 208°), holding at this temp. ca 15 min after crystals are melted. Protect from dust during prepn. Cool in desiccator, remove product from beaker, powder in mortar, dry 0.5 hr at 105°, and store in brown g-s bottle in dark over good desiccant.

(**b**) *Reference soln.*—To mixt. of 5 mL HNO_3 (1+1), 2 mL Fe alum soln, **50.030(a)**, and 115 mL H_2O, add ca 0.02 mL 0.1*N* thiocyanate, **50.003**, noting exact vol. used.

50.003 ***Preparation of Standard Solution***

Prep. ca 0.1*N* soln from reagent that shows no Cl, using 7.612 g NH_4SCN or 9.718 g KSCN/L.

50.004 ***Standardization***

Accurately weigh, on tared watch glass, enough purified $AgNO_3$ to give titrn of ca 40 mL (ca 0.7 g for 0.1*N* soln) and transfer with H_2O thru glass funnel to 250 mL g-s erlenmeyer. Dissolve in ca 75 mL H_2O (halogen-free), and add 5 mL HNO_3 (1+1) and 2 mL Fe alum soln, **50.030(a)**. Titr. with thiocyanate soln until titrd soln is reddish brown, which remains after shaking vigorously 1 min. Record buret reading and set flask aside 5 min, shaking occasionally and maintaining end point color by addn of thiocyanate soln as required. Then add addnl thiocyanate soln, if necessary, to produce permanent end point color, matching with color of ref. soln, **50.002(b)**. From total vol. thiocyanate soln used in titrn, subtract vol. contained in ref. soln.

Normality = g $AgNO_3$ × 1000/mL titer × 169.87.

Arsenious Oxide (*3*)—Official Final Action

50.005 ***Reagent***

Arsenious oxide.—Use NBS SRM 83. Dry 1 hr at 105° immediately before using.

50.006 ***Preparation of Standard Solution***

Accurately weigh As_2O_3 by difference from small g-s weighing bottle (use ca 4.95 g/L for 0.1*N*). Dissolve in 1*N* NaOH (50 mL/5 g As_2O_3) in flask or beaker by heating on steam bath. Add ca same vol. 1*N* H_2SO_4. Cool, quant. transfer mixt. to vol. flask, and dil. to vol. (Soln must be neut. to litmus, not alk.)

Normality = g As_2O_3 × 4000/mL final vol. × 197.84.

Buffer Solutions for Calibration of pH Equipment (*4*)
Official Final Action

50.007 ***Preparation of Standard Buffer Solutions***

Use H_2O with pH of ≥6.5 but ≤7.5, obtained by boiling H_2O 15 min and cooling under CO_2-free conditions. Store std buffer solns except $Ca(OH)_2$ in bottles of chem. resistant glass. Protect phosphate, borax, and $Ca(OH)_2$ buffers from CO_2. pH values as function of temp. are given in Table **50:02**.

(**a**) *Potassium tetroxalate buffer soln.*—0.0496*M*; 0.05*m*. Transfer 12.61 g $KHC_2O_4.H_2C_2O_4.2H_2O$ (air wt) (NBS SRM 189) to 1 L vol. flask, dil. to vol. with H_2O, and mix thoroly. (It is not necessary to remove dissolved CO_2 from the H_2O or to dry salt before weighing.) Prep. fresh every 2 months.

(**b**) *Potassium hydrogen tartrate buffer soln.*—Satd soln at 25°, 0.034*M*. Add excess (ca 100%) of $KHC_4H_4O_6$ (NBS SRM 188) to H_2O in g-s bottle or flask, and shake vigorously; few min shaking is enough for satn (100 mL H_2O at 25° dissolves ca 0.7 g $KHC_4H_4O_6$). Adjust to 25°, let solid settle, and decant clear soln, or filter if necessary. Discard when mold appears. Few crystals of thymol added during prepn will retard mold growth, and will alter pH by <0.01 unit. For accuracy of ±0.01 pH unit, temp. of soln at satn must be between 20 and 30°.

(**c**) *Acid potassium phthalate buffer soln.*—0.0496*M*; 0.05*m*. Dissolve 10.12 g dried (2 hr at 110°) $KHC_8H_4O_4$ (NBS SRM 185) in H_2O and dil. to 1 L. (Elaborate precautions for exclusion of atm. CO_2 are unnecessary, altho soln should be protected

Table 50:01 Temperature Corrections for Volume of Aqueous Solutions

	Correction in Milliliters at—												
Vol. Std Soln	6°	8°	10°	12°	14°	16°	18°	20°	22°	24°	26°	28°	30°
mL													
10	0.01	0.01	0.01	0.01	0.01	0.01	0.00	0.00	0.00	0.00	−0.01	−0.02	−0.02
20	0.03	0.03	0.03	0.02	0.02	0.01	0.01	0.00	−0.01	−0.02	−0.03	−0.03	−0.03
25	0.04	0.03	0.03	0.03	0.02	0.02	0.01	0.00	−0.01	−0.02	−0.03	−0.04	−0.05
30	0.04	0.04	0.04	0.03	0.03	0.02	0.01	0.00	−0.01	−0.02	−0.04	−0.05	−0.07
40	0.06	0.06	0.05	0.04	0.04	0.03	0.01	0.00	−0.02	−0.03	−0.05	−0.07	−0.09
50	0.07	0.07	0.06	0.06	0.05	0.03	0.02	0.00	−0.02	−0.04	−0.06	−0.09	−0.12

against evapn and contamination with molds. Replace soln if mold appears.)

(d) *Phosphate buffer soln.*—0.0249*M*; 0.025*m*. Dissolve 3.387 g KH_2PO_4 and 3.533 g Na_2HPO_4 (NBS SRM 186-I and II) in H_2O and dil. to 1 L. (Dry salts 2 hr at 110–130° before use.)

(e) *Phosphate buffer soln.*—0.008663*M*, 0.008695*m* KH_2PO_4 and 0.03030*M*, 0.03043*m* Na_2HPO_4. Dissolve 1.179 g KH_2PO_4 and 4.303 g Na_2HPO_4 (NBS SRM 186-I and II) in H_2O and dil. to 1 L. (Dry salts 2 hr at 110–130° before use.)

(f) *Borax buffer soln.*—0.00996*M*; 0.01*m*. Dissolve 3.80 g $Na_2B_4O_7.10H_2O$ (NBS SRM 187) in H_2O and dil. to 1 L. (Salt must not be dried in oven before use.) To avoid contamination with CO_2, stopper bottle except when in use or protect with soda-lime tube. Use buffer soln within 10 min after removal from bottle.

(g) *Sodium bicarbonate-carbonate buffer soln.*— 0.0249*M*; 0.025*m* (each). Transfer 2.092 g $NaHCO_3$ (NBS SRM 191; do not heat) and 2.640 g Na_2CO_3 (NBS SRM 192; dry 2 hr at 275°) to 1 L vol. flask. Dissolve and dil. to vol. with CO_2-free H_2O.

(h) *Calcium hydroxide buffer soln.*—Satd soln at 25°, 0.02025*M*. Slowly heat finely granular $CaCO_3$, Low in Alkalies, to 1000° in Pt dish and maintain at this temp. 45–60 min. Cool in desiccator, and add to H_2O with stirring. Heat to bp with continuous stirring. Cool, and filter on medium fritted glass filter. Dry at 110°, cool, and crush to fine, granular powder.

Place crushed CaO in polyethylene bottle, add H_2O, shake vigorously, let settle, and record temp. (Keep large excess of $Ca(OH)_2$ in bottle.) For use, filter soln thru medium fritted glass filter. Use at same temp. at which satn took place, and discard filtered soln if it becomes turbid. When more buffer soln is needed, add addnl H_2O to suspension, re-sat., and filter as above.

Standard Buffers and Indicators for Colorimetric pH Comparisons (5)—Official Final Action

50.008 ***Preparation of Sulfonphthalein Indicators***

	X	pH
Bromocresol green	14.3	3.8–5.4
Chlorophenol red	23.6	4.8–6.4
Bromothymol blue	16.0	6.0–7.6
Phenol red	28.2	6.8–8.4

X = mL 0.01*N* NaOH/0.1 g indicator required to form mono-Na salt. Dil. to 250 mL for 0.04% reagent.

50.009 ***Preparation of Stock Solutions***

Use recently boiled and cooled H_2O.

(a) *Acid potassium phthalate soln.*—0.2*M*. Dry to const wt at 110–115°. Dissolve 40.836 g in H_2O and dil. to 1 L.

(b) *Monopotassium phosphate soln.*—0.2*M*. Dry KH_2PO_4 to const wt at 110–115°. Dissolve 27.232 g in H_2O and dil. to 1 L. Soln should be distinctly red with Me red, and distinctly blue with bromophenol blue.

(c) *Boric acid-potassium chloride soln.*—0.2*M*. Dry H_3BO_3 to const wt in desiccator over $CaCl_2$. Dry KCl 2 days in oven at 115–120°. Dissolve 12.405 g H_3BO_3 and 14.912 g KCl in H_2O, and dil. to 1 L.

(d) *Sodium hydroxide std soln.*—0.2*M*. Prep. and stdze as in **50.032–50.035**; 0.04084 g $KHC_8H_4O_4$ = 1 mL 0.2*M* NaOH. It is preferable to use factor with soln rather than try to adjust to exactly 0.2*M*.

50.010 ***Preparation of Buffer Solutions***

Prep. std buffer solns from designated amts stock solns, **50.009**, and dil. to 200 mL. For use as colorimetric std, mix 20 mL buffer soln with 0.5 mL indicator soln, **50.008**.

Phthalate-NaOH Mixtures

pH	0.2*M* KH Phthalate (mL)	0.2*M* NaOH (mL)
5.0	50	23.65
5.2	50	29.75
5.4	50	35.25
5.6	50	39.70
5.8	50	43.10
6.0	50	45.40
6.2	50	47.00

KH_2PO_4-NaOH Mixtures

pH	0.2*M* KH_2PO_4 (mL)	0.2*M* NaOH (mL)
5.8	50	3.66
6.0	50	5.64
6.2	50	8.55
6.4	50	12.60
6.6	50	17.74
6.8	50	23.60
7.0	50	29.54
7.2	50	34.90
7.4	50	39.34
7.6	50	42.74
7.8	50	45.17
8.0	50	46.85

H_3BO_3-KCl-NaOH Mixtures

pH	0.2*M* H_3BO_3, KCl (mL)	0.2*M* NaOH (mL)
7.8	50	2.65
8.0	50	4.00
8.2	50	5.90
8.4	50	8.55
8.6	50	12.00

Hydrochloric Acid—Official Final Action

50.011 ***Preparation of Standard Solutions***

Following table gives approx. vols of 36.5–38% HCl required to make 10 L std solns:

Approx. normality	*mL HCl to be dild to 10 L*
0.01	8.6
0.02	17.2
0.10	86.0
0.50	430.1
1.0	860.1

50.012 ***Standard Sodium Hydroxide Method (6)***

Titr. 40 mL against std alkali soln, **50.034–50.036**, of ca same concn as acid being stdzd in 300 mL flask that has been swept free from CO_2, using CO_2-free H_2O and 3 drops phthln.

Normality = (mL std alkali × normality of alkali)/mL HCl.

If more concd than desired, dil. soln to required normality value by following formula:

$$V_1 = V_2 \times N_2/N_1$$

where N_2 and V_2 represent normality and vol. of stock soln, resp., and V_1 = vol. to which stock soln should be dild to obtain desired normality, N_1.

Check exact concn of final soln by titrn as above. Normality will be exact only if same indicator is used in detn as in stdzn. Restdze if indicators other than phthln are used.

50.013 ***Constant Boiling Method (7)***

Dil. 822 mL HCl (36.5–38% HCl) with 750 mL H_2O. Check sp gr with spindle and adjust to 1.10. Place 1.5 L in 2 L flat-bottom distg flask, add ca 10 SiC grains (ca "20 mesh"), and connect to long, straight inner-tube condenser. Heat on elec. hot plate and distil at 5–10 mL/min, keeping end of condenser open to air. When 1125 mL has distd, change receivers and catch next 225

Table 50:02 pH Values for Standard Buffer Solutions as Function of Temperature

Temperature	0.05m Potassium Tetroxalate	Satd Potassium Hydrogen Tartrate	0.05m Acid Potassium Phthalate	0.025m Phosphate	0.008695m and 0.03043m Phosphate	0.01m Borax	0.025m $NaHCO_3$ and 0.025m Na_2CO_3	Satd Calcium Hydroxide
°C	pH	pH	pH	pH	pH	pH	pH	pH
0	1.666	—	4.003	6.982	7.534	9.460	10.321	13.423
5	1.668	—	3.998	6.949	7.501	9.392	10.248	13.207
10	1.670	—	3.996	6.921	7.472	9.331	10.181	13.003
15	1.672	—	3.996	6.898	7.449	9.276	10.120	12.810
20	1.675	—	3.999	6.878	7.430	9.227	10.064	12.627
25	1.679	3.557	4.004	6.863	7.415	9.183	10.014	12.454
30	1.683	3.552	4.011	6.851	7.403	9.143	9.968	12.289
35	1.688	3.549	4.020	6.842	7.394	9.107	9.928	12.133
37	1.691	3.548	4.024	6.839	7.392	9.093	–	12.043
40	1.694	3.547	4.030	6.836	7.388	9.074	9.891	11.984
45	1.700	3.547	4.042	6.832	7.385	9.044	9.859	11.841
50	1.707	3.549	4.055	6.831	7.384	9.017	9.831	11.705
55	1.715	3.554	4.070	–	–	–	–	11.574
60	1.723	3.560	4.085	–	–	–	–	11.449

mL, which is const boiling HCl, in erlenmeyer with end of condenser inserted into flask, but above surface of liq. Read barometer to nearest mm at beginning and end of collection of 225 mL portion and note barometer temp. Average readings.

Calc. air wt in g (G) of this const boiling HCl required to give one equiv. wt of HCl from one of following equations:

For $P_0 = 540–669$ mm Hg:
$$G = 162.255 + 0.02415\ P_0$$
For $P_0 = 670–780$ mm Hg:
$$G = 164.673 + 0.02039\ P_0,$$

where P_0 = barometric pressure in mm Hg corrected to 0°C for expansion of Hg and of barometer scale. For brass scale barometer, following correction is accurate enough:

$P_0 = P_t(1 - 0.000162t)$, where t = barometer temp. in °C.

Weigh required amt of const boiling HCl in tared, stoppered flask to at least 1 part in 10,000. Dil. immediately, and finally dil. to vol. with CO_2-free H_2O at desired temp.

Standard Borax Method (8)

50.014 ***Reagents***

(**a**) *Methyl red indicator*.—Dissolve 100 mg Me red in 60 mL alcohol and dil. with H_2O to 100 mL.

(**b**) *Reference soln*.—Prep. ref. soln of H_3BO_3, NaCl, and indicator corresponding to composition and vol. of soln at equivalence point. For use in detn of end point of titrn with 0.1N HCl, ref. soln should be 0.1M in H_3BO_3 and 0.05M in NaCl.

(**c**) *Std borax*.—Sat. 300 mL H_2O at 55° (not higher) with $Na_2B_4O_7.10H_2O$ (ACS) (ca 45 g). Filter at this temp. thru folded paper into 500 mL erlenmeyer. Cool filtrate to ca 10°, with continuous agitation during crystn. Decant supernate, rinse ppt once with 25 mL cold H_2O, and dissolve crystals in just enough H_2O at 55° to ensure complete soln (ca 200 mL). Recrystallize by cooling to ca 10°, agitating flask during crystn.

Filter crystals onto small buchner with suction, wash ppt once with 25 mL ice-cold H_2O, and dry crystals by washing with two 20 mL portions alcohol, drying after each washing with suction. Follow with two 20 mL portions ether. (Just before use, free alcohol and ether from any possible reacting acids by vigorously shaking each with 2–3 g of the pure, dry $Na_2B_4O_7.10H_2O$ and then filtering.) Spread crystals on watch glass, immediately place dried $Na_2B_4O_7.10H_2O$ in closed container over soln satd with respect to both sucrose and NaCl, and let it remain ≥24 hr before using. Then transfer the pure $Na_2B_4O_7.10H_2O$ to g-s container and store in closed container over soln satd with respect to both sucrose and NaCl (stable under these conditions 1 year).

50.015 ***Standardization***

Accurately weigh enough std $Na_2B_4O_7.10H_2O$ to titr. ca 40 mL and transfer to 300 mL flask. Add 40 mL CO_2-free H_2O, **50.033(a)**, and stopper flask. Swirl gently until sample dissolves. Add 4 drops Me red and titr. with soln that is being stdzd to equivalence point as indicated by ref. soln.

Normality = g $Na_2B_4O_7.10H_2O$ × 1000/mL acid × 190.69.

Standard Sodium Carbonate Method (8)

50.016 ***Reagents***

(**a**) *Methyl orange indicator*.—0.1% in H_2O.

(**b**) *Reference soln*.—80 mL CO_2-free H_2O contg 3 or 4 drops Me orange.

(**c**) *Anhydrous sodium carbonate* (**9**).—Heat 250 mL H_2O to 80° and add $NaHCO_3$ (ACS), stirring until no more dissolves. Filter soln thru folded paper (use of hot H_2O funnel is desirable) into erlenmeyer. Cool filtrate to ca 10°, swirling constantly during crystn. Fine crystals of trona that sep. out have approx. composition: $Na_2CO_3.NaHCO_3.2H_2O$. Decant supernate, drain crystals by suction, and wash once with cold H_2O.

Transfer ppt, being careful not to include any paper fibers, to large flat-bottom Pt dish. Heat 1 hr at 290° in elec. oven or furnace with pyrometer control. Stir contents occasionally with Pt wire. Cool in desiccator. Place the anhyd. Na_2CO_3 in g-s container and store in desiccator contg efficient desiccant. Dry at 120° and cool just before weighing.

50.017 ***Standardization***

Accurately weigh enough anhyd. Na_2CO_3, (**c**), to titr. ca 40 mL, transfer to 300 mL erlenmeyer, and dissolve in 40 mL H_2O. Add 3 drops Me orange and titr. until color begins to deviate from H_2O tint (ref. soln). (Equivalence point has not been reached.) Boil soln gently 2 min, and cool. Titr. until color is barely different from H_2O tint of indicator.

Normality = g Na_2CO_3 × 1000/mL acid × 52.994.

Iodine (*3*)—Official Final Action

50.018 ***Preparation of Standard Solution***

Dissolve weighed amts of I (12.7 g/L for 0.1N soln) and KI, in proportion of 20 g KI to 13 g I, in 50 mL H_2O. When I dissolves, transfer soln to g-s vol. flask. Dil. to vol. with H_2O and mix thoroly. Store in dark brown, g-s bottle away from light and restdze as frequently as necessary.

50.019 ***Standardization***

Transfer accurately measured portion of std As_2O_3 soln, **50.006** (40–50 mL ca 0.1*N* soln for 0.1*N* I soln), to erlenmeyer. Acidify slightly with H_2SO_4 (1+10), neutze with solid $NaHCO_3$, and add ca 2 g excess. Titr. with I soln, using ca 0.2% starch soln (5 mL/100 mL) as indicator. Sat. soln with CO_2 at end of titrn by adding 1 mL H_2SO_4 (1+10) just before end point is reached.

Normality = mL As_2O_3 × normality As_2O_3/mL I.

Potassium Bromide-Bromate (*10*)—Official Final Action

50.020 ***Preparation of Standard Solution***

Dissolve ca 2.8 g $KBrO_3$ and 12 g KBr in boiled H_2O and dil. to 1 L with boiled H_2O for ca 0.1*N* soln.

50.021 ***Standardization***

Measure 40 mL std As_2O_3 soln, **50.006**, from buret into 300 mL erlenmeyer. Add 10 mL HCl and 3 drops Me orange, **50.016(a)**. Titr. with KBr-$KBrO_3$ soln until $\leq$1 drop causes color of Me orange to fade completely. Swirl soln constantly and add last mL dropwise, swirling between drops.

Normality = mL As_2O_3× normality As_2O_3/mL KBr-$KBrO_3$.

Potassium Dichromate (*11*)—Official Final Action

50.022 ***Reagent***

Starch soln.—Mix ca 1 g arrowroot starch with 10 mL H_2O and pour slowly, with const stirring, into 200 mL boiling H_2O. Boil until thin, translucent fluid is obtained. Let settle and use clear supernate. Preserve with Hg.

50.023 ***Assay of Stock Potassium Dichromate***

If $K_2Cr_2O_7$ is in small crystals, mix by shaking thoroly in large, clean jar; if it is in lumps, grind representative sample to pass No. 60 sieve, and then mix by shaking. Dry portion for weighings 2 hr at 100°.

Weigh, into each of 3 g-s erlenmeyers, enough $K_2Cr_2O_7$ (NBS SRM 136) to give titer of 100.5–102.0 mL 0.1*N* $Na_2S_2O_3$, **50.037** (0.4928–0.5001 g for 0.1*N* soln). Completely dissolve in 100 mL H_2O, add 4.0 g KI, and swirl mixt. until dissolved. With buret, add 4.0 mL HCl, stopper flask, mix by swirling, and let stand in dark 10 min. Cool flask ca 1 min in ice-H_2O.

While swirling flask, pipet in 100 mL $Na_2S_2O_3$ soln. Add 5 mL starch soln and complete titrn with $Na_2S_2O_3$ soln added from 10 mL microburet (graduated in 0.05 mL). End point is from bluish green to clear green; change takes place within 0.01 mL. Record vol. to nearest 0.01 mL. Calc. apparent normality of $Na_2S_2O_3$ soln for each of the 3 titrns, and average. Designate this av. as N_{NBS}.

Similarly titr. 3 portions of stock $K_2Cr_2O_7$ and calc. the 3 apparent normalities. Designate each of these results as N_{stock}. Calc. % purity of stock $K_2Cr_2O_7$ = (N_{NBS} × 100)/N_{stock}.

Take av. of the 3 results as % purity of stock $K_2Cr_2O_7$.

50.024 ***Preparation of Standard Solution***

Dissolve theoretical wt $K_2Cr_2O_7$ (NBS SRM 136) (4.9032 g for 0.1*N* soln), or wt stock $K_2Cr_2O_7$, **50.023**, found to have oxidimetric value 99.95–100.05% of NBS SRM, in enough H_2O to make 1 L. (Dry $K_2Cr_2O_7$ 2 hr at 100° before using.)

Potassium Permanganate (*12*)—Official Final Action

50.025 ***Preparation of Standard Solution***

Dissolve slightly more than desired equiv. wt (3.2 g for 0.1*N*) of $KMnO_4$ in 1 L H_2O. Boil soln 1 hr. Protect from dust and let stand overnight. Thoroly clean 15 cm glass funnel, perforated porcelain plate from Caldwell crucible, and g-s bottle (preferably of brown glass) with warm chromic acid cleaning soln. Digest asbestos for use in gooches on steam bath 1 hr with ca 0.1*N* $KMnO_4$ that has been acidified with few drops H_2SO_4 (1+3). Let settle, decant, and replace with H_2O. To prep. glass funnel, place porcelain plate in apex, make pad of asbestos ca 3 mm thick on plate, and wash acid-free. (Pad should not be too tightly packed and only moderate suction should be applied.) Insert stem of funnel into neck of bottle and filter $KMnO_4$ soln directly into bottle without aid of suction.

50.026 ***Standardization***

For 0.1*N* soln, transfer 0.3 g dried (1 hr at 105°) Na oxalate (NBS SRM 40) to 600 mL beaker. Add 250 mL H_2SO_4 (5+95), previously boiled 10–15 min and then cooled to 27±3°.

Stir until $Na_2C_2O_4$ dissolves. Add 39–40 mL $KMnO_4$ soln at rate of 25–35 mL/min, stirring slowly. Let stand until pink disappears (ca 45 sec). If pink persists because $KMnO_4$ soln is too concd, discard and begin again, adding few mL less of $KMnO_4$ soln. Heat to 55–60°, and complete titrn by adding $KMnO_4$ soln until faint pink persists 30 sec. Add last 0.5–1 mL dropwise, letting each drop decolorize before adding next.

Det. excess of $KMnO_4$ soln required to turn soln pink by matching with color obtained by adding $KMnO_4$ soln to same vol. of boiled and cooled dil. H_2SO_4 at 55–60°. This correction is usually 0.03–0.05 mL. From net vol. $KMnO_4$, calc. normality:

Normality = g $Na_2C_2O_4$ × 1000/mL $KMnO_4$ × 66.999.

Silver Nitrate (*13*)—Official Final Action

50.027 ***Preparation of Standard Solution***

Dissolve slightly more than theoretical wt of $AgNO_3$ (equiv. wt, 169.87) in halogen-free H_2O and dil. to vol. Thoroly clean glassware, avoid contact with dust, and keep prepd soln in amber g-s bottles away from light.

Mohr Method

50.028 ***Reagents***

(a) *Potassium chloride.*—Recrystallize KCl 3 times from H_2O, dry at 110°, and then heat at ca 500° to const wt. Equiv. wt KCl = 74.555. Or, preferably, use NBS SRM 999.

(b) *Potassium chromate soln.*—5% soln of K_2CrO_4 in H_2O.

50.029 ***Standardization***

Accurately weigh enough KCl to yield titrn of ca 40 mL (ca 0.3 g for 0.1*N* soln), and transfer to 250 mL g-s erlenmeyer with 40 mL H_2O. Add 1 mL K_2CrO_4 soln and titr. with $AgNO_3$ soln until first perceptible pale red-brown appears. From titrn vol., subtract mL of the $AgNO_3$ soln required to produce end point color in 75 mL H_2O contg 1 mL K_2CrO_4 soln. From net vol. $AgNO_3$, calc. normality:

Normality = g KCl× 1000/mL $AgNO_3$ × 74.555.

Volhard Method

50.030 ***Reagents***

(a) *Ferric alum indicator soln.*—Satd soln of $FeNH_4(SO_4)_2.12H_2O$ in H_2O.

(**b**) *Potassium or ammonium thiocyanate std soln.*—Prep. ca 0.1*N* soln, **50.003**. Det. working titer by accurately measuring 40–50 mL std $AgNO_3$ soln, adding 2 mL Fe alum soln and 5 mL HNO_3 (1+1), and titrg with the thiocyanate soln until soln appears pale rose after vigorous shaking.

50.031 ***Standardization***

Accurately weigh enough KCl, **50.028(a)**, to yield titrn of ca 40 mL (ca 0.3 g for 0.1*N* soln) and transfer to 250 mL g-s erlenmeyer with 40 mL H_2O. Add 5 mL HNO_3 (1+1) and excess $AgNO_3$ soln. Mix, and let stand few min protected from light. Filter thru gooch prepd with medium pad of asbestos previously rinsed with 2% HNO_3. Wash flask and ppt with several small portions of 2% HNO_3, passing washings thru crucible until filtrate and washings measure ca 150 mL. Add 2 mL Fe alum soln and titr. residual $AgNO_3$ with thiocyanate soln. From titrn, together with ratio of the 2 solns, calc. net vol. $AgNO_3$ soln. (Errors of blank are compensating and may be disregarded.) From net vol. $AgNO_3$, calc. normality as in **50.029**.

Sodium Hydroxide—Official Final Action

Standard Potassium Hydrogen Phthalate Method (14)

50.032 ***Apparatus***

Use buret and pipet calibrated by NBS or by analyst. Protect exits to air of automatic burets from CO_2 contamination by suitable guard tubes contg soda-lime. Use containers of alkali-resistant glass.

50.033 ***Reagents***

(**a**) *Carbon dioxide-free water.*—Prep. by one of following methods: (*1*) Boil H_2O 20 min and cool with soda-lime protection; (*2*) bubble air, freed from CO_2 by passing thru tower of soda-lime, thru H_2O 12 hr.

(**b**) *Sodium hydroxide soln.*—(1+1). To 1 part NaOH (reagent quality contg <5% Na_2CO_3) in flask add 1 part H_2O and swirl until soln is complete. Close with rubber stopper. Set aside until Na_2CO_3 has settled, leaving perfectly clear liq. (ca 10 days).

(**c**) *Acid potassium phthalate.*—NBS SRM for Acidimetry 84. Crush to pass No. 100 sieve. Dry 2 hr at 120°. Cool in desiccator contg H_2SO_4.

50.034 ***Preparation of Standard Solution***

Following table gives approx. vols of NaOH soln (1+1) necessary to make 10 L of std solns:

Approx. normality	*mL NaOH to be dild to 10 L*
0.01	5.4
0.02	10.8
0.10	54.0
0.50	270.0
1.0	540.0

Add required vol. of NaOH soln (1+1) to 10 L CO_2-free H_2O. Check normality, which should be slightly high, as in **50.035**, and adjust to desired concn by following formula:

$$V_1 = V_2 \times N_2/N_1$$

where N_2 and V_2 represent normality and vol. stock soln, resp., and V_1, vol. to which stock soln should be dild to obtain desired normality, N_1. Stdze final soln as in **50.035** or **50.036**.

50.035 ***Standardization***

Accurately weigh enough dried $KHC_8H_4O_4$ to titr. ca 40 mL and transfer to 300 mL flask that has been swept free from CO_2. Add 50 mL cool CO_2-free H_2O. Stopper flask and swirl gently until sample dissolves. Titr. to pH 8.6 with soln being stdzd, taking precautions to exclude CO_2 and using as indicator either glass-electrode pH meter or 3 drops phthln. In latter case, det. end point by comparison with pH 8.6 buffer soln, **50.010**, contg 3 drops phthln. Det. vol. NaOH required to produce end point of blank by matching color in another flask contg 3 drops phthln and same vol. CO_2-free H_2O. Subtract vol. required from that used in first titrn and calc. normality.

$$\text{Normality} = \text{g } KHC_8H_4O_4 \times 1000/\text{mL NaOH} \times 204.229.$$

50.036 ***Constant Boiling Hydrochloric Acid Method (7)***

Accurately weigh from weighing buret enough const boiling HCl, **50.013**, to titr. ca 40 mL, into erlenmeyer previously swept free from CO_2. Add ca 40 mL CO_2-free H_2O, then 3–5 drops desired indicator, and titr. with soln being stdzd.

$$\text{Normality} = \text{g HCl} \times 1000/\text{mL titer} \times G,$$

where G has value given in **50.013**.

Sodium Thiosulfate (*15*)—Official Final Action

50.037 ***Preparation of Standard Solution***

Dissolve ca 25 g $Na_2S_2O_3.5H_2O$ in 1 L H_2O. Boil gently 5 min and transfer while hot to storage bottle previously cleaned with hot chromic acid cleaning soln and rinsed with warm boiled H_2O. (Temper bottle, if not heat-resistant, before adding hot soln.) Store soln in dark, cool place; do not return unused portions to stock bottle. If solns less concd than 0.1*N* are desired, prep. by diln with boiled H_2O. (More dil. solns are less stable and should be prepd just before use.)

50.038 ***Standardization***

Accurately weigh 0.20–0.23 g $K_2Cr_2O_7$ (NBS SRM 136 dried 2 hr at 100°) and place in g-s I flask (or g-s flask). Dissolve in 80 mL Cl-free H_2O contg 2 g KI. Add, with swirling, 20 mL ca 1*N* HCl and immediately place in dark 10 min. Titr. with $Na_2S_2O_3$ soln, **50.037**, adding starch soln after most of I has been consumed.

$$\text{Normality} = \text{g } K_2Cr_2O_7 \times 1000/\text{mL } Na_2S_2O_3 \times 49.032.$$

Sulfuric Acid—Official Final Action

50.039 ***Preparation of Standard Solution***

Following table gives approx. vols of 95–98% H_2SO_4 necessary to make 10 L std solns:

Approx. normality	*mL H_2SO_4 to be dild to 10 L*
0.01	2.8
0.02	5.6
0.10	27.7
0.50	138.1
1.0	276.1

Standard Borax Method (8)

50.040 ***Standardization***

See **50.015**.

50.041 ***Specific Gravity Method (16)***

Dil. H_2SO_4 with enough H_2O to make convenient vol. of ca 70% H_2SO_4 by wt. Det. sp gr in air at convenient temp. (0–40°) as in **9.011** (or sp gr may be detd with Sprengel pycnometer), protecting soln from contact with air. Calc. exact % H_2SO_4 by wt,

$$P = S(85.87 + 0.05T - 0.0004t^2) - 69.82,$$

where S = sp gr (in air) at T°, compared with H_2O at t°.

Weigh exactly *W* g prepd acid contg *P*% H_2SO_4 and dil. to *n* L to make required soln contg *G* g H_2SO_4/L. Calc. *W* from equation:

$$W = nG \times 100/P.$$

Titanium Trichloride (*17*)—Official Final Action

50.042 ***Preparation of Standard Solution***

To 200 mL com. 15% $TiCl_3$ soln add 150 mL HCl and dil. to 2 L. Make soln ca 0.1*N*, place in container with H atm. provision (e.g., JAOAC **5**, 207(1921)), and let stand 2 days for absorption of residual O.

50.043 ***Standardization***

Weigh 3 g $FeSO_4(NH_4)_2SO_4.6H_2O$ and transfer to 500 mL flask. Introduce stream of CO_2, and add 50 mL recently boiled H_2O and 25 mL 40% (by wt) H_2SO_4. Then, without interrupting current of CO_2, rapidly add 40 mL 0.1*N* $K_2Cr_2O_7$, **50.024**. Add $TiCl_3$ soln until near calcd end point. Then quickly add 5 g NH_4SCN, and complete titrn. Det. blank on 3 g $FeSO_4(NH_4)_2SO_4.6H_2O$, using same vols of H_2O, H_2SO_4, and NH_4SCN, and current of CO_2. From net vol. $TiCl_3$, calc. normality:

$$\text{Normality} = \text{mL } K_2Cr_2O_7 \times \text{normality } K_2Cr_2O_7/\text{ mL } TiCl_3.$$

SELECTED REFERENCES

(*1*) JAOAC **25**, 650(1942).
(*2*) JAOAC **25**, 661(1942); **30**, 105, 496(1947).
(*3*) JAOAC **22**, 568(1939); **24**, 100, 639(1941).
(*4*) NBS Certificates for Standard Samples 185e, 186c, 187b, 188, 189, 191, and 192; JAOAC **33**, 223(1950); **41**, 302(1958); **47**, 43(1964).
(*5*) JAOAC **24**, 583(1941); Clark, "Determination of Hydrogen-ions," 3rd Ed., pp. 91, 94, 192–202.
(*6*) JAOAC **19**, 107, 194(1936); **49**, 250(1966); Kolthoff & Stenger, "Volumetric Analysis," **II**, 52(1947).
(*7*) JAOAC **25**, 653(1942); **36**, 96, 354(1953); **37**, 122, 462(1954).
(*8*) JAOAC **22**, 102, 563(1939).
(*9*) Kolthoff & Stenger, "Volumetric Analysis," **II**, 80(1947); Ind. Eng. Chem., Anal. Ed. **9**, 141(1937); JAOAC **22**, 563(1939).
(*10*) JAOAC **30**, 502(1947); **31**, 119, 572(1948).
(*11*) JAOAC **32**, 587(1949); **33**, 225(1950).
(*12*) JAOAC **23**, 543(1940); **31**, 568(1948); J. Research NBS **15**, 493(1935), Research Paper No. 843.
(*13*) JAOAC **24**, 100, 631(1941).
(*14*) JAOAC **19**, 107, 194(1936); NBS Certificate for Standard Reference Material 84.
(*15*) JAOAC **25**, 659(1942); **27**, 557(1944); **28**, 594(1945); **38**, 382(1955); **47**, 43, 46(1964); **48**, 103(1965).
(*16*) J. Chem. Soc. Trans. **57**, 64(1890); J. Soc. Chem. Ind. (1899), 1091; JAOAC **24**, 636(1941).
(*17*) JAOAC **31**, 573(1948); **32**, 589(1949).

51. Laboratory Safety

Introduction

This chapter is not intended to be an exhaustive treatise on laboratory safety. These precautionary notes serve only as a reminder of possible hazards involved in the use of particular operations or substances. Refer to std texts on laboratory safety for fuller treatment of subject. Follow safety requirements of laboratory and rules issued by voluntary organizations and government agencies expert in the field of occupational safety. These notes do not meet all requirements of U.S. Occupational Safety and Health Act of 1970.

Nature and amt of each chemical and its prescribed use were criteria used in detg if cautionary statement for method was indicated.

Safety hazard was considered to exist when nature, amt, and use of chemical or equipment specified in method appeared likely to produce any of following:

(**a**) Concn of vapors from flammable liq. exceeding 25% of lower flammability limit of that liq. described by National Fire Protection Association, Boston, MA.

(**b**) Contact between analyst and amts of material highly active physiologically or toxic to man in excess of Threshold Limit Values published by American Conference of Governmental Industrial Hygienists, P.O. Box 1937, Cincinnati, OH 45201.

(**c**) Contact between analyst and amts of highly corrosive material sufficient to produce serious injury.

(**d**) Contact between analyst and radiations which could be harmful.

(**e**) Explosion or violent reaction.

(**f**) Injury to analyst by hazards in equipment or processes which are not readily detectable by analyst.

When in doubt about possible hazards not covered in this chapter, consult refs at end of chapter or other sources of information such as hazard warnings on labels and manufacturers' data sheets.

Equipment

Use equipment only for purposes for which it was designed. Some common hazards associated with equipment specified in this book are described below (*7, 9*).

51.001 *Refrigerators*

Should be explosion proof or explosion resistant when used for storage of ether and other highly volatile, flammable liqs. Ordinary refrigerator can be made explosion resistant by removal of light switch, receptacle, and associated wiring and placing thermoregulation controls on outside of refrigerator.

51.002 *Glass*

Dispose of chipped or broken glassware in special containers; minor chips may be fire-polished and glassware retained. If glassware is to be repaired, mark defective area plainly and store in special location until repairs are completed.

Use heat-resistant glassware for prepn of solns that generate heat (e.g., not bottles or graduates).

51.003 *Fire Extinguishers*

Class B and C dry chemical fire extinguishers (for flammable liq. and elec. fires) should be conveniently available to each laboratory room. Carbon dioxide fire extinguishers should be used on fires in electronic equipment.

Become familiar with their location and methods for effective use.

51.004 *Blenders*

Motor on high-speed blenders used to mix flammable solv. with other materials should be explosion proof. Blend toxic or flammable liqs in effective fume removal device.

51.005 *Centrifuges*

Adjust all tubes to equal wt before loading them into centrf. Make certain that stoppers of tubes placed in pivot-type head will clear center when tubes swing to horizontal. Do not open centrf. cover until machine stops completely. Before removing tubes, turn elec. switch to "off." Do not rely on zero-set rheostat. Use only tubes specially designed for centrfg. Do not exceed safe speed for various tube materials (glass, cellulose nitrate, polyethylene, etc.) recommended by tube manufacturer. Cellulose nitrate tubes may explode if autoclaved. Heating cellulose nitrate tubes $>60°$ may cause them to produce harmful nitrogen oxide fumes.

51.006 *Atomic Absorption Spectrophotometer*

Use effective fume removal device to remove gaseous effluents from burner. Use especially designed exhausts when N_2O is used as fuel oxidant. If instrument has drain trap, check to ensure it is filled with H_2O before igniting burner. Explosions of fuel gas accumulated thru this drain line have been reported.

51.007 *Flame Photometer*

Use effective fume removal device to remove gaseous burner effluents.

51.008 *Photofluorometer*

Considerable amts of O_3 are formed by UV light radiated by quartz lamp. Ozone is toxic even in low concns; remove thru effective fume removal device placed near quartz lamp.

51.009 *Monitoring Equipment*

Monitor unattended operations with equipment that will automatically shut down process if unsafe condition develops (*9*).

51.010 *Compressed Gas Cylinders*

Identify by name(s) of gas(es) contents of compressed gas cylinders on attached decal, stencil, or tag, instead of by color codes. Secure cylinders in upright position by means of strap, chain, or non-tip base. Use only correct pressure gages, pressure regulator, and flow regulator for each size of gas cylinder and type of gas as specified by supplier. Use toxic gases only in effective fume removal device. When burning gas, use back flow prevention device in gas line to prevent flame being sucked back into cylinder.

51.011 *Distillation, Extraction, and Evaporations*

(**a**) *Flammable liquids.*—Perform operations behind safety barrier with hot H_2O, steam, or elec. mantle heating. Use effective fume removal device to remove flammable vapors as produced. Set up app. on firm supports and secure all connections. Leave ample headroom in flask and add boiling chips *before* heating is begun. All controls, unless vapor sealed, should be located outside vapor area. Dispose of waste flammable solvs by evapn as above unless other provisions for safe disposal are available.

(**b**) *Toxic liquids.*—Use effective fume removal device to remove toxic vapors as produced. Avoid contact with skin. Set up app. on firm supports and secure all connections. Dispose of waste toxic solvs by evapn, using effective fume removal device unless other provisions for safe disposal are available.

51.012 ***Electrical Equipment***

Accidents involving elec. equipment may result in *mech. injury,* e.g., fingers being caught in chopping mill knives; *elec. shock,* which may be due to lack of or improper grounding, defective equipment, exposed wiring, or inadequate maintenance; and *fire* thru ignition of flammable vapors by electrically produced spark. Ground all elec. equipment to avoid accidental shock. Installation, maintenance, and repair operations should be performed by qualified electricians.

51.013 ***Parr Bomb***

Follow manufacturer's directions closely to avoid explosion.

51.014 ***Pressure***

Do not conduct pressure operations with std glassware. In certain circumstances, glassware specifically designed to withstand pressure may be used. Observe manufacturer's recommended safeguards when using pressure app. such as calorimeter bomb, hydrogenator, etc.

51.015 ***Vacuum***

Tape or shield with safety barrier containers and app. to be used under vac. to minimize effects of possible implosion. Vac. pump drive belts must have effective guards.

51.016 ***Hazardous Radiations***

UV radiation is encountered in AA spectrophotometry, fluorometry, UV spectrophotometry, germicidal lamps, and both long- and shortwave UV lamps used to monitor chromatgc sepns. Never expose unprotected eyes to UV light from any source either direct or reflected (e.g., flames in flame photometer, lamps, elec. arcs, etc.). Always wear appropriate eye protection such as goggles having uranium oxide lenses, welder's goggles, etc., when such radiations are present and unshielded. Keep skin exposure to UV radiations to min.

Technics and Practices

51.017 ***Spraying Chromatograms***

When strong corrosive and toxic reagents are sprayed on chromatograms, use gloves, face shield, respiratory protection, and appropriate fume removal device to protect skin, eyes, and respiratory tract against mists or fumes generated by spraying device.

51.018 ***Pipets***

Do not pipet hazardous liqs by using mouth suction to fill pipet. Use pipet fillers or rubber tubing connected thru trap to vac. line for this purpose.

51.019 ***Wet Oxidation***

This technic is among most hazardous uses of acids but can be performed safely. Observe precautions in this chapter for particular acids used and rigorously follow directions given in specific method being used.

51.020 ***Hazardous or After Hours Work***

Anyone working alone after hours or on hazardous procedures should arrange for someone to contact him periodically as safety measure.

51.021 ***Glass Tubing***

Protect hands with heavy towel or gloves when inserting glass tubing into cork or rubber stopper. Fire polish all raw glass cuts.

Open ampules in fume removal device over tray large enough to hold contents if ampule should break. If contents are volatile, cool before opening.

Acids

Use effective *acid-resistant* fume removal device whenever heating acids or performing reactions which liberate acid fumes. In dilg, always add acid to H_2O unless otherwise directed in method. Keep acids off skin and protect eyes from spattering. If acids are spilled on skin, wash immediately with large amts of H_2O.

51.022 ***Acetic Acid and Acetic Anhydride***

React vigorously or explosively with CrO_3 and other strong oxidizers. Wear face shield and heavy rubber gloves when using.

51.023 ***Chromic and Perchromic Acids***

Can react explosively with Ac_2O, HOAc, EtOAc, isoamyl alcohol, and benzaldehyde. Less hazardous with ethylene glycol, furfural, glycerol, and MeOH. Conduct reactions behind safety barrier. Wear face shield and heavy rubber gloves.

51.024 ***Formic and Performic Acids***

Strong reducing agents; react vigorously or explosively with oxidizing agents. Irritating to skin, forming blisters. Performic acid (formyl hydroperoxide) has detonated for no apparent reason while being poured. Wear face shield and heavy rubber gloves when using.

51.025 ***Hydrofluoric Acid***

Very hazardous with NH_3. It can cause painful sores on skin and is extremely irritating to eyes. Use effective removal device. Wear goggles and acid-resistant gloves.

51.026 ***Nitric Acid***

Reacts vigorously or explosively with aniline, H_2S, flammable solvs, hydrazine, and metal powders (especially Zn, Al, and Mg). Gaseous nitrogen oxides from HNO_3 can cause severe lung damage. Copious fumes are evolved when concd HNO_3 and concd HCl are mixed. Avoid premixing. Use effective fume removal device when fumes are generated. Handle with disposable polyvinyl chloride, not rubber, gloves.

51.027 ***Oxalic Acid***

Forms explosive compd with Ag and Hg. Oxalates are toxic. Avoid skin contact and ingestion.

51.028 ***Perchloric Acid***

Contact with oxidizable or combustible materials or with dehydrating or reducing agents may result in fire or explosion. Persons using this acid should be thoroly familiar with its hazards. Safety practices should include following:

(**a**) Remove spilled $HClO_4$ by immediate and thoro washing with large amts of H_2O.

(**b**) Hoods, ducts, and other devices for removing $HClO_4$ vapor should be made of chem. inert materials and so designed that they can be thoroly washed with H_2O. Exhaust systems should discharge in safe location and fan should be accessible for cleaning.

(**c**) Avoid use of org. chems in hoods or other fume removal devices used for $HClO_4$ digestions.

(**d**) Use goggles, barrier shields, and other devices as necessary for personal protection; use polyvinyl chloride, not rubber, gloves.

(**e**) In wet combustions with $HClO_4$, treat sample first with HNO_3 to destroy easily oxidizable org. matter unless otherwise specified. *Do not evap. to dryness.*

(**f**) Contact of $HClO_4$ soln with strong dehydrating agents such as P_2O_5 or concd H_2SO_4 may result in formation of anhyd. $HClO_4$ which reacts explosively with org. matter and with reducing agents. Exercise special care in performing analyses requiring use of $HClO_4$ with such agents. Extremely sensitive to shock and heat when concn is >72%.

(**g**) Also observe precautions outlined in (1) "Perchloric Acid Solution," Chemical Safety Data Sheet SD-11 (1965), Manufacturing Chemists Association of the US, 1825 Connecticut Ave, NW, Washington, DC 20009; (2) "Applied Inorganic Analysis," W. F. Hillebrand, G. E. F. Lundell, H. A. Bright, and J. I. Hoffman, 2nd ed. (1953), pp. 39–40, John Wiley and Sons, Inc., New York, NY; (3) "Notes on Perchloric Acid and Its Handling in Analytical Work," Analyst **84**, 214–216(1959); (4) "Perchlorates," ACS Monograph No. 146, J. C. Schumacher, ed., Reinhold (1960). *See also* refs at end of this chapter.

51.029 ***Picric Acid***

Highly sensitive to shock when in dry state. In contact with metals and NH_3, it produces picrates which are more sensitive to shock than picric acid. Readily absorbed thru skin and irritating to eyes. Wear heavy rubber gloves and eye protection.

51.030 ***Sulfuric Acid***

Always add H_2SO_4 to H_2O. Wear face shield and heavy rubber gloves to protect against splashes.

51.031 ***Fuming Acids***

Prep. and use with effective fume removal device. Wear acid-resistant gloves and eye protection.

Alkalies

Alkalies can burn skin, eyes, and respiratory tract severely. Wear heavy rubber gloves and face shield to protect against concd alkali liqs. Use effective fume removal device or gas mask to protect respiratory tract against alkali dusts or vapors.

51.032 ***Ammonia***

Extremely caustic liq. and gas. Wear skin, eye, and respiratory protection when handling in anhyd. liq. or gaseous state. NH_3 vapors are flammable. Reacts violently with strong oxidizing agents, halogens, and strong acids.

51.033 ***Ammonium Hydroxide***

Caustic liq. Forms explosive compds with many heavy metals such as Ag, Pb, Zn, and their salts, especially halide salts.

51.034 ***Sodium, Potassium, Lithium, and Calcium Metals***

Violently reactive with H_2O or moisture, CO_2, halogens, strong acids, and chlorinated hydrocarbons. Emit corrosive fumes when burned. Can cause severe burns. Wear skin and eye protection when handling. Use only dry alcohol when preparing Na alcoholate and add metal directly to alcohol, one small piece at a time. Avoid adding metallic Na to reaction thru condenser.

51.035 ***Sodium Peroxide***

Less caustic than Na and K hydroxides but reacts violently with H_2O, org. matter, charcoal, glycerol, Et_2O, or P. Wear skin, eye, and respiratory protection when handling multigram amts.

51.036 ***Calcium Oxide (Burnt Lime)***

Strongly caustic! Reacts violently with H_2O. Protect skin, eyes, and respiratory tract against contact with dust.

51.037 ***Sodium and Potassium Hydroxides***

Extremely caustic. Can cause severe burns. Protect skin and eyes when working with these alkalies as solids or concd solns. Add pellets to H_2O, not vice versa.

51.038 ***Sodium Biphenyl, Sodium Methylate, and Sodium Ethylate***

Less caustic than NaOH but can be injurious. React vigorously with H_2O. Protect skin and eyes when handling.

Organic Solvents

(Do not mix waste solvs.)

51.039 ***Flammable Solvents***

Do not let vapors conc. to flammable level in work area, since it is nearly impossible to eliminate all chance of sparks from static electricity even tho elec. equipment is grounded. Use effective fume removal device to remove these vapors when released.

51.040 ***Toxic Solvents***

Vapors from some volatile solvs are highly toxic (***1–3, 9, 10***). Several of these solvs are readily absorbed thru skin. Use effective fume removal device to remove vapors of these solvs as they are liberated.

Special Chemical Hazards

51.041 ***Pesticides***

Many pesticide chemicals are extremely toxic. These chemicals include org. Cl, carbamate, and org. P insecticides, mercurials, arsenicals, cyanides, nicotine, and other chemicals (***1, 6***). Observe following min. precautions at all times. Consult safety data sheets or labels for addnl information.

(**a**) Do all laboratory sampling, mixing, weighing, etc., under effective fume removal device in area having good forced ventilation of nonrecirculated air, or wear gas mask of proper type. If mask is used, replace cartridges as recommended, since using contaminated mask may be worse than no mask.

(**b**) Keep off skin. Wear clean protective clothing and non-permeable gloves (such as polyethylene gloves) as necessary.

Wash thoroly with soap and water to avoid contaminating food and smoking materials.

(**c**) Label all sample containers with name and approx. content of all pesticides.

(**d**) Have readily available and study information on symptoms of poisoning and first aid treatment for each type of pesticide being handled (***1, 6***).

(**e**) Consult physician about preventive measures and antidotes for use in emergencies when pesticide poisoning is suspected.

(**f**) Follow your organization's procedures when disposing of waste pesticides. The manufacturer can be contacted for advice on disposal problems.

(**g**) Do not enter pesticide *residue* or other laboratories after handling pesticide formulations until protective clothing and gloves have been removed and face and hands thoroly washed with soap and water.

51.042 ***Aniline***

Toxic. Avoid contact with skin and eyes. Use effective fume removal device. Highly toxic when heated to decomposition. Flammable. May react vigorously with oxidizing agents. Ignites in presence of fuming HNO_3. May react violently with O_3.

51.043 ***Acetonitrile***

Toxic. Avoid contact with skin and eyes. Use effective fume removal device. HCN is liberated on contact with acid.

51.044 ***Ammoniacal Silver Nitrate***

Use soon after prepn and do not allow to stand for long periods of time.

51.045 ***Benzene***

Toxic. Highly flammable. Avoid contact with skin. Do not breath vapors. Use effective fume removal device. Decomposes violently in presence of strong oxidizing agents. Reacts violently with Cl. Considered to be tumor producing agent.

51.046 ***Acetone***

Highly flammable. Forms explosive peroxides with oxidizing agents. Use effective fume removal device. Do not mix with $CHCl_3$.

51.047 ***Bromine and Chlorine***

Hazardous with NH_3, H, petroleum gases, turpentine, benzene, and metal powders. Extremely corrosive. Use effective fume removal device. Protect skin against exposure.

51.048 ***Carbon Disulfide***

Extremely flammable with low ignition temp. Toxic. Use effective fume removal device. Can react vigorously to violently with strong oxidizing agents, azides, and Zn. Avoid static electricity.

51.049 ***Carbon Tetrachloride***

Reacts violently with alkali metals. Toxic. Fumes may decompose to phosgene when heated strongly. Use effective fume removal device.

51.050 ***Cyanides***

React with acids to form highly toxic and rapid acting HCN gas. Use only in effective fume removal device. Destroy residues with alk. NaOCl soln.

51.051 ***Cyclohexane***

Highly flammable. Use effective fume removal device. Can react vigorously with strong oxidizing agents.

51.052 ***Di- and Triethylamine***

Flammable. Toxic. Corrosive to skin and eyes. Use effective fume removal device. Can react vigorously with oxidizing materials.

51.053 ***Dimethylformamide***

Toxic. Flammable. Avoid contact with skin and eyes. Use effective fume removal device. Can react vigorously with oxidizing agents, halogenated hydrocarbons, and inorg. nitrates.

51.054 ***Diethyl Ether***

Store protected from light. Extremely flammable. Unstable peroxides can form upon long standing or exposure to sunlight in bottles. Can react explosively when in contact with Cl, O_3, $LiAlH_4$, or strong oxidizing agents. Use effective fume removal device. Avoid static electricity. See also **51.070(b)**.

51.055 ***Ethanol***

Flammable. Use effective fume removal device when heating or evapg.

51.056 ***Chloroform***

Can be harmful if inhaled. Forms phosgene when heated to decomposition. Use effective fume removal device. Can react explosively with Al, Li, Mg, Na, K, disilane, N_2O_4, and NaOH plus MeOH. Considered to be tumor producing agent.

51.057 ***Ethyl Acetate***

Flammable, especially when being evapd. Irritating to eyes and respiratory tract. Use effective fume removal device.

51.058 ***Formaldehyde***

Exposure to high concns may cause skin irritation and inflammation of mucous membranes, eyes, and respiratory tract. Use skin protection and effective fume removal device.

51.059 ***Hydrogen Sulfide***

Hazardous with oxidizing gases, fuming HNO_3, and Na_2O_2. Forms explosive mixts with air. Toxic. Use effective fume removal device.

51.060 ***Hypophosphorus Acid***

Reacts violently with oxidizing agents. On decomposition, emits highly toxic fumes (phosphine) and may explode. Use effective fume removal device.

51.061 ***Hexane***

Highly flammable. Use effective fume removal device.

51.062 ***Isooctane***

Highly flammable. Use effective fume removal device.

51.063 ***Magnesium***

When finely divided, liberates H in contact with H_2O. Burns in air when exposed to flame. Can be explosive in contact with $CHCl_3$ or CH_3Cl.

51.064 ***Magnesium Perchlorate***

Explodes on contact with acids and reducing materials. Use as drying agent on inorg. gases and materials only.

51.065 ***Mercury***

Hazardous in contact with NH_3, halogens, and alkali. Vapors are extremely toxic and cumulative. Regard spills on hot surfaces as extremely hazardous and clean up promptly. Powd S sprinkled over spilled Hg can assist in cleaning up spills. High degree of personal cleanliness is necessary for persons who use Hg. Handle only in locations where any spill can be readily and thoroly cleaned up. When Hg evapn is necessary, use effective fume removal device.

To avoid environmental contamination, dil. liq. remaining in Kjeldahl distn flask to ca 300 mL with H_2O, cool to room temp., and add 50 mL 30% H_2O_2. (If Raney powder method is used, 6 mL is enough.) Warm gently to initiate reaction, let reaction go to completion in warm flask, and sep. pptd HgS. Reserve ppt in closed labeled container for recovery of Hg or disposal appropriate for Hg.

See also **51.079**.

51.066 ***Methanol***

Flammable. Toxic. Avoid contact with eyes. Avoid breathing vapors. Use effective fume removal device. Can react vigorously with NaOH plus $CHCl_3$, and KOH plus $CHCl_3$ or $HClO_4$.

51.067 ***Methyl Cellosolve***

Vapors can be harmful. Use effective fume removal device.

51.068 ***Nitrobenzene and Other Nitroaromatics***

Readily absorbed thru skin. Symptoms of intoxication are sense of well-being and bluish tint on tongue, lips, and fingernails. Wear resistant rubber gloves when handling. Heat or evap. in effective fume removal device.

51.069 ***Oxidizers***

(Perchlorates, peroxides, permanganates, persulfates, perborates, nitrates, chlorates, chlorites, bromates, iodates, concd H_2SO_4, concd HNO_3, CrO_3)

Can react violently with most metal powders, NH_3, and NH_4 salts, P, many finely divided org. compds, flammable liqs, acids, and S. Use exactly as specified in method. Handle in effective fume removal device from behind explosion-resistant barrier. Use face shield.

51.070 ***Peroxides***

(**a**) *Hydrogen peroxide.*—30% strength is hazardous; can cause severe burns. Drying H_2O_2 on org. material such as paper or cloth can lead to spontaneous combustion. Cu, Fe, Cr, other metals, and their salts cause rapid catalytic decomposition of H_2O_2. Hazardous with flammable liqs, aniline, and nitrobenzene. Since it slowly decomposes with evolution of O, provide stored H_2O_2 with vent caps. Wear gloves and eye protection when handling.

(**b**) *Ether peroxides.*—These peroxides form in Et_2O, dioxane, and other ethers during storage. They are explosive and must be destroyed chem. before distn or evapn. Exposure to light influences peroxide formation in ethers. Filtration thru activated alumina is reported to be effective in removing peroxides. Store over Na ribbon to retard peroxide formation.

51.071 ***Phosphotungstic Acid***

Emits highly toxic fumes when heated to decomposition or in strong alkali.

51.072 ***Pyridine***

Toxic. Flammable. Use effective fume removal device. Releases toxic cyanides when heated to decomposition.

51.073 ***Petroleum Ether***

Extremely flammable. Use effective fume removal device. Avoid static electricity.

51.074 ***Pentane***

Extremely flammable. Use effective fume removal device. Avoid static electricity.

51.075 ***Radioactive Chemicals***

Consult NBS Handbook No. 92, "Safe Handling of Radioactive Materials" (available as NCRP Report No. 30 from National Council on Radiation Protection, Publications Dept., 4201 Conn. Ave. NW, Washington, DC 20008) and NCRP Report No. 39 "Basic Radiation Protection Criteria," before handling these materials.

51.076 ***Silver Nitrate***

Powerful oxidizing agent; strongly corrosive. Dust or solid form is hazardous to eyes. Handle as in **51.069**.

51.077 ***Silver Iodate***

Powerful oxidizing agent. Can initiate combustion in contact with org. material (e.g., paper or cloth). Can react vigorously with reducing agents. Handle as in **51.069**.

51.078 ***Arsenic Trioxide***

Toxic. Forms toxic volatile halides in contact with halide acids. Forms volatile, highly toxic arsine when reduced in acid soln. Protect skin and respiratory tract when handling. Use effective fume removal device when arsine or arsenic trihalide is formed.

51.079 ***Mercury Salts***

Mercuric salts are quite toxic and mostly H_2O-sol. Use skin and respiratory protection when dry mercuric salts are to be used. Use skin protection when concd aq. solns of mercuric salts are used. Mercurous salts are generally less toxic than mercuric salts. Use of personal protection is advisable when handling these salts and their concd solns.

See also **51.065**.

51.080 ***Permanganates***

Moderately toxic. Readily sol. in H_2O. Strong oxidizing agent. May form explosive mixt. with H_2SO_4 or $HClO_4$. When using with strong acids to destroy org. matter, perform reaction behind safety barrier.

51.081 ***Sulfur Dioxide***

Toxic gas. Forms H_2SO_3 in contact with moisture. Use effective fume removal device to remove SO_2 vapors released by reaction or from gas cylinder. Avoid contact with skin, eyes, and respiratory tract.

51.082 ***Di- and Trichloroacetic and Trifluoroacetic Acids***

Protein precipitants. Can cause severe burns to skin and respiratory tract. Use rubber gloves, eye protection, and effective fume removal device to remove vapors generated.

51.083 ***Uranyl Acetate***

Highly toxic. Avoid skin contact and breathing dusts.

51.084 ***Toxic Dusts***

Use gloves and goggles to avoid contact with skin and eyes. Use effective fume removal device or other respiratory protection.

51.085 ***Carcinogens***

Regulations of U.S. Department of Labor require special precautions to avoid exposure of persons to carcinogenic chems. Consult 29CFR1910.93c (U.S. Government Printing Office, Washington, DC 20402) for these precautions.

51.086 ***Asbestos***

Dry asbestos fibers are hazardous when inhaled. Wet fibers form a mat which does not constitute a hazard. Transfer dry fibers in hood to container of distd H_2O and store under H_2O until needed, e.g., for prepn of mats in Gooch crucibles. Do not dry asbestos in forced draft oven, only in convection oven. Open oven doors slowly to avoid developing convection currents that will make fibers airborne. Reuse of filtering mats is often possible by washing, drying, and ignition, as appropriate.

REFERENCES

(*1*) Gleason, Gosselin, and Hodge, "Clinical Toxicology of Commercial Products (Home and Farm)," 4th ed. (1976); The Williams & Wilkins Co., 428 E Preston St, Baltimore, MD 21202.

(*2*) American Conference of Governmental Industrial Hygienists, "Threshold Limit Values"; PO Box 1937, Cincinnati, OH 45201.

(*3*) Sax, "Dangerous Properties of Industrial Materials," 5th ed. (1979); Reinhold Publishing Corp., New York, NY 10022.

(*4*) National Fire Protection Association, "Fire Protection Guide on Hazardous Materials," 7th ed. (1978); 470 Atlantic Dr, Boston, MA 02210.

(*5*) C. Marsden, "Solvents Guide" (1963); Wiley-Interscience Publishers, New York, NY 10016.

(*6*) Brown, "Pesticides in Clinical Practice: Identification, Pharmacology and Therapeutics" (1966); Charles C. Thomas Publishers, 301–327 E Lawrence, Springfield, IL 62717.

(*7*) National Institutes of Health, Handbook No. 3, "Chemical and Biological Safety Guide," Bethesda, MD 20014.

(*8*) Ind. Eng. Chem., Anal. Ed. **18,** 52(1946).

(*9*) N. V. Steere, "Handbook of Laboratory Safety" (1971); CRC Press, Inc., 2255 Palm Beach Lakes Blvd, West Palm Beach, FL 33409.

(*10*) Journal of the American Society of Safety Engineers **7,** Feb. 1964.

52. Reference Tables

SURPLUS TABLES

w Element for which known variations in isotopic composition in normal terrestrial material prevent a more precise atomic weight being given; $A_r(E)$ values should be applicable to any "normal" material.

x Element for which geological specimens are known in which the element has an anomalous isotopic composition, such that the difference between the atomic weight of the element in such specimens and that given in the Table may exceed considerably the implied uncertainty.

y Element for which substantial variations in A_r from the value given can occur in commercially available material because of inadvertent or undisclosed change of isotopic composition.

z Element for which the value of A_r is that of the radioisotope of longest half-life.

52.001 Table of atomic weights 1977; from Commission on Atomic Weights, International Union of Pure and Applied Chemistry

Scaled to the relative atomic mass, $A_r(^{12}C) = 12$

The atomic weights of many elements are not invariant but depend on the origin and treatment of the material. The footnotes to this Table elaborate the types of variation to be expected for individual elements. The values of $A_r(E)$ given here apply to elements as they exist naturally on earth and to certain artificial elements. When used with due regard to the footnotes, they are considered reliable to ±1 in the last digit or ±3 when followed by an asterisk*. Values in parentheses are used for certain radioactive elements whose atomic weights cannot be quoted precisely without knowledge of the origin of the elements; the value given is the atomic mass number of the isotope of that element of longest known half life.

Name	Symbol	Atomic Number	Atomic Weight	Footnotes	Name	Symbol	Atomic Number	Atomic Weight	Footnotes
Actinium	Ac	89	227.0278	z	Mercury	Hg	80	200.59*	
Aluminum	Al	13	26.98154		Molybdenum	Mo	42	95.94	
Americium	Am	95	(243)		Neodymium	Nd	60	144.24*	x
Antimony	Sb	51	121.75*		Neon	Ne	10	20.179*	y
Argon	Ar	18	39.948*	w,x	Neptunium	Np	93	237.0482	z
Arsenic	As	33	74.9216		Nickel	Ni	28	58.70	
Astatine	At	85	(210)		Niobium	Nb	41	92.9064	
Barium	Ba	56	137.33	x	Nitrogen	N	7	14.0067	
Berkelium	Bk	97	(247)		Nobelium	No	102	(259)	
Beryllium	Be	4	9.01218		Osmium	Os	76	190.2	x
Bismuth	Bi	83	208.9804		Oxygen	O	8	15.9994*	w
Boron	B	5	10.81	w,y	Palladium	Pd	46	106.4	x
Bromine	Br	35	79.904		Phosphorus	P	15	30.97376	
Cadmium	Cd	48	112.41	x	Platinum	Pt	78	195.09*	
Calcium	Ca	20	40.08	x	Plutonium	Pu	94	(244)	
Californium	Cf	98	(251)		Polonium	Po	84	(209)	
Carbon	C	6	12.011	w	Potassium	K	19	39.0983*	
Cerium	Ce	58	140.12	x	Praseodymium	Pr	59	140.9077	
Cesium	Cs	55	132.9054		Promethium	Pm	61	(145)	
Chlorine	Cl	17	35.453		Protactinium	Pa	91	231.0359	z
Chromium	Cr	24	51.996		Radium	Ra	88	226.0254	x,z
Cobalt	Co	27	58.9332		Radon	Rn	86	(222)	
Copper	Cu	29	63.546*	w	Rhenium	Re	75	186.207	
Curium	Cm	96	(247)		Rhodium	Rh	45	102.9055	
Dysprosium	Dy	66	162.50*		Rubidium	Rb	37	85.4678*	x
Einsteinium	Es	99	(252)		Ruthenium	Ru	44	101.07*	x
Erbium	Er	68	167.26*		Samarium	Sm	62	150.4	x
Europium	Eu	63	151.96	x	Scandium	Sc	21	44.9559	
Fermium	Fm	100	(257)		Selenium	Se	34	78.96*	
Fluorine	F	9	18.998403		Silicon	Si	14	28.0855*	
Francium	Fr	87	(223)		Silver	Ag	47	107.868	x
Gadolinium	Gd	64	157.25*	x	Sodium	Na	11	22.98977	
Gallium	Ga	31	69.72		Strontium	Sr	38	87.62	x
Germanium	Ge	32	72.59*		Sulfur	S	16	32.06	w
Gold	Au	79	196.9665		Tantalum	Ta	73	180.9479*	
Hafnium	Hf	72	178.49*		Technetium	Tc	43	(98)	
Helium	He	2	4.00260	x	Tellurium	Te	52	127.60*	x
Holmium	Ho	67	164.9304		Terbium	Tb	65	158.9254	
Hydrogen	H	1	1.0079	w	Thallium	Tl	81	204.37*	
Indium	In	49	114.82	x	Thorium	Th	90	232.0381	x,z
Iodine	I	53	126.9045		Thulium	Tm	69	168.9342	
Iridium	Ir	77	192.22*		Tin	Sn	50	118.69*	
Iron	Fe	26	55.847*		Titanium	Ti	22	47.90*	
Krypton	Kr	36	83.80	x,y	Tungsten (Wolfram)	W	74	183.85*	
Lanthanum	La	57	138.9055*	x	Uranium	U	92	238.029	x,y
Lawrencium	Lr	103	(260)		Vanadium	V	23	50.9415*	
Lead	Pb	82	207.2	w,x	Xenon	Xe	54	131.30	x,y
Lithium	Li	3	6.941*	w,x,y	Ytterbium	Yb	70	173.04*	
Lutetium	Lu	71	174.967*		Yttrium	Y	39	88.9059	
Magnesium	Mg	12	24.305	x	Zinc	Zn	30	65.38	
Manganese	Mn	25	54.9380		Zirconium	Zr	40	91.22	x
Mendelevium	Md	101	(258)						

(*See* preceeding page for footnotes.)

52.002 Various strength solutions of the common acids, alkalies, and alcohol[a]

(a) *Ammonia solns:* Specification requires $\geq$28–$\leq$30% NH_3 by wt. Sp gr of 28.0% NH_3 soln = 0.9 at 15°. Mix and dil. to 1 L.

NH_3 Strength Desired	Reagent NH_3 Required	
g/L	g	ml
5	17.86	19.8
10	35.71	39.7
15	53.57	59.5
20	71.43	79.4
25	89.29	99.2
50	178.57	198.4
75	267.86	297.6
100	357.14	396.8
150	535.71	595.2
200	714.29	793.7

(b) *Sodium hydroxide solns:* Specification requires $\geq$97% NaOH in sticks or pellets of caustic soda. Dissolve and dil. to 1 L.

NaOH Strength Desired	NaOH Required	
g/L	g	
12.5	12.89	For crude fiber
30	30.93	
40	41.24	1*N* soln
50	51.55	
75	77.32	
100	103.09	
150	154.64	
200	206.19	
250	257.73	
300	309.28	

(c) *Hydrochloric acid solns:* Specification requires $\geq$36.5–$\leq$38.0% HCl by wt. Sp gr of 37.2% HCl soln = 1.19 at 15°. Mix with H_2O and dil. to 1 L.

HCl Strength Desired	HCl Required		
g/L	g	ml	
5	13.44	11.29	
10	26.88	22.59	
15	40.32	33.88	
20	53.77	45.18	
36.46	98.01	82.36	1*N* soln
50	134.41	112.95	
100	268.82	225.90	
150	403.23	338.85	
200	537.63	451.79	
222.6	598.39	502.85	Constant boiling
278.4	748.39	628.90	Sp gr 1.125
300	806.45	677.69	

(d) *Nitric acid solns:* Specification requires $\geq$69.0–$\leq$71.0% HNO_3 by wt. Sp gr of 70.4% HNO_3 soln = 1.42 at 15°. 1 ml concd HNO_3 contains ca 1.00 g HNO_3. Mix with H_2O and dil. to 1 L.

HNO_3 Strength Desired	HNO_3 Required		
g/L	g	ml	
5	7.10	5.0	
10	14.20	10.0	
20	28.41	20.0	
30	42.61	30.0	
40	56.82	40.0	
50	71.02	50.0	
63	89.49	63.0	1*N* soln
70	99.43	70.0	
100	142.05	100.0	
150	213.07	150.0	
200	284.09	200.1	
300	426.14	300.1	

(e) *Sulfuric acid solns:* Specification requires $\geq$95.0–$\leq$98.0% H_2SO_4 by wt. Sp gr of 96.0% soln = 1.84 at 15°. Pour acid into excess of H_2O and dil. to 1 L.

H_2SO_4 Strength Desired	H_2SO_4 Required		
g/L	g	ml	
5	5.21	2.8	
12.5	13.02	7.1	For crude fiber
20	20.83	11.3	
30	31.25	17.0	
40	41.67	22.6	
49	51.04	27.7	1*N* soln
100	104.17	56.6	
150	156.25	84.9	
250	260.42	141.5	
300	312.50	169.8	
400	416.67	226.5	

(f) *Alcoholic solns:*[b] Specification requires 95% C_2H_5OH by vol. Sp gr = 0.810 at 25°. Mix and dil. to 1 L.

Alcohol Strength Desired	Alcohol Required	
ml/L	g	ml
50	42.63	52.6
100	85.26	105.3
150	127.89	157.9
200	170.52	210.5
250	213.16	263.2
300	255.78	315.9
400	341.04	421.1
500	426.32 (proof)	526.3
700	596.84	736.8

[a] Prepd by G. C. Spencer and H. J. Fisher, 1935 and updated by W. D. Hubbard, 1970.

[b] Alcohol of any desired strength may be obtained by taking number of ml 95% alcohol equiv. to desired strength and dilg soln to 95 ml; e.g., to obtain soln of 70% alcohol, take 70 ml 95% alcohol and dil. to 95 ml.

52.003 Percentages by volume at 15.56°C (60°F) of ethyl alcohol corresponding to apparent specific gravity at various temperatures[a]

Apparent Specific Gravity	15.56/15.56	20/20	22/22	24/24	25/25	26/26	28/28	30/30	32/32	34/34	35/35	36/36
1.0000	0.00	0.00	0.00	0.00	0.00	0.00	0.00	0.00	0.00	0.00	0.00	0.00
0.9999	.07	.07	.07	.07	.07	.07	.07	.07	.07	.07	.07	.07
98	.13	.13	.13	.13	.13	.13	.13	.13	.13	.13	.13	.13
97	.20	.20	.20	.20	.20	.20	.20	.20	.20	.20	.20	.20
96	.27	.26	.26	.26	.26	.26	.26	.26	.26	.26	.26	.26
95	.33	.33	.33	.33	.33	.33	.33	.33	.33	.33	.33	.33
94	.40	.40	.40	.40	.40	.40	.40	.40	.40	.40	.40	.40
93	.47	.46	.46	.46	.46	.46	.46	.46	.46	.46	.46	.46
92	.53	.53	.53	.53	.53	.53	.53	.53	.53	.53	.53	.53
91	.60	.60	.60	.60	.60	.60	.60	.60	.60	.60	.60	.60
90	.67	.66	.66	.66	.66	.66	.66	.66	.66	.66	.66	.66
89	.73	.73	.73	.73	.73	.73	.73	.73	.73	.73	.73	.73
88	.80	.80	.80	.80	.80	.80	.79	.79	.79	.79	.79	.79
87	.87	.87	.87	.87	.87	.87	.86	.86	.86	.86	.86	.86
86	.93	.93	.93	.93	.93	.93	.93	.93	.93	.93	.93	.93
85	1.00	1.00	1.00	1.00	1.00	1.00	.99	.99	.99	.99	.99	.99
84	.07	.07	.07	.07	.07	.07	1.06	1.06	1.06	1.06	1.06	1.06
83	.14	.14	.14	.13	.13	.13	.13	.13	.13	.13	.13	.13
82	.20	.20	.20	.20	.20	.20	.20	.19	.19	.19	.19	.19
81	.27	.27	.27	.27	.27	.27	.26	.26	.26	.26	.26	.26
80	.34	.34	.34	.34	.34	.33	.33	.32	.32	.32	.32	.32
79	.41	.41	.41	.40	.40	.40	.40	.39	.39	.39	.39	.39
78	.48	.48	.48	.47	.47	.47	.47	.46	.46	.46	.46	.46
77	.54	.54	.54	.54	.54	.53	.53	.53	.53	.53	.52	.52
76	.61	.61	.61	.60	.60	.60	.60	.59	.59	.59	.59	.59
75	.68	.68	.68	.67	.67	.67	.67	.66	.66	.66	.66	.66
74	.75	.75	.75	.74	.74	.73	.73	.73	.73	.72	.72	.72
73	.82	.81	.81	.81	.81	.80	.80	.80	.80	.79	.79	.79
72	.88	.88	.88	.87	.87	.87	.86	.86	.86	.85	.85	.85
71	.95	.95	.95	.94	.94	.94	.93	.93	.93	.92	.92	.92
70	2.02	2.02	2.02	2.01	2.01	2.01	2.00	2.00	2.00	.99	.99	.99
69	.09	.09	.09	.08	.08	.08	.07	.07	.06	2.05	2.05	2.05
68	.16	.15	.15	.14	.14	.14	.14	.14	.13	.12	.12	.12
67	.23	.22	.22	.21	.21	.21	.20	.20	.20	.19	.19	.19
66	.30	.29	.29	.28	.28	.28	.27	.27	.27	.26	.26	.26
65	.37	.36	.36	.35	.35	.35	.34	.34	.33	.32	.32	.32
64	.43	.43	.43	.42	.42	.42	.41	.41	.40	.39	.39	.39
63	.50	.50	.50	.49	.49	.49	.48	.48	.47	.46	.46	.46
62	.57	.57	.57	.56	.56	.56	.55	.54	.54	.53	.53	.53
61	.64	.64	.64	.63	.63	.63	.62	.61	.60	.60	.59	.59
60	.71	.70	.70	.70	.70	.70	.69	.68	.67	.67	.66	.66
59	.78	.77	.77	.77	.77	.77	.76	.75	.74	.74	.73	.73
58	.85	.84	.84	.83	.83	.83	.82	.82	.81	.81	.80	.80
57	.92	.91	.91	.90	.90	.90	.89	.88	.87	.87	.86	.86
56	.99	.98	.98	.97	.97	.97	.96	.95	.94	.94	.93	.93
55	3.06	3.05	3.05	3.04	3.04	3.04	3.03	3.02	3.01	3.01	3.00	3.00
54	.13	.12	.12	.11	.11	.11	.10	.09	.08	.08	.07	.07
53	.20	.19	.19	.18	.18	.18	.17	.16	.15	.15	.14	.14
52	.27	.26	.26	.25	.25	.25	.24	.23	.22	.22	.21	.21
51	.34	.33	.33	.32	.32	.32	.31	.30	.29	.28	.27	.27
50	.41	.40	.40	.39	.39	.39	.38	.37	.36	.35	.34	.34
49	.49	.47	.47	.46	.46	.46	.45	.44	.43	.42	.41	.41
48	.56	.54	.54	.53	.53	.53	.52	.51	.50	.49	.48	.48
47	.63	.61	.61	.60	.60	.60	.59	.58	.57	.56	.55	.55
46	.70	.68	.68	.67	.67	.67	.66	.65	.64	.63	.62	.62
45	.77	.76	.75	.74	.74	.74	.73	.72	.70	.69	.68	.68
44	.84	.83	.82	.81	.81	.81	.79	.78	.77	.76	.75	.75
43	.91	.90	.89	.88	.88	.88	.86	.85	.84	.83	.82	.82
42	.99	.97	.96	.95	.95	.95	.93	.92	.91	.90	.89	.89
41	4.06	4.04	4.03	4.02	4.02	4.02	4.00	.99	.98	.97	.96	.96
40	.13	.11	.10	.10	.09	.09	.07	4.06	4.05	4.04	4.03	4.03
39	.20	.18	.17	.17	.16	.16	.14	.13	.12	.11	.10	.10
38	.28	.26	.25	.25	.24	.23	.21	.20	.19	.18	.17	.17
37	.35	.33	.32	.32	.31	.30	.28	.27	.26	.25	.24	.24
36	.42	.40	.39	.39	.38	.37	.36	.35	.33	.32	.31	.30
35	.50	.48	.47	.46	.45	.44	.43	.42	.40	.39	.38	.37
34	.57	.55	.54	.53	.52	.51	.50	.49	.47	.46	.45	.44
33	.64	.62	.61	.60	.59	.58	.57	.56	.54	.53	.52	.51
32	.71	.69	.68	.67	.66	.65	.64	.63	.61	.60	.59	.58
31	.79	.77	.76	.75	.74	.73	.72	.70	.68	.67	.66	.65

(Continued)

[a] Compiled at National Bureau of Standards. Table is based on data published in *Bull. Natl. Bur. Std.* 9(3) (1913), (Sci. Paper No. 197).

52.003 Percentages by volume at 15.56°C (60°F) of ethyl alcohol corresponding to apparent specific gravity at various temperatures[a]—*Continued.*

Apparent Specific Gravity	15.56/15.56	20/20	22/22	24/24	25/25	26/26	28/28	30/30	32/32	34/34	35/35	36/36
0.9930	4.86	4.84	4.83	4.82	4.81	4.80	4.79	4.77	4.75	4.74	4.73	4.72
29	.93	.91	.90	.89	.88	.87	.86	.84	.82	.81	.80	.79
28	5.01	.98	.97	.96	.95	.94	.93	.91	.89	.88	.87	.86
27	.08	5.06	5.04	5.03	5.02	5.01	5.00	.98	.96	.95	.94	.93
26	.16	.13	.12	.11	.10	.09	.07	5.05	5.03	5.02	5.01	5.00
25	.23	.21	.19	.18	.17	.16	.14	.12	.10	.09	.08	.07
24	.31	.28	.26	.25	.24	.23	.21	.20	.18	.16	.15	.14
23	.39	.36	.34	.33	.32	.31	.29	.27	.25	.23	.22	.21
22	.46	.43	.41	.40	.39	.38	.36	.34	.32	.30	.29	.28
21	.54	.51	.49	.48	.47	.46	.44	.42	.40	.38	.37	.36
20	.61	.58	.56	.55	.54	.53	.51	.49	.47	.45	.44	.43
19	.69	.66	.64	.62	.61	.60	.58	.56	.54	.52	.51	.50
18	.77	.73	.71	.70	.69	.68	.66	.64	.62	.59	.58	.57
17	.84	.81	.79	.77	.76	.75	.73	.71	.69	.66	.65	.64
16	.92	.88	.86	.85	.84	.83	.80	.78	.76	.74	.73	.72
15	.99	.96	.94	.92	.91	.90	.87	.85	.83	.81	.80	.79
14	6.07	6.03	6.01	6.00	.99	.98	.95	.93	.91	.88	.87	.86
13	.15	.11	.09	.07	6.06	6.05	6.02	6.00	.98	.95	.94	.93
12	.23	.18	.16	.15	.14	.13	.10	.08	6.05	6.02	6.01	6.00
11	.30	.26	.24	.22	.21	.20	.17	.15	.12	.10	.09	.08
10	.38	.34	.32	.30	.29	.28	.25	.23	.20	.17	.16	.15
09	.46	.41	.39	.37	.36	.35	.32	.30	.28	.25	.24	.23
08	.54	.49	.47	.45	.44	.43	.40	.38	.35	.32	.31	.30
07	.62	.57	.55	.53	.52	.51	.48	.45	.42	.39	.38	.37
06	.70	.65	.63	.60	.59	.58	.55	.53	.50	.47	.46	.45
05	.77	.73	.71	.68	.67	.66	.63	.60	.57	.54	.53	.52
04	.85	.80	.78	.75	.74	.73	.70	.68	.65	.62	.60	.59
03	.93	.88	.86	.83	.82	.81	.78	.75	.72	.69	.68	.67
02	7.01	.96	.93	.90	.89	.88	.85	.83	.80	.77	.75	.74
01	.09	7.04	7.01	.98	.97	.95	.92	.90	.87	.84	.82	.81
00	.17	.12	.09	7.06	7.05	7.03	7.00	.98	.94	.91	.90	.88
0.9899	.25	.19	.16	.13	.12	.10	.07	7.05	7.01	.98	.97	.95
98	.33	.27	.24	.21	.20	.18	.15	.13	.09	7.06	7.04	7.02
97	.41	.35	.32	.29	.28	.26	.23	.21	.17	.14	.12	.10
96	.50	.43	.40	.37	.36	.34	.31	.28	.24	.21	.19	.17
95	.58	.51	.48	.45	.44	.42	.39	.36	.32	.29	.27	.25
94	.66	.59	.56	.53	.52	.50	.47	.44	.40	.36	.34	.32
93	.74	.67	.64	.60	.59	.57	.54	.51	.47	.44	.42	.40
92	.82	.75	.72	.68	.67	.65	.62	.59	.55	.51	.49	.47
91	.90	.82	.79	.76	.75	.73	.70	.66	.62	.59	.57	.55
90	.98	.90	.87	.84	.83	.81	.78	.74	.70	.66	.64	.62
89	8.07	.98	.95	.92	.91	.89	.86	.82	.78	.74	.72	.70
88	.15	8.06	8.03	8.00	.98	.96	.93	.89	.85	.81	.79	.77
87	.23	.15	.11	.08	8.06	8.04	8.01	.97	.93	.89	.87	.85
86	.32	.23	.19	.16	.14	.12	.09	8.05	8.01	.96	.94	.92
85	.40	.31	.27	.24	.22	.20	.16	.12	.08	8.04	8.02	8.00
84	.48	.39	.35	.32	.30	.28	.24	.20	.16	.11	.09	.07
83	.57	.47	.43	.40	.38	.36	.32	.27	.23	.19	.17	.15
82	.65	.55	.51	.48	.46	.44	.40	.35	.31	.26	.24	.22
81	.73	.63	.59	.56	.54	.52	.48	.43	.39	.34	.32	.30
80	.82	.71	.67	.63	.61	.59	.55	.50	.46	.41	.39	.37
79	.90	.79	.75	.71	.69	.67	.63	.58	.54	.49	.47	.45
78	.98	.88	.84	.79	.77	.75	.71	.66	.61	.56	.54	.52
77	9.07	.96	.92	.87	.85	.83	.78	.73	.69	.64	.62	.60
76	.15	9.04	9.00	.95	.93	.91	.86	.81	.76	.71	.69	.67
75	.24	.13	.08	9.03	9.01	.99	.94	.89	.84	.79	.77	.75
74	.32	.21	.16	.11	.09	9.07	9.02	.96	.91	.86	.84	.82
73	.40	.29	.24	.19	.17	.15	.10	9.04	.99	.94	.92	.90
72	.49	.38	.33	.27	.25	.23	.18	.12	9.07	9.02	.99	.97
71	.57	.46	.41	.35	.33	.31	.26	.20	.15	.10	9.07	9.05
70	.66	.54	.49	.43	.41	.38	.33	.27	.22	.17	.14	.12
69	.74	.62	.57	.51	.49	.46	.41	.35	.30	.25	.22	.19
68	.82	.70	.65	.59	.57	.54	.49	.43	.37	.32	.29	.26
67	.91	.79	.74	.68	.65	.62	.57	.51	.45	.40	.37	.34
66	.99	.87	.82	.76	.73	.70	.65	.59	.53	.47	.44	.41
65	10.08	.95	.90	.84	.81	.78	.72	.66	.60	.54	.51	.48
64	.16	10.03	.98	.92	.89	.86	.80	.74	.68	.62	.59	.56
63	.25	.11	10.06	10.00	.97	.94	.88	.82	.76	.69	.66	.63
62	.33	.20	.14	.08	10.05	10.02	.96	.90	.84	.77	.74	.71
61	.42	.28	.22	.16	.13	.10	10.04	.98	.91	.84	.81	.78

(Continued)

52.003 Percentages by volume at 15.56°C (60°F) of ethyl alcohol corresponding to apparent specific gravity at various temperatures[a]—*Continued.*

Apparent Specific Gravity	15.56/15.56	20/20	22/22	24/24	25/25	26/26	28/28	30/30	32/32	34/34	35/35	36/36
0.9860	10.50	10.36	10.30	10.24	10.21	10.18	10.11	10.05	9.99	9.92	9.89	9.86
59	.59	.44	.38	.32	.29	.26	.19	.13	10.06	.99	.96	.93
58	.68	.53	.47	.40	.37	.34	.27	.21	.14	10.07	10.04	10.00
57	.76	.61	.55	.48	.44	.41	.34	.28	.21	.14	.11	.07
56	.85	.69	.63	.56	.52	.49	.42	.36	.29	.22	.19	.15
55	.93	.78	.71	.64	.60	.57	.50	.44	.37	.30	.26	.23
54	11.02	.86	.79	.72	.68	.65	.58	.52	.45	.38	.34	.31
53	.11	.94	.87	.80	.76	.73	.66	.59	.52	.45	.41	.38
52	.19	11.03	.96	.88	.84	.81	.74	.67	.60	.53	.49	.45
51	.28	.11	11.04	.96	.92	.89	.82	.75	.67	.60	.56	.52
50	.37	.19	.12	11.04	11.00	.96	.89	.82	.74	.67	.63	.59
49	.46	.28	.20	.12	.08	11.04	.97	.90	.82	.75	.71	.67
48	.54	.36	.28	.20	.16	.12	11.05	.98	.90	.82	.78	.74
47	.63	.45	.36	.28	.24	.20	.13	11.05	.97	.90	.86	.82
46	.72	.53	.45	.37	.33	.29	.21	.13	11.05	.97	.93	.89
45	.81	.61	.53	.45	.41	.37	.29	.21	.13	11.05	11.01	.97
44	.89	.70	.62	.53	.49	.45	.37	.29	.21	.12	.08	11.04
43	.98	.78	.70	.61	.57	.53	.44	.36	.28	.20	.16	.12
42	12.07	.87	.78	.69	.65	.61	.52	.44	.36	.27	.23	.19
41	.16	.95	.86	.78	.73	.69	.60	.52	.44	.35	.31	.27
40	.25	12.04	.95	.86	.81	.77	.68	.60	.51	.42	.38	.34
39	.34	.12	12.03	.94	.89	.85	.76	.67	.58	.50	.46	.42
38	.43	.21	.12	12.03	.98	.93	.84	.75	.66	.57	.53	.49
37	.52	.29	.20	.11	12.06	12.01	.92	.83	.74	.65	.61	.57
36	.61	.38	.28	.19	.14	.09	12.00	.91	.82	.73	.68	.64
35	.70	.47	.37	.27	.22	.17	.07	.98	.89	.80	.76	.72
34	.79	.55	.45	.35	.30	.25	.15	12.06	.97	.88	.83	.79
33	.88	.64	.54	.44	.39	.34	.24	.14	12.05	.96	.91	.86
32	.97	.73	.63	.52	.47	.42	.32	.22	.12	12.03	.98	.93
31	13.06	.81	.71	.60	.55	.50	.40	.30	.20	.11	12.06	12.01
30	.16	.90	.79	.68	.63	.58	.48	.38	.28	.19	.14	.09
29	.25	.99	.88	.77	.71	.66	.56	.46	.36	.26	.21	.16
28	.34	13.07	.96	.85	.80	.74	.64	.54	.44	.34	.29	.24
27	.43	.16	13.05	.93	.88	.82	.72	.62	.52	.42	.37	.32
26	.52	.25	.13	13.01	.96	.90	.80	.70	.59	.49	.44	.39
25	.61	.34	.22	.10	13.04	.99	.88	.78	.67	.57	.52	.47
24	.71	.43	.31	.19	.13	13.08	.97	.86	.75	.65	.60	.55
23	.80	.51	.39	.27	.21	.16	13.05	.94	.83	.72	.67	.62
22	.89	.60	.47	.35	.29	.24	.13	13.02	.91	.80	.75	.70
21	.98	.68	.56	.44	.38	.33	.22	.10	.99	.88	.82	.77
20	14.08	.77	.64	.52	.46	.40	.29	.18	13.06	.95	.90	.85
19	.17	.86	.73	.61	.55	.49	.37	.26	.15	13.04	.98	.93
18	.26	.95	.82	.69	.63	.57	.45	.34	.22	.11	13.05	13.00
17	.36	14.04	.91	.78	.72	.66	.54	.42	.30	.19	.13	.08
16	.45	.13	14.00	.87	.80	.74	.62	.50	.38	.27	.21	.16
15	.55	.22	.08	.95	.88	.82	.70	.58	.46	.34	.28	.23
14	.64	.30	.17	14.04	.97	.91	.78	.66	.54	.42	.36	.30
13	.74	.39	.25	.12	14.05	.99	.86	.74	.62	.50	.44	.38
12	.83	.48	.34	.20	.13	14.07	.94	.82	.70	.58	.52	.46
11	.92	.57	.43	.29	.22	.16	14.03	.90	.77	.65	.59	.53
10	15.02	.66	.51	.37	.30	.24	.11	.98	.85	.73	.67	.61
09	.11	.75	.60	.46	.39	.32	.19	14.06	.93	.81	.75	.69
08	.21	.84	.69	.54	.47	.40	.27	.14	14.01	.88	.82	.76
07	.30	.93	.77	.62	.55	.48	.35	.22	.09	.96	.90	.84
06	.40	15.02	.86	.71	.64	.57	.43	.30	.17	14.04	.98	.92
05	.49	.11	.95	.79	.72	.65	.51	.38	.25	.12	14.05	.99
04	.58	.20	15.04	.88	.81	.74	.60	.46	.33	.20	.13	14.07
03	.67	.28	.12	.96	.89	.82	.68	.54	.41	.28	.21	.15
02	.77	.37	.21	15.05	.97	.90	.76	.62	.49	.36	.29	.23
01	.87	.46	.30	.14	15.06	.99	.84	.70	.56	.43	.36	.30
00	.96	.55	.39	.23	.15	15.07	.92	.78	.64	.51	.44	.38
0.9799	16.06	.64	.48	.32	.24	.16	15.01	.86	.72	.59	.52	.46
98	.15	.73	.46	.40	.32	.24	.09	.94	.80	.67	.60	.54
97	.25	.82	.55	.49	.41	.33	.17	15.02	.88	.74	.67	.61
96	.35	.91	.64	.57	.49	.41	.26	.11	.96	.82	.75	.68
95	.44	16.00	.83	.66	.58	.50	.34	.19	15.04	.90	.83	.76
94	.54	.10	.92	.75	.66	.59	.43	.27	.12	.98	.91	.84
93	.63	.19	16.01	.84	.75	.67	.51	.35	.20	15.05	.98	.91
92	.73	.28	.10	.93	.84	.76	.59	.43	.28	.13	15.06	.99
91	.83	.37	.19	16.01	.92	.84	.67	.51	.36	.21	.14	15.07

(Continued)

52.003 Percentages by volume at 15.56°C (60°F) of ethyl alcohol corresponding to apparent specific gravity at various temperatures[a]—*Continued.*

Apparent Specific Gravity	15.56/15.56	20/20	22/22	24/24	25/25	26/26	28/28	30/30	32/32	34/34	35/35	36/36
0.9790	16.92	16.46	16.27	16.09	16.00	15.92	15.75	15.59	15.44	15.29	15.22	15.15
89	17.02	.55	.26	.18	.09	16.01	.84	.67	.52	.37	.30	.23
88	.12	.64	.45	.27	.18	.10	.93	.76	.61	.45	.38	.31
87	.22	.73	.54	.36	.27	.18	16.01	.84	.68	.52	.45	.38
86	.32	.83	.63	.44	.35	.26	.09	.92	.76	.60	.53	.46
85	.42	.92	.72	.53	.44	.35	.17	16.00	.84	.68	.61	.53
84	.51	17.01	.81	.62	.53	.44	.26	.08	.92	.76	.69	.61
83	.61	.10	.90	.70	.61	.52	.34	.17	.10	.84	.77	.69
82	.71	.20	.99	.79	.70	.61	.43	.25	16.08	.92	.84	.76
81	.81	.29	17.08	.88	.78	.69	.51	.33	.16	16.00	.92	.84
80	.91	.38	.17	.97	.87	.78	.59	.41	.24	.08	16.00	.92
79	18.01	.47	.26	17.06	.96	.87	.68	.50	.33	.16	.08	16.00
78	.11	.57	.35	.14	17.04	.95	.76	.58	.41	.24	.16	.08
77	.21	.66	.44	.23	.13	17.04	.85	.66	.49	.32	.24	.16
76	.31	.75	.53	.32	.22	.12	.93	.74	.57	.40	.32	.24
75	.41	.84	.62	.40	.30	.20	17.01	.83	.65	.48	.40	.32
74	.51	.94	.72	.50	.39	.29	.10	.91	.73	.56	.48	.40
73	.61	18.03	.81	.59	.48	.38	.18	.99	.81	.64	.56	.48
72	.71	.12	.90	.68	.57	.47	.27	17.07	.89	.72	.63	.55
71	.81	.22	.99	.76	.65	.55	.35	.16	.97	.80	.71	.63
70	.91	.31	18.08	.85	.74	.63	.43	.24	17.05	.88	.79	.71
69	19.01	.40	.16	.94	.83	.72	.52	.32	.14	.96	.87	.79
68	.11	.50	.25	18.02	.91	.80	.60	.40	.22	17.04	.95	.86
67	.21	.59	.34	.11	18.00	.89	.69	.49	.30	.12	17.03	.94
66	.32	.69	.44	.20	.09	.98	.78	.57	.38	.20	.11	17.02
65	.42	.78	.53	.29	.18	18.07	.86	.65	.46	.28	.19	.10
64	.52	.88	.63	.38	.27	.16	.95	.74	.55	.36	.27	.17
63	.62	.97	.71	.47	.35	.24	18.03	.82	.62	.43	.35	.25
62	.72	19.07	.81	.56	.44	.33	.11	.90	.70	.51	.43	.33
61	.83	.16	.80	.65	.53	.42	.20	.98	.78	.59	.50	.41
60	.93	.26	.99	.74	.62	.50	.28	18.07	.87	.67	.58	.49
59	20.03	.35	19.08	.83	.71	.60	.37	.15	.95	.75	.66	.56
58	.13	.45	.18	.92	.80	.69	.46	.23	18.03	.83	.74	.64
57	.23	.54	.27	19.01	.88	.77	.54	.32	.11	.91	.82	.72
56	.33	.64	.36	.10	.97	.86	.62	.40	.19	.99	.90	.80
55	.43	.73	.45	.19	19.06	.94	.70	.48	.27	18.07	.98	.88
54	.53	.83	.55	.28	.15	19.03	.79	.57	.36	.15	18.06	.96
53	.63	.92	.64	.37	.24	.12	.88	.65	.44	.23	.13	18.04
52	.73	20.02	.73	.46	.33	.21	.96	.73	.52	.31	.21	.12
51	.83	.11	.82	.55	.42	.30	19.05	.82	.60	.39	.29	.19
50	.93	.20	.91	.64	.50	.38	.13	.90	.68	.47	.37	.27
49	21.03	.30	20.01	.73	.59	.47	.22	.98	.76	.55	.45	.35
48	.13	.39	.10	.82	.68	.56	.31	19.07	.85	.64	.53	.43
47	.23	.48	.19	.91	.77	.65	.39	.15	.93	.72	.61	.51
46	.33	.58	.28	20.00	.86	.74	.48	.24	19.01	.80	.69	.59
45	.43	.67	.37	.09	.95	.82	.56	.32	.09	.88	.77	.67
44	.52	.76	.46	.17	20.03	.90	.64	.40	.17	.96	.85	.75
43	.62	.86	.55	.26	.12	.99	.73	.49	.26	19.04	.93	.83
42	.72	.95	.64	.35	.21	20.08	.82	.57	.34	.12	19.01	.91
41	.82	21.04	.73	.44	.30	.17	.91	.66	.42	.20	.09	.98
40	.92	.14	.82	.53	.38	.25	.99	.74	.50	.28	.17	19.06
39	22.02	.23	.91	.62	.47	.34	20.07	.82	.58	.35	.24	.23
38	.12	.32	21.00	.71	.56	.43	.16	.90	.66	.43	.32	.31
37	.22	.41	.09	.79	.64	.51	.24	.98	.74	.51	.40	.29
36	.31	.50	.18	.88	.73	.59	.32	20.06	.82	.59	.48	.37
35	.41	.60	.27	.97	.82	.68	.41	.15	.90	.67	.56	.45
34	.51	.69	.36	21.05	.90	.77	.50	.24	.99	.75	.64	.53
33	.61	.78	.45	.14	.99	.85	.58	.32	20.07	.83	.72	.61
32	.71	.87	.54	.23	21.08	.94	.66	.40	.15	.91	.80	.68
31	.80	.96	.63	.32	.16	21.02	.74	.48	.23	.99	.87	.76
30	.90	22.05	.72	.41	.25	.11	.83	.56	.31	20.07	.95	.84
29	23.00	.14	.81	.50	.34	.20	.91	.64	.39	.15	20.03	.92
28	.10	.24	.90	.58	.42	.28	.99	.72	.47	.23	.11	20.00
27	.19	.33	.99	.67	.51	.36	21.07	.80	.55	.31	.19	.08
26	.29	.42	22.08	.76	.59	.45	.16	.89	.63	.39	.27	.16
25	.38	.51	.17	.84	.68	.53	.24	.97	.71	.46	.34	.23
24	.48	.60	.26	.93	.77	.62	.33	21.05	.79	.54	.42	.30
23	.58	.69	.34	22.01	.85	.70	.41	.13	.87	.62	.50	.38
22	.67	.78	.43	.10	.94	.78	.49	.21	.95	.70	.58	.46
21	.77	.87	.52	.19	22.03	.87	.58	.30	21.03	.78	.66	.54

(Continued)

52.003 Percentages by volume at 15.56°C (60°F) of ethyl alcohol corresponding to apparent specific gravity at various temperatures[a]—*Continued.*

Apparent Specific Gravity	15.56/15.56	20/20	22/22	24/24	25/25	26/26	28/28	30/30	32/32	34/34	35/35	36/36
0.9720	23.87	22.96	22.61	22.27	22.11	21.96	21.66	21.38	20.11	20.86	20.73	20.61
19	.96	23.06	.70	.36	.19	22.04	.74	.46	.19	.94	.81	.69
18	24.06	.15	.79	.45	.28	.12	.82	.54	.27	21.02	.89	.77
17	.15	.24	.88	.54	.36	.21	.91	.62	.35	.10	.97	.85
16	.25	.33	.96	.62	.45	.30	.99	.70	.43	.17	21.05	.92
15	.34	.42	23.05	.70	.53	.38	22.08	.79	.51	.24	.12	.99
14	.43	.51	.14	.79	.62	.46	.16	.87	.59	.33	.20	21.08
13	.53	.60	.22	.87	.70	.54	.24	.95	.67	.40	.27	.15
12	.62	.69	.31	.96	.79	.63	.32	22.03	.75	.88	.35	.22
11	.72	.78	.40	23.04	.87	.71	.40	.11	.83	.56	.43	.30
10	.81	.87	.49	.13	.96	.8[illegible]	.49	.19	.91	.64	.50	.37
09	.91	.95	.57	.21	23.04	.88	.57	.27	.99	.72	.58	.45
08	25.00	24.04	.66	.30	.13	.97	.65	.35	22.07	.80	.66	.53
07	.09	.13	.74	.38	.21	23.05	.73	.43	.14	.87	.73	.60
06	.19	.22	.83	.47	.29	.13	.81	.51	.22	.95	.81	.68
05	.28	.31	.92	.56	.38	.22	.90	.59	.30	22.03	.89	.76
04	.38	.40	24.00	.64	.46	.30	.98	.67	.38	.10	.96	.83
03	.47	.49	.09	.73	.55	.38	23.06	.75	.46	.18	22.04	.91
02	.57	.58	.18	.81	.63	.46	.14	.83	.53	.25	.11	.98
01	.66	.66	.26	.89	.71	.54	.21	.90	.61	.33	.19	22.06
00	.75	.75	.35	.98	.80	.63	.30	.98	.69	.41	.27	.14
0.9699	.85	.84	.44	24.06	.88	.72	.38	23.06	.77	.48	.34	.21
98	.94	.93	.53	.15	.97	.80	.46	.14	.84	.55	.42	.28
97	26.04	25.01	.61	.23	24.05	.88	.54	.22	.92	.63	.49	.35
96	.13	.10	.69	.31	.13	.96	.62	.30	23.00	.71	.57	.43
95	.22	.19	.78	.40	.22	24.05	.70	.38	.08	.78	.64	.50
94	.31	.28	.86	.48	.30	.13	.78	.45	.15	.86	.72	.58
93	.41	.36	.95	.57	.38	.21	.86	.53	.23	.94	.80	.66
92	.50	.45	25.04	.65	.47	.29	.94	.61	.31	23.01	.87	.74
91	.59	.54	.13	.74	.55	.37	24.02	.69	.38	.08	.95	.81
90	.69	.62	.21	.82	.63	.45	.10	.77	.46	.16	23.02	.88
89	.78	.71	.29	.90	.72	.53	.18	.84	.53	.23	.10	.96
88	.87	.80	.38	.98	.80	.61	.26	.92	.61	.31	.17	23.03
87	.96	.89	.46	25.07	.88	.69	.34	24.00	.68	.38	.24	.10
86	27.05	.98	.55	.15	.97	.77	.42	.08	.76	.46	.32	.18
85	.15	26.06	.63	.23	25.05	.85	.50	.16	.84	.53	.39	.25
84	.24	.15	.72	.32	.13	.94	.58	.23	.92	.61	.47	.33
83	.33	.24	.80	.40	.21	25.02	.66	.31	.99	.68	.54	.40
82	.42	.33	.89	.48	.29	.10	.74	.39	24.06	.75	.61	.47
81	.51	.41	.97	.57	.37	.18	.81	.47	.14	.83	.69	.54
80	.60	.50	26.06	.65	.45	.26	.89	.54	.21	.90	.76	.61
79	.69	.59	.14	.73	.53	.34	.97	.62	.30	.98	.84	.69
78	.78	.67	.22	.81	.61	.42	25.05	.70	.37	24.06	.91	.77
77	.87	.76	.31	.89	.69	.50	.13	.78	.45	.14	.99	.84
76	.96	.84	.39	.97	.77	.58	.21	.85	.52	.21	24.06	.91
75	28.05	.93	.47	26.05	.85	.66	.29	.93	.60	.29	.13	.99
74	.14	27.01	.56	.14	.94	.74	.37	25.01	.68	.36	.21	24.06
73	.23	.10	.64	.22	26.02	.82	.45	.09	.75	.43	.28	.13
72	.32	.19	.73	.30	.10	.90	.53	.16	.83	.51	.36	.20
71	.41	.27	.81	.38	.18	.98	.60	.24	.90	.58	.43	.28
70	.50	.36	.89	.46	.26	26.06	.68	.32	.98	.66	.50	.35
69	.59	.44	.97	.54	.34	.14	.76	.40	25.06	.73	.58	.42
68	.68	.52	27.05	.63	.42	.22	.84	.47	.13	.81	.65	.50
67	.77	.61	.14	.71	.50	.30	.92	.55	.20	.88	.73	.57
66	.86	.69	.22	.79	.58	.38	.99	.63	.28	.95	.80	.64
65	.95	.77	.30	.87	.66	.46	26.07	.70	.36	25.03	.87	.72
64	29.04	.86	.39	.95	.74	.54	.15	.78	.44	.11	.95	.79
63	.12	.94	.47	27.03	.82	.62	.23	.86	.51	.18	25.02	.86
62	.21	28.02	.55	.11	.90	.70	.31	.94	.59	.25	.09	.93
61	.30	.11	.64	.19	.98	.77	.38	26.02	.66	.33	.17	25.01
60	.39	.19	.72	.27	27.06	.85	.46	.09	.74	.40	.24	.08
59	.47	.28	.81	.35	.13	.93	.54	.17	.82	.48	.31	.15
58	.56	.36	.89	.43	.21	27.01	.61	.24	.89	.56	.39	.23
57	.65	.44	.97	.51	.29	.09	.69	.32	.97	.63	.46	.30
56	.74	.53	28.05	.59	.37	.17	.77	.39	26.04	.70	.53	.37
55	.82	.61	.13	.67	.45	.25	.85	.47	.11	.77	.61	.45
54	.91	.69	.21	.75	.53	.33	.93	.55	.19	.85	.68	.52
53	30.00	.78	.29	.83	.61	.41	27.00	.62	.26	.92	.75	.59
52	.09	.86	.37	.91	.69	.49	.08	.70	.34	.99	.82	.66
51	.17	.94	.45	.99	.77	.56	.16	.78	.41	26.06	.90	.74

(Continued)

52.003 Percentages by volume at 15.56°C (60°F) of ethyl alcohol corresponding to apparent specific gravity at various temperatures[a]—*Continued.*

Apparent Specific Gravity	15.56/15.56	20/20	22/22	24/24	25/25	26/26	28/28	30/30	32/32	34/34	35/35	36/36
0.9650	30.26	29.03	28.53	28.07	27.85	27.64	27.23	26.85	26.49	26.14	25.97	25.81
49	.34	.11	.61	.15	.93	.72	.31	.92	.56	.21	26.04	.89
48	.43	.19	.69	.23	28.01	.79	.38	27.00	.64	.29	.11	.96
47	.52	.27	.73	.31	.09	.87	.46	.07	.71	.36	.19	26.03
46	.60	.35	.85	.39	.16	.95	.53	.15	.78	.43	.26	.10
45	.69	.44	.93	.47	.24	28.03	.61	.22	.85	.51	.33	.17
44	.78	.52	29.02	.55	.32	.10	.69	.30	.93	.58	.40	.24
43	.86	.60	.10	.63	.40	.18	.76	.37	27.00	.65	.47	.31
42	.95	.68	.18	.71	.47	.26	.84	.44	.07	.72	.54	.38
41	31.03	.76	.26	.79	.55	.34	.91	.52	.14	.79	.61	.45
40	.11	.85	.34	.86	.63	.41	.99	.59	.22	.86	.69	.52
39	.20	.93	.42	.93	.71	.49	28.06	.67	.29	.93	.76	.59
38	.28	30.01	.50	29.01	.78	.56	.14	.74	.37	27.01	.83	.66
37	.36	.09	.58	.09	.86	.64	.21	.81	.44	.08	.90	.73
36	.44	.17	.66	.17	.94	.72	.29	.89	.51	.15	.97	.80
35	.52	.25	.74	.25	29.02	.80	.37	.96	.58	.22	27.04	.87
34	.61	.34	.28	.33	.09	.87	.44	28.04	.66	.29	.11	.94
33	.69	.42	.90	.41	.17	.95	.52	.11	.73	.36	.18	27.01
32	.77	.50	.98	.49	.25	29.03	.60	.19	.80	.43	.25	.08
31	.85	.58	30.06	.57	.33	.11	.67	.26	.87	.50	.32	.15
30	.93	.66	.13	.64	.40	.18	.74	.33	.95	.58	.39	.22
29	32.02	.74	.21	.72	.48	.26	.82	.41	28.02	.65	.46	.29
28	.09	.82	.29	.79	.56	.33	.89	.48	.01	.72	.54	.36
27	.17	.89	.36	.87	.64	.41	.97	.56	.17	.79	.61	.43
26	.25	.97	.44	.95	.71	.48	29.04	.63	.24	.86	.68	.50
25	.33	31.05	.52	30.03	.79	.56	.12	.70	.31	.93	.75	.57
24	.41	.13	.60	.10	.87	.64	.20	.78	.38	28.00	.82	.64
23	.49	.20	.67	.17	.95	.71	.27	.85	.45	.07	.89	.71
22	.57	.28	.75	.25	30.02	.79	.35	.93	.52	.14	.96	.78
21	.65	.36	.83	.33	.10	.86	.42	29.00	.59	.21	28.03	.85
20	.72	.44	.91	.41	.17	.94	.50	.07	.67	.29	.10	.92
19	.80	.52			.25	30.01	.57	.14	.74	.36	.17	.99
18	.88	.59			.32	.09	.65	.22	.82	.43	.24	28.06
17	.96	.67			.40	.16	.72	.29	.89	.50	.31	.13
16	33.04	.75			.47	.24	.79	.36	.96	.57	.38	.20
15	.12	.82			.54	.31	.86	.43	29.03	.64	.45	.27
14	.19	.90			.62	.39	.94	.51	.10	.71	.52	.43
13	.27	.98			.69	.46	30.01	.58	.17	.78	.59	.41
12	.35	32.05			.77	.53	.08	.65	.24	.85	.66	.48
11	.43	.13			.84	.61	.15	.72	.31	.92	.73	.55
10	.50	.21			.92	.68	.23	.80	.39	.99	.80	.62
09	.58	.28			.99	.75	.30	.87	.46	29.06	.87	.69
08	.66	.36			31.07	.83	.38	.94	.53	.13	.94	.76
07	.74	.43			.13	.90	.45	30.01	.60	.20	29.01	.83
06	.81	.51			.21	.98	.52	.09	.67	.27	.08	.90
05	.89	.58			.29	31.05	.59	.16	.74	.34	.15	.97
04	.97	.66			.36	.13	.66	.23	.81	.41	.22	29.04
03	34.05	.73			.43	.20	.73	.30	.88	.48	.29	.11
02	.12	.81			.51	.28	.80	.37	.95	.55	.36	.18
01	.20	.88			.58	.35	.88	.44	30.02	.62	.43	.25
00	.27	.96			.65	.42	.95	.51	.09	.69	.50	.31
0.9599	.35	33.03			.73			.58	.16	.76	.57	.38
98	.42	.10			.80			.65	.23	.83	.63	.45
97	.50	.18			.87			.72	.30	.90	.70	.51
96	.57	.25			.95			.79	.37	.97	.77	.58
95	.65	.32			32.02			.87	.44	30.04	.84	.65
94	.72	.40			.09			.94	.51	.11	.91	.72
93	.80	.47			.16			31.01	.58	.18	.98	.79
92	.87	.54			.23			.08	.65	.25	30.05	.86
91	.95	.62			.30			.15	.72	.32	.12	.93
90	35.02	.69			.37			.22	.79	.38	.18	.99
89	.09	.76			.44			.38			.25	30.06
88	.17	.84			.51			.35			.23	.13
87	.24	.91			.58			.42			.39	.20
86	.31	.98			.65			.49			.46	.27
85	.38	34.05			.73			.56			.52	.33
84	.46	.12			.80			.63			.59	.40
83	.53	.20			.87			.70			.66	.47
82	.60	.27			.94			.77			.73	.54
81	.67	.34			33.01			.84			.80	.61

(Continued)

52.003 Percentages by volume at 15.56°C (60°F) of ethyl alcohol corresponding to apparent specific gravity at various temperatures[a]—*Continued.*

Apparent Specific Gravity	15.56/15.56	20/20	25/25	30/30	35/35
0.9580	35.75	34.41	33.08	31.91	30.86
79	.82	.48	.15	.98	.93
78	.89	.56	.22	32.05	31.00
77	.96	.63	.29	.11	.07
76	36.04	.70	.36	.18	.13
75	.11	.77	.43	.25	.20
74	.18	.84	.50	.32	.26
73	.25	.91	.57	.38	.33
72	.32	.98	.64	.45	.39
71	.39	35.05	.71	.52	.46
70	.46	.12	.78	.58	.53
69	.53	.19	.85	.65	.59
68	.60	.26	.92	.72	.66
67	.67	.33	.99	.79	.72
66	.74	.40	34.05	.85	.79
65	.81	.47	.12	.92	.86
64	.88	.54	.19	.99	.92
63	.95	.61	.26	33.05	.99
62	37.02	.68	.32	.12	32.05
61	.09	.75	.39	.19	.12
60	.16	.82	.46	.25	.18
59	.22	.88	.53	.32	.25
58	.29	.95	.59	.39	.31
57	.36	36.02	.66	.45	.37
56	.43	.09	.73	.52	.44
55	.50	.15	.80	.59	.50
54	.56	.22	.86	.65	.57
53	.63	.29	.93	.72	.63
52	.70	.36	35.00	.79	.70
51	.77	.42	.07	.85	.76
50	.84	.49	.13	.92	.83
49	.90	.56	.20	.99	.89
48	.97	.63	.26	34.05	.95
47	38.04	.69	.33	.12	33.02
46	.11	.76	.39	.18	.08
45	.17	.83	.46	.25	.15
44	.24	.89	.53	.31	.21
43	.31	.96	.59	.38	.27
42	.37	37.03	.66	.44	.34
41	.44	.09	.72	.51	.40
40	.51	.16	.79	.57	.46
39	.57	.23	.86	.64	.53
38	.64	.29	.92	.70	.59
37	.71	.36	.99	.77	.66
36	.77	.42	36.05	.83	.72
35	.84	.49	.12	.90	.78
34	.91	.56	.18	.96	.85
33	.97	.62	.25	35.03	.91
32	39.04	.69	.31	.09	.97
31	.10	.75	.38	.15	34.04
30	.17	.82	.44	.22	.10
29	.23	.88	.51	.28	.16
28	.30	.95	.57	.34	.22
27	.36	38.01	.64	.41	.29
26	.43	.07	.70	.47	.35
25	.49	.14	.77	.53	.41
24	.56	.20	.83	.59	.47
23	.62	.27	.90	.66	.53
22	.69	.33	.96	.72	.60
21	.75	.39	37.02	.78	.66
20	.82	.46	.09	.85	.72
19	.88	.52	.15	.91	.78
18	.95	.59	.21	.97	.84
17	40.01	.65	.28	36.04	.91
16	.08	.72	.34	.10	.97
15	.14	.78	.40	.16	35.04
14	.20	.84	.46	.22	.10
13	.27	.91	.52	.28	.16
12	.33	.97	.59	.35	.22
11	.39	39.04	.65	.41	.28
0.9510	40.46	39.10	37.71	36.47	35.34
09	.52	.16	.78	.53	.40
08	.58	.23	.84	.59	.46
07	.65	.29	.90	.65	.52
06	.71	.35	.96	.72	.58
05	.77	.41	38.02	.78	.64
04	.84	.48	.09	.84	.71
03	.90	.54	.15	.90	.77
02	.96	.60	.21	.96	.83
01	41.02	.67	.27	37.02	.89
00	.09	.73	.33	.09	.95
0.9499	.15	.79	.40	.15	36.01
98	.21	.85	.46	.21	.07
97	.27	.91	.52	.27	.13
96	.33	.98	.58	.33	.19
95	.40	40.04	.64	.39	.25
94	.46	.10	.70	.45	.31
93	.52	.16	.77	.51	.37
92	.58	.22	.83	.57	.43
91	.64	.29	.89	.63	.49
90	.70	.35	.95	.70	.55
89	.77	.41	39.01	.76	.61
88	.83	.47	.07	.82	.67
87	.89	.53	.13	.88	.73
86	.95	.59	.20	.94	.79
85	42.01	.65	.26	38.00	.85
84	.07	.71	.32	.06	.91
83	.13	.78	.38	.12	.97
82	.19	.84	.44	.18	37.03
81	.25	.90	.50	.24	.09
80	.31	.96	.56	.30	.15
79	.37	41.02	.62	.36	.21
78	.43	.08	.68	.42	.26
77	.49	.14	.74	.48	.32
76	.55	.20	.80	.54	.38
75	.61	.26	.87	.60	.44
74	.67	.32	.93	.66	.50
73	.73	.38	.99	.72	.56
72	.80	.44	40.05	.78	.62
71	.86	.50	.11	.84	.68
70	.92	.56	.17	.90	.74
69	.98	.62	.22	.96	.79
68	43.04	.68	.28	39.02	.85
67	.09	.74	.34	.08	.91
66	.15	.80	.40	.13	.97
65	.21	.86	.46	.19	38.03
64	.27	.92	.52	.25	.09
63	.33	.98	.58	.31	.15
62	.39	42.04	.64	.37	.20
61	.45	.09	.70	.43	.26
60	.51	.15	.76	.49	.32
59	.57	.21	.82	.54	.38
58	.63	.27	.88	.60	.44
57	.69	.33	.93	.66	.49
56	.75	.39	.99	.72	.55
55	.80	.45	41.05	.78	.61
54	.86	.51	.11	.84	.67
53	.92	.57	.17	.89	.73
52	.98	.63	.23	.95	.78
51	44.04	.69	.28	40.01	.84
50	.10	.74	.34	.07	.90
49	.16	.80	.40	.13	.96
48	.21	.86	.46	.18	39.02
47	.27	.92	.51	.24	.07
46	.33	.98	.57	.30	.13
45	.39	43.04	.63	.35	.19
44	.45	.09	.69	.41	.24
43	.50	.15	.75	.47	.30
42	.56	.21	.80	.53	.36
41	.62	.27	.86	.58	.41

(Continued)

52.003 Percentages by volume at 15.56°C (60°F) of ethyl alcohol corresponding to apparent specific gravity at various temperatures[a]—*Continued.*

Apparent Specific Gravity	15.56/15.56	20/20	25/25	30/30	35/35	Apparent Specific Gravity	15.56/15.56	20/20	25/25	30/30	35/35
0.9440	44.68	43.33	41.92	40.64	39.47	0.9370	48.53	47.20	45.81	44.52	43.33
39	.73	.39	.98	.70	.53	69	.58	.26	.86	.58	.38
38	.79	.44	42.03	.75	.59	68	.63	.31	.91	.63	.43
37	.85	.50	.09	.81	.64	67	.69	.36	.97	.68	.49
36	.91	.56	.15	.87	.70	66	.74	.42	46.02	.74	.54
35	.97	.62	.21	.93	.76	65	.79	.47	.07	.79	.59
34	45.02	.67	.26	.98	.81	64	.85	.52	.13	.84	.65
33	.08	.73	.32	41.04	.87	63	.90	.58	.18	.90	.70
32	.14	.78	.38	.10	.93	62	.95	.63	.23	.95	.75
31	.19	.85	.43	.15	.98	61	49.01	.68	.29	45.01	.81
30	.25	.90	.49	.21	40.04	60	.06	.73	.34	.06	.86
29	.31	.96	.55	.27	.09	59	.11	.79	.39	.11	.91
28	.36	44.02	.61	.32	.15	58	.16	.84	.45	.16	.97
27	.42	.07	.66	.38	.21	57	.21	.89	.50	.22	44.02
26	.47	.13	.72	.44	.26	56	.26	.94	.55	.27	.07
25	.53	.18	.78	.49	.32	55	.32	48.00	.61	.32	.13
24	.59	.24	.83	.55	.37	54	.37	.05	.66	.37	.18
23	.64	.30	.89	.60	.43	53	.42	.10	.71	.43	.23
22	.70	.35	.95	.66	.48	52	.47	.15	.77	.48	.28
21	.76	.41	43.01	.72	.54	51	.52	.21	.82	.53	.34
20	.81	.46	.06	.77	.59	50	.58	.26	.87	.58	.39
19	.87	.52	.12	.83	.65	49	.63	.31	.93	.64	.44
18	.93	.58	.17	.89	.71	48	.68	.36	.98	.69	.49
17	.98	.63	.23	.94	.76	47	.73	.41	47.03	.74	.54
16	46.04	.69	.29	42.00	.82	46	.78	.47	.08	.79	.60
15	.09	.74	.34	.06	.87	45	.83	.52	.14	.85	.65
14	.15	.80	.40	.11	.93	44	.89	.57	.19	.90	.70
13	.20	.86	.46	.17	.98	43	.94	.62	.24	.95	.75
12	.26	.91	.51	.22	41.04	42	.99	.68	.29	46.01	.81
11	.31	.97	.57	.28	.09	41	50.04	.73	.34	.06	.86
10	.37	45.03	.62	.33	.15	40	.09	.78	.40	.11	.91
09	.43	.08	.68	.39	.20	39	.14	.83	.45	.16	.96
08	.48	.14	.74	.44	.26	38	.19	.88	.50	.21	45.02
07	.54	.19	.79	.50	.31	37	.24	.94	.55	.27	.07
06	.59	.25	.85	.56	.37	36	.30	.99	.60	.32	.12
05	.65	.30	.90	.61	.42	35	.35	49.04	.66	.37	.17
04	.70	.36	.96	.67	.48	34	.40	.09	.71	.42	.22
03	.76	.42	44.02	.72	.53	33	.45	.14	.76	.47	.27
02	.81	.47	.07	.78	.59	32	.50	.19	.81	.53	.33
01	.87	.53	.13	.83	.64	31	.55	.25	.86	.58	.38
00	.92	.58	.18	.89	.70	30	.60	.30	.92	.63	.43
0.9399	.98	.64	.23	.94	.75	29	.65	.35	.97	.68	.48
98	47.03	.69	.29	43.00	.81	28	.70	.40	48.02	.73	.53
97	.09	.74	.34	.05	.86	27	.75	.45	.07	.79	.59
96	.14	.80	.40	.11	.92	26	.81	.50	.12	.84	.64
95	.19	.85	.45	.16	.97	25	.86	.55	.17	.89	.69
94	.25	.91	.51	.22	42.03	24	.91	.60	.22	.94	.74
93	.30	.96	.56	.27	.08	23	.96	.65	.28	.99	.79
92	.35	46.01	.62	.33	.14	22	51.01	.70	.33	47.05	.84
91	.41	.07	.67	.38	.19	21	.06	.75	.38	.10	.90
90	.46	.12	.73	.44	.24	20	.11	.80	.43	.15	.95
89	.52	.18	.78	.49	.30	19	.16	.85	.48	.20	46.00
88	.57	.23	.84	.55	.35	18	.21	.90	.53	.25	.05
87	.62	.29	.89	.60	.41	17	.26	.95	.58	.30	.10
86	.68	.34	.95	.66	.46	16	.31	50.00	.63	.35	.15
85	.73	.39	45.00	.71	.52	15	.36	.05	.68	.40	.20
84	.78	.45	.05	.77	.57	14	.41	.10	.73	.45	.26
83	.84	.50	.11	.82	.63	13	.46	.16	.79	.50	.31
82	.89	.56	.16	.87	.68	12	.51	.21	.84	.55	.36
81	.95	.61	.22	.93	.73	11	.56	.26	.89	.60	.41
80	48.00	.67	.27	.98	.79	10	.61	.31	.94	.65	.46
79	.05	.72	.32	44.04	.84	09	.66	.36	.99	.71	.51
78	.11	.77	.38	.09	.90	08	.71	.41	49.04	.76	.56
77	.16	.83	.43	.15	.95	07	.76	.46	.09	.81	.61
76	.21	.88	.48	.20	43.01	06	.81	.51	.14	.86	.66
75	.26	.94	.54	.25	.06	05	.86	.56	.19	.91	.71
74	.32	.99	.59	.31	.11	04	.91	.61	.24	.96	.77
73	.37	47.04	.65	.36	.17	03	.96	.66	.29	48.01	.82
72	.42	.10	.70	.41	.22	02	52.01	.71	.34	.06	.87
71	.48	.15	.75	.47	.27	01	.06	.76	.39	.11	.92

(Continued)

52.003 Percentages by volume at 15.56°C (60°F) of ethyl alcohol corresponding to apparent specific gravity at various temperatures[a]—*Continued.*

Apparent Specific Gravity	15.56/15.56	20/20	25/25	30/30	35/35
0.9300	52.11	50.81	49.44	48.16	46.97
0.9299	.16	.86	.49	.21	47.02
98	.21	.91	.54	.26	.07
97	.26	.96	.59	.31	.12
96	.31	51.01	.64	.36	.17
95	.36	.06	.69	.41	.22
94	.41	.11	.74	.46	.27
93	.46	.16	.79	.51	.32
92	.51	.21	.84	.56	.37
91	.56	.26	.89	.61	.42
90	.61	.31	.94	.66	.47
89	.66	.36	.99	.71	.52
88	.71	.41	50.04	.76	.57
87	.76	.46	.09	.81	.62
86	.81	.50	.14	.86	.67
85	.86	.55	.19	.91	.72
84	.91	.60	.24	.96	.77
83	.96	.65	.29	49.01	.82
82	53.00	.70	.34	.06	.87
81	.05	.75	.39	.11	.92
80	.10	.80	.44	.16	.97
79	.15	.85	.49	.21	48.02
78	.20	.90	.54	.26	.07
77	.25	.95	.59	.31	.12
76	.30	52.00	.64	.36	.17
75	.35	.05	.68	.41	.22
74	.40	.10	.73	.46	.27
73	.45	.15	.78	.51	.32
72	.50	.20	.83	.56	.37
71	.54	.25	.88	.61	.42
70	.59	.29	.93	.66	.47
69	.64	.34	.98	.71	.52
68	.69	.39	51.03	.76	.57
67	.74	.44	.08	.81	.62
66	.79	.49	.13	.86	.67
65	.84	.54	.18	.91	.71
64	.89	.59	.23	.96	.76
63	.94	.64	.27	50.00	.81
62	.99	.69	.32	.05	.86
61	54.03	.74	.37	.10	.91
60	.08	.79	.42	.15	.96
59	.13	.84	.47	.20	49.01
58	.18	.89	.52	.25	.06
57	.23	.93	.57	.30	.11
56	.28	.98	.62	.35	.15
55	.32	53.03	.67	.40	.20
54	.37	.08	.72	.44	.25
53	.42	.13	.76	.49	.30
52	.47	.18	.81	.54	.35
51	.52	.22	.86	.59	.40
50	.57	.27	.91	.64	.44
49	.61	.32	.96	.69	.49
48	.66	.37	52.01	.74	.54
47	.71	.42	.06	.79	.59
46	.76	.47	.11	.83	.64
45	.81	.52	.16	.88	.69
44	.86	.56	.20	.93	.73
43	.90	.61	.25	.98	.78
42	.95	.66	.30	51.03	.83
41	55.00	.71	.35	.08	.88
40	.05	.76	.40	.13	.93
39	.10	.81	.45	.17	.98
38	.14	.85	.50	.22	50.02
37	.19	.90	.54	.27	.07
36	.24	.95	.59	.32	.12
35	.29	54.00	.64	.37	.17
34	.33	.05	.69	.42	.22
33	.38	.09	.74	.46	.27
32	.43	.14	.79	.51	.31
31	.48	.19	.83	.56	.36
0.9230	55.52	54.24	52.88	51.61	50.41
29	.57	.29	.93	.66	.46
28	.62	.33	.98	.71	.51
27	.67	.38	53.03	.75	.56
26	.71	.43	.08	.80	.60
25	.76	.48	.12	.85	.65
24	.81	.53	.17	.90	.70
23	.86	.57	.22	.95	.75
22	.90	.62	.27	52.00	.80
21	.95	.67	.31	.04	.85
20	56.00	.72	.36	.09	.89
19	.05	.77	.41	.14	.94
18	.09	.81	.46	.19	.99
17	.14	.86	.50	.23	51.04
16	.19	.91	.55	.28	.09
15	.24	.96	.60	.33	.13
14	.28	55.00	.65	.38	.18
13	.33	.05	.70	.43	.23
12	.38	.10	.74	.47	.27
11	.43	.15	.79	.52	.32
10	.47	.19	.84	.57	.37
09	.52	.24	.89	.62	.42
08	.57	.29	.93	.67	.46
07	.62	.34	.98	.71	.51
06	.66	.38	54.03	.76	.56
05	.71	.43	.08	.81	.61
04	.76	.48	.12	.86	.65
03	.81	.53	.17	.90	.70
02	.85	.57	.22	.95	.75
01	.90	.62	.26	53.00	.80
00	.95	.67	.31	.05	.84
0.9199	57.00	.71	.36	.09	.89
98	.04	.76	.41	.14	.94
97	.09	.81	.45	.19	.99
96	.13	.86	.50	.23	52.03
95	.18	.90	.55	.28	.08
94	.23	.95	.59	.33	.13
93	.27	56.00	.64	.37	.17
92	.32	.04	.69	.42	.22
91	.37	.09	.74	.47	.27
90	.41	.14	.78	.51	.32
89	.46	.18	.83	.56	.36
88	.51	.23	.88	.61	.41
87	.55	.28	.92	.65	.46
86	.60	.32	.97	.70	.50
85	.65	.37	55.02	.75	.55
84	.69	.42	.07	.79	.60
83	.74	.46	.11	.84	.65
82	.79	.51	.16	.89	.69
81	.83	.56	.21	.93	.74
80	.88	.60	.25	.98	.79
79	.93	.65	.30	54.03	.83
78	.97	.70	.35	.07	.88
77	58.02	.74	.39	.12	.93
76	.06	.79	.44	.17	.98
75	.11	.84	.49	.21	53.02
74	.16	.88	.53	.26	.07
73	.20	.93	.58	.31	.12
72	.25	.97	.63	.36	.16
71	.29	57.02	.67	.40	.21
70	.34	.07	.72	.45	.26
69	.38	.11	.77	.50	.30
68	.43	.16	.81	.54	.35
67	.47	.21	.86	.59	.40
66	.52	.25	.91	.64	.44
65	.57	.30	.95	.68	.49
64	.61	.35	56.00	.73	.53
63	.66	.39	.05	.78	.58
62	.70	.44	.09	.82	.63
61	.75	.48	.14	.87	.67

(Continued)

52.003 Percentages by volume at 15.56°C (60°F) of ethyl alcohol corresponding to apparent specific gravity at various temperatures[a]—*Continued.*

Apparent Specific Gravity	15.56/15.56	20/20	25/25	30/30	35/35
0.9160	58.79	57.53	56.18	54.92	53.72
59	.84	.58	.23	.96	.77
58	.89	.62	.28	55.01	.81
57	.93	.67	.32	.06	.86
56	.98	.71	.37	.10	.91
55	59.02	.76	.41	.15	.95
54	.07	.81	.46	.19	54.00
53	.11	.85	.51	.24	.05
52	.16	.90	.55	.29	.09
51	.20	.94	.60	.33	.14
50	.25	.99	.65	.38	.18
49	.29	58.03	.69	.42	.23
48	.34	.08	.74	.47	.28
47	.38	.13	.78	.52	.32
46	.43	.17	.83	.56	.37
45	.47	.22	.88	.61	.41
44	.52	.26	.92	.65	.46
43	.56	.31	.97	.70	.51
42	.61	.35	57.01	.75	.55
41	.65	.40	.06	.79	.60
40	.70	.44	.10	.84	.65
39	.74	.49	.15	.88	.69
38	.79	.53	.20	.93	.74
37	.83	.58	.24	.98	.78
36	.88	.62	.29	56.02	.83
35	.92	.67	.33	.07	.88
34	.97	.71	.38	.11	.92
33	60.01	.76	.42	.16	.97
32	.06	.80	.47	.21	55.01
31	.10	.85	.51	.25	.06
30	.15	.89	.56	.30	.11
29	.19	.94	.60	.34	.15
28	.24	.98	.65	.39	.20
27	.28	59.03	.70	.44	.24
26	.33	.07	.74	.48	.29
25	.37	.12	.79	.53	.33
24	.42	.16	.83	.57	.38
23	.46	.21	.88	.62	.42
22	.50	.25	.92	.67	.47
21	.55	.30	.97	.71	.52
20	.59	.34	58.01	.76	.56
19	.64	.39	.06	.80	.61
18	.68	.43	.10	.85	.65
17	.73	.48	.15	.89	.70
16	.77	.52	.19	.94	.74
15	.82	.57	.24	.99	.79
14	.86	.61	.28	57.03	.84
13	.91	.66	.33	.08	.88
12	.95	.70	.37	.12	.93
11	61.00	.75	.42	.17	.97
10	.04	.79	.46	.21	56.02
09	.08	.84	.51	.26	.06
08	.13	.88	.55	.30	.11
07	.17	.92	.60	.35	.15
06	.22	.97	.64	.39	.20
05	.26	60.01	.69	.44	.25
04	.30	.06	.73	.48	.29
03	.35	.10	.78	.53	.34
02	.39	.15	.82	.57	.38
01	.44	.19	.87	.62	.43
00	.48	.24	.91	.66	.47
0.9099	.52	.28	.96	.71	.52
98	.57	.33	59.00	.75	.56
97	.61	.37	.04	.80	.61
96	.66	.41	.09	.84	.65
95	.70	.46	.13	.89	.70
94	.74	.50	.18	.93	.75
93	.79	.55	.22	.98	.79
92	.83	.59	.27	58.02	.84
91	.88	.64	.31	.07	.88

Apparent Specific Gravity	15.56/15.56	20/20	25/25	30/30	35/35
0.9090	61.92	60.68	59.36	58.11	56.93
89	.96	.72	.40	.15	.97
88	62.01	.77	.45	.20	57.02
87	.05	.81	.49	.24	.06
86	.10	.86	.53	.29	.11
85	.14	.90	.58	.33	.15
84	.18	.94	.63	.38	.19
83	.23	.99	.67	.42	.24
82	.27	61.03	.71	.46	.28
81	.31	.08	.76	.51	.33
80	.36	.12	.80	.55	.37
79	.40	.17	.85	.60	.42
78	.45	.21	.89	.64	.46
77	.49	.25	.94	.69	.50
76	.53	.30	.98	.73	.55
75	.58	.34	60.03	.77	.59
74	.62	.39	.07	.82	.64
73	.66	.43	.11	.86	.68
72	.71	.47	.16	.91	.73
71	.75	.52	.20	.95	.77
70	.79	.56	.25	59.00	.81
69	.84	.60	.29	.04	.86
68	.88	.65	.33	.08	.90
67	.93	.69	.38	.13	.95
66	.97	.74	.42	.17	.99
65	63.01	.78	.46	.21	58.04
64	.06	.82	.51	.26	.08
63	.10	.87	.55	.30	.12
62	.14	.91	.60	.35	.17
61	.19	.96	.64	.39	.21
60	.23	62.00	.68	.43	.26
59	.27	.04	.73	.48	.30
58	.32	.09	.77	.52	.34
57	.36	.13	.82	.57	.39
56	.40	.17	.86	.61	.43
55	.45	.22	.90	.65	.48
54	.49	.26	.95	.70	.52
53	.53	.30	.99	.74	.56
52	.58	.35	61.03	.79	.61
51	.62	.39	.08	.83	.65
50	.66	.43	.12	.87	.70
49	.71	.48	.16	.92	.74
48	.75	.52	.21	.96	.78
47	.79	.56	.25	60.00	.83
46	.84	.60	.29	.05	.87
45	.88	.65	.34	.09	.92
44	.92	.69	.38	.14	.96
43	.97	.73	.42	.18	59.00
42	64.01	.78	.47	.22	.05
41	.05	.82	.51	.27	.09
40	.09	.86	.55	.31	.13
39	.14	.91	.60	.35	.18
38	.18	.95	.64	.40	.22
37	.22	.99	.68	.44	.27
36	.27	63.04	.73	.48	.31
35	.31	.08	.77	.53	.35
34	.35	.12	.81	.57	.40
33	.40	.17	.86	.62	.44
32	.44	.21	.90	.66	.48
31	.48	.25	.94	.70	.53
30	.53	.30	.99	.75	.57
29	.57	.34	62.03	.79	.61
28	.61	.38	.07	.83	.66
27	.66	.43	.12	.88	.70
26	.70	.47	.16	.92	.74
25	.74	.51	.20	.97	.79
24	.78	.56	.24	61.01	.83
23	.83	.60	.29	.05	.87
22	.87	.64	.23	.09	.92
21	.91	.69	.37	.14	.96

(Continued)

52.003 Percentages by volume at 15.56°C (60°F) of ethyl alcohol corresponding to apparent specific gravity at various temperatures[a]—*Continued*.

Apparent Specific Gravity	15.56/15.56	20/20	25/25	30/30	35/35
0.9020	64.96	63.73	62.42	61.18	60.00
19	65.00	.77	.46	.22	.05
18	.04	.82	.50	.27	.09
17	.09	.86	.55	.31	.13
16	.13	.90	.59	.35	.18
15	.17	.94	.63	.40	.22
14	.21	.99	.67	.44	.26
13	.26	64.03	.72	.48	.30
12	.30	.07	.76	.53	.35
11	.34	.11	.80	.57	.39
10	.38	.16	.85	.61	.43
09	.43	.20	.89	.66	.48
08	.47	.24	.93	.70	.52
07	.51	.28	.97	.74	.56
06	.55	.33	63.02	.78	.61
05	.60	.37	.06	.83	.65
04	.64	.41	.10	.87	.69
03	.68	.45	.15	.91	.73
02	.72	.50	.19	.96	.78
01	.77	.54	.23	62.00	.82
00	.81	.58	.27	.04	.86
0.8999	.85	.62	.32	.09	.91
98	.89	.67	.36	.13	.95
97	.94	.71	.40	.17	.99
96	.98	.75	.44	.21	61.03
95	66.02	.79	.49	.26	.08
94	.06	.84	.53	.30	.12
93	.10	.88	.57	.34	.16
92	.15	.92	.62	.38	.21
91	.19	.96	.66	.43	.25
90	.23	65.01	.70	.47	.29
89	.27	.05	.74	.51	.33
88	.31	.09	.79	.55	.38
87	.36	.13	.83	.60	.42
86	.40	.18	.87	.64	.46
85	.44	.22	.91	.68	.50
84	.48	.26	.96	.72	.55
83	.52	.30	64.00	.77	.59
82	.56	.35	.04	.81	.63
81	.61	.39	.08	.85	.68
80	.65	.43	.13	.89	.72
79	.69	.47	.17	.94	.76
78	.73	.51	.21	.98	.80
77	.77	.56	.25	63.02	.85
76	.82	.60	.30	.06	.89
75	.86	.64	.34	.11	.93
74	.90	.68	.38	.15	.97
73	.94	.72	.42	.19	62.02
72	.98	.77	.47	.23	.06
71	67.03	.81	.51	.28	.10
70	.07	.85	.55	.32	.14
69	.11	.89	.59	.36	.19
68	.15	.94	.64	.40	.23
67	.19	.98	.68	.44	.27
66	.23	66.02	.72	.49	.31
65	.28	.06	.76	.53	.36
64	.32	.10	.81	.57	.40
63	.36	.15	.85	.61	.44
62	.40	.19	.89	.66	.48
61	.44	.23	.93	.70	.53
60	.48	.27	.97	.74	.57
59	.53	.31	65.02	.78	.61
58	.57	.36	.06	.83	.65
57	.61	.40	.10	.87	.69
56	.65	.44	.14	.91	.74
55	.69	.48	.18	.95	.78
54	.73	.52	.23	64.00	.82
53	.78	.56	.27	.04	.86
52	.82	.60	.31	.08	.91
51	.86	.65	.35	.12	.95
0.8950	67.90	66.69	65.39	64.16	62.99
49	.94	.73	.44	.21	63.03
48	.98	.77	.48	.25	.08
47	68.02	.81	.52	.29	.12
46	.07	.85	.56	.33	.16
45	.11	.90	.60	.37	.20
44	.15	.94	.64	.42	.24
43	.19	.98	.69	.46	.28
42	.23	67.02	.73	.50	.33
41	.27	.06	.77	.54	.37
40	.31	.10	.81	.58	.41
39	.35	.15	.85	.63	.45
38	.39	.19	.90	.67	.49
37	.43	.23	.94	.71	.54
36	.48	.27	.98	.75	.58
35	.52	.31	66.02	.79	.62
34	.56	.35	.06	.84	.66
33	.60	.39	.10	.88	.70
32	.64	.43	.15	.92	.74
31	.68	.47	.19	.96	.79
30	.72	.52	.23	65.00	.83
29	.76	.56	.27	.05	.87
28	.80	.60	.31	.09	.91
27	.84	.64	.35	.13	.95
26	.89	.68	.39	.17	64.00
25	.93	.72	.44	.21	.04
24	.97	.76	.48	.25	.08
23	69.01	.80	.52	.29	.12
22	.05	.84	.56	.34	.16
21	.09	.89	.60	.38	.21
20	.13	.93	.64	.42	.25
19	.17	.97	.68	.46	.29
18	.21	68.01	.73	.50	.33
17	.25	.05	.77	.54	.37
16	.29	.09	.81	.59	.41
15	.33	.13	.85	.63	.46
14	.37	.17	.89	.67	.50
13	.41	.21	.93	.71	.54
12	.46	.26	.98	.75	.58
11	.50	.30	67.02	.79	.62
10	.54	.34	.06	.83	.67
09	.58	.38	.10	.88	.71
08	.62	.42	.14	.92	.75
07	.66	.46	.18	.96	.79
06	.70	.50	.22	66.00	.83
05	.74	.54	.26	.04	.87
04	.78	.58	.30	.08	.92
03	.82	.62	.34	.12	.96
02	.86	.67	.39	.17	65.00
01	.90	.71	.43	.21	.04
00	.94	.75	.47	.25	.08
0.8899	.98	.79	.51	.29	.12
98	70.02	.83	.55	.33	.17
97	.06	.87	.59	.37	.21
96	.10	.91	.63	.41	.25
95	.14	.95	.67	.45	.29
94	.18	.99	.71	.50	.33
93	.22	69.03	.75	.54	.37
92	.27	.07	.80	.58	.41
91	.31	.11	.84	.62	.45
90	.35	.15	.88	.66	.50
89	.39	.19	.92	.70	.54
88	.43	.23	.96	.74	.58
87	.47	.27	68.00	.79	.62
86	.51	.32	.04	.83	.66
85	.55	.36	.08	.87	.70
84	.59	.40	.12	.91	.74
83	.63	.44	.16	.95	.79
82	.67	.48	.20	.99	.83
81	.71	.52	.24	67.03	.87

(Continued)

52.003 Percentages by volume at 15.56°C (60°F) of ethyl alcohol corresponding to apparent specific gravity at various temperatures[a]—*Continued*.

Apparent Specific Gravity	15.56/15.56	20/20	25/25	30/30	35/35
0.8880	70.75	69.56	68.28	67.07	65.91
79	.79	.60	.33	.11	.95
78	.83	.64	.37	.15	.99
77	.87	.68	.41	.20	66.03
76	.91	.72	.45	.24	.07
75	.95	.76	.49	.28	.11
74	.99	.80	.53	.32	.16
73	71.03	.84	.57	.36	.20
72	.07	.88	.61	.40	.24
71	.11	.92	.65	.44	.28
70	.15	.96	.69	.48	.32
69	.19	70.00	.73	.52	.36
68	.23	.04	.77	.56	.40
67	.27	.08	.81	.60	.44
66	.31	.12	.85	.64	.48
65	.35	.16	.89	.68	.52
64	.38	.20	.93	.72	.56
63	.42	.24	.98	.76	.60
62	.46	.28	69.02	.80	.64
61	.50	.32	.06	.85	.69
60	.54	.36	.10	.89	.73
59	.58	.40	.14	.93	.77
58	.62	.44	.18	.97	.81
57	.66	.48	.22	68.01	.85
56	.70	.52	.26	.05	.89
55	.74	.56	.30	.09	.93
54	.78	.60	.34	.13	.97
53	.82	.64	.38	.17	67.01
52	.86	.68	.42	.21	.05
51	.90	.72	.46	.25	.09
50	.94	.76	.50	.29	.13
49	.98	.80	.54	.33	.17
48	72.02	.84	.58	.37	.21
47	.06	.88	.62	.41	.25
46	.10	.92	.66	.45	.29
45	.14	.96	.70	.49	.33
44	.18	71.00	.74	.53	.38
43	.22	.04	.78	.57	.42
42	.25	.08	.82	.61	.46
41	.29	.12	.86	.65	.50
40	.33	.16	.90	.69	.54
39	.37	.20	.94	.73	.58
38	.41	.24	.98	.77	.62
37	.45	.27	70.02	.81	.66
36	.49	.31	.06	.85	.70
35	.53	.35	.10	.89	.74
34	.57	.39	.13	.93	.78
33	.61	.43	.17	.97	.82
32	.65	.47	.21	69.01	.86
31	.69	.51	.25	.05	.90
30	.73	.55	.29	.09	.94
29	.76	.59	.33	.13	.98
28	.80	.63	.37	.17	68.02
27	.84	.67	.41	.21	.06
26	.88	.71	.45	.25	.10
25	.92	.75	.49	.29	.14
24	.96	.79	.53	.33	.18
23	73.00	.83	.57	.37	.22
22	.04	.87	.61	.41	.26
21	.08	.91	.65	.45	.30
20	.12	.95	.69	.49	.34
19	.16	.99	.73	.53	.38
18	.19	72.03	.77	.57	.42
17	.23	.07	.81	.61	.46
16	.27	.10	.85	.65	.50
15	.31	.14	.89	.69	.54
14	.35	.18	.93	.73	.58
13	.39	.22	.97	.77	.62
12	.43	.26	71.01	.81	.66
11	.47	.30	.05	.85	.70

Apparent Specific Gravity	15.56/15.56	20/20	25/25	30/30	35/35
0.8810	73.50	72.34	71.09	69.89	68.74
09	.54	.38	.13	.93	.78
08	.58	.42	.16	.97	.82
07	.62	.46	.20	70.01	.86
06	.66	.50	.24	.05	.90
05	.70	.53	.28	.09	.94
04	.74	.57	.32	.13	.98
03	.78	.61	.36	.17	69.02
02	.81	.65	.40	.21	.06
01	.85	.69	.44	.25	.10
00	.89	.73	.48	.29	.14
0.8799	.93	.77	.52	.33	.18
98	.97	.81	.56	.37	.22
97	74.01	.85	.60	.41	.26
96	.05	.88	.64	.44	.30
95	.08	.92	.67	.48	.34
94	.12	.96	.71	.52	.38
93	.16	73.00	.75	.56	.42
92	.20	.04	.79	.60	.45
91	.24	.08	.83	.64	.49
90	.28	.12	.87	.68	.53
89	.32	.16	.91	.72	.57
88	.36	.19	.95	.76	.61
87	.39	.23	.99	.80	.65
86	.43	.27	72.03	.84	.69
85	.47	.31	.07	.88	.73
84	.51	.35	.11	.92	.77
83	.55	.39	.14	.96	.81
82	.59	.43	.18	71.00	.85
81	.63	.47	.22	.04	.89
80	.66	.50	.26	.07	.93
79	.70	.54	.30	.11	.97
78	.74	.58	.34	.15	70.01
77	.78	.62	.38	.19	.05
76	.82	.66	.42	.23	.09
75	.86	.70	.46	.27	.13
74	.90	.74	.49	.31	.16
73	.93	.78	.53	.35	.20
72	.97	.81	.57	.39	.24
71	75.01	.85	.61	.42	.28
70	.05	.89	.65	.46	.32
69	.09	.93	.69	.50	.36
68	.13	.97	.73	.54	.40
67	.16	74.01	.77	.58	.44
66	.20	.05	.81	.62	.48
65	.24	.08	.84	.66	.52
64	.28	.12	.88	.70	.56
63	.32	.16	.92	.74	.60
62	.35	.20	.96	.77	.64
61	.39	.24	73.00	.81	.67
60	.43	.28	.04	.85	.71
59	.47	.32	.08	.89	.75
58	.51	.35	.12	.93	.79
57	.54	.39	.15	.97	.83
56	.58	.43	.19	72.01	.87
55	.62	.47	.23	.05	.91
54	.66	.51	.27	.08	.95
53	.70	.55	.31	.12	.99
52	.73	.58	.35	.16	71.03
51	.77	.62	.38	.20	.07
50	.81	.66	.42	.24	.10
49	.85	.70	.46	.28	.14
48	.89	.74	.50	.32	.18
47	.92	.77	.54	.36	.22
46	.96	.81	.58	.39	.26
45	76.00	.85	.62	.43	.30
44	.04	.89	.65	.47	.34
43	.07	.93	.69	.51	.38
42	.11	.97	.73	.55	.41
41	.15	75.00	.77	.59	.45

(Continued)

52.003 Percentages by volume at 15.56°C (60°F) of ethyl alcohol corresponding to apparent specific gravity at various temperatures[a]—*Continued.*

Apparent Specific Gravity	15.56/15.56	20/20	25/25	30/30	35/35
0.8740	76.19	75.04	73.81	72.63	71.49
39	.22	.08	.85	.66	.53
38	.26	.12	.88	.70	.57
37	.30	.16	.92	.74	.61
36	.34	.19	.96	.78	.65
35	.37	.23	74.00	.82	.69
34	.41	.27	.04	.86	.72
33	.45	.31	.08	.90	.76
32	.49	.35	.11	.93	.80
31	.52	.38	.15	.97	.84
30	.56	.42	.19	73.01	.88
29	.60	.46	.23	.05	.92
28	.64	.50	.27	.09	.96
27	.67	.54	.31	.13	72.00
26	.71	.57	.34	.16	.03
25	.75	.61	.38	.20	.07
24	.79	.65	.42	.24	.11
23	.82	.69	.46	.28	.15
22	.86	.73	.50	.32	.19
21	.90	.76	.53	.35	.23
20	.94	.80	.57	.39	.27
19	.97	.84	.61	.43	.30
18	77.01	.88	.65	.47	.34
17	.05	.91	.69	.51	.38
16	.09	.95	.73	.55	.42
15	.12	.99	.76	.58	.46
14	.16	76.03	.80	.62	.50
13	.20	.06	.84	.66	.53
12	.23	.10	.88	.70	.57
11	.27	.14	.92	.74	.61
10	.31	.18	.95	.77	.65
09	.34	.22	.99	.81	.69
08	.38	.25	75.03	.85	.73
07	.42	.29	.07	.89	.77
06	.46	.33	.10	.93	.80
05	.49	.37	.14	.97	.84
04	.53	.40	.18	74.00	.88
03	.57	.44	.22	.04	.92
02	.60	.48	.25	.08	.96
01	.64	.52	.29	.12	73.00
00	.68	.55	.33	.16	.03
0.8699	.71	.59	.37	.19	.07
98	.75	.63	.40	.23	.11
97	.79	.66	.44	.27	.15
96	.83	.70	.48	.31	.19
95	.86	.74	.52	.35	.22
94	.90	.78	.55	.38	.26
93	.94	.81	.59	.42	.30
92	.97	.85	.63	.46	.34
91	78.01	.89	.67	.50	.38
90	.05	.92	.70	.54	.41
89	.08	.96	.74	.57	.45
88	.12	77.00	.78	.61	.49
87	.16	.03	.82	.65	.53
86	.19	.07	.85	.69	.56
85	.23	.11	.89	.73	.60
84	.27	.14	.93	.76	.64
83	.30	.18	.97	.80	.68
82	.34	.22	76.00	.84	.72
81	.38	.26	.04	.88	.75
80	.41	.29	.08	.92	.79
79	.45	.33	.12	.95	.83
78	.49	.37	.15	.99	.87
77	.52	.40	.19	75.03	.91
76	.56	.44	.23	.07	.94
75	.60	.48	.26	.10	.98
74	.63	.51	.30	.14	74.02
73	.67	.55	.34	.18	.06
72	.71	.59	.38	.22	.09
71	.74	.62	.41	.25	.13

Apparent Specific Gravity	15.56/15.56	20/20	25/25	30/30	35/35
0.8670	78.78	77.66	76.45	75.29	74.17
69	.82	.70	.49	.33	.21
68	.85	.73	.53	.37	.24
67	.89	.77	.56	.40	.28
66	.93	.81	.60	.44	.32
65	.96	.84	.64	.48	.36
64	79.00	.88	.68	.51	.39
63	.04	.92	.71	.55	.43
62	.07	.96	.75	.59	.47
61	.11	.99	.79	.63	.51
60	.14	78.03	.82	.66	.55
59	.18	.07	.86	.70	.58
58	.22	.10	.90	.74	.62
57	.25	.14	.94	.78	.66
56	.29	.17	.97	.81	.70
55	.32	.21	77.01	.85	.73
54	.36	.25	.05	.89	.77
53	.40	.28	.08	.93	.81
52	.43	.32	.12	.96	.85
51	.47	.36	.16	76.00	.88
50	.51	.39	.19	.04	.92
49	.54	.43	.23	.07	.96
48	.58	.47	.27	.11	75.00
47	.61	.50	.30	.15	.03
46	.65	.54	.34	.19	.07
45	.69	.57	.38	.22	.11
44	.72	.61	.41	.26	.15
43	.76	.65	.45	.30	.18
42	.79	.68	.49	.33	.22
41	.83	.72	.52	.37	.26
40	.87	.76	.56	.41	.29
39	.90	.79	.60	.44	.33
38	.94	.83	.63	.48	.37
37	.97	.86	.67	.52	.41
36	80.01	.90	.71	.56	.44
35	.05	.94	.74	.59	.48
34	.08	.97	.78	.63	.52
33	.12	79.01	.82	.67	.56
32	.15	.05	.85	.70	.59
31	.19	.08	.89	.74	.63
30	.22	.12	.93	.78	.67
29	.26	.16	.96	.81	.71
28	.30	.19	78.00	.85	.74
27	.33	.23	.04	.89	.78
26	.37	.26	.07	.93	.82
25	.40	.30	.11	.96	.85
24	.44	.34	.14	77.00	.89
23	.47	.37	.18	.04	.93
22	.51	.41	.22	.07	.97
21	.55	.45	.25	.11	76.00
20	.58	.48	.29	.15	.04
19	.62	.52	.33	.18	.08
18	.65	.55	.36	.22	.11
17	.69	.59	.40	.26	.15
16	.72	.63	.43	.29	.19
15	.76	.66	.47	.33	.23
14	.80	.70	.51	.36	.26
13	.83	.73	.54	.40	.30
12	.87	.77	.58	.44	.34
11	.90	.80	.62	.47	.37
10	.94	.84	.65	.51	.41
09	.97	.88	.69	.55	.45
08	81.01	.91	.72	.58	.48
07	.05	.95	.76	.62	.52
06	.08	.98	.80	.66	.56
05	.12	80.02	.83	.69	.59
04	.15	.05	.87	.73	.63
03	.19	.09	.91	.77	.67
02	.22	.13	.94	.80	.70
01	.26	.16	.98	.84	.74

(Continued)

52.003 Percentages by volume at 15.56°C (60°F) of ethyl alcohol corresponding to apparent specific gravity at various temperatures[a]—*Continued.*

Apparent Specific Gravity	15.56/15.56	20/20	25/25	30/30	35/35
0.8600	81.29	80.20	79.01	77.88	76.78
0.8599	.33	.23	.05	.91	.82
98	.36	.27	.09	.95	.85
97	.40	.30	.12	.99	.89
96	.43	.34	.16	78.02	.93
95	.47	.38	.19	.06	.96
94	.51	.41	.23	.09	77.00
93	.54	.45	.27	.13	.04
92	.58	.48	.30	.17	.07
91	.61	.52	.34	.20	.11
90	.65	.55	.37	.24	.14
89	.68	.59	.41	.27	.18
88	.72	.62	.44	.31	.22
87	.75	.66	.48	.35	.25
86	.79	.69	.52	.38	.29
85	.82	.73	.55	.42	.33
84	.86	.77	.59	.45	.36
83	.89	.80	.62	.49	.40
82	.93	.84	.66	.53	.43
81	.96	.87	.70	.56	.47
80	82.00	.91	.73	.60	.51
79	.03	.94	.77	.64	.54
78	.07	.98	.80	.67	.58
77	.10	81.01	.84	.71	.62
76	.14	.05	.87	.74	.65
75	.17	.08	.91	.78	.69
74	.21	.12	.95	.82	.72
73	.24	.16	.98	.85	.76
72	.28	.19	80.02	.89	.80
71	.31	.23	.05	.92	.83
70	.35	.26	.09	.96	.87
69	.38	.30	.12	79.00	.91
68	.42	.33	.16	.03	.94
67	.45	.37	.20	.07	.98
66	.49	.40	.23	.10	78.01
65	.52	.44	.27	.14	.05
64	.56	.47	.30	.17	.09
63	.59	.51	.34	.21	.12
62	.63	.54	.37	.25	.16
61	.66	.58	.41	.28	.19
60	.70	.61	.44	.32	.23
59	.73	.65	.48	.35	.27
58	.77	.68	.51	.39	.30
57	.80	.72	.55	.42	.34
56	.84	.75	.59	.46	.37
55	.87	.79	.62	.49	.41
54	.91	.82	.66	.53	.45
53	.94	.86	.69	.57	.48
52	.98	.89	.73	.60	.52
51	83.01	.93	.76	.64	.55
50	.04	.96	.80	.67	.59
49	.08	82.00	.83	.71	.63
48	.11	.03	.87	.74	.66
47	.15	.07	.90	.78	.70
46	.18	.10	.94	.81	.73
45	.22	.14	.98	.85	.77
44	.25	.17	81.01	.89	.81
43	.29	.21	.05	.92	.84
42	.32	.24	.08	.96	.88
41	.35	.28	.12	.99	.91
40	.39	.31	.15	80.03	.95
39	.42	.35	.19	.06	.99
38	.46	.38	.22	.10	79.02
37	.49	.42	.26	.13	.06
36	.53	.45	.29	.17	.09
35	.56	.49	.30	.20	.13
34	.59	.52	.36	.24	.16
33	.63	.55	.40	.28	.20
32	.66	.59	.43	.31	.23
31	.70	.62	.47	.35	.27
0.8530	83.73	82.66	81.50	80.38	79.30
29	.77	.69	.54	.42	.34
28	.80	.73	.57	.45	.38
27	.84	.76	.61	.49	.41
26	.87	.80	.64	.52	.45
25	.90	.83	.68	.56	.48
24	.94	.87	.71	.59	.52
23	.97	.90	.75	.63	.55
22	84.01	.94	.78	.66	.59
21	.04	.97	.82	.70	.62
20	.07	83.01	.85	.73	.66
19	.11	.04	.89	.77	.70
18	.14	.07	.92	.81	.73
17	.18	.11	.96	.84	.77
16	.21	.14	.99	.88	.80
15	.24	.18	82.03	.91	.84
14	.28	.21	.06	.95	.87
13	.31	.25	.10	.98	.91
12	.34	.28	.13	81.02	.94
11	.38	.32	.16	.05	.98
10	.41	.35	.20	.09	80.01
09	.45	.39	.23	.12	.05
08	.48	.42	.27	.16	.08
07	.51	.45	.30	.19	.12
06	.55	.49	.34	.23	.15
05	.58	.52	.37	.26	.19
04	.61	.56	.41	.30	.23
03	.65	.59	.44	.33	.26
02	.68	.62	.47	.37	.30
01	.72	.66	.51	.40	.33
00	.75	.69	.54	.44	.37
0.8499	.78	.73	.58	.47	.40
98	.82	.76	.61	.51	.44
97	.85	.79	.65	.54	.47
96	.89	.83	.68	.57	.51
95	.92	.86	.71	.61	.54
94	.95	.90	.75	.64	.58
93	.99	.93	.78	.68	.61
92	85.02	.97	.82	.71	.65
91	.05	84.00	.85	.75	.68
90	.09	.03	.89	.78	.72
89	.12	.07	.92	.82	.75
88	.15	.10	.96	.85	.79
87	.18	.14	.99	.89	.82
86	.22	.17	83.02	.92	.86
85	.25	.20	.06	.96	.89
84	.28	.24	.09	.99	.93
83	.32	.27	.13	82.03	.96
82	.35	.31	.16	.06	81.00
81	.38	.34	.20	.10	.03
80	.42	.37	.23	.13	.07
79	.45	.41	.26	.17	.10
78	.48	.44	.30	.20	.14
77	.51	.47	.33	.24	.17
76	.55	.51	.37	.27	.21
75	.58	.54	.40	.30	.24
74	.61	.57	.43	.34	.28
73	.65	.61	.47	.37	.31
72	.68	.64	.50	.41	.35
71	.71	.67	.54	.44	.38
70	.75	.71	.57	.48	.42
69	.78	.74	.61	.51	.45
68	.81	.78	.64	.55	.49
67	.84	.81	.67	.58	.52
66	.88	.84	.71	.62	.56
65	.91	.88	.74	.65	.59
64	.94	.91	.78	.69	.63
63	.98	.94	.81	.72	.66
62	86.01	.98	.85	.75	.70
61	.04	85.01	.88	.79	.73

(Continued)

52.003 Percentages by volume at 15.56°C (60°F) of ethyl alcohol corresponding to apparent specific gravity at various temperatures[a]—*Continued.*

Apparent Specific Gravity	15.56/15.56	20/20	25/25	30/30	35/35	Apparent Specific Gravity	15.56/15.56	20/20	25/25	30/30	35/35
0.8460	86.08	85.04	83.91	82.82	81.77	0.8390	88.33	87.33	86.24	85.18	84.16
59	.11	.08	.95	.86	.80	89	.36	.36	.28	.22	.19
58	.14	.11	.98	.89	.84	88	.39	.39	.31	.25	.22
57	.17	.14	84.02	.93	.87	87	.43	.43	.34	.28	.26
56	.21	.18	.05	.96	.91	86	.46	.46	.37	.31	.29
55	.24	.21	.08	83.00	.94	85	.49	.49	.40	.35	.32
54	.27	.24	.12	.03	.98	84	.52	.52	.44	.38	.36
53	.30	.28	.15	.06	82.01	83	.55	.55	.47	.41	.39
52	.34	.31	.18	.10	.04	82	.58	.58	.50	.45	.42
51	.37	.34	.22	.13	.08	81	.61	.62	.53	.48	.46
50	.40	.38	.25	.17	.11	80	.65	.65	.57	.51	.49
49	.43	.41	.29	.20	.15	79	.68	.68	.60	.54	.52
48	.47	.44	.32	.23	.18	78	.71	.71	.63	.58	.55
47	.50	.48	.35	.27	.22	77	.74	.74	.66	.61	.59
46	.53	.51	.39	.30	.25	76	.77	.78	.70	.64	.62
45	.57	.54	.42	.34	.28	75	.80	.81	.73	.68	.65
44	.60	.57	.45	.37	.32	74	.83	.84	.76	.71	.69
43	.63	.61	.49	.40	.35	73	.87	.87	.79	.74	.72
42	.66	.64	.52	.44	.39	72	.90	.90	.83	.77	.75
41	.70	.67	.55	.47	.42	71	.93	.94	.86	.81	.79
40	.73	.71	.59	.51	.46	70	.96	.97	.89	.84	.82
39	.76	.74	.62	.54	.49	69	.99	88.00	.92	.87	.85
38	.79	.77	.65	.57	.52	68	89.02	.03	.95	.90	.89
37	.83	.80	.69	.61	.56	67	.05	.06	.99	.94	.92
36	.86	.84	.72	.64	.59	66	.08	.09	87.02	.97	.95
35	.89	.87	.76	.68	.63	65	.11	.13	.05	86.00	.99
34	.92	.90	.79	.71	.66	64	.14	.16	.08	.04	85.02
33	.96	.94	.82	.74	.70	63	.18	.19	.11	.07	.05
32	.99	.97	.86	.78	.73	62	.21	.22	.15	.10	.08
31	87.02	86.00	.89	.81	.76	61	.24	.25	.18	.13	.12
30	.05	.03	.92	.85	.80	60	.27	.29	.21	.16	.15
29	.09	.07	.96	.88	.83	59	.30	.32	.24	.20	.18
28	.12	.10	.99	.91	.87	58	.33	.35	.27	.23	.22
27	.15	.13	85.02	.95	.90	57	.36	.38	.31	.26	.25
26	.18	.16	.06	.98	.93	56	.39	.41	.34	.29	.28
25	.22	.20	.09	84.02	.97	55	.42	.44	.37	.33	.31
24	.25	.23	.12	.05	83.00	54	.45	.47	.40	.36	.35
23	.28	.26	.16	.08	.04	53	.48	.50	.43	.39	.38
22	.31	.30	.19	.12	.07	52	.51	.54	.46	.42	.41
21	.34	.33	.22	.15	.11	51	.54	.57	.50	.45	.44
20	.38	.36	.25	.18	.14	50	.58	.60	.53	.49	.48
19	.41	.39	.29	.22	.17	49	.61	.63	.56	.52	.51
18	.44	.43	.32	.25	.21	48	.64	.66	.59	.55	.54
17	.47	.46	.35	.28	.24	47	.67	.69	.62	.58	.58
16	.50	.49	.39	.32	.28	46	.70	.72	.66	.62	.61
15	.54	.52	.42	.35	.31	45	.73	.75	.69	.65	.64
14	.57	.56	.45	.38	.34	44	.76	.79	.72	.68	.67
13	.60	.59	.49	.42	.38	43	.79	.82	.75	.71	.71
12	.63	.62	.52	.45	.41	42	.82	.85	.78	.75	.74
11	.67	.65	.55	.48	.45	41	.85	.88	.82	.78	.77
10	.70	.68	.59	.52	.48	40	.88	.91	.85	.81	.80
09	.73	.72	.62	.55	.51	39	.91	.94	.88	.84	.84
08	.76	.75	.65	.59	.55	38	.94	.97	.91	.87	.87
07	.79	.78	.69	.62	.58	37	.98	89.00	.94	.91	.90
06	.83	.81	.72	.65	.62	36	90.01	.04	.97	.94	.93
05	.86	.85	.75	.69	.65	35	.04	.07	88.01	.97	.97
04	.89	.88	.78	.72	.68	34	.07	.10	.04	87.00	86.00
03	.92	.91	.82	.75	.72	33	.10	.13	.07	.04	.03
02	.95	.94	.85	.79	.75	32	.13	.16	.10	.07	.06
01	.99	.98	.88	.82	.79	31	.16	.19	.13	.10	.10
00	88.02	87.01	.92	.85	.82	30	.19	.22	.16	.13	.13
0.8399	.05	.04	.95	.89	.85	29	.22	.25	.19	.16	.16
98	.08	.07	.98	.92	.89	28	.25	.28	.23	.19	.19
97	.11	.10	86.02	.95	.92	27	.28	.31	.26	.23	.23
96	.14	.14	.05	.99	.96	26	.31	.35	.29	.26	.26
95	.18	.17	.08	85.02	.99	25	.34	.38	.32	.29	.29
94	.21	.20	.11	.05	84.02	24	.37	.41	.35	.32	.32
93	.24	.23	.15	.09	.06	23	.40	.44	.38	.35	.35
92	.27	.27	.18	.12	.09	22	.43	.47	.41	.39	[illegible]
91	.30	.30	.21	.15	.12	21	.46	.50	.45	.42	[illegible]

(Cor

52.003 Percentages by volume at 15.56°C (60°F) of ethyl alcohol corresponding to apparent specific gravity at various temperatures[a]—*Continued.*

Apparent Specific Gravity	15.56/15.56	20/20	25/25	30/30	35/35
0.8320	90.49	89.53	88.48	87.45	86.45
19	.51	.56	.51	.48	.48
18	.54	.59	.54	.51	.52
17	.57	.62	.57	.54	.55
16	.60	.65	.60	.58	.58
15	.63	.68	.64	.61	.61
14	.66	.71	.67	.64	.65
13	.69	.74	.70	.67	.68
12	.72	.77	.73	.70	.71
11	.75	.80	.76	.74	.74
10	.78	.83	.79	.77	.77
09	.81	.86	.82	.80	.81
08	.84	.89	.85	.83	.84
07	.87	.93	.88	.86	.87
06	.90	.96	.92	.89	.90
05	.93	.99	.95	.93	.94
04	.96	90.02	.98	.96	.97
03	.99	.05	89.01	.99	87.00
02	91.02	.08	.04	88.02	.03
01	.05	.11	.07	.05	.06
00	.08	.14	.10	.08	.10
0.8299	.11	.17	.13	.12	.13
98	.14	.20	.16	.15	.16
97	.17	.23	.19	.18	.19
96	.20	.26	.22	.21	.22
95	.23	.29	.25	.24	.25
94	.26	.32	.28	.27	.29
93	.28	.35	.31	.30	.32
92	.31	.38	.35	.34	.35
91	.34	.41	.38	.37	.38
90	.37	.44	.41	.40	.41
89	.40	.47	.44	.43	.44
88	.43	.50	.47	.46	.48
87	.46	.53	.50	.49	.51
86	.49	.56	.53	.52	.54
85	.52	.59	.56	.55	.57
84	.55	.62	.59	.59	.60
83	.58	.65	.62	.62	.63
82	.60	.67	.65	.65	.67
81	.63	.70	.68	.68	.70
80	.66	.73	.71	.71	.73
79	.69	.76	.74	.74	.76
78	.72	.79	.77	.77	.79
77	.75	.82	.80	.81	.83
76	.78	.85	.83	.84	.86
75	.81	.88	.87	.87	.89
74	.84	.91	.90	.90	.92
73	.87	.94	.93	.93	.95
72	.90	.97	.96	.96	.98
71	.92	91.00	.99	.99	88.02
70	.95	.03	90.02	89.02	.05
69	.98	.06	.05	.06	.08
68	92.01	.09	.08	.09	.11
67	.04	.12	.11	.12	.14
66	.07	.15	.14	.15	.17
65	.10	.18	.17	.18	.20
64	.13	.21	.20	.21	.23
63	.15	.24	.23	.24	.26
62	.18	.27	.26	.27	.30
61	.21	.29	.29	.30	.33
60	.24	.32	.32	.33	.36
59	.27	.35	.35	.36	.39
58	.30	.38	.38	.39	.42
57	.33	.41	.41	.42	.45
56	.35	.44	.44	.45	.48
55	.38	.47	.47	.48	.51
54	.41	.50	.50	.51	.55
53	.44	.53	.53	.54	.58
52	.47	.56	.56	.57	.61
51	.50	.59	.59	.61	.64

Apparent Specific Gravity	15.56/15.56	20/20	25/25	30/30	35/35
0.8250	92.53	91.62	90.61	89.64	88.67
49	.55	.64	.64	.67	.70
48	.58	.67	.67	.70	.73
47	.61	.70	.70	.73	.76
46	.64	.73	.73	.76	.79
45	.66	.76	.76	.79	.83
44	.69	.79	.79	.82	.86
43	.72	.82	.82	.85	.89
42	.75	.85	.85	.88	.92
41	.78	.87	.88	.91	.95
40	.80	.90	.91	.94	.98
39	.83	.93	.94	.97	89.01
38	.86	.96	.97	90.00	.04
37	.89	.99	91.00	.03	.07
36	.92	92.02	.03	.06	.10
35	.94	.05	.06	.09	.13
34	.97	.08	.09	.12	.16
33	93.00	.10	.12	.15	.20
32	.03	.13	.15	.18	.23
31	.05	.16	.18	.21	.26
30	.08	.19	.21	.24	.29
29	.11	.22	.23	.27	.32
28	.14	.25	.26	.30	.35
27	.16	.28	.29	.33	.38
26	.19	.31	.32	.36	.41
25	.22	.33	.35	.39	.44
24	.25	.36	.38	.42	.47
23	.27	.39	.41	.45	.50
22	.30	.42	.44	.48	.53
21	.33	.45	.47	.51	.56
20	.36	.48	.50	.54	.59
19	.38	.50	.52	.57	.62
18	.41	.53	.55	.60	.65
17	.44	.56	.58	.63	.68
16	.47	.59	.61	.66	.71
15	.49	.62	.64	.69	.74
14	.52	.65	.67	.72	.77
13	.55	.67	.70	.75	.80
12	.58	.70	.73	.78	.84
11	.60	.73	.76	.81	.87
10	.63	.76	.79	.84	.90
09	.66	.79	.81	.87	.93
08	.68	.81	.84	.90	.96
07	.71	.84	.87	.93	.99
06	.74	.87	.90	.96	90.02
05	.76	.90	.93	.99	.05
04	.79	.92	.96	91.01	.08
03	.82	.95	.99	.04	.11
02	.84	.98	92.02	.07	.14
01	.87	93.01	.05	.10	.17
00	.90	.04	.07	.13	.20
0.8199	.92	.06	.10	.16	.23
98	.95	.09	.13	.19	.26
97	.98	.12	.16	.22	.29
96	94.01	.14	.19	.25	.32
95	.03	.17	.22	.27	.35
94	.06	.20	.24	.30	.38
93	.08	.23	.27	.33	.40
92	.11	.25	.30	.36	.43
91	.14	.28	.33	.39	.46
90	.16	.31	.36	.42	.49
89	.19	.34	.39	.45	.52
88	.22	.36	.41	.48	.55
87	.24	.39	.44	.51	.58
86	.27	.42	.47	.53	.61
85	.30	.44	.50	.56	.64
84	.32	.47	.53	.59	.67
83	.35	.50	.56	.62	.70
82	.38	.53	.58	.65	.73
81	.40	.55	.61	.68	.76

(Continued)

52.003 **Percentages by volume at 15.56°C (60°F) of ethyl alcohol corresponding to apparent specific gravity at various temperatures[a]**—*Continued.*

Apparent Specific Gravity	15.56/15.56	20/20	25/25	30/30	35/35
0.8180	94.43	93.58	92.64	91.71	90.79
79	.46	.61	.67	.74	.82
78	.48	.64	.70	.77	.85
77	.51	.66	.72	.79	.88
76	.53	.69	.75	.82	.91
75	.56	.72	.78	.85	.94
74	.59	.74	.81	.88	.97
73	.61	.77	.84	.91	91.00
72	.64	.80	.86	.94	.03
71	.66	.82	.89	.97	.06
70	.69	.85	.92	92.00	.09
69	.72	.88	.95	.03	.12
68	.74	.90	.97	.05	.14
67	.77	.93	93.00	.08	.17
66	.79	.96	.03	.11	.20
65	.82	.98	.06	.14	.23
64	.84	94.01	.09	.17	.26
63	.87	.04	.11	.20	.29
62	.90	.06	.14	.22	.32
61	.92	.09	.17	.25	.35
60	.95	.12	.20	.28	.38
59	.97	.14	.22	.31	.40
58	95.00	.17	.25	.34	.43
57	.03	.20	.28	.36	.46
56	.05	.22	.30	.39	.49
55	.08	.25	.33	.42	.52
54	.10	.28	.36	.45	.55
53	.13	.30	.39	.48	.58
52	.15	.33	.41	.51	.61
51	.18	.36	.44	.54	.64
50	.20	.38	.47	.56	.66
49	.23	.41	.50	.59	.69
48	.25	.44	.52	.62	.72
47	.28	.46	.55	.65	.75
46	.30	.49	.58	.68	.78
45	.33	.51	.60	.70	.81
44	.36	.54	.63	.73	.84
43	.38	.57	.66	.76	.87
42	.41	.59	.69	.79	.90
41	.43	.62	.71	.82	.92
40	.46	.64	.74	.84	.95
39	.48	.67	.77	.87	.98
38	.51	.70	.79	.90	92.01
37	.53	.72	.82	.93	.04
36	.56	.75	.85	.96	.07
35	.58	.77	.87	.98	.10
34	.61	.80	.90	93.01	.13
33	.63	.83	.93	.04	.15
32	.66	.85	.95	.07	.18
31	.68	.88	.98	.09	.21
30	.71	.90	94.01	.12	.24
29	.73	.93	.03	.15	.27
28	.76	.95	.06	.18	.30
27	.78	.98	.09	.20	.33
26	.81	95.01	.11	.23	.35
25	.83	.03	.14	.26	.38
24	.86	.06	.17	.29	.41
23	.88	.08	.19	.31	.44
22	.91	.11	.22	.34	.47
21	.93	.14	.24	.37	.50
20	.96	.16	.27	.40	.53
19	.98	.19	.30	.42	.55
18	96.01	.21	.32	.45	.58
17	.03	.24	.35	.48	.61
16	.06	.26	.38	.51	.64
15	.08	.29	.40	.53	.66
14	.10	.32	.43	.56	.69
13	.13	.34	.46	.59	.72
12	.15	.37	.48	.61	.75
11	.18	.39	.51	.64	.78

Apparent Specific Gravity	15.56/15.56	20/20	25/25	30/30	35/35
0.8110	96.20	95.42	94.53	93.67	92.80
09	.23	.44	.56	.69	.83
08	.25	.47	.59	.72	.86
07	.28	.49	.61	.75	.89
06	.30	.52	.64	.77	.92
05	.32	.54	.65	.80	.94
04	.35	.57	.69	.83	.97
03	.37	.59	.72	.85	93.00
02	.40	.62	.74	.88	.03
01	.42	.64	.77	.91	.05
00	.45	.67	.79	.94	.08
0.8099	.47	.69	.82	.96	.11
98	.50	.72	.85	.99	.14
97	.52	.74	.87	94.02	.16
96	.54	.77	.90	.04	.19
95	.57	.79	.92	.07	.22
94	.59	.82	.95	.10	.25
93	.61	.84	.98	.12	.27
92	.64	.87	95.00	.15	.30
91	.66	.89	.03	.17	.33
90	.69	.92	.05	.20	.36
89	.71	.94	.08	.23	.38
88	.73	.97	.10	.25	.41
87	.76	.99	.13	.28	.44
86	.78	96.02	.16	.31	.46
85	.81	.04	.18	.33	.49
84	.83	.07	.21	.36	.52
83	.85	.09	.23	.39	.55
82	.88	.11	.26	.41	.57
81	.90	.14	.28	.44	.60
80	.93	.16	.31	.47	.63
79	.95	.19	.33	.49	.65
78	.97	.21	.36	.52	.68
77	97.00	.24	.39	.54	.71
76	.02	.26	.41	.57	.73
75	.04	.29	.44	.60	.76
74	.07	.31	.46	.62	.79
73	.09	.33	.49	.65	.81
72	.11	.36	.51	.67	.84
71	.14	.38	.54	.70	.87
70	.16	.41	.56	.73	.90
69	.18	.43	.59	.75	.92
68	.21	.46	.61	.78	.95
67	.23	.48	.64	.80	.98
66	.25	.50	.66	.83	94.00
65	.28	.53	.69	.86	.03
64	.30	.55	.71	.88	.06
63	.32	.58	.74	.91	.08
62	.35	.60	.76	.93	.11
61	.37	.63	.79	.96	.14
60	.39	.65	.81	.99	.16
59	.42	.67	.84	95.01	.19
58	.44	.70	.86	.04	.22
57	.46	.72	.89	.06	.24
56	.49	.75	.91	.09	.27
55	.51	.77	.94	.11	.30
54	.53	.79	.96	.14	.32
53	.55	.82	.99	.17	.35
52	.58	.84	96.01	.19	.38
51	.60	.86	.04	.22	.40
50	.62	.89	.06	.24	.43
49	.64	.91	.09	.27	.45
48	.67	.94	.11	.29	.48
47	.69	.96	.14	.32	.51
46	.71	.98	.16	.34	.53
45	.73	97.01	.19	.37	.56
44	.76	.03	.21	.40	.59
43	.78	.05	.24	.42	.61
42	.80	.08	.26	.45	.64
41	.82	.10	.28	.47	.66

(Continued)

52.003 Percentages by volume at 15.56°C (60°F) of ethyl alcohol corresponding to apparent specific gravity at various temperatures[a]—*Continued.*

Apparent Specific Gravity	15.56/15.56	20/20	25/25	30/30	35/35
0.8040	97.85	97.12	96.31	95.50	94.69
39	.87	.15	.33	.52	.72
38	.89	.17	.36	.55	.74
37	.91	.19	.38	.57	.77
36	.94	.22	.41	.60	.79
35	.96	.24	.43	.62	.82
34	.98	.26	.46	.65	.85
33	98.00	.29	.48	.67	.87
32	.03	.31	.50	.70	.90
31	.05	.33	.53	.72	.92
30	.07	.36	.55	.75	.95
29	.09	.38	.58	.77	.98
28	.11	.40	.60	.80	95.00
27	.14	.43	.62	.82	.03
26	.16	.45	.65	.85	.05
25	.18	.47	.67	.87	.08
24	.20	.49	.70	.90	.11
23	.22	.52	.72	.92	.13
22	.25	.54	.74	.95	.16
21	.27	.56	.77	.97	.18
20	.29	.59	.79	96.00	.21
19	.31	.61	.82	.02	.23
18	.33	.63	.84	.05	.26
17	.35	.66	.86	.07	.28
16	.38	.68	.89	.10	.31
15	.40	.70	.91	.12	.34
14	.42	.72	.94	.15	.36
13	.44	.75	.96	.17	.39
12	.46	.77	.98	.20	.41
11	.48	.79	97.01	.22	.44
10	.50	.81	.03	.25	.46
09	.53	.84	.05	.27	.49
08	.55	.86	.08	.29	.52
07	.57	.88	.10	.32	.54
06	.59	.90	.12	.34	.57
05	.61	.92	.15	.37	.59
04	.63	.95	.17	.39	.62
03	.65	.97	.19	.42	.64
02	.67	.99	.22	.44	.67
01	.70	98.01	.24	.47	.69
00	.72	.03	.26	.49	.72
0.7999	.74	.06	.29	.51	.74
98	.76	.08	.31	.54	.77
97	.78	.10	.33	.56	.79
96	.80	.12	.36	.59	.82
95	.82	.14	.38	.61	.84
94	.84	.17	.40	.63	.87
93	.86	.19	.43	.66	.89
92	.88	.21	.45	.68	.92
91	.90	.23	.47	.71	.94
90	.92	.26	.50	.73	.97
89	.95	.28	.52	.75	.99
88	.97	.30	.54	.78	96.02
87	.99	.32	.57	.80	.04
86	99.01	.34	.59	.83	.07
85	.03	.36	.61	.85	.09
84	.05	.39	.63	.87	.12
83	.07	.41	.66	.90	.14
82	.09	.43	.68	.92	.16
81	.11	.45	.70	.95	.19
80	.13	.47	.72	.97	.21
79	.15	.49	.75	97.00	.24
78	.17	.51	.77	.02	.26
77	.19	.54	.79	.04	.29
76	.21	.56	.81	.07	.31
75	.23	.58	.84	.09	.34
74	.25	.60	.86	.11	.36
73	.27	.62	.88	.14	.38
72	.29	.64	.90	.16	.41
71	.31	.66	.93	.18	.43

Apparent Specific Gravity	15.56/15.56	20/20	25/25	30/30	35/35
0.7970	99.33	98.68	97.95	97.21	96.46
69	.35	.70	.97	.23	.48
68	.37	.72	.99	.25	.51
67	.39	.75	98.02	.28	.53
66	.42	.77	.04	.30	.56
65	.44	.79	.06	.32	.58
64	.46	.81	.08	.35	.60
63	.48	.83	.10	.37	.63
62	.50	.85	.12	.39	.65
61	.52	.87	.15	.42	.68
60	.54	.89	.17	.44	.70
59	.56	.91	.19	.46	.72
58	.58	.93	.21	.49	.75
57	.60	.95	.23	.51	.77
56	.61	.97	.26	.53	.80
55	.63	99.00	.28	.56	.82
54	.65	.02	.30	.58	.84
53	.67	.04	.32	.60	.87
52	.69	.06	.34	.62	.89
51	.71	.08	.36	.65	.92
50	.73	.10	.39	.67	.94
49	.75	.12	.41	.69	.96
48	.77	.14	.43	.71	.99
47	.79	.16	.45	.74	97.01
46	.81	.18	.47	.76	.04
45	.83	.20	.49	.78	.06
44	.85	.22	.51	.80	.08
43	.87	.24	.54	.83	.11
42	.89	.26	.56	.85	.13
41	.91	.28	.58	.87	.15
40	.93	.30	.60	.89	.18
39	.95	.32	.62	.92	.20
38	.97	.34	.64	.94	.22
37	.99	.36	.66	.96	.25
36	100.00	.38	.68	.98	.27
35		.40	.70	98.01	.29
34		.42	.73	.03	.32
33		.44	.75	.05	.34
32		.46	.77	.07	.36
31		.48	.79	.09	.39
30		.50	.81	.12	.41
29		.52	.83	.14	.43
28		.54	.85	.16	.46
27		.56	.87	.18	.48
26		.58	.89	.20	.50
25		.60	.91	.23	.52
24		.62	.93	.25	.55
23		.64	.96	.27	.57
22		.66	.98	.29	.59
21		.68	99.00	.31	.62
20		.70	.02	.33	.64
19		.72	.04	.36	.66
18		.74	.06	.38	.68
17		.76	.08	.40	.71
16		.78	.10	.42	.73
15		.80	.12	.44	.75
14		.82	.14	.46	.77
13		.84	.16	.48	.80
12		.86	.18	.51	.82
11		.88	.20	.53	.84
10		.90	.22	.55	.86
09		.92	.24	.57	.89
08		.94	.27	.59	.91
07		.96	.29	.61	.93
06		.98	.31	.63	.95
05		100.00	.33	.66	.98
04			.35	.68	98.00
03			.37	.70	.02
02			.39	.72	.04
01			.41	.74	.07

(Continued)

52.003 Percentages by volume at 15.56°C (60°F) of ethyl alcohol corresponding to apparent specific gravity at various temperatures[a]—*Concluded.*

Apparent Specific Gravity	25/25	30/30	35/35
0.7900	99.43	98.76	98.09
.7899	.45	.78	.11
98	.47	.80	.13
97	.49	.82	.15
96	.51	.84	.18
95	.53	.87	.20
94	.55	.89	.22
93	.57	.91	.24
92	.59	.93	.26
91	.61	.95	.29
90	.63	.97	.31
89	.65	.99	.33
88	.67	99.01	.35
87	.69	.03	.37
86	.71	.05	.40
85	.73	.07	.42
84	.75	.09	.44
83	.77	.12	.46
82	.79	.14	.48
81	.81	.16	.50
80	.83	.18	.53
79	.85	.20	.55
78	.86	.22	.57
77	.88	.24	.59
76	.90	.26	.61
75	.92	.28	.63
74	.94	.30	.65
73	.96	.32	.67
72	.98	.34	.70
71	100.00	.36	.72
70		.38	.74
69		.40	.76
68		.42	.78
67		.44	.80
66		.46	.82
65		.48	.84
64		.50	.86
63		.52	.89
62		.54	.91
61		.56	.93
60		.58	.95
59		.60	.97
58		.62	.99
57		.64	99.01
56		.66	.03
55		.68	.05
54		.70	.07
53		.72	.09
52		.74	.12
51		.76	.14
50		.78	.16
49		.80	.18
48		.82	.20
47		.84	.22
46		.86	.24
45		.88	.26
44		.90	.28
43		.92	.30
42		.94	.32
41		.96	.34
40		.98	.36
39		100.00	.38
38			.40
37			.42
36			.44
35			.46
34			.48
33			.50
32			.52
31			.54

Apparent Specific Gravity	35/35
0.7830	99.56
29	.58
28	.60
27	.62
26	.64
25	.66
24	.68
23	.70
22	.72
21	.74
20	.76
19	.78
18	.80
17	.82
16	.84
15	.86
14	.88
13	.90
12	.92
11	.94
10	.96
09	.98
08	100.00

52.004 Alcohol table for calculating percentages of alcohol by volume at 15.56°C (60°F) in mixtures of ethyl alcohol and water from Zeiss immersion refractometer readings and refractive indices at 17.5–25°C[a]

Scale Reading[b]	Refractive Index	Temp., °C								
		17.5	18	19	20	21	22	23	24	25
13.2	1.33250									0.00
.4	3257									0.18
.6	3265								0.14	0.35
.8	3273							0.10	0.31	0.53
14.0	3281						0.08	0.28	0.49	0.70
.2	3288					0.04	0.24	0.45	0.67	0.88
.4	3296					0.21	0.41	0.63	0.84	1.06
.6	3304				0.16	0.38	0.59	0.80	1.02	1.24
.8	3312			0.14	0.34	0.55	0.77	0.98	1.19	1.40
15.0	3319	0.00	0.10	0.31	0.52	0.73	0.94	1.16	1.36	1.55
.2	3327	0.17	0.27	0.48	0.69	0.91	1.12	1.32	1.51	1.71
.4	3335	0.34	0.44	0.65	0.85	1.07	1.29	1.47	1.66	1.86
.6	3343	0.51	0.60	0.82	1.03	1.24	1.44	1.62	1.82	2.01
.8	3350	0.68	0.78	0.99	1.21	1.40	1.60	1.77	1.97	2.17
16.0	3358	0.84	0.94	1.17	1.36	1.55	1.75	1.92	2.12	2.33
.2	3366	1.02	1.12	1.32	1.51	1.70	1.90	2.08	2.27	2.48
.4	3374	1.18	1.29	1.47	1.66	1.85	2.05	2.24	2.43	2.62
.6	3381	1.34	1.43	1.62	1.81	2.00	2.20	2.39	2.57	2.77
.8	3389	1.49	1.57	1.77	1.96	2.15	2.35	2.53	2.72	2.92
17.0	3397	1.63	1.72	1.92	2.11	2.30	2.50	2.69	2.87	3.06
.2	3405	1.77	1.87	2.06	2.26	2.45	2.65	2.82	3.02	3.21
.4	3412	1.92	2.01	2.21	2.41	2.59	2.79	2.97	3.17	3.36
.6	3420	2.07	2.16	2.36	2.56	2.74	2.94	3.12	3.32	3.51
.8	3428	2.21	2.31	2.51	2.70	2.89	3.09	3.27	3.46	3.66
18.0	3435	2.36	2.45	2.66	2.85	3.04	3.23	3.42	3.61	3.81
.2	3443	2.50	2.60	2.81	3.00	3.19	3.37	3.57	3.76	3.96
.4	3451	2.65	2.75	2.96	3.15	3.34	3.52	3.71	3.91	4.11
.6	3459	2.80	2.90	3.10	3.30	3.48	3.66	3.86	4.06	4.26
.8	3466	2.95	3.05	3.25	3.45	3.63	3.81	4.01	4.21	4.41
19.0	3474	3.10	3.19	3.40	3.59	3.77	3.96	4.16	4.36	4.56
.2	3482	3.25	3.34	3.55	3.73	3.92	4.11	4.31	4.51	4.70
.4	3489	3.39	3.48	3.70	3.88	4.07	4.26	4.46	4.65	4.85
.6	3497	3.53	3.63	3.84	4.03	4.22	4.41	4.61	4.80	5.00
.8	3505	3.68	3.78	3.98	4.17	4.37	4.56	4.75	4.95	5.15
20.0	3513	3.83	3.93	4.13	4.32	4.52	4.72	4.90	5.10	5.29
.2	3520	3.97	4.07	4.27	4.47	4.66	4.87	5.05	5.24	5.44
.4	3528	4.12	4.22	4.42	4.61	4.82	5.01	5.20	5.38	5.58
.6	3536	4.26	4.36	4.56	4.75	4.96	5.15	5.34	5.52	5.72
.8	3543	4.41	4.51	4.70	4.90	5.10	5.29	5.48	5.67	5.87
21.0	3551	4.56	4.65	4.85	5.04	5.24	5.44	5.62	5.82	6.02
.2	3559	4.70	4.80	4.99	5.19	5.39	5.58	5.77	5.96	6.16
.4	3566	4.84	4.94	5.14	5.33	5.53	5.72	5.91	6.11	6.30
.6	3574	4.99	5.09	5.28	5.47	5.67	5.87	6.06	6.25	6.44
.8	3582	5.13	5.23	5.43	5.61	5.82	6.01	6.20	6.39	6.59
22.0	1.33590	5.27	5.37	5.57	5.76	5.96	6.15	6.34	6.54	6.73
.2	3597	5.41	5.51	5.71	5.90	6.11	6.29	6.49	6.68	6.87
.4	3605	5.56	5.65	5.85	6.05	6.25	6.43	6.63	6.82	7.01
.6	3613	5.70	5.80	6.00	6.19	6.39	6.57	6.77	6.96	7.16
.8	3620	5.85	5.94	6.14	6.33	6.53	6.71	6.91	7.10	7.31

(Continued)

[a] Rearranged from table of B. H. St. John, which is based upon data of Doroschevskii and Dvorzhanchik, *J. Russ. Phys. Chem. Soc.* **40**, 101(1908). Scale readings were converted into refractive indices by using $n_D = 1.327338 + 0.00039347X - 0.00000020446X^2$.

[b] Scale readings refer only to scale of arbitrary units proposed by Pulfrich, *Z. Angew. Chem.* 1168(1899). According to this scale, 14.5 = 1.33300, 50.0 = 1.34650, and 100.0 = 1.36464. If immersion refractometer used is calibrated to another arbitrary scale, readings must be converted into refractive indices before table is used to determine per cent alcohol.

52.004 Alcohol table for calculating percentages of alcohol by volume at 15.56°C (60°F) in mixtures of ethyl alcohol and water from Zeiss immersion refractometer readings and refractive indices at 17.5–25°C[a]—*Continued.*

Scale Reading[b]	Refractive Index	Temp., °C								
		17.5	18	19	20	21	22	23	24	25
23.0	1.33628	5.99	6.08	6.28	6.47	6.67	6.86	7.06	7.24	7.45
.2	3636	6.13	6.22	6.42	6.61	6.81	7.00	7.20	7.39	7.59
.4	3643	6.27	6.36	6.56	6.75	6.95	7.14	7.34	7.53	7.73
.6	3651	6.41	6.50	6.70	6.90	7.09	7.28	7.48	7.67	7.87
.8	3659	6.55	6.64	6.85	7.04	7.23	7.42	7.62	7.81	8.00
24.0	3666	6.69	6.78	6.99	7.18	7.38	7.56	7.76	7.95	8.14
.2	3674	6.83	6.92	7.13	7.32	7.52	7.70	7.90	8.09	8.28
.4	3682	6.97	7.06	7.27	7.46	7.66	7.84	8.04	8.23	8.42
.6	3689	7.11	7.20	7.41	7.60	7.80	7.98	8.17	8.37	8.55
.8	3697	7.25	7.35	7.55	7.74	7.93	8.12	8.31	8.51	8.69
25.0	3705	7.39	7.49	7.68	7.88	8.06	8.26	8.45	8.64	8.84
.2	3712	7.53	7.63	7.82	8.01	8.20	8.40	8.59	8.78	8.98
.4	3720	7.66	7.76	7.95	8.14	8.34	8.54	8.73	8.92	9.12
.6	3728	7.80	7.90	8.09	8.28	8.48	8.68	8.86	9.06	9.26
.8	3735	7.94	8.03	8.22	8.42	8.62	8.82	9.00	9.20	9.39
26.0	3743	8.07	8.16	8.36	8.55	8.75	8.95	9.14	9.34	9.53
.2	3751	8.21	8.30	8.50	8.69	8.89	9.09	9.28	9.48	9.67
.4	3758	8.34	8.44	8.63	8.82	9.03	9.22	9.42	9.61	9.81
.6	3766	8.48	8.57	8.77	8.96	9.16	9.36	9.55	9.75	9.95
.8	3774	8.62	8.71	8.91	9.10	9.30	9.49	9.69	9.89	10.09
27.0	3781	8.75	8.85	9.05	9.23	9.44	9.63	9.83	10.03	10.23
.2	3789	8.89	8.98	9.18	9.37	9.58	9.76	9.97	10.17	10.37
.4	3796	9.02	9.12	9.32	9.51	9.71	9.90	10.10	10.31	10.51
.6	3804	9.16	9.26	9.45	9.65	9.85	10.03	10.24	10.45	10.65
.8	3812	9.29	9.39	9.59	9.79	9.98	10.17	10.38	10.58	10.79
28.0	3820	9.43	9.53	9.72	9.92	10.12	10.31	10.51	10.72	10.93
.2	3827	9.57	9.66	9.86	10.06	10.25	10.45	10.65	10.86	11.06
.4	3835	9.70	9.80	9.99	10.19	10.39	10.59	10.79	11.00	11.20
.6	3842	9.84	9.93	10.13	10.32	10.52	10.72	10.93	11.13	11.33
.8	3850	9.97	10.07	10.26	10.46	10.66	10.86	11.06	11.27	11.47
29.0	3858	10.10	10.19	10.40	10.59	10.79	11.00	11.20	11.40	11.61
.2	3865	10.24	10.33	10.52	10.73	10.93	11.13	11.33	11.54	11.75
.4	3873	10.36	10.46	10.66	10.86	11.06	11.27	11.47	11.67	11.88
.6	3881	10.50	10.59	10.79	10.99	11.20	11.39	11.60	11.81	12.01
.8	3888	10.63	10.72	10.93	11.12	11.33	11.53	11.74	11.94	12.15
30.0	3896	10.76	10.86	11.05	11.26	11.46	11.66	11.87	12.08	12.29
.2	3904	10.89	10.99	11.18	11.38	11.59	11.79	12.00	12.21	12.42
.4	3911	11.02	11.12	11.31	11.51	11.72	11.93	12.13	12.34	12.56
.6	3919	11.15	11.25	11.44	11.64	11.85	12.06	12.27	12.48	12.70
.8	3926	11.28	11.38	11.58	11.78	11.99	12.19	12.40	12.61	12.84
31.0	3934	11.41	11.51	11.71	11.91	12.12	12.32	12.54	12.75	12.97
.2	3942	11.54	11.64	11.84	12.04	12.25	12.46	12.67	12.89	13.11
.4	3949	11.66	11.77	11.97	12.17	12.38	12.59	12.81	13.02	13.24
.6	3957	11.79	11.90	12.10	12.30	12.51	12.72	12.94	13.15	13.37
.8	3964	11.92	12.03	12.23	12.43	12.64	12.85	13.07	13.29	13.51
32.0	3972	12.05	12.15	12.36	12.57	12.78	12.99	13.20	13.42	13.64
.2	3980	12.18	12.28	12.49	12.70	12.91	13.12	13.34	13.55	13.77
.4	3987	12.31	12.40	12.62	12.83	13.04	13.25	13.47	13.69	13.91
.6	3995	12.43	12.54	12.75	12.96	13.17	13.38	13.60	13.82	14.04
.8	4002	12.56	12.67	12.88	13.09	13.30	13.51	13.73	13.95	14.17
33.0	4010	12.69	12.79	13.01	13.22	13.43	13.64	13.86	14.09	14.31
.2	4018	12.82	12.92	13.13	13.35	13.56	13.78	13.99	14.22	14.44
.4	4025	12.95	13.05	13.26	13.48	13.69	13.91	14.13	14.35	14.58
.6	4033	13.08	13.18	13.39	13.61	13.82	14.04	14.26	14.48	14.71
.8	4040	13.20	13.30	13.52	13.74	13.95	14.17	14.39	14.62	14.85

(Continued)

52.004 Alcohol table for calculating percentages of alcohol by volume at 15.56°C (60°F) in mixtures of ethyl alcohol and water from Zeiss immersion refractometer readings and refractive indices at 17.5–25°C[a]—*Continued.*

Scale Reading[b]	Refractive Index	Temp., °C								
		17.5	18	19	20	21	22	23	24	25
34.0	1.34048	13.33	13.43	13.64	13.86	14.08	14.30	14.52	14.75	14.98
.2	4056	13.45	13.56	13.77	13.99	14.21	14.43	14.65	14.88	15.11
.4	4063	13.58	13.68	13.90	14.12	14.34	14.57	14.78	15.01	15.25
.6	4071	13.70	13.81	14.02	14.25	14.47	14.70	14.91	15.14	15.38
.8	4078	13.83	13.94	14.14	14.37	14.59	14.83	15.05	15.28	15.51
35.0	4086	13.96	14.06	14.27	14.50	14.72	14.96	15.18	15.41	15.65
.2	4094	14.08	14.19	14.39	14.62	14.85	15.09	15.31	15.54	15.78
.4	4101	14.21	14.31	14.52	14.75	14.97	15.22	15.44	15.67	15.91
.6	4109	14.33	14.44	14.65	14.87	15.10	15.34	15.56	15.80	16.05
.8	4116	14.46	14.56	14.78	15.00	15.23	15.47	15.69	15.93	16.18
36.0	4124	14.58	14.69	14.90	15.13	15.35	15.59	15.82	16.06	16.31
.2	4131	14.71	14.81	15.03	15.25	15.48	15.72	15.95	16.19	16.44
.4	4139	14.83	14.94	15.16	15.38	15.61	15.85	16.08	16.32	16.56
.6	4146	14.96	15.06	15.28	15.51	15.73	15.97	16.21	16.45	16.69
.8	4154	15.08	15.19	15.41	15.63	15.86	16.10	16.34	16.58	16.82
37.0	4162	15.20	15.31	15.53	15.76	15.99	16.23	16.47	16.71	16.95
.2	4169	15.33	15.44	15.66	15.89	16.11	16.35	16.60	16.84	17.08
.4	4177	15.45	15.56	15.79	16.01	16.24	16.48	16.72	16.97	17.21
.6	4184	15.57	15.69	15.91	16.14	16.37	16.61	16.85	17.09	17.34
.8	4192	15.70	15.81	16.04	16.26	16.49	16.73	16.98	17.22	17.46
38.0	4199	15.82	15.94	16.16	16.39	16.62	16.86	17.11	17.35	17.59
.2	4207	15.94	16.06	16.29	16.51	16.75	16.99	17.23	17.47	17.72
.4	4215	16.07	16.18	16.41	16.64	16.87	17.11	17.36	17.60	17.85
.6	4222	16.19	16.31	16.53	16.76	17.00	17.24	17.48	17.73	17.97
.8	4230	16.31	16.43	16.66	16.89	17.13	17.36	17.61	17.85	18.10
39.0	4237	16.44	16.55	16.78	17.01	17.25	17.49	17.74	17.98	18.23
.2	4245	16.56	16.67	16.91	17.14	17.38	17.62	17.86	18.11	18.35
.4	4252	16.68	16.80	17.03	17.26	17.50	17.74	17.99	18.23	18.48
.6	4260	16.80	16.92	17.15	17.39	17.63	17.87	18.11	18.36	18.61
.8	4267	16.93	17.04	17.28	17.51	17.75	17.99	18.24	18.48	18.73
40.0	4275	17.05	17.16	17.40	17.63	17.88	18.12	18.36	18.61	18.86
.2	4282	17.17	17.29	17.52	17.76	18.00	18.24	18.49	18.74	18.99
.4	4290	17.29	17.41	17.64	17.88	18.12	18.37	18.61	18.86	19.11
.6	4298	17.41	17.53	17.77	18.01	18.25	18.49	18.74	18.99	19.24
.8	4305	17.54	17.65	17.89	18.13	18.37	18.61	18.86	19.11	19.37
41.0	4313	17.66	17.77	18.01	18.25	18.49	18.74	18.99	19.24	19.49
.2	4320	17.78	17.90	18.13	18.37	18.62	18.86	19.11	19.36	19.62
.4	4328	17.90	18.03	18.26	18.50	18.74	18.99	19.24	19.49	19.75
.6	4335	18.02	18.14	18.38	18.62	18.86	19.11	19.36	19.61	19.87
.8	4343	18.14	18.26	18.50	18.74	18.99	19.23	19.48	19.74	20.00
42.0	4350	18.27	18.38	18.62	18.87	19.11	19.36	19.61	19.86	20.13
.2	4358	18.39	18.50	18.74	18.99	19.23	19.48	19.73	19.99	20.25
.4	4365	18.51	18.62	18.87	19.11	19.36	19.60	19.86	20.11	20.38
.6	4373	18.63	18.75	18.99	19.23	19.48	19.72	19.98	20.24	20.50
.8	4380	18.75	18.87	19.11	19.36	19.60	19.85	20.10	20.36	20.63
43.0	4388	18.87	18.99	19.23	19.48	19.72	19.97	20.23	20.49	20.75
.2	4395	18.99	19.11	19.35	19.60	19.85	20.09	20.35	20.61	20.88
.4	4403	19.11	19.23	19.47	19.72	19.97	20.21	20.47	20.74	21.01
.6	4410	19.23	19.35	19.59	19.85	20.09	20.34	20.60	20.86	21.13
.8	4418	19.35	19.47	19.72	19.97	20.21	20.46	20.72	20.99	21.25
44.0	4426	19.46	19.59	19.84	20.09	20.34	20.58	20.84	21.11	21.38
.2	4433	19.58	19.71	19.96	20.21	20.46	20.71	20.96	21.23	21.50
.4	4440	19.70	19.83	20.08	20.33	20.58	20.83	21.09	21.36	21.63
.6	4448	19.82	19.95	20.20	20.45	20.70	20.95	21.21	21.48	21.75
.8	4456	19.94	20.07	20.32	20.58	20.82	21.07	21.33	21.60	21.88

(Continued)

52.004 Alcohol table for calculating percentages of alcohol by volume at 15.56°C (60°F) in mixtures of ethyl alcohol and water from Zeiss immersion refractometer readings and refractive indices at 17.5–25°C[a]—*Continued.*

Scale Reading[b]	Refractive Index	Temp., °C								
		17.5	18	19	20	21	22	23	24	25
45.0	1.34463	20.06	20.18	20.44	20.70	20.95	21.19	21.45	21.73	22.00
.2	4470	20.18	20.30	20.56	20.82	21.07	21.31	21.58	21.85	22.13
.4	4478	20.29	20.42	20.68	20.94	21.19	21.43	21.70	21.98	22.25
.6	4486	20.41	20.54	20.80	21.06	21.31	21.55	21.82	22.10	22.38
.8	4493	20.53	20.66	20.92	21.18	21.43	21.67	21.94	22.23	22.51
46.0	4500	20.65	20.78	21.04	21.30	21.54	21.79	22.07	22.35	22.64
.2	4508	20.76	20.89	21.16	21.42	21.66	21.91	22.19	22.48	22.76
.4	4516	20.88	21.01	21.28	21.54	21.78	22.03	22.32	22.61	22.89
.6	4523	21.00	21.13	21.40	21.66	21.90	22.16	22.44	22.73	23.02
.8	4530	21.12	21.25	21.52	21.78	22.02	22.28	22.57	22.86	23.15
47.0	4538	21.24	21.37	21.64	21.90	22.15	22.41	22.69	22.99	23.28
.2	4545	21.36	21.49	21.76	22.02	22.27	22.53	22.82	23.12	23.41
.4	4553	21.48	21.61	21.88	22.15	22.39	22.66	22.94	23.24	23.54
.6	4560	21.60	21.73	22.00	22.27	22.51	22.78	23.07	23.37	23.67
.8	4568	21.72	21.85	22.12	22.39	22.64	22.91	23.20	23.50	23.80
48.0	4575	21.84	21.97	22.24	22.51	22.76	23.03	23.32	23.63	23.93
.2	4583	21.96	22.09	22.36	22.63	22.88	23.16	23.45	23.76	24.06
.4	4590	22.08	22.21	22.48	22.75	23.01	23.28	23.58	23.89	24.19
.6	4598	22.20	22.33	22.60	22.87	23.13	23.41	23.71	24.02	24.32
.8	4605	22.32	22.45	22.72	22.99	23.26	23.54	23.83	24.14	24.45
49.0	4613	22.44	22.57	22.84	23.12	23.38	23.66	23.96	24.27	24.59
.2	4620	22.56	22.69	22.96	23.24	23.51	23.79	24.09	24.40	24.72
.4	4628	22.68	22.81	23.08	23.36	23.63	23.92	24.22	24.53	24.85
.6	4635	22.80	22.93	23.21	23.48	23.76	24.04	24.35	24.66	24.98
.8	4643	22.92	23.05	23.33	23.61	23.88	24.17	24.48	24.79	25.11
50.0	4650	23.04	23.17	23.45	23.73	24.01	24.30	24.61	24.92	25.25
.2	4658	23.16	23.30	23.57	23.85	24.13	24.43	24.74	25.05	25.38
.4	4665	23.28	23.42	23.69	23.98	24.26	24.56	24.86	25.18	25.51
.6	4672	23.40	23.54	23.81	24.10	24.38	24.69	24.99	25.32	25.65
.8	4680	23.51	23.66	23.93	24.22	24.51	24.81	25.12	25.45	25.78
51.0	4687	23.63	23.78	24.05	24.35	24.64	24.94	25.25	25.58	25.91
.2	4695	23.75	23.90	24.18	24.47	24.76	25.07	25.38	25.71	26.05
.4	4702	23.87	24.02	24.30	24.59	24.89	25.20	25.51	25.84	26.18
.6	4710	23.99	24.14	24.42	24.72	25.01	25.33	25.64	25.97	26.32
.8	4717	24.11	24.26	24.54	24.84	25.14	25.46	25.77	26.11	26.45
52.0	4724	24.23	24.38	24.66	24.96	25.27	25.58	25.90	26.24	26.59
.2	4732	24.36	24.50	24.79	25.09	25.39	25.71	26.03	26.37	26.72
.4	4740	24.48	24.62	24.91	25.21	25.52	25.84	26.16	26.51	26.86
.6	4747	24.60	24.74	25.03	25.34	25.65	25.97	26.29	26.64	26.99
.8	4754	24.72	24.86	25.15	25.46	25.77	26.10	26.42	26.77	27.13
53.0	4762	24.84	24.98	25.28	25.59	25.90	26.23	26.56	26.91	27.27
.2	4769	24.96	25.10	25.40	25.71	26.03	26.35	26.69	27.04	27.40
.4	4777	25.08	25.23	25.52	25.84	26.15	26.48	26.82	27.17	27.54
.6	4784	25.20	25.35	25.65	25.96	26.28	26.61	26.95	27.31	27.67
.8	4792	25.32	25.47	25.77	26.09	26.41	26.74	27.08	27.44	27.81
54.0	4799	25.44	25.59	25.90	26.22	26.54	26.87	27.21	27.58	27.95
.2	4806	25.56	25.71	26.02	26.34	26.67	27.00	27.35	27.71	28.08
.4	4814	25.68	25.84	26.14	26.47	26.79	27.13	27.48	27.85	28.22
.6	4821	25.81	25.96	26.27	26.59	26.92	27.26	27.61	27.98	28.36
.8	4829	25.93	26.08	26.39	26.72	27.05	27.39	27.75	28.11	28.49
55.0	4836	26.05	26.20	26.52	26.85	27.18	27.52	27.88	28.25	28.63
.2	4844	26.17	26.32	26.64	26.97	27.31	27.65	28.01	28.38	28.77
.4	4851	26.29	26.45	26.76	27.10	27.43	27.78	28.15	28.52	28.90
.6	4858	26.41	26.57	26.89	27.23	27.55	27.92	28.28	28.65	29.04
.8	4866	26.53	26.69	27.01	27.35	27.69	28.05	28.41	28.78	29.18

(Continued)

52.004 Alcohol table for calculating percentages of alcohol by volume at 15.56°C (60°F) in mixtures of ethyl alcohol and water from Zeiss immersion refractometer readings and refractive indices at 17.5–25°C[a]—*Continued.*

Scale Reading[b]	Refractive Index	Temp., °C 17.5	18	19	20	21	22	23	24	25
56.0	1.34873	26.65	26.81	27.14	27.48	27.82	28.18	28.54	28.92	29.31
.2	4880	26.78	26.93	27.26	27.60	27.94	28.31	28.68	29.05	29.45
.4	4888	26.90	27.05	27.38	27.73	28.07	28.44	28.81	29.19	29.58
.6	4895	27.02	27.18	27.51	27.85	28.20	28.56	28.94	29.32	29.72
.8	4903	27.14	27.30	27.63	27.98	28.33	28.69	29.07	29.46	29.86
57.0	4910	27.26	27.42	27.75	28.10	28.46	28.82	29.20	29.59	29.99
.2	4918	27.38	27.54	27.88	28.23	28.59	28.95	29.34	29.73	30.13
.4	4925	27.50	27.66	28.00	28.35	28.72	29.08	29.47	29.86	30.27
.6	4932	27.62	27.79	28.13	28.48	28.85	29.21	29.60	30.00	30.41
.8	4940	27.75	27.91	28.25	28.60	28.97	29.34	29.73	30.14	30.55
58.0	4947	27.87	28.03	28.38	28.73	29.10	29.47	29.87	30.27	30.69
.2	4954	27.99	28.15	28.50	28.86	29.23	29.60	29.99	30.41	30.83
.4	4962	28.11	28.28	28.62	28.98	29.36	29.73	30.13	30.54	30.97
.6	4969	28.23	28.40	28.75	29.11	29.48	29.86	30.26	30.68	31.11
.8	4977	28.35	28.52	28.88	29.23	29.61	29.99	30.40	30.82	31.25
59.0	4984	28.47	28.64	29.00	29.36	29.74	30.13	30.53	30.95	31.40
.2	4991	28.59	28.77	29.12	29.49	29.87	30.26	30.67	31.09	31.54
.4	4999	28.71	28.89	29.25	29.61	29.99	30.39	30.81	31.23	31.68
.6	5006	28.84	29.01	29.37	29.74	30.13	30.53	30.94	31.38	31.83
.8	5014	28.96	29.13	29.50	29.87	30.26	30.66	31.08	31.52	31.97
60.0	5021	29.08	29.26	29.62	29.99	30.39	30.79	31.22	31.66	32.12
.2	5028	29.20	29.38	29.74	30.12	30.52	30.93	31.36	31.80	32.27
.4	5036	29.32	29.50	29.87	30.25	30.65	31.06	31.50	31.94	32.41
.6	5043	29.45	29.63	29.99	30.38	30.78	31.20	31.64	32.09	32.56
.8	5050	29.57	29.75	30.12	30.51	30.91	31.33	31.78	32.23	32.71
61.0	5058	29.69	29.87	30.25	30.64	31.05	31.47	31.92	32.38	32.86
.2	5065	29.81	29.99	30.38	30.77	31.18	31.61	32.06	32.52	33.01
.4	5073	29.93	30.12	30.50	30.90	31.32	31.74	32.20	32.67	33.16
.6	5080	30.06	30.25	30.63	31.03	31.45	31.88	32.34	32.81	33.31
.8	5087	30.18	30.37	30.76	31.16	31.59	32.01	32.49	32.96	33.46
62.0	5095	30.31	30.50	30.89	31.29	31.72	32.16	32.63	33.10	33.60
.2	5102	30.43	30.63	31.01	31.43	31.86	32.30	32.77	33.25	33.75
.4	5110	30.56	30.75	31.14	31.56	31.99	32.44	32.91	33.40	33.90
.6	5117	30.69	30.88	31.28	31.69	32.13	32.58	33.06	33.55	34.05
.8	5124	30.81	31.01	31.41	31.83	32.27	32.72	33.20	33.70	34.21
63.0	5132	30.94	31.14	31.54	31.96	32.41	32.87	33.35	33.84	34.36
.2	5139	31.06	31.26	31.67	32.10	32.55	33.01	33.50	33.99	34.52
.4	5146	31.19	31.39	31.80	32.23	32.69	33.15	33.64	34.15	34.67
.6	5154	31.32	31.52	31.93	32.37	32.83	33.30	33.79	34.30	34.83
.8	5161	31.45	31.65	32.07	32.51	32.97	33.44	33.93	34.45	34.98
64.0	5168	31.58	31.78	32.20	32.65	33.11	33.59	34.08	34.61	35.15
.2	5176	31.70	31.91	32.34	32.79	33.25	33.73	34.23	34.76	35.31
.4	5183	31.83	32.04	32.47	32.92	33.39	33.88	34.39	34.92	35.48
.6	5190	31.96	32.17	32.60	33.06	33.53	34.02	34.54	35.07	35.64
.8	5198	32.09	32.30	32.74	33.20	33.67	34.17	34.69	35.23	35.80
65.0	5205	32.22	32.43	32.87	33.34	33.82	34.32	34.84	35.39	35.97
.2	5212	32.35	32.57	33.01	33.48	33.96	34.47	34.99	35.55	36.13
.4	5220	32.48	32.70	33.15	33.62	34.10	34.61	35.15	35.71	36.30
.6	5227	32.61	32.83	33.28	33.76	34.25	34.76	35.30	35.87	36.46
.8	5234	32.75	32.96	33.42	33.90	34.40	34.91	35.46	36.02	36.63
66.0	5242	32.88	33.10	33.56	34.04	34.54	35.06	35.62	36.19	36.79
.2	5249	33.01	33.23	33.70	34.18	34.69	35.22	35.77	36.35	36.96
.4	5256	33.14	33.37	33.84	34.33	34.84	35.38	35.93	36.52	37.13
.6	5264	33.28	33.51	33.98	34.47	34.99	35.53	36.09	36.68	37.30
.8	5271	33.41	33.65	34.12	34.62	35.14	35.69	36.25	36.84	37.48
67.0	5278	33.55	33.79	34.26	34.76	35.29	35.84	36.41	37.01	37.65
.2	5286	33.69	33.92	34.41	34.91	35.44	36.00	36.57	37.18	37.83
.4	5293	33.82	34.06	34.55	35.05	35.60	36.16	36.73	37.35	38.00
.6	5300	33.96	34.20	34.69	35.20	35.75	36.32	36.90	37.52	38.18
.8	5308	34.09	34.34	34.84	35.35	35.90	36.48	37.06	37.69	38.35

(Continued)

52.004 Alcohol table for calculating percentages of alcohol by volume at 15.56°C (60°F) in mixtures of ethyl alcohol and water from Zeiss immersion refractometer readings and refractive indices at 17.5–25°C[a]—*Concluded.*

Scale Reading[b]	Refractive Index	Temp., °C								
		17.5	18	19	20	21	22	23	24	25
68.0	1.35315	34.23	34.48	34.98	35.50	36.05	36.63	37.23	37.86	38.53
.2	5322	34.36	34.62	35.13	35.65	36.21	36.79	37.39	38.03	38.70
.4	5329	34.50	34.76	35.27	35.80	36.37	36.95	37.56	38.21	38.88
.6	5337	34.64	34.90	35.42	35.95	36.52	37.12	37.73	38.38	39.06
.8	5344	34.77	35.04	35.57	36.10	36.68	37.28	37.90	38.56	39.24
69.0	5351	34.91	35.19	35.71	36.25	36.84	37.45	38.07	38.73	39.43
.2	5359	35.04	35.33	35.86	36.41	36.99	37.61	38.24	38.90	39.61
.4	5366	35.19	35.47	36.01	36.56	37.15	37.78	38.41	39.08	39.80
.6	5373	35.34	35.62	36.16	36.72	37.32	37.94	38.58	39.26	39.98
.8	5381	35.49	35.76	36.31	36.87	37.48	38.11	38.75	39.45	40.17
70.0	5388	35.64	35.91	36.46	37.02	37.64	38.28	38.92	39.63	40.35
.2	5395	35.78	36.05	36.61	37.19	37.80	38.45	39.10	39.81	40.53
.4	5402	35.93	36.20	36.76	37.35	37.97	38.61	39.28	39.99	40.72
.6	5410	36.08	36.35	36.92	37.51	38.13	38.78	39.46	40.17	40.90
.8	5417	36.23	36.50	37.07	37.67	38.30	38.95	39.64	40.35	41.08
71.0	5424	36.38	36.65	37.23	37.83	38.47	39.12	39.82	40.54	41.27
.2	5432	36.53	36.80	37.39	37.99	38.63	39.30	40.00	40.72	41.46
.4	5439	36.68	36.95	37.55	38.16	38.80	39.48	40.18	40.90	41.64
.6	5446	36.83	37.11	37.71	38.32	38.97	39.65	40.36	41.08	41.83
.8	5454	36.98	37.27	37.87	38.49	39.14	39.83	40.54	41.27	42.02
72.0	5461	37.13	37.42	38.02	38.65	39.31	40.01	40.72	41.45	42.21
.2	5468	37.29	37.58	38.19	38.82	39.49	40.18	40.90	41.64	42.40
.4	5475	37.44	37.73	38.35	38.98	39.66	40.36	41.08	41.82	42.58
.6	5483	37.60	37.89	38.51	39.16	39.83	40.54	41.26	42.01	42.77
.8	5490	37.75	38.05	38.67	39.33	40.01	40.71	41.45	42.19	42.96
73.0	5497	37.91	38.21	38.84	39.50	40.18	40.88	41.63	42.38	43.15
.2	5504	38.06	38.37	39.00	39.67	40.36	41.06	41.81	42.56	43.33
.4	5512	38.22	38.53	39.17	39.84	40.53	41.24	41.99	42.75	43.52
.6	5519	38.38	38.69	39.34	40.02	40.70	41.42	42.17	42.93	43.70
.8	5526	38.54	38.85	39.50	40.19	40.88	41.60	42.36	43.12	43.89
74.0	5533	38.70	39.01	39.67	40.36	41.05	41.78	42.54	43.31	44.08
.2	5541	38.86	39.18	39.84	40.53	41.23	41.96	42.72	43.49	44.28
.4	5548	39.02	39.34	40.01	40.71	41.41	42.15	42.91	43.68	44.48
.6	5555	39.18	39.51	40.18	40.88	41.59	42.33	43.09	43.86	44.67
.8	5563	39.35	39.68	40.35	41.05	41.77	42.51	43.28	44.05	44.87
75.0	5570	39.51	39.84	40.53	41.23	41.95	42.70	43.46	44.25	45.07
.2	5577	39.68	40.01	40.70	41.41	42.13	42.88	43.65	44.44	45.29
.4	5584	39.84	40.18	40.87	41.58	42.31	43.07	43.83	44.63	45.50
.6	5592	40.01	40.35	41.04	41.76	42.49	43.25	44.02	44.83	45.71
.8	5599	40.18	40.53	41.22	41.94	42.67	43.44	44.21	45.03	45.92
76.0	5606	40.35	40.70	41.40	42.12	42.85	43.63	44.41	45.24	46.12
.2	5613	40.53	40.87	41.57	42.30	43.04	43.81	44.60	45.44	46.34
.4	5621	40.70	41.04	41.75	42.48	43.22	44.00	44.80	45.65	46.56
.6	5628	40.87	41.22	41.92	42.66	43.41	44.19	44.99	45.86	46.78
.8	5635	41.04	41.39	42.10	42.84	43.60	44.38	45.19	46.07	47.00
77.0	5642	41.22	41.57	42.28	43.02	43.79	44.57	45.40	46.29	47.23
.2	5650	41.39	41.74	42.46	43.20	43.97	44.76	45.60	46.51	47.45
.4	5657	41.57	41.91	42.63	43.39	44.16	44.95	45.81	46.73	47.68
.6	5664	41.75	42.09	42.81	43.57	44.35	45.15	46.01	46.95	47.91
.8	5671	41.92	42.26	42.99	43.76	44.54	45.35	46.23	47.17	48.14
78.0	5678	42.09	42.43	43.17	43.94	44.73	45.56	46.45	47.40	48.37
.2	5686	42.26	42.61	43.36	44.13	44.92	45.76	46.67	47.63	48.60
.4	5693	42.44	42.78	43.54	44.32	45.12	45.96	46.89	47.85	48.84
.6	5700	42.61	42.96	43.72	44.51	45.32	46.17	47.11	48.08	49.07
.8	5707	42.78	43.14	43.91	44.70	45.52	46.39	47.34	48.31	49.31
79.0	5715	42.95	43.32	44.09	44.89	45.72	46.61	47.56	48.53	49.54
.2	5722	43.13	43.50	44.28	45.08	45.92	46.83	47.79	48.76	49.77
.4	5729	43.31	43.68	44.47	45.28	46.13	47.04	48.01	48.99	50.01
.6	5736	43.49	43.86	44.65	45.48	46.34	47.26	48.23	49.22	50.24
.8	5744	43.67	44.05	44.84	45.68	46.56	47.48	48.46	49.45	50.48
80.0	5751	43.85	44.24	45.04	45.88	46.77	47.70	48.68	49.68	50.71

52.005 Percentages by weight corresponding to various percentages by volume at 15.56°C (60°F) in mixtures of ethyl alcohol and water[a]

% Alcohol			% Alcohol		
by Vol.	by Wt	Difference	by Vol.	by Wt	Difference
0	0.000		50	42.487	
1	0.795	0.795	51	43.428	0.941
2	1.593	.798	52	44.374	.946
3	2.392	.799	53	45.326	.952
4	3.194	.802	54	46.283	.957
		.804			.962
5	3.998		55	47.245	
6	4.804	.806	56	48.214	.969
7	5.612	.808	57	49.187	.973
8	6.422	.810	58	50.167	.980
9	7.234	.812	59	51.154	.987
		.813			.993
10	8.047		60	52.147	
11	8.862	.815	61	53.146	.999
12	9.679	.817	62	54.152	1.006
13	10.497	.818	63	55.165	.013
14	11.317	.820	64	56.184	.019
		.821			.024
15	12.138		65	57.208	
16	12.961	.823	66	58.241	.033
17	13.786	.825	67	59.279	.038
18	14.612	.826	68	60.325	.046
19	15.440	.828	69	61.379	.054
		.829			.062
20	16.269		70	62.441	
21	17.100	.831	71	63.511	.070
22	17.933	.833	72	64.588	.077
23	18.768	.835	73	65.674	.086
24	19.604	.836	74	66.768	.094
		.839			.102
25	20.443		75	67.870	
26	21.285	.842	76	68.982	.112
27	22.127	.842	77	70.102	.120
28	22.973	.846	78	71.234	.132
29	23.820	.847	79	72.375	.141
		.850			.151
30	24.670		80	73.526	
31	25.524	.854	81	74.686	.160
32	26.382	.858	82	75.858	.172
33	27.242	.860	83	77.039	.181
34	28.104	.862	84	78.233	.194
		.867			.208
35	28.971		85	79.441	
36	29.842	.871	86	80.662	.221
37	30.717	.875	87	81.897	.235
38	31.596	.879	88	83.144	.247
39	32.478	.882	89	84.408	.264
		.886			.281
40	33.364		90	85.689	
41	34.254	.890	91	86.989	.300
42	35.150	.896	92	88.310	.321
43	36.050	.900	93	89.652	.342
44	36.955	.905	94	91.025	.373
		.910			.398
45	37.865		95	92.423	
46	38.778	.913	96	93.851	.428
47	39.697	.919	97	95.315	.464
48	40.622	.925	98	96.820	.505
49	41.551	.929	99	98.381	.561
		.936			1.619
50	42.487		100	100.000	

[a] *Natl. Bur. Std.* Circ. 19, p. 18 (1924).

52.006 Density of carbon dioxide (Parr)[a]

(Wt in mg of 1 ml CO_2 at 700–770 mm pressure and 10–30°C. Corrected for aq. vapor and barometer readings on glass scale. Calcd from 1.976 equals wt of 1 L CO_2 at 0°C, 760 mm pressure, and 41° latitude.)

mm	10°	11°	12°	13°	14°	15°	16°	17°	18°	19°	inches
700	1.7288	1.7201	1.7113	1.7020	1.6927	1.6863	1.6799	1.6716	1.6632	1.6547	27.56
702	338	252	164	072	980	914	848	765	680	595	27.64
704	388	302	215	124	.7033	965	897	813	729	644	27.72
706	438	353	266	176	086	.7016	946	862	778	692	27.80
708	488	403	317	228	139	067	995	911	826	741	27.87
710	538	453	368	280	192	118	.7044	960	874	789	27.95
712	588	504	419	332	245	169	092	.7008	922	837	28.03
714	638	555	470	384	298	220	141	057	970	886	28.11
716	688	605	521	436	351	271	190	106	.7019	934	28.19
718	738	656	572	488	404	322	239	154	068	983	28.27
720	788	706	623	540	457	373	288	203	117	.7031	28.35
722	838	756	673	590	506	422	337	252	166	079	28.43
724	888	806	723	639	555	471	386	301	215	128	28.50
726	938	856	773	689	605	520	435	349	263	176	28.58
728	988	905	822	738	654	569	484	398	312	225	28.66
730	.8038	955	872	788	703	618	533	447	360	273	28.74
732	089	.8005	921	837	752	667	582	496	409	321	28.82
734	139	055	971	887	802	717	631	545	458	370	28.90
736	189	105	.8021	936	851	766	680	593	506	418	28.98
738	239	155	071	986	901	815	729	642	555	467	29.06
740	288	204	120	.8035	950	864	778	691	603	515	29.13
742	338	254	170	085	999	913	827	740	652	564	29.21
744	388	304	219	134	.8048	962	875	788	700	612	29.29
746	439	354	269	184	098	.8011	924	837	749	661	29.37
748	489	404	319	233	147	060	973	886	798	709	29.45
750	539	454	368	282	196	109	.8022	934	846	757	29.53
752	589	504	418	332	246	159	072	984	895	806	29.61
754	639	554	468	382	295	208	120	.8032	944	854	29.69
756	689	603	517	431	344	257	169	081	992	902	29.76
758	739	653	567	481	394	306	218	130	.8041	951	29.84
760	789	703	617	530	443	355	267	178	089	999	29.92
762	839	753	667	580	492	404	316	227	138	.8048	30.00
764	890	803	716	629	541	453	365	276	187	096	30.08
766	940	853	766	679	591	503	414	325	235	144	30.16
768	990	903	816	728	640	552	463	374	284	193	30.24
770	.9040	953	865	777	689	601	512	422	332	241	30.31

mm	20°	21°	22°	23°	24°	25°	26°	27°	28°	29°	30°	inches
700	1.6462	1.6370	1.6278	1.6195	1.6112	1.6021	1.5930	1.5837	1.5744	1.5649	1.5554	27.56
702	510	419	327	243	160	068	977	884	791	696	600	27.64
704	558	467	376	292	207	116	.6025	931	838	742	647	27.72
706	607	516	425	340	254	163	072	979	885	789	693	27.80
708	655	564	474	388	302	211	119	.6026	932	836	740	27.87
710	703	613	522	436	350	258	166	073	978	882	786	27.95
712	751	662	571	485	397	305	214	120	.6025	929	832	28.03
714	799	710	620	533	444	353	261	167	072	976	879	28.11
716	848	759	670	581	492	400	308	215	119	.6023	925	28.19
718	896	807	718	629	540	448	356	262	166	069	972	28.27
720	944	856	767	678	587	495	403	309	213	116	.6018	28.35
722	992	904	815	726	635	543	450	356	.6260	163	065	28.43
724	.7041	953	863	773	682	590	497	403	307	210	.6111	28.50
726	089	.7001	911	821	730	638	544	450	354	256	157	28.58
728	137	049	959	869	778	685	591	497	401	303	204	28.66
730	185	097	.7007	917	825	732	638	544	448	350	251	28.74
732	233	145	055	964	872	779	685	591	494	396	297	28.82
734	282	193	103	.7012	920	827	733	638	541	443	343	28.90
736	330	241	151	060	968	875	780	685	588	490	390	28.98
738	378	289	199	107	.7015	922	827	732	635	537	437	29.06
740	426	337	247	155	063	969	874	778	681	583	483	29.13
742	475	385	295	203	111	.7017	922	826	729	630	530	29.12
744	523	433	342	250	158	064	969	873	776	677	577	29.29
746	571	481	390	298	206	112	.7016	920	822	723	623	29.37
748	619	529	438	346	253	159	063	967	869	770	670	29.45
750	667	577	486	394	301	206	110	.7014	916	817	716	29.53
752	716	625	534	441	348	254	158	061	963	864	763	29.61
754	764	673	582	489	396	301	205	108	.7010	910	809	29.69
756	812	721	630	537	443	348	252	155	057	957	856	29.76
758	861	770	678	585	491	396	300	202	104	.7004	903	29.84
760	909	818	725	632	538	443	347	249	150	050	949	29.92
762	957	866	773	680	586	490	394	296	197	097	996	30.00
764	.8005	914	821	728	633	538	441	343	244	144	.7042	30.08
766	053	962	869	776	681	585	488	390	291	191	089	30.16
768	102	.8010	917	823	728	633	535	437	338	237	135	30.24
770	150	058	965	871	776	680	582	484	385	284	182	30.31

[a] *J. Am. Chem. Soc.* **31**, 237(1909). Values of 700–718 mm were calcd by formula given by Parr.

52.007 Correction factors for gasometric determination of carbon dioxide[a]

(Based on sample weighing 1.7000 g)

(Multiply number of ml gas evolved from 1.7000 g sample by factor that corresponds with existing atmospheric conditions and divide by 10 to obtain % CO_2 by wt in sample.)

mm	15.0°C 59.0°F	15.5°C 59.9°F	16.0°C 60.8°F	16.5°C 61.7°F	17.0°C 62.6°F	17.5°C 63.5°F	18.0°C 64.4°F	18.5°C 65.3°F	19.0°C 66.2°F	19.5°C 67.1°F	inches
700	0.99194	0.99006	0.98818	0.98573	0.98329	0.98082	0.97835	0.97585	0.97335	0.97085	27.56
702	0.99494	0.99300	0.99106	0.98862	0.98618	0.98368	0.98118	0.97868	0.97618	0.97368	27.64
704	0.99794	0.99544	0.99394	0.99147	0.98900	0.98653	0.98406	0.98156	0.97906	0.97653	27.72
706	1.00094	0.99886	0.99682	0.99435	0.99188	0.98941	0.98694	0.98406	0.98188	0.97938	27.80
708	1.00394	1.00183	0.99971	0.99723	0.99476	0.99226	0.98976	0.98726	0.98476	0.98224	27.87
710	1.00694	1.00477	1.00259	1.00012	0.99765	0.99512	0.99259	0.99009	0.98759	0.98506	27.95
712	1.00994	1.00767	1.00541	1.00294	1.00047	0.99795	0.99541	0.99291	0.99041	0.98788	28.03
714	1.01294	1.01061	1.00829	1.00582	1.00335	1.00080	1.99824	0.99576	0.99329	0.99073	28.11
716	1.01594	1.01356	1.01118	1.00871	1.00624	1.00368	1.00112	0.99861	0.99612	0.99358	28.19
718	1.01894	1.01650	1.01406	1.01156	1.00906	1.00653	1.00400	1.00150	0.99900	0.99644	28.27
720	1.02194	1.01949	1.01694	1.01444	1.01194	1.00941	1.00688	1.00435	1.00182	0.99925	28.35
722	1.02482	1.02232	1.01982	1.01732	1.01482	1.01229	1.00976	1.00720	1.00465	1.00209	28.43
724	1.02771	1.02521	1.02271	1.02021	1.01771	1.01518	1.01265	1.01009	1.00753	1.00497	28.50
726	1.03059	1.02809	1.02559	1.02306	1.02053	1.01800	1.01574	1.01291	1.01035	1.00779	28.58
728	1.03347	1.03097	1.02847	1.02594	1.02341	1.02088	1.01835	1.01580	1.01324	1.01065	28.66
730	1.03635	1.03385	1.03135	1.02882	1.02629	1.02374	1.02118	1.01862	1.01606	1.01347	28.74
732	1.03924	1.03674	1.03424	1.03171	1.02918	1.02662	1.02406	1.02147	1.01888	1.01629	28.82
734	1.04218	1.03915	1.03712	1.03459	1.03206	1.02950	1.02694	1.02435	1.02176	1.01919	28.90
736	1.04506	1.04253	1.04000	1.03744	1.03488	1.03232	1.02976	1.02718	1.02459	1.02200	28.98
738	1.04794	1.04541	1.04288	1.04037	1.03776	1.03521	1.03265	1.03006	1.02747	1.02486	29.06
740	1.05082	1.04829	1.04576	1.04321	1.04065	1.03806	1.03547	1.03288	1.03029	1.02768	29.13
742	1.05371	1.05118	1.04865	1.04609	1.04353	1.04094	1.03835	1.03577	1.03318	1.03056	29.21
744	1.05659	1.05403	1.05147	1.04991	1.04635	1.04377	1.04118	1.03859	1.03600	1.03338	29.29
746	1.05947	1.05691	1.05435	1.05180	1.04924	1.04665	1.04406	1.04147	1.03888	1.03624	29.37
748	1.06235	1.05929	1.05724	1.05418	1.05212	1.04953	1.04694	1.04433	1.04171	1.03906	29.45
750	1.06524	1.06218	1.06012	1.05748	1.05494	1.05235	1.04976	1.04715	1.04453	1.04189	29.53
752	1.06818	1.06512	1.06306	1.06047	1.05788	1.05527	1.05265	1.05003	1.04741	1.04477	29.61
754	1.07106	1.06847	1.06588	1.06330	1.06071	1.05812	1.05553	1.05289	1.05024	1.04759	29.69
756	1.07394	1.07135	1.06876	1.06618	1.06359	1.06197	1.05835	1.05571	1.05306	1.05041	29.76
758	1.07682	1.07423	1.07165	1.06906	1.06647	1.06386	1.06124	1.05859	1.05594	1.05330	29.84
760	1.07971	1.07712	1.07453	1.07191	1.06929	1.06668	1.06406	1.06141	1.05876	1.05612	29.92
762	1.08259	1.08050	1.07741	1.07480	1.07218	1.06956	1.06694	1.06430	1.06165	1.05897	30.00
764	1.08547	1.08288	1.08029	1.07768	1.07506	1.07244	1.06982	1.06715	1.06447	1.06179	30.08
766	1.08841	1.08580	1.08318	1.08056	1.07794	1.07530	1.07265	1.06997	1.06729	1.06462	30.16
768	1.09129	1.08868	1.08606	1.08344	1.08082	1.07818	1.07553	1.07285	1.07018	1.06750	30.24
770	1.09418	1.09156	1.08894	1.08630	1.08365	1.08100	1.07835	1.07567	1.07300	1.07032	30.31

mm	20.0°C 68.0°F	20.5°C 68.9°F	21.0°C 69.8°F	21.5°C 70.7°F	22.0°C 71.6°F	22.5°C 72.5°F	23.0°C 73.4°F	23.5°C 74.3°F	24.0°C 75.2°F	24.5°C 76.1°F	inches
700	0.96835	0.96564	0.96294	0.96023	0.95753	0.95509	0.95265	0.95020	0.94776	0.94508	27.56
702	0.97118	0.96850	0.96582	0.96311	0.96041	0.95794	0.95547	0.95303	0.95059	0.94788	27.64
704	0.97400	0.97132	0.96865	0.96597	0.96329	0.96082	0.95835	0.95585	0.95335	0.95067	27.72
706	0.97688	0.97420	0.97153	0.96888	0.96624	0.96371	0.96118	0.95865	0.95612	0.95344	27.80
708	0.97971	0.97703	0.97435	0.97173	0.96912	0.96656	0.96400	0.96147	0.95894	0.95626	27.87
710	0.98253	0.97988	0.97724	0.97459	0.97195	0.96938	0.96682	0.96429	0.96176	0.95905	27.95
712	0.98535	0.98273	0.98012	0.97747	0.97483	0.97227	0.96971	0.96712	0.96453	0.96182	28.03
714	0.98818	0.98556	0.98294	0.98032	0.97771	0.97512	0.97253	0.96991	0.96729	0.96461	28.11
716	0.99106	0.98844	0.98582	0.98323	0.98065	0.97800	0.97535	0.97273	0.97012	0.96741	28.19
718	0.99388	0.99126	0.98865	0.98606	0.98348	0.98083	0.97818	0.97556	0.97294	0.97023	28.27
720	0.99671	0.99412	0.99153	0.98894	0.98636	0.98371	0.98106	0.97838	0.97571	0.97300	28.35
722	0.99953	0.99694	0.99435	0.99176	0.98918	0.98653	0.98388	0.98120	0.97853	0.97582	28.43
724	1.00241	0.99982	0.99724	0.99462	0.99200	0.98932	0.98665	0.98397	0.98129	0.97858	28.50
726	1.00524	1.00265	1.00006	0.99746	0.99483	0.99215	0.98947	0.98679	0.98412	0.98141	28.58
728	1.00806	1.00547	1.00288	1.00027	0.99765	0.99497	0.99229	0.98961	0.98694	0.98420	28.66
730	1.01088	1.00829	1.00571	1.00306	1.00041	0.99781	0.99512	0.99241	0.98971	0.98697	28.74
732	1.01371	1.01112	1.00853	1.00588	1.00324	1.00056	0.99788	0.99517	0.99247	0.98973	28.82
734	1.01659	1.01497	1.01135	1.00870	1.00606	1.00338	1.00071	0.99799	0.99529	0.99255	28.90
736	1.01941	1.01679	1.01418	1.01153	1.00888	1.00620	1.00353	1.00083	0.99812	0.99538	28.98
738	1.02224	1.01962	1.01700	1.01435	1.01171	1.00900	1.00629	1.00359	1.00088	0.99815	29.06
740	1.02506	1.02244	1.01982	1.01717	1.01453	1.01182	1.00912	1.00643	1.00371	1.00095	29.13
742	1.02794	1.02529	1.02265	1.02000	1.01735	1.01464	1.01194	1.00923	1.00653	1.00377	29.21
744	1.03076	1.02811	1.02547	1.02279	1.02212	1.01752	1.01471	1.01200	1.00929	1.00643	29.29
746	1.03359	1.03094	1.02829	1.02561	1.02294	1.02024	1.01753	1.01482	1.01212	1.00936	29.37
748	1.03641	1.03376	1.03112	1.02844	1.02576	1.02306	1.02035	1.01762	1.01488	1.01212	29.45
750	1.03924	1.03659	1.03394	1.03126	1.02859	1.02589	1.02318	1.02045	1.01771	1.01492	29.53
752	1.04212	1.03944	1.03676	1.03408	1.03141	1.02868	1.02594	1.02321	1.02047	1.01771	29.61
754	1.04494	1.04226	1.03959	1.03691	1.03424	1.03150	1.02876	1.02603	1.02329	1.02050	29.69
756	1.04776	1.04508	1.04241	1.03973	1.03706	1.03433	1.03159	1.02883	1.02606	1.02326	29.76
758	1.05065	1.04797	1.04529	1.04259	1.03988	1.03715	1.03441	1.03165	1.02888	1.02608	29.84
760	1.05347	1.05079	1.04812	1.04539	1.04265	1.03992	1.03718	1.03442	1.03165	1.02886	29.92
762	1.05629	1.05361	1.05094	1.04821	1.04547	1.04274	1.04000	1.03724	1.03447	1.03164	30.00
764	1.05912	1.05644	1.05376	1.05103	1.04829	1.04556	1.04282	1.04003	1.03723	1.03444	30.08
766	1.06194	1.05926	1.05659	1.05386	1.05112	1.04839	1.04565	1.04285	1.04005	1.03723	30.16
768	1.06482	1.06212	1.05941	1.05668	1.05394	1.05118	1.04841	1.04562	1.04282	1.04003	30.24
770	1.06765	1.06424	1.06224	1.05950	1.05676	1.05400	1.05123	1.04844	1.04564	1.04282	30.31

(Continued)

[a] Calcd from 1.976 = wt 1 L CO_2 at 0°C, 760 mm pressure, and 41° latitude. Formula given by W. Parr, *J. Am. Chem. Soc.* **31**, 237(1909).

52.007 Correction factors for gasometric determination of carbon dioxide[a]—*Concluded.*

(Based on sample weighing 1.7000 g)

(Multiply number of ml gas evolved from 1.7000 g sample by factor that corresponds with existing atmospheric conditions and divide by 10 to obtain % CO_2 by wt in sample.)

mm	25.0°C 77.0°F	25.5°C 77.9°F	26.0°C 78.8°F	26.5°C 79.7°F	27.0°C 80.6°F	27.5°C 81.5°F	28.0°C 82.4°F	28.5°C 83.3°F	29.0°C 84.2°F	29.5°C 85.1°F	inches
700	0.94241	0.93973	0.93706	0.93432	0.93159	0.92885	0.92612	0.92332	0.92053	0.91773	27.56
702	0.94518	0.94250	0.93982	0.93708	0.93435	0.92161	0.92888	0.92608	0.92329	0.92047	27.64
704	0.94800	0.94532	0.94256	0.93988	0.93712	0.93438	0.93165	0.92882	0.92600	0.92320	27.72
706	0.95076	0.94808	0.94541	0.94267	0.93994	0.93717	0.93441	0.93158	0.92876	0.92594	27.80
708	0.95359	0.95088	0.94818	0.94544	0.94271	0.93994	0.93718	0.93435	0.93153	0.92870	27.87
710	0.95635	0.95364	0.95094	0.94820	0.94547	0.94267	0.93988	0.93706	0.93424	0.93141	27.95
712	0.95812	0.95644	0.95376	0.95100	0.94824	0.94544	0.94265	0.93982	0.93700	0.93414	28.03
714	0.96194	0.95923	0.95653	0.95376	0.95100	0.94820	0.94541	0.94258	0.93976	0.93691	28.11
716	0.96471	0.96200	0.95929	0.95655	0.95382	0.95100	0.94818	0.94535	0.94253	0.93964	28.19
718	0.96753	0.96482	0.96212	0.95935	0.95659	0.95376	0.95094	0.94809	0.94524	0.94238	28.27
720	0.97029	0.96758	0.96488	0.96213	0.95939	0.95655	0.95371	0.95085	0.94800	0.94512	28.35
722	0.97312	0.97038	0.96765	0.69488	0.96212	0.95929	0.95647	0.95361	0.95076	0.94788	28.43
724	0.97588	0.97314	0.97041	0.96764	0.96488	0.96206	0.95924	0.95638	0.95353	0.95062	28.50
726	0.97871	0.97594	0.97318	0.97041	0.96765	0.96482	0.96200	0.95912	0.95624	0.95332	28.58
728	0.98147	0.97870	0.97594	0.97319	0.97041	0.96758	0.96476	0.96188	0.95900	0.95609	28.66
730	0.98424	0.98147	0.97871	0.97594	0.97318	0.97036	0.96753	0.96464	0.96176	0.95885	28.74
732	0.98700	0.98423	0.98147	0.97871	0.97594	0.97309	0.97024	0.96735	0.96447	0.96156	28.82
734	0.98982	0.98705	0.98429	0.98165	0.97871	0.97585	0.97300	0.97012	0.96724	0.96429	28.90
736	0.99265	0.98985	0.98706	0.98426	0.98147	0.97861	0.97576	0.97288	0.97000	0.96706	28.98
738	0.99541	0.99261	0.98982	0.98703	0.98424	0.98138	0.97835	0.97564	0.97276	0.96982	29.06
740	0.99818	0.99538	0.99259	0.98976	0.98694	0.98409	0.98124	0.97835	0.97547	0.97253	29.13
742	1.00100	0.99820	0.99541	0.99258	0.98976	0.98691	0.98406	0.98115	0.97824	0.97529	29.21
744	1.00376	1.00097	0.99818	0.99535	0.99253	0.98967	0.98682	0.98391	0.98100	0.97806	29.29
746	1.00659	1.00376	1.00094	0.99809	0.99529	0.99241	0.98953	0.98662	0.98371	0.98076	29.37
748	1.00935	1.00653	1.00371	1.00088	0.99806	0.99517	0.99229	0.98938	0.98647	0.98353	29.45
750	1.01212	1.00936	1.00659	1.00370	1.00082	0.99796	0.99506	0.99215	0.98924	0.98626	29.53
752	1.01494	1.01211	1.00929	1.00644	1.00359	1.00071	0.99782	0.99491	0.99200	0.98903	29.61
754	1.01771	1.01483	1.01206	1.00921	1.00635	1.00342	1.00059	0.99738	0.99471	0.99173	29.69
756	1.02047	1.01764	1.01482	1.01197	1.00912	1.00624	1.00335	1.00041	0.99747	0.99450	29.76
758	1.02329	1.02047	1.01765	1.01477	1.01188	1.00900	1.00612	1.00318	1.00024	0.99724	29.84
760	1.02606	1.02323	1.02041	1.01753	1.01465	1.01174	1.00882	1.00588	1.00294	0.99995	29.92
762	1.02882	1.02600	1.02318	1.02030	1.01741	1.01450	1.01159	1.00865	1.00571	1.00274	30.00
764	1.03165	1.02880	1.02594	1.02306	1.02018	1.01727	1.01435	1.01141	1.00847	1.00547	30.08
766	1.03441	1.03156	1.02871	1.02583	1.02294	1.02003	1.01712	1.01418	1.01124	1.00824	30.16
768	1.03724	1.03435	1.03147	1.02859	1.02571	1.02280	1.01988	1.01611	1.01394	1.01094	30.24
770	1.04000	1.03712	1.03424	1.03136	1.02847	1.02556	1.02265	1.01968	1.01671	1.01371	30.31

mm	30.0°C 86.0°F	30.5°C 86.9°F	31.0°C 87.8°F	31.5°C 88.7°F	32.0°C 89.6°F	32.5°C 90.5°F	33.0°C 91.4°F	33.5°C 92.3°F	34.0°C 93.2°F	34.5°C 94.1°F	35.0°C 95.0°F	inches
700	0.91494	0.91203	0.90912	0.90620	0.90329	0.90082	0.89735	0.89432	0.89129	0.88821	0.88512	27.56
702	0.91765	0.91476	0.91188	0.90894	0.90600	0.90303	0.90006	0.89703	0.89400	0.89091	0.88782	27.64
704	0.92041	0.91750	0.91459	0.91165	0.90871	0.90576	0.90282	0.89976	0.89671	0.89362	0.89053	27.72
706	0.92312	0.92024	0.91735	0.91441	0.91147	0.90847	0.90547	0.90241	0.89935	0.89627	0.89318	27.80
708	0.92588	0.92297	0.92006	0.91712	0.91418	0.91118	0.90818	0.90512	0.90206	0.89897	0.89588	27.87
710	0.92859	0.92567	0.92276	0.91982	0.91688	0.91388	0.91088	0.90782	0.90476	0.90168	0.89859	27.95
712	0.93129	0.92841	0.92553	0.92256	0.91959	0.91659	0.91359	0.91053	0.90747	0.90438	0.90129	28.03
714	0.93406	0.93115	0.92824	0.92529	0.92235	0.91932	0.91629	0.91323	0.91018	0.90706	0.90394	28.11
716	0.93676	0.93388	0.93100	0.92803	0.92506	0.92203	0.91900	0.91594	0.91288	0.90976	0.90665	28.19
718	0.93953	0.93662	0.93371	0.93078	0.92776	0.92474	0.92171	0.91865	0.91559	0.91247	0.90935	28.27
720	0.94224	0.93932	0.93641	0.93344	0.93047	0.92744	0.92441	0.92135	0.91829	0.91517	0.91206	28.35
722	0.94500	0.94209	0.93918	0.93618	0.93318	0.93015	0.92712	0.92412	0.92100	0.91785	0.91471	28.43
724	0.94771	0.94479	0.94188	0.93897	0.93606	0.93294	0.92982	0.92676	0.92371	0.92056	0.91741	28.50
726	0.95041	0.94750	0.94459	0.94159	0.93859	0.93556	0.93253	0.92944	0.92635	0.92323	0.92012	28.58
728	0.95318	0.95026	0.94735	0.94435	0.94135	0.93830	0.93544	0.93215	0.92906	0.92591	0.92276	28.66
730	0.95594	0.95300	0.95006	0.94706	0.94406	0.94103	0.93800	0.93488	0.93176	0.92861	0.92547	28.74
732	0.85865	0.95578	0.95282	0.94979	0.94676	0.94373	0.94071	0.93759	0.93447	0.93132	0.92818	28.82
734	0.96135	0.95844	0.95553	0.95250	0.94947	0.94644	0.94341	0.94034	0.93718	0.93403	0.93088	28.90
736	0.96412	0.96118	0.95824	0.95521	0.95218	0.94915	0.94612	0.94300	0.93988	0.93670	0.93353	28.98
738	0.96688	0.96394	0.96100	0.95797	0.95494	0.95188	0.94882	0.94570	0.94259	0.93941	0.93624	29.06
740	0.96959	0.96665	0.96371	0.96068	0.95765	0.95459	0.95153	0.94841	0.94529	0.94211	0.93894	29.13
742	0.97235	0.96941	0.96647	0.96341	0.96035	0.95730	0.95424	0.95112	0.94800	0.94482	0.94165	29.21
744	0.97512	0.97215	0.96918	0.96615	0.96312	0.96003	0.95694	0.95382	0.95071	0.94750	0.94429	29.29
746	0.97782	0.97485	0.97188	0.96885	0.96582	0.96273	0.95965	0.95653	0.95341	0.95020	0.94700	29.37
748	0.98059	0.97762	0.97465	0.97159	0.96853	0.96544	0.96235	0.95925	0.95606	0.95288	0.94971	29.45
750	0.98329	0.98032	0.97735	0.97429	0.97124	0.96815	0.96506	0.96191	0.95876	0.95558	0.94251	29.53
752	0.98606	0.98306	0.98006	0.97703	0.97400	0.97088	0.96776	0.96461	0.96147	0.95826	0.95506	29.61
754	0.98876	0.98579	0.98282	0.97976	0.97671	0.97359	0.97047	0.96732	0.96418	0.96097	0.95776	29.69
756	0.99153	0.98853	0.98553	0.98247	0.97941	0.97629	0.97318	0.97003	0.96688	0.96367	0.96047	29.76
758	0.99429	0.99129	0.98829	0.98521	0.98212	0.97900	0.97588	0.97273	0.96959	0.96638	0.96318	29.84
760	0.99700	0.99400	0.99100	0.98794	0.98488	0.98176	0.97865	0.97547	0.97229	0.96908	0.96588	29.92
762	0.99976	0.99673	0.99371	0.99065	0.98759	0.98443	0.98135	0.97817	0.97500	0.97176	0.96853	30.00
764	1.00247	0.99948	0.99647	0.99338	0.99029	0.98717	0.98406	0.98088	0.97771	0.97447	0.97124	30.08
766	1.00524	1.00221	0.99918	0.99609	0.99300	0.98988	0.98676	0.98356	0.98053	0.97714	0.97394	30.16
768	1.00794	1.00491	1.00188	0.99880	0.99571	0.99259	0.98947	0.98629	0.98312	0.97986	0.97659	30.24
770	1.01071	1.00768	1.00465	1.00156	0.99847	0.99532	0.99218	0.98897	0.98576	0.98252	0.97929	30.31

52.008 Degrees Brix, specific gravity, and degrees Baumé of sugar solutions (Plato Table)[a]

°Brix or % by Wt of Sucrose	Specific Gravity at: 20/20°	Specific Gravity at: 20/4°	°Baumé (Modulus 145)	°Brix or % by Wt of Sucrose	Specific Gravity at: 20/20°	Specific Gravity at: 20/4°	°Baumé (Modulus 145)
0.0	1.00000	0.998234	0.00	9.0	1.03586	1.034029	5.02
.2	078	9010	.11	.2	668	4850	.13
.4	155	9786	.22	.4	750	5671	.24
.6	233	1.000563	.34	.6	833	6494	.35
.8	311	1342	.45	.8	915	7318	.46
1.0	389	2120	.56	10.0	998	8143	.57
.2	467	2897	.67	.2	4081	8970	.68
.4	545	3675	.79	.4	164	9797	.80
.6	623	4453	.90	.6	247	40626	.91
.8	701	5234	1.01	.8	330	1456	6.02
2.0	779	6015	.12	11.0	413	2288	.13
.2	858	6796	.23	.2	497	3121	.24
.4	936	7580	.34	.4	580	3954	.35
.6	1015	8363	.46	.6	664	4788	.46
.8	093	9148	.57	.8	747	5625	.57
3.0	172	9934	.68	12.0	831	6462	.68
.2	251	10721	.79	.2	915	7300	.79
.4	330	1510	.90	.4	999	8140	.90
.6	409	2298	2.02	.6	5084	8980	7.02
.8	488	3089	.13	.8	168	9822	.13
4.0	567	3881	.24	13.0	252	50665	.24
.2	647	4673	.35	.2	337	1510	.35
.4	726	5467	.46	.4	422	2356	.46
.6	806	6261	.57	.6	506	3202	.57
.8	886	7058	.68	.8	591	4050	.68
5.0	965	7854	.79	14.0	677	4900	.79
.2	2045	8652	.91	.2	762	5751	.90
.4	125	9451	3.02	.4	847	6602	8.01
.6	206	20251	.13	.6	933	7455	.12
.8	286	1053	.24	.8	6018	8310	.23
6.0	366	1855	.35	15.0	104	9165	.34
.2	447	2659	.46	.2	190	60022	.45
.4	527	3463	.57	.4	276	0880	.56
.6	608	4270	.69	.6	362	1738	.67
.8	689	5077	.80	.8	448	2598	.78
7.0	770	5885	.91	16.0	534	3460	.89
.2	851	6694	4.02	.2	621	4324	9.00
.4	932	7504	.13	.4	707	5188	.11
.6	3013	8316	.24	.6	794	6054	.22
.8	095	9128	.35	.8	881	6921	.33
8.0	176	9942	.46	17.0	968	7789	.45
.2	258	30757	.58	.2	7055	8658	.56
.4	340	1573	.69	.4	142	9529	.67
.6	422	2391	.80	.6	229	70400	.78
.8	504	3209	.91	.8	317	1273	.89

(Continued)

[a] *Natl. Bur. Std. Circ.* C440, pp. 614, 626(1942). Based upon figures prepared by Kaiserliche Normal-Eichungs-Kommission and accepted by International Commission for Uniform Methods of Sugar Analysis.

52.008 Degrees Brix, specific gravity, and degrees Baumé of sugar solutions (Plato Table)[a]—*Continued.*

°Brix or % by Wt of Sucrose	Specific Gravity at: 20/20°	Specific Gravity at: 20/4°	°Baumé (Modulus 145)	°Brix or % by Wt of Sucrose	Specific Gravity at: 20/20°	Specific Gravity at: 20/4°	°Baumé (Modulus 145)
18.0	1.07404	1.072147	10.00	27.0	1.11480	1.112828	14.93
.2	492	3023	.11	.2	573	3763	15.04
.4	580	3900	.22	.4	667	4697	.15
.6	668	4777	.33	.6	761	5635	.26
.8	756	5657	.44	.8	855	6572	.37
19.0	844	6537	.55	28.0	949	7512	.48
.2	932	7419	.66	.2	2043	8453	.59
.4	8021	8302	.77	.4	138	9395	.69
.6	110	9187	.88	.6	232	20339	.80
.8	198	80072	.99	.8	327	1284	.91
20.0	287	0959	11.10	29.0	422	2231	16.02
.2	376	1848	.21	.2	517	3179	.13
.4	465	2737	.32	.4	612	4128	.24
.6	554	3628	.43	.6	707	5079	.35
.8	644	4520	.54	.8	802	6030	.46
21.0	733	5414	.65	30.0	898	6984	.57
.2	823	6309	.76	.2	993	7939	.67
.4	913	7205	.87	.4	3089	8896	.78
.6	9003	8101	.98	.6	185	9853	.89
.8	093	9000	12.09	.8	281	30812	17.00
22.0	183	9900	.20	31.0	378	1773	.11
.2	273	90802	.31	.2	474	2735	.22
.4	364	1704	.42	.4	570	3698	.33
.6	454	2607	.52	.6	667	4663	.43
.8	545	3513	.63	.8	764	5628	.54
23.0	636	4420	.74	32.0	861	6596	.65
.2	727	5328	.85	.2	958	7565	.76
.4	818	6236	.96	.4	4055	8534	.87
.6	909	7147	13.07	.6	152	9506	.98
.8	.10000	8058	.18	.8	250	40479	18.08
24.0	092	8971	.29	33.0	347	1453	.19
.2	183	9886	.40	.2	445	2429	.30
.4	275	.100802	.51	.4	543	3405	.41
.6	367	1718	.62	.6	641	4384	.52
.8	459	2637	.73	.8	739	5363	.63
25.0	551	3557	.84	34.0	837	6345	.73
.2	643	4478	.95	.2	936	7328	.84
.4	736	5400	14.06	.4	5034	8313	.95
.6	828	6324	.17	.6	133	9298	19.06
.8	921	7248	.28	.8	232	50286	.17
26.0	1014	8175	.39	35.0	331	1275	.28
.2	106	9103	.49	.2	430	2265	.38
.4	200	10033	.60	.4	530	3256	.49
.6	293	0963	.71	.6	629	4249	.60
.8	386	1895	.82	.8	729	5242	.71

(Continued)

52.008 Degrees Brix, specific gravity, and degrees Baumé of sugar solutions (Plato Table)[a]—*Continued.*

°Brix or % by Wt of Sucrose	Specific Gravity at: 20/20°	Specific Gravity at: 20/4°	°Baumé (Modulus 145)	°Brix or % by Wt of Sucrose	Specific Gravity at: 20/20°	Specific Gravity at: 20/4°	°Baumé (Modulus 145)
36.0	**1.15828**	1.156238	19.81	45.0	1.20467	1.202540	24.63
.2	**928**	7235	.92	.2	573	3603	.74
.4	**6028**	8233	20.03	.4	680	4668	.85
.6	128	9233	.14	.6	787	5733	.95
.8	228	60233	.25	.8	894	6801	25.06
37.0	329	1236	.35	46.0	1001	7870	.17
.2	430	2240	.46	.2	108	8940	.27
.4	530	3245	.57	.4	215	10013	.38
.6	631	4252	.68	.6	323	1086	.48
.8	732	5259	.78	.8	431	2162	.59
38.0	833	6269	.89	47.0	538	3238	.70
.2	934	7281	21.00	.2	646	4317	.80
.4	7036	8293	.11	.4	755	5395	.91
.6	138	9307	.21	.6	863	6476	26.01
.8	239	70322	.32	.8	971	7559	.12
39.0	341	1340	.43	48.0	2080	8643	.23
.2	443	2359	.54	.2	189	9729	.33
.4	545	3379	.64	.4	298	20815	.44
.6	648	4400	.75	.6	406	1904	.54
.8	750	5423	.86	.8	516	2995	.65
40.0	853	6447	.97	49.0	625	4086	.75
.2	956	7473	22.07	.2	735	5180	.86
.4	8058	8501	.18	.4	844	6274	.96
.6	162	9527	.29	.6	954	7371	27.07
.8	265	80560	.39	.8	3064	8469	.18
41.0	368	1592	.50	50.0	174	9567	.28
.2	472	2625	.61	.2	284	30668	.39
.4	575	3660	.72	.4	395	1770	.49
.6	679	4696	.82	.6	506	2874	.60
.8	783	5734	.93	.8	616	3979	.70
42.0	887	6773	23.04	51.0	727	5085	.81
.2	992	7814	.14	.2	838	6194	.91
.4	9096	8856	.25	.4	949	7303	28.02
.6	201	9901	.36	.6	4060	8414	.12
.8	305	90946	.46	.8	172	9527	.23
43.0	410	1993	.57	52.0	284	40641	.33
.2	515	3041	.68	.2	395	1757	.44
.4	620	4090	.78	.4	507	2873	.54
.6	726	5141	.89	.6	619	3992	.65
.8	831	6193	24.00	.8	731	5113	.75
44.0	936	7247	.10	53.0	844	6234	.86
.2	.20042	8303	.21	.2	956	7358	.96
.4	148	9360	.32	.4	5069	8482	29.06
.6	254	.200420	.42	.6	182	9609	.17
.8	360	1480	.53	.8	295	50737	.27

(Continued)

52.008 Degrees Brix, specific gravity, and degrees Baumé of sugar solutions (Plato Table)[a]—*Continued.*

°Brix or % by Wt of Sucrose	Specific Gravity at: 20/20°	Specific Gravity at: 20/4°	°Baumé (Modulus 145)	°Brix or % by Wt of Sucrose	Specific Gravity at: 20/20°	Specific Gravity at: 20/4°	°Baumé (Modulus 145)
54.0	1.25408	1.251866	29.38	63.0	1.30657	1.304267	34.02
.2	521	2997	.48	.2	778	5467	.12
.4	635	4129	.59	.4	898	6669	.23
.6	748	5264	.69	.6	1019	7872	.33
.8	862	6400	.80	.8	139	9077	.43
55.0	976	7535	.90	64.0	260	10282	.53
.2	6090	8674	30.00	.2	381	1489	.63
.4	204	9815	.11	.4	502	2699	.74
.6	319	60955	.21	.6	623	3909	.84
.8	433	2099	.32	.8	745	5121	.94
56.0	548	3243	.42	65.0	866	6334	35.04
.2	663	4390	.52	.2	988	7549	.14
.4	778	5537	.63	.4	2110	8766	.24
.6	893	6686	.73	.6	232	9983	.34
.8	7008	7837	.83	.8	354	21203	.45
57.0	123	8989	.94	66.0	476	2425	.55
.2	239	70143	31.04	.2	599	3648	.65
.4	355	1299	.15	.4	722	4872	.75
.6	471	2455	.25	.6	844	6097	.85
.8	587	3614	.35	.8	967	7325	.95
58.0	703	4774	.46	67.0	3090	8554	36.05
.2	819	5936	.56	.2	214	9785	.15
.4	936	7098	.66	.4	337	31017	.25
.6	8052	8262	.76	.6	460	2250	.35
.8	169	9428	.87	.8	584	3485	.45
59.0	286	80595	.97	68.0	708	4722	.55
.2	404	1764	32.07	.2	832	5961	.66
.4	520	2935	.18	.4	957	7200	.76
.6	638	4107	.28	.6	4081	8441	.86
.8	755	5281	.38	.8	205	9684	.96
60.0	873	6456	.49	69.0	330	40928	37.06
.2	991	7633	.59	.2	455	2174	.16
.4	9109	8811	.69	.4	580	3421	.26
.6	227	9991	.79	.6	705	4671	.36
.8	346	91172	.90	.8	830	5922	.46
61.0	464	2354	33.00	70.0	956	7174	.56
.2	583	3539	.10	.2	5081	8427	.66
.4	701	4725	.20	.4	207	9682	.76
.6	820	5911	.31	.6	333	50939	.86
.8	940	7100	.41	.8	459	2197	.96
62.0	.30059	8291	33.51	71.0	585	3456	38.06
.2	178	9483	.61	.2	711	4717	.16
.4	298	.300677	.72	.4	838	5980	.26
.6	418	1871	.82	.6	964	7245	.35
.8	537	3068	.92	.8	6091	8511	.45

(Continued)

52.008 Degrees Brix, specific gravity, and degrees Baumé of sugar solutions (Plato Table)[a]—*Continued.*

°Brix or % by Wt of Sucrose	Specific Gravity at: 20/20°	Specific Gravity at: 20/4°	°Baumé (Modulus 145)	°Brix or % by Wt of Sucrose	Specific Gravity at: 20/20°	Specific Gravity at: 20/4°	°Baumé (Modulus 145)
72.0	1.36218	1.359778	38.55	81.0	1.42088	1.418374	42.95
.2	346	61047	.65	.2	222	9711	43.05
.4	473	2317	.75	.4	356	21049	.14
.6	600	3590	.85	.6	490	2390	.24
.8	728	4864	.95	.8	625	3730	.33
73.0	856	6139	39.05	82.0	759	5072	.43
.2	983	7415	.15	.2	894	6416	.53
.4	7111	8693	.25	.4	3029	7761	.62
.6	240	9973	.35	.6	164	9109	.72
.8	368	71254	.44	.8	298	30457	.81
74.0	496	2536	.54	83.0	434	1807	.91
.2	625	3820	.64	.2	569	3158	44.00
.4	754	5105	.74	.4	705	4511	.10
.6	883	6392	.84	.6	841	5866	.19
.8	8012	7680	.94	.8	976	7222	.29
75.0	141	8971	40.03	84.0	4112	8579	.38
.2	270	80262	.13	.2	249	9938	.48
.4	400	1555	.23	.4	385	41299	.57
.6	530	2851	.33	.6	521	2661	.67
.8	660	4148	.43	.8	658	4024	.76
76.0	790	5446	.53	85.0	794	5388	.86
.2	920	6745	.62	.2	931	6754	.95
.4	9050	8045	.72	.4	5068	8121	45.05
.6	180	9347	.82	.6	205	9491	.14
.8	311	90651	.92	.8	343	50860	.24
77.0	442	1956	41.01	86.0	480	2232	.33
.2	573	3263	.11	.2	618	3605	.42
.4	704	4571	.21	.4	755	4980	.52
.6	835	5881	.31	.6	893	6357	.61
.8	966	7192	.40	.8	6031	7735	.71
78.0	.40098	8505	.50	87.0	170	9114	.80
.2	230	9819	.60	.2	308	60495	.89
.4	361	.401134	.70	.4	446	1877	.99
.6	493	2452	.79	.6	585	3260	46.08
.8	625	3771	.89	.8	724	4645	.17
79.0	758	5091	.99	88.0	862	6032	.27
.2	890	6412	42.08	.2	7002	7420	.36
.4	1023	7735	.18	.4	141	8810	.45
.6	155	9061	.28	.6	280	70200	.55
.8	288	10387	.37	.8	420	1592	.64
80.0	421	1715	.47	89.0	559	2986	.73
.2	554	3044	.57	.2	699	4381	.83
.4	688	4374	.66	.4	839	5779	.92
.6	821	5706	.76	.6	979	7176	47.01
.8	955	7039	.85	.8	8119	8575	.11

(Continued)

52.008 Degrees Brix, specific gravity, and degrees Baumé of sugar solutions (Plato Table)[a]—*Concluded.*

°Brix or % by Wt of Sucrose	Specific Gravity at: 20/20°	20/4°	°Baumé (Modulus 145)	°Brix or % by Wt of Sucrose	Specific Gravity at: 20/20°	20/4°	°Baumé (Modulus 145)
90.0	1.48259	1.479976	47.20	95.0	1.51814	1.515455	49.49
.2	400	81378	.29	.2	958	6893	.58
.4	540	2782	.38	.4	2102	8332	.67
.6	681	4187	.48	.6	246	9771	.76
.8	822	5593	.57	.8	390	21212	.85
91.0	963	7002	.66	96.0	535	2656	.94
.2	9104	8411	.75	.2	680	4100	50.03
.4	246	9823	.84	.4	824	5546	.12
.6	387	91234	.94	.6	969	6993	.21
.8	529	2647	48.03	.8	3114	8441	.30
92.0	671	4063	.12	97.0	260	9891	.39
.2	812	5479	.21	.2	405	31342	.48
.4	954	6897	.30	.4	551	2794	.57
.6	.50097	8316	.40	.6	696	4248	.66
.8	239	9736	.49	.8	842	5704	.75
93.0	381	.501158	.58	98.0	988	7161	.84
.2	524	2582	.67	.2	4134	8618	.93
.4	667	4006	.76	.4	280	40076	51.02
.6	810	5432	.85	.6	426	1536	.10
.8	952	6859	.94	.8	573	2998	.19
94.0	1096	8289	49.03	99.0	719	4462	.28
.2	239	9720	.12	.2	866	5926	.37
.4	382	11151	.22	.4	5013	7392	.46
.6	526	2585	.31	.6	160	8861	.55
.8	670	4019	.40	.8	307	50329	.64
				100.0	454	1800	.73

52.009 Specific gravity and degrees Plato of sugar solutions or per cent extract by weight[a]

Specific Gravity at 20/20°	g Extract in 100 g Soln	Specific Gravity at 20/20°	g Extract in 100 g Soln	Specific Gravity at 20/20°	g Extract in 100 g Soln	Specific Gravity at 20/20°	g Extract in 100 g Soln	Specific Gravity at 20/20°	g Extract in 100 g Soln
1.00000	0.000	1.00300	0.770	1.00600	1.539	1.00900	2.305	1.01200	3.067
05	13	05	83	05	52	05	17	05	80
10	26	10	96	10	65	10	30	10	93
15	39	15	.808	15	78	15	43	15	.105
20	52	20	21	20	90	20	56	20	18
25	64	25	34	25	.603	25	69	25	31
30	77	30	47	30	16	30	81	30	43
35	90	35	59	35	29	35	94	35	56
40	.103	40	72	40	41	40	.407	40	69
45	16	45	85	45	54	45	19	45	81
1.00050	29	1.00350	98	1.00650	67	1.00950	32	1.01250	94
55	41	55	.911	55	80	55	45	55	.207
60	54	60	24	60	93	60	58	60	19
65	67	65	37	65	.705	65	70	65	32
70	80	70	49	70	18	70	83	70	45
75	93	75	62	75	31	75	96	75	57
80	.206	80	75	80	44	80	.508	80	70
85	19	85	88	85	57	85	21	85	82
90	31	90	1.001	90	69	90	34	90	95
95	44	95	14	95	82	95	47	95	.308
1.00100	57	1.00400	26	1.00700	95	1.01000	60	1.01300	21
05	70	05	39	05	.807	05	72	05	33
10	83	10	52	10	20	10	85	10	46
15	96	15	65	15	33	15	98	15	58
20	.309	20	78	20	46	20	.610	20	71
25	21	25	90	25	59	25	23	25	84
30	34	30	.103	30	72	30	36	30	96
35	47	35	16	35	84	35	49	35	.409
40	60	40	29	40	97	40	61	40	21
45	73	45	42	45	.910	45	74	45	34
1.00150	86	1.00450	55	1.00750	23	1.01050	87	1.01350	47
55	98	55	68	55	35	55	99	55	59
60	.411	60	80	60	48	60	.712	60	72
65	24	65	93	65	61	65	25	65	85
70	37	70	.206	70	73	70	38	70	97
75	50	75	19	75	86	75	50	75	.510
80	63	80	32	80	99	80	63	80	23
85	76	85	44	85	2.012	85	76	85	35
90	88	90	57	90	25	90	78	90	48
95	.501	95	70	95	38	95	.801	95	61
1.00200	14	1.00500	83	1.00800	53	1.01100	14	1.01400	73
05	27	05	96	05	65	05	26	05	86
10	40	10	.308	10	78	10	39	10	98
15	52	15	21	15	91	15	52	14	.611
20	65	20	34	20	.101	20	64	20	24
25	78	25	47	25	14	25	77	25	36
30	91	30	60	30	27	30	90	30	49
35	.604	35	72	35	39	35	.903	35	62
40	16	40	85	40	52	40	15	40	74
45	29	45	98	45	65	45	28	45	87
1.00250	42	1.00550	.411	1.00850	78	1.01150	40	1.01450	99
55	55	55	24	55	91	55	53	55	.712
60	68	60	37	60	.203	60	66	60	25
65	80	65	50	65	16	65	79	65	37
70	93	70	62	70	29	70	91	70	50
75	.706	75	75	75	41	75	3.004	75	62
80	19	80	88	80	54	80	17	80	75
85	32	85	.501	85	67	85	29	85	88
90	45	90	14	90	80	90	42	90	.800
95	57	95	26	95	.292	95	55	95	13

[a] From the American Society of Brewing Chemists.

(Continued)

52.009 Specific gravity and degrees Plato of sugar solutions or per cent extract by weight[a]—*Continued*.

Specific Gravity at 20/20°	g Extract in 100 g Soln	Specific Gravity at 20/20°	g Extract in 100 g Soln	Specific Gravity at 20/20°	g Extract in 100 g Soln	Specific Gravity at 20/20°	g Extract in 100 g Soln	Specific Gravity at 20/20°	g Extract in 100 g Soln
1.01500	3.826	1.01800	4.580	1.02100	5.330	1.02400	6.077	1.02700	6.819
05	38	05	92	05	43	05	89	05	31
10	51	10	.605	10	55	10	.101	10	44
15	63	15	17	15	67	15	14	15	56
20	76	20	30	20	80	20	26	20	68
25	88	25	42	25	92	25	39	25	81
30	.901	30	55	30	.405	30	51	30	93
35	14	35	68	35	18	35	63	35	.905
40	26	40	80	40	30	40	76	40	18
45	39	45	92	45	43	45	88	45	30
1.01550	51	1.01850	.705	1.02150	55	1.02450	.200	1.02750	43
55	64	55	18	55	67	55	13	55	55
60	77	60	30	60	80	60	25	60	67
65	89	65	43	65	92	65	38	65	79
70	4.002	70	55	70	.505	70	50	70	92
75	14	75	68	75	17	75	63	75	7.004
80	27	80	80	80	30	80	75	80	17
85	39	85	92	85	42	85	87	85	29
90	52	90	.805	90	55	90	.300	90	41
95	65	95	18	95	67	95	12	95	53
1.01600	77	1.01900	30	1.02200	80	1.02500	25	1.02800	66
05	90	05	43	05	92	05	37	05	78
10	.102	10	55	10	.605	10	50	10	91
15	15	15	68	15	17	15	62	15	.103
20	28	20	80	20	29	20	74	20	15
25	40	25	93	25	42	25	87	25	27
30	53	30	.905	30	54	30	99	30	40
35	65	35	18	35	67	35	.411	35	52
40	78	40	30	40	79	40	24	40	64
45	90	45	43	45	92	45	36	45	77
1.01650	.203	1.01950	55	1.02250	.704	1.02550	49	1.02850	89
55	16	55	68	55	16	55	61	55	.201
60	28	60	80	60	29	60	73	60	14
65	41	65	93	65	41	65	85	65	26
70	53	70	5.006	70	54	70	98	70	38
75	66	75	18	75	66	75	.510	75	51
80	78	80	30	80	79	80	23	80	63
85	91	85	43	85	91	85	35	85	75
90	.304	90	55	90	.803	90	47	90	87
95	16	95	68	95	16	95	60	95	.300
1.01700	29	1.02000	80	1.02300	28	1.02600	72	1.02900	12
05	41	05	93	05	41	05	84	05	24
10	54	10	.106	10	53	10	97	10	37
15	66	15	18	15	65	15	.609	15	49
20	79	20	30	20	78	20	21	20	61
25	91	25	43	25	90	25	34	25	74
30	.404	30	55	30	.903	30	46	30	86
35	17	35	68	35	15	35	59	35	98
40	29	40	80	40	28	40	71	40	.411
45	42	45	93	45	40	45	83	45	23
1.01750	54	1.02050	.205	1.02350	52	1.02650	96	1.02950	35
55	67	55	18	55	65	55	.708	55	47
60	79	60	30	60	77	60	20	60	60
65	92	65	43	65	90	65	33	65	72
70	.505	70	55	70	6.002	70	45	70	84
75	17	75	68	75	15	75	57	75	97
80	29	80	80	80	27	80	70	80	.509
85	42	85	93	85	39	85	82	85	21
90	55	90	.305	90	52	90	94	90	33
95	67	95	18	95	64	95	.807	95	46

(*Continued*)

52.009 Specific gravity and degrees Plato of sugar solutions or per cent extract by weight[a]—*Continued*.

Specific Gravity at 20/20°	g Extract in 100 g Soln	Specific Gravity at 20/20°	g Extract in 100 g Soln	Specific Gravity at 20/20°	g Extract in 100 g Soln	Specific Gravity at 20/20°	g Extract in 100 g Soln	Specific Gravity at 20/20°	g Extract in 100 g Soln
1.03000	7.558	1.03300	8.293	1.03600	9.024	1.03900	9.751	1.04200	10.475
05	70	05	.305	05	36	05	64	05	87
10	83	10	17	10	48	10	76	10	99
15	95	15	30	15	60	15	88	15	.511
20	.607	20	42	20	73	20	.800	20	23
25	19	25	54	25	85	25	12	25	36
30	32	30	66	30	97	30	24	30	48
35	44	35	78	35	.109	35	36	35	59
40	56	40	91	40	21	40	48	40	71
45	68	45	.403	45	33	45	60	45	84
1.03050	81	1.03350	15	1.03650	45	1.03950	73	1.04250	96
55	93	55	27	55	58	55	85	55	.608
60	.705	60	39	60	70	60	97	60	20
65	17	65	52	65	82	65	.909	65	32
70	30	70	64	70	94	70	21	70	44
75	42	75	76	75	.206	75	33	75	56
80	54	80	88	80	18	80	45	80	68
85	67	85	.500	85	30	85	57	85	80
90	79	90	13	90	43	90	69	90	92
95	91	95	25	95	55	95	81	95	.704
1.03100	.803	1.03400	37	1.03700	67	1.04000	93	1.04300	16
05	16	05	49	05	79	05	10.005	05	28
10	28	10	61	10	91	10	17	10	40
15	40	15	74	15	.303	15	30	15	52
20	53	20	86	20	16	20	42	20	64
25	65	25	98	25	28	25	54	25	76
30	77	30	.610	30	40	30	66	30	88
35	89	35	22	35	52	35	78	35	.800
40	.901	40	34	40	64	40	90	40	12
45	14	45	47	45	76	45	.102	45	24
1.03150	26	1.03450	59	1.03750	88	1.04050	14	1.04350	36
55	38	55	71	55	.400	55	26	55	48
60	50	60	83	60	13	60	38	60	60
65	63	65	95	65	25	65	50	65	72
70	75	70	.708	70	37	70	62	70	84
75	87	75	20	75	49	75	74	75	96
80	8.000	80	32	80	61	80	86	80	.908
85	12	85	44	85	73	85	98	85	20
90	24	90	56	90	85	90	.210	90	32
95	36	95	68	95	98	95	23	95	44
1.03200	48	1.03500	81	1.03800	.509	1.04100	34	1.04400	56
05	61	05	93	05	22	05	46	05	68
10	73	10	.805	10	34	10	59	10	80
15	85	15	17	15	46	15	71	15	92
20	98	20	30	20	58	20	83	20	11.004
25	.110	25	42	25	70	25	95	25	16
30	22	30	54	30	82	30	.307	30	27
35	34	35	66	35	94	35	19	35	39
40	46	40	78	40	.606	40	31	40	51
45	59	45	90	45	18	45	43	45	63
1.03250	71	1.03550	.902	1.03850	31	1.04150	55	1.04450	75
55	83	55	15	55	43	55	67	55	87
60	95	60	27	60	55	60	79	60	.100
65	.207	65	39	65	67	65	91	65	12
70	20	70	51	70	79	70	.403	70	23
75	32	75	63	75	91	75	15	75	35
80	44	80	75	80	.703	80	27	80	47
85	56	85	88	85	15	85	39	85	59
90	69	90	9.000	90	27	90	51	90	71
95	81	95	12	95	40	95	63	95	83

(Continued)

52.009 Specific gravity and degrees Plato of sugar solutions or per cent extract by weight[a]—*Continued.*

Specific Gravity at 20/20°	g Extract in 100 g Soln	Specific Gravity at 20/20°	g Extract in 100 g Soln	Specific Gravity at 20/20°	g Extract in 100 g Soln	Specific Gravity at 20/20°	g Extract in 100 g Soln	Specific Gravity at 20/20°	g Extract in 100 g Soln
1.04500	11.195	1.04800	11.912	1.05100	12.624	1.05400	13.333	1.05700	14.039
05	.207	05	23	05	36	05	45	05	51
10	19	10	35	10	48	10	57	10	62
15	31	15	47	15	60	15	69	15	74
20	43	20	59	20	72	20	80	20	86
25	55	25	71	25	84	25	92	25	97
30	67	30	83	30	95	30	.404	30	.109
35	79	35	95	35	.707	35	16	35	21
40	91	40	12.007	40	19	40	28	40	33
45	.303	45	19	45	31	45	39	45	44
1.04550	15	1.04850	31	1.05150	43	1.05450	51	1.05750	56
55	27	55	42	55	55	55	63	55	68
60	39	60	54	60	67	60	75	60	79
65	51	65	66	65	78	65	87	65	91
70	63	70	78	70	90	70	99	70	.203
75	75	75	90	75	.802	75	.510	75	15
80	87	80	.102	80	14	80	22	80	26
85	99	85	14	85	26	85	34	85	38
90	.411	90	26	90	38	90	46	90	50
95	23	95	38	95	49	95	57	95	61
1.04600	35	1.04900	50	1.05200	61	1.05500	69	1.05800	73
05	46	05	62	05	73	05	81	05	85
10	58	10	73	10	85	10	93	10	97
15	70	15	85	15	97	15	.604	15	.308
20	82	20	97	20	.909	20	16	20	20
25	94	25	.209	25	20	25	28	25	32
30	.506	30	21	30	32	30	40	30	43
35	18	35	33	35	44	35	51	35	55
40	30	40	45	40	56	40	63	40	67
45	42	45	56	45	68	45	75	45	79
1.04650	54	1.04950	68	1.05250	79	1.05550	87	1.05850	90
55	66	55	80	55	91	55	98	55	.402
60	78	60	92	60	13.003	60	.710	60	14
65	90	65	.304	65	15	65	22	65	25
70	.602	70	16	70	27	70	34	70	37
75	14	75	28	75	39	75	46	75	49
80	26	80	40	80	50	80	57	80	60
85	38	85	51	85	62	85	69	85	72
90	50	90	63	90	74	90	81	90	84
95	61	95	75	95	86	95	92	95	95
1.04700	73	1.05000	87	1.05300	98	1.05600	.804	1.05900	.507
05	85	05	99	05	.109	05	16	05	19
10	97	10	.411	10	21	10	28	10	31
15	.709	15	23	15	33	15	39	15	42
20	21	20	35	20	45	20	51	20	54
25	33	25	47	25	57	25	63	25	65
30	45	30	58	30	68	30	75	30	77
35	57	35	70	35	80	35	86	35	89
40	68	40	82	40	92	40	98	40	.601
45	80	45	94	45	.204	45	.910	45	12
1.04750	92	1.05050	.506	1.05350	15	1.05650	21	1.05950	24
55	.804	55	18	55	27	55	33	55	36
60	16	60	30	60	39	60	45	60	47
65	28	65	42	65	51	65	57	65	59
70	40	70	53	70	63	70	68	70	71
75	52	75	65	75	74	75	80	75	82
80	64	80	77	80	86	80	92	80	94
85	76	85	89	85	98	85	14.004	85	.706
90	88	90	.601	90	.310	90	15	90	17
95	.900	95	13	95	22	95	27	95	29

(Continued)

52.009 Specific gravity and degrees Plato of sugar solutions or per cent extract by weight[a]—*Concluded*.

Specific Gravity at 20/20°	g Extract in 100 g Soln	Specific Gravity at 20/20°	g Extract in 100 g Soln	Specific Gravity at 20/20°	g Extract in 100 g Soln	Specific Gravity at 20/20°	g Extract in 100 g Soln	Specific Gravity at 20/20°	g Extract in 100 g Soln
1.06000	14.741	1.06200	15.207	1.06400	15.671	1.06600	16.134	1.06800	16.595
05	52	05	18	05	83	05	45	05	.606
10	64	10	30	10	94	10	57	10	18
15	76	15	41	15	.706	15	69	15	30
20	87	20	53	20	17	20	80	20	41
25	99	25	65	25	29	25	91	25	52
30	.811	30	76	30	41	30	.203	30	64
35	22	35	88	35	52	35	15	35	76
40	34	40	.300	40	64	40	26	40	87
45	46	45	11	45	76	45	38	45	99
1.06050	57	1.06250	23	1.06450	87	1.06650	49	1.06850	.710
55	69	55	34	55	99	55	61	55	22
60	81	60	46	60	.810	60	72	60	33
65	92	65	58	65	22	65	84	65	44
70	.904	70	69	70	33	70	95	70	56
75	16	75	81	75	45	75	.307	75	68
80	27	80	93	80	57	80	19	80	79
85	39	85	.404	85	68	85	30	85	91
90	50	90	16	90	80	90	41	90	.802
95	62	95	27	95	91	95	53	95	13
1.06100	74	1.06300	39	1.06500	.903	1.06700	65	1.06900	25
05	86	05	51	05	14	05	76	05	36
10	97	10	62	10	26	10	88	10	48
15	15.009	15	74	15	38	15	99	15	59
20	20	20	86	20	49	20	.411	20	71
25	32	25	97	25	61	25	22	25	82
30	44	30	.509	30	72	30	34	30	94
35	55	35	20	35	84	35	45	35	.905
40	67	40	32	40	95	40	57	40	17
45	79	45	44	45	16.007	45	68	45	28
1.06150	90	1.06350	55	1.06550	19	1.06750	80	1.06950	40
55	.102	55	67	55	30	55	91	55	51
60	14	60	78	60	41	60	.503	60	63
65	25	65	90	65	53	65	14	65	74
70	37	70	.602	70	65	70	26	70	86
75	48	75	13	75	76	75	37	75	97
80	60	80	25	80	88	80	49	80	17.009
85	72	85	37	85	99	85	61	85	20
90	83	90	48	90	.111	90	72	90	32
95	95	95	60	95	22	95	83	95	43

51.010 Temperature corrections for readings of saccharometers (standard at 20°C)

(Calcd from data on thermal expansion of sugar solns by Plato[a] and assumed that instrument is of Jena 16[III] glass. Table should be used with caution and only for approx. results when temp. differs much from standard temp. or from temp. of surrounding air.)

Temp., °C	Observed Percentage of Sugar 0	5	10	15	20	25	30	35	40	45	50	55	60	70
	Subtract from Per Cent Sugar													
0	0.30	0.49	0.65	0.77	0.89	0.99	1.08	1.16	1.24	1.31	1.37	1.41	1.44	1.49
5	.36	.47	.56	.65	.73	.80	0.86	0.91	0.97	1.01	1.05	1.08	1.10	1.14
10	.32	.38	.43	.48	.52	.57	.60	.64	.67	0.70	0.72	0.74	0.75	0.77
11	.31	.35	.40	.44	.48	.51	.55	.58	.60	.63	.65	.66	.68	.70
12	.29	.32	.36	.40	.43	.46	.50	.52	.54	.56	.58	.59	.60	.62
13	.26	.29	.32	.35	.38	.41	.44	.46	.48	.49	.51	.52	.53	.55
14	.24	.26	.29	.31	.34	.36	.38	.40	.41	.42	.44	.45	.46	.47
15	.20	.22	.24	.26	.28	.30	.32	.33	.34	.36	.36	.37	.38	.39
16	.17	.18	.20	.22	.23	.25	.26	.27	.28	.28	.29	.30	.31	.32
17	.13	.14	.15	.16	.18	.19	.20	.20	.21	.21	.22	.23	.23	.24
18	.09	.10	.10	.11	.12	.13	.13	.14	.14	.14	.15	.15	.15	.16
19	.05	.05	.05	.06	.06	.06	.07	.07	.07	.07	.08	.08	.08	.08
17.5	.11	.12	.12	.14	.15	.16	.16	.17	.17	.18	.18	.19	.19	.20
15.56 (60°F)	.18	.20	.22	.24	.26	.28	.29	.30	.30	.32	.33	.33	.34	.34
	Add to Per Cent Sugar													
21	0.04	0.05	0.06	0.06	0.06	0.07	0.07	0.07	0.07	0.08	0.08	0.08	0.08	0.09
22	.10	.10	.11	.12	.12	.13	.14	.14	.15	.15	.16	.16	.16	.16
23	.16	.16	.17	.17	.19	.20	.21	.21	.22	.23	.24	.24	.24	.24
24	.21	.22	.23	.24	.26	.27	.28	.29	.30	.31	.32	.32	.32	.32
25	.27	.28	.30	.31	.32	.34	.35	.36	.38	.38	.39	.39	.40	.39
26	.33	.34	.36	.37	.40	.40	.42	.44	.46	.47	.47	.48	.48	.48
27	.40	.41	.42	.44	.46	.48	.50	.52	.54	.54	.55	.56	.56	.56
28	.46	.47	.49	.51	.54	.56	.58	.60	.61	.62	.63	.64	.64	.64
29	.54	.55	.56	.59	.61	.63	.66	.68	.70	.70	.71	.72	.72	.72
30	.61	.62	.63	.66	.68	.71	.73	.76	.78	.78	.79	.80	.80	.81
35	.99	1.01	1.02	1.06	1.10	1.13	1.16	1.18	1.20	1.21	1.22	1.22	1.23	1.22
40	1.42	1.45	1.47	1.51	1.54	1.57	1.60	1.62	1.64	1.65	1.65	1.65	1.66	1.65
45	1.91	1.94	1.96	2.00	2.03	2.05	2.07	2.09	2.10	2.10	2.10	2.10	2.10	2.08
50	2.46	2.48	2.50	2.53	2.56	2.57	2.58	2.59	2.59	2.58	2.58	2.57	2.56	2.52
55	3.05	3.07	3.09	3.12	3.12	3.12	3.12	3.11	3.10	3.08	3.07	3.05	3.03	2.97
60	3.69	3.72	3.73	3.73	3.72	3.70	3.67	3.65	3.62	3.60	3.57	3.54	3.50	3.43
27.5	0.43	0.44	0.46	0.48	0.50	0.52	0.54	0.56	0.58	0.58	0.59	0.60	0.60	0.60

[a] Charlottenberg. Physikalisch-technische reichsanstalt. Wiss. Abhandl. Kaiserliche Normal-Eichungs-Kommission, **2**, 140(1900).

52.011 Jackson-Mathews table of densities of fructose solutions and mean density and expansion coefficients between 20 and 25°C[a]

(All wts corrected to vac.)

Fructose, %	D_4^{20}	D_4^{25}	$-\Delta D/\Delta t$	$\Delta v/\Delta t$
			$\times10^{-6}$	$\times10^{-6}$
0	0.99823	0.99708	231	231
1	.00214	.00095	238	237
2	0607	0484	245	243
3	1003	0877	252	249
4	1402	1272	259	255
5	1803	1670	266	261
6	2207	2071	273	267
7	2614	2475	280	273
8	3024	2881	287	278
9	3437	3290	294	284
10	3853	3702	301	290
11	4271	4118	308	295
12	4692	4535	315	300
13	5116	4955	323	307
14	5543	5378	330	313
15	5972	5804	337	318
16	6405	6233	345	324
17	6840	6664	352	329
18	7278	7098	360	336
19	7719	7535	367	341
20	8162	7975	375	347
			$\times10^{-5}$	$\times10^{-5}$
21	8606	842	38	35
22	9055	886	38	35
23	9507	931	39	36
24	9962	976	40	36
25	.10420	.1022	41	37
26	088	0675	41	37
27	1345	1135	42	38
28	181	160	43	38
29	229	207	43	39
30	276	254	44	39
31	324	3015	45	40
32	372	349	46	40
33	4205	397	46	40
34	469	446	47	41
35	5185	495	48	41
			$\times10^{-5}$	$\times10^{-5}$
36	1.1568	1.1544	48	42
37	618	593	49	42
38	668	643	50	43
39	718	693	50	43
40	769	7435	51	43
41	820	794	52	44
42	872	845	53	44
43	923	897	53	45
44	975	9485	54	45
45	.2028	.20005	55	45
46	0805	053	55	46
47	134	106	56	46
48	187	159	57	46
49	241	212	57	47
50	295	266	58	47
51	349	320	59	47
52	404	374	59	48
53	459	429	60	48
54	514	484	60	48
55	570	539	61	49
56	626	595	62	49
57	682	651	62	49
58	739	707	63	50
59	796	764	64	50
60	853	821	64	50
61	911	878	65	50
62	969	936	66	51
63	.3027	994	66	51
64	086	.3052	67	51
65	145	111	67	51
66	204	170	68	51
67	263	229	69	52
68	323	289	69	52
69	384	349	70	52
70	444	409	70	52
71	505	470	71	53

[a] *J. Res. Natl. Bur. Std.* **8**, 437(1932), RP 426; Natl. Bur. Std. Circ. 440(1942).

52.012 Refractive indices (*n*) of sucrose solutions at 20°[a]

n 20°	Sucrose, %	*n* 20°	Sucrose, %	*n* 20°	Sucrose, %	*n* 20°	Sucrose, %	*n* 20°	Sucrose, %
1.3330	0.009	1.3380	3.463	1.3430	6.831	1.3480	10.116	1.3530	13.321
1.3331	.078	1.3381	3.532	1.3431	6.898	1.3481	10.181	1.3531	13.384
1.3332	.149	1.3382	3.600	1.3432	6.964	1.3482	10.246	1.3532	13.448
1.3333	.218	1.3383	3.668	1.3433	7.031	1.3438	10.311	1.3533	13.511
1.3334	.288	1.3384	3.736	1.3434	7.097	1.3484	10.375	1.3534	13.574
1.3335	0.358	1.3385	3.804	1.3435	7.164	1.3485	10.440	1.3535	13.637
1.3336	.428	1.3386	3.872	1.3436	7.230	1.3486	10.505	1.3536	13.700
1.3337	.498	1.3387	3.940	1.3437	7.296	1.3487	10.570	1.3537	13.763
1.3338	.567	1.3388	4.008	1.3438	7.362	1.3488	10.634	1.3538	13.826
1.3339	.637	1.3389	4.076	1.3439	7.429	1.3489	10.699	1.3539	13.890
1.3340	0.707	1.3390	4.144	1.3440	7.495	1.3490	10.763	1.3540	13.953
1.3341	.776	1.3391	4.212	1.3441	7.561	1.3491	10.828	1.3541	14.016
1.3342	.846	1.3392	4.279	1.3442	7.627	1.3492	10.892	1.3542	14.079
1.3343	.915	1.3393	4.347	1.3443	7.693	1.3493	10.957	1.3543	14.141
1.3344	.985	1.3394	4.415	1.3444	7.759	1.3494	11.021	1.3544	14.204
1.3345	1.054	1.3395	4.483	1.3445	7.825	1.3495	11.086	1.3545	14.267
1.3346	1.124	1.3396	4.550	1.3446	7.891	1.3496	11.150	1.3546	14.330
1.3347	1.193	1.3397	4.618	1.3447	7.957	1.3497	11.215	1.3547	14.393
1.3348	1.263	1.3398	4.686	1.3448	8.023	1.3498	11.279	1.3548	14.456
1.3349	1.332	1.3399	4.753	1.3449	8.089	1.3499	11.343	1.3549	14.518
1.3350	1.401	1.3400	4.821	1.3450	8.155	1.3500	11.407	1.3550	14.581
1.3351	1.470	1.3401	4.888	1.3451	8.221	1.3501	11.472	1.3551	14.644
1.3352	1.540	1.3402	4.956	1.3452	8.287	1.3502	11.536	1.3552	14.707
1.3353	1.609	1.3403	5.023	1.3435	8.352	1.3503	11.600	1.3553	14.769
1.3354	1.678	1.3404	5.091	1.3454	8.418	1.3504	11.664	1.3554	14.832
1.3355	1.747	1.3405	5.158	1.3455	8.484	1.3505	11.728	1.3555	14.894
1.3356	1.816	1.3406	5.225	1.3456	8.550	1.3506	11.792	1.3556	14.957
1.3357	1.885	1.3407	5.293	1.3457	8.615	1.3507	11.856	1.3557	15.019
1.3358	1.954	1.3408	5.360	1.3458	8.681	1.3508	11.920	1.3558	15.082
1.3359	2.023	1.3409	5.427	1.3459	8.746	1.3509	11.984	1.3559	15.144
1.3360	2.092	1.3410	5.494	1.3460	8.812	1.3510	12.048	1.3560	15.207
1.3361	2.161	1.3411	5.562	1.3461	8.878	1.3511	12.112	1.3561	15.269
1.3362	2.230	1.3412	5.629	1.3462	8.943	1.3512	12.176	1.3562	15.332
1.3363	2.299	1.3413	5.696	1.3463	9.008	1.3513	12.240	1.3563	15.394
1.3364	2.367	1.3414	5.763	1.3464	9.074	1.3514	12.304	1.3564	15.456
1.3365	2.436	1.3415	5.830	1.3465	9.139	1.3515	12.368	1.3565	15.518
1.3366	2.505	1.3416	5.897	1.3466	9.205	1.3516	12.431	1.3566	15.581
1.3367	2.574	1.3417	5.964	1.3467	9.270	1.3517	12.495	1.3567	15.643
1.3368	2.642	1.3418	6.031	1.3468	9.335	1.3518	12.559	1.3568	15.705
1.3369	2.711	1.3419	6.098	1.3469	9.400	1.3519	12.623	1.3569	15.767
1.3370	2.779	1.3420	6.165	1.3470	9.466	1.3520	12.686	1.3570	15.829
1.3371	2.848	1.3421	6.231	1.3471	9.531	1.3521	12.750	1.3571	15.891
1.3372	2.917	1.3422	6.298	1.3472	9.596	1.3522	12.813	1.3572	15.953
1.3373	2.985	1.3423	6.365	1.3473	9.661	1.3523	12.877	1.3573	16.016
1.3374	3.053	1.3424	6.432	1.3474	9.726	1.3524	12.940	1.3574	16.078
1.3375	3.122	1.3425	6.498	1.3475	9.791	1.3525	13.004	1.3775	16.140
1.3376	3.190	1.3426	6.565	1.3476	9.856	1.3526	13.067	1.3576	16.201
1.3377	3.259	1.3427	6.632	1.3477	9.921	1.3527	13.131	1.3577	16.263
1.3378	3.327	1.3428	6.698	1.3478	9.986	1.3528	13.194	1.3578	16.325
1.3379	3.395	1.3429	6.765	1.3479	10.051	1.3529	13.258	1.3579	16.387

(Continued)

[a] Values in this table are calcd from equation developed by K. Rosenhauer for ICUMSA, programmed and computed by Frank G. Carpenter of USDA, and published in *Sugar J.* **33,** 15–22(June 1970). Refractive index was measured at 20° with D line of Na; Brix (% sucrose by wt) was obtained by weighing at 20° in air at 760 Torr (mm Hg) pressure and 50% relative humidity. It replaces previous table, **47.012,** 11th ed., taken from *Intern. Sugar J.* **39,** 22s (1937).

52.012 Refractive indices (*n*) of sucrose solutions at 20°—*Continued.*

n 20°	Sucrose, %	*n* 20°	Sucrose, %	*n* 20°	Sucrose, %	*n* 20°	Sucrose, %	*n* 20°	Sucrose, %
1.3580	16.449	1.3630	19.503	1.3680	22.487	1.3730	25.403	1.3780	28.253
1.3581	16.511	1.3631	19.564	1.3681	22.546	1.3731	25.460	1.3781	28.310
1.3582	16.573	1.3632	19.624	1.3682	22.605	1.3732	25.518	1.3782	28.366
1.3583	16.634	1.3633	19.684	1.3683	22.664	1.3733	25.576	1.3783	28.422
1.3584	16.696	1.3634	19.745	1.3684	22.723	1.3734	25.633	1.3784	28.479
1.3585	16.758	1.3635	19.805	1.3685	22.781	1.3735	25.691	1.3785	28.535
1.3586	16.819	1.3636	19.865	1.3686	22.840	1.3736	25.748	1.3786	28.591
1.3587	16.881	1.3637	19.925	1.3687	22.899	1.3737	25.806	1.3787	28.648
1.3588	16.943	1.3638	19.985	1.3688	22.958	1.3738	25.863	1.3788	28.704
1.3589	17.004	1.3639	20.045	1.3689	23.017	1.3739	25.921	1.3789	28.760
1.3590	17.066	1.3640	20.106	1.3690	23.075	1.3740	25.978	1.3790	28.816
1.3591	17.127	1.3641	20.166	1.3691	23.134	1.3741	26.035	1.3791	28.872
1.3592	17.189	1.3642	20.226	1.3692	23.193	1.3742	26.093	1.3792	28.928
1.3593	17.250	1.3643	20.286	1.3693	23.251	1.3743	26.150	1.3793	28.984
1.3594	17.311	1.3644	20.346	1.3694	23.310	1.3744	26.207	1.3794	29.040
1.3595	17.373	1.3645	20.406	1.3695	23.369	1.3745	26.265	1.3795	29.096
1.3596	17.434	1.3646	20.466	1.3696	23.427	1.3746	26.322	1.3796	29.152
1.3597	17.496	1.3647	20.525	1.3697	23.486	1.3747	26.379	1.3797	29.208
1.3598	17.557	1.3648	20.585	1.3698	23.544	1.3748	26.436	1.3798	29.264
1.3599	17.618	1.3649	20.645	1.3699	23.603	1.3749	26.493	1.3799	29.320
1.3600	17.679	1.3650	20.705	1.3700	23.661	1.3750	26.551	1.3800	29.376
1.3601	17.741	1.3651	20.765	1.3701	23.720	1.3751	26.608	1.3801	29.432
1.3602	17.802	1.3652	20.825	1.3702	23.778	1.3752	26.665	1.3802	29.488
1.3603	17.863	1.3653	20.884	1.3703	23.836	1.3753	26.722	1.3803	29.544
1.3604	17.924	1.3654	20.944	1.3704	23.895	1.3754	26.779	1.3804	29.600
1.3605	17.985	1.3655	21.004	1.3705	23.953	1.3755	26.836	1.3805	29.655
1.3606	18.046	1.3656	21.063	1.3706	24.011	1.3756	26.893	1.3806	29.711
1.3607	18.107	1.3657	21.123	1.3707	24.070	1.3757	26.950	1.3807	29.767
1.3608	18.168	1.3658	21.183	1.3708	24.128	1.3758	27.007	1.3808	29.823
1.3609	18.229	1.3659	21.242	1.3709	24.186	1.3759	27.064	1.3809	29.878
1.3610	18.290	1.3660	21.302	1.3710	24.244	1.3760	27.121	1.3810	29.934
1.3611	18.351	1.3661	21.361	1.3711	24.302	1.3761	27.178	1.3811	29.989
1.3612	18.412	1.3662	21.421	1.3712	24.361	1.3762	27.234	1.3812	30.045
1.3613	18.473	1.3663	21.480	1.3713	24.419	1.3763	27.291	1.3813	30.101
1.3614	18.534	1.3664	21.540	1.3714	24.477	1.3764	27.348	1.3814	30.156
1.3615	18.595	1.3665	21.599	1.3715	24.535	1.3765	27.405	1.3815	30.212
1.3616	18.655	1.3666	21.658	1.3716	24.593	1.3766	27.462	1.3816	30.267
1.3617	18.716	1.3667	21.718	1.3717	24.651	1.3767	27.518	1.3817	30.323
1.3618	18.777	1.3668	21.777	1.3718	24.709	1.3768	27.575	1.3818	30.378
1.3619	18.837	1.3669	21.836	1.3719	24.767	1.3769	27.632	1.3819	30.434
1.3620	18.898	1.3670	21.896	1.3720	24.825	1.3770	27.688	1.3820	30.489
1.3621	18.959	1.3671	21.955	1.3721	24.883	1.3771	27.745	1.3821	30.544
1.3622	19.019	1.3672	22.014	1.3722	24.941	1.3772	27.802	1.3822	30.600
1.3623	19.080	1.3673	22.073	1.3723	24.998	1.3773	27.858	1.3823	30.655
1.3624	19.141	1.3674	22.132	1.3724	25.056	1.3774	27.915	1.3824	30.711
1.3625	19.201	1.3675	22.192	1.3725	25.114	1.3775	27.971	1.3825	30.766
1.3626	19.262	1.3676	22.251	1.3726	25.172	1.3776	28.028	1.3826	30.821
1.3627	19.322	1.3677	22.310	1.3727	25.230	1.3777	28.084	1.3827	30.876
1.3628	19.382	1.3678	22.369	1.3728	25.287	1.3778	28.141	1.3828	30.932
1.3629	19.443	1.3679	22.428	1.3729	25.345	1.3779	28.197	1.3829	30.987

(Continued)

52.012 Refractive indices (*n*) of sucrose solutions at 20°—*Continued.*

n 20°	Sucrose, %	*n* 20°	Sucrose, %	*n* 20°	Sucrose, %	*n* 20°	Sucrose, %	*n* 20°	Sucrose, %
1.3830	31.042	1.3880	33.771	1.3930	36.442	1.3980	39.059	1.4030	41.623
1.3831	31.097	1.3881	33.825	1.3931	36.495	1.3981	39.111	1.4031	41.674
1.3832	31.152	1.3882	33.879	1.3932	36.548	1.3982	39.163	1.4032	41.725
1.3833	31.207	1.3883	33.933	1.3933	36.601	1.3983	39.214	1.4033	41.776
1.3834	31.262	1.3884	33.987	1.3934	36.654	1.3984	39.266	1.4034	41.826
1.3835	31.317	1.3885	34.040	1.3935	36.706	1.3985	39.318	1.4035	41.877
1.3836	31.372	1.3886	34.094	1.3936	36.759	1.3986	39.370	1.4036	41.928
1.3837	31.428	1.3887	34.148	1.3937	36.812	1.3987	39.421	1.4037	41.978
1.3838	31.482	1.3888	34.202	1.3938	36.865	1.3988	39.473	1.4038	42.029
1.3839	31.537	1.3889	34.256	1.3939	36.917	1.3989	39.525	1.4039	42.080
1.3840	31.592	1.3890	34.310	1.3940	36.970	1.3990	39.576	1.4040	42.130
1.3841	31.647	1.3891	34.363	1.3941	37.023	1.3991	39.628	1.4041	42.181
1.3842	31.702	1.3892	34.417	1.3942	37.075	1.3992	39.679	1.4042	42.231
1.3843	31.757	1.3893	34.471	1.3943	37.128	1.3993	39.731	1.4043	42.282
1.3844	31.812	1.3894	34.524	1.3944	37.180	1.3994	39.782	1.4044	42.332
1.3845	31.867	1.3895	34.578	1.3945	37.233	1.3995	39.834	1.4045	42.383
1.3846	31.922	1.3896	34.632	1.3946	37.286	1.3996	39.885	1.4046	42.433
1.3847	31.976	1.3897	34.685	1.3947	37.338	1.3997	39.937	1.4047	42.484
1.3848	32.031	1.3898	34.739	1.3948	37.391	1.3998	39.988	1.4048	42.534
1.3849	32.086	1.3899	34.793	1.3949	37.443	1.3999	40.040	1.4049	42.585
1.3850	32.140	1.3900	34.846	1.3950	37.495	1.4000	40.091	1.4050	42.635
1.3851	32.195	1.3901	34.900	1.3951	37.548	1.4001	40.142	1.4051	42.685
1.3852	32.250	1.3902	34.953	1.3952	37.600	1.4002	40.194	1.4052	42.736
1.3853	32.304	1.3903	35.007	1.3953	37.653	1.4003	40.245	1.4053	42.786
1.3854	32.359	1.3904	35.060	1.3954	37.705	1.4004	40.296	1.4054	42.836
1.3855	32.414	1.3905	35.114	1.3955	37.757	1.4005	40.348	1.4055	42.887
1.3856	32.468	1.3906	35.167	1.3956	37.810	1.4006	40.399	1.4056	42.937
1.3857	32.523	1.3907	35.220	1.3957	37.862	1.4007	40.450	1.4057	42.987
1.3858	32.577	1.3908	35.274	1.3958	37.914	1.4008	40.501	1.4058	43.037
1.3859	32.632	1.3909	35.327	1.3959	37.967	1.4009	40.553	1.4059	43.088
1.3860	32.686	1.3910	35.380	1.3960	38.019	1.4010	40.604	1.4060	43.138
1.3861	32.741	1.3911	35.434	1.3961	38.071	1.4011	40.655	1.4061	43.188
1.3862	32.795	1.3912	35.487	1.3962	38.123	1.4012	40.706	1.4062	43.238
1.3863	32.849	1.3913	35.540	1.3963	38.175	1.4013	40.757	1.4063	43.288
1.3864	32.904	1.3914	35.593	1.3964	38.228	1.4014	40.808	1.4064	43.338
1.3865	32.958	1.3915	35.647	1.3965	38.280	1.4015	40.860	1.4065	43.388
1.3866	33.013	1.3916	35.700	1.3966	38.332	1.4016	40.911	1.4066	43.439
1.3867	33.067	1.3917	35.753	1.3967	38.384	1.4017	40.962	1.4067	43.489
1.3868	33.121	1.3918	35.806	1.3968	38.436	1.4018	41.013	1.4068	43.539
1.3869	33.175	1.3919	35.859	1.3969	38.488	1.4019	41.064	1.4069	43.589
1.3870	33.230	1.3920	35.912	1.3970	38.540	1.4020	41.115	1.4070	43.639
1.3871	33.284	1.3921	35.966	1.3971	38.592	1.4021	41.166	1.4071	43.689
1.3872	33.338	1.3922	36.019	1.3972	38.644	1.4022	41.217	1.4072	43.739
1.3873	33.392	1.3923	36.072	1.3973	38.696	1.4023	41.268	1.4073	43.789
1.3874	33.446	1.3924	36.125	1.3974	38.748	1.4024	41.318	1.4074	43.838
1.3875	33.500	1.3925	36.178	1.3975	38.800	1.4025	41.369	1.4075	43.888
1.3876	33.555	1.3926	36.231	1.3976	38.852	1.4026	41.420	1.4076	43.938
1.3877	33.609	1.3927	36.284	1.3977	38.904	1.4027	41.471	1.4077	43.988
1.3878	33.663	1.3928	36.337	1.3978	38.955	1.4028	41.522	1.4078	44.038
1.3879	33.717	1.3929	36.389	1.3979	39.007	1.4029	41.573	1.4079	44.088

(*Continued*)

52.012 Refractive indices (*n*) of sucrose solutions at 20°—*Continued*.

n 20°	Sucrose, %	*n* 20°	Sucrose, %	*n* 20°	Sucrose, %	*n* 20°	Sucrose, %	*n* 20°	Sucrose, %
1.4080	44.138	1.4130	46.604	1.4180	49.023	1.4230	51.399	1.4280	53.733
1.4081	44.187	1.4131	46.652	1.4181	49.071	1.4231	51.446	1.4281	53.779
1.4082	44.237	1.4132	46.701	1.4182	49.119	1.4232	51.493	1.4282	53.825
1.4083	44.287	1.4133	46.750	1.4183	49.167	1.4233	51.540	1.4283	53.871
1.4084	44.337	1.4134	46.799	1.4184	49.215	1.4234	51.587	1.4284	53.918
1.4085	44.386	1.4135	46.848	1.4185	49.263	1.4235	51.634	1.4285	53.964
1.4086	44.436	1.4136	46.896	1.4186	49.311	1.4236	51.681	1.4286	54.010
1.4087	44.486	1.4137	46.945	1.4187	49.359	1.4237	51.728	1.4287	54.056
1.4088	44.535	1.4138	46.994	1.4188	49.407	1.4238	51.775	1.4288	54.102
1.4089	44.585	1.4139	47.043	1.4189	49.454	1.4239	51.822	1.4289	54.148
1.4090	44.635	1.4140	47.091	1.4190	49.502	1.4240	51.869	1.4290	54.194
1.4091	44.684	1.4141	47.140	1.4191	49.550	1.4241	51.916	1.4291	54.241
1.4092	44.734	1.4142	47.188	1.4192	49.598	1.4242	51.963	1.4292	54.287
1.4093	44.783	1.4143	47.237	1.4193	49.645	1.4243	52.010	1.4293	54.333
1.4094	44.833	1.4144	47.286	1.4194	49.693	1.4244	52.057	1.4294	54.379
1.4095	44.882	1.4145	47.334	1.4195	49.741	1.4245	52.104	1.4295	54.425
1.4096	44.932	1.4146	47.383	1.4196	49.788	1.4246	52.150	1.4296	54.471
1.4097	44.981	1.4147	47.431	1.4197	49.836	1.4247	52.197	1.4297	54.517
1.4098	45.031	1.4148	47.480	1.4198	49.884	1.4248	52.244	1.4298	54.563
1.4099	45.080	1.4149	47.528	1.4199	49.931	1.4249	52.291	1.4299	54.609
1.4100	45.130	1.4150	47.577	1.4200	49.979	1.4250	52.338	1.4300	54.655
1.4101	45.179	1.4151	47.625	1.4201	50.027	1.4251	52.384	1.4301	54.701
1.4102	45.228	1.4152	47.674	1.4202	50.074	1.4252	52.431	1.4302	54.746
1.4103	45.278	1.4153	47.722	1.4203	50.122	1.4253	52.478	1.4303	54.792
1.4104	45.327	1.4154	47.771	1.4204	50.169	1.4254	52.524	1.4304	54.838
1.4105	45.376	1.4155	47.819	1.4205	50.217	1.4255	52.571	1.4305	54.884
1.4106	45.426	1.4156	47.868	1.4206	50.264	1.4256	52.618	1.4306	54.930
1.4107	45.475	1.4157	47.916	1.4207	50.312	1.4257	52.664	1.4307	54.976
1.4108	45.524	1.4158	47.964	1.4208	50.359	1.4258	52.711	1.4308	55.022
1.4109	45.574	1.4159	48.013	1.4209	50.407	1.4259	52.758	1.4309	55.067
1.4110	45.623	1.4160	48.061	1.4210	50.454	1.4260	52.804	1.4310	55.113
1.4111	45.672	1.4161	48.109	1.4211	50.502	1.4261	52.851	1.4311	55.159
1.4112	45.721	1.4162	48.158	1.4212	50.549	1.4262	52.897	1.4312	55.205
1.4113	45.770	1.4163	48.206	1.4213	50.596	1.4263	52.944	1.4313	55.250
1.4114	45.820	1.4164	48.254	1.4214	50.644	1.4264	52.990	1.4314	55.296
1.4115	45.869	1.4165	48.302	1.4215	50.691	1.4265	53.037	1.4315	55.342
1.4116	45.918	1.4166	48.350	1.4216	50.738	1.4266	53.083	1.4316	55.388
1.4117	45.967	1.4167	48.399	1.4217	50.786	1.4267	53.130	1.4317	55.433
1.4118	46.016	1.4168	48.447	1.4218	50.833	1.4268	53.176	1.4318	55.479
1.4119	46.065	1.4169	48.495	1.4219	50.880	1.4269	53.223	1.4319	55.524
1.4120	46.114	1.4170	48.543	1.4220	50.928	1.4270	53.269	1.4320	55.570
1.4121	46.163	1.4171	48.591	1.4221	50.975	1.4271	53.316	1.4321	55.616
1.4122	46.212	1.4172	48.639	1.4222	51.022	1.4272	53.362	1.4322	55.661
1.4123	46.261	1.4173	48.687	1.4223	51.069	1.4273	53.408	1.4323	55.707
1.4124	46.310	1.4174	48.735	1.4224	51.116	1.4274	53.455	1.4324	55.752
1.4125	46.359	1.4175	48.784	1.4225	51.164	1.4275	53.501	1.4325	55.798
1.4126	46.408	1.4176	48.832	1.4226	51.211	1.4276	53.548	1.4326	55.844
1.4127	46.457	1.4177	48.880	1.4227	51.258	1.4277	53.594	1.4327	55.889
1.4128	46.506	1.4178	48.928	1.4228	51.305	1.4278	53.640	1.4328	55.935
1.4129	46.555	1.4179	48.976	1.4229	51.352	1.4279	53.686	1.4329	55.980

(*Continued*)

52.012 Refractive indices (*n*) of sucrose solutions at 20°—*Continued.*

n 20°	Sucrose, %	*n* 20°	Sucrose, %	*n* 20°	Sucrose, %	*n* 20°	Sucrose, %	*n* 20°	Sucrose, %
1.4330	56.026	1.4380	58.279	1.4430	60.496	1.4480	62.677	1.4530	64.823
1.4331	56.071	1.4381	58.324	1.4431	60.540	1.4481	62.720	1.4531	64.865
1.4332	56.116	1.4382	58.369	1.4432	60.584	1.4482	62.763	1.4532	64.908
1.4333	56.162	1.4383	58.413	1.4433	60.628	1.4483	62.806	1.4533	64.950
1.4334	56.207	1.4384	58.458	1.4434	60.672	1.4484	62.849	1.4534	64.993
1.4335	56.253	1.4385	58.503	1.4435	60.716	1.4485	62.893	1.4535	65.035
1.4336	56.298	1.4386	58.547	1.4436	60.759	1.4486	62.936	1.4536	65.078
1.4337	56.343	1.4387	58.592	1.4437	60.803	1.4487	62.979	1.4537	65.120
1.4338	56.389	1.4388	58.637	1.4438	60.847	1.4488	63.022	1.4538	65.163
1.4339	56.434	1.4389	58.681	1.4439	60.891	1.4489	63.065	1.4539	65.205
1.4340	56.479	1.4390	58.726	1.4440	60.935	1.4490	63.108	1.4540	65.248
1.4341	56.525	1.4391	58.770	1.4441	60.979	1.4491	63.152	1.4541	65.290
1.4342	56.570	1.4392	58.815	1.4442	61.023	1.4492	63.195	1.4542	65.333
1.4343	56.615	1.4393	58.859	1.4443	61.066	1.4493	63.238	1.4543	65.375
1.4344	56.660	1.4394	58.904	1.4444	61.110	1.4494	63.281	1.4544	65.417
1.4345	56.706	1.4395	58.948	1.4445	61.154	1.4495	63.324	1.4545	65.460
1.4346	56.751	1.4396	58.993	1.4446	61.198	1.4496	63.367	1.4546	65.502
1.4347	56.796	1.4397	59.037	1.4447	61.241	1.4497	63.410	1.4547	65.544
1.4348	56.841	1.4398	59.082	1.4448	61.285	1.4498	63.453	1.4548	65.587
1.4349	56.887	1.4399	59.126	1.4449	61.329	1.4499	63.496	1.4549	65.629
1.4350	56.932	1.4400	59.170	1.4450	61.372	1.4500	63.539	1.4550	65.672
1.4351	56.977	1.4401	59.215	1.4451	61.416	1.4501	63.582	1.4551	65.714
1.4352	57.022	1.4402	59.259	1.4452	61.460	1.4502	63.625	1.4552	65.756
1.4353	57.067	1.4403	59.304	1.4453	61.503	1.4503	63.668	1.4553	65.798
1.4354	57.112	1.4404	59.348	1.4454	61.547	1.4504	63.711	1.4554	65.841
1.4355	57.157	1.4405	59.392	1.4455	61.591	1.4505	63.754	1.4555	65.883
1.4356	57.202	1.4406	59.437	1.4456	61.634	1.4506	63.797	1.4556	65.925
1.4357	57.247	1.4407	59.481	1.4457	61.678	1.4507	63.840	1.4557	65.967
1.4358	57.292	1.4408	59.525	1.4458	61.721	1.4508	63.882	1.4558	66.010
1.4359	57.337	1.4409	59.569	1.4459	61.765	1.4509	63.925	1.4559	66.052
1.4360	57.382	1.4410	59.614	1.4460	61.809	1.4510	63.968	1.4560	66.094
1.4361	57.427	1.4411	59.658	1.4461	61.852	1.4511	64.011	1.4561	66.136
1.4362	57.472	1.4412	59.702	1.4462	61.896	1.4512	64.054	1.4562	66.178
1.4363	57.517	1.4413	59.746	1.4463	61.939	1.4513	64.097	1.4563	66.221
1.4364	57.562	1.4414	59.791	1.4464	61.983	1.4514	64.139	1.4564	66.263
1.4365	57.607	1.4415	59.835	1.4465	62.026	1.4515	64.182	1.4565	66.305
1.4366	57.652	1.4416	59.879	1.4466	62.070	1.4516	64.225	1.4566	66.347
1.4367	57.697	1.4417	59.923	1.4467	62.113	1.4517	64.268	1.4567	66.389
1.4368	57.742	1.4418	59.967	1.4468	62.156	1.4518	64.311	1.4568	66.431
1.4369	57.787	1.4419	60.011	1.4469	62.200	1.4519	64.353	1.4569	66.473
1.4370	57.832	1.4420	60.056	1.4470	62.243	1.4520	64.396	1.4570	66.515
1.4371	57.877	1.4421	60.100	1.4471	62.287	1.4521	64.439	1.4571	66.557
1.4372	57.921	1.4422	60.144	1.4472	62.330	1.4522	64.481	1.4572	66.599
1.4373	57.966	1.4423	60.188	1.4473	62.373	1.4523	64.524	1.4573	66.641
1.4374	58.011	1.4424	60.232	1.4474	62.417	1.4524	64.567	1.4574	66.683
1.4375	58.056	1.4425	60.276	1.4475	62.460	1.4525	64.609	1.4575	66.725
1.4376	58.101	1.4426	60.320	1.4476	62.503	1.4526	64.652	1.4576	66.767
1.4377	58.145	1.4427	60.364	1.4477	62.547	1.4527	64.695	1.4577	66.809
1.4378	58.190	1.4428	60.408	1.4478	62.590	1.4528	64.737	1.4578	66.851
1.4379	58.235	1.4429	60.452	1.4479	62.633	1.4529	64.780	1.4579	66.893

(Continued)

52.012 Refractive indices (*n*) of sucrose solutions at 20°—*Continued.*

n 20°	Sucrose, %	*n* 20°	Sucrose, %	*n* 20°	Sucrose, %	*n* 20°	Sucrose, %	*n* 20°	Sucrose, %
1.4580	66.935	1.4630	69.016	1.4680	71.065	1.4730	73.084	1.4780	75.074
1.4581	66.977	1.4631	69.057	1.4681	71.106	1.4731	73.124	1.4781	75.114
1.4582	67.019	1.4632	69.098	1.4682	71.146	1.4732	73.164	1.4782	75.153
1.4583	67.061	1.4633	69.139	1.4683	71.187	1.4733	73.204	1.4783	75.193
1.4584	67.103	1.4634	69.181	1.4684	71.228	1.4734	73.244	1.4784	75.232
1.4585	67.145	1.4635	69.222	1.4685	71.268	1.4735	73.285	1.4785	75.272
1.4586	67.186	1.4636	69.263	1.4686	71.309	1.4736	73.325	1.4786	75.311
1.4587	67.228	1.4637	69.304	1.4687	71.349	1.4737	73.365	1.4787	75.350
1.4588	67.270	1.4638	69.346	1.4688	71.390	1.4738	73.405	1.4788	75.390
1.4589	67.312	1.4639	69.387	1.4689	71.431	1.4739	73.445	1.4789	75.429
1.4590	67.354	1.4640	69.428	1.4690	71.471	1.4740	73.485	1.4790	75.469
1.4591	67.396	1.4641	69.469	1.4691	71.512	1.4741	73.524	1.4791	75.508
1.4592	67.437	1.4642	69.510	1.4692	71.552	1.4742	73.564	1.4792	75.547
1.4593	67.479	1.4643	69.551	1.4693	71.593	1.4743	73.604	1.4793	75.587
1.4594	67.521	1.4644	69.593	1.4694	71.633	1.4744	73.644	1.4794	75.626
1.4595	67.563	1.4645	69.634	1.4695	71.674	1.4745	73.684	1.4795	75.666
1.4596	67.604	1.4646	69.675	1.4696	71.714	1.4746	73.724	1.4796	75.705
1.4597	67.646	1.4647	69.716	1.4697	71.755	1.4747	73.764	1.4797	75.744
1.4598	67.688	1.4648	69.757	1.4698	71.795	1.4748	73.804	1.4798	75.784
1.4599	67.729	1.4649	69.798	1.4699	71.836	1.4749	73.844	1.4799	75.823
1.4600	67.771	1.4650	69.839	1.4700	71.876	1.4750	73.884	1.4800	75.862
1.4601	67.813	1.4651	69.880	1.4701	71.917	1.4751	73.924	1.4801	75.901
1.4602	67.854	1.4652	69.921	1.4702	71.957	1.4752	73.963	1.4802	75.941
1.4603	67.896	1.4653	69.962	1.4703	71.998	1.4753	74.003	1.4803	75.980
1.4604	67.938	1.4654	70.003	1.4704	72.038	1.4754	74.043	1.4804	76.019
1.4605	67.979	1.4655	70.044	1.4705	72.078	1.4755	74.083	1.4805	76.058
1.4606	68.021	1.4656	70.085	1.4706	72.119	1.4756	74.123	1.4806	76.098
1.4607	68.063	1.4657	70.126	1.4707	72.159	1.4757	74.162	1.4807	76.137
1.4608	68.104	1.4658	70.167	1.4708	72.199	1.4758	74.202	1.4808	76.176
1.4609	68.146	1.4659	70.208	1.4709	72.240	1.4759	74.242	1.4809	76.215
1.4610	68.187	1.4660	70.249	1.4710	72.280	1.4760	74.282	1.4810	76.254
1.4611	68.229	1.4661	70.290	1.4711	72.320	1.4761	74.321	1.4811	76.294
1.4612	68.270	1.4662	70.331	1.4712	72.361	1.4762	74.361	1.4812	76.333
1.4613	68.312	1.4663	70.372	1.4713	72.401	1.4763	74.401	1.4813	76.372
1.4614	68.353	1.4664	70.413	1.4714	72.441	1.4764	74.441	1.4814	76.411
1.4615	68.395	1.4665	70.453	1.4715	72.482	1.4765	74.480	1.4815	76.450
1.4616	68.436	1.4666	70.494	1.4716	72.522	1.4766	74.520	1.4816	76.489
1.4617	68.478	1.4667	70.535	1.4717	72.562	1.4767	74.560	1.4817	76.528
1.4618	68.519	1.4668	70.576	1.4718	72.602	1.4768	74.599	1.4818	76.567
1.4619	68.561	1.4669	70.617	1.4719	72.643	1.4769	74.639	1.4819	76.607
1.4620	68.602	1.4670	70.658	1.4720	72.683	1.4770	74.678	1.4820	76.646
1.4621	68.643	1.4671	70.698	1.4721	72.723	1.4771	74.718	1.4821	76.685
1.4622	68.685	1.4672	70.739	1.4722	72.763	1.4772	74.758	1.4822	76.724
1.4623	68.726	1.4673	70.780	1.4723	72.803	1.4773	74.797	1.4823	76.763
1.4624	68.768	1.4674	70.821	1.4724	72.843	1.4774	74.837	1.4824	76.802
1.4625	68.809	1.4675	70.861	1.4725	72.884	1.4775	74.876	1.4825	76.841
1.4626	68.850	1.4676	70.902	1.4726	72.924	1.4776	74.916	1.4826	76.880
1.4627	68.892	1.4677	70.943	1.4727	72.964	1.4777	74.956	1.4827	76.919
1.4628	68.933	1.4678	70.984	1.4728	73.004	1.4778	74.995	1.4828	76.958
1.4629	68.974	1.4679	71.024	1.4729	73.044	1.4779	75.035	1.4829	76.997

(*Continued*)

52.012 Refractive indices (*n*) of sucrose solutions at 20°—*Concluded.*

n 20°	Sucrose, %	*n* 20°	Sucrose, %	*n* 20°	Sucrose, %	*n* 20°	Sucrose, %	*n* 20°	Sucrose, %
1.4830	77.036	1.4880	78.969	1.4930	80.876	1.4980	82.755	1.5030	84.609
1.4831	77.075	1.4881	79.008	1.4931	80.913	1.4981	82.793	1.5031	84.645
1.4832	77.113	1.4882	79.046	1.4932	80.951	1.4982	82.830	1.5032	84.682
1.4833	77.152	1.4883	79.084	1.4933	80.989	1.4983	82.867	1.5033	84.719
1.4834	77.191	1.4884	79.123	1.4934	81.027	1.4984	82.905	1.5034	84.756
1.4835	77.230	1.4885	79.161	1.4935	81.065	1.4985	82.942	1.5035	84.792
1.4836	77.269	1.4886	79.199	1.4936	81.103	1.4986	82.979	1.5036	84.829
1.4837	77.308	1.4887	79.238	1.4937	81.140	1.4987	83.016	1.5037	84.866
1.4838	77.347	1.4888	79.276	1.4938	81.178	1.4988	83.054	1.5038	84.903
1.4839	77.386	1.4889	79.314	1.4939	81.216	1.4989	83.091	1.5039	84.939
1.4840	77.425	1.4890	79.353	1.4940	81.254	1.4990	83.128	1.5040	84.976
1.4841	77.463	1.4891	79.391	1.4941	81.291	1.4991	83.165	1.5041	85.013
1.4842	77.502	1.4892	79.429	1.4942	81.329	1.4992	83.202	1.5042	85.049
1.4843	77.541	1.4893	79.468	1.4943	81.367	1.4993	83.240	1.5043	85.086
1.4844	77.580	1.4894	79.506	1.4944	81.405	1.4994	83.277	1.5044	85.123
1.4845	77.619	1.4895	79.544	1.4945	81.442	1.4995	83.314	1.5045	85.159
1.4846	77.657	1.4896	79.582	1.4946	81.480	1.4996	83.351	1.5046	85.196
1.4847	77.696	1.4897	79.620	1.4947	81.518	1.4997	83.388	1.5047	85.233
1.4848	77.735	1.4898	79.659	1.4948	81.555	1.4998	83.425	1.5048	85.269
1.4849	77.774	1.4899	79.697	1.4949	81.593	1.4999	83.463	1.5049	85.306
1.4850	77.812	1.4900	79.735	1.4950	81.631	1.5000	83.500	1.5050	85.343
1.4851	77.851	1.4901	79.773	1.4951	81.668	1.5001	83.537	1.5051	85.379
1.4852	77.890	1.4902	79.811	1.4952	81.706	1.5002	83.574	1.5052	85.416
1.4853	77.928	1.4903	79.850	1.4953	81.744	1.5003	83.611	1.5053	85.452
1.4854	77.967	1.4904	79.888	1.4954	81.781	1.5004	83.648	1.5054	85.489
1.4855	78.006	1.4905	79.926	1.4955	81.819	1.5005	83.685	1.5055	85.525
1.4856	78.045	1.4906	79.964	1.4956	81.856	1.5006	83.722	1.5056	85.562
1.4857	78.083	1.4907	80.002	1.4957	81.894	1.5007	83.759	1.5057	85.598
1.4858	78.122	1.4908	80.040	1.4958	81.932	1.5008	83.796	1.5058	85.635
1.4859	78.160	1.4909	80.078	1.4959	81.969	1.5009	83.833	1.5059	85.672
1.4860	78.199	1.4910	80.116	1.4960	82.007	1.5010	83.870	1.5060	85.708
1.4861	78.238	1.4911	80.154	1.4961	82.044	1.5011	83.907	1.5061	85.744
1.4862	78.276	1.4912	80.192	1.4962	82.082	1.5012	83.944	1.5062	85.781
1.4863	78.315	1.4913	80.231	1.4963	82.119	1.5013	83.981	1.5063	85.817
1.4864	78.353	1.4914	80.269	1.4964	82.157	1.5014	84.018	1.5064	85.854
1.4865	78.392	1.4915	80.307	1.4965	82.194	1.5015	84.055	1.5065	85.890
1.4866	78.431	1.4916	80.345	1.4966	82.232	1.5016	84.092	1.5066	85.927
1.4867	78.469	1.4917	80.383	1.4967	82.269	1.5017	84.129	1.5067	85.963
1.4868	78.508	1.4918	80.421	1.4968	82.307	1.5018	84.166	1.5068	86.000
1.4869	78.546	1.4919	80.459	1.4969	82.344	1.5019	84.203	1.5069	86.036
1.4870	78.585	1.4920	80.497	1.4970	82.381	1.5020	84.240	1.5070	86.072
1.4871	78.623	1.4921	80.534	1.4971	82.419	1.5021	84.277	1.5071	86.109
1.4872	78.662	1.4922	80.572	1.4972	82.456	1.5022	84.314	1.5072	86.145
1.4873	78.700	1.4923	80.610	1.4973	82.494	1.5023	84.351	1.5073	86.182
1.4874	78.739	1.4924	80.648	1.4974	82.531	1.5024	84.388	1.5074	86.218
1.4875	78.777	1.4925	80.686	1.4975	82.569	1.5025	84.424	1.5075	86.254
1.4876	78.816	1.4926	80.724	1.4976	82.606	1.5026	84.461	1.5076	86.291
1.4877	78.854	1.4927	80.762	1.4977	82.643	1.5027	84.498	1.5077	86.327
1.4878	78.892	1.4928	80.800	1.4978	82.681	1.5028	84.535	1.5078	86.363
1.4879	78.931	1.4929	80.838	1.4979	82.718	1.5029	84.572	1.5079	86.399

52.013 Table for determining per cent sucrose in sugar solutions from readings of Zeiss immersion refractometer at 20°C[a]

Reading[b] at 20°	n_D^{20}	Sucrose, %	Reading[b] at 20°	n_D^{20}	Sucrose, %	Reading[b] at 20°	n_D^{20}	Sucrose, %
14.47	1.33299	0	45	1.34463	7.91	76	1.35606	15.24
15	3320	0.15	46	4500	8.15	77	5642	15.47
16	3358	0.41	47	4537	8.39	78	5678	15.69
17	3397	0.68	48	4575	8.64	79	5714	15.91
18	3435	0.94	49	4612	8.89			
19	3474	1.21				80	5750	16.14
			50	4650	9.13	81	5786	16.36
20	3513	1.48	51	4687	9.38	82	5822	16.58
21	3551	1.74	52	4724	9.62	83	5858	16.81
22	3590	2.01	53	4761	9.86	84	5894	17.03
23	3628	2.27	54	4798	10.10	85	5930	17.25
24	3667	2.54	55	4836	10.34	86	5966	17.47
25	3705	2.80	56	4873	10.58	87	6002	17.69
26	3743	3.07	57	4910	10.82	88	6038	17.91
27	3781	3.33	58	4947	11.06	89	6074	18.12
28	3820	3.59	59	4984	11.30			
29	3858	3.85				90	6109	18.34
			60	5021	11.54	91	6145	18.56
30	3896	4.11	61	5058	11.78	92	6181	18.78
31	3934	4.36	62	5095	12.01	93	6217	19.00
32	3972	4.62	63	5132	12.25	94	6252	19.21
33	4010	4.88	64	5169	12.48	95	6287	19.42
34	4048	5.14	65	5205	12.72	96	6323	19.63
35	4086	5.40	66	5242	12.95	97	6359	19.85
36	4124	5.65	67	5279	13.18	98	6394	20.06
37	4162	5.91	68	5316	13.41	99	6429	20.27
38	4199	6.16	69	5352	13.64			
39	4237	6.41				100	6464	20.48
			70	5388	13.87	101	6500	20.69
40	4275	6.66	71	5425	14.10	102	6535	20.90
41	4313	6.91	72	5461	14.33	103	6570	21.11
42	4350	7.16	73	5497	14.56	104	6605	21.32
43	4388	7.41	74	5533	14.79	105	6640	21.53
44	4426	7.66	75	5569	15.01			

[a] Values in this table were calcd by J. A. Mathews from five-place indices of Schönrock as given by Landt, *Z. Ver. Deut. Zucker-Ind.* **83**, 692(1933).

[b] Scale readings refer only to scale of arbitrary units proposed by Pulfrich, *Z. Angew. Chem.* 1168(1899). According to this scale 14.5 = 1.33300, 50.0 = 1.34650, and 100.0 = 1.36464. If immersion refractometer used is calibrated according to another arbitrary scale, readings must be converted into refractive indices before this table is used to determine per cent sugar.

52.014 Refractive indices of glucose, fructose, and raffinose hydrate solutions at 20°C

% by Wt in Air	Refractive Index			% by Wt in Air	Refractive Index	
	Glucose[a]	Fructose	Raffinose Hydrate[b]		Glucose[a]	Fructose
0	1.33299	1.33299	1.33299	50	1.41826	1.41819
1	3442	3441	3422	51	2029	2022
2	3586	3583	3546	52	2233	2228
3	3731	3727	3671	53	2439	2434
4	3877	3872	3797	54	2646	2642
5	4024	4017	3924	55	2855	2851
6	4173	4164	4052	56	3065	3062
7	4322	4312	4181	57	3276	3273
8	4472	4461	4311	58	3488	3487
9	4623	4611	4443	59	3702	3701
10	4775	4762	4576	60	3918	3917
11	4928	4914	4709	61	4135	4135
12	5082	5067	4844	62	4354	4353
13	5237	5221	4979	63	4574	4573
14	5393	5377	5116	64	4796	4794
15	5551	5534	5253	65	5019	5017
16	5710	5692	5391	66	5244	5241
17	5870	5851	5530	67	5470	5466
18	6031	6011	5670	68	5697	5693
19	6193	6172	5811	69	5926	5921
20	6356	6335	5953	70	6156	6150
21	6520	6499	6096	71	6388	6380
22	6685	6664	6239	72	6621	6612
23	6852	6830	6384	73	6856	6845
24	7020	6998	6529	74	7092	7079
25	7189	7167	6676	75	7330	7315
26	7359	7337	6824	76	7569	7551
27	7530	7508	6972	77	7810	7789
28	7702	7681	7121	78	8052	8028
29	7876	7855	7272	79	8296	8269
30	8051	8030	7424	80	8542	8510
31	8228	8207	7577	81		8753
32	8406	8385	7730	82		8997
33	8585	8564	7884	83		9242
34	8765	8745	8040	84		9488
35	8946	8927	8197	85		9735
36	9129	9110	8356	86		9984
37	9313	9295	8516	87		.50233
38	9498	9481	8677	88		0484
39	9684	9668	8840[b]	89		0736
40	9872	9857	9004	90		0988
41	.40061	.40047				
42	0251	0238				
43	0443	0431				
44	0636	0625				
45	0831	0821				
46	1028	1018				
47	1226	1216				
48	1425	1415				
49	1625	1616				

[a] Zerban and Martin, *JAOAC* **27**, 295(1944). Glucose values graphically smoothed, Young and Jones, *JAOAC* **37**, 932 (1954).
[b] Zerban and Martin, *JAOAC* **34**, 808(1951).

52.015 Refractive indices of invert sugar solutions[a]

% Invert Sugar by Wt in Air (*p*)	n_D at 15°C	n_D at 20°C	n_D at 25°C	n_D at 30°C
0	1.33339	1.33299	1.33250	1.33194
1	1.33482	1.33441	1.33392	1.33335
2	1.33627	1.33584	1.33535	1.33476
3	1.33772	1.33728	1.33678	1.33619
4	1.33919	1.33873	1.33823	1.33763
5	1.34066	1.34020	1.33969	1.33908
6	1.34215	1.34167	1.34116	1.34054
7	1.34364	1.34315	1.34264	1.34201
8	1.34516	1.34465	1.34413	1.34349
9	1.34668	1.34616	1.34563	1.34498
10	1.34821	1.34768	1.34714	1.34648
11	1.34975	1.34920	1.34866	1.34800
12	1.35130	1.35075	1.35020	1.34952
13	1.35286	1.35230	1.35174	1.35106
14	1.35444	1.35386	1.35330	1.35260
15	1.35603	1.35544	1.35487	1.35416
16	1.35762	1.35702	1.35644	1.35573
17	1.35923	1.35862	1.35803	1.35731
18	1.36085	1.36023	1.35964	1.35891
19	1.36248	1.36185	1.36125	1.36051
20	1.36413	1.36348	1.36287	1.36213
21	1.36578	1.36513	1.36451	1.36375
22	1.36745	1.36679	1.36616	1.36539
23	1.36913	1.36846	1.36782	1.36705
24	1.37082	1.37014	1.36949	1.36871
25	1.37252	1.37183	1.37118	1.37038
26	1.37424	1.37354	1.37287	1.37207
27	1.37596	1.37525	1.37458	1.37377
28	1.37770	1.37698	1.37630	1.37548
29	1.37945	1.37873	1.37803	1.37721
30	1.38122	1.38048	1.37978	1.37895
31	1.38299	1.38225	1.38154	1.38070
32	1.38478	1.38403	1.38331	1.38246
33	1.38658	1.38582	1.38509	1.38423
34	1.38840	1.38763	1.38689	1.38602
35	1.39022	1.38944	1.38869	1.38782
36	1.39206	1.39128	1.39052	1.38964
37	1.39391	1.39312	1.39235	1.39146
38	1.39578	1.39498	1.39420	1.39330
39	1.39766	1.39685	1.39606	1.39515
40	1.39955	1.39873	1.39793	1.39702
41	1.40145	1.40063	1.39982	1.39890
42	1.40337	1.40254	1.40172	1.40079
43	1.40530	1.40446	1.40363	1.40270
44	1.40724	1.40640	1.40556	1.40462
45	1.40920	1.40835	1.40750	1.40655
46	1.41117	1.41031	1.40945	1.40849
47	1.41315	1.41229	1.41142	1.41045
48	1.41515	1.41428	1.41340	1.41243
49	1.41716	1.41628	1.41539	1.41442
50	1.41919	1.41830	1.41740	1.41642
51	1.42122	1.42033	1.41942	1.41843
52	1.42328	1.42238	1.42146	1.42046
53	1.42534	1.42444	1.42351	1.42251
54	1.42742	1.42651	1.42558	1.42457
55	1.42952	1.42860	1.42766	1.42664
56	1.43163	1.43070	1.42975	1.42873
57	1.43375	1.43282	1.43186	1.43083
58	1.43589	1.43495	1.43398	1.43294
59	1.43804	1.43710	1.43612	1.43507
60	1.44020	1.43926	1.43827	1.43722
61	1.44238	1.44143	1.44043	1.43938
62	1.44458	1.44362	1.44262	1.44155
63	1.44679	1.44582	1.44481	1.44374
64	1.44901	1.44804	1.44702	1.44595
65	1.45125	1.45027	1.44925	1.44817
66	1.45350	1.45252	1.45149	1.45040
67	1.45577	1.45479	1.45375	1.45265
68	1.45805	1.45706	1.45602	1.45492
69	1.46035	1.45936	1.45830	1.45720
70	1.46266	1.46166	1.46060	1.45950
71	1.46499	1.46399	1.46292	1.46181
72	1.46734	1.46633	1.46525	1.46414
73	1.46970	1.46868	1.46760	1.46648
74	1.47207	1.47105	1.46997	1.46884
75	1.47446	1.47343	1.47235	1.47121
76	1.47687	1.47583	1.47474	1.47360
77	1.47929	1.47825	1.47715	1.47601
78	1.48172	1.48068	1.47958	1.47843
79	1.48418	1.48313	1.48203	1.48087
80	1.48664	1.48559	1.48449	1.48333
81	1.48913	1.48807	1.48696	1.48580
82	1.49163	1.49057	1.48945	1.48828
83	1.49414	1.49308	1.49196	1.49079
84	1.49668	1.49560	1.49449	1.49331
85	1.49922	1.49815	1.49703	1.49584

[a] Snyder and Hattenburg, NBS Monograph 64, June 7, 1963, p. 4. A condensed form of this table was published in the Proceedings of the Twelfth Session of the International Commission for Uniform Methods of Sugar Analysis, 1958, p. 26.

$n_D^{15} = 1.3333872 + 1.4292 \times 10^{-3}p + 0.515855 \times 10^{-5}p^2 + 0.1153 \times 10^{-7}p^3$

$n_D^{20} = 1.3329877 + 1.4149 \times 10^{-3}p + 0.52729 \times 10^{-5}p^2 + 0.1105 \times 10^{-7}p^3$

$n_D^{25} = 1.3325026 + 1.4114 \times 10^{-3}p + 0.51088 \times 10^{-5}p^2 + 0.1244 \times 10^{-7}p^3$

$n_D^{30} = 1.3319403 + 1.4016 \times 10^{-3}p + 0.5134 \times 10^{-5}p^2 + 0.1249 \times 10^{-7}p^3$

52.016 Temperature corrections for readings of per cent sucrose in sugar solutions by either Abbé or immersion refractometer at temperatures other than 20°C[a]

(International Temperature Correction Table, 1936)[a]

Temp., °C	Per Cent Sucrose 0	5	10	15	20	25	30	40	50	60	70
	Subtract from Per Cent Sucrose										
10	0.50	0.54	0.58	0.61	0.64	0.66	0.68	0.72	0.74	0.76	0.79
11	.46	.49	.53	.55	.58	.60	.62	.65	.67	.69	.71
12	.42	.45	.48	.50	.52	.54	.56	.58	.60	.61	.63
13	.37	.40	.42	.44	.46	.48	.49	.51	.53	.54	.55
14	.33	.35	.37	.39	.40	.41	.42	.44	.45	.46	.48
15	.27	.29	.31	.33	.34	.34	.35	.37	.38	.39	.40
16	.22	.24	.25	.26	.27	.28	.28	.30	.30	.31	.32
17	.17	.18	.19	.20	.21	.21	.21	.22	.23	.23	.24
18	.12	.13	.13	.14	.14	.14	.14	.15	.15	.16	.16
19	.06	.06	.06	.07	.07	.07	.07	.08	.08	.08	.08
	Add to Per Cent Sucrose										
21	0.06	0.07	0.07	0.07	0.07	0.08	0.08	0.08	0.08	0.08	0.08
22	.13	.13	.14	.14	.15	.15	.15	.15	.16	.16	.16
23	.19	.20	.21	.22	.22	.23	.23	.23	.24	.24	.24
24	.26	.27	.28	.29	.30	.30	.31	.31	.31	.32	.32
25	.33	.35	.36	.37	.38	.38	.39	.40	.40	.40	.40
26	.40	.42	.43	.44	.45	.46	.47	.48	.48	.48	.48
27	.48	.50	.52	.53	.54	.55	.55	.56	.56	.56	.56
28	.56	.57	.60	.61	.62	.63	.63	.64	.64	.64	.64
29	.64	.66	.68	.69	.71	.72	.72	.73	.73	.73	.73
30	.72	.74	.77	.78	.79	.80	.80	.81	.81	.81	.81

[a] *Intern. Sugar J.* **39**, 24s (1937).

52.017 Total reducing sugar required for complete reduction of 10 ml Soxhlet solution to be used in conjunction with Lane-Eynon general volumetric method

Titer	Invert Sugar, No Sucrose	g Sucrose/100 ml Invert Sugar				Glucose	Fructose	Maltose		Lactose	
		1	5	10	25			Anhyd.	$C_{12}H_{22}O_{11}.H_2O$	Anhyd.	$C_{12}H_{22}O_{11}.H_2O$
	Required for Reduction of 10 ml Soxhlet Soln										
15	50.5	49.9	47.6	46.1	43.4	49.1	52.2	77.2	81.3	64.9	68.3
16	.6	50.0	.6	.1	.4	.2	.3	.1	.2	.8	.2
17	.7	.1	.6	.1	.4	.3	.3	.0	.1	.8	.2
18	.8	.1	.6	.1	.3	.3	.4	.0	.0	.7	.1
19	.8	.2	.6	.1	.3	.4	.5	76.9	80.9	.7	.1
20	.9	.2	.6	.1	.2	.5	.5	.8	.8	.6	.0
21	51.0	.2	.6	.1	.2	.5	.6	.7	.7	.6	.0
22	.0	.3	.6	.1	.1	.6	.7	.6	.6	.6	.0
23	.1	.3	.6	.1	.0	.7	.7	.5	.5	.5	67.9
24	.2	.3	.6	.1	.9	.8	.8	.4	.4	.5	.9
25	.2	.4	.6	.0	.8	.8	.8	.4	.4	.5	.9
26	.3	.4	.6	.0	.8	.9	.9	.3	.3	.5	.9
27	.4	.4	.6	.0	.7	.9	.9	.2	.2	.4	.8
28	.4	.5	47.7	.0	.7	50.0	53.0	.1	.1	.4	.8
29	.5	.5	.7	.0	.6	.0	.1	.0	.0	.4	.8
30	.5	.5	.7	.0	.5	.1	.2	.0	.0	.4	.8
31	.6	.6	.7	45.9	.5	.2	.2	75.9	79.9	.4	.8
32	.6	.6	.7	.9	.4	.2	.3	.9	.9	.4	.8
33	.7	.6	.7	.9	.3	.3	.3	.8	.8	.4	.8
34	.7	.6	.7	.8	.2	.3	.4	.8	.8	.4	.9
35	.8	.7	.7	.8	.2	.4	.4	.7	.7	.5	.9
36	.8	.7	.7	.8	.1	.4	.5	.6	.6	.5	.9
37	.9	.7	.7	.7	.0	.5	.5	.6	.6	.5	.9
38	.9	.7	.7	.7	.0	.5	.6	.5	.5	.5	.9
39	52.0	.8	.7	.7	41.9	.6	.6	.5	.5	.5	.9
40	.0	.8	.7	.6	.8	.6	.6	.4	.4	.5	.9
41	.1	.8	.7	.6	.8	.7	.7	.4	.4	.6	68.0
42	.1	.8	.7	.6	.7	.7	.7	.3	.3	.6	.0
43	.2	.8	.7	.5	.6	.8	.8	.3	.3	.6	.0
44	.2	.9	.7	.5	.5	.8	.8	.2	.2	.6	.0
45	.3	.9	.7	.4	.4	.9	.9	.2	.2	.7	.1
46	.3	.9	.7	.4	.4	.9	.9	.1	.1	.7	.1
47	.4	.9	.7	.3	.3	51.0	.9	.1	.1	.8	.2
48	.4	.9	.7	.3	.2	.0	54.0	.1	.1	.8	.2
49	.5	.0	.7	.2	.1	.0	.0	.0	.0	.8	.2
50	.5	.0	.7	.2	.0	.1	.0	.0	.0	.9	.3

52.018 Total reducing sugar required for complete reduction of 25 ml Soxhlet solution to be used in conjunction with Lane-Eynon general volumetric method

Titer	Invert Sugar, No Sucrose	1 g Sucrose/ 100 ml Invert Sugar	Glucose	Fructose	Maltose Anhyd.	Maltose $C_{12}H_{22}O_{11}.H_2O$	Lactose Anhyd.	Lactose $C_{12}H_{22}O_{11}.H_2O$
	Required for Reduction of 25 ml Soxhlet Soln							
15	123.6	122.6	120.2	127.4	197.8	208.2	163.9	172.5
16	.6	.7	.2	.4	.4	207.8	.5	.1
17	.6	.7	.2	.5	.0	.4	.1	171.7
18	.7	.7	.2	.5	196.7	.1	162.8	.4
19	.7	.8	.3	.6	.5	206.8	.5	.1
20	.8	.8	.3	.6	.2	.5	.3	170.9
21	.8	.8	.3	.7	195.8	.1	.0	.6
22	.9	.9	.4	.7	.5	205.8	161.8	.4
23	.9	.9	.4	.8	.1	.4	.6	.2
24	124.0	.9	.5	.8	194.8	.1	.5	.0
25	.0	123.0	.5	.9	.5	204.8	.4	169.9
26	.1	.0	.6	.9	.2	.4	.2	.7
27	.1	.0	.6	128.0	193.9	.1	.0	.5
28	.2	.1	.7	.0	.6	203.8	160.8	.3
29	.2	.1	.7	.1	.3	.5	.7	.2
30	.3	.1	.8	.1	.0	.2	.6	.0
31	.3	.2	.8	.1	192.8	202.9	.5	168.9
32	.4	.2	.8	.2	.5	.6	.4	.8
33	.4	.2	.9	.2	.2	.3	.2	.6
34	.5	.3	.9	.3	191.9	.0	.1	.5
35	.5	.3	121.0	.3	.7	201.8	.0	.4
36	.6	.3	.0	.4	.4	.5	159.8	.2
37	.6	.4	.1	.4	.2	.2	.7	.1
38	.7	.4	.2	.5	.0	.0	.6	.0
39	.7	.4	.2	.5	190.8	200.8	.5	167.9
40	.8	.4	.2	.6	.5	.5	.4	.8
41	.8	.5	.3	.6	.3	.3	.3	.7
42	.9	.5	.4	.6	.1	.1	.2	.6
43	.9	.5	.4	.7	189.8	199.8	.2	.6
44	125.0	.6	.5	.7	.6	.6	.1	.5
45	.0	.6	.5	.8	.4	.4	.0	.4
46	.1	.6	.6	.8	.2	.2	.0	.4
47	.1	.7	.6	.9	.0	.0	158.9	.3
48	.2	.7	.7	.9	188.9	198.9	.8	.2
49	.2	.7	.7	129.0	.8	.7	.8	.2
50	.3	.8	.8	.0	.7	.6	.7	.1

52.019 Hammond table for calculating glucose, fructose, and invert sugar and lactose alone and in the presence of sucrose[a], with values for maltose from the Munson and Walker table[b]; values expressed as mg

					Invert Sugar and Sucrose				Lactose. H_2O and Sucrose			
Cu[c]	Cu_2O[c]	Glucose	Fructose	Invert Sugar	0.3 g Total Sugar	0.4 g Total Sugar	2.0 g Total Sugar	Lactose . H_2O	1 Lactose 4 Sucrose	1 Lactose 12 Sucrose	Cu_2O[d]	Maltose . H_2O
10	11.3	4.6	5.1	5.2	3.2	2.9		7.7	7.7	6.6	10	6.2
11	12.4	5.1	5.6	5.7	3.7	3.4		8.5	8.5	7.3		
12	13.5	5.6	6.1	6.2	4.2	3.9		9.3	9.2	8.0	12	7.9
13	14.6	6.0	6.7	6.7	4.8	4.4		10.0	10.0	8.7		
14	15.8	6.5	7.2	7.2	5.3	4.9		10.8	10.7	9.4	14	9.5
15	16.9	7.0	7.7	7.7	5.8	5.4		11.5	11.5	10.1		
16	18.0	7.5	8.3	8.2	6.3	5.9		12.3	12.2	10.8	16	11.2
17	19.1	8.0	8.8	8.7	6.8	6.4		13.1	12.9	11.5		
18	20.3	8.5	9.3	9.2	7.3	6.9		13.8	13.7	12.2	18	12.9
19	21.4	8.9	9.9	9.7	7.8	7.4		14.6	14.4	12.9		
20	22.5	9.4	10.4	10.2	8.3	7.9	1.9	15.4	15.2	13.6	20	14.6
21	23.6	9.9	10.9	10.7	8.8	8.4	2.4	16.1	15.9	14.4		
22	24.8	10.4	11.5	11.2	9.3	8.9	2.9	16.9	16.7	15.1	22	16.2
23	25.9	10.9	12.0	11.7	9.9	9.5	3.4	17.7	17.4	15.8		
24	27.0	11.4	12.5	12.3	10.4	10.0	3.9	18.4	18.2	16.5	24	17.9
25	28.1	11.9	13.1	12.8	10.9	10.5	4.4	19.2	18.9	17.2		
26	29.3	12.3	13.6	13.3	11.4	11.0	4.9	19.9	19.7	17.9	26	19.6
27	30.4	12.8	14.2	13.8	11.9	11.5	5.5	20.7	20.4	18.6		
28	31.5	13.3	14.7	14.3	12.4	12.0	6.0	21.5	21.1	19.3	28	21.2
29	32.6	13.8	15.2	14.8	12.9	12.5	6.5	22.2	21.9	20.0		
30	33.8	14.3	15.8	15.3	13.4	13.0	7.0	23.0	22.6	20.7	30	22.9
31	34.9	14.8	16.3	15.8	14.0	13.5	7.5	23.8	23.4	21.4		
32	36.0	15.3	16.8	16.3	14.5	14.1	8.0	24.5	24.1	22.2	32	24.6
33	37.2	15.7	17.4	16.8	15.0	14.6	8.5	25.3	24.9	22.9		
34	38.3	16.2	17.9	17.3	15.5	15.1	9.0	26.1	25.6	23.6	34	26.2
35	39.4	16.7	18.4	17.8	16.0	15.6	9.5	26.8	26.4	24.3		
36	40.5	17.2	19.0	18.3	16.5	16.1	10.1	27.6	27.1	25.0	36	27.9
37	41.7	17.7	19.5	18.9	17.0	16.6	10.6	28.4	27.9	25.7		
38	42.8	18.2	20.1	19.4	17.6	17.1	11.1	29.1	28.6	26.4	38	29.6
39	43.9	18.7	20.6	19.9	18.1	17.6	11.6	29.9	29.4	27.1		
40	45.0	19.2	21.1	20.4	18.6	18.2	12.1	30.6	30.1	27.8	40	31.3
41	46.2	19.7	21.7	20.9	19.1	18.7	12.6	31.4	30.8	28.6		
42	47.3	20.1	22.2	21.4	19.6	19.2	13.1	32.2	31.6	29.3	42	32.9
43	48.4	20.6	22.8	21.9	20.1	19.7	13.7	32.9	32.3	30.0		
44	49.5	21.1	23.3	22.4	20.7	20.2	14.2	33.7	33.1	30.7	44	34.6
45	50.7	21.6	23.8	22.9	21.2	20.7	14.7	34.5	33.8	31.4		
46	51.8	22.1	24.4	23.5	21.7	21.3	15.2	35.2	34.6	32.1	46	36.3
47	52.9	22.6	24.9	24.0	22.2	21.8	15.7	36.0	35.3	32.8		
48	54.0	23.1	25.4	24.5	22.7	22.3	16.2	36.8	36.1	33.5	48	37.9
49	55.2	23.6	26.0	25.0	23.2	22.8	16.8	37.5	36.8	34.3		
50	56.3	24.1	26.5	25.5	23.8	23.3	17.3	38.3	37.6	35.0	50	39.6
51	57.4	24.6	27.1	26.0	24.3	23.8	17.8	39.1	38.3	35.7		
52	58.5	25.1	27.6	26.5	24.8	24.3	18.3	39.8	39.1	36.4	52	41.3
53	59.7	25.6	28.2	27.0	25.3	24.9	18.8	40.6	39.8	37.1		
54	60.8	26.1	28.7	27.6	25.8	25.4	19.3	41.4	40.6	37.8	54	42.9
55	61.9	26.5	29.2	28.1	26.3	25.9	19.9	42.1	41.3	38.5		
56	63.0	27.0	29.8	28.6	26.9	26.4	20.4	42.9	42.1	39.3	56	44.6
57	64.2	27.5	30.3	29.1	27.4	26.9	20.9	43.7	42.8	40.0		
58	65.3	28.0	30.9	29.6	27.9	27.5	21.4	44.4	43.6	40.7	58	46.3
59	66.4	28.5	31.4	30.1	28.4	28.0	21.9	45.2	44.3	41.4		

[a] *J. Res. Natl. Bur. Std.* **24**, 589–596(1940); **41**, 217–220(1948).

[b] **43.012**, *Official Methods of Analysis*, 10th Ed. (Cu_2O = Cu × 1.1259).

[c] Applicable to all sugars except maltose.

[d] Applicable only to maltose.

(Continued)

52.019 Hammond table for calculating glucose, fructose, and invert sugar and lactose alone and in the presence of sucrose[a], with values for maltose from the Munson and Walker table[b]; values expressed as mg —*Continued*.

					Invert Sugar and Sucrose				Lactose. H_2O and Sucrose			
Cu[c]	Cu_2O[c]	Glucose	Fructose	Invert Sugar	0.3 g Total Sugar	0.4 g Total Sugar	2.0 g Total Sugar	Lactose . H_2O	1 Lactose 4 Sucrose	1 Lactose 12 Sucrose	Cu_2O[d]	Maltose . H_2O
60	67.6	29.0	31.9	30.6	28.9	28.5	22.5	46.0	45.1	42.1	60	48.0
61	68.7	29.5	32.5	31.2	29.5	29.0	23.0	46.7	45.8	42.8		
62	69.8	30.0	33.0	31.7	30.0	29.5	23.5	47.5	46.5	43.6	62	49.6
63	70.9	30.5	33.6	32.2	30.5	30.1	24.0	48.3	47.3	44.3		
64	72.1	31.0	34.1	32.7	31.0	30.6	24.5	49.0	48.0	45.0	64	51.3
65	73.2	31.5	34.7	33.2	31.6	31.1	25.1	49.8	48.8	45.7		
66	74.3	32.0	35.2	33.7	32.1	31.6	25.6	50.6	49.5	46.4	66	53.0
67	75.4	32.5	35.8	34.3	32.6	32.1	26.1	51.3	50.3	47.1		
68	76.6	33.0	36.3	34.8	33.1	32.7	26.6	52.1	51.0	47.9	68	54.6
69	77.7	33.5	36.8	35.3	33.6	33.2	27.1	52.9	51.8	48.6		
70	78.8	34.0	37.4	35.8	34.2	33.7	27.7	53.6	52.5	49.3	70	56.3
71	79.9	34.5	37.9	36.3	34.7	34.2	28.2	54.4	53.3	50.0		
72	81.1	35.0	38.5	36.8	35.2	34.7	28.7	55.2	54.0	50.7	72	58.0
73	82.2	35.5	39.0	37.4	35.7	35.3	29.2	55.9	54.8	51.4		
74	83.3	36.0	39.6	37.9	36.3	35.8	29.8	56.7	55.5	52.2	74	59.6
75	84.4	36.5	40.1	38.4	36.8	36.3	30.3	57.5	56.3	52.9		
76	85.6	37.0	40.7	38.9	37.3	36.8	30.8	58.2	57.0	53.6	76	61.3
77	86.7	37.5	41.2	39.4	37.8	37.4	31.3	59.0	57.8	54.3		
78	87.8	38.0	41.7	40.0	38.4	37.9	31.9	59.8	58.5	55.0	78	63.0
79	88.9	38.5	42.3	40.5	38.9	38.4	32.4	60.5	59.3	55.7		
80	90.1	39.0	42.8	41.0	39.4	38.9	32.9	61.3	60.0	56.5	80	64.6
81	91.2	39.5	43.4	41.5	39.9	39.5	33.4	62.1	60.8	57.2		
82	92.3	40.0	43.9	42.0	40.5	40.0	34.0	62.8	61.6	57.9	82	66.3
83	93.4	40.5	44.5	42.6	41.0	40.5	34.5	63.6	62.3	58.6		
84	94.6	41.0	45.0	43.1	41.5	41.0	35.0	64.4	63.1	59.3	84	68.0
85	95.7	41.5	45.6	43.6	42.0	41.6	35.5	65.1	63.8	60.1		
86	96.8	42.0	46.1	44.1	42.6	42.1	36.1	65.9	64.6	60.8	86	69.7
87	97.9	42.5	46.7	44.7	43.1	42.6	36.6	66.7	65.3	61.5		
88	99.1	43.0	47.2	45.2	43.6	43.1	37.1	67.4	66.1	62.2	88	71.3
89	100.2	43.5	47.8	45.7	44.1	43.7	37.6	68.2	66.8	62.9		
90	101.3	44.0	48.3	46.2	44.7	44.2	38.2	69.0	67.6	63.7	90	73.0
91	102.5	44.5	48.9	46.7	45.2	44.7	38.7	69.7	68.3	64.4		
92	103.6	45.0	49.4	47.3	45.7	45.2	39.2	70.5	69.1	65.1	92	74.7
93	104.7	45.5	50.0	47.8	46.3	45.8	39.8	71.3	69.8	65.8		
94	105.8	46.0	50.5	48.3	46.8	46.3	40.3	72.1	70.6	66.5	94	76.3
95	107.0	46.5	51.1	48.8	47.3	46.8	40.8	72.8	71.3	67.3		
96	108.1	47.0	51.6	49.4	47.8	47.4	41.3	73.6	72.1	68.0	96	78.0
97	109.2	47.5	52.2	49.9	48.4	47.9	41.9	74.4	72.8	68.7		
98	110.3	48.0	52.7	50.4	48.9	48.4	42.4	75.1	73.6	69.4	98	79.7
99	111.5	48.5	53.3	50.9	49.4	48.9	42.9	75.9	74.3	70.2		
100	112.6	49.0	53.8	51.5	50.0	49.5	43.5	76.7	75.1	70.9	100	81.3
101	113.7	49.5	54.4	52.0	50.5	50.0	44.0	77.4	75.8	71.6		
102	114.8	50.0	54.9	52.5	51.0	50.5	44.5	78.2	76.6	72.3	102	83.0
103	116.0	50.6	55.5	53.0	51.6	51.1	45.1	79.0	77.3	73.1		
104	117.1	51.1	56.0	53.6	52.1	51.6	45.6	79.7	78.1	73.8	104	84.7
105	118.2	51.6	56.6	54.1	52.6	52.1	46.1	80.5	78.8	74.5		
106	119.3	52.1	57.1	54.6	53.1	52.7	46.7	81.3	79.6	75.2	106	86.3
107	120.5	52.6	57.7	55.2	53.7	53.2	47.2	82.1	80.4	76.0		
108	121.6	53.1	58.2	55.7	54.2	53.7	47.7	82.8	81.1	76.7	108	88.0
109	122.7	53.6	58.8	56.2	54.7	54.2	48.3	83.6	81.9	77.4		

(Continued)

52.019 Hammond table for calculating glucose, fructose, and invert sugar and lactose alone and in the presence of sucrose[a], with values for maltose from the Munson and Walker table[b]; values expressed as mg —*Continued.*

					Invert Sugar and Sucrose				Lactose. H_2O and Sucrose			
Cu[c]	Cu_2O[c]	Glucose	Fructose	Invert Sugar	0.3 g Total Sugar	0.4 g Total Sugar	2.0 g Total Sugar	Lactose .H_2O	1 Lactose 4 Sucrose	1 Lactose 12 Sucrose	Cu_2O[d]	Maltose .H_2O
110	123.8	54.1	59.3	56.7	55.3	54.8	48.8	84.4	82.6	78.1	110	89.7
111	125.0	54.6	59.9	57.3	55.8	55.3	49.3	85.1	83.4	78.9		
112	126.1	55.1	60.4	57.8	56.3	55.8	49.9	85.9	84.1	79.6	112	91.3
113	127.2	55.6	61.0	58.3	56.9	56.4	50.4	86.7	84.9	80.3		
114	128.3	56.1	61.6	58.9	57.4	56.9	50.9	87.4	85.6	81.0	114	93.0
115	129.5	56.7	62.1	59.4	57.9	57.4	51.5	88.2	86.4	81.8		
116	130.6	57.2	62.7	59.9	58.5	58.0	52.0	89.0	87.1	82.5	116	94.7
117	131.7	57.7	63.2	60.4	59.0	58.5	52.5	89.8	87.9	83.2		
118	132.8	58.2	63.8	61.0	59.5	59.0	53.1	90.5	88.6	84.0	118	96.4
119	134.0	58.7	64.3	61.5	60.1	59.6	53.6	91.3	89.4	84.7		
120	135.1	59.2	64.9	62.0	60.6	60.1	54.1	92.1	90.2	85.4	120	98.0
121	136.2	59.7	65.4	62.6	61.2	60.7	54.7	92.8	90.9	86.1		
122	137.4	60.2	66.0	63.1	61.7	61.2	55.2	93.6	91.7	86.9	122	99.7
123	138.5	60.7	66.5	63.6	62.2	61.7	55.8	94.4	92.4	87.6		
124	139.6	61.3	67.1	64.2	62.8	62.3	56.3	95.2	93.2	88.3	124	101.4
125	140.7	61.8	67.7	64.7	63.3	62.8	56.8	95.9	93.9	89.0		
126	141.9	62.3	68.2	65.2	63.8	63.3	57.4	96.7	94.7	89.8	126	103.0
127	143.0	62.8	68.8	65.8	64.4	63.9	57.9	97.5	95.5	90.5		
128	144.1	63.3	69.3	66.3	64.9	64.4	58.4	98.2	96.2	91.2	128	104.7
129	145.2	63.8	69.9	66.8	65.4	64.9	59.0	99.0	97.0	92.0		
130	146.4	64.3	70.4	67.4	66.0	65.5	59.5	99.8	97.7	92.7	130	106.4
131	147.5	64.9	71.0	67.9	66.5	66.0	60.1	100.6	98.5	93.4		
132	148.6	65.4	71.6	68.4	67.1	66.6	60.6	101.3	99.2	94.1	132	108.0
133	149.7	65.9	72.1	69.0	67.6	67.1	61.1	102.1	100.0	94.9		
134	150.9	66.4	72.7	69.5	68.1	67.6	61.7	102.9	100.7	95.6	134	109.7
135	152.0	66.9	73.2	70.0	68.7	68.2	62.2	103.6	101.5	96.3		
136	153.1	67.4	73.8	70.6	69.2	68.7	62.8	104.4	102.3	97.1	136	111.4
137	154.2	68.0	74.3	71.1	69.8	69.3	63.3	105.2	103.0	97.8		
138	155.4	68.5	74.9	71.6	70.3	69.8	63.9	106.0	103.8	98.5	138	113.0
139	156.5	69.0	75.5	72.2	70.8	70.3	64.4	106.7	104.5	99.3		
140	157.6	69.5	76.0	72.7	71.4	70.9	64.9	107.5	105.3	100.0	140	114.7
141	158.7	70.0	76.6	73.2	71.9	71.4	65.5	108.3	106.0	100.7		
142	159.9	70.5	77.1	73.8	72.5	72.0	66.0	109.0	106.8	101.4	142	116.4
143	161.0	71.1	77.7	74.3	73.0	72.5	66.6	109.8	107.5	102.2		
144	162.1	71.6	78.3	74.9	73.5	73.0	67.1	110.6	108.3	102.9	144	118.0
145	163.2	72.1	78.8	75.4	74.1	73.6	67.7	111.4	109.1	103.6		
146	164.4	72.6	79.4	75.9	74.6	74.1	68.2	112.1	109.8	104.4	146	119.7
147	165.5	73.1	80.0	76.5	75.2	74.7	68.7	112.9	110.6	105.1		
148	166.6	73.7	80.5	77.0	75.7	75.2	69.3	113.7	111.3	105.8	148	121.4
149	167.8	74.2	81.1	77.6	76.3	75.7	69.8	114.4	112.1	106.6		
150	168.9	74.7	81.6	78.1	76.8	76.3	70.4	115.2	112.8	107.3	150	123.0
151	170.0	75.2	82.2	78.6	77.3	76.8	70.9	116.0	113.6	108.0		
152	171.1	75.7	82.8	79.2	77.9	77.4	71.5	116.8	114.4	108.8	152	124.7
153	172.3	76.3	83.3	79.7	78.4	77.9	72.0	117.5	115.1	109.5		
154	173.4	76.8	83.9	80.3	79.0	78.5	72.6	118.3	115.9	110.2	154	126.4
155	174.5	77.3	84.4	80.8	79.5	79.0	73.1	119.1	116.6	111.0		
156	175.6	77.8	85.0	81.3	80.1	79.6	73.7	119.9	117.4	111.7	156	128.0
157	176.8	78.3	85.6	81.9	80.6	80.1	74.2	120.6	118.2	112.4		
158	177.9	78.9	86.1	82.4	81.2	80.6	74.8	121.4	118.9	113.2	158	129.7
159	179.0	79.4	86.7	83.0	81.7	81.2	75.3	122.2	119.7	113.9		

(Continued)

52.019 Hammond table for calculating glucose, fructose, and invert sugar and lactose alone and in the presence of sucrose[a], with values for maltose from the Munson and Walker table[b]; values expressed as mg —*Continued*.

					Invert Sugar and Sucrose				Lactose.H_2O and Sucrose			
Cu[c]	Cu_2O[c]	Glucose	Fructose	Invert Sugar	0.3 g Total Sugar	0.4 g Total Sugar	2.0 g Total Sugar	Lactose .H_2O	1 Lactose 4 Sucrose	1 Lactose 12 Sucrose	Cu_2O[d]	Maltose .H_2O
160	180.1	79.9	87.3	83.5	82.2	81.7	75.9	122.9	120.4	114.6	160	131.4
161	181.3	80.4	87.8	84.0	82.8	82.3	76.4	123.7	121.2	115.4		
162	182.4	81.0	88.4	84.6	83.3	82.8	77.0	124.5	121.9	116.1	162	133.0
163	183.5	81.5	89.0	85.1	83.9	83.4	77.5	125.3	122.7	116.8		
164	184.6	82.0	89.5	85.7	84.4	83.9	78.1	126.0	123.5	117.6	164	134.7
165	185.8	82.5	90.1	86.2	85.0	84.5	78.6	126.8	124.2	118.3		
166	186.9	83.1	90.6	86.8	85.5	85.0	79.2	127.6	125.0	119.1	166	136.4
167	188.0	83.6	91.2	87.3	86.1	85.6	79.7	128.4	125.7	119.8		
168	189.1	84.1	91.8	87.8	86.6	86.1	80.3	129.1	126.5	120.5	168	138.0
169	190.3	84.6	92.3	88.4	87.2	86.7	80.8	129.9	127.3	121.3		
170	191.4	85.2	92.9	88.9	87.7	87.2	81.4	130.7	128.0	122.0	170	139.7
171	192.5	85.7	93.5	89.5	88.3	87.8	81.9	131.5	128.8	122.7		
172	193.6	86.2	94.0	90.0	88.8	88.3	82.5	132.2	129.5	123.5	172	141.4
173	194.8	86.7	94.6	90.6	89.4	88.9	83.0	133.0	130.3	124.2		
174	195.9	87.3	95.2	91.1	89.9	89.4	83.6	133.8	131.1	124.9	174	143.0
175	197.0	87.8	95.7	91.7	90.5	90.0	84.1	134.6	131.8	125.7		
176	198.1	88.3	96.3	92.2	91.0	90.5	84.7	135.3	132.6	126.4	176	144.7
177	199.3	88.9	96.9	92.8	91.6	91.1	85.2	136.1	133.4	127.2		
178	200.4	89.4	97.4	93.3	92.1	91.6	85.8	136.9	134.1	127.9	178	146.4
179	201.5	89.9	98.0	93.8	92.7	92.2	86.3	137.7	134.9	128.6		
180	202.7	90.4	98.6	94.4	93.2	92.7	86.9	138.4	135.6	129.4	180	148.0
181	203.8	91.0	99.2	94.9	93.8	93.3	87.4	139.2	136.4	130.1		
182	204.9	91.5	99.7	95.5	94.3	93.8	88.0	140.0	137.2	130.8	182	149.7
183	206.0	92.0	100.3	96.0	94.9	94.4	88.6	140.8	137.9	131.6		
184	207.2	92.6	100.9	96.6	95.4	94.9	89.1	141.5	138.7	132.3	184	151.4
185	208.3	93.1	101.4	97.1	96.0	95.5	89.7	142.3	139.4	133.1		
186	209.4	93.6	102.0	97.7	96.5	96.0	90.2	143.1	140.2	133.8	186	153.0
187	210.5	94.2	102.6	98.2	97.1	96.6	90.8	143.9	141.0	134.5		
188	211.7	94.7	103.1	98.8	97.6	97.1	91.3	144.6	141.7	135.3	188	154.7
189	212.8	95.2	103.7	99.3	98.2	97.7	91.9	145.4	142.5	136.0		
190	213.9	95.7	104.3	99.9	98.7	98.2	92.4	146.2	143.3	136.8	190	156.4
191	215.0	96.3	104.8	100.4	99.3	98.8	93.0	147.0	144.0	137.5		
192	216.2	96.8	105.4	101.0	99.9	99.4	93.6	147.7	144.8	138.2	192	158.0
193	217.3	97.3	106.0	101.5	100.4	99.9	94.1	148.5	145.5	139.0		
194	218.4	97.9	106.6	102.1	101.0	100.5	94.7	149.3	146.3	139.7	194	159.7
195	219.5	98.4	107.1	102.6	101.5	101.0	95.2	150.1	147.1	140.5		
196	220.7	98.9	107.7	103.2	102.1	101.6	95.8	150.8	147.8	141.2	196	161.4
197	221.8	99.5	108.3	103.7	102.6	102.1	96.4	151.6	148.6	142.0		
198	222.9	100.0	108.8	104.3	103.2	102.7	96.9	152.4	149.3	142.7	198	163.0
199	224.0	100.5	109.4	104.8	103.7	103.2	97.5	153.2	150.1	143.4		
200	225.2	101.1	110.0	105.4	104.3	103.8	98.0	153.9	150.9	144.2	200	164.7
201	226.3	101.6	110.6	106.0	104.9	104.4	98.6	154.7	151.6	144.9		
202	227.4	102.2	111.1	106.5	105.4	104.9	99.2	155.5	152.4	145.7	202	166.4
203	228.5	102.7	111.7	107.1	106.0	105.5	99.7	156.3	153.2	146.4		
204	229.7	103.2	112.3	107.6	106.5	106.0	100.3	157.0	153.9	147.1	204	168.0
205	230.8	103.8	112.9	108.2	107.1	106.6	100.9	157.8	154.7	147.9		
206	231.9	104.3	113.4	108.7	107.6	107.2	101.4	158.6	155.5	148.6	206	169.7
207	233.1	104.8	114.0	109.3	108.2	107.7	102.0	159.4	156.2	149.4		
208	234.2	105.4	114.6	109.8	108.8	108.3	102.5	160.2	157.0	150.1	208	171.4
209	235.3	105.9	115.2	110.4	109.3	108.8	103.1	160.9	157.7	150.9		

(Continued)

52.019 Hammond table for calculating glucose, fructose, and invert sugar and lactose alone and in the presence of sucrose[a], with values for maltose from the Munson and Walker table[b]; values expressed as mg *—Continued.*

					Invert Sugar and Sucrose				Lactose. H_2O and Sucrose			
Cu[c]	Cu_2O[c]	Glu-cose	Fruc-tose	Invert Sugar	0.3 g Total Sugar	0.4 g Total Sugar	2.0 g Total Sugar	Lactose .H_2O	1 Lactose 4 Su-crose	1 Lactose 12 Su-crose	Cu_2O[d]	Maltose .H_2O
210	236.4	106.5	115.7	110.9	109.9	109.4	103.7	161.7	158.5	151.6	210	173.0
211	237.6	107.0	116.3	111.5	110.4	110.0	104.2	162.5	159.3	152.4		
212	238.7	107.5	116.9	112.1	111.0	110.5	104.8	163.3	160.0	153.1	212	174.7
213	239.8	108.1	117.5	112.6	111.6	111.1	105.4	164.0	160.8	153.8		
214	240.9	108.6	118.0	113.2	112.1	111.6	105.9	164.8	161.6	154.6	214	176.4
215	242.1	109.2	118.6	113.7	112.7	112.2	106.5	165.6	162.3	155.3		
216	243.1	109.7	119.2	114.3	113.2	112.8	107.1	166.4	163.1	156.1	216	178.0
217	244.3	110.2	119.8	114.9	113.8	113.3	107.6	167.1	163.9	156.8		
218	245.4	110.8	120.3	115.4	114.4	113.9	108.2	167.9	164.6	157.6	218	179.7
219	246.6	111.3	120.9	116.0	114.9	114.4	108.8	168.7	165.4	158.3		
220	247.7	111.9	121.5	116.5	115.5	115.0	109.3	169.5	166.2	159.1	220	181.4
221	248.8	112.4	122.1	117.1	116.1	115.6	109.9	170.3	166.9	159.8		
222	249.9	112.9	122.6	117.6	116.6	116.1	110.5	171.0	167.7	160.6	222	183.0
223	251.1	113.5	123.2	118.2	117.2	116.7	111.0	171.8	168.5	161.3		
224	252.2	114.0	123.8	118.8	117.7	117.3	111.6	172.6	169.2	162.1	224	184.7
225	253.3	114.6	124.4	119.3	118.3	117.8	112.2	173.4	170.0	162.8		
226	254.4	115.1	125.0	119.9	118.9	118.4	112.7	174.2	170.8	163.6	226	186.4
227	255.6	115.7	125.5	120.4	119.4	119.0	113.3	174.9	171.5	164.3		
228	256.7	116.2	126.1	121.0	120.0	119.5	113.9	175.7	172.3	165.1	228	188.0
229	257.8	116.7	126.7	121.6	120.6	120.1	114.4	176.5	173.1	165.8		
230	258.9	117.3	127.3	122.1	121.1	120.7	115.0	177.3	173.8	166.5	230	189.7
231	260.1	117.8	127.9	122.7	121.7	121.2	115.6	178.1	174.6	167.3		
232	261.2	118.4	128.4	123.3	122.3	121.8	116.2	178.8	175.3	168.0	232	191.3
233	262.3	118.9	129.0	123.8	122.8	122.4	116.7	179.6	176.1	168.8		
234	263.4	119.5	129.6	124.4	123.4	122.9	117.3	180.4	176.9	169.5	234	193.0
235	264.6	120.0	130.2	124.9	124.0	123.5	117.9	181.2	177.6	170.3		
236	265.7	120.6	130.8	125.5	124.5	124.1	118.4	181.9	178.4	171.0	236	194.7
237	266.8	121.1	131.3	126.1	125.1	124.6	119.0	182.7	179.2	171.8		
238	268.0	121.7	131.9	126.6	125.7	125.2	119.6	183.5	180.0	172.5	238	196.3
239	269.1	122.2	132.5	127.2	126.2	125.8	120.2	184.3	180.7	173.3		
240	270.2	122.7	133.1	127.8	126.8	126.3	120.7	185.1	181.5	174.0	240	198.0
241	271.3	123.3	133.7	128.3	127.4	126.9	121.3	185.8	182.3	174.8		
242	272.5	123.8	134.2	128.9	127.9	127.5	121.9	186.6	183.0	175.5	242	199.7
243	273.6	124.4	134.8	129.5	128.5	128.0	122.5	187.4	183.8	176.3		
244	274.7	124.9	135.4	130.0	129.1	128.6	123.0	188.2	184.6	177.0	244	201.3
245	275.8	125.5	136.0	130.6	129.6	129.2	123.6	189.0	185.3	177.8		
246	277.0	126.0	136.6	131.2	130.2	129.8	124.2	189.7	186.1	178.5	246	203.0
247	278.1	126.6	137.2	131.7	130.8	130.3	124.8	190.5	186.9	179.3		
248	279.2	127.1	137.7	132.3	131.3	130.9	125.3	191.3	187.6	180.1	248	204.7
249	280.3	127.7	138.3	132.9	131.9	131.5	125.9	192.1	188.4	180.8		
250	281.5	128.2	138.9	133.4	132.5	132.0	126.5	192.9	189.2	181.6	250	206.3
251	282.6	128.8	139.5	134.0	133.1	132.6	127.1	193.6	189.9	182.3		
252	283.7	129.3	140.1	134.6	133.6	133.2	127.6	194.4	190.7	183.1	252	208.0
253	284.8	129.9	140.7	135.1	134.2	133.8	128.2	195.2	191.5	183.8		
254	286.0	130.4	141.3	135.7	134.8	134.3	128.8	196.0	192.2	184.6	254	209.7
255	287.1	131.0	141.8	136.3	135.3	134.9	129.4	196.8	193.0	185.3		
256	288.2	131.6	142.4	136.8	135.9	135.5	130.0	197.5	193.8	186.1	256	211.3
257	289.3	132.1	143.0	137.4	136.5	136.0	130.5	198.3	194.6	186.8		
258	290.5	132.7	143.6	138.0	137.1	136.6	131.1	199.1	195.3	187.6	258	213.0
259	291.6	133.2	144.2	138.6	137.6	137.2	131.7	199.9	196.1	188.3		

(Continued)

52.019 Hammond table for calculating glucose, fructose, and invert sugar and lactose alone and in the presence of sucrose[a], with values for maltose from the Munson and Walker table[b]; values expressed as mg —*Continued*.

					Invert Sugar and Sucrose				Lactose. H_2O and Sucrose			
Cu[c]	Cu_2O[c]	Glucose	Fructose	Invert Sugar	0.3 g Total Sugar	0.4 g Total Sugar	2.0 g Total Sugar	Lactose . H_2O	1 Lactose 4 Sucrose	1 Lactose 12 Sucrose	Cu_2O[d]	Maltose . H_2O
260	292.7	133.8	144.8	139.1	138.2	137.8	132.3	200.7	196.9	189.1	260	214.7
261	293.8	134.3	145.4	139.7	138.8	138.3	132.9	201.4	197.6	189.8		
262	295.0	134.9	145.9	140.3	139.4	138.9	133.4	202.2	198.4	190.6	262	216.3
263	296.1	135.4	146.5	140.8	139.9	139.5	134.0	203.0	199.2	191.4		
264	297.2	136.0	147.1	141.4	140.5	140.1	134.6	203.8	199.9	192.1	264	218.0
265	298.3	136.5	147.7	142.0	141.1	140.7	135.2	204.6	200.7	192.9		
266	299.5	137.1	148.3	142.6	141.7	141.2	135.8	205.3	201.5	193.6	266	219.7
267	300.6	137.7	148.9	143.1	142.2	141.8	136.3	206.1	202.2	194.4		
268	301.7	138.2	149.5	143.7	142.8	142.4	136.9	206.9	203.0	195.1	268	221.3
269	302.9	138.8	150.1	144.3	143.4	143.0	137.5	207.7	203.8	195.9		
270	304.0	139.3	150.6	144.8	144.0	143.5	138.1	208.5	204.6	196.7	270	223.0
271	305.1	139.9	151.2	145.4	144.5	144.1	138.7	209.2	205.3	197.4		
272	306.2	140.4	151.8	146.0	145.1	144.7	139.3	210.0	206.1	198.2	272	224.6
273	307.4	141.0	152.4	146.6	145.7	145.3	139.8	210.8	206.9	198.9		
274	308.5	141.6	153.0	147.1	146.3	145.9	140.4	211.6	207.6	199.7	274	226.3
275	309.6	142.1	153.6	147.7	146.8	146.4	141.0	212.4	208.4	200.4		
276	310.7	142.7	154.2	148.3	147.4	147.0	141.6	213.2	209.2	201.2	276	228.0
277	311.9	143.2	154.8	148.9	148.0	147.6	142.2	214.0	210.0	202.0		
278	313.0	143.8	155.4	149.4	148.6	148.2	142.8	214.7	210.7	202.7	278	229.6
279	314.1	144.4	156.0	150.0	149.2	148.8	143.4	215.5	211.5	203.5		
280	315.2	144.9	156.5	150.6	149.7	149.3	143.9	216.3	212.3	204.2	280	231.3
281	316.4	145.5	157.1	151.2	150.3	149.9	144.5	217.1	213.0	205.0		
282	317.5	146.0	157.7	151.8	150.9	150.5	145.1	217.9	213.8	205.7	282	233.0
283	318.6	146.6	158.3	152.3	151.5	151.1	145.7	218.7	214.6	206.5		
284	319.7	147.2	158.9	152.9	152.1	151.7	146.3	219.4	215.4	207.3	284	234.6
285	320.9	147.7	159.5	153.5	152.6	152.2	146.9	220.2	216.1	208.0		
286	322.0	148.3	160.1	154.1	153.2	152.8	147.5	221.0	216.9	208.8	286	236.3
287	323.1	148.8	160.7	154.6	153.8	153.4	148.1	221.8	217.7	209.5		
288	324.2	149.4	161.3	155.2	154.4	154.0	148.6	222.6	218.4	210.3	288	238.0
289	325.4	150.0	161.9	155.8	155.0	154.6	149.2	223.3	219.2	211.1		
290	326.5	150.5	162.5	156.4	155.5	155.2	149.8	224.1	220.0	211.8	290	239.6
291	327.6	151.1	163.1	157.0	156.1	155.7	150.4	224.9	220.8	212.6		
292	328.7	151.7	163.7	157.5	156.7	156.3	151.0	225.7	221.5	213.4	292	241.3
293	329.9	152.2	164.3	158.1	157.3	156.9	151.6	226.5	222.3	214.1		
294	331.0	152.8	164.9	158.7	157.9	157.5	152.2	227.3	223.1	214.9	294	242.9
295	332.1	153.4	165.4	159.3	158.5	158.1	152.8	228.0	223.9	215.6		
296	333.3	153.9	166.0	159.9	159.0	158.7	153.4	228.8	224.6	216.4	296	244.6
297	334.4	154.5	166.6	160.5	159.6	159.3	154.0	229.6	225.4	217.2		
298	335.5	155.1	167.2	161.0	160.2	159.9	154.6	230.4	226.2	217.9	298	246.3
299	336.6	155.6	167.8	161.6	160.8	160.4	155.2	231.2	227.0	218.7		
300	337.8	156.2	168.4	162.2	161.4	161.0	155.7	232.0	227.7	219.5	300	247.9
301	338.9	156.8	169.0	162.8	162.0	161.6	156.3	232.7	228.5	220.2		
302	340.0	157.3	169.6	163.4	162.5	162.2	156.9	233.5	229.3	221.0	302	249.6
303	341.1	157.9	170.2	164.0	163.1	162.8	157.5	234.3	230.1	221.7		
304	342.3	158.5	170.8	164.5	163.7	163.4	158.1	235.1	230.8	222.5	304	251.3
305	343.4	159.0	171.4	165.1	164.3	164.0	158.7	235.9	231.6	223.3		
306	344.5	159.6	172.0	165.7	164.9	164.6	159.3	236.7	232.4	224.0	306	252.9
307	345.6	160.2	172.6	166.3	165.5	165.1	159.9	237.4	233.1	224.8		
308	346.8	160.7	173.2	166.9	166.1	165.7	160.5	238.2	233.9	225.6	308	254.6
309	347.9	161.3	173.8	167.5	166.7	166.3	161.1	239.0	234.7	226.3		

(Continued)

52.019 Hammond table for calculating glucose, fructose, and invert sugar and lactose alone and in the presence of sucrose[a], with values for maltose from the Munson and Walker table[b]; values expressed as mg —*Continued.*

					Invert Sugar and Sucrose				Lactose.H_2O and Sucrose			
Cu[c]	Cu_2O[c]	Glucose	Fructose	Invert Sugar	0.3 g Total Sugar	0.4 g Total Sugar	2.0 g Total Sugar	Lactose .H_2O	1 Lactose 4 Sucrose	1 Lactose 12 Sucrose	Cu_2O[d]	Maltose .H_2O
310	349.0	161.9	174.4	168.0	167.2	166.9	161.7	239.8	235.5	227.1	310	256.3
311	350.1	162.5	175.0	168.6	167.8	167.5	162.3	240.6	236.3	227.9		
312	351.3	163.0	175.6	169.2	168.4	168.1	162.9	241.4	237.0	228.6	312	257.9
313	352.4	163.6	176.2	169.8	169.0	168.7	163.5	242.2	237.8	229.4		
314	353.5	164.2	176.8	170.4	169.6	169.3	164.1	243.0	238.6	230.2	314	259.6
315	354.6	164.7	177.4	171.0	170.2	169.9	164.7	243.7	239.4	230.9		
316	355.8	165.3	178.0	171.6	170.8	170.5	165.3	244.5	240.1	231.7	316	261.2
317	356.9	165.9	178.6	172.2	171.4	171.1	165.9	245.3	240.9	232.5		
318	358.0	166.5	179.2	172.8	172.0	171.7	166.5	246.1	241.7	233.2	318	262.9
319	359.1	167.0	179.8	173.3	172.6	172.2	167.1	246.9	242.5	234.0		
320	360.3	167.6	180.4	173.9	173.1	172.8	167.7	247.7	243.2	234.8	320	264.6
321	361.4	168.2	181.0	174.5	173.7	173.4	168.3	248.5	244.0	235.5		
322	362.5	168.8	181.6	175.1	174.3	174.0	168.9	249.2	244.8	236.3	322	266.2
323	363.6	169.3	182.2	175.7	174.9	174.6	169.5	250.0	245.6	237.1		
324	364.8	169.9	182.8	176.3	175.5	175.2	170.1	250.8	246.3	237.8	324	267.9
325	365.9	170.5	183.4	176.9	176.1	175.8	170.7	251.6	247.1	238.6		
326	367.0	171.1	184.0	177.5	176.7	176.4	171.3	252.4	247.9	239.4	326	269.6
327	368.2	171.6	184.6	178.1	177.3	177.0	171.9	253.2	248.7	240.1		
328	369.3	172.2	185.2	178.7	177.9	177.6	172.5	253.9	249.5	240.9	328	271.2
329	370.4	172.8	185.8	179.2	178.5	178.2	173.1	254.7	250.2	241.7		
330	371.5	173.4	186.4	179.8	179.1	178.8	173.7	255.5	251.0	242.4	330	272.9
331	372.7	173.9	187.0	180.4	179.7	179.4	174.3	256.3	251.8	243.2		
332	373.8	174.5	187.6	181.0	180.3	180.0	174.9	257.1	252.6	244.0	332	274.6
333	374.9	175.1	188.2	181.6	180.9	180.6	175.5	257.9	253.3	244.8		
334	376.0	175.7	188.8	182.2	181.5	181.2	176.1	258.7	254.1	245.5	334	276.2
335	377.2	176.3	189.4	182.8	182.1	181.8	176.7	259.4	254.9	246.3		
336	378.3	176.8	190.1	183.4	182.6	182.4	177.3	260.2	255.7	247.1	336	277.9
337	379.4	177.4	190.7	184.0	183.2	183.0	178.0	261.0	256.5	247.8		
338	380.5	178.0	191.3	184.6	183.8	183.6	178.6	261.8	257.2	248.6	338	279.5
339	381.7	178.6	191.9	185.2	184.4	184.2	179.2	262.6	258.0	249.4		
340	382.8	179.2	192.5	185.8	185.0	184.8	179.8	263.4	258.8	250.2	340	281.2
341	383.9	179.7	193.1	186.4	185.6	185.4	180.4	264.2	259.6	250.9		
342	385.0	180.3	193.7	187.0	186.2	186.0	181.0	265.0	260.4	251.7	342	282.9
343	386.2	180.9	194.3	187.6	186.8	186.6	181.6	265.8	261.1	252.5		
344	387.3	181.5	194.9	188.2	187.4	187.2	182.2	266.6	261.9	253.3	344	284.5
345	388.4	182.1	195.5	188.8	188.0	187.8	182.8	267.4	262.7	254.0		
346	389.5	182.7	196.1	189.4	188.6	188.4	183.4	268.1	263.5	254.8	346	286.2
347	390.7	183.2	196.7	190.0	189.2	189.0	184.0	268.9	264.2	255.6		
348	391.8	183.8	197.3	190.6	189.8	189.6	184.6	269.7	265.0	256.4	348	287.9
349	392.9	184.4	197.9	191.2	190.4	190.2	185.3	270.5	265.8	257.1		
350	394.0	185.0	198.5	191.8	191.0	190.8	185.9	271.3	266.6	257.9	350	289.5
351	395.2	185.6	199.2	192.4	191.6	191.4	186.5	272.1	267.4	258.7		
352	396.3	186.2	199.8	193.0	192.2	192.0	187.1	272.9	268.2	259.4	352	291.2
353	397.4	186.8	200.4	193.6	192.8	192.6	187.7	273.7	268.9	260.2		
354	398.5	187.3	201.0	194.2	193.4	193.2	188.3	274.4	269.7	261.0	354	292.8
355	399.7	187.9	201.6	194.8	194.0	193.8	188.9	275.2	270.5	261.8		
356	400.8	188.5	202.2	195.4	194.6	194.4	189.5	276.0	271.3	262.6	356	294.5
357	401.9	189.1	202.8	196.0	195.2	195.0	190.2	276.8	272.1	263.3		
358	403.1	189.7	203.4	196.6	195.8	195.7	190.8	277.6	272.8	264.1	358	296.2
359	404.2	190.3	204.0	197.2	196.4	196.3	191.4	278.4	273.6	264.9		

(Continued)

52.019 Hammond table for calculating glucose, fructose, and invert sugar and lactose alone and in the presence of sucrose[a], with values for maltose from the Munson and Walker table[b]; values expressed as mg —*Continued.*

					Invert Sugar and Sucrose				Lactose.H_2O and Sucrose			
Cu[c]	Cu_2O[c]	Glucose	Fructose	Invert Sugar	0.3 g Total Sugar	0.4 g Total Sugar	2.0 g Total Sugar	Lactose .H_2O	1 Lactose 4 Sucrose	1 Lactose 12 Sucrose	Cu_2O[d]	Maltose .H_2O
360	405.3	190.9	204.7	197.8	197.1	196.9	192.0	279.2	274.4	265.7	360	297.8
361	406.4	191.5	205.3	198.4	197.7	197.5	192.6	280.0	275.2	266.4		
362	407.6	192.0	205.9	199.0	198.3	198.1	193.2	280.8	276.0	267.2	362	299.5
363	408.7	192.6	206.5	199.6	198.9	198.7	193.9	281.6	276.8	268.0		
364	409.8	193.2	207.1	200.2	199.5	199.3	194.5	282.4	277.5	268.8	364	301.2
365	410.9	193.8	207.7	200.8	200.1	199.9	195.1	283.2	278.3	269.6		
366	412.1	194.4	208.3	201.4	200.7	200.5	195.7	284.0	279.1	270.3	366	302.8
367	413.2	195.0	209.0	202.0	201.3	201.1	196.3	284.8	279.9	271.1		
368	414.3	195.6	209.6	202.6	201.9	201.7	196.9	285.6	280.7	271.9	368	304.5
369	415.4	196.2	210.2	203.2	202.5	202.4	197.6	286.3	281.5	272.7		
370	416.6	196.8	210.8	203.8	203.1	203.0	198.2	287.1	282.2	273.5	370	306.1
371	417.7	197.4	211.4	204.4	203.7	203.6	198.8	287.9	283.0	274.2		
372	418.8	198.0	212.0	205.0	204.3	204.2	199.4	288.7	283.8	275.0	372	307.8
373	419.9	198.5	212.6	205.7	204.9	204.8	200.0	289.5	284.6	275.8		
374	421.1	199.1	213.3	206.3	205.6	205.4	200.7	290.3	285.4	276.6	374	309.5
375	422.2	199.7	213.9	206.9	206.2	206.0	201.3	291.1	286.2	277.4		
376	423.3	200.3	214.5	207.5	206.8	206.6	201.9	291.9	286.9	278.2	376	311.1
377	424.4	200.9	215.1	208.1	207.4	207.3	202.5	292.7	287.7	278.9		
378	425.6	201.5	215.7	208.7	208.0	207.9	203.1	293.5	288.5	279.7	378	312.8
379	426.7	202.1	216.3	209.3	208.6	208.5	203.8	294.3	289.3	280.5		
380	427.8	202.7	217.0	209.9	209.2	209.1	204.4	295.0	290.1	281.3	380	314.5
381	428.9	203.3	217.6	210.5	209.8	209.7	205.0	295.8	290.9	282.1		
382	430.1	203.9	218.2	211.1	210.4	210.3	205.6	296.6	291.7	282.9	382	316.1
383	431.2	204.5	218.8	211.8	211.1	211.0	206.3	297.4	292.4	283.6		
384	432.3	205.1	219.5	212.4	211.7	211.6	206.9	298.2	293.2	284.4	384	317.8
385	433.5	205.7	220.1	213.0	212.3	212.2	207.5	299.0	294.0	285.2		
386	434.6	206.3	220.7	213.6	212.9	212.8	208.1	299.8	294.8	286.0	386	319.4
387	435.7	206.9	221.3	214.2	213.5	213.4	208.8	300.6	295.6	286.8		
388	436.8	207.5	221.9	214.8	214.1	214.0	209.4	301.4	296.4	287.6	388	321.1
389	438.0	208.1	222.6	215.4	214.7	214.7	210.0	302.2	297.2	288.4		
390	439.1	208.7	223.2	216.0	215.4	215.3	210.6	303.0	298.0	289.2	390	322.8
391	440.2	209.3	223.8	216.7	216.0	215.9	211.3	303.8	298.8	290.0		
392	441.3	209.9	224.4	217.3	216.6	216.5	211.9	304.6	299.5	290.7	392	324.4
393	442.5	210.5	225.1	217.9	217.2	217.1	212.5	305.4	300.3	291.5		
394	443.6	211.1	225.7	218.5	217.8	217.8	213.2	306.2	301.1	292.3	394	326.1
395	444.7	211.7	226.3	219.1	218.5	218.4	213.8	307.0	301.9	293.1		
396	445.8	212.3	226.9	219.8	219.1	219.0	214.4	307.8	302.7	293.9	396	327.7
397	447.0	212.9	227.6	220.4	219.7	219.6	215.1	308.6	303.5	294.7		
398	448.1	213.5	228.2	221.0	220.3	220.3	215.7	309.4	304.3	295.5	398	329.4
399	449.2	214.1	228.8	221.6	220.9	220.9	216.3	310.2	305.1	296.3		
400	450.3	214.7	229.4	222.2	221.5	221.5	217.0	311.0	305.9	297.1	400	331.1
401	451.5	215.3	230.1	222.9	222.2	222.1	217.6	311.8	306.7	297.9		
402	452.6	215.9	230.7	223.5	222.8	222.8	218.2	312.6	307.5	298.7	402	332.7
403	453.7	216.5	231.3	224.1	223.4	223.4	218.9	313.4	308.3	299.5		
404	454.8	217.1	232.0	224.7	224.0	224.0	219.5	314.2	309.1	300.3	404	334.4
405	456.0	217.8	232.6	225.4	224.7	224.7	220.1	315.0	309.9	301.1		
406	457.1	218.4	233.2	226.0	225.3	225.3	220.8	315.9	310.7	301.9	406	336.0
407	458.2	219.0	233.9	226.6	225.9	225.9	221.4	316.7	311.5	302.7		
408	459.3	219.6	234.5	227.2	226.6	226.5	222.0	317.5	312.3	303.5	408	337.7
409	460.5	220.2	235.1	227.9	227.2	227.2	222.7	318.3	313.1	304.3		

(Continued)

52.019 Hammond table for calculating glucose, fructose, and invert sugar and lactose alone and in the presence of sucrose[a], with values for maltose from the Munson and Walker table[b]; values expressed as mg —*Concluded*.

					Invert Sugar and Sucrose				Lactose.H_2O and Sucrose			
Cu[c]	Cu_2O[c]	Glucose	Fructose	Invert Sugar	0.3 g Total Sugar	0.4 g Total Sugar	2.0 g Total Sugar	Lactose .H_2O	1 Lactose 4 Sucrose	1 Lactose 12 Sucrose	Cu_2O[d]	Maltose .H_2O
410	461.6	220.8	235.8	228.5	227.8	227.8	223.3	319.1	313.9	305.1	410	339.4
411	462.7	221.4	236.4	229.1	228.4	228.4	224.0	319.9	314.7	305.9		
412	463.8	222.0	237.1	229.7	229.1	229.1	224.6	320.7	315.5	306.7	412	341.0
413	465.0	222.6	237.7	230.4	229.7	229.7	225.3	321.6	316.3	307.6		
414	466.1	223.3	238.4	231.0	230.4	230.4	225.9	322.4	317.1	308.4	414	342.7
415	467.2	223.9	239.0	231.7	231.0	231.0	226.6	323.2	317.9	309.2		
416	468.4	224.5	239.7	232.3	231.6	231.7	227.2	324.0	318.7	310.0	416	344.4
417	469.5	225.1	240.3	232.9	232.3	232.3	227.8	324.9	319.5	310.8		
418	470.6	225.7	241.0	233.6	232.9	232.9	228.5	325.7	320.3	311.7	418	346.0
419	471.7	226.3	241.6	234.2	233.5	233.6	229.1	326.5	321.2	312.5		
420	472.9	227.0	242.2	234.8	234.2	234.2	229.8	327.4	322.0	313.4	420	347.7
421	474.0	227.6	242.9	235.5	234.8	234.9	230.4	328.2	322.8	314.2		
422	475.1	228.2	243.6	236.1	235.5	235.5	231.1	329.1	323.6	315.0	422	349.3
423	476.2	228.8	244.3	236.8	236.2	236.2	231.8	329.9	324.5	315.9		
424	477.4	229.5	244.9	237.5	236.8	236.9	232.4	330.8	325.3	316.8	424	351.0
425	478.5	230.1	245.6	238.1	237.5	237.5	233.1	331.7	326.2	317.6		
426	479.6	230.7	246.3	238.8	238.2	238.2	233.8	332.6	327.0	318.5	426	352.7
427	480.7	231.4	247.0	239.5	238.8	238.9	234.5	333.5	327.9	319.4		
428	481.9	232.0	247.8	240.2	239.5	239.6	235.1	334.4	328.8	320.4	428	354.3
429	483.0	232.7	248.5	240.8	240.2	240.3	235.8	335.3	329.7	321.3		
430	484.1	233.3	249.2	241.5	240.9	241.0	236.5	336.3	330.6	322.3	430	356.0
431	485.2	234.0	250.0	242.3	241.7	241.7	237.2	337.3	331.5	323.3		
432	486.4	234.7	250.8	243.0	242.4	242.5	238.0	338.3	332.5	324.4	432	357.6
433	487.5	235.3	251.6	243.8	243.2	243.3	238.7	339.4	333.5	325.5		
434	488.6	236.1	252.7	244.7	244.1	244.2	239.6	340.7	334.6	326.7	434	359.3
435	489.7	236.9	253.7	245.6	245.1	245.1	240.4	342.0	335.8	328.1		
											436	361.0
											438	362.6
											440	364.3
											442	365.9
											444	367.6
											446	369.3
											448	370.9
											450	372.6
											452	374.2
											454	375.9
											456	377.6
											458	379.2
											460	380.9
											462	382.5
											464	384.2
											466	385.9
											468	387.5
											470	389.2
											472	390.8
											474	392.5
											476	394.2
											478	395.8
											480	397.5
											482	399.1
											484	400.8
											486	402.4
											488	404.1
											490	405.8

52.020 Density of sucrose solutions at 0–100°C and 0–70%, in mg/ml[a]

% Sugar	Temperature, °C										
	0[b]	10[b]	20[b]	30	40	50	60	70	80	90	100[c]
0	0.99987	0.99973	0.99823	0.99567	0.99224	0.98807	0.98324	0.97781	0.97183	0.96534	0.95838
10	1.04135	1.04016	1.03814	1.03529	1.03156	1.02713	1.02207	1.01648	1.01039	1.00381	0.9968
20	1.08546	1.08353	1.08096	1.07766	1.07366	1.06898	1.06365	1.05790	1.05169	1.04503	1.0379
30	1.13274	1.13014	1.12698	1.12325	1.11888	1.11395	1.10847	1.10257	1.09626	1.08956	1.0825
40	1.18349	1.18020	1.17645	1.17231	1.16758	1.16238	1.15675	1.15073	1.14432	1 13746	1 1301
50	1 23775	1 23382	1 22957	1 22501	1 21996	1 21455	1.20875	1.20260	1.19615	1.18939	1.1823
60	1.29560	1.29117	1.28646	1.28149	1.27616	1.27035	1.26464	1.25844	1.25191	1.24511	1.2378
70	1.35719	1.35230	1.34717	1.34185	1.33635	1.33056	1.32454	1.31834	1.31190	1.30527	

[a] Schneider, Schliephake, and Klimmek, *Zucker Beih.* **4**(2), 72–76(1962).
[b] Values taken from Plato *et al.*, Charlottenberg. Physikalisch-technische reichsanstalt. Wiss. Abhandl. Kaiserliche Normal-Eichungs-Kommission, No. 2, and *Z. Ver. Deut. Zucker-Ind.* **50,** 982 and 1079(1900).
[c] Extrapolated.

52.021 Volume factors for thermal expansion of sucrose solutions up to 100°C[a]; volumes at 20°C = 1.0000

% Sugar	Temperature, °C										
	0	10	20	30	40	50	60	70	80	90	100
0	0.9984	0.9985	1.0000	1.0026	1.0060	1.0102	1.0152	1.0209	1.0274	1.0342	1.0411
10	0.9969	0.9981	1.0000	1.0027	1.0064	1.0107	1.0157	1.0213	1.0274	1.0342	1.0416
20	0.9958	0.9976	1.0000	1.0030	1.0068	1.0112	1.0163	1.0218	1.0278	1.0344	1.0416
30	0.9949	0.9972	1.0000	1.0033	1.0072	1.0117	1.0167	1.0221	1.0280	1.0343	1.0411
40	0.9941	0.9969	1.0000	1.0036	1.0076	1.0121	1.0170	1.0224	1.0280	1.0343	1.0410
50	0.9934	0.9966	1.0000	1.0038	1.0079	1.0123	1.0172	1.0224	1.0279	1.0338	1.0400
60	0.9929	0.9963	1.0000	1.0039	1.0081	1.0125	1.0173	1.0223	1.0276	1.0332	1.0391

[a] Schneider, Schliephake, and Klimmek, *Zucker Beih.* **4**(2), 72–76 (1962).

52.022 Table for determining total solids in milk from any given specific gravity and percentage of fat (Shaw and Eckles); results expressed as per cent total solids

% Fat	Lactometer Reading at 60°F (Quévenne Degrees)										
	26	27	28	29	30	31	32	33	34	35	36
2.00	8.90	9.15	9.40	9.65	9.90	10.15	10.40	10.66	10.91	11.16	11.41
.05	.96	.21	.46	.71	.96	.21	.46	.72	.97	.22	.47
.10	9.02	.27	.52	.77	10.02	.27	.52	.78	11.03	.28	.53
.15	.08	.33	.58	.83	.08	.33	.58	.84	.09	.34	.59
.20	.14	.39	.64	.89	.14	.39	.64	.90	.15	.40	.65
.25	.20	.45	.70	.95	.20	.45	.70	.96	.21	.46	.71
.30	.26	.51	.76	10.01	.26	.51	.76	11.02	.27	.52	.77
.35	.32	.57	.82	.07	.32	.57	.82	.08	.33	.58	.83
.40	.38	.63	.88	.13	.38	.63	.88	.14	.39	.64	.89
.45	.44	.69	.94	.19	.44	.69	.94	.20	.45	.70	.95
.50	.50	.75	10.00	.25	.50	.75	11.00	.26	.51	.76	12.01
.55	.56	.81	.06	.31	.56	.81	.06	.32	.57	.82	.07
.60	.62	.87	.12	.37	.62	.87	.12	.38	.63	.88	.13
.65	.68	.93	.18	.43	.68	.93	.18	.44	.69	.94	.19
.70	.74	.99	.24	.49	.74	.99	.24	.50	.75	12.00	.25
.75	.80	10.05	.30	.55	.80	11.05	.31	.56	.81	.06	.31
.80	.86	.11	.36	.61	.86	.11	.37	.62	.87	.12	.37
.85	.92	.17	.42	.67	.92	.17	.43	.68	.93	.18	.43
.90	.98	.23	.48	.73	.98	.23	.49	.74	.99	.24	.49
.95	10.04	.29	.54	.79	11.04	.30	.55	.80	12.05	.30	.55
3.00	.10	.35	.60	.85	.10	.36	.61	.86	.11	.36	.61
.05	.16	.41	.66	.91	.17	.42	.67	.92	.17	.42	.68
.10	.22	.47	.72	.97	.23	.48	.73	.98	.23	.48	.74
.15	.28	.53	.78	11.03	.29	.54	.79	12.04	.29	.55	.80
.20	.34	.59	.84	.09	.35	.60	.85	.10	.35	.61	.86
.25	.40	.65	.90	.16	.41	.66	.91	.16	.42	.67	.92
.30	.46	.71	.96	.22	.47	.72	.97	.22	.48	.73	.98
.35	.52	.77	11.03	.28	.53	.78	12.03	.28	.54	.79	13.04
.40	.58	.83	.09	.34	.59	.84	.09	.34	.60	.85	.10
.45	.64	.89	.15	.40	.65	.90	.15	.40	.66	.91	.16
.50	.70	.95	.21	.46	.71	.96	.21	.46	.72	.97	.22
.55	.76	11.02	.27	.52	.77	12.02	.27	.52	.78	13.03	.28
.60	.82	.08	.33	.58	.83	.08	.33	.58	.84	.09	.34
.65	.88	.14	.39	.64	.89	.14	.39	.64	.90	.15	.40
.70	.94	.20	.45	.70	.95	.20	.45	.70	.96	.21	.46
.75	11.00	.26	.51	.76	12.01	.26	.51	.76	13.02	.27	.52
.80	.06	.32	.57	.82	.07	.32	.57	.82	.08	.33	.58
.85	.12	.38	.63	.88	.13	.38	.63	.88	.14	.39	.64
.90	.18	.44	.69	.94	.19	.44	.69	.94	.20	.45	.70
.95	.24	.50	.75	12.00	.25	.50	.75	13.00	.26	.51	.77
4.00	.30	.56	.81	.06	.31	.56	.81	.06	.32	.57	.83
.05	.36	.62	.87	.12	.37	.62	.87	.12	.38	.63	.89
.10	.42	.68	.93	.18	.43	.68	.93	.18	.44	.69	.95
.15	.48	.74	.99	.24	.49	.74	.99	.25	.50	.76	14.01
.20	.54	.80	12.05	.30	.55	.80	13.05	.31	.56	.82	.07
.25	.60	.86	.11	.36	.61	.86	.12	.37	.62	.88	.13
.30	.66	.92	.17	.42	.67	.92	.18	.43	.68	.94	.19
.35	.72	.98	.23	.48	.73	.98	.24	.49	.74	14.00	.25
.40	.78	12.04	.29	.54	.79	13.04	.30	.55	.80	.06	.31
.45	.84	.10	.35	.60	.85	.10	.36	.61	.86	.12	.37
.50	.90	.16	.41	.66	.91	.16	.42	.67	.92	.18	.43
.55	.97	.22	.47	.72	.97	.22	.48	73	98	.24	.49
.60	12.03	.28	.53	.78	13.03	.28	.54	.79	14.04	.30	.55
.65	.09	.34	.59	.84	.09	.34	.60	.85	.10	.36	.61
.70	.15	.40	.65	.90	.15	.40	.66	.91	.16	.42	.67
.75	.21	.46	.71	.96	.21	.46	.72	.97	.22	.48	.73
.80	.27	.52	.77	13.02	.27	.52	.78	14.03	.28	.54	.79
.85	.33	.58	.83	.08	.33	.58	.84	.09	.34	.60	.85
.90	.39	.64	.89	.14	.39	.64	.90	.15	.40	.66	.91
.95	.45	.70	.95	.20	.45	.70	.96	.21	.46	.72	.97

(Continued)

52.022 Table for determining total solids in milk from any given specific gravity and percentage of fat (Shaw and Eckles); results expressed as per cent total solids—*Concluded.*

% Fat	Lactometer Reading at 60°F (Quévenne Degrees)										
	26	27	28	29	30	31	32	33	34	35	36
5.00	12.51	12.76	13.01	13.26	13.51	13.76	14.02	14.27	14.52	14.78	15.03
.05	.57	.82	.07	.32	.57	.83	.08	.33	.58	.84	.09
.10	.63	.88	.13	.38	.63	.89	.14	.39	.64	.90	.15
.15	.69	.94	.19	.44	.69	.95	.20	.45	.70	.96	.21
.20	.75	13.00	.25	.50	.75	14.01	.26	.51	.76	15.02	.27
.25	.81	.06	.31	.56	.81	.07	.32	.57	.82	.08	.33
.30	.87	.12	.37	.62	.87	.13	.38	.63	.88	.14	.39
.35	.93	.18	.43	.68	.93	.19	.44	.70	.95	.20	.45
.40	.99	.24	.49	.74	14.00	.25	.50	.76	15.01	.26	.51
.45	13.05	.30	.55	.80	.06	.31	.56	.82	.07	.32	.57
.50	.11	.36	.61	.86	.12	.37	.62	.88	.13	.38	.63
.55	.17	.42	.67	.93	.18	.43	.69	.94	.19	.44	.69
.60	.23	.48	.73	.99	.24	.49	.75	15.00	.25	.50	.75
.65	.29	.54	.79	14.05	.30	.55	.81	.06	.31	.56	.81
.70	.35	.60	.85	.11	.36	.61	.87	.12	.37	.62	.87
.75	.41	.66	.91	.17	.42	.68	.93	.18	.43	.68	.93
.80	.47	.72	.97	.23	.48	.74	.99	.24	.49	.74	.99
.85	.53	.78	14.04	.29	.54	.80	15.05	.30	.55	.80	16.06
.90	.59	.84	.10	.35	.60	.86	.11	.36	.61	.86	.12
.95	.65	.90	.16	.41	.66	.92	.17	.42	.67	.92	.18
6.00	.71	.96	.22	.47	.72	.98	.23	.48	.73	.98	.24
.05	.77	14.02	.28	.53	.78	15.04	.29	.54	.79	16.04	.30
.10	.83	.08	.34	.59	.84	.10	.35	.60	.85	.10	.35
.15	.89	.14	.40	.65	.90	.16	.41	.66	.91	.16	.42
.20	.95	.20	.46	.71	.96	.22	.47	.72	.97	.22	.48
.25	14.01	.26	.52	.77	15.02	.28	.53	.78	16.03	.28	.54
.30	.07	.32	.58	.83	.08	.34	.59	.84	.09	.34	.60
.35	.13	.38	.64	.90	.14	.40	.65	.90	.15	.40	.66
.40	.19	.44	.70	.96	.20	.46	.71	.96	.21	.46	.72
.45	.25	.50	.76	15.02	.26	.52	.77	16.02	.27	.52	.78
.50	.31	.56	.82	.08	.32	.58	.83	.08	.33	.58	.84
.55	.37	.62	.88	.14	.38	.64	.89	.14	.39	.64	.90
.60	.43	.68	.94	.20	.44	.70	.95	.20	.45	.70	.96
.65	.49	.74	15.00	.26	.50	.76	16.01	.26	.51	.76	17.02
.70	.55	.80	.06	.32	.56	.82	.07	.32	.57	.82	.08
.75	.61	.86	.12	.38	.62	.88	.13	.38	.63	.88	.14
.80	.67	.92	.18	.44	.68	.94	.19	.44	.69	.94	.20
.85	.73	.98	.24	.50	.74	16.00	.25	.50	.75	17.00	.26
.90	.79	15.04	.30	.56	.80	.06	.31	.56	.81	.06	.32
.95	.85	.10	.36	.62	.86	.12	.37	.62	.87	.12	.38

Proportional Parts

Lactometer Fraction	Fraction to Be Added to Total Solids	Lactometer Fraction	Fraction to Be Added to Total Solids	Lactometer Fraction	Fraction to Be Added to Total Solids
0.1	0.03	0.4	0.10	0.7	0.18
.2	.05	.5	.13	.8	.20
.3	.08	.6	.15	.9	.23

Table giving proportional parts shows amount to be added when lactometer readings are in whole numbers and decimals.

52.023 Correction table for specific gravity of milk (Quévenne lactometer)[a]

Lactometer	Temperature (°F) 51	52	53	54	55	56	57	58	59	60
20	19.3	19.4	19.4	19.5	19.6	19.7	19.8	19.9	19.9	20.0
21	20.3	20.3	20.4	20.5	20.6	20.7	20.8	20.9	20.9	21.0
22	21.3	21.3	21.4	21.5	21.6	21.7	21.8	21.9	21.9	22.0
23	22.3	22.3	22.4	22.5	22.6	22.7	22.8	22.8	22.9	23.0
24	23.3	23.3	23.4	23.5	23.6	23.6	23.7	23.8	23.9	24.0
25	24.2	24.3	24.4	24.5	24.6	24.6	24.7	24.8	24.9	25.0
26	25.2	25.2	25.3	25.4	25.5	25.6	25.7	25.8	25.9	26.0
27	26.2	26.2	26.3	26.4	26.5	26.6	26.7	26.8	26.9	27.0
28	27.1	27.2	27.3	27.4	27.5	27.6	27.7	27.8	27.9	28.0
29	28.1	28.2	28.3	28.4	28.5	28.6	28.7	28.8	28.9	29.0
30	29.1	29.1	29.2	29.3	29.4	29.6	29.7	29.8	29.9	30.0
31	30.0	30.1	30.2	30.3	30.4	30.5	30.6	30.8	30.9	31.0
32	31.0	31.1	31.2	31.3	31.4	31.5	31.6	31.7	31.9	32.0
33	31.9	32.0	32.1	32.3	32.4	32.5	32.6	32.7	32.9	33.0
34	32.9	33.0	33.1	33.2	33.3	33.5	33.6	33.7	33.9	34.0
35	33.8	33.9	34.0	34.2	34.3	34.5	34.6	34.7	34.9	35.0

Lactometer	Temperature (°F) 61	62	63	64	65	66	67	68	69	70
20	20.1	20.2	20.2	20.3	20.4	20.5	20.6	20.7	20.9	21.0
21	21.1	21.2	21.3	21.4	21.5	21.6	21.7	21.8	22.0	22.1
22	22.1	22.2	22.3	22.4	22.5	22.6	22.7	22.8	23.0	23.1
23	23.1	23.2	23.3	23.4	23.5	23.6	23.7	23.8	24.0	24.1
24	24.1	24.2	24.3	24.4	24.5	24.6	24.7	24.9	25.0	25.1
25	25.1	25.2	25.3	25.4	25.5	25.6	25.7	25.9	26.0	26.1
26	26.1	26.2	26.3	26.5	26.6	26.7	26.8	27.0	27.1	27.2
27	27.1	27.3	27.4	27.5	27.6	27.7	27.8	28.0	28.1	28.2
28	28.1	28.3	28.4	28.5	28.6	28.7	28.8	29.0	29.1	29.2
29	29.1	29.3	29.4	29.5	29.6	29.7	29.9	30.1	30.2	30.3
30	30.1	30.3	30.4	30.5	30.7	30.8	30.9	31.1	31.2	31.3
31	31.2	31.3	31.4	31.5	31.7	31.8	31.9	32.1	32.2	32.4
32	32.2	32.3	32.5	32.6	32.7	32.9	33.0	33.2	33.3	33.4
33	33.2	33.3	33.5	33.6	33.8	33.9	34.0	34.2	34.3	34.5
34	34.2	34.3	34.5	34.6	34.8	34.9	35.0	35.2	35.3	35.5
35	35.2	35.3	35.5	35.6	35.8	36.9	36.1	36.2	36.4	36.5

[a] Paul G. Heineman, *Milk*, W. B. Saunders Co., Philadelphia, 1921, p. 144.

52.024 Optical crystallographic properties of some crystalline drugs[a]

Compound	α	β	γ	Optic Sign	Extinction	Elongation	2V	Remarks
Alkaloids and Related Amines								
Aconitine	1.560	—	1.575	+		−	36°	
Alphaprodine.HCl	1.499	1.572	1.597	−	p, i		63°	
Apomorphine.HCl	1.638	1.658	1.701	+				
Arecoline.HBr	1.555	1.590	1.655	+	p	−		
Atropine	1.550	1.583	1.595	−				n_α very common
Atropine sulfate	1.555	—	1.60					
Benzethonium chloride	1.560	1.565	1.589	+			48°	Most fragments do not extinguish completely
Berberine	1.490	1.701	>1.734	−	p	−		Yellow needles and rods
Berberine.HCl.2H_2O	1.500	1.535	>1.733	+	p			
Brucine	1.562	—	>1.65		p			
Brucine sulfate	1.512	1.595	1.688	+	p	+		6-sided plates and rods
Cetylpyridinium chloride	1.509	1.566	1.613	−	i		88°	Op. ax. fig. common
Cinchonidine	1.610	1.625	1.675	+	p	+	59°	r>v weak
Cinchonidine sulfate	1.562	1.604	1.660	+	p	+		
Cinchonine	1.570	1.685	1.690	−	p	+	21°	Plates and rods
Cinchonine.HCl.2H_2O	1.545	1.617	1.661	−		+	large	
Cocaine.HCl	1.570	1.596	1.618	−				
Codeine	1.543	1.636	1.684	−			53°	
Codeine.HCl	1.559	1.580	1.676	+				
Codeine sulfate	1.561	1.642	1.661	−	p	−		Rods
Desipramine.HCl	1.586	1.622	1.698	+	p, s	−	large	Elongate prisms, many 6-sided in outline; op. ax. figs. rare, flash figs. common
Dextropropoxyphene napsylate	1.568	1.636	1.638	−			23°	Marked dispersion, r<v
Diacetylmorphine (Heroin)	1.556	1.607	1.627	−				Sl. sol. in R. I. oils
Diacetylmorphine.HCl.H_2O	1.578_ω		1.613_ϵ	+				Uniaxial
Diphenylhydantoin	1.600	—	1.635		p	−		
l-Ephedrine.HCl	1.530	1.603	1.638	−	p	−	70°	Prisms and rods
Ethoheptazine citrate	1.537	—	1.556					
Ethylhydrocupreine.HCl	1.513	—	1.619					
Hydrastine	1.550	1.734	>1.734					n_α common
Hyoscyamine	1.562	—	1.581		p, i	+		
Isobucaine.HCl	1.522	1.574	1.612	−	p, i	±	82°	
Levallorphan tartrate	1.545	1.595	1.653	+			86°	
Meperidine.HCl	1.545	1.581	1.618	+	p	+		
Methaqualone.HCl	1.568	1.659	sl >1.800	+	p	−		Long rods and rectangular plates; α lengthwise, β and γ crosswise
Methscopolamine bromide	1.580	1.615	1.617	−			33°	

[a] Abbreviations: p = parallel; s = symmetrical; i = inclined; n = index; n_i = intermediate index; Bx.ac. = acute bisectrix; Bx.ob. = obtuse bisectrix; Op.ax. = optic axis; fig. = figure; sl = slightly; r = red; v = violet.

(Continued)

52.024 Optical crystallographic properties of some crystalline drugs[a]—*Continued.*

Compound	α	β	γ	Optic Sign	Extinc-tion	Elonga-tion	2V	Remarks
			Alkaloids and Related Amines—*Continued*					
Methylphenidate.HCl	1.558	1.581	1.585	−			43°	
O^6-Monoacetylmorphine.HCl	1.526	1.597	1.639	−	p	−	fairly large	Elongate prisms; α lengthwise, β and γ crosswise
Morphine.HCl, anhyd.	1.612	1.637	1.644	−	p	−	med. to large	Irregular plates, some rectangular or lath-shaped showing α and γ
Morphine.H_2O	1.580	1.625	1.645	−	p	±		
Morphine.HCl.$3H_2O$	1.540	n_i1.590	1.635	−	p	−		
Morphine sulfate.$5H_2O$	1.545	1.620	1.632	−	p	−		
Papaverine	1.625	1.690	>1.690		p	−	large	Orthorhombic
Papaverine.HCl	1.555	n_i1.733	>1.733					n_α common
Pentazocine	1.575	1.590	1.627	+	p	−		α lengthwise, γ crosswise
Pentazocine.HCl	1.577	—	1.594		p, i	+		Mostly inclined extinction; flash figs. common; α crosswise, γ lengthwise
Phenmetrazine.HCl	1.508	1.516	1.628	+				
Phensuximide	1.536	1.617	>1.673		p, i		very large	
Phenylbutazone	1.600	—	1.620	+	p	−		
Quinidine	1.580	1.665	1.690	−	p	+	55°	
Quinidine sulfate	1.565	1.607	1.670	+	p	+		
Quinine	1.620	1.625	1.630		p	−	very large	
Quinine.HCl	1.590	1.610	1.669	+	p	+	61°	r>v
Racephedrine.HCl	1.570	1.608	1.630	−				Irregular fragments; op. ax. figs. occasional
Scopolamine.HBr	1.567	1.585	1.623	+	p		medium	Rods and prisms
Strychnine	1.617	1.660	>1.690	−	p	+	large	
Strychnine.HCl.$2H_2O$	1.610	1.626	1.668	+		−	large	
Syrosingopine	1.529	1.538	1.646	+	p	−	34°	
Yohimbine	1.548	1.563	1.688	+			42°	
Yohimbine.HCl	1.57	1.61	1.69	+				
			Antibiotics					
Carbomycin	1.474	1.484	1.513	+	p	±		
Chloramphenicol	1.523	1.608	1.659	−	p	−	70–80°	
Chloramphenicol palmitate	1.527	—	1.569		p	±		
Chlortetracycline.HCl	1.635	1.706	1.730	−	p, s		59°	

(Continued)

52.024 Optical crystallographic properties of some crystalline drugs[a]—*Continued.*

Compound	α	β	γ	Optic Sign	Extinc- tion	Elonga- tion	2V	Remarks
Antibiotics—*Continued*								
Cycloserine	1.583	—	1.630					Rod-shaped aggregates
Dihydrostreptomycin.3HCl	1.522	1.548	1.566	−	p	+	80°	
Dihydrostreptomycin sulfate	1.552	1.558	1.566	+	p, i		89°	Ext. angle = 18°
Erythromycin estolate	1.483	1.488	1.515	+	p	−	52°	
Erythromycin ethylcarbonate	1.496	1.506	1.510	−	p	+	medium	Op. ax. figs. common
Erythromycin ethylsuccinate	1.490	1.515	1.567	+	p	−		n_γ rare
Erythromycin gluceptate	1.506	—	1.528		p	+		
Erythromycin.HI.H_2O	1.528	1.536	1.550	+	p	+	75°	
Erythromycin.$2H_2O$	1.512	1.523	1.532	−	p	−	84°	
Erythromycin oxalate.$2H_2O$	1.484	1.492	1.516	+	p	+	60°	
Erythromycin stearate	1.498	1.507	1.563	+	p	±	small	n_γ rare
Fumagillin	1.518	ca 1.572	>1.780	+	p, i		small	
Gramicidin	1.541	ca 1.553	1.573	+				
Neomycin sulfate	n 1.541							Isotropic
Novobiocin acid, form 2	1.608	1.638	1.654	−			71°	r>v
Novobiocin sodium	1.565	—	1.629		p	−		Tiny needles
Nystatin	1.512	1.583	1.682	+	p	−		Small, pale yellow rods
Oxytetracycline.$2H_2O$	1.634	1.646	>1.700	+	p		28°	
Oxytetracycline.HCl	1.546	1.635	1.730	+	p, i	+	very large	Op. ax. figs. common
Penicillin G benzathine	1.523	1.622	1.630	−	p	+	very small	n_α and n_γ common
Penicillin G dibenzylamine	1.567	—	1.613		p	+		
Penicillin G *l*-ephedrine	1.575	—	1.610		p	−		
Penicillin G *l*-ephenamine	1.583	1.590	1.648	+	i		very small	Bx. ac. figs.
Penicillin G hydrabamine	1.556	ca 1.590	1.619		p, i	−		
Penicillin G.HI diethylaminoethyl ester	1.601	1.608	1.632	+	p	−	medium	
Penicillin G potassium	1.550	—	1.603	−	p	+		Elongated rectangular plates
Penicillin G procaine	1.545	1.570	1.685	+	p, i	±		n_β common
Penicillin G sodium	1.550	1.609	1.620	−	p	+	large	n_β common
Penicillin O chloroprocaine	1.541	1.585	1.656	+	p	±	large	
Penicillin O potassium	1.545	—	1.593		p	+		
Tetracycline.HCl	1.603	1.685	1.714	−	p		large	Bx. ac. and op. ax. figs.
Tetracycline.$3H_2O$	1.538	1.646	sl >1.787	+	p, i		large	Occasional op. ax. figs.
Tyrocidine.HCl	1.553	—	1.584		p	+		

(*Continued*)

52.024 Optical crystallographic properties of some crystalline drugs[a]—*Continued.*

Compound	α	β	γ	Optic Sign	Extinc-tion	Elonga-tion	2V	Remarks
				Antihistamines				
Anthallan®.HCl	1.505	1.585	1.617	−	p	−		Small rods & irregular fragments; no figs.
Bromothen.HCl	1.617	1.654	1.734	+	i	+		Very small rods
Chlorcyclizine.HCl	1.590	1.610	1.665	+				Thin platy fragments; op. ax. figs. common
Chlorcyclizine.2HCl	1.610	1.660	1.665	−	p		very small	Short rods & thin 6-sided plates; op. ax. figs. common
Chlorothen citrate	1.583	1.603	1.645					Minute plates & shreds; op. ax. figs. rare
Chlorothen.HCl	1.553	1.625	>1.734					Massive fragments, some rectangular; op. ax. figs. occasional
Chlorpheniramine maleate	1.533	n_i1.668	l<1.734					Box-like prisms & irregular fragments; figs. infrequent
Cyproheptadine.HCl	1.620	1.647	1.738	+	p		60°	
Dexchlorpheniramine maleate	1.509	1.564	1.683	+	p		70°	
Dimenhydrinate (unsatisfactory for optical crystallographic study)								
Diphenhydramine.HCl	1.602	1.625	1.630	−	p	−		Platy material & rods
Doxylamine succinate	ca 1.525	1.563	1.598	−				6-sided plates
p-Fluorotripelennamine.HCl	1.585	1.600	1.668	+	p	−	86° large	Rods & square plates; op. ax. figs. occasional
Methaphenilene.HCl	1.604	1.675	1.733	−				Elongated 6-sided rods with obtuse ends; op. ax. figs. frequent
Methapyrilene.HCl	1.588	1.654	>1.695–<1.734	−				Thick hexagonal plates
2-(4-Morpholinyl) ethyl benzhydryl ether.HCl (Linadryl.HCl)	1.577	1.631	1.672	−	p, i	±		Elongated 6-sided & irregular fragments; figs. rare
Phenbenzamine.HCl	1.587	1.635	1.734	+				Short prisms
Pheniramine maleate	1.548	1.574	1.665	+	p	+	small	Rods & plates
Promethazine.HBr	1.667	1.675	>1.733	+			small	Massive prisms; elongated or short & stubby
Promethazine.HCl	1.617	1.691	1.733	−	p	+		Rods & irregular fragments
Pyrathiazine.HCl	1.690	—	1.737					Stout prismatic forms; no figs.
Pyrilamine maleate (unsatisfactory for optical crystallographic study)								
Pyrrobutamine phosphate	1.566	1.614	1.653					Rods & irregular fragments
Thenyldiamine.HCl	1.590	—	1.680				82° large	Square plates & stubby prisms
Thonzylamine.HCl	1.612	1.679	1.691	−	p	+		Rods & platy material
Tripelennamine.HCl	1.580	1.655	1.705	−				Rectangular plates & prisms from water; op. ax. figs. common

(Continued)

52.024 Optical crystallographic properties of some crystalline drugs[a]—*Continued.*

Compound	α	β	γ	Optic Sign	Extinc-tion	Elonga-tion	2V	Remarks
Barbiturates								
Allobarbital	1.516	1.572	1.625	−	s		large	Op. ax. fig. common
Alphenal (5-allyl-5-phenylbarbituric acid)	1.551	1.578	1.645	+	p	−	67°	Op. ax. fig. common
Amobarbital	1.467	1.533	1.560	−	p	+		
Amobarbital sodium	n 1.505							Isotropic
Aprobarbital	1.520	1.581	1.600	−	i		medium	Rods
Barbital	1.445	1.548	1.580					All n's common
Barbital sodium	1.512	1.532	1.615				40°	
Butabarbital sodium	1.465	1.529	1.532	−	p	+	very small	
Butalbital	1.508	n_i1.521	1.577	+	p	+	medium	Rods and plates
Butallylonal	1.524	1.577	1.603	−	p	+	medium	Rosettes of tiny rods and blades; bx. ac. figs. occasional
Butethal	1.454	1.518	1.556	−	i		large	Rods & needles; op. ax. and bx. ac. figs. common
Cyclobarbital	1.515	1.546	1.621	+		±	69°	Bx. ac. & bx. ob. figs. common
Cyclopal® (5-allyl-5-(2-cyclopenten-1-yl) barbituric acid)	1.520	1.575	1.626	−		−	85°	Bx. ac. fig. common
Hexethal (5-ethyl-5-*n*-hexylbarbituric acid)	1.473	1.519	1.549	−		−	76°	
Hexobarbital	1.546	1.608	1.634	−	p	+	64°	Bx. ac. & op. ax. figs. common
Mephobarbital	1.594	1.610	1.651	+	p	−	65°	Bx. ac. fig. common
Pentobarbital	1.465	—	1.565	−	i		very large	
Pentobarbital sodium	1.477	—	1.523					
Phenobarbital	1.557	1.620	1.667		p	−		β very common
Phenobarbital sodium (unstable)								
Probarbital	1.477	1.573	1.624	−	i	+	73°	Rods
Probarbital sodium	1.532	—	1.629		p	+		Rods & needles
Secobarbital	1.487	1.557	1.563	−	p	+	31°	
Secobarbital sodium	1.490	n_i1.500	1.525					
Sigmodal® (5-(2-bromoallyl)-5-(1-methyl-butyl) barbituric acid)	1.519	1.583	1.634	−		+	80°	
Thiopental	1.534	1.634	—	−	i		40–45°	Lamellar
Vinbarbital	1.506	1.544	1.672	+	p	−	61°	

(Continued)

52.024 Optical crystallographic properties of some crystalline drugs[a]—*Continued.*

Compound	α	β	γ	Optic Sign	Extinction	Elongation	2V	Remarks
			Hallucinogens					
d-Lysergic acid diethylamide tartrate (LSD-25)	1.540	1.596	1.676	+	i		83°	
4-Methyl-2,5-dimethoxyamphetamine.HCl ("STP".HCl) (DOM®)	1.518	1.622	1.632	−			33°	Bx. ob. figs. common
3,4-Methylenedioxyamphetamine carbonate (MDA carbonate)	1.564	1.586	1.598	−	p or sl i	−		α lengthwise, γ crosswise
3,4-Methylenedioxyamphetamine.HCl (MDA.HCl)	1.517	1.612	1.679	−	i, s		large	Broad plates; extinction sl i and almost symmetrical
3,4-Methylenedioxyamphetamine sulfate (MDA sulfate)	1.537	—	1.629					Uniaxial figs. and biaxial figs. with small 2V
Phencyclidine.HBr	1.572	1.620	1.654					
Phencyclidine.HCl	1.572	1.618	1.654	−			80°	
Psilocybin	1.527	1.554	1.672	+			55°	n_β and n_γ common
			Steroids					
Betamethasone	1.554	—	1.667		p	+		Very small rods
Cholesterol	1.520	1.532	1.566	+			60°	Elongated plates
Cortisone	1.552	1.572	1.625	+	p	+	medium	n_α and n_β most common
Cortisone acetate	1.512	1.552	1.621	+	p	±	medium	
Dehydrocholic acid	1.510	1.542	1.572	−	p, i	±	80°	
Desoxycorticosterone acetate	1.529	1.550	1.630	+			54°	r > v
Dexamethasone	1.553	1.572	1.648	+			52°	Bx. ac. common
Diethylstilbestrol, trans	1.594	1.611	1.73	+	p	−		Orthorhombic system
Equilin	1.534	1.677	1.705	−			40°	Plates
Estradiol benzoate	1.586	1.603	1.633	+	p	−	large	
Estradiol dipropionate	1.506	—	1.598	−				2E = 46°
Estrone, phase 1	1.520	1.642	1.692	−	i		60°	Ext. angle = 12°; r>v
Estrone, phase 2	1.511	1.621	1.697	−			75°	r>v weak
Estrone, phase 3	1.594	1.628	1.647	−	p		73°	Metastable crystals, 6-sided plates
Ethisterone	1.576	1.625	1.645	−			67°	2E = 127°
Fluorometholone	1.562	1.568	1.704	+			26°	r > v strong
Hydrocortisone	1.531	1.550	1.638	+	p	n		Tiny rods & plates
Hydrocortisone acetate	1.543	1.589	1.627	−	p, i	±	83°	Monoclinic; r>v
Methylprednisolone acetate	1.562	1.575	1.700	+			38°	v > r
Methylprednisolone sodium succinate	1.552	—	1.561	+			very small	
Methyltestosterone	1.555	ca 1.565	1.620	+	p	−	medium	

(Continued)

52.024 Optical crystallographic properties of some crystalline drugs[a]—*Continued.*

Compound	α	β	γ	Optic Sign	Extinction	Elongation	2V	Remarks
			Steroids—*Continued*					
Prednisone	1.587	1.590	1.651	+	p		very small	Bx. ac. common
Progesterone, alpha	1.542	1.554	1.663	+			40°	Platy fragments with brilliant interference colors
Progesterone, beta	1.529	1.575	1.676	+	p	−	68°	Crystals acicular
Testosterone	1.548	1.565	1.670	+	p	−	medium	
Triamcinolone acetonide	1.546_{ϵ}		1.595_{ω}	−				
Triamcinolone diacetate	1.517	1.567	1.592	−			69°	
			Sulfonamides					
Succinylsulfathiazole	1.578	1.676	1.710	−	i		58°	Rods
Sulfacetamide	1.559	1.564	1.727	+	s		21°	
Sulfadiazine	1.596	1.675	1.830	+	p, i	±	76°	
Sulfadiazine[b]	1.615	1.663	>1.734		p	±		Rods
Sulfaguanidine	1.606	1.663	1.734					Op. ax. fig.
Sulfaguanidine. H_2O	1.586	1.649	1.731	+	p, i	±	86°	
Sulfallantoin® (sulfanilamide+allantoin-addition product)	1.513	1.590	>1.690 <1.733					Op. ax. fig.
Sulfamerazine	1.568	1.657	1.687	−	p	±	58°	
Sulfamerazine[b]	1.587	—	1.675					
Sulfamethazine	1.584	1.623	>1.778		p	−		Rods
Sulfamidazole® (sulfanilamide+sulfathiazole-double crystal)[c]	1.661	1.678	>1.733	+			small	Bx. ac. fig.
Sulfanilamide phase B (anhyd.)	1.555	1.672	1.85	+	p	−		Stable form com. prepns
Sulfanilamide. HCl	1.540	1.655	1.690		p	−		Rods
Sulfapyridine[b]	1.680	1.733	>1.733					Op. ax. fig.
Sulfapyridine, phase I	1.670	1.736	1.813	+	p, i	±	88°	Tabular to equant; stable form com. prepns
Sulfapyridine sodium. H_2O	1.590	—	1.700		p	−		
Sulfathiazole, phase I	1.674	1.685	>1.733	+			small	α & β common
Sulfathiazole, phase II	1.598	1.741	1.780	−	p, i	±	52°	Lath shaped
Sulfathiazole[b]	1.695	n_i1.733	>1.733					
Sulfathiazole sodium. $1\frac{1}{2}H_2O$	1.596	—	1.621					
Sulfisoxazole	1.605	1.642	1.697	+	p	±	large	Plates & rods

(Continued)

[b] The second set of optical properties in each case represents intermediate data which are quite commonly found in some commercial samples. They probably represent an anhydrous form or merely a different common orientation of the crystal.

[c] Equimolecular proportions.

52.024 Optical crystallographic properties of some crystalline drugs[a]—*Continued.*

Compound	α	β	γ	Optic Sign	Extinction	Elongation	2V	Remarks
Sympathomimetic Amines								
dl-Amphetamine.HCl	1.508	1.582	1.611		p	−		Rods and plates
dl-Amphetamine phosphate, dibasic	1.549	1.589	1.665	+			large	Small platy crystals; bx. ac. figs. common
dl-Amphetamine sulfate	1.520	1.531	1.614	+		−	very small	
Dextroamphetamine.HCl	1.560	1.592	1.622	+	p, i	±	very large	Large plates & rods; op. ax. figs. occasional
Dextroamphetamine phosphate, dibasic	1.546	1.583	1.664	+	p	±	medium	Plates with truncated corners
Dextroamphetamine sulfate	1.501	1.545	1.603	+		−	small	6–8-sided plates
l-Ephedrine.HCl	1.530	1.603	1.638	−	p	−	70°	Elongated prisms & rods
l-Ephedrine sulfate	1.540	1.565	1.587		p		large	6-sided plates & rods
Epinephrine	1.548	1.597	>1.735	+	p	−	medium	Thin, blade-like, 6-sided crystals in rosettes; bx. ac. figs. common
Hydroxyamphetamine.HBr	1.560	1.680	1.734	−				Irregular fragments
p-Hydroxyephedrine.HCl	1.507	1.604	1.668	−	p	±		Rectangular rods; bx. ob. figs. common
p-Hydroxymethamphetamine sulfate	1.516	1.552	1.645	+	s	+		Rhombohedral or 6-sided plates
Isoxsuprine.HCl	1.508	1.648	1.670	−	p, i		40°	
Levamfetamine succinate	1.572	1.587	1.650	+	p, i		52°	Bx. ac. figs. common
Mephentermine sulfate	1.530	1.585	1.596	−	p, i		46°	
Methamphetamine.HCl	1.530	1.537	1.615	+				Irregular fragments; op. ax. figs. frequent
dl-Methamphetamine.HCl	1.535	1.540	1.620	+	p	−	small	Small 6-sided platy or rod-like crystals; no figs.
Naphazoline nitrate	1.560	1.619	>1.740	+	s, i			6-sided plates & irregular fragments; bx. ac. figs. common
Phendimetrazine.HCl	1.535	1.602	1.607	—			fairly small	Small, rounded crystals
Phendimetrazine tartrate	1.544	1.594	1.614	—	p	—	fairly large	Platy crystals; α lengthwise, β and γ crosswise
Phenylpropanolamine.HCl	1.563	1.618	1.650	−			large	
Phenylpropylmethylamine.HCl	1.577	—	1.603		p	−		Small rod-like fragments; no figs.
Pseudoephedrine.HCl	1.543	—	1.632		p	−		
Racephedrine.HCl	1.570	1.608	1.630	−				Irregular fragments; op. ax. figs. occasional
dl-Synephrine base (Desoxyepinephrine)	1.546	1.604	ca 1.725	+	s, i		large	Platy crystals, often diamond-shaped; op. ax. figs. common
Synephrine.HCl	1.549	1.605	1.664	+	p, i		large	Large plates; bx. ac. figs. frequent
dl-Synephrine (+) tartrate (neutral salt)	1.516	n_i1.620	1.689	+	i	+	large	Rods & plates; partial op. ax. figs. common
Tolazoline.HCl	1.586	1.604	1.703	+	i			6-sided plates; inclined op. ax. figs. common
Tuaminoheptane sulfate	1.458_{ω}		1.468_{ϵ}	+	p			Irregular-shaped plates & fibrous flakes; figs. frequent

(Continued)

52.024 Optical crystallographic properties of some crystalline drugs[a]—*Concluded*.

Compound	α	β	γ	Optic Sign	Extinction	Elongation	2V	Remarks
				Tranquilizers				
Azacyclonol.HCl	1.638	1.647	1.674	+			medium	
Chlordiazepoxide.HCl	1.634	ca 1.710	>1.780	+			large	6-sided prisms; n_β rare
Chlorpromazine.HCl	1.584	—	>1.735	+	i			
Ethinamate	1.530	1.536	1.546	+			76°	Recrystallized from dil. alcohol
Glutethimide	1.572	1.585	1.590	−	p, i	+	large	6-sided rods and plates
Meprobamate	ca 1.515	—	ca 1.544		p	+		Fibers and irregular thin platy fragments with wavy extinction
Thiopropazate.2HCl	1.589	1.609	1.700					Irregular platy fragments

52.025 Table of refractive indices for drugs, arranged according to ascending value of the lowest index[a]

α	β	γ	Compound
		Alkaloids and Related Amines	
1.490	1.701	>1.734	Berberine
1.499	1.572	1.597	Alphaprodine.HCl
1.500	1.535	>1.733	Berberine.HCl.2H_2O
1.508	1.516	1.628	Phenmetrazine.HCl
1.509	1.566	1.613	Cetylpyridinium chloride
1.512	1.595	1.688	Brucine sulfate
1.513	—	1.619	Ethylhydrocupreine.HCl
1.522	1.574	1.612	Isobucaine.HCl
1.526	1.597	1.639	O^6-Monoacetylmorphine.HCl
1.529	1.538	1.646	Syrosingopine
1.530	1.603	1.638	*l*-Ephedrine.HCl
1.536	1.617	>1.673	Phensuximide
1.537	—	1.556	Ethoheptazine citrate
1.540	1.590	1.635	Morphine.HCl.H_2O
1.543	1.636	1.684	Codeine
1.545	1.581	1.618	Meperidine.HCl
1.545	1.595	1.653	Levallorphan tartrate
1.545	1.617	1.661	Cinchonine.HCl.2H_2O
1.545	1.620	1.632	Morphine sulfate.5H_2O
1.548	1.563	1.688	Yohimbine
1.550	1.583	1.595	Atropine
1.550	1.734	>1.734	Hydrastine
1.555	—	1.60	Atropine sulfate
1.555	1.590	1.655	Arecoline.HBr
1.555	n_i1.733	>1.733	Papaverine.HCl
1.556	1.607	1.627	Diacetylmorphine
1.558	1.581	1.585	Methylphenidate.HCl
1.559	1.580	1.676	Codeine.HCl
1.560	—	1.575	Aconitine
1.560	1.565	1.589	Benzethonium chloride
1.561	1.642	1.661	Codeine sulfate
1.562	—	1.581	Hyoscyamine
1.562	—	>1.65	Brucine
1.562	1.604	1.660	Cinchonidine sulfate
1.565	1.607	1.670	Quinidine sulfate
1.567	1.585	1.623	Scopolamine.HBr
1.568	1.636	1.638	Dextropropoxyphene napsylate
1.568	1.659	sl >1.800	Methaqualone.HCl
1.57	1.61	1.69	Yohimbine.HCl
1.570	1.596	1.618	Cocaine.HCl
1.570	1.608	1.630	Racephedrine.HCl
1.570	1.685	1.690	Cinchonine
1.575	1.590	1.627	Pentazocine
1.577	—	1.594	Pentazocine.HCl
1.578_ω		1.613_ϵ	Diacetylmorphine.HCl.H_2O
1.580	1.615	1.617	Methscopolamine bromide
1.580	1.625	1.645	Morphine.H_2O
1.580	1.665	1.690	Quinidine
1.586	1.622	1.698	Desipramine.HCl
1.590	1.610	1.669	Quinine.HCl
1.600	—	1.620	Phenylbutazone
1.600	—	1.635	Diphenylhydantoin
1.610	1.625	1.675	Cinchonidine
1.610	1.626	1.668	Strychnine.HCl.2H_2O
1.612	1.637	1.644	Morphine.HCl, anhyd.
1.617	1.660	>1.690	Strychnine
1.620	1.625	1.630	Quinine
1.625	1.690	>1.690	Papaverine
1.638	1.658	1.701	Apomorphine.HCl
		Antibiotics	
1.474	1.484	1.513	Carbomycin
1.483	1.488	1.515	Erythromycin estolate
1.484	1.492	1.516	Erythromycin oxalate.2H_2O
1.490	1.515	1.567	Erythromycin ethylsuccinate
1.496	1.506	1.510	Erythromycin ethylcarbonate
1.498	1.507	1.563	Erythromycin stearate

[a] *See* **52.023** for symbols.

(Continued)

52.025 Table of refractive indices for drugs, arranged according to ascending value of the lowest index[a] —Continued.

α	β	γ	Compound
			Antibiotics—*Continued*
1.506	—	1.528	Erythromycin gluceptate
1.512	1.523	1.532	Erythromycin.$2H_2O$
1.512	1.583	1.682	Nystatin
1.518	ca 1.572	>1.780	Fumagillin
1.522	1.548	1.566	Dihydrostreptomycin.3HCl
1.523	1.608	1.659	Chloramphenicol
1.523	1.622	1.630	Penicillin G benzathine
1.527	—	1.569	Chloramphenicol palmitate
1.528	1.536	1.550	Erythromycin.HI.H_2O
1 538	1.646	sl >1.787	Tetracycline.$3H_2O$
n 1.541			Neomycin sulfate
1.541	ca 1.553	1.573	Gramicidin
1.541	1.585	1.656	Penicillin O chloroprocaine
1.545	—	1.593	Penicillin O potassium
1.545	1.570	1.685	Penicillin G procaine
1.546	1.635	1.730	Oxytetracycline.HCl
1.550	—	1.603	Penicillin G potassium
1.550	1.609	1.620	Penicillin G sodium
1.552	1.558	1.566	Dihydrostreptomycin sulfate
1.553	—	1.584	Tyrocidine.HCl
1.556	ca 1.590	1.619	Penicillin G hydrabamine
1.565	—	1.629	Novobiocin sodium
1.567	—	1.613	Penicillin G dibenzylamine
1.575	—	1.610	Penicillin G *l*-ephedrine
1.583	—	1.630	Cycloserine
1.583	1.590	1.648	Penicillin G *l*-ephenamine
1.601	1.608	1.632	Penicillin G.HI diethylaminoethyl ester
1.603	1.685	1.714	Tetracycline.HCl
1.608	1.638	1.654	Novobiocin acid, form 2
1.634	1.646	>1.700	Oxytetracycline.$2H_2O$
1.635	1.706	1.730	Chlortetracycline.HCl
			Antihistamines
1.505	1.585	1.617	Anthallan®.HCl
1.509	1.564	1.683	Dexchlorpheniramine maleate
ca 1.525	1.563	1.598	Doxylamine succinate
1.533	n_i1.668	sl <1.734	Chlorpheniramine maleate
1.548	1.574	1.665	Pheniramine maleate
1.553	1.625	>1.734	Chlorothen.HCl
1.566	1.614	1.653	Pyrrobutamine phosphate
1.577	1.631	1.672	2(4-Morpholinyl) ethyl benzhydryl ether.HCl
1.580	1.655	1.705	Tripelennamine.HCl
1.583	1.603	1.645	Chlorothen citrate
1.585	1.600	1.668	*p*-Fluorotripelennamine.HCl
1.587	1.635	1.734	Phenbenzamine.HCl
1.588	1.654	>1.695–<1.734	Methapyrilene.HCl
1.590	—	1.680	Thenyldiamine.HCl
1.590	1.610	1.665	Chlorcyclizine.HCl
1.602	1.625	1.630	Diphenhydramine.HCl
1.604	1.675	1.733	Methaphenilene.HCl
1.610	1.660	1.665	Chlorcyclizine.2HCl
1.612	1.679	1.691	Thonzylamine.HCl
1.617	1.654	1.734	Bromothen.HCl
1.617	1.691	1.733	Promethazine.HCl
1.620	1.647	1.738	Cyproheptadine.HCl
1.667	1.675	>1.733	Promethazine.HBr
1.690	—	1.737	Pyrathiazine.HCl
			Barbiturates
1.445	1.548	1.580	Barbital
1.454	1.518	1.556	Butethal
1.465	—	1.565	Pentobarbital
1.465	1.529	1.532	Butabarbital sodium
1.467	1.533	1.560	Amobarbital
1.473	1.519	1.549	Hexethal

(Continued)

52.025 Table of refractive indices for drugs, arranged according to ascending value of the lowest index[a] —*Continued*.

α	β	γ	Compound
			Barbiturates—*Continued*
1.477	—	1.523	Pentobarbital sodium
1.477	1.573	1.624	Probarbital
1.487	1.557	1.563	Secobarbital
1.490	n_i1.500	1.525	Secobarbital sodium
n 1.505			Amobarbital sodium
1.506	1.544	1.672	Vinbarbital
1.508	n_i1.521	1.577	Butalbital
1.512	1.532	1.615	Barbital sodium
1.515	1.546	1.621	Cyclobarbital
1.516	1.572	1.625	Allobarbital
1.519	1.583	1.634	Sigmodal®
1.520	1.575	1.626	Cyclopal®
1.520	1.581	1.600	Aprobarbital
1.524	1.577	1.603	Butallylonal
1.532	—	1.629	Probarbital sodium
1.534	1.634	—	Thiopental
1.546	1.608	1.634	Hexobarbital
1.551	1.578	1.645	Alphenal
1.557	1.620	1.667	Phenobarbital
1.594	1.610	1.651	Mephobarbital
			Hallucinogens
1.517	1.612	1.679	3,4-Methylenedioxyamphetamine.HCl
1.518	1.622	1.632	4-Methyl-2,5-dimethoxyamphetamine.HCl
1.527	1.554	1.672	Psilocybin
1.537	—	1.629	3,4-Methylenedioxyamphetamine sulfate
1.540	1.596	1.676	*d*-Lysergic acid diethylamide tartrate
1.564	1.586	1.598	3,4-Methylenedioxyamphetamine carbonate
1.572	1.618	1.654	Phencyclidine.HCl
1.572	1.620	1.654	Phencyclidine.HBr
			Steroids
1.506	—	1.598	Estradiol dipropionate
1.510	1.542	1.572	Dehydrocholic acid
1.511	1.621	1.697	Estrone, phase 2
1.512	1.552	1.621	Cortisone acetate
1.517	1.567	1.592	Triamcinolone diacetate
1.520	1.532	1.566	Cholesterol
1.520	1.642	1.692	Estrone, phase 1
1.529	1.550	1.630	Desoxycorticosterone acetate
1.529	1.575	1.676	Progesterone, beta
1.531	1.550	1.638	Hydrocortisone
1.534	1.677	1.705	Equilin
1.542	1.554	1.663	Progesterone, alpha
1.543	1.589	1.627	Hydrocortisone acetate
1.546_ϵ		1.595_ω	Triamcinolone acetonide
1.548	1.565	1.670	Testosterone
1.552	—	1.561	Methylprednisolone sodium succinate
1.552	1.572	1.625	Cortisone
1.553	1.572	1.648	Dexamethasone
1.554	—	1.667	Betamethasone
1.555	ca 1.565	1.620	Methyltestosterone
1.562	1.575	1.700	Methylprednisolone acetate
1.562	1.568	1.704	Fluorometholone
1.576	1.625	1.645	Ethisterone
1.586	1.603	1.633	Estradiol benzoate
1.587	1.590	1.651	Prednisone
1.594	1.611	1.73	Diethylstilbestrol, trans
1.594	1.628	1.647	Estrone, phase 3
			Sulfonamides
1.513	1.590	>1.690–<1.733	Sulfallantoin®
1.540	1.655	1.690	Sulfanilamide.HCl
1.555	1.672	1.85	Sulfanilamide, phase B (anhyd.)
1.559	1.564	1.727	Sulfacetamide

(Continued)

52.025 Table of refractive indices for drugs, arranged according to ascending value of the lowest index[a] —*Concluded*.

α	β	γ	Compound
		Sulfonamides—*Continued*	
1.568	1.657	1.687	Sulfamerazine
1.578	1.676	1.710	Succinylsulfathiazole
1.584	1.623	>1.778	Sulfamethazine
1.586	1.649	1.731	Sulfaguanidine.H_2O
1.587	—	1.675	Sulfamerazine[b]
1.590	—	1.700	Sulfapyridine sodium.H_2O
1.596	—	1.621	Sulfathiazole sodium.1½H_2O
1.596	1.675	1.830	Sulfadiazine
1.598	1.741	1.780	Sulfathiazole, phase II
1.605	1.642	1.697	Sulfisoxazole
1.606	1.663	1.734	Sulfaguanidine
1.615	1.663	>1.734	Sulfadiazine[b]
1.661	1.678	>1.733	Sulfamidazole®
1.670	1.736	1.813	Sulfapyridine, phase I
1.674	1.685	>1.733	Sulfathiazole, phase I
1.680	1.733	>1.733	Sulfapyridine[b]
1.695	n_i1.733	>1.733	Sulfathiazole[b]
		Sympathomimetic Amines	
1.458$_\omega$		1.468$_\epsilon$	Tuaminoheptane sulfate
1.501	1.545	1.603	Dextroamphetamine sulfate
1.507	1.604	1.668	*p*-Hydroxyephedrine.HCl
1.508	1.582	1.611	*dl*-Amphetamine.HCl
1.508	1.648	1.670	Isoxsuprine.HCl
1.516	1.552	1.645	*p*-Hydroxymethamphetamine sulfate
1.516	n_i1.620	1.689	*dl*-Synephrine (+) tartrate (neutral salt)
1.520	1.531	1.614	*dl*-Amphetamine sulfate
1.530	1.537	1.615	Methamphetamine.HCl
1.530	1.585	1.596	Mephentermine sulfate
1.530	1.603	1.638	*l*-Ephedrine.HCl
1.535	1.540	1.620	*dl*-Methamphetamine.HCl
1.535	1.602	1.607	Phendimetrazine.HCl
1.540	1.565	1.587	*l*-Ephedrine sulfate
1.543	—	1.632	Pseudoephedrine.HCl
1.544	1.594	1.614	Phendimetrazine tartrate
1.546	1.583	1.664	Dextroamphetamine phosphate, dibasic
1.546	1.604	ca 1.725	*dl*-Synephrine base
1.548	1.597	>1.735	Epinephrine
1.549	1.589	1.665	*dl*-Amphetamine phosphate, dibasic
1.549	1.605	1.664	Synephrine.HCl
1.560	1.592	1.622	Dextroamphetamine.HCl
1.560	1.619	>1.740	Naphazoline nitrate
1.560	1.680	1.734	Hydroxyamphetamine.HBr
1.563	1.618	1.650	Phenylpropanolamine.HCl
1.570	1.608	1.630	Racephedrine.HCl
1.572	1.587	1.650	Levamfetamine succinate
1.577	—	1.603	Phenylpropylmethylamine.HCl
1.586	1.604	1.703	Tolazoline.HCl
		Tranquilizers	
ca 1.515	—	ca 1.544	Meprobamate
1.530	1.536	1.546	Ethinamate
1.572	1.585	1.590	Glutethimide
1.584	—	>1.735	Chlorpromazine.HCl
1.589	1.609	1.700	Thiopropazate.2HCl
1.634	ca 1.710	>1.780	Chlordiazepoxide.HCl
1.638	1.647	1.674	Azacyclonol.HCl

[b] The second set of optical properties in each case represents intermediate data which are commonly found in some commercial samples. They probably represent an anhydrous form or merely a different common orientation of the crystal.

52.026 Nomograph relating absorbance, concentration, and absorptivity (1 cm cell)

(A straight edge placed at known values on two appropriate axes (i.e., absorbance and absorptivity) will intersect the corresponding value on the third axis (i.e., concentration).)

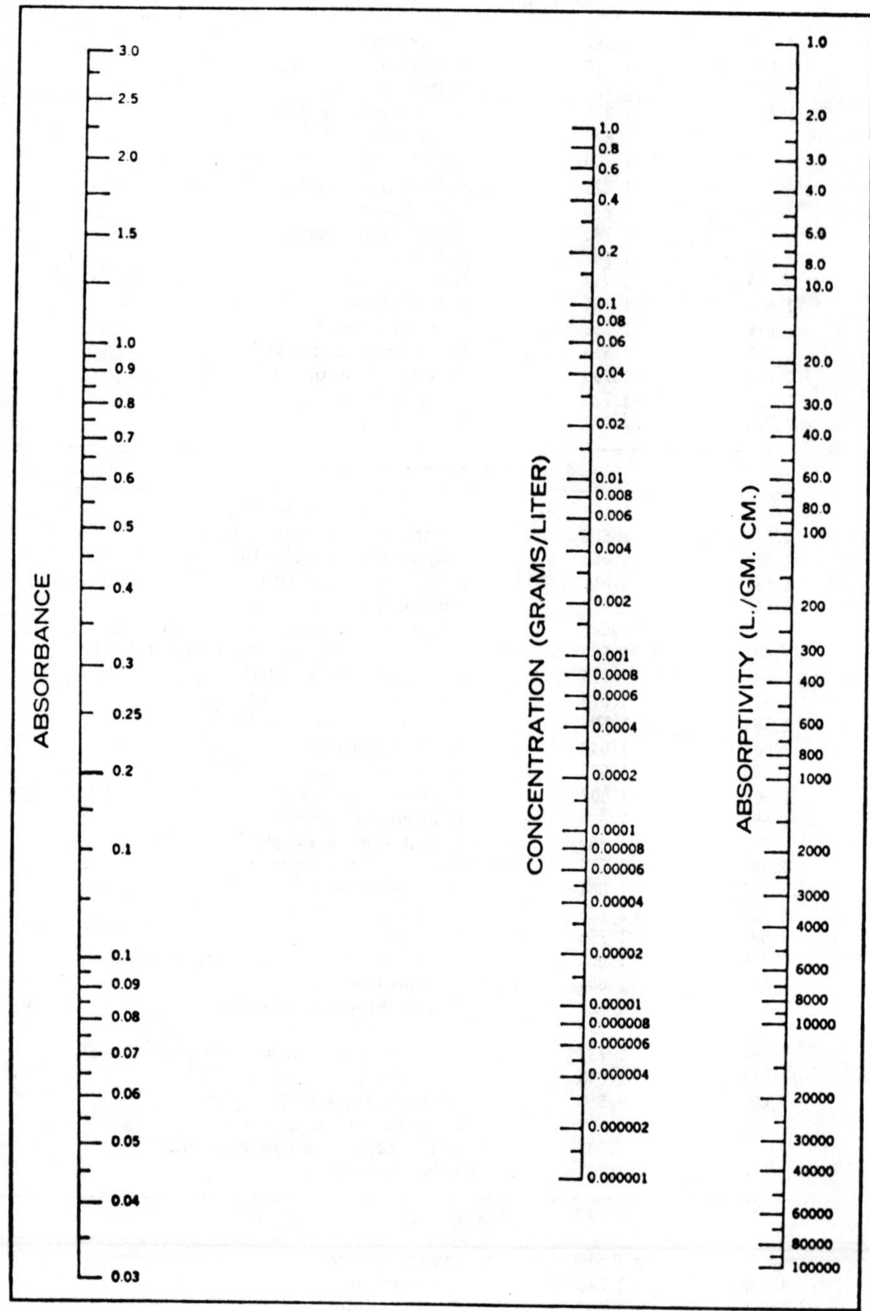

Reprinted from *The Analyzer* **4**, No. 2 (1963)
Beckman Instruments, Inc., Fullerton, Calif.

Index

Entries are located by section numbers, rather than by page numbers. A single number refers to the first section of a multiple section method; an inclusive set of numbers refers to several methods included within the group of numbers.

Entries usually will be found under the constituent sought rather than under the product in which it is to be determined, *e.g.,* the determination of potassium in fruits will be found under potassium rather than under fruits. Commodities and products may often be located more easily through the Table of Contents when basic composition methods are desired. They are entered here when commodities and products are a part of a general topic, *e.g.,* filth or pesticide residue analysis.

Secondary determinations (*e.g.,* water-soluble ash) have been included with the primary determination (ash). Negative prefixes (*e.g., non*sugar, *un*fermentable) are usually not indexed when there is a corresponding positive entry for the same determination.

Ordinary reagents are not indexed unless they are "named" (*e.g.,* Keller-Kiliani reagent) or are likely to be useful in other methods (*e.g.,* coupling reagent). Buffer solutions are indexed only if a specific pH is given in the description.

The number in brackets at the end of a line listing a chemical is the *Chemical Abstracts Service* registry number. For synonyms, the CAS registry number is given with the common name. If two compounds are listed on the same line, the registry number refers to the first.

In placing entries, positional prefixes are ignored (*e.g.,* numerals, Greek letters unless spelled out, *o-, m-, p-,* atomic symbols, etc.). The alphabetical order is word by word with hyphenated words treated as closed up.